India Handbook

David Stott
Vanessa Betts
Victoria McCulloch

India strikes its visitor with a sensory, intellectual, spiritual and philosophical assault that's unmatched by any other place on earth, all set in an awesome physical environment teeming with a resilient, indefatigable 1.2 billion-strong population. Every expectation – be it of beauty, mysticism, poverty, bigotry or bureaucracy – will be outdone by what hits you on the ground. When VS Naipaul wrote "there is little subtlety to India", it was itself an understatement: whether measured in passion for cricket, film, faith or politics, India revels in the extreme, and rejects all apathy, minimalism and restraint.

The subcontinent's sheer diversity is staggering: India ranges from tropical beach paradises to primary forests of teak and jackfruit trees where elephants roam and macaques leap, desert tundras broken by fairytale forts ruled by haughty princes with Rajput moustaches, chilly foothills clad in tea plantations and dotted with British clubhouses, opening onto vistas of the world's highest mountain peaks, through outsized metropoles whose infrastructure buckles under the weight of the unceasing movement of their vast human populations, right down to atavistic village life of tapping toddy, ploughing seed, tilling soil.

And despite the fact that India is embracing modernity with open arms, it has shunned secularism. Most of Indian society remains fiercely religious, a religiosity which remains a source of both social harmony and sporadic tension. The north holds hushed Tibetan Buddhist monasteries of frugal understatement, their air thick with incense, lit with ghee lamps, hewn into jagged Himalaya cliff faces, where prayer wheels chime and flags flutter in the high-altitude granite desert. The south answers with riotous candy-pop Hindu confections, crammed with gaudy gods, flanked by painted festival elephants and bugle-playing Brahmins. In between lie Muslim mausoleums, mosques of vast proportions, sprawling Sikh temple complexes plated with gold and the tombs of Sufi mystics peopled by pilgrims of every denomination.

This page Holi, a colourful spring festival celebrating the love between Krishna and Radha.

Previous page Panoramic view of the Taj Mahal at sunrise.

CHINA
JAMMU &
KASHMIR
Leh
Dharamshala
Manali
HIMACHAL
PRADESH
Shimla
PUNJAB
UTTAR-
AKHAND
(TIBET)
PAKISTAN
HARYANA
4
Corbett
National
Park
DELHI
1
NEPAL
SIKKIM
Darjeeling
7
RAJASTHAN
UTTAR
PRADESH
Jaisalmer
5
Agra
2
Lucknow
Jodhpur
Jaipur
Gwalior
BIHAR
Varanasi
3
Orchha
Deogarh
Udaipur
Khajuraho
JHARKHAND
WEST
BENGAL
GUJARAT
Dungarpur
Sanchi
Bhopal
Jabalpur
Kolkata
6
Ahmedabad
Mandu
MADHYA
PRADESH
CHHATTISGARH
Aurangabad
12
MAHARASHTRA
ORISSA
Bhubaneswar
Puri
Mumbai
11
Hyderabad
10
Nagarjunakonda
9
Hampi
ANDHRA
PRADESH
GOA
Arabian
Sea
KARNATAKA
Hassan
Bengaluru
Chennai
Mysore
TAMIL
NADU
Chidambaram
Coonoor
KERALA
Tiruchirappalli
Thanjavur
Munnar
Kochi
8
Madurai
Thiruvananthapuram
Kovalam
SRI
LANKA
N
200 km
200 miles
The Government of India states that "the external boundaries of India are neither correct nor authenticated"

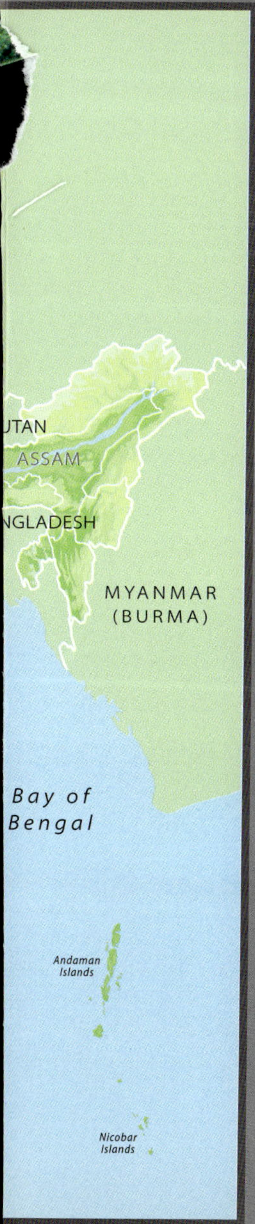

Highlights

See colour maps at the end of book

1 Delhi India's capital city is brash, chaotic, dynamic and a perfect introduction to the country. See page 71.

2 Taj Mahal The romance of the world's most famous building still astonishes in its power and beauty. See page 149.

3 Varanasi The holiest of cities defies easy description. This is India in the raw: utterly fascinating, deeply spiritual and often uncomfortable. See page170

4 Corbett National Park India's first national park, and one of its finest; a great place to see tigers – from the top of an elephant. See page 242.

5 Jaisalmer This magical medieval city shimmers like a mirage in the desert and has an incredible atmosphere. See page 399.

6 Kolkata The country's intellectual hub also retains many of her most striking colonial buildings. See page 601.

7 Darjeeling Tea gardens, trekking and the perfect escape from the steamy summer heat of the plains. See page 641.

8 Madurai This noisy, dusty and overcrowded Tamil centre is a heady cocktail of temple elephants, crumbling buildings, flower sellers, cycle-rickshaws and musicians. See page 946.

9 Hampi The former capital of the Vijayanagar Empire is a place of hugely impressive ruins and a hypnotic, chilled-out vibe. See page 1093.

10 Nagarjunakonda Island Board a boat to reach one of India's oldest Buddhist sites. See page 1129.

11 Mumbai Maximum City is the home of Bollywood, where you can take tea at the Taj and see 'Queen Victoria's necklace'. See page 1157.

12 Aurangabad The best starting point for visiting the amazing Ellora and Ajanta caves. See page 1190.

On the way to work in one of Darjeeling's tea plantations.

One of Varanasi's many ghats, on the banks of the sacred River Ganga.

Contents

Essentials

Contents

Footprint features

Planning your trip

Where to go

The heart of India

The heart of India beats in the densely populated plains of the River Ganga, settled and cultivated for millennia, and the home of great civilizations which shape the lives of more than 1.2 billion people today. To the south lies the peninsula, politically always more fragmented than the plains and agriculturally less fertile, but with mineral resources that have supplied empires from the Indus Valley Civilization over 4000 years ago to the present. Beyond lies one of India's great natural frontiers, the palm-fringed Indian Ocean, stretching from the Arabian Sea in the west to the Bay of Bengal in the east, and offering nothing but scattered island chains between Kanniyakumari and Antarctica.

From snowfields to deserts

To the north of the plains stand the Himalaya, what a 19th-century Surveyor General of India described as "the finest natural combination of boundary and barrier that exists in the world. It stands alone. For the greater part of its length only the Himalayan eagle can trace it. It lies amidst the eternal silence of vast snowfield and icebound peaks". In the eastern foothills of the Himalaya, for example, are some of the wettest regions in the world, still covered in dense rainforest, while in their western ranges are the high-altitude deserts of Ladakh. Similarly the Gangetic plains stretch from the fertile and wet delta of Bengal to the deserts of North Rajasthan. Even the peninsula ranges from the tropical humid climate of the western coast across the beautiful hills of the Western Ghats to the dry plateau inland.

Land of sacred rivers

India's most holy river, the Ganga, runs across the vital heartland of the country and through the mythology of Hinduism. Joined by other holy rivers along its route, its waters are a vital source of irrigation. Its path is dotted with towns and settlements of great sanctity, and it is a vital economic asset as well as the focus of devotion for hundreds of millions of people. To the south the great rivers of the peninsula – the Narmada, Krishna, Tungabhadra and Kaveri to name only the largest – also have a spiritual significance to match their current role as providers of water and power.

Golden sands

Goa's palm-fringed golden beaches on the sun-drenched tropical west coast have long provided a magical getaway for travellers from around the world. But there are still many less well-known hideaways up and down the often sandy coastline. Lushly vegetated and densely populated, Kerala in the far southwest adds idyllic backwaters to its coastal fringe, while offshore the almost unvisited Lakshadweep Islands offer a coral paradise for divers equalling that of the better-known Maldives to the south. Far to the east in the Bay of Bengal the Andamans add another dimension to the exotic character of India's coast, its scattered islands being home to some of the world's most primitive aboriginal tribes.

Itineraries

First-time visitors are often at a loss when faced with the vast possibilities for travel in India. We have made a few suggestions for two- to three-week trips on the basis that some journeys will be flown and that tickets have been booked in advance. Two or three of these itineraries could be combined to make a longer trip. However, since travelling times are often quite long compared to Western standards, it is advisable to stick to a particular region rather than trying

New on iPad
tripadvisor®
tripadvisor
Find places travellers trust
Hotels
Restaurants
Things to do
Flights
Forums
Write a Review
The #1 Essential Travel Download*
Get TripAdvisor Mobile - **FREE**
• Browse millions of traveller reviews, photos & maps
• Find hotels, restaurants & things to do
• See what's nearby
• Apps available for iPhone, Android, Nokia, Palm Pre, & Windows Mobile
* From "iPhone Travel Apps: 10 Essential Downloads" on Frommers.com

Packing for India

Travel light: it's possible to get most essentials in larger cities and shops in five-star hotels. Here are some items you might find helpful: loose-fitting, light cotton clothes including a sarong. Remember that women should dress modestly at all times; brief shorts and tight vest tops are best avoided, though on the beach modest swimwear is fine. Locally bought inexpensive and cool *kurta pyjama* for men, and *shalwar kameez* for women are excellent options on the plains but it can be cold in the north December to February and everywhere over 1500 m, where heavier clothing is essential. Comfortable sandals or trainers are impotant. Take high-factor sun screen and a sun hat.

Indian pharmacies can be very cheap but aren't always reliable, so take a supply of medicines from home, including inhalers and anti-malarial drugs (Proguanil is not available). Take repellent for protection against mosquitoes. See Health, page 52.

Photocopies of passport and visa pages, and spare photos are useful when applying for permits or in case of loss or theft.

For budget travellers: nets aren't always provided in cheap hotels so take an impregnated mosquito net. Earplugs are indispensable, and eyeshades can come in handy. Take a good padlock to secure your budget room too, though these can be cheaply bought in India hardware stores. A cotton or silk sheet sleeping bag are useful when you can't be sure of clean linen.

to cover too much ground in a short time. Listed throughout the book are reliable travel agencies who can make arrangements for a relatively small fee, saving you time and bother. Air tickets can be difficult to get at short notice for some trips, eg Leh–Delhi and Varanasi–Delhi. Railway tickets can be just as elusive, especially during school holidays. Indian railways are divided into regions, and despite computerized booking and the growing number of booking offices where All-India reservations can be made, there are still places where it is impossible to book tickets for travel to regions outside the one you are in. Allow more time if you are planning to travel entirely by road and rail. On the plus side, however, if you use overnight trains for longer journeys you can cover almost as much ground in the same time as flying (**figures in brackets are the number of nights we suggest you spend**).

Himalayan foothills

Two weeks Delhi (**2**) has both the British-built New Delhi and Shah Jahan's 17th-century capital. The city also provides access to some of the most beautiful sights in the Himalayan foothills and awe-inspiring mountain peaks. You can fly to Shimla (**2**), the British summer capital, then continue by road to Dharamshala (**3**) associated with the Dalai Lama and the Tibetan settlement. Spend a night in Mandi (**1**) en route to Naggar (**2**) and Manali (**4**) for some trekking. Fly back to Delhi from Kullu and take the fast *Shatabdi Express* to Agra (**1**) for the Taj Mahal and splendid fort.

Three weeks Between late June and September the tour could be altered to take in the Tibetan-Buddhist area of Ladakh (**3**) (instead of Dharamshala) by travelling to Leh (**5**) by the stunning road from Manali (**2**).

The Northwest

Three weeks This route taking in Mughal and Rajput India starts in Delhi (**2**) and moves to Agra (**2**) and Jaipur (**2**). Relax at the sleepy village of Samode (**2**) before flying across the desert to Jaisalmer (**3**) and then head for Jodhpur (**2**). On the way to lakeside Udaipur (**3**) you can visit the exquisite Jain temples at Ranakpur and the impressive fort at Kumbhalgarh from restful Deogarh (**2**). As a bonus, you can sample the charming hospitality at heritage hotels in former palaces and forts in both Rajasthan and Gujarat. Stop at Poshina Fort (2) or Balaram Palace en route to Ahmadabad (2) with its architectural heritage and Calico Museum, before flying back.

Central North India

Three weeks Across the heart of central North India you can see some of the best examples of Buddhist, Hindu and Muslim art and architecture. Travelling partly by road or rail, you also experience the varied scenery and agriculture, going first across the Deccan plateau, with its rich black lava soils, then over Rajasthan and Khajuraho on the northern edge of the peninsula. Mumbai (2) to Aurangabad (3) for Ajanta, Ellora and Daulatabad Fort. Then to Udaipur (3) and Deogarh (2) visiting Ranakpur Jain temples and Kumbhalgarh Fort. Onwards to Jaipur (2), Agra (2), Khajuraho (2) and Varanasi (3) before returning to Delhi (2).

Central India

Two weeks This tour of India is characterized by prehistoric interest and palaces. It starts in the centre of Muslim influence in Delhi (2) and Agra (1), and passes through some of the great Rajput palaces and forts in Gwalior (3), visiting Datia and idyllic Orchha (2) via Jhansi en route to Bhopal (3). Around Bhopal are impressive prehistoric rock art at Bhimbetka, and early Hindu and Buddhist remains at Bhojpur and Sanchi. On the way to Mumbai (2) a brief diversion from Indore takes you to the quaint fortified site at Mandu (2) with its picturesque past.

East India

Two weeks This tour, characterized by mountains and temples, starts in Kolkata (2), a vibrant city that was once the capital of the raj, and then takes you to the foothills of the Himalaya starting with Darjeeling (3), famous for its tea estates and magnificent views of Khangchendzonga. Distant Sikkim (3) with its distinctive Buddhist influence is a fascinating side trip. Magnificent Orissan temples can be seen at Bhubaneswar (3) and Konark, with a possible beach diversion near the pilgrimage centre of Puri (3), and on to the holy city of Varanasi (2) to see India laid bare for the first-time visitor. The tour winds up with a visit to see the fabulous carvings at Khajuraho (2) and concludes in Delhi (2) with a stop en route at Agra (1) to see the finest of the Mughal buildings, the Taj Mahal.

South India

Three weeks The historical South India circuit starts at Mumbai (2) where you can first visit the rock-cut caves rich in frescoes and carvings at Ajanta and Ellora and the rugged Daulatabad fort near Aurangabad (3). Then on to Hyderabad (3), with the former capital of the Muslim Nizam with Golconda fort and the tombs nearby. You then visit centres of ancient Tamil culture at Chidambaram, Gangaikondacholapuram and Thanjavur (3) after Chennai (1), fitting in a visit to Mahabalipuram's shore temple (2). The tour returns through southern Karnataka via Mysore (3), visiting the exquisite carvings in the Hindu and Jain temples at Belur and Halebid from Hassan or Chikmagalur (2), and finally to Bengaluru (Bangalore) (2).

Far South

Three weeks From Chennai (2) drive to Swamimalai (2) known for traditional bronze casting and continue south to the ancient Tamil temples at Thanjavur (2) and Madurai (2). A morning start allows a stop at Padmanabhapuram Palace on the way across to Kerala on the west coast to relax on the beach at Kovalam (3) near Thiruvananthapuram. Take a boat along the backwaters as you move to Kochi (3), a fascinating meeting point of Eastern and European cultures. Then drive across to the tea estates of Munnar (2), high in the Western Ghats before dropping to the Tamil plains to visit the ancient fort and temples at Trichy (2) and Srirangam. Before returning home from Chennai, stop by the sea for the rock-cut cave temples at Mahabalipuram (3).

Wildlife

Northern tour This starts in Delhi (**2**) and goes via Bhopal (**2**) and Jabalpur (**1**) to Kanha (**3**), one of the most outstanding reserves in Central India, with a very rich habitat and still little visited. It continues to Khajuraho (**2**), where there is a chance to see magnificent 10th-century temples, en route to Agra's (**2**) magnificent Taj Mahal and the abandoned city of Fatehpur Sikri before arriving at the peaceful bird sanctuary at Bharatpur (**2**), excellent for waterside birds.

Southern tour This starts in Chennai (**2**) to visit the bird sanctuary of Vedanthangal and Mahabalipuram (**2**), by the sea, with its ancient temples. Then travel down to Trichy (**2**) to climb up the rock fort and see the great temple of Srirangam on the banks of the Kaveri. From there the route continues to the hill station of Coonoor (**1**) going up to Udhagamandalam (Ooty) (**1**) on the *Blue Mountain Railway* (if it is running), then on to the rich wildlife sanctuary of Mudumalai-Bandipur (**3**). Travelling north into Karnataka, you can visit the beautiful national park of Nagarhole (**3**).

When to go

India is divided almost exactly in half by the Tropic of Cancer, stretching from the near-equatorial Kanniyakumari to the Mediterranean latitudes of Kashmir – roughly the same span as from the Amazon to San Francisco, or from Melbourne to Darwin. Not surprisingly, climate varies considerably and high altitudes further modify local climates.

In most of India, by far the best time to visit is from the end of the monsoon in October to the end of March. However, there are important exceptions. The hill stations in the Himalaya and the Western Ghats are beautiful in the hot months of April to early June. Parts of the western Himalaya can be excellent until September though it can be very cold and sometimes wet in spring.

The monsoon season lasts from between three and five months depending on the region. If you are travelling in the wetter parts of India during the monsoon you need to be prepared for extended periods of torrential rain and disruption to travel. However, many parts of India receive a total of under 1000 mm a year, mainly in the form of heavy isolated showers. Rainfall generally decreases towards the northwest, Rajasthan and northern Gujarat merging imperceptibly into genuine desert. Tamil Nadu in the southeast has an exceptional rainfall pattern, receiving most of its rain in the period of the retreating monsoon, October to December.

Some of the country's great festivals such as **Dasara** and **Diwali** (celebrated across India) and **Pongal** (celebrated in Tamil Nadu) take place in the autumn and winter. In Rajasthan, local camel and cattle fairs and the **Desert Festival** among the dunes are added attractions during these seasons.

What to do

India has a wealth of opportunities for adventure sports. Such thrills can be combined with more conventional sightseeing. Apart from the activities listed here, you can also try ballooning, heli-skiing, hang-gliding, mountain or rock climbing and even motor rallying. There are even ski resorts in Himachal Pradesh (namely Manali and Narkanda) but don't expect them to compare to Western resorts. ▸▸ *For tour operators, see page 63.*

Birdwatching

The country's diverse and rich natural habitats harbour over 1200 species of bird of which around 150 are endemic. Visitors to all parts of the country can enjoy spotting oriental species whether it is in towns and cities, in the countryside or more abundantly in the national parks and sanctuaries. On the plains, the cooler months (Nov-Mar) are the most comfortable for a chance to see migratory birds from the hills, but the highlands themselves are ideal between May and Jun and again after the monsoons when visibility improves in Oct and Nov. Water bodies large and small draw visiting waterfowl from other continents during the winter.

It is easy to get to some parks from the important tourist centres. *A Birdwatcher's Guide to India,* by Krys Kazmierczak and Raj Singh (published by Prion Ltd, Sandy, Bedfordshire, UK, 1998), is well researched and comprehensive, with helpful practical information and maps.

Some prime spots include: Chilika Lake in Orissa; Keoladeo Ghana National Park in Rajasthan; Nalsarovar Bird Sanctuary in Gujarat; Pulicat Lake in Andhra Pradesh; Ranganathittu Bird Sanctuary in Karnataka; Saharanpur Bird Sanctuary in Delhi; Taroba National Park in Maharashtra; and Vedanthangal Bird Sanctuary in Tamil Nadu.

For information, **Bird Link**, biks@giasdl01.vsnl.net.in, is concerned with conservation of birds and their habitat. Useful websites include: www.delhibird.net, www.orientalbirdclub.org, www.sacon.org.

Camel safaris

Today's camel safaris try to recreate something of the atmosphere of the early camel trains. The guides are expert navigators and the villages that are passed through along the way add colour to an unforgettable experience, if you are prepared to sit out the somewhat uncomfortable ride.

For information, see the Thar Desert National Park in Rajasthan, page 403.

Cycling

Cycling offers a peaceful and healthy alternative to cars, buses or trains. Touring on locally hired bicycles is possible along country roads – ideal if you want to see village life in India and the lesser-known wildlife parks. Consult a good Indian agent for advice. For example, a week's cycling trip could cover about 250 km in the Garhwal foothills, starting in Rishikesh, passing through the Corbett and Rajaji national parks over easy gradients, to finish in Ramnagar. Expert guides, cycles and support vehicle, accommodation in simple rest houses or tents, are included.

For local operators, see the listings section of the relevant town.

Horse safaris

Gaining in popularity, the conditions are similar to camel safaris with grooms (and often the horse owner) accompanying. The best months are Nov-Mar when it is cooler in the day (and often cold at night). The trails chosen usually enable you to visit small villages, old forts and temples, and take you through a variety of terrain and vegetation from scrub-covered arid plains to forested hills. The charges can be a lot higher than for a camel safari but the night stays are often in comfortable palaces, forts or *havelis*.

For information see Kumbhalgarh Wildlife Sanctuary (page 363) and Shekhawati (page 445).

Trekking

The Himalaya offers unlimited opportunities to view the natural beauty of mountains, unique flora and fauna and the diverse groups of people who live in the ranges and valleys, many of whom have retained cultural identities because of their isolation. The treks described in this book are only for guidance. They try to give a flavour of an area or a destination. Some trails fall within the 'Inner Line' for which special permits are required (see page 488).

Types of trekking There are some outstandingly beautiful treks, though they are often not through the wilderness that 'trekking in the Himalaya' conjures up. Nevertheless, trekking alone is not recommended as you will be in unfamiliar territory where you may not be able to communicate with the local people and if injured help may not be at hand. Independent trekkers should get a specialist publication with detailed route descriptions and a good map. Remember, mountain topography is subject to constant change, and tracks and crossings can be affected very rapidly. Speak to those who know the area well and have been trekking to the places you intend to visit.

Backpacking/camping Hundreds of people arrive each year with a pack and some personal equipment, buy some food and set off trekking, carrying their own gear and choosing their own campsites or places to stay. Serious trekkers will need a framed backpack. Supplies of fuel wood are scarce and flat ground suitable for camping rare. It is not always easy to find isolated and 'private' campsites.

Trekking without a tent Although common in Nepal, only a few trails in India offer the ease and comfort of this option.

Exceptions are the Singalila Ridge trail in the Darjeeling area, the Sikkim Khangchendzonga trek, the Markha Valley trek in Ladakh and some lower-elevation trails around Shimla and Manali. On these, it is often possible to stay in trekking huts or in simple village homes. You carry clothes and bedding, as with youth hostelling and, for a few rupees a night you get a space on the floor, a wooden pallet or a camp bed or, in the more luxurious inns, a room and shower. The food is simple, usually vegetable curry, rice and dhal which, although repetitive, is healthy and often tasty. This approach brings you into closer contact with the local population, the limiting factor being the routes where accommodation is available.

Locally organized treks Porters can usually be hired through an agent in the town or village at the start of a trek. Porters hired in the bazar may be cheaper than agency porters but can be unreliable. Make sure they are experienced in carrying loads over distances at high altitude. They will help carry your baggage, sometimes cook for you, and communicate with the local people. A good porter will know the area and some can tell you about local customs and point out interesting details en route. Away from roads, the footpath is the principal line of communication between villages. Tracks tend to be well graded and in good condition. In remoter areas away from all habitation, tracks may be indistinct and a local guide is recommended. Although some porters speak a little English (or another foreign language) you may have communication problems and misunderstandings. Remember, you may be expected to provide your porter's warm clothing and protective wear including shoes, gloves and goggles on high-altitude treks.

Hiring a *sardar* (mountain guide) and crew is more expensive but worthwhile since they will speak some English, take care of engaging porters and cooks, arrange for provisions and sort out all logistical problems. A *sardar* will cost more and although they may be prepared to carry a load, their principal function will be as a guide and overseer for the porters. Make sure your *sardar* is experienced in the area you will be travelling in and can provide references which are their own and not borrowed.

Using a trekking agent Trekking agents based in Delhi or at hill stations (eg Dehradun, Shimla, Manali, Dharamshala, Leh, Darjeeling, Gangtok) will organize treks for a fee and provide a *sardar*, porters, cooks, food and equipment, but it requires effort and careful thought on your part. This method can be excellent and is recommended for a group, preferably with some experience, that wants to follow a specific itinerary. In some areas, a pre-arranged itinerary must be followed, as required by the government, and to allow porters to arrive at certain points on schedule. You can make arrangements from abroad in advance; often a protracted business with faxes and emails. Alternatively, wait until you get to India but allow at least a week to make arrangements.

Fully organized and escorted treks This is where a company or individual with local knowledge and expertise organizes a trip and sells it. Some or all camping equipment, food, cooking, decision-making based on progress and weather conditions, liaison with porters, shopkeepers, etc, are taken care of. When operating abroad, the agency may take care of all travel arrangements, ticketing, visas and permits. This option has the advantage of being a good, safe introduction to the country. You will be able to travel with limited knowledge of the region and its culture and get to places you may not have reached alone and without the expense of completely kitting yourself out. You should take full note of any advice in the preparatory material you are sent, as your enjoyment greatly depends on it.

An escorted trek will involve going with a group; you will camp together but not necessarily walk together. If you are willing to trade some of your independence for careful, efficient organization and make the effort to ensure the group works well together, the experience can be very rewarding. Ideally there should be no more than 20 trekkers (preferably around 12). Companies have reputations to maintain and try to comply with Western concepts of hygiene. Before booking, check the itinerary – is it too demanding, or not adventurous enough? Is the leader qualified and familiar with the route? Also make sure both you and the trekking company understand exactly who is to provide what equipment.

Himalayan environment trust code of practice

Deforestation Do not make open fires and discourage others from making one for you. Limit use of firewood and heated water and use only permitted dead wood. Choose accommodation where kerosene or fuel-efficient wood-burning stoves are used.
Litter Remove it. Burn or bury paper and carry away non-degradable litter. If you find other people's litter, remove it too. Pack food in biodegradable containers.
Plants Do not take cuttings, seeds and roots – it is illegal in all parts of the Himalaya.
Water Keep local water clean. Do not use detergents and pollutants in streams and springs. Where there are no toilets be sure you are at least 30 m away from a water source and bury or cover. Do not allow cooks or porters to throw rubbish in streams and rivers.
Begging Giving to children can encourage begging. Donations to a project, health centre or school may be more constructive.
Etiquette Be aware of local traditions and cultures; respect peoples' privacy, and ask permission before taking photographs; respect holy places, never touching or removing religious objects, and removing shoes before entering temples; be aware of local etiquette, dressing modestly particularly when visiting temples and shrines and, while walking through villages, avoiding shorts, skimpy tops and tight-fitting outfits.

For further information, see Responsible travel, page 46.

Trekking seasons These vary with the area you plan to visit and the elevation. Autumn is best in most parts of the Himalaya though Mar- May can be pleasant. The monsoons (mid-Jun to end-Sep) can obviously be very wet and localized thunderstorms can occur at any time, particularly in the spring and summer. Start your trek early in the morning as the monsoon approaches. It often continues to rain heavily up to mid-Oct in the eastern Himalaya. The Kullu valley is unsuitable for trekking during the monsoons but areas beyond the central Himalayan range, eg Ladakh, Zanskar, Lahul and Spiti, are largely unaffected. Be prepared for extremes in temperatures in all seasons and come prepared with light clothing as well as enough waterproof protection. Winters can be exceptionally cold; high passes can be closed and you will need more equipment. Winter treks on all but a few low-altitude ones (up to 3200 m) are only recommended for the experienced trekker accompanied by a knowledgeable local guide.

Trekking permits Trekking is permitted in all areas other than those described as Restricted or Protected and within the 'Inner Line'; you may not go close to the international boundary in many places. Often, destinations falling within these 'sensitive' zones, which have recently been opened for trekking, require treks to be organized by a recognized Indian travel agent for groups of at least 4, travelling on a specified route, accompanied by a representative/liaison officer. Sometimes there are restrictions on the maximum number of days, season and type of transport used. The 'Inner Line' runs parallel and 40 km inside the international boundary. Kaza (Himachal Pradesh) , however, is now open to group trekkers though overnight stays are not allowed at Puh, Khabo or Sumdo. Other areas now open to tourists include Kalindi Khal (Garhwal), Milam Glacier (Kumaon), Khardung La, Tso Moriri and Pangong (Ladakh), Tsangu Lake, Lachung and Yumthang (Sikkim) and Kameng Valley (Arunachal Pradesh). On arrival in India, government-approved trekking agencies can obtain permits relatively easily, usually within 3 or 4 days. It can be much slower applying for trekking permits from abroad and may also slow down your visa application. Some restricted areas are still totally closed to foreigners. For other restricted areas, permits are issued at the Foreigners' Regional Registration Offices in Delhi, Mumbai, Kolkata and Chennai (and sometimes at a local FRRO), from immigration officers at some points of entry, and sometimes at the district magistrate's. There are also entrance fees for the various national parks and conservation areas which can be as much as Rs 350 for foreigners.

Watersports

Snorkelling, parasailing, windsurfing and waterskiing are popular along the long stretches of unspoilt coastal India. Scuba-diving centres are on Vainguinim Beach and Bogmalo in Goa, on Havelock Island and the Marine National Park in the Andamans, and on Bangaram in the Laccadives. Courses are well run and cost US$85 for an introductory dive, US$400 for 4 days, or US$600 for a 2-week Dive Master course. Coastal resorts in Kerala and Goa also offer fishing trips and dolphin viewing.

For information, see the Andaman Islands, page 833; Lakshadweep, Minicoy and Amindivi Islands, page 1040; Goa, page 1231.

Whitewater rafting

The snow-fed rivers that flow through regions such as Sikkim and Arunachal Pradesh offer excellent whitewater rafting. The popular waters range from Grades II-III for amateurs (Zanskar, Indus) to the greater challenges of Grades IV-VI for the experienced (eg Chenab, Beas, Sutlej, Rangit, Tons). Trips range from a half day to several days and allow a chance to see scenery, places and people off the beaten track. The trips are organized and managed by professional teams who have trained abroad. The rivers can sometimes be dangerous in Aug and Sep when the water levels are high.

For local operators, see the listings section of the relevant town.

Getting there

Air

India is accessible by air from virtually every continent. Most international flights arrive in Delhi, Mumbai, Chennai or Kolkata. There are also international airports in several other cities (eg Ahmedabad, Bengaluru (Bangalore), Hyderabad, Thiruvananthapuram, Goa), some of which allow customs formalities to be completed there although the flight may be routed through a principal airport. Some carriers permit 'open-jaw' travel, arriving in, and departing from, different cities in India. Some (eg **Air India**, **British Airways**) have convenient non-stop flights from Europe, eg from London to Delhi, takes only nine hours.

Alternatively, you can fly to numerous destinations across India with **Jet Airways** or **Kingfisher**. The prices are very competitive if domestic flights are booked in conjunction with Jet on the international legs. In 2011 the cheapest return flights to Delhi from London started from around £400, but leapt to £800+ as you approached the high season of Christmas, New Year and Easter.

Buying a ticket

Discounts The cheapest fares from Europe tend to be with Central European, Central Asian or Middle Eastern airlines. With these airlines it pays to confirm your return flight as early as possible. You can also get good discounts from Australasia, Southeast Asia and Japan. If you plan to visit two or more South Asian countries within three weeks, you may qualify for a 30% discount on your international tickets.

Ticket agents Companies dealing in volume and taking reduced commissions for ticket sales can offer better deals than the airlines themselves. The national press carry their advertisements. **Trailfinders**, T0845-058 5858, www.trailfinders.com, has worldwide agencies; **STA**, T0871-230 0040, www.statravel.co.uk, with over 100 offices worldwide, offers special deals for under-26s; **Travelbag**, T0871-703 4700, www.travelbag.co.uk, quotes competitive fares and is part of ebookers. **General Sales Agents** (GSAs) for specific airlines can sometimes

First impressions

On arrival at any of India's major cities the first impressions can take you aback. The exciting images of an ancient and richly diverse culture which draw many visitors to India can be overwhelmed by the immediate sensations which first greet you:

Pollution All cities seriously suffer.

Noise Many find India incredibly noisy, as radios, videos and loudspeakers blare at all times.

Smells India has a baffling mix of smells, from the richly pungent and unpleasant to the delicately subtle.

Pressure On stepping out of your hotel everybody seems to clamour to sell you their services. Taxi and rickshaw drivers are always there when you don't want them, much less often when you do. There often seems to be no sense of personal space or privacy. Young women are often stared at.

Public hygiene (or lack of it) It is common to see people urinating in public places and defecating in the open countryside.

These can be daunting. Even on a short visit to India, give yourself time and space to adjust.

offer attractive deals: **Jet Air**, for Gulf Air, Kuwait Airways, etc, and **Welcome Travel**, for Air India (for contact details, see page 24).

Charter flights Several tour operators from Europe, especially from Britain (eg **First Choice**, T0871-200 7799, www.firstchoice.co.uk, **Charter Flight Centre**, T0845-045 0153, www.charter flights.co.uk, **Jewel in the Crown**, T01293-533338, www.jewel holidays.com, **Somak**, T020-8423 3000, www.somak.com, **Thomas Cook** www.thomascook. com, flying from Gatwick and Manchester), offer package holidays from October to April to Goa and Kerala. They are often exceptional value (especially in November and from mid-January to mid-March). Government rules protect **Air India**'s monopoly on flight-only deals to Goa, but you can sidestep these by searching for holiday deals, rather than just flight-only deals, which can work out cheaper than flight-only deals, though the bargains are no longer as outrageous as they used to be; a week's bed-and-breakfast in a reasonable resort may cost around £500 per person. During high season it's sometimes cheaper to book a scheduled flight (most often to Mumbai, but worth looking at Hyderabad and Bengaluru as less hectic entry points).

The following rules apply to package holiday flights: 1) They are not available to Indian nationals. 2) The deal must include accommodation. If you take the cheap 'dorm house' option, it may be necessary to change to a more comfortable room. It may be difficult to find a room during the peak Christmas and New Year period so it is worth paying a little extra on booking, to ensure accommodation of a reasonable standard. 3) Officially, charter passengers can only stay for a maximum of 45 days, although this restriction can be circumvented somewhat if you have a valid visa to cover the duration of your proposed extension. You may not travel on a non-charter international flight (eg to Sri Lanka) while in India.

Stopovers and Round-the-World (RTW) tickets You can arrange several stopovers in India on RTW and long-distance tickets. RTW tickets allow you to fly in to one and out from another international aiport. You may be able to arrange some internal flights using international carriers eg **Air India** sometimes allows stopovers within India for a small extra charge.

From Europe

Despite the increases to Air Passenger Duty, Britain remains the cheapest place in Europe for flights to India. **Virgin Atlantic**, **British Airways** and **Kingfisher** fly to Delhi in 8½ hours or Mumbai in 9½ hours. From mainland Europe, **Jet Airways** flies to India from Brussels and Milan, while major European flag carriers including **KLM** and **Lufthansa** fly to Delhi and/or Mumbai from their respective hub airports. In most cases the cheapest flights are with Middle Eastern or Central Asian airlines, transiting via airports in the Gulf. Several airlines from the Middle East (eg **Emirates, Gulf Air, Kuwait Airways, Royal Jordanian, Qatar Airways, Oman Air**) offer good discounts to Mumbai and other Indian regional capitals from London, but fly via their hub cities, adding to the journey time. Consolidators in the UK can quote some competitive fares, such as: **Flight bookers**, T0871-223 5000, www.ebookers. com; **North South Travel**, T01245-608291, www.northsouth travel.co.uk (profits to charity).

From North America

From the east coast, several airlines including **Air India, Jet Airways, Continental** and **Delta** fly direct from New York to Delhi and Mumbai. **American** flies to both cities from Chicago. Discounted tickets on **British Airways, KLM, Lufthansa, Gulf Air** and **Kuwait Airways** are sold through agents although they will invariably fly via their country's capital cities. From the west coast, **Air India** flies from Los Angeles to Delhi and Mumbai, and **Jet Airways** from San Francisco to Mumbai via Shanghai. Alternatively, fly via Hong Kong, Singapore or Bangkok using one of those countries' national carriers. **Air Canada** operates between Vancouver and Delhi. **Air Brokers International**, www.air brokers.com, is competitive and reputable. **STA**, www.statravel.co.uk, has offices in many US cities, Toronto and Ontario. Student fares are also available from **Travel Cuts**, www.travelcuts.com, in Canada.

From Australasia

Qantas, Singapore Airlines, Thai Airways, Malaysian Airlines, Cathay Pacific and **Air India** are the principal airlines connecting the continents, although Qantas is the only one that flies direct, with services from Sydney to Mumbai. **Tiger Airways** run a no-frills service from Darwin to Kochi via Singapore, and **Air Asia X** operates from Melbourne and the Gold Coast to several South Indian cities via Kuala Lumpur; these flights can be much cheaper than standard airlines, at the cost of extended layovers and the usual extra charges for checked luggage, food etc. **STA** and **Flight Centre** offer discounted tickets from their branches in major cities in Australia and New Zealand. **Abercrombie & Kent, Adventure World, Peregrine** and **Travel Corporation of India**, organize tours; see Ticket agents and airlines, page 24.

Airport information

Departure tax Rs 500 is payable for all international departures other than those to neighbouring SAARC countries, when the tax is Rs 250 (not reciprocated by Sri Lanka). This is normally included in your international ticket; check when buying. (To save time 'Security Check' your baggage before checking in at departure.)

Ticket agents and airlines

Agents

Abercrombie & Kent, www.abercrombie kent.com, www.abercrombiekent.com.au. Luxury travel company.
Adventure Company, T0845-287 5820, www.adventurecompany.co.uk. Treks and adventure tours.
Adventure World, www.adventureworld.com.au.
Ebookers, T0871-223 5000, www.ebookers.com.
Flight Centres, www.flightcentre.co.uk.
Hari World Travels, www.hariworld.com.
Jet Air, 188 Hammersmith Rd, London T0871-910 1000. For Gulf Air, Kuwait Airways.
North South Travel, T01245-608291, www. northsouthtravel.co.uk. Profits go to charity.
Peregrine, www.peregrineadventures.com.
Red Dot Tours, T0870-231 7892, www.reddottours.com.
Southall Travel, T0844-855 8001, www.southalltravel.co.uk.
STA, London, T0871-230 0040, www.sta travel.co.uk. Over 100 offices worldwide.
Trailfinders, London, T0845-058 5858, www.trailfinders.com. Worldwide agencies.
Travel Corporation of India, www.tcindia.com.
Travel Cuts, www.travelcuts.com. US and Canadian agent.

Welcome Travel, 106 Great Portland St, Marylebone, London W1W 6PF, T020-7788 6450. For Air India.
www.cheapairticketsindia.com, **www.expedia.co.uk**, **www.lastminute.com** **www.travelocity.com**, **www.yatra.com**.

Airlines

Air India, www.airindia.in.
British Airways, www.ba.com.
Cathay Pacific, www.cathaypacific.com.
Emirates, www.emirates.com.
Gulf Air, www.gulfair.com.
Indian Airlines, www.indianairlines.in.
Jet Airways, www.jetairways.com.
Kingfisher, www.flykingfisher.com.
KLM, www.klm.com.
Kuwait Air, www.kuwait-airways.com.
Lufthansa, www.lufthansa.com.
Malaysian Airlines, www.malaysiaairlines.com.
Qantas, www.qantas.com.au.
Royal Jordanian, www.rja.com.jo.
Singapore Airlines, www.singaporeair.com.
Thai Airways, www.thaiair.com.
Tiger Airways, www.tigerairways.com.
Virgin Atlantic, www.virgin-atlantic.com.

Road

Crossings between India and its neighbours are affected by the political relations between them. Get your Indian visa in advance, before arriving at the border. Several road border crossings are open periodically, but permission to cross cannot be guaranteed. Those listed below are the main crossings which are usually open all year to tourists. Direct 'friendship' buses have been introduced between Lahore and Delhi and between Dhaka and Kolkata. Note also that you are not allowed to take any Indian currency from India into Pakistan. Indian rupees can be changed on a 1:1 basis at the border.

From Bangladesh To Kolkata from Dhaka and Jessore. The Bangaon–Benapol crossing is the most reliable. On the Bangladesh side rickshaws are available from Benapol, while buses and minibuses go to Bangaon railway station from the border. To Tripura from Dhaka is only four hours by road from the border crossing, just 2 km from the centre of Agartala, with flights to Kolkata. The border post is efficient when open but arrive there before 1500, as formalities often take time. Regulations are subject to change so find out in advance. In London, contact the Bangladesh High Commission on T020-7584 0081.

From Bhutan From Bagdogra, the nearest airport, it's a three- to four-hour drive to Jaigaon, the rather unkempt Indian border town. The Indian Immigration checkpost is on the main street, about 1 km from the 'Bhutan Gate' at the border town of Phuntsholing, where it is possible to spend a night. Accommodation ranges from the simple Central Hotel to the moderate government-run Druk Hotel. To enter Bhutan you need an entry permit and a visa from a Bhutanese tour agent.

From Nepal Four crossings are in common use: To Delhi via Banbassa is the shortest direct route between Kathmandu and Delhi, via the Nepali town of Mahendranagar and Banbassa – www.nepembassy.org.uk.

To Varanasi via Gorakhpur you must go to the Sonauli–Bhairawa crossing, the shortest and fastest route to Varanasi; many continue to Delhi from there. From Kathmandu or Pokhara you can get to Bhairawa, 6 km inside the Nepal border, Sonauli on the border itself, and Nautanwa on the Indian side. From there, buses take 3½ hours to Gorakhpur, with train connections for Delhi, or 5½ hours by bus to Varanasi. ▸▸ *See box, page 146.*

To Patna via Raxaul-Birganj several buses run daily from Raxaul to Patna (five to seven hours) but timings are unreliable and the buses are crowded and uncomfortable. Night buses from Patna reach the border in the early morning; morning buses from Patna connect with the night bus to Kathmandu. Either way you have to have at least one night bus journey unless you stay overnight at Birganj or Raxaul, which is not recommended. The bus journey between Kathmandu or Pokhara and the border takes about 11-12 hours. Even Express buses are slow and packed. Tourist minibuses are the only moderately comfortable option. ▸▸ *See box, page 816.*

Kakarbhitta (Kakarvita) is on the Nepalese side of a wide river which forms the border here between India and Nepal. A kilometre-long road bridge links it to the Indian town of Panitanki on the east bank. Cycle rickshaws run between the two. A small notice and an Indian flag are all that mark the Indian Immigration checkpost which is in a shady grove of trees by the road. The larger Indian town of Bagdogra is 15 km away. ▸▸ *See box, page 663.*

From Pakistan The **Wagah border**, 23 km from Lahore, is the only crossing open. Vans from central Lahore take you to the border where you walk across through Pakistani and Indian immigration and customs. There are taxis and rickshaws on the Indian side to take you to Attari; buses from there go to **Amritsar** (see page 476). The only **train crossing** is an uncertain one. The Lahore to Amritsar train via the Wagah border post runs twice weekly but it can take five hours to clear customs. It is normally much slower than the bus and is not recommended – http://pakistan.embassyhomepage.com. ▸▸ *See box, page 474.*

From Europe The reopening of Iran to travellers of most nationalities has reinstated the Istanbul–Tehran–Quetta route when the political situation in the region is stable.

Sea

A few cruise ships stop at some ports like Mumbai, Margao, Kochi and Chennai. Operators include **Swan Hellenic**, T0845-246 9700, www.swanhellenic.com.

From Sri Lanka amd Maldives After many years of speculation, a ferry service has finally been approved connecting Colombo with Tuticorin in far south Tamil Nadu. The ferry began operating in June 2011, with crossings taking eight to nine hours.

Getting around

Air

India has a comprehensive network linking the major cities of the different states. Deregulation of the airline industry has had a transformative effect on travel within India, with a host of low-budget private carriers offering sometimes unbelievably cheap fares on an ever-expanding network of routes in a bid to woo the train-travelling middle class. Promotional fares as low as Rs 9 (US$0.20) are not unknown, though such numbers are rendered somewhat meaningless by additional taxes and fuel charges – an extra US$30-50 on most flights. On any given day, booking a few days in advance, you can expect to fly between Delhi and Mumbai for around US$100 one way including taxes, while a month's notice and flying with a no-frills airline can reduce the price to $70-80; regional routes, eg Mumbai–Kozhikode in north Kerala, are often cheaper than routes between main cities.

Competition from the efficiently run private sector has, in general, improved the quality of services provided by the nationalized airlines. It also seems to herald the end of the two-tier pricing structure, meaning that ticket prices are now usually the same for foreign and Indian travellers. The airport authorities too have made efforts to improve handling on the ground.

Although flying is expensive, for covering vast distances or awkward links on a route it is an option worth considering, though delays and re-routing can be irritating. For short distances, and on some routes (eg Delhi–Agra–Delhi), it makes more sense to travel by train. If you don't want to take a connecting flight down to Goa, the Konkan railway makes a pretty, and increasingly speedy, alternative. Don't be tempted to take the bus.

The best way to get an idea of the current routes, carriers and fares is to use a third-party booking website such as **www.cheapairticketsindia.com** (toll-free numbers: UK T0800-101 0928, USA T1-888 825 8680), **www.cleartrip.com**, **www.makemytrip.co.in**, or **www.yatra. com**. Booking with these is a different matter: some refuse foreign credit cards outright, while others have to be persuaded to give your card special clearance. Tickets booked on these sites are typically issued as an email ticket or an SMS text message – the simplest option if you have an Indian mobile phone, though it must be converted to a paper ticket at the relevant carrier's airport offices before you will be allowed into the terminal. Makemytrip.com and Travelocity.com both accept international credit cards.

Indian airlines

The following were well established at the time of writing, although the pace of change is rapid:

Go Air, T(0)9223-222111, www.goair.in. Comparable to **SpiceJet**, flies Delhi–Jaipur–Mumbai among other routes.

Indian Airlines, www.indianairlines.in. The nationalized carrier, with the widest network of routes. Subsidiary **Alliance Air** flies some of the oldest aircraft in Indian skies and has a poor safety record.

IndiGo, T(0)9910-383838, www.goindigo.in. Comparable to **SpiceJet**.

Jagson Airlines, T011-2372 1593, www.jagsonairline.com. Flies from Delhi to a variety of Himalayan destinations, but a real challenge to book. Has a reputation for cancelling flights.

Jet Airways, T1800-225522, T011-3989 3333, www.jetairways.com. The longest-established of the private airlines, offering full-service domestic flights.

Kingfisher, T0124-284 4700 (toll free T1-800-209 3030, www.flykingfisher.com. Similar service and prices to **Jet.**

SpiceJet, T1800-180 3333, T(0)9871-803333, www.spicejet.com. No-frills service between major cities.

Airport information The formalities on arrival in India have been increasingly streamlined during the last few years and the facilities at the major international airports greatly improved. However, arrival can still be a slow process. Disembarkation cards, with an attached customs declaration, are handed out to passengers during the inward flight. The immigration form should be handed in at the immigration counter on arrival. The customs slip will be returned, for handing over to the customs on leaving the baggage collection hall. You may well find that there are delays of over an hour at immigration in processing passengers passing through immigration who need help with filling in forms.

Pre-paid taxis to the city are available at all major airports. Some airports have up to three categories, 'limousine', 'luxury' and 'ordinary'. The first two usually have prominent counters, so you may have to insist if you want the standard service. Insist on being taken to your chosen destination even if the driver claims the city is unsafe or the hotel has closed down. For more details on getting from the airport into the city centre, see the following cities: Delhi (see page 74), Kolkata (see page 601), Chennai (see page 867), Tiruvananthapuram (see page 975), Bengaluru (see page 1050), Hyderabad (see page 1119) and Mumbai (see page 1157).

Air tickets All the major airlines are connected to the local travel agents who will book your tickets for a fee if you don't want to spend precious time searching online or waiting in a queue. Remember that tickets are in great demand in the peak season on some sectors (eg Delhi–Leh–Delhi) so it is essential to get them weeks or months ahead. If you are able to pre-plan your trip, it is even possible to book internal flights at home when you buy your international air ticket. This can done through an agent or direct with the airline (eg **Air India** or **Jet Airways**). Both Jet and Indian offer a variety of flight passes (details available on their respective websites), valid on certain sections of their networks; these can be useful if you plan to travel extensively and quickly in areas beyond the reach of the budget airlines.

Indian Airlines and **Jet Airways** offer special seven-, 15- and 21-day unlimited travel deals (some are limited to one sector) from around US$300 to US$800. A 25% discount is given on US dollar fares for travellers aged 12-30 years and 25% discount fares exist on some late-night flights (between 2000 and 0800) between metropolitan cities. Air India has relaunched the companion-free scheme for routes between USA/Canada and UK/Europe.

Delays Be prepared for delays, especially in North India during the winter. Nearly all northern routes originate in Delhi where from early December to February smog has become a common morning hazard, sometimes delaying departures by several hours.

Air travel tips Security: Major airports continue to streamline the check-in process in line with international norms, but it's still possible that you'll need to have your luggage screened at a separate x-ray machine before going to the counter, and in some cases even personally identify it after passing through security check.

Telephone: There is a free telephone service at major airports (occasionally through the tourist office counter) to contact any hotel of your choice.

Wait-lists: If you don't have a confirmed booking and are 'wait-listed' it pays to arrive early at the airport and be persistent in enquiring about your position.

Rail

Trains can still be the cheapest and most comfortable means of travelling long distances saving you hotel expenses on overnight journeys. It gives access to booking station Retiring Rooms, which can be useful from time to time (see page 40). Above all, you have an ideal opportunity to meet local travellers and catch a glimpse of life on the ground. Remember the dark glass on air-conditioned coaches does restrict vision. See also www.indianrail.gov.in.

High-speed trains There are several air-conditioned 'high-speed' **Shatabdi** (or 'Century') **Express** for day travel, and **Rajdhani Express** ('Capital City') for overnight journeys. These cover large sections of the network but due to high demand you need to book them well in advance (up to 90 days). Meals and drinks are usually included.

Royal trains You can travel like a maharaja on the **Palace on Wheels** (www.palaceonwheels.net), the famous seven-nighter which has been running for many years and gives visitors an opportunity to see some of the 'royal' cities in Rajasthan during the winter months for around US$2500. A wonderful way to travel but time at the destinations is a little compressed for some. Two other seven-nighters are the **Deccan Odyssey** (www.indiarail.co.uk/do.htm), a train running in Maharashtra, and the **Golden Chariot** (www.indiarail.co.uk/gt.htm), a relatively new option running in Karnataka covering Belur, Halebid, Shravanabelagola and then Hampi and Badami/Aihole/Pattadakal. The **Heritage on Wheels** (www.heritageonwheels.org.in) a meter-gauge train covering the Shekawati region, Tal Chappar and Bikaner, starts and concludes in Jaipur. Bookings and more information for all these heritage style trains is available at www.indrail.co.uk.

Riding the rails

High-class, comfortable and, by Indian standards, quick new Express trains have brought many journeys within daytime reach. But while they offer an increasingly functional means of covering long distances in comfort, it is the overnight trips that retain something of the feel of early Indian train travel. The bedding carefully prepared – and now available on air- conditioned second-class trains – the early- morning light illuminating another stretch of hazy Indian landscape, spontaneous conversations with fellow travellers – these are still on offer, giving a value far beyond the modest prices.

Steam For rail enthusiasts, the steam-hauled narrow-gauge trains between Kurseong and Darjeeling in North Bengal (a World Heritage Site), and between Mettupalayam and Coonoor, and a special one between Ooty and Runnymede in the Nilgiris, are an attraction. See the IRCTC and Indian Railways website, www.irctc.co.in. **Williams Travel**, 18/20 Howard St, Belfast BT1 6FQ, Northern Ireland, T028-9023 0714, and **SDEL** (see page 29) are recommended for tailor-made trips.

Classes **A/c First Class**, available only on main routes, is very comfortable (bedding provided). It will also be possible for tourists to reserve special coaches (some air conditioning) which are normally allocated to senior railway officials only. **A/c Sleeper**, two and three-tier configurations (known as 2AC and 3AC), are clean and comfortable and popular with middle class families; these are the safest carriages for women travelling alone. **A/c Executive Class**, with wide reclining seats, are available on many *Shatabdi* trains at double the price of the ordinary **a/c Chair Car** which are equally comfortable. **First Class (non-a/c)** is gradually being phased out, and is now restricted to a handful of routes in the south, but the run-down old carriages still provide a pleasant experience if you like open windows. **Second Class (non-a/c)** two and three-tier (commonly called **Sleeper**), provides exceptionally cheap and atmospheric travel, with basic padded vinyl seats and open windows that allow the sights and sounds of India (not to mention dust, insects and flecks of spittle expelled by passengers up front) to drift into the carriage. On long journeys Sleeper can be crowded and uncomfortable, and toilet facilities can be unpleasant; it is nearly always better to use the Indian-style squat loos rather than the Western-style ones as they are better maintained. At the bottom rung is **Unreserved Second Class**, with hard wooden benches. You can travel long distances for a trivial amount of money, but unreserved carriages are often ridiculously crowded, and getting off at your station may involve a battle of will and strength against the hordes trying to shove their way on.

Indrail passes These allow travel across the network without having to pay extra reservation fees and sleeper charges but you have to spend a high proportion of your time on the train to make it worthwhile. However, the advantages of pre-arranged reservations and automatic access to 'Tourist Quotas' can tip the balance in favour of the pass for some travellers.

Tourists (foreigners and Indians resident abroad) may buy these passes from the tourist sections of principal railway booking offices and pay in foreign currency, major credit cards, travellers' cheques or rupees with encashment certificates. Fares range from US$57 to US$1060 for adults or half that for children. Rail-cum-air tickets are also to be made available.

Indrail passes can also conveniently be bought abroad from special agents. For people contemplating a single long journey soon after arriving in India, the Half- or One-day Pass with a confirmed reservation is worth the peace of mind; two- or four-day passes are also sold.

The UK agent is **SDEL**, 103 Wembley Park Drive, Wembley, Middlesex HA9 8HG, UK, T020-8903 3411, www.indiarail.co.uk. They make all necessary reservations and offer excellent advice. They can also book Indian Airlines and Jet Airways internal flights.

A White Pass allows first class a/c travel (the top rung); a Green, a/c two-tier Sleepers and Chair Cars; and the Yellow, only second-class travel. Passes for up to four days' duration are only sold abroad.

Cost A/c first class costs about double the rate for two-tier shown below, and non a/c second class about half. Children (aged five to 12) travel at half the adult fare. The young (12-30 years) and senior citizens (65 years and over) are allowed a 30% discount on journeys over 500 km (just show your passport).

Period	US$ A/c 2-tier	Period	US$ A/c 2-tier
½ day	26	21 days	198
1 day	43	30 days	248
7 days	135	60 days	400
15 days	185	90 days	530

Fares for individual journeys are based on distance covered and reflect both the class and the type of train. Higher rates apply on the Mail and Express trains and the air-conditioned *Shatabdi* and *Rajdhani Expresses*.

Rail travel tips **Bedding**: It can get cold in air-conditioned coaches when travelling at night. Bedding is provided on second class air-conditioned sleepers. On others it can be hired for Rs 30 from the Station Baggage Office for second class.

Berths: It is worth asking for upper berths, especially in second class three-tier sleepers, as they can also be used during the day when the lower berths are used as seats. Once the middle berth is lowered for sleeping the lower berth becomes too cramped to sit on. Passengers with valid tickets but no berth reservations are sometimes permitted to travel overnight, causing great discomfort to travellers occupying lower berths.

Credit cards: Some main stations now have separate credit card booking queues – even shorter than women's queues!

Delays: Always allow plenty of time for booking and for making connections. Delays are common on all types of transport. The special **Shatabdi** and **Rajdhani Express** are generally quite reliable. Ordinary Express and Mail trains have priority over local services and occasionally surprise by being punctual, but generally the longer the journey time, the greater the delay. Delays on the rail network are cumulative, so arrivals and departures from mid-stations are often several hours behind schedule. Allow at least two hours for connections, more if the first part of the journey is long distance.

Food and drink: It is best to carry some, though tea, bottled water and snacks are sold on the platforms (through the windows). Carry plenty of small notes and coins on long journeys. Rs 50 and Rs 100 notes can be difficult to change when purchasing small food items. On long-distance trains, the restaurant car is often near the upper-class carriages (bogies).

Getting a seat: It is usually impossible to make seat reservations at small 'intermediate' stations as they don't have an allocation. You can sometimes use a porter in a second-class carriage; for about Rs 20 he will take the luggage and ensure that you get a seat.

Internet services: Much information is available online via www.railtourismindia.com, www.indianrail.gov.in and www.trainenquiry.com, where you can check timetables (which change frequently), numbers, seat availability and even the running status of your train. Internet e-tickets can be bought and printed on www.irctc.in – a great time-saver when the system works properly. The credit card process can be complicated, and at time of writing is off-limits to credit cards issued outside India. The best option is to use third-party agent such as makemytrip.com or www.cleartrip.com, which provide an easily-understood booking engine and accept foreign cards. An alternative is to seek a local agent who can sell e-tickets, which can cost as little as Rs 5-10 (plus Rs 20 reservation fee, some agents charge up to Rs 150 a ticket,

Train touts

Many railway stations – and some bus stations and major tourist sites – are heavily populated with touts. Self-styled 'agents' will board trains before they enter the station and seek out tourists, often picking up their luggage and setting off with words such as "Madam!/Sir! Come with me madam/sir! You need top-class hotel ...". They will even select porters to take your luggage without giving you any say.

If you have succeeded in getting off the train or even in obtaining a trolley you will find hands eager to push it for you.

For a first-time visitor such touts can be more than a nuisance. You need to keep calm and firm. Decide in advance where you want to stay. If you need a porter on trains, select one yourself and agree a price **before** the porter sets off with your baggage. If travelling with a companion one can stay guarding the luggage while the other gets hold of a taxi and negotiates the price to the hotel. It sounds complicated and sometimes it feels it. The most important thing is to behave as if you know what you are doing!

however), and can save hours of hassle; simply present the printout to the ticket collector. However, it is tricky if you then want to cancel an e-ticket which an agent has bought for you on their account.

Ladies' compartments: A woman travelling alone, overnight, on an unreserved second-class train can ask if there is one of these. Lone female travellers may feel more comfortable in air-conditioned sleeper coaches, which require reservations and are used by Indian families.

Ladies' and seniors' queues: Separate (much shorter) ticket queues may be available for women and senior citizens. Travellers over 60 can ask for a 30% discount on the ticket price.

Left luggage: Bags can be left for up to 30 days in station cloakrooms. These are especially useful when there is time to go sightseeing before an evening train. The bags must be lockable and you are advised not to leave any food in them.

Overbooking: Passengers with valid tickets but no berth reservations are sometimes permitted to travel overnight, causing great discomfort to travellers occupying lower berths. Wait-listed passengers should confirm the status of their ticket in advance by calling enquiries at the nearest computerised reservation office. If you have access to www.irctc.in you can also check the waitlist status of your ticket using the PNR number or a travel agent can do this online. At the station, check the reservation charts (usually on the relevant platform) and contact the Station Manager or Ticket Collector.

Porters: These can carry prodigious amounts of luggage. Rates vary from station to station (sometimes listed on a board on the platform) but are usually around Rs 10-25 per item of luggage. Establish the rate first.

Pre-paid taxis: Many main stations have a pre-paid taxi (or auto-rickshaw) service which offers a reliable service at a fair price. If there are no pre-paid ask your hotel for a guide price.

Quotas: A large number of seats are technically reserved for various groups of travellers (civil servants, military personnel, etc), and booking under one of these quotas may allow you to get on board a theoretically 'full' train. Two quotas are particularly useful to travellers. **Foreign Tourist Quota** is available at main stations, and at tourist destinations off the rail network (eg Darjeeling). As a tourist you are not obliged to use it, but it can be the best way to get a seat at short notice. To book, find the Foreigners counter at the station booking office, and fill in the details of the train you want (see Tickets and reservations, below). You will need your passport. You can pay in US dollars or pounds sterling, or in rupees accompanied by a currency encashment certificate or ATM receipt (in practice these are rarely requested). Tourist Quota fills up early on popular routes (eg Mumbai–Goa). If you have an Indrail Pass (see page 29) you have a better chance of getting a seat. **'Tatkal' Quota** releases a small percentage of seats at 0800 two days before a train departs; you pay an extra Rs 75-200 (depending on class and season) to get on an otherwise heavily booked train. Unlike most tickets, Tatkal tickets are non-refundable if you cancel. In addition, many stations have their own quota for particular trains so that a train may be 'fully booked' when there are still some tickets available from the special quota of other stations. These are only sold on the day of departure so wait-listed passengers are often able to travel at the last minute. Ask the ticket superintendent to try the 'Special' or 'VIPQuota'.

Note All train numbers changed to five-digit numbers in 2010-2011; in most cases, adding a '1' to the start of an old four-figure number will produce the new number. Otherwise, try your luck with the 'train number enquiry' search at www.indianrail.gov.in/inet_trnno_enq.html.

Security: Keep valuables close to you, securely locked, and away from windows. For security, carry a good lock and chain to attach your luggage.

Tickets and reservations: Unreserved tickets are available at any station by queueing at the window – a skill in itself – and represent the quickest way to get on a train that is about to depart. On most trains (not *Rajdhani* or *Shatabdi Express*) you can attempt to upgrade an unreserved ticket by seeking out the station manager's office, or the black-suited TTE (Travelling Ticket Examiner) if the train is at the platform, and asking if a seat is available; an upgrade fee is payable. This can save time waiting in the slower line for reservations.

It is now possible to reserve tickets for virtually any train on the network from one of the 1000 computerized reservation centres across India. It is always best to book as far in advance as possible (usually up to 60 days). To reserve a seat on a particular train, note down the train's name, number and departure time and fill in a reservation form while you line up at the ticket window; you can use one form for up to four passengers. At busy stations the wait can take an hour or more. You can save a lot of time and effort by asking a travel agent to get your tickets for a fee of Rs 50-100. If the class you want is full, ask if special 'quotas' are available (see above). If not, consider buying a 'wait list' ticket, as seats often become available close to the train's departure time; phone the station on the day of departure to check your ticket's status. If you don't have a reservation for a particular train but carry an Indrail Pass, you may get one by arriving three hours early. Be wary of touts at the station offering tickets, hotels or exchange.

Timetables: Regional timetables are available cheaply from station bookstalls; the monthly 'Indian Bradshaw' is sold in principal stations. The handy 'Trains at a Glance' (Rs 30) lists popular trains likely to be used by most foreign travellers and is available at stalls at Indian railway stations and in the UK from SDEL (see page 29).

Road

Road travel is often the only choice for reaching many of the places of outstanding interest in which India is so rich. For the uninitiated, travel by road can also be a worrying experience because of the apparent absence of conventional traffic regulations and also in the mountains, especially during the rainy season when landslides are possible. Vehicles drive on the left – in theory. Routes around the major cities are usually crowded with lorry traffic, especially at night, and the main roads are often poor and slow. There are a few motorway-style expressways, but most main roads are single track. Some district roads are quiet, and although they are not fast they can be a good way of seeing the country and village life if you have the time.

Bus Buses now reach virtually every part of India, offering a cheap, if often uncomfortable, means of visiting places off the rail network. Very few villages are now more than 2-3 km from a bus stop. Services are run by the State Corporation from the State Bus Stand (and private companies which often have offices nearby). The latter allow advance reservations, including booking printable e-tickets online (check www.redbus.in and www.viaworld.in) and, although tickets prices are a little higher, they have fewer stops and are a bit more comfortable. In the absence of trains, buses are often the only budget option, into the Himalaya for example. There are many sleeper buses (a contradiction in terms) running Mumbai–Goa or into the Himalaya – if

The hazards of road travel

On most routes it is impossible to average more than 50-60 kph in a car. Journeys are often very long, and can seem an endless succession of horn blowing, unexpected dangers, and unforeseen delays. Villages are often congested – beware of the concealed spine-breaking speed bumps – and cattle, sheep and goats may wander at will across the road. Directions can also be difficult to follow. Drivers frequently don't know the way, maps are often hopelessly inaccurate and map reading is an almost entirely unknown skill. Training in driving is negligible and the test often a farce. You will note a characteristic side-saddle posture, one hand constantly on the horn, but there can be real dangers from poor judgement, irresponsible overtaking and a general philosophy of 'might is right'.

you must take a sleeper bus, choose a lower berth near the front of the bus. The upper berths are almost always really uncomfortable.

Bus categories Though comfortable for sightseeing trips, apart from the very best 'sleeper coaches' even **air-conditioned luxury coaches** can be very uncomfortable for really long journeys. Often the air conditioning is very cold so wrap up. Journeys over 10 hours can be extremely tiring so it is better to go by train if there is a choice. **Express buses** run over long distances (frequently overnight), these are often called 'video coaches' and can be an appalling experience unless you appreciate loud film music blasting through the night. Ear plugs and eye masks may ease the pain. They rarely average more than 45 kph. **Local buses** are often very crowded, quite bumpy, slow and usually poorly maintained. However, over short distances, they can be a very cheap, friendly and easy way of getting about. Even where signboards are not in English someone will usually give you directions. Many larger towns have **minibus** services which charge a little more than the buses and pick up and drop passengers on request. Again very crowded, and with restricted headroom, they are the fastest way of getting about many of the larger towns.

Bus travel tips Some towns have different bus stations for different destinations. Booking on major long-distance routes is now computerized. Book in advance where possible and avoid the back of the bus where it can be very bumpy. If your destination is only served by a local bus you may do better to take the Express bus and 'persuade' the driver, with a tip in advance, to stop where you want to get off. You will have to pay the full fare to the first stop beyond your destination but you will get there faster and more comfortably. When an unreserved bus pulls into a bus station, there is usually an unholy scramble for seats, whilst those arriving have to struggle to get off! In many areas there is an unwritten 'rule of reservation' using handkerchiefs or bags thrust through the windows to reserve seats. Some visitors may feel a more justified right to a seat having fought their way through the crowd, but it is generally best to do as local people do and be prepared with a handkerchief or 'sarong'. As soon as it touches the seat, it is yours! Leave it on your seat when getting off to use the toilet at bus stations.

Car A car provides a chance to travel off the beaten track, and gives unrivalled opportunities for seeing something of India's great variety of villages and small towns. Until recently, the most widely used hire car was the Hindustan Ambassador. However, except for the newest model, they are often very unreliable, and although they still have their devotees, many find them uncomfortable for long journeys. For a similar price, Maruti cars and vans (Omni) are much more reliable and are now the preferred choice in many areas. Gypsy 4WDs and Jeeps are also available, especially in the hills, where larger Sumos have made an appearance. Maruti Esteems and Toyota Qualis are comfortable and have optional reliable air-conditioning. A specialist operator can be very helpful in arranging itineraries and car hire in advance.

Car hire With a driver, car hire is cheaper than in the West. A car shared by three or four can be very good value. Be sure to check carefully the mileage at the beginning and end of the trip. Two- or three-day trips from main towns can also give excellent opportunities for sightseeing off the beaten track in reasonable comfort. Local drivers often know their way much better than drivers from other states, so where possible it is a good idea to get a local driver who speaks the state language, in addition to being able to communicate with you. In the mountains, it is better to use a driver who knows the roads. Drivers may sleep in the car overnight although hotels (especially pricier ones) should provide a bed for them. They are responsible for their expenses, including meals. Car (and auto) drivers increase their earnings by taking you to hotels and shops where they get a handsome commission (which you will pay for). If you feel inclined, a tip at the end of the tour of Rs 100 per day in addition to their daily allowance is perfectly acceptable. Check beforehand if fuel and inter-state taxes are included in the hire charge.

Cars can be hired through private companies. International companies such as **Hertz**, **Europcar** and **Budget** operate in some major cities and offer reliable cars; their rates are generally higher than those of local firms (eg **Sai Service**, **Wheels**). The price of an imported car can be three times that of the Ambassador.

Car with driver	**Economy** **Maruti 800** **Ambassador**	**Regular a/c** **Maruti 800** **Contessa**	**Premium a/c** **Maruti 1000** **Opel**	**Luxury a/c** **Esteem** **Qualis**
8 hrs/80 km	Rs 800	Rs 1000	Rs 1400	Rs 1800+
Extra km	Rs 4-7	Rs 9	Rs 13	Rs 18
Extra hour	Rs 40	Rs 50	Rs 70	Rs 100
Out of town				
Per km	Rs 7	Rs 9	Rs 13	Rs 18
Night halt	Rs 100	Rs 200	Rs 250	Rs 250

Importing a car Tourists may import their own vehicles into India with a Carnet de Passage (Triptyques) issued by any recognized automobile association or club affiliated to the Alliance Internationale de Tourisme in Geneva. In the UK contact Paul Gowan at the RAC ⓘ *Carnet Dept, RAC, Great Park Rd, Bradley Stoke, Bristol, BS32 4QN, T01454-208304.*

Self-drive car hire This is still in its infancy and many visitors may find the road conditions difficult and dangerous so take great care. Pedestrians, cattle and a wide range of other animals roam at will. This can be particularly dangerous when driving after dark especially as even other vehicles often have no lights.

Car travel tips When booking emphasize the importance of good tyres and general roadworthiness. On main roads across India **petrol stations** are reasonably frequent, but some areas are poorly served. Some service stations only have diesel pumps though they may have small reserves of petrol. Always carry a spare can. Diesel is widely available and normally much cheaper than petrol. Petrol is rarely above 92 octane. Drivers must have third party **insurance**. This may have to be with an Indian insurer, or with a foreign insurer who has a national guarantor. You must also be in possession of an International Driving Permit, issued by a recognised driving authority in your home country (eg the AA in the UK, apply at least six weeks before leaving). **Asking the way** can be very frustrating as you are likely to get widely conflicting advice each time you stop to ask (this happens to Indians asking directions too, it's not just a game to play on foreigners!). On the main roads, 'mile' posts periodically appear in English and can help. Elsewhere, it is best to ask directions often and follow the average direction. **Accidents** often produce large and angry crowds very quickly. It is best to leave the scene of the accident and report it to the police as quickly as possible thereafter. Ensure that you have adequate provisions, plenty of food and drink and a basic tool set in the car.

The **Automobile Association** (AA) offers a range of services to members. Chennai: AA of Southern India, AASI Centre, 187 Anna Salai, T044-2852 1162, www.aasindia.in. Mumbai: Western India AA, Lalji Narainji Memorial Building, 76, Vir Nariman Rd, Churchgate, T022-2204 1085, www.wiaaindia.com. New Delhi: AA of Upper India, C-8 Qutab Institutional Area, behind Qutab Hotel, T011-2696 5397, www.aaui.org.

Taxi Yellow-top taxis in cities and large towns are metered, although tariffs change frequently. These changes are shown on a fare chart which should be read in conjunction with the meter reading. Increased night time rates apply in some cities, and there is a small charge for luggage. Insist on the taxi meter being flagged in your presence. If the driver refuses, the official advice is to contact the police. This may not work, but it is worth trying. When a taxi doesn't have a meter, you will need to fix the fare before starting the journey. Ask at your hotel desk for a guide price. As a foreigner, it is rare to get a taxi in the big cities to use the meter – if they are eager to, watch out as sometimes the meter is rigged and they have a fake rate card. Also watch the note shuffle – you pay with a Rs 500 note, but they only have a Rs 100 note in their hand – David Blaine style sleight-of-hand – this happens frequently at the pre-paid booth outside New Delhi train station too, no matter how small the transaction.

At stations and airports it is often possible to share taxis to a central point. It is worth looking for fellow passengers who may be travelling in your direction and get a pre-paid taxi. At night, always have a clear idea of where you want to go and insist on being taken there. Taxi drivers may try to convince you that the hotel you have chosen 'closed three years ago' or is 'completely full'. Say that you have a reservation.

Rickshaw **Auto-rickshaws** (autos) are almost universally available in towns across India and are the cheapest and most convenient way of getting about. It is best to walk a short distance away from a hotel gate before picking up an auto to avoid paying an inflated rate. In addition to using them for short journeys it is often possible to hire them by the hour, or for a half or full day's sightseeing. In some areas younger drivers who speak some English and know their local area well may want to show you around. However, rickshaw drivers are often paid a commission by hotels, restaurants and gift shops so advice is not always impartial. Drivers generally refuse to use a meter, often quote a ridiculous price or may sometimes stop short of your destination. If you have real problems it can help to note down the vehicle license number and threaten to go to the police. Beware of some rickshaw drivers who show the fare chart for taxis, especially in Mumbai.

Cycle-rickshaws and **horse-drawn tongas** are more common in the more rustic setting of a small town or the outskirts of a large one. You will need to fix a price by bargaining. The animal attached to a tonga usually looks too undernourished to have the strength to pull the driver, let alone passengers.

Cycling Cycling is an excellent way of seeing the quiet byways of India. It is easy to hire bikes in most small towns for about Rs 30-50 per day. Indian bikes are heavy and without gears, but on the flat they offer a good way of exploring comparatively short distances outside towns. In the more prosperous tourist resorts, mountain bikes are now becoming available, but at a higher charge. It is also quite possible to tour more extensively and you may then want to buy a cycle.

There are shops in every town and the local Hero brand is considered the best, with Atlas and BSA good alternatives; expect to pay around Rs 1200-1500 for a second-hand Indian bike but remember to bargain. At the end of your trip you could sell it easily at half price. Imported bikes have lighter weight and gears, but are more difficult to get repaired and carry the much greater risk of being stolen or damaged. If you wish to take your own, it is quite easy if you dismantle it and pack it in its original shipping carton; be sure to take all essential spares including a pump. It is possible to get Indian spares for 26" wheel cycles. All cyclists should take bungy cords (to strap down a backpack) and good lights from home, although cycling at night is not recommended; take care not to leave

On the road on a motorbike

An experienced motorbiker writes: unless you bring your own bike (Carnet de passage, huge deposit) the only acceptable machine is the legendary Enfield Bullet 350 or 500 cc. Humming along the Indian roads or tracks this four stroke classic machine is a must. Also available in diesel version (1½ litres per 100 km and much cheaper fuel) the 500 cc is much better for travelling with luggage and easier to take home as brakes and 12v lights conform with EC regulations.

Expect a cruising speed of around 50 kph. Riding above 70 kph gets very tiring due to the lack of silent blocks and the nerve-wracking Indian roads. A good average distance is 200 km per day. Riding at night furthers the excitement – practise at home on a death race video first, but bear in mind that accidents can turn into a first-hand lynching experience! If you stop, prepare to settle quickly in cash, but while third party insurance is cheap refunds are less than guaranteed.

Buying In Delhi, Karol Bagh is the biker's den, where you can have your second hand bike assembled to order. It's also good for arranging shipping (Rs 13,000 to Europe), and for spares and gear. You can now find good helmets at a fraction of the European price (Studds Rs 300-2000 for a full face type), also goggles, sturdy panniers and extras. A Bullet will cost from Rs 25,000 to Rs 40,000 second hand, or Rs 50,000-Rs 60,000 new. Allow plenty of time to shop around.

Papers Many Indians and tourists don't bother changing the name on the ownership papers. If you are driving through more than one state this is rash, as it is essential to have the papers in your name, plus the NOC (No Objection Certificate) from the Motor Vehicles Department if you intend to export the vehicle home. Regardless of the dealer's assertions to the contrary, demand the NOC as otherwise you will have to apply for it in the state of origin. You have to allow 15 days.

Spares Before buying, negotiate the essential extras: mirrors, luggage carriers, better saddle, battery. Spares are cheap and readily available for the 350cc model. Take along a spare throttle and clutch cable, a handful of nuts and bolts, puncture repair kit and pump or emergency canister so you don't have to leave the bike unattended while hitching a lift to the nearest puncture wallah – and of course a full set of tools. Check the oil level daily. Finally, remember that for long distances you can load your bike on a night train (Rs 100 per 100 km). Just turn up at the parcel office with an empty petrol tank at least two hours before departure.

your bike parked anywhere with your belongings. Bike repair shops are universal and charges are nominal; you are usually not far from a 'puncture wallah' who can also make minor repairs cheaply.

It is possible to cover 50-80 km a day quite comfortably. One cyclist reported that the national highways are manic but country roads, especially along the coast, can be idyllic, if rather dusty and bumpy. You can even put your bike on a boat for a backwater trip or on top of a bus. If you want to take your bike on the train, allow plenty of time for booking it in on the brake van at the Parcels office and for filling in forms.

It is best to start a journey early in the morning, stop at midday and then resume in the late afternoon. Night riding, though cooler, can be hazardous because of lack of lighting and poor road surfaces. Try to avoid major highways as far as possible. Fortunately, foreign cyclists are usually greeted with cheers, waves and smiles and truck drivers are sometimes happy to give lifts to cyclists (and their bikes). This is a good way of taking some of the hardship out of cycling round India. For expert advice contact the **Cyclists' Touring Club** ⓘ *T0844-736 8450, www.ctc.org.uk.*

Motorcycling (For general advice, see under Car and Cycling, above.) This is a particularly attractive way of getting around. It is easy to buy new Indian-made motorcycles including the 350cc Enfield Bullet and several 100cc Japanese models, including Suzukis and Hondas made in collaboration with

Indian firms; Indian Rajdoots are less expensive but have a poor reputation for reliability. Buying new at a fixed price ensures greater ease and reliability. Buying second hand in rupees takes more time but is quite possible (expect to get a 30-40% discount) and repairs are usually easy to arrange and quite cheap. You can get a broker to help with the paperwork involved (certificate of ownership, insurance, etc) for a fee (see also Insurance, page 55). They charge about Rs 5000 for a No Objection Certificate (NOC), essential for reselling; it's easier to have the bike in your name. Bring your own helmet and an International Driving Permit. Vespa, Kinetic Honda and other makes of scooters in India are slower than motorbikes but comfortable for short hauls of less than 100 km and have the advantage of a 'dicky' (small, lockable box) for spares, and a spare tyre. See also box, above. Motorbikes and scooters for hire in Goa must have black and yellow numberplates. Bikes with other numberplates will be cheaper to hire but you will get stopped by the police. Expect to pay between 150 and 400 a day to rent a scooter or bike in Goa.

Chandertal Tours & Himalayan Folkways, 20 The Fridays, East Dean, Eastbourne, BN20 0DH, UK, T01323-422213, www.chandertaltours.co.uk. Himachal, Ladakh and Rajasthan.
Mountain Adventures, T0129-411 7492, www.mountainindia.com. Based in Delhi, for motorbike and cycling tours.
Peter and Friends Classic Adventures, www.classic-bike-india.com, see page 66. Organized motorbike tours in Rajasthan and the Himalaya with good back-up. Well organized, friendly and popular. Also hires Enfield motorbikes in Goa (US$120-165 per week).
Royal Enfield, www.royalenfield.com. Indian website with information on pilgrim tours by motorbike and how to buy a new Bullet. Also, www.indax.com has useful information on motorbike touring hazards in India.

Hitchhiking Hitchhiking is uncommon, partly because public transport is so cheap. If you try, you are likely to spend a very long time on the roadside. However, getting a lift on scooters and on trucks in areas with little public transport can be worthwhile, whilst those riding motorbikes or scooters in Goa can be expected to pick up the occasional hitchhiking policeman. It is not recommended for women on their own.

Maps

For anyone interested in the geography of India, or even simply getting around, trying to buy good maps is a depressing experience. For security reasons it is illegal to sell large- scale maps of areas within 80 km of the coast or national borders.

The **Bartholomew** 1:4 m map sheet of India is the most authoritative, detailed and easy to use map available. It can be bought worldwide. **GeoCenter World Map** 1:2 m, covers India in three regional sections and are clearly printed. **Nelles'** regional maps of India at the scale of 1:1.5 m offer generally clear route maps, though neither the road classifications nor alignments are wholly reliable. The same criticism applies to the attractively produced and easy-to-read **Lonely Planet Travel Atlas of India and Bangladesh** (2001).

State and town plans are published by the **TTK Company**. These are often the best available though they are not wholly reliable. For the larger cities they provide the most compact yet clear map sheets (generally 50 mm by 75 mm format). The **Indian Map Service** publishes a limited number of maps of both Rajasthan and Maharashtra.

Stanfords, 12-14 Long Acre, London, WC2, T020-7836 1321, www.stanfords.co.uk, offers a mail order service. **The Survey of India** publishes large scale 1:10,000 town plans of some 70 cities. These detailed plans are the only surveyed town maps in India, and some are over 20 years old. The Survey also has topographic maps at the scale of 1:25,000 and 1:50,000 in addition to its 1:250,000 scale coverage, some of which are as recent as the late 1980s. However, maps are regarded as highly sensitive and it is only possible to buy these from main agents of the Survey of India. The export of large-scale maps from India is prohibited.

Sleeping

India has an enormous range of accommodation. You can stay safely and very cheaply by Western standards right across the country. In all the major cities there are also high-quality hotels, offering a full range of facilities; in small centres hotels are much more variable. In Rajasthan and Gujarat, old Maharajas' palaces and forts have been privately converted into comfortable, unusual hotels. Hotels in beach resorts and hill stations, because of their location and special appeal, often deviate from the description of our different categories. In the peak season (October to April for most of India) bookings can be extremely heavy in popular destinations. It is sometimes possible to book in advance by phone, fax or email, but double check your reservation, and always try to arrive as early as possible in the day.

Hotels → *For Sleeping price codes, see box, page 39.*

Price categories The category codes used in this book are based on prices of double rooms excluding taxes. They are **not** star ratings and individual facilities vary considerably. The most expensive hotels charge in US dollars only. Modest hotels may not have their own restaurant but will often offer 'room service', bringing in food from outside. In South and West India, and in temple towns, restaurants may only serve vegetarian food. Many hotels operate a 24-hour checkout system. Make sure that this means that you can stay 24 hours from the time of check-in. Expect to pay more in Delhi, Mumbai and, to a lesser extent, in Bengaluru (Bangalore), Chennai and Kolkata for all categories; Kerala, too, is becoming quite expensive. Prices away from large cities tend to be lower for comparable hotels. Away from the metropolitan cities, in South India, room rates tend to be lower than the North, and the standard of cleanliness is higher.

Off-season rates Large reductions are made by hotels in all categories out-of-season in many resorts. Always ask if any is available. You may also request the 10-15% agent's commission to be deducted from your bill if you book direct. Clarify whether the agreed figure includes all taxes.

Taxes In general most hotel rooms rated at Rs 1200 or above are subject to a tax of 10%. Many states levy an additional luxury tax of between 10 and 25%, and some hotels add a service charge of 10% on top of this. Taxes are not necessarily payable on meals, so it is worth settling your meals bill separately. Most hotels in the **C** category and above accept payment by credit card. Check your final bill carefully. Visitors have complained of incorrect bills, even in the most expensive hotels. The problem particularly afflicts groups, when last-minute extras appear mysteriously on some guests' bills. Check the evening before departure, and keep all receipts.

Hotel facilities You have to be prepared for difficulties which are uncommon in the West. It is best to inspect the room and check that all equipment (air conditioning, TV, water heater, flush) works before checking in at a modest hotel. Many hotels try to wring too many years' service out of their linen, and it's quite common to find sheets that are stained, frayed or riddled with holes. Don't expect any but the most expensive or tourist-savvy hotels to fit a top sheet to the bed.

In some states **power cuts** are common, or hot water may be restricted to certain times of day. The largest hotels have their own generators but it is best to carry a good torch. Usually, only category **C** and above have **central air conditioning**. Elsewhere air conditioned rooms are cooled by individual units and occasionally by large 'air-coolers' which can be noisy and unreliable. When they fail to operate tell the management as it is often possible to get a rapid repair done, or to transfer to a room where the unit is working. During power cuts generators may not be able to cope with providing air conditioning. Fans are provided in all but the cheapest of hotels.

Apart from those in the **A** category and above, 'attached bath' does not necessarily refer to a bathroom with a bathtub. Most will provide a **bathroom** with a toilet, basin and a shower. In the lower priced hotels and outside large towns, a bucket and tap may replace the shower, and an Indian squat toilet instead of a Western WC (squat toilets are very often cleaner). Even mid-price hotels, which are clean and pleasant, don't always provide towels, soap and toilet paper.

Sleeping and eating price codes

Sleeping

LL	over US$200	B	US$46-65	E	US$12-20
L	US$151-200	C	US$31-45	F	US$7-11
AL	US$101-150	D	US$21-30	G	under US$7
A	US$66-100				

For a double room in high season, excluding taxes.

Eating

🍴🍴🍴	over US$12	🍴🍴	US$6-12	🍴	under US$6

For a two-course meal for one person, excluding drinks and service charge.

In some regions **water supply** is rationed periodically. Keep a bucket filled to use for flushing the toilet during water cuts. Occasionally, tap water may be discoloured due to rusty tanks. During the cold weather and in hill stations, hot water will be available at certain times of the day, sometimes in buckets, but is usually very restricted in quantity. Electric water heaters may provide enough for a shower but not enough to fill a bath tub. For details on drinking water, see page 41.

At some times of the year and in some places **mosquitoes** can be a real problem, and not all hotels have mosquito-proof rooms or mosquito nets. If you have any doubts check before confirming your room booking. In cheap hotels you need to be prepared for the presence of flies, cockroaches, spiders, ants and geckos (harmless house lizards). Poisonous insects and scorpions are extremely rare in towns. Hotel managements are nearly always prepared with insecticide sprays. Few small hotels in mosquito-prone areas supply nets so it is best for budget travellers to take one from home. An impregnated, wedge-shaped one (for single-point fixing) is preferable, available in all good camping/ outdoor shops. Remember to shut windows and doors at dusk. Electrical mats and pellets are now widely available, as are mosquito coils that burn slowly. One traveller recommends Dettol soap to discourage mosquitoes. Dusk and early evening are the worst times for mosquitoes so trousers and long-sleeved shirts are advisable, especially outdoors. At night, fans can be very effective in keeping mosquitoes off; remember to tuck the net under the mattress all round. As well as insects, expect to find spiders larger and hairier than those you see at home; they are mostly harmless and more frightened of you than you are of them.

Hotels close to temples can be very **noisy**, especially during festivals. Music blares from loudspeakers late at night and from very early in the morning, often making sleep impossible. Mosques call the faithful to prayers at dawn. Some find ear plugs helpful.

Hotels in hill stations often supply **wood fires** in rooms. Usually there is plenty of ventilation, but ensure that there is always good air circulation, especially when charcoal fires are provided in a basket.

Where staff training is lacking, the person who brings up your cases may proceed to show you light switches, room facilities, TV tuning, and hang around waiting for a **tip**. Room boys may enter your room without knocking or without waiting for a response to a knock. Both for security and privacy, it is a good idea to lock your door when you are in the room. At the higher end, you should expect to tip bellboys a little for every favour.

Tourist 'bungalows'

The different state tourism development corporations run their own hotels and hostels which are often in places of special interest. These are very reasonably priced, though they may be rather institutional, restaurant menus may be limited and service is often slow.

Railway and airport Retiring Rooms

Railway stations often have 'Retiring Rooms' or 'Rest Rooms' which may be hired for periods of between one and 24 hours by anyone holding an onward train ticket. They are cheap and simple though often heavily booked. Some major airports (eg Mumbai) have similar facilities.

Government rest houses

Rest houses may be available for overnight stays, especially in remote areas. They are usually very basic, with a caretaker who can sometimes provide a simple meal, with notice. Check the room rate in advance as foreigners can be overcharged. Government officials always take precedence, even over guests who have booked.

Indian-style hotels

These, catering for Indian businessmen, are springing up fast in or on the outskirts of many small- and medium-sized towns. Most have some air-conditioned rooms and attached showers. They are variable in quality but it is increasingly possible to find excellent value accommodation even in remote areas.

Hostels

The Department of Tourism runs 16 youth hostels, each with about 50 beds, usually organized into dormitory accommodation. The YHA also have a few sites all over India. Travellers may also stay in religious hostels (*dharamshalas*) for up to three days. These are primarily intended for pilgrims and are sometimes free, though voluntary offerings are welcome. Usually only vegetarian food is permitted; smoking and alcohol are not.

Camping

Mid-price hotels with large grounds are sometimes willing to allow camping. Regional tourist offices have details of new developments. For information on YMCA camping facilities contact: YMCA, The National General Secretary, National Council of YMCAs of India, PB No 14, Massey Hall, Jai Singh Rd, New Delhi 1.

Homestays

At the upmarket end, increasing numbers of travellers are keen to stay in private homes and guesthouses, opting not to book large hotel chains that keep you at arm's length from a culture. Instead, travellers get home-cooked meals in heritage houses and learn about a country through conversation with often fascinating hosts. Kerala leads the way in this field, but Delhi is catching up fast, with dozens of new and smart family-run B&Bs springing up. Tourist offices have lists of families with more modest homestays. Companies specializing in homestays include **Kerala Connections**, **MAHout**, **Pyramid Tours** and **Sundale Vacations**. See tour operators, page 63.

Eating → *For Eating price codes, see box, page 39.*

Food

ⓘ *See page 1447 for a food glossary.* *Regional cuisine is covered in the introduction to each state.*

You find just as much variety in dishes and presentation crossing South India as you would on an equivalent journey across Europe. Combinations of spices give each region its distinctive flavour.

The larger hotels, open to non-residents, often offer **buffet** lunches with Indian, Western and sometimes Chinese dishes. These can be good value (Rs 250-300; but Rs 450 in the top grades) and can provide a welcome, comfortable break in the cool. The health risks, however, of food kept warm for long periods in metal containers are considerable, especially if turnover at the buffet is slow. We have received several complaints of stomach trouble following a buffet meal, even in five-star hotels.

It is essential to be very careful since food hygiene may be poor, flies abound and refrigeration in the hot weather may be inadequate and intermittent because of power cuts. It is best to eat only freshly prepared food by ordering from the menu (especially meat and fish dishes). Avoid salads and cut fruit.

If you are unused to spicy food, go slow. Stick to Western or mild Chinese meals in good restaurants and try the odd Indian dish to test your reaction. Food is often spicier when you eat with families or at local places. Popular local restaurants are obvious from the number of people eating in them. Try a traditional *thali*, which is a complete meal served on a large stainless steel plate (or very occasionally on a banana leaf). Several preparations, placed in small bowls, surround the central serving of wholewheat chapati and rice. A vegetarian *thali* would include dhal (lentils), two or three curries (which can be quite hot) and crisp poppadums, although there are regional variations. A variety of pickles are offered – mango and lime are two of the most popular. These can be exceptionally hot, and are designed to be taken in minute quantities alongside the main dishes. Plain *dahi* (yoghurt) in the south, or *raita* in the north, usually acts as a bland 'cooler'. Simple *dhabas* (rustic roadside eateries) are an alternative experience for sampling authentic local dishes.

Many city restaurants offer a choice of so-called **European options** such as toasted sandwiches, stuffed pancakes, apple pies, fruit crumbles and cheesecakes. Italian favourites (pizzas, pastas) can be very different from what you are used to. In the big cities, Goa and Dharamshala, the Western food is generally pretty good. Western confectionery, in general, is disappointing. **Ice creams**, on the other hand, can be exceptionally good; there are excellent Indian ones as well as some international brands.

India has many delicious tropical **fruits**. Some are seasonal (eg mangoes, pineapples and lychees), while others (eg bananas, grapes and oranges) are available throughout the year. It is safe to eat the ones you can wash and peel.

Drink

Drinking water used to be regarded as one of India's biggest hazards. It is still true that water from the tap or a well should never be considered safe to drink since public water supplies are often polluted. Bottled water is now widely available although not all bottled water is mineral water; most are simply purified water from an urban supply. Buy from a shop or stall, check the seal carefully (some companies now add a second clear plastic seal around the bottle top) and avoid street hawkers; when disposing bottles puncture the neck which prevents misuse but allows recycling for storage.

There is growing concern over the mountains of plastic bottles that are collecting and the waste of resources needed to produce them, so travellers are being encouraged to use alternative methods of getting safe drinking water. In some towns such as Dharamshala and Leh, purified water is now sold for refilling your own container. You may wish to purify water yourself. A portable water filter is a good idea, carrying the drinking water in a plastic bottle in an insulated carrier. Always carry enough drinking water with you when travelling. It is important to use pure water for cleaning teeth.

Tea and **coffee** are safe and widely available. Both are normally served sweet, and with milk. If you wish, say 'no sugar' (*chini nahin*), 'no milk' (*dudh nahin*) when ordering. Alternatively, ask for a pot of tea and milk and sugar to be brought separately. Freshly brewed coffee is a common drink in South India, but in the North, ordinary city restaurants will usually serve the instant variety. Even in aspiring smart cafés, espresso or cappuccino may not turn out quite as you'd expect in the West.

Bottled **soft drinks** such as Coke, Pepsi, Teem, Limca, Thums Up and Gold Spot are universally available but always check the seal when you buy from a street stall. There are

Two masala dosai and a pot of tea

One traveller to Ooty reported that a hotel bar had closed, apparently permanently. He found, however, that it was still possible to obtain alcoholic drinks from the restaurant. Having ordered and been served a beer, he was intrigued that when the bill came it was made out for "two masala dosai". The price was, of course, correct for the beer.

Another traveller found that a well-known hotel in the heart of New Delhi also appeared to have been forced to adapt its attitude to serving alcohol to the prevailing laws. Asked in the early evening for a double whisky the barman was very happy to comply until he was asked to serve it in the garden. On being told that he could only drink it in the bar the visitor expressed great disappointment, on which the barman relented, whispering that if the visitor really wanted to drink it outside he would serve it to him in a tea pot.

If you are thirsting for alcohol in a prohibitionist area perhaps you need to order two masala dosai and a pot of tea.

also several brands of fruit juice sold in cartons, including mango, pineapple and apple – Indian brands are very sweet. Don't add ice cubes as the water source may be contaminated. Take care with fresh fruit juices or *lassis* as ice is often added.

Indians rarely drink **alcohol** with a meal. In the past wines and spirits were generally either imported and extremely expensive, or local and of poor quality. Now, the best Indian whisky, rum and brandy (IMFL or 'Indian Made Foreign Liquor') are widely accepted, as are good Champagnoise and other wines from Maharashtra. If you hanker after a bottle of imported wine, you will only find it in the top restaurants for at least Rs 800-1000.

For the urban elite, refreshing Indian beers are popular when eating out and so are widely available. 'Pubs' have sprung up in the major cities. Elsewhere, seedy, all-male drinking dens in the larger cities are best avoided for women travellers, but can make quite an experience otherwise – you will sometimes be locked into cubicles for clandestine drinking. If that sounds unsavoury then head for the better hotel bars instead; prices aren't that steep. In rural India, local rice, palm, cashew or date juice *toddy* and *arak* is deceptively potent. However, the Sikkimese *chhang* makes a pleasant change drunk out of a wooden tankard through a bamboo straw.

Most states have alcohol-free dry days or enforce degrees of Prohibition. Some upmarket restaurants may serve beer even if it's not listed, so it's worth asking. In some states there are government approved wine shops where you buy your alcohol through a metal grille. For dry states and liquor permits, see page 69.

Entertainment

Despite an economic boom in cities like and Bengaluru (Bangalore), Chennai, Delhi, Hyderabad and Mumbai and the rapid growth of a young business class, India's nightlife remains meagre and is mainly focused on discos in the biggest hotels. In Goa, beach trance parties usually take place in makeshift venues and continue to attract large groups of young foreigners particularly during Christmas and New Year. However, the government has threatened to close down these venues and has imposed a 2200 music curfew (although this is not always rigorously imposed), so now there are more day parties. More traditional, popular entertainment is widespread across Indian villages in the form of folk drama, dance and music, each region having its own styles, and open-air village performance are common. The hugely popular local film industry comes largely out of this tradition. It's always easy to find a cinema, but prepare for a long sitting with a standard story line and set of characters and lots of action.

Festivals and events

India has a wealth of festivals with many celebrated nationwide, while others are specific to a particular state or community or even a particular temple. Many fall on different dates each year depending on the Hindu lunar calendar so check with the tourist office.

The Hindu calendar

Hindus follow two distinct eras: The *Vikrama Samvat* which began in 57 BC and the *Salivahan Saka* which dates from AD 78 and has been the official Indian calendar since 1957. The *Saka* new year starts on 22 March and has the same length as the Gregorian calendar. The 29½ day lunar month with its 'dark' and 'bright' halves based on the new and full moons, are named after 12 constellations, and total a 354-day year. The calendar cleverly has an extra month (*adhik maas*) every 2½ to three years, to bring it in line with the solar year of 365 days coinciding with the Gregorian calendar of the West.

Some major national and regional festivals are listed below; details of these and others appear under the particular state or town. A few count as national holidays: **26 January**: Republic Day; **15 August**: Independence Day; **2 October**: Mahatma Gandhi's Birthday; **25 December**: Christmas Day.

Major festivals and fairs

Jan New Year's Day (1 Jan) is accepted officially when following the Gregorian calendar but there are regional variations which fall on different dates, often coinciding with spring/harvest time in Mar and Apr: **Losar** in Ladakh, **Naba Barsha** in Bengal (14 Apr), **Goru** in Assam, **Ugadi** in Andhra, **Vishu** in Kerala and **Jamshed Navroj** for the Parsi community. **14 Jan Makar Sankranti** marks the end of winter and is celebrated with kite flying, especially in Gujarat. **Pongal** is Tamil Nadu's harvest festival.

26 Jan Republic Day Parade in New Delhi. Communist-style display of military strength.

Feb Vasant Panchami, the spring festival when people wear bright yellow clothes to mark the advent of the season with singing, dancing and feasting. In Bengal it is also **Saraswati Puja** when the goddess of learning is worshipped. **Desert Festival** – Jaisalmer, Rajasthan. **Nagaur Camel Fair** in Rajasthan. **Surajkund Crafts Mela** in Haryana. **International Yoga Festival** in Rishikesh, Uttarakhand. **Elephanta Festival** in Maharashtra. **Konark Festival** in Orissa.

Feb-Mar Maha Sivaratri marks the night when Siva danced his celestial dance of destruction (*Tandava*), which is celebrated with feasting and fairs at Siva temples, but preceded by a night of devotional readings and hymn singing. **Carnival** in Goa. Spectacular costumes, music and dance, float processions and feasting mark the 3-day event.

Mar Ellora Festival of Classical Dance and Music in Maharashtra. **Khajuraho Dance Festival** in Madhya Pradesh. **Gangaur Mela** in Rajasthan. **Holi**, the festival of colours, marks the climax of spring. The previous night bonfires are lit in parts of North India symbolizing the end of winter (and conquering of evil). People have fun throwing coloured powder and water at each other and in the evening some gamble with friends. If you don't mind getting covered in colours, you can risk going out but celebrations can sometimes get very rowdy (and unpleasant). Some worship Krishna who defeated the demon Putana.

Apr Mahavir Jayanti. **Baisakhi** in North India.

Apr/May Buddha Jayanti, the 1st full moon night in Apr/May marks the birth of the Buddha. **Pooram** in Thrissur, Kerala; a grand spectacle staged by rival temples with elaborately ornamented elephants.

Jun/Jul Rath Yatra in Puri, Orissa. **Hemis Festival** in Leh, Ladakh. **Teej** in Jaipur, Rajasthan.

Jul/Aug Raksha (or Rakhi) Bandhan symbolizes the bond between brother and sister, celebrated mainly in North India at full moon. A sister says special prayers for her brother and ties coloured threads around his wrist to remind him of the special bond. He in turn gives a gift and promises to protect and care for her. Sometimes *rakshas* are exchanged as a mark of friendship. **Narial Purnima** on the same full moon. Hindus,

Purnima (Full Moon)

Many religious festivals depend on the phases of the moon. Full moon days are particularly significant and can mean extra crowding and merrymaking in temple towns throughout India, and are sometimes public holidays.

particularly in coastal areas of West and South India, make offerings of *narial* (coconuts) to the Vedic god Varuna (Lord of the waters) by throwing them into the sea. **15 Aug** is **Independence Day**, a national secular holiday is marked by special events, and in Delhi there is an impressive flag-hoisting ceremony at the Red Fort. **Ganesh Chaturthi** was established just over 100 years ago by the Indian nationalist leader Tilak. The elephant-headed God of good omen is shown special reverence. On the last of the 5-day festival after harvest, clay images of Ganesh are taken in procession with dancers and musicians, and are immersed in the sea, river or pond.

Aug/Sep Janmashtami, the birth of Krishna is celebrated at midnight at Krishna temples. Special festivities are held in Mathura his birth place and nearby at Vrindavan where *Rasalilas* (dance dramas) are performed all night.

Sep/Oct Dasara has many local variations. In North India, celebrations for the 9 nights *(navaratri)* are marked with **Ramlila**, various episodes of the Ramayana story (see page 1402) are enacted with particular reference to the battle between the forces of good and evil. In some parts of India it celebrates *Rama*'s victory over the Demon king *Ravana* of Lanka with the help of loyal *Hanuman* (Monkey). Huge effigies of *Ravana* made of bamboo and paper are burnt on the 10th day (*Vijaya dasami*) of **Dasara** in public open spaces. other regions the focus is on Durga's victory over the demon *Mahishasura*. Bengal celebrates **Durga** puja. **Onam** in Kerala.

Oct/Nov Gandhi Jayanti (2 Oct), Mahatma Gandhi's birthday, is remembered with prayer meetings and devotional singing.

Diwali/Deepavali (*Sanskrit ideepa* lamp), the festival of lights, is celebrated particularly in North India. Some Hindus celebrate Krishna's victory over the demon *Narakasura*, some Rama's return after his 14 years' exile in the forest when citizens lit his way with oil lamps. The festival falls on the dark *chaturdasi* (14th) night (the one preceding the new moon), when rows of lamps or candles are lit in remembrance, and *rangolis* are painted on the floor as a sign of welcome. Fireworks have become an integral part of the celebration which are often set off days before Diwali. Equally, Lakshmi, the Goddess of Wealth (as well as Ganesh) is worshipped by merchants and the business community who open the new financial year's account on the day. Most people wear new clothes; some play games of chance.

In Bengal **Kali Puja** is celebrated the day before Diwali but is a distinct festival. **Pushkar Fair** in Rajasthan. **Guru Nanak Jayanti** commemorates the birth of Guru Nanak. **Akhand Path** (unbroken reading of the holy book) takes place and the book itself (*Guru Granth Sahib*) is taken out in procession. **Sonepur Fair** in Bihar.

Dec Christmas Day (25 Dec) sees Indian Christians celebrate the birth of Christ in much the same way as in the West; many churches hold services/mass at midnight. There is an air of festivity in city markets which are specially decorated and illuminated. Over **New Year's Eve** (**31 Dec**) hotel prices peak and large supplements are added for meals and entertainment in the upper category hotels. Some churches mark the night with a Midnight Mass. **Shekhavati Festival** in Rajasthan. **Hampi-Vijaynagar Festival** in Karnataka.

Muslim holy days

These are fixed according to the lunar calendar, see page 1422. According to the Gregorian calendar, they tend to fall 11 days earlier each year, dependent on the sighting of the new moon.

Ramadan is the start of the month of fasting when all Muslims (except young children, the very elderly, the sick, pregnant women and travellers) must abstain from food and drink, from sunrise to sunset.
Id ul Fitr is the 3-day festival that marks the end of Ramadan.
Id-ul-Zuha/Bakr-Id is when Muslims commemorate Ibrahim's sacrifice of his son according to God's commandment; the main time of pilgrimage to Mecca (the Hajj). It is marked by the sacrifice of a goat, feasting and alms giving.
Muharram is when the killing of the Prophet's grandson, Hussain, is commemorated by Shi'a Muslims. Decorated *tazias* (replicas of the martyr's tomb) are carried in procession by devout wailing followers who beat their chests to express their grief. Hyderabad and Lucknow are famous for their grand *tazias*. The Shi'as fast for the 10 days.

Shopping

India excels in producing fine crafts at affordable prices through the tradition of passing down of ancestral skills. You can get handicrafts of different states from the government emporia in the major cities which guarantee quality at fixed prices (no bargaining), but many are poorly displayed, a fact not helped by reluctant and unenthusiastic staff. Private upmarket shops and top hotel arcades offer better quality, choice and service but at a price. Vibrant and colourful local bazars are often a great experience but you must be prepared to bargain.

Bargaining can be fun and quite satisfying but it is important to get an idea of prices being asked by different stalls for items you are interested in, before taking the plunge. Some shopkeepers will happily quote twice the actual price to a foreigner showing interest, so you might well start by halving the asking price. On the other hand it would be inappropriate to do the same in an established shop with price tags, though a plea for the 'best price' or a 'special discount' might reap results even here. Remain good humoured throughout. Walking away slowly might be the test to ascertain whether your custom is sought and you are called back.

Taxi/rickshaw drivers and tour guides get a commission when they deliver tourists to certain shops, but prices are invariably inflated. Small private shops can't always be trusted to pack and post your purchases: unless you have a specific recommendation from a person you know, only make such arrangements in government emporia or a large store. Don't enter into any arrangement to help 'export' marble items, jewellery, etc, no matter how lucrative your 'cut' of the profits may sound. Many's the traveller that's been cheated through misuse of credit card account, and left with unwanted goods. Make sure, too, that credit cards are run off just once when making a purchase.

The country is a vast market place but there are regional specializations. If you are planning to travel widely, wait to find the best places to buy specific items. Export of certain items is controlled or banned (see page 50).

Carpets and dhurries

The superb hand-knotted carpets of Kashmir, using old Persian designs woven in wool or silk or both, are hard to beat for their beauty and quality. Kashmiri traders can now be found throughout India, wherever there is a hint of foreign tourism. Agra too has a long tradition of producing wool carpets and welcomes visitors to their factories. Tibetan refugees in Karnataka, Darjeeling and Gangtok produce excellent carpets which are less expensive but of very high quality. They will make carpets to order and parcel post them safely. Flat woven cotton dhurries in subtle colours are best seen in Rajasthan.

Jewellery

Whether it is chunky tribal necklaces from the Himalaya, heavy 'silver' bangles from Rajasthan, fine Orissan filigree, legendary pearls from Hyderabad, Jaipuri uncut gems set in gold or semi-precious stones in silver, or glass bangles from Varanasi, you will be drawn to the arcade shop window as much as the wayside stall. It's best to buy from reputable shops as street stalls often pass off fake ivory, silver, gems and stones as real. Gold and silver should have a hallmark, but antique pieces often do not. Be warned, gold prices have doubled in the last three years and in early 2011 silver prices increased by 45% in just three months. Naturally jewellery prices will reflect this price hike.

Metal work

The choice is vast, from brass, copper and white-metal plates and bowls from the North, with ornate patterns or plain polished surfaces, exquisite Jaipuri enamelled silver pill boxes, tribal lost-wax *dhokra* toys from Orissa, Bihar and Bengal, Nawabi silver-on-gunmetal Bidri pieces from around Hyderabad, to copies of Chola bronzes cast near Thanjavur.

Paintings

Contemporary Indian art is exhibited in modern galleries in the state capitals often at a fraction of London or New York prices. Traditional 'Mughal' miniatures, sometimes using natural pigments on old paper (don't be fooled) and new silk, are reaching mass production levels in Rajasthan's back alleys. Fine examples can still be found in good craft shops.

Stoneware

Artisans inspired by the Taj Mahal continue the tradition of inlaying tiny pieces of gem stones on fine white marble, to produce something for every pocket, from a small coaster to a large table top. Softer soapstone is cheaper. Stone temple carvings are produced for sale in Tamil Nadu (try Mahabalipuram), Orissa (Puri, Konark) and Uttar Pradesh (near Hamirpur).

Textiles

Handlooms produce rich shot silk from Kanchipuram, skilful *ikat* from Gujarat, Orissa and Andhra, brocades from Varanasi, golden *muga* from Assam, printed silks and batiks from Bengal or opulent *Himroo* shawls from Aurangabad. Sober handspun *khadi*, colourful Rajasthani block-printed cottons using vegetable dyes, tribal weaving from remote Himalayan villages and tie-dyed Gujarati *bandhni* are easier on the pocket. Unique pieces also from Kashmiri embroidery on wool, Lucknowi *chickan* shadow-work on fine voil or *zari* (gold/silver thread) work on silk. The *pashmina* shawl and scarf from Kashmir have travelled to every continent and are available in dozens of colours at less inflated prices. They come in various widths and quality (often mixed with silk). See page 560. All trade in tush (toosh) wool is banned.

Wood craft

Each region of India has its special wood – walnut in Kashmir, sandalwood in Mysore, rosewood in the South, sheesham in the North. Carving, inlay and lacquerwork are particular specialities. The southern states produce fine carved wooden panels and images which are sold through the state emporia (they offer a posting service).

Responsible travel

Customs

Most travellers experience great warmth and hospitality. With it comes an open curiosity about personal matters. You should not be surprised if total strangers ask for details of your job, income and family circumstances or discuss politics and religion.

Conduct

Respect for the foreign visitor should be reciprocated by a sensitivity towards local customs and culture. How you dress is how people will judge you; cleanliness, modest clothes and a smile go a

How big is your footprint?

As well as respecting local cultural sensitivities, travellers can take a number of simple steps to reduce, or even improve, their impact on the local environment. Environmental concern is relatively new in India. Don't be afraid to pressurize businesses by asking about their policies.

Litter Many travellers think that there is little point in disposing of rubbish properly when the tossing of water bottles, plastic cups and other non-biodegradable items out of train windows is already so widespread. Don't follow an example you feel to be wrong. You can immediately reduce your impact by refusing plastic bags and other excess packaging when shopping – use a small backpack or cloth bag instead – and if you do collect a few, keep them with you to store other rubbish until you get to a litter bin.

Plastic mineral water bottles, an inevitable corollary to poor water hygiene standards, are a major contributor to India's litter mountain. However, many hotels, including nearly all of the upmarket ones, most restaurants and bus and train stations, provide drinking water purified using a combination of ceramic and carbon filters, chlorine and UV irradiation. Ask for '*filter paani*'; if the water tastes like a swimming pool it is probably quite safe to drink, though it's best to introduce your body gradually to the new water. If purifying water yourself, bringing it to a boil at sea level will make it safe, but at altitude you have to boil it for longer to ensure that all the microbes are killed. Various sterilizing methods can be used that contain chlorine (eg Puritabs) or iodine (eg Pota Aqua) and there are a number of mechanical or chemical water filters available on the market.

Bucket baths or showers The biggest issue relating to responsible and sustainable tourism is water. Much of northwest India is afflicted by severe water restrictions, with certain cities in Rajasthan and Gujarat having water supply for as little as 20 minutes a day. The traditional Indian 'bucket bath', in which you wet, soap then rinse off using a small hand-held plastic jug dipped into a large bucket, uses on average around 15 litres of water, as compared to 30-45 for a shower. These are commonly offered except in four- and five-star hotels.

Support responsible tourism Spending your money carefully can have a positive impact. Sleeping, eating and shopping at small, locally owned businesses directly supports communities, while specific community tourism concerns, such as those operated by The Blue Yonder in Kerala and Village Ways in Uttarakhand (see next page), provide an economic motivation for people to stay in remote communities, protect natural areas and revive traditional cultures, rather than exploit the environment or move to the cities for work.

Transport Choose walking, cycling or public transport over fuel-guzzling cars and motorbikes.

long way. Scanty, tight clothing draws unwanted attention. Nudity is not permitted on beaches in India and although there are some places where this ban is ignored, it causes much offence. Public displays of intimacy are inappropriate in public. You may at times be frustrated by delays, bureaucracy and inefficiency, but displays of anger and rudeness will not achieve anything positive, and often make things worse. People's concept of time and punctuality is also often rather vague so be prepared to be kept waiting.

Courtesy

It takes little effort to learn common gestures of courtesy and they are greatly appreciated. The greeting when meeting or parting, used universally among the Hindus across India, is the palms joined together as in prayer, sometimes accompanied with the word *namaste* (North and West), *namoshkar* (East) or *vanakkam* in Tamil. Muslims use the greeting *assalām aleikum*, with the response *waleikum assalām*, meaning 'peace be with you'; 'please' is *mehrbani-se*; 'thank you' is often expressed by a smile, or with the somewhat formal *dhannyabad*, *shukriya* (Urdu), and *nandri* in Tamil.

Hands and eating

Traditionally, Indians use the right hand for giving, receiving, shaking hands and eating, as the left is considered to be unclean since it is associated with washing after using the toilet. In much of rural India cutlery is alien at the table except for serving spoons, and at most humble restaurants you will be offered only small spoonsto eat with. If you visit an ashram or are lucky enough to be invited to a temple feast day, you will almost certainly be expected to eat with your hands. Watch and copy others until the technique becomes familiar.

Women → *See also page 69.*

Indian women in urban and rural areas differ in their social interactions with men. To the Westerner, Indian women may seem to remain in the background and appear shy when approached. Yet you will see them working in public, often in jobs traditionally associated with men in the West, in the fields or on construction sites. It is not considered polite for men to photograph women without their consent, so ask before you start snapping.

Women do not usually shake hands with men as physical contact between the sexes is not acceptable. A westernized city woman, however, may feel free to shake hands with a foreign visitor. In certain, very traditional rural circles, it is still the custom for men to be offered food first, separately, so don't be surprised if you, as foreign guest (man or woman), are awarded this special status when invited to an Indian home.

Visiting religious sites

Visitors to all religious places should be dressed in clean, modest clothes; shorts and vests are inappropriate. Always remove shoes before entering (and all leather items in Jain temples). Take thick socks for protection when walking on sun-baked stone floors. Menstruating women are considered 'unclean' and should not enter places of worship. It is discourteous to sit with one's back to a temple or shrine. You will be expected to sit cross-legged on the floor – avoid pointing your feet at others when attending prayers at a temple. Walk clockwise around a shrine (keeping it to your right).

Non-Hindus are sometimes excluded from the inner sanctum of **Hindu** temples and occasionally even from the temple itself. Look for signs or ask. In certain temples and on special occasions you may enter only if you wear unstitched clothing such as a *dhoti*.

In **Buddhist** shrines, turn prayer wheels in a clockwise direction. In **Sikh** gurudwaras, everyone should cover their head, even if it is with a handkerchief. Tobacco and cigarettes should not be taken in. In **Muslim** mosques, visitors should only have their face, hands and feet exposed; women should also cover their heads. Mosques may be closed to non-Muslims shortly before formal prayers.

Some temples have a register or a receipt book for **donations** which works like an obligatory entry fee. The money is normally used for the upkeep and services of the temple or monastery. In some pilgrimage centres, priests can become unpleasantly persistent. If you wish to leave a donation, put money in the donation box; priests and Buddhist monks often do not handle money. It is also not customary to shake hands with a priest or monk. *Sanyasis* (holy men) and some pilgrims depend on donations.

Guide fees

Guides at tourist sites vary considerably in their knowledge and ability. Government trained and licensed guides are covered by specified fees. Local temple and site guides should charge less. Charges for four people for half a day are Rs 280, for a full day Rs 400; for five to 15 people for half a day Rs 400, for a full day Rs 530. Rs 125 for a language other than English.

Begging and charitable giving

Beggars are often found on busy street corners in large Indian cities, as well as at bus and train stations where they often target foreigners. In the larger cities, beggars are often exploited by syndicates which cream off most of their takings. Yet those seeking alms near religious sites are another matter, and you may see Indian worshippers giving freely to those less fortunate than themselves, since this is tied up with gaining 'merit'. How you deal with begging is a matter of personal choice. Young children sometimes offer to do 'jobs' such as call a taxi, carry shopping or pose for a photo. You may want to give a coin in exchange. While travelling, some visitors prefer to hand out fruit to the many open-palmed children they encounter.

A pledge to donate a part of one's holiday budget to a local charity could be an effective formula for 'giving'. Some visitors like to support self-help cooperatives, orphanages, refugee centres, disabled or disadvantaged groups, or international charities like Oxfam, Save the Children or Christian Aid which work with local partners, by either making a donation or by buying their products. Some of these charities are listed under the appropriate towns. A few (which also welcome volunteers) are listed here.

Akanksha, T022-2370 0253, www.akanksha.org. Mumbai-based charity working with slum kids who have fallen out of formal education.
Concern India Foundation, 6 K Dubash Marg, Mumbai, T022-2202 9708, www.concernindia.org. An umbrella organization working with local charities.
El Shaddai Charitable Trust, www.childrescue.net, www.scanindia.in. Charity providing food, clothing, shelter and education for orphans and economically deprived children in India.
Oxfam, 2nd floor, 1 Community Centre, New Friends Colony, New Delhi 110065, T011-4653 8000; 274 Banbury Rd, Oxford OX2 7D2, UK, www.oxfamindia.org (400 grassroots projects).
Salaam Baalak Trust, several centres in Mumbai and Delhi, www.salaambaalaktrust.com. Set up by the team who made the movie *Salaam Bombay* 20 years ago, Salaam Baalak's mission is to give streetkids the joys of childhood and prepare them for a productive adulthood – they offer food, shelter, education, vocational training. They hold dramas and dance events to raise awareness about community and health issues.
Save the Children India, Vardhaman Trade Centre, 9-10-11 Nehru Place, New Delhi 110019, T011-4229 4900.
Share and Care Children's Welfare Society, 4/28 Arumugam St, near Perambur station, Chennai, T044-2537 6338, www.shareandcare.org.in. A small but highly regarded organization that runs an orphanage, self-help groups for women, aged care and environmental education programs.
Trek-Aid, 2 Somerset Cottages, Stoke Villages, Plymouth, Devon, PL3 4AZ, www.a38.com/trekaid. Health, education, etc, through self-help schemes for displaced Tibetan refugees.
Urmul Trust, Urmul Dairy, Ganganagar Rd, Bikaner, Rajasthan, T0151-252 2139. Healthcare, education and rural crafts in Rajasthani villages.
Very Special Arts India, Plot 3, Sector C, Institutional Area, Nelson Mandela Marg, Vasant Kunj, New Delhi 110070, T011-2613 4983, www.vsaindia.org. This organization promotes the creative power in people with disabilities and works towards enriching their lives through remedial therapies.

Photography

Many monuments and national parks charge a camera fee ranging from Rs 20-100 for still cameras, and as much as Rs 500 for video cameras (more for professionals). Special permits are needed from the Archaeological Survey of India, New Delhi, for using tripods and artificial lights. When photographing people, it is polite to first ask – they will usually respond warmly with smiles. Visitors often promise to send copies of the photos – don't unless you really mean to do so. Photography of airports, military installations, bridges and in tribal and 'sensitive border areas', is not permitted.

Essentials A-Z

Accident and emergency

Contact the relevant emergency service (police T100, fire T101, ambulance T102) and your embassy (see under Directory in major cities such as Delhi, Chennai, Mumbai, etc). Make sure you obtain police/medical reports required for insurance claims.

Children

Children of all ages are widely welcomed. However, care should be taken when travelling to remote areas where health services are primitive. It's best to visit in the cooler months since you need to protect children from the sun, heat, dehydration and mosquito bites. Cool showers or baths help; avoid being out during the hottest part of the day. Diarrhoea and vomiting are the most common problems, so take the usual precautions. Breastfeeding is best and most convenient for babies. In the big cities you can get safe baby foods and formula milk. It doesn't harm a baby to eat an unvaried and limited diet of familiar food carried in packets for a few weeks if local dishes are not acceptable, but it may be an idea to give vitamin and mineral supplements. Wet wipes and disposable nappies are difficult to find. The biggest hotels provide babysitting. Many European families have permanently relocated to Goa and the facilities here are accordingly good. See also Health, page 52.

Customs and duty free

Duty free

Tourists are allowed to bring in all personal effects 'which may reasonably be required', without charge. The official customs allowance includes 200 cigarettes or 50 cigars, 0.95 litres of alcohol, a camera and a pair of binoculars. Valuable personal effects and professional equipment including jewellery, special camera equipment and lenses, laptop computers and sound and video recorders must be declared on a Tourist Baggage Re-Export Form (TBRE) in order for them to be taken out of the country. These forms require the equipment's serial numbers. It saves considerable frustration if you know the numbers in advance and are ready to show them on the equipment. In addition to the forms, details of imported equipment may be entered into your passport. Save time by completing the formalities while waiting for your baggage. It is essential to keep these forms for showing to the customs when leaving India, otherwise considerable delays are very likely at the time of departure.

Currency regulations

There are no restrictions on the amount of foreign currency or TCs a tourist may bring into India. If you are carrying more than US$5000 in cash or US$10,000 or its equivalent in cash and TCs you need to fill in a currency declaration form. This could change with a relaxation in the currency regulations.

If you are travelling to Nepal, note that it is illegal to take Indian Rs 500 and Rs 1000 notes into the country. These notes will be confiscated, and offenders are liable to fines or imprisonment.

Prohibited items

The import of dangerous drugs, live plants, gold coins, gold and silver bullion and silver coins not in current use are either banned or subject to strict regulation. It is illegal to import firearms into India without special permission. Enquire at consular offices abroad for details.

Export restrictions

Export of gold jewellery purchased in India is allowed up to a value of Rs 2000 and other jewellery (including settings with precious stones) up to a value of Rs 10,000. Export of antiquities and art objects over 100 years old is restricted. Ivory, musk, skins of all animals, *toosh* and *pashmina* wool, snakeskin and articles made from them are banned, unless you get permission for export. For further information, contact the Indian High Commission or consulate, or access the Central Board of Excise and Customs website, www.cbec.gov.in/travellers.htm.

Disabled travellers

India is not geared up to making provisions for the physically handicapped or wheelchair-bound traveller. Access to buildings, toilets (sometimes squat), pavements, kerbs and public transport can prove frustrating, but it is easy to find people to give a hand to help with lifting and carrying. Provided there is an able-bodied companion to help and you are prepared to pay for at least mid-price accommodation, car hire and taxis, India should be rewarding, even if in a somewhat limited way.

Some travel companies are beginning to specialize in exciting holidays, tailor-made for individuals depending on their level of disability. **Global Access**, Disabled Travel Network, www.globalaccessnews.com, dedicated to providing travel information for 'disabled adventurers' and includes a number of reviews and tips from members of the public. *Nothing Ventured*, edited by Alison Walsh (HarperCollins), gives personal accounts of worldwide journeys by disabled travellers, plus advice and listings. **Accessible Journeys Inc**, 35 West Sellers Av, Ridley Park, PA 19078, T610-521 0339, www.disabilitytravel.com, runs some packages to India. **ResponsibleTravel.com**, 3rd floor, Pavillion House, 6 Old Steine, Brighton, BN1 1EJ, UK, T01273-600030, www.responsibletravel.com, created by Body Shop founder Anita Roddick, specializes in eco-friendly holidays and has some tailored to the needs of disabled travellers.

Drugs

Certain areas, such as Goa's beaches, Kovalam, Gokarna and Hampi, have become associated with foreigners who take drugs. These are likely to attract local and foreign drug dealers but be aware that the government takes the misuse of drugs very seriously. Anyone charged with the illegal possession of drugs risks facing a fine of Rs 100,000 and a minimum 10 years' imprisonment. Several foreigners have been imprisoned for drugs-related offences in the last decade.

Electricity

Inida supply is 220-240 volts AC. Some top hotels have transformers. There may be pronounced variations in the voltage, and power cuts are common. Power back-up by generator or inverter is becoming more wide- spread, even in humble hotels, though it may not cover a/c. Socket sizes vary so take a universal adaptor; low-quality versions are available locally. Many hotels, even in the higher categories, don't have electric razor sockets. Invest in a stabilizer for a laptop.

Embassies and consulates

For information on visas and immigration, see page 68. For a comprehensive list of embassies (but not all consulates), see http://india.gov.in/overseas/indian_missions.php. Many embassies around the world are now outsourcing the visa process which might affect how long the process takes.

Indian embassies abroad

Australia 3-5 Moonah Pl, Yarralumla, Canberra T02-6273 3999, www.hcindia-au.org; Level 27, 25 Blight St, Sydney T612-9223 9239; Melbourne, 344 St Kilda Rd, T03-9682 7836.
Canada 10 Springfield Rd, Ottawa, Ontario K1M 1C9, T613-744 3751, www.hciottawa.ca. Toronto, T416-960 0751, Vancouver, T604-662 8811.
France 15 Rue Alfred Dehodencq, Paris, T01-4050 7070, www.amb-inde.fr.
Germany Tiergartenstrasse 17, 10785 Berlin, T030-257950. Consulates: Bonn T0228-540132; Frankfurt T069-7408 7646 (outsourced through IGCS), Hamburg T040-324744, Munich T089-210 2390, Stuttgart T0711-153 0050.
Ireland 6 Leeson Park, Dublin 6, T01-497 0843, www.indianembassy.ie.
Nepal 336 Kapurdhara Marg, Kathmandu, T+9771-441 0900, www.south-asia.com/embassy-india.
Netherlands Buitenrustweg-2, 2517 KD, The Hague, T070-346 9771, www.indianembassy.nl.
New Zealand 180 Molesworth St, Wellington, T+64-4473 6390, www.hicomind.org.nz.
Singapore India House, 31 Grange Rd, T6737 6777, www.embassyofindia.com.
South Africa 852 Schoeman St, Arcadia, Pretoria 0083, T012-342 5392; Cape Town T021-419 8110, www.indiainsouthafrica.com.
Sri Lanka 36-38 Galle Rd, PO Box No. 882, Colombo 3, T+94-11-2327587, www.hcicolombo.org.
Switzerland Kirchenfeldstrasse 28, CH-3005 Bern, T031-351 1110, www.indembassybern.ch.
Thailand For visas call T026-652968, www.ivac-th.com.
UK India House, Aldwych, London, T020-7836 8484, www.hcilondon.net. Since May 2008, the visa application process has been outsourced

to VF Service UK with offices throughout UK (several in London, Birmingham, Manchester, Cardiff, Edinburgh, Glasgow). Submit visa applications online at http://in.vfsglobal.co.uk. Call centre T0905-757 0045.

USA 2107 Massachusetts Av, Washington DC 20008, T202-939 7000, www.indianembassy.org. Consulates: New York, T212-774 0600, San Francisco, T415-668 0662, Chicago, T312-595 0405, Houston, T713-840 0489. Outsource process for visa application.

Gay and lesbian travellers

In 2009 the Delhi High Court reversed a 148-year-old law criminalizing homosexual acts between men. Whilst this was a major breakthrough for the gay community, attitudes to homosexuality outside the big cities remain mired in religious conservatism and distrust. Although it is common to see young males holding hands in public, this rarely indicates a gay relationship and is usually an expression of friendship. Overt displays of affection between homosexuals (and indeed between heterosexuals) cause offence.

Health

Local populations in India are exposed to a range of health risks not encountered in the Western world. Many of the diseases are major problems for the local poor and destitute and, although the risk to travellers is more remote, they cannot be ignored. Obviously 5-star travel is going to carry less risk than backpacking on a budget.

Health care in the region is varied. There are many excellent private and government clinics/hospitals. As with all medical care, first impressions count. It's worth contacting your embassy or consulate on arrival and asking where the recommended (ie those used by diplomats) clinics are. You can also ask about locally recommended medical do's and don'ts. If you do get ill, and you have the opportunity, you should also ask your medical insurer whether they are satisfied that the medical centre/hospital you have been referred to is of a suitable standard.

Before you go

Ideally, you should see your GP or travel clinic at least 6 weeks before your departure for general advice on travel risks, malaria and vaccinations. Make sure you have travel insurance, get a dental check (especially if you are going to be away for more than a month), know your own blood group and if you suffer a long-term condition such as diabetes or epilepsy make sure someone knows or that you have a Medic Alert bracelet/necklace with this information on it. Remember that it is risky to buy medicinal tablets abroad because the doses may differ and India has a huge trade in false drugs.

A-Z of health risks

Altitude sickness can creep up on you as just a mild headache with nausea or lethargy during your visit to the Himalaya. The more serious disease is caused by fluid collecting in the brain in the enclosed space of the skull and can lead to coma and death. There is also a lung disease version with breathlessness and fluid infiltration of the lungs. The best cure is to descend as soon as possible. Preventative measures include getting acclimatized and not reaching the highest levels on your first few days of arrival. Try to avoid flying directly into the cities of highest altitude. Climbers like to take treatment drugs as protective measures but this can lead to macho idiocy and death. The peaks are still there and so are the trails, whether it takes you a bit longer than someone else does not matter as long as you come back down alive.

If you are unlucky (or careless) enough to receive a venomous **bite or sting** by a snake, spider, scorpion or sea creature, try to identify the creature, without putting yourself in further danger (do not try to catch a live snake). Snake bites in particular are very frightening, but in fact rarely poisonous – even venomous snakes bite without injecting venom. Victims should be taken to a hospital or a doctor without delay. Commercial snake bite and scorpion kits are available, but are usually only useful for the specific types of snake or scorpion. Most serum has to be given intravenously so it is not much good equipping yourself with it unless you are used to making injections into veins. It is best to rely on local practice in these cases, because the particular creatures will be known about locally and appropriate treatment can be given. To prevent bites, do not walk in snake territory in bare feet or sandals – wear proper shoes or boots. For scorpions and spiders, keep beds away from the walls and look inside your shoes and under the toilet seat every morning. Certain tropical sea fish when trodden upon inject venom into bathers' feet. This can be very painful. Wear plastic shoes if such creatures are reported. The pain can be relieved by immersing the foot in hot water (as hot as you can bear) for as long as the pain persists. Citric acid juices in fruits such as lemon are reported as being useful.

Chikungunya is a relatively rare mosquito-borne disease has become prevalent in several parts of India, including Kerala, Goa and Gujarat, particularly during the monsoon when flooded areas encourage the carrier mosquitoes to breed. The disease manifests within 12 days of infection and symptoms resemble a severe fever, with headaches, joint pain, arthritis and exhaustion lasting from several days to several weeks; in vulnerable sections of the population it can be fatal. Neither vaccine nor treatment are available, so rest is the best cure.

Unfortunately there is no vaccine against **dengue fever** and the mosquitoes that carry it bite during the day. You will be ill for 2-3 days, then get better for a few days and then feel ill again. It should all be over in 7-10 days. Heed all the anti-mosquito measures that you can.

The standard advice for **diarrhoea** prevention is to be careful with water and ice for drinking. If you have any doubts about where the water came from then boil it or filter and treat it. There are many filter/treatment devices now available on the market. Food can also transmit disease. Be wary of salads (what were they washed in, who handled them), re-heated foods or food that has been left out in the sun having been cooked earlier in the day. There is a simple adage that says wash it, peel it, boil it or forget it. Also be wary of unpasteurized dairy products, these can transmit a range of diseases from brucellosis (fevers and constipation), to listeria (meningitis) and tuberculosis of the gut (constipation, fevers and weight loss).

The key treatment with all diarrhoea is rehydration. Try to keep hydrated by taking the right mixture of salt and water. This is available as Oral Rehydration Salts (ORS) in ready-made sachets or can be made up by adding a teaspoon of sugar and a half teaspoon of salt to a litre of clean water. You can also use flat carbonated drinks. Drink at least 1 large cup of this drink for each loose stool. Alternatively, Immodium (or Pepto-Bismol, used a lot by Americans) is good if you have a long coach/train journey or on a trek, although is not a cure. Antibiotics like Ciproxin (Ciprofloaxcin) – obtained by private prescription in the UK – can be a useful antibiotic for some forms of travellers' diarrhoea. If it persists beyond 2 weeks, with blood or pain, seek medical attention. One good preventative is taking probiotics like Vibact or Bifilac which are available over the counter.

If you go **diving** make sure that you are fit to do so. The **British Sub-Aqua Club (BSAC)**, Telford's Quay, South Pier Rd, Ellesmere Port, Cheshire CH65 4FL, UK, T01513-506200, www.bsac.com, can put you in touch with doctors who do medical examinations. Protect your feet from cuts, beach dog parasites (larva migrans) and sea urchins. The latter are almost impossible to remove but can be dissolved with lime or vinegar. Keep an eye out for secondary infection. Check that the dive company know what they are doing, have appropriate certification from BSAC or **PADI**, Unit 7, St Philips Central, Albert Rd, St Philips, Bristol, BS2 OTD, T0117-300 7234, www.padi.com, and that the equipment is well maintained.

Hepatitis means inflammation of the liver. The most obvious symptom is a yellowing of your skin or the whites of your eyes. However, prior to this all that you may notice is itching and tiredness. Early on, depending on the type of hepatitis, a vaccine or immunoglobulin may reduce the duration of the illness. There are vaccines for hepatitis A and B; the latter spread through blood and unprotected sexual intercourse, both of these can be avoided. Unfortunately there is no vaccine for hepatitis C or the increasing alphabetical list of other hepatitis viruses.

If infected with **leishmaniasis**, you may notice a raised lump, which leads to a purplish discoloration on white skin and a possible ulcer. The parasite is transmitted by the bite of a sandfly. Sandflies do not fly very far and the greatest risk is at ground levels, so if you can avoid sleeping on the jungle floor do so, under a permethrin- treated net and use insect repellent. Seek advice for any persistent skin lesion or nasal symptom. Several weeks of treatment is required under specialist supervision.

Various forms of **leptospirosis** occur throughout the world, transmitted by a bacterium which is excreted in rodent urine. Fresh water and moist soil harbour the organisms, which enter the body through cuts and scratches. If you suffer from any form of prolonged fever consult a doctor.

Malaria has some seasonality but it is too unpredictable to not take malaria prophylaxis. In the UK we still believe that Chloroquine and Paludrine are sufficient for most parts of India, but the US disagree and recommend either Malarone, Mefloquine or Doxycycline.

For **mosquito repellents**, remember that DEET (Di-ethyltoluamide) is the gold standard. Apply the repellent 4-6 hrs but more often if you are sweating heavily. If a non-DEET product is used check who tested it. Validated products (tested at the London School of Hygiene and Tropical Medicine) include Mosiguard, Non-DEET Jungle formula and non-DEET Autan. If you want to use citronella remember that it must be applied very frequently (hourly) to be effective. If you are a target for insect bites or develop lumps quite soon after being bitten, carry an Aspivenin kit.

Prickly heat is a common intensely itchy rash, avoided by frequent washing and by wearing loose clothing. It is cured by allowing skin to dry off through use of powder – and spending a few nights in an a/c hotel.

Remember that **rabies** is endemic throughout certain parts of India, so avoid dogs that are behaving strangely and cover your toes at night from the vampire bats, which also carry the disease. If you are bitten by a domestic or wild animal, do not leave things to chance: scrub the wound with soap and water and/or disinfectant, try to at least determine the animal's ownership, where possible and seek medical assistance at once. The course of treatment depends on whether you have already been satisfactorily vaccinated against rabies. If you have (and this is worthwhile if you are spending lengths of time in developing countries) then some further doses of vaccine are all that is required. If you are not already vaccinated then anti-rabies serum (immunoglobulin) may be required in addition. It is important to finish the course of treatment.

The range of visible and invisible **sexually transmitted diseases** is awesome. Unprotected sex can spread HIV, hepatitis B and C, gonorrhea (green discharge), chlamydia (nothing to see but may cause painful urination and later female infertility), painful recurrent herpes, syphilis and warts, just to name a few. You can cut down the risk by using condoms, a femidom or avoiding sex altogether.

Make sure you protect yourself from the **sun** with high-factor sun screen and don't forget to wear a hat.

Ticks usually attach themselves to the lower parts of the body often after walking in areas where cattle have grazed. They swell up as they start to suck blood. The important thing is to remove them gently, so that they do not leave their head parts in your skin, because this can cause a nasty allergic reaction later. Do not use petrol, Vaseline, lighted cigarettes, etc to remove the tick, but, with a pair of tweezers remove the gently by gripping it at the attached (head) end and rock it out in very much the same way that a tooth is extracted.

Certain **tropical flies** which lay their eggs under the skin of sheep and cattle also occasionally do the same thing to humans with the unpleasant result that a maggot grows under the skin and pops up as a boil or pimple. The best way to remove these is to cover the boil with oil, Vaseline or nail varnish to stop the maggot breathing, then to squeeze it out gently the next day.

Vaccinations

If you need vaccinations, see your doctor well in advance of your travel. Most courses must be completed by a minimum of 4 weeks. Travel clinics may provide rapid courses of vaccination, but are likely to be more expensive. The following vaccinations are recommended: typhoid, polio, tetanus, infectious hepatitis and diptheria. For details of malaria prevention, see above.

The following vaccinations may also be considered: rabies, possibly BCG (since TB is still common in the region) and in some cases meningitis and diphtheria (if you're staying in the country for a long time). Yellow fever is not required in India but you may be asked to show a certificate if you have travelled from Africa or South America. Japanese encephalitis may be required for rural travel at certain times of the year (mainly rainy seasons). An effective oral cholera vaccine (Dukoral) is now available as 2 doses providing 3 months' protection.

Further information

Websites

Blood Care Foundation (UK), www.bloodcare.org.uk A Kent-based charity 'dedicated to the provision of screened blood and resuscitation fluids in countries where these are not readily available'. They will dispatch certified non-infected blood of the right type to your hospital/clinic. The blood is flown in from various centres around the world.

British Travel Health Association (UK), www.btha.org This is the official website of an organization of travel health professionals.

Fit for Travel, www.fitfortravel.scot.nhs.uk This site from Scotland provides a quick A-Z of vaccine and travel health advice requirements for each country.

Foreign and Commonwealth Office (FCO) (UK), www.fco.gov.uk This is a key travel advice site, with useful information on the country, people, climate and lists the UK embassies/consulates. The site also promotes the concept of 'know before you go' and encourages travel insurance and appropriate travel health advice. It has links to Department of Health travel advice site, see above.

The Health Protection Agency, www.hpa.org.uk Up-to-date malaria advice guidelines for travel around the world. It gives specific advice about the right drugs for each location. It also has useful information for those who are pregnant, suffering from epilepsy or planning to travel with children.

Medic Alert (UK), www.medicalalert.com This is the website of the foundation that produces bracelets and necklaces for those with existing medical problems. Once you have ordered your bracelet/necklace you write your key medical details on paper inside it, so that if you collapse, a medic can identify you as having epilepsy or a nut allergy, etc.

Travel Screening Services (UK), www.travelscreening.co.uk A private clinic dedicated to integrated travel health. The clinic gives vaccine, travel health advice, email and SMS text vaccine reminders and screens returned travellers for tropical diseases.

World Health Organisation, www.who.int The WHO site has links to the WHO Blue Book on travel advice. This lists the diseases in different regions of the world. It describes vaccination schedules and makes clear which countries have yellow fever vaccination certificate requirements and malarial risk.

Books

International Travel and Health World Health Organisation Geneva ISBN 92 4 158026 7.

Lankester, T, *The Travellers Good Health Guide*, ISBN 0-85969-827-0.

Warrell, D and Anderson, A (eds), *Expedition Medicine (The Royal Geographic Society)*, ISBN 1 86197 040-4.

Young Pelton, R, Aral, C and Dulles, W, *The World's Most Dangerous Places*, ISBN 1-566952-140-9.

Insurance

Buying insurance with your air ticket is the most costly way of doing things: better go to an independent. Ask your bank too; some now offer travel insurance for current account holders. See also the website www.dh.gov.uk/policyandguidance/healthadvicefortravellers.

If you are carrying specialist equipment – expensive cameras, VCRs, laptops – you will probably need to get separate cover for these items (otherwise you risk claims for individual items being limited to £250, not a good return on a digital SLR) unless they are covered by existing home contents insurance. It is always best to dig out all the receipts for these expensive personal effects. Take photos of the items and note down all serial numbers. Also check exactly what your medical cover includes, eg ambulance, helicopter rescue or emergency flights back home. Most importantly check for exclusions in the policy before you travel. You may find that even activities such as mountain biking are not covered and travellers would do well to note that drinking alcohol is likely to invalidate a claim in the event of an accident. Also check the payment protocol. You may have to pay first – known as an excess charge – before the insurance company reimburses you.

Always carry the telephone number of your insurer's 24-hr emergency helpline and your insurance policy number (and details).

Most annual policies have a trip limit of around a month. If you plan to be abroad for longer insurers including **Columbus, Direct Travel Insurance**, **Flexicover** and **Insure and Go** offer suitable cover. If travelling abroad several times in a year, an annual, worldwide insurance policy will save you money. A 45-year-old buying no-frills annual, worldwide cover can expect to pay between £55-110. A family of 4 should expect to pay £100-200. Prices vary widely so it is best to get several quotes before you buy.

Senior travellers should note that some companies will not cover people over 65, or may charge higher premiums.

Insurance companies

In North America

Young travellers from North America can try the **International Student Insurance Service** (**ISIS**), which is available through **STA Travel**, T1-800-777 0112, www.sta-travel.com. Other recommended travel insurance companies include: **Access America**, T1-800-284 8300, www.accessamerica.com; **Travel Assistance International**, T1-800-821 2828; **Travel Guard**, T1-800- 826 1300, www.noelgroup.com; **Travel Insurance Services**, T1-800-937 1387.

In the UK

STA Travel and other reputable student travel organizations offer good-value policies for students. There are also several companies who specialize in gap year travel insurance such as **Columbus Direct**, www.columbusdirect.com, **Down Under Travel Insurance**, www.duinsure.com, **Endsleigh**, www.endsleigh.co.uk, and **World Nomads**, www.worldnomads.com.

For standard insurance, you can compare policies from a wide selection of providers at www.moneysupermarket.com.

The best policies for UK senior travellers are offered by **Age Concern**, T0845-600 3348 and **Saga**, T0800-015 8055, www.saga.co.uk. Travellers with pre-existing medical conditions can try **MIA**, www.miatravelinsurance.co.uk, or **Medici**, www.medicitravel.com.

Internet

India is at the forefront of the technology revolution and raced to embrace the internet. In 2010, 100 million Indians were online, making it the 3rd largest user in the world, behind only the USA and China. You're never far from an internet café or PCO (public call office), which also offers the service. Note that internet cafés now require you to produce ID.

In small towns there is less internet access and it is recommended to take precautions: write lengthy emails in Word, save frequently, then paste them into your web-based email server rather than risking the loss of missives home when the power fails or the connection goes down. Browsing costs vary dramatically depending on the location: these can be anything from Rs 20-100, with most charging somewhere in between. As a rule, avoid emailing from upmarket hotels as their prices can be exorbitant unless you are a guest, in which case it's often free. Wi-Fi is spreading fast. Virtually all business-grade hotels, and an increasing number of mid-range and budget places, now boast a Wi-Fi connection, as do the Barista chain of cafés, major airports, and certain multinational fast food outlets.

If you intend to stay in India for a while, sign up for membership with the internet chain **I-way**.

Language

Hindi, spoken as a mother tongue by over 400 million people, is India's official language. The use of English is also enshrined in the Constitution for a wide range of official purposes, notably communication between Hindi and non-Hindi speaking states. The most widely spoken Indo-Aryan languages are: Bengali (8.3%), Marathi (8%), Urdu (5.7%), Gujarati (5.4%), Oriya (3.7%) and Punjabi (3.2%). Among the Dravidian languages Telugu (8.2%), Tamil (7%), Kannada (4.2%) and Malayalam (3.5%) are the most widely used. Most of these languages have their own scripts. In all, there are 15 major and several hundred minor languages and dialects.

English now plays an important role across India. It is widely spoken in towns and cities and even in quite remote villages it is usually not difficult to find someone who speaks at least a little English. Outside of major tourist sites, other European languages are almost completely unknown. The accent in which English is spoken is often affected strongly by the mother tongue of the speaker and there have been changes in common grammar which sometimes make it sound unusual. Many of these changes have become standard Indian English usage, as valid as any other varieties of English used around the world. It is possible to study a number of Indian languages at language centres.

See also page 1400. For Hindi words and phrases, food and drink and a glossary of terms, see page 1446.

Laundry

Laundry services are generally speedy and can be arranged very cheaply (eg a shirt washed and pressed for Rs 15-20 in **C-D** category; but Rs 50 or more in **LL-AL** hotels) and quickly (in 12-24 hrs). It is best not to risk delicate fibres, though luxury hotels can usually handle these and also dry clean items.

Media

International **newspapers** (mainly English language) are sold in the bookshops of top hotels in major cities and occasionally by booksellers elsewhere. India has a large and lively English language press. They all have extensive analysis of contemporary Indian and some international issues. The major papers now have websites, excellent for keeping track of events, news and weather.

The best known are the traditionalist *The Hindu*, www.hinduonline.com/today. *The Hindustan Times*, www.hindustantimes.com, the slightly more tabloid-establishment *Times of India*, www.timesofindia.com, and *The Statesman*, www.thestatesman.org. *The Economic Times* is good for world coverage. *The Telegraph*, www.telegraphindia.com, has good foreign coverage. *The Indian Express*, www.expressindia.com, stands out as being consistently critical of the Congress Party and the government. *The Asian Age* is now published in the UK and India simultaneously and gives good coverage of Indian and international affairs. Of the news weeklies, some of the most widely read are current affairs *India Today*, *Frontline* and *The Week*, which are journals in the *Time* or *Newsweek* mould. *Business Today* is of course economy-based, while *Outlook* has a broader remit and has good general interest features. There is also *Outlook Traveller*, probably the best of the domestic travel titles.

India's national **radio** and **television** network, *Doordarshan*, broadcasts in national and regional languages but things have moved on. The advent of cabel and satellite TV has brought live cricket, Bollywood music videos and vapid soap operas to the most remote corners of the country, and there are over 500 local broadcast television stations – each state has its own local-language current affairs broadcaster plus normally at least one other channel for entertainment. Even modest hotels in small towns now come with a cable connection as standard, making it easy for travellers to keep in touch with world news via *CNN* and *BBC World*, to waste time with Hollywood movies – even to learn yoga (see Guru TV box in Uttarakhand chapter, page 213).

Money

Indian currency is the Indian Rupee (Re/Rs). It is **not** possible to purchase these before you arrive. If you want cash on arrival it is best to get it at the airport bank (see page 27 for details of international airport facilities), although see if an ATM available as airport rates are not very generous. Rupee notes are printed in denominations of Rs 1000, 500, 100, 50, 20, 10. The rupee is divided into 100 paise. Coins are minted in denominations of Rs 5, Rs 2, Rs 1 and 50 paise. **Note** Carry money, mostly as travellers' cheques, in a money belt worn under clothing. Have a small amount in an easily accessible place.

Exchange rates *(Jun 2011)*

US$1 = Rs 44.7; UK £1 = Rs 73.5; AUS$1 = Rs 48; CAN$1 = Rs 45.6; NZ$1 = Rs 36.5; €1 = Rs 65.4.

Traveller's cheques (TCs)

TCs issued by reputable companies (eg **Thomas Cook**, **American Express**) are widely accepted. They can be easily exchanged at small local travel agents and tourist internet cafés but are rarely used directly for payment. Try to avoid

Money matters

It can be difficult to use torn or very worn notes. Check notes when you are given them and refuse any that are damaged.

Request some Rs 100 and 50 notes. Rs 500 (can be mistaken for Rs 100) notes reduce 'wallet bulge' but can be difficult to change. A good supply of small denomination notes always comes in handy for bus tickets, cheap meals and tipping. Remember that if offered a large note, the recipient will never have any change.

It can be worth carrying a few clean, new sterling or dollar notes for use where traveller's cheques and credit cards are not accepted. It is likely to be quite a while before euro notes are widely accepted.

changing at banks, where the process can be time consuming; opt for hotels and agents instead, take large denomination cheques and change enough to last for some days. Most banks, but not all, will accept US dollars, pounds sterling and euro TCs so it is a good idea to carry some of each. Other major currency TCs are also accepted in some larger cities. One traveller warns that replacement of lost Amex TCs may take weeks. If travelling to remote areas it can be worth buying Indian rupee TCs from a major bank, these are more widely accepted than foreign currency ones.

Credit cards

Major credit cards are increasingly acceptable in the main centres, though in smaller cities and towns it is still rare to be able to pay by credit card. Payment by credit card can sometimes be more expensive than payment by cash, whilst some credit card companies charge a premium on cash withdrawals. **Visa** and **MasterCard** have a growing number of ATMs in major cities and several banks offer withdrawal facilities for Cirrus and Maestro cardholders. It is however easy to obtain a cash advance against a credit card. Railway reservation centres in major cities take payment for train tickets by Visa card which can be very quick as the queue is short, although they cannot be used for Tourist Quota tickets.

ATMs

By far the most convenient method of accessing money, ATMs are all over India, usually attended by security guards, with most banks offering some services to holders of overseas cards. Banks whose ATMs will issue cash against Cirrus and Maestro cards, as well as Visa and MasterCard, include **Bank of Baroda**, **Citibank**, **HDFC**, **HSBC**, **ICICI**, **IDBI**, **Punjab National Bank**, **State Bank of India** (**SBI**), **Standard Chartered** and **UTI**. A withdrawal fee is usually charged by the issuing bank on top of the conversion charges applied by your own bank. Fraud prevention measures quite often result in travellers having their cards blocked by the bank when unexpected overseas transactions occur; advise your bank of your travel plans before leaving.

Changing money

The **State Bank of India** and several others in major towns are authorized to deal in foreign exchange. Some give cash against Visa/MasterCard (eg **ANZ**, **Bank of Baroda** who print a list of their participating branches, **Andhra Bank**). American Express cardholders can use their cards to get either cash or TCs in Mumbai and Chennai. They also have offices in Coimbatore, Goa, Hyderabad, and Thiruvananthapuram. The larger cities have licensed money changers with offices usually in the commercial sector. Changing money through unauthorized dealers is illegal. Premiums on the currency black market are very small and highly risky. Large hotels change money 24 hrs a day for guests, but banks often give a substantially better rate of exchange. It is best to exchange money on arrival at the airport bank or the Thomas Cook counter. Many international flights arrive during the night and it is generally far easier and less time consuming to change money at the airport than in the city. You should be given a foreign currency encashment certificate when you change money through a bank or authorized dealer; ask for one if it is not automatically given. It allows you to change Indian rupees back to your own currency on departure. It also enables you to use rupees to pay hotel bills or buy air tickets for which payment in foreign exchange may be required. The certificates are only valid for 3 months.

Transferring money to India

HSBC, **Barclays** and **ANZGrindlays** and others can make 'instant' transfers to their offices in India but charge a high fee (about US$30). **Standard Chartered Bank** issues US$ TCs. Sending a bank draft (up to US$1000) by post is the cheapest option.

Cost of living

The cost of living in India remains well below that in the West. The average wage per capita is about Rs 34,000 per year (US$800). Manual, unskilled labourers (women are often paid less than men), farmers and others in rural areas earn considerably less. However, thanks to booming global demand for workers who can provide cheaper IT and technology support functions and many Western firms transferring office functions or call centres to India, salaries in certain sectors have sky rocketed. An IT specialist can earn an average Rs 500,000 per year and upwards – a rate that is rising by around 15% a year.

Cost of travelling

Most food, accommodation and public transport, especially rail and bus, is exceptionally cheap, although inflation in 2010 was 16.3% and basic food items such as rice, lentils, tomatoes and onions have skyrocketed. There is a widening range of moderately priced but clean hotels and restaurants outside the big cities, making it possible to get a great deal for your money. Budget travellers sharing a room, taking public transport, avoiding souvenir stalls, and eating nothing but rice and dhal can get away with a budget of Rs 400-600 (about US$8-12 or £5-8) a day. This sum leaps up if you drink alcohol (still cheap by European standards at about US$2, £1 or Rs 80 for a pint), smoke foreign-brand cigarettes or want to have your own wheels (you can expect to spend between Rs 150 and 200 to hire a Honda per day). Those planning to stay in fairly comfortable hotels and use taxis sightseeing should budget at US$50-80 (£30-50) a day. Then again you could always check into **Ananda Spa** or the **Taj Falaknuma** for Christmas and notch up an impressive US$600 (£350) bill on your B&B alone. India can be a great place to pick and choose, save a little on basic accommodation and then treat yourself to the type of meal you could only dream of affording back home. Also, be prepared to spend a fair amount more in Mumbai, Hyderabad, Bengaluru (Bangalore) and Chennai, where not only is the cost of living significantly higher but where it's worth coughing up extra for a half-decent room: penny-pinch by the beach when you'll be spending precious little time indoors anyway. A newspaper costs Rs 5 and breakfast for 2 with coffee can come to as little as Rs 50 in a South Indian 'hotel', but if you intend to eat banana pancakes or pasta beside a Goan beach, you can expect to pay more like Rs50-150 a plate.

Opening hours

Banks are open Mon-Fri 1030-1430, Sat 1030-1230. Top hotels sometimes have a 24-hr money changing service. Post offices open Mon-Fri 1000-1700, often shutting for lunch, and Sat mornings. Government offices Mon-Fri 0930-1700, Sat 0930-1300 (some open on alternate Sat only). Shops open Mon-Sat 0930-1800. Bazars keep longer hours.

Post

The post is frequently unreliable, and delays are common. It is best to use a post office where you can hand over mail for franking across the counter, or a top hotel post box. Valuable items should only be sent by registered mail. Government emporia or shops in the larger hotels will send purchases home if the items are difficult to carry. Seamail and Book Post have been on hold since Jan 2008 because of the Somali pirate situation – best to check for availability.

Airmail services to Europe, Africa and Australia take at least a week and a little longer for the Americas. Speed post (which takes about 4 days to the UK) is available from major towns. Speed post to the UK from Tamil Nadu costs Rs 675 for the first 250g sent and an extra Rs 75 for each 250g thereafter. Specialist shippers deal with larger items, normally around US$150 per cubic metre. Courier services (eg **DHL**) are available in the larger towns. At some main post offices you can send small packages under 2 kg as **letter post** (rather than parcel post), which is much cheaper at Rs 220. Check that the post office holds necessary customs declaration forms (2-3 copies needed). Write 'No commercial value' if returning used clothes, books etc. **Sea mail**, see above, costs Rs 800 for 10 kg. 'Packers' at or near the post office do necessary cloth covering, sealing etc for Rs 20-50; you address the parcel, obtain stamps from a separate counter; stick stamps and a customs form to the parcel with the provided glue (the other form/s must be partially sewn on). Post at the Parcels Counter and obtain a registration slip. Cost varies by destination and is normally displayed on a board beside the counter. Sea Mail is currently being phased out to be replaced by **SAL** (Surface Air Lifted). The prices are fractionally lower than airmail, Rs 500-600 for the first kg and Rs 150-250 per extra kg. Delivery can take up to 2 months.

Poste restante facilities are widely available in even quite small towns at the GPO where mail is held for 1 month. Ask for mail to be addressed to you with your surname in capitals and underlined. When asking for mail at Poste Restante check under surname as well as christian name.

Safety

Personal security

In general the threats to personal security for travellers in India are remarkably small. However, incidents of petty theft and violence directed specifically at tourists have been on the increase so care is necessary in some places, and basic common sense needs to be used with respect to looking after valuables. Follow the same precautions you would when at home. There have been incidents of sexual assault in and around the main tourist beach centres, particularly after full moon parties in South India. Avoid wandering alone outdoors late at night in these places. During daylight hours be careful in remote places, especially when alone. If you are under threat, scream loudly. Be very cautious before accepting food or drink from casual acquaintances, as it may be drugged.

Some parts of India are subject to political violence. The Vale of Kashmir and Jammu remains under tight military control. Even when the border area is relatively quiet, very few hotels are open in Srinagar and the army is massively deployed and on constant alert. Despite the promises of travel touts that Kashmir is completely safe, tourists who visit do so at considerable risk and are subjected to regular curfews. There is no prospect of an early solution to the political problem or of a quick return to normality. Some areas have long been noted for banditry.

The left-wing Maoist extremist Naxalites are active in east central and southern India. They have a long history of conflict with state and national authorities, including attacks on police and government officials. The Naxalites have not specifically targeted Westerners, but have attacked symbolic targets including Western companies. As a general rule, travellers are advised to be vigilant in the lead up to and on days of national significance, such as Republic Day (26 Jan) and Independence Day (15 Aug) as militants have in the past used such occasions to mount attacks.

Following a major explosion on the Delhi to Lahore (Pakistan) train in Feb 2007 and the Mumbai attacks in Nov 2008, increased security has been implemented on many trains and stations. Similar measures at airports may cause delays for passengers so factor this into your timing. Also check your airline's website for up-to-date information on luggage restrictions. In Mumbai, the UK's Foreign and Commonwealth Office warns of a risk of armed robbers holding up taxis travelling along the main highway from the airport to the city in the early hours of the morning (0200-0600) when there is little traffic on the roads. If you are using the route during these times, you should, if possible, arrange to travel by coach or seek advice at the airport on arrival.

That said, in the great majority of places visited by tourists, violent crime and personal attacks are extremely rare.

Travel advice

It is better to seek advice from your consulate than from travel agencies. Before you travel you can contact: **British Foreign & Commonwealth Office Travel Advice Unit**, T0845-850 2829 (Pakistan desk T020-7270 2385), www.fco.gov.uk. **US State Department's Bureau of Consular Affairs** Overseas Citizens Services, Room 4800, Department of State, Washington, DC 20520-4818, USA, T202-647 1488, http://travel.state.gov. **Australian Department of**

Foreign Affairs Canberra, Australia, T02-6261 3305, www.smartraveller.gov.au. Canadian official advice is on www.voyage.gc.ca.

Theft

Theft is not uncommon. It is best to keep TCs, passports and valuables with you at all times. Don't regard hotel rooms as being automatically safe; even hotel safes don't guarantee secure storage. Avoid leaving valuables near open windows even when you are in the room. Use your own padlock in a budget hotel when you go out. Pick-pockets and other thieves operate in the big cities. Crowded areas are particularly high risk. Take special care of your belongings when getting on or off public transport.

If you have items stolen, they should be reported to the police as soon as possible. Keep a separate record of vital documents, including passport details and numbers of TCs. Larger hotels will be able to assist in contacting and dealing with the police. Dealings with the police can be very difficult and in the worst regions such as Bihar even dangerous. The paperwork involved in reporting losses can be time consuming and irritating and your own documentation (eg passport and visas) may be demanded.

In some states the police occasionally demand bribes, though you should not assume that if procedures move slowly you are automatically being expected to offer a bribe. The traffic police are tightening up on traffic offences in some places. They have the right to make on-the-spot fines for speeding and illegal parking. If you face a fine, insist on a receipt. If you have to go to a police station, try to take someone with you.

If you face really serious problems (eg in connection with a driving accident), contact your consular office as quickly as possible. You should ensure you always have your international driving licence and motorbike or car documentation with you.

Confidence tricksters are particularly common where people are on the move, notably around railway stations or places where budget tourists gather. A common plea is some sudden and desperate calamity; sometimes a letter will be produced in English to back up the claim. The demands are likely to increase sharply if sympathy is shown. See also Shopping, page 45.

Travel safety

Motorcycles don't come fitted with helmets and accidents are commonplace so exercise caution, the horn and the brake. Horns carry their own code: pip to make pedestrians, stray dogs and other bikers (you hear little over your own engine) aware you're about to overtake or hold a screaming continuous note to communicate urgent alarm to anything fast bearing down on you – even then be prepared to dive from the tarmac.

First-class compartments on **trains** are self-contained and normally completely secure, although nothing of value should be left close to open train windows. 2- and 3-tier a/c compartments are larger, allowing more movement of passengers and are therefore not so secure. Most thefts occur in non-a/c sleeper class carriages. Attendants may take little notice of what is going on, and thefts – particularly on the Goa–Hampi and Delhi–Varanasi–Kolkata train route – are on the rise, so luggage should be chained to a seat for security overnight and care taken in daylight. Locks and chains are easily available at main stations and bazars. Travelling bags and cases should be made of tough material, and external pockets (both on bags and on clothing) should never be used for carrying either money or important documents. Strong locks for travelling cases are invaluable. Use a leather strap around a case for extra security. Some travellers prefer to reserve upper berths, which offer some added protection against theft and also the benefit of allowing daytime sleeping. If you put your bags on the upper berth during the day, beware of fellow passengers climbing up for a 'sleep'. Be guarded with new friends on trains who show particular interest in the contents of your bag and be extra wary of accepting food or drink from casual acquaintances; travellers have reported being drugged and then robbed. Pickpockets and other thieves operate in crowded areas.

Senior travellers

Travellers over 60 can take advantage of several discounts on travel, including 30% on train fares and up to 50% on some air tickets. Ask at the time of booking, since these will not be offered automatically.

Smoking

Several state governments have passed a law banning smoking in all public buildings and transport but exempting open spaces. To avoid fines, check for notices.

Student travellers

Full-time students qualify for an ISIC (International Student Identity Card) which is issued by student travel and specialist agencies (eg Usit, Campus, STA) at home. The card allows certain travel benefits such as reduced prices and concessions into certain sites. For details see www.isic.org or contact **STIC** in Imperial Hotel, Janpath, New Delhi, T011-2334 3302. Those intending to study in India may get a year's student visa (see page 68). For details of student travel insurance, see page 55.

Telephone

The international code for India is +91. International Direct Dialling is widely available in privately run call booths, usually labelled on yellow boards with the letters 'PCO-STD-ISD'. You dial the call yourself, and the time and cost are displayed on a computer screen. Cheap rate (2100-0600) means long queues may form outside booths. Telephone calls from hotels are usually more expensive (check price before calling), though some will allow local calls free of charge. Internet phone booths, usually associated with cybercafés, are the cheapest way of calling overseas.

A double ring repeated regularly means it is ringing; equal tones with equal pauses means engaged (similar to the UK). If calling a mobile, rather than ringing, you might hear music while you wait for an answer.

One disadvantage of the tremendous pace of the telecommunications revolution is the fact that millions of telephone numbers go out of date every year. Current telephone directories themselves are often out of date and some of the numbers given in this book will have been changed even as we go to press. Our best advice is if the number in the text does not work, add a '2'. **Directory enquiries**, T197, can be helpful but works only for the local area code.

Mobile phones are for sale everywhere, as are local SIM cards that allow you to make calls within India and overseas at much lower rates than using a 'roaming' service from your normal provider at home – sometimes for as little as Rs 0.5 per min. Arguably the best service is provided by the government carrier **BSNL/MTNL** but security provisions make connecting to the service virtually impossible for foreigners. Private companies such as **Airtel**, **Vodafone**, **Reliance** and **Tata Indicom** are easier to sign up with, but the deals they offer can be befuddling and are frequently changed. To connect you'll need to complete a form, have a local address or receipt showing the address of your hotel, and present photocopies of your passport and visa plus 2 passport photos to an authorized reseller – most phone dealers will be able to help, and can also sell top-up. **Univercell**, www.univercell.in, and **The Mobile Store**, www.themobilestore.in, are 2 widespread and efficient chains selling phones and sim cards.

India is divided into a number of 'calling circles' or regions, and if you travel outside the region where your connection is based, eg from Delhi into Rajasthan, you will pay higher charges for making and receiving calls, and any problems that may occur – with 'unverified' documents, for example – can be much harder to resolve.

Time

India doesn't change its clocks, so from the last Sun in Oct to the last Sun in Mar the time is GMT +5½ hrs, and the rest of the year it's +4½ hrs (USA, EST +10½ and +9½ hrs; Australia, EST -5½ and -4½ hrs).

Tipping

A tip of Rs 10 to a bellboy carrying luggage in a modest hotel (Rs 20 in a higher category) would be appropriate. In upmarket restaurants, a 10% tip is acceptable when service is not already included, while in places serving very cheap meals, round off the bill with small change. Indians don't normally tip taxi drivers but a small extra is welcomed. Porters at airports and railway stations often have a fixed rate displayed but will usually press for more. Ask fellow passengers what a fair rate is.

Tourist information

There are **Government of India** tourist offices in the state capitals, as well as state tourist offices (sometimes **Tourism Development Corporations**) in the major cities and a few important sites. They produce their own tourist literature, either free or sold at a nominal price, and some also have lists of city hotels and paying guest options. The quality of material is improving though maps are often poor. Many offer tours of the city, neighbouring sights and overnight and regional packages. Some run modest hotels and midway motels with restaurants and may also arrange car hire and guides. The staff in the regional and local offices are usually helpful.

Tourist offices overseas

Australia Level 5, Glasshouse,135 King St, Sydney, NSW 2000, T02-9221 9555, info@indiatourism.com.au.
Canada 60 Bloor St West, Suite No 1003, Toronto, Ontario, T416-962 3787, indiatourism@bellnet.ca.
Dubai 6 Post Box 12856, NASA Building, Al Maktoum Rd, Deira, T04-227 4848, goirto@emirates.net.ae.
France 11-13 Bis Boulevard Hausmann, 75009, Paris T01-4523 3045.
Germany Baserler St 48, 60329, Frankfurt AM-Main 1, T069-242 9490, www.india-tourism.de.
Italy Via Albricci 9, Milan 20122, T02-805 3506, info@indiatourismmilan.com.
Japan B9F Chiyoda Building, 1-8-17 Ginza, Chuo-Ku, Tokyo 104-0061, T03-3561 0651, indiatourt@smile.ocn.ne.jp.
The Netherlands Rokin 9-15, 1012 KK Amsterdam, T020-620 8991, info@indiatourismamsterdam.com.
Singapore 20 Kramat Lane, 01-01A United House, 228773, Singapore, T6235-3800, indtour.sing@pacific.net.sg.
South Africa Hyde Lane, Lancaster Gate, Johannesburg, T011-325 0880, goito@global.co.za.
UK 7 Cork St, London WIS 3LH, T020-74373677, T08700-102183, london5@indiatouristoffice.org.
USA 3550 Wilshire Blvd, Room 204, Los Angeles, California 90010, T213-380 8855, goitola@aol.com; Suite 1808, 1270 Av of Americas, New York, NY 10020-1700, T212-5864901, ny@itonyc.com.

Also check out www.incredibleindia.org for information.

Tour operators

In the UK

Ace, T01223-835055, www.acestudytours.co.uk. Expert-led cultural study tours.
The Adventure Company, Cross and Pillory House, Cross and Pillory Lane, Alton, GU34 1HL, T0845-450 5316, www.adventurecompany.co.uk. Adventure tours, small groups.
Colours Of India, Marlborough House, 298 Regent's Park Rd, London, N3 2TJ, T020- 8347 4020, www.partnershiptravel.co.uk. Tailor-made cultural, adventure, spa and cooking tours.
Cox & Kings (Taj Group), T020-7873 5000, www.coxandkings.co.uk.
Dragoman, T01728-861133, www.dragoman.com. Overland, adventure, camping.
Exodus, T0208-675 5550, www.exodus.co.uk. Small group overland and trekking tours.
Greaves Tours, 53 Welbeck St, London, T020-7487 9111, www.greavesindia.com. Luxury, tailor-made tours using only scheduled flights. Traditional travel such as road and rail preferred to flights between major cities.
Guerba Expeditions, T01373-826611, www.guerba.co.uk. Adventure, treks and aiming to be carbon neutral.
India Beat, B-4 Vijay Path, Tilak Nagar, Jaipur 302004, T0141-651 9797, www.indiabeat.co.uk. Winner of the Conde Nast Traveler Top Travel Specialist Award for the last few years, you are in good hands with Victoria and Bertie at Indiabeat. They offer a unique insight into India and have a reliable team to help you with tours all over India.
Indian Explorations, Afex House, Holwell, Burford, Oxfordshire, OX18 4JS, T01993-822443, www.indianexplorations.com. Bespoke holidays, including to the Andaman Islands and Rajasthan.
Kerala Connections, School House Lane, Horsmonden, Kent, TN12 8BP, T01892-722 440, www.keralaconnections.co.uk. Excellent tailor-made tours throughout India, including Lakshadweep and Andaman Islands, with great homestays. Also trades under the name **Select Connections**, www.selectconnections.co.uk.

Kuoni, Kuoni House, Dorking, Surrey, RH5 4AZ, T01306-747002, www.kuoni.co.uk, and subsidiary upmarket brand **Voyage Jules Vernes**, www.vjv.co.uk. Runs week-long culture and relaxation tours.
MAHout, The Manor, Manor Rd, Banbury, T01295-758 150, www.mahoutuk.com. Boutique hotels representation specialist.
Master Travel, T0800-587 7329, www.mastertravel.co.uk. History, Ayurveda.
Metropole Travel Services, 224, Defence Colony Flyover Market, New Delhi-110024, T011-2431 0313, www.metrovista.co.in. Years of experience and a wide range of tours throughout North India. Also offers car hire, reliable information and has a couple of great B&Bs in Delhi.
On the Go Tours, 68 North End Rd, London, W14 9EP, T020-7371 1113, www.onthego tours.com. Legendary tours and tailor-made itineraries at amazing prices.
Palanquin Travels, T020-7436 9343, www.palanquin.co.uk. Historical and cultural tours led by expert academics.
Pettitts, T01892-515966, www.pettitts.co.uk. Unusual locations.
Red Dot Tours, Orchard House, Folly Lane, Bramham, Leeds, LS23 6RZ, T0113-815 1864, www.reddottours.com. Tailor-made specialist in Kerala and Rajasthan. Also organizes flights and cricket tours.
STA Travel, T0871-230 0040, www.statravel. co.uk. Student and young persons' travel agent.
Steppes Discovery, 51 Castle St, Cirencester, GL7 1QD, T01285-643333, www.steppes discovery.co.uk. Wildlife safaris, tiger study tours and cultural tours with strong conservation ethic.
Steppes Travel, 51 Castle St, Cirencester, Gloucestershire, GL7 1QD, T01285-880980, www.steppestravel.co.uk.
Trans Indus, 75 St Mary's Rd and the Old Fire Station, Ealing, London, W5 5RH, T020-8566 3739, www.transindus.com. Upmarket India travel specialists offering tailor-made and group tours and holidays. Unusual locations.
Travel the Unknown, T020-8823 0705, www.traveltheunknown.com. Excellent tours to rarely travelled destinations especially in Northeast India.
W&O Travel, Welby House, 96 Wilton Rd, London, SW1V 1DW, T0845-277 3344, www.wandotravel.com. Specialist tour company covering India and the Indian Ocean.

In India

Aquaterra Adventures, S-507, ground floor, Greater Kailash-II, New Delhi, T011-2921 2641, www.treknraft.com. Trekking, rafting, kayaking, etc, in all Indian Himalayan states.
Banyan Tours and Travels, www.banyan tours.com. Pan-Indian operator specializing in bespoke, upmarket travel, with strength in culture, heritage, adventure and wildlife.
The Blue Yonder, T080-4115 2218, www.theblueyonder.com. Highly regarded and award-winning sustainable and community tourism operators, active in Kerala, Sikkim, Orissa and Rajasthan.
Dynamic Tours, Suite 206, Rakesh Deep, 11 Commercial Complex, Gulmohar Enclave, New Dehli 110 049, T011-2685 3760,

www.adventure-india.com, www.indian tiger.com. Members of WelcomHeritage and TOFT. Resident naturalist on site. Offers jungle safaris, birdwatching and tailor-made holidays.

Help Tourism, Kolkata/Siliguri/Guwahati, T033-2455 0917, www.helptourism.com. Eco-tours in Assam, Arunachal and North Bengal, involving local communities.

Ibex Expeditions, 30 Community Centre, East of Kailash, New Delhi 110 065, T011-2646 0244, T011-2646 0246, www.ibexexpeditions.com. Award-winning eco-aware tour operator for tours, safaris and treks.

Indebo India, 116-117 Aurobindo Pl, Hauz Khas, New Delhi 110016, T011-4716 5500, www.indebo.com. Customized tours and travel-related services throughout India.

KOKO India, www.kokoindia.com. Based in Goa, but offering unique holidays around India – from yoga and reiki to belly dancing and horse safaris, also creative retreats for aspiring writers and photographers.

Paradise Holidays, 312 Ansals Classique Tower, Rajouri Garden, New Delhi 110027, T011-4552 0735/6/7/8, www.paradiseholidays.com. Wide range of tailor-made tours, from cultural to wildlife.

Parul Tour & Travels, 32 Lal Ghat, Udaipur 313001, T0294-242 1697, www.rajasthan travelbycab.com. Ticketing, reservations and escorted tours in Rajasthan and South India.

Pepper Tours, House No 127, Subash Chandra Bose Rd, Jawahar Nagar, Kadavanthara, PO Cochin 682020, T0484-405 8886, www.peppertours.com. Memorable journeys in Kerala, Rajasthan and Goa.

Peter and Friends Classic Adventures, Casa Tres Amigos Assagao 403 507, Goa, www.classic-bike-india.com. An Indo-German company which arranges high-octane tours around South India, Rajasthan and the Himalaya and Nepal on Enfield motorbikes.

Purple Valley Yoga Center, Assagao, www.yogagoa.com. Retreats of 1-2 weeks and drop-in yoga classes with international ashtanga teachers like John and Lucy Scott.

Purvi Discovery, Jalannagarh, Dibrugarh, Assam, T0373-230 1120, www.purviweb.com, www.assamteatourism.com. Experienced in tours to Arunachal, Assam and other northeast destinations. A quality outfit with quality accommodation.

Pyramid Tours, 'Deccan Dreams', B-3, Jyothi Complex, 134/1, Infantry Rd, Bangalore, T080-2286 7589, www.pyramidsdeccan.com. Academics as guides. Heritage, nature, culture and rejuvenation packages. Specialists in homestays.

Royal Expeditions, 26 Community Center (11th floor), East of Kailash, New Delhi 110065, T91-11-2623 8545; USA T1-404-993 6116, Latin America T55-11-9209 9720), www.royalexpeditions.com. Tailor-made tours in culture, wildlife and photography. Specializes in easy options for senior travellers.

Sundale Vacations, 39/5955A, Atlantis Jn, MG Rd, Cochin-682015, Kerala, T0484-235 9127/235 8735, www.sundale.com. A mix of unusual accommodation, cultural activities and sightseeing tours in Kerala.

Weeks Tours, T12/1463A, Cochin, Kerala, T0484-222 0168, www.weekstour.com. Good tours.

In North America

Adventures Abroad, T1-800-665 3998, www.adventures-abroad.com.

Absolute Asia, 180 Varick St, 16th floor, New York, T1-800-736-8187, www.absoluteasia.com. Luxury custom-designed tours: culinary, pilgrimage of the south, honeymoon, 'Jewish India' tour plus Tamil tour combining Tamil Nadu with Sri Lanka.

General Tours, 53 Summer St, Keene, New Hampshire, T1-800-221-2216, www.general tours.com. Packages include Kerala spas, houseboats and wildlife, South India and Karnataka, South India and Tamil Nadu, Goa.

Greaves Tours, 121 W Wacker Dr, Chicago, T1-800-318 7801. See under UK entry, above.

Myths and Mountains, T1-800-670 6984, www.mythsandmountains.com. Culture, crafts and religion.

Relief Riders International, T1-413-329 5876, www.reliefridersinternational.com. Unique horseback tours through the Thar Desert of Rajasthan, with guests working as support staff to a full-scale aid mission.
Sita World Travel, 350 Fifth Av, Suite 1421, New York, T1-800-421-5643, www.sitatours.com. Top-end packages like 7-day Ayurveda programmes and Trails of South India tour.
Spirit of India, USA T1-888-3676147, www.spirit-of-india.com. General and spirituality-focused tours, local experts.

In Australia and New Zealand

Adventure World, 73 Walkers St, North Sydney, T1300-295049, www.adventureworld.com.au. Independent tour operator with packages from 7 nights in Kerala. Also 101 Great South Rd, Remuera, Auckland, T64-9524 5118, www.adventureworld.co.nz.
India Unbound, 40 Leithead St, Brunswick, Victoria, T1300-889513, www.indiaunbound.com.au. Intriguing range of small-group trips and bespoke private tours.
Intrepid Travel, 11-13 Spring St, Fitzroy, Victoria 3065, T1300-364 512, www.intrepidtravel.com. Cookery courses to village stays.
Peregrine Adventures, Australia, T03-8601 4444, www.peregrineadventures.com. Small group overland and trekking tours.

In Europe

Academische Reizen, World Travel Holland, Academische Reizen BV, Prinsengracht 783-785, 1017 JZ Amsterdam, T020-589 2940, www.academischereizen.nl. All-India group culture tours.
Chola Voyages, 190, rue du Faubourg St Denis, 75010 Paris, T01-4034 5564, delamanche@hotmail.com.
La Maison Des Indes, 7 Place St Sulpice, 75006 Paris, T01-5681 3838, www.maisondesindes.com. Bespoke or group cultural tours.
The Shoestring Company, Meidoornweg 2, 1031 GG Amsterdam, T020-685 0203, info@shoestring.nl. Group leisure and adventure tours.

Visas and immigration

For embassies and consulates, see page 51. Virtually all foreign nationals, including children, require a visa to enter India. Nationals of Bhutan and Nepal only require a suitable means of identification. The rules regarding visas change frequently and arrangements for application and collection also vary from town to town so it is essential to check details and costs with the relevant embassy or consulate. These remain closed on Indian national holidays. Now many consulates and embassies are outsourcing the visa process, it's best to find out in advance how long it will take. For example, in London where you used to be able to get a visa in person in a morning if you were prepared to queue, it now takes 2-3 working days and involves 2 trips to the office.

At other offices, it can be much easier to apply in advance by post, to avoid queues and frustratingly low visa quotas. Postal applications can 15 working days to process.

Visitors from countries with no Indian representation may apply to the resident British representative, or enquire at the **Air India** office. An application on the prescribed form should be accompanied by 2 passport photographs and your passport which should be valid 6 months beyond the period of your visit. Note that visas are valid from the date granted, not from the date of entry. For up-to-date information on visa requirements visit www.india-visa.com.

No foreigner needs to register within the 180-day period of their tourist visa. All foreign visitors who stay in India for more than 180 days need to get an income tax clearance exemption certificate from the Foreign Section of the Income Tax Department in Delhi, Mumbai, Kolkata or Chennai.

Currently the following visa rules apply:
Transit For passengers en route to another country (no more than 72 hrs in India).
Tourist Normally valid for 3-6 months from date of issue, though some nationalities may be granted visas for up to 5 years. Multiple entries permitted, but a new rule requires a 2-month wait before you can return to India. The rule doesn't apply if you plan to visit neighbouring countries as part of your trip (eg Nepal, Sri Lanka), but you need clear documentation proving your itinerary.
Business 3-6 months or up to 2 years with multiple entry. A letter from the company giving the nature of business is required.

5 year For those of Indian origin only, who have held Indian passports.

Student Valid up to 1 year from the date of issue. Attach a letter of acceptance from Indian institution and an AIDS test certificate. Allow up to 3 months for approval.

Visa extensions Applications should be made to the Foreigners' Regional Registration Offices at New Delhi, Mumbai, Kolkata or Chennai, or an office of the Superintendent of Police in the District Headquarters. After 6 months, you must leave India and apply for a new visa – the Nepal office is known to be difficult. Anyone staying in India for a period of more than 180 days (6 months) must register at a convenient Foreigners' Registration Office.

Permits and restricted and protected areas

Some areas are politically sensitive and special permits may be needed to visit them though the government is relaxing its regulations. The border regions, tribal areas and Himalayan zones are subject to restrictions and special permits may be needed to visit them.

Currently, only Arunachal Pradesh requires foreigners to have a Restricted Area Permit (RAP) to enter. Apply to the Under Secretary, Ministry of Home Affairs, Foreigners Division, Lok Nayak Bhavan, Khan Market, New Delhi 110003, at least 4 weeks in advance. Since Jan 2011, special permission is no longer required for foreign nationals to enter Manipur, Mizoram or Nagaland on a year's trial basis. For more information, see box page 693. For the **Andaman Islands**, permits are issued for 30 days to visit some of the islands on arrival at Port Blair, see page 838. Of the **Lakshadweep Islands**, foreigners may visit Bangaram and Suheli Islands only; permits from the Lakshadweep Administration, Willingdon Island, Harbour Rd, Cochin 3. For **Sikkim**, permits for 15 days are issued by a large number of government offices; see box, pages 661 and 669.

Work permits

Foreigners should apply to the Indian representative in their country of origin for the latest information about work permits.

Liquor permits

Periodically some Indian states have tried to enforce prohibition. To some degree it is in force in Gujarat, Manipur, Mizoram and Nagaland. When applying for your visa you can ask for an All India Liquor Permit. Foreigners can also get the permit from any Government of India Tourist Office in Delhi or the state capitals. Instant permits are issued by some hotels.

Weights and measures

Metric is in universal use in the cities. In remote areas local measures are sometimes used. One lakh is 100,000 and 1 crore is 10 million.

Women travellers

Independent travel is still largely unheard of for Indian women. Although it is relatively safe for women to travel around India, most people find it an advantage to travel with a companion. Even then, privacy is rarely respected and there can be a lot of hassle, pressure and intrusion on your personal space, as well as some outright harassment. Backpackers setting out alone often meet like-minded travelling companions at budget hotels. Cautious women travellers recommend dying blonde hair black and wearing wedding rings, but the most important measure to ensure respect is to dress appropriately, in loose-fitting, non-see-through clothes, covering shoulders, arms and legs (such as a *salwaar kameez*, which can be made to fit in around 24 hrs for around Rs 400-800). Take advantage, too, of the gender segregation on public transport, to avoid hassle and to talk to local women. In mosques women should be covered from head to ankle. **Independent Traveller**, T0870-760 5001, www.independenttraveller.com, runs women-only tours to India.

'Eve teasing', the euphemism for physical harassment, is an unfortunate result of the sexual repression latent in Indian culture, combined with a young male population whose only access to sex education is via the dingy cybercafés. Unaccompanied women are most vulnerable in major cities, crowded bazars, beach resorts and tourist centres where men may follow them and touch them; festival nights are particularly bad for this. Women have reported that they have been molested while being measured for clothing in tailors' shops. If you are harassed, it can be effective to make a scene. Be firm and clear if you don't wish to speak to someone. The best response to staring, whether lascivious or curious, is to avert your eyes down and away. This is not the submissive gesture it might seem, but an effective tool to communicate that you have no interest in any further interaction. Aggressively staring back or confronting the starer can be construed as a come-on. It is best to be accompanied at night, especially when travelling by rickshaw or taxi in towns. Be prepared to raise an alarm if anything unpleasant threatens.

Most railway booking offices have separate women's ticket queues or ask women to go to the head of the general queue. Some buses have seats reserved for women. See also page 48.

Working in India

See also Visas and immigration, page 68.
It is best to arrange voluntary work well in advance with organizations in India (addresses are given in some towns, eg Delhi, Darjeeling, Dharamshala, Kolkata and Leh); alternatively, contact an organization abroad.

Students may spend part of their year off helping in a school or teaching English

Voluntary work

Some charitable organizations, including **Share and Care** and **Salaam Baalak** (see page 49) also take volunteers.

In the UK

i to i, Woodside House, 261 Low Lane, Leeds, LS18 5NY, T0800-011 1156, www.i-to-i.com.
International Voluntary Service IVS GB, Thorn House, 5 Rose St, Edinburgh, EH2 2PR, T0131-243 2745.
VSO, 317 Putney Bridge Rd, London, SW15 2PN, www.vso.org.uk.
Volunteer Work Information Service, T01273 479 047, www.workingabroad.com.

In the USA

Amerispan, 1334 Walnut St, 6th floor, Philadelphia, PA 19107, T1-800-879 6640, www.amerispan.com. Volunteer placements in Delhi and Jaipur.
Council for International Programs, 1700 East 13th St, Suite 4ME, Cleveland, Ohio, T216-566-1088, www.cipusa.org.

In Australia

www.ampersand.org.au has links to volunteer organizations, of which the biggest is:
Australian Volunteers International, 71 Argyle St, Fitzroy, VIC 3065, T03-9279 1788, www.australianvolunteers.com.

Delhi

Contents

Footprint features

At a glance

Getting around Metro, taxi and bus (the latter only off peak). Hiring a car and driver saves much haggling with rickshaw drivers.

Time required At least 3 days to explore Old Delhi and the key museums and archaeological sites.

Weather Cold winters and foggy mornings, staggeringly hot in May and Jun. Oct and Mar are best.

When not to go It's too hot to enjoy Delhi in the weeks prior to the monsoon.

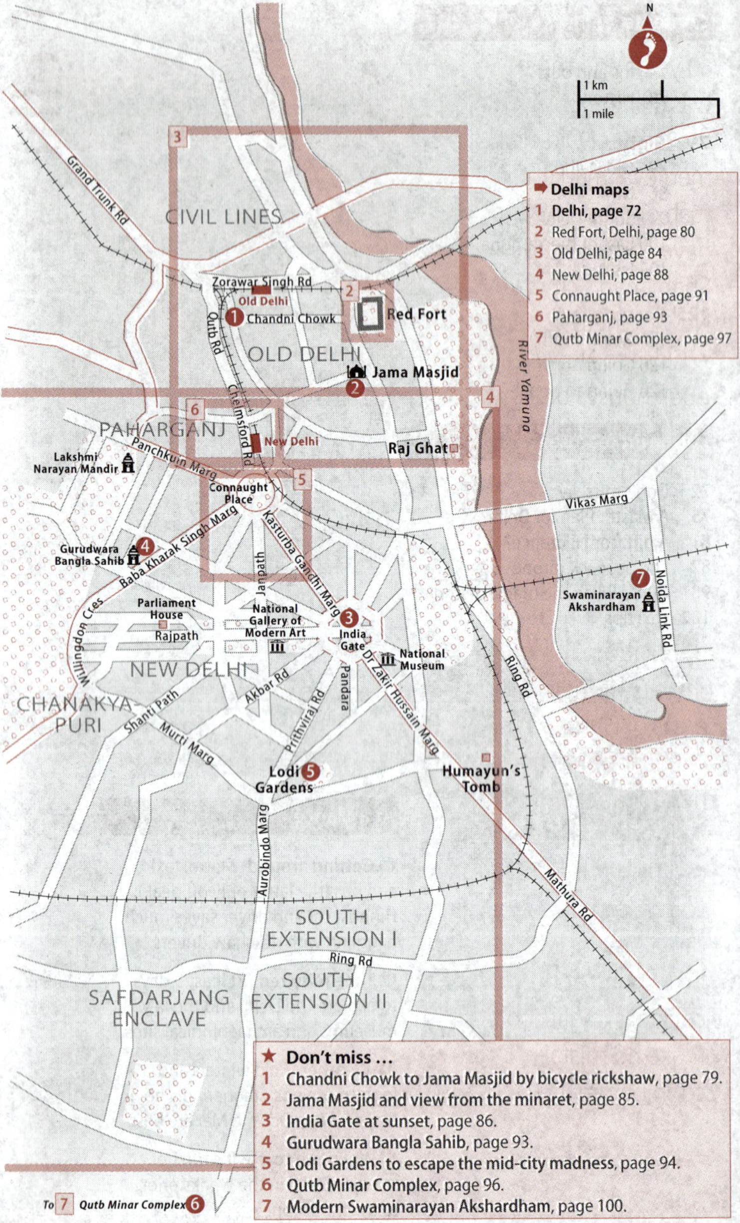

Delhi maps

★ **Don't miss ...**

1. Chandni Chowk to Jama Masjid by bicycle rickshaw, page 79.
2. Jama Masjid and view from the minaret, page 85.
3. India Gate at sunset, page 86.
4. Gurudwara Bangla Sahib, page 93.
5. Lodi Gardens to escape the mid-city madness, page 94.
6. Qutb Minar Complex, page 96.
7. Modern Swaminarayan Akshardham, page 100.

Delhi can take you aback with its vibrancy and growth. Less than 60 years ago the spacious, quiet and planned city of New Delhi was still the pride of late colonial British India, while to its north, the lanes of Old Delhi resonated with the sounds of a bustling medieval market. Today, both worlds have been overtaken by the rush of modernization. As Delhi's population surges, its tentacles have spread in all directions – from both the ancient core of Shahjahan's city in the north and the late British capital of New Delhi to its south.

Close to New Delhi Railway Station, the cheap hotels and guesthouses of Paharganj squeeze between cloth merchants and wholesalers. In Old Delhi, further north, with the Red Fort and Jama Masjid, the old city is still a dense network of narrow alleys and tightly packed markets and houses. Your senses are bombarded by noise, bustle, smells and apparent chaos. A 'third city' comprises the remorselessly growing squatter settlements (*jhuggies*), which provide shelter for more than a third of Delhi's population. To the south is another, newer, chrome-and-glass city, the city of the modern suburbs and urban 'farms', where the rural areas of Gurgaon have become the preserve of the prosperous, with shopping malls, banks and private housing-estates. Old and new, simple and sophisticated, traditional and modern, East and West are juxtaposed. Whatever India you are looking for, the capital has it all – getting lost in warrens of crowded streets, wandering through spice markets, eating kebabs by the beautiful Jama Masjid, lazing among Mogul ruins, listening to Sufi musicians by a shrine at dusk or shopping in giant shining malls, drinking cocktails in glitzy bars and travelling on the gleaming metro. But make no mistake, Delhi is developing at breakneck speed – visit soon before it changes beyond recognition (see box, page 75).

Ins and outs → *Phone code: 011; dial 1952, then the old number, to get the new phone number. Colour map 1, C3. Population: 16.8 million. Area: 434 sq km. Directory enquiries: T197/1952.*

Getting there

Delhi is served by **Indira Gandhi International (IGI) Airport**, which handles both international and domestic traffic. The Domestic Terminal 1, 15 km from the centre, handles flights from two separate sections: 'A', exclusively for **Air India** and 'B' for others. The new T3 has one of the longest runways in Asia and is connected to the city centre by metro. It is about 23 km from the centre. During the day, it can take 30-45 minutes from the Domestic Terminal and 45 minutes to an hour from the International Terminal to get to the centre. With the metro, it should take 20 minutes. A free shuttle runs between the terminals. To get to town take a pre-paid taxi (see Transport, page 120) or an airport coach or ask your hotel to collect you.

The **Inter State Bus Terminus (ISBT)** is at Kashmere Gate, near the Red Fort, about 30 minutes by bus from Connaught Place. Local buses connect it to the other ISBTs.

There are three main railway stations. The busy **New Delhi Station**, a 10-minute walk north of Connaught Place, can be maddeningly chaotic; you need to have all your wits about you. The quieter **Hazrat Nizamuddin** (which has some south-bound trains) is 5 km southeast of Connaught Place. The overpoweringly crowded **Old Delhi Station** (2 km north of Connaught Place) has a few important trains. ▸▸ *See Transport, page 119.*

Getting around

The new Metro is making the sprawling city very navigable: it's now possible to get from Connaught Place to Old Delhi in a cool five minutes; while CP to Qutb Minar is about 30 minutes and all the way down to the final stop in Gurgaon is about one hour. It is a strange experience to go from air-conditioned high tech to the bustling streets of Chandi Chowk. Out to the airport from New Delhi train station in about 20 minutes. There is a women-only carriage at the front of each train, clearly marked inside and on the platform – this prevents women from having to succumb to the crush of the other carriages. There is a fine of Rs 250 for men ignoring all the signs in pink and in early 2011, a posse of women made men do sit-ups on the train for trespassing into the pink zone! Like any city metro service, try and avoid rush hour if you can. At each metro station you have to go through airport-like security and have your bag x-rayed, etc.

Auto-rickshaws and taxis are widely available, though few are prepared to use their meters, especially for foreigners. It's best to use pre-paid stands at stations, airport terminals and at the junction of Radial Road 1 and Connaught Place if possible, otherwise be sure to agree a fare before you get in. The same applies to cycle rickshaws, which ply the

A Master Plan for Delhi?

A tale of two cities – anyone arriving in Delhi in the few months building up to the 2010 Commonwealth Games who got stuck in endless detours, had to dodge falling masonry in Connaught Place and negotiate piles of rubble while staring into the open fronts of buildings sliced off in Paharganj's Main Bazar would have to pinch themselves now as they arrive in the sparkly new T3 at Indira Gandhi Airport and jump on the metro into downtown Delhi.

The going did not look good at the start of the Commonwealth Games with the media reporting on the shoddy workmanship, collapsing flyovers and the words "filthy and unhygenic" imprinted in the memories of incoming travelers from all over the world. Chief Minister Sheila Dikshit announced plans to clear Delhi of 60,000 beggars in a move reminiscent of the 'beautification' dreamt up by Indira Gandhi during the state of emergency back in 1975. In the aftermath, there have been investigations into every backhander, kickback and dodgy dealing.

"When the world came visiting, we could've showcased how we manage poverty, instead of pretending it doesn't exist", says Shoma Chaudhury, managing editor of *Tehelka* magazine. "We could have showcased how we live in a proud, integrated city, instead of pretending it was a doll's house. Those who wish to turn Delhi into Dubai and Mumbai into Shanghai must remember: a great and unsustainable ugliness underpins their artificial beauty."

Thing is the average guy on the street in India knows that their politicians are corrupt and as they secured an unprecedented medal tally and the games closed without incident, President Pratibha Patil and Delhiites at large saw the whole shenanigans as a great success.

And beyond that Delhi is a new city post CWG. The games were a catalyst in improving the city's infrastructure. As well as T3 and the metro taking the pressure off the streets, three million new trees were planted, 1100 new low floorboard buses have taken to the avenues and the road network of Delhi has been widened and lengthened by about 25%. Surekha Narain who conducts walking tours in Delhi feels "Delhi is a much more polished city than it was".

Delhi's population is expected to exceed 23 million by 2021. In a city that averages six power cuts a day during summer, where almost half the population lacks access to an organized sewerage system, and which may have already outgrown its capacity to supply water, the recent wave of hectic growth is unlikely to prove sustainable.

The Delhi Development Authority (DDA) has released a marvelously quixotic Master Plan, which prescribes solutions to the problems of housing, land acquisition for industry and commercial developments, provision of green space, air and noise pollution, waste disposal and parking. But with 75% of Delhi already violating previous Master Plans, it is difficult to see how enforcing such a plan in the face of endemic corruption and vested interests will ever be possible.

Delhi 2050 is a think tank led by Dutch architect Anne Feenstra – they have created an exhibition of architectural models and scenarios showcasing Delhi in 40 years time. One future scenario is a Delhi which is 'copy-paste Dubai, more inequality, less healthy, more aggression', but this is counterbalanced by four positive scenarios including 'heritage city', 'profit city' and 'self-sustained city'. Feenstra does not want to create another Master Plan, but they do want to create debate, ultimately they want to get people thinking about the future of their city.

streets of Old Delhi. City buses are usually packed and have long queues. Be on your guard from thieves around New Delhi Station. State Entry Road runs from the southern end of Platform 1 to Connaught Place. This is a hassle-free alternative to the main Chelmsford Road during the day (gate closed at night). Also watch your change or cash interactions even at the prepaid booths – sometimes they do a switch of a Rs 100 note for a Rs 10 for example. Fleets of Radio Taxis are the

Delhi Metro

Jahangir Puri
Ardash Nagar
Azadpur
Rithala
Rohini West
Model Town
GTB Nagar
Rohini East
Pitampura
Vishwavidyalaya
Kohat Enclave
Netaji Subhash Place
Vidhan Sabha
Keshav Puram
Kanhaiya Nagar
Nangloi Railway Station
Pratap Nagar
Civil Lines
Surajmal Stadium
Paschim Vihar East
Shivaji Park
Ashok Park Main
Inderlok
Tis Hazari
Kashmere Ga
Mundka
Peeragarhi
Rajdhani Park
Nangloi
Udyog Nagar
Paschim Vihar West
Madipur
Punjabi Bagh
Shastri Nagar
Pulbangash
Shastri Pa
Chandni Chowk
Satguru Ram Singh Marg
Pulbangash
Moti Nagar
Kirti Nagar
Chawri Baza
Shadipur
Rajendra Place
Jhandewalan
New Delhi
Rajouri Garden
Ramesh Garden
Patel Nagar
Karol Bagh
Ramakrishna Ashram Marg
Rajiv Chowk
Barakhamb Road
Tagore Garden
Subhash Nagar
Shivaji Stadium
Patel Chowk
Central Secretariate
Mandi House
Janakpuri East
Tilak Nagar
Udyog Bhawan
Khan Marke
Uttam Nagar West
Janakpuri West
Race Course
Dwarka Mor
Nawada
Uttam Nagar East
Jor Bagh
JLN Stadium
Dwarka
INA
Dhaula Kuan
Dwarka Sector 14
Dwarka Sector 13
AIIMS
Dwarka Sector 11
Delhi Aero City
Green Park
Dwarka Sector 12
Hauz Khas
Dwarka Sector 9
Dwarka Sector 10
Malviya Nagar
IGI Airport
Dwarka Sector 8
Saket
Dwarka Sector 21
Qutab Minar
Chhattarpur
Sultanpur
Ghitorni
IFFCO Chowk
Sikanderpur
Arjangarh
MG Road
Guru Dronacharya
HUDA City Centre

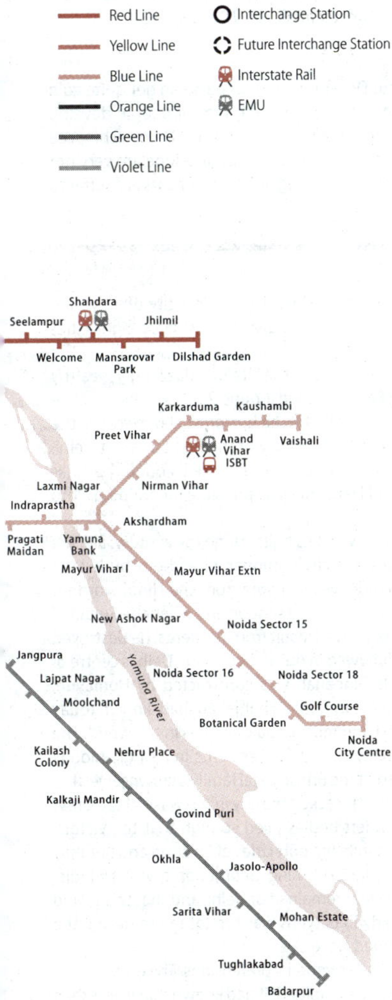

newest additions to the city's transport options. These include: **Mega Cabs**, T011-4141 4141; **Delhi Cab**, T011-4433 3222; **Easy Cab**, T011-4343 4343; **Quick Cab**, T011-4533 3333. ▸▸ *See Transport, page 119.*

Orientation

The **Red Fort** and **Jama Masjid** are the focal point of Old Delhi, 2 km northeast of Connaught Place. Chandni Chowk, the main commercial area, heads west from the fort. Around this area are narrow lanes packed to the rafters with all different types of wares for sale. To the southeast are **New Delhi Railway Station** and the main backpackers' area, **Paharganj**, with **Connaught Place**, the notional 'centre' of New Delhi, about 1 km south. Running due south of Connaught Place is **Janpath** with small shops selling craft products, and hotels like the **Imperial**. Janpath is intersected by **Rajpath** with all the major state buildings at its western end. Immediately south is the diplomatic enclave, **Chanakyapuri**. Most of the upmarket hotels are scattered across the wide area between Connaught Place and the airport to the southwest. As Delhi's centre of gravity has shifted southwards, a series of new markets has grown up to serve extensive housing colonies such as **South Extension**, **Greater Kailash** and **Safdarjang Enclave**. This development has brought one of the major historic sites, the **Qutb Minar**, within the limits of the city, about half an hour by taxi south of Connaught Place. **Gurgaon** which is strictly not in Delhi but in Haryana, is the new business hub with many shopping malls to boot.

Tourist information

Most tourist offices are open Monday-Friday 1000-1800 www.delhitourism.com. **Government of India Tourist Office** ⓘ *88 Janpath, T011-332 0005, Mon-Sat 0900-1800*, helpful, issues permits for visits to Rashtrapati Bhavan and gardens. Also at International Airport. **Delhi Tourism** ⓘ *N-36 Connaught Pl, T011-2331 5322*, (touts pester you to use one of many imposters; correct office is directly opposite 'Competent House'); **Coffee Home Annexe** ⓘ *Baba Kharak Singh Marg, T011-336 5358; hotel, transport and tour bookings*

T011-2462 3782, 0700-2100; also at Airport Terminals; Inter-State Bus Terminal; **New Delhi Railway Station** ⓘ *T011-2373 2374*; **Nizamuddin Railway Station** ⓘ *T011-2251 1083*. **India Tourism Development Corporation** (ITDC) ⓘ *L-1 Connaught Circus, T011-2332 0331*.

Best time to visit

October to March are the best months to visit, but December and January can get quite cold and foggy at night. Pollution can affect asthma sufferers – in fact a lot of people develop respiratory problems and sore throats if they spend more than a few days in Delhi; echinacea can help. Monsoon lasts from the end of June to mid-September. May and June are very hot and dry and with the whole city switching on its air-condioning units, power cuts are suffered more frequently at this time.

History

In the modern period, Delhi has only been India's capital since 1911. It is a city of yo yo-ing fortunes and has been repeatedly reduced to rubble. There have been at least eight cities founded on the site of modern Delhi.

According to Hindu mythology, Delhi's first avatar was as the site of a dazzlingly wealthy city, Indraprastha, mentioned in the Mahabharata and founded around 2500 BC. The next five cities were to the south of today's Delhi. First was Lalkot, which, from 1206, became the capital of the Delhi Sultanate under the Slave Dynasty. The story of the first Sultan of Delhi, Qutb-ud-din Aybak, is a classic rags-to-riches story. A former slave, he rose through the ranks to become a general, a governor and then Sultan of Delhi. He is responsible for building Qutb Minar, but died before its completion.

The 1300s were a tumultuous time for Delhi, with five cities built during the century. Siri, the first of these, has gruesome roots. Legend has it that the city's founder, Ala-ud-din, buried the heads of infidels in the foundation of the fort. Siri derives its name from the Hindi word for 'head'. After Siri came Tughlaqabad, whose existence came to a sudden end when the Sultan of Delhi, Muhammad Tughlaq, got so angry about a perceived insult from residents, he destroyed the city. The cities of Jahanpanah and Ferozebad followed in quick succession. Delhi's centre of gravity began to move northwards. In the 1500s Dinpanah was constructed by Humayun, whose wonderful tomb (1564-1573) graces Hazrat Nizamuddin. Shahjahanabad, known today as Old Delhi, followed, becoming one of the richest and most populous cities in the world. The Persian emperor Nadir Shah invaded, killing as many as 120,000 residents in a single bloody night and stealing the Kohinoor Diamond (now part of the British royal family's crown jewels).

The next destroyers of Delhi were the British, who ransacked the city in the wake of the Great Uprising/Mutiny of 1857. The resulting bloodbath left bodies piled so high that the victors' horses had to tread on them. For the next 50 years, while the port cities of Calcutta and Bombay thrived under the British, Delhi languished. Then, in 1911, King George, on a visit to India, announced that a new city should be built next to what remained of Delhi, and that this would be the new capital of India. The British architect Edwin Lutyens was brought in to design the city. You could argue that the building hasn't stopped since ...

The central part of New Delhi is an example of Britain's imperial pretensions. The government may have been rather more reticent about moving India's capital, if it had known that in less than 36 years time, the British would no longer be ruling India. Delhi's population swelled after the violence of partition, with refugees flooding to the city. In 10 years the population of Delhi doubled, and many well-known housing colonies were built during this period.

The economic boom that began in the 1990s has lead to an explosion of construction and soaring real estate prices. Delhi is voraciously eating into the surrounding countryside. It is a city changing at such breakneck speed that shops, homes and even airports seem to appear and disappear almost overnight. Go now and witness the changes as they happen.

Sights

The sites of interest are grouped in three main areas. In the centre is the British-built capital of New Delhi, with its government buildings and wide avenues. The heart of Shahjahanabad (Old Delhi) is about 2 km north of Connaught Circus. Ten kilometres to the south is the Qutb Minar complex, with the old fortress city of Tughluqabad, 8 km to its east. Across the Yamuna River is the remarkable new Akshardham Temple. You can visit each separately, or link routes together into a day-tour to include the most interesting sites. ▸▸ *For listings, see pages 102-124.*

Old Delhi

Shah Jahan (ruled 1628-1658) decided to move back from Agra to Delhi in 1638. Within 10 years the huge city of **Shahjahanabad**, now known as Old Delhi, was built. The plan of Shah Jahan's new city symbolized the link between religious authority enshrined in the Jama Masjid to the west, and political authority represented by the Diwan-i-Am in the Fort, joined by Chandni Chowk, the route used by the emperor. The city was protected by rubble-built walls, some of which still survive. These walls were pierced by 14 main gates. The **Ajmeri Gate**, **Turkman Gate** (often referred to by auto-rickshaw wallahs as 'Truckman Gate'), **Kashmere Gate** and **Delhi Gate** still survive.

Chandni Chowk

Shahjahanabad was laid out in blocks with wide roads, residential quarters, bazars and mosques. Its principal street, Chandni Chowk, had a tree-lined canal flowing down its centre which became renowned throughout Asia. The canal is long gone, but the jumble of shops, alleys crammed with craftsmen's workshops, food stalls, mosques and temples, cause it to retain some of its magic. A cycle rickshaw ride gives you a good feel of the place. Make sure you visit Naughara Street, just off Kinari Bazar, one of the most atmospheric streets in Delhi, full of brightly painted and slowly crumbling *havelis*.

The impressive red sandstone façade of the **Digambar Jain Mandir** (temple) standing at the eastern end of Chandni Chowk, faces the Red Fort. Built in 1656, it contains an image of Adinath. The charitybird hospital within this compound releases the birds on recovery instead of returning them to their owners; many remain within the temple precincts (www.charity birdshospital.org). Beyond Shahjahanabad to its north lies Kashmiri Gate, Civil lines and the Northern Ridge. The siting of the railway line which effectively cut Delhi into two unequal parts was done deliberately. The line brought prosperity, yet it destroyed the unity of the walled city forever. The northern ridge was the British cantonment and Civil Lines housed the civilians. In this area the temporary capital of the British existed from 1911-1931 till New Delhi came. The Northern ridge is a paradise for birds and trees. Follow the **Mutiny Trail** by visiting Flagstaff Tower, Pir Ghaib, Chauburj, Mutiny Memorial. Around Kashmire Gate and Civil Lines, you can discover the Old Residency, St James Church, Nicholson's cemetery and Qudsia Bagh.

Red Fort (Lal Qila)

ⓘ *Tue-Sun sunrise to sunset, Rs 250 foreigners, Rs 10 Indians, allow 1 hr. The entrance is through the Lahore Gate (nearest the car park) with the admission kiosk opposite; keep your ticket as you will need to show it at the Drum House. There are new toilets inside, best to avoid ones in Chatta Chowk. You must remove shoes and cover all exposed flesh from your shoulders to your legs.*

Between the new city and the River Yamuna, Shah Jahan built a fort. Most of it was built out of red *lal* (sandstone), hence the name **Lal Qila** (Red Fort), the same as that at Agra on which the Delhi Fort is modelled. Begun in 1639 and completed in 1648, it is said to have cost Rs 10 million, much of which was spent on the opulent marble palaces within. In recent years much effort has been put into improving the fort and gardens, but visitors may be saddened by the neglected state of some of the buildings, and the gun-wielding soldiers lolling around do nothing to improve the ambience. However, despite the modern development of roads and shops and the never-ending traffic, it's an impressive site.

The approach The entrance is by the Lahore Gate. The defensive barbican that juts out in front of it was built by Aurangzeb, see page 1389. A common story suggests that Aurangzeb built the curtain wall to save his nobles and visiting dignitaries from having to walk – and bow – the whole length of Chandni Chowk, for no one was allowed to ride in the presence of the emperor. When the emperor sat in the Diwan-i-Am he could see all the way down the Chowk, so the addition must have been greatly welcomed by his courtiers. The new entrance arrangement also made an attacking army more vulnerable to the defenders on the walls.

2 Red Fort, Delhi

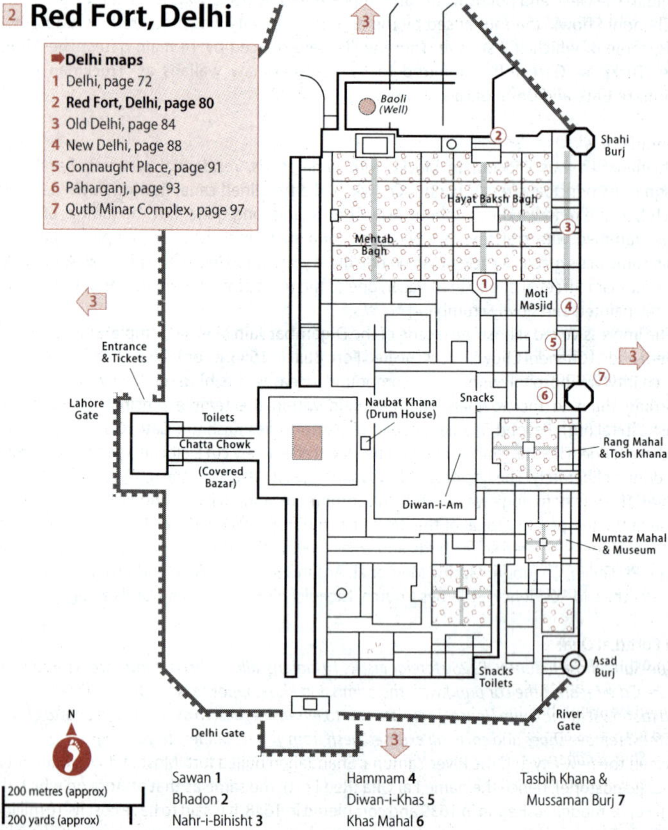

A gift from Florence?

There are 318 Florentine pietra dura plaques in the niche behind the throne, showing flowers, birds and lions as well as the central figure of Orpheus, playing to the beasts. In between these Italian panels are Mughal pietra dura works with flowery arabesques and birds. Ebba Koch argues that the techniques employed by the Mughal artisans are exactly the same as the Italian ones, so there must have been a direct connection.

This is not to say that there was no independent development of Mughal inlay craftsmanship. Such a view has been described by Tillotson as the result of wishful thinking by Europeans, eager to claim a stake in the superb work. In fact the Mughals had an equally fine tradition of stone carving and of inlay work on which to draw as the Florentine princes, as can be seen from the work in the Jama Masjid in Ahmedabad, built in 1414.

Chatta Chowk and the Naubat Khana Inside is the **Covered Bazar**, which was quite exceptional in the 17th century. In Shah Jahan's time there were shops on both upper and lower levels. Originally they catered for the Imperial household and carried stocks of silks, brocades, velvets, gold and silverware, jewellery and gems. There were coffee shops too for nobles and courtiers.

The **Naubat Khana** (Naqqar Khana) (Drum House or music gallery) marked the entrance to the inner apartments of the fort. Here everyone except the princes of the royal family had to dismount and leave their horses or *hathi* (elephants), hence its other name of **Hathi Pol** (Elephant Gate). Five times a day ceremonial music was played on the kettle drum, *shahnais* (a kind of oboe) and cymbals, glorifying the emperor. In 1754 Emperor Ahmad Shah was murdered here. The gateway with four floors is decorated with floral designs. You can still see traces of the original panels painted in gold or other colours on the interior of the gateway.

Diwan-i-Am Between the first inner court and the royal palaces at the heart of the fort, stood the **Diwan-i-Am** (Hall of Public Audience), the furthest point the normal visitor would reach. It has seen many dramatic events, including the destructive whirlwind of the Persian Nadir Shah in 1739 and of Ahmad Shah the Afghan in 1756, and the trial of the last 'King of Delhi', **Bahadur Shah II** in 1858.

The well-proportioned hall was both a functional building and a showpiece intended to hint at the opulence of the palace itself. In Shah Jahan's time the sandstone was hidden behind a very thin layer of white polished plaster, *chunam*. This was decorated with floral motifs in many colours, especially gilt. Silk carpets and heavy curtains hung from the canopy rings outside the building, such interiors reminders of the Mughals' nomadic origins in Central Asia, where royal durbars were held in tents.

At the back of the hall is a platform for the emperor's throne. Around this was a gold railing, within which stood the princes and great nobles separated from the lesser nobles inside the hall. Behind the throne canopy are 12 marble panels inlaid with motifs of fruiting trees, parrots and cuckoos. Figurative workmanship is very unusual in Islamic buildings, and these panels are the only example in the Red Fort.

As well as matters of official administration, Shah Jahan would listen to accounts of illness, dream interpretations and anecdotes from his ministers and nobles. Wednesday was the day of judgement. Sentences were often swift and brutal and sometimes the punishment of dismemberment, beating or death was carried out on the spot. The executioners were close at hand with axes and whips. On Friday, the Muslim holy day, there would be no business.

Shah Jahan spent two hours a day in the Diwan-i-Am. According to Bernier, the French traveller, the emperor would enter to a fanfare and mount the throne by a flight of movable steps.

The peacock throne

In the centre of the Diwan-i-Khas (5) is a marble pedestal on which stood the Peacock Throne that Shah Jahan commissioned on his accession in 1627. It took seven years to make. The throne was designed with two peacocks standing behind with a parrot carved out of a single emerald between them. It was inlaid with a vast number of precious stones – sapphires, rubies, emeralds, pearls and diamonds. Over the top was a gem-encrusted gold canopy edged with pearls, supported by 12 pillars.

The throne was carried off by Nadir Shah, a Turk, who after conquering Persia sacked Delhi in 1739. Soon after his occupation of Delhi a riot broke out in which 900 of his soldiers were killed. Nadir Shah himself rode through the streets of Delhi to assess the situation when some residents were rash enough to throw stones at him. Enraged, Nadir Shah ordered the entire population of Delhi to be massacred, resulting in 30,000 dead. In the evening the 'Great' Mughal (Mohammad Shah) begged for mercy, and such was Nadir Shah's control over his troops that he was able immediately to halt the carnage. The invaders took with them as much as they could extort from all the nobles. Bahadur Shah later replaced the throne with a poor copy. The Peacock Throne itself was broken up by Nadir Shah's assassins in 1747; some of the jewels are believed to have been incorporated into the late Shah of Iran's throne.

Inner palace buildings Behind the Diwan-i-Am is the private enclosure of the fort. Along the east wall, overlooking the River Yamuna, Shah Jahan set six small palaces (five survive). Also within this compound are the Harem, the Life-Bestowing Garden and the Nahr-i-Bihisht (Stream of Paradise).

Life-Bestowing Gardens (Hayat Baksh Bagh) The original gardens were landscaped according to the Islamic principles of the Persian *char bagh*, with pavilions, fountains and water courses dividing the garden into various but regular beds. The two pavilions **Sawan** and **Bhadon**, named after the first two months of the rainy season (July-August), reveal something of the character of the garden. The garden used to create the effect of the monsoon and contemporary accounts tell us that in the pavilions, some of which were especially erected for the **Teej** festival, which marks the arrival of the monsoon, the royal ladies would sit in silver swings and watch the rains. Water flowed from the back wall of the pavilion through a slit above the marble shelf and over the niches in the wall. Gold and silver pots of flowers were placed in these alcoves during the day whilst at night candles were lit to create a glistening and colourful effect.

Shahi Burj From the pavilion next to the Shahi Burj (**Royal Tower**) the canal known as the **Nahr-i-Bihisht** (Stream of Paradise) began its journey along the Royal Terrace. The three- storey octagonal tower was seriously damaged in 1857 and is still unsafe. In Shah Jahan's time the Yamuna lapped the walls. Shah Jahan used the tower as his most private office and only his sons and a few senior ministers were allowed with him.

Moti Masjid To the right are the three marble domes of Aurangzeb's 'Pearl Mosque' (shoes must be removed). Bar the cupolas, it is completely hidden behind a wall of red sandstone, now painted white. Built in 1662 of polished white marble, it has some exquisite decoration. All the surfaces are highly decorated in a fashion similar to rococo, which developed at the same time as in Europe. Unusually the prayer hall is on a raised platform with inlaid outlines of individual *musallas* ('prayer mats') in black marble. While the outer walls were aligned to the cardinal points like all the other fort buildings, the inner walls were positioned so that the mosque would correctly face Mecca.

Hammam The **Royal Baths** have three apartments separated by corridors with canals to carry water to each room. The two flanking the entrance, for the royal children, had hot and cold baths. The room furthest away from the door has three basins for rose water fountains.

Diwan-i-Khas Beyond is the single-storeyed **Hall of Private Audience**, topped by four Hindu-style *chhattris* and built completely of white marble. The *dado* (lower part of the wall) on the interior was richly decorated with inlaid precious and semi-precious stones. The ceiling was silver but was removed by the Marathas in 1760. Outside, the hall used to have a marble pavement and an arcaded court. Both have gone.

This was the Mughal office of state. Shah Jahan spent two hours here before retiring for a meal, siesta and prayers. In the evening he would return to the hall for more work before going to the harem. The hall's splendour moved the 14th-century poet Amir Khusrau to write the lines inscribed above the corner arches of the north and south walls: "*Agar Firdaus bar rue Zamin-ast/Hamin ast o Hamin ast o Hamin ast*" (If there be a paradise on earth, it is here, it is here, it is here).

Royal palaces Next to the Diwan-i-Khas is the three-roomed **Khas Mahal** (Private Palace). Nearest the Diwan-i-Khas is the **Tasbih Khana** (Chamber for the Telling of Rosaries) where the emperor would worship privately with his rosary of 99 beads, one for each of the mystical names of Allah. In the centre is the Khwabgah (Palace of Dreams) which gives on to the octagonal **Mussaman Burj** tower. Here Shah Jahan would be seen each morning. A balcony was added to the tower in 1809 and here George V and Queen Mary appeared in their Coronation Durbar of 1911. The **Tosh Khana** (Robe Room), to the south, has a beautiful marble screen at its north end, carved with the scales of justice above the filigree grille. If you are standing with your back to the Diwan-i-Khas you will see a host of circulating suns (a symbol of royalty), but if your back is to the next building (the Rang Mahal), you will see moons surrounding the scales. All these rooms were sumptuously decorated with fine silk carpets, rich silk brocade curtains and lavishly decorated walls. After 1857 the British used the Khas Mahal as an officer's mess and sadly it was defaced.

The **Rang Mahal** (Palace of Colours), the residence of the chief *sultana*, was also the place where the emperor ate most of his meals. It was divided into six apartments. Privacy and coolness were ensured by the use of marble *jali* screens. Like the other palaces it was beautifully decorated with a silver ceiling ornamented with golden flowers to reflect the water in the channel running through the building. The north and south apartments were both known as **Sheesh Mahal** (Palace of Mirrors) since into the ceiling were set hundreds of small mirrors. In the evening when candles were lit a starlit effect would be produced.

Through the palace ran the **Life-bestowing Stream** and at its centre is a lotus-shaped marble basin which had an ivory fountain. As might be expected in such a cloistered and cosseted environment, the ladies sometimes got bored. In the 18th century the **Empress of Jahandar Shah** sat gazing out at the river and remarked that she had never seen a boat sink. Shortly afterwards a boat was deliberately capsized so that she could be entertained by the sight of people bobbing up and down in the water crying for help.

The southernmost of the palaces, the **Mumtaz Mahal** (Palace of Jewels) ⓘ *Tue-Sun 1000-1700*, was also used by the harem. The lower half of its walls are of marble and it contains six apartments. After the Mutiny of 1857 it was used as a guardroom and since 1912 it has been a museum with exhibits of textiles, weapons, carpets, jade and metalwork as well as works depicting life in the court. It should not be missed.

Spice market

Outside the Red Fort, cycle rickshaws offer a trip to the spice market, Jama Masjid and back through the bazar. You travel slowly westwards down Chandni Chowk passing the town hall. Dismount at Church Road and follow your guide into the heart of the market on Khari Baoli

3 Old Delhi

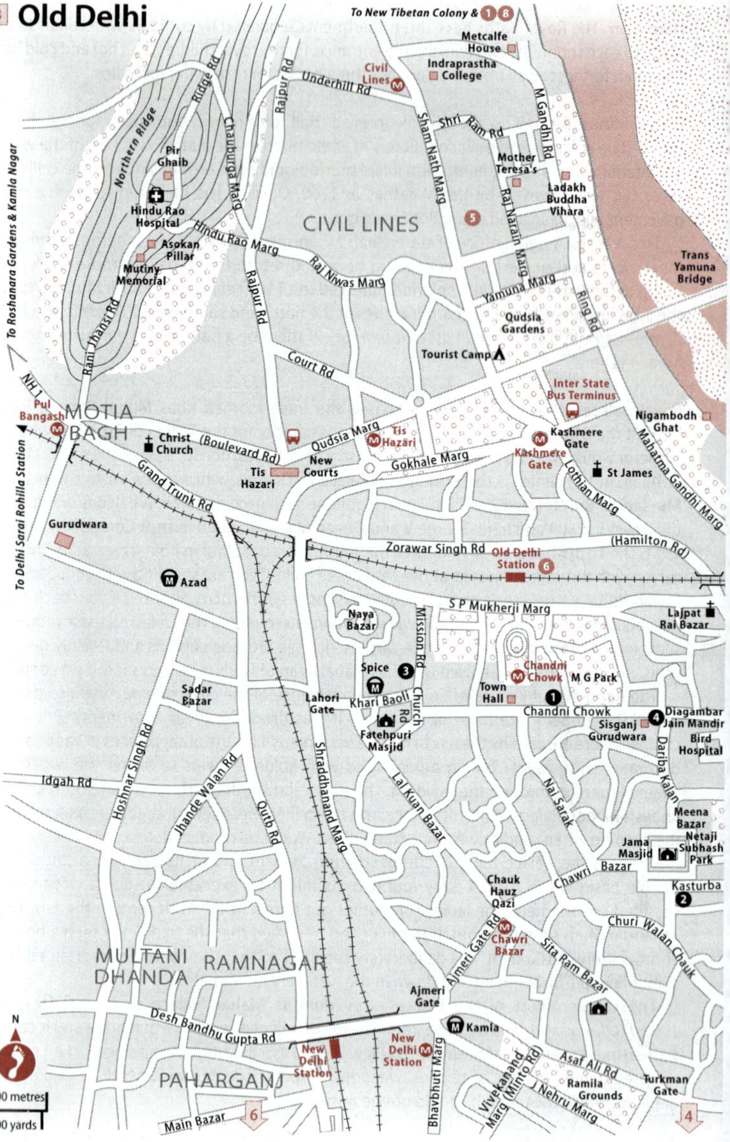

Sleeping
Broadway & Chor Bizarre Restaurant **2**
Oberoi Maidens **5**
Peace House **1**
Railway Retiring Rooms **6**
Wongdhen House **8**

Eating
Haldiram's **1**
Karim's **2**

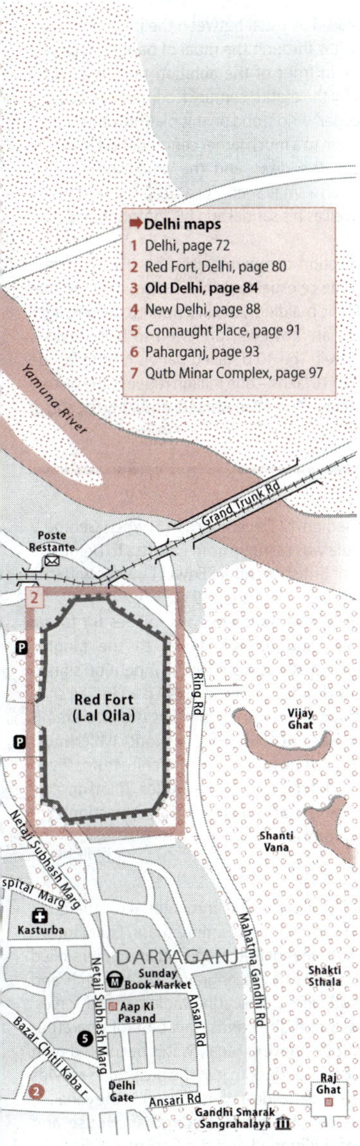

➡Delhi maps

Mahalaxmi Misthan Bhanohar **3**
Old Famous Jalebiwala **4**
Peshawari **5**

where wholesalers sell every conceivable spice. Ask to go to the roof for an excellent view over the market and back towards the Red Fort. The ride back through the bazar is equally fascinating – look up at the amazing electricity system. The final excitement is getting back across Netaji Subhash Marg. Panic not, the rickshaw wallahs know what they are doing. Negotiate for one hour and expect to pay about Rs 100. The spice laden air may irritate your throat.

Jama Masjid (Friday Mosque)

ⓘ *Visitors welcome from 30 mins after sunrise until 1215; and from 1345 until 30 mins before sunset, free, still or video cameras Rs 150, tower entry Rs 20.*

The magnificent Jama Masjid is the largest mosque in India and the last great architectural work of Shah Jahan, intended to dwarf all mosques that had gone before it. With the fort, it dominates Old Delhi. The mosque is much simpler in its ornamentation than Shah Jahan's secular buildings – a judicious blend of red sandstone and white marble, which are interspersed in the domes, minarets and cusped arches.

The gateways Symbolizing the separation of the sacred and the secular, the threshold is a place of great importance where the worshipper steps to a higher plane. There are three huge gateways, the largest being to the east. This was reserved for the royal family who gathered in a private gallery in its upper storey. Today, the faithful enter through the east gate on Fridays and for **Id-ul-Fitr** and **Id-ul-Adha**. The latter commemorates Abraham's (Ibrahim's) sacrificial offering of his son Ishmael (Ismail). Islam (unlike the Jewish and Christian tradition) believes that Abraham offered to sacrifice Ishmael, Isaac's brother.

The courtyard The façade has the main *iwan* (arch), five smaller arches on each side with two flanking minarets and three bulbous domes behind, all perfectly proportioned. The *iwan* draws the worshippers' attention into the building. The minarets have great views from the top; well worth the climb for Rs 10 (women may not be allowed to climb alone). The **hauz**, in the centre of the courtyard, is an ablution tank placed as usual between the inner and outer parts of the building to remind the worshipper that it is through the ritual of baptism that one first enters the community of believers. The **Dikka**, in front of the ablution tank, is a raised platform. Muslim communities grew so rapidly that by the eighth century it sometimes became necessary to introduce a second *muballigh* (prayer leader) who stood on this platform and copied the postures and chants of the *imam* inside to relay them to a much larger congregation. With the introduction of the loudspeaker and amplification, the *dikka* and the *muballigh* became redundant. In the northwest corner of the masjid there is a small shed. For a small fee, the faithful are shown a hair from the beard of the prophet, as well as his sandal and his footprint in rock.

The Kawthar Inscription Set up in 1766, the inscription commemorates the place where a worshipper had a vision of the Prophet standing by the celestial tank in paradise. It is here that the Prophet will stand on Judgment Day. In most Islamic buildings, the inscriptions are passages from the Koran or Sayings of the Prophet. Shah Jahan, however, preferred to have sayings extolling the virtues of the builder and architect as well. The 10 detailed panels on the façade indicate the date of construction (1650-1656), the cost (10 lakhs – one million rupees), the history of the building, the architect (Ustad Khalil) and the builder (Nur Allah Ahmed, probably the son of the man who did most of the work on the Taj Mahal).

New Delhi

Delhi's present position as capital was only confirmed on 12 December 1911, when George V announced at the Delhi Durbar that the capital of India was to move from Calcutta to Delhi. The new city, New Delhi, planned under the leadership of British architect Edwin Lutyens with the assistance of his friend Herbert Baker, was inaugurated on 9 February 1931.

The city was to accommodate 70,000 people and have boundless possibilities for future expansion. The king favoured something in form and flavour similar to the Mughal masterpieces but fretted over the horrendous expense that this would incur. A petition signed by eminent public figures such as Bernard Shaw and Thomas Hardy advocated an Indian style and an Indian master builder. Herbert Baker had made known his own views even before his appointment when he wrote "first and foremost it is the spirit of British sovereignty which must be imprisoned in its stone and bronze". Lutyens himself despised Indian architecture. "Even before he had seen any examples of it", writes architectural historian Giles Tillotson, "he pronounced Mughal architecture to be 'piffle', and seeing it did not disturb that conviction". Yet in the end, Lutyens was forced to settle for the compromise.

India Gate and around

A tour of New Delhi will usually start with a visit to India Gate. This war memorial is situated at the eastern end of **Rajpath**. Designed by Lutyens, it commemorates more than 70,000 Indian soldiers who died in the First World War. Some 13,516 names of British and Indian soldiers killed on the Northwest Frontier and in the Afghan War of 1919 are engraved on the arch and foundations. Under the arch is the Amar Jawan Jyoti, commemorating Indian armed forces' losses in the Indo-Pakistan War of 1971. The arch (43 m high) stands on a base of Bharatpur stone and rises in stages. Similar to the Hindu *chhattri* signifying regality, it is decorated with nautilus shells symbolizing British maritime power. Come at dusk to join the picnicking crowds enjoying the evening. You may even be able to have a pedalo ride if there's water in the canal.

To the northwest of India Gate are two impressive buildings, **Hyderabad House** and **Baroda House**, built as residences for the Nizam of Hyderabad and the Gaekwar of Baroda. Now used as offices, both were carefully placed to indicate the paramountcy of the British Raj over the Princely States. The Nizam, reputed to be the richest man in the world, ruled over an area equal to that of France. The Gaekwar belonged to the top level of Indian princes and both, along with the maharajas of Mysore, Jammu and Kashmir and Gwalior were entitled to receive 21-gun salutes.

Rajpath leads west from India Gate towards **Janpath**. To the north are the Lutyens-designed **National Archives**, formerly the Imperial Record Office. To the south is the National Museum (see below).

National Gallery of Modern Art

ⓘ *Jaipur House, near India Gate, T011- 2338 4640, www.ngmaindia.gov.in, Tue-Sun 1000-1700, Rs 150 foreigners, Rs 10 Indians.*

There is now a new a/c wing of this excellent gallery and select exhibits in the old building housed in a former residence of the Maharaja of Jaipur. **In the Seeds of Time** traces the trajectory of modern Indian art. Artists include: Amrita Shergil: over 100 exhibits, synthesizing the flat treatment of Indian painting with a realistic tone; Rabindranath Tagore (ground floor): examples from a brief but intense spell in the 1930s; The Bombay School or Company School (first floor): includes Western painters who documented their visits to India. Realism is reflected in Indian painting of the early 19th century represented by the schools of Avadh, Patna, Sikkim and Thanjavur; The Bengal School (the late 19th-century Revivalist Movement): artists such as Abanindranath Tagore and Nandalal Bose have their works exhibited here. Western influence was discarded in response to the nationalist movement. Inspiration derived from Indian folk art is evident in the works of Jamini Roy and YD Shukla. Prints from the gallery shop are incredibly good value – up to Rs 80 for poster size prints of famous works.

National Museum

ⓘ *Janpath, T011-2301 9272, www.nationalmuseumindia.gov.in, daily 1000-1700, foreigners Rs 300 (including audio tour), Indians Rs 10, camera Rs 300; free guided tours 1030, 1130, 1200, 1400, films are screened every day (1430), marble squat toilets, but dirty.*

The collection was formed from the nucleus of the Exhibition of Indian Art, London (1947). Now merged with the Asian Antiquities Museum it displays a rich collection of the artistic treasure of Central Asia and India including ethnological objects from prehistoric archaeological finds to the late Medieval period. Replicas of exhibits and books on Indian culture and art are on sale. There is a research library.

Ground floor **Prehistoric**: seals, figurines, toy animals and jewellery from the Harappan civilization (2400-1500 BC). **Maurya Period**: terracottas and stone heads from around the third century BC include the *chaturmukha* (four-faced) *lingam*. **Gandhara School**: stucco heads showing the Graeco Roman influence. **Gupta terracottas** (circa AD 400): include two life-size images of the river goddesses Ganga and Yamuna and the four-armed bust of Vishnu from a temple near Lal Kot. **South Indian sculpture**: from Pallava and early Chola temples and relief panels from Mysore. Bronzes from the Buddhist monastery at Nalanda. Some of Buddha's relics were placed in the Thai pavilion in 1997.

First floor **Illustrated manuscripts**: include the *Babur-i-nama* in the emperor's own hand-writing and an autographed copy of Jahangir's memoirs. **Miniature paintings**: include the 16th-century Jain School, the 18th-century Rajasthani School and the Pahari Schools of Garhwal, Basoli and Kangra. **Aurel Stein Collection** consists of antiquities recovered by him during his explorations of Central Asia and the western borders of China at the turn of the 20th century.

Second floor **Pre-Columbian and Mayan artefacts**: anthropological section devoted to tribal artefacts and folk arts. **Sharad Rani Bakkiwal Gallery of Musical Instruments**: displays over 300 instruments collected by the famous *sarod* player.

4 New Delhi

Delhi maps
1 Delhi, page 72
2 Red Fort, Delhi, page 80
3 Old Delhi, page 84
4 New Delhi, page 88
5 Connaught Place, page 91
6 Paharganj, page 93
7 Qutb Minar Complex, page 97
To Karol Bagh
Patel Nagar East
Daryaganj
Patel Rd
Guru Ravi Das Marg
Saraswati M
Arya Samaj Rd
A Khan Rd
Desh Bandhu Gupta Rd
Pusa Rd
Qutb Rd
New Delhi Station
Jama Masjid
Netaji Subhash Marg
Rajendra Place
Karol Bagh
Jhandewalan
Panchkuin Marg
Paharganj
Chelmsford Rd
J Nehru Marg
JP Narain
Shankar Rd
Roberdra Ranga Shala Rd
Lakshmi Narayan Mandir
RK Ashram Marg
Minto Bridge
GB Pant
Gandhi Darshan
Rajendra Nagar
Bhagat Singh Marg
Connaught Place
Rajiv Chowk
Natural History Museum
Deen Dayal Rd
Barakhamba Rd
Bengali
Mandir Marg
Bangla Sahib
Upper Ridge Rd
Buddha Jayanti Park
R M Lohia
Baba Kharak Singh Marg
Gurudwara Bangla Sahib
Sansad Marg
Janpath
Kasturba Gandhi Marg
Jantar Mantar
Patel Chowk
Ashoka Rd
Barakhamba M
Tansen Rd
College
Mandi House
Mathura Rd
Nepal Embassy
F Shah Rd
Talkatora Rd
Willingdon Cres
Raisina Rd
Baroda House
Tilak Rd
Pragati Maidan
North Block Secretariat
Parliament House
National Archives
Mansingh Rd
Hyderabad House
Rashtrapati Bhavan
Central Secretariat
Rajpath
India Gate
Shastri Marg
South Block Secretariat
National Museum
Martyrs' Memorial
Teen Murti Mg
Kushak Rd
Rafi Marg
Akbar Rd
National Gallery of Modern Art
Purana Qila
Gandhi Museum
Pandara
Kautilya Marg
Nehru Museum
Indira Gandhi Museum
Aurangzeb Rd
Khan
S Bharati Rd
Dr Zakir Hussain Marg
Lal Bahadur
Sardar Patel Marg
Panchsheel Marg
Prithviraj Rd
Full Circle Book Store
Sujan Singh Park
Dhaula Kuan
Naya Marg
Shanti Path
Niti Marg
Santushti Complex
Safdarjung Rd
Tughlak Rd
Lodi Tombs
Lodi Gardens
Indian Int Centre
Race Course
Nehru Park
Lodi Rd
Chanakyapuri
Jorbagh
Tibet House
Safdarjang's Tomb
Jor Bagh
Bian
Pratap
India Habitat Centre
Vinay
Safdarjang Airport
Nehru Stadium
Ring Rd
Lodi Estate Rd No 3
Link Rd
Shanti Path
Sarojini Nagar
Aurobindo Marg
INA
To Airport & Gurgaon
Rao Tularam
Dilli Haat
South Extension I
Lala Lajpat Rai Marg
R K Puram
Defence Colony
Lajpat Nagar
Olof Palme Marg
Swamimlai Temple
Ring Rd
Safdarjang
MG Marg
AIIMS
Vivekanand Marg
Africa Av
Safdarjang Enclave
Pacific Sports Complex
East of Kailas
South Extension II
Vasant Vihar
Yusuf Sarai
Ansal Plaza
Arjun Nagar
Deer Park
Moth ki Masjid
Poorvi Marg
Priya Cinema
N Mandela Marg
Green Park
Siri Fort Marg
Josef Brod Tito Marg
Ekasur Vithi Marg
Jawaharlal Nehru University
Gamel Abdul Nasser Marg
Hauz Khas Village
Khel Gaon Marg
Siri Fort Sports Club
Asiad Village
Greater Kailash
A Asaf Ali Marg
Siri
Indian Institute of Technology
Sri Aurobindo Ashram
Bijai Mandal
Panchsheel Marg
Outer Ring Rd
Vasant Kunj
To Anupam Cinema, 12 19 46 (at Qutb Minar), Garden of 5 Senses & 35 36 48
Begumpuri Masjid
Panchsheel South
To Khirki Masjid & Saket

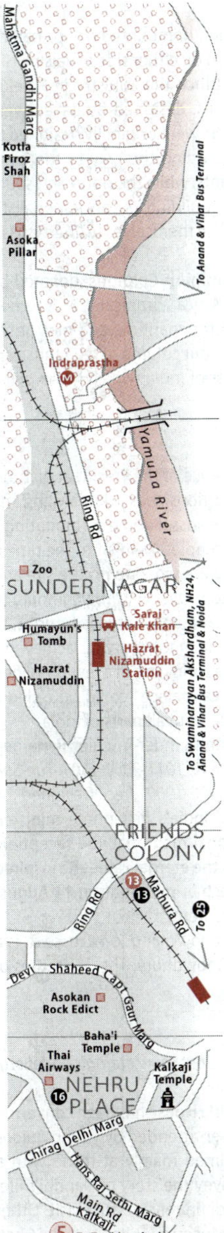

Sleeping

'27' Jorbagh **1** *D3*
Aman New Delhi **23** *C2*
Amarya Haveli **24** *F2*
Amarya Villa **3** *E2*
Bajaj Indian Homestay **4** *A2*
Basera **11** *C4*
Casa Delhi **7** *E4*
Claridges **5** *C3*
Clark International **31** *A2*
Colonel's Retreat **27** *E4*
Diplomat **6** *C2*
ITC Maurya Sheraton **8** *C1*
Jukaso Inn **9** *C4*
K One One **28** *D4*
Life Tree **12** *E4*
Lutyens Bungalow **10** *D3*
Manor **13** *E5*
Master **14** *B2*
Murad Baig **29** *F3*
Oberoi **15** *C4*
On the House **30** *E2*
Shervani **26** *C4*
Taj Mahal **19** *C3*
Taj Palace **20** *C1*
Tree of Life **16** *F3*
Vivanta by Taj **2** *C4*
Yatri Paying Guest House **21** *A2*
Youth Hostel **22** *C2*

Eating

All American Diner **29** *D4*
Choko La/Mamagoto **26** *C4*
Andhra Bhavan **1** *B4*
Baci **21** *C4*
Big Chill **11** *E4*
Chopsticks **2** *F3*
Colonelz Kebabz **5** *E4*
Diva **15** *F4*
Flavors **30** *E4*
Gunpowder **3** *F2*
Indian Accent **13** *D5*
Kainoosh **34** *E1*
Khan Cha Cha **33** *C4*
Le Café **32** *E4*
Living Room **7** *F2*
Lodi **10** *D3*
Magique **35** *F2*
Market Café & Latitude **27** *C3*
Moti Mahal Deluxe **20** *C2*
Naivedyam **4** *F2*
Nathu's & Bengali Sweet House **18** *B4*
Oh! Calcutta **16** *F5*
Olive Tree **12** *F2*
Park Baluchi **6** *F2*
Ploof **24** *D3*
Sagar **8** *E4*
Sakura **17** *B3*
Sanchos **31** *E3*
Smokehouse Bar & Grill **22** *F4*
Swagath **9** *E4*
Thai High **19** *F2*
Yum Yum Tree **25** *E5*

Bars & clubs

Blue Frog **36** *F2*
Bohemia **37** *F4*
Café Morrisons **38** *E3*
Grey Garden **39** *F2*
Keya **40** *E1*
Kuki **41** *F4*
Ministry of Sound **42** *F1*
Pegs-n-Pints **43** *D1*
Shalom **44** *F4*
Stone **45** *D4*
Trishna **46** *F2*
Urban Pind **47** *E4*
Zoo **48** *F2*

Metro Stops (Yellow Line)
Metro Stops (Videt Line)

The Secretariats

At the Secretariat and Rashtrapati Bhavan gates, the mounted and unmounted troops parade in full uniform on Saturdays at 1030 are worth attending. Standing on either side of Raisina Hill, **North Block** houses the Home and Finance Ministries, **South Block** the Ministry of Foreign Affairs. These long classical buildings topped by Baroque domes, designed by Baker, were derived from Wren's Royal Naval College at Greenwich. The towers were originally designed to be twice the height of the buildings and to act as beacons guarding the way to the inner sanctum. The domes are decorated with lotus motifs and elephants, while the north and south gateways are Mughal in design. On the northern Secretariat building is the imperialistic inscription "Liberty will not descend to a people: a people must raise themselves to liberty. It is a blessing that must be earned before it can be enjoyed".

In the **Great Court** between the Secretariats are the four **Dominion Columns**, donated by the governments of Australia, Canada, New Zealand and South Africa – ironically, as it turned out. Each is crowned by a bronze ship sailing east, symbolizing the maritime and mercantile supremacy of the British Empire. In the centre of the court is the Jaipur column of red sandstone topped with a white egg, bronze lotus and six-pointed glass star of India (which has evolved into today's five-pointed star).

Rashtrapati Bhavan and Nehru Memorial Museum

Once the Viceroy's House, Rashtrapati Bhavan is the official residence of the President of India. The Viceroy's House, New Delhi's centrepiece of imperial proportions, was 1 km around the foundations, bigger than Louis XIV's palace at Versailles. It had a colossal dome surmounting a long colonnade and 340 rooms in all. It took nearly 20 years to complete, similar to the time it took to build the Taj Mahal. In the busiest year, 29,000 people were working on the site and buildings began to take shape. The project was surrounded by controversy from beginning to end. Opting for a fundamentally classical structure, both Baker and Lutyens sought to incorporate Indian motifs, many entirely superficial. While some claim that Lutyens achieved a unique synthesis of the two traditions, Tillotson asks whether "the sprinkling of a few simplified and classicized Indian details (especially *chhattris*) over a classical palace" could be called a synthesis. The Durbar Hall, 23 m in diameter, has coloured marble from all parts of India.

To the south is Flagstaff House, formerly the residence of the commander-in-chief. Renamed Teen Murti Bhawan it now houses the **Nehru Memorial Museum** ⓘ *T011-2301 4504, Tue-Sun 1000-1500, planetarium Mon-Sat 1130-1500, library Mon-Sat 0900-1900, free*. Designed by Robert Tor Russell, in 1948 it became the official residence of India's first prime minister, Jawaharlal Nehru. Converted after his death (1964) into a national memorial, the reception, study and bedroom are intact. A *Jyoti Jawahar* (torch) symbolizes the eternal values he inspired and a granite rock is carved with extracts from his historic speech at midnight on 14 August 1947; an informative and vivid history of the Independence Movement.

The **Martyr's Memorial**, at the junction of Sardar Patel Marg and Willingdon Crescent, is a magnificent 26-m-long, 3-m-high bronze sculpture by DP Roy Chowdhury. The 11 statues of national heroes are headed by Mahatma Gandhi.

Eternal Gandhi Multimedia Museum

ⓘ *Birla House, 5 Tees Jan Marg (near Claridges Hotel), T011-3095 7269, www.eternalgandhi.org, closed Mon and 2nd Sat, 0930-1730, free, film at 1500.*

Gandhi's last place of residence and the site of his assassination, Birla House has been converted into a whizz-bang display of 'interactive' modern technology. Over-attended by young guides eager to demonstrate the next gadget, the museum seems aimed mainly at those with a critically short attention span, and is too rushed to properly convey the story of Gandhi's life. However, a monument in the garden marking where he fell is definitely worth a visit. Other museums in the city related to Gandhi include **National Gandhi Museum** ⓘ *opposite Raj Ghat,*

T011-2331 1793, www.gandhimuseum.org, Tue-Sat 0930-1730, with five pavilions – sculpture, photographs and paintings of Gandhi and the history of the *Satyagraha* movement, the philosophy of non-violence; **Gandhi Smarak Sangrahalaya** ⓘ *Raj Ghat, T011-2301 1480, Fri-Wed 0930-1730*, displays some of Gandhi's personal belongings and a small library includes

5 Connaught Place

➡Delhi maps
1 Delhi, page 72
2 Red Fort, Delhi, page 80
3 Old Delhi, page 84
4 New Delhi, page 88
5 Connaught Place, page 91
6 Paharganj, page 93
7 Qutb Minar Complex, page 97

Sleeping
Alka **1** *B1*
Asian Guest House **9** *C3*
Choudhary **3** *A2*
Hans Plaza **5** *C3*
Imperial, Spice Route Restaurant & 1911 Bar **6** *D2*
Palace Heights **7** *B3*
Park & Agni Bar **8** *C1*
YMCA Tourist Hostel **10** *D1*

Eating
Amber **1** *C2*
Bonsai **11** *A2*
Chinese **15** *B2*
Embassy **4** *A3*
Kake da Hotel **5** *A3*
Kwality **6** *C2*
Nizam's Kathi Kebabs **8** *A2*
Q'BA **9** *B3*
Rodeo **10** *B2*
Saravana Bhavan **19** *B1, D2*
Ten at YWCA International Guesthouse **16** *D1*
United Coffee House **13** *B3*
Veda **20** *A2*
Zen **14** *A2*

Bars & clubs
24/7 Lalit **3** *B3*

Shopping
Bookworm **1** *A2*
Central Cottage Industries Emporium **2** *D2*
Hidesign **3** *B1*
Khadi Gramodyog Bhawan **4** *B1*
Oxford Bookstore **5** *C3*

recordings of speeches; **Indira Gandhi Museum** ⓘ *1 Safdarjang Rd, T011-2301 0094, Tue-Sun 0930-1700, free*, charts the phases of her life from childhood to the moment of her death. Fascinating if rather gory exhibits- you can see the blood-stained, bullet-ridden sari she was wearing when assassinated.

Parliament House and around

Northeast of the Viceroy's House is the **Council House**, now **Sansad Bhavan**. Baker designed this based on Lutyens' suggestion that it be circular (173 m diameter). Inside are the library and chambers for the Council of State, Chamber of Princes and Legislative Assembly – the **Lok Sabha**. Just opposite the Council House is the **Rakabganj Gurudwara** in Pandit Pant Marg. This 20th-century white marble shrine, which integrates the late Mughal and Rajasthani styles, marks the spot where the headless body of Guru Tegh Bahadur, the ninth Sikh Guru, was cremated in 1657. West of the Council House is the Cathedral **Church of the Redemption** (1927-1935) and to its north the Italianate Roman Catholic **Church of the Sacred Heart** (1930-1934), both conceived by Henry Medd.

Connaught Place and Connaught Circus

Connaught Place and its outer ring, Connaught Circus (now officially named **Rajiv Chowk** and **Indira Chowk**, but still commonly referred to by their old names), comprise two-storey arcaded buildings, arranged radially around a circular garden that was completed after the Metro line was installed. Designed by Robert Tor Russell, they have become the main commercial and tourist centre of New Delhi. Sadly, the area also attracts bands of insistent touts ready to take advantage of the unwary traveller by getting them into spurious 'official' or 'government' shops and travel agencies. The area (and Palika Bazar, a humid and dingy underground market hidden beneath it) has long been renowned for its shoe-shine tricksters. Large wadges of slime appear mysteriously on shoes and are then pointed out eagerly by attendant boys or men who offer to clean them off at a price. This can just be the start of 'necessary repairs' to the shoes for which bills of over Rs 300 are not unknown. If caught – increasingly unlikely as the scammers seem to be on the way out – insist politely but firmly that the dirt is cleaned off free of charge.

Paharganj

Delhi's backpacker ghetto occupies a warren of lanes and dingy alleys immediately to the west of New Delhi railway station, a few hundred metres north of Connaught Circus. The crowded Main Bazar offers an instant immersion into the chaos of which India is capable, as stray cows and cycle rickshaws tangle with a throng of pedestrians, hotel touts, and salesmen hawking knock-off handbags, books and cheap clothing. Though there's little other than shopping to hold your interest, the hundreds of guesthouses here offer the greatest concentration of genuinely cheap accommodation in the city, and the area contains a number of appealing rooftop cafés that provide a respite from the madness below. In 2010, the Main Bazar had an overhaul. Ignoring the strikes of the shopkeepers, bulldozers moved in and widened the road by essentially cutting off the front of the buildings that were encroaching onto it. Now the streets are wider and the businesses are giving themselves a facelift.

Northwest of Paharganj, the grid of streets comprising **Karol Bagh** contains what is, by some definitions, the biggest market in Asia. Conveniently linked to the city by Metro, the area is full of mid-range hotels, but mainly populated by Indians.

Lakshmi Narayan Mandir

To the west of Connaught Circus is the Lakshmi Narayan **Birla Temple** in Mandir Marg. Financed by the prominent industrialist Raja Baldeo Birla in 1938, this is one of the most popular Hindu shrines in the city and one of Delhi's few striking examples of Hindu architecture. Dedicated to Lakshmi, the goddess of well-being, it is commonly referred to as **Birla Mandir**. The design is in the Orissan style with tall curved *sikharas* (towers) capped by large *amalakas*. The exterior is faced with red and ochre stone and white marble. Built around a central courtyard, the main shrine has images of Narayan and his consort Lakshmi while two separate cells have icons of Siva (the Destroyer) and Durga (the 10-armed destroyer of demons). The temple is flanked by a *dharamshala* (rest house) and a Buddhist *vihara* (monastery).

Gurudwara Bangla Sahib

ⓘ *Baba Kharak Singh Rd, free.*

This is a fine example of Sikh temple architecture, featuring a large pool reminiscent of Amritsar's Golden Temple. The 24-hour reciting of the faith's holy book adds to the atmosphere, and there's free food on offer, although don't be surprised if you're asked to help out with the washing up! You must remove your shoes and cover your head to enter – suitable scarves are provided if you arrive without.

Further northeast on Baba Kharak Singh Marg is **Hanuman Mandir**. This small temple was built by Maharaja Jai Singh II of Jaipur. **Mangal haat** (Tuesday Fair) is a popular market.

N

200 metres
200 yards

Sleeping
Ajay's **1**
Ajanta **2**
Anoop **3**
Gush **19**
Heritage Inn **6**
Jyoti Mahal & White Klove **7**
Metropolis Tourist Home **18**
Namaskar **8**
Payal **10**
Prince Polonia **17**
Railway Retiring Rooms **9**
Rak International **11**
Relax **4**
Star Plaza **5**

Eating
Appetite **1**
Café Sim Tok **8**
Everest Bakery Café **5**
Madan's **2**
Malhotra's **3**
Open Hand Café **7**
Southern **4**
Tadka **6**

Jantar Mantar

Just to the east of the Hanuman Mandir in Sansad Marg (Parliament Street) is Jai Singh's **observatory** (Jantar Mantar) ⓘ *sunrise to sunset, Rs 100 foreigners, Rs 5 Indians.* The Mughal Emperor Mohammad Shah (ruled 1719-1748) entrusted the renowned astronomer Maharaja Jai Singh II with the task of revising the calendar and correcting the astronomical tables used by contemporary priests. Daily astral observations were made for years before construction began and plastered brick structures were favoured for the site instead of brass instruments. Built in 1725 it is slightly smaller than the later observatory at Jaipur.

Memorial Ghats

Beyond Delhi Gate lies the **Yamuna River**, marked by a series of memorials to India's leaders. The river itself, a kilometre away, is invisible from the road, protected by a low rise and banks of trees. The most prominent memorial, immediately opposite the end of Jawaharlal Nehru Road, is that of Mahatma Gandhi at **Raj Ghat**. To its north is **Shanti Vana** (Forest of Peace), landscaped gardens where Prime Minister Jawaharlal Nehru was cremated in 1964, as were his grandson Sanjay Gandhi in 1980, daughter Indira Gandhi in 1984 and elder grandson, Rajiv, in 1991. To the north again is **Vijay Ghat** (Victory Bank) where Prime Minister Lal Bahadur Shastri was cremated.

South Delhi

South Delhi is often overlooked by travellers. This is a real pity as it houses some of the city's most stunning sites, best accommodation, bars, clubs and restaurants, as well as some of its most tranquil parks. However be warned, South Delhi can be hell during rushhour when the traffic on the endless flyovers comes to a virtual standstill. But with the metro, you can explore all the way down to Gurgaon with relative ease.

Lodi Gardens

These beautiful gardens, with mellow stone tombs of the 15th- and 16th-century Lodi rulers, are popular for gentle strolls and jogging. In the middle of the garden facing the east entrance from Max Mueller Road is **Bara Gumbad** (Big Dome), a mosque built in 1494. The raised courtyard is provided with an imposing gateway and *mehman khana* (guest rooms). The platform in the centre appears to have had a tank for ritual ablutions.

The **Sheesh Bumbad** (Glass Dome, late 15th century) is built on a raised incline north of the Bara Gumbad and was once decorated with glazed blue tiles, painted floral designs and Koranic inscriptions. The façade gives the impression of a two-storeyed building, typical of Lodi architecture. **Mohammad Shah's Tomb** (1450) is that of the third Sayyid ruler. It has sloping buttresses, an octagonal plan, projecting eaves and lotus patterns on the ceiling. **Sikander Lodi's Tomb**, built by his son in 1517, is also an octagonal structure decorated with Hindu motifs. A structural innovation is the double dome which was later refined under the Mughals. The 16th-century **Athpula** (Bridge of Eight Piers), near the northeastern entrance, is attributed to Nawab Bahadur, a nobleman at Akbar's court.

Safdarjang's Tomb

ⓘ *Sunrise to sunset, Rs 100 foreigners, Rs 5 Indians.*

Safdarjang's Tomb, seldom visited, was built by Nawab Shuja-ud-Daulah for his father Mirza Mukhim Abdul Khan, entitled Safdarjang, who was Governor of Oudh (1719-1748), and Wazir of his successor (1748-1754). Safdarjang died in 1754. With its high enclosure walls, *char bagh* layout of gardens, fountain and central domed mausoleum, it follows the tradition of Humayun's tomb. Typically, the real tomb is just below ground level. Flanking the mausoleum are pavilions used by Shuja-ud-Daulah as his family residence. Immediately to its south is the battlefield where Timur and his Mongol horde crushed Mahmud Shah Tughluq on 12 December 1398.

Hazrat Nizamuddin

ⓘ *Dress ultra-modestly if you don't want to feel uncomfortable or cause offence.*

At the east end of the Lodi Road, Hazrat Nizamuddin Dargah (Nizamuddin 'village') now tucked away behind the residential suburb of Nizamuddin West, off Mathura Road, grew up around the shrine of Sheikh Nizamuddin Aulia (1236-1325), a Chishti saint. This is a wonderfully atmospheric place. *Qawwalis* are sung at sunset after *namaaz* (prayers), and are particularly impressive on Thursdays – be prepared for crowds. Highly recommended.

West of the central shrine is the **Jama-at-khana Mosque** (1325). Its decorated arches are typical of the Khalji design also seen at the Ala'i Darwaza at the Qutb Minar. South of the main tomb and behind finely crafted screens is the grave of princess Jahanara, Shah Jahan's eldest and favourite daughter. She shared the emperor's last years when he was imprisoned at Agra Fort. The grave, open to the sky, is in accordance with the epitaph written by her: "Let naught cover my grave save the green grass, for grass suffices as the covering of the lowly". Pilgrims congregate at the shrine twice a year for the **Urs** (fair) held to mark the anniversaries of Hazrat Nizamuddin Aulia and his disciple Amir Khusrau, whose tomb is nearby.

Humayun's Tomb

ⓘ *Sunrise to sunset, Rs 250 foreigners, Rs 10 Indians, video cameras Rs 25, located in Nizamuddin, 15-20 mins by taxi from Connaught Circus, allow 45 mins.*

Eclipsed later by the Taj Mahal and the Jama Masjid, this tomb is the best example in Delhi of the early Mughal style of tomb. Superbly maintained, it is well worth a visit, preferably before visiting the Taj Mahal. Humayun, the second Mughal emperor, was forced into exile in Persia after being heavily defeated by the Afghan Sher Shah in 1540. He returned to India in 1545, finally recapturing Delhi in 1555. The tomb was designed and built by his senior widow and mother of his son Akbar, Hamida Begum. A Persian from Khurasan, after her pilgrimage to Mecca she was known as Haji Begum. She supervised the entire construction of the tomb (1564-1573), camping on the site.

The plan The tomb has an octagonal plan, lofty arches, pillared kiosks and the double dome of Central Asian origin, which appears here for the first time in India. Outside Gujarat, Hindu temples make no use of the dome, but the Indian Muslim dome had until now, been of a flatter shape as opposed to the tall Persian dome rising on a more slender neck. Here also is the first standard example of the garden tomb concept: the **char bagh** (garden divided into quadrants), water channels and fountains. This form culminated in the gardens of the Taj Mahal. However, the tomb also shows a number of distinctively Hindu motifs. Tillotson has pointed out that in Humayun's tomb, Hindu *chhattris* (small domed kiosks), complete with temple columns and *chajjas* (broad eaves), surround the central dome. The bulbous finial on top of the dome and the star motif in the spandrels of the main arches are also Hindu, the latter being a solar symbol.

The approach The tomb enclosure has two high double-storeyed gateways: the entrance to the west and the other to the south. A *baradari* occupies the centre of the east wall, and a bath chamber that of the north wall. Several Moghul princes, princesses and Haji Begum herself lie buried here. During the 1857 Mutiny Bahadur Shah II, the last Moghul emperor of Delhi, took shelter here with his three sons. Over 80, he was seen as a figurehead by Muslims opposing the British. When captured he was transported to Yangon (Rangoon) for the remaining four years of his life. The tomb to the right of the approach is that of Isa Khan, Humayun's barber.

The dome Some 38 m high, the dome does not have the swell of the Taj Mahal and the decoration of the whole edifice is much simpler. It is of red sandstone with some white marble to highlight the lines of the building. There is some attractive inlay work, and some *jalis* in the balcony fence and on some of the recessed keel arch windows. The interior is austere and consists of three storeys of arches rising up to the dome. The emperor's tomb is of white marble and quite plain without any inscription. The overall impression is that of a much bulkier, more squat building than the Taj Mahal. The cavernous space under the main tombs is home to great colonies of bats.

Hauz Khas

ⓘ *1-hr cultural show, 1845, Rs 100 (check with Delhi Tourism, see page 77).*

South of Safdarjang's Tomb, and entered off either Aurobindo Marg on the east side or Africa Avenue on the west side, is Hauz Khas. Ala-ud-din Khalji (ruled 1296-1313) created a large tank here for the use of the inhabitants of Siri, the second capital city of Delhi founded by him. Fifty years later Firoz Shah Tughluq cleaned up the silted tank and raised several buildings on its east and south banks which are known as Hauz Khas or Royal Tank.

Firoz Shah's austere tomb is found here. The multi-storeyed wings, on the north and west of the tomb, were built by him in 1354 as a *madrasa* (college). The octagonal and square *chhattris* were built as tombs, possibly to the teachers at the college. Hauz Khas is now widely used as a park for early-morning recreation – walking, running and yoga *asanas*. Classical music concerts, dance performances and a *son et lumière* show are held in the evenings when monuments are illuminated by thousands of earthen lamps and torches. Wandering the streets of Haus Khaz village, you can almost forget that you are in India. Labyrinthine alleys lead to numerous galleries, boutiques and restaurants. There are a lot of little design studios here and a more boho vibe.

Qutb Minar Complex

ⓘ *Sunrise to sunset, Rs 250 foreigners, Rs 10 Indians. The metro goes to Qutb Minar. Bus 505 from New Delhi Railway Station (Ajmeri Gate), Super Bazar (east of Connaught Circus) and Cottage Industries Emporium, Janpath. Auto Rs 110, though drivers may be reluctant to take you. This area is also opening up as a hub for new chic restaurants and bars.*

Muhammad Ghuri conquered northwest India at the very end of the 12th century. The conquest of the Gangetic plain down to Benares (Varanasi) was undertaken by Muhammad's Turkish slave and chief general, Qutb-ud-din-Aibak, whilst another general took Bihar and Bengal. In the process, temples were reduced to rubble, the remaining Buddhist centres were dealt their death blow and their monks slaughtered. When Muhammad was assassinated in 1206, his gains passed to the loyal Qutb-ud-din-Aibak. Thus the first sultans or Muslim kings of Delhi became known as the **Slave Dynasty** (1026-1290). For the next three centuries the Slave Dynasty and the succeeding Khalji (1290-1320), Tughluq (1320-1414), Sayyid (1414-1445) and Lodi (1451-1526) dynasties provided Delhi with fluctuating authority. The legacy of their ambitions survives in the tombs, forts and palaces that litter Delhi Ridge and the surrounding plain. Qutb-ud- din-Aibak died after only four years in power, but he left his mark with the **Qutb Minar** and his **citadel**. Qutb Minar, built to proclaim the victory of Islam over the infidel, dominates the countryside for miles around. Visit the *minar* first.

Qutb Minar (1) In 1199 work began on what was intended to be the most glorious tower of victory in the world and was to be the prototype of all *minars* (towers) in India. Qutb-ud-din-Aibak had probably seen and been influenced by the brick victory pillars in Ghazni in Afghanistan, but this one was also intended to serve as the minaret attached to the Might of Islam Mosque. From here the muezzin could call the faithful to prayer. Later every mosque would incorporate its minaret.

As a mighty reminder of the importance of the ruler as Allah's representative on earth, the Qutb Minar (literally 'axis minaret') stood at the centre of the community. A pivot of Faith, Justice and Righteousness, its name also carried the message of Qutb-ud-din's (Axis of the Faith) own achievements. The inscriptions carved in Kufi script tell that "the tower was erected to cast the shadow of God over both east and west". For Qutb-ud-din-Aibak it marked the eastern limit of the empire of the One God. Its western counterpart is the Giralda Tower built by Yusuf in Seville.

The Qutb Minar is 73 m high and consists of five storeys. The diameter of the base is 14.4 m and 2.7 m at the top. Qutb-ud-din built the first three and his son-in-law Iltutmish embellished these and added a fourth. This is indicated in some of the Persian and Nagari (North Indian) inscriptions which also record that it was twice damaged by lightning in 1326 and 1368. While repairing the damage caused by the second, Firoz Shah Tughluq added a fifth storey and used marble to face the red and buff sandstone. This was the first time contrasting colours were used decoratively, later to become such a feature of Mughal buildings. Firoz's fifth storey was topped by a graceful cupola but this fell down during an earthquake in 1803. A new one was added by a Major Robert Smith in 1829 but was so out of keeping that it was removed in 1848 and now stands in the gardens.

The original storeys are heavily indented with different styles of fluting, alternately round and angular on the bottom, round on the second and angular on the third. The beautifully carved honeycomb detail beneath the balconies is reminiscent of the Alhambra Palace in Spain. The calligraphy bands are verses from the Koran and praises to its patron builder.

Quwwat-ul-Islam Mosque (2) The Quwwat-ul-Islam Mosque (The Might of Islam Mosque), the earliest surviving mosque in India, is to the northwest of the Qutb Minar. It was begun in 1192, immediately after Qutb-ud-din's conquest of Delhi and completed in 1198, using the remains of no fewer than 27 local Hindu and Jain temples.

7 Qutb Minar Complex

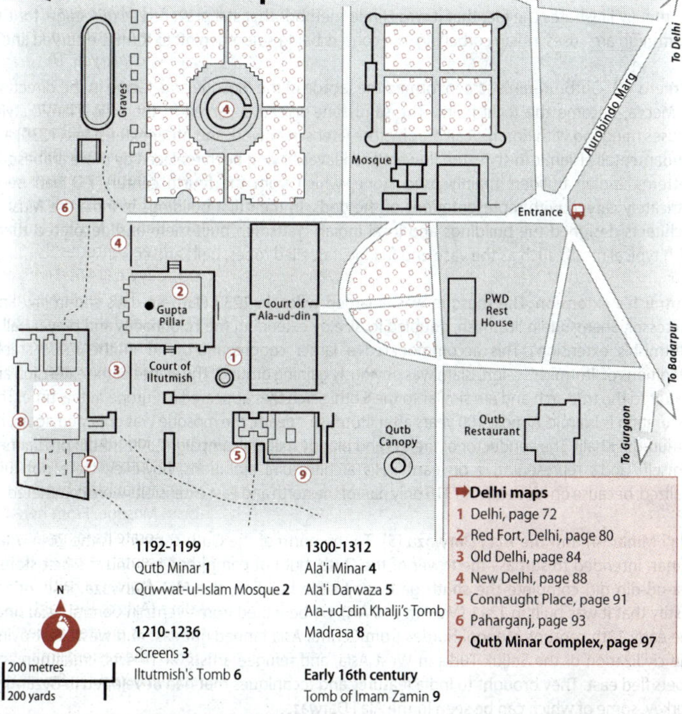

1192-1199
Qutb Minar **1**
Quwwat-ul-Islam Mosque **2**

1210-1236
Screens **3**
Iltutmish's Tomb **6**

1300-1312
Ala'i Minar **4**
Ala'i Darwaza **5**
Ala-ud-din Khalji's Tomb
Madrasa **8**

Early 16th century
Tomb of Imam Zamin **9**

➡Delhi maps
1 Delhi, page 72
2 Red Fort, Delhi, page 80
3 Old Delhi, page 84
4 New Delhi, page 88
5 Connaught Place, page 91
6 Paharganj, page 93
7 Qutb Minar Complex, page 97

Gupta Pillar: the magic of iron

In the courtyard of the Quwwat-ul-Islam Mosque (2) is the fourth-century iron pillar. The Sanskrit inscription states that it was erected as a flagstaff in honour of Vishnu and in memory of the Gupta King Chandragupta II (AD 375-413). Originally the pillar was topped by an image of Vishnu's *vahana* (carrier or vehicle) Garuda, the mythical half bird of prey, half man, and probably stood facing a Vishnu temple. The purity of its wrought iron (98%) is extraordinary, and it has survived 1600 years virtually without blemish. A local tradition regards the pillar as having magical qualities. Anyone who can encircle it with their hands behind their back will have good fortune – quite a challenge now the pillar is fenced off.

The architectural style contained elements that Muslims brought from Arabia, including buildings made of mud and brick and decorated with glazed tiles, *squinches* (arches set diagonally across the corners of a square chamber to facilitate the raising of a dome and to effect a transition from a square to a round structure), the pointed arch and the true dome. Finally, Muslim buildings came alive through ornamental calligraphy and geometric patterning. This was in marked contrast to indigenous Indian styles of architecture. Hindu, Buddhist and Jain buildings relied on the post-and-beam system in which spaces were traversed by corbelling, ie shaping flat-laid stones to create an arch. The arched screen that runs along the western end of the courtyard beautifully illustrates the fact that it was Hindu methods that still prevailed at this stage, for the 16-m-high arch uses Indian corbelling, the corners being smoothed off to form the curved line.

Screens (3) Qutb-ud-din's screen formed the façade of the mosque and, facing in the direction of Mecca, became the focal point. The sandstone screen is carved in the Indo-Islamic style, lotuses mingling with Koranic calligraphy. The later screenwork and other extensions (1230) are fundamentally Islamic in style, the flowers and leaves having been replaced by more arabesque patterns. Indian builders mainly used stone, which from the fourth century AD had been intricately carved with representations of the gods. In their first buildings in India the Muslim architects designed the buildings and local Indian craftsmen built them and decorated them with typical motifs such as the vase and foliage, tasselled ropes, bells and cows.

Iltutmish's extension The mosque was enlarged twice. In 1230 Qutb-ud-din's son-in-law and successor, Shamsuddin Iltutmish, doubled its size by extending the colonnades and prayer hall – 'Iltutmish's extension'. This accommodated a larger congregation, and in the more stable conditions of Iltutmish's reign, Islam was obviously gaining ground. The arches of the extension are nearer to the true arch and are similar to the Gothic arch that appeared in Europe at this time. The decoration is Islamic. Almost 100 years after Iltutmish's death, the mosque was enlarged again, by Ala-ud-din Khalji. The conductor of tireless and bloody military campaigns, Ala-ud-din proclaimed himself 'God's representative on earth'. His architectural ambitions, however, were not fully realized, because on his death in 1316 only part of the north and east extensions were completed.

Ala'i Minar (4) and the Ala'i Darwaza (5) To the north of the Qutb complex is the 26-m **Ala'i Minar**, intended to surpass the tower of the Qutb, but not completed beyond the first storey. Ala-ud-din did complete the south gateway to the building, the **Ala'i Darwaza**; inscriptions testify that it was built in 1311 (Muslim 710 AH). He benefited from events in Central Asia: since the early 13th century, Mongol hordes from Central Asia fanned out east and west, destroying the civilization of the Seljuk Turks in West Asia, and refugee artists, architects, craftsmen and poets fled east. They brought to India features and techniques that had developed in Byzantine Turkey, some of which can be seen in the Ala'i Darwaza.

The gatehouse is a large sandstone cuboid, into which are set small cusped arches with carved *jali* screens. The lavish ornamentation of geometric and floral designs in red sandstone and white marble produced a dramatic effect when viewed against the surrounding buildings.

The inner chamber, 11 sq m has doorways and, for the first time in India, true arches. Above each doorway is an Arabic inscription with its creator's name and one of his self- assumed titles – 'The Second Alexander'. The north doorway, which is the main entrance, is the most elaborately carved. The dome, raised on squinched arches, is flat and shallow. Of the effects employed, the arches with their 'lotus-bud' fringes are Seljuk, as is the dome with the rounded finial and the façade. These now became trademarks of the **Khalji style**, remaining virtually unchanged until their further development in Humayun's Tomb.

Iltutmish's Tomb (6) Built in 1235, Iltutmish's Tomb lies in the northwest of the compound, midway along the west wall of the mosque. It is the first surviving tomb of a Muslim ruler in India. Two other tombs also stand within the extended Might of Islam Mosque. The idea of a tomb was quite alien to Hindus, who had been practising cremation since around 400 BC. Blending Hindu and Muslim styles, the outside is relatively plain with three arched and decorated doorways. The interior carries reminders of the nomadic origins of the first Muslim rulers. Like a Central Asian *yurt* (tent) in its decoration, it combines the familiar Indian motifs of the wheel, bell, chain and lotus with the equally familiar geometric arabesque patterning. The west wall is inset with three *mihrabs* that indicate the direction of Mecca.

The tomb originally supported a dome resting on *squinches* which you can still see. The dome collapsed (witness the slabs of stone lying around) suggesting that the technique was as yet unrefined. From the corbelled squinches it may be assumed that the dome was corbelled too, as found in contemporary Gujarat and Rajput temples. The blocks of masonry were fixed together using the Indian technology of iron dowels. In later Indo- Islamic buildings lime plaster was used for bonding.

Other tombs To the southwest of the uncompleted Quwwat-ul-Islam mosque, an L-shaped ruin marks the site of **Ala-ud-din Khalji's Tomb (7)** within the confines of a **madrasa** (college) **(8)**. This is the first time in India that a tomb and *madrasa* are found together, another custom inherited from the Seljuks. Immediately to the east of the Ala'i Darwaza stands the **Tomb of Imam Zamin (9)**, an early 16th-century *sufi* 'saint' from Turkestan. It is an octagonal structure with a plastered sandstone dome and has *jali* screens, a characteristic of the Lodi style of decoration.

Tughluqabad

ⓘ *Sunrise to sunset, foreigners Rs100, Indians Rs 5, video camera Rs 25, allow 1 hr for return rickshaws, turn right at entrance and walk 200 m. The site is often deserted so don't go alone. Take plenty of water.*

Tughluqabad's ruins, 7.5 km east from Qutb Minar, still convey a sense of the power and energy of the newly arrived Muslims in India. From the walls you get a magnificent impression of the strategic advantages of the site. **Ghiyas'ud-Din Tughluq** (ruled 1321-1325), after ascending the throne of Delhi, selected this site for his capital. He built a massive fort around his capital city which stands high on a rocky outcrop of the Delhi Ridge. The fort is roughly octagonal in plan with a circumference of 6.5 km. The vast size, strength and obvious solidity of the whole give it an air of massive grandeur. It was not until Babur (ruled 1526-1530) that dynamite was used in warfare, so this is a very defensible site.

East of the main entrance is the rectangular **citadel**. A wider area immediately to the west and bounded by walls contained the **palaces**. Beyond this to the north lay the **city**. Now marked by the ruins of houses, the streets were laid out in a grid fashion. Inside the citadel enclosure is the **Vijay Mandal tower** and the remains of several halls including a long underground passage. The fort also contained seven tanks.

A causeway connects the fort with the tomb of Ghiyas'ud-Din Tughluq, while a wide embankment near its southeast corner gave access to the fortresses of **Adilabad** about 1 km away, built a little later by Ghiyas'ud-Din's son Muhammad. The tomb is very well preserved and has red sandstone walls with a pronounced slope (the first Muslim building in India to have sloping walls), crowned with a white marble dome. This dome, like that of the Ala'i Darwaza at the Qutb, is crowned by an *amalaka*, a feature of Hindu architecture. Also Hindu is the trabeate arch at the tomb's fortress wall entrance. Inside are three cenotaphs belonging to Ghiyas'ud-Din, his wife and son Muhammad.

Ghiyas'ud-Din Tughluq quickly found that military victories were no guarantee of lengthy rule. When he returned home after a victorious campaign the welcoming pavilion erected by his son and successor, Muhammad-bin Tughluq, was deliberately collapsed over him. Tughluqabad was abandoned shortly afterwards and was thus only inhabited for five years. The Tughluq dynasty continued to hold Delhi until Timur sacked it and slaughtered its inhabitants. For a brief period Tughluq power shifted to Jaunpur near Varanasi, where the Tughluq architectural traditions were carried forward in some superb mosques.

Baha'i Temple (Lotus Temple)

ⓘ *1 Apr-30 Sep 0900-1900, 1 Oct-31 Mar Tue-Sun 0930-1730, free entry and parking, visitors welcome to attend services, at other times the temple is open for silent meditation and prayer. Audio-visual presentations in English are at 1100, 1200, 1400 and 1530, remove shoes before entering. Bus 433 from the centre (Jantar Mantar) goes to Nehru Place, within walking distance (1.5 km) of the temple at Kalkaji, or take a taxi or auto-rickshaw.*

Architecturally the Baha'i Temple is a remarkably striking building. Constructed in 1980-1981, it is built out of white marble and in the characteristic Baha'i temple shape of a lotus flower – 45 lotus petals form the walls – which internally creates a feeling of light and space (34 m high, 70 m in diameter). It is a simple design, brilliantly executed and very elegant in form. All Baha'i temples are nine-sided, symbolizing 'comprehensiveness, oneness and unity'. The Delhi Temple, which seats 1300, is surrounded by nine pools, an attractive feature also helping to keep the building cool. It is particularly attractive when flood-lit. Baha'i temples are "dedicated to the worship of God, for peoples of all races, religions or castes. Only the Holy Scriptures of the Baha'i Faith and earlier revelations are read or recited".

The Baha'i faith was founded by a Persian, Baha'u'llah (meaning 'glory of God'; 1817-1892), who is believed to be the manifestation of God for this age. His teachings were directed towards the unification of the human race and the establishment of a permanent universal peace.

East of the Yamuna

Designated as the site of the athletes' village for the 2010 Commonwealth Games, East Delhi has just one attraction to draw visitors across the Yamuna.

Swaminarayan Akshardham

ⓘ *www.akshardham.com, Apr-Sep Tue-Sun 1000-1900, Oct-Mar Tue-Sun 0900-1800, temple free, Rs 125 for 'attractions', musical fountain Rs 20, no backpacks, cameras or other electronic items (bag and body searches at entry gate). Packed on Sun; visit early to avoid crowds.*

Opened in November 2005 on the east bank of the Yamuna, the gleaming Akshardham complex represents perhaps the most ambitious construction project in India since the foundation of New Delhi itself. At the centre of a surreal 40-ha 'cultural complex' complete with landscaped gardens, cafés and theme park rides, the temple-monument is dedicated to the 18th-century saint Bhagwan Swaminarayan, who abandoned his home at the age of 11 to embark on a lifelong quest for the spiritual and cultural uplift of Western India. It took 11,000 craftsmen, all volunteers, no less than 300 million hours to complete the temple using traditional building and carving techniques.

If this is the first religious site you visit in India, the security guards and swarms of mooching Indian tourists will hardly prepare you for the typical temple experience. Yet despite this, and the boat rides and animatronic shows which have prompted inevitable comparisons to a 'spiritual Disneyland', most visitors find the Akshardham an inspiring, indeed uplifting, experience, if for no other reason than that the will and ability to build something of its scale and complexity still exist.

The temple You enter the temple complex through a series of intricately carved gates. The Bhakti Dwar (Gate of Devotion), adorned with 208 pairs of gods and their consorts, leads into a hall introducing the life of Swaminarayan and the activities of BAPS (Bochasanwasi Shri Akshar Purushottam Swaminarayan Sanstha), the global Hindu sect-cum-charity which runs Akshardham. The main courtyard is reached through the Mayur Dwar (Peacock Gate), a conglomeration of 869 carved peacocks echoed by an equally florid replica directly facing it.

From here you get your first look at the central monument. Perfectly symmetrical in pink sandstone and white marble, it rests on a plinth encircled by 148 elephants, each sculpted from a 20-tonne stone block, in situations ranging from the literal to the mythological: mortal versions grapple with lions or lug tree trunks, while Airavatha, the eight-trunked mount of Lord Indra, surfs majestically to shore after the churning of the oceans at the dawn of Hindu creation. Above them, carvings of deities, saints and *sadhus* cover every inch of the walls and columns framing the inner sanctum, where a gold-plated *murti* (idol) of Bhagwan Swaminarayan sits attended by avatars of his spiritual successors, beneath a staggeringly intricate marble dome. Around the main dome are eight smaller domes, each carved in hypnotic fractal patterns, while paintings depicting Swaminarayan's life of austerity and service line the walls (explanations in English and Hindi).

Surrounding the temple is a moat of holy water supposedly taken from 151 sacred lakes and rivers visited by Swaminarayan on his seven-year barefoot pilgrimage. 108 bronze *gaumukhs* (cow heads) representing the 108 names of God spout water into the tank, which is itself hemmed in by a 1-km-long *parikrama* (colonnade) of red Rajasthani sandstone.

The exhibition halls and grounds Much of the attention paid to Akshardham revolves around the Disneyesque nature of some of its attractions. Deliberately populist, they aim to instil a sense of pride in the best of Indian values and cultural traditions, and may come across to some as overly flag-waving and patriotic. **Sahajanand Darshan** is an animatronic rendition of Swaminarayan's life, told over a series of rooms through which you are shepherded by an attendant. A beautifully shot Imax movie, *Neelkanth Darshan*, tells the story of the young yogi's seven-year pilgrimage, with dance routines and scenic set pieces worthy of a Bollywood ad campaign. **Sanskruti Vihar** is a 14-minute boat ride along the mythical Saraswati River where visitors are introduced to Indian pioneers in the fields of science, technology, medicine and philosophy.

A similar message imbues the **Cultural Garden**, an avenue of bronze statues extolling the cardinal virtues of prominent figures from Hindu mythology and Indian history. Between the exhibition halls and the main Akshardham is the **Yagnapurush Kund**, an enormous step well (claimed to be the biggest in the world) overlooked by a 9-m bronze statue of Neelkanth. This is the scene for a dramatic and popular musical fountain show each evening.

Delhi listings

Hotel prices

LL over US$200	**L** US$151-200	**AL** US$101-150
A US$66-100	**B** US$46-65	**C** US$31-45
D US$21-30	**E** US$12-20	**F** US$7-11
G under US$7		

Restaurant prices

ΨΨΨ over US$12	ΨΨ US$6-12	Ψ under US$6

Sleeping

Avoid hotel touts. Airport taxis may pretend not to know the location of your chosen hotel so give full details and insist on being taken there. Around Paharganj particularly, you might be followed around by your driver trying to eek a commission out of the guest house once you have checked in. It really saves a lot of hassle if you make reservations. Even if you change hotel the next day, it is good to arrive with somewhere booked especially if you are flying in late at night. Hotel prices in Delhi are significantly higher than in most other parts of the country. Smaller **C-D** guesthouses away from the centre in **South Delhi** (eg Kailash, Safdarjang) or in **Sunder Nagar**, are quieter and often good value but may not provide food. **E-F** accommodation is concentrated around **Janpath** and **Paharganj** (New Delhi), and **Chandni Chowk** (Old Delhi) – well patronized but basic and usually cramped yet good for meeting other backpackers. Some have dormitory beds for less than Rs 100. Some city centre rooms are windowless. Signs in some hotels warn against taking drugs as this is becoming a serious cause for concern. Police raids are frequent.

Old Delhi and beyond *p79, map p84*

L-AL Oberoi Maidens, 7 Sham Nath Marg, T011-2397 5464, www.oberoihotels.com. 54 large well-appointed rooms, restaurant (slow), barbecue nights are excellent, coffee shop, old-style bar, attractive colonial style in quiet area, spacious gardens with excellent pool, friendly welcome, personal attention. Recommended.

AL-B Broadway, 4/15A Asaf Ali Rd, T011-4366 3600, www.oldworldhospitality.com. 36 rooms, some wonderfully quirky. The 'coloured' rooms are designed for children, complete with inventive fairy lights, miniature furniture and psychedelic bathroom tiles. **Chor Bizarre** restaurant and bar is highly regarded, as is the unfortunately named '**Thugs**' pub. Morning and afternoon walking tours of Old Delhi – book in advance. Easily one of the best options.

C-E Peace House, 20A New Tibetan Colony, Manju-ka-Tilla, T011-2393 9415. Clean, basic rooms in friendly guesthouse.

C-E Wongdhen House, 15A New Tibetan Colony, Manju-ka-Tilla, T011-2381 6689, wongdhenhouse@hotmail.com. Very clean rooms, some with a/c and TV, safe, cosy, convivial, good breakfast and great Tibetan meals, an insight into Tibetan culture, peacefully located by Yamuna River yet 15 mins by auto-rickshaw north of Old Delhi Station. Recommended. For more information on the Tibetan colony of Manju-ka-Tilla, check out www.tibetcity.com.

Connaught Place *p92, maps p88 and p91*

LL Imperial, Janpath, T011-2334 1234, www.theimperialindia.com. 230 rooms and beautiful 'deco suites' in supremely elegant Lutyens-designed 1933 hotel. Unparalleled location, great bar, antiques and art everywhere, corridors scented with jasmine oil, gardens with spa and secluded pool, amazing **Spice Route** restaurant, classy and knows it but still quite an experience. Highly recommended.

LL-L Park, 15 Sansad Marg, T011-2374 3000, www.theparkhotels.com. 224 of the best contemporary-style rooms in town, good views, friendly, award-winning restaurant and funky, modern bar, **Aqua**, by the pool, new glass-walled spa overlooking Jantar Mantar. There is a great shop, **The Box**, on ground floor. Recommended.

L Hans Plaza, 15 Barakhamba Rd (16th-20th floor), T011-2331 6868, www.hanshotels.com. 67 slightly uninspired rooms, not a 'boutique hotel' as advertised but clean and quiet with superb views. There is very little difference between the 'deluxe' and the 'executive' rooms, so go for the cheapest.

AL-A Palace Heights, D26-28 Connaught Pl, T011-4358 2610, www.hotelpalaceheights.com. Recently given a complete facelift, the bright, modern rooms with good attention to detail, represent the best choice in Connaught Pl in this price bracket. There's also an attractive glass-walled restaurant overlooking the street.

A Hotel Alka, P Block, Connaught Circus, T011-2334 4328, www.hotelalka.com. 21 well-appointed rooms including 2 spotless restaurants but it's nothing special. Next door to the great restaurant **Saravana Bhavan** for dosas.

C-D YMCA Tourist Hostel, Jai Singh Rd, T011-2336 1915, www.newdelhiymca.org. 120 rooms, for both sexes, a/c rooms with bath (B-Block, non a/c and shared bath), some reported dirty, common areas have been recently refurbished. Restaurant (breakfast included but disappointing), cybercafé, travel agent, peaceful gardens, tennis, good pool (Rs 200 extra), luggage storage (Rs 10 per day), pay in advance but check bill, reserve ahead, very professional.

D-E Asian Guest House, 14 Scindia House (upstairs from Religare Arts Gallery and Café), off Kasturba Gandhi Marg, the sign is a bit hidden behind petrol pump, T011-2331 3393, www.asianguesthouse.com. Friendly faces greet you here, although it's a bit tricky to find – call ahead for directions. Great central location. Clean basic rooms, some with a/c, some with TV.

D-F Choudhary, H 35/3 Connaught Circus, T011-2332 2043, hkc_guesthouse@hotmail.com. Tucked away but worth seeking out; very clean but basic rooms in a central location with a friendly manager who knows his stuff.

Paharganj *p92, maps p88 and p93*

Parharganj is where backpackers congregate. Its back lanes hide one of Asia's biggest markets for export-quality goods. Sandwiched between the main sights and near the main railway station, it's noisy, dirty and a lot of hassle. Its chief virtues are economy and convenience, with plenty of shops selling souvenirs and cheap clothes, travel agents, budget hotels and cafés catering for Western tastes. For a more sedate, 'authentic' experience, you might like to try elsewhere. Rooms tend to be cheap, often with shared baths. Avoid **Hotel Bright**.

AL White Klove, 1563 Laxmi Narayan St, near Imperial Cinema, T011-4100 0358, www.thewhiteklove.com. Lovely lobby leads up to stylish, but small boutique-style rooms with all the mod cons. Nice little roof terrace. However if this is your budget, why stay in Paharganj?

AL-B Jyoti Mahal, 2488 Nalwa St, behind Imperial Cinema, T011-2358 0524, www.jyotimahal.net. An oasis in Paharganj with large and atmospheric rooms in a beautiful converted *haveli* and new deluxe rooms in stylish new wing. Cool and quiet with nice antique pieces dotted around and bowls of floating rose petals lining the staircases. They have given their rooftop restaurant a bit of a facelift and added new continental dishes to the menu, but their Indian fare is top-notch. It's a very atmospheric place to dine. Highly recommended.

B-C Star Plaza, 5158 Main Bazar, although is slightly off the Bazar, T011-2358 1731, www.hotelstarplaza.in, It's close to the Main Bazar without being right in the thick of it and you can take back streets to metro station – very handy. Clean a/c rooms with all the mod cons including Wi-Fi. Pretty smart looking place for this part of town.

C Hotel Relax, 4970 Ram Dwara Rd, Nehru Bazar, T011-2356 2811, vidur109@hotmail.com. Off main bazar down the veg market road is a little gem of a hotel. Good clean rooms, nice vibe – a cut above the rest.

C Metropolis Tourist Home, 1634-35 Main Bazar, T011-2358 5766, metropolistouristhome @yahoo.co.in. More expensive rooms have ornate heavy wooden furniture, but walls are grubby throughout. Nice rooftop restaurant, and wonderful wooden espresso bar in the lobby. Has another branch close to the metro station.

C-D Hotel Ajanta, 36 Arakashan Rd, Ram Nagar (opposite New Delhi railway station), T011-4176 4563, www.ajantahotel.com. A few blocks removed from the madness of the Main Bazar, 70 well-maintained rooms, most a/c, good service and lobby and restaurant. If you make a reservation be sure to stress you want to stay in their main hotel. Enormous suites and family rooms. Spanish quilts, spring mattresses; they stress their use of fabric softener! IATA travel agency on site for tickets and tours.

C-D Prince Polonia, 2325-26 Tilak Gali (behind Imperial Cinema), T011-4762 6600, www.hotelprincepolonia.com. Very unusual for Paharganj in that it has a rooftop pool (small, but good for a cool down). Breezy rooftop café. Attracts a slightly more mature crowd. Safe, clean. Ignore claims from their site about being a 'boutique' hotel – it's standard Indian fare.

D-E Anoop, 1566 Main Bazar, T011-2358 9366, www.anupamhoteliersltd.com. 43 rooms with bath, some with air-cooler, very clean though basic, noisy at times, safe. Good 24-hr rooftop restaurant.

D-E Railway Retiring Rooms, New (and Old) Delhi Railway Station. For 12 hrs and 24 hrs, dorm beds, 10 rooms (6 a/c are usually pre-booked), only for train ticket-holders, basic and noisy, but convenient.

D-F Ajay's, 5084A Main Bazar, T011-2358 3125, www.ajayguesthouse.com. 48 fairly clean (windowless) rooms with bath, dorm, good bakery, restaurant, friendly, popular backpackers' hangout.

D-F Heritage Inn, 2374 Raj Guru Rd, Chuna Mandi, T011-2358 8222. New building with 20 simple, spotless rooms and friendly staff.

D-F Hotel Gush, 626, Main Bazar, Chowk Bawli, T011-2356 1758, hotelgushinternational@ gmail.com. New hotel with same friendly manager as neighbouring **Rak International** (see below). Neetu, runs the hotels with his brothers (they also have the bindi shop on the corner their side street and Main Bazar). Steel and marble themed. Basic, clean rooms. Might win most unfortunate name though.

D-F Rak International, 820 Main Bazar, Chowk Bowli, T011-2358 6508, www.hotelrak international.com. 27 basic but clean rooms in professionally run. Quiet, friendly hotel with a rooftop restaurant and water feature.

D-F Star Palace, 4590 Dal Mandi, off Main Bazar (lane opposite Khalsa Boots), T011-2358 4849, www.stargroupofhotels.com. 31 clean, well-kept rooms (some a/c) with "fantastic showers", quiet, friendly, safe, airport pick-up.

E-F Hotel Payal, 1182 Main Bazar, T011-2356 2867, hotelpayalsharmaji@yahoo.com. As you would expect for main bazar, but clean with attached bathrooms and friendly reception.
F-G Namaskar, 917 Chandiwalan, Main Bazar, T011-2358 3456, namaskarhotel@yahoo.com. Owner is a fount of knowledge, friendly and helpful 32 small basic rooms (2-4 beds), all have showers, clean but some windowless, newer **D** a/c rooms in extension, generator, safe, friendly service, good atmosphere, quiet at night, free luggage storage, car rental, reserve ahead.

Karol Bagh and Rajendra Nagar

West of Pahar Ganj on the Metro line, **Karol Bagh** is full of identikit modern hotels, albeit a degree more upmarket than Paharganj. There are plentiful good eating places, and the area is handy for Sarai Rohilla station. Nearby **Rajendra Nagar**, a residential suburb, has one of Delhi's best homestays.
AL Hotel Clark International, 5/47 WEA, Saraswati Mark, Karol Bagh, T011-4500 5500, www.hotelclarkindia.com. Business hotel with 32 elegant spacious rooms. If you have this budget though there are many more interesting options in quieter parts of town.
A Bajaj Indian Home Stay, 8A/34 WEA, Karol Bagh, T011-2573 6509, www.indianhomestay.com. 10 comfortable rooms, all have a different theme, from gods to holy cities. Mod cons include telephones in all the bathrooms. Homely touches and atmosphere. Tricky to find – tell the taxi driver, the turn-off is by "Pusa Road metro pillar 122".
A Yatri Paying Guest House, corner of Panchkuin and Mandir Margs, T011-2362 5563, www.yatrihouse.com. A quiet, peaceful oasis with beautiful gardens. 6 large, attractive rooms all with 42-inch televisions, nice bathrooms, Wi-Fi, fridge and a/c. Free airport pick-up or drop off. Breakfast, tea/coffee and afternoon snack included. A bit overpriced.
B Master Guest House, R-500 New Rajendra Nagar (Shankar Rd and GR Hospital Rd crossing), T011-2874 1089, www.masterbedandbreakfast.com. 3 clean rooms, a/c, with private bathroom, Wi-Fi, rooftop for breakfast, *thalis*, warm welcome, personal attention, secure, recommended. Each room has the theme of a different god, complete with appropriate colour schemes. Very knowledgeable, caring owners run excellent tours of 'hidden Delhi'.

South Delhi *p94, map p88*

Most of the city's smartest hotels are located south of Rajpath, in a broad rectangle between Chanakyapuri and Humayun's Tomb. The southern residential suburbs are also peppered with homestays; a list is available from **Delhi Tourism**, BK Singh Marg (see page 77), or arrange with the reliable **Metropole** (see Car hire, page 121).
LL Aman New Delhi, Lodhi Rd, T011-4363 3333, www.amanresorts.com. This serene and stylish hotel takes luxury to new levels. Come for the suites with private pools, exquisite contemporary design and fantastic spa.
LL Claridges, 12 Aurangzeb Rd, T011-3955 5000, www.claridges.com. 138 refurbished, classy rooms, art deco-style interiors, colonial atmosphere, attractive restaurants (**Jade Garden** is good), slick **Aura** bar, impeccable service, more atmosphere than most. Recommended.
LL Oberoi, Dr Zakir Hussain Marg, T011-2436 3030, www.oberoihotels.com. 300 rooms and extremely luxurious suites overlooking golf club, immaculate, quietly efficient, beautiful touches, eg carved Tree of Life in lobby, all 5-star facilities including 2 pools and spa, superb business centre, good restaurants.
LL Taj Mahal, 1 Mansingh Rd, T011-2302 6162, www.tajhotels.com. 1 of 3 Taj hotels in Delhi. 300 attractive rooms, comfortable, new club levels outstanding, excellent restaurants and service (**Haveli** offers wide choice and explanations for the newcomer; **Ming House**'s spicing varies; **Machan** overlooks palm trees and has wildlife library), good Khazana shop, lavishly finished with 'lived-in' feel, friendly 1920s-style bar, good city views but lacks atmosphere.
LL-L ITC Maurya Sheraton, Sardar Patel Marg, T011-2611 2233, www.itcwelcom group.com. 484 rooms, those in ITC block exceptional with private butler, electric massage chairs, excellent decor and service, splendid pool (solar heated), disco (noisy late at night, so avoid rooms nearby), good restaurants.
LL-L Vasant Continental, Vasant Vihar, T011-2614 8800, www.jaypeehtoels.com. 110 rooms in recently renovated, contemporary-

style hotel, convenient for airports (free transfer), large pool and gardens near Basant Lok Market, good service, interesting range of restaurants. Recommended.

LL-L Vivanta by Taj , Sujan Singh Park, T011-2463 2600, www.tajhotels.com. Close to Khan Market and Lodhi Gardens, 81 rooms in period property, pleasant garden, quirky bar and coffee shop, calm atmosphere, quiet and convenient location. There is also the more business-oriented **Taj Palace** on Sardar Patel Marg.

L Manor, 77 Friends Colony, T011-2692 5151, www.themanordelhi.com. Contemporary boutique hotel with 10 stylish rooms, heavenly beds, polished stone surfaces and chrome, relaxing garden, a haven. This is where Sir Terence Conran stays so you can be guaranteed of quality. Beautiful artwork and relaxed vibe. Charming service.

L-AL Casa Delhi, C-56 Defence Colony, T(0)9971-425558, www.casaboutiquehotels.com. Some of the most beautiful rooms you will find in Delhi. A true boutique hotel with sumptuous decor – a true oasis. The sister hotel, **Casa Friends**, in Friends Colony East, was having a facelift at the time of writing.

L-AL Jukaso Inn, 50 Sunder Nagar, T011-2435 0308, www.jukasohotels.com. Pleasant, quiet, not much character, friendly staff, restaurant, room service. Country house style atrium which is at odds with the quite lovely red or gold bedrooms. Not to be confused with cheaper **Jukaso Inn Downtown**.

AL Amarya Haveli, P5 Hauz Khas Enclave, T011-4175 9268, www.amaryagroup.com. Luxury, boutique, hip guesthouse, run by 2 Frenchmen. Unique, bright, en suite rooms, with TV, Wi-Fi. Fantastic roof garden. Great home cooked food. Book ahead. Slightly cheaper than their newer hotel. Highly recommended.

AL Amarya Villa A2/20 Sardarjung Enclave, T011-4103 6184, , www.amaryagroup.com. Stunning rooms with different vibrant colour themes and great attention to detail. Hip vibe with lovely lounge area downstairs and stylish roof garden at the top from the same team as delivered the lovely **Amarya Haveli**.

AL Diplomat, 9 Sardar Patel Marg, T011-2301 0204, www.thehoteldiplomat.com. 25 rooms, all different. Good attention to detail. The delicious **Olive Beach** restaurant (see Eating) is in the garden. No pool, quietly located.

AL Lutyens Bungalow, 39 Prithviraj Rd, T011-2469 4523, www.lutyensbungalow.co.in. Private guesthouse in a bungalow that has been running for over 35 years – it's looking a little faded around the edges. Eccentric, rambling property with 15 a/c rooms, a wonderful pool and beautiful gardens with a garden accessory shop on-site. free airport pickup/drop off, full services, used for long-stays by NGOs and foreign consultants.

AL-A Basera, 10 Sunder Nagar, T011-2435 8276, avvkhanna@gmail.com. Billed as a B&B, this place has a relaxed vibe and charmingly decorated rooms. There are also weekly and monthly rates for rooms and furnished apartments. Lovely green location.

AL-A Shervani, 11 Sundar Nagar, T011-4250 1000, www.shervanihotels.com. Swish, business boutique hotel in quiet Sundar Nagar. All mod cons. Quiet location – opposite communal gardens. Stylish and relaxed atmosphere.

A Colonel's Retreat, D 418 Defence Colony, T011-4660 4927, www.colonelsretreat.com. New B&B. En suite rooms, all mod cons, well located, lively atmosphere.

A-B K One One, K11, Jangpura Extn, 2nd floor, T011-4359 2583, www.parigold.com. Homely guesthouse in quiet, central residential area. Run by wonderful ex-TV chef, who also gives cooking lessons. All rooms en suite with ac, mini-bar, Wi-Fi, some with balconies. Wonderful roof terrace with views of Humayan's Tomb. Rooftop room is lovely. Book ahead.

B '27' Jorbagh, 27 Jorbagh (2 mins from Lodi tombs), T011-2469 4430, www.jorbagh27.com. 20 a/c rooms, car hire, not plush but very quiet hassle free, book ahead.

B Murad Baig, R-block, Hauz Khas Enclave (phone for exact address), T(0)9899-555704. A real find. Just one beautiful bedroom with attached bathroom, leads out onto a large green roof terrace. The owner is an oracle when it comes to Delhi history and his wife, author of 16 cookbooks, gives cookery lessons. They make you part of the family. The room gets booked up, so reserve well ahead.

B On the House B-4/120 Safdarjung Enclave, T011-4602 4897, www.bedandbreakfastnew delhi.com. Popular B&B in quiet, residential area. Colourful en suite rooms, all with a/c, Wi-Fi, TV.

B Tree of Life B&B, D-193, Saket, T(0)9810-277699, www.tree-of-life.in. Stylish B&B with beautifully decorated rooms, simple but chic. Kitchen access, excellent on-site reflexology and yoga – really good atmosphere. The owner also runs **Metropole Tourist Service**. Close to Saket metro station and to **PVR** cinema (see page 121) and malls.

B-C Life Tree, G 14 Lajpat Nagar Part II, T(0)9910-460898, lifetreebnb@gmail.com. A more simple but charming B&B from the **Tree of Life** family – well located for Khan Market and centre.

D-F Youth Hostel, 5 Naya Marg, Chanakyapuri, T011-2611 6285, www.yhaindia.org. Wide range of room from a/c doubles to a basic dorm (a/c dorms much better). Meals available at restaurant if ordered in advance. Soulless but clean and comfortable. Great location. You need YHA membership to stay (Rs 250 foreigners, Rs 100 Indians).

Airport

Unless you can afford a 5-star, hotels around the airport are overpriced and best avoided.

LL-L Radisson National Highway 8, T011-2677 9191. Plush, if slightly soulless 5-star, with all mod cons.

L-A Hotel Saptagiri L-322, Mahipalpur Extension, National Highway 8, T011-4616 0000, www.hotelsaptagiri.com. 5-10 mins from the airports. The cheapest rooms have no windows. Suites with balconies overlook the the noisy National Highway. Clean, secure. Wi-Fi.

A-C Sam's Snooze at My Space T3 IGI Airport, opposite Gate 17, T(0)8800-230013, www.newdelhiairport.in. You can book a snooze pod for $9 per hr – only if you are flying out of T3. There's Wi-Fi, TV and DVD, work stations.

C Hotel Eurostar International, A 27/1 Street No 1, near MTNL office, Mahipalpur Extension, T011-4606 2300, www.hoteleurostar.in. Good-value option near the airport.

Gurgaon

Although technically in Haryana, Gurgaon is the new New Delhi, dubbed the new face of Corporate India. On the metro it takes less than an hour from Connaught Place, by road it really depends. There are a lot of new 5-stars.

LL The Leela Kempinski, Ambience Island, National Highway, www.theleela.com. One of the newer **Leela's** to open in the country and ready to pick up awards. The rooms and suites are everything you can imagine in style and substance. There are several restaurants on-site. The main restaurant caters for every taste and has semi-live kitchens, where you can see your teppenyaki being made or your pancakes being tossed. Should you get bored, there is a stunning spa and it is right next door to the latest mall, **Ambience**. Recommended.

A-B Ahuja Residency, N3/36 DLF City, Phase II, T0124-401 9335, www.ahujaresidency.com. Comfortable smart rooms with 24-hr room service and business facilities – a more homely feel. They also have another in Gurgaon at Park Lane, Phase 1 and 2 guesthouses in the city in Sunder Nagar and Defence Colony.

A-B Crowne Plaza, Site 2 Sector 29, opposite Signature Tower, T124-453 4000, www.ichotels group.com. Smart rooms from this established global chain. Swimming pool, sauna and gym on-site.

A-B Harry's Bed and Breakfast, Plot 40, Silver Oaks Av, DLF 1, T(0)9871-699996, www.harrysbedandbreakfast.com. Elegant rooms here with beautiful dining area and common living room, as well as study and meeting room.

Eating

The larger hotel restaurants are often the best for cuisine, decor and ambience. Buffets (lunch or dinner) cost Rs 700 or more. Sun buffets are becoming quite the thing in the top-notch hotels. Others may only open around 1930 for dinner; some close on Sun. Alcohol is served in most top hotels, but only in some non-hotel restaurants eg **Amber**, **Ginza** and **Kwality**.

The old-fashioned 'tea on the lawn' is still served at the **Imperial** and in **Claridges** (see Sleeping). **Aapki Pasand**, at 15 Netaji Subhash Marg, offers unusual tea-tasting in classy and extremely professional surroundings; it's quite an experience.

Old Delhi *p79, map p84*

In **Paranthewali Gali**, a side street off Chandni Chowk, stalls sell a variety of *paranthas* including *kaju badam* (stuffed with dry fruits and nuts). Although a few local Delhi folks say this place is overrated. Other good places to try local foods like *bedmi aloo* puri with spiced potato are **Mahalaxmi Misthan Bhandhar** at 659 Church Mission street and **Natraj Chowk** 1396 Chandni Chowk for *dahi balli* and *aloo tikki*. For sweets you have to seek out **Old Famous Jalebi Wala** 1797 Dariba Corner, Chandni Chowk – as they are old and famous.

TTT **Chor Bizarre**, **Broadway Hotel** (see Sleeping), T011-2327 3821. Tandoori and Kashmiri cuisine (Wazwan, Rs 500). Fantastic food, quirky decor, including salad bar that was a vintage car. Well worth a visit.

T **Haldiram's**, 1454/2 Chandni Chowk. Stand-up counter for excellent snacks and sweets on the run (try *dokhla* with coriander chutney from seller just outside), and more elaborate sit-down restaurant upstairs.

T **Karim's**, Gali Kababiyan (south of Jama Masjid), Mughlai. Authentic, busy, plenty of local colour. The experience, as much as the food, makes this a must. Not a lot to tempt vegetarians though.

T **Peshawari**, 3707 Subhash Marg, Daryaganj. Closed Tue. Tiny, with tiled walls, serves delicious chicken.

Connaught Place *p92, maps p88 and p91*

TTT **Bonsai, Chorus Hotel**, B49 Connaught Pl, T011-4365 2240. Tranquil garden, imaginative, good-value food. Perfect for when you want to escape the noise of CP.

TTT **Rodeo**, 12-A, T011-2371 3780. Excellent Mexican (3-course and beer, Rs 350), Italian, continental, "heavenly". Fast service, fully stocked bar, Wild West decor.

TTT **Sakura, Hotel Metropolitan Nikko**, Bangla Sahib Rd, T011-2334 2000. Top Japanese royal cuisine in classic, uncluttered surroundings. One of the best in the city, priced accordingly.

TTT **Spice Route, Imperial Hotel** (see Sleeping). Extraordinary temple-like surroundings (took 7 years to build), Kerala, Thai, Vietnamese cuisines, magical atmosphere but expensive food doesn't always thrill.

TTT **Veda**, 27-H, T011-4151 3535. Owned by fashion designer Rohit Bal with appropriately beautiful bordello-style decor, done out like a Rajasthani palace with high-backed leather chairs and candles reflecting from mirror work on ceilings. Food is contemporary Indian. Great atmosphere at night.

TTT **Zen**, B-25, T011-2335 7455. Stylish, a little impersonal, but popular, generous portions for Chinese, more expensive Japanese and seafood.

TT **Amber**, N-Block, T011-2331 2092. High-class decor, lightly spiced Mughlai cuisine, beer.

TT **The Chinese**, F14/15, T011-2370 8888. Rivals **Q'BA** (see below) for the most authentic Chinese food in Connaught Pl, but service is a few degrees better; beers are poured like fine wines.

TT **Embassy**, D-11, T011-2341 7480. International food. Popular with artistic-intellectual-political crowd, good food, long-standing local favourite.

TT **Kwality**, 7 Regal Building, near **Park Hotel**, T011-2374 2352. International. Spicy Punjabi dishes with various breads. Try *chhole bhature*.

TT **Q'BA**, E-42 Connaught Pl, T011-4151 2888. Dodgy decor, slow service but attractive menu, excellent Chinese section, and a superb terrace overlooking Connaught Pl (reserve ahead). Live jazz on Sun.

TT **United Coffee House**, E-15 Connaught Pl, T011-2341 1697. Recommended more for the colonial-era cake-icing decor than for the fairly average food. Often someone waxing lyrical over a Casio keyboard. Always attracts a mixed crowd, well worth a visit.

Ⴤ **Kake da Hotel**, Outer Circle opposite L-block. Famous Punjabi *dhaba*. *Handi* dishes and delicious green masala fish, not the cleanest but very cheap and popular.

Ⴤ **Nathu's**, and **Bengali Sweet House**, both in Bengali Market (east of Connaught Pl). Sweet shops also serving vegetarian food. Good dosa, *iddli*, *utthapam* and North Indian *chana bathura*, *thalis*, clean, functional. Try *kulfi* (hard blocks of ice cream) with *falooda* (sweet vermicelli noodles).

Ⴤ **Nizam's Kathi Kebabs**, H-5 Plaza, T011-2371 3078. Very good, tasty filled *parathas*, good value, clean, excellent '3-D toilets' (note the emergency button!).

Ⴤ **Saravana Bhavan**, P-15/90, near McDonalds, T011-2334 7755; also at 46 Janpath, T011-2331 7755. Chennai-based chain, light and wonderful South Indian, superb chutneys, unmissable *kaju anjeer* ice cream with figs and nuts. Can take hours to get a table at night or at weekends. If your name's not on the list, you're not getting a dosa. Highly recommended.

Ⴤ **Street stalls**, at entrance to Shankar Market. Stalls dish out *rajma chawal* (bean stew and rice) to a vast, appreciative crowd on weekdays.

Ⴤ **Triveni Tea Terrace**, Triveni Kala Sangam, 205 Tansen Marg, near Mandi House metro station (not Sun). Art galleries, an amphitheatre and this little café in quite an unusual building close to CP – the tea terrace is a bit of an institution.

Paharganj *p92, maps p88 and p93*

The rooftop restaurants at **Jyoti Mahal** and **Shelton** are great locations for a bite to eat.

ႤႤ-Ⴤ **Café Sim Tok**, Tooti Chowk, above Hotel Navrang, near Hotel Rak, T(0)9810-386717. You could stay in this area for years and never know this little gem of a Korean restaurant even exists. No signage to guide you, ask for **Hotel Navrang** and ignore the squalor that is the Navrang, keep going up stairs and find delicious *kimbab* (Korean sushi), *kimchi* and all sorts of soups, in a sweet little café.

Ⴤ **Appetite**, 1575 Main Bazar, T011-2753 2079. Chinese, Nepali, Italian. Rather grim-looking backpacker den, good bakery items and *lassis*.

Ⴤ **Everest Bakery Café**, Dal Mandi, near **Star Palace Hotel**. Fantastic *momos*, cakes and pies, green teas, sociable. Recommended.

Ⴤ **Madan's**, 1601 Main Bazar. International. Everything from egg and chips to *thalis*, not special but friendly, popular and good value.

Ⴤ **Malhotra's**, 1833 Laxmi Narayan St, T011-2358 9371. Good Indian and Chinese, wide choice, a/c section; also takeaway. Also has a South Indian *dosa* joint next door.

Ⴤ **Open Hand Café**, Main Bazar, near RK Ashram Metro station. An oasis in the midst of the mayhem of Paharganj. Beautiful café serving international portions of cappuccino, carrot cake, salads and sandwiches. A few tables, but also mezzanine level of floor cushions. Recommended.

Ⴤ **Southern Restaurant**, opposite **Ajanta**, Arakashan Rd. Spartan but clean and very cheap café for excellent fresh *dosas*, friendly Indian clientele, atmosphere better downstairs than in fan-cooled upstairs room.

Ⴤ **Tadka**, off Main Bazar. Good option for tasty food in this area. Great range of all the usual Indian favourites, with nice decor, friendly staff and good hygiene levels.

South Delhi *p92, map p88*

ႤႤႤ **Ai**, MGF Metropolitan Mall, Saket, T011-4065 4567. This glamorous uber-trendy 200-seater restaurant serves top-quality sushi. Stylish decor and great terrace, jazz bar and some fantastic DJ nights. Hang out with the beautiful people.

ႤႤႤ **Baci**, 23 Sunder Nagar Market, Near HDFC Bank, T011-4150 7445. Classy, top-quality Italian food, run by gregarious Italian-Indian. There is also a cheaper café **Amici** run by the same team in Khan Market.

ႤႤႤ **Bukhara**, **ITC Maurya Sheraton** (see Sleeping), T011-2611 2233. Stylish Northwest Frontier cuisine amidst rugged walls draped with rich rugs (but uncomfortable seating). Outstanding meat dishes and dhal. Also tasty vegetable and *paneer* dishes, but vegetarians will miss out on the best dishes.

ႤႤႤ **Diva**, M8, M-Block Market, Greater Kailash II, T011-2921 5673. Superb Italian in minimalist space popular with celebrity crowd. Great fish dishes, inventive starters, dedicated vegetarian section, extensive wine list.

Indian Accent, at **The Manor**, 77 Friends Colony West, T011-4323 5151. With a menu designed by Manish Mehotra, who runs restaurants in Delhi and London, this acclaimed restaurant offers up Indian food with a modern twist. Your *dosas* will reveal masala morel mushrooms, rather than the traditional Goan prawns *balchao* here you will find it with roasted scallops. Or how about toffee chyawanprash cheesecake with badam milk (*chyawanprash* is a health elixir from the amla fruit)? The menu reflects the changing of the seasons and there is live fusion music on Sat. Highly recommended.

Kainoosh, 122-124 DLF Promenade Mall, Vasant Kunj, T(0)9560-715544. Under the watchful eye of celebrity chef Marut Sikka, delicious *thalis* marry the traditional and modern faces of Indian food. This is *thali* with a difference – bespoke with giant morel mushrooms, sea bass mousse and chicken cooked in orange juice and saffron in a terracotta pot. There is a chic and sexy bar next door **Keya** offering up signature cocktails like *Keya Magic* (vodka, sambuca and beetleleaf) or *India Pink* (vodka, rosewater, cardamom and lemon juice).

Latitude, 9 Khan Market, above Good Earth, T011-2462 1013. Like sitting in someone's very posh, very chic living room and getting served delicious Italian numbers like bruschetta, yummy salads and pastas. Topped off with top-notch coffees.

Line of No Control, **Qutab Hotel**, Shahid Jeet Singh Marg, T011-4168 8963/62. Well worth braving the outer edges of South Delhi for this blend of Indian and Pakistani cuisine. Sit on the breezy terrace or enjoy the lavish interiors.

Lodi, Lodi Gardens, T011-2465 5054. Continental lunch, Indian dinner menu in pleasant, Mediterranean-style surroundings, nice terrace and garden. Come more for the setting than the food which can be mediocre.

Magique, Gate No 3, Garden of 5 Senses, Mehrauli Badarpur Rd, T011-2953 6767. High-class quality food, in a magical setting. Sit outside among the candles and fairy lights. One of Delhi's most romantic restaurants.

Olive at the Qutb, www.olivebarand kitchen.com. Branch of the ever popular Mumbai restaurant and some people say the Delhi version wins hands down. Serving up delicious platters of Mediterranean food and good strong cocktails. Or head to their sister restaurant in the **Diplomat Hotel – Olive Beach** especially for their legendary blow-out Sun brunches: for Rs 1900 you get open access to a mind-boggling buffet and as many martini's as you can drink.

Orient Express, **Taj Palace Hotel**, T011-2611 0202. Continental. Recreated luxury of the famous train carriages, formal dress code, expensive but different.

Park Baluchi, inside Deer Park, Hauz Khas Village, T011-2685 9369. Atmospheric dining in Hauz Khas Deer Park. The lamb wrapped in chicken served on a flaming sword comes highly recommended. Can get crowded, book ahead.

Ploof, 13 Main Market, Lodhi Colony, T011-2464 9026. The place to come for seafood. Very popular. Bright, comfortable restaurant.

Smokehouse Bar & Grill, No 2, VIPPS Centre, Masjid Moth Greater Kailash II, T011-4143 5530. Classy joint, great continental food, fine wines, an enviable cigar selection and a stylish bar. In the same square as **Mainland China** (see below). They are also opening another branch near Qutb Minar.

Trishna, near Qutb Minar. Alas no contact details at time of writing, but the acclaimed seafood restaurant **Trishna** (Bombay and London) is coming to the Qutb Minar. Well worth further investigations.

Yum Yum Tree, 1st floor, Friends Colony Community Centre (opposite Nathu Sweets), T011-4260 2020. Excellent Chinese, with an enormous menu. Very popular. Great decor.

All American Diner, India Habitat Centre, Lodhi Rd, T011-4366 3333, ext 3162. The place to come if you feel like a shake and a burger. A perfect mock-up of a 1950s diner, in the surreal setting of the Habitat Centre.

The Big Chill, F-38 East of Kailash (off Lala Lajpat Rai Path near Spring Meadows Hospital), also in Khan Market. 1230 till late. A bright café with a wide range of carefully prepared, wholesome meals of grills, bakes, fresh pasta, home-made desserts and ice creams.

Choko la, Khan Market, T011-4175 7570. According to this chocolate boutique, 'there is no love more sincere than the love of chocolate' and they prove it with their chocolate croissants and home-made pieces of decadence. They serve up a great cappuccino and have a more savoury menu too in this chic little café which is actually jolly good value compared to some of the other Khan Market eateries.

Grey Garden, 13a Hauz Khaz Village, near the lake, T011-2651 6450. New kid on the block in the lovely Hauz Khaz village, this boho chic little number serves up a small menu but with great attention to detail. Delicious banana-wrapped fish or thin-crust pizzas, lotus stem chips and other assorted goodies. There is an excellent clothes shop run by the same team next door too. If you are heading there at the weekend, book ahead. Highly recommended.

Gunpowder, 22 Hauz Khaz Village, 3rd floor. Wander around the labyrinthine streets of Hauz Khaz and hopefully stumble upon this great restaurant. Specializing in spicy flavours from South India, these are tastes you don't often find north of Mumbai. Try the *Toddy Shop Meen Curry*, *Malabar parotta* and spicy dry pickle *Vepilakkati*. Great views from the terrace and deservedly popular, so book ahead. Recommended.

Flavors, 52-C, Flyover Complex, Defence Colony, T011-2464 5644. Ignore the bizarre location next to a flyover and enjoy some good Italian food. If you're lucky you may even get serenaded by a man with a synthesizer.

Le Café, N1, N-Block Market, GK1, T011-4173 1935. Stylish café, with wonderful roof garden, hidden on the 3rd floor above **Ravi Bajaj** clothes shop (corner of N-block market).

The Living Room, 31 Haus Khaz, T011-4608 0533, www.tlrcafe.com. Funky laid-back atmosphere day and night at this three-tiered restaurant. By day there's cosy armchairs and sofas and a delicious menu of Indian and Western treats, all done to perfection. There's a 'reading nook' (library) sponsored by Penguin books. By night, things kick up a gear with live music, open mics and DJs spinning electronica and dubstep, and all manner of themed nights. Recommended.

Mamagoto, 53 Khan Market, T011-4516 6060, www.mamagoto.in. Manga style restaurant serving up asian food like *Chicken Broth for the Hungry Soul* and *Chiang Mai Train Station Noodles*. *Mamagoto* means 'play with your food' and the fantastic cartoon decor definitely gives a funky playful vibe. There is another branch at **PVR Select Citywalk** mall in Saket.

Market Café, 2nd floor, Middle Lane, Khan Market, T011-4175 7703. Free Wi-Fi, large menu and a great roof terrace, make this a popular choice.

Moti Mahal Deluxe, 20/48 Malcha Marg, Chanakyapuri (near **Diplomat**), T011-2611 8698. Closed Tue. Excellent Mughlai, short on ambience but food makes up for it.

Naivedyam, Hauz Khas Village, T011-2696 0426. Very good South Indian, great service and very good value

Oh! Calcutta, E-Block, ground floor, International Trade Towers, Nehru Pl, T011-2646 4180. Authentic Bengali cuisine, with excellent vegetarian and fish options, somewhat odd location but not far from the Baha'i temple.

Sanchos, E 3, 3rd floor, South Extension II, T011-4607 6422. Good Mexican, lethal sangria, the sizzling *fajitas* are recommended.

Swagath, 14 Defence Colony Market, T011-2433 0930. Neighbouring, some say superior rival to the famous **Sagar** (see below), with a variety of cuisines (Chinese, Tamil, Mangalore) and a strong emphasis on seafood.

Andhra Bhavan, near India Gate. Crowded and rushed but atmospheric place for extra-spicy Chettinad (South Indian) food, vegetarian and non-vegetarian options, superb *thalis*.

Colonelz Kebabz, Defence Colony Market. Tandoori. 1000-2200. Excellent tikkas and kebabs. Several others, including **RK Puram**, serving delicious, safe, street food.

Khan Cha Cha, Khan Market, 75 Middle Lane. This no-frills joint serves some of the best kebabs in the city from a window in the middle lane of Khan Market. Fantastic value. You can recognize the place from the crowd clamouring at the counter.

Sagar, 18 Defence Colony Market, T011-2433 3110. Other branches in Vasant Kunj, Malviya Nagar and NOIDA. Excellent South Indian. Cheap and "amazing" *thalis* and coffee, very hectic (frequent queues). One of the best breakfasts in Delhi.

Ten, YWCA International GH, Sansad Marg. Mexican, continental. Cheery café popular with long-stay foreigners, pleasant tree-shaded garden, clean, modern, well run. Recommended.

Bars and clubs

Many national holidays are 'dry' days. Delhi's bar/club scene has exploded over the last few years. Expect to pay a lot for your drinks and, when in doubt, dress up as some clubs have strict dress codes. Delhi's 'in' crowd is notoriously fickle; city magazines (*Time Out, First City*) will point you towards the flavour of the month. For more insight into Delhi check out the website www.bringhomestories.com.

Connaught Place *p92, maps p88 and p91*

1911, **Imperial Hotel** (see Sleeping). Elegantly styled colonial bar, good snacks.

Agni, **Park Hotel** (see Sleeping). Terence Conran-style bar, sharply dressed staff, reliable party atmosphere that can descend into bar-top dancing.

Aqua, also in **Park Hotel**, is Delhi's first poolside bar.

South Delhi *p92, map p88*

24/7, **Lalit Hotel**, Barakhamba Av, Connaught Pl. Boasting molecular mixology with their cocktails and regular turns by prominent DJs and more alternative acts, 24/7 is putting itself in the scene.

Baci, ground floor of classy Italian eatery (see Eating). Hosts some stomping DJ nights, especially on Thu.

Blue Frog, near Qutb Minar, www.bluefrog.co.in. For years, Blue Frog has been the best venue in Mumbai with supreme live acts and star DJs doing a turn and now it's coming to Delhi. Check the website for details.

Bohemia, opposite **Shalom** (see below), T011-2924 3328. Relaxed, contemporary bar, friendly staff plus a good Indian restaurant upstairs.

Café Morrisons, Shop E-12, South Extension Part II, T011-2625 5652. Very popular sticky rock bar. Come for live bands or just to mosh to the DJ.

The F-Bar, **Ashok Hotel** (see Sleeping), Chanakyapuri, T011-2611 1066. Glitzy, glamorous A-list bar. Generally plays house or electronica. Dress smart. Expensive.

The Living Room (see Eating). Fondly known as TLR, they have a range of themed nights – there is live music, open mic and DJs spinning electronica and dubstep over 3 floors, with a rooftop terrace.

The Love Hotel, part of **Ai** (see Eating). Super-hip, elegant bar. Some of the best visiting DJs play here.

Ministry of Sound, LSC Sector C, Pocket 6/7, Vasant Kunj, T011-4604 5319. Sleek steel-and-glass pyramid, variable crowd and music, large dance floor, expensive entry (Rs 2500 per couple) and drinks, but goes until early hours.

Pegs-n-Pints, Chanakya Lane, Chanakyapuri (tucked away behind Akbar Bhawan), T011-2687 8320. On Tue evenings it hosts Delhi's only gay club. Western and Indian pop. It gets packed. A lot of fun.

Rick's, **Taj Mahal Hotel** (see Sleeping). Suave Casablanca-themed bar with long martini list, a long-time fixture on Delhi's social scene.

Shalom, 'N' Block Market, Greater Kailash 1, T011-4163 2280. Comfortable, stylish lounge bar serving Lebanese cuisine; the resident DJ plays ambient music at a pleasantly low volume.

Smokehouse Bar & Grill (see Eating). Stylish downstairs bar is generally busy, but on a Thu evening it is heaving. Enjoy the bling and some of the most expensive drinks in Delhi.

Stone, Moets Complex, 50 Defence Colony Market, T011-4155 0571. Cool and calm bar in busy South Delhi neighbourhood, coffee table books, terrace, decent food, good atmosphere.

Urban Pind, N4, N-block market, GK1, T011-3951 5656. Multi-level bar, with large roof terrace, popular. Hosts a controversial expat/journalist night on Thu with an 'all-you-can-drink' entry fee, unsurprisingly this normally features a lot of drunk foreigners.

Zoo, at **Magique** (see Eating), one of the latest and most popular places on the scene serving up big portions of beats in a beautiful location.

Entertainment

Delhi *p74, maps p72, p84 p88, p91 and p93*

For advance notice of upcoming events see www.delhievents.com. Current listings and reviews can be found in *First City* (monthly, Rs 30), *Time Out* (fortnightly, Rs 30), *Delhi City Info* (fortnightly, free) and *Delhi Diary*(weekly). Also check out www.bringhomestories.com for inspiration on what to do in Delhi.

Cinema

For programmes see cinema listings in the daily *Delhi Times*.

PVR is a multiplex chain with branches everywhere, mostly screening Hindi movies, including **PVR Plaza** in Connaught Pl. Now with the metro, it's pretty easy to get to PVR Saket for example where as once it was extremely unlikely you would bother.

Music, dance and culture

The Attic, 36 Regal Building, Connaught Pl, T011-5150 3436, www.theatticdelhi.org. Hosts an eclectic range of lectures, films and workshops on art, culture and philosophy.
Goethe Institute, 3 Kasturba Gandhi Marg, T011-2332 9506. Recommended for arts, film festivals, open-air cinema, plays and events.
India Habitat Centre, Lodi Rd, T011-2468 2222. Good programme of lectures, films, exhibitions, concerts, excellent restaurant.
Indian International Centre, 40 Lodhi Estate, Max Mueller Marg, T011-2461 9431, www.iic delhi.nic.in. Some fantastic debates and performances, well worth checking the 'forth-coming programmes' section of their website.
Kingdom of Dreams, Great Indian Nautanki Company Ltd. Auditorium Complex, Sector 29, Gurgaon, Metro IFFCO, T0124-452 8000, www.kingdomofdreams.in. Ticket Prices 750-3000 depending on where you sit and more pricey at the weekend. The highlight is a much acclaimed all-singing, all-dancing Bollywood style performance. A little like an Indian Disneyland showcasing Indian tastes, foods, culture, dress and dance all in one a/c capsule, but done impeccably.
Triveni Kala Sangam, 205 Tansen Marg (near Mandi House Metro station), T011-2371 8833. Strong programme of photography and art exhibitions, plus an excellent North Indian café.

Son et lumière

Red Fort (see page 79), Apr-Nov 1800-1900 (Hindi), 1930-2030 (English). Entry Rs 50. Tickets available after 1700. Take mosquito cream.

Festivals and events

Delhi *p74, maps p72, p84 p88, p91 and p93*

For exact dates consult the weekly *Delhi Diary* available at hotels and many shops and offices around town.

Muslim festivals of **Ramadan**, **Id-ul-Fitr**, **Id-ul-Zuha** and **Muharram** are celebrated according to the lunar calendar.

January

Lohri (13 Jan) The climax of winter, is celebrated with bonfires and singing.
Republic Day Parade (26 Jan) Rajpath. A spectacular fly-past and military march-past, with colourful pageants and tableaux from every state, dances and music. Tickets through travel agents and most hotels, Rs 100. You can see the full dress preview free, usually 2 days before; week-long celebrations during which government buildings are illuminated.
Beating the Retreat (29 Jan) Vijay Chowk, a stirring display by the armed forces' bands marks the end of the Republic Day celebrations.
Martyr's Day (30 Jan) Marks the anniversary of Mahatma Gandhi's death; devotional *bhajans* and Guard of Honour at Raj Ghat.
Kite Flying Festival Makar Sankranti above Palika Bazar, Connaught Pl.

February

Vasant Panchami (2 Feb) Celebrates the 1st day of spring. The Mughal Gardens are opened to the public for a month.
Delhi Flower Show Purana Qila.
Thyagaraja Festival South Indian music and dance, Vaikunthnath Temple.

March

Basant Ritu Sammelan North Indian music.

April

Amir Khusrau's Birth Anniversary A fair in Nizamuddin celebrates this with prayers and *qawwali* singing.

May

Buddha Jayanti (1st full moon night in May) Marks the birth of the Buddha; prayer meetings are held at Ladakh Buddha Vihara, Ring Rd and Buddha Vihara, Mandir Marg.

August

Janmashtami Celebrates the birth of the Hindu god Krishna. Special *puja*, Lakshmi Narayan Mandir.
Independence Day (15 Aug) Impressive flag-hoisting ceremony and prime ministerial address at the Red Fort.
Vishnu Digambar Sammelan North Indian music and dance festival.

October-November

Gandhi Jayanti (2 Oct) Mahatma Gandhi's birthday; devotional singing at Raj Ghat.

Dasara With over 200 Ramlila performances all over the city recounting the Ramayana story (see page 1402).
Ramlila Ballet The ballet, which takes place at Delhi Gate (south of Red Fort) and Ramlila Ground, is performed for a month and is most spectacular. Huge effigies of Ravana are burnt on the 9th night; noisy and flamboyant.
National Drama Festival Shri Ram Centre.
Diwali The festival of lights; lighting of earthen lamps, candles and firework displays.
National Drama Festival Rabindra Bhavan.
Dastkar Nature Bazaar (Oct/Nov) Working with over 25,000 crafts people from across India, **Dastkar's** main objective is to empower rural artisans and keep alive the traditional crafts of India. They hold many events each year, but this is the pinnacle. Knowing that shopping here will bring a difference to the lives of rural people.

December

Christmas (25 Dec) Special Christmas Eve entertainments at major hotels and restaurants; midnight mass and services at all churches.
Ayyappa Temple Festival Ayyappa Swami Temple, Ramakrishnapuram; South Indian music.
New Year's Eve (31 Dec) Celebrated in most hotels and restaurants offering special food and entertainment.

O Shopping

Delhi *p74, maps p72, p84 p88, p91 and p93*

There are several state emporia around Delhi including the **Cottage Industries Emporium (CIE)**, a huge department store of Indian handicrafts, and those along Baba Kharak Singh Marg (representing crafts from most states of India). In this stretch, there are several places selling products from women's collectives or rural artisans, like **Mother Earth** and **Hansiba**). It is a convenient way of shopping, as the shelves are packed with a huge choice of goods from all over India, and everything has a fixed price. You may have to pay a little more but it is hassle-free. Shops generally open 1000-1930 (winter 1000-1900). Food stores and chemists stay open later. Most shopping areas are closed on Sun.

Art galleries

Galleries exhibiting contemporary art are listed in *First City*.
Delhi Art Gallery, Hauz Khas Village. A newly expanded gallery with a good range of moderately priced contemporary art.
Devi Art Foundation, Sirpur House, plot 39, sector 44 Gurgaon, www.deviartfoundation.org. You might need a degree in navigating Gurgaon to find this place, but it's well worth the adventure. Check the website for current exhibitions.
Espace, 16 Community Centre, New Friends Colony, T011-2683 0499. Group and solo shows by artists from all over India.
Nature Morte, A-1 Neethi Bagh, near Kamla Nehru College, www.naturemorte.com. With a twin gallery in Berlin, you can expect the most profound and inspiring of contemporary art here.
Photo Ink, Hyundai MGF building, 1 Jhandewalan Faiz Rd, www.photoink.net. Close to Paharganj, this gallery offers up top notch contemporary photography.
Religare Art, 7 Atmaram Mansion, Level One, Scindia House, off Connaught Pl, below **Asian Guest House** (see Sleeping), www.religare arts.com. Right in the heart of things just off CP, this is a moveable feast of art and photography. There is a good café and terrace too.

Books and music

Hotel booksellers often carry a good selection of imported books about India, though some charge inflated prices. Among those with specialist academic and art books focusing on India are: **Jainson's**, Janpath Hotel; **Krishan**, Claridges; **Khazana**, Taj Mahal and Taj Palace hotels (0900-2000).

Serious bibliophiles should head to the Sun book market in Daryaganj, Old Delhi, when 2 km of pavement are piled high with books – some fantastic bargains to be had.
Bahri & Sons, opposite Main Gate, Khan Market. One among many in the booklovers' heaven of Khan Market. Wide choice.
Bookworm, B-29, Connaught Pl. Wide selection, including art, Indology, fiction.
Central News Agency, P 23/90, Connaught Pl. Carries national and foreign newspapers and journals.
Full Circle, 5 B, Khan Market, T011-2465 5641. Helpful knowledgeable staff. Sweet café upstairs for a quick drink – food is hit and miss though.
Jacksons, 5106, Main Bazar, Paharganj, T011-5535 1083. Selection in many languages, mostly

second hand at half original price (also buys used books).
Kabaadi Bazaar, Netaji Subhash Marg, Old Delhi. Sun market with thousands of very cheap used books, great for browsing.
Manohar, 4753/23 Ansar Rd, Daryaganj, Old Delhi. A real treasure trove for books on South Asia and India especially, most helpful, knowledgeable staff. Highly recommended.
Motilal Banarsidass, Bungalow Rd, Kamla Nagar (northwest of Old Delhi, opposite Kirorimal College). Far flung, but good for spirituality and Indology.
Munshiram Manoharlal, Nai Sarak, Chandni Chowk. Books on Indology.
Music World, **Ansal Plaza** (see Malls, below); also in Plaza PVR, Connaught Pl. Excellent for Indian and Western music, a good place to listen before buying.
New Book Depot, 18B, Connaught Pl. Highly recommended.
Prabhu & Sons, Hauz Khas Village, well-hidden on 1st-floor balcony down side street, for antiquarian/second-hand books.
Rikhi Ram, G Block Connaught Circus, T011-2332 7685. This is the place to come if you've wondered about how easy it is to learn to play and travel with a sitar. Has a range of guitars and other stringed instruments too.
Timeless, 46 The Housing Society, 3rd floor and basement, Part 1, South Extension. Full of coffee tables, art books and novels.
Yodakin, 2 Hau Khaz Village, T011-4178 7201, www.yodakin.com. Excellent alternative bookshop stocking independent publishers including Yoda Press in the heart of the village with talks at the weekends.

Carpets

Carpets can be found in shops in most top hotels and a number round Connaught Pl, not necessarily fixed price. If you are visiting Agra, check out the prices here first.

Clothing

For serious designer-wear that may well break the bank, go to **Lodhi Colony Main Market**. There you'll find: **Bian**, T011-2464 2914, run by New York-based stylist, this is the place to come to ogle at Swarovski crystal-studded saris; and **Pratap**, T011-2463 8788, for sleek designs in an industrial-chic gallery.

For other designer wear, try **Ogaan** and for more contemporary, less budget blowing try **Grey Garden** both in **Hauz Khas Village**, **Sunder Nagar Market** near the Oberoi hotel, or the Crescent arcade near the Qutab Minar.

For inexpensive (Western and Indian) clothes, try shops along Janpath and between Sansad Marg and Janpath; you can bargain down 50%.

The **Central Cottage Industries Emporium** (see below) has a good selection of clothing and fabrics. The **Khadi shop** (see Emporia, below) has Indian-style clothing.
Fab India, 14N-Gt Kailash I (also in B-Block Connaught Pl, Khan Market and Vasant Kunj). Excellent shirts, Nehru jackets, *salwar kameez*, linen, furnishing fabrics and furniture. The most comprehensive collection is in N block.

Earthenware

Unglazed earthenware *khumba matkas* (water pots) are sold round New Delhi Railway Station (workshops behind main road).

Emporia

Most open 1000-1800 (close 1330-1400).
Central Cottage Industries Emporium, corner of Janpath and Tolstoy Marg. Offers hassle-free shopping, exchange counter (spend at least 50% of amount to be cashed, take bills to till and use TCs/credit card to pay), gift wrapping, will pack and post overseas; best if you are short of time.
Dilli Haat, opposite INA Market. Rs 15, 1100-2200. Well-designed open-air complex with rows of brick alcoves for craft stalls from different states; local craftsmen's outlets (bargaining obligatory), occasional fairs (tribal art, textiles, etc). Also good regional food – hygienic, safe, weighted towards non-vegetarian. Pleasant, quiet, clean (no smoking) and uncrowded, not too much hassle.
Khadi Gramodyog Bhawan, near the Regal building, Baba Kharak Singh Marg. For inexpensive homespun cotton *kurta pajama* (loose shirt and trousers), cotton/silk waistcoats, fabrics and Jaipuri paintings.
Khazana, **Taj Mahal** and **Taj Palace** hotels (daily 0900-2000). High class.
Santushti, Chanakyapuri, opposite **Hotel**

Samrat. Mon-Sat 1000-1800, some shops close for lunch. Attractive a/c units in a garden setting, hassle free. Shops sell good-quality clothes, crafts, linen, saris, silver, etc. **Basil and Thyme** serves trendy Western snacks.

Food

Aap ki Pasand, opposite Golcha cinema, Netaji Subhash Marg, Old Delhi. Excellent place to taste and buy a variety of Indian teas.
Altitude Store, 16 Shanti Niketan Market, T(0)9811-755222, www.thealtitudestore.com. Offering up organic foods, teas and candles. Pioneering.
Bhim Sen's, Bengali Market, end of Tansen Marg, near Connaught Pl. For some of the best, freshest (hence safest) Indian sweets.
Darjeeling Tea Bureau, Kaka Nagar Market (opposite Delhi Golf Club), nathmulls@goldentipstea.com. Charming, reliable and good selection. Highly recommended.
Haldiram's, Chandni Chowk near Metro. Wide selection of sweet and salty snack foods.
Khari Baoli, Chandni Chowk, lined with colourful shops. Spices and dried fruit, etc. **MDH**, **Everest** brands are reliable.
Steak House, Jorbagh Market. Cold meats, cheeses, yoghurts.

Jewellery

Traditional silver and goldsmiths in Dariba Kalan, off Chandni Chowk (north of Jama Masjid). Cheap bangles and along Janpath; also at Hanuman Mandir, Gt Kailash I, N-Block. Also Sunder Nagar market. Bank St in Karol Bagh is recommended for gold.

Amrapali, Khan Market has an exceptional collection from affordable to mind-blowing.
Ashish Nahar, 1999 Naughara St, Kinari Bazaar, Chandni Chowk, T011-2327 2801. On quite possibly the prettiest street in Delhi, full of brightly painted and slowly crumbling *havelis*, you will find a little gem of a jewellery shop.
Silverline, 18 Babar Rd, Bengali Market, T011-2335 0454. Contemporary silver jewellery at wholesale prices.

Leather

Cheap sandals from stalls on Janpath (Rs 100). **Yashwant Place Market** next to Chanakya Cinema Hall, Chanakyapuri. **Khan Market** (see below) sells leather goods and shoes.
Da Milano, South Extension and Khan Market.
Hidesign, G49, Connaught Pl. High class.

Markets and malls

Beware of pickpockets in markets and malls.
Ansal Plaza, HUDCO, Khelgaon Marg (south of South Extension). Delhi's first European-style shopping mall. Very smart, lots of chains.
Basant Lok, Vasant Vihar. Has a few upmarket shops attracting the young.
Hauz Khas village, South Delhi. Authentic, old village houses converted into designer shops selling handicrafts, ceramics, antiques and furniture in addition to luxury wear. Many are expensive, but some are good value. A good place to pick up old Hindi film posters with many art galleries and restaurants.
Jorbagh, Gt Kailash Pt I-M. Western travellers hankering for the familiar, and prepared to pay the price, will find a good range of food and toiletries here.
Khan Market, South Delhi. Great bookshops, cafés, restaurants and boutiques. Full of expats so expect expat prices.
Main Bazar, Paharganj. Good range of food and toiletries for Westerners with enough cash.
Sarojini Nagar, South Delhi. Daily necessities as well as cheap fabric and clothing. Come for incredible bargains. This is where a lot of the Western brands dump their export surplus or end-of-line clothes. Haggle hard.
Select City Walk, Saket. An enormous, glitzy mall for the ultimate in upmarket shopping. Lots of chains, cinemas, etc.
Shahpur Jat, is a new up and coming shopping area, south of **South Extension**.
South Extension, South Delhi. Good for clothes, shoes, jewellery, music, etc.
Sunder Nagar, South Delhi. Has a few shops selling Indian handicrafts and jewellery (precious and semi-precious); some quite original.
Tibetan Market, North Delhi. Stalls along Janpath have plenty of curios – most are new but rapidly aged to look authentic.

Tailoring

Small shops charge around Rs 100-150 to copy a dress or shirt; trousers Rs 150-200. **Khan Market** has several tailors and cloth stores. **Shankar**

Market, near Connaught Pl, has good suiting, corduroys, denim, etc.
Mohan Singh Place, Baba Kharak Singh Mg opposite the government emporia. Hundreds of tailors; insist on a good job, and allow 24 hrs for stitching. Nearly all big hotels have upmarket boutiques and also fabric/tailor's shops (some may allow fabric purchased elsewhere).

Unique souvenirs

Dastkari Haat, 39 Khan Market, www.indiancraftsjourney.in. Charming selection of conscious crafts from around India working with rural artisans and women's collectives.
Gulabsingh Johrimal Perfumers, 467 Chandni Chowk, T011-2326 3743. Authentic *attars* (sandalwood based perfumes), perfumes and incense. High-quality oils are used.
Khazana India, 50A Hauz Khaz Village. Little treasure trove of Bollywood posters, old photographs and all sorts of interesting bric-a-brac.
People Tree, 8 Regal Building, Connaught Pl. Handmade clothing, mostly T-shirts with arty and people conscious slogans. Great posters made up of all those weird signs that you see around India and wide-range of ecological books. A real find.
Playclan, F51 Select Citywalk, Saket, www.theplayclan.com. Fantastic shop selling all manner of clothes, notebooks, lighters and pictures with great colourful cartoon designs created by a collective of animators and designers – giving a more animated view of India's gods, goddesses, gurus, Kathakali dancers and the faces of India.
Purple Jungle, 16 Hauz Khaz Village, T(0)9650-973039, www.purple-jungle.com. Offering up kitsch India with bollywood pictures and curious road signs refashioned onto bags, clothes, cushions, etc.

▲ Activities and tours

Delhi *p74, maps p72, p84 p88, p91 and p93*

Body and soul

Hatha Art Studio, 24/1 Hauz Khaz Village, opposite **Yodakin Books** hathastudio@gmail.com. Regular yoga classes, on the 'village roof' in the winter. And also you can learn guitar here and there are art studios and exhibitions with Hugo and Tara.
Integral Yoga, Sri Aurobindo Ashram, Aurobindo Marg, T011-2656 7863. Regular yoga classes (Tue-Thu and Sat 0645-0745 and 1700-1800) in *asana* (postures), *pranayama* (breathing techniques) and relaxation.
Laughter Club of Delhi, various locations, T011-2721 7164. Simple yogic breathing techniques combined with uproarious laughter. Clubs meet early morning in parks throughout the city – a bright start to the day.
Morarji Desai National Institute of Yoga, 68 Ashoka Rd, T011-2371 8301. Classes run throughout the day, some aimed at particular physical ailments.
Sari School, Jangpura Extension, near Lajpat Nagar, T011-4182 3297. Author of *Saris in India* Rta Christi Kapur holds classes every Sat in different styles of sporting a sari.
Tree of Life Reflexology, T(0)9810-356677. Reflexology with acclaimed teacher Suruchi. She also does private and group yoga classes on the roof and in the park.
Yogalife, Shapur Jat main market, T(0)9811-863332, www.yogalife.org. Closed Mon. Bright, friendly centre.

Sport

Members only clubs, but maybe you can find a willing member to take you.
Delhi Gymkhana Club, 2 Safdarjang Rd, T011-2301 5533. Mostly for government and defence personnel, squash, tennis, swimming, bar and restaurant.
Pacific Sports Complex, next to Central School, Andrews Ganj, T011-6507 9552. Can be hard to find – it's near Lady Sri Ram College.
SIri Fort Club, August Kranti Marg, New Delhi, near Siri Fort Auditorium, T011-2649 7482. You can get temporary membership – wonderful outdoor swimming pool (summer only), tennis, squash, basketball, reiki, taekwando, etc.

Tours and tour operators

Local sightseeing tours can be arranged through approved travel agents and tour operators. For approved tourist guides/agencies contact **Government of India Tourist Office** and travel agents. There are many small agents, eg opposite New Delhi Railway Station, seemingly offer unusual itineraries, but their standards can't be guaranteed and their rates are not significantly lower.

Rates Delhi only, half day Rs 90, full day Rs 160. **India Tourism Development Corporation** (ITDC) and **Delhi Tourism** (see page 77) both run city sightseeing tours. Combining Old and New Delhi tours on the same day can be very tiring. A/c coaches are particularly recommended during the summer months. The price includes transport and guide services, but all are whistle-stop tours. Check whether entrance fees to many sights are included in the price of the tour. A group of 3 or 4 people could consider hiring a car and doing the tour at their own pace. Another alternative is to hire an auto-rickshaw for the day (around Rs 200). It will entail visiting gift shops for the driver to get a commission, but you don't have to buy.

Delhi Tourism tours

Departs from **Delhi Tourism**, Baba Kharak Singh Mg near State Govt Emporia, T011-2336 3607, www.delhitourism.nic.in. Book a day in advance. Check time.

Evening Tour (Tue-Sun 1830-2200): Rajpath, India Gate, Kotla Firoz Shah, Purana Qila, *son et lumière* (Red Fort). Rs 150.

New Delhi Tour (0900-1400): Jantar Mantar, Qutb Minar, Lakshmi Narayan Temple, Baha'i Temple (Safdarjang's Tomb on Mon only).

Old Delhi Tour (1415-1715): Jama Masjid, Red Fort, Raj Ghat, Humayun's Tomb. Both Rs 100 plus entry fees.

ITDC Tours

Guides are generally good but tours are rushed, T011-2332 0331. Tickets can be booked from **Hotel Indraprastha**, T011-2334 4511.

New Delhi Tour: departs from L-1 Connaught Circus and **Hotel Indraprastha** (0800-1330), Rs 125 (a/c coach): Jantar Mantar, Lakshmi Narayan Temple, India Gate,Nehru Pavilion, Pragati Maidan (closed Mon), Humayun's Tomb, Qutb Minar.

Old Delhi Tour: departs **Hotel Indraprastha**. (1400-1700), Rs 100: Kotla Firoz Shah, Raj Ghat, Shantivana, Jama Masjid and Red Fort.

Taj Mahal tours

Many companies offer coach tours to Agra (eg **ITDC**, from L1 Connaught Circus, Sat-Thu 0630-2200, Rs 600, a/c coach). However, travelling by road is slow and uncomfortable; by car, allow at least 4 hrs each way. Train is a better option: either *Shatabdi* or *Taj Express*, but book early.

Tour operators

There are many operators offering tours, ticketing, reservations, etc, for travel across India. Many are around Connaught Circus, Parharganj, Rajendra Pl and Nehru Pl. Most belong to special associations (IATA, PATA) for complaints.

Capital City Travels and Tours, 36 Arakashan Rd, Ram Nagar, behind Sheila Cinema, T011-2956 2097, www.tourism-india.com. Fixed and tailor-made tours throughout India.

Creative Travel, 27-30 Creative Plaza, Nanak Pura, Moti Bagh, T011-2687 2257, www.travel 2india.com. Efficient, reliable, helpful.

Highland, N-29 Middle Circus, Connaught Pl, T011-2331 8236, highlandtravels@usa.net. Friendly, competent and reasonably priced.

Ibex Expeditions, 30 Community Centre East of Kailash, New Delhi, T011-2682 8479, www.ibexexpeditions.com. Offers a wide range of tours and ticketing, etc.

Kunzum Travel Café, T-49 Hauz Khaz Village, T011-2651 3949. Unusual little place to plan trips, meet travellers and swap stories. Possibly the most unusual travel centre – there's free Wi-Fi, walls lined with photographic exhibitions, coffee, magazines and usually buzzing with people.

India Tours International, 206 Victoria Cross, 4/54-55 WEA, Saraswati Marg, Karol Bag, New Delhi, T011-2576 2190, www.indiatours web.com. Quality tours, hotels and resorts.

Namaste Voyages, I-Block 28G/F South City, 2 Gurgaon, 122001, T0124-221 9330, www.namastevoyages.com. Specializes in tailor-made tours, tribal, treks, theme voyages.

Paradise Holidays, 312 Ansal Classique Tower, J block, Rajouri Garden, T011-4552 0736, www.paradiseholidays.com. All India tours, value for money. Highly recommended.

Potala Tours & Travels, 101 Antriksh Bhavan, 22 K Ghandi Marg, T011-2373 1620, www.potala tours.com. Excellent staff, car tours, ticketing.

Shanti Travel, F-189/1A Main Rd Savitri Nagar, T011-4607 7800, www.shantitravel.com. Delhi-based travel agency specializing in tailor-made tours throughout India.

Wanderlust Travels, G-18, 2nd floor, Masjid Moth, Greater Kailash Part-II, New Delhi T011-4053 7116, www.wanderlustindia.com. Tailor-made tours throughout India, groups and individuals.

Walking tours

Chor Bizarre, Hotel Broadway, T011-2327 3821. Special walking tours of Old Delhi, with good lunch, 0930-1330, 1300-1630, Rs 350 each, Rs 400 for both.

Delhi Metro Walks, T(0)9811-330098, www.delhi metrowalks.com. With the charismatic Surekha Narain guiding your every step, she offers informative heritage walks around all of Delhi. Check her website for all the possibilities.

Master Guest House (see Sleeping, page 105). Highly recommended walking tours for a more intimate experience of Delhi.

Salaam Baalak Trust, T(0)9873-130383, www.salaambaalaktrust.com. NGO-run tours of New Delhi station and the streets around it, guided by Javed, himself a former street child. Your Rs 200 goes to support the charity's work with street children.

Transport

Delhi *p74, maps p72, p84 p88, p91 and p93*

Air

All international flights arrive at the shiny new terminal of **Indira Gandhi International Airport**, 20 km south of Connaught Pl. Terminal 1 (Domestic) enquiries T011-2567 5126, www.newdelhiairport.in; Terminal 3 (International) T0124-377 6000. At check-in, be sure to tag your hand luggage, and make sure it is stamped after security check, otherwise you will be sent back at the gate to get it stamped.

The domestic air industry is in a period of massive growth, so check a 3rd-party site such as www.flightraja.com or www.makemy trip.com for the latest flight schedules and prices. Delhi has connections (many direct) with the following domestic destinations:

Daily flights **Ahmedabad**; **Amritsar**; **Bagdogra** (for Darjeeling); **Bengaluru** (Bangalore); **Bhopal**; **Bhubaneshwar**; **Kolkata**; **Chandigarh**; **Chennai** (Madras); **Cochin**; **Goa**; **Guwahati**; **Hyderabad**; **Jaipur**; **Jammu**; **Kathmandu**; **Khajuraho**; **Kullu**; **Lucknow**; **Mumbai** (Bombay); **Nagpur**; **Patna**; **Pune**; **Raipur**; **Rajkot**; **Ranchi**; **Srinagar**; **Trivandrum**; **Udaipur**; **Vadodara**; and **Varanasi**.

Non-daily flights **Aurangabad**; **Dhaka**; **Dibrugarh**; **Gwalior**; **Indore**; **Imphal**; **Jodhpur**; **Leh**; **Lucknow**; **Paro**; and **Shimla**.

The most extensive networks are with **Indian Airlines**, T140/T011-2562 2220, www.indianairlines.in; **Jet Airways**, T011-3989 3333, airport T011-2567 5404, www.jetairways.com; and **Kingfisher**, T1-860-266 9000, www.flykingfisher.com. Other budget airlines fly to the most popular destinations. Many domestic airlines have their offices in N-Block, Connaught Pl, including: **Jet Airways**, **Indigo**, T(0)9910-383838, www.goindigo.in, and **Spicejet**, T(0)9871-803333, www.spicejet.com.

For a complete list of international airline offices see *First City* magazine.

Transport to and from the airport

The metro is up and running and runs from the airport to New Delhi train station. There is a booth just outside 'Arrivals' at the International and Domestic terminals for the **bus** services. It is a safe, economical option. A free **shuttle** runs between the 2 terminals every 30 mins during the day. Some hotel buses leave from the Domestic terminal. **Bus 780** runs between the **airport** and **New Delhi Railway Station**.

The International and Domestic terminals have **pre-paid taxi** counters outside the baggage hall (3 price categories) which ensure that you pay the right amount (give your name, exact destination and number of items of luggage). Most expensive are white 'DLZ' **limousines** and then white 'DLY' **luxury taxis**. Cheapest are 'DLT' **ordinary Delhi taxis** (black with yellow top Ambassador/Fiat cars and vans, often very old). 'DLY' taxis charge 3 times the DLT price. A 'Welcome' desk by the baggage reclamation offers expensive taxis only. Take your receipt to the ticket counter outside to find your taxi and give it to the driver when you reach the destination; you don't need to tip, although they will ask. From the International terminal DLT taxis charge about Rs 240 for the town centre (Connaught Pl area); night charges double 2300-0500. Rates from the Domestic terminal are slightly lower.

Bus

Local

The city bus service run by the **Delhi Transport Corporation (DTC)** connects all important points in the city and has more than 300 routes. Information is available at www.dtc.nic.in, at DTC assistance booths and at all major bus stops. Don't be afraid to ask conductors or fellow passengers. Buses are often hopelessly overcrowded so only use off-peak.

Long distance

Delhi is linked to most major centres in North India. Services are provided by **Delhi Transport Corporation (DTC)** and State Roadways of neighbouring states from various **Inter-State Bus Termini (ISBT)**. Allow at least 30 mins for buying a ticket and finding the right bus.

Kashmere Gate, north of Old Delhi, T011-2296 0290 (general enquiries), is the main terminus, with a restaurant, left luggage, bank (Mon-Fri 1000-1400; Sat 1000-1200), post office (Mon-Sat 0800-1700) and telephones (includes international calls). The following operators run services to neighbouring states from here: **Delhi Transport Corp**, T011-2386 5181. **Haryana Roadways**, T011-2296 1262; daily to **Agra** (5-6 hrs, quicker by rail), **Chandigarh** (5 hrs), **Jaipur** (Rs 150, 6½ hrs), **Mathura**, etc, **Himachal Roadways**, T011-2296 6725; twice daily to **Dharamshala** (12 hrs), **Manali** (15 hrs), **Shimla** (10 hrs), etc. **J&K Roadways**, T011-2332 4511; **Punjab Roadways**, T011-2296 7892, to **Amritsar**, **Chandigarh**, **Jammu**, **Pathankot**. **UP Roadways**, T011-2296 8709, city office at Ajmeri Gate, T011-2323 5367; to **Almora** (5 hrs), **Dehradun**, **Haridwar**, **Mussoorie**, **Gorakhpur**, **Kanpur**, **Jhansi**, **Lucknow**, **Nainital**, **Varanasi**.

Sarai Kale Khan Ring Rd, smaller terminal near Nizamuddin Railway Station, T011-2469 8343 (general enquiries), for buses to Haryana, Rajasthan and UP: **Haryana Roadways**, T011-2435 1084. **Rajasthan Roadways**, T011-2435 3731. For **Agra**, **Mathura** and **Vrindavan**; **Ajmer**; **Alwar**; **Bharatpur** (5 hrs); **Bikaner** (11 hrs); **Gwalior**; **Jaipur**; **Jodhpur**; **Pushkar**; **Udaipur**, etc.

Anand Vihar, east side of Yamuna River, T011-2214 8097, for buses to Uttar Pradesh, Uttarakhand and Himachal Pradesh.

Bikaner House, Pandara Rd (south of India Gate), T011-2338 1884; for several 'Deluxe' a/c buses to **Jaipur** (6 hrs, Rs 300); ask for 'direct' bus (some buses stop at Amber for a tour of the fort). Also to **Udaipur** via **Ajmer**, and to **Jodhpur**.

HPTDC, Chandralok Bldg, 36 Janpath, T011-2332 5320, hptdcdelhi@hub.nic.in, runs a/c Volvo and Sleeper buses to **Manali** and **Dharamshala**. Of the myriad private bus operators, **Raj National Express** has by far the best buses, and highest prices.

To Nepal See also page 126. Direct private buses run to **Kathmandu**, though the 36-hr journey is quite exhausting. A much shorter route to Nepal is to the Indian border town of **Banbassa** via Tanakpur or Khatima (more relaxed, good hotels) and crossing to the western Nepal border town of Mahendranagar. **UP Roadways** and private buses for Banbessa leave daily from Anand Vihar bus station and take around 9 hrs (but check details carefully). The onward journey to Kathmandu is about 20 hrs; it is best done via Royal Bardia National Park or Nepalganj.

To Pakistan A direct 'Friendship' bus to **Lahore** runs on Tue, Wed, Fri and Sat at 0600, departing from Ambedkar Stadium terminal, near Delhi Gate, Old Delhi (reserve ahead, T011-2331 8180 (14 hrs, Rs 1250), for Indians with valid visas and relations in Pakistan, and for Pakistanis.

Car hire

The main roads out of Delhi are very heavily congested; the best time to leave is in the very early morning.

Hiring a car is an excellent way of getting about town either for sightseeing or if you have several journeys to make during the day.

Full day local use with driver (non a/c) is about Rs 700-800, 80 km/8 hrs, driver overnight *bata* Rs 150 per day; self-drive 24 hrs/150 km Rs 1200. Airport to city centre Rs 400-500. To Jaipur, about Rs 3000; return Rs 5400. The **Tourist Office**, 88 Janpath, has a list of approved agents.

Cozy Travels, N1 BMC House, Middle Circle, Connaught Pl, T011-2331 1593, cozytravels@vsnl.net.com. For Ambassador or similar, Rs 650 non-a/c, Rs 850 a/c.

Metropole Tourist Service, 224 Defence Colony Flyover Market, (Jangpura Side), New Delhi, T011-2431 2212, T(0)9810-277699, www.metrovista.co.in. Car/ jeep (US$45-70 per day), safe, reliable and recommended, also hotel bookings and can help arrange homestays around Delhi. Highly recommended.

Mohindra Tourist Taxis, Vasant Vihar Block D, T011-2614 3188. "Excellent service, safe driving".

Western Court Tourist Taxis, 36 Janpath, **Hotel Imperial**, T011-2336 8036. Helpful.

Metro

The sparkling new Metro system (T011-2436 5202, www.delhimetrorail.com) is set to revolutionize transport within Delhi. For travellers, the yellow line is the main aorta and useful as it stops Chandni Chowk, Connaught Place and Qutb Minar. The blue line connects to Paharganj. The violet line for Khan Market. And the Orange Line linking airport to New Delhi train station.

Line 1 (Red) Running northwest to east, of limited use to visitors; from Rithala to Dilshad Garden.

Line 2 (Yellow) Running north-south through the centre from Jahangipuri to Huda City via Kashmere Gate, Chandni Chowk, New Delhi Station, Connaught Pl (Rajiv Chowk), Hauz Khaz, Qutb Minar and Saket – probably the most useful line for visitors.

Line 3 (Blue) From Dwarka 21 to Valshall or City Centre (splits after Yamuna Bank) Intersecting with Line 2 at Rajiv Chowk and running west through Paharganj (RK Ashram station) and Karol Bagh.

Line 4 (Orange) Just 4 stations for now including I.G.I Airport to New Delhi Train Station.

Line 5 (Green) From Mundka to Inderlok.

Line 6 (Violet) From Central Secretariat to Badarpur, including Khan Market and Lajpat Nagar. Useful.

Trains run 0600-2200. Fares are charged by distance: tokens for individual journeys cost Rs 6-19. **Smart Cards**, Rs 100, Rs 200 and Rs 500, save queuing and money. **Tourist Cards** valid for 1 or 3 days (Rs 70/200) are useful if you plan to make many journeys. Luggage is limited to 15 kg; guards may not allow big backpacks on board. Look out for the women-only carriages at the front of each train, clearly marked in pink. For an insight into the construction of the metro, there is a metro museum at **Patel Chowk** on the yellow line.

Motorcycle hire

Chawla Motorcycles, 1770, Shri Kissan Dass Marg, Naiwali Gali, is very reliable, trustworthy, highly recommended for restoring classic bikes.

Ess Aar Motors, Jhandewalan Extn, west of Paharganj, T011-2367 8836; and **Nanna Motors**, 112 Press Rd (east of Connaught Circus), T011-2335 1769. Both recommended for buying Enfields, very helpful. Also for scooter rentals **U Ride**, T(0)9711-701932, www.uride.in.

Rickshaw

Auto-rickshaws Widely available at about half the cost of taxis (Rs 4 per km). Normal capacity for foreigners is 2 people (3rd person extra); very few will use meter so agree fare in advance; see www.delhigovt.nic.in for a 'fare calculator' – slightly out of date. Expect to pay Rs 20 for the shortest journeys. Allow Rs 120 for 2 hrs' sightseeing/shopping. It is best to walk away from hotels and tourist centres to look for an auto.

Taxi tips

First-time visitors can be vulnerable to exploitation by taxi drivers at the airport. If arriving at night, you are very strongly advised to have a destination in mind and get a pre-paid taxi. Be firm about being dropped at the hotel of your choice and insist that you have a reservation; you can always change hotels the next day if you are unhappy. Don't admit to being a first-time visitor.

If you don't take a pre-paid taxi, the driver will demand an inflated fare. He may insist that the hotel you want to go to has closed or is full and will suggest one where he will get a commission (and you will be overcharged).

Some travellers have been told that the city was unsafe with street fighting, police barricades and curfews and have then been taken to Agra or Jaipur. In the event of taxi trouble, be seen to note down the licence plate number and threaten to report the driver to the police; if you need to do this, the number is T011-2331 9334.

Cycle-rickshaws Available in the Old City. Be prepared to bargain: Chandni Chowk Metro to Red Fort Rs 8-10. They are not allowed into Connaught Pl.

Taxi

Yellow-top taxis, which run on compressed natural gas, are readily available at taxi stands or you can hail one on the road. Meters should start at Rs 13; ask for the conversion card. Add 25% at night (2300-0500) plus Rs 5 for each piece of luggage over 20 kg.

Easy Cabs, T011-4343 4343. Runs clean a/c cars and claim to pick up anywhere within 15 mins; Rs 15 per km.

Train

Delhi stations from which trains originate have codes: **OD** – Old Delhi, **ND** – New Delhi, **HN** – Hazrat Nizamuddin, **DSR** – Delhi Sarai Rohilla. The publication *Trains at a Glance'* (Rs 30) lists important trains across India, available at some stations, book shops and newsagents,

New Delhi Railway Station and **Hazrat Nizamuddin Station** (500 m north and 5 km southeast of Connaught Pl respectively) connect Delhi with most major destinations. The latter has many important southbound trains. **Old Delhi Station**, 6 km north of the centre, has broad and metre-gauge trains. **Delhi Sarai Rohilla**, northeast of CP, serves Rajasthan.

Train enquiries T131. Reservations T1330. Each station has a computerized reservation counter where you can book any Mail or Express train in India. Allow time (1-2 hrs) and be prepared to be very patient as it can be a nightmare. Have your train's name and number ready and, if necessary, politely muscle your way in to get a reservation form before lining up. Separate queues for ladies and for credit card payments can save barging. Smaller suburban booking offices (eg Sarojini Nagar) are less fraught and worth the detour; alternatively, you can use a recommended travel agent for tickets and pay Rs 50-100 fee.

International Tourist Bureau (ITB), 1st floor, Main Building, New Delhi Station, T011-2340 5156, Mon-Fri 0930-1630, Sat 0930-1430, provides assistance with planning and booking journeys, for foreigners only; efficient and helpful if slow. You need your passport; pay in US$, or rupees (with an encashment certificate/ ATM receipt). Those with **Indrail** passes should confirm bookings here. At the time of writing the station was under renovation, so the layout may change, but be wary of rickshaw drivers/ travel agents who tell you the ITB has closed or moved elsewhere. (There are also counters for foreigners and NRIs at **Delhi Tourism**, N-36 Connaught Pl, 1000-1700, Mon-Sat, and at the airport; quick and efficient.)

New Delhi and Hazrat Nizamuddin stations have pre-paid taxi and rickshaw counters with official rates per km posted: expect to pay around Rs 30 for up to 4 km. Authorized *coolies* (porters), wear red shirts and white *dhotis;* agree the charge, around Rs 20 per bag, before engaging one. For left luggage, you need a secure lock and chain.

Some principal services are: **Agra**: *Shatabdi Exp 12002*, ND 0615, 2 hrs; *Taj Exp 12280*, HN, 0715, 2¾ hrs. **Ahmedabad**: *Rajdhani Exp 12958, ND, 1935*, Wed-Mon, 14½ hrs. **Amritsar**: *Shatabdi Exp 12013*, ND, 1630, 6 hrs; *New Delhi-Amritsar Exp 12459*, ND, 1340, 8 hrs; *Shan-e-Punjab Exp 12497*, ND, 0650, 7½ hrs. **Bengaluru (Bangalore)**: *Rajdhani Exp 12430*, Mon, Tue, Fri, Sat, HN, 2050, 34 hrs; **Bhubaneswar**: *Rajdhani Exp 12422*, ND, 1715, 24 hrs. **Bhopal**: *Shatabdi Exp 12002*, ND, 0615, 8¾ hrs. **Bikaner**: *Bikaner Exp 12463*, Wed, Fri, Sun, DSR, 0835, 10¼ hrs. **Chandigarh**: *Shatabdi Exp 12011*, ND, 0740, 3½ hrs; *Shatabdi Exp 12005*, ND, 1715, 3 hrs. **Chennai**: *Rajdhani Exp 12434*, Wed, Fri, HN, 1600, 29 hrs; *GT Exp 12616*, ND, 1840, 36¼ hrs; *Tamil Nadu Exp 12622*, ND, 2230, 33¼ hrs. **Dehradun**: *Shatabdi Exp 12017*, ND, 0655, 5¾ hrs. **Goa**: see Madgaon, below. **Guwahati**: *Rajdhani Exp 12424*, ND, Mon, Tue, Wed, Fri, Sat, 1400, 28 hrs; *Rajdhani Exp 12436*, ND, Thu, Sun, 0930, 32 hrs. **Gwalior**: *Shatabdi Exp 12002*, ND, 0615, 3¼ hrs. **Haridwar**: *Shatabdi Exp 12017*, ND, 0655, 4¼ hrs; *Mussoorie Exp 14041*, DSR, 2110, 8¾ hrs. **Jabalpur**: *Gondwana Exp 12412*, HN, 1525, 16 hrs. **Jaipur**: *Shatabdi Exp 12015*, Thu-Tue, ND, 0610, 4¾ hrs; *Ashram Exp 12916*, OD, 1505, 5 hrs. **Jammu**: *Rajdhani Exp 12425*, ND, Fri, 2100, 9½ hrs. **Jhansi**: *Shatabdi Exp 12002*, ND, 0615, 4½ hrs; *Lakshadweep Exp 12618*, HN, 0920, 6 hrs. **Jodhpur**: *Mandore Exp 12461*, OD, 2045, 11 hrs. **Kalka**: see Shimla, below. **Kanpur**: *Shatabdi Exp 12004*, ND, 0615, 5 hrs. **Kolkata**: *Rajdhani Exp 12302*, ND, 1700, 17½ hrs (via Gaya; except Fri, *12306* via Patna, 19½ hrs); *Kalka-Howrah Mail 12312*, OD, 0730, 24 hrs. **Lucknow**: *Shatabdi Exp 12004*, ND, 0615, 6½ hrs. **Madgaon** (Goa): *Rajdhani Exp 12432*, Tue, Sun, HN, 1105, 26 hrs. **Mathura**: *Taj Exp 12280*, HN, 0715, 2 hrs. **Mumbai (Central)**: *Rajdhani Exp 12952*, ND, 1630, 16 hrs; *Paschim Exp 12926*, ND, 1655, 22 hrs; *Golden Temple Mail 12904*, ND, 0750, 22 hrs. **New Jalpaiguri** (for **Darjeeling**): *Rajdhani Exp 12424*, Mon-Wed, Fri, Sat, ND, 1400, 21½ hrs. **Patna**: *NE Exp 15622*, ND, 0640, 17 hrs. **Secunderabad** *Rajdhani Exp 12430*, Mon, Tue, Fri, Sat (12438 Sun), HN, 2050, 22 hrs. **Shimla**: to **Kalka** on *Himalayan Queen 14095*, ND, 0600, 5¼ hrs, or *Shatabdi Exp 12011*, ND, 0740, 4¼ hrs; change to narrow gauge *255*, 1210, total 12 hrs (see Shimla and Kalka, page 494). **Thiruvananthapuram**: *Rajdhani Exp 12432*, Sun, Tue, HN, 1105, 31 hrs. **Udaipur**: *Mewar Exp 12963*, HN, 1900, 12 hrs. **Varanasi** (take extra care with possessions): *Poorva Exp 12382*, Mon, Tue, Fri, ND, 1625, 12¼ hrs; *Farakka Exp 13414*, Mon, Wed, Sat (*13484* other days), OD, 12145, 18 hrs.

For special diesel *Palace on Wheels* and other tours, see page 28.

Directory

Delhi *p74, maps p72, p84 p88, p91 and p93*

Banks Open Mon-Fri 1000-1400, Sat 1000-1200. It is usually quicker to change foreign cash and TCs at hotels. ATMs for International Visa/ Plus/Cirrus/Maestro card-holders at **HDFC**, **HSBC**, **Standard Chartered**, **UTI**, **State Bank of India**, **ICICI** and **Citibank** all over Delhi. Foreign banks and money changers include: **American Express**, A-Block Connaught Pl, excellent; small branch in Paharganj; **Standard Chartered Grindlays**, 15 K Gandhi Marg; **Thomas Cook**, Hotel Imperial, Janpath; New Delhi Railway station (24 hrs). Indian banks (dealing in foreign exchange) open 24 hrs: **Central Bank of India**, Ashok Hotel, **State Bank of India**, Palam Airport. Swift transfers from overseas through **Western Union**, SITA, F-12, Connaught Pl. **Embassies and consulates** Most are in the diplomatic enclave/Chanakyapuri. **Australia**, 1/50-G Shantipath, T011-4139 9900. **Canada**, 7-8 Shantipath, T011-4178 2000. **France**, 2/50-E Shantipath, T011-2419 6100. **Ireland**, 230 Jor Bagh, T011-2462 6733. **Netherlands**, 6/50F Shantipath, T011-2419 7600. **New Zealand**, 50-N Nyaya Marg, T011-688 3170. **South Africa**, B/18 Vasant Marg, T011-2614 4911. **UK**, Shantipath, T011-2419 2100. **USA**, Shantipath, T011-2419 8000. **Medical services Ambulance** (24 hrs): T102. **Hospitals**: Embassies and high commissions have lists of recommended doctors and dentists. Doctors approved by IAMAT (International Association for Medical Assistance to Travellers) are listed in a directory. Casualty and emergency wards in both private and government hospitals are open 24 hrs. **Ram Manohar Lohia**, Willingdon Crescent, T011-2336 5525, 24-hr A&E. **Bara Hindu Rao**, Sabzi Mandi, T011-2391 9476. **JP Narayan**, J Nehru Marg, Delhi Gate, T011-2323

2400. **Safdarjang General**, Sri Aurobindo Marg, T011-2616 5060. **S Kripalani**, Panchkuin Rd, T011-2336 3728. **Chemists**: Many hospitals have 24-hr services: **Hindu Rao Hospital**, Sabzi Mandi; **Ram Manohar Lohia Hospital**, Willingdon Crescent; **S Kripalani Hospital**, Panchkuin Rd. In Connaught Pl: **Nath Brothers**, G-2, off Marina Arcade; **Chemico**, H-45. **Post** Stamps are often available from the reception in the larger hotels. **Speedpost** from 36 centres. Head post offices at **Sansad Marg**, Mon-Sat 1000-1830, **Eastern Court**, Janpath, 24 hrs, **Connaught Pl**, A-Block, Mon-Sat 1000-1700 (parcel packing service outside). **New Delhi GPO** at Ashoka Pl, southwest of Connaught Pl, 24 hrs, poste restante available; make sure senders specify 'New Delhi 110001'; collect from the counter behind sorting office, Mon-Fri 0900-1700, Sat 0900-1300. Take your passport. **Useful contacts** Fire: T101. **Foreigners' Registration Office**: East Block-VIII, Level 2, Sector 1, RK Puram, T011-2671 1443. **Police**: T100.

Leaving Delhi

Going south

Surajkund

Surajkund (meaning 'sun pool') is a perennial lake surrounded by rock-cut steps, built by the Rajput king Surajpal Tomar. According to tradition this is where the Rajputs first settled near Delhi in the 11th century AD. At the head of the reservoir, to the east, are the ruins of what is believed to have been a sun temple. A little south is **Siddha Kund**, a pool of fresh water trickling from a rock crevice which is said to have healing properties.

The annual **Craft Mela**, held in February, draws potters, weavers, metal and stone workers, painters, printers, wood carvers and embroiderers from all over India.

Gurgaon and Saharanpur Bird Sanctuary

Eight kilometres southwest of Indira Gandhi Airport, Gurgaon is as good a place as any to witness the rising of the 'New India'. A succession of multinational corporations have set up call centres, offices and factories, taking advantage of cheap land and labour prices and proximity to Delhi, and this one-time rural backwater is now a mushrooming city with closer links to the USA than to the rest of India. Shopping malls, fast-food chains, hotels and nightclubs have sprouted, the yellow line of the metro extends down to three stations in Gurgaon MG Road, IFFCO terminating at Huda City. For the new extravaganza of Kingdom of Dreams, you need IFFCO station. If you feel the need to explore, it's best to visit by car or taxi.

Beyond Gurgaon, 46 km from Delhi, is the small **Saharanpur Bird Sanctuary** with a *jheel* (shallow lake) surrounded by reeds. The large and handsome Sarus, the only indigenous Indian crane, breeds here. The migratory demoiselle, the smallest member of the crane family, flock to the lakeside in winter. White (rosy) pelicans, flamingos and waders can be seen, as can indigenous birds including grey pelican, cormorant, painted stork, grey and pond heron and egret. Take a blue Haryana bus to Gurgaon from Delhi (every 10 minutes from Dhaula Khan). At Gurgaon take a Chandu bus (three to four daily) and get off at Sultanpur.

The Delhi–Jaipur Road

The NH8 is the main route between Delhi and Jaipur. Although it is very busy there are some attractive stops en route, notably **Neemrana**. Another rural escape is **Tikli**, 8 km off the Sonah road (turn off at Badshapur), about an hour's drive from Delhi towards the Aravalli Hills. Lovingly conceived by an English couple, the exclusive 'farmhouse' stands in a flower- and bird-filled garden, has an inviting pool and is a place to spoil yourself. Ask for Manender Farm, Gairatpur Bass village. **Rewari**, 83 km from Delhi, was founded in AD 1000 by Raja Rawat but there are the ruins of a still older town east of the 'modern' walls. It has been a prosperous centre for the manufacture of iron and brass vessels, and now serves as a rail hub for much of Rajasthan; many trains that once ran to Delhi now start and finish here.

On a rocky outcrop just above a village is the beautiful **Neemrana Fort** ⓘ *T01494-246006, sales@neemrana.com, Rs 100*, built in 1464 by Prithvi Raj Chauhan III and converted into an exceptional hotel. It is quiet and peaceful (occasional chanting from village below), full of character and beautifully furnished with collectors' pieces. Particularly recommended are Baag, Dakshin, Jharoka, Surya Mahals, though some (eg Moonga) are a testing climb up to the seventh level. Superb Rajasthani and French cuisine is served (non-residents Rs 350, which allows looking around). It has a magical atmosphere and is highly recommended; reservations essential. The village and the fort ruins above are worth exploring.

Going north

Meerut ➔ *Colour map 1,C4. Phone code: 0121. Population: 850,000.*

Meerut, known to this day as the place where the Indian Mutiny broke out in 1857, is a busy marketing, commercial and administrative town. It reputedly produces 80% of the world's cricket equipment. Although the old city is compact, the cantonment to the north is typically spaced out with some attractive broad tree-lined streets, including a particularly fine mall.

On 10 May 1857 the first revolt that was to end the East India Company's rule and usher in the era of the British Indian Empire rocked the streets of Meerut. However, the town's history goes back as early as Asoka's time: the modern town contains various Hindu and Muslim buildings from the 11th century onwards. The **cemetery of St John's**, the old garrison church (1821) contains interesting memorials. The **Baleshwar Nath Temple** and several old Hindu shrines surround the **Suraj Kund tank** (1714) which is fed by a canal from the Ganga. The mausolea and mosques indicate strong Mughal influence. The **Jama Masjid** (1019, later restored by Humayun), is one of the oldest in India. The red sandstone **Shah Pir Maqbara** (1628) on Hapur Road was built by the Empress Nur Jahan and further west on Delhi Road is the **Abu Maqbara**, with a large tank. Qutb-ud-din Aibak is believed to have built the *maqbara* of **Salar Masa-ud Ghazi** (1194). The **Nauchandi Mela** is held in March. The train takes 1½ hours from Delhi, the bus takes two hours. The railway stations are to the west and the City Bus Stand nearly 2 km to the southeast.

Saharanpur, 70 km north of Meerut, is famous for carved wood furniture. It was founded in 1340 as a summer retreat for the Mughals. The **Eastern Yamuna Canal**, one of the first great 19th-century canals to irrigate the Ganga-Yamuna doab, transformed the landscape of what had been a heavily overpopulated region. It has become a particularly important source of fruit trees. The **Mango Festival** is held in June/July when hundreds of varieties are displayed. Woodcarvers can be seen at work in Lakdi Bazar and the old market place.

Going to Nepal

The road east from Delhi to the Nepal border gives access to some popular hill stations of the Uttarakhand Himalaya and to the Corbett National Park.

Ghaziabad is a modern satellite town for Delhi, with a population of 520,000 but little of aesthetic appeal. Beyond Ghaziabad is countryside, an area where two crops are cultivated each year, mostly rice in the monsoon and wheat in winter, but also sugarcane. Countless bullock carts trundle along the highway and line up outside the refineries.

The small town of **Garmukhteswar**, with some typical North Indian temples, stands on the west bank of the Ganga, with riverside ghats. According to the *Mahabharata*, this is where King Santanu met the Goddess Ganga in human form. Each year at the full moon in October and November, thousands of pilgrims converge to bathe in the holy waters. From the road bridge you may see turtles swimming around in the waters below.

Rampur was founded in 1623 by two Afghan Rohillas who served under the Mughals. Subsequently, the Rohillas united and expanded their empire (Rohilkhand, see page 139), but in 1772 the region was invaded by the Marathas. The Nawab of Rampur remained loyal to the British during the Mutiny and supported them in the second Afghan War. There is an extensive palace and fort here. The State Library has an excellent collection of 16th- to 18th-century portraits, plus a small book of Turkish verse with notes by both Babur and Shah Jahan.

Banbassa is a small town on the India–Nepal border with a large Nepali population and a friendly feel. ▸▸ *See Transport, page 119.*

Uttar Pradesh

Contents

Footprint features

Border crossings

At a glance

Getting around Trains are best for getting between major cities. Domestic flights to Lucknow and Varanasi. Agra is a standard feature on 'Golden Triangle' car tours.

Time required Minimum 1 day for Agra's main sights, 2 days each for Lucknow and Dudhwa NP, a week for Varanasi and nearby sites.

Weather Dry and dusty with bitterly cold mornings Nov-Feb, hot and muggy in Apr and May. Best in autumn and spring.

When not to go Avoid Agra during public holidays, and on Fri when the Taj Mahal is free to Indian tourists.

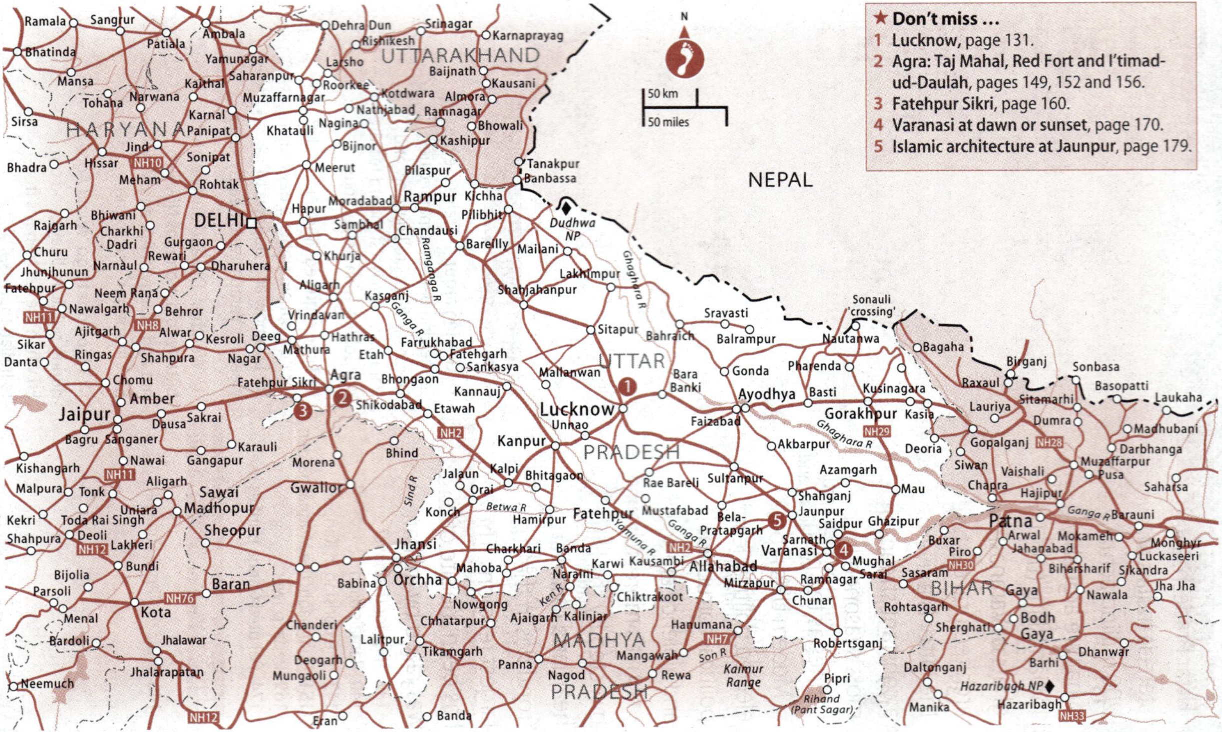

★ Don't miss …

1. **Lucknow**, page 131.
2. **Agra: Taj Mahal, Red Fort and I'timad-ud-Daulah**, pages 149, 152 and 156.
3. **Fatehpur Sikri**, page 160.
4. **Varanasi at dawn or sunset**, page 170.
5. **Islamic architecture at Jaunpur**, page 179.

Uttar Pradesh, a vast, socially conservative and deeply agricultural state, is India's answer to Texas – although its population of 200 million actually exceeds that of most nations. The state holds what are arguably the most famous cultural landmarks of both Indian Islam (the Taj Mahal at Agra) and Hinduism (the bathing ghats of Varanasi). While the former is the world's greatest architectural gesture to a single instance of inconsolable grief, the latter is a riverbank that has for centuries born witness to a constant stream of death at its funeral pyres. Many – from the most seasoned Indophile to the first-time traveller -- count these shrines as the high-water marks of any trip to the subcontinent.

Modern UP's reputation is less enviable domestically: many of India's elected political leaders have 'colourful' histories, but the level of political corruption in the state is exceptional, and casual criminality and violence are so high that some question the rule of law.

What's more, the state's position as both cradle of Hinduism, bisected by the Hindu spiritual life-force River Ganga, and cultural heartland of Indian Islam has spawned one of the most febrile frontlines in the contemporary conflict between India's two largest religions. The contested sacred ground at Ayodhya has been the site of bloody conflict since the Babri Mosque was razed by militant Hindus in 1992.

Background → *Population: 200 million. Area: 238,155 sq km. Language: Hindi.*

The land

Geography The landscape of Uttar Pradesh (Northern Province) is dominated by the flat alluvial plains of the Ganga and its tributaries. The north of the state runs along the southern margins of the **Shiwalik Hills**, which parallel the Himalaya. These are succeeded on their south by the often marshy tropical **Terai**, which, until they were cleared for cultivation in the 1950s, formed a belt of jungle 65 km wide from the Ganga gorge at Haridwar to Bihar. The **Gangetic Plain** occupies most of the state; flat and almost featureless, it is stiflingly hot, dry and dusty in summer. Further south are the northern margins of the peninsula, including the outer slopes of the **Vindhyan Mountains** in the southeast, which in places rise to more than 600 m.

Climate Although winter nights are cold everywhere in Uttar Pradesh, daytime temperatures can reach 25°C on the plains even in December and January. Between April and June temperatures soar and can reach 50°C. A desiccating hot wind, known as the Loo, often blows from the west. Despite a drop of temperature between June and September humidity increases, making it a very uncomfortable season.

Culture

The majority of the population is Hindu but nearly one fifth is Muslim, concentrated between Aligarh and Faizabad in what is called 'The Muslim Belt'. Today, adherents of Buddhism, Jainism, Christianity and Sikhism together constitute less than 3% of the state's population. Ethnically, the great majority of people on the plains are of Indo-Aryan stock. Most people speak Hindi, but Urdu is still quite widely used among Muslims. There are numerous local dialects.

Modern Uttar Pradesh

Uttar Pradesh has produced eight of India's 14 prime ministers since Independence, including Jawaharlal Nehru, his daughter Indira Gandhi and grandson Rajiv Gandhi. However, after three decades of Congress dominance, politics in Uttar Pradesh have become like a frequently shaken kaleidoscope. Lower caste groups have become more effectively mobilized, and in the 1990s transferred their votes from the Congress to alternatives, mainly the Janata Party and the Bahujan Samaj Party.

The rout of the Congress was seemingly completed by the emergence in the state of the BJP, but in the 2007 State Assembly elections the BSP, under the leadership of the 'Dalit Queen' Ms Mayawati, gained an overall majority. In the 2009 Lok Sabha elections, however, the BSP won only 20 of the 80 seats, one fewer than the newly resurgent Congress, reducing her influence at the centre.

The state legislative assembly meets at Lucknow, the capital. Uttar Pradesh has 80 seats in the Lok Sabha (Lower House) and 32 seats in the Rajya Sabha (Upper House), more than any other state. Both Rajiv Gandhi's widow, Sonia, who has proved a highly effective Congress president, and their son Rahul, an increasingly important figure in the Congress, hold UP seats.

Lucknow

→ *Colour map 3, A2. Population: 4,588,455.*

In Kipling's Kim *"no city – except Bombay, the queen of all – was more beautiful in her garish style than Lucknow". The capital of the state sprawls along the banks of the Gomti River in the heart of Uttar Pradesh. The ordered Cantonment area contrasts with the cream-washed buildings of the congested city centre, dotted with an incredible variety of decaying mansions and historic monuments, the best of which are breathtaking. In the heart of the old city traditional craftsmen continue to produce the rich gold zari work, delicate* chikan *embroidery and strong attar perfume. The arts still flourish and the bookshops do brisk trade in serious reading. Veils have largely disappeared as progressive college girls speed along on their scooters weaving between cows, cars and rickshaws.* ▸▸ *For listings, see pages 136-138.*

Ins and outs

Getting there

The modern airport, connected by direct flights to Delhi, Kolkata, Mumbai and Patna, is 14 km south of the city, about half an hour by taxi (pre-paid Rs 310) or auto (available outside for about Rs 150). Lucknow is well connected by train and road to other major cities of the north. The Junction Railway Station is in the southeast corner of the Hussainabad area, close to the historic sights, while the Charbagh Railway Station is to the south. The Kaiserbagh Bus Stand near the centre is for long-distance services, while most interstate buses terminate at the Charbagh Station Bus Stand near the stations. ▸▸ *See Transport, page 138.*

Getting around

The main sites are close enough to the centre to visit by cycle-rickshaw, or by hopping on a cheap shared *tempo* which run on fixed routes. However, the city is quite spread out and for extended sightseeing it is worth hiring a taxi.

Tourist information

Tourist office ⓘ *Charbagh Railway Station, Main Hall, daily 0600-2200, also at the airport*, has brochures and enthusiastic staff. UP Tours ⓘ *Gomti Hotel (see page 136), Mon-Sat 0900-1800.*

Background

Today Lucknow is a major administrative centre and market city, growing rapidly on both sides of the Gomti River from its historic core along the river's right bank. Although the discovery of **Painted Grey Ware** and **Northern Black** pottery demonstrates the long period over which the site has been occupied, its main claim to fame is as the capital of the cultured Nawabs of **Oudh** (*Avadh*), and later the scene of one of the most remarkable episodes in the 'Uprising' of 1857. Lucknow developed rapidly under the Mughal Emperor Akbar's patronage in the 16th century. In the early 18th century, Nawab Saadat Khan Burhan-ul-Mulk, a Persian courtier, founded the Oudh Dynasty. The city's growing reputation as a cultural centre attracted many others from Persia, leaving an indelible Shi'a imprint on the city's life. The builder of 'modern' Lucknow was Nawab Asaf-ud-Daula who shifted his capital here from Faizabad in 1775. In the attempt to build a wonderful city he emptied the regal coffers.

Jobs for the boys?

In 1784 Lucknow and its region suffered an appalling famine, and thousands of starving people flocked into the city. In a spectacular example of 'food for work' (pre-Keynes Keynesian economics) Asaf-ud-Daula decided to build the Great Imambara. He offered work night and day, reputedly employing 22,000 men, women and children. However, in order to ensure that the task was not finished too quickly, he divided it into two parts. During the day, normal building proceeded. At night the workmen destroyed one quarter of what had been built the previous day. Nobles were allowed to work at night to spare them the embarrassment of being seen as having to labour to survive. To the labourers this was a life-saving act of charity, even if the building itself is widely reported as something of a monstrosity.

In the mid-1850s under **Lord Dalhousie**, the British annexed a number of Indian states. He evolved a policy of lapse whereby the states of Indian princes without direct heirs could be taken over on the ruler's death. Chronic mismanagement was also deemed just cause for takeover, the justification given for the annexation of Oudh. The novelist Premchand in *The Chess Players* attributes the fall of Oudh to the fact that "small and big, rich and poor, were dedicated alike to sensual joys ... song, dance and opium". History suggests that Nawab Wajid Ali Shah continued with his game of chess even as British soldiers occupied his capital. A strong British presence was established in the city as it became a key administrative and military centre. **Satyajit Ray**'s film *'Satranj Ki Khilari (The Chess Players)'* is an excellent portrayal of these times.

When the '**Uprising**' (previously referred to as the Mutiny) broke in 1857, Sir Henry Lawrence gathered the British community into the Residency which rapidly became a fortress. The ensuing siege lasted for 87 days. When the relieving force under Sir Colin Campbell finally broke through, the once splendid Residency was a blackened ruin, its walls pockmarked and gaping with cannonball holes. Today it is a mute witness to a desperate struggle.

Under the **Nawabs**, Lucknow evolved specialized styles of dance, poetry, music and calligraphy. The Lucknowi *gharana* (house) of music and the exquisite crafts are reminders of its splendid past as it remains the regional cultural capital. Today, of the vintage modes of travel, only the *ekka* (one-horse carriage) has survived. To trace its Muslim heritage, visit the Bara and Chhota Imambaras, Shah Najaf Imambara and take a look at the Rumi Darwaza, Clock Tower and Chattar Manzil. Among the colonial monuments, the Residency and Constantia are the most rewarding.

Parivartan Chowk and the black **Mayawati monument**, which faces **Clarks Avadh Hotel**, symbolize *parivartan* (the spirit of 'change') which the 1997-1998 government of the fiery Chief Minister Mayawati hoped to encourage by giving increasing power to the scheduled castes. Recently Lucknow has been through periods of violent communal tension which is partly explained by the important BJP presence here. ▸▸ *See Books, page 1441, for further reading.*

Sights

The original city centre is believed to be the high ground crowned by the Mosque of Aurangzeb on the right bank of the Gomti. Tillotson, an architectural historian, suggests that the major buildings of Asaf-ud-Daula, built after 1775 – the **Bara Imambara**, the **Rumi Darwaza** (Turkish Gate) and the **mosque** – between them dramatically illustrate the 'debased Mughal' style of 'Indo-European' architecture in decline. The monuments have been divided into three main groups. They usually open between 0600 and 1700.

North West and Hussainabad

Just south of the Hardinge Bridge was the **Machhi Bhavan** (Fish House) enclosure. Safdarjang, Governor of Oudh (1719-1748), was permitted to use the fish insignia (a royal/imperial symbol/crest) by the Mughal Emperor Akbar. The Machhi Bhavan itself, once a fort, was blown up by the British in 1857, the only surviving part being the *baoli* which escaped because it was sunk into the hillside. Allow two to three hours for the Hussainabad tour.

The **Bara Imambara** ⓘ *foreigners Rs 350, ticket also allows access to the Chhota Imambara and the Baradari, guide fees are posted outside, foreigners not permitted in the Asifi Mosque,* is a huge vaulted hall which, like all *imambaras*, serves as the starting point for the Muharram procession (see page 44). The vast hall (50 m long and 15 m high), built by Asaf-ud-Daula to provide employment during a famine, is one of the largest in the world, unsupported by pillars. Look out for the notice: "Spiting (sic), smoking and call of nature strictly prohibited"! The remarkable *bhul-bhulaya*, a maze of interconnecting passages above, is reached by stairs; a delightful diversion. One visitor spent over an hour trying to find his way out. The five-storeyed *baoli* is connected directly with the River Gomti. Legends suggest that secret tunnels connect the lower steps, which are always under water, with a treasure stored beneath the *imambara* itself.

1 Lucknow

Sleeping
Deep Avadh **2**
Lucknow Homestay **4**
Mayur **5**
Vishwanath **1**
Vivanta by Taj & Oudhyana Restaurant **3**

At the end of the avenue leading up to the *imambara* from the river is the **Rumi Darwaza** (1784), a spectacular gate that resembles a conch-shell, built in the Byzantine style. Further along is the 19th-century Gothic 67-m-high Hussainabad **clock tower** (1880s) designed by Roskell Payne, which contains the largest clock in India though three of the four faces have been smashed. Next to it is the attractive octagonal Hussainabad Tank (1837-1842), around which is the Taluqdar's Hall and the incomplete Satkhanda (1840) seven-storeyed watchtower. There are excellent views of Lucknow from the top. Also worth a look is the restored **Baradari** ⓘ *Tue-Sun 0800-1800, entrance included in the Bara Imambara ticket,* housing a picture gallery with portraits of the Nawabs of Oudh.

Hussainabad Imambara (Chhota Imambara) ⓘ *sunrise-sunset, entrance included in the Bara Imambara ticket*, with its golden dome and elaborate calligraphy and containing beautiful chandeliers, gilt-edged mirrors and a silver throne (1837), is illuminated during Muharram. Further west is the extensively renovated **Jami Masjid** begun by Muhammad Shah and finished by his wife in the mid-1840s. **Victoria Park** (1890) with several British tombs is nearby. South of the park is the Chowk, the Old City bazar, where there are some interesting old buildings including the **Dargah of Hazrat Abbas** which contains a relic, a metal crest from the battle at Kerbala. Nearby is **Nadan Mahal** (c 1600), with the tomb of Shaikh Abdur Rahim, Akbar's Governor of Oudh, and son of Ibrahim Chishti. This is a fine building, built in the Mughal style and faced with red sandstone.

2 Lucknow centre

Lucknow maps
1 Lucknow, page 133
2 Lucknow centre, page 134

500 metres
500 yards

Sleeping
Arif Castles **1**
Capoor's **2**
Carlton **3**
Clarks Avadh, Falaknuma Restaurant & Indian Airlines **4**
Gomti & UP Tours **5**
Grand **6**
Le Place Sarovar Portico **8**
NRK **7**
Tekarees Inn & Koolbreak **9**

Eating
Moti Mahal **1**
Royal Inn/Royal Café **2**
Ritz Continental **3**

Residency and Hazratganj area

The Residency's 3000 mostly European occupants, hastily brought there by **Sir Henry Lawrence**, came under siege on 30 June 1857. Two days later Lawrence was fatally injured. After 90 days, General Sir Henry Havelock and General Sir James Outram appeared through the battered walls with a column of Highlanders. However, the siege was intensified and sepoy engineers began tunnelling to lay mines to blow the place up. From quite early on, there was a shortage of food and eventually smallpox, cholera and scurvy set in. Havelock was slowly dying of dysentery. The heroic Irishman, Henry Kavanagh, had sat in the tunnels and shot mutineers as they wriggled forward to lay more mines. He then volunteered to run the gauntlet through the enemy lines to find Sir Colin Campbell's relieving force, which he did by swimming the Gomti. On 17 November, Lucknow was finally relieved. Of the 2994 men, women and children who had taken refuge in the Residency, only 1000 marched out.

The **Residency Compound** is now a historic monument. You enter through the Bailey Guard gate. The **Treasury** on your right served as an arsenal while the grand Banquet Hall next door housed the wounded during the 'Uprising'. On the lawn of **Doctor Fayrer's House**, to your left, stands a marble cross to Sir Henry Lawrence. **Begum Kothi**, which belonged to Mrs Walters who married the Nawab of Oudh, can be reached through the long grass, but the old officers' mess has made way for flats and apartments.

The **Residency** (1800) ⓘ *foreigners Rs 100, cameras Rs 25*, to the northeast, built by Saadat Ali Khan, has *tykhanas* (cool underground rooms) where there is a museum, the highlight of which is an 1873 model of the complex, which gives you a good idea of how extensive and self-sufficient the original settlement was. At the time of the 'Uprising' the Residency was overlooked by high houses, now all destroyed, which gave cover to snipers firing into the compound. There are many etchings and records including Tennyson's *Relief of Lucknow*. Suggestions of a wooden staircase for officers, an underground passage to the palace, a secret room hidden in the wall behind false doors, all conjure up images of the past. The graves of Lawrence, Neill and others are in the church **cemetery**. Women visitors should not visit the cemetery alone. Just outside the Residency on the banks of the Gomti is a white obelisk commemorating the 'Nationalist Insurgents' who lost their lives in 1857.

Southeast of the Residency, near the Hanuman Setu, is the **Chattar Manzil** (Umbrella Palace) now the Central Drug Research Institute, where the submerged basement provided natural air conditioning. There are also the sad remains of the **Kaisarbagh Palace** (1850) conceived as a grand chateau. Better preserved are the almost twin **tombs** of Saadat Ali Khan (1814) and Khurshid Begum. To its east again are **Nur Bakhsh Kothi** and Tarawali Kothi (circa 1832), the observatory of the royal astronomer Colonel Wilcox, which is now the **State Bank of India**.

Eastern Group

Shah Najaf Imambara (1814-1827) ⓘ *free entry*, near the Gomti, has the tombs of Nawab Ghazi-ud-Din Haidar and his three wives, with its white dome and elaborate interior decorations, including a huge array of chandeliers, mirrors and paintings. It was used by sepoy mutineers as a stronghold in 1857. Wajid Ali Shah's (ruled 1847-1856) pleasure garden **Sikander Bagh**, created for his favourite wife, retains the original gateway and mosque.

To the south of these are **Wingfield Park**, laid out in the 1860s, which contains a marble pavilion and some statues. Within the **Zoo** ⓘ *Tue-Sun 0830-1730, foreigners Rs 100*, off Park Rd, is the **State Museum** ⓘ *Banarsi Bagh, T0522-220 6158, Tue-Sun 1000-1700 (last entrance at 1600), foreigners Rs 50*, the oldest in Uttar Pradesh and one of the richest in India, exhibits Hindu, Buddhist and Jain works including stone sculptures from Mathura, and busts and friezes from Allahabad and Garhwal, dating from the first to 11th centuries. Also marble sculptures, paintings, natural history and anthropology. Marvellous relics of the British Raj, removed at the time of Independence, languish in the backyard. **Christchurch** (1860), a memorial to the British killed during the 'Uprising' is nearby, along with the imposing Legislative Council Chamber (1928) and **Raj Bhawan** (Government House), enlarged in 1907.

To the east is Constantia, now **La Martinière College**, planned as the country residence of Major-General Claude Martin (1735-1800), a French soldier of fortune who is buried in the crypt. He ran highly successful indigo and money-lending businesses. The curious wedding cake of a building was completed after Martin's death from the endowment set aside by him for a school here and at Kolkata for 'Anglo-Indians' (Kipling's *Kim* being one of them). For the students' bravery during the siege of the Residency, the school was unique in being awarded Battle Honours. The chapel, historical photos and the crypt are interesting. You may ask to look around both outside and within. The office is at the east end.

Further south is **Dilkusha** (Heart's Delight), once a royal shooting lodge in what was a large deer park. There are graves of soldiers who died here during the 'Uprising', including that of General Havelock; his grave obelisk is in Alam Bagh, 100 m northeast of the garden's main gateway.

Lucknow listings

For Sleeping and Eating price codes and other relevant information, see Essentials pages 38-42.

Sleeping

Lucknow *p131, maps p133 and p134*

LL Clarks Avadh, 8 MG Marg, T0522-262 0131, www.hotelclarks.com. 98 rooms, modern, clean, comfortable, efficient, attentive service, good restaurants. Recommended.

LL Vivanta by Taj, Vipin Khand, Gomti Nagar, 5 km east of railway station, T0522-671 1000, www.vivantabytaj.com. 110 rooms in elegant colonial-style modern building, excellent restaurants, good pool, attractive gardens (transplanted mature palms), city's most luxurious hotel and the only really quiet one.

L Le Place Sarovar Portico, 6 Shahnajaf Rd, T0522-400 4040, www.sarovarhotels.com. 50 large contemporary-styled rooms in a modern, friendly chain hotel, very well maintained, attractive grill resto-bar on the roof, 24-hr coffee shop, breakfast included. Good location and atmosphere.

AL Arif Castles, 4 Rana Pratap Marg, Hazratganj, T0522-409 8777, www.arifcastles.com. The exterior is uninspiring, but inside is since it re-opened in 2010 as a boutique hotel, 42 rooms and suites with full amenities and chic furnishings. 2 good restaurants, specializing in Nawabi and Italian food. Also in a good location, efficient.

A-B Tekarees Inn, 17/3 Ashok Marg, T0522-221 5409, www.tekareesinn.com. Tiled floors, TV, fridge, rooms feel bright but layout varies so look at a few. Disappointing shower rooms for the price. Good restaurant (see Eating, page 137).

B-E Gomti (UP Tourism), 6 Sapru Marg, T0522-262 0624, www.up-tourism.com. 65 rooms covering a range of categories, all with TV, some a/c, but getting shabby and fusty at the lower end of the spectrum. However, the location is good, as is the restaurant and bright attractive bar (open 1100-2400, beer Rs 120), plus service is attentive.

C Capoor's, 52 Hazratganj, T0522-405 4300, www.hotelcapoors.com. 30 rooms, central a/c, some without windows, gloomy corridors, old world charm obliterated by bad re-fits and furnishings, but very central. Good 'Nawabs' restaurant, **Strokes** sports bar attracts a crowd (1200-2400).

C Carlton, Rana Pratap Marg, T0522-262 2445. Charming ex-British residency, large rooms and huge lawn, undergoing complete renovation at the time of research.

C-E Grand, 4 Lalbagh, T0522-262 4229. Modern anonymous-looking hotel with a/c rooms that are clean and bright, laminate floors and decent bathrooms, quieter at the rear, restaurant, correctly priced for the standard. Don't be put off by the exterior, it's a decent choice.

D Vishwanath, Subhash Marg, Charbagh, T0522-245 0879, vishwanath_04@yahoo.com. A/c rooms are not bad value at Rs 950 per double, also has restaurant and car parking plus friendly staff. Recommended.

E-F Mayur, Subhash Marg, T0522-245 1824. One of few hotels close to the station that welcomes foreigners, the Mayur has cheap rooms that are about acceptable, singles Rs 350, doubles Rs 450. Pay significantly more for a/c. English spoken.

E-F New Ram Krishna (NRK), 17/2 Ashok Marg, Hazratganj, T0522-228 7491. Clean rooms with bath with hot water and TV, rates decrease the higher up the building you go (there's no lift), some a/c but others have air-cooler.

F Lucknow Homestay, 10 Mall Av, T0522-223 5460, naheed2k@gmail.com. 7 modest rooms a couple of kilometres southeast of the city centre (and expect train noise), but homely and clean, attracts any backpackers passing through. Use of fridge/kettle, free Wi-Fi, breakfast included, lunch/dinner available (Rs 50), good library. Doubles Rs 450/500. Recommended.

Eating

Lucknow p131, maps p133 and p134

The better hotels serve good Lucknowi food - rich *biryanis*, *roomali roti* and *kebabs* and *kulfis* to end the meal. Special *cum pukht* (steam cooked) dishes are worth trying. 1st and 7th of month and public holidays are 'dry' days.

TTT **Falaknuma**, on rooftop of **Clarks Avadh**. Serves tasty, spicy Nawabi cuisine by candle light, good views, beer available, attentive service and live *ghazals* of exceptionally high quality. Recommended.

TTT **Oudhyana**, at **Vivanta by Taj** (see Sleeping). Special Avadhi food, lovely surroundings, the finest fine dining in town. Book in advance.

TT **Royal Inn/Royal Café**, 9/7 Shahnajaf Rd, T0522-409 5555. Open 1100-2300. Excellent and huge menu of mainly Indian and Chinese dishes, veg or non-veg. Large hygienic modern surrounds, attracts families, deservedly popular. It's not cheap but expect quality.

T **Koolbreak**, **Tekarees Inn** (see Sleeping). Good menu of Chinese and Indian food, plus a few continental dishes, in a modern cafe-style restaurant.

T **Moti Mahal**, 75 Hazratgang, T0522-262 33375. Open 0800-2330. Huge menu, mainly North Indian but some Chinese and South Indian, good ice-creams, family-friendly split-level surroundings.

T **Ritz Continental**, Ashok Marg, opposite Jawahar Bhavan, Gole Market. Good vegetarian, recently refurbished.

T **Tunde Kababi**, branches in the main Chowk and Aminabad Chowk. Kebabs (named after a one-armed ancestor) are sought after locally and famed throughout the city.

Festivals and events

Lucknow p131, maps p133 and p134

Oct-Nov National Kite Flying Competition at the Patang Park, MG Marg the day after **Diwali**.

25 Nov-5 Dec Mahotsav Festival with emphasis on Indian classical music: song, drama and dance, processions, boating and *ekka* races, crafts and cuisine.

Shopping

Lucknow p131, maps p133 and p134

Lucknow is famous for fine floral *chikan* or 'shadow' embroidery in pastel colours, produced around the chowk. You will also find gold *zari* and sequin work and prized *attar*. Shops usually open 1000-1930, markets until 2000. **Janpath market**, Hazratganj, is closed on Sun; **Aminabad**, Chowk, Sadar, Super Bazar closed on Thu.

The following are in Hazratganj.

Asghar Ali, near Chowk. For *attar* perfume.

Gangotri, 31/29. Handloom and crafts, and other government emporia.

Lal Behari Tandon, 17 Ashok Marg. Good-quality *chikan*.

Ram Advani, Mayfair Cinema Building, Hazratganj, T0522-306 0990. Lucknow's best bookshop since 1951. Mon-Sat 1000-1930.

Universal Booksellers, Hazratganj. Large stock covering all subjects.

Activities and tours

Lucknow p131, maps p133 and p134

Golf

Golf course at **La Martinière Boys College**, open to public (one of the hazards is the tomb of Augustus Nayne – a British officer who fell in the 'Uprising' and was reputedly buried with his monocle still in place).

Horse racing

Race course at Cantonment.

Tour operators

Tornos, Tornos House, C-2016 Indira Nagar, T(0)9935-538105, toll free T1800-1022882, www.tornosindia.com. Very reliable, whole host of special interest tours, including culinary, reasonable prices.

UP Tours, Hotel Gomti, T0522-261 4708. For air/rail tickets, car hire (Rs 800, 8 hrs, 80 km; Rs 8 per km for longer trips, minimum 200 km), *tonga* sightseeing tours (Rs 400, 4 hrs, 2 hrs advance notice required) and **Heritage Walks** which start near the Hardinge Bridge and take in lesser-known sights in the Chowk (daily starting 0800, 3 hrs, Rs 10, can contact direct on T(0)9415-013047). Interesting and unbelievable value.

Transport

Lucknow *p131, maps p133 and p134*

Air **Amausi Airport** (recently renamed Chaudhry Charan Singh International Airport), 14 km; pre-paid taxis available, Rs 310; autos Rs 150. Flights to most Indian cities, daily to **Delhi** with **Air India**, **Kingfisher** and **IndiGo**, also to **Mumbai**, **Kolkata** and **Patna**. Thrice weekly flights to **Kathmandu** with **Buddha Air**, www.buddhaair.com,

Long distance bus **UP Roadways, Charbagh Bus Stand**, T0522-245 0988 (left luggage, 0600-2200, Rs 5-10 per piece). Frequent services to **Allahabad** (4½ hrs), **Faizabad** (3 hrs), **Gorakhpur** (9 hrs), **Kanpur** (2½ hrs) and **Varanasi** (9 hrs). From **Kaisarbagh Bus Stand**, T0522-222 2503. Bus to **Delhi** (12-13 hrs), also services to **Gorakhpur**.

Rickshaw Tempo-rickshaws on fixed routes are cheap (Rs 3 minimum) and easy to use (from station, cross the road and ask for a landmark nearby, eg GPO). Cycle-rickshaws are widely available; Rs 10-15 for 2 km.

Train Take special care of belongings at the railway station. Theft is common.

Lucknow is on the Northern and Northeastern railway lines with 2 main railway stations, **Charbagh** and **Lucknow Junction**, both about 3 km southwest of town centre. **Northern Railway** trains leave from both stations: enquiries T131 (Arrivals T1331, Departures T1332); reservations Charbagh T0522-263 5841. **Northeastern Railway** trains leave from Junction station: enquiries T0522-263 5877. **Agra Fort**: *Marudhar Exp 14853/14863/14865*, 0030, 5½ hrs. **Allahabad**: *Nauchandi Exp 14512*, 0525, 4½ hrs; *Ganga-Gomti Exp 14216*, 1800, 4¼ hrs; *Intercity Exp 14210*, 0730, 4¼ hrs. **Bhopal**: *GKP Exp 12589/12591*, 1150 except Mon, 9½ hrs; *Pushpak Exp 12533*, 1945, 10¼ hrs. **Gorakhpur** (for Nepal): several, best are *Kathgodam Howrah Bagh Exp 13020*, 0620, 6 hrs; *Krishak Exp 15008*, 2305, 7¼ hrs. **Jabalpur** (for Kanha): *Chitrakoot Exp 15009*, 1730, 14¼ hrs. **Jhansi**: *Kushinagar Exp 11016*, 0040, 6¼ hrs; *Pushpak Exp 12533*, 1945, 6 hrs. **Kanpur**: *Gomti Exp 12419*, 0525, 1½ hrs; *Shatabdi Exp 12003*, 1535, 1¼ hrs. **Kolkata (H)**: *Amritsar-Howrah Mail 13006*, 1050, 20½ hrs; *Doon Exp 13010*, 0835, 22½ hrs. **Kathgodam** (for **Nainital**): *Bagh Exp 13019*, 0030, 9 hrs. **New Delhi**: *Gomti Exp 12419*, 0525, 8½ hrs; *Shatabdi Exp 12003*, 1535, 6½ hrs; *Lucknow New Delhi Mail 12229*, 2210, 9 hrs. **Varanasi**: *Kashi Vishwanath Exp 14258*, 2150, 7 hrs; *Varuna Exp 14228/24228*, 1750, 5½ hrs.

Directory

Lucknow *p131, maps p133 and p134*

Banks **State Bank**, Hazratganj, and **Punjab National Bank**, Ashok Marg change money. Many ATMs on MG Rd and **HSBC** on Shahnajaf Marg. **Internet** **Cybernet**, off MG Rd, Rs 20 per hr; **Lucknow Homestay** has free wireless. **Hospitals** **Balrampur District Hospital**, Hospital Rd, Golaganj, T0522-222 4040. **Post** **GPO**: Vidhan Sabha Marg, 0930-1730. Also in Chowk and Mahanagar. **Useful contacts** **Archaeological Survey of India**: Amirud Daula Kothi, Kaisarbagh. **Foreigners' Registration Office**: 5th floor, Jawahar Bhavan, Ashok Marg. **Wildlife Office**: 17 Rana Pratap Marg.

Around Lucknow

The area around Lucknow has been involved in some of the most turbulent events in modern Indian history, from the 1857 Uprising in Kanpur, now the state's largest industrial city, to the clashes in 2002 between Hindus and Muslims over the holy site of Ayodhya. East of Ayodhya, Gorakhpur makes a convenient base for exploring a number of key Buddhist sites, as well as being a popular jumping-off point for the crossing to Nepal, while north of Lucknow in the Himalayan foothills, the rarely visited Dudhwa National Park protects a handful of tigers and a reintroduced population of Indian one-horned rhino. ▸▸ *For listings, see pages 143-146.*

Dudhwa National Park → *Colour map 3, A2. 220 km north of Lucknow.*

ⓘ *Open mid-Nov to mid-Jun, foreigners Rs 500 per day; Indians and students pay reduced rates; camera free, video Rs 500; road fees for light vehicles, Rs 150 per day. Night driving is not allowed in the park so arrive before sunset. Reception Centre, Dudhwa National Park, Lakhimpur Kheri, near Dist Magistrate's house, T05871-252106. Wildlife Warden, Dudhwa National Park, Palia, T05871-233485. Tours available in season.*

A reserve since 1879, Dudhwa was designated a national park in 1977 and Project Tiger Reserve in 1988 by adding 200 sq km of the Kishanpur Sanctuary, 30 km away. Bordering the Sarda River in the Terai, it is very similar to the Corbett National Park. It has sal forest (in addition to sheesham, asna, khair and sagaun), tall savannah grasslands and large marshy areas watered by the Neora and Sohel rivers.

The swamps are the ideal habitat of the barasingha (swamp deer with 12 tined antlers, *Cervus duvanceli*), now numbering about 2000, which are best seen in the Sathiana and Kakraha blocks. The tiger population is believed to be about 140 though they are rarely spotted. Dudhwa also has sambar, nilgai, some sloth bears (*Melursus ursinus*), the endangered hispid hare, fishing cats and a few leopards. The one-horned rhino was reintroduced from northeast India in 1985 but visitors are not allowed into the enclosure. The 400 species of avifauna includes *Bengal floricans*, pied and great Indian hornbills, owls and king vultures. It also attracts a wide variety of water birds (swamp partridge, eastern white stork) addition to birds of prey (osprey, hawks, fishing eagles). Banke Tal is good for birdwatching.

To view the wildlife you can hire a jeep or minibus (Rs 20-30 per km), from the park office at Dudhwa. However, elephants are recommended and are available at Dudhwa only. Each carries four (Rs 50 per person for 2½ hours; minimum charge Rs 200). Elephant rides should be booked on arrival at the park.

The best time to visit is February to April; from April to June it becomes very hot, dry and dusty, but it is good for viewing big game. In summer the maximum temperature is 35°C, minimum 10°C. In winter the maximum is 30°C, minimum 4°C. Annual rainfall is 1500 mm; the wettest months are June to September. Palia has a bank, a basic health centre and a post office. Dudhwa has a dispensary.

Bareilly → *Colour map 3, A2. Phone code: 0581.*

Bareilly, the capital of Rohilkhand (an empire built by two Afghan Rohillas who served under the Moghals), was founded in 1537 by the Bas Deo and Barel Deo brothers (hence Bareilly) and traces of their fortress remain. It was ceded to the British in 1801 and later contributed to the drama of the 'Uprising'. There are three 17th-century mosques and two churches in town. Bareilly is known for its iron industry and its gold *zari* work. It is an important rail junction with a population of around 4.4 million.

Rama's birth

Rama's father, Dasaratha, unable to have children by any of his wives, was instructed to perform a great sacrifice in order that his wives might conceive. At the same time there was great trouble in the home of the gods, for Ravana, the king of the demons, had been assured by Brahma that he could never be harmed by a human, or by "devas and other supernatural beings". When the gods learned of this promise they turned to Vishnu and begged him to be born as a man so that he could put an end to Ravana. Vishnu agreed that he would be born as four sons of Dasaratha, who was then performing his sacrifice.

The sacred fire was lit and ghee poured on. Out of the flames emerged a startling figure. He held out a bowl of *payasam* (a milk dessert) to Dasaratha and said: "The gods are pleased with your sacrifice. If your wives drink this payasam they will be blessed with sons".

Dasaratha was overjoyed. He immediately gave the *payasam* to his wives. In due course all three became pregnant. Kausalya gave birth to Rama and Kaikeyi gave birth to Bharata. Sumitra, having taken two portions of the divine payasam, gave birth to the twins, Lakshmana and Satrughuna.

Faizabad → *Colour map 3, A3. Phone code: 05278. Population: 2.47 million.*

Faizabad, 124 km east of Lucknow, is handy for visiting Ayodhya. It was once the capital of Oudh. Shuja-ud-Daula (1754-1775), the third Nawab of Oudh, built Fort Calcutta here after his defeat by the British at Buxar in 1764. The 42-m-high white marble **Mausoleum of Bahu Begum** (circa 1816), his widow, is particularly fine. Gulab Bari (Mausoleum of Shuja-ud-Daula, circa 1775) nearby, contains the tombs of his mother and father.

Ayodhya → *Colour map 3, A3. Phone code: 05276. Population: 50,000.*

Ayodhya ('a place where battles cannot take place'), 9 km from Faizabad on the banks of the **Saryu River**, is one of the seven holy Hindu cities (the others are Mathura, Haridwar, Varanasi, Ujjain, Dwarka and Kanchipuram). It is regarded by many Hindus as the birthplace of Rama and where he once reigned, though the historian Romila Thapar stresses that there is no evidence for such a belief. Jains regard it as the birthplace of the first and fourth Tirthankars, and the Buddha is also thought to have stayed here.

The **Archaeological Survey of India** and the **Indian Institute of Advanced Study** began excavation in 1978. The ruins have a circumference of between 4 km and 5 km, rising at some places to 10 m above the ground. According to Professor BB Lal, the site was occupied from at least the seventh century BC if not earlier, when both iron and copper were in use. Later finds include a Jain figure from the fourth to third century BC, possibly the earliest Jain figure found in India. Houses during this period were built in kiln-baked brick, and various coins have been found from periods up to the fourth century AD, some indicating extensive trade with East India. BB Lal goes on: "many of the now standing temples having been erected during the past two centuries only".

In accordance with Muslim practice elsewhere, a number of temples were razed and mosques were built on the site, often using the same building material. In recent years Ayodhya has become the focus of intense political activity by the Vishwa Hindu Parishad, an organization asserting a form of militant Hinduism, and the BJP, its leading political ally. They claim that Ayodhya was '**Ramajanambhumi**' (Rama's birthplace) and that this holy site is beneath the remains of the **Babri Mosque**, built by **Babur** and deserted now for many years. On 6 December 1992, the mosque was destroyed by militant Hindus. This was followed by widespread disturbances resulting in over 2500 deaths across the country. Ayodhya remains a potential flashpoint, so check conditions first if you plan to visit. The massacre of young Hindu activists returning from Ayodhya to Gujarat in February 2002 resulted in over 1000 deaths in the following months.

Other sites include **Lakshmana Ghat**, 3 km from the station, where Rama's brother committed suicide. **Hanumangarh** takes its name from the Hanuman and Sita temple and the massive walls surrounding it.

Gorakhpur ➔ *Colour map 3, A4. Phone code: 0551. Population: 4.44 million.*

Gorakhpur, at the confluence of the Rapti and Rohini rivers, is the last major Indian town before the Nepali border. The British and the Gurkha armies clashed nearby in the early 18th century. Later it became the recruitment centre for Gurkha soldiers enlisting into the British and Indian armies. The **Gorakhnath Temple** attracts Hindu pilgrims, particularly *Kanfata sadhus* who have part of their ears cut. Unusual terracotta pottery figures and animals are made here. **Tourist office** ⓘ *Park Rd, Civil Lines, T0551-233 5450; counter on Platform 1, railway station.*

Kushinagar ➔ *Colour map 3, A4.*

Kushinagar, 50 km east of Gorakhpur, is celebrated as the place where the Buddha died and was cremated and passed into *parinirvana*; the actual site is unknown. Originally called Kushinara, it is one of four major Buddhist pilgrimage sites (see page 1422). Monasteries established after the Buddha's death flourished here until the 13th century.

In the main site, the core of the Main Stupa possibly dates from Asoka's time with the **Parinirvana Temple.** The restored 6-m recumbent sandstone figure of the dying Buddha in a shrine in front may have been brought from Mathura by the monk Haribala during King Kumargupta's reign (AD 413-455). The *stupas*, *chaityas* and *viharas*, however, were 'lost' for centuries. The Chinese pilgrims Fa Hien, Hiuen Tsang, and I Tsing, all recorded the decay and ruins of Kushinagar between 900 and 1000 years after the Buddha's death. The *stupa* and the temple were rediscovered only in the 1880s. The **Mathakuar shrine** to the southwest has a large Buddha in the *bhumisparsha mudra* and marks the place where the Buddha last drank water. **Rambahar stupa** (Mukutabandhana), 1 km east, was built by the Malla Dynasty to house the Buddha's relics after the cremation. Some of the bricks (which have holes for easier firing) were carved to form figures.

Excavations were begun by the Archaeological Survey of India in 1904-1905, following clues left by the Chinese travellers. A shaft was driven through the centre of the Nirvana *stupa* "which brought to light a copper plate placed on the mouth of a relic casket in the form of a copper vessel with charcoal, cowries, precious stones and a gold coin of Kumaragupta I". The whole area was occupied until the 11th century. In all there are eight groups of monasteries, *stupas* and images, indicating that Kushinagar was a substantial community.

Kanpur ➔ *Colour map 3, B2. Phone code: 0512.*

With a population of over 2.5 million people, Kanpur is the largest city of Uttar Pradesh and the most important industrial centre in the state. Cotton mills were first established in 1869, some of the first in India. It is now one of the major industrial cities in India with aviation, woollen and leather industries, cotton, flour and vegetable oil mills, sugar refineries and chemical works. As a result of this high level of industry, the city is extremely polluted, and has become one sprawling, congested market, with seemingly every street constantly choked with traffic. As an example of industry run riot it somehow has a perverse attraction, and perhaps needs to be experienced once in a lifetime. Tourist information is available at UPTDC ⓘ *26/51 Birhana Rd, opposite the post office, T0512-235 8186.*

The principal British monuments are in the southeast of the city in the old cantonment area. Stone posts mark the lines of the trenches near **All Souls' Memorial Church** (1862-1875), a handsome Gothic-style building designed by Walter Granville. A tiled pavement outside marks the graves of those executed on 1 July 1857, soon after the Satichaura Ghat massacre. To the east, the **Memorial Garden** has a statue by Marochetti and a screen designed by Sir Henry Yule, which were brought here after Independence. The infamous **Satichaura Ghat**, 1 km northeast of the church by the Ganga, has a small Siva temple. You can walk along the river from the Lucknow Road bridge (about 200 m, but dirty) which leads to the site of the boat massacre just upstream of the temple, where cannons were stationed on the high banks. The temple is altered but the landing ghats are still used by fishermen's boats and for washing clothes.

At the siege site, remains of the walls are still visible – as is the privy drain system and the well. The Massacre House was north of the canal about 250 m from the Ganga, and north of the Arms Factory, now marked by a statue of Nana Sahib. In the city centre there is the King Edward VII **Memorial (KEM) Hall** and **Christ Church** (1848). The higher-grade hotels are along the Mall, some within reach of Meston Road with its interesting, faded, colonial architecture and cheap leather goods shops.

Bithur

Nana Sahib's home town, 20 km north of Kanpur, has pleasant ghats by the Ganga. His opulent palace was destroyed by the British in 1857 and is now marked by a memorial bust. Ruins of a few large well heads survive in a park west of the main road into town from Kanpur. 'Enthusiasts' should allow two hours.

Sleeping
Ashoka 1
Attic 2
Gaurav 4
Geet 4
Grand Palace 3
Landmark 4
Meera Madhuvan 5
Vaishali 6

Eating
Kwality 1
Little Chef 2

The uprising in Kanpur

Kanpur was one of the most important British garrisons on the Ganga. During the 'Uprising' the insurgents rallied under Nana Sahib, who bore a grievance against the British because he had received only a small pension. They laid siege to the British community of around 400 men, women and children who had been gathered together under General Sir Hugh Wheeler. Inadequately protected and without enough food, after 18 days the defenders were severely reduced through gunshot wounds, starvation and disease. Nana Sahib then offered a truce and arranged for boats to take the survivors downstream to Allahabad. When they were boarding at Satichaura Ghat, they were raked with fire and hacked down by horsemen. One boat escaped. The survivors were either butchered and thrown down a well or died of cholera and dysentery. The reprisals were as horrible. General Sir James Neill "was seized with an Old Testamental vision of revenge" (Moorhouse). To break a man's religion and caste, pork and beef were stuffed down his throat, thus condemning him to eternal damnation. More often than not, suspected mutineers were bayoneted on sight. Nana Sahib escaped after pretending to commit suicide in the Ganga and is believed to have died in Nepalin 1859. For further reading, see Books, page 1441.

Around Lucknow listings

For Sleeping and Eating price codes and other relevant information, see Essentials pages 38-42.

Sleeping

Dudhwa National Park *p139*

All hotels are basic and foreigners pay more than Indians. Advance booking (15 days), and full payment (bank draft/postal order) is needed. Bedding is available at Dudhwa and Sathiana which have electricity; generators available on request at Sathiana, Sonaripur and Belrayan, at extra charge. For reservations at any of the places listed below, call Chief Wildlife Warden, UP, 17 Rana Pratap Marg, Lucknow, T0522-220 6584, or Dy Director, Dudhwa Project Tiger, Palia, Lakhimpur Kheri, T05871-233485.

The accommodation is 4 km from Dudhwa railway station, 10 km from Palia and 37 km from Mailani.

D Forest Resthouse, Dudhwa. 5 suites, 1 a/c.
D Forest Resthouse, Sathiana. 2 suites.
D-E Tiger Haven, Palia. Lodges.
E Forest Resthouse, Bankatti. 4 suites.
E Log huts, Dudhwa. 2 huts.
E Log huts, Sathiana. 6 huts.
E Tharu huts, Dudhwa. 12 huts.
G Dorm beds, Dudhwa. 25 beds. Reserve with Field Director, T05872-252106.

Bareilly *p139*

AL-B Swarn Towers, Station Rd, 5-min walk from station, T0581-242 6666, www.hotelswarntowers.in. 30 a/c rooms, bit overpriced, modern, friendly **Cheers** bar for drinks and snacks, swimming pool and 3 restaurants.
B-D Uberoi Anand, 46 Civil Lines, T0581-257 0838. 88 rooms, some a/c or air-cooled, restaurant, money exchange, terrace garden.
E-G Civil and Military, Station Rd, T0581-257 0879. Central hotel, 22 rooms, some a/c, dorm beds, restaurant, bar.
G Railway Retiring Rooms. 2 rooms, clean, hot and cold water, secure.

Faizabad *p140*

C-F Shan-e-Avadh, near Civil Lines Bus Stand, T05278-223586. Clean hotel, 52 rooms with bath, hot water, good restaurant, clean.
C-F Tirupati, Main Rd, T05278-223231. Next door to **Shan-e-Avadh**, 35 rooms with bath (bucket hot water), some a/c, best upstairs at rear, good restaurant, modern.
F Railway Retiring Rooms. 2 rooms, dorm.

Ayodhya *p140*

There are better hotels in Faizabad.
E-G Rahi Tourist Bungalow (UPTDC), turn right from railway station, T05278-232435, www.up-

tourism.com. Very clean, basic rooms, 1 a/c, simple restaurant, tourist information, friendly.

Gorakhpur *p141*

Budget hotels opposite the railway station can be noisy.

AL-A The Grand, 6 Park Rd, Civil Lines, T0551-220 5016, www.clarksinngrand.in. Upmarket hotel with all the mod cons, bit faceless. New family restaurant on-site.

C-D Ganges Delux, Cinema Rd, T0551-233 6330. Comfortable, 10 a/c rooms.

D Avantika, Airport Rd (NH28), beyond cross-roads 3 km from railway station, T0551-220 0765. Modern, good rooms and restaurant.

D Ganges, Tarang Crossing, T0551-233 3530. Some a/c rooms, good restaurant and ice cream parlour, well managed. Recommended.

D-F Upvan, Nepal Rd, T0551-233 8003. Ask rickshaw for **Bobina** next door. Some a/c or good air-cooled rooms, Indian restaurant, clean, efficient room service. Recommended.

F-G Kailash, Nepal Rd, 1 km from railway station, T0551-233 6406. All air-cooled rooms, clean linen and bath, good management, no restaurants nearby.

G Railway Retiring Rooms, upstairs from Platform 1. Some a/c (best deluxe) and 3 dorms, restaurant, quiet. Recommended.

Kushinagar *p141*

C-E Pathik Niwas, UPTDC, near ASI office, T05564-273045, www.up-tourism.com. 8 rooms, tourist office, restaurant.

G Dharamshalas, T05564-273093. The Chinese temple's new block is recommended.

Kanpur *p141, map p142*

Some budget hotels are reluctant to take foreigners as it means filling up forms. There are pools in hotels **Meghdoot**, **Grand Trunk** and **Landmark**.

AL Landmark, Som Datta Plaza, 10 The Mall, T0512-230 5305, www.thehotellandmark.com. 131 plain but comfortable rooms, smart restaurants, casual coffee lounge, station/airport pick-up, large pool and a huge games room including a 4-lane bowling alley.

B-C Attic, 15/198 V Singh Rd, Civil Lines, T0512-230 6691, www.theattickanpur.com. Probably the most peaceful place in town. 13 a/c rooms in a modern block behind a charming colonial house in a secluded setting and a beautifully kept garden. Recommended.

C-D Ashoka, 24/16 Birhana Rd, T0512-231 2742. Very centrally located, 30 rooms on a relatively quiet backstreet.

D-E Gaurav, 18/54 The Mall, T0512-231 8531, www.gauravhotel.com. 33 a/c rooms, restaurant, pleasant garden.

D-E Geet, 18/174-5 The Mall, T0512-231 1042, www.geethotel.com. 40 a/c rooms, restaurant good, exchange. Slightly cheaper than **Gaurav**.

D-E Meera Madhuvan, 37/19 The Mall, T0512-207 5300. Clean, modern and friendly, 50 rooms, some a/c, restaurant (Indian snacks, drinks), good value, recommended.

D-F Grand Palace, 45/98 Moolganj Crossing, T0512-235 3405. The 29 rooms on a busy main road are unexceptional, but the staff are extremely friendly and helpful.

F Vaishali, Meston Rd, Tilak Hall Lane, T0512-235 3404. The 85 rooms are decent but baths are small.

Eating

Dudhwa National Park *p139*

Only Dudhwa has a canteen (Ÿ) serving meals and snacks. Other places have facilities (crockery and utensils). Provisions must be brought in. **Palia**, 10 km away, has eating places.

Faizabad *p140*

Ÿ **Gulnar**, Main Rd 'T' junction. Good curries.

Gorakhpur *p141*

ŸŸ-Ÿ Recommended hotel restaurants include **Avantika**, **Ganges** and **President** (see Sleeping), also fast-food outlets near Indira Children's Park.

Ÿ **Bobi's**, over the road from **President Hotel**. Tasty Indian and friendly staff.

Ÿ **Ganesh**. South Indian vegetarian.

Kanpur *p141, map p142*

ŸŸ **Fu-Tu**, The Mall. Chinese.

ŸŸ **Kwality**, 16/97 The Mall. International, bar.

ŸŸ **Little Chef**, 15/198-A, Civil Lines. Specializes in outdoor catering, a little soulless but very clean.

ŸŸ **Shanghai**, The Mall. Chinese.

Ÿ **Kabab Corner**, Sarvodaya Nagar. North Indian.

Ÿ **Sarovar**, Sarvodaya Nagar. North Indian food.

Ÿ **Shalaka**, in shopping arcade opposite **Landmark**. Pizzas and South Indian snacks.

Festivals and events

Kushinagar *p141*

Apr/May Buddha Jayanti (1st full moon) marks the Buddha's birth. A huge fair is held when his relics (on public display at this time only) are taken out in procession.

Shopping

Kanpur *p141, map p142*

The main shopping areas are **The Mall**, Birhana Rd, and **Navin Market**. Kanpur is famous for cotton and leather products, which an be found along **Meston Rd**.

Activities and tours

Kanpur *p141, map p142*

Tour operators

Jet Air, 24/1, LIC Building, 1st floor, The Mall, T0512-231 2559, yugesh@jetair.co.in. (GSA for several foreign airlines). Very efficient. Recommended.

Sita, 18/53 The Mall, T0512-235 2980, www.sitaindia.com. For **Indian Airlines** as well as several international airlines, plus package tours.

Transport

Dudhwa National Park *p139*

Air The nearest airports are Lucknow (219 km); and Bareilly (260 km) in India, and Dhangari (35 km) in Nepal.

Bus **UP Roadways** and private buses connect Palia with **Lakhimpur Kheri** and **Lucknow** (219 km), **Shahjahanpur** (107 km), **Bareilly** (260 km) and **Delhi** (420 km).

Train Dudhwa is on the **Northeast Railway**, metre gauge line, and is connected with Bareilly via **Mailani** (45 km from the park). Mailani to **Bareilly**: *Rohilkand Exp 15309*, 0750, 3½ hrs. From Bareilly: *Rohilkand Exp 15310*, 1315, 3½ hrs. A branch line from Mailani links places in the park. Transport is not always available at **Dudhwa Station**; best to get off at **Palia** (10 km) and take the hourly bus or taxi.

Bareilly *p139*

Bus Extensive connections with all major cities on the plains.

Train The station is 3 km from the centre with frequent *tempo* transfer, Rs 5. **Dehra Dun**: *Doon Exp 13009*, 2245, 8 hrs; *Varanasi Dehra Dun Exp 14265*, 0030, 9 hrs. **Delhi**: *Bareilly Delhi Exp 14555*, OD, 1600, 5 hrs; *Shramjeevi Exp 12401*, ND, 0010, 5½ hrs; *Kashi-Viswanath Exp 14257*, ND, 0100, 5¾ hrs; *Lucknow New Delhi Mail 12229*, ND, 0140, 5½ hrs. **Lucknow**: *Barwadih Triveni Exp 4370*, 1200, 4 hrs. **Varanasi**: *Shramjeevi Exp 2402*, 1730, 9 hrs; *Kashi-Viswanath Exp 14258*, 1833, 10¾ hrs.

Faizabad *p140*

Bus Bus Stand, T05278-222964, bus to **Lucknow**, 3 hrs, Rs 47; **Varanasi**, 0630, 6 hrs, Rs 156.

Train Railway station, T05278-244119.

Ayodhya *p140*

Train T05278-232023. **Jodhpur**, via **Agra** and **Jaipur**: *Marudhar Exp 14853*, 2015 (Mon, Wed, Sat), 10 hrs (Agra), 15½ hrs (Jaipur), 21¼ hrs (Jodhpur). **Varanasi**: *Marudhar Exp 14854*, 0529 (Tue, Fri, Sun), 4 hrs.

Gorakhpur *p141*

Bus The **main bus stand** is a 3-min walk from the railway station, with services to **Lucknow** (6-7 hrs), **Faizabad** (4 hrs), **Kushinagar** (on the hr, 2 hrs), and **Patna** (10 hrs). Buses for **Varanasi** (205 km, 6 hrs) leave from Katchari Stand.

To Nepal (See border box, page 146.) UP Government buses (green and yellow) are 'Express' and depart the main bus stand from 0500, for **Nautanwa** (95 km; 2½ hrs) or **Sonauli**, just beyond, on the border (102 km; Rs 40; 3 hrs). Private buses leave from opposite the railway station; touts will try to sell you tickets all the way to Kathmandu or Pokhara, but there's no guarantee of bus quality across border. Buses to **Kathmandu** (Rs 200, 12 hrs), **Pokhara** (Rs 180; 10 hrs), **Nepalganj** (Rs 220) or **Narayanghat** (Rs 35 for national park). Most depart at 0700. Beware of ticket touts in Gorakhpur (private buses opposite railway station) and Nepal border. Some overcharge and others demand excessive 'luggage charge'. When buying a ticket, make absolutely sure which bus, what is included in ticket (meals, overnight accommodation), when and from where it departs (may be 2 hrs' delay). Avoid **International Tourism Agency** opposite railway station; its buses are very poorly maintained.

Train **Gorakhpur Junction**, NE Railway HQ station, has tourist information, left luggage (only with padlocks, Rs 15 per piece) and computerized reservations; good waiting rooms. **Old Delhi**: *Barauni-Katihar Amritsar Exp 15707*,

Border essentials: India–Nepal

From Gorakhpur, the usual route to Nepal is to take a bus or shared jeep north to Nautanwa via Pharenda, crossing the Nepal border at **Sonauli** (see Transport, below). At Sonauli you need to fill in a form and get your Exit stamp at the Indian Immigration office (close to the bus stand). You then proceed to the Nepalese Immigration counter to get your Entry stamp (starting date of visa noted); the counter is open 0530-2100. If you leave Gorakhpur after 1400 you will arrive at Sonauli after 1700 and it might be better to stay overnight on the Indian side (**E-F** Rahi Tourist Bungalow, T05522-238201, grim looking and has a mosquito problem) and walk across or get a rickshaw in the morning to maximize visa days. From the Nepali side you can take a bus/jeep (Rs 5) to **Bhairawa** (6 km) where onward buses to **Kathmandu** (0630, 0730, 0830, 235 km, Rs 150-200) and flights are available. From Bairawa, buses run every 30 minutes to the Buddha's birthplace at **Lumbini** (Rs 10 for a day trip). Indian rupees are exchanged on the Nepal side. Coming in from Nepal, the last bus from Sonauli to Gorakhpur leaves at around 2000.

1230, 15½ hrs; *Assam Exp 15609*, 2345, 16 hrs. **New Delhi**: *Vaishali Exp 12553*, 1655, 13½ hrs (often longer, up to 20 hrs); several others. **Kolkata** (**H**): *Howrah Bagh Exp 13020*, 1300, 22½ hrs. **Lucknow**: *Lucknow Exp 15007*, 2300, 7 hrs. **Varanasi**: *Krishak Exp 15008*, 0638, 6¼ hrs; *Manduadih Exp 15103*, 1700, 5½ hrs; *Chauri Chaura Exp 15004*, 2245, 6½ hrs. **Nautanwa**: the most convenient are 2 *Fast Passenger trains 95*, 0615, 2½ hrs (return departs Nautanwa, *96*, 0910); *93*, 1230, 3¼ hrs (return *94*, 1700). No need to book ahead (1st class, Rs 100; 2nd class, Rs 35). See above for bus services to Kathmandu and Pokhara from Nautanwa.

Kushinagar *p141*

Bus and taxi From **Gorakhpur** (30 mins).

Kanpur *p141, map p142*

Air **Indian Airlines**, opposite MG College, Civil Lines, T0512-231 1430, www.indian-airlines.nic.in.
Bus **UP Roadways Bus Stand**, Fazalganj, T0512-229 6657, for **Lucknow**, **Allahabad**, etc; **Chunniganj**, T0512-253 0646, for **Delhi**, **Agra**. **City Bus Service** has extensive network for getting around the city.
Rickshaw *Tempos*, auto-rickshaws, cycle-rickshaws and horse *tongas* are available.
Taxi Private taxis from Canal Rd taxi stand, hotels and agencies. Full day (8 hrs) about Rs 250.
Train Kanpur is on the main broad gauge Delhi–Kolkata line and also has lines from Lucknow, Agra and Central India. **Central Station**, T131, T0512-2032 8170; **Anwarganj**, T0512-254 5488. **Agra**: *Toofan Exp 13007*, 0835, 7 hrs (Agra Cantt); *Jodhpur/Bikaner Exp 12307*, 1530, 4 hrs (Agra Fort). **Kolkata** (**H**): *Rajdhani Exp* (via Gaya) *12302/12306*, 2140, 12½ hrs; *Kalka-Howrah Mail 12312*, 1445, 16¼ hrs. **Lucknow**: *Shatabdi Exp 12004*, 1125, 1¼ hrs; *Pratapgarh Exp 14124*, 1735, 1½ hrs. **New Delhi**: *Shatabdi Exp 12003*, 1645, 5 hrs; *Rajdhani Exp 12301/12305*, 0505, 5 hrs. **Patna**: *Rajdhani Exp 12302/12306*, 2135, 8 hrs; *Poorva Exp 12304*, 2315, Wed, Thu, Sat, Sun, 8½ hrs; *Northeast Exp 15622*, 1310, 9¼ hrs. **Varanasi**: *Lichhavi Exp 15206*, 2330, 6 hrs; *Farakka Exp 13484/13414*, 0540, 9¾ hrs.

Directory

Gorakhpur *p141*

Telephone ISD and fax services from **Door Sanchar**, The Target, opposite Vijay Cinema.

Kanpur *p141, map p142*

Banks Usually open 1030-1430. **Standard Chartered Grindlays**, 16 Mahatma Gandhi Rd, T0512-236 8253. Changes TCs. **Allahabad Bank**, Mahatma Gandhi Rd. **Medical services** **Regency Hospital**, T0512-229 5789. **Dufferin**, T0512-231 1510. **KPM**, T0512-235 8538.
Post **Head GPO**: Bara Chauraha, The Mall, T0512-236 0493 (open 24 hrs). **Useful contacts** Police: T100.

Agra and around

→ *Colour map 3, A1. Phone code: 0562. Population: 4.38 million.*

The romance of what is arguably the world's most famous building still astonishes in its power. In addition to the Taj Mahal, Agra also houses the great monuments of the Red Fort and the I'timad-ud-Daulah, but to experience their beauty you have to endure the less attractive sides of one of India's least prepossessing towns. A big industrial city, the monuments are often covered in a haze of polluted air, while visitors may be subjected to a barrage of high-power selling. Despite it all, the experience is unmissable. The city is also the convenient gateway to the wonderful, abandoned capital of Fatehpur Sikri, the beautifully serene Akbar's Mauseuleum and some of Hinduism's most holy sites. ▸▸ *For listings, see pages 165-169.*

Ins and outs

Getting there By far the best way to arrive is by the *Shatabdi Express* train from Delhi, which is much faster than travelling by car and infinitely more comfortable than the frequent 'express' buses, which can take five tiring hours.

Getting around Buses run a regular service between the station, bus stands and the main sites. See Entrances, page 150. Cycle-rickshaws, autos and taxis can be hired to venture further afield, or hire bike if it's not too hot. ▸▸ *See Transport, page 168.*

Tourist information **Government of India tourist office** ⓘ *191 The Mall, T0562-222 6378.* Guides available (Rs 100), helpful and friendly. **UPTDC** ⓘ *64 Taj Rd, T0562-236 3377, also at Agra Cantt, T0562-242 1204,* and **Tourist Bungalow** ⓘ *Raja-ki-Mandi, T0562-285 0120.* **UP Tours** ⓘ *Taj Khema, Taj East Gate, T0562-233 0140.*

Note that there is an **Agra Development Authority** Tax of Rs 500 levied on each day you visit the Taj Mahal, with lesser fees for the Red Fort, Fatehpur Sikri and other attractions. This is in addition to the individual entry fees.

Climate The best time to visit is between November and March.

History

With minor interruptions Agra alternated with Delhi as the capital of the Mughal Empire. **Sikander Lodi** seized it from a rebellious governor and made it his capital in 1501. He died in Agra but is buried in Delhi (see page 94). Agra was Babur's capital. He is believed to have laid out a pleasure garden on the east bank of the River Yamuna and his son Humayun built a mosque here in 1530. **Akbar** lived in Agra in the early years of his reign. Ralph Fitch, the English Elizabethan traveller, described a "magnificent city, with broad streets and tall buildings". He also saw Akbar's new capital at Fatehpur Sikri, 40 km west, describing a route lined all the way with stalls and markets. Akbar moved his capital again to Lahore, before returning to Agra in 1599, where he spent the last six years of his life. **Jahangir** left Agra for Kashmir in 1618 and never returned. Despite modifying the Red Fort and building the Taj Mahal, **Shah Jahan** also moved away in 1638 to his new city Shah Jahanabad in Delhi, though he returned in 1650, taken prisoner by his son Aurangzeb and left to spend his last days in the Red Fort. It was **Aurangzeb**, the last of the Great Mughals, who moved the seat of government permanently to Delhi. In the 18th century Agra suffered at the hands of the Jats, was taken, lost and retaken by the Marathas who, in turn, were ousted by the British in 1803. It was the centre of much fighting in the 'Uprising' and was the administrative centre of the Northwest Provinces and Oudh until that too was transferred to Allahabad in 1877. ▸▸ *See Background, page 1389.*

1 Agra

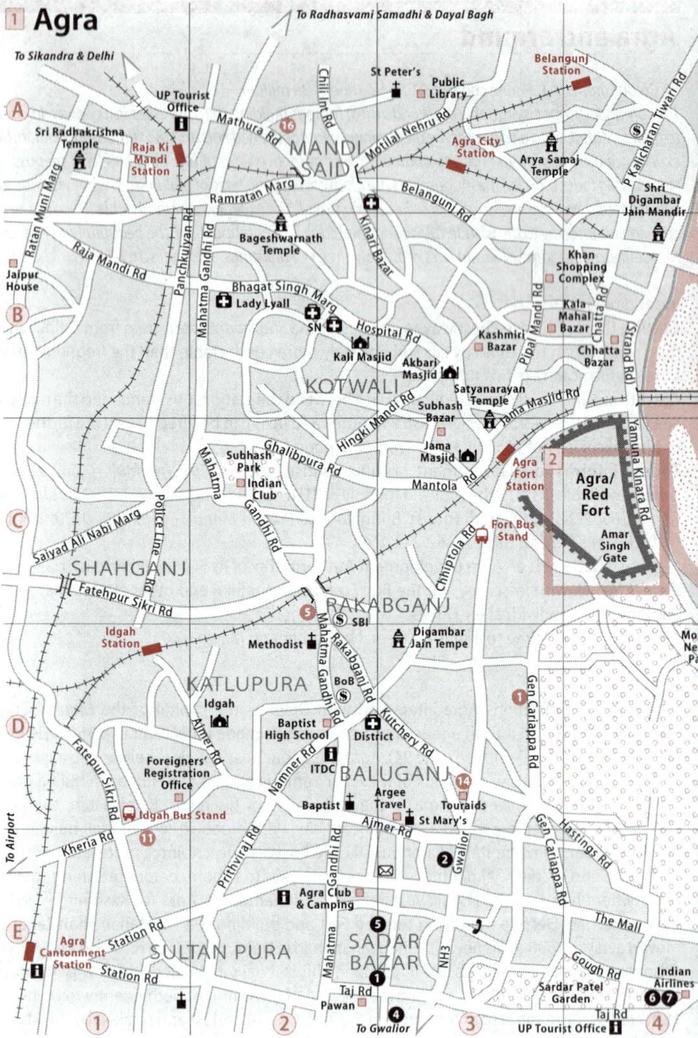

Sleeping
Agra **1** *D3*
Amar **3** *E5*
Amar Vilas & Esphahan Restaurant **2** *D6*
Garden Villa Homestay **6** *E5*
Gateway **12** *E6*
Grand Imperial **5** *C2*
Host **4** *D6*
Mayur Tourist Complex **8** *E6*
Mughal & Peshawari Restaurant **9** *E6*
Sakura **11** *E1*
Sheela **18** *D6*
Tourists Rest House **14** *D3*
Trident **13** *E6*
Youth Hostel **16** *A2*

Eating
Café Coffee Day **1** *E2*
Dasaprakash **2** *E3*
Joney's Place **8** *D6*
Maya Hotel **11** *E6*

N
400 metres
400 yards

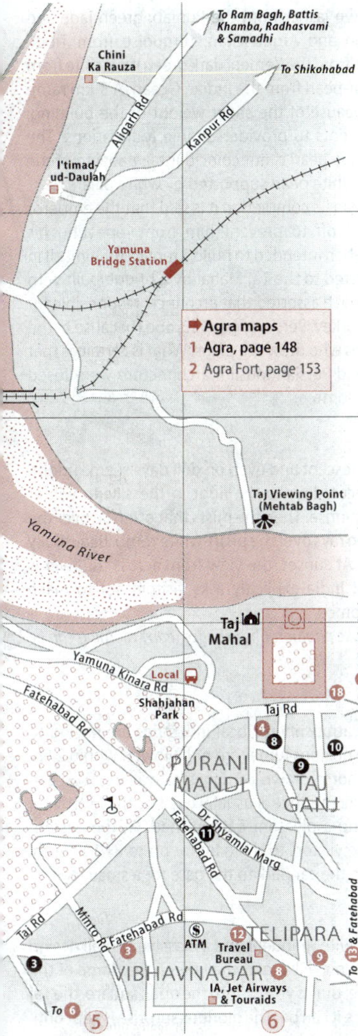

Mughal Room & Mercury Travel at Clarks Shiraz Hotel **7** *E4*
Only **3** *E5*
Park **4** *E3*
Riao **6** *E4*
Shankara Vegis **9** *D6*
Yash Café **10** *D6*
Zorba the Buddha **5** *E2*

Taj Mahal

ⓘ *Sat-Thu sunrise to sunset (last entry 1700), foreigners Rs 750 (including Development Tax), Indians Rs 20, cash only, includes still camera, video cameras, tripods, other electronic items eg mobile phones not allowed, lockers at East and West Gates Rs 1. No photos inside the tomb (instant fines). Allow at least 1 hr. Full moon viewing 2 nights either side of full moon (see www.stardate.org/nightsky/moon for full moon dates), 2030-0030, separate entry fee of foreigners Rs 750, Indians Rs 510, book tickets day before at Architectural Survey of India, 22 The Mall, T0562-222 7261.*

Of all the world's great monuments, the Taj Mahal is one of the most written about, photographed, televized and talked about. To India's Nobel Laureate poet, Tagore, the Taj was a "tear drop on the face of humanity", a building to echo the cry "I have not forgotten, I have not forgotten, O beloved" and its mesmerizing power is such that despite the hype, no one comes away disappointed.

Shah Jahan, the fifth of the Great Mughals, was so devoted to his favourite wife, Mumtaz Mahal (Jewel of the Palace) that he could not bear to be parted from her and insisted that she always travel with him, in all states of health. While accompanying him on a military campaign, she died at the age of 39 giving birth to their 14th child. On her deathbed, it is said, she asked the emperor to show the world how much they loved one another.

The grief-stricken emperor went into mourning for two years. He turned away from the business of running the empire and dedicated himself to architecture, resolving to build his wife the most magnificent memorial on earth. On the right bank of the River Yamuna in full view of his fortress palace, it was to be known as the Taj-i-Mahal (Crown of the Palace).

According to the French traveller Tavnier, work on the Taj commenced in 1632 and took 22 years to complete, employing a workforce of 20,000. The red sandstone was available locally but the white marble was quarried at Makrana in Rajasthan and transported 300 km by a fleet of 1000 elephants. Semi-precious stones for the inlay came from far and wide:

red carnelian from Baghdad; red, yellow and brown jasper from the Punjab; green jade and crystal from China; blue lapis lazuli from Ceylon and Afghanistan; turquoise from Tibet; chrysolite from Egypt; amethyst from Persia; agates from the Yemen; dark green malachite from Russia; diamonds from Central India and mother-of-pearl from the Indian Ocean. A 3-km ramp was used to lift material up to the dome and, because of the sheer weight of the building; boreholes were filled with metal coins and fragments to provide suitable foundations. The resemblance of the exquisite double dome to a huge pearl is not coincidental; a saying of the Prophet describes the throne of God as a dome of white pearl supported by white pillars.

Myths and controversy surround the Taj Mahal. On its completion it is said that the emperor ordered the chief mason's right hand to be cut off to prevent him from repeating his masterpiece. Another legend suggests that Shah Jahan intended to build a replica for himself in black marble on the other side of the river, connected to the Taj Mahal by a bridge built with alternate blocks of black and white marble. Some have asserted that architects responsible for designing this mausoleum must have come from Turkey, Persia or even Europe (because of the pietra dura work on the tomb). In fact, no one knows who drew the plans. What is certain is that in the Taj Mahal, the traditions of Indian Hindu and Persian Muslim architecture were fused together into a completely distinct and perfect art form.

Viewing

The white marble of the Taj is extraordinarily luminescent and even on dull days seems bright. The whole building appears to change its hue according to the light in the sky. In winter (December to February), it is worth being there at sunrise. Then the mists that often lie over the River Yamuna lift as the sun rises and casts its golden rays over the pearl-white tomb. Beautifully lit in the soft light, the Taj appears to float on air. At sunset, the view from across the river is equally wonderful. The **Archaeological Survey of India** explicitly asks visitors not to make donations to anyone including custodians in the tomb.

Visit at sunrise and sunset to avoid crowds and take photographs in peace (early morning can be misty). Hiring a guide isn't necessary.

Entrances

To reduce damage to the marble by the polluted atmosphere, local industries are having to comply with strict rules now and vehicles emitting noxious fumes are not allowed within 2 km of the monument. People are increasingly using horse-drawn carriages or walking. You can approach the Taj from three directions. The western entrance is usually used by those arriving from the fort and is an easy 10-minute walk along a pleasant garden road. At the eastern entrance, rickshaws and camel drivers offer to take visitors to the gate for up to Rs 100 each; however, an official battery bus ferries visitors from the car park to the gate for a small fee.

The approach

In the unique beauty of the Taj, subtlety is blended with grandeur and a massive overall design is matched with immaculately intricate execution. You will already have seen the dome of the tomb in the distance, looking almost like a miniature, but as you go into the open square, the Taj itself is so well hidden that you almost wonder where it can be. The glorious surprise is kept until the last moment, for wholly concealing it is the massive red sandstone gateway of the entrance, symbolizing the divide between the secular world and paradise.

The gateway was completed in 1648, though the huge brass door is recent. The original doors (plundered by the Jats) were solid silver and decorated with 1100 nails whose heads were contemporary silver coins. Although the gateway is remarkable in itself, one of its functions is to prevent you getting any glimpse of the tomb inside until you are right in the doorway itself. From here only the tomb is visible, stunning in its nearness, but as you move forward the minarets come into view.

Char bagh: the Mughal garden

In the Koran, the garden is repeatedly seen as a symbol for paradise. Islam was born in the deserts of Arabia. Muslims venerate water, without which plants will not grow – the old Persian word *pairidaeza* means 'garden'. It is no coincidence then that green is the colour of Islam.

Four main rivers of paradise are also specified: water, milk, wine and purified honey. This is the origin of the quartered garden (*char bagh*). The watercourses divided the garden into quadrats and all was enclosed behind a private wall. To the Muslim the beauty of creation and of the garden was held to be a reflection of God. The great Sufi poet **Rumi** used much garden imagery: "The trees are engaged in ritual prayer and the birds in singing the litany". Thus, the garden becomes as important as the tomb.

The four minarets at each corner of the plinth provide balance to the tomb - see how each slants outwards. Familiar with the disastrous effects of earthquakes on mosques in Gujarat, the architects deliberately designed the minarets so they would fall away from the tomb, not onto it.

The garden

The Taj garden, well kept though it is nowadays, is nothing compared with its former glory. The guiding principle is one of symmetry. The *char bagh*, separated by the watercourses (rivers of heaven) originating from the central, raised pool, were divided into 16 flower beds, making a total of 64. The trees, all carefully planted to maintain the symmetry, were either cypress (signifying death) or fruit trees (life). The channels were stocked with colourful fish and the gardens with beautiful birds. It is well worth wandering along the side avenues for not only is it much more peaceful but also good for framing photos of the tomb with foliage. You may see bullocks pulling the lawnmowers around.

The mosque and its jawab

On the east and west sides of the tomb are identical red sandstone buildings. On the west (left-hand side) is a mosque. It is common in Islam to build one next to a tomb. It sanctifies the area and provides a place for worship. The replica on the other side is known as the **Jawab** (answer). This can't be used for prayer as it faces away from Mecca.

The tomb

There is only one point of access to the **plinth** and tomb, where shoes must be removed (socks can be kept on; remember the white marble gets very hot) or cloth overshoes worn (Rs 2, though strictly free).

The **tomb** is square with bevelled corners. At each corner smaller domes rise while in the centre is the main dome topped by a brass finial. The dome is actually a double dome and this device, Central Asian in origin, was used to gain height. The resemblance of the dome to a huge pearl is not coincidental. The exterior ornamentation is calligraphy (verses of the Koran), beautifully carved panels in bas relief and superb inlay work.

The **interior** of the mausoleum comprises a lofty central chamber, a *maqbara* (crypt) immediately below this, and four octagonal corner rooms. The central chamber contains replica tombs, the real ones being in the crypt. The public tomb was originally surrounded by a jewel-encrusted silver screen. Aurangzeb removed this, fearing it might be stolen, and replaced it with an octagonal screen of marble carved from one block of marble and inlaid with precious stones. It is an incredible piece of workmanship. This chamber is open at sunrise, but may close during the day.

Above the tombs is a **Cairene lamp** whose flame is supposed never to go out. This one was given by Lord Curzon, Governor General of India (1899-1905), to replace the original which was stolen by Jats. The tomb of Mumtaz with the 'female' slate, rests immediately beneath the dome. If you look from behind it, you can see how it lines up centrally with the main entrance. Shah Jahan's tomb is larger and to the side, marked by a 'male' pen-box, the sign of a cultured or noble person. Not originally intended to be placed there but squeezed in by Aurangzeb, this flaws the otherwise perfect symmetry of the whole complex. Finally, the acoustics of the building are superb, the domed ceiling being designed to echo chants from the Koran and musicians' melodies.

The **museum** ⓘ *above the entrance, Sat-Thu 1000-1700*, has a small collection of Mughal memorabilia, photographs and miniatures of the Taj through the ages but has no textual information. Sadly, the lights do not always work.

Agra Fort (Red Fort)

ⓘ *0600-1800, foreigners Rs 300 (Rs 250 if you've been to the Taj on the same day), Indians Rs 15, video Rs 25; allow a minimum of 1½ hours for a visit. The best route round is to start with the building on your right before going through the gate at the top of the broad 100 m ramp; the gentle incline made it suitable for elephants.*

On the west bank of the River Yamuna, Akbar's magnificent fort dominates the centre of the city. Akbar erected the walls and gates and the first buildings inside. **Shah Jahan** built the impressive imperial quarters and mosque, while Aurangzeb added the outer ramparts. The outer walls, just over 20 m high and faced with red sandstone, tower above the outer moat. The fort is crescent-shaped with a long, nearly straight wall facing the river, punctuated at regular intervals by bastions. The main entrance used to be in the centre of the west wall, the **Delhi Gate**, facing the bazar. It led to the Jami Masjid in the city but is now permanently closed. You can only enter now from the **Amar Singh Gate** in the south. Although only the southern third of the fort is open to the public, this includes nearly all the buildings of interest. At the gate you will have to contend with vendors of cheap soapstone boxes and knick-knacks. If you want to buy something, bargain hard. Guides will offer their services – most are not particularly good.

Fortifications

The fortifications tower above the 9-m-wide, 10-m-deep moat (still evident but containing stagnant water) formerly filled with water from the Yamuna River. There is an outer wall on the riverside and an imposing 22-m-high inner, main wall, giving a feeling of great defensive power. Although it served as a model for Shah Jahan's Red Fort in Delhi, its own model was the Rajput fort built by Raja Man Singh Tomar of Gwalior in 1500, see page 279. If an aggressor managed to get through the outer gate they would have to make a right-hand turn and thereby expose their flank to the defenders on the inner wall. The inner gate is solidly powerful but has been attractively decorated with tiles. The similarities with Islamic patterns of the tilework are obvious, though the Persian blue was also used in the Gwalior Fort and may well have been imitated from that example. The incline up to this point and beyond was suitable for elephants and as you walk past the last gate and up the broad brick-lined ramp with ridged slabs, it is easy to imagine arriving on elephant back. At the top of this 100-m ramp is a gate with a map and description board on your left.

Jahangiri Mahal (1) Despite its name, this was built by Akbar (circa 1570) as women's quarters. It is all that survives of his original palace buildings. In front is a large **stone bowl**, with steps both inside and outside, which was probably filled with fragrant rose water for bathing. Almost 75 m sq, the palace has a simple stone exterior. Tillotson has pointed out that the blind arcade of pointed arches inlaid with white marble which decorate the façade is copied from 14th-century monuments of the Khaljis and Tughluqs in Delhi. He notes that they are complemented by some features derived from

Hindu architecture, including the *jarokhas* (balconies) protruding from the central section, the sloping dripstone in place of *chajja* (eaves) along the top of the façade, and the domed *chhattris* at its ends. The presence of distinctively Hindu features does not indicate a synthesis of architectural styles at this early stage of Mughal architecture, as can be seen much more clearly from inside the Jahangiri Mahal. Here most of the features are straightforwardly Hindu; square-headed arches and extraordinarily carved capitals and brackets illustrate the vivid work of

2 Agra Fort

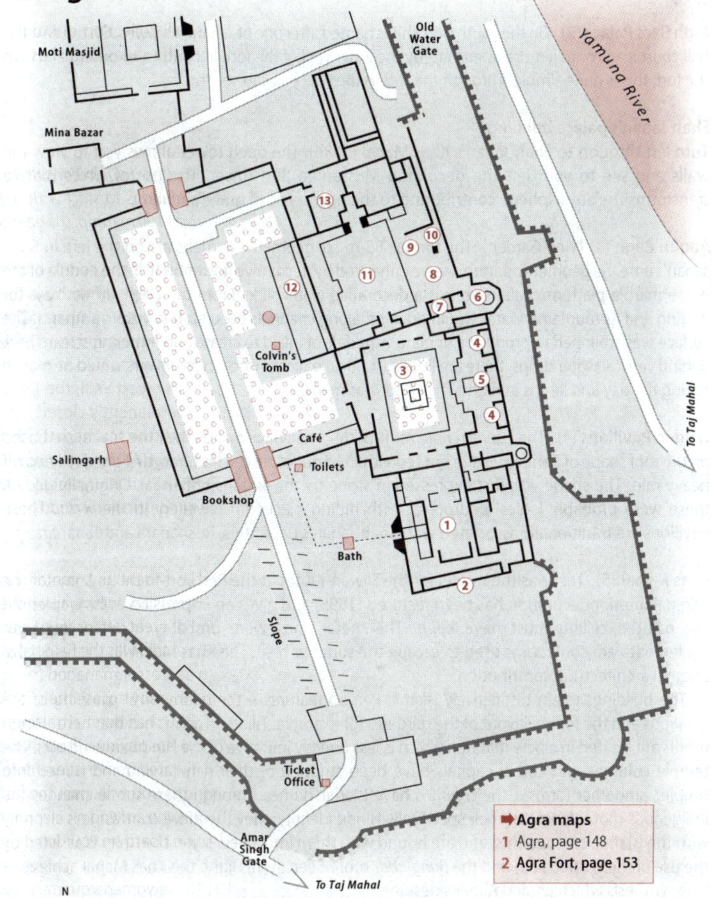

N
50 metres
50 yards

Jahangiri Mahal 1
Jodh Bai's Palace 2
Anguri Bagh 3
Golden Pavilions 4
Khas Mahal 5
Mussaman Burj 6
Sheesh Mahal & Hammams 7
Diwan-i-Khas 8
Terrace 9
Black Marble Throne 10
Machhi Bhavan 11
Diwan-i-Am 12
Nagina Masjid 13

local Hindu craftsmen employed by Akbar without any attempt either to curb their enthusiasm for florid decoration and mythical animals nor to produce a fusion of Hindu and Islamic ideas. Tillotson argues that the central courtyard is essentially Hindu, in significant contrast with most earlier Indo-Islamic buildings. In these, an Islamic scheme was modified by Hindu touches. He suggests, therefore, that the Jahangiri Mahal marks the start of a more fundamental kind of Hinduization, typical of several projects during Akbar's middle period of rule, including the palace complex in Fatehpur Sikri. However, it did not represent a real fusion of ideas – something that only came under Shah Jahan – simply a juxtaposition of sharply contrasting styles.

Jodh Bai's Palace (2) On the south side, this is named after one of Jahangir's wives. On the east the hall court leads onto a more open yard by the inner wall of the fort. In contrast to other palaces in the fort, this is quite simple. Through the slits in the wall you can see the Taj.

Shah Jahan's palace buildings

Turn left through to Shah Jahan's Khas Mahal (1636). The open tower allows you to view the walls and see to your left the decorated Mussaman Burj tower. The use of white marble transforms the atmosphere, contributing to the new sense of grace and light.

Anguri Bagh (3) (Vine Garden) The formal, 85-m-sq, geometric gardens are on the left. In Shah Jahan's time the geometric patterns were enhanced by decorative flower beds. In the middle of the white marble platform wall in front is a decorative water slide. From the pool with its bays for seating and its fountains, water would drain off along channels decorated to mimic a stream. The surface was scalloped to produce a rippling waterfall, or inlaid to create a shimmering stream bed. Behind vertical water drops, there are little cusped arch niches into which flowers would be placed during the day and lamps at night. The effect was magical.

Golden Pavilions (4) The curved *chala* roofs of the small pavilions by the Khas Mahal are based on the roof shape of Bengali village huts constructed out of curved bamboo, designed to keep off heavy rain. The shape was first expressed in stone by the Sultans of Bengal. Originally gilded, these were probably ladies' bedrooms, with hiding places for jewellery in the walls. These pavilions are traditionally associated with Shah Jahan's daughters, Roshanara and Jahanara.

Khas Mahal (5) This was the model for the Diwan-i-Khas at the Red Fort in Delhi. Some of the original interior decoration has been restored (1895) and gives an impression of how splendid the painted ceiling must have been. The metal rings were probably used for *punkhas*. Underneath are cool rooms used to escape the summer heat. The Khas Mahal illustrates Shahs' original architectural contribution.

The buildings retain distinctively Islamic Persian features – the geometrical planning of the pavilions and the formal layout of the gardens, for example. Tillotson points out that here "Hindu motifs are treated in a new manner, which is less directly imitative of the Hindu antecedents. The temple columns and corbel capitals have been stripped of their rich carving and turned into simpler, smoother forms ... the *chhattris* have Islamic domes. Through these subtle changes the indigenous motifs have lost their specifically Hindu identity; they therefore contrast less strongly with the Islamic components, and are bound with them into a new style. The unity is assisted by the use of the cusped arch and the *Bangladar* roof". Seen in this light, the Khas Mahal achieves a true synthesis which eluded Akbar's designs.

Mussaman Burj (6) On the left of the Khas Mahal is the Mussaman Burj (Octagonal Tower, though sometimes corrupted into Saman Burj, then translated as Jasmine Tower). It is a beautiful octagonal tower with an open pavilion. With its openness, elevation and the benefit of cooling evening breezes blowing in off the Yamuna River, this could well have been used as the emperor's bedroom. It has been suggested that this is where Shah Jahan lay on his deathbed, gazing at the Taj. Access to this tower is through a magnificently decorated and intimate apartment with a scalloped fountain in the centre. The inlay work here is exquisite, especially above the pillars. In front of the fountain is a sunken courtyard which could be filled by water carriers, to work the fountains in the pool.

Sheesh Mahal (7) (Mirror Palace) Here are further examples of decorative water engineering in the *hammams*; the water here may have been warmed by lamps. The mirrors, which were more precious than marble, were set into the walls, often specially chiselled to accommodate their crooked shape. The defensive qualities of the site and the fortifications are obvious. In the area between the outer rampart and the inner wall gladiatorial battles were staged pitting man against tiger, or elephant against elephant. The tower was the emperor's grandstand seat.

Diwan-i-Khas (8) (Hall of Private Audience, 1637) This is next to the Mussaman Burj, approached on this route by a staircase which brings you out at the side. The interior of the Diwan-i-Khas, a three-sided pavilion with a terrace of fine proportions, would have been richly decorated with tapestries and carpets. The double columns in marble inlaid with semi-precious stones in delightful floral patterns in pietra dura have finely carved capitals.

Terrace and Machhi Bhavan

In front of the Diwan-i-Khas are two throne 'platforms' on a **terrace (9)**. Gascoigne recounts how Shah Jahan tried to trick a haughty Persian ambassador into bowing low as he approached the throne by erecting a fence with a small wicket gate so that his visitor would have to enter on hands and knees. The ambassador did so, but entered backwards, thus presenting his bottom first to the Emperor. The **black marble throne (10)** at the rear of the terrace was used by Jahangir when claiming to be Emperor at Allahabad. The emperor sat on the white marble platform facing the **Machhi Bhavan (11)** (Fish Enclosure), which once contained pools and fountains, waiting to meet visiting dignitaries.

Diwan-i-Am (12) Go down an internal staircase and you enter the Diwan-i-Am from the side. The clever positioning of the pillars gives the visitor arriving through the gates in the right- and left-hand walls of the courtyard an uninterrupted view of the throne. On the back wall of the pavilion are *jali* screens to enable the women of the court to watch without being seen. The open-sided, cusped arched hall built of plaster on red stone, is very impressive. The throne alcove of richly decorated white marble completed in 1634 after seven years' work used to house the Peacock Throne. Its decoration made it extraordinary: "the canopy was carved in enamel work and studded with individual gems, its interior was thickly encrusted with rubies, garnets and diamonds, and it was supported on 12 emerald covered columns" writes Tillotson. When Shah Jahan moved his capital to Delhi he took the throne with him to the Red Fort, only for it to be taken back to Persia as loot by Nadir Shah in 1739.

Nagina Masjid (13) From the corner opposite the Diwan-i-Khas two doorways lead to a view over the small courtyards of the *zenana* (harem). Further round in the next corner is the Nagina Masjid. Shoes must be removed at the doorway. Built by Shah Jahan, this was the private mosque of the ladies of the court. Beneath it was a *mina* bazar for the ladies to make purchases from the marble balcony above. Looking out of the Diwan-i-Am you can see the domes of the **Moti Masjid** (Pearl Mosque, 1646-1653), an extremely fine building closed to visitors because of structural problems. Opposite the Diwan-i-Am are the barracks and **Mina Bazar**, also closed to the public. In the paved area in front of the Diwan-i-Am is a large well and the **tomb of Mr John Russell Colvin**, the Lieutenant Governor of the Northwest Provinces who died here during the 1857 'Uprising'. Stylistically it is sadly out of place. The yellow buildings date from the British period.

Jama Masjid

The mosque built in 1648, near the fort railway, no longer connected to the fort, is attributed to Shah Jahan's dutiful elder daughter Jahanara. In need of repair and not comparable to buildings within the fort, its symmetry has suffered since a small minaret fell in the 1980s. The fine marble steps and bold geometric patterns on the domes are quite striking.

I'timad-ud-Daulah and Sikandra

I'timad-ud-Daulah

ⓘ *0630-1830 (last entry 1700), foreigners Rs 100 plus Rs 10 tax, Indians Rs 10, video Rs 25.*

The tomb of I'timad-ud-Daulah (or 'Baby Taj'), set a startling precedent as the first Mughal building to be faced with white marble inlaid with contrasting stones. Unlike the Taj it is small, intimate and has a gentle serenity, but is just as ornate. The tomb was built for **Ghiyas Beg**, a Persian who had obtained service in Akbar's court, and his wife, see page 1389. On Jahangir's succession in 1605 he became *Wazir* (chief minister). Jahangir fell in love with his daughter, **Mehrunissa**, who at the time was married to a Persian. When her husband died in 1607, she entered Jahangir's court as a lady-in-waiting. Four years later Jahangir married her. Thereafter she was known first as **Nur Mahal** (Light of the Palace), later being promoted to **Nur Jahan** (Light of the World), see page 1389. Her niece Mumtaz married Shah Jahan.

Nur Jahan built the tomb for her father in the *char bagh* that he himself had laid out. It is beautifully conceived in white marble, mosaic and lattice. There is a good view from the roof of the entrance. Marble screens of geometric lattice work permit soft lighting of the inner chamber. The yellow marble caskets appear to have been carved out of wood. On the engraved walls of the chamber is the recurring theme of a wine flask with snakes as handles - perhaps a reference by Nur Jahan, the tomb's creator, to her husband Jahangir's excessive drinking. Stylistically, the tomb marks a change from the sturdy and manly buildings of Akbar's reign to softer, more feminine lines. The main chamber, richly decorated in pietra dura with mosaics and semi-precious stones inlaid in the white marble, contains the tomb of I'timad-ud-Daulah (Pillar of the Goverment) and his wife. Some have argued that the concept and skill must have travelled from its European home of 16th-century Florence to India. However, Florentine pietra dura is figurative whereas the Indian version is essentially decorative and can be seen as a refinement of its Indian predecessor, the patterned mosaic.

Sikandra

ⓘ *Sunrise-sunset, foreigners Rs 100, Indians Rs 10, includes camera, video Rs 25. Morning is the quietest time to visit.*

Following the Timurid tradition, Akbar (ruled 1556-1605) had started to build his own tomb at Sikandra. He died during its construction and his son **Jahangir** completed it in 1613. The result is an impressive, large but architecturally confused tomb. A huge gateway, the **Buland Darwaza**, leads to the great garden enclosure, where spotted deer run free on the immaculate lawns. The decoration on the gateway is strikingly bold, with its large mosaic patterns, a forerunner of the pietra dura technique. The white minarets atop the entrance were an innovation which reappear, almost unchanged, at the Taj Mahal. The walled garden enclosure is laid out in the *char bagh* style, with the mausoleum at the centre.

A broad paved path leads to the 22.5-m-high tomb with four storeys. The lowest storey, nearly 100 m sq and 9 m high, contains massive cloisters. The entrance on the south side leads to the tomb chamber. Shoes must be removed or cloth overshoes worn (hire Rs 2). In a niche opposite the entrance is an alabaster tablet inscribed with the 99 divine names of Allah. The sepulchre is in the centre of the room, whose velvety darkness is pierced by a single slanting shaft of light from a high window. The custodian, in expectation of a donation, makes "Akbaaarrrr" echo around the chamber.

Some 4 km south of Sikandra, near the high gateway of the ancient **Kach ki Sarai** building, is a sculptured horse, believed to mark the spot where Akbar's favourite horse died. There are also *kos minars* (marking a *kos*, about 4 km) and several other tombs on the way.

Mathura → *For listings see pages 165-169. Colour map 2, A6. Phone code: 0565. Population: 2.54 million.*

Mathura, 50 km from Agra on the west bank of the Yamuna, is one of the most sacred cities of Hinduism dating back to 600 BC. For Vaishnavites, it is perhaps the supremely sacred city of India, being the reputed birthplace of **Krishna**, the most human aspect of Vishnu. Krishna is widely seen as the embodiment of the ideal lover, soldier, statesman, as well as the adorable baby, or wayward child. Many places around are associated with episodes in his life. Mathura's ancient structures were mostly destroyed by Muslims but its religious association draws thousands of pilgrims.

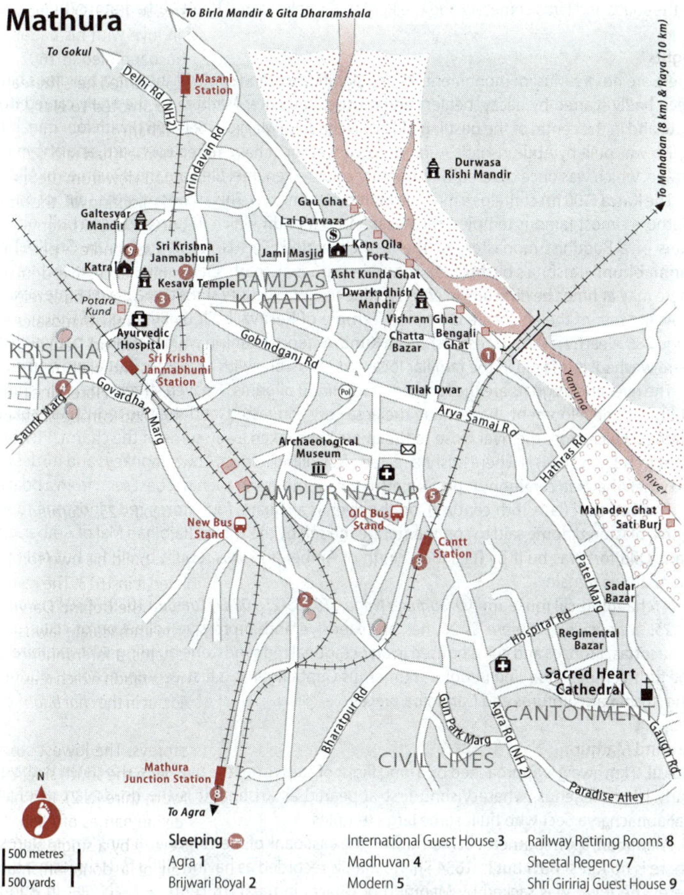

Today, it is also an important industrial city with much evidence of modernizing on the approach from the highway. The opening of a big oil refinery on the outskirts of the city in 1975 caused great concern among environmentalists that atmospheric pollution would irreversibly damage the Taj Mahal, only 50 km away. UPTDC ⓘ *near Old Bus Stand, T0565-250 5351.*

History

Ptolemy mentioned the town and it assumed the importance of a capital city during the first to second century **Kushan Empire**. When the Chinese traveller Hiuen Tsang visited it in AD 634 it was an important Buddhist centre with several monasteries. However, **Mahmud of Ghazni** sacked the city and desecrated its temples in 1017, followed by **Sikander Lodi** in 1500, whilst the Mughal **Emperor Aurangzeb** used a local revolt in which his governor was killed as an excuse to destroy the main temples. Jats and Marathas fought over the city as the Mughal Empire declined, but at the beginning of the 19th century it came under British control. They laid out a cantonment in the south and left a cemetery and the Roman Catholic Sacred Heart Cathedral (1870).

Sights

There are no pre-Muslim monuments of any significance, and some of the finest buildings have been badly scarred by decay, neglect and misuse. You enter Mathura by the finely carved **Holi Gate** and in the centre of the bustling old city is the **Jami Masjid** (1660-1661) with four minarets, which was built by Abd-un-Nadi, Aurangzeb's governor. It has a raised courtyard, and above the façade, which was once covered with brightly coloured enamel tiles, are the 99 names of Allah.

The **Katra** (500 m) contains a mosque built by Aurangzeb. This stands over the ruins of one of Mathura's most famous temples, the **Kesava Deo Mandir** which in turn had been built on the ruins of a Buddhist monastery of the Kushan period. This is considered to be **Sri Krishna Janmabhumi** (Krishna's birthplace). The main statues are particularly serene and attractive but there may at times be difficulty in entering due to extra security since there is a mosque next to it. At the rear of the enclosure is a newer **Temple of Kesava**, built by Bir Singh of Orchha, see page 286. Nearby is the impressive **Potara Kund**, a stepped tank in which Krishna's baby clothes were washed. It is faced in the familiar local red sandstone with access for cattle and horses.

The river and its ghats are the focal point for Hindu pilgrims. A paved street runs their length, but recent developments have made the area very congested, and the two industrial-looking bridges which cross the river close to the ghats have taken away some of the charm. **Vishram Ghat** (rebuilt in 1814) is where Krishna rested after killing Kamsa. Cows, monkeys and turtles are fed when the *Arati* ceremony is performed in the morning and evening; best seen from a boat.

The **Sati Burj** (late 16th century), on the river, is a square, four-storey red sandstone tower with a plastered dome said to commemorate the *sati* by the wife of Rajbihari Mal of Amber. The **Kans Qila** fort was built by Raja Man Singh of Amber and was rebuilt by Akbar but only the foundations remain.

Archaeological museum ⓘ *Dampier Nagar, T0565-250 0847, Tue-Sun 1030-1630, foreigners Rs 25, Indians Rs 5, camera Rs 20*, has an extensive and impressive collection of sculptures, terracottas, bronzes and coins housed in an octagonal red sandstone building. Also exhibited is the fifth-century 'Standing Buddha', numerous Gupta figures, a first-century headless Buddha, and Kushana sculptures and Gandhara pieces.

Around Mathura

Gokul, 2 km away, is approached by a long flight of steps from the river. It is associated with very early Hindu legends, where Vishnu first appeared as Krishna. It is the headquarters of the Vallabhacharya Sect who built some large temples.

Mahaban, 9 km southeast of Mathura on the east bank of the Yamuna, means 'a great forest'. There is no forest now but in 1634 Shah Jahan is recorded as having killed four tigers in a hunt here. The town was sacked by Mahmud of Ghazni in the 11th century. Each year in August

Vaishnavite pilgrims come to the **Nanda Krishna Palace** where Krishna was believed to have been secretly raised. His cradle stands in the hall, the hole in the wall is where the *gopis* hid his flute, and the place where his mother stood churning butter is marked by a polished pillar.

Baradari of Sikander Lodi, 28 km south of Mathura, is the 12 pillared pavilion of Sikander Lodi, one time King of Delhi, built in 1495, and the 1611 **tomb of Mariam uz Zamani**, Akbar's Hindu Rajput wife who is said to have been converted to Christianity, though there is little supporting evidence. There are beautiful carvings on the red sandstone structure.

Govardhan, 26 km west of Mathura, lies in the narrow range of the Girraj Hills. In legend, when Indra caused a tremendous flood, Krishna raised these hills up above the flood for seven days so that people could escape. The **Harideva Temple**, by the Manasi Ganga River, was built by Raja Bhagwan Das in the reign of Akbar. On the opposite bank are the *chhattris* of Ranjit Singh and Balwant Singh, both rulers of Bharatpur. There are stone ghats on all sides, built in 1817. Krishna is believed to have ritually bathed at the temple to purify himself after killing the demon bull Arishta.

Vrindavan → *For listings, see pages 165-169. Colour map 2, A6.* *Phone code: 0565.*

ⓘ *The temples are open morning and evening usually 0900-1200 and 1800-2100 when visitors are welcome to attend worship.*

Vrindavan - 'Forest of Tulsi (basil) Plants' - is the most famous of the holy sites around Mathura. In Vrindavan, Krishna played with the *gopis* (cowgirls), stealing their clothes while they bathed.

Vrindavan

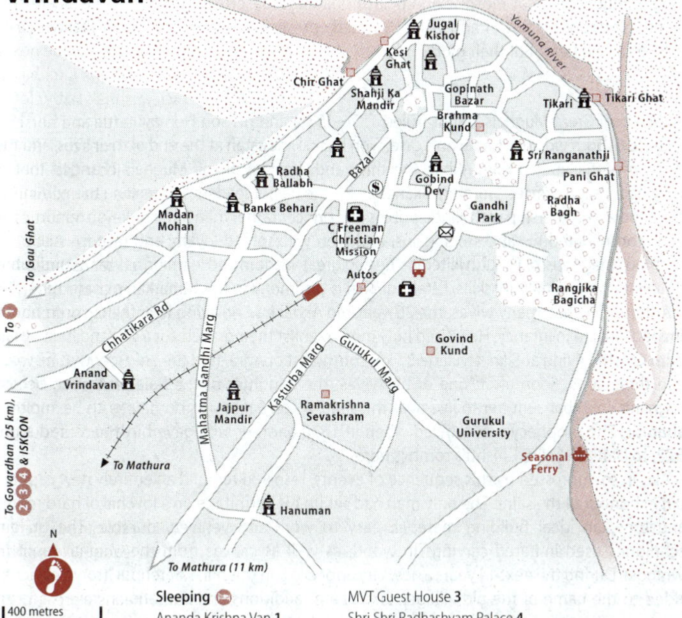

Sleeping
Ananda Krishna Van **1**
International Rest House **2**
MVT Guest House **3**
Shri Shri Radhashyam Palace **4**

You are entering perhaps the most sacred region of India for Vaishnavite Hindus, where many of the stories surrounding Krishna are set, see page 1411). The town retains a tranquil, welcoming atmosphere, and offers an interesting mix of stunning temples, narrow medieval alleyways and beautiful river scenes, observed by an equally interesting mix of local Sadhus and international devotees of Hare Krishna.

At the entrance to the town is the 16th-century **temple of Gobind Dev** (1590), the 'Divine Cowherd', Krishna. Built by Man Singh of Jaipur during Akbar's reign, it was severely damaged by the less tolerant Aurangzeb. Nearby there is a Dravidian-style temple dedicated to **Sri Ranganathji** (Vishnu), with three *gopura*, each nearly 30 m high. There is an annual 10-day **Rath** (car) **festival** in March/April. The 16th-century **Madan Mohan temple** stands above a ghat on an arm of the river; there is a pavilion decorated with cobra carvings. Siva is believed to have struck Devi here and made it a place for curing snake bites. The octagonal tower is similar to the one on the 16th-century **Jagat Krishna temple.**

Other temples include **Jugal Kishor** (reputedly 1027) near Kesi Ghat, **Banke Behari** near Purana Bazar where great excitement builds up each time the curtain before the deity is opened for *darshan* and **Radha Ballabh**, partly demolished by Aurangzeb, close by. **International Society for Krishna Consciousness** (ISKCON) with the Shri Krishna Balaram Temple, has a modern marble memorial. The centre runs yoga and meditation courses.

Fatehpur Sikri → *For listings, see pages 165-169.* *Colour map 2, A6. Phone code: 05613. Population: 2.63 million.*

The red sandstone capital of Emperor Akbar, one of his architectural achievements, spreads along a ridge. The great mosque and palace buildings, deserted after only 14 years are still a vivid reminder of his power and vision. Perfectly preserved, it conjures up the lifestyle of the Mughals at the height of their glory.

History

The first two Great Mughals, Babur (ruled 1526-1530) and his son Humayun (ruled 1530-1540, 1555-1556) both won (in Humayun's case, won back) Hindustan at the end of their lives, and they left an essentially alien rule. Akbar, the third and greatest of the Mughals changed that. By marrying a Hindu princess, forging alliances with the Rajput leaders and making the administration of India a partnership with Hindu nobles and princes rather than armed foreign minority rule, Akbar consolidated his ancestors' gains, and won widespread loyalty and respect. Akbar had enormous magnetism. Though illiterate, he had great wisdom and learning as well as undoubted administrative and military skills. Fatehpur Sikri is testimony to this remarkable character.

Although he had many wives, the 26-year-old Akbar had no living heir; the children born to him had all died in infancy. He visited holy men to enlist their prayers for a son and heir. **Sheikh Salim Chishti**, living at Sikri, a village 37 km southwest of Agra, told the emperor that he would have three sons. Soon after, one of his wives, the daughter of the Raja of Amber, became pregnant, so Akbar sent her to live near the sage. A son Salim was born, later to be known as **Jahangir**. The prophecy was fulfilled when in 1570 another wife gave birth to Murad and in 1572, to Daniyal. Salim Chishti's tomb is here.

Akbar, so impressed by this sequence of events, resolved to build an entirely new capital at Sikri in honour of the saint. The holy man had set up his hermitage on a low hill of hard reddish sandstone, an ideal building material, easy to work and yet very durable. The building techniques used imitated carvings in wood, as well as canvas from the Mughal camp (eg awnings). During the next 14 years a new city appeared on this hill – 'Fatehpur' (town of victory) added to the name of the old village, 'Sikri'. Later additions and alterations were made and debate continues over the function and dates of the various buildings. It is over 400 years old and yet perfectly preserved, thanks to careful conservation work carried out by the

Archaeological Survey of India at the turn of the century. There are three sections to the city: the 'Royal Palace', 'Outside the Royal Palace' and the 'Jami Masjid'.

When Akbar left, it was slowly abandoned to become ruined and deserted by the early 1600s. Some believe the emperor's decision was precipitated by the failure of the water supply, whilst local folklore claims the decision was due to the loss of the court singer Tansen, one of the 'nine gems' of Akbar's court. However, there may well have been political and strategic motives. Akbar's change in attitude towards orthodox Islam and his earlier veneration of the Chishti saints supplanted by a new imperial ideology, may have influenced his decision. In 1585 he moved his court to Lahore and when he returned south again, it was to Agra. But it was at Fatehpur Sikri that Akbar spent the richest and most productive years of his 49-year reign.

The entrance

ⓘ *Sunrise to sunset, foreigners US$5/Rs 250, Indians Rs 5. It is best to visit early, before the crowds. Official guides are good (about Rs 100; Rs 30 off season) but avoid others. Avoid the main entrance (lots of hawkers); instead, take the right-hand fork after passing through Agra gate to the hassle-free 2nd entrance. Allow 3 hrs and carry plenty of drinking water.*

Entry to Fatehpur Sikri is through the **Agra Gate**. The straight road from Agra was laid out in Akbar's time. If approaching from Bharatpur you will pass the site of a large lake, which provided one defensive barrier. On the other sides was a massive defensive wall with nine gates

Fatehpur Sikri

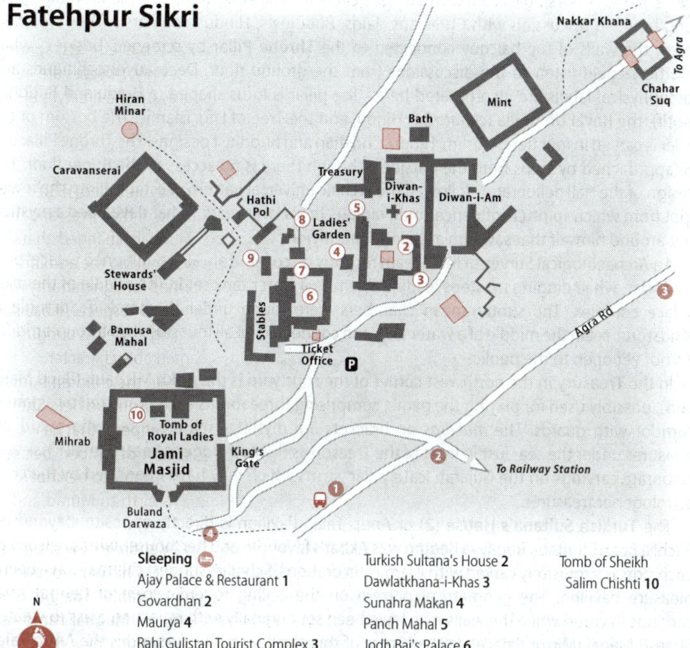

Sleeping
Ajay Palace & Restaurant 1
Govardhan 2
Maurya 4
Rahi Gulistan Tourist Complex 3

Sights
Pachisi Board 1
Turkish Sultana's House 2
Dawlatkhana-i-Khas 3
Sunahra Makan 4
Panch Mahal 5
Jodh Bai's Palace 6
Hawa Mahal 7
Nagina Masjid 8
Raja Birbal's Palace 9
Tomb of Sheikh Salim Chishti 10

(clockwise): Delhi, Lal, Agra, Bir or Suraj (Sun), Chandar (Moon), Gwaliori, Tehra (Crooked), Chor (Thief's) and Ajmeri. Sadly there are men with 'performing' bears along the road from Agra – they should be discouraged – avoid stopping to photograph or tip.

From the Agra Gate you pass the sandstone **Tansen's Baradari** on your right and go through the triple-arched **Chahar Suq** with a gallery with two *chhattris* above which may have been a **Nakkar khana** (Drum House). The road inside the main city wall leading to the entrance would have been lined with bazars. Next on your right is the square, shallow-domed **Mint** with artisans' workshops or animal shelters, around a courtyard. Workmen still chip away at blocks of stone in the dimly lit interior.

Royal Palace

The **Diwan-i-Am** (Hall of Public Audience) was also used for celebrations and public prayers. It has cloisters on three sides of a rectangular courtyard and to the west, a pavilion with the emperor's throne, with *jali* screens on either side separating the court ladies. Some scholars suggest that the west orientation may have had the added significance of Akbar's vision of himself playing a semi-divine role.

This backed onto the private palace. In the centre of the courtyard behind the throne is the **Pachisi Board (1)** or Chaupar. It is said that Akbar had slave girls dressed in yellow, blue and red, moved around as 'pieces'!

The **Diwan-i-Khas** (Hall of Private Audience) to your right, is a two-storey building with corner kiosks. It is a single room with a unique circular throne platform. Here Akbar would spend long hours in discussion with Christians, Jains, Buddhists, Hindus and Parsis. They would sit along the walls of the balcony connected to the **Throne Pillar** by screened 'bridges', while courtiers could listen to the discussions from the ground floor. Decorative techniques and metaphysical labels are incorporated here - the pillar is lotus shaped (a Hindu and Buddhist motif), the Royal Umbrella (*chhattri*) is Hindu, and the Tree of Life, Islamic. The bottom of the pillar is carved in four tiers; Muslim, Hindu, Christian and Buddhist designs. The Throne Pillar can be approached by steps from the outside although there is no access to the upper floor. The design of the Hall deliberately followed the archaic universal pattern of establishing a hallowed spot from which spiritual influence could radiate. In his later years, Akbar developed a mystical cult around himself that saw him as being semi-divine.

An Archaeological Survey of India team recently discovered an 'air-conditioned palace' built for Akbar, while digging up steps leading down to a water tank set in the middle of the main palace complex. The subterranean chambers were found under the small quadrangle in sandstone, set in the middle of a water tank and connected on all four sides by narrow corridors. It's not yet open to the public.

In the **Treasury** in the northwest corner of the courtyard is the **Ankh Michauli** (Blind Man's Buff), possibly used for playing the game, comprising three rooms each protected by a narrow corridor with guards. The *makaras* on brackets are mythical sea creatures who guard the treasures under the sea. Just in front of the Treasury is the **Astrologer's Seat**, a small kiosk with elaborate carvings on the Gujarati 'caterpillar' struts which may have been used by the court astrologer or treasurer.

The **Turkish Sultana's House (2)** or Anup Talao Pavilion is directly opposite, beyond the Pachisi Board. Sultana Ruqayya Begum was Akbar's favourite and her 'house', with a balcony on each side, is exquisitely carved with Islamic decorations. Scholars suggest this may have been a pleasure pavilion. The geometrical pattern on the ceiling is reminiscent of Central Asian carvings in wood while the walls may have been set originally with reflecting glass to create a Sheesh Mahal (Mirror Palace). In the centre of this smaller south courtyard is the **Anup Talao** where the Emperor may have sat on the platform, surrounded by perfumed water. The *Akbarnama* mentions the emperor's show of charity when he filled the Talao with copper, silver and gold coins and distributed them over three years.

Dawlatkhana-i-Khas (3), the emperor's private chambers, are next to the rose-water fountain in the corner. There are two main rooms on the ground floor. One housed his library - the recesses in the walls were for manuscripts. Although unable to read or write himself, Akbar enjoyed having books read to him. Wherever he went, his library of 50,000 manuscripts accompanied him. The larger room behind was his resting area. On the first floor is the **Khwabgah** (Palace of Dreams) which would have had rich carpets, hangings and cushions. This too was decorated with gold and ultramarine paintings. The southern window (Jharokha Darshan) was where the emperor showed himself to his people every morning.

Leaving the Dawlatkhana-i-Khas you enter another courtyard which contained the **Ladies' garden** for the *zenana*, and the **Sunahra Makan (4)** or the Christian wife **Maryam's** House, a two-storeyed affair for the emperor's mother, which was embellished with golden murals in the Persian style. The inscriptions on the beams are verses by **Fazl**, Akbar's poet laureate, one of the '*Navaratna*' (Nine Jewels) of the Court. Toilets in the corner of the garden are quite clean.

The **Panch Mahal (5)** is an elegant, airy five-storeyed pavilion just north of this, each floor smaller than the one below, rising to a single domed kiosk on top. The horizontal line of this terraced building is emphasized by wide overhanging eaves (for providing shade), parapets broken by the supporting pillars of which there are 84 on the ground floor (the magic number of seven planets multiplied by 12 signs of the zodiac). The 56 carved columns on the second floor are all different and show Hindu influence. Originally dampened scented *khuss* (grass screens) which were hung in the open spaces, provided protection from the heat and sun, as well as privacy for the women who used the pavilion.

Jodh Bai, the daughter of the Maharaja of Amber, lived in Raniwas. The spacious **palace (6)** in the centre, assured of privacy and security by high walls and a 9-m-high guarded gate to the east. Outside the north wall is the 'hanging' **Hawa Mahal (7)** (Palace of Winds) with beautiful *jali* screens facing the *zenana* garden which was once enclosed, and the bridge (a later addition) led to the Hathipol. Through the arch is the small **Nagina Masjid (8)**, the mosque for the ladies of the court. The *hammams* (baths) are to the south of the palace. The centre of the building is a quadrangle around which were the harem quarters, each section self-contained with roof terraces. The style, a blend of Hindu and Muslim (the lotus, chain and bell designs being Hindu, the black domes Muslim), is strongly reminiscent of Gujarati temples, possibly owing to the craftsmen brought in (see *jarokha* windows, niches, pillars and brackets). The upper pavilions north and south have interesting ceiling structure (imitating the bamboo and thatch roof of huts), here covered with blue glazed tiles, adding colour to the buildings of red sandstone favoured by Akbar. Jodh Bai's vegetarian kitchen opposite the palace has attractive chevron patterns.

Raja Birbal's Palace (9) is a highly ornamented house to the northwest of Jodh Bai's Palace. It has two storeys – four rooms and two porches with pyramidal roofs below, and two rooms with cupolas and screened terraces above. Birbal, Akbar's Hindu prime minister, was the brightest of Akbar's 'Nine Jewels'. Again the building combines Hindu and Islamic elements (note the brackets, eaves, *jarokhas*). Of particular interest is the insulating effect of the double-domed structure of the roofs and cupolas which kept the rooms cool, and the diagonal positioning of the upper rooms which ensured a shady terrace. Some scholars believe that this building, *Mahal-i-Ilahi*, was not for Birbal, but for Akbar's senior queens.

South of the Raja's house are the **stables**, a long courtyard surrounded by cells which probably housed zenana servants rather than the emperor's camels and horses, though the rings suggest animals may have been tied there.

Jami Masjid

Leaving the Royal Palace you proceed across a car park to the Jami Masjid and the sacred section of Fatehpur Sikri. The oldest place of worship here was the **Stone Cutters' Mosque** (circa 1565) to the west of the Jami Masjid. It was built near Sheikh Salim Chishti's cell which was later incorporated into it by stonecutters who settled on the ridge when quarrying for the Agra Fort began. It has carved monolithic 'S' brackets to support the wide sloping eaves.

The **Badshahi Darwaza** (King's Gate) is the entrance Akbar used. Shoes must be left at the gate but there are strips of carpet cross the courtyard to save burning your feet. The porch is packed with aggressive salesmen. The two other gates on the south and north walls were altered by subsequent additions. Built in 1571-1572, this is one of the largest mosques in India. Inside is the congregational courtyard (132 m by 111 m). To your right in the corner is the **Jamaat Khana Hall** and next to this the **Tomb of the Royal Ladies** on the north wall. The square nave carries the principal dome painted in the Persian style, with pillared aisles leading to side chapels carrying subsidiary domes. The **mihrab** in the centre of the west wall orientates worshippers towards Mecca. The sanctuary is adorned with carving, inlay work and painting.

The **Tomb of Sheikh Salim Chishti (10)**, a masterpiece in brilliant white marble, dominates the northern half of the courtyard. The Gujarati-style serpentine 'S' struts, infilled with *jali*, are highly decorative while the carved pillar bases and lattice screens are stunning pieces of craftsmanship. The canopy over the tomb is inlaid with mother of pearl. On the cenotaph is the date of the saint's death (1571) and the date of the building's completion (1580); the superb marble screens enclosing the veranda were added by Jahangir's foster brother in 1606. Around the entrance are inscribed the names of God, the Prophet and the four Caliphs of Islam. The shrine inside, on the spot of the saint's hermitage, originally had a red sandstone dome, which was marble veneered around 1806. Both Hindu and Muslim women pray at the shrine, tying cotton threads, hoping for the miracle of parenthood that Akbar was blessed with.

Next to it, in the courtyard, is the larger, red, sandstone tomb of **Nawab Islam Khan**, Sheikh Salim's grandson, and other members of the family.

Buland Darwaza (Triumphal Gate) dominates the south wall but it is a bit out of place. Built to celebrate Akbar's brilliant conquest of Gujarat (circa 1576), it sets the style for later gateways. The high gate is approached from the outside by a flight of steps which adds to its grandeur. The decoration shows Hindu influence, but is severe and restrained, emphasizing the lines of its arches with plain surfaces. You see an inscription on the right of a verse from the Qur'an:

Said Jesus Son of Mary (on whom be peace):
The world is but a bridge;
pass over it but build no houses on it. He
who hopes for an hour, hopes for
Eternity. The world is an hour. Spend it
in prayer, for the rest is unseen.

Outside the Royal Palace

Between the Royal Palace and the Jami Masjid, a paved pathway to the northwest leads to the **Hathipol** (Elephant Gate). This was the ceremonial entrance to the palace quarters, guarded by stone elephants, with its *nakkar khana* and bazar alongside. Nearby are the **waterworks**, with a deep well which had an ingenious mechanism for raising water to the aqueducts above ridge height. The **caravanserai** around a large courtyard fits on the ridge side, and was probably one of a series built to accommodate travellers, tradesmen and guards. Down a ramp immediately beyond is the **Hiran Minar**, an unusual tower studded with stone tusks, thought to commemorate Akbar's favourite elephant, Hiran. However, it was probably an *Akash Diya* (lamp to light the sky) or the 'zero point' for marking road distances in *kos*. You can climb up the spiral staircase inside it but take care as the top has no rail. This part of Fatehpur Sikri is off the main tourist track, and though less well preserved it is worth the detour to get the 'lost city' feeling, away from the crowds.

Agra and around listings

For Sleeping and Eating price codes and other relevant information, see Essentials pages 38-42.

Sleeping

Agra *p147, map p148*

The most atmospheric place to stay is in the busy lanes of **Taj Ganj**, where the basic hotels are clustered. Most of the upscale hotels are along **Fatehabad Rd**, a rather charmless strip of pricey restaurants, international fast-food outlets and handicrafts emporia.

LL Amar Vilas, near Taj East Gate, T0562-223 1515, www.amarvilas.com. 105 rooms, all Taj-facing. The modern-day equivalent of the most luxurious of maharaja's palaces, designed in strict adherence to the Mughal style. Stunning swimming pool, superb rooms, extraordinary ambience. Guests are entertained at sunset with traditional dancing and musicians. Expensive, but a magical experience.

LL-L The Mughal, Fatehabad Rd, T0562-233 1701, www.itcwelcomgroup.in. 285 rooms. Stunning suites, a palatial spa and beautiful gardens. Low-rise construction means only rooftop observatory offers good views of the Taj. Excellent restaurant.

LL-AL Gateway Hotel (formerly **Taj View**), Fatehabad Rd, T0562-223 2400, www.thegatewayhotels.com. 100 rooms. Tasteful Mughal-style interiors, large pool surrounded by lovely gardens, comfortable rooms some Taj facing, puppet shows. Friendly staff, but all round a bit average for the Taj chain.

LL-AL Trident, Fatehabad Rd, T0562-233 1818, www.tridenthotels.com. 138 bright, comfortable rooms, good pool, beautiful gardens, lovely zen minimalist foyer which has recently been renovated. Child friendly, kids' club with splash pool and activities. Friendly staff. Good restaurant. Recommended.

L Grand Imperial, Mahatma Gandhi Rd, T0562-225 1190, www.hotelgrandimperial.com. Agra's first bid at a genuine heritage hotel, with 30 opulent rooms, some still displaying their original red brickwork, arcaded around a pleasant lawn in a 100-year-old neoclassical mansion, all modern facilities, smart international restaurant with live classical Indian music at dinner. Swimming pool and small spa. Charming staff. The only drawback is the distance from the Taj and the proximity to a loud main road. Highly recommended.

A-B Hotel Amar, Fatehabad Rd, T0562-2331884, www.hotelamar.com. Although located in the busy city centre, this hotel is a haven for the mid-range traveller or good for business; lively, buzzy yet friendly feel; 66 comfortably furnished, a/c rooms with satellite TV; quiet gardens with swimming pool, health club and Ayurvedic massage; bar and restaurant, plus the opportunity to purchase home-baked brown bread. Recommended.

C Garden Villa Homestay, Kaveri Vihar, Chamrauli Village, T(0)9719-113626, www.gardenvillahomestay.com. Friendly homestay in a tiny gated community 7 km outside the city; 7 spacious, homely rooms with TV and a/c fronting onto a small, sunny garden; owned and run by charming retired couple who are passionate about tourism and gardening; very accommodating, can arrange cookery demo's, transport and sightseeing, yoga. Recommended.

C-D Mayur Tourist Complex, Fatehabad Rd, T0562-233 2302, www.mayurcomplex.com. 24 a/c rooms in slightly run-down bungalows. The complex has a campground feel with bucket showers and children's park. Built in 1970s, decor unchanged since. Internet. Restaurant, beer-only bar, large pool, relaxing garden setting.

D Agra Hotel, 165 FM Cariappa Rd, T0562-246 3331, agrahotel@yahoo.com. Backpacker hotel away from the main hub. 18 rooms in 1926 'British-time' bungalow. Basic, old-fashioned, good food, pleasant garden. Very friendly family-run hotel. Views from the terrace.

D Lauries, Mahatma Gandhi Rd, T0562-242 1447, lauries hotel@hotmail.com. A piece of history, alas very unloved and looking like it hasn't been redecorated or really cleaned since the 1961 visit from Queen Elizabeth II. Dating back to 1880, you can see its former elegance but it is a little faded.

D-E Sakura, 49 Old Idgah Colony, T0562-242 0169, www.hotelsakuraagra.com. No-frills rooms on noisy street, but handy for train station and Jaipur buses (which leave from outside the door). Manager is also a tour guide who has lots of tips. Hotel provides free pick-up from train or bus station.

E-F Sheela, East Gate, 2 mins' walk from the Taj, T0562-233 1194, www.hotelsheelaagra.com. 25 decent rooms with bath, pleasant garden, good restaurant, clean, peaceful, reliable laundry, secure (ask for gates to be unlocked for sunrise), very helpful manager. Good location in low pollution area. May be moved to sister hotel **Sheela Inn**, which is a 10-min bicycle rickshaw ride away if the hotel is full (no commission to rickshaws), reserve ahead.

E-F Tourists Rest House, 4/62 Kutchery Rd, Balugunj, T0562-246 3961. 28 basic but reasonably clean rooms, bucket baths some a/c, vegetarian restaurant, knowledgeable manager, often full. Runs popular 2-week trips to Rajasthan.

F-G Host, West Gate, T(0)9219-143409. 15 spartan but spacious and quite clean rooms with bath and hot water, rooftop restaurant with great view of the Taj, some rooms have no windows but very good location.

G Youth Hostel, Sanjay Pl, Mahatma Gandhi Rd, T0562-215 4462. 4 double rooms, 2 singles, 6 dorms. Clean if a little drab, good value but a long way from the Taj. Usual YHA rules apply.

Mathura *p157, map p157*

Hotels serve vegetarian food only. No alcohol.

A-B Brijwasi Royal, Station Rd, T0565-240 1225, www.brijwasiroyal.com. 40 comfortable, well appointed rooms in this busy, friendly hotel in the heart of the city. Professionally run, a very popular pure veg restaurant serves delicious north Indian food, and there are 2 bars (including a sheeshar room). Recommended.

B Sheetal Regency, near Krishna Janmabhoomi, Deeg Gate, Masani Rd, T0565-240 4401, www.hotelsheetalregency.com. 28 passable rooms in friendly, modern hotel. Changes money.

C Madhuvan, Krishna Nagar, T0565-242 0064, madhuvanhotel@indiatimes.com. 28 clean, fragrant rooms, some a/c with bath, restaurant, exchange, travel, pool, a little gloomy but friendly.

D-F Agra, near Bengali Ghat, T0565-240 3318. 15 clean, basic rooms, some a/c, traditional, friendly, well run.

D-F Tourist Reception Centre, (UPTDC), State Bank Crossing, near Railway Station Rd, T(0)9415-902719, www.up-tourism.com. All you expect from a government run place – clean but uninspiring. Restaurant on-site.

F-G International Guest House, Katra Keshav Deo, T0565-242 3888. Some air-cooled rooms, interesting place to stay.

G Railway Retiring Rooms, at Cantt and Junction stations.

Vrindavan *p159, map p159*

B Ananda Krishna Van, Parikrama Marg, near ISKCON, T0565-329 8855, www.anandakrishnavan.com. Sprawling new construction complete with waterfall, bathing pool, temple and restaurants, many rooms taken on timeshare basis, but some 4 bed a/c rooms available to visitors, remarkable undertaking.

D-E MVT Guest House, next to ISKCON, T0565-320 7578, www.mvtindia.com. Comfortable rooms, some a/c, set around pleasant gardens. Highly rated restaurant.

E International Rest House (ISKCON), Raman Reti, T0565-254 0022. Clean rooms, good, reasonably priced vegetarian restaurant, very popular, book well ahead.

E Shri Shri Radheshyam Palace, signposted behind ISKCON, T0565-254 0729. 22 clean rooms in friendly, well-located hotel.

Fatehpur Sikri *p160, map p161*

It is worth spending a night here to make an early start.

D-E Rahi Gulistan Tourist Complex (UP Tourism), Agra Rd, 1 km from bus stand, T05613-282490, www.up-tourism.com. Reasonable rooms with modern facilities, Campground feel, quiet, pleasant grounds, restaurant, bar.

D-F Govardhan, Buland Darwaza Rd Crossing, T05613-882643, www.hotelfatehpursikriviews.com. Clean shared bathroom, air-cooled suites with fridge, camping (Rs 20), 20% student discount, garden restaurant, pool, badminton, well maintained, lively and conscientious owner. Recommended.

E-F Hotel Vrinduvan, Bulund Gate Crossing, T05613-282 318, www.hotelvrindavanfts.com. Hospitable place with good value rooms. There's internet on-site, campfires in the winter, music and tours can also be provided.

Eating

Agra *p147, map p148*

₹₹₹ Esphahan, **Amar Vilas** (see Sleeping). Outstanding, rich Avadhi food in high-class setting, but non-residents will find it hard to get a table.

₹₹₹ Jhanka, **Gateway Hotel** (see Sleeping). Tasty Indian food, pleasant surroundings and good service.

₹₹₹ Mughal Room, **Hotel Clarks Shiraz**, 54 Taj Rd. Pretty standard 5-star fare, rich and meaty, mainly distinguished by glassed-in rooftop setting with great views over the city.

₹₹₹ Peshawari, **Mughal Sheraton** (see Sleeping). Regarded as the city's best, refined North Indian cuisine, smart surroundings, vegetarian offerings less inspired.

₹₹ Dasaprakash, Meher Theatre Complex, 1 Gwalior Rd, T0562-246 3535. Comprehensive range of South Indian offerings, *thalis* and dosas a speciality, slightly sterile chain-style interior but good hygiene and service.

₹₹ Only, 45 Taj Rd, T0562-236 4333. Interesting menu, attractive outside seating, popular with tour groups, live entertainment.

₹₹ Riao, next to **Clarks Shiraz**, 44 Taj Rd, T(0)9412-154311. Good North Indian food, puppet shows and live music, great garden and atmosphere.

₹₹ Sonam, 51 Taj Rd. Indian, Chinese. A/c, good food, well-stocked bar, large garden, popular with locals.

₹ Joney's Place, near South Gate, Taj Ganj. The original and, despite numerous similarly named imitators, still the best. Tiny place but the food is consistently good. Can produce Israeli and Korean specialities. Recommended.

₹ Maya, 18 Purani Mandi Circle, Fatehabad Rd. Varied menu, good Punjabi *thalis*, pasta, 'special tea', friendly, prompt service, hygienic, tasty, Moroccan-style decor. Recommended.

₹ Shankara Vegis, Taj Ganj. Vegetarian food prepared in reassuringly clean, open kitchen. Rooftop seats have obscured view of Taj, vies with **Joney's Place** for the best *lassis* in Agra.

₹ Shivam, **Raj Hotel**, near Taj south gate. Quality Indian, clean.

₹ Yash Café. Indian/Western menu, cheap but freshly prepared, very tasty *malai kofta*.

₹ Zorba the Buddha, E-19 Sadar Bazaar, T0562-222 6091, zorbaevergreen@yahoo.com. 1200-1500, 1800-2100. Run by disciples of Osho, one of India's more popular, and most libidinous, gurus. Unusual menu (in a good way), naan breads a speciality, very clean, undersize furniture gives doll's house feel, an enjoyably quirky experience.

Cafés

Café Coffee Day, A7 Sadar Bazar. Part of the nationwide chain, good coffee and Western snacks, nice escape.

Park, Taj Rd, Sadar Bazar. Standard North Indian menu, decor and service above average.

Festivals and events

Agra *p147, map p148*

18-27 Feb Taj Mahotsav, a celebration of the region's arts, crafts, culture and cuisine.

Aug/Sep A **fair** at Kailash (14 km away). A temple marks the spot where Siva is believed to have appeared in the form of a stone lingam.

Mathura *p157, map p157*

Mar Rang Gulal, the colourful Holi festival. Similar festivities at **Janmashtami**.

Aug/Sep Banjatra (Forest Pilgrimage). During the monsoon, episodes from Krishna's life are enacted.

Shopping

Agra *p147, map p148*

Agra specializes in jewellery, inlaid and carved marble, carpets and clothes. The main shopping areas are Sadar Bazar (closed Tue), Kinari Bazar, Gwalior Rd, Mahatma Gandhi Rd and Pratap Pura. Beware, you may order a carpet or an inlaid marble piece and have it sent later but it may not be what you ordered. Never agree to any export 'deals' and take great care with credit card slips (scams reported). Many rickshaws, taxi drivers and guides earn up to 40% commission by taking tourists to shops. Insist on not being rushed away from sights and shop independently. To get a good price you have to bargain hard anyway.

Carpets

Silk/cotton/wool mix hand-knotted carpets and woven *dhurries* are all made in Agra. High quality and cheaper than in Delhi.

Kanu Carpet Factory, Purani Mandi, Fetehabad Rd, T0562-233 0167. A reliable source.

Mughal Arts Emporium, Shamshabad Rd. Also has marble. Artificial silk is sometimes passed off as pure silk.

Handlooms and handicrafts

Government emporia in **Taj. UP Handlooms** and **UPICA**, Sanjay Place, Hari Parbat.

Marble

Delicately inlaid marble work is a speciality. Sometimes cheaper alabaster and soapstone is used and quality varies.

Akbar International, Fatehabad Rd. Good selection, inlay demonstration, fair prices.

Handicrafts Inn, 3 Garg Niketan, Fatehabad Rd, Taj Ganj.

Krafts Palace, 506 The Mall. Watch craftsmen working here.

UP Handicrafts Palace, 49 Bansal Nagar. Wide selection from table tops to coasters, high quality and good value.

Activities and tours

Agra *p147, map p148*

Tour operators

Aargee, Fatehabad Rd, T0562-272 0914.

Mercury, Hotel Clarks Shiraz, 54 Taj Rd, T0562-222 6531. Helpful and reliable.

Travel Bureau, near **Taj View Hotel**, T0562-233 0245, www.travelbureauagra.com. Long-established local company, highly experienced (handle ground arrangements for most foreign travel agents), helpful, can arrange anything. Reliable and recommended.

UP Tours, Taj Khema (5 mins' walk from Taj East Gate), T0562-233 0140, tajkhema@up-tourism.com. Coach tours: Fatehpur Sikri-Taj Mahal-Agra Fort (full day) 1030-1830, Rs 1700 (Indian Rs 400) including guide and entry fees; half-day Fatehpur Sikri tour ends at 1300 which only gives 45 mins at the site, not worthwhile, better take a taxi if you can afford it. Sikandra-Fatehpur Sikri (half day) 0930-1400, Rs 100 (excludes entry fees); Sikandra-Fatehpur Sikri-Taj Mahal-Agra Fort (full day), 1030-1830. Tours start and finish at Agra Cantt Railway Station and tie in with arrival/departure of *Taj Express* (see Transport); check times. Pickup also possible from **India Tourism** office on The Mall (advance notice).

World Ways, Taj East Gate, T(0)9358-499616, worldways@mail.com. Arrangements for budget travellers.

Transport

Agra *p147, map p148*

Air Kheria airport is 7 km from city centre. At the time of writing all flights were suspended. Several airlines have offices in Clarks Shiraz Hotel, including **Indian**, T0562-222 6801, and **Jet Airways**, T0562-222 6529.

Auto rickshaw Pre-paid stand at Agra Cantt Station has prices clearly listed for point-to-point rates and sightseeing. Expect to pay Rs 60-70 to Fatehabad Rd or Taj Ganj, or Rs 300 for a full day.

Cycle rickshaw Negotiate (pay more to avoid visiting shops); Taj Ganj to Fort Rs 30; Rs 80-200 for visiting sights.

Local bus City Bus Service covers most areas and main sights. Plenty leave from the Taj Mahal area and the **Fort Bus Stand**.

Long distance bus Most long-distance services leave from the **Idgah Bus Stand**, T0562-242 0324, including to: **Delhi** (4-5 hrs) via **Mathura** (1 hr); **Fatehpur Sikri** (40 km, 1 hr); **Bharatpur** (2 hrs); **Khajuraho** (10 hrs). **Agra Fort Stand**, T0562-236 4557, has additional buses to **Delhi**, **Lucknow** (10 hrs) and **Haridwar** (minimum 12 hrs). Deluxe buses for **Jaipur** arrive and depart from a stop near **Hotel Sakura**: closer to most hotels and where there is less hassle from touts. **Delhi** from tourist office, 0700, 1445, deluxe, 4 hrs.

Motorbike/bicycle hire Firoz Motorcycle House, Cariappa Rd, Enfield Bullets Rs 500 per day. Bike hire from Sadar Bazar, near police station and near **Tourist Rest House**, Rs 30-40 per day.

Taxi/car hire Tourist taxis from travel agents, remarkably good value for visiting nearby sights. Non-a/c car Rs 5 per km, full day Rs 1000 (100 km), half day Rs 500/600 (45 km); a/c rates double; to Fatehpur Sikri Rs 1500-2200 return depending on car). **Travel Bureau**, T0562-233 0230; **UP Tours**, T0562-233 0140.

Train From Delhi train is the quickest and most reliable way. Most trains use **Agra Cantonment Railway Station**, 5 km west of Taj Mahal, enquiries T131, reservations T0562-242 1039, open 0800-2000. Foreigners' queue at Window 1.

Pedal power

To achieve a 'greener', cleaner Agra and reducing pollution by vehicle emissions, a new model of cycle rickshaw has been developed by the Institute for Transportation and Development Policy, an Indian NGO, with help from the US Agency for International Development, after consulting local organizations and the men who will be pedalling them. The much lighter (and easier to operate), more comfortable and faster transport for two, is an attractive alternative to fume-emitting engines. The concerned visitor can opt to hire one from outside a top hotel for around Rs 150, to be wheeled around the city to see the Taj Mahal, the Red Fort, sample local cuisine and also reduce approaches by hawkers and beggars.

Pre-paid taxi/auto-rickshaw kiosk outside the station. Some trains to Rajasthan from quieter **Agra Fort Station**, T132, T0562-236 9590. Trains mentioned arrive and depart from **Agra Cantt** unless specified. To **Delhi**: *Shatabdi Exp 12001*, (**ND**), 2040, 2½ hrs; *Taj Exp 12279*, (**HN**), 1855, 3¼ hrs (CC/II); *Intercity Exp 11103*, (**HN**), 0600, 3½ hrs (2nd class only). To **Jaipur**: *Intercity Exp 12307*, 1645, 6 hrs (from Agra Fort); *Marudhar Exp 14853/63*, 0715, 6¾ hrs. **Jhansi** (via Gwalior): *Taj Express 12280*, 1015, 3 hrs, (Gwalior 1¾ hrs), **Mumbai** (**CST**): *Punjab Mail 12138*, 0855, 2¼ hrs. **Sawai Madhopur** (for Ranthambore) at 0600, 0900, 1800.

Mathura *p157, map p157*

Bus Frequent service to **Delhi**, **Jaipur** and neighbouring towns from the **New Bus Stand** opposite Hotel Nepal. Buses to **Govardhan** and **Agra** from **Old Bus Stand** near the railway station, T0565-240 6468.

Taxi From opposite District Hospital. Also, buses, auto and cycle rickshaws.

Train **Mathura Junction** is the main station, T0565-240 5830. **Cantt Station** is at Bahadurganj (metre gauge). **Sri Krishna Janmabhumi** is at Bhuteshwar. For Delhi and Agra, the best is to **Agra Cantt**: *Taj Exp 12280*, 0900, 47 mins. **New Delhi** (**HN**): *Taj Exp 12279*, 1930, 2¼ hrs. **Sawai Madhopur**: *Golden Temple Mail 12904*, 1025, 3 hrs; *Bandra Exp 19020*, 0140, 3½ hrs; *Janata Exp 19024*, 1735, 4 hrs. **Vrindavan**: see below.

Vrindavan *p159, map p159*

Bus/taxi Buses, *tempos* and rickshaws to and from **Mathura**.

Train Services from **Mathura Junction** at 0627, 0850, 1457, 1655, 1925, takes 35 mins; returns from **Vrindavan** at 0725, 0940, 1610, 1740, 2015.

Fatehpur Sikri *p160, map p161*

Bus Frequent buses from **Agra Idgah Bus Stand** (1 hr) Rs 17.

Taxi Taxis from **Agra** include the trip in a day's sightseeing (1500-2200 return depending on car).

Directory

Agra *p147, map p148*

Banks Several ATMs on Fatehabad Rd (Cirrus, Maestro, Visa cards, etc). **Andhra Bank**, Taj Rd, opposite **Kwality's** gives cash against card. **Thomas Cook**, Crystal Tower, Fatehabad Rd, TCs and cash against card. **Internet** The Mall (24 hrs). Many in Taj Ganj and around hotel areas, Rs 40-50/hr. **Khurana Cyber Café**, 805 Sadar Bazar, opposite Cantt Hospital. **Medical services** **Ambulance:** T102. **District Hospital**, Chhipitola Rd/Mahatma Gandhi Rd, T0562-236 2043. **Dr VN**, Kaushal, opposite Imperial Cinema, T0562-236 3550. Recommended. **Post** **GPO** opposite India Tourist Office, with **Poste Restante**. **Useful contacts** **Fire:** T101. **Police:** T100.

Mathura *p157, map p157*

Medical services **District Hospital**, near Agra Rd, T0565-240 3006. **Methodist Hospital**, Vrindavan Rd, T0565-273 0043.

Varanasi and around

→ *Colour map 3, B4. Population: over 3.14 million.*

Perhaps the holiest of India's cities, Varanasi defies easy description. A highly congested maze of narrow alleys winds behind its waterfront ghats, at once highly sacred yet physically often far from clean. As an image, an idea and a symbol of Hinduism's central realities, the city draws pilgrims from around the world, to worship, to meditate, and above all to bathe. It is a place to be born and a place to die. In the cold mists of a winter's dawn, you can see life and death laid bare. For an outside observer it can be an uncomfortable, albeit unmissable experience, juxtaposing the inner philosophical mysteries of Hinduism with the practical complications of living literally and metaphorically on the edge.

More holy places surround Varanasi: Sarnath, one of Buddhism's major centres, Jaunpur, a city with a strong Islamic history, and Allahabad, a sacred place for Hindus due to its position at the confluence of the Ganja and Yamuna rivers. ▸▸ *For listings, see pages 184-191.*

Varanasi → *For listings, see pages 184-191. Colour map 3, B4.*

The riverside city, and the focus for most tourists and pilgrims, extends from Raj Ghat in the north to Assi Ghat in the south. At dawn the riverbank's stone steps begin to hum with activity. Early risers immerse themselves in the water as they face the rising sun, boatmen wait expectantly on the waterside, pilgrims flock to the temples, flower sellers do brisk business, astrologers prepare to read palms and horoscopes while families carry the dead to their last rites by the holy river. A few steps away from the ghats, motorbikers speed through the lanes past wandering *sadhus*, hopeful beggars, curious visitors and wandering cows, while packs of stray dogs scavenge among the piles of rubbish.

Ins and outs

Getting there Several airlines link Varanasi with Delhi, Khajuraho, Kathmandu, Mumbai and other cities. From Babatpur airport, 22 km away, there is an unreliable airport bus to the Indian Airlines office in the Cantonment area. Better to take a taxi from the prepaid booth. Most trains stop at Junction Station near the Cantonment, about 5 km northwest of the Old City and the budget hotels. Some trains (eg Delhi–Kolkata *Rajdhani* and *Expresses* to New Jalpaiguri and Guwahati) do not pass through Varanasi itself but stop at Mughal Sarai, 17 km away, which is accessible by road from Varanasi. Shared jeeps cost Rs 20 between the two stations, or a taxi is Rs 220. Most long-distance buses arrive at the bus stands near Junction Station.

Note On arrival at Junction Station, you will be accosted by rickshaw-wallahs who are desperate to get you to a hotel which pays them commission. It can be stressful; don't believe touts who say your chosen hotel is closed or full – such things rarely change in Varanasi. Several budget hotels offer free pick-up from the station (call on arrival), or try to get at least 50 m outside of the station area before bargaining for an auto (Rs 70) or cycle-rickshaw (Rs 40). Shared autos leave from the far side of the main road outside the station to Godoulia (Rs 10) near Main Ghat. Note that autos are not permitted into the narrow lanes near the main ghats, and you will have to walk the last stretch (10-20 minutes to hotels). However, autos can get close to Assi Ghat (one of the ghats furthers south), from where it's a two-minute walk to hotels.

Getting around The only way to see the heart of the Old City is on foot, though no visit is complete without an early-morning boat trip along the ghats. Varanasi is quite spread out: the university to the south is nearly 7 km from the spacious Cantonment area and the Junction Station to the north. Around town, cycle-rickshaws and autos are plentiful. Shared autos run along main routes, though it is difficult (as a tourist) to avoid being pressured into private hire. Unmetered taxis are best for longer sightseeing trips. The city has some of the disadvantages of

1 Varanasi

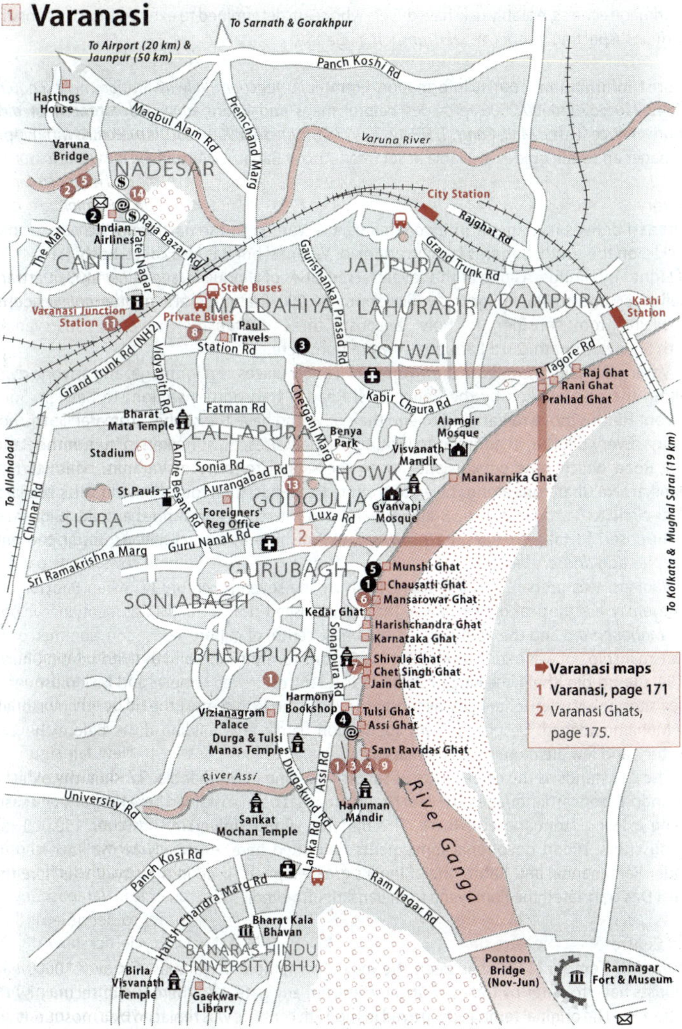

Sleeping
Chaitanya Guest House 4
Clarks Varanasi 2
Ganges View 1
Gateway Ganges 14
Palace on Ganges 3
Radisson 5
Rahi Tourist Bungalow 8
Railway Retiring Rooms 11
Sahi River View Guest House 9
Shiva Ganga Lodge 7
Shiva Ganges View 6
Sun Shiv 13

Eating
Brownie 2
Lotus Lounge 1
Pizzeria Café Vaatika 4
Poonam 3
Shiva Café & German Bakery 5

pilgrimage centres, notably rickshaw drivers who seem determined to extort as much as possible from unsuspecting visitors. ▸▸ *See Transport, page 189.*

Tourist information Tourist Information Counter ⓘ *Junction Railway Station, near 'Enquiry', T0542-250 6670, 0600-2000*, provides helpful maps and information. **Government of India Tourist Office** ⓘ *The Mall, Cantt, T/F0542-250 1784, Mon-Sat 0900-1630*, is well run, with helpful manager and staff; **guides** available at set rates. Also at Babatpur Airport.

History

Varanasi derives its name from two streams, the Varuna to the north and the Assi, a small trickle, on the south. **Banaras** is a corruption of Varanasi but it is also called **Kashi** (Siva's 'City of Light') by Hindus. As one of the seven sacred cities of Hinduism, see page 1409, it attracts well over one million pilgrims while about 50,000 Brahmins are permanent residents. The Jains too consider it holy because three *tirthankars* (seventh Suarsvanath, 11th Shyeyanshnath, 23rd Parsvanath) were born here.

Varanasi is said to combine the virtues of all other places of pilgrimage, and anyone dying within the area marked by the **Panch Kosi Road** is transported straight to heaven. Some devout Hindus move to Varanasi to end their days and have their ashes scattered in the holy Ganga. Every pilgrim, in addition to visiting the holy sites, must make a circuit of the Panch Kosi Road which runs outside and round the sacred territory of Varanasi. This starts at Manikarnika Ghat, runs along the waterfront to Assi Ghat, then round the outskirts in a large semi-circle to Barna Ghat. The 58-km route is lined with trees and shrines and the pilgrimage is supposed to take six days, each day's walk finishing in a small village, equipped with temples and *dharamshalas*.

Varanasi was probably an important town by the seventh century BC when Babylon and Nineveh were at the peak of their power. The Buddha visited in 500 BC and it was mentioned in both the *Mahabharata* and the *Ramayana*. It became a centre of culture, education, commerce and craftsmanship but was raided by **Mahmud of Ghazni's** army in 1033 and by Qutb-ud-din Ghuri in 1194. **Ala-ud-din Khalji**, the King of Delhi (1294-1316), destroyed temples and built mosques on their sites. The Muslim influence was strong so even in the 18th century the city was known briefly as Mohammadabad. Despite its early foundation hardly any building dates before the 17th century, and few are more than 200 years old.

The city stands as the chief centre of Sanskrit learning in North India. Sanskrit, the oldest of the Indo-European languages, used for Hindu ritual has been sustained here long after it ceased to be a living language elsewhere. The **Banaras Hindu University** has over 150,000 rare manuscripts. Hindu devotional movements flourished here, especially in the 15th century under Ramananda, and **Kabir**, one of India's greatest poets, lived in the city. It was here that **Tulsi Das** translated the Ramayana from Sanskrit into Hindi.

Old Centre

Visvanath Temple (1777) has been the main Siva temple in Varanasi for over 1000 years. Tourists have to enter by Gate 2, but can exit from any gate, and there is stiff security by the entrances. The original temple, destroyed in the 12th century, was replaced by a mosque. It was rebuilt in the 16th, and again destroyed within a century. The present **'Golden' temple** was built in 1777 by Ahilya Bai of Indore. The gold plating on the roof was provided by Maharaja Ranjit Singh in 1835. Its pointed spires are typically North Indian in style and the exterior is finely carved. The 18th-century **Annapurna Temple** (*anna* food; *purna* filled) nearby, built by Baji Rao I, has shrines dedicated to Siva, Ganesh, Hanuman and Surya. Ask for directions as you make your way through the maze of alleys around the temples.

The **Gyan Kup** (Well of Knowledge) next door is said to contain the Siva lingam from the original temple – the well is protected by a stone screen and canopy. The nearby **Gyanvapi**

Mosque (Great Mosque of Aurangzeb), with 71-m-high minarets, shows evidence of the original Hindu temple, in the foundations, the columns and at the rear.

The 17th-century **Alamgir Mosque** (Beni Madhav ka Darera), impressively situated on Panchganga Ghat, was Aurangzeb's smaller mosque. It was built on the original Vishnu temple of the Marathas, parts of which were used in its construction. Two minarets are missing – one fell and killed some people and the other was taken down by the government as a precaution. You can climb to the top of the mosque for fantastic views (donation expected); again, bags are prohibited and you may be searched.

Back lanes

The maze of narrow lanes, or *galis*, along the ghats through the old quarters exude the smells and sounds of this holy city. They are fascinating to stroll through though easy to get lost in. Some find it too over-powering. Near the Town Hall (1845) built by the Maharaja of Vizianagram, is the **Kotwali** (Police Station) with the Temple of **Bhaironath**, built by Baji Rao II in 1825. The image inside is believed to be of the Kotwal (Superintendent) who rides on a ghostly dog. Stalls sell sugar dogs to be offered to the image. In the temple garden of **Gopal Mandir** near the Kotwali is a small hut in which Tulsi Das is said to have composed the *Binaya Patrika* poem.

The **Bhelupura Temple** with a museum marks the birthplace of the 23rd Jain Tirthankar **Parsvanath** who preached non-violence. The **Durga Temple** (18th-century) to the south along Durga Kund Road, was built in the Nagara style. It is painted red with ochre and has the typical five spires (symbolizing the elements) merging into one (Brahma). Non-Hindus may view from the rooftop nearby. Next door in a peaceful garden, the **Tulsi Manas Temple** (1964) in white marble commemorates the medieval poet Tulsi Das. It has walls engraved with verses and scenes from the *Ramcharitmanas*, composed in a Hindi dialect, instead of the conventional Sanskrit, and is open to all (closed 1130-1530). Good views from the second floor of 'Disneyland-style' animated show. **Bharat Mata Temple**, south of Varanasi Junction Station, has a relief map of 'Mother India' in marble.

Riverfront

The hundred and more **ghats** on the river are the main attraction for visitors to Varanasi. Visit them at first light before sunrise (0430 in summer, 0600 in winter) when Hindu pilgrims come to bathe in the sacred Ganga, facing the rising sun, or at dusk when synchronized *pujas* are performed, culminating in leaf-boat lamps being floated down the river, usually from 1800 (later in summer). Large crowds gather at Dasasvamedha (Main) Ghat and Mir Ghat every night, or there's a more low-key affair at Assi Ghat. Start the river trip at Dasasvamedha Ghat where you can hire a boat quite cheaply especially if you can share (bargain to about Rs 100-150 per hour for two to eight people, at dawn). You may go either upstream (south) towards Harishchandra Ghat or downstream to Manikarnika Ghat. You may prefer to have a boat on the river at sunset and watch the lamps floated on the river, or go in the afternoon at a fraction of the price quoted at dawn. For photographs, visit the riverside between 0700-0900. The foggy sunshine early in the morning often clears to produce a beautiful light.

Kite flying is a popular pastime, as elsewhere in India, especially all along the riverbank. The serious competitors endeavour to bring down other flyers' kites and so fortify their twine by coating it with a mix of crushed light bulbs and flour paste to make it razor sharp. The quieter ghats, eg Panchganga, are good for watching the fun: boys in their boats on the river scramble to retrieve downed kites as trophies that can be re-used even though the kites themselves are very cheap. Cricket is also played on the ghats, particularly those to the north which are more spacious and less crowded.

Dasasvamedha Ghat Commonly called 'Main Ghat', Dasasvamedha means the 'Place of Ten Horse Sacrifices' performed here by Brahma, God of Creation. Some believe that in the age of the

Polluted Ganga purifies itself

All along the Ganga, the major problem of waste disposal (of human effluent and industrial toxins) has defied the best efforts of the Ganga Action Plan set up in 1986 to solve it. The diversion and treatment of raw sewage in seven main cities was planned. In Varanasi however, the inadequate 17th-century sewers, the increased waterflow during the monsoons and the erratic electricity supply (essential for pumping) have all remained problems. In addition, although most Hindus are cremated, an estimated 45,000 uncremated or partially cremated bodies are put in the Ganga each year. A breed of scavenger turtles which dispose of rotting flesh was introduced down river but the turtles disappeared. The Uttar Pradesh Water Board (Jal Nigam) put forward a Ganga Action Plan II, but critics of the first failed scheme are proposing an alternative under the guidance of a Banaras Hindu University engineering professor, Veer Bhadra Mishra. It remains to be seen whether his proposal of a massive educational programme backed by engineering will help the city purify the filth that enters it every day.

Although the Ganga may be one of the world's most polluted rivers, like many tropical rivers it can cleanse itself quickly. Scientists discovered the river's exceptional self- purification properties in the last century: the cholera microbe did not survive three hours in Ganga water whereas in distilled water it survived 24 hours. Good news for Varanasi's 60,000 daily bathers!

gods when the world was in chaos, Divodasa was appointed King of Kashi by Brahma. He accepted, on condition that all the gods would leave Varanasi. Even Siva was forced to leave but Brahma set the test for Divodasa, confident that he would get the complex ceremony wrong, allowing the gods back into the city. However, the ritual was performed flawlessly, and the ghat has thus become one of the holiest, especially at eclipses. Bathing here is regarded as being almost as meritorious as making the sacrifice.

Moving south You will pass **Munshi Ghat**, where some of the city's sizeable Muslim population (25%) come to bathe. The river has no religious significance for them. Close by is **Darbhanga Ghat** where the mansion had a hand-operated cable lift. Professional washermen work at the **Dhobi Ghat**; there is religious merit in having your clothes washed in the Ganga. Brahmins have their own washermen to avoid caste pollution. The municipality has built separate washing facilities away from the ghat.

Narad Ghat and **Chauki Ghat** are held sacred since the Buddha received enlightenment here under a *peepul* tree. Those who bathe together at Narad, supposedly go home and quarrel! The pink water tower here is for storing Ganga water. High water levels are recorded at **Raj Ghat**. The flood levels are difficult to imagine when the river is at its lowest in January and February. **Mansarovar Ghat** leads to ruins of several temples around a lake. **Kedar Ghat** is named after Kedarnath, a pilgrimage site in the Uttarakhand, with a Bengali temple nearby.

The **Harishchandra Ghat** is particularly holy and is dedicated to King Harishchandra. It is now the most sacred *smashan* or cremation ghat although Manikarnika is more popular. Behind the ghat is a *gopuram* of a Dravidian-style temple. The **Karnataka Ghat** is one of many regional ghats which are attended by priests who know the local languages, castes, customs and festivals.

The **Hanuman Ghat** is where Vallabha, the leader of a revivalist Krishna bhakti cult was born in the late 15th century. **Shivala Ghat** (Kali Ghat) is privately owned by the ex-ruler of Varanasi. **Chet Singh's Fort**, Shivala, stands behind the ghat. The fort, the old palace of the Maharajas, is where the British imprisoned him but he escaped by climbing down to the river and swimming away. **Anandamayi Ghat** is named after the Bengali saint Anandamayi Ma (died 1982) who received 'enlightenment' at 17 and spent her life teaching and in charitable work. **Jain Ghat** is near the birthplace of Tirthankar Shyeyanshnath. **Tulsi Ghat** commemorates the great saint-poet Tulsi Das who lived here (see Tulsi Manas Temple, page 173). Furthest upstream is the **Assi Ghat**, where the River Assi meets the Ganga, one of the five that pilgrims should bathe from in a day. The order is Assi, Dasasvamedha, Barnasangam, Panchganga and Manikarnika. Upstream on the east bank is the Ramnagar Fort, the Maharaja of Varanasi's residence (see page 177). Here the boat will turn to take you back to Dasasvamedha Ghat.

Moving north Leaving Dasasvamedha Ghat, you come to **Man Mandir Ghat** dominated by a Rajput palace ⓘ *open dawn till dusk, Rs100 foreigners, Rs 5 Indians*, built by Maharajah Man Singh of Amber in 1600 and one of the oldest in Varanasi. The palace was restored in the last century with brick and plaster. The beautiful stone balcony on the northeast corner gives an indication of how the original looked. Maharaja Jai Singh of Jaipur converted the palace into an **observatory** in 1710 (see also Jaipur, page 327). Like its counterparts in Delhi, Jaipur and Ujjain, the rooftop observatory comprises a collection of instruments built of brick, cement and stone. At the entrance is the Bhittiyantra, or wall quadrant, over 3 m high and in the same plane as the line of longitude. Similarly placed is the Samratyantra which is designed to slope upwards pointing at the Pole Star. From the top of the Chakra Yantra there is a superb view of the ghats and the town. Near the entrance to the palace is a small **Siva Temple** whose shrine is a lingam immersed in water. During droughts, water is added to the cistern to make it overflow for good luck.

2 Varanasi Ghats

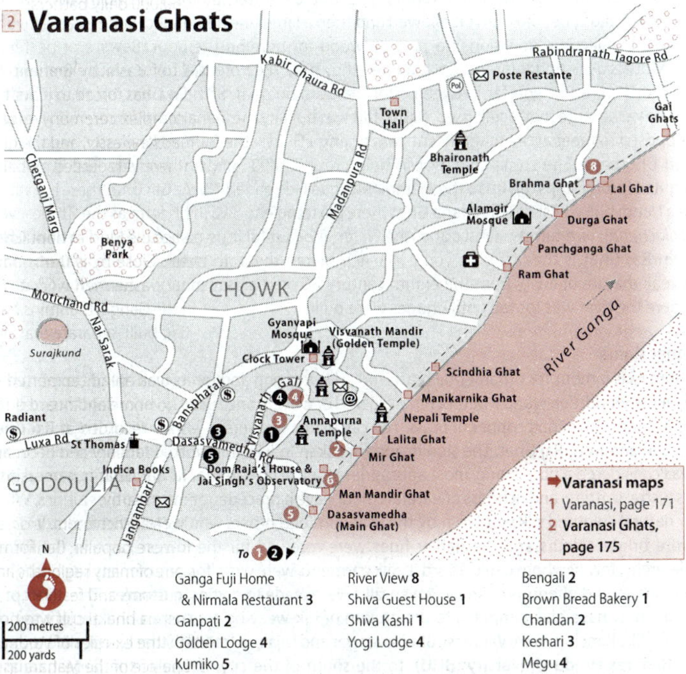

Varanasi maps
1 Varanasi, page 171
2 Varanasi Ghats, page 175

Sleeping
Alka 2
Baba Guest House 1
Ganga Fuji Home & Nirmala Restaurant 3
Ganpati 2
Golden Lodge 4
Kumiko 5
Monu Family Guest House 4
Rashmi Guest House & Dolphin Restaurant 6
River View 8
Shiva Guest House 1
Shiva Kashi 1
Yogi Lodge 4

Eating
Ankita 2
Aroma 5
Bengali 2
Brown Bread Bakery 1
Chandan 2
Keshari 3
Megu 4
Monalisa 2

The **Dom Raja's House** is next door, flanked by painted tigers. The *doms* are the 'Untouchables' of Varanasi and are integral to the cremation ceremony. As Untouchables they can handle the corpse, a ritually polluting act for Hindus. They also supply the flame from the temple for the funeral pyre. Their presence is essential and also lucrative since there are fees for the various services they provide. The Dom Raja is the hereditary title of the leader of these Untouchables.

Mir Ghat leads to a sacred well; widows who dedicate themselves to prayer, are fed and clothed here. Then comes **Lalita Ghat** with the distinctive Nepalese-style temple with a golden roof above ⓘ *entrance Rs 10* and wood carvings decorating the exterior. Above **Manikarnika Ghat** is a well into which Siva's dead wife Sati's earring is supposed to have fallen when Siva was carrying her after she committed suicide (see page 1411). The Brahmins managed to find the jewel from the earring (*manikarnika*) and returned it to Siva who blessed the place. Offerings of *bilva* flowers, milk, sandalwood and sweetmeats are thrown into the tank where pilgrims come to bathe. Between the well and the ghat is *Charanpaduka*, a stone slab with Vishnu's footprint. Boatmen may try to persuade you to leave a 'private' offering to perform a *puja* (a ploy to increasing their earnings).

The adjoining **Jalasayin Ghat** is the principal burning ghat of the city. The expensive scented sandalwood which the rich alone can afford is used sparingly; usually not more than 2 kg. You may see floating bundles covered in white cloth; children, and those dying of 'high fever', or smallpox in the past, are not cremated but put into the river. This avoids injuring Sitala the goddess of smallpox. **Note** Photography is not permitted at the burning ghats, though travellers might be told that it is allowed and then a large fine demanded. Other scams involve conmen collecting 'donations' to provide wood for burning the poor. Beware of pestering individuals declaring they are "not a guide", they have the potential to ruin your experience.

Tourists are few and far between after the burning ghat. **Scindia Ghat**, originally built in 1830, was so large that it collapsed. **Ram Ghat** was built by the Maharaja of Jaipur. Five rivers are supposed to meet at the magnificent **Panchganga Ghat** – the Ganga, Sarasvati, Gyana, Kirana and Dhutpapa. The stone column can hold around 1000 lamps at festivals. The impressive flights of stone steps run up to the Alamgir Mosque (see page 173). At **Gai Ghat** there is a statue of a Nandi bull whilst at **Trilochana Ghat** there is a temple to Siva in his form as the 'Three-eyed' (*Trilochana*); two turrets stand out of the water. A beautiful little palace is found at **Rani Ghat**, then **Raj Ghat** is the last ghat you can reach before the path peters out. Excavations have revealed a site of a city from the eighth century BC on a grassy mound nearby. Raj Ghat was where the river was forded until bridges were built.

Other sights

Varanasi is famous for ornamental brasswork, silk weaving and for its glass beads, exported all over the world. *Zari* work, whether embroidered or woven, once used silver or gold thread but is now done with gilded copper or brass. You can watch weavers at work in Piti Kothi, the Muslim area inland from Raj Ghat. The significance of **silk** in India's traditional life is deep-rooted. Silk was considered a pure fabric, most appropriate for use on ceremonial and religious occasions. Its lustre, softness and richness of natural colour gave it precedence over all other fabrics. White or natural coloured silk was worn by the Brahmins and others who were 'twice born'. Women wore bright colours and the darker hues were reserved for the lowest caste in the formal hierarchy, few of whom could afford it. Silk garments were worn for ceremonials like births and marriages, and offerings of finely woven silks were made to deities in temples. This concept of purity may have given impetus to the growth of silk-weaving centres around ancient temple towns like Kanchipuram, Varanasi, Bhubaneswar and Ujjain, a tradition that is kept alive today.

Banaras Hindu University (**BHU**), to the south of the city, is one of the largest campus universities in India and enjoys a pleasant, relaxed atmosphere. Founded at the turn of the 19th century, it was originally intended for the study of Sanskrit, Indian art, music and culture. The **New Visvanath Temple** (1966), one of the tallest in India, is in the university semicircle and was financed by the Birla family. It was planned by Madan Mohan Malaviya (1862-1942), chancellor of the university, who believed in Hinduism without caste distinctions. The marble Siva temple modelled on the old Visvanath Temple, is open to all.

Bharat Kala Bhavan ⓘ *BHU, T0542-230 7621, Mon-Sat 1100-1630, closed holidays, foreigners Rs 100, Indians Rs 10, camera Rs 20 (lockers at entrance)*, exhibits include sculptures from Mathura and Sarnath, excellent Mughal miniature paintings and Benarasi brocades.

Across the river in a dramatic setting on the edge of narrow crowded streets is the run-down 17th-century **Ramnagar Fort**, the former home of the Maharaja of Varanasi. The ferry costs Rs 10 return, or there are rickshaws from the main gate of BHU which cross a bone-jarring pontoon bridge to the fort (under water June to October), Rs 10 each way, or take a boat back or else walk over the pontoon bridge. The **museum** ⓘ *T0542-233 9322, 1000-1700, Rs 16*, has palanquins, elephant *howdahs* and headdresses, costumes, arms and furniture gathering dust. Look out for the amazing locally made astrological clock and peer inside the impressive Durbar Hall, cunning designed to remain cool in the summer heat, with lifesize portraits lining one wall. Nearby Ramnagar village has *Ramlila* performances during Dasara (October to November) and has some quieter backalleys which make for a relaxing hours wandering.

Chunar → *Colour map 3, B4.*

Chunar, 35 km southwest of Varanasi, is famous for Chunar sandstone, the material of the Asoka pillars, highly polished in a technique said to be Persian. The town is also noted for its **fort** built on a spur of the Kaimur Hills, 53 m above the surrounding plain. It was of obvious strategic importance and changed hands a number of times. The army occupies the fort today, but you can look around. There is an impressive well with steps leading down to a water gate; watch out for snakes. The **British cemetery** below the fort overlooks the Ganga. **Islamic tombs** of Shah Kasim Suleiman and his son here, feature in paintings by Daniells and others. Buses from Varanasi's City Station take 1½ hours.

Sarnath → *For listings, see pages 184-191.* *Colour map 3, B4.*

Sarnath, 10 km northeast of Varanasi, is one of Buddhism's major centres in India. The museum houses some superb pieces, including the famed four-lion capital that is the symbol of the Indian Union. The *stupas*, monasteries and Buddha statues make an interesting contrast to nearby Hindu Varanasi.

Tourist information Modern Reception Centre ⓘ *T0542-259 5965, T(0)9580-574420, Mon-Sat 1000-1700*, provides a map and information.

History

When he had gained enlightenment at Bodhgaya, the Buddha came to the deer park at Sarnath and delivered his first sermon (circa 528 BC), usually referred to as *Dharmachakra* (The Wheel of Law). Since then, the site has been revered. The Chinese traveller Hiuen Tsang described the *sangharama* (monastery) in AD 640 as having 1500 monks, a 65-m-high *vihara*, a figure of the Buddha represented by a wheel, a 22-m-high stone *stupa* built by Asoka, a larger 90-m-high *stupa* and three lakes. The remains here and the sculptures now at the Indian Museum, Kolkata and the National Museum, Delhi, reveal that Sarnath was a centre of religious activity, learning and art, continuously from the fourth century BC until its abandonment in the ninth century AD and ultimate destruction by Muslim armies in 1197.

Archaeological Museum

The **Archaeological Museum** ⓘ *Sat-Thu 0900-1700, entrance Rs 5, cameras and bags must be left outside*, has a well-displayed collection of pieces from the site, including the famous lion capital from the Asokan Column. The four lions sitting back to back are of highly polished sandstone and show Mauryan sculpture at its best. Also on display are a Sunga period (first century BC) stone railing, Kushana period (second century AD) Boddhisattvas and Gupta period (fifth century AD) figures including a magnificent seated Buddha.

Enclosure

ⓘ *Open sunrise-sunset, foreigners Rs 100, video Rs 25*

The **Dhamekh Stupa** (Dharma Chakra) dating to fifth to sixth century AD, is the most imposing monument at Sarnath, built where the Buddha delivered his first sermon to his five disciples. Along with his birth, enlightenment and death, this incident is one of the four most significant. The *stupa* consists of a 28-m-diameter stone plinth which rises to a height of 13 m. Each of the eight faces has an arched recess for an image. Above this base rises a 31-m-high cylindrical tower. The upper part was probably unfinished. The central section has elaborate Gupta designs, eg luxuriant foliation, geometric patterns, birds and flowers. The Brahmi script dates

Sarnath

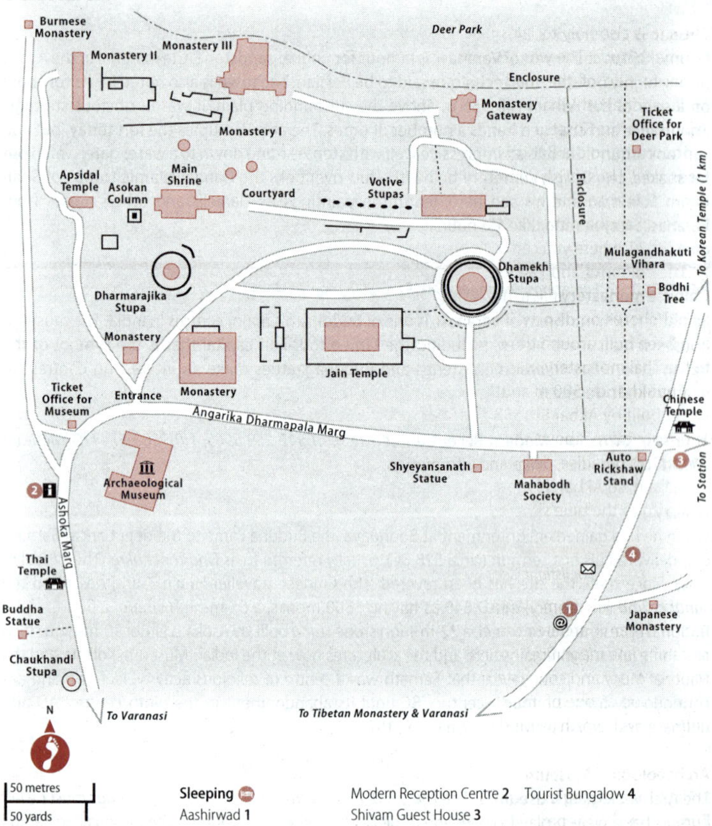

Sleeping
Aashirwad 1
Modern Reception Centre 2
Shivam Guest House 3
Tourist Bungalow 4

from the sixth to ninth centuries. The *stupa* was enlarged six times and the well-known figures of a standing Boddhisattva and the Buddha teaching were found nearby.

The **Dharmarajika Stupa** was built by the Emperor Asoka to contain relics of the Buddha. It was enlarged on several occasions but was destroyed by Jagat Singh, Dewan of the Maharaja of Benares, in 1794, when a green marble casket containing human bones and pearls was found. The British Resident at the maharaja's court published an account of the discovery thereby drawing the attention of scholars to the site.

The **main shrine**, marking the place of the Buddha's meditation, is attributed to Asoka and the later Guptas. To the rear is the 5-m lower portion of a polished sandstone **Asokan Column** (third century BC). The original was about 15 m high and was topped by the lion capital which is now in the Archaeological Museum (see above). The column was one of many erected by Asoka to promulgate the faith and this contained a message to the monks and nuns not to create any schisms and to spread the word. The monastery (fifth century onwards) in the southwest corner is one of four (the others are along the north edge of the enclosure). All are of brick, with cells off a central courtyard that are in ruins.

Other sights

The site is also holy to Jains because **Shyeyanshnath**, the 11th Tirthankar, was born near the Dhamekh *stupa*. The word 'Sarnath' may be derived from his name. A large temple and (on the opposite side of the road) a statue have been built to commemorate him. The modern **Mulagandhakuti Vihara** ⓘ *open 0400-1130, 1330-2000,* (1929-1931) contains frescoes by the Japanese artist Kosetsu Nosu depicting scenes from the Buddha's life. An urn in the ground is supposed to hold a Buddha relic obtained from Taxila (Pakistan). The wall around the **Bodhi tree** (*pipal, Ficus religiosa*) is thick with prayer flags. The tree, planted in 1931, is a sapling of the one in Sri Lanka that was grown from a cutting taken there circa 236 BC by Mahinda's sister Princess Sanghamitta. Past the Mulagandhakuti temple is the **deer park/zoo** ⓘ *open 0800-dusk, Rs 20,* where you can see birds, deer and crocodiles.

The colourful and peaceful **Burmese monastery** is worth the detour from the road. The **Chinese monastery** has a map showing Hiuen Tsang's route to India during AD 629-644, as well as old photos on display. Tibetan, Japanese, Cambodian, Korean and Thai monasteries have also been built around the old complex. The 24-m-high **standing statue** of Lord Buddha, next to the Thai monastery, was completed in March 2011.

Chaukhandi, 500 m south, has a fifth-century *stupa*. On top of this is an octagonal brick tower built by Akbar in 1588 to commemorate the visit his father Humayun made to the site. The inscription above the doorway reads "As Humayun, king of the Seven Climes, now residing in paradise, deigned to come and sit here one day, thereby increasing the splendour of the sun, so Akbar, his son and humble servant, resolved to build on this spot a lofty tower reaching to the blue sky".

Jaunpur → *For listings, see pages 184-191.* *Colour map 3, B4. Population: 4.47 million.*

Jaunpur, 58 km from Varanasi, is a uniquely important centre of 14th- and 15th-century regional Islamic architecture. Once the short-lived capital of the Sharqi Dynasty, today only the ruins of some magnificent mosques and its famous Akbari Bridge distinguish it from hundreds of other dusty and congested Uttar Pradesh towns. The buildings that remain remind us of its brief period as one of India's main centres of political, architectural and artistic development and so is well worth a visit if you can spare the time.

History

Located at a strategic crossing point of the Gomti River, Jaunpur was established by Feroz Shah Tughluq in 1360 as part of his drive to the East. Earlier Hindu and Jain structures were destroyed to provide material for the mosques with which the Sharqi Dynasty rapidly embellished their capital. The Sharqi kings (named 'Kings of the East' by Feroz Shah) established effective independence from the Tughluqs who had been crushed in Timur's sack of Delhi in 1398. They maintained it until 1479, when Husain Shah, the last Sharqi king, was violently deposed by Ibrahim Lodi. Although all the secular buildings, including palaces and courts, were razed to the ground, Ibrahim Lodi spared at least some of the mosques. Some of the city's destruction visible today can be put down to much later events - floods in 1773 and 1871 and an earthquake in 1934. According to Rushbrook Williams this last catastrophe destroyed seven of the 15 arches in the great 200-m-long Akbari Bridge, designed by the Afghan architect Afzal Ali and built between 1564-1568. The stone lion above an elephant at the end of the bridge marks the point from which distances from the city were measured.

Sights

The **bridge** emphasized Jaunpur's role as the centre of a pre-Mughal trading network. In the 17th century the Gomti allowed ships up to 18 tonnes to navigate over 200 km upstream. Under the great king Shams-ud-din-Ibrahim (1402-1436) Jaunpur became a centre of the arts and university education. Today, however, it is the remains of the fort and the mosques which are most worth visiting.

The **Old Shahi Fort** ⓘ *Rs 100*, just north of the Akbari Bridge, is an irregular grassy quadrangle enclosed by ruined stone walls. It shelters the oldest **mosque** in Jaunpur (1377), a narrow arcade (40 m by 7 m) supported by carved pillars, named after its builder, Ibrahim Naib Barbak, Feroz Shah Tughluq's brother. In the mid-19th century Fergusson described some distinctive yellow and blue enamelled bricks on the fine 15-m-high stone gateway, and an inscribed monolith (1766) at the entrance, still visible today. Of particular interest is the almost perfect model of a **hammam** (Turkish bath) which you can wander around.

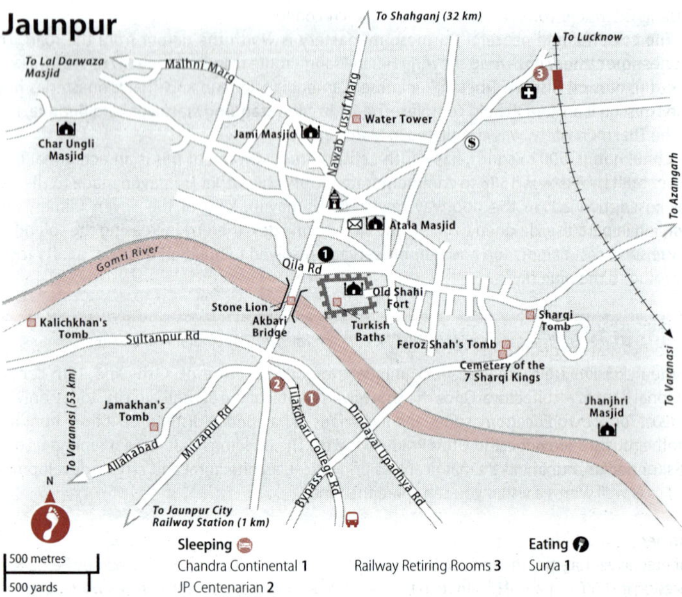

Perhaps the most striking of the surviving mosques, the **Atala**, stands less than 400 m north of the fort. Built in 1408 on the site of the Hindu Atala Devi temple, it marks the triumphant beginning of Shams-ud-din-Ibrahim's reign and introduces unique features of Jaunpuri style. An arched gateway or 'pylon' fronts the sanctuary on the west side of the 50-m-sq court; the remaining three sides are spacious cloisters, two-storeyed and five aisles deep. The pylon has sloping sides, as in other Tughluq building, and its central arch is over 22 m high – along with the arch of the great Jami Masjid nearby, the highest in India. Other features borrowed from the Tughluq style are a recessed arch with its ornamented fringe, and tapering turrets on the west wall. Although artisans were brought in from Delhi, Jaunpur builders soon articulated their Tughluq traditions in a highly distinctive way. Note the beautiful sanctuary interior with its decorated nave and transepts, and the perforated stone screens. At the far end, the transepts are two-storeyed, with the upper section screened off for the zenana.

The same weakness applies to the 'most ambitious' of Jaunpur's mosques: the **Jami Masjid**, about 1 km north of the fort. Begun by Shah Ibrahim in 1438 it was completed by Husain Shah, the last Sharqi king, in 1470. Raised about 6 m on an artificial platform, the worshipper is forced to climb a steep flight of steps to enter the 60-m-sq courtyard. Built on an even grander scale than the Atala Mosque, the 25-m-high central pylon dominates the sanctuary. Note the unsupported transept halls which create a remarkable clear covered open space. Despite the lack of pillars they have survived earthquakes as well as normal ageing. Allow three hours on foot for the main sights.

Allahabad

→ *For listings see pages 184-191. Colour map 3, B3.* *Population 5.96 million.*

The narrow spit of land at the confluence of the Ganga and Yamuna rivers, normally an almost deserted river beach of fine sand, becomes home for two weeks once every 12 years to the **Kumbh Mela**, when more than 70 million pilgrims converge to bathe in the holy waters. Allahabad has grown around this spot and is today a rapidly expanding commercial and administrative city. It is particularly sacred for Hindus because it is at the confluence of three rivers, the Ganga, Yamuna and the mythological underground Saraswati. For the Muslims and the British too, this became a strategically vital centre; they have left their imprint on the landmarks of the city, making it an interesting city to explore, particularly the Civil Lines area to the north.

Ins and outs

Getting there Bamrauli airport is 18 km west of town. The Civil Lines (MG Marg) Bus Stand is used by buses arriving from the north and west, while Zero Road Bus Stand, halfway between the Junction and City railway stations, serves local and southern routes, including Khajuraho. Just south of the Civil Lines, Allahabad Junction Station is the main stop for Delhi and Kolkata trains. There are also direct trains from Mumbai and key cities of South India.

Getting around Many of the city's hotels are in Civil Lines, within easy reach of the Junction station (rear exit) and the bus stands. Although this centre is quite compact you need an auto-rickshaw to get to some of the main sights, including the Fort and the Sangam. Taxis and cycle-rickshaws are also easily available. » *See Transport, page 191.*

Tourist information Ilawart Tourist Bungalow ⓘ *35 MG Marg, T0532-2440 8873, Mon-Sat 1000-1700 (closed 2nd Sat in month); also at the railway station, daily 0800-1800*, has competent staff and can provide city maps and numerous leaflets. Car hire can be arranged here (Rs 6.5 per km, minimum 200 km).

History

Ancient sites here point to Allahabad's early history. Draupadi Ghat has revealed signs of extensive habitation and quantities of pottery, Northern Black Polished Ware, dated between 1100 and 800 BC. Remains of the the **Kushans** were found on the Bharadwaj Ashram site. The Muslims first conquered it in 1194 and renamed it Allahabad in 1584. It later became the headquarters of the British government of the Northwest Provinces and Oudh, and here the transfer of government from the East India Company to the crown was announced by Lord Canning in 1858.

Sights

Prayag (The confluence) The purifying power of a sacred river is strongest at a confluence. In addition, the mythical underground **Sarasvati River** is also said to surface here. Bathing here is auspicious at all times of the year, more so at **Magh Mela** which occurs every year for 15 days (January/February) and longer at the **Kumbh Mela** when pilgrims bathe at *prayag* to wash away a lifetime's sins. In legend, Hindu gods and demons vied for the *kumbha* (pot) that held the *amrit* (nectar of immortality). During the 12-day fight for possession, Vishnu spilt four drops of *amrit* which fell to earth, making four sacred places: Allahabad, Haridwar (Uttarakhand), Ujjain (MP) and Nasik (Maharashtra). Holiest of all is Allahabad, the site of the **Maha** (great) **Kumbh Mela**. This festival moves every three years returning to Allahabad every 12th year (next in Allahabad in 2013). There are still rows of tents at the *prayag*, which give a good indication of the sheer size of

Allahabad

Sleeping
Allahabad Regency **1**
Grand Continental **2**
Ilawart Tourist Bungalow & Tourist Office **3**
JK Palace **4**
Kanha Shyam **5**
Milan Palace **6**
NC Continental **7**
Prayag **8**
Sun City **10**
Yatrik **11**

Eating
El Chico **2**

the Kumbh Mela, when the area becomes a canvas city, home to over a million people. Boats leave from nearby ghats, the nearest being the one by the fort.

Mughal Period Allahabad has few monuments pre-dating the Muslim period. The **fort**, begun in 1583, was the largest of Akbar's forts. It has three massive gateways and 7-m-high walls, seen to advantage from across the river. The Marathas held it from 1739 to 1750, then the Pathans, and finally the British from 1801. Most of the fort is closed to visitors, including the third-century BC Asoka pillar, moved there from Kaushambi under Akbar's orders. Under the fort's east wall is the **Undying Banyan Tree** (*Akshaivata*), an underground temple from which pilgrims threw themselves to achieve salvation in death. To see, ask for a permit at the tourist office.

Khusrau Bagh This typical Mughal garden enclosure makes a peaceful retreat from the city, and houses the handsome tomb of Prince Khusrau. After staging an unsuccessful rebellion against his father Jahangir in 1607, Khusrau spent the next year in chains. When freed, he encouraged a plot to assassinate his father but was discovered. Partially blinded and kept a captive, he was murdered in 1615 by his own brother, who became the Emperor Shah Jahan (ruled 1627-1658). Of the three impressive mausoleums, Khusrau's is the furthest east with decorative plasterwork, stone lattice windows and his burial chamber underground. The central tomb is thought to be his sister's and is beautifully painted inside. Furthest west is the tomb of his Rajput mother, whose cenotaph of white marble is located at the top of the building; she committed suicide in 1603 by over-dosing on opium. On arrival someone will appear with the keys to the mausoleums, and expect a bit of baksheesh. The southern gate to the gardens remains impressively intact, the large wood door covered with horseshoes.

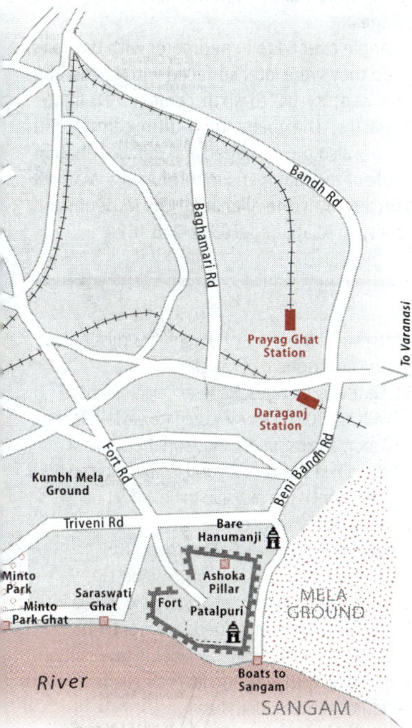

Hot Stuff **3**
Jade Garden at Tepso Hotel **4**

Buildings from the British Period Canning Town, opposite Junction Railway Station, was laid out on a grid in the 1860s. Within it are the Old High Court and Public Offices, classical-style buildings from the late 19th century including the Gothic-style **All Saint's Cathedral**. At the east end of the Civil Lines is Alfred Park (now Chandra Sekhar Azad Park), north of which stands **Muir College**, a fine example of 'Indo-Saracenic' architecture. It was later established as the University of Allahabad. West of this is the extraordinary **Mayo Hall** with **St Joseph's Roman Catholic Cathedral** (1879) to its south. **Holy Trinity Church** (early 19th century) on J Nehru Marg, contains memorials from the Gwalior Campaign (1843) and the 'Uprising' (1857).

Allahabad Museum ⓘ *Chandra Sekhar Azad Park, Kamla Nehru Rd, T0532-260 1200, closed Mon and 2nd Sun of month, 1000-1700, foreigners Rs 100, Indians Rs 5, 18 galleries*, contains a wide range of stone sculptures (second century BC from Bharhut and Kaushambi; first century AD Kushana from Mathura; fourth to sixth century Gupta and 11th-century carvings from Khajuraho). It also has a fine collection of Rajasthani miniatures, terracotta figurines, coins and paintings by Nicholas Roerich. **Anand Bhavan** ⓘ *T0532-246 7071, Tue-Sun 1000-1700, Rs 50*, the former Nehru family home, contains many interesting items. These relate to: Motilal Nehru (1861-1931), active in the Independence Movement; Jawaharlal Nehru (1889-1964), Independent India's first prime minister; Indira Gandhi (1917-1984; prime minister 1966-1977, 1980-1984); and her sons Sanjay Gandhi who died 1980 and Rajiv Gandhi (prime minister 1984-1989) who was assassinated in 1991. The **garden** ⓘ *free*, is pleasant to relax in. Next to it stands **Swaraj Bhawan** ⓘ *Tue-Sun 1000-1700, Rs 50*, where Indira Gandhi was born; it is interesting to wander through.

Kaushambi → *Colour map 3, B3.*

Kaushambi is 60 km southwest of Allahabad. According to the epics, Kausam was founded by a descendant of the *Pandavas* who left Hastinapur when it was destroyed by floods from the Ganga. It is one of the earliest historical cities of the region. According to Hiuen Tsang the Buddha preached here and two *viharas* (monasteries) were built to commemorate the event. The enormous ruins are spread through several villages.

The ramparts of a fort form an approximate rectangle over 6 km in perimeter with bastions that tower up to nearly 23 m. Originally made of mud they were later surfaced with bricks. The town was occupied continuously from the eighth century BC to sixth century AD. In the southwest corner are possibly the remains of a palace. The main *stupa* (fifth century BC) measured 25 m in diameter and 25 m in height. There is also the damaged and defaced shaft of a sandstone column, probably erected during the rule of the Mauryan Emperor Asoka. Many of the coins and terracottas discovered here are now on display in the Allahabad City Museum and Ancient History Department Museum at the University of Allahabad, T0532-246 1694.

Varanasi and around listings

For Sleeping and Eating price codes and other relevant information, see Essentials pages 38-42.

Sleeping

Varanasi *p170, maps p171 and p175*

Off-season discounts are available in Jun and Jul. Be prepared for power cuts and carry a torch at night. Some rickshaw drivers insist on taking you to hotels where they get a commission; check whether your hotel arranges pick-up from the station to avoid this hassle. Hotels on the riverfront can be difficult to locate, particularly at night when walking along the minor ghats is not advisable. Auto- and cycle-rickshaws cannot go down the narrow lanes of the old city, which are a confusing maze on first arrival. Look for hotel signs (with arrows) painted on walls to find your way, or ask shopkeepers. Most **E** hotels have rooms with TV and attached baths. Rooms with river view are worth the extra. Staying in the Cantonment area can be more comfortable and better value for money but it means missing out on the atmosphere of the city.

LL Gateway Ganges, Nadesar Palace Ground, T0542-250 3001-19, www.thegatewayhotels.com. 130 rooms (plus suites), those on the 3rd floor have walk-in showers, 2 good restaurants serve alcohol, pool is the nicest in town, busy but formal efficient service.

L Radisson, The Mall, Cantonment, T0542-250 1566, www.radisson.com/varanasi.in. The grandest rooms in town, large with quality furnishings, wide white beds, sofas and good bathrooms. Good health facilities, disappointing pool (small with few loungers), excellent restaurant and modern bar.

L-AL Clarks Varanasi, The Mall, T0542-250 1011-20, www.clarkshotels.com. In the quieter Cantonment area, not as plush as other high-end options, with rooms that feel a bit dated, but the facilities are good and it has some character. The pool itself is uninviting but the surroundings of established trees and plants is pleasing (non-residents, Rs 300 includes food), restaurant and nice bar. Discounts available (10%).

AL Palace on Ganges, B-1/158 Assi Ghat, T0542-231 5050, www.palaceonganges.com. Set in a converted former palace, each room is decorated in the style of a different Indian state. Restaurant with live Indian classical music plus a small rooftop dining area. The most luxurious hotel on the banks of the Ganga, but some rooms are faded.

A Ganges View, Assi Ghat, T0542-231 3218, www.hotelgangesview.com. Old patrician home converted into a welcoming guesthouse with a tastefully decorated range of small rooms, more expensive on the upper level with the better views, very pleasant atmosphere, interesting clientele, lovely riverside verandas, beautiful artwork adorns the public spaces, vegetarian restaurant (guests only), Wi-Fi Rs 25 per hr. Deservedly popular so book ahead.

A-B Rashmi Guest House, Manmandir Ghat, T0542-240 2778, www.palaceonriver.com. This modern tower has an excellent loation close to Main Ghat, rooms are clean and modern, a good place for families. The rooftop restaurant is reliable and hygienic. A/c, hot water, TV, advisable to book in advance.

A-B Shiva Ganges View, Mansarovar Ghat, T0542-245 0063, www.varanasiguesthouse.com. In a British-built old family house, 8 large spotless rooms have high ceilings, multiple windows, mosquito nets and coolers – but strange furniture and clashing decor. Great views from the front upstairs rooms, which share a balcony and have a/c; lower rooms have air-coolers and are cheaper. Chatty owner.

C-F Alka, Mir Ghat, T0542-240 1681, www.hotelalkavns.com. Wide variety of clean rooms in a modern building, though some are in need of a lick of paint. Expect towels, a/c and TV in the more expensive rooms, cheaper end share bathrooms. The prime riverside location means it is often full, book ahead. Handy access down to the ghats from the courtyard.

D-F Ganpati, next to **Alka** on Mir Ghat, T0542-239 0059, www.ganpatiguesthouse.com. Atmospheric old building, rooms range from cubby holes to spacious, private or shared baths, no a/c. Great views from rooftop, very good restaurant, but reports of unpleasant staff.

D-F Tourist Bungalow (UP Tourism), off Parade Kothi, opposite railway station, T0542-220 8545, www.up-tourism.com. A/c, air-cooled or fan (cheap at Rs 350 per double) rooms and dorm (Rs 150) in barrack-style 2-storey building, restaurant, bar, shady veranda, pleasant garden, simple, clean and efficient, popular – definitely wise to phone ahead. Can arrange cars for the day (minimum Rs 1100 for 200 km).

D-G Ganga Fuji Home, Shakarkand Gali, near Golden Temple, T0542-239 7333, www.gangafujihomevaranasi.com. An excellent choice with a wide range of price categories, from very cheap with shared bath up to comfortable deluxe rooms with a/c and TV. Free Wi-Fi, hot water, decent pillows and mattresses, competent management, **Nirmala** restaurant on rooftop (see Eating). A new 3-star building next door will be completed in 2012, with swimming pool and elevator. They can pick up from the train station – call on arrival.

E Sun Shiv, D 54/16-D Ravi Niketan, Jaddumandi Rd (off Aurangabad Rd), T0542-241 0468, hotelsunshiv@rediffmail.com. 16 modest but charming rooms with balconies in unusual, art deco-inspired 1960s family house, room service, quiet, no commission to rickshaws. Highly engaging, multi-lingual owner.

E-F Chaitanya Guest House, B1/158-A, Assi Ghat, T0542-231 3686, knpsahi@yahoo.com. A cosy family place with only 4 rooms, attached bathrooms, in an old building with moulded ceilings, coloured glass windows and tiny terrace at the front. Sadly views are over a car park rather than the Ganga. Rooms with a/c cost significantly more, or air coolers provided in summer.

E-F Monu Guest House, Kalika Lane, near Golden Temple, T0542-240 0908, T(0)9335-668877, www.monuguesthouse.com. Sweet, atmospheric and a bargain, 5 rooms, cheap singles with outside bath, doubles with bathrooms of a decent size, hot water, free Wi-Fi, various members of the family give music, language and cookery lessons. Rooms soon to be remodelled, and hopefully will not lose their character.

E-F Sahi River View Guest House, Assi Ghat, T0542-236 6730, sahi_rvgh@sify.com. 12 rooms of all standards, great views from balcony and rooftop, food from spotless kitchen, free local and received calls, owner eager to please, no commission given to touts.

F Baba Guest House, D20/15 Munshi Ghat, T0542-245 5452, babaguesthouse@yahoo.com. Basic, freshly painted rooms, some with bath, dorm, huge Korean menu, food served in downstairs café when it's too hot to use rooftop restaurant.

F Golden Lodge, Kalika Lane, near Golden Temple, T0542-239 8788, www.goldenlodge.canalblog.com. Small clean rooms have character, 3 on roof are the best, common or private bath, some doubles with TV and a/c, triples available, 24-hr hot water, enthusiastic proprietor, a/c restaurant (**Fagin's**), free use of washing machine, free Wi-Fi.

F Kumiko, riverside near Dasasvamedha Ghat, T0542-309 1356, kumiko_house@hotmail.com. Rooms and dorm, breakfast and dinner, Japanese spoken, friendly and quirky owners. Very welcoming. Recommended.

F River View, Brahma Ghat, T(0)9415-697507, hotel_riverview@hotmail.com. 9 rooms (more underway) in peaceful, clean and friendly hotel, away from tourist scene but still ghat-side, some with bath, TV, air cooler, great views (watch dawn from front rooms), cute breezy restaurant, discounts on longer stay. Ask to be picked up from GPO.

F Shiva Kashi Guesthouse, Chausatti Ghat, T(0)9235-512294, shivakashiguesthousevaranasi@gmail.com. Very respectable rooms, quite modern, some with balcony, not on the river but very close, free Wi-Fi, peaceful and comfortable. Good choice.

F-G Shiva Guest House, D20/14 Munshi Ghat, T0542-245 2108, shiva_guest_house@hotmail.com. 17 simple, clean rooms in an old building, some with tiny private bathrooms, hot water, great views from the rooftop, family-run, friendly, popular with Japanese and Korean backpackers. Recommended.

F-G Suraj Guest House, Lalita Ghat near Nepali Temple, T0542-239 8560. Tucked away behind a tiny temple, quaint simple rooms owned by eccentric family, extremely cheap, nice vibe.

F-G Yogi Lodge, D8/29 Kalika Gali, near Golden Temple, T0542-240 4224, yogilodge@yahoo.com. Simple rooms, shared bath, dorm (Rs 80), meals on roof terrace or in pleasant courtyard, open kitchen, internet, friendly staff, recommended.

G Railway Retiring Rooms, Varanasi Junction. Some a/c rooms and dorm.

G Shiva Ganga Lodge, Niranjani Ghat, T0542-227 7755. Super little budget place, 10 rooms with common bath around a sweet courtyard, fabulous views from a nearby terrace, friendly owner. They have rooms with private bath in a hotel nearby (same name) but it lacks the atmosphere.

Sarnath *p177, map p178*

As Varanasi is only 10 km away, most people visit Sarnath for the day. Should you wish to overnight there are several options, and the Chinese monastery has plenty of beds.

D-E Tourist Bungalow (UP Tourism), T0542-259 5965, www.up-tourism.com. Old but clean rooms, some with a/c, are rather overpriced, dorm (Rs 175, awful bathrooms), antique Indian restaurant.

E Modern Reception Centre, T(0)9580-574420. Clean rooms with attached bath and TV, even those without a/c are cool. Nothing special, but new furniture and fittings that haven't had time to deteriorate yet. Restaurant.

E Shivam Guest House, opp Chinese Temple, T0542-259 5450, shivamguesthouse.pandey38@gmail.com. Smart new place, clean and tiled, TV, pay more for larger rooms with balconies. Good choice.

There are also several paying guesthouses on the road south of the Chinese temple, of which **F Aashirwad**, T0542-259 5475, is a fair bet with clean rooms. Not much Eng spoken.

Jaunpur *p179, map p180*

E-G Hotel JP Centenarian, Olandganj, T05452-268056. Cleanish rooms in central location, helpful staff, singles Rs 250, doubles Rs 300 or with a/c 700.

G Railway Retiring Rooms, cheap but bearable rooms.

Allahabad *p181, map p182*

AL-A Grand Continental, Sardar Patel Marg, Civil Lines, T0532-260 0631-5, www.birhotel.com. Modern but fussy rooms (carpets and patterned curtains) in smart hotel in central location, attractive restaurant and bar, swimming pool, perhaps a little overpriced.

A Allahabad Regency, 16 Tashkent Marg, Civil Lines, T0532-240 7835, www.hotelallahabad

regency.com. A red-and-white heritage bungalow with arched portico dating from 1866, modernized rooms capture a period atmosphere with cream walls and dark furniture, probably worth paying the extra for the pleasing duplexes, excellent shower rooms. Delightful manicured gardens, wood-panelled reception hall, salubrious bar (beer Rs 170). The pool was under renovation at the time of research.

A Kanha Shyam, Civil Lines, T0532-256 0123, www.hotelkanhashyam.com. 85 comfortable rooms, pool, 2 huge restaurants, one on the rooftop next to the cosy bar.

A Milan Palace, 4/2 Strachy Rd, Civil Lines, T0532-242 1505, www.hotelmilanpalace.com. Very modern, lively hotel in good location, spotless rooms, contemporary-styled restaurant and bar, professional staff. Recommended.

A-B Yatrik, 33 Sardar Patel Marg, Civil Lines, T0532-226 0921-6, www.hotelyatrik.com. The stark modernist facade hides a lovely back garden with sizable pool (closed in winter), 38 a/c rooms are smart and homely, if not fashionably decorated; deluxe ones are fresher and larger than standard doubles, but all have good shower rooms. Public areas are pleasant with airy terraces, good service, restaurant but no bar. Well-priced for what you get.

C-D Ilawart Tourist Bungalow (UP Tourism), 35 MG Marg, T0532-240 7440, rahiilawart@up-tourism.com. Rooms are clean and of a good size, a/c with bath and hot water, but standard are very costly for shabby furnishings and dirty corridors. 8-bed dorm Rs 125. Restaurant, bar, pleasant garden but can be noisy, helpful staff. Next to main bus station, which can be handy.

C-E JK Palace, Tashkant Marg, Civil Lines, T0532-226 0615, www.hoteljkpalace.com. Eager staff, good location, clean rooms with TV, Indian toilets, nothing special but an OK mid-range choice.

D Sun City, 19/21 Leader Rd, T0532-240 5130. Fairly modern hotel, 19 clean and comfortable rooms with a/c, helpful staff, on a busy road but recommended. Close to the station.

E-F NC Continental, Katju Rd, T0532-265 2058. One of better options close to the station, 70 reasonably well-maintained rooms, staff wary of lone female travellers.

E-G Prayag, 73 Noorullah Rd (opposite railway station), T0532-265 6416, akashgupta25@gmail.com. Vast range of rooms, from bargain-basic with shared bath (clean sheets on request) to those with a/c, most have TV. Very handy if travelling by train, efficient staff, 24-hr check-out. Pay Rs 50 for air-cooler. A safe bet and well used to foreigners.

F Railway Retiring Rooms and dorm.

Eating

Varanasi *p170, maps p171 and p175*

Restaurants outside hotels tend to be vegetarian and are not allowed to serve alcohol (though a couple do). Dry days are on the 1st and 7th of each month, and on some public holidays. Many tourist-oriented eateries are on **Bengali Tola** (large alley running from Main Ghat to Assi Ghat), and there are some excellent and cheap South Indian places at its southern end.

TT **Poonam**, **Pradeep Hotel**, Jagatganj, T0542-220 4963/220 4994. Good variety of fabulous Indian dishes, served by professional staff in classy surroundings. **Eden** restaurant on the roof is equally good – and has a garden.

TT-T **Brown Bread Bakery**, Tripura Bhairavi (near Golden Temple. Excellent salads and unusually diverse menu (Thai, Italian, etc) in attractive *haveli* setting, with cushions for lounging and live sitar music every evening. Organic ingredients used where possible. The service can be abominable, however, and food comes in long drawn-out stages – never expect to eat all together. Always, packed, nonetheless.

TT-T **Brownie**, Bungalow No 53-1, between TV tower and India Tourism, Canttonment, T0542-251 1500. Open 0730-2230. If you find yourself in the area, head here for good mix of Indian and international menus (attentive to Western tastes), coffee, live music in the evenings, free Wi-Fi. The wicker booths are cosy.

TT-T **Dolphin**, on the rooftop of **Rashmi Guest House** (see Sleeping). Huge menu, plenty of mutton, fish and chicken, food is tasty and covers more continents. The breeze is welcome or there's a/c indoors during summer. Indifferent staff, but beer (Rs 150) ensures it's busy.

TT-T **Lotus Lounge**, Mansarovar Ghat, T(0)9838-567717. Top spot for Ganga views from chilled-out terrace, prices are reasonable for inventive Asian and Western dishes, interesting salads and decent breakfasts. A perfect place if you need to get away from the bustle, plus a clean toilet.

Ankita, Bengali Tola, near Pandey Ghat. The usual tourist menu but the environment is more cheerful than most with a mix of colourful patterns, fairy lights and a mash-up of iconography on the walls.

Aroma, Dasasvamedha Rd, Godoulia, T0542-326 4564. Bland pastel decor and low ceilings but a clean a/c environment off the tourist circuit, best for south Indian meals. Free delivery 0800-2200 on orders over Rs 200.

Bengali Restaurant, Bengali Tola. The lighting is warm in this cosy hideaway, and the tomato kofta and sumptuous *lassis* are memorable.

Chandan, Bengali Tola. Popular for breakfasts (good coffee and real toast), evening meals, and great shakshuka.

Keshari, Teri Neem, Godoulia (off Dasasvamedha Rd), T0542-240 1472. Excellent vegetarian *thalis* (Rs 100-150) plus north and south Indian dishes and some Chinese, "the longest menu in town" but not every item is available, efficient service, generous portions. Recommended.

Ganpati (see Sleeping). Has a rooftop restaurant with sublime river views and downstairs courtyard with Mediterranean feel, both serving quality food. Great place for hanging out.

Megu, Kalika Lane near Golden Temple. This tiny restaurant specializes in Japanese food and is incredibly popular.

Monalisa, Bengali Tola. Western favourites as well as East Asian, always busy, nice atmosphere, opens earlier than most and so is good for breakfast, PCs available.

Nirmala, Ganga Fuji Home (see Sleeping). Hygienic kitchen, food tempered down for Western palate, live classical music every evening at 1930. Recommended for the exceptional city views, ambiance and hospitality, serves beer (Rs 150).

Pizzeria Café Vaatika, Assi Ghat. Wonderful shady plant-filled terrace on the Ganga, friendly staff, Italian and Indian food, excellent coffee. A perfect place to relax.

Shiva Café and German Bakery, Bengali Tola near Naraol Ghat. Open from 0800. Very popular, especially for breakfasts which are excellent (proper porridge). Spartan decor on the ground floor but the 2nd storey is a bit jazzier with low seating and a Nepalese theme. Staff are delightful.

Jaunpur *p179, map p180*

Surya, Qila Rd, for snacks, clean.

Allahabad *p181, map p182*

El Chico, 24 MG Marg. Good quality and choice of Indian and Chinese food (veg and non), with bakery next door, over 40 years of service.

Jade Garden, **Tepso Hotel**, MG Marg, T0532-256 1408. For upmarket Chinese and Indian, recommended.

Hot Stuff, 21C LB Shastri Mg. Smart, fast food, also good ices.

Entertainment

Allahabad *p181, map p182*

Prayag Sangeet Samiti, near Hanuman temple, Civil Lines, presents music and dance programmes in the evenings.

Festivals and events

Varanasi *p170, maps p171 and p175*

Feb **Ganga Water Rally**, organized by UP Tourism, is an international and national kayak get-together from Allahabad to Chunar Fort. A 40-km race from Chunar to Varanasi takes place on the final day. Also **International Yoga Week**.

Late Feb/early Mar 3 days at Sivaratri, **festival of Dhrupad music** attracts performers from near and far, beginners and stars, in a very congenial atmosphere, a wonderful experience, many *naga babas* (naked *sadhus*) set up camp on ghats.

Mar/Apr **Holi** is celebrated with great fervour.

Apr Pilgrims walk around 'Kashi', as laid down in the scriptures. Jain **Mahavir Jayanti**.

Apr/May **Sankat Mochan Music Festival**, Sankat Mochan Mandir. Non-stop temple music, open to all.

May **Ganga Dasara** celebrates the day the waters of the Ganga reached Haridwar.

Jul/Aug Month-long **carnival** with funfair opposite Monkey Temple, monsoon fever makes it particularly crazy.

Oct/Nov **Dasara Ramlila** at Ramnagar. **Ganga Festival** is organized by UP Tourism alongside a 10-day craft fair. **Nagnathaiya** draws up to 50,000 worshippers to Tulsi Ghat, re-enacting the story of Krishna jumping into the Yamuna to overcome Kalija, the King of the Serpents. **Nakkataiya** A fair at Chetganj recalling Rama's brother, Lakshmana, cutting off Ravana's sister's nose when she attempted to force him into a marriage. At Nati Imli, **Bharat Milap**, the meeting of Rama and Bharat after 14 years' separation is celebrated – the Maharaja of Varanasi attends in full regalia on elephant back.

Dec-Feb Music festivals.

Sarnath *p177, map p178*

May On 1st full-moon, **Buddha Jayanti** marks the Buddha's birthday. A fair is held and relics which are not on public display at any other time are taken out in procession.

Allahabad *p181, map p182*

Jan/Feb **Maha Kumbh Mela** every 12 years, next in 2013. Also **International Yoga Week**.

Shopping

Varanasi *p170, maps p171 and p175*

Varanasi is famous for silks including brocades (Temple Bazar, Visvanath Gali), brassware, gold jewellery, sitar making and hand-block printed goods. The main shopping areas are Chowk, Godoulia, Visvanath Gali, Gyanvapi and Thatheri Bazar.

Books

Harmony, B1/158 Assi Ghat. Best selection in town, excellent fiction, coffee-table books and travel guides.

Indica Books, D 40/18 Godoulia, near crossing. Specialist Indological bookshop.

Universal Book Co, D40/60 Godoulia, nearby. Wide range of English-language books.

Handloom and handicrafts

Benares Art Culture, 2/114 Badhaini Assi. Aims to promote local artists, interesting selection of sculpture, paintings and silks at fixed prices.

Bhagwan Stores, in Visvanath Gali and K37/32 Golghar. Recommended.

Brijraman Das, in Visvanath Gali and K37/32 Golghar. Recommended.

Ganga Handlooms, D10/18 Kohli Katra, off Viswanath Gali, near Golden Temple (ask locally). 1100-2000. Large selection of beautiful cotton fabrics, *ikats*, vegetable dyes, good tailors, great patterns (Western).

Activities and tours

Varanasi *p170, maps p171 and p175*

Body and soul

International Yoga Clinic and Meditation Centre, Man Mandir Ghat, T0542-239 7139. Hour-long classes, maximum 3 students.

Panch Mandir, Assi Ghat. Drop-in classes each morning 0600-0930, reasonably priced.

Satya Foundation, B-37/54B Rukma Bhawan, Birdopur, T(0)9336-877455, www.satyafoundation.com. Music, meditation and yoga, highly authentic teachings. Recommended.

Siddhartha Yoga Centre, below Lotus Lounge, Mansarowar Ghat, T(0)9236-830966. 2-hr classes at 0800 and 1530, Rs 300, you can 'drop-in' but better to call ahead as there is only room for 4-5 people.

Yoga Institute, BHU, T0542-230 7208. 1-month courses.

Language courses

'Tourist Hindi' courses are advertised in several hotels and restaurants.

Swimming

Pools at hotels **Radisson**, **Gateway Ganges**, and **Clarks Varanasi**.

Tour operators

Many small travel agents in laneways of Old City, usually charge Rs 50-70 commission on railway tickets.

TCI, Sri Das Foundation, S20/51-5 and S20/52-4, The Mall, T0542-250 0866, www.tcindia.com. Highly recommended.

Tiwari Tours and Travel, Assi Ghat, T0542-236 6727, www.tiwaritravel.com. Good service, bus tickets to high-end tours.

Allahabad *p181, map p182*

Sports centre

Mayo Hall Complex, Stanley Rd. One of the largest training centres in India for table tennis, basketball, badminton and volleyball.

Transport

Varanasi *p170, maps p171 and p175*

Air Transfer from the airport by taxi, a/c Rs 500, non-a/c Rs 400. Some taxis offer free transfer and claim a commission from hotel on arrival. A minibus to the airport runs from Assi Ghat for Rs 200 per person, contact **Tiwari Tours**.

Indian Airlines flies daily to **Delhi** and **Mumbai**; to **Khajuraho** Wed, Fri, Sun; **Kathmandu**, Mon, Tue, Thu, Sat. **Jet Airways**, S20/56D Kennedy Rd, The Mall, T0542-250 6444; airport T0542-262 2544, www.jetairways.com, flies to **Delhi**, **Khajuraho** and **Kathmandu** daily. **Kingfisher**, T1800-

1800 101, and **Spicejet**, T1800-180 3333, both fly to Delhi and Mumbai. **Thai Airways** have 3 flights per week to **Bangkok**, Oct-Mar only, and **Mihin Lanka** have flights to **Colombo**.

Bicycle Enquire at your guesthouse about bicycle hire.

Boat This is the best way to enjoy Varanasi. It is necessary to bargain especially for an early-morning ghats visit; shared boat, Rs 50 per person per hr is the official rate for a boat carrying up to 10 people, but bargaining is possible. Ask around for others to share boat; river crossing about Rs 40 return. A boat ride at dusk is also recommended.

Bus UP Roadways Bus Stand, Sher Shah Suri Marg, is opposite Junction Station, open 24 hrs, T(0)9415-049623. Buses to **Sarnath**, 10 km (Rs 5). To **Allahabad**, every 15 mins from 0330-2300 (3 hrs, Rs 83), better than train; to **Gorakhpur**, hourly from 0400-0030 (7 hrs, Rs 145, see page 145, for information on private bus to Nepal). For **Delhi** go via **Kanpur**, frequent service from 0700 (8 hrs, Rs 172); **Lucknow**, every 30 mins (8 hrs), also an a/c sleeper bus at 2300. **Agra**, at 1230, 1700 and 2000 (14 hrs). **Gaya**: better by rail. Private buses from opposite the railway station go frequently to **Allahabad** and **Jaunpur** (1-1½ hrs, Rs 35).

Rickshaw *Tempos* and auto-rickshaws run on fixed routes; those near hotel gates overcharge (fix the fare before hiring). They are not allowed in the narrow streets of the old city but will go to **Godoulia** in the centre near Dasasvamedha Ghat, Rs 70 from station, or Rs 80 to **Assi Ghat**. There is a pre-paid taxi and rickshaw booth near the station reservations office.

Taxi Private taxis from agents and hotels. **Uttar Pradesh Tourist Bungalow**, Parade Kothi, T0542-220 6638, is a good place to start.

Train The official Reservations office is outside the station on the left as you exit. Be extra careful with your possessions on trains bound for Varanasi as theft is common.

Most trains stop at the **Junction** (or **Cantonment**) **Station**, T0542-234 8031 or T131, with 24-hr left luggage; to reach a Cantonment hotel on foot, use the back exit. **Mughal Sarai** station, T0542-225 5703, has the **Delhi/Kolkata** *Rajdhani Exp* (though some go via Patna); see below. Get your tickets (preferably a day in advance) from the **Foreign Tourist Assistance** inside the main hall which is very helpful and efficient, passport required (0800-2200, Sun 0800-1400). When it is closed use the computerized railway reservations (0800-1400, 1430-2000). **Agra Fort**: *Marudhar Exp 14853/14863/14865*, 1720/1815/1745, 12½/11¾/12¼ hrs (book ahead); or go to Tundla from Mughal Sarai Station (see below). **Allahabad**: *Vibhuti Exp 12333*, 0955, 2½ hrs. *Mahanagari Exp 11094*, 1130, 3¼ hrs; *Kamayani Exp 11072*, 1550, 3½ hrs. **Chennai**: *Ganga-Kaveri Exp 12670*, 0125, Tue, Thu, 37 hrs, reserve early. **Dehra Dun**: *Doon Exp 13009*, 1036, 20½ hrs, book in advance (no tourist quota); *Janta Exp 14265*, 0830, 22¼ hrs. **Gaya**: *Dehra Dun Exp 13010*, 1625, 5 hrs. **Gorakhpur** (for Nepal): *Krishak Exp 15003*, 0035, 6¼ hrs; *Manduadih Gorakhpur Exp 15104*, 0545, 5½ hrs; **Jaunpur**: *Sutlej Doon Exp 13307*, 0530 1¼ hr; *Farakka Exp 13483*, 1120, 1¼ hrs. **Kolkata** (**H**): *Amritsar-Howrah Mail 13006*, 1700, 14¼ hrs; *Doon Exp 13010*, 1625, 14¼ hrs. **Lucknow**: *Varuna Exp 14227/24227*, 0455, 5 hrs; *Kashi-Visvanath Exp 14257*, 1345, 7 hrs. **Mahoba** (for **Khajuraho**): *Bundelkhand Exp 11108*, 1710, 10¼ hrs (take onward bus). **Satna** (for **Khajuraho**): *Satna Mahanagari Exp 11094*, 1130, 6¾ hrs (from Satna, bumpy bus next day, 5 hrs). **Mumbai** (**CST**): *Varanasi Lokmanya Tilak Exp 11066*, 2320, Tue, Thu, Sat, 28½ hrs. **New Delhi**: *Shramjeevi Exp 12401*, 2220, 13½ hrs.

Mughal Sarai Station (with retiring rooms and left luggage). Take a connecting train from Varanasi (45 mins), or allow plenty of time as you need to cross the Ganga and there are huge jams. Easiest to take a taxi from Varanasi, although shared autos leave from the railway station. Mughal Sarai has several trains to **Gaya**; a good one is *Purushottam Exp 12802*, 1040, 3 hrs. Also to: **Kolkata** (**H**): *Rajdhani Exp 12302/12306*, 0155, 8-11 hrs; *Kalka Howrah Mail 12312*, 2040, 10¾ hrs. **New Delhi**: *Poorva Exp 12381/12303*, 1805 (13¼ hrs) and 1950 (11½ hrs); *Rjpb Rajdhani Exp 12309*, 2240, 9 hrs. *Rajdhani Exp 12301/12305*, 0100, 9 hrs. **New Jalpaiguri** (for **Darjeeling**): *Mahananda Exp 14084*, 2120, 16¼ hrs; *NE Exp 12506*, 1830, 14 hrs and to **Guwahati**, 22¼ hrs.

Transport to Nepal

See box, page 146, for border crossing.

Payment for Nepalese visa at border in cash only. Try to carry exactly US$30 (other currencies not accepted), as money changers at the border give terrible exchange rates. It is illegal to carry Rs 500 and Rs 1000 notes into Nepal.

To **Kathmandu**, the journey requires an overnight stay near the border plus about 20 hrs on the road so can be tiring. **UP Roadways** buses go via **Gorakhpur** to **Sonauli**, every 1-2 hrs, check at bus stand for timings, 7-9 hrs, Rs 135; from Sonauli, 0600. Private buses (agents near **UP Tourist Bungalow**, around Bengali Tola/Assi Ghat and opposite railway station), often demand inclusive fares for hotel stay; you may prefer to opt for their deluxe buses to the border. The best bet is the well-organized bus service by **Paul Travels**, T0542-220 8137, T(0)9335-852757, near **UP Tourist Bungalow**, buy tickets at the office (or through agents such as Ganga Fuji Home, Shanti Guesthouse, Yogi Lodge), Rs 800; departs Mon, Wed and Sat at 0830 (report at the office at 0700), reaches **Sonauli** 1700, overnight in Paradise Hotel on the Nepali side, next morning depart 0830 for **Kathmandu** (8-9 hrs). Also possible to buy tickets direct to **Chitwan National Park** and **Pokhara** (also Rs 800).

Sarnath *p177, map p178*

Bus/taxi Infrequent bus service from the Roadways bus stand; also included in coach tours. From Varanasi, autos from opposite railway station (Rs 100), *tempo* seat (Rs 10), you might have to change to another *tempo* halfway. Taxis take 30 mins (Rs 800 including wait).

Jaunpur *p179, map p180*

Bus Frequent service along NH56 to/from **Varanasi** and **Lucknow** including *Express* (under 2 hrs). Ask to be dropped at the Akbari Bridge (crossroads north of the bus stand) where you can pick up a cycle rickshaw.
Taxi To **Varanasi**, Rs 850 return.
Train To **Varanasi**: *Sutlej Exp 13308*, 1838, 2 hrs; *Varuna Exp 14228*, 2136, 1¾ hrs.

Allahabad *p181, map p182*

Air **Bamrauli Airport** is 14 km from the city with **Air India** flights to **Delhi** and **Kanpur**.
Bus **UP Roadways** buses leave from the bus station in Civil Lines, and link Allahabad with **Delhi** at 1230 (643 km), **Jaunpur**, **Jhansi**, **Kanpur**, **Lucknow** every 45 mins 0630-2100 (4½ hrs, Rs 274, a/c), and **Varanasi** every 15 mins from 0600-2000 (3½ hrs, Rs 83); Zero Rd, buses to **Rewa**. **Private bus stands** at Ram Bagh and Civil Lines for frequent luxury coaches to **Lucknow** and **Varanasi**.
Train Allahabad is on the major broad-gauge route from Delhi to Kolkata. **Allahabad Junction** is the main station, T0532-260 0179. **Allahabad City**, mostly for Varanasi. **Jhansi**: *Bundelkhand Exp 11108*, 2225, 8¾ hrs. **Lucknow**: *Ganga- Gomti Exp 14215*, 0600, 4 hrs (CC class only); *Nauchandi/Link Exp 14511*, 1740, 5¼ hrs. **Kolkata**: *Kalka-Howrah Mail 12312*, 1730, 14 hrs; *Rajdhani Exp 12302/12306*, 2345, 10¼/13 hrs. **Mumbai** (**CST**): *Mumbai Mail 12321*, 1140, 24 hrs; *Mahanagiri Exp 11094*, 1540, 23 hrs. **New Delhi**: *Prayagraj Exp 12417*, 2130, 9½ hrs; *Poorva Exp 12303/12381*, 2205, 9 hrs. **Patna**: *Magadh Exp 12402*, 0520, 6 hrs; *Udyan Abha Toofan Exp 13008*, 2215, 8 hrs; *Lal Quila Exp 13112*, 1100, 8½ hrs. **Varanasi**: *Gorakhpur Kashi Exp 15017*, 0835, 4½ hrs; *Bundelkhand Exp 11107*, 0710, 3¾ hrs.

Directory

Varanasi *p170, maps p171 and p175*

Banks **State Bank of India** ATM at **Godoulia** (near Indica Books), many in Canttonment area.
Internet Several along Bengali Tola and around Assi Ghat, about Rs 30 per hr.
Hospitals **Heritage Hospital, Lanka** (near BHU main entrance), T0542-236 8888. Private hospital, out-patients 0830-2000. Many hotels, even budget ones, have a doctor on call.
Post **Head Post Office**: Bisheshwarganj (parcel packing outside). Post office in Cantt, Mon-Sat 1000-1800. A man offers to 'help' get a parcel posted for a fee (Rs 100), but you can do this yourself. Also a small post office on Bengali Tola.

Allahabad *p181, map p182*

Banks **Bank of India**, ATMs all over town.
Hospitals **Motilal Nehru Hospital**, Colvin, T0532-265 2141. **Swaroop RaniHospital**, off MG Marg.

Uttarakhand

Contents

Footprint features

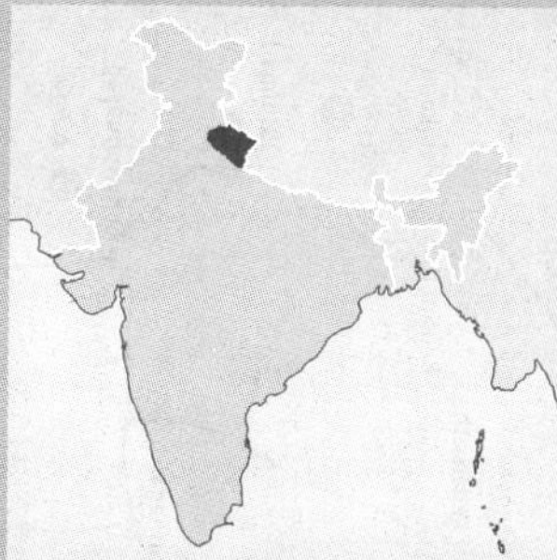

At a glance

Getting around Trains reach the foot of the Himalaya; use buses, share jeeps or car hire on mountain routes.

Time required 1-2 weeks for eastern hill stations and a retreat around Rishikesh; 12 days for Char Dham pilgrimage; 3-4 days for Corbett NP; 7 days for the Kumaon hill stations.

Weather Warm to steamy in the lowlands, cool and fresh to snowy in the mountains.

When not to go During the rambunctious Siva festival in Aug, when towns by the Ganges become crowded beyond belief.

★**Don't miss …**

1 Mussoorie and Landour, page 200.
2 Haridwar at sunset, page 206.
3 Rishikesh, page 208.
4 Trekking in the Valley of Flowers, page 221.
5 Walk the Curzon Trail, page 231.
6 Follow in Timothy Leary's footsteps at Cranks' Ridge above Almora, page 236.
7 Tiger-spotting Corbett National Park, page 242.

With Himachal Pradesh to the west, Tibet to the north and Nepal to the east, it's small wonder that the Himalayan hill-state of Uttarakhand holds some of India's most magnificent mountain scenery.

Garhwal and Kumaon's thickly wooded hillsides break softly towards a stunning range of snow-capped Himalayan peaks, including India's second highest mountain Nanda Devi, forming one of the world's most awesome natural borders. Were it not for travel restrictions imposed following hostilities between India and China in the 1960s, trekking in this remote and still relatively untouched region might now be as popular as in Nepal, whose natural beauty and variety of routes it easily matches.

Many of Uttarakhand's most stunning treks are in fact age-old pilgrimage routes (or 'yatra' routes). As the source of the Ganga and Yamuna rivers, the state looms large in India's mythological history – it is the setting for much of the *Mahabharata* – and contains some of India's holiest shrines.

On the banks of the Ganga, the holy cities of Haridwar and Rishikesh have served as spiritual magnets for millennia, and receive a continuous stream of pilgrims from all over India seeking to fill plastic bottles with precious holy water, and foreign visitors who come to study yoga or the *vedas*.

Further east, Almora and Nainital have long served as charming, cool holiday resorts in the hills, while the great tiger reserve of Corbett National Park stands as a beacon of successful wildlife management. With India's whitewater rafting capital just north of Rishikesh at Shivpuri, and the development of skiing facilities at Auli, Uttarakhand is now establishing a reputation for adventure sports, too.

Background → *Population: 8.5 million. Area: 53,480 sq km.*

The land

Geography The extraordinarily contorted geology of the Garhwal and Kumaon Himalaya reflects the fierce uplifting and the complex movements that have happened since the great mountain range first started to form. The outer ranges of the Shiwaliks, generally less than 2500 m high, are a jumble of deeply dissected sediments. In places these are separated from the Lesser Himalayan ranges by great longitudinal valleys, or *duns*, such as Dehra Dun. The Lesser Himalayan towns immediately to the north of the Shiwaliks, such as Mussoorie, Almora and Nainital, offer coolness from the overpowering summer heat of the plains. Forming a massive barrier to their north are the permanent snows of **Nanda Devi** (7816 m), **Shivling** (6543 m) and other peaks over 6000 m. The high peaks are surrounded by deep valleys, with some of the world's largest glaciers at their heads. Some meteorologists predict that the Himalaya will be glacier-free within 30 years or so. Although partly attributed to a 10,000-year retreat of the last northern hemisphere Ice Age, the speed of glacial melt has accelerated since the 1970s. The Gangotri Glacier, one of the 'water towers' of the River Ganga, is receding at a rate of 23 m per year, a pattern repeated across all of the great Himalayan ice sheets. The resultant loss of river flow threatens irrigation and drinking water supplies to 500 million people in the Gangetic Basin.

Climate The climate of Uttarakhand is dominated by the monsoon, with over three quarters of the rainfall coming between June and September, but temperature is controlled both by height and by season. In the lower valleys, such as Dehra Dun, summers are hot and sticky and temperatures reach 45°C. Towns on the ridges up to 2000 m, such as Almora and Ranikhet, experience maximum summer temperatures of 34°C, while in winter they experience snow, and temperatures even in the outer valleys fall to as low as 3-4°C. June and September are uncomfortably humid in the foothills, despite lower temperatures. The high peaks are under permanent snow and in the higher hills the air can be very cold. Late April to early June and September to October tend to be the best times for trekking.

Culture

Ethnically, the people of the plains are largely of Indo-Aryan origin, with stronger Mongoloid influences closer to the border with Tibet. Hindi and Urdu are widely spoken, but there are numerous local dialects such as Garhwali and Kumaoni (hill) dialects.

History

The 14th century ruler Ajai Pal (1358-1370) consolidated a number of petty principalities that made up Garhwal (Land of the Forts) to become the region's raja. The area was a popular plundering ground for Sikh brigands. The **Gurkhas** overran it in 1803, taking women and children into slavery and conscripting men into their army. Gurkha encroachments on the land around Gorakhpur prompted the British to expel them from Garhwal and Kumaon in 1814. They took the eastern part of Garhwal as British Garhwal and returned the western part, Tehri Garhwal, to the deposed raja. The hillsmen here have long resented their political domination by the plainsmen of Uttar Pradesh, so the creation of Uttarakhand (Sanskrit for 'northern section', but initially called Uttaranchal) on 9 November 2000 was the fulfilment of a long cherished dream. In the first state elections, held in February 2002, the Congress swept the BJP from power, and the veteran Congress leader ND Tiwari became chief minister. The question of the capital is still contentious. Dehra Dun has initially been given the status of 'interim capital', but there are still demands that it should be transferred to Gairsain, a hill town in the heart of the new state.

In the State Assembly elections of February 2007 the BJP took 34 of the state's 70 seats against the Congress party's 21 and the BSP's eight, and the BJP formed a government under the Chief Minister B C Khanduri. Uttarakhand has five members of the Lok Sabha (India's lower house), all of which went to the Congress in the 2009 elections.

Economy

Scattered farming villages among picturesque terraces show the skill with which Uttarakhand's mountain people have adapted to their environment. Agriculture is still by far the most important economic activity for people in the hills, often carried out with considerable sophistication, both of engineering and of crop selection. On many of the hillsides terracing is wonderfully intricate, and a wide variety of crops are grown: paddy, wheat, barley, hemp and lentils on the low-lying irrigated terraces; sugar cane, chilli, buckwheat and millet higher up. Market gardening and potato cultivation have spread around all the townships. Rotation of crops is widely practised and intensive use of animal manure helps to fertilize the soil. The terraces themselves, sometimes as high as 6 m, may have as many as 500 flights, and some villages have up to 6000 individual terraces. Given that it takes one man a day to build a wall 1 m high and 2 m long, it is easy to see the vast amount of labour that has gone into their construction, and how much care is lavished on their maintenance. Drought-like conditions in 90% of the state since November 2008 have devastated farmers, whose irrigation entirely depends on rain.

The forests supply vital wealth. Apart from the timber itself, resin is often a valuable export, and woodcarving is a widely practised skill. Horticulture, fruit cultivation and the production of medicinal plants are potentially of great value, though transport remains a huge problem. Today tourism is an increasingly important source of income, thought to bring in over US$50 million a year from domestic and foreign visitors. Development of the new state's massive hydroelectric potential is highly controversial. The Tehri Dam, at over 250 m high the eighth tallest dam in the world, was the focus of intense opposition from environmental campaigners for more than 30 years. The lower tunnels were closed in 2001 and the upper tunnel in October 2005, allowing the first electricity to be generated in 2006. The stored water provides little benefit to the state, being primarily used to enhance irrigation and supply urgent water needs of Delhi and other rapidly growing cities on the plains. In 2009, a 77-year-old retired academic, GD Agrawal, staged a month-long hunger strike in his fight to halt work on the Lohari Nag Pala hydroelectric project, a series of six dams and numerous tunnels, which environmentalists argued would dry up 125 km of the Bhagirathi River, the source stream of the Ganges, between Gangotri and Uttarkashi. The central government has now established a Ganga River Basin Authority to manage the basin's development, and Environment Minister Jairam Ramesh has declared that "India is a civilization of rivers, and it should not become a land of tunnels", yet work proceeds apace on a huge new dam on the Alaknanda, the second of the Ganges' two key tributaries, with plans in place for up to 30 more dams in the Ganga basin, which if completed would see several of the sacred confluences inundated under metres of water.

Eastern hill stations

The quickest cool escape from Delhi's sweltering summer, the old Raj hill stations of Mussoorie and Landour still make a popular getaway, with their crumbling bungalows, pine-scented pathways and grand Himalayan panoramas. The state capital, Dehra Dun, sprawls across the valley below and is home to some of India's most important educational, research and military facilities. ▸▸ *For listings, see pages 202-205.*

Dehra Dun → *For listings see pages 202-205. Colour map 1, B4. Phone code: 0135. Population: 370,000. Altitude: 640 m.*

Dehra Dun (*dera* – camp; *dun* – valley, pronounced 'doon'), lies in a wooded valley in the Shiwalik Hills. In Hindu legend the Dun Valley was part of Siva's stamping ground. Rama and his brother are said to have done penance for killing Ravana, and the five Pandavas stopped here on their way to the mountains. It makes a pleasant and relaxing stop on the way to the hills, and its mild climate has made it a popular retirement town. The cantonment, across the seasonal Bindal Rao River, is spacious and well wooded, while the Mussoorie road is lined with very attractive houses.

There is not much to recommend the town other then a place to stay if you are caught late at night on your way to a hill station. It is busy, with some international chain stores and coffee shops recently opened on the Rajpur road up to Mussoorie. If you happen to be caught in traffic on your way through, keep your eyes open for the very unique miniature suits of armour displayed in the iron shops along the main roads.

Ins and outs

Getting there The railway station, off Haridwar Road to the south of town, has trains from Delhi, Varanasi, Rajasthan and Kolkata. Buses and shared taxis heading for the Mussoorie and the Garhwal hills use the Mussoorie Bus Stand, just outside the station, while those bound for the plains and the Kumaon hills use the new inter-state bus terminal (ISBT, often referred to as the 'New' Delhi Bus Stand) 5 km southwest of the centre. Shared *tempos* and rickshaws (Rs 50-60) can take you into town.

Getting around The City Bus Stand, also used by private buses, is just north of the clock tower in the busy town centre, about 10 minutes on foot from the railway station. Although the town centre is compact it is best to get a taxi or auto-rickshaw for visiting the various sights, which are between 4 km and 8 km away. ▸▸ *See Transport, page 204.*

Tourist information GMVN ⓘ *74/1 Rajpur Rd, T0135-274 7898.* **Uttarakhand Tourism** ⓘ *45 Gandhi Rd, next to Drona Hotel, T0135-265 3217, Mon-Sat 1000-1700.*

History

A third century BC Asoka rock inscription found near Kalsi suggests that this area was ruled by the emperor. During the 17th and 18th centuries Dehra Dun changed hands several times. The Gurkhas overran it on their westward expansion from Kumaon to Kangra, finally ceding it in 1815 to the British, who developed it as a centre of education and research. It is still a major centre for government institutions like the Survey of India and the Royal Indian Military College, and in November 2000 it became the provisional state capital of Uttaranchal (re-named in 2007 as Uttarakhand), but there is still no sign of agreement of an alternative state capital.

Sights

The **Survey of India** (founded 1767), has its headquarters on Rajpur Road, 4 km north of the clock tower. **Robber's Cave** (8 km), **Lakshman Sidh** (12 km), the snows at **Chakrata** (9 km) and sulphur springs at **Shahasradhara** (14 km) are also within easy reach. The springs were threatened by limestone quarrying until the High Court forced the closure of the quarries. Replanting of the deforested hills has been allowing the water table to recover.

In the west of town, off Kaulagarh Road, the **Doon School**, India's first public school, is still one of its most prestigious. Further along, the highly regarded **Forest Research Institute** (1914), an impressive red-brick building which was designed by Lutyens, is surrounded by the fine lawns of the **Botanical Gardens** and forests. It has excellent **museums** ⓘ *Mon-Fri 0900-1730*. The **Tapkesvar Cave Temple** ⓘ *5 km northwest of town, open sunrise to sunset*, is in a pleasant setting with cool sulphur springs for bathing. There is a simple Indian café nearby. Buses stop 500 m from the temple.

Dehra Dun

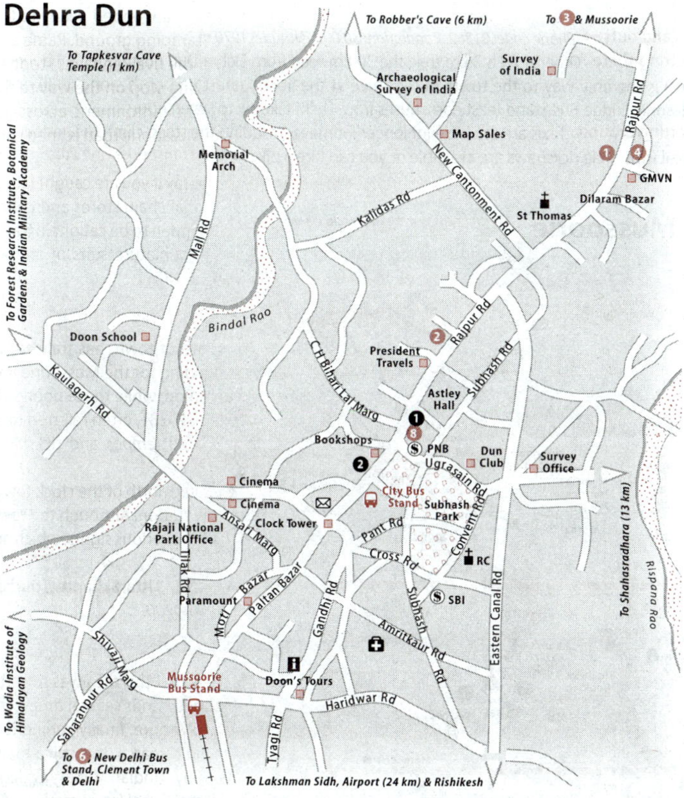

Sleeping
Ajanta Continental **1**
Deepshikha **2**
Great Value Dehradun **4**
President **8**
Shaheen Bagh **3**
Tibetan Colony Private Guest Houses **6**

Eating
Bossa Nova **1**
Daddys **1**
Kumar **2**
Vegetarian **1**

Six kilometres south of town, close to the ISBT, the Tibetan enclave of Clement Town is home to **Mintokling Monastery**, with a striking new 60-m-high *stupa*. The nearby **Dhe Chen Chokhor Kagyupa Monastery** has a similarly tall statue of the Buddha.

Mussoorie and Landour → *For listings see pages 202-205. Colour map 1, B4.*

Mussoorie, named after the Himalayan shrub mansoor, has commanding views over the Doon Valley to the south and towards the High Himalaya to the north. It is spread out over 16 km along a horseshoe-shaped ridge up to which run a series of buttress-like subsidiaries. Being the nearest hill station to Delhi, it is very popular with Indian tourists though no longer as clean as it was once, and it has nothing over other hill stations. Landour, 300 m higher and away from the crowds, by contrast has fresh, pine-scented air.

Ins and outs → *Phone code: 01362. Population: 30,000. Altitude: 1970 m.*

Getting there Other than a 7-km trek, the 30-km road from Dehra Dun (just under 1¾ hours by bus) is the only way to the town. Buses arrive at the library (west end of the long Mall) or the Masonic Lodge Bus Stand (east end). Buses from Delhi take six to seven hours.

Getting around Taxis are available for longer journeys, including the steep climb to Landour. For local trips cycle rickshaws are available or you can hire a bike. ▸▸ *See Transport, page 205.*

Mussoorie

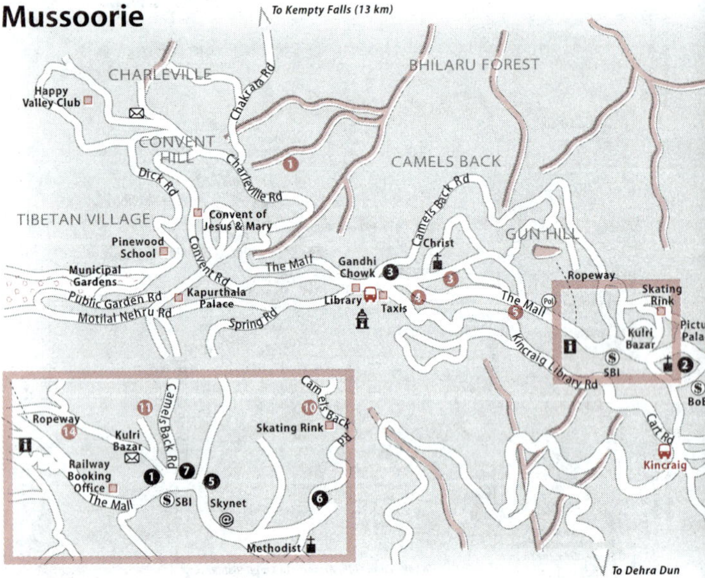

N

400 metres

400 yards

Sleeping
Broadway 10
Carltons Plaisance 1
Connaught Castle 11
Dev Dar Woods 8
Garhwal Terrace 5
Golden Heaven 2
Kasmanda Palace 3
Nabha Palace 6
Padmini Nivas 4
Residency Manor 7
Shiva Continental 9
Valley View 14

Eating
Café Coffee Day 1
Char Dukan 4
City Point 3

Tourist information GMVN ⓘ *Library Bus Stand, T0135-263 1281*. Uttarakhand Tourism ⓘ *The Mall, T0135-263 2863*.

Sights

Captain Young 'discovered' Mussoorie in 1826 and it developed as an escape from the heat of the plains for the British troops. To the east, **Landour**, at 2270 m, has the old barracks area. The first British residence was built here, followed by The Mall, Club, Christ Church (1837) and the library. It's a very pleasant walk up through the woods and away from the crowds of The Mall. There are good views, though the weather can change quickly. 'Char Dukan' is a small junction in the cantonment area with two snack bars/shops and a post office; the road to the right leads to the **International Language School** and the one to the left to **Lal Tibba** – a nice view point (take binoculars). The Woodstock School and the Language School are in a magnificent location, and some of the guesthouses have stunning views. To the west are **Convent Hill, Happy Valley** (where Tibetan refugees have settled; the school may welcome volunteers to teach English), and the pleasant **Municipal Garden**.

Walks

From the tourist office, it is 5 km to **Lal Tibba** and nearby **Childe's Lodge** on the highest hill. **Gun Hill**, where before Independence a midday gun fire enabled residents to set their watches, has a stunning view of snow-capped peaks, best at sunrise. It can be reached in around half an hour on foot or horseback by a bridle path leaving from the Kutchery on The Mall, or by a 400-m **ropeway** ⓘ *0900-1900, Rs 50 return*. However, the mess of souvenir stalls, cafés and photographers later in the day may not appeal to all. The **Camel's Back Road**, from Kulri to the library, is a pleasant 3-km walk.

Excursions from Mussoorie

Kempty Falls, 15 km away on the Chakrata Road, is a rather dispiriting 'beauty spot', with fabulous ribbon-like falls spoiled by mounds of rubbish and a pair of resorts gaudily advertising soft drink brands. A taxi is about Rs 250 with a one-hour stop. Heading to **Dhanolti**, 25 km away, you can go on a further 3 km to find the **Surkhanda Devi Temple** at 3030 m. There are superb views of several high peaks over 6500 m. A taxi is Rs 600 with a two- to three-hour stop. Buses between Mussoorie and Chamba take you within 2 km of the hill top.

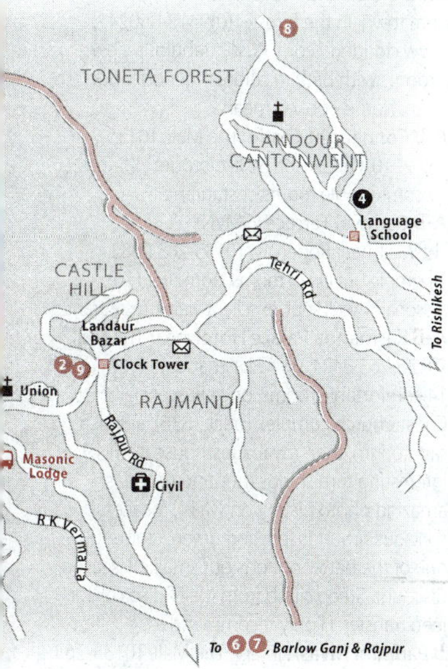

Kalsang-Tibetan **1**
Kwality **5**
Madras Cafi **6**
Prakash **4**
Rice Bowl **7**
Swiss Café **3**
Tavern **2**
Whispering Windows **3**

Eastern hill stations listings

For Sleeping and Eating price codes and other relevant information, see Essentials pages 38-42.

Sleeping

Dehra Dun *p198, map p199*

There are good discounts out of season (Aug-Feb). The cheaper hotels are near the station and the clock tower; the upmarket ones are north, along **Rajpur Rd**.

AL-A Great Value Dehradun (Clarks), 74C Rajpur Rd, 4 km from the railway station, T0135-274 4765, www.greatvaluehotel.com. 53 standard rooms with a restaurant (Indian singing in the evening), and business centre.

AL-A Shaheen Bagh, Upper Dehradun, T0135-210 8199, T(0)9897-046353, www.shaheenbagh.in. Price includes breakfast and dinner. Beautiful guesthouse on a 3-ha property by the river, with lovely interior spaces in grand country-house style, large canopied beds, pretty gardens (370 bird species recorded) with mountain views in the Ton River valley, fruit trees and pool. DVD players are in all the rooms and guests can choose from a 400+ DVD library. Distant from town; a refuge. Service has gone downhill under new ownership but recommended.

A Ajanta Continental, 101 Rajpur Rd, T0135-274 9595, www.ajanta continental.com. 29 clean rooms, good restaurant/bar, pleasant family-run.

A President, 6 Astley Hall, Rajpur Rd, T0135-265 7082, www.hotelpresidentdehradun.com. Has 22 smallish a/c rooms, excellent restaurant, bar, coffee shop, exchange, travel, golf and riding arranged, pleasant service.

D-E Deepshikha, 57/1 Rajpur Rd, T0135-265 9888. 22 Basic rooms (some a/c) that overlook a busy road. Restaurant.

G Private guesthouses, Clement Town (Tibetan Colony), 6 km south of centre near ISBT. Spacious, clean rooms (Rs 250). Quiet and peaceful atmosphere, but somewhat ad hoc; no phone for bookings, so best to show up and ask at the monasteries.

Mussoorie and Landour *p200, map p200*

Some hotels are old-fashioned but full of character. There are also a string of modern **B-C** hotels west of Gandhi Chowk on **The Mall** and **Motilal Nehru Rd**. The Mall is closed to cars and buses. You may have to walk to your hotel; porters are available at the bus stands. Prices are based on high-season tariffs, which are often quite ridiculous; most offer big off-season discounts. The options below are situated in Mussoorie unless otherwise stated.

LL Residency Manor, Barlow Ganj, 4 km southeast of town, T0135-263 1800, www.jaypeehotels.com. Great family hotel with spa, pool and bowling alley. The 90 rooms are smart, large and impressive. Views of the valley, children's playground and amazing terraces.

L-AL Nabha Residence (Claridges), Airfield, Barlow Ganj Rd, 2 km from town centre, T0135-263 1426, www.claridges.com. 22 rooms with veranda arranged around attractive garden in converted hill palace, superb views, Raj-style but with all mod cons. Very good family rooms with lofts. Includes half-board.

AL-B Cloud End Forest Resort, 7 km from town, in the forest, T(0)9412-050242, www.cloudend.com. Rustic, fabulous views, 7 rooms with bath in colonial-period lodge, clean, Home-cooked meals.

A-B Connaught Castle, The Mall, T0135-263 2210. Off-season 50% discount, 29 comfortable rooms, restaurant.

A-B Garhwal Terrace (GMVN), The Mall, near Ropeway, T0135-263 2682. 24 simple but clean rooms, dorm (Rs 130), reasonably well kept, excellent views, restaurant.

A-B Kasmanda Palace Hotel, near The Mall, T0135-263 2424, www.kasmandapalace.com. 14 comfortable rooms, once Basset Hall of the Christ Church complex (built 1836), a British sanatorium, then royal guesthouse from 1915, interesting furnishings (hunting trophies, amazing photo history on walls), peaceful, spacious grounds (putting green, croquet), one of the better options but small off-season discount. Steep climb from Mall Rd so call for jeep transfer. Highly recommended.

B Padmini Nivas, Library, The Mall, T0135-263 1093, www.hotelpadmini nivas.com. 27 rooms in former palace with character, some with good views, also (**A**) cottages, not grand but pleasant ambience, good restaurant (pure vegetarian Gujarati). Car parking and access before the gated mall area. Highly recommended.

B-D Hotel Shiva Continental, next to clock tower, The Mall, Kulri, T0135-263 2174, T(0)9897-057885. Pretty patio, some rooms with views, basic rooms but relatively clean.
C-D Broadway, 3 km from main mall, Camels Back Rd, next to rink, T0135-263 2243, www.hotelbroadwaymussoorie.com. Renovated 19th-century hotel, 10 rooms with bath, best with views and geyser, some with bucket hot water, Indian meals, cheap and atmospheric.
C-E Carltons Plaisance, 1.5 km from main mall, Charleville Rd, T0135-263 2800, T(0)9358-120911, www.carltonplaisance.com. Victorian house converted into a hotel with period furniture, peaceful, spacious, 12 rooms (some with fine views), pretty suites, good restaurant (includes Tibetan).
C-E The Hermitage, on a ridge near Surkhanda Devi Temple, 35 km north of Mussoorie, T(0)991-767 4830, sumenb@hotmail.com. 16 comfortable rooms, pleasant lawns and restaurant, nightly bonfire with music. Price includes breakfast and dinner
C-E Valley View, The Mall (Kulri) near Ropeway, T0135-263 2324. Friendly, with 14 clean rooms (some with kitchenette), Great open-air terrace and all the rooms have a shared balcony, restaurant, bakery, garden, good service.
C-E Wolfsburn Estate Cottages, Landour, T01362-263 1440. Basic studios and apartments for language school students. Beautiful views, quiet location. No children.
F Shalimar, 1.5 km from main mall, Charleville Rd, T0135-263 2410. An eccentric family-run hotel. 10 pokey rooms with a/c, pleasant atmosphere with some antique furniture. Steep hike down to hotel. Closed in winter.
F-G Hotel Dev Dar Woods, Fair View, Sisters Bazaar, Landour Cant, T0135-263 2644. A great trekkers' hotel, clean rooms in a period house, budget hotel in woods, secluded but next to a well-stocked shop with local honey, jam and cheese. Surprisingly good pizza is the only thing on the menu. Recommended.

Eating

Dehra Dun *p198, map p199*

TT Kumar, 15B Rajpur Rd (towards **Kwality**, see below). Tasty Punjabi dishes, friendly staff.
T Bossa Nova, Astley Hall. Ice cream, snacks.
T Daddys, above **The Vegetarian** (see below). Serves travellers favourites.
T Osho, 111 Rajpur Rd. Good snacks in roadside café.
T Sheetal Restaurant, west of town on canal bank. Attractive setting.
T The Vegetarian, 3 Astley Plaza, Rajpur Rd. Non-vegetarian.

Bakeries

Ellora and **Grand**, both on Rajpur Rd, Paltan Bazar. Fresh bread, biscuits and sticky toffees.

Mussoorie and Landour *p200, map p200*

Restaurants may be closed off-season, and to non-residents. Carltons **Plaisance** and **Valley View** have good restaurants. **Kasmanda Palace Hotel** (near the mall, past the Anglican church) has affordable and delicious Western and Indian food. Eat on the grass terrace and enjoy views over the valley. Very pleasant ambience and friendly service.
TTT Prakash, Landour (above Woodstock School). Really good sandwiches, omelettes, etc; also beer and cheese but at a silly price.
TT Bhelpuri. *Chaat*, kababs, chicken curry with *pulao*, *kulchas*, dosas, ice cream.
TT Char Dukan, Landour (above Woodstock School). Great sandwiches and omelettes.
TT Deo Van, Lal Tibba. Famous for pizzas baked in a stone oven.
TT Hotel Dev Dar Woods (see Sleeping). A lovely stop for a fantastic pizza, which is the only thing on the menu but worth it for the mountain views and pine-scented air.
TT Kwality, above Bank of Baroda, Kulri. International. Dependable quality.
TT Tavern, Kulri. Respectable Thai and roasts, live music and dancing some nights.
TT Whispering Windows, Library Bazar, Gandhi Chowk. International. Popular bar.
T Kalsang-Tibetan Restaurant, near bank on main mall. Tasty Tibetan food, lively ambience.
T Madras Cafi, Kulri. Very good South Indian.
T Rice Bowl, The Mall. Tibetan and Chinese.

Cafés

Café Coffee Day Le-Chef, Mall Rd, Kurli. Lovely iced and hot coffee in a well-known chain, serves *momos* with a view.
City Point and **Swiss Café**, Gandhi Chowk. Reasonable fast food.

Clocktower Café, clock tower, Landour T(0)9997-055999. Italian/Chinese food, with stunning views. Packed with students. Fantastic coffee. Recommended.

Shopping

Dehra Dun *p198, map p199*

Shops around the clock tower, on Rajpur Rd, Paltan Bazar and Astley Hall, sell handwoven woollens, brassware and jewellery.

English Book Depot, 15 Rajpur Rd, T0135-265 5192, www.englishbookdepot.com. Extensive collection of English fiction and non-fiction.

The Green Bookshop, Rajpur Rd.

Paramount or **Mountain Equipment**, both in Moti Bazar (west of Paltan Bazar). For trekking equipment.

Mussoorie and Landour *p200, map p200*

The main areas are Library, Kulri and Landour Bazars and Shawfield Rd near Padmini Niwas. Several shops on The Mall sell handcrafted walking sticks. For woollen goods try **Garhwal Wool House**, near GPO; **Natraj**, Picture Palace; or the **Tibetan market**, near Padmini Nivas.

Banaras House, The Mall. Silks.

Baru Mal Janki Dass. Tribal silver jewellery.

Activities and tours

Dehra Dun *p198, map p199*

GMVN, Old Survey Chowk, 74/1 Rajpur Rd, T0135-274 6817, www.gmvnl.com. Runs the following tours: City sights, 1030, Rs 120; Mussoorie and Kempty Falls, 1000, Rs 150; Haridwar and Rishikesh, 1000, Rs 200.

President Travel, T0135-265 5111, prestrav@sancharnet.in. Ticketing and general travel arrangements.

Mussoorie and Landour *p200, map p200*

Fishing

Fishing is popular in the Aglar and Yamuna rivers for mahseer and hill trout. A permit is required; available from Division Forest Officer, Yamuna Division.

Horse riding

1-hr ride (7 km) around Camels Back Rd, Rs 250. Off-season, Rs 100.

Language classes

Landour Language School, 41/2 Landour Cantt, Mussoorie, T0135-263 1487, http://landour languageschool.com. One of the best schools in India, including Urdu, Garhwali and Sanskrit as well as Hindi. Courses for all levels and timescales. Rs 325 per class (one-to- one tuition), Rs 210-240 per person for group classes.; max 4 lessons per day. Standard of teachers varies so try a few till you are happy.

Paragliding

Snowbird Flying Club, near the lake, T0135-263 1366. Open 1000-1700.

Tours and tour operators

Tours operated by **GMVN**. Kempty Falls: Rs 50, at 0900, 1200, 1500 (off-season: 1000, 1300). Dhanolti, Surkhanda Devi Temple, Mussoorie Lake: full day (0900), Rs 130, season only. Tickets from **KMVN** and **Uttarakhand Tourism**.

Garhwal Alpine Tours, Masonic Lodge, T0135-263 2507.

Kulwant Travels, Masonic Lodge Bus Stand, T0135-263 2717.

Yoga

Yog Ganga Centre, 101 Old Rajpur, near Shahenshah Ashram, Dehra Dun, T0135-273 3653, www.yog-ganga.com. Highly regarded Iyegnar yoga school established by a couple who have advised the Indian government on the yogic syllabus for India's education system.

Transport

Dehra Dun *p198, map p199*

Air **Jolly Grant air strip** (24 km), enquiry T0135-241 2412; limited flights to/from **Delhi** with **Jet Airways** and **Kingfisher**.

Bus Local buses leave from Rajpur Rd, near clock tower. Long-distance buses leave from **New Delhi Bus Stand** (**ISBT**), Clement Town, T0135-309 3367, for most hill destinations and the plains, including **Chandigarh** (5 hrs), **Delhi** (7-8 hrs), **Dharamshala** (14 hrs), **Haridwar** (1 hr) **Kullu/Manali** (14 hrs), **Nainital** (12 hrs); **Ramnagar** for **Corbett** (7 hrs), **Rishikesh** (1 hr; board inside terminal as buses fill to bursting at the main gate), **Shimla** (8-9 hrs). **Mussoorie Bus Stand**, outside the railway station, T0135-262 3435. Half hourly to **Mussoorie**, 0600-2000, tickets from counter No 1, Rs 22. Private buses from **City Bus Stand**, Parade Ground. Regular services to **Mussoorie**, 1 hr. **Drona Travels** (GMVN), 45 Gandhi Rd, T0135-265 3309, or **Doon Tours & Travels**, 16 Bhatt Shopping Complex, 1 Haridwar Rd, T0135-262 4520. Rs 800-1000 per day, friendly, professional.

Taxi/rickshaw Taxi, T0135-262 7877. Auto-rickshaw Rs 50 from station to centre. Cheaper but crowded *vikrams* easily available.

Train Railway Station, T0135-262 2131. Reservations opposite, 0800-2000, Sun 0800-1400; book early for Haridwar. **New Delhi**: *Shatabdi Exp 12018*, 1700, 5 hrs; *Dehradun Bandra Exp 19020*, 1035, 10 hrs; *Mussoorie Exp 14042*, 2115, 9 hrs. **Allahabad**: *Link Exp 14114*, 1320, 19 hrs. **Kolkata**: *Doon Exp 13010*, 2020, 34 hrs (via **Varanasi**, 19 hrs). **Varanasi**: *Dehra Dun-Varanasi Exp 14266*, 1815, 24 hrs.

Mussoorie and Landour *p200, map p200*

Bus Long-distance stands: **Library** (Gandhi Chowk), T0135-263 2258; **Masonic Lodge** (Kulri), T0135-263 2259. Frequent service to **Chamba**, scenic trip via **Dhanolti**, 3 hrs; **Dehra Dun** through Ghat roads, Rs 22, 1 hr. Private buses **to Delhi**, are Rs 200-250 depending on a/c facility. Direct buses **from Delhi** ISBT, dep 0515, 2230, 6-7 hrs, about Rs 120; stop for snacks at **Cheetal Grand**. Also buses from **Saharanpur Railway** and **Tehri**.

Taxi/rickshaw Cycle rickshaws for The Mall, fixed-fare chart from tourist office. Taxi stand at Library, T0135-263 2115; stand at Masonic Lodge, T0135-263 1407; **Kulwant Travels**, Masonic Lodge Bus Stand, T0135-263 2717. To **Dehra Dun**, Rs 400; **Delhi** Rs 2800.

Train See above for trains from **Dehra Dun**. **Railway Out Agency** (computerized all-India reservations), near GPO, **Kulri**, 0800-1100, 1200-1500, Sun 1800-1400, T0135-263 2846.

Directory

Dehra Dun *p198, map p199*

Banks **Punjab National Bank**, Ashley Hall, Ugrasain Rd, with exchange; ATMs nearby on Rajpur Rd. **State Bank of India**, Convent Rd, 1st floor. **President Travels**, 45 Rajpur Rd, changes TCs. Medical services **Doon Hospital**, Amrit Kaur Rd, T0135-265 9355. **Useful contacts** **Rajaji National Park**, 5/1 Ansari Marg, T0135-262 1669. For permits. **Wildlife Institute of India**, PO Box 18, Chandrabani, T0135-264 0111, www.wii.gov.in.

Mussoorie and Landour *p200, map p200*

Banks Exchange can be difficult. Try **Bank of Baroda**, Kulri. ATMs in Gandhi Chowk. **Internet** Above **Tavern** restaurant, Rs 30 per hr. **Library** Gandhi Chowk, small fee. **Medical services** **Civil Hospital** at Landour, T0135-263 2891. **Community**, South Rd, T0135-263 2053. **St Marys**, Gun Hill Rd, T0135-263 2891. **Post** GPO: Kulri.

Haridwar, Rishikesh and around

The sacred cities of Haridwar and Rishikesh abound in Hindu religious history and seethe with modern-day pilgrims. Yet, although only a few kilometres apart, they share little in tempo or atmosphere. One of the oldest cities in the world, dilapidated, heady Haridwar, fabled for holding Vishnu's footprint and the site of numerous scenes from the Mahabharata, is one of Hinduism's seven holiest cities and correspondingly overrun with Indian pilgrims – between February and June 2010 an estimated 10 million devotees arrived as the city played host to the epic Kumbh Mela festival. Meanwhile, ashram and swami-filled Rishikesh, upriver, is much more geared towards Western spiritual seekers: a place one writer summed up as a hybrid of Blackpool and Lourdes. Along with an array of sound hatha yoga and vedanta classes come all the accoutrements of international budget travel: internet cafés, self-help bookshops, clothes and mantra CD shops. Further upstream, the sacred Ganga has a new following, hungry for adventure not enlightenment: they are drawn to Shivpuri in its role as India's unofficial whitewater rafting capital. The Char Dham pilgrimage route begins at Rishikesh, and the town makes a good base from which to arrange treks in the Garhwal Himalaya or elephant-spotting trips into the nearby Rajaji National Park.
▸▸ *For listings, see pages 210-215.*

Haridwar → *For listings see pages 210-215. Colour map 1, C4. Phone code: 0133. Population: 175,000.*

Haridwar lies at the base of the Shiwalik Hills where the River Ganga begins a 2000-km journey across the plains. In setting foot on the western bank here (Hari-Ki-Pairi), Vishnu made it one of Hinduism's seven holy cities (see Hindu Holy places, page 1409), a place where pilgrims bathe to cleanse themselves of sins, where *swamies* sermonize, Brahmin priests preside over spectacular sunset ceremonies, *sadhus* sit at makeshift shelters under trees and beggars huddle and urchins dart between the crowds.

Ins and outs

Getting there and around The nearest airport is at Jolly Grant, 30 km away on the Dehra Dun road. Haridwar is connected by rail to all major cities. It is 214 km from Delhi by road on NH 45, but the train is much faster. Locally there are private buses, tempos, autos, *tongas*, cycle rickshaws and taxis. Haridwar is also the stepping off point for Rishikesh. ▸▸ *See Transport, page 214.*

Tourist information **Uttarakhand tourist office** ⓘ *Motel Rahi, T01334-265304, Mon-Sat 1000-1700.* **GMVN** ⓘ *Lalta Rao Bridge, T01334-224240, 1000-1700.* **UP Tourism** ⓘ *Lalta Rao Bridge, T01334-227370.* **Ganga Sabha** ⓘ *near Hari-ki Pairi, T01334-227925.* Only vegetarian food is available in town and there is no alcohol.

History

Seventh-century Chinese traveller Hiuen Tsang mentioned the city in his writing, and Timur (Tamburlaine) sacked it in AD 1399, see page 1386.

Hari-ki-Pairi, where Vishnu trod, is now where some of the Ganga is drawn off as irrigation water for the Upper Ganga Canal system and for a hydroelectric power station.

Sights

Near the steps at Hari-ki-Pairi is a modern clock tower and some temples, none particularly old. Further down, foodstalls and shrines line alleyways leading off into the bazar. There are six bridges to take you across the river, where it is quieter. A new footbridge leads directly to Hari-ki-Pairi. Foreign visitors are likely to be approached for donations for its construction and upkeep. There are many *ashrams* here, including Shatikunj, Ananda Mayee Ma, said by some to have the most authentic Ganga arati, and Premnagar. Many have herb gardens producing Ayurvedic medicines.

Moti (Lower) Bazar, parallel to the Jawalapur–Haridwar road, is interesting, colourful, invariably crowded and surprisingly clean and tidy. Stalls sell coloured powder piled high in carefully made cones (for *tikas*). Others sell saris, jewellery, brass and aluminium pots, sweets and snacks. **Mansa Devi Temple** is worth visiting for the view. Set on the southernmost hill of the Shiwaliks, it is accessible on foot or by the crowded cable car (0630-2030, Rs 80 return; or take the package ticket to include Chanda Devi temple, 4 km away on the other side of the Ganga). Towards Rishikesh, 5 km from Haridwar, are the newer temples: **Pawan Dham** with a Hanuman temple, its spectacular glittering glass interior and the seven-storey **Bharat Mata Mandir** to Mother India.

Kankhal, 3 km downstream, with the **Temple of Dakseshwara**, is where legend holds that Siva's wife, Sati, burned herself to death, irked at her father Daksa's failure to invite her husband Siva to a grand sacrifice. Siva temporarily destroyed the sacrifice, and gave Daksa (himself a son of Brahma) the head of a goat. Professor Wendy Doniger says that when Siva learned that of Sati's suicide, "he took up her body and danced in grief, troubling the world with his dance and his tears until the gods cut the corpse into pieces. When the *yoni* fell, Siva took the form of a *linga*, and peace was re-established in the universe".

Haridwar

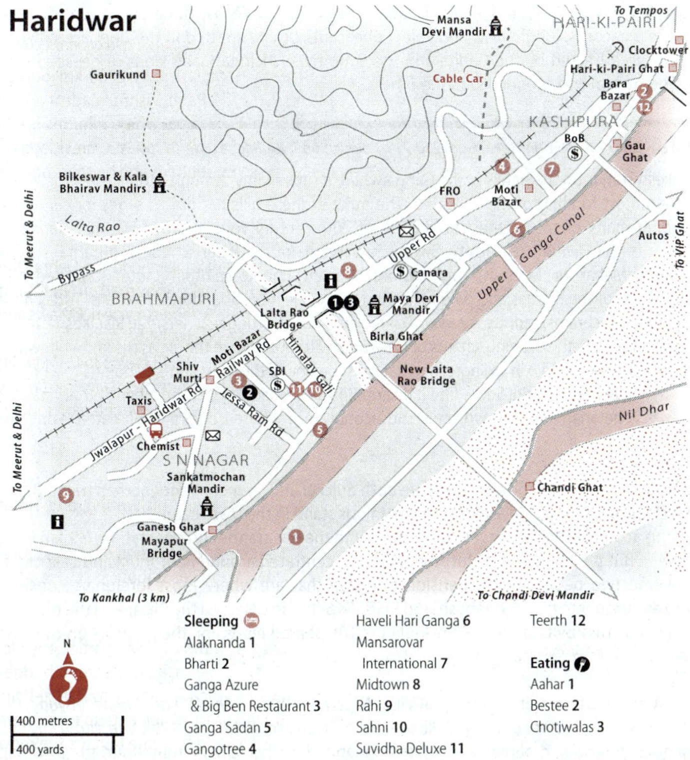

Sleeping
- Alaknanda 1
- Bharti 2
- Ganga Azure & Big Ben Restaurant 3
- Ganga Sadan 5
- Gangotree 4
- Haveli Hari Ganga 6
- Mansarovar International 7
- Midtown 8
- Rahi 9
- Sahni 10
- Suvidha Deluxe 11
- Teerth 12

Eating
- Aahar 1
- Bestee 2
- Chotiwalas 3

Rajaji National Park → *For listings see pages 210-215. Colour map 1, B4. Altitude: 302-1000 m.*

ⓘ *The park can be reached from Haridwar, Rishikesh and Dehra Dun (see Transport, page 214). Permits from Director 5/1 Ansari Rd, Dehra Dun, T0135-262 1669, Mohan's Adventure, T01334-265543, or at the Chilla park office, T01382-266757. Open 15 Nov-15 Jun between sunrise and sunset. Entry first 3 days: foreigners Rs 350, Indians Rs 40; additional day Rs 175/Rs 20; camera Rs 50; video, Rs 5000. Elephant rides from Chilla, Rs 200, 2 hrs. Chilla, 7 km from Haridwar, is the best for viewing. Car permit Rs 100-500. Jeep hire from Haridwar, Rishikesh or Dehradun.*

Uttarakhand's largest park, 820 sq km, is named after C Rajagopalachari, the only Indian to hold the post of governor general. Spread across the rugged and dangerously steep slopes of the Shiwaliks, the park's vegetation ranges from rich *sal, bhabbar* tracts, broad- leaf mixed forest to *chir* pine forests interspersed with areas of scrub and pasture which provide a home for a wide variety of wildlife including over 23 mammal and 438 species of bird. On foot, however, you are likely to see very little. Even by car or jeep many are disappointed as few animals are spotted.

A large number of **elephants**, together with the rarely seen **tiger**, are found, here at the northwest limit of their range in India. The elephants move up into the hills when the water holes are dry. A census taken in 2001 recorded 453 elephants, 30 tigers and 236 **leopards** in the park. Other animals include spotted deer, sambar, muntjac, nilgai and ghoral. Along the tracks, you may spot wild boar, langur and macaque; the Himalayan yellow-throated marten and civet are rare. Peacocks, jungle fowl and kaleej pheasants can be spotted in the drier areas, while waterbirds attracted by the Ganga and the Song rivers include many kinds of geese, ducks, cormorant, teal and spoonbill, among others.

Rishikesh → *For listings see pages 210-215. Colour map 1, B4. Phone code: 01350. Population: 72,000.*

Rishikesh stands on the banks of the Ganga where it runs swiftly through a forested gorge in the southernmost foothills of the Shiwaliks. The quiet of these hills has drawn sages for centuries, including many of the greatest luminaries of 20th-century yoga, such as Swami Sivananda, founder of the Divine Life Society, Swami Satyananda of the Bihar school, and perhaps most famously Maharishi Mahesh Yogi, whose Western-tinged spiritual patter captured the imagination of the Beatles and paid for a then space age, now abandoned, ashram. Today it's a mixed bag of ashrams, sadhus, Ayurveda clinics and globetrotting teachers, yet, Rishikesh still has a certain magic. In the evening, chants of *Om Namoh Shivaya* drift on the air, as the last whitewater rafters of the day paddle in to shore, in what must be one of the most surreal endings to a rafting trip anywhere in the world. Some find it disappointing and lacking in atmosphere; others stay for weeks. A vegetarian temple town, meat and alcohol are prohibited; eggs are only eaten in private.

Ins and outs

Getting there From Haridwar, buses are both quicker and far more frequent than trains. Buses from Delhi and Dehra Dun arrive at the main bus stand in the town centre.

Getting around The compact town centre, with the bus stands and bus station, is 1 km from the river. But it is the ashrams further north, concentrated around Ram Jhula and Lakshman Jhula (the two pedestrian suspension bridges), that are where most foreigners consider Rishikesh proper to be. Frequent shared taxis (Rs 5-10) go between the Bazar and the bridges, or you can cross by boat near Ram Jhula (Rs 10). Shared jeeps link the quarters on the east bank (Rs 5-10) . ▸▸ *See Transport, page 215.*

Tourist information **Garhwal Mandal Vikas Nigam (GMVN)** ⓘ *Shail Vihar, Haridwar Bypass Rd, T0135-243 2648, also at Yatra Office, Kailash Gate, Bypass Rd, T0135-243 1793, yatra@gmvnl.com*, organizes trekking, mountaineering, rafting and the Char Dham tour (four to 12 days). **Uttarakhand Tourism** ⓘ *162 Railway Rd, T0135-243 0209*, is helpful. During the *yatra* season, tourist information is also available from the **Uttarakhand Guest House** next to the Yatra Bus Stand, T094-1010 6800.

Sights

Many travel to Rishikesh (Hair of Sages) to study in one of its numerous ashrams, seats of spiritual learning often housed in bizarrely colourful architectural curiosities. As a result, the town has become something of a yoga supermarket. Evening *aarti* is popular at Parmath Niketan, but the Triveni ghat (which has striking statues of Siva) is where local pilgrims perform the ritual. The trees along the east bank between Lakshman and Ram Jhula shade scores of bungalows, the homes to the ubiquitous saffron-robed sadhus you'll find sitting at every pathside, swinging tiffins and sparking up chillums. Follow the track northeast, beyond Lakshman Jhula, to reach beautiful, secluded swimming beaches.

Rishikesh is the base for several pilgrimages and treks, including the **Char Dham Pilgrimage** (see box, page 217), or going to the Garhwal hills and Hemkund Sahib.

Rishikesh

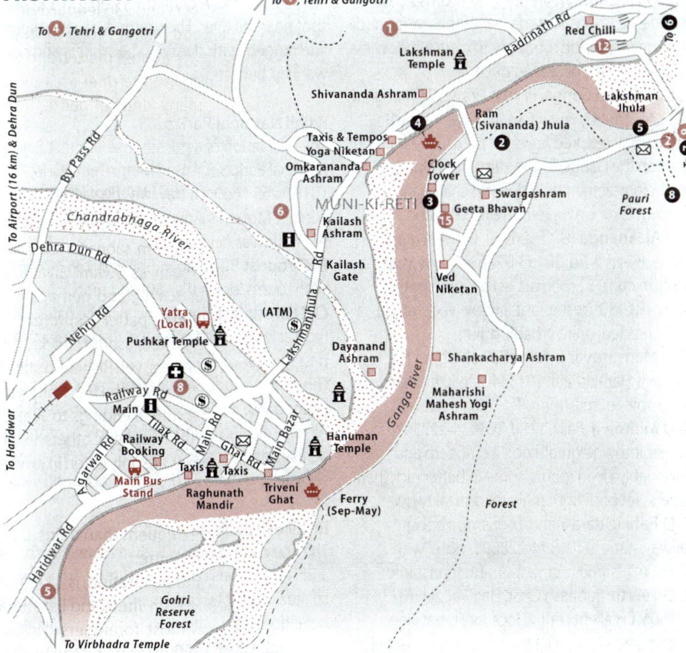

Sleeping
Ananda-in-the-Himalayas **4**
Bhandari Swiss Cottage **1**
Bombay Guesthouse **9**
Divya **2**
Ganga Banks **7**
Ganga Kinare **5**
Glasshouse on the Ganges **14**
Inderlok **8**
Ishan **12**
Parmarth Niketan **15**
Rainforest House **3**
Rishilok **6**

Eating
Chotiwalas **2**
Ganga Freedom Café **5**
Madras Café **4**
Moksha **7**
Pyramid Café **8**
Ramana's Garden **6**
The Office **3**

N

500 metres
500 yards

Haridwar, Rishikesh and around listings

For Sleeping and Eating price codes and other relevant information, see Essentials pages 38-42.

Sleeping

Haridwar *p206, map p207*

There are more than 100 places to stay. Many offer off-season discounts outside Jun and Jul, up to 50% Nov-Feb.

LL-L Ganga Sadan, opposite Chintamani Ashram, Sharvan Nath Nagar, T01334-228322, www.gangasadan.com. Sleek new boutique hotel right on the Ganga, with a private bathing ghat and atmospheric rooftop cafe. The more expensive of the well-equipped rooms boast a wonderful unobstructed view of the river; avoid the cheaper inside rooms, which are windowless and not worth the asking price.

A Haveli Hari Ganga, Pilibhit House, 21 Ramghat, T01334-226443, www.haveliharigangа.com. Attractively restored *haveli* with exclusive bathing ghat on the Ganga, rooms decorated along mythological themes, old-world charm and modern luxury, Ayurvedic treatments and yoga.

B-E Alaknanda (UP Tourism), Belwala (east bank), By-pass Rd, T01334-226379, www.up-tourism.com. 32 rooms, best a/c with bath, dorm (Rs 150), restaurant (simple vegetarian), small garden, on riverbank, quiet.

C-D Mansarovar International, Upper Rd, towards Hari-ki-Pairi, T01334-226501. Clean, 64 simple rooms, dorm (Rs 100), restaurant.

C-D Midtown, Railway Rd, T01334-227507, hotelmidtown@gmail.com. 23 modern and reasonably clean rooms, some in better nick than others. Set back from main road so fairly quiet.

C-D Rahi (Uttarakhand Tourism), opposite railway station, T01334-228606. Hotel with 19 rooms (some a/c), restaurant, tourist info.

C-D Teerth, Subhash Ghat, Hari-ki-Pairi, T01334-228506. Excellent central location, great views over ghats, 32 reasonable rooms, some air-cooled, but not the value it once was.

C-E Ganga Azure, Railway Rd, T01334-227101, www.hotelgangaazure.com. 32 adequate rooms, TV, hot water, some (**B**) a/c, decent restaurant.

C-E Suvidha Deluxe, SN Nagar, T01334-227423, www.hotelsuvidhadeluxe.com. Somewhat dark and dated but clean and central hotel with 28 reasonably good rooms, some a/c, the best of which have balconies overlooking the quiet street. Restaurant.

D-E Inder Kutir, Niranjani Akhara Rd, SN Nagar, T01334-226336. A good new budget option, with bright and airy rooms opening on to a terrace. One room has a balcony from which you can peep through to the river.

E Gangotree, Upper Rd, T01334-224407. 14 simple rooms, attached bath.

F-G Bharti, Hari ki Pairi, T01334-224396, hotel_bharti@yahoo.co.in. Basic but very well-kept rooms with bucket hot water, family atmosphere.

G Sahni, Niranjani Akhara Rd, SN Nagar, T01334-227906. A genuine cheapie in a quiet spot near the river. The rooms are pretty gloomy and ragged, with decaying bedsheets and hot water in buckets.

Rajaji National Park *p208*

For reservation of a guesthouse, contact Rajaji National Park, 5/1 Ansari Marg, Dehra Dun, T0135-262 1669. To stay in a tribal village, contact **Mohan's Adventure**, T01334-220910, see Haridwar Activities and tours, page 213.

B-C Tourist Bungalow, Chilla, T01382-266697. With rooms, dorm (Rs 150) and tents.

C-E Forest Rest Houses, near all the gates. All have at least 2 suites. Those at Chilla (apparently best spot for wildlife) and Motichur cost Rs 1000. Others at Asarodi, Beribara, Kansrao, Kunnao, Phandowala, Ranipur and Satyanarain are Rs 600. All have electricity and water supply except Beribara and Kansrao. Very basic, 'concrete boxes', self-catering (utensils provided), not good value.

Rishikesh *p208, map p209*

The noisy and congested town around the bazar and Triveni ghats couldn't be further from the spiritual calm for which many travel to Rishikesh, but it does hold some good accommodation if you're less eager to immerse yourself in *sadhus* and *swamis*. The best options across Ram Jhula Bridge, in Swargashram, are within ashrams themselves, which can be safe and clean but impose curfews and some moderate constraints on behaviour. The best independent hostels and guesthouses are dotted on either riverbank of Lakshman Jhula, 30 mins north of Ram Jhula on foot (unadvisable at night).

Clean Himalaya, www.cleanhimalaya.com, is an award-winning environmental group, established by members of the **Divine Life Society** (contact Susan T(0)9897-946696) running local rubbish collections and campaigning for greater public awareness of green issues. Volunteer, donate, and encourage local businesses to sign up.

LL Ananda-in-the-Himalayas, The Palace, Narendra Nagar, T01378-227500, www.anandaspa.com. Exclusive destination spa with 75 rooms (including a literally palatial suite in the Viceregal Palace, which has its own open-air hot tub and 3 cottages with their own infinity pools and saunas), in a superb location 30 mins above Rishikesh with panoramic views across the valley. There's golf, yoga, vendanta lectures, a swimming pool and hikes, but many come for the treatments (ayurveda and international) at the beautiful spa, or just to relax and enjoy the outstanding food. Winner of many international awards.

L-A Glasshouse on the Ganges, 23rd Milestone Rishikesh–Badrinath Rd, Gular Dogi District, T01378-269224, www.neemranahotels.com, 23 km from Rishikesh towards Badrinath. A lovely riverside retreat in lychee and mango tree garden once used by the Rajas of Garwhal. Rooms either in main block or cottages. The property has its own beach and yoga is complimentary.

A-B Rainforest House, below Neer Gaddu forest *chowkie*, Badrinath Rd, 3 km from Tapovan, T(0)9258-053013, www.rainforest-house.com. Charming, isolated guesthouse upstream from Rishikesh on the Ganga with 9 rustic but beautifully designed double rooms set around a central court. Very peaceful forested retreat without phones or TVs, run by English and Indian husband and wife, with small child.

A Ganga Kinare, 237 Virbhadra Rd, on quiet riverside 2 km south of centre, T0135-243 1658, www.uttrakhandhotels.com. 36 Ganga-facing rooms, slightly dog-eared but with good service and a lovely lawn by the water.

B Ganga Banks, Shivpuri, contact Wanderlust in Delhi, T011-4163 6896, www.wanderlustindia.com. A 'green' resort with 28 comfortable, eco-friendly cottages with bath, built using local raw materials, restaurant, pool, health spa, in natural surroundings employing recycling techniques (no plastics), solar heating, well placed for trekking, rafting, etc.

C-D Inderlok, Railway Rd, T0135-243 0555. inderlokhotel@hotmail.com. Best budget choice in the town centre is this faded block: spotless and airy, set around a huge central atrium. The rooftop has a terrace lawn with mountain views. 22 clean rooms.

C-E Rishilok (GMVN), Badrinath Rd, Muni-ki-Reti, T0135-243 0373. Within walking distance of Ram Jhula, set far enough from the main road and taxi stand to be quiet, is this charming 1970s government guesthouse. Although its fading upholstery is as old as the building, it holds 46 clean rooms, some with bath, in blocks set around a beautifully kept garden of bamboo, bougainvillea and butterflies. Excellent service.

F Ishan, west end of Lakshman Jhula, T0135-243 3271. Clean and pleasant rooms, some with balconies overlooking river, internet downstairs and an excellent restaurant.

Several other **F** hotels near main bus stand.

F-G Bhandari Swiss Cottage, High Bank, off Lakshman Jhula Rd, T0135-243 2939. Most rooms here are gifted with a heavenly view over the Ganga and to the hills beyond. Big rooms, clean and basic and a tranquil setting. Internet café and little restaurant.

F-G Divya, near taxi stand, Lakshman Jhula, T0135-243 5998, divyanew@yahoo.com. 22 clean, but small rooms, attached hot bath, restaurant with travellers' favourites, filtered drinking water available.

G Bombay Guest House, Laxman Jhulla T0135-325 0038, T(0)9897-543224. Funky heritage house from 1958 with 20 somewhat grubby rooms set around a courtyard. Safe and friendly.

Ashrams and yoga shalas

There are scores of visiting teachers, both of hatha yoga and of meditation. Check fly posters and ask fellow travellers for the latest details.

Dayananda, Purani Jhadi near Chandrabhaga River, T0135-243 0769, www.dayananda.org. Has daily lectures on Vedanta, and rooms with marble floors and tiled bathrooms.

Parmarth Niketan, Swargashram, T0135-243 4301, www.parmarth.com/home. Large scale ashram, with well attended sunset *aarti* on the Ganga. Tidy rooms in blocks set around pleasant leafy gardens full of stucco deities and friezes of passages from the *Gita*.

Eating

Haridwar p206, map p207

Cheap stalls on Railway Rd provide simple food for pilgrims.

Aahar, Railway Rd. Punjabi, Chinese and continental. Excellent meals.

Big Ben, **Ganga Azure** (see Sleeping). Decent, large range of Indian, Chinese and continental.

Bestee, Railway Rd. Mughlai and South Indian. Stuffed *parathas* are recommended.

Chotiwalas, several (including on Railway Rd, opposite tourist office) of varying quality.

Rishikesh p208, map p209

Madras Café, on the West Bank, and **Chotiwalas**, on the East Bank, are Ram Jhula's 2 long-running, cheap fast food joints. **Amrita Little Italian Café** is a sweet stop off for proper espresso coffee to the right of the boat jetty crossing on the West bank. Lakshman Jhula has more atmospheric and Western options, including a handful of German bakeries. Safe drinking water is sold to refill bottles near the Ram Jhula, and the mini-markets all sell prized international supplies including Lindt dark chocolate, 'yogi' bread, cakes and home-made peanut butter.

Ramana's Garden, uphill from Lakshman Jhula then right at **Tapovan Resort**, 5 mins' walk, www.ramanasgarden.org. Open 1100-1530 and Sat, 1830-2100. If the organic home-grown salad plates and scrumptious cakes weren't enough in themselves, this pleasant garden restaurant funds a school for local orphan children, who spill out across its grounds during breaks and help Ramana's multinational team of volunteers in the kitchen. Pricier than most but well worth it. Film nights on Sat.

Ganga Freedom Café, behind Dr Kothari clinic, Lakshman Jhula. Easily the tastiest scran on the East Bank – serving the likes of rosemary roast tatties and ratatouille, a little pricier than some local *dabhas* but food comes in big portions. Lovely atmosphere and views along the river.

Hotel Jaipur, opposite Lakshman Jhula bridge, near Ashoka. Great rooftop restaurant serving up good range of Indian food, including healthy Ayurvedic options like *kichadi* (dahl and rice). Atmospheric with great views and lots of clanging temple bells.

Moksha, near Goa Beach, Lakshman Jhula, T(0)9897-460487. Handmade noodle soups, *kimchi* and regional specials in a chilled-out bamboo and tatami-mat-strewn villa heading north on the east bank of the Ganga.

Mount Valley Mama Cottage, next to **Bhandari Swiss Cottage**. All-you-can-eat *thalis* are much famed among travellers. Delicious and highly recommended.

New Bhandari Swiss Cottage, behind Bhandari Swiss Cottage. Great range of food and generous portions of Indian, Tibetan and Continental dishes, including marinated tofu steaks with mushroom sauce.

The Office, Swargashram ghats near clock tower. Although postage-stamp sized, this is so much more than a chai joint: a lovely tiny caff turning out a few excellent specials, such as fresh chick pea salad or houmous and apple and chocolate banana samosas. Minimalist bulletin board for upcoming courses, yoga cookery, Ayurveda. Plus a teeny balcony on the Ganges. Lovely.

Pyramid Café, Lakshman Jhula. Offers all sorts of veggie and vegan health food, such as tofu brown rice *kombucha* and spirulina. The atmosphere and soundtrack in the mellow tipi garden make it well worth the short walk up the hill for. There's Wi-Fi too.

Festivals and events

Haridwar p206, map p207

Thousands of pilgrims visit the city when the birth of the river (*Dikhanti*) is celebrated in spring. **Kumbh Mela**, held here every 12th year (next in Mar-Apr 2021), and **Ardha Kumbh** also every 12 years (next in 2016), attract millions of devotees who come to bathe in the confined area near Hari-ki-Pairi.

Rishikesh p208, map p209

Feb-Mar International Yoga Festival, hosted by the Parmarth Niketan ashram. An opportunity to meet and learn from some of the leading lights in the yoga community.

Shopping

Rishikesh p208, map p209

Rishikesh has several excellent bookshops specializing in yoga and the spiritual life; good places to rummage for reading material are on the east bank of the Ganga near Ram Jhula and the west bank at Lakshman Jhula. The central market area around Dehra Dun, Haridwar, Ghat and Railway Rds has markets and curio shops.

Guru TV

In today's India, where even renounced *Swamis* communicate with their devotees via smartphones, some of the more pro-active yogis have adopted television as a means to spread their message. Far and away the most successful has been a young guru named Baba Ramdev, whose yoga camps, aired live on several national TV channels every day, attract the devoted and the curious in their thousands.

Guru TV offers an illuminating contrast to morning TV elsewhere in the world. The photogenic Ramdev sits in *padmasana* (cross-legged pose) on a stage, microphones rigged up before him, and with vivid demonstrations expounds upon the virtues of stomach rolling exercises that strengthen the digestive system and *anuloma viloma pranayama*, a breathing technique in which one breathes through each nostril in turn, focusing the mind.

Baba Ramdev's fame has, inevitably, earned him the scorn of some *swamis*, not to mention unwanted media attention, particularly after his ill-advised acceptance of an offer from the Madhya Pradesh government to build a college campus on tribal land. Yet despite making some high-profile enemies, including the makers of certain carbonated soft drinks whose products he publicly compares to toilet cleaning fluid, Ramdev has had a significant impact on the popularity of yoga, particularly among housewives and young children – the core viewers of morning TV. His new 'five-star' ashram and Yogic hospital, **Patanjali Yogpeeth**, on the Haridwar–Delhi highway (www.divyayoga.com), is one of the most visited in India.

Alternatively you can catch him on tour, live at a stadium near you.

Gecko, under **Hotel Ishan**, Lakshman Jhula. Intriguing and colourful range of Nepali-made dresses and winter jackets.

Gandhi Ashram Khadi Bhandar, Haridwar Rd.

Activities and tours

Haridwar *p206, map p207*

Body and soul

Patanjali Yogpeeth, near Bahadarabad, Delhi–Haridwar National Highway, T01334-240008, www.divyayoga.com. Rooms **E-G**. Enormous and exceptionally well-equipped ashram/yogic hospital, offering yoga camps and treatments for diseases from diabetes to impotence. See box, above. However, daily yoga classes are taught in Hindi only

Tours and tour operators

Daily tours of Haridwar-Rishikesh, 0930, Rs 80; Dehra Dun–Mussoorie, 0800, Rs 140; Rajaji National Park, 1000, 1430.

Ashwani Travels, 3 Railway Rd, T01334- 224581, ashwanitravels@hotmail.com. Official agent of GMVN, specializing in pilgrimage tours, also trekking.

Mohan's Adventure, next to Chitra Cinema, Railway Rd, T01334-265543, www.mohans adventure.in. Very reliable trips run by Sanjeev Mehta. Trekking, jeep safaris, rafting. Jungle trips into Rajaji National Park, with night stay in tribal village. Highly recommended.

Rishikesh *p208, map p209*

Boat rides

On the Ganga from from Lakshman Jhula. Fix rates with local boatmen.

Body and soul

Yoga classes, meditation courses and instruction in Ayurveda and Vedanta are Rishikesh's stock-in-trade. Most hotels can put you in touch with courses, though both style and quality are highly variable. The following institutions are well-established and reliable.

Omkarananda Ashram (Durga Mandir) above Yoga Niketan, Ram Jhula, T0135-243 0883. Good Iyengar yoga courses, also offers music and classical dance.

Parmarth Niketan, T0135-243 4301.

Sivananda Ashram (Divine Life Society), T0135-243 0040. Short to 3-month courses (apply 1 month ahead); holds music classes and produces herbal medicines. Forest Academy open to male students; non-Indians can attend classes informally, but are not given certificates.

Swami Rama Sadhaka Grama, south of town centre on Virbhadra Rd, T0135-245 0093, www.ahymsin.org. Yoga training with a strong focus on meditation, based on the Himalayan tradition laid out by Sankaracharya. There's a rigorous 600-hr yoga teacher training program, or you can simply use the cottages for a few days' retreat.

Ved Niketan, south end of Swargashram ghats, T0135-2430279. Has a flexible programme of yoga; also Hindi, Sanskrit, music and dance classes and basic rooms.

Music

Sivananda Ramesh, towards Muni-ki-Reti Taxi Stand, T(0)98971-73406. Lessons in tabla, sitar, santoor, singing, etc.

Rafting and trekking

There are more than 60 whitewater rafting outfits in town, and Shivpuri, 17 km north, has become an adventure sports playground. You can book onto daily trips on the Grade III waters the day before, or go for more adventurous, longer-haul expeditions with meals and overnights at camps. Below are 3 companies known for their sound environmental records. Ask the government office for a full list of operators.

De-N-Ascent Expeditions, Tapovan Sarai T0135-244 2354, www.kayakhimalaya.com. Excellent equipment and stringent safety, with a background in kayaking. Runs day trips and more adventurous routes through less charted waters, also trekking.

Himalayan River Runners, with an office in Delhi, T011-2685 2602, www.hrrindia.com. Mar-May, Sep-Oct. Highly recommended.

Red Chilli, Tapovan, above Lakshman Jhula, T0135-243 4021, www.redchilliadventure.com. Enthusiastic local outfit with good environmental standards.

Swimming

Hotel Natraj, Dehra Dun Rd, has a pool (non-residents Rs 250).

Tour operators

Garhwal Himalayan Exploration, Muni Ki Reti, T0135-243 3478, www.thegarhwalhimalayas.com. Wide range of trekking and rafting trips.

GMVN, Yatra Office, T0135-243 1793, www.gmvnl.com. Char Dham pilgrimage tours, plus 4- to 5-day adventure tours and yoga at **Parmarth Niketan** (see Ashrams under Sleeping).

Triveni, Haridwar Rd, T0135-243 0989, www.triveniindia.com. Recommended for rafting and trekking.

Transport

Haridwar *p206, map p207*

Bus The long-distance bus stand is opposite the railway station. Frequent buses to/from **Delhi** (5-7 hrs) and **Dehra Dun** (1¾ hrs). Buses for **Rishikesh** leave irregularly and only when enough passengers turn up; better to take a tempo or taxi.

Rickshaw, jeep and taxi The taxi stand is outside railway station, rates negotiable. To **Rishikesh** costs Rs 600-800. Tempos shuttle around town and to nearby destinations; to **Rishikesh**, Rs 25 (more for Lakshman Jhula). Catch them outside the railway station where the chance of getting a seat is highest.

Tata Sumo Union, outside bus stand, T01334-221017, has share jeeps to **Joshimath** (Rs 320 a seat) via **Deoprayag**, **Rudraprayag** (Rs 180) and **Karanprayag** (Rs 220). Private jeeps (for up to 9 passengers) cost around Rs 2500 per day in May-Jun, or around Rs 1800 outside pilgrimage season.

Train Railway Station, T131. Reservation office 0800-2000. 3 trains per day to **Rishikesh**, 0515, 0845, 1715, better to take road transport; **Delhi** (**OD**): *Dehra Dun Bandra Exp 19020*, 1255, 8½ hrs (**HN**); *Mussoorie Exp 14042*, 2310 (**OD**), 8 hrs (beware of thieves); *Shatabdi Exp 12018*, 1810, 4½ hrs (**ND**). **Dehra Dun**: *Shatabdi Exp 12017*, 1125, 1¼ hrs, among several others. **Varanasi**: *Dehra Dun Varanasi Exp 14266*, 2035, 20 hrs. For **Nainital**: *Dehradun-Kathgodam Exp 14120*, 0020, 7 hrs. For **Shimla**, travel via Ambala and Kalka (train is better than bus).

Rajaji National Park *p208*

The park has 8 entry gates. From **Dehra Dun**: **Mohan** (25 km on Delhi–Dehra Dun highway, 5-hr drive from Delhi), **Ramgarh** (14 km, Delhi–Dehra Dun highway, via Clement Town) and **Lachhiwala** (18 km, Dehra Dun–Haridwar route, right turn before Doiwala). From **Haridwar**: **Chilla** (7 km, via private bus route to Rishikesh),

Motichur (9 km, Haridwar– Rishikesh or Dehra Dun–Haridwar highways) and **Ranipur** (9 km, Haridwar–BHEL–Mohand Rd). From **Rishikesh**: **Kunnao** (6 km, via private bus route on Rishikesh–Pashulok route). From **Kotdwara**: **Laldhang** (25 km, via private bus route Kotdwara to Chilla).

Rishikesh *p208, map p209*

Rishikesh is the main staging post for visiting the Himalayan pilgrim centres of of **Badrinath** (301 km); **Gangotri** (258 km); **Kedarnath** (228 km); **Uttarkashi** (154 km); **Yamunotri** (288 km).

Bus Long-distance buses use **main bus stand**, Haridwar Rd, T0135-243 0066. Various State Government bus services (**DTC, Haryana Roadways, Himachal RTC, UP Roadways** serve destinations including: **Chandigarh** (252 km), **Dehra Dun** (42 km, every 30 mins), **Delhi** (238 km, 6 hrs), **Haridwar** (24 km, every 30 mins), **Mussoorie** (77 km). For **Shimla**, stay overnight in Dehra Dun and catch 0600 bus. Share taxis for Dehra Dun and Haridwar leave from outside the bus stand.

The **Yatra Bus Stand**, Dehra Dun Rd, has buses for local destinations and the mountain pilgrimage sites. Reserve tickets the day before (especially during *yatra* season, May-Nov); open 0400-1900, 0400-1400 out of season. To **Char Dhams**: buses leave early for the very long routes to Hanuman Chatti (for Yamunotri), **Badrinath, Gangotri, Gaurikund** (for Kedarnath); best to take a luxury bus, and break your journey. For **Badrinath** and **Hemkund** stop overnight at Joshimath (after 1630 road to Govindghat is southbound only). Although the *yatra* season ends in late Oct (Yamunotri, Gangotri, Kedarnath) to mid-Nov (Badrinath), bus frequency drops drastically during Oct. Even light rains can cause severe road blocks, mainly due to landslides. Bus for Badrinath departs from **Tehri Bus Stand** (100 m right from station), 1600, Rs 180, but noisy, crowded and uncomfortable. **Garhwal Motor Owners Union**, T0135-243 0076; **Tehri Garhwal MOU, Triveni**, Haridwar Rd, T0135-243 0989. Also worth a try, though no cheaper than buses, are 'Newspaper taxis', eg Joshimath, Rs 200 per person; ask at **Sanjay News Agency**, Main Rd (before turn-off to Ghat Rd) or travel agent.

Ferry Ferry boat from near Ram Jhula for river crossing, Rs 10, return Rs 15.

Jeep Hire for **Badrinath** (1-way), Rs1500- 2000, is the best option. Book the night before.

Motorbike Motorbike mechanic at **Bila**, opposite **Ganga View Hotel**, Lakshman Jhula.

Rickshaw Auto-rickshaw rates are negotiable; allow around Rs 30 to **Ram Jhula**, Rs 35-40 for **Lakshman Jhula**.

Taxi Fixed rates from from taxi stands south of **Ram Jhula** and in the market near **Lakshman Jhula**.

Tempo Mostly fixed routes. From Ram Jhula shared, to Rishikesh Bazar Rs 5; from Lakshman Jhula Rs 10; to **Haridwar** Rs 25, 50 mins. Foreigners may be asked for more.

Train There is a branch line from **Haridwar** to **Rishikesh**, but the bus is quicker.

Directory

Haridwar *p206, map p207*

Banks ATMs around Hari ki Pauri Ghat. **State Bank of India**, Station Rd, 1030-1430. Pounds, euro and US$ cash only. **Bank of Baroda**, Upper Rd. Cash on Visa cards only. **Canara Bank**, Upper Rd. Changes TCs. **Medical services** District **Hospital**, Upper Rd, T01334-226060. **RK Mission**, Kankhal, T01334-247141. **Chemists**: on Railway and Upper Rd. **Post** Railway Rd. 1000-1630. **Useful contacts** Police: T01334-227775.

Rishikesh *p208, map p209*

Banks ATMs in town centre and near east end of Ram Jhula. **Bank of Baroda**, Dehra Dun Rd, T0135-243 0653. Accepts Visa and MasterCard. **State Bank of India**, Railway Rd. Mon-Fri 1000-1400, Sat 1000-1200. **Internet** Several in town. **Blue Hills Travels** has best facilities in Ram Jhula area (Rs 50 per hr), but queueing often necessary. **Red Chilli** (see Rafting, above) is cool and quiet and has Wi-Fi. **Medical services** **Ambulance**: T102. **Govt Hospital**, Dehra Dun Rd, T0135-243 0402. **Nirmal Ashram**, T0135-243 2215. **Sivananda**, Muni-ki-Reti, T0135-243 0040. **Post** Open 0700-2200. **GPO**: at Harilal Marg, Lakshman Jhula and Muni-ki-Reti. Ghat Rd. Swargashram GPO by **Chotiwalas**. **Useful contacts** Fire: T101. Police: T100.

Garhwal and the Pilgrimage (Yatra)

The shrines of Kedarnath, Yamunotri, Gangotri and Badrinath are visited by hundreds of thousands of Hindu pilgrims each summer. They come from all corners of the subcontinent to engage in what Dalrymple calls "a modern-day Indian Canterbury Tales". Garhwal's fragmented political history gives no clue as to the region's religious significance. The sources of the Yamuna and the Ganga, and some of Hinduism's holiest mountains, lie in the heart of the region. Since the seventh-century Tamil saint Sankaracharya travelled north on his mission to reinvigorate Hinduism's northern heartland, some have been watched over permanently by South Indian priests. The most famous is the Rawal – head priest – at the Badrinath temple, who to this day comes from Kerala. Badrinath is one of the four dhams, 'holiest abodes' of the gods. Along with Dwarka, Puri and Rameswaram, they mark the cardinal points of Hinduism's cultural geography. After a ritual purificatory bathe in the Ganga at Haridwar and, preferably, Rishikesh, the pilgrim begins the 301-km journey to Badrinath. The purpose is to worship, purify and acquire merit. Roads go all the way to Gangotri and Badrinath, and to within 14 km of Yamunotri and Kedarnath. The correct order for pilgrims is to visit the holy places from west to east: Yamunotri, Gangotri, Kedarnath and Badrinath. ▸▸ *For listings, see pages 222-224.*

Ins and outs

Temples and trekking routes open from the end of April to mid-November (October for Badrinath). June is very crowded; heavy rains from July to mid-September may trigger landslips. The best time to visit is May and mid-September to mid-October. *Yatra* tourists on public buses are required to register with the Yatra Office at the Yatra (Local) Bus Stand, Rishikesh (0600-2200). A certificate of immunization against cholera and typhoid is needed. In practice, 'Registration' is often waived, but the immunization certificate is checked. Accommodation prices are higher than average. **GMVN** (www.gmvnl.com) organizes 12-day pilgrimage tours from Delhi and Rishikesh during season. ▸▸ *For trekking, see page 224.*

Yamunotri and Gangotri → *For listings, see pages 222-224.*

Yamunotri can be reached from Rishikesh or from Dehra Dun via Yamuna Bridge and Barkot. The former is the more popular. From Rishikesh it is 83 km to Tehri, or 165 km via Deoprayag. **Tehri**, northeast of Rishikesh, the capital of the former princely state, will eventually be submerged by the waters behind the controversial and still unfinished Tehri Dam. **New Tehri**, 24 km from the original town, is a 'planned' town and the new district headquarters. Note that it is an offence to photograph sensitive installations, troop movements and bridges on most routes. Offenders can be treated very severely.

Yamunotri → *Colour map 1, B4. Altitude: 3291 m.*

Dominated by **Banderpunch** (6316 m), Yamunotri, the source of the Yamuna, is believed to be the daughter of Surya (the sun) and the twin sister of Yama (the 'Lord of Death'). Anyone who bathes in her waters will be spared an agonizing death.

To begin the trek to reach the temple take a jeep from **Hanuman Chatti** (large vehicles also stop here and pick up) to **Janki Chatti**, 8 km further up, which is more pleasant and where you can leave luggage. The trek along the riverbank is exhilarating with the mountains rising up on each side, the last 5 km somewhat steeper. The source itself is a difficult 1-km climb from the 19th-century **Yamunotri Temple** ⓘ *0600-1200, 1400-2100*, with a black marble deity. The modern temple was rebuilt this century after floods and snow destroyed it. There are **hot springs** nearby (the most sacred being Surya Kund) in which pilgrims cook potatoes and rice tied in a piece of cloth. The meal, which takes only a few minutes to cook is first offered to the deity and then distributed as *prasad*. On the return to Hanuman Chatti, you can visit the

Purification and piety

Bad karma (see page 1407), the impurity caused by bad actions in previous births, and death itself, is the focus of some of Hinduism's most important rituals. Rivers are believed to have great purifying power, stronger at the source, at their confluence, and at the mouth. There are five *prayags* (confluences) in the Himalayan section of the Ganga – Deoprayag, Rudraprayag, Karnaprayag, Nandaprayag and Vishnuprayag, called Trayagraj (King of Prayags). On the plains, Allahabad is the most important confluence of all, where the Yamuna, the Ganga and the mythical underground river, the Sarasvati, all meet.

Hardship enhances the rewards of the *yatra* pilgrims. The really devout prostrate themselves either for the whole distance or around the temple, lying face down, stretching the arms forwards, standing up, moving up to where their fingertips reached and then repeating the exercise, each one accompanied by a chant. Most pilgrims today make the journey by bus or by car.

Someshwar Temple at **Kharsali**, 3 km across the river from Janki Chatti. The temple is one of the oldest and finest in the region.

Uttarkashi and around → *Colour map 1, B4. Altitude: 3140 m.*

This busy town, en route to Gangotri, 155 km from Rishikesh, has several places to stay but all are full during the season. There's a **tourist office** ⓘ *T01374-222290*, and the **Nehru Institute of Mountaineering** offers courses and you can trek to **Dodital** (see page 227); porters can be hired. You can buy provisions from the bazar near the bus stand. If you are in town on 14 January you will see the **Makar Sankranti Garhwal festival** of music and dance.

Gangotri and around → *Colour map 1, B5. Altitude: 3140 m.*

Gangotri, 240 km from Rishikesh, is the second of the major shrines in the Garhwal Himalaya. A high bridge now takes the road across the Jad Ganga River joining the Bhagirathi which rushes through narrow gorges, so buses travel all the way. The 18th-century granite **temple** is dedicated to the goddess Ganga, where she is believed to have descended to earth. It was built by a Gurkha commander, Amar Singh Thapa, in the early 18th century and later rebuilt by the Maharaja of Jaipur. Hindus believe that Ganga (here Bhagirathi) came down from heaven after **King Bhagirath**'s centuries-long penance. He wanted to ensure his dead relatives' ascent to heaven by having their ashes washed by the sacred waters of the Ganga. When the tempestuous river arrived on earth, the force of her flow had to be checked by Siva who received her in the coils of his hair, lest she sweep all away. A submerged lingam is visible in the winter months.

Rishikund, 55 km from Uttarkashi, has hot sulphur springs near **Gangnani** suitable for bathing, and a 15th-century temple. The **Gaurikund waterfall** here is one of the most beautiful in the Himalaya. Below Gangotri are **Bhojbasa** and **Gaumukh**, which are on a gradual but scenically stunning trek. You can continue to trek another 6 km to Nandanvan (4400 m), base camp for Bhagirathi peak, and continue 4 km to Tapovan (4463 m), known for its meadows that encircle the base of Shivling peak. ▸▸ *For trekking, see page 225.*

Rishikesh to Kedarnath → *For listings, see pages 222-224. Colour map 1, B4-B5.*

From Rishikesh the road follows the west bank of the Ganga and enters forest. At the 23rd milestone, at **Gular-dogi village**, is the orchard and garden of the Maharaja of Tehri Garhwal, close to a white-sand and rock beach, which is now home to a luxury hotel.

The section up to **Deoprayag** (68 km) is astonishingly beautiful. The folding and erosion of the hills can be clearly seen on the mainly uninhabited steep scarps on the opposite bank. Luxuriant forest runs down to the water's edge which in many places is fringed with silver sand beaches. In places the river rushes over gentle rapids. A few kilometres before Byasi is **Vashisht Gufa** (the cave where the saint meditated) which has an ashram. About 5 km after **Byasi** the road makes a gradual ascent to round an important bluff. At the top, there are fine views down to the river. The way tiny fields have been created by terracing is marvellous. Jeeps can be hired from here to Badrinath or Rishikesh.

Deoprayag is the most important of the hill *prayags* because it is here, where the frothing Bhagirathi from Gangotri joins the calm Alaknanda flowing down from Badrinath, that the Ganga herself is born. The town tumbles down the precipitous hillside in the deeply cut 'V' between the rivers, with houses almost on top of one another. Where the rivers meet is a pilgrims' bathing ghat, artificially made into the shape of India. From Deoprayag, the road is flat as far as Srinagar (35 km) and the land is cultivated. The Siva and Raghunath temples here attract pilgrims.

The old capital of Tehri Garhwal, **Srinagar** was devastated when the Gohna Lake dam was destroyed by an earthquake in the mid-19th century. The most attractive part of Srinagar, which is a university town, runs from the square down towards the river. There are some typical hill houses with elaborately carved door jambs. The 35-km route from Srinagar to **Rudraprayag**, at the confluence of the Mandakini and Alaknanda, passes through cultivated areas, wild ravines, and the vast construction works for a new dam. Halfway, an enormous landslip indicates the fragility of the mountains. Some 5 km before reaching Rudrapayag, in a grove of trees by a village, is a tablet marking the spot where the 'man-eating leopard of Rudraprayag' was killed by Jim Corbett, see box, page 243. Rudraprayag with its temples is strung out along a narrow part of the Alaknanda Valley.

For Kedarnath, leave the Pilgrim road at Rudraprayag, cross the Alaknanda River, and go through a tunnel before following the Mandakini Valley through terraced cultivation and green fields. The road goes past **Tilwara**, 9 km, then **Kund**, to **Guptakashi** where Siva proposed to Parvati. If time permits and you have hired a jeep from Guptakashi, stop at **Sonprayag**, 26 km, a small village at the confluence of the Mandakini and Son Ganga rivers, to visit the **Triyuginarayan Temple** where the gods were married. Enjoy the viewpoint here before continuing to **Gaurikund**, 4 km away, where the motorable road ends. Hundreds of pilgrims bathe in the hot sulphur springs in season. From here you either trek (start early) or ride a mule to **Kedarnath**, 14 km away. The ascent, which is steep at first, is through forests and green valleys to **Jungle Ghatti** and **Rambara** (over 1500 m); the latter part goes through dense vegetation, ravines and passes beautiful waterfalls. Beyond Rambara the path is steep again. At intervals tea stalls sell refreshments.

Kedarnath Temple and around → *For listings, see pages 222-224. Colour map 1, B5.*

The area around Kedarnath is known as Kedarkhand (the Abode of Siva). Kedarnath has one of the 12 *jyotirlingas* (luminous energy of Siva manifested at 12 holy places, miraculously formed lingams). In the *Mahabharata*, the **Pandavas** built the temple to atone for their sins after the battle at Kurukshetra, see page 462.

Kedarnath Temple → *Altitude: 3584 m. 77 km from Rudraparyag. Pujas at 0600 and 1800.*

The Kedarnath Temple is older and more impressive than Badrinath. Some claim it is originally more than 800 years old. Built of stone, unpainted but carved outside, it comprises a simple, squat, curved tower and a wooden-roofed *mandapa*. Set against an impressive backdrop of snow-capped peaks, the principal one being the Kedarnath peak (6970 m), the view from the forecourt is ruined by ugly 'tube' lights. At the entrance to the temple is a large Nandi statue.

Vasuki Tal → *A guide is necessary. Altitude: 4235 m.*

Vasuki Tal, about 6 km away, the source of Son Ganga, is to the west up along a goat track. It has superb views of the Chaukhamba Peak (7164 m). A short distance northwest is the beautiful Painya Tal where through the clear water you can see the rectangular rocks which form the lake bottom.

Kedarnath Musk Deer Sanctuary

ⓘ *Permits to visit from DFO, Kedarnath Wildlife Division in Gopeshwar, T01372-252149, dfokedarnath@rediffmail.com; Rs 100, Indians Rs 40.*

The area bounded by the Mandal–Ukhimath road and the high peaks to the north (the Kedarnath Temple is just outside) was set aside in 1972 principally to protect the endangered Himalayan musk deer – the male carries the prized musk pod. There is a **breeding centre** at Khanchula Kharak about 10 km from Chopta. The diversity of the park's flora and fauna are particular attractions. Dense forested hills of chir pine, oak, birch and rhododendron and alpine meadows with the presence of numerous Himalayan flowering plants, reflect the diverse climate and topography of the area while 40% of the rocky heights remain under permanent snow. Wildlife includes jackal, black bear, leopard, snow leopard, sambar, *bharal* and Himalayan tarh, as well as 146 species of bird. A 2-km trek from Sari village near Chopta leads to Deoriatal, at 2438 m, overlooking Chaukhamba Peak.

The Panch Kedars

There are five temples visited by pilgrims: Kedarnath, Madhmaheswar, Tungnath, Rudranath and Kalpeshwar. These vary in altitude from 1500 m to 3680 m in the Rudra Himalaya and make an arduous circuit. Kedarnath and Badrinath are 41 km apart with a tiring *yatra* (pilgrim route) between the two; most pilgrims take the longer but easier way round by bus or car. The myth of the 'five Sivas' relates how parts of the shattered Nandi Bull fell in the five places: the humped back at Kedarnath, the stomach at Madhmaheswar, the legs at Tungnath, the face at Rudranath and the hair at Kalpeshwar. Since all but Kalpeshwar and Tungnath are inaccessible in winter, each deity has a winter seat in a temple at Ukhimath. The images are brought down in the autumn and returned to their temples in the spring.

Panch Kedars trek

If you wish to undertake the 170 km, 14-day trek, start at Rishikesh, visiting Kedarnath first (see above). Return to Guptakashi and proceed to Kalimath to start the 24-km trek to **Madhmaheswar** from Mansuna village. You can stop overnight at **Ransi**, 1 km southwest of Madhmaheswar, and continue following the Ganga through the Kedarnath Musk Deer Sanctuary (see above). From near the temple at 3030 m, which has three streams flowing by it, you can see Chaukhamba Peak (7164 m).

Tungnath, at 3680 m the highest temple, is surrounded by the picturesque Nanda Devi, Neelkanth and Kedarnath mountains. You reach it by a 3-km trek from Chopta, on a driving route from Ukhimath to Gopeshwar, passing through villages, fields and wooded hills before reaching meadows with rhododendrons. The two-hour climb, though steep, is not difficult since it is along a good rocky path with occasional benches.

For **Rudranath**, at 3030 m, get to Gopeshwar by road and then on to Sagar (5 km) for the 24-km trek covering stony, slippery ground through tall grass, thick oak and rhododendron forests. Landslides are quite common. The grey stone Rudranth temple has the Rudraganga flowing by it. The views of the Nandadevi, Trisul and Hathi Parbat peaks and down to the small lakes glistening in the surroundings are fantastic.

Kalpeshwar, at 2100 m, near Joshimath, is the only one of the Panch Kedars accessible throughout the year. Its position, overlooking the Urgam Valley, offers beautiful views of the Garhwal's most fertile region with its terraced cultivation of rice, wheat and vegetables. Trekking across the Mandakini starts from Tangni.

Rudraprayag to Badrinath → *For listings, see pages 222-224.*

→ *For listings, see pages 222-224.*

The road to Joshimath → *Colour map 1, B5.*

Along the Pilgrim road, about midway between Rudraprayag and Karnaprayag, you pass **Gauchar**, famous locally for its annual cattle fair. The valley is wider here providing the local population with very good agricultural land. The beautiful Pindar River joins the Alaknanda at **Karnaprayag**, 17 km, while **Nandaprayag** is the confluence with the Nandakini River. All these places have GMVN accommodation. **Chamoli**, 40 km further on, is the principal market for the Chamoli district though the administrative headquarters is at Gopeshwar on the hillside opposite. By this point, the valley walls have become much higher and steeper and the road twists and turns more. Troop movements up to the border with Tibet/China are common and military establishments are a frequent sight on the Pilgrim road. From Chamoli onwards the road is an impressive feat of engineering.

Joshimath → *Colour map 1, B5. Phone code: 01389. Altitude: 1875 m.*

Joshimath is at the junction of two formerly important trans-Himalayan trading routes. Travellers to Govindghat and beyond may be forced to spend a night here as the road closes to northbound traffic at 1630. Joshimath is now the base for India's longest and highest **cable car route** ⓘ *generally begins 0800 or 0900, Rs 200 one way to Auli Ski Resort,* with beautiful views of Nanda Devi, Kamet, Mana Parvat and Dunagiri peaks, all above 7000 m. There is a restaurant in the meadow. The **tourist office** ⓘ *in the annexe above Neelkanth Motel, T01389-222181,* is helpful.

Vishnuprayag

Vishnuprayag is at the bottom of the gorge at the confluence of the Alaknanda and Dhauliganga rivers. Some 12 km and a steep downhill stretch brings the road from Joshimath to the winter headquarters of the Rawal of Badrinath. Buses for Badrinath, along the narrow hair-raising route start around 0600, the one-way flow regulated by police. You travel through precipitous gorges, past another Hanuman Chatti with a temple and climb above the tree-line to reach the most colourful of the *Char Dhams*, in the valley.

The **Bhotias** (Bhutias), a border people with Mongoloid features and strong ties with Tibet live along these passes (see page 668). The women wear a distinctive Arab-like headdress. Like their counterparts in the eastern Himalaya, they used to combine high-altitude cultivation with animal husbandry and trading, taking manufactured goods from India to Tibet and returning with salt and borax. When the border closed following the 1962 Indo-Chinese War, they were forced to seek alternative income and some were resettled.

Auli → *Colour map 1, B5. Altitude: 2519 m. By road it is16 km from Joshimath, or a 5-km trek; there is also a cable car (see Transport, page 224).*

The extensive meadows at Auli on the way to the Kauri Pass had been used for cattle grazing by the local herders. After the Indo-Chinese War (1962), a road was built from Joshimath to Auli and a Winter Craft Centre set up for the border police in the 1970s. With panoramic views of mountains, particularly Nanda Devi and others in the sanctuary, and Mana and Kamet on the Indo-Tibet border, and good slopes, Auli has been developed as a **ski resort** by GMVN and **Uttarakhand Tourism** operating from mid-December to early March. Though not a spectacularly equipped resort by world standards, Auli offers a 500-m ski lift (Rs 30) and 800-m chair lift (Rs 200), and has cheap lessons and gear hire.

Badrinath and around → *For listings, see pages 222-224. Colour map 1, B5. Phone code: 01389. Altitude: 3150 m.*

According to Hindu Shastras, no pilgrimage is complete without a visit to Badrinath, the abode of Vishnu. Along with Ramesvaram, Dwarka and Puri, it is one of the four holiest places in India, see page 1409. Guarding it are the Nar and Narayan ranges and in the distance towers the magnificent pyramid-shaped peak of Neelkanth, at 6558 m; a hike to its base takes two hours. Badri is derived from a wild fruit that Vishnu was said to have lived on when he did penance at Badrivan, the area which covers all five important temples including Kedarnath. Shankaracharya, the monist philosopher from South India, is credited with establishing the four great pilgrimage centres in the early ninth century AD, see page 1408.

Badrinath Temple

The main Badrinath Temple is small and brightly painted in green, blue, pink, yellow, white, silver and red. The shrine is usually crowded with worshippers. The *Rawal* (Head Priest) always comes from a Namboodri village in Kerala, the birthplace of Shankaracharya. Badrinath is snowbound over winter, when the images are transferred to Pandukeshwar, and is open late April to October. Along with worshipping in the temple and dispensing alms to the official (sometimes wealthy) temple beggars outside, it is customary to bathe in **Tapt Kund**, a hot pool nearby below the temple. This is fed by a hot sulphurous spring in which Agni (the god of fire) resides by kind permission of Vishnu. The temperature is around 45°C. **Badrinath Festival** takes place 3-10 June.

Hemkund and the Valley of Flowers → *Colour map 1, B5.*

ⓘ *Permits to enter the park are issued at the police post at the road head of Govindghat and the Forest Check Post at Ghangharia, Rs 350, camera fee Rs 50; may be negotiable in the off-season. Camping overnight in the valley or taking back plants or flowers is prohibited.*

Govindghat, 20 km from Joshimath, is on the road to Badrinath. A bridle track leads to Ghangharia, for the Valley of Flowers, 19 km further on, and Hemkund Sahib. This trail-head is very crowded in peak season (May-June). You can trek or hire mules for the two-day journey; there are several tea-stalls along the route.

Ghangharia, at 3048 m, is a 14-km walk from Govindghat. May to June are very busy. Those arriving late without a reservation may only find floor space in the Sikh Gurudwara.

To reach **Hemkund** (6 km further on, 4329 m) after 1 km from Ghangharia leave the main Valley of Flowers track, up a path to the right. **Guru Gobind Singh** is believed to have sat here in meditation during a previous incarnation, see page 1426. It is an important Sikh pilgrimage site. On the shore of the lake where pilgrims bathe in the icy cold waters, is a modern *gurudwara*; well worth the long trek though some may suffer from the high altitude. Hemkund is also a Hindu pilgrimage site, referred to as **Lokpal**. Lakshman, the younger brother of Rama, meditated by the lake and regained his health after being severely wounded by Ravana's son, Meghnath. A small Lakshman temple stands near the *gurudwara*. Despite its ancient connections, Hemkund/Lokpal was 'discovered' by a Sikh *Havildar*, Solan Singh, and only became a major pilgrimage centre after 1930.

The 14-km trail from Govindghat to Ghangharia runs along a narrow forested valley past the villages of **Pulna** and **Bhiyundar**. The **Valley of Flowers** (3000-3600 m; best July-August), is a further 5 km. **Hathi Parbat** (Elephant Peak), at 6700 m, rises dramatically at the head of the narrow side valley. Close views of mountains can be seen from Bhiyundar. The trek has beautifully varied scenery. After crossing the Alaknanda River by suspension bridge the winding path follows the Laxman Ganga as its constant companion, passing dense forests and commanding panoramic views of the lovely Kak Bhusundi Valley on its way to the hamlet of **Ghangaria** (Govind Dham), the base for the Valley of Flowers, nestling amidst giant deodars. As the path from Ghangaria gradually climbs to the Valley of Flowers, glaciers, snow bridges, alpine flowers and wildlife appear at intervals. The 6-km-long and 2-km-wide U-shaped valley is laced by waterfalls. The River Pushpati and many other small streams wind across it, and its floor, carpeted with alpine flowers during the monsoons, is particularly beautiful. It is especially popular because of its accessibility. The valley was popularized by **Frank Smythe**, the well-known mountaineer, in 1931. Local people had always kept clear of the valley because of the belief that it was haunted, and any who entered it would be spirited away. A memorial stone to Margaret Legge, an Edinburgh botanist, who slipped and fell to her death in 1939 reads, "I will lift up mine eyes unto the hills from whence cometh my strength".

Satopanth → *25 km from Badrinath. Take a guide.*

Satopanth, a glacial lake, takes a day to reach from Badrinath via the track along the Alaknanda Valley; it's a gentle climb up to **Mana** village (6 km north) near the border, inhabited by Bhotias. Foreigners need to register here and deposit their cameras since they are not permitted to take photographs. Nearby is the cave where Vyasa is said to have written the epic *Mahabharata*. The track disappears and you cross a snowbridge, trek across flower-filled meadows before catching sight of the impressive 144-m **Vasudhara Falls**. The ascent becomes more difficult as you approach the source of the Alaknanda near where the Satopanth and Bhagirathi Kharak glaciers meet. The remaining trek takes you across the **Chakra Tirth** meadow and over the steep ridge of the glacier till you see the striking green Satopanth Lake. According to legend its three corners mark the seats of Brahma, Vishnu and Siva. The peaks of **Satopanth** (7084 m) from which the glacier flows, **Neelkanth** (6558 m) and **Chaukhamba** (7164 m) make a spectacular sight.

Garhwal and the Pilgrimage (Yatra) listings

For Sleeping and Eating price codes and other relevant information, see Essentials pages 38-42.

Sleeping

Contact **GMVN**, T0135-243 1793, www.gmvnl.com, for reservations in their **B-F** resthouses along the routes. Some have 'deluxe' rooms which are still basic, with toilet and hot water, and most have dorms (Rs 200). There are also simple guesthouses in places. Room prices everywhere blow out during *yatra* season, and advance reservations are essential; **GMVN** places may only be available if you book their organized tour. Carry bottled water or a filter and take a good torch.

Yamunotri *p216*

There are other lodges and *dharamshalas* and also places to eat.

E Rest House, Janki Chatti, GMVN, T01375-235639. Closed Dec-Mar.

D Rest House, Yamunotri, GMVN. On a hill.

D-E Tourist Rest House, by the river, Hanuman Chatti. Closed Dec-Mar. GMVN, clean, simple rooms, dorm (Rs 200), hot water in buckets, the only decent place.

Uttarkashi and around *p217*

A Shikhar Nature Resort, 5 km out of town, by the Bhagirathi River, T01374-223762, www.naturecampsindia.com. Luxury tents with mod cons in scenic setting.

Dodital

E-F hotels are clustered near the bus stand.

D-E Shivam, T01374-222 525. Some a/c.

D-F Monal Tourist Home, near Kot Bungalow, T01374-222270, www.monaluttarkashi.com. Pleasant rooms and atmosphere, a little out of town. Friendly owner leads good day treks, plus yoga and Hindi classes.

E GMVN Tourist Bungalow, near bridge, T01374-222 271. Small, 33 rooms with bath, few a/c, vegetarian meals.

Gangotri *p217*

B-D Tourist Rest House (GMVN), T01377-238021, across the footbridge. 20 rooms and dorm, meals.

E Birla Niketan, near **Shikhar Nature Resort**. Rooms with bath. Other lodges have rooms without bath or electricity for less than Rs 100.

E Ganga Niketan, across the road bridge. Good rooms and a simple terrace restaurant.

Rishikesh to Kedarnath *p217*
A-E Tourist Rest House, near bus stop in central square, Srinagar, T01346-252199, www.gmvnl.com. 90 rooms, deluxe en suite, cabins and dorm, restaurant, tourist office, clean and quiet.
A-B New Tourist Bungalow, on a hill 1 km south of village centre, Rudraprayag, T01364-233347, www.gmvnl.com. 25 rooms with bath, all with excellent views of prayag, plus dorm.
B Glasshouse on the Ganges, 23 km north of Rishikesh on Badrinath Rd, Gular-dogi, T01378-269 224, www.neemranahotels.com. 16 rooms, best in the glass house itself, others in cottages in beautifully maintained gardens. Extremely peaceful location by the side of the river, wonderful place to relax.
C-D Tourist Bungalow, Gaurikund, T01364-269202, www.gmvnl.com. May-Nov. 10 rooms.
C-D Tourist Bungalow, Guptakashi, T01364-267221, www.gmvnl.com. 6 basic, clean rooms.
E Chandrapuri Camp, north Rudraprayag, by the river. 10 safari-type tents for 4.
E Tourist Bungalow, on a hillside, 1.5 km from the main bazar and bus stand, Deoprayag, T01378-266013, www.gmvnl.com. 16 rooms, some with bath, meals.

Kedarnath Temple *p218*
D Tourist Rest House, T01364-263210. 16 rooms, some with bath, and dorm.

The road to Joshimath *p220*
D Tourist Bungalow, Gauchar, T01363-240611, www.gmvnl.com. Open all year.
E Tourist Bungalow, Nandaprayag, T01372-261215, www.gmvnl.com. Open all year. Small but clean rooms.
D-E Tourist Bungalow, Karnaprayag, T01363-244210, www.gmvnl.com. Open all year. Attractive setting.

Joshimath *p220*
Hotel prices rise in high season.
E Neelkantha Motel, Upper Mall, by bus stand, T01389-222226. Often full, 15 comfortable rooms, some deluxe with bath, dorm, restaurant (acceptable though limited menu), helpful staff (will arrange jeep, porter).
F Kamet, by Ropeway, Lower Mall, T01389-222155. Not great value but cheaper rooms in annexe.
G Auli Paying Guest House, opposite the police station, has an 8-bed dorm (Rs 100).
G Nanda Devi, between Upper and Lower Mall, in the bazar, T01389-222170. Basic, cheap, porter agents.
G Shailja, behind **Neelkanth Motel**. Basic but friendly, good food but check the bill.

Auli *p220*
A-B Tourist Bungalow, T01389-223208, www.gmvni.com. Wide range, including huts and a dorm (Rs 150), large restaurant.

Badrinath *p221*
For pilgrims: *dharamshalas* and *chattis* (resthouses), T01381-225204.
B-C Devlok (GMVN), near bus stand, T01381-222212. The best option in the trekking area with 30 large rooms and a restaurant.

Hemkund and Valley of Flowers *p221*
C-D Tourist Lodge, Ghangharia. Overpriced rooms, dorm (Rs 100), tent (Rs 60).
F Bharat Lodge, at the far end of Govindghat. With bucket hot water.
F Merry Lodge. Rooms with bath.
G Krishna, Ghangharia. Rooms with bath.
Forest Rest House and **Govind Singh Gurudwara**, Govindghat, free beds and food to all (donations accepted) and reliable cloakroom service for trekkers.

Eating

Uttarkashi and around *p217*
In **Dodital**, simple *dhabas* in the bazar serve vegetarian *thalis*.

Gangotri *p217*
Numerous tea and food stalls near the temple.

Joshimath *p220*
Several places serve vegetarian meals. **Pindari** serves delicious *thalis*. Also, **Paradise**, nearby.

Activities and tours

Uttarkashi and around *p217*
Crystal Adventure, **Hotel Tapovan**, near Tourist Bungalow, Dodital, T01374-222 566.
Mount Support, Nautial Bhawan, Bhatwari Rd, near bus stand, does foreign exchange at monopoly rates.

Joshimath p220

Eskimo Travels, next to GMVN. Recommended for trekking, climbing and skiing.
Garhwal Mountain Services, T01389-222 288. For porters.
Great Himalayan Expeditions are trekking agents at **Nanda Devi Hotel**. Highly recommended for "local knowledge, good humour, high spirits and reliability".
Mountain Shepherds, Lata village, T(0)971-931 6777, www.mountainshepherds.com. Unique community tourism venture, with treks around the Nanda Devi region led by properly trained guides, plus unusual options including the chance to accompany local shepherds on their daily rounds.

Transport

For further details of getting to the region, see Rishikesh Transport, page 215.

Yamunotri p216

Bus Early bus (0600) best from Rishikesh to **Hanuman Chatti** (210 km, 9 hrs).

Uttarkashi and around p217

Bus Frequent buses from Dodital to **Rishikesh** (140 km) and **Gangotri** (100 km) during the *yatra* season.
Taxi For a return trip in a taxi to **Gangotri**, Rs 1300.

Kedarnath Temple p218

Bus From **Rishikesh** to **Rudraprayag** and **Gaurikund**.

Joshimath p220

Bus Frequent buses to **Badrinath**, 4 hrs, via **Govindghat**, 1 hr, Rs 15; to **Kedarprayag**, 1300, 4 hrs; **Rishikesh**, 0400, 0600, 10 hrs; **Rudraprayag**, 1100, 5 hrs.

Auli p220

Bus Regular buses from **Rishikesh** (253 km), **Haridwar** (276 km) up to **Joshimath**.
Cable car A modern 25-seater cable car carries people from Joshimath. It costs Rs 300 return in season, Rs 200 off season.
Jeeps/taxis Between **Joshimath** and Auli.

Trekking in Garhwal and Kumaon Himalaya

This region contains some of the finest mountains in the Himalaya and is highly accessible and yet surprisingly very few Westerners visit it, many preferring to go to Nepal. Of the many treks available, eight routes are included here. The scenic splendour of these ranges lies partly in the fact that the forests around the big peaks are still wonderfully untouched and the local population unaffected by the ravages of mass tourism. It is easy to get up into the mountain ranges of Garhwal and Kumaon, enabling a feeling of intimacy with the alpine giants. The mountains have been described as "a series of rugged ranges tossed about in the most intricate confusion" (Walton, 1910). ▸▸ *For listings, see pages 222-224.*

Ins and outs

Reliable local agents who will make all arrangements including accommodation and porters, are in Haridwar, Dehra Dun and Rishikesh. Porter agents in Uttarkashi, Joshimath, Munsiari, etc, who act as trekking agents, may not be as reliable; negotiate rates for specific services and insist on reliable porters. The Forest Office charges an entry fee and a camping fee that varies for each trek. Different months offer different things: at lower altitudes in February and March there are spectacular displays of rhododendrons; April and May allows access to higher altitudes but can get very hot and views can be restricted due to large-scale burning; July and August sees the monsoon and is good for alpine flowers but wet, humid and mostly cloudy. If the monsoon is heavy, roads and tracks can become impassable; in September the air is beautifully rain-washed, but early-morning clear skies can give way by 1000 to cloud, and views may completely disappear; in October and November temperatures are lower, the skies clearer and the vegetation greener following the monsoon.

Background

This region had been open since the British took over in 1815 but it was closed in 1960 due to political troubles with China, and during this period Nepal became popular with climbers and trekkers. Garhwal and Kumaon Himalaya have gradually been opened to explorers since 1975, though parts bordering Tibet remain closed. Much of the early Himalayan exploration was undertaken here. **Trisul**, 7120 m, after it had been climbed by Doctor Tom Longstaff in 1906, remained the highest mountain climbed for the next 30 years.

Trekking

Trekking in this region is not highly organized so you need to be well prepared. Topo- graphical maps are not available locally. A good map for the area is Leomann's *Indian Himalya Sheet 8, Kumaon Garhwal.* On most treks you need a tent (though not for the Pindari Glacier trek, for example). Very few villagers speak English, and the rewards for the well-equipped trekker, who has planned carefully, are great – especially the feeling of being far from the madding crowd. If you are travelling in small groups of three to four it is often possible to find lodgings in villagers' houses but despite their hospitality, this is uncomfortable. Where available, GMVN and KMVN lodges provide rustic but clean rooms and some have deluxe rooms with bath. Caretakers cook simple meals. If you would like to leave the logistics to someone else, hire a government-recognized specialist tour operator.

Around **Gangotri** and **Yamunotri** in Garhwal there are a number of good treks, some suitable for the independent or 'go-it-alone' trekker. **Nanda Devi** is the other area and this forms a ring that includes both Garhwal and Kumaon. There are many more treks than those indicated here. The lower part of the Niti Valley, and the Darma Valley, are open to groups of four with requisite permits. You are not allowed to go beyond Badrinath.

Gangotri and Yamunotri area → *For listings, see pages 222-224. Colour map 1, B4/5.*

Gangotri to Gaumukh

The best-known trek here is to Gaumukh (Cow's Mouth) and, if desired, beyond onto the Gangotri Glacier. Gaumukh can easily be managed in three days with minimal equipment but carry provisions.

From Gangotri, at 3046 m, follow the well-defined, gradually ascending path for 14 km to **Bhojbasa** at 3792 m. It takes about five hours. There is a **Tourist Rest House** here which has fours rooms and a dorm without bedding. This is, however, often full. You can hire good- value two-person tents for Rs 160 a night. There is also an *ashram* where trekkers and pilgrims can stay and there is tented accommodation at **Chirbasa**, 5 km before Bhojbasa.

The 4 km to **Gaumukh** (the last section is across boulder scree and moraine), takes about one hour so it is quite feasible to go from Bhojbasa to Gaumukh, spend some time there, then return the same day. There are plenty of tea houses en route. Gaumukh, the present source of the Bhagirathi (Ganga) River, is at the mouth of the Gangotri Glacier where blocks of glacier ice fall into the river and pilgrims cleanse themselves in freezing water. There are breathtaking views. There is basic tent accommodation.

Beyond Gaumukh more care and camping equipment is required. The **Gangotri Glacier** is in an amphitheatre of 6500- to 7000-m peaks which include Satopanth (7084 m), Vasuki (6792 m), Bhagirathi (6556 m), Kedar Dome and the prominent trio of Bhagirathi I, II and III; Shivling (6543 m), standing alone, is one of the most spectacular peaks in the Himalaya.

Tapovan → *Altitude: 4463 m.*

In a breathtaking setting in a grassy meadow on the east bank of the Gangotri Glacier, this is the base camp for climbing expeditions to the stunningly beautiful **Shivling** (6543 m), Siva's lingam and the 'Matterhorn of the Himalaya'. You can either return the same way or make a round trip by crossing over the glacier for 3 km to **Nandanvan**, at 4400 m, and continuing upwards for a further 6 km to Vasuki Tal beneath **Vasuki** peak (6792 m). Since the trek involves crossing a glacier crossing, it is recommended that you go with a guide. The return is via Nandanvan, the west bank of the Gangotri Glacier crossing the Raktvarn Glacier to Gaumukh-Raktvarn, so called because of the rust-coloured boulders in its moraine. Full camping equipment is necessary on this trek.

Gangotri to Kedartal

This is an excellent short trek with scenic variety and spectacular views but be aware of the problems associated with altitude and allow time for acclimatization. It requires a tent, stove and food. It is 17 km to Kedartal (5000 m), a small glacial lake surrounded by Meru (6672 m), Pithwara (6904 m) and Bhrigupanth (6772 m).

Leaving Gangotri you proceed up the gorge of the Kedar Ganga (Siva's contribution to the Bhagirathi River). It is 8 km to Bhoj Kharak and then a further 4 km to Kedar Kharak, passing through some beautiful Himalayan birch forest en route. The bark from the trees (*bhoj* in

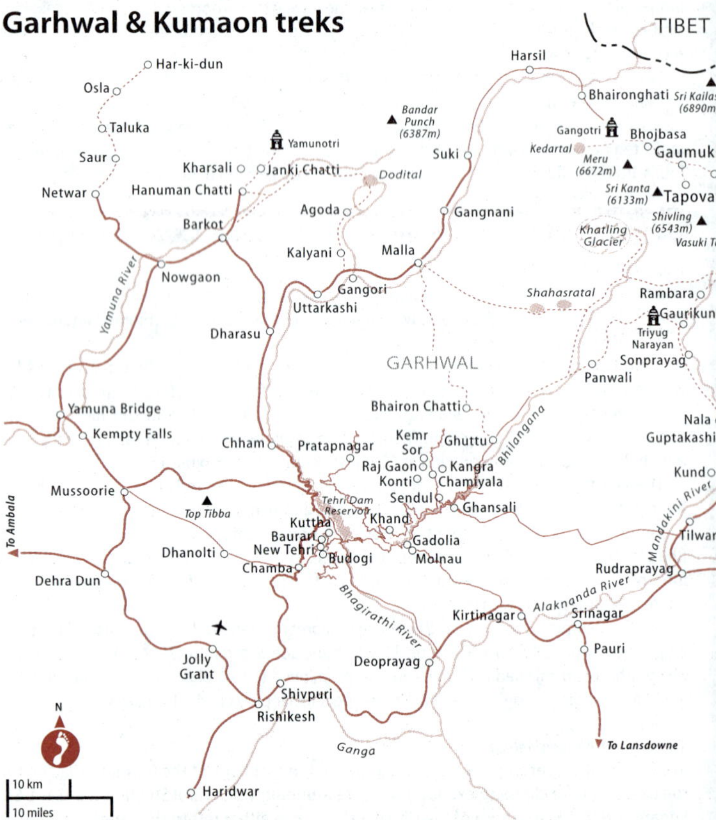

Garhwali) was used by sages and hermits for manuscripts. From Kedar Kharak, where you can camp, it is a laborious 5-km ascent to Kedartal. Besides the peaks surrounding the lake you can also see the Gangotri range.

You return to Gangotri the same way. **Rudugaira Kharak** is the base camp for the peaks at the head of the Rudugaira Valley. Coming down towards Gangotri you must cross to the opposite bank near Patangnidhar to avoid the cliffs on the west bank. Nearer Gangotri cross back to the west bank.

Gangotri to Yamunotri via Dodital

This is a beautiful trek between Kalyani and Hanuman Chatti, a distance of 49 km. You can do a round trip from either end. It takes five days.

From **Uttarkashi** take a local bus to Kalyani via **Gangori**, 3 km away, or walk it. At **Kalyani**, 1829 m, the recognized starting point of the trek, you take a track to the right. From here it gets steeper as the path climbs through forest to **Agoda**, 5 km away. There is a suitable camping or halting place 2 km beyond Agoda. The next day carry on to **Dodital**, 16 km away at 3024 m, picturesquely set in a forest of pine, deodar and oak. This is the source of the Asi Ganga and is stocked with trout. There is a dilapidated **Forest Rest House** and several cheap lodges. Above the lake there are fine views of Bandar Punch (Monkey's Tail, 6387 m). To reach **Hanuman Chatti** at 2400 m, walk for 6 km up to the Aineha Pass, 3667 m, which also has splendid views. Then it is a 22-km walk down to Hanuman Chatti, the roadhead for Yamunotri.

Har-ki-Dun Trek

Har-ki-Dun (God's Valley) nestles in the northwest corner of Garhwal near the Sutlej-Yamuna watershed. The people of the area have the distinction of worshipping **Duryodhana**, head of the crafty royal family in the *Mahabharata*, rather than siding with the pious Pandavas, see page 1401. The valley is dominated by Swargarohini (6096 m) and Kalanag. From **Nowgaon**, 9 km south of Barkot, take a bus to the roadhead of **Sankri**. From here it is a gradual ascent over 12 km to **Taluka**, and **Osla** (2559 m), 11 km further. Another 8 km and 1000 m higher is **Har-ki-Dun** (3565 m), an ideal base for exploring the valley. Allow three days to Har-ki-Dun. There are **Forest** and **Tourist Rest Houses** at all these places.

You can return to Nowgaon or, if properly equipped and provisioned, trek for 29 km on to **Yamunotri** via the Yamunotri Pass (5172 m). You will need to allow time for acclimatization. The views from the pass are well worth the effort.

Nanda Devi area → *Colour map 1, B5.*

Nanda Devi (7816 m), named after the all-encompassing form of the female deity, dominates the Garhwal and Kumaon Himalaya. With its two peaks separated by a 4-km-long ridge, the second-highest mountain in India is incredibly beautiful. She is also the most important of

Nanda Devi area treks

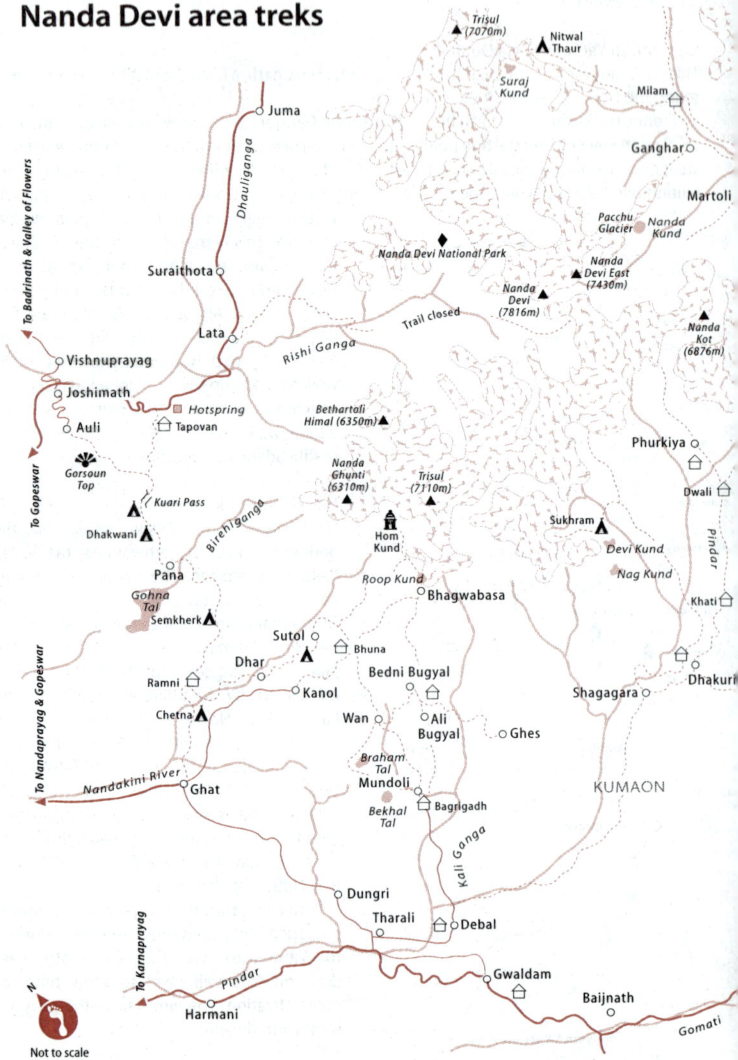

Garhwal's deities, protected by a ring of mountains, 112 km in circumference, containing 12 peaks over 6400 m high. In only one place is this defensive ring lower than 5500 m, at the **Rishi Gorge**, one of the deepest in the world. It is the place of ascetic sages (*rishis*). The Nanda Devi Sanctuary is a World Biosphere Reserve.

Pindari Glacier Trek

This trek along the southern edge of the Sanctuary is an 'out and back' trek, ie you return by the same route. **KMVN Tourist Lodges** (www.kmvn.gov.in, some with only four beds, none with telephones) are dotted along the route so this trek can be done with little equipment, although a sleeping bag is essential. Book your accommodation early or take your own tent. The trek is 66 km from Song, which has the last bus terminus.

From **Bageshwar**, see page 237, take a local bus to **Bharari**, at 1524 m, which has a **PWD Rest House**, a cheap hotel and **Tourist Bungalow** (T01372-260465, www.gmvnl.com); open all year. From here you can walk 16 km along the Saryu Valley to **Song** or take another bus. It is just over 1.5 km further to **Loharkhet**, at 1829 m, which also has a **PWD Bungalow** in the village and a basic **KMVN Tourist Rest House** overlooking it. There are good views of the hillside opposite and the head of the Saryu Valley. It is 11 km from Loharkhet to **Dhakuri** via the Dhakuri Pass (2835 m) which has a wonderful view of the south of the Nanda Devi Sanctuary including Panwali Dhar (6683 m) and Maiktoli (6803 m). The walk to the pass is mostly through forest on a well-graded path. About 100 m below the pass on the north side is a clearing with a **PWD Bungalow** and a **KMVN Tourist Rest House**. The views are great, especially at sunrise and sunset.

In the Pindar Valley you descend to **Khati**, 8 km away at 2194 m, first through rhododendron, then mixed forests dominated by stunted oak. Khati is a village with over 50 households situated on a spur that runs down to the river, some 200 m below. There is a **PWD Bungalow**, **KMVN Tourist Rest House** and a village hotel. You can buy biscuits, eggs and chocolate, brought in by mule from Bharari.

From Khati follow the Pindar 8 km to **Dwali**, 2580 m, which is at the confluence of the Pindar and the Kaphini rivers. Here there is a **KMVN Travellers' Lodge** and a run-down **PWD Bungalow**. If you have a tent, camp in front.

The next stop, 6 km on, is **Phurkiya**, 3260 m, which also has a **KMVN Travellers' Lodge**. This can be used as a base for going up to Zero Point (4000 m), a viewpoint from where the steep falling glacier can be seen (it is difficult for trekkers to go up to the snout of the glacier itself). On either side there are impressive peaks, including Panwali Dwar (6683 m) and Nanda Kot (6876 m). Return to Bharari the same way.

From Dwali, however, a side trip to the **Kaphini Glacier** is worthwhile. Alternatively, you could trek up to **Sundar Dhunga Glacier** from Khati. Including either of these, the trek can be accomplished in a week but for comfort allow nine days.

Roopkund Trek → *Altitude: 4800 m. Kund means lake in Garhwali.*

A legend relates Nanda Devi, the wife of Siva, to this small lake. When her sister Balpa accompanied her husband King Jasidhwal of the medieval Kingdom of Kanauj on a pilgrimage to Kailash (Mount Trisul), she delivered a child at Balpa de Sulera (adjoining Bhagwabasa), thus polluting the entire mountain. Nanda Devi's herald Latu (who has a temple at Wan), at the command of the goddess, hurled the royal pilgrimage party into the small tarn called Roopkund; hence the remains of the 300 bodies found in the lake. Thirty years ago the Indian anthropologist DN Majumdar discovered a number of frozen bodies around this small mountain tarn, the remains of a party of pilgrims on a *yatra* who died when bad weather closed in. Carbon-dating suggests the bones are 600 years old.

This is a highly varied and scenic trek which can be undertaken by a suitably equipped party. A week is sufficient – nine days if you want to take it more comfortably with a rest day for acclimatization. The trek can start in Debal where you can pick up provisions, or at Bagrigadh (see below). You can usually get porters at Gwaldam or Debal.

Gwaldam → *Colour map 1, C5. Altitude: 1950 m.*

Gwaldam is a small market strung out along a ridge surrounded by orchards. The British established tea plantations which have since been abandoned. **GMVN Tourist Bungalow** ⓘ *T01363-274244, www.gmvnl.com*, has splendid views from the garden, especially at dawn and dusk, of Trisul (7120 m) and Nanda Ghunti (6310 m).

From Gwaldam, at 1950 m, walk down through attractive pine forest, cross the River Pindar and continue 8 km to **Debal**, at 1350 m, where there is a **KMVN Tourist Rest House**, a **Forest Rest House** and *dharamshalas*. From here you can either walk 12 km along a dirt road through villages with views of Trishul (6855 m), or go by cramped jeep-taxi to **Bagrigadh**, which is 500 m below the **Lohajung Pass** (2350 m) where there is an attractive **GMVN Travellers' Lodge** and two cheap lodges, right on the ridge beside a pretty shrine. The best option is **Patwal Tourist Lodge**, PO Mundoli, Chamoli, which has spotless, comfortable rooms, immaculate toilet and showers (bucket hot water), and treks arranged by a retired army officer. There are good views here of Nanda Ghunti and Trisul from the terrace. If time is at a premium, you can save a day by going by bus from Gwaldam to Tharali, taking another bus to Debal, catching the jeep-taxi to Bagrigadh and walking up to Lohajung in one long day.

From **Lohajung** you walk down through stunted oak forest and along the *Wan Gad* (river) 12 km to the village of **Wan**, 2400 m, which has a **Forest Rest House** and **GMVN Travellers' Lodge**. From Wan it is essentially wilderness travel as you make the ascent to Roopkund, first walking through thick forest to **Bedni Bugyal** (*bugyal* – meadow) which is used as summer pasture. This is at 3550 m and has good views of Trisul, Nandaghunti and the Badrinath range to the north. There are some shepherds' stone huts which you may be able to use but it is better to take a tent.

From Bedni it is a gradual 7-km climb along a well-defined path over the 4500-m **Kalwa Vinayak** to more shepherds' huts at Bhagwabasa which, at 4000 m, is the base for the final walk up to Roopkund. A stove is necessary for cooking and it can be very cold at night, but water is available about 150 m northeast and up the slope from the campsite. From here, it is two to three hours up to **Roopkund**. Immediately after the monsoon the views can disappear

Conquering Nanda Devi on apricot brandy

For half a century the problems that engaged the attention of many experienced explorers and mountaineers was not so much how to climb the mountain but how to get to it. Various attempts were made from a number of places to gain entry into what became known as the Nanda Devi Sanctuary. The riddle was finally solved by the 'Terrible Twins', Bill Tilman and Eric Shipton in a characteristically lightweight expedition (these two great mountaineers would agonize over whether to take one shirt or two on an expedition lasting a few months!). The route they discovered was up the Rishiganga and through the difficult Rishi Gorge. They made two trips into the Sanctuary during their five-month expedition in the Garhwal Himalaya in 1934. Bill Tilman returned in 1936 (Shipton was on Hugh Rutledge's Everest Expedition) with a small party and climbed the mountain with little real difficulty.

In *The Ascent of Nanda Devi*, Tilman, a purist, wrote: "mountaineering is in danger of becoming mechanized. It is therefore pleasing to record that in climbing Nanda Devi no climbing aids were used, apart, that is, from the apricot brandy we took. Our solitary oxygen apparatus was fortunately drowned, pitons were forgotten at base camp and crampons were solemnly carried up only to be abandoned".

In 1936 the monsoon was particularly heavy. The Pindar River rose dramatically. In the village of Tharali 40 lives were lost on 29 August, the day that Tilman's party reached the summit. Some say the anger of the goddess was provoked by the violation of her sanctuary. See Books, page 1440, for recommended reading.

in cloud by 1000, so it is best to leave early. In the final steep part the ground can be icy. Roopkund Lake itself is small and unimpressive, but from the 4900-m ridge approximately 50 m above Roopkund there is a magnificent view of the west face of Trisul rising over 3500 m from the floor of the intervening hanging valley to the summit. Return to Gwaldam by the same route or via **Ali Bugyal** and village Didina which bypasses Wan.

Curzon Trail

The Curzon Trail is an incomparably beautiful trek. However, rapid ascent follows equally steep descent from one valley to the next, and at no point does the trek get close to the high snow-covered peaks. It was the route followed by Tilman and Shipton on their way to the Rishi Gorge (see box, above), and by other mountaineers en route to the peaks on the Indo-Tibetan border. The crossing of the Kuari Pass is a fitting conclusion to a trek that takes in three lesser passes and five major rivers – the Pindar, Kaliganga, Nandakini, Birehiganga and Dhauliganga. The trail was named after Lord Curzon, a keen trekker, and the path may have been specially improved for him. After 1947 it was officially renamed the 'Nehru Trail'. Take camping equipment. Some stopping off places have no suitable accommodation.

This trek begins at **Joshimath** via Auli, or at **Gwaldam** and ends at **Tapovan** in the Dhauliganga Valley on the Joshimath–Niti Pass road. It crosses the **Kuari Pass** (4268 m), one of the finest vantage points in the Himalaya.

From Gwaldam proceed to **Wan** as in the previous trek. Then, go over the Kokinkhal Pass to **Kanol** (2900 m) through thick mixed forest for 10 km to **Sutol**, at 2100 m, in the Nandakini Valley. There is a good campsite by the river. The next two stages follow the Nandakini downstream 10 km to Padergaon, 2500 m, via Ala. The trail to Tapovan leads up over the rhododendron forest-clad **Ramni Pass** (3100 m) with a good view of the Kuari Pass. The trail southwest of Ramni goes to the nearby road head at **Ghat**, from where you can also start the trek. To reach Tapovan from Ramni is a good three days' walk, down through lush forest to cross the Birehiganga River by an impressive suspension bridge, up around the horseshoe-shaped hanging valley around Pana Village, over an intervening spur and into the forested tributary valley of the Kuari nallah. There is no settlement in this area; *bharal* (mountain goats) and the rarely seen Himalayan black bear inhabit the rich forest. Waterfalls tumble down over steep crags. There is a camp and a cave (about one hour) before the Kuari Pass at **Dhakwani** (3200 m).

Leave early to get the full effect of sunrise over the peaks on the Indo-Tibetan border. Some of the peaks seen are Kamet, Badrinath (7040 m), Dunagiri (7066 m) and Changabang (6863 m). There is a wonderful wooded campsite with marvellous views about 300 m below the pass. From here one trail leads along a scenic ridge to Auli, where you can finish with a cable car ride to Joshimath, while another drops down over 2000 m to **Tapovan** and the Joshimath–Niti road. There is a hot sulphur spring (90°C) here and a bus service to **Joshimath**. Allow 10 days for the trek.

Nanda Devi East Base Camp and Milam Glacier Trek

Much of this area was only reopened to trekkers in 1993 after more than 30 years of seclusion. The Milam Valley, incised by the 36-km-long Gori Ganga Gorge, was part of the old trade route between Kumaon and Tibet, only interrupted by the Indian-Chinese War of 1962. Milam, which once had 500 households, many occupied by wealthy traders and surrounded by barley and potato fields, has been reduced to a handful of occupied cottages. The trek is moderate, with some sustained steady walking but no really steep gradients or altitude problems. The route is through some of the remotest regions of the Himalaya with spectacular scenery and rich wildlife.

Day 1 From **Munsiari**, a 10-hour drive from Almora, takes you down to Selapani where the trail up the Milam Valley begins. **Lilam** (1800 m) is an easy 7-km walk (2½ hours) where the tiny **Rest House** offers a convenient halt or camping ground for the first night. See page 237 for details about Munsiari.

Day 2 (14 km; seven hours) From Lilam the trail enters the spectacular 25-km-long gorge. Etched into the cliff face above the Gori Ganga the hillsides above are covered in dense bamboo thickets and mixed rainforest. After the junction of the Ralam and Gori Ganga rivers the track climbs to a tea shop at Radgari, then goes on to a small **Rest House** at **Bugdiar** (2700 m). A memorial commemorates villagers and army personnel lost in the avalanche of 1989. Only a few houses remain on the edge of a wasteland.

Day 3 (16 km; six hours) The valley opens up after climbing quite steeply to a huge overhanging cliff, which shelters a local deity. The route enters progressively drier terrain, but there are two waterfalls of about 100 m, one opposite a tea shop at Mapang. The track climbs to **Rilkote** (3200 m).

Day 4 (13 km; six hours) Passing deserted villages in the now almost arid landscape the track goes through the large village of **Burphu**, backed by the Burphu Peak (6300 m). Nanda Devi East comes into view before reaching **Ganghar** village (3300 m) where only three of the former 60 families remain. Some of the houses have beautiful carved wooden door and window frames; the carefully walled fields below are deserted.

Day 5 (7 km; three hours) A steep narrow track leads into the **Pachhu Valley**, dominated by the northeast face of Nanda Devi East, 3800 m above the Pachhu Glacier. Dwarf rhododendron and birch, with anemones and primulas below, line the first section of the track before it emerges into alpine meadows below the debris of the glacier itself. **Tom Longstaff** came through this valley in his unsuccessful attempt to climb Nanda Devi East in 1905 before trying the parallel valley to the south of Pachhu via what is now known as Longstaff's Col. There is a campsite (3900 m), 3 km from the base of Nanda Devi East, with both the col and the summit clearly visible in good weather.

Day 6 Side treks are possible up to the Pachhu Glacier and along its edge to the glacial lake **Nanda Kund**.

Day 7 (17 km; six hours) Returning via Ghanghar at Burfu, the track crosses the Gori Ganga on a wooden bridge then climbs to the former staging post of **Milam** (3300 m).

Day 8 Another 'excursion' (10 km; eight hours) is possible from Milam to the **Milam Glacier** (4100 m). There are superb views of the clean ice uncovered by debris from the track which runs along the left bank of the Milam Glacier. Three tributary glaciers join the main Milam Glacier.

Day 9 (13 km; five hours) The track runs along the left bank of the river via Tola village to the base of the 4750 m Brijganga Pass, outside **Sumdu** village (3400 m).

Day 10 (12 km; seven hours) Superb views characterize this steady climb to the top of the pass. The razor sharp Panchchulis dominate the south while the twin peaks of Nanda Devi are straight ahead. **Ralam** village is a steep drop below the pass (3700 m).

Day 11 (10 km; six hours) This can be a rest day or a day trek up to the **Shankalpa Glacier** along the watershed between the rarely visited Ralam and Darma valleys.

Day 12-14 (six hours each day) The trek runs steadily down through the thickly forested Ralam Valley, passing Marjhali, Bhujani, Buria, Sarpa and Besani villages.

Day 15 (11 km; four hours) Return from Lilam to Munsiari via a number of villages.

Darma Valley Trek

The easternmost of the Kumaon valleys, the Darma Valley is now also open to trekkers but you need permission. Separated from western Nepal by the Kaliganga River and with Tibet to the north, the valley is one of the least explored in the Himalaya. From the roadhead at **Dharchula** (on the India/Nepal border) it is possible to trek for four or five days up to Sipu and also to spend time exploring the numerous side valleys. Buses are available from Pithoragarh, see page 237, and Almora up to Dharchula from where it is often possible to get local transport for a further 32 km up to **Sobala**. Then it is a three- to four-day trek up to Sipu, the northernmost point allowed under present regulations.

Nainital and around

Kumaon's hill stations offer access to some relatively unexplored sections of the Himalaya. Nainital itself is a congested Indian holiday town set around a steadily diminishing lake, albeit in the midst of some excellent birdwatching territory. Further northeast, the lush hillsides around Almora have inspired some of India's greatest mystics, and now provide a venue for some interesting projects in sustainable tourism. ▸▸ *For listings, see pages 238-242.*

Nainital →

For listings, see pages 238-242. Colour map 1, C5. Phone code: 05942. Population: 40,000. Altitude: 1938 m. See map, page 234.

Much of Nainital's historic appeal has waned with the influx of mass tourism. Its villas, bungalows and fine houses are swamped with Indian holiday-makers in the summer season, and although it holds some attractive walks and only a few foreign tourists, congestion and pollution is taking its toll, particularly on the fragile ecosystem of the lake. It can be very cold in winter, and depressions sometimes bring cloud and rain obscuring the views of the mountains. Many now prefer to break the journey to Almora from Corbett or Rishikesh at Ranikhet instead.

Ins and outs

Getting there The nearest railway station is 1¾ hours away at Kathgodam, linked to Nainital by frequent buses. The climb from Kathgodam to Nainital is dramatic, rising 1300 m over 30 km. The road follows the valley of the Balaya stream then winds up the hillsides through forests and small villages. After the long drive the town around the *tal* (lake) appears suddenly; the land south and on the plains side falls away quite steeply so you only see the lake when you are at its edge. Buses from Delhi and the surrounding hill stations use the Tallital Bus Stand at the southern end of the lake, while some buses from Ramnagar (for Corbett National Park) use the Mallital Bus Stand at the northern end.

Getting around The Mall, pedestrianized at peak times, is the hub of Nainital's life. You can hire a cycle-rickshaw if the walk feels too much, or take a taxi for travelling further afield. ▸▸ *See Transport, page 241.*

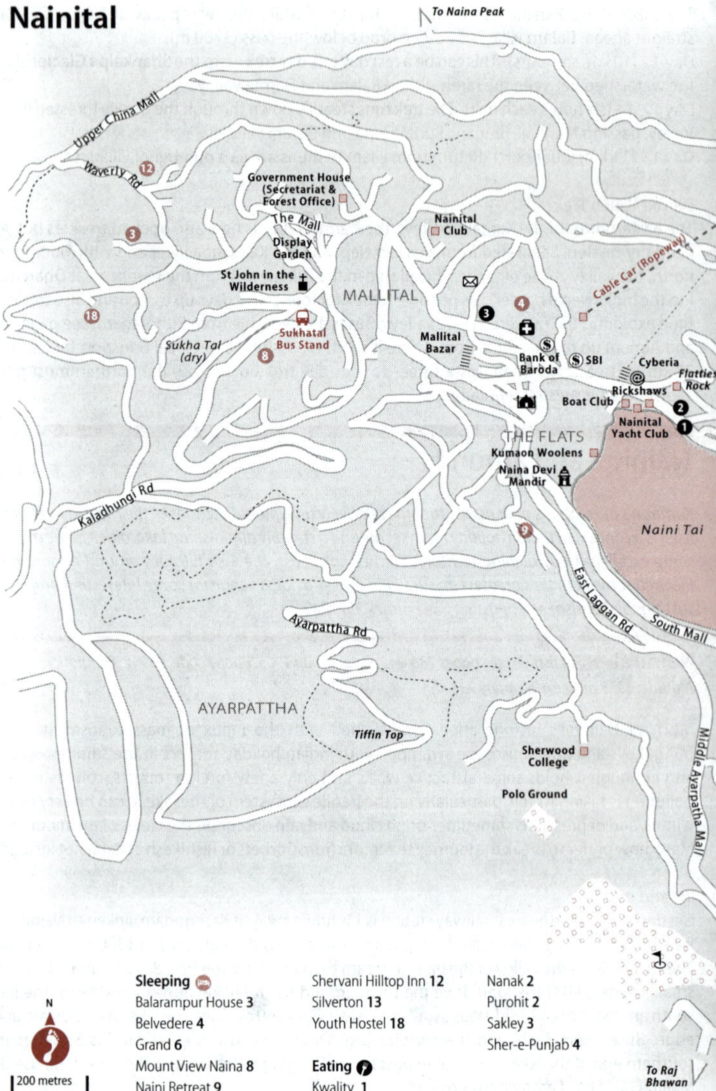

Tourist information KMVN Information Centre ⓘ *Parvat Tours; at Secretariat, Mallital, T/F05942-231436*. Uttarakhand Tourism ⓘ *Mall Rd, Mallital, T05942-235337*. Tourist Bungalow ⓘ *T05942-235400*.

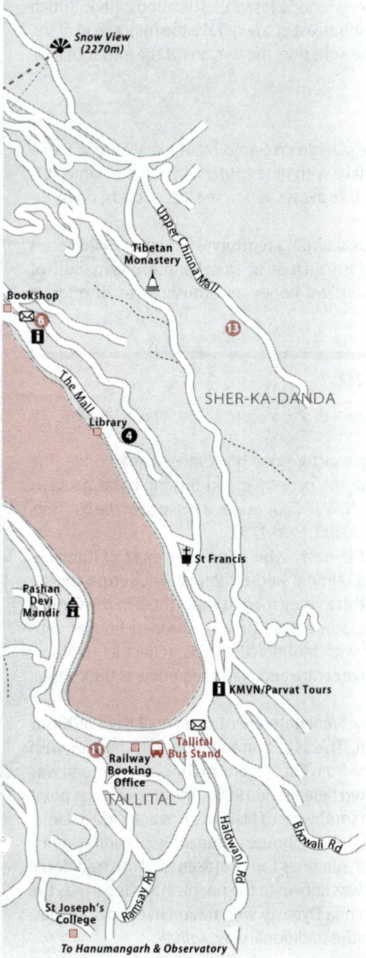

History

In 1839 the small hamlet of Nainital was 'discovered' by a Mr P Barron, a sugar manufacturer from Saharanpur. He was so impressed by the 1500-m-long and 500-m-wide lake that he returned with a sailing boat a year later, carried up in sections from the plains. In due course Nainital became the summer capital of the then United Provinces. An old legend of Siva and Sati, see page 207, associates the place as where Sati's eyes fell (hence *naini*). The *tal* (lake) is surrounded by seven hills, the Sapta-Shring. On 18 September 1880 disaster struck the town. At the north end of the lake, known now as Mallital (the southern part is Tallital) stood the **Victoria Hotel**. In two days nearly 1000 mm of rain fell leading to a landslip which crushed some outhouses, burying several people. The cliff overhanging the hotel collapsed, burying the soldiers and civilians engaged in rescue work and making it impossible to save the 150 buried. Later the area was levelled, became known as The Flats, and was used for public meetings and impromptu games of football and cricket. Today it is more a bus park in the tourist season, though sports tournaments are held here in June, August and December.

Sights

There is little of architectural interest other than the colonial-style villas overlooking the lake (walking is the major attraction of this town). The **Church of St John in the Wilderness** (1846), one of the earliest buildings, is beyond Mallital, below the Nainital Club. The most distinctive building is **Government House** (1899, now the Secretariat) which was designed in stone by FW Stephens who was also responsible for VT (now CST) and Churchgate Stations in Mumbai. Early in the season it is pleasant to walk round (the Lower Mall is pedestrianized) or take a boat across the lake; remember it can still be very cold in March.

Naina (Cheena) Peak (2610 m) is a 5-km walk from the lake. From the top, there are stunning views of the Himalaya including Nanda Devi (7816 m) and the mountains on the Tibetan border. In season there is a '**cable car**' (ropeway) ⓘ *0900-1700, winter 1000-1600, Rs 65 return,* which runs from the Mallital end of the lake to Snow View (2270 m), another good vantage point for viewing the snow-capped peaks. It is also possible to make the 2-km steep climb up to the viewpoint from the north end of the lake, passing the small Tibetan *gompa* which has fluttering prayer flags marking it.

Hanumangarh with a small temple off Haldwani Road, and the **Observatory** ⓘ *3 km from the lake, Mon-Sat 1400-1600 and 1930-2100,* further along the path, have lookouts for watching the sun set over the plains. The opposite side has only a few cottages and much higher up near the ridge are two private boys' schools – Sherwood College and St Joseph's. The atmospheric **British Cemetery** with its crumbling graves is about 3 km southeast of town. Take the minor road at the south end of the lake (not the Rampur Road); on the right side, the remains of the entrance gate are just visible behind some trees.

Excursions from Nainital

Sat Tal, 24 km away, has seven lakes including the jade green Garud Tal, the olive green Rama Tal and Sita Tal. **Naukuchiyatal**, 26 km away, is a lake with nine corners, hence the name. It is beautifully unspoilt and quiet paddling round the lake allows you to see lots of birds; boats for hire. Tour buses stop around 1630.

Pangot, 15 km from Nainital via Kilbury, is in ideal birding territory where over 580 species have been recorded. **Jeolikote**, a small hamlet on the main road up from Ranpur, 18 km south of Nainital, is known for its health centre and butterflies, honey and mushrooms. It offers a peaceful weekend retreat.

Around Nainital → *For listings, see pages 238-242.*

Almora and around → *Phone code: 05962. Colour map 1, C5. Population: 32,500. Altitude: 1646 m. 66 km northeast of Nainital.*

Almora is a charming bustling hill town occupying a picturesque horseshoe-shaped ridge. The Mall runs about 100 m below the ridge line, while the pedestrianized historic bazar above is jostling and colourful. For information contact: **KMVN** ⓘ *Holiday Home, 2 km west of the bus stop,* or **Uttarakhand Tourism** ⓘ *opposite GPO, T05962-230180, 1000-1700.*

The town was founded in 1560 by the Chand Dynasty who ruled over most of Kumaon, which comprises the present districts of Nainital, Almora and Pithoragarh. Overrun by the Gurkhas in 1798, it was heavily bombed by the British as they tried to expel them in the Gurkha Wars of 1814-1815. Traces of an old Chand fort, stone-paved roads, wooden houses with beautifully carved façades and homes decorated with traditional murals, reflect its heritage. Today an important market town and administrative centre and is also regarded as the cultural capital of the area it richly rewards exploring.

Swami Vivekenanda came to Almora and gained enlightenment in a small cave at **Kasar Devi** on Kalimatiya Hill, 7 km northeast of town. This is a tranquil mountain hamlet with stunning views, which has been visited by everyone from Cat Stevens to DH Lawrence, and was dubbed '**Crank's Ridge**' after Timothy Leary streaked here in the 1960s. Another vantage point for sunrise and sunset is **Bright End Corner**, 2.5 km southwest of Mall Road, near All India Radio. The stone **Udyotchandesvar Temple**, above Mall Road, houses Kumaon's presiding deity, Nanda Devi, whose festival is in August/ September. Almora's Tamta artisans still use traditional methods to work with copper. Copper metallurgy was known to the people here as early as the second century BC and is associated with the Kuninda Dynasty who traded in copper articles. The hand-beaten copper pots are 'silver plated' in the traditional way, *kalhai*.

Jageswar, 34 km northeast, lies beside a brook in a dappled clearing in the nape of a serene cedar wooded gorge. It is famous for the 164 ornamented temples built by the Chand rajas and also holds one of the 12 *jyotirlingas*. The scores of temples here, shaded by the trees' canopy, and in nearby Gandeswar are very fine examples of early medieval hill temple architecture but are rarely visited by outsiders. Some elegant examples of vernacular architecture lie in the village. The temple dedicated to Jogeswar with finely carved pillars has a small museum; 6 km before Jageswar, a roadside sign points to stone-age **cave paintings**, about 50 m off the road. These are in red, white and black, depicting human figures, trees, animals and possibly water courses. Though several paintings were damaged by storage of cement bags during bridge-building work nearby, many can be seen and are worth the short stop. Once the capital of the Chand rajas, **Binsar** has a bird sanctuary sited at 2410 m with superb views of valleys around and panoramic mountain views. It is 28 km away.

Kausani → *Colour map 1, C5. Altitude: 1892 m. 50 km north of Almora.*

Kausani sits on a narrow ridge among pine forests with wonderfully wide views of the **Nanda Devi** group of mountains stretching over 300 km along the horizon; the view is particularly stunning at sunrise. Modern Kausani has a strong military presence, so be careful with your camera. You may trek from here to Bageswar, Gwaldam and the Pindari Glacier. In 1929 **Mahatma Gandhi** spent 12 days at what is now Anashakti Ashram.

Baijnath and Garur → *Colour map 1, C5. 17 km northwest of Kausani.*

From Kausani, the road descends to Garur and Baijnath. The small town of **Baijnath** on the banks of the Gomti River has distinctively carved 12th- and 13th-century Katyuri temples. They are now mostly ruined, but its houses have intricately carved wooden doors and windows, see also page 508. The main 10th-century temple houses a beautiful image of Parvati. Siva and Parvati are believed to have married at the confluence of the Gomti and Garur Ganga. The Katyur Dynasty, which ruled the valley for 500 years, took their name from Siva and Parvati's mythical son, Karttikeya. **Garur** has plenty of buses and taxis northwards. Just north of Garur a road runs northwest to Gwaldam, see Roopkund Trek, page 230, and another east to Bageshwar.

Bageshwar and the Saryu Valley → *Altitude: 960 m. 90 km north of Almora, 23 km east of Baijnath.*

Bageshwar, meaning Siva as 'Lord of Eloquent Speech', stands at the confluence of the Gomti and Saryu rivers. It is Kumaon's most important pilgrimage centre and has several temples, the most important of which is the 17th-century Bhagnath temple, overlooking the confluence. From Bageshwar a jeep road runs northwards along the Saryu, through beautiful wooded gorges where lammergeiers and griffon vultures soar overhead, to Talai. This is an alternative trailhead for treks to the **Pindari Glacier** (see page 229), and also gives access to a string of beautiful villages perched on mountainsides among terraced fields and rhododendron forests: Supi, Basham and Khal Jhuni. This area has virtually no tourist infrastructure, but is being developed by the communities in association with **Village Ways** (see page 241)

Munsiari → *Altitude: 2300 m. 207 km from Almora.*

This is a quiet hill town overlooked by the majestic five peaks of **Panchchuli** which, in legend, served as the five *chulis* (stoves) used to cook the last meal of the five Pandava brothers before they ascended to heaven. Munsiari is a base for treks into the Milam, Ralam and Namik glaciers, and towards Panchchuli. It is also the start of an easy trek (three to four days) via Namik to Dwali in the Pindar Valley.

Pithoragarh → *Colour map 1, C5.*

Sitting in a small valley with some fine temples built by the Chands, it is overlooked by a hill fort, 7 km away, dating from times when the town was at the crossroads of trade routes. The district, separated from Almora in 1962, borders Nepal and Tibet and has a number of high peaks such as Nanda Devi East (7434 m) and West (7816 m), and offers trekking to many glaciers including

Milam, **Namik**, **Ralam** and **Panchchuli**. See page 228 (no permit needed). There are good views from **Chandak Hill** (1890 m), 7 km away. It is on the Pilgrim road to **Mount Kailash** and **Mansarovar Lake**. The Mount Kailash trek (Indian nationals only) starts from Askot. The place is known for its fine gold and silver jewellery and bowls carved out of *sal* wood.

Nainital and around listings

For Sleeping and Eating price codes and other relevant information, see Essentials pages 38-42.

Sleeping

The regional tourist office, **Kumaon Mandal Vikas Nigam**, T05942-236374, www.kmvn.gov.in, has rest houses throughout the state, including: Bhimtal; Ramnagar; Almora; Ranikhet; Jageshwar; Binsar, Munsyari; Dharchula; Kausani; Pindari Glacier route; and Kashipur. The office also runs budget treks to Pindari, Panchachuli, Adi Kailash (from Rs 3000 for a 1-week trek).

Nainital *p233, map p234*

Peak rates (given here) can be high. Off-season discounts of up to 60% are usual but may mean inadequate heating.

LL Abbotsford, Prasada Bhawan, T05942-236188, www.abbotsford.in. Just 4 rooms in the stunning former summer mansion for the Agra and Oudh's ruler. A classic mountain house with tinned roof and pinewood flooring and art deco interiors. Library with antiquarian books.

LL Shervani Hilltop Inn, Waverly Rd, T05942-233800, www.shervanihotels.com. 21 rooms in old royal home, some in cottages, peaceful, lovely garden, free jeep to centre.

LL-L Naini Retreat, Ayarpattha Slopes, 2 km from Mallital Bazar, T05942-235105, www.leisurehotels.co.in. 34 rooms, good restaurant, service and location.

L-AL Belvedere (WelcomHeritage), above **Bank of Baroda**, Mallital, T05942-237434, www.welcomheritagehotels.com. 19 large, comfortable rooms (good-value family suite) with lake views, in former raja's summer palace, a colonial building with pleasant garden, restaurant, well located, quiet, friendly owners, helpful staff.

AL-B Grand, The Mall, near Flatties Rock, T05942-235406. Family-run and friendly with 31 basic but clean rooms, colonial style but faded, good food served on lake-facing veranda (order 3 hrs in advance), good service. Recommended.

A-B Balarampur House, Mallital, T05942-236236, www.balrampurhotelsnainital.com. A royal summer retreat converted to a luxury hotel with 10 well-furnished rooms, pleasant location.

A-C Silverton, Sher-ka-Danda, 2.5 km to centre, T05942-235249, www.hotelsilverton.com. 27 rooms in 'chalets', some with good views, peaceful, vegetarian restaurant.

C-F Sarovar, near Tallital Bus Stand, T05942-235570. Good value, with 30 (**C**) rooms, 8-bed dorms (Rs 75), hot water.

E-G Mount View (KMVN), near Sukhatal Bus Stand, T05942-235400, www.kmvn.org. Good value, 42 small, grubby rooms with bath, some with TV, restaurant, gardens.

G Youth Hostel, west of Mallital Bazar, T05942-236353. Book 15 days ahead 5 and 8-bed dorms, open to non-members (Rs 25), cheap meals, quiet, "showers a mess".

Excursions from Nainital *p236*

AL The Cottage, nestled on the hillside, Jeolikote, T05942-224013, www.thecottagejeolikot.com. Swiss-chalet style, with 3 beautiful spacious rooms with good valley views, meals included. Highly recommended.

B-C Jungle Lore Birding Lodge, Pangot, T011-4412 8785, www.pangot.com. A cottage and hut with baths, 2 tents with shared facilities, meals included (from home-grown produce), library, naturalist guides. Over 200 species of bird on property.

C Lake Side, Naukuchiyatal, T05942-247138, www.kmvn.org. Well maintained and attractive. 12 rooms and dorm (Rs 100).

D-E KMVN Rest Houses, www.kmvn.org. Good-value outside May to mid-Jul.

Almora and around *p236*

Most hotels give off-season discount of 50%.

D Savoy, up hill opposite GPO, near Uttarakhand Tourism, T05962-230329. 17 good-sized but basic rooms, some with hot bath, restaurant, pleasant terrace and quiet garden.

D-E Holiday Home (KMVN), 2 km southwest of bus stand, T05962-230250, www.kmvn.gov.in. 14 simple cottages and 18 rooms with hot bath, dorm (Rs 60), restaurant, garden, good mountain views.
D-E Konark, just east of bus stand on Mall Rd, T05962-231217. Good views, 13 clean rooms, TV, hot water in mornings.
E Shyam, east and uphill from bus stand on LR Shah Rd, T05962-235467, www.hotelshyam.com. 18 small but clean rooms, good terrace views.

Around Almora

L-AL Binsar Valley Resort, Binsar, T05962-253028, www.clubmahindra.com. Just outside the sanctuary, with 32 modern cottages, pleasant, clean, in spacious grounds, good food, exceptional service, good riding, river fishing and trekking.
C Deodars Guest House, Papparsalli village (4 km uphill from Almora), T05962-233025, rwheeler@rediffmail.com. Just 3 rooms in a charming 150-year-old former missionary's residence, stunning views across the mountains set off by carefully tended flower gardens. Stuffed leopards, tigers and bears adorn the characterful interiors. Shared sitting room has a TV, stacks of books.
C-D Tourist Rest House (KMVN), Binsar, T05962- 280176. On a thickly wooded spur near Nanda Devi, 1920s with antique cutlery and table linen lists still hanging on the walls. The furniture and decor are evocative of the Raj, and the caretaker may occasionally be persuaded to open the house for a viewing.
D Kalmatia Sangam, Kalimat Estate, T05962-251176, www.kalmatia-sangam.com. 10 cottages with stunning mountain views spread across hillside on the approach to Kesar Devi. Some cottages' beds are on a mezzanine from where you can see Nanda Devi.
D Nanda Devi (KMVN), in the heart of the sanctuary, Binsar, T05962-251110. Only filtered rainwater, electricity from solar batteries for few hours each evening.
F Tara, Papersallie Village, T05962-231036. www.taraguesthouse.com. Guesthouse, simple restaurant and shop, each run by one of 3 brothers. Rooms come with valley views, tiled bathrooms and solar showers.

Jageswar

E-F Pilgrim's Lodge, Kashipur House, T(0)97597-50136. 8 simple rooms, 4 of which count as deluxe thanks to the addition of a TV, all have hot water. Prices double during the pilgrimage season (Apr-Jun).
F Tara, T05962-263068, mesutara@hotmail.com. A cottage set in a garden with 6 simple rooms on the hillside above the tourist office bungalow, overlooking the temple.

Kausani *p237*

AL-B Krishna Mountview, near Gandhi Ashram, T05962-258008, www.kumaonindia.com. 30 smart rooms, some with good views, fine location, credit cards accepted.
B-E Uttarakhand, 5-min walk from bus stand, T05962-258012, www.uttarakhand kausani.com. Clean and spacious rooms in a freshly upgraded hotel.
C-D Trishul (KMVN), 2 km from town, T05962-258006, www.kmvn.org. 12 deluxe rooms plus 12 separate cottages, food available with a few hours' notice. Superb views and compass on the lawn to spot the peaks.

Baijnath *p237*

E Tourist Bungalow, T05963-250101, and Inspection House.

Bageshwar and the Saryu Valley *p237*

LL 360 Leti, in the village of Leti, near to Sharma village, 2 hrs north of Bageshwar, T0124-456 3899, www.shaktihimalaya.com. 4 understated, but exquisitely deluxe cottages on a 2700-m plateau at the very brink of the Himalaya in the Ramganga Valley. Electricity is solar, there are en suites, private sit outs, Indian, Tibetan and continental food, private guides on hand to take you around the local terrain, yoga and meditation by appointment, but the main prize is the glorious views of sky and mountains. Absolutely unique.
C Wayfarer Retreat, Vijaypur, 13 km before Chaukori, T011-2610 7715 (bookings), www.wayfareradventures.com.
C-E Gomati, Pindari Rd, 2-min walk from bus stand, T05963-220071. Smart, newly refurbished rooms, some with views over mango orchards and river. Good room service meals and obliging staff.
E Bagnath, 20 rooms, where you can hire trekking equipment, restaurant.

Munsiari *p237*

C Wayfarer Mountain Resort, 1 km beyond town, T011-4412 8785, www.himalayanlodges.com. Comfortable Swiss tents, toilets, electricity, phone, forest walks, treks, trout fishing, jeeps, professionally run.

D Tourist Rest House, main road just before the town, T05961-222339. Comfortable, welcome hot showers, good value; also 2 other cheap lodges.

Pithoragarh *p237*

D-E Ulka Devi (KMVN), T05964-225434. Has a restaurant. Others near the bus station are very basic.

Eating

Nainital *p233, map p234*

Most restaurants are at the north of the lake, on the Mall. Some have a limited off-season menu.

Udupi Wala, opposite the train railway in Kathgodam, offers packed meals for train/road journeys. Delicious south Indian food is also available on Nanital Rd, T(0)9219-421600.

TT Kwality, on the lake. Western and good Indian. Ideally located.

TT Machan, The Mall. Good Indian/Chinese and pizzas.

TT Sakley, The Mall, near GPO. Western dishes and confectionery.

T Kumaon Farm Products, towards Ropeway. Good for vegetarian snacks.

T Nanak. Vegetarian Western fast food.

T Purohit, The Mall, opposite Kwality. Recommended for *thalis*.

T Sher-e-Punjab, Mallital Bazar. Tasty, North Indian. Halfway to Tallital, with one serving very good local Kumaon dishes.

Almora *p236*

Plenty of choice along the busy Mall Rd.

TT Glory, good North Indian, but a bit pricey.

T Dolma's Place, Papersallie village near Kasar Devi. Fluffy pancakes, good Tibetan, lemon ginger tea, spring rolls.

T Madras Café, beyond the bus stand. Good Indian meals and snacks.

T Mohan's, Binsar Rd, Kasar Devi, T05962-251215, mohan_rayal72@hotmail.com. Popular backpacker hangout with excellent pizza, internet and confectionary and travel services. Also has 4 rooms down the hill side with kitchenettes.

Kausani *p237*

TT-T Hill Queen, above **Uttarakhand Tourist Lodge**. Serves reasonably priced meals.

Festivals and events

Almora *p236*

Sep-Oct Dasara is celebrated with colourful Ramlila pageants. Also **Kumaon Festival of Arts**.

Shopping

Nainital *p233, map p234*

Bazars sell local woollens and candles at Tallital and Mallital. Also souvenir shops on the Mall, Mallital, including **UP Handlooms**, the excellent, fixed price **Gandhi Ashram**. Along the far edges of the flats, Tibetan refugees sell wool and acrylic shawls; you can try steaming *momos*.

Almora *p236*

Almora Kithab Ghar, The Mall. Has a good selection of books.

Anokhe Lal Hari Kishan Karkhana, Bazar Almora, T05962-230158. Traditional copper ware manufacturer.

Ashok Traders, LR Shah Rd. Sells local copper articles.

Panchachuli Women Weavers Cooperative, T05962-232310, www.panchachuli.com. 10-year-old self-sufficient artisan cooperative turning high-quality raw materials into beautiful pashmina, lambswool, merino and sheepwool stoles, fabrics, scarves and tweeds. Expensive but stunning.

Activities and tours

Nainital *p233, map p234*

Boating

Boat Club, Mallital, T05942-235153. Sail on the lake for Rs 80 per hr; pedal boat Rs 40.

Fishing

Permits for the lake from Executive Officer, Nagar Palika. For other lakes, contact the Fisheries Officer in Bhimtal.

Horse riding

There is a horse stand in Mallital, opposite State Bank of India. Various treks: Snow View, Rs 40; Tiffin Top Rs 60; Naina (Chinna) Peak, Rs 150 (2½-3 hrs; can leave at 0500 to see sunrise from the top, but dress warmly); Naina Devi, Rs 30; horses are generally fit and well cared for.

Mountaineering and trekking

Equipment can be hired from **Nainital Mountaineering Club**, T05942-222051, and **KMVN**, Tourist Office, Mallital, T05942-236356. The club organizes rock climbing at Barapathar, 3 km away.

Tour operators

Parvat Tours & Information (KMVN), Dandi House, Tallital, near rickshaw stand, T05942-236356, among others on the Mall. Day tours: Sat tal; Ranikhet; Mukteshwar (with the Veterinary Research Centre); Kaladhungi. 2-day trips: Kausani; Ranikhet/Almora; Corbett.

Shakti Experience, T0124-456 3899, www.shaktihimalaya.com. Educated guides steer you through the pristine mountain terrain between villages in the Kumaon. Food is immaculate and cooked by local villagers. Accommodation is with local families, in rooms that are adapted to an elegantly understated high standard. A highly recommended way to immerse yourself in rural India.

Vibgyor, 56 Tallital Bazar.

Almora *p236*

High Adventure, Mall Rd, opposite the Post Office, T05962-232277. Organizes treks, cave tours, bus tickets.

Village Ways, Khali Estate, Ayapani, Almora, T01164-623175 (in the UK T01223-750049), www.villageways.com. This community-based enterprise runs walking tours of 9-12 days through the Binsar Wildlife Sanctuary, staying in specially constructed guesthouses managed by locals. The tours take in beautiful scenery and provide an interesting insight into village life, while bolstering economic opportunities for the villagers.

Bageshwar and the Saryu Valley *p237*

Village Ways (see above for contact details). In a similar vein to the company's tours in Binsar, but here the walking is through wilder country around Supi village, with the high Himalaya almost at your fingertips. Nights in cosy village guesthouses are combined with a campout on alpine meadows at 3000 m, with exhilarating sunrise views of the Nanda Devi range. Guiding, accommodation and food are all of a high standard

Munsiari *p237*

Nanda Devi Mountaineering Institution is in the SBI Building. In the main bazar is **Panchuli Trekking** and **Nanda Devi Trekking**, the former run by an elderly Milam tribal villager who has vast and accurate knowledge of the area.

Transport

Nainital *p233, map p234*

Wherever possible, avoid night driving. The hill roads can be dangerous. Flat, straight stretches are rare, road lighting does not exist and villagers frequently drive their animals along them or graze them at the curbside. During the monsoon (Jun-Sep) landslides are fairly common. Usually these are cleared promptly but in the case of severe slips requiring days to clear, bus passengers are transferred.

On the Mall Rd there is an **access toll** of Rs 50. Access is barred, May, Jun, Oct: heavy vehicles, 0800-1130, 1430-2230; light vehicles, 1800-2200; Nov-Apr: all vehicles, 1800-2000.

Air The nearest airport is Pantnagar (71 km) on the plains; **Jagsons** theoretically fly from **Delhi**, but flights are painful to book and frequently cancelled. **Parvat Tours** (see Tour operators) offer transfer by coach to Nainital (2 hrs).

Bus **Roadways**, Tallital, for major inter-city services, T05942-235518, 0930-1200, 1230-1700; **DTC**, Hotel Ashok, Tallital, T35180. **Kumaon Motor Owners' Union (KMOU)**, bus stand near tourist office, Sukhatal, Mallital, T05942-235451; used by private operators. Regular services to **Almora** (66 km, 3 hrs); **Dehra Dun** (390 km); **Delhi** (322 km), a/c night coach, 2100 (Rs 240, 8-9 hrs), or via Haldwani. **Haridwar** (390 km, 8 hrs); **Kausani** (120 km, 5 hrs); **Ranikhet** (60 km, 3 hrs) and **Ramnagar** for **Corbett** (66 km, 3½ hrs plus 3½ hrs).

Rickshaw Cycle-rickshaw and *dandi* Rs 5-10 along The Mall.

Ropeway Cable car/gondola, T05942-235772, from 'Poplars', Mallital (near GB Pant Statue) to Snow View, summer 0800-1730 in theory, but usually opens at 1000, winter 1000-1630, return fare Rs 65, advance booking recommended in season, tickets valid for a 1-hr halt at the top. Some claim its anchorage is weak.

Taxi From **Parvat Tours** (see Tour operators). Full day for around Rs 800-900 (120 km).

Train All India computerized reservation office, Tallital Bus Stand, T05942-235518. Mon-Fri,

0900-1200, 1400-1700, Sat, 0900-1200. The nearest railhead is **Kathgodam** (35 km), taxi, Rs 450 (peak season), bus Rs 30. **Delhi (OD)**: *Ranikhet Exp 15014*, 2040, 8 hrs. Towards **Dehradun** and **Haridwar (OD)**: *Dehradun-Kathgodam Exp 14321*, 1940, 9 hrs. **Kolkata (H)** via **Lucknow** and **Gorakhpur**, *Howrah Bagh Exp 13020*, 2155, 40 hrs (Lucknow 8 hrs, Gorakhpur 15 hrs).

Almora *p236*

Bus Connect Almora with **Kathgodam** (90 km, 3 hrs) for rail links, and with **Nainital** (3 hrs) and **Ranikhet** (2½ hrs). Hourly buses to **Kausani** (3 hrs). For the **Nepal border**, take a bus from the Dhara Naula bus stand (4 km from town centre) to Champawat, and change there for Banbassa. **Jeep** Share jeeps to **Ranikhet**, Rs 70; **Kathgodam**, Rs 120. For **Nainital**, take **Haldwani** jeep as far as **Bhowali**, then bus or jeep to Nainital.

Kausani *p237*

Bus From **Almora** and **Ranikhet** (2½-3½ hrs). **Joshimath** is a tough but spectacular 10-hr journey.

Bageshwar and the Saryu Valley *p237*

Buses and share jeeps to **Almora**. To reach the far end of the Saryu Valley, take jeeps bound for Kapkot, and change there for Song or Munar.

Munsiari *p237*

Bus From Almora, change at Thal; from **Haldwani** or **Nainital**, take a bus to Pithoragarh and change. To **Almora** (11 hrs) and **Pithoragarh** (8 hrs), 0500 and another for Pithoragarh in the afternoon.

Directory

Nainital *p233, map p234*

Banks In Mallital: **State Bank of India** has an international ATM and foreign exchange. **Bank of Baroda**, below Belvedere Hotel, for cash against Visa card. **Internet** Try **Cyberia**, The Mall, near ropeway. Reasonably reliable connection if a bit pricy at Rs 2 per min. **Library** The Mall, by the lake. Open weekdays (closed mid-morning to mid-afternoon). Pleasant for dropping in. **Medical services** Ambulance: T05942-235022. **BD Pande Govt Hospital**, Mallital, T05942-235012. **Post** Mallital. Branch at Tallital. **Useful contacts** Fire: T05942-235626. **Police**: T05942-235424 (Mallital), T05942-235525 (Tallital).

Almora *p236*

Banks **State Bank of India**, Mall Road. May change Amex TCs, but don't rely on this. Best to change in advance. **Medical services** **District Hospital**, Chowk Bazar, T05962-230322. **Post** GPO on Mall Rd.

Corbett National Park

→ *Colour map 1, C5. Phone code: 05945. Altitude: 400-1200 m.*

The journey from Delhi to one of the finest wildlife parks in India offers excellent views of the almost flat, fertile and densely populated Ganga-Yamuna doab, one of the most prosperous agricultural regions of North India. Corbett is India's first national park and one of its few successfully managed tiger reserves. As well as rich and varied wildlife and birdlife it is also extremely picturesque with magnificent sub-montane and riverain views. ▸▸ *For listings, see pages 247-248.*

Ins and outs

Entry fees

ⓘ *Corbett Tiger Reserve Reception Centre, T05947-251489, www.corbett nationalpark.in.* Current fees and opening hours are available from the website. At **Dhikala Gate**: foreigners Rs 1000, Indians Rs 200, valid for three days (two nights); each additional day, Rs 450, Indians Rs 100. At **Bijrani, Sonanadi, Jhirna and Doumunda** gates: Rs 450, Indians Rs 100 per visit (four hours). Entrance permits are not transferable between gates (eg a morning visit to Bijrani and a night halt at Dhikala will require separate payment). **Vehicle fees**: Dhikala Rs 1500 per

Tiger, tiger, burning bright?

Jim Corbett was born in 1875 into the large family of the postmaster of Nainital. Fascinated as a child by the jungles surrounding his home, he developed a considerable knowledge of the eco-system's workings, while at the same time honing his rifle skills on the local population of tigers and leopards; he killed his first big cat at the age of eight, and continued to hunt throughout his career in the Bengal Northeast Railway.

But from the 1920s Corbett turned from hunting to photography, only picking up his gun to kill the man-eating cats that from time to time terrorized the Kumaon hills. Later in life he recounted his exploits in a series of books: *The Man-Eating Leopard of Rudraprayag*, *The Man-eaters of Kumaon* and *Jungle Lore*. These classic adventure stories were a major source of inspiration to Indian conservationists, who in 1973 instituted **Project Tiger** to protect the country's dwindling population of tigers.

The elder Corbett would rightfully be proud of the park that today bears his name. With a committed Field Director and motivated staff, the tiger population has, according to the latest census, climbed steadily over the last few years to reach 160 in early 2008.

Unfortunately, Corbett National Park seems to be one of Project Tiger's few success stories. As each park depends on its director's will and ability to use funds earmarked for conservation, poaching in many areas goes ignored, unchecked, and often denied.

According to figures published by the **Wildlife Institute of India**, the tiger population in Madhya Pradesh, which holds two of the country's most important reserves in Kanha and Bandhavgarh, dropped from an official (and probably inflated) 700 tigers in 2005 to just 300 in early 2008, with at least 22 animals being poached over that period from one park alone.

Worldwide, tigers are vanishing at an alarming rate. Of a global population of around 3500 wild tigers, India currently holds roughly 1400 – a decline of 60% in the last 10 years. Many tigers live in parks. Many live in parks surrounded by human settlements, from which poaching gangs can easily gain access to the animals. A male tiger fetches up to Rs 60,000, and a tigress Rs 45,000, on the illegal international market, which is most heavily concentrated in China. If China goes through with its threat to contravene the CITES Treaty (Convention on the International Trade in Endangered Species) by lifting a ban on the use of tiger parts in medicine, pressure on the tiger is likely to become critical within the next decade.

If travellers can have any impact on this situation, it is by paying the ever-increasing entry fees to visit one or two national parks, and where possible staying in lodges that spread wealth to the local community. The UK-based organization **Travel Operators for Tigers** (T01285-643333, www.toftiger.org) offers a number of useful pointers to encourage pro-tiger tourism.

car/jeep, Indians Rs 500 (covers overnight stay). Bijrani, Sonanadi, Jhirna and Doumunda: Rs 500 per car/jeep, Indians Rs 250.

Access

The main gate at Dhangarhi (for Dhikala) is approximately 16 km north of Ramnagar on the Ranikhet road. Only visitors who are staying overnight may enter Dhikala. Day visits are allowed at the Amdanda and Laldhang gates for Bijrani and Jhirna respectively. There are also entry gates for the Sonanadi Wildlife Sanctuary, which borders Corbett to the north and forms part of the larger tiger reserve, at Sonanadi and Doumunda. A limit of 30 vehicles per day at each entrance is applied, half of which can be booked in advance – try to reserve at the time of booking your accommodation, with several months' notice. Prior reservation to enter is recommended for day visits, although not always necessary at dawn, when half the entry is determined on a first-come-first-served basis. This can mean queuing for hours in the dark in Ramnagar, being shuffled from one office to another, and still not getting in – you may be refused entry when the quota is filled. Travel agents cannot help as they are not allowed to apply for permits. A reservation at the Bijrani or Dhela **Forest Rest Houses** does not entitle visitors to enter by the Dhangari Gate. From 1 March until the monsoon all roads around Dhikala, except the main approach road, are closed between 1100 and 1500 when visitors are not allowed to move about the forest. Most of the park is closed 30 June to 15 October; the Dhikala section is closed 15 June to 15 November.

Viewing

Elephant rides are available from Dhikala, Khinanauli, Bijrani, Gairal and Jhirna. Each elephant can carry four people. This is the best way to see the jungle and the wildlife. Morning and evening, two hours, Rs 1000, Indians Rs 300 from government, more with private operators; book at Dhikala or Bijrani reception (whichever is relevant). Book as early as possible on arrival since these rides are very popular. **Cars** and **jeeps** may drive round part of the park. A seat in a

Corbett National Park

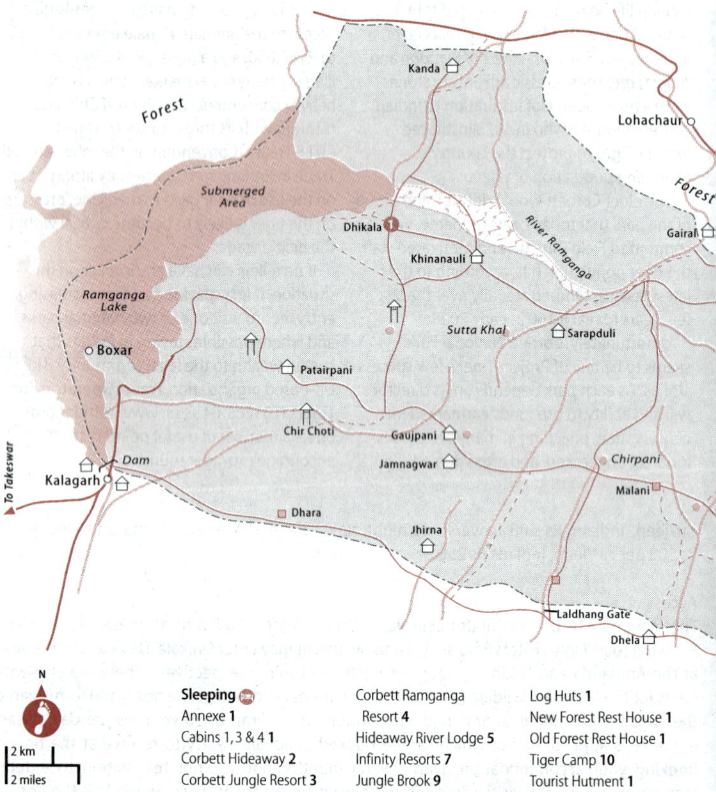

cantor (large open-topped truck) costs Rs 1500 for foreigners, Rs 620 Indians for a full-day tour (0800- 1800). Apart from the immediate area within the complex at Dhikala, **don't go walking in the park**. Tiger and elephant attacks are not unknown. The two watch towers are good vantage points for spotting wildlife. Night driving is not allowed in the park.

Climate

Rainfall is heavier in the higher hills, on average the valley receives 1550 mm, the bulk from July to mid-September. Summer days are hot but the nights quite pleasant. Winter nights can get very cold and there is often a frost and freezing fog in the low-lying tracts. Birdwatching is best between December and February. Summer is the best time for seeing the larger mammals, which become bolder in leaving the forest cover to come to the river and water holes; early summer is best for scenic charm and floral interest.

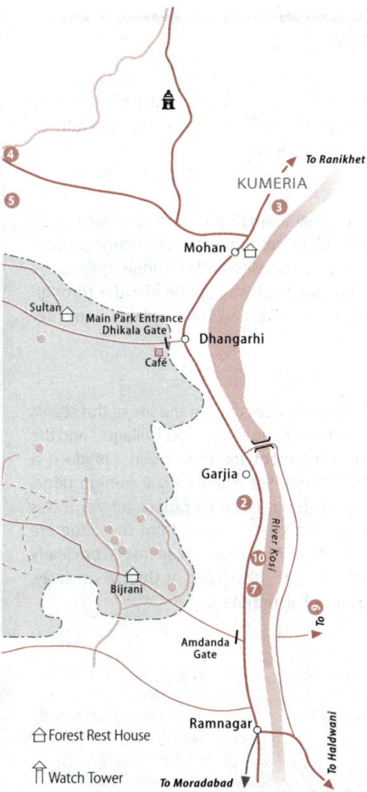

Wildlife and vegetation

Wildlife

The park has always been noted for its tigers; there are now over 150 but they are not easily spotted. About 10% of visitors see one – usually entering at the Bijrani Gate. There are leopards too but they are seldom seen. Sambar, chital, para (hog deer) and muntjac (barking deer) are the main prey of the big cats and their population fluctuates around 20,000. Some, like the chital, are highly gregarious whilst the large sambar, visually very impressive with its antlers, is usually solitary. The two commonly seen monkeys of North India are the rhesus (a macaque – reddish face and brownish body) and the common langur (black face and silvery coat). Elephants are now permanent inhabitants since the Ramganga Dam has flooded their old trekking routes. There are a few hundred of them and they are seen quite often. Other animals include porcupine and wild boar (often seen around Dhikala – some can be quite dangerous, attacking unsuspecting visitors who have food with them). In total there are more than 50 species of mammal alone, though the dam appears to have caused significant losses. The last swamp deer was seen in March 1978, and the loss of habitat has been keenly felt by the cheetal, hog deer and porcupine, all of which appear to be declining.

There are 26 species of reptile and seven of amphibian. In certain stretches of the river and in the Ramganga Lake are the common mugger crocodile: notices prohibiting swimming warn "Survivors will be prosecuted"! The fish-eating gharial can also be found, as can soft-shelled tortoises, otters and river fish. The python is quite common.

The birdlife is especially impressive with over 600 species including a wide range of water birds, birds of prey such as the crested serpent eagle, harriers, Pallas' fishing eagle, osprey, buzzards and vultures. Woodland birds include: Indian and great pied hornbills, parakeets, laughing thrushes, babblers and cuckoos. Doves, bee-eaters, rollers, bulbuls, warblers, finches, robins and chats are to be seen in the open scrub from the viewing towers. The rarer ibisbill is one of the main attractions for serious twitchers.

Vegetation

There are 110 species of trees, 51 species of shrubs, three species of bamboos and 27 species of climbers. The valley floor is covered with tall elephant grass (*Nall* in the local terminology), lantana bushes and patches of *sal* and *sheesham* (*Dalbergia sissoo*) forest, whilst the enclosing hills on both sides are completely forest covered, with *sal*, *bakli*, *khair*, *jhingan*, *tendu*, *pula* and *sain*. *Charas* grows wild in the fields. Nullahs and ravines running deep into the forests are dry for much of the year, but there are swift torrents during the monsoon. These hold brakes of bamboo and thick scrub growth.

Around the park → *For listings, see pages 247-248.*

Ramnagar → *Colour map 1, C5.*

Ramnagar, with a railway station, 134 km from Moradabad, is 18 km from the park boundary and 50 km from **Dhikala**. It is a noisy town with the Project Tiger Office for Corbett reservations, and provides a night halt. They will receive faxes and hold them.

Kaladhungi

At Kaladhungi visit **Jim Corbett's house** ⓘ *Rs 10*, now a small museum. The area is an extension of the Tiger Reserve with equally good wildlife but minus the restrictions, and is also excellent for birdwatching. If you turn up the road opposite and continue up into the hills, travelling along a delightful, metalled road that winds its way up the hillsides through *chir* pine forest and the occasional village, you'll see impressive views of the plains. You enter Nainital at the north end of the lake.

Ranikhet → *Colour map 1, C5. Phone code: 05966.*

Rani Padmadevi, the queen of Raja Sudhardev is believed to have chosen the site of this scenic place, hence Ranikhet (Queen's Field). In 1869 the land was bought from local villagers and the British established a summer rest and recreation settlement for their troops, made it a cantonment town and developed it as a quiet hill station. Set along a 1800-m-high ridge, Ranikhet sprawls out through the surrounding forest without having a proper centre. This is one of its attractions and there are many enjoyable walks. The views from the ridge are magnificent and the twin peaks of Nanda Devi (at a height of 7816 m and 7434 m) can be clearly seen. **Uttarakhand Tourist Office** ⓘ *The Mall, T05966- 220227, 1000-1700*. At **Upat**, 6 km away, there is a beautifully located nine-hole golf course and a Kali temple.

Corbett National Park listings

For Sleeping and Eating price codes and other relevant information, see Essentials pages 38-42.

Sleeping

Corbett National Park *p242, map p244*
Corbett is hugely popular, and it's essential to book your accommodation as far ahead as possible – up to 2 months in high season. If you are travelling to the park without reserved accommodation, you must go to Ramnagar first to make a booking. Dhikala is the park centre and has accommodation. Remember to get a clearance card from Dhikala from the office here before leaving in the morning. There is a decent restaurant (big portions) and a small *dhaba* with cheaper food and basic necessities (biscuits, chocolate, soap, etc).

Within the park

Reservations for all accommodation, except the Annexe at Dhikala, can be booked at the **Corbett Tiger Reserve Reception Centre** in Ramnagar, T05947-251489. Office open daily 0830-1300, 1500-1700. For the Annexe, book through **Uttarakhand Tourism**, Indraprakash Bldg, Barakhamba Rd, Delhi, T011-2371 2246, www.kmvn.gov.in. Foreigners pay 2-3 times the price of Indians, and prices are raised frequently. Entry permits and vehicle charges are payable at the respective gate.

For information on the various rest houses, see www.corbettnationalpark.in and follow links to 'Permits and Reservations'. Rates range from Rs 400 per night for a dorm bed in Dhikala's Log Hut to Rs 5000 for a room in the **Old Forest Rest House**.

Outside the park

LL Hideaway River Lodge, on the periphery of the park, T05947-284132, www.corbetthideaway.com. 1.2 ha of luxury tented accommodation actually inside the tiger sanctuary. The jungle cacophony is incredibly atmospheric, and staying a number of nights overlooking the stunning Ramganga river plain gets you a ringside seat to the park's wildlife.
LL Infinity Resorts, 8 km north of Ramnagar, T05947-251279, www.infinityresorts.com. Established by the **Corbett Foundation**, who have done pioneering work in compensating farmers for lost livestock to prevent revenge killings of big cats. 24 rooms, pool, lawns, mango orchards, good food, old world feel, charming staff. Elephant safaris and excellent birdlife.
AL Corbett Hideaway, Garjia, above the river (10-min drive from gate), T05947-284132, www.leisurehotels.co.in. 30 upmarket lodges in orchard on riverside, 20 luxury tents, jeep transfer to park, good food, very good naturalist in Imran Khan, well-run, own elephant for viewing, pool.
AL Corbett Jungle Resort (Quality Inn), Kumeria Reserve Forest, Mohan, about 13 km from the Dhangarhi entrance, T05947-287820, www.corbettjungleresort.com. Among mango and sal trees. 18 small cottages, imaginatively designed, restaurant, elephant rides, jeeps, jungle walks, swimming in river, eco-friendly.
AL Corbett Ramganga Resort, Jhamaria, 17 km from Dhangarhi, T(0)9310-510582, www.ramganga.com. 10 well-appointed rooms in cottages, 8 Swiss cottage tents, safe spring water, river rafting, riding, climbing, gliding, fishing (fighting fish in the river pools below), excellent pool and ground, friendly service, picturesque position on river edge.
AL Jungle Brook, Tera Village, T(0)9811-095698, www.jungle brook.com. Choice of luxury tents or beautifully and originally designed cottages, whole place has an innovative but friendly feel, all meals included. Highly recommended.
AL-A Tiger Camp, Dhikuli, T05974-287901. Book through **Asian Adventures**, Delhi, T011-4412 8785, www.tiger-camp.com. 20 cottages in Kumaoni Village style but modern interiors, rooms with fan and bath (**E**), tents (shared bath), electricity (plus generator), good food, lovely garden, jeep, hiking, friendly owner. Recommended.

Ramnagar *p246*
C-D KMVN Lodge, T05947-251225. 12 rooms in 3 different categories.
E Govind, 100 m down the road.
F Also cheap, basic guesthouses in town.

Kaladhungi *p246*
AL Camp Corbett, 25 km east of Corbett, T05942-242126, www.campcorbett.net.

Cottages and tents, wonderful meals, an outstanding resort run by the hospitable Anand family, relaxing and totally hassle free, pick-up from Haldwani station arranged.

Ranikhet *p246*

A West View, Mahatma Gandhi Rd, 5 km from centre, T05966-220261, www.westviewhotel.com. 19 rooms in old-fashioned hotel, restaurant, exchange, large grounds.

A-B Chevron Rosemount, The Mall (2 km centre), T05966-221391, www.chevronhotels.com. Refurbished old colonial building, stylish, croquet lawn, tennis.

B-D Parwati Inn, above bus stand, T05966-220325. Good choice from 32 large rooms, restaurant, friendly staff, credit cards accepted, best in the town itself.

C Moon, Sadar Bazar, T05966-220382. 14 clean rooms plus 2 (**B**) cottages, TV, restaurant.

D-E Kalika, upper cantonment, T05966-220893, www.kmvn.gov.in. Pleasant rooms with bath, some 'super deluxe', restaurant (mostly Indian), attractive location, good views.

D-E Tourist Rest House, Chilianaula, 7 km west, T05966-220588, www.kmvn.gov.in. New unit next to the temple complex, rooms, dorm, restaurant, stunning mountain views.

Activities and tours

Corbett National Park *p242, map p244*

KMVN runs 3-day tours from Delhi departing every Fri in season, around Rs 6500 for foreigners, Rs 4700 Indians, taxes extra. **Reservations**: 1st floor, Indraprastha Building, Barakhamba Rd, New Delhi, T011-2371 2246, www.kmvn.gov.in, or from **Uttar Pradesh Tourist Office**, Chandralok Building, 36 Janpath, New Delhi, T011-2332 2251.

Reception Centre in Ramnagar runs day tours to Dhikala – the only access to this part of the park wihout reserved accommodation.

Tigerland Safaris, T05947-284173, www.tigerlandsafaris.com. Well-organized safaris, professional service. Recommended.

Transport

Corbett National Park *p242, map p244*

Air Phoolbagh airport at Pantnagar (130 km) may have flights with **Jagsons Airlines**, T011-237231593, www.jagsonairlines.com, to **Delhi** and **Shimla**.

Bus The **Delhi–Dhikala** road (260 km) passes through Moradabad (turn left after Moradabad, towards Kashipur and Ramnagar), 5½-6 hrs – strewn with bus/lorry/car crashes. Frequent buses from Ramnagar **Delhi, Dehra Dun**, **Moradabad**, **Nainital** and **Ranikhet** (if coming from Dhikala wait outside Dhangarhi gate, no need to return to Ramnagar). Bus to **Dhikala**, 1530, not reliable; return leaves 1000 from Dhikala after elephant ride.

Jeep Becoming very expensive. Expect to pay Rs 1800-2500 for a day. Hire from near Ramnagar park office. Petrol vehicles are cheaper (up to Rs 2000 per day) and quieter. You also pay Rs 50 admission for the driver.

Train Nearest station is at Ramnagar (50 km), for **Moradabad** and Delhi. **To Delhi (OD)**: *Ramnagar Delhi Link Exp 25036*, 0950, 5½ hrs; *Corbett Park Link Exp 25014*, 2145, 6¼ hrs. **From Delhi (OD)**: *Uttarakhand Sampark Kranti Exp 15035*, 1600, 4½ hrs; *Ranikhet Exp 15013*, 2240, 6¼ hrs.

Ranikhet *p246*

Bus Regular buses to **Ramnagar**, **Almora** and **Nainital**, with bus stands at each end of the Mall.

Directory

Ranikhet *p246*

Banks **State Bank of India**, at the top end of The Mall. Changes Amex and Thomas Cook TCs only. **Medical services** **Civil Hospital**, near bus stand, T05966-220422. **Post** The Mall.

Madhya Pradesh & Chhattisgarh

Contents

Footprint features

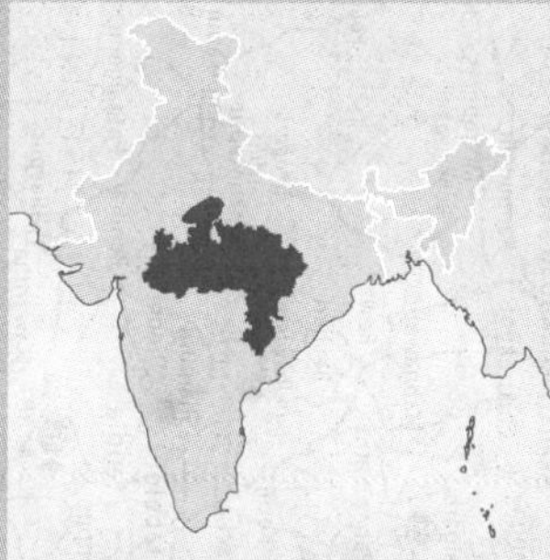

At a glance

Getting around Bhopal, Indore and Jabalpur are the transport hubs, with buses and trains to all points. Car hire/taxis are advisable on long road journeys eg Satna-Khajuraho-Orchha. There is a major overhaul of the road network going on in the state and fingers crossed roads should be a lot better by 2013.

Time required 7-10 days for a western circuit; 5 days for Northern MP; minimum 3-4 days for each of the tiger parks; 4 days for a trek in tribal Chhattisgarh.

Weather Best in Oct-Nov and spring. Chilly mornings in winter.

When not to go Diwali, Christmas and Holi, when the tiger parks are packed with tourists, and 1 Jul-30 Sep, when they're closed altogether.

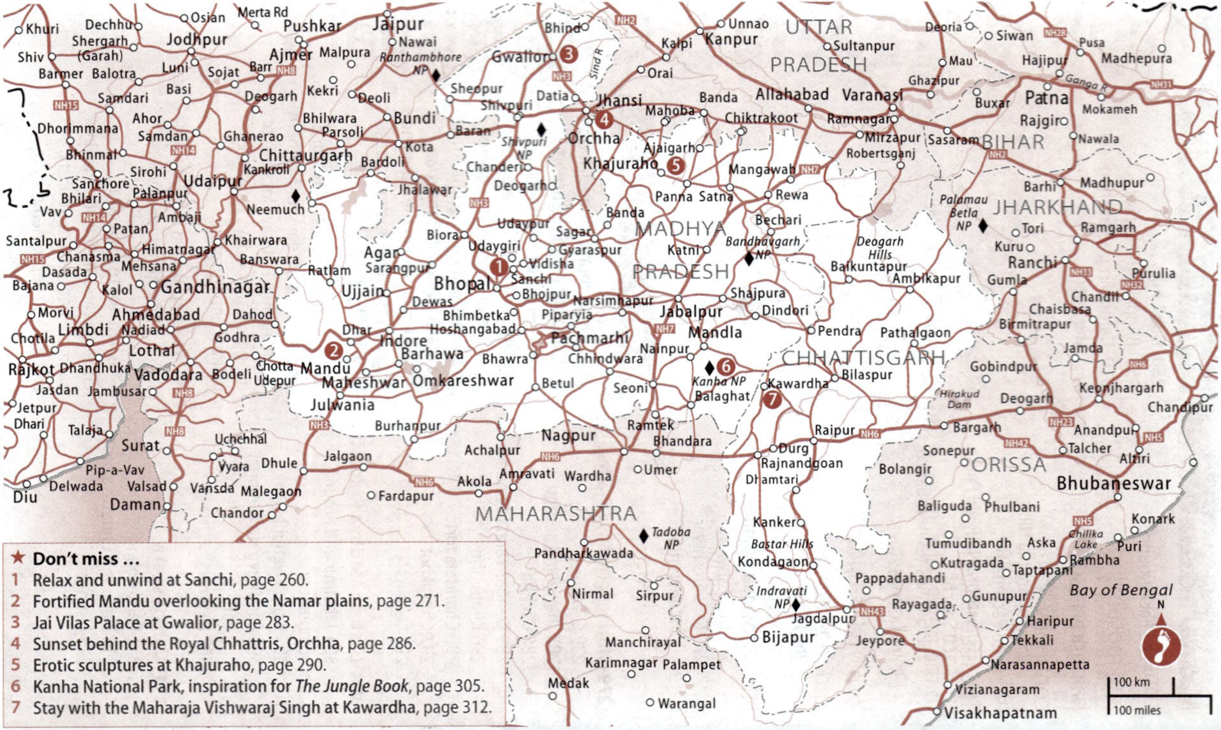

★ **Don't miss …**

1 Relax and unwind at Sanchi, page 260.
2 Fortified Mandu overlooking the Namar plains, page 271.
3 Jai Vilas Palace at Gwalior, page 283.
4 Sunset behind the Royal Chhattris, Orchha, page 286.
5 Erotic sculptures at Khajuraho, page 290.
6 Kanha National Park, inspiration for *The Jungle Book*, page 305.
7 Stay with the Maharaja Vishwaraj Singh at Kawardha, page 312.

Madhya Pradesh and Chhattisgarh are at the heart of India. They contain many of the tribal groups least touched by modernization and most of India's remaining genuine forest. The magnificent paintings made in rock shelters at Bhimbetka illustrate the continuity of settlement for over half a million years, while Buddhism left a still-visible mark in the glories of Sanchi's 2000-year-old *stupas*. The magnificent palaces of Orchha and temples of Khajuraho testify to the power of Rajput dynasties for over a thousand years.

Flowing westwards along the southern edge of the great Vindhyan ranges runs the Narmada, the site of one of the largest – and most controversial – dam development programmes in the world. Yet Madhya Pradesh remains largely unindustrialized and little visited, allowing the dense forests and grasslands of the east to house two of India's best national parks at Kanha and Bandhavgarh.

On 1 November 2000, 16 districts in the southeast of Madhya Pradesh were carved out to create the new state of Chhattisgarh. One of the least accessible areas of peninsular India, it is a largely tribal state, currently in the throes of a modern-day peasant rebellion.

Background → *Population: 60.39 million. Area: 308,000 sq km.*

The land

Geography Madhya Pradesh has some magnificent scenery. The dominating **Vindhyan mountains** run diagonally across the heart of Madhya Pradesh while the Kaimur range runs to the north and east, overlooking the Gangetic plain around Varanasi and Allahabad. Both rise to 600 m but are frequently cut by deep forest-clad ravines. Behind the Kaimur range is the **Baghelkhand plateau** while the Hazaribagh range juts into the state in the east. The **Narmada** rising in the east, flows west to the Arabian Sea, along with the Tapti to its south. Black volcanic soils are often visible across the state, but in some places the land is stony and inhospitable. Between Gwalior and Jhansi the Chambal River has dug deep gorges, creating a *badlands* area which **dacoits** have enjoyed as hideouts. Wildlife wise, things seem to be looking up for the tigers of Madhya Pradesh. In the 2010 Tiger Census, the tiger population of this state is up by 43 to 257. Some say that the improved numbers nationwide (1706 up 295 since last count) is due to improved counting, but the results are good. On a mixed note, Madhya Pradesh, along with Gujarat have been at the centre of protests around the Narmada River project. The extensive damming of the Narmada river over the last 25 years has displaced thousands of villagers with little or no consideration, let alone compensation. However on the flip side, electricity and clean water now gets to the outer reaches of India, the little villages. Supported by authors and activists Arundhati Roy and Vandana Shiva, this story shines a light on the changing face of India, geographically and culturally. Check out www.narmada.org or Roy's essay *The Greater Common Good*.

Climate Most rain falls between June and September, increasing from about 1000 mm in the west to 2000 mm in the east. March to May is hot and dry: average maximum temperatures exceed 33°C and often reach 44°C. The average daily maximum during the monsoon is 30°C and the minimum 19°C, when the landscape turns green and places like Mandu are particularly attractive. Winters are dry and pleasant. The average daily maximum temperature from November to February is 27°C and the minimum 10°C.

History

Rock paintings and stone artefacts prove the existence of Stone Age cultures. Although the region was incorporated into successive states from the empire of Asoka to that of the Mughals, it was rarely the centre of a major power.

In the 10th century a number of dynasties controlled different parts of the region, most notably the Chandelas at Khajuraho. Gwalior was conquered in the 11th century by the Muslims, whose influence spread southeast under the Khaljis into Malwa during the 13th century. Akbar annexed this into his empire in the mid-16th century. The Scindia and Holkar dynasties of Marathas ruled independently at Gwalior and Indore respectively during the 18th century.

Under the British the region became known as the Central Provinces and under the state re-organization after Independence the modern state of Madhya Pradesh was created.

Culture

Even though the majority of the former state of Madhya Pradesh's tribal people now have their own state of Chhattisgarh, Madhya Pradesh remains the home of many tribals, including Bhils, Gonds and Baigas. Many have been painfully absorbed into the mainstream of Indian life. Hindi is the most widely spoken language. On each of the borders the languages of neighbouring states – particularly Marathi and Gujarati in the west – are quite commonly used. The Bhils speak **Bhili** and the Gonds **Gondi**, independent in origin to the Indo-European and Dravidian language groups.

Bhopal – the legacy

The legacy of the 1984 **Union Carbide** disaster continues today. People are still suffering from the after effects of the poisonous gas (500 times more toxic than cyanide) which escaped from the US-owned pesticide plant on 3 December 1984. More than 50,000 people were exposed to the gas, over 3800 were killed instantly and today the death toll stands at over 20,000. Safety systems were not in place to contain the disaster. Many children continue to be born suffering from deformities and chronic health problems. Shockingly, the plant continues to operate today and campaigners say that toxic waste and pollution still contaminate the water of the local residential areas to the north and just outside Bhopal. After a legal battle lasting many years, during which the victims received hardly any compensation, finally in 2001, Bhopal Memorial hospital and research centre was set up from the sale of Union Carbide's shares. **Sambhavna Trust** has been set up to help victims and Westerners are welcome to volunteer – www.bhopal.org. With 10-km runs in London in 2011 for Bhopal and support from celebrities, this story needs to remain in the headlines. The people of Bhopal cannot be forgotten. It's a story that will not go away. For more insight into the tragedy read the book *Five past Midnight in Bhopal* (royalties go to support the victims).

Textiles are important but Madhya Pradesh also has a strong traditional village handicraft industry. Handloom *Chanderi* and *Maheshwar* silks are especially sought after. The tribal people produce attractive handicrafts.

Modern Madhya Pradesh

Under the leadership of Digvijay Singh's, the last Congress Party Chief Minister, Madhya Pradesh was one of the first states to tackle its huge government overspend problem. By June 2002 the policy had led Madhya Pradesh to being one of the first states to return to financial surplus. However, the policies proved electorally suicidal, and the BJP swept the INC aside in both the Assembly elections of 2003 and the Lok Sabha elections of 2004. In the 2004 Lok Sabha elections the BJP bucked the national trend, winning 25 of the 29 seats, the INC taking the other four. With the formation of Chhattisgarh the state legislative assembly lost 90 of its seats to the new state, reducing the total to 230. Here the BJP also formed a majority government, and took 10 of the 11 Lok Sabha seats. In 2005 Shivraj Singh Chauhan became MP's chief minister.

In the Lok Sabha elections in spring 2009 the BJP won 16 of the 29 seats in Madhya Pradesh, down from 25 in 2004 but still better than the party's performance elsewhere in India. Congress took 12 seats. The state's chief minister Shivraj Singh Chouhan, who had been mooted as a potential prime ministerial candidate in the case of victory, was openly critical of his party's election strategy, and, unlike fellow prominent BJP leader, Gujarat's Narendra Modi, has called for a radical redefinition of 'Hindutva' along developmental rather than communal lines.

Central Madhya Pradesh

Rarely visited by travellers, this section of the Indian interior features a number of hidden jewels, including the Palaeolithic cave paintings of Bhimbetka, the silent Buddhist ruins of Sanchi, and Pachmarhi, one of India's most unassuming hill stations. The hub of the region is Bhopal, an enjoyable and relatively prosperous city of lakes and atmospheric warren-like bazars. *▸▸ For other listings, see pages 264-267.*

Bhopal → *For listings, see pages 264-267. Colour map 2, C6.* *Phone code: 0755. Population: 1,450,000.*

Perhaps most unfortunately well known for the tragic Union Carbide disaster, Bhopal today is a surprisingly pleasant Indian City with its own quite unusual and interesting character.Situated around two huge artificial lakes and on gently rolling hills, parts of Bhopal, the state capital of Madhya Pradesh, have a spacious feel with some pleasant parks, ambitious royal palaces and modern public buildings. In contrast, to the north, is the far busier and crowded Old city, with its strong Muslim character, filled with mosques and bazars, as well as the crowded commercial centre in the New Market area of TT Nagar beyond the lakes to the southwest.

Ins and outs

Getting there The airport is about 20 minutes by bus from the town centre. There are direct flights from Delhi, Gwalior and Mumbai. Bhopal is on the main train line to South India and is just seven hours by the *Shatabdi Express* from Delhi. There is an extensive bus network; the bus stand is on Hamidia Road. *▸▸ See Transport, page 266.*

Getting around The town is quite spread out: it takes about 15 minutes to walk through the Old City centre from the railway station to the bus station. Local buses go to all parts of town but the best bet is an auto-rickshaw. You will have to pay a surcharge to go to the Shamla Hills or other points on the edge of town.

Tourist information Madhya Pradesh Tourism ⓘ *Gangotri, 4th floor, TT Nagar, T0755-277 4340, www.mptourism.com*. Railway Station ⓘ *T0755-274 6827*.

History

Legend suggests that Bhopal stands on an 11th-century site created by Raja Bhoja, who is believed to have built a *pal* (dam) which created the lakes. The modern city was developed by **Dost Mohammad Khan**, one of Aurangzeb's Afghan governors, who planned to set out wide roads, adorn it with monuments and replant the gardens. After his death Bhopal remained almost an island state in Malwa. Loyal to the British throughout the 18th century, from 1857 until 1926, Bhopal was ruled by two Muslim women, Sultan Shahjahan Begum and her mother Sikander Begum It still retains a strong Muslim character. In 1984, the city hit international news headlines with the **Union Carbide** disaster (see box, page 253).

Sights

In 1878 Shah Jahan Begum (ruled 1868-1901), began work on the pink **Taj-ul Masjid**, one of the largest mosques in India, but it was left unfinished for over a century. It is a striking sight, with three white domes, two massive minarets and an impressive hall with attractive pillars. Today it is used as a *madrassa* (religious school). The main Chote Talao entrance, which has steps, is closed, so enter by the Lall Market gate. The smaller **Jama Masjid** (1837) in the bazar, with its minarets topped by gold spikes, was built by Qudsia Begum, and the **Moti Masjid** (1860, based on the Jama Masjid in Delhi), was built by her daughter, Sikander Begum. At the entrance to the Chowk in the old city area is **Shaukat Mahal**, designed by a Frenchman, combining post-Renaissance and Gothic styles. Nearby is the **SadarManzil**, the Hall of Public Audience of the former rulers of Bhopal. South of the Lower Lake is the modern **Lakshmi Narayan** (Birla) **Temple** (Vaishnavite), Arera Hills. There are good views from here and in the evening from Shamla Hills. There are pedalo and sailing boats for hire on the Upper Lake.

State Archaeological Museum ⓘ *Banganga Rd, Tue-Sun 1000-1800, foreigners Rs 50, Indians Rs 10, camera Rs 10*, houses sculptures, antiquities and tribal handicrafts, stone sculptures in gallery grounds and an interesting collection of 87 small Jain bronzes of the Paramar period (12th century) from a single site in Dhar District. **Birla Museum** ⓘ *Tue-Sun 1000-1700, foreigners Rs 50, Indians Rs 10*, by the Lakshmi Narayan Temple, complements the former. It has a small collection of well-displayed rare sculptures (seventh to 12th centuries) in Siva, Vishnu and Devi galleries. **Bharat Bhawan** ⓘ *Tue-Sun 1000-1700, foreigners Rs 20, Indians Rs 10*, a centre for creative and performing arts, is in the Shamla Hills. Designed by the Indian architect Charles Correa in unobtrusive low-rise buildings, it houses an impressive collection of rural and tribal arts, a modern art gallery, crafts gallery, print maker's studio, library and theatre for performing arts, and a café. **Indira Gandhi Rashtriya Manav Sangrahalaya (Museum of Man)** ⓘ *www.igrms.com, Tue-Sun, Mar-Aug 1100-1830, Sep-Feb 1000-1730, Rs 10*, south of Shamla Hills, is the largest open air anthropological museum in India with a permanent exhibition of tribal huts in typical village settings from across India, from desert to the Himalayas, coastal belt to the plains, with details of interiors. A shop sells good tribal crafts. There are also a whole host of music and drama programmes here too. Check website for details.

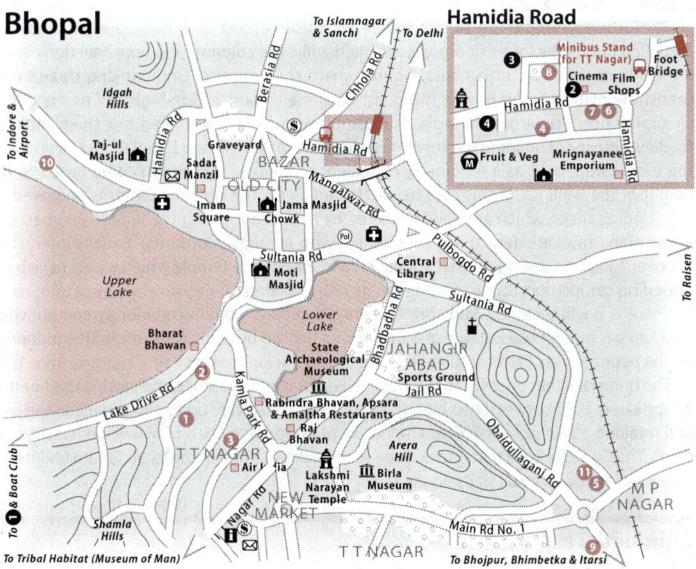

N

200 metres

200 yards

Sleeping
Amer Palace **5**
Jehan Numa Palace **1**
Lake View Ashok **2**
Motel Shiraz **9**
Noor-us-Sabah **10**
Palash (MP Tourism) **3**
Rama International **6**
Ranjit's **7**
Residency **11**
Shrimaya **8**
Sonali **4**

Eating
Indian Coffee House **2**
Jyoti **3**
Manohar Place **4**
Wind & Waves **1**

Excursions from Bhopal

Islamnagar, 11 km from the town centre on a drive north past the former Union Carbide factory, is an attractive little oasis of calm in a tiny village. The palace at the heart of the gardens was built by Dost Mohammad Khan, the early Afghan ruler of Bhopal. The pavilion pillars are decorated with floral patterns. The two-storeyed Rani Mahal and the *hammam* (baths) of the Chaman Mahal can also still be seen. The gardens are lovingly tended by the elderly *chowkidar* who, despite his limited English, is a very helpful guide. The gate is normally locked but as the village is very small it is usually easy to find him.

A cluster of sites to the northeast of Bhopal – **Sanchi, Vidisha, Gyaraspur**, the **Udaygiri caves** and **Udaypur** – can be visited on a day trip (see pages 260-263). Equally, **Bhimbetka** to the south can be combined with Bhojpur, 28 km from Bhopal (see below). If you just have a day to spare, hire a car and visit Bhimbetka in the morning and Sanchi in the afternoon. If you have an afternoon, you can fit in a four-hour excursion by taxi from Bhopal to Bhojpur and Bhimbetka – it's the best way to visit.

Bhojpur → *Colour map 2, C6.*

Bhojpur is famous for its Siva temple, sometimes referred to as the 'Somnath of the North', and for its dams, a testimony to the crucial importance of irrigation water for agriculture in this region. Both the religious and civil functions implicit in these buildings owed their origin to the 11th-century Paramar king of Dhar, **Raja Bhoj** (1010-1053), who was noted not only as a great builder but also as a scholar.

Bhojeshwar Temple is a simple square with sides of just over 20 m. Surmounted by a corbelled dome, the lower doorposts are plain while the columns and upper sections inside are richly carved. Two ornamental figures guard the entrance. On a striking three-tiered sandstone platform over 6 m sq is a polished stone lingam 2.35 m high and nearly 6 m in circumference, the largest in India. The temple was never completed but the traditional medieval means of building the towering structures of great Hindu temples are still visible in the earth ramp, built as a temporary expedient to enable large stones to be raised to the height of the wall, yet in this case never cleared away. The gigantic patterns engraved on surrounding rocks, which are now protected by rails, suggest that the temple was part of a grand plan (note one depicting a Siva temple with pilgrims' footprints). Equally interesting are over 1300 masons' marks that appear on and around the temple which would have been erased on completion. Stone masons can be seen working on site.

There is a whitewashed **Jain shrine** nearby, behind a modern community centre, which encloses a 6-m-high black statue of a Tirthankara flanked by two smaller ones. The inscription on the pedestal uses 11th-century script. A caretaker holds the keys.

The huge lake that once lay to the west behind two massive stone and earth dams has now disappeared. Built between two hills, the Cyclopean dams were up to 100 m wide at the base and retained a lake of over 700 sq km, but in 1430 Hoshang Shah of Malwa demolished the dams. The Gonds believe that it took three years to drain, and that the local climate underwent a major change as a result of its drying out.

Bhimbetka Hill → *Colour map 2, C6.*

ⓘ *A taxi from Bhopal is the easiest way to visit the caves and Bhojpur Temple. Alternatively, from Bhopal, take the Hoshangabad bus and ask to be dropped at the Bhimbetka turning (the caves are a 3-km walk). You may get a lift from a truck on the main road to Bhojpur, or from Bhopal take a bus to Obaidullaganj, 7 km north of the Bhimbetka turning, and hire a bicycle there. There is no obvious signpost to Bhimbetka on the main road. At a Hindi sign (on the left), a lane turns right with a railway crossing just after the turn. The caves are to the right, off this lane.*

Bhimbetka has South Asia's richest collection of prehistoric paintings and many other archaeological discoveries. The site was discovered by VS Wakanker of the Vikram University, Ujjain, in 1957. In the middle of a dense deciduous forest, there are over 30 species of tree with edible fruit, flower seeds and tubers – a vital food for tribal people even today. You may notice teak and *tendu*, the latter harvested in May and June to make *bidis* for smoking. The area is also rich in wildlife including several species of deer, wild boar, sloth bear, antelope, leopard, jackal, scaly anteater and many birds. Perennial springs provide the essential year-round water supply. This is the setting for a total of more than 1000 shelters which were occupied from the early Stone Age to the late Stone Age perhaps less than 2000 years ago. Some enthusiasts and visitors have found the site disappointing.

Background

Dating of the occupation is far from complete. In the bottom layers of the settlement sequence were a few pebble tools. There was a thin layer of bare material above this, followed by a thick layer of **Acheulian deposits**. Over 2.5 m of accumulated material were excavated in Cave III F-23, bringing to light successive floors paved with stone and large quantities of stone implements that were clearly being made in the cave. This period is dominated by flake tools – blades, scrapers, cleavers and hand axes. Some of the core tools, often beautifully executed, were found to weigh up to 40 kg.

This level is followed in many caves by **Middle Palaeolithic** materials (circa 40,000-12,000 BC), suggesting that this culture developed on the same site out of the preceding Acheulian culture. The same raw materials are used, although the tools are generally smaller. The **Upper Palaeolithic** period (circa 12,000-5500 BC) was even shorter than the Middle, again growing out of it. Short thin blades made their appearance for the first time. It was in the **Mesolithic** period, immediately following the Upper Palaeolithic, that the largest number of caves were occupied. A Ghosh suggests that during this period there was a huge increase in population and some of the cave paintings can be correlated with this period. There may have been improvement in the climate, although there is evidence for climatic change even within the Mesolithic period, which at Bhimbetka has been Carbon-14 dated as running from 5500-1000 BC. A brand new technology was introduced. Tiny stone tools – microliths – were made: knives, arrow heads, spearheads and sickles. Hard, fine-grained rocks like chert and chalcedony were the basic material. The raw materials for the new industry had to be brought in – the nearest source is near Barkhera, 7 km to the southeast. The dead were buried in caves still occupied by the living, usually, though not always, in a crouched position with the head to the east. Antlers and stone tools were buried alongside them. In the middle level of the deposits are copper tools and pottery. The site seems to have been largely deserted by the end of the first millennium BC. Several circular structures on the hills around have been interpreted as Buddhist *stupas* of a much later era, a view supported by Asokan inscription, found 20 km west of Bhimbetka.

The caves

ⓘ *Take drinking water with you; there are no facilities. The area is often virtually deserted and it is not easy to find specific caves with worthwhile paintings outside the enclosure.*

By far the most striking remains today are the paintings covering walls and ceilings in over 500 shelters and in rocky hollows. Some are quite small, while others are up to 10 m long. Red and white are the dominant colours used, but green and yellow are also found. These were obtained from manganese, haematite, soft red stone and charcoal, sometimes combined with animal fat and leaf extract. The site has been enclosed to allow visitors to be taken around nine representative caves by Archaeological Survey guides during daylight hours. The tour, along a well-made path linking the major shelters, takes about 45 minutes; allow longer if you wish to explore independently (there are about 130 caves along 4 km). The caretaker will expect a small tip. There are plans to build a picnic area and water supply.

The **paintings**belong to three periods. The Upper Palaeolithic paintings, usually in white, dark red and green lines, depict large animals, eg bison, rhinoceros and tiger. The Mesolithic figures and animals, usually in red, are smaller but they lose their proportions and naturalism. Hunting is a common theme – 'stick men' appear; they are shown grazing, riding and hunting animals, dancing in groups. Women are sometimes seen with a child or appear pregnant. The later period, probably dating from the early centuries AD when green and yellow colours are also used, is quite different, showing battle scenes with men riding on elephants and horses, holding spears, shields, bows and arrows. Religious symbols, Ganesh and Siva, trees and flowers also appear. Some shelters were used over several periods and you can spot interesting details: **Auditorium 3** has deer, peacock, leopard, old men and dancers; **Rock Shelter 1** shows two elephants and a nilgai; **No 8** has a garlanded king on horseback with hunters and a cheetah; **No 9** has a flower pot, elephant and an old man; **No 10** shows Ganesh, Siva lingam and a tree; **No 7**, stylized hunters on horseback based on simple crosses; **No 6**, drummer, group dancers, tree roots and branches and bison.

Pachmarhi → *For listings, see pages 264-267. Colour map 3, C1. Phone code: 07578.*

Population: 11,300. Altitude: 1100 m.

Pachmarhi is one of the most beautiful and friendly hill stations in Central India and rarely sees Western visitors. Except at the height of summer, the air remains pleasantly fresh and cool. The massive iron-rich sandstones, which rise steeply from the trough of the Narmada Valley floor to form the Satpura Range, offer plenty of scope for quiet, wooded walks, with several view points, waterfalls, rock pools and hills to climb within easy reach. The Gondwana series, known locally as Pachmarhi sandstones, are rich in plant fossils, notably of ferns. The area is also known for its ancient cave paintings.

Ins and outs

Getting there Pachmarhi can easily be reached by bus from Bhopal in about six hours. It is similarly accessible from Nagpur. Pipariya (see Sleeping, page 265), between Jabalpur and Itarsi on the Mumbai–Kolkata line, is the nearest railway station. ▸▸ *See Transport, page 267.*

Getting around Most hotels are either near the bus stand or in the bazar. You can share a jeep to the more far-flung hotels and major points of interest.

Tourist information Tourist office ⓘ *near Hotel Amaltas, T07578-252100*. Helpful.

History

In 1857 Captain Forsyth of the Bengal Lancers 'discovered' the spot on which Pachmarhi came to be built. He was said to have headed a column of troops but in fact was accompanied by just two others. The beautiful landscape of the plateau of the Satpura range impressed him with its tranquil forests of wild bamboo, *sal*, *yamun*, *amla* and *gular* trees, interspersed with deep pools fed by the streams that ran across the iron-stained sandstone hills. Later, the British developed Pachmarhi as a military sanatorium and hot weather resort.

Sights

The **Panch Pandav** 'caves', south of the town centre beyond the Cantonment, are believed to have sheltered Buddhist monks in the first century BC, a fact confirmed by the recent discovery at the caves of the remains of a *stupa* from this period (6 m in circumference). There are several delightful spots nearby. The small natural bathing pool **Apsara Vihar** is along a path to the left. The pool has a broad shallow edge, suitable for children to paddle. There is a short scramble from there to the top of **Rajat Pratap** (the 'big fall'), over 110 m high.

There are other falls in the area, some of which fall within the bounds of the **Satpura National Park** ⓘ *sunrise-sunset, foreigners Rs 200 per person on foot (Indians Rs 20), foreigners Rs 1500 per car (Indians Rs 400)*, a tiger and leopard reserve. Attractive outings include **Jalwataran** (Duchess Fall), 3 km along the path from Belle Vue. It is a strenuous 4-km walk to the base of the first cascade, perhaps the most attractive in Pachmarhi. Wildlife safaris into the park can be arranged by some Pachmarhi hotels.

Short one-day treks are possible to Mahadeo and Dhupgarh peaks, and the spectacular hilltop temple of Chauragarh. The square-topped hill at **Chauragarh**, on the southern edge of the Pachmarhi plateau, is 10 km away. The ridge-top temple draws crowds of tribals and pilgrims for **Sivaratri** in February and March. It owes its sanctity to a legend in which Siva and Vishnu defeated the demon Bhasmasur by tricking him into turning himself to stone. A remarkable spring flows out of the **Cave of Mahadeo**, nearly 100 m inside the hillside. The temple itself is reached by a 3-km walk through beautiful forest culminating in a climb up 1300 steps, and there are superb views from the top. Take a jeep to the start of the walk as the road is too steep for bikes. **Priyadarshini Point**, on the way, from which Captain Forsyth is said to have first set eyes on the Pachmarhi region, still gives a commanding view over the town and the region. You can look back at the **Handi Khoh** ravine from this vantage point.

To the north of the bazar, a 3-km hike past some ancient rock shelters leads to the **Jatashankar Cave** where the Siva lingam bears the likeness of the god's coiled matted hair.

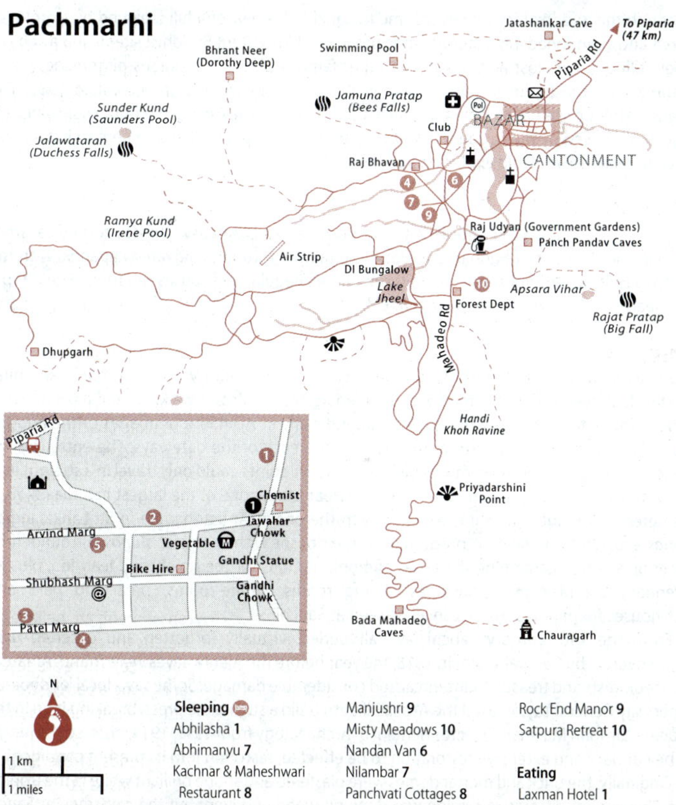

Satpura National Park

Joined with Pachmarhi and Bori National Parks, Satpura is close to Pachmarhi town and around 200 km from Bhopal and is still a relatively unknown wildlife reserve of over 524 sq km of dry, deciduous forest landscape, rugged sandstone peaks, deep gorges and ravines. A wide range of animals, birds and plant life inhabit the terrain, including leopards, sloth bears, gaur, deer, flying squirrels, crocodiles and the increasingly elusive tiger. If you want a much more off the beaten track National park experience, then this is definitely the place. Set up in 1981 and still with only a few lodges in the surrounding areas, you can cruise around the park by Jeep, on elephant, by boat or even on foot (not allowed in most other parks but then this probably indicates the lack of tigers and leopards!), knowing that you won't be seeing hoards of other enthusiasts desperately on the lookout for now elusive 'Stripes'. The park is open Nov-May, sunrise-sunset, foreigners Rs 200 per person on foot (Indians Rs 20), foreigners Rs 1500 per car (Indians Rs 400).

Sanchi → *For listings, see pages 264-267. Colour map 2, C6.* *Phone code: 07482.*

Although the Buddha himself never came to Sanchi, this peaceful hill crowned by a group of *stupas* and abandoned monasteries is one of the most important Buddhist sites in India. It has a quiet stillness now, lost at many of the other famous places of religious pilgrimage, yet in keeping with the Buddhist faith. It was included on the World Heritage list in 1989. The imposing hilltop site has commanding views. Sitting under the trees in the bright sunshine, it is easy to be moved by the surroundings. Comparatively few people venture here so it is a good place to relax, unwind and explore the countryside.

Ins and outs

Getting there Some 47 km northeast of Bhopal, Sanchi is an easy half-day trip by car from Bhopal. The road out of Bhopal runs along the railway through cultivated flatlands, with the Vindhya Hills to your right, covered in scrub jungle. Regular local buses run from both Bhopal and nearby Vidisha. ▸▸ *See Transport, page 267.*

Background

The first *stupa* was built during **Asoka's** reign in the third century BC, using bricks and mud mortar. Just over a century later it was doubled in size; a balcony/walkway and a railing were added. The gateways were built 75 years later. Finally in AD 450 four images of the Buddha (belonging to the later period), were placed facing each of the gateways. The entrances are staggered because it was commonly believed that evil spirits could only travel in a straight line. The wall was built for the same purpose. The **Great Stupa**, one of the largest in India (37 m in diameter, 16 m high), does not compare with the one at Anuradhapura in Sri Lanka. Indian *stupas* evolved to be taller in proportion to their bases with the great *stupas* surrounded by lesser ones, often containing the ashes of monks famous for their piety and learning, plus an attendant complex of monasteries, dining rooms, shrine-rooms, preaching halls and rest-houses for pilgrims. These can all be seen at Sanchi.

From the 14th century Sanchi lay half buried, virtually forgotten and deserted until 'rediscovered' by General Taylor in 1818, the year before the Ajanta caves were found. Amateur archaeologists and treasure hunters caused considerable damage. Some say a local landholder, others say General Taylor, used the Asoka Pillar to build a sugarcane press, breaking it up in the process. Sir John Marshall, Director General of Archaeology from 1912-1919, ordered the jungle to be cut back and extensive restoration to be effected, restoring it to its present condition.

Originally, the brick and mortar domes were plastered and shone brilliant white in the tropical sun. The earliest decorative carving was done on wood and ivory but the craftsmen at Sanchi readily transferred their skills to the yellow sandstone here, which lends itself to intricate carving. The **carvings** illustrate scenes from the life of Buddha, events in the history of Buddhism and the *Jataka* stories (legends about the Buddha's previous lives). ▸▸ *See Books, page 1441.*

The site

ⓘ *Sunrise-sunset, foreigners Rs 250. The main gate at the bottom of the hill is within walking distance from the railway station. For a better appreciation of the site, make the short pilgrimage up the hill and if possible visit at the most spectacular times of either sunrise or sunset. Allow at least 1½ hrs. If in a hurry, visit Stupas 1, 2 and 3, Gupta Temple (17), Temple 18, and Monasteries 45 and 51.*

The Gateways The basic model consists of two pillars joined by three architraves (cross beams), sculpted as if they actually passed through the upright posts. They are regarded as the finest of all Buddhist *toranas*. The **East Gate** shows the young prince Siddhartha Gautama, leaving his father's palace and setting off on his journey towards enlightenment, and the dream his mother had before Gautama's birth. The **West Gate** portrays the seven incarnations of the Buddha. The **North Gate**, crowned by a wheel of law, illustrates the miracles associated with the Buddha as told in the *Jatakas*. The **South Gate** reveals the birth of Gautama in a series of

Sanchi

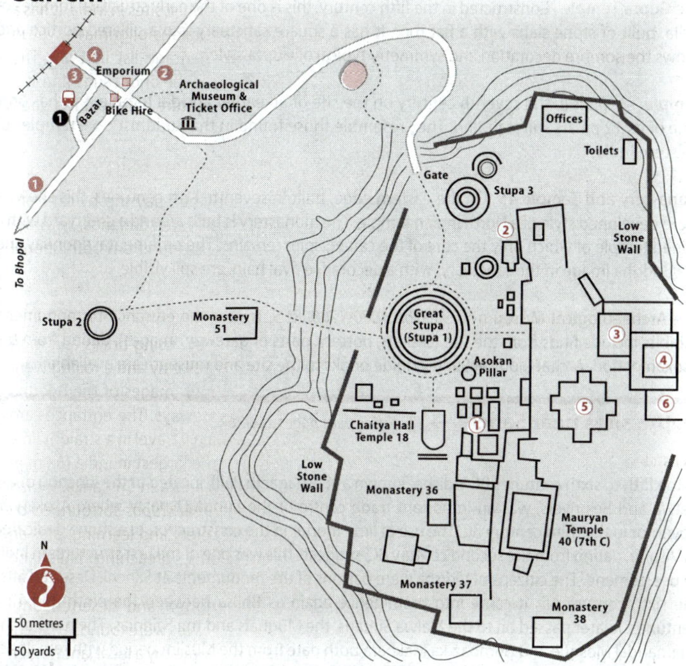

Sleeping
Gateway Retreat **1**
Krishna/Jaiswal Lodge **2**
New Jaiswal Lodge **3**
Sri Lanka Mahabodhi Society Guest House **4**

Eating
Kapil **1**

Sights
Gupta Temple **1**
Temple 31 (7th C) **2**
Monastery 46 & 47 **3**
Monastery & Temple 45 **4**
Monastery Structure 43 **5**
Temple 44 **6**

dramatically rich carvings. Just to the right of the south gate is the stump of the pillar erected by Asoka in the third century BC. The capital, with its four lion heads, is in the local museum. It recalls the one in the Sarnath Museum, of superior workmanship, that was adopted as the national symbol of Independent India.

Monastery 51 This is reached by steps opposite the west gateway of the Great Stupa. It is well preserved with thick stone walls faced with flat bricks and is typical in plan. A raised, pillared veranda with 22 monastic cells behind, surrounds a brick-paved courtyard. The discovery of charred wood suggested that roofs and pillars may have been constructed with wood. There was possibly a chapel at the centre of the west side; the massive 'bowl' beyond the west gate was caused by removal of a large boulder which you can see on your way to Stupa 2.

Stupa 2 This *stupa* stands on a terrace down the slope. The original balustrade has been dated to the second century BC with later additions. The decoration, though interesting, is much simpler than on Stupa 1, especially when dealing with the human form. The relic chamber of the *stupa* contained valuable relics of 10 saints belonging to three generations after the Buddha's immediate disciples, which may explain the choice of this site, below the main terrace.

The Gupta Temple Constructed in the fifth century, this is one of the early structural temples of India, built of stone slabs with a flat roof. It has a square sanctuary and a pillared portico and shows the sombre decoration and symmetry typical of Gupta style.

Temple 18 Built in the seventh century on the site of an earlier apsidal temple, this has only nine of its 12 pillars still standing. They resemble those found in the Buddhist cave temples of Western India.

Monastery and Temple 45 On the eastern edge, built in seventh-11th centuries, this shows a more developed style of a North Indian temple. The monastery is built around a courtyard with a ruined temple of which only the core of the carved spire remains. The ornamental doorway and the Buddha image in the sanctuary, with a decorative oval halo, are still visible.

The **Archaeological Museum** ⓘ *Sat-Thu 1000-1700, Rs 5*, is near the entrance to monument. Exhibits include finds from the site (caskets, pottery, parts of gateway, images), dating from the Asokan period. Archaeological Survey guide books to the site and museum are available.

Gupta sites near Sanchi → *For listings, see pages 264-267.*

Vidisha

In the fifth to sixth centuries BC Vidisha (known as Besnagar in Pali), located at the junction of the Betwa and Bes rivers, was an important trade centre of the Sunga Dynasty where Asoka was governor in the third century BC. The use of lime mortar in the construction of a shrine dedicated to Vishnu, dating from the second century BC, suggests this was one of the first structures in India to use 'cement'. The citizens of Vidisha were patrons of the monuments at Sanchi. Deserted after the sixth century AD, it came into prominence again as Bhilsa between the ninth and 12th centuries. It later passed on to the Malwa Sultans, the Mughals and the Scindias. The ruins of the Bijamandal Mosque and Gumbaz-ka Makbara both date from the Muslim period with remains of votive pillars nearby. The small museum contains some of Vidisha's earliest antiquities.

Heliodorus Pillar, the 'Khambha Baba', is a free-standing monolithic column, similar to Asokan pillars but much smaller, dated to 140 BC. It is 3 km after crossing the Betwa River. The inscription demonstrates that relations existed between the Greeks in the Punjab and the kings of this area and that Heliodorus had become a follower of Vishnu.

Udaygiri Caves

ⓘ *From Vidisha take a tonga or auto-rickshaw, or cycle from Bhopal and visit Vidisha and Udaygiri (an enjoyable 20 km each way).*

The group of rock-cut sanctuaries, 4 km north of Vidisha, are carved into the sandstone hillside, an inscription in one indicating that they were produced during the reign of **Chandragupta II** (AD 382-401). The caves possess all the distinctive features that gave Gupta art its unique vitality, vigour and richness of expression: the beautifully moulded capitals, the design of the entrance, and the system of continuing the architrave as a string-course around the structure. The caves have been numbered, probably in the sequence in which they were excavated.

Cave 1 has a frontage created out of a natural ledge of rock. The row of four pillars bear the 'vase and foliage' pattern about which Percy Brown wrote: "the Gupta capital typifies a renewal of faith, the water nourishing the plant trailing from its brim, an allegory which has produced the vase and flower motif". The shrines become progressively more ornate. **Cave 5** depicts Vishnu in a massive carving in his Varaha (Boar) incarnation holding the earth goddess Prithvi aloft on one tusk. Another large sculpture is of the reclining Vishnu. Both reflect the grand vision and aspirations of the carvers. **Cave 19** is notable for its high pillars, its long portico and pillared hall.

Udaypur

At Udaypur, 60 km north from Udaygiri, is the colossal **Neelkantheswara Temple**. Built of red sandstone and set on a high platform, it has a delicately carved, beautifully proportioned spire, and is an outstanding example of 11th-century Paramara architecture. **Basoda** is 24 km away and has accommodation.

Gyaraspur

Some 64 km northeast of Bhopal, Gyaraspur is an attractive and important site of medieval Jain and Hindu activity. The late ninth-century **Maladevi Temple**, on the hill above the village, is the most striking of the remains with the ruins of a *stupa* to its west. Partly rock cut (the sanctum conveniently set in a cave at the back), it has served as both a Hindu and a Jain shrine. There are ruins of an eight-pillared temple, *Athakhambe*, and a four-pillared *Chaukhambe*.

Eran

Eran, north of Gyaraspur, has the only extant standing Gupta column (AD 485) near today's small village (once the fortified **Airikina**) which is reached by dusty tracks. The large (5-m-long) late fifth-century Vishnu Varaha here (represented wholly as a boar) is carved with tiny figures of *sadhus* who are believed to have sheltered in its bristles during the Flood.

Central Madhya Pradesh listings

For Sleeping and Eating price codes and other relevant information, see Essentials pages 38-42.

Sleeping

Bhopal *p254, map p255*

Mid-price hotels are in Hamidia Rd and Berasia Rd (15-min walk from bus and train station). Better hotels in the quiet Shamla Hills, 5 km from railway, 2 km from centre. Most budget hotels are dire and infested with mosquitoes. Some refuse to take foreigners. The cheap hotels on Station Rd are best avoided.

LL-AL Noor-us-Sabah (WelcomHeritage), VIP Rd, Koh-e-Fiza, T0755-422 3333, www.noorussabahpalace.com. 39 beautifully decorated rooms in a wonderfully atmospheric 1920s palace perched up and away on the top of a hill with fantastic views of Bhopal lake. 3 restaurants, one of which is outside, fitness centre, swimming pool, Wi-Fi, currency exchange.

LL-B Amer Palace, 209 Zone 1, MP Nagar, T0755-3918110-14 , www.hotelamerpalace.com. 60 a/c rooms, good restaurant, "best pastry shop in town", pleasant and far more aesthetically pleasing business hotel than others in the area.

L-A Jehan Numa Palace, 157 Shamla Hill, T0755-266 1100, www.hoteljehanumapalace.com. Pristinely converted 19th- century palace with 100 luxurious, rooms set around 2 courtyards of immaculately kept gardens. Newly built area has rooms with balconies overlooking a large swimming pool and spa/fitness centre. 3 superb restaurants, coffee shop/bakery and 2 bars, all with a thriving and international atmosphere. Outstanding service and a complimentary breakfast buffet fit for kings. Internet, currency exchange and very helpful travel desk. Trips to the newly opened **Reni Pani** jungle lodge can also be booked from here. Highly recommended.

L-A Residency, 208 MP Nagar, T0755-255 6001, hoteltheresidency@yahoo.com. 58 a/c rooms in modern, business style hotel, excellent restaurant. Hopefully the shockingly dirty swimming pool will be given a clean soon!

AL-A Lake View Ashok (ITDC), Shamla Hills, opposite TV Tower, T0755-266 0090, www.lakeviewashok.com. Modern business style hotel now somewhat in need of a refurb. 45 comfortable but slightly shabby rooms (hot water erratic), good restaurant, theoretical Wi-Fi, car hire, pool, health club. Redeeming feature is the quiet location with great lake views of Upper Lake.

AL-B Nisarga, 211 Zone 1, MP Nagar, T0755-255 5701, www.hotelnisarga.com. 41 rooms, very good restaurant (tasty Chinese), comfortable although dark and mostly windowless rooms in business-style hotel.

AL-B Palash, near '45 Bungalows', TT Nagar, T0755-255 3006, www.mptourism.com. 37 pleasant rooms in recently renovated business hotel, very helpful staff, restaurant, handy for tourist office and MPTDC buses.

C-E Rama Internationa, Hamidia Rd, T0755-253 5542. Peaceful place nicely tucked back from the busy main road. 12 large, clean, simple, rooms, some a/c.

B-D Motel Shiraz, Hamidia Rd, T0755-255 2513. A good lower budget option for the area in this basic motel, 22 rooms, best are on the 2nd floor at the back overlooking garden. Curiously much more expensive are the a/c cottages that are not much larger and pretty dark, dismal and mouldy. 24-hr checkout.

D-F Hotel Ranjeet, Hamidia Rd, T0755-274 0501. 28 clean, simple, but good sized rooms, attached bath (bucket hot water), TV, good restaurant and bar, complimentary breakfast.

E-F Shrimaya, No 3 Hamidia Rd (actually in side street off the main road), T0755-274 7401, shrimaya@sancharnet.in. 27 modern rooms in bright and friendly hotel some a/c. Recommended

F Sonali, near Radha Talkies, Hamidia Rd, T0755-274 0880, www.sonalihotel.com. Decent, clean rooms (best a/c), good food (room service), professional, courteous staff. Recommended.

Pachmarhi *p258, map p259*

Prices increase tenfold during Diwali, Christmas and other holidays. Most hotels have wood boilers which provide hot water for a few hours morning and evening.

A Rock End Manor, Pachmarhi, 2 km from the market area, T07578-252079, www.mptourism.com. 6 deluxe rooms, 3 a/c, some with 6-m-high ceilings in restored colonial building, lovely views of old golf course and polo fields. Recommended.

A Satpura Retreat, Mahadeo Rd, 2 km from centre, T07578-252097, www.mptourism.com. 6 rooms, 2 a/c, attractive old bungalow with veranda, in pleasant if rather far-flung setting.

C Panchvati Cottages, near Tehsil, T07578-252096. Quiet and well-maintained, with 5 2-bedroom cottages and 5 huts, all with TV and hot water, good-value restaurant, bar.

D-E Kachnar, Arvind Marg, T07578-252323. 11 spacious, clean, comfortable rooms with bath, good views from upper-floor terraces, very friendly and helpful. Wildlife safaris in Satpura from travel desk downstairs.

D-E Nilambar, T07578-252039. Good views from 6 attractive twin-bed cottages, hot water.

D-F Misty Meadows, Patel Marg, T07578-252136, www.pachmarhihotels.info. Pleasant, spacious rooms (some renovated), 2 with access to terrace, peaceful garden, home-cooked food. Mr Bhakshi is a friendly and knowledgeable host.

D-F Nandan Van (SADA), T07578-252018. 12 old-fashioned but well-kept cottages in spacious peaceful gardens. Friendly, though little English spoken.

F Abhilasha, T07578-252203. Hotel with 10 rooms, bucket hot water, 24-hr check-out.

F-G Abhimanyu, Arvind Rd, T07578-252126, kapil_juneja81@hotmail.com. Spacious and clean enough rooms, enthusiastic owner, lively atmosphere, simple rooftop restaurant with good hill views. Willing local guides hang out in lobby.

G Manjushri, Patel Marg, T07578-252347. 24 grimy but acceptable rooms, better with marble floor instead of carpet, friendly.

Pipariya

F-G Alka, across footbridge from station, T07576-224222. Range of simple rooms, some a/c, some amazingly cheap, handy for trains and buses, very popular restaurant (although little competition).

Satpura National Park *p260*

L-A Reni Pani Lodge, Village Reni Pani, Tehsil Sohagpur, Dist Hoshangabad. 135 km from Bhopal and 45 km from Hoshangabad. Nearest railway Pipariya (35 km), T0755-266 1100, www.renipanijunglelodge.com. In a refreshingly remote location a few kilometres outside the park, brothers Faiz and Ali are impeccable hosts at this luxuriously rustic, yet newly built lodge. 12 immaculately designed ethnic-style cottages which even come with your very own locally employed butler. Swimming pool, library, souvenir shop selling local handicrafts, fantastic cuisine and evening fireside candlelit drinks where you can discuss the various animal, bird and local tribal village sightings of the day. All activities in the park are arranged and enthusiastically guided by either one of the brothers or the highly knowledgable local naturalist. Visits can be arranged directly or through **Jehan Numa Palace Hotel** in Bhopal. Highly recommended.

Sanchi *p260, map p261*

C Gateway Retreat, T07482-266723, www.mptourism.com. The smartest place in town although quite overpriced.18 rooms set around attractive gardens some a/c, plus bar and restaurant. Complimentary breakfast.

C-G Sri Lanka Mahabodhi Society Guest House, near railway station, T07482-266739. Often full with large groups of Sri Lankan Buddhist pilgrims, there are 2 options, a newly built quite overpriced hotel with clean, spacious but spartan rooms with bath and a/c or a more humble place next door with smaller, simpler and cheaper rooms set around a couple of courtyards and gardens, also dorm, often full.

E Tourist Cafeteria, by the museum, T07482-266743. Café with 2 basic but clean rooms.

E-F Krishna/Jaiswal Lodge, T07482-266610, Bhopal–Vidisha road. Brother of the owner of **New Jaiswal Lodge**, this place is a very similar budget option. Often filled with Sri Lankan pilgrims, who sometimes take over the large upstairs hall as a mass dorm.

E-F New Jaiswal Lodge, next to railway station, T07482-266508. Cheaper and more cheerful family-run place with small and simple cleanish rooms, some with attached bathroom, restaurant.

Gupta sites near Sanchi *p262*

E-F Hotel Kumud Palace, Kala Bag, Bareth Rd, T07594-222223. Hotel with 16 clean air-cooled or a/c rooms, hot water, TV and a restaurant.

Eating

Bhopal *p254, map p255*

¥¥¥ Jehan Numa Palace (see Sleeping). International, 3 superb restaurants, one under a giant mango tree, excellent Indian, garden barbecues, 24-hr coffee shop with Western snacks and an impressive coffee selection. Vibrant, modern atmosphere.

¥¥¥ Lake View Ashok (see Sleeping). International cuisine, some excellent dishes, pleasant ambience but service can be slow.

¥¥ Kwality, Hamidia Rd and New Market. Indian, Chinese, continental. Dark but cool and comfortable.

¥¥ Wind and Waves, Boat Club, Lake Drive Rd, T0755-266 1523. Unrivalled location delivers everything the name promises. Food is predictable MP Tourism multi-cuisine fare. Well known for the bar.

¥ Indian Coffee House, Hamidia Rd, Sivaji Nagar and New Market. Indian. Good *thalis* but uninspired greasy *dosas*.

¥ Jyoti, 53 Hamidia Rd. Indian. Spartan but excellent cheap vegetarian *thalis*.

¥ Manohar Place, 6 Hamidia Rd. *Dosas* and snacks (fantastic *pakoras*), very reasonable, excellent sweets, delicious fresh fruit juices, an Indian café.

Pachmarhi *p258, map p259*

MP Tourism hotels have bland restaurants serving Indian and a few Chinese dishes:

¥¥ Satpura Retreat (see Sleeping). Very pleasant.

¥ Laxman Hotel (sign in Hindi only), Jawahar Chowk. Rightly popular for *chai*, snacks (try *dal pakora*) and Indian sweets.

¥ Maheshwari, Kachnar Hotel (see Sleeping). Excellent vegetarian dishes, *thalis*, clean and bright, best in the bazar area.

Sanchi *p260, map p261*

¥ Kapil, New Bus Stand. Good, cheap vegetarian food.

¥ Tourist Cafeteria, by the museum. Clean, pricey average meals, bit oily, small tidy garden.

¥ Travellers' Lodge (see Sleeping). Indian and Chinese. Non-residents with advance notice.

Festivals and events

Bhopal *p254, map p255*

26-30 Jan Lok Rang features local crafts and cultural performances.

Feb Bhopal Mahotsav is similar. **Summer Festival**, Bharat Bhawan centre stages art exhibitions, theatre and music.

Shopping

Bhopal *p254, map p255*

Most shops open 0930-2000 and close on Sun (some on Mon). **Chowk** and **New Market** are the main shopping centres.

Handicrafts Emporium, Hamidia Rd. Souvenirs and local handicrafts.

MP State Emporium, GTB Complex, TT Nagar. Specializes in local *chanderi* (cotton/silk mix, so sheer that Aurangzeb insisted that his daughter wear 7 layers of it) as well as *tussar* and other raw silks.

Mrignayanee Emporium, 23 New Shopping Centre. Stock souvenirs and local handicrafts.

Books

Landmark, Arera Colony. Also near water tower in the Old City.

Variety Bookhouse, GTB Complex, New Market, has an extensive choice in English.

Activities and tours

Bhopal *p254, map p255*

Boat Club, Lake Drive Rd, T0755-266 1523. Boat and canoe hire, windsurfing.

MP Tourism, 4th floor, Gangotri, TT Nagar, T0755-277 4340. Tours to Islamnagar, Sanchi and Udaigiri (Sat and Sun), Sanchi, Bhimbetka and Bhojpur (Sat), Rs 200 plus admission fees.

Safari Travel, 2 Van Vihar Rd, T(0)755-273 9997. Travel agent.

Transport

Bhopal *p254, map p255*

Air The airport is 11 km from centre. Transport to town by taxi, about Rs 200 (non a/c). **Indian Airlines** bus to the airport from City Office, 0700. **Air India**, GTB Complex, TT Nagar, T0755-522 0666; **Indian Airlines**, Bhad Bhada Rd, T0755-277 8434, airport T0755-264 6123, flies to **Mumbai** daily via **Indore**; also **Delhi** (2 via Gwalior). **Jet Airways**, T0755-276 0371, airport T0755-264 5676, to **Mumbai**.

Bus Hamidia Rd Bus Stand, T0755-254 0841. Daily services include: **Agra** 541 km; **Gwalior** 422 km, 0600, 1900; **Indore** 187 km, frequent, good a/c coach 0700, 1330, 4 hrs; **Jaipur**

572 km; **Khajuraho** better to take train; **Nagpur** 345 km; **Pachmarhi** 0230-1615, a/c 0800; **Sanchi** 45 km, 1½ hrs, hourly; **Shivpuri**, 1130-1500. For **Ujjain** take bus to Devas (about 3 hrs) then jeep or bus to Ujjain. MP Tourism buses to **Indore** and **Pachmarhi** can be more comfortable, T0755-255 3076.
Car MP Tourism (Transport) a/c and non a/c cars; full day Rs 575-750 non-a/c, Rs 800-900 a/c. Out of town: Rs 6-14 per km, depending on vehicle, plus night halt charge, Rs 250 (minimum 200 km average per day).
Taxi **Bhojpur** and **Bhimbetka** cost about Rs 600 by taxi, 4 hrs round trip. Unmetered.
Train City Booking T0755-255 3599. Railway Station, enquiry T131, reservation T1335. Booking office and tourist information outside Platform 1. **Agra Cantt**: see Delhi, and deduct 4-5 hrs. **Amritsar**: *Dadar Amritsar Exp 11057*, 1520, 26 hrs. **Bengaluru** (**Bangalore**): *Rajdhani Exp 12430*, 0450, Mon, Tue, Fri, Sat, 26 hrs. **Chennai**: *Tamil Nadu Exp 12622*, 0805, 23 hrs. **Delhi** (**ND**): *Chhattisgarh Exp 18237*, 0720, 13¾ hrs; *Punjab Mail 12137*, 0915, 12 hrs; *Dadar Amritsar Exp 11057*, 1520, 13¾ hrs; *GT Exp 12615*, 1930, 11½ hrs; *AP Exp 12723*, 2210, 10 hrs. **Gwalior**: *Punjab Mail 12137*, 0915, 5½ hrs; *Dadar Amritsar Exp 11057*, 1520, 6½ hrs. **Jabalpur**: *Narmada Exp 18233*, 2335, 7 hrs; *Amarkantak Exp 12854*, 1545, 6 hrs. **Jalgaon** (for **Ajanta**/**Ellora**): *Karnataka Exp 12628*, 0700, 6½ hrs. **Kolkata**: *Shipra Exp 19305*, 0420, Mon, Thu, Fri, 28 hrs. **Lucknow**: *Pushpak Exp 12533*, 2155, 11½ hrs; *Kushinagar Exp 11015*, 1420, 11½ hrs. **Mumbai** (**CST**): *Punjab Mail 12138*, 17000, 15 hrs; *Pushpak Exp 12534*, 0615, 14½ hrs. **Ujjain**: *Narmada Exp 18234*, 0435, 5½ hrs, continues to **Indore**; *Intercity Exp 19304*, 1700, 3½ hrs (2nd class only).

Pachmarhi *p258, map p259*

4WD Most hotels can arrange 4WD Gypsys. Can usually get seat in shared jeep for cheaper.
Bus Bus stand, T07578-252058. Daily services to **Bhopal** 0730, 1530, 5-6 hrs; **Indore** 0630; **Khargon** 1830; **Nagpur** 0700 (returns 1000), 12 hrs; **Pipariya** every 30 mins until 2000, 1½ hrs. Also share jeeps, frequent but crowded.
Train The nearest station is Pipariya, 47 km. Computerized reservations at DI Bungalow near lake, 0800-1400 (closed Tue). To **Kolkata**: *Howrah Mail 12322*, 1049, 25 hrs (via **Jabalpur** (2½ hrs), **Satna** (5 hrs) and **Allahabad** (10½ hrs). **Mumbai**: *Mumbai Mail 12321*, 2012, 15 hrs (via **Jalgaon**, 7½ hrs). **Satna**: *Ranchi Exp 18610*, 0644, 5-6 hrs.

Sanchi *p260, map p261*

Bus Frequent buses from **Bhopal**, Hamidia Rd, 0630-1930, 1½ hrs direct or over 2 hrs via **Raisen**; latter more attractive; also to **Vidisha**.
Taxi Hire in Bhopal; allow Rs 600 for visit and 1½ hrs each way.
Train Some trains on the Jhansi-Itarsi section of the Central Railway stop in Sanchi. Slow local passenger trains run to and from **Bhopal** a couple of times a day, 1 hr, and to **Vidisha**, 20 mins.

Gupta sites near Sanchi *p262*

Add on Rs 150 to include **Vidisha** and **Udaygiri** in a day trip by car to Sanchi. Regular buses from Vidisha to Bhopal and Raisen), and local trains to Sanchi. For **Udaipur**, take a train from Bhopall to Basoda (the station is Ganjbasoda), then bus (Rs 10) or *tonga*to Udaypur.

Directory

Bhopal *p254, map p255*

Banks Indian Overseas Bank, near Surya Hotel for foreign exchange. ATMs everywhere.
Cultural centres British Council Library, GTB Complex, Roshanpura Naka, New Market, Tue-Sat 1100-1900. English periodicals and newspapers in cool reading room.
Internet Jehan Numa Palace Hotel (Rs 100 per hr). **Medical services** Ambulance: T0755-255 3355. **Carewell Hospital**, Mahadev Mandir Rd, T0755-254 3983. **Mayo Hospital**, Shahjahanabad, T0755-253 5584. **Post** Central GPO: TT Nagar; Sultania Rd for Poste Restante.

Pachmarhi *p258, map p259*

Internet Anurag Photostat, Shubhash Marg.

Sanchi *p260, map p261*

Useful contacts Chief Conservator of Forests, Van Bhawan, Tulsi Nagar, T0755-267 4318.

Western Madhya Pradesh

The pearl of western Madhya Pradesh is Mandu, an abandoned citadel littered with empty palaces, gazing out over the Narmada River plains from the top of a craggy plateau. Temple ghats line the Narmada banks in the holy towns of Omkareshwar and Maheshwar, while Ujjain, further north on the river Shipra, is one of Hinduism's seven holiest cities, and a venue of the Maha Kumbh Mela.
▸▸ *For listings, see pages 275-278.*

Indore → *For listings, see pages 275-278. Colour map 2, C5. Phone code: 0731. Population: 1,600,000.*

A rapidly growing and rather characterless industrial city, Indore is on the banks of the rivers Sarasvati and Khan. A major centre for cotton textiles and the automobile industry, the city is also notable for Hindustani classical music.

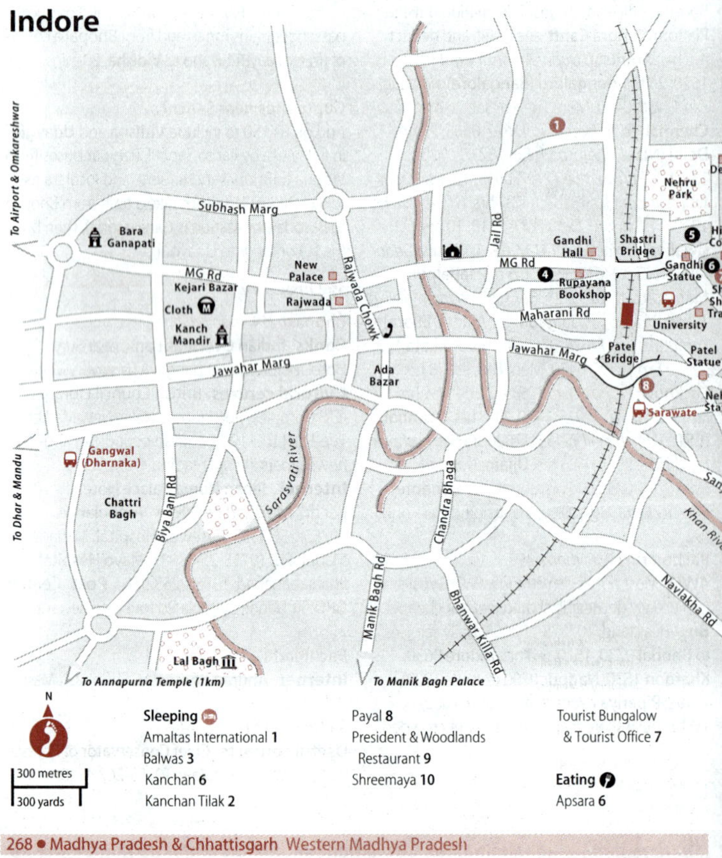

Sleeping
Amaltas International **1**
Balwas **3**
Kanchan **6**
Kanchan Tilak **2**
Payal **8**
President & Woodlands Restaurant **9**
Shreemaya **10**
Tourist Bungalow & Tourist Office **7**

Eating
Apsara **6**

Ins and outs

Getting there Indore has direct flights to Bhopal, Delhi, Gwalior and Mumbai. It is under five hours by the fastest train from Bhopal. The railway station and the Sarwate Bus Stand are near the town centre, but buses to Mandu go from the Gangwal Bus Stand, a 10-minute auto ride away. ▸▸ *See Transport, page 277.*

Getting around Indore is quite spread out and very congested so it is best to take an auto to visit the sights away from the centre.

Tourist information Madhya Pradesh Tourism ⓘ *RN Tagore Rd opposite Ravindra Natyagrih, T0731-252 8653.*

History

The land on which Indore was built was given to **Malhar Rao Holkar** in 1733 by the Maratha Peshwas, see page 1154, in appreciation of his help in many of their battles. Malhar Rao left much of the statecraft in the highly gifted hands of his widowed daughter-in-law who succeeded him on the throne. The city was destroyed in 1801 but recovered and was the British headquarters of their Central India Agency. The ruling family of Indore, the **Holkars**, took the British side during the Mutiny in 1857. Indore was one of the first states to open temples and schools to *Harijans*, in support of Gandhi's campaign against untouchability.

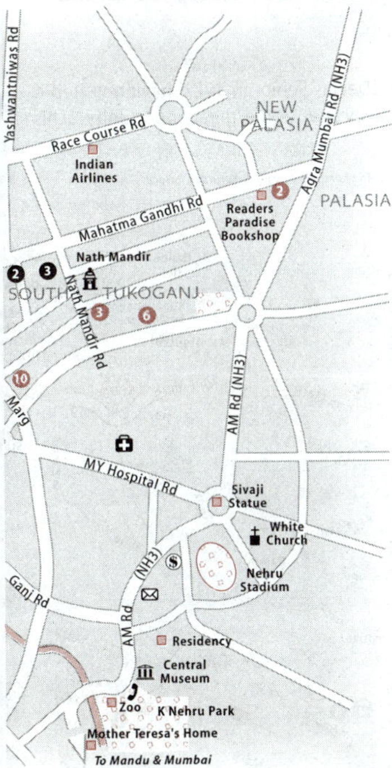

Ding Ding **2**
Gypsy **3**
Indian Coffee House **4**
Landmark **1**
Statue **5**

Sights

The **Rajwada** (Old Palace) with its seven-storeyed gateway, faces the main square. A fire in 1984 destroyed most of it; now only the façade remains. On the north side is the **New Palace** and garden. In the streets are some good timber houses with deep recessed verandas and carved pillars.

Kanch Mandir ⓘ *allow 30 mins, shoes to be left at door*, is on Jawahar Marg next to **Hotel Sheesh Mahal**. Inside this Jain temple thousands of mirrors adorn the walls, floor and ceilings, supplemented by brightly patterned ceramic tiles, Chinese lantern- type glass lamps and cut-glass chandeliers, all exquisitely crafted. There are about 50 murals depicting scenes of conversion to Jainism and 19th-century courtly life. The use of glass beads and raised figures produces a pleasing 3D effect. The image of Mahavir is in plain black onyx. This mirrored palace is at variance with the austerity and simplicity of the Mahavir's supposed existence and teachings.

Lal Bagh (Nehru Centre) ⓘ *Tue-Sun 1000-1700, small entry fee*, southwest of town, once the residence of the maharaja, built and decorated in a confusion of styles, is now a museum and cultural centre. The rooms have been restored and furnished to pleasing effect. Queen Victoria looks on to the main 'entrance portico' (you leave through this and enter through a side entrance). There are a number of sporting trophies including stuffed tigers. The maharaja, a keen sportsman, is seen in photographs rowing on a lake, and flying in an early aeroplane. Both these are in fact 'backdrop paintings' with a hole for him to stand in to be photographed! There are also good prints of the Old Palace. The entrance hall is in marble and gilt rococo with a display of prehistoric artefacts. Two attractive rooms are predominantly 'Indian' and include Mughal exhibits. On the first floor is the coin collection which dates mostly from the Muslim period. Exhibits include miniatures, contemporary Indian sculptures and paintings, Italian sculptures and intricately inlaid boxes. If your time is limited, visit this riotously varied and fascinating museum rather than the Cental Museum.

Central Museum ⓘ *Agra–Mumbai Rd, near GPO, Tue-Sun 1100-1800, free, guides available, allow 30 mins*, has two main galleries: **Gallery I** with artefacts from circa 50,000- 4000 BC, some from west Malwa including stone tools, quartz sickles, ornaments. Also a model of the first Hindu temple at Bharhut. **Gallery II** contains Hindu mythological carvings. Sculptures stand in the grounds, which were possibly a battlefield during the Mutiny.

Around Indore → *For listings, see pages 275-278.*

Dewas → *Colour map 2, C5.*

EM Forster 'worked' here in the court of the Raja of Dewas Senior in 1921, having visited it earlier in 1912. Forster came to regard his stay in this dusty town as the 'great opportunity' of his

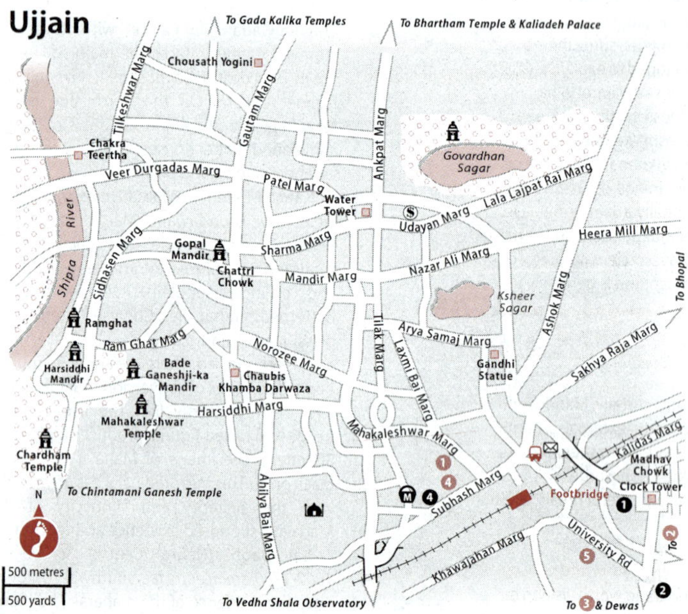

Sleeping
Ajay 1
Ramkrishna 4
Shipra 5
Surana Palace 2
Yatri Niwas 3

Eating
5 Star 1
Ashnol 2
Sudama 4

life and used this experience to good effect with the autobiographical *The Hill of Devi* and his most famous novel, *A Passage to India*. It is worth going up the 'Hill of Devi' overlooking the town for the views; you can drive all the way to the temple at the top. Dewas today is an important industrial centre.

Ujjain → *Colour map 2, C5. Phone code: 0734. Population: 430,000.*

Ujjain, one of the best-known cities of ancient India and one of Hinduism's seven sacred cities, see page 1409, is one of the four centres of the **Kumbh Mela**, see page 182, attracting about three million pilgrims every 12 years. At other times, a constant stream come to bathe in the River Shipra and worship at the temples. Despite its sanctity and its age, it has few remarkable buildings. In its heyday, Ujjain was on a flourishing trade route to Mesopotamia and Egypt. Nowadays, it is little more than a provincial town. The **Madhya Pradesh Tourism** ⓘ *T0734-2561544*, is at the railway station.

Many dynasties ruled over this prosperous city and it is said to have been the seat of the viceroyalty of Asoka in 275 BC. His sons were born here, and it was from here that they set out to preach Buddhism. The poet **Kalidasa**, one of the *Nava Ratna* (Nine Gems) of Hindu literature, wrote some of his works here. Ujjain stands on the first meridian of longitude for Hindu astronomers, who believed that the **Tropic of Cancer** also passed through the site. This explains the presence of the **Vedha Shala** observatory, southwest of town, built by Raja Jai Singh II of Jaipur around 1730 when he was the Governor of Malwa under the Mughals. Small, compared to the Jantar Mantars, it has only five instruments. Even today the *Ephemeris* tables (predicted positions of the planets), are published here.

Mahakaleshwar Temple, dedicated to Siva, was rebuilt by Marathas in the 18th century. The temple lingam is one of the 12 *jyotirlingas* (in India, believed to be *swayambhu* – born of itself). The myths surrounding the 'linga of light' go back to the second century BC and were developed to explain and justify linga worship, see page 1412. The **Chaubis Khambha Darwaza** (circa 11th century) has 24 carved pillars which probably belonged to the medieval temple.

Close to the tank near Mahakaleshwar is a large sculpted image of Ganesh in the **Bade Ganeshji-ka Mandir**. A rock covered with turmeric is worshipped as the head of a legendary king Vikramaditya in the centre of the **Harsiddhi Mandir. Gopal Mandir** in the bazar contains a silver image of Krishna and an ornamental silver door. The **Bina-Niv-ki- Masjid** in Anantpeth, originally a Jain temple (see entrance porch), was converted to a mosque (circa 1400), by the first independent Sultan of Malwa. The **Chintamani Ganesh Temple** across the river is believed to have ancient medieval origins. There are other temples and shrines along the river where the atmosphere is generally very relaxed.

Mandu (Mandav) → *For listings, see pages 275-278. Colour map 2, C5. Phone code: 07292. Population: 5000.*

Architecturally, Mandu represents the best in a provincial Islamic style, restrained and lacking in elaborate external ornamentation. Fine buildings are spread over the naturally defensible plateau with a sheer drop towards the Namar plains to the south and waterfalls flowing into the Kakra Khoh Gorge. You can visit Mandu from Indore on a long day excursion, but it is better to have a peaceful break here for a couple of days.

Ins and outs

Getting there and around Indore is the nearest centre for air, bus and train connections. Everything worth visiting can be reached on foot or bike. Cars can be hired informally for day trips. ⏩ *See Transport, page 278.*

History

Perched along the Vindhya ranges, Mandu was fortified as early as the sixth century. By 1261, King Jayavaram transferred the Paramara capital from Dhar to Mandu itself. The whole area fell to the Muslims in 1293, though Mandu remained under Hindu rule until 1305, when it came under the Khaljis in Delhi. The first of these Pathan sultans re-named Mandu **Shadiabad** (City of Joy). Hoshang Shah (1405-1435) made it his capital and as Mandu's strategic importance grew he embellished it with its most important civic buildings. Under his successor, the liberal Mahmud Khalji, a resurgence of art and literature followed, fostering Hindu, Jain as well as Muslim development. Mandu remained a prosperous centre of peace and stability under his son Ghiyasuddin until 1500. Several early Mughal rulers enjoyed visiting Mandu, but by the end of the Mughal period it had effectively been abandoned, and in 1732 it passed into Maratha hands.

Sights

The road leading up to the fort passes through a series of well fortified gates, most notable of which is the **Delhi Gate** (1405-1407), the main entrance to the city. The 45-km parapet wall with 12 gates was built from rubble and boulders. Most of the buildings inside date from 1401 to 1526 – some have stones salvaged from desecrated local Hindu temples. There are six groups of buildings at Mandu, the first three being the most important. The return trip taking in Roopmati's Pavilion is about 14 km.

Royal Enclave ⓘ *Rs 100.* The **Mosque of Dilwar Khan** (1405) is the earliest Islamic building, comprising a central colonnaded courtyard. There are Hindu influences in the main entrances. **Hathi Pol** (Elephant Gate) is the main entrance to the royal enclosure. **Hindola Mahal** (Swing Palace, circa 1425), built on a 'T' plan, was the audience hall, acquiring its name from its inward sloping walls which give the impression of swaying. Behind and to the west of the Hindola Mahal is a jumble of ruins which was once the palace of the Malwa sultans.

Here is the 6.5-m-deep **Champa Baoli**, an underground well (its water is said to have smelt like the *champak* flower), cool vaulted *tyhkhanas* (rooms for summer use), a *hammam* (hot bath) and a water pavilion.

The late 15th-century **Jahaz Mahal** (Ship Palace), reflects the spirit of romantic beauty characteristic of the palace life of the Muslim rulers of India. Built between two artificial lakes, Munj and Kapur Talaos, it is 122 m long and only 15 m wide. Its shape and kiosks give it the impression of a stately ship. Built to house Ghiyas'ud-Din's increasing *harem*, it was 'crewed' entirely by women, some from as far afield as Turkey and Abyssinia, and consists of three great halls with a beautiful bath.

Other places of interest in this enclave are **Taveli Mahal (1)** (stables and guardhouse), which has a wonderful panorama of the Mandu ruins; it has a small **museum** ⓘ *Sat-Thu 0900-1700.* Nearby are two deep, bat-filled wells – the *Ujala* (bright) and *Andheri* (dark) **baolis** – and **Gada Shah's Shop (2)**. The last, in ruins, retains a romantic second name, the Kesar Kasturi Mahal. Gada Shah taking pity on a group of gypsies trying to sell their perfumed *kesar* and *kasturi* which had been ruined by a downpour, bought their wares and then had to use it all in his palace since it was unsaleable.

Central Group **Hoshang Shah's Tomb (3)** (circa 1440) ⓘ *Mandu Bazar, Rs 100,* is India's first marble monument, a refined example of Afghan architecture. It has a well-proportioned dome, delicate marble latticework and porticoed courts and towers. The square base of the interior changes to an octagon through being raised by arches to the next level, and then becomes 16-sided further up. Shah Jahan sent four of his architects, including Ustad Ahmed, who is associated with the Taj Mahal, to study it for inspiration. The adjoining **Jama Masjid (3)** (1454), which took three generations to complete, was inspired by the great mosque at Damascus.

Conceived by Hoshang Shah on a grand scale, it is on a high plinth (4.6 m), with a large domed porch ornamented with jali screens and bands of blue enamel tiles set as stars. The courtyard is flanked by colonnades. The western one is the Prayer Hall, the most imposing of all with numerous rows of arches and pillars which support the ceilings of the three great domes and 58 smaller ones. The central *mihrab* (niche) is beautifully designed and ornamented along its sides with a scroll of interwoven Arabic letters containing quotations from the Koran.
Ashrafi Mahal (4) (Palace of Gold Coins, circa 1436-1440) was conceived as the first *madrassa* of Persian studies. Its builder Mahmud Shah Khilji (1436-1469) constructed the seven-storey tower to celebrate his victory over Rana Khumba of Mewar. Only one storey survives. Also in ruins is the tomb, intended to be the largest building in Mandu.

Sagar Talao Group To the east of the road between the village and Sagar Talao is the **Hathi Mahal** (Elephant Palace). It takes its names from its stumpy pillars supporting the dome and was probably a *baradari* (pleasure pavilion), turned into a tomb with a mosque by it. The **Tomb of Darya Khan** (circa 1526), a red masonry mausoleum once embellished with rich enamel patterns, is nearby.

In the large group of monuments around the picturesque **Sagar Talao** (lake) is the **Malik Mughith Mosque (5)** built in 1432. Its west wall retains blue tile decoration in carved niches. In front is the **caravanserai** (also 1432), an open courtyard with two halls with rooms at both ends. The **Dai-ka-Mahal (6)** (Gumbad) to the south is the tomb belonging to the wet-nurse of a

Mandu Fort

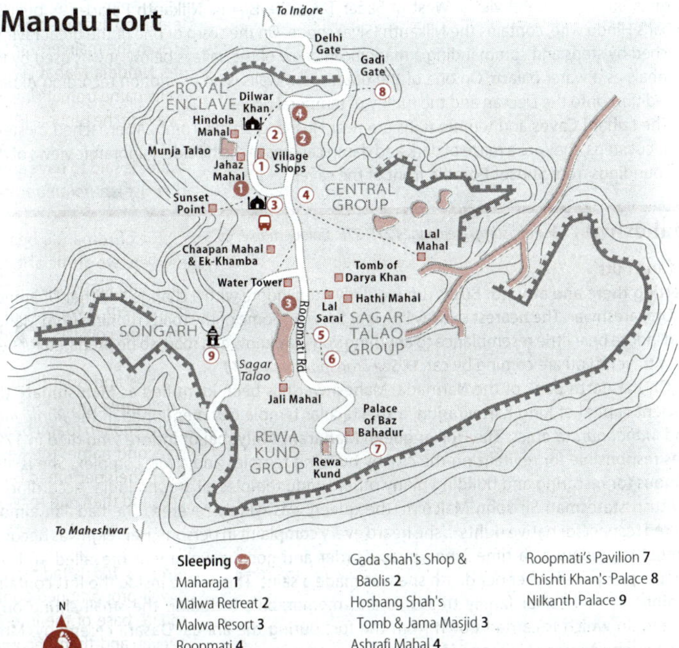

Sleeping
Maharaja **1**
Malwa Retreat **2**
Malwa Resort **3**
Roopmati **4**

Sights
Taveli Mahal & Museum **1**
Gada Shah's Shop & Baolis **2**
Hoshang Shah's Tomb & Jama Masjid **3**
Ashrafi Mahal **4**
Malik Mughith Mosque & Caravansarai **5**
Dai-ka-Mahal **6**
Roopmati's Pavilion **7**
Chishti Khan's Palace **8**
Nilkanth Palace **9**

1 km
1 mile

Mandu prince. Alongside, the ruins of a pretty mosque include a fine octagonal base decorated with small kiosks.

Rewa Kund Group ⓘ *foreigners Rs 100.* This is a sacred tank, 3.2 km south of the village, whose waters were lifted to supply the **Palace of Baz Bahadur** (1508-1509), the musician prince, on the rising ground above. The palace was built before Baz Bahadur, the last Sultan of Malwa (1555), came to occupy it. The main portion of the palace consists of a spacious open court with halls and rooms on all sides and a beautiful cistern in its centre. On the terrace above are two *baradaris* (pavilions) from which there are lovely views.

On higher ground at the southern edge of the plateau is **Roopmati's Pavilion (7)**, built as a military observation post but later modified and added to as a palace, so that Baz Bahadur's mistress could have her view of the sacred **Narmada River**, seen 305 m below winding like a white serpent across the plains. The shepherdess **Roopmati**, the story goes, so impressed Baz Bahadur with her singing that he captured her. She agreed to go to Mandu with Baz Bahadur when he promised that she would live in a palace within sight of her beloved river. He built the Rewa Kund so that she could practise her Hindu rites. The pavilions, square with hemispherical domes, are the latest additions.

Other palaces On the edge of the plateau is the **Lal Mahal** (Red/Ruby Palace) or Lal Bungalow, once used as a royal summer retreat. **Chishti Khan's Palace (8)**, used during the monsoon, is now in ruins but offers good views. West of Sagar Talao the Islamic **Nilkanth Palace (9)**, built for Akbar's Hindu wife, contains the Nilkanth (Siva) shrine. On the scarp of one of the great ravines, reached by steps and commanding a magnificent view of the valleys below, it was used by the Mughals as a water palace. On one of the outer room walls is an inscription recording Akbar's expeditions into the Deccan and the futility of temporal riches.

The **Lohani Caves** and temple ruins are near Hoshang Shah's Tomb. Approached by steep rock-cut steps, they are a maze of dark and damp caverns in the hillside. Panoramic views of the surroundings from **Sunset Point** in front of the caves.

Maheshwar → *For listings, see pages 275-278. Colour map 2, C5.*

Ins and outs

Getting there and around Buses run regularly from Indore with a change at either Dhamnod or Omkareshwar. The nearest railway link is at Barwah. Some of the roads running from Mandu and Indore bear little resemblance to anything you may know as a road, so be prepared for very slow travel if you are coming by car. ▸▸ *See Transport, page 278.*

On the north bank of the Narmada, Maheshwar has been identified as **Mahishmati**, the ancient capital of King Kartivirarjun, a spectacular temple city mentioned in the *Ramayana* and *Mahabharata* epics. The Holkar queen **Maharani Ahilyabai of Indore** who died in 1795 was responsible for revitalizing the city by building temples and a fort complex. She is also famous for restoring and building many other Hindu temples all around India. According to Scottish statesman Sir John Malcolm, the queen was widely revered. She had "an almost sacred respect for native rights ... she heard every complaint in person". Her reign has become almost legendary as a time when peace, order and good government prevailed and the people prospered. After her death she was made a saint. The palace inside the fort contains exhibits of the Holkar family treasures and memorabilia including the small shrine on a palanquin which is carried down from the fort during the annual Dasara ceremony. Most Indians who come to Maheshwar always visit and pay their respects at this shrine.There is also a statue of the Rani seated on her throne.

The small town is renowned for its *Maheshwar* saris woven in a unique way for over 200 years. At one time almost lost, the tradition has been revived by the Holkar family and today, the

Rehwa Society (www.rehwasociety.org) is a thriving cottage industry, the profits of which go to fund both the housing of the local female weavers, their families and a thriving school for local children from poorer families.The **ghats** on the riverbank are perhaps some of the cleanest and un-touristy in India. Local women wash clothes along the ghats and sadhus quietly go about their day. Lining the banks are many small temples, lingams and stone memorials to the *satis*(recently widowed women who would commit suicide by throwing themselves onto their husbands funeral pyre. The practice has been outlawed since 1829). The temples to see are **Kaleshwara**, **Rajarajeshwara**, **Vithaleshwara** and **Ahileshwar**. In the middle of the river, on a small island is Baneshwar temple, which, rumour has it, is located at the centre of the Universe. Indore's Prince Richard Holkar's daughter recently had the temple restored and got married there.

Omkareshwar (Mandhata) → *For listings, see pages 275-278. Colour map 2, C5.*

A sacred island shaped like the holy Hindu symbol 'Om' at the confluence of the Narmada and the Kaveri, Omkareshwar has drawn pilgrims for centuries. Over 2 km long and 1 km wide the island is divided north to south by a deep gully. The ground slopes gently along the north edge but in the south and east there are cliffs over 150 m high forming a gorge. The village spreads to the south bank from the island, now linked by a bridge. The river is reputedly very deep and has crocodiles.

Sri Omkareshwar Mahadeo Temple has one of the 12 *jyotirlingas* in India, natural rock features that are believed to be representations of Siva. The oldest temple is at the east end of the island. **SiddhnathTemple** on the hill is a fine example of early medieval temple architecture, its main feature being a frieze of elephants over 1.5 m high carved on a stone slab at its outer perimeter. Craftsmen have carved elaborate figures on the upper portion of the temple and its roof. Encircling the shrine are verandas with columns carved in circles, polygons and squares. A gigantic Nandi bull is carved in the hillside opposite the temple to **Gauri Somnath** at the west end of the island.

The temples were severely damaged after the Muslim invasions of **Mahmud of Ghazni**. Every dome was overturned and the sculptured figures mutilated. They became completely overgrown, and *Murray's Guide* records that when the Peshwa Baji Rao II wanted to repair the temple it could not be found, so he built a new one.

Western Madhya Pradesh listings

For Sleeping and Eating price codes and other relevant information, see Essentials pages 38-42.

Sleeping

Indore *p268, map p268*

AL-B President, 163 RN Tagore Marg, T0731-252 8866, www.hotelpresidentindore.com. 65 comfortable a/c rooms, good South Indian restaurant, modern, friendly, good travel desk.

A-C Mashal, Jhoomerghat, Rasalpura, A-B Rd, T0731-531 391. Comfortable a/c rooms on a hilltop out of town, gardens, pool, squash.

A-C Shreemaya, 12/1 RNT Marg (near railway), T0731-251 5555, www.shreemaya.com. 52 a/c rooms with bath, good popular South Indian café, exchange, Indian-style hotel, 1000 check-out.

B-C Balwas, 30/2 S Tukoganj, T0731-252 4934, balwasmp@sancharnet.in. 38 a/c rooms, good restaurant, travel desk, popular with tours from the Gulf, quiet, good value.

B-D Kanchan Tilak, 585/2 Mahatma Gandhi Rd, Palasia, T0731-253 8606, www.hotelkanchantilak.com. Has 39 rooms, a good restaurant, garden, clean, modern, family atmosphere, pleasant lobby. Good service and value but noisy.

C-D Amaltas International, Agra–Mumbai Rd, 2 RK Puram, T0731-243 2631. 30 small rooms, some a/c, restaurant claustrophobic but good value, bar, garden, far from centre.

C-E Kanchan, Kanchan Bagh, T0731-251 8501, hotelkanchan@yahoo.co.in. 28 comfortable rooms, some a/c with bath, restaurant, bar, good value. Recommended.

D-F Tourist Bungalow, behind Ravindra Natya Griha, RN Tagore Marg, T0731-252 1818, www.mptourism.com. 6 rooms, 2 a/c with bath, Nos 4 and 5 are larger, breakfast only, tourist office, safe, peaceful.

F Payal, Chhoti Gwaltoli, opposite Sarawate bus station, T0731-247 8460. Neat rooms with bath, some air-cooled with TV.

Ujjain *p271, map p270*

C Surana Palace, 23 GDC Rd, southeast of Madhav Chowk, T0734-253 0045, palacehotel surana@yahoo.co.in. Comfortable rooms, good food.

C-F Shipra (MP Tourism), University Rd, T0734-255 1495, www.mptourism.com. 30 rooms (10 a/c), restaurant, beer bar, travel, garden, quiet but run-down and major mosquito menace.

E-G Yatri Niwas (MP Tourism), LB Shastri Marg, 2.5 km south of station, T0734-251 1398, www.mptourism.com. 4 rooms, 60 dorm beds, canteen, clean, quiet.

F-G Ajay, opposite railway station, T0734-2550856. Some rooms air-cooled with bath.

G Ramkrishna, Subhash Marg, T0734-255 7012. Basic rooms, some with bath, vegetarian restaurant.

Mandu *p271, map p273*

Severe water shortage is likely before the monsoon – buckets are provided.

C-D Malwa Resort (MP Tourism), Roopmati Rd, 20-min walk from bus stand, T07292-263235, www.mptourism.com. 20 rooms (10 a/c), spacious cottages with small lounge, No 16 best a/c, No 18 best non-a/c (avoid Nos 1, 2, 7 and 8), good restaurant, gardens, peaceful setting by Sagar Talao Lake.

C-E Rupmati, 500 m beyond entrance, T07292-263270. 19 clean rooms with attached bath, mostly a/c, with balcony and set around spacious garden. Stunning gorge views, very pleasant outdoor garden restaurant, beer.

B-E Malwa Retreat (MP Tourism), next to **Roopmati**, T07292-263221, www.mptourism.com. 8 rooms some a/c and 3 tents restaurant (order ahead), bright, cheerful, very pleasant, excellent view of plateau. Negotiate if quiet.

E-G Maharaja, opposite police post, T07292-263288. With present hygiene levels scary enough to make your hair stand on end, thankfully a new block of rooms is currently being built that should remain habitable as a budget option for the next few years. Set around a large grassy courtyard that hopefully will also be receiving some attention. Friendly owner.

Maheshwar *p274*

LL-AL Ahilya Fort, at top of walled city, T07283-273329, T(0)114-155 1575, www.ahilyafort.com. One of the most atmospheric heritage hotels in central India, this 18th-century former home of highly revered Queen Ahilyabhai has an enchanting rustic charm as well as a welcoming, family atmosphere. It is in fact still the home of Prince Richard Holkar, 22nd generation descendent of Ahilyabhai, who will even cook meals for the guests when he is home! Each room has its own style, tastefully decorated with antique furniture and beautifully retaining its original character. Many rooms have stunning views out over the Ghats of the Narmada river. Rambling antique filled courtyards, tranquil seating areas with fountains and flower filled Urns, a family temple, large swimming pool, organic veggie and herb gardens grown in preparation for the delicious communal evening dinner. Sunset boat ride with optional dip in the river and evening drinks at the candle lit fort ramparts all make for a very special and highly memorable experience. Highly recommended.

C Narmada Retreat, T07283-273455, www.mptourism.com. Set a few kilometres away from the centre, bungalows and family tents set in well-tended gardens with nice views of the river. Restaurant.

F-G Akash Deep, at bottom of walled city, before the hill going up to the fort T07283-273326, Good budget option with clean simple rooms, some with TV.

Eating

Indore *p268, map p268*

Several places near bus stand and train station.

Ding Ding, 18/5 Mahatma Gandhi Marg. Open-air eating.

Gypsy, 17 Mahatma Gandhi Rd. Fast food. Good Western snacks, cakes and ice cream.

Landmark, RN Tagore Marg, by **President**. Indian, continental. Good ambience, unusual offerings.

Woodlands, **President** (see Sleeping). Vegetarian. South Indian. A/c, bar, good food.
Apsara, RN Tagore Marg. Indian vegetarian. A/c and outdoors (evening).
Indian Coffee House, off Mahatma Gandhi Rd. Indian. Light snacks, dated decor.
Sarafa Bazar and **Chhappan Bazar**. These streets come alive at night with stalls selling delicious, authentic local Malwa specialities: try *bafla* (wheat flour balls soaked in dhal) and the charmingly named *bhutta kis* (fried grated corn tossed with coconut and coriander).
Statue, 565 Mahatma Gandhi Rd. Indian vegetarian. Large *thalis*.

Ujjain *p271, map p270*
Ashnol, University Rd. Indian vegetarian in pleasant a/c surroundings.
Surana Palace (see Sleeping). Indian, Chinese. Pleasant outdoor seating option, best in town.
5 Star, 1st floor, by Madhav Chowk Clock Tower. Mainly South Indian. Tasty snacks and meals, roof top is more pleasant.
Sudama, next to Ramkrishna, Subhash Marg. Good Indian meals.

Festivals and events

Ujjain *p271, map p270*
Kumbh Mela takes place here every 12 years, see page 182. The next one is in 2016.
Feb/Mar **Mahasivaratri Fair** is held at the Mahakaleshwar Temple.
Nov **Kartik Mela**, the month-long fair, draws large crowds from surrounding villages.

Activities and tours

Indore *p268, map p268*
MP Tourism, T0731-252 1818, tours Jul-Sep: **Mandu** Wed, Fri, Sat and Sun, Rs 100; **Omkareshwar** and **Maheshwar** Mon and Thu, Rs 75. Both depart from Tourist Bungalow, 0730, return 1900. Tours of **Mandu** from Vijayant, 165 RN Tagore Marg, T0731-243 0771, every Sun.

Ujjain *p271, map p270*
MP Tourism, T0734-256 1544. **Ujjain Darshan** bus covers 11 temples and sights, Rs 100, 3½ hrs.

Mandu *p271, map p273*
Malwa Resort (see Sleeping), T07292-263235. Runs tours from Bhopal and Indore.

Transport

Indore *p268, map p268*
Air The airport is 9 km west of town; taxis charge Rs 150-300. **Air India**, Race Course Rd, T0731-253 1176; airport T0731-241 1758, www.home.airindia.in, flies to **Bhopal**, **Mumbai** and **Delhi** daily. **Jet Airways**, G2 Vidyapathi, Race Course Rd, T0731-254 4590, airport T0731-262 0819, www.jetairways.com, to **Delhi** and **Mumbai**. **Air Deccan**, T3900 8888, to **Delhi** via **Gwalior**, daily.
Bus **Sarwate Bus Stand** (south of railway station, through Exit 1), timetables in Hindi only but helpful enquiry desk, T0731-246 5688, has buses to **Bhopal** (187 km) 0800-2300, **Gwalior** 0500-1830; **Ujjain** (2 hrs) and Omkareshwar Rd (hourly, 3 hrs); change at the last for **Jhansi**, **Khajuraho** and **Omkareshwar**.

Gangwal Bus Stand (3 km west of town), T0731-238 0688, serves **Ahmedabad**, **Aurangabad** (for Ajanta and Ellora), **Amrawati** and **Dhar** (hourly). 1 bus a day goes direct to **Mandu** (99 km, 4-5 hrs); otherwise change at Dhar.

Private bus companies serving Rajasthan operate from east of the railway station. Most are overnight services.
Train Indore is on a spur of the Mumbai–Delhi line to Ujjain. Station has pre-paid rickshaws. Enquiries, T131/132, Reservations opposite, in front of Railway Hospital, T0731-243 0275. **Bhopal**: *Malwa Exp 12919*, 1225, 5¼ hrs. **Kolkata (H)**: *Shipra Exp 19305*, 2300, Tue, Thu, Sat, 31 hrs. **Delhi (ND)**: *Malwa Exp 12919*, 1225, 19¼ hrs; *Indore Nizamuddin Exp 12415*, 1620, 14 hrs (HN). **Mumbai (Central)**: *Avantika Exp12962*, 1550, 14¾ hrs. **Ujjain**: *Narmada Exp 18233*, 1700, 2 hrs; *Malwa Exp 12919*, 1225, 2 hrs.

Ujjain *p271, map p270*
Air The nearest airport is at Indore (53 km), connected by regular flights with **Delhi**, **Gwalior**, **Bhopal** and **Mumbai**.
Bus Hindi timetables only. Direct to **Bhopal**; regular to: **Dhar**, **Indore** (53 km, 1½ hrs), **Gwalior**, **Mandu** (149 km, 6 hrs), **Omkareshwar**.
Taxi and rickshaw Sights by taxi (Rs 600-800), auto-rickshaw (Rs 200-300), *tempos* and cycle-rickshaws.
Train **Ahmedabad**: *Sabarmati Exp 19164/66/68*, 1830, 10½ hrs. **Bhopal**: *Narmada Exp*

18233, 1920, 5½ hrs; *Malwa Exp 12919*, 1412, 4¾ hrs. **Indore**: *Narmada Exp18234*, 0835, 2¾ hrs; *Malwa Exp 12920*, 1125, 1¾ hrs. **Mumbai (Central)**: *Avantika Exp 12962*, 1735, 13¼ hrs. **New Delhi**: *Malwa Exp 12919*, 1412, 17¼ hrs; *Indore-Nizamuddin Exp 12415*, 1755, 12¼ hrs (**HN**).

Mandu *p271, map p273*

Air The nearest airport is at Indore.
Bus Just off NH3, Mandu is most accessible from Indore. You can get day return taxis Indore to Mandu. Regular bus services to **Dhar** (35 km, 1½ hrs), 1st depart 0530; change there for **Indore** (99 km, 4-5 hrs) and **Ujjain**. There is 1 direct bus per day to Indore at 0720, but it's very slow. Also to **Bhopal** (286 km), **Ratlam** (124 km) and **Ujjain** (152 km).
Bicycle and rickshaw Cycle-rickshaws (Rs 20 for 'sights') and bicycles are available (Rs 30, 24 hrs).
Car A private car from Indore should charge around Rs 500-600 one way. Some local car owners offer day trips to Maheshwar and Omkareshwar.
Train Most convenient railheads are **Ratlam** (124 km) on Mumbai-Delhi line, and **Indore** (99 km) on branch route. Ratlam has connections from **Vadodara**, **Bhopal**, **Kanpur**.

Maheshwar *p274*

Regular bus services from **Barwaha**, **Khandwa**, **Dhar** and **Dhamnod**. The nearest railhead is **Barwaha** (39 km) on the Western Railway.

Omkareshwar *p275*

Bus and train Omkareshwar is connected to Indore, Ujjain, Khandhwa and Omkareshwar Rd railway station (12 km) by regular bus services. The railhead is on the Ratlam–Khandwa section of the Western Railway.

Directory

Indore *p268, map p268*

Banks **State Bank of India**, 13 Ranade Complex, Old Palasia. **Medical services** **Ambulance**: T102. **Lifeline Hospital**, Meghdoot Gdns, T0731-257 5611. **CHL Apollo Hospital**, Manikbagh Rd, T0731-254 9090. Recommended. **Chemists**: on Maharani Rd. **Post** **CTO**: K Nehru Park, Fax, 0700-2000. **GPO**: AB Rd. **Useful contacts** **Fire**: T101. **Police**: T100.

Ujjain *p271, map p270*

Banks **State Bank**, Budhwariya off Udayan Marg, near Water Tower, changes cash (not TCs); after 1030.

Mandu *p271, map p273*

Bank **State Bank of India** (no exchange), 1100-1500, closed Thu and Sun.

Northern Madhya Pradesh

The boulder-strewn, thinly wooded Vindhya hills stretch across the north of the state, connecting some of the most fascinating historic monuments in central India. Foremost among them are the fascinating Tantric temples of Khajuraho, the sole raison d'être of a touristy village rendered slightly seedy by a cadre of boys who assume that anyone willing to endure the bus odyssey required to get here must be desperate for something. Further west, the riverside village of Orchha has all the ingredients for a relaxing break from the road, with palaces and lots of ruined mausoleums to explore, while Gwalior, a couple of hours by train from Agra, has one of the most awesome palace forts in the state. ▸▸ *For listings, see pages 297-303.*

Gwalior → *For listings, see pages 297-303. Colour map 3, B1. Phone code: 0751. Population: 827,000.*

Surrounded by attractive open plateau country immediately to the north of the Vindhyas, Gwalior is set in one of the state's driest regions. The majestic hill fort, formerly the key to control of the Central Provinces, dominates a ridge overlooking the town spread out below. It contains awe-inspiring Jain sculptures, Jain and Hindu temples and the charming sandstone palace. The Jai Vilas Palace, within its walls, bears testimony to the idiosyncratic tastes of the Scindia Maharajas. Much of the town, which sees few tourists, is very busy, noisy and crowded.

Ins and outs

Getting there There are a daily flights from Delhi and Indore, but the *Shatabdi Express* gives Gwalior excellent train connections with Agra and Delhi to the north and Jhansi and Bhopal to the south. The railway station and Madhya Pradesh State Bus Stand are southeast of the fort. From there, it is 6 km along the dusty MLB Road to the Jayaji Chowk area of Lashkar, the New Town. ▸▸ *See Transport, page 301.*

Getting around In addition to a *tempo* stand near the station, there are unmetered autos and taxis. Gwalior is quite spread out and the fort is a stiff climb.

Tourist information Tourist office ⓘ *Platform 1, railway station, T0751-504 0777.*

History

In legend, Gwalior's history goes back to AD 8 when the chieftain **Suraj Sen** was cured of leprosy by a hermit saint, Gwalipa. In gratitude he founded and named the city after him. An inscription in the fort records that during the fifth-century reign of Mihiragula the Hun, a temple of the sun was erected here. Later, Rajput clans took and held the fort. Muslim invaders like **Qutb-ud-din-Aibak** (12th century) ruled Gwalior before it passed through a succession of Tomar Rajput, Mughal, Afghan and Maratha hands. During the 1857 **Mutiny**, the Maharaja remained loyal to the British but 6500 of his troops mutinied on 14 June. The next year, there was fierce fighting round Gwalior, the rebels being led by Tantia Topi and the **Rani of Jhansi**. When the fort was taken by the British, the Rani was found, dressed in men's clothes, among the slain.

The Maharaja (Scindia) of Gwalior was one of five Maharajas awarded a 21-gun salute by the British.

The fort

ⓘ *Sunrise-sunset, Foreigners Rs 100, Indians Rs 5 allow at least 2-3 hrs. Palaces open 0930-1700. English-speaking guides here expect Rs 200 (hotel guides charge more).*

The fort stands on a sandstone precipice 91 m above the surrounding plain, 2.8 km long and 200-850 m wide. In places the cliff overhangs, elsewhere it has been steepened to make it unscaleable. The main entrance to the north comprised a twisting, easily defended approach. On the west is the **Urwahi Gorge** and another well-guarded entrance. The fort's size is impressive but the eye cannot capture all of it at once. Apart from its natural defences, Gwalior had the advantage of an unlimited water supply with many tanks on the plateau.

Approach The fort is a long walk from the town. You may enter from the northeast by the Gwalior or Alamgiri Gate but it is quite a steep climb. Mineral water is sold at the ticket counter; decline the booklet. Alternatively, take a taxi or an auto-rickshaw and enter from the west by the Urwahi Gate, where there are interesting Jain sculptures. After visiting the temples and palaces, you can descend to the Gujari Mahal in the northeast and pick up an auto from the Gwalior Gate. Visitors to the fort, particularly young women, should be prepared and aware that they may receive some unwanted attention from bored local teenage boys who often hang around inside the fort. Dressing modestly is definitely recommended.

Western entrance Above the **Urwahi Gate** there are 21 Jain sculptures dating from the seventh to 15th centuries, some up to 20 m tall. An offended Babur ordered their faces and genitalia to be destroyed. Modern restorers have only repaired the faces. There is a paved terrace along one side (ask to be dropped near the steps to view the sculptures since vehicles may not park along the road).

Northeast entrance A 1-km steep, rough ramp, with good views, leads to the main palace buildings. You pass through the **Gwalior Gate** (1660), the first of several gates, mostly built between 1486 and 1516. Next is the Badalgarh or **Hindola Gate (1)**, named because of the swing which was once here. It is (unusually) a true structural arch, flanked by two circular towers. Note the use of material from older buildings.

At the base of the ramp the **Gujari Mahal Palace** (circa 1510) containing the **Gujari Mahal Archaeological Museum (2)** ⓘ *Tue-Sun 1000-1700, Rs 30*. The pretty palace has an interesting collection including sculptures and archaeological pieces (second and first century BC), terracottas (Vidisha, Ujjain), coins and paintings and copies of frescoes from the Bagh caves. Ask the curator to show you the beautiful 10th-century Shalbhanjika (Tree Goddess) miniature. Some museums and palaces are closed on Monday. Some distance from the fort above, this palace was built by Raja Man Singh for his Gujar

1 Gwalior Fort

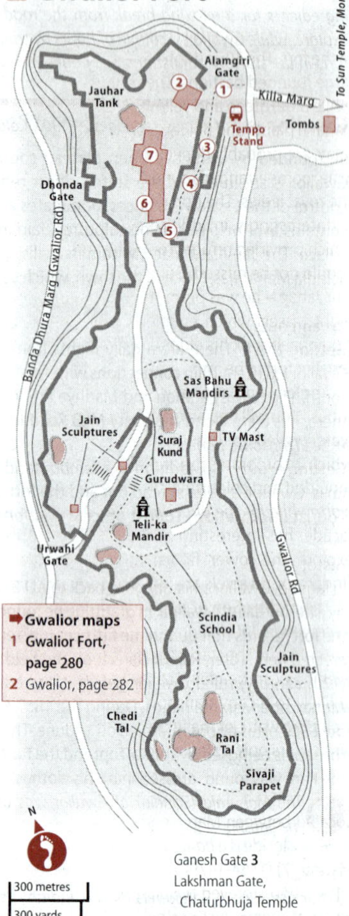

➡ **Gwalior maps**
1 Gwalior Fort, page 280
2 Gwalior, page 282

Hindola Gate **1**
Gujari Mahal Palace & Archaeological Museum **2**
Ganesh Gate **3**
Lakshman Gate, Chaturbhuja Temple & Jain Sculptures **4**
Hathia Paur **5**
Man Mandir Palace **6**
Vikramaditya Palace & Karan Mandir **7**

queen Mrignayani. The exterior is well preserved. The 'Bhairon' Gate no longer exists and the fourth is the simple **Ganesh Gate (3)** with a *kabutar khana* (pigeon house) and a small tank nearby. The mosque beyond stands on the site of an old shrine to the hermit Gwalipa, the present temple having been built later with some of the original material. Before the **Lakshman Gate** (circa 14th century) is the ninth-century Vishnu **Chaturbhuja Temple (4)**, with later additions, in a deep gap. A Muslim tomb and the northeast group of Jain sculptures are nearby. **Hathia Paur (5)** (Elephant Gate, 1516), the last, is the entrance to the main Man Mandir palace which also had a Hawa gate, now demolished.

Man Mandir Palace (6) (1486-1516) Built by Raja Man Singh, this is the most impressive building in the fort. The 30-m-high eastern retaining wall is a vast rock face on the cliff-side interrupted by large rounded bastions. The palace had ornamental parapets and cupolas, once brightly gilded, while blue, green and yellow tile-work with patterns of elephants, human figures, ducks, parrots, banana plants and flowers covered the exterior walls. The remarkable tiles, and the style of their inlay, are probably derived from Chanderi (200 km south) or Mandu. The beautifully decorated little rooms arranged round two inner courts have small entrances, suggesting they were built for the royal ladies. The iron rings here were used for swings and decorative wall hangings.

Interestingly, in addition to the two storeys above ground there are two underground floors which provided refuge from hot weather and acted as circular dungeons when required; these should not be missed. Guru Har Gobind who was once detained here was freed at the behest of Nur Jahan – he was permitted to take out any others who could touch his shawl so he attached eight tassels which enabled 56 prisoners to be freed with him. On 24 June 1658 Emperor Aurangzeb took his elder brother Murad captive en route to Delhi and then transferred him to Gwalior fort to be imprisoned. In December of the same year Aurangzeb ordered his execution.

Angled ventilation ducts allowed in fresh air while pipes in the walls were used as 'speaking tubes'. You will find an octagonal bath which would have been filled with perfumed water – the water welled up through inlet holes in the floor which have now been blocked. The south wall which incorporates the arched Hathia Paur with its guardroom above is particularly ornate with moulded and colourfully tiled friezes. A small **museum** ⓘ *Sat-Sun 0800-1800, guides available, worthwhile for the underground floors if you don't have a torch; give a small tip,* opposite the façade, has interesting archaeological pieces of Hindu deities. **Note** A torch is essential to explore the lower floors: there are holes in the floor, some of which are quite deep. Underground levels are infested with bats (easily disturbed) and so there is a revolting smell.

The nightly **Son et Lumière** ⓘ *Hindi at 1830, English at 1930 (1 hr later in summer), 45 mins, foreigners Rs 150, Indians Rs 40,* is well worth attending for stunning illumination of Man Mandir. The colourful spectacle traces the history of Gwalior fort through interesting anecdotes. Winter evenings can be chilly, so bring warm clothes; a torch is useful at any time of year. There is unlikely to be any transport available at the end of the show, so hire a taxi (Rs 250-300 return including wait), or make the fort your last stop when hiring a car for the day in the summer (day hire covers only a single fort visit).

Vikramaditya Palace (7) (1516) ⓘ *Tue-Sun 0800-1700 (1 Apr-30 Sep, 0700-1000, 1500-1800), free.* Located between Man Mandir and Karan Mandir, the palace is connected with them by narrow galleries. Inside is a *baradari* (open hall) with a domed roof. Opposite the Dhonda Gate is the **Karan Mandir (7)** (1454-1479), more properly called the Kirtti Mandir after its builder Raja Kirtti Singh. It is a long, two-storeyed building with a large, pillared hall and fine plaster moulding on ceilings of adjacent rooms. Just northwest is the **Jauhar Tank** where the Rajput women performed *jauhar* (mass suicide) just before the fort was taken by Iltutmish in 1232 (see page 1385), and also at Chittaurgarh (see page 374). The two unremarkable Muslim palaces, Jahangiri and Shah Jahan Mahals are further north. Moving south from Hathia Paur, towards the east wall, are the **Sas Bahu Mandirs**. Dedicated to Vishnu, the 11th-century 'Mother and Daughter-in-law' pair of temples built by Mahipala Kachhawaha (1093) still preserve fine carvings in places. The larger 12-sided temple is more interesting although only the *Mahamandapa* (Assembly Hall) remains. The smaller temple has an ornately carved base with a frieze of elephants, and a vaulted ceiling under the pyramidal roof. The wide ridged stone 'awning' is well preserved. An impressive modern marble **gurudwara** (1970) in memory of Sikh Guru Har Gobind (1595-1644), who had been imprisoned in the fort, is to its south, providing a haven of cool respite for visitors; the Guru Granth Sahib is read throughout the day. West of the *gurudwara* is **Suraj Kund**, a large tank, first referred to in the fifth century, where Suraj Sen's leprosy was cured. The water is now green and stagnant.

Teli-ka Mandir Teli-ka Mandir probably means 'oil man's temple'. It is the earliest temple in Gwalior, and architecturally has more in common with some early Orissan temples than those in the south (though sometimes guides suggest a link with Telangana in modern Andhra Pradesh indicating the fusion of Dravidian and North Indian architectural styles). This unique 25-m-high Pratihara (mid-eighth century) Vishnu Temple is essentially a sanctuary with a *Garuda* at the entrance. The oblong vaulted roof rather resembles a Buddhist *chaitya* and the Vaital Deul (Bhubaneswar). Tillotson records how after the 'Mutiny' "this great medieval temple, for example, was put to service as a soda-water factory and coffee shop. By such acts of desecration the British showed Indian rulers how the ancient Hindu heritage was then regarded by those who laid claim to power and authority". It was reconstructed in 1881-1883. The Katora Tal behind was excavated when the fort was built, like many others here. The Ek-khamba Tal has a single stone column standing in it.

Rani Tal (12), further south, was supposedly intended for the royal ladies; it is connected underground to the neighbouring **Chedi Tal**. Jain sculptures in the southeast corner can be seen from a path below the wall.

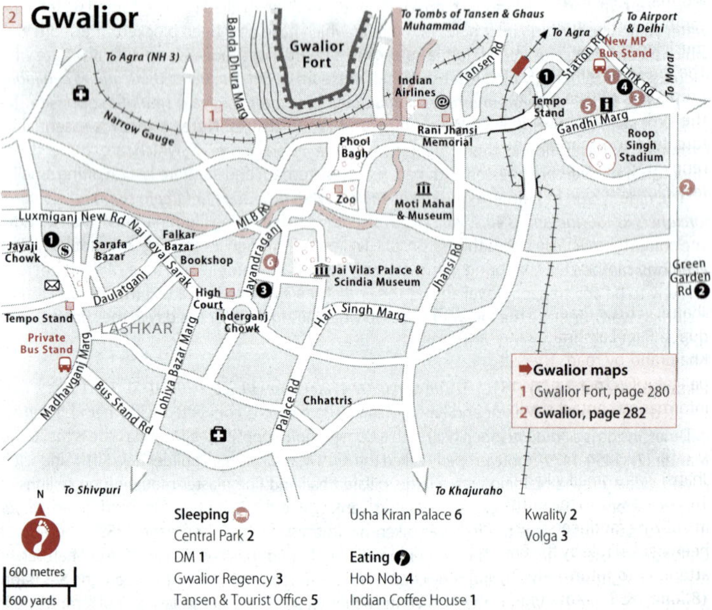

➡Gwalior maps
1 Gwalior Fort, page 280
2 Gwalior, page 282

Sleeping
Central Park 2
DM 1
Gwalior Regency 3
Tansen & Tourist Office 5
Usha Kiran Palace 6

Eating
Hob Nob 4
Indian Coffee House 1
Kwality 2
Volga 3

The town

After Daulat Rao Scindia acquired Gwalior in 1809 he pitched camp to the south of the fort. The new city that arose was **Lashkar** (The Camp) with palaces, King George Park (now Gandhi Park) and the *chhattris* of the Maharajas. **Jayaji Chowk**, once an elegant square, dominated by late 19th- and early 20th-century buildings, notably the Regal Cinema, and the Chowk Bazar can still be a pleasant place to watch people going about their business from one of the good little restaurants.

Jai Vilas Palace (1872-1874) ⓘ *Tue-Sun 0930-1700, tickets at gate: foreigners Rs 100, Indians Rs 25, camera Rs 25, video Rs 75, guided tours (1 hr) sometimes compulsory*, designed by Lieutenant-Colonel Sir Michael Filose, resembles an Italian palazzo in places, using painted sandstone to imitate marble. Part of the palace is the present maharaja's residence but 35 rooms house the **Scindia Museum**, an idiosyncratic collection of royal possessions, curiosities (eg 3-D mirror portraits), carpets (note the Persian rug with royal portraits) and interesting memorabilia.

In a separate building opposite (show ticket) is the extraordinary **Durbar Hall**. It is approached by a crystal staircase, gilded in 56 kg of gold, and in it hang two of the world's largest chandeliers each weighing 3.5 tonnes; before they were hung the ceiling was tested by getting 10 elephants to climb on to it via a 2-km ramp. Underneath is the dining room. The battery-operated silver train set transported cigars, dry fruit and drinks round the table, after dinner. The lifting of a container or bottle would automatically reduce pressure on the track, and so stop the train. Southeast of the fort is the spot where **Rani Lakshmi Bai** of Jhansi was cremated, marked by a stirring statue.

The **Royal Chhattris**, south of town, are each dedicated to a Gwalior Maharaja. These ghostly pavilions are in various stages of neglect. The lighted images are still clothed and 'fed' daily. Be there at 1600 when they are shown again by the guardians after their afternoon nap.

In the crowded Hazira in the **Old Town**, northeast of the fort, is the **Tomb of Ghaus Muhammad**, a 16th-century Afghan prince who helped Babur to win the fort. It is in an early Mughal style with finely carved *jali* screens. Hindus and Muslims both make pilgrimage to the tomb. Nearby, in an attractive garden setting, is the **Tomb of Tansen**, the most famous musician of Akbar's court. It is the venue for the annual music festival (November/December). The present tamarind tree replaces the old one which was believed to have magical properties. Tansen was an exponent of the *dhrupad* style, and laid the foundations for what in the 19th century became the Gwalior *ghurana* style, noted for its stress on composition and forceful performance. One of the best-known contemporary exponents is Amjad Ali Khan, a renowned sarod player. A recently built **Sun Temple** similar in style to Konark is at Morar, a few kilometres east of the tombs.

Jhansi and around → *For listings, see pages 297-303.* *Colour map 3, B1. Phone code: 0517. Population: 405,000.*

Jhansi, in Uttar Pradesh, is best known for its fort and the involvement in the 1857 Mutiny of its queen Rani Lakshmi Bai. Today, it is a useful stop on the train from Delhi en route to visiting Khajuraho by road. There is plenty to explore nearby, though this is just as easily done from peaceful Orchha which offers a happy escape from the busy small town atmosphere. For information contact **Madhya Pradesh Tourism** ⓘ *at the railway station, T0510-244 2620.*

Jhansi

Jhansi was a small village until taken in 1742 by the Marathas, who extended the old Fort. In 1853 it 'lapsed' to the British, when the raja died without leaving a male heir. The fort was seized in 1857 by mutineers and most of the occupants were slaughtered. The young Rani, who had been denied rule by the British, joined the rebels but had to retire to Gwalior. She continued her attempts to return after the British regained control of Jhansi. She was killed in action on 18 June 1858 at Kotah-ki-Sarai "dressed like a man ... holding her sword two-handed and the reins of her horse in her teeth ..." (Hibbert). The British ceded the fort to the Maharaja of Scindia and exchanged it for Gwalior in 1866.

Shankar Fort ⓘ *sunrise-sunset*, was built by Bir Singh Deo in 1613. The nucleus of the fort, which has concentric walls up to 9 m high with 10 gates, was breached by the British in 1858. There are good views from the walls. Rani Mahal, once Lakshmi Bai's home, is an **archaeological museum** (ninth to 12th century). **Retribution Hill** ⓘ *Tue-Sun 1030-1630 (6 Apr-30 Jun 0730-1230), closed 2nd Sun each month, foreigners US$2*, marks the last stand of the Mutineers in 1858. The **State Museum** ⓘ *Tue-Sun 1000- 1700*, near the fort in a vast modern building, has a good collection of stone sculptures in addition to weapons and ethnography.

Barua Sagar

Some 24 km east along the Khajuraho road are the ruins of a historic fort where the Maratha Peshwas fought the Bundelas. The deserted sandstone fort has excellent views over the *sagar* (lake) created by a dam across the Betwa River. The ninth-century early **Pratihara Temple** (Jarai-ka-Math), dedicated to Siva and Parvati, is built in red sandstone and highly ornamented. Yet the place is rarely visited and is wonderfully peaceful; you can swim in the lake. Buses from Jhansi travelling to Khajuraho will stop here on request (about one hour from Jhansi). It is then a five-minute walk along a narrow tree-lined canal to the fort; ask locally for keys. To return, wave down any bus to Jhansi (frequent service).

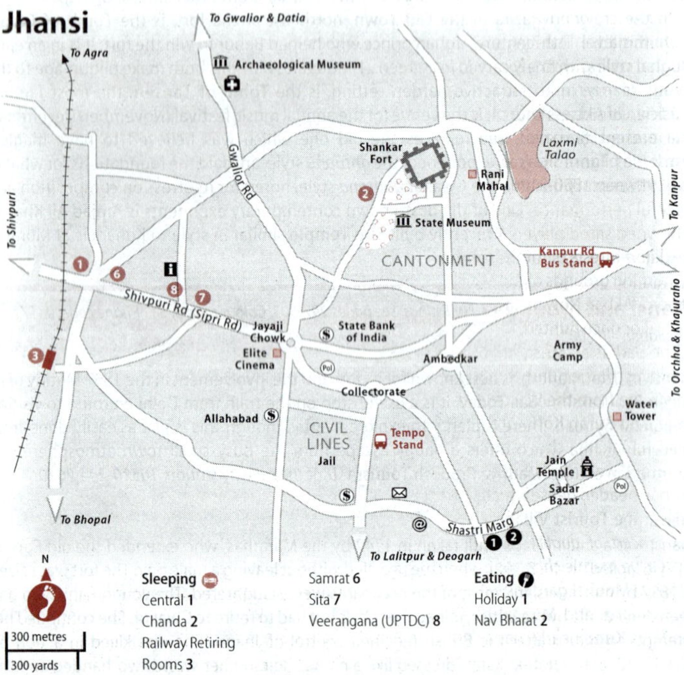

Sleeping
Central 1
Chanda 2
Railway Retiring Rooms 3
Samrat 6
Sita 7
Veerangana (UPTDC) 8

Eating
Holiday 1
Nav Bharat 2

Datia and Sonagiri → *75 km south of Gwalior, 34 km from Jhansi.*

Datia itself is not nearly as attractive as Orchha but is interesting to visit nevertheless, particularly as there is hardly a tourist in sight. The forgotten palace lies on the edge of the lively town with a significant Muslim population.

Bir Singh Deo's **Govind Mandir Palace** (circa 1620) ⓘ *0800-1700, caretaker 'guide' (speaks little English but holds keys), expects Rs 50 for a tour*, unlike other Bundelkhand palaces, was conceived as an integrated whole, its form and decoration blending Mughal and Rajput styles. Standing on an uneven rocky ridge, the palace has five storeys visible, while several cool underground floors excavated out of the rock remain hidden. The lower floors are very dark – carry a torch. Dilapidated and deserted, it is still imposing and atmospheric. The Bundela chief Bir Singh Deo supported Salim (later Jahangir) against his father Akbar, and may have been responsible for robbing and killing Abul Fazl in an ambush. His successors, however, were loyal to the Mughals.

The main entrance is on the east side, approached through very narrow crowded streets, while the south overlooks the lake Karna Sagar. There is a profusion of arches, *chhattris*, ornamental *jali* screens, coloured tiling, balconies and oriel windows which open up delightful views. Within the square plan which surrounds the central courtyard, a separate five-storey 'tower' houses the royal apartments which are connected with the surrounding palace by four colonnaded flying bridges, completing this unusual architectural marvel. Strangely it was occupied only intermittently (possibly never by the royal family). The paintings – in deep red, orange and green – though few, are lovely. The first floor has a Dancing Room with stucco figures, the second floor the Queen's Room and a Dancing Room with beautiful wall and ceiling paintings of peacocks, elephants and kings, while the third floor has bridges and the Diwan-i-khas, for private audience (note the Mughal tomb in the corner). Keys are needed to go above this level. The King's Room on the fourth floor with its shallow dome has a beautifully sculpted ceiling with geometric designs of flower petals and stars while the roof parapet has remains of green and blue tiles. There are excellent views all round.

A few kilometres north of Datia, just off the main road, **Sonagiri** has 77 white Jain temples on a hill reached by a paved path. Some date from the 17th century: the one to Chatranatha is the best. It is a pilgrim site for *Digambara* Jains, see page 1425, many of whom attend the evening *arati* between 1800-2100.

Shivpuri National Park → *Colour map 3, B1. Phone code: 07492.*

The dense forests of the Shivpuri or Madhav National Park, 114 km southwest of Gwalior, were the hunting grounds of the Mughal emperors when great herds of elephants were captured for Emperor Akbar. Now mainly a deer park in forested hill territory, this was also where Maharajas of Gwalior once hunted.

The park is a 156-sq-km dry deciduous forest, with Sakhya Sagar, a large perennial lake, attracting a large number of migratory birds in the winter. Stop where the forest track crosses the stream from the Waste Wier. **George Castle** on high ground, once the Scindias' hunting lodge, and **Burah Koh** watchtower have good views over the lake at sunset. Animals include nilgai, chinkara, chowsingha, sambar, cheetal and wild pig. **Chandpata Lake** attracts numerous waterbirds including migratory pochard, pintail, teal, mallard, demoiselle crane and bar-headed geese which remain until May. The best time to visit is from January to March.

Near the **Tourist Village**, the pink **Madhav Vilas summer palace** ⓘ *evening prayers (arati) and concert of quality classical singing around 1900*, is now a government building. The impressive marble *chhattris* of the Scindia rulers, with fine pietra dura inlay and *jali* work, are set in formal Mughal gardens with flowering trees. They synthesize Hindu and Islamic styles with their *sikharas* and Mughal pavilions. Curiously, meals are still prepared for the past rulers. **Bhadaiya Kund** nearby has a spring rich in minerals.

From Jhansi to Khajuraho

This route, across the mainly agricultural hill region of Bundelkhand, runs along the northern edge of the peninsula, crossing a number of significant rivers such as the Betwa and Dhasan as they flow off the plateau. Before Independence this was a land of small Rajput and Muslim states, struggling to maintain and expand their power against the greater forces from the plains to the north. Much is now open farmland pimpled with rock outcrops and forested hills, making for very attractive scenery – best appreciated from a car, or from the roof of one of the notoriously overcrowded buses that ply this busy road. For a stop-off, **Nowgong** has a pleasant breezy restaurant in a pretty garden, on the Jhansi side of town.

Orchha → *For listings, see pages 297-303.* *Colour map 3, B1. Phone code: 07680. Population: 8500.*

Highly picturesque, in the middle of nowhere, abandoned and somewhat neglected, Orchha is an ideal stop between Gwalior and Khajuraho. Set on an island on a bend in the Betwa River, the fort palace from a bygone era is raised on a rocky promontory above the surrounding wooded countryside. This largely untouched island of peace and calm is approached from the congested, increasingly touristy village centre by a remarkable early 17th-century granite bridge built by Bir Singh Deo, while all around, the forest encroaches on the tombs and monuments.

Ins and outs

Getting there Orchha is quite easily reached by road from Jhansi. After travelling 9 km southeast along the Khajuraho Road, a minor road turns south for the remaining 7 km to Orchha. There are taxis, *tempos* or buses from Jhansi station, but it is best to travel during daylight hours, and book and enquire about onward buses well ahead.

Getting around The fort palace complex and the village are all easily seen on foot. The riverside is a 10-minute stroll away. If you are laden with luggage you can get a rickshaw from the village centre to your hotel. Women are advised not to wander around the site alone.

History

The Bundela chief **Raja Rudra Pratap** (1501-1531) chose an easily defended and beautiful site for his capital. In the 11th century, a Rajput prince is said to have offered himself as a sacrifice to the mountain goddess Vrindavasini; she prevented his death and named him '*Bundela*' (one who offered blood). The dynasty ruled over the area between the Yamuna and Narmada rivers, having stepped into the vacuum left by the Tughlaqs and extended their power, moving their base to Orchha (meaning hidden). Raja Rudra Pratap threw a wall around the existing settlement and began work on the palace building (circa 1525- 1531) and an arched bridge to it. This was completed by his successor Bharti Chand (1531-1554) who was installed in the Raj Mahal with great ceremony.

The continuing fortunes of the dynasty may have stemmed from the rulers' diplomatic skills. Though the third ruler, the religious **Madhukar Shah**, was defeated in battle by Akbar and was exiled in 1578 (died 1592), he nevertheless won the Mughal emperor's friendship. Later **Bir Singh Deo** (1605-1627, see Datia, page 285), while opposing Akbar, aligned himself with Prince Salim (Jahangir), who later rewarded him with the throne of Orchha, thus ensuring its ongoing prosperity. The Jahangir Mahal was built to commemorate the emperor's visit to Orchha. However, Bir Singh's first son, Jhujan, ran foul of Shah Jahan and, ignoring orders, treacherously killed the neighbouring chief of Chauragarh. The imperial army routed Jhujan and Orchha was pillaged. In 1783 the Bundela capital was moved to Tikamgarh, leaving Orchha to the *dhak* forests, the Betwa River and its guardian eagles.

The site

ⓘ *Foreigners Rs 250, Indians Rs 5, camera (no flash) Rs 20, video Rs 50; ticket office at palace, 0800-1800. Allow 2 hrs. Audio tour from Sheesh Mahal hotel, Rs 50. Highly recommended. The buildings are in a bad state of repair. If you go to the top take extra care and carry a torch.*

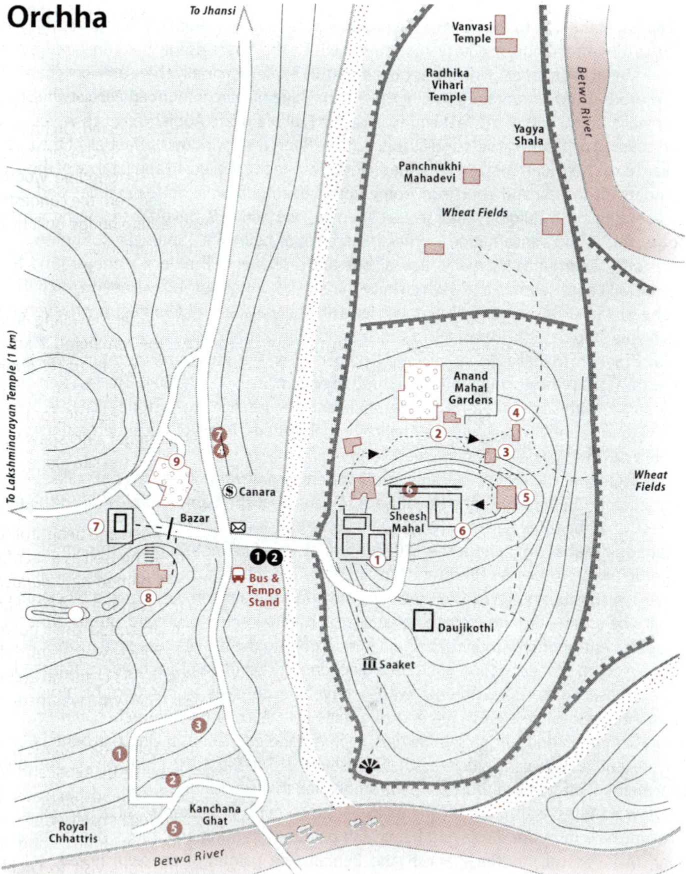

N

200 metres

200 yards

Sleeping
Amar Mahal **1**
Bhandan Guesthouse **3**
Betwa Retreat **2**
Fort View **4**
Ganpati **7**
Orchha Resort **5**
Sheesh Mahal **6**

Eating
Betwa Tarang **1**
Milan **2**

Sights
Raj Mahal **1**
Rai Praveen Mahal **2**
Hamaam **3**
Royal Gate **4**
Camel Stables **5**
Jahangir Mahal **6**
Ram Raja Temple **7**
Chaturbhuj Temple **8**
Phool Bagh **9**

Orchha is a wonderful example of a medieval fort palace. Within the turreted walls are gardens, gateways, pavilions and temples, near the Betwa and Jamni rivers. On a moonlit night, the view across the palaces with their *chhattris* and ornamented battlements is enchanting. A suggested route is to visit the Raj Mahal with its Hall of Private Audience then go through the doorway to the Hall of Public Audience. From here go down the ramp and follow the path to the Rai Praveen Mahal. Continue along the path to the Jahangir Mahal, arriving back at the courtyard of the Sheesh Mahal.

The **Raj Mahal (1)**, to the right of the quadrangle, exemplifies Bundela Rajput architecture. There are two rectangular courtyards around which the floors rise in tiers (inspired by the Koshak Mahal in Chanderi, which was built a century earlier); typically there are cool chambers below ground and a fountain. Some of the original blue tile decoration remains on the upper outer walls. To the left of the first courtyard is the Hall of Private Audience which would have been covered with rich carpets and cushions (note floor- level windows). The Hall of the Public Audience has two quarter-size plaster elephants. Despite the neglected appearance of the royal chambers off the second courtyard, some have beautiful murals on the ceilings and walls. Representing both religious and secular themes, one series is devoted to the *Ramayana*, another to Vishnu's incarnations, others to scenes of court life – musicians, hunters, river excursions, fairground. Normally locked, but the caretaker will unlock some ground floor rooms. Don't miss Rooms 5 and 6 which have the best paintings but you will need a torch. There is a Sheesh Mahal upstairs as well as good views of other palaces and temples from the very top; watch your step though, especially in strong winds.

Rai Praveen Mahal (2) was probably named after the musician-courtesan who was a favourite at the princely court of Indrajit, brother of Ram Shah (1592-1604). The low two-storey brick palace with cool underground chambers and beautifully carved stone niches is built to scale with surrounding trees and the Anand Mandal gardens. To get to the underground rooms, turn left down steps on exiting the main rooms.

The octagonal flowerbeds are ingeniously watered from two wells. A new path takes you via the **hamaam (3)**, bypassing the **Royal Gate (4)**, and past the **Camel Stables (5)** to the most impressive of the three palaces.

Jahangir Mahal (6), built in the 17th century by Raja Bir Singh Deo to commemorate the Emperor's visit, synthesizes Hindu and Muslim styles as a tribute to his benefactor. The 70-m-sq palace, which is best entered from the east, the original main entrance flanked by elephants, can also be entered from the south. It has a large square interior courtyard, around which are the apartments in three storeys. The guided tour goes to the top of these up narrow and dark stairways. Each corner bastion and the projection in the middle of each side is topped by a dome. These contain apartments with intervening terraces – hanging balconies with balustrades and wide eaves create strong lines set off by attractive arches and brackets, decorative cobalt and turquoise blue tiles, *chhattris* and *jali* screens giving this huge palace a delicate and airy feel. There is a small **museum** ⓘ *Sat-Thu 1000-1700*, with a run-down assortment of photos, sculptures and *sati* stones; labels are in Hindi.

A few minutes' walk south of the main palace complex is **Saaket** ⓘ *1000-1700, Rs 40*, an excellent new museum displaying Ramayana paintings in traditional folk styles from Orissa, Bihar, Maharashtra, Andhra Pradesh and Bengal. The paintings, on palm leaves, silk and organically dyed cotton, are of the highest quality, and the stories behind them fascinating.

The village

Just south of the crossroads is the **Ram Raja Temple (7)** ⓘ *0800-1230, 1900-2130 (1 hr later on summer evenings), cameras and leather articles must be left outside*, which forms a focus for village life. The temple courtyard and the narrow lane leading to it have stalls selling souvenirs and the area occasionally swells with pilgrims and *sanyasis*. The pink and cream paint is not in keeping with the other temples. It is interesting to visit during *arati*; otherwise there is little to see inside. Following the appearance of Rama in a dream, the pious Madhukar Shah brought an image of the god from Ayodhya and placed it in this palace prior to its installation in a temple. However, when the temple was ready it proved impossible to shift the image and the king remembered, only too late, the divine instruction that the deity must remain in the place where it was first installed. It is the only palace-turned-temple in the country where Rama is worshipped as king.

Chaturbhuj Temple (8) ⓘ *usually open 0800-1700*, up the steps from the Ram Raja Temple courtyard, was built by King Madhukar Shah for his Queen Kunwari to house the image of Rama brought from Ayodhya. Laid out in the form of a cross, a symbolic representation of the four-armed god Krishna, there is a triple-arched gate with attractive *jharokas* on the exterior. The tallest *sikhara* is over the Garbagriha shrine, to the left of which you will see a Ganesh and a set of kettle drums. The high arches and ceilings with vaulting and lotus domes painted in a rich red in places, are particularly striking. You can climb up any of the corner staircases, which lead up, by stages, to the very top of the temple. The second level gives access to tiny decorated balconies which provided privileged seating. There are good views of the nine palaces from the top, reached by the mini labyrinth of narrow corridors and steps. On the roof are langurs, wild bee hives and vultures nesting in corner towers.

A 1-km paved path links the Ram Raja with Bir Singh Deo's early 17th-century **Lakshminarayan Temple** ⓘ *0900-1700, 15-min walk*, on a low hill, which incorporates elements of fort architecture. The ticket attendant gives a 'tour', naming the characters illustrated; go up the tower, the steps are steep but there are very good views of the entire area. The typical village houses along the path are freshly whitewashed for Diwali. The diagonal plan enclosing the central square temple structure is most unusual. The excellent murals (religious and secular), on the interior walls and ceilings of the four cool galleries around the temple here, are well-preserved examples of the Bundela school. The paintings in red, black, yellow, grey and turquoise portray Hindu deities, scenes from the epics, historical events including the early British period (note the interesting details of Lakshmi Bai's battle against the British), as well as giving an insight into the domestic pleasures of royalty.

Phool Bagh (9) is a formal garden and an eight-pillared pavilion which has a cool underground apartment. Well worth a visit.

Of the 15 **Royal Chhattris** to former rulers grouped by the Kanchana Ghat by the river, about half are neglected and overgrown but pleasant for walking around in the late afternoon. A few are well preserved; ask the watchman if you want to look inside. He will take you to the upper levels by some very narrow, dark stairs: good fun but take a torch and be careful. He will expect a small tip. The chhattris are best photographed from the opposite bank: take a stick as dogs can be a problem.

The small but busy **village bazar**, with some interesting temples nearby, is about 10 minutes walk from the riverside where a series of royal *chhattris* still stand as sentinels. The riverside is ideal for lazing under a shady tree. Cross the bridge and head upstream for better spots for swimming (watch out for currents).

Deogarh and Chanderi → *For listings, see pages 297-303. Colour map 3, B1.*

Deogarh

On the Uttar Pradesh side of the Betwa River, the small village of Deogarh (Fort of the Gods), offers the chance to rest and enjoy cliff-top views of the Betwa River, go hiking and wildlife watching in the forest, and visit numerous temples. Impressive cliffs overlook the river with shrines and reliefs carved into the cliff walls. On the southern fringes of the great Gupta Empire (fourth to sixth century AD), its relative isolation has meant that some fine temples survive.

The temples were built of local stone (and occasionally granite), rather than the more easily destroyed brick. The sixth-century red sandstone, ruined in parts but otherwise well-preserved

Dasavatara Temple is the finest here. The central sanctum had four flat-roofed entrance porticoes in place of the normal one, and the first northern pyramidal temple *sikhara*, though little of it remains. There are fine sculptures on the three walls, of Vishnu legends and a doorway with carvings of Ganga and Yamuna. The remarkable Anantashayi Vishnu, in Harle's phrase, lies "dreaming another aeon into existence". While Lakshmi gently holds Vishnu, the sacred lotus with Brahma rises from his navel.

The dramatic **hilltop fort** encloses 31 Jain temples dating from the ninth to 10th centuries with sculpted panels, images and 'thousand image pillars'; the best examples are in temples 11 and 12. Nearby, the Sahu Jain Sangrahalaya has some fine 10th- to 11th-century carvings. A well-marked path from the parking lot here leads to the river and the shrines; it is a fairly long walk.

Chanderi

The road climbs steeply to approach Chanderi, 37 km west of Lalitpur, an important town under the Mandu sultans, which was dominated by a hill fort. It is attractively placed in an embayment in the hills overlooking the Betwa River and contains the 15th-century Koshak Mahal and other ruined palaces, market places, mosques and tombs. The old town, 8 km north and buried in jungle, has Jain temples dating from the 10th century. Chanderi is famous for very fine saris and brocades. Visitors can stay in the **Dak Bungalow**.

Khajuraho → *For listings, see pages 297-303. Colour map 3, B2. Phone code: 07686. Population: 6500.*

Khajuraho, home to what are now perhaps the most famous of India's temples on account of their remarkable erotic sculptures, lies in a rich, well-watered plain. Set miles from the nearest town in an open forested and cultivated landscape with the striking Vindhyan ranges as a backdrop, it is listed as a World Heritage Site. Sadly, Khajuraho's drastically defined rich and lean seasons have bred a particular culture, and you may find yourself subjected to a barrage of sleazy salesmen, touts and junior con artists capable of sweet-talking you in three different languages. Nevertheless, the village away from the tourist areas maintains a pleasant laid-back feel, and early mornings even at the main temples can be wonderfully calm and peaceful. The best time to visit is between October and March. From April to June it becomes very hot, dry and dusty.

Ins and outs

Getting there Daily flights connect Khajuraho with Delhi and Varanasi. The airport is only 5 km from most hotels, with cycle-rickshaws and taxis available for transfer. Buses travel to Jhansi and Satna, both with good railway connections, but they become horrifically packed: if you can afford only one taxi ride in India, let it be here. We hope that MP Tourism and the local governments get around to doing something about the roads. There is a railway station around 7 km north of town, on the line to Mahoba and Varanasi with daily trains between Jhansi and Khajuraho. ▸▸ *See Transport, page 302.*

Getting around Khajuraho is still a small village though the temples are scattered over 8 sq km. Although some are within walking distance, hiring a bike is a good alternative to getting a cycle-rickshaw to visit the temples to the east and south.

Tourist information Government of India Tourist Office ⓘ *opposite W Group, T07686-272347, Mon-Fri 0930-1800*. Madhya Pradesh Tourism ⓘ *at bus stand, T07686-274163*.

Background

Khajuraho was formerly the capital of the old kingdom of Jajhauti, the region now known as **Bundelkhand**. The name Khajuraho may be derived from *khajura* (date palm), which grows freely in the area and perhaps because there were two golden *khajura* trees on a carved gate here. The old name was Kharjuravahaka (scorpion bearer), the scorpion symbolizing poisonous lust.

Khajuraho's temples were built under later Chandela kings between AD 950 and 1050 in a truly inspired burst of creativity, but were 'lost' for centuries until they were accidentally 'discovered' by a British army engineer in 1839. Of the original 85 temples, the 20 surviving are among the finest in India.

Basham suggested that India's art came from secular craftsmen who, although they worked to instructions, loved the world they knew, their inspiration not so much a ceaseless quest for the absolute as a delight in the world as they saw it.

The gods and demi-gods in temples all over India are young and handsome, their bodies rounded, often richly jewelled. They are often smiling and sorrow is rarely portrayed. Temple sculpture makes full use of the female form as a decorative motif. Goddesses and female attendants are often shown naked from the waist up, with tiny waists and large, rounded breasts, posing languidly – a picture of well-being and relaxation. ▸▸ *See Books, page 1441.*

Khajuraho

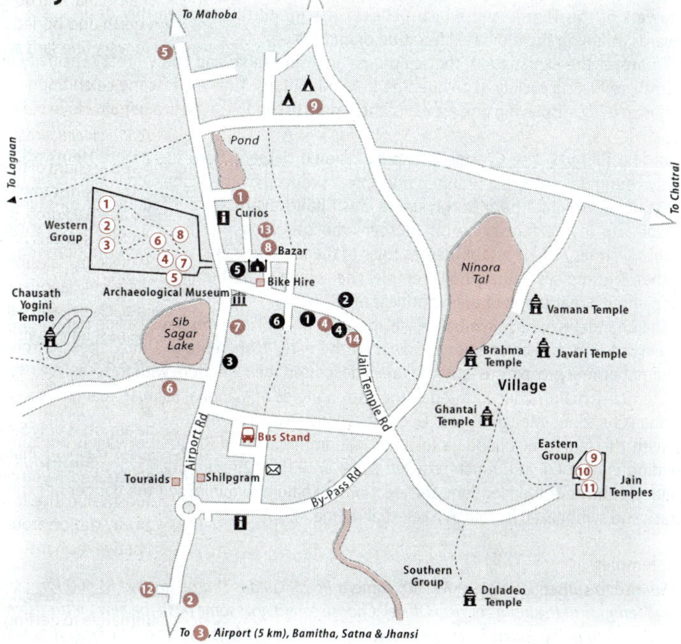

N

300 metres
300 yards

Sleeping
Casa di William **1**
Chandela **2**
Clarks Khajuraho **3**
Lakeside **7**
Lalit **5**
Marble Palace **8**
Payal **9**
Shanti **6**
Surya **4**
Tourist Village **11**
Usha Bundela **12**
Yogi Lodge **13**
Zen **14**

Eating
Agrawal **1**
Chai & Paratha Stalls **6**
Garden View **4**
Mediterraneo **2**
Paradise **3**
Safari **5**

Temples
Chitragupta **1**
Jagadambi **2**
Kandariya Mahadeva **3**
Lakshmana **4**
Matangesvara **5**
Parvati **6**
Varaha **7**
Vishvanatha **8**
Adinatha **9**
Parsvanatha **10**
Santinatha **11**

Shakti worship and erotic sculptures Although each temple here is dedicated to a different deity, each expresses its own nature through the creative energy of Shakti. Tantric beliefs within Hinduism led to the development of Shakti cults which stressed that the male could be activated only by being united with the female in which sexual expression and spiritual desire were intermingled. Since this could not be suppressed it was given a priestly blessing and incorporated into the regular ritual. Romila Thapar traces its origin to the persisting worship of the Mother Goddess (from the Indus Valley civilization, third millennium BC), which has remained a feature of religion in India. Until last century, many temples kept *devadasis* (literally, servants of God), women whose duty included being the female partner in these rituals.

The presence of erotic temple sculptures, even though they account for less than 10% of the total carvings, have sometimes been viewed as the work of a degenerate society obsessed with sex. Some believe they illustrate the Kama Sutra, the sensuality outside the temple contrasting with the serenity within. Yet others argue that they illustrate ritual symbolism of sexual intercourse in **Tantric belief**, see page 1413. The Chandelas were followers of the Tantric cult which believes that gratification of earthly desires is a step towards attaining the ultimate liberation or *moksha*.

Whatever the explanation, the sculptures are remarkable and show great sensitivity and warmth, reflecting society in an age free from inhibitions. They express the celebration of all human activity, displaying one aspect of the nature of Hinduism itself, a genuine love of life.

Chandela Rajputs The Chandela Rajputs claimed descent from the moon. **Hemwati**, the lovely young daughter of a Brahmin priest, was seduced by the Moon God while bathing in a forest pool. The child born of this union was **Chandravarman**, the founder of the dynasty. Brought up in the forests by his mother who sought refuge from a censorious society, Chandravarman, when established as ruler of the local area, had a dream visitation from his mother. She implored him to build temples that would reveal human passions and in doing so bring about a realization of the emptiness of desire.

The Chandelas, whose symbol recalls the 16-year-old king who slayed a lion bare- handed, developed into a strong regional power in the early 10th century. Under their patronage Jajhauti became prosperous, and the rulers decorated their kingdom with forts, palaces, tanks and temples, mainly concentrated in their strongholds of Mahoba, Kalinjar, Ajaigarh and also Dudhai, Chandpur, Madanpur and Deogarh (Jhansi District).

With the fading of Chandela fortunes, the importance of Khajuraho waned but temple building continued, at a much reduced pace, until the 12th century. Far removed from the political centres of the kingdom, the location of Khajuraho minimized the danger of external attack and symbolized its role as a celestial refuge.

The temples

ⓘ *Sunrise to sunset. Foreigners Rs 250, camera Rs 25. Guides charge around Rs 400 for a small group (enquire at the India Tourism Office). Choose carefully as some push the new Cultural Centre, souvenir shop and puppet show (overpriced atRs 250) and others can be a little leary around the sculptures. Audio tours Rs 50 plus Rs 500 deposit. Avoid the toilets. Son et lumière every evening at the Western group of temples, in English at 1900, Hindi at 2000, foreigners Rs 250, Indians Rs 50.*

The temples, built mostly of a fine sandstone from Panna and Ajaigarh – although granite was used in a few – can be conveniently divided into three groups: the **Western** (opposite bazar), **Eastern** (30 minutes away on foot) and **Southern**. The Western Group, which dominates the village, is the most impressive and the gardens the best kept. The temples in the other two groups are remarkable and pleasing in their own right but if you feel that temple fatigue is likely to set in, then the Western Group is the one to see, especially the Lakshmana Temple. Allow a day (minimum five hours) for sightseeing. Naturally early morning offers the best light – grab a chai in the square opposite the entrance and get in the temples before the crowds.

The temples here are compact and tall, raised on a high platform with an ambulatory path around, but with no enclosure wall. Each follows an east-west axis and has the essential *garbha-griha* (sanctum) containing the chief image, joined to the hall for *mandapa* (worshippers) by a *antarala* (vestibule). The hall is approached through an *ardha mandapa* (porch); both have pyramidal towers. Larger temples have lateral transepts and balconied windows, an internal ambulatory and subsidiary shrines. The sanctuary is surmounted by a tall *sikhara* (tower), while smaller towers rise from other parts of the temple, imitating mountain peaks culminating in the highest. The sanctum is usually *sapta-ratha* (seven projections in plan and elevation), while the cubical section below the *sikhara* repeats the number, having seven bands, *sapta-bada*. The whole, studded with sculptured statues with clear lines of projections and recesses, makes most effective use of light and shade. The sculptures themselves are in the round or in high or medium relief depicting cult images, deities, celestial nymphs, secular figures and animals or mythical beasts.

In India's medieval period of temple building, simple stonework techniques replaced previous wooden and brick work. Temples were heavily and ornately decorated. Heavy cornices, strong, broad pillars and the wide base of the *sikhara* (tower) give them the feeling of strength and solidity, only partly counteracted by the ornate friezes.

Western Group **Varaha Temple** (circa AD 900-925), a shrine dedicated to Vishnu in his third incarnation as Varaha, the boar. Vishnu, the preserver, is usually depicted resting on a bed of serpents, until summoned to save the world from disaster. The rat-demon Hiranyaksha stole the earth and dragged it down to his underwater home. The gods begged for Vishnu's help. The demon created 1000 replicas of himself to confuse any pursuer, but Vishnu incarnated himself as a boar and was able to dig deep and seek out the real demon. Thus, Hiranyaksha was destroyed and the world saved. The 2.6-m-long Varaha is of highly polished sandstone covered with 674 deities. He is the Lord of the Three Worlds - water, earth and heaven, and under him is the serpent *Sesha* and the feet of the broken figure of *Prithvi*, the earth goddess. The lotus ceiling shows superb relief carving.

The temples are in a peaceful setting of a beautiful park. The area covered by the Western Group was originally a sacred lake – perhaps a reason for the high plinths.

Lakshmana Temple (circa AD 950) best preserves the architectural features that typify the larger temples here. The **platform** has friezes of hunting and battle scenes with soldiers, elephants and horses as well as scenes from daily life including the erotic. The **basement** again has bands of carvings – processional friezes showing animals, soldiers, acrobats, musicians, dancers, domestic scenes, festivities, ceremonies, loving couples and deities. The details differentiate between an **officer** (beard), **general** (beard and belly) and **priest** (beard, belly and stick). An ordinary soldier has none of these. You might spot the occasional error – a camel with legs jointed like a horse, for example. Note the beautifully carved elephants at shoulder height, each one different. On the **walls** are the major sculptures of gods and goddesses in two rows, with *sura-sundaris* or *apsaras* in attendance on the raised sections and loving couples discreetly placed in the recesses. All the figures are relaxed, resting their weight on one leg, thus accentuating their curves. The bands are broken by ornate balconied windows with carved pillars and overhanging eaves. The nymphs shown attending to their toilet, bearing offerings, dancing, playing musical instruments or as sensual lovers, are executed with great skill. They are graceful and fluid (note the taut muscle or creased skin), with expressive faces and gestures. The best examples are seen in the recesses below the main tower. The **façades** are covered in superb sculpture. On the south façade are a couple of minstrels, their faces expressing devotional ecstasy, a dancing Ganesh, ladies attending to their toilet, and groups of lovers. Moving to the southwest, a *sura-sundari* applies vermilion while another plays with a ball. In the northwest corner is a nymph after her bath in her wet clothes. The south face of the northwest shrine has a fine Ganesh panel. On the north face, returning towards the porch, there is a group of *apsaras* accomplished in art and music (one plays the flute, another paints, yet another writes a letter). The east face of the subsidiary shrine in the southeast corner has a master architect with his apprentices. Leave shoes at the entrance and enter the **interior** through a simple *makara-torana* flanked by gladiators. The circular ceiling of the porch (*ardha mandapa*) is a superbly carved open lotus blossom. In the hall (*mandapa*) is a raised platform possibly used for dancing and tantric rituals. At each corner of the platform are pillars with carved brackets with *apsaras* which are among the finest sculptures at Khajuraho. There are eight figures on each column, representing the eight sects of Tantra. The sanctum (*garba-griha*) doorway has a panel showing incarnations of Vishnu while the lintel has Lakshmi with Brahma and Siva on either side. A frieze above depicts the nine planets including *Rahu*, while Krishna legends and innumerable carvings of animals, birds and humans, appear on the wall. The *pancha-ratha* sanctum has a three-headed Vishnu as Vaikuntha, and around it are 10 incarnations and 14 forms of Vishnu.

Kandariya Mahadeva Temple (circa 1025-1050) is the most developed, the largest and tallest of the Khajuraho temples. Dedicated to Siva, the elaborately carved *makara torana* doorway leads to a porch with an ornate ceiling and a dark inner sanctum with a marble linga. The temple roof rises in a series of seven bands of peaks to the summit of the central, 31-m-high *sikhara*. There are 84 smaller, subsidiary towers which are replicas. The architectural and sculptural genius of Khajuraho reaches its peak in this temple where every element is richly endowed. The platform is unique in the way it projects to the sides and rear, reflecting the plan of the transepts. It also has the highest and most ornamental basement with intricately carved processional friezes. Leaving the temple, walk to the rear of the delightful gardens to the other two temples.

Along the same platform, to Kandariya's north is the **Jagadambi Temple** (early 11th century), which is similar in layout and predates the next temple, the Chitragupta. It has a standing Parvati image in the sanctum but was originally dedicated to Vishnu. The outer walls have no projecting balconies but the lavish decorations include some of the best carvings of deities – several of Vishnu, a particularly fine *Yama*, numerous nymphs and amorous couples. In between is the ruined **Mahadeva Shrine** (11th century). Little remains except a porch, under which Sardula, a mythical lion, towers over a half-kneeling woman.

Chitragupta Temple (early 11th century) is the only one here dedicated to Surya, the Sun God. Longer and lower than its companions, it has been much restored (platform, steps, entrance porch, northeast façade). Unlike the simple basement mouldings of the Jagadambi, here there are processional friezes; the *maha-mandapa* ceiling too has progressed from the simple square in the former to an ornate octagonal ceiling. The *garbha griha* has Surya driving his chariot of seven horses, while on the south façade is a statue of Vishnu with 11 heads signifying his 10 incarnations, see page 1410.

Vishvanatha Temple (1002) is dedicated to Siva. According to the longer inscription on the wall, it originally had an emerald linga in addition to the stone one present today. Built before the Kandariya Mahadeva, they are similar in design and plan. The high, moulded basement has fine scrollwork and carvings of processions of men and animals as well as loving couples. On the nine principal basement niches of both are the *Sapta-matrikas* (seven 'Mothers') with Ganesha and Virabhadra. The excellent carvings include a fine musician with a flute and amorous couples inside the temple, and divinities attended by enchanting nymphs in innumerable poses (one removing a thorn from her foot), on the south façade. Only two subsidiary shrines of the original four remain. Sharing the same raised platform and facing the temple is the **Nandi Pavilion** with a fine elephant frieze on the basement. It houses a 2.2-m polished sandstone Nandi bull (Siva's vehicle). Before coming down the steps note the sleeping *mahout* on an elephant!

Outside this garden complex of temples and next to the Lakshmana temple is the **Matangesvara Temple** (AD 900-925), simpler in form and decoration than its neighbour and unlike all the others, still in everyday use. It has an interesting circular interior which contains a large Siva linga dating back 1000 years. You do not need to pay to get into this temple and morning or evening *puja* is very beautiful and very welcoming.

Chausath Yogini (late ninth century) is a ruined Jain temple in coarse granite on a platform. It stands apart from the rest of the Western Group beyond the tank. Only 35 of the original *chausath* (64) shrines to the *yoginis* (attendants of Kali), of the 'open-air' temple, remain.

Eastern Group South of the village is the ruined **'Ghantai' Temple** (late 10th century). The fine carvings of *ghanta* (chains-and-bells) on the pillars, the richly ornamented doorway and ceiling of the entrance porch can only be seen from the road. Walk through Khajuraho village to the small **Javari Temple** (late 11th century), with its tall, slender *sikhara*. It has a highly decorative doorway and finely sculpted figures on the walls. About 200 m north is the **Vamana Temple** (late 11th century), with a four-armed Vamana incarnation of Vishnu in the sanctum. This is in the fully developed Chandela style and has a single tower and no ambulatory. The walls are adorned with sensuous *sura-sundaris*. Returning to the modern part of Khajuraho, you pass the early 10th-century so-called **Brahma Temple** on the bank of Ninora-tal. A Vishnu temple, wrongly attributed to Brahma, it has a sandstone *sikhara* on a granite structure.

Three Jain temples stand within an enclosure about 500 m southeast of the Ghantai Temple; others are scattered around the village. The **Parsvanatha Temple** (mid-10th century), is the largest and one of the finest. The curvilinear tower dominates the structure and is beautifully carved. There are no balconies but light enters through fretted windows. Although a Jain temple, there are numerous Vaishnav deities, many of them excellently carved on the three wall panels. Some of the best known non-erotic sculptures too are found here, particularly the graceful *sura-sundaris* (one applying kohl and another removing a thorn, on the south façade; one tying ankle-bells on the north façade), as well as the fine *Dikpalas* in the corners. The interior is richly carved with elephants, lions, sea goddesses and Jain figures. The temple was originally dedicated to Adinatha, but the modern black marble image of Parsvanatha was placed in the sanctum in 1860. Next, is the smaller and simpler **Adinatha Temple** (late 11th century), where only the sanctum (containing a modern image) and vestibule have survived – the porch is modern. The sculptures on three bands again depict attractive *sura-sundaris*, the niches have *yakshis*, the corners, *Dikpalas*. **Santinatha Temple** with its 4.5-m statue of Adinatha is the main place of Jain worship. An inscription dating it at AD 1027-1028 is covered with plaster – the thoroughly renovated temple retains its ancient heart and medieval sculptures. The small sand-coloured structures around the temples are reconstructions around remains of old shrines. There is also a small Jain museum and picture gallery here.

Southern Group The two temples stand on open land. The setting, attractive at sunset, lacks the overall ambience of the Western Group but the backdrop of the Vindhyas is impressive. **Duladeo Temple**, 800 m southwest of the Jain temples down a path off the road, is the last the Chandelas built here, when temple building was already in decline. There are 20 *apsara* brackets but the figures are often repetitive and appear to lack the quality of carving found in earlier temples. The shrine door and *mandapa* ceiling have some fine carving while the linga has 11 rows of 100 lingas. **Chaturbhuja Temple** (circa 1100), 3 km south of the village, anticipates the Duladeo but lacks erotic sculptures. The sanctum contains an exceptional 2.7-m four-armed *Dakshina-murti* Vishnu image while outside there are some fine *Dikpalas*, nymphs and mythical beasts in niches.

Excursions from Khajuraho

At **Rajgarh**, 5 km south, is the imposing ruined 19th-century hilltop fort-palace of the Maharaja which the Oberoi Group will convert to a heritage hotel. It is particularly interesting when villagers congregate for the Tuesday Market. Get there by auto-rickshaw or car. **Panna National Park** ⓘ *Nov-May, for fees, see box,* *page 310*, is accessed along the Satna Road with attractive waterfalls (Rs 100) on the way. Ken River, parts of which have been declared a sanctuary for fish eating gharials, flows across the Panna National Park, which is a Project Tiger Reserve. The park, rich in biodiversity, covers dense forest, open meadows, plateaus and gorge with waterfalls, and supports chinkara, sambar, nilgai and the big cats. Although tiger sightings are rare, it is pleasant to visit in winter. There is little wildlife to be seen in the dry season (when the gharials are removed for their own protection). Access is easiest from Madla, 27 km from Khajuraho. Jeep or motorbike hire from Khajuraho, or bus; tour of park can be arranged in Madla.

Chandela forts

The Chandela kings' main defensive bases were Mahoba and Kalinjar, but as the kingdom expanded these were complemented by other forts at Ajaigarh, Orchha, Datia, Deogarh and Chanderi. Like other kings, they donated villages to maintain the families of soldiers who had died in war. Heroic virtues were instilled into a child from birth and women admired men who fought well; *sati* became common practice throughout the region. After the mid-10th century the independent Chandelas joined a Hindu confederacy to repel Afghan invasions. **Mahmud of Ghazni**, the 'Idol Breaker', made at least 17 of his plunder raids into India between 1000-1027, ultimately taking the title, albeit briefly, Lord of Kalinjar. The forts suffered varied fortunes until the British took them over in the early 19th century. Now the area is being invaded by forests of teak and ebony but offer an insight into totally unspoilt territory. Ajaigarh and Kalinjar are quite 'primitive' but a visit, particularly to the former, is worthwhile. A tour of these and Chitrakoot is really worthwhile. Enlist a local guide to show you the best spots. Take water with you.

Ajaigarh

Ajaigarh, 36 km north of Panna, surrounded by dense forest, stands on a granite outcrop crowned by a 15-m perpendicular scarp. Ajaigarh was a self-contained hill fort, intended to withstand long sieges and to house the entire population of the region, which accounts for its great size. Despite its inaccessibility and the difficult 250-m climb involved (allow about 40 minutes on the way up), the fort is worth visiting for its peaceful atmosphere and wonderful views. Two of the original five gates are accessible; the large stone steps here once helped elephants in their steep ascent. Encircling the hill, the fort wall encloses part-ruined temples; only four of the original 22 temples remain. Rock carvings, pillars and sculptures from Hindu and Jain temples, some later used by Muslims to reinforce the fortifications, today lie scattered amongst woodland. The old stone quarry now filled by a lake is said to have provided stone for Khajuraho.

Some believe it is auspicious to eat here, hence the remains of bonfires and presence of picnickers; but the town is dirty with few facilities; it's best to bring your own food and water.

Kalinjar

Some 20 km from Ajaigarh this fort stands on the last spur of the Vindhya hills overlooking the Gangetic plains, a plateau with a steep scarp on all sides. One of the most ancient sites in Bundelkhand (Ptolemy's Kanagora), it combines the sanctity of remote hilltops with natural defensive strength. One legend names Kalinjar after Siva, the Lord of Destruction (*kal* = death, *jar* = decay). The ancient hill has long been a place of pilgrimage and worship for Hindu *sadhus*, *rishis* and pilgrims. It is rarely visited by other travellers.

The design of the fort has a mystical significance. The only approach is from the north and entry is through **seven gates** with barbicans corresponding to the seven known planets and stations through which the soul must pass before being absorbed into Brahma. At the crest, crumbling Hindu and Muslim monuments stand side by side on the 1.5-km-long plateau. Beyond the last gate, a drop of about 3.6 m leads to **Sita Sej**, a stone couch set in a rock-cut chamber (fourth century). Beyond, a passage leads to Patalganga (underground Ganga), believed to run through Kalinjar.

Mahoba

Some 63 km north of Khajuraho, Mahoba was reputedly founded by Raja Chandra- varman, in AD 800. Today, it is a small town with a fort on a low hill, several ancient tanks and a thriving 'Dariba' or betel market. The vines are grown under traditional shelters to produce high quality *paan* (betel leaf) for which the area is famous.

After winning Bundelkhand, the Chandela kings dedicated themselves not only to building temples for their gods, but also to bringing water to the land. They created large tanks by damming shallow valleys. Mahoba's oldest tank, **Rahila Sagar** (circa AD 900) has impressive ruins of a ninth-century granite Sun Temple. The 12th-century **Madan Sagar** has a granite Siva temple nearby and a ruined Vishnu temple on one of its rocky islets. Along its embankment is the old fort, **Qila Mismar**, with ruins of palaces, Hindu temples and a tomb. In the fields, remains of Buddhist and Jain sculptures lie abandoned. **Gokhar Hill**, near Madan Sagar, with 24 Jain Tirthankaras figures carved out of sheer rock, is worth exploring. There is a *Tourist Bungalow* here with a restaurant and bar. The station is 3 km from the bus stand. To Jhansi (four hours); to Varanasi via Allahabad (11 hours).

Chitrakoot → *For listings, see pages 297-303. Colour map 3, B2.*

On the north flank of the Vindhyas where they dip gently beneath the Ganges Plains, 175 km from Khajuraho, Chitrakoot's forests and peaceful rivers were home to Rama and Sita in 11 of their 14 years of exile. **Ramghat**, the principal bathing ghat on the banks of the beautiful Mandakini River, is widely revered in India and the site of countless pilgrimages, though scarcely known to foreigners. Like the much more famous waters of the Yamuna at Allahabad or the Ganga at Varanasi, the River Mandakini is lined with temples. A good way to see the ghats is to hire a boat. Upstream from Ramghat the Mandakini passes through a beautiful stretch of wooded valley.

Northern Madhya Pradesh listings

For Sleeping and Eating price codes and other relevant information, see Essentials pages 38-42.

Sleeping

Gwalior *p279, map p282*

LL-AL Usha Kiran Palace, Jayendraganj Lashkar, T0751-244 4000-05, www.tajhotels.com. 36 unique and very atmospheric a/c rooms (some vast suites) in 120-year-old maharaja's palace. Beautiful spa (musicians play live behind jali screens) and gardens, swimming pool, good restaurant, billiards and bar. It retains character of charming royal guesthouse, with all the trimmings and attention to detail you would expect from somewhere where members of various royal families do actually come and stay sometimes. Recommended.

L-B Central Park, Madhav Rao Scindia Marg, City Centre, T0751-2232440, www.thecentralpark.net. Modern a/c rooms in Gwalior's top business hotel. Pool, health club, coffee shop, good restaurant and bar, currency exchange and breakfast included. Recommended.

AL-C Gwalior Regency, Link Rd, near New Bus Stand, T0751-234 0670. http://www.hotelregencygroup.com/. 51 modern rooms, smallish but well maintained, restaurant, coffee shop, pool.

A-C Tansen, 6A Gandhi Rd, T0751-4056789, www.mptourism.com. 36 rooms, mostly a/c, good restaurant, bar, garden, car hire, tourist information, quiet location and handy for bus and train.

F-G DM, Link Rd, near New Bus Stand, T0751-234 2083. Small and pretty shabby rooms with attached bath (hot water) and small garden at the back. Reasonably quiet and handy for bus stand.

Jhansi *p283, map p284*

It is better to stay at Orchha.

B-D Sita, Shivpuri Rd, T0510-244 4690. 29 smart, clean a/c rooms with bath, good restaurant, car hire, exchange.

C-E Chanda, 365/1A Civil Lines, T0510-2450027. Opposite Laxmi Bai Park, 24 comfortable a/c or air-cooled rooms with bath, restaurant.

C-E Samrat, Chitra Chauraha near railway station, T0510-244 4943. Rooms with fan, some with a/c, mosquito menace, check rooms before you commit, some are fine, some are hideous so that extra Rs 100 could make a big difference on what you get.

F-G Central, 701 Civil Lines (500 m from raillway station), T0510-244 0509. 39 rooms (some 4-bed), some air-cooled, with bath, Indian meals.

G Railway Retiring Rooms and 6-bed dorm. Other hotels near the station are dirty.

Datia *p285*

C-D Datia Motel (MP Tourism), 2 km from town on Gwalior Rd, T07522-238125, www.mptourism.com. Overlooks the palace and lake with 4 spotless, airy rooms and a restaurant.

G Shri Raghunath Ganga Hotel, Station Rd, opposite Pitambra Peeth Temple, T07522-236754. Owners helpful and very welcoming. 9 air-cooled rooms, baths, clean, secure.

Shivpuri National Park *p285*

C-D Chinkara Motel, NH3, 4 km south of Shivpuri, T07492-221297. Motel with 19 clean rooms, some a/c, restaurant.

C-D Tourist Village (MP Tourism), Jhansi Rd, 5 km east of town, Bhadaiya Kund, T07492-223760, www.mptourism.com. 19 rooms in cottages, 5 a/c, 2 with 4 beds, pleasant restaurant, attractive location overlooking lake, jeep hire, close to the park.

E-F Delhi Hotel, Madhav Chowk, A-B Rd, T07492-233093. Hotel with 12 simple rooms with bath, some a/c, vegetarian restaurant.

Orchha *p286, map p287*

Hotels are best on the idyllic riverside.

AL-A Amar Mahal, T07680-252102, www.amarmahal.com. Experience how a Maharaja palace would have looked back in its day in this modern day version built and decorated in traditional Bundelkhand architectural style. Luxurious, attractively decorated and extremely spacious rooms with four-poster beds arranged around 2 courtyards, one with pool. Well-maintained and tranquil gardens where local musicians play during the evening, perfect for relaxing after a day walking around the sites. Excellent buffet style restaurant with 24-carat gold-painted ceiling, Ayurvedic massage, gym and doctor on call. Recommended.

AL-A Orchha Resort, Kanchanghat, on riverside, T07680-252222, www.orchharesort.com. 32 immaculate although characterless a/c rooms and12 musty tents arranged around parched tennis court with the redeeming feature of an extraordinary backdrop of the royal *chhatris*. Reasonable pool and excellent restaurant (strict vegetarian)

AL-C Betwa Retreat (MP Tourism), overlooking river, 10-min walk from bus stand, T07680-252618, betwa@mptourism.com. 15 clean and bright, typically dated government style cottages, some a/c, the best (**AL**) in beautiful high-ceilinged Maharaja Villa, plus 10 'luxury' tents, in serious need of mould fumigation. Spacious well-kept gardens, scattered ruins, nightly folk music and dance, average restaurant.

AL-D Sheesh Mahal (MP Tourism), In a breathtakingly stunning location inside the fort, T07680-252624 (book in advance). 8 beautiful ornate rooms and 2 majestic suites (**AL-A**) with terrace, antique fittings and furniture, huge marble tub, panoramic view from toilet. Full of character and atmospheric charm, restaurant has great views, friendly staff. Recommended.

C-F Ganpati, just north of main crossroads, T07680-252765. www.hotelganpati.com. A wide range of clean rooms (even more were being built at time or writing). Best are the large, amusingly named 'sweet rooms' with a/c, murals and great views of the fort. Hot showers, small courtyard and gardens, great views of palace and very friendly owner. Recommended.

D-G Fort View, next to **Ganpati**, T07680-252701. Retired school teacher's clean and friendly guesthouse, hot water, dorm, same good views. Negotiable price for longer stay.

F Bhandari Guesthouse, 5 mins' walk south near river bridge, T07680-252745/ T(0)9425-342559. Fairly newly built, very clean rooms with attached bathrooms set around a small courtyard. Good value for price.

Deogarh *p289*

E Tourist Bungalow, opposite Dasavatara Temple. Clean air-cooled rooms, water from nearby pump, kitchen. The caretaker will prepare meals and escort you on hikes to half a dozen temples, in woods 5-10 km away.

Khajuraho *p290, map p291*

Most hotels are within 1 km of the western temples, notably along Jain Temples Rd. They are subject to frequent power cuts but top hotels have generators.

LL The Lalit, opposite Circuit House, T0786-272111, www.thelalit.com. Slightly soulless top-notch hotel with all the trimmings including sparkling new rooms and extravagant suites. Here you can comfortably forget the outside world watching 42"plasma TV screens, enjoying the luxury spa, eating at the 24-hr multi-cuisine restaurant, shopping at the overpriced gift store or lounging by the pool.

LL-AL Chandela (Taj), Airport Rd, T07686-272355, www.tajhotels.com. 94 comfortable rooms in this bustling but slightly dated complex. 2 restaurants, nice pool and fitness centre, best bookshop in town though pricey, currency exchange, pleasant gardens.

LL-AL Clarks Khajuraho, Khajuraho Village, T07686-274038, www.hotelclarks.com. With a deceptively plain exterior, inside are 104 tastefully decorated, modern rooms with views of the pool and extensive well kept grounds, badminton and tennis courts, large restaurant, massage and gym.

AL-A Usha Bundela, Airport Rd, T07686-272386. Full of character, although in need of some maintenance, Comfy rooms, well managed, restaurant, bar and good pool.

C Tourist Village, T07686-274062. Veering away from the norm,13 well-equipped attractive 2-room 'ethnic' huts, bathroom and a/c, outdoor restaurant, bike useful, campsite nearby.

C-E Payal, 10-min walk from centre, T07686-274076, www.mptourism.com. 25 reasonable rooms with bath, some a/c, restaurant (good breakfast and tea), bar, very quiet garden, small pool, helpful staff.

D-E Lakeside, by Sib Sagar Lake, T07686-274120. Beautiful evening views, 18 functional rooms and dorm, clean but noisy and often full.

D-E Marble Palace, opposite Gole Market, Jain Temples Rd, T07686-274353 www.hotelmarblepalace.com. 9 spacious rooms, best upstairs facing street, others dark.

D-E Surya, Jain Temple Rd, T07686-274145, www.hotelsuryakhajuraho.com. 40 comfortable, very pleasant rooms, best in newly built block, attached bath, balconies and a/c. Set around a lovely garden. Excellent vegetarian restaurant, bike hire, extremely helpful travel desk and staff. Very good value. Highly Recommended.

D-F Hotel Shanti, opposite Shiv Sagar Lake, T07686-274560, shanti.hotelkhajuraho@yahoo.com. Great location by lake, spacious, clean and light rooms with bath, temple views and TV, restaurant. Good value.

D-G Zen, Jain Temple Rd, T07686-274228, oshozen62@hotmail.com. Large, bright ramshackle rooms with clean attached bath, nice garden with water features, a good place to stay but strange atmosphere – beware of attempts to charge spurious 'luxury tax' on cheap rooms. Spectacularly overpriced Italian restaurant in garden although owner now promises 10% discount for all Footprint readers.

E-F Casa di William, opposite western group of temples, T07686-274244. Very conveniently located,15 pleasant and clean rooms with bath, some a/c. Absolutely stunning sunset views of temples from roof restaurant, massage, internet, bike rental. Very friendly and helpful staff, Italian management. Good value

F Sunset View, south of bazar, alongside Chandela Emporium, T07686-274077. Well located near lake and bus stand, unimposing entrance, 12 simple rooms (6 air-cooled with tubs), fairly clean, pleasant terrace and garden, good value.

G Yogi Lodge, western temples, T07686-274158. Excellent budget option, spartan but clean rooms, rooftop café, internet, bike hire, yoga classes, well run, links to nearby ashram for a quiet retreat

Excursions from Khajuraho *p295*

Panna National Park

LL Pashan Ghar, 12 km from park entrance, www.tajsafaris.com. Newly opened, this is at the supreme luxe end of the spectrum with beautifully decorated stone cottages with a nod to traditional style and a watchtower overlooking the water hole. This is the place for a romantic getaway with candlelit suppers in a palanquin or dinners delivered through the 'butler hatch' to your own private veranda.

A Ken River Lodge, Village Madla, T07732-275235, www.kenriverlodge.com. In a beautiful location with both cottages and 'Swiss' tents, tree-top restaurant, fishing, boating, swimming.

D-E Gilles' Treehouse, 3 km from Madla, serves food (chilled beers are sent 20 m up a tree by a pulley system). Camping possible, contact **Raja's Café**, Khajuraho.

E Rest Houses, ask at gate or park office, Panna National Park. Take provisions.

Chitrakoot *p297*

D-E Tourist Bungalow, near bus stand, T07670-265326, www.mptourism.com. 17 rooms (2 a/c), restaurant (prior ordering), not very welcoming, women not allowed.

G Pitri Smriti Visram Grih, Ramghat, Hathi Darwaza, T07670-265314. Pleasant place, 16 basic rooms with fairly clean bath, friendly manager. Vegetarian; no alcohol.

Eating

Gwalior *p279, map p282*

TTT Usha Kiran Palace, International. Good rich Mughlai meals and snacks, live classical music, bar, attentive service, pleasant ambience in ornate surroundings looking out over attractive gardens.

TT Kwality, Green garden road behind SP Office. Pretty decent and tasty mainly Indian and snacks. Clean but rather dark helpful staff.

T Hob Nob, next to **DM Hotel** (see Sleeping). A good option for large and tasty dosas, handy for bus stand.

T Indian Coffee House, **India Hotel**, just off Jayaji Chowk. Great for South Indian breakfasts, snacks and *thalis*.

T Volga, near Inderganj Chowk. Indian. Popular locally.

Jhansi *p283, map p284*

Hotels **Sita** and **Samrat** are recommended.

TT Holiday, Shastri Marg. Indian and Western. Clean, a/c, reasonably priced.

T Nav Bharat, Shastri Marg. Indian snacks.

Orchha *p286, map p287*

TTT Orchha Resort (see Sleeping). Vegetarian. Pleasant decor, à la carte or buffet (breakfast Rs 200, lunch/dinner Rs 400).

TT Betwa Tarang, near fort bridge (upstairs). Good food, pleasant roof terrace or indoor, clean toilets. Also 'picnic' meals by the river.

TT Sheesh Mahal (see Sleeping). International, non-vegetarian served in a large foyer in the fantastic and atmospheric palace location. Great North Indian, chilled beer, good service.

T Milan restaurant, small, clean and well cared for place just before the fort bridge. Serves a range of cuisines and lives up to its name serving 'real' Expresso coffee, not so easy to find in these parts. Great breakfast. Recommended.

Khajuraho *p290, map p291*

*Chai*and *parathas* cooked fresh at stalls in the market square on Jain Temples Rd make a good quick breakfast before the temples.

TT Blue Sky Restaurant, Main Rd, overlooking Western Temples. Pop in here for a good sundowner over the temples, but the food is pretty ropey. They will be always be busy because of their location and they know this. There's a surcharge to sit in the tree house.

TT Mediterraneo, opposite **Hotel Surya**. Good bruschetta, fresh pasta dishes, tasty pizza, good desserts, Indian chefs. Beware of imitators – a "branch" has opened in Orchha but has nothing to do with this great place.

TT Paradise, Main Rd, opposite Shiv Sagar Lake, T(0)9893-138049. Western, Indian. Good meals reasonably priced, excellent biryanis and banana pancakes, pleasant rooftop with lake views, family-run, friendly and inviting.

TT Raja's Café, Main Rd, near Western Temples entrance. Probably the best food you will get in Khajuraho and great coffee too all with the backdrop of the temples. There's a nicely designed a/c room downstairs on days that swelter or head up the spiral staircase for great views. Highly recommended.

T Agrawal, near **Hotel Surya**. The only local-feeling place in town, good *thalis* (vegetarian only), not too oily.

TT Garden View Restaurant, inside **Hotel Surya**, Jain temple Rd. Western, Fantastic Indian local recipes served in pleasant garden surroundings, family-run, friendly and inviting. Recommended.

Safari, opposite Western Group. Bizarre array of menus, good food but specify if you want vegetarian dishes (may be made with meat gravy), large helpings, good *lassis*, supreme *thalis*, amazing Indian muesli but very slow service.

Chitrakoot *p297*

Annapurna, Ramghat. Excellent *thalis*.
Digbeah, near bridge on Ramghat. Lunchtime *thalis* recommended.

Entertainment

Khajuraho *p290, map p291*

Shilpgram, Airport Rd. Interesting programme of cutural performances in season, 1900-2100, often free. A more rustic, less commercial experience than the similarly named cultural centre across the street, which attracts tour buses.

Festivals and events

Orchha *p286, map p287*

Nov/Dec Ram Vivah (Rama's marriage). Colourful processions draw crowds particularly as superbly trained horses perform extraordinary feats where one removes a horseman's eye make-up with a hoof.

Khajuraho *p290, map p291*

Feb-Mar Dance Festival. Many of the country's most accomplished dancers perform in the spectacular setting of the Western Group. Ask at the tourist office for details.

Shopping

Gwalior *p279, map p282*

Ganpatlal Krishna Lal, Sarafa Bazar. Jewellery and antiques. Closed Tue.
Kothari, Sarafa Bazar. Brocade, *chanderi* (light and flimsy cotton and silk material), silk saris.
Loyal, near High Court, Nai Sarak. Books.
MD Fine Arts, Subhash Market. Paintings and objets d'art.
MP Emporium, Sarafa Bazar. Handlooms.
MP Khadi Sangh, Sarafa Bazar. Handlooms.
Mrignayani's, an MP State Emporium, in Patankar Bazar also recommended.

Khajuraho *p290, map p291*

Gift shops sell cheap stone and bronze sculptures, handicrafts and gems in the bazar near the Western Group (**Panna diamond mines**, the largest in the country, are nearby).
Chandela Emporium, near Sibsagar. Large selection of gifts, crafts and jewellery.
Ganesh Garments, Jain Temples Rd. Reasonable Western clothes (quick alterations).
Karan Jewellers, for diamonds.
MP Emporium for fixed prices; small craft shops on way to Javeri temple cheaper than the bazar.

Activities and tours

Gwalior *p279, map p282*

Travel Bureau, 6/788 Devasheesh Enclave, near Kailash Vihar, T0751-223 3765, www.travelbureauagra.com. Tours to Orchha and Shivpuri, Rs 1600 (car for 5), same day return. City sights, Rs 600, contact tourist office at **Tansen Hotel**.

Jhansi *p283, map p284*

Touraids, Jai Complex, Civil Lines, T0510-244 0490. Helpful and reliable manager with a fleet of cars for hire.
Travel Bureau, 197 Chand Gate, Nai Basti, T0510-244 9355, www.travelbureauagra.com.

Orchha *p286, map p287*

River rafting trips (Oct-Feb) can be organized by **MP Tourism**, or contact manager of **Betwa Retreat** or **Sheesh Mahal** (see Sleeping). Scenic 90-min and 3-hr trips on the Betwa with a few fairly gentle rapids (around Rs 1200/2000). The Jamuni River has more adventurous runs (Rs 3000).

Khajuraho *p290, map p291*

Touraids, Bamitha Rd, near Shilpgram, T07686-274060. Reliable cars with drivers.
Travel Bureau, Holiday Inn, T07686-274037, www.travelbureauagra.com.

Transport

Gwalior *p279, map p282*

Air The airport is 9 km from town. **Kingfisher**, T1 860 266 9000, flies to **Delhi** and **Indore** daily. Taxi to town, about Rs 150.
Bus Bus stand, Link Rd, T0751-234 0192. Frequent buses to **Agra**, **Bhopal**, **Indore** and **Shivpuri**. Daily to **Khajuraho**.
Rickshaw Prepaid auto-rickshaw stand at the railway station. Cycle-rickshaw charge around

Rs 25 for rides within town. *Tempos* on fixed routes, Rs 3-8.

Train Tickets for the *Shatabdi Express*are usually sold in the separate, 'non-computerized' queue. Gwalior is on the main Delhi–Mumbai and Delhi–Chennai lines. Enquiries T131, reservations T135. For **Agra Cantt**, take any Delhi train, 1¾ hrs. **Bhopal**: *Shatabdi Exp 12002,* 0930 (Fri 0945), 5 hrs; *Punjab Mail 12138,* 1040, 6¼ hrs; *Lakshadweep Exp 12618,* 1400, 6 hrs. **Delhi**: *Lakshadweep Exp 12617,* 0822, 6 hrs (**HN**); *Punjab Mail 12137,* 1518, 5½ hrs (**ND**); *Taj Exp 12279,* 1655, 5 hrs (**HN**); *Dadar Amritsar Exp 11057,* 2150, 5½ hrs (**ND**). **Jabalpur** (for **Kanha**): *Gondwana Exp 12412,* 2022, 11 hrs; *Mahakoshal Exp 12190,* 2108, 13¼ hrs. **Jhansi**: see Bhopal, journey time 1-1½ hrs. **Mumbai** (**CST**): *Punjab Mail 12138,* 1040, 21¼ hrs, plus others to Dadar. **Varanasi**: *Bundelkhand Exp 11107,* 1950, 14½ hrs (calling at **Allahabad** 4 hrs earlier).

Jhansi *p283, map p284*

Bus From **Kanpur Rd Bus Stand**, 3 km east of railway station: **Gwalior** 0645-1800 via Datia; **Khajuraho**, bumpy and crowded, 0530, 1100, 1145, 1330, 1545 (tickets from booth on Platform 1, claim your seat early; Rs 100, plus luggage Rs 5, 5-6 hrs); **Lalitpur** 0730, 1025, 2100, 2300. **Shivpuri** 0500-1800. **Orchha** half-hourly during daylight, about 30 mins, Rs 8. *Tempos* leave when full, 30 mins, Rs 15.

Car Car hire with driver: about Rs 6 per km, minimum 200 km per day; night halt Rs 150. To **Khajuraho**, **Travel Bureau** or **Touraids** charge around Rs 2400, reliable drivers.

Rickshaw and taxi Rickshaws can be found at the station; use the prepaid counter or aim for Rs 20-30 to the bus stand; drivers visiting **MP Tourism** office at station quote "friends" rate, around Rs 40. *Tempo* to bus stand Rs 5 each. To Orchha from station, allow Rs 200; return after sightseeing Rs 340-400. Taxis are equally overpriced, about Rs 300- 450; to **Khajuraho**, around Rs 1500-1800.

Train **Agra Cantt**: see Delhi, 3-3½ hrs. **Bhopal**: *Shatabdi Exp 12002,* 1047, 3¾ hrs; *Punjab Mail 12138,* 1230, 4½ hrs; *Lakshadweep Exp 12618,* 1532, 4¼ hrs. **Delhi**: *Lakshadweep Exp 12617,* 0700, 7¼ hrs (**HN**); *Punjab Mail 12137,* 1340, 6¾ hrs (**ND**); *Shatabdi Exp 12001,* 1755, 5 hrs (**HN**). **Jabalpur** (for **Kanha**): *Gondwana Exp 12412,* 2200, 9½ hrs. **Jalgaon** (for **Ajanta**/**Ellora**): *Amritsar Dadar Exp 11058,* 0505, 14¼ hrs; *Punjab Mail 12138,* 1230, 11¾ hrs. **Lucknow**: *Kushinagar Exp 11015,* 1930, 7 hrs (continues to **Gorakhpur**, 5¼ hrs), plus several non-daily services. **Mumbai**: *Punjab Mail 12138,* 1230, 19½ hrs, plus several to Dadar. **Varanasi**: *Bundelkhand Exp 11107,* 2135, 15 hrs.

Datia and Sonagiri *p285*

Bus Frequent from **Jhansi** (1 hr, Rs 10), and **Gwalior** (Rs 30).

Rickshaw *Tempos* and cycle-rickshaws run the 2 km between Datia station and the fort/palace (10 mins, Rs 20), and the 5 km between Sonagiri station and the temples.

Train Datia and Sonagiri are on the Delhi-Mumbai main line, with frequent trains to both **Gwalior** and **Jhansi**.

Shivpuri National Park *p285*

Air Nearest airport is at **Gwalior** (112 km).

Bus Regular bus services from **Bhopal**, **Chanderi**, **Indore**, **Jhansi** (101 km, 3 hrs by car) and **Ujjain**. Auto-rickshaws available at bus stand.

Train Nearest stations are **Jhansi** and **Gwalior**.

Deogarh *p289*

Bus/train **Jakhlaun** (13 km) is the nearest station, with buses to **Deogarh** and **Lalitpur**. Lalitpur (30 km away) has auto-rickshaws for transfer to Deogarh (1 hr, Rs 200). It also has trains to **Jhansi**: *Kushinagar Exp* 11015, 1840, 1½ hrs; *Jhelum Exp 11077,* 1230, 1½ hrs; *Amritsar Exp 11457,* 1818, 1½ hrs. **Bina-Etawa**, south of Deogarh, is an important railway junction.

Khajuraho *p290, map p291*

Air The airport is 5 km south of the village centre, T07686-274041. Flights are heavily booked in season: confirm onward flight on arrival. Transport to town: taxi Rs 150, auto-rickshaw Rs 100 (overpriced; difficult to bargain). **Indian Airlines**: Usha Bundela, T07686-274035, Airport T07686-274036; no credit cards. **Jet Airways**: T07686-274406 (airport). Both fly daily to/from **Delhi** and **Varanasi**. **Kingfisher** operate out of here too.

Bicycle Cycle hire in Gole Market behind museum and along Jain Temples Rd; Rs 50 per day, recommended mode though not allowed in temple complex.

Bus Long-distance buses arrive at a newish bus stand 1.5 km south of the main bazar on Airport Rd, with a computerized counter for reservations on buses and trains elsewhere. Daily buses to **Agra** 391 km, 0700, 0800, 0900, 1800 (an exhausting 10-12 hrs via Jhansi and Gwalior); **Bhopal** 350 km, 0600, 0700; **Indore** 480 km, 0600; **Jhansi** 176 km, several 0500-1800 (4½-5 hrs), semi-deluxe via Orchha 1115; **Mahoba** (stops 3 km from the railway station), several 0600-1700 (3 hrs); **Satna** (for rail connections to **Jabalpur**, **Allahabad** and **Kolkata**), 0745, 0830, 0930, 1400, 1500, 4 hrs (very uncomfortable).
Car Car hire with driver to **Jhansi**, Rs 2000-3500, arranged through hotels or by **Touraids** and Travel Bureau, 4 hrs. **Satna**, Rs 1500-2400. **Agra** or **Varanasi**, Rs 5000-7000, 8-9 hrs.
Rickshaw and taxi Cycle-rickshaws try to charge Rs 30 for shortest journey; approx local price from bazar to bus stand, Rs 15. Rs 75-100 per half day. Taxis are from **MP Tourism** or **Touraids** near Usha Hotel, but overpriced. To Satna, cheaper fares can be had from drivers who have dropped off passengers in Khajuraho.
Train The station at Khajuraho opened in 2008 and now is much more connected to the rest of India with regular trains running between Delhi, Agra, Varanasi, Udaipur, Jhansi and Allahabad. Computerized reservations at bus stand, T07686-274416.

Excursions from Khajuraho *p295*

Bus **Satna** is a transport link to Khajuraho. Khajuraho buses depart from the railway bridge, 2 km north of the station (*tempo* Rs 5, rickshaw Rs 20). Several uncomfortable buses daily with **MPSRTC**, 0630-1530, 4-5 hrs; after 1530 catch bus to **Bamitha** (hourly until 1800) then taxi (Rs 100) or share jeep to **Khajuraho**. Other buses go to **Amarkantak** 0750; **Chitrakoot** 0500, 1200, 1530; **Tala** for **Bandhavgarh**, daily, 0800, 4 hrs, but better to take train to Katni then bus to park.
Train Reservations from office on right outside main entrance; enquiries T131. The 0745 bus from Khajuraho connects with several useful trains. **Kolkata**, *Howrah Mumbai Mail 12322*, 1630, 20¼ hrs. **Mumbai** (**CST**) (all via Katni, Jabalpur and Pipariya): *Howrah Mumbai Mail12321*, 1455, 21¼ hrs; *Mahanagri Exp 11094*, 1825, 21¼ hrs. **Varanasi**: *Sarnath Exp 15159*, 0805, 8 hrs; *Mahanagri Exp 11093*,1930, 8¼ hrs; plus many at awkward times, on certain days only.

Chitrakoot *p297*

Bus Regular services to **Jhansi**, **Mahoba**, **Satna** and **Chhattarpur**.
Train The nearest station is Karwi (Chitrakoot Dham) with services between **Delhi** (**HN**) and **Jabalpur** and to **Lucknow**, then tempo to **Chitrakoot**, 30 mins, Rs 10. **Delhi** (**HN**) via Agra: *Nizamuddin Mahakosal Exp 12189*, 2316, 14 hrs (**Agra** 9½ hrs).

Directory

Gwalior *p279, map p282*

Post GPO: Jayaji Chowk, Birla Nagar, Morar and Residency.

Jhansi *p283, map p284*

Banks **State Bank of India**, Jayaji Chowk, 1030-1430, Sat 1030-1230.

Orchha *p286, map p287*

Banks **Orchha Resorts** for residents; **Canara Bank**, main street, changes TCs.

Khajuraho *p290, map p291*

Banks **State Bank of India**, opposite Western Group, foreign exchange, can be busy. Several ATMs. **Police** T07686-274032. **Post** Bus stand, 0900-1700.

Eastern Madhya Pradesh

The modern city of Jabalpur makes a convenient jumping-off point for some of India's quintessential wildernesses. Kanha and Bandhavgarh national parks protect the landscapes that inspired Kipling's Jungle Book *and, despite the continued predations of poachers, Bandhavgarh at least still offers the possibility of tracking a tiger from the back of an elephant. Facilities for wildlife viewing in the parks are improving and a number of new safari resorts have opened: some massively luxurious, others working to involve local communities in the conservation effort.* ▸▸ *For listings, see pages 307-310.*

Jabalpur and around → *For listings, see pages 307-310. Colour map 3, C2. Phone code: 0761. Population: 952,000.*

On the upper reaches of the River Narmada in the heart of India's forested tribal belt, Jabalpur receives remarkably few visitors. It serves as the main gateway to two of India's finest wildlife reserves, Kanha and Bandhavgarh. Jabalpur town was the capital and pleasure resort of the Gond kings during the 12th century. It was later the seat of the Kalchuri Dynasty until it fell to the Marathas. The British took it in 1817 and left their mark with the cantonment residences and barracks.

Ins and outs

Getting there Although there are long-distance buses to Jabalpur from the surrounding large cities, it is most comfortable to travel here by train. Under eight hours from Bhopal or Allahabad, there are also good connections to Nagpur and South India. The main station is on the edge of the Civil Lines, under 2 km from the town centre. The cheaper hotels are easily reached from the main bus stand. **Warning** Hotel touts are very active round the station and bus stand so it is best to have a hotel in mind. Rickshaws offer cheap fares to hotel and then charge a commission. ▸▸ *See Transport, page 309.*

Getting around The town is too spread out to cover on foot easily but there are plenty of taxis, unmetered autos and cheap shared *tempos* for sights further afield.

Sleeping
Anand **2**
Kalchuri Residency **4**
Krishna **5**
Rishi Regency **6**
Samdariya & Restaurant **7**
Sidharth **8**
Satyam Shivam Sundaram **2**

Eating
Indian Coffee House **1**

Tourist information Madhya Pradesh Tourism ⓘ *railway station, T0761-267 7690, car hire, runs daily bus to Kanha, departs at 0800, return 1900.*

Sights

Madan Mahal Fort (1116) ⓘ *Tue-Sun 1000-1700, closed holidays, free*, built by the Gond ruler Madan Shah on a hill just to the west of the city, has superb views. To get there take a tempo from the stand near the **Krishna Hotel** to Sharda Chowk (Rs 5), then walk up the left-hand hill. **Rani Durgavati Museum and Memorial** houses a collection of sculptures and prehistoric relics, and the **Tilwara Ghat** where **Mahatma Gandhi's** ashes were immersed in the Narmada, are all places of interest. There are also Jain temples.

The **Marble Rocks** are 22 km west of Jabalpur. Captain J Forsyth wrote of them: "The eye never wearies of the effect produced by the broken and reflected sunlight, glancing from a pinnacle of snow-white marble reared against the deep blue of the sky and again losing itself in the soft bluish greys of their recesses". These white rocks, with views of black/dark green volcanic seams, rise to 30 m on either side of the Narmada River and in moonlight produce a magical effect; floodlights have been added, though boating may not be possible. Stalls sell cheap soap-stone carvings. There's lodging nearby in Bhedaghat, if needed. To get to the rocks take a *tempo* from the stand near **Krishna Hotel** to Bhedaghat, Rs 8, which takes you right to the Marble Rocks car park. Walk up to see the waterfalls, or go past the Mandir to the town and follow steps down for boat trips (30 minutes, Rs 10, recommended, though if you're alone and hire the whole boat it costs Rs 200).

Other sights nearby are the **Dhuandhar Falls** (smoke cascade), where the Narmada plunges through a narrow chasm, **Hathi-ka-paon** (Elephant's Foot Rock) and **Monkey's Leap** ledge. Nearby is the **Chausath Yogini Mandir**, a 10th-century temple with stone carvings. Legend suggests that it is connected to the Gond queen Durgavati's palace by an **underground passage**. Approached by a long flight of steps, there is an excellent view of the Narmada from the top. The British era **Pariyat tank**, 12 km from Jabalpur, is a popular picnic and fishing spot for locals.

Mandla → *Colour map 3, C2.*

The capital of the ancient Gond Kingdom of Garha-Mandla early in the Christian era, Mandla is of great historical significance to the Gond tribal peoples. The Gond Queen Rani Durgavati took her life here when her army was cornered by Mughal forces under Asaf Khan in 1564. The **fort** was built in the 17th century and is surrounded on three sides by the Narmada River. It passed to the Marathas and then to the British in 1818. The jungle has since taken over the ruins (only a few towers remain), though there are some temples and ghats in the town. The Gond Raja Hirde Shah built a large **palace** in a commanding site nearby in Ramnagar (15 km), of which little remains.

Kanha National Park → *For listings, see pages 307-310.* *Colour map 3, C2.*

This is the country about which Kipling wrote so vividly in his *Jungle Book*. The area was famed as a hunter's paradise but now the valley has been well developed as a national park. It is worth spending a couple of days here. Lying in the Maikal hills in the eastern part of the Satpura Range, 40 km from Mandla, the park has deciduous hardwoods, rolling grasslands and meandering streams of the Banjar River. The park forms the core of the Kanha Tiger Reserve. It was created in 1974 and also protects the rare hardground-adapted barasingha (swamp deer). George Schaller, the zoologist, conducted the first ever scientific study of the tiger here and research is also being done on deer and langur habitat.

Ins and outs

Getting there The journey by car takes about five hours from Jabalpur on a poor road. The main gates are at Kisli and Mukki. If arriving in the evening, stop overnight at Khatia or Kisli as vehicles are not allowed into the park after dark. From Nagpur or Raipur enter via Mukki Gate. Diesel vehicles, motorcycles and bicycles are not allowed in the park. ▸▸ *See Transport, page 309.*
Getting around Visitors may not walk around inside the park, but you can walk in the peaceful forest between the gate at Kanha and the park itself. ▸▸ *See box, page 310.*
Park information Area: 1945 sq km. Visitor centres at Khatia and Mukki gates and at Kanha (the largest). Open 0700-1030, 1600-1800. Informative displays, short films, audio-visual shows and books for sale. Recommended minimum stay two nights.
Climate It can get very cold on winter nights. Summer: maximum 43°C, minimum 11°C; winter: maximum 29°C, minimum 2°C. Annual rainfall: 1250 mm; monsoon July- September. The best time to visit is January to June. The park is closed 1 July-31 October.

Wildlife

Kanha has 22 species of mammal, the most easily spotted of which are the three-striped palm squirrel, common langur monkey, jackal, wild boar, cheetal, sambar, Branden barasingha and blackbuck. Less commonly seen are Indian hare, *dhole* (Indian wild dog) and gaur. Rarely seen are Indian fox, sloth bear, striped hyena, tiger (estimated at about 100), leopard, *nilgai* (blue bull), Indian porcupine, wolf (outside park proper) and the Indian pangolin (sometimes called a scaly anteater).

As for birds, Kanha has 230 species recorded. Good vantage points are in the hills where the mixed and bamboo forest harbours many species. Commonly seen species are: leaf warblers, minivets, black ibis, common peafowl, racket-tailed drongo, hawk eagle, red-wattled lapwing, various species of flycatcher, woodpecker, pigeon, dove, parakeet, babbler, mynah, Indian roller, white-breasted kingfisher and grey hornbill.

Viewing

Forest Department guides accompany visitors around the park on mapped-out circuits to see a cross-section of wildlife from a jeep (see box, page 310); there are two viewing sessions a day, the first beginning 30 minutes before sunrise and the second ending 30 minutes after sunset; confirm locally for the exact times. However, one traveller comments that "vehicles chase each other round, their paths crossing and re-crossing and their noisy engines presumably driving the more timid wildlife way back from the tracks". It is better to stop the vehicle on the forest track and in front of the grasslands.

The *sal* forests do not normally allow good viewing. The best areas are the meadows around Kanha. **Bamni Dadar** (Sunset Point) affords a view of the dense jungle and animals typical of the mixed forest zone: sambar, barking deer and chausingha (four- horned antelope). Early morning and late afternoon are ideal times and binoculars are invaluable. *Machans* (viewing platforms/observation towers), are available for use during daylight; those above waterholes (eg **Sravantal**), are recommended.

Elephants, once used for tiger tracking, are now only available for 'joy rides' outside the park at Kisli. MP Tourism hires out Gypsy 4WDs and jeeps from the **Baghira Log Huts**, Kisli in the park (for maximum six), Rs 9 per kilometre. Book the previous day. Petrol is often not available at Kisli; nearest pumps at Mandla.

Bandhavgarh National Park → *For listings, see pages 307-310. Colour map 3, C2.*

Phone code: 07653. Altitude: 800 m.

The park is set in extremely rugged terrain with many hills. The marshes which used to be perennial now support a vast grassland savannah. Though it involves quite a journey you may be rewarded with sighting one of the few tigers; a three-day stay gives you a 90% chance of seeing one. There are also interesting cave shrines scattered around the park, with Brahmi inscriptions dating from the first century BC. You can visit the remains of a fort believed to be 2000 years old where you may spot crag martins and brown rock thrush.

Bandhavgarh (pronounced Bandogarh) is not very far from Rewa, famous as the original home of the white tiger, now only found in zoos. Before becoming a national park in 1968, it was the game reserve of the Maharajas of Rewa. The conservation programme helps to protect wildlife from disease, fire, grazing and poaching.

Ins and outs

This compact park is in the Vindhya hills with a core area of 105 sq km and a buffer zone of 437 sq km. The main entrance and park office is at Tala to the north of the park. The park is open 1 October-30 June. Temperature range: 42-42°C. Rainfall: 1500 mm. For information, contact Field Director, Bandhavgarh Tiger Reserve, Umaria, T07653-222214. » *For admission fees, see box, page 310; for Transport, see page 309.*

Wildlife

The park has a wide variety of game and has a longer 'season' than Kanha. Its main wild beasts are tiger, leopard, sloth bear, gaur, sambar, chital, muntjac, *nilgai*, chinkara and wild pigs. There are over 60 tigers, but they remain very elusive. The flowering and fruit trees attract woodland birds which Include green pigeon, Jerdon's leaf bird, crested serpent eagle and variable hawk eagle.

Viewing

Jeeps are available from dawn to 1000 and from 1600 until dusk when the animals are most active. The short way round is 18 km, the long way is 37 km. The fort, 18 km away, requires a 4WD vehicle; ask at the **White Tiger Forest Lodge** about MP Tourism Jeeps (Rs 9 per kilometre). **Jeep Tours** (up to six passengers) cost around Rs 2000; private hire from Talu is Rs 400 (each entry) after bargaining; vehicle entry is Rs 25 per day.

Forest Department elephants are a good way of seeing wildlife, but present challenges to the photographer; lodges sell vouchers entitling you to a place in the waiting list for 'tiger show', in which visitors are rushed by jeep to an elephant which has tracked a tiger. Some feel the constant traffic of elephants and jeeps is affecting wildlife – "a bit like a circus". Nevertheless, the forest authorities are making efforts to improve the experience for visitors, by encouraging a code of respect for wildlife and the environment and constructing new *machans* (viewing platforms/ observation towers). The watchtower at Bhadrashila is a good place to look for gaur.

Eastern Madhya Pradesh listings

For Sleeping and Eating price codes and other relevant information, see Essentials pages 38-42.

Sleeping

Jabalpur and around *p304, map p304*

B-C Satya Ashoka, Wright Town, T0761-241 5111, www.hotelsatyaashoka.com. 50 rooms, central a/c, restaurant, bar, garden, tours. Recommended.

C Samdariya, off Russell Chowk, T0761-500 4137, www.thesamdariyahotel.com. Modern, quiet, with a/c rooms (some cheaper), good **Woodlands** South Indian restaurant.

C-E Rishi Regency, opposite State Bank of India, T0761-262 1804, www.hotelrishiregency.com. 42 rooms, a/c or air-cooled, restaurant, bar, exchange, free internet.

D Kalchuri Residency (MP Tourism), 20 km from airport, and 2.5 km from railway, T0761-267 8491, www.mptourism.com. 36 clean rooms (14 a/c), good restaurant, bar, good value but close to noisy temple.

D-E Krishna, near Rani Durgavati Museum, T0761-500 4023, www.krishnahotels.com. 25 rooms, some a/c, restaurant, garden, pool.

E Sidharth, Russell Chowk, T0761-240 9247. Some a/c rooms, modern.
G Anand, near Nassdera Bridge. Clean rooms with bath though noisy, helpful staff.

Kanha National Park *p305*

Some hotels offer pick-up from Jabalpur. Most offer the option of a 'Jungle Plan', including all meals, 2 safaris a day, entry fees and a naturalist guide. Reserve rooms in advance; most are open 1 Nov-30 Jun. Private lodges are outside the park and usually offer good discounts in May-Jun when visitors are few.
LL The Baagh Forest Retreat, Village Gudma, Mukki Gate, T07637-296 340, www.thebaagh.com. A sister property to the beautiful **Bagh** in Bharatpur, Rajasthan, this certainly does not disappoint with 16 deluxe cottages and 8 suites. There's a nice swimming pool, multi-cuisine restaurant and barbecue, dinners can also be arranged in special outdoor nooks, guided walks, tribal dancing and bonfires. And giving back to the community, rainwater harvesting at the resort has created new arable land for the local farmers.
LL Kanha Jungle Lodge, Balaghat–Raipur Rd, just south of Mukki, 12 km from Baihar and main road, T07637-216015, www.tiger-resorts.com. Beautifully decorated cottages with private patios overlooking the forest. Modern facilities, attached bathroom, hot water, comfortably furnished. Even a hot water bottle to keep you warm at night.
LL Shergarh, Bahmni Village, T(0)9098-187346. Nov-May. Beautiful new camp run by Anglo-Indian couple, 6 tents surrounding picturesque lake, 2 safaris and all meals included, plus possibilities to birdwatch, visit local markets and even paint elephants. Highly recommended.
L Kipling Camp, near Khatia, T07649-277218, bookings T011-6519 6377, www.kiplingcamp kanha.com. 18 chalets, pleasant ambience and well run, all-inclusive package.
B Wild Chalet Resort, Mocha Village, T07649-277203. Reservations **Asian Adventures**, T0120-255 1963, www.indianwildlife.com. Cottages with shower over looking river, good food and park tours, helpful and efficient manage. Recommended.

Inside the park

Arrive by sunset as no entry after dark. Reservations can be made through **MP Tourism**, Bhopal, T0755-277 4340.
C Baghira Log Huts, Kisli, T07649-277227, www.mptourism.com. 16 rooms, restaurant, cheaper canteen, restaurant.
F Tourist Hostel, Kisli, opposite bus stand, www.mptourism.com. 24 dorm beds (roof may leak), no nets (mosquito ridden), Uninspiring vegetarian meals in a grim canteen on offer.

Bandhavgarh National Park *p306*

LL Bagh Sarai, Parasi village, 6 km from Ghori Gate, T011 3-2957881, www.baghsarai.com. In the same area as Anant Van, with 12 very new and stylish luxury tented bungalows, run by Neeraj Pathania, who has worked on wildlife films for *National Geographic* among others, excellent levels of comfort and service and good wildlife knowledge. Recommended.
LL Samode Safari Lodge, www.samode.com. This stunning addition to the **Samode** chain in Rajasthan is the ultimate in luxury, while still leaving a light footprint on the earth. Designed to blend with the surroundings, no trees were cut down in this new build and there is a good nod to eco-tourism with rainwater harvesting, solar energy and villas made from local materials with local craftsmen. Recommended.
LL Treehouse Hideaway, T(0)8800-637711, www.treehousehideaway.com. World's apart from any tree house you might have had as a kid, these are boutique treehouses made of regularised dark wood with beautiful décor and stunning views. They also have a hide overlooking the water hole. They have a 2-tiered restaurant in a large *mahua* tree. Very special.
LL-AL Bandhavgarh Jungle Lodge, within walking distance of the park gates, T07627-265317, www.tiger-resorts.com/bandhavgarh_jungle_lodge.html. 8 rooms in 2 separate villas with typical Indian village theme, modern facilities with attached bathroom, hot water. Also 13 spacious, comfortable cottages.
A Anant Van, near Ghori Gate, www.anantvan.com. Billed as a homestay, this is an unusual new camp on little-visited side of park, with 2 rustic but comfy mud-brick cottages and 2 tent-cottages, guests can get involved in project working with local villages to regenerate

over-grazed land, eco- and community-friendly. Recommended.

B-C White Tiger Forest Lodge (MP Tourism), Tala, overlooking river, T07627-265366, www.mptourism.com. Reservations: **MP Tourism**, Bhopal, T0755-277 4340. Also **Forest Rest House**. 26 rooms (8 a/c), restaurant (expensive, tiny portions, but good), bar, jeep hire (for residents), modest but good value, the best rooms are in detached cottages by the river, "in need of a good sweep".

D-E Patel Lodge, near **Natural Heritage Lodge**. Rooms with bath, and 3 meals, pleasant location, good food.

E V Patel Resort, off Umaria Rd, T07653-265323. Clean rooms with hot water, meals in garden; 4 rooms, also complete packages.

F Kum-kum, opposite **White Tiger**, T07627-265324. Very basic, 4 large, clean rooms with fan, hot water, excellent vegetarian food, friendly, helpful, well-run, jeep driver Saleem is an expert tiger spotter. Recommended.

Eating

Jabalpur *p304, map p304*

TT Samdariya. International. Smart decor, meals or snacks.

T Indian Coffee House, near clock tower. South Indian, good breakfasts, snacks, coffee.

T Satyam Shivam Sundaram, 1st floor, near **Krishna Hotel**. Air-cooled, vegetarian Indian. Very good value, tasty *thalis*.

Kanha National Park *p305*

Most lodges include meals.

Baghira Log huts, Kisli, have a restaurant and bar (see above). Ask for boiled water specifically; water served at the private lodges is generally filtered. Cold drinks are usually available but fresh fruit is not.

Shopping

Jabalpur *p304, map p304*

Universal Book Service, opposite **India Coffee House**. Interesting stock. Recommended.

Activities and tours

Jabalpur *p304, map p304*

Chadha Travels, **Jackson's Hotel**, T0761-232 2178. Reliable service. Recommended.

Transport

Jabalpur *p304, map p304*

Air **Kingfisher**, www.flykingfisher.com, daily to **Delhi** and 3 times weekly to **Bhopal**.

Bus Services for **Kanha** via Mandla; **MP Tourism** bus from their railway station office at 0800 (6 hrs, Rs 100), is much faster than 1100, Rs 50 (see Kanha, below). **Khajuraho**, 0900. Also to **Allahabad**, **Bhopal**, **Nagpur**, **Varanasi** and other main centres by private coach.

Train Jabalpur is on the Mumbai–Allahabad–Kolkata railway line. **Allahabad**: *Howrah Mail 12322*, 1335, 6½ hrs. **Bhopal**: *Narmada Exp 18234*, 2100, 8 hrs. **Delhi (HN)**: *Mahakosal Exp 12189*, 1805, 19¾ hrs; *Gondwana Exp 12411*, 1550, 15¾ hrs (both stopping at **Agra Cantt** 4-4½ hrs earlier). **Lucknow**: *Chitrakoot Exp 15009*, 1915, 15 hrs. **Kolkata**: *Howrah Mail 12322*, 1335, 22 hrs.

Kanha National Park *p305*

Air **Indian Airlines**, **Kingfisher** and **Jet Airways** fly to Nagpur (226 km) from **Mumbai**, **Kolkata** and **Bhubaneswar**, **Hyderabad**, **Delhi** and **Bhopal**.

Bus Kanha is connected with **Jabalpur**, **Nagpur** and **Bilaspur** by motorable, but often poor roads. From Jabalpur buses daily to **Kisli** (via Mandla and Chiraidongri, 0800, 1100) and **Mukki** (0900).

Jeep Private hire to **Jabalpur** around US$55.

Train **Jabalpur** (173 km) is on the **Mumbai-Allahabad–Kolkata**, **Delhi–Jabalpur** and **Chennai–Varanasi** main lines; or via **Raipur**, 230 km. A wonderful narrow gauge (diesel) train runs between **Mandla** and **Jabalpur**.

Bandhavgarh National Park *p306*

Air Jabalpur is the nearest airport.

Bus From Tala buses go to **Umaria**, **Rewa**, **Satna** and **Katni**, all with rail connections.

Jeep From Tala it's possible to get a jeep seat (Rs 100) to **Satna** (insist on your full seat); poor road, bumpy and dusty 3-hr ride. From **Umaria**: jeep to Tala for park, Rs 500, good for sharing. From **Jabalpur** drive to Shajpura (144 km) then take a country road (fairly hilly) to Umaria. From **Khajuraho** (237 km) 6-7 hrs.

Taxi Available from **Satna** (129 km) 3 hrs, **Katni** and **Umaria**.

Train **Umaria** (35 km) is the nearest station, on the Katni-Bilaspur sector (1 hr by road). Rickshaw to bus stand (Rs 20-30), from where you can get

Carpooling: a new hope for the tiger?

A uniform fee structure applies to Kanha and every other tiger reserve in Madhya Pradesh, but the mercurial nature of the state's Forest Department means that it changes with the frequency and unpredictability of backdrops in a Bollywood dance sequence.

The latest version, aimed at reducing congestion and pollution in the parks, does away with individual entry fees and instead charges a levy on each vehicle that enters the gates, with a strict quota system limiting the number of cars allowed into each park on a given day. (Diesel vehicles older than five years are banned altogether.) A car or jeep carrying up to eight passengers, including the driver, costs Rs 2000 per 'round', or visit, with two rounds being available per day – one beginning just before sunrise, the other ending half an hour after sunset. In addition, each vehicle has to carry a qualified guide, who will charge between Rs 150 and Rs 400 per round depending on their level of experience and wildlife knowledge.

Further fees apply to elephant rides and 'tiger shows' (Rs 600 for an hour), in which you ride on elephant back to see a tiger that has been tracked by forest guards; though touristy these are a uniquely organic way to get close to the quarry. Where watchtowers and hides have been constructed, as in Bandhavgarh, access to them costs Rs 1500 per group for up to four hours.

The greatest innovation to be introduced in the latest wave of changes is the ability to book and pay for your slot weeks in advance on the internet: follow the 'National Parks' link from **www.mponline.gov.in**. One thing that remains firmly entrenched, however, is the dual pricing system, with Indian visitors paying 10-25% of the price paid by foreigners for most fees – Rs 100 for an elephant ride, Rs 150 for a watchtower session, and Rs 500 for a full vehicle. Note that the presence of a single foreign face in a jeep will invoke the higher charge.

Nevertheless, the potential benefits of this scheme are clear: more people in your jeep means a less costly safari, and fewer cars churning up dust in tiger country ought to create a better experience for everyone – not least of all the tigers themselves.

a bus to Tala. Direct train from Umaria to **Delhi**: *Utkal Express 18477*, 2300, 17¼ hrs. To **Bhubaneswar**, *Utkal Express 18478*, 0430, 28¼ hrs. To **Jabalpur**, *Mahakosal Exp 12190*, 0815, 1½ hrs. **Varanasi**, *Sarnath Exp 15159*, 0630, 9 hrs (book well ahead for a berth). From Satna to **Katni**, Mahakoshal Exp 12190, 0650, 1 hr). From Katni to **Umaria**, 0955, 2 hrs.

Directory

Jabalpur *p304, map p304*

Banks **State Bank of India**, Jackson's Hotel advise on getting cash against credit cards.

Kanha National Park *p305*

Banks You can't cash TCs at Kanha, Kisli or Mukki, nor at any of the lodges. The nearest bank for exchange is in Mandla. **Medical services** Basic hospitals are **Mandla Civil Hospital** and **Katra Mission Hospital**. Only basic first aid at Mukki, Mocha and Baihar. **Post** At Mocha and Mukki. **Telephone** At Khatia (non-STD). Nearest STD at Mandla.

Chhattisgarh

→ *Population: under 21 million. Area: 135,000 sq km.*

A mixture of heavy industrial belts and untouched forest, India's second-newest state remains terra incognita for most tourists, and the relative lack of infrastructure makes travelling here a genuine adventure. Though potentially hugely rewarding for anyone interested in tribal culture, parts of the state have in recent years been consumed by violent struggle between Maoist Naxalites and state-sponsored militias. It is imperative to check local conditions and wise to seek advice from your government before travelling beyond the main towns. ▸▸ *For listings, see pages 313-314.*

Background

The land

The hilly and forested region of Chhattisgarh (36 forts), one of the least densely populated and urbanized regions of peninsular India, retains a strongly rural character. The ancient granites, gneisses and sedimentaries which comprise the major geological formations of the state contain an abundance of minerals, from gold and diamonds to coal and iron ore, dolomite and bauxite. Chhattisgarh is estimated to have reserves of nearly 27 billion tonnes of coal and nearly 200 million tonnes of top quality iron ore. Yet there is also fertile agricultural land, and where the brown forest soils have been converted to agricultural land they yield good rice harvests, lending the state the reputation of being India's 'rice bowl'. Forest cover extends up to 40% of the state's area, with 70% of India's *tendu* leaf production, used for making *bidis*.

Industry

Despite the poverty which still characterizes much of Chhattisgarh, the new state already has a wide range of mineral-based industries. It earns approximately US$400 million a year from mining alone and the state has over 75 large or medium scale plants producing such goods as cement, steel, iron and rails. The chief minister, Raman Singh of the right-wing Hindu BJP, has followed his predecessor's lead in pushing for large-scale multinational investment in the mining industry. Chhattisgarh is also a significant power surplus state, and is continuing to develop its thermal electricity capacity to export to other states.

Modern Chhattisgarh

Chhattisgarh became an independent state on 1 November 2000, though the first demand for the creation of a state for the region can be traced back to 1925. It comprises the largely tribal districts of the southeast corner of Madhya Pradesh. Some suggested that the long-standing tribal demand for a separate state was finally ceded by Madhya Pradesh because of the difficulty of controlling the violent Naxalites, groups of revolutionary guerrillas. The political and economic challenge facing the young state's government is huge, but its policy of arming a counter militia, the Salwa Judum (Peace March), and granting it the powers of an emergency police force, has achieved little but to entirely polarize rural tribal communities between the Naxalites and those who violently oppose them. Parts of the state have effectively become consumed by a civil war in which the rule of law has dissolved. Many villages have been depopulated, their inhabitants forced to move to refugee camps in fear of being seen by either side to be supporters of the other.

The challenge to Chhattisgarh is equally obvious in terms of social and economic development. Literacy rates are among the lowest in India, with 43% literate across the state as a whole, 58% of men but only 28% of women, and Bastar District having over 80% still illiterate. Half the households have no drinking water, only one third have any electricity connection, over 40% of girls are married before they are 20 and infant mortality is still 84%.

Exploring Chhattisgarh → *For listings, see pages 313-314.*

Raipur → *Colour map 6, A3. Phone code: 0771. Population: 605,000.*

Raipur is the rapidly growing state capital of Chhattisgarh, and also the regional transport centre. Water tanks and a temple date from the 17th and 18th centuries. Jai Stambh Chowk (Chhattisgarh Circle) is generally regarded to be the centre of town with the Head Post Office, State Bank and several hotels close by. The **tourist office** ⓘ *Chhattisgarh Hotel, Teli Bandha (4 km), T0771-506 6415, www.chhattisgarhtourism.net*, provides minimal information.

Durg → *Colour map 6, A2.*

Durg, west of Raipur on the NH6, is now joined to the Hindustan steel works town at **Bhilainagar**. Durg is the only place with reasonable accommodation in the area.

Kawardha → *Colour map 6, A2.*

Kawardha is a small town in the Rajnandgaon region of Chhattisgarh. In this remote area Maharaja Vishwaraj Singh welcomes visitors to his late 1930s palace. It provides a delightfully quiet unspoiled contrast with India's big cities and with the much busier tourist route of Rajasthan's 'palace circuit'. The Radha Krishna family temple with underground rooms is nearby. You can visit the 11th-century Chandela-style temples at Bhoramdev with beautiful carvings, step wells, enjoy excellent birdwatching or explore the area's natural beauty on foot with the Yuvraj. The Gonds and the gentle Baiga tribe continue to follow a primitive lifestyle in the surrounding forests; ecologically sensitive visits are arranged.

Bilaspur → *Colour map 6, A3.*

Unless you have a passionate interest in cement production, or have chosen a particularly circuitous train routing to reach a cricket match, there is little reason to stop here. However, if forced to stay overnight there are a number of reasonable hotels and an excellent restaurant (at **Shyama Hotel**) about 2 km from the railway station.

Kanker → *Colour map 6, A3.*

Some 140 km south of Raipur, Kanker is a district headquarters town, with some fine century-old colonial buildings. It nestles by a tributary of the Mahanadi River, amidst unspoilt forests and hills, the home of several tribal groups who continue to practise age-old crafts and traditions. Kanker's royal family, who trace their ancestors back to the 12th century, welcomes guests to their palace to share their region's culture and history.

Bastar District

Lying in the southern tip of Chhattisgarh, Bastar district is home to several indigenous tribal groups in one of the state's more densely forested areas. There are two national parks within driving distance of Jagdalpur, the district headquarters, which also serves as a useful base for visiting the region's tribal areas. To visit the area, car hire costs around Rs 3000 per day from Kanker Palace.

Jagdalpur, 160 km south of Kanker, is the centre of the tribal heartland of Bastar where you can see the Gond, Halba, Muriya, Madia, Dhurwa and Bhattra people. *Mrignayani* emporium collects and sells their arts and crafts. There is a small **tribal museum** maintained by the Anthropological Society of India, and a **tourist office** ⓘ *Snajay Market, T07782-221686.*

Situated 35 km south west of Jagdalpur, in the transition zone marking the natural southern limit of *sal* and the northern limit of teak, **Kanger Valley National Park** is a narrow stretch of mixed virgin forest, playing host to tiger, panther, sambhar, wild pig, flying squirrel as well as a wide range of reptiles and birds. Within the park the **Kailash** and **Kutumsar Gupha** are attractive limestone caves which are popular with visitors. Forest guides are available. The 30-m

Tirathgarh Falls, 39 km southwest of Jagdalpur, sees the Kanger River descend the valley in a series of steps. Overnight stay is possible in basic forest rest houses at Kutumsar, Netanar and Teerathgarh. Contact Director Kangerghati NP, Jagdalpur, T07782-222261.

Indravati National Park

This park along the Indravati River was designated a Project Tiger reserve in 1982. The dense monsoon forest interspersed with grassy glades is known as ancient Dandakaranya, cited in the *Ramayana* as the place where Rama was exiled. Apart from increasing tiger protection, the park is seen as the best reserve for the wild buffalo (*Bubalus amee*) and an ideal alternative home for the endangered Branden barasingha (hardground swamp deer), which is only found in Kanha further north. The NH43 is a good, scenic road, ideal for seeing the Bastar tribal area. Following the Indravati west from Jagdalpur, the popular waterfalls at **Chitrakote** (38 km) drop some 30 m in a horseshoe curve and provide an attractive diversion.

Barnawapara Sanctuary

ⓘ *Permission to enter from DFO, Wildlife Division, Old Chhattisgarh College Campus, Raipur, T0771-242 5064.*

Occupying 245 sq km in the northern part of Mahasamund District, near Sirpur, this sanctuary offers the chance to see several species of deer in the hilly *sal* forest as well as sloth bear and bison; tigers and panthers are present though rarely seen. Migratory birds are attracted by artificial waterholes in the winter. **Dev Travels** (see Activities and tours, below) organizes tours. The best time to visit is from November to April.

You can stay in forest rest houses on the outskirts of the sanctuary or inside at Barnawapara which has two basic rooms.

Chhattisgarh listings

For Sleeping and Eating price codes and other relevant information, see Essentials pages 38-42.

Sleeping

Raipur *p312*

There are several **F-G** hotels near railway station, although earplugs may be needed for a good sleep.

A-B Hotel Grand International, behind Gurudwara, Station Rd, T0771-403 9401, www.hotelgrandinternational.com. Top notch hotel with all the mod cons and some nice decorative features. There's a multi-cuisine restaurant and bar.

A-B Mayura, GE Rd, near Raj Talkies, 2 km from stations, T0771-253 6001, www.hotelmayuraraipur.com. 50 good rooms, central a/c, TV, excellent **Kapri** restaurant, airport pickup.

B-C Piccadilly, Mohaba Bazar, 5 km from town towards Durg, T0771-257 5210. 54 comfortable rooms, a/c, attached bath with tubs, TV, airport/station pickup, pool (roadside), friendly staff, well run, out-of-town location is the only drawback.

B-D Aditya, KK Rd, T0771-403 2941, www.hoteladityaraipur.com. 34 decent rooms, central a/c, TV.

E-F Chhattisgarh, Tehbanda, 4 km from centre towards airport, T0771-244 2769, visitcg@mantrafreenet.com. 21 rooms, some a/c, hot bath, TV, restaurant.

F-G Radhika, Jai Stambh Chowk, T0771-223 3806. Rooms at front suffer from road noise. 26 rather scruffy rooms with TV and bath, some a/c, good restaurant.

Durg *p312*

E-F Sagar, opposite railway station, T0788-323 465. Has 60 clean rooms with bath (some a/c), a/c restaurant, friendly. Recommended but often full.

E-F Sheela, Indira Market, T0788-322 265. Clean, well-furnished rooms (some a/c), good a/c restaurant, bar, friendly. Cycle-rickshaws offer free transfer from station (paid by hotel).

Kawardha p312

AL-A Palace Kawardha, Kawardha 120 km from Raipur in Chattisgar, T07741-232085, www.kawardhapalace.com. 5 large suites with pleasant verandas, Western baths, imposing Durbar Hall, attractive gardens, a unique experience visiting tribal settlements, temples, jeep excursions, short treks into surrounding hills (5-8 km, 2½-5 hrs), longer treks into the jungle with advance notice, very warm hospitality. Reservations essential.

Kanker p312

AL Royal Palace, in a garden setting, T07868-222005, www.kankerpalace.com. Once residency of British Agent, has 3 modern suites but aims to retain 'earthy flavour' with cottages on site too. Maharajkumar Surya Pratap Deo arranges interesting excursions to explore both the natural surroundings as well as the area's rich tribal heritage. Reserve well ahead.

Bastar District p312

For cheaper options look out for **Akash**, **Anand** and **Athithi**.

AL Royal Bastar Farm, in a village near Jagdalpur, T07782-242285, www.royalbasrar farm.com. Owned by the Kanker royal family, it has 3 comfortable cottages for visitors who wish to experience rural living with a difference (advance notice needed).

E-FHotel Akansha Deluxe, Jagdalpur, T07782-225335. Rooms, some a/c, and a restaurant.

Activities and tours

Raipur p312

Dev Travels, behind Netaji Subhash Stadium, Ahmedji Colony, T0771-242 1303, www.dev travelindia.com. Professional agency, can arrange cars for visiting tribal areas, wildlife sanctuaries, etc.

Oberoi Tours & Travels, KK Rd, opposite **Aditya**, T0771-253 9977, oberoitours@hotmail.com. Efficient air ticketing office.

Transport

Raipur p312

Air Mana Airport, 15 km southeast of town. Taxis take around 30 mins to the centre; the better hotels provide free pickup with advance notice. **Kingfisher** and **Indigo** fly to Raipur, www.flykingfisher.com and www.goindigo.in. Daily flights to **Delhi** via **Jabalpur** or **Nagpur**, and to **Mumbai** via **Bhubaneswar**.

Bus New Bus Stand, 3 km from the railway station, has services to all towns in Chhattisgarh and Madhya Pradesh.

Train Enquiry, T0771-252 8130/131. **Ahmedabad**: *Howrah Ahmedabad Exp 12834*, 1345, 24 hrs. **Allahabad**: *Sarnath Exp 15159*, 2120, 16½ hrs (to **Varanasi**, 20½ hrs). **Kolkata** (**H**): *Gitanjali Exp 12859*, 2340, 14 hrs; *Mumbai Howrah Mail 12809*, 1640, 15 hrs. **Mumbai** (**CST**): *Gitanjali Exp 12860*, 0230, 19½ hrs; *Howrah Mumbai Mail 12810*, 0905, 21½ hrs. **New Delhi**: *Chhattisgarh Exp 18237*, 1610, 30½ hrs (via **Bhopal**, 16 hrs).

Kawardha p312

Bus and car Express buses run from **Raipur** and **Bilaspur**, where cars can also be hired, or ask for pick- up from either city (4½ hrs) or **Kanha National Park** (5½ hrs).

Jeep Ask at **Palace Kawardha**, **Raipur** US$40, **Kanha** US$50.

Train From **Raipur** (140 km) and **Bilaspur** (124 km).

Directory

Raipur p312

Banks ICICI, opposite Raj Kumar College, GE Rd. Exchanges cash and TCs, also ATM. **State Bank of India**, Jai Stambh Chowk. Cash and TCs. **Internet** At **Planet Café**, opposite Old Bus Stand, has good connection. **Medical services** **Government Medical College Hospital**, T0771-251 1101. Private **MMI**, T0771- 241 2310. **Post** **Head Post Office**, Jai Stambh Chowk.

Rajasthan

Contents

Footprint features

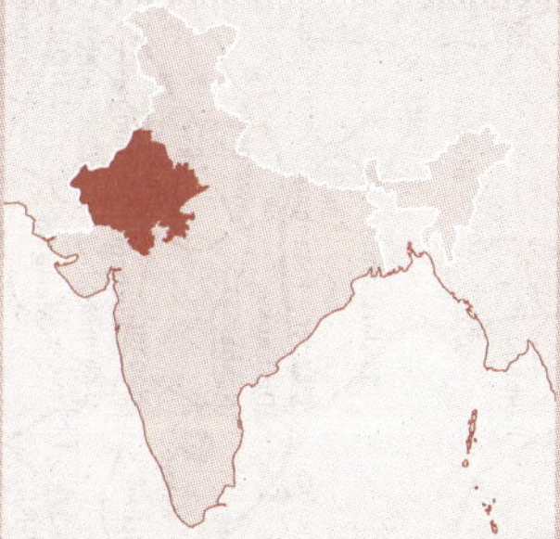

At a glance

Getting around Trains, buses and 'sleeper' buses cover all major towns. A car is worthwhile to explore more obscure areas.

Time required Infinite. Minimum 2-3 days each for Jaipur, Jodhpur, Jaisalmer, Udaipur, Mt Abu, Bundi and Ranthambhore.

Weather Desert climate: hot days and cool nights most of the year; summer is stiflingly hot.

When not to go The heat in May and Jun can be draining.

★ Don't miss ...

1 Sundown at Nahargarh (Tiger Fort), page 328.
2 Juna Mahal, page 358.
3 A stroll through Bundi, page 378.
4 Meherangarh, the Majestic Fort, page 386.
5 Jaisalmer, fairytale fort in the desert, page 399.
6 Camel safari in Kakoo, page 441.

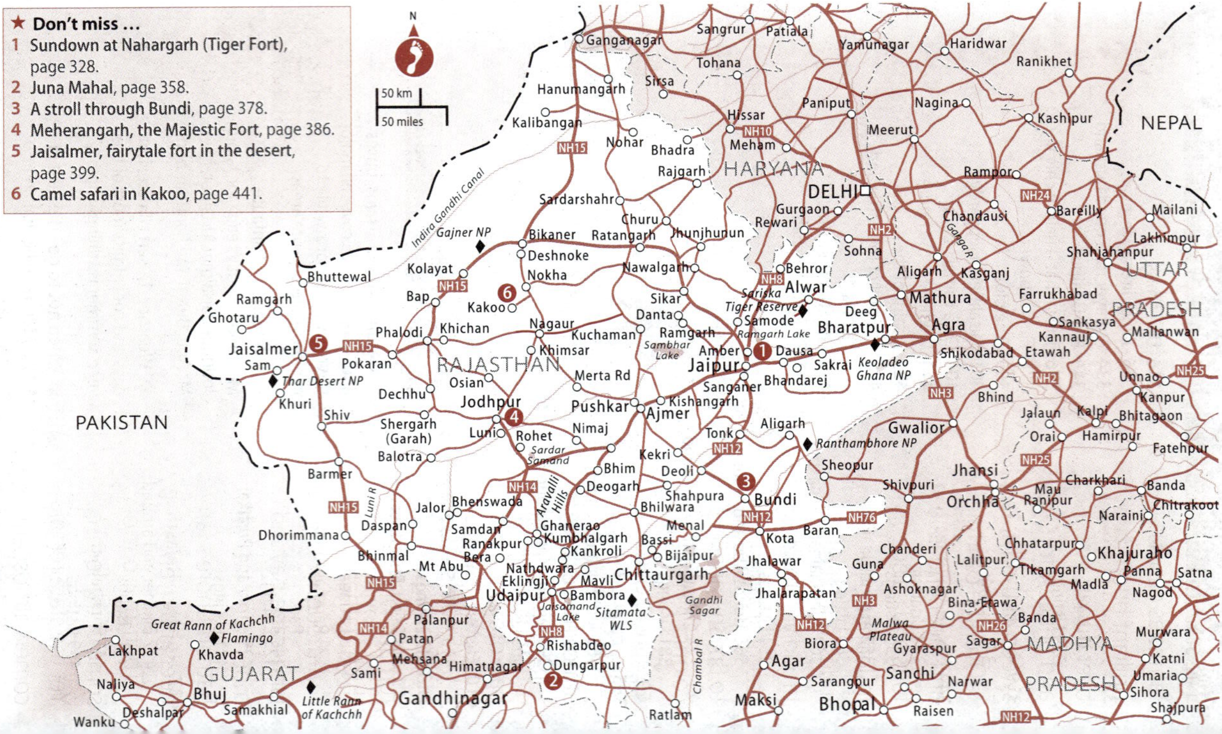

The state of Rajasthan exceeds even the most far-fetched fantasies of what India might be: women dazzle in swathes of brilliant bright fabrics; luxuriously mustachioed men drive camels over dunes; tigers and leopards prowl through ancient forests; and princely forts and palaces loom up from the crushingly hot sweep of the Thar Desert.

Over the centuries, and in testament to their tradition of chivalry and independence, Rajasthan's rulers have built scores of evocative forts and palaces, such as those at Samode, Deogarh and Udaipur. In Jodhpur, the majestic Meherangarh sits high above a moat of iridescent blue houses, while the far-flung wonder of Jaisalmer rises proudly from the surrounding sands. But much of Rajasthan's more recent architectural bounty – and its predilection for pomp – is due to British imperial policy towards the state's then maharajas. The colonial regime allowed them great wealth but little power, thus creating a civilization characterized by great extravagance. It is this surfeit of opulence that you'll see everywhere so sadly but atmospherically crumbling into decay.

Rajasthan's people are as theatrical as their architectural backdrop, and in today's cities and villages you'll encounter an eye-popping cast of characters: everyone from suave polo-playing Rajputs to tall, peasant camel-drivers in incandescent turbans with a gold hoop in each ear, and tribal women whose thick, gathered skirts are a shock of colour against the sands.

Although it is synonymous with desert dunes, Rajasthan has landscape beyond the Thar: it holds some of the world's oldest mountains; has green, rolling hills; and dense jungle that hides Rathambhore's famous tigers, along with monkeys, leopards, deer and hyenas.

Tourism is one of the main engines of Rajasthan's economy, and some of the local colour can seem correspondingly stage-managed. Yet the state remains a sumptuous feast for the senses with many corners almost entirely untouched by tourist development.

Background → *Population: 56.47 mllion. Area: 342,000 sq km.*

The land

Geography Running like a spine through Rajasthan, the Aravalli Hills are some of the oldest mountains in the world. A series of jagged, heavily folded ranges, they stretch from Mount Abu in the southwest (1720 m) to Kota and Bundi in the east. In the northwest is the forbidding Thar Desert, with its shifting sand dunes and crushingly high summer temperatures. In the south the average elevation is higher (330-1150 m). In the northeast the landscape forms part of the nearly flat Yamuna drainage basin.

Wildlife The natural jungle is ideal territory for tigers, leopards, sloth bear, sambhar (large deer) and chital (smaller spotted deer), now normally restricted to game reserves. Nilgai (blue bulls), blackbuck and ravine deer are fairly numerous on the plains and there's a great variety of birds. Bharatpur and other low-lying swampy areas in the southeast are popular winter grounds for migratory birds from Siberia and Northern Europe.

Climate Rajasthan is one of the driest regions in India. Apart from in the hills, summer temperatures are very high with a maximum of 46°C and an average from May to August of 38°C. In winter the daily maximum in most low-lying areas is 22-28°C and the minimum 8-14°C. January nights in the desert can feel very cold. Over three-quarters of the rainfall occurs between July and September.

History

Early origins Humans lived along the **Banas River** 100,000 years ago. **Harappan** and post-Harappan (third to second millennium BC) cultures have been discovered, as at Kalibangan where pottery has been dated to 2700 BC. The Mauryan Emperor Asoka controlled this part of the state in the third century BC, to be succeeded by the Bactrian Greeks (second century BC), the Sakas (Scythians, second to fourth centuries AD), the Guptas (fourth to sixth centuries) and the Huns (sixth century). Rajput dynasties rose from the seventh to the 11th centuries and until the end of the 12th century they controlled much of North India.

Rajputs Rajputs claimed to be the original *kshatriyas* (warriors) of the ancient *varna* system, born out of the fire offering of the Gods on Mount Abu. They were probably descended from the Huns and Scythians who had entered India in the sixth century, and they modelled themselves on Rama (the hero of the *Ramayana* epic), seeing themselves as protectors of the Hindu *dharma* against invaders. The Brahmins made considerable efforts to give them royal lineages and accorded them *kshatriya* status. The Rajputs went to great lengths to insist on their *kshatriya* status – a means of demonstrating to their subjects that not only was it foolhardy, but also sacrilegious to oppose their authority. Associated with this was promotion of those qualities ascribed to the martial castes: chivalry, bravery and unquestioning loyalty.

The Mughals and the Rajputs Rather than engage in costly campaigns to crush the Rajputs, the Mughal Emperor **Akbar** (ruled 1556-1605) sought conciliation. Many Rajput princes were given high office in return for loyalty and Akbar sealed this important strategic alliance by marrying a Rajput princess, **Jodha Bai**, the daughter of the Maharaja of Amber. The relationship between the Rajput princes and the Mughals did not always remain so close, and in the later Mughal period several Rajput princes sought to secure their autonomy from Mughal rule. Such autonomy was brought to an end by the spread of British colonial power. After the quelling of the Mutiny in 1858 and establishment of the British Indian Empire, the Rajput Princely States gained in show of power, with 21-gun salutes, royal polo matches and durbars, just as they lost its reality.

Culture

Tribals Today tribals constitute 12% of the state population, nearly double the national average. The Bhils and Minas are the largest groups, but Sahariyas, Damariyas, Garasias and Gaduliya Lohars are all important. The tribes share many common traits but differ in their costumes and jewellery; their gods, fairs and festivals also set them apart from one another. The **Bhils** comprise nearly 40% of Rajasthan's tribal population with their stronghold in Baneshwar. *Bhil* (meaning 'bow') describes their original skill at hunting. Physically short, stocky and dark with broad noses and thick lips, the Bhils once lived off roots, leaves and fruits of the forest and the increasingly scarce game. Most now farm land and keep cattle, goats and sheep, or work as day labourers. Thousands congregate near the confluence of the Mahi and Som rivers for the Baneshwar fair in January and February. The **Minas** are Rajasthan's largest and most widely spread tribal group. Tall, with an athletic build, light brown complexion and sharp features, men wear a loincloth round the waist, a waistcoat and a brightly coloured turban while the women wear a *ghaghra* (long gathered skirt), a *kurti-kanchali* (small blouse) and a large scarf. Most Minas are cultivators who measure their wealth in cattle and other livestock. Like other tribal groups they have a tradition of giving grain, clothes, animals and jewellery to the needy.

Language The principal language is Rajasthani, a close relative of Hindi.

Crafts **Bandhani** is an ancient technique of tie-dyeing whereby the fabric is pinched together in selected places, tied round with twine or thread and then dyed. **Miniature paintings** on old paper or silk, use natural colours derived from minerals, rocks and vegetables and follow old techniques; their quality varies. The princely states were important patrons of medieval miniature painting and several schools developed in different areas drawing from local traditions and combining them with Mughal art. '**Jaipur Blue Pottery**' uses a coarse grey clay that is quite brittle even when fired. It is then decorated with floral and geometric patterns along Persian lines utilizing rich ultra- marines, turquoise and lapis.

Modern Rajasthan

After Independence the region's 18 princely states were ultimately absorbed into the new state of Rajasthan on 1 November 1956. The successors of royal families have lost power but retain considerable political influence. The palaces, many of them converted to hotels with varying degrees of success, maintain the memory of princely India. In its political life Rajasthan has alternated between Congress- or BJP-led state governments. Its current State assembly is dominated by the Indian National Congress Party. The state Chief Minister is Ashok Gehlot, who originally held the post between 1998 and 2003 and started his current term in December 2008. In the 2009 Lok Sabha elections Congress won 20 of the 25 seats.

Economy Rajasthan is one of the least densely populated and poorest states in India. Primarily an agricultural and pastoral economy, it does have good mineral resources. Tourism makes a large contribution to the regional economy. The main industries are textiles, the manufacture of rugs and woollen goods, vegetable oil and dyes. Heavy industry includes the construction of railway rolling stock, copper and zinc smelting. The chemical industry also produces caustic soda, calcium carbides and sulphuric acid, fertilizer, pesticides and insecticides. There is a rapidly expanding light industry which includes television assembly. Traditional handicrafts such as pottery, jewellery, marble work, embossed brass, block printing, embroidery and decorative painting are now very good foreign exchange earners.

Jaipur and around

The sandstone 'pink city' of Jaipur, Rajasthan's capital, is the heady gateway to the state. Its poetic landmarks and icons of antiquity, such as the Palace of the Winds, lie amid the overwhelming sprawl that characterizes most large Indian metropolises galloping towards modernity. Outside the city lies a tranquil agrarian landscape, in which there are many hunting lodges, palaces and forts.

Jaipur

→ *Colour map 2, B5. Phone code: 0141. Population: 2,600,000.*

The 'pink city', gateway to the state, is on the popular 'Golden Triangle' route (Delhi–Agra–Jaipur–Delhi), which, for many short-haul visitors, is their only experience of Rajasthan. The steady stream of tourists means the city has to make little effort to attract visitors; as a result its pastel-hued buildings are not what they used to be and many of the sights are poorly maintained. Nonetheless it's a worthwhile stopover in itself, as well as a staging post for the surrounding area. The old city, with its bazars, palaces and havelis, *along with a couple of forts and the ancient city of Amber nearby, are well worth a wander. Knotted, narrow streets hold cupboard-sized workshops where elderly women dash out clothes on rusty Singers; men energetically stuff mattresses with piles of rags; boys mend bicycles next to old men rolling pellets of paste into sweets; whole families carve table legs or hammer bed headboards out of sheet metal; and 'gold men' leave the old city's textile houses sprinkled with metallic pigment from a day's work rubbing the powder into fabric patterned with resin glue. Escape the bustle and head up to the Tiger Fort (Nahargarh) for sunset, where proud peacocks pick among the ruins and monkeys scamper about in the twilight against the backdrop of Man Sagar Lake and its Jal Mahal (Water Palace).* ▸▸ *For listings, see pages 329-338.*

Ins and outs

Getting there Sanganer Airport, 15 km south of town, has flights from Ahmedabad, Chennai, Delhi, Jodhpur, Mumbai, Rajkot and Udaipur. Airport buses, taxis and auto- rickshaws take 30 minutes to the centre. The railway station has links with most major cities. The Main Bus Terminal at Sindhi Camp is used by state and private buses. Buses from Delhi use the dramatically improved NH8; the journey now takes under four hours by car. The alternative Gurgaon–Alwar–Jaipur route is more interesting but much slower. Most hotels are a short auto-rickshaw ride away from the station and bus terminal.

Getting around The walled Old City, to the northeast of town, holds most of the sights and the bazar. Take a rickshaw to the area, then explore on foot. What few attractions the new town holds are spread out so it's best explored by rickshaw, bus or taxi. There is also a new metro system under construction which should ease the traffic above ground. ▸▸ *See Transport, page 337.*

Tourist information **Government of India Tourism** ⓘ *Hotel Khasa Kothi, T0141-237 2200, Rajasthan, Paryatan Bhavan, Tourist Hotel, Mirza Ismail Rd, T0141-511 0598*, also has counters at the **Railway Station** ⓘ *T0141-231 5714*, and **Central Bus Stand** ⓘ *T0141-506 4102*. Guides for four to eight hours cost Rs 250-400 (Rs 100 extra for French, German, Japanese, Spanish). *'Jaipur for Aliens'*, a free miniature guidebook created by the owner of the **Hotel Pearl Palace**, has regularly updated information on transport and attractions; available at the hotel (see Sleeping, page 332).

History

Jaipur ('City of Victory') was founded in 1727 by **Maharaja Jai Singh II**, a Kachhawaha Rajput, who ruled from 1699 to 1744. He had inherited a kingdom under threat not only from the last great Mughal Emperor Aurangzeb, but also from the Maratha armies of Gujarat and Maharashtra. Victories over the Marathas and diplomacy with Aurangzeb won back the favour

Jaipur

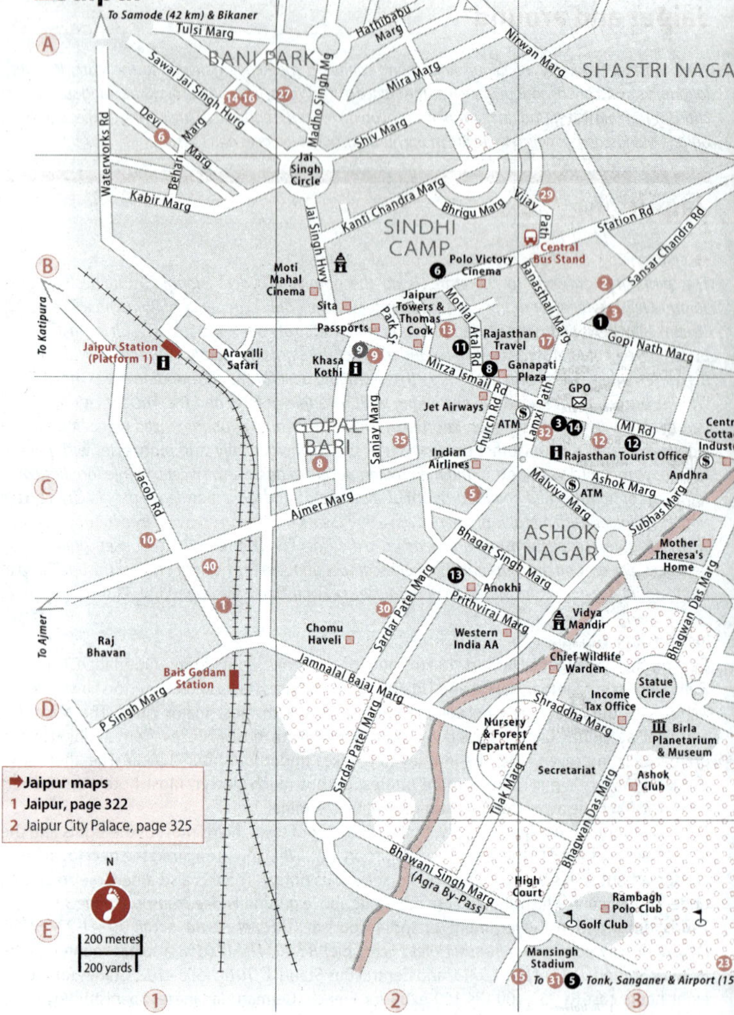

➡Jaipur maps
1 Jaipur, page 322
2 Jaipur City Palace, page 325

Sleeping

Alsisar Haveli **2** *B3*
Arya Niwas **3** *B3*
Atithi **13** *B2*
Bissau Palace **4** *A4*
Chirmi Palace **5** *C2*
Dera Rawatsar **29** *B3*
Diggi Palace **7** *C4*
Gangaur **9** *B2*
General's Retreat **30** *D2*
Hari Mahal Palace **1** *D1*
Jai Mahal Palace **10** *C1*
Jas Vilas **18** *A1*
Karauli House **31** *E3*
LMB **11** *B5*
Madhuban **16** *A1*
Mansingh Tower **17** *B3*
Nana-ki-Haveli **20** *D5*
Narain Niwas **33** *E4*
Pearl Palace & Peacock Restaurant **35** *C2*
Pearl Palace Heritage **8** *C2*
Pink Sun & Cocoon **12** *C3*
Rajasthan Palace **37** *E5*
Rajvilas **38** *C6*
Rambagh Palace **23** *E3*
Samode Haveli Gangapole **42** *A6*
Santha Bagh **24** *E4*
Shahar Palace **40** *C1*
Shahpura House **6** *A1*
Tourist **32** *C3*

Umaid Bhawan **27** *A2*
Umaid Mahal **14** *A1*
Youth Hostel **15** *E2*

Eating
BMB **2** *C5*
Chaitanya **1** *B3*
Chokhi Dhani **5** *E2*
Copper Chimney **3** *C3*
Dasaprakash **12** *C3*
Four Seasons **13** *C2*
Handi **14** *C3*
Kanji **6** *B2*
Lassiwala **4** *C4*
Mohan **11** *B2*
Natraj **10** *C4*
Niros & Book Corner **7** *C4*
Suriya India **8** *B2*
Surya Mahal **15** *C4*

Bars & clubs
Sheesha **9** *B2*

of the ageing Mughal, so that the political stability that Maharaja Jai Singh was instrumental in creating was protected, allowing him to pursue his scientific and cultural interests. Jaipur is very much a product of his intellect and talent. A story relates an encounter between the **Emperor Aurangzeb** and the 10-year-old Rajput prince. When asked what punishment he deserved for his family's hostility and resistance to the Mughals, the boy answered "Your Majesty, when the groom takes the bride's hand, he confers lifelong protection. Now that the Emperor has taken my hand, what have I to fear?" Impressed by his tact and intelligence, Aurangzeb bestowed the title of *Sawai* (one and a quarter) on him, signifying that he would be a leader.

Jai Singh loved mathematics and science, and was a keen student of astronomy, via Sanskrit translations of Ptolemy and Euclid. A brilliant Brahmin scholar from Bengal, Vidyadhar Bhattacharya, helped him to design the city. Work began in 1727 and it took four years to build the main palaces, central square and principal roads. The layout of streets was based on a mathematical grid of nine squares representing the ancient Hindu map of the universe, with the sacred Mount Meru, home of Siva, occupying the central square. In Jaipur the royal palace is at the centre. The three-by-three square grid was modified by relocating the northwest square in the southeast, allowing the hill fort of Nahargarh (Tiger Fort) to overlook and protect the capital. At the southeast and southwest corners of the city were squares with pavilions and ornamental fountains. Water for these was provided by an underground aqueduct with outlets for public use along the streets. The main streets are 33 yds wide (33 is auspicious in Hinduism). The pavements were deliberately wide to promote the free flow of pedestrian traffic and the shops were also a standard size. Built with ancient Hindu rules of town planning in mind, Jaipur was advanced for its time. Yet many of its buildings suggest a decline in architectural power and originality. The architectural historian Giles Tillotson argues that the "traditional architectural details lack vigour and depth and are also flattened so that they become relief sculpture on the building's surface, and sometimes they are simply drawn on in white outline".

In addition to its original buildings, Jaipur has a number of examples of late 19th- century buildings which marked an attempt to revive Indian architectural skills. A key figure in this movement was Sir Samuel Swinton Jacob. A school of art was founded in 1866 by a group of English officers employed by Maharaja Sawai Madho Singh II to encourage an interest in Indian tradition and its development. In February 1876 the Prince of Wales visited Jaipur, and work on the Albert Hall, now the Central Museum, was begun to a design of Jacob. It was the first of a number of construction projects in which Indian craftsmen and designers were employed in both building and design. This ensured that the Albert Hall was an extremely striking building in its own right. The opportunities for training provided under Jacob's auspices encouraged a new school of Indian architects and builders. One of the best examples of their work is the Mubarak Mahal (1900), now Palace Museum, designed by Lala Chiman Lal.

A good insight into the worlds of maharajahs and the Jaipur of yesteryear is the memoir of Maharani Gayatri Devi, A Princess Remembers.

Sights

Hawa Mahal

ⓘ *Enter from Tripolia Bazar, Sat-Thu 0900-1630, Rs 5, cameras Rs 30, video Rs 70; for the best views accept invitations from shop owners on upper floors across the street.*

The 'Palace of the Winds' (circa 1799) forms part of the east wall of the City Palace complex and is best seen from the street outside. Possibly Jaipur's most famous building, this pink sandstone façade of the palace was built for the ladies of the harem by Sawai Pratap Singh. The five storeys stand on a high podium with an entrance from the west. The elaborate façade contains 953 small casements in a huge curve, each with a balcony and crowning arch. The windows enabled *hawa* (cool air) to circulate and allowed the women who were secluded in the *zenana* to watch processions below without being seen. The museum has second-century BC utensils and old sculpture.

City Palace (1728-1732)

ⓘ 0930-1700 (last entry 1630). Foreigners Rs 300 (includes still camera and a good audio guide), Indians Rs 35 (camera Rs 50 extra); includes Sawai Man Singh II Museum and Jaigarh Fort, valid for 1 week. Video (unnecessary) Rs 200; doorkeepers expect tips when photographed. Photography in galleries prohibited.

The City Palace occupies the centre of Jaipur, covers one seventh of its area and is surrounded by a high wall – the *Sarahad*. Its style differs from conventional Rajput fort palaces in its separation of the palace from its fortifications, which in other Rajput buildings are integrated in one massive interconnected structure. In contrast the Jaipur Palace has much more in common with Mughal models, with its main buildings scattered in a fortified campus. To find the main entrance, from the Hawa Mahal go north about 250 m along the Sireh Deori Bazar past the Town Hall (Vidhan Sabha) and turn left through an arch – the *Sireh Deori* (boundary gate). Pass under a second arch – the *Naqqar* Darwaza (drum gate) – into Jaleb Chowk, the courtyard which formerly housed the palace guard. Today it is where coaches park. This is surrounded by residential quarters which were modified in the 19th century under Sawai Ram Singh II. A gateway to the south leads to the Jantar Mantar, the main palace buildings and museum and the Hawa Mahal.

In Jai Singh's day, the buildings were painted in a variety of colours, including grey with white borders. Pink, a traditional colour of welcome, was used in 1853 in honour of the visit by Prince Albert, and the colour is still used.

Mubarak Mahal The main entrance leads into a large courtyard at the centre of which is the Mubarak Mahal, faced in white marble. Built in 1890, originally as a guesthouse for the Maharaja, the Mubarak Mahal is a small but immaculately conceived two-storeyed building, designed on the same cosmological plan in miniature as the city itself – a square divided into a three by three square grid, see page 324.

The **Textile and Costume Museum** on the first floor has fine examples of fabrics and costumes from all over India, including some spectacular wedding outfits, as well as musical instruments and toys from the royal nursery. In the northwest corner of the courtyard is the

2 Jaipur City Palace

➡Jaipur maps
1 Jaipur, page 322
2 Jaipur City Palace, page 325

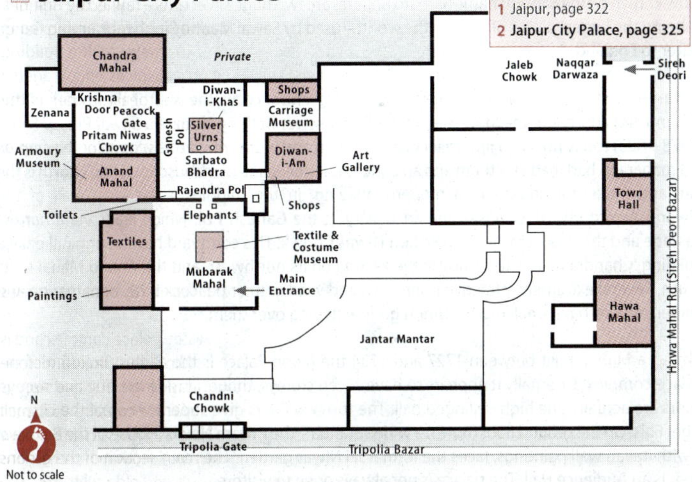

Jaipur literary festival

Started in 2006, the Jaipur Literary Festival is an exciting gathering of writers and musicians with readings, workshops and performances. The Creative Directors are William Dalrymple and Namita Gokhale and speakers have included – Vikram Seth, Pico Iyer, Hanif Kureshi and Simon Shama. At the last event in 2011, the local news estimated that 50,000 people had passed through the gates to hear the authors who included Patrick French, author of the new *India: A Portait*, Nobel laureate Orhan Pamuk, Booker winner Kiran Desai and founder of *Tehelka* magazine Tarun Tejpal. All held in the beautiful and relaxed atmosphere of **Hotel Diggi Palace**. There are music events in the evening including performances from musicians all over India and the world - like Susheela Raman, Natacha Atlas and DJ Cheb I Sabbah. The 2012 event will run from the 20-24 January. For more information on this fantastic new annual event check out http://jaipurliteraturefestival.org.

Armoury Museum containing an impressive array of weaponry – pistols, blunderbusses, flintlocks, swords, rifles and daggers, as well as some fascinating paintings on the way in. This was originally the common room of the harem. From the north-facing first-floor windows you can get a view of the Chandra Mahal (see below). Just outside the Armoury Museum is **Rajendra Pol**, a gate flanked by two elephants, each carved from a single block of marble, which leads to the inner courtyard. There are beautifully carved alcoves with delicate arches and *jali* screens and a fine pair of patterned brass doors.

Diwan-i-Khas (Sarbato Bhadra) The gateway leads to the courtyard known variously as the Diwan-i-Am, the Sarbato Bhadra or the Diwan-i-Khas Chowk. Today, the building in its centre is known as the Diwan-i-Khas (circa 1730). Originally the Diwan-i-Am, it was reduced to the hall of private audience (Diwan-i-Khas) when the new Diwan-i-Am was built to its southeast at the end of the 18th century. The courtyard itself reflects the overwhelming influence of Mughal style, despite the presence of some Hindu designs, a result of the movement of Mughal-trained craftsmen from further north in search of opportunities to practise their skills. In the Diwan-i-Khas (now known by the Sanskrit name Sarbato Bhadra) are two huge silver urns – ratified by Guinness as being the largest pieces of silver in the world – used by Sawai Madho Singh for carrying Ganga water to England.

Diwan-i-Am (Diwan Khana) Art Gallery With its entrance in the southeast corner of the Diwan-i-Am courtyard, the 'new' Hall of Public Audience built by Maharaja Sawai Pratap Singh (1778-1803) today houses a fine collection of Persian and Indian miniatures, some of the carpets the maharajas had made for them and an equally fine collection of manuscripts. To its north is the **Carriage Museum**, housed in a modern building. In the middle of the west wall of the Diwan-i-Am courtyard, opposite the art gallery, is the **Ganesh Pol**, which leads via a narrow passage and the Peacock Gate into **Pritam Niwas Chowk**. This courtyard has the original palace building 'Chandra Mahal' to its north, the *zenana* on its northwest, and the Anand Mahal to its south. Several extremely attractive doors, rich and vivid in their peacock blue, aquamarine and amber colours, have small marble Hindu gods watching over them.

Chandra Mahal Built between 1727 and 1734 the Moon Palace is the earliest building of the palace complex. Externally it appears to have seven storeys, though inside the first and second floors are actually one high-ceilinged hall. The top two floors give superb views of the city and Tiger Fort. On the ground floor (north) a wide veranda – the **Pritam Niwas** (House of the Beloved) – with Italian wall paintings, faces the formal Jai Niwas garden. The main section of the ground floor is an Audience Hall. The palace is not always open to visitors.

The hall on the first and second floors, the **Sukh Niwas** (House of Pleasure), underwent a Victorian reconstruction. Above it are the **Rang Mandir** and the **Sobha Niwas**, built to the same plan. The two top storeys are much smaller, with the mirror palace of the **Chavi Niwas** succeeded by the small open marble pavilion which crowns the structure, the **Mukat Niwas**.

In the northeast corner of the Pritam Niwas Chowk, leading into the *zenana*, is the **Krishna door**, its surface embossed with scenes of the deity's life. The door is sealed in the traditional way with a rope sealed with wax over the lock.

Govind Deo Temple and beyond North of the Chandra Mahal, the early 18th-century Govind Deo Temple, which was probably built as a residence, has been restored by an ancient technique using molasses, curd, coconut water, fenugreek, rope fibres and lime, but is again not always open to visitors. The furniture is European – Bohemian glass chandeliers – the decoration Indian. Following the steps around you will see a *mandala* (circular diagram of the cosmos), made from rifles around the royal crest of Jaipur. The ceiling of this hall is in finely worked gold. Further on are the beautiful Mughal-style fountains and the **Jai Niwas gardens** (1727), laid out as a *char bagh*, the **Badal Mahal** (circa 1750) and the **Tal Katora** tank. The view extends across to the maharaja's private Krishna temple and beyond the compound walls to the Nahargarh (Tiger Fort) on the hills beyond.

Jantar Mantar (Observatory)

ⓘ *1000-1630, foreigners Rs 100, Indians Rs 10, camera Rs 50, video Rs 100 (stills better).*
Literally 'Instruments for measuring the harmony of the heavens', the Jantar Mantar was built between 1728 and 1734. Jai Singh wanted things on a grand scale and chose stone with a marble facing on the important planes. Each instrument serves a particular function and each gives an accurate reading. Hindus believe that their fated souls move to the rhythms of the universe, and the matching of horoscopes is still an essential part in the selection of partners for marriage. Astrologers occupy an important place in daily life and are consulted for all important occasions and decision-making. The observatory is fascinating. We recommend you hire a guide to explain the functions of the instruments. There is little shade so avoid the middle of the day. Moving clockwise the *yantras* (instruments) are as follows:

Small 'Samrat' is a large sundial (the triangular structure) with flanking quadrants marked off in hours and minutes. The arc on your left shows the time from sunrise to midday, the one on the right midday to sundown. Read the time where the shadow is sharpest. The dial gives solar time, so to adjust it to Indian Standard Time (measured from Allahabad) between one minute 15 seconds and 32 minutes must be added according to the time of year and solar position as shown on the board.

'Dhruva' locates the position of the Pole Star at night and those of the 12 zodiac signs. The graduation and lettering in Hindi follows the traditional unit of measurement based on the human breath, calculated to last six seconds. Thus: four breaths = one *pala* (24 seconds), 60 *palas* = one *gati* (24 minutes), 60 *gatis* = one day (24 hours).

'Narivalya' has two dials: south facing for when the sun is in the southern hemisphere (21 September-21 March) and north facing for the rest of the year. At noon the sun falls on the north-south line.

The Observer's Seat was intended for Jai Singh.

Small 'Kranti' is used to measure the longitude and latitude of celestial bodies.

'Raj' (King of Instruments) is used once a year to calculate the Hindu calendar, which is based on the Jaipur Standard as it has been for 270 years. A telescope is attached over the central hole. The bar at the back is used for sighting, while the plain disk is used as a blackboard to record observations.

'Unnathamsa' is used for finding the altitudes of the celestial bodies. Round-the-clock observations can be made and the sunken steps allow any part of the dial to be read.

'Disha' points to the north.

'Dakshina', a wall aligned north-south, is used for observing the position and movement of heavenly bodies when passing over the meridian.
Large 'Samrat' is similar to the small one (see above) but 10 times larger and thus accurate to two seconds instead of 20 seconds. The sundial is 27.4 m high. It is used on a particularly holy full moon in July/August, to predict the length and heaviness of the monsoon for the local area.
'Rashivalayas' has 12 sundials for the signs of the zodiac and is similar to the Samrat yantras. The five at the back (north to south), are Gemini, Taurus, Cancer, Virgo and Leo. In front of them are Aries and Libra, and then in the front, again (north-south), Aquarius, Pisces, Capricorn, Scorpio and Sagittarius. The instruments enable readings to be made at the instant each zodiacal sign crosses the meridian.
'Jai Prakash' acts as a double check on all the other instruments. It measures the rotation of the sun, and the two hemispheres together form a map of the heavens. The small iron plate strung between crosswires shows the sun's longitude and latitude and which zodiacal sign it is passing through.
Small 'Ram' is a smaller version of the Jai Prakash Yantra (see above).
Large 'Ram Yantra' Similarly, this finds the altitude and the azimuth (arc of the celestial circle from Zenith to horizon).
'Diganta' also measures the azimuth of any celestial body.
Large 'Kranti' is similar to the smaller Kranti (see above).

Gatore Ki Chhatriyan (Royal Gaitor)

ⓘ *Foreigners Rs 30, Indians Rs 20, camera Rs20.*

The gaitor is a complex of temples and tombs in the foothills of the the Nahargarh (Tiger Fort), see below. It has a dramatic rocky setting and good views of the crenellated city wall snaking up and over the dusty hills behind. Creamy marble domes with interiors of beautiful stonework encrusted with carvings of elephants, battle scenes and wild flowers. The site is barely maintained and the lawns are parched lawns, but endearingly so. It's a very peaceful, restful spot.

Nahargarh (Tiger Fort)

ⓘ *1000-1630, foreigners Rs 30, Indians Rs 5, camera Rs 30, video Rs 70. Rickshaw for sunset Rs 300-400 return. Snacks and drinks are available at the Durg Café.*

The small fort with its immense walls and bastions stands on a sheer rock face. The city at its foot was designed to give access to the fort in case of attack. To get there on foot you have to first walk through some quiet and attractive streets at the base of the hill, then 2 km up a steep, rough winding path to reach the top. Alternatively, it can also be reached by road via Jaigarh Fort. Beautifully floodlit at night, it dominates the skyline by day. Much of the original fort (1734) is in ruins but the walls and 19th-century additions survive, including rooms furnished for maharajas. This is a 'real fort', quiet and unrushed, and well worth visiting for the breathtaking views, to look inside the buildings and to walk around the battlements. However, it is an active fort used as a training ground for soldiers; women alone may feel quite vulnerable here. You can combine this visit with Jaigarh Fort (see page 341), 7 km away along the flat-topped hill, which is part of the same defensive network.

Central Museum and Modern Art Gallery

ⓘ *Museum Sat-Thu 1000-1630, Rs 30 (Mon free); gallery 1000-1700, free, closed 2nd Sat of month and Sun; garden 0900-1700, foreigners Rs 100, Indians Rs 10.*

Within the Ram Niwas Gardens you can visit the museum, gallery and a zoological garden. Housed in the beautiful Albert Hall is the **Central Museum**, displaying mainly excellent decorative metalware, miniature portraits and other art pieces. It also features Rajasthani village life – including some gruesome torture techniques – displayed through costumes, pottery, woodwork, brassware, etc. The first-floor displays are covered in dust and poorly labelled. **Modern Art Gallery**, Ravindra Rang Manch, has an interesting collection of contemporary Rajasthani art. Finally, in the gardens is the **Zoological Garden** containing lions, tigers, panthers, bears, crocodiles and deer, plus a bird park opposite.

SRC Museum of Indology

ⓘ *24 Gangwal Park, 0800-1600, foreigners Rs 40, Indians Rs 20.*

Further south, along J Nehru Marg, is the extraordinarily eclectic, and not a little quirky, SRC Museum of Indology. It houses a collection of folk and tantric art including all manner of manuscripts, textiles, paintings, Hindi written on a grain of rice, Sanskrit on a rabbit hair, fossils, medals, weapons and so on.

Birla Mandir

Something of an architectural curiosity, the modern temple built by the Birla family in the southeast of the city is impressive in scale and in the eclecticism of its religious art. The quality of the marble used can be seen in its near transparency.

Surya Mandir

ⓘ *Galta Pol can be reached by taking a bus or by walking 2 km east from the Hawa Mahal; from there it is about 600 m uphill and then downhill. A rickshaw costs Rs 200-250 return.*

From Galta Pol take a walk to the 'Valley of the Monkeys' to get a view of the city from the Surya Mandir (Sun Temple), which is especially impressive at sunset. It is not on the tourist circuit and so you are less likely to get hassled here. There are plenty of monkeys on the way up to the temple and you can buy bags of nuts to feed them. Walk down the steps from the top of the ridge to the five old temples, with impressive wall paintings, dedicated to Rama-Sita and Radha-Krishna. Hundreds of monkeys can be seen playing in the water tank below.

Jaipur listings

For Sleeping and Eating price codes and other relevant information, see Essentials pages 38-42.

Sleeping

Jaipur *p321, map p322*

The city's popularity has meant that foreigners are targeted by hotel and shop touts, many of whom drive rickshaws, so be on your guard. Look out for new hotel and convention centre under construction at the time of writing in the stunning floating Jal Mahal on the way to Amber – www.jalmahal.com.

LL Devi Ratn Jamdoli, Agra Rd, www.deviresorts.in. This all-suite property is inspired by the **Jantar Mantar** observatory using domes, arches and towers. Stunningly designed restaurant with domed ceiling and beautiful Chakra Bar. The stylish suites are as decadent as you would imagine – unique design. Spectacular achievement.

LL Jai Mahal Palace (Taj), Jacob Rd, Civil Lines, T0141-222 3636, www.tajhotels.com. 100 rooms in 250-year-old palace that has managed to maintain a real sense of authenticity. Bathrooms not as good as some but rooms are tastefully decorated and set in very attractive, peaceful gardens. Attentive staff. Pool is lovely.

LL Rajvilas (Oberoi), 8 km from town on Goner Rd, T0141-268 0101, www.oberoi hotels.com. This award-winning hotel is housed in a low-lying recreated fort-palace within large, exquisitely landscaped gardens with orchards, pools and fountains. There are 71 rooms including 13 'tents' and 3 private villas with their own pools. Room interiors are not especially imaginative, but the safari-style 'tents' in a desert garden area are delightful. Bathrooms are impressive. There is also an Ayurvedic spa in a restored *haveli*. Indulgent and atmospheric, but slightly lacking in buzz.

LL Rambagh Palace (Taj), Bhawani Singh Rd, T0141-221 1919, www.tajhotels.com. 90 luxuriously appointed rooms and extraordinary suites arranged around a courtyard in the former maharaja's palace, still feels like the real thing. Set in 19 ha of beautifully maintained garden, larger groups are invited to participate in elephant polo on the back lawn! Stunning indoor pool and a new tented spa, but the real pièce de résistance is the spectacular dining hall, reminiscent of Buckingham Palace. Pleasant, relaxed atmosphere, good food and friendly staff. Extremely pricey but unforgettable.

LL-L Samode Haveli Gangapole, T0141-263 2407, www.samode.com. 150-year-old, beautifully restored *haveli* with a leafy courtyard and gardens. 30 rooms and 2 suites (the spectacular Maharaja and Maharani suites have original mirrored mosaics, faded wall paintings, pillars, lamp-lit alcoves, cushions and carved wooden beds). Evening meals are served in the peaceful, atmospheric courtyard or in the magnificent, somewhat over-the-top dining room. Large pool with bar. Excellent food, including a good Western selection, huge wine list.

L Mansingh Tower, Sansar Chandra Rd, T0141-237 8771, www.mansinghhotels.com. 45 rooms in modern business hotel, tastefully and imaginatively designed. A good option if palaces don't appeal.

A Alsisar Haveli, Sansar Chandra Rd, T0141-236 8290, www.alsisarhaveli.com. 36 intricately painted a/c rooms, modern frescoes, excellent conversion of 1890s character home, attractive courtyards, beautiful pool, but average food and below par service can be frustrating (try nearby **Chaitanya**, see Eating, below), village safaris available.

A Narain Niwas, Kanota Bagh, Narain Singh Rd, T0141-256 1291, www.hotelnarainniwas.com. The well-presented rooms pale in comparison to the suites in this characterful old mansion. There's a great dining room and lounge area, and clean pool in beautiful gardens, with lots of room to sit around the pool (which is rare). Patchy reports on food and service. The beautiful boutique **Hot Pink** is in the grounds and offers designer names.

A-B Bissau Palace, outside Chandpol Gate, T0141-230 4371, www.bissaupalace.com. 45 a/c rooms, some charming, in the home of the Rawal of Bissau (built 1919) with library and royal museum, drawing room is crammed with memorabilia, antiques and hunting trophies. There's a bookshop, pleasant garden and good views from terrace of city but it could all do with a bit of sprucing up. The onsite agent **Karwan Tours** offer excellent tours and camel safaris and money exchange, but temple music may irritate. Good summer discounts.

A-B Royal Heritage Haveli, Khatipura Jhotwara Rd, T0141-408 2121, www.royalheritagehaveli.com. This thoughtfully restored *haveli* has many original features which were rediscovered during renovation. The bathrooms are tiled with the local pottery tiles and each room has unique features. Although a little far out of town, this can also be a blessing.

A-B Shahpura House, Devi Marg, Bani Park, T0141-220 2293, www.shahpurahouse.com. The only genuine 'heritage' option in the area, this 1950s maharaja's residence is still run by the family and has with many original features including mirrored *thekri* ceilings, comfortable individually decorated suites, old-fashioned bathrooms, lovely canopied rooftop restaurant (pricey meals), and a pool.

A-C Dera Rawatsar, D-194/C, Vijay Path, behind Sindhi Camp Bus Station, T0141-236 0717, www.derarawatsar.com. Beautiful rooms and **A-B** suites in smart new premises, all kept to a high standard. Outside areas are more understated than others in the area so has a more relaxed, family-run vibe.

A-C Hari Mahal Palace, Jacob Rd, Civil Lines, T0141-222 1399, www.harimahalpalace.com. 11 large, quirky rooms with big bath tubs, period furniture in old mansion, large lawn, old world feel.

B Jas Vilas, C-9 Sawai Jai Singh Highway, Bani Park, T0141-220 4638, www.jasvilas.com. A charming family-run hotel. 12 a/c rooms with bath (tub, power shower), internet, delicious home-cooked meals, very pretty pool surrounded by a lawn, friendly family. Their suite has a particularly amazing tiled bathtub. This road is getting busier and noisier, however. Recommended.

B Karauli House, New Sanganer Rd, Sodala (towards the airport), T0141-229 0763, www.karauli.com. 6 rooms in a family 'retreat', large garden, pool, personal attention, home-cooked meals.

B LMB, Johari Bazar, Old City, T0141-256 5844, www.hotellmb.com. Centrally a/c rooms above a famous restaurant/sweet shop, comfortable but dingy rooms with traffic noise, but certainly at the heart of everything and in walking distance of major sites.

B-C Diggi Palace, SMS Hospital Rd, T0141-237 3091, www.hoteldiggipalace.com. 43 attractive rooms in charming 125-year-old building. Not as glitzy as some but effortlessly chic with large range of rooms. Lovely open restaurant, great home-grown food, peaceful garden, enthusiastic, helpful owners who host the **Jaipur Literature and Heritage Festival** with co-host William Dalrymple. Calming atmosphere; you can really feel at home here. Highly recommended.

B-C Madhuban, D237 Behari Marg, Bani Park, T0141-220 0033, www.madhuban.net. Elegant, characterful hotel, 25 beautifully furnished rooms, small courtyard pool, pleasant garden, helpful staff, good food. Recommended.

B-C Nana-ki-Haveli, Fateh Tiba, Moti Dungri Rd, near Old City, T0141-261 5502, nanakihavelijaipur@yahoo.com. 12 spacious a/c rooms in a modernized 1918 garden house, the grounds are not as nice as others in this range, very hospitable, friendly family, excellent home cooking.

B-C Umaid Bhawan, D1-2A Bani Park, T0141-231 6184, www.umaidbhawan.com. 28 beautifully decorated and ornately furnished rooms, many with balconies, one of the most charming *haveli*-style guest houses with a lovely pool and friendly, knowledgeable owners. Highly recommended.

B-C Umaid Mahal, B2 Bihari Marg, Bani Park, T0141-220 1954, www.umaidmahal.com. A new heritage-style development with good modern facilities and stunning architectural features. Beautiful courtyard pool and Wi-Fi.

C General's Retreat, 9 Sardar Patel Rd, T0141-237 7134, www.generalsretreat.com. 8 rooms with bath, some with kitchenettes, attractive bungalow of a retired general, airy rooms, pleasant gardens and nice communal areas, restaurant.

C Santha Bagh, Kalyan Path, Narain Singh Rd, T0141-256 6790. 12 simple, comfortable rooms (a/c or air-cooled), very friendly, helpful and charming staff, excellent meals, lawn, quiet location. Recommended.

C-E Chirmi Palace, Dhuleshwar Garden, Sardar Patel Marg, T0141-236 5063, www.chirmi.com. 23 spacious but variable a/c rooms in 150-year-old *haveli* conversion. Traditional Rajasthani decor, attractive dining room, lawns, pool (summer only), email, gentle staff, standard rooms are good value, but the deluxe rooms are not.

C-E Rajasthan Palace, 3 Peelwa Gardens, 1 km from Sanganeri Gate, Moti Dungri Rd, T0141-261 1542, rajasthanmotel@yahoo.co.in. 40 rooms, some old-fashioned and wacky, others modern and clean, plus budget rooms with shared bathroom, around pleasant gardens and small pool. In a city of palaces, this isn't in the same league.

C-E Shahar Palace, Barwada Colony, Civil Lines, T0141-222 1861, www.shaharpalace.com. 9 rooms in a separate annexe of a residential home. Well-maintained gardens, home-cooked food and friendly but discreet staff make this a soothing retreat. Recommended.

D Arya Niwas, Sansar Chandra Rd (behind Amber Tower), T0141-237 2456, www.arya niwas.com. 95 very clean, simple rooms but not always quiet, modernized and smart, good very cheap vegetarian food, pleasant lounge, travel desk, tranquil lawn, friendly, helpful, impressive management, book ahead (arrive by 1800), great value.

D Gangaur (RTDC), Mirza Ismail Rd, T0141-237 1641. 63 rooms, some a/c, restaurant, coffee shop, in need of a lick of paint and an airing, but convenient for bus/railway stations.

D-E Atithi, 1 Park House Scheme, T0141-237 8679, atithijaipur@hotmail.com. This place has had a recent stylish facelift – well thought out design. The 24 rooms offer up wonderful hot showers; there's a relaxing roof terrace, internet, good vegetarian food, helpful, friendly staff. Recommended.

D-E Pearl Palace Heritage, 54 Gopal Bari Lane 2, T0141-237 5242, www.pearlpalaceheritage.com. An amazing new heritage-style property from the charming Mr Singh who also runs the extremely popular **Hotel Pearl Palace**. With an armful of books on Indian architecture and art, Mr Singh has gathered artisans from all over India to create the beautiful stone carvings that line the walls of his new hotel. Each room is themed, so using the golden stone from Jaisalmer he has created a desert room; there is a mirrored Udaipur room and a wooden Victoriana room.

The rooms are large here with big sitting areas, TVs and beautifully tiled bathrooms. Attention to detail is key here. Exceptionally good value. Whole-heartedly recommended.

E Shri Sai Nath, 1233 Mali Colony, outside Chandpol Gate, T0141-230 497. 10 clean, quiet rooms, meals on request, very hospitable, helpful and warm.

E Tiger Fort, T0141-236 0238. For an atmospheric stay. Here, you'll find 2 simple rooms with bath. Enquire at the **Durg Café** (see page 328).

E-F Hotel Pearl Palace, Hari Kishan Somani Marg, Hathroi Fort, Ajmer Rd, T0141-237 3700, www.hotelpearlpalace.com. A real gem. Rooms are quirky and all slightly different with art pieces gathered or designed by the charming owner, modern, comfortable, some with a/c, Wi-Fi, lots of character. The pinnacle is the **Peacock** restaurant on the roof serving excellent food with great views of Jaipur, surrounded by plants and artworks. There is a little rooftop shop and money exchange at good rates. Book ahead. Great value you have to pinch yourself at the prices. Whole-heartedly recommended.

F Cocoon, Chameliwala market, near Petrol Pump off Mirza Ismail Rd, www.the-cocoon.com, T0141-221 6964. A warrantine group of alleyways makes up Chameliwala Jewellery market – a small alley by the petrol pump on MI road leads you into the market where there are a few low-budget guest houses. Cocoon offers up clean basic rooms and there is a popular rooftop restaurant.

F Hotel Pink Sun, Chameliwala market, off Mirza Ismail Rd, T0141-237 6753. Clean, simple rooms in busy location, right at the heart of things, good for doing business in the market. Good rooftop restaurant.

F Shakuntalam, D-157 Durga Marg, Bani Park, T0141-220 3225. 16 adequate rooms, family-run, attentive service, meals available.

F Tourist Hotel (RTDC), Mirza Ismail Rd, same building as tourist office, T0141-236 0238. 47 simple rooms with bath, dorm (Rs 50), little atmosphere, beer bar, tours, well located.

G Youth Hostel, near the SMS Stadium, out of town, T0141-274 1130. 8 clean double rooms plus 3 dorms (Rs 40), renovated, good value. Discounts for YHA members.

Eating

Jaipur *p321, map p322*

TTT **Jai Mahal Palace** (see Sleeping). International cuisine in beautiful surroundings, buffet breakfast and dinner recommended; but snack bar inadequate.

TTT **Rambagh Palace** (see Sleeping). Royal Indian cuisine from 4 regions in the beautiful **Suvarna Mahal** restaurant, attractive light-filled coffee shop, popular for lunch, pricey (Rs 2500 minimum for non-residents) but generous.

TTT-T **Chokhi Dhani**, 19 km south on Tonk Rd, T0141-277 0555, www.chokhidhani.com. Enjoyable 'village' theme park with camel and elephant rides, traditional dancing and puppet shows popular with families from Delhi. If you are only coming to Jaipur, this gives you a Disney view of the rest of Rajasthan, but it is done very well. Food-wise there are 2 options, the 1st for Rs 350 gets you a traditional Rajasthani thali and you sit on the floor in a vibey outdoor space. The Royal Rajasthani Dinner is Rs 650 and offers up a huge menu, not for the faint-hearted. A taxi will cost around Rs 400 return. There's also good accommodation, *haveli*-style or in huts, and a pool.

TT **Anokhi Café**, KK Square Shopping Complex, Prithviraj Rd, C-Scheme, T0141-400 7244. Great café offering up international tastes like Thai Green Bean salad, quiches and sandwiches. Try the pomegranate and pineapple juice, great filter coffee and an array of cakes and biscuits. A little oasis and right next door to the beautiful Anokhi shop.

TT **Chaitanya**, Sansar Ch Rd, 100 m from **Alsisar Haveli** (see Sleeping), in shopping complex on opposite side of road. Excellent vegetarian in civilized surroundings. Extensive menu includes Rajasthani, Italian and Mexican specialities.

TT **Copper Chimney**, Mirza Ismail Rd, T0141-237 2275. Open for lunch and dinner. A/c, quality international food, large non-vegetarian selection including seafood from Sep to Mar. Incessant *muzak*.

TT **Dasaprakash**, Mirza Ismail Rd. Upmarket and modern South Indian chain restaurant, serving first-rate *utthapam* and *upma* alongside the usual range of dosas. A/c can be a bit fierce.

TT **Four Seasons**, D-43A2 Subhash Mg, C-Scheme, T0141-227 5450. High-quality vegetarian Indian and Chinese, with an extensive menu, pleasantly smart ambience and good staff. A worthwhile detour.

TT **Handi**, back of Maya Mansion on Mirza Ismail Rd, T0141-236 4839. Indian. Partly open-air, simple canteen style.

TT **LMB**, Johari Bazar. Rajasthani vegetarian in slightly confused contemporary interior matched by upbeat dance tunes. Tasty (if a little overpriced) *thalis*; (*panchmela saag* particularly good). Popular sweet shop and egg-free bakery attached. During **Diwali**, this is a feast for the senses.

TT **Natraj**, Mirza Ismail Rd. Rajasthani, some Chinese, vegetarian only. A/c, much smarter inside than out. Good range of *thalis* and sweets, Western classical on stereo.

TT **Niros**, Mirza Ismail Rd, T0141-2374493. International. With its bland decor you could be anywhere, but there's a good choice of Indian, Chinese and continental dishes, all set to blasting a/c and *popzak*.

TT **Suriya India**, B Ganpati Plaza, Motilal Atal Rd, T0141-360749. Good selection of pure vegetarian North Indian, live music.

TT **Surya Mahal**, Mirza Ismail Rd, T0141-236 9840. East meets west in chaotic clash of interiors. Wide variety including Mexican and pizzas, food far superior to music.

T **BMB**, Sanganeri Gate. Excellent value dosas and snacks on the edge of the Old City; dingy but clean a/c section upstairs. Good sweets too.

T **Kanji**, opposite Polo Victory Cinema, Station Rd. Clean and extremely popular sweets-and-snacks joint, a good place to experiment with exotica such as *Raj kachori* or *aloo tikki*, both of which come smothered in yoghurt and mild sweet chutney. Stand-up counters downstairs, a/c seating upstairs.

T **Lassiwala**, Mirza Ismail Rd, opposite Niro's. The unrivalled best *lassis* in the city, served in rough clay cups and topped off with a crispy portion of milk skin. Of the 3 'original' Lassiwalas parked next to each other, the genuine one is on the left, next to the alley. Come early; they run out by afternoon.

T **Mohan**, Motilal Atal Rd, opposite **Neelam Hotel**. Simple restaurant with good pan-Indian food accompanied by Punjabi prayer music, *thalis* recommended.

T **Peacock**, on roof of **Hotel Pearl Palace** (see Sleeping). Excellent Indian and continental dishes plus backpacker fare, with vegetarian and non-vegetarian food prepared in separate kitchens. Superb views by day and night from

A prayer for a good husband

Ishar and Gangaur are the mythical man and wife who embody marital harmony. During the **Gangaur Fair**, colourfully dressed young women carrying brass pitchers on their heads make their way through the streets to the temple of Gauri (another name for Parvati). Here they ceremonially bathe the deity who is then decked with flowers. Young women pray for good husbands, or the long life of their husbands if they are already married. The ceremony ends with singing and rejoicing as it is believed that if a woman is unhappy while she sings she will be landed with an ill-tempered husband. The festivities end when Ishar arrives, accompanied by elephants, to escort his bride Gangaur home. The fair has been made very tourist-friendly, for foreigners in particular, and offers plenty of photo opportunities with painted elephants and dancers/musicians in traditional dress.

this 2-tiered restaurant, eclectic collection of quirky furniture designed by the owner watched over by a giant peacock. Worth seeking out if you're not staying. Very atmospheric – highly recommended.

Bars and clubs

Jaipur *p321, map p322*

Nawabganj Safari, Crystal Palm Mall, Level 3, Sardar Patel Parg. A little bit like a Disney jungle ride with moving plastic animals and with bar stools designed on the rear ends of zebra and ostriches (which can make for very unflattering photographs) this bar is a sight to behold. Grab a cocktail and enjoy your safari.

Sheesha, City Pearl, near Khasa Kothi, M I Rd. Get giddy with great views and cocktails at this vibey bar spread over 4 levels (outdoor and indoor seating).

Entertainment

Jaipur *p321, map p322*

Raj Mandir Cinema, off Mirza Ismail Rd. 'Experience' a Hindi film in shell pink interior.

Ravindra Rang Manch, Ram Niwas Garden. Hosts cultural programmes and music shows.

Festivals and events

Jaipur *p321, map p322*

See page 43 for nationwide festivals.

14 Jan Makar Sankranti The kite-flying festival is spectacular. Everything closes down in the afternoon and kites are flown from every rooftop, street and even from bicycles. The object is to bring down other kites to the deafening cheers of huge crowds.

Feb/Mar Elephant Festival (7 Mar 2012, 26 Mar 2013) at Chaugan Stadium, procession, elephant polo, etc.

Mar/Apr Gangaur Fair (25-26 Mar 2012, 13-14 Apr 2013) about a fortnight after **Holi**, when a colourful procession of women starts from the City Palace with the idol of Goddess Gauri. They travel from the Tripolia Gate to Talkatora, and these areas of the city are closed to traffic during the festival. See box, above.

Jul/Aug Teej (22-23 Jul 2012, 9-10 Aug 2013). The special celebrations in Jaipur have elephants, camels and dancers joining in the processions.

Shopping

Jaipur *p321, map p322*

Jaipur specializes in printed cotton, handicrafts, carpets and *durries* (thick handloomed rugs); also embroidered leather footwear and blue pottery. You may find better bargains in other cities in Rajasthan.

Antiques and art

Art Palace, Chomu Haveli. Specializes in 'ageing' newly crafted items – alternatives to antiques. Also found around Hawa Mahal.

Manglam Arts, Amer Rd. Sells modern miniature paintings and silver.

Mohan Yadav, 9 Khandela House, behind Amber Gauer, SC Rd, T0141-378 009. Visit the workshop to see high-quality miniatures produced by the family.

Royale Treasure, 5 Jacob Rd, Civil Lines, www.royaletreasure.com. If you are inspired to redecorate, **Royale Treasure** offers up an eclectic mix of hand-painted cabinets, decorative lamps, jewellery boxes, textiles and wall hangings.

Bazars

Traditional bazars and small shops in the Old City are well worth a visit; cheaper than Mirza Ismail Rd shops but may not accept credit cards. Most open Mon-Sat 1030-1930.
Bapu Bazar specializes in printed cloth.
Chaupar and **Nehru Bazars** for textiles.
Johari Bazar for jewellery.
Khajanewalon-ka-Rasta, off Chandpol bazar, for marble and stoneware.
Maniharon-ka-Rasta for lac bangles which the city is famous for.
Ramganj Bazar has leather footwear while opposite Hawa Mahal you will find the famous featherweight Jaipuri *rezais* (quilts).
Tripolia Bazar (3 gates), inexpensive jewellery.

Blue pottery

Blue Pottery Art Centre, Amer Rd, near Jain Mandir. For unusual pots.
Kripal Kumbha, B-18, Shiv Marg, Bani Park, T0141-220 0127. Gives lessons by appointment. Recommended.

Books

Book Corner, Mirza Ismail Rd, by **Niros Restaurant** (see Eating). Good selection.
Bookwise, **Rajputana Sheraton Hotel**, also in Mall 21 opposite Rajmandir Cinema. Vast range, excellent service, fair price.
City Books and Art Palace, just inside gate at City Palace, T0141-261 0970. Wide range of reference and coffee-table books on Rajasthan.
Crosswords , C-11, KK Square, Prithviraj Rd. Great branch of this bookshop with good travel section and DVDs.
Photo Service, **Rambagh Palace Hotel** (see Sleeping), T0141-238 5030, bookshop506@hotmail.com. Has old and obscure Rajasthani titles as well as typical holiday reading.

Carpets

Channi Carpets and Textiles, Mount Rd opposite Ramgarh Rd. Factory shop, watch carpets being hand-knotted, then washed, cut and quality checked with a blow lamp.
Maharaja, Chandpol (near **Samode Haveli**). Watch carpet weavers and craftsmen, good-value carpets and printed cotton.
The Reject Shop, Bhawani Singh Rd. For 'Shyam Ahuja' *durrie* collections.

Fabrics

Chirag International, 771 Khawasji ka Rasta, Hawa Mahal Rd. Wholesale warehouse, with a corresponding vast selection.
Ridhi Sidhi Textiles, 9 East Govind Nagar, Amber Rd.

Handicrafts

Anokhi, KK Shopping Complex, Prithviraj Rd, C-Scheme, T0141-400 7244. Beautifully crafted clothes, great designs. Some mens and childrens clothes, attractive block- printed homeware and bags. Recommended.
Handloom Haveli, Lalpura House, Sansar Ch Rd.
Handloom House, Rituraj Building, Mirza Ismail Rd (near **Tourist Hostel**).
Rajasthali, Government Handicrafts, Mirza Ismail Rd, 500 m west of Ajmeri Gate.
Rajasthan Fabrics & Arts, near City Palace gate. Exquisite textiles.

Clothing and Lifestyle

Hot Pink, **Narain Niwas** (see Sleeping) T0141-510 8932, www.hotpinkindia.com. Beautiful boutique in the grounds of Narain Niwas Palace in the south of city with pieces from Indian designers including Manish Arora (the master of Kitsch chic), Abraham & Thakore (for true elegance) and Tarun Tahliani (for Bollywood style). Homeware also available. There is also a lovely small branch in Amber Fort.

Jewellery

Jaipur is famous for gold, jewellery and gem stones (particularly emeralds, rubies, sapphires and diamonds, but diamonds require special certification for export). Semi-precious stones set in silver are more affordable (but check for loose settings, catches and cracked stones); sterling silver items are rare in India and the content varies widely. **Johari Bazar** is the scene of many surreptitious gem deals, and has backstreet factories where you may be able to see craftsmen at work. Bargaining is easier on your own so avoid being taken by a 'guide'. For about Rs 40 you can have gems authenticated and valued at the **Gem Testing Laboratory**, off Mirza Ismail Rd, near New Gate, T0141-256 8221 (reputable jewellers should not object).

Do not use credit cards to buy these goods and never agree to 'help to export' jewellery. There have been reports of misuse of credit card accounts at **Apache Indian Jewellers** (also operating as **Krishna Gems** or **Ashirwad Gems & Art**) opposite Samodia Complex, Loha Mandi, SC Rd; and **Monopoli Gems**, opposite Sarga Sooli, Kishore Niwas (1st floor) Tripolia Bazar.

Reputable places include **Beg Gems**, Mehdi-ka-Chowk, near Hawa Mahal.

Bhuramal Rajmal Surana, 1st floor, between Nos 264 and 268, Haldiyon-ka-Rasta. Highly recommended.

Dwarka's, H20 Bhagat Singh Marg. Crafts high-quality gemstones in silver, gold and platinum in modern and traditional designs.

Gem Palace, Mirza Ismail Rd, opposite Natraj and Niros, T0141-237 4175, www.gempalace jaipur.com. Exceptional range of jewellery in diverse styles, from traditional Indian bridal to chic modern pieces. It's a great place to see the unique styles of Indian jewellery from tribal regions to high society. Recommended.

Pearl Palace Silver Shop, at **Hotel Pearl Palace** (see Sleeping). Great value jewellery and bits and pieces of traditional crafts from Jaipur from a trusted source.

Photography

Sentosa Colour Lab, Ganpati Plaza, Mirza Ismail Rd. Good fast printing service and limited range of supplies.

Silverware

Amrapali Silver Shop, corner of Mirza Ismail and Mahavir Marg, opposite Thomas Cook and Natraj.

Arun's Emporium, Mirza Ismail Rd.

Mona Lisa, Hawa Mahal Rd.

Nawalgarh Haveli, near Amber Fort bus stop.

▲ Activities and tours

Jaipur *p321, map p322*

Some hotels (such as the **Rambagh Palace**, see Sleeping) will arrange golf, tennis, squash, or elephant polo.

Body and soul

Kerala Ayurveda Kendra, T0141-510 6743, www.keralaayurvedakendra.com. Ayurvedic treatments, clean and hygienic, recommended for massages, also constitution analysis, Panchkarma, classes in Ayurveda. Phone for free pick-up.

Vipasana Centre, Dhammathali, Galta, 3 km east of centre, T0141-268 0220. Meditation courses for new and experienced students.

City tours

RTDC City Sightseeing Half day: 0800-1300, Rs 150; Central Museum, City Palace, Amber Fort and Palace, Gaitore, Laxmi Narayan Temple, Jantar Mantar, Jal Mahal, Hawa Mahal. **Full day**: 0900-1800, Rs 200; including places above, plus Jaigarh Fort, Nahargarh Fort, Birla Planetarium, Birla Temple and Kanak Vrindavan. **Pink City by Night**: 1830-2230, Rs 250. Includes views of Jai Mahal, Amber Fort, etc, plus dinner at Nahargarh Fort. Call T0141-220 3531 or book at railway station, **Gangaur Hotel** or **Tourist Hotel** (see Sleeping).

Virasat Journeys Heritage Walks, T0141-510 9090, www.virasatjourneys.com. Virasat Journeys offer a fantastic range of walks to offer you unique insight into Jaipur. They make a lot of effort to show you the real Jaipur. On the Bazars and Cuisines tour, you get to watch local artisans at work and try the best samosas and most famous lassi in town. You will hear fascinating stories about the buildings and families that populate the labyrinthine lanes of the old town. Highly recommended.

Other operators also offer city sightseeing: half/full day, Rs 100-150. The tours are worthwhile, but may miss out promised sights claiming they are closed. Some may find the guides' English difficult to follow and the obligatory shopping trips tedious.

General tours

Aravalli Safari, opposite **Rajputana Palace Hotel**, Palace Rd, T0141-236 5344, aravalli2@ datainfosys.net. Very professional.

Chetan, 17 Muktanand Nagar, Gopalpura Bypass, Tonk Rd, T0141-254 5302. Experienced, reliable car tours.

Forts & Palaces Tours Ltd, S-1, Prabhakar Apartment, Vaishali Nagar, T0141-235 4508,

www.palaces-tours.com. A very friendly, knowledgeable outfit offering camel safaris, sightseeing tours, hotel reservations, etc.
Karwan Tours, **Bissau Palace Hotel**, Chandpol Gate, T0141-230 8103, karwantours@mailcity.com. For camel safaris, tours, taxis, ticketing, exchange; very helpful.
Pepper Tours, T0484-405 8886/(0)9847-322802, www.peppertours.com. Creates memorable journeys in Kerala, Rajasthan and Goa.
Rajasthan Travel, 52 Ganpati Plaza, Mirza Ismail Rd, T0141-236 5408, rtsjaipur@bhaskarmail.com. Ticketing, reliable guides. Recommended.

Transport

Jaipur *p321, map p322*

Air **Sanganer Airport**, T0141-272 1333, has good facilities. Transport to town: taxi, 30 mins, Rs 250-300; auto-rickshaw Rs 150. **Indian Airlines**, Nehru Pl, Tonk Rd, T0141-274 3324; airport, T0141-272 1519, flies to **Delhi**, **Mumbai**, **Udaipur**, **Ahmedabad**, **Kolkata**, **Dubai**. **Jet Airways**, T0141-511 2222; airport T0141-255 1352, flies to **Delhi**, **Mumbai** and **Udaipur**. **Go Air**, T0141-650 0801, flies to **Delhi** and **Mumbai**. **Spicejet**, T18000-180 3333, to **Ahmedabad**, **Chennai**, **Hyderabad** and **Mumbai**. **Air Deccan**, T3900 8888, to **Bengaluru** (**Bangalore**) and **Mumbai**. **Kingfisher**, T0141-272 3485 or T1800-180 0101 to **Goa**, **Hyderabad**, **Kolkata** and **Mumbai**.

Auto-rickshaw Avoid hotel touts and use the pre-paid auto-rickshaw counter to get to your hotel. Persistent auto-rickshaw drivers at railway station may quote Rs 10 to anywhere in town, then overcharge for city tour.

Station to city centre hotel, about Rs 30; sightseeing (3-4 hrs) Rs 200, 6-7 hrs, Rs 360. From railway and bus stations, drivers (who expect to take you to shops for commission) offer whole-day hire including Amber for Rs 150; have your list of sights planned and refuse to go to shops.

Local bus Unless you have plenty of time and a very limited budget, the best way to get around the city is by auto-rickshaw. To **Amber**, buses originate from Ajmeri Gate, junction with Mirza Ismail Rd, so get on there if you want a seat.

Long distance bus **Central Bus Stand**, Sindhi Camp, Station Rd. Enquiries: *Deluxe*, Platform 3, T0141-511 6031, *Express*, T0141-511 6044 (24 hrs). Left luggage, Rs 10 per item per day. When arriving, particularly from Agra, you may be told to get off at Narain Singh Chowk, a bus stand some distance south of the centre; to avoid paying an inflated auto-rickshaw fare, insist on staying on until you reach the bus stand. Private buses will drop you on Station Rd but are not allowed inside the terminal. State and private *Deluxe* buses are very popular so book 2 days in advance. To **Agra** 12 buses a day 0600-2400, 6½ hrs with 1 hr stop, a/c buses at 0800 and 1415, Rs 194/316, a/c, pay when seat number is written on ticket; (230 km, 5 hrs, via Bharatpur) – get off at the 2nd (last) stop to avoid being hassled by rickshaw drivers; **Ajmer** (131 km, regular service 0400-2330, 3 hrs, Rs 94/135 for a/c); **Bharatpur** 5 buses a day, but all deluxe and a/c buses to Agra go through Bharatpur but you have to pay Agra fare Rs 119; **Delhi** (261 km, half hourly, 5½ hrs, almost hourly service with deluxe, Pink Line and Volvo buses running Rs 300/500 for a/c; **Jaisalmer** (654 km, 2145, 13 hrs via Jodhpur, Rs 391). **Jodhpur** (332 km, frequent, 7 hrs, Rs 219/322); **Udaipur** (374 km, 12 hrs, Rs 267 for a/c, 4 a/c and sleeper buses Rs 419 for a/c and sleeper); **Kota** via **Bundi** (7 daily, 4-5 hrs); **Chittaurgarh** (deluxe, 1200, 2115, 2400). 1 daily to **Shimla** (2000); and **Haridwar** (2200) – mixed reports on Shimla and Haridwar service, often you have to change in Delhi and pay again.

Cycle rickshaw (Often rickety) station to central hotels, Rs 15-20; full day Rs 100.

Taxi Unmetered taxis; 4 hrs costs Rs 450 (40 km), 8 hrs costs Rs 750 (city and Amber). Extra hill charge for Amber, Raigarh, Nahargarh. Out of city Rs 5-8 per km; **Marudhar Tours** (see Activities and tours) recommended; or try **RTDC**, T0141-220 3531. Also **Pink City Taxis**, T0141-511 5100, excellent radio cab service.

Train Enquiry, T131, T0141-220 4536, reservation T135. Computerized booking office in separate building to front and left of station; separate queue for foreigners. Use pre-paid rickshaw counter. **Abu Rd** (for **Mount Abu**): *Ahmedabad Mail 19106*, 0455, 8½ hrs, *Aravali Exp 19708* (goes on to Mumbai), 0835, 8 hrs; **Agra Cantt**: *Marudhar Exp 14854/14864*, 1550, 7 hrs. **Ahmedabad**: *Aravali Exp 19708*, 0845, 14 hrs; *Ashram Exp 12916*, 2045, 11½ hrs. *Rajdhani Exp 12958*, not Tue 0045, 9 hrs. **Ajmer**:

Aravali Exp 19708, 0845, 2½ hrs; **Bikaner**: *Bikaner Exp 14737*, 2210, 10 hrs; *Intercity Exp 12468*, 1550, 7 hrs. **Chittaurgarh**: *Chittaurgarh Exp 19769*, 1200, 7½ hrs; *Chetak Exp 14715*, 1945, 8½ hrs. **Delhi**: *Shatabdi 12016*, 1745, 4 hrs 25 mins, Jaipur JAT Exp 12413, 1635, 5½ hrs; *Haridwar Mail 19105*, 2310, 5½ hrs. **Indore**: *Jaipur Indore Exp 12974*, Fri and Sun 2115, 9½ hrs; **Jodhpur**: *Ranthambhore Exp 12465*, 1705, 5½ hrs; *Intercity Exp 12465*, 1740, 5½ hrs. **Mumbai** (**C**): *Jaipur BCT Superfast 12956*, 1410, 18½ hrs; **Udaipur** : *Udaipur City Exp 12965*, 2240, 10 hrs. **Varanasi** via **Lucknow**: *Marudhar Exp 14864*, 1540, 20 hrs.

Directory

Jaipur *p321, map p322*

Banks Several on Mirza Ismail Rd and Ashok Marg. Open 1030-1430, 1530-1630; most change money and have ATMs. ATMs also scattered along Johari Bazar and in C scheme **Thomas Cook**, Jaipur Towers, 1st floor, Mirza Ismail Rd (500 m from railway station, T0141236 0801, 0930-1800, open Sun). No commission on own TCs, Rs 20 for others. Recommended. Often easier to use hotels, eg Hotel Pearl Palace (24-hr, fast, good rates). **Karwan Tours**, Bissau Palace (sunrise until late). Jewellery shops opposite Hawa Mahal often hold exchange licences but travellers report misuse of credit cards at some. **Internet** Most hotels have a computer or 2. Handy new facility at railway station near platform ticket office, plus many others scattered around city, eg Ganpati Plaza basement, Rs 1 per min; Mirza Ismail Rd opposite Niro's, Rs 25-30 per hr; **Mewar**, near Central Bus Stand, 24 hrs, also has faxing. **Medical services Ambulance:** T102. **Santokba Durlabhji Hospital**, Bhawani Singh Rd, T0141-256 6251. **SMS Hospital**, Sawai Ram Singh Marg, T0141-256 0291. **Post** GPO, Mirza Ismail Rd. Excellent parcel service. Take parcels to Customs counter upstairs for quick dispatch. Parcel-wallah to left of gate stitches packages, Rs 50-150. **Useful contacts** **Fire:** T101. **Police:** T100. **Directory enquiries** T197. **Foreigners' Registration Office:** Hazari Garden, behind Hawa Mahal.

Around Jaipur

Amber Fort is one of Jaipur's biggest draws, with an elephant ride to the top a priority on many people's 'to do' list. It's still an impressive building but has been poorly maintained in recent years. Sanganer and Bagru offer good opportunities to see handicrafts in production, while Samode is perhaps the last word in elegant living. ▸▸ *For listings, see pages 342-343.*

Amber (Amer) → *For listings, see pages 342-343.* *Colour map 2, A5. 11 km north of Jaipur.*

Today there is no town to speak of in Amber, just the palace clinging to the side of the rocky hill, overlooked by the small fort above, with a small village at its base. In the high season this is one of India's most popular tourist sites, with a continuous train of colourfully decorated elephants walking up and down the ramp to the palace. One penalty of its popularity is the persistence of the vendors.

History

Amber, which takes its name from Ambarisha, a king of the once-famous royal city of Ayodhya, was the site of a Hindu temple built by the Mina tribes as early as the 10th century. Two centuries later the Kachhawaha Rajputs made it their capital, which it remained until Sawai Jai Singh II moved to his newly planned city of Jaipur in 1727. Its location made Amber strategically crucial for the Mughal emperors as they moved south, and the Maharajahs of Amber took care to establish close relations with successive Mughal rulers. The building of the fort palace was begun in 1600 by Raja Man Singh, a noted Rajput general in Akbar's army, and Mughal influence was strong in much of the subsequent building.

The approach

ⓘ *Around Rs 550 per elephant carrying 4, no need to tip, though the driver will probably ask, takes 10 mins. Jeeps Rs 100 each way, or Rs 10 per seat. It can be quite a long wait in a small garden with little shade and you will be at the mercy of the hawkers. If you do want to buy, wait until you reach the steps when the price will drop dramatically.*

From the start of the ramp you can either walk or ride by elephant; the walk is quite easy and mainly on a separate path. Elephants carry up to four people on a padded seat. The ride can be somewhat unnerving when the elephant comes close to the edge of the road, but it is generally perfectly safe. You have to buy a 'return ticket' even if you wish to walk down later. The elephants get bad tempered as the day wears on. If you are interested in finding out more about the welfare of Amber's elephants, or indeed any of Jaipur's street animals, you should contact an organization called **Help in Suffering** ⓘ *T0141-276 0803, www.his-india.org.au.*

The Palace

ⓘ *0900-1630 (it's worth arriving at 0900), foreigners Rs 150, Indians Rs 10, camera Rs 75, video Rs 150 (tickets in the Chowk, below the steps up to Shila Mata). Take the green bus from the Hawa Mahal, Rs 5. Auto-rickshaw Rs 80 (Rs 200 for return, including the wait). Guides are worth hiring, Rs 400 for a half day (group of 4), find one with a government guide licence.*

After passing through a series of five defensive gates, you reach the first courtyard of the **Raj Mahal** built by Man Singh I in 1600, entered through the **Suraj Pol** (Sun Gate). Here you can get a short ride around the courtyard on an elephant, but bargain very hard. There are some toilets near the dismounting platform. On the south side of this Jaleb Chowk with the flower beds, is a flight of steps leading up to the **Singh Pol** (Lion Gate) entrance to the upper courtyard of the palace.

A separate staircase to the right leads to the green marble-pillared **Shila Mata Temple** (to Kali as Goddess of War), which opens at certain times of the day and then only allows a limited number of visitors at a time (so ask before joining the queue). The temple contains a black marble image of the goddess that Man Singh I brought back from Jessore (now in Bangladesh; the chief priest has always been Bengali). The silver doors with images of Durga and Saraswati were added by his successor.

In the left-hand corner of the courtyard, the **Diwan-i-Am** (Hall of Public Audience) was built by Raja Jai Singh I in 1639. Originally, it was an open pavilion with cream marble pillars supporting an unusual striped canopy-shaped ceiling, with a portico with double red sandstone columns. The room on the east was added by Sawai Ram Singh II. **Ganesh Pol** (circa 1700-1725), south of the chowk, colourfully painted and with mosaic decoration, takes its name from the prominent figure of Ganesh above the door. It separates the private from the public areas.

This leads onto the **Jai Singh I** court with a formal garden. To the east is the two- storeyed cream-coloured marble pavilion – **Jai Mandir** (Diwan-i-Khas or Hall of Private Audience) below and **Jas Mandir** (1635-1640) with a curved Bengali roof, on the terrace above. The former, with its marble columns and painted ceiling, has lovely views across the lake. The latter has colourful mosaics, mirrors and marble *jali* screens which let in cooling breezes. Both have **Shish Mahals** (Mirror Palaces) faced with mirrors, seen to full effect when lit by a match. To the west of the chowk is the **Sukh Niwas**, a pleasure palace with a marble water course to cool the air, and doors inlaid with ivory and sandalwood. The Mughal influence is quite apparent in this chowk.

Above the Ganesh Pol is the **Sohag Mandir**, a rectangular chamber with beautiful latticed windows and octagonal rooms to each side. From the rooftop there are stunning views over the palace across the town of Amber, the long curtain wall surrounding the town and further north, through the 'V' shaped entrance in the hills, to the plains beyond. Beyond this courtyard is the **Palace of Man Singh I**. A high wall separates it from the Jai Singh Palace. In the centre of the chowk which was once open is a *baradari* (12-arched pavilion), combining Mughal and Hindu influences. The surrounding palace, a complex warren of passages and staircases, was turned into *zenana* quarters when the newer palaces were built by Jai Singh. Children find it great fun to explore this part.

Old Palace and Anokhi Museum

Old Palace of Amber (1216) lies at the base of Jaigarh Fort. A stone path (currently being restored) from the Chand Pol in the first courtyard of Amber Palace leads to the ruins. Though there is little interest today, nearby are several worthwhile temples. These include the **Jagatsiromani Temple** dedicated to

Amber Palace

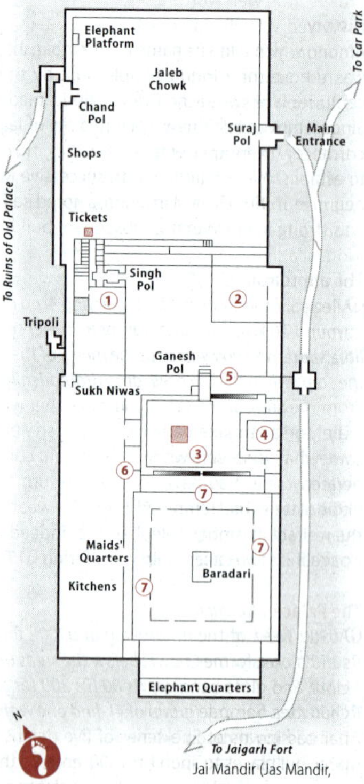

Not to scale

Shila Mata Temple **1**
Diwan-i-Am **2**
Jai Singh I Garden **3**
Jai Mandir (Jas Mandir, 1st floor) **4**
Sohag Mandir (1st floor) **5**
Palace of Man Singh I (1st floor) **6**
Zenana **7**

Krishna, with carvings and paintings; it is associated with Mira Bai. Take time to visit the fantastic Anokhi Museum of hand-printing. Great textile collection and you can even try your hand at handblock printing.

North of Jaipur → *For listings, see pages 342-343. Colour map 2, A5.*

Jaigarh Fort

ⓘ *0900-1630. Foreigners Rs 35, Indians Rs 20, free with City Palace entry ticket (use within 48 hrs), still camera Rs 40, video Rs150, vehicle entry Rs 50. To reach the fort, from Amber Palace turn right out of the Suraj Pol and follow a stone road past the old elephant quarters. This is the start of the ascent – a steady climb of about 25 mins, or take a taxi. What appears at first to be 2 adjoining forts is in fact all part of the same structure. There is also a good road from the Jaipur–Amber road which goes straight to Jaigarh Fort and on to Nahargarh.*

Above the palace on the hill top stands the gigantic bulk of Jaigarh, impressively lit at night; its *parkotas* (walls), bastions, gateways and watchtowers a testimony of the power of the Jaipur rulers. It is well worth a visit. The forbidding medieval fort was never captured and so has survived virtually intact which makes it particularly interesting. In the 16th-century cannon foundry you can see the pit where the barrels were cast, the capstan-powered lathe which bored out the cannon and the iron-workers' drills, taps and dies. The armoury has a large collection of swords and small arms, their use in the many successful campaigns having been carefully logged. There is an interesting photograph collection and a small café outside the armoury. There are gardens, a granary, open and closed reservoirs; the ancient temples of Ram Harihar (10th century) and Kal Bhairava (12th century) are within the fort. You can explore a warren of complicated dark passageways among the palaces. Many of the apartments are open and you can see the collections of coins and puppets (shows on demand). The other part of the fort, at a slightly higher elevation, has a tall watch tower. From here there are tremendous views of the surrounding hills. The massive 50-tonne **Jai Ban cannon** stands on top of one tower. Allegedly the largest cannon on wheels in the world, with an 8-m barrel, it had a range of around 20 km, but it was never used. Some 7 km further along the top of the hill is the smaller Nahargarh Fort overlooking Jaipur itself (see page 328).

Ramgarh Lake and Jamwa Sanctuary → *30 km northeast of Jaipur.*

The 15-sq-km lake of Jamwa Ramgarh attracts large flocks of waterfowl in winter, and lies within a game sanctuary with good boating and birdwatching. Built to supply Jaipur with water, it now provides less than 1% of the city's needs and in years of severe drought may dry up completely. The 300-sq-km Jamwa Sanctuary, which once provided the Jaipur royal family with game, still has some panthers, nilgai and small game. Contact the tourist office in Jaipur (see page 321) for details of public buses. It is about a 45-minute drive.

Samode → *Colour map 2, A5. Phone code: 01423. 42 km northwest of Jaipur.*

At the head of the enclosed valley in the dry rugged hills of the northern Aravallis, Samode stands on a former caravan route. The sleepy village, with its local artisans producing printed cloth and glass bangles, nestles within a ring of old walls. The painted *havelis* are still full of character. Samode is well worth the visit from Jaipur, and makes a good stop en route to the painted towns of Shekhawati (see page 445). Both the palace and the *bagh* are wonderful, peaceful places to spend a night.

The **palace** ⓘ *now a heritage hotel, entry Rs 500 for non-residents includes tea/coffee,* which dominates the village, is fabulously decorated with 300-year-old wall paintings (hunting scenes, floral motifs, etc) which still look almost new. Around the first floor of the Darbar Hall are magnificent alcoves, decorated with mirrors like *shish mahal* and *jali* screens through which the royal ladies would have looked down into the grand jewel-like Darbar Hall.

Towering immediately above the palace is **Samode Fort**, the maharajah's former residence, reached in times of trouble by an underground passage. The old stone zigzag path has been replaced by 300 steps. Though dilapidated, there are excellent views from the ramparts; a caretaker has the keys. The main fort gate is the starting point of some enticing walks into the Aravallis. A paved path leads to a shrine about 3 km away. There are two other powerful forts you can walk to, forming a circular walk ending back in Samode. Allow three hours, wear good shoes, a hat and carry water.

Samode Bagh, a large 400-year-old Mughal-style formal garden with fountains and pavilions, has been beautifully restored. It is 3 km southeast of Samode, towards the main Jaipur-Agra road. Within the grounds are modest-sized but elaborately decorated tents.

South of Jaipur → *For listings, see pages 342-343.*

Sanganer

Sanganer is 16 km south of Jaipur. Sanganer is a beautiful little town dedicated traditional crafts like paper making and handblock printing. There's also a blue pottery factory and several old *havelis*.

Madhogarh → *45 km southeast of Jaipur, off the Jaipur–Agra Rd.*

Madhogarh is a small but impressive fort, with a strong medieval flavour, and a pleasant place to break your journey between Jaipur and Ranthambore if you have your own transport. It is located on a hillock, and has huge walls, bastions, wells and turrets. The Rajput-Maratha battle of Tunga was fought at the nearby village, with the Jaipur army based at Madhogarh, during the mid-18th century.

Around Jaipur listings

For Sleeping and Eating price codes and other relevant information, see Essentials pages 38-42.

Sleeping

Ramgarh Lake and Jamwa Sanctuary *p341*

LL-L Ramgarh Lodge (Taj), overlooking the lake, T01426-252217, www.tajhotels.com. 18 elegant a/c rooms (3 enormous suites) in the former royal hunting lodge with a museum and library, furnished appropriately, hunting trophies, limited restaurant, delightful walks, fishing and boating plus ruins of old Kachhawaha fort nearby. **AL** in summer.

E-F Jheel Tourist Village (RTDC), Mandawa Choraha, T01426-252170. Pleasant surroundings for 10 not especially well-maintained rustic huts.

Samode *p342*

LL-L Samode Palace, T01423-240014, www.samode.com. Reservations essential. Half price 1 May-30 Sep. Contact Samode Haveli, T0141-263 2407, to reserve and arrange taxi from Jaipur. 42 a/c rooms, tastefully modernized without losing any of the charm, magnificent setting with gardens and beautiful secluded pool with plenty of space to lounge, courtyard and modern indoor restaurants (international menu), also buffets for groups, shop with good textiles, camel rides around village and to Samode Bagh (but some animals are in poor condition). Really remarkable for its setting and atmosphere,generally friendly and exceptional service. Well worth a visit even if not staying. Highly recommended.

L-AL Samode Bagh, 3 km from the palace T01423-240235, www.samode.com. 44 luxury a/c tents decorated in the Mughal-style, each with a beautiful modern bath room and its own veranda. *Darbar* tent, al fresco meals, pool with slide, tennis, volleyball, badminton, lovely setting in peaceful walled Mughal gardens, plenty of birdwatching, safaris to sand dunes, amazing. Reservations essential. Recommended.

B-C Maharaja Palace, modern hotel. 18 rooms (some a/c) in mock *haveli*, restaurant, garden with village-style huts. Staff look a little shabby, but generally friendly.

E Prem Devi Artist's Homestay, CB Mugal Art Galary, Shilp Colony, Samode T(0)982-864 3924, sureshmdw1983@yahoo.com. Simple, friendly homestay run by a lovely family of artists – the ever cheerful Prem Devi, her husband and 2 grown-up children. 5 sparse but very clean rooms with attached bathrooms. Exterior and lobby of house beautifully decorated with traditional art and miniature paintings. 3 home-cooked vegetarian meals per day available for an extra Rs 250 (no restaurants in Samode); free art classes.

Madhogarh *p342*

C Fort Madhogarh, T01428-281141, www.fortmadhogarh.in. A **Rajput Special Hotels** with 25 quaint rooms (some in the tower) with views of the countryside. Good (though rather spicy) food, interesting temples nearby, family-run, recently converted so still finding its feet. Great atmosphere on the ramparts in the evening when the family and guests enjoy tea.

Shopping

Amber *p339*

Near the *baoli* and temples, you can see demonstrations of block printing and other handicrafts, simple snacks, shops selling gems, jewellery, textiles, handicrafts and 'antiques' (objects up to 90 years old; genuine 100-year-old antiques may not be exported). Amber is a tax holiday zone, and products manufactured by industries here are 10-15% cheaper than at Jaipur (though the benefit may not be passed on to the customer).

Samode *p342*

A small artists' colony in the village produces good-quality miniature paintings on old paper. Contact Krishan Kumar Khari, often found at the hotel entrance.

Activities and tours

Ramgarh Lake and Jamwa Sanctuary *p341*

Polo can be played at **Ramgarh Resort** (HRH), T0294-252 8016, www.hrhindia.com. An exclusive facility for polo enthusiasts with a full-size polo field near the lake, occasional matches and polo training camps run by World Cup Indian captain Lokendra Singh. **A** deluxe tented accommodation for participants, restaurant, pool and riding stable.

Samode *p342*

Contact **Samode Bagh** (see Sleeping), for activities around this Moghul garden/hotel. See also **Samode Palace** for camel safaris. Birdwatching around this area is good.

Transport

Samode *p342*

Samode is a 1-hr drive from **Jaipur**. Buses from Chandpol Gate go to Chomu where you can pick up a local bus to Samode. Taxi Rs 950.

Southern Rajasthan

Possibly the most varied region in Rajasthan, the main draw is incomparable Udaipur. The area around is equally appealing however, from time-warped, just-becoming-touristy Bundi and Chittaurgarh in the east to the quirky charms of Mount Abu, Rajasthan's only hill station and a great escape from the heat of the summer, in the west. To the south lie delightful Dungarpur and a range of small heritage hotels dotted around the countryside, perfect places to unwind away from the tourist fray. To the north is the majestic Kumbhalgarh Fort, its mammoth walls so vast they're visible from space, and the exquisite Jain temples at Ranakpur, comparable to those in Mount Abu but in a far more tranquil setting. Fascinating drives through the surprisingly green Aravalli hills link one place to the next, passing through picturesque rural villages and agricultural areas unlike those anywhere else in Rajasthan along the way.

Udaipur

➔ *Colour map 2, B4. Phone code: 0294. Population: 500,000.*

Enchanting Udaipur, set in the Girwa Valley in the Aravalli Hills of south Rajasthan, must be one of the most romantic cities in India, with white marble palaces, placid blue lakes, attractive gardens and green hills that are a world away from the surrounding desert. High above the lake towers the massive palace of the Maharanas. From its rooftop gardens and balconies, you can look over Lake Pichola, the Lake Palace "adrift like a snowflake" in its centre. The monsoons that deserted the city earlier in the decade have returned – though water shortage remains a threat – to replenish the lakes and ghats, where women gently thrash wet heaps of washing with wooden clubs, helped by splashing children. The houses and temples of the old city stretch out in a pale honeycomb, making Udaipur an oasis of colour in a stark and arid region. Sunset only intensifies the city's beauty, turning the city palace's pale walls to gold, setting the lake to shimmer in silvery swathes against it, while mynah birds break out into a noisy twilight chorus. Ochre and orange skies line the rim of the westernmost hills while countless roof terraces light up and the lake's islands appear to float on waters dancing in the evening breeze and turning purple in the fading light. ▸▸ *For listings, see pages 350-357.*

Ins and outs

Getting there The airport, about 30-45 minutes by taxi or city bus, is well connected. The main bus stand is east of Udai Pol, 2-3 km from most hotels, while Udaipur City Railway Station is another 1 km south. Both have auto-rickshaw stands outside as well as pushy hotel touts.

Getting around The touristy area around the Jagdish temple and the City Palace, the main focus of interest, is best explored on foot but there are several sights further afield. Buses, shared tempos, auto-rickshaws and taxis cover the city and surrounding area; some travellers prefer to hire a scooter or bike. ▸▸ *See Transport, page 356.*

Tourist information Be prepared for crowds, dirt and pollution and persistent hotel touts who descend on new arrivals. It is best to reserve a hotel ahead or ask for a particular street or area of town. Travellers risk being befriended by someone claiming to show you the city for free. If you accept, you run the risk of visiting one shop after another with your 'friend'. **Rajasthan Tourism Development Corporation** (RTDC) ⓘ *Tourist Reception Centre, Fateh Memorial, Suraj Pol, T0294-241 1535, 1000-1700, guides 4-8 hrs, Rs 250-400.*

History

The legendary **Ranas of Mewar** who traced their ancestry back to the Sun, first ruled the region from their seventh-century stronghold Chittaurgarh. The title 'Rana', peculiar to the rulers of **Mewar**, was supposedly first used by Hammir who reoccupied Mewar in 1326. In 1568, **Maharana Udai Singh** founded a new capital on the shores of Lake Pichola and named it

1 Udaipur

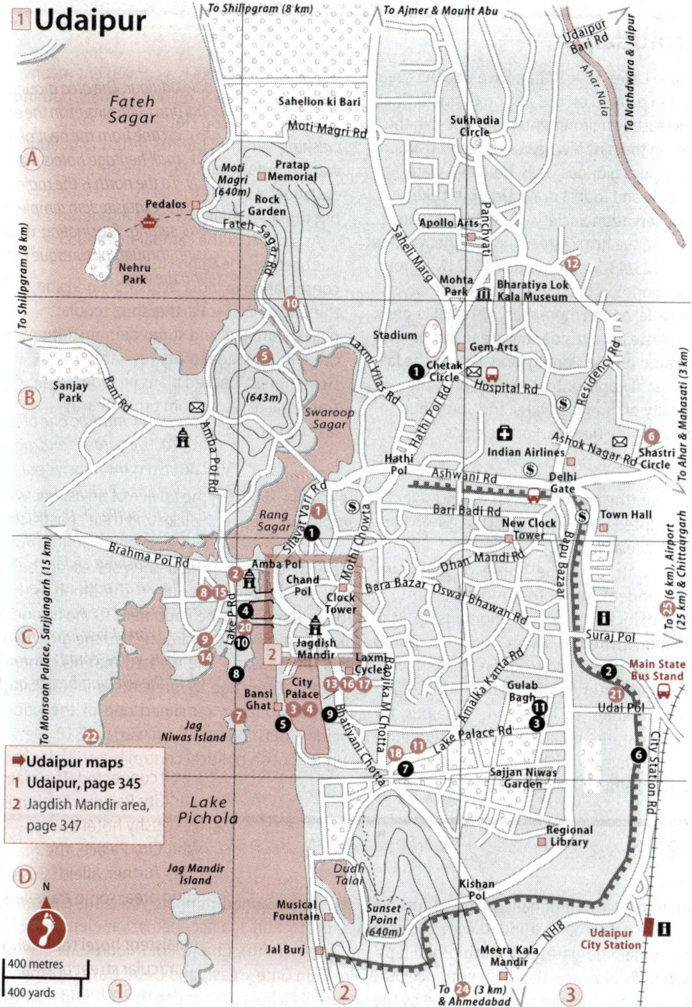

Sleeping

Dream Heaven **2** *C1*
Fateh Prakash **3** *C2*
Hibiscus **9** *C1*
Hill Lake **1** *B2*
Hilltop Palace **5** *B2*
Kajri **6** *B3*
Kumbha Palace **13** *C2*
Lake Palace **7** *C2*
Lake Pichola **20** *C2*
Laxmi Vilas Palace **10** *B2*
Leela Palace Kempinski **14** *C1*
Mahendra Prakash **11** *C2*
Mewar Inn **12** *A3*
Mona Lisa **16** *C2*
Pratap Country Inn **25** *C3*
Queen Café **8** *C1*
Raj Palace **17** *C2*
Rang Niwas Palace **18** *C2*
Shikarbadi **24** *D3*
Shiv Niwas **4** *C2*
Udai Kothi **15** *C1*
Udaivilas **22** *C1*
Yatri Guest House **21** *C3*

Eating

Ambrai **8** *C2*
Food Club **10** *C2*
Garden Hotel **3** *C3*
Green Room **1** *B2*
Hariyali **11** *C3*
Little Prince **4** *C2*
Natraj **6** *C3*
Samore Garden **7** *C2*
Sankalp **2** *C3*
Sunset Terrace **5** *C2*
Whistling Teal **9** *C2*

Eco-Udaipur

"Save Lakes, Save Water, Save Udaipur", reads a sign painted on the wall on Gangaur Ghat. Increased environmental awareness in the city in the past few years has centred around Udaipur's glorious lakes, both as a water supply and tourist draw. **Udaipur Lake Conservation Society** (Jheel Sanrakshan Samiti, see http://green ingindia.net/content/view/23/43) was formed in 1992 by a group of volunteers in order to protect the city's six large lakes and more than 100 smaller ones.

Waste from residential areas and hotels located on the sloping land around the lake, can easily drain into it, threatening the quality of drinking water and spreading waterborne disease. For the city's population, the lake is a convenient means of rubbish disposal, religious rituals, bathing, ablutions, washing clothing, and even washing vehicles, but the resulting pollution, water shortage and eutrophication endanger not only the lakes' ecosystems but threaten their existence altogether.

As a result of the campaign, the JSS has become a leading NGO on water conservation in India. Working alongside the **Global Water Partnership**, regular rallies, seminars and street demonstrations bring its message to city residents. Government-backed plans include the transferal of water from other nearby lakes and basins.

Udaipur (the city of sunrise) having selected the spot in 1559. On the advice of an ascetic who interrupted his rabbit hunt, Udai Singh had a temple built above the lake and then constructed his palace around it.

In contrast to the house of Jaipur, the rulers of Udaipur prided themselves on being independent from other more powerful regional neighbours, particularly the Mughals. In a piece of local princely one-upmanship, **Maharana Pratap Singh**, heir apparent to the throne of Udaipur, invited Raja Man Singh of Jaipur to a lakeside picnic. Afterwards he had the ground on which his guest had trodden washed with sacred Ganga water and insisted that his generals take purificatory baths. Man Singh reaped appropriate revenge by preventing Pratap Singh from acceding to his throne. Udaipur, for all its individuality, remained one of the poorer princely states in Rajasthan, a consequence of being almost constantly at war. In 1818, Mewar, the Kingdom of the Udaipur Maharanas, came under British political control but still managed to avoid almost all British cultural influence.

Sights

Old City

Udaipur is a traditionally planned fortified city. Its bastioned rampart walls are pierced by massive gates, each studded with iron spikes as protection against enemy war elephants. The five remaining gates are: **Hathi Pol** (Elephant Gate – north), **Chand Pol** (Moon Gate – west), **Kishan Pol** (south), the main entrance **Suraj Pol** (Sun Gate – east) and **Delhi Gate** (northeast). On the west side, the city is bounded by the beautiful Pichola Lake and to the east and north, by moats. To the south is the fortified hill of Eklingigarh. The main street leads from the Hathi Pol to the massive City Palace on the lake side.

The walled city is a maze of narrow winding lanes flanked by tall whitewashed houses with doorways decorated with Mewar folk art, windows with stained glass or *jali* screens, majestic *havelis* with spacious inner courtyards and shops. Many of the houses here were given by the Maharana to retainers – barbers, priests, traders and artisans while many rural landholders (titled jagirdars), had a *haveli* conveniently located near the palace.

The **Jagdish Mandir** ⓘ *150 m north of the palace, 0500-1400, 1600-2200,* was built by Maharana Jagat Singh in 1651. The temple is a fine example of the Nagari style, and contrasts with the serenity of Udaipur's predominantly white-washed buildings, surrounded as it often is by chanting Sadhus, gambolling monkeys and the smell of incense. A shrine with a brass Garuda stands outside and stone elephants flank the entrance steps; within is a black stone image of Vishnu as Jagannath, the Lord of the Universe.

A quiet, slightly eccentric museum, including what they claim is the world's largest turban, now lies in the lovely 18th- century **Bagore ki Haveli** ⓘ *1000-1900, Rs 25, camera Rs 10*, has 130 rooms and was built as a miniature of the City Palace. There are cool shady courtyards containing some peacock mosaics and fretwork, and carved pillars made from granite, marble and the local blueish-grey stone. A slightly forlorn but funny puppet show plays several times a day on the ground floor.

City Palace

ⓘ *0930-1730, last entry 1630. From Ganesh Deori Gate: Rs 50 (more from near Lake Palace Ghat). Camera Rs 100, video Rs 300. From 'Maharajah's gallery', you can get a pass for Fateh Prakash Palace, Shiv Niwas and Shambu Niwas, Rs 75. Guided tour, 1 hr, Rs 100 each. Guides hang around the entrance; standards vary wildly and they can cause a scene if you already have hired a guide. Ask at the ticket office. Rs 25 gets you access to the complex and a nice walk down to the jetty.*

This impressive complex of several palaces is a blend of Rajput and Mughal influences. Half of it, with a great plaster façade, is still occupied by the royal family. Between the **Bari Pol** (Great Gate, 1608, men traditionally had to cover their heads with a turban from this point on) to the north, and the **Tripolia Gate** (1713), are eight *toranas* (arches), under which the rulers were weighed against gold and silver on their birthdays, which was then distributed to the poor. One of the two domes on top of the Tripolia originally housed a water clock; a glass sphere with a small hole at the base was filled with water and would take exactly one hour to empty, at which point a gong would be struck and the process repeated. The gate has three arches to allow the royal family their private entrance, through the middle, and then a public entry and exit gate to either side. Note the elephant to the far left (eastern) end of the gate structure; they were seen as bringers of good fortune and appear all over the palace complex. The Tripolia leads in to the **Manak Chowk**, originally a large courtyard which was converted in to a garden only in 1992. The row of lumps in the surface to the left are original, and demarcate elephant parking bays! Claiming descent from Rama,

2 Jagdish Mandir area

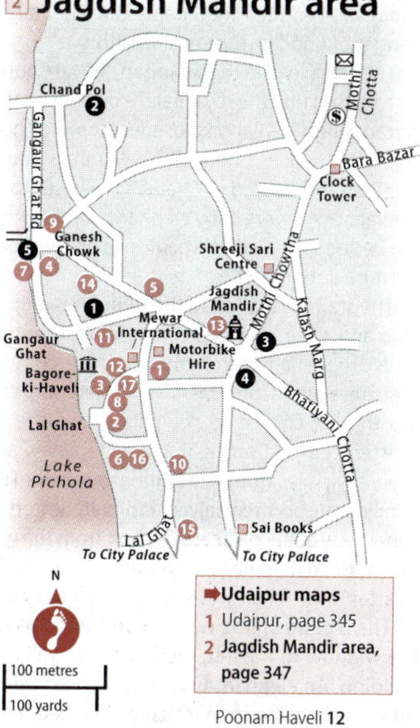

➡Udaipur maps
1 Udaipur, page 345
2 Jagdish Mandir area, page 347

Sleeping

Anjani **5**
Devraj Niwas **2**
Jagat Niwas **6**
Jheel Guest House **7**
Kankarwa Haveli **16**
Lake Ghat **8**
Lal Ghat Haveli **17**
Lalghat Guest House **3**
Lehar **1**
Minerva **14**
Nayee Haveli **4**
Nukkad Guest House **9**
Poonam Haveli **12**
Pratap Bhawan **10**
The Tiger **11**
Udai Garh **15**
Udai Niwas **13**

Eating

Café Edelweiss **1**
Mayur **3**
Papu's Juice Bar **5**
Savage Garden **2**
Si Palace Rd **4**

and therefore the sun, the Mewars always insured that there was an image of the sun available for worship even on a cloudy day, thus the beautiful example set in to the exterior wall of the palace. The large step in front of the main entrance was for mounting horses, while those to the left were for elephants. The family crest above the door depicts a Rajput warrior and one of the Bhil tribesmen from the local area whose renowned archery skills were much used in the defence of the Mewar household. The motto translates as 'God protects those who stand firm in upholding righteousness'.

As you enter the main door, a set of stairs to the right leads down to an armoury which includes an impressive selection of swords, some of which incorporate pistols in to their handles. Most people then enter the main museum to the right, although it is possible to access the government museum from here (see below). The entrance is known as **Ganesh Dori**, meaning 'Ganesh's turn'; the image of the elephant God in the wall as the steps start to turn has been there since 1620. Note the tiles underneath which were imported from Japan in the 1930s and give even the Hindu deities an Oriental look to their eyes. The second image is of Laxmi, bringer of good fortune and wealth.

The stairs lead in to **Rai Angan**, 'Royal Court' (1559). The temple to the left is to the sage who first advised that the royal palace be built on this side. Opposite is a display of some of Maharana Pratap Singh's weapons, used in some of his many battles with the Mughals, as well as his legendary horse, Chetak. The Mughals fought on elephants, the Mewars on horses; the elephant trunk fitted to Chetak's nose was to fool the Mughal elephants in to thinking that the Mewar horses were baby elephants, and so not to be attacked. A fuller version of this nosepiece can be seen in one of the paintings on the walls, as indeed can an elephant wielding a sword in its trunk during battle.

The stairs to the left of the temple lead up to **Chandra Mahal**, featuring a large bowl where gold and silver coins were kept for distribution to the needy. Note that the intricately carved walls are made not from marble but a combination of limestone powder, gum Arabic, sugar cane juice and white lentils. From here steps lead up in to **Bari Mahal** (1699-1711), situated on top the hill chosen as the palace site; the design has incorporated the original trees. The cloisters' cusped arches have wide eaves and are raised above the ground to protect the covered spaces from heavy monsoon rain. This was an intimate 'playground' where the royal family amused themselves and were entertained. The painting opposite the entrance is an aerial view of the palace; the effect from the wall facing it is impressive. The chair on display was meant for Maharana Fateh Singh's use at the Delhi Darbar, an event which he famously refused to attend. The chair was sent on and has still never been used.

The picture on the wall of two elephants fighting shows the area that can be seen through the window to the left; there is a low wall running from the Tripolia Gate to the main palace building. An elephant was placed either side of the wall, and then each had to try to pull the other until their opponent's legs touched the wall, making them the victor.

The next room is known as **Dil Kushal Mahal** ('love entertainment room'), a kind of mirrored love nest. This leads on to a series of incredibly intricate paintings depicting the story of life in the palace, painted 1782-1828. The **Shiv Vilas Chini ki Chatar Sali** incorporates a large number of Chinese and Dutch tiles in to its decoration, as well as an early petrol-powered fan. Next is the Moti Mahal, the ladies' portion of the men's palace, featuring a changing room lined with mirrors and two game boards incorporated into the design of the floor.

Pritam Niwas was last lived in by Maharana Gopal Singh, who died in 1955 having been disabled by polio at a young age. His wheel armchair and even his commode are on display here. This leads on to **Surya Chopar**, which features a beautiful gold-leaf image of the sun; note the 3D relief painting below. The attractive **Mor Chowk** court, intended for ceremonial darbars, was added in the mid-17th century, and features beautiful late 19th-century peacock mosaics. The throne room is to its south, the **Surya Chopar**, from which the Rana (who claimed descent from the Sun) paid homage to his divine ancestor. The **Manak Mahal** (Ruby Palace) was filled with figures of porcelain and glass in the mid-19th century. To the north, the **Bari Mahal** or Amar Vilas (1699-1711) was added on top of a low hill. It has a pleasant garden with full grown trees around a square water tank in the central court.

A plain, narrow corridor leads in to the **Queen's Palace**, featuring a series of paintings, lithographs and photographs, and leading out in to **Laxmi Chowk**, featuring two cages meant for trapping tigers and leopards. The entrance to the **government museum** ⓘ *Sat-Thu 1000-1600, Rs 3*, is from this courtyard. The rather uncared for display includes second century BC inscriptions, fifth- to eighth-century sculptures and 9000 miniature paintings of 17th- and 19th-century Mewar schools of art but also a stuffed kangaroo and Siamese twin deer.

On the west side of the Tripolia are the **Karan Vilas** (1620-1628) and **Khush Mahal**, a rather grotesque pleasure palace for European guests, whilst to the south lies the **Shambhu Niwas Palace** the present residence of the Maharana.

Maharana Fateh Singh added to this the opulent **Shiv Niwas** with a beautiful courtyard and public rooms, and the **Fateh Prakash Palace**. Here the Darbar Hall's royal portrait gallery displays swords still oiled and sharp. The Bohemian chandeliers (1880s) are reflected by Venetian mirrors, the larger ones made in India of lead crystal. Both, now exclusive hotels (see Sleeping, below), are worth visiting.

On the first floor is the **Crystal Gallery** ⓘ *0900-2000, Rs 500 for a guided tour with a talk on the history of Mewar, followed by a cup of tea (overpriced with a cold reception according to some; avoid the cream tea as the scones are so hard they will crack your teeth)*. The gallery has an extensive collection of cut-crystal furniture, vases, etc, made in Birmingham, England in the 1870s, supplemented by velvet, rich 'zardozi' brocade, objects in gold and silver and a precious stone-studded throne.

'The Legacy of honour', outlining the history of the Mewar dynasty, is a good **Son et Lumière**, the first privately funded one in India. There are two shows daily at 1930 and 2030, Rs 100 for ground seating, Rs 300 on terrace; book at the City Palace ticket office.

Lake Pichola

Fringed with hills, gardens, *havelis*, ghats and temples, Lake Pichola is the scenic focus of Udaipur though parts get covered periodically with vegetation, and the water level drops considerably during the summer. Set in it are the Jag Niwas (Lake Palace) and the Jag Mandir Palaces.

Jag Mandir, built on an island in the south of the lake, is notable for the Gul Mahal, a domed pavilion started by Karan Singh (1620-1628) and completed by Jagat Singh (1628-1652). It is built of yellow sandstone inlaid with marble around an attractive courtyard. Maharajah Karan Singh gave the young Prince Khurram (later Shah Jahan), refuge here when he was in revolt against his father Jahangir in 1623, cementing a friendly relationship between the Mewar Maharaja and the future Mughal Emperor. Refugee European ladies and children were also given sanctuary here by Maharana Sarap Singh during the Mutiny. There is a lovely pavilion with four stone elephants on each side (some of the broken trunks have been replaced with polystyrene!). You get superb views from the balconies. It's possible to take an enjoyable **boat trip** ⓘ *Apr-Sep 0800-1100, 1500-1800, Oct-Mar 1000-1700, on the hour, Rs 300 for 1-hr landing on Jag Mandir, Rs 200 for boat ride without stop*, from Rameshwar Ghat, south of City Palace complex. It's especially attractive in the late afternoon light. Rates from the boat stand at Lal Ghat may be slightly cheaper. There is a pricey bar/restaurant on the island but it's worth stopping for the stunning views.

Jag Niwas Island (Lake Palace) ⓘ *it is no longer possible to go to the Lake Palace for lunch or dinner unless you are a resident at Lake Palace, Leela or Oberoi*. The Dilaram and Bari Mahal Palaces were built by **Maharana Jagat Singh II** in 1746 and cover the whole island. Once the royal summer residences and now converted into a hotel, they seem to float like a dream ship on the blue waters of the lake. The courtly atmosphere, elegance and opulence of princely times, the painted ceilings, antique furniture combined with the truly magical setting make it one of the most romantic buildings in India. There are, of course, superb views.

Jal Burj is on the water's edge, south of the town. From the small **Dudh Talai** nearby, there is an attractive walk alongside the main lake (especially pleasant in the evening; large fruit bats can also often be seen). A left turn up a new road leads to **Manikya Lal Verma Park** ⓘ *Rs 5 during the day, Rs 10 evening*, which has great lake views and a delightfully kitsch 'musical fountain', switched on in the evening – a favourite with Indian families.

On the hill immediately to the east of Dudh Talai, a pleasant two-hour walk to the south of the city, is **Sunset Point** which has excellent free views over the city. The path past the café (good for breakfast) leads to the gardens on the wall; a pleasant place to relax. Although it looks steep it is only a 30-minute climb from the café.

Fateh Sagar and around

This lake, north of Lake Pichola, was constructed in 1678 during the reign of Maharana Jai Singh and modified by Maharana Fateh Singh. There is a pleasant lakeside drive along the east bank but, overall, it lacks the charm of the Pichola. **Nehru Park** on an island (accessible by ferry) has a restaurant.

Overlooking the Fateh Sagar is the **Moti Magri (Pearl Hill)** ⓘ *0900-1800, Rs 20, camera free*. There are several statues of local heroes in the attractive rock gardens including one of Maharana Pratap on his horse Chetak, to which he owed his life. Local guides claim that Chetak jumped an abyss of extraordinary width in the heat of the battle of Haldighati (1576) even after losing one leg. To find out more look at *Hero of Haldighati*.

Sahelion ki Bari (Garden of the Maids of Honour) ⓘ *0900-1800, Rs 10, plus Rs 2 for 'fountain show'*, a little north from Moti Magri, is an ornamental pleasure garden; a great spot, both attractive and restful. There are many fountains including trick ones along the edge of the path which are operated by the guide clapping his hands! In a pavilion in the first courtyard, opposite the entrance, a children's museum has curious exhibits including a pickled scorpion, a human skeleton and busts of Einstein and Archimedes. Beautiful black marble kiosks decorate the corners of a square pool. An elegant round lotus pond has four marble elephants spouting water. To the north is a rose garden with over 100 varieties.

At **Ahar** (3 km east) are the remains of the ancient city which has some Jain *chhatris* set on high plinths in the Mahasati (royal cremation ground). A small **museum** ⓘ *1000-1700, closed Fri and holidays, Rs 3*, contains pottery shards and terracotta toys from the first century BC and 10th-century sculptures. Nearby are the temples of Mira Bai (10th century), Adinatha (11th century) and Mahavira (15th century).

Udaipur listings

For Sleeping and Eating price codes and other relevant information, see Essentials pages 38-42.

Sleeping

Udaipur *p344, map p345 and p347*

Frenzied building work continues to provide more hotels while restaurants compete to offer the best views from the highest rooftop. The area around the lake is undeniably the most romantic place to stay, but also the most congested. The hotels on Lake Palace Rd and on the hilltop above Fateh Sagar Lake offer more peaceful surroundings, while Swaroop Sagar offers a good compromise between calmness and convenience. **Tourist Reception Centre**, Fateh Memorial, has a list of accommodation.

LL Fateh Prakash (HRH), City Palace, T0294-252 8016, www.hrhindia.com. Well-appointed lake-facing rooms in modern 'Dovecote' wing and 7 superb suites in main palace building. Original period furniture, great views from **Sunset Terrace** restaurant, facilities of Shiv Niwas, good service (residents may ask for a pass at City Palace entrance for a short cut to hotel).

LL Lake Palace (Taj), Lake Pichola, T0294-252 8800, www.tajhotels.com. 84 rooms, most with lake view, in one of the world's most spectacularly located hotels. Standard rooms are tasteful but unremarkable, suites are outstanding and priced to match, spa and small pool, quite an experience, service can be slightly abrupt. Location for the 1980s Bond film *Octopussy*.

LL Leela Palace Kempinski, T0294-670 1234, www.theleela.com. The newest palace in Udaipur, this award-winning hotel is inspired by Mughal architecture – the inner courtyard is stunning. After arriving by boat, you are greeted by musicians and then taken to your beautiful room with views over the lake or over the Aravali hills.

LL Udaivilas (Oberoi), Lake Pichola, T0294-243 3300, www.oberoihotels.com. The elegant but monochrome exterior of this latter-day palace does nothing to prepare you for the opulence within; the stunning entry courtyard sets the scene for staggeringly beautiful interiors. The 87 rooms are the last word in indulgence; some have one of the hotel's 9 swimming pools running alongside their private balcony. The setting on the lake, overlooking both the lake and city palaces, is superb, as are the food and service. Outstanding.

LL-L Shiv Niwas (HRH), City Palace (turn right after entrance), T0294-252 8016, www.hrhindia.com. 19 tasteful rooms, 17 luxurious suites including those stayed in by Queen Elizabeth II and Roger Moore, some with superb lake views, very comfortable, good restaurant, very pleasant outdoor seating for all meals around a lovely marble pool (non-residents pay Rs 300 to swim), tennis, squash, excellent service, beautiful surroundings, reserve ahead in season. Recommended.

L-AL Shikarbadi (HRH), Govardhan Vilas, Ahmedabad Rd, 5 km from centre, T0294-258 3201, www.hrhindia.com. 26 good, refurbished a/c rooms, pool, horse riding, attractive 100-year-old royal hunting lodge and stud farm with lake, lovely gardens, deer park, charming and peaceful.

A Hilltop Palace, 5 Ambavgarh near Fateh Sagar, T0294-243 2245, www.hotelhilltoppalace.net. Above Fateh Sagar lake, 62 pleasant but unremarkable rooms (large rooms upstairs with balcony), restaurant (visit for a view from the roof), bar, exchange, pool, good food, friendly and efficient service.

A The Tiger, 33 Gangaur Ghat, T0294-242 0430, www.thetigerudaipur.com. Stylish new rooms, funky decor and vibe. Fantastic in-house spa with steam room, sauna, jacuzzi and traditional massage. Great sunset view from rooftop restaurant. Recommended.

A Udai Kothi, Hanuman Ghat, T0294-243 2810, www.udaikothi.com. 24 attractive rooms and beautiful rooftop pool. Great restaurant; book the poolside table for maximum romance. A real treat.

A-C Udai Garh, 21 Lal Ghat, behind Jagdish Temple, T0294-242 1239, www.udaigarh.com. Beautiful rooms with classic furniture, but the crowning glory here is the rooftop swimming pool with great views across the lake. Seductive rooftop restaurant too.

A-D Anjani Hotel, 77 Gangour Ghat, T0294-242 1770, www.anjanihotel.com. Plush Rajasthani-themed rooms – nice artwork and stained-glass features. Small courtyard swimming pool to cool off in. Good views from rooftop restaurant.

A-D Jagat Niwas, 24-25 Lal Ghat, T0294-242 0133, www.jagatniwaspalace.com. 30 individual, very clean rooms in beautifully restored 17th-century 'fairy tale' *haveli*, good restaurant (see Eating), helpful staff, good travel desk, excellent service. Lots of groups, though, so book well in advance. Recommended.

A-D Kankarwa Haveli, 26 Lal Ghat, T0294-241 1457, khaveli@yahoo.com. Wide range of rooms in renovated 250-year-old *haveli* on lake shore, some with views and some with beautiful original artwork and features – each room is unique. 2 new stunning suites have been built – modern glass-fronted design but fitting in seamlessly with this classic building. The roof terrace has also had a revamp and you can sample some great home cooking. Lots of cosy nooks to sit in with owner's massive magazine collection. Highly recommended.

B-E Hibiscus Guest House, 190 Naga Nagri, Chandpol, follow signs to **Leela Palace Hotel**, T0294-280 3490, www.hibiscusinudaipur.com. Tucked away on the Chandpol side of the lake, this lovely guest house has a relaxed vibe run by Carol and Babu. Beautifully decorated rooms, lovely dining room, pretty garden, massive dog.

B-E Rang Niwas Palace, Lake Palace Rd, T0294-252 3890, www.rangniwaspalace.com. 20 beautifully renovated a/c rooms in 200-year-old building, some with charming balconies facing garden, some with beautiful window seats, old-world charm, restaurant, pool, pretty gardens, helpful staff, good location, but some road noise.

C Hotel Hill Lake, Purohit Ji Ka Khurra, inside Chandpole, T0294-241 9412, www.hotelhilllake.com. Stylish rooms in new build, but with exceptional views across both Fateh Sagar lake and across to City Palace and Lake Pichola from atmospheric rooftop restaurant.

C Lake Pichola, Hanuman Ghat, overlooking lake, T0294-243 1197, www.lakepicholahotel.com. 32 rooms, some a/c, fantastic views from some rooms with lots of beautiful window seats sitting over lake, boat rides, friendly, relatively cheap food.

C-D Devraj Niwas, 32 Lal Ghat, T0294-241 6132. Stylish rooms, some with a/c – not many with views, although there are commanding views from the recommended rooftop restaurant **Natural View**.

C-D Raj Palace, 103 Bhatiyani Chotta, T0294-241 0364, rajpalaceudr@yahoo.com. 26 beautiful rooms arranged around pleasant courtyard garden, lovely rooftop restaurant, excellent service with views of City Palace.

C-E Jheel Guest House, 56 Gangaur Ghat (behind temple), T0294-242 1352, www.jheelguesthouse.com. Friendly owner and fantastic views. Don't be deceived by the unremarkable entrance, one room in particular practically hangs over the ghats with a spectacular view all the way towards the **Lake Palace** hotel. New extension has 6 pleasant rooms with bath and hot water; 8 rooms in older part, good rooftop restaurant. Recommended.

C-E Mahendra Prakash, Lake Palace Rd, T0294-241 9811, udai99@hotmail.com. 20 large, spotless, well-furnished rooms in an attractive mansion, some a/c, pleasant patio garden, excellent pool and poolside restaurant, plus pool table. Owner/manager is of the Maharana's family, friendly, excellent service.

C-F Gangaur Palace, 339 'Ashoka Haveli' Gangaur Rd, T0294-242 2303, www.ashokahaveli.com. Attractive, clean rooms around an interesting courtyard – nice design features, although most lake views have been obscured by new hotels. Good rooftop restaurant, but pretty café downstairs is blighted by traffic noise. Recommended.

D Pratap Country Inn, Airport Rd, Titadhia Village, T0294-258 3138. 20 rooms, few a/c, restaurant, horse and camel safaris, riding, pool (sometimes empty), old royal country house in attractive grounds, 6 km from centre (free transfer from railway station).

D-E Kajri (RTDC), Shastri Circle, T0294-241 0501. 53 rooms, some a/c, and dorm, typical institutional RTDC feel, money is better spent elsewhere, restaurant (dull food), bar, travel, Tourist Reception Centre.

D-E Lake Ghat, 4/13 Lalghat, 150 m behind Jagdish Mandir, T0294-252 1636. 13 atmospheric, well-decorated rooms, friendly, lots of greenery cascading down inner staircase, light and airy great views from terraces, good food.

D-E Pratap Bhawan, 12 Lal Ghat, T0294-256 0566, pratapbhawan@yahoo.co.in. 10 large, very clean rooms with a bit of a Raj feel, lots of English hunting scenes, lake-facing terrace restaurant, excellent, home-cooked meals, warm welcome from retired army colonel and his wife.

D-F Minerva, 5/13 Gadiya Devra, Gangaur Ghat (behind temple), T0294-252 3471. Good range of rooms for many budgets, decorative touches. Atmospheric rooftop restaurant. Good, speedy internet.

D-G Udai Niwas, near Jagdish Temple, Gangaur Marg, T0294-512 0789, www.hoteludainiwas.com. 14 renovated rooms in friendly hotel with a pleasant rooftop and good views, new 'penthouse' with lake view with 4-poster bed, all are well decorated with Rajasthani touches. Recommended.

E Poonam Haveli, 39 Lal Ghat, T0294-241 0303, poonamhaveli@hotmail.com. 16 modern, attractive, clean rooms all with nice touches of Rajasthani decor, plus large roof terrace.

E-F Yatri Guest House, 3/4 Panchkuin Rd, Udaipol, near the bus stand, T0294-242 1959. 13 simple rooms, helpful, knowledgeable owner, best option in area.

E-G Dream Heaven, just over Chandpol, on the edge of the lake, T0294-243 1038, deep_rg@yahoo.co.uk. 6 clean, simple rooms with bath, family-run, no frills but excellent rooftop restaurant – exceptional overflowing *thalis* and very good lasagne. Great views.

F-G Kumbha Palace, 104 Bhatiyani Chotta, T0294-242 2702. Run by Dutch-Indian family.

9 clean and quiet rooms with quality linen, good but not particularly busy rooftop restaurant (see Eating), a little way from the heart of things, horse riding arranged.

F-G Lalghat Guest House, 33 Lal Ghat, T0294-252 5301. The best dorm in town (good clean beds with curtains). Some of the 24 rooms have lake views. Very relaxed and sociable, good place to meet people, but indifferent management, reports that you often show up and the great room with a view you were promised has already been taken.

G Lehar, 86 Gangaur Ghat, T0294-241 7651. 5 small rooms with bath, best with lake view. Run by a charming lady.

G Lal Ghat Haveli, 4 Lal Ghat, T0294-241 3666. 8 well-maintained rooms, particularly charming lower down, cheap but with character. Disappointing food in restaurant.

G Mewar Inn, 42 Residency Rd (pleasantly away from centre), T0294-241 1590, mewarinn@hotmail.com. 27 spotless rooms, some with hot shower, street side very noisy, no commission to rickshaws (if they refuse to go try a horse carriage), **Osho** vegetarian restaurant, good cheap bike hire, rickshaw to town Rs 30, very friendly, YHA discounts. Cheap but very out of the way.

G Mona Lisa, 104 Bhatiyani Chotta, T0294-256 1562. Pleasant and quiet, 8 rooms, some air-cooled, with bath, good breakfast, garden, newspaper, cooking lessons, beauty parlour, family-run, good value.

G Nayee Haveli, 55 Gangaur Marg, T(0)982-951 1573, nayee.haveli.udaipur@newyork.com. 5 clean, basic rooms in friendly family home, home-cooked food. Recommended.

G Nukkad Guest House, 56 Ganesh Chowk (signposted from Jagdish Temple), T0294-241 1403, nukkad_raju@yahoo.com. 10 small, simple rooms, some with bath, in typical family house, home-cooked meals, rooftop, very friendly and helpful, clean. Although building work was going on at time of writing.

G Queen Café, 14 Bajrang Marg, T0294-243 0875. 2 decent rooms, shared bath, roof terrace with good views, home-cooked meals (including continental Swiss), informal, welcoming family. Meenu teaches cooking and Hindi. Highly recommended.

Eating

Udaipur *p344, map p345 and p347*

The local belly-buster to try is *dhal-bhatti-choorma*. Plush heritage hotels have expensive menus, but the non-vegetarian buffet food can be kept warm for long periods and can therefore be risky. Many of the budget places are attached to hotels in the Lal Ghat area; the usual fare includes pancakes, macaroni, falafel, etc, for the homesick visitor, and an amazing number still wheel out the TV for a nightly showing of *Octopussy*. Those near Jagdish Mandir do not serve alcohol. Note it is no longer possible to go for lunch or dinner at Lake Palace Hotel unless you are a guest at the hotel itself or staying at the Leela or the Oberoi.

TTT **Ambrai**, Lake Pichola Rd. Magical garden restaurant with tables under trees by lake shore, superb views of City Palace, good at sunset. Recommended by everyone you speak to in Udaipur.

TTT **Gallery Restaurant**, **Fateh Prakash** (see Sleeping). Beautiful restaurant, superb views but pretty tasteless continental food, English cream teas.

TTT **Savage Garden**, up alley near east end of Chandpol bridge. Good in the evenings: striking blue interior and superior food including Indian-style pasta dishes, fish dishes, risottos and great mezze. Recommended.

TTT **Shiv Niwas**, see Sleeping. Wonderful buffet followed by disappointing desserts, eat in the bar, or dine in luxury by the pool listening to live Indian classical music; bar expensive but the grand surroundings are worth a drink.

TT **51 Palace Road**, near Jagdish Temple, T(0)9829-361640. Super stylish glass-fronted three-tiered restaurant overlooking the comings and goings of the Jagdish Temple and the Palace Rd.

TT **Food Club**, Bada Ramayan Chowk, Chandpol side, T(0)9352-320103. The food doesn't quite live up to the fantastic setting, but they serve up tasty Indian fare. And it's a beautifully decorated restaurant with great views.

TT **Jagat Niwas** (see Sleeping). Mainly Indian food. Jarokha rooftop restaurant with fabulous lake views, excellent meals, breakfast, ice cream. Fluorescent lighting can be a mood-killer at night.

Sankalp, outside Suraj Pol, City Station Rd, T0294-510 2686. Upmarket South Indian, modern, great range of chutneys.

Whistling Teal, Jhadol Haveli, 103 Bhattiyana Chohatta, T0294-242 2067. Delicious traditional Rajasthani food as well as a bit of everything from around the globe in lovely garden restaurant.

Café Edelweiss, 73 Gangaur Ghat, opposite The Tiger. Great coffee! Small patisserie – sometimes you just have to sit on the side of the road – but the coffee is that good. Recommended.

Dream Heaven (see Sleeping). Excellent, never-ending *thalis* on rooftop "watch the sun go down over the lake listening to the drums from the Jagdish Mandir".

Garden Hotel, opposite Gulab Bagh, Excellent Gujarati/Rajasthani vegetarian *thalis*, Rs 50, served in the former royal garage of the Maharanas of Mewar, an interesting circular building. The original fuel pumps can still be seen in the forecourt where 19 cars from the ancestral fleet have been displayed. Packed at lunch, less so for dinner, elderly Laurel-and-Hardyesque waiters shout at each other and forget things, food may arrive cold, but worth it for the experience. Recommended.

The Green Room, Hathi Pol. A bit of a hike past Chandpol, past the horse stables and a bit further and you find this lovely little café serving up healthy salads, momos and delicious desserts.

Gokul, on roof of **Minerva Hotel** (see Sleeping). Good range of international cuisines, decent burgers and Israeli food, well-run and good views. Great divans for lounging. Recommended.

The Little Prince, Hanuman Ghat, near footbridge. At this charming little café you can sit right at water's edge and get big portions of the usual travellers fare from around the globe. Very popular.

Kumbha Palace (see Sleeping), T0294-242 2702. Closed 1500-1800. Excellent Indian and Western food (chocolate cake, baked potato, pizzas, milk shakes) on rooftop from where you can sneak a distant view of the City Palace sound-and-light show, friendly, helpful.

Natraj, near Town Hall. Rajasthani. Excellent *thalis* in family-run simple dining hall, very welcoming.

Papu's Juice Stand, by footbridge. Extremely popular hole in the wall juice stand serving up great juice combos and fantastic fruit salads.

Queen Café, 14 Bajrang Marg. Fantastic menu of unusual curries (mango, pumpkin and irresistible chocolate balls. Also offers cooking lessons. Highly recommended.

Samore Garden, opposite **Rang Niwas Palace**, Lake Palace Rd. Wide international menu, open later than most, no beer.

Entertainment

Udaipur *p344, map p345 and p347*

Bagore-ki-Haveli, T0294-242 3610 (after 1700). Daily cultural shows 1900-2000. Enjoyable music and dance performances, including traditional dances with women balancing pots of fire on their heads. No need to book.

Bharatiya Lok Kala Museum, T0294-252 5077. The 20-min puppet demonstrations during the day are good fun. Evening puppet show and folk dancing Sep-Mar 1800-1900, Rs 30, camera Rs 50. Recommended.

Festivals and events

Udaipur *p344, map p345 and p347*

Mar/Apr Mewar Festival (13-15 Apr 2013, 2-4 Apr 2014). See page 43 for state-wide festivals.

Shopping

Udaipur *p344, map p345 and p347*

The local handicrafts are wooden toys, colourful portable temples (*kavad*), Bandhani tie-dye fabrics, embroidery and Pichchwai paintings. Paintings are of 3 types: miniatures in the classical style of courtly Mewar; phads or folk art; and pichchwais or religious art (see Nathdwara, page 359). The more expensive ones are 'old' – 20-30 years – and are in beautiful dusky colours; the cheaper ones are brighter.

The main shopping centres are Chetak Circle, Bapu Bazar, Hathipol, Palace Rd, clock tower, Nehru Bazar, Shastri Circle, Delhi Gate, Sindhi Bazar, Bada Bazar.

Books

BA Photo and Books, 708 Palace Rd. Very good selection in several languages, also has internet access.

Mewar International, 35 Lalghat. A wide selection of English books, exchange, films.

Pustak Sadan (Hindi sign), Bapu Bazar, near Town Hall. Good for Rajasthani history.
Sai, 168 City Palace Rd, 100 m from palace gate. Good English books (new and second-hand), internet, exchange, travel services.
Suresh, Hospital Rd. Good fiction, non-fiction and academic books.

Fabric and tailoring

Ashoka, opposite entrance to **Shiv Niwas**. Good quality but very expensive.
Monsoon Collection, 55 Bhatiyani Chotta. Quick, quality tailoring. Recommended.
Shree Ji Saree Centre, Mothi Chowtha, 200 m from temple. Good value, very helpful owner. Recommended.
Udaipur New Tailors, inside Hathipol. Gents tailoring, reasonably priced, excellent service.

Handicrafts and paintings

Some shops sell old pieces of embroidery turned into bags, cushion covers, etc. Others may pass off recent work as antique.
Apollo Arts, 28 Panchwati; **Ashoka Arts** and **Uday Arts** on Lake Palace Rd, for paintings on marble paper and 'silk'; bargain hard. Hathipol shop has good silk scarves (watch batik work in progress).
Gallery Pristine, Kalapi House, Bhatiyani Chotta, Palace Rd, T0294-242 3916. Good collection of contemporary art, including original 'white on brown' paintings, pleasant ambience. Recommended.
Ganesh Handicraft Emporium, City Palace Rd, ganeshemporium@yahoo.com. Through the dull entrance of Ganesh on the main road, you disappear down an alley and come out at a huge old *haveli* spilling with traditional Udaipur and Gujarati embroideries, wooden horses and all manner of textiles. Maybe not the cheapest place, but great selection and ask for a tour of the building.
Honest Art Gallery, inside Chanpol 18, www.honestart.orgHonest Art supports Indian artists who receive 60% for each piece – find unique artworks.
KK Kasara, opposite Nami Gali, 139 Mothi Chowtha. Good religious statues, jewellery.
Modern Art Gallery, outside Chandpol, near footbridge. Beautiful collection of artwork by local artists, including Sharmila Rathore who runs the shop.
Sadhna Women's Collective, Jagdish Temple Rd. www.sadhna.org. Sadhna started in 1988 with 15 women and has grown to include the work of 600 women today as artisans and co-owners. On offer is a beautiful variety of clothes, *kurtas* and scarves as well as a homeware range with traditional appliqué, tanka and patchwork. The patterns incorporated in the pieces reflect rural life in Rajasthan.
Shivam Ayurvedic, Lake Palace Rd. Also art store, interesting, knowledgeable owner.
Sisodia Handicrafts, entrance of Shiv Niwas Palace. Miniature 'needle paintings' of high quality – see the artists at work, no hard sell.

▲ Activities and tours

Udaipur *p344, map p345 and p347*

Art, cooking and Hindi classes

Ashoka Arts, 339 'Ashoka Haveli' Gangaur Ghat. In the courtyard of Gangaur Palace, art classes are available.
Hare Krishna Arts, City Palace Rd, T0294-242 0304. Rs 450 per 2-hr art lesson, miniature techniques a speciality. Cooking classes, too.
Queen Café, 14 Bajrang Marg, T0294-243 0875. Rs 2000 for 5-hr introductory class in basics of Indian cooking: tiny kitchen but very good class. Also Hindi lessons. Both are highly recommended.

Body and soul

Bharti Guesthouse, Lake Pichola Rd, T0294-243 3469. Therapeutic, Swedish-style massage.
The Tiger, 33 Gangaur Ghat, T0294-242 0430. Great spa, with real sauna and steam rooms, jacuzzi and a range of traditional massages on offer. Recommended.

Elephant, camel and horse riding

Travel agencies (eg **Namaskar**, **Parul** in Lalghat) arrange elephant and camel rides, Rs 200 per hr but need sufficient notice. Horse riding through **Pratap Country Inn**, or **Princess Trains**, T(0)9829-042012, www.princesstrails.com, a German-Indian company that offers Marwari horses for 3 trips from 2 hrs to 8 days.

Sightseeing tours

Offered by **RTDC Fateh Memorial**, Suraj Pol. City sightseeing: half day (0830-1300) Rs 90 (reported as poor). Excursion: half day

(1400-1900), Haldighati, Nathdwara, Eklingji, Rs 130. Chittaurgarh (0830-1800), Rs 350 (with lunch); Ranakpur, Kumbhalgarh (0830-1900) Rs 330; Jagat–Jaisamand–Chavand–Rishabdeo (0830-1900) Rs 330 (with lunch).

In addition to sightseeing tours, some of the following tour operators offer accommodation bookings and travel tickets.

Aravalli Safari, 1 Sheetla Marg, Lake Palace Rd, T0294-242 0282. Very professional. Recommended.

Parul, **Jagat Niwas Hotel**, Lalghat, T0294-242 1697, parul_tour@rediffmail.com. Air/train, palace hotels, car hire, exchange. Highly recommended.

People & Places, 34-35 Shrimal Bhawan, Garden Rd, T0294-241 7359, www.palaces-tours.com.

Tourist Assistance Centre, 3 Paneri House, Bhatiyani Chotta, T0294-252 8169. Government guides charge Rs 350-400 per day for a group of 1-4 people.

Swimming

Some hotel pools are open to non-residents: **Lakshmi Vilas** (Rs 175); **Mahendra Prakash** (Rs 125); **Rang Niwas** (Rs 100); **Shiv Niwas** (Rs 300). Also at Shilipgram Craft Village, Rs 100.

Transport

Udaipur *p344, map p345 and p347*

Air Dabok airport is 25 km east, T0294-265 5453. Security check is thorough; no batteries allowed in hand luggage. 3 airlines fly in daily Kingfisher, Jet airways and Indian Airlines. Transport to town: taxis, Rs 190. **Indian Airlines**, Delhi Gate, T0294-241 0999, open 1000-1315, 1400-1700; airport, T0294-265 5453, enquiry T142. Reserve well ahead. **Indian Airlines** flights to **Delhi**, via **Jodhpur** and **Jaipur**; **Mumbai**. **Jet Airways**, T0294-256 1105, airport T0294-265 6192: **Delhi** via **Jaipur**, **Mumbai**; **Kingfisher**, T0294-510 2468: **Jodhpur** via **Jaisalmer**, **Aurangabad**, and **Agra**.

Auto-rickshaw Agree rates: about Rs 40 from bus stand to Jagdish Mandir.

Bicycle **Laxmi Bicycles**, halfway down Bhatiyani Chotta, charges Rs 30 per day for hire, well maintained and comfortable. Also shops near **Kajri Hotel**, Lalghat and Hanuman Ghat area, which also have scooters (Rs 200 per day).

Long distance bus Main State Bus Stand, near railway line opposite Udai Pol, T0294-248 4191; reservations 0700-2100. State RTC buses to **Agra**, 15 hrs; **Ahmedabad**, 252 km, 6 hrs; **Ajmer**, 274 km, 7 hrs; **Bhopal**, 765 km, 15 hrs; **Bikaner**, 500 km, 13 hrs; **Chittaurgarh**, 2½ hrs; **Delhi**, 635 km, 17 hrs; **Indore**, 373 km, 12 hrs; **Jaipur**, 405 km, 9 hrs; **Jaisalmer**, 14 hrs; **Jodhpur**, 8 hrs (uncomfortable, poorly maintained but scenic road); **Mount Abu**, 270 km, 0500-1030, 6 hrs; **Mumbai**, 802 km, very tiring, 16 hrs; **Pushkar**, tourist bus, 7 hrs; **Ujjain**, 7 hrs. Private buses and luxury coaches run mostly at night; ticket offices offices on City Station Rd, from where most buses depart. **Ahmedabad** with **Bonney Travels**, Paldi, Ahmedabad, has a/c coaches with reclining seats (contact **Shobha Travels**, City Station Rd), departs 1400 (5½ hrs), Rs 325, with drink/snack stops every 2 hrs. Highly recommended. **Shrinath**, T0294-242 2204, and **Punjab Travels** have non a/c buses to **Ahmedabad** and **Mount Abu**. **Jaipur**: several 'deluxe' buses (computerized booking) with reclining seats, more expensive but better. For **Jaisalmer**: change at Jodhpur. **Jodhpur**: several options but best to book a good seat, a day ahead, Rs 180. Tour operators have taxis for **Kumbhalgarh** and **Ranakpur**.

Motorbike Scooters and bikes can be hired from **Heera Tours & Travels** in a small courtyard behind Badi Haveli (Jagdish Temple area), Rs 250-500 per day depending on size of machine.

Taxi RTDC taxis from Fateh Memorial, Suraj Pol. Private taxis from airport, railway station, bus stands and major hotels; negotiate rates. **Taxi Stand**, Chetak Circle, T0294-252 5112. **Tourist Taxi Service**, Lake Palace Rd, T0294-252 4169.

Train Udaipur City station, 4 km southeast of centre, T0294-252 7390, T131, reservations T135. **Ahmedabad**: *Ahmedabad Exp 19943*, 1945, 8½ hrs. **Chittaurgarh**: 5 local trains daily. **Delhi (HN)**: *Mewar Exp 12964*, 1835, 12 hrs, via Chittaurgarh, Kota and Bharatpur. **Jaipur**: *Jaipur Exp 12966*, 2220, 9½ hrs, and on to **Agra** (12 hrs) and **Gwalior** (14 hrs) via **Kota** (5 hrs) and **Sawai Madhopur** (7 hrs); **Mumbai**: *Jaipur Exp 12966*,

Directory

Udaipur *p344, map p345 and p347*

Banks Many ATMs on Town Hall Rd. Chetak circle and around Bapu Bazar. Foreign exchange at **Andhra Bank**, Shakti Nagar. Cash advance against Visa/MasterCard, efficient. **Bank of Baroda**, Bapu Bazar. For Amex. **Thomas Cook**, Lake Palace Rd. Poor rates. **Trade Wings**, Polo Ground Rd, **Vijaya Bank**, City Palace entrance. **Internet** Many options around Jagdish Mandir and Hanuman Ghat, Rs 30-50 per hr. Wireless at **Whistling Teal**, next to Raj Palace Hotel, pleasant garden cafe but poor service, overpriced. **Medical services** Ambulance: T102. **General Hospital**, Chetak Circle. **Aravali Hospital** (private), 332 Ambamata Main Rd, opposite **Charak Hostel**, T0294-243 0222, very clean, professional. Recommended. **Chemist** on Hospital Rd. **Post** The GPO is at Chetak Circle. Posting a parcel can be a nightmare. **Poste Restante**: Shastri Circle Post Office. **Useful contacts** Fire: T0294-227 111. **Police**: T100. **Tourist Assistance Force**: T0294-241 1535.

Around Udaipur

The area around Udaipur is dotted with a wide range of attractions, from some of the grandest of Rajasthan's heritage hotels to some of its cosiest castles, from secluded forest lakes, surrounded by wildlife, to one of the largest reservoirs in Asia. It's also home to some ancient temples and perhaps the most evocative of Rajasthan's plentiful palaces, the Juna Mahal near Dungarpur. ▸▸ *For listings, see pages 360-361.*

Ins and outs

Most of the sights in this area are a little isolated and so not well connected by train. However, the quality of the region's roads has greatly improved recently, making travel either by bus or taxi both quick and convenient. ▸▸ *See Transport, page 361.*

Monsoon Palace

ⓘ *15 km west. Foreigners Rs 80 plus Rs 65 road toll. Taxis minimum Rs 250 (tourist taxis Rs 450 including toll), auto-rickshaws Rs 200 return including toll. Allow about 3 hrs for the round trip.*

There are good views from this deserted palace on a hilltop. The unfinished building on **Sajjangarh**, at an altitude of 335 m, which looks picturesque from the west-facing battlements, was named after Sajjan Singh (1874-1884) and was planned to be high enough to see his ancestral home, Chittaurgarh. Normally, you need a permit from the police in town to enter, though many find a tip to the gateman suffices. It offers panoramic views of Udaipur (though the highest roof is spoilt by radio antennas); the windows of the Lake Palace can be seen reflecting the setting sun. The palace itself is very run down but the views from the hill top are just as good. A visit in the late afternoon is recommended; take binoculars.

Jaisamand Lake → *Colour map 2, B4. 52 km southeast of Udaipur.*

Before the building of huge modern dams in India, Jaisamand was the second largest artificial lake in Asia, 15 km by 10 km. Dating from the late 17th century, it is surrounded by the summer palaces of the Ranis of Udaipur. The two highest surrounding hills are topped by the **Hawa Mahal** and **Ruti Rani palaces**, now empty but worth visiting for the architecture and views. A small sanctuary nearby has deer, antelope and panther. Tribals still inhabit some islands on the lake while crocodiles, keelback water snakes and turtles bask on others.

Bambora → *Colour map 2, B4. 45 minutes' drive southeast of Udaipur.*

The imposing 18th-century hilltop fortress of Bambora has been converted to a heritage hotel by the royal family of Sodawas at an enormous restoration cost yet retaining its ancient character. The impressive fort is in Mewari style with domes, turrets and arches. To get here from Udaipur, go 12 km east along the airport road and take the right turn towards Jaisamand Lake passing the 11th-century Jagat Temple (38 km) before reaching Bambora.

Sitamata Wildlife Sanctuary → *Colour map 2, B4. 117 km from Udaipur.*

The reserve of dense deciduous forests covers over 400 sq km and has extensive birdlife (woodpeckers, tree pies, blue jays, jungle fowl). It is one of the few sanctuaries between the Himalaya and the Nilgiris where giant brown flying squirrels have been reported. Visitors have seen hordes of langur monkey, nilgai in groups of six or seven, four-horned antelope, jackal and even panther and hyena, but the thick forests make sighting difficult. There are crocodiles in the reservoirs.

Rishabdeo → *Colour map 2, C4. 63 km south of Udaipur along the NH8.*

Rishabdeo, off the highway, has a remarkable 14th-century Jain temple with intricate white marble carving and black marble statuary, though these are not as fine as at Dilwara or Ranakpur. Dedicated to the first Jain Tirthankar, Adinath or Rishabdev, Hindus, Bhils as well as Jains worship there. An attractive bazar street leads to the temple, which is rarely visited by tourists. Special worship is conducted several times daily when Adinath, regarded as the principal focus of worship, is bathed with saffron water or milk. The priests are friendly; a small donation (Rs 10-20) is appreciated.

Dungarpur → *Colour map 2, C4. Phone code: 02964. Population 50,000.*

Dungarpur (City of Hills) dates from the 13th century. The district is the main home of the Bhil tribal people, see page 320. It is also renowned for its stone masons, who in recent years have been employed to build Hindu temples as far afield as London. The attractive and friendly village has one of the most richly decorated and best-preserved palaces in Rajasthan, the Juna Mahal. Surrounded on three sides by Lake Gaibsagar and backed by picturesque hills, the more recent **Udai Bilas Palace** (now a heritage hotel, see page 360) was built by Maharawal Udai Singhji in the 19th century and extended in 1943. The huge courtyard surrounds a 'pleasure pool' from the centre of which rises a four-storeyed pavilion with a beautifully carved wooden chamber.

The **Juna Mahal**, above the village, dates from the 13th century when members of the Mewar clan at Chittaur moved south to found a new kingdom after a family split. It is open to guests staying at Udai Bilas and by ticket (Rs 150) for non-residents, obtainable at the hotel. The seven-storeyed fortress-like structure with turrets, narrow entrances and tiny windows has colourful and vibrant rooms profusely decorated over several centuries with miniature wall paintings (among the best in Rajasthan), and glass and mirror inlay work. There are some fine *jarokha* balconies and sculpted panels illustrating musicians and dancers in the local green-grey parava stone which are strikingly set against the plain white walls of the palace to great effect. The steep narrow staircases lead to a series of seven floors giving access to public halls, supported on decorated columns, and to intimate private chambers. There is a jewel of a Sheesh Mahal and a cupboard in the Maharawal's bedroom on the top floor covered in miniatures illustrating some 50 scenes from the Kama Sutra. Windows and balconies open to the breeze command lovely views over the town below. Perhaps nowhere else in Rajasthan gives as good an impression of how these palaces must have been hundreds of years ago; it is completely unspoilt and hugely impressive. It is amazing, but not very accessible to elderly people. There is no actual path.

Some interesting temples nearby include the 12th-century Siva temple at **Deo Somnath**, 12 km away, and the splendid complex of temple ruins profusely decorated with stone sculptures.

Dungarpur is a birdwatchers' paradise with lots of ducks, moorhens, waders, ibises at the lake, tropical green pigeons and grey hornbills in the woods.

Khempur

This small, attractive village is conveniently located midway between Udaipur and Chittaurgarh. To find it turn off the highway, 9 km south of Mavli and about 50 km from Udaipur. The main reason for visiting is to eat or stay in the charming heritage hotel, see Sleeping, page 360.

Eklingji and Nagda → *Colour map 2, B4. 22 km north of Udaipur.*

ⓘ *0400-0700, 1000-1300 and 1700-1900. No photography.*

The white marble **Eklingji Temple** has a two-storey mandapa to Siva, the family deity of the Mewars. It dates from AD 734 but was rebuilt in the 15th century. There is a silver door and screen and a silver Nandi facing the black marble Siva. The evenings draw crowds of worshippers and few tourists. Many smaller temples surround the main one and are also worth seeing. Nearby is the large but simple **Lakulisa Temple** (AD 972), and other ruined semi-submerged temples. The back-street shops sell miniature paintings, see page 320. It is a peaceful spot attracting many waterbirds. Occasional buses go from Udaipur to Eklingji and Nagda which are set in a deep ravine containing the Eklingji Lake. The RTDC (see page 344) run tours from Udaipur, 1400-1900.

At Nagda, are three temples: the ruined 11th-century Jain temple of **Adbhutji** and the **Vaishnavite Sas-Bahu** (Mother-in-law/Daughter-in-law) temples. The complex, though comparatively small, has some very intricate carving on pillars, ceiling and mandapa walls. You can hire bicycles in Eklingji to visit them. There are four 14th-century Jain Temples at **Delwara** about 5 km from Eklingji, which also boast the **Devi Garh**, one of India's most luxurious hotels.

Nathdwara → *Colour map 2, B4. 48 km from Udaipur.*

This is a centre of the Krishna worshipping community of Gujarati merchants who are followers of Vallabhacharya (15th century). Non-Hindus are not allowed inside the temple, which contains a black marble Krishna image, but the outside has interesting paintings. **Shrinathji Temple** is one of the richest Hindu temples in India. At one time only high caste Hindus (Brahmins, Kshatriyas) were allowed inside, and the *pichhwais* (temple hangings) were placed outside, for those castes and communities who were not allowed into the sanctum sanctorum, to experience the events in the temple courtyard and learn about the life of lord Krishna. You can watch the 400-year-old tradition of *pichhwai* painting which originated here. The artists had accompanied the Maharana of Mewar, one of the few Rajput princes who still resisted the Mughals, who settled here when seeking refuge from Aurangzeb's attacks. Their carriage carrying the idol of Shrinathji was stuck at Nathdwara in Mewar, 60 km short of the capital Udaipur. Taking this as a sign that this was where God willed to have his home, they developed this into a pilgrim centre for the worship of lord Krishna's manifestation, Shrinathji. Their paintings, *pichhwais*, depict Lord Krishna as Shrinathji in different moods according to the season. The figures of lord Krishna and the *gopis* (milkmaids) are frozen on a backdrop of lush trees and deep skies. The bazar sells *pichhwais* painted on homespun cloth with mineral and organic colour often fixed with starch.

Rajsamand Lake → *Colour map 2, B4. 56 km north of Udaipur.*

At **Kankroli** is the Rajsamand Lake. The **Nauchoki Bund**, the embankment which contains it, is over 335 m long and 13 m high, with ornamental pavilions and *toranas*, all of marble and exquisitely carved. Behind the masonry bund is an 11-m-wide earthen embankment, erected in 1660 by Rana Raj Singh who had defeated Aurangzeb on several occasions. He also commissioned the longest inscription in the world, "Raj Prashasthi Maha Kavyam", which tells the story of Mewar on 24 granite slabs in Sanskrit. Kankroli and its beautiful temple are on the southeast side of the lake.

Deogarh → *Colour map 2, B4. 2 km off the NH8. Altitude: 700 m.*

Deogarh (Devgarh) is an excellent place to break journey between Udaipur and Jaipur or Pushkar. It is a very pleasant, little frequented town with a dusty but interesting bazar (if you are interested in textiles, visit **Vastra Bhandar** ⓘ *T02904-252187*, for reasonably priced and good-quality textiles). Its elevation makes it relatively cool and the country- side and surrounding hills are good for gentle treks. There is an old fort on a hill as well as a magnificent palace on a hillock in the centre with murals illustrating the fine local school of miniature painting. **Raghosagar Lake**, which is very pleasant to walk around, has an island with a romantic ruined temple and centotaphs (poor monsoons leave the lake dry). It attracts numerous migratory birds and is an attractive setting for the charming 200-year-old palace, **Gokal Vilas**, the home of the present Rawat Saheb Nahar Singhji and the Ranisahiba. Their two sons have opened the renovated 17th-century **Deogarh Mahal Palace** to guests, see Sleeping, page 361. The Rawat, a knowledgeable historian and art connoisseur, has a private collection of over 50 paintings which guests may view, advance notice required. The shop at the hotel has good modern examples to buy. There is plenty to do here including an excellent 45-minute train journey from Deogarh to Phulud which winds down through the Aravalli hills to the plain below through tunnels and bridges.

Around Udaipur listings

For Sleeping and Eating price codes and other relevant information, see Essentials pages 38-42.

Sleeping

Jaisamand Lake *p357*

A Jaisamand Island Resort, Baba Island on Jaisamand Lake, T02906-234723, http://jaisamand.com. 40 well-equipped a/c rooms in an unsubtle concrete castle, pool, garden, excellent location, great views, restaurant (international menu), mixed reports on food and service.

Bambora *p357*

AL-A Karni Fort, Bambora, T0291-2512101, www.karnihotels.com. Heritage hotel with 30 beautifully decorated rooms (circular beds) in large, imposing fort, marble bathrooms, modern facilities, impressive interiors, enthusiastic and friendly manager, exceptional marble pool, folk concerts, great beer bar, delicious food, hugely enjoyable. Recommended.

Sitamata Wildlife Sanctuary *p358*

B-C Fort Dhariyawad, at the sanctuary, T02950-220050. 14 rooms and 4 suites in restored and converted, mid-16th-century fort (founded by one of Maharana Pratap's sons) and some in contemporary cottage cluster, meals (international menu), period decor, medieval flavour, great location by sanctuary (flying squirrels, langur monkeys in garden, crocodiles in reservoir), tribal village tours, jeeps to park, horse safaris, treks.

D Forest Lodge, at the sanctuary, Dhariyawad, contact District Forest Officer, Chittorgarh, T01472-244915. Rather expensive considering lack of amenities, but fantastic location and views, a paradise for birders.

Dungarpur *p358*

A Udai Bilas Palace, 2 km from Dungarpur, T02964-230808, www.udaibilas palace.com. 22 unique a/c rooms (including 16 suites of which 6 are vast 'grand suites') mirror mosaics, some dated with art deco furniture, marble bathrooms. With quite possibly the most stunning restaurant in India, charming host Harshvardhan Singh has built a beautiful restaurant around a central water feature. He has also created a very eccentric bar to appeal to every car fanatic which compliments his great vintage car collection. There is a lovely relaxing pool area too. Highly recommended.

E-F Vaibhav, Saghwara Rd, T02964-230244. Simple rooms, tea stall/restaurant, owner very friendly and helpful.

Khempur *p359*

C Ravla Khempur, T02955-237154, www.ravla khempur.com. The former home of the village chieftain, this is a charming, small-scale heritage property. The rooms have been sensitively renovated with modern bathrooms, pleasant lawns, horse rides a speciality.

Eklingji and Nagda *p359*

LL Devi Garh, Delwara, 5 km from Eklingji, T02953-289211, www.deviresorts.com. For the ultimate in luxury. It specializes in letting all 30 individually decorated suites for fabulous weddings or parties.

A Heritage Resort, Lake Bagela, Eklingji, T(0)9829-252507, www.heritageresort.com. Fabulously located by the lake and ringed by hills. 30 excellent a/c rooms, contemporary building in traditional design, good food (organic vegetarian grown on property, pool, jacuzzi, boating, riding, good walking and cycling. Recommended.

Nathdwara *p359*

E Gokul (RTDC), near Lalbagh, 2 km from bus stand, Nathdwara, T02953-230917. 6 rooms and dorm (Rs 50), restaurant.

F Yatrika Mangla (RTDC), Nathdwara, T02953-231119. Hotel with 5 rooms and dorm (Rs 50).

Deogarh *p360*

AL-B Deogarh Mahal, T02904-252777, www.deogarhmahal.com. This labyrinthine fort dates back to 1617 and boasts 50 beautifully restored rooms, including atmospheric suites furnished in traditional style with good views, best have balconies with private jacuzzis, but not all are up to the same standard. Fabulous lotus-flower-shaped pool, Keralan massage, Mewari meals, home-grown produce (room service 50% extra), bar, good gift shop, log fires, folk entertainment, boating, birdwatching, jeep safaris, audio tour by William Dalrymple, talks on art history, hospitable and delightful hosts. They can organize romantic dinners in private courtyards around the mahal or out in abandoned forts in the surrounding countryside or gala dinners with camel cart rides and fireworks. Outstanding hotel; highly recommended. Reserve well ahead. The family have also renovated the **Fort Singh Sagar** fort, 5 km from Deogarh. This is where the man of the house of Deogarh Mahal used to bring his shooting parties. With more contemporary décor, there are 4 stylish suites and amazing sunken bathrooms. It is in the middle of a small lake, very serene and is an ideal hideaway. Prices start at US$350 per night. Stunning.

AL-B Deogarh Khayyam, 4 km from Deogarh, T02904-252777, www.deogarhmahal.com. These stunning tents are perched on a jungle plateau – you are utterly surrounded by nature. The 16 luxurious tents are fairly spread out so you feel the birds and wildlife are your neighbours not your fellow guests. Log fires and starry skies in the evening and the same amazing food as Deogarh Mahal served up. Camping was never so exciting.

Festivals and events

Dungarpur *p358*

Feb Baneshwar Fair (21-25 Feb 2013 and 10-14 Feb 2014). The tribal festival at the Baneshwar Temple, 70 km from Dungarpur, is one of Rajasthan's largest tribal fairs when Bhils gather at the temple in large numbers for ritual bathing at the confluence of rivers. There are direct buses to Baneshwar during the fair. The temporary camp during the fair is best avoided. **Vagad Festival** in Dungarpur offers an insight into local tribal culture. Both are uncommercialized and authentic. Details from **Udai Bilas Palace**, see Sleeping, page 360.

Transport

Around Udaipur *p357*

Bus For **Nathdwara**, several buses from Udaipur from early morning. Buses also go to **Nagda**, **Eklingji** and **Rajsamand**. Private transport only for Khempur and Deogarh. From Dungarpur buses travel to/from **Udaipur** (110 km), 2 hrs, **Ahmedabad** (170 km), 4 hrs. You will need to hire a taxi to get to the other destinations.

Kumbhalgarh, Ranakpur and around

Little-known Kumbhalgarh is one of the finest examples of defensive fortification in Rajasthan. You can wander around the palace, the many temples and along the walls – 36 km long in all – to savour the great panoramic views. It is two hours north (63 km) of Udaipur through the attractive Rajasthani countryside. The small fields are well kept and Persian wheels and 'tanks' are dotted across the landscape. In winter, wheat and mustard grow in the fields, and the journey there and back is as magical as the fort.

The temples of Ranakpur are incredibly ornate and amazingly unspoilt by tourism, having preserved a dignified air which is enhanced by the thick green forests that surround them. There are a number of interesting villages and palaces in the nearby area; if time allows this is a great region to explore at leisure, soaking in the unrushed, rural way of life. ▸▸ *For listings, see pages 364-366.*

Kumbhalgarh → *For listings, see pages 364-366. Colour map 2, B4.*

Kumbhalgarh Fort → *Phone code: 02954. Altitude: 1087m. 63 km from Udaipur.*

ⓘ *Foreigners Rs 100, Indians Rs 5.*

Kumbhalgarh Fort, off the beaten tourist track, was the second most important fort of the Mewar Kingdom after Chittaurgarh. Built mostly by Maharana Kumbha (circa 1485), it is situated on a west-facing ridge of the Aravalli hills, commanding a great strategic position on the border between the Rajput kingdoms of Udaipur (Mewar) and Jodhpur (Marwar). It is accessible enough to make a visit practicable and getting there is half the fun. There are superb views over the lower land to the northwest, standing over 200 m above the pass leading via Ghanerao towards Udaipur.

The approach Passing though charming villages and hilly terrain, the route to the fort is very picturesque. The final dramatic approach is across deep ravines and through thick scrub jungle. Seven gates guarded the approaches while seven ramparts were reinforced by semicircular bastions and towers. The 36-km-long black walls with curious bulbous towers exude a feeling of power as they snake their way up and down impossibly steep terrain. They were built to defy scaling and their width enabled rapid deployment of forces – six horses could walk along them side by side. The walls enclose a large plateau containing the smaller Katargarh Fort with the decaying palace of Fateh Singh, a garrison, 365 temples and shrines, and a village. The occupants (reputedly 30,000) could be self-sufficient in food and water, with enough storage to last a year. The fort's dominant location enabled defenders to see aggressors approaching from a great distance. Kumbhalgarh is believed to have been taken only once and that was because the water in the ponds was poisoned by enemy Mughals during the reign of Rana Pratap.

The gates The first gate **Arait Pol** is some distance from the main fort; the area was once thick jungle harbouring tigers and wild boar. Signals would be flashed by mirror in times of emergency. **Hulla Pol** (Gate of Disturbance) is named after the point reached by invading Mughal armies in 1567. **Hanuman Pol** contains a shrine and temple. The **Bhairava Pol** records the 19th-century chief minister who was exiled. The fifth gate, the **Paghra (Stirrup) Pol** is where the cavalry assembled; the Star tower nearby has walls 8 m thick. The Top-Khana (Cannon Gate) is alleged to have a secret escape tunnel. The last, **Nimbu (Lemon) Pol** has the Chamundi temple beside it.

The palace It is a 30-minute walk (fairly steep in parts) from the car park to the roof of the Maharana's darbar hall. Tiers of inner ramparts rise to the summit like a fairytale castle, up to the appropriately named Badal Mahal (19th century) or 'palace in the clouds', with the interior painted in pastel colours. Most of the empty palace is usually unlocked (a *chaukidar* holds the keys). The views over the walls to the jungle-covered hillsides (now a wildlife reserve) and across the deserts of Marwar towards Jodhpur, are stunning. The palace rooms are decorated in a 19th-century style and some have attractive coloured friezes, but are unfurnished. After the maze-like palace at Udaipur, this is very compact. The Maharana's palace has a remarkable blue darbar hall with floral motifs on the ceiling. Polished *chunar* (lime) is used on walls and window sills, but the steel ceiling girders give away its late 19th-century age. A gap separated the *mardana* (men's) palace from the *zenana* (women's) palace. Some of the rooms in the *zenana* have an attractive painted frieze with elephants, crocodiles and camels. A circular Ganesh temple is in the corner of the *zenana* courtyard. A striking feature of the toilets was the ventilation system which allowed fresh air into the room while the toilet was in use.

Kumbhalgarh Wildlife Sanctuary

ⓘ *Foreigners Rs 100, Indians Rs 10, car Rs 65, open sunrise to sunset.*

The sanctuary to the west of the fort covering about 600 sq km has a sizeable wildlife population but you have to be extremely lucky to spot any big game in the thick undergrowth. Some visitors have seen bear, panther, wolf and hyena but most have to be contented with seeing nilgai, sambhar deer, wild boar, jackal, jungle cat and birds. Crocodiles and water fowl can be seen at **Thandi Beri Lake**. Jeep and horse safaris can be organized from hotels in the vicinity including **Aodhi, Ranakpur, Ghanerao** and **Narlai**. The rides can be quite demanding as the tracks are very rough. There is a 4WD jeep track and a trekking trail through the safari area can be arranged through Shivika Lake Hotel, Ranakpur (http://shivikalakehotel.com).

The tribal Bhils and Garasias – the latter found only in this belt (see page 320) – can be seen here, living in their traditional huts. The Forest Department may permit an overnight stay in their Rest House in **Kelwara**, the closest town, 6 km from sanctuary. With steep, narrow streets devoid of cars it is an attractive little place.

Ghanerao and Rawla Narlai → *For listings, see pages 364-366.* *Colour map 2, B4.*

Ghanerao was founded in 1606 by Gopal Das Rathore of the Mertia clan, and has a number of red sandstone *havelis* as well as several old temples, *baolis* and marble *chhatris*, 5 km beyond the reserve. The village lay at the entrance to one of the few passes through the Aravallis between the territories held by the Rajput princes of Jodhpur and Udaipur. The beautiful 1606 **royal castle** has marble pavilions, courtyards, paintings, wells, elephant stables and walls marked with canon balls. The present Thakur Sajjan Singh has opened his castle to guests (see Sleeping, page 365), and organizes two- to three-day treks to Kumbhalgarh Fort, 50 km by road accessible to jeep, and Ranakpur.

The **Mahavir Jain Temple**, 5 km away, is a beautiful little 10th-century temple. It is a delightful place to experience an unspoiled rural environment.

Rawla Narlai, 25 km from Kumbhalgarh Fort, and an hour's drive from Ranakpur, is a Hindu and Jain religious centre. It has a 17th-century fort with interesting architecture, right in the heart of the village, which is ideal for a stopover.

Ranakpur → *For listings, see pages 364-366.* *Colour map 2, B4. Phone code: 02934. 90 km Udaipur, 25 km Kumbhalgarh.*

ⓘ *Daily; non-Jains are only allowed to visit the Adinatha 1200-1700, free. Photos with permission from Kalyanji Anandji Trust office next to the temple, camera Rs 50, video Rs 150, photography of the principal Adinatha image is prohibited. Shoes and socks must be removed at the entrance. Black clothing and shorts are not permitted. No tips, though unofficial 'guides' may ask for baksheesh.*

One of five holy Jain sites and a popular pilgrimage centre, it has one of the best-known Jain temple complexes in the country. Though not comparable in grandeur to the Dilwara temples in Mount Abu, it has very fine ornamentation and is in a wonderful setting with peacocks, langurs and numerous birds. The semi-enclosed deer park with spotted deer, nilgai and good birdlife next to the temple, attracts the occasional panther! You can approach Ranakpur from Kumbhalgarh through the wildlife reserve in 1½ hours although you will need to arrange transport from the Sanctuary entrance. A visit is highly recommended.

The **Adinatha** (1439), the most noteworthy of the three main temples here, is dedicated to the first Tirthankar. Of the 1444 engraved pillars, in Jain tradition, no two are the same, each individually carved. The sanctuary is symmetrically planned around the central shrine and is within a 100-sq-m raised terrace enclosed in a high wall with 66 subsidiary shrines lining it, each with a spire; the gateways consist of triple-storey porches. The sanctuary with a clustered centre tower contains a *chaumukha* (four-fold) marble image of Adinatha. The whole complex, including the extraordinary array of engraved pillars, carved ceilings and arches are intricately decorated, often with images of Jain saints, friezes of scenes from their lives and holy sites. The lace-like interiors of the corbelled domes are a superb example of western Indian temple style. The **Parsvanatha** and **Neminath** are two smaller Jain temples facing this, the former with a black image of Parsvanatha in the sanctuary and erotic carvings outside. The star-shaped **Surya Narayana Temple** (mid-15th century) is nearby.

There is a beautiful 3.7-km trek around the wildlife sanctuary, best attempted from November to March, contact sanctuary office next to temples for information.

Kumbhalgarh, Ranakpur and around listings

For Sleeping and Eating price codes and other relevant information, see Essentials pages 38-42.

Sleeping

Kumbhalgarh *p362*

AL Aodhi (HRH), 2 km from fort gate, T02954-242341, www.eternalmewar.in. Closest place to fort, great location set in to the rock face. 27 rooms in modern stone 'cottages' decorated in colonial style to good effect with attached modern bathrooms. Beautiful restaurant and coffee shop, pool, relaxing atmosphere, very helpful staff, fabulous views, very quiet, superb horse safaris (US$200 per night), trekking, tribal village tours. Highly recommended.

A-B Club Mahindra Fort Kumbhalgarh, Kelwara–Kumbhalgarh Rd, T1800-425 2737, www.clubmahindra.com. Part of the Club Mahindra chain, this beautifully designed hotel caters mainly for Indian tourists, but would be great for families as it has a lovely pool and lots of activities like archery and a children's play area. This is a big place with 80 odd rooms, there are regular theme nights and several restaurants on-site.

C-E Dera, Kelwara, T02954-242200, www.derakumbhalgarh.com. Great array of tents in three categories – some with a/c. Some of the tents are semi-permanent so are beautifully furnished, others are a fabulous purple inside rather than the standard white. Great views. Recommended.

D-E Ratnadeep, Kelwara, in the middle of a bustling village, T02954-242217, hotelratnadeep@yahoo.co.in. 14 basic rooms, some deluxe with cooler and marble floors, Western toilets, small lawn, restaurant, camel, horse and jeep safaris, friendly, well run.

E Forest Department Guest House, near the Parsram Temple, about 3 km from **Aodhi** by road then 3 km by 4WD jeep or on foot. Basic facilities but fantastic views over the Kumbalgarh sanctuary towards the drylands of Marwar.

G Lucky, 2 km from fort at bottom of hill by Kelwara turn-off, T02593-513965. Simple, quite new guesthouse, some rooms with shared bath, good cheap food in generous portions, friendly and keen owner.

Ghanerao and Rawla Narlai *p363*

AL Fort Rawla Narlai, Rawla Narlai, T02934-282425. Overlooked by a huge granite boulder, this place is rather special. The energy of the boulder and the temples and caves that are dotted around it, plus the beautifully renovated fort create a very serene place to hideaway. 20 rooms (11 a/c) individually decorated with antiques, new showers, plus 5 luxurious, well-appointed 'tents', good simple meals under the stars, helpful, friendly staff, attractive garden setting, good riding. You can wander up to the temple on top of the boulder by scaling 700 steps. Highly recommended.

B Kotri Raola, Ghanerao, T02934-240224, www.kotriraola.com. 8 rooms, 2 suites in 18th-century royal 'bungalow', excellent horse safaris run by Thakur Mahendra Singh, an expert on Marwari horses and his son, a well-known polo player.

B-C Ghanerao Royal Castle, see page 363, reservations, T022-404 2211 (Mumbai), www.nivalink.com/ghanerao. Suites and a restaurant serving simple food, slightly run-down but has nostalgic appeal of faded glory, charming hosts, expensive local guide (bargain hard if buying paintings), jeeps and camping arranged.

C Bagha-ka-Bagh (Tiger's Den), Ghanerao. Spartan hunting lodge among tall grass jungle near wildlife sanctuary gate. 8 basic rooms, 5 with bucket hot water, dorm, generator for electricity, breathtaking location, wildlife (including panther, nilgai), rich in birdlife, 5-day treks including Kumbhalgarh, Ranakpur. Contact **North West Safaries**, T079-2630 8031, ssibal@ad1.vsnl.net.in.

Ranakpur *p363*

AL Fateh Bagh Palace (HRH), on the highway near the temple, T02934-286186, www.eternalmewar.in. A 200-year-old fort was dismantled in to 65,000 pieces and transported here from its original site 50 km away in order to make this palace. The result is a beautiful property, cleverly combining old and new. There are 20 tastefully decorated, well-appointed rooms, including 4 suites, the best of which have attached jacuzzis. Good pool, friendly staff.

A Maharani Bagh (WelcomHeritage), Ranakpur Rd, T02934-285105, www.marudharhotels.com. 18 well- furnished modern bungalows with baths in lovely 19th-century walled orchard of Jodhpur royal family, full of bougainvillea and mangos, outdoor Rajasthani restaurant (traditional Marwari meals Rs 400), pool, jeep safaris, horse riding. Wake up call is care of the peacocks or langur monkeys tap dancing on the roof.

C Ranakpur Hill Resort, Ranakpur Rd, T02934-286411, www.ranakpurhillresort.com. 16 good-sized, well-appointed rooms, 5 a/c, in new construction, pleasant dining room, clean pool.

D-F Roopam, Ranakpur Rd, T02934-285321, www.roopamresort.com. 12 well-maintained rooms, some a/c, pleasant restaurant, attractive lawns.

E-F Shilpi (RTDC), T02934-285074. 12 clean-ish rooms, best with hot water and a/c, dorm (dirty), vegetarian meals.

F Dharamshala, T02934-285119. Some comfortable rooms, simple and extremely cheap vegetarian meals.

Eating

Kumbhalgarh *p362*

TTT Aodhi (see Sleeping). Thatched restaurant with central barbecue area. Good Indian (try *laal maas*, a mutton dish), authentic 7-course Mewari meal but service can be very slow.

TT Ratnadeep. À la carte vegetarian menu.

Ranakpur *p363*

There are no eateries near the temple, only a tea stall, but the *dharamshala* serves very good cheap food at lunchtime and sunset.

TT Roopam, Ranakpur-Maharani Bagh Rd, near Shivika. Good Rajasthani food. Pleasant village theme setting, modern, popular.

TT Shivika Lake, part open-air restaurant by lake with hill views. Delicious Rajasthani lunches, non-spicy curries possible, barbecued chicken, excellent breakfasts, tea by the lake, family-run, clean.

Transport

While most of the places in this section do have bus links, a private car is indispensable and makes the most of the scenic drives on offer. A round-trip from Udaipur could also take in Eklingji, Nagda and Nathdwara.

Kumbhalgarh *p362*

Bus and taxi For the fort: buses (irregular times) from Chetak Circle, Udaipur go to **Kelwara**, Rs 20, 3 hrs (cars take 2 hrs); from there a local bus (Rs 6) can take you a further 4 km up to a car park; the final 2-km climb is on foot; the return is a pleasant downhill walk of 1 hr. Jeep taxis charge Rs 50-100 from Kelwara to the fort (and say there are no buses). Return buses to Udaipur from Kelwara until 1730. Buses to **Saira** leave in the afternoon.

From Udaipur, a taxi for 4, about Rs 2500 depending on car, can cover the fort and Ranakpur in 11 hrs; very worthwhile.

Ranakpur *p363*
Bus From Udaipur, there are 6 buses daily (0530-1600), slow, 3 hrs. Also buses from **Jodhpur** and **Mount Abu**. To get to **Kumbhalgarh**, take Udaipur bus as far as **Saira** (20 km, 45 mins), then catch a bus or minibus to the Kumbhalgarh turn-off (32 km, 1 hr).
Taxi For taxi options, see above.
Train The nearest railway line is Falna Junction on the Ajmer–Mount Abu line, 39 km away.

Mount Abu and around

Mount Abu, Rajasthan's only hill resort, stretches along a 20-km plateau. Away from the congestion and traffic of the tourist centres on the plains, Mount Abu is surrounded by well-wooded countryside filled with flowering trees, numerous orchids during the monsoon and a good variety of bird and animal life. Many of the rulers from surrounding princely states had summer houses built here and today it draws visitors from Rajasthan and neighbouring Gujarat who come to escape the searing heat of summer (and Gujarat's alcohol prohibition) and also to see the exquisite Dilwara Jain temples. Alas it is a bit like Margate with softy ice creams, pedalos on Nakki Lake and portrait sketches, but is great for a birds' eye view of Indians at play – it is overrun in the hot months between April and June and around Diwali when hotel prices can triple. There are some fabulous heritage hotels in the area, well off the beaten track and worthwhile experiences in themselves. ▸▸ *For listings, see pages 371-374.*

Ins and outs

Getting there and around The nearest railway station is at Abu Road, 27 km away. It is usually quicker to take a bus directly to Mount Abu, instead of going to Abu Road by train and then taking a bus up the hill. The compact area by Nakki Lake, with hotels, restaurants and shops, is pedestrianized. Taxis are available at a stand nearby. A form of transport unique to Mount Abu is the *baba gari*, a small trolley generally used to pull small children up the steepest of Mount Abu's hills. ▸▸ *See Transport, page 373.*
Tourist information RTDC ⓘ *opposite the bus stand, T02974-235151, 0800-1100, 1600- 2000.* Guides available, four to eight hours, Rs 250-400.

Mount Abu → *For listings, see pages 371-374. Colour map 2, B3. Phone code: 02974. Population: 15,600. Altitude: 1720 m.*

Mount Abu was the home of the legendary sage Vasishtha. One day Nandini, his precious wish-fulfilling cow, fell into a great lake. Vasishtha requested the gods in the Himalaya to save her so they sent Arbuda, a cobra, who carried a rock on his head and dropped it into the lake, displacing the water, and so saved Nandini. The place became known as Arbudachala, the 'Hill of Arbuda'. Vasishtha also created the four powerful 'fire-born' Rajput tribes, including the houses of Jaipur and Udaipur at a ritual fire ceremony on the mount. Nakki Talao (Lake), sacred to Hindus, was, in legend, scooped out by the *nakki* (fingernails) of gods attempting to escape the wrath of a demon. Abu was leased by the British government from the Maharao of Sirohi and was used as the headquarters for the Resident of Rajputana until 1947, and as a sanatorium for troops.

Dilwara Jain Temples

ⓘ *Free (no photography), shoes and cameras, mobile phones, leather items and backpacks (Rs 1 per item) are left outside, tip expected; 1200-1800 for non-Jains; some guides are excellent, it's a 1-hr uphill walk from town, or share a jeep, Rs 5 each.*
Set in beautiful surroundings of mango trees and wooded hills, 5 km from the town centre, the temples have superb marble carvings. The complex of five principal temples is surrounded by a

high wall, dazzling white in the sunlight. There is a resthouse for pilgrims on the approach road, which is also lined with stalls selling a collection of tourist kitsch lending a carnival atmosphere to the sanctity of the temples. It would be beautiful and serene here, but noisy guides and visitors break the sanctity of the magnificent temples.

Chaumukha Temple The grey sandstone building is approached through the entrance on your left. Combining 13th- and 15th-century styles, it is generally regarded as inferior to the two main temples. The colonnaded hall (ground floor) contains four-faced images of the Tirthankar Parsvanatha (hence *chaumukha*), and figures of *dikpalas* and *yakshis*.

1 Mount Abu

Mount Abu maps
1 Mount Abu, page 367
2 Dilwara Temples, page 368

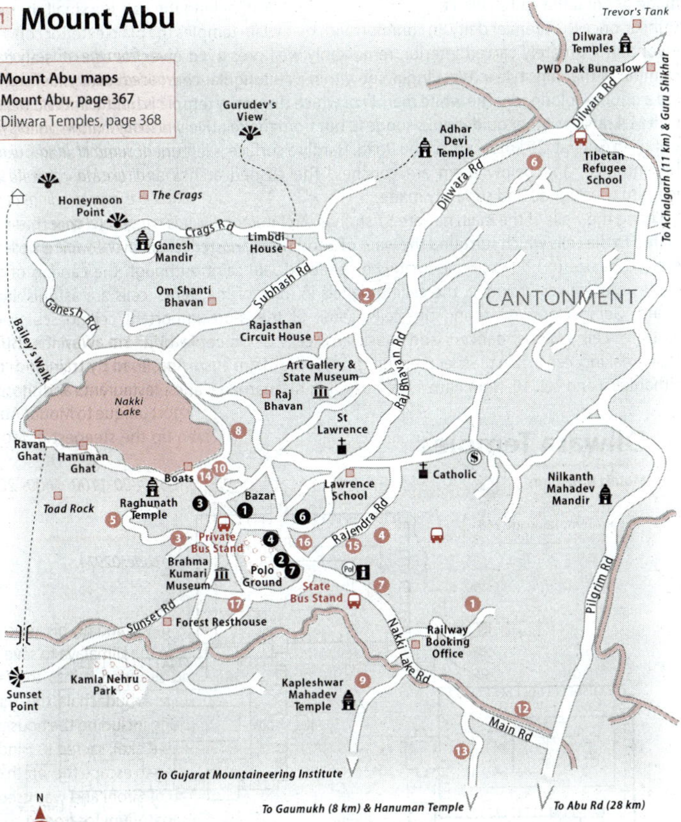

Sleeping
Aradhana 13
Aravalli 1
Cama Rajputana Club Resort 2
Chacha Inn 12
Connaught House 4
Hilltop 7
Jaipur House 5
Lake Palace 8
Lake View 10
Palace 6
Panghat 14
Rajendra 15
Samrat International 16
Saraswati 17
Shri Ganesh 3
Sunrise Palace 9

Eating
Chunky Bites 1
Coffee Day 2
King's Food 3
Madras Café 4
Sankalp 2
Shere-e-Punjab 6
Veena 7

Adinatha Temple (Vimala Shah Temple) This temple lies directly ahead; the oldest and most famous of the Dilwara group. Immediately outside the entrance to the temple is a small portico known as the Hastishala (elephant hall), built by Prithvipal in 1147-1159 which contains a figure of the patron, Vimala Shah, the Chief Minister of the Solanki King, on horseback. Vimala Shah commissioned the temple, dedicated to Adinatha, in 1031-1032. The riders on the 10 beautifully carved elephants that surround him were removed during Alauddin Khilji's reign. Dilwara belonged to Saivite Hindus who were unwilling to part with it until Vimala Shah could prove that it had once belonged to a Jain community. In a dream, the goddess Ambika (Ambadevi or Durga) instructed him to dig under a champak tree where he found a huge image of Adinatha and so won the land. To the southwest, behind the hall, is a small shrine to Ambika, once the premier deity. In common with many Jain temples the plain exterior conceals a wonderful ornately carved interior, remarkably well preserved given its age. It is an early example of the Jain style in West India, set within a rectangular court lined with small shrines and a double colonnade. The white marble of which the entire temple is built was brought not from Makrana, as other guidebooks suggest, but from the relatively nearby marble quarries of Ambaji in Gujarat, 25 km south of Abu Road. Hardly a surface is left unadorned. Makaras guard the entrance, and below them are conches. The cusped arches and ornate capitals are beautifully designed and superbly made.

Lining the walls of the main hall are 57 shrines. Architecturally, it is suggested that these are related to the cells which surround the walls of Buddhist monasteries, but in the Jain temple are reduced in size to house simple images of a seated Jain saint. Although the carving of the images themselves is simple, the ceiling panels in front of the saints' cells are astonishingly ornate. Going clockwise round the cells, some of the more important ceiling sculptures illustrate: cell 1, lions, dancers and musicians; cells 2-7, people bringing offerings, birds, music-making; cell 8, Jain teacher preaching; cell 9, the major auspicious events in the life of the Tirthankars; and cell 10, Neminath's life, including his marriage, and playing with Krishna and

2 Dilwara Temples

➡Mount Abu maps
1 Mount Abu, page 367
2 Dilwara Temples, page 368

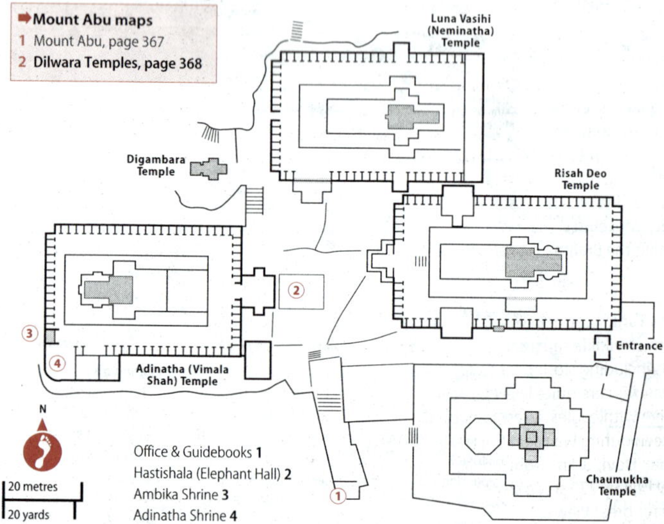

the *gopis*. In the southeast corner of the temple between cells 22 and 23 is a large black idol of Adinath, reputedly installed by Vimal Shah in 1031.

Cell 32 shows Krishna subduing Kaliya Nag, half human and half snake, and other Krishna scenes; cell 38, the 16-armed goddess Vidyadevi (goddess of knowledge); cells 46-48, 16-armed goddesses, including the goddess of smallpox, Shitala Mata; and cell 49, Narasimha, the 'man-lion' tearing open the stomach of the demon Hiranya-Kashyapa, surrounded by an opening lotus.

As in Gujarati Hindu temples, the main hall focuses on the sanctum which contains the 2.5-m image of Adinatha, the first Tirthankar. The sanctum with a pyramidal roof has a vestibule with entrances on three sides. To its east is the Mandapa, a form of octagonal nave nearly 8 m in diameter. Its 6-m-wide dome is supported by eight slender columns; the exquisite lotus ceiling carved from a single block of marble, rises in 11 concentric circles, carved with elaborately repeated figures. Superimposed across the lower rings are 16 brackets carved in the form of the goddesses of knowledge.

Risah Deo Temple Opposite the Vimala Visahi, this temple is unfinished. It encloses a huge brass Tirthankar image weighing 4.3 tonnes and made of *panchadhatu* (five metals) – gold, silver, copper, brass and zinc. The temple was commenced in the late 13th century by Brahma Shah, the Mewari Maharana Pratap's chief minister. Building activity was curtailed by war with Gujarat and never completed.

Luna Vasihi or Neminatha Temple (1231) To the north of the Adinatha Temple, this one was erected by two wealthy merchants Vastupala and Tejapala, and dedicated to the 22nd Tirthankar; they also built a similar temple at Girnar. The attractive niches on either side of the sanctum's entrance were for their wives. The craftsmanship in this temple is comparable to the Vimala Vasahi; the decorative carving and *jali* work are excellent. The small domes in front of the shrine containing the bejewelled Neminatha figure, the exquisitely carved lotus on the sabhamandapa ceiling and the sculptures on the colonnades are especially noteworthy.

There is a fifth temple for the Digambar ('Sky-Clad') Jains which is far more austere.

Spiritual University, Art Gallery and State Museum and Spiritual Museum

The headquarters of the Spiritual University movement of the Brahma Kumaris is **Om Shanti Bhavan** ⓘ *T02974-238268*, with its ostentatious entrance on Subhash Road. You may notice many residents dressed in white taking a walk around the lake in the evening. It is possible to stay in simple but comfortable rooms with attached baths and attend discourses, meditation sessions, yoga lessons, and so on. The charitable trust runs several worthy institutions including a really good hospital. **Art Gallery and State Museum** ⓘ *Raj Bhavan Rd, Sat-Thu 1000-1700, free*, has a small collection which includes some textiles and stone sculptures (ninth to 10th centuries). The **Spiritual Museum** ⓘ *near the pony stand by the lake, 0800-2000*, has a Disney-like diorama explaining the Brahma Kumari vision of the universe, including a laser show.

Walks around Mount Abu

Trevor's Tank ⓘ *50 m beyond the Dilwara Jain temples, Rs 5, car/jeep taken up to the lake Rs 125*, is the small wildlife sanctuary covering 289 sq km with the lake which acts as a watering hole for animals including sloth bear, sambhar, wild boar, panther. Most of these are nocturnal but on your walk you are quite likely to see a couple of crocodiles basking on the rocks. The birdlife is extensive with eagles, kites, grey jungle fowl, red spurfowl, francolin, flycatchers, bulbuls and more seen during walks on the trails in the sanctuary. There are superb views from the trails.

Adhar Devi, 3 km from town, is a 15th-century Durga temple carved out of a rock and approached by 220 steep steps. There are steep treks to Anandra point or to a Mahadev temple nearby for great views.

Around Nakki Lake **Honeymoon Point** and **Sunset Point** to the west, afford superb views across the plains. They can both be reached by a pleasant walk from the bus stand (about 2 km). You can continue from Honeymoon Point to **Limbdi House**. If you have another 1½ hours, walk up to **Jai Gurudev's meditation eyrie**. If you want to avoid the crowds at Sunset Point, take the **Bailey's Walk** from the **Hanuman Temple** near Honeymoon Point to **Valley View Point**, which joins up with the Sunset Point walk. You can also walk from the Ganesh temple to the Crags for some great views. The owner of **Shri Ganesh Guest House** advises his guests only to do this walk, and others in the area, when there are other people around as attacks by animals and robberies do occur.

Excursions from Mount Abu

The Aravalli hills, part of the subcontinent's oldest mountain range, look more like rocky outcrops, in places quite barren save for date palms and thorny acacias. From Mount Abu it is possible to make day-treks to nearby spots.

Achalgarh, 11 km away, has superb views. The picturesque **Achaleshwar Temple** (ninth century) is believed to have Siva's toeprint, a brass Nandi and a deep hole claimed to reach into the underworld. On the side of **Mandakini tank** near the car park is an image of Adi Pal, the Paramara king and three large stone buffaloes pierced with arrows. In legend, the tank was once filled with ghee and the buffaloes (really demons in disguise) came every night to drink from it until they were shot by Adi Pal. A path leads up to a group of carved Jain temples (10 minutes' climb).

Guru Shikhar is the highest peak in the area (1720 m) with a road almost to the top. It is 15 km from Mount Abu; taxis take about an hour. To get to the small Vishnu temple you must climb 300 steps or hire a palanquin. Good views especially at dawn.

Gaumukh (Cow's Mouth), 8 km southeast, is on the way to Abu Road. A small stream flows from the mouth of a marble cow. There is also a Nandi bull, and the tank is believed to be the site of Vasishtha's fire from which the four great Rajput clans were created. An image of the sage is flanked by ones of Rama and Krishna.

The **Arbuda Devi Temple** carved out of the rocky hillside is also worth walking to for the superb views over the hills.

Around Mount Abu → *For listings, see pages 371-374. Colour map 2, B3.*

Bera → *34 km from Sirohi.*

The large panther population in the surrounding hills of Bera and the Jawai River area draws wildlife photographers. Antelopes and jackals also inhabit the area. Visit the **Jawai Dam**, 150 km from Mount Abu towards Jodhpur, to see historic embankments, numerous birds and basking marsh crocodiles. A bed for the night is provided by **Leopard's Lair** in a colourful Raika village near the lake and jungle (see Sleeping, page 372).

Jalor → *160 km north of Mount Abu.*

Jalor is a historic citadel. In the early 14th century, during court intrigues, the Afghani Diwan of Marwar, Alauddin Khilji, took over the town and set up his own kingdom. Later, the Mughal emperor Akbar captured it and returned the principality to his allies, the Rathores of Marwar by means of a peaceful message to the Jalori Nawabs, who moved south to Palanpur in Gujarat. The medieval fort straddles a hill near the main bazar and encloses Muslim, Hindu and Jain shrines. It is a steep climb up but the views from the fort are rewarding. The old Topkhana at the bottom of the fortified hill has a mosque built by Alauddin Khilji using sculptures from a Hindu temple. Of particular interest are the scores of domes in different shapes and sizes, the symmetry of the columns and the delicate arches. Jalor bazar is good for handicrafts, silver jewellery and textiles, and is still relatively unaffected by tourist pricing.

Bhenswara → *16 km east of Jalor.*

Bhenswara is a small, colourful village on the Jawai River. It has another Rajput country estate whose 'castle' has been converted into an attractive hotel. The jungles and the impressive granite Esrana hills nearby have leopard, nilgai, chinkara, blackbuck, jungle cat, porcupines, jackals and spiny-tailed lizards. It's a good place to stay for a couple of nights.

Bhinmal → *95 km northwest of Mount Abu.*

Bhinmal has some important archaeological ruins, notably one of the few shrines in the country to Varaha Vishnu. It is also noted for the quality of its leather embroidered *mojdis*. Nearby, at **Vandhara**, is one of the few marble *baolis* (step wells) in India, while the historic **Soondha Mata Temple** is at a picturesque site where the green hills and barren sand dunes meet at a freshwater spring fed by a cascading stream.

Daspan → *25 km north of Bhinmal.*

Daspan is a small village where the restored 19th-century castle built on the ruins of an old fort provides a break between Mount Abu and Jaisalmer.

Mount Abu and around listings

For Sleeping and Eating price codes and other relevant information, see Essentials pages 38-42.

Sleeping

Mount Abu *p366, map p367*

Touts can be a nuisance to budget travellers at the bus stand. Prices shoot up during Diwali, Christmas week and summer (20 Apr-20 Jun) when many **D-F** hotels triple their rates; meals, ponies and jeeps cost a lot more too. Off-season discounts of 30-50% are usual, sometimes up to 70% in mid-winter (when it can get very cold). For a list of families receiving paying guests visit the tourist office.

A Cama Rajputana Club Resort, Adhar Devi Rd, T02974-238205, www.camahotelsindia.com. Refurbished old club house (1895) for Mt Abu's royal and British residents, guests become temporary members, 42 rooms in split-level cottages with views and modern decor, 2 period suites, lounge with fireplaces and old club furniture, average restaurant, eco-friendly (recycled water, alternative energy, drip irrigation), beautifully landscaped gardens, billiards, tennis, etc, efficient service, immaculate pool.

A Connaught House (WelcomHeritage), Rajendra Marg, take track uphill opposite the bus stand, T02974-238560, www.welcomheritage.com. British Resident of Jodhpur's colonial bungalow, 5 good, old-fashioned rooms (royal memorabilia), good bathrooms, 8 modern a/c rooms in quieter new cottage, comfortable, restaurant (average à la carte, good Rajasthani meals), trekking with guide (Rs 2000 plus), beautiful gardens filled with birds, interesting old retainer of the Jodhpur family, efficient management. Recommended.

A The Jaipur House, above Nakki Lake, T02974-235176. 9 elegant rooms and 14 new cottages in the Maharaja of Jaipur's former summer palace, unparalleled hilltop location, fantastic views, especially from terrace restaurant, friendly, professional staff. Recommended.

A Palace Hotel, Bikaner House, Dilwara Rd, 3 km from centre, T02974-235121, www.palacehotelbikanerhouse.com. 33 large renovated rooms with period and reproduction furniture in Swinton Jacob's imposing 1894 hunting lodge, also a new annexe, atmospheric public rooms, grand dining hall (good English breakfast, Rajasthani meals, memorable à la carte, expensive set menu), tennis, etc, civilized but average service, very quiet, set in sprawling grounds and backdrop of hills.

A-B Hilltone, set back from road near petrol pump, T02974-238391, www.hotelhilltone.com. 66 tastefully decorated rooms (most a/c), attractive Handi (a style of cooking using baking/steaming in covered pots) restaurant, pool, garden, quiet, most stylish of Mt Abu's hotels, helpful staff. Recommended.

B-C Aravalli, Main Rd, T(0)931-003 4583, http://hotelaravalimountabu.com/. 40 rooms

(12 in cottages, 10 in new wing) on different levels, good restaurant, very well maintained, landscaped garden, pool, gym, good off-season discount, very helpful staff.

B-C Sunrise Palace, Bharatpur Kothi, T02974-235573. 20 large, sparsely furnished rooms, great bathrooms, in a grand, slightly unloved converted mansion, good small restaurant, open-air BBQ, elevated with excellent views from the restaurant.

B-D Aradhana, St Mary's Rd, T02974-237227, T(0)9829-827755. Modern rooms, some a/c, large terraces, pleasant atmosphere, 10 mins' walk from town.

B-D Samrat International, near bus stand, T02974-235173, www.mountabu.com. 50 comfortable rooms with some incredibly kitsch suites, Bollywood restaurant, and terraces. Noise from the road can be irritating.

C Chacha Inn, Main Rd (2 km from centre), T02974-235374, www.mountabu.com. Attractive though a bit brash, with lots of artefacts on display, 22 good a/c rooms with modern facilities, some with balconies offering hill views, restaurant, bar, garden really good fun; dining lawns with magic and puppet shows, dancing and music.

C-E Lake Palace, facing lake, T02974-237154, www.savshantihotels.com. 13 rooms (some a/c), garden restaurant, beautifully situated with great lake views from terrace, rear access to hill road for Dilwara, well run and maintained. Recommended.

E-F Saraswati, west of Polo Ground, T02974-238887. Best of many options in area, 36 rooms (some with balconies), better in annexe, good views from upstairs, simple, clean, large rooms with bath and hot water, smart restaurant (Gujarati *thalis* only).

E-G Lake View, on a slope facing the lake, T02974-238659. Beautiful location, 15 basic rooms, Indian WC, helpful staff.

F Krishna, Raj Bhawan Rd, T02974-238045. 12 clean, simple rooms, quiet and homely.

F Rajendra, Rajendra Rd, T02974-238174. Well-designed, clean rooms with bucket hot water, *thalis*, huge balcony, friendly.

F-G Panghat, overlooking Nakki Lake, T02974-238886. Great location, 10 small but adequate rooms and friendly staff.

F-G Shri Ganesh, west of the polo ground, uphill behind Brahma Kumari, T02974-237292, lalit_ganesh@yahoo.co.in. 23 clean, simple rooms, plenty of solar-heated hot water, very quiet, cookery classes, wildlife walks in morning and afternoon (Rs 100), one of the few places catering specifically for foreigners, 16 years' experience shows in the service, recommended. Ring ahead for free pick-up.

Around Mount Abu *p370*

A Leopard's Lair, in a colourful Raika village, Bera, T(0)9828-889093, www.leopardslair resort.com. Well-designed stone cottages, 6 a/c rooms modern amenities, delicious meals included (fresh fish from lake), bar, pool, garden, riding, birdwatching, panther-viewing 'safaris' with owner.

C Ravla Bhenswara (Rajput Special Hotel), Bhenswara, T02978-282187, www.hotelravla bhenswara.com. 20 rooms with bath, painted exterior, inspired decor ('Badal Mahal' with cloud patterns, 'Hawa Mahal' with breezy terrace, etc), breakfast treats of masala cheese toast or vegetarian *parathas*, delicious Marwari meals. Courtyard lawns. Walk to parakeet-filled orchards and pool at the nearby Madho Bagh. Hospitable family are very knowledgeable and enterprising. Visits to Rabari herdsmen, Bhil tribal hamlets, night safaris for leopards, camping safaris including the Tilwara cattle fair or even treks to Mt Abu. Highly recommended.

D Castle Durjan Niwas, Daspan, T0141-222 6126 (Jaipur). Pleasant sitting areas, 11 rooms, folk entertainment, knowledgeable owners, camel rides (Rs 200 per hr; Rs 800 per day).

Eating

Mount Abu *p366, map p367*

Small roadside stalls sell tasty local vegetarian food. You can also get good *thalis* (Rs 30-40) at simple restaurants.

TTT Handi, Hilltone Hotel (see Sleeping). 0900-2300. Gujarati, Punjabi, Western. Plenty of choice, very comfortable but pricey. Has a bar.

TT Sankalp, opposite **Samrat International** (see Sleeping), excellent South Indian chain restaurant with amazing chutneys.

TT Shere-e-Punjab, near the taxi stand. One of the best in town for vegetarian/non-vegetarian Indian (some Chinese/Western).

Chunky Bites, on main drag. Good selection of Punjabi, pizza, pasta and *chaat*.

Coffee Day, next to **Sankalp** (see above). Coffee chain but best coffee in town.

King's Food, near MK, Nakki Lake Rd. Very popular for North Indian vegetarian (Rs 40); Chinese, South Indian and Western snacks.

Madras Café, Nakki Lake Rd. Indian, vegetarian 'hot dog', *thalis*, juices, real coffee and milk shakes in a garden, meals indoors.

Maharaja, near bus stand. Gujarati. Simple, clean, produces excellent value *thalis*.

Veena, near taxi stand. Brews real coffee, serves traditional Indian meals and a few Western favourites, very clean, outdoors, loud music, best of many on same strip.

Festivals and events

Mount Abu *p366, map p367*

Diwali is especially colourful here.

May An annual **Summer Festival** (23-25 May 2013, 12-14 May 2014) features folk music, dancing, fireworks, etc.

29-31 Dec Winter Festival.

Around Mount Abu *p370*

Sep The **Navratri Festival** is held in Bhinmal. Despan also holds special Navratri celebrations.

Shopping

Mount Abu *p366, map p367*

Shopping is less hassle here than in the tourist towns; most places are open daily 0900-2100. Ready-made Indian clothing and silver jewellery are particularly good value. For Garasia tribal jewellery try stalls near the GPO.

Chacha Museum, good metal, wood, stone crafts, paintings and odd curios (fixed price but may give a discount).

Khadi Gramudyog, by pony hire. Handloom fabric, carved agate boxes, marble figures.

Roopali, near Nakki Lake. Silver jewellery.

Saurashtra and **Rajasthan Emporia**, Raj Bhavan Rd, opposite the bus stand, sell a good selection.

Activities and tours

Mount Abu *p366, map p367*

Mountain sports

For rock climbing and rapelling, contact the **Mountaineering Institute**, near Gujarat Bhawan Hostel. Equipment and guide/instructors are available.

Polo

Occasional matches and tournaments have begun to take place at the long-abandoned polo ground in the town centre. Entry is free, with local investors keen to generate income from 'polo tourism'. Ask the tourist office for information on upcoming matches.

Swimming, tennis and billiards

Non-residents can use facilities at the **Cama Rajputana** and **Bikaner House Palace** hotels.

Tour operators

RTDC, and **Rajasthan SRTC**, run daily tours to Dilwara, Achalgarh, Guru Shikhar, Nakki Lake, Sunset Point, Adhar Devi and Om Shanti Bhavan, 0830-1300, 1330-1900, Rs 80. **Gujarat**, **Maharajah**, **Shobha** (T02974-238302) and **Green Travels** also offer similar tours for Rs 40-60; Ambaji-Kumbhairyaji tours Rs 120.

A wildlife guide who comes very highly recommended is **Charles**, T(0)9414-154854, mahendradan@yahoo.com, also contactable through **Lake Palace Hotel**. He offers a wide range of treks from 3- to 4-hr excursions at Rs 150 per person to longer overnight camping trips, very knowledgeable.

Transport

Mount Abu *p366, map p367*

Toll on entering town, Rs 10 per head. Frequent rockfalls during the monsoon makes the road from Mount Abu hazardous; avoid night journeys. The nearest airport is Udaipur.

Bus Local buses go to **Dilwara** and **Achalgarh** at 1100 and 1500, go early if doing a day-trip. **State Bus Stand**, Main Rd (opposite tourist office, T02974-235434); **Private Bus Stand**, south of Govt Bus Stand on Petrol Pump road. Many 'direct' long distance buses involve a change at Abu Rd bus stand, T02974-222323. To **Abu Rd**: every 30 mins (45 mins-1 hr) Rs 20. **Ahmedabad**: several (7 hrs, Rs 200) via Palanpur (3 hrs, change here for Bhuj); **Delhi**: overnight. **Jaipur** (overnight, 9 hrs), **Jodhpur** morning and afternoon (7 hrs). **Mumbai**, **Pune**: early morning (18 hrs). **Udaipur**: 0830, 1500, 2200 (5-6 hrs, Rs 80). **Vadodara**: 0930, 1930 (5 hrs). **Shobha**,

T02974-235302, and **Gujarat Travels**, T02974-235564, run private buses.

Taxi and jeep Posted fares for sightseeing in a jeep; about Rs 800 per day, but open to negotiation; anywhere in town Rs 40; to Sunset Point Rs 70. Taxi (for sharing) Abu Rd Rs 300; shared taxis for Jain Temples from Dilwara stand near the bazar opposite Chacha Museum (from Rs 5).

Train **Western Railway Out Agency**, Tourist Reception Centre, has a small reservation quota, Mon-Sat 0900-1600, Sun 0900-1230. Book well in advance; you may have to wait 2-3 days even in the off-season. Abu Rd, T02974-222222, is the railhead with frequent buses to Mt Abu. To **Ahmedabad**: *Ashram Exp 12916*, 0355, 3½ hrs; *Ahmedabad Mail 19106*, 1248, 5 hrs; *Aravalli Exp 19708*, 1710, 5 hrs (continues to **Mumbai**, further 8½ hrs). **Jaipur**: *Aravalli Exp 19707*, 0958, 9 hrs, via **Ajmer**, 6 hrs; *Ahmedabad-Delhi Mail 19105*, 1405, 9 hrs. **Jodhpur**: *Ranakpur Exp 14708*, 0427, 5½ hrs; *Surya Nagari Exp 12480*, 0122, 5½ hrs. **Delhi**: *Ahmedabad Delhi Mail 19105*, 1405, 15¾ hrs; *Ashram Exp 12915*, 2120, 13¾ hrs; **Margao Goa**: *BKN TVC Express 16311* on Wed. There are additional trains at Diwali and New Year.

Around Mount Abu *p370*

Train/bus To Bera from **Mumbai** and **Ajmer** via Abu Rd (*Aravalli* and *Ranakpur Exp*) stop at Jawai Dam and Mori Bera. For **Bhenswada**, trains and buses from Abu Rd. For **Bhinmal**, trains from **Jodhpur**. From **Ahmedabad**, 2130 (12 hrs); to Ahmedabad, 1940.

Directory

Mount Abu *p366, map p367*

Internet Yanj-Ya, Hotel Mount Winds, Raj Bhavan Rd. Friendly place with free chai.

Chittaurgarh and around

This is a relatively undiscovered corner of Rajasthan but is home to some of the state's oldest and most interesting treasures. Chittaurgarh's 'Tower of Victory' has become well known in recent years, but the whole of this ancient, historically important city is worth exploring. Kota and the area around Jhalawar contain some of the oldest and most impressive temples and cave paintings in India, while nowhere takes you back in time as far as Bundi, seemingly untouched for centuries. There are limited rail connections in this area, but a new highway being built pretty much across the whole of southern Rajasthan will greatly improve travel in this region. Limited transport links mean that a visit to this region does require a little more time and effort than to other areas in Rajasthan, but also that the region has remained uncrowded, unspoilt and hugely hospitable. ▸▸ *For listings, see pages 381-384.*

Ins and outs

Getting there All of the region's major towns are served by the railway, but often by branch lines some way off the main routes. Buses starting from all the major cities surrounding the area give quick access to the main towns; from Udaipur to Chittaurgarh takes 2½ hours.

Getting around Most of the principal sights are fairly close together, making travel by road a convenient option. Frequent buses criss-cross the area, but a private taxi might be worth considering as some of the sights and most interesting places to stay are somewhat off the beaten track. ▸▸ *See Transport, page 384.*

Tourist information Tourist office ⓘ *Janta Avas Grih, Station Rd, T01472-241089.*

Chittaurgarh → *For listings, see pages 381-384. Colour map 2, B5. Phone code: 01472. Population: 100,000.*

The hugely imposing Chittaurgarh Fort stands on a 152-m-high rocky hill, rising abruptly above the surrounding plain. The walls, 5 km long, enclose the fascinating ruins of an ancient civilization, while the slopes are covered with scrub jungle. The modern town lies at the foot of the hill with access across a limestone bridge of 10 arches over the Gambheri River.

History

One of the oldest cities in Rajasthan, Chittaurgarh was founded formally in AD 728 by Bappu Rawal, who according to legend was reared by the Bhil tribe. However, two sites near the River Berach have shown stone tools dating from half a million years ago and Buddhist relics from a few centuries BC. From the 12th century it became the centre of Mewar. Excavations in the Mahasati area of the fort have shown four shrines with ashes and charred bones, the earliest dating from about the 11th century AD. This is where the young Udai Singh was saved by his nurse Panna Dai; she sacrificed her own son by substituting him for the baby prince when, as heir to the throne, Udai Singh's life was threatened.

Chittaurgarh

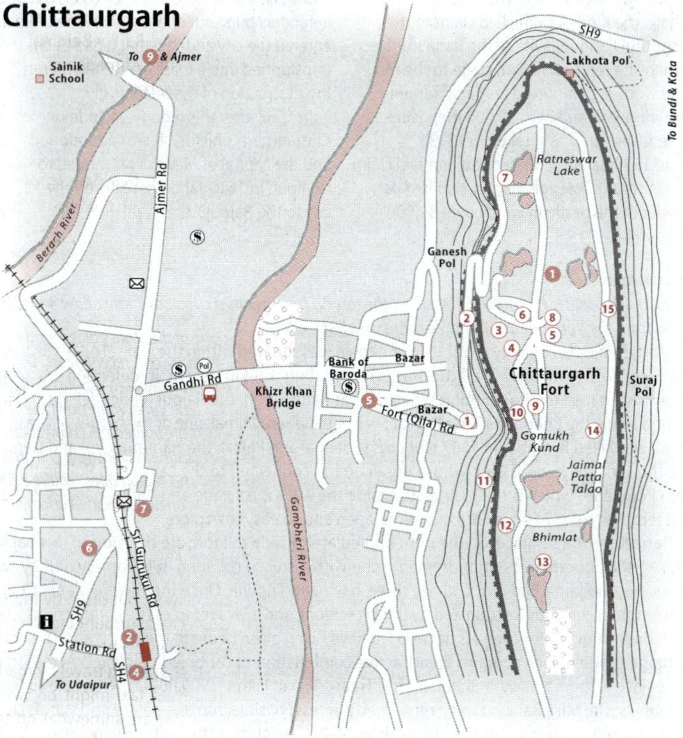

Sleeping

Birla 1
Chetak 2
Ganesh Guest House 5
Meera 4
Padmini 9
Panna 6
Pratap Palace & Padmini Haveli 7

Sights

Padal Pol 1
Tuta Pol 2
Rana Kumbha's Palace, Nau Lakha Bandar & Archaeological Office 3
Khumbha Shyama & Mira Bai Temples 4
Sat Bis Deori Temple 5
Shringara Chauri Temple 6
Rana Ratan Singh's Palace 7
Fateh Prakash Palace & Museum 8
Vijay Stambha & Mahasati 9
Samadhishvara Temple 10
Palaces of Jaimal & Patta 11
Kalika Mata Temple & Chonda's House 12
Padmini's Palace 13
Adbhutanatha Temple 14
Kirti Stambha 15

The jauhar – Rajput chivalry

On three occasions during Chittaurgarh's history its inhabitants preferred death to surrender, the women marching en masse into the flames of a funeral pyre in a form of ritual suicide known as *jauhar* before the men threw open the gates and charged towards an overwhelming enemy and annihilation.

The first was in 1303 when Ala-ud-din Khalji, the King of Delhi, laid claim to the beautiful Padmini, wife of the Rana's uncle. When she refused, he laid siege to the fort. The women committed *jauhar*, Padmini entering last, and over 50,000 men were killed. The fort was retaken in 1313.

In 1535 Bahadur Shah of Gujarat laid claim to Chittaurgarh. Every Rajput clan lost its leader in the battle in which over 32,000 lives were lost, and 13,000 women and children died in the sacred *jauhar* which preceded the final charge.

The third and final sack of Chittaurgarh occurred only 32 years later when Akbar stormed the fort. Again, the women and children committed themselves to the flames, and again all the clans lost their chiefs as 8000 defenders burst out of the gates. When Akbar entered the city and saw that it had been transformed into a mass grave, he ordered the destruction of the buildings.

In 1567 after this bloody episode in Chittaurgarh's history, it was abandoned and the capital of Mewar was moved to Udaipur. In 1615 Jahangir restored the city to the Rajputs.

Chittaurgarh Fort

ⓘ *0600-1800, entry Rs 100/US$2. Visiting the fort on foot means a circuit of 7 km; allow 4 hrs. The views from the battlements and towers are worth the effort.*

The fort dominates the city. Until 1568 the town was situated within the walls. Today the lower town sprawls to the west of the fort. The winding 1.5-km ascent is defended by seven impressive gates: the **Padal Pol** is where Rawat Bagh Singh, the Rajput leader, fell during the second siege; the Bhairon or **Tuta Pol** (broken gate) where Jaimal, one of the heroes of the third siege, was killed by Akbar in 1567 (*chhatris* to Jaimal and Patta); the Hanuman Pol and Ganesh Pol; the Jorla (or Joined) Gate whose upper arch is connected to the Lakshman Pol; finally the **Ram Pol** (1459) which is the main gate. Inside the walls is a village and ruined palaces, towers and temples, most of which are out in the open and so easy to explore.

Rana Kumbha's Palace, on the right immediately inside the fort, are the ruins of this palace (1433-1468), originally built of dressed stone with a stucco covering. It is approached by two gateways, the large Badi Pol and the three-bay deep Tripolia. Once there were elephant and horse stables, *zenanas* (recognized by the *jali* screen), and a Siva temple. The *jauhar* committed by Padmini and her followers is believed to have taken place beneath the courtyard. The north frontage of the palace contains an attractive combination of canopied balconies. Across from the palace is the Nau Lakha Bhandar (The Treasury; nau lakha – 900,000). The temple to Rana Kumbha's wife **Mira Bai** who was a renowned poetess is visible from the palace and stands close to the Kumbha Shyama Temple (both circa 1440). The older 11th-century Jain **Sat Bis Deori** with its 27 shrines, is nearby. The **Shringara Chauri Temple** (circa 1456), near the fort entrance, has sculptured panels of musicians, warriors and Jain deities.

Rana Ratan Singh's Palace is to the north by the Ratneshwar Lake. Built in stone around 1530 it too had stucco covering. Originally rectangular in plan and enclosed within a high wall, it was subsequently much altered. The main gate to the south still stands as an example of the style employed.

The early 20th-century **Fateh Prakash Palace** built by Maharana Fateh Singh (died 1930) houses an interesting **museum** ⓘ *Sat-Thu 0800-1630, Rs 3*. To the south is the **Vijay Stambha** (1458-1468), one of the most interesting buildings in the fort, built by Rana Kumbha to celebrate his victory over Mahmud Khilji of Malwa in 1440. Visible for miles around, it stands on a base

14 sq m and 3 m high, and rises 37 m. The nine-storeyed sandstone tower has been restored; the upper section retains some of the original sculpture. For no extra charge you can climb to the top. Nearby is the Mahasati terrace where the ranas were cremated when Chittaurgarh was the capital of Mewar. There are also numerous *sati* stones. Just to the south is the **Samdhishvara Temple** to Siva (11th and 15th centuries), which still attracts many worshippers and has some good sculptured friezes. Steps down lead to the deep Gomukh Kund, where the sacred spring water enters through a stone carved as a cow's mouth (hence its name).

Of the two palaces of **Jaimal and Patta**, renowned for their actions during the siege of 1567, the latter, based on the *zenana* building of Rana Kumbha's Palace, is more interesting. You then pass the Bhimtal before seeing the **Kalika Mata Temple** (originally an eighth-century Surya temple, rebuilt mid-16th) with exterior carvings and the ruins of Chonda's House with its three-storey domed tower. Chonda did not claim the title when his father, Rana Lakha, died in 1421.

Padmini's Palace (late 13th century, rebuilt end of the 19th) is sited in the middle of the lake surrounded by pretty gardens. Ala-ud-din Khilji is said to have seen Padmini's beautiful reflection in the water through a mirror on the palace wall. This striking vision convinced him that she had to be his.

You pass the deer park on your way round to the **Suraj Pol** (Sun Gate) and pass the **Adbhutanatha Temple** to Siva before reaching the second tower, the **Kirti Stambha**, a Tower of Fame (13th and 15th centuries). Smaller than the Vijay Stambha (23 m) with only seven storeys, but just as elegant, it is dedicated to Adinath, the first Jain Tirthankar. Naked figures of Tirthankars are repeated several hundred times on the face of the tower. A narrow internal staircase goes to the top.

Of particular interest are the number of tanks and wells in the fort that have survived the centuries. Water, from both natural and artificial sources, was harnessed to provide an uninterrupted supply to the people.

Chittaurgarh to Kota → *For listings, see pages 381-384. Colour map 2, B5.*

Bassi, 28 km from Chittaurgarh, is famous for handicrafts and miniature wooden temples painted with scenes from the epics. The palace, a massive 16th-century fort, has been opened as a hotel (see Sleeping, page 381).

Bijaipur is a feudal village with a 16th-century **castle**, set among the Vindhya hills and now open as a hotel (see Sleeping, page 381). It has a splendid location near the **Bassi- Bijaipur wildlife sanctuary**, which is home to panther, antelope and other wildlife. The forests are interspersed with lakes, reservoirs, streams and waterfalls with good birdlife in the winter months. The ruined **Pannagarh Fort** facing a lily covered lake is believed to be one of the oldest in Rajasthan.

Menal, further east, has a cluster of Siva temples believed to date from the time of the Guptas. They are associated with the Chauhans and other Rajput dynasties. Though neglected the temples have some fine carvings and a panel of erotic sculptures somewhat similar to those at Khajuraho in Madhya Pradesh. Behind is a deep, wooded ravine with a seasonal waterfall.

Kota

Kota's attractive riverside location and decent hotels make it a comfortable place to stay. The town itself is of no special appeal, but can be used as a base from which to visit nearby Bundi if you're short on time. There's a **tourist office** ⓘ *Hotel Chambal (see Sleeping, page 382), T0744-232 7695.*

At the south end of the town, near the barrage, is the vast, strongly fortified **City Palace** (1625) which you enter by the south gate having driven through the bustling but quite charming old city. There are some striking buildings with delicate ornamental stonework on the balconies and façade, though parts are decaying. The best-preserved murals and carved marble panels are in the chambers upstairs and in the Arjun Mahal. These murals feature motifs

Flower power

Crossing the high plateau between Bundi and Chittaurgarh the landscape is suddenly dotted with tiny patches of papery white flowers. These two Rajasthani districts, along with the neighbouring districts of Madhya Pradesh, are India's opium poppy growing belt, accounting for over 90% of production. As early as the 15th century this region produced opium for trade with China. Today the whole process is tightly monitored by the government. Licences to grow are hard won and easily lost. No farmer can grow more than half a *bigha* of opium poppy (less than one-twentieth of a hectare), and each must produce at least 6 kg of opium for sale to the government. Failure to reach this tough target results in the loss of the licence to grow. Laying out the field, actual cultivation and sale are all government controlled. Between late February and early April the farmers harvest the crop by incising fine lines in one quarter of each poppy head in the evening, and collecting the sap first thing in the morning. The harvesting has to be so precise that each evening a different quarter of the seed head will be cut on a different face – north, south, east or west. Finally the government announces the collection point for the harvested opium just two or three days in advance, and farmers have to travel miles to the centre selected for weighing and final payment.

characteristic of the Kota School of Art, including portraiture (especially profiles), hunting scenes, festivals and the Krishna Lila.

The 15th-century **Kishore Sagar** tank between the station and the palace occasionally has boats for hire. **Jag Mandir Island Palace**, closed to visitors, is in the centre of the lake. The **Chambal Gardens** by Amar Niwas, south of the fort, is a pleasant place for a view of the river, although the rare fish-eating gharial crocodiles with which the pond was stocked are rarely seen these days. A variety of birds, occasionally including flamingos, can be seen at the river and in nearby ponds.

The **Umed Bhawan** (1904), 1 km north of town, was built for the Maharao Umaid Singh II and designed by Sir Samuel Swinton Jacob in collaboration with Indian designers. The buff-coloured stone exterior with a stucco finish has typical Rajput detail. The interior, however, is Edwardian with a fine drawing-room, banquet hall and garden. It has now been converted into a heritage hotel (see Sleeping, page 382).

Bundi → *For listings, see pages 381-384. Colour map 2, B5. Phone code: 0747. Population: 100,000.*

Bundi lies in a beautiful narrow valley with Taragarh Fort towering above. The drive into the town is lovely as the road runs along the hillside overlooking the valley opposite the fort. You might feel 'forted out' by the time you reach Bundi, but this beautiful old town nestles under the palace and fort and offers spectacular views and a unique charm. Much less developed than the other fort towns, Bundi is starting to blossom – now more classic *havelis* are being 'boutiqued', and there are plenty of more down-home family guest houses springing up too. Popular with backpackers and now increasingly tour buses, Bundi is relaxed and friendly and still a long way off the bazar bustle of Pushkar and the speed and hustle of the more developed fort towns of Jodhpur and Jaisalmer, but good cafés serving cappuccinos cannot be too far along the line. It is well worth spending a day or two here to soak in the atmosphere. Bundi is especially colourful and interesting during the many festivals, see page 384. **Tourist office** ⓘ *Circuit House, near Raniji ki Baori, T0747-244 3697.*

History

Formerly a small state founded in 1342, Bundi's fortunes varied inversely with those of its more powerful neighbours. Neither wealthy nor powerful, it nevertheless ranked high in the Rajput hierarchy since the founding family belonged to the specially blessed Hada Chauhan clan. After Prithviraj Chauhan was defeated by Muhammad Ghuri in 1193, the rulers sought refuge in Mewar. However, adventurous clan members overran the Bhils and Minas in the Chambal valley and established the kingdom of Hadavati or **Hadoti** which covers the area around Bundi, Kota and Jhalawar in southeastern Rajasthan. It prospered under the guidance of the able 19th-century ruler Zalim Singh, but then declined on his death. The British reunited the territory in 1894.

Bundi

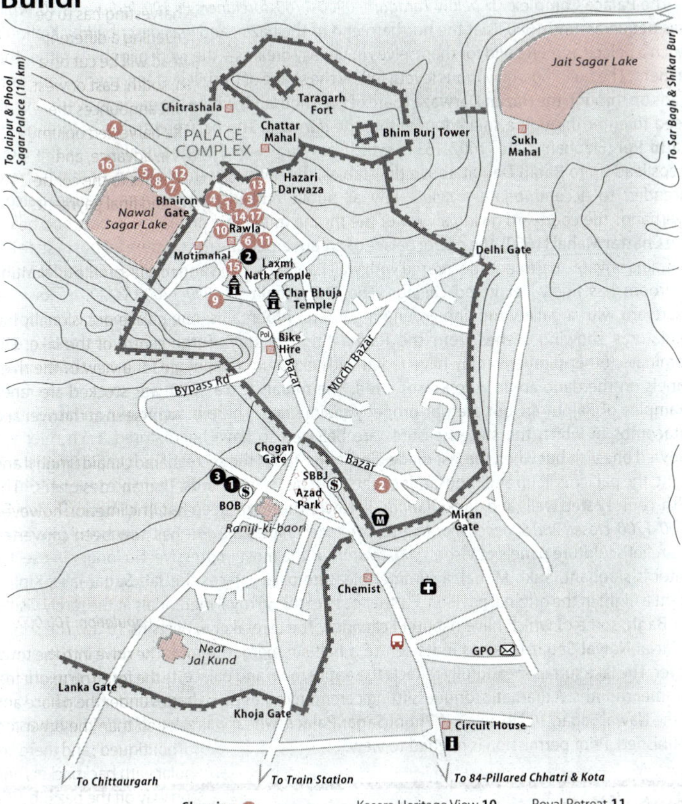

Sleeping
Bundi Haveli **16**
Bundi Inn **6**
Bundi Vilas **1**
Govindam **12**
Haveli Braj Bhushanjee **4**
Haveli Elephant Stables **3**
Kasera & Rooftop Restaurant **2**
Kasera Heritage View **10**
Kasera Paradise **14**
Lake View Paying Guest House **5**
Mangalam **17**
Nawal Sagar Palace **7**
Rainbow Heritage Paying Guest House **15**
RN Haveli **9**
Royal Retreat **11**
Shivam Guesthouse **4**
Tara Home Stay **13**
Uma Megh Haveli **8**

Eating
Diamond **1**
Sathi Cold Drinks **2**
Sher-e-Punjab **3**

Sights

Taragarh Fort (1342) ⓘ *0600-1800, foreigners Rs 100, Indians Rs 20, camera Rs 50, video Rs 100,* stands in sombre contrast to the beauty of the town and the lakes below. There are excellent views but it is a difficult 20-minute climb beset in places by aggressive monkeys; wear good shoes and wield a big stick. The eastern wall is crenellated with high ramparts while the main gate to the west is flanked by octagonal towers. The **Bhim Burj** tower dominates the fort and provided the platform for the Garbh Ganjam ('Thunder from the Womb'), a huge cannon. A pit to the side once provided shelter for the artillery men, and there are several stepped water tanks inside. Cars can go as far as the TV tower then it is 600 m along a rough track.

The **Palace Complex** ⓘ *below Taragarh, 0900-1700, foreigners Rs 100, Indians Rs 20,* which was begun around 1600, is at the northern end of the bazar, and was described by Kipling as "such a palace as men build for themselves in uneasy dreams – the work of goblins rather than of men". The buildings, on various levels, follow the shape of the hill. A steep, rough stone ramp leads up through the **Hazari Darwaza** (Gate of the Thousand) where the garrison lived; you may need to enter through a small door within the *darwaza*. The palace entrance is through the **Hathi Pol** (Elephant Gate, 1607-1631), which has two carved elephants with a water clock. Steps lead up to **Ratan Daulat** above the stables, the unusually small Diwan-i-Am which was intended to accommodate a select few at public audience. A delicate marble balcony overhangs the courtyard giving a view of the throne to the less privileged, who stood below. The **Chattar Mahal** (1660), the newer palace of green serpentine rock, is pure Rajput in style and contains private apartments decorated with wall paintings, glass and mirrors. The **Badal Mahal** bedroom has finely decorated ceilings. The **Chitrashala** ⓘ *0900-1700, Rs 20,* a cloistered courtyard with a gallery running around a garden of fountains, has a splendid collection of miniatures showing scenes from the Radha Krishna story. Turquoise, blues and greens dominate (other pigments may have faded with exposure to sunlight) though the elephant panels on the dado are in a contrasting red. The murals (circa 1800) are some of the finest examples of Rajput art but are not properly maintained. There is supposedly a labyrinth of catacombs in which the state treasures are believed to have been stored. Each ruler was allowed one visit but when the last guide died in the 1940s the secret of its location was lost. At night, the palace is lit up and thousands of bats pour out of its innards. There are several 16th- to 17th-century step wells and 'tanks' (*kunds*) in town. The 46-m-deep **Raniji-ki-baori** ⓘ *Mon-Sat 1000-1700, closed 2nd Sat each month, free, caretaker unlocks the gate,* with beautiful pillars and bas relief sculpture panels of Vishnu's 10 *avatars*, is the most impressive. No longer in use, the water is stagnant. **Sukh Mahal**, a summer pleasure palace, faces the **Jait Sagar** lake; Kipling spent a night in the original pavilion. Further out are the 66 royal memorials at the rarely visited **Sar Bagh**, some of which have beautiful carvings. The caretaker expects Rs 10 tip. The square artificial **Nawal Sagar** lake has in its centre a half-submerged temple to Varuna, the god of water. The lake surface beautifully reflects the entire town and palace, but tends to dry up in the summer months. A dramatic tongue-slitting ceremony takes place here during Dussehra. West of the Nawal Sagar, 10 km away, is **Phool Sagar Palace**, which was started in 1945 but was left unfinished. Prior permission is needed to view.

South of Kota → *For listings, see pages 381-384. Colour map 2, B5.*

Jhalawar, 85 km southeast of Kota, was the capital of the princely state of the Jhalas, which was separated from Kota by the British in 1838. It lies in a thickly forested area on the edge of the Malwa plateau with some interesting local forts, temples and ancient cave sites nearby. The **Garh Palace** in the town centre, now housing government offices, has some fine wall paintings which can be seen with permission. The **museum** ⓘ *Sat-Thu 1000-1630, Rs 3,* established in 1915, has a worthwhile collection of sculptures, paintings and manuscripts. **Bhawani Natyashala** (1921) was known for its performances ranging from Shakespearean plays to Shakuntala dramas. The stage with a subterranean driveway allowed horses and chariots to be brought on stage during performances. The **tourist office** ⓘ *T07432-230081*, is at the Hotel Chandravati.

The small walled town of **Jhalarapatan**, 7 km south of Jhalawar, has several fine 11th-century Hindu temples, the **Padmanath Sun Temple** on the main road being the best. The **Shantinath Jain** temple has an entrance flanked by marble elephants. There are some fine carvings on the rear façade and silver polished idols inside the shrines.

About 7 km away, **Chandrawati**, on the banks of the Chandrabhaga River, has the ruins of some seventh-century Hindu temples with fragments of fine sculpture.

Chittaurgarh and around listings

For Sleeping and Eating price codes and other relevant information, see Essentials pages 38-42.

Sleeping

Chittaurgarh *p374, map p375*

B Padmini Haveli Anna Poorna Temple Rd, Shah Chowk T01472-241 251, www.thepadminihaveli.com. Newly restored *haveli* within the fort walls provides a rare opportunity to stay within Chittaurgarh fort. 9 beautifully furnished rooms built around a central courtyard. Home-cooked meals available, full board Rs 800.

C-D Pratap Palace (Rajput Special Hotels), Sri Gurukul Rd, near GPO, T01472-240099, hpratapp@hotmail.com. Recently spruced up. Clean, well-maintained rooms, some a/c, 2 with ornately painted walls, good fun, good food in restaurant or in the pleasant garden, jeep and horse safaris visiting villages. Recommended.

C-E Padmini, Chanderiya Rd, near Sainik School, T01472-241718, hotel_padmini@rediffmail.com. 46 clean, modern rooms, 30 a/c, Indian-style furniture, gloomy restaurant, quiet, airport transfer from Udaipur.

D-E Panna (RTDC), Udaipur Rd, near railway station, T01472-241238. Indian business hotel, popular with those visiting quarries/mines. 31 simple rooms, some a/c, best with fort view, dorm (Rs 50), vegetarian dining hall, bar, run-down but attentive service.

D-F Meera, near railway station, Neemuch Rd, T01472-240266. Modern, 24 a/c and non-a/c rooms with TV and phone, Gujarati/Punjabi restaurant, bar, laundry, car rental, travel assistance, internet, characterless but efficient.

F Chetak, opposite railway station, T01472-241589. Modern, 23 clean, fairly pleasant rooms, 'deluxe' have Western toilets and hot showers.

F-G Ganesh Guest House, New Fort Rd, opposite Sukhadiya Park, T01472-248240. 20 basic and yet still overpriced rooms, Indian and Western toilets.

G Birla, near the Kirti Stambh in the fort, T01472-246939. Has been opened by the dharamshala group. 17-room guesthouse, very basic but only Rs 50 per double, great location, water a problem in the summer.

Chittaurgarh to Kota *p377*

B Castle Bijaipur (Rajput Special Hotels), Bijaipur, T01472-240099, www.castlebijaipur.com. 25 simple rooms in traditional style with comfortable furniture and modern bathrooms in castle and a new wing, lawns and gardens, hill views from breezy terrace, superb pool, delicious Rajasthani meals, also tea on medieval bastion, jeep/horse safaris with camping, jungle trekking. You may find yoga groups bedding down and bending here.

C Bassi Fort Palace, Bassi, T01472-225321, www.bassifortpalace.com. 16 unpretentious rooms in a family-run 16th-century fort. Same family has an abandoned fort on top of the nearby hill (where dinner can be arranged) and a hunting lodge 6 km away accessible by boat or horse. Safaris to this lodge and local tribal villages can be arranged. Refreshingly informal. Recommended.

E-F Menal Motel, Menal. One simple room – handy for a cup of tea or a simple meal.

Kota *p377*

Kota has a good selection of mid-range hotels, but little for budget travellers; there's a far better choice in Bundi. Budget hotels (**G**) near the bus station can be noisy and dirty.

B Umed Bhawan (WelcomHeritage), Palace Rd, T0744-232 5262, www.welcomheritage.com. 32 large, comfortable rooms, impressive building and interesting memorabilia and billiards rooms with more stuffed animals than you can shake a stick at, it's not such a great surprise that there are so few tigers left in the wild when you come to some of these Raj-era establishments. Elegant dining room, great beer bar, sunny terraces, behind woods (langurs, deer, parakeets, peacocks), tennis, attentive staff.

B-C Brijraj Bhawan Palace, Civil Lines, T0744-245 0529, www.indianheritagehotels.com. With a great location overlooking the river, this is an old British Residency with bags of character. Once patronized by Queen Mary, you will find 7 spacious a/c rooms with verandas, stately drawing and dining rooms (regal memorabilia), immaculate gardens, croquet, tennis, very civilized.

C Palkiya Haveli, Mokha Para (in walled city), near Suraj Pol, T0744-238 7497, www.alsisarhaveli.com A beautifully restored haveli, with a nice family vibe. 6 traditionally furnished a/c rooms with bath (tubs), carved wood furniture, exquisite murals, very good fixed meals, peaceful courtyard garden (full of birds). Recommended.

C-D Navrang, Collectorate Circle, Civil Lines, T0744-232 3294. Much more ornate inside than out, 25 rooms, deluxe much better than standard, air-cooled or a/c, TV, **C** suites, new a/c vegetarian restaurant, well managed. Maybe a bit pricey for what you get. Handy for ATMs there are 3 nearby.

C-D Sukhdham Kothi, Civil Lines, T0744-232 0081, www.sukdhamkothi.com. 15 elegant rooms (size varies), 10 a/c, in a 19th-century British residence with sandstone balconies and screens, good homemade Rajasthani food, large, private garden well set back from road, family-run, friendly. Peacocks in the garden. Recommended.

E Chambal (RTDC), Nayapura, T0744-232 6527. 12 rooms, nothing special but clean, friendly staff, well located close to old city.

Bundi *p378, map p379*

A-E Haveli Braj Bhushanjee, below the fort, opposite Ayurvedic Hospital, T0747-244 2322, www.kiplingsbundi.com. 16 quaint rooms with clean bath (hot showers), in 19th-century 4-storey *haveli* covered in frescos, plenty of atmosphere and memorabilia but a bit stuffy and overpriced, although some of the cheaper rooms are good value. Home-cooked vegetarian meals (no alcohol), pleasant terrace, good fort views, pick-up from station on request, good craft shop below, mixed reports on service. Also modern rooms in attached, newly restored 17th-century Badi Haveli.

B Bundi Haveli, 107 Balchand Parra, near Naval Sagar Lake, T0747-244 7861, www.hotelbundihaveli.com. Chic and beautiful rooms around a central courtyard in restored *haveli*. Large rooms with beautiful furniture, divans and fantastic artwork. Good shop of collectibles and fabrics in courtyard.

B Bundi Vilas, below palace, behind Haveli Braj Bhushanjee, T(0)9414-175280, www.bundivilas.com. Wander up a beautiful atmospheric alleyway and you find yourself at a super stylish boutique hotel. Newly restored sumptuous *haveli* with good views from rooftop. Great attention to detail, rose petals everywhere scenting the way, Wi-Fi, stylishly furnished. Good tasty food – brown bread is brought daily from Delhi, jams from the Himalaya and the lady of the house makes a great sesame dessert. Highly recommended.

C-D Bundi Inn near Elephant Memorial, Bundi Palace Road, www.bundiinn.com, T0747-244 2612. Borrowing a little from the style of Bundi Vilas and jumping on the 'boutique' bandwagon is Bundi Inn. It has lots of character and offers up boutique on a budget.

C-F Nawal Sagar Palace, Balchandpada, T0747-230 0644, nawalsagarpalace@hotmail.com. Through an imposing door, you find charming, comfortable rooms. Beautifully decorated. New restaurant planned in adjacent wing. Friendly owner, friendly dog.

E-F Kasera Heritage View, below palace, T0747-244 4679, www.kaseraheritageview.com. Good rooms with attached bathrooms and some with good views, enjoy the rooftop restaurant for a beer and a good view of the palace, but poor reports on the food. Same family owns **Kasera** and **B-D Kasera Paradise**, with 10 a/c rooms, marble bathrooms and a rooftop restaurant 5 storeys up in an old *haveli*.

E-F R N Haveli, behind Laxmi Nath Temple, T0747-512 0098, rnhavelibundi@yahoo.co.in. 5 rooms in a friendly family home run exclusively by 'woman power', a little persistent but the home cooking is excellent. Recommended.
F-G Haveli Elephant Stables, at base of palace near gate, T(0)9928-154064, elephant stable_guesthouse@hotmail.com. Formerly used to house royal elephants, the 4 simple but huge rooms have mosquito nets and basic Indian toilets, beneath a huge peepal tree in a dusty courtyard. Good home cooking, relaxed.
F-G Lake View Paying Guest House, Bohra Meghwan Ji Ki Haveli, Balchand Para, below the palace, by Nawal Sagar, T0747-244 2326, lakeviewbundi@yahoo.com. 7 simple clean rooms (3 in separate, basic garden annexe with shared bath) in 150-year-old *haveli* with wall paintings, private terrace shared with monkeys and peacocks, lovely views from rooftop, warm welcome, popular, very friendly hosts.
F-G Shivam Guesthouse, outside the walls near the Nawal Sagar, T0747-244 7892, shivam_pg@yahoo.com. Simple, comfortable rooms around a shaded blue courtyard, exceptionally friendly, come for food even if you're not staying.
F-G Uma Megh Haveli, Balchand Para, T0747-244 2191. Very atmospheric, 11 unrestored rooms, 7 with basic attached bathrooms, plus a pleasant garden and restaurant.
G Govindam, opposite Nawal Sagar Palace, T(0)9887-332761. Basic rooms. Friendly family.
G Mangalam, next to Kasera Paradise, T0747-244 2555, mangalam_bundi@yahoo.com. Basic clean rooms, family-run, good reports on food and service.
G Rainbow Heritage Paying Guest House, Nahar Ka Couhatta, opposite Sathi Cold Drinks, T(0)988-721 0334. Backpacker hangout with basic rooms with more being built.
G Tara Home Stay, near Elephant Stables, T(0)9829-718554, tarahomestay@gmail.com, Only a couple of rooms, but exceptional views of the palace.

South of Kota *p380*

E Purvaj, centre of Jhalawar. A delightful old *haveli*, owned by an interesting family, delicious and simple home-cooked meals.

Eating

Chittaurgarh *p374, map p375*

For the best places to eat, visit the hotels. There are several cheap options near the bus stand.
Pratap Palace (see Sleeping). Tasty Indian in pleasant surroundings.
RTDC Café, near the Vijay Stambha. Handy for visitors to the fort.

Kota *p377*

The best places to eat are the hotels; those listed below offer cheaper alternatives. Good *kulfis* and home-made ices in Sindhi shops.
Payal, Nayapura. Good Indian. Also some Chinese, and Indian-style continental.
Venue, Civil Lines. A/c, good but very spicy Indian, disappointing Western.
Hariyali, Bundi Rd. Good Punjabi, some Chinese/continental. Pleasant garden restaurant, outdoors or under a small shelter, very popular but some way out of town.
Jodhpur Sweets, Ghumanpura Market. Saffron *lassis* and flavoured milks.
Palace View, outdoor meals/snacks. Handy for visitors to the City Palace.
Priya, Nayapura. Popular Indian vegetarian.

Bundi *p378, map p379*

Several of the hotels have pleasant rooftop restaurants, see Sleeping.
Diamond, Suryamahal Chowk. Very popular locally for cheap vegetarian meals, handy when visiting step wells.
Sathi Cold Drinks, Palace Rd. Excellent *lassis* (saffron, spices, pistachio and fruit), pleasant.
Sher-e-Punjab, near **Diamond**. Non-vegetarian.

Festivals and events

Chittaurgarh *p374, map p375*

Oct/Nov Mira Utsav, 2 days of cultural evening programmes and religious songs in the fort's Mira temple.

Kota *p377*

Mar/Apr Colourful **Gangaur**.
Jul/Aug Teej.
Sep/Oct Dasara Mela (22-24 Oct 2012, 12-14 Oct 2013). Great atmosphere, with shows in lit up palace grounds.

Bundi *p378, map p379*

Aug Kajli Teej (22-23 Aug 2013, 12-13 Aug 2014), and **Bundi Utsav**, which takes place 3 days after the Pushkar fair has finished, see box, page 435.

Nov Jhalawar sees the **Chandrabhaga Fair** (27-29 Nov 2012) a cattle and camel fair with all the colour and authenticity of Pushkar but less commercialization. Animals are traded in large numbers, pilgrims come to bathe in the river as the temples become the centre of religious activity and the town is abuzz with all manner of vendors.

Transport

Chittaurgarh *p374, map p375*

Bicycle hire By railway station, Rs 5 per hr.

Bus Enquiries, T01472-241177. Daily buses to **Bundi** (4 hrs), **Kota** (5 hrs), **Ajmer** (5 hrs) and frequent buses to **Udaipur**.

Train Enquiries, T01472-240131. A 117-km branch line runs from Chittaurgarh to **Udaipur**. At **Mavli Junction** (72 km) another branch runs down the Aravalli scarp to **Marwar Junction** (150 km). The views along this line are very picturesque, though trains are slow, with hard seats. By taking this route you can visit Udaipur, Ajmer and Jodhpur in a circular journey. Call for times as services have been scaled back in recent years. **Jaipur**: *Jaipur Exp 19770*, 0515, 8½ hrs; *Chetak Exp 19616*, 2200, 8½ hrs; both call at **Ajmer** (4½-5 hrs).

Kota *p377*

Bus At least hourly to **Bundi** (45 mins) and a few daily to **Ajmer**, **Chittaurgarh**, **Jhalarapatan** (2½ hrs) and Udaipur; also to **Gwalior**, **Sawai Madhopur** and **Ujjain**.

Train From **Kota Junction**: **Bharatpur**: *Golden Temple Mail 12903*, 1125, 4 hrs (continues to **Mathura**, 5 hrs). **Mumbai (Central)**: *Rajdhani Exp 12952*, 2105, 11¾ hrs; *Paschim Exp 12926*, 2345, 15½ hrs; *Golden Temple Mail 12904*, 1440, 15¼ hrs. **New Delhi**: *Rajdhani Exp 12951*, 0330, 5½ hrs; *Golden Temple Mail 12903*, 1125, 7½ hrs; *Dehra Dun Exp 19019*, 1945, 10½ hrs, all via **Sawai Madhopur**, 1½ hrs.

Bundi *p378, map p379*

Bus Enquiries: T0747-244 5422. To **Ajmer** (165 km), 5 hrs; **Jaipur**, several daily, 4 deluxe, 4-5 hrs; **Kota** (37 km), 45 mins; **Chittaurgarh** (157 km), 5 hrs; **Udaipur** (120 km), 3 hrs. For **Jhalarapatan** catch a bus from **Kota** to **Jhalawar**; then auto-rickshaw or local bus for sights. The Ujjain–Jhalawar road is appalling.

Train Enquiries: T0747-244 3582. The station south of town has a train each way between **Kota** and **Neemuch** via **Chittaurgarh**. A direct Delhi service may be running, but involves hours waiting in Kota; better to take the bus to Kota and board trains there.

Directory

Kota *p377*

Internet Acme, 2nd floor, Kalawati Paliwal Market, Gumantpura. **Medical services** MBS Hospital, T0744-232 3261. **Police** T0744-245 0066. ATMs dotted around, but 3 near Hotel Navrang (see Sleeping).

Bundi *p378, map p379*

Banks Exchange can be a problem; try **Bank of Baroda**, T0747-244 3706.

Internet Dotted around town. **Medical services** City Hospital, T0747-244 2333.

Western Rajasthan

The Rajasthan of most people's imagination is found in this part of the state; camels crossing windswept sand dunes, colourful tribes dancing against a stark desert landscape, and some imperious buildings surveying the scene from on high. Jaisalmer is perhaps the ultimate expression of these romantic desert images. However, no other fort in Rajasthan exudes the same authority as Jodhpur's Meherangarh, watching over the town with unmatched majesty. The area south of Jodhpur is dotted with some of the state's most secluded heritage hotels, while to the north lie the utterly authentic attractions of Nagaur and Osian.

Jodhpur and around

→ *Colour map 2, B3. Phone code: 0291.*

Rajasthan's second largest city, Jodhpur is entirely dominated by its spectacular Meherangarh fort, towering over proceedings below with absolute authority. You could spend most of a day wandering this grand stone edifice on its plinth of red rock, pausing in the warm shafts of sunlight in its honey-coloured courtyards and strolling its chunky, cannon-lined ramparts high above the moat of blue buildings which make up the old city. Up there, birds of prey circle on the thermals, close to eye level, while the city hums below, its rickshaw horns and occasional calls to prayer still audible. Jodhpur's fascinating old city is a hive of activity, the colourful bazars, narrow lanes, and bustling Sardar Market frequented by equally colourful tribal people from the surrounding areas. South of the railway line things are altogether more serene, and nowhere more so than the impressive Umaid Bhawan Palace, its classic exterior belying the art deco extravaganza within. There are also some remarkable sights around Jodhpur: the temples of Osian and Nagaur are well worth a visit and there are some great heritage hotels set in quiet nearby villages. ▸▸ *For listings, see pages 392-398.*

Ins and outs

Getting there Jodhpur has good air, rail and road links with the other major cities of Rajasthan as well as Delhi and Mumbai. Many visitors stop here either on the way to or from Jaisalmer, or on their way down to Udaipur.

Getting around The train and bus stations are conveniently located close to the old city, with most hotels a Rs 20-30 rickshaw ride away, while the airport is 5 km south of town. The old city is small enough to walk around, although many people find a rented bicycle the best way to get about. ▸▸ *See Transport, page 398.*

Tourist information The government tourist office is on the grounds of the RTDC ⓘ *Hotel Ghoomar, High Court Rd, T0291-254 5083*. As well as the usual supply of maps and pamphlets, it also organize half-day city tours and village safaris. Also, **Tourist Assistance Force** has a presence at the railway station bus stand and clock tower.

History

The **Rathore** Rajputs had moved to Marwar – the 'region of death' – in 1211, after their defeat at Kanauj by Muhammad Ghori. In 1459 Rao Jodha, forced to leave the Rathore capital at Mandore, 8 km to the north, chose this place as his capital because of its strategic location on the edge of the Thar Desert. The Rathores subsequently controlled wide areas of Rajasthan. Rao Udai Singh of Jodhpur (died 1581) received the title of Raja from Akbar, and his son, Sawai Raja Sur Singh (died 1595), conquered Gujarat and part of the Deccan for the emperor. Maharaja Jaswant Singh (died 1678), having supported Shah Jahan in the Mughal struggle for succession in 1658, had a problematic relationship with the subsequent Mughal rule of Aurangzeb, and his son Ajit Singh was only able to succeed him after Aurangzeb's own death in 1707. In addition to driving the Mughals out of Ajmer he added substantially to the Meherangarh Fort in Jodhpur.

His successor, Maharaja Abhai Singh (died 1749) captured Ahmedabad, and the state came into treaty relations with the British in 1818.

Jodhpur lies on the once strategic Delhi-Gujarat trading route and the Marwaris managed and benefited from the traffic of opium, copper, silk, sandalwood, dates, coffee and much more besides.

Jodhpur → *For listings, see pages 392-398. Colour map 2, B3.*

The Old City

The Old City is surrounded by a huge 9.5-km-long wall which has 101 bastions and seven gates, above which are inscribed the names of the places to which the roads underneath them lead. It comprises a labyrinthine maze of narrow streets and lively markets, a great place to wander round and get lost. Some of the houses and temples are of richly carved stone, in particular the red sandstone buildings of the Siré (Sardar) Bazar. Here the **Taleti Mahal** (early 17th century), one of three concubines' palaces in Jodhpur, has the unique feature of *jarokhas* decorated with temple columns.

Meherangarh

ⓘ *T0291-254 8790, 0900-1700, foreigners Rs 250, students Rs 200, Indians Rs 20, includes excellent MP3 audio guide and camera fee, video Rs 200, allow at least 2 hrs, there is a pleasant restaurant on the terrace near the ticket office.*

The 'Majestic Fort' sprawls along the top of a steep escarpment with a sheer drop to the south. Originally started by Rao Jodha in 1459, it has walls up to 36 m high and 21 m wide, towering above the plains. Most of what stands today is from the period of Maharajah Jaswant Singh (1638-1678). On his death in 1678, Aurangzeb occupied the fort. However, after Aurangzeb's death Meherangarh returned to Jaswant Singh's son Ajit Singh and remained the royal residence until the Umaid Bhavan was completed in 1943. It is now perhaps the best preserved and presented palace in Rajasthan, an excellent example which the others will hopefully follow.

The summit has three areas: the palace (northwest), a wide terrace to the east of the palace, and the strongly fortified area to the south. There are extensive views from the top. One approach is by a winding path up the west side, possible by rickshaw, but the main approach and car park is from the east. The climb is quite stiff; those with walking difficulties may use the elevator (Rs 15 each way).

The fort is used for film shoots and adverts and hosts the Rajasthan Folk Music Festival which is patronized by Mick Jagger. The 2008 event was cancelled in memory of the 249 people killed in the stampede at Chamunda Devi temple in the fort complex who were gathered for Navratri.

The gateways There were originally seven gateways. The first, the **Fateh Gate**, is heavily fortified with spikes and a barbican that forces a 45° turn. The smaller **Gopal Gate** is followed by the **Bhairon Gate**, with large guardrooms. The fourth, **Toati Gate**, is now missing but the fifth, **Dodhkangra Gate**, marked with cannon shots, stands over a turn in the path and has loopholed battlements for easy defence. Next is the **Marti Gate**, a long passage flanked by guardrooms. The last, **Loha (Iron) Gate**, controls the final turn into the fort and has handprints (31 on one side and five on the other) of royal *satis*, the wives of maharajas, see page 1402. It is said that six queens and 58 concubines became *satis* on Ajit Singh's funeral pyre in 1724. *Satis* carried the Bhagavad Gita with them into the flames and legend has it that the holy book would never perish. The main entrance is through the **Jay (Victory) Pol**.

The palaces From the Loha Gate the ramp leads up to the Suraj (Sun) Pol, which opens onto the Singar Choki Chowk, the main entrance to the museum, see below. Used for royal ceremonies such as the anointing of rajas, the north, west and southwest sides of the Singar Choki Chowk date from the period immediately before the Mughal occupation in 1678. The upper storeys of the chowk were part of the *zenana*, and from the **Jhanki Mahal** (glimpse palace) on the upper floor of the north wing the women could look down on the activities of the courtyard. Thus the chowk below has the features characteristic of much of the rest of the *zenana*, *jarokhas* surmounted by the

Sleeping

Ajit Bhawan **2** *B2*
Bal Samand Palace **1** *A3*
Blue House **27** *B1*
Chauhan's Guest House **4** *A2*
Cosy Guest House **5** *A1*
Devi Bhavan **6** *C2*
Durag Niwas Guest House **7** *B2*
Ghoomar **10** *B2*
Govind **11** *B1*
Hare Krishna Guest House **9** *A1*
Haveli **28** *A1*
Haveli Inn Pal **16** *A1*
Inn Season **17** *C1*
Karni Bhawan **12** *C3*
Krishna Prakash Haveli **9** *A1*
Madho Niwas **3** *C3*
Pal Haveli **29** *A1*
Raas **13** *A1*
Raman Palace **15** *B2*
Ratan Vilas **24** *C1*
Saji Sanwri **18** *B1*
Shahi Guest House **8** *B1*
Singhvi's Haveli **25** *B1*
Sun City Guest House **23** *C2*
Umaid Bhawan Palace **20** *B3*
Yogi's Guest House **14** *A1*
Youth Hostel **22** *C2*

Eating

Café Sheesh Mahal **12** *A1*
Gypsy **8** *C1*
Hotel Priya **5** *B1*
Jhankar **13** *A1*
Jodhpur Coffee House **10** *B1*
Kalinga **3** *B1*
Mishrilal **4** *B1*
New Jodhpur Lodge **9** *B1*
On the Rocks **11** *B2*
Poonam **2** *B2*
Sankalp **7** *C1*
Shandar **6** *B1*
Softy & Softy **14** *B2*
Uttam **1** *B1*

distinctive Bengali-style eaves and beautifully ornate *jali* screens. These allowed cooling breezes to ventilate rooms and corridors in the often stiflingly hot desert summers.

Also typical of Mughal buildings was the use of material hung from rings below the eaves to provide roof covering, as in the columned halls of the **Daulat Khana** and the **Sileh Khana** (armoury), which date from Ajit Singh's reign. The collection of Indian weapons in the armoury is unequalled, with remarkable swords and daggers, often beautifully decorated with calligraphy. Shah Jahan's red silk and velvet tent, lavishly embroidered with gold thread and used in the Imperial Mughal campaign, is in the **Tent Room**. The **Jewel House** has a wonderful collection of jewellery, including diamond eyebrows held by hooks over the ears. There are also palanquins, howdahs and ornate royal cradles, all marvellously well preserved.

The **Phool Mahal** (Flower Palace), above the Sileh Khana, was built by Abhai Singh (1724-1749) as a hall of private audience. The stone *jali* screens are original and there are striking portraits of former rulers, a lavishly gilded ceiling and the Jodhpur coat of arms displayed above the royal couch; the murals of the 36 musical modes are a late 19th-century addition.

The **Umaid Vilas**, which houses Rajput miniatures, is linked to the **Sheesh Mahal** (Mirror Palace), built by Ajit Singh between 1707 and 1724. The room has characteristic large and regularly sized mirror work, unlike Mughal 'mirror palaces'. Immediately to its south, and above the Sardar Vilas, is the **Takhat Vilas**. Added by Maharajah Takhat Singh (1843-1873), it has wall murals of dancing girls, love legends and Krishna Lila, while its ceiling has two unusual features: massive wooden beams to provide support and the curious use of colourful Belgian Christmas tree balls.

The **Ajit Vilas** has a fascinating collection of musical instruments and costumes. On the ground floor of the Takhat Vilas is **Sardar Vilas**, and to its south the **Khabka** and **Chandan Mahals** (sleeping quarters). The **Moti Vilas** wings to the north, east and south of the Moti Mahal Chowk, date from Jaswant Singh's reign. The women could watch proceedings in the courtyard below through the *jali* screens of the surrounding wings. Tillotson suggests that the **Moti Mahal (Pearl Palace)** ⓘ *Rs 150 for 15 mins*, to the west, although placed in the *zenana* of the fort, was such a magnificent building that it could only have served the purpose of a Diwan-i-Am (Hall of Public Audience). The Moti Mahal is fronted by excellently carved 19th-century woodwork, while inside waist-level niches housed oil lamps whose light would have shimmered from the mirrored ceiling. A palmist reads your fortune at Moti Mahal Chowk (museum area).

Meherangarh Fort Palace Museum is in a series of palaces with beautifully designed and decorated windows and walls. It has a magnificent collection of the maharajas' memorabilia – superbly maintained and presented.

Jaswant Thada ⓘ *off the road leading up to the fort, 0900-1700, Rs 30*, is the cremation ground of the former rulers with distinctive memorials in white marble which commemorate Jaswant Singh II (1899) and successive rulers of Marwar. It is situated in pleasant and well- maintained gardens and is definitely worth visiting on the way back from the fort.

The new city

The new city beyond the walls is also of interest. Overlooking the Umaid Sagar is the **Umaid Bhawan Palace** on Chittar Hill. Building started in 1929 as a famine relief exercise when the monsoon failed for the third year running. Over 3000 people worked for 14 years, building this vast 347-room palace of sandstone and marble. The hand-hewn blocks are interlocked into position, and use no mortar. It was designed by HV Lanchester, with the most modern furnishing and facilities in mind, and completed in 1943. The interior decoration was left to the artist JS Norblin, a refugee from Poland; he painted the frescoes in the Throne Room (East Wing). For the architectural historian, Tillotson, it is "the finest example of Indo-Deco. The forms are crisp and precise, and the bland monochrome of the stone makes the eye concentrate on their carved shapes". The royal family still occupy part of the palace.

True blue

As you approach the fort you will notice the predominance of blue houses which are often inaccurately referred to as 'Brahmin houses' – the colour being associated with the high caste. In fact they are blue due to termites (white ants). It appears that the white limewash used originally did not deter the pests which have caused havoc, making unsightly cavities in local homes. The addition of chemicals (eg copper sulphate), which resulted in turning the white lime to a blue wash, was found to be effective in limiting the pest damage and so was widely used in the area around the fort. This also happens to be a part of town where large numbers of the Brahmin community live.

The **Umaid Bhawan Palace Museum** ⓘ *T0291-251 0101, 0900-1700, Rs 50*, includes the Darbar Hall with its elegantly flaking murals plus a good collection of miniatures, armour and quirky old clocks as well as a bizarre range of household paraphernalia; if it was fashionable in the 1930s, expensive and not available in India, it's in here. Many visitors find the tour and the museum in general disappointing with not much to see (most of the china and glassware you could see in your grandma's cabinets). The palace hotel which occupies the majority of the building has been beautifully restored, but is officially inaccessible to non-residents; try sneaking in for a cold drink and a look at the magnificent domed interior, a remarkable separation from the Indian environment in which it is set (see Sleeping, page 392).

Government Museum ⓘ *Umaid Park, Sat-Thu 1000-1630, Rs 3*, is a time-capsule from the British Raj, little added since Independence, with some moth-eaten stuffed animals and featherless birds, images of Jain Tirthankars, miniature portraits and antiquities. A small zoo in the gardens has a few rare exotic species.

Just southeast of Raikabagh Station are the **Raikabagh Palace** and the **Jubilee Buildings**, public offices designed by Sir Samuel Swinton Jacob in the Indo-Saracenic style. On the Mandore Road, 2 km to the north, is the large **Mahamandir Temple**.

In 1886, before steam engines were acquired, the Jodhpur Railway introduced camel-drawn trains. The maharaja's luxurious personal saloons (1926) are beautifully finished with inlaid wood and silver fittings and are on display near the Umaid Bhawan Palace.

Excursions from Jodhpur

A village safari visiting a **Bishnoi village** is recommended, although they have naturally become more touristy over the years. Most tours include the hamlets of **Guda**, famous for wildlife, **Khejarali**, a well-known Bishnoi village, **Raika** cameleers' settlement and **Salawas**, see page 391.

Majestic Marwar – Rural Villages Tours created by the excellent Virasat Journeys (Jaipur) they run a very intesting non-touristy trip into the villages around Jodhpur with an interesting twist. The tour costs Rs 2500 per person, but Rs 500 of that goes to the villages to create rainwater harvesting projects and improve hygiene. You are really giving something back here, in contrast to some of the other 'tribal' tours touted locally which are exploitative – www.virasatjourneys.com.

The small, semi-rural village of **Jhalamand**, 12 km south of Jodhpur, is a good alternative to staying in the city, particularly if you have your own transport. It works especially well as a base from which to explore the Bishnoi and Raika communities.

Marwar, 8 km north of Jodhpur, is the old 14th-century capital of Mandore, situated on a plateau. Set around the old cremation ground with the red sandstone *chhatris* of the Rathore rulers, the gardens are usually crowded with Indian tourists at weekends. The **Shrine of the 33 Crore Gods** is a hall containing huge painted rock-cut figures of heroes and gods, although some of the workmanship is a little crude. The largest deval, a combination of temple and cenotaph, is Ajit Singh's (died 1724); worth a closer look but is unkempt. The remains of an eighth-century Hindu temple is on a hilltop nearby.

Bal Samand Lake is the oldest artificial lake in Rajasthan, 5 km north. Dating from 1159, it is surrounded by parkland laid out in 1936 where the 19th-century **Hawa Mahal** was turned into a royal summer palace. Although the interior is European in style, it has entirely traditional red sandstone filigree windows and beautifully carved balconies. The peaceful and well-maintained grounds exude calm and tranquillity, while the views over the lake are simply majestic.

Around Jodhpur → *For listings, see pages 392-398.*

The temples of Osian are remarkable as much for their location in the middle of the desert as their architecture, while Nagaur is one of Rajasthan's busiest but most unaffected cities. The area south of Jodhpur is refreshingly green and fertile compared to the desert landscapes of most of Western Rajasthan (although it can be very dry from March until the monsoon). Leaving the city, the landscape soon becomes agricultural, punctuated by small, friendly villages, some housing stunning heritage hotels.

Osian → *Colour map, 2, B3.*

Surrounded by sand dunes, this ancient town north of Jodhpur in the Thar Desert contains the largest group of eighth- to 10th-century Hindu and Jain temples in Rajasthan. The typical Pratihara Dynasty **temple complex** is set on a terrace whose walls are finely decorated with mouldings and miniatures. The sanctuary walls have central projections with carved panels' and above these rise curved towers. The doorways are usually decorated with river goddesses, serpents and scrollwork. The 23 temples are grouped in several sites north, west and south of the town. The western group contains a mixture of Hindu temples, including the **Surya Temple** (early eighth century) with beautifully carved pillars. The Jain **Mahavira Temple** (eighth to 10th centuries) the best preserved, 200 m further on a hillock, rises above the town, and boasts a fantastically gaudy interior. The 11th- to 12th-century **Sachiya Mata Temple** is a living temple of the Golden Durga. Osian is well worth visiting.

Khimsar → *Colour map, 2, A4.*

On the edge of the desert, 80 km northeast of Jodhpur, Khimsar was founded by the Jain saint Mahavir 2500 years ago. The isolated, battle scarred, 16th-century moated castle of which a section remains, had a *zenana* added in the mid-18th century and a regal wing added in the 1940s. See Sleeping, page 394, for one of the best hotels in the state.

Nagaur → *Colour map, 2, A4.*

ⓘ *Foreigners Rs 50, Indians Rs 10, camera Rs 25, video Rs 50.*

Nagaur, 137 km north of Jodhpur, was a centre of Chishti Sufis. It attracts interest as it preserves some fine examples of pre-Mughal and Mughal architecture. The dull stretch of desert is enlivened by Nagaur's fort palace, temples and *havelis*. The city walls are said to date from the 11th- to 12th-century Chauhan period. Akbar built the mosque here and there is a shrine of the disciple of Mu'inuddin Chishti of Ajmer, see page 427. **Ahhichatragarh Fort**, which dominates the city, is absolutely vast, contains palaces of the Mughal emperors and of the Marwars, and is being restored with help from the Paul Getty Foundation. The Akbar Mahal is stunningly elegant and perfectly proportioned. The fort also has excellent wall paintings and interesting ancient systems of rainwater conservation and storage, ably explained by a very knowledgeable curator. It was awarded a UNESCO Heritage Award in 2000.

Khichan → *Colour map, 2, A3.*

Four kilometres from Phalodi, southwest of Bikaner just off the NH15, is a lovely, picturesque village with superb red sandstone *havelis* of the Oswal Jains. Beyond the village are sand dunes and mustard fields, and a lake which attracts ducks and other waterfowl. The once small quiet village has grown into a bustling agricultural centre and a prominent bird-feeding station. Jain villagers put out grain behind the village for winter visitors; up to 8000 demoiselle cranes and occasionally common eastern cranes can be seen in December and January on the feeding grounds. At present you can go along and watch without charge.

Pokaran → *Colour map, 2, A2.*

Pokaran, between Jaisalmer and Jodhpur, stands on the edge of the great desert with dunes stretching 100 km west to the Pakistan border. It provides tourists with a mid-way stopover between Bikaner/Jodhpur and Jaisalmer as it did for royal and merchant caravans in the past. The impressive 16th-century yellow sandstone **Pokaran fort** ⓘ *foreigners Rs 50, Indians Rs 10, camera Rs 50,* overlooking a confusion of streets in the town below, has a small museum with an interesting collection of medieval weapons, costumes and paintings. There are good views from the ramparts. Pokaran is also well known for its potters who make red-and-white pottery and terracotta horses/elephants. **Ramdeora**, the Hindu and Jain pilgrim centre nearby, has Bishnoi hamlets and a preserve for blackbuck antelope, Indian gazelle, bustards and sand grouse. **Ramdeora Fair** (September) is an important religious event with cattle trading.

Khetolai, about 25 km northwest of Pokaran, is the site of India's first nuclear test explosion held underground on 18 March 1974, and of further tests in May 1998.

Balotra and around → *Colour map, 2, B3.*

The small textile town, 100 km southwest of Jodhpur, is known for its traditional weaving using pit looms and block prints, although many are now mechanized causing pollution of the Luni River. Nearby is the beautiful Jain temple with elephant murals at **Nakoda**. **Kanana**, near Balotra, celebrates **Holi** with stage shows and other entertainment. There is a *dharamshala* at Nakoda and guesthouses at Balotra. At **Tilwara**, 127 km from Jodhpur, the annual Mallinathji **cattle fair** is a major event, which takes place just after **Holi** on the dry Luni riverbed. Over 50,000 animals are brought (although this has declined in recent years due to the drought), including Kapila (Krishna's) cows and Kathiawari horses, making it Rajasthan's largest. Few tourists make it this far as so it is much less commercial than Pushkar. Try and go with a Rajasthani-speaking guide as the farmers and traders are very happy to allow you in on the negotiations as well as describing the key things to look for when buying a camel (the front legs should not rub against its belly, for instance). There are some interesting trade stalls including sword makers.

Salawas

Salawas, about 30 minutes' drive south from Jodhpur, is well known for its pit loom weaving. The village produces *durries*, carpets, rugs, bed covers and tents using camel hair, goat hair, wool and cotton in colourful and interesting patterns. You can visit the weavers' co-operatives such as **Roopraj** and **Salawas Durry Udhyog** (anyone on a Bishnoi village tour is normally frogmarched into one of them), where you can buy authentic village crafts, but watch out for high prices and pushy salesmen.

Luni → *Colour map, 2, B3.*

The tiny bustling village of Luni, 40 km from Jodhpur, sits in the shadow of the 19th- century red sandstone Fort Chanwa which has been converted to a hotel. With its complex of courtyards, water wheels, and intricately carved façades, the fort and its village offer an attractive and peaceful alternative to the crowds of Jodhpur. The village of **Sanchean**, which you will pass through on the way, is worth exploring.

Rohet and Sardar Samand → *Colour map 2, B4.*

Rohet, 50 km north of Jodhpur, was once a picturesque hamlet settled by the Bishnoi community. It is now a busy highway village although it has a busy bazar and is pleasant to wander around. At the end of the village a lake attracts numerous winter migrants in addition to resident birds. Here also are the family cenotaphs. Rohetgarh, a small 'castle' beside the lake, which has been converted in to a hotel, has a collection of antique hunting weapons. The hotel will organize trips to the local Bishnoi villages. It is quite usual to see blue bull, black buck and other antelopes in the fields. Village life can be very hard in this arid environment but the Bishnoi are a dignified people who delight in explaining their customs. You can take part in the opium tea ceremony which is quite fun and somewhat akin to having a pint with the locals down at the pub.

The lake nearby is a beautiful setting for the royal 1933 art deco hunting lodge, **Sardar Samand Palace**, see page 395. The lake attracts pelicans, flamingos, cranes, egrets and kingfishers and the wildlife sanctuary has blackbuck, gazelle and nilgai, but the water level drops substantially during summer; the lake has actually dried up from April to June in recent years. Sardar Samand is 60 km southeast of Jodhpur.

Nimaj → *Colour map, 2, B4.*

A small feudal town 110 km east of Jodhpur on the way to the Jaipur-Udaipur highway, the real attraction is the artificial lake, **Chhatra Sagar**, 4 km away. The ex-ruling family have recreated a 1920s-style tented hunting lodge on the lake's dam, which offers amazing views over the water and a genuine family welcome (see Sleeping, page 395).

Jodhpur and around listings

For Sleeping and Eating price codes and other relevant information, see Essentials pages 38-42.

Sleeping

Jodhpur *p386, map p387*

Certain budget hotels, including some of those listed below, may quote low room prices that depend on you booking a tour or camel safari with them; some have been known to raise the price dramatically or even evict guests who refuse. Confirm any such conditions before checking in.

LL Umaid Bhawan Palace, T0291-251 0101, www.tajhotels.com. Freshly renovated in stunning contemporary art deco, with 36 rooms and 40 beautifully appointed suites, best with garden-view balconies and unforgettable marble bathrooms, rather cool and masculine, far removed from the typical Rajasthani colour-fest, soaring domed lobbies, formal gardens and an extraordinary underground swimming pool with smart new spa treatment rooms to one side. Good for once-in-a-lifetime indulgence (this is where Liz Hurley tied the knot), but money perhaps better spent elsewhere.

LL-L Raas, Tunvarji Ka Jhalra, Makrana Mohalla, www.raasjodhpur.com, T0291-263 6455. Raas is a gem at the heart of the city. Built from the same warm rose-red sandstone as the fort that towers above it; stunning balconies with carved stone shutters discreetly open up to reveal exceptional fort views. There is a contemporary vibe inspired by the essence of Rajasthan, rather than the traditional 'heritage-style' and yet it blends into the old city – it looks chic and stylish without looking out of place. As well as all the mod cons, you will find sumptuous fabrics and evocative photographs in every room. There are 2 restaurants, one open for non-residents as well as a very inviting pool. Recommended.

L Ajit Bhawan, Circuit House Rd, T0291-251 3333, www.ajitbhawan.com. With a rather imposing palace façade, it is hard to imagine the variety of rooms, cottages and tents at this fantastic property. All luxuriously kitted out, the cottages are particularly beautiful. There is a very ornate swimming pool, several restaurants on-site, an opulent bar and heaps of character. This is India's first heritage hotel started in 1927 and still leads the way.

A-C Inn Season, PWD Rd, T0291-261 6400, www.innseasonjodhpur.com. 11 classy a/c rooms with interesting layout and private areas in, well-run hotel, good pool in beautiful gardens, a definite cut above the rest.

A-C Karni Bhawan, Palace Rd, T0291-251 2101, www.karnihotels.com. 30 clean, simple, classy rooms (20 a/c), each with a different theme and period furniture to match, in 1940s sandstone 'colonial bungalow' (on 3 floors). Village-theme restaurant, peaceful lawns, clean pool, unhurried helpful staff. More expensive and lacking the charm of its neighbour **Devi Bhavan** (see below).

B-C Pal Haveli, behind clock tower in the middle of town, T0291-329 3328, www.palhaveli.com. 20 chic and atmospheric rooms in authentic 200-year-old *haveli* with stylishly decorated drawing room/mini-museum, attractive courtyard dining area plus good views from roof bar/restaurant of both the fort and clock tower. Occasional theme nights are held. Massage available, friendly staff and chilled vibe. Recommended.

B-D Krishna Prakash Haveli, Killikhana, T0291-320 0254, www.kpheritage.com. Pleasant and spacious rooms with bath in 100-year-old building, "heartfully decorated" with repro antique furniture, some facing fort, slightly less inspired ones in recently added block, quite close to base of fort so impressive views from stylish shaded rooftop restaurant. One extra special suite with a swimming-pool size bathtub and 3 rooms.

C-D Devi Bhavan, 1 Ratanada Circle, T0291-251 1067, www.devibhawan.com. Beautiful rooms with bath and most with a/c, delightful shady garden with lovely new pool, excellent Indian dinner (set timings), Rajput family home. Popular with independent travellers, this is a very special place. Recommended.

C-D Haveli Inn Pal, T0291-261 2519, www.haveliinnpal.com. Quirkily designed rooms, some with huge windows overlooking fort, some with lake views and unusual marble shower troughs, others with beds you need a ladder to get into, fantastic furniture, rooftop restaurant with commanding views and a rare patch of lawn, pleasant, Recommended.

C-D Madho Niwas, New Airport Rd, Ratanada, T0291-251 2486, madhoniwas@satyam.net.in. 16 simple rooms in art deco 1920s bungalow. Thakur Dalvir Singh oversees excellent Marwari meals in garden, small plunge pool. His family at Bhenswar and Ranakpur can organize excellent safaris, treks, etc.

C-D Ratan Vilas, Loco Shed Rd, Ratanada, T0291-261 4418, www.ratanvilas.com. 15 rooms, some a/c, arranged around beautiful courtyard in elegant period property. Peaceful as no TVs. Very well maintained, lovely gardens with seated areas, friendly family. Recommended.

C-E Hotel Ghoomar (RTDC), High Court Rd, T0291-254 4010. Most rooms not worth considering, but 'super-deluxe' a/c rooms have been renovated to a high standard.

C-E Shahi Guest House, City Police, Gandhi St, opposite Narsingh Temple, T0291-262 3802, www.shahiguesthouse.com. Enchanting 350-year-old mughal-style *haveli* with 6 quirky rooms (4 a/c, 2 with air-coolers) set around central courtyard. The building was traditionally the *janana dodi*, or women's area, of Rajput officers' quarters. The Queen's Palace room and Honeymoon Suite are particularly lovely. Friendly family and little rooftop restaurant with beautiful views of the old city and the fort. Charming young family hosts.

C-E Sun City Guest House, 1/C High Court Colony, Ratanada, T0291-262 5880. 8 good-sized, clean, basic rooms run by very enthusiastic and friendly family.

C-F Hotel Haveli (formerly **Haveli Guest House**), Makaran Mohalla, opposite Turjika Jhalra, T0291-261 4615, www.haveliguesthouse.com. Attractive sandstone building with 22 simple, clean rooms, prices vary according to view, cheerful decor, breezy roof terrace with vegetarian restaurant and great views of fort, particularly atmospheric in the evening with trickling fountains, comfy lounges and nightly live music and dance.

C-G Singhvi's Haveli, Navchokiya, Ramdevjika Chowk, T0291-262 4293, singhvi15adhaveli@hotmail.com. 11 rooms in charming, 500-year-old *haveli* (one of the oldest), tastefully decorated, friendly family. New extra-special suite with mirror-work ceiling reminiscent of the fort that towers above. Nice chill-out area. Recommended.

D-F Saji Sanwri, Gandhi St, near City Police Station, T0291-244 0305, sajisanwri@rediffmail.com. The rooms here are getting a little dog-eared for the price, but there is bags of charm. The lady owner is hugely enthusiastic and a little eccentric. No commission.

D-G Blue House, Sumer Bhawan, Moti Chowk, T0291-262 1396,www.bluehousejodhpur.com. 11 clean rooms with bath (hot water all day), home-cooked meals, great views from rooftop restaurant, mixed reports on food and service. Be wary of trips to cousin's overpriced handicrafts shop.

D-G Yogi's Guest House, Raj Purohit Ji Ki Haveli, Manak Chowk, old town, T0291-264 3436, yogiguesthouse@hotmail.com. 12 rooms, most in 500-year-old *haveli*, clean, modern bathrooms, camel/jeep safaris, experienced management. Lovely atmosphere.
E-G Cosy Guest House, Novechokiya Rd, in Brahm Puri, a narrow lane full of cheap guesthouses just west of the fort, T0291-261 2066, www.cosyguesthouse.com. 6 clean and simple little rooms, good if slightly pricey home-cooked meals (other restaurants 15-min walk), outstanding roof- top views of old city, sociable atmosphere, can be good for meeting other travellers.
E-G Govind, Station Rd, opposite GPO, T0291-262 2758, www.govindhotel.com. 12 cleanish rooms, recently smartened up, some a/c, good rooftop vegetarian restaurant with real coffee, fort views, camel safaris, bus and rail ticketing, luggage storage, internet, friendly, very helpful owner but noisy location.
E-G Hare Krishna Guest House, Killi Khana, Mehron Ka Chowk, T0291-263 5307, www.harekrishnaguesthouse.net. Run by the President of the Jodhpur Guest House Association, you are definitely looked after here. With a variety of rooms, lots of character and great views from the restaurant and chill-out space on the roof. They also run excellent Bishnoi village safaris.
E-G Raman Palace, opposite Keshar Bagh, Shiv Rd, T0291-251 3980. Family atmosphere, 20 clean though simply furnished rooms with bath (hot water) in nice building made of Jaisalmer sandstone, 3 with a/c, traditional meals, quiet area, pleasant rooftop, friendly and efficient owner.
F Durag Niwas Guest House, Old Public Park Lane, near Circuit House, T0291-251 2385, www.durag-niwas.com. Cheaper and more character than **Durag Vilas** next door. Runs a women's craft collective 'Sambhali' on-site.
F Youth Hostel, Bhatia Circle, Ratanada, T0291-251 0160. Attractive, well-located building with 5 rooms and 6 dorms. Friendly staff, camping.
F-G Chauhan's Guest House, Fort Rd, T0291-254 1497. Quirky homestay offering courses in Hindi, yoga, music, painting, relaxing café, family-run, set above large art shop where you can watch painters at work, book exchange.

Excursions from Jodhpur *p389*

A Bal Samand Palace (WelcomHeritage), T0291-257 2321, www.welcomheritage hotels.com. Essentially this is 2 properties together, the Palace and the Garden Retreat. In extensive grounds on the lake, there are 10 attractively furnished suites in an atmospheric palace and 26 'garden retreat' rooms in the imaginatively renovated stables, restaurant (mainly buffet), lovely pool, boating, pleasant orchards which attract nilgai, jackals and peacocks, has a calming, tranquil atmosphere.
B Jhalamand Garh, Jhalamand, T0291-272 0481, www.heritagehotelsindia.com. 18 comfortable rooms in whitewashed, family-run period property. Good local dishes, atmospheric dining hall, jeep, horse and camel safaris arranged, perhaps not the most professional set-up but charming.

Osian *p390*

Also some **E** and **F** guesthouses in town.
L Camel Camp, on the highest sand dunes, T0291-243 7023, www.camelcamposian.com. A beautiful complex of 50 double-bedded luxury tents with modern conveniences (attached baths, hot showers), superb restaurant and bar plus an amazing pool – quite a sight at the top of a sand dune. Tariff inclusive of meals and camel safaris, ask in advance for jeep/camel transfers to avoid a steep climb up the dunes. Recommended.

Khimsar *p390*

AL Khimsar Fort, T01585-262 345, www.khimsar.com. Popular with tours, this is a well run venture with 48 large, comfortable a/c rooms, good restaurant on breezy rooftop with lovely views, fabulous pool, yoga, gym, beautiful large gardens, fire dances at the illuminated medieval fort, this is an award-winning heritage hotel, but lacks some of the charm of other fort hotels. It's a bit too polished.
AL Khimsar Sand Dunes Village, 6 km from the fort, contact fort as above. 16 ethnically styled luxury huts in the heart of the dunes around a small lake, unbeatable setting, 'safaris' by camel cart.

Nagaur *p390*

LL-AL Ranvas, T0291-257 2321 (Jodhana Heritage), www.ranvasnagaur.com. Stunningly restored *havelis* within the magical fort of Nagaur. This new venture is extremely stylish and yet comfortable. Beautiful furnishings, sumptuous fabrics, rare artefacts, charming courtyards and secluded spots, Ranvas is effortlessly chic. There is an amazing pool and great restaurant – highly recommended.

AL Royal Camp, T0291-257 2321, www.jodhanaheritagehotels.com. Operates from October to March and during the camel fair (when the price rises to **L**) 20 delightful deluxe 2-bed furnished tents (hot water bottles, heaters, etc), flush toilets, hot water in buckets, stunning dining area, all inside fort walls. Although you seem very secluded, Nagaur fort is right in the middle of the city and not elevated, so you do get traffic and mosque noise. An experience.

D-E Shree Aditya, Ajmer Rd, near Vyas petrol pump, T01582-245438. Uninspiring building with 24 modern rooms, 12 a/c. Restaurant.

D-F Mahaveer International, Vijay Vallabh Chowk, near bus stand, T01582-243158. 15 reasonable rooms, 7 a/c, huge dining hall, friendly knowledgeable manager.

Pokaran *p391*

A Desert Tented Resort, 61 km from Pokaran, Manwar, 2.5 km away on a sand dune, www.manvar.com, T02928-268011. Good 2-bed tents with hot showers, flush toilets, meals, camel, jeep safaris and visits to Bishnoi villages.

A-B Fort Pokaran, T02994-222274, www.fortpokaran.com. 19 quaint, quirky rooms with bath (some run-down), old 4-posters, some carved columns, good hot lunches Rs 200-250 (order ahead if passing through town), service a little detached.

B-C Manwar Desert Camp, 61 km from Pokaran in Manwar off Jodhpur–Jaisalmer highway, www.manvar.com, T02928-268011. Beautifully designed cottages with attractive interiors, some a/c, restaurant (a good lunch stop), great handicrafts shop. They run the Desert Camp above.

E Motel Pokaran (RTDC), on NH15, T02994-222275. A ramshackle building with 8 sparse rooms, plus 5 passable garden cottages.

Luni *p391*

A Fort Chanwa, T02931-284 216, www.fortchanwa.com. 47 good rooms in 200-year-old fort, not large but well furnished, individually designed, excellent Rajasthani meals in impressive dining room, pleasant lawn for drinks, excellent pool and well managed.

Rohet and Sardar Samand *p391*

LL-L Mihirgarh, an hour from Rohet, T982-902 3453, www.mihirgarh.com. The 'sun fortress' is a new venture from the team at **Rohetgarh** (see below) offering stunning suites with private courtyards and plunge pools. There is also an infinity pool, spa, beautiful restaurant and barbeque area and 360-degree views of the desert landscape.

A Rohetgarh, Rohet, T02936-268 231, www.rohetgarh.com. Come here to write a book. Both William Dalrymple and Bruce Chatwin have used the inspiring Rohetgarh to put pen to paper. Dating to 1622, there are a range of rooms (avoid rooms near outdoor restaurant). Fine Rajasthani food, ordinary architecture but in beautiful environment, pleasant lake view terraces, lovely pool, health club, riding and safaris to Bishnoi, Raika and artisans' villages, boating on the lake, a relaxing getaway.

A Sardar Samand Palace, Sardar Samand, Pali, T02960-245001, www.heritagehotelsofindia.com. 19 colonial-style rooms (11 a/c), in a slightly forbidding-looking building. Built in 1933 as a hunting lodge, much of the furniture is original, and lends a very un-Indian feel. Safaris and boating trips arranged in the season, Nov best time for birdwatching on the lake, good pool and tennis court, isolated but atmospheric.

Nimaj *p392*

LL Chhatra Sagar, 4 km from Nimaj, T02939-230118, www.chhatrasagar.com. Open 1 Oct-31 Mar. 11 beautiful colonial-style tents on the banks of a very picturesque reservoir. The ex-rulers of Nimaj have recreated the hunting lodge of their forefathers to great effect, and still live on the lake themselves, so a very convivial family atmosphere. Safaris arranged, all meals included in the tariff. Recommended.

Eating

Jodhpur *p386, map p387*

The best restaurants are in hotels; reserve ahead. Rooftop restaurants in most budget and mid-range hotels welcome non-residents. For *Daal-bhatti, lassi* and *kachoris* head for Jalori and Sojati gates. Great food at **Pal Haveli** and **Hotel Haveli** (see Sleeping).

TTT **Ajit Bhawan**, Airport Rd, T0291-251 1410. Evening buffet, excellent meal in garden on a warm evening with entertainment, but lacking atmosphere if eating indoors in winter.

TTT **Mehran**, T0291-255 5389, www.mehrangarh.org. What a backdrop. Great Rajasthani food as you sit perched over the city of Jodhpur at the majestic Mehrengarh fort. Breathtaking.

TTT **Raas**, (see Sleeping), Offering a fine dining experience at the heart of the old city. Recommended.

TTT **Umaid Bhavan**, T0291-251 0101. Fabulous setting and fine food make it a great place for dinner. **Pillars**, a tiny garden restaurant, can be hired for one couple for Rs 2000, the most romantic setting in town.

TT **Gypsy**, PWD Colony, T0291-510 3888. 1130-1530 and 1900-2300. Good range of Indian, continental and Mexican dishes, choice of indoor or outdoor seating, swanky place popular with well-off locals.

TT **Kalinga**, opposite station. Western and Indian. A/c, good food (try butter chicken and aubergine dishes), friendly service, music may not please, breakfast good value.

TT **On the Rocks**, near **Ajit Bhawan**, T0291-510 2701. Good mix of Indian and continental, plus a relaxing bar, patisserie, ice cream parlour and lovely gardens.

TT **Sankalp**, 12th Rd (west of city centre), 1030-2300. Upmarket a/c South Indian, dosas come with a fantastic range of chutneys, good service. Recommended.

T **Café Sheesh Mahal**, behind clock tower and next to **Pal Haveli**. Great cappuccino and macchiato in stylish coffee lounge. You can get sandwiches and hot chocolate brownie too.

T **Hotel Priya**, 181 Nai Sarak. Fantastic special *thalis* for Rs 55 and extra quick service.

T **Jhankar**, follow signs to next to **Ganesh Guest House** or as it's run by the owner of **Blue Guest House** you can ask there. This little courtyard café has great character – very pretty and a menu of all the usual traveller favourites to boot.

T **Jodhpur Coffee House**, Sojati Gate. Good South Indian snacks and *thalis*.

T **Mishrilal**, Clocktower. The best *lassis* in town, if not the world.

T **New Jodhpur Lodge**, a real challenge to find, ask for Golion ki Haveli in Tripoliya Bazar in the old city, T0291-261 3340. A family home which offers good, basic *thalis* for Rs 30 in a shaded courtyard, quite an experience.

T **Poonam**, High Court Rd. Pure vegetarian Indian. "Gorgeous 4-ft masala dosas".

T **Shandar**, Jalori Gate. Indian vegetarian. Good food and sweets.

T **Softy and Softy**, High Court Rd. Excellent sweets and *namkeen*, thick shakes, fun for people-watching.

T **Uttam**, High Court Rd, near Sojati Gate. Good a/c *thali* restaurant friendly, fast service.

Festivals and events

Jodhpur *p386, map p387*

Jul/Aug Nag Panchami, when Naga (*naag*), the cobra, is worshipped. The day is dedicated to Sesha, the 1000-headed god or *Anant* (infinite) Vishnu, who is often depicted reclining on a bed of serpents. In Jodhpur, snake charmers gather for a colourful fair in Mandore.

Oct Marwar Festival (28-29 Oct 2012, 17-18 Oct 2013, 7-8 Oct 2014), held at full moon, includes music, puppet shows, turban-tying competitions, camel polo and ends with a fire dance on the dunes at Osian.

Oct Jodhpur RIFF, www.jodhpurfolkfestival.org. Coinciding with Kartik Purnima, the brightest full moon of the year, Jodhpur's Rajasthan International Folk Festival (RIFF) is an eclectic mix of master musicians from local Rajasthan communities, acts from around the world and cutting-edge global dance music at Club Mehran. There are workshops and interactive daytime sessions for visitors. Some performances are around the city, while the main stage and club are in the stunning Mehrangahr Fort itself. www.jodhpurfolkfestival.org – held every Oct.

Nagaur *p390*

Jan/Feb The popular **Cattle and Camel Fair** (17-20 Feb 2013, 6-9 Feb 2014) is held just outside the town. There are camel races, cock fights, folk dancing and music. The fields become full of encampments of pastoral communities, tribal people and livestock dealers with their cattle, camels, sheep, goats and other animals.

Shopping

Jodhpur *p386, map p387*

Jodhpur is famous for its once-popular riding breeches although it is pricey to get a pair made these days, tie-dye fabrics, lacquer work and leather shoes. Export of items over 100 years old is prohibited. The main areas are: **Sojati Gate** for gifts; **Station Rd** and Sarafa Bazar for jewellery; **Tripolia Bazar** for handicrafts; **Khanda Falsa** and Kapra Bazar for tie-dye; **Lakhara Bazar** for lac bangles. **Raj Rani** has a nice selection of more unusual designed clothes (probably from Pushkar) at Makrana Mohalla, near clock tower. Shoes are made in **Mochi Bazar**, **Sardarpura** and **Clock Tower**, *bandhanas* in **Bambamola**, and around **Siwanchi** and **Jalori Gates**. *Durries* are woven at **Salawas**, 18 km away. In most places you'll need to bargain.

Antiques

Shops on road between Umaid and Ajit Bhawans, flourishing trade though pricey.
Kirti Art Collection, T0291-251 2136. Has a good selection. Recommended.

Books

Radha Krishan Arts, Clock Tower, near Police Choki. Great selection of secondhand books in this general souvenir shop.

Clothing and lifestyle

New parade of shops next to Ajit Bhawan (Circuit House Road) including beautiful designer jewellery shop **Amrapali**, clothes and prints from **Anokhi**Anokhi and **Pahnava**.

Handloom and handicrafts

Chauhan's (see Sleeping). Great range of artworks and miniatures at fair prices. You can also watch artists at work.
Krishna Arts and Crafts, by Tija Mata temple on main road running west from clock tower. Interesting shop by temple, fixed prices.
Marasthaly, High Court Rd.
Marwar Heritage Art School, 116 Kamal, T0291-5132187, are among many shops keeping the miniature painting tradition alive.
Rajasthan Khadi Sangathan, BK ka Bagh.
Shriganesham, 1st floor, outside **Pal Haveli**, behind clock tower. Wide selection.

Jewellery

Amrapali, near Ajit Bhawan, Circuit House Rd. Beautiful designer jewellery in gold and silver with a range of traditional pieces. Recommended.
Gems & Art Plaza, Circuit House Rd. As patronized by Angelina Jolie. Some nice pieces in Kundan and Minakari styles, gaudy rings.

Spices

Mohanlal Verhomal Spices, 209-B, Kirana Merchant Vegetable Market (inside the market to the left of clock tower), T0291-261 5846, www.mvspices.com. Sought after for hand-mixed spices, but quality assured and is simply the best spice outlet in the city. Usha, along with her 6 sisters and mother, runs the shop. Insist your guide takes you here as many have tried to pass themselves off as her shop.

Pokaran *p391*

Kashida, just outside town, Jaisalmer-Bikaner Rd, T02994-222 511. Excellent handwoven crafts from the desert region, clean, well laid out, reasonably priced, profits help local self-help projects, part of the **URMUL** trust (see box, page 439).

Activities and tours

Jodhpur *p386, map p387*

Body and soul

Ayurvedic massages are offered by **Pal Haveli**, page 393, **Khimsar Fort**, page 394, and **Ajit Bhawan**, page 396.

Tour operators

Many of the hotels organize village safaris, as does the tourist office, which charges Rs 1100 for 4 people including car, guide and tips given to villagers. City sightseeing, starts from tourist office at **Ghoomar Hotel**, T0291-254 5083: half day (0830-1300, 1400-1800). Fort and palaces, Jaswant Thada, Mandore Gardens, Government Museum, bazar around Old City Clock Tower.

Aravalli Safari, 4 Kuchaman House Area, Airport Rd, T0291-262 6799.
Exclusive India, Kishan Villas, Police Line Rd, Ratanada, T0291-342006, exclinjdh@datainfosys.net. Ask for Rajendra Singh Rathore who is very knowledgeable and an excellent companion.
Forts & Palaces, 15 Old Public Park, T0291-251 1207, www.palaces-tours.com.
Marwar Eco-Cultural Tours, Makrana Mohalla near **Haveli Guest House**, T0291-513 2409, www.nativeplanet.org/tours/india. NGO-run tours into tribal country, connecting with a mix of settled and nomadic tribes. Profits divided between the NGO and communities.

Transport

Jodhpur *p386, map p387*
Air Transport to town: by taxi, Rs 300/400; auto-rickshaw, Rs 150. **Indian Airlines**, near Bhati crossroads, T0291-2510757, 1000-1300, 1400-1700; airport enquiries T0291-251 2617, flies to **Delhi**, **Jaipur**, **Mumbai**, **Udaipur**. **Jet Airways**, T0291-510 2222, airport T0291-251 5551, to **Delhi** and **Mumbai**.
Local bus Minibuses cover most of the city except Fort and Umaid Bhavan Palace. For **Mandore**, frequent buses leave from **Paota Bus Stand**. Also several daily buses to **Salawas**, **Luni** (40 km), **Rohet** (450 km) and **Osian** (65 km).
Long distance **RST Bus Stand**, near Raikabagh Railway Station, T0291-254 4989. 1000-1700; bookings also at tourist office. A convenient bus route links Jodhpur with **Ghanerao** and **Ranakpur**, **Kumbhalgarh** and **Udaipur**. Other daily services include: **Abu Rd**, 6 hrs; **Ahmedabad**, 10 hrs; **Ajmer**, 5 hrs; **Jaipur**, frequent, 8 hrs; **Jaisalmer**, 0530 (depart Jaisalmer, 1400), 5-6 hrs; faster than train but scenically tedious; **Pali**, 1 hr; **Udaipur**, 7 hrs by rough road, best to book a good seat a day ahead.

Private operators arrive at Barakuttulah Stadium west of town, to a scrum of rickshaw drivers: pay around Rs 30 to the old city. Some companies have offices opposite railway station, eg **HR Travels**, **Sun City Tours**, and **Sethi Yatra**, or book at **Govind Hotel** (see Sleeping, page 394).

Car and taxi Car hire from tourist office, **Ghoomar Hotel**, whole day about Rs 900; half day Rs 500. For a taxi, T0291-262 0238.
Rickshaw Railway station to fort should be about Rs 25 (may demand Rs 50; try walking away).
Train Jodhpur Station enquiries: T131. Open 0800-2400. Reservations: T0291-263 6407. Open 0900-1300, 1330-1600. Advance reservations, next to GPO. Tourist Bureau, T0291-254 5083 (0500-2300). **International tourist waiting room** for passengers in transit (ground floor), with big sofas and showers; clean Indian toilets in 2nd-class waiting room on the 1st floor of the station Foyer.
To: **Agra**: *Jodhpur-Howrah Exp 2308*, 1945, 12¾ hrs, continues via **Varanasi** to **Kolkata**. **Ahmedabad** via **Abu Rd (Mount Abu)**: *Ranakpur Exp 14707*, 1510, 5½ hrs; *Surya Nagari Exp 12479*, 1845, 9½ hrs (Abu Rd 4½-5½ hrs), both continue to **Mumbai** (17 hrs). **Barmer**: *Barmer Exp 14059*, 0645, 3½ hrs. **Delhi**: *Mandore Exp 12462*, 1930, 11 hrs (OD); *Jodhpur Delhi Exp 14060*, 2230, 12½ hrs (OD). **Kalka/Haridwar** via **Bikaner**: *Kalka Exp 14888/ Link Exp 14888A*, 1045, 23 hrs; **Jaipur**: *Inter-City Exp 12467*, 0500, 6 hrs; *Mandore Exp 12462*, 1930, 5 hrs; *Marudhar Exp 14854/14864*, 0915, 5 hrs. **Jaisalmer** (via **Osian**): *Jodhpur Jaisalmer Exp*, and *Jaisalmer Exp 14059*, 0645, 6½ hrs; *Jaisalmer Exp 14810*, 2330, 6½ hrs. **Varanasi** via Agra and Lucknow: *Marudhar Exp 14854/14864*, 0915, 12 hrs (**Agra**) 19 hrs (**Lucknow**), 26 hrs (**Varanasi**).

Directory

Jodhpur *p386, map p387*
Banks 1030-1400. Plenty of ATMs around Sojati Gate. For TC: **State Bank of India**, High Court Rd (inside High Court complex). Currency and TCs. **Internet** Sify i-Way, Ratanada Rd behind Raman Guest House and behind clock tower, near Café Sheesh Mahal. Also at **Ghoomar Hotel** and most guesthouses. **Medical services** Ambulance: T102. **MG Hospital**, T0291- 636437. **Dispensary**: Paota, Residency. Mon-Sat 0800-1200, 1700-1900, Sun 0800-1200. **Post** GPO, south of railway station, 1000-2000, Sat 1000-1600. **Useful contacts** Fire: T101. Police: T100.

Jaisalmer and around

→ *Phone code: 02992. Population: 80,000.*

The approach to Jaisalmer is magical as the city rises out of the vast barren desert like an approaching ship. With its crenellated sandstone walls and narrow streets lined with exquisitely carved buildings, through which camel carts trundle leisurely, it has an extraordinarily medieval feel and an incredible atmosphere. The fort inside, perched on its hilltop, contains some gems of Jain temple building, while beautifully decorated merchants' havelis are scattered through the town. Once inside the fort walls looking out to the desert, it's easy to imagine caravans and camels sweeping across towards you in a dream of Arabian nights, but what you actually see are growing legions of windmills flanking the dunes in the distance. Unlike the other forts you visit in Rajasthan, Jaisalmer's is fully alive with shops, restaurants and guesthouses inside its walls and labyrinthine alleyways. It's beautiful to wander the tiny streets always finding a new nook or a great view.

All this has not failed to attract the attention of mass tourism, and at times Jaisalmer can feel overrun with package tourists, being swept from one shop to the next in a whirlwind of rapid consumption by insistent guides. Over the years, increased development of guesthouses and businesses within the walls has put pressure on the sewage, drainage and foundations of the fort. Three of the 99 bastions crumbled a couple of years ago and several people were killed. These bastions have now been replaced, but if you look at the fort bastions from the outside you can see signs of water discolouration (see box, page 401).

If you find Jaisalmer's magic diminished there's always the romantic desolation of the Thar Desert, easily accessible beyond the edge of the city. Many of the settlements close to the city have become well used to tourists, so it's worth venturing a little further out to get an idea of life in the desert. Highlights include the remarkable ghost city of Khuldera and, of course, the chance to take it all in from on top of a camel.
▸▸ *For listings, see pages 405-409.*

Ins and outs

Getting there The nearest airport is at Jodhpur, 275 km away, which is connected to Jaisalmer by buses and several daily trains. Most long-distance buses arrive at the bus stand, a 15-minute walk from the fort. Your hotel may offer a pick-up. If not, have a place in mind and prepare for a barrage of competing touts.

Getting around Unmetered jeeps and auto-rickshaws can be hired at the station but they are no help inside the fort so you may have to carry your luggage some distance uphill if you choose a fort hotel. Rickshaws are allowed into the fort at certain times. You can hire a bike from Gopa Chowk (Rs 30) though the town is best explored on foot. Most hotels and restaurants are clustered around the two chowks and inside the fort. ▸▸ *See Transport, page 409.*

Tourist information RTDC ⓘ *near TRC, Station Rd, Gadi Sagar Pol, T02992-252406, 0800-1200, 1500-1800*. Counter at railway station.

Background

Founded by Prince Jaisal in 1156, Jaisalmer grew to be a major staging post on the trade route across the forbidding Thar Desert from India to the West. The merchants prospered and invested part of their wealth in building beautiful houses and temples with the local sandstone. The growth of maritime trade between India and the West caused a decline in trade across the desert which ceased altogether in 1947. However, the wars with Pakistan (1965 and 1971) resulted in the Indian government developing the transport facilities to the border to improve troop movement. This has also helped visitors to gain access. Today, the army and tourism are mainstays of the local economy; hotel touts and pushy shopkeepers have become a problem in recent years.

The fort

ⓘ *Best light for photography is late afternoon.*

On the roughly triangular-shaped Trikuta Hill, the fort stands 76 m above the town, enclosed by a 9-km wall with 99 bastions (mostly 1633-1647). Often called the Golden Fort because of the colour of its sandstone walls, it dominates the town. You enter the fort from the east from Gopa Chowk. The inner, higher fort wall and the old gates up the ramp (Suraj Pol, Ganesh Pol, Hawa Pol and Rang Pol) provided further defences. The Suraj Pol (1594), once an outer gate, is flanked by heavy bastions and has bands of decoration which imitate local textile designs. Take a walk through the narrow streets within the fort, often blocked by the odd goat or cow, and see how even today about 1000 of the town's people live in tiny houses inside the fort often with beautiful carvings on doors and balconies. It is not difficult to get lost.

As with many other Rajput forts, within the massive defences are a series of palaces, the product of successive generations of rulers' flights of fancy. The local stone is relatively easy to carve and the dry climate has meant that the fineness of detail has been preserved through the centuries. The *jali* work and delicately ornamented balconies and windows with wide eaves break the solidity of the thick walls, giving protection from the heat, while the high plinths of the buildings keep out the sand. '**Sunset Point**', just north of the fort, is popular at sundown for views over Jaisalmer.

1 Jaisalmer

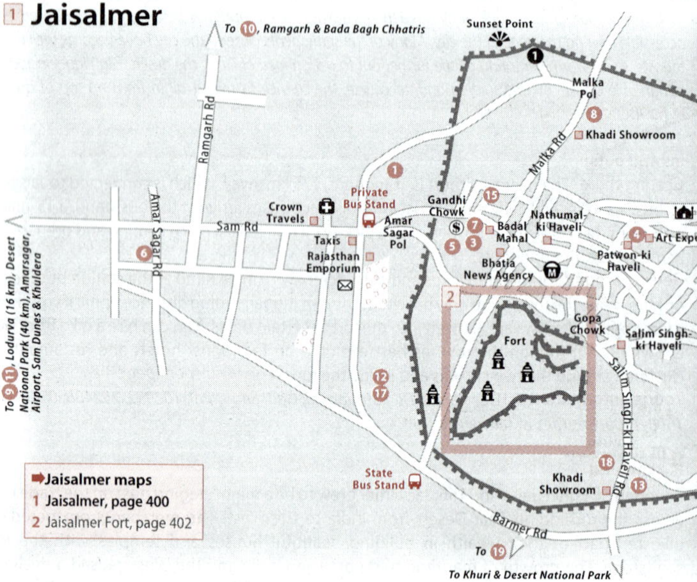

200 metres
200 yards

Sleeping
Ashoka **23**
Fifu Guest House **19**
Fort Rajwada **25**
Golden City **13**
Himmatgarh Palace **10**
Jaisal Palace **3**
Killa Lodge **4**
Mandir Palace **5**
Moomal **6**
Nachana Haveli **7**
Narayan Niwas Palace **8**
Pol Haveli **1**
Rawal **18**
Residency Centre Point **9**
Serai **2**
Shahi Palace **12**
Star Haveli & Oasis Haveli **17**

Jaisalmer in jeopardy

Jaisalmer in Jeopardy is a UK-based charity fighting to preserve the unique historical architecture of the city. Through raising awareness and funds, it has achieved the restoration of buildings such as the Rajput Palace and Rani-ka Mahal (Maharani's Palace) and helped ensure that Jaisalmer Fort is listed on the World Monuments Fund '100 Most Endangered Sites in the World'.

Some visitors feel that it is unethical to stay in the fort guesthouses and add to the problems of water consumption and waste disposal. As far back as the late 1990s guesthouses inside the fort were offered incentives to start their businesses in new locations outside the walls, although only one, Shahi Palace Guest House, took up the offer. Nowadays, thanks to greater awareness, there are many beautiful guesthouses both within the walls of the fort and outside gazing up at the fairytale. Jaisalmer in Jeopardy want to ensure that the Jaisalmer Fort can be enjoyed for another 400 years. Check out www.jaisalmer-in-jeopardy.org and www.intach.org (Indian National Trust for Art and Cultural Heritage) for further information.

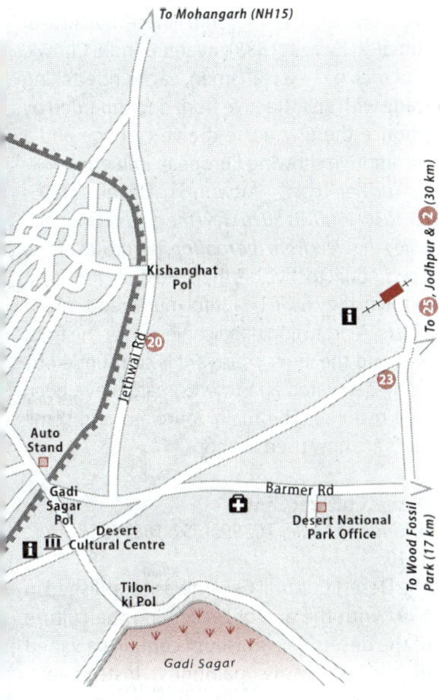

Suryagarh **11**
Swastika **15**

Eating
Junction Palace **1**

The entire **Fort Palace Museum and Heritage Centre** ⓘ *0800-1800 summer, 0900-1800 winter, foreigners Rs 250 includes an excellent audio guide and camera, Indians Rs 10, video Rs 150*, has been renovated and an interesting series of displays established, including sculpture, weapons, paintings and well-presented cultural information. The view from the roof, the highest point inside the fort, is second to none. The **Juna Mahal** (circa 1500) of the seven-storey palace with its *jali* screens is one of the oldest Rajasthani palaces. The rather plain *zenana* block to its west, facing the *chauhata* (square) is decorated with false *jalis*. Next to it is the *mardana* (men's quarters) including the Rang Mahal above the Hawa Pol, built during the reign of Mulraj II (1762-1820), which has highly detailed murals and mirror decoration. **Sarvotam Vilas** built by Akhai Singh (1722-1762) is ornamented with blue tiles and glass mosaics. The adjacent **Gaj Vilas** (1884) stands on a high plinth. Mulraj II's **Moti Mahal** has floral decoration and carved doors.

The open square beyond the gates has a platform reached by climbing some steps; this is where court was held or royal visitors entertained. There are also fascinating **Jain temples** (12th-16th centuries) ⓘ *0700-1200, Rs 10, camera Rs 50, video Rs 100, leather shoes not permitted*, within the fort. Whilst the Rajputs were devout Hindus they permitted the practice of Jainism. The **Parsvanatha**

(1417) has a fine gateway, an ornate porch and 52 subsidiary shrines surrounding the main structure. The brackets are elaborately carved as maidens and dancers. The exterior of the **Rishbhanatha** (1479) has more than 600 images as decoration whilst clusters of towers form the roof of the **Shantinatha** built at the same time. **Ashtapadi** (16th century) incorporates the Hindu deities of Vishnu, Kali and Lakshmi into its decoration. The **Mahavir Temple** ⓘ *view 1000-1100*, has an emerald statue. The **Sambhavanatha** (1431) ⓘ *1000-1100*, has vaults beneath it that were used for document storage. The **Gyan Bhandar** here is famous for its ancient manuscripts.

Havelis

There are many exceptional *havelis* (see box, page 447) in the fort and in the walled town. Many have beautifully carved façades, *jali* screens and oriel windows overhanging the streets below. The ground floor is raised above the dusty streets and each has an inner courtyard surrounded by richly decorated apartments. An unofficial 'guide' will usually show you the way for about Rs 20. When the *havelis* are occupied, you may be allowed in on a polite request, otherwise, your 'guide' will help you gain access for a small fee (though this may just get you as far as the shops in the courtyard!).

Inside Amar Sagar Pol, the former ruler's 20th-century palace **Badal Mahal** with a five-storeyed tower, has fine carvings. Near the fort entrance, the 17th-century **Salim Singh-ki Haveli** ⓘ *0800-1800, Rs 10, good carvings but is being poorly restored, over-long guided tour*, is especially attractive with peacock brackets; it is often referred to as the 'Ship Palace' because of its distinctive and decorative upper portion. **Nathumal-ki Haveli** (1885), nearer Gandhi Chowk, was built for the prime minister. Partly carved out of rock by two craftsmen, each undertaking one half of the house, it has a highly decorative façade with an attractive front door guarded by two elephants. Inside is a wealth of decoration; notice the tiny horse-drawn carriage and a locomotive showing European influence.

Further east, **Patwon-ki Haveli** (1805) ⓘ *1030-1700, Rs 50 to view the gold ceilings and enjoy the view from the rooftop*, is a group of five *havelis* built for five brothers. Possibly the finest in town, they have beautiful murals and carved pillars. A profusion of balconies cover the front wall and the inner courtyard is surrounded by richly decorated apartments; parts have been well restored. The main courtyard and some roofs are now used as shops.

Desert Cultural Centre

ⓘ *Gadisar Circle, T02992-252 188, 1000-1700, Rs 10.*

The Desert Cultural Centre was established in 1997 with the aim of preserving the culture of the desert. The museum contains a varied display of fossils, paintings, instruments, costumes and textiles which give an interesting glimpse in to life in the desert. The charismatic founder, Mr Sharma, is a fount of information and has written several books on Jaisalmer.

2 Jaisalmer Fort

➡Jaisalmer maps
1 Jaisalmer, page 400
2 Jaisalmer Fort, page 402

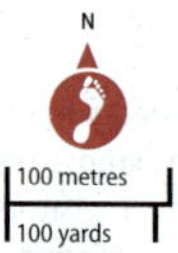

Sleeping
Desert Boy's Guest House **1**
Desert Haveli **9**
Jaisal Castle **3**
Killa Bhawan **2**
Simla **8**
Suraj **10**
Temple View **7**

Eating
8th July **1**
Kanchan Shree **5**
La Purezza **3**
Little Tibet **2**
Palace View **6**
Vyas **4**

Gadi Sagar tank

The Gadi Sagar (Gadisar or Gharisar) tank, southeast of the city walls, was the oasis which led Prince Jaisal to settle here. Now connected by a pipe to the Indira Gandhi Canal, it has water all year. It attracts migratory birds and has many small shrines around it and is well worth visiting, especially in the late afternoon. The delightful archway is said to have been constructed by a distinguished courtesan who built a temple on top to prevent the king destroying the gate. Pedalos are available for trips round the lake from Rs 50 for half an hour.

Around Jaisalmer → *For listings, see pages 405-409.*

Amar Sagar and Lodurva

The pleasant **Amar Sagar** ⓘ *5 km northwest of Jaisalmer, foreigners Rs 30, Indians free, camera Rs 50, video Rs 100*, was once a formal garden with a pleasure palace of Amar Singh (1661-1703) on the bank of a lake which dries up during the hot season. The Jain temple there has been restored.

A further 10 km away is **Lodurva** ⓘ *0630-1930, foreigners Rs 20, Indians free, camera Rs 50, video Rs 100*, which contains a number of Jain temples that are the only remains of a once-flourishing Marwar capital. Rising honey-coloured out of the desert, they are beautifully carved with *jali* outside and are well maintained and worth visiting. The road beyond Lodurva is unsealed.

Khuldera

This is a fascinating ghost town, and well worth stopping at on the way to Sam. The story goes that 400 or so years ago, Salim Singh, the then prime minister of Jaisalmer, took a distinct shine to a Paliwal girl from this village. The rest of the Paliwal people did not want this beautiful girl taken away from them, and so after intense pressure from the prime minister decided to abandon the village one night, with everyone dispersing in different directions, never to return. It is remarkably well preserved, and best visited with a guide who can point out the most interesting buildings from the many still standing. **Khabha**, just south of here, is also recommended.

Sam dunes (Sain) → *Colour map 2, B2.*

ⓘ *Rs 10, car Rs 20 (camera fees may be introduced), camel rates start at Rs 50 per hr but can be bargained down.*

Sam dunes, 40 km west of Jaisalmer, is popular for sunset camel rides. It's not a remote spot in the middle of the desert but the only real large stretch of sand near town; the dunes only cover a small area, yet they are quite impressive. Right in the middle of the dunes, **Sunset View** is like a fairground, slightly tacky with lots of day-trippers – as many as 500 in the high season; the only escape from this and the camel men is to walk quite a way away.

Khuri → *Colour map 2, B2.*

ⓘ *Rs 10, car Rs 20, buses from Jaisalmer take 1½ hrs, jeep for 4 people Rs 450 for a sunset tour.*

Khuri, 40 km southwest of Jaisalmer, is a small picturesque desert village of decorated mud-thatched buildings which was ruled by the Sodha clan for four centuries. Visitors are attracted by shifting sand dunes, some 80 m high, but the peace of the village has been spoilt by the growing number of huts, tents and guesthouses which have opened along the road and near the dunes. Persistent hotel and camel agents board all buses bound for Khuri. The best months to visit are from November to February.

Thar Desert National Park → *Colour map 2, B2.*

ⓘ *Rs 150 per person; car permits Rs 500; permits are required, apply 2 days in advance to Forest Department, T02992-252489, or through travel agents.*

The Thar Desert National Park is near Khuri, the core being about 60 km from Jaisalmer (the road between Sam and Khuri is passable with a high-clearance vehicle). The park was created to

On a camel's back

Camel safaris draw many visitors to Jaisalmer. They allow an insight into otherwise inaccessible desert interiors and a chance to see rural life, desert flora and wildlife. The 'safari' is not a major expedition into the middle of nowhere. Instead, it is often along tracks, stopping off for sightseeing at temples and villages along the way. The camel driver/owner usually drives the camel or rides along- side (avoid one sharing your camel), usually for two hours in the morning and three hours in the afternoon, with a long lunch stop in between. There is usually jeep or camel cart backup with tents and 'kitchen' close by, though thankfully out of sight. It can be fun, especially if you are with companions and have a knowledgeable camel driver.

Camel safaris vary greatly in quality with prices ranging from around Rs 500 per night for the simplest (sleeping in the open, vegetarian meals) to those costing Rs 4500 (deluxe double-bedded tents with attached Western baths). Bear in mind that it is practically impossible for any safari organizer to cover his costs at anything less than Rs 500 – if you're offered cheaper tours, assume they'll be planning to get their money back by other means, ie shopping/drug selling along the way. Safaris charging Rs 500-1000 can be adequate (tents, mattresses, linen, cook, jeep support, but no toilets). It's important to ascertain what is included in the price and what are extras.

The popular 'Around Jaisalmer' route includes Bada Bagh, Ramkunda, Moolsagar, Sam dunes, Lodurva and Amar Sagar with three nights in the desert. Some routes now include Kuldhara's medieval ruins and the colourful Kahla village, as well as Deda, Jaseri lake (good birdlife) and Khaba ruins with a permit. Most visitors prefer to take a two days/one night or three days/two nights camel safari, with jeep transfer back to Jaisalmer. A more comfortable alternative is to be jeeped to a tented/hut camp in the desert as a base for a night and enjoy a camel trek during the day without losing out on the evening's entertainment under the stars. A short camel ride in town up to Sunset Point (or at Sam/Khuri) is one alternative to a 'safari' before deciding on a long haul, and also offers great views of upper levels of *havelis* – but watch out for low – slung electric wires! Pre-paid camel rides have now been introduced – Rs 80 for a 30-minute ride. For some, "half an hour is enough on a tick-ridden animal". For a selection of tour operators offering camel safaris, see page 408.

Make sure you cover up all exposed skin and use sunscreen to avoid getting burnt.

protect 3000 sq km of the Thar Desert, the habitat for drought resistant, endangered and rare species which have adjusted to the unique and inhospitable conditions of extreme temperatures. The desert has undulating dunes and vast expanses of flat land where the trees are leafless, thorny and have long roots. Fascinating for birdwatching, it is one of the few places in India where the **great Indian bustard** is proliferating (it can weigh up to 14 kg and reach a height of 40 cm). In winter it also attracts the migratory **houbara bustard**. You can see imperial black-bellied and common Indian sand grouse, five species of vulture, six of eagle, falcons, and flocks of larks at Sudasari, in the core of the park, 60 km from Jaisalmer. Chinkaras are a common sight, as are desert and Indian foxes. Blackbuck and desert cat can be seen at times. Close to sunset, you can spot desert hare in the bushes.

While most hotels will try to sell you a tour by 4WD vehicle, this is no longer necessary. You can hire any jeep or high-clearance car (Ambassador, Sumo) for the trip to the park. Off-the-road journeys are by camel or camel cart (park tour Rs 50 and Rs 150 respectively).

Barmer → *Colour map 2, B2.*

This dusty desert town, 153 km south of Jaisalmer, is surrounded by sand dunes and scrublands. It is a major centre for wood carving, *durrie* rug weaving, embroidery and block printing (you can watch printers in Khatriyon ki galli). The 10th- to 11th-century Kiradu temples, though badly damaged, are interesting. **Someshvara** (1020), the most intact, has some intricate carving but the dome and the tower have collapsed. The town itself is surprisingly industrial and not especially charming; those interested in seeking out handicrafts are well advised to locate **Gulla**, the town's only guide. He can normally be contacted at the **KK Hotel** (see Sleeping, page 407), or emailed in advance on gulla_guide@yahoo.com. The small number of visitors to Barmer means that he doesn't get too many opportunities to practice his profession; be sure to explain exactly what you would like to see, and try to fix a price before starting the tour.

Dhorimmana → *Colour map 2, B2.*

The area further south of Barmer has some of the most colourful and traditional Bishnoi villages and a large population of *chinkaras* and desert fauna. The village women wear a lot of attractive jewellery but may be reluctant to be photographed so it is best to ask first. **PWD Rest house** has clean and comfortable rooms.

Jaisalmer and around listings

For Sleeping and Eating price codes and other relevant information, see Essentials pages 38-42.

Sleeping

Jaisalmer *p400, maps p400 and p402*

Some hotels close in Apr-Jun. Very low room prices may be conditional on taking the hotel's camel safari – check; refusal may mean having to move out. Some budget places allow travellers to sleep on the roof for Rs 30-50. The tourist office has a Paying Guest list. Negative reports on **Himalayan Guest House** and **Peacock Hotel.**

LL The Serai, near Chandan village, 30 km outside Jaisalmer, T02997-200014, www.sujanluxury.com. Already guest starring on the front cover of *Condé Nast Traveller* magazine, this luxurious resort is inspired by the colours of the desert, with warm sandstone and beautiful natural textiles. The beautiful swimming pool is based on an Indian step-well and 6 of the luxury tents have their own plunge pools. Sit by the swimming pool and get treated to sorbet and ice cold nimbu pani, while the restaurant serves up global fusion food. This is the most stylish way to experience desert life.

LL Suryagarh, Kahala Phata, Sam Rd, T02992-269269, www.suryagarh.com. With the arrival of **Suryagarh** and **The Serai** on the Jaisalmer scene, things are starting to look particularly luxe. This is a stunning new project but based on traditional ideas and the outer façade of the hotel mirrors the famous Jaisalmer fort. Beautiful suites, vibey bar area and lovely indoor pool.

LL-AL Fort Rajwada, 1 Hotel Complex, Jodhpur Rd, T02992-253533, www.fortrajwada.com. 65 top-class, central a/c rooms and 4 suites conceived by an opera set designer, in a modern luxury hotel, deceptively old looking from the outside. Architectural features have been recovered from crumbling local *havelis* and incorporated in to the stylish interior, of which the exquisite bar is particularly worthy of mention. Friendly management, eager staff.

L-A Killa Bhawan, Kotri Para, T02992-251204, www.killabhawan.com. 7 rooms, 2 a/c, in characterful old building, beautiful interiors but teeny tiny rooms, classiest place in fort by some margin.

AL-A Narayan Niwas Palace, opposite Jain Temple, Malka Rd, T02992-252408, www.narayan niwas.com. A converted caravanserai with 51 lacklustre rooms; however the common areas are beautiful with lovely seated areas Pillared indoor pool is remarkable, and views from rooftop restaurant exceptional.

A Himmatgarh Palace, 1 Ramgarh Rd, 2.5 km from town, T02992-252002, himmatgarh@sancharnet.in. 40 a/c rooms and cottages in attractive, quirky sandstone building, great views from garden and pool.

A Mandir Palace, T02992-252788, www.welcomheritagehotels.com. Well-maintained a/c rooms and beautiful atmospheric suites in exclusive location inside royal palace. Not very well run but an experience.

B Killa Lodge, opposite Patwon-ki Haveli, T02992-253833, www.killabhawan.com. Small boutique hotel with only 6 rooms run by the same team as **Killa Bhawan** in the fort. Good style, but pricey. Great location opposite beautiful *haveli*. Lovely café on top and bookshop downstairs – great collection of coffee table books.

B-C Nachana Haveli, Gandhi Chowk, T02992-252 110, nachana_haveli@yahoo.com. Converted 18th-century Rajput *haveli* with carved balconies and period artefacts. Rooms are stylishly done with great bathrooms, particularly upstairs suites. Rooftop restaurant in the season, has very authentic feel overall. Friendly family. Highly recommended.

C-D Desert Boy's Guest House, Vyasa Para in fort, T02992-253091, desert_p@yahoo.com. 14 jauntily furnished rooms in attractive property that feels quite new, good if pricey Italian rooftop restaurant with seating on the floor, camel safaris have a good reputation.

C-D Jaisal Castle, in fort, T02992-252362, www.naryanniwas.com. 11 quirky rooms in rambling, characterful old *haveli*. Room 101 is particularly lovely, ironically. Beautiful communal areas.

C-E Moomal (RTDC), Amar Sagar Rd, T02992-252392. Better than RTDC average but still has institutional air. 60 rooms (17 a/c), could be cleaner, mediocre restaurant, bar, tours, friendly and helpful. 12 tribal-style circular huts offer a great alternative although in slightly scrubby grounds – they have a lot more character.

C-F Hotel Pol Haveli (RTDC), near Geeta Ashram, Dedansar Rd, T02992-250131. New *haveli*-style building with stylish decor and chilled-out vibe. Beautiful furnishings, especially the beds. Run by same family as **Shahi Palace**. Slightly odd area as it feels you are staying in a dusty village, but it is just a short walk from Gandhi Chowk and the heart of things. Good views of sunset point and the fort in the distance from their attractive rooftop café.

C-F Shahi Palace, Shiv St, near SBBJ bank, outside fort, T02992-255920, www.shahipalacehotel.com. 16 super stylish rooms in a beautiful sandstone building with outstanding bathrooms. The team of 4 brothers here work hard to make everyone feel at home. Beautiful chic rooftop restaurant with lots or archways and even a wooden boat from Karnataka masquerading as a flowerpot. The view of the fort is outstanding as is their food and a cappuccino machine is promised. Excellent reports on their camel safaris. Whole-heartedly recommended.

D-E Fifu Guest House, opposite Nagarpalika (1 km out of town), T02992-254317, www.fifutravel.com. 8 well-decorated rooms in modern building with excellent rooftop views. Location slightly inconvenient but hosts are charming and free bike hire for guests. Ring ahead for free pickup.

D-E Jaisal Palace, near Gandhi Chowk, behind SBI, T02992-252717, www.hoteljaisalpalace.com. 14 clean, simple rooms with bath, 6 a/c, 8 air-cooled, 1st-floor balconies with views, Rajasthani food on roof terrace in season, train/bus bookings. Bit pricey for what's on offer.

D-E Oasis near Shahi Palace, Shiv St, T02992-250871. Another offering from the brothers at Shahi Palace, Oasis boasts bigger rooms than its older sibling and some of the 7 rooms have a/c. It's beautifully decorated with sumptuous fabrics and there's a lovely chill-out area downstairs. Next door, they have 6 more big rooms in **Star Haveli**.

D-E Rawal, Salim Singh-ki Haveli Marg, Dibba Para, T02992-252570. Pleasant and relaxed with 20 large, clean albeit a bit dreary rooms, all with attached bathrooms, Indian restaurant, good views from rooftop.

D-E Suraj, behind Jain Temple, T02992-251623, hotelsurajjaisalmer@hotmail.com. Suraj boasts beautiful rooms in this 530-year-old *haveli* overlooking the Jain temple. It may have seen better days and can get quite chilly in winter, but very atmospheric.

D-F Simla, Kund Para, T02992-253061, simlahaveli@yahoo.co.in. 5 clean rooms in thoughtfully renovated 550-year-old *haveli*, attractive wall hangings, 1 large with bath, others minute with bath downstairs, no safari pressure, friendly management, a cut above the norm.

E-F Golden City, Dibba Para, T02992-251664, hotelgoldencity@hotmail.com. Clean comfortable air-cooled rooms with hot shower, 3 **D** a/c, rooftop restaurant with good views, free station transfer, exchange, internet, family atmosphere with pool (open to non-residents). Away from the heart of things.

E-G The Desert Haveli, near Jain Temple, T02992-251555, desert_haveli@yahoo.com. 7 characterful rooms in charming, 400-year-old *haveli*, honest, friendly owner. Very atmospheric. Recommended.

F-G Swastika, Chainpura St, T02992-252483. 9 clean, well-kept rooms, all with bath, reasonable view, free tea and pickups.

F-G Temple View, next to Jain Temple, T02992-252832, jaisalmertempleview@hotmail.com. 7 well-decorated rooms, 3 with attached bath, attention to detail, great view of temples from roof, entertaining owner.

G Ashoka, opposite railway station, T02992-256021. 20 cleanish rooms, in quiet location, good option as close to the station.

G Residency Centre Point, near Patwon-ki Haveli, T02992-252883. Quiet family-run hotel with 5 basic but characterful rooms, good views from roof. Excellent value.

Sam dunes *p403*

D Sam Dhani (RTDC), T02992-252392. 8 huts facing the dunes, very busy in late afternoon and sunset but very pleasant at night and early morning. Includes all meals.

Khuri *p403*

E-F Khuri Guest House, reservations T022-240 42211, www.nivalink.com/khuri. Simple rooms or huts, friendly management. Recommended.

E-F Mama's, T01304-274 023. Cool, thatched huts, tasty meals. Recommended.

Thar Desert National Park *p403*

F Rest Huts, facing the park. Adequate. Contact Park Director on T02992-252489.

Barmer *p405*

E-F KK Hotel, Station Rd, T02982-230038. 24 reasonable rooms, some a/c, very similar to Krishna nearby.

E-F Krishna, Station Rd, a few mins' walk from station, T02982-220785. The biggest and best in town with 32 decent rooms, some a/c, but no restaurant.

Eating

Jaisalmer *p400, maps p400 and p402*

TT 8th July, just inside fort (another opposite Fort Gate). Vegetarian. Pleasant rooftop seating – popular for breakfast, pizzas, food average, 'famous' apple pie a letdown, pleasant for evening drink, mixed reports on service.

TT La Purezza, Vyas Para. Excellent salads, Italian cheese veggies and other unusual offerings. Has another outlet in Manali.

TT Little Tibet, beyond the palace chowk. Momos and much more of travellers' choice, generous, hygienic, enthusiastic staff, popular.

TT Nachana Haveli (see Sleeping), another hotel with great views of fort at night. Beautiful decor, lovely food and relaxed vibe.

TT Shahi Palace (see Sleeping). Great food from this beautiful rooftop restaurant with amazing views of fort. Try traditional Rajasthani meals like *kej sangari* (desert beans) and *kadi pakoda* (yoghurt turmeric curry) and, if they're not busy, you can go in the kitchen and watch how they make it. And if you need a little oomph, they have a cappuccino machine.

T Junction Palace, T0921412349. A little out of the way, this place is close to Sunset point, so a great place for sundowners. People come here for the good food and live entertainment.

T Little Italy, in the main fort gate: charming, cool interiors with windows looking up the pathway to the fort: excellent bruschetta and a great meeting point before or after fort walks.

T Palace View Restaurant, Gandhi Chowk, near Jain Temples. Varied selection but main attraction is the home-made apple pie.

T Vyas, Fort. Simple, good vegetarian *thalis* (Rs 20-30), pleasant staff.

Snacks and drinks

Chai stalls at **Gopa Chowk** make good masala tea before 1730. Hot and crisp *kachoris* and samosas opposite Jain temples near **Narayan Niwas**, are great for breakfast or tea.

Dhanraj Bhatia. Scrumptious Indian sweets including Jaisalmeri delights (try *godwa*).

Doodh bhandars, in Hanuman Chauraya. Sells a delicious mix of creamy milk, cardamom and sugar, whipped up with a flourish, between sunset and midnight.

Kanchan Shree, Gopa Chowk, 250 m from Salim Singh-ki Haveli. *Lassis* (19 varieties) and

ice cream floats, as well as cheap, tasty *thalis*. Many recommendations for this place.
Mohan Juice Centre, near **Sunil Bhatia Rest House**. Delicious *lassis*, good breakfasts.

Entertainment

Jaisalmer *p400, maps p400 and p402*
The more expensive hotels have bars.
Desert Cultural Centre, Gadisar Circle. 2 puppet shows every evening, at 1830 and 1930, Rs 30 entry, Rs 20 camera, Rs 50 video.

Festivals and events

Jaisalmer *p400, maps p400 and p402*
Feb/Mar **Holi** is especially colourful but gets riotous.

Sam dunes *p403*
Feb 3-day **Desert Festival** (23-25 Feb 2013, 12-13 Feb 2014) with *son et lumière* amid the sand dunes at Sam, folk dancing, puppet shows and camel races, camel polo and camel acrobatics, Mr Desert competition. You can also watch craftsmen at work. Rail and hotel reservations can be difficult.

Barmer *p405*
Mar **Thar Festiva** highlights desert culture and handicrafts.

Shopping

Jaisalmer *p400, maps p400 and p402*
Shops open 1000-1330 and 1500-1900. Jaisalmer is famous for its handicrafts – stone-carved statues, leather ware, brass enamel engraving, shawls, tie-dye work, embroidered and block printed fabrics, but garments are often poorly finished. Look in **Siré Bazar**, **Sonaron-ka-Bas** and shops in the narrow lanes of the old city including **Kamal Handicrafts**, **Ganpati Art Home**, and **Damodar** in the fort. In Gandhi Chowk: **Rajasthali**, closed Tue; the good, fairly priced selection at **Khadi Emporium** at the end of the courtyard just above Narayan Niwas Hotel. **Jaisalmer Art Export**, behind Patwon-ki Haveli has high-quality textiles. For textiles try **Amrit Handprint Factory**, just inside Sagar Gate on the left. **Geeta Jewellers** on Aasni Rd near Fort Gate is recommended, good value and no hard sell.

For tailors try **Mr Durga**, small shop near fort entrance on Kacheri Rd, Bansari Bazar, "beware imitations". Excellent Western-style tailoring. Shirts made to measure, around Rs 200. Also **Nagpur**, Koba Chowk, and **Raju**, Kachari Rd, outside Amar Sagar Pol, for Western-style tailoring.

Activities and tours

Jaisalmer *p400, maps p400 and p402*

Camel safaris

Thar Safaris, T02992-252722, www.derajaisalmer.com, charges Rs 950. Upscale options include: **Safari Tours**, T02992-251058. 10 'desert huts' with shared facilities and 10 tents with private bathrooms, about 8 km from Sam; **Rajasthan Desert Safaris**, T(0)9414-140109, Swiss-cottage tents with attached toilets near the dunes, Rs 4500 per night. **Ganesh Travels**, T02992-252538, and **Trotters' Independent Travels**, Gopa Chowk, near Bhang Shop, T(0)9414-469292, www.trotterscamelsafari jaisalmer.com, come well recommended for less fancy safaris. Also: **Sahara Travels**, run by local identity "Mr Desert" (see Tour operators, below); **Comfort Tours** (Gorbandh Palace); **Travel Plan**. Less upmarket, but still reliable options include those from **Shahi Palace**, **Fifu Guesthouse** and **Desert Haveli**.

Cooking

Karuna, Ishar Palace, in the fort near the Laxminath Temple, T02992-253062, karunaacharya@yahoo.com. Learn Indian cookery with Karuna, Courses of any length can be arranged. Highly recommended.

Music

Anyone interested in learning to play a Rajasthani musical instrument, or to hear a performance, should contact Kamru Deen on T02992-254181, arbamusic@yahoo.co.in.

Paragliding

SPS Kaushik, T94143-05121. Paragliding in the desert, with participants being towed behind a jeep for Rs 750 a go. An unusual way to see the desert.

Swimming

Gorbandh Palace (non-residents Rs 350); also **Heritage Inn** (meal plus swim deals) and **Fort Rajwada**.

Tour operators

Aravalli Safari, near Patwon-ki Gali, T02992-252 632. Professional. Recommended.
Rajasthan Tourism, T02992-252406. City sightseeing: half day, 0900-1200. Fort, *havelis*, Gadisagar Lake. Sam sand dunes: half day, 1500-1900.
Royal Desert Safaries, Nachna Haveli, Gandhi Chowk, T02992-252538, www.palaces-tours.com. Experienced and efficient.
Sahara Travels, Gopa Chowk, right of the 1st Fort gate, T02992-252609. Mr (Desert) Bissa's reliable camel safaris with good food.
Thar Safari, Gandhi Chowk, near **Trio**, T02992-252722. Reliable tours.

Transport

Jaisalmer *p400, maps p400 and p402*
Jaisalmer is on NH15 (Pathankot-Samakhiali). Transport to town from train and bus station is by auto-rickshaws or jeeps; police are on duty so less harassment.
Bus Touts may board buses outside town to press you to take their jeep; it is better to walk 10-15 mins from Amar Sagar Pol and choose a hotel. Most hotels offer station pick-up too so call ahead.

State Roadways buses, from near the station, T02992-251541, and at SBBJ Bank Government Bus Stop. There is now a new Volvo bus running daily Jaisalmer to Delhi, via Jodhpur and Jaipur, but takes a whopping 18 hrs – leaves 1730 from Jaisalmer (From Delhi to Jaisalmer starts at 1730 too). sevice Services to **Ajmer**, **Barmer**, **Bikaner** (330 km on good road, 8 hrs, Rs 160), **Jaipur** (638 km); Abu Rd for **Mount Abu**. **Jodhpur** (285 km, 0500, 0600, 0630, 0730 and 2230, 5 hrs, Rs 130). **Udaipur** (663 km, a tiring 14 hrs). **Bikaner** 0600 and 2130 from Hanuman Chowk; Private deluxe coaches from outside Amar Sagar Pol or Airforce Circle, to a similar range of destinations. Most hotels can reserve bus tickets. Operators: **Marudhara Travels**, Station Rd, T02992-252351. **National Tours**, Hanuman Choraha, T02992-252348.
Train The military presence can make getting tickets slow; book in advance if possible. Foreign Tourist Bureau with waiting room, T02992-252354, booking office T02992-251301. *Jsm Bkn Exp 14071* to **Bikaner** 2245 (5½ hrs) *Jaisalmer Delhi Exp 14060*, to **Jodhpur** (6 hrs) and **Delhi** (19 hrs). *Jodhpur Exp 14809*, 2315, 7 hrs. Can get very cold (and dusty) try and book 3AC where bedding is provided.

Barmer *p405*
From Barmer, the hot and dusty bus journey to **Jaisalmer** takes 4 hrs; **Mt Abu**, 6 hrs.

Directory

Jaisalmer *p400, maps p400 and p402*
Banks Mon-Fri 1030-1430, Sat 1030-1230. On Gandhi Chowk: **Bank of Baroda** with ATM and **SBBJ** with ATM (there is also ICICI ATM nearby), TCs and cash against credit cards; **State of Bank of India**, Nachna Haveli, currency only. There is also an ATM which accepts international cards close to Hanuman Chowk on the road which leads to Sam and one opposite Government Hospital. **Internet** Slow, expensive dial-up connections are the norm in the fort. **Joshi Travel**, opposite PO, Central Market, Gopa Chowk, T02992-250455, joshitravel@hotmail.com. Cybercafé, modern equipment, also STD, fax, etc. **Desert Cyber Inn**, inside fort close to Little Tibet restaurant. **Medical services** **Maheshwan Hospital**, Barmer Rd, T02992-250024. **Post** The GPO is near Police Station, T02992-252407. With Poste Restante. **Useful contacts** **Fire**: T02992-252352. **Police**: T02992-252668.

Eastern Rajasthan

This is one of the most visited regions of Rajasthan, lying as it does on the well-trodden 'Golden Triangle' route of Delhi-Agra-Jaipur, yet it retains several hidden treasures, all within easy range of Delhi. There is an amazing variety of towns and villages, from the busy pilgrimage centre of Ajmer in the south, and its laid-back neighbour Pushkar, to the unspoilt towns of Alwar and Deeg in the north. These human settlements are surrounded by a natural world in which wild animals and birds continue to find a protected home in sanctuaries and wildlife parks, including the magnificent Bharatpur-Keoladeo Ghana National Park, home to the rare Siberian crane during its migratory season and a great place for a cycle, and the incomparable Ranthambhore National Park, one of the world's top venues for tiger spotting, but also a beautiful landscape to explore even when the tigers don't show.

Alwar, Sariska and around

Alwar has fascinating monuments including the Bala Quilla fort, overlooking the town, and the Moti Doongri fort, in a garden. The former, which was never taken by direct assault, has relics of the early Rajput rulers, the founders of the fort, who had their capital near Alwar. Over the centuries it was home to the Khanzadas, Mughals, Pathans, Jats and finally the Rajputs. There are also palaces and colonial period parks and gardens. The town itself is very untouristy and spread over a large area, making navigation difficult at times, but is generally very welcoming.

The 480-sq-km Sariska reserve is a dry deciduous forest set in a valley surrounded by the barren Aravalli hills. The princely shooting reserve of the Maharajah of Alwar was declared a sanctuary in 1955. Exactly 50 years later it acquired the dubious honour of being the first Project Tiger reserve to be declared free of tigers, the last ones presumably having been poached to feed the Chinese demand for erectile function in old age. Nevertheless, the park still holds some wildlife, and a certain rugged appeal. ▸▸ *For listings, see pages 412-413.*

Ins and outs

Getting there and around Alwar is well connected to both Delhi and Jaipur by bus and train, and is only a three-hour drive from Delhi, or 1½ hours from Jaipur. Sariska is an easy 35-km drive from Alwar. ▸▸ *See Transport, page 413.*

Tourist information **Rajasthan Tourist Reception Centre** ⓘ *Nehru Marg, opposite railway station, Alwar, T0144-234 7348, closed weekends.*

Background

As Mughal power crumbled Rao Pratap Singhji of Macheri founded Alwar as his capital in 1771. He shook off Jat power over the region and rebelled against Jaipur suzerainty making Alwar an independent state. His successors lent military assistance to the British in their battles against the Marathas in AD 1803, and in consequence gained the support of the colonial power. The Alwar royals were flamboyant and kept a fleet of custom-made cars (including a throne car and a golden limousine), and collected solid silver furniture and attractive walking sticks.

Alwar → *For listings, see pages 412-413. Colour map 2, A6. Phone code: 0144. Population: 211,000.*

Alwar is protected by the hilltop **Bala Quilla** which has the remains of palaces, temples and 10 tanks built by the first rulers of Alwar. It stands 308 m above the town, to the northwest, and is reached by a steep 4WD track (with permission from the police station). There are splendid views.

The City Palace, **Vinai Vilas Mahal** (1840) ⓘ *closed Mon, 1000-1700, free, museum Rs 50 foreigners, Rs 5 for Indians*, with intricate *jali* work, ornate *jarokha* balconies and courtyards, houses government offices on the ground floor, and a fine museum upstairs. The palace is impressive but is poorly maintained, with dusty galleries (you may find children playing cricket in the courtyard). The Darbar Room is closed, and the throne, miniatures and gilt-edged mirrors can only be viewed through the glass doors and windows or by prior permission of the royal family (not easily obtained). The museum is interesting, housing local miniature paintings, as well as some of the Mughal, Bundi and other schools, an array of swords, shields, daggers, guns and armour, sandalwood carvings, ivory objects, jade art, musical instruments and princely relics. Next to the city palace are the lake and royal cenotaphs. On the south side of the tank is the Cenotaph of Maharaja Bakhtawar Singh (1781-1815) which is of marble on a red sandstone base. The gardens are alive with peacocks and other birds. To the right of the main entrance to the palace is a two-storey processional elephant carriage designed to carry 50 people and be pulled by four elephants.

The **Yeshwant Niwas**, built by Maharaja Jai Singh in the Italianate style, is also worth seeing. Apparently on its completion he disliked it and never lived in it. Instead he built the **Vijay Mandir** in 1918, a 105-room palace beside Vijay Sagar, 10 km from Alwar. Part of it is open with prior permission from the royal family or their secretary, but even without it is worth seeing from the road, with its façade resembling an anchored ship. When not in Delhi, the royal family now live in Phool Bagh, a small 1960s mansion opposite the New Stadium.

Alwar to Sariska → *For listings, see pages 412-413. Colour map 2, A6.*

At **Siliserh**, 15 km to the west, runs an aqueduct which supplies the city with water. The lake, a local picnic spot, has boats for hire. **Kesroli**, 10 km northeast, has a seven-turreted 16th-century fort atop a rocky hillock, now sympathetically (though more modestly) restored. It is a three-hour drive from Delhi and convenient for an overnight halt. Turn left off the NH8 at Dharuhera for Alwar Road and you will find it. **Kushalgarh Fort** is en route to Sariska. Near Kushalgarh is the temple complex of **Talbraksha** (or Talvriksh) with a large population of rhesus macaque monkeys. Guides report panthers having been seen near the **Cafeteria Taal** here, probably on the prowl for monkeys near the canteen.

Sariska Tiger Reserve → *For listings, see pages 412-413. Colour map 2, A6.* *Phone code: 0144.*

ⓘ *Rs 450 including still camera, Indians Rs 60, video Rs 200; vehicle Rs 250 per trip. Early-morning jeep trips from Sariska Palace Hotel or Tiger Den (see Sleeping, page 413) venture into the park as far as the Monkey Temple, where you can get a cup of tea and watch monkeys and peacocks. Jeep hire for non-standard trips in the reserve, Rs 1050 for 3 hrs, excluding entry fees. Compulsory guide Rs 150. You need to get permit from Forest Registry Office for early morning and late afternoon safaris (0600-1000/1500-1800). Closed Jul-Sep.*

Despite the lack of tigers, Sariska provides plenty of opportunities to see wildlife. The main rhesus monkey population lives at Talvriksh near Kushalgarh, while at Bhartri-Hari you will see many langurs. The chowsingha, or four-horned antelope, is found here, as are other deer including chital and sambar. You may see nilgai, wild boar, jackals, hyenas, hares and porcupines; leopards are present but rarely seen since the reserve is closed at night to visitors. During the monsoons many animals move to higher ground, but the place is alive with birds. There are ground birds such as peafowl, jungle fowl, spur fowl and grey partridge. Babblers, bulbuls and treepies are common round the lodges. Some tigers were taken from Ranthambhore National Park further south starting in 2008 with the hope of repopulating Sariska, only time will tell. There is an interesting campaign **Save Our Tigers** sponsored by communication company Aircel with a big TV and billboard campaign to raise awareness – www.saveourtigers.com. In the 2011 Tiger Census, numbers were up across the country to 1706, but only by four in Rajasthan.

Unlike most national parks, Sariska is open all year round. During the monsoon travel through the forest may be difficult. The best season to visit is between November and April. In the dry season, when the streams disappear, the animals become dependant on man-made water holes at Kalighatti, Salopka and Pandhupol.

Sariska, the gateway for Sariska National Park, is a pleasant, quiet place to stay and relax. Excursions by jeep are possible to forts and temples nearby. The **Kankwari Fort** (2 km), where Emperor Aurangzeb is believed to have imprisoned his brother **Dara Shikoh**, the rightful heir to the Mughal throne, is within the park. The old **Bhartrihari** temple (6 km) has a fair and six-hour dance-drama in September to October. **Neelkanth** (33 km) has a complex of sixth- to 10th-century carved temples. **Bhangarh** (55 km), on the outskirts of the reserve, is a deserted city of some 10,000 dwellings established in 1631. It was abandoned 300 years ago, supposedly after it was cursed by a magician.

Alwar, Sariska and around listings

For Sleeping and Eating price codes and other relevant information, see Essentials pages 38-42.

Sleeping

Alwar *p410*

L-A Clarks Inn, Shanti Kunj , 3 km from Alwar railway station, T01444-270 0600/01, www.clarksinn.in. 32 contemporary-style rooms with chic bathrooms in smart, new hotel, peaceful area of city, very friendly and professionally run, great value for money (especially the Club Rooms). Weekend packages include dinner and jeep safari. Recommended.

A Dadhikar Fort, Village Dadhikar, T(0)9950-449900, www.dadhikar.com. Nestling in the Aravali hills 6 km outside Alwar, is the ancient site of the Dadhikar Fort, now restored from ruin into a deluxe hotel. 11 individually styled rooms have been comfortably furnished with bespoke heavy wooden furniture and antique objets d'art, and include a rooftop suite, an underground chamber and a family duplex. Dining takes place in the cosy central courtyard (with individual bonfires in winter) and breakfast is served on the rooftop to take in unparalleled views across the colourful mustard fields and lush green hills. Highly recommended.

B-C Hotel Hill View, Moti Doongri, T0144-270 0989/0969-454 8080, hillviewalwar@gmail.com, Excellent value for money, mid-range hotel run by enthusiastic and helpful manager. 11 very comfortable, clean rooms ranging from deluxe to suites, all with Sky TV and fridge. Most rooms have views across to Moti Doongri. There is internet, billiards and a small gym. Cosy and comfortable seating areas scattered around, including a small garden and rooftop; multi-cuisine restaurant. The hotel will happily arrange a tiger safari and guide, all international credit and debit cards accepted.

C Alwar, 26 Manu Marg, T0144-270 0012, www.hotelalwar.com. Set off the road in an attractive garden, 16 rooms, 7 in new block, attached baths (hot showers), TV, fridge, phone, revamped restaurant **Angeethi**, use of pool and tennis courts at nearby club (rs50), efficient service, popular.

C-E Hotel Yuvraj, 31 Moti Dungri, T0144-270 0741, kothirao@yahoo.com. Formerly Kothi Rao. Dubbed a 'House Hotel' by the very charming family of owners who offer up home cooked meals and take great pride in their home style hospitality. It's a bit shabby around the edges for the price.

D-F Ankur, Manu Marg, T0144-233 3025. The same hotel occupies 2 buildings on opposite sides of square. The one closest to **Imperial Hotel** is significantly better than the other; the pick of the nearby options.

D-G Ashoka, Manu Marg, T0144-234 6780. 30 rooms, clean and comfortable, deluxe rooms have TV, running hot water and Western toilets, cheaper rooms have Indian toilets and hot water in buckets, restaurant (Rs 35 *thalis*), good value.

E Meenal (RTDC), near Circuit House, T0144-234 7352. 6 rooms with bath (2 a/c), restaurant, bar, quiet location.

Delhi to Alwar

L-A Neemrana Fort Palace, Delhi-Jaipur Highway, T01494-246 006, www.neemrana hotels.com. The pinnacle of the Neemrana properties, this palace looks like it has come straight out of a fairy-tale, with many tiers and turreted rooms. There are many rooms with their own private rooftop terraces. Ziplining available

Alwar to Sariska *p411*

AL-B Hill Fort Kesroli (Heritage Hotel), Alwar Rd, Kesroli, T01468-289352, www.neemranahotels.com. Comfortable, if eccentric, airy rooms and plush suites, set around a courtyard, delicious lunch and dinner buffet included, some of the best food in Rajasthan, relaxing, and in a lovely isolated rural location. Often overrun by groups though.

Sariska Tiger Reserve *p411*

A Alwar Bagh, T0144-288 5231, next door to **Sariska Tiger Camp** (see below). Extremely well run hotel in a peaceful location. Formerly **Baba Resorts** there are 32 newly decorated, deluxe rooms and suites in 2 separate villas and a traditional 'haveli style' building; all with TV, air con and great walk in showers; suites offer such delights as hanging beds and private rooftop terraces; most rooms overlook pretty orchard gardens and a beautiful pool; very child friendly; rooftop used for cocktail parties and dining, or modern restaurant in grounds serves excellent cuisine; solar panels and an opportunity to become involved in village social projects for a day. Highly recommended.

A Sariska Tiger Camp, 19 km towards Alwar on main road, T0144-288 5311. Eccentric design with 20 simply furnished 'mud concept' rooms in traditional 'village style with wall paintings'; well tended garden and swimming pool; restaurant has lovely terrace; again feels like it caters for groups and bit 'empty' without them.

A-C Lake Palace (RTDC), Siliserh, T0144-288 6322. 10 rooms, 5 a/c, restaurant, Includes all meals. This RTDC hotel looks untouched since it first opened twenty years ago; very basic rooms and general shabby decor, yet a truly amazing location overlooking an enormous lake. Boating trips possible. Worth it for the incredible views from the terrace alone.

A-C Tiger Den (RTDC), in the sanctuary, T0144-284 1342. Superbly located tourist bungalow with views of hill and park, 30 rooms with attached baths (hot showers) but shabby, dirty public areas, vegetarian restaurant (Indian buffets Rs 130-150), bar and shop sells cards and souvenirs, nice garden, friendly management.

D-E Forest Rest House, Main Rd, opposite turning to Kushalgarh, T0144-284 1333. 6 simple rooms, only open during the winter season.

Eating

Alwar *p410*

¶¶ Ice and Spice, **Hotel Aashyana**, Nangli Circle. Popular (if windowless) meeting place for locals; extensive lunch and dinner menus, and coffees a speciality.

¶ Baba, Hope Circle. Popular for *kalakand* ('milk cake') and other Rajasthani sweets.

¶ Moti Doongri Park. Has a number of stalls selling cheap South Indian snacks in the evening. Some Chinese and North Indian.

Transport

Alwar *p410*

Bus Regular buses to/from **Delhi** (4½-5 hrs) and **Jaipur**. Frequent service to **Bharatpur** (2½ hrs), **Deeg** (1½ hrs) and **Sariska** (1 hr).

Train **New Delhi**: *Shatabdi Exp 12016*, not Sun, 1941, 2½ hrs. **Delhi**: *Jodhpur Delhi Exp 14860*, 0835, 3 hrs; *Jaipur-JAT Exp 12413*, 1900, 3 hrs.

Sariska Tiger Reserve *p411*

Train The nearest station is at Alwar (36 km), with buses to the sanctuary.

Deeg, Bharatpur and around

For a typical dusty and hot North Indian market town, Deeg gained the somewhat surprising reputation as the summer resort of the Raja of Bharatpur. Located on the plains just northwest of Agra, the raja decided to develop his palace to take full advantage of the monsoon rains. The fort and the 'monsoon' pleasure palace have ingenious fountains and are of major architectural importance, their serenity in stark contrast to the barely controlled chaos of the rest of the town. One of the most popular halting places on the 'Golden Triangle', Bharatpur is best known for its Keoladeo Ghana Bird Sanctuary. Once the hunting estate of the Maharajas of Bharatpur, with daily shoots recorded of up to 4000 birds, the 29-sq-km piece of marshland, with over 360 species, is potentially one of the finest bird sanctuaries in the world, but has suffered badly in recent years from water deprivation. Lesser visited are the sights off the road which connects Agra to Jaipur, NH11, which sees huge volumes of tourist traffic. The Balaji temple is particularly remarkable.
▸▸ *For listings, see pages 418-420.*

Ins and outs

There are regular bus services from both Mathura and Bharatpur to Deeg, with the road from Bharatpur being by far the smoother of the two. Bharatpur, 40 km south of Deeg, has good bus and train connections from Agra, Jaipur and Delhi. Keoladeo Ghana National Park is 4 km south of Bharatpur town.

Deeg → *For listings, see pages 418-420. Colour map 2, A6. Phone code: 05641. Population: 38,000.*

The rubble and mud walls of the square **fort** are strengthened by 12 bastions and a wide, shallow moat. It has a run-down *haveli* within, but is otherwise abandoned. The entrance is over a narrow bridge across the moat, through a gate studded with anti-elephant spikes. Negotiating the undergrowth, you can climb the ramparts which rise 20 m above the moat; some cannons are still in place on their rusty carriages. You can walk right around along the wide path on top of the walls and climb the stairs to the roof of the citadel for good views.

The **palaces** ⓘ *opposite the fort, Sat-Thu 0930-1730, Rs 200*, are flanked by two reservoirs, Gopal (west) and Rup Sagar (east), and set around a beautifully proportioned central formal garden in the style of a Mughal *char bagh*. The main entrance is from the north, through the ornamental, though unfinished, Singh (Lion) Pol; the other gates are Suraj (Sun) Pol (southwest) and Nanga Pol (northeast). The impressive main palace **Gopal Bhavan** (1763), bordering Gopal Sagar, is flanked by Sawon and Bhadon pavilions (1760), named after the monsoon months (mid-July to mid-September). Water was directed over the roof lines to create the effect of sheets of monsoon rain. The palace still retains many of the original furnishings, including scent and cigarette cases made from elephant's feet and even a dartboard. There are vegetarian and non-vegetarian dining rooms, the former particularly elegant, with floor seating around a low-slung horseshoe-shaped marble table. Outside, overlooking the formal garden, is a beautiful white marble *hindola* (swing) which was brought as booty with two marble thrones (black and white) after Suraj Mal attacked Delhi.

To the south, bordering the central garden, is the single-storey marble **Suraj Bhavan** (circa 1760), a temple, and **Kishan Bhavan** with its decorated façade, five arches and fountains. The water reservoir to its west was built at a height to operate the fountains and cascades effectively; it held enough water to work all the fountains for a few hours, though it took a week to fill from four wells with bullocks drawing water up in leather buckets. Now, the 500 or so fountains are turned on once a year for the **Monsoon festival** in August. All these are gravity fed from huge holding tanks on the palace roof, with each fountain jet having its own numbered pipe leading from the tank. Coloured dyes are inserted into individual pipes to create a spectacular effect. The (old) **Purana Mahal** beyond, with a curved roof and some fine architectural points, was begun by Badan Singh in 1722. It now houses government offices but the simple wall paintings in the entrance chamber of the inner court are worth seeing.

Keshav Bhavan, a *baradari* or garden pavilion, stands between the central garden and Rup Sagar with the **Sheesh Mahal** (Mirror Palace, 1725) in the southeast corner. **Nand Bhavan** (circa 1760), north of the central garden, is a large hall 45 m long, 24 m wide and 6 m high, raised on a terrace and enclosed by an arcade of seven arches. There are frescoes inside but it has a deserted feel. The pavilion's ingenious double-roof design took the monsoon theme further: water was channelled through hollow pillars to rotate heavy stone balls, mimicking the sound of thunder.

Bhandarej to Bharatpur → *For listings, see pages 418-420. Colour map 2, B6-A6.*

Bhandarej, 62 km from Jaipur, south of NH11 after Dausa, is a relaxing place to stop for the night. From here the NH11 goes through a series of small towns and villages to **Sakrai** (77 km) which has a good roadside RTDC restaurant. Some 15 km after Sakrai is the turning for Balaji, home to the truly extraordinary **Balaji Temple**. People who believe themselves to have been possessed by demons come here, to have the evil spirits exorcized. The scenes on the first floor in particular are not for the faint-hearted; methods of restraining the worst afflicted include chaining them to the walls and placing them under large rocks. Most exorcisms take place on Tuesdays and Saturdays, when there are long queues to get in. From **Mahuwa** a road south leads through Hindaun to Karauli (64 km).

Bharatpur

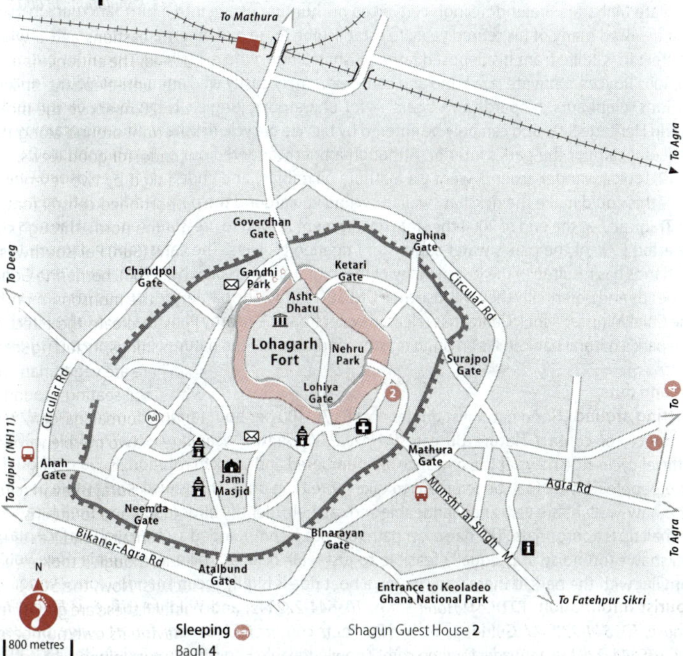

Sleeping
Bagh 4
Laxmi Vilas Palace 1
Shagun Guest House 2

Noted for its pale red sandstone, **Karauli** (1348), was the seat of a small princely state which played a prominent part in support of the Mughal emperors. The impressive **City Palace** has some fine wall paintings, stone carvings and a fine Darbar Hall. Fairs are held at nearby temples lasting a week to a fortnight (see Festivals and events, page 419). Mahavirji, associated with the 24th Tirthankar Mahavir, is an important Jain pilgrimage centre.

Bharatpur → *For listings, see pages 418-420. Colour map 2, A6. Phone code: 05644. Population: 157,000.*

Built by Suraj Mal, the **Lohagarh Fort**, which occupies the island at the centre of Bharatpur village, appears impregnable, but the British, initially repulsed in 1803, finally took it in 1825. There are double ramparts, a 46-m-wide moat and an inner moat around the palace. Much of the wall has been demolished but there are the remains of some of the gateways. Inside the fort are three palaces (circa 1730) and Jewel House and Court to their north. The **museum** ⓘ *1000-1630, closed Fri, Rs 3,* in the Kachhari Kalan exhibits archaeological finds from villages nearby, dating from the first to 19th centuries as well as paintings and artefacts; the armoury is upstairs.

Peharsar ⓘ *23 km away, Rs 30 to 'headman' secures a tour,* with a carpet weaving community, makes a very interesting excursion from Bharatpur.

Keoladeo Ghana National Park → *For listings, see pages 418-420. Colour map 2, A6.*

ⓘ *www.knpark.org, Rs 400, video Rs 200, professional video Rs 1500, payable each time you enter. Park closed May and Jun. Cafés inside, or ask your hotel to provide a packed lunch.*

The late Maharaja Brajendra Singh converted his hunting estate into a bird sanctuary in 1956 and devoted many of his retired years to establishing it. He had inherited both his title and an interest in wildlife from his deposed father, Kishan Singh, who grossly overspent his budget – 30 Rolls Royces, a private jazz band and some extremely costly wild animals including "dozens of lions, elephants, leopards and tigers" – for Bharatpur's jungles. It has been designated a World Heritage Site, and can only be entered by bicycle or cycle rickshaw, thus maintaining the peaceful calm of the park's interior. Although a tiger wandered out of Ranthambhore Park in 2010, took a wander around, went via Mathura oil refinery and ended up in Keoloadeo Ghana NP – this could make the rickshaw wallah cycling you around the park peddle a little faster!

Tragically, at the end of 2004 the state government bowed to pressure from local farmers and diverted 97% of the park's water supply for irrigation projects. The catastrophic damage to its wetlands has resulted in the loss of many of the migratory birds on which Bharatpur's reputation depends and potentially they will lose their UNESCO status. The battle goes on and in recent years the Chief Minister Ashok Gehlot has released water from the nearby Panchna Dam to help restore the park's natural habitat. It's an ongoing story and certainly the nature of the park is changing.

Ins and outs

Getting around Good naturalist guides cost Rs 70-100 per hour (depending on group size) at entrance, or contact **Nature Bureau** ⓘ *Haveli SVP Shastri, Neemda Gate, T/F05644-225498.* Official cycle-rickshaws at the entrance are numbered and work in rotation, Rs 50 per hour for two people (drivers may be reluctant to take more than one). This is well worthwhile as some rickshaw-wallahs are very knowledgeable and can help identify birds (and know their location): a small tip is appropriate. The narrower paths are not recommended as the rough surface makes rickshaws too noisy. It is equally feasible to just walk or hire a bike, particularly once you're familiar with the park. If there's any water, a boat ride is highly recommended for viewing.

Tourist information RTDC ⓘ *Hotel Saras, T05644-222542,* and **Wildlife Office** ⓘ *Forest Rest House, T05644-222777.* Guides available. For tours contact **GTA** ⓘ *near Tourist Lodge, Gol Bagh Rd, T05644-228188, vfauzdar@yahoo.com.* Knowledgeable English-speaking guides, Rs 300 for two hours. It is worth buying the well-illustrated *Collins Handguide to the Birds of the Indian*

Sub-continent (available at the reserve and in bookshops in Delhi, Agra, Jaipur, etc). *Bharatpur: Bird Paradise* by Martin Ewans (Lustre Press, Delhi) is extremely good.

Best time to visit Winters can be very cold and foggy, especially in the early morning. It is traditionally best November to February when it is frequented by northern hemisphere

Keoladeo Ghana National Park

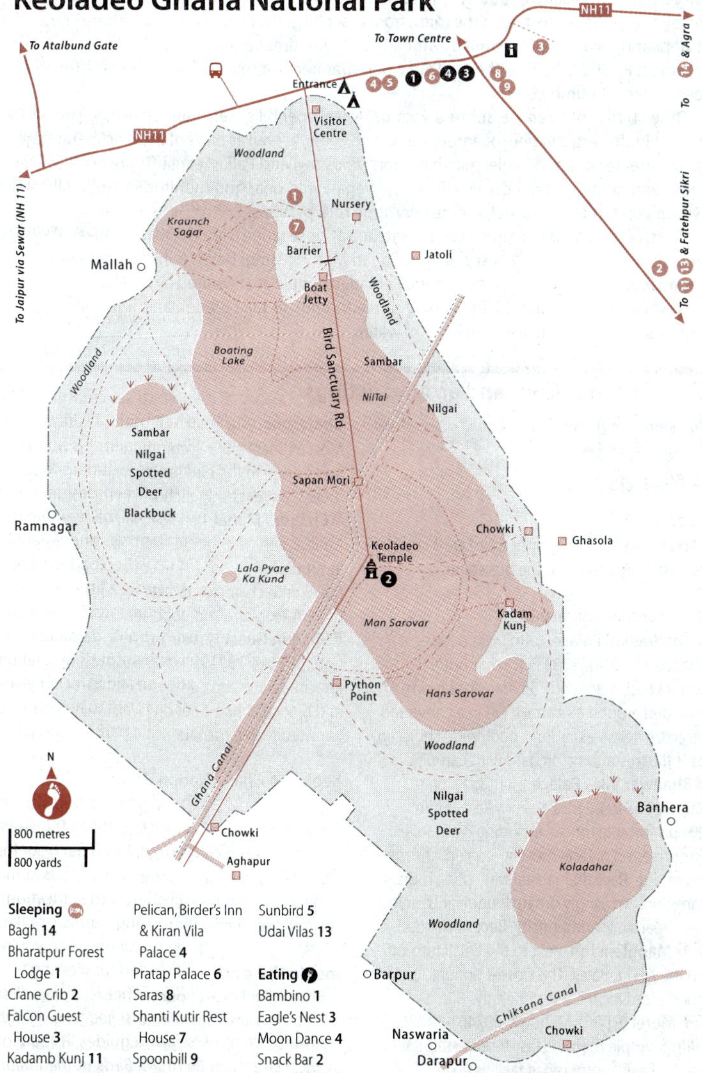

migratory birds. To check in advance whether there is any water, try contacting the tourist information numbers above, or use the contact form on www.knpwhs.org.

Sights

The handful of rare Siberian cranes that used to visit Bharatpur each year have been missing since 2003. The ancient migratory system, some 1500 years old, may have been lost completely, since young cranes must learn the route from older birds (it is not instinctive). These cranes are disappearing worldwide – eaten by Afghans and sometimes employed as fashionable 'guards' to protect Pakistani homes (they call out when strangers approach). The Sarus crane can still be seen in decent numbers.

Other birds that can be spotted include Asian openbills, Ferruginous ducks, spoonbills, storks, kingfishers, a variety of egrets, ducks and coots, as well as birds of prey including Laggar falcon, greater-spotted eagle, marsh harrier, Scops owl and Pallas' eagle. There are also chital deer, sambar, nilgai, feral cattle, wild cats, hyenas, wild boar and monitor lizards, whilst near Python Point, there are usually some very large rock pythons.

Birds, accustomed to visitors, can be watched at close range from the road between the boat jetty and Keoladeo temple, especially at Sapan Mori crossing. Dawn (which can be very cold) and dusk are the best times; trees around Keoladeo temple are favoured by birds for roosting, so are particularly rewarding. Midday may prove too hot so take a book and find a shady spot. Carry a sun hat, binoculars and plenty of water.

Deeg, Bharatpur and around listings

For Sleeping and Eating price codes and other relevant information, see Essentials pages 38-42.

Sleeping

Deeg *p414*

If you have to spend a night there are a couple of very basic options near the bus stand.

Bhandarej to Bharatpur *p415*

B Bhadrawati Palace, 5 km from palace, Bhandarej, T01427-283351, www.hotelbhadrawatipalace.com. 35 adequate rooms arranged around a central lawn in a converted palace, extensive gardens, pool, wide choice in beautiful restaurant; orchard with camping.

B Bhanwar Vilas Palace (Heritage Hotel), Karauli, T07464-220024, www.karauli.com. 29 comfortable rooms, including 4 a/c suites in converted palace, most air-cooled, cheaper in cottage, Rajasthani restaurant, pool, tours, camping, amazingly ornate lounge and dining halls, real air of authenticity. Recommended.

C-D Manglam Inn, next to the Balaji turn-off on the NH11, Balaji. The closest option, 10 clean, good-sized rooms, 3 a/c, friendly.

E-F Motel (RTDC), Mahuwa, T07461-240260. With 5 simple rooms, a fast-food restaurant, toilets, basic motor repair facilities.

Bharatpur *p416, map p415*

Most of Bharatpur's accommodation is out of town, close to the bird sanctuary. However, there is a great budget choice in the old city.

B Chandra Mahal, Peharsar, Jaipur–Agra Rd, Nadbai, Peharsar, T05643-264336. 23 rooms in simply furnished, 19th-century Shia Muslim *haveli* with character, quality set meals (from Rs 250), jeep hire and good service.

F Shagun Guest House, just inside Mathura Gate, T05644-232455. Has 6 basic rooms, 1 with attached bathroom, all under Rs 100, bicycle and binocular hire. Friendly, welcoming and knowledgeable manager.

Keoladeo Ghana National Park *p416, map p417*

Some budget hotels have tents. The NH11 past the park is being widened, affecting the hotels near the park entrance, some of which will have to be partly demolished; prepare for a degree of construction/traffic disturbance.

Inside the park

B Bharatpur Forest Lodge (Ashok), 2.5 km from gate, 8 km from railway and bus stand, T05644-222760, itdchba@sancharnet.in, book in advance. 17 comfortable a/c rooms with balconies, pricey restaurant and bar, very friendly staff, peaceful, boats for birdwatching, animals (eg wild boar) wander into the compound. Entry fee each time you enter park.

E Shanti Kutir Rest House, near boat jetty. 5 clean rooms in old hunting lodge, mostly used by guests of the park director.

Outside the park

LL-A Udai Vilas, Fatehpur Sikri Rd, 3 km from park, T05644-233161, www.udaivilaspalace.com. Contemporary rooms plus 10 luxurious suites in impressively run hotel, excellent restaurant, pleasant gardens. Recommended.

L-AL The Bagh, Agra Rd, 4 km from town, T05644-228 333, www.thebagh.com. Set in a beautiful orchard, space is everything here. There are 14 elegant, well decorated, centrally a/c rooms with outstanding bathrooms. Attractive dining room, lovely pool , beautiful 200-year-old gardens, some may find facilities rather spread out.

B-C Birders' Inn, near park entrance, T05644-227 346, www.birdersinn.com. Beautifully designed hotel set back from the road. Great décor and by the time you are reading this, there should be a new restaurant and 6 new rooms. Recommended.

B-C Park Regency, opposite park, T05644-224232, www.hotelparkregency.com. 8 large, modern, clean rooms, 24-hr room service, lawns, friendly, good value.

B-C Sunbird, near park gate, T05644-225701, www.hotelsunbird.com. Attractive red-brick building with clean rooms with hot shower, better on 1st floor. Now also 4 deluxe cottages, pleasant restaurant, friendly staff, bike hire, good value, well maintained. Highly recommended.

C-E Crane Crib, Fatehpur Sikri Rd, 3 km from park, T05644-222224. Attractive sandstone building, 25 rooms of wide- ranging standards and tariffs, all reasonable value. Small cinema where wildlife films are shown nightly, bonfires on the lawn during winter and welcoming staff. Run by the Honorary warden of the park. Recommended.

D-F Kiran Vila Palace, Saras Circle, 300 m from park gate, T(0)9314-364030. Nicely decorated rooms set back from the road, so a little quieter.

D-F Pratap Palace, near park gate, T05644-224245, www.hotelpratappalace.net. 30 rooms (10 a/c) with bath, whole place feels slightly run-down, mediocre restaurant but helpful management, good value.

E Saras (RTDC), Fatehpur Sikri Rd, T05644-223700. Hotel with 25 simple clean rooms, some a/c (limited hot water), dorm (Rs 50), restaurant (indifferent food), lawns, camping, dull, but helpful tourist information.

E-F Falcon Guest House, near **Saras**, T05644-223815. 10 clean, well-kept rooms, some a/c with bath, owned by naturalist, good information, bike hire, quiet, very helpful, warm welcome, off-season discount.

F-G Pelican, near park gate, T05644-224221. 9 clean rooms with fan, best No 8 with hot (salty) shower, quite modern with tiny balcony, restaurant, friendly, bike hire (Rs 40 per day), good information.

F-G Spoonbill, near **Saras**, T05644-223 571, www.hotelspoonbill.com. Good-value rooms with shared facility (hot water in buckets), dorm (Rs 60), run by charming ex-army officer, courteous and friendly service, good food, bike hire, also 4 more good-size rooms in **New Spoonbill** down the road.

Eating

Keoladeo Ghana National Park

p416, map p417

Inside the park

TTT Forest Lodge, overpriced buffets feeding the many tour groups.

T Snack Bar, dirty, serving drinks and biscuits.

Outside the park

All restaurants offer Indian and Western dishes.

TTT Laxmi Vilas, wide choice but some find it disappointing, standard fare for Westerners.

TT Eagle's Nest, new 100-seater restaurant with the promise of a/c to come.

TT Moon Dance tent, near **Pratap Palace**. Good food, lively atmosphere, beer.

T Bambino, open-air dining in a garden.

T Pelican, good choice, chicken, vegetarian, Israeli dishes, 'Westernized'.

T Spoonbill, good food, obliging (beer and special *kheer* on request). Recommended.

Festivals and events

Bhandarej to Bharatpur *p415*

Feb/Mar In Karauli, **Sivaratri**.

Mar/Apr Kaila Devi (7 Mar 2013, 26 Mar 2014). Held in Karauli.

Bharatpur *p416, map p415*

2-4 Feb Brij Festival, honours lord Krishna with folk dances and drama relating the love story of Radha-Krishna.

Transport

Bhandarej to Bharatpur *p415*

Train Nearly all trains on the main Delhi-Mumbai line stop at Gangapur City, 30 km from Karauli.

Bharatpur *p416, map p415*

Air The nearest airport is at Jaipur (175 km).
Bus Buses to Bharatpur tend to get very crowded but give an insight into Indian rural life. The main stand is at Anah Gate just off NH11 (east of town). To **Agra** (55 km, 1½ hrs), **Deeg**; **Delhi**, 185 km, 6 hrs; and **Jaipur** 175 km, 5 hrs.
Train From: **Delhi** (**ND**): *Paschim Exp 12925*, 0635, 4 hrs; *Golden Temple Mail 12903*, 1513, 3½ hrs; *Mumbai-Firozepur Janata Exp 19023*, 0805, 5½ hrs. **Sawai Madhopur**: *Paschim Exp 12926*, 1945, 2½ hrs; *Golden Temple Mail 12904*, 1045, 2½ hrs.

An auto-rickshaw from train station (6 km) to park Rs 50; from bus stand (4 km), Rs 20.

Keoladeo Ghana National Park *p416, map p417*

Cycle There are bikes for hire near Saras or ask at your hotel; Rs 40 per day; hire on previous evening for an early start next day.

Directory

Bharatpur *p416, map p415*

Banks SBBJ, near Binarayan Gate, may ask for proof of purchase, or refuse to change TCs.

Ranthambhore National Park

→ *Colour map 2, B6. Phone code: 07462.*

The park is one of the finest tiger reserves in the country, although even here their numbers have dwindled due to poachers. Most visitors spending a couple of nights here are likely to spot one of these wonderful animals, although many leave disappointed. Set in dry deciduous forest, some trees trailing matted vines, the park's rocky hills and open valleys are dotted with small pools and fruit trees. The reserve covers 410 sq km between the Aravalli and Vindhya hills. Scrubby hillsides surrounding Ranthambhore village are pleasantly peaceful, their miniature temples and shrines glowing pink in the evening sun before they become silhouetted nodules against the night sky. Once the private tiger reserve of the Maharajah of Jaipur, in 1972 the sanctuary came under the Project Tiger scheme following the government Wildlife Protection Act. By 1979, 12 villages inside the park had been 'resettled' into the surrounding area, leaving only a scattering of people still living within the park's boundaries. Should the tigers evade you, as you pass along misty dust tracks as the crisp morning air disperses with the sunrise, you may well spot leopard, hyena, jackal, marsh crocodile, wild boar, langur monkey, bear, and many species of deer and birdlife. The park's 10th-century fort, proudly flanked by two impressive gateways, makes a good afternoon excursion after a morning drive. ▸▸ *For listings, see pages 423-425.*

Ins and outs

Getting there and around The national park is 10 km east of Sawai Madhopur, with the approach along a narrow valley; the main gate is 4 km from the boundary. The park has good roads and tracks. Entry is by park jeep (gypsy) or open bus (canter) on four-hour tours; 16 jeeps and 20 canters are allowed in at any one time to minimize disturbance. You can book online. Some lodges can organize trips for you or there are a couple of jeeps and canters reserved for same-day bookings, which involves a queue and elbows and you may get gazumped by hotels paying over the odds for a private jeep. Jeeps are better but must be booked in advance so request one at the time of booking your lodge (passport number and personal details required) or try online. Visitors are picked up from their hotels.

The park is open 1 October-30 June for two sessions a day: winter 0630-1030, 1400-1800; summer 0600-1000, 1430-1830, but check as times change. Jeep hire: Rs 800-1200 per person for up to five passengers; jeep entry Rs 125; guide Rs 150. A seat in a canter, Rs 500-550, can often be arranged on arrival, bookings start at 0600 and 1330 for same-day tours; advance bookings from 1000-1330. Individual entry fees are extra: foreigners Rs 200, Indians Rs 25, camera free, video Rs 200. ▸▸ *See Transport, page 425.*

Tourist information Rajasthan Tourism ⓘ *Hotel Vinayak, T07462-220808. Conservator of Forests/Field Director, T07462-220223.* Forest Officer ⓘ *T07462-221142.* A very informative background with photography tips is available on www.ranthambhore.com.

Climate Best from November to April, though vegetation dies down in April exposing tigers. Maximum temperatures from 28-49°C. It can be very cold at dawn in winter.

History

Much of the credit for Ranthambhore's present position as one of the world's leading wildlife resorts goes to India's most famous 'tiger man', Mr Fateh Singh Rathore. His enthusiasm for all things wild has been passed on to his son, Dr Goverdhan Singh Rathore, who set up the Prakratik Society in 1994. This charitable foundation was formed in response to the increasing

Ranthambhore National Park

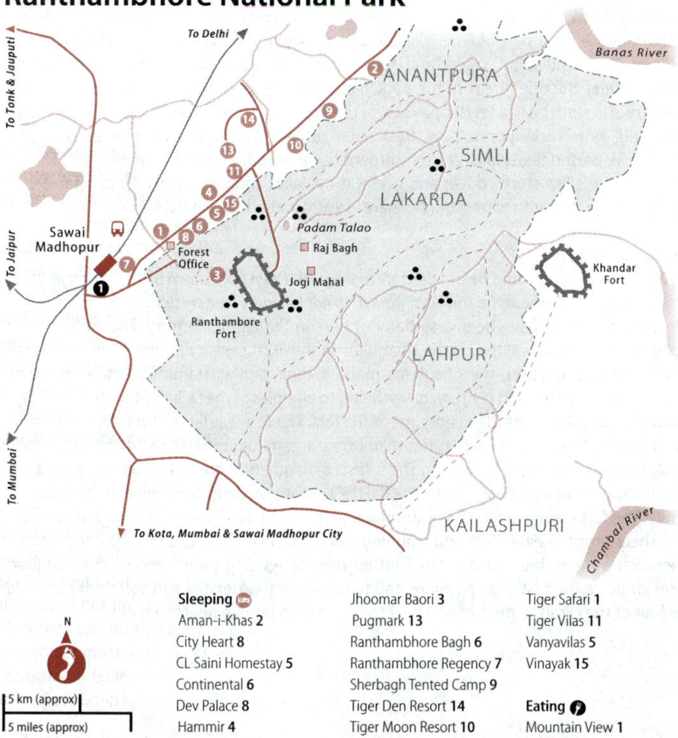

Sleeping
Aman-i-Khas 2
City Heart 8
CL Saini Homestay 5
Continental 6
Dev Palace 8
Hammir 4
Jhoomar Baori 3
Pugmark 13
Ranthambhore Bagh 6
Ranthambhore Regency 7
Sherbagh Tented Camp 9
Tiger Den Resort 14
Tiger Moon Resort 10
Tiger Safari 1
Tiger Vilas 11
Vanyavilas 5
Vinayak 15

Eating
Mountain View 1

human encroachment on the tiger's natural forest habitat; in 1973 there were 70,000 people living around Ranthambhore Park, a figure which has now increased to 200,000.

The human population's rapidly increasing firewood requirements were leading to ever-more damaging deforestation, and the founders of the Prakratik Society soon realized that something needed to be done. Their solution was as brilliant as it was simple; enter the 'biogas digester'. This intriguingly named device, of which 225 have so far been installed, uses cow dung as a raw material, and produces both gas for cooking, negating the need for firewood, and organic fertilizer, which has seen crop yields increase by 25%. The over-whelming success of this venture was recognized in June 2004, when the Prakratik Society was presented with the prestigious Ashden Award for Sustainable Energy in London.

Wildlife

Tiger sightings are recorded almost daily, usually in the early morning, especially from November to April. Travellers report the tigers seem "totally unconcerned, ambling past only 10 m away". Sadly, poaching is prevalent: between 2003 and 2005, 22 tigers were taken out of the park by poachers operating from surrounding villages, a wildlife scandal that spotlighted official negligence in Ranthambhore. Since then the population has recovered somewhat, with about six cubs being born each year. In 2011, two new cubs were spotted in April. Across the country the Tiger Census of 2010 has revealed that tiger numbers are up by 295 making a total of 1706 tigers. Current estimate is 31 adult tigers in the park. As well as Save the Tiger campaigns from Aircel, there is a Travel Operators for Tigers group who many of the hotels in Ranthambhore are a part of. The lakeside woods and grassland provide an ideal habitat for herds of chital and sambar deer and sounders of wild boar. Nilgai antelope and chinkara gazelles prefer the drier areas of the park. Langur monkeys, mongoose and hare are prolific. There are also sloth bear, a few leopards, and the occasional rare caracal. Crocodiles bask by the lakes, and some rocky ponds have freshwater turtles. Extensive birdlife includes spurfowl, jungle fowl, partridges, quails, crested serpent eagle, woodpeckers, flycatchers, etc. There are also water birds like storks, ducks and geese at the lakes and waterholes. Padam Talao by the Jogi Mahal is a favourite water source; there are also water holes at Raj Bagh and Milak.

Ranthambhore Fort

ⓘ *The entrance to the fort is before the gate to the park. Open from dawn to dusk, though the Park Interpretation Centre near the small car park may not be open. Free entry.*

There is believed to have been a settlement here in the eighth century. The earliest historic record is of it being wrested by the Chauhans in the 10th century. In the 11th century, after Ajmer was lost to Ghori, the Chauhans made it their capital. Hamir Chauhan, the ruler of Ranthambhore in the 14th century, gave shelter to enemies of the Delhi sultanate, resulting in a massive siege and the Afghan conquest of the fort. The fort was later surrendered to Emperor Akbar in the 16th century when Ranthambhore's commander saw resistance was useless, finally passing to the rulers of Jaipur. The forests of Ranthambhore historically guarded the fort from invasions but with peace under the Raj they became a hunting preserve of the Jaipur royal family. The fort wall runs round the summit and has a number of semi-circular bastions, some with sheer drops of over 65 m and stunning views. Inside the fort you can see a Siva temple – where Rana Hamir beheaded himself rather than face being humiliated by the conquering Delhi army – ruined palaces, pavilions and tanks. Mineral water, tea and soft drinks are sold at the foot of the climb to the fort and next to the Ganesh temple near the tanks.

Ranthambhore National Park listings

For Sleeping and Eating price codes and other relevant information, see Essentials pages 38-42.

Sleeping

Ranthambhore National Park
p420, map p421

Book well ahead. Hotels tend to be overpriced, with dusty rooms and erratic electricity. Take a torch. Most **B** category and above are geared for tour groups so may neglect independent travellers. Heavy discounts are offered May-Jun. Sawai Madhopur has a few seedy hotels in the market area, but little else going for it.

LL Aman-i-Khas, close to park, T07462-252052, www.amanresorts.com. 6 super luxury a/c tents in beautiful surroundings, minimum 3-night stay on all-inclusive basis.

LL Dev Vilas Village Khilchipur, Ranthambhore Rd, Sawai Madhopur, T07462-252168, www.devvilas.com. 21 rooms and 7 a/c tents. Tiger safaris, 5-min drive to park entrance. Nice pool, lawns, large bedrooms. Meals included. Evening buffet hit and miss. Very friendly and attentive. Member of TOFT (see box, page 424).

LL Sherbagh Tented Camp, Sherpur-Khiljipur, T07462-252120, www.sujanluxury.com. Open 1 Oct-30 Mar. Award-winning eco-camp with luxury tents and hot showers, bar, dinner around fire, lake trips for birders, stunning grounds and seated areas for quiet contemplation, jungle ambience, well organized. All meals included. Beautiful shop on site. Highly recommended.

LL Vanyavilas (Oberoi), T07462-223999, www.oberoihotels.com. Very upmarket 8-ha garden resort set around a recreated *haveli* with fantastic frescoes. 25 unbelievably luxurious a/c tents (wooden floors, marble baths), billiards, elephant rides, wildlife lectures, dance shows in open-air auditorium, "fabulous spa", friendly and professional. Elephants greet you at the door.

LL-L The Pugmark, Khilchipur, T07462-252205, www.thepugmark.net. 22 luxury a/c cottages (one with its own pool), in an entertainingly over-the-top resort. Defining feature is the "imaginatively landscaped" garden, replete with waterways, illuminations and plastic rocks. Rooms are modern and uninspiring.

L Tiger Moon Resort, near Sherpur on the edge of the park, 12 km from railway, T07462-252284, www.indianadventures.com. 32 stone (25 a/c), and 5 simple bamboo cottages, all with modern fittings, hot water, some tents are added in the peak season, buffet meals, bar, library, pool, pleasant "jungle ambience". All meals and 2 safaris included.

AL Ranthambhore Regency, T07462- 223456, www.ranthambhor.com. 39 a/c rooms in cottages in swanky modern surroundings. Very clean pool and huge, 100-cover dining hall, plus evening folk performances.

AL Tiger Den Resort, 6 km from park, Khilchipur, Ranthambhore Rd, T07462-252070, www.tigerdenresort.com. 40 modern a/c rooms in brick cottages around a well-kept lawn, evening meals (Indian buffet) seated around braziers, surrounded by farmland and guava groves. Lacks character. Meals included.

A-B Jhoomar Baori (RTDC), Ranthombore Rd, T07462-220495. Set high on a hillside, this former hunting lodge is an interesting building and offers fantastic views of the area. 12 quirky rooms, varying in size, plus a small bar, reasonable restaurant and beautifully decorated communal lounges on each floor.

B Ranthambore Bagh, Ranthambhore Rd, T07462-221728, www.ranthambhore.com. 12 luxury tents and 12 simple but attractive rooms in this pleasantly laid-back property owned by a professional photographer. Family-run, pride has been taken in every detail; the public areas and dining hall are particularly well done. Fantastic food including traditional Rajasthani and atmospheric suppers around the campfire. Highly recommended.

B-C Tiger Vilas, Ranthambore Rd, T07462-221121, www.tigervilla.in. 10 clean, modern rooms in convenient location for park, beautiful decor, reasonably priced veggie food.

C-D Hammir, T07462-220562. One of the oldest hotels, in interesting building fresh from much-needed renovation, forgettable rooms (some a/c) plus a new pool and a friendly, cheerful manager. Nice Vibe.

C-E Tiger Safari, T07462-221137, www.tigersafariresort.com. 14 cosy rooms, 4 attractive a/c cottages, very clean, hot shower, quiet, jeep/bus to park, very helpful, good value, ordinary food but few other options. Recommended.

Wildlife for the future

Travel Operators for Tigers (TOFT), www.toftigers.org, was established in 2002 to promote responsible wildlife tourism across India. In partnership with **Global Tiger Patrol**, www.globaltigerpatrol.org, TOFT counts accommodation providers and international and domestic tour operators among its members, and works across Rajasthan, Madhya Pradesh and Uttarakhand. Funded through a small levy imposed by participating operators, TOFT aims to reverse the decline in tiger numbers, to support the park's efforts against poaching, to assist local community employment, as well as to cover the costs of running park tours. To ensure such tourism is sustainable, there are 'best practice' guidelines for tour operators, service providers and visitors. Visitors are urged to book lodges and tours with TOFT members and to abide by a code of conduct when visiting conservation areas. TOFT also seeks to empower and inspire local communities to become involved in wildlife tourism projects to benefit themselves and to help park conservation. Also among the organization's initiatives are waste and water management, trade cooperatives and fair wage plans. They hold an annual TOFT Wildlife Tourism Awards in Delhi. In the 2010 Tiger Census, tiger population was on the up – a rise of 295 to 1706. So initiatives like TOFT are hopefully raising awareness amongst the travel industry and individuals.

D-E Vinayak (RTDC), Ranthambhore Rd, close to park, T07462-221333. Good location. 14 adequate rooms, including 5 a/c, bit institutional, but pleasant lawns. Gloomy restaurant serves fantastic vegetarian *thalis*.

E C L Saini Homestay, Ranthambhore Rd. T(0)9828-214049, op_ranthambhore@yahoo.co.in. Ranthambhore's 1st homestay – decent size rooms with hot water, garden and rooftop views of the forest and food served on request.

E-G City Heart, Ranthambhore Rd, 100 m from Ranthambhore Bagh, T07462-223402. Good, clean rooms, some with TV.

E-G Continental, set back from Ranthambhore Rd, next to Ranthambhore Bagh, T(0)9414-727157. Beautiful gardens with 4 simple but big rooms and 2 rooftop tents. Pretty, good home-cooked food; great reports from guests.

F-G Dev Palace, Ranthambhore Rd, near City Heart, T(0)9413-023628, ranthambhoresafari@rediffmail.com. Only 4 rooms, but one of the cheapest options; simple but sweet. Friendly.

F-G Rajeev Resort, 16 Indira Colony, Civil Lines, Sawai Madhopur, T07462-221413. 12 fairly decent rooms, 2 a/c (some with Western toilets), and larger 4-bed rooms, simple meals to order.

Eating

Ranthambhore National Park

p420, map p421

ΨΨ **Mountain View Restaurant**, Ranthambhore Rd. Standard menu but pleasant lawns to sit out on and a friendly welcome.

Ψ **Asha**, T07462-220803. Don't be put off by uninviting exterior, this is a great little eatery, friendly, fast service, cheap and scrumptious.

Shopping

Ranthambhore National Park

p420, map p421

Dastkar, the original women's collective shop is near Sherbagh, with another branch on Ranthambhore Rd near Ranthambhore Regency. Many locals have jumped on the 'Women's Collective Crafts' bandwagon but **Dastkar** is the only genuine one. The collective empowers women by making them self sufficient. They started with just 6 women, but now employ 360 women to do quilting, patchwork, block printing and sequin embroidery based on traditional local skills that were dying out. Beautiful fabrics, clothes, toys and collectibles are sold at extremely fair prices. Highly recommended.

Transport

Ranthambhore National Park

p420, map p421

Bus Stand is 500 m from Sawai Madhopur Railway Station. Buses go to **Kota** and **Jaipur**, but trains are quicker and more pleasant.

Train The railway station at Sawai Madhopur, T07462-220222, is on the main Delhi–Mumbai line. To **Jaipur**: *Mumbai–Jaipur Exp 12955*, 1045, 2 hrs. From Jaipur to **Mumbai**: *Jaipur–Mumbai Exp 12956*, 1410, 2 hrs. **Jodhpur**: *Ranthambore Exp 12465*, 1435. **Mumbai** via **Kota**: *Jaipur Mumbai Exp 12956*, 1610, 16 hrs; *Paschim Exp 12926*, 2205, 17¼ hrs; *Golden Temple Mail 12904*, 1310, 15 hrs (Kota 1½ hrs). **New Delhi** (via Bharatpur and Mathura) *Golden Temple Mail 12903*, 1240, 6 hrs; *Dehra Dun Exp 19019*, 2130, 8 hrs.

Directory

Ranthambhore National Park

p420, map p421

Internet Cyber Café on Ranthambhore Rd near to Ankur Resort. **Useful contacts** Police, T07462-220456. Tiger Watch, T07462-220811.

Ajmer and Pushkar

Although geographically close, these towns could hardly be more different. Situated in a basin at the foot of Taragarh Hill (870 m), Ajmer is surrounded by a stone wall with five gateways. Renowned throughout the Muslim world as the burial place of Mu'inuddin Chishti, who claimed descent from the son-in-law of Mohammad, seven pilgrimages to Ajmer are believed to equal one to Mecca. Every year, especially during the annual Islamic festivals of Id and Muharram, thousands of pilgrims converge on this ancient town on the banks of Ana Sagar Lake. Many visitors are discouraged by the frantic hustle of Ajmer on first arrival, but it's worth taking time to explore this underrated city.

Separated from Ajmer by Nag Pahar (Snake Mountain), Pushkar lies in a narrow valley overshadowed by rocky hills, which offer spectacular views of the desert at sunset. The lake at its heart, almost magically beautiful at dawn and dusk, is one of India's most sacred. The village is transformed during the celebrated camel fair into a colourful week of heightened activity, but a visit outside this annual extravaganza is also worthwhile.

The village has been markedly changed in recent years by the year-round presence of large numbers of foreigners originally drawn by the Pushkar Fair, but there are still plenty of chances for an unhurried stroll around the lake that uncovers a very holy site: ghats dotted with shrines to the elephant-god Ganesh; little alcoves filled with candles, flowers and burning incense; here and there a wild-haired, spindly sadhu sits in repose by a tiny charcoal fire, knees brought up to his chin ...

Dozens of hotels, restaurants, cafés and shops cater to Western tastes and many travellers find it hard to drag themselves away from such creature comforts. The village's main bazar, though busy, has banned rickshaws so is relieved of revving engines and touting drivers. Take the short trek up to the Savitri Temple (3 km along a sandy track and jagged stone steps cut into the mountain), and you can swap village activity for open swathes of valley and fringes of desert beyond. From on high, the houses crowd the lake's edges as if it's a plug-hole down which all of Pushkar is slowly being drawn. Come the evening, groups of women promenade the bazars, the clashing colours of their saris all flowing together. Men dry their turbans in the evening sun after washing them in the lake, wafting the metres of filmy fabric in the breeze or draping it on nearby trees. Note that Pushkar is not to everybody's taste as there is a high hassle factor from cash-seeking ubiquitous Brahmin 'priests' requesting a donation receipt for the 'Pushkar Passport' (a red string tied around the wrist as part of a puja/blessing). After a two year lake cleaning project started in 2009, hopefully now the lake is healthy and thriving. ▸▸ *For listings, see pages 431-436.*

Ins and outs

Getting there Pushkar has relatively few direct buses, but Ajmer is well connected by bus and train to the main towns and cities. The station is in the centre, while the main bus stand is 2 km east. Buses to Pushkar leave from the State Bus Stand, and also from a general area 1 km northwest of the station, near the Jain temple. In Pushkar, most buses arrive at the Central

(Marwar) Bus Stand, to the usual gauntlet of touts; others pull in at a separate stand 10 minutes' walk east of the lake.

Getting around The main sights and congested bazars of Ajmer, which can be seen in a day at a pinch, are within 15 to 20 minutes' walk of the railway station but you'll need a rickshaw to get to Ana Sagar. Pushkar is small enough to explore on foot. Hire a bike to venture further. ▸▸ *See Transport, page 436.*

Tourist information In Ajmer, there are offices at the railway station and next to **Khadim Hotel** ⓘ *T0145-262 7426, tourismajmer@rediffmail.com, Mon-Sat 0800-1800, closed 2nd Sat of the month*. Both are very helpful. In Pushkar, at the **Sarovar Hotel** ⓘ *T0145-277 2040.*

Jaipur to Ajmer → *For listings, see pages 431-436.*

Sambhar Lake → *Colour map 2, A5.*

The salt lake, one of the largest of its kind in India, until recently attracted thousands of flamingos and an abundance of cranes, pelicans, ducks and other waterfowl; some 120 species of bird have been recorded. However, the poor monsoons of recent years have caused the lake to dry up leaving only a few marshy patches. Check the situation before visiting. Nilgai, fox and hare are spotted around the lake. The saline marshes are used for the production of salt. **Sakambari Temple**, nearby, dedicated to the ancestral deity of the Chauhans, is believed to date from the sixth century.

Kuchaman

Kuchaman is a large village with temples and relics. Many visitors stop here for tea and snacks between Shekhawati and Ajmer. If you do stop, make time for a visit to the fort; it is a unique experience. Before the eighth century, Kuchaman lay on the highly profitable Central Asian caravan route. Here Gurjar Pratiharas built the massive **cliff-top fort** with 10 gates leading up from the Meena bazar in the village to the royal living quarters. The Chauhans drove the Pratiharas out of the area and for some time it was ruled by the Gaurs. From 1400, it has been in the hands of the Rathores who embellished it with mirrors, mural and gold work in superb palaces and pavilions such as the golden Sunheri Burj and the mirrored Sheesh Mahal, both in sharp contrast to the fort's exterior austerity. The Sariska Palace Group have restored and renovated the fort at enormous cost. You can also visit the **Krishna temple** with a 2000-year-old image, and the **Kalimata ka Mandir** which has an eighth-century black stone deity and you can shop in the **Meena Bazar** or watch local village crafts people.

Kishangarh → *Colour map 2, A6. Population: 22,000.*

Enormous blocks of marble in raw, polished and sculpted forms line the road into Kishangarh, the former capital of a small princely state founded by Kishan Singh in 1603, with a fort facing Lake Gundalao. Local artists – known for their depiction of the Krishna legend and other Hindu themes – were given refuge here by the royal family during the reign of the Mughal emperor, Aurangzeb, who, turning his back on the liberal views of earlier emperors, pursued an increasingly zealous Islamic purity. Under their patronage the artists reached a high standard of excellence and they continue the tradition of painting Kishangarh miniatures which are noted for sharp facial features and elongated almond-shaped eyes. Most of those available are cheap copies on old paper using water colours instead of the mineral pigments of the originals. The town has a bustling charm, and is an interesting place to wander around.

The fort palace stands on the shores of Lake Gundalao. Its **Hathi Pol** (Elephant Gate) has walls decorated with fine murals and, though partly in ruins, you can see battlements, courtyards with gardens, shady balconies, brass doors and windows with coloured panes of glass. The temple has a fine collection of miniatures.

Roopangarh

About 20 km from Kishangarh, Roopangarh was an important fort of the Kishangarh rulers founded in AD 1649 on the old caravan route along the Sambhar Lake. The fort stands above the village which is a centre for craft industries – leather embroidery, block printing, pottery and handloom weaving can all be seen. The Sunday market features at least 100 cobblers making and repairing *mojdi* footwear.

Ajmer → *For listings, see pages 431-436. Colour map 2, B5. Phone code: 0145. Population: 490,000. Altitude: 486 m.*

The **Dargah of Khwaja Mu'inuddin Chishti** (1143-1235) is the tomb of the Sufi saint (also called 'The Sun of the Realm') which was begun by Iltutmish and completed by Humayun. Set in the heart of the old town, the main gate is reached on foot or by *tonga* or auto-rickshaw through the bazar. The Emperor Akbar first made a pilgrimage to the shrine to give thanks for conquering Chittor in 1567, and the second for the birth of his son Prince Salim. From 1570 to 1580 Akbar made almost annual pilgrimages to Ajmer on foot from Agra, and the *kos minars* (brick marking pillars at about two-mile intervals) along the road from Agra are witness of the popularity of the pilgrimage route. It is considered the second holiest site after Mecca. On their first visit, rich Muslims pay for a feast of rice, ghee, sugar, almonds, raisins and spices to be cooked in one of the huge pots in the courtyard inside the high gateway. These are still in regular use. On the right is the Akbar Masjid (circa 1570); to the left, an assembly hall for the poor. In the inner courtyard is the white marble Shah Jahan Masjid (circa 1650), 33 m long with 11 arches and a carved balustrade on three sides. In the inner court is the square *dargah* (tomb), also white marble, with a domed roof and two entrances. The ceiling is gold-embossed velvet, and silver rails and gates enclose the tomb. At festival times the tomb is packed with pilgrims, many coming from abroad, and the crush of people can be overpowering.

The whole complex has a unique atmosphere. The areas around the tomb have a real feeling of community; there is a hospital and a school on the grounds, as well as numerous shops. As you approach the tomb the feeling of religious fervour increases – as does the barrage of demands for 'donations' – often heightened by the music being played outside the tomb's ornate entrance. For many visitors, stepping into the tomb itself is the culmination of a lifetime's ambition, reflected in the ardour of their offerings.

Nearby is the **Mazar** (tomb) of Bibi Hafiz Jamal, daughter of the saint, a small enclosure with marble latticework. Close by is that of Chimni Begum, daughter of Shah Jahan. She never married, refusing to leave her father during the seven years he was held captive by Aurangzeb in Agra Fort. She spent her last days in Ajmer, as did another daughter who probably died of tuberculosis. At the south end of the Dargah is the **Jhalra** (tank).

The **Arhai-din-ka Jhonpra Mosque** ('Hut of Two and a Half Days') lies beyond the Dargah in a narrow valley. Originally a Jain college built in 1153, it was partially destroyed by Muhammad of Ghori in 1192, and in 1210 turned into a mosque by **Qutb-ud-din-Aibak** who built a massive screen of seven arches in front of the pillared halls, allegedly in 2½ days (hence its name). The temple pillars which were incorporated in the building are all different. The mosque measures 79 m by 17 m with 10 domes supported by 124 columns and incorporates Hindu and Jain masonry. Much of it is in ruins though restoration work was undertaken at the turn of the century; only part of the 67-m screen and the prayer hall remain.

Akbar's Palace, built in 1570 and restored in 1905, is in the city centre near the east wall. It is a large rectangular building with a fine gate. Today it houses the **Government Museum** ⓘ *Sat-Thu 1000-1630, Rs 3, no photography*, which has a dimly presented collection of fine sculpture from sixth to 17th centuries, paintings and old Rajput and Mughal armour and coins.

The ornate **Nasiyan Jain Temple (Red Temple)** ⓘ *Prithviraj Marg, 0800-1700, Rs 5*, has a remarkable museum alongside the Jain shrine, which itself is open only to Jains. It is well worth visiting. Ajmer has a large Jain population (about 25% of the city's total). The Shri Siddhkut Chaityalaya was founded in 1864 in honour of the first Jain Tirthankar, Rishabdeo, by a Jain diamond merchant, Raj Bahadur Seth Moolchand Nemichand Soni (hence its alternative name, the Soni temple). The opening was celebrated in 1895. Behind a wholly unimposing exterior, on its first floor the Svarna Nagari Hall houses an astonishing reconstruction of the Jain conception of the universe, with gold-plated replicas of every Jain shrine in India. Over 1000 kg of gold is estimated to have been used, and at one end of the gallery diamonds have been placed behind decorative coloured glass to give an appearance of backlighting. It took 20 people 30 years to build. The holy mountain, Sumeru, is at the centre of the continent, and around it are such holy sites as Ayodhya, the birthplace of the Tirthankar, recreated in gold plate, and a remarkable

Ajmer

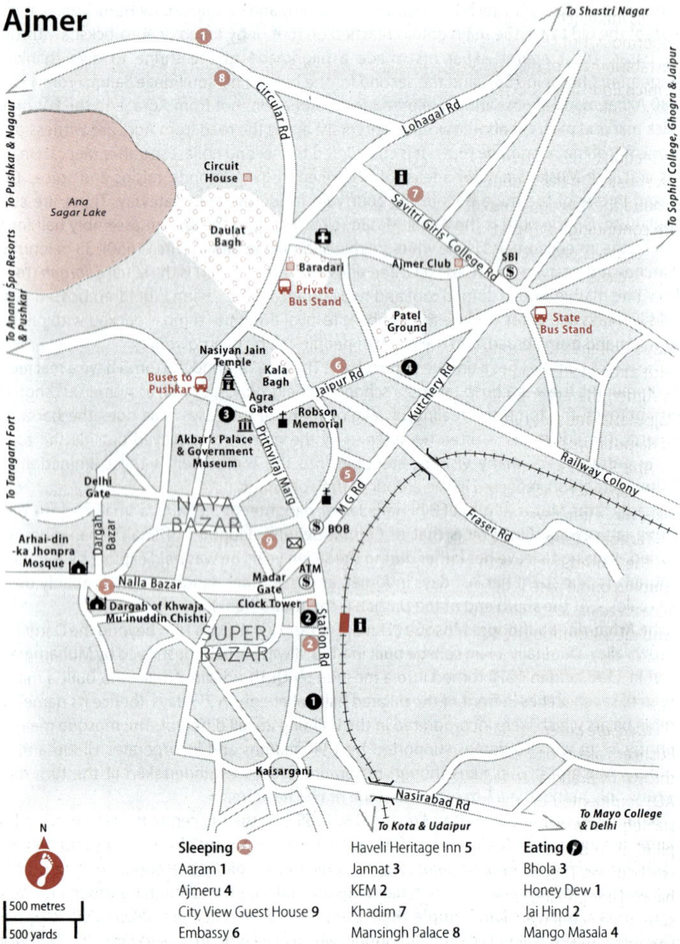

Sleeping
Aaram **1**
Ajmeru **4**
City View Guest House **9**
Embassy **6**
Haveli Heritage Inn **5**
Jannat **3**
KEM **2**
Khadim **7**
Mansingh Palace **8**

Eating
Bhola **3**
Honey Dew **1**
Jai Hind **2**
Mango Masala **4**

A saint of the people

Khwaja Mu'inuddin Chishti probably came to India before the Turkish conquests which brought Islam sweeping across Northern India. A sufi, unlike the Muslim invaders, he came in peace. He devoted his life to the poor people of Ajmer and its region. He was strongly influenced by the Upanishads; some reports claim that he married the daughter of a Hindu raja.

His influence during his lifetime was enormous, but continued through the establishment of the Chishti school or *silsila*, which flourished "because it produced respected spiritualists and propounded catholic doctrines". Hindus were attracted to the movement but did not have to renounce their faith, and Sufi khanqah (a form of hospice) were accessible to all.

Almost immediately after his death Khwaja Mu'innuddin Chishti's followers carried on his mission. The present structure was built by Ghiyasuddin Khalji of Malwa, but the embellishment of the shrine to its present ornate character is still seen as far less important than the spiritual nature of the Saint it commemorates.

collection of model temples. Suspended from the ceiling are *vimanas* (airships of the gods) and silver balls. On the ground floor, beneath the model, are the various items taken on procession around the town on the Jain festival day of 23 November each year. The trustees of the temple are continuing to maintain and embellish it.

From Station Road, a walk through the bazars, either to Dargah/Masjid area or to Akbar's Palace/Nasiyan Temple area, is interesting.

Excursions from Ajmer

Mayo College (1873), only 4 km from the centre, was founded to provide young Indian princes with a liberal education, one of two genuinely Indo-Saracenic buildings designed by De Fabeck in Ajmer, the other being the **Mayo Hospital** (1870). The college was known as the 'Eton of Rajputana' and was run along the lines of an English public school. Access is no longer restricted to Rajput princes.

Ana Sagar, an artificial lake (circa 1150), was further enhanced by emperors Jahangir and Shah Jahan who added the baradari and pavilions. The **Foy Sagar**, 5 km away, another artificial lake, was a famine relief project.

Taragarh (Star Fort), built by Ajaipal Chauhan in 1100 with massive 4.5-m-thick walls, stands on the hilltop overlooking the town. There are great views of the city but the walk up the winding bridle path is tiring. A road accessible by road has reduced the climb on foot and made access easier. Jeeps charge Rs 500 for the trip. Along the way is a graveyard of Muslim 'martyrs' who died storming the fort.

Pushkar

→ *For listings, see pages 431-436.* *Colour map 2, B5. Phone code: 0145. Population: 15,000.*

ⓘ *There are dozens of temples here, most of which are open 0500-1200, 1600-2200.*

Pushkar Lake is one of India's most sacred lakes. It is believed to mark the spot where a lotus thrown by Brahma landed. Fa Hien, the Chinese traveller who visited Pushkar in the fifth century AD, commented on the number of pilgrims, and although several of the older temples were subsequently destroyed by Aurangzeb, many remain. Ghats lead down to the water to enable pilgrims to bathe, cows to drink, and the town's young folk to wash off after the riotous Holi celebrations. They also provide a hunting ground for Brahmin 'priests', who press a flower into the hand of any passing foreigner and offer – even demand – to perform *puja* (worship) in return for a sum of money. If this hard-sell version of spirituality appeals, agree your price in advance – Rs 50 should be quite sufficient – and be aware that a proportion of so-called priests are no such thing.

The **Brahma temple** ⓘ *0600-1330, 1500-2100 (changes seasonally)*, beyond the western end of the lake, is a particularly holy shrine and draws pilgrims throughout the year. Although it isn't the only Brahma temple in India, as people claim, it is the only major pilgrim place for followers of the Hindu God of Creation. It is said that when Brahma needed a marital partner for a ritual, and his consort Saraswati (Savitri) took a long time to come, he married a cow-girl, Gayatri, after giving her the powers of a goddess (Gayatri because she was purified by the mouth of a cow or *gau*). His wife learnt of this and put a curse on him – that he would only be worshipped in Pushkar.

There are 52 ghats around the lake, of which the Brahma Ghat, Gan Ghat and Varah Ghat are the most sacred. The medieval **Varah Temple** is dedicated to the boar incarnation of Vishnu. It is said the idol was broken by Emperor Jahangir as it resembled a pig. The **Mahadev Temple** is said to date from 12th century while the **Julelal Temple** is modern and jazzy. Interestingly enough the two wives of Brahma have hilltop temples on either side of the lake, with the Brahma temple in the valley. A steep 3-km climb up the hill which leads to the **Savitri Temple** (dedicated to Brahma's first wife), offers excellent views of the town and surrounding desert.

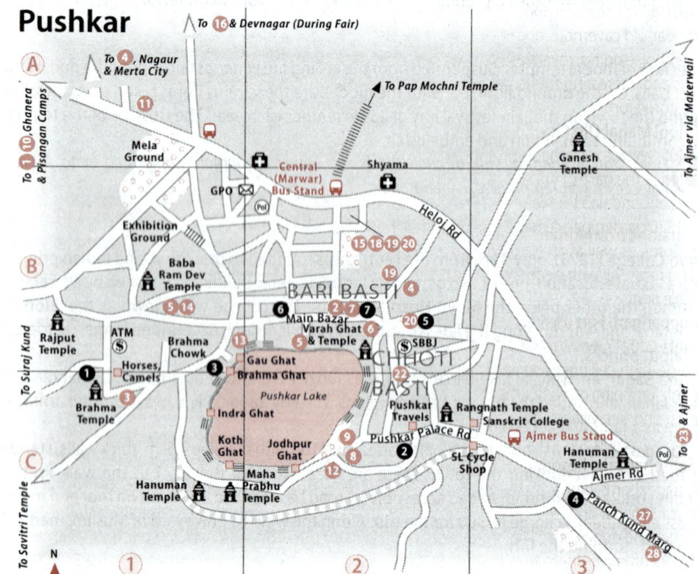

300 metres

300 yards

Sleeping
Bharatpur Palace **13** *B1*
Colonel's Camp **10** *A1*
Dia **28** *C3*
Greenhouse Resort **4** *A1*
Inn Seventh Heaven & Sixth Sense **4** *B2*
Jagat Palace **23** *C3*
JP's Tourist Village Resort **1** *A1*
Kanhaia **19** *B2*
Kohinoor **15** *B2*
Lake View **6** *B2*
Little Tibet **2** *B2*
Masters Paradise **28** *C3*
Milkman **18** *B2*
Navratan Palace **3** *C1*
Paramount Palace **5** *B1*
Payal Guest House **7** *B2*
Peacock International Camp Resort **16** *A1*
Pushkar Palace **9** *C2*
Raghav Resort **19** *B2*
Sai Baba Haveli **17** *B2*
Sarovar **12** *C2*
Shannu's Ranch & Horse Rides **27** *C3*
Shanti Palace **20** *B2*
Shiva Guesthouse **17** *B2*
Shyam Krishna Guest House **22** *B2*
Sunset & Sunset Café **8** *C2*
Tourist Village (RTDC) **11** *A1*
U-turn Guest House **14** *B1*
White House **20** *B2*

Eating
Halwai Ki Gali **6** *B2*
Honey & Spice Café **7** *B2*
Karmima **1** *C1*
La Pizzeria **5** *B2*
Little Italy Pizzeria **4** *C3*
Moondance **2** *C2*
Rainbow **3** *B1*

Ghat ≡

The **Main (Sadar) Bazar** is full of shops selling typical tourist, as well as pilgrim knick-knacks and is usually very busy. At full moon, noisy religious celebrations last all night so you may need your ear plugs here.

Ajmer and Pushkar listings

For Sleeping and Eating price codes and other relevant information, see Essentials pages 38-42.

Sleeping

Jaipur to Ajmer *p426*

AL-A Kuchaman Fort (Heritage Hotel), Kuchaman, T022-2404 2211, www.nivalink.com/kuchaman. 35 distinctive a/c rooms in a part of the fort, attractively furnished, restaurant, bar, jacuzzi, gym, luxurious pools (including a 200-year-old cavernous one underground), camel/horse riding, royal hospitality, superb views and interesting tour around the largely unrestored fort.

B Phool Mahal Old City, Kishangarh, T01463-247405, www.royalkishangarh.com. Superbly located at the base of Kishangarh Fort on the banks of Gundalao lake (dries up in summer), this 1870 garden palace has 21 well-maintained a/c rooms, as well as an elegant lounge and dining room, all with period furnishings and marble floors.

B Roopangarh Fort (Heritage Hotel), Roopangarh, T01497-220217, www.royalkishangarh.com. 20 large, high-ceilinged rooms, rich in character though furnishing can be a bit basic. Marwar decor and cuisine, free village safaris plus excursions, good sunrise and sunset views, friendly staff.

D Sambhar Lake Resorts, Sambhar Lake. 6 cottage rooms, bath with hot showers, friendly staff, camel rides and jeep safaris across the saline marshes and dunes, also short rail journey on diesel locomotive-driven trolleys that carry salt from the pans to the towns. Price includes meals and safaris. Day visit (Rs 500) includes vegetarian lunch, tea and a tour of the salt marshes.

Ajmer *p427, map p428*

Prices rise sharply, as much as 10 times, during the week of the **mela**. Many hotels are booked well in advance. The tourist office has a list of Paying Guest accommodation.

AL-A Mansingh Palace, Ana Sagar Circular Rd, T0145-242 5702, www.mansinghhotels.com. 54 rooms in attractive sandstone modern building, most comfortable in town. Pleasant restaurant, comfortable bar.

B-D Hotel Embassy, Jaipur Rd, T0145-262 3859, www.hotelembassyajmer.com. 31 smart a/c rooms in building newly renovated to 3-star standard. Enthusiastic, professional staff, elegant restaurant.

C-E Khadim (RTDC), Savitri Girls' College Rd, near bus station, T0145-262 7490. Pleasant setting 55 rooms, some a/c (**C** suites), best are the uncarpeted, renovated rooms, dorm (Rs 50), gloomy restaurant, bar, tourist information, car hire, usual RTDC service.

C-F Haveli Heritage Inn, Kutchery Rd, T0145-262 1607. 12 good-sized, clean, comfortable rooms in homely 125-year-old building, no hot water in cheaper rooms. Rooms are quite expensive for what you get. Family-run, good home cooking, located on busy main road but set back with a pleasant courtyard, very charming owner.

D-F Aaram, off Ana Sagar Circular Rd, opposite Mansingh, T0145-242 5250. 22 slightly grubby rooms, some a/c, restaurant, small garden, friendly manager.

D-F Hotel Ajmeru, Khailand Market, near Akbar Fort, T0145-243 1103, www.hotel ajmeru.com. 12 very clean, light, modern rooms, 8 a/c, in relatively quiet location.

E-F Hotel Jannat, very close to Durgah, T0145-243 2494, www.ajmerhoteljannat.com. 36 clean, modern rooms in great location, find yourself in labyrinthine alleys, friendly staff, a/c restaurant, all mod cons.

E-G KEM, Station Rd, T0145-242 9936. 45 rooms in period building near the railway station, 1st-class rooms are clean and acceptable, 2nd-class ones are less so. Service practically non-existent. Attached bath.

G City View Guest House, 133/17 Nalla Bazar, T0145-263 0958. Very basic but charmingly run guesthouse in warrens of the Old City, Indian toilets, atmospheric building, friendly hosts.

Northwest of Ajmer

There are 2 good options on the road towards Nagaur.

D Fort Khejarla, Khejarla, T02930-258311, madhoniwas@satyam.net.in. A Rajput Special Hotels. Simple rooms in the old part the fort, meals (Rs 180), excursions to Raika and Bishnoi tribal villages. Contact Curvet India, Delhi, T011-2684 0037.

D Raj Palace Motel, Merta Rd, T01590-220202. 25 clean rooms with bath, 6 a/c, friendly family. Recommended.

Pushkar *p429, map p430*

The town suffers from early-morning temple bells. During the fair, hotel charges can be 10 times the normal rate. Booking in advance is essential for the better places. Some budget hotels offer views of the lake from communal rooftops; however, local authorities periodically threaten to close down all commercial properties within 100 m of the lake, including hotels and restaurants. To escape the noise of the Main Bazar, choose one in a back street of Bari Basti or near Ajmer Bus Stand.

L-A Ananta Spa and Resorts, Ajmer Rd, 4 km from Pushkar, www.anantaindia.in, T0800-309 3901. Certainly not to be confused with the Ananda Spa near Rishikesh, this is a lovely crafted resort but as yet not so focused on the spa facilities. Great view of the hills around, nice rooms with all mod cons away from the bustle of Pushkar and Ajmer.

L-A Greenhouse Resort, Tilora village, 8 km from Pushkar, www.thegreenhouseresort.com, T0145-230 0079. This is a truly unique place with luxurious tents mixed with giant greenhouses growing roses and strawberries and lots of organic vegetables for the kitchen. With a nod to the environment, they are experimenting with water conservation, innovative irrigation and solar panels and the resort is staffed mainly with local people. The beds are stunning and there are all mod cons in the tents. This is a serene place, relaxing and inspiring. Recommended.

L-A Pushkar Palace (WelcomHeritage), on lakeside, T0145-277 2001, www.hotelpushkar palace.com. 52 overpriced rooms including 25 suites overlooking the lake, in beautifully renovated old palace, attractive gardens. It looks good but is rather uncomfortable and lakeside rooms have very small windows. Alas, too the terrace restaurant is now closed, so the restaurant is in the courtyard with no lake view.

A Jagat Palace (WelcomHeritage), Ajmer Rd, T0145-277 2953, www.jagatpalace.co.in. Rooms of various sizes in new building made to resemble a Rajput fort, colourful, naturally lit interiors, beautiful pool and gardens, a bit lacking in atmosphere.

B Dia, Panch Kund Rd, T0145-510 5455, www.inn-seventh-heaven.com/dia. Fantastic big rooms in new chic building. Offering just 4 stylish a/c rooms and plenty of open spaces to curl up with a book or look out at Pushkar and the surrounding hills, this is in a quiet part of town away from the bustle. Highly recommended.

B-C Master Paradise, Panch Kund Rd, T0145-277 3933, www.pushkarmasterparadise.com. Spacious modern rooms, some suites, slightly extravagant decor, pool is the highlight.

C-E JP's Tourist Village Resort, Ganhera, 2 km from town, T0145-277 2067, www.pushkarhotel booking.com. 30 very rustic, basic rooms built in traditional style with mud walls, quirky feel, great gardens with dusty pool, outside town so a popular retreat for those seeking non-vegetarian food and a tipple.

C-F Inn Seventh Heaven, next to Mali ka Mandir, T0145-510 5455, www.inn-seventh-heaven.com. Beautiful rooms spiral out from the inner courtyard in this fantastically well-restored 100-year-old *haveli*, plus a handful of ascetic but much cheaper rooms in neighbouring building. Lots of seating areas dotted throughout the 3-storey building, even some lovely swinging diwans. Very friendly, informal, excellent rooftop restaurant (baked potatoes from open coal fire in winter), charming owner and a sociable atmosphere. Exceptionally good value. Whole-heartedly recommended.

D-E U-Turn, Lake Vahara Ghat Choti Basti, T(0)992-873 7798. A new chic little number right on the lake. The rooms are small due to the age of the building, but with bags of charm. Formerly the **Bhola Guest House**, the 2nd oldest guest house in Pushkar. Of the 6 beautifully decorated rooms, you can choose from the 'Princess Villa' or the 'Kama Sutra Villa'. The rooftop café is also a cut above, with nice fabrics and comfy chairs and serves up the usual global fare.

D-E Navratan Palace, near Brahma temple, T0145-277 2145. Comfortable though not particularly attractive. 33 clean rooms, some a/c with hot showers (Rs 300-600), clean pool, small garden with views, well kept.

D-E Sarovar (RTDC), on lakeside, T0145-277 2040. 38 clean rooms (best with amazing lake view, in old part), some a/c with bath, new rooms good but no atmosphere, cheap 6-bed dorm, set around courtyard in former lakeside palace, indifferent vegetarian restaurant, attractive gardens.

D-F Sunset, on the lake, T0145-277 2382, hotelsunset@hotmail.com. 20 plain, clean rooms, 3 a/c, around a lovely garden, lots of flowers and papaya trees. Well located close to lake, plus access to **Sunset Café**.

E-G Paramount Palace, Bari Basti, T0145-277 2428, hotelparamountpalace@ hotmail.com. 16 clean, basic rooms, some with bath, best with balcony, elevated site with splendid views from rooftop, highest in Pushkar. Very friendly host.

F-G Bharatpur Palace, lakeside, T0145-277 2320. Exceptional views of the ghats, 1 very simple room practically hangs over the ghat, 18 unusually decorated rooms, clean bathrooms.

F-G Kanhaia, near Mali Mandir, T0145-277 2146. Friendly staff, good value, 14 small rooms with more coming, recently renovated, best has sofa, with good bathrooms.

F-G Lake View, lakefront, Sadar Bazar, T0145-277 2106. Basic rooms some with shared bath, but great views and relaxed atmosphere perched right on the lake. Restaurant serves up the usual fare, but lovely view.

F-G Milkman, near White House, T0145-277 3452. Mostly cheap and basic rooms, some bigger.

F-G Payal Guest House, opposite Municipality, Sadar Bazar, T0145-277 2163. Pushkar standard room fare but with great view from rooftop and great Tibetan restaurant in the courtyard.

F-G Raghav Resort, Panday Nursery Farm, T0145-277 2207, www.lakeviewpushkar.com. 14 reasonable rooms surrounded by beautiful nursery gardens, attractive outdoor restaurant, a peaceful retreat.

F-G Sai Baba Haveli, near market post office, T0145-510 5161, lola_singh_modiano@ hotmail.com. Nice big rooms around a central courtyard, lots of greenery and hanging plants, lots of potential but needs a lick of paint.

F-G Shannu's Ranch, Panch Kund Rd, T0145-277 2043. On the edge of town, with nice quirky, 'rustique' cottages in a garden, owned by French-Canadian riding instructor, good for a longer stay but could get cold in winter.

G Shanti Palace, near Varah temple, T(0)9414-415351, shantipalace@hotmail.com. 12 basic rooms in very peaceful surroundings, plus a friendly owner and good views of town.

G Shiva Guest house, near market post office, T0145-277 2120. Basic but clean rooms in calm environment enhanced by free-range tortoises in central courtyard, 7 of them at last count

G Shyam Krishna Guest House, Chhoti Basti, T0145-277 2461. Part of 200-year-old temple complex with 25 rooms around a courtyard, some with *jali* work on upper floor, run by friendly Brahmin family.

G White House, in narrow alley near Marwar Bus Stand, T0145-277 2147, hotelwhitehouse@ hotmail.com. Very clean, impressively white rooms in well- maintained building overlooking nursery gardens. Good views from pleasant rooftop restaurant with excellent food, free and very tasty mango tea. Also nice cheaper rooms available at their sister guesthouse, **Kohinoor**. Recommended.

During the fair

It is best to visit early in the week when toilets are still reasonably clean.

Tourist village Erected by **RTDC**, this is a remarkable feat, accommodating 100,000 people. Conveniently placed with deluxe/ super deluxe tents (Rs 6000-6500 with meals), ordinary/dorm tents (Rs 300 per bed), 30 'cottages', some deluxe (Rs 4000-5000). Beds and blankets, some running water, Indian toilets are standard. Meals are served in a separate tent (or eat cheap, delicious local food at the tribal tented villages near the show ground). Reservation with payment, essential (open 12 months ahead); contact **RTDC** in Jaipur, T0141-220 3531, www.rajasthantourism.gov.in.

Private camps Privately run camps charge about US$150-250 including meals for Regular and 'Swiss' double tent. They might be some distance from fair ground and may lack security: **Colonel's Camp**, Motisar Rd, Ghanera, T0141-220 2034, www.meghniwas.com. 120 deluxe tents with toilet and shower in attractive gardens.

Peacock International Camp Resort, at Devnagar (2 km from Mela Ground), T0145-277 2689. Common facilities for the 25 tents among orchards with pool, free transport.
Pushkar Palace (see page 432). Sets up 50 'Swiss' tents and 50 deluxe.
Royal Tents Camp, www.welcomheritage.com, T0291-257 2321. Comfortable tents with veranda, flush toilet, hot water in buckets or shower of sorts, Rajasthani cuisine, very well organized.
Wanderlust Desert Camp, T011-2467 9059, www.wanderlustindia.cim. 120 Swiss tents with bath, electricity, varied meals.

Eating

Ajmer *p427, map p428*

Son halwa, a local sweet speciality, is sold near the Dargah and at the market. Delicious street snacks can be found in the back lanes between Delhi and Agra gates.
TTT **Mansingh Palace**, Ana Sagar Circular Rd. International. Pricey, unexciting food, popular with meat-seeking Pushkaris.
TT **Mango Masala**, Sandar Patel Marg, T0145-242 2100. American diner-styled place with wide-ranging menu including pizzas, sizzlers, Indian and sundaes. Standard is high, portions large and service outstanding.
TT **Silver Leaf, Hotel Embassy** (see Sleeping). Good range of multi-cuisine choices in sophisticated surroundings.
T **Bhola**, Agra Gate. Good vegetarian food, no nonsense service.
T **Honey Dew**, Station Rd. Indian, continental. Pleasant shady garden, good Indian snacks all day, disappointing Western.
T **Jai Hind**, in alley by clock tower, opposite railway station. Best for Indian vegetarian. Delicious, cheap meals.
T **Madeen**, opposite station. Simple but tasty.

Pushkar *p429, map p430*

No meat, fish or eggs are served in this temple town, and alcohol is banned, as are 'narcotics' – in theory. Take special care during the fair: eat only freshly cooked food and drink bottled water. Long-stay budget travellers have resulted in an increase of Western and Israeli favourites like falafel, granola and apple pie, while Nepali and Tibetan immigrants have brought their own specialities. Roadside vendors offer cheap, filling *thalis* close to Ajmer Bus Stand.
TT **Little Italy Pizzeria**, Panch Kund Rd. High-quality Italian dishes plus Israeli and Indian specialities, pleasant garden setting. They have opened another restaurant **La Pizzeria** near Varah Temple and **Shanti Palace** (see Sleeping), Chhoti Basti.
TT **Moondance**, just by the turning to **Pushkar Palace**. Western food. Highly rated café run by friendly Nepalese, popular and occasionally slow, but the food hits the mark.
TT **Sixth Sense**, perched at the top of **Inn at Seventh Heaven** (see Sleeping) this is by far the most stylish dining experience in Pushkar. Serving up the usual Indian fare and beyond, with baked potatoes, pastas and fantastic home-baked desserts. Highly recommended.
T **Halwai ki gali** (alley off Main Bazar). Sweet shops sell *malpura* (syrupy pancake), as well as other Rajasthani/Bengali sweets.
T **Honey and Spice**, Laxmi Market. Only open during the day, this little café offers up great coffees like aniseed and cinnamon, renowned banana bread and steaming plates of brown rice and veggies.
T **Karmima**, and other small places opposite Ashish-Manish Riding. Home-cooked *thalis* (Rs 15/20) and excellent fresh, orange/sweet lime juice.
T **Little Tibet Garden Restaurant**, Sadar Bazar, **Payal Guest House** (see Sleeping). Very good Tibetan food and a bit of everything else. Pretty courtyard restaurant. Very popular. Recommended.
T **Rainbow**, near Brahma Ghat. Wide choice (pizzas, jacket potatoes, enchiladas, humous, falafel, Indian dishes), tasty muesli, fruit crumble with choc sauce and ice cream, long climb but good lake view.
T **Sunset Café** by **Pushkar Palace**. Particularly atmospheric in the evening when crowds gather to listen to music and watch sunset, lacklustre food. Recommended for ambience.

Festivals and events

Ajmer *p427, map p428*

Urs Festival, commemorating Khwaja Mu'inuddin Chishti's death in 1235, is celebrated with 6 days of almost continuous music, and devotees from all over India and the Middle East

The pull of the cattle and camels

The huge **Mela** is Pushkar's biggest draw. Over 200,000 visitors and pilgrims and hordes of cattle and camels with their semi-nomadic tribal drivers, crowd into the town. Farmers, breeders and camel traders buy and sell. Sales in leather whips, shoes, embroidered animal covers soar while women bargain over clay pots, bangles, necklaces and printed cloth.

Events begin four to five days before the full moon in November. There are horse and camel races and betting is heavy. In the **Ladhu Umt** race teams of up to 10 men cling to camels, and one another, in a hilarious and often chaotic spectacle. The Tug-of-War between Rajasthanis and foreigners is usually won by the local favourites. There are also sideshows with jugglers, acrobats, magicians and folk dancers. At nightfall there is music and dancing outside the tents, around friendly fires – an unforgettable experience despite its increasingly touristy nature, even including a laser show. The cattle trading itself actually takes place during the week before the fair; some travellers have reported arriving during the fair and there being no animals left.

make the pilgrimage. Qawwalis and other Urdu music developed in the courts of rulers can be heard. Roses cover the tomb. The festival starts on sighting the new moon in Rajab, the 7th month of the Islamic year. The peak is reached on the night between the 5th and 6th days when tends of thousands of pilgrims pack the shrine. At 1100 on the last morning, pilgrims and visitors are banned from the dargah, as the khadims, who are responsible through the year for the maintenance of worship at the shrine, dressed in their best clothes, approach the shrine with flowers and sweets. On the final day, women wash the tomb with their hair, then squeeze the rose water into bottles as medicine for the sick.

Pushkar *p429, map p430*

Oct/Nov Kartik Purnima is marked by a vast **cattle and camel fair** (28 Nov 2012, 17 Nov 2013, 6 Nov 2014), see box, above. Pilgrims bathe in the lake – the night of the full moon being the most auspicious time – and float 'boats' of marigold and rose petals in the moonlight. Camel traders often arrive a few days early to engage in the serious business of buying and selling and most of the animals disappear before the official starting date. Arrive 3 days ahead if you don't want to miss this part of the fair. The all-night drumming and singing in the Mela Ground can get tiring, but the fair is a unique spectacle. Travellers warn of pickpockets.

O Shopping

Ajmer *p427, map p428*

Fine local silver jewellery, tie-dye textiles and camel hide articles are best buys. The shopping areas are Madar Gate, Station Rd, Purani Mandi, Naya Bazar and Kaisarganj. Some alleys in the old town have good shopping.

Pushkar *p429, map p430*

There is plenty to attract the Western eye; check quality and bargain hard. Miniatures on silk and old paper are everywhere. Cheap clothes, baba pants and bags are aplenty here. Most interesting are:

Manu Maloo Antiques and Collectibles, Badi Basti (sweet street) take street opposite Gau Ghat past the array of bubbling sweet stalls and you will discover a little hole-in-the-wall shop with a great range of framed pictures and all manner of wooden and bronze objets. Bargain hard, they are interesting but not hugely valuable.

Also a cut above the other numerous tailors are:

Essar, shop 6, Sadar Bazar, opposite Narad Kunj. Excellent tailoring (jacket Rs 250-300 including fabric).

Harish, Brahma Temple Rd. For lightweight *razai* quilts, bedsheets, cloth bags.

JP Dhabai's, opposite Shiva Cloth Store near **Payal Guest House**, Main Bazar. Offers fine quality (painted with a single squirrel hair!) miniatures at a price. Recommended.

Activities and tours

Pushkar *p429, map p430*

Horse and camel safaris

Hiring a horse costs Rs 1500 per day, camels around Rs 400 per day, at most hotels and near the Brahma temple. **Ashish-Manish**, opposite Brahma Temple, T0145-277 2584, or **Shannu's Riding School**, owned by a French Canadian, Panch Kund Rd, T0145-277 2043. For lessons, Rs 150 per hr (minimum 10 hrs over 5 days).

Body and Soul

Pushkar Yoga Garden, Vamdev Rd, near Gurudwara, www.pushkaryoga.org. Regular hatha classes with Yogesh Yogi and also longer courses. **Shakti School of Dance**, Old Rangi Temple Complex, near Honey and Spice, www.colleenashakti.com. You can learn traditional Odissi style dance, tribal fusion belly dance and local Khalbelia Rajasthani gypsy dance.

Swimming

Sarovar, **Oasis**, **Navratan** hotels, non-residents pay Rs 40-50.

Tour operators

Ekta Travels, opp Marwar Bus Stand, T0145-277 2131, www.ektatravelspushkar.com. Tours, excellent service, good buses, reliable.

Transport

Jaipur to Ajmer *p426*

Train and jeep For **Sambhar Lake** take the train to **Phulera**, 7 km from Sambhar village, 9 km from the lake. Jeeps charge Rs 50 for the transfer.

Kishangarh is an important railway junction between Jaipur and Ajmer, with regular trains from both places.

Ajmer *p427, map p428*

Bus The **State Bus Stand** is 2 km east of centre, enquiries T0145-242 9398. Buses to **Agra**, 9 hrs; **Delhi**, 9 hrs; **Jaipur**, 2½ hrs; **Jodhpur**, 5 hrs; **Bikaner**, 7 hrs; **Chittaurgarh**, 5 hrs; **Udaipur**, 7 hrs via Chittaurgarh; **Kota** via Bundi; **Pushkar**, 45 mins, frequent. Private buses for **Pushkar** leave from near the Jain Temple.

Train Ajmer Station is seemingly overrun with rats and is not a great place to wait for a night train. Taxis outside the station charge Rs 200-250 to **Pushkar**.

Reservations, T0145-243 2535, 0830-1330, 1400-1630, enquiries, T131/132. **Ahmedabad**: *Aravali Exp 19708*, 1125, 11½ hrs; *Ahmedabad Mail 19106*, 0740, 10 hrs; *Ashram Exp 12916*, 2320, 8½ hrs. **Jaipur**: *Ajmer Jaipur Exp 19652*, 0640, 3 hrs. *Aravali Exp 19707*, 1733, 2½ hrs; *Shatabdi Exp 12016*, 1530, not Sun, 2 hrs. **Delhi** (all via **Jaipur**): *Ahmedabad Delhi Mail 19105*, 2028, 9 hrs; *Shatabdi Exp 12016* not Sun, 1550, 6½ hrs; (**OD**) *Ashram Exp 12915*, 0155, 8 hrs.

Pushkar *p429, map p430*

Bicycle/car/motorbike hire Rs 10 entry 'tax' per vehicle. **Michael Cycle SL Cycles**, Ajmer Bus Stand Rd, very helpful, Rs 30 per day; also from the market. **Hotel Oasis** has Vespa scooters, Rs 300 per day. **Enfield Ashram**, near Hotel Oasis, Rs 400 per day for an Enfield.

Bus Frequent service to/from **Ajmer**, Rs 10. Long-distance buses are more frequent from Ajmer, and tickets bought in Pushkar may involve a change. Direct buses to **Jaipur**, **Jodhpur** via Merta (8 hrs), **Bikaner**, and **Haridwar**. Sleeper bus to **Delhi**, Rs 250, 1930 (11 hrs); **Agra**, Rs 250, 1930 (11 hrs); **Jaisalmer** Rs 450, 2200 (11 hrs), **Udaipur**, Rs 250, 2200 (8 hrs) and 2300 (8 hrs). Many agents in Pushkar have times displayed. **Pushkar Travels**, T0145-277 2437, reliable for bookings.

Directory

Ajmer *p427, map p428*

Banks ATMs are on Station Rd but can run out on weekends. **Bank of Baroda**, opposite GPO, accepts Visa, MasterCard; **State Bank of India** near bus stand, changes cash, TCs. Government-approved money changers in Kavandas Pura main market.

Pushkar *p429, map p430*

Banks ATM near Brahma temple, accepts some overseas cards. **SBBJ** changes TCs; **Hotels Peacock** and **Oasis** offer exchange for a small commission. **Internet** All over town, Rs 30-40. Inn **Seventh Heaven** rooftop café for wireless. **Medical services** Shyama Hospital, Heloj Rd, T0145-277 2029. **Post** One at the Chowk with a very helpful postmaster, east end of Main Bazar.

Northern Rajasthan

This is one of the less-visited regions of Rajasthan, but is well worth passing through on your way to the better-known areas. Bikaner, perhaps the least touristy big city in Rajasthan, has until now been somewhat overshadowed by the state's other cities, but is gaining popularity both as an interesting city, and as a place to go for a camel safari – as scenic as Jaisalmer but far less commercial. Even further off the beaten track, desert villages such as Kakoo offer an accessible insight into rural desert life, while wildlife enthusiasts will find plenty of interest in Gajner National Park and Tal Chappar Wildlife Sanctuary.

Shekhawati has its own quirky charm; still largely undeveloped, its outdoor treasures sit as silent testimony to an illustrious past, strangely at odds with the day-to-day bustle on their doorsteps. The region's boom days, when the indigenous Marwari businessmen were trading with the four corners of the globe, constantly vying to outdo each other in the elaborateness of their haveli *homes, are long gone. Marwari traders still enjoy a reputation as astute businessmen, but today operate in India's major business centres – many of their* havelis *having fallen into disrepair, yet still intact enough to give a fascinating glimpse of a time gone by.*

Bikaner and around

Bikaner is something of a dusty oasis town among the scrub and sand dunes of northwest Rajasthan. Its rocky outcrops in a barren landscape provide a dramatic setting for the Junagarh Fort, one of the finest in western Rajasthan. The old walled city retains a medieval air, and is home to over 300 havelis, while outside the walls some stunning palaces survive. Well off the usual tourist trail, Bikaner is en route to Jaisalmer from Jaipur or Shekhawati, and is well worth a visit. ▸▸ *For listings, see pages 441-444.*

Ins and outs → *Phone code: 0151. Population: 530,000.*

Getting there Bikaner is a full day's drive from Jaipur so it may be worth stopping a night in Samode or the Shekhawati region (see pages 342 and 445). The railway station is central and has services from Delhi (Sarai Rohilla), Jaipur and Jodhpur. The New Bus Stand is 3 km to the north, so if arriving from the south you can ask to be dropped in town. There are regular bus services to Desnok, but to get to Gajner, Kakoo or Tal Chappar you'll need to hire private transport. ▸▸ *See Transport, page 444.*

Getting around The fort and the Old City are within easy walking distance from the station. Auto- and cycle rickshaws transfer passengers between the station and the New Bus Stand. Taxis can be difficult to get from the Lalgarh Palace area at night.

Tourist information Dhola-Maru Tourist Bungalow ⓘ *Poonam Singh Circle, T0151-252 9621, Oct-Mar 0800-1800*. As well as information, car hire is available.

Bikaner → *For listings, see pages 441-444. Colour map 2, A4.*

Junagarh Fort

ⓘ *1000-1630 (last entry), Rs 100 foreigners, Rs 10 Indians; camera Rs 30, video Rs 100 (limited permission), guided tours in Hindi and English, private guides near the gate offer better 'in- depth' tours; Rs 100 for 4 people, 2 hrs.*

This is one of the finest examples in Rajasthan of the paradox between medieval military architecture and beautiful interior decoration. Started in 1588 by Raja Rai Singh (1571-1611), a strong ally of the Mughal Empire, who led Akbar's army in numerous battles, it had palaces added for the next three centuries.

You enter the superbly preserved fort by the yellow sandstone **Suraj Prole** (Sun Gate, 1593) to the east. The pale red sandstone perimeter wall is surrounded by a moat (the lake no longer exists) while the Chowks have beautifully designed palaces with balconies, kiosks and fine *jali* screens. The interiors are beautifully decorated with shell-work, lime plaster, mirror-and-glass inlays, gold leaf, carving, carpets and lacquer work. The ramparts offer good views of the elephant and horse stables and temples, the old city with the desert beyond, and the relatively more recent city areas around the medieval walls. The walls of the **Lal Niwas**, which are the oldest, are elaborately decorated in red and gold. Karan Singh commemorated a victory over Aurangzeb by building the **Karan Mahal** (1631-1639) across the Chowk. Successive rulers added the **Gaj Mandir** (1745-1787) with its mirrored Shish Mahal, and the **Chattra Niwas** (1872-1887) with its pitched roof and English 'field sport' plates decorating the walls. The magnificent **Coronation Hall**, adorned with plaster work, lacquer, mirror and glass, is in Maharaja Surat Singh's **Anup Mahal** (1788-1828). The decorative façades around the Anup Mahal Chowk, though painted white, are in fact of stone. The fort also includes the **Chetar**

Bikaner

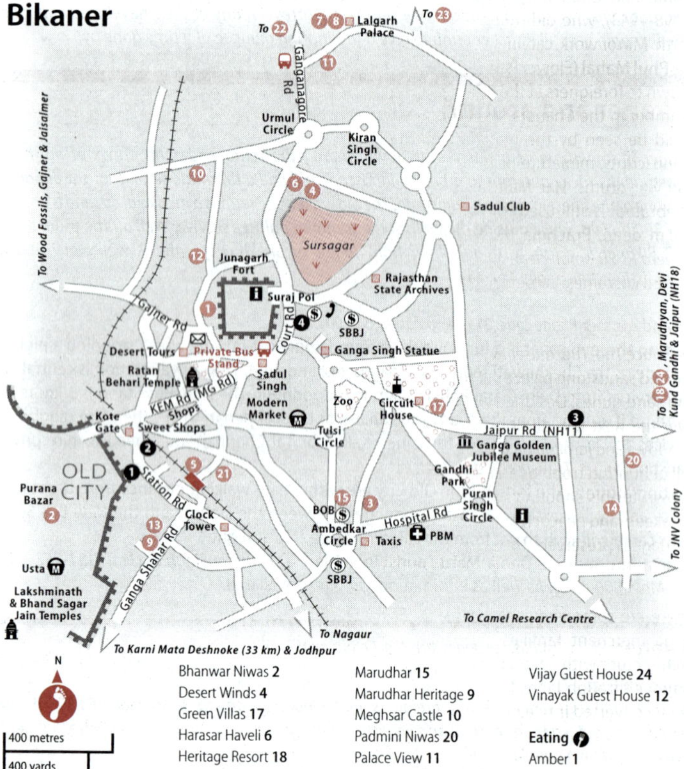

Sleeping

Basant Vihar Palace **22**
Bhairon Vilas **1**
Bhanwar Niwas **2**
Desert Winds **4**
Green Villas **17**
Harasar Haveli **6**
Heritage Resort **18**
Jaswant Bhawan **21**
Karni Bhawan Palace **23**
Lallgarh Palace **7**
Laxmi Niwas **8**
Marudhar **15**
Marudhar Heritage **9**
Meghsar Castle **10**
Padmini Niwas **20**
Palace View **11**
Railway Retiring Rooms **5**
Regent **3**
Sri Ram **14**
Suraj **13**
Vijay Guest House **24**
Vinayak Guest House **12**

Eating

Amber **1**
Gallops **4**
Kesria **3**
Lalji **2**

Life after the rains

When in Bikaner, drop in at URMUL's showroom, **Abhiviyakyi**, opposite the New Bus Stand. A fair trade NGO, URMUL works with the marginalised tribespeople of the Thar Desert. The droughts of the 1980s made farming, the traditional source of livelihood for the majority of these people, no longer a viable option. URMUL was formed in 1991 with the aim to teach people new skills which could bring them the income that the absent rains had taken away. As the range of products on offer testifies, the project has been a huge success. All the items on sale, including clothing, tablecloths, bed linen, shoes and bags, have been made by the project's participants, and are of a quality previously unseen in the often all-too-amateur 'craft' sector. Visit the shop before agreeing to go with rickshaw drivers or touts to a 'URMUL' village; scams are not unknown.

Mahal and **Chini Burj** of Dungar Singh (1872-1887) and **Ganga Niwas** of Ganga Singh (1898-1943), who did much to modernize his state and also built the Lalgarh Palace to the north. Mirror work, carving and marble decorate the ornate **Chandra Mahal** (Moon Palace) and the **Phul Mahal** (Flower Palace), built by Maharaja Gaj Singh. These last two, the best rooms, are shown to foreigners at the end as a 'special tour' when the guide expects an extra tip. The royal chamber in the Chandra Mahal has strategically placed mirrors so that any intruder entering could be seen by the maharaja from his bed. The fort **museum** has Sanskrit and Persian manuscripts, miniature paintings, jewels, enamelware, silver, weapons, palanquins, howdahs and war drums. **Har Mandir**, the royal temple where birth and wedding ceremonies were celebrated, is still used for Gangaur and other festivities. The well nearby is reputedly over 130 m deep. **Prachina Museum** ⓘ *1000-1700, foreigners Rs 50 (guided tour), Indians Rs10, camera Rs 20, small clean café outside is open-air but shady*, in the grounds, exhibits beautifully crafted costumes, carpets and ornamental objects.

Lalgarh Palace

ⓘ *Palace Thu-Tue, museum Mon-Sat 1000-1700, Rs 40 (museum extra Rs 20).*

The red sandstone palace stands in huge grounds to the north of the city, surrounded by rocks and sand dunes. Designed by Sir Swinton Jacob in 1902, the palace complex, with extensions over the next few decades, has attractive courtyards overlooked by intricate *zenana* screen windows and *jarokha* balconies, columned corridors and period furnishings. The banquet hall is full of hunting trophies and photographs. His Highness Doctor Karni Singh of Bikaner was well known for his shooting expertise – both with a camera and with a gun. The bougainvillea, parakeets and peacocks add to the attraction of the gardens in which the Bikaner State Railway Carriage is preserved. The Lalgarh complex has several hotels (see Sleeping, page 441).

Rampuria Street and the Purana Bazar

There are some exquisite *havelis* in Bikaner belonging to the Rampuria, Kothari, Vaid and Daga merchant families. The sandstone carvings combine traditional Rajasthani *haveli* architecture with colonial influence. Around Rampuria Street and the Purana Bazar you can wander through lanes lined with fine façades. Among them is **Bhanwar Niwas** which has been converted into a heritage hotel.

Ganga Golden Jubilee Museum

ⓘ *Public Park, 1000-1630, Rs 3.*

This museum has a fine small collection of pottery, massive paintings, stuffed tigers, carpets, costumes and weapons. There are also some excellent examples of Bikaner miniature paintings which are specially prized because of their very fine quality.

Around Bikaner → *For listings, see pages 441-444.*

Bhand Sagar

ⓘ *Free but caretakers may charge Rs 10 for cameras.*

Some 5 km southwest of Bikaner, Bhand Sagar has a group of Hindu and Jain temples which are believed to be the oldest extant structures of Bikaner, dating from the days when it was just a desert trading outpost of Jodhpur. The white-painted sandstone **Bandeshwar Temple** with a towering *shikhara* roof and painted sculptures, murals and mirrorwork inside, is the most interesting. The **Sandeshwar Temple**, dedicated to Neminath, has gold-leaf painting, *meenakari* work and marble sculptures. They are hard to find and difficult to approach by car but rickshaw wallahs know the way. There are numerous steps but wonderful views.

Camel Research Centre

ⓘ *10 km from Bikaner in Jorbeer, 1500-1730, foreigners Rs 50, Indians Rs 5, camera Rs 20.*

This 800-ha facility is dedicated to scientific research into various aspects of the camel, with the aim of producing disease-resistant animals that can walk further and carry more while consuming less water. As well as genetically increasing the camel's tolerances, researchers are investigating the nutritional benefits of drinking camel milk; camel ice cream is for sale if you want to test for yourself – and coming soon are camel milk moisturizers! It's particularly worth being here between 1530 and 1600, when the camels return to the centre for the evening: the spectacle of 100 or more camels ambling out of the desert towards you is quite unforgettable.

On the way to the Camel Research Centre, you will find the **Museum of Turbans and Cooking Utensils** ⓘ *near Shiv Bari Temple, Camel Farm Rd, T(0)9829-867323*, run by a French NGO. This quirky museum contains traditional musical instruments, cooking utensils and turbans for every occasion – you can even learn to tie one.

Gajner National Park → *Colour map 2, A3.*

Now part of a palace hotel, this park, 30 km west of Bikaner, used to be a private preserve which provided the royal family of Bikaner with game. It is a birder's paradise surrounded by 13,000 ha of scrub forest which also harbours large colonies of nilgai, chinkara, blackbuck, wild boar and desert reptiles. Throughout the day, a train of antelope, gazelle and pigs can be seen arriving to drink at the lake. Winter migratory birds include the Imperial black-bellied sand grouse, cranes and migratory ducks. Some visitors have spotted great Indian bustard at the water's edge. It is worth stopping for an hour's mini-safari if you are in the vicinity.

Kolayat → *Colour map 2, A3.*

Some 50 km southwest via Gajner road, Kolayat is regarded as one of the 58 most important Hindu pilgrimage centres. It is situated around a sacred lake with 52 ghats and a group of five temples built by Ganga Singhji (none of which is architecturally significant). The oasis village comes alive at the November full moon when a three-day festival draws thousands of pilgrims who take part in ritual bathing.

Karni Mata Mandir

ⓘ *Closed 1200-1600, free, camera Rs 40.*

This 17th-century temple, 33 km south of Bikaner at Deshnoke, has massive silver gates and beautiful white marble carvings on the façade. These were added by Ganga Singh (1898-1943) who dedicated the temple to a 15th-century female mystic Karniji, worshipped as an incarnation of Durga. A gallery describes her life. Mice and rats, revered and fed with sweets and milk in the belief that they are reincarnated saints, swarm over the temple around your feet; spotting the white rat is supposed to bring good luck. Take socks as the floor is dirty, but note that the rats are far less widespread than they are made out to be. Sensationalised accounts give the impression of a sea of rats through which the visitor is obliged to walk barefoot, whereas in reality, while there are a good number of rats, they generally scurry around the outskirts of the temple courtyard – you're very unlikely to tread on one. The temple itself is beautiful, and would be well worth visiting even without the novelty of the rats.

Kakoo → *Colour map 2, A3.*

This picturesque village, 75 km south of Bikaner, with attractive huts and surrounded by sand dunes, is the starting point for desert camel safaris costing Rs 1500 per day with tented facilities. Staying here makes a fantastic introduction to the practicalities of life in the desert; this is probably the most authentic desert settlement in this area that can be easily reached by road. Good trips to Kakoo are organized by Mr Bhagwan Singh T(0)9829-218237, www.kakusafari.com. You can travel to Kakoo by bus changing at Nokhamandi (62 km) from Bikaner.

Kalibangan and Harappan sites → *Colour map 1, C1.*

One of North India's most important early settlement regions stretches from the Shimla hills down past the important Harappan sites of **Hanumangarh** and **Kalibangan**, north of Bikaner. Late Harappan sites have been explored by archaeologists, notably A Ghosh, since 1962. They were identified in the upper part of the valley, the easternmost region of the Indus Valley civilization. Across the border in Pakistan are the premier sites of Harappa (200 km) and Moenjo Daro (450 km). Here, the most impressive of the sites today is that of Kalibangan (west off the NH15 at Suratgarh). On the south bank of the Ghaggar River it was a heavily fortified citadel mound, rising about 10 m above the level of the plain. There were several pre-Harappan phases. Allchin and Allchin record that the bricks of the early phase were already standardized, though not to the same size as later Harappan bricks. The ramparts were made of mud brick and a range of pottery and ornaments have been found. The early pottery is especially interesting, predominantly red or pink with black painting.

Bikaner and around listings

For Sleeping and Eating price codes and other relevant information, see Essentials pages 38-42.

Sleeping

Bikaner *p437, map p438*

Budget hotel rooms usually have shared bath; often serve Indian vegetarian food only. The tourist office has a list of Paying Guest hotels.

LL-AL Laxmi Niwas, Lalgarh Palace Complex, T0151-2252 1188, www.laxminiwaspalace.com. 60 large rooms and suites which once formed Maharaja Ganga Singh's personal residence, with fabulous carvings and beautifully painted ceilings, all arranged around the stunningly ornate courtyard. Superb bar, restaurant and lounge, discreet but attentive service, absolutely one-off. Recommended. You can also pay Rs 100 to have a tour if you are not staying here.

AL-A Bhanwar Niwas, Rampuria St, Old City (500 m from Kote Gate), ask for Rampuria Haveli, T0151-252 9323, www.bhanwarniwas.com. 26 beautifully decorated rooms (all different) around a fantastic courtyard in an exquisite early 20th-century *haveli*. Original decor has been painstakingly restored to stunning effect, takes you back to another era, great service. Recommended.

AL-A Karni Bhawan Palace (HRH), Gandhi Colony behind Lalgarh Palace, T0151-252 4701, www.hrhindia.com. 12 comfortable a/c rooms and spacious suites in original art deco mansion. Elegant furniture, modern fittings, fantastic artwork, good restaurant, large garden, peaceful, attentive service, feels like the original inhabitants have just stepped out for a while.

AL-B Lallgarh Palace, 3 km from the railway, T0151-254 0201, www.lallgarhpalace.com. Large a/c rooms in beautiful and authentic surroundings (see page 439), indoor pool needs some attention, atmospheric dining hall, mixed reports on food and service unfortunately.

A Heritage Resort, along the Jaipur highway, '9 km' post, T0151-275 2393, www.carnival hotels.com. 36 modern, well-appointed cottage rooms in a pleasant location. Attractive gardens, outdoor coffee shop, pool, 3-hole golf course, friendly.

C Basant Vihar Palace, Ganganagar Rd, T0151-225 0675, www.basantviharpalace.com. Rooms in attractive early 20th-century palatial sandstone mansion built by Maharajah Ganga Singhji albeit a little faded today, magnificent darbar hall, pool, large gardens, old lily ponds.

C-D Bhairon Vilas, near fort, T0151-254 4751, www.hotelbhaironvilas.com. Restored 1800s aristocratic *haveli*, great atmosphere, 18 eclectic rooms decorated with flair – you can spend hours simply exploring the antiquities in your own room, excellent rooftop restaurant (musicians, dancers), great views across the city and fort and funky boutique shop. Kitsch chic, whole-heartedly recommended.

C-D Palace View, near Lalgarh Palace, T0151-2543625. 15 clean, comfortable rooms (some a/c), good views of palace and gardens, food to order, small garden, courteous, hospitable family.

C-E Meghsar Castle, 9 Gajner Rd, T0151-252 7315, www.hotelmeghsarcastle.com. 16 air-cooled rooms in modern hotel built in traditional Rajput sandstone style, some bigger family rooms, attractive garden, friendly manager and Dalmatian.

C-F Harasar Haveli, opposite Karni Singh Stadium, T0151-220 9891, www.harasar.com. Notorious for paying hefty commissions to rickshaw drivers; often full when others empty. Otherwise nice enough; rooms in converted mansion, some with verandas and good views, TVs, dining room with period memorabilia, plus great rooftop restaurant, garden, internet, clean, friendly.

D-E Desert Winds, opposite Karni Stadium, next to **Harasar Haveli**, T0151-254 2202. www.hoteldesertwinds.in. 22 clean, comfortable rooms with TV, good food, pleasant balcony and garden, friendly family. Run by knowledgable ex-tourist officer.

D-E Jaswant Bhawan, Alakh Sagar Rd, near railway station, T(0)9829-436491, jaswant bhawan@yahoo.co.in.15 rooms in a charming old building, quiet location, restaurant, lawn, good value. Recommended.

D-F Marudhar Heritage, Bhagwan Mahaveer Marg, near Station Rd, T0151-252 2524, hmheritage20000@yahoo.co.in. 27 variable rooms, air-cooled or a/c, bath with hot showers (am), TV, clean and comfortable, generous *thalis* (Rs 50), friendly owner.

D-F Sri Ram, A-228, Sadul Ganj, T0151-252 2651, www.hotelshriram.com. A hotel, guest-house and youth hostel in one. 20 rooms, all clean and well-maintained, some a/c, run by a knowledgeable, entertaining ex-army man and family, free pickups. More rooms being built. Recommended.

E Marudhar, Ambedkar Circle, T0151-220 2444, www.hotelmarudhar.com. 26 clean, well maintained rooms, 9 a/c, friendly staff. Better than **Thar** and **Ashoka** next door.

E Padmini Niwas, 148 Sadul Ganj, T0151-252 2794, www.hotelpadmininiwas.com. Clean, basic, comfy rooms (some a/c) in laid-back bungalow in quiet location, only outdoor pool in town, pleasant lawn, includes 1 hr free internet, free pickup. Recommended.

E-F Hotel Regent, Sadul Colony, near PBM Hospital, T0151-254 1598, bituharisingh@ yahoo.com. 11 modern, clean, comfortable rooms, 4 a/c, in quiet area. Excellent home-cooked meals, owner Hari is a most hospitable and knowledgeable host, good value, recommended. Camel safaris also arranged.

E-F Suraj Hotel, near railway station, Rani Bazar, T(0)9414-142174, surajhotel@vsnl.com. 20 rooms in modern building, well run, slightly shabby but good value. Attached vegetarian restaurant recommended.

F Railway Retiring Rooms and dorm are good value.

F-G Green Villas, behind **Raj Vilas**, T0151-252 1877. A friendly homestay with 3 simple, clean rooms, home-cooked meals great value.

F-G Vijay Guest House, opposite Sophia School, Jaipur Rd, T0151-223 1244, www.camelman.com. 6 clean rooms with attached bathrooms, plus 2 with common bath. Slightly distant location compensated for by free use of bicycles or scooter, free pickups from bus/train, Rs 5 in shared rickshaw to town. Delicious home-cooked meals, pleasant garden, quiet, very hospitable (free tea and rum plus evening parties on lawn), knowledgeable host, great value. Good camel safaris. Recommended.

F-G Vinayak Guest House, near Junagarh fort, Hanuman Temple, Old Ginani, T0151-220 2634, vinayakguesthouse@gmail.com. Friendly homestay run by manager of URMUL shop and his wildlife expert son who cannot do enough for you, excellent home cooking and cooking lessons, also runs camel safaris, photography classes, village and wildlife tours. Highly recommended.

Around Bikaner *p440*

L-A Gajner Palace, Gajner National Park, T01534-275061, www.hrhindia.com. 44 a/c rooms in the elegant palace and its wings, set by a beautiful lake. Rooms in main building full of character (Edwardian Raj nostalgia), those in wings well maintained but very middle England. Sumptuous lounge bar and restaurant overlooking lake, magnificent gardens, boating, good walking, pleasantly unfrequented and atmospheric, friendly manager and staff, no pool. Visitors are welcome 0800-1730, Rs 100.

E Dr Karni Singh's Rest House, adjoining the home of his forefathers, Kakoo, T01532-253006. Resthouse with 6 simple rooms and 4 rustic huts with attached baths, hot water in buckets, a great experience. Good camel safaris arranged, with the advantage of getting straight in to the desert rather than having to get out of town first as in Jaisalmer/Bikaner.

F Yatri Niwas, near Karni Mata Mandir. Simple rooms.

Eating

Bikaner *p437, map p438*

You can dine in style at several of the hotels. Try the local specialities – *Bikaneri bhujia/sev/ namkeen* – savoury snacks made from dough. Purana Bazar sells ice-cold *lassis* by day, hot milk, sugar and cream at night.

🍴🍴 **Amber**, Station Rd. Indian, some Western dishes. Popular, vegetarian *thali* is exceptional but some reports of falling standards.

🍴🍴 **Bhairon Vilas** (see Sleeping). Breezy rooftop for Rajasthani meals, atmospheric, order ahead. Come here to eat even if you don't stay here – special place.

🍴🍴 **Bhanwar Niwas** (see Sleeping). Amazingly ornate dining hall, good way of having a look around if you're not staying there.

🍴🍴 **Gallops**, Court Rd. Excellent views of the fort, but overpriced and disappointing food but good for a rest after exploring the fort.

🍴🍴 **Kesria**, Jaipur Rd. Pleasant countryside location, popular on breezy summer evenings but disappointing food.

🍴🍴 **Padmini Niwas** (see Sleeping). An average hotel restaurant, but eating here buys you the right to use the swimming pool.

🍴 **Lalji**, Station Rd near **Evergreen**. Popular local joint serving good dosas and sweets.

🍴 **Vijay Guest House** (see Sleeping). Delicious home-cooked vegetarian *thalis*, non-vegetarian set menu (Rs 60-100).

Festivals and events

Bikaner *p437, map p438*

Both the following are especially spectacular in Junagarh Fort in the Old City near Kote Gate and some smaller palaces.

Oct/Nov Diwali.

Dec/Jan Camel Fair (26-27 Jan 2013, 15-16 Jan 2014)

Around Bikaner *p440*

Oct/Nov In Kolayat, the **Cattle and Camel Fair** (26-27 Jan 2013, 15-16 Jan 2014) is very colourful and authentic but it can get quite riotous after dark. Since facilities are minimal, it is best to arrive before the festival to find a local family with space to spare, or ask a travel agent in Bikaner.

Shopping

Bikaner *p437, map p438*

Bikaner is famous for *Usta* work including footwear, purses and cushions. Local carpets and woodwork available too. Main shopping centres are on KEM (MG) Rd and around Kote Gate in the Old City, Modern Market.

Abhivyakti, URMUL Desert Craft, Sri Ganga nagar Rd, next to New Bus Stand, T0151-252 2139. Run by **URMUL** trust, see box, page 439.

Kalakar Arts, Sardar Hall, Lalgarh Palace Rd, T0151-220 4477. Good selection of silver jewellery and other artefacts.

Activities and tours

Bikaner *p437, map p438*

Camel safaris must be arranged through private operators. Budget tours (Rs 500-600 per day) for groups of 4 or more; bring water.

Aravalli Tours, opposite Municipal Council Hall, Junagarh Rd, T0151-220 1124. Rs 1800 per person (toilet tent shared between 10 people) for upmarket experience. Other tours too.

Camel Man, **Vijay Guest House**, Jaipur Rd, T0151-223 1244, www.camelman.com. Good value, reliable, friendly and professional safaris, jeep tours, cycling. Lightweight 'igloo' tents, clean mattresses, sheets, good food and guidance. Safaris to see antelopes, colourful villages and potters at work; from 1- to 2-hr rides to 5-day trips; Rs 800-1000 per person per day.

Thar Desert Safari, Ganganagar Rd, behind New Bus Stand, T0151-252 1661, www.thardesert safari.com. Honest, unpretentious outfit offering simple, no frills camel tours.

Vinayak Desert Safari, T(0)9414-430948, vinayakguesthouse@gmail.com. Eco-friendly camel trekking with Jitu Solanki who has a Masters degree in wildlife and specializes in the study of reptiles. Offer camel, jeep and wildlife safaris and village homestays. Highly informed and friendly guide.

Vino Desert Safari, Gangashahar, T0151-227 0445, www.vinodesertsafari.com. Good-value low-key safaris, including some longer distance 'inter-city' treks, eg 12-day Bikaner–Osian.

Transport

Bikaner *p437, map p438*

Bus The New Bus Stand is 3 km north of town. Private buses leave from south of the fort. **Rajasthan Roadways**, enquiries, T0151-252 3800; daily deluxe buses to **Ajmer**, **Jodhpur**, **Jaisalmer** (8 hrs), **Udaipur**. 2 daily to **Delhi** via Hissar (12 hrs).

Rickshaw/taxi Autos between station and bus stand or Lalgarh Palace, Rs 25. Taxis are unmetered. Shared *tempos* run on set routes, Rs 5.

Train Enquiries, T0151-220 0131, reservations, Mon-Sat 0800-1400, 1415-2000, Sun 0800- 1400. For tourist quota (when trains are full) apply to Manager's Office by Radio Tower near **Jaswant Bhawan Hotel**. There are 2 direct trains to **Delhi**: *Assam Awadh Express 15610*, 2000 (12 hrs) arrives Old Delhi station; *Sampark Kranti Express 12464*, 1720 (12 hrs Tue, Thu, Sat) or take a train to Rewari and change. **Rewari**: *Link Exp 14710*, 1750, 8 hrs; *Rewari Mail 14792*, 1955, 8 hrs; *Rewari Exp 14790*, 0835, 8½ hrs. **Jaipur**: *Intercity Exp 12467*, 0500, 6½ hrs. **Jodhpur**: *Ranakpur Exp 14707*, 0945, 5½ hrs, continues to **Ahmedabad**, 16 hrs, and **Mumbai** (Bandra), 27 hrs.

Around Bikaner *p440*

Bus For **Karni Mata Mandir**, buses leave from Bikaner New Bus Stand, Rs 15, or on Ganga Shahar Rd and at Ambedkar Circle. Taxis charge around Rs 300 return. For **Kalibangan** catch a bus to **Suratgarh** then change; this junction town also has connections to Hanumangarh, Sirsa (Haryana) or Mandi Dabwali (Punjab).

Train The broad-gauge train line from Suratgarh to **Anupgarh**, about 15 km from the Pakistan border, calls at Raghunathgarh, the closest station to Kalibangan; travel from there to Kalibangan is difficult (check at Suratgarh). Trains from Suratgarh: **Anupgarh**: *Passenger*, *10755*, 2¼ hrs. **Bikaner** (Lalgarh Junction): *Chandigarh Exp 14887*, 0835, 3¼ hrs. **Bhat- inda**: *Chandigarh Exp 14888*, 1955, 3¼ hrs.

Directory

Bikaner *p437, map p438*

Banks **Bank of Baroda**, Ambedkar Circle, cash against Visa; **State Bank of Bikaner & Jaipur**, Ambedkar Circle; also near fort's Suraj Pol. Changes TCs but may charge up to 10% commission. **Harasar Haveli Hotel** charges 1%. **Internet** **Meghsar Castle**, **Hotel Sagar** and **Harasar Haveli**, Rs 2 per min; others at Sadulganj, Sagar Rd, Jaipur Rd and near the fort. **Medical services** PBM Hospital, Hospital Rd, T0151-252 5312. **Post** GPO: behind Junagarh Fort. **Useful contacts** Police: T100/T0151-252 2225.

Shekhawati

Covering an area of about 300 sq km on the often arid and rock-studded plains to the northwest of the Aravalli mountain range, Shekhawati is the homeland of the Marwari community. The area is particularly rich in painted havelis; Sikar district in the southwest and Jhunjhunun in the northeast form an 'open-air art gallery' of paintings dating from the mid-19th century. Although a day trip gives you an idea of its treasures, it is better to spend two or three nights in Shekhawati to see the temples, frescoed forts, chhatris and step wells at leisure. There are other diversions laid on such as horse or camel safaris and treks into the hills. Shekhawati sees far fewer visitors than the better-known areas of Rajasthan, and as such retains something of a 'one pen/rupee' attitude to tourists. This is generally quite innocent and should not be a deterrent to potential visitors.

Ramgarh has the highest concentration of painted havelis, though they are not as well maintained as those of Nawalgarh which has the second largest selection. It is easier to visit havelis in towns that have hotels, such as Nawalgarh, Mandawa, Dundlod, Mukundgarh, Mahansar, Fatehpur, Baggar and Jhunjunun, and where the caretakers are used to visitors, though towns like Bissau, Alsisar, Malsisar and Churu have attractive havelis as well. ▸▸ *For listings, see pages 449-452.*

Ins and outs

Getting there You can get to the principal Shekhawati towns by train but road access is easier. A car comes in handy, though there are crowded buses from Delhi, Jaipur and Bikaner to some towns. Buses leave every 30 minutes from 0500-2000 from Jaipur's Main Bus Station and take three hours. ▸▸ *See Transport, page 451.*

Getting around You can get from one Shekhawati town to another by local bus, which run every 15 to 20 minutes. Within each town it is best to enlist the help of a local person (possibly from the hotels listed below) to direct you to the best *havelis*, as it can be very difficult to find your way around.

The *havelis* are often occupied by the family or retainers who will happily show you around, either for free or for a fee of about Rs 20. Many *havelis* are in a poor state of repair with fading paintings which may appear monotonously alike to some.

Tourist information RTDC ⓘ *Mandawa Circle, Jhunjhunun, T01592-232909*. Recommended reading includes *The painted towns of Shekhawati*, by Ilay Cooper, a great Shekhawati enthusiast, with photos and maps.

History

The 'Garden of Shekha' was named after Rao Shekhaji of Amarsar (1433-1488) who challenged the Kachhawahas, refusing to pay tribute to the rulers at Amber. These Rajput barons made inroads into Muslim territory even during Mughal rule, and declared Shekhawati independent from the Jaipur suzerainty until 1738. During this period the merchants lavishly decorated their houses with paintings on religious, folk and historical themes. As Mughal power collapsed Shekhawati became a region of lawless banditry. In the early 19th century the British East India Company brought it under their control, bringing peace but also imposing taxes and tolls on trade which the Marwaris resented. Many of the merchants migrated to other parts of the country to seek their fortune and those who flourished returned their wealth to their homeland and took over as patrons of the arts.

Sikar District → *For listings, see pages 449-452. Colour map 2, A5.*

Sikar

The late 17th-century fort was built when Sikar was an important trading centre and the wealthiest *thikana* (feudatory) under Jaipur. It now has a population of 148,000. You can visit the old quarter and see the Wedgwood blue 'Biyani' (1920) and 'Mahal' (1845), Murarka and Somani *havelis* and murals and carvings in Gopinath, Raghunath and Madan Mohan temples. From Jaipur take the NH11 to Ringas (63 km) and Sikar (48 km).

Laksmangarh

Founded early 19th century, the town plan was based on Jaipur's model; this can be seen by climbing up to the imposing old fort which has now been renovated by the Jhunjhunwala family. The fine *havelis* include one of the area's grandest – Ganeriwala with *char chowks* (four courtyards). Others include the 'Rathi' *haveli* near the clock tower in the market, and several in the Chowkhani.

Pachar

This is a little town west of Jaipur in the middle of the sand dunes with a golden sandstone castle scenically situated on a lakeshore. A road north from Bagru on the NH8 also gives access.

Ramgarh

Ramgarh was settled by the Poddars in the late 18th century. In addition to their many *havelis* and that of the Ruias, visit the *chhatris* with painted entrances near the bus stand, as well as the temples to Shani (with mirror decoration) and to Ganga. Ramgarh has the highest concentration of painted *havelis*, though they are not as well maintained as those of Nawalgarh which has the second largest assemblage. The town has a pleasantly laid-back feel. Look for handicrafts here.

Fatehpur

Fatehpur has a whole array of *havelis*, many are rather dishevelled. Fatehpur is worth a visit simply for the **Nadine Le Prince Haveli Cultural Centre**, near Chauhan Well, www.cultural-centre.com, T0157-123 1479. Following a visit to the area, Nadine Le Prince took it upon herself to safeguard the cultural heritage of Fatehpur and the restoration of this *haveli* is exceptional. The frescoes here are exquisite and have served as an inspiration to Nadine's own artwork. As well as the restored *haveli*, there is a fine art gallery, sculpture garden and tribal art gallery and she hopes to create an artistic exchange between local and international artists. Although there are a couple of lacklustre accommodation options in Fatehpur, it would be better to visit from Mandawa.

Danta

Originally a part of Marwar, Danta was given to Thakur Amar Singhji in the mid-17th century. It is well off the beaten track and as such is completely unspoilt. Two empty *kilas* (forts) and the residential wing (early 18th-century) combine Mughal and Rajput art and architectural styles.

Jhunjhunun District → *For listings, see pages 449-452. Colour map 2, A5.*

Jhunjhunun

A stronghold of the Kayamkhani Nawabs, Jhunjhunun was defeated by the Hindu Sardul Singh in 1730. The Mohanlal **Iswardas Modi** (1896), **Tibriwala** (1883) and the Muslim **Nuruddin Farooqi Haveli** (which is devoid of figures) and the *maqbara* are all worth seeing. The *Chhe* Haveli complex, Khetri Mahal (1760) and the Biharilal temple (1776), which has attractive

Fit for a merchant

The *havelis* in Shekhawati were usually built around two courtyards – one for general use, and the other a *zenana* courtyard for the women. The latter was also used for laundry and so often had a well and occasionally a play area for children. Security was a prime concern so a *haveli* was typically entered by a solid gate with a smaller door in it for regular use by residents. Watchmen had rooms on either side of the entrance. The *baithak* (reception room) had mattresses and bolsters for sitting on the floor while others were set aside for sleeping or storage. The *havelis* were enlarged as the families grew larger or wealthier, and with the onset of peaceful times, they became more palatial and lavished with decoration.

The *haveli* was made from brick or local stone. It was plastered in two layers with decorations on the second layer – a polished lime plaster finish often set with agate and other semi-precious stones. Murals were either painted on dry surfaces or on wet plaster. Mineral colours were derived from indigo, ochre, lead, copper, lapis lazuli, lime and even gold. Synthetic blue was imported and only the wealthiest could afford strong blue tones on their *havelis*. Some of the finest frescoes were near the door separating the courtyard from the main chambers and these were often restored or repainted during weddings and festivals. The subject of the paintings varied. The 10 avatars of Vishnu were popular, especially scenes from *Krishna Lila* and the *Ramayana*. The *Mahabharata*, the *Ragamala* (depicting musical modes of different seasons), folk tales, historic events, daily life in Shekhawati and floral and faunal themes were also popular, and there was a fascination for portraying the British and their curious ways.

frescoes (closed during lunch time), are also interesting. The **Rani Sati** temple commemorates Narayana Devi who is believed to have become a *sati*; her stone is venerated by many of the wealthy *bania* community and an annual Marwari fair is held (protesting women's groups feel it glorifies the practice of *sati*). Since 1947, 29 cases of *sati* have been recorded in Jhunjhunun and its two neighbouring districts. Jhunjhunun is the most bustling town in Shekhawati and serves as the district's headquarters – it is preferable to stay in Nawalgarh or Mandawa.

Mukundgarh

The market for textiles and brass betel cutters, Mukundgarh lies 10 km south of Jhunjhunun. The Ganeriwala *havelis* (1860s and 1870s) are worth visiting as well as the Jhunjhunwala (1859) *haveli* with Krishna stories and Sukhdev *haveli* (circa 1880).

Nawalgarh

Some 25 km southeast of Mandawa, Nawalgarh was founded in 1737 by Thakur Nawal Singh. There are numerous fine *havelis* worth visiting here. The town has a colourful bazar - though lone tourists have been harassed here – and two forts (circa 1730). **Nawalgarh fort** has fine examples of maps and plans of Shekhawati and Jaipur. The **Bala Kila**, which has a kiosk with beautiful ceiling paintings, is approached via the fruit market in the town centre and entered through the **Hotel Radha**. It also has the **Roop Niwas Palace** (now a hotel) and some 18th-century temples with 19th- and early 20th-century paintings. There are other interesting temples in town including Ganga Mai near Nansa Gate.

The **Anandilal Poddar Haveli**, now converted to the **Poddar Haveli Museum** ⓘ *foreigners Rs 100, includes camera and guide*, is perhaps the best restored *haveli* of Shekhawati. The 1920s *haveli* has around 700 frescoes including a Gangaur procession, scenes from the Mahabharata, trains, cars, the avatars of Vishnu, bathing scenes and British characters. Exceptionally well restored throughout, some of the best paintings frame the doors leading from the courtyard to the rooms. The upper storey of the *haveli* is now a school but the ground floor has been opened as a museum. The photo-gallery records the life of congressman and freedom fighter Anandilal Poddar, and the merchant-turned- industrialist Poddar family. There is a diorama of costumes of various Rajasthani tribes and communities, special bridal attires and a gallery of musical instruments.

Other remarkable Murarka *havelis* include the 19th-century **Kesardev Murarka**, which has a finely painted façade and the early 20th-century **Radheshyam Murarka**. The latter portrays processions, scenes from folk tales and various Hindu and Christian religious themes, sometimes interspersed with mirror-work. Other fine *havelis* are those of the Bhagat, Chokhani, Goenka, Patodia, Kedwal, Sangerneria, Saraogi, Jhunjhunwala, Saha and Chhauchuria families. The paintings here depict anything from European women having a bath to Hindu religious themes and Jesus Christ. Some of the *havelis* are complexes of several buildings which include a temple, dharamshala, cenotaph and a well). Most charge Rs 15-20 for viewing.

Mandawa

Similar to Nawalgarh, Mandawa has a high density of *havelis* in its pleasant streets and is one of the preferred places to stay in the area with plenty of characterful accommodation. Even the State Bank of Bikaner and Jaipur is an old *haveli*.

Parasarampura

About 12 km southeast of Nawalgarh, Parasarampura has a decorated *chhatri* to Sardul Singh (1750) and the adjacent **Gopinath** temple (1742); these are the earliest examples of Shekhawati frescoes painted with natural pigments (the caretaker has the keys, and will point things out with a peacock feather).

Dundlod

West of Nawalgarh, the best of Dundlod's murals are in the **castle** (1750) ⓘ *Darbar Hall, Rs 20 for non-residents*, now a poorly run heritage hotel. At the time of writing, Dundlod Castle was seriously unloved and badly looked after. Make a detour here only if you are a real mural enthusiast. The **Goenk** *haveli* near the fort has three painted courtyards, and the **Satyanarayan temple** has religious paintings but both these may be closed in the low season. The interesting deep step well now has an electric pump. The **Polo Centre** provides an opportunity to see camel, horse and bicycle polo, tent pegging, etc. Mukundgarh is the nearest station, from where you can take a jeep or taxi.

Baggar

The grand *haveli* of the **Makharias**, 10 km north east of Jhunjhunun, has rooms along open corridors around grassy courtyards; worth seeing if only for the wall paintings of gods and angels being transported in motor cars.

Mahansar

Founded in the mid-18th century, Mahansar, 30 km northeast of Jhunjhunun, has a distinctly medieval feel. It has the Poddar *haveli* of **Son Chand**, the **Rama Temple** (ask for the key to the Golden Room; expensive at Rs 100 but very well preserved) and the large **Raghunath Temple** with some of the finest paintings of the region. The fort (1768) has palaces and a *baradari* which were added later.

Churu

Set in semi-desert countryside, Churu, northwest of Baggar, was believed to have been a Jat stronghold in the 16th century. In the 18th century it was an important town of Bikaner state and its fort dates from this period. The town thrived during the days of overland desert trade.

The town has some interesting 1870s Oswal Jain *havelis* like those of the Kotharis and the Suranas. Also worth a look are the **Banthia** (early 20th century), **Bagla** (1880), **Khemka** (1800s), **Poddar** and **Bajranglal Mantri** *havelis*. The main attraction, however, is the extraordinary **'Malji-ka-Kamra'**, a crumbling, colonnaded *haveli* which houses some amazing interior scenes.

Tal Chappar

A possible day excursion from one of the castle hotels is a visit to **Tal Chappar Wildlife Sanctuary** near Sujjangarh covering 71 sq km of desert scrubland with ponds and salt flats. It has some of the largest herds of Blackbuck antelope in India (easily seen at the watering point near the park gate itself during the dry season), besides chinkara gazelle, desert cat, desert fox and other dryland wildlife. Huge flocks of demoiselle and common cranes can be seen at nearby lakes and wetlands during the winter months (September to March) where they feed on tubers and ground vegetation. Some 175 different species of bird visit the park over the course of a year, including sandgrouse, quails, bar-headed geese and cream-coloured desert courser.

Ins and outs The best time to visit is just after the rainy season, generally August and September. The enthusiastic and charming forest guard, Brij Dansamor, is a good guide to the area. A local NGO, **Krishna Mirg**, is active in tree plantation and in fundraising for the eco-development of Tal Chappar, providing support fodder during dry months to blackbuck and cranes. **Forest Department Rest House** has five basic but adequate rooms at Rs 300 per double. To book ahead call the head office in Churu on T01562-250938. Try **Hanuman** tea stall for delicious *chai* and the local sweet, *malai laddoo*. the drive to Tal Chappar can be long and tiring. If you are travelling between Bikaner and Shekhawati in a jeep, it is worth making a detour.

Shekhawati listings

For Sleeping and Eating price codes and other relevant information, see Essentials pages 38-42.

Sleeping

Sikar District *p446*

B-C Ashirwad Palace, Churu Bypass, NH11, 2 km from Fatehpur, T01571-222635. 12 basic rooms around a small lawn, quite overpriced. If you want to visit Fatehpur, better to do as a day-trip from Mandawa.

B-C Castle Pachar, Pachar, T0141-222 6920 (Jaipur office) www.castlepachar.com. 16 well-decorated rooms in a fascinating old property with portraits, paintings and weaponry, delicious if very rich food, charming hosts, swimming pool under construction. Recommended.

C Dera, off the high street, Danta, T01577-270 041. Open 1 Oct-31 Mar. 14 large, characterful rooms in residential wing below the 2 old forts, good restaurant (meals Rs 160), peacocks at dawn, camel rides (Rs 350 per hr, Rs 6050 for 3 hrs), horse safaris, jeep safaris (minimum 4 people), Rs 1400 each per day.

D-E Hotel Niros, Station Rd, Sikar, T01572-241 0060. An upmarket establishment with 31 rooms including an a/c restaurant boasting some unusual water features.

D-F Hotel Haveli (RTDC), Sikar Rd, 500 m south of bus stand, Fatehpur, T01571-230293. Typical RTDC fare with clean rooms, some a/c with bath, pleasant building, dull restaurant, best bet in town.

F Aravalli Resort, NH11, Sikar. Simple and shabby with 2 air-cooled rooms with bath, inexpensive Indian restaurant.

Jhunjhunun District *p446*

AL-A Castle Mandawa, Mandawa, T0141-237 1194 (Jaipur office), www.mandawahotels.com. Huge castle with lots of character 68 a/c rooms, some in tower, complete with swing, most with 4-posters and period trappings but rooms vary and beds can be hard so select with care, excellent views, atmospheric, lovely swimming pool, interesting miniature shop with on-site artist, mixed reports, some disappointed with meals (Rs 450-500).

AL-A Desert Resort, 1 km south of Mandawa, T01592-223151, www.mandawahotels.com. Palatial mud-huts with serene swimming pool and inspiring views. This unique resort puts a new spin on traditional mud huts with interiors ornamented with mirrorwork and glass beads and all the mod cons. Very beautiful, highly recommended.

AL-B Grand Haveli, Bawari Gate, Nawalgahr, T01594-225301, www.grandhaveli.com. Stunning newly restored *haveli* with 19 deluxe rooms and several suites and duplexes. This impressive building is ornately decorated with frescoes and each room has its own *jhakora* with diwan and stained glass windows. Beautiful restaurant and cocktail bar.

A-C Singhasan Haveli (Heritage Hotel), T01592-223137, www.singhasanhaveli.com. 19 restored rooms and 5 suites in beautifully painted *haveli*. Fantastic views of Mandawa from the roof – you really get to see the extent of exquisite buildings here from this vantage point. Also offering up gala dinners with fireworks and sand dune dinners with camel cart rides and a BBQ under the stars.

B Mukundgarh Fort (Heritage Hotel), T01594-252397, www.crosscountry.co.in. 45 rooms in converted mid-18th-century fort. Extensive renovation work at time of writing.

B Roop Vilas Palace, Rawal Sab Ki Kothi, T01594-224321, www.roopvilas.com. Elegant heritage-style hotel with 21 rooms and 3 luxury tents. Beautifully set around an open courtyard, stylish rooms, and good locally grown food.

B-C Mandawa Haveli, near Sonthaliya Gate, Mandawa, T01592-223088, http://hotel mandawa.free.fr. 18 stunning rooms with modernized baths in a 3- storeyed, characterful *haveli* with original 19th-century frescoes in courtyard, every aspect is beautiful inside and out, great Rajasthani meals, museum and library. Friendly staff, authentic feel, but water can be a problem. Recommended.

B-C Piramal Haveli, Baggar, T0159-221220, www.neemranahotels.com. Stunning 100-year-old home, restored sensitively with a few roaming peacocks, excellent vegetarian meals and attentive service, quirky original frescoes.

B-C Roop Niwas Kothi, 1 km north of Nawalgarh, T01594-222008, www.roopniwas kothi.com. 25 rooms in sunny colonial-style buildings. Beautiful grounds with peacocks, Good food, large gardens with peacocks, pool, horse safaris are highly recommended, qualified guides, good food but service is disappointing.

B-D Heritage Mandawa, off Mukundgarh Rd, 200 m from the main bazar street and the bus stand, Mandawa, T01592-223742, www.hotel heritagemandawa.com. 13 rooms with local 'ethnic' furnishings in an opulent, fresco-covered *haveli*, attached baths, dining hall, clean and pleasant, manager and staff very friendly and accommodating (good discounts in the low-season), camel rides, guides, taxis. Camping possible in grounds.

B-D Jamuna Resort, Baggar Rd, Jhunjhunun, T01592-232871, www.shivshekawati.com. 14 a/c cottage rooms with attractive mirror work and murals, 'Golden Room' with painted ceiling "like a jewel box", frescos, open-air Rajasthani vegetarian/non-vegetarian restaurant serving delicious food, gardens, pool (open to hotel/ restaurant guests only), local guided tours. Recommended.

C-D Hotel Shekhawati Heritage, off Station Rd, Jhunjhunun, T01592-237134, www.hotel shekhawatiheritage.com. 22 rooms, 10 a/c, certainly not heritage clean and friendly, but overpriced. You can get better accommodation at this price and cheaper in Nawalgarh.

C-D Narayan Niwas Castle, near bus stand, Mehansar, T01565-264322, www.mehansar castle.com. Rooms in the fort, converted by Thakur Tejpal Singh. Only 16 rooms are open (out of a total of 500); Nos 1 and 5 are really exceptional. Attractive wall paintings, pleasingly unspoilt but poor bathrooms. Delicious meals (cooked by Mrs Singh), home-made liqueurs, charming owners, a *Fawlty Towers* experience.

C-D Thikana, T01594-222152, www.heritage thikana.com. Comfortable rooms in attractive building. Family-run and welcoming, good locally grown food.

D Apani Dhani, Jhunjhunu Rd, 1 km from railway station, 500 m north of bus stand, Nawal garh, T01594-222239, www.apanidhani.com. 8 environmentally friendly huts and 3 beautiful tents on an ecological farm run by the charming and authoritative Ramesh Jangid. Attractive, comfortable, solar-lit thatched cottages traditionally built using mud and straw, modern bathrooms (some with 'footprint' toilets), home-grown vegetarian, immaculately presented, relaxing atmosphere.

Accommodation and education in one enticing package. Cooking lessons also possible. Very special place. No alcohol permitted and modest respectful dress requested. Recommended.

D-E Natraj Hotel, Churu, T01562-257245. 28 clean, modern rooms, best bet in town.

D-F Shiv Shekhawati, Muni Ashram, Khemi Sati Rd, Jhunjhunun, T0159-223 2651, www.shivshekhawati.com. 20 simple clean rooms, 8 a/c, bath and hot water, good vegetarian restaurant, tourist office (guides). Same owner as **Jamuna Resort** (see above). Friendly.

E Shekawati Guest House, near Roop Niwas, Nawalgarh, T01594-224 658, www.shekawati restaurant.com. 6 clean, well-presented rooms and also now a circle of simple, yet beautiful thatched cottages, as well as an attractive thatched restaurant run by the friendly qualified cook Kalpana Singh. The food is exceptional and cooking classes can be arranged, as can local tours. Check out their organic garden. Recommended.

E Tourist Pension, behind Maur Hospital, Nawalgarh, T01594-224060, www.apanidhani.com. 8 rooms, some family-sized, in modern house run by Rajesh, the son of the owner of **Apani Dhani** (see above), and his wife Sarla, an excellent cook. Some nice big rooms, beautiful old furniture made by Rajesh's grandfather, very welcoming. Another guesthouse has opened up calling itself Tourist Pension near Roop Niwas, make sure you come to this one.

E-F Hotel Shekawati, off Mukandgarh Rd, Mandawa, T01592-223036. Simple, basic rooms, only budget place in town, adequate.

E-G Neelam, opposite Khetan Hospital, Jhunjhunun, T01592-234278. 24 rooms, a/c and air-cooled, economical with shared facilities, restaurant serving snacks, best budget option.

Eating

Sikar District *p446*

Natraj Restaurant, Main Rd, Sikar. Good meals and snacks, clean, reasonable.

Jhunjhunun District *p446*

Roop Niwas Kothi, Nawalgarh. For heritage experience (and unreliable service).

Shekawati Guest House, Nawalgarh. For delicious, hygienically prepared fare.

Activities and tours

Shekhawati *p445*

Camel safaris

A typical 5-day safari might include Nawalgarh–Mukundgarh–Mandawa–Mahansar–Churu (crossing some of the finest sand dunes in Shekhawati); 3-day safaris might include Nawalgarh-Fatehpur. Also 1-week country safaris to Tal Chappar Wildlife Sanctuary. The cost depends on the number in the group and the facilities provided ranging from Rs 800-1500 per day. 1-day safaris arranged by the heritage hotels cost about Rs 800 with packed lunch and mineral water. **Roop Niwas Palace**, **Apani Dhani** (Nawalgarh), and **Mandawa** (see Sleeping) offer trips.

Horse safaris

Roop Niwas at Nawalgarh (see Sleeping) offer 1-week safaris staying overnight in royal tents (occasionally in castles or heritage hotels) to cover the attractions of the region. The most popular take in the Pushkar or Tilwara fairs. You can expect folk music concerts, camp-fires, guest speakers, masseurs, and sometimes even a barber, all with jeep support. You ride 3 hrs in the morning and 2 hrs in the afternoon, and spend time visiting eco-farms, rural communities and *havelis* en route.

Trekking

There are some interesting treks in the Aravalli hills near Nawalgarh starting from Lohargal (34 km), a temple with sacred pools. Local people claim that this is the place recorded in the *Mahabharata* where Bhim's mace is said to have been crafted. A 4- to 5-day trek would take in the Bankhandi Peak (1052 m), Krishna temple in Kirori Valley, Kot Reservoir, Shakambari mata temple, Nag Kund (a natural spring) and Raghunathgarh Fort. The cost depends on the size of the group and the facilities. **Apani Dhani**, see Sleeping, arranges highly recommended treks with stays at the temple guesthouses and villages for US$50 per person per day (minimum 2 people).

Transport

Shekhawati *p445*

Bicycle Apani Dhani, Nawalgarh. Arranges cycle tours in Shekhawati.

Bus All major towns in the region including Sikar, Nawalgarh and Jhunjhunun are linked by bus with **Jaipur** (3-6 hrs) and **Bikaner**, and some have a daily service to **Delhi** (7-10 hrs); it's best to book a day ahead for these as buses fill up.
Jeep For hire in Nawalgarh, Mandawa and Dundlod, about Rs 1500 per day.
Taxi From **Jaipur**, a diesel Ambassador costs around Rs 3000 for a day tour of parts of Shekhawati; with detours (eg Samode) and a/c cars coming in around Rs 5000.

Local hire is possible in Mandawa, Mukundgarh and Nawalgarh. Also see Car hire in Delhi, page 121, as Shekhawati lies on a sensible if slightly elongated route between there and Jaipur.

Train Most trains through Shekhawati are slow passenger services, which tend to run to their own schedule. Most begin their journeys at **Rewari** (see Bikaner, page 444), and connect with **Bikaner** and **Jaipur**. Check locally for current schedules.

Directory

Jhunjhunun District *p446*

Banks SBBJ and **Bank of Baroda**, Mandawa. In Nawalgarh, **SBBJ** changes currency and TCs, but poor rate. **Roop Niwas** can help get better rates. **UCO Bank** changes currency in Dundlod.

Haryana & Punjab

Contents

Footprint features

Border crossings

At a glance

Getting around Chandigarh and Amritsar have frequent train connections with Delhi and buses to Himachal Pradesh.

Time required One day in Chandigarh is enough for most people. Allow at least a day for the Golden Temple.

Weather Dry, dusty and hot most of the year, with numbingly cold winter mornings.

When not to go Avoid the middle of summer.

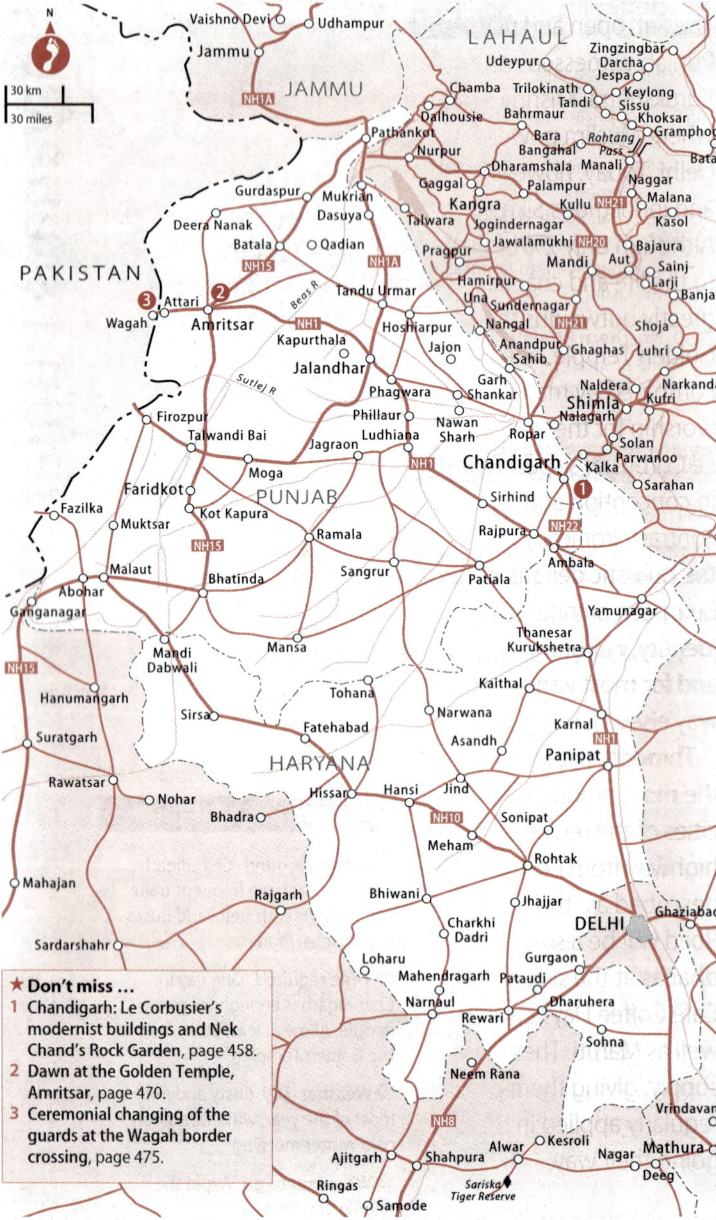

★ **Don't miss ...**

1. Chandigarh: Le Corbusier's modernist buildings and Nek Chand's Rock Garden, page 458.
2. Dawn at the Golden Temple, Amritsar, page 470.
3. Ceremonial changing of the guards at the Wagah border crossing, page 475.

The flat, open and richly cultivated plains of Haryana and Punjab witnessed some of ancient India's most significant battles. Kurukshetra, Krishna's battlefield in the *Mahabharata*, and Panipat, where Muslim power was established, lie in Haryana just north of Delhi. Today, however, it is the Punjab, peopled by the gregarious and industrious Sikhs, which is the foremost of the two states. Although only 2% of the Indian population, the Sikh contribution to the life and character, not to mention cuisine, of Northern India, greatly outweighs their relatively meagre numbers. Amritsar's Golden Temple, one of the great treasures of North India and compared by many to the Taj Mahal, is the holiest centre of worship for the Sikhs, whose roots lie in the soil of the Punjab. Le Corbusier's specially designed capital, Chandigarh, modernist in conception and secular in spirit, could scarcely stand in greater contrast. Ironically many now seem to visit Chandigarh more for the quixotic delights of Nek Chand's 'Rock Garden' than for its European architect's alien buildings. Haryana has a less distinct identity, culturally subsumed by the capital city which it surrounds, and for most visitors will simply serve as a transit state on their way elsewhere.

Through extensive irrigation Haryana and Punjab have become the most productive states of India. Most of the major towns and cities of the region are close to the Grand Trunk Road, the great highway from Peshawar to Kolkata which Rudyard Kipling described as "the backbone of all Hind". By 2013, the Grand Trunk Road will be a six-lane highway and joining the numerous Punjabi dhabas at the side of the road, there are drive-thru McDonalds and Café Coffee Days emerging. And you can spy Audi dealerships as well as Maruti. These two states also hold the key to Delhi's water supply, giving them powerful political leverage that has been regularly applied in the past when things have not been going their way.

Background → *Haryana Population: 21.1 million. Area: 44,200 sq km.*
Punjab Population: 24.29 million. Area: 50,300 sq km.

The land

Punjab and Haryana occupy the strategic borderlands between the Indus and Yamuna-Ganga river systems. Well over 1000 km from the sea, their gently sloping plains are less than 275 m above sea level. In the southwest, on the arid borders of Rajasthan, sand dunes form gentle undulations in the plain.

History

Before Independence The Ghaggar Valley, running from the Shiwalik Hills down to the Rajasthan desert, was the home of fortified urban settlements before 3000 BC and the rise of the Harappan civilization. The rising tide of Aryan influence steadily became the dominant force. It was here that the Vedas took shape. The region became vital for the Muslim kings of the Delhi sultanate; 1500 years later it was part of the Mughals' core region of power.

Sikhism became an increasingly powerful force after Guru Nanak, who lived in the Punjab from 1469 to 1539, first established his community of 'seekers'. See page 1427. Aurangzeb tried to put down Sikhism by force, encouraging the Sikhs to become militant. In 1799 **Ranjit Singh** set up a Sikh confederacy, which governed until the late 1830s. Two wars with the British ended in 1849, after which the Sikh community played an important role in British India, see page 1426. In 1857 they took the British side in the Mutiny, and were given prominent positions in the Indian armed services throughout the later period of British rule. However, many Sikhs also joined the struggle for Independence, and suffered grievously at the **Jallianwala Bagh massacre** in 1919, see page 473.

In 1947 Punjab was torn apart by the massacres that accompanied **Partition**. In the atmosphere of increasing communal violence, the Punjab was divided in two, leaving over five million Sikhs and Hindus in Muslim West Pakistan and 40 million Muslims in predominantly Hindu India. Many people, terrified by the prospect of losing all that they had worked for, turned on each other. Amritsar, 24 km from the border and the main railway station between Delhi and Lahore, witnessed some of the worst carnage. In six terrible weeks from August to mid-September at least half a million people died, and more than 13 million people crossed the new borders of India and Pakistan.

After Independence Sikh political opinion in Punjab continued to stress the need for a measure of autonomy within India's federal constitution. The creation of linguistic states in 1956 encouraged the Sikh Akali Dal to press for the further division of Punjab. Religious identity in itself was inadmissible under the Indian Constitution as a basis for separate statehood, and the Akalis therefore argued the distinctiveness of Punjabi from Hindi. Punjabi agitation in 1966 succeeded in achieving the further subdivision of the Punjab into the present states of Punjab (predominantly Sikh), Haryana (predominantly Hindu) and Himachal Pradesh (a purely mountain state, 96% Hindu).

Government In 1947, the Indian government built Chandigarh as the modern administrative capital for the Punjab. When Haryana was created in 1966 Chandigarh became the capital for both states. Arbitration was promised to decide its ultimate allocation, but its future remains undecided.

Recent political developments **Punjab** has 13 seats in the Lok Sabha (Lower House) and seven seats in the Rajya Sabha (Upper House) in the national parliament in New Delhi. In recent years Punjab has had several periods of direct rule from New Delhi. After the decade of political turmoil in the 1980s, marked by widespread violence surrounding the emergence of an Independence movement in Punjab, normality has returned. The Shiromani Akali Dal (SAD) and the BJP combine recaptured power from Congress in the February 2007 elections, with 63 of the 117 seats between them, but the Lok Sabha elections of 2009 saw the Congress win eight of the 13 seats.

Haryana has five seats in the Rajya Sabha and 10 seats in the Lok Sabha in New Delhi. Following a trend seen in many states, recent assembly elections have seen regional parties gain increasing strength at the expense of national parties like the Congress. In the February 2000 Assembly elections the Indian National Lok Dal came to power. However, the 2005 assembly elections saw Congress candidates returned in 67 of the 90 seats, a result which saw Sri Bhupinder Singh Hooda become chief minister. Congress also dominated the 2009 Lok Sabha elections, winning nine of the 10 seats.

Culture

Despite the strong influence of Hinduism and to a much lesser extent Islam, Sikhism displays a distinctive character of its own. Its literature has strong connections with Sufism. Guru Nanak travelled the region with two musicians and delivered his sermons to music as poetry through the sacred language *gurmukhi*. Typically Hindu celebrations and festivals such as **Dasara** and **Diwali** are enthusiastically observed, as are the birth and death anniversaries of the gurus and saints. Sikh music, much of it like the Mughal *ghazal* and *qawwali*, is immensely popular.

The long *kurta* (shirt) and baggy trousers drawn in at the ankle are traditional and popular forms of dress with Punjabi men. Women usually wear a similar *salwar kamiz* with a *dupatta* (long scarf). Sikh men are distinctive for their turbans and beards. The Sikhs are often thought of as enterprising and practical people, using machines from tractors to tubewells, threshing machines to grinders. They are now found driving buses, taxis and hire cars. They were the drivers in the Indian army and have maintained this role ever since.

Two-thirds of the 21 million people in Punjab speak **Punjabi**, closely related to Hindi, while the remainder speak **Hindi**.

The Punjab consumes more than twice as much butter and chicken than any other state, perhaps one reason for the average Sikh being heavier than the average Indian. Such is the esteem in which butter, in particular, is held that car stickers bearing nothing but the word 'butter' can be bought in Amritsar.

Chandigarh and around

→ *Phone code: 0172. Population: 900,900.*

In 1947 when Lahore, Punjab's former capital, was allocated to Pakistan, the Indian government decided to build a new capital for the Indian state of the Punjab. The result is Chandigarh, a planned city in the post-war modernist style, acting as the dual capital of Punjab and Haryana states. Some critics describe Chandigarh as soulless; anyone familiar with England may find themselves reminded of Milton Keynes. Not quite the garden city it was dreamt to be, it is nevertheless a convenient stop en route to Himachal Pradesh, or before flying to Leh. ▸▸ *For listings, see pages 464-468.*

Chandigarh → *For listings, see pages 464-468. Colour map 1, B3.*

Ins and outs

Getting there The airport and railway stations are some distance from the centre with pre-paid auto rickshaws to town. From the large Inter-State Bus Terminus (ISBT) in the busy Sector 17, you can walk to several budget hotels and restaurants. ▸▸ *See Transport, page 467.*

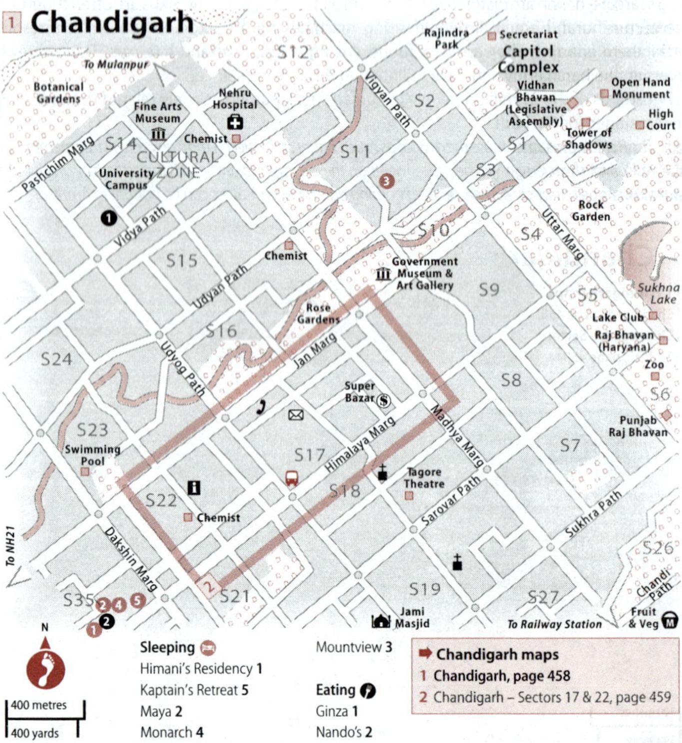

Sleeping
Himani's Residency **1**
Kaptain's Retreat **5**
Maya **2**
Monarch **4**
Mountview **3**

Eating
Ginza **1**
Nando's **2**

➡ **Chandigarh maps**
1 Chandigarh, page 458
2 Chandigarh – Sectors 17 & 22, page 459

Getting around Buses serve the different sectors but if you are only here for a few hours, it is best to hire transport as there are long distances to cover in this widely spread out city and it is not always easy to find a taxi or auto-rickshaw for single journeys. Half-day tours 'Fun on Wheels' offer a hop-on hop-off service around the attractions; contact CITCO (below) for information.

Tourist information **Chandigarh Tourism** ⓘ *ISBT, Sector 17, T0172-270 3839, www.chandigarhtourism.gov.in*. **Chandigarh Industrial and Tourism Development Corporation (CITCO)** ⓘ *T0172-464 4430, www.citcochandigarh.com*. **Himachal Tourism** ⓘ *1st floor, ISBT, T0172-270 8569*. **Uttarakhand and Uttar Pradesh Tourism** ⓘ *ISBT, T0172-271 3988*.

Climate Temperatures in summer reach a maximum 39°C/minimum 25°C; in winter, maximum 20°C/minimum 7°C. Over 250 mm of rain falls from June to August. The best time to visit is November to March.

Background

The initial plans for the creation of the city were drawn in New York by Mayer and Novicki. When the latter died in 1950 the work was entrusted to the internationally renowned architect **Le Corbusier** who supervised the layout and was responsible for the grand buildings. Fry and Drew designed the residential and commercial areas.

Jawaharlal Nehru said of Chandigarh "Let this be a new town symbolic of the freedom of India, unfettered by the traditions of the past, an expression of the nation's faith in the future". Its detractors describe it as a concrete prairie, the product of "the ivory tower school of architecture" and, despite its planning, many regard Chandigarh as a characterless failure. Today there is a growing scarcity of land, despite the complete ban on industrial activity. However, the ban has had the advantage of greatly limiting air pollution.

Sights

Chandigarh's major centres are: the **Capitol Complex** consisting of the Secretariat, Legislative Assembly and High Court in the northeast with the Shiwalik Hills as a backdrop; **Sector 17**, the central business district with administrative and state government offices, shopping areas and

2 Chandigarh – Sectors 17 & 22

Chandigarh maps
1 Chandigarh, page 458
2 Chandigarh – Sectors 17 & 22, page 459

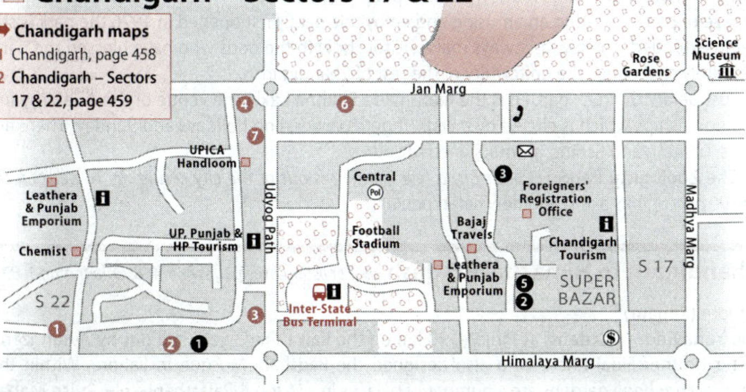

300 metres
300 yards

Sleeping
Aroma 1
Divyadeep & Bhoj Restaurant 2
Green View 7
Jullunder 3
Pankaj 4
Shivalik View 6

Eating
Chopsticks 1
Ghazal 2
Hot Millions 3
Mehfil 5
Tasty Bite 1

banks; a **Cultural Zone** in Sector 14, for education which includes a museum and a campus university with institutions for engineering, architecture, Asian studies and medicine. A vast colonnaded **Shopping Mall** has opened in Sector 35, with hotels, restaurants, banks, a well-stocked supermarket and internet/international phones. Sector 7 also has a high density of shops.

The multi-pillared **High Court** stands nearby with a reflective pool in front. Primary colour panels break up the vast expanses of grey concrete but this classic work of modernist architecture looks stark and bleak. The **Legislative Assembly** has a removable dome and a mural by Le Corbusier that symbolizes evolution. In the same sector is the **Open Hand Monument**. The insignia of the Chandigarh Administration, it symbolizes "the hand to give and the hand to take; peace and prosperity, and the unity of humankind". The metal monument, 14 m high and weighing 50 tonnes, rotates in the wind and sometimes resembles a bird in flight. The geometrical hill nearby, known as the **Tower of Shadows** ⓘ *tours 1030-1230 and 1420-1630, ask at Secretariat reception desk (you may need special permission to enter)*, was designed to beautify the complex, breaking its symmetrical lines.

The **Government Museum and Art Gallery** ⓘ *Sector 10, Tue-Sun 1000-1630*, has a collection of stone sculptures dating back to the Gandhara period, as well as miniature paintings, modern art, prehistoric fossils and artefacts. The **Museum of Evolution of Life** ⓘ *Sector 10, Tue-Sun 1000-1630*, has exhibits covering 5000 years from the Indus Valley Civilization to the present day. The **Fine Arts Museum** ⓘ *Punjab University, Sector 14 (all the faculties of the university are in Gandhi Bhavan, Sector 14), Mon-Fri 1000-1700 (closed between 1300-1400)*, specializes in Gandhi studies. The **Chandigarh Architecture Museum** ⓘ *Sector 10-C, Tue-Sun 1000-1645* charts the planning and creation of Chandigarh.

The **Rose Gardens** ⓘ *Sector 16, until sunset*, are one of the largest in Asia (25 ha), contains over 1500 varieties of rose; well worth visiting in spring. There's a rose show in early March.

The **Rock Garden** or **Garden of Nek Chand** ⓘ *Apr-Sep 0900-1300, 1500-1900, Oct-Mar 1400-1800, Rs 15, allow 3 hrs*, an unusual place, is the creation of Nek Chand, a road inspector in the Capitol City project. The 'garden' comprises an extraordinary collection of stones from the nearby Shiwaliks (carried on his bike) and domestic rubbish transformed into sculptures. Nek Chand dreamed of "creating a temple to Gods and Goddesses" out of discarded items of everyday use, for example bottle tops, fluorescent lights, mud guards, tin cans, and by highly imaginative re-assembling made models of people and animals. These have been set out along a maze of paths, creating an amusing and enjoyable park. First opened in 1976 the park is still being extended. The low archways make visitors bow to the gods who have blessed the park. Definitely challenges the uniformity of the rest of Chandigarh.

Just below the rock garden is the man-made **Sukhna Lake**, the venue of the Asian rowing championships which is circled by a walk. It gets crowded on holidays and Sunday. There are cafés, boating and fishing (permits needed).

The **Zoological Park** ⓘ *Chaat Bir, a few kilometres out of the city centre, Rs 10 per person, Rs 100 per car*, has a lion and deer safari park.

Chandigarh to Himachal Pradesh

→ *For listings, see pages 464-468. Colour map 1, B3.*

Pinjore (Pinjaur)

The **Yadavindra Gardens**, at Pinjore, 20 km on the Kalka road, were laid out by Aurangzeb's foster brother Fidai Khan, who also designed the Badshahi Mosque in Lahore. Within the Mughal *char bagh* gardens are a number of palaces in a Mughal-Rajasthani style: **Shish Mahal**, which has mirror-encased ceiling and is cooled by water flowing underneath (remove a slab to see!); **Rang Mahal**, a highly decorated pavilion; and **Jal Mahal**, set among fountains, cool and delightful. There are also camel rides and fairground attractions to tempt city dwellers. Keep a close eye on your belongings at all times; thefts have been reported.

Kalka, beyond Pinjore, is the starting point for the mountain railway to Shimla; see page 487. The quickest route to Dharamshala is via Ropar and Anandpur Sahib.

Anandpur Sahib

Anandpur Sahib (City of Divine Bliss), in a picturesque setting at the foot of the Shiwaliks by the River Sutlej, was established by the ninth guru, Tegh Bahadur, in 1664, when the Sikhs had been forced into the foothills of the Himalaya by increasing Mughal opposition. Guru Tegh Bahadur himself was executed in Chandni Chowk, Delhi, and his severed head was brought to Anandpur Sahib to be cremated. The event added to the determination of his son, Guru Gobind Singh, to forge a new body to protect the Sikh community. The Khalsa Panth was thus created on Baisakhi Day in 1699. Anandpur Sahib became both a fortress and a centre of Sikh learning. **Hola Mohalla** is celebrated the day after **Holi** when battles are re-enacted by *nihangs* (Guru Gobind Singh's army) on horseback, dressed in blue and huge turbans, carrying old weapons. The stunning blossom of The Khalsa Heritage Complex is a dramatic addition to the architecture of Anandpur Sahib – it will house galleries, a state of the art museum, a research library, 400-seat auditorium, water gardens and restaurant. www.khalsaheritagecomplex.org. Opening in 2012. Anandpur Sahib is also the home of Dashmesh Sadan – former residence of Yogi Bhajan and now popular with students of Kundalini Yoga as a retreat and training space, www.dashmeshsadan.org.

Patiala

Patiala, a neatly kept town southwest of Chandigarh, was once the capital of an independent state, along with Jind and Nabha, whose ruling houses were all Sikh. The Maharaja of Patiala's treaty with the British in 1809 kept Ranjit Singh out. In due course the maharaja became a premier Sikh prince and remained so until 1947.

Surrounded by a moat, the huge concentric **Bahadurgarh Fort** was built by Maharaja Ala Singh in the late 18th century. It is a good example of a *nara durg*, a large fort built on a plain, housing a garrison large enough to repulse strong attacks such as the fierce Maratha attempt in 1794. Now a Police Commando Training School, it is closed to visitors but you may request the guards at the back gate to allow you to sign in and look around. The Sikh palace is almost in ruins and the Moghul mosque survives through the amateur conservation efforts of the Fort Commandant.

The **Old Motibagh Palace** (late 19th century) ⓘ *3 km to the south, at the end of Mall Rd*, is one of the largest residences in Asia with 15 dining halls. The grotesquely oversized rambling central building is surrounded by lawns and trees. A combination of European, Rajput and Mughal styles, part of it is now the National Institute for Sports. The Sheesh Mahal has a **Museum and Art Gallery** housing ethnography, arms, natural history and miniature paintings. There is an unusual sunken lake and a curious 19th-century suspension bridge.

Chandigarh to Delhi → *For listings, see pages 464-468. Colour map 1, B3 and C3.*

From December to March the fields are green with wheat, though towards Delhi many are now planted with vegetables for the Delhi market. If travelling by train through this area at harvest time, expect to find your nostrils, clothes and luggage filled with dust and chaff. The Grand Trunk Road through Haryana is one of the busiest in India. By 2013, this will be a six-lane highway. It has long stretches lined with magnificent trees, and villagers have to buy rights to the leaves and wood. Check out www.haryanatourism.gov.in for unique experiences staying on farms – 'farm retreats' undoubtedly more aimed at Indians, but maybe worth a look into.

Ambala

Ambala, now the district headquarters, became a large British cantonment, laid out from 1843 onwards in grid fashion. The famous Gupta iron pillar now at the Qutb Minar in Delhi was originally on the hill just outside town.

Kurukshetra

The battlefield where Arjuna learned the meaning of *dharma* has left no trace. See page 1401. The plain around Kurukshetra is described in Sanskrit literature as "Brahmavarta" (Land of Brahma). Like many other sacred sites it becomes the special focus of pilgrimage at the time of exceptional astronomical events. In Kurukshetra, eclipses of the sun are marked by special pilgrimages, when over one million people come to the tank. It is believed that the waters of all India's sacred tanks meet together at the moment of eclipse, giving extra merit to anyone who can bathe in it at that moment.

Brahmasar Lake, 1 km west, a pilgrim site, is visited by a wide range of wildfowl, particularly from December to February. Temples and ghats surround the tank. The modern temple can best be described as kitsch, a reproduction of earlier temple styles. But the site is important for its influence on the development of Hindu ideas, not Hindu architecture. There are also the remains of a **Muslim Fort**, including the **Tomb of Shaikh Chilli Jalal** (died 1582) and **Lal Masjid**, a small red sandstone mosque. The carving on the domes is similar to that at Fatehpur Sikri.

Karnal

Karnal was taken by the British in 1797 who established a cantonment here in 1811. At **Uchana**, 3 km north, **Haryana Tourism** has created an artificial lake.

Panipat

Panipat is the site of three great battles which mark the rise and fall of the Mughal Empire. It stands on the higher ground made up of the debris of earlier settlements near the old bank of the River Yamuna. Today it is an important textile town with over 30,000 looms. A high proportion of the products, carpets, curtains and tablewear, is exported.

In the first battle of Panipat on 21 April 1526 Babur, the first Mughal emperor, fought Ibrahim Lodi, the Sultan of Delhi, reputedly resulting in the death of 20,000 of the sultan's army, including Ibrahim Lodi. The second battle, on 5 November 1556, changed the course of India's history, as it secured Mughal power. Akbar, who had just succeeded his father Humayun and his general, defeated Hemu, the nephew of the Afghan Sher Shah. There was a mass slaughter of the captives, and in the gruesome tradition of Genghis Khan, a victory pillar was built with their heads plastered in. The third battle took place on 13 January 1761. The once great Mughal Empire was threatened from the west by the resurgent Rajputs and from the northwest by the Afghans. The distracted Mughal minister called in the Marathas. Despite their numbers, the Marathas lost and their soldiers fled. However, the Afghan leader Ahmad Shah Durrani was unable to take advantage of his victory as his followers mutinied for the two years' arrears of pay he owed them. North India was thus left in a political vacuum which adventurers tried to fill during the next 40 years. The main old building in Panipat is a **shrine** to the Muslim saint Abu Ali Kalandar.

Southwestern Haryana → *For listings, see pages 464-468. Colour map 2, A5/A6.*

Road and rail criss-cross the largely flat plain where irrigation sustains lushly cultivated fields. Further west dry land predominates, shading into the deserts of Rajasthan. The NH10 gives access to several remote archaeological sites and India's most important early settlement region but it is rarely visited.

Rohtak → *77 km from Delhi.*

The archaeological sites at **Khokhra Kot** and **Ramala Ala** have revealed pottery from pre-Harappan and early historical times after 1500 BC. Coin moulds from the first century have thrown valuable light on the processes of minting coins. Today, it is well known for its turbans, interwoven with gold and silver thread.

Hissar

Hissar was founded in 1354 by Firuz Shah Tughlaq who constructed a canal to bring water to his hunting ground. This was renovated in the 19th century and incorporated into the West Yamuna Canal. The Gujari Mahal in the old fort was built from the remains of a Jain temple. The citadel contains the Mosque of Firuz Shah (late 14th century) and the *Jahaz* (ship) east of the city, which takes its name from its shape (reminiscent of that at Mandu – see page 271). Hissar exports cattle all over India and is widely known for its biennial **cattle fairs**.

Sirsa

Sirsa was settled from around 1500 BC with pottery known as Rang Mahal Ware. Thus it was clearly occupied long before the traditional date of its founding – the sixth century AD – when it was known as Sarasvati. Just north of Sirsa the road crosses the usually dry bed of the Ghaggar River, one of North India's most important early settlement regions. The **Kalibangan** Harappan site is just beyond Suratgarh to the west, see page 441. There is a large cattle fair here in August/September.

Chandigarh to Amritsar → *For listings, see pages 464-468. Colour map 1, B2/3.*

Many of the small towns along this route show signs of Punjab's rapid industrialization; steel rolling, textiles, sugar mills, food processing and a whole range of small industrial services from computers to advertising.

Sirhind

Mahmud of Ghazni extended his control to the town in the 11th century when it became the border town for Muslim possessions in India, hence Sar-i-Hind (Frontier of India). Later it became Sher Shah Suri's capital, whose army was defeated by Humayun in 1555.

The town's period of greatest splendour was between 1556 and 1707. The stone-built **Tomb of Mir Miran** is an octagon topped by a dome. Another octagonal tomb, ornately decorated with painted flowers, is that of Pirbandi Nakshwala, with its pear-shaped dome covered in glazed tiles. **Salabat Beg Haveli** is a large and well-preserved Mughal house whilst the Sarai of the Mughal emperors, in the southeast of the town, is now a **public hall**. For the Sikhs, Sirhind is associated with the brutal execution of the two younger sons of the 10th Guru, who were bricked up alive in the fort in 1705 for refusing to convert to Islam.

Ludhiana

A major textile (hosiery) and light engineering centre, Ludhiana's predominantly concrete grey hue bears testimony to both the rapid pace of its development and its somewhat unfinished feel. Here you can get good-quality fabric from the market and garments copied cheaply by expert tailors. The rich agricultural area around it supports a large grain market. Founded in 1480 by Lodi princes from Delhi (hence its name), Ludhiana subsequently passed through a number of hands. The surrounding area was fiercely fought over during the First Sikh War with the British in 1845-1846. The three major battlefields at **Mudki, Firozshah** and **Sobraon** all have commemorative obelisks. The town is also the home of the **Christian Medical College Hospital**, which is in partnership with the CMC hospital in Vellore. The world famous **Punjab Agricultural University**, on the edge of town, has a good museum. In Februrary, a show of Rural Games of Punjab is organized at Kila Raipur nearby.

Jalandhar

Jalandhar (Jullundur) is an ancient city of which very little survives, although it retains a more established, settled feel than nearby Ludhiana. It was sacked by Mahmud of Ghazni and under the Mughals it was an important administrative centre. Today, it is a major road and rail junction with a busy market, the Rainik Bazar, a network of narrow, atmospheric alleys which are worth exploring. It's main claim to fame is cricket – it's a massive manufacturer of cricket bats. The cantonment area to the southeast was established in 1846 to house army units after the treaties signed in Lahore in March and December 1846 which ended the First Sikh War.

Kapurthala

Kapurthala is the capital of the former Sikh princely state and the home town of the Ahluwalia family who conquered it in 1747. Its army fought against the British at Aliwal in the First Sikh War but took the British side during the Second Sikh War (1848) and the Mutiny (1857). There are buses from Jalandhar and Amritsar.

Later governed as a model city-state, the French-educated ruler Jagajit Singh, who ascended the throne in 1890, tried to make his capital city a Parisian replica. His palace, the **Jalaukhana**, might have come straight out of the French Renaissance, except that the red sandstone with which it was started had to give way to pink stucco when funds ran out. The palace is now a boys' school. The maharaja's international preferences changed when he married a Spanish dancer, however, and the **Villa Buena Vista** (1894) has an Iberian flavour.

Goindwal and Tarn Taran

On the way from Jalandhar to Amritsar there are important *gurudwaras* where Sikhs on pilgrimage traditionally stop. There are separate bathing places for men and women at Goindwal, with a small market place outside the temple. The *gurudwara* at Taran Tarn is surrounded by a busy bazar. The *gurudwara* itself is very beautiful, with a very large water tank and cloisters providing welcome shade.

Chandigarh and around listings

For Sleeping and Eating price codes and other relevant information, see Essentials pages 38-42.

Sleeping

Chandigarh *p458, maps p458 and p459*

Rickshaw drivers act as hotel touts.

AL Mountview, S10, T0172-464 4400, www.citcochandigarh.com. 156 centrally a/c rooms, pool, government-run business hotel boasting all 5-star amenities.

AL-A Lemontree, Chandigarh Industrial and Business Park Phase-I, www.lemontreehotels.com. Opened in Sep 2011, Lemontree offers citrus smelling rooms with all the mod cons – piped pop music plays through reception and in the common areas. It's a fresh approach to hospitality. Extensive buffet breakfasts on offer as well as multi-cuisine restaurant for the rest of the day.

AL-A Maya , SCO 325-28, S35-B, T0172-260 0547, After quite the nip and tuck, Maya has recently become a very stylish hotel. At the time of writing, rooms were still under renovation but if they mirror the chic lobby and restaurant, they will be very 'boutique' indeed. Definitely worth checking out.

A Shivalik View, S17, T0172-270 0001, www.citcochandigarh.com. 108 rooms with all mod cons in government-run hotel, business centre, good Chinese restaurant, friendly, well located.

A-B Kaptain's Retreat, 303 S35-B, T0172-500 5599, kaptainsretreat@hotmail.com. Owned by the legendary cricketer, Kapil Dev, this is Chandigarh's first boutique hotel. Each room is named after one of the great man's achievements, eg 'nine wickets', although the interiors are more than cricket chic with nice décor and excellent attention to detail. There's also an attractive bar and restaurant. Good value. Recommended.

B Aroma, Himalaya Marg, S22, T0172-401 0000, www.hotelaroma.com. 30 clean, a/c rooms, plus a cavernous 'water-featured' restaurant which is pretty naff looking but the staff are friendly. There are another 30 premium rooms in their new wing and there is a branch of **Café Coffee Day** on site.

B-C Jullunder, S22, opposite ISBT, T0172-270 6777, www.jullunderhotel.com. 17 average a/c rooms with restaurant on site.

B-C Monarch, 351-352, S35-B, T0172-260 9991. Efficiently run, modern hotel with popular, well-priced basement bar. Rates negotiable.
B-D Himani's Residency, 469-70, S35-C, T0172-266 1070, www.himanihotels.com. 17 adequate rooms in a good location close to bars and restaurants, friendly, good value.
C North Park, out of town at Pachkula, near Ghaggar Bridge, T0172-256 1212. 43 comfortable rooms in business-class hotel.
C-D Classic, S35-C, T0172-260 6092, Comfortable modern hotel (buffet breakfast included), bar, reasonable value, lively bar and disco.
D Divyadeep, S22-B, Himalaya Marg. T0172-270 5191. 15 rooms, some a/c, neat and clean, great value, good **Bhoj** restaurant. Recommended
D Pankaj, S22-A, T0172-270 9891, colharsharam@yahoo.com. 14 comfortable rooms, some a/c rooms with bath, good restaurant, exchange, slightly out on a limb.
F Green View, halfway along Udyog Path, 1st floor, S22. T0172-508 5681. Few clean rooms, hot shower, meals.

Anandpur Sahib *p461*

It is possible to stay in one of the many *gurudwaras* in town. Also at time of writing a three star government (PTDC) hotel is under construction, all to help accommodate people visiting the stunning **Khalsa Heritage Complex**.
C Dashmesh Sadan, Bani Village, 4 km from Anandpur Sahib, www.dashmeshsadan.org. For students and teachers of Kundalini Yoga, this is Yogi Bhajan's home and it's doors have reopened as an ashram and teaching centre. It's possible to come and stay here independently, but there are also regular retreats, yatras and teacher trainings. You must book in advance. Beautiful gardens and inspiring vibration. Within walking distance of the main *gurudwaras*. "Walk where the gurus walked". Check the website for full programme.
C-E Kissan Haveli, Dashmesh Academy Rd, T01887-232 650. 10 rooms in this characterful 'heritage-style' property.
E-F Holy City, Dashmesh Academy Rd, T01887-232 330, www.hotelholycity.com. Clean basic rooms and good value restaurant.

Patiala *p461*

AL-A Baradari Palace, Baradari Gardens, near Circuit House, T0175-230 4433, www.neemranahotels.com. Beautifully restored palace with period furniture and many with lovely verandahs or massive terraces. Common areas and restaurant are elegant.
E-F Harpawittar International, Sirhind Rd, T0175-235 6874. Basic rooms, those at the front would have great view of the *gurudwara* if they hadn't stuck hulking great a/c units in the windows. There are cheaper hotels near the bus station, not very appealing to solo women.

Ambala *p461*

D Kingfisher (Haryana Tourism), 5 km north of town (near junction of Amritsar–Chandigarh road), T0171-443732. 13 rooms, 2 a/c, restaurant, attractive gardens and pool.
D-E Batra Palace, Lawrence Rd, behind bus station, T0171-500 7501, www.batrapalace.com. Comfortable rooms with 'proper' bathroom (hot water), friendly room service with good food. Recommended.

Kurukshetra *p462*

D-E Neelkanthi Yatri Niwas, well sign-posted, T01744-291 1615. Haryana Tourism offers over-priced simple rooms, but there are dorm beds at Rs 300 a pop, restaurant.

Panipat *p462*

C-D Skylark, GT Rd, T0180-264 1051. 16 a/c rooms and dorm (Rs 100), restaurant, fast food.
D Midtown, GT Rd, town centre, T0181-266 7901. With restaurant and 28 a/c rooms.
D-E Gold, GT Rd, south of town, T0180-266 0012, www.hotelgoldpanipat.com. 30 a/c rooms, restaurants, bar, pool.

Rohtak *p462*

C-D Tilyar, T01262-273119. 12 a/c rooms and dorms (Rs 100), restaurant and boating.

Hissar *p463*

C-D Flamingo, T01662-225702. 6 a/c rooms, restaurant and bar.

Sirhind *p463*

D Bougainvillea Tourist Complex, GT Rd towards Mandi Gobindgarh, outside town,

T01763-555570. 8 rooms, 4 a/c, floating restaurant, camping and showers.

D Mulsari Tourist Complex, Aam Khas Bagh, in town centre, T01763-222250. Old caravanserai conversion, 8 rooms (4 a/c), restaurant, beer bar, Mughal garden, archaeological ruins nearby.

E Queens Flower Tourist Resort, on Sirhind canal at Neelon, T0161-283 3832. 6 rooms, some a/c, restaurant, bar, garden.

Ludhiana *p463*

There are numerous **D-E** options, all much of a muchness, close to railway station.

AL Park Plaza, Ferozepur Rd, T0161-277 3000, www.sarovarhotels.com. 120 elegant rooms plus usual 5-star facilities including pool, part of nationwide chain.

A-B Friends Regency, Ferozepur Rd, T0161-277 1111, hotelfriendsregency@yahoo.com. 21 classy rooms, impressive building, all the mod cons.

A-B Gulmor, Ferozepur Rd, T0161-277 1700, www.hotelgulmor.com. 28 rooms, central a/c, **Saffron**restaurant, exchange, pleasant gardens, relaxed atmosphere, well maintained. Recommended.

B Nagpal Regency, Bhaibala Chowk, Ferozepur Rd, T0161-277 2394. 30 well-presented rooms in modern building plus friendly staff and a well-stocked bar.

Jalandhar *p463*

A Kamal Palace, EH-192, Civil Lines, T0181-245 8473, www.kamalpalace.com. 41 very comfortable rooms, central a/c, modern and well presented.

B Leo Fort, GT Rd, T0181-224 4890, www.leoforthotel.com. 61 modern rooms, central a/c, health club, pool, great bar, outstanding value, recommended.

D-E Plaza, Old Court Rd, New Plaza Chowk, near Friends Cinema, T0181-222 5833, hotelplaza@vsnl.net. 38 rooms, some a/c with bath, restaurant, bar.

Kapurthala *p464*

D Magnolia Tourist Complex, western edge of town, T0181-278 2322. 4 rooms, restaurant, bar, garden, very pleasant for a break or an overnight stop.

Eating

Chandigarh *p458, maps p458 and p459*

TTT Curry's, Piccadily Hotel , Himalaya Marg, Sector 22-B. Upmarket Indian in luxurious surroundings.

TTT Elevens, Kaptain's Retreat (see Sleeping). Unusual combination of Pakistani, Indian and Thai cuisines in Mediterranean-style interior. Recommended.

TTT Mehfil, 183, S17-C, T0172-270 4224. International. Upmarket, a/c, comfortable seating, spicy meals.

TTT Nando's, 339, S35-B, T0172-405 2501. International chain serving up decidedly good spicy chicken. They also have some of the best veggie burgers on the planet and everything can be tweaked to your own tolerance of spiciness.

TT Bhoj, S22-B, **Divyadeep** (see Sleeping). Indian Vegetarian. Good set *thalis* only, pleasant, clean, busy at lunch, good value.

TT Chopsticks, Himalaya Marg. Chinese. Smart, cool, reasonable food.

TT Ghazal, 189, S17-C. International. Comfortable, good Indian, popular with families, separate bar.

TT Khyber, S35-B. Excellent frontier-style cuisine in pleasant ground-floor restaurant plus 'Wild West' bar in basement, complete with cowboy waiters. Recommended.

TT Sagar Ratna, S35-C. High-quality South Indian. Well-presented, nationwide chain, very professional.

T Ginza, 40, S14 (University Campus). Chinese.

Cafés and snacks

Coffee Day, S35-C. Nationwide coffee chain, plus good snacks in relaxing surroundings.

Down Under, 183-4, S17. A pleasant bar.

Hot Millions, S17. Wide choice. 3 places.

Tasty Bite, Himalaya Marg. Good South Indian eats and burgers.

Ludhiana *p463*

TT City Heart Hotel. International. Wide choice, well prepared, generous portions, chilled beer, genial, helpful and prompt service.

T Café 33, 33 SCF, Sarabha Nagar Market. Indian.

T Chicken Plaza, Ghumar Mandi. Fantastic chicken with naan, try *haryali* chicken.

T Gazebo, 15 Bhadaur House Market. International menu in a/c comfort.

Larks, City Market. Punjabi. Typical *dhaba*, but clean, chicken dishes recommended.

Jalandhar *p463*

La Roma, next to **Radisson Hotel**, "Italian by flavour, Indian by heart".

Clock Tower, Nehru Garden. Also has a bar.

Eat Well, close to **Clock Tower**. Quick and clean; also **DearNear** juice bar next door.

Festivals and events

Chandigarh *p458, maps p458 and p459*

Apr All the Hindu festivals are celebrated especially **Baisakhi**, celebrated by both Hindus and Sikhs as **New Year's Day** (13-14 Apr). Bhangra dancers perform.

Shopping

Chandigarh *p458, maps p458 and p459*

Most shops open Mon-Sat 1000-1330, 1530-1945. Small shops in S19 and S22 open on Sun. A large new mall has been built in S35 with all the usual brands. S17 is relaxed as there is no traffic. S17 and 22 have **State Govt Emporia**. There is a small branch of **Anokhi** for great hand-block print clothes and textiles in S7-C inner market.

Patiala *p461*

Lacquerware at 94 Bichittar Nagar.

Activities and tours

Chandigarh *p458, maps p458 and p459*

Swimming

Lake Pool Complex, S23. Temporary membership available.

Tour operators

Chandigarh Tourism, T0172-505 5462, www.chandigarhtourism.com, or book at ISBT (see page 458). Local tours including good-value open-top bus (Rs 75 all day), and further afield to Pinjore Gardens, Bhakra Dam, Amritsar, Shimla, Kullu and Manali. They do half-day tours of the city in their double decker fun bus.

Cozy Tours, SCF I Sector 10, T0172-274 0850.

Transport

Chandigarh *p458, maps p458 and p459*

Air Airport, 11 km. Taxis charge Rs 300 to centre. **Indian Airlines**: reservations, S17, T0172-265 6029, airport, T0172-622 4941, 1000-1630. Daily to **Mumbai** and **Delhi**. **Jet Airways**, 14 S 9D Madhya Marg, T0172- 274 0550, airport T0172-265 8935, daily to **Delhi**. **Air Deccan**, T0172-265 1748, daily to **Mumbai** and **Jammu**.

Bicycle hire Free to CITCO hotel guests.

Bus It is easier to get a seat on the **Shimla** bus from Chandigarh than from Kalka. Many buses daily from **ISBT**, S17. A 2nd terminal in S43 has some buses to **Himachal Pradesh**, **Jammu** and **Srinagar**; city buses connect the 2. Transport offices: ISBT, S17, 0900-1300, 1400-1600; Chandigarh, T0172-270 0006; Haryana, T0172-270 4104; Himachal, T0172-266 8943; Punjab, T0172-260 6672. Buy bus tickets from the designated booths next to platforms before boarding. Seat numbers (written on the back of tickets) are often assigned. **Shimla** buses (via Kalka) leave from platform 10. To **Amritsar**, 6 hrs (from Aroma Hotel, T0172-270 0045); **Pathankot**, 7 hrs; **Dharamshala**, 10 hrs; **Kalka** (from Platform 10), Rs 11-28. Buses to **Shimla** also stop at **Kalka**; **Kullu** 12 hrs. Also **Himachal Tourism** coaches during the season, to **Delhi**, 5 hrs, Rs 180; **Manali**, 0800, 10 hrs, Rs 280; **Shimla**, 5 hrs, Rs 100.

Motorcycle Sikhs are officially exempt from wearing motorcycle helmets, although strictly speaking the length of cloth used to form the turban should be not less than 5 m as anything less is not deemed to give adequate protection.

Rickshaw Auto-rickshaws are metered with a minimum fare, but you can bargain. Stands at bus station, railway station and the Rock Garden. Cycle rickshaws are unmetered.

Taxi Private taxi stands in S22, S17, S35. **Chandigarh Tourism (CITCO)**, S17, T0172-270 3839. **Mega Cabs**, T0172-414 1414. To **Kalka**, up to Rs 400.

Train The station (8 km) has a clean waiting room but a poor bus service to the city. Pre-paid auto-rickshaws, Rs 45 to S22; to bus stand Rs 34; to Kalka (for the brave) Rs 200. Enquiries/ reservations, T1333, T0172-264 1651, 1000-1700; City Booking Office, 1st floor, Inter-State Bus Terminal (ISBT), S17, T0172-270 8573, Mon-Sat 0800-1345, 1445-2000, Sun 0800-1400. Tourist office, 0600-2030. **New Delhi**: *Shatabdi Exp 12006*, 0650, 3¾ hrs; *Shatabdi Exp 12012*, 1820, 3¼ hrs; *Himalayan Queen 14096*, 1728, 4½ hrs.

Old Delhi: *Kalka-Howrah Mail 12312*, 0110, 5½ hrs. **Shimla**: *Himalayan Queen 14095*, 1028, 1 hr to **Kalka**, then 40 mins' wait for *Exp 255* to **Shimla** (1210, 6 hrs, book ahead).

Anandpur Sahib *p461*

Bus From **Chandigarh** and **Ropar**.
Train To **Ambala**, *Himachal Exp 4544*, 2210, 3½ hrs. To **Nangal Dam**, *Exp 4553*, 0620, 30 mins.

Patiala *p461*

Bus and train The railway and bus stations are at the north end of Mall Rd, 1 km from the centre. Daily buses to **Delhi**, other towns in Punjab and neighbouring states. Patiala is on the branch line to **Bhatinda**.

Ambala *p461*

Train New Delhi: *Shatabdi Exp 2006*, 0723, 2½ hrs. *Shatabdi Exp 2012*, 1900, 2½ hrs. Frequent trains to **Chandigarh**. Northern Railway connects **Shimla** trains with those from **Jammu Tawi** and **Lucknow**.

Ludhiana *p463*

Bus Long-distance daily bus services connect Ludhiana with **Delhi** and towns in Punjab and neighbouring states.
Train To **Amritsar**: *Shatabdi Exp 2013*, 2035, 2 hrs; *Katihar Amritsar Exp 5707*, 0915, 2½ hrs; *Paschim Exp 2925*, 1635, 2½ hrs; *New Delhi-Amritsar Exp 2459*, 1840, 2½ hrs. To **Delhi**: *Shatabdi Exp 2014*, 0708, 3¾ hrs; *Paschim Express, 2926*, 1050, 5½ hrs; *Golden Temple Mail 2904*, 0015, 7 hrs.

Jalandhar *p463*

Air A/c coach connects with **Air India** flights from **Delhi** airport to **London**, 1700 (9 hrs), return 0400; Rs 350.
Train The City and Cantt train stations are on the same line, though not all trains stop at both. There are many trains to Amritsar and Ludhiana. From City Station: **Amritsar**: *Katihar Amritsar Exp 5705*, 1025, 1½ hrs; *Shatabdi Exp 2013*, 2130, 1 hr; *Paschim Exp 2925*, 1745, 1 hr. **Kolkata**: via Ludhiana and Varanasi, *Amritsar-Howrah Mail 3006*, 0050, 34 hrs. **Delhi**: via Ludhiana and Meerut, *Shatabdi Exp 2014*, 0615, 4½ hrs; *Paschim Exp 2926*, 0930, 7 hrs; *Golden Temple Mail 2904*, 2255, 8½ hrs.

❶ Directory

Chandigarh *p458, maps p458 and p459*

Banks ATMs easily found everywhere. Exchange: **Paul's Merchants**, S22-A, T0172-270 4279, speedy, efficient, good rates, will send rep to hotel. Recommended. **American Express** TCs only. **Medical services** Ambulance: T102. 24-hr chemists. **General Hospital**, S16, T0172-278 0756; **PG Institute**, S12, T0172-274 7610. **Useful contacts** Fire: T101. Police: T100. **Foreigners' Registration Office**: Town Hall Bldg, S17 (1000-1700), T0172-2741100.

Patiala *p461*

Banks **State Bank of Patiala**, in the centre, changes money reasonably quickly.

Jalandhar *p463*

Banks **Thomas Cook**, for exchange, 2 Alpha Estate, 39 GT Rd, T0181-223 8790.

Northern Punjab

Northern Punjab is defined more than anything by its proximity to the Pakistan border, with a heavy military presence always in attendance. Before Partition, the Punjab extended well in to present-day Pakistan and many families still have members or property on both sides of the divide, some of whom have not seen each other for generations. Today the area is dominated by agriculture, with the efficiently farmed plains providing a stark contrast to the soaring peaks of neighbouring Kashmir, and by Amritsar's incomparable Golden Temple. ▸▸ *For listings, see pages 475-477.*

Amritsar → *For listings, see pages 475-477. Colour map 1, B2. Phone code: 0183. Population: 976,000.*

Amritsar ('Pool of the Nectar of Immortality') is named after the sacred pool in the Golden Temple, the holiest of Sikh sites. The temple itself, the city's singular attraction, is a haven of peace amidst an essentially congested city. The atmosphere is particularly powerful during *amritvela* (dawn to early light), when the surrounding glistening white-marble pavement is still cold under foot and the gold begins to shimmer on the lightening water. Sunset and evening prayers are also a special time to visit. You cannot help but be touched by the sanctity and radiance of the place, the friendly welcome of the people and the community spirit. Music constantly plays from within the inner sanctum of the Hari Mandir.

Ins and outs

Getting there Rajasansi Airport is 11 km away with taxi or auto-rickshaw transfers. The railway is central, the bus station 2 km east; both are a 15-minute auto-rickshaw ride from the Golden Temple to the south. If you have a couple of hours to spare between connections, you can fit in a visit. ▸▸ *See Transport, page 476.*

Getting around The city is quite spread out. Cycle-rickshaws squeeze through the crowded lanes. Auto-rickshaws are handy for longer journeys unless you get a bike.

Tourist information Tourist office ⓘ *opposite the railway station, T0183-240 2452.*

Background

The original site for the city was granted by the Mughal Emperor Akbar (ruled 1556-1605) who visited the temple, and it has been sacred to the Sikhs since the time of the fourth guru, Guru Ram Das (1574-1581). He insisted on paying its value to the local Jats who owned it, thereby eliminating the possibility of future disputes on ownership. Guru Ram Das then invited local merchants to live and trade in the immediate vicinity. In 1577 he heard that a cripple had been miraculously cured while bathing in the pool here. The pool was enlarged and named Amrit Sarovar (Immortality). Guru Arjan Dev (1581-1601), Guru Ram Das' son and successor, enlarged the tank further and built the original temple at its centre from 1589-1601. The Afghan Ahmad Shah Durrani, desecrated the Golden Temple in 1757. The Sikhs united and drove him out, but four years later he defeated the Sikh armies, sacking the town and blowing up the temple. Later, the Sikhs re-conquered the Punjab and restored the temple and tank. Under their greatest secular leader, Maharaja Ranjit Singh, the temple was rebuilt in 1764. In 1830 he donated 100 kg (220 lbs) of gold which was applied to the copper sheets on the roof and much of the exterior of the building, giving rise to the name the 'Golden Temple'. Now Punjab's second largest town, Amritsar was a traditional junction of trade routes. The different peoples, Yarkandis, Turkomans, Kashmiris, Tibetans and Iranians indicate its connections with the Old Silk Road.

Golden Temple

The spiritual nerve centre of the Sikh faith, every Sikh tries to make a visit and bathe in the holy water. It is immensely powerful, spiritual and welcoming to all, with an all-pervasive air of strength and self-sufficiency.

Visiting the temple Shoes, socks, sticks and umbrellas can be left outside the cloakroom free of charge. Visitors should wash their feet outside the entrance. It is best to go early as for much of the year the marble gets too hot by noon. Dress appropriately and cover your head in the temple precincts. Head scarves are available during the day but not at night; a handkerchief suffices. Avoid sitting with your back towards the temple or with your legs stretched out. Tobacco, narcotics and intoxicants are not permitted. The community kitchen provides food all day, for a donation. The **information office** ⓘ *near the main entrance, T0183-255 3954*, is very helpful.

Worship Singing is central to Sikh worship, and the 24-hour chanting at the Golden Temple adds greatly to the reverential atmosphere. After building the temple, Guru Arjan Dev compiled a

1 Amritsar

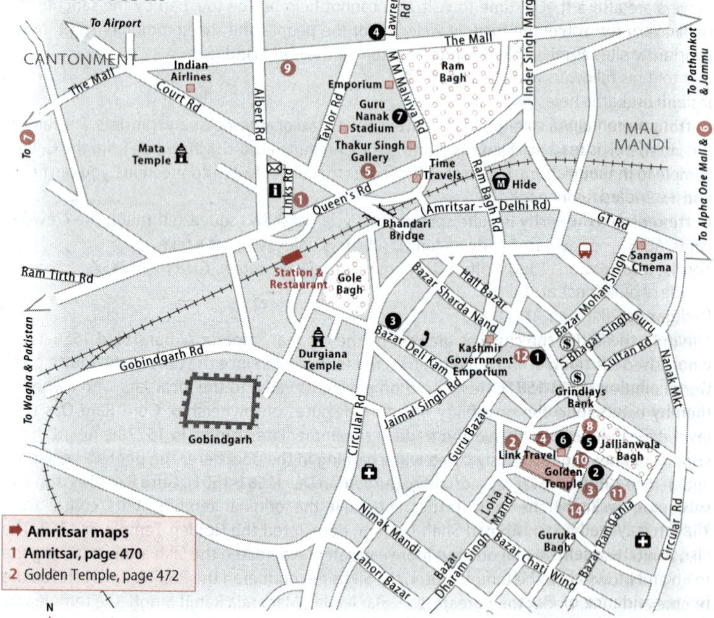

Sleeping
CJ International 4
Golden Tower 8
Grace 3
Grand 1
Ista 6
Kishore Castle 5
Le Golden 2
Lucky 10
MK Sood 14
Mrs Bhandari's Guest House 7
Ramada 12
Ranjit's Svaasa 9
Sita Niwas 11

Eating
Bharawan's 1
Curd Stall 2
Kesar da Dhaba 3
Kwality 4
Neelam 6
Punjabi Rasoi 5
Salads Plus 4
Sindhi Coffee House 7

collection of hymns of the great medieval saints and this became the *Adi Granth* (Original Holy book). It was installed in the temple as the focus of devotion and teaching. Guru Gobind Singh, the 10th and last Guru (1675-1708) revised the book and also refused to name a successor saying that the book itself would be the Sikh Guru. It thus became known as the *Guru Granth Sahib* (The Holy Book as Guru).

The temple compound Entering the temple compound through the main entrance or clock tower you see the **Harmandir** (the Golden Temple itself, also spelt Harimandir, and known by Hindus as the Durbar Sahib) beautifully reflected in the stunning expanse of water that surrounds it. Each morning (0400 summer, 0500 winter) the *Guru Granth Sahib* is brought in a vivid procession from the **Akal Takht** at the west end to the Harmandir, to be returned at night (2200 summer, 2100 winter). The former represents temporal power, the latter spiritual – and so they do not quite face each other. Some like to attend **Palki Sahib** (night ceremony).

All pilgrims walk clockwise round the tank, stopping at shrines and bathing in the tank on the way round to the Harmandir itself. The tank is surrounded by an 8-m-wide white marble pavement, banded with black and brown Jaipur marble.

East End To the left of the entrance steps are the bathing ghats and an area screened off from public view for women to dip. Also on this side are the **68 Holy Places** representing 68 Hindu pilgrimage sites as referenced in Guru Nanak's Japji Sahib. When the tank was built, Guru Arjan Dev told his followers that rather than visit all the orthodox Hindu places of pilgrimage, they should just bathe here, thus acquiring equivalent merit.

A shrine contains a copy of the **Guru Granth Sahib**. Here and at other booths round the tank the Holy Book is read for devotees. Sikhs can arrange with the temple authorities to have the book read in their name in exchange for a donation. The *granthi* (reader) is a temple employee and a standard reading lasts for three hours, while a complete reading takes 48 hours. The tree in the centre at the east end of the tank is popularly associated with a healing miracle.

Dining Hall, Kitchen, Assembly Hall and Guesthouses The surrounding *bunghas* (white arcade of buildings), are hostels for visitors. Through the archway a path leads to the **Guru Ram Das Langar** (kitchen and dining hall) immediately on the left, while two tall octagonal minarets, the 18th-century **Ramgarhia Minars**, provide a vantage point over the temple and inner city. At the far end of the path are a series of guesthouses including **Guru Ram Das Sarai**, where pilgrims can stay free for up to three nights. Sikhs have a community kitchen where all temple visitors, regardless of their religious belief, can eat together. The third Guru, Guru Amar Das (1552-1574), abolished the custom of eating only with others of the same caste. He even refused to bless the Mughal Emperor Akbar unless he was prepared to eat with everyone else who was present. *Seva* (voluntary service), which continues to be a feature of modern Sikhism, extends to the kitchen staff and workers; visitors are also welcome to lend a hand. The Amritsar kitchen may feed up to 10,000 people a day, with 3000 at a sitting and up to 1 Lakh (100,000) visitors at the weekends. It is free of charge and vegetarian, though Sikhs are not banned from eating meat. Lunch is 1100-1500 and dinner 1900 onwards. Next to the Guru Amar Das Langar is the **residence of Baba Kharak Singh** who is hailed by Sikhs as a saint. His followers are distinguished by their orange turbans while temple employees and members of the militant Akali sect wear blue or black turbans.

Returning to the temple tank, the **shrine** on the south side is to Baba Deep Singh. When Ahmad Shah Durrani attacked Amritsar in 1758, Baba Deep Singh was copying out the *Guru Granth Sahib*. He went out to fight with his followers, vowing to defend the temple with his life. He was mortally wounded, 6 km from town; some say that his head was hacked from his body. Grimly determined and holding his head on with one hand he fought on. On his way back to the temple he died on this spot. The story is recounted in the picture behind glass.

West end The complex to the west has the Akal Takht, the flagstaffs, and the Shrine of Guru Gobind Singh. The **flagstaffs** symbolize religion and politics, in the Sikh case intertwined. They are joined in the middle by the emblem of the Sikh nation, the two swords of Hargobind, representing spiritual and temporal authority. The circle is inscribed with the Sikh rallying call *Ek Onkar* (God is One).

Started when Arjan Dev was Guru (1581-1605), and completed by Guru Hargobind in 1609, the **Akal Takht** is the seat of the Sikhs' religious committee. It is largely a mixture of 18th- and early 19th-century building, the upper storeys being the work of Ranjit Singh. It has a first-floor room with a low balcony which houses a gilt-covered ark, central to the initiation of new members of the Khalsa brotherhood.

To the side of the flagstaffs is a **shrine** dedicated to the 10th and last guru, Gobind Singh (Guru 1675-1708). In front of the entrance to the temple causeway is a square, a gathering place for visitors.

Sometimes you may see Nihang (meaning 'crocodile') Sikhs, followers of the militant Guru Gobind Singh, dressed in blue and armed with swords, lances and curved daggers.

At the centre of the tank stands the most holy of all Sikh shrines, the **Harmandir** (The Golden Temple). Worshippers obtain the sweet *prasad* before crossing the causeway to the temple where they make their offering. The 60-m-long bridge, usually crowded with jostling worshippers, is built out of white marble like the lower floor of the temple. The rest of the temple is covered in copper gilt. On the doorways verses from the *Guru Granth Sahib* are inscribed in Gurumukhi script while rich floral paintings decorate the walls and excellent silver work marks the doors. The roof has the modified onion-shaped dome, characteristic of Sikh temples, but in this case it is covered in the gold that Ranjit Singh added for embellishment.

The ground floor of the three-storey temple contains the Holy Book placed on a platform under a jewel-encrusted canopy. *Guru Granth Sahib* contains approximately 3500 hymns. Professional singers and musicians sing verses from the book continuously from 0400-2200 in the summer and 0500-2130 in winter. An excited crowd of worshippers attempts to touch the serpent horn. Each evening the holy book is taken ceremoniously to the Akal Takht and brought back the next morning; visitors are welcome. The palanquin used for this, set with emeralds, rubies and diamonds with silver poles and a golden canopy, can be seen in the treasury on the

2 Golden Temple

Amritsar maps
1 Amritsar, page 470
2 Golden Temple, page 472

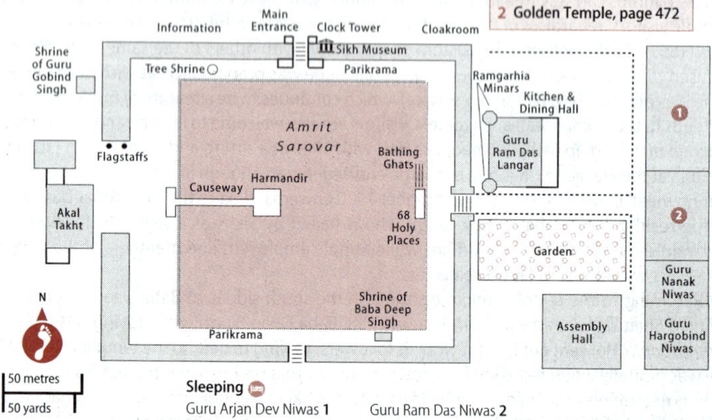

first floor of the entrance to the temple. Throughout the day, pilgrims place offerings of flowers or money around the book. There is no ritual in the worship or pressure from temple officials to donate money. The marble walls are decorated with mirror-work, gold leaf and designs of birds, animals and flowers in semi-precious stones in the Mughal style.

On the first floor is a balcony on which three respected Sikhs always perform the **Akhand Path** (Unbroken Reading). In order to preserve unity and maintain continuity, there must always be someone practising devotions. The top floor is where the gurus used to sit and here again someone performs the *Akhand Path*; this is the quietest part of the building and affords a good view over the rest of the complex.

On the edge of the tank just west of the entrance is the **Tree Shrine**, a gnarled, 450-year-old *jubi* tree, reputed to have been the favourite resting place of the first chief priest of the temple. Women tie strings to the ingeniously supported branches, hoping to be blessed with a son by the primaeval fertility spirits that choose such places as their home. It is also a favourite spot to arrange and sanctify marriages, despite the protests of the temple authorities. The **Sikh Museum** ⓘ *at the main entrance to the temple (just before steps leading down to the parikrama), 0700-1830, free*, is somewhat martial, reflecting the struggles against the Mughals, the British and the Indian Army. The **Sikh Library** ⓘ *in the Guru Nanak Building, Mon-Sat 0930-1630*, has a good selection of books in English as well as current national newspapers.

The town

The old city is south of the railway station encircled by a ring road, which traces the line of the city walls built during the reign of Ranjit Singh. **Jallianwala Bagh**, noted for the most notorious massacre under British rule (see below), is 400 m north of the Golden Temple.

Relations with the British had soured in 1919. *Hartals* (general strikes) became a common form of demonstration. The Punjab, which had supplied 60% of Indian troops committed to the First World War, was one of the hardest hit economically in 1918 and tension was high. The lieutenant governor of the province decided on a 'fist force' to repulse the essentially non-violent but vigorous demonstrations. Some looting occurred in Amritsar and the British called in reinforcements. These arrived under the command of General Dyer.

Dyer banned all meetings but people were reported to be gathering on Sunday 13 April 1919 as pilgrims poured into Amritsar to celebrate **Baisakhi**, the Sikh New Year and the anniversary of the founding of the *khalsa* in 1699. That afternoon thousands were crammed into Jallianwala Bagh, a piece of waste ground popular with travellers, surrounded on all sides by high walls with only a narrow alley for access. Dyer personally led some troops to the place, gave the crowd no warning and ordered his men to open fire leaving 379 dead and 1200 wounded. Other brutal acts followed.

The **Jallianwala Bagh massacre** was hushed up and the British government in London was only aware of it six months later at which time the Hunter Committee was set up to investigate the incident. It did not accept Dyer's excuse that he acted as he did in order to prevent another insurrection on the scale of the Mutiny of 1857. He was asked to resign and returned to England where he died in 1927. However, he was not universally condemned. A debate in the House of Lords produced a majority of 126 to 86 in his favour and the *Morning Post* newspaper launched a fund for "The Man who Saved India". More than £26,000 was raised to comfort the dying general.

India was outraged by Dyer's massacre. **Gandhi**, who had called the nationwide *hartal* in March, started the Non Co-operation Movement, which was to be a vital feature of the struggle for Independence. This was not the end of the affair. O'Dwyer, the governor of the province, was shot dead at a meeting in Caxton Hall, London, by a survivor of Jallianwala Bagh who was hanged for the offence. For a modern take on the whole story, check out the Bollywood movie *Rang de Basanti.*

Today the gardens are a pleasant enclosed park. They are entered by a narrow path between the houses, opening out over lawns. A **memorial plaque** recounts the history at the entrance,

Border essentials: India–Paksitan

→ *Pakistan time is 30 mins behind IST.*

It is best to cross in the morning; allow an hour for formalities although it can take longer, especially for a bus load (five different passport and customs checks on the Indian side; three on the Pakistan side taking nearly three hours to process 15 travellers). The border check post is nominally open 1000-1500, Indian time, but is subject to change. Unless you have your own vehicle or are on the new through-coach from Delhi to Lahore, you have to walk from the Indian check post to the Pakistani check post. Indian porters can carry your luggage to the border line, where it is transferred to a Pakistani porter; expect to pay Rs 25-50 after bargaining (Indian side) and Rs 30-50 (Pakistani) respectively. There is a bank within the customs area with foreign currency exchange facilities. Beyond Pakistani immigration and customs there is a taxi and minicab park; you can usually share one to Lahore (30 km). Amritsar to Lahore usually takes three to five hours though there can be unexpected delays. A luxury coach now runs between Delhi and Lahore. At the border, **Niagra Falls Restaurant** has four air-cooled rooms, restaurant and a beer bar.

and a large memorial dominates the east end of the garden. There is an interesting museum. On the north side is a well in which many who tried to escape the bullets were drowned, and remnants of walls have been preserved to show the bullet holes.

The old town has a number of mosques and Hindu temples – the **Durgiana Temple** (16th century), and the new **Mata Lal Devi Temple**, which imitates the difficult access to the famous Himalayan Mata Vaishno Devi Cave Temple of Katra by requiring the worshipper to wade awkwardly through water and crawl through womb-like tunnels is well worth a visit. The whole temple area is Disneyesque with plastic grottoes and statues. Women who wish to have children come here to pray, there is community food and a charity hospital run from the temple's trust. It's a very popular and lively temple, definitely worth a visit. Northeast of the railway station are the **Ram Bagh gardens**, the Mall and Lawrence Road shopping areas.

To Pakistan → *For listings, see pages 475-477.*

From Amritsar, the road continues west to the Pakistan border. Despite the easing in the political situation in Punjab there are numerous police check posts so motorbikes and cars may be stopped several times. It is better to take Pakistani rupees into Pakistan to avoid being hassled. You can change money in Amritsar (Link Road/Albert Road) or just across the border. The **road crossing** for foreigners is currently through the Wagah check post (see box, opposite), 35 km from Amritsar along the attractive and tree-lined GT Road to **Attari**, the last town before the border, just 2 km from Wagah. From Amritsar, frequent minibuses take about one hour to Attari, where you get a rickshaw or taxi, Rs 500 (Rs 550 return, to see flag ceremony), take 30 minutes; auto-rickshaw Rs 250 (Rs 350 return); tourist bus Rs 70 return. A **train** goes from Attari to Lahore in Pakistan, but services are dependent on the state of political relations between India and Pakistan. At the end of November when Sikhs visit shrines in Pakistan the train may be restricted to Sikh pilgrims. When running, it can be a very slow journey with customs and immigration formalities taking four hours or more. Crossing the border by road is more convenient than by train.

Wagah → *Colour map 1, B2.*

The changing of the guards and the ceremonial lowering of the flags ceremony at sundown, carried out with great pomp and rivalry, are quite a spectacle. There is much synchronized foot stamping, gate slamming and displays of scorn by colourful soldiers! It is the ministry of funny walks. New viewing galleries have been built but crowds still clamour to get the best view. Women are allowed to get to the front, and there is a VIP section (open to foreign visitors) next to the gate. It is best to get there near closing time though photography is difficult with the setting sun.

Pathankot → *Colour map 1, B2.*

Pathankot, a crossroads town and trading centre on the border with Himachal Pradesh, is the gateway to Jammu and Kashmir and western Himachal. It is also the starting point for the Kangra Valley Railway but has little else to offer. **Shapur Kandi Fort** (16th century), 13 km to the north, was once the stronghold of the Rajas of Pathan but is now no more than a ruin. It sits on the banks of the Ravi River, which has a hydroelectricy power station at **Ranjit Sagar Dam**.

Northern Punjab listings

For Sleeping and Eating price codes and other relevant information, see Essentials pages 38-42.

Sleeping

Amritsar *p469, map p470*

Local Sikh families welcome guests – Contact **Time Travels** (see Activities and tours, below).

L-AL Ista, next to Alpha One Mall, GT Rd, T0183-270 8888, www.istahotels.com. Part of the new **Ista** chain within India, this is a beautiful boutique hotel offering up the most stylish rooms in Amritsar. There is a stunning spa with all the usual ayurvedic fare, but also rose quartz and amethyst facials. Food-wise, you can choose between the all-day **Collage** with food from around the globe and a *teppenyaki* station or **Thai-Chi**, evenings only.

L-AL Ramada, near Town Hall, www.ramada.com. More chain hotels are opening up in Amritsar, there is also a **Radisson** near the airport. The **Ramada** has a great location, closer to the centre of town than any other 4star. All the mod cons are here in this attractive hotel.

AL-A Ranjit's Svaasa, 47-A The Mall Rd, T0183-256 6618, www.welcomheritage.com. Tastefully restored rooms with huge windows in a 250-year-old red-brick manor surrounded by palms and lawns, elegant service, great food, , beautiful Spa Pavilion offering Ayurvedic and international treatments. Recommended.

A-C CJ International, opposite the Golden Temple, T0183-254 3478, www.cjhotel.net. 25 clean, modern rooms close to temple.

B-C Hotel Le Golden, clock tower Extension, outside Golden Temple complex, T0183-502 8000, www.hotellegolden.com. Modern rooms close to the temple, with views of Akal Takht, rooftop restaurant **The Glass** has view of Siri Harmandir Sahib.

C Kishore Castle, 10 Queens Rd, T0183-240 2818, kishorecastle_hotel@yahoo.com. 25 rooms, room service only, friendly staff.

C Mrs Bhandari's Guest House, 10 Cantonment, northwest of town, T0183-222 8509, http://bhandari_guesthouse. tripod.com. Unusual guest house, feels like barracks. 9 a/c rooms with bath in 1930s building, no TV, Heath Robinson baths, fireplaces, hot water bottles, sepia prints, 'English' meals, pool (Mar-Nov), large grounds, quiet, camping (Rs 150).

C-D Grand, Queens Rd, opposite train station, T0183-256 2424, www.hotelgrand.in. 32 modern but characterful rooms, some a/c, set around attractive garden, popular restaurant and attractive bar with Kingfisher on draught, good food, very friendly management.

C-E Golden Tower, near Jallianwala Bagh, T0183-253 4446, www.hotelgoldentower.com. Modern, comfortable, a/c rooms close to the Golden Temple and Jallianwala Bagh.

C-E Grace, 35 Braham Buta Market, close to Golden Temple, T0183-255 9355. Good range of rooms, friendly management.

D-G Sita Niwas, east of Golden Temple, T0183-254 3092, sitaniwas@yahoo.co.in. 100 rooms from very basic to all mod cons, fans or a/c, hot water in buckets, bit run-down, room service (cheap Indian meals), can be noisy at dawn (pilgrims), very helpful, friendly manager. Recommended.

E-F Lucky, Mahna Singh Rd, near Golden Temple and Jallianwala Bagh, T0183-254 2175. Basic rooms some with a/c. Good value.

E-F MK Sood, off Bharam Butta Market, opposite PN Bank near Golden Temple, T0183-509 3376 Range of clean and comfortable a/c and non a/c rooms near the temple.

G Rest houses, in/near the Golden Temple, eg **Guru Ram Das Niwas** and **Guru Arjan Dev Niwas**. Some free (up to 3 nights), very simple food; please leave a donation. Guru Ram Das Niwas has small foreigner only enclave with guard. Tobacco, alcohol and drugs are prohibited. Can be noisy as sometimes so busy people stay in the courtyard, but an eye-opening experience.

Eating

Amritsar *p469, map p470*

Eating with pilgrims in the *langar* (Golden Temple community kitchen) can be a great experience. Remember to hold out both hands (palms upwards) when receiving food. The corner of the Mall and Malaviya Rd comes alive with ice cream and fast-food stalls in the evening. *Dhabas* near the station and temple sell local *daal*, *saag paneer* and mouthwatering stuffed *parathas*.

TTT **The Glass**, at **Le Golden Hotel** close to Golden Temple. Glass rooftop restaurant serves up range of foods and great views of the temple.

TTT **Mrs Bhandari's** (see Sleeping). For unexpected Raj tones, ring ahead for a table.

TT **Crystal**, Queens Rd, T0183-222 5555. Good international food, excellent service, pleasant ambience, huge portions. There is **Crystal** on the ground floor proclaiming that there is only one branch. And there is **Crystal** on the 2nd floor proclaiming the same thing – the two brothers have fallen out and both refuse to change the name.

TT **Kwality**, The Mall, T0183-222 4849. International with good following. Under renovation at time of writing.

TT **Punjabi Rasoi**, near Jallianwala Bagh, T0183-254 0140. The best option near the Golden Temple. Very good *thalis*, south Indian food and traditional Punjabi fare. Internet café upstairs too. Recommended.

T **Bharawan's**, near Town Hall. Excellent breakfast and lunch *thalis* and good vegetarian.

T **Curd stall**, opposite **Ashar Guest House**. Excellent, safe *lassis*.

T **Gagan**, 34 Sita Niwas Rd, near the Golden Temple. Simple, good Indian, not spicy.

T **Kesar da Dhaba**, Passian Darwaza, near Durgiana Temple. Serves extremely popular sweet *phirni* in small earthenware bowls for Rs 6. Also Punjabi *thalis*.

T **Neelam**, near Jallianwalla Bagh. Indian, Chinese. Cheap, plentiful and really tasty.

Bakeries

Bakewell, Cooper Rd. Good for cakes and fruit puddings.

Blue Baker, Circular Rd, opposite Medical College. Has good reputation.

Festivals and events

Amritsar *p469, map p470*

The birth anniversaries of the 10 gurus are observed as holy days and those of Guru Nanak (**Oct/Nov**), and Guru Gobind Singh (**Dec/Jan**), are celebrated as festivals with *Akhand Path* and processions.

Apr Baisakhi, for Sikhs, the Hindu New Year marks the day in 1699 Guru Gobind Singh organized the Sikhs into the Khalsa, see page 1426. The vigorous *bhangra* dance is a common sight in the villages. Falls on 13 or 14 Apr.

Oct/Nov Diwali Illumination of the Golden Temple, fireworks.

Activities and tours

Amritsar *p469, map p470*

Time Travels, 14 Kapoor Plaza, Crystal Sq, T0183-240 0131, www.travelamritsar.com. Organizes homestays, tours to Dharamshala, Manali, Shimla, etc, local villages, as well as to important Gurudwaras in the state. Very efficient, helpful. Recommended.

Transport

Amritsar *p469, map p470*

Air Rajsansi Airport, T0183-259 2166; taxi (Rs 550) or auto-rickshaw (Rs 200) to town.

Domestic flights Daily flights to **New Delhi** with **Indian Airlines**, 39A Court Rd, T0183-

221 3393, **Kingfisher** T0183-2214227 and **Jet Airways** T0183-2214033.

International flights Weekly flights to/from **London** and **Birmingham** on **Uzbek and Turkmenistan Airways**. Contact in UK T0207-935 4775. **Singapore Airlines**, T0183-250 0330.

Bicycle hire A bicycle is worthwhile here; available for hire from Hide Market.

Bus Daily services to **Delhi** (tiring 10 hrs); **Dharamshala** (7 hrs); **Dalhousie** (8 hrs), **Jammu** (5 hrs); **Pathankot** (3 hrs); **Chandigarh** (5 hrs); **Shimla** 0530 and 0730, 10 hrs. **Link Travels** and other private operators leave for Delhi from outside railway station, 2200; for **Jammu** and **Chandigarh** from Hall Gate. Cross-border bus service to **Lahore** (Tue, Wed, Fri and Sat). Contact International Bus Terminal, T0183-258 7070. Advance booking must).

Rickshaw Auto-rickshaw/*tonga*: full day, Rs 500, half day Rs 300.

Taxi Non-a/c car from **Time Travels** near Crystal restaurant, Queens Rd, T0183-240 0131/4, www.travelamritsar.com, and **Link Travels**, outside Golden Temple Clock Tower Car Park: full day, Rs 1200, half day Rs 800, Wagah Rs 900. To **Delhi** Rs 6200, **Dharamshala** Rs 3000.

Train Enquiries T131. There is a free shuttle bus from the station to the Golden Temple. Computerized reservations in the Golden Temple Complex (far right of the office), open until 2000 on weekdays. **Kolkata**: via **Lucknow** (16½ hrs) and **Varanasi** (22¼ hrs); *Amritsar-Howrah Mail 13006*, 1845, 37¼ hrs. **Mumbai (Central)**: *Golden Temple Mail 12904*, 2140, 32½ hrs; *Paschim Exp 12926*, 0815, 31½ hrs. **New Delhi**: *Shatabdi Exp 12014*, 0510, 5¾ hrs; *Shan-e-Punjab Exp 12498*, 1510, 8 hrs (HN); *Amritsar Shatabdi 12032*, 1700, 5¾ hrs. **Pathankot**: *Ravi Exp 14633*, 0915, 2¼ hrs; *Jammu Tawi Exp 18101/18601*, 0545, 2¾ hrs, continues to Jammu, 6 hrs.

Pathankot *p475*

Bus Some trains to and from Jammu don't stop at Pathankot Junction but at Chakki Bank. There is a tempo service between the 2 stations. Bus and railway stations are 100 m apart. Buses to all important towns nearby. To **Dharamshala**, several buses 0415-1730, 3½ hrs.

Taxi Shared taxis available at the railway station if the prospect of a hill bus journey fails to thrill. Depending on size of car, around Rs 1500 to McLeodganj.

Train The spectacular narrow-gauge Kangra Valley Railway, built in 1928, runs to **Jogindernagar**, 56 km northwest of Mandi in HP. See page 534.

Baijnath Paprola: *3PB Passenger*, 0835, 5½ hrs. **Baijnath and Jogindernagar**: *3PBJ Passenger*, 0920, 6½ hrs and 8¾ hrs. **Amritsar**: several, including *Ravi Exp 14634*, 1415, 2¾ hrs (2nd class only); *Tatanagar Exp 18102/18602*, 1625, 2¾ hrs, continues to **Delhi** (**ND**), 12 hrs.

Directory

Amritsar *p469, map p470*

Bank **Punjab Bank**, next door to Golden Temple, quick. ATMs everywhere.

Himachal Pradesh

Contents

Footprint features

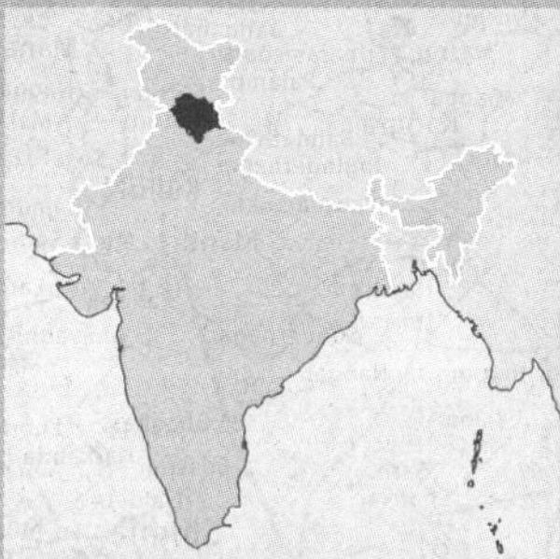

At a glance

Getting around Buses or cars are the only way to get around most of this mountainous state; Kalka–Shimla narrow-gauge train and the Kangra Valley Railway.

Time required 2-3 days each for Shimla and Manali; many people spend weeks in Dharamshala.

Weather The hills are a mercifully cool retreat in Apr and May.

When not to go Monsoon rains can bring landslides and closed roads.

★ **Don't miss …**

1. Stroll around the faded streets of Shimla, page 484.
2. Climb behind Bhimakali Temple in Sarahan, page 489.
3. Chos Khor Gompa, page 497.
4. Kullu Valley and Naggar, page 510.
5. Manali to Leh road, page 523.
6. Dharamshala: wonderful trekking, spectacular railway journey and home of the Dalai Lama, page 528.
7. Pragpur, India's first 'heritage village', page 533.

Himachal Pradesh is defined more than anything by the mighty Himalaya, towering over its northern periphery with implacable dominance, both feared and revered by the state's sparse population. The mountains have long attracted nature lovers, climbers and trekkers, while in recent years a number of more adrenalin-inducing sports have also come to prominence. Manali has become a centre for adventurous activities: from heli-skiing to rafting, mountain biking to paragliding and horse riding, there's a huge range on offer. The arrival of the Tibetans after the Chinese invasion of Tibet in 1959 has added attractions of an altogether more mellow manner. McLeodganj (Dharamshala), home to His Holiness the Dalai Lama, has become a mecca for those after more spiritual pursuits; many come to follow courses in yoga, meditation, Buddhism, or to learn about the Tibetan cause.

Some of the state's finest mountain views can be seen from Dalhousie, a popular hill station during the Raj and today a quaint if anachronistic reminder of how the British used to build their homes. Himachal's other Raj relic, and its capital city, Shimla, is part quaint English village, part traffic, touts and mayhem. Arriving via the 'toy train' from Kalka is by far the best way and the scenery is almost painfully picturesque. Although most people come to Himachal to see the mountains, the plains also have much to offer. Kangra Valley is especially pretty, with charming villages connected by quiet, windy roads. Those in search of more rugged adventures should head for Kinnaur, Spiti and Lahaul, accessible only in the summer when the snow melts on the higher passes, meaning they can be crossed by road, giving access to the barren but spectacular scenery beyond. This area also forms the start of the incomparable Manali–Leh road, the highway from Himachal to Ladakh and one of the world's best road trips.

Background → *Population: over 6 million. Area: 55,673 sq km.*

The land

Geography Himachal Pradesh (Himalayan Province) is wholly mountainous, with peaks rising to over 6700 m. The **Dhaula Dhar** range runs from the northwest to the Kullu Valley. The **Pir Panjal** is further north and parallel to it. High, remote, arid and starkly beautiful, Lahaul and Spiti are sparsely populated. They contrast strongly with the well-wooded lushness of those areas to the south of the Himalayan axis.

Climate At lower altitudes the summers can be very hot and humid whereas the higher mountains are permanently under snow. In Shimla, the Kangra Valley, Chamba and the Kullu Valley, the monsoon arrives in mid-June and lasts until mid-September, giving periods of very heavy rain; in the Kullu Valley there can be sudden downpours in March and early April. To the north, Lahaul and Spiti are beyond the influence of the monsoon, and consequently share the high-altitude desert climatic characteristics of Ladakh.

History

Originally the region was inhabited by a tribe called the Dasas who were later assimilated by the Aryans. From the 10th-century parts were occupied by the Muslims. Kangra, for example, submitted to Mahmud of Ghazni and later became a Mughal province. The Gurkhas of Nepal invaded Himachal in the early 19th century and incorporated it into their kingdom as did the Sikhs some years later. The British finally took over the princely states in the middle of the 19th century.

Culture

Religion Although the statistics suggest that Himachal is one of the most Hindu states in India, its culture reflects the strong influence of Buddhism, notably in the border regions with Tibet and in the hill stations where many Tibetan refugees have made their homes. In the villages many of the festivals are shared by Hindus and Buddhists alike. There are also small minorities of Sikhs, Muslims and Christians.

People Hill tribes such as the Gaddis, Gujars, Kinnaurs, Lahaulis and Pangwalas have all been assimilated into the dominant Hindu culture though the caste system is simpler and less rigid than elsewhere. The tribal peoples in Lahaul and Spiti follow a form of Buddhism while Kinnauris mix Buddhism with Hinduism in their rituals. Their folklore has the common theme of heroism and legends of love. *Natti*, the attractive folk dance of the high hills, is widely performed.

Language The dominant local language is Pahari, a Hindi dialect derived from Sanskrit and Prakrit but largely unintelligible to plains dwellers. Hindi is the medium for instruction in schools and is widely spoken.

Handicrafts Handicrafts include woodcarving, spinning wool, leather tanning, pottery and bamboo crafts. Wool products are the most abundant and it is a common sight in the hills to see men spinning wool by hand as they watch over their flocks or as they are walking along. Good-quality shawls made from the fine hair from pashmina goats, particularly in Kullu, are highly sought after. *Namdas* (rugs) and rich pile carpets in Tibetan designs are also produced. Buddhist *thangkas*, silverware and chunky tribal silver jewellery are popular with tourists and are sold in bazars.

Modern Himachal Pradesh

Himachal Pradesh was granted full statehood in 1970. There are 68 seats in the State Assembly, but as one of India's smallest states Himachal Pradesh elects four members of the

The seasonal move of government

So beneficial were the effects of the cooler mountain air that Shimla (see page 484), 'discovered' by the British in 1819, became the summer seat of government from 1865 to 1939. The capital was shifted there from Calcutta and later from Delhi (1912 onwards) and all business was transacted from this cool mountain retreat.

Huge baggage trains were needed to transport the mountains of files and the whole operation cost thousands of rupees. At the end of the season back they would all go.

Women heavily outnumbered men, as wives of many British men who ran the empire escaped to the hills for long periods. Army officers spent their leave there. Social life in hill stations became a round of parties, balls, formal promenades along The Mall and brief flirtations.

Lok Sabha and three representatives to the Rajya Sabha. Since 1966 Shimla has been the state capital. Dharamshala (McLeodganj) has been the home of His Holiness the Dalai Lama and the Tibetan government in exile since 1959, following the Chinese takeover of Tibet. With the long-term closure of routes through Kashmir, Himachal Pradesh has seen a sharp rise in tourism, and is the main land route to Ladakh. The new strategically important tunnel under the Rohtang Pass is scheduled for completion in 2014.

Current political developments Even though Himachal is quite close to Delhi, it still has the feel of a political backwater. News from the state rarely makes the national newspapers and, while the contest for representation in the Lok Sabha and in the Assembly is intense, the two-horse race between Congress and the BJP rarely attracts much attention. The Congress party gained power in March 2003 under Chief Minister Shri Virbhadra Singh, his third appointment to the post after earlier tenures covering much of the 1980s and 1990s, but the BJP won three of the four Lok Sabha seats in 2009.

Southern Himachal

Southern Himachal offers an intriguing mix of experiences. Shimla's colonial past, with its Little England architecture and anachronistic air, seems to be fighting for survival amidst the modern-day bustle of Himachal's capital city. The area around Shimla offers stunning views of the foothills of the Himalaya and plenty of attractive places to stay nestled amongst the cool pine forests. This area is also the gateway to the altogether more rugged landscapes of Kinnaur, a world far less affected by the advance of time.
▸▸ For listings, see pages 490-494. For trekking, see page 546.

Shimla → *For listings, see pages 490-494. Colour map 1, B3. Phone code: 0177. Population: 150,000. Altitude: 2213 m.*

Once a charming hill station and the summer capital of the British, an air of decay hangs over many of Shimla's Raj buildings, strung out for 3 km along a ridge. Below them a maze of narrow streets, bazars and shabby 'local' houses with corrugated-iron roofs cling to the hillside. Some find it delightfully quaint and less spoilt than other hill stations. There are some lovely walks with magnificent pines and cedars giving a beautifully fresh scent to the air.

Ins and outs

Getting there Despite the romance of the narrow-gauge railway from Kalka, see page 487, most arrive in Shimla by bus or taxi as it is so much quicker. The bus stand and the station are on Cart Road, where porters and hotel touts jostle to take your luggage up the steep hill – possibly

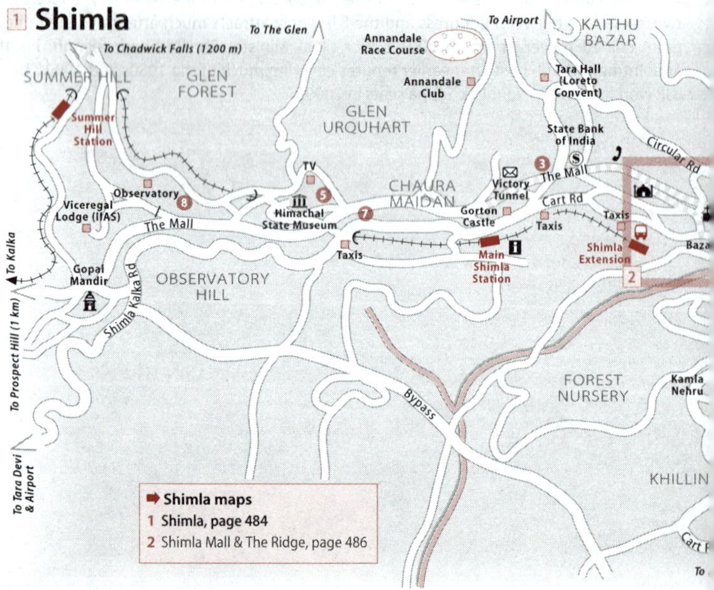

Sleeping
Chapslee House 1
Clarkes 2
Dalziel 3
Harsha 5
Oberoi Cecil 7
Peterhoff 8
Springfields 9

the best few rupees you will ever spend. If you are staying on the western side of town it is worth getting off the bus at the railway station. Buses from the east, including Rampur and Kinnaur, stop at the Rivoli Bus Stand. Shimla (Jabbarhatti) airport has a coach (Rs 50) in season, and taxis (Rs 400-500) for transfer.

Getting around The Mall can only be seen on foot; it takes about half an hour to walk from the Viceroy's Lodge to Christ Church. The main traffic artery is Cart Road, which continues past the station to the main bus stand, taxi rank and the two-stage lift which goes to The Mall above. The Victory Tunnel cuts through from Cart Road to the north side of the hill. ▸▸ *See Transport, page 493.*

Tourist offices Himachal Pradesh Tourism Development Corportation (HPTDC) ⓘ *The Mall, T0177-265 2561, www.hptdc.nic.in, 0900-1800, in season 0900-1900; also at Cart Rd, near Victory Tunnel, T0177-265 4589, 1000-1700*, is very informative and helpful.

Climate October and November are very pleasant, with warm days and cool nights. December-February is cold and there are snowfalls. March and April are changeable; storms are not infrequent and the air can feel very chilly. Avoid May-June, the height of the Indian tourist season prior to the monsoon.

Sights

Shimla is strung out on a long crescent-shaped ridge that connects a number of hilltops from which there are good views of the snow-capped peaks to the north: Jakhu (2453 m), Prospect Hill (2176 m), Observatory Hill (2148 m), Elysium Hill (2255 m) and Summer Hill (2103 m). For the British, the only way of beating the hot weather on the plains in May and June was to move to hill stations, which they endowed with mock-Tudor houses, churches, clubs, parks with bandstands of English county towns, and a main street invariably called The Mall.

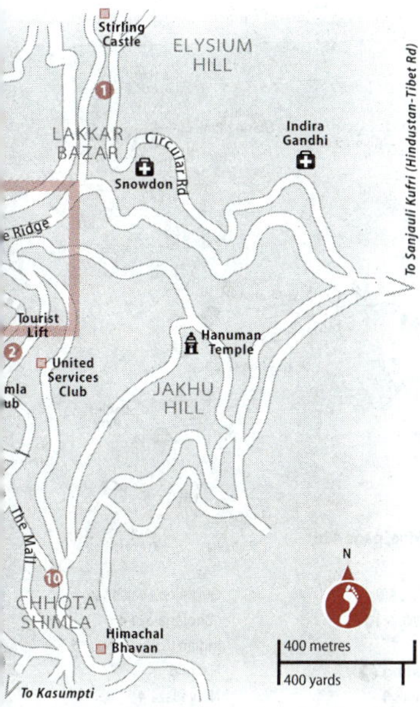

Woodville Palace **10**

Christ Church (1844), on the open area of The Ridge, dominates the eastern end of town. Consecrated in 1857, a clock and porch were added later. The original chancel window, designed by Lockwood Kipling, Rudyard's father, is no longer there. The mock tudor **library** building (circa 1910) is next door. The Mall joins The Ridge at Kipling's **'Scandal Point'**, where today groups gather to exchange gossip. Originally the name referred to the stir caused by the supposed 'elopement' of a lady from the Viceregal Lodge and a dashing Patiala prince after they arranged a rendezvous here.

The **Gaiety Theatre** (1887) and the **Town Hall** (circa 1910) are reminiscent of the 'arts and crafts' style, as well as the timbered **General Post Office** (1886). Beyond, to the west, is the **Grand Hotel**. Further down you pass the sinister-looking **Gorton Castle**, designed by Sir Samuel Swinton Jacob, which was once the Civil Secretariat. A road to the left leads to the railway station, while one to the right goes to Annandale, the racecourse and cricket ground. The Mall leads to the rebuilt **Cecil Hotel**. On

Observatory Hill, the **Viceregal Lodge** (1888) is the most splendid of Shimla's surviving Raj-era buildings, built for Lord Dufferin in the Elizabethan style. Now the **Rashtrapati Niwas** ⓘ *1000-1630, Rs 10 including a brief tour*, it stands in large grounds with good views of the mountains. Reminders of its British origins include a gatehouse, a chapel and the meticulously polished brass fire hydrants imported from Manchester. Inside, you can visit the main reception rooms and the library which are lined from floor to ceiling with impressive teak panelling. It is a long up the hill walk from the gate.

Himachal State Museum ⓘ *near Chaura Maidan, Tue-Sun 1000-1330, 1400-1700, free*, is a 30-minute walk west from the GPO along The Mall; then it's a short climb from the Harsha Hotel. Small, with a good sculpture collection and miniatures from the Kangra School, it also houses contemporary art including work by Roerich, costumes, jewellery, bronzes and textiles (everything is well labelled).

Walks

Jakhu Temple on a hill with excellent views (2455 m), dedicated to Hanuman the monkey god, is 2 km from Christ Church. Walking sticks (handy for warding off monkeys, which can be vicious – keep all food out of sight) are available at *chai* shops at the start of the ascent. **The Glen** (1830 m), to the northwest, is a 4-km walk from the centre past the **Cecil Hotel**. **Summer Hill** (1983 m), a pleasant 'suburb' 5 km from town, is a stop on the Shimla-Kalka railway. **Chadwick Falls** (1586 m), 3 km further, drops 67 m during the monsoon season.

Prospect Hill (2175 m) is 5 km from The Ridge and a 20-minute walk from Boileauganj to the west. **Tara Devi** (1851 m), with a hilltop temple, 11 km southwest from the railway station, can also be reached by car or train.

2 Shimla Mall & The Ridge

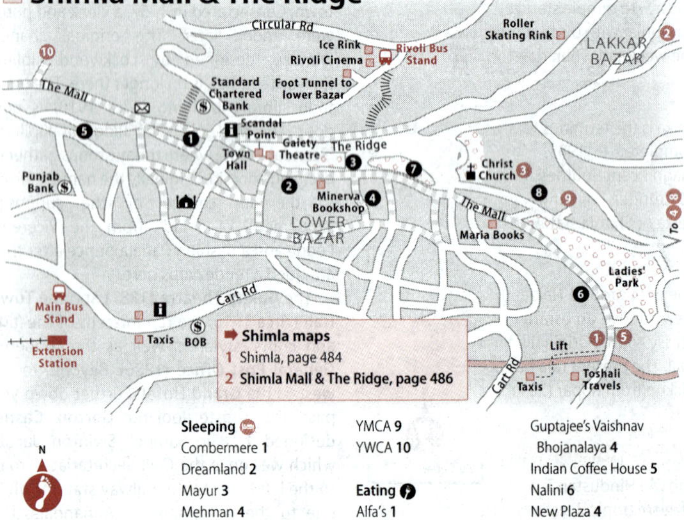

Sleeping
Combermere 1
Dreamland 2
Mayur 3
Mehman 4
Samrat Regency 5
Woodland 8
YMCA 9
YWCA 10

Eating
Alfa's 1
Baljee's 2
Goofa 3
Guptajee's Vaishnav Bhojanalaya 4
Indian Coffee House 5
Nalini 6
New Plaza 4
Park 7
Ridge Café 8

Around Shimla → *For listings, see pages 490-494. Colour map 1, B3.*

Kufri

About 16 km from Shimla, at 2500 m, Kufri hosts a winter sports festival in January which includes the **National Snow Statue Competition**. Don't expect European or American resort standards though. There are some attractions around and about the town. At **Danes Folly** (2550 m), 5 km away, is a government-run orchard. A 10-minute walk uphill takes you to a mini zoo of Himalayan wildlife. **Mahasu Peak** (bus, Rs 15) 20 minutes from a path behind the Kufri Resort cottages, offers fabulous mountain views on a clear day and there is a small but interesting temple at the start of the walk. The best time to visit is in January and February.

Chharabra

Chharabra is an enjoyable 3-km forest walk down from Kufri. The Wildflower Hall which once stood here was the residence of **Lord Kitchener**, commander-in-chief of the Indian Army. The original building was replaced; its successor was converted into a hotel which burnt down in 1993. **Oberoi** has opened a new luxury hotel (see Sleeping, page 490).

Naldera

Off the Hindusthan-Tibet road, 26 km north of Shimla, Naldera has a nine-hole golf course, possibly the oldest in India and one of the highest in the world, and the beautiful Mahung temple. The colourful **Sipi Fair** in June attracts handicraft-sellers from surrounding villages.

Chail

In a superb forest setting with fine snow views, 45 km southeast of Shimla (2½ hours by bus), off the NH22, Chail was once the Maharaja of Patiala's summer capital. Built across three hills, it claims to have the country's highest cricket ground at 2444 m, a 2-km walk from the bus stand. The old palace on Rajgarh Hill has been converted to a hotel while the old residency, Snow View, and a Sikh temple stand on the other hills. The **Chail Sanctuary**, once a private hunting reserve, is popular with birders and has a Cheer pheasant-breeding programme. It is an idyllic spot until the weekend when day-trippers descend on the tiny resort.

Kalka

Kalka is the terminus for the narrow-gauge railway from Shimla. The Kalka-Shimla line (0.76 m), completed in 1903, runs 97 km from Kalka in the foothills to Shimla at over 2000 m. The magnificent journey takes just over five hours. The steepest gradient is 1:33; there are 107 tunnels covering 8 km and 969 bridges over 3 km. Take snacks or order a meal in advance at Kalka or Shimla station.

Nalagarh

The area around Nalagarh was once ruled by the Chandela Rajputs. The fort has wonderful views above an estate of forests and orchards and is built on five levels around manicured grassy courts. Originally built in the 15th century; the **Diwan-i-Khas** (1618) is now the Banquet Hall. The present raja has opened his home to guests. You can request the **Nalagarh Fort** hotel pickup from Ropar (20 km) or Kalka (40 km).

Old Hindustan Tibet Road → *For listings, see pages 490-494. Colour map 1, B3/4.*

The Old Hindustan Tibet road runs east from Shimla to the Tibetan border through a landscape of lush tropical valleys, snow-clad peaks and precipitous gorges. Connecting a string of prosperous-looking farms, villages and towns, it passes through terraced slopes covered with orchards before entering the high-altitude deserts of Spiti. As the narrow road winds even deeper towards the Tibetan border its unprotected sides plunge hundreds of metres to the roaring monsoon-swollen River Sutlej below, grasping at huge boulders brought down by thundering landslides into the gloomy gorges. By bus or jeep, this road is not for the faint-hearted. The road may be severely damaged in the rains.

Ins and outs

Inner Line Permits, which are needed for travel close to the Tibetan border (essentially the area between Kaza and Jangi), are easy enough to get. Permits are issued free to individuals for seven days from the date of issue (easily renewable for three days at Kaza or Recong Peo). Take your passport, two copies of the details and Indian visa pages, and three passport photos and complete the form from the **Sub-Divisional Magistrate's office** (SDM) in **Shimla** ⓘ *T0177-265 5988*; **Recong Peo** ⓘ *T01786-222452*; or **Kaza** ⓘ *T01906-222212*, where you need the additional 'No Objection' certificate from the chief of police (a mere formality of a stamp and signature). In Recong Peo, the whole process takes about an hour, which may include *chai* or breakfast with the SDM. Permits are also available (in theory) from the **Resident Comissioner of Himachal Pradesh** ⓘ *Himachal Bhavan, 27 Sikandra Rd, New Delhi, T011-2371 6574*, and other magistrates offices. In Shimla, travel agents charge Rs 150. Permits are checked at Jangi if coming from Shimla and at Sumdo coming from Spiti. Carry about 10 photocopies as some checkpoints demand to keep one. Rules regarding overnight stays have been relaxed considerably; it is now possible to sleep in Puh and Nako. Accommodation is limited to simple rest houses, lodges or tents. In some places enterprising local families are opening their modest homes to paying guests. Local village shops often stock canned food and bottled water. It is virtually impossible to get foreign exchange in this area.

Narkanda

The small market town at 2700 m occupies a superb position. The town offers a base from which to ski but the skiing does not compare with that found in Western resorts. Enquire at the Marketing Office in Shimla for skiing excursions in winter and the seven-day beginners' course (Rs 4500-5000).

Nirath

The road drops sharply through woodland interspersed with apple orchards from Narkanda, down to Kingel from where it zig-zags down to Sainj. The seasonal route is best by 4WD though buses cover this route very carefully. Some 5 km beyond Sainj there are superb views both across the valley, and of a wall of eroded outwash deposits at least 50 m thick. The main road passes through Nirath where there is a **Surya Temple** believed to date from the eighth century which still has some fine carving preserved on the outer walls and has carved wooden panels within. At an altitude of 800-900 m the Sutlej Valley towards Rampur has a subtropical summer climate, with mango trees and bananas replacing apples.

Rampur Bushahr

This is one of Himachal's most important market towns. **Padam Palace** (1920s), opposite the bus stand, once the residence of the raja, has interesting carved wooden panels and wall murals, but is difficult to enter. **Sat Narain Temple** in the main bazar (1926) has a beautiful but decaying façade. **Lavi Fair** (November) draws large crowds of colourful hill people who bring their produce – handicrafts, carpets, rugs, fruit and nuts and animals – to the special market. There are sporting competitions in the day, and dancing and making music around bonfires after dark.

Rampur to Sarahan

From Rampur the highway enters one of the most exciting (and geologically active) stretches of road in the region. During the rains, the Sutlej River is a surging torrent of muddy water,

The stuff of epics

The *bhoj patra*, found distinctively in the Sangla Valley, is a revered product. The extraordinarily fine waterproof layers just beneath the bark of the *bhoj patra* tree were used for writing centuries ago, particularly where palm leaves were not available. Renowned for its suppleness, strength and apparent indestructibility, bark from this valley was used for some of Hinduism's most ancient writings, including the epics, and it is still highly valued for copying sacred texts. Genealogies which trace the descent of some families in the Sangla Valley to the legendary Pandavas are still widely accepted, and connections between the residents of the valley and the early roots of Hinduism are treasured.

dropping over 450 m in under 30 km and passing through gorges and deeply incised valleys. Although an ancient trade route, the road is comparatively recent and is constantly being upgraded particularly in connection with the Nathpa-Jhakhri HEP scheme, with a 28-km-long tunnel from **Nathpa**, near Wangtu, to **Jhakhri**, about 10 km beyond Rampur. When completed this will be one of the largest Hydel schemes in the world. The blasting both for the shafts and for road widening has further destabilized the already landslide-prone hillsides and during the rains the road may be blocked. Blockages are usually cleared within hours, though travelling times are wholly unpredictable. You also need a strong stomach, both for the main road and for diversions, especially up the Baspa Valley to Sangla. Some 9 km west of Jeori the river passes through a dramatic gorge. On the north side of the river isolated tiny pockets of cultivated land cling to the hillside. **Jeori** is the junction for Sarahan, 21 km south, an hour away. There are several provisions stores to pick up the basics here since Sarahan has very limited supplies.

Sarahan →

For listings, see pages 490-494. *Colour map 1, B4. Phone code: 01782. Population: 1200. Altitude: 2165 m.*

An important market for traders of neighbouring regions, Sarahan is an attractive town, surrounded by high peaks, with a pheasant-breeding centre nearby (see below). The bazar is interesting: friendly villagers greet travellers, shops sell flowers, bright red and gold scarves and other offerings for worshippers among local produce, fancy goods, clothes and jewellery. It is also a stop on the trekkers' route.

Sarahan was the old capital of the local Rampur Bushahr rulers and has a palace complex containing the strikingly carved wood-bonded **Bhimakali Temple** (rebuilt circa 1927), in a mixture of Hindu and Buddhist styles. The two temples stand on a slope among apple and apricot orchards behind the bazar. The Bhimakali is dedicated to Durga as the destroyer of the *asuras* (demons) and has a Brahmin priest in attendance. Plan for an early-morning visit to the temple to see morning prayers; evening prayers are around 1900. Leave shoes and leather objects with the attendant and wear the saffron cap offered to you before entering. You may only photograph the outside of the temples. It is worth climbing around the back of the complex for a picturesque view.

According to some sources the ancient temple on the right (closed for safety reasons) is many centuries olde. Built in traditional timber-bonded style it has whitewashed dry stone and rubble masonry alternating with horizontal deodar or spruce beams to withstand earthquakes. The upper floors have balconies and windows with superb ornamental woodcarving; the silver repoussée-work doors are also impressive. The first floor has a 200-year-old gold image of goddess Bhimkali which is actively worshipped only during the **Dasara festival** when animals and birds are sacrificed in the courtyard, while on the second floor daily early-morning *puja* is carried out to a second image. The sacrificial altar and the old well are in the courtyard with three other shrines. The palace of the Rampur rajas behind the temple has a drawing room with ornate furniture and a painted ceiling; the caretaker may let you in.

Pheasant Breeding Centre ⓘ *summer 0830-1830, winter 0930-1630, free*, on a hill, a 1-km strenuous walk from the main road, on a wooded trail, has Monal, Khalij, Western Tragopan and other varieties in cages.

A pilgrimage route encircles **Shrikhand Mahadev peak** (5227 m), which takes pilgrims seven days to go round. On a clear day you get fantastic panoramic views of the snow- covered peaks.

Southern Himachal listings

For Sleeping and Eating price codes and other relevant information, see Essentials pages 38-42.

Sleeping

Shimla *p484, maps p484 and p486*

Prices soar May-Jun when modest rooms can be difficult to find especially after midday, so book ahead. Some places close off-season; those that remain open may offer discounts of 30-50%. From the railway or bus station it is a stiff climb up to hotels on or near the Ridge. Porters are available (Rs 20 per heavy bag).

LL Chapslee House (Heritage), Lakkar Bazar, T0177-280 2542, www.chapslee.com. 6 suites only, charming, full of bygone-era character, large grounds, exquisite interior, good views, excellent meals (disappointing *thali* though) and excellent service, if you can get in.

LL Oberoi Cecil, Chaura Maidan (quiet end of The Mall), T0177-280 4848, www.oberoi hotels.com. 79 sumptuous rooms, colonial grandeur on the edge of town, with superb views, beautifully renovated, stylishly furnished, good restaurant, special ultra-modern pool, full-board. Recommended.

AL Clarkes, The Mall, near Lift, T0177-265 1010, www.clarkesshimla.com. 39 large, comfortable rooms, those with mountain views at rear may suffer from traffic noise at night, front rooms with town views quieter, impressive dining room (good buffets), pleasant bar, has character, well run but lacks some **AL** facilities (eg no pool).

AL-A Woodville Palace (Heritage), Raj Bhavan Rd, The Mall, T0177-262 4038, www.woodville palace.com. 30 rooms (variable), some good **L** suites with period furniture (freezing in winter), dining hall worth visiting for eclectic mixture of portraits, weapons and hunting trophies (non-residents on advance notice), owned by the Raja of Jubbal's family and featured in *Jewel in the Crown*. Good views, spacious, large grounds, one of the quietest.

A Springfields (Quality Inn), opposite Tibetan School, Chhota Shimla, T0177-262 1297, www.ushalexushotels.com. 11 huge, light and airy rooms with modern bathrooms in old maharaja's bungalow "where staff refused to be tipped". Superb views, lawns, restaurant.

A-B Combermere, 2 entrances, next to the lift at top and bottom, T0177-265 1246, www.hotelcombermere.com. Good central location, 40 decent rooms (including penthouses) on 6 levels (partly served by lift), well located, friendly, efficient, very helpful, pleasant terrace café and bar, games room, central heating/a/c, super deluxe rooms worth the extra Rs 200.

A-C Peterhoff (HPTDC), Chaura Maidan, near All India Radio, T0177-265 2538, www.hptdc. nic.in. 35 sombre but spacious rooms in very quiet location with beautiful lawn terrace and friendly, helpful staff.

B-C Harsha, The Mall, next to State Museum, T0177-265 8442, www.hotelharshashimla.com. 21 rooms, restaurant, rather uninspired but friendly service, pleasant and quiet location.

C-D Dalziel, The Mall, above station, T0177-645 1306, www.dalzielhotel.com. 30 clean enough, comfy, creaky valley-facing rooms with bath (hot water) in heritage building, Indian meals, prices depend on size of TV.

C-D Samrat Regency, near upper lift station on The Mall, T0177-265 8272, samratregency@ hotmail.com. 20 rooms, restaurant, helpful.

C-D Spars Lodge, museum road up the hill from the Oberoi, T0177-265 7908, www.spars lodge.com. 12 rooms. Simple and clean, with good views from the top floors and excellent hospitality. Recommended.

C-F Mayur, above Christ Church, T0177-265 2393, www.hotelmayur.com. 30 rooms in 1970s style, some with mountain views, some with tub, good restaurant but check bill, modern and clean, lift, helpful staff.

D-E Mehman, above Christ Church, T0177-281 3692. Modern with 21 rooms (some with mirrored ceilings), plumbing suspect, very clean, great views from the front, very helpful staff.

D-F Dreamland, The Ridge, T0177-280 6897, www.hoteldreamlandshimla.com. 31 clean rooms that vary in size and quality of bathroom, check first, plus good views.

E-F Woodland, Daisy Bank, The Ridge, T0177-281 1002, www.hotelwoodlandshimla.com. 21 rooms, some wood-panelled, some with great views, all with bath, cleanliness varies, avoid noisy downstairs rooms near reception, friendly, room service, safe luggage storage, off-season bargain.

E-F YMCA, The Ridge, above Christ Church, T0177-265 2375. 40 rooms (**E** in annexe best with bath), clean linen, hot water in mornings, clean bathrooms on 2nd floor, avoid west side near noisy cinema, mediocre meals (breakfast included), quiet, relaxed, popular but very efficient/institutionalized, gym and billiards.

G YWCA, Constantia, T0177-280 3081. Superb position, 11 clean if musty rooms for both sexes, heavily booked May-Jun, off-season discounts, water at certain times of day, safe and very good value, but now starting to crumble slightly.

Kufri *p487*

LL-A Kufri Holiday Resort, T0177-264 8341, www.kufriholidayresorts.com. 30 rooms (**A**) and 8 modern cottages (**LL**, 2-3 bedrooms), limited hot water, cold in winter, but attractive design and setting with flower-filled gardens, outstanding views from cottages above and good walks.

Chharabra *p487*

LL Wildflower Hall, T0177-264 8585, www.oberoihotels.com. Former residence of Lord Kitchener, retains period exterior but has been completely refurbished inside. 87 sumptuous rooms, beautifully decorated, mountain views, good restaurants and lovely gardens surrounded by deodar forest with beautifully peaceful walks, plus extensive spa, yoga classes under pine trees, Ayurvedic treatments.

Naldera *p487*

L-AL The Chalets Naldehra, Durgapur Village, T0177-274 7715, www.chaletsnaldehra.com. 14 alpine-style pine chalets plus restaurant and a wide range of outdoor activities including world's highest golf course.

AL-D Golf Glade (HPTDC), T0177-274 7739, www.hptdc.nic.in. 5 simple rooms, plus 7 log huts (2 bedrooms), restaurant, bar, golfing requirements including clubs and instructors.

B Koti Resort, T0177-274 0177, www.kotiresort.net. 40 modern, if slightly spartan rooms in beautifully located hotel surrounded by deodar forest, friendly manager, very relaxing.

D-E Mitwa Cottage, near **Koti Resort**, T0177-201 2279. Sweet little homestay with kitchens and balconies.

Chail *p487*

A Tarika's Jungle Retreat, Chail, T01792-248684/691, www.tarikasjungleretreat.com. 35 well-appointed 'suite' cottages with lots of wood panelling. Geodesic glass reception. Popular family resort.

A Toshali Royal View Resort, Shilon Bagh (5 km outside Chail), T(0)9350-599084, www.toshaliroyalview.com. 77 modern rooms in this huge alpine-style lodge, great views from dining terrace, friendly staff.

A-C Chail Palace, T01792-248141, www.hptdc.nic.in. 19 rooms and 3 suites in old stone-built mansion; avoid basement rooms 21, 22, 23, dark, dingy wooden chalets but others OK, billiards, tennis, orchards, well-maintained lawns and gardens, slightly institutional feel, interesting museum.

E Himneel, T01792-248141, www.hptdc.nic.in. 16 rooms, modest but full of character. **Kailash** restaurant serves good-value breakfasts and lunches.

Kalka *p487*

If using your own transport, there are many hotels, guesthouses and *dhabas* along the Kalka-Shimla road. **Kasauli** is an attractive hill resort with a distinctly English feel, 16 km off the main road with a few hotels, notably:

A Baikunth, Village Chabbal, near Kasauli, T01792-272 712, www.baikunth.com. Red brick building in the hills. Sunny rooms with all mod cons. Recommended for its spa.

A Kasauli Resorts, T01792-273651, www.kasauliresort.net. 33 luxurious rooms in a modern, upmarket development in the hills, extra clean, gym, mountain views.

B Alasia, T01792-272008. 13 rooms in hugely atmospheric Raj-era hotel, remarkably authentic English cuisine, impeccable staff.

G Railway Retiring Rooms. Good for early-morning departures. Reserve ahead at Kalka or Shimla.

Nalagarh *p487*

A-B Nalagarh Fort, T01795-223179, www.nalagarh.com. 15 comfortable rooms (some suites), with modern baths, traditional furniture, good food (buffets only), small pool, tennis, rural surroundings, plenty of atmosphere. Recommended. Book ahead.

Narkanda *p488*

L-AL Banjara Orchard Retreat, Thanedar Village, 15km from Narkanda (80 km from Shimla), T(0)9418-077180, www.banjara camps.com. 6 double rooms, 2 suites and 2 lovely log cabins, set in apple orchards with stunning views down the Sutlej Valley. Evenings round the fire under the stars, trekking and excellent food. Recommended.

A-B Tethy's Narkanda Resort, T01782-242641. Comfortable rooms and some swiss cottage tents with stunning views. They organize snow skiing, hiking, mountain biking, river rafting, horse riding.

A-C The Hatu, (HPTDC), T01782- 242430. Typical government fare, but with great views.

Rampur Bushahr *p488*

C-E Bushehar Regency, 2 km short of Rampur on NH22, T01782-234103. 20 rooms, some a/c, well positioned. Restaurant, huge lawn, bar nearby.

F-G Bhagwati, below bus stand near river, T01782-233117. Friendly hotel, 24 clean rooms with bath (hot water), TV, restaurant.

Sarahan *p489*

C-E Srikhand (HPTDC), T01782-274234, www.hptdc.nic.in. Superb hilltop site, over-looking the Sutlej Valley, Srikhand peak and beyond. 19 rooms with bath and hot water (3 large with balcony, 8 smaller with views, 4 in annexe cheaper), dorm (Rs 75), 2-bedroom royal cottage, restaurant but limited menu. Very close to stunning temple.

E Sangrika, near Police Assistance, T01782-274491. 8 rooms with Indian toilets, 6 planned with Western toilets on 1st floor, family-run, home-cooked meals.

F-G Bhimakali Temple. Basic rooms with clean bathrooms and shared balconies, highly atmospheric.

Eating

Shimla *p484, maps p484 and p486*

Below The Mall, towards Lower Bazar, good cheap *dhabas* sell snacks (eg *tikki channa*).

TTT **Cecil, Oberoi Cecil** (see Sleeping). Atmospheric, plush, modernized.

TTT **Chapslee**. Old-fashioned.

TTT **Woodville Palace** (see Sleeping). Intimate.

TT **Alfa's**, The Mall. Modern interior, range of continental dishes in addition to good *thalis*, courteous service.

TT **Baljees**, 26 The Mall, opposite Town Hall. Good snacks, justifiably packed, cakes and sweets available from takeaway counter.

TT **Goofa** (below Ashiana), the Ridge. Dimly lit cavern under the bandstand, with decent pizzas, *thalis*, and a couple of unusual Himachali dishes.

TT **Nalini**, The Mall. International food. Pleasant, good service, salty but delicious tandoori dishes, pizzas; also ice creams and sweets counters.

T **Guptajee's Vaishnav Bhojanalaya**, 62 Middle Bazar. 1st-class Indian vegetarian fare including tasty stuffed tomatoes, great *thali*. Recommended.

T **Indian Coffee House**, The Mall. International. South Indian snacks, excellent coffee, some Western dishes, old-world feel, uniformed waiters, spartan and dim. Recommended.

T **New Plaza**, 60/61 Middle Bazar, down steps. Excellent value, friendly, simple but clean, serves a variety of Western dishes.

T **Park Café**, in hidden park below Christ Church. Indian. Continental menu. Student and traveller hangout, great pizzas, excellent espresso coffee.

T **Sagar Ratna**, 6/1 The Mall, upstairs, T0177-280 0526. Good vegetarian South Indian food, *dosas*, *idlis*, good value.

Sarahan *p489*
Dhabas in town serve basic food (rice, dhal and snacks).

Festivals and events

Shimla *p484, maps p484 and p486*
May-Jun Summer Festival includes cultural programmes from Himachal and neighbouring states, and art and handicrafts exhibitions.
25 Dec An **ice skating carnival** is held on Christmas Day.

Shopping

Shimla *p484, maps p484 and p486*
The main shopping areas are The Mall, Lower Bazar and Lakkar Bazar.
Himachal Emporium, The Mall, opposite Telegraph Office. Woollen items, fixed prices.
Maria Brothers, 78 The Mall. 1030-1300, 1700-2000. Good selection of antiquarian books, maps and prints.
Minerva, 46 The Mall, opposite Gaiety Theatre. Good range of books and maps.
Tibetan Self-Help Handicrafts Centre, near Kusumpti, 6 km. Produces carpets and woven goods, keeping Tibetan traditions alive, sold through other outlets in town.

Activities and tours

Shimla and around *p484, maps p484 and p486*

Golf

There is a 9-hole course in Naldera. Casual members: green fee and equipment, about Rs 100, see page 487.

Ice skating

Skating rink: below Rivoli, winter only, Rs 50 to skate all day to loud Indian film hits.

Skiing

Early Jan to mid-Mar. Ski courses at Narkanda (64 km) organized by **HPTDC**, 7- and 15-day courses, Jan-Mar, Rs 1700-3000; see page 488.

Tour operators

Tour companies charge Rs 800-900 per car.
Band Box, 9 The Mall, T0177-265 8157, bboxhv@satyam.net.in. Jeep safaris round Kinnaur and Spiti (around Rs 1800 per day), helpful advice, safe drivers and guides who clearly love the mountains. Recommended.
Hi-Lander, 62 The Mall, T0177-280 1565, www.hilandertravels.com. Adventure tours and treks, hotel and transport bookings.
HPTDC's various tours during the season are well run, usually 1000-1700 (Rs 160-250). All start from Rivoli, enquire when booking for other pickup points. Return drop at Lift or Victory Tunnel. 2 tours visit Kufri, Chini Bungalow and Nature Park; 1 returns to Shimla via Fagu, Naldehra and Mashobra, the other by Chail and Kairighat. A further tour visits Fagu, Theog, Matiana and Narkanda. Book in advance at HPTDC office on The Mall.
Nature Beckons, T0177-2640 2471, www.naturebeckons.com. Competently organized trekking, camping, jeep and horse safaris in Shimla and Kullu environs.

Transport

Shimla *p484, maps p484 and p486*
Air Shimla (Jabbarhatti) airport (23 km from town) has daily flights to **Delhi** and **Kullu** all year round, as well as some extra flights during summer. **Air India**, T1-800-180 1407, www.airindia.in; **Kingfisher Red**, T1-800-209 3030, www.flykingfisher.com. Flights can be badly disrupted by the weather especially during the monsoon. Taxis charge Rs 500 to town.
Local bus From Cart Rd. Lift: 2-stage lift from the Taxi Stand on Cart Rd and near **Hotel Samrat** on The Mall, takes passengers to and from The Mall, 0800-2200, Rs 8. Porters at bus stand and upper lift station will ask anything from Rs 10 to Rs 50 per bag; lower prices mean hotel commission.
Long distance bus From main bus stand, Cart Rd, T0177-265 8765. Buy tickets from counter before boarding bus (signs in Hindi so ask for help) some long-distance buses can be reserved in advance: HPTDC coaches during the season are good value and reliable. **Kalka**, 3 hrs, Rs 80, quicker than train but requires strong stomach; **Chandigarh**, 4 hrs, Rs 90, **Dehra Dun**, 9 hrs, Rs 168; **Delhi**, 10-12 hrs, Rs 380; overnight to **Dharamshala**, 10 hrs, Rs 180. **Manali**, departs outside the 'Tunnel', 8-10 hrs, Rs 220, tickets from main bus stand. HPTDC deluxe buses between Shimla and **Delhi** in the summer, 9 hrs, Rs 415.

From **Rivoli Bus Stand** (Lakkar Bazar) T0177-281 1259: frequent buses to **Kufri**, **Rampur**, hourly from 0530, 8 hrs, and **Chitkul**, 2 daily; **Jeori** for **Sarahan** (8 hrs).

Car hire HPTDC (see page 485), has a/c cars.

Taxi Local taxis have fixed fares and run from near the lift on Cart Rd, T0177-265 7645. Long-distance taxis run from Union Stands near the lift, T0177-280 5164, and by the main bus stand on Cart Rd. **Chandigarh**, Rs 1400; **Kalka** (90 km), Rs 1100; **Mussoorie**, Rs 4500, 8 hrs, including stops; **Rekong-Peo**, around Rs 4500 (11 hrs).

Train Enquiry T131. Computerized reservations at main station (T0177-265 2915), 1000-1330, 1400-1700, Sun 1000-1400, and by tourist office on The Mall. The newer extension station, where some trains start and terminate, is just below the main bus stand. Travel to/from Shimla involves a change of gauge to the slow and cramped but extremely picturesque 'toy train' at Kalka. To reach Shimla from **Delhi** in a day by train, catch the *Himalayan Queen* or *Shatabdi Exp* to arrive in Kalka by 1200 (see Kalka, below). In the reverse direction, the 1030 train from Shimla has you in Kalka at 1600 in time to board the Delhi-bound *Himalayan Queen*. Book tickets for the toy train in advance; the 'Ticket Extension Booth' on Kalka station sells out by 1200 when the *Shatabdi* arrives, and the train often arrives on the Kalka platform already full of locals who board it while it waits in the siding. Worth paying Rs 150-170 plus reservation fee of Rs 20 to guarantee a seat on 1st class. **Kalka to Shimla**: *1 KS*, 0400, 5½ hrs; *Shiwalik Exp Deluxe 241*, 0530, 4¾ hrs; *Shimla Mail 251*, 0600, 5 hrs; *Shimla Exp 255*, 1210, 5¼ hrs. Extra trains in season (1 May-15 Jul; 15 Sep-30 Oct; 15 Dec-1 Jan): *Shiwalik Deluxe 253*, 0630, 5 hrs, boasts "toilet fittings of latest variety" and "curtains of latest design", pricier ticket (Rs 305) includes tea and breakfast/dinner at Barog; *Exp 251*, 1235, 5 hrs. The quicker 16-seater glass-top *Rail Car 0730* and 1135 on demand, 3½ hrs, can only be booked at Kalka. **Shimla to Kalka**: *Shimla-Kalka Exp 256*, 1030, 5½ hrs; *2 KS*, 1425, 5¾ hrs; *Shiwalik Exp Deluxe 242*, 1740, 4¾ hrs; *Shimla Mail 11815*, 5 hrs.

Kalka *p487*

Bus or taxi Easily reached from **Shimla**, by bus or taxi (Rs 1100), and from **Chandigarh** by taxi (Rs 500).

Train Kalka to Delhi: *Shatabdi Exp 2006*, 0600, 4 hrs; *Shatabdi Exp 12012*, 1730, 4 hrs; *Himalayan Queen 14096*, ND, 1640, 5½ hrs; *Kalka Howrah Mail 12312*, OD, 2345, 6¾ hrs; day trains are better). All via Chandigarh, 45 mins. **Delhi to Kalka**: *Himalayan Queen 14095*, ND, 0600, 5¼ hrs; *Shatabdi Exp 12011*, ND, 0740, to Kalka 1200; *Howrah Kalka Mail 12311*, OD, 2215, to Kalka 0455.

Rampur Bushahr *p488*

Bus Buses are often late and overcrowded. To **Chandigarh**, **Delhi**; **Mandi** (9 hrs); **Recong Peo** (5 hrs) and **Puh**; **Sarahan** (2-3 hrs), better to change at Jeori; **Shimla**, several (5-6 hrs); **Tapri** (and Kalpa) 0545 (3¼ hrs), change at Karchham for Sangla and Chitkul.

Sarahan *p489*

Bus Daily buses between **Shimla** (**Rivoli Bus Stand**) and **Jeori** on the Highway (6 hrs), quicker by car. Local buses between Jeori and the army cantonment below Sarahan.

❶ Directory

Shimla *p484, maps p484 and p486*

Banks Several international ATMs along The Mall. Changing foreign currency outside Shimla is not easy except in Manali or McLeodganj. Do not depend on credit cards for cash. Exchange procedure is awkward; photocopies of passport and visa needed. **Grindlays**, The Mall, and **UCO** quick and efficient. **Internet** HPTDC, The Mall, Rs 50 per hr; better deal on The Mall from "Internet Telephony" place, upstairs opposite Gaiety Theatre, Rs 30. **Medical services** **Tara Hospital**, The Ridge, T0177-280 3785: Dr Puri, Mehghana Complex, The Mall, T0177-280 1936, speaks fluent English, is efficient, and very reasonable. **Post** GPO, The Mall, T0177-265 2518. Open Sun 1000-1600. **Poste Restante**: Counter 10 (separate entrance), chaotic, 0800-1700, Sun 1000-1600. **CTO** nearby. **Useful contacts** **Police**: T0177-265 2860.

Kinnaur and Spiti

The regions of Kinnaur and Spiti lie in the rainshadow of the outer Himalayan ranges. The climate in Spiti is much drier than in the Kullu Valley and is similar to that of Ladakh. The temperatures are more extreme both in summer and winter and most of the landscape is barren and bleak. The wind can be bitingly cold even when the sun is hot. The annual rainfall is very low so cultivation is restricted to the ribbons of land that fringe rivers with irrigation potential. The crops include potatoes, wheat, barley and millet. The people are of Mongol origin and almost everyone follows a Tibetan form of Buddhism.

Kinnaur and Spiti can only be seen by following a circular route, first along the Old Hindustan Tibet Road by the Sutlej River, then crossing into the wild Spiti Valley, which has the evocative Tibetan Buddhist sites of Tabo and Kaza set against the backdrop of a rugged mountain landscape. The road continues round to the Rohtang Pass and Manali, or on up to Ladakh. It's also worth making a side trip up the Baspa Valley via Sangla to Chitkul for its views and landscapes, villages, pagodas and culture.
▸▸ *For listings, see pages 503-506.*

Kinnaur and around → *For listings, see pages 503-506. Colour map 1, B3.*

Most Kinnauri Buddhist temples only accept visitors at around 0700 and 1900. You must wear a hat and a special belt available locally. ▸▸ *For trekking, see page 546.*

Along the Sutlej

An exciting mountain road runs through cliffside cuttings along the left bank of the Sutlej – frequently blocked by rockfalls and landslides during the monsoons. At **Choling** the Sutlej roars through a narrow gorge, and at **Wangtu** the road re-crosses the river where vehicle details are checked. Immediately after crossing the Wangtu bridge a narrow side road goes to **Kafnoo village** (2427 m), in the Bhabha Valley (a camping site and the start for an attractive 10-day trek to the Pin Valley). From Wangtu the road route runs to **Tapri** (1870 m) and **Karchham** (1899 m) both of which have hot springs. Here the Baspa River joins the Sutlej from the south. A hair-raising excursion by a precipitous winding rough road leads 16 km up the Baspa Valley to Sangla; buses take approximately 1½ hours.

Baspa Valley

The valley carries the marks of a succession of glacial events which have shaped it, although the glaciers which formed the valley have now retreated to the high slopes above Chitkul at over 4500 m. Recently the valley has been terribly scarred by the Baspa Hydroelectric Project, with blasting, dust and truck logjams commonplace, but persevere and carry on up the valley and the rewards are worth it. All villages in Baspa are characterized by exaggerated steeply sloping slate roofs, rich wood carving and elaborate pagoda temples. Although Kinner Kailash (sacred to Hindus and Buddhists) is not visible from here, the valley is on the circumambulating **Parikrama/Kora** route which encircles the massif. Fields of the pink coloured *ogla*, a small flower seed grown specifically in the Baspa Valley for grinding into grain, add a beautiful colouring in the season.

Sangla, at 2680 m, is built on the massive buttress of a terminal moraine which marks a major glacial advance of about 50,000 years ago. The Baspa River has cut a deep trench on its south flank. Immediately above is the flat valley floor, formed on the dry bed of a lake which was once dammed behind the moraine. The village has excellent carving and is full of character. No foreign exchange is available but there are telephone facilities. Sangla is famous for its apples, while a **saffron farm** just north of the village is claimed to be better than that at Pampore in Kashmir.

The old seven-storey **Killa** (Fort) ⓘ *0800-0900, 1800-1900*, where the Kinnaur rajas were once crowned, is 1 km north of new Sangla just before the road enters the village. It was occupied by the local rulers for centuries. It now has a temple to Kamakshi where the idol is from Guwahati, Assam, see page 693.

Barseri, 8 km from Sangla, is situated on an outwash cone which has engulfed part of the Baspa's valley floor. This well-kept 'green village' is happy to show visitors its solar heaters, *chakkis* (water mills) and water-driven prayer wheels. The Buddha Mandir, with *Shakyamuni* and other images and a large prayer wheel, is beautiful inside. Villagers weave shawls and do woodcarving.

The beautifully carved pagoda-style Rakcham temple is dedicated to Shamshir Debta, Devi and Naga, combining Buddhist and Hindu deities. The ibex horns on the roof are ancient male fertility symbols. There is also a pre-Buddhist, animist Bon cho shrine and a Siva temple.

Chitkul, some 18 km from Barseri, at an altitude of 3450 m, is the furthest point foreigners can travel without special permits. With its typical houses, Buddhist temple and a small tower, it

Kinnaur & Spiti

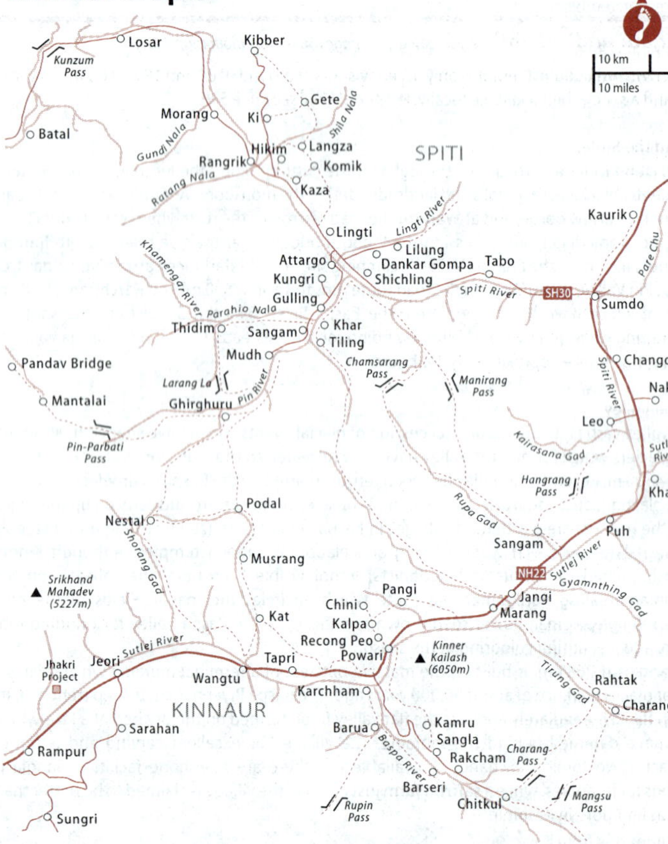

is worth the trip. The Kagyupa (Oral Transmission School), has a highly valued, old image of the Shakyamuni Buddha. There are four directional kings on either side of the door as well as a Wheel of Life. You can walk along the Baspa River which has paths on both sides. The rough path along the tributary starting at the bridge across the river, below the bus stand, is very steep in places with loose stones. Do not attempt alone. A shop sells a few provisions.

Recong Peo to the Spiti River

Recong Peo, also called 'Peo', at 2290 m, is the District HQ and a busy little market town. The Sub-Divisional Magistrate's office in a three-storey building below the bus stand deals with Inner Line Permits (see page 488). A short walk above the town takes you to the Kalachakra Temple with a large Buddha statue outside and good views of Kinner Kailash. A shop here sells provisions, medicines and has a telephone, but there's nowhere to change money.

Kothi village, reached by a path from the Kalachakra Temple, has ancient Hindu temples associated with the Pandavas. One has a tank of sacred fish, 30 minutes' walk from the bazar.

Kalpa (Chini), 12 km from Recong Peo at 2960 m, is reached after a stiff climb. It has an interesting temple complex and Budh mandir and is surrounded by apple, *bemi* (wild apricot) and plum orchards and chilgoza pine forests, with striking views across to Kinner Kailash (6050 m).

A high road from Kalpa/Recong Peo with little traffic passes through Chilgoza pine forests, north to the hamlet of **Pangi**, 10 km away. Pangi is surrounded by apple orchards. The colourful Sheshri Nag temple at the top of the village has an inscription in a strange script above the entrance and standing stones in the courtyard. Apart from two Buddhist temples, the carved pagoda temple to Sheshri's mother encloses a huge boulder representing the Devi. The road then goes over bare and rugged hills beyond to **Morang** which has impressive monasteries with wood carvings and sculptures.

Inner Line Permits are checked at **Jangi**. From here the road goes to Puh, a steep climb with hairpin bends.

Spiti → *For listings, see pages 503-506. Colour map 1. B4. For trekking information, see page 546.*

The bridge at **Khab**, 11 km beyond Puh, marks the confluence of the Sutlej and Spiti rivers. The entry into the Spiti Valley at Khab is a rare example of crossing from the Himalaya to the Trans-Himalaya without going over a major pass. The Sutlej now disappears east towards the Tibet border, while the road follows the Spiti. Major deforestation of the mountain slopes has resulted in sections of the road being washed away. The new road, a remarkable feat of engineering, hairpins up to the village of **Nako**, with some basic guesthouses, and rejoins the river at Chango.

Sumdo, the last village of Kinnaur, has a border police checkpost and a tea shop, and is the starting point of State Highway 30, which passes through an arid valley with small patches of cultivation of peas and barley near the snow melt streams. It is 31 km from Sumdo to Tabo.

Tabo → *Colour map 1, B4. Altitude: 3050 m.*

At the crossroads of two ancient trade routes, Tabo was one of the great centres of Buddhist learning and culture. Founded in 996, the **Chos Khor Gompa** (see below) is the oldest living Buddhist establishment in this part of the world. Today, the small town is rapidly being modernized with paved streets and electric lights. Government offices have appeared alongside traditional mud homes and the local shops stock basic provisions for trekkers. There is a post office.

Chos Khor Gompa Founded in AD 996 as a scholastic institution, the monastery's original layout was planned as a *mandala* centred around a **Du khang** (Assembly Hall). The deodar wood used was imported from Kullu, Kinnaur, Chamba and Kashmir while the lack of quality structural stone resulted in the extensive use of earth, strengthened with gypsum for the high walls. Today the *gompa* houses 60 *lamas* and has a good collection of scriptures, *thangkas* and art pieces. It is most important and has an immense sense of the spiritual. Carry a torch. No photography allowed.

Many of the **colourful murals** come close to the pure Indian style identified with Ajanta. The technique required the surface to be coated with several thin layers of lime and yak-skin glue and burnished vigorously to provide the 'ground' which was then smoothed and freshened with animal fat and butter. Natural vegetable dyes and powdered stone colours were mixed with *dzo* milk and yak urine for painting. The early Indian style murals used a profusion of reds and yellows with little stress on landscaping, the area around the principal figures being filled with small divinities. These images wear seraphic smiles and have half-shut dreamy eyes denoting introspective meditation. The later 17th-century paintings illustrate the Central Tibetan/Chinese art form where ultramarine takes over from the earlier dominance of reds and yellows, and landscapes become lively and vivid with the appearance of cliffs, swirling clouds, stylized flames, flora and fauna. Here the twists and turns of the limbs and the flowing elaborate drapery show great fluency. This is one of the few *gompas* in the Tibetan Buddhist-influenced areas of Ladakh, Lahaul and Spiti where the highly structured art of painting the complex Tibetan religious iconography is taught. What appears outwardly as a free art form is taught on lined paper where each shape and form is closely measured.

Nine Temples **Tsuglhakhang** (academy) The 'resplendent' central *Mahavairochana* – a composite of four figures, each facing a cardinal direction, represents the unity of all Buddhas. On the walls inside are stucco figures of different Buddhas and Bodhisattvas. The floral ceiling decorations are in the Ajanta style.

Dri Tsang khang (Inner Sanctum) and **Kora** (Circumambulatory Path) At the centre of the 'mandala', the five *Dhyani* Buddhas escorted here by four Bodhisattvas, emerge from the darkness lit by a shaft of sunlight.

Masks, weapons and ritual costumes are stored in the **Gon Khang** which is closed to visitors. **Zhalma** (Picture Hall) has a 17th-century entrance temple where the murals are recent and in pure Tibetan style.

Dromton Lhakhang Chenpo (17th century) Dominated by Medicine Buddhas. The ceiling, in high Tibetan style, is exceptional, depicting *nagas*, titans, peacocks and parrots amongst rainbows.

Ser Khang (Golden Temple) The walls were believed to have been coated with a layer of gold dust as thick as a yak's skin for painting the numerous larger-than-life figures. They were renewed in the 16th and 17th centuries.

Chamba Chenpo La Khang Dedicated to the Maitreya (Future) Buddha, this temple has a 6-m-high seated statue. The murals of the eight Buddhas may be some of the earliest in Tabo.

Buddhist caves To the north, the small natural caves above the road were an integral part of the monastic complex. **Pho Gompa**, the only surviving, with early murals showing pure Indian influence, has been restored. These post-Ajantan paintings, however, are already fading. On open ground to the east, on both sides of a dyke, there are pre-Buddhist rock carvings on metamorphosed igneous rocks showing ibex, swastikas, *yonis*, horses, panthers and human figures.

Dankar

Once the capital of Spiti, Dankar is a tiny village. The early 16th-century fort/monastery **Dankar Gompa** (3890 m), which once served as a jail, stands on an impressive overhang, perched on crumbling towers. Today it has more than 160 *lamas* in residence. The 'highest temple' has a collection of Bhotia Buddhist scriptures, a four-in-one *Dhyani Buddha* and interesting murals of Medicine Buddhas and protector deities. The *gompa* is a very steep two-hour climb from a point 2 km away, beyond Shichling on the main road. The 4WD road from the SH30, about 1 km west of Shichling, winds up 8 km to Dankar (a two-hour walk) and is easier. A beautiful large pond at just under 4100 m is reached by a 2.5-km track.

A large Mala (sacrificial wood) tree at the northwest corner of the monastery, the only one of four to survive, is held sacred by the villagers.

Lalung Gompa

Lalung Gompa, known for its carved wood panelling, is off the SH30, 22 km from Kaza, reached by 8-km narrow, drivable track. From Dankar Gompa this is a two-hour trek. Carry plenty of water as there are no streams and it can get very hot.

Pin Valley

About 5 km from Dankar is a sign for the Pin Valley National Park which is on the other side of the river. The Pin River joins the Spiti at Attargo. Above Attargo, 10 km along the Pin Valley, is the **Kungri Gompa** (circa 1330), which though not old is in an established monastic site with old carved wooden sculptures and is commonly understood to be a Bon monastery still practising elements of the pre-Buddhist Bon religion. The trek from the Bhabha Valley ends at the road head at Kungri, see page 547. One bus a day departs from Kaza at 1200, goes along the Pin Valley as far as Mikkim and turns straight back at 1400, not allowing enough time to visit the *gompa*. You therefore face a long walk unless you can hitch a lift on a passing tractor, truck or yak.

At the confluence of the Pin River and one of its tributaries, 1 km from Mikkim, **Sangam** can be reached by car over a new iron bridge, or more adventurously by a pulley system with a person-sized bucket, 750 m west of the bus stop along the river. It requires a reasonable degree of fitness to negotiate, especially if crossing alone. The local greeting is *joolay, joolay*!

Pin Valley National Park is described as the "land of ibex and snow leopard" and was created to conserve the flora and fauna of the cold desert. It adjoins the Great Himalayan National Park (southwest), and Rupi Bhabha Sanctuary (south) with the Bara Shigri Glacier forming its north boundary. The park covers 675 sq km with a buffer zone of 1150 sq km mainly to its east where there are villages, and varies in altitude from 3600 m to 6630 m. The wildlife includes Siberian ibex, snow leopard, red fox, pika, weasels, lammergeier, Himalayan griffon, golden eagle, Chakor partridge, Himalayan snow cock and a variety of rose finches. The Siberian ibex can be sighted at high altitudes, beyond Hikim and Thango village. From July to September the young ibex kids need protection and so the females move up to the higher pastures near cliffs while the adult males concentrate on feeding lower down. The 60-km-long Lingti Valley is famous for its fossils.

Although rugged, the summer brings more rain here than the rest of Spiti resulting in a profusion of wild flowers.

Kaza

Kaza, at 3600 m, is 13 km from Lingti village. Old Kaza has village homes while New Kaza sports government offices. It is a busy bus terminus with a small market, a basic health centre and jeeps for hire. Inner Line Permits are issued by the SDM's office. Tourist facilities are open May to October. No foreign exchange is available. If you are in need of supplies, **Kibber**, 19 km away, has post, a bank and several provisions stores for trekkers. For an exceptional insight into the area, check out www.spitiecosphere.com with a focus on conservation.

There is an attractive one-day circular trek from here to **Hikim** and **Komik** villages visiting the monastery midway. **Hikim Gompa** (early 14th century), modelled on a Chinese castle, was built under Mongol patronage. ▸▸ *For trekking in Himachal, see page 546.*

Kibber-Gete Wildlife Sanctuary

One of the world's highest wildlife sanctuaries, covering an area of 98 sq km, Kibber-Gete has **Mount Gya** (6754 m) to the north and **Kamelong** (5867 m) to the south. On the drive from Kibber to Tashigang, you may spot musk deer and bharal sheep but to see larger mammals (bear, wolf and the rare snow leopard) you would need to trek. Also to be seen are Himalayan birds of prey as well as snowcock and other high-altitude birds. Buses from Kaza take about an hour.

Tashigang

Tashigang, 18 km away, is one of the highest villages in the world connected by road. **Ki Monastery** on the way is the largest in Spiti and houses 300 *lamas*. Although it has suffered from wars, fires and earthquakes it still has a good collection of *thangkas* and *kangyurs* (scriptures). Although no permit is needed, the monks have instituted their private 'entrance fee' system which, by all accounts, appears quite flexible and linked to the visitor's perceived ability to pay. There are a few cheap guesthouses and camping is possible. If you cannot stay take a bus up and walk down via the Ki Monastery, 11 km from Kaza.

To Lahaul

Losar, at 4079 m, is the last village in Spiti, reached after driving through fields growing peas and cabbage among poplars, willows and apple orchards. There is a rest house and guesthouse and a couple of cafés serving Tibetan/Spitian food.

The road continues up for 18 km to the **Kunzum La** (Pass) at 4551 m. It means 'meeting place for ibex' and gives access to Lahaul and good views of some of the highest peaks of the Chandrabhaga group that lies immediately opposite the Kunzum La to the west. To the southeast is the Karcha Peak (6271 m). The pass has an ancient *chorten* marker. The temple to **Gyephang**, the presiding deity, is circumambulated by those crossing the pass; the giver of any offering in cash which sticks to the stone image receives special blessing.

The road descends through 19 hairpin curves to reach the rock strewn valley of the River Chandra at **Batal**, where a tea shop serves noodles and sells biscuits and bottled water. It continues to **Chhota Dhara** and **Chhatru**, with rest houses and eateries, and then **Gramphoo** joining the Manali-Keylong-Leh highway around three hours after leaving the pass. From Gramphoo to Manali is 62 km.

Shimla to the Kullu Valley → *For listings, see pages 503-506.*

Bilaspur and Bhakra-Nangal Dam → *Colour map 1, B3.*

Bilaspur used to be the centre of a district in which the tribal Daora peoples panned in the silts of the Beas and Sutlej for gold. Their main source, the Seer Khud, has now been flooded by the Bhakra Nangal Lake and they have shifted their area of search upstream. For a bite to eat visit the **Lake View Café**.

The dam on the River Sutlej is one of the highest dams in the world at 225 m and was built as part of the Indus Waters Treaty between India and Pakistan (1960). The Treaty allocated the water of the rivers Sutlej, Beas and Ravi to India. The dam provides electricity for Punjab, Haryana and Delhi. It is also the source for the Rajasthan Canal project, which takes water over 1500 km south to the Thar Desert. There is accommodation should you wish to stay.

Una to Mandi

Having passed through Una, along the main bus route, **Ghanahatti**, 18 km further on, has the adequate **Monal Restaurant**. There are some magnificent views, sometimes across intensively cultivated land, sometimes through plantations of chilgoza, khir and other species. In **Shalaghat**, further on, accommodation is available. The road descends into a deep valley before climbing again to the small market town of **Bhararighat**. A jeep can take over two hours for this part of the journey. In **Brahmpukar** the road to Beri and Mandi is a very attractive country lane. The more heavily used though still quiet road to the main Bilaspur-Manali road joins it at **Ghaghas**. During the monsoons landslides on the NH21 may cause long delays. Carry plenty of water and some food. The tree-lined and attractive approach to **Sundernagar** from the south gives some indication of the town's rapid growth and prosperity.

Mandi (Sahor) → *Colour map 1, B3. Phone code: 01905. Population: 26,900. Altitude: 760 m.*

Founded by a Rajput prince in circa 1520, Mandi is held sacred by both Hindus and Buddhists. The old town with the main (Indira) bazar is huddled on the left bank of the Beas at the southern end of the Kullu Valley, just below its junction with the River Uhl. The Beas bridge – claimed to be the world's longest non-pillar bridge – is across Sukheti Khad at the east end of town. The main bus station is across the river, just above the open sports ground. It is worth stopping a night in this quaint town with 81 temples, a 17th-century palace and a colourful bazar. **Tourist information** ⓘ *T01905-225036.*

Triloknath Temple (1520), on the riverbank, built in the Nagari style with a tiled roof, has a life-size three-faced Siva image (Lord of Three Worlds), riding a bull with Parvati on his lap. It is at the centre of a group of 13th- to 16th-century sculpted stone shrines. The Kali Devi statue which emphasizes the natural shape of the stone, illustrates the ancient Himalayan practice of stone worship.

Panchavaktra Temple, at the confluence of the Beas and a tributary with views of the Trilokinath, has a five-faced image (*Panchanana*) of Siva. The image is unusually conceived like a temple *shikhara* on an altar plinth. Note the interesting frieze of yogis on a small temple alongside.

Bhutnath Temple (circa 1520) by the river in the town centre is the focus at **Sivaratri fair** (see page 505). The modern shrines nearby are brightly painted.

In lower Sumkhetar, west of the main bazar, is the 16th-century **Ardhanarishvara Temple** where the Siva image is a composite male/female form combining the passive Siva (right) and the activating energy of Parvati (left). Although the *mandapa* is ruined, the carvings on the *shikhara* tower and above the inner sanctum door are particularly fine.

From the old suspension bridge on the Dharamshala road, if you follow a narrow lane up into the main market you will see the slate roof over a deep spring which is the **Mata Kuan Rani Temple**, dedicated to the 'Princess of the Well'. The story of this Princess of Sahor (Mandi) and her consort **Padmasambhava**, who introduced Mahayana Buddhism in Tibet, describes how the angry king condemned the two to die in a fire which raged for seven days and when the smoke cleared a lake appeared with a lotus – Rewalsar or *Tso Pema* (Tibetan 'Lotus Lake').

Around Mandi

The small dark **Rewalsar Lake**, 24 km southeast, with its floating reed islands, is a popular pilgrimage centre. The colourful Tibetan Buddhist monastery was founded in the 14th century, though the pagoda-like structure is late 19th century. The Gurudwara commemorates Guru Gobind Singh's stay here. Start early for the hilltop temples by the transmission tower as it is a steep and hot climb. The **Sisu fair** is held in February/March. There are many buses to the lake from Mandi Bus Stand, one hour, Rs 17; you can also board them below the palace in Indira Bazar.

At **Prashar**, a three-tiered pagoda Rishi temple sits beside a sacred lake in a basin surrounded by high mountains with fantastic views of the Pir Panjal range. The rich woodcarvings here suggest a date earlier than the Manali Dhungri Temple (1553), which is not as fine. No smoking, alcohol or leather items are allowed near the temple or lake. There are basic pilgrim rest houses. A forest rest house is 1 km west of temple. To reach the temple, follow a steep trail from Kandi, 10 km north of Mandi, through the forest of rhododendron, oak, deodar and kail (three hours). After arriving at a group of large shepherd huts the trail to the left goes to the temple, the right to the forest rest house.

You can walk to **Aut**, see below, from Prashar in six to seven hours. A level trail east crosses a col in under a kilometre. Take the good path down to the right side of the *nullah* (valley) and cross the stream on a clear path. Climb a little and then follow a broad path on the left bank to the road. Turn right and down to **Peon village** in the *Chir nullah* and continue to Aut.

Tirthan Valley and Jalori Pass

From Mandi the NH21 runs east then south along the left bank of the Beas, much diminished in size by the dam at **Pandoh**, 19 km from Mandi, from which water is channelled to the Sutlej. The dam site is on a spectacular meander of the Beas (photography strictly prohibited). The NH21 crosses over the dam to the right bank of the Beas then follows the superb **Larji Gorge**, in which the Beas now forms a lake for a large part of the way upstream to Aut. A large hydroelectric project is being constructed along this stretch. At **Aut** (pronounced 'out') there is trout fishing (season March to October, best in March and April); permits are issued by the Fishery Office in Largi, Rs 100 per day. The main bazar road has a few cheap hotels and eating places. It is also a good place to stop and stock up with trekking supplies such as dried apricots and nuts.

From Aut, a road branches off across the Beas into the **Tirthan Valley** climbing through beautiful wooded scenery up to the Jalori Pass. Allow at least 1½ hours by jeep to **Sojha**, 42 km from Mandi, and another 30 minutes to Jalori. Contact tourist office in Kullu for trekking routes. One suggested trek is Banjar–Laisa–Paldi–Dhaugi/Banogi–Sainj, total 30 km, two days.

Banjar, with attractive wood-fronted shops lining the narrow street, has the best examples in the area of timber-bonded Himalayan architecture in the fort-like rectangular temple of **Murlidhar** (Krishna). Halfway to **Chaini**, 3 km away, the large **Shring Rishi Temple** to the deified local sage is very colourful with beautiful wooden balconies and an impressive 45-m-tall tower which was damaged in the last earthquake. The entrance, 7 m above ground, is reached by climbing a notched tree trunk. Such free-standing temple towers found in eastern Tibet were sometimes used for defence and incorporated into Thakur's castles in the western Himalaya. The fortified villages here even have farmhouses like towers.

From Banjar the road climbs increasingly steeply to **Jibhi**, 9 km away, where there are sleeping options and trekking. Two kilometres beyond is **Ghayaghi**, also with accommodation. A few kilometres on is **Sojha**, a Rajput village in the heart of the forest, which offers a base for treks in the Great Himalayan National Park.

Finally you reach the **Jalori Pass** (altitude: 3350 m), open only in good weather from mid-April, which links Inner and Outer Seraj and is 76 km from Kullu. You may wish to take the bus up to the pass and walk down, or even camp a night at the pass. Check road conditions before travelling. A ruined fort, **Raghupur Garh**, sits high to the west of the pass and from the meadows there are fantastic views, especially of the Pir Panjal range. Take the path straight from the first hairpin after the pass and head upwards for 30-40 minutes. The road is suitable for 4WD vehicles. There is a very pleasant, gradual walk, 5 km east, through woodland (one hour), starting at the path to the right of the temple. It is easy to follow. **Sereuil Sar** (Pure Water) is where local women worship Burhi Nagini Devi, the snake goddess, and walk around the lake pouring a line of *ghee*. It is claimed that the lake is kept perpetually clear of leaves by a pair of resident birds. *Dhabas* provide simple refreshments and one has two very basic cheap rooms at the pass.

Great Himalayan National Park and Tirthan Sanctuary ⓘ *foreigners Rs 200 per day, Indians Rs 10, students half price, camera Rs 150/50, video Rs 5000/2500*, lies southeast of Kullu town in the Seraj Forest Division, an area bounded by mountain ridges (except to the west) and watered by the upper reaches of the rivers Jiwa, Sainj and Tirthan. The hills are covered in part by dense forest of blue pine, deciduous broadleaved and fir trees and also shrubs and grassland; thickets of bamboo make it impenetrable in places. Attractive species of iris, frittilaria, gagea and primula are found in the high-altitude meadows. Wildlife include the panther, Himalayan black bear, brown bear, tahr, musk deer, red fox, goral and bharal. The rich birdlife includes six species of pheasant. The park is 60,561 ha with an altitude of 1500-5800 m and the sanctuary covers 6825 ha; its headquarters are in Shamshi. Access is easiest from April to June and September to October. Check it out at www.greathimalayannationalpark.com. **Goshiani** is the base for treks into the park. The first 3 km along the river are fairly gentle before the track rises to harder rocky terrain; there are plenty of opportunity to see birds and butterflies. The trout farm here sells fresh fish at Rs 150 per kg. Fishing permits, Rs 100, are obtainable from the Fisheries Department.

Kinnaur and Spiti listings

For Sleeping and Eating price codes and other relevant information, see Essentials pages 38-42.

Sleeping

Baspa Valley *p495*

A Banjara Camps, Barseri, 8 km beyond Sangla, T01786-242536, www.banjaracamps.com. Superb riverside site with impressive mountains looming above you. 18 twin-bed rooms and some 4-bed deluxe tents, delicious meals included, hot water bottles in the bed, friendly staff, mountain biking, trekking, Lahaul, Spiti, Ladakh tours. Buses stop 2 km from the site, where road drops down to right, car park at foot of hill is 500-m walk from camp (horn will summon porters). Highly recommended.

B-C Hotel River Rupin View, Rakcham Village, 12 km from Sangla, T(0)9816-686789. Pretty little place well off the beaten track, set in garden with basic rooms.

B-C Kinner Camp, Barseri, T(0)9418-339866, www.kinnerkamps.com. Small tents with beds/sleeping bags, shared baths, birdwatching, trekking, jeep safaris, meals, cafeteria, superb location.

D-G Mount Kailash, Sangla, T01786-242527. 8 clean, pleasant rooms (hot shower), 4-bed dorm, too.

E-F Thakur Guest House, Chitkul. 4 rooms with bath, 3 with shared bath, varied meals.

G Amar Guest House, Chitkul. Clean double rooms (Rs 100), hot water, friendly family atmosphere. Recommended.

G Hotel Apple Pie, Sangla, T07186-226304. Run by a veteran mountaineer.

G PWD Rest House, Chitkul. 4 rooms, lawns, attractive.

G Sangla Guest House, T01786-242401, Sangla, near shops. Clean rooms with bath (hot water), restaurant.

Recong Peo to the Spiti River *p497*

A-C Inner Tukpa between Kalpa and Recong Peo, T01786-223077, hotelinnertukpa@gmail.com. Nestled in the woods between Kalpa and Recong Peo, this is a stylish little number from the fine front door down to the fittings.

A-D Kinner Kailash Cottage (HPTDC), Kalpa, T01786-226159, www.hptdc.nic.in. Open May-Nov. Commanding position, 5 rooms (bath tub Rs 1100), limited menu, camping.

B-D Chine Resort Roshi Rd, 1.5 km from Kalpa, T01786-226572, www.kinnaurgeotourism.com. 6 spacious swiss cottage tents in pretty surroundings.

C-E Kinner Villa, 4 km outside Kalpa, T01786-226006, circuits@vsnl.net.in. 20 rooms with bath, attractively located, seasonal tents and a 6-bed dorm.

E Forest Rest House, Chini, 2 km from Kalpa. Caretaker can prepare meals, modern building, camping overnight (with permission) in school grounds 1600-1000.

E-F Aucktong Guest House ('Aunties'), near Circuit House, 1 km north on Pangi road, Kalpa, T01786-226019. Pleasant, 6 clean spacious rooms, large windows, restaurant, very friendly ("arrived for one night and stayed a week!").

E-F Shivling View, near bus stand, Recong Peo, T01786-222421. Good view of Shivling peak. OK but better to stay up near Kalpa.

Tabo *p497*

Guesthouses in the village allow camping.

D-E Millennium Guest House, run by monks in monastery complex, 13 colourful rooms, shared dirty toilets, hot water on request, meals.

E-F Tanzin, near monastery. Tibetan food, friendly, family-run, best in village.

Dankar *p498*

G The *gompa* has 2 rooms; only 1 has a bed.

G Dolma Guest House. 8 perfectly fine rooms.

Pin Valley *p499*

G Norzang Guest House. Rooms for Rs 100.

G PWD Rest House.

Kaza *p499*

Kaza is ideal for camping.

A Kaza Retreat, T01906-222236, www.banjaracamps.com. 11 clean, modern rooms with attached bathrooms. You can expect high standards here, good food and relaxing atmosphere. Recommended.

B-D Spiti Valley Resorts, T01786-226572, www.kinaurgeotourism.com. 8 spacious swiss cottage tents in pretty location surrounded by flowers. They have other camps in Nako and Kalpa.

C-D Sakya's Abode, T01906-222254. 10 rooms in a fine-looking building with a wide range of rooms and a cheap dorm (Rs 80).

C-D Snow Lion Guest House, T01906-222525. 8 large, prefectly comfortable rooms.

E Kaycee Lodge. Simple rooms, good service.

F Mahabuddha Guest House. Basic but large room, shared bath, very clean, meals. Recommended.

Una to Mandi *p500*

D Mehman, Shalaghat. Occupies an extraordinarily bold setting. Restaurant.

E-F Relax Inn, Sundernagar, on Mandi side of town, T01907-262409. Modern, clean.

Mandi *p501*

A-C Hotel Regent Palms, near Kargil Park, close to Raj Mahal, T01905-222 777. Bright new hotel with all the mod cons and nice decor.

A-D Raj Mahal, lane to right of palace, Indira Bazar, T01905-222401, www.rajmahal palace.com. Former 'palace' has character but in need of attention. 14 rooms, including atmospheric deluxe rooms with bath (sharpened sword in one might be mistaken for a towel rail). Rooms in palace are charismatic, in the other block they are quite dull, but cheap. Restaurant, bar, garden temple. Recommended. Although be persistent – they don't always answer phone.

A-D Visco Resorts, 2 km south of Mandi, T01905-225057, www.viscoresorts.com. 18 large rooms (some for 4) in modern resort, by the river, good cheap vegetarian restaurant, extremely well run.

D-E Munish Resorts, on hillside 2 km above New Beas Bridge, T01905-235035, www.munishresorts.com. 15 clean rooms with bath, restaurant, lovely views, colourful garden with tempting fruit, friendly family.

E-F Evening Plaza, Indira Bazar, T01905-225123. 14 reasonable rooms, some a/c, TV, changes cash and TCs at a good rate.

E-F Rewalsar Inn (HPTDC), above the lake, T01905-280252, www.hptdc.nic.in. 12 reasonable rooms with bath, some with TV and balcony, dorm (Rs 75), good lake views.

G Vyas, 5-min walk from bus stand, past sports ground, T01905-235556. 6 small rooms, 4-bed dorm (Rs 40), clean enough, quiet location overlooking Beas, good value.

Tirthan Valley and Jalori Pass *p502*

AL-A Hymalayan Trout House, below Banjar, T01903-225112, www.mountainhighs.com. All-weather eco-cabins, mud hut suites and stone cottage suites. Stunning location, fine food, great hospitality. Artists studio, gazebo with fire and library. Trekking and fishing. Little shop selling organic wares. Highly recommended.

A Sojha Retreat, Sojha, T01902-276070, www.banjaracamps.com. 5 basic double rooms and 4 lovely suites in wooden lodge with fantastic views, good food and trekking information. You can see all the way to the mountains above Manali from here.

E Doli Guest house, Jhibi village, T01903-227 034. Nice little rooms in traditional building. Sweet little café by the river in very pretty little village. Ask about the cottages above the village with sitting rooms and woodburning stove. Recommended.

E Raju's Place, Goshaini, is a family-run river-facing guesthouse, 3 rooms with bath. They offer meals, treks and safaris. Access by zip wire over the river.

E-F Dev Ganga, 9 km from Banjar in Jibhi, T01903-227 005. 8 double rooms, friendly, comfortable, with exceptional views.

E-F Fort View Home Stay, Sojha, just by entrance to Banjara Camp, T(0)9418-626634. Traditional building with four rooms inside – shared bathroom. Atmospheric.

E-F Whispering Woods, Jibhi village, T(0)9418-776699. Lovely views right by the river, nice little sit-outs. Basic clean rooms.

F Forest Rest House, near Sojha, spectacular and isolated just below the Jalori Pass.

F Meena, beyond bus stand, Banjar, T01902-222258, 4 double rooms.

Eating

Baspa Valley *p495*

Sonu, Sangla. Good Tibetan and travellers' fare, *momos* and pancakes.

Kaza *p499*

There are several bakeries and cafés.

German Bakery, serves up the usual fare.

Layul, does Chinese, Tibetan and Indian dishes, and cold beer.

Mandi *p501*
There are some *dhabas* by the bus terminal.
Mayfair. Efficient and tasty North Indian food, some continental and Chinese.
Café Shiraz, HPTDC, Gandhi Chowk, near Bhutnath Temple. Snacks, bus ticketing.
Gomush Tibetan Restaurant, near *gompa* at Rewalsar Lake. Excellent *momos*.
Raj Mahal. Quiet, peaceful (interesting photos and antiques), pleasant garden, good value but limited menu and surly waiters.

Festivals and events

Mandi *p501*
Feb/Mar Sivaratri Fair, a week of dance, music and drama as temple deities from surrounding hills are taken in procession with chariots and palanquins to visit the Madho Rai and Bhutnath temples.

Activities and tours

Kaza *p499*
Tour operators
Spiti Ecospheres, www.spitiecospheres.com. Based in Kaza, this is an exceptional project with a nod towards conservation, environmental and livelihoods; also volunteering projects, unique treks and promoting organic agriculture.

Transport

Baspa Valley *p495*
Sangla
Bus To **Chitkul** (often 2-3 hrs late); **Shimla** via Tapri (9 hrs); **Recong Peo**, 0630; from Tapri, 0930. 4WD recommended between Karchham and Chitkul in bad weather.

Chitkul
Bus Twice daily to/from **Karchham** (0930) via **Sangla** (1100) and **Rakcham**; from **Tapri**, 0930; from **Recong Peo** 0600 (prompt).

Recong Peo to the Spiti River *p497*
Recong Peo
Bus Reserve tickets from booth shortly before departure. Bus to **Chandigarh**; **Delhi** 1030; **Kalpa**, occasional; **Kaza** (9 hrs), gets very crowded so reserve seat before 0700; **Puh**; **Rampur**, frequent (5 hrs); **Sangla/Chitkul** (4 hrs); **Shimla**; **Tabo**, via Kaza (9-10 hrs).

Kalpa
Bus To **Shimla**, 0730; **Chitkul**, 1300. To get to Peo for Kaza bus at 0730, walk down (40 mins) or arrange taxi from Peo. Travellers may not be allowed beyond Jangi without an 'Inner Line' permit. Contact **SDM** in Recong Peo a day ahead (see page 488).

Tabo *p497*
Bus To **Chandigarh** via Kinnaur, 0900; **Kaza**, 1000.

Kaza *p499*
Bus Reserve a seat at least 1 hr ahead or night before. The road via Kunzum-La and Rohtang Pass can be blocked well into Jul. New bus stand, bottom end of village. In summer: from **Manali** (201 km), 12 hrs via Rohtang Pass and Kunzum La; **Shimla** (412 km) on the route described, 2 days. Approximate times shown: daily to **Chango**, 1400; **Kibber** 0900, **Losar** 0900; **Mikkim** (19 km from Attargo), in the Pin Valley, 1200 (2 hrs); returns 1400. Long-distance buses to **Kullu**, 0400; **Manali** (from Tabo), 0500; **Chandigarh** 0630. The last 3 are heavily used.

Mandi *p501*
Bus Bus information T01905-235538. **Chandigarh** 1100 (203 km, 5 hrs). **Dharamshala** 1215, 6 hrs; **Kullu/ Manali** every 30 mins, 3 hrs, Rs 80 (Kullu), 4 hrs (Manali); **Shimla** (5½ hrs,). Book private buses in town or opposite the bus stand at least 1 day in advance; they do not originate in Mandi. **Dharamshala**, 5 hrs; **Kullu/Manali**, 2 hrs (Kullu), 3½ hrs (Manali).
Taxi Rs 700 to **Kullu**; Rs 1200 to **Manali**; Rs 1200 to **Dharamshala**.
Train **Jogindernagar** (55 km), T01908-222088, is on the narrow gauge from Pathankot.

Tirthan Valley and Jalori Pass *p502*
Bus From **Jibli** the bus to **Jalori** can take 1 hr. Some go via **Ghayaghi** (approximate times): **Kulla–Bagipul**, 0800; **Manali–Rampur**, 1000; **Kullu–Dalash**, 1100; **Manali–Ani**, 1100. If heading for Shimla or Kinnaur, change buses at Sainj on NH22.

Bus from **Ani** and **Khanag** to the south, runs to **Jalori Pass** and back. 4 buses daily traverse the pass in each direction when it is open (8-9 months). Bus to **Sainj**, 3½ hrs, and on to **Shimla**, 5 hrs.

Taxi From **Banjar** to **Jalori Pass** costs Rs 800 (Rs 1200 return), to **Jibhi/Ghayaghi**, Rs 300, to **Kullu**, Rs 600, to **Manali**, Rs 1200, to **Mandi** Rs 700, to **Shimla**, Rs 3000. Buses are rare.

Directory

Mandi *p501*

Banks Bank of Baroda, Hospital Rd, in the old town centre, can take over 1 hr to change Visa; **Indian Overseas Bank** changes TCs. **Evening Plaza Hotel** is the only place to change cash (see Sleeping). **Medical services** Hospital, T01905-222102. **Useful contacts** Police: T01905-235536.

Kullu Valley

The Kullu Valley was the gateway to Lahaul for the Central Asian trade in wool and borax. It is enclosed to the north by the Pir Panjal range, to the west by the Bara Bangahal and to the east by the Parvati range, with the Beas River running through its centre. The approach is through a narrow funnel or gorge but in the upper part it extends outwards. The name Kullu is derived from Kulantapith 'the end of the habitable world'. It is steeped in Hindu religious tradition; every stream, rock and blade of grass seemingly imbued with some religious significance. Today, the main tourist centre is Manali, a hive of adventurous activity in the summer months, a quiet and peaceful place to relax in the winter snow.

▸▸ *For listings, see pages 514-522. For trekking, see page 546.*

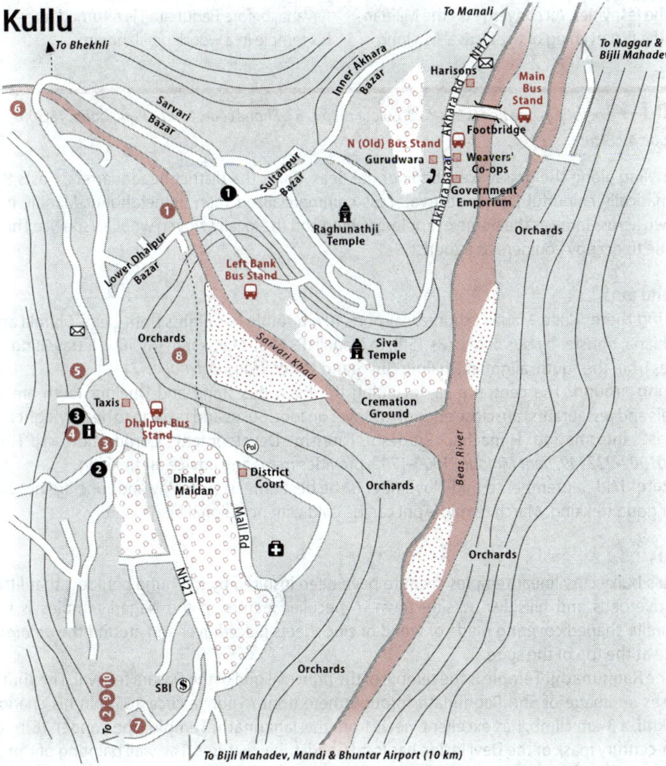

Sleeping
Aaditya 1
Apple Valley Resorts 2
Bijleshwar View 3
Gaur Niwas 4
Ramneek 5
Rock'n'River 6
Sarwari 7
Shobla 8
Silver Moon 9
Vaishali 10

Eating
Ashiyana 1
Hot Stuff Food Junction 2
Monal Café 3
Planet Food 2

Dasara in Kullu

The festival of Dasara celebrates Rama's victory over the demon Ravana. From their various high mountain homes about 360 gods come to Kullu, drawn in their *raths* (chariots) by villagers to pay homage to Raghunathji who is ceremoniously brought from his temple in Kullu.

The goddess Hadimba, patron deity of the Kullu Rajas has to come before any other lesser deities are allowed near. Her chariot is the fastest and her departure marks the end of the festivities. All converge on the Maidan on the first evening of the festival in a long procession accompanied by shrill trumpeters. Thereafter there are dances, music and a market. During the high point of the fair a buffalo is sacrificed in front of a jostling crowd. Jamlu, the village God of Malana, high up in the hills, follows an old tradition. He watches the festivities from across the river, but refuses to take part. See box, page 550. On the last day Raghunathji's *rath* is taken to the riverbank where a small bonfire is lit to symbolize the burning of Ravana, before Ragunathji is returned to his temple in a wooden palanquin.

Kullu → *For listings, see pages 514-522. Colour map 1, B3. Phone code: 01902. Population: 18,300. Altitude: 1219 m.*

Sprawling along the grassy west bank of the Beas, Kullu, the district headquarters, hosts the dramatically colourful **Dasara festival**. Less commercialized than its neighbour Manali, it is known across India as the home of apple-growing and the locally woven woollen shawls. There is little to occupy you here as a tourist.

Ins and outs

Getting there Kullu-Manali (Bhuntar) airport, 10 km south, has flights from Delhi, Shimla and Ludhiana; transfer by bus or taxi (Rs 150), to Manali (Rs 650), Manikaran (Rs 500). If travelling on buses from the south, alight at Dhalpur Bus Stand. ▸▸ *See Transport, page 521.*

Getting around The central area, including the main bus stand and Dhalpur (with ample hotels and restaurants) are close enough to cover on foot. Buses and taxis go to nearby sights.

Tourist information Himachal Pradesh Tourism Development Corporation (HPTDC) ⓘ *T01902-222349, near Maidan, 1000-1700*, provides maps and advice on trekking.

Climate Mid-September to mid-November is the best time to visit. May and June are hot but offer good trekking. March to mid-April can be cold with occasional heavy rain.

Sights

Kullu's bulky curvilinear temples seem to have been inspired by the huge boulders that litter the riverbeds and hillsides outside town. A peculiar feature of the Nagari temples is the umbrella-shaped covering made of wood or zinc sheets placed over and around the *amalaka* stone at the top of the spire.

The **Raghunathji Temple** is the temple of the principal god of the **Dasara festival**. The shrine houses an image of Shri Raghunath (brought here from Ayodhya circa 1657) in his chariot. **Bhekhli**, a 3-km climb, has excellent views from the **Jagannathi Temple**. The copper 16th- to 17th-century mask of the Devi inside has local Gaddi tribal features. The wall painting of Durga is in traditional folk style. There are also superb views on the steep but poorly marked climb to the tiny **Vaishno Devi Temple**, 4 km north, on Kullu-Manali road.

Around Kullu

Bijli Mahadev, 11 km from Kullu at 2435 m, is connected by road most of the way with a 2-km walk up steps from the road head. The temple on a steep hill has a 20-m rod on top which is reputedly struck by *bijli* (lightning) regularly, shattering the stone *lingam* inside. The priests put the *lingam* together each time with *ghee* (clarified butter) and a grain mixture until the next strike breaks it apart again. Several buses until late afternoon from Left Bank Bus Stand, the road to Bijli is rough and the buses are in a poor state.

Bajaura Temple, on the banks of the Beas River, about 200 m off the NH21 at **Hat** (Hatta), is one of the oldest in the valley. The massive pyramidal structure is magnificently decorated with stone images of Vishnu, Ganesh and Mahishasuramardini (Durga as the Slayer of the Buffalo Demon, see page 1412) in the outer shrines. The slender bodies, elongated faces and limbs suggest East Indian Pala influence. Floriated scrollwork decorate the exterior walls.

Parvati Valley → *For listings, see pages 514-522. Colour map 1, B3. See also map, page 548.*
Phone code: 01902.

The Parvati (Parbati) Valley runs northeast from Bhuntar. Attractive orchards and the fresh green of terraced rice cultivation line the route. Known for its hot springs at Manikaran, more recently the valley has become infamous for the droves of chillum-smoking Israelis and Europeans who decamp here in the summer months attracted by the intensive cultivation of narcotics.

Several local buses (and jeep taxis) travel daily to the valley from Kullu via Bhuntar, taking about two hours to Manikaran, which also has buses from Manali. The area is prone to landslides and flash floods – take special care. ▸▸ *See Transport, page 521. For trekking, see page 550.*

Jari
Jari is the point where the deep Malana Nala joins the Parvati River. It is a popular resting place for trekkers but also for drug users. The guesthouses vary; a few away from the village centre have better views.

Kasol
Kasol is the next village en route to Manikaran. The rapidly expanding village has spread on both sides of the road bridge which crosses a tributary that flows into the Parvati, not far from the village itself. About 500 m beyond the village, a narrow side road leads to the river and the location of a fine hot spring on the riverbank. Kasol is the main destination for long-stay visitors, many of whom sit in a haze of *charas* smoke by day, repeating the process by night. **Chhalal** is a 20-minute walk from Kasol. It is a quiet village where families take in guests. A couple of guesthouses have also sprung up here.

Manikaran
Manikaran, 45 km from Kullu, is at the bottom of a dark gorge with **hot sulphur springs** emerging from the rock-strewn banks of the Parvati. A local legend describes how while Parvati bathed in the river, Naga, the serpent god stole her *manikaran* (earrings). At Siva's command Naga angrily blew them back from underground causing a spring to flow. Hindu and Sikh pilgrims come to the Rama temple and the *gurdwara* and gather to cook their food by the springs, purportedly the hottest in the world. There are separate baths for men and women. Manikaran, though not attractive in itself, provides a brief halt for trekkers. Short treks go to Pulga and Khirganga beyond while a footpath (affected by landslips in places), leads to the Pin Valley in Spiti. If trekking this route, always go with a registered guide; do not attempt it alone (see box, page 510). A road continues for 15 km to **Barseni**, which has become a popular place with long-term travellers.

Pulga and Khirganga
Pulga, a noisy village seemingly overrun by giggling children, is in a beautiful location with some cheap guesthouses. It is a good four-hour walk east of Manikaran. Some long-stay travellers prefer the basic airy guesthouses outside the village which offer meals.

Disappearances in the valley

Cases of Western travellers going missing in the Kullu Valley in recent years continue to be reported. They seem to have occurred mostly when trekking alone or camping. Some suggest that there have been genuine accidents in the mountains or that some drug users have 'opted out' and chosen to sever their ties and remain with *sadhus* in remote caves. However, the threat to personal safety is very real so if you're trekking beyond Manikaran, or from Naggar across the Chandrakhani Pass to the Malana Valley, you should not walk alone. Only use registered guides through local trekking agents.

Khirganga is along the trek which winds through the lush Parvati Valley, east of Pulga. It is known for its sacred ancient hot springs marking the place where Siva is thought to have meditated for 2000 years. There is an open bathing pool for men and an enclosed pool for women, next to the humble shrine at the source. A few tents may be hired. *Dhabas* sell vegetarian food. This is the last village in this valley.

Kullu to Manali → *For listings, see pages 514-522. Colour map 1, B3.*

The NH21 continues north along the west side of the Beas. The older road to the east of the river goes through terraced rice fields and endless apple orchards, and is rougher and more circuitous but more interesting. Sections of both roads can be washed away during the monsoon.

Kullu to Katrain

As you wind out the centre of Kullu along the right bank you'll pass the **Sitaramata Temple** embedded in the conglomerate cliff and **Raison**, a grassy meadow favoured by trekkers. **Katrain**, in the widest part of the Kullu Valley, mid-way between Kullu and Manali, is overlooked by **Baragarh Peak** (3325 m). There are plenty of options for an overnight stay. Across the bridge at **Patli Kuhl**, the road climbs through apple orchards to Naggar.

Naggar → *Colour map 1, B3. Phone code: 01902.*

Naggar's (Nagar) interesting castle sits high above Katrain. Built in the early 16th century, it withstood the earthquake of 1905 and is a fine example of the timber-bonded building of West Himalaya. It was built around a courtyard with verandas, from where there are enchanting views over the valley. With a pleasant, unhurried atmosphere, it is a good place to stop a while. It is also an entry for treks to Malana, see page 550.

The **castle**, probably built by Raja Sidh Singh, was used as a royal residence and state headquarters until the 17th century when the capital was transferred to Sultanpur (see Kullu). It continued as a summer palace until the British arrived in 1846, when it was sold to Major Hay, the first assistant commissioner, who Europeanized part of it, fitting staircases, fireplaces and so on. Extensive renovations have produced fine results, especially in the intricately carved woodwork. In the first courtyard are several black *barselas* (sati stones) with primitive carvings. Beyond the courtyard and overlooking the valley the **Jagti Pat Temple** houses a cracked stone slab measuring 2.5 m by 1.5 m by 2 m believed to be a piece of Deo Tibba, which represents the deity in 'the celestial seat of all the gods'. A priest visits the slab every day.

The small **museum** ⓘ *Rs 10*, has some interesting exhibits, including examples of local *pattu* and *thippu* (women's dress and headdress) and *chola* (folk dance costumes). There are also local implements for butter and tea making, and musical instruments like the *karnal* (broad bell horn) and *singa* (long curled horn).

Roerich Art Gallery ⓘ *Tue-Sun 0900-1300 (winter from 1000), 1400-1700, Rs 30*, a 2-km climb from the castle, is Nicholas Roerich's old home in a peaceful garden with excellent views. The small museum downstairs has a collection of photos and his distinctive stylized paintings of the Himalaya using striking colours. It's a beautiful collection from an inspiring family. Nicholas Roerich created the Roerich Pact in the 1930s in order to preserve culture and the arts in the wake of WWI. It was originally signed by 21 countries.

Uruswati Institute ⓘ *uphill from the main house, Rs 15*, was set up in 1993. The **Himalayan Folk and Tribal Art Museum** is well presented, with contemporary art upstairs. One room upstairs is devoted to a charming collection of Russian traditional costumes, dolls and musical instruments.

There are a number of **temples** around the castle including the 11th-century Gauri Shankar Siva near the bazar, with some fine stone carving. Facing the castle is the Chaturbhuj to Vishnu. Higher up, the wooden Tripura Sundari with a multi-level pagoda roof in the Himachal style celebrates its fair around mid-May. Above that is the Murlidhar Krishna at Thawa, claimed as the oldest in the area which has a beautifully carved stone base. Damaged in the 1905 earthquake, it is now well restored. There are fine mountain views from here.

Manali and around → *For listings, see pages 514-522. Colour map 1, B3. Phone code: 01902. Population: 6300. Altitude: 1926 m.*

Manali occupies the valley of the Beas, now much depleted by hydroelectric projects, with the once-unspoilt Old Village to the north and Vashisht up on the opposite hillside across the river. Set amidst picturesque apple orchards, Manali is packed with Pahari-speaking Kullus, Lahaulis, Nepali labourers and enterprising Tibetan refugees who have opened guesthouses, restaurants and craft shops. The town has become increasingly built-up with dozens of new hotel blocks. It is a major tourist destination for Indian holidaymakers and adventure-seeking foreigners, attracted by the culturally different hill people and the scenic treks this part of the Himalaya offers. In summer months Manali is the start of an exciting two-day road route to Leh.

Ins and outs

Getting there Kullu-Manali (Bhuntar) airport is 50 km away with bus and taxi transfers. The bus and taxi stands are right in the centre (though many private buses stop short of the centre) within easy reach of some budget hotels – the upmarket ones are a taxi ride away. ▸▸ *See Transport, page 521. For trekking in the Himachal, see page 546.*

Getting around Manali, though hilly, is ideal for walking. For journeys outside taxi rates are high, so it is worth hiring a motorcycle to explore.

Tourist information HPTDC ⓘ *next to Kunzam Hotel, The Mall, T01902-252175*, is helpful.

Climate The best season is March-April but there is occasional heavy rain and snow in the villages. May-June and mid-September to mid-November offer better trekking.

Sights

The **Tibetan Monastery**, built by refugees, is not old but is attractive and is the centre of a small carpet-making industry. Rugs and other handicrafts are for sale. The colourful **bazar** sells Kullu shawls, caps and Tibetan souvenirs.

Old Manali is 3 km away, across Manalsu Nala. Once a charming village of attractive old farmsteads with wooden balconies and thick stone-tiled roofs, Old Manali is rapidly acquiring the trappings of a tourist economy: building work continues unchecked in the lower reaches of the village, as ever more guesthouses come up to thwart those seeking an escape from the crowds of modern Manali, while the arrival of the drugs and rave scene in summer extinguishes most of Old Manali's remaining charm. The main road continues through some unspoilt villages to the modern **Manu Mandir**, dedicated to Manu, the Law Giver from whom Manali took its name and who, legend tells, arrived here by boat when fleeing from a great flood centuries ago. Aged rickshaws may not make it up the hill, so visitors might have to get off and walk.

Vashisht is a small hillside village that can be reached by road or a footpath, a 30- to 40-minute walk from the tourist office. Note the carvings on the houses of the wealthy farmers. Below the village, there is a temple to Rama and Vashisht, with sulphur springs (small fee);

1 Manali

➡Manali maps
1 Manali, page 512
2 Manali centre, page 513

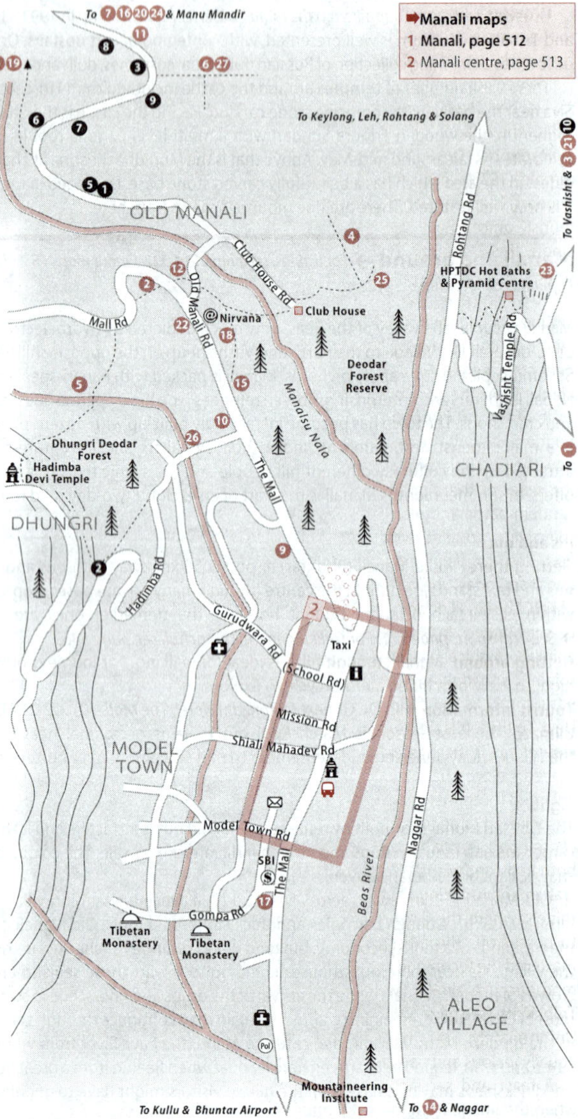

Sleeping
Baikunth **18**
Bodh **3**
Cairn Lodge **4**
Casa Bella Vista **2**
Chetna **5**
Cottage Cad Corner **7**
Dharma/Arohi **21**
Dragon **6**
Drifters **11**
Himalaya Cottage **8**
Jimmy Johnson Lodge **9**
John Banon's Guest House **10**
Leela Huts **12**
Log Huts **13**
Manali Resorts **14**
Manu Allaya **1**
Mayflower **15**
Monal **16**
Piccadilly **17**
Rockway Cottage **19**
Rohtang Manalsu **26**
Shiv Shakti **20**
Sunshine **22**
Surabhi **23**
Surya Cottage **24**
Tourist Nest **27**
Upcountry Lodge **25**

Eating
Bee's Knees **3**
Café Sang Sang **4**
Dylan's **5**
German Bakery **1**
Il Forno **2**
Lazy Dog **6**
Open Hand **8**
Pizza Olive **9**
Shiva Garden Café **7**
Sushi Yeon **10**

remove shoes at the entrance. **Hot springs** at the top of the hill lead to free communal baths in the village centre.They can get dirty and are best in the morning. The village, with its messy jumble of old village houses and newer buildings, has cheap places to stay which attract young travellers. A two-hour walk past the village up the hillside leads to a **waterfall**.

Dhungri Village is at the top of Hadimba Road. Follow the road uphill, past the gates leading to the temple and take the path 50 m further to arrive at the village centre. The village houses have cedar wood carving and balconies with superb views across the valley. Travellers are welcomed into family homes and traditional village life carries on around the guests, although several new developments, including a fun fair, are starting to change the flavour of the lower half of the village.

Hadimba Devi Temple, the Dhungri temple (1553), in a clearing among ancient deodars, is an enjoyable 2-km walk from the tourist office. Built by Maharaja Bahadur Singh, the 27-m-high pagoda temple has a three-tier roof and some fine naturalistic wood carving of animals and plants, especially around the doorway. The structure itself is relatively crude, and the pagoda is far from perfectly perpendicular. Massive deodar planks form the roof but in contrast to the scale of the structure the brass image of the goddess Hadimba inside, is tiny. A legend tells how the God Bhima fell in love with Hadimba, the sister of the demon Tandi. Bhima killed Tandi in battle and married Hadimba, whose spirituality, coupled with her marriage to a god, led to her being worshipped as a goddess. Today, she is seen as an incarnation of Kali. The small doorway, less than 1 m high, is surrounded by wood-carved panels of animals, mythical beasts, scrolls, a row of foot soldiers and deities, while inside against a natural rock is the small black image of the Devi. To the left is a natural rock shelter where legend has it that Hadimba took refuge and prayed before she was deified. The greatly enlarged footprints imprinted on a black rock are believed to be hers. Hadimba Devi plays a central part in the annual festival in May, at both Kullu and Manali. To prevent the master craftsman producing another temple to equal this elsewhere, the king ordered his right hand to be cut off. The artist is believed to have mastered the technique with his left hand and reproduced a similar work of excellence at Trilokinath (see page 525) in the Pattan Valley. Unfortunately, his new master became equally jealous and had his head cut off.

A **feast and sacrifice** is held in mid-July when the image from the new temple in Old

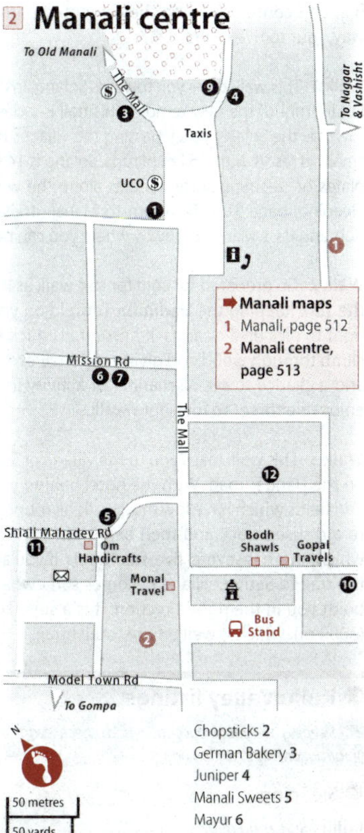

Sleeping
Beas 1
Monarch 2

Eating
Adarsh 1
Chopsticks 2
German Bakery 3
Juniper 4
Manali Sweets 5
Mayur 6
Mehak 7
Palan Sher-e-Punjab 1
Sa Ba 9
Tibetan Dhaba 10
Tibetan Friends' Corner 11
Superbake 12

Manali is carried to the Hadimba Temple where 18 ritual blood sacrifices are performed. Sacrifices include a fish and a vegetable, and culminate with the beheading of an ox in front of a frenzied crowd. This ceremony is not for the faint-hearted. Pickpockets are known to take advantage of awestruck tourists, so take care.

Walks

Manali is the trail-head for a number of interesting and popular treks (see below). Beyond Old Manali, the **shepherd trail**, which winds its way up and down the hillside, allows you to capture a picture of Himalayan life as well as see some superb birdlife. The path starts at some concrete steps (after The Lazy Dog lounge/bar) on the first hairpin bend along the paved road to Old Manali (or you can pick it up where the road ends and taxis turn around at the top of the hill) and continues along the cemented path, which turns into a dirt trail. Return the same way, four to five hours.

Walk 1 This walk takes you towards Solang. In Old Manali Village take the right fork and then turn left in front of the new temple. This trail is a classic, following the right bank of the Beas River up towards the Solang Valley passing the villages of **Goshal**, **Shanag**, **Buruwa** to **Solang** (2480 m), a small ski resort with 2.5 km of runs. Solang is 14 km (five hours). You can get tea, biscuits, nuts and plates of steaming spicy noodles along the walk, and there are also places to stay (see Manali Sleeping, page 516). To return to Manali it is a steady walk down the valley side to the main Rohtang Pass-Manali Highway where you can pick up a bus (Rs 5) or shared jeep (Rs 10).

Walk 2 Go prepared for cold for this walk as it takes you through woodland shading you from the sun. Keeping the **Hadimba Temple** on your right follow the contour of the hill and bear right to pick up a clear pack-horse trail which heads up the steep valley. This is a steady uphill climb through woodland giving superb views of the river below, abundant Himalayan birdlife and a chance to see all manner of activity in the woods, chopping, cutting and burning. An enjoyable three- to four-hour walk.

Walk 3 This walk takes you to the village of **Sethan** (12 km). Take a local bus to the Holiday Inn on the Naggar road. With the hotel behind you, cross the road and pass through the orchard and fields which have low mud walls all round which can be walked on. Bear east till you come to a disused track and then bear right and follow it to the once-untouched village of **Prini** which now has several five-star hotels. If you are lucky the *chai* shop will be open. Further east, the trail to Sethan village becomes somewhat indistinct, though local people are at hand to point you in the right direction. It is a superb three-hour hike up a wooded valley to Sethan (3000 m), which is well off the tourist trail.

Kullu Valley listings

For Sleeping and Eating price codes and other relevant information, see Essentials pages 38-42.

Sleeping

Kullu *p508, map p507*

The choice of hotels is widening, some good hotels in all ranges, though very full during Dasara. Large off-season discounts (30-50%).

L-B Apple Valley Resorts, Mohal, NH21, on the Beas River, 6 km from airport, T01902-260001, www.applevalley-resorts.co.in. 36 comfortable, very well-designed modern chalets in landscaped grounds, excellent food, friendly reception, rafting nearby.

C-D Gaur Niwas, Dhalpur, close to tourist office, T01902-240555. Charming period property with 4 spacious, comfortable rooms, beautiful balconies. Easily the most atmospheric place in town.

C-D Shobla, Dhalpur, T01902-222800, www.shoblainternational.com. 25 rooms, flashy exterior, central, clean, pleasant atmosphere, airy restaurant, overlooking river.

C-E Sarwari (HPTDC), 10-min walk south of Dhalpur Bus Stand, T01902-222471. Peaceful hotel with 16 simple but comfortable rooms (10 in more spacious new wing), 8-bed dorm (Rs 75), good-value restaurant, beer, pleasant gardens, elevated with good views.

D-E Silver Moon (HPTDC), perched on a hill, 2 km south of centre, T01902-222488, www.hptdc.nic.in. 6 rooms with bath and heaters, each with small sitting room in traditional style, very clean, good food, has character (enhanced because Mahatma Gandhi stayed here). Taxis Rs 50 from Kullu centre, buses stop at gate if requested – ask for the last barrier south out of Kullu.

E Vaishali, Gandhinagar, 1 km south of bus stand No 2, T01902-224225, www.vaishali hotel.com. 33 chintzy rooms, excellent restaurant, immaculate kitchen, pleasant small garden running down to river, rafting 4 km south.

E-G Aaditya, Lower Dhalpur, T01902-224263. Decently furnished rooms with bath (hot shower), some with river-facing balcony, others cheaper, smart, room service meals, bar.

Jari *p509*

G The Himalayan Village , Doonkhara, between Jari and Kasol, T01902-276266, www.thehimalayanvillage.in. Inspiring new construction based on traditional principles, in fact builders had to be trained in how to build this old-style property with layered wood and stone. Beautiful rooms with great attention to detail – door handles and mirrors for example. Planning to expand with more rooms and tented area but seamlessly blending into the forest. Good restaurant and spa. Recommended.

G Village Guest House, 10-min walk beyond the village, follow signs, T01902-276070. One of several **G** options that are springing up along the main road. This one is in the most peaceful setting and has 5 simple rooms with clean, shared hot bath and a restaurant. An excellent location on the edge of a traditional farming village, very friendly, good value.

Kasol *p509*

There are now at least 30 guesthouses and family houses that take in paying guests in this expanding village

E-F Alpine, T01902-273710, www.alpineguest house.net. By far the best place in town right next to the river and deservedly popular. Friendly and welcoming with good clean rooms.

E-F Green Valley, T01902-273869. Friendly place although genuinely surprised if you are not Israeli – clean basic rooms on the way into town.

E-G Panchali Holiday Home, T01902-273095. Good range of rooms.

G Bhoj, close to **Green Valley**. Basic rooms in an interesting family-home environment.

G Sasi, new Kasol riverside, T(0)9817-009523. Cheap and cheerful place with basic rooms, often full. Good terrace by the river.

Manikaran *p509*

There are a large number of **E-F** guesthouses in the lower part of the village, some with baths fed by the hot springs. However, prices in season rise to unbelievable rates given that most rooms are basic at best. Some obviously cater for the drug-induced end of the market, so choose carefully. Local families also take paying guests.

C-D Country Charm, main bus stand, T01902-273703. Not really in the country, and not all that charming, but one of the smarter places in town, with 10 brand new rooms, good-value off season.

E-F Shivalik, T01902-273817. Restaurant with good choice of dishes. 20 acceptable rooms with TV.

F Parvati, near the temple, T01902-273735. 10 simple rooms, sulphur baths, restaurant.

F-G Padha Family Guest House, Manikaran bazar, near Gurudwara, T(0)9817-044874. Cheap rooms, super basic but clean with hot shower. Downstairs separate hot bathing room. **Moon Guest House** nearby offers much the same.

Katrain *p510*

AL-A Span Resort, Manali Highway, T01902-240138, www.spanresorts.com. 25 rooms in 8 attractive stone cottages overlooking the river, sports, riding, huge grounds, good views, trout hatchery nearby ensures good river fishing, very comfortable, but some **C** category facilities.

B Ramgarh Heritage Villa, near Raison between Kullu and Manali, T(0)9816-248514, www.ramgarhheritagevillamanali.com. A farm since 1928, nicely furnished rooms with TV and Wi-Fi, but beyond the front door there are orchards of pear, pomegranate and walnut trees and great views of the mountains. You can do trips to their kiwi plantation and they can organize paragliding, river rafting, yoga and picnics.

E Orchard Resorts, Dobhi, 2 km south of Katrain, T01902-240160. Good off-season discount. 16 attractive wood-panelled 'cottages', with hot water, TV, heaters.

E River View (HPTDC), near Beas Bridge, T01902-240836, www.hptdc.nic.in. 2 family-sized cottages, attractive decor, comfortable.

G Anglers' Bungalow, (HPTDC) Katrain, T01902-240136. Superb views from 6 spartan rooms.

Naggar *p510*

B-F Castle, T01902-248316, www.hptdc.nic.in. Built in 1460, has been a hotel since 1978, 13 rooms, stylish but traditional decor and furniture, comfortable beds, fireplaces, modernized baths, best (**B**) overlook valley, some share bath (**F**), very basic dorm (Rs 75), restaurant, good service. May-Jun add Rs 150 for vegetarian meals. Absolutely beautiful property with amazing temple.

D-E Poonam Mountain Lodge, close to Castle, T01902-248248, www.poonam mountain.in. 6 spotless rooms, hot water, very good food. Friendly family.

D-E Ragini, T01902-248185, raginihotel@ hotmail.com. 16 smart rooms with modernized baths (hot water), large windows, good views from rooftop restaurant, excellent breakfasts, Ayurvedic massage and yoga, good value, friendly.

E-F Sheetal, T01902-248319. Overlooking valley, clean and spacious, 14 very pleasant rooms with bath, hot water (some tubs), TV, use of kitchen.

E-F Snow View, down steps past Tripura Sundari Temple, T(0)9481-388335, snowviewhomestay@gmail.com. Weaving co-op outlet, 7 rooms and restaurant.

F-G Alliance, 200 m above castle, T01902-248263, www.allianceguesthouse.com. Run by French ex-pat, 6 rooms, hot water, meals, clean, simple, homely, very good value. Good for families.

G Chand Kulvi, near bus stand. Away from road, 8 rooms, some with bath, lovely garden.

Manali and around

p511, maps p512 and p513

Hotels are often full in May and Jun so better to visit off-season when most offer discounts. Winter heating is a definite bonus. There are many cheap hotels on **School Rd** and in **Model Town** offering modest rooms often with shared baths and hot water in buckets.

Families in **Dhungri** village offer rooms with basic facilities (Rs 50-70). Several are in traditional houses, clean rooms, bedding, small stove (fuel for sale), some have balconies with fantastic views.

In **Old Manali**, generally the further you walk, the greater the reward. Those above the Club House are almost out of Old Manali and are in a great location overlooking the valley but still close enough to town.

Vashisht village is another popular choice.

AL Manu Allaya, Sunny Side, Chadiari, overlooking Old Manali, T01902-252235, www.manuallaya.com. Formerly **Ambassador Resorts** – 53 smart, imaginative rooms, most done in a contemporary design using wood and marble, stunning views and good facilities, a definite cut above the rest, ie an architect has been involved. Recommended.

AL Manali Resorts, 5 km south of Manali on Kullu Rd, T01902-252274, www.manali resorts.com. 37 rooms, a luxury base for winter sports, lovely position with landscaped gardens by Beas River.

AL-A Piccadily, The Mall, T01902-252113, www.piccadilyhotel.com. 70 rooms, clean, modern though signs of wear, welcoming reception, good restaurant but very slow service, many facilities including pool and gym. Multiplex cinema.

A Baikunth Magnolia, Circuit House Rd, The Mall, T01902-250118, www.baikunth.com. Definitely the most stylish place to stay in Manali – beautiful décor, heavy wooden doors and floors, chic 4-posters. Come in Apr to catch the magnolia tree in bloom. Great place for a romantic getaway. Highly recommended.

A Leela Huts, Sunshine Orchards, The Mall (N), T01902-252464, www.leelahuts.com. Not really huts but small stone houses, 3 with 3 bedrooms and 2 with 2, plus drawing/dining room and kitchen of a good standard, not bad value for its size, set in well-tended gardens.

A Log Huts (HPTDC), top of Circuit House Rd high above Manalsu Nala, T01902-253225. 2-bedroom cottages, 12 newer and modern, 6 spacious though dated and somewhat musty (built in 1965), kitchen, attractive views, cafeteria nearby and room service.

A-B Casa Bella Vista, Log Hut Area, just above Old Manali Rd, T01902-251985, www.casabellavistamanali.com. Pretty cottages with nice garden – you can even get your own cook. Or depending on how lazy you want to be there is also a Spanish café on site and wood-oven pizzas.

B-C Banon Resort, The Mall, opposite Mayflower, T01902-253026, www.banonresortsmanali.com. 32 plush rooms, including 12 suites and 6 snazzy stone and wooden cottages set in stunning gardens.

B-C Jimmy Johnson Lodge, The Mall, T01902-253023, johnsonshotel@gmail.com. 12 very elegant rooms (cottages also available), great bathrooms, pretty gardens, great views, outstanding restaurant (see Eating, below). Recommended.

B-C Strawberry Garden Cottages, below Sersai village on the Manali–Nagar road, T01902-257032, www.strawberrygardenmanali.com. Stunning location, 4 self- contained, cute, 2-floor cottages in a beautiful garden with great views. Friendly, helpful English owner. Recommended.

C Mayflower, The Mall, opposite Circuit House, T01902-252104, www.negismayflower.com. 18 rooms, spacious, tastefully decorated wood-panelled suites, TV, good patio restaurant, friendly, well run, but perhaps not the value it once was.

C Shanti Guest House, Prini Village, 10 km south of Manali towards Naggar, T(0)9816-929704, www.highmountainstourism.org. In a cluster of little hotels in Prini, near **Club Mahindra** this is a place to feel at home. Comfy rooms, nice living rooms and open terrace, Spanish and Chilean food.

C-D Hymalayan Country House, near Manu Temple, T01902-252294. 15 smart double rooms, plenty of marble and pine, with great views over Old Manali. Popular, specializes in trekking and motorbike safaris. Getting a bit pricey though.

C-E Beas (HPTDC), near bridge, T01902-252832, www.hptdc.nic.in. 31 somewhat run-down rooms with bath, TV, breakfast, room service meals, magnificent river views. Bit overpriced now for what you get.

C-E Chetna, near **Log Huts**, T01902-252245. 13 comfortable rooms with balconies, hot water, good open-air restaurant, lawns, elevated, with beautiful views. Not such a nice area to stay though – many many hotels clustered here, not much space.

C-E Rohtang Manalsu (HPTDC), near Circuit House, The Mall, T01902-252332, www.hptdc.nic.in. 27 large rooms, good restaurant, garden, superb views.

D-E Dragon, Old Manali, T01902-252290, www.dragontreks.com. This hardy perennial of the Old Manali scene has had a chic facelift and offers a smarter alternative in this part of town. Nice décor, lovely outdoor sitting areas, great vibe. There's a good family suite. Recommended.

D-E Drifters' Inn, Old Manali, T01902-251077, www.drifersinn.in. In the heart of Old Manali, comfortable rooms with TV, free Wi-Fi and popular café downstairs.

D-F Dharma Guest House, above Vashist, T01902-252354, www.hoteldharmamanali.com. Perched high on the hill above Vashist, this place has great views. Rooms are clean and comfortable. Buns of steel guaranteed climbing up there.

E-F Arohi, Vashisht, T01902-254421, www.arohiecoadventures.com. Clean, attractive rooms, big windows facing mountains, owner good for trekking knowledge.

E-F Sunshine, The Mall, next to **Leela Huts**, T01902-252320. Lots of character, 9 rooms in old traditional house, others in newer cottage, log fires, restaurant, lovely garden, peaceful, family atmosphere, friendly, such good value you might need them to repeat the price! Highly recommended.

F-G Cairn Lodge, above Club House, Old Manali, T01902-252861. Pleasant and comfortable, 3 wood-panelled rooms, attached hot bath, good café.

F-G Tourist Nest Guest House, near Dragon, Old Manali, T01902-252383. Bright clean rooms with balconies – top floors still have views, whereas building in front obscures views from lower floors.

G Bodh, Vashisht, T01902-254165, bunteee23@hotmail.com. 5 clean, tidy rooms, shared bath (hot shower), good views from terrace. A good choice among many in this village.

G Cottage Cold Corner, Old Manali, T01902-252312. Strange name and certainly not the vibe, very warm and friendly welcome indeed. Basic rooms, little outdoor seating area.

G Didi Guest House, Vashisht. Through the village and above the school. 10 wood panelled bedrooms. Cheap, chilled and cheerful with yoga and excellent views up and down the valley.

G Mango Guest House, Vashisht. The highest up the hill above the temple baths. 6 basic bedrooms. Well worth the walk.

G Monal, above Old Manali, beyond Manu Temple, T01902-253848. Up steep cemented steps, 9 rooms, some with hot showers, others shared, café, pretty garden, superb views all round. Recommended.

G Rockway Cottage, above Old Manali, the last one before the wilderness, a 10-min walk from the road, T01902-254328. Very friendly, 10 well-crafted, but simple rooms, most with woodburners, clean common bath, excellent location. Recommended.

G Shiv Shakti, above Old Manali, beyond Manu Temple, T01902-254170. Fine views across valley and mountains beyond, 4 pleasant rooms and café, attached hot bath, friendly farming family. Reiki courses and treatments.

G Upcountry Lodge, above Club House, Old Manali, T01902-252257. Quiet location in orchards, 9 clean rooms, attached hot bath, pleasant garden.

Eating

Kullu *p508, map p507*

Ashiyana in hotel, Sarvari Bazar. Clean, good south Indian.

Planet Food, next door to **Hot Stuff Food Junction**. Similar but slightly more upmarket with beer bar as well, good-value *thalis*.

Hot Stuff Food Junction, near tourist information. Good for snacks, light meals, outdoor seating.

Monal Café, next to the tourist office. Simple meals.

Shobla (see Sleeping). Pleasant.

Vaishali (see Sleeping). Excellent, a/c.

Kasol *p509*

Evergreen Restaurant. The most popular with a wide choice of Indian and Western food including all the travellers' favourites plus more. A major meeting place in season.

Moondance, centre of village. A pleasant building with good German bakery.

Manikaran *p509*

Wayside stalls serve local food, while some near the springs cater for Westerners; there are also a couple of reasonable *dhabas* by the bus stand. There is a classier sister concern of **Evergreen** in Kasol, similar menu.

Holy Palace, in bazar. Look for the finely carved doors.

Gurudwara, near the temple, Excellent meals, steam-cooked at the springs (donation only).

Pulga *p509*

Paradise Restaurant, in the village. Great vegetarian dishes. Also has information on guides and equipment for treks up the valley and over the Pin-Parvati Pass (5300 m). If you are lucky, you may be able to persuade the watchman of the old **Forest Rest House** to let you in. The 'visitors' registration book' contains entries that date back to the 1930s and include several well-known mountaineers who have passed by.

Naggar *p510*

There is also a dhaba up at the Jana waterfall recommended for trying real Himachal food – *dhal* made with sour milk, corn flour *rotis*.

Nightingale, 200 m above bus stand. Serves trout and Italian.

Ragini, roof terrace at hotel of the same name. Excellent for breakfast.

Ristorante Italiano, bus stand. Open in season, Fri-Sun.

German Bakery, next to **Ragini**. Sweet little café offering up the usual GB fare, good photography on walls.

Manali and around

p511, maps p512 and p513

Hotels may need advance notice from non-residents. Some close in the off-season.

In **Dhungri** village, there is a bakery and restaurant opposite the temple. Stalls sell snacks, drinks and provisions. In **Old Manali** there are plenty of Israeli dishes and music which can range from techno to Tibetan.

¶¶¶ **Johnson Café**, Circuit House Rd, T01902-253023. Western (varied menu). Elegant restaurant in a large garden, specializes in trout – you can have it oven-baked, curried, masalad or smoked, excellent home-made pasta, good filter coffee, delicious ice creams. Beautiful lighting, quite magical at night. Highly recommended.

¶¶¶ **La Plage**, Old Manali, Opening in 2012, this is the 1st franchise of the renowned **La Plage** from Goa. You can expect nothing but the best from this slick French operation – with great tastes and great ambience.

¶¶¶ **The Lazy Dog**, Old Manali, on left past shops going uphill (before road swings to right). Funky interior design with excellent food, good music, filter coffee, free Wi-Fi and a lovely terrace overlooking the river. Highly recommended.

¶¶ **Adarsh**, The Mall (opposite Kunzam). One of many Punjabi places, but has more style and better menu than others.

¶¶ **Café Sang Sang**, Old Manali. Korean café with lovely vibe serving up trout *sushi* and *sashimi*, as well as other Korean delights and plenty of veggie options.

¶¶ **Chopsticks**, The Mall, opposite bus stand. Tibetan, Chinese, Japanese. Good food, although some say with its growing popularity, its portions have downsized.

¶¶ **Il Forno**, Hadimba Rd. Italian. Attractive pizzeria in traditional building, halfway up hill.

¶¶ **Mayur**, Mission Rd. Vast international menu. Excellent food, smart, efficient service, subdued decor, very pleasant with linen table cloths and candles on tables, Indian classical music, great ambience, cosy with wood-burning stove and generator.

¶¶ **Mehak**, next to **Mayur**. Cheaper imitation but does very tasty Gujarati and Punjabi food.

¶¶ **Peace Café**, behind post office. Good Tibetan, Japanese, some Chinese. Unpretentious, pleasant, warm (wood- burning stove), friendly owner.

¶¶ **Sa Ba**, Nehru Park. Excellent Indian, snacks, pizzas, cakes, some outdoor seating for people-watching. Recommended.

¶¶ **Sushi Yoon**, Vashist. Chic little hole-in-the-wall café with just 12 seats serving up tasty sushi, delicious teas and coffees and the ultimate – green tea ice cream. Highly recommended.

¶¶ **Vibhuti's**, The Mall, corner of Model Town Rd, up short flight of steps. South Indian vegetarian. Delicious *masala dosas*.

¶ **Bee's Knees**, Old Manali. Under the watchful eye of Avi – the man with the greatest smile, you can get big plentiful plates of Mexican food and all the usual Indian fare. Recommended.

¶ **Dylan's Toasted and Roasted**, Old Manali, www.dylanscoffee.com. The best coffee this side of Delhi, served up by the affable Raj. The cookies are legendary as is his 'Hello to the Queen' – great atmosphere. Highly recommended.

¶ **Green Forest**, Dhungri village, on the forest path, past temple down towards Old Manali, just after leaving the forest. Vegetarian. Excellent breakfasts and meals.

¶ **Manali Sweets**, Shiali Mahadev Rd. Excellent Indian sweets (superb *gulab jamuns*), also good *thalis* (Rs 40).

¶ **Palan Sher-e-Punjab**, near taxis, The Mall. Good Punjabi vegetarian.

¶ **Pizza Olive**, Old Manali. Very tasty wood-oven pizzas, great range of pastas and even tiramisu. Recommended.

¶ **River Music**, by bridge. Popular hangout, travellers' staples plus Israeli.

¶ **Tibetan Dhaba**, back of bus station. Very small and cosy, great *momos*.

¶ **Yangkhor**, past **Moondance**. Tibetan and Western favourites.

Cafés and snacks

Café Amigos, opposite Nehru Park, good cakes, breads, real coffee, friendly, popular.

Lhasa Café, Vashisht, above **Vashisht Video Hall** (which shows 2-3 films daily).

Open Hand, Old Manali. Sweet little branch of the stylish Delhi based café serving up large cappuccinos and wedges of carrot cake

Shiva Garden Café, 100 m further uphill in Old Manali. Good food with an adventurous international flavour plus 'German bakery', delightful spot, pleasant ambience, open-air seating, restful music, good views over Manalsu Nala, very reasonable.

Superbake, Vashisht. Good bread, cakes, biscuits and chilled drinks.

Rainbow Café, Vashisht. For food, music and wonderful cinnamon *chai*, great for meeting other travellers. Internet.
Tibetan Kitchen, just beyond Manalsu bridge, and left, Old Manali. German Bakery, reasonably priced cakes, breads, real coffee, trekkers' supplies.

Festivals and events

Kullu *p508, map p507*

End Apr Colourful 3-day **Cattle Fair** attracts villagers from the surrounding area. Numerous cultural events accompany.
Oct-Nov **Dasara** is sacred to the Goddess Durga which, elsewhere in India, tends to be overshadowed by **Diwali** which follows a few weeks later. In this part of the Himalaya it is a big social event and a get-together of the gods.

Manali and around *p511, maps p512 and p513*

Mid-Feb Week-long **Winter Sports Carnival**.
May 3-day colourful **Dhungri Forest festival** at Hadimba Devi Temple, celebrated by hill women.

Shopping

Kullu *p508, map p507*

Best buys are shawls, caps, *gadmas*. The state weaving cooperative, **Bhutti Weavers Colony**, 6 km south, has retail outlets; **Bhuttico**, 1 store 2 km south of Apple Valley Resorts.

Akhara Bazar has a **Government Handicrafts Emporium**, **Himachal Khadi Emporium** and **Khadi Gramudyog**. **Charm Shilp** is good for sandals.

Manali and around *p511, maps p512 and p513*

Books

Bookworm, NAC Market, behind Bus Station. Huge stock of quality paperbacks, reasonably priced. Highly recommended. New branch near Manali Post, 1000-1800.

Crafts and local curios

Bhutico Bodh, by the Hindu temple in Traders, Gulati Complex. Sikh tailors, quick, good quality, copies and originals (caps to order, ready in hours, Rs 75). There's another branch by the Hindu temple in the bazar, with good range of shawls.
Charitable Trust Tibetan Handicrafts, The Mall. Government shop.
Great Hadimba Weaver's, near Manu Temple, Old Manali. Excellent value, hand-woven, co-op produced shawls/scarves and there is a little workroom to the side where you can watch them at work. Recommended.
Manushi, in the market. Women's co-op producing good quality shawls, hats, socks.
Om Collection, The Mall. Good Tibetan T-shirts, dresses, jewellery, jumpers.
Shree-la Crafts, near the main taxi stand. Friendly owner, good value silver jewellery.
Tibetan Bazar and Tibetan Carpet Centre.
Hyund Manu Market. Curios, woollen clothing, arts and crafts.

Tailors

Gulati Traders, Gulati Complex. Sikh tailors, quick, good quality, copies and originals.

Trekking equipment

Ram Lal and Sons, E9 Manu Market, behind bus stand. Good range of well-made products, friendly, highly recommended.

Activities and tours

Kullu *p508, map p507*

Look East, c/o Bajaj Autos, Manikaran Chowk, Shamshi, T01902-065771. Operator recommended for river rafting and bike hire.

Naggar *p510*

For trekking to Malana, it is best to employ a local guide. Pawan, from the old *chai* shop in the main village, is recommended.

Manali and around *p511, maps p512 and p513*

Body and Soul

Shri Hari Yoga Ashram, below Vashist, T(0)9418-240369. Swami Yogananda has a great following and offers down-to-earth spirituality with your downward dog. Recommended.
Spa Magnolia at **Johnson's Lodge** Circuit House Road. T(0)9816-100023. Stylish little spa with pricy little treatments – but a bit of a treat. Ayurvedic and Western treatments available.

Skiing and mountaineering

Mountaineering and Allied Sports Institute, 1.5 km out of town, T01902-252342. Organizes courses in mountaineering, skiing, watersports, high-altitude trekking and mountain rescue courses; 5- and 7-day ski courses, Jan-Mar. There is a hostel, an exhibition of equipment and an auditorium.

Tour operators

Himalayan Adventurers, opposite tourist office, T01902-252750, www.himalayan adventurersindia.com. Wide range of itineraries and activities.
HPTDC, T01902-253531/252116. Daily, in season by luxury coach (or car for 5): to Nehru Kund, Rahla Falls, Marhi, Rohtang Pass, 1000-1700, Rs 200 (car Rs 1200); to Solang, Jagatsukh and Naggar; 1000-1600, Rs 190 (car Rs 1200); to Manikaran, 0900-1800, Rs 250 (car Rs 1100).
Swagatam, opposite **Kunzam**, The Mall, T01902-252990. Long-distance buses, trekking, rafting, very efficient.

Trekking

Clarify details and number of trekkers involved and shop around before making any decisions.
Above 14000ft, log huts area, www.above 14000.ft.com, T(0)98166-32281. Expert, environmentally conscious adventure organizers, specializing in treks, mountain biking, climbing expeditions and mountaineering courses throughout the region. Paperless office. Highly recommended.
Himalayan Journeys, Park View Building, The Mall, T01902-254397, www.himalayanjourneys india.com. Good range, experienced guides.
Magic Mountain, no office as such, but call Raju on T(0)9816-056934, www.magic mountainadventures.com. Manali's most experienced cycling guide, Raju also offers trekking and jeep safaris, and is honest, friendly and reliable. Highly recommended.
Shangri-la Adventures, Tibetan Colony, Rohtang Rd, T01902-252734, shang-adv@ hotmail.com. Treks to Zanskar, Ladakh, Spiti, fishing, rafting, experienced Tibetan guides, competitive pricing for small groups, excellent service from Jigme, honest, friendly.
WH Adventure Travel, Hotel D'Chalet, The Mall, T(0)9816-166680, www.whadventures.com. Mr Ghosh is knowledgeable, advises on routes; organizes treks, jeep safaris, mountaineering in Lahaul, Spiti, Zanskar and Ladakh.

Transport

Kullu *p508, map p507*

Air Bhuntar Airport, T01902-265727. **Air India**, T1-800-180 1407, www.airindia.in; **Kingfisher Red**, T1-800-209 3030, www.flykingfisher.com.
Bus Most buses coming to Kullu continue to Manali. Most long-distance buses use main bus stand, **Sarvari Khad**, with a booking office. For long distance and to **Manali**, left bank bus stand across the bridge: buses for **Naggar** (every 30 mins in summer) and **Bijli Mahadev**, and several to **Manali**; HPTDC deluxe bus to **Chandigarh** (270 km), 0800, 8 hrs, Rs 340; **Delhi**, 512 km, 15 hrs, extra buses during season, often better than private buses, you will pay more for a/c, Volvo service is pricier; **Dharamshala**, 0800-0900, 8 hrs; **Shimla** (235 km), 0900, 8 hrs, Tickets from tourist office.

Parvati Valley *p509*

Bus There are frequent buses from **Bhuntar Bus Stand**, outside the airport, with many connections to/from **Kullu** and **Manali**. To **Manikaran**, 2½ hrs, Rs 28.

Naggar *p510*

Bus The bus stop is in the bazar, below the castle. Several daily between **Kullu** and **Manali** via scenic east bank route (1½ hrs, Rs 24). From Manali, more frequent buses to **Patli Kuhl** (6 km from Naggar, 45 mins, Rs 16), where you can get a local bus (half hourly in summer) or rickshaw (around Rs 90).

Manali and around

p511, maps p512 and p513

Air Flights connect **Bhuntar Airport** near Kullu T01902-265037, with **Delhi**, **Shimla** and **Ludhiana**. **Jagsons**, T01902-252843. Transport to town: taxi to Manali, Rs 1100 for 4 persons. **Himachal Transport** (green) bus, every 15 mins, Rs 25 (allow 2½ hrs travel time from Manali).
Bus Local bus stand, T01902-252323. Various state RTCs offer direct services to major towns. **HRTC Bus Stand**, the Mall, T01902-252116, reservations 1000-1200, 1400-1600. HPTDC coaches in season (fewer in winter); deluxe have

2 seats on either side: **Harisons** and **Swagatam** (see Tour operators, above), run their own buses. **Chandigarh** 0700, 10 hrs, Rs 415; **Delhi** a/c 1830, 15 hrs, Rs 825; a/c sleeper Rs 1100; non a/c, 1700, Rs 425. **Dharamshala** 0530, 0810, Rs 210, **Keylong** 0600, 6 hrs, Rs 145. **Kullu** via **Naggar**: 2 daily, Rs 30, 1 hr; most Kullu buses go via the national highway and stop at **Patli Kuhl** (see Naggar, above). **Mandi**, Rs 112. **Rohtang Pass** 0900, day trip with photo-stops, striking scenery (take sweater/jacket), 1½ hrs at pass, Rs 120. **Shimla** (280 km), 0830, 1900, 9 hrs, Rs 415.

To **Leh** HPTDC and private coaches run ordinary and luxury buses during the season (mid-Jun to end Sep), but not always daily; usually based on demand. Seats should be reserved ahead. Front seats are best though the cab gets filled by locals wanting a 'lift'. Those joining the bus in Keylong must reserve from Manali to be certain of a seat. Rs 400-850 (Rs 1600 including tent and meals); usual overnight stop is at Sarchu where other cheaper tents may be available (some choose to sleep on the bus). The 530 km takes about 24-28 hrs on the road, so leave 0600, arrive Leh next afternoon. There are reports of some drivers getting drunk, hence unsafe.

Motorbike The uncrowded Kullu-Manali road via Naggar is an ideal place for a test ride. **Anu Auto Works**, halfway up the hill to Vashisht. Excellent selection; insurance and helmets provided. Mechanical support and bike safaris organized throughout the region.

Bike Point, Old Manali. Limited choice of bikes in good condition, mechanical support and competitive rates.

Bony Sony Motors, Old Manali, T01902-253967. Good service, knowledgeable and experienced mechanics. Recommended.

Enfield Club, Vashisht Rd, T01902-254090. Enfields and Hondas for hire; reasonable charges, friendly, honest service.

Local taxi The local union is very strong, office near tourist office, T01902-254032. Fares tend to be high; from bus stand: Rs 50 for hotels (2-3 km). To Vashisht or top of Old Manali Rd, Rs 60; auto-rickshaws Rs 30.

Long distance taxi **Aut**, Rs 900, Rs 1200 (return); **Darcha**, Rs 3000; **Keylong**, Rs 2400; **Kullu**, Rs 550 (Rs 800 return); **Mandi**, Rs 1200 (Rs 1500 return); **Naggar**, Rs 350 (Rs 400 return); **Rohtang Pass**, Rs 900, Rs 1200.

Train Reservations at HPTDC office, T01902-251925.

❶ Directory

Kullu *p508, map p507*

Banks **State Bank of Patiala**, T01902-222457 (1100-1400), Akhara Bazar (north of town) for foreign exchange (cash and TCs only); **State Bank of India**, off NH21, south of town, T01902-225902. Nearest Visa exchange at Mandi. **Internet** Facilities are growing.

Manali and around
p511, maps p512 and p513

Banks **State Bank of India**, the Mall, 100 m above Picadilly Hotel, T01902-252405. ATM. **UCO Bank**, The Mall, opposite Nehru Park (1000-1430, closed Tue), T01902-252330, changes TCs, quicker and more polite than the SBI. Signs indicate exchanges on the Mall; try **Swagatam** opposite Kunzam, changes major TCs, cash against Visa; or **Paul Merchants Office** who apparently have the best rates among the private money changers. **Internet** **Nirvana Café**, Circuit House Rd, Old Manali, T01902-253222. 9 machines, well run. Several others in town and Old Manali. **Medical services** **Mission Hospital**, T01902-252379. **Men Tsee Khang Hospital**, Gompa Rd, highly recommended for Tibetan herbal/ mineral treatments. **Chemists**: opposite NAC Market. **Post** GPO, off Model Town Rd, T01902-252324, Mon-Sat 0900-1700. Very efficient. **Telephone** **Telecom office**, south of Shiali Mahadev Rd. **Gopal Travels**, opposite temple in bazar. Friendly, ISD phone, receives faxes, photocopies.

Lahaul and the Manali–Leh road

→ *Colour map 1, A3/B3.*

Lying between the green alpine slopes of the Kullu and Chamba valleys to the south and the dry, arid plateau of Ladakh, the mountainous arid landscapes of Lahaul manage to get enough rain during the monsoon months to allow extensive cultivation, particularly on terraces, of potatoes, green peas and hops (for beer making). Lahaul potatoes are some of the best in the country and are used as seed for propagation. These and rare herbs have brought wealth to the area. Most people follow a curious blend of both Hindu and Buddhist customs though there are a few who belong wholly to one or the other religion.
▸▸ *For listings, see pages 527-528. For trekking, see page 546.*

Ins and outs

The whole region can be approached by road from three directions: Shimla via the Spiti Valley; Manali over the Rohtang Pass (3985 m) into Upper Lahaul; and from Zanskar and Ladakh over the Shingo La and Baralacha La (passes). The Shingo La gives access to Lahaul from Zanskar (see page 587), while the Baralacha La (4880 m) on the Leh–Manali road provides access from Ladakh. There is a trekking route from Manali to Zanskar. Streams cross the road at several places. These may be impassable during heavy rain, and those fed by snow-melt swell significantly during the day as meltwater increases, so travel in the late afternoon can be more difficult than in the early morning when the flow is at its lowest. Rockfalls are also a common hazard. ▸▸ *See Transport, page 528.*

History

Historically there are similarities between this region and Ladakh since in the 10th century Lahaul, Spiti and Zanskar were part of the Ladakh Kingdom. The Hindu rajas in Kullu paid tribute to Ladakh. In the 17th century Ladakh was defeated by a combined Mongol-Tibetan force. Later Lahaul was separated into Upper Lahaul which fell under the control of Kullu, and Lower Lahaul which came under the Chamba rajas. The whole region came under the Sikhs as their empire expanded, whilst under the British Lahaul and Kullu were part of the administrative area centred on Kangra.

Manali to Leh → *For listings, see pages 527-528. Colour map 1, B3-A3.*

This stunningly beautiful road, one of the highest in the world, is currently the main route for foreigners into the region of Lahaul and on to Leh. The 530-km highway is usually open from July to September, depending on snow fall; most buses stop in mid-September. The first 52 km runs up the Kullu Valley, then climbs through the Rohtang Pass. The pass itself normally opens at the end of May and is the only way into Lahaul, pending the completion of a delayed tunnel, which is currently scheduled to open in 2014. No permits are necessary.

Leaving Manali

From Manali the NH21 goes through the village of Palchan and then begins a sharp climb to **Kothi**, at 2530 m, set below towering cliffs. Beautiful views of coniferous hillsides and meadows unwind as the road climbs through 2800 m, conifers giving way to poplars and then banks of flowers. The 70-m-high **Rohalla Falls**, 19 km from Manali at an altitude of 3500 m, are a spectacular sight.

The landscape, covered in snow for up to eight months of the year, becomes totally devoid of trees above Marrhi, a seasonal settlement and restaurant stop, as the road climbs through a series of tight hairpins to the Rohtang Pass.

Rohtang Pass → *Colour map 1, B3.*

From the pass you get spectacular views of precipitous cliffs, deep ravines, large glaciers and moraines. Buses stop for photos. From June until mid-October, when **Himachal Tourism** (HPTDC) runs a daily bus tour from Manali, the pass becomes the temporary home to a dozen or more noisy roadside 'cafés'.

The descent to **Gramphoo** (Gramphu), which is no more than a couple of houses at the junction of the road from Tabo and Kaza, offers superb views of the glaciated valley of the Chandra River, source of the Chenab. To the north and east rise the peaks of Lahaul, averaging around 6000 m and with the highest, Mulkila, reaching 6520 m. As the road descends towards Khoksar there is an excellent view of the Lumphu Nala coming down from the Tempo La glacier. An earlier glacial maximum is indicated by the huge terminal moraine visible halfway up the valley.

There is a police check post in **Khoksar**, at 3140 m, where you may be required to show your passport and sign a register. This can take some time if more than one bus arrives at the same time. About 8 km west of Khoksar work is in progress on the Rohtang tunnel, which will link the Solang Valley with the Chandra Valley. If you cross the bridge here you find an attractive waterfall.

Manali to Leh

Gondhla to Keylong and the Pattan Valley

It is worth stopping here to see the 'castle' belonging to the local *thakur* (ruler), built around 1700. The seven-storey house with staircases made of wooden logs has a veranda running around the top and numerous apartments on the various floors. The fourth floor was for private prayer, while the Thakur held court from the veranda. There is much to see in this neglected, ramshackle house, particularly old weapons, statues, costumes and furniture. The 'sword of wisdom', believed to be a gift from the His Holiness the Dalai Lama, is of special interest. On close inspection you will notice thin wires have been hammered together to form the blade, a technique from Toledo, Spain. The huge rock near the Government School, which some claim to be of ancient origin, has larger-than-life figures of *Bodhisattvas* carved on it.

As the road turns north approaching **Tandi**, the Chandra rushes through a gorge, giving a superb view of the massively contorted, folded and faulted rocks of the Himalaya. Tandi itself is at the confluence of the Chandra and Bhaga rivers, forming the Chandrabhaga or Chenab. Keylong is 8 km from here, see page 526. At Tandi you can take a left turn and visit the Pattan Valley before heading to Keylong to continue on the journey.

Pattan Valley → *For listings, see pages 527-528. Colour map 1, A3/B3.*

The Pattan Valley has a highly distinctive agricultural system which despite its isolated situation is closely tied in to the Indian market. Pollarded willows are crowded together all around the villages, offering roofing material for the flat-roofed houses and fodder for the cattle during the six-month winter. Introduced by a British missionary in the 19th century to try and help stabilize the deeply eroded slopes, willows have become a vital part of the valley's village life, with the additional benefit of offering shade from the hot summer sun. Equally important are the three commercial crops which dominate farming: hops, potatoes and peas, all exported, while wheat and barley are the most common subsistence grain crops.

Tandi to Trilokinath

Just out of **Tandi** after crossing the Bhaga River on the Keylong road, the Udeypur road doubles back along the right bank of the Chenab running close to but high above the river. The road passes through **Ruding**, **Shansha**, 15 km from Tandi, **Jahlma**, 6 km and **Thirot**, another 11 km on (rest house here). A bridge at **Jhooling** crosses the Chenab. Some 6 km further on, the road enters a striking gorge where a bridge crosses the river before taking the road up to **Trilokinath**, 6 km away.

Trilokinath

Trilokinath, at 2760 m, is approached by a very attractive road which climbs up the left bank of the Chenab. The glitteringly white-painted Trilokinath temple stands at the end of the village street on top of a cliff. The **Siva temple** has been restored by Tibetan Buddhists, whose influence is far stronger than the Hindu. Tibetan prayer-flags decorate the entrance to the temple which is in the ancient wooden-pagoda style. In the courtyard is a tiny stone Nandi and a granite lingam, Saivite symbols which are dwarfed in significance by the Buddhist symbols of the sanctuary, typical prayer-wheels constantly being turned by pilgrims, and a 12th-century six-armed white marble Avalokiteshwara image (Bodhisattva) in the shrine, along with other Buddhist images. The original columns date from Lalitaditya's reign in the eighth century, but there has been considerable modernization as well as restoration, with the installation of bright electric lights including a strikingly garish and flickering *chakra* on the ceiling. Hindus and Buddhists celebrate the three-day **Pauri Festival** in August.

Udeypur

Ten kilometres from the junction with the Trilokinath road is Udeypur (Udaipur). Visited in the summer it is difficult to imagine that the area is completely isolated by sometimes over 2 m of snow during the six winter months. It is supplied by weekly helicopter flights (weather permitting). The helipad is at the entrance to the village. Trekking routes cross the valley here and further west, see page 547.

The unique **Mrikula** (Markula) **Devi temple** (AD 1028-1063) is above the bazar. The temple dedicated to Kali looks wholly unimposing from the outside with a battered-looking wood-tiled 'conical' roof and crude outside walls. However, inside are some beautiful, intricate deodar-wood carvings belonging to two periods. The façade of the shrine, the *mandapa* (hall) ceiling and the pillars supporting it are earlier than those beside the window, the architraves and two western pillars. Scenes from the *Mahabharata* and the *Ramayana* epics decorate the architraves, while the two *dvarapalas* (door guardians), which are relatively crude, are stained with the blood of sacrificed goats and rams. The wood carvings here closely resemble those of the Hadimba Temple at Manali and some believe it was the work of the same 16th-century craftsman (see page 513). The silver image of Kali (*Mahisha-shurmardini*) 1570, inside, is a strange mixture of Rajasthani and Tibetan styles (note the *lama*-like head covering), with an oddly proportioned body.

Motorcycling from Manali to Leh

Allow four days on the way up, to help acclimatize as the 500 km road will take you from 2000 m to 5420 m and down to 3500 m (Leh). The last petrol station is in Tandi, 7 km before Keylong. A full tank plus five to 10 litres of spare petrol will take you to Leh. Above 3500 m, you should open the air intake on your carb to compensate for the loss of power.

Apart from Keylong, there are no hotels, only a few tented camps, providing basic food and shelter from mid-June to mid-September. Some will be noisy and drafty. The lack of toilet facilities leads to pollution near the camps (don't forget your lighter for waste paper). A tent and mini-stove plus pot, soups, tea, biscuits, muesli, will add extra comfort, allowing you to camp in the wild expanses of the Moray Plains (4700 m).

Unless you plan to sleep in the camp there, you must reach Pang before 1300 on the way up, 1500 on the way down, as the police will not allow you to proceed beyond the checkpoint after these times. The army camp in Pang has helpful officers and some medical facilities.

Keylong → *For listings, see page 527-528. Colour map 1, B3. Phone code: 01900. Altitude: 3350 m.*

The principal town of the district of Lahaul, Keylong is set amidst fields of barley and buckwheat surrounded by brown hills and snowy peaks and was once the home of Moravian missionaries. Only traders and trekkers can negotiate the pass out of season. Keylong is an increasingly widely used stopping point for people en route to Leh or trekking in the Lahaul/Spiti area. Landslides on the Leh–Manali road can cause quite long delays and the town can be an unintended rest halt for a couple of days. It has little to offer, though the views are very attractive and there are pleasant walks.

There is a pleasant circuit of the town by road which can be done comfortably in under two hours. Tracks run down into the town centre. The **local deity** 'Kelang Wazir' is kept in Shri Nawang Dorje's home which you are welcome to visit. There is a **Tibetan Centre for Performing Arts**. A statue in the centre of Keylong commemorates the Indian nationalist **Rash Behari Bose**, born 15 May 1886 near Kolkata.

Khardong Monastery, 3 km away across the Chandra River up a steep tree-shaded path, is the most important in the area. It is believed to have been founded 900 years ago and was renovated in 1912. Nuns and monks enjoy equality; married *lamas* spend the summer months at home cultivating their fields and return to the monastery in winter. The monastery contains a huge barrel drum, a valuable library and collections of *thangkas*, Buddha statues, musical instruments, costumes and ancient weapons.

Sha-Shur Monastery, a kilometre away, was in legend reputedly founded as early as AD 17 by a Buddhist missionary from Zanskar, Lama Deva Tyatsho who was sent by the Bhutanese king. It has ancient connections with Bhutan and contains numerous wall paintings and a 4.5-m *thangka*. The annual **festival** is held in June/July.

Tayul Monastery, above Satingri village, has a 4-m-high statue of Padma Sambhava, wall paintings and a library containing valuable scriptures and *thangkas*. The *mani* wheel here is supposed to turn on its own marking specially auspicious occasions, the last time having been in 1986.

Keylong to Leh → *For listings, see page 528-528. Colour map 1, B3-A3.*

From Keylong the road passes through very high-altitude desert with extraordinary mountain views. **Jispa**, 21 km on at an altitude of 3200 m, has a hotel, a campsite, a few tea stalls and a mountaineering institute. **Himachal Tourism**'s concrete 'lodge' has three basic rooms with toilets and cheap camping in the yard. About 2 km beyond Jispa is **Teh** which has accommodation. There is a 300-year-old palace, built in the Tibetan style, comprising 108 rooms over four storeys – apparently the largest traditional structure in Lahaul. It is 3.5 km off the main highway (turn off at Ghemur, between Keylong and Jispa) in a village called **Kolong**, and has recently been converted in to a heritage hotel (see Sleeping, page 528). A museum has also been opened there, with some interesting exhibits depicting the traditional and ceremonial life of the local rulers, who still own the property.

All vehicles must stop for passport checks at **Darcha** checkpost where the Bhaga River is bridged. Tents appear on the grassy riverbank in the summer to provide a halt for trekkers to Zanskar. The road climbs to **Patseo** where you can get a view back of Darcha. A little further is **Zingzingbar.** Icy streams flow across the road while grey and red-brown scree reach down from the bare mountainside to the road edge. The road then goes over the **Baralacha La** (54 km; 4880 m), 107 km from Keylong, at the crossroads of Lahaul, Zanskar, Spiti and Ladakh regions before dropping to **Sarchu** (on the state border). There are a dozen or so tented camps in Sarchu, including on run by **Himachal Tourism** (HPTDC), mostly with two-bed tents (sometimes reported dirty), communal toilet tents, late-night Indian meal and breakfast; private bus passengers without reservations are accommodated whenever possible (Rs 150 per person); open mid-June to mid-September.

The road runs beyond Brandy Nala by the Tsarap River before negotiating 22 spectacular hairpin bends, known as the 'Gata Loops', to climb up to the **Nakli La** (4950 m) and **Lachalung La** (5065 m). It then descends past tall earth and rock pillars to **Pang**, a summer settlement in a narrow valley where you can stop for an expensive 'breakfast' (usually roti, vegetables and omelettes to order). The camp remains open beyond 15 September; an overnight stop is possible in communal tents. The 40-km-wide Moray plains (4400 m) provide a change from the slower mountain road. The road then climbs to **Taglang La** (5370 m), the highest motorable pass along this route and the second highest in the world; the altitude is likely to affect many travellers at this point. You descend slowly towards the Indus valley, passing small villages, before entering a narrow gorge with purple coloured cliffs. The road turns left to continue along the Indus basin passing **Upshi** with a sheep farm and a checkpost, and then **Thikse**, before reaching **Leh**.

Lahaul and the Manali–Leh road listings

For Sleeping and Eating price codes and other relevant information, see Essentials pages 38-42.

Sleeping

Udeypur *p525*

Camping is possible in an attractive site about 4 km beyond the town (permission from Forest Officer) but since there is no water supply, water has to be carried in from a spring about 300 m further up the road. Carry provisions too as there is little in the bazar.

F Amandeep Guest House, T01909-222256. 7 semi deluxe rooms with limited hot water. Good dhaba opposite serves good Indian food.

F Forest Rest House, off the road in a pleasant raised position. 2 rooms with bath, very basic, bring your own sleeping bag.

Keylong *p526*

C-D Chandrabhaga (HPTDC), T01900-222247. Open mid-Jun to mid-Oct, reserve ahead. 3 rooms with bath, 2-bed tents, dorm (Rs 150), meals to order, solar-heated pool, rates include vegetarian meals.

E-F Tashi Deleg, on main road through town. Does well from being the first place you come to from Tandi, slightly overpriced as a result. Rooms are comfortable though, and the restaurant is one of the best in town. Also has a car park.

F Snowland, above Circuit House, T01900-222219. Modest but adequate, 15 rooms with bath, friendly reception. Recommended.

G Dekyid, below police station. 3-storey hotel, friendly, helpful reception, decent-sized rooms with bath, quiet, excellent views over fields, good restaurant but service very slow.

G Gyespa, on main road, T01900-222873. 11 basic but adequate rooms plus a good restaurant.

Keylong to Leh *p526*

B Khangsar Sarai, Kolong, T01900-233329. 4 deluxe rooms in a recently converted 300-year-old palace, unique in the area and well worth a visit, highly recommended.

D-E Ibex Hotel, Jispa, T01900-233204, nomad_adventures@yahoo.com. Glass and cement block, 27 comfortable rooms, dorm (Rs 100), whole place in need of a lick of paint but the location is impressive. Reserve ahead.

Transport

Keylong *p526*

Bus State and private luxury buses are most comfortable but charge more than double the 'B'-class fare. To **Manali** (6-8 hrs); to **Leh** (18 hrs). To board deluxe buses to Leh in Keylong, reserve ahead and pay full fare from Manali (Rs 1300, plus Rs 300 for tent and meals in Sarchu).

Jeep To **Manali** by jeep, 4 hrs, weather permitting; **Sarchu** 6 hrs, **Leh** 14 hrs.

Directory

Keylong *p526*

Banks State Bank of India, but no foreign exchange.

Northern Himachal

Dominated by Dharamshala, this is a region replete with some of the most breathtaking mountain views imaginable. From Dalhousie eastwards there are tantalizing glimpses of snow-capped peaks, while McLeodganj has been attracting Western travellers for decades, coming in search of peace, tranquillity, the Dalai Lama and sometimes even themselves. The Kangra Valley sees far fewer visitors, but has an unhurried charm all of its own, epitomized by Pragpur, India's first heritage village. *▸▸ For listings, see pages 537-545. For Trekking, see page 546.*

Dharamshala

→ For listings, see pages 537-545. *Colour map 1, B3. Phone code: 01892. Population: 8600. Altitude: 1250-2000 m.*

Dharamshala has a spectacular setting along a spur of the Dhauladhar range, varying in height from 1250 m at the 'Lower Town' bazar to 1768 m at McLeodganj. It is this 'Upper' and more attractive part of town that attracts the bulk of visitors. Although the centre of the town itself has now become somewhat overdeveloped, it is surrounded by forests, set against a backdrop of high peaks on three sides, with superb views over the Kangra Valley and Shiwaliks, and of the great granite mountains that almost overhang the town.

Ins and outs

Getting there Flights to Gaggal Airport (13 km). Lower Dharamshala is well connected by bus with towns near and far. You can travel from Shimla to the southeast or from Hoshiarpur to the southwest along the fastest route from Delhi. The nearest station on the scenic mountain railway is at Kangra, while Pathankot to the west is on the broad gauge.

Getting around From Dharamshala, it is almost 10 km by the bus route to McLeodganj but a shorter, steeper path (3 km) takes about 45 minutes on foot. Local jeeps use this bumpy, potholed shortcut. Compact McLeodganj itself, and its surroundings, are ideal for walking.

Tourist information HPTDC ⓘ *behind post office, McLeodganj, T01892-221205, Mon-Sat 1000-1700*. Foreign volunteers are often accepted at the hospital and other units. Try contacting LHA meaning 'innate goodness' for volunteer options, www.lhasocialwork.org; or **Khana Nirvana** or check the free monthly magazine *Contact*, T(0)98161-55523, contactmag@hotmail.com. English-language teachers are in high demand to teach newly arrived refugees, for short or long term. There are a couple of places for teaching and conversation near **Dokebi** restaurant.

Background

The hill station was established by the British between 1815 and 1847, but remained a minor town until the **Dalai Lama** settled here after Chinese invasion of Tibet in October 1959. There is an obvious Tibetan influence in McLeodganj. The Tibetan community has tended to take over the hospitality business, sometimes a cause of friction with the local population. Now many Westerners come here because they are particularly interested in Buddhism, meditation or the Tibetan cause. A visitor's attempt to use a few phrases in Tibetan is always warmly responded to: *tashi delek* (hello, good luck), *thukje-chey* (thank you), *thukje-sik* (please), *gong-thag* (sorry), and *shoo-den-jaa-go* (goodbye).

Sights

Church of St John-in-the-Wilderness (1860) ⓘ *1000-1700*, with attractive stained-glass windows, is a short distance below McLeodganj. Along with other buildings in the area, it was destroyed by the earthquake of 1905 but has been rebuilt. In April 1998 thieves tried to steal the

1 Dharamshala

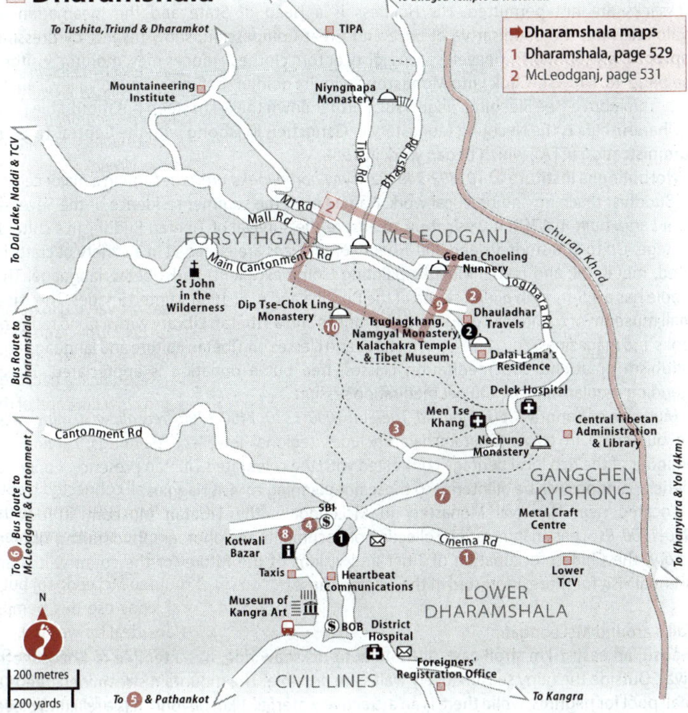

Sleeping
Chamunda 1
Chonor House 2
Clouds End Villa 3
Dhauladhar 4
Dip Tse-Chok Ling 10
Dream 5
Grace 6
Kashmir House 7
Rainbow Lodge 8
Tara 9

Eating
Midtown 1
Namgyal Café 2

old bell, cast in London, which was installed in 1915, but could only move it 300 m. The eighth Lord Elgin, one of the few viceroys to die in office, is buried here according to his wish as it reminded him of his native Scotland.

Namgyal Monastery at McLeodganj, with the Buddhist School of Dialectics, mostly attended by small groups of animated 'debating' monks, is known as 'Little Lhasa'. This *tsuglagkhang* (cathedral) opposite the Dalai Lama's residence resembles the centre of the one in Lhasa and is five minutes' walk from the main bazar. It contains large gilded bronzes of the Buddha, Avalokitesvara and Padmasambhava. To the left of the Tsuglagkhang is the **Kalachakra Temple** with very good modern murals of *mandalas*, protectors of the Dharma, and Buddhist masters of different lineages of Tibetan Buddhism, with the central image of Shakyamuni. Sand *mandalas* (which can be viewed on completion), are constructed throughout the year, accompanied by ceremonies. The temple is very important as the practice of Kalachakra Tantra is instrumental in bringing about world peace and harmony.

The **Dalai Lama** usually leads the prayers on special occasions – 10 days for **Monlam Chenmo** following **Losar, Saga Dawa** (May) and his own birthday (6 July). If you wish to have an audience with him, you need to sign up in advance at the Security Office (go upstairs) by **Hotel Tibet**. On the day, arrive early with your passport. Cameras, bags and rucksacks are not permitted. His Holiness is a Head of State and the incarnation of Avalokitesvara, the Bodhisattva of Love and Great Compassion; show respect by dressing appropriately (no shorts, sleeveless tops, dirty or torn clothes); monks may 'monitor' visitors. See page 48. **Dip Tse-Chok Ling Monastery**, with its golden roof in a wooded valley, can be seen from above (see Sleeping, page 538). Further down the 3-km steep but motorable road to Dharamshala is the Nechung Monastery in **Gangchen Kyishong** with the **Central Tibetan Administration** (CTA), which began work in 1988.

Norbulingka Institute ⓘ *T01892-246402, www.norbulingka.org*, is becoming a major centre for Buddhist teaching and practical work. Named after the summer residence of the Seventh Dalai Lama built in 1754, it was set up to ensure the survival of Tibetan Buddhism's cultural heritage. Up to 100 students and 300 Tibetan employees are engaged in a variety of crafts in wood, metal, silk and metal, *thangka* painting (some excellent) and Tibetan language. The temple has a 4.5-m-high gilded statue of the Buddha and over 1000 painted images. There is a small **museum** of traditional 'dolls' made by monks and a **Tibetan Library** with a good range of books and magazines. You can attend lectures and classes on Tibetan culture and language and Buddhism or attend two **meditation** classes, free but a donation is appreciated. Those attending regularly pay Rs 100 per meditation session.

Museum of Kangra Art ⓘ *Main Rd, Tue-Sun 1000-1330, 1400-1700, free, allow 30 mins*, near the bus stand in Lower Dharamshala, includes regional jewellery, paintings, carvings, a reminder of the rich local heritage contrasted with the celebrated Tibetan presence. Copies of Roerich paintings will be of interest to those not planning to visit Naggar.

Located near Namgyal Monastery in McLeodganj, the **Tibetan Museum** ⓘ *Tue-Sun 0900-1700, Rs 5*, has an interesting collection of documents and photographs detailing Tibetan history, the Chinese occupation of Tibet and visions of the future for the country. It is an essential visit for those interested in the Tibetan cause.

Walks around McLeodganj

Bhagsu, an easy 2-km stroll east, or Rs 40 auto-rickshaw ride, has a temple to Bhagsunath (Siva). Outside the rainy season lovely walks are possible. The mountain stream here feeds a small pool for pilgrims, while there is an attractive waterfall 1 km beyond. It is a relaxing place with great views, and so attracts some to stay here. Unfortunately this has resulted in it becoming very touristy, with increasing building activity up the valley towards Dharamkot and an influx of noisy day-trippers.

2 McLeodganj

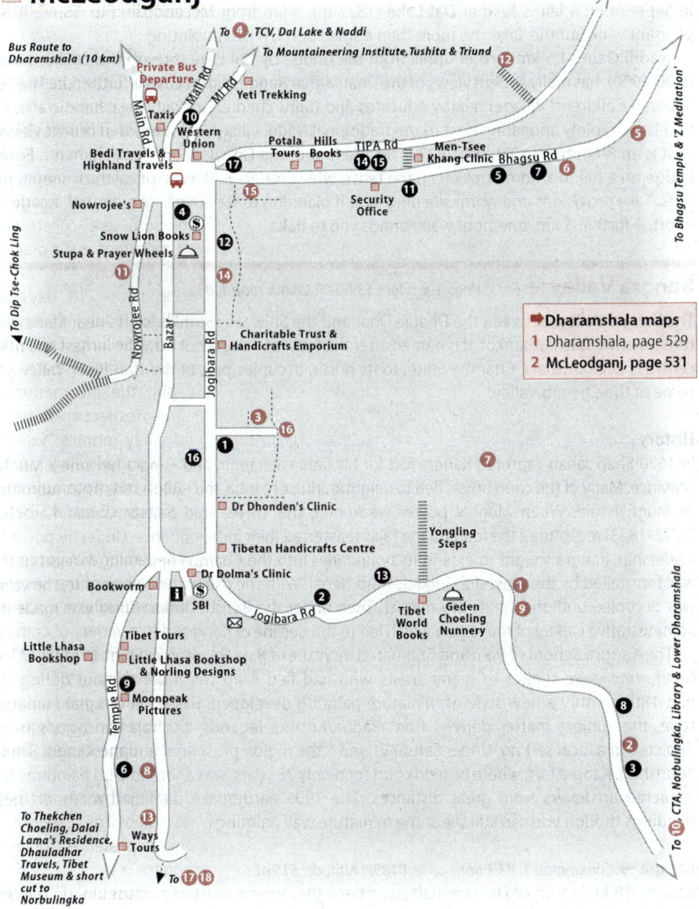

50 metres
50 yards

Sleeping
Cheryton Cottage 1
Chonor House 17
Drepung Loseling 3
Glenmoor Cottages 4
Green 5
Himalaya 6
Ladies Venture 9
Norling Guest House 10
Om 11
Paljor Gakyil 12
Pawan House 2
Pema Thang 13
Sidharth House 7
Snow Lion 14
Surya 8
Tara 18
Tibet 15
Yongten 16

Eating
Carpe Diem 2
Dokebi 3
Gakyi 1
German Bakery 10
Khana Nirvana 6
Kunga's/Nick's Italian Kitchen 7
Lhamo's Croissant 5
Lhasa 17
Lung-Ta 8
McLlo 4
Moonlight & Sunrise 14
Moonpeak Espresso 9
Rangzen 11
Rogpa Café 13
Shambala 12
Tara Café 15
Tibetan Dasang/Lhoka 16

Dharamkot, 3 km away, has very fine views and you can continue on towards the snowline. In September, a fair is held at **Dal Lake** (1837 m), 3 km from McLeodganj Bus Stand; it is a pleasant walk but the 'lake', no more than a small pond, is disappointing.

Naddi Gaon, 1.5 km further uphill from the bridge by Dal Lake (buses from Dharamshala, 0800-1900), has really superb views of the Dhauladhar Range. **Kareri Lake** is further on. The TCV (Tibetan Childrens' Village) nearby educates and trains children in traditional handicrafts. Big hotels are rapidly appearing next to the traditional Naddi village. Most enjoy excellent views.

It is an 8-km trek to **Triund**, 2827 m, at the foot of the Dhauladhar where there is a **Forest Lodge** on a hill top. Some trekkers pitch tents, whilst others make use of caves or shepherds' huts. Take provisions and warm sleeping gear if planning to stay overnight. It's well worth the effort. A further 5 km, one-hour walk, brings you to **Ilaka**.

Kangra Valley → *For listings, see pages 537-545.* *Colour map 1, B3.*

The Kangra Valley, between the Dhaula Dhar and the Shiwalik foothills, starts near Mandi and runs northwest to Pathankot. It is named after the town of Kangra but now the largest and main centre is Dharamshala. Chamba State, to its north, occupies part of the Ravi River Valley and some of the Chenab Valley.

History

In 1620 Shah Jahan captured Kangra fort for his father Jahangir, and Kangra became a Mughal province. Many of the court artists fled to neighbouring Chamba and Kullu as the Rajas submitted to Mughal rule. When Mughal power weakened, the 16-year-old **Sansar Chand Katoch II** (1775-1823) recaptured the fort and the rajas reasserted their independence. Under his powerful leadership, Kangra sought to extend its boundaries into the Chamba and Kullu Valleys but this was forestalled by the powerful Gurkhas from Nepal. With the rise of the Sikh empire, the valley was occupied until the Treaty of Amritsar. Then under the British, Dharamshala was made the administrative capital of the region which led to the decline of Kangra.

The **Kangra School of Painting** originated by virtue of Raja Goverdhan Singh (1744-1773) of Guler, who gave shelter to many artists who had fled from the Mughals, and during the mid-18th century a new style of miniature painting developed. Based on Mughal miniature style, the subject matter derived from Radha/Krishna legends, the rajas and gods being depicted in a local setting. Under Sansar Chand II the region prospered and the Kangra School flourished. Kangra fort, where he held court for nearly 25 years, was adorned with paintings and attracted art lovers from great distances. The 1905 earthquake damaged many of these buildings though you can still see some miniature wall paintings.

Kangra → *Colour map 1, B3. Phone code: 01892. Altitude: 615 m.*

Kangra, 18 km south of Dharamshala, was once the second most important kingdom in the West Himalaya after Kashmir. Kangra town, the capital, was also known as Bhawan or Nagarkot. It overlooks the Banganga River and claims to have existed since the Vedic period with historical reference in Alexander's war records.

Kangra Fort ⓘ *foreigners US$2, Indians Rs 5, auto-rickshaw Rs 70 return, taxi Rs 100*, stands on a steep rock dominating the valley. A narrow path leads up to the fort which was once protected by several gates and had the palace of the Katoch kings at the top. The fort, 5 km from the road bridge, is worth the effort. At its foot is a large modern Jain temple which has pilgrim accommodation (worth considering for its peaceful location). There is also a British cemetery nearby. Inside the fort itself is an old Jain temple which is still in use. At the very top, the remains of Sansar Chand's palace offer commanding views.

Brajesvari Devi Temple, in Kangra Town, achieved a reputation for gold, pearls and diamonds and attracted many Muslim invaders from the 11th century, including Mahmud of

Fight over the flight of the living Buddha

Rival claims by two boy-gods to the position of the 17th Karmapa, the head of the Kagyu Buddhist sect and the inheritor of the coveted black hat "woven from the hair of 10,000 angels", has created a rift in high Buddhist clerical circles. The Indian headquarters of the powerful and affluent Kagyu sect is in Rumtek in Sikkim. On 5 January 2000, the dramatic appearance of the 14-year-old Urgyen Thinley in Dharamshala after a strenuous mountain crossing having escaped from captivity in Tibet, has put the cat among the pigeons. The older claimant, Thaye Dorje now 19, who escaped from Tibet as the 17th incarnation of a 12th-century spiritual leader in 1994, is being groomed in the quiet backwaters of Kalimpong, away from the warring monks of Rumtek, for the third highest position (after the Dalai Lama and the Panchen Lama) in Tibetan Buddhism. Thaye Dorje's supporters are ready to oppose any move by the Karmapa to usurp the 'throne' they feel rightfully belongs to their earlier find.

Ghazni, the Tughlaqs and the Lodis, who periodically plundered its treasures and destroyed the idols. In the intervening years the temple was rebuilt and refurbished several times but in the great earthquake of 1905 both the temple and the fort were badly damaged. The Devi received unusual offerings from devotees. According to Abul Fazal, the pilgrims "cut out their tongues which grew again in the course of two or three days and sometimes in a few hours"! The present temple in which the deity sits under a silver dome with silver *chhatras* (umbrellas) was built in 1920 and stands behind the crowded, colourful bazar. The State Government maintains the temple; the priests are expected to receive gifts in kind only. The area is busy and quite dirty, with mostly pilgrim-oriented stalls. Above these is **St Paul's Church** and a Christian community. Along the river between Old Kangra and Kangra Mandir is a pleasant trail, mostly following long-disused roads past ruined houses and temples which evidence a once sizeable town.

Masrur → *Colour map 1, B3. 34 km southwest of Dharamshala. Altitude: 800 m.*

A sandstone ridge to the northeast of the village has 15, ninth- to 10th-century *sikhara* temples excavated out of solid rock. They are badly eroded and partly ruined. Even in this state they have been compared with the larger rock-cut temples at Ellora in Maharashtra and at Mamallapuram south of Chennai. Their ridge-top position commands a superb view over the surrounding fertile countryside, but few of the original *shikharas* stand, and some of the most beautifully carved panels are now in the State Museum, Shimla. There are buses from Kangra.

Jawalamukhi → *Colour map 1, B3.*

This is one of the most popular Hindu pilgrimage sites in Himachal and is recognized as one of 51 *Shakti pitha*. The **Devi temple**, tended by the followers of Gorakhnath, is set against a cliff and from a fissure comes a natural inflammable gas which accounts for the blue 'Eternal Flame'. Natural springs feed the two small pools of water; one appears to boil, the other with the flame flaring above the surface contains surprisingly cold water. Emperor Akbar's gift of gold leaf covers the dome. In March/April there are colourful celebrations during the **Shakti Festival**; another in mid-October. There is accommodation here, and buses to/from Kangra.

Pragpur → *Colour map 1, B3.*

Pragpur, across the River Beas, 20 km southwest of Jawalamukhi, is a medieval 'heritage village' with cobbled streets and slate-roofed houses. The fine 'Judges Court' (1918) nearby has been carefully restored using traditional techniques. A three- to four-day stay is recommended here and it is advisable to reserve ahead.

Stops along the Kangra Valley Railway

Jogindernagar is the terminus of the beautiful journey by narrow-gauge rail (enquiries Kangra, T01892-252279) from Pathankot via Kangra. The hydro-power scheme here and at nearby Bassi channels water from the River Uhl. Paragliding and hang-gliding is possible at Billing (33 km), reached via Bir (19 km, see below).

Baijnath's temples are old by hill standards, dating from at least 1204. Note the Lakshmi/Vishnu figure and the graceful balcony window on the north wall. The **Vaidyanatha Temple** (originally circa 800), which contains one of 12 *jyotirlingas*, stands by the roadside on the Mandi-Palampur road, within a vast rectangular enclosure. Originally known as **Kirangama**, its name was changed after the temple was dedicated to **Siva** in his form as the Lord of Physicians. It is a good example of the Nagari style; the walls have the characteristic niches enshrining images of Chamunda, Surya and Karttikeya and the *sikhara* tower is topped with an *amalaka* and pot. A life-size stone Nandi stands at the entrance. There is a bus to and from Mandi taking 3½ hours, Rs 50.

Palampur, 16 km from Baijnath, 40 km from Dharamshala (via Yol), is a pleasant little town for walking, with beautiful snow views, surrounded by old British tea plantations, thriving on horticulture. It is a popular stop with trekkers; see page 551. The Neugal Khad, a 300-m-wide chasm through which the Bandla flows is very impressive when the river swells during the monsoons. It holds a record for rainfall in the area.

Bir, 30 km east of Palampur, has a fast-growing reputation as one of the best paragliding locations in the world. Bordered by tea gardens and low hills, it also has four Buddhist monasteries worth visiting. Most prominent among these are Choling. You can also pick up fine Tibetan handicrafts from Bir. The village of Billing is 14 km up sharp, hair-raising hairpins and has the hilltop from where paragliders launch. Although unsuitable for beginners, there are courses available for intermediate fliers and a few residential pilots with tandem rigs.

Andretta is an attractive village 13 km from Palampur. It is associated with **Norah Richards**, a follower of Mahatma Gandhi, who popularized rural theatre, and with the artist **Sardar Sobha Singh** who revived the Kangra School of painting. His paintings are big, brightly coloured, ultra-realistic and often devotional, incorporating Sikh, Christian and Hindu images. There is an art gallery dedicated to his work and memory; prints, books and soft drinks are sold in the shop. The **Andretta Pottery** (signposted from the main road), is charming. It is run by an artist couple (Indian/English), who combine village pottery with 'slipware'. The Sikh partner is the son of Gurcharan Singh (of Delhi Blue Pottery fame) and is furthering the tradition of studio pottery; works are for sale.

Chamba Valley → *For listings, see pages 537-545. Colour map 1, B2.*

Dalhousie → *Phone code: 01899. Population: 7400. Altitude: 2030 m.*

Dalhousie, named after the governor-general (1848-1856), was developed on land purchased by the British in 1853 from the Raja of Chamba. It sprawls out over five hills just east of the Ravi River. By 1867 it was a sanatorium and reached its zenith in the 1920s and 1930s as a cheaper alternative to Shimla, and the most convenient hill station for residents of Lahore. Rabindranath Tagore wrote his first poem in Dalhousie as a boy and Subhash Chandra Bose came secretly to plan his strategies during the Second World War. Its popularity declined after 1947 and it became a quiet hill station with old colonial bungalows, surrounded by thick pine forests interspersed with oak and rhododendron. Its spectacular mountain views mean that it remains a popular bolt hole for tourists from the plains, but its importance today is mainly due to the number of good schools and the presence of the army.

The three Malls laid out for level walks are around Moti Tibba, Potreyn Hill and Upper Bakrota. The last, the finest, is about 330 m above **Gandhi Chowk** around which the town centres. From there two rounds of the Mall lead to Subhash Chowk. Tibetans make and sell handicrafts, woollens, jackets, cardigans and rugs. Their paintings and rock carvings can be seen along Garam Sarak Mall.

The HPTDC ⓘ *near bus stand, T01899-242136, 1000-1700*, is helpful, but opening hours are irregular, especially out of season.

Just over 2 km from Gandhi Chowk is **Martyr's Memorial** at Panchpulla (five bridges), which commemorates Ajit Singh, a supporter of Subhash Bose and the Indian National Army during the Second World War. On the way you can see the **Satdhara** (seven springs), said to contain mica and medicinal properties. **Subhash Baoli** (1.5 km from the square), is another spring. It is an easy climb and offers good views of the snows. Half a kilometre away **Jhandri Ghat**, the old palace of Chamba rulers, is set among tall pine trees. For a longer walk try the Bakrota Round (5 km), which gives good views of the mountains and takes you through the Tibetan settlement.

Kalatope and Khajjiar

Kalatope, 9 km from Dalhousie, with good mountain views, is a level walk through a forest sanctuary with accommodation. The road is accessible by jeep. **Khajjiar**, 22 km further along the motorable road, is a long, wide glade ringed by cedars with a small lake. You can explore the area in a pleasant three-day walk. Alternatively you can extend the day's walk to Khajjiar into a short trek to Dharamshala over two days. A 30-km path through dense deodar forest leads to Chamba. Buses to Khajjiar from Dalhousie leave at 0930 and return 1530. They take an hour and cost Rs 13.

Chamba → *Colour map 1, B2. Phone code: 01899. Altitude: 996 m.*

Picturesque Chamba is on the south bank of the Iravati (Ravi), its stone houses clinging to the hillside. Some see the medieval town as having an almost Italian feel, surrounded by lush forests and with its Chaugan or grassy meadow in the centre, although recent developments have somewhat diminished its appeal. Most hotels, temples and palaces are within walking distance of the bus stand.

Dalhousie

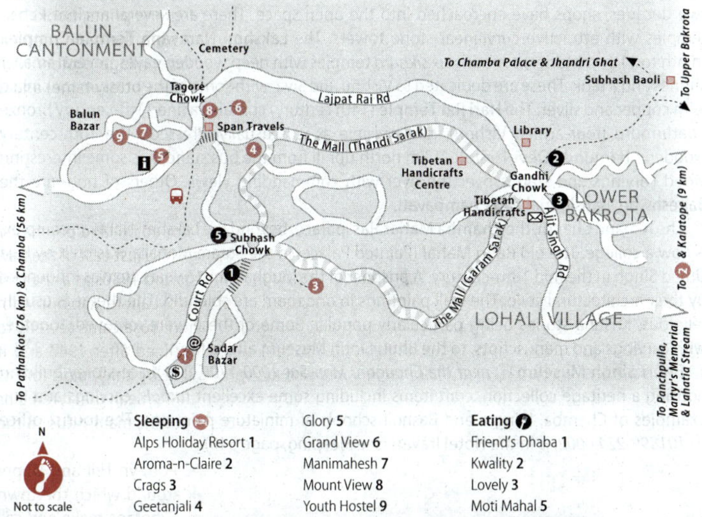

The little-known 'mountain' railway

A superb narrow-gauge railway links Pathankot in the west with Jogindernagar via Kangra (near Dharamshala) and Baijnath. The views of the Kangra Valley are quite spectacular. This is very much a working service and not a 'relic' (this train can be packed with ordinary users). Sadly, it is often very late as it is incredibly slow, and very uncomfortable because of the hard seats. 'Tourists' would do better to sample short sections of the line, and allow for delays – any purposeful journey is better done by bus. See page 545 for an optimistic timetable.

Founded in the 10th century, Chamba State was on an important trade route from Lahaul to Kashmir and was known as the 'Middle Kingdom'. Though Mughal suzerainty was accepted by the local rajas, the kingdom remained autonomous but it came under Sikh rule from 1810-1846. Its relative isolation led to the nurturing of the arts – painting, temple sculpture, handicrafts and unique 'rumal'. These pieces of silk/cotton with fine embroidery imitate miniature paintings; the reverse is as good as the front.

Chamba is the centre of the **Gaddis**, shepherds who move their flocks of sheep and goats, numbering from a couple of hundred to a thousand, from lower pastures at around 1500 m during winter to higher slopes at over 3500 m, after snow-melt. They are usually only found in the Dhaula Dhar range which separates Kangra from Chamba. Some believe that these herdsmen first arrived in this part of Himachal in the 10th century though some moved from the area around Lahore (Pakistan) in the 18th century, during the Mughal period. Their religious belief combines animism with the worship of Siva; Bahrmaur with its distinctive Manimahesh Temple is their principal centre of worship (see below). In the winter the Gaddis can be seen round Kangra, Mandi and Bilaspur and in the small villages between Baijnath and Palampur. The men traditionally wear a *chola* (a loose white woollen garment), tied at the waist with a black wool rope and a white embroidered cap.

The **Chaugan**, almost a kilometre long, is the central hub of the town but sadly, over the last two decades, shops have encroached into the open space. There are several ancient Pahari temples with attractive curvilinear stone towers. The **Lakshmi Narayana Temple Complex** (ninth to 11th centuries) contains six *sikhara* temples with deep wooden eaves, several smaller shrines and a tank. These are dedicated to Vishnu and Siva, with some of the brass images inlaid with copper and silver. The **Hari Rai Temple** (14th century) contains a fine 11th-century bronze Chaturmurti (four-armed Vishnu), rarely visible as it is usually 'dressed'. The 10th-century wooden **Chamunda Devi Temple**, 1 km north uphill from the bus stand, has some interesting wood carvings and stands over the river with commanding views. Others of note are the Bajreshwari, Bansigopal and Champavati.

The Akhand Chandi, the **Chamba Maharajas' palace**, beyond the Lakshmi Narayan complex, is now a college. The old **Rang Mahal** (Painted Palace) in the Surara Mohalla was built by Raja Umed Singh in the mid 18th-century. A prisoner of the Mughals for 16 years, he was influenced by their architectural style. The wall paintings in one room are splendid. The theme is usually religious, Krishna stories being particularly popular. Some of these were removed, together with carvings and manuscripts, to the Bhuri Singh Museum after a fire.

Bhuri Singh Museum ⓘ *near the Chaugan, Mon-Sat 1000-1700*, is a three-storey building housing a heritage collection, craft items including some excellent *rumals*, carvings and fine examples of Chamba, Kangra and Basholi schools of miniature paintings. The **tourist office** ⓘ *T01899-224 0002*, is in the **Hotel Iravati** (see Sleeping, page 540).

Northern Himachal listings

For Sleeping and Eating price codes and other relevant information, see Essentials pages 38-42.

Sleeping

Dharamshala *p528, maps p529 and p531*

Most visitors stay in McLeodganj (see below). In Mar, May and early Jun accommodation may be hard to find. A 40% seasonal discount is usually given from mid-Jun to Aug. Check what time the gate closes at night to avoid being locked out. With the new IPL cricket ground in Dharamshala, more 3-star and up hotels are under construction in the area.

LL-L White Haven Tea Estate, below Dharamshala. T01892-226162, www.hotelwhitehavendharamshala.com. Charming working colonial tea estate set in 2.8 ha of beautiful gardens. 7 sumptuous rooms with creaking floorboards, log fires, lots of wood panelling and period antiques, exceptional service and tons of history. Recommended.

L Eagles Nest, Upper Dharamkot, T(0)9218-402822, www.hoteleaglesnest.com. 8 lovely themed rooms and suites in a beautiful old colonial house set in 20 ha of forest. Perched on top of the hill with spectacular views over Kangra and Kullu valleys. All inclusive, with excellent food and plenty of activities. Price includes all meals, horse-riding and guides for trekking. Recommended.

AL-A Blossom Village, Sidhpur, near Dharamshala, T(0)9816-561213, www.blossomvillage.com. 19 rooms including cottages and suites. Stylishly decorated using local timber and solar energy.

B-D Dhauladhar (HPTDC), Kotwali Bazar, T01892-224926, www.hptdc.nic.in. 23 rooms, 2 suites (**B**), cheaper in annexe, clean, large rooms, restaurant, bar, pleasant garden, billiard table, terrace for meals, friendly staff.

C Clouds End Villa, north of Dharamshala, steep approach off Naoroji Rd, T01892-222109, www.cloudsendvilla.com. 7 rooms and 1 bungalow in Raja of Lambagraon's bungalow (Raj period), not luxurious but very clean, annexe has excellent valley views, authentic local cuisine (everything home-made), tours, peaceful, very friendly, excellent service.

C Grace Hotel, 558 Old Chari Rd, Kotwali Bazar, T01892-223265, www.welcomheritage.com. 11 comfortable rooms in a 200-year-old wooden manor, formerly the residence of India's first Chief Justice. Pleasantly situated slightly out of town, a good place to relax and admire the views.

C-E Kashmir House (HPTDC), Kotwali Bazar, T01892-222977, www.hptdc.nic.in. 10 large rooms, 1 suite (**C**) in beautiful period property, hot water, TV, good value.

F-G Chamunda, Khanyara Rd, T01892- 225608. Good views, 15 basic rooms including 2 singles, hot water.

McLeodganj

AL-A Glenmoor Cottages, off Mall Rd, T01892-221010, www.glenmoorcottages.com. Very peaceful, 7 large, modern, well-equipped 'cottages' with bedroom, kitchen, veranda, secluded old colonial house surrounded by forest, good valley views, great walks from doorstep.

A Surya, near **Hotel Bhagsu** (HPTDC), T01892-221418, www.suryamcleod.com. Upmarket hotel with good views, nothing special though. Restaurant has good reputation locally for tip-top north Indian fare.

B Norling Guest House, Norbulingka Institute, Gangchen Kyishong, T01892-246406, normail@norbulingka.org. Clean, comfortable rooms, in modern facilities in a Tibetan-style house. Café accepts Master/Visa cards.

B-C Chonor House, Thekchen Choeling Rd, T01892-221006, www.norbulingka.org. 11 very comfortable, stylish rooms furnished in Tibetan style (murals of lost monasteries and mythical beasts), good restaurant, clean, well managed, popular with foreign diplomats, beautiful garden, a quiet and lovely place. Book ahead. Accepts credit cards. Highly recommended.

C Sahil Plaza, Temple Rd, T01892-220 430, www.hotelsahilplaza.com. Clean but uninspiring rooms with good views down the valley.

D Cheryton Cottage, Jogibara Rd, T01892-221237. Enquire at **Chocolate Log**. 4 very smart octagonal rooms with bath and garden. Slightly overshadowed by new buildings around it.

D-E Pema Thang, opposite **Hotel Bhagsu**, T01892-221871, www.pemathang.net. 15 rooms with a bit more character than the average, good view, quiet, friendly, cooking facilities possible, hot water, good pizza and pasta restaurant. Recommended.

D-E Tibet, behind bus stand, T01892-221587, htdshala@sancharnet.in. 20 well-maintained rooms with bath and TV, not much difference between standard and deluxe, those on roadside can be noisy, good restaurant, cosy bar, accepts credit cards.

E Pawan House, next to Dokebi, Jogibara Rd, T01892-220069. Good views across the valley. Nice spacious clean rooms – good vibe. Recommended.

E-F Dip Tse-Chok Ling Monastery, below McLeodganj, climb down 300 steps, TT01892-221726. 20 clean rooms, 3 attached, some singles, hot showers, breakfast and dinner at set times, 'wonderfully peaceful'.

E-F Green Hotel, Bhagsu Rd, T01892-221200, www.greenhotel.biz. Popular with backpackers, 30 variable rooms (avoid ground floor ones near the noisy courtyard), restaurant with comfy sofas, good internet.

E-F Shambhala Guest House, next to Snow Lion, Jogibara Rd. Cosy family run place. Small rooms but nicely decorated, lots of warm blankets, hot shower, TV.

E-G Ladies Venture, Jogibara Rd, T01892-221559. Peaceful hotel with 13 clean rooms, some with bath, good dorm (Rs 100), small restaurant (good Chinese and Western food), terrace, very friendly, good place to meet people, often full so book ahead

F Om, western edge of bazar, T01892-221322. Friendly hotel with 18 spartan but clean rooms, excellent shower, very good restaurant, great views at sunset.

F Sidharth House, bottom of Yongling School Steps off Jogibara Rd, T(0)9736-211095, www.sidharthhouse.in. Great guest house with conscious eco-vibe who established the 'Clean McLeodganj Project' and they have bins for compost as well as encouraging recycling. Much needed. Highly recommended.

F Snow Lion, near prayer wheels, T01892-221289. Good view from rear, friendly hotel, 8 rooms with bath, good Tibetan restaurant (excellent cakes).

F Yonten, next to **Tibetan Ashoka**, T01892-221509. 10 comfortable, basic but clean rooms with excellent views from the top floor. Rooftop restaurant.

F-G Drepung Loseling, Jogibara Rd, T01892-220085. Friendly hotel, 17 clean, well-maintained rooms with bath (some with hot water), dorm (Rs 90), terrace. Profits to Loseling Moanstery in Karnataka.

F-G Paljor Gakyil, TIPA Rd, up steps, T01892-221343. 14 clean rooms with bath (hot shower), dorm (Rs 25), excellent views, charming owners speak French and German, best of nearby bunch.

Walks around McLeodganj *p530*

B-D Udechee Huts, Naddi Gaon, T01892-221781, www.udecheehuts.com. Blending in with local style, 10 pleasantly furnished circular huts with bath (hot water), restaurant plus dining terrace, well kept, friendly hosts.

C Nishaad Resorts, Cantt area, Naddi Gaon, T01892-221707, www.nishaadresorts.com. 10 rooms, 6 in cottages, some with great views, large tiered gardens, good for kids, somewhat spartan overall.

D-E Hotel High Land, Bhagsu Main Drag, T01892-220501. Big rooms with a bit of a view, TV.

E-F Hill View, Naddi Gaon, T01892-221432. 6 rooms with good attached bathrooms plus great views from balconies, good value.

E-F 9 Chimes, Upper Bhagsu, near Tree House, T(0)9736-130284, www.9chimes.com. 8 spacious rooms with balconies and nice views. Recommended.

F-G Sapna House, above Bhagsu, just above Unity Pizza, T01892-221594. Perennial favourite of the area – friendly family run place with pleasant rooms and garden.

F-G Sky Pie, Bhagsu, T01892-220497. 25 good-value, clean, basic rooms in 2 blocks (one old, one new) with balconies, roof terraces and great views. Restaurant with excellent multinational food, filter coffee and the famous banoffee pie. Friendly and helpful owner.

G DK House, Upper Bhagsu, T01892-220671. 14 comfortable, spacious and clean rooms with big terrace and **Evergreen Restaurant** attached. Friendly family. Popular and good value.

G Pink House, between Dharamkot and Bhagsu, T(0)9805-642060. Excellent value place with great views. Really peaceful and run by president of local women's group – she is quite right-on. Recommended.

G Orion, above Bhagsu, T01892-220643. 4 rooms, 1 'duplex' self-catering studio. Homestay style, astounding good value and very friendly family. Charming.

G Shiv Shakti Rishi Bhawan, off Dharamkot Rd, T01892-221875. Run by friendly father and son, 18 basic rooms with attached bath plus a stand alone, well-equipped cottage available on a daily or monthly (Rs 5000) basis. New restaurant and internet.

G Trimurthi Garden Cafe, above Unity Pizza, Bhagsu. Favourite haunt with simple rooms, café and numerous workshops.

G ZKL Guesthouse, above Bhagsu Rd, 500 m before Bhagsu itself, T01892-221581, www.zkl-monastery.com. 12 very basic but clean rooms in this charming monastery, Buddhist teachings and a café in the summer, outstanding value.

Kangra *p532*

Most hotels on the busy main road are noisy, even at night.

E-F Jannat, Chamunda Rd, T01892-265479. 5 rooms, restaurant, TV, hot water, closest to Kangra Mandir railway station.

G Dilraj Guest House, near Tehsil Chowk (taxi stand), T01892-265362. Friendly family house with 5 simple rooms, meals available. Recommended.

G Gupt Ganga Dharamshala, T01892-265021. Donation expected, 30 rooms and 3 halls.

Pragpur *p533*

A-B Judge's Court (Heritage), set in a large orchard, T01970-245035, www.judgescourt.com. 10 tastefully decorated rooms in a fine mansion, 1 in an annexe, 1 large private modernized suite with veranda overlooking the Dhauladhar in a separate building. Family hospitality, home-grown vegetables and fruit, fresh river fish, authentic Himachali meals, tours of Kangra Fort and other sights included (a ride on a part of the narrow-gauge mountain railway is possible) friendly, efficient management. Pragpur very pretty village with lovely atmosphere. Recommended.

Stops along the Kangra Valley Railway *p534*

A Taragarh Palace, Al-hilal, 11 km southeast of Palampur, T01894-242034, www.taragarh.com. 26 rooms in 1930s summer resort, period furniture, atmospheric, tastefully decorated, tennis, pool, lovely gardens and mango orchards, luxury Swiss tents in summer. Great service, but food a bit hit and miss.

B-G Yamini, Ghaggar Rd, Palampur, T01894-230631. Quality varies among the 25 rooms with bath and the 8-bed dorm.

C-E Darang Tea Estate, 10 km from Palampur, T01894-240231, www.darangtea estate.com. 2 cottages and 1 room in the main house. Family run homestay in beautiful working tea estate. Exceptional food and hospitality. Recommended.

C-E Silver Oaks, Bandla Tea Estate, 2 km from Palampur, T01894-232 442. 18 large rooms, dorm for budget travellers, welcoming, quiet, scenic location with views of Dhaula Dhar peaks, friendly, knowledgeable manager.

C-E T-Bud (HPTDC), 1 km from bus stand, Palampur, T01894-231298. Beautiful setting, 31 rooms but only deluxe category (**C-D**) are worth considering, hot water, restaurant, pleasant lawn, clean, quiet, good service.

E-F Colonel's Retreat, 1 km out of Bir on the Billing road, T(0)9805-534220, www.colonels resort.com. 4 simple, comfortable rooms and 2 cottages with 2 rooms in each. Set in pear orchards and working tea plantation, with sublime views down the valley and behind into Dhauladhar mountains. Good food, warm hospitality, great value. Popular with paragliders.

E-F Uhl, on hill outside Jogindernagar, T01908-222002. Simple, clean and peaceful hotel, 16 rooms with bath, best upstairs with balcony, restaurant.

G Standard, Baijnath, behind bus station. 5 fairly clean and surprisingly tidy rooms with bath and hot water.

Dalhousie *p534, map p535*

Some hotels look neglected and run-down, often because the cost of maintaining the Raj-built structures is prohibitive. Most have good mountain views and discounts out of season.

B-C Mount View, next to bus stand, T01899-242120, www.hotelmountview.com. The elegant, period, oak-panelled reception flatters to deceive; all 24 rooms are in a modern block to the rear, only the cramped restaurant is in the older building.

B-C Silverton Estate Guest House, near Circuit House, the Mall, T01899-240674, www.heritagehotels.com/silverton. Old colonial building in large grounds, rooms with phone, TV, closed off season.

C Grand View, near bus stand, T(0)9418-010659, www.grandviewdalhousie.in. 30 spacious, well-equipped rooms in the best-preserved of Dalhousie's many Raj-era hotels. The views from the terrace are stunning, while the restaurant and lounge bar are quintessentially British. Recommended.

C-D Alps Holiday Resort, Khajjiar Rd, Bakrota Hills, T01899-240781, www.alpsresort.in. 19 smart rooms in modern hotel, with large lawns, fine views, 2-km climb.

C-D Manimahesh (HPTDC), near bus stand, T01899-242793, www.hptdc.nic.in. 18 well-maintained, carpeted rooms, restaurant, bar, good mountain views.

D-E Aroma-n-Claire, Court Rd, T01899-242199. If the exterior looks quirky, wait until you get inside: kitsch collectables adorn every available space in this unusual hotel. The rooms are spartan, the bathrooms remarkable, worth a visit.

E Geetanjali (HPTDC), Thandi Sarak, near bus stand, T01899-242155. 10 rooms with bath, simple restaurant in run-down building.

E-F Crags, off the Mall, T01899-242124. The 100 steps separating this place from the Mall are the only real disadvantage. The rooms are dated but clean with bath (hot water), meals, good views down the valley, friendly, well used to catering to foreign travellers.

G Glory, near bus stand, T01899-242533. 4 rooms with bath, good restaurant.

G Youth Hostel, behind Manimahesh, T01899-242189, www.youthhosteldalhousie.org. Well-maintained, modern building with 2 double rooms (Rs 200) and 6 dorms (Rs 60 adult/Rs 40 student).

Kalatope and Khajjiar *p535*

A-C Mini Swiss, Khajjiar, T01899-236365, www.hotelminiswiss.com. 34 comfortable, very clean rooms, great views, good restaurant, boating lake.

C-E Devdar (HPTDC), Khajjiar, T01899-236333, www.hptdc.nic.in. 12 clean rooms, dorm and beds in cottage, simple restaurant, horse riding, beautiful setting.

Chamba *p535*

A-C Aroma Palace, near Pink Palace, Court Lane, T01899-225577, www.hotelaromapalace chamba.com. The best hotel here by some margin; range from dorm rooms to sumptuous honeymoon suite, all spotless, plus there's a restaurant, internet facility, camping and trekking, and the friendly manager even accepts credit cards. Breakfast included.

C-E Iravati (HPTDC), Court Rd, near bus stand, T01899-222671. Friendly management, 19 variable but mostly clean rooms with bath and hot water, restaurant.

E Akhand Chandi, College Rd, Dogra Bazar, T01899-222371. Attractive stone building with 8 rooms.

F The Orchard Hut, 8 km out of town (book through **Mani Manesh Travels** next to Lakshmi Narayana Temple, T01899-222607, www.himalayanlap.com. Also contact for **Ridgemore Cottage**. Idyllic location (20 mins from nearest road), 4 rooms in guesthouse set in delightful garden, clean shared shower and toilets, pitch a tent in the garden for Rs 100, superb home cooking (great all-inclusive deal), very friendly family, book at office in town first. Recommended.

G Rishi, opposite Lakshmi Narayana Temple, T01899-224343. Rooms with bath (hot water), TV, good-value meals, friendly owner.

Eating

Dharamshala *p528, maps p529 and p531*

Most memorable food is in McLeodganj.

City Heart, Kotwali Bazar. Vast menu and quirky, fun vibe.

Midtown, Kotwali Bazar. Indian and Chinese, some continental, best in town.

McLeodganj

Enterprising Tibetans in the upper town offer good traveller favourites for those tired of curries; some serve beer. Try *thukpa* (Tibetan soups), noodle dishes, steamed or fried *momos* and *shabakleb*. Save plastic waste (and money) by refilling your bottles with safe filtered, boiled water at the eco-friendly **Green shop** on Bhagsu Rd, Rs 5 per litre; also recycle used batteries.

Carpe Diem, past Post Office, Jogibara Rd. Nepali run joint with excellent Indian, Thai and continental flavours. Good vibe, nice rooftop, beer under the table and open mic nights. Recommended.

Dokebi Seven Hills, near **Lung Ta**, Jogibara Road. Wonderful cosy restaurant with delicious

range of vegetarian food including spicy hotpot style soups and Kimchi (Korean sushi). Upstairs there is lovely airy room with floor seating. Great fresh juices and smoky green tea. Highly recommended.
Jimmy's Italian Kitchen, near prayer wheels, Jogibara Rd. Tibetan run with excellent food and views and a rooftop terrace. Live music most weekends even a contestant from **American Idol** once!
Kunga's/Nick's Italian Kitchen, Bhagsu Rd. Good vegetarian food, Italian including excellent gnocchi plus quiches, pies, cakes, etc, but some small portions, now has a huge terrace, deservedly popular, recommended.
McLlo, near bus stand. Indian, Western. Glassed in, beer, good value.
Namgyal, Namgyal Monastery, bottom of Temple Rd. You can hear the monks debating while you scoff amazing pizzas like roquefort and walnut or smoked cheese and spinach – best pizza in the area. Good salads and Tibetan dishes too. Highly recommended.
Amdo Chachung, Jogibara Rd. Good Tibetan. Nice terrace, cable TV.
Gakyi, Jogibara Rd. Tibetan. Also excellent porridge, fruit muesli. Lovely lady owner.
Hotel Tibet, behind bus stand (see Sleeping). Good Tibetan/Japanese restaurant and take-out bakery.
Khana Nirvana, Temple Rd. Open Sun-Fri. Well-prepared Mexican/Italian dishes, juices, organic coffee, herb teas, excellent ambience, good service, talks on Sun (1800) from Tibetan prisoners of conscience, music/poetry on Mon evening. Stunning views at sunset. Highly recommended.
Lhamo's Croissant, Bhagsu Rd. Beautiful café with furniture from **Norbulingka** serving up tip top cappuccino, healthy salads, monumental club sandwiches, home-made soups and outrageously good cakes and tarts all served up by the eponymous Lhamo. They show films about the Tibetan cause every evening. Highly recommended.
Lhasa, on 1st floor opposite **Hotel Tibet**. Tucked away, very mellow interior serving good Tibetan dishes, well worth a visit.
Lung-Ta, Jogibara Rd. Mon-Sat 1200-2030. Classy Japanese vegetarian restaurant, not for profit, daily set menu or à la carte, good breads and cakes. Great value and very popular. Little shop on-site too. Highly recommended.
Om, west end of bazar. Indian. Very good meals.
Pema Thang (see Sleeping). Good vegetarian buffet brunch (Rs 150) on Sun 1000-1400, plus normal menu featuring great pasta, salads and pizza.
Shambala, Jogibara Rd. Excellent breakfasts, Western cakes and pancakes, try apple pie and lemon curd, good portions, very good value, pleasant atmosphere (records on request), quick and friendly. Recommended.
Snow Lion (see Sleeping). Offers good Tibetan and Western meals, excellent cakes.

Cafés and snacks

German Bakery, Mirza Ismail Rd, steep road to Dharamkot. Open till 0100. Best bread, brown rice.
Moonlight and **Sunrise**, opposite Tibetan Welfare Office, Bhagsu Rd. Small *chai* shops adjacent to each other with basic food. Excellent for meeting other travellers, especially in the evenings when overspill occupies benches opposite.
Moonpeak, Temple Rd, on the way to Tibet Museum. Very atmospheric hole in the wall café where people spill out onto outside tables to enjoy great cappuccinos, sandwiches and fantastic cakes. The first of the many coffee shops. Often shows photographic exhibitions.
Rangzen (Freedom), Bhagsu Rd. Good health food, cakes.
Rogpa Jogibara Rd. Tiny little café serving up lovely cakes and tasty coffee – all for charity. Recommended.
Tara Café, Bhagsu Rd. Huge pancakes, friendly.
Tenyang, Temple Rd. Delicious coffee and cakes. Recommended.

Walks around McLeodganj *p530*

Tree of Life, Bhagsu. Fantastic range of dishes in this cosy restaurant – really the heart of Bhagsu. Healthy salads can be counteracted by potato wedges and garlic mayo, meanwhile leave room for the epic Sunday roast with nut roast and yorkshire pudding. Run in conjunction with a popular yoga space and healing studio. Highly recommended.
Unity, Dharamkot towards Bhagsu. English owner creates amazing food, well presented and now a larger restaurant so more opportunity for pizza.

Family Pizzeria, between Upper Bhagsu and Dharamkot. Excellent pizzas, French pastries, quiches and desserts, friendly staff and cider.
Sansu's, Upper Bhagsu. Renowned for its epic 'fruit-muesli-curd' – the best on the hillside.
Singh Corner, Bhagsu. Deservedly popular place with a bit of everything on the menu – but all done well.
Wa Blu, Upper Bhagsu. Climb the steps for tempting Japanese food, miso soups and juices.

Kangra *p532*

Chicken Corner, Dharamshala Rd, near the main bazar. An eccentric though fairly clean little hut does chicken dinners.

Dalhousie *p534, map p535*

Kwality, Gandhi Chowk. Good Indian and Chinese if a bit pricey. Nice place with TV.
Snow Lion, near **Grand View**. Serves Tibetan dishes.
Friend's Dhaba, Subhash Chowk. Good, unpretentious Punjabi, *paneer burji* to die for.
Jim's Italian Kitchen, by **Aroma-n-Claire** (see Sleeping). Varied Italian vegetarian and non-vegetarian pizzas and pastas, hard to find a seat at lunchtime.
Lovely, near Gandhi Chowk. Funky mirrored interiors, tasty North Indian.
Moti Mahal, Subhash Chowk. North Indian.
Napoli, near Gandhi Chowk. Similar to **Kwality**. Very friendly. Large portions.

Chamba *p535*

There are a number of really atmospheric little *dhabas* in the alleys through Dogra Market.
Park View and Jagaan, 1st floor above main drag. Reasonable selection, relatively calm.
Ravi View Café, 1st floor above main drag. Reasonable food plus beer and in a pleasant location.

Entertainment

Dharamshala *p528, maps p529 and p531*

See *Contact*, a free, monthly publication. With everyone travelling with laptops now, there is only 1 film-club on the strip now on Jogibara Rd with a programme of Western films at a rather pricey Rs 150. **Lhamos Croissant**shows documentaries on Tibet. There are open mics at **Carpe Diem** and **Khana Nirvana**. Indian classical music and Tibetan traditional music often at Yongling School.
One Nest, Bhagsu, past the swimming baths. Regular live music in the evenings (Indian Classical and Western nomads), contact dance and free dance sessions.
Tibetan Institute of Performing Arts (**TIPA**), www.tibetanarts.org, McLeodganj, stages occasional music and dance performances; details at Tourist Office.

Festivals and events

Chamba *p535*

Apr **Suhi Mela**, lasts 3 days, commemorates a Rani who consented to be buried alive in a dry stream bed in order that it could flow and provide the town with water. Women and children in traditional dress carry images of her to a temple on the hill, accompanied by songs sung in her praise. Men are strictly prohibited from participating.
Jul-Aug **Gaddis** and **Gujjars** take part in many cultural events to mark the start of harvesting. **Minjar** is a 7-day harvest festival when people offer thanks to Varuna the rain god. Decorated horses and banners are taken out in procession through the streets to mark its start. Sri Raghuvira is followed by other images of gods in palanquins and the festival ends at the River Irawati where people float *minjars* (tassels of corn and coconut).

Shopping

Dharamshala *p528, maps p529 and p531*

It is pleasantly relaxed to shop here, although competition and prices have increased in recent years. Many items on sale have been imported from the Tibetan market in New Delhi. McLeodganj Bazar is good for Tibetan handicrafts (carpets, metalware, jewellery, jackets, handknitted cardigans, gloves); special market on Sun.
Bookworm, near **Surya Resort**, has a good selection of paperbacks, some second-hand.
Doritsang Tibetan Culture Centre, Temple Rd, near SBBI. Great range of books, CDs, clothes and Tibetan bits and pieces.
Jewel of Tibet, opposite prayer wheels. Best selection of singing bowls, jewellery and Tibetan arts. Maybe not the cheapest, but certainly the best value.

Green Shop, Bhagsu Rd. Sells recycled and handmade goods including cards and paper. Also sells filtered drinking water for half the price of bottled water.
Norbulingka Shop, Temple Rd, close to Moonpeak. Well-crafted bags, cushion covers and clothes from **Norbulingka** – preserving Tibetan cultural arts.
Rogpa, Jogibara Rd. Charity based shop selling great gifts, notebooks, cards, bags and wallets. And second hand clothes.
Tibet Book World, Jogibara Rd, near Yongling School steps. Best bookshop in town – great range.
Tibetan Children's Villages (TCVs), Main office on Temple Rd and workshops at various locations around town. Fabrics and jewellery at fixed prices.
Tibetan Handicrafts Centre, Jogibara Rd, near the tourist office. Ask at the office for permission to watch artisans working on carpets, *thangkas*, etc, reasonable prices.

Chamba *p535*
Handicrafts Centre, Rang Mahal. Rumal embroidery and leather goods.

Activities and tours

Dharamshala *p528, maps p529 and p531*

Body and soul

See also **Tibetan Library**, page 530 and **Tibet Tours**, below.
Dr Gonpo Kyi Acupuncture, 2nd floor, **Hotel Mountview**, Jogibara Rd, T(0)9857-119800. Attentive and reliable healer working with acupuncture, massage and Tibetan medicine.
Himachal Vipassana Centre, Dhamma Sikhara, next to Tushita, T01892-221309, www.sikhara.dhamma.org. 10-day retreat, meditation in silence, donations only, reserve in advance, information and registration Mon-Sat 1600-1700.
Himalayan Iyengar Yoga Centre, Dharamkot, www.hiyogacentre.com. Offers 5-day course in Hatha yoga, starting every Thu at 0830. Information and registration Mon 1330. Now has retreat centre too.
Himalaya Yoga Valley, bottom of Yongling School stairs, www.yogagoaindia.com. Top quality teacher training at this excellent school who also run trainings in Goa. Led by teacher Lalit Kumar with back up from excellent team teaching philosophy, anatomy and business management. Highly recommended.
Tree House, Upper Bhagsu, T(0)9805-717533. Exceptional reiki and reflexology with the lady of the house and yoga studio with internationally qualified teachers. Also massage and reiki courses. Connected to the perennially popular **Tree of Life** restaurant. Highly recommended.
Tushita Meditation Centre, Dharamkot village 2 km north of McLeodganj, T01892-221866, www.tushita.info. Quiet location, offers individual and group meditation; 10-day 'Introduction to Buddishm' including lectures and meditation (residential courses get fully subscribed), enquiries Mon-Sat 0930-1130, 1230-1600, simple accommodation on site.
"Z Meditation", past post office, down stairs of Yongling School, follow ZM signs, T01892-220621. Interesting course including yoga and meditation. Retreats offered in silence with separate discussion sessions, 5 days (Mon 1600-Sat 1100), Rs 3500 includes a 'humble' breakfast; highly recommended for beginners, run by friendly couple in peaceful location with beautiful views. Information and registration at 1230 only.

Horse trekking

Highpoint Adventures at **Sagar Book Shop**, Bhagsu Rd, also at **Kareri Hotel**, T01892-221132, www.trek.123himachal.com. Half- or full-day round trips, Rs 500-800, also offers treks and jeep safaris.

Tibetan cookery

Lhamo's Kitchen Next to **Green Shop**, Bhagsu Rd T(0)9816-468719. Runs 3 courses (soups, bread, *momos*), 1100-1300, 1700-1900, Rs 200 each. Friendly, fun, eat what you cook.

Tour operators

Dhauladhar Travels, Temple Rd, McLeodganj, T01892-221158, dhauladhar@hotmail.com. Agents for **Indian Airlines**.
HPTDC luxury coach in season: Dharamshala to McLeodganj, Kangra Temple and Fort, Jawalamukhi, 1000-1900, Rs 200; Dharamshala to McLeodganj, Bhagsunath, Dal Lake, Talnu, Tapovan, Chamunda, 1000-1700, Rs 200. Tickets from HPTDC Marketing Office, near SBI, Kotwali Bazar in Dharamshala, T01892-0224 928.
Skyways Travels , just off main square, Temple Rd, T01892-221 501, www.skywaystravels.com.

Reliable travel agent who is a mine of knowledge and even has paypal. Can make travelling in India a whole lot easier. Also for tours to Jammu and Kashmir, Rajasthan; trekking, camping and paragliding locally.

Summit Adventures, main square, Bhagsu Nag, McLeodganj, T01892-221679, www.summit-adventures.net. Specialist in trekking and climbing, also cultural trips.

Tibet Tours, Temple Rd, T01892-220383, www.tibettours.com. Comprehensive range of tours, very professional, include pilgrimage tours, with lectures by eminent Buddhist *lamas*. Recommended.

Trans Himalaya, 6 Skye Cres, Crieff, PH7 3FB, T01764-650604, www.trans-himalaya.com. This UK-based company specializes in touring the Himalayan region. With an indepth knowledge of Buddhist heritage, it offers cultural tours and eco-trekking.

Ways Tours & Travels, Temple Rd, T01892-221910, waystour@vsnl.net. Most reliable, Mr Gupta is very experienced, and provides professional service.

Trekking

Best season Apr-Jun and Sep-Oct. Rates upwards of Rs 1400 per person per day.

Highland Trekkers, opposite Taxi Union, T01892-221740, hltrekkers@hotmail.com. Organize treks for smaller groups and a range of package tours.

Himalayan Trekkers, Dharamkot, T01892-221260, anilsingh143@hotmail.com. Good range of treks and other mountain activities including climbing.

Mountaineering Institute, Mirza Ismail Rd, T01892-221787. Invaluable advice on routes, equipment, accommodation, campsites, etc. Equipment and porters can be hired for groups of 8 or more, reasonable charges. The deputy director (SR Saini) has described many routes in *Treks and Passes of Dhauladhar and Pir Pinjal* (Rs 150) although the scale of maps can be misleading. Consult the author for detailed guidance. Mon-Sat 1000-1700.

Dalhousie *p534, map p535*

HPTDC has daily tours during the tourist season to Khajjiar, 0900-1500, Rs 600 (car for 5) or Rs 85 by luxury coach; to Chamba, 1000-1900, Rs 120 by luxury coach; to Pathankot (one way) by luxury coach, Rs 120.

Transport

Dharamshala *p528, maps p529 and p531*

It is dangerous to drive at night in the hills. The roads are not lit and the risks of running off the edge are great.

Air Nearest airport is at Gaggal, T01892-232374, 13 km (taxi Rs 650). To/from **Delhi** with **Kingfisher**, www.flykingfisher.com.

Local bus Buses and share jeeps between Dharamshala and McLeodganj, 10 km, 30 mins' ride, Rs 10.

Long distance bus Most originate in Dharamshala, T01892-224903, but some super and semi-deluxe buses leave from below the taxi stand in McLeodganj. **HRTC** enquiries, T01892-221750. **HPTDC** run luxury coaches in season). **Delhi** (Kashmir Gate, 521 km), semi-deluxe coach departs McLeodganj 1700, 14 hrs, Rs 445; deluxe coach 1830, Rs 595, 1945, Rs 740; super deluxe coach, 1900 (Volvo), Rs 1025. From Delhi at same times. 1930 arrives Lower Dharamshala 1000, recommended for best morning views of the foothills (stops en route). **Dalhousie** and **Chamba**, 0730, 0830, 1730, Rs150, 8 hrs; **Manali**, 1700, Rs 300, 8 hrs; luxury coach 2030, Rs550, **Pathankot**, from Mcleod 1000, 1100, 1320, 1450, 1600, Rs110. HRTC buses to **Baijnath**, 2½ hrs; **Chandigarh** (248 km), 9 hrs, via Una (overnight stop possible); also deluxe buses to **Dehra Dun**, 1420, Rs 570 and 2000, Rs 410 and **Shimla**, 6000, 0820 and 2130 (from Dharamshala), Rs 280/300/415 (deluxe). **Kangra**, 50 mins, Rs 14; **Kullu** (214 km) 10 hrs; **Manali** (253 km) 11 hrs; best to travel by day (0800), fabulous views but bus gets overcrowded; avoid sitting by door where people start to sit on your lap! Always keep baggage with you; **Pathankot** (90 km), several 1000-1600, 4 hrs, connection for **Amritsar**, 3 hrs; **Shimla** (317 km, via Hamirpur/Bilaspur), 10 hrs.

Private bus service **Dalhousie**, 0740, 6 hrs, Rs 125; **Delhi** (Connaught Pl), 1800, 1900, 11 hrs. **Dehra Dun**, 1900, 12 hrs, Rs 350; **Manali**, 0900, 2100, 8 hrs, Rs 250. Several private agents, see **Sky Travels**.

Local taxi Shared by 4, pick up shuttle taxi at Kotwali Bazar on its way down before it turns around at the bus stand, as it is usually full when it passes the taxi stand.

Long distance taxo Can be hired from near the bus stands, T01892-221205. Full day (80 km),

Rs 800; between Dharamshala and McLeodganj, Rs 100; to Pathankot around Rs 1500-2000 depending on size of vehicle.
Train Nearest broad-gauge railhead is at Pathankot. Booking office at bus stand, below tourist office, 1000-1100. For narrow gauge, see below.

Kangra *p532*

Air **Gaggal Airport**, see Dharamshala, above.
Bus To **Dharamshala**, Rs 10, under 1 hr.
Taxi A taxi to **Dharamshala** costs Rs 400.
Train Narrow-gauge **Kangra Valley Railway**, enquiries T01892-265026. From **Pathankot** to **Jogindernagar** or **Baijnath**, reaching Kangra after 4½ hrs: 0430, 0710, 0925, 1300, 1640, 1740, 5 hrs (often 1 hr late). **Jogindernagar to Pathankot**: 0720, 1220, reaches Kangra in 5-6 hrs; **Baijnath to Pathankot**: 0420, 0735, 1425, 1800, to Kangra in 3-4 hrs. Kangra station serves Old Kangra with the fort, near the main road, while Kangra Mandir station is near the temple, bazar and most of the hotels. During the day there are regular **rickshaw** shuttles between Kangra Mandir station and Tehsil Chowk, Rs 5.

Dalhousie *p534, map p535*

Bus Dalhousie is on NH1A. **Delhi**, 559 km; **Chandigarh**, 336 km; **Shimla**, 414 km. Long distance to **Chamba** (56 km via Khajjiar) 1½ hrs; **Dharamshala** (180 km, 7 hrs via Gaggal on the Shimla bus, change at Gaggal, 30 mins from Dharamshala); **Pathankot** 120 km, 3 hrs.
Jeep From bus stand up to **Gandhi Chowk**, Rs 50, **Bakrota**, Rs 90.
Taxi **Taxi Union**, T01899-240220.
Train Nearest station is at Pathankot, 2 hrs by taxi.

Stops along the Kangra Valley Railway *p534*

Air The nearest airport is at Gaggal, see Dharamshala, above.
Bus **Chandigarh**, 265 km (via Nangal, Una, Kangra), 5½ hrs; **Delhi**, 535 km, 10 hrs. From **Delhi ISBT**, overnight deluxe service. To **Andretta** (Private) from the bus station. **Dharamshala**, State buses from near the Nehru statue at the top of the main street. The town is 5 km from the railway station (taxi Rs 50). From **Pathankot** (narrow gauge) *Kangra Queen*, 0820, 4½ hrs, return departs Palampur 1345, via Kangra and Jawalamukhi.

Chamba *p535*

Bus Arrive at the north end of the Chaugan. **Dalhousie** (2 hrs plus stop in Khajjiar); direct to **Amritsar**, 0745, 8 hrs.
Jeep hire is relatively expensive. Special service during **Manimahesh Yatra**.

Directory

Dharamshala *p528, maps p529 and p531*

Banks **Bank of Baroda**, Kotwali Bazar. For Visa/MasterCard cash advances, T01892-223175, collect on next working day (Rs 100, plus 1% commission). **State Bank of India**, Kotwali Bazar, with ATM sometimes not keen on foreign cards; branch in McLeodganj changes TCs, 1000-1400. **Western Union**, near bus stand, McLeodganj, T01892- 221745. Money transfer and exchange, 1000-1930. **Internet** Dozens of places: Awasthi recommended, Dogga and Cloud 9 plush but drop outs not uncommon. **Medical services** **Delek Hospital**, T01892-220 053/223 381, often foreign volunteer doctors, good for dentistry. **District Hospital**, T01892-222133. **Men Tse Khang** (Tibetan Medical Institute) T01892-222484, Gangchen Kyishong, for Tibetan herbal medicine. **Dr Dolma's** and **Dr Dhonden's** clinics, near McLeodganj Bazar for Tibetan treatment. **Post** **GPO**, 1 km below tourist office on Main Rd T01892-222912, Mon-Sat 1000-1630, another in Kotwali Bazar. In McLeodganj, the post office, Jogibara Rd, has poste restante. **Useful contacts** **Foreigners' Registration Office**: Civil Lines, beyond GPO, near petrol pump. **Police**: T01892-224893.

Dalhousie *p534, map p535*

Banks **Punjab Bank**, Court Rd, changes TCs.
Hospital **Civil Hospital**, T01899-242125.
Post **GPO**: Gandhi Chowk.

Chamba *p535*

Banks **State Bank of India**, Court Rd, **Punjab Bank**, Hospital Rd, change Amex TCs.

Trekking in Himachal

Himachal has something to offer every type of trekker. From short, leisurely walks through the pine forests that surround Shimla, with ample food and accommodation options meaning that nothing need be carried, to demanding treks over the high passes of Lahaul, Kinnaur and Spiti, the choice is almost as staggering as the views. ▸▸ *For listings, see pages 514-522, 527-528 and 537-545.*

Trekking from Shimla

From Shimla on the Hindustan-Tibet Highway, there are opportunities for short and long treks. These include **Chharabra**, 13 km beyond Shimla at 2593 m, and **Naldera**, 23 km from Shimla, which was Curzon's summer retreat, see page 487.

Still further on at **Narkanda**, 64 km from Shimla, is another trek with very good walks, especially up Hattu Peak. From Narkanda the road runs down to the Sutlej Valley and enters Kinnaur and Spiti. Foreigners are allowed into Spiti if they have a permit.

From just beyond Narkanda you can trek northwest over the **Jalori Pass** (3350 m) in the **Seraj** region. Starting from Ani village reached by bus/jeep from Luhri in the Sutlej Valley below Narkanda, you trek into the lower part of the Kullu Valley, joining the Kullu–Manali road at Aut. There is a road, accessible to jeeps, over much of this route. An alternative is to proceed 65 km from Narkanda to **Rampur** and then trek into the Kullu Valley via the **Bashleo Pass** (3600 m). There are forest rest houses en route so a tent is not essential. The pass is crossed on the third day of this five-day trek. Both treks end at **Banjar** in the Tirthan Valley from where there are buses to Kullu.

Trekking in Lahaul, Kinnaur and Spiti

The border areas are being opened to trekkers with permits. At the same time the local tribal people are being exposed to outside influences which started with the introduction of television in these valleys. Now enterprising families open their homes to paying guests, youths offer their services as guides and muleteers and shops stock bottled drinks and canned food. However, anyone trekking in this region is advised to carry food, tents and all essentials.

Lahaul → *Colour map 1, A3.*

Lahaul, like Zanskar and Ladakh immediately to the north, is an ideal trekking destination during the monsoon, as it is not nearly as wet as most other regions. The best time to go is from mid-June to mid-October but some passes, eg Shingo-La, Parvati Pass, may remain snow bound until mid-July or even later.

You can take a trek from **Darcha**, see page 527, up the valley over the **Shingo La** and on to **Padum**, the capital of the Zanskar region. Padum is linked with Leh. Shingo-La is over 5000 m so some acclimatization is desirable. The route is well marked.

An alternative route to Zanskar is up the Chandra valley and over **Baralacha La**. From here a trail leads over a high pass Phitsela to Phuktal, where you join the main trail coming from Darcha. Most travellers drive into Darcha; however, a fine trek past the 'Lake of the Moon' or Chandratal makes a nice and less known addition for those with a little more time. The route taken from **Manali** is over the **Hamta Pass** with good views of Deo Tibba (6001 m), weather permitting, to **Chhatru** village in the Chandra Valley. Here, there is camping in the grounds of a rest house and local families can put up visitors in very basic homes. It is four days' trek from Manali. Two days along the dirt road brings you to **Batal** (to save time you can take the bus from Manali over the Rohtang Pass). The next stage of both variations is to Chandratal.

Chandratal (4270 m) is 18 km from Batal. The first section up to Kunzum Pass is on the bus route. The remaining 8.5-km trail is open June-October and brings you to the beautiful clear blue-water lake, about 1 km long and 500 m wide, which lies on a glacial bowl. Carry your own tent and provisions. The lake can also be reached on a lower 14-km trail that directly runs from Batal (no regular buses from Manali). From Chandratal the route crosses several fast flowing streams before reaching the Baralacha La (usually three days). You need to be very careful and take adequate safety precautions while negotiating these stream crossings. It then goes over another pass along the same ridge as the Shingo-La, to join the main Darcha-Padum trail. From here you can continue on to **Padum** or return to Darcha in Lahaul. This second option makes for a very good circular trek.

Another possibility is to trek down the Chenab Valley and either cross the Pir Panjal by one of a number of passes into the Ravi Valley via Bahrmaur, to Chamba or carry on to Kishtwar.

Around lower Lahaul, you can trek from the district town of **Udeypur** at the base of the Miyar Nullah, the upper section of which is glaciated. To the east, high passes give access to the Bhaga valley and to the west to the Saichu Nala (Chenab tributary). The Trilokinath Temple nearby is well worth a visit, see page 525.

Trails run into the Miyar Nullah, renowned for flowers, then over the 5100-m Kang La Pass to Padum. Alternatively, you can follow the Chandrabhaga River to the scarcely visited Pangi valley with its rugged scenery, then over the 4240-m Sach Pass leading to Chamba District.

In the Pangi Valley, the Chandrabhaga flows at over 2400 m after the two rivers meet in this desolate and craggy region. The cheerful and good-looking Pangiwals keep their unique heritage alive through their singing and dancing. The Mindhal temple to Devi is their focus of worship. **Kilar** is the HQ which has a rest house and the Detnag Temple nearby. From Kilar a wide trail follows the steep slopes above the Chandrabhaga (Chenab) River to Dharwas on the Himachal/Kashmir border and then onwards to **Atholi** in the Paddar region of Kishtwar, known for its sapphire mines.

Kinnaur → *Colour map 1, B3. See also page 495.*

Close to the Tibetan border on its east, Kinnaur has the Sutlej flowing through it. Garhwal is to the south, Spiti Valley to the north and Kullu to the west. The rugged mountains and sparse rainfall make Kinnaur resemble Lahaul. The Kinners (Kinnauris) are Hindu but the Tibetan Buddhist influence is evident in the numerous *gompas* that can be seen alongside the temples. The **Phulaich** (Festival of Flowers) takes place in September when some villagers leave for the mountains for two days and nights to collect scented blossoms, then return on the third day to celebrate with singing and dancing. Kinnaur, including the lovely side valleys of **Sangla** and **Bhabha**, is now open and permits are easily available from the District Magistrates in Shimla, Kullu or Keylong. These treks are immensely enjoyable; although there are stone huts and the occasional rest house, always carry a tent in this area.

Baspa Valley Starting from **Sangla** (2680 m), you can take a fairly level forest walk up to Batrseri (5 km), then along the road up to Rakcham (8 km; 3130 m) and climb gradually to reach **Chitkul** (18 km; 3450 m), passing through Mastrang. Another option is to start at **Morang**, see page 497, which has a bus from Kalpa. The trail follows the Sutlej River bank for a short distance until the Tirung Gad meets it. Here it turns southeast and after going through a narrow valley reaches **Thangi**, a village connected to Morang by road (4WD only) where mules are available for hire. The track continues along barren hills to Rahtak (camping possible), before rising steeply to Charang Pass (5266 m), then drops down following a mountain stream to Chitkul.

Bhabha Valley Starting from **Kafnoo** (2427 m), 22 km from Wangtu, this is another beautiful valley to trek. Permit details have to be entered and stamped at the police post 1 km before Kafnoo reservoir. They are checked at Tabo.

There is level ground at the end of the road by the reservoir suitable for camping, but it can get flooded. Local guides are available. From Kafnoo, the trail follows the right bank of the river for about 1 km before crossing to the left bank over a new bridge. From here, the trail gradually ascends to **Chokhapani**, about a five-hour walk away. The riverside trail is slippery and not recommended. The upper trail climbs past Yangpa II then through fields around Musrang hamlet. There is an adequate campsite at Chokhapani (10 km, 3000 m).

From Chokhapani to **Upper Mulling** (3470 m) is a beautiful 8 km, four hours' walk (including lunch stop), following the left bank of the Bhabha stream. Initially going through forests the track then crosses open meadows. At the far end of the meadows is an ideal camping site by the river. The trail from Mulling enters a forested section leading to a snow bridge across the stream. Cross the stream and follow the steeply rising trail to the **Kara** meadows where the Government Animal Husbandry Department has a merino sheep breeding centre. Ford the Bhabha River with care (either on horseback or by wading across with support from a fixed line), to the campsite at Pasha. This section takes three hours, so you can continue to the **Kara-Taria Pass Base**. The 5-km walk up a steep trail along the right fork of the Bhabha stream takes

Kullu Valley treks

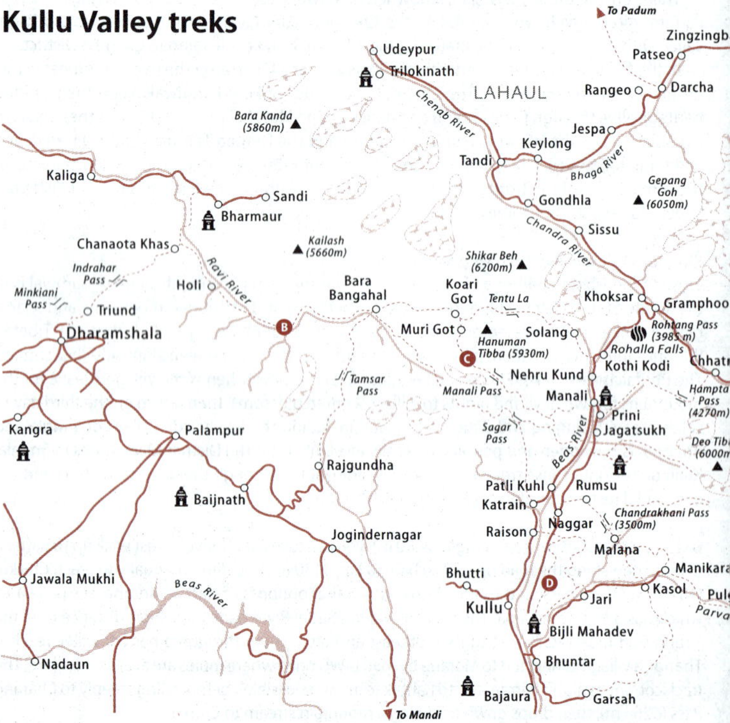

N

5 km
5 miles

Principal Trekking Routes

Ⓐ Manali - Hamta Pass - Chhatru - Batal - Chandratal Lake - Baralacha La - Darcha - Shingola - Padum (21 Days - 240 km)

Ⓑ Manali - Sagordug Thach - Bara Bangahal - Holi - Chanaota Khas - (detour to Brahmaur) - Indrahar Pass - Triund - Dharamshala (18 Days - 180 km)

Ⓒ Manali - Solang - Tentu La - Manali Pass - Manali (8 Days - 75 km)

another four hours. Taria Base Pass (4290 m) camp is below the steep slope leading to the Pass. Camp well away from the slope as it is prone to rock falls.

Pin Valley There is a steep descent over scree for the first kilometre from **Taria Pass**, followed by a five-hour 15-km walk along a narrow but clear trail to the first camp in the Pin Valley. None of the apparently promising campsites on the way has a good water source. The **Bara Boulder** site has a stream and good grazing for horses.

The 11-km stretch from Bara Boulder to **Mudh** (3925 m) takes four hours. It is the highest permanently inhabited village in the Pin Valley and is surrounded by summer cultivation. Log bridges cross several streams feeding into the Pin River. There are places to stay and food is available but some villagers charge up to Rs 200-300 for a room. It is possible to camp outside the village. One campsite is on the flat plateau overlooking the river near the summer hut of the lay *lama* (before crossing the narrow foot bridge on the river), another is near the fields immediately below the village where a side stream runs below the old monastery into the Pin. It is worth visiting the old *gompas* in the village.

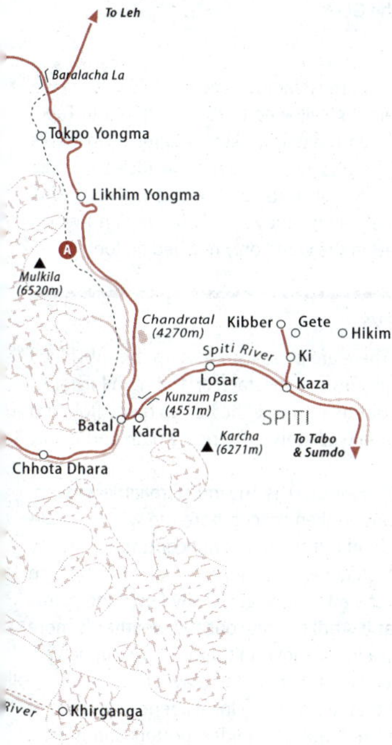

D Manali - Naggar - Malana - Manikaran - Kasol - Jari - Bijli Mahadev - Naggar - Manali (9 Days - 140 km)

From Mudh to **Gulling** is a gentle five-hour trek (15 km) along the right bank of the Pin. A single log bridge takes the path into Tilling village, followed by a gentle climb to the big village of **Sagnam** on the opposite bank, see page 499. The track crosses a rocky spur and descends steeply to some small fields beside the river. Descend to the sandy riverbed and cross diagonally to the single wire rope strung across the river. A makeshift pulley and harness crossing has to be rigged up here unless a suitable shallow spot can be found further downstream. Camp can be set up in the fields just below the road immediately above the crossing point.

From this point arrange to be picked up to drive to (Kaza) Spiti. You can visit the small but locally important Nyingmapa Gompa of Kungri (Ghungri), just above the road, and if you have an extra day based here you can walk up the short stretch of dirt road towards Sagnam, then turn right into the virtually unknown Parahio River valley, an important tributary of the Pin.

Spiti → *Colour map 1, B4.*

Spiti is a high-altitude desert, bare, rugged and inhospitable, with the Spiti River running from the slopes of Kunzum La (4551 m) to Sumdo (3230 m). Kunzum La offers seasonal access by road to Kullu from the valley, and it is also directly connected with Shimla via the NH22 and the SH30. Like neighbouring Lahaul, Spiti is famous for its *gompas*. Foreigners are allowed to trek in this region up to Kibber with permits.

The valley of the gods

No one knows the origin of the village of Malana. People believe that a band of renegade soldiers who deserted Alexander's army in the fourth century BC settled here (some wooden houses have soldiers carved on them); it is more probable that their antecedents were from the Indian plains. Their language, Kanashi, has no script but is linked to Tibetan. The villagers are directly involved in taking decisions on important matters affecting them, thus operating as an ancient democratic 'city state'. Language, customs and religious practices also differ from neighbouring hill tribes, polygamy being permitted.

A charming myth is associated with Jamlu, the principal deity in the valley. Jamlu, possibly of pre-Aryan origin, was carrying a casket containing all the important deities of Hinduism and while crossing the mountains through the Chandrakhani Pass into Kullu, a strong gust of wind blew open the box and spread the deities all over the valley. Since then Malana has been known as 'The Valley of the Gods'.

At **Tabo**, the Buddhist monastery is one of the region's most famous, see page 497. There is a dispensary and two adequate teashops. Foreigners are now allowed to stay overnight in Tabo. There are other important *gompas* at Dankar, Ki, Kungri and Lalung. Trekkers interested in **fossils** choose a trail starting at **Kaza** and travel to **Langza** (8.5 km), which has a narrow track accessible to 4WD. The trek goes to Hikim, the Tangyut monastery, Komik (8 km) and returns to Kaza (6 km). From Kibber (4205 m) there is a 6-km track through alpine meadows to **Gete** (4520 m) which claims to be one of the highest permanent settlements in the world only reached on foot.

Trekking in the Kullu and Parvati valleys

Treks here vary in duration and degree of difficulty. There are pleasant walks up the subsidiary valleys from Aut and Katrain with the opportunity to camp in spectacular and high locations without having to spend very long getting there. An option is to take the bus up to the Rohtang Pass, 51 km from Manali, which is spectacular and then walk down. There is a path and it only takes a few hours.

The post-monsoon period (September to mid-November) is the most reliable **season**. Longer treks with crossings of high passes can be undertaken then, before the winter snows arrive. During the monsoon (June to September) it is wet but the rain is not continuous. It may rain all day or for only an hour or two. Visibility is affected and glimpses of mountains through the clouds are more likely than broad clear panoramic views. However, many flowering plants are at their best. There is trekking in the spring, that is April to May, but the weather is more unsettled and the higher passes may still have quite a lot of snow on them. There can be very good spells of fine weather during this period and it can get quite hot in May.

You will need to take your own **equipment** since that hired out by local agencies is often of an inferior quality. Kullu now has pony unions with fixed rates for guides, porters and horses. Ask at the tourist office and the **Mountaineering Institute** for information and assistance.

Routes

From **Manali** you can go north into **Lahaul** (Map trek **A**) and **Spiti** Valleys by crossing the Rohtang (3985 m) or the Hampta Pass (4270 m). Once over the great divide of the Pir Panjal the treks are briefly described – see Trekking in Lahaul, Kinnaur and Spiti, above. West of Manali there are routes into the **Chamba** and **Kangra** Valleys (Map trek **B**).

The trek to Malana Valley offers an opportunity to see a relatively isolated and comparatively unspoilt hill community. From Manali you go to Naggar (28 km, which can also be reached by bus) and stay at **Rumsu** (2377 m), which is higher. The Chandrakhani Pass (3500 m) takes you into the Malana Valley at the head of which is the glacier. On the third day you can reach **Malana** (2650 m, 20 km from Naggar), which has two guesthouses. In the past you could only enter with permission from the villagers but this is no longer needed. On the fourth day you trek to **Jari** (1500 m) where you can catch a bus to Kullu. The road from Jari to Malana may destroy the distinct character of the community. The whole of the Malana Valley is dominated by **Deo Tibba** peak in the north.

Parvati Valley

To extend the trek from Malana it is possible to continue to **Manikaran** and onwards to Pulga and beyond in the scenic Parvati Valley. You can also get to Manikaran by bus from Kullu, see page 509. Up to **Khirganga** the trail is fairly clear but take care since the area is prone to heavy rain and land slips. Beyond Khirganga, the trek follows the valley up-river passing the tree line to Pandav Bridge and eventually arriving at the sacred lake and shrine at **Mantalai**. Here it splits leading up and over the Pin-Parvati Pass, and down into the dry Pin Valley.

Alternatively, you can explore the lower Parvati Valley by walking to **Kasol**, and then to Jari and Naggar via the temple of Bijli Mahadev (Map trek **D**).

Pin Valley → *Colour map 1, B4. See also page 499.*

The difference between the Parvati and the Pin Valley is striking. Immense glaciers and bizarre moonscape rock formations here contrast with the verdant pastures and evergreen forests of the Parvati Valley behind. The trek leads down to the traditional village of **Mudh**, see page 549. The road to Mudh is still incomplete so it takes about five hours to walk to Sangam and Chatral, leading to Kinnaur and Spiti. There are buses from Chatral to Kaza, see page 499. The trek from Manikaran to Kaza with passes over 5300 m, can take 10 to 14 days. Guides and porters are necessary.

Trekking in Kangra → *Colour map 1, B3. See also page 532.*

Baijnath, **Palampur** and **Dharamshala** are popular starting points. See pages 528 and 532. From here you go over the **Dhaula Dhar** at passes such as the Indrahar and Minkiani (both from Dharamshala) and the Waru (from Palampur), then enter a feeder of the Upper Ravi Valley.

Midway up the valley, which lies between the Manimahesh Dhar and Dhaula Dhar ranges, is Bara Bangahal. From there you can go downstream to **Chamba** or upstream which offers the choice of at least three passes for crossing into the Kullu Valley. The northernmost of these is the Taintu Pass which passes Beas Kund beneath Hanuman Tibba. In the middle is the Manali Pass whilst the southernmost is Kalihani Pass. A good trip which includes the upper part of this valley is the round trip trek from Manali, see page 550.

There are very pleasant day walks throughout the Kangra Valley. Longer, more arduous treks are north over the Dhaula Dhar to Chamba or the Kullu Valley.

Trekking from Chamba → *Colour map 1, B2.*

The Chamba region receives less rain than the Kangra Valley to the south. A trek, particularly over the Pir Panjal into Lahaul is possible during the monsoon months (June to September). The ideal season, though, is just after the monsoon. There are several short and longer treks from Chamba and Bahrmaur in the Upper Ravi Valley.

To the north there are three main passes over the **Pir Panjal** into Lahaul: the Kalicho, Kugti and Chobia passes. At least five days should be allowed for crossing them as their heights are around 5000 m and acclimatization is highly desirable. All the first stages of the walks are along the Budhil River. After the first two days, the services of a guide or porters are recommended for picking the right trail. Views from the passes are very good both of the Himalaya to the north and the Chenab Valley to the south. The descent from the passes is very steep. On reaching the road you can take a bus from **Udeypur** or **Trilokinath** in the Pattan Valley, to the Kullu Valley over Rohtang Pass. Several trails cross the high passes over the Pir Panjal range to give access to the Pattan Valley of Lahaul. The semi-nomadic Gaddi shepherds regularly use these to take their flocks across to the summer grazing grounds located in the high-sided valleys of Lahaul.

Bahrmaur (1981 m), also spelt Brahmaur or Bharmaur, is 65 km from Chamba and can be reached by bus. It was the original capital Brahmapura for four centuries and has 8th-10th-century *Pahari* style temples. The best known are the Lakshminarayan group which is the centre of worship for the semi-nomadic Gaddi tribe. From Bahrmaur a three-day trek is possible to **Manimahesh Lake** (3950 m), 34 km, in the Manimahesh Kailash (5575 m), a spur running off the Pir Panjal. The **Manimahesh Yatra** begins in Chamba and ends at the lake, revered by local people as a resting place of Siva. Pilgrims arrive at the Manimahesh temple here and take a holy bath a fortnight after *Janmashtami* (September/October). The temple has a brass *Mahisasuramardini* image. During the *yatra* period buses, minibuses and taxis are laid on from Chamba to Bahrmaur. Many pilgrims trek the next 12 km to Hadsar although jeeps are available. From here it is a two-day climb to the lake with a night halt at Dhanchho. Himachal Tourism tents available at Bahmaur and there is also a rest house, Hadsar, Dhanchho and Manimahesh; contact tourist office, Dalhousie, T01899-242736. Ponies and porters can be hired at each place. The nine-day trek starting from Chamba includes **Rakh** (20 km) on Day 1, **Bahrmaur** on Day 2, a rest stop there, then continuing to **Hadsar** (12 km), **Dhanchho** (7 km) and **Manimahesh** (7.5 km) with a brief halt at **Bhairon Ghati**. The return is by the same route.

Jammu & Kashmir

Contents

Footprint features

At a glance

Getting around Trains run as far as Jammu. Buses and jeeps go to Srinagar and on to Leh, which also has a spectacular road connection to Manali in Himachal Pradesh. Domestic flights to Srinagar and Leh.

Time required At least a week for the Vale of Kashmir and a houseboat stay; 2 days for Vaishno Devi; 10 days in Ladakh to acclimatize and visit sights – more if you want to add in a trek.

Weather Ladakh is best May-Oct, and drops far below freezing over winter. The snow season in Gulmarg runs Dec-Apr.

When not to go Avoid the harsh mid-winter in Ladakh, and the Vale of Kashmir on contentious dates such as Republic Day (26 Jan).

★ Don't miss ...

1 Witness *yatra* at Vaishno Devi, page 565.
2 Bargain hard at Leh bazar, page 574.
3 Leh to Manali road, page 577.
4 An overnight stay at Hemis monastery, page 579.
5 Alchi monastery, page 581.
6 Spituk to Hemis trek, page 584.

The lakes, fertile valleys and remote, snow-covered peaks of Jammu and Kashmir have had a magnetic appeal to rulers, pilgrims and humble travellers, from the Mughals onwards.

Yet tragically, extended and bitter political violence has put the beauty of the Vale of Kashmir either literally or psychologically out of bounds for almost 20 years. Despite the prominent marketing of houseboats, golf courses and ski resorts and the fact that visitors are beginning to return to Srinagar in numbers, there remains a very obvious military presence. While levels of violence have gone down over the years as the insurgency went underground, the Indian army and Kashmiri militants continue their grim battle with each other today. Although the major pilgrimage to Amarnath is open, and conspicuously guarded by the army, trekking elsewhere in the region is limited and should only be undertaken after careful research and with a reliable guide. However, foreigners will find themselves warmly welcomed by the Kashmiris and in Srinagar alone there is plenty to see and do – not to mention to buy and to eat.

However, the state has other fascinating and accessible regions, set in some of the world's most beautiful scenery. The spectacular high-altitude deserts of Ladakh and Zanskar provide the setting for a hardy Buddhist culture, whose villages and monasteries retain strong links with Tibet. Alchi, Hemis and Thikse are just three of the most striking of the many monasteries clinging to mountainsides. Here you can trek to your heart's content among some of the highest-altitude passes in the world, in one of India's least-known regions.

Background → *Population: 10.1 million. Area: 222,000 sq km.*

The land

Geography The largest of India's Himalayan states comprises three regions of stark geographical and cultural diversity. **Jammu**, in the southwest, is a predominantly Hindu region bordering the **Punjab**, its foothills forming the transitional zone between the plains and the mountains. To the north the Shiwalik mountains give way to the Pir Panjal, which attain heights of 5000 m. Between the Pir Panjal and the High Himalaya, at an average altitude of 1580 m, lies the largely Islamic **Vale of Kashmir**, where snow-capped peaks form a backdrop to the capital, Srinagar, and the Nagin and Dal lakes. Rising behind the Vale are the Great Himalaya which culminate in the west with Nanga Parbat (Naked Mount) at 8125 m.

To the west and north are the Buddhist mountain provinces of **Ladakh** and **Zanskar**, crossed by four mountain ranges – Great Himalaya, Zanskar, Ladakh and Karakoram – as well as by the River Indus and its tributaries the Zanskar, Shingo and Shyok. The Zanskar cuts an impressive course of 120 km before slicing through the Zanskar range in a series of impressive gorges to join the Indus at Nimmu near Leh, the capital of Ladakh. During the winter months, the frozen Zanskar provides the only access for Zanskaris into Ladakh. Combined with its two subsidiary valleys, the Stod (Doda Chu) and the Lung-Nak (Tsarap Chu or 'Valley of Darkness'), which converge below Padum, the main valley is approximately 300 km long and is ringed by mountains, so access to it is over one of the high passes. The most important are the Pensi La connecting Zanskar with the Suru Valley in the west, the Umasi La with the Chenab Valley in the south and the Shingo La with Lahul in the east. Ladakh also has the world's largest glaciers outside the polar regions, and the large and beautiful lake Pangong Tso, 150 km long and 4 km wide, at a height of over 4000 m. This makes for spectacular trekking country.

Climate Even in the Vale, the air in summer is fresh and at night can be quite brisk. The highest daytime temperatures in July rarely exceed 35°C but may fall as low as -11°C in winter. A short climb quickly reduces these temperatures. In Ladakh the sun cuts through the thin atmosphere, and daily and seasonal temperature variations are even wider. The rain-bearing clouds drifting in from the Arabian Sea never reach Ladakh; while Srinagar receives over 650 mm per annum, Leh has only 85 mm, much as snow. Over half Srinagar's rain comes with westerly depressions in the winter.

History

Ruled for many years by Scythian and then Tartar princes, **Kashmir** was captured in 1341 by Shams ud Dinwho spread Islam across the Vale. In 1588 the Mughal Emperor Akbar conquered Kashmir and his son Jahangir (1605-1627), captivated by the beauty of the Vale of Kashmir, planted chenar trees and constructed pleasure gardens. Later, the area fell under Sikh rule and when they were defeated by the British at the end of the first Sikh War in 1846, Jammu, the Vale of Kashmir, Ladakh, Baltistan and Gilgit were assigned to the Maharaja Gulab Singh of Jammu, who had aided the British victory. He founded a dynasty of Dogra Rajputs, descended from the Katoch branch of the lunar race of Rajputs. Thus began a period of Hindu rule over the mainly Muslim population of the Vale of Kashmir.

Rock carvings in Ladakh indicate that the region has been used for thousands of years by nomadic tribesmen who include the Mons of North India, the Dards, the Mongols and Changpa shepherds from Tibet. In Roman times Kashmir and Ladakh lay on a feeder of the great Silk Road that ran from China to the Mediterranean. By the end of the 10th century, Ladakh was controlled by the Thi Dynasty which founded a capital at Shey and built many forts. Tibetan Lamaistic Buddhism took hold at the same time and over 100 gompas were built. In 1533 Soyang Namgyal united the whole region up to the outskirts of Lhasa and made his capital at Leh. The Namgyal Dynasty still exists today and the Rani (Queen) of Stok was elected to the Indian Parliament. During the reigns of Senge Namgyal (circa 1570-1620) and Deldan Namgyal

Warning

Visitors to India have been advised not to travel to the Kashmir Valley. Several of the splinter groups opposed to the Indian government have taken hostages as a means of putting pressure on the government so the risks of travel in Kashmir are still real.

An increasing number of tourists are visiting the valley; take advice from your own consulate, and be aware that travelling against their advice can render your travel insurance void. All foreigners visiting Kashmir or Ladakh must register on arrival.

(circa 1620-1660) Ladakh was threatened from the south and west by the Baltis, who had enlisted the assistance of the Mughals. They were beaten back and the Namgyals extended Ladakhi power. The expansionist era came to an end when the fifth Dalai Lama of Tibet, Nawang Lobsang Gyatso (1617-1682) persuaded the Mongols, whom he had converted to Buddhism, to enter a military campaign against West Tibet and Ladakh. The Ladakhis were unable to repel the invading Mongol forces and in desperation Delegs Namgyal turned to Kashmir for help. The Mughal Governor of Kashmir sent troops to help the King of Leh regain his throne but in return he had to pay regular tribute and build a mosque. From then on the country became an extension of the Mughal Empire. In 1834 Zorwar Singh, an Army General, conquered Ladakh and brought the area under the control of the Dogra Maharajah of Kashmir. The dethroned royal family received the Stok Palace where they still live today.

Zanskar became an administrative part of Ladakh under Senge Namgyal whose three sons became the rulers of Ladakh, Guge and Zanskar/Spiti. This arrangement collapsed after Ladakh's war with Tibet and the Zanskar royal house divided, one part administering Padum, the other Zangla. Under the Dogras, the rulers were reduced to puppets as the marauding army wreaked havoc on the villages, monasteries and people.

When India gained Independence from Britain, rulers of 'princely states' such as Kashmir were given the choice of whether to stay with India or join Pakistan. But Kashmir's maharajah, Hari Singh, played for time, in the hope that Kashmir could remain independent of both countries. In October 1947, Kashmir was invaded by tribesmen from Pakistan's North West Frontier Province, with the support of the Pakistani army. Singh, supported by popular leader Sheikh Abdullah, had to turn to India for help. Nehru sent in the Indian army and 18 months of fighting followed until 1949, when the state was split by a UN-monitored cease-fire line, much of which remains the de facto border between India and Pakistan today. Of the total area of the pre-Independence State, over which India continues to claim the legitimate right to govern, 78,000 sq km are currently controlled by Pakistan and a further 42,600 sq km by China. Kashmir has remained the single most important cause of conflict between India and Pakistan since 1949, while arguments for autonomy within the Kashmir Valley have periodically dominated the political agenda, erupting in 1987, when – it is widely accepted – India rigged the state elections to bring about a favourable result. Widespread unrest followed and hundreds of young men fled over the border to receive arms training in Pakistan. The militancy started in earnest in1988 and continues today, although it is now much less overt than during the early years.

Following India's Independence and partition in 1947, Ladakh, like Kashmir, was divided. Indian and Chinese troops have been stationed on the eastern border since the Chinese invasion of Tibet in 1950-1951. From the early 1950s Chinese troops were stationed in the Aksai Chin, which India also claimed, and without Indian knowledge built a road linking Tibet with Xinjiang. This was one of the two fronts in China's war with India in 1962, which confirmed China's de facto hold on the territory. India still disputes its legality. Since the 1962 war the Indian army has maintained a very strong presence in Ladakh. The strategic requirements of better links with the rest of India were primarily responsible for Ladakh being 'opened up' to some influences from outside.

The current political situation

The insurgency that started in the late 1980s has gone through several evolutions. Until the mid-1990s, it was overt and highly visible, with parts of Srinagar being held by the militants, openly carrying arms. Fierce counter-insurgency measures forced them underground, but the violence continued. Meanwhile, in May 1999, war broke out between Pakistan and India, in the Kargil area, lasting two months. Even after the cease-fire, the two countries continued shelling each other across the border, badly affecting the Jammu border districts of Poonch and Rajouri.

The tension reached a peak in June 2002 after an attack on the Indian parliament in December 2001 – allegedly carried out by Pakistan based militants. Internationally, there were serious fears that the two countries were on the brink of nuclear war but thankfully the situation was wound down following a new agreement between India and Pakistan to try and find a peaceful solution to the problem. India and Pakistan embarked on a dialogue that saw some improvement in relations.

On 8 October 2005 a massive 7.6 magnitude earthquake struck Kashmir, killing 73,000 people and injuring hundreds of thousands more on either side of the Line of Control. While border controls were loosened to allow families to search or grieve for loved ones, the potential longer-term benefits of international cooperation have not yet been realized. By April 2007 only 1600 people had availed of the Peace Bus (set up in 2005 to enable Kashmiris to visit their relatives on the other side of the Line of Control, and as a "confidence-building measure" between India and Pakistan), in part due to the bureaucracy involved in making the crossing.

In December 2008, state elections saw the highest voter turnout since the militancy began. The National Conference won, in a coalition with the Indian National Congress party and Omar Abdullah, aged 38, became the state's youngest ever chief minister. However, the early part of 2009 saw regular protests against alleged violations by security forces.

Instability and the rise of the Taliban in Pakistan's North-West Frontier through 2009, along with the holding of peaceful elections for the state assembly and the Lok Sabha in Indian-held Kashmir have relegated Kashmir to the back pages, but a solution which meets with the full support of Kashmiris in both Indian and Pakistani Kashmir is still a distant prospect.

Modern government

The state enjoys a special status within the Indian nation. As defined in Article 370 of the constitution, since 1956 Jammu and Kashmir has had its own constitution affirming its integrity. The central government has direct control over defence, external affairs and communications within the state and indirect influence over citizenship, Supreme Court jurisdiction and emergency powers. In normal times the state sends six representatives to the Lok Sabha and two members who are nominated by the governor to the Rajya Sabha.

In Ladakh, the local government body, the Ladakh Hill Council, has once again put forth a demand to the Indian government to separate the district from the rest of the state of Jammu and Kashmir. Citing reasons of cultural uniqueness and the fact that they do not wish to be part of any separatist movement in Kashmir, the Ladakhis demand they be made into a 'Union Territory' directly funded by the central government.

Culture

Culturally, the people of Jammu, Kashmir and Ladakh could scarcely be more different from each other. The 10 million population is unevenly scattered. The Vale of Kashmir has more than half the population, whilst Ladakh is the most sparsely populated region. Jammu was traditionally the seat of Dogra power and serves a largely Hindu population whose affinities lie more with the Punjab than the Vale. Kashmir marks the northernmost advance of Islam in the Himalaya while Ladakh is aptly named 'Little Tibet'. Ethnically the Ladakhis are of Tibetan stock. Indeed, it was once a province of Tibet and was governed in secular matters by an independent prince and in spiritual affairs by the Dalai Lama. Tibetan Changpas form the bulk of the

Ladakhi dress

Ladakhis dress in *gonchas*, loose woollen robes tied at the waist with a wide coloured band. Buddhists usually wear dark red while Muslims and nomadic tribes often use undyed material. The headdress varies from the simple Balti woollen cap with a rolled brim and the traditional *gonda* (a high embroidered hat) to the snake-shaped ornate black lambskin *perak* worn by some women. Studded with turquoise and lapis lazuli these are precious enough to be handed down as heirlooms.

population in central and eastern Ladakh. These nomadic herdsmen can be seen living in black yak-hair tents on the mountains with their yaks, goats and sheep. They still provide the fine pashm goat wool. The Mons, nomads of Aryan stock, introduced Buddhism and established settlements in the valleys. The Droks or Dards from the Gilgit area settled along the Indus Valley and introduced irrigation; many converted to Islam 300 years ago. Most are cultivators speaking a language based on Sanskrit. The Baltis with Central Asian origins mostly live in the Kargil region. The Zanskaris are of the same stock as the Ladakhis and because of the sheer isolation of their homeland were able to preserve their Buddhist culture against the onslaughts of Mughal India. The majority of Zanskaris are Buddhist, though there are Muslim families in Padum, the capital, dating from the Dogra invasion.

Kashmiri is influenced by Sanskrit and belongs to the Dardic branch of the Indo-Aryan languages. Linguistically and physically Kashmiris are similar to the tribes around Gilgit in Pakistan. The Ladakhis physically reveal Tibetan-Mongolian and Indo-Aryan origins while their language belongs to the Tibetan-Burmese group.

Religion

In the Vale of Kashmir, 95% of the people are **Muslim**, the majority being Sunnis, while in Jammu over 65% are **Hindu**. In Ladakh, 52% are Lamaistic **Buddhists**. Most follow Mahayana Buddhism of the Vajrayana sect with a mixture of Bon animism and Tantric practices. The Red Hat Drukpa (or Kagyupa) sect of Tibetan monastic Buddhists enjoy royal patronage. The reformist Yellow Hat sect are Gelugpa Buddhists and, like the Dalai Lama, wear a yellow headdress with their maroon robes. The more ancient Nyingmapa Buddhists have their seat in Tak-thok. Ladakhi *lamas* may also be physicians, teachers and astrologers; they also work in the fields, as do the *chomos* (nuns). Nearly every family has a member who chooses to become a *lama* (often the third son) or a *chomo*. The most important in the Tibetan tradition are recognized reincarnate *lamas* (Trulku), who are born to the position. The Buddhist *gompas* (monasteries) are places of worship, meditation and religious instruction and the structures, often sited on spectacular mountain ridges, add to the attraction of the landscape while remaining a central part of Ladakhi life. Ladakh also has a large number of Shi'a Muslims, mainly in Kargil District, many being immigrant Kashmiris and Dards. Their mosques and *imambaras*, influenced by Persian architecture, can be found in Leh proper and villages nearby.

The foundation of Sani in the 11th century is recognized as the first monastery in Zanskar. Phugtal and Karsha date from the same period. The sects developed alongside those in Ladakh. The Gelugpa (Yellow Hat) order was established in the 15th century and monasteries at Karsha, Lingshet and Mune belong to this. The Drukpa sect set up monasteries at Bardan and Zangla and 'occupied' that at Sani. These have links with Stakna near Leh and the Gelugpa is associated with the Lekir monastery. Traditional Ladakhi and Zanskari life, even today, comes close to Gandhi's idealized vision of life in ancient India.

Handicrafts

Kashmir is deservedly famous for its distinctive and fine handicrafts. Many of these developed when Srinagar was a trading post on the ancient trans-Himalayan trade route. High-quality craftsmanship in India initially owed much to the patronage of the court and Kashmir was no exception. From the 15th century onwards, carpet making, shawl weaving and embroidery and decorative techniques were actively encouraged and the tradition grew to demands made at home and abroad. Since tourism has been severely affected in the Vale since 1989, Kashmiri tradesmen have sought markets in other parts of India.

Kashmir **shawls** are world renowned for their softness and warmth. The best are pashmina and shahtush, the latter being the warmest, the rarest and, consequently, the most expensive. Prized by Moghuls and maharajas they found their way to Europe and, through Napoleon's Egyptian campaign, became an item of fashion in France. The craft was possibly introduced from Persia in the 15th century. Originally a fine shawl would take months to complete especially if up to 100 colours were used. The soft fleece of the pashmina goat or the fine under hairs of the Tibetan antelope were used, the former for pashmina (cashmere) shawls, the latter for shahtush. The very best were soft and warm and yet so fine that they could be drawn through a finger ring. The designs changed over the years from floral patterns in the 17th century to Paisley in the 19th century. The Mughals, especially Akbar, used them as gifts. However, with the introduction of the Jacquard loom, cheap imitations were mass produced at a fraction of the price of hand woven shawls. Kashmiri shawls thus became luxury items, their manufacture remaining an important source of employment in the Vale, but they ceased to be the major export.

All trade in shahtush and articles made from the wool of the chiru (Tibetan antelope) is banned, hence buying and exporting an article is illegal.

Hand-knotted **carpets** were traditionally made in either pure wool or mixed with cotton or silk. However, nowadays pure wool carpets are hardly produced in the valley, the preference being for silk. The patterns tend to the traditional, the Persian and Bukhara styles being common, though figurative designs such as The Tree of Life are becoming increasingly popular. A large carpet will take months to complete, the price depending on the density of knots and the material used, silk being by far the most expensive. The salesmen usually claim that only vegetable dyes are used and whilst this is true in some instances, more readily available and cheaper chemical dyes are commonplace. After knotting, the pile is trimmed with scissors, loose threads burnt off and the carpet washed and dried. Young boys work with a master and it is common to hear them calling out the colour changes in a chant. Child labour in carpet making across North India is increasingly widely criticized, but government attempts to insist on limiting hours of work and the provision of schooling are often ignored. Look for the rug mark awarded when no child labour is used.

Papier mâché boxes, trays, coasters make ideal gifts. Paper is soaked, dried in a mould, then painted and lacquered. Traditionally, natural colouring was used (lapis lazuli for blue, gold leaf for gold, charcoal for black) but this is unlikely today. The patterns can be highly intricate and the finish exquisite.

Other crafts include **crewel** work (chain stitching) on fabric, Kashmiri silver **jewellery**, silk and fine **woodcarving**, particularly on walnut wood.

Kashmir Valley

The beauty of the Vale of Kashmir, with its snow-dusted mountains looming in shades of purple above serene lakes and wildflower meadows, still has the power to reduce grown poets to tears. Nonetheless, the reality of military occupation pervades many aspects of daily life, with army camps, bunkers and checkposts positioned every few hundred metres along the highways and throughout the countryside. Travellers not dissuaded by the ever-present threat of violence or the official warnings to stay away can expect to encounter extremes of beauty and friendliness, not to mention hard salesmanship, in an economy that's been starved of tourist income for over 20 years.
▸▸ *For listings, see pages 567-572.*

Srinagar

→ *For listings, see pages 567-572.* *Colour map 1, A2. Population: 894,900. Altitude: 1730 m.*

Founded by Raja Pravarasen in the sixth century, ringed by mountains and alluringly wrapped around the Dal and Nagin lakes, Srinagar ('beautiful city') is divided in two by the River Jhelum. Once known as the city of seven *kadals* (bridges), there are now 12 that connect the two sides, the older ones giving their names to their adjoining neighbourhoods. It is the largest city in the state and the summer seat of government. Sadly the troubles of the past 20 years have scarred the town, leading to the desertion and neglect of many of its fine houses, buildings and Hindu temples. The famous Dal Lake has shrunk to a sixth of its former size and has become badly polluted. Older Srinagaris lament the passing of the formerly spruce city, yet even so, Srinagar is a charming city with a strong character, unique in India for its Central Asian flavour.

Ins and outs

Getting there The airport is 14 km south of town; a taxi to the main tourist areas takes 30-45 minutes and costs Rs 300. Srinagar has several daily direct flights from Delhi and weekly flights from Leh. Direct buses from New Delhi take 24 hours, but this is an arduous trip. If you want to travel overland, it's more comfortable to take the train as far as Jammu (12 hours), stop for the night and then travel to the valley by bus the next day (nine hours, including stops for lunch and tea). It's a stunning journey through the mountains as the bus winds its way up to the Jawahar tunnel that burrows through the Pir Panjal, the jade-green Chenab river flowing hundreds of feet below. Emerging from the tunnel on the other side, high in the hills of south Kashmir, travellers are treated to a breathtaking view of the valley spread before out before them. There are several bus stations; tourist buses from Jammu and Delhi arrive and leave from the Tourist Reception Centre, see below.

Getting around There are government taxi stands with fixed rates at the Tourist Reception Centre (Residency Road), Dal Gate and Nehru Park, and an abundance of auto-rickshaws. Local buses are cheap, but can be crowded and slow. The days of dusk-to- dawn curfews are over, but even so, the city shuts down relatively early; by 2100 the streets are deserted and it can be tricky to find transport. ▸▸ *See Transport, page 572.*

Tourist information The **Tourist Reception Centre** ⓘ *Residency Rd, close to the tourist area of Dalgate, T0194-245 2690*, houses the state department of tourism, the **Jammu and Kashmir Tourism Development Corporation** (JKTDC), www.jktdc.co.in, and **Adventure Tourism** ⓘ *T0194-245 7927*, for booking accommodation and tours. Also within the complex is the **J&K Transport Corporation** for bus tickets.

Safety At time of writing the British **Foreign and Commonwealth Office**, www.fco.gov.uk, advises against all rural travel in Jammu and Kashmir, except in Ladakh, and against non-essential travel to Srinagar. For an on-the-ground perspective, check www.greaterkashmir.com, www.kashmirtimes.com and www.kashmirobserver.com. Travellers continue to visit Srinagar, some using the road to Leh to enter Ladakh. Most report no problems, but it is essential to be careful and keep informed about the situation.

Shrine etiquette

Before entering a shrine or mosque, check when you are required to remove your shoes. Most places have a cloakroom, where you can leave them for a few rupees until you have finished looking around. Women should cover their heads and both sexes should wear long sleeves. You can make a contribute to the shrines' upkeep by putting a donation in the green *tameer* (building) fund box, usually at the entrance of the shrine.

Grenade attacks on army bunkers in the city used to be common, but are currently rare. However, in 2006 six Indian tourists were killed during grenade attacks on two bus loads of tourists from West Bengal. Given the tensions between Kashmir and the Indian government, Indian tourists are more likely to be directly targeted than foreigners.

Since the uprising in 2008, demonstrations, stone throwing and daytime curfews – particularly in the old city – have been increasing in frequency. The Dal and Nagin lake areas are hardly affected on such occasions – at worst, you might not be able to get transport during a *bandh* (general shutdown).

If you are in town and see the shop shutters coming down before closing time, this is generally a sign that a protest is approaching. Either beat a hasty retreat in an auto- rickshaw, or take shelter in a shop until the demonstrators and police have passed. Always ask how the situation is before heading to the old city ('Downtown') and don't go there on Fridays, when spontaneous demonstrations following afternoon prayers are common.

In view of the present political situation this edition of the *India Handbook* carries limited details of places to visit outside Srinagar.

Sights

The city falls into three parts; the commercial area (**Uptown**), the old city (**Downtown**) and the area around the lakes (**Dalgate**, the **Boulevard**, **Nehru Park**). Downtown can be reached from Uptown either directly, by driving through Dalgate or by driving all the way around Dal Lake, which takes you past the gardens of Cheshma Shahi, Nishat and the turning for the road to Shalimar. This route also takes you past the Grand Palace Hotel, the village of Brein, the Char Minar Island restaurant and reaches Downtown via the Hazrat Bal mosque and Makhdoom Sahib. Uptown is the place for shopping, particularly Polo View and the Bund, which is a footpath that runs along the Jhelum. Residency Road and Lal Chowk are also in Uptown.

Hotels on the Boulevard are popular – particularly with Indian tourists – but tend to be huge, impersonal and overpriced. The city is famous for its houseboats and staying on one can be a very pleasant experience, but it is necessary to book carefully; if the deal sounds too good to be true, then it probably is and you will end up paying in other ways (ie by being coerced into shopping trips, from which your hosts will take a hefty commission). Don't be bullied into booking a trip by pushy, Kashmiri travel agents in New Delhi – better to book through the **Houseboat Owners Association**. Try and find a boat with good references from other travellers, through sites such as www.tripadvisor.com. Also be aware that many boats in the Dal and Nagin lakes can only be accessed by *shikara*. While boat owners will always insist that a *shikara* will always be at your disposal, some tourists have found that this has not been the case and have found themselves marooned on boats with hosts they don't particularly like.

The Uptown area is good to stay in if you are interested in exploring the city and prefer to be away from the tourist rush. There are also some houseboats on the Jhelum, with walk-on/walk-off access. You can hear the noise of the traffic from these boats, but there are no hawkers in this area.

Hotels around Dalgate tend to offer more budget options and can be very enjoyable. Those actually inside the lake are a good choice (Heaven Canal, Akbar) as the area is interesting with good views, but less hassle than the Boulevard.

Old City

Srinagar's old city (known locally as 'Downtown') is a fascinating area to wander around. Once the manufacturing and trade hub of Kashmir, each *mohalla* (neighbourhood) had its own speciality, such as carpet weaving, goldsmithery and woodcarving. It was said that you could find even the milk of a pigeon in the thriving bazars and its traders grew rich, building themselves impressive brick and wood houses, in a style that is a charming fusion of Mughal and English Tudor.

In the north of the Old City, on the southern side of the Hari Parbat hill, the **Makhdoom Sahib shrine** is dedicated to Hazrat Sultan and affords wonderful views of the city. The actual shrine is off-limits to women and non-Muslims, but you can peek through the ornate, carved screen from outside and marvel at the fabulous array of chandeliers.

From Makhdoom Sahib take an auto-rickshaw (or walk 15 minutes) to the **Jama Masjid** (1674). The mosque is notable for the 370 wooden pillars supporting the roof, each is made from a single *deodar* tree. The building forms a square around an inner courtyard, with a beautiful fountain and pool at its centre. Its four entrance archways are topped by the striking, pagoda-like roofs that are an important architectural characteristic of the valley's mosques and shrines. The mosque is famed as the place where the sacred hair of the Prophet Mohammed was kept before being moved to the Hazratbal Mosque.

About 10 minutes' walk, to the southeast lies the 17th-century **tomb of Naqash Band Sahib**, a sufi saint. Next to the shrine lie the graves of the 'martyrs' who died in the 1931 uprising against the Dogras. They are claimed as heroes by both the state government and the separatists – one of the few things both sides agree on.

Continue further in the same direction and you will reach the **Dastagir Sahib shrine**, which houses the tomb of Abdul Qazi Geelani. The papier mâché decoration in this friendly shrine is delightful and there is a 300-year-old, giant, handwritten Qu'ran. Watch what you wear; perhaps hailing back to a more permissive age, a sign at the entrance requests visitors "not to enter the shrine naked"!

A minute's walk away is the peaceful **Rozahbal Masjid**, which claims to contain the 'tomb of Jesus' (Holger Kersten's *Jesus Lived in India* recounts the legend; also see www.tombofjesus.com). Head west, towards the river for the **Shah-i-Hamdan Masjid**, the site of Srinagar's first mosque, built in 1395 by Mir Sayed Ali Hamadni. The original building was destroyed by fire, the current structure dating back to the 1730s. The entrance is worth seeing for its exquisite papier mâché work and woodcarving, but non-Muslims are not allowed inside the shrine area.

Facing Shah-i-Hamdan, across the river is the **Pattar Masjid** (1623), built for the Empress Nur Jahan and renamed Shahi Mosque. Further up the river, on the same side as Shah-i-Hamdan lies the **tomb of Zain-ul-Abidin**, a sultan of Kashmir. The area, Zaina Kadal, is interesting to walk around – carved copperwork is still produced here and you can see the craftsmen at work. It's the best place to buy your souvenir samovar.

South of the old city and the river is the remarkable **Sri Pratap Singh Museum** ⓘ *Lal Mandi, summer 1030-1630, winter 1100-1700, foreigners Rs 50, Indians Rs 10.* Kashmir's Hindu and Buddhist past literally stares you in the face as 1000-year-old statues of Siva, Vishnu and the Buddha, excavated from all over the valley, casually line the walls. A second room houses an eclectic mix of stuffed animals, bottled snakes and birds eggs, topped off by the skeleton of a woolly mammoth and looked down on by a collection of stags heads, mounted on the papier mâché walls. This is only a small part of the collection, which will be displayed in full when the museum moves to the larger building being constructed next door.

Dal Lake and the floating gardens

Of all the city's sights, **Dal Lake** must be its trademark. Over 6.5 km long and 4 km wide, it is divided into three parts by manmade causeways. The small islands are willow covered, while round the lake are groves of *chinar*, poplar and willow. The Mihrbahri people have lived around the lakes for centuries and are market gardeners, tending the floating beds of vegetables and flowers that they have made and cleverly shielded with weeds to make them unobtrusive. Shikaras, the gondola-like pleasure boats that ply the lake, can be hired for around Rs 50 an hour for trips around the Dal. The morning vegetable market is well worth seeing by boat and if you're curious about the city, take one up the Jhelum as far as Shah-i-Hamdan, where you can get out for a walk. If you do this, it's worth taking a guide with you who can speak English.

Set up on a hill, behind the Boulevard (known as Takht-i-Sulaiman or 'Throne of Soloman'), is the **Shankaracharya Temple**. The walk up the hill is fairly steep but affords great views and is a good place to orientate yourself. The temple was constructed during Jahangir's reign but is said to be on the same site as a second-century BC temple built by Asoka's son.

Set in front of a triangle of the lake created by the intersecting causeways with a slender bridge at the centre lies the famous **Nishat Bagh** (Garden of Gladness). Sandwiched between the hills and the lake, it was laid out by Asaf Khan, Nur Jahan's brother, in 1632 (see page 156).

The **Shalimar Bagh** gardens are about 4 km away and set back from the lake. A channel extends up to their edge. Built by Jahangir for his wife, Nur Jahan, the gardens are distinguished by a series of terraces linked by a water channel. These are surrounded by decorative pools, which can only be reached by stepping stones. The uppermost pavilion has elegant black marble pillars and niches in the walls for flowers during the day and candles or lamps at night. **Chashma Shahi** (Royal Spring, 1632) is a much smaller garden built around the course of a renowned spring and is attributed to Shah Jahan though it has been altered over the centuries. Rather wilder than the other gardens, its tucked- away location makes it a good place for runners to stretch their legs.

West of Chashmi Shahi, nestling in the hills, is the smallest and sweetest of the Mughal gardens, the charmingly named **Pari Mahal** (Fairy Palace). Built in the 17th century by the ill-fated prince Dara Shikoh, who was later beheaded by his brother Aurangzeb, the garden has six terraces and the best sunset views of Srinagar.

Close to Nagin Lake, **Hazratbal** (Majestic Place) is on the western shore of Dal Lake and commands excellent views. The modern mosque stands out for its white, marble dome and has a special sanctity as a hair of the prophet Mohammad is preserved here. Just beyond is the **Nazim Bagh** (Garden of the Morning Breeze), one of the earliest Mughal gardens and attributed to Akbar.

Dachigam National Park

ⓘ *22 km east, past the Shalimar gardens. Passes available from the Tourist Reception Centre.*
This national park is home to the endangered Hangul deer as well as black and brown bears, leopards, musk deer and various migratory birds. Permits and further information about the best time to see the wildlife can be obtained from the Tourist Reception Centre in Srinagar.

Around Srinagar → *For listings, see pages 567-572.*

Gulmarg → *Colour map 1, A2. 56 km west of Srinagar. Altitude: 2650 m.*

India's premier winter sports resort, Gulmarg attracts a colourful mix of characters, from the off-piste powder-addict adventurers who stay for months each year to the coach- loads of Indian tourists eager to see snow for the first time. Host of the country's annual Winter Games, it is one of the cheapest places in the world to learn to ski, although there are only a few beginners' runs. The resort is served by three ski lifts and boasts the world's highest **gondola** ⓘ *daily 1000-1800, Rs 800 return*, which stops at the Kangdori mid- station before rising up to Apharwat Top (4000 m), from where you can ski the 6 km back to Gulmarg. Check with JKTDC (see page 561) about opportunities for heli-skiing. The season runs from December to April, and equipment is available for hire for around Rs 300 a day. Lift passes cost Rs 700-1250. Outside the winter season, Gulmarg is a popular day trip from Srinagar, with pony rides, walks and golf being the main attractions.

Sonamarg → *Colour map 1, A2. 84 km northeast of Srinagar.*
Literally meaning the 'golden valley' gets its name from the yellow crocus blooms that carpet the valley each spring. At an altitude of 2740 m, it's the last major town in Kashmir before the Zoji La Pass – the gateway to Ladakh. The area is highly regarded for its trekking and fishing; trout were introduced here by the British in the 19th century. Accommodation is available through JK TDC (see page 561) in the summer months.

Pahalgam → *Colour map 1, A2. 100 km east of Srinagar.*
Pahalgam ('village of shepherds') sits at an altitude of 2133 m and is the base for the yearly 'Amarnath Yatra' pilgrimage, which sees thousands of Hindu pilgrims climbing to a cave housing an 'ice lingam'. During the Yatra season, which now runs from June to August, the town gets very busy. There are many short walks you can take from here and it is also a good base for longer treks. A wide selection of accommodation caters for all budgets.

Jammu → *For listings, see pages 567-572. Colour map 1, A2. Phone code: 0191. Population: 378,400.*

Jammu, the second largest city in the state, is the winter capital of government and main entry point for Kashmir by train. While it doesn't possess the charm of Srinagar, it is a pleasant enough city to spend a day in.

Ins and outs

Getting there The airport is within the city; a pre-paid taxi to the centre (Ragunath Bazar) costs around Rs 200. There are flights from Delhi and Srinagar. The railway station is in the New Town, across the Tawi River, and a few kilometres from the old hilltop town where most of the budget hotels are located. The general bus stand, where inter-state buses come in, is at the foot of the steps off the Srinagar Road in the Old Town. ▸▸ *See Transport, page 572.*
Getting around The frequent, cheap city bus service or an auto-rickshaw comes in handy as the two parts of the town and some sights, are far apart.
Tourist information **Jammu and Kashmir Tourist Reception Centre** ⓘ *Vir Marg, T0191-254 8172.* **Jammu Tawi** ⓘ *railway station, T0191-247 6078.* **JKTDC** ⓘ *T0191-257 9554.*
Climate Temperatures in summer reach a maximum of 40°C, minimum 28°C. Rainfall in July and August is 310 mm, with other months measuring an average 40 mm. The best time to visit is from November to March.

Sights

Raghunath Temple (1857) in the old centre is one of the largest temple complexes in North India. The temple has seven shrines, with gold-plated interiors. **Rambiresvar Temple** (1883), centrally located about 500 m from the Dogra Art Gallery on the Shalimar Road, is dedicated to Siva. It has a 75-m tower and extraordinary crystal lingams and is the largest Siva temple in North India.

The **Amar Mahal Museum** ⓘ *winter Tue-Sun 1000-1200, 1500-1700, summer Tue-Sat 1000-1200, 1700-1900, Sun 1000-1200, Rs 5, great views of the river but no photography allowed, Rs 50-80 by auto-rickshaw from the centre of town,* is superbly sited on the bend of the Tawi, just off Srinagar Road. There is a portrait gallery, Pahari paintings of *Mahabharata* scenes and royal memorabilia. The early 20th-century palace is a curiosity; its French designer gave it château-like roofs and turrets. Four rooms are open but you can look into others through the windows.

Vaishno Devi → *For listings, see pages 567-572. Colour map 1, A2.*

The Vaishno Devi cave, 61 km north of Jammu, is one of the region's most important pilgrimage sites. As the temple draws near you hear cries of 'Jai Matadi' (Victory to the Mother Goddess). Then at the shrine entrance, pilgrims walk in batches through cold ankle-deep water to the low and narrow cave entrance to get a glimpse of the deity. Visitors joining the *yatra* find it a very moving experience.

The main pilgrimage season is March to July. The arduous climb along the 13-km track to the cave temple has been re-laid, widened and tiled, and railings provided. Another road from Lower Sanjichat to the Darbar brings you 2 km closer with 300 m less to climb. Ponies, *dandies* (a kind of local palanquin for carrying tourists) and porters are available from Katra at fixed rates. Auto-rickshaws and taxis can go as far as the Banganga. Yatra slips are issued free of charge by the **Yatra Registration Counter** (YRC) in the bus stand in Katra. The slip must be presented at the Banganga checkpoint within six hours (or face disciplinary action if caught). One slip can be used for up to nine people. Tea, drinks and snacks are available on the route.

Visitors should leave all leather items in a cloakroom at Vaishno Devi before entering the cave; take bottled water and waterproofs. If you are on your own or in a small group, you can usually avoid having to wait for a group if you present yourself at Gates 1 or 2, and smile.

Katra is an attractive town at the foot of the Trikuta Hills where visitors to the Vaishno Devi cave can stay.

Srinagar to Leh road

The road to Leh from Srinagar must be one of the most fascinating journeys in the world as it negotiates high passes and fragile mountainsides. There are dramatic scenic and cultural changes as you go from verdant Muslim Kashmir to ascetic Buddhist Ladakh. Because of political unrest in Kashmir, the route, which runs very close to the Line of Control, may be closed to travellers. The alternative route to Leh from Manali is equally fascinating, see page 523.

After passing through **Sonamarg** (see page 565), you reach **Zoji La** where a traffic control system operates: vehicles on the one-lane road bound for Leh are allowed through 1400-0700, while traffic for Srinagar can travel 0700-1400; check times before departing, or prepare for a lengthy wait at the pass. From Zoji La the road descends to **Minamarg meadow** and **Dras**. The winter temperatures go down to -50°C, and heavy snow and strong winds cut off the town. The broad Kargil basin and its wide terraces are separated from the Mulbekh Valley by the 12-km-long **Wakha Gorge**.

On the bank of the River Suru, **Kargil**, at 2740 m, was an important trading post on two routes, from Srinagar to Leh, and to Gilgit and the lower Indus Valley. Before 1990 it was the main overnight stop on the Srinagar–Leh highway, and in 1999 the Pakistan army took control briefly of the heights surrounding the town before being forced to retreat.

From Kargil the road continues 30 km to **Shergol** – the cultural boundary between Muslim and Buddhist areas – and then passes **Mulbek**, after another 9 km, and **Namika La**, at 3720 m (known as the 'Pillar in the Sky'), before climbing to **Photu La** at 4093 m, the highest pass on the route. From here you can catch sight of the monastery at Lamayuru. The road does a series of loops to descend to **Khaltse** where it meets the milky green Indus River.

In **Lamayuru**, 10 km from Khaltse, the famous monastery is perched on a crag overlooking the Indus in a striking setting between a drained lake and high mountains. The complex, which includes a library, thought to be the oldest in the region, was founded in the 11th century and belongs to the Tibetan Kagyupa sect. The present monastery dating from the 16th century was partly destroyed in the 19th. You can still see some of the murals, the 11-headed and 1000-armed Avalokiteshvara image, along with the redecorated *Dukhang* (assembly hall). There are caves carved out of the mountain wall and some of the rooms are richly furnished with carpets, Tibetan tables and butter lamps. Overnight stays and meals can be arranged at the **Monastery Hotel** and a few other guesthouses; it's also possible to camp near the stream in a willow grove. Festivals are held in February/March and July. There are daily buses from Leh.

Rizong, 53 km away, east towards Leh, has a monastery and nunnery, which may accommodate visitors. **Saspul** village marks the wide valley from which you can reach **Alchi**

by taking a branch road across the Indus after passing some caves. **Lekir** is off the main road, 8 km after Saspul.

Further along the road you catch sight of the ruins of **Basgo** before it crosses the Chargyal Thang plain with *chortens* and *mani* walls and enters **Nimmu**. The road rejoins the Indus Valley and rises to a bare plateau to give you the first glimpse of Leh, 30 km away. **Phyang** is on a hill and finally **Spituk** is reached. See page 579 for details of monasteries.

There are check points on some routes and foreigners will need to stop and register at **Khaltse**. Visitors from Leh approach Lamayaru along this road.

Kashmir Valley listings

For Sleeping and Eating price codes and other relevant information, see Essentials pages 38-42.

Sleeping

Srinagar *p561*

The room costs quoted reflect peak-season prices; if you go in the winter, you can expect to get a hefty discount. Be prepared to haggle.

LL The Lalit Grand Palace, Gupkar Rd, a few kilometres outside the city, T0194-250 1001, www.thelalit.com. This former palace was once the residence of Kashmir's last maharajah, Hari Singh. Situated on a hillside overlooking Dal Lake, it has been tastefully kitted out with antiques befitting its history, including India's largest handmade carpet. One wing houses enormous, classically styled suites, while the other has 70 recently refurbished modern rooms. The restaurant, bar and health club are open to non-guests. It's a good place to go on a summer evening for the al fresco buffet.

AL Hotel Broadway, Maulana Azad Rd, T0194-245 9001, www.hotelbroadway.com. One of Srinagar's oldest and best-known hotels, the **Broadway**'s original 1970s interior has been well maintained. With lots of wood panelling, rooms can be a little dark. The staff are professional and polite, while the comfortable, centrally heated rooms, Wi-Fi service and city location make it popular with business travellers and journalists. It houses one of the city's only drinking spots, has an informal cinema and is attached to the city's 1st coffee shop, **Café Arabica**.

A-B Hotel Malik, Boulevard Rd, T0194-247 3692, mas_inc786@yahoo.com. One of the smaller hotels on the Boulevard, its size gives it a more personal feel. 25 decent rooms with TV, hot water and telephone. There's also travel desk for sightseeing trips.

A-C Hotel Akbar, Dal Gate, T0194-250 0507, www.hotelakbar.com. Smart, clean hotel with 36 spacious rooms arranged around a pretty rose garden. 8 of the rooms have a balcony and all come with attached bath. Restaurant, currency exchange and travel desk.

A-C Hotel Madhuban, Gagribal Rd, T0194-245 3800, www.hotelmadhuban-kashmir.net. The **Madhuban** has bags of character, with a lot of wood going on in its homely rooms. The restaurant has an attractive veranda where guests can sit out in the summer and there is a small, but well-kept garden.

C Ahdoos, Residency Rd, T0194-250 0861, ahdooshotel@yahoo.com. A Srinagar institution, **Ahdoos** backs onto the Jhelum river and is well situated for the city's classiest handicraft and shawl shops, on and around Polo view. The deluxe rooms are huge, the standard rooms are not much smaller and all have bathtubs. A good choice for those who want to get a feel of the city, rather than the more touristy area around the lake. Staff are friendly and the restaurant is renowned among locals for its Kashmiri food.

C-E Hotel Heaven Canal, Dal Gate, T0194-250 0943, sayeedyousuf@yahoo.com. A funky little place, reached via a crooked footbridge over a canal. Both upstairs and downstairs rooms front onto a shared terrace, with chairs and tables facing out over the lake – a great spot for watching the world float by over a cup of *kahwa*, out of reach of the hawkers. Recommended.

D-E Swiss Hotel Kashmir, Gagribal Rd, T0194-2472766, www.swisshotelkashmir.com. Describing itself as an 'eco-hotel' the **Swiss** has 24 rooms with attached bath and running hot water in an attractive red-painted house with a big front garden. One of the few hotels with a stated environmental policy, owner Rouf makes a point of shopping locally and using energy efficient lighting. A plan to install solar panels is on the drawing board and he's open to new ideas from travellers. Recommended.

E-F Cathay Hotel, Dal Gate, T0194-1902 5339. Stands out among the other budget guesthouses mainly for its pleasant, large garden. A row of single storey rooms with a shared terrace lie adjacent to the lawn, while the rest are in a converted house. All rooms have running hot water.

Houseboats

Houseboats are peculiar to Srinagar and can be seen moored along the shores of Dal Lake, the quieter and distant Nagin Lake and along the busy Jhelum River. They were originally thought up by the British as a ruse to get around the law that foreigners could not buy land in the state: being in the water, the boats didn't technically count as property.

In the valley's heyday the boats were well kept and delightfully cosy; today some are still lavishly decorated with antiques and traditional Kashmiri handicrafts, but others have become distinctly shabby. Still mostly family-run, they usually include all meals and come in 5 categories: deluxe, A, B, C and D. The tariff for each category is given by the **Houseboat Owners Association**, T0194-245 0326, www.houseboatowners.org, through whom you can also make bookings.

Most tourists enjoy their houseboat holidays, however a significant number complain of being ripped off in various ways. It's better to spend extra on a boat with a good reputation than to go for a bargain that is probably too good to be true.

The following all quote **AL-A**, but prices are generally negotiable if you go in person.

Chapri Tours and Travels, Nagin Lake, T(0)9418-023936, www.chapritoursandtravels.com. Recommended for houseboats and local tours.

Gurkha Houseboats, Nagin Lake, T0194-242 1001, www.nivalink.com/gurkha. The **Gurkha** group are renowned for their comfortable rooms and stylish boats on peaceful Nagin Lake. Good service and food.

Mantana, Dal Lake, Gate 2, T0194-250 1488, www.mantanakashmirtours.com. If you want to experience the old-style opulence of a traditional Kashmiri houseboat, the *Mantana* is a good option. As well as the carefully preserved, sumptuous interior, there is also an ingeniously constructed floating garden. Owned and run by a reliable family.

Marguerite, The Bundh, T0194-247 6699. A charming boat with some lovely woodcarving. The trustworthy Thulla family are great fun and as the boat is moored to riverbank, guests can come and go as they please with no need to take a *shikara*. Recommended.

Gulmarg *p564*

As with Srinagar, prices can be negotiated in the winter months, particularly for longer stays.

L-A Hotel Highlands Park, T01954-254430, www.hotelhighlandspark.com. Oozing with old-world charm, rooms and suites are decorated with Kashmiri woodcraft and rugs. Renowned for its atmosphere – the best bar in Gulmarg is here, a large yet cosy lounge, straight out of the 1930s – it's a wonderful place to unwind after a hard day on the slopes. Rooms have *bukharis* (wood stoves) to keep you warm and electric blankets are available on request. Recommended.

L-A Grand Mumtaz, near Gondola, T9013-527195, www.grandmumtazkashmir.com. Part of a Kashmir chain with big hotels and tour packages.

AL-A Nedou's Hotel, T01954-254428, www.nedoushotel.com. The oldest hotel in Gulmarg, the **Nedous** has the same cosy colonial charm as **Highlands Park**. Its rooms and suites are comfortingly old-fashioned, with spotless bathrooms. The food isn't flash, but it's home-cooked, wholesome and delicious.

B-C Hotel Yemberzal, T01954-254523, www.yemberzalhotel.com. Rooms are on the small side, but at least this means they heat up quickly. Each has its own gas heater and the bathrooms have 24-hr running hot water. If you ask for the corner room, you can enjoy a panoramic view of the mountains. The restaurant is very good and the management are extremely helpful. It's a 10-min walk to the lifts, but there's a taxi stand next door if you feel lazy.

B-D JK Tourism Huts, T(0)9419-488181. These comfortable huts come with 1-2 bedrooms, a living room and kitchen. Very good value and close to the drag-lift.

C Green Heights, T01954-254404. Slightly shabby, but the quirky staff more than compensate, making this a budget choice with character. The decent-sized rooms come with wood stoves and if you ask nicely, you might get a hot-water bottle. Close to the gondola.
D-E Raja's, T(0)9797-008107. Buried in the woods, **Raja's** colourful shack consists of 3 rooms with shared bath and can accommodate up to 9 people. Popular with long-stayers.

Pahalgam *p565*

AL Pahalgam Hotel, T01936-243252, www.pahalgamhotel.com. Tastefully decorated, upper-end hotel dating back to the 1930s spread over 1 ha, with 25 doubles and 20 suites. Swimming pool, sauna and steam room.
C-E Himalaya Hotel, T(0)9418-020814, gulzarhakeem@hotmail.com. A cosy hotel on the river with an enchanting island garden and a restaurant of repute. 12 rooms, all with attached bath and hot water some with bathtub and balcony. The comfortable sitting room has a fireplace and is a good place to make friends. The hotel is linked to a recommended trekking company, www.himalayafunandtours.com.
C-E Hotel Brown Palace, T01936-211076, www.brownpalace.in. Another decent budget option. All rooms have attached bath with hot water. Bungalows available.

Jammu *p565*

LL-A Hari Niwas Palace, Palace Rd, T0191-254 3303, www.hariniwaspalace.com. 40 a/c rooms and suites in a heritage property with elegant bar, classy restaurant and spa. Meals and drinks can be enjoyed on the immaculate lawns, with a sweeping view of the city.
A-B Asia Jammu-Tawi, Nehru Market, north of town, T0191-243 5757, www.asiahotels jammu.com. The 44 rooms are beginning to show their age a little, but this Jammu stalwart has an excellent Chinese restaurant, bar, currency exchange and a clean pool. There is also a function room, so if you need peace and quiet it's worth checking if there are any weddings going on. Close to the airport.
A-B Jehlum Resorts, Bahu Plaza, T0191-247 0079, www.traveltokashmir.com. A comfortable option near the railway station with a bar, multi-cuisine restaurant, travel desk and ATM.
B KC Residency, Vir Marg, T0191-252 0770, www.kcresidency.com. Rising from the heart of Jammu, the KC tower is a good place to stay if you have a day or so to check out the city. There are 61 good-quality a/c rooms, a currency exchange, and health club specializing in Ayurvedic massage, all extraordinarily crowned by a superb, multi-cuisine revolving restaurant.
C-E Tourist Reception Centre, Vir Marg, T0191-257 9554. Set back from the main road, the TRC has 173 rooms with bath ranging in price and quality arranged around well-kept gardens. The best accommodation is in Blocks NA and A. The restaurant has a very good reputation, in particular for its Kashmiri food.
D Jewel's, Jewel Chowk, T0191-252 0801, jewels@vsnl.com. Located in a busy, congested area, however, the 18 a/c rooms are good value in an increasingly expensive city. There's a fast-food restaurant and bar.
E Kranti Hotel, near the railway station, T0191-247 0525. One of the better budget hotels in the railway area with 45 clean rooms with attached bath and a restaurant.

Vaishno Devi *p565*

B Asia Vaishnodevi, Katra, T01991-232061, www.asiavaishnodevi.com. 37 a/c rooms, restaurant, transport to Banganga.
C-D Ambica, Katra, T01991-232062, www.hotelambika.com. 58 rooms, a/c, *puja* shop and health centre.
E Prem, Main Bazar, Katra, T01991-232014. Rooms with hot water and a fire, adequate.
E Tourist Bungalow, Katra, T01991-232009. 42 basic but clean rooms.
F Dormitories, at the halfway point to Vaishno Devi. Simple rooms provide sheets.
F Retiring Centre, Katra, T01991-232309. Rooms and very cheap dorm, near bus stand.

Eating

Srinagar *p561*

While Kashmiris generally prefer to eat at home, being a tourist town, Srinagar has its fair share of good restaurants catering for all tastes.

Traditional Kashmiri food is centred around meat, with mutton generally being the favoured flesh. The traditional 36-course banquet served at weddings is known as a *wazwan* and you will find several of its signature dishes on the menu in restaurants where Kashmiri food is served. *Yakhnee* is a delicious mutton stew cooked in a spiced curd sauce. *Goshtabas* and *rishtas* are meatballs made from pounded (not ground) meat, which makes a big difference in consistency. *Goshtabas* come in a curd sauce; *rishtas* in red sauce. *Roganjosh* is made with chicken or mutton and is curd based, owing its red colour to red Kashmiri chilies. *Hakh* is the Kashmiri version of spinach and *nadroo* are lotuses, usually served in a *yakhnee* sauce.

Qayaam Chowk street, close to Dalgate, is locally known as 'the barbeque'. It's lined with small restaurants serving *sheesh* and *seekh* kebabs, accompanied by an array of delicious, homemade Kashmiri chutneys. Recommended.

TT Café Robusta, Maulana Azad Rd, near Polo View. Competes with nearby **Café Arabica** (in the Broadway Hotel) to attract Srinagar's latte lovers. Aside from pizza, kebabs and cake, you can also sample a *shisha* (Middle Eastern water pipe) with a range of flavoured tobaccos on offer. Bring your laptop and make use of the Wi-Fi.

TT Char Chinar, Boulevard Rd, near Brein village. You'll need to take a *shikara* to get to this houseboat restaurant, moored on a tiny island in Dal Lake. Named after the 4 giant *chinar* trees that grow there, the food is average, but it's a perfect place to sit in peace with a good book on a sunny day.

TT Mughal Darbar, Residency Rd. Popular with middle-class locals, the cosy Mughal Darbar offers multi-cuisine fare, specializing in Kashmiri *wazwan*.

TT Tao Café, Residency Rd. A popular hangout with local journalists, politicians and artists, the **Tao** serves decent Kashmiri and Chinese food, as well as Tibetan *momos* and various snacks. Its attractive gardens make it a good summer spot.

TT Vishal Punjabi Vaishno Bhojanalaya, Boulevard Rd. A haven for vegetarians in a city of meat-eaters, the Vishal gets the thumbs-up from fastidious Indian tourists for its cleanliness and pure veg fare.

T Shakti Sweets and **Modern Sweets**, Residency Rd. If you are invited to a Kashmiri home, a box of *burfi* will go down well as a gift. Both serve great snack food, such as *channa bhatura* and *masala dosa*.

Gulmarg *p564*

Most hotels serve their own food but some close their kitchens in low season. In the bazar there is a row of *dhabas* serving a wide variety of Indian vegetarian food including *thalis*, *dosas* and *punjabi*. Outside seating.

TT Sahara Hotel, next to **Yemberzal Hotel**. Well worth venturing out in the cold for. The owner spent 15 years working as a chef in Saudi Arabia, Japan and China, so has a wide repertoire. If you need a break from Indian food, the continental choice here is good, especially the chicken champion.

T Lala's, close to the JK Tourism Huts (see Sleeping). Good, honest home-cooked food.

Jammu *p565*

The best eateries tend to be found in the upmarket hotels. However, there are some good snack places dotted around town, which can be fun to check out.

TT Smokin' Joes Pizza, Bahu Plaza, near the railway station. Very acceptable veg and non-veg pizza and pasta, but strictly no pork. Take away and home delivery also available.

T Amritsarian di Hatti, Raghunath Bazar. Good and popular vegetarian, also sells sweets.

T Barista, KC Cineplex and City Square Mall. Popular Indian café chain, also sells sandwiches and cakes.

T India Coffee House, Exhibition Ground.

T Kailash, in Raghunath Bazar. Vegetarian.

Vaishno Devi *p565*

Excellent vegetarian food is available – curd and *paneer* (curd cheese) dishes are especially good. For non-*dhaba* food try the 2 vegetarian fast food places on the main street. Both are clean and good. No alcohol.

O Shopping

Srinagar *p561*

If you arrived in Srinagar without your thermals or you're craving a bar of chocolate, a bowl of cornflakes, marmite on toast or just about any other Western goods, then look no further than **Harker's Pick** and **Choose Supermarket** on Residency Rd, for all your expat needs.

Gulshan Bookstore, a few mins' walk from Residency Rd, towards Lal Chowk. Here you will find all manner of books about Kashmir, some of

The most expensive spice in the world

Pampore, 16 km from Srinagar, is the centre of Kashmir's saffron industry. Saffron, a species of crocus (*Crocus sativus*), grows here in abundance, and in a few other places in the world, and is harvested by hand. Within each purple bloom, the three orange-red anthers yield pure saffron. Over 4500 blooms make one ounce (28 g) of the spice, so the price of this delicate flavouring and colouring in cooking is high (once far more valuable than gold). Its value has led the Indian government to set up a saffron research farm at Sangla in Himachal Pradesh.

The precious orange-coloured dye was used by royalty and the colour saffron was chosen by monks for their robes after the Buddha's death.

Enterprising traders have found a way to disguise dyed shreds of newspaper as saffron. You can test by rubbing a strand or two in a few drops of water on your palm: fake saffron will turn to red paste almost immediately, while the genuine article takes longer to stain and remains yellow.

them extremely rare. If you are interested in the political situation, it's an excellent place for books on Kashmir's history.

Mahatta's Photographic Store, next to **Suffering Moses**. Worth stopping by for its old-world charm, its history and above all for the priceless visual memory of old Srinagar it houses. Founded in 1918, this was once the place to have your portrait taken and was patronized by the elite of the day. The walls are lined with large prints of the city, taken up in the 1930s and 1940s. They are not for sale, but they have produced a booklet, 'Srinagar Views 1934-1965' for Rs 300.

Handicrafts

There are plenty of handicraft shops, particularly around Dal Lake and Dalgate, but beware of touts who are on commission. Much of what is sold is not even Kashmiri: inferior quality papier mâché products from Bihar and shawls from Amritsar have flooded the market and are bought merrily by tourists who don't know the difference. As a result, along with the troubles of the past 20 years, the valley's handicraft industry has been tragically eroded.

For a real understanding of Kashmiri craftwork and to support the local industry, call into any of the quality shops on **Polo View** or the **Bund**. The prices may seem high, but the quality, authenticity is guaranteed and shopkeepers here do not usually pay commission. Shopkeepers here are rather more restrained than the average Kashmiri salesman making it a pleasant place to wander around.

Asia Crafts, next to **Suffering Moses**, (see below). Very fine embroidery and genuine Kashmiri carpets, but much of its stock is now sold in New Delhi.

Habib Asian Carpets, Zaldagar Chowk, Downtown, T0194-247 8640. If you are serious about buying a genuine Kashmiri carpet, this is one of the few companies that has its workshop in the city.

Heritage Woodcrafts, on the way to Shalimar gardens. It's worth making the trip here for the carved walnut wood. Stuffed with fine pieces including some antiques, the authenticity of the work is guaranteed by the on-site workshop.

Sadiq's Handicrafts, next to **Tao Café** (see Eating). Owned by the same family as **Suffering Moses** and is almost as much a museum as a shop; many of the antique treasures are not for sale and Mr Sadiq, a man passionate about art, will happily explain their history to you. Prices in both shops are fixed and there is no pressure to buy.

Suffering Moses, next to **Mughal Darbar** restaurant (see Eating). Famous for its exquisite papier mâché goods. The curious name was apparently awarded to the owner's father by the British, who were impressed by the amount of suffering that went into each work.

▲ Activities and tours

Srinagar *p561*

Athena Houseboats, opposite **Hotel Duke**, Dal Lake, Srinagar, T0194-476957. One of the larger houseboat operators on Dal Lake, **Athena** has voluminous boats that can comfortably sleep larger groups. Excellent service, with real integrity: discourages hawkers and tries to support only legitimate retail and onward tourism. Recommended.

Transport

Srinagar *p561*

Air **Srinagar Airport**, 14 km south, T0194-230 3000. Taxi to town: Rs 300. Stringent security checks on roads plus 2 hrs' check-in at airport. Tight on hand luggage but you can generally get away with a laptop. Daily flights to **Delhi**, most via **Jammu**, with: **Air India**, T0194-245 0257, airport T0194-243 0334; **Jet Airways**, T0194-248 0801, airport T0194-243 1521; **Kingfisher**, T1-800 180 0101; **Spicejet**, T1600-180 3333, 4 per week; **GoAir** T1800-222111, 6 a week. To **Leh** with **Air India**, daily. **Mumbai**, with **Kingfisher**, T0124-284 4700.

Bus Srinagar is on NH1A linked to the rest of India by 'all-weather' roads, some through superb scenery. To **Jammu** (293 km), by a narrow mountain road, often full of lorries and military convoys, takes 12 hrs; few stops for food.

Some long-distance **State Roadways** buses to Delhi, Chandigarh and Amritsar to Jammu continue to Srinagar. **J&KSRTC**, TRC, Srinagar, T0194-245 5107. Summer 0600-1800, winter 0700-1700.

Bus to **Kargil** (alternate days in summer), **Leh** (434 km). **Gulmarg**, daily bus in ski season from Tourist Reception Centre, returning in the evening. Taxis charge around Rs 1200 for same-day return. Or take **J&KSRTC** bus to **Tangmarg**, 8 km before Gulmarg and take a *sumo* from there, Rs 20.

Ferry *Shikaras* (boats): Rs 50 per hr.

Train The most convenient railhead is **Jammu Tawi** with coach (12 hrs) and taxi transfer (9 hrs). **Govt TRC**, 0700-1900. T0191-243 1582 for reservation of 2nd-class sleeper and a/c only. Summer 0830-1900, winter 1000-1800. Connections with several cities including **Guwahati**, **Kolkata**, **Mumbai**, **Chennai** and **Delhi**.

Jammu *p565*

Air **Rambagh Airport**, 6 km. Transport to town: taxis (Rs 200) and auto-rickshaws. No hand luggage allowed. **Air India**, TRC, Vir Marg, T0191-254 2735, airport T0191-243 0449, flies to **Delhi** and **Srinagar** daily; **Leh** (Thu, Sat). **Jet Airways, KC Residency Hotel**, T0191-257 4312, airport T0191-245 3999; to **Delhi** and **Srinagar** daily. Also **Spicejet**, T1600-180 3333, and **Kingfisher**, T1-800-180 0101.

Bus *Sumos* run to **Katra** from the station cost Rs 900 (Rs 1200 a/c). **J&KSRTC**, TRC, Vir Marg, T0191-257 9554 (1000-1700), general bus stand, T0191-257 7475 (0400-2000) direct buses to **Srinagar** (293 km), **Katra** (for Vaishno Devi), **Pathankot** and **Kishtwar**. Punjab Roadways T0191-254 2782. To **Delhi** (586 km), daily. **Srinagar** buses leave from the railway station, usually 0600-0700.

Taxi Unmetered, T0191-243 3485. Tourist taxis, T0191-254 6266.

Train 5 km from centre; allow at least 30 mins by auto. Enquiries T0191-245 3027. To **Delhi** (**OD**): *Jammu Tawi Mail 14034*, 1545, 14¼ hrs; *Jaipur Exp 12414*, 1815, 10½ hrs. **Delhi** (**ND**): *Jammu Tawi Indore Malwa Exp 12920*, 0900, 10½ hrs; *Jhelum Exp 11078*, 2145, 12¼ hrs; *Shalimar Exp 14646*, 2100, 13¼ hrs; *Rajdhani Exp 12426*, Sat 2030, 9 hrs. **Kolkata** (**Kolkota**): *Jammu Tawi Exp 13152*, 1915, 45 hrs.

Vaishno Devi *p565*

Buses and taxis leave from the general bus stand, Jammu (or the railway station at peak season) and go to **Katra** (48 km); Rs 25, a/c Rs 55; taxi Rs 500 for 4.

Directory

Srinagar *p561*

Useful contacts Ambulance: T0194-247 4591. **Fire**: T0194-247 2222. **Police**: T100. **Foreigners' Registration Office**: Supt of Police, Residency Rd. 1000-1600.

Jammu *p565*

Banks State Bank of India, Hari Market, among several. **Post** GPO: Pacca Danga. Post Offices in Old Palaces, near Dogra Art Gallery and Raghunath Temple. **Medical services** Hospital: T0191-254 7637. **Useful contacts** Fire: T101. **Police**: T100. **Foreigners' Registration Office**: Supt of Police, Canal Rd, T0191-254 2676. Foreigners must register.

Ladakh

→ Colour map 1, A3. Population: 175,000. Altitude: 2500-4500 m, passes 4000-6000 m, peaks up to 7500 m. The mountains of Ladakh – literally 'many passes' – may not be as typically spectacular as some parts of the high Himalaya for, as even the valleys are at an altitude of 3500 m, the summits are only 3000 m higher. Because it is desert there is little snow on them and they look like big brown hills, dry and dusty, with clusters of willows and desert roses along the streams. Yet for thousands of visitors Ladakh is a completely magical place, remote, with delightful, gentle, ungrasping people. *▸▸ For listings, see pages 588-594.*

Ins and outs

Getting there and around **Inner Line Permits** are available for areas that would normally be restricted but are open to tourists include Rizong, Likir, Phyang, Shey, Thiksey, Chemrey and Tak-thok *gompas*. Permits are available from the District Commissioner's office in Leh (see Directory, page 594). **Special Entry Permits** for the Nubra and Shyok Valleys, Dha Hanu, Khardung La, Tso-moriri and Pangong Tso cost US$20, while trekkers in the Hemis High Altitude Park must pay Rs 25 (Indians Rs 10) per day. As a matter of course you should carry your passport with you since Ladakh is a sensitive border region. It's also worth carrying several photocopies of your passport and permits, as some checkpoints demand a copy. **Note** Given the darkness of many buildings even at midday it is worth taking a torch wherever you go; a must at night. *▸▸ See Transport, page 593.*

Climate The temperature can drop to -30°C in Leh and Kargil and -50°C in Dras, remaining sub-zero from December to February. Yet on clear sunny days in the summer, it can be scorching hot and you can easily get sunburnt; take plenty of sun cream. Rainfall is only 50 mm annually and there are even occasional dust storms.

Background

Until recently Ladakhi society has generally been very introverted and the economy surprisingly self-sufficient. An almost total lack of precipitation has meant that cultivation must rely on irrigation. The rivers have been harnessed but with difficulty as the deep gorges presented a problem. Altitude and topography determine the choice of crop and farming is restricted to the areas immediately around streams and rivers. Barley forms the staple food while peas are the most common vegetable and apples and apricots the most popular fruits – the latter are dried for winter sustenance, while the kernel yields oil for burning in prayer-lamps. Because of the harshness of the climate and lack of rain, the cropping season usually lasts from April to October. At lower altitudes, grape, mulberry and walnut are grown.

Livestock is precious, especially the yak which provides meat, milk for butter, hair and hide for tents, boots, ropes and dung for fuel. Goats, especially in the eastern region, produce fine *pashm* for export. Animal transport is provided by yaks, ponies, Bactrian camels and the broad-backed *hunia* sheep. The Zanskar pony is fast and strong and used for transport – and for the special game of Ladakhi polo. Travellers venturing out of Leh are likely to see villagers using traditional methods of cultivation with the help of *dzos* and donkeys and using implements that have not changed for centuries.

Cut off from the outside world for six months a year, Ladakh also developed a very distinct culture. Polyandry (where a woman has more than one husband) was common but many men became *lamas* (monks) and a few women *chomos* (nuns). Most people depended on subsistence agriculture but the harsh climate contributed to very high death rates and a stable population. That is rapidly changing. Imported goods are increasingly widely available and more and more people are taking part in the monetary economy. Ladakh and its capital Leh have only been open to tourists since 1974, but some feel there are already too many; the pitfalls of modern society are all too evident in the mounds of plastic rubbish strewn along the roadsides.

Leh → *For listings, see pages 588-594. Colour map 1, A3. Phone code: 01982. Population: 27,500. Altitude: 3500 m.*

Mysterious dust-covered Leh sits in a fertile side valley of the Indus, about 10 km from the river. Encircled by stark awe-inspiring mountains with the cold desert beyond, it is the nearest experience to Tibet in India. The old Palace sits precariously on the hill to the north and looms over Leh. The wide Main Bazar Street (circa 1840s), which once accommodated caravans, has a colourful vegetable market where remarkably unpushy Ladakhi women sell local produce on the street side while they knit or chat. Makeshift craft and jewellery stalls line parts of Fort Road to the east to attract summer visitors along with Kashmiri shopkeepers who have come in search of greener pastures. The Old Village, mainly to the east of the Main Street, with its maze of narrow lanes, sits on the hillside below the palace and is worth exploring.

Ins and outs

Getting there For seven to eight months in the year Leh is cut off by snow and the sole link with the outside world is by air. Tickets are in high demand so it is essential to book well ahead (you can do this from home on the internet). From mid-June to the end of September (weather permitting) the Manali-Leh highway opens to traffic, bringing travellers to the New Bus Stand south of town. Jeeps wait at both the airport and bus stand to take you to town.

Getting around Most hotels are within a few minutes' walk of the Main Bazar Street around which Leh's activities are concentrated. All the places of interest in Leh itself can also be tackled on foot by most visitors though those arriving by air are urged to acclimatize for 48 hours before exerting themselves. For visiting monasteries and spots out of town arrange a jeep or taxi. ▸▸ *See Transport, page 593.*

Tourist information Jammu and Kashmir Tourism ⓘ *2 km south on Airport Rd, T01982-252094, www.jktourism.org; or try the more convenient office on Fort Rd, T01982- 253462, 1000-1600.*

History

The city developed as a trading post and market, attracting a wide variety of merchants – from Yarkand, Kashgar, Kashmir, Tibet and North India. Tea, salt, household articles, wool and semi-precious stones were all traded in the market. Buddhism travelled along the Silk Road and the Kashmir and Ladakh feeder, which has also seen the passage of soldiers, explorers and pilgrims, forerunners of the tourists who today contribute most to the urban economy.

Sights

Leh Palace ⓘ *sunrise to sunset, and sometimes 1500-1800, Rs 100*, has been described as a miniature version of Lhasa's Potala Palace. Built in the mid-16th century, the palace was partly in ruins by the 19th century. It has nine storeys, sloping buttresses and projecting wooden balconies. From the town below it is dazzling in the morning sun and ghostly at night. Built by King Singe Namgyal and still owned by the royal family, it is now unoccupied – they live in the palace at Stok. Visible damage was caused during Zorawar Singh's invasion from Kashmir in the last century. Be careful of the hazardous holes in the floor. After a steep climb some find the palace disappointing, but the views from the roof are exceptional. A part of the palace is a **museum**. Like the Lhasa Potala Palace it has numerous rooms, steps and narrow passages lined with old *thangkas*, paintings and arms. The central prayer room (not in use; usually locked but opened on request), has religious texts lining the walls. The Archaeological Survey of India is responsible for restoration and you may be able to watch work in progress. There are many painted scrolls, murals and old manuscripts in the ruined palace.

South of the palace, the architecturally striking **Leh Mosque** in the main bazar is worth visiting – the inner section is not open to women visitors. The Sunni Muslim mosque is believed to stand on land granted by King Deldan Namgyal in the 1660s; his grandmother was the Muslim Queen of Ladakh.

1 Leh orientation

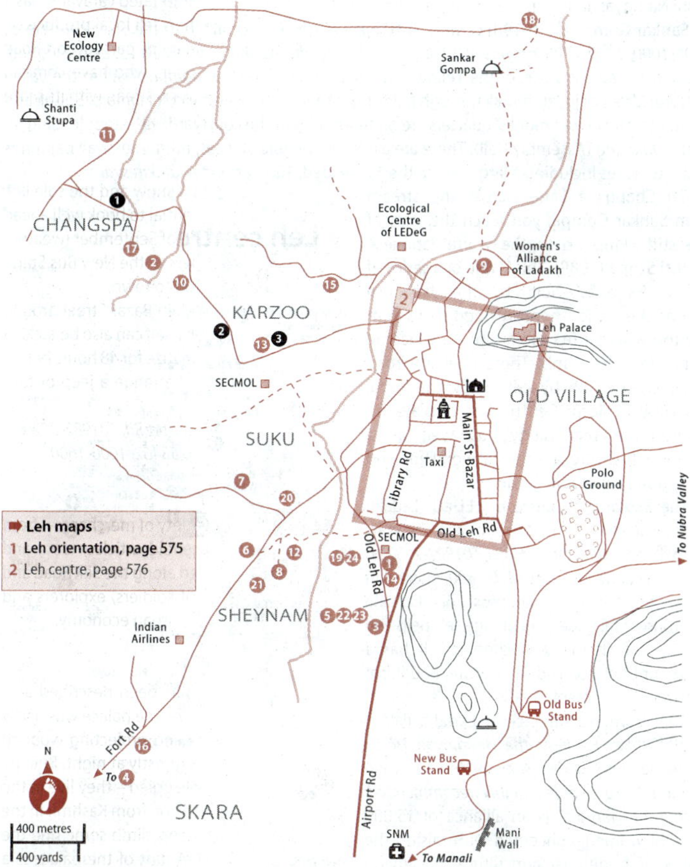

Sleeping
Grand Dragon **1**
Goba **2**
Harmit Hut **5**
Hills View **3**
Larisa **4**
Kangla **22**
Lharimo **6**
Lhung-Se-Jung **7**
Lung Snon **8**
New Antelope Guest House **9**
Omasila **10**
Oriental **11**
Padma **12**
Padmaling **13**
Rainbow **15**
Remo **16**
Ri-Rab **17**
Shambhala **14**
Shynam **19**
Silver Cloud **18**
Spic-n-Span **24**
Tsomo-Ri **20**
Wari-La **23**
Zarla **21**

Eating
Booklovers **1**
Elements **2**
Mona Lisa & Bakery **3**

The **Soma Gompa** (New Monastery, 1957) in the main street of the Old Village was built to commemorate the 2500th anniversary of the birth of Buddha. The remains of the **Leh Gompa** houses a large golden Buddha.

The 15th-century **Tsemo Gompa** ('Red' Temple) ⓘ *0700-0900, Rs 25*, is a strenuous walk north of the city and has a colossal two-storey-high image of Maitreya, flanked by figures of Avalokitesvara (right) and Manjusri (left). It was founded by the Namgyal rulers and a portrait of Tashi Namgyal hangs on the left at the entrance.

Sankar Gompa (17th-18th centuries) ⓘ *3 km north of the centre, past the Himalayan Hotel, 0700-1000, 1700-1900, prayers at 1830 with chanting, drums and cymbals, Rs 25; before visiting, check at the tourist office*, of the Yellow Hat Sect, is one of the few *gompas* built in the valley bottom; it's an enjoyable walk through fields from town. It houses the chief *lama* of Spituk and 20 others. The newer monks' quarters are on three sides of the courtyard with steps leading up to the *dukhang* (Assembly Hall). There are a number of gold statues, numerous wall paintings and sculptures including a large one of the 11-headed, 1000-armed *Avalokitesvara*.

On Changspa Lane, across the stream from Sankar Gompa, you reach the start of the stiff climb up to the white Japanese **Shanti Stupa** (1989). This is one of a series of 'Peace Pagodas' built by the Japanese around the world. There are good views from the top where a tea room offers a welcome sight after the climb. There is also a road which is accessible by jeep. Below the *stupa*, the **New Ecology Centre**, has displays on 'appropriate technology', as well as a handicrafts centre, a technical workshop and an organic vegetable garden.

The **Ecological Centre of LEDeG** (Ladakh Ecological Development Group) and the **craft shop** ⓘ *next to Tsemo La Hotel, T01982-253221, www.ledeg.org, Mon-Sat 1400-1800*, opened in 1984 to spread awareness of Ladakhi environmental issues, encourage self-help and the use of alternative technology. It has a library of books on Ladakhi culture, Buddhism and the environment.

The **Women's Alliance of Ladakh** (WAL) ⓘ *off Sankar Rd near the Himalayan Hotel, T01982-250293, video shown Mon-Sat 1500 (minimum 10 people), highly recommended, restaurant Mon-Sat*, is an alliance of 15,000 Ladakhi women, concerned with raising the status of traditional agriculture, preserving the traditionally high status of women which is being eroded in the modern sector, and creating an alternative development model based on self-reliance for Ladakh. The centre has a restaurant selling local and organic foods, and a craft shop. They hold spectacular festivals, cultural shows, dances, etc which are advertised around Leh; it's mainly aimed at

2 Leh centre

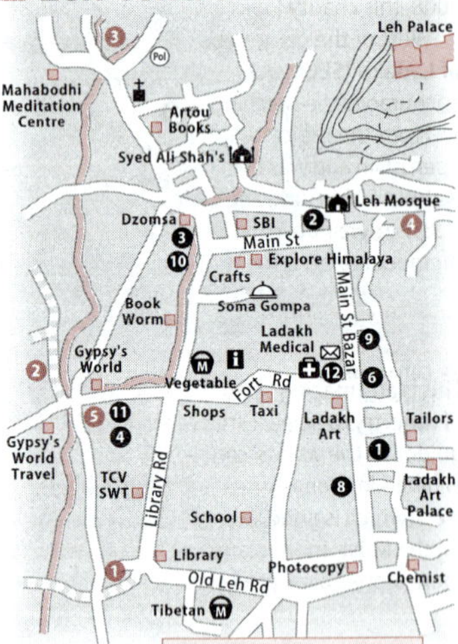

➡ **Leh maps**
1 Leh orientation, page 575
2 **Leh centre, page 576**

Not to scale

Sleeping
Bijoo **1**
Indus **2**
Kang-lha Chen **3**
Old Ladakh **4**
Yak Tail **5**

Eating
Amdo II **1**
Budshah Inn **2**
Devi Tibetan **3**
Dreamland **4**
Hi Life **4**
Kokonor **6**
La Montessori **8**
Nepali **9**
Pumpernickel **10**
Summer Harvest **11**
Tibetan Friend's Corner **12**

Volunteering

If you are interested in voluntary work, get in touch with the various organizations in Leh, such as **SECMOL**, or **LEDeG** (see below). There is a range of possibilities in and around Leh for potential volunteers, from teaching English to construction work. Alternatively, contact **Ladakh Project**, Apple Barn, Week, Dartington, Devon TQ9 6JP, UK, or 850 Talbot Avenue, Albany, CA 94796, USA. Farm volunteers with the Ladakh Project are welcome from May to October, for a minimum of a one-month to stay and work with a Ladakh farming family. A contribution of about US$200 plus a nominal amount for daily lodging is expected.

local people, but all visitors are welcome. In conjunction with the Ladakh Project, WAL runs a **Farm Volunteer Scheme** (see box, above). Western volunteers live and work on a Ladakhi farm, helping to boost the status of traditional agriculture. An interesting video 'Ancient Futures' tracing ecologically sensitive Ladakh's changing face over 20 years.

The **The Donkey Sanctuary**, www.donkeysanctuary.in, is highly recommended. Opened in 2008, this charity looks after 40-60 donkeys at any one time – well worth a visit.

West of the centre, the non-profit making **Students' Educational and Cultural Movement of Ladakh (SECMOL)** ⓘ *Karzoo, with an office on Old Leh Rd, T01982-252421, www.secmol.org*, encourages the teaching of Ladakhi history, culture and crafts.

From the radio station there are two long *mani* walls. **Rongo Tajng** is in the centre of the open plain and was built as a memorial to Queen Skalzang Dolma by her son Dalden Namgyal. It is about 500 m long and was built in 1635. The stones have been meticulously carved. The other, a 350-m wall down the hill, is believed to have been built by Tsetan Namgyal in 1785 as a memorial to his father the king.

Leh to Manali road → *For listings, see pages 588-594. Colour map 1, A3.*

This is an amazing stretch of road with some fascinating monasteries en route. If you are short of time, try to at least stop at Thiksey and Hemis. On all trips, it's best to go with a local Ladakhi guide as the *lamas* can refuse admission if unaccompanied. Camera flash is usually not allowed in monasteries to reduce damage to wall paintings and *thangkas*. If you hire a car or jeep (which is good value when shared by four), you can visit the places below in a day. Carry a torch. Most monasteries expect a donation of Rs 25. The same advice applies to the monasteries along the Srinagar Road.

Choglamsar

Choglamsar, south of Leh on the east bank of the Indus, is a green oasis with poplars and willows where there are golf links and a polo ground as well as horticultural nurseries. Some village houses use solar energy. The Central Institute of Buddhist Studies is here with a specialist library. Past the Tibetan refugee camps, children's village and the arts and crafts centre, the Choglamsar Bridge crosses the Indus. The **Chochot Yugma Imambara**, a few minutes' walk from the bridge, is worth a visit. Buses depart Leh hourly from 0800-1800.

Stok

Across Choglamsar Bridge, 16 km south of Leh, is the royal palace dating from the 1840s when the King of Ladakh was deposed by the invading Dogra forces. The last king died in 1974 but his widow continues to live here. His son continues the royal line and ascended to the throne in July 1993. The palace is a rambling building where only a dozen of the 80 rooms are used. The small **Palace Museum** ⓘ *May-Oct 0800-1900, Rs 25*, with three rooms, is a showpiece for the royal *thangkas*, many 400 years old, crown jewels, dresses, coins, *peraks* (headdresses) encrusted with turquoise and lapis lazuli as well as religious objects.

The **gompa**, a short distance away, has some ritual dance masks. Tsechu is in February. A three-hour walk up the valley behind Stok takes you to some extraordinary mountain scenery dominated by the 6121-m-high Stok Kangri.

There is an **archery contest** in July. Below the museum there is a clean hotel with good views. Buses to Stok leave Leh at 0730 and 1700. Taxis from the Leh central taxi stand are available at fixed rates at any time.

Shey

ⓘ *Palace open all day; try to be there 0700-0900, 1700-1800 when prayers are chanted, Rs 15.*

Until the 16th century, Shey was the royal residence, located at an important vantage point in the Indus Valley. Kings of Leh were supposed to be born in the monastery. The royal family moved to Stok in order to escape advancing Dogra forces from Kashmir who came to exploit the trade in pashmina wool. Shey, along with Thikse, is also regarded as an auspicious place for cremation.

Much of the palace and the fort high above it have fallen into disrepair and are dirty though the wall paintings in the palace have now been restored. The palace *gompa* with its 17.5-m-high blue-haired Maitreya Buddha, imitating the one at Tsemo Gompa, is attended by Drukpa monks from Hemis. It is made of copper and brass but splendidly gilded and studded with precious gem stones. The large victory *stupa* is topped with gold. Extensive grounds covering the former lake bed to the east contain a large number of *chortens* in which cremated ashes of important monks, members of the royal family and the devout were buried. A newer temple houses another old giant Buddha statue. There are several rock carvings; particularly noteworthy is that of five *dhyani* Buddhas (circa eighth century) at the bottom of the hill. The small hotel below the *gompa* has spartan but clean rooms. It is 15 km southeast of Leh on the Indus River or can be reached along a stone path from Thikse. Hourly buses depart Leh 0800-1800.

Thikse

ⓘ *Rs 25, hourly buses from Leh 0800-1800.*

Situated 25 km south of Leh on a crag overlooking the flood plain on the east bank of the Indus, this is one of the most imposing monasteries in Ladakh and was part of the original Gelugpa order in the 15th century. The 12-storey monastery, with typical tapering walls painted deep red, ochre and white, has 10 temples, a nunnery and 60 *lamas* in residence whose houses cling to the hillside below. The complex contains numerous *stupas*, statues, *thangkas*, wall paintings (note the fresco of the 84 Mahasiddhas, high above) swords and a large pillar engraved with the Buddha's teachings.

The new temple interior is dominated by a giant 15-m-high Buddha figure near the entrance. The principal *Dukhang* (assembly hall) right at the top of the building has holes in the wall for storing religious texts; views from the roof are good. The temple with the Guardian Deities, which in other monasteries may be closed to women, is open to all since parts of the offending figures are covered. The *Dukhang* lower down has Tibetan-style wall paintings. Thikse is a good place to watch religious ceremonies, usually at 0630 or 1200. An early start by taxi makes even the first possible, or it's possible to stay overnight (see Sleeping, page 590). They are preceded by the playing of large standing drums and long horns similar to *alpenstock*. Masked dances are performed during special festivals.

Stakna

Across the valley on a hill, Stakna is the earliest Drukpa monastery, built before Hemis though its decorations are not as ancient. It is also called 'Tiger's nose' because of the shape of the hill site. This small but well-kept monastery has a beautiful silver-gilt *chorten* in the assembly hall, installed around 1955, and some interesting paintings in the dark temple at the back. No need for a local guide as the *lamas* are always willing to open the doors. There are excellent views of the Indus Valley and the Zanskar range.

Hemis

On the west bank of the Indus, 45 km south of Leh, the monastery, built on a green hillside surrounded by spectacular mountain scenery, is hidden in a gorge. The **Drukpa Monastery** was founded by Stagsang Raspa during the reign of Senge Namgyal (circa 1630). It is the biggest and wealthiest in Ladakh and is a 'must' for visitors. You walk past *chortens* and sections of *mani* walls to enter the complex through the east gate which leads into a large 40 m by 20 m courtyard. Colourful flags flutter in the breeze from the four posts against the white walls of the buildings. On the north side are two assembly halls approached by a flight of steep stone steps. The large *Dukhang* to the right used for ceremonies is rather plain; the smaller *Tshogskhang* (main temple) contains some silver gilt *chortens* and a Kashmiri lacquered-wood throne. The murals in the verandas depicting guardian deities, the *kalachakra* (wheel of life) and 'Lords of the four quarters' are well preserved. A staircase alongside the *Tshogskhang* leads to a roof terrace where there are a number of shrines including a bust of the founder. The *Lakhang* (chapel) has ancient Kashmiri bronzes and silver *chortens*, an important library of Tibetan-style books and an impressive collection of *thangkas*, the largest of which is displayed every 12 years (next 2016). The heavy silk *thangka* is beautifully embroidered in bright coloured threads and pearls.

There is a pleasant 3-km walk uphill to another *gompa*. A stay in Hemis overnight enables you to attend early-morning prayers, a moving experience and strongly recommended. Bus services have improved making a day trip possible.

Along the Srinagar road → *For listings, see pages 588-594. Colour map 1, A3.*

The Srinagar road out of Leh passes through a flat dusty basin mostly occupied by army encampments with mile after mile of wire fencing. The scenery is stunning and as with the Leh-Manali Road, is punctuated with monasteries. A bus leaves Leh each afternoon for Alchi (see below), allowing access to most of the sites described in this section.

Spituk

Standing on a conical hill, some 8 km from Leh, Spituk was founded in the 11th century. The buildings themselves, including three chapels, date from the 15th century and are set in a series of tiers with courtyards and steps. The Yellow-Hat Gelugpa monks created the precedent in Ladakh for building on mountain tops rather than valley floors. You can get good views of the countryside around.

The long 16th- to 17th-century *dukhang* (assembly hall) is the largest building and has two rows of seats along the length of the walls to a throne at the far end. Sculptures and miniature *chortens* are displayed on the altar. Spituk has a collection of ancient Jelbagh masks, icons and arms including some rescued from the Potala Palace in Lhasa.

Also 16th- to 17th-century, the **Mahakal Temple**, higher up the hill, contains a shrine of Vajrabhairava, often mistaken for the Goddess Kali. The terrifying face is only unveiled in January, during the **Gustor festival**. The Srinagar buses can drop you on the highway (four daily, 20 minutes).

Phyang

Phyang, 16 km from Leh, dominates a side valley with a village close by. It belongs to the Red-Hat Kagyupa sect, with its 16th-century Gouon monastery built by the founder of the Namgyal Dynasty which is marked by a flagstaff at the entrance. It houses hundreds of statues including some Kashmiri bronzes (circa 14th century), *thangkas* and manuscript copies of the

Kangyur and Tengyur. The temple walls have colourful paintings centering on the eight emblems of happiness. Phyang is the setting for a spectacular July **Tseruk festival** with masked dancing. There are three buses daily (one hour); the morning bus allows you to explore the valley and walk back to Leh, but the afternoon bus only allows 20 minutes for visit (last return, around 1700).

Phyang to Nimmu

About 2 km before Nimmu the Indus enters an impressive canyon before the Zanskar joins it, a good photo opportunity. As the road bends, a lush green oasis with lines of poplars comes into view. The mud brick houses of Nimmu have grass drying on the flat rooftops to provide fodder for the winter. A dry stone *mani* wall runs along the road; beyond Nimmu the walls become 2 m wide in places with innumerable *chortens* alongside. The rocky outcrops on the hills to the right appear like a natural fortress.

Basgo

The road passes through Basgo Village with the ruins of a Buddhist citadel impressively sited on a spur overlooking the Indus Valley. It served as a royal residence for several periods between the 15th and 17th centuries. The **fort palace** was once considered almost impregnable having survived a three-year siege by Tibetan and Mongol armies in the 17th century.

Among the ruins only two temples have survived. The higher **Maitreya Temple** (mid-16th century) built by Tashi Namgyal's son contains a very fine Maitreya statue at the rear of the hall, flanked by *bodhisattvas*. Some murals from the early period illustrating the Tibetan Buddhist style have also survived on the walls and ceiling; among the Buddhas and *bodhisattvas* filled with details of animals, birds and mermaids, appear images of Hindu divinities. The 17th-century **Serzang Temple** (gold and copper), with a carved doorway, is the other and contains another large Maitreya image whose head rises through the ceiling into a windowed box-like structure which can be seen by climbing up to the gallery above. The murals look faded and have been damaged by water.

Lekir (Likir)

Some 5.5 km from Basgo, a road on the right leads to Lekir via a scenic route. The picturesque whitewashed monastery buildings rise in different levels on the hillside across the Lekir River. A huge saffron-coloured Maitreya Buddha towers over the fields below. Lekir was built during the reign of Lachen Gyalpo who installed 600 monks here, headed by Lhawang Chosje (circa 1088). The *gompa* was invested with a collection of fine images, *thangkas* and murals to vie with those at Alchi. The present buildings date mainly from the 18th century since the original were destroyed by fire. A rough path up leads to the courtyard where a board explains the origin of the name: Klu-Khyil (snake coil) refers to the *nagas* here, reflected in the shape of the hill. Lekir was converted to the Gelugpa sect in the 15th century. The head *lama*, the younger brother of the Dalai Lama, has his apartments here, which were extended in the mid-1990s.

The **dukhang** (assembly hall) contains huge clay images of the Buddhas (past, present and future) and Kangyur and Tengyur manuscripts, the Kangyur having been first compiled in Ladakh during Lachen Gyalpo's reign. The **Nyenes-Khang** contains beautiful murals of the 35 confessional Buddhas and 16 arahats. The **Gon-Khang** houses a statue of the guardian deity here. A small but very interesting **museum** ⓘ *Rs 15, opened on request (climb to a hall above, up steep wooden stairs),* displays *thangkas*, old religious and domestic implements, costumes, etc, which are labelled in English.

Village craftsmen produce *thangkas*, carved wooden folding seats and clay pottery. If you wish to stay overnight, **Norbu Spon Guest House**, 3 km off main road towards Lekir, also allows camping and the two-storeyed whitewashed **Lhankay Guest House** is located amongst the fields.

Alchi

The road enters Saspul, 8 km from the Lekir turn-off. About 2 km beyond the village, a link road with a suspension bridge over the river leads to Alchi, which is hidden from view as you approach. A patchwork of cultivated fields surrounds the complex. A narrow path from the car park winds past village houses, donkeys and apricot trees to lead to the Dharma Chakra monastery. You will be expected to buy a ticket from one of the *lamas* on duty. The whole complex, about 100 m long and 60 m wide, is enclosed by a whitewashed mud and straw wall. Alchi's large temple complex is regarded as one of the most important Buddhist centres in Ladakh and a jewel of monastic skill. A path on the right past two large prayer wheels and a row of smaller ones leads to the river which attracts deer down to the opposite bank in the evenings. At the rear, small *chortens* with inscribed stones strewn around them, line the wall. From here, you get a beautiful view of the Indus River with mountains as a backdrop. For accommodation options, see Sleeping, page 590.

Founded in the 11th century by Rinchen Zangpo, the 'Great Translator', it was richly decorated by artists from Kashmir and Tibet. Paintings of the mandalas, which have deep Tantric significance, are particularly fine; some decorations are reminiscent of Byzantine art. The monastery is maintained by monks from Lekir and is no longer a place for active worship.

The temple complex The three entrance *chortens* are worth looking in to. Each has vividly coloured paintings within, both along the interior walls as well as in the small *chorten*-like openings on the ceilings. The first and largest of these has a portrait of the founder Rinchen Zangpo. Some of the paintings here are being restored by researchers.

The oldest temple is the **dukhang**, which has a courtyard (partially open to the sky) with wooden pillars and painted walls; the left wall shows two rowing boats with fluttering flags, a reminder perhaps of the presence in ancient times of lakes in this desert. The brightly painted door to the *dukhang*, about 1.5 m high, and the entrance archway has some fine woodcarving; note the dozen or so blue pottery Buddhas stuck to the wall. The subsidiary shrines on either side of the doorway contain *Avalokitesvaras* and *Bodhisattvas* including a giant four-armed Maitreya figure to the extreme right. This main assembly hall, which was the principal place of worship, suffers from having very little natural light so visitors need a good torch. The 'shrine' holds the principal gilded *Vairocana* (Resplendent) Buddha (traditionally white, accompanied by the lion) with ornate decorations behind, flanked by four important Buddha postures among others. The walls on either side are devoted to fine *Mandala* paintings illustrating the four principal manifestations of the *Sarvavid* (Omniscient) Buddha – *Vairocana*,

Alchi Choskor

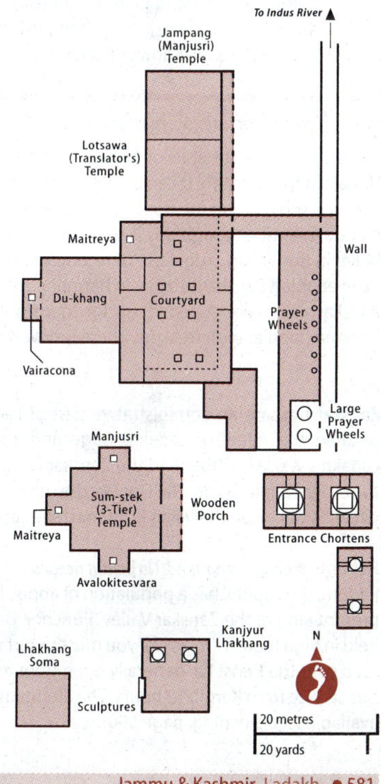

Sakyamuni (the Preacher), *Manjusri* (Lord of Wisdom) andas *Prajna Paramita* (Perfection of Wisdom) described in detail by Snellgrove and Skorupski. There are interesting subsidiary panels, friezes and inscriptions. Note the terrifying figure of *Mahakala* the guardian deity above the door with miniature panels of royal and military scenes. The one portraying a drinking scene shows the royal pair sanctified with haloes with wine-cups in hand, accompanied by the prince and attendants – the detail of the clothing clearly shows Persian influence.

The **Lotsawa** (Translator's) and **Jampang** (Manjusri) *Lhakhangs* were built later and probably neglected for some time. The former contains a portrait of Rinchen Zangpo along with a seated Buddha while the latter has *Manjusri* where each directional face is painted in the colour associated with the cardinal directions of north (dark green), south (yellow), east (blue) and west (red). There are two small temples beyond.

Sum-stek, the three-tier temple with a carved wooden gallery on the façade, has triple arches. Inside are three giant four-armed, garlanded stucco figures of *Bodhisattvas*: the white *Avalokitesvara* on the left, the principal terracotta-red *Maitreya* in the centre at the back, and the ochre-yellow *Manjusri* on the right; their heads project to the upper storey which is reached by a rustic ladder. The remarkable features here are the brightly painted and gilded decorations on the clothing of the figures which include historical incidents, musicians, palaces and places of pilgrimage. Quite incongruous court scenes and Persian features appear on *Avalokitesvara* while the figures on *Maitreya* have Tantric connotations illustrating the very different styles of ornamentation on the three figures. The walls have numerous *mandalas* and inscriptions.

Lhakhang Soma (New Temple) is a square hall with a *chorten* within; its walls are totally covered with *mandalas* and paintings portraying incidents from the Buddha's life and historic figures; the main figure here is the preaching Buddha. There is an interesting panel of warriors on horseback near the door. **Kanjyur Lhakhang** in front of the Lhakhang Soma houses the scriptures.

Zanskar → *For listings, see pages 588-594. Colour map 1, A2/3.*

Zanskar is a remote area of Ladakh contained by the Zanskar range to the north and the Himalaya to the south. It can be cut off by snow for as much as seven months each year when access is solely along the frozen Zanskar River. This isolation has helped Zanskar to preserve its cultural identity, though this is now being steadily eroded. Traditional values include a strong belief in Buddhism, frugal use of resources and population control: values which for centuries have enabled Zanskaris to live in harmony with their hostile yet fragile environment. The long Zanskar Valley was 'opened' up for tourism even later than the rest of Ladakh and quickly became popular with trekkers. There is now river rafting on the Zanskar River.

History

Zanskar became an administrative part of Ladakh under Senge Namgyal whose three sons became the rulers of Ladakh, Guge and Zanskar/Spiti. This arrangement collapsed after Ladakh's war with Tibet and the Zanskar royal house divided, one part administering Padum, the other Zangla. Under the Dogras, the rulers were reduced to puppets as the marauding army wreaked havoc on the villages, monasteries and population.

Padum → *Colour map 1, A3. No permit needed.*

Padum, the capital, has a population of about 1000 of whom about 40% are Sunni Muslim. The present king of the Zanskar Valley, Punchok Dawa, who lives in his modest home in Padum, is held in high regard. On arrival you must report to the Tourist Officer. Access is either by the jeep road over the **Pensi La**, generally open from mid-June to mid-October with an alternate days' bus service from Kargil, 18 hours. The alternative method is to trek in. There is accommodation available (see Sleeping, page 590).

Nubra Valley, Nyona and Drokhpa area → *For listings, see pages 588-594.*

Colour map 1, A4.

These once-restricted areas are now open to visitors. Permits are freely issued by the District Magistrate (District Development Commissioner) in Leh to groups of four or more travelling together by jeep, for a maximum of seven days. Allow a day to get a permit, which costs Rs 250. A lot of ground can be covered in the period but it is necessary to consult a Leh-based trekking and travel agent. Traffic into and out of the Nubra Valley is controlled by the army at Pulu: entry is allowed 1000-1200, exit 1300-1500. There are a few rest houses, and temporary lakeside tented camps are occasionally set up by tour companies, but make sure you are fully equipped with tents, food and sleeping bags.

Tso-Moriri → *Colour map 1, A4.*

The Rupshu area, a dry, high-altitude plateau to the east of the Leh-Manali Highway, is where the nomadic Changpas live (see page 558), in the bleak and windswept Chamathang highlands bordering Tibet. The route to the beautiful Tso-Moriri (*tso* – lake), the only nesting place of the bar-headed geese on the Indus, is open to visitors. It is 220 km from Leh; jeeps make the journey. To the south of the 27-km-long lake is the land of the Tibetan wild ass.

You can travel either via **Chhumathang**, 140 km, visiting the hot spring there or by crossing the high pass at Taglang La, leaving the Manali-Leh Highway at Debring. The route takes you past the **Tsokar** basin, 154 km, where salt cakes the edges. A campsite along the lake with access to fresh water is opposite **Thukje** village which has a *gompa* and a 'wolf-catching trap'. The road then reaches the hot sulphur springs at **Puga** before arriving at the beautiful Tso-Moriri, about four hours' drive from Tsokar. You can follow the lake bank and visit the solitary village of **Karzog**, at 4500 m, north of the lake, which also has a *gompa*. There are some rest houses and guesthouses at Chhumathang and Karzog and camping at Tsokar and Karzog as well as a tent camp at Chhumathang.

Pangong-Tso → *Colour map 1, A4.*

From Leh you can also get a permit to visit the narrow 130-km-long Pangong-Tso, at 4250 m, the greater part of which lies in Tibet. The road, which is only suitable for 4WD in places, is via **Karu** on the Manali-Leh Highway, where the road east goes through **Zingral** and over the Chang La pass. Beyond are **Durbuk**, a small village with low-roofed houses, and **Tangste**, the 'abode of Chishul warriors' with a Lotswa Temple, which is also an army base with a small bank. The rough jeep track takes you through an impressive rocky gorge which opens out to a valley which has camping by a fresh water stream in the hamlet of **Mugleb** and then on to **Lukung**, the last check-point and finally **Spangmik**, 153 km from Leh. On the way you will be able to see some Himalayan birds including *chikhor* (quail) which may end up in the cooking pot.

An overnight stop on the lake shore allows you to see the lake in different lights. You can walk between Lukung and Spangmik, 7 km, on the second day, passing small settlements growing barley and peas along the lake shore. Both villages have yaks which you can experience a ride on. You return to Leh on the third day. There are tented camps at Durbuk, Tangtse, Lukung and Spangmik. Jeeps make the journey from Leh.

Nubra Valley → *Colour map 1, A3/A4.*

For an exhilarating high-altitude experience over possibly the highest motorable pass in the world, travel across the Ladakh range over the 5600-m **Khardung La**. North of Leh, this is along the old Silk Route to the lush green Nubra Valley up to **Panamik**, 140 km from Leh, which has reddish, sulphurous hot springs nearby. It is best to visit this region after mid-June.

Camel caravans once transported Chinese goods along this route for exchanging with Indian produce. The now highly prized and rare camels can occasionally be seen on the sand dunes near Nubra (see page 587). The relatively gentle climate here allows crops, fruit and nuts to grow, so some call it 'Ldumra' (orchard). You can visit the **Samstaling**, **Sumur** and **Deskit** *gompas*. There are rest houses at **Deskit**, **Panamik** and **Khardung** village with permission from the Executive Engineer, PWD, in Deskit. Local families take in guests and tented camps are sometimes set up by tour companies (double tents Rs 800 including food) during the season. Should you need medical help, there is a health centre at Deskit and a dispensary at Panamik.

From Leh there are two buses per week from June to September taking eight hours; a few have tried by bike, which can be put on the roof of the bus for the outward journey.

Drokhpa area → *Colour map 1, A3.*

Dah and **Biama** (Bema) are two Drokhpa villages where the so-called pure Aryan tribe speaking a distinct dialect live in a fair degree of isolation; Buddhism here is mixed with animist practices. You may reach these Indus Valley villages from **Khaltse** on the Leh-Srinagar road via Dumkhar, Tirit, Skurbuchan and Hanudo. There is a rest house at Biama and guesthouses and a campsite.

Trekking in Ladakh → *Colour map 1, A3.*

Make sure your trekking guide is experienced and competent. See Books, page 1444, for recommended reading. Some treks, eg Spituk to Hemis and Hemis High Altitude National Park, charge a fee of Rs 25 per person per day or Rs 10 for Indians. Leh is the major town in the Indus Valley. For trekking, July and August are pleasant months. Go earlier and you will be trudging through snow much of the time. September and October are also good months, though colder at night.

Spituk to Hemis

Both places are in the Indus Valley, just 30 km apart. A very satisfying nine to 10 days can be undertaken by traversing the Stok range to the Markha Valley, walking up the valley and then back over the Zanskar range to Hemis. The daily walking time on this trek is five to six hours so you must be fit.

There is an interesting monastery at **Spituk**, a short drive from Leh (see page 579). From Spituk proceed southwest of the Indus along a trail passing through barren countryside. After about 7 km you reach the **Zingchen Valley** and in a further five hours, the beautiful village of **Rumbak**. Camp below the settlement. You can also trek here from Stok which takes two days and a steep ascent of the **Namlung La** (4570 m).

From Rumbak it is a five-hour walk to **Utse** village. The camp is two hours further on at the base of the bleak **Gandha La** (4700 m), open, bare and windswept. To go over the pass takes about three hours, then the same time again to negotiate the wooded ravine to **Skiu**. Here the path meets the Markha Valley. You can make a half-day round trip from Skiu to see the impressive gorges on the Zanskar River. The stage to **Markha**, where there is an impressive fort, is a six-hour walk. The monastery, while not particularly impressive from the outside, has some superb wall paintings and *thangkas*, some dating from the 13th century. You need to take a torch.

The next destination is **Hankar** village, whose ruined fort forms an astonishing extension of the natural rock face, an extremely impressive ruin. From here the path climbs quite steeply to a plateau. There are good views of Nimaling Peak (6000 m) and a number of *mani* walls en route. From **Nimaling** it is a two-hour climb to **Gongmaru La** (5030 m) with views of the Stok range and the Indus Valley. The descent is arduous and involves stream crossings. There is a lovely campsite at **Shogdu** and another at **Sumda** village, 3 km further on. The final stage is down the valley to **Martselang** from where you can walk down 5 km to **Karu** village on the Leh-Manali road or take a 2-km diversion to visit **Hemis** monastery.

Hemis High Altitude National Park

Set up in 1981, the park adjoining the monastery covers 600 sq km, comprising the catchments of Markha, Rumbak and Sumda *nalas*, with plans to extend across another 1670 sq km. The rugged terrain with valleys often littered with rocks and rimmed by high peaks (some over 6000 m), supports limited vegetation but contains some rare species of flora and fauna, including the ibex, Pallas' cat, *bharal* and *shapu*. A new reserve is being planned to protect the endangered snow leopard. It is also hoped that the activities of local villagers, who graze livestock within the park, can be restricted to a buffer zone so that their animals can be kept safe from attack by wolves and snow leopards.

There are camping sites within the park, which can be reserved through the Wildlife Warden in Leh. Since most of the park lies within 'restricted' areas, you need a special Group Permit for entry, also issued in Leh. Contact a local travel agent for advice.

Ladakh & Zanskar treks

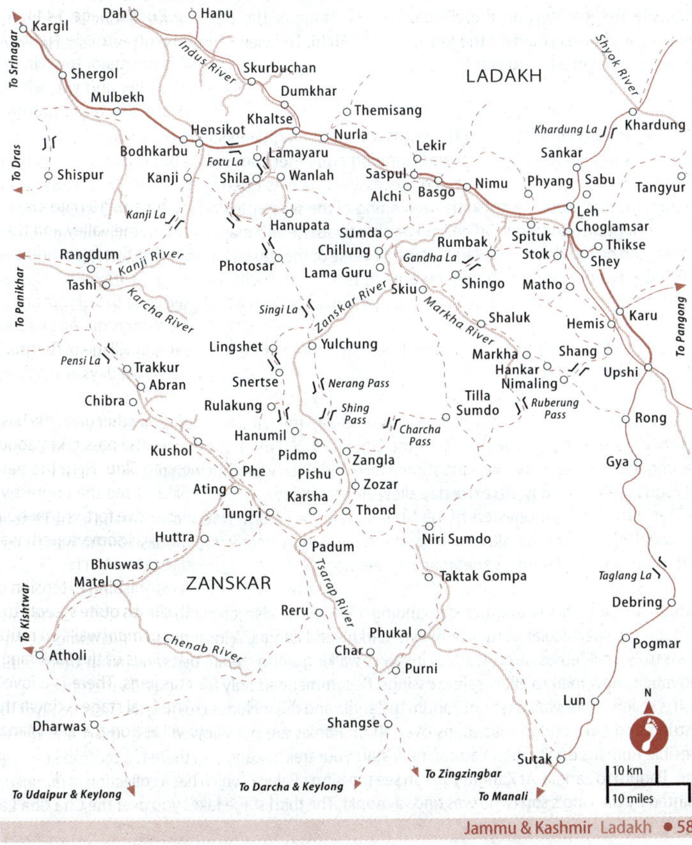

Lamayaru to Alchi

This is a shorter trek of five to six days, however, the average daily walking time is 6½ hours so don't think that the shortness of the trek means less effort. Three passes, the **Printiki La** (3500 m), **Konze La** (4570 m) and **Stapski La** (5200 m) are crossed rewarding the exertion of reaching them with excellent views.

The first stage involves walking from the campsite just below the monastery down the valley for 2 km then over the **Printiki La**. You then descend the Shillakong Valley and climb to **Phangi** village, passing huge boulders brought down by a landslide, and impressive irrigation in such a forbidding landscape. From Phangi you walk up the Ripchar Valley to **Khaltse**, crossing the river a number of times. The trek passes a number of small settlements until you reach the summer grazing ground a few kilometres below the pass. The **Konze La** is a steep two-hour climb. From here you will see the Zanskar River and gorge and the Stok range.

The fourth stage should be with a guide since the trail splits, one path leading to **Chillung** on the Zanskar River, the other to **Sumdahchenmo**. The latter being quite treacherous as it involves many river crossings (about three hours below Sumdahchenmo there is a path which climbs the ridge above the river; it is quite easy to miss this, hence the guide). There is a monastery here with an impressive statue of the Buddha and some attractive wall paintings. A campsite lies just beyond the village. The last stage of the trek is long, about eight hours' walking, and takes you over the **Stapski La** to **Alchi**. The views from the top are superb. From Alchi you can get a bus to Leh.

Trekking in Zanskar

Trekking in Zanskar is not easy. The paths are often rough and steep, the passes high and the climate extreme. Provisions, fuel and camping equipment should be bought in advance from Kishtwar, Manali or Leh. You may get necessities such as dried milk, biscuits and sugar from Padum, though probably not at the beginning of the season. In Padum the Tourism Officer and Government Development Officer will be able to advise and maybe even assist in hiring horses. Porters can be hired at **Sani** village for the traverse of the **Umasi La** into Kishtwar. Horses cannot use this pass. In Padum you may be able to hire porters with whom you can cover rougher terrain. It is best to contact a trekking agent in advance. ▸▸ *See Activities and tours, page 592.*

Pensi La to Padum You can trek this three-day route before the road opens (June- October) when it is free of vehicles.

Karsha to Lamayaru This is a demanding nine-day trek which includes seven passes, five of which are over 4500 m. The highest is the Singi La (5060 m). It is essential to be very fit before starting the trek. Each day's walking should take under six hours, but with time for rests and lunch this adds up to a full day. An extra day allows for flexibility.

The 16th-century monastery of the Tibetan Gelugpa (Yellow Hat) sect at **Karsha** is the largest and wealthiest in the Zanskar Valley and is occupied by nearly 200 monks. Karsha has an inn with dormitory beds and a vegetarian canteen.

Padum to Leh This is another demanding trek which also takes about 10 days. Some are through the spectacular gorges between Markha and Zangla. A local guide is recommended as this is truly a wilderness area. The trek involves walking along stream beds and in July there is still too much snow melt to allow safe crossings. Recommended only for August/September.

It is seven hours' walking from Padum to Zangla and this includes crossing the Zanskar River by a string and twig bridge that spans over 40 m. Ponies are not allowed on it and if it is windy sensible humans don't cross. You can now start your trek at Zangla as there is a motorbike route from Padum to Zangla. At **Zangla** you can see the King's Palace, which has a collection of *thangkas* painted by the king's son (who was once a monk). The third stage takes you over the **Cha Cha La**

(5200 m). On the next stage river crossings are again necessary. This is time consuming and if you are travelling in mid-summer, an extra day may be called for.

You then follow the **Khurna River** to a narrow gorge that marks the ancient border between Zanskar and Ladakh, and end up below the **Rubarung La**. When you cross this you get good views of the Stok range. You then descend into the Markha Valley and from here you can reach Leh in six stages by heading west into the heart of the valley and then crossing the Ganda La to Spituk, or in three stages by crossing the Gongmaru La and descending to Martselang and nearby Hemis.

Padum to Darcha This is a week-long trek and starts with a walk along the Tsarap Chu to **Bardan**, which has *stupas* and interesting idols, and **Reru**. There is a now a motorable road till Mune from where the trek starts towards Darcha.

After two stages you reach **Purni** (with a couple of shops and a popular campsite), where you can stay two nights and make a side trip to the impressive 11th-century **Phugtal monastery** (a two-hour walk). On a spectacular site, it has been carved out of the mountainside round a limestone cave. Usually there are about 50 monks in attendance. From Purni you continue on to Kargiakh, the last village before the **Shingo La**. It's another day's walk to the camp below this high pass (5200 m).

The mountain scenery is stunning with 6000 m-plus peaks all around. Once over the pass you can stop at **Rumjack** where there is a campsite used by shepherds or you can continue to the confluence of the **Shingo** and the **Barai** rivers where there is now a bridge. From here the trail passes through grazing land and it is about 15 km to **Darcha**, the end of the trek. Keen trekkers can combine this with a trek from Darcha to **Manali**. The average daily walking time of the Padum-Darcha trek is six hours so you have to be very fit. There is now a motorable road from Darcha all the way to Zanskar Sumdo which is after the Shingo La Pass.

Trekking in the Nubra and Shyok valleys

The gradual easing of controls to visit the Nubra-Shyok valleys has now made possible treks that start from points in the Indus Valley not far from Leh, cross the Ladakh Range to enter the Shyok River valley and then re-cross the Ladakh range further to the west to re-enter the Indus Valley near Phyang monastery. Ask a good local trekking agent for advice on how to get the required 'Restricted Area Permits'.

Day 1 Drive from Leh south along the Manali road to Karu, near Hemis, where you turn left and drive about 10 km to the roadhead at the village of Sakti, just past **Takthak monastery**. Trek about 90 minutes to **Chumchar** and camp.
Day 2 Cross the Ladakh range at the **Wari La** (4400 m) and descend to Junlez on the northern flank.
Day 3 Walk downhill to **Tangyar** (3700 m) with a nice *gompa*.
Days 4, 5, 6 A level walk along the **Shyok River** valley takes you to **Khalsar** from where you follow the military road west to the confluence of the Shyok and Nubra rivers at **Deskit**. On a hill above the village is a Gelugpa sect **monastery** (the largest in Nubra) built by the Ladakhi king Sohrab Zangpo in the early 1700's. There is large statue of Tsongkhapa and the Rimpoche of Thikse monastery south of Leh oversees this monastery also. The Rimpoche was nominated to the Rajya Sabha in 1998. The next biggest monastery in Nubra is near **Tiggur** halfway along the road north of Deskit to **Panamik** in the Nubra Valley. Called the **Samtanling** *gompa*, it was founded in 1842 and belongs to the Gelugpa sect. The Permit allows travel only up to the village of Panamik (see Nubra Valley, above).
Days 7, 8, 9 Three days to gradually ascend the northern flanks of the Ladakh Range passing the hamlets of **Hundar**, **Wachan** and **Hundar Dok** to the high pastures of **Thanglasgo** (4700 m).
Days 10, 11 Trek back over the Ladakh Range via the Lasermo La pass (5150 m) to a campsite on the southern base of the pass.
Day 12 Camp at Phyang village about 1 km above Phyang monastery before driving back to Leh.

Ladakh listings

For Sleeping and Eating price codes and other relevant information, see Essentials pages 38-42.

Sleeping

Lamayuru *p566*

F-G Moonland Guest House, basic, shared bathrooms but clean. Great view and good food.

Leh *p574, maps p575 and p576*

Mid-range hotels are getting better at honouring advance reservations, although it used to be a problem as arrival and departure times can be unpredictable, especially with large groups. Hotel touts can be a nuisance during the 14-day Ladakh festival. **Grand Dragon**, **Hotel Lasermo**, **Omasila** , **Oriental** remain open throughout the year. There are now several guest houses and many traditional Ladakhi homes offer rooms during the summer. Outside the peak period expect discounts. Those in Karzoo and Changspa (some way from the bus stand) are quieter and preferable to those near the bazar. In some hotels, meals are included. There are a growing number of restaurants in Leh.

There is some budget accommodation along the Old Rd and in the Changspa area; some are very basic with cold water only. Fleas and bed bugs can be a problem; use your own sleeping bag if possible. But generally you will find a clean basic room.

AL-A Grand Dragon, Old Road Sheynam, T01982-257 786, www.thegranddragonladakh.com. Big hotel with all mod cons, Wi-Fi and great views. Stunning dining room and a nod to eco tourism with double-glazing, under-floor heating and solar panels. Open all year round.

AL-A Lharisa, Skara, T01982-252 000, www.ladakh-larisa.com. With a boutique vibe, they offer stylish rooms and the outside of the building is simply beautiful. In the restaurant they serve up flavours from all over India as well as traditional Ladakhi food. Recommended.

AL-A Shambhala, Skara, T01982-251 100, www.hotelshambhala.com (Welcome Heritage). 24 large airy rooms, good restaurant (often caters for German packages), meals included, very pleasant, friendly staff, peaceful away from crowds, attractive garden with hammocks, free transport to centre.

A Lharimo, Fort Rd, T01982-252101. Attractive, central hotel, 30 simple but comfortable rooms with baths, good views from balconies, restaurant. Recently renovated.

A-B Kang-lha Chen, T01982-252144, klcleh@sancharnet.in. Open May-Oct. 25 simple rooms, with attached bathrooms. Recently renovated with larger dining area, lobby done in traditional style with old family furniture and carpets, restaurant, pleasant shaded inner courtyard garden and lawns with sitting area at hotel entrance, own spring, quiet and peaceful and centrally located, old fashioned but well maintained. Recommended.

A-C Omasila, Changspa, T01982-252119, hotelomasila@yahoo.com. 34 luxurious rooms, ornate restaurant (garden vegetables), garden, pleasant quiet location, own spring water. Open throughout the year, run very well with the owner, Mr Nawang taking personal attention all the time. Highly recommended.

B Shynam, Old Rd, T01982-252345. 15 comfortable rooms, huge dining hall, beautiful gardens, very well run.

B Spic-n-Span, Old Rd, T01982-252765. 29 rooms which actually live up to the name, good views from roof, attractive building. Recently renovated with new wing having modern fixtures and amenities.

B Tsomo-Ri, Fort Rd, T01982-253611, www.ladakhtsomori.com. 15 surprisingly quiet rooms around central courtyard, very hospitable manager.

B-C Yak Tail, Fort Rd, T01982-252118, www.hotelyaktail.com. Open Apr-Sep. 30 rooms, some 'houseboat style' (newer ones have balconies), nice courtyard garden restaurant (good, reasonably priced Indian food), money exchange, pleasant atmosphere.

B-D Padma, off Fort Rd at end of an alley, T01982-252630, www.padmaladakh.net. 6 clean, charming rooms with common bath in guesthouse, upstairs has mountain views, plus 15 rooms in newer hotel, beautiful, peaceful garden, cheap meals to order, outstanding hospitality. Highly recommended.

C Bijoo, near Library, 100 m from bazar, T01982-252131, hotel_bijoo@rediffmail.com.

Prepare for a different lifestyle in Leh

The whitewashed sun-dried brick walls of a typical two-storey, flat-roofed Ladakhi house, often with decorative woodwork around doors and windows and a carefully nurtured garden, look inviting to a traveller after a long hard journey. Local families are opening their homes to provide for the increasing demand for accommodation over a very short peak season and new hotels are springing up. These are listed by the Tourism Department as A- to D-class hotels, or as guesthouses, and must charge fixed rates. However, prices do not reflect the type of furniture, furnishings and plumbing you might expect elsewhere in India although on the whole the rooms are kept clean. There is usually a space for sitting out – a 'garden' with a tree or two, some flower beds and some grass struggling to establish itself.

Electricity is limited, so expect power cuts, which are random and unpredictable. Some hotels have generators. Those without may run out of tap water but buckets are always at hand. Hot water is a luxury, available only during mornings and evenings. Plumbing allows for flush WCs in at least D-category hotels but the water from the basin disappears down the plughole only to emerge around your feet as there is only one drain in a corner of the bathroom!

Guests are encouraged to economize on water and electricity – you will notice the low-power bulbs and scarcity of lights in rooms and public areas, so put away your reading material until sunrise.

2-storey white building hidden by wall, 18 good rooms with bath, good restaurant, pleasant flower-filled garden and shady seating, treks and tours.

C **Ri-Rab**, Changspa, T01982-253108, chhospel@hotmail.com. 18 clean simple rooms with baths, restaurant (own fresh garden vegetables), parking.

C-D **Lhung-Se-Jung**, Fort Rd, T01982-252193, modhalileh@yahoo.com. 14 charming, old-fashioned rooms with bath, 2-storey old building and small annexe, upstairs better, restaurant, small garden, quiet location, student discount, good service, friendly manager. Recommended.

D **Padmaling**, Changspa, T01982-252933. 10 clean, well-maintained rooms with bath, hot water morning and evening, helpful manager, **Mona Lisa** restaurant next door, pleasant garden, good views over Stok Kangri.

D-E **Goba**, in Changspa down side alley, T01982-253670. Very peaceful garden, home-cooked food, lovely family and 15 simple but attractive rooms. Recommended. New block built. They have 30 more rooms in new wing with attached bathrooms. Very busy and popular. No group bookings as most people stay long-term or are walk-in guests. Recommended.

D-E **Hills View**, T01982-252058, adventure hills@vsnl.net. 12 clean, charming rooms, 12 more coming, authentically rickety, some with good views, breakfast and snacks, pleasant staff, pretty garden, relaxing, safe, stores luggage.

D-E **New Antelope Guest House**, Main St, T01982-252086. Guesthouse with 11 simple, clean rooms, some with bath, good food, quiet, shady garden. Recently renovated.

D-E **Silver Cloud**, on the road opposite Sankar Gompa, 15 mins' walk from centre, T01982-253128. Ladakhi guesthouse with 15 very clean rooms, 9 with bath (1 room C), friendly, helpful family, excellent food, large garden. Recommended.

D-F **Oriental**, below Shanti Stupa, T01982-253153, www.orientalguesthouse.com. 35 very clean rooms in traditional family home, good home cooking, great views across the valley, friendly, treks and travel arrangements reliable. Open all year. Recommended.

E-F **Old Ladakh**, in the Old Town. 8 rooms, varying in comfort, has character, pleasant atmosphere, good place to meet others.

E-F **Rainbow**, Karzoo. Big, clean rooms with wonderful views of mountains and Shanti Stupa, hot water in buckets, great hospitality, good breakfasts. Recommended.

F **Harmit Hut**, Old Road Chulung, T01982-251348. Quiet and charming, 9 cosy rooms with attached bathrooms.

Staying healthy in Leh

The supply of clean water and the sewage system can come under heavy pressure in the tourist season. Drink pressure-boiled water from Dzomsa only or use water purification tablets. Bottled water can sometimes be more than a year old and doesn't always conform to safety standards. Meat is sometimes brought in unrefrigerated lorries having travelled two days, so is best avoided.

F Kangla, Airport Rd, T01982-252506. 14 slightly tatty rooms but very friendly and helpful, organize treks.
F Shanti Guest House, below Shanti Stupa, T01982-253084. Guesthouse with 9 well-heated rooms, most with great views, very good food, summer/winter treks arranged with guide, friendly Ladakhi family.
F Zarla, Sheynam Old Rd, down dirty alley but worth the effort, T01982-252 672. 10 simple rooms in friendly family house.
F-G Indus, off Fort Rd, T01982-252502, masters_adv@yahoo.co.in. 17 large rooms some with bath (hot water in buckets), better upstairs, food, simple but homely, peaceful garden.
F-G Lung Snon, Sheynam Chulli Chan. 8 rooms, delightful guesthouse in peaceful countryside, clean and friendly, but simple, earth toilet.
G Remo, Fort Rd, T01982-253336. Clean, quiet, simple rooms, shared toilets, bucket hot water (no charge), very kind family.
G Wari-La, Old Road near **Hotel Horzey**, T01982-253302. Good views, 6 charming rooms, home-cooked food on demand.

Thikse *p578*

F Shalzang Chamba, with outdoor restaurant.

Hemis *p579*

Many householders take in guests. Not ideal.
G Tourist, camp or sleep on the floor, own sleeping bag, Rs 25. Basic, grubby tented restaurant.

Alchi *p581*

Near Alchi car/bus park there are tea stalls and a few guesthouses. A couple of kilometres away in Saspul are **Carefree Travels Camp** and **Worldroof Camping Resort** and **Restaurant**.
F-G Lotsava, on the path. Simple.
G Samdrupling Guest house, Basic, clean with attached bathrooms.
G Uley Ethnic Resort, Uletokpo, T01982-253640. Mud huts and simple tents.
G Zimskhang, very clean rooms, walled-in open-air restaurant for light meals and snacks, camping. Highly recommended. There is also a German Bakery on the way to the temple.

Nubra Valley *p583*

F-G Snow Leopard, Hundar Village. Cosy place with garden and fruit trees.

Padum *p582*

Places to stay are limited, being mostly dormitory style. There is a **tourist complex** with basic rooms and meals; you can camp.
E Ibex has the best rooms and a restaurant.

Eating

Leh *p574, maps p575 and p576*

TTT Mona Lisa, Changspa, T01982-252687. International. Good atmosphere, quiet garden with shady trees, hanging lanterns, excellent food (try pizzas, *momos*, garlic cheese with bread), scrawny chickens, no desserts, service can be indifferent.
TT Booklovers' Retreat, Changspa. Perennial favourite as cosy place for food and hanging out. There's a roof terrace.
TT Dreamland, Fort Rd. International. Good atmosphere and food especially Chinese, excellent breakfasts.
TT Elements, Changspa Rd. New kid on the block with top chef Stanzin Namgyal who moonlights at the renowned **Sublime** in Goa during the winter. Dishing up trout, lamb and as much organic produce as possible, both local and exotic grown by local farmers in Changspa and Sankar. You can also get a dose of culture here with classical music, storytelling, documentaries, stone carving workshops and crafts. Highly recommended.
TT Hi Life, Fort Rd. Exceptional range of high-quality food, friendly owners, seating indoor and out. Highly recommended.

Gompas and festivals

Buddhist festivals usually take place in the bleak winter months when villagers gather together, stalls spring up around the *gompas* and colourful dance dramas and masked dances are performed in the courtyards. Musical instruments, weapons and religious objects are brought out during these dance performances. The Kushak (high priest) is accompanied by monks in monotonous recitation while others play large cymbals, trumpets and drums. The serious theme of victory of Good over Evil is lightened by comic interludes. A few monasteries celebrate their festivals in the summer months, for example Lamayuru, Hemis and Phyang.

🍴🍴 **Ibex**, near taxi stand. Tandoor oven and good helpings of *mughlai* food. Popular.

🍴🍴 **Il Forno**, Zangsti Rd. Serves up pretty decent pizzas, pastas and there's beer too.

🍴🍴 **La Montessori**, Main St Bazar. Excellent Tibetan and Chinese. Filling soups, interesting local clientele.

🍴🍴 **Lamuyara**, Changspa. Exceedingly popular for North Indian fare and Ladakhi specials.

🍴🍴 **Penguin Garden**, just off Main St. Good garden café with nice atmosphere care of Nepali owners.

🍴🍴 **Summer Harvest**, Fort Rd, 1st floor, next to **Dreamland**. Mainly Indian, also Chinese, Tibetan. Extensive menu of local and 'tourist' dishes from mutton *thukpa* (Rs 30) to tandoori chicken (Rs 160).

🍴🍴 **Women's Alliance Café**, see page 576. Serves good Ladakhi breakfast, while promoting traditional farming methods threatened by the modern cash economy. Recommended.

🍴 **Amdo II**, Main Bazar. Tibetan. Good fried *momos*, Rs 25-35 per dish, friendly (better than **Amdo Café** opposite).

🍴 **Budshah Inn**, Lal Chowk, top floor. North Indian fare. Lacks ambience but excellent Kashmiri (Rs 45, dish).

🍴 **Devi Tibetan**, Library Rd, by Dzomsa. Traditional meals, refreshing spiced teas.

🍴 **Nepali**, Main St Bazar. Nepali, Tibetan. Excellent vegetarian *momos*.

🍴 **Tibetan Friend's Corner**, Fort Rd and Main St Bazar. Clean, simple, delicious *kothay* (fried *momos*) Rs 25, huge pancakes, friendly, locally popular.

🍴 Also recommended the kebab places near the mosque.

Bakeries

Four German bakeries sell good bread (trekking bread keeps for a week) and excellent cakes and muesli.

Pumpernickel, Main St Bazar. The original German bakery is the best and friendliest, indoor/outdoor seating, excellent apricot and apple crumble/pie, message board for trekkers.

Entertainment

Leh *p574, maps p575 and p576*

The **Ecological Centre** shows films, see page 576. Ladakhi dancing and singing, below entrance to the palace, 1800 (1 hr), Rs 50.

The **Elements** (see Eating) shows films, has live classical music, traditional storytelling and craft workshops.

Festivals and events

Leh *p574, maps p575 and p576*

Dates vary depending on the lunar calendar.

Apr-May Buddha Purnima marks the Buddha's birth, at full moon.

10-15 Sep Ladakh Festival. The main events are held in the Leh polo grounds with smaller events in other districts. Usually during the 1st week in Sep, there are 4 days of dances, displays of traditional costumes, Ladakhi plays and polo matches.

Dec Celebration of **Losar** which originated in the 15th century to protect people before going to battle.

Hemis *p579*

Jun Hemis Tsechu is perhaps the biggest cultural festival in Ladakh. It commemorates the birth of **Guru Padmasambhava** who is believed to have fought local demons to protect the people. Young and old of both sexes join *lamas* in masked dance-dramas, while stalls sell handicrafts A colourful display of Ladakhi Buddhist culture, it attracts large numbers of foreign visitors.

Shopping

Leh p574, maps p575 and p576

Please use your own bags. Plastic bags are not allowed in the bazar as they were finding their way into streams when not piled on unsightly heaps.

Leh Bazar is full of shops selling curios, clothes and knick-knacks. Tea and *chang* (local barley brew) vessels, cups, butter churns, knitted carpets with Tibetan designs, Tibetan jewellery, prayer flags, musical bowls, are all available. Prices are high especially in Kashmiri shops so bargain vigorously. It is better to buy Ladakhi jewellery and souvenirs from Ladakhis who generally ask a fair price. There are tight restrictions on the export of anything over 100 years old. Baggage is checked at the airport partly for this reason. However, even though most items are antique-looking, they are, in fact, fresh from the backstreet workshops. If you walk down the narrow lanes, you will probably find an artisan at work from whom you can buy direct.

In **Dzomsa** you can get water refill. Place to dispose batteries etc. Laundry and organic stuff available. **Ecological Shop for Organic Products** Stock up on local produce here including apricot jam.

Books

Artou Books, opposite Post Office, Zangsti and in Main Bazar. Good selection, especially on trekking in the region, also fax and international phone.
Book Worm, near **Galdan Hotel**.
Second-hand books.

Crafts

A group of Ladakhis have stalls off the Fort Rd.
Chan Gali, behind Main Bazar. Worth exploring for curios.
Cottage Emporium, Fort Rd. Many carpets and pashminas.
Ladakh Arts & Craft House, top of Fort Rd, opposite PO. Some interesting bric-a-brac.
Ladakhi Village Curios. Selection of *thangkas*, inlaid bowls, baubles, bangles and beads.
LEDeG Craft Shop, at the Ecology Centre, and opposite **State Bank** in the Main Bazar.
Sonam Bongo, Main Bazar St. Local costumes.
Tibetan Arts. Has a selection of *thangkas*, inlaid bowls, baubles, bangles and beads.

Fruit and nuts

Available in season. Dried apricots can be bought along any roadside in Aug and Sep. Bottled juice is sold by the **Dzomsa** Laundry.

Photography

Syed Ali Shah's Postcard Shop, Choterantag St, is worth a visit. An authentic photographer's studio; collection of old photocopies sold, postcards, camera films.

Tailor

Next to **Budshah Inn** near mosque, excellent shirt maker, made-to-measure. Also several in Nowshara Gali.

Activities and tours

Leh p574, maps p575 and p576

Archery

The **Archery Stadium** is nearby where winter competitions attract large crowds; the target is a hanging white clay tablet.

Meditation

Mahabodhi Meditation Centre is in town. Enquire about short courses.

Polo

Polo, the 'national' sport, is popular in the summer and is played in the polo ground beyond the main bus stand. The local version which is fast and rough appears to follow no rules! The **Polo Club** is the highest in the world and worth a visit.

Tour operators

Women on their own should take special care when arranging a tour with a driver/guide.
Discovery Initiatives (UK), T01285-643333, www.discoveryinitiatives.co.uk. Runs conservation-minded 14-day 'Snow Leopard treks' in search of Ladakhi wildlife.
Eco-Adventures, 8 Malcha Marg Shopping Centre, Diplomatic Enclave, New Delhi, T011-2611 5504, www.magical-india.com. Tailor-made and group tours.

To fly or not to fly

Ecological implications aside, travel by road gives you an advantage over flying into Leh as it enables you to acclimatize to a high-altitude plateau and if you are able to hire a jeep or car it will give you the flexibility of stopping to see the several sights on the way. However, some people find the bus journey from Manali or Srinagar terrifying and very uncomfortable, and most healthy people find that if they relax completely for two days after flying in, they acclimatize without difficulty. If you have a heart condition, consult your doctor on the advisability of going to Leh.

Explore Himalayas, Main Bazar (opposite SBI), T/F01982-253354, wangchuks@hotmail.com. Recommended, normally excellent crew though some reports of inept guides, friendly, good to animals, environment conscious.
K2, Main Bazar, T01982-253532. Good rates for treks (Markha Valley), very friendly, environment conscious.
Mountain Experience, **Hotel Saser**, T01982-250162. 20 years of trekking experience.
Rimo Expeditions, **Kang-lha Chen Hotel**, T01982-253348, www.rimoexpeditions.com Insightful and informative about the local area, running a whole host of treks, as well as mountain biking, mountaineering, river rafting, cultural tours and family holidays. The best of the lot. Highly recommended.
Shakti Experiences, www.shaktihimalaya.com. Sensitively run sustainable tours and personalized treks to remote villages 30 km from Leh in the rugged high mountains of Ladakh. A 7-night tour includes jeep safaris, and a 2-night, 3-day rafting experience on the Shyok River, with overnight stays in African style safari-tents. Luxurious but understated.

Whitewater rafting and kayaking

Possible on the Tsarap Chu and Zanskar rivers from mid-Jun; the upper reaches of the former (Grade IV rapids) are suitable for experienced rafters only, though the remaining stretch can be enjoyed by all. Along the Indus: Hemis to Choglamsar (easy, very scenic); Phey-Nimmu (Grade III); Nimmu-Khaltse (professional). Ensure the trip is organized by a well-experienced rafter and that life jackets and wet suits are provided. Half to full day, including transport and lunch, Rs 800-1400.

Zanskar *p582*

Ibex in Delhi organizes trekking and rafting in Zanskar. See page 114.
Zanskar Tours and Travels, T01983-245064, in Padum.

Transport

Leh *p574, maps p575 and p576*

Air The small airport is 5 km away on Srinagar Rd. It is surrounded by hills on 3 sides and the flight over the mountain ranges is spectacular. Transport to town: buses, and jeep-taxis for sharing, or around Rs 200 for charter.

Allow 2 hrs for check in; no hand luggage allowed. Weather conditions may deteriorate rapidly even in the summer resulting in flight cancellations (especially outside Jul and Aug) so always be prepared for a delay or to take alternative road transport out of Ladakh. Furthermore, the airlines fly quite full planes into Leh but can take fewer passengers out because of the high-altitude take-off. This adds to the difficulty of getting a flight out. **Book your tickets as soon as possible** (several months ahead for Jul and Aug). You can book on the internet before you depart for India (eg www.welcometravel.com).

Air India, office near Shambhala Hotel (often chaotic), T01982-252076, airport T01982-252255, www.airindia.in, flies to/from **Delhi**, Tue-Sun in season (Jul-Sep); to **Jammu**, Sun, Fri; **Srinagar**, Wed. **Jet Airways**, T01982-250999; airport T01982-250324, www.jetairways.com, to **Delhi** daily except Sat. **Kingfisher**, www.flykingfisher.com, **Spicejet**, T1800-180 3333, also fly to **Delhi**.
Local bus The **New Bus Stand** is near the cemetery. The vehicles are ramshackle but the fares are low. See under monasteries for details. Enquiries **J&KSRTC**, T01982-252285.

Long distance Himachal Tourism runs regular (not daily) Deluxe and Ordinary buses between Manali and Leh, usually mid-Jun to end Sep. To **Manali**, 530 km, 'Deluxe', booked at HPTDC, Fort Rd, or at travel agents, Rs 1600 includes camp bed and meals in Keylong); Ordinary bus Rs 425, gruelling journey departs 0400 Ordinary (Private) booked at bus stand, 'A' Rs 500, and 'B', Rs 425, stop overnight at Keylong. **J&KSRTC** bus **Kargil**, 230 km (alternate days in summer) Rs 110-180, **Srinagar** 434 km, Rs 200-360.

Road If you have travelled by road you may already be better acclimatized, but a mild headache is common and can be treated with aspirin or paracetamol. Drink plenty of fluids on journeys.

Leh is connected to Manali via Keylong (closed Oct to mid-Jun or longer) and to Srinagar, via Kargil, by a State Highway. Both can be seriously affected by landslides, causing long delays. The Leh–Srinagar road is also often blocked by army convoys. Information on road conditions from the Traffic Police HQ, Maulana Azad Rd, Srinagar.

The road to **Manali**, crossing some very high passes, is open mid-Jun or early Jul, until end Sep (depending on the weather) and takes 2 days. Road conditions may be poor in places. Departure from Leh can be early (0400) with overnight stop in Keylong; next day to Manali. Alternatively, camp in Sarchu (10 hrs from Leh), or Jespa; next day 14 hrs to Manali (charge Rs 800-1200 per night in Sarchu). Roadside tents provide food en route during the tourist season; carry snacks, water and a good sleeping bag when planning to camp. Many travellers find the mountain roads extremely frightening and they are comparatively dangerous. Some are cut out of extremely unstable hillsides, usually with nothing between the road's edge and the near-vertical drop below; parts remain rough and pot- holed and during the monsoons, landslides and rivers can make it impassable for 2-3 days. It is also a long and uncomfortable journey, but there is some spectacular scenery.

Taxi 4WD between Leh and Manali are expensive but recommended if you want to stop en route to visit monasteries. 2-day trip, about Rs 13,000. Taxis often return empty to Manali (some visitors choose to fly out of Leh) so may agree a much reduced fare for the return leg. Officially, Manali (or Srinagar) taxis are allowed to carry their passengers to and from Leh but are not permitted to do local tours, a rule fiercely monitored by the Leh Taxi Operators' Union.

Tourist taxi and jeep Ladakh Taxi Operators' Union, Fort Rd, T01982-252723. Fixed fares point-to-point. From the airport to Main Bazar, about Rs 150; from bus stand Rs 60. A day's taxi hire to visit nearby *gompas* costs about Rs 1000-1200; Rs 7500 for a 2-night trip. Taxi union has fixed rate.

Alchi *p581*

Bus One daily direct bus from **Leh** in summer, 1500, 3 hrs, returns around 0700. **Srinagar**-bound buses (0630, 0900) stop at **Saspol**; from there it is a 2.5-km walk across the bridge.

Directory

Leh *p574, maps p575 and p576*

Banks **J&K Bank**, Main Bazar, with Maestro ATM; **State Bank of India**, slow exchange and temperamental ATM, next to tourist office. Large hotels and **Amex** (1030-1430, Sat 1030-1230) in Kangri and **Yak Tail**, charge a steep commission. **Internet** Several on Fort Rd, but email very erratic, slow and poor value at over Rs 100 an hr. Phone connections with the rest of India are unpredictable. **Medical services** Ambulance: T102. **SNM Hospital**, T01982-252014, 0900-1700 (also for advice on mountain sickness), after hours, T01982-253629. During the day, doctors have little time; better at clinics in evenings. **Soway Clinic**, in Bazar; **Kunfan Octsnang Clinic**; **Ladakh Medicate**, behind post office (ask for Dr Norbu, Old Leh Rd). **Post** Head Post Office and Telegraph Office: Airport Rd, 3 km from Leh centre (1000-1500); parcels often disappear. Mail may be sent via **Gypsy's World**, Fort Rd, T01982-252935 (not fail safe); make sure addressed c/o Gypsy's World, PO Box 160, Leh, Ladakh 194101, India. **Telephone** Pick up faxes here for a small fee; **Useful contacts** **Police**: T01982-252018. **Foreigners' Registration Office**: T01982-252200. **Deputy Commisioner's Office** for Inner Line Permits: T01982-252010, F01982-252106. Take passport, copies of visa and personal details pages and 2 photos.

West Bengal

Contents

Footprint features

Border crossing

At a glance

Getting around Trains link Kolkata to Siliguri, which has buses and jeeps to Darjeeling and Kalimpong. Domestic flights to Kolkata and Bagdogra.

Time required 3-4 days to get to grips with Kolkata, 2-3 days for a Sunderbans visit, and a week for a trek in the hills around Darjeeling.

Weather Best Oct-Feb in Kolkata; Oct and Mar-May in the hills. Extremely humid in the lowlands from Apr until the monsoon arrives in early Jun.

When not to go The middle of summer, when steamy Kolkata evacuates en-masse to the hills.

★ **Don't miss ...**

1. King prawn cutlets at Kolkata's Bengali restaurants, page 619.
2. Sunderbans Tiger Reserve, page 631.
3. A peaceful weekend at Murshidabad, page 635.
4. A visit to a tea estate in Darjeeling and trekking in the spring, page 641.
5. Wednesday and Sunday market in Kalimpong, page 650.

No visit to India is complete without some time spent in West Bengal; this cultured corner of the subcontinent has added immeasurably to India's overall identity.

Kolkata is considered by many to be the country's cultural hub. Many visitors have a preconceived idea of this oft-maligned city, but a little time spent here is often enough for those ideas to be rapidly dispelled and gives a fascinating glimpse of the way in which more than 15 million people live together. From rich to poor and educated to illiterate, Kolkatans melt together in a way that isn't seen in other cities.

Travelling north takes you through a land that has been left wonderfully fertile by both the ever-shifting course of the great Ganga River and by run-off from the Himalaya. Intensely populated and cultivated, the area contains treasures such as the terracotta temples at Bishnupur, Shantiniketan, home of the great Bengali poet Rabindranath Tagore, and Murshidabad, the delightful old capital of the Nawabs of Bengal.

Darjeeling is synonymous with tea the world over. Made popular by the British, the hill station has always been a holiday destination, particularly during the summer months, when the cool mountain air provides relief from the heat of the plains. With large Tibetan and Nepali populations, Darjeeling and the region around it have a very different feel from the India of the plains. The monasteries and prayer flags give a taste of the land and its peoples that lie deeper within the Himalaya.

If the mountains are too cold, head south from Kolkata to the Sunderbans. A World Heritage Site, these mangrove forests are home to a large Bengal tiger population.

Background → *Population: 91,347,736. Area: 88,752 sq km.*

The land

Geography Graphically described as being made up of "new mud, old mud and marsh", most of West Bengal lies on the western delta of the Ganga. Its limited higher ground, the basalt **Rajmahal Hills** just west of Murshidabad, are an extension of the ancient rocks of the peninsula. All that remains of the dense forests that once covered the state are the mangrove swamps of the **Sunderbans** in the far south and a narrow wooded belt along the southern slopes of the Himalaya. The apparently unchanging face of the Bengali countryside is highly misleading. Rivers have constantly changed their courses and over the last 300 years the Ganga has shifted progressively east, leaving the Hugli as a relatively minor channel. Minor variations in height make enormous differences to the quality of land for farming. The chief variety in the landscape of the plains of Bengal, however, comes from the contrasting greens of the different varieties of rice, often producing startlingly attractive countryside. The dominating mountains to the north and the plateau and hills of the southwest provide far greater scenic contrasts though. The gently rising slopes which lead from the delta to the peninsular rocks of Bihar and Orissa, are the home of some of India's most isolated tribal peoples, though their forest habitat has been severely degraded.

Climate Hot and oppressively humid summers are followed by much cooler and clearer winters. Heavy storms occur in late March and April. These electric storms are marked by massive cloud formations, strong winds and heavy rain. Occasionally tropical cyclones also strike coastal areas at this time of year, though they are far more common between October and December. The monsoon hits between June and September, when large parts of Kolkata are knee-deep in water for hours at a time. Asthma sufferers find the traffic pollution in Kolkata very trying.

History

In **prehistoric times** Bengal was home to Dravidian hunter-gatherers. In the first millennium BC, the Aryans from Central Asia, who had learned the agricultural techniques and the art of weaving and pottery, arrived in Bengal, bringing with them the Sanskrit language. From about the fifth century BC trade in cotton, silk and coral from Ganga Nagar flourished. In the third century BC, Bengal was part of the Mauryan Empire, but it remained densely forested and comparatively sparsely populated.

The **Guptas** conquered Bengal in the fourth century AD and trade with the Mediterranean expanded for the next 200 years, particularly with Rome. The fall of the Roman Empire in the fifth century led to a decline in Bengal's fortunes. Only with the founding of the **Pala Dynasty** in AD 750 was the region united once again. Bengal became a centre of Buddhism and art and learning flourished. The **Senas** followed. They were great patrons of the arts and ruled for 50 years until deposed by the invading Turks, who began a century of Muslim rule under the Khaljis of the Delhi Sultanate. The most notable of the Pathan kings who followed the Khaljis was **Sher Shah**, who extended his territory from Bihar into Bengal, which was taken back by the Mughal emperor Akbar, anxious to obtain the rich resources of rice, silk and saltpetre in 1574-1576.

The increasing power of the Muslims spurred the **Portuguese** towards the subcontinent and they began trading with Bengal in the mid-16th century. Before long they faced competition from the Dutch and the British and in 1632 an attack on their port near Kolkata by Emperor Shah Jahan reduced their merchant power.

In 1690 the purchase of the three villages which grew into Calcutta enabled the British to build a fort and consolidate their power. In 1700, Bengal became an independent presidency and Calcutta prospered. The *firmans* (permits) granted were for trading from the ports but the British took the opportunity of gaining a monopoly over internal trade as well. After the death of Emperor Aurangzeb, the authority of Delhi slowly crumbled. In 1756, Siraj-ud-Daula, the then

Nawab of Bengal, began to take note of Kolkata's growing wealth. Finding the British strengthening the fortifications he attacked Fort William, finding little difficulty in capturing the city. Within a year, however, Clive took the city back and then defeated the Nawab at Plassey; a turning point for the British in India. Through the 19th century West Bengal became the economic and political centre of **British India**.

Calcutta developed as the principal centre of cultural and political activity in modern India. Bengali literature, drama, art and music flourished. Religious reform movements such as the **Brahmo Samaj**, under the leadership of **Raja Ram Mohan Roy** in the 1830s, developed from the juxtaposition of traditional Hinduism with Christian missionary activity at the beginning of the 19th century. Later, one of India's greatest poets, Nobel Prize winner **Rabindranath Tagore** (1861-1941), dominated India's cultural world, breathing moral and spiritual life into the political movement for independence.

Until 1905 Bengal had included much of modern Bihar and Orissa, as well as the whole of Bengal. Lord Curzon's short-lived Partition of Bengal in 1905 roused fierce opposition, and also encouraged the split between Muslims and Hindus which finally resulted in Bengali Muslim support for the creation of Pakistan in 1947. The division into the two new states was accompanied by the migration of over five million people and appalling massacres as Hindus and Muslims fled. West Bengal was again directly affected by the struggle to create Bangladesh, when about 10 million refugees arrived from East Pakistan after 25 March 1971. Most returned after Bangladesh gained its Independence in December 1971.

Modern West Bengal

From the mid-1960s until the 2009 Lok Sabha elections political life was dominated by the confrontation between the Communist Party of India (Marxist) (the CPI(M)) and the Congress Party. The CPI(M) has held power in the State Assembly since June 1977, making it the world's longest-running democratically elected Communist government. The Congress, the second largest party, has performed better in the Lok Sabha parliamentary elections. Although the CPI(M) has lost some of its share of the urban vote, especially in Kolkata, Assembly elections have continued to be won convincingly by the CPI(M)-led Left Front under Chief Minister Buddhadeb Bhattacharjee. This pattern continued in the 2006 State Assembly elections, when the CPM won 233 of the 293 Assembly seats. Dismayed by the slow pace of industialisation in West Bengal compared with many other Indian states the CPM decided to create Special Economic Zones (SEZs) in rural areas. However, the policy of acquiring farm land led to vigorous communal agitation, erupting in the village of Nandigram on 14 March 2007, when at least 12 protesters were killed in police firing. Proposed developments by both foreign and Indian companies, most notably the Indian multinational Tata's plans to produce a new small car at Singur, were aborted. The CPM's popularity slumped, and at the Lok Sabha elections of 2009 the CPM won only nine of the 42 seats, the Trinamool Congress winning 19 and the Congress six.

Culture

The majority of the people are Bengalis. Tribal groups include Santals, Oraons and Mundas in the plains and the borders of Chota Nagpur and Lepchas and Bhotias in the Himalaya. Over 85% of the population speak Bengali. Hindi, Urdu and tribal languages account for most of the remainder.

Bengalis are said to be obsessed about what they eat. The men often take a keen interest in buying the most important elements of the day's meal, namely fresh fish. Typically, it is river fish, the most popular being *hilsa* and *bekti* or the widely available shellfish, especially king prawns. *Bekti* is grilled or fried and is tastier than the fried fish of the west as it has often been marinated in mild spices first. The prized smoked *hilsa*, although delicious, has thousands of fine bones. *Maachh* (fish) comes in many forms as *jhol* (in a thin gravy), *jhal* (spicy and hot), *malai curry* (in coconut milk, mildly spiced), chop (in a covering of mashed potato and crumbs) or *chingri maachher* cutlet (flattened king prawn 'fillets', crumbed and fried). Bengali cooking uses mustard oil and mustard which grows in abundance, and a subtle mixture of spices. *Mishti* (sweetmeats) are another distinctive feature. Many are milk based and the famous *sandesh*, *roshogolla, roshomalai*, *pantua* and *ledikeni* (named after Lady Canning, the wife of the first Viceroy of India) are prepared with a kind of cottage cheese, in dozens of different textures, shapes, colours and tastes. Pale pinkish brown, *mishti doi*, is an excellent sweet yoghurt eaten as a dessert, typically sold in hand-thrown clay pots.

You will only find the true flavour of Bengali cooking in someone's home or at a few special Bengali restaurants.

Crafts

Silk has been woven in India for more than 3500 years and continues today with the weaving of the natural-coloured wild silk called *tassar*. Bengal silk, found as block-printed saris, has had a revival in the exquisite brocade weaving of *baluchari*, produced in the past under royal patronage, and is now carried out in Bankura. The saris are woven in traditional style with untwisted silk and have beautiful borders and *pallu* (the end section), which depict peacocks, flowers and human figures. Fine **cotton** is woven also.

The Bankura horse has become a symbol of **pottery** in West Bengal which still flourishes in the districts of Bankura, Midnapore and Birbhum. Soft **soap stone** is used for carving copies of temple images, while **shell** bangles are considered auspicious. **Ivory** carvers once produced superb decorative items, a skill developed in the Mughal period. Today, bone and plastic have largely replaced ivory in inlay work. **Metal** workers produce brass and bell- metal ware while the tribal *dhokra* casters still follow the ancient *cire perdue* method, see page 767. Kalighat *pat* paintings are in a primitive style using bold colours.

Kolkata (Calcutta)

→ *Colour map 4, C2. Population: 13.22 million.*

To Bengalis Kolkata is the proud intellectual capital of India, with an outstanding contribution to the arts, services, medicine and social reform in its past, and a rich contemporary cultural life. As the former imperial capital, Kolkata retains some of the country's most striking colonial buildings, yet at the same time it is truly an Indian city. Unique in India in retaining trams, and the only place in the world to still have hand-pulled rickshaws, you take your life in your hands each time you cross Kolkata's streets. Hugely crowded, Kolkata's Maidan, the parkland, give lungs to a city packed with some of the most densely populated slums, or bustees, anywhere in the world. ▸▸ *For listings, see pages 615-630.*

Ins and outs

Getting there Subhas Chandra Bose airport at Dum Dum serves international and domestic flights. Taxis to the city centre take 45-60 minutes and there is a pre-paid taxi booth before exiting the airport (to Sudder Street, the backpacker hub, costs Rs 235). There are new buses which leave from outside Terminal 1, some of which go to Howrah and Esplanade (for Sudder St), about Rs 40. Arrival at Howrah station, on the west bank of the Hugli, can be daunting and the taxi rank outside is often chaotic; the prepaid taxi booth is to the right as you exit – check the price chart near the booth, note that Sudder St is less than 5 km. Trains to/from the north use the slightly less chaotic Sealdah terminal east of the centre, which also has prepaid taxis. Long-distance buses arrive at Esplanade, 15 minutes' walk from most budget hotels. ▸▸ *See Transport, page 627.*

Getting around You can cover much of Central Kolkata on foot. For the rest you need transport. You may not fancy using hand-pulled rickshaws, but they become indispensable when the streets are flooded. Buses and minibuses are often jam packed, but routes comprehensively cover the city – conductors and bystanders will help you find the correct bus. The electric trams can be slightly better outside peak periods. The Metro, though on a limited route and very crowded, is the easiest way of getting from north to south. Taxis are relatively cheap (note that the meter reading is not the true fare – they have conversion charts which work out at about double the meter) but allow plenty of time to get through very congested traffic. Despite the footpath, it is not permitted to walk across the Vidyasagar Bridge (taxi drivers expect passengers to pay the Rs 10 toll).

Tourist information India Tourism ⓘ *4 Shakespeare Sarani, T033-2282 5813, Mon-Fri 0930-1800, Sat 0900-1300*, can provide a city map and information for all India. More useful is **West Bengal Tourism Development Corporation (WBTDC)** ⓘ *BBD Bagh, T033-2248 8271, Mon-Fri 1030-1630, Sat 1030-1300; also a counter at the station in Howrah.*

Background

Calcutta, as it came to be named, was founded by the remarkable English merchant trader **Job Charnock** in 1690. He was in charge of the East India Company factory (ie warehouse) in Hugli, then the centre of British trade from eastern India. Attacks from the local Muslim ruler forced him to flee – first down river to Sutanuti and then 1500 km south to Chennai. However, in 1690 he selected three villages – Kalikata, Sutanuti and Govindpur – where Armenian and Portuguese traders had already settled, leased them from Emperor Aurangzeb and returned to what became the capital of British India.

The first fort here, named after King William III (completed 1707), was on the site of the present BBD Bagh. A deep defensive moat was dug in 1742 to strengthen the fort – the Maratha ditch. The Maratha threat never materialized but the city was captured easily by the 20-year-old **Siraj-ud-Daula**, the new Nawab of Bengal, in 1756. The 146 British residents who failed to escape by the fort's river gate were imprisoned for a night in a small guard room about 6 m by 5 m with

1 Kolkata

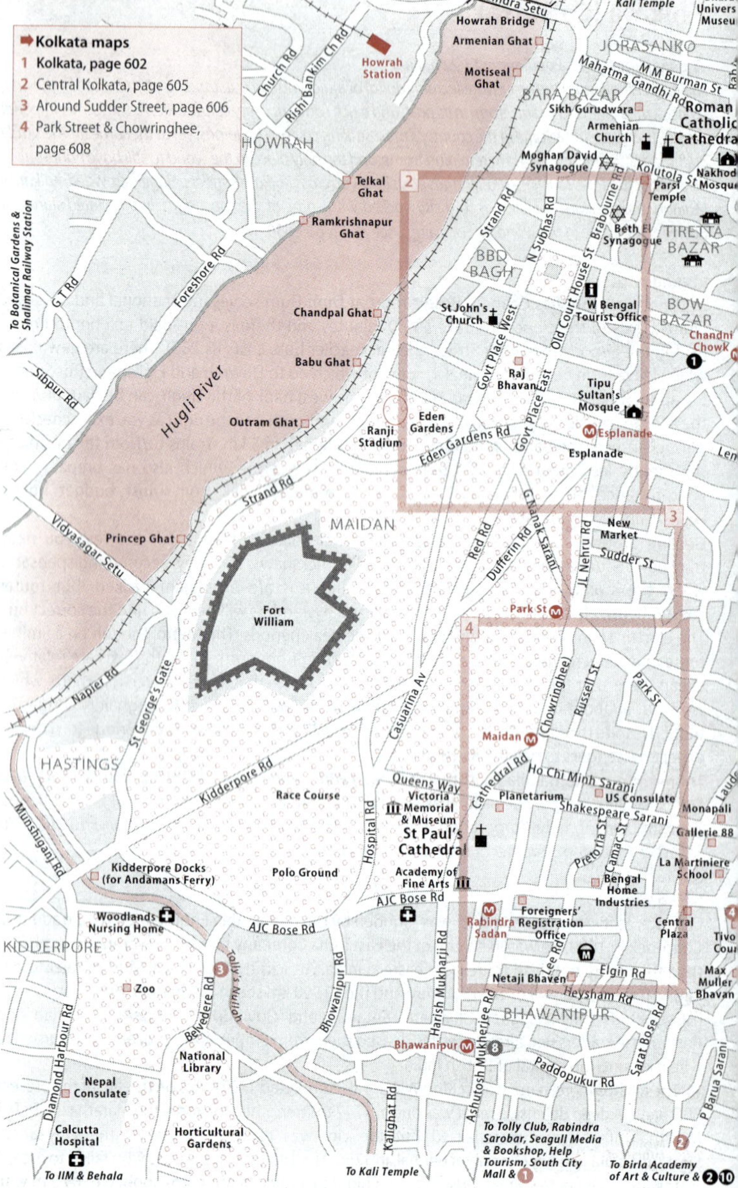

Kolkata maps
1 Kolkata, page 602
2 Central Kolkata, page 605
3 Around Sudder Street, page 606
4 Park Street & Chowringhee, page 608
To Belur Math
To Kumartuli & Dakshineshwar Kali Temple
Rabindra Bharati University Museum
Rabindra Setu
Howrah Bridge
Armenian Ghat
Howrah Station
Motiseal Ghat
JORASANKO
Mahatma Gandhi Rd
M M Burman St
BARA BAZAR
Sikh Gurudwara
Roman Catholic Cathedral
Armenian Church
Church Rd
Rishi Bankim Ch Rd
HOWRAH
Moghan David Synagogue
Kolutola St
Nakhoda Mosque
Parsi Temple
Telkal Ghat
Ramkrishnapur Ghat
Strand Rd
N Subhas Rd
Brabourne Rd
Beth El Synagogue
TIRETTA BAZAR
To Botanical Gardens & Shalimar Railway Station
G T Rd
Foreshore Rd
BBD BAGH
Old Court House St
W Bengal Tourist Office
BOW BAZAR
Chandpal Ghat
St John's Church
Govt Place West
Chandni Chowk
Sibpur Rd
Babu Ghat
Hugli River
Raj Bhavan
Govt Place East
Tipu Sultan's Mosque
Outram Ghat
Ranji Stadium
Eden Gardens
Eden Gardens Rd
Esplanade
Strand Rd
Vidyasagar Setu
Princep Ghat
MAIDAN
G Nanak Sarani
New Market
JL Nehru Rd
Sudder St
Red Rd
Dufferin Rd
Fort William
Park St
Napier Rd
St George's Gate
Casuarina Av
Chowringhee
Russell St
Park St
Maidan
HASTINGS
Kidderpore Rd
Cathedral Rd
Ho Chi Minh Sarani
Queens Way
Planetarium
US Consulate
Race Course
Victoria Memorial & Museum
Shakespeare Sarani
Monapali
Munshiganj Rd
Hospital Rd
St Paul's Cathedral
Gallerie 88
Pretoria St
Camac St
La Martiniere School
Kidderpore Docks (for Andamans Ferry)
Polo Ground
Academy of Fine Arts
Bengal Home Industries
AJC Bose Rd
Woodlands Nursing Home
Foreigners' Registration Office
Central Plaza
Rabindra Sadan
KIDDERPORE
Tolly's Nullah
Bhowanipur Rd
Harish Mukharji Rd
Lee Rd
Elgin Rd
Tivoli Court
Max Muller Bhavan
Zoo
Belvedere Rd
Netaji Bhavan
Heysham Rd
BHAWANIPUR
Ashutosh Mukherjee Rd
Sarat Bose Rd
Bhawanipur
Diamond Harbour Rd
National Library
Paddopukur Rd
P Barua Sarani
Nepal Consulate
Kalighat Rd
Calcutta Hospital
Horticultural Gardens
To Tolly Club, Rabindra Sarobar, Seagull Media & Bookshop, Help Tourism, South City Mall & 1
To IIM & Behala
To Kali Temple
To Birla Academy of Art & Culture & 2 10

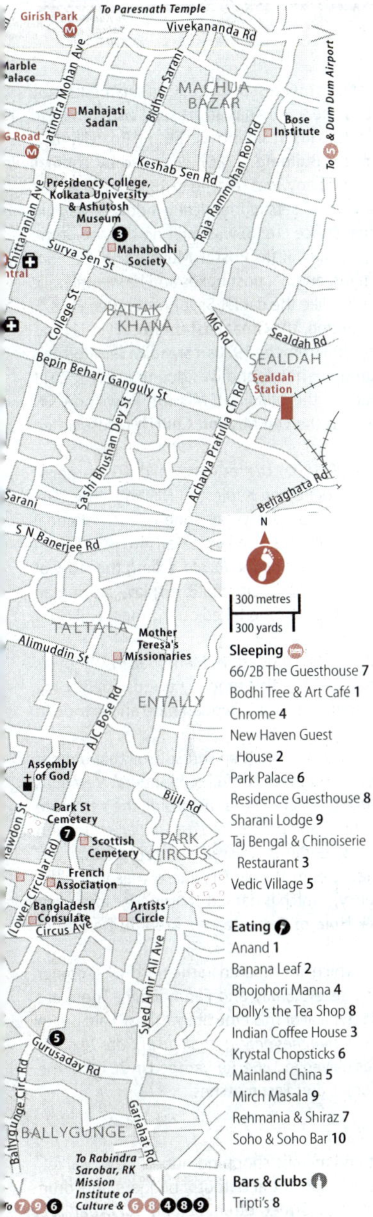

only one window – the infamous '**Black Hole of Calcutta**'. Some records suggest 64 people were imprisoned and only 23 survived.

The following year **Robert Clive** re-took the city. The new Fort William was built and in 1772 Calcutta became the capital of British administration in India with Warren Hastings as the first Governor of Bengal, see page 1391. Some of Calcutta's most impressive colonial buildings were built in the years that followed, when it became the first city of British India. It was also a time of Hindu and Muslim resurgence.

Colonial Calcutta grew as new traders, soldiers and administrators arrived, establishing their exclusive social and sports clubs. Trade in cloth, silk, lac, indigo, rice, areca nut and tobacco had originally attracted the Portuguese and British to Bengal. Later Calcutta's hinterland producing jute, iron ore, tea and coal led to large British firms setting up headquarters in the city. Calcutta prospered as the commercial and political capital of British India up to 1911, when the capital was transferred to Delhi.

Kolkata had to absorb huge numbers of migrants immediately after Partition in 1947. When Pakistan ceased trading with India in 1949, Kolkata's economy suffered a massive blow as it lost its supplies of raw jute and its failure to attract new investment created critical economic problems. In the late 1960s the Communist Party of India Marxist, the CPI(M), was elected – and their dominance was to last over 30 years. Since 2000, the CPI(M) were committed to a mixed economy and sought foreign private investment, and the city's economy has experienced a much needed upturn.

Central Kolkata

BBD Bagh (Dalhousie Square) and around

Many historic Raj buildings surround the square, which is quietest before 0900. Renamed Benoy Badal Dinesh (BBD) Bagh after three Bengali martyrs, the square has an artificial lake (tank) fed by natural springs that used to supply water to Calcutta's first residents. On Strand Road North is the dilapidated **Silver Mint** (1824-1831). The **Writers' Building** (1780), designed by Thomas Lyon as the trading headquarters of the East India Company, was refaced in 1880. It is now the state Government Secretariat. The classical block with 57 sets of identical windows was built like barracks inside. The white domed **General Post Office** (1866) was built on the site of the first Fort William. Around the corner, there is a quaint little **Postal Museum** ⓘ *Mon-Sat 1100-1600, entrance free*, which displays shabby maps, original post boxes and has a philatelic library. Elegant **St Andrew's Kirk** (1814) ⓘ *0900-1400*, like the earlier St John's Church (1787), was modelled partially on St Martin-in-the-Fields, London. The **Great Eastern Hotel** (1841) was in Mark Twain's day "the best hotel East of the Suez", but from the 1970s it steadily declined. It is now undergoing major restoration by the LaLit group of hotels and was due to open in 2011 (though that looks unlikely from the present state of the building). **Mission Row** (now RN Mukharji Road) is Kolkata's oldest street, and contains the **Old Mission Church** (consecrated 1770), built by the Swedish missionary Johann Kiernander.

South of BBD Bagh is the imposing **Raj Bhavan** (1799-1802), the residence of the Governor of West Bengal, formerly Government House. It was modelled on Kedleston Hall in Derbyshire, England (later Lord Curzon's home), and designed by Charles Wyatt, one of many Bengal engineers who based their designs on famous British buildings. The **Town Hall** (1813) has been converted into a **museum** ⓘ *1100-1800, foreigners Rs 10, no bags allowed*, telling the story of the independence movement in Bengal through a panoramic, cinematic display, starring an animatronic Rabindranath Tagore. The **High Court** (1872) was modelled on the medieval cloth merchants' hall at Ypres in Flanders.

The **Ochterlony Monument** (1828), renamed Shahid Minar (Martyrs' Memorial) in 1969, was built as a memorial to Sir David Ochterlony, who led East India Company troops against the Nepalese in 1814-1816. The 46-m-tall Greek Doric column has an Egyptian base and is topped by a Turkish cupola.

St John's Church (1787) ⓘ *0800-1700, entrance Rs 10*, was built on soft subsoil that did not allow it to have a tall spire and architecturally it was thought to be 'full of blunders'. Verandas were added to the north and south in 1811 to reduce the glare of the sun. Inside the vestry are Warren Hastings's table and chair, plus Raj-era paintings and prints. *The Last Supper*, by Johann Zoffany was restored in 2010 and shows the city's residents dressed as the Apostles. Job Charnock is buried in the grounds. His octagonal mausoleum, the oldest piece of masonry in the city, is of Pallavaram granite (from Madras Presidency), which is named charnockite after him. The monument built by Lord Curzon to the **Black Hole of Calcutta** was brought here from Dalhousie Square (BBD Bagh) in 1940.

Eden Gardens ⓘ *daily 1200-1700, entrance free*, which are situated in the northwest corner of the Maidan, were named after Lord Auckland's sisters Emily and Fanny Eden. There are pleasant walks, a lake and a small Burmese pagoda (typical of this type of Pyatthat). Laid out in 1834, part forms the Ranji Stadium ⓘ *usually open for matches only, a small tip at Gate 14 gains entry on other days* where the first cricket match was played in 1864. Re-vamped in 2011 for the Cricket World Cup, massive crowds are attracted for IPL and Test matches.

Around Sudder Street

Conveniently close to Chowringhee and the vast and archaic shopping hub of New Market, Sudder Street is the focus for Kolkata's backpackers and attracts touts, beggars and drug pushers aplenty. Beggars on Chowringhee and Park Street often belong to organized syndicates who have to pay a large percentage of their 'earnings' for the privilege of working the area. Women asking for milk or rice for their baby is the most popular ruse.

Around the corner from Sudder Street is the **Indian Museum** ⓘ *27 Chowringhee (JL Nehru Rd), T033-2286 1679, www.indianmuseumkolkata.org, Mar-Nov Tue-Sun 1000-1700, Dec-Feb*

2 Central Kolkata

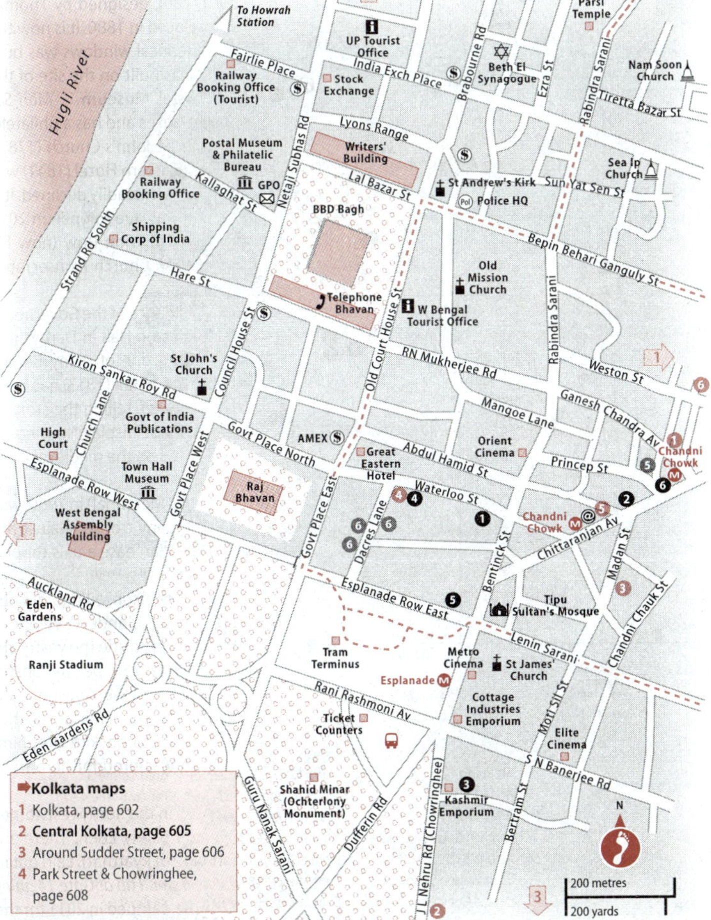

Sleeping
Broadway & Bar **1**
Buddha Dharmankur Sabha **6**
Cosmos Guest House **5**
Majestic **3**
Manthan **4**
Oberoi Grand & Baan Thai Restaurant **2**

Eating
Aaheli at Peerless Inn **3**
Amber **1**
Anand **2**
Bhojohori Manna **5**
Madras **6**
Song Hay **4**

Bars & clubs
Embassy **5**
Local Bars **6**

Tram Line - - - -

3 Around Sudder Street

➡ **Kolkata maps**
1 Kolkata, page 602
2 Central Kolkata, page 605
3 Around Sudder Street, page 606
4 Park Street & Chowringhee, page 608

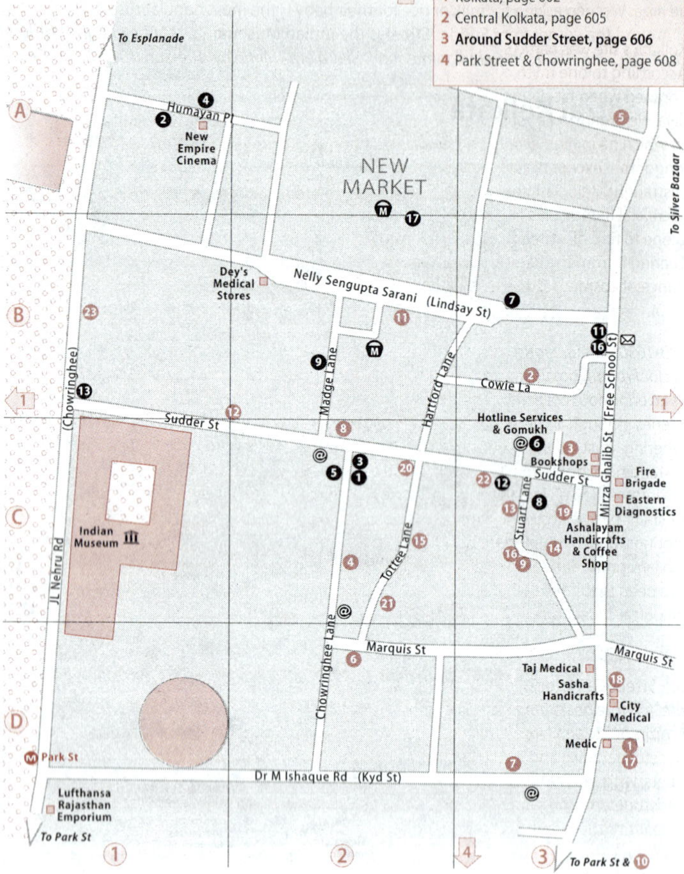

Sleeping
Afraa 1 *D3*
Al-Sana 5 *A3*
Ashreen Guest House 2 *B3*
Astoria 3 *C3*
Bawa Walson Spa'o'tel 22 *C3*
Capital Guest House 4 *C2*
Emirates 7 *D3*
Fairlawn 8 *C2*
Galaxy 9 *C3*
Housez 43 10 *D3*
Lindsay & Blue Beyond 11 *B2*
Lytton 12 *B2*
Maria 13 *C3*
Modern Lodge 14 *C3*
Paragon 16 *C3*
Paramount 17 *D3*
Pioneer International 6 *D2*
Sonali Resort 18 *D3*
Super Guest House 19 *C3*
Times Guest House 20 *C2*
Timestar 15 *C2*
YMCA 23 *B1*

Eating
Blue Sky Café 1 *C2*
Brothers Snacks 2 *A1*
Curd Corner 3 *C2*
Family Home 4 *A1*
Fresh & Juicy 5 *C2*
Jimmy's 7 *B3*
Jo-jo's 8 *C3*
Kathleen's 16 *B3*
Khalsa 9 *B2*
Nahoum 17 *B2*
NV Stores & Maa Kalai 11 *B3*
Raj's Spanish Café 6 *C3*
Tirupati 12 *C3*
Zaranj & Jong's 13 *B1*

Kolkata's place in the cosmic dance

Kolkata's site was particularly holy to Hindus. According to one myth, King Daksa was enraged when his daughter Sati married Siva. He organized a *yajna* (grand sacrifice) to which he invited everyone in the kingdom – except his son-in-law. Distraught, Kali (Sati) threw herself on the sacrificial flames. Siva in turn arrived on the scene to find his wife's body already burnt. Tearing it from the flames, he started his dance of cosmic destruction. All the other gods, witnessing the devastation that Siva was causing in his anguish, pleaded with Vishnu to step in and end the chaos. Vishnu intercepted him with his *chakra* (discus-like weapon) and, in order to dislodge Kali's body from Siva's shoulder, chopped it into 51 pieces, which were flung far and wide. The place where each one fell became a *pithasthana* (place of pilgrimage). Kali's little toe fell at Kali Ghat. The place, Kalikshetra or Kalikata, gave the city its name.

1000-1630, foreigners Rs 150, Indians Rs 10, cameras Rs 50/100 with tripod; no bags allowed (there is a cloakroom), possibly Asia's largest. The Jadu Ghar (House of Magic) was founded in 1814 and has an enormous collection. The colonnaded Italianate building around a central courtyard has 36 galleries (though large sections are often closed off for restoration). Parts are poorly lit and gathering dust so it is best to be selective. Highlights include: the stone statutory with outstanding exhibits from the Harappa and Moenjodaro periods; the Cultural Anthropology room with information on India's tribes; and the excellent new Mask Gallery (hidden on the 4th floor, up the stairs past the ground floor coin collection and library). There are some lovely miniature paintings, the Egyptian room has a popular mummy and the Plant gallery is curiously beautiful, with jars, prints and samples filling every inch of space. The animals in the Natural History gallery have been there since 1878 while the birds are so dirty they are all uniformly black in colour. The geological collection with Siwalik fossils is mind-bogglingly huge. Allow a couple of hours.

Park Street

Park Street Cemetery ⓘ *daily 0800-1630, free, information booklet Rs 100, security guard opens gate for foreigners and will expect you to sign the visitors' book,* was opened in 1767 to accommodate the large number of British who died 'serving' their country. The cemetery is a peaceful paradise and a step into history, located on the south side of one of Kolkata's busiest streets, with a maze of soaring obelisks shaded by tropical trees. The heavily inscribed decaying headstones, rotundas, pyramids and urns have been restored, and gardeners are actively trying to beautify the grounds. Several of the inscriptions make interesting reading. Death, often untimely, came from tropical diseases or other hazards such as battles, childbirth and even melancholia. More uncommonly, it was an excess of alcohol, or as for Sir Thomas D'Oyly, through "an inordinate use of the hokkah". Rose Aylmer died after eating too many pineapples! Tombs include those of Col Kyd, founder of the Botanical Gardens, the great oriental scholar Sir William Jones, and the fanciful mausoleum of the Irish Major-General 'Hindoo' Stuart. Across AJC Bose Road, on Karaya Road, is the smaller and far more derelict **Scottish Cemetery** ⓘ *daily 0700-1730, free, pamphlet by donation to the caretaker*. The Kolkata Scottish Heritage Trust begun work in 2008 to restore some of the 1600 tumbledown graves but the undergrowth is rampant and jungle prevails. It is also known as the 'dissenters' graveyard', as this was where non-Anglicans were buried.

The **Asiatic Society** ⓘ *1 Park St, T033-2229 0779, www.asiaticsocietycal.com, Mon-Fri 1000-1800, free,* the oldest institution of Oriental studies in the world, was founded in 1784 by the great Orientalist, Sir William Jones. It is a treasure house of 150,000 books and 60,000 ancient manuscripts in most Asian languages, although permission is required to see specific pieces. The museum includes an Ashokan edict, rare coins and paintings. The library is worth a

4 Park Street & Chowringhee

Sleeping
Astor 1
Chrome 10
Golden Parkk & Fusion Bar/Club 2
Gulshan International 3
Hindustan 11
Middleton Inn 5
New Kenilworth 6
Park 7
Sunflower 4
YWCA 9

Eating
Amber 17
Bar-B-Q 1
Bistro by the Park 16
Café Thé 18
Fire & Ice 2
Flury's 3
Gangaur 4
Gupta's 6
Hamro Momo 11
Ivory 5
Kewpies 15
Maya Ram 13
Mocambo 7
Momo Plaza 14
Peter Cat 8
Pure Milk Centre 9
Teej 21
Tung Fong 10
Waldorf & Sam's Pub 12

Bars & clubs
Oly Pub 19
Shisha Reincarnated 20

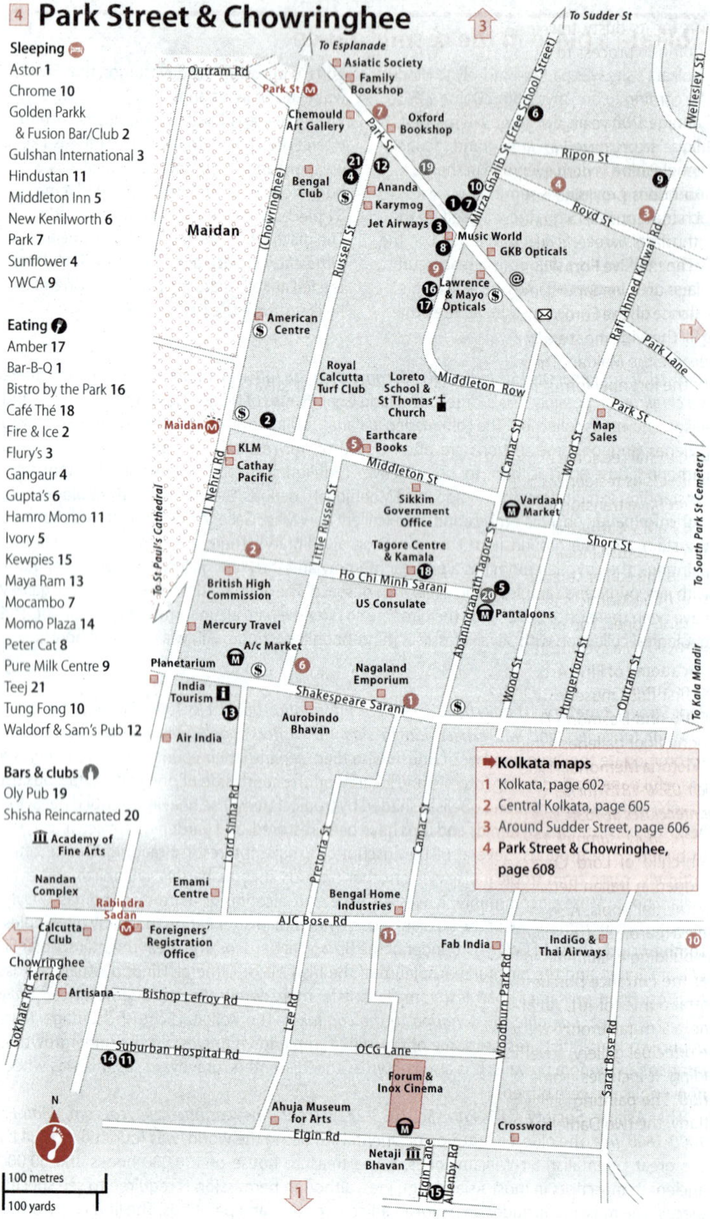

visit for its dusty travelogues and titles on the history of Calcutta. Bring a passport, as the signing-in process to visit the building is (at least) a triplicate process.

The Maidan

This area, 200 years ago, was covered in dense jungle. Often called the 'lungs of the city', it is a unique green, covering over 400 ha along Chowringhee (JL Nehru Road). Larger than New York's Central Park, it is perhaps the largest urban park in the world. In it stands Fort William and several clubhouses providing tennis, football, rugby, cricket and even crown green bowls. Thousands each day pursue a hundred different interests – from early-morning yogis, model plane enthusiasts, weekend cricketers and performers earning their living, to vast political gatherings.

The massive **Fort William** was built by the British after their defeat in 1756, on the site of the village of Govindapur. Designed to be impregnable, it was roughly octagonal and large enough to house all the Europeans in the city in case of an attack. Water from the Hugli was channelled to fill the wide moat and the surrounding jungle was cleared to give a clear field of fire; this later became the Maidan. The barracks, stables, arsenal, prison and St Peter's Church are still there, but the fort now forms the Eastern Region's Military Headquarters and entry is forbidden.

Chowringhee and around

You can still see some of the old imposing structures with pillared verandas (designed by Italian architects as residences of prominent Englishmen), though modern high-rise buildings and a flyover have transformed the skyline of what was the ancient pilgrim route to Kalighat.

St Paul's Cathedral ⓘ *0900-1200, 1500-1800, 5 services on Sun*, is the original metropolitan church of British India. Completed in 1847, its Gothic tower (dedicated in 1938) was designed to replace the earlier steeples which were destroyed by earthquakes. The cathedral has a fine altar piece, three 'Gothic' stained-glass windows, two Florentine frescoes and the great West window by Burne-Jones. The original stained-glass East window, intended for St George's Windsor, was destroyed by a cyclone in 1964 and was replaced by the present one four years later.

Academy of Fine Arts ⓘ *2 Cathedral Rd, open 1500-2000, entrance free*, was founded in 1933. The first floor museum, which includes miniature paintings, textiles and works of Jamini Roy, Tagore and Desmond Doig, has been closed for years and shows no sign of reopening. The ground floor galleries exhibit contemporary paintings and sculptures by Indian artists.

Victoria Memorial (1906-1921) ⓘ *T033-2223 1889-91, www.victoriamemorial-cal.org. Gardens open 0530-1815 (ticket counter closes at 1745), Rs 4; museum open Tue-Sun 1000-1700 (ticket counter closes at 1630, very crowded on Sun), foreigners Rs 150, cameras not permitted inside; son et lumière show, summer 1945, winter 1915, 45 mins, Rs 20 front seats, Rs 10 elsewhere*, was the brain-child of Lord Curzon. The white marble monument to Queen Victoria and the Raj designed in Italian Renaissance/Indo-Saracenic style stands in large, well-kept grounds with ornamental pools. A seated bronze Queen Victoria dominates the approach from the north, while a marble statue stands in the main hall where visitors sometimes leave flowers at her feet. The building is illuminated in the evening; the musical fountain is a special draw. The statues over the entrance porches (including Motherhood, Prudence and Learning), and around the central dome (of Art, Architecture, Justice, Charity) came from Italy. The impressive weather vane, a 5-m-tall bronze winged Angel of Victory weighing three tonnes, looks tiny from below. The principal gallery, covering the history of the city, is well-presented and makes interesting reading. It includes some fascinating lithographs and illustrations of the city during the Raj period. The painting galley has works by European artists in India from 1770-1835, including Zoffany, the two Daniells and Samuel Davis.

North Kolkata

College Street

This is the heart of intellectual Kolkata with the **university** and several academic institutions, including the old **Sanskrit College** and the elite **Presidency College**. Europeans and Indian benefactors established the Hindu College (1817) to provide a liberal education. In 1855, this became the Presidency College. A centre for 19th-century Bengali writers, artists and reformers, it spawned the early 20th-century Swadeshi Movement. The famous **Indian Coffee House** (opened in 1944), cavernous haunt of the city's intelligentsia, has tonnes of atmosphere and is always packed despite the average coffee and food. Along the pavements are interesting second-hand book stalls. The **Asutosh Museum of Indian Art** ⓘ *University Centenary Building, Mon-Fri 1100-1600, closed university holidays, entrance Rs 10*, is well maintained and worth a look. The ground floor is packed with eastern Indian pieces of sculpture and terracotta tiles depicting figures. The first floor has colourful Bengali and Orissan folk art, textiles, and a hoard of paintings including 14th-19th century miniatures, Kalighat paintings, Nepalese art and Tibetan *thankas*. Also look out for the model of the Senate Hall which was pulled down to make way for the concrete monster of the present Centenary block, in the days before heritage buildings were accorded any value.

Marble Palace

ⓘ *46 Muktaram Babu St, closed Mon and Thu, 1000-1600. Free pass from WBTDC (see page 601), 24 hrs ahead, or baksheesh (Rs 20 per person) to the security man at the gate, shoes must be removed, no photography allowed.*

Located in *Chor Bagan* ('Thieves' Garden'), the one-man collection of Raja Rajendra Mullick is in his ornate home (1835) with an Italianate courtyard, classical columns and Egyptian sphinxes. Family members still inhabit a portion of the house while servants' descendants live in the huts that encircle the grounds. Six sleeping marble lions and statuary grace the lawns and there is a veritable menagerie at the back of the garden. The galleries are crammed with statues, porcelain, clocks, mirrors, chandeliers and English (Reynolds), Dutch (Reubens) and Italian paintings, disorganized and gathering dust. The pink, grey and white Italian marble floors are remarkable, as is the solid rosewood statue of Queen Victoria. Allow one hour, or take a book and relax in the garden. The rambling museum on two floors has more than curiosity appeal – it is one of Kolkata's gems.

Howrah Bridge area

North of the Marble Palace on Baghbazar Street is the **Girish Mancha**, the government theatre complex. The gorgeously well-kept **Armenian Church** of Holy Nazareth (1724) is a reminder of the important trading role the small Armenian community who mostly came from Iran, played from the 17th century. The church is open 0600-1200 on weekdays or you can ask someone to open up in order to view the beautifully maintained interior. A gravestone in the compound is inscribed with the date 1630. The 150 or so Armenians in the city still hold a service in Armenian in one of their two churches in the city every Sunday. Their college on Mirza Ghalib Street (also the birthplace of William Makepeace Thackery in 1811) has boarding pupils from Armenia who are usually orphans. To the east of the Church of Holy Nazareth is the **Roman Catholic Cathedral** (1797) built by the Portuguese. The Jewish community, mostly Sephardic, of Baghdadi origin, was also once very prominent in commerce. Their two synagogues are well maintained with stained glass windows. The grander of the two is the church-like and cavernous **Moghan David Synagogue** (1884) in Canning Street (daily 0900-1700). The smaller **Beth El Synagogue** is at 26/1 Pollock Street nearby (Sunday-Friday 1000-1700). There are only around 20-30 elderly Jews left in the city who continue to congregate at Nahoum's bakery in the New Market; the Jewish Girls School in Park Street has no pupils from the community. To view the interior of the synagogues, it is necessary to get permission from Mr DE Nahoum, either at the bakery or from the office at 1 Hartford Lane.

A few reminders that there was once a Chinatown in Kolkata remain in the form of Chinese 'churches'. Seek out the **Sea Ip Church** (1905) which has an intricately carved wooden altar and the **Nam Soon Church**, with a school at the rear; gorgeously maintained with bright paint, a huge bell and drum, and a little courtyard with trees. Both are willingly opened by the custodians. At the top of Bentinck Street, where it meets BB Ganguly Street, are several tiny old-fashioned shoe-shops run by aging members of the Chinese community.

Howrah Bridge (Haora), or Rabindra Setu, was opened in 1943. This single-span cantilever bridge, the quintessential image of Calcutta, replaced the old pontoon (floating) bridge that first joined the city of Kolkata with Howrah and the railway station. To avoid affecting river currents and silting, the two 80-m-high piers rise from road level; the 450-m span expands by a metre on a hot day. It is the busiest bridge in the world in terms of foot passengers, with over 3.5 million pedestrians per day (many with improbable loads on their heads). Wrestlers can be seen underneath and there is a daily **flower market** beneath the eastern end at Mullik Ghat, with piles of marigolds glowing against the mud. At night the bridge is illuminated, which makes a fine sight – if waiting for a night train at Howrah station go to first floor waiting rooms for a good aspect. The pedestrian-free **Vidyasagar Setu**, further south, has eased the traffic burden slightly.

Rabindra Bharati University Museum

ⓘ *6/4 Dwarakanath Tagore Lane (red walls visible down lane opposite 263 Rabindra Sarani), Mon-Fri 1000-1700, Sat 1000-1330, Sun and holidays 1100-1400.*

This museum, in a peaceful enclave away from the teeming chaos of Rabindra Sarani, occupies the family home of Rabindranath Tagore, who won the Nobel Prize for Literature in 1913. It showcases Tagore's life and works, as well as the 19th-century Renaissance movement in Bengal.

Kumartuli

South of the Dakshineshwar temple is Kumartuli. Off Chitpur Road, the *kumars* or potters work all year, preparing clay images around cores of bamboo and straw. For generations they have been making life-size idols for the *pujas* or festivals, particularly of goddess Durga on a lion, slaying the demon. The images are usually unbaked since they are immersed in the holy river at the end of the festival. As the time of the *pujas* approaches, you will see thousands of images, often very brightly painted and gaudily dressed, awaiting the final finishing touch by the master painter. There are also *shola* artists who make decorations for festivals and weddings. The potters' area of Kumartuli is being rebuilt currently, and concrete structures are replacing the towering bamboo workshops that were so very photogenic.

Northeast of the city centre

Just north of the Belgachia Metro station is a cluster of three Digambar Jain temples, one of the most tranquil spots in the city. The meticulously maintained and ornate **Paresnath Temple** ⓘ *0700-1200, 1500-2000, no leather*, is dedicated to the 10th Tirthankara. Consecrated around 1867, it is richly decorated with mirrors, Victorian tiles and Venetian glass mosaics.

Difficult to find (and perhaps not worth the effort unless you are a true aficionado of Raj history) is **Clive's House**, off Jessore Rd in Nagarbajar, Dum Dum. This was the country home of the first governor-general of the East India Company and is the oldest colonial monument in Kolkata. For years, Bangladeshi immigrants lived in and around the derelict property until it was restored in 2008. Already the brick walls are being re-consumed by plant life and it requires some imagination to envisage its former glory.

Belur Math and the Dakshineshwar Kali Temple

Some 16 km north of the city is **Belur Math** ⓘ *0600-1200, 1600-1900*, the international headquarters of the **Ramakrishna Mission**, founded in 1899 by Swami Vivekananda, a disciple of the 19th-century Hindu saint Ramakrishna. He preached the unity of all religions and to symbolize this the *Math* ('monastery') synthesizes Hindu, Christian and Islamic architectural styles in a peaceful and meditative atmosphere.

On the opposite side of the river from Belur Math is the **Dakshineshwar Kali Temple** ⓘ *0600-1200, 1500-1800, 1830-2100, no photography allowed inside*. This huge Kali temple was built in 1847 by Rani Rashmoni. The 12 smaller temples in the courtyard are dedicated to Siva and there are also temples to Radha and Krishna. Because of the Rani's low caste, no priest would serve there until Ramakrishna's elder brother agreed and was succeeded by Ramakrishna himself. Here, Ramakrishna achieved his spiritual vision of the unity of all religions. The temple is crowded with colourfully clad devotees, particularly on Sundays when there are lengthy queues, and is open to all faiths. A boat (Rs 8) takes 20 minutes to/from to Belur Math across the Hooghly. Buses from BBD Bagh go to Dunlop Intersection, from where it's a short auto ride to the temple; trains run from Sealdah to Dakshineshwar.

South Kolkata

Netaji Museum

ⓘ *Netaji Bhavan, 38/1 Elgin Rd, entrance Rs 5, daily (except Mon) 1100-1430 (last entry 1615), no photography.*

This museum remembers the mission of Subas Chandra Bose, the leader of the INA (Indian National Army), and is in the house where he lived before he had to flee the British oppressors. On the first floor, you can view his bedroom and study (where walls are painted with the tricolours of the Congress flag), although panes of glass prevent close inspection of his possessions. A detailed video is played in the second floor rooms showing old footage and giving a detailed explanation of his life's work. Interesting is the German Room, with a photo of Netaji meeting Hitler and information on Azad Hind and the Indo-German Friendship Society.

Kali Temple

ⓘ *Off Ashok Mukherjee Rd, 0500-1500, 1700-2200.*

This is the temple to Kali (1809), the patron goddess of Kolkata, usually seen in her bloodthirsty form garlanded with skulls. There was an older temple here, where the goddess's little toe is said to have fallen when Siva carried her charred corpse in a frenzied dance of mourning, and she was cut into pieces by Vishnu's *chakra* (see box, page 607). Non-Hindus have limited access to this important Hindu pilgrimage centre. Where once human sacrifices were made, the lives of goats are offered daily on two wooden blocks to the south of the temple. When visiting the temple, priests will attempt to snare foreigners for the obligatory *puja*. A barrage may start as far away as 500 m from the temple. Don't be fooled in to handing over your shoes and succumbing to any priests until you are clearly inside the temple, despite being shown 'priest ID' cards. Once settled with a priest the experience can be well worth the initial hassle. An acceptable minimum donation is Rs 50-60. Books showing previous donations of Rs 1000 are probably faked. Having done the *puja*, you'll probably be left alone to soak up the atmosphere.

Mother Teresa's Homes

Mother Teresa, an Albanian by birth, came to India to teach as a Loreto nun in 1931. She started her Order of the Missionaries of Charity in Kalighat to serve the destitute and dying 19 years later. **Nirmal Hriday** ('Pure Heart'), near the Kali Temple, the first home for the dying, was opened in 1952. Mother Teresa died on 5 September 1997 but her work continues. You may see nuns in their white cotton saris with blue borders busy working in the many homes, clinics and orphanages in the city.

Birla Mandir and Birla Academy of Art and Culture

ⓘ *Birla Mandir, Gariahat Rd, 0600-1100 and 1630-2030; Birla Academy of Art and Culture, 108/109 Southern Av, T033-2466 2843, Tue- Sun 1600-2000.*

Housed in a modern high rise, the Birla Academy of Art and Culture concentrates on medieval and contemporary paintings and sculpture. It is worth visiting. Taking 22 years to complete, the shiny white edifice of Birla Mandir pulls in a lot of devotees and it is particularly impressive when lit up at night. Another gift of the Birla family, it is modelled on the Lingaraj Temple at Bhubaneshwar and is covered with carvings both inside and out. No photos are permitted inside.

Botanical Gardens

ⓘ *20 km south from BBD Bagh, 0700-1700, Rs 50, avoid Sun and public holidays when it is very crowded.*

Kolkata's Botanical Gardens, on the west bank of the Hugli, were founded in 1787 by the East India Company. The flourishing 250-year-old banyan tree, with a circumference of over 300 m, is perhaps the largest in the world. The original trunk was destroyed by lightning in 1919 but over 1500 offshoots form an impressive sight. The gardens are peaceful and deserted during the week and make a welcome change from the city. To reach the Botanical Gardens catch a bus from Esplanade; minibuses and CTC buses (No C-12) ply the route.

Around Kolkata

There are several interesting places for a day's outing north of Kolkata. It's best to take a train (buses are slow); avoid peak hours, and keep an eye on your possessions.

Barrackpur and Hugli District → *25 km away.*

Many European nations had outposts along the River, and Hugli District has a rich history. When the Mughals lost power, several of the ancient seats of earlier rulers of Bengal became centres of foreign trade. The Portuguese and British settled at Hugli, the Dutch chose Chinsura, the French Chandernagore, the Danes Serampore, the Greeks had an outpost at Rishra, and the Germans and Austrians one at Bhadreswar.

In Barrackpur, the riverside **Gandhi Ghat** has a museum and there is a pleasant garden in memory of Jawaharlal Nehru. The bronze raj statues removed from their pedestals in Central Kolkata after Independence have found their way to the gardens of the bungalow of the former governor (now a hospital). The tower was part of the river signalling system. The town is accessed by train from Sealdah station.

Shrirampur (Serampore) → *24 km north of Kolkata.*

Founded by the Danes in 1616 as Fredricnagore, Serampore, became a Danish colony in 1755. From the early 19th century it was the centre of missionary activity, until sold to the East India Company in 1845. The Government House, two churches (one of which is closed and unsafe to enter), the Old Court House (which is being renovated) and a Danish cemetery remain. There is a **College of Textile Technology** ⓘ *12 Carey Rd, 1000-1630 (Sat 1000-1300).* The Baptist missionaries Carey, Marshman and Ward came to Serampore since they were not welcomed by the English administrators in Calcutta. They set up the Baptist Mission Press, which by 1805 was printing in seven Indian languages. **Serampore College** (1818) ⓘ *T033-2662 2322, Mon-Fri 1000-1600, Sat 1000-1300, with permission from the principal,* India's first Christian Theological college and still operating as such, was allowed to award degrees by the Danish king in 1829. The library has rare Sanskrit, Pali and Tibetan manuscripts and the Bible in over 40 Asian languages. Serampore is half an hour on a local train from Howrah station.

Chandernagore

The former French colony, which dates back to 1673, was one of the tiny pockets of non-British India that did not gain Independence in 1947, but was handed over to India after a referendum in 1950. The churches, convents and cemeteries of the French are still there, although the old French street names have been replaced by Bengali. The former Quai de Dupleix, with its riverfront benches, still has a somewhat Gallic air. The Bhubanesvari and Nandadulal **temples** are worth visiting, especially during **Jagaddhatri Puja**. The **Institute Chandernagore** ⓘ *at the Residency, Mon-Sat except Thu 1600-1830, Sun 1100-1700*, has interesting documents and relics of the French in India. The orange-painted Italian missionary **church** (1726) also stands witness to Chandernagore's European past.

Chinsura and Hugli

The Dutch acquired Chinsura from the Nawab of Murshidabad in 1628 and built the **Fort Gustavus**, but it was exchanged with Sumatra (Indonesia) and became British in 1825. The octagonal **Dutch church** (1678) with its cemetery nearby, a 17th-century Armenian church and three East India Company barracks remain. The Dutch are still remembered at the **Shandesvar Siva Temple** on special occasions, when the lingam is bizarrely decked in Western clothes and a Dutch sword!

The Portuguese set up a factory in Hugli in 1537 but Emperor Shah Jahan took the important trading post in 1632. The East India Company built their factory in 1651, destroyed in skirmishes marking the following six years, but Clive regained Hugli for the Company in 1757.

The **Shi'a Imambara of Hazi Mohammed Mohasin** (1836-1876) has fine marble inlay decoration, a silver pulpit and elaborate lanterns. In **Chota Pandua** nearby, interesting Muslim buildings include the ruins of the 14th-century Bari Masjid that has elements of Buddhist sculpture. In Rajbalhat, the **Amulya Pratnasala Museum** ⓘ *closed 2nd and 4th Tue, Wed 1400-2100*, exhibits sculpture, coins, terracottas and manuscripts.

Bandel

Bandel (Portuguese *bandar* or wharf) is now a railway junction town. The Portuguese built **Bandel Church** to Our Lady of the Rosary around 1660, on the site of an older Augustinian monastery. The keystone of the original church (1599), perhaps the earliest in Bengal, is on the riverside gate. Destroyed in 1640 by Shah Jahan, the church was reinstated 20 years later. The seafaring Portuguese believed that the statue of Our Lady of Happy Voyages in the bell tower could work miracles. Lost in the river, while being carried to save it from Shah Jahan's soldiers, it miraculously reappeared two centuries later. The 18th-century stone and terracotta **Hanseswari Temple** is 4 km away.

Tribeni and Pandua

Originally *Saptagram* (seven villages), **Tribeni** (three rivers) is particularly holy, being at the confluence of the Ganga, Saraswati and Kunti. It has many Hindu temples and 11th- to 12th-century Vaishnavite and Buddhist structures. The remains of the **Mazar of Zafarkhan Ghazi** (1313), the earliest mausoleum in eastern India, shows how black basalt sculpture and columns of earlier Hindu temples and palaces were incorporated into Muslim buildings. **Pandua** (Hugli District) has several remains of the Pala and Sena periods. Shah Sufi-ud-din is thought to have built the 39-m **Victory Tower** after defeating the local Hindu ruler in 1340. Its circular base had a court house. Outside, a staircase spirals up the fluted surface, while inside there is enamelled decoration. Hoards of Kushana and Gupta Dynasty gold coins have been found in nearby **Mahanad**.

Kalna

The town north of Pandua, centred on the **Maharaja of Burdwan's palace**, has several fine 18th-century terracotta temples. Look for the *Ramayana* scenes on the large Lalji (1739), Krishna panels on the Krishnachandra (1752), assorted friezes on the Ananta Vasudeva (1754) and the later Pratapesvara (1849). Across the way is the unusual circular Siva temple (1809) with 108 small double-vaulted shrines. Kalna has trains from Kolkata and rickshaws at the station, 3 km from the temples.

Nabadwip

The birthplace of Sri Chaitanya (see page 637) is a pilgrimage centre for his followers and the river ghats are lined with temples where devotees worship by singing *keertans* and *bhajans*. International Society for Krishna Consciousness (ISKCON) has a **Chandrodaya Mandir** ⓘ *Mayapu, across the river, until 1300*, and a guesthouse (inexpensive dorms, a/c rooms and cheap meals). Nabadwip has trains from Sealdah and Howrah, and ferries across to Mayapur.

Kolkata listings

Hotel prices

LL over US$200	**L** US$151-200	**AL** US$101-150
A US$66-100	**B** US$46-65	**C** US$31-45
D US$21-30	**E** US$12-20	**F** US$7-11
G under US$7		

Restaurant prices

TTT over US$12	TT US$6-12	T under US$6

Sleeping

Watch out for 10% luxury tax, 10% service charge and 20% expenditure tax in the higher price brackets. Medium price and budget hotels attracting foreigners are concentrated in the **Sudder St** area. Mid-priced hotels often have a few a/c rooms but may not have a generator and so have power cuts, especially in summer.

Central Kolkata *p604, map p605*

LL Oberoi Grand, 15 Chowringhee (JL Nehru), T033-2249 2323, www.oberoihotels.com. Atmospheric Victorian building opposite the Maidan, exquisitely restored, range of rooms and suites which have giant 4-posters, all are spacious, those with balconies overlooking the raised garden and pool are charming, bathrooms a tad old-fashioned but in keeping with the colonial style, excellent Thai restaurant and 24-hr **Le Terrasse** with international cuisine, billiards in the bar, lovely pool for guests, wonderful spa. Can get a reasonable price online for a standard room.

B-C Manthan, 3 Waterloo St, T033-2248 9577, manthanhotel@gmail.com. Only 4 rooms, spacious and well-appointed, TV, a/c and pleasantly subtle furnishings. The bar/restaurant and banquet service mean it's fairly bustling. Bargaining is most certainly possible from the Rs 2400 quoted.

C-D Majestic, 4C Madan St, T033-2212 6518/7701, www.hotelmajestickolkata.com. An old building with large a/c rooms, tiled floors, geysers and TVs, but some oversights such as curtains being too short. A couple of rooms have balconies, try for these. 1st-floor bar can be noisy.

D-E Cosmos Guest House, ground floor, 9 Chittaranjan Ave, T033-2236 1383. Decent simple rooms aren't huge but have fresh paint, clean bedding, TV and good bathrooms. At the rear of the building, so surprisingly quiet. A good choice for single travellers (Rs 400), also a/c rooms (Rs 1000). 2 other hotels in the same building should Cosmos be full (which they often are).

E Broadway, 27A Ganesh Chandra Ave, T033-2236 3930, www.broadwayhotel.in. Amazingly good-value hotel in a characterful building that hasn't changed much since it opened in 1937. Very clean rooms are non-a/c but airy with powerful fans, antique furniture and Bengali-red floors, towels, some with common bath, plus 24-hr checkout. Noisy on the lower levels at the front. The bar is appealing (see Bars, page 622). Highly recommended.

E-G Buddha Dharmankur Sabha, 1 Buddhist Temple St, Bow Bazar, T033-2211 7138, www.bengalbuddhist.com. Run by the Bengal Buddhist Association and with plenty of monks wandering around, cheap clean rooms with twin beds, fans, share decent bathrooms (Rs 250). Also a/c option with bath attached, a bit larger and with a few sticks of furniture. The compound gates are locked at 2230, call ahead to reserve.

Around Sudder Street *p604, map p606*

Kyd St has changed its name to Dr Md Ishaque Rd and **Free School St** is now called Mirza Ghalib St.

AL Bawa Walson Spa'o'tel, 5A Sudder St, T033-2252 1512, www.bawahotels.com. An unlikely situation for a Spa'o'tel, but the new Walson is immaculate with Thai accents throughout. Rooms are wood and white, swish shower rooms, free Wi-Fi, Arabic restaurant. Huge discounts possible.

AL Lytton, 14 Sudder St, T033-2249 1872, www.lyttonhotelindia.com. Comfortable, tastefully furnished rooms with flatscreen TVs, a/c bar, efficient and attracts businessmen, breakfast included.

A Housez 43, 43 Mirza Ghalib St, T033-2227 6020-2, www.housez43.com. Attractive 'value boutique' hotel making a slightly wide-of-the-mark attempt at contemporary, well-presented rooms, nice public areas with leather beanbags and seats, restaurant, elevator, and breakfast included in the colourful cafe, pleasant staff.

A Lindsay, 8-A Lindsay St, T033-2252 2237/8, www.hotellindsay.com. Recently refurbished hotel towering over Newmarket, mainly for business travellers, Wi-Fi in rooms, good breakfast. **Blue & Beyond** rooftop restaurant/bar has panoramic city views and great food.

B Fairlawn, 13A Sudder St, T033-2252 1510/8766, www.fairlawnhotel.com. Old-fashioned rooms but characterful rooms (including breakfast and afternoon tea) have a/c, TV, hot water, and are comfortable. Semi-formal meals at set times aren't the best. The hotel and management provide a throwback to the Raj, bric-a-brac everywhere, photos cover all the communal spaces, quite a place and the garden terrace is great for a beer. Wi-Fi Rs 250 per day.

C-D Astoria Hotel, 6 Sudder St, near firestation, T033-2252 2241. Offers 41 rooms of various standards. Closed at the time of writing for renovations, so may well reopen in a higher price category. Great top-floor room with a terrace.

D Super Guest House, 30A Mirza Ghalib St, T033-2252 0995, super_guesthouse@hotmail.com. This guesthouse has some of the cleanest rooms in the area for Rs 1100-1300 per double, all a/c with hot bath, tiled and simple box rooms. Be sure to ask for a room that does not suffer noise from the daily live music in Super Pub Bar. No single rates.

D YMCA, 25 JI Nehru Rd, T033-2249 2192, www.calcuttaymca.org. 17 rooms, some a/c, all with bath, geyser and TV, in large, rambling colonial building, clean linen, recently renovated but check room first as some are nicer than others. Helpful staff, rates include bed tea and breakfast. The oldest YMCA in Asia.

D-E Al-Sana, Futnani Chamber (near Society Cinema), 6A SN Banerjee Rd, T033-2265 6210, hotel_alsana@yahoo.com. Go for one of the refurbished rooms with clean white paint, TV and new furniture, push for a window. It's close to the chaos of Newmarket and out of the backpacker scene. Some rooms have a/c.

D-E Emirates, 11/1 Dr Md Ishaque Rd (Kyd St), T033-2217 8487. Fresh, bright rooms in a building with character, some a/c, bathrooms are a bit jaded but there's a pleasant terrace.

E Afridi Guest House, opposite **Ashreen Guest House** and under the same management (see below), calcutta_guest house@yahoo.com. Recently remodelled, most rooms share bathrooms (some of which have hot water), some have a/c, most have TV, but many rooms are windowless. Sheets are clean and standards better than many Sudder St options. Try and book ahead, though that is easier said than done.

E Ashreen Guest House, 2 Cowie Lane, T033-2252 0889, ashreen_guesthouse@yahoo.com. Modern rooms of above-average standard with TV and hot water, a suitable place to break yourself into Kolkata gently, or to put up the parents, though prices are ever escalating. Pickup for late night flights, Rs 500.

E Pioneer International, 1 Marquis St, T033-2252 0557, hotelpioneerinternational@rediffmail.com. Decent sized rooms with private bath, clean, quieter than many, one of the cheapest a/c options (Rs 750 double), try to ignore the shabby exterior and the odd hole in the ceiling. Negotiation possible.

E Sonali Resort, 21A Mirza Ghalib St (Free School St), T033-2252 3223, sonaliguesthouse@yahoo.in. Set back from the main road, with 13 pokey but clean rooms with bath and TV, some with a/c for a reasonable price, roof for drying washing.

E-F YWCA, 1 Middleton Row, T033-2229 2494. Old colonial building with good atmosphere, airy verandas and tennis courts. Some rooms with bath (Rs 555) but doubles with shared bath have windows (Rs 305), dorm, all spotless, very friendly staff. Rates include breakfast, alcohol forbidden, a pleasant oasis in the city. A recommended alternative to Sudder St for women travellers.

E-F Afraa, B/33/H/3 Mirza Ghalib St (Free School St), 3rd floor, T033-2217 7222, manager@hotelafraa.8k.com. Clean, small rooms in this warren are good value starting from Rs 300 for a double, TV, ask for one with a window. Some rooms with a/c. In the same building, the **Milan**, T033-3022 8621, is the same price but slightly better and often full. Brightest of all is the **Paramount**, T033-2229 4295, which is marginally more expensive.

E-F Capital Guest House, 11B Chowringhee Lane, T033-2252 0598. Tucked away from the road in a freshly painted old building, Capital is relatively quiet and all rooms have TV and private bath, though ones with windows are more expensive. Good value compared to nearby options butnot a place to meet other travellers.

E-F Galaxy, 3 Stuart Lane, T033-2252 4565, hotelgalaxy@vsnl.net. 12 good tiled rooms with attached bath and TV, singles Rs 400, doubles Rs 600/800 without/with a/c, a decent choice but often full of long-stayers. Try at around 1030 just after checkout.

F Timestar Hotel, 2 Tottee Lane (off Sudder St), T033-2252 3817, timestarhotel@yahoo.co.in. An old-fashioned building, creaking but kept clean, rooms all have bathrooms, fans, TV and tiled floors. Set back off a quieter lane, the scene is more sedate and the management professional.

F-G Maria, 5/1 Sudder St, T033-2252 0860. 24 clean, basic rooms (hard beds), some with bath, dorm (Rs 80), internet, TV in the lobby, hot water, water filter, pleasant staff. Popular budget place with a good atmosphere.

F-G Modern Lodge, 1 Stuart Lane, T033-2252 4960. Very popular, almost always full with long-term volunteers, 14 rooms, attached or shared bath, breezy rooftop, pleasant lobby with plants but sinister 'lounge', quirky staff, no reservations so try at 1000.

F-G Paragon, 2 Stuart Lane, T033-2252 2445. Textbook backpacker haunt with 45 rooms, some tiny and prison-like but it's clean just about (some doubles have attached bath) and mixed sex dorms (Rs 120/150 with shared/private bath), rooftop rooms are better. Water heater to fill buckets. Open communal spaces, indifferent management.

F-G Times Guest House, 3 Sudder St, T033-2252 1796. Get a room at the front with balcony to view the action on the street below. Has character, jolly staff, cheap singles (Rs 150) with shared bath.

Park St and Chowringhee *pp607-609, map p608*

LL-L Park, 17 Park St, T033-2249 9000, www.theparkhotels.com. Trendy designer hotel, one of Kolkata's most reputable, good restaurants, nightclubs, health club, 24-hr café, service can be disappointing, entrance themed on underground car park. Go online for the best discounts.

LL-AL Astor, 15 Shakespeare Sarani, T033-2282 9957-9, www.astorkolkata.com. In a red-brick colonial building, comfortable a/c rooms with bath tubs, inferior annexe, have not retained original features, although public areas have fared better. The tiny blue-lit bar (**Cheers**, daily 1100-2300) is a nice place to be, and **Plush** lounge-bar is also fun (every night except Mon, liveliest on Wed, Fri and Sun). Breakfast included, mini-bar, off- season discounts, Wi-Fi Rs 331 per 24 hrs.

LL-AL Golden Parkk, 13 Ho Chi Minh Sarani, T033- 2288 3939, www.goldenparkk.com. Stylish hotel has an atrium lobby with classical statues, rooms with all facilities and black marble floors, breakfast included, 24-hr business centre and free internet, good restaurants and **Fusion** club (see Entertainment). 40% discounts usually available.

LL-AL New Kenilworth, 1 & 2 Little Russell St, T033-2282 3939/40, www.kenilworthhotels.com. A very comfortable and attractive hotel, though overpriced at rack rates. The foyer is all marble and chandeliers, but modern rooms are neutrally furnished with soft lighting, flatscreen TV, minibar, nice bathrooms. The older period building contains suites and the **Big Ben**

English-style pub, which has appeal as a dark den with a pool table and sports TV.

B Gulshan International, 21B Royd St, T033-2229 0566. Efficient staff, 21 clean, comfortable rooms, complimentary breakfast.

B-C Middleton Inn, 10 Middleton St, T033-2216 0452, mchamber@vsnl.net. Closed for refurbishment at the time of writing, but expect pleasantly furnished a/c rooms with hot bath (fridge, TV), not particularly spacious though spotlessly clean, original art, quiet and convenient, breakfast included.

D-E Sunflower Guest House, 7 Royd St, T033-2229 9401, www.sunflowerguest house.com. An airy 1950s building with very clean well-maintained rooms, TV, hot water, more costly with a/c and newer bathrooms. Spacious lounge area, the numerous staff are kindly. Good location, near Sudder St but out of the backpacker scene. No single room rates.

South Kolkata *p612, map p602*

South Kolkata is a more salubrious area than elsewhere in the city, where quiet residential streets hide some good (mainly mid-range) guesthouses. Excellent little restaurants and vibrant markets are in plentiful supply.

LL-L Chrome, 226 AJC Bose, T033-3096 3096, www.chromehotel.in. Space-age hotel opened Jan 2009, with, slick modern rooms, dense with gadgetry, 'adrenalin' showers and trendy colour schemes. 3 categories, The 'Edge' suites being the zenith, but all are supremely comfortable. Good city-scapes from the higher levels. Minimalist **Khana Sutra** restaurant is North Indian, with huge set lunch/dinner menus as well as à la carte, rooftop bar/club **Pulp** has a pure white Zen theme, and **Nosh** café in the lobby is good for speciality coffee. Swimming pool is planned. Discounts possible, especially for stays of a few days.

LL-L Hindusthan International, 235/1 AJC Bose Rd, T033-2283 0505, www.hindusthan.com. Comfortable quiet rooms on 8 floors are priced right, but staff are distracting with their demands for tips. The food is nothing special although there's an almost cool bar/coffee shop and **Underground** nightclub is popular, pool (non-residents Rs 500). Huge discounts are possible.

A-B The Bodhi Tree, 48/44 Swiss Park (near Rabindra Sarovar metro, exit Swiss Park), T033-2424 6534, www.bodhitree-cal.spaces.live.com. Simply beautiful little boutique hotel with just 6 rooms, each uniquely furnished in a different regional style (eg rural Bengal, with mud-plastered walls), flatscreen TVs, 1 Penthouse. The owners are active promoters of young artistic talent, the in-house cafe is a delight (see Coffee shops, page 621), dinner is available, business centre, free wireless, small library. Prices are entirely reasonable for the special experience. Discounts for single women travellers/social workers. Recommended.

A-B Park Palace, Singhi Villa, 49/2 Gariahat Rd, T033-2461 9108-11, www.parkpalace hotel.com. The main draws are the peaceful residential area, **Mirch Masala** restaurant/bar next door, and the roof terrace with excellent views. Rooms have fitted furniture and are large yet cosy, if twee. Ask for the 20% discount. Staff delightful. Behind Pantaloons, off Gariahat Rd.

B The Residency Guest House, 50/1C Purna Das Rd, T033-2466 9382, r_singla@vsnl.net. A very appealing mid-range hotel, with clean tiled rooms, quality furnishings, a/c, TV, good bathrooms, comfortable beds. Close to Gariahat Market but on a quiet street.

B-C 66/2B The Guest House, 66/2B Purna Das Rd, T033-2464 6422/1, tgh662B@rediffmail.com. On a tree-lined street with some great restaurants a 2-min walk away, 66/2B is well furnished, with decent baths, all rooms have a/c, geysers and flatscreen TV. A more relaxing area to stay in. Breakfast included. Some rooms being refurbished at the time of writing.

C-D New Haven Guest House, 19B Ritchie Rd, T033 2475 4462. Simply furnished, clean rooms with bath, small front garden, only breakfast, residential area with good *dhaba* and Chinese restaurants within 10 mins' walk.

D-E Sharani Lodge, 71/K Hindustan Park, T033-2463 5717, gautam_sharani@rediffmail.com. In a quiet area, yet close to hectic Rash Behari Av, this well-maintained and well-run lodge is very Indian in ambiance. The a/c rooms are not worth really worth the extra money, but non-a/c are a good deal (Rs 660-770), ones with common bath also share balconies at the front, all have TV, towels and plenty of space.

Other areas *map p602*

LL Taj Bengal, 34B Belvedere Rd, Alipore, T033-2223 3939, www.tajhotels.com. Opulent and modern, restaurants are plush, imaginative, intimate, with good food (ground floor Indian cheaper than 5th floor), leisurely service, unusual Bengali breakfast, *Khazana* shop for excellent textiles, *Baluchari* saris, *kantha* embroidery, etc.

LL-L Vedic Village, T033-22802071, www.thevedicvillage.com. In Rajarhat, 20 mins from the airport on the eastern edge of the city, but a world away from the rest of Kolkata. The appeal is the clean air and rural surrounds as much as the luxurious rooms, fabulous pool and of course the spa. Top-end villas and suites are stunning while studio rooms are not unreasonable when compared to other options in the city.

Eating

Licensed restaurants serve alcohol (some are no longer pleasant places to eat in since the emphasis is on drink). Be prepared for a large surcharge for live (or even recorded) music. This, plus taxes, can double the price on the menu. Many restaurants outside hotels do not accept credit cards. Special Bengali sweets are made fresh every afternoon at thousands of sweet shops (1600-1730): try *shingaras*, *kochuris* and *nimkis*.

Central Kolkata *p604, map p605*

TTT Baan Thai, Oberoi Grand (see Sleeping), T033-2249 2323. Excellent selection, imaginative decor, Thai-style seating on floor or chairs and tables.

TT Aaheli and **Oceanic**, at the **Peerless Inn**, 12 JL Nehru Rd, T033-2228 0301. Aaheli has an excellent menu of Bengali specialities, carefully selected from around the state by the chef, open from 1900. Oceanic has interesting seafood and is more pricey, open lunch and dinner. Both are comfortable with a/c and serve alcohol.

TT Amber, 11 Waterloo St, T033-2248 3477. Open 1100-2330. 2 floors of North Indian and continental gourmet delights (best for meat *tandoori*), generous helpings, fast service. **Essence** on 2nd floor fancies itself as a cocktail bar, but alcohol is served in both. There's also a functional bar on the ground floor (strictly no women). They also have a smaller restaurant on Middleton Row (T033-4000 7490), open 1200-1600 and 1900-2300.

TT-T Bhojohori Manna, Esplanade. Open 1130-2130 (closed for cleaning 1630-1800). The newest branch of the Bengali chain, with budget prices for veg dishes and pricier fish items. Ticks on the whiteboard indicate availability, choice can be limited in the evenings as they sell out.

TT-T Song Hay, 3 Waterloo St, T033-2248 0794. This small a/c restaurant is functional with formica tables and efficient staff. Hugely popular and with a huge menu, it attracts a varied clientele, (cheap) alcohol served. Highly recommended. Women not permitted in the downstairs bar.

T Anand, 19 Chittaranjan Av, T033-2212 9757. Open 0900-2130, Sun from 0700, closed Wed. Great South Indian food. Mammoth *dosas*, stuffed *idly*, all-vegetarian, family atmosphere and warmly decorated. Barefoot waiters are efficient. Queues at weekends.

T Madras Restaurant, 25/B Chittaranjan Av, T033-2237 9764. A simpler setting than nearby Anand and slightly cheaper, but still has a/c. The list of dosa and uttampams is endless, plus there are a few Chinese dishes. Go between 1130-1530 for the South Indian thalis (only Rs 45).

Around Sudder Street *p604, map p606*

TTT Zaranj and **Jong's**, 26 JL Nehru Rd. Adjacent restaurants, both tasteful, stylish, subdued decor, excellent food. Try *pudina paratha*, *murgh makhani*, *tandoori* fish in Zaranj, or delectable Burmese fare in Jong's.

TT-T Jimmy's, 14D Lindsay St. Chinese. Small, a/c, good *momos*, Szechuan dishes, ice cream. Alcohol served.

T Blue Sky Café, 3 Sudder St. Chiefly Western. Very popular travellers' meeting place, a/c, always full and cramped, opinions on the food vary.

T Curd Corner, 3 Sudder St. Reliable breakfasts, they do a good muesli fruit curd but there is plenty more to choose from. Strong coffee.

T Family Home, Humayan Place, near New Market. Excellent Indian veg meals, particularly recommended for South Indian, good lassis, cheap and busy.

T Fresh and Juicy, Chowringhee Lane, T033-2286 1638. Newly renovated with a/c and first floor seating, good place for a sociable breakfast with some of the best coffee around, reasonably authentic Indian meals, attracts a loyal following. Phone ahead for parcel-order.

Jo-jo's, Stuart Lane. Average Indian snacks and meals but superb juices, 1st floor a/c, good escape during summer.

Khalsa, 4C Madge Lane, T033-2249 0075. Excellent *lassis*, Western breakfasts, Indian mains, all super-cheap, and beyond excellent service from the utterly charming Sikh owners.

NV Stores, T033-2252 9661, and Maa Kali, 12/2 Lindsay St. Closed Sun. Stand-up street eateries making surprisingly good sandwiches from any possible combination of ingredients; great *lassis* too.

Tirupati, street stall next to **Hotel Maria**. A Sudder St institution; find a spot on the busy benches and enjoy enormous helpings of food from every continent. Closes out of season.

Park Street *p607, map p608*

Visitors craving Western fast food will find plenty of familiar names in this area.

Ivory, Block D 5th Fl, 22 Camac St, T033-2281 1313, www.ivorykitchen.com. Daily 1230-1500, 1900-2230. Slightly formal and functional, yet pleasingly decorated in ivory tones, dishes encompass a wide selection of Oriental and international dishes, with an Indian twist. Top-class dining.

Bar-B-Q, 43 Park St, T033-2229 9916. Always popular, always delicious. 3 sections serving Indian and Chinese food, bar.

Bistro by the Park, 2A Middleton Row, T033-2229 494, www.bistrobythepark.com. Daily 1200-1700 and 1900-2300. It's not near any park, but this attractive contemporary place serves world cuisine (including Southeast Asian, Middle Eastern) with the main focus on Italian fare (salads, pockets, pizzas, etc). Look online for the full menu.

Fire and Ice, Kanak Building, Middleton St, T033-2288 4073, www.fireandicepizza.com. Open 1100-2330. Pizzas here are the real deal, service is excellent, and the ambience relaxing. Decor is very much what you would expect from a pizza-place at home. Definitely worth it.

Flury's, 18 Park St. Classic Kolkata venue with hit-and-miss Western menu, but pastries and afternoon tea are winners and the bakery has brown bread. It's an institution.

Gangaur, 2 Russell St. A wide menu of Indian delights, if you can resist the superb Rs 100 (plus tax) *thali* (1130-1530). Afterwards head next door for Bengali sweets.

Mocambo, 25B Park St. International. A/c, pleasant lighting, highly descriptive menu. Long-standing reliable favourite.

Peter Cat, 18A Park St (entrance on Middleton Row), T033-2229 8841. Chiefly Indian, with some international dishes. Good kebabs and sizzlers, hilarious menu of cheap cocktails, pleasant ambience but can rush you on busy weekend nights. No booking system, expect to queue outside.

Teej, 2 Russell St, T033-2217 0730. Pure vegetarian Rajasthani delights washed down with cold beer, colourful *haveli*-esque setting.

Tung Fong, Mirzah Ghalib St. Quality Chinese food for a reasonable price, the setting spacious and subtly Asian, white linens and Ming vases. Great Manchurian dishes, good fish and chilli garlic paneer, excellent desserts. Super-swift service.

Waldorf, 13D Russell St, T033-6535 4952. Open 1200-2230. Excellent Chinese and Thai. Extensive menu, speciality fish and prawn dishes in a kitschy but cosy setting with white faux leather seats, fish tanks and other Chinese trinkets.

Gupta's, 53C Mirza Ghalib St, T033-2229 6541. Open 1100-2300 for excellent Indian and Chinese. More intimate and softly lit upstairs, low ceilings (beware of the fans), try fish *tikka peshwari* and *bekti tikka*, alcohol reasonably priced.

Hamro Momo, Suburban Hospital Rd (near **Momo Plaza**, see below). Open 1300-2100. Cheap and good Chinese and Tibetan dishes, in simple eat-and-run surroundings, always packed out and there's very little space.

Maya Ram, 1 Lord Sinha Rd, T033-6515 5837. Open 1100-2300. A good place to try 'snacks' such as *paw bhaji*.

Momo Plaza, 2A Suburban Hospital Rd, T033-2287 8260. Open 1200-2200. With black half-tiling and pastel pink walls accentuated by kitsch ornaments, this place could be intentionally bohemian. Recommended for plentiful and delicious Tibetan and Chinese meals. Try the soups, chilli chicken, huge *momos* and *thukpa*.

South Kolkata *p612, map p602*

Mainland China, 3A Gurusaday Rd, T033-2283 7964; also at South City Mall,

3rd floor. Sublime Chinese. Unusual offerings, especially fish and seafood, tastefully decorated with burnished ceiling and evocative wall mural, pleasant ambience, courteous. Book ahead.

Kewpie's, 2 Elgin Lane (just off Elgin Rd), T033-2486 1600/9929. Tue-Sun 1200-1500, 1700-2245. Authentic Bengali, home cooking at its best, add on special dishes to basic *thali* (Rs 200), unusual fish and vegetarian. Few tables in rooms in a residence, a/c, sells recipe book. Highly recommended, book in advance.

Krystal Chopsticks, 71H Hindustan Park, T033-2464 3449. Open 1200-2230. Attractive East Asian decor and an excellent menu (chiefly Chinese) attracts well-heeled Bengalis. It's not outrageously priced, plenty of interesting vegetarian as well as chicken, fish and meat dishes.

Soho, Ideal Plaza, 11/1 Sarat Bose Rd, T033-2289 6059. Daily 1200-1530 and 1930-2330. Mainly Mediterranean cuisine in a recently refurbished space with a cafe atmosphere, good wine list, Sun brunch buffet with North Indian and mezze choices, candlelit at night, adjacent bar/club (see Discos and nightclubs, page 623).

Bhojohori Manna, 13 PC Sorcar Sarani (aka Ekdalia Rd); also at JD Park. Budget prices and a perfect little place to sample pure Bengali cuisine, veg and non-veg. Ticks on the wall menu indicate availability, try *echor dalna* (jackfruit curry) and *bhekti paturi* (mustard-drenched fish steamed in banana leaves). 2 people should order 4-5 different dishes to share. Much better than the newer 'Bhojohori 6' outlet nearby. Decent toilet.

Mirch Masala, 49/2 Gariahat Rd, Gariahat, T033-2461 8900. Lunch 1200-1500, dinner 1900-2230. This popular restaurant-bar has walls decorated with *pukkah* murals depicting Bollywood stars. Food can be a bit heavy (mainly Indian, non-veg) but the atmosphere is lively and staff competent.

Tero Parbon, 49C Purna Das Rd, T033-2463 2016. Daily 1200-2230, but best to go in the evening when a wider choice is available. Experiment with Bengali food in attractive Asian-colonial surrounds, reed blinds, dark wood ceiling fans and bamboo – no doubt inspired by the pricier **Oh Calcutta**. The emphasis is on fish, veg dishes are seasonal.

Banana Leaf, 73-75 Rash Behari Av, T033-2464 1960. Open 0730-2200. Vegetarian South Indian, top-notch *dosas* and *thalis* plus superb *mini-idli* and decent southern-style coffee.

Bliss, 53 Hindustan Park, T033-2463 5962. For Chinese in a fast-food environment, Bliss is ideal. Portions are generous, the soups delicious, it's tiny but there's seating.

South India Club, off Rash Behari Ave. Daily 0700-2130. An authentic taste of the South in a canteen environment, full meals for Rs 35, and a good place to experiment with less commonly seen dishes such as *pongal* or *upma*. Highly recommended.

Other areas

Chinoiserie, **Taj Bengal** (see Sleeping), T033-2223 3939. Good for a splurge on excellent Chinese. Connoisseurs of Chinese cuisine also go to South Tangra Rd off EM bypass, east of the city centre. The approach is none too picturesque, past tanneries and open drains, but among the maze of lanes (in places lit by lanterns) many eateries are quite swanky.

Beijing, 77/1A Christopher Rd, T033-2328 1001. Try garlic chicken, sweet and sour fish, chop suey, steamed fish, generous portions.

Golden Joy, **Kafulok** and **Sin Fa**, to name but a few, offer excellent soups, jumbo prawns and honey chicken, best to go early (1200 for lunch, 2000 for dinner).

Coffee shops, sweets and snacks

Art Cafe, at the Bodhi Tree (see Sleeping). Open Tue-Sat, 1400-1830. Half-inside/half-outside, this beautiful slate-floored cafe is lit by green lights and decorated with Buddhas, palm trees and original works of art (exhibitions are occasionally held). There's a tempting drinks menu in addition to light meals. Something quite out of the ordinary for Kolkata.

Ashalayam, 44 Mirza Ghalib St. Peaceful oasis run by NGO, sells handicrafts made by street children.

Café Thé, Tagore Centre, 9A Ho Chi Min Sarani, T033-4003 5878. Daily 0900-2100. Modern, clean cafe serving Western/Indian/Chinese snacks and meals, with an interesting menu of hot/cold teas.

Dolly's, The Tea Shop, Dakshinapan market, (just after Dhakuria Bridge). The quaintest place in the city for a variety of teas, refreshing iced-teas (try watermelon) and decent toasties. Tea-chest tables, low basket chairs, indoor and outdoor

seating, even the walls are lined with old tea-crates. Dolly is a formidable lady.
Indian Coffee House, Albert Hall, just off College St (see page 610).
Indthalia, 12a Hindustan Park (off Rash Behari Ave), Gariahat, T033-4008 6657. Daily 1000-2300. Low-key unpretentious coffee shop for proper (cheap) latte and tasty multi-cuisine food. Try the Thai soup or tomato *kofta*.
Raj's Spanish Cafe, 7 Sudder St. Daily 0800-2200. Great Spanish nibbles, real coffee from a real machine, salads, pastries and sandwiches also good. Wi-Fi Rs 30 per hr.

Confectionary

Kathleen's, several branches, including 12 Mirza Ghalib St, corner of Lord Sinha Rd.
Nahoum, Shop F20, New Market, T033-6526 9936. Good pastries, cakes, savouries and brown bread. The original 1930s till and some fixtures still *in situ*.
Nepal Sweets, 16B Sarat Bose Rd. *Chandrakala*, almond *pista barfi*, mango *roshogolla*, *kheer mohan* (also savouries). Recommended.
Pure Milk Centre, near Rafi Ahmed Kidwai St/Ripon St corner. Good sweet 'curd' (*mishti doi*), usually sold out by lunchtime. Excellent hot *roshogollas*.

Kathi-rolls

Kathi-rolls (tender kebabs wrapped in *parathas*) are hard to beat. Try mutton/ chicken egg roll (if you don't want raw onions and green chillis, order *'no piaaz e mirchi'*) There are also plenty of great veg options.
Brothers Snacks, 1 Humayun Pl, Newmarket. Safe, tasty bet with outdoor seats.
Rehmania and **Shiraz Golden Restaurant**, on opposite corners of Park St/AJC Bose Rd crossing. Muslim joints famed for their mutton rolls and kebabs.

Bars and clubs

Kolkata *p601, maps p602, p605, p606, p608*

Bars

The larger hotels have pleasant bars and upmarket restaurants serve alcohol. The top hotels are well stocked, luxurious but pricey. In Sudder St, **Fairlawn's** pleasant garden terrace is popular at dusk attracting anyone seeking a chilled beer. The clientele is quite mixed, fairy lights set the greenery glowing and it's perfect for a first night drink to acclimatize – but beware the below-average food and stiff charges for snacks. **Sunset Bar** in the **Lytton Hotel** nearby has a/c and a recognisable pub ambience (last orders 2230). **Super Pub Bar**, Sudder St, is always busy and sociable, but expect gruff service and check your change. The first floor has live music (Hindi and Bengali singing) every night from 1600-2400. (If you need a beer after hours, Super Chicken next door has take-away beers and is open later than the wine-shops). The 9th floor bar **Blue & Beyond** at the **Lindsay Hotel**, is a rooftop bar/restaurant with great views over New Market and Kolkata and some excellent Indian and Chinese food (quite pricey), plus a few Western dishes. The 'ceiling' is composed of blue fairy lights, there is an indoor a/c section, beer is Rs 130. **Sam's Pub**, off Park St, is open later than most (last orders at 2330 on weekend nights) and still permits smoking in a curious indoor gazebo; football and cricket matches are shown on the flatscreen. 'Local' bars, open usually from 1100-2230, often lack atmosphere or have deafening live singing; some are positively men only – there is a seedy choice down **Dacres Lane**, just north of Esplanade. A friendlier place to hear live acts is the **Hotel Embassy Bar**, which accepts females; some vintage elements remain despite the plastic tabletops and veneer walls. Women are also welcome in the **Broadway Bar** at the **Broadway Hotel** (last orders 2230), where marble floors, polished retro seating, soft lighting, whirring fans and windows open to the street make it one of the best choices in the city. The bar at the **New Empire Cinema**, between New Market and Chowringhee, is pleasant, blue-lit and efficiently staffed. **Oly Pub**, 21 Park St, is an institution: very noisy, serves steak and eggs, no women allowed downstairs. Another classic is **Tripti's**, SP Mukerjee Rd (next to Netaji

Bhavan metro), Mon-Sat 1100-2300, Sun 1100-2230. Established in 1935, Tripti's is styled like a canteen, no smoking but still smoke-stained, 1950s flooring and shuttered windows, expect rowdiness and cheap booze. It's on the 1st floor up hidden steps, look for the sign; take a wander round sprawling and atmospheric **Jadu Babu Bazar** to the rear while in the area.

Discos and nightclubs

At hotels: **Incognito (Taj Bengal)**, closed Mon, understated, relaxed ambience, 30-plus crowd, good food, taped music, fussy dress codes. **Someplace Else (Park Hotel)**. Pub, live bands play loud music to the same crowd each week. **Tantra (Park Hotel)**. Taped music, large floor, young crowd, no shorts or flip-flops, cover charge. Next door **Roxy** is less popular, but has free entry and is more relaxed, with slouchy sofas upstairs. **Underground (Hindusthan International)**. Good live band, young crowd, good sizzlers, pool tables. The fairly swish bar beneath **Ginger** restaurant (106 SP Mukerjee Rd, T033-2486 3052/3, near JD Park metro) accommodates same-sex couples, open 1130-2330. **Fusion (Golden Parkk Hotel)**, has cool minimal lighting and small dance-floor, plush seating and disco (week nights 2000-2400, Sat/Sun -0200).
Shisha Reincarnated, Block D 6th Fl, 22 Camac St, T033-2281 1313, www.shishareincarnated.com. Dark and stylish with a chilled atmosphere and low red lights, huge bar lined with spirits, and DJs every night (varying music styles) and a decent sized dancefloor. Hookahs cost Rs 300, the roof-deck is the best place to hang out. Open 1800-2400, Wed, Fri and Sat -0200.
Soho, Ideal Plaza, 11/1 Sarat Bose Rd. Open until 0230 Fri and Sat (Rs 600 per couple on Sat). A good late night hangout with a curved bar, funky lighting, a mix of Western and Hindi tunes and flatscreen TVs showing big sporting events.

Private clubs

Some are affiliated to a number of Indian and foreign clubs including Royal Overseas League, Travellers, St James's, National Liberal, Oxford and Cambridge universities. To use the facilities you need to be a member of these clubs, or the guest of a local member.

Bengal Club, 1/1 Russell St, T033-2226 6954. The former house of Lord Macaulay, has an excellent dining room.
Tollygunge Club, 120 DP Sasmal Rd, T033-2473 2316. Built on an old indigo plantation, 18-hole golf course, riding, tennis, pool, away from centre, atmosphere and location make up for average rooms and restaurant.

Entertainment

Kolkata *p601, maps p602, p605, p606, p608*

The English-language dailies (*Telegraph*, *Times of India*, etc) carry a comprehensive list.

Cinema

A/c and comfortable cinemas showing English-language films are a good escape from the heat, and many are still very cheap. Check the newspapers for timings, programmes change every Fri. **Elite**, SN Banerjee Rd, and **New Empire Cinema**, New Market St, are conveniently close to Sudder St. **Nandan Complex**, AJC Bose Rd, T033-2223 1210, shows classics and art-house movies; the **Kolkata International Film Festival** is held here in Nov, an excellent event. Swish **Inox** multiplexes (www.inoxmovies.com) are scattered around town (Forum, City Centre); tickets for these are Rs 100-150 and can be booked by credit card over the phone. **Fame cinema**, www.famecinemas.com, Rs 100-250, in South City Mall is open 1000-0100, ticket line T4010-5555.

Dance, music, theatre and art

Regular performances at **Rabindra Sadan**, Cathedral Rd. Kala Mandir, 48 Shakespeare Sarani. **Gorky Sadan**, Gorky Terrace, near Minto Park. **Sisir Mancha**, 1/1 AJC Bose Rd. Some of these also hold art exhibitions as at **Academy of Fine Arts**, Cathedral Rd, and **Ramakrishna Mission**, Gol Park. **Seagull Arts and Media Centre**, 36C SP Mukherjee Rd (just off Mukherjee on a smaller street), T033-2455 6492/3, www.seagullindia.com, holds regular photography exhibitions (see listings in the daily papers) from 1400-2000. They also have a bookshop on the opposite side of SP Mukherjee). You can see Bengali theatre of a high standard at **Biswaroopa**, 2A Raja Raj Kissen St, and **Star Theatre**, 79/34 Bidhan Sarani.

Worship of the clay goddess

Durga Puja, the 17th-century festival in honour of the clay goddess, precedes the full moon in late September/early October, when all offices and institutions close down and the Metro only operates from the late afternoon.

Images of the 10-armed, three-eyed goddess, a form of Shakti or Kali (see page 1412) astride her 'vehicle' the lion, portray Durga slaying Mahisasura, the evil buffalo demon. Durga, shown with her four children Lakshmi, Sarasvati, Ganesh and Kartik, is worshipped in hundreds of brightly illuminated and beautifully decorated *pandals* (marquees) made of bamboo and coloured cloth. The priests perform prayers at appointed times in the morning and evening. On the fourth and last day of festivities, huge and often emotionally charged processions follow devotees who carry the clay figures to be immersed in the river at many points along the banks. The potters return to collect clay from the river bank once again for the following year.

You can see the image makers in Kumartuli (see page 611) a few days earlier and visit the *pandals* early in the evening, before they become crowded. Local communities are immensely proud of their *pandals* and no effort is spared to put on the most impressive display. The images are decorated with intricate silver, golden or *shola* (white pith) ornaments, there are moving electric light displays and huge structures are built (sometimes resembling a temple) in order to win competitions. WBTDC offers an all-night bus tour as well as a two-hour launch trip on the Hugli to watch the immersion ceremony on the last night.

Performing arts

English-language productions staged by British Council and theatre clubs. **Sangeet Research Academy**, near Mahanayak Uttam (Tollygunge) Metro station, a national centre for training in Indian Classical music, stages free concert on Wed evenings. **Rabindra Bharati University**, 6/4 Dwarakanath Tagore Lane, holds performances, particularly during the winter, including singing, dancing and *jatras*. *Jatra* is community theatre, highly colourful and exaggerated both in delivery and make-up, drawing for its subject romantic favourites from mythology or more up to date social, political and religious themes.

Festivals and events

Kolkata *p601, maps p602, p605, p606, p608*

Jan Ganga Sagar Mela at Sagardwip, 105 km south of Kolkata, where the River Hugli joins the sea, draws thousands of Hindu pilgrims. See page 631.

Mar/Apr Holi (*Dol Purnima*) spring festival.

Jun-Jul Ratha Yatra at Mahesh, nearby.

Sep-Oct Durga Puja, Bengal's celebration of the goddess during **Dasara**.

Oct-Nov Diwali (*Kali Puja* in Bengal) is the festival of lights.

Dec Christmas. Many churches hold special services, including Midnight Mass, and the New Market takes on a new look in Dec as **Barra Din** (Big Day) approaches with stalls selling trees and baubles. Other religious festivals are observed as elsewhere in India.

Galleries

Ahuja Museum for Arts, 26 Lee Rd (Elgin Rd crossing with AJC Bose), T033-2289 4645, www.ahujaptm.com/museum. The private collection of Mr SD Ahuja contains over 1200 works of art, which are displayed here in rotation. Entrance is free, coffee is distributed, and the toilets are handy.

Artists' Circle, 46 Circus Av, T033-2283 3176. Interesting exhibitions by emerging artists.

Centre Art Gallery, 87C Park St. Mainly works by Bengali artists.

Chemould Art Gallery, 12F Park St. One of the big names in contemporary art, and worth keeping an eye on.

CIMA, 2nd floor, Sunny Towers, 43 Ashutosh Chowdhury Av, T033-2485 8717, www.cimaart india.com. Tue-Sat 1100-1900, closed Sun, Mon 1500-1900. The best exhibition space in the city and the shop has a good stock in wall-hangings, metalwork, clothes, stoles, ornaments, etc.

Galerie 88, 28B Shakespeare Sarani, www.galerie88.in. 1200-2000. Contemporary art.
Studio 21, 17/L Dover Terrace (off Ballygunge Phari), T033-2486 6735, studio21.gallery@gmail.com. A minimalist new space for emerging artists from all disciplines, art/photography exhibitions change regularly. Hard to find in a residential area, best accessed from Dover Lane (take 2nd turning on right then ask). Same opening hours as **CIMA**, to which the gallery is affiliated.

O Shopping

Kolkata *p601, maps p602, p605, p606, p608*
Most shops open Mon-Fri 1000-1730 or later (some break for lunch), Sat 1000-1300. New Market stalls, and most shops, close on Sun.

Books

College St, a wealth of second-hand pavement bookstalls along this street mainly for students but may reveal an interesting first edition for a keen collector (see page 610).
Crossword, Elgin Rd. Deservedly popular chain store, with 2 floors of books, CDs , good selection of magazines and films and a busy coffee shop.
Earthcare Books, 10 Middleton St (by Drive Inn), T033-2229 6551, www.earthcare books.com. Excellent selection of children's books, Indian-focussed titles, socially conscious books, plenty of fiction, has small photo exhibitions. Mon-Fri 1100-1900, Fri 1100-1600.
Family Book Shop, 1A Park St. Good selection of guidebooks. 10-15% discounts offered (without your asking).
Kolkata Book Fair, check venue with tourist office. End of Jan for a fortnight, stalls sell paperback fiction to antiquarian books.
Mirza Ghalib St. Has a string of small shops selling new, used and photocopied versions of current favourites. Bargaining required.
Oxford Book Shop, Park St. Huge selection of English titles, postcards and films, nice café upstairs where you can browse through titles. Excellent for books on Kolkata, and a good children's bookshop next door.
Seagull, 31A SP Mukherjee Rd, T033-2476 5869/5, www.seagullindia.com. Large and unusual stock of art-related books, coffee-table tomes, etc. Open 1030-1930, except Sun.
Starmark, top floor, Emami Centre, 3 Lord Sinha Rd, T033-2282 2617-9; also City Centre and South City Mall. Mon 1200-2030, Tue-Sun 1000-2030. The best selection of fiction in Kolkata, plus imported magazines, films.

Clothes and accessories

Ananda, 13 Russell St. Fancy saris.
Anokhi, Shop 209 Forum Shopping Mall, 10/3 Lala Lajpat Rai Sarani, near AJC Bose Rd. Beautiful block-print bed-linens, floaty bed-wear, scarves, accessories, clothes and more. Made in Jaipur, mid-range prices.
Biba, South City Mall, Prince Anwar Shar Rd, www.bibaindia.com; also has franchises in **Pantaloons** department stores. Chic cotton print dresses, tasteful *salwar*.
Fabindia, 16 Hindustan Park (also branches at Woodburn Park Rd, near AJC Bose Rd, and City Centre Mall in Salt Lake). 1000-2030. Clothes, textiles, toiletries, rugs and home furnishings from fair-trade company. Hugely successful due to their tasteful and high-quality selection. Well worth a visit.
Gomukh, 7 Sudder St. Traveller wear, plus a range of scarves and wall-hangings, cheap and well-stocked.
Monapali, 15 Louden St. Designer *salwar*.
Ogaan, P545 Lake Rd Extension. High-quality clothes including swimwear and lingerie.
Ritu's Boutique, 46A Rafi Ahmed Kidwai Rd. *Kurtas* and saris.
Taj Bengal arcade. For pricey leather goods.

Government emporia

Government emporia are mainly in the town centre and are fixed price shops. Several at **Dakshinapan**, near Dhakuria Bridge, Mon-Fri 1030-1930, Sat 1030-1400, convenient, excellent selection of handloom and handicrafts. **Central Cottage Industries**, 7 JL Nehru Rd. **Kashmir Art**, 12 JL Nehru Rd. **Phulkari**, Punjab Emporium, 26B Camac St. **Rajasthali**, 30E JL Nehru Rd. **Tripura**, 58 JL Nehru Rd. **UP**, 12B Lindsay St.

Handicrafts and handloom

There are many handicraft shops around Newmarket St, selling batik prints, handloom, blockprints and embroidery, but starting prices are usually excessive so bargain hard. Shops listed below are all either fair trade-based or associated with self-help groups.

Artisana, 13 Chowringhee Place (off Gokhale Rd), T033-2223 9422. Handloom and handicrafts, traditional hand-block textiles, designer jewellery, metalware and more. Mon-Sat 1100-1900.

Ashalayam Handicrafts, 1st floor, 44 Mirza Ghalib St. Products made by street children who have been trained and given shelter by the **Don Bosco Ashalayam Project**. Proceeds are split between the artisans and the trust.

Bengal Home Industries Association, 11 Camac St. Good selection of printed cotton (bedspreads, saris) and assorted knick-knacks. Relaxed, fixed price.

Calcutta Rescue Handicrafts, **Fairlawn Hotel**. Thu 1830-2030. Medical NGO sells great selection of cards, bags and trinkets made and embroidered by former patients.

Kamala, 1st floor, Tagore Centre, 9A Ho Chi Min Sarani, T033-2223 9422. Outlet shop for the Crafts Council of West Bengal; great selection of textiles, jewellery, gifts and trinkets at very reasonable prices (sourced directly from the artisans). Mon-Sat 1000-1900.

Karmyog, 12B Russell St. Gorgeous handcrafted paper products.

Sasha, 27 Mirza Ghalib St, T033-2252 1586, www.sashaworld.com. Mon-Sat 1000-1900, Sun 1000-0100. Attractive range of good-quality, fair trade textiles, furnishings, ceramics, metalwork, etc, but not cheap, welcome a/c.

Jewellery

Bepin Behari Ganguly St (Bow Bazar) is lined with mirrored jewellers' shops; **PC Chandra, BB Dutt, B Sirkar** are well known. Also many on Rash Behari Av. **Silver market** (*Rupa bajar*) is off Mirza Ghalib St opposite Newmarket. Gold and silver prices are listed daily in the newspapers.

Markets

The **New Market**, Lindsay St, behind the original Hogg Market (largely rebuilt since a fire in 1985 and recently revamped), has more than 2500 shops. It used to be said that you could buy anything from a needle to an elephant (on order) in one of its stalls. Today it's still worth a visit; come early morning to watch it come alive. You will find mundane everyday necessities to exotic luxuries, from fragrant florists to gory meat stalls. Be prepared to deal with pestering basket-wallahs.

For conventional shopping try **Air-Conditioned Market**, Shakespeare Sarani, for imported food and toiletries (closed Sun); **The Forum**, Elgin Rd, has Anokhi, Western clothing, cinema and restaurants; plus **City Centre**, Salt Lake, and **Planet M**, on Camac St. The newest to open is **South City Mall**, Prince Anwar Shar Rd, closest metro Rabindra Sarovar, open 1100-2030 for shopping (Body Shop, Marks and Spencer, huge Spencers supermarket, etc), later for restaurants and cinema. On Free School St, **More** supermarket is convenient and well-stocked, Mon-Fri 0730-2200, weekends 1000-2100.

Kolkata has a number of **bazars**, each with a character of its own. In **Bentinck St** are Muslim tailors, Chinese shoemakers plus Indian sweetmeat shops and tea stalls. **Gariahat market** early in the morning attracts a diverse clientele (businessmen, academics, cooks) who come to select choice fresh fish. In **Shyambazar** the coconut market lasts from 0500 to 0700. **Burra Bazar** is a hectic wholesale fruit market held daily. The colourful **flower market** is on Jagannath Ghat on the river bank. The old **China Bazar** no longer exists although **Tiretta Bazar** area still retains its ethnic flavour; try an exceptional Chinese breakfast from a street stall.

Music

Music World, 18G Park St, T033-2217 0751. Sells a wide range of all genres. For musical instruments (sitars, tablas, etc) head to the southern end of Rabindra Sarani.

Tailors

Garments can be skilfully copied around New Market and on Madge Lane. Tailors will try to overcharge foreigners as a matter of course.

▲ Activites and tours

Kolkata *p601, maps p602, p605, p606, p608*

Body and soul

Look out for adverts around Sudder St for yoga classes held on hotel rooftops.

Aurobindo Bhavan, 8 Shakespeare Sarani, T033-2282 3057. Very informal drop-in classes, women on Mon/Wed/Fri 1530-1930, men on

Tue/Thu/Sat 130-1930 (Rs 200). Bring a copy of your passport and visa.

Cricket
Occasional Test matches and One-Day Internationals and regular IPL fixtures at Eden Gardens, see page 604, 100,000 capacity; get tickets in advance.

Football
The season starts in May and continues through the monsoons. The club grounds are on the Maidan (try **East Bengal Football Club**, T033-2248 4642).

Golf
Royal Calcutta Golf Club, 18 Golf Club Rd, T033-2473 1352, founded in 1829, the oldest golf club in the world outside the UK. It moved to its present course in 1910 having taken the radical step of admitting women in 1886.
The Tollygunge Club, 120 Despran Sasmal Rd, T033-2473 5954. The course is on land that was once an indigo plantation.

Horse racing
Royal Calcutta Turf Club, T033-2229 1104. Racing takes place in the cool season (Nov to early Apr) and monsoon (Jul-Sep); tote, bookmakers available. The Derby is in the 1st week of Jan.The history of racing goes back to the time of Warren Hastings and the 1820s grandstand is especially handsome. It's a fun, cheap day out in the public stands, better still if you can access the members enclosure to get up close to the racehorses and enjoy a drink in the bar with antlers mounted on the wall.

Sightseeing tours
WBTDC tours, departure point is Tourism Centre, 3/2 BBD Bagh E, 1st floor, T033-2248 8271. Daily tours, 0830-1730, Rs 150 in non a/c bus, Rs 200 in a car for 4-5 passengers. Tour stops at: Eden Gardens, High Court, Writers' Building, Belur Math, Dakshineswar Kali Temple, Jain Temple, Netaji Bhavan, Kolkata Panorama and Esplanade, Victoria Memorial, St Paul's Cathedral and Kali Ghat. Entry fees not included. Private tour operators also offer city tours. Approved guides from **Govt of India Tourist Office**, T033-2582 5813.

Swimming
The **Hindustan International Hotel** pool is open to non-residents (Rs 500).

Tour operators
Best deals in air tickets to/from the East (through Bangkok) are offered by agents in the Sudder St area.
American Express, 21 Old Court House St, T033-2248 9491.
The Brothers, 278 CR Ave, T/F033-4008 1723, www.brothershorizons.com. Tours to Darjeeling.
Cox & Kings, 6 Little Russel St, T033-4018 3600/1, www.coxandkings.com.
Help Tourism, Sadananda Kothi (1st floor), 67A Kali Temple Rd, Kalighat, T033-2455 0917, www.helptourism.com. Wide variety of wildlife and adventure tours in Assam, Arunachal and North Bengal, with strong eco credentials and involvement of local communities. Recommended.
Thomas Cook, 19B Shakespeare Sarani, T033-2282 6719.

Volunteer work
Many people come to Kolkata to work with one of the many NGOs. The following organizations accept volunteers, though it's wise to contact them in advance (except for the Missionaries of Charity, where you only need to attend one of the registration days, see below).
Don Bosco Ashalayam Project, T033-2643 5037, www.ashalayam.org. Rehabilitates young homeless people by teaching skills.
Hope Kolkata Foundation, 39 Panditya Pl, T033-2474 2904, www.hopechild.org. An Irish charity focussing on the needs of disadvantaged children.
Missionaries of Charity (**Mother Teresa**), The Mother House, 54A AJC Bose Rd, T033-2249 7115. The majority of volunteers work at one of the Mother Teresa homes. Induction/registration sessions are at 1500 on Mon, Wed and Fri in various languages.

Transport

Kolkata *p601, maps p602, p605, p606, p608*
Kolkata is at the eastern end of the Grand Trunk Rd (NH2). Many city centre roads become one way or change direction from 1400 to 2100 so expect tortuous detours.

Air Enquiries T033-2511 8787. The spacious terminals are well organized and have been recently renovated; a new terminal is being built.A reservation counter for rail (same-day travel only) is found in the Arrivals hall. There are money changers at the exit of the International terminal.

For transport to town, pre-paid taxis (office closes at 2200) to the city centre cost about Rs 350 (de luxe cars, Rs 550-700). From the city centre to the airport costs the same or less if you bargain hard. New a/c buses leave from directly outside Arrivals, going to Howrah station (via the city centre) and Esplanade (from where it is a 15 min walk to Sudder St), taking at least 1 hr and costing Rs 40. They also go to Tollygunge. The old public bus is not recommended for new arrivals as it's a 400-m walk across the car park to main the road, and then changing for the nearest Metro station which is at Dum Dum (Rs 8 to city centre); auto-rickshaws to the Metro cost about Rs 80.

Domestic For schedules and prices it's best to visit a 3rd-party booking site such as www.yatra.com or www.makemytrip.com. Airlines include: **Air India**, 50 Chowringhee Rd, T033-2282 2356, airport T033-2248 2354. **Jet Airways**, 18D Park St, T033-3989 3333, airport T033-2511 9894. **IndiGo**, Crescent Tower, 229 AJC Bose Rd, T033-4003 6208, www.goindigo.com; **Kingfisher**, T1800-180 0101, www.flykingfisher.com; and **Spicejet**, T1800-180 3333, www.spicejet.com.

International For international flights, see page 22. Airlines include: **Biman Bangladesh**, airport, T033-2511 8772. **Cathay Pacific**, 1 Middleton St, T033-2288 4312. **China Eastern**, 1st floor, Landmark Building, 228A AJC Bose Rd, T033-4044 8887. **Druk Air**, 51 Tivoli Court, 1A Ballygunge Circular Rd T033-2240 2419. **Emirates**, Trinity Tower, 83 Topsia Rd Sth, T033-4009 9555. **Gulf Air**, 3rd floor, 230A AJC Bose Rd, T033-4006 3741, airport T033-2511 1612. **KLM**, 1 Middleton St, T033-2283 0151. **Kuwait Airways**, 230A AJC Bose Rd, T033-2240 3575. **Lufthansa**, Tower 2, 8A, Millennium City, DN62, Sec V, Salt Lake, T033- 4002 4200. **Qatar Airways**, 24 Park St, T033-3242 2416, has a daily flight to Doha connecting with cities in Europe and USA. **Singapore Airlines**, Tower 2, 9A, Millennium City, DN-62, Sector V, Salt Lake, T033-2367 5417. **Thai Airways**, 8th floor, Crescent Tower, 229 AJC Bose Rd, T033-2283 8865.

Bicycle Bike hire is not easy; ask at your hotel if a staff bike is free. Spares are sold along Bentinck St, north of Chowringhee.

Local bus State transport services run throughout the city and suburbs from 0500-2030; usually overcrowded after 0830, but very cheap (minimum Rs 4 on the big blue-yellow buses, which are noteworthy for their artwork) and a good way to get around. Maroon minibuses (little more expensive, minimum Rs 5) cover major routes. South Bengal minibuses are bigger and will often stop on request. Newer a/c buses are becoming commonplace.

Long distance bus An extensive hub and spoke bus operation from Kolkata allows cheap travel within West Bengal and beyond, but long bus journeys in this region are gruelling as roads are generally terrible, and are a last resort when trains are full. The tourist office, 3/2 BBD Bagh, has timetables. Advance bookings at computerized office of **Calcutta State Transport Corp** (CSTC), Esplanade, T033-2248 1916: To **Digha** from 0530-1600; **Cooch Behar**; **Malda**; **Siliguri**, 12 hrs; **Bishnupur**; and other towns in West Bengal. More comfortable private a/c buses with push-back seats to Siliguri also depart from Esplanade; good are Royal Cruisers, T(0)9903-400926, Rs 900, who also have buses to **Puri** via **Bhubaneswar** at 2100, Rs 750. **Orissa & Bihar STC**, Babu Ghat: to **Ranchi**; **Dhaka**, **Gaya**, **Puri**, 11 hrs. **Bhutan Govt**, **Phuntsholing** via Siliguri, 1900, 16 hrs.

To Bangladesh Private buses to **Dhaka**) can be booked from numerous agencies on Marquis St, from where they also depart.

Local ferry To cross the Hugli, between Howrah station and Babu Ghat, Rs 4, except Sun. During festivals a ferry goes from Babu Ghat to Belur Math, 1 hr.

Long distance ferry **Shipping Corp of India**, 1st floor, 13 Strand Rd (enter from Hare St), T033-2248 4921 (recorded information T033-2248 5420), 1000-1300 (for tickets), 1400-1745 (information only), operates a steamer to **Port Blair** in the Andamans. Some 3 or 4 sailings a month (66 hrs), Rs 1961 to Rs 7631 one way. For tickets go 4 days in advance, and be there by 0830; huge queue for 'bunk class'. See page 845.

Metro The Metro is usually clean, efficient and punctual. The recently extended metro line runs for 25 km from Dum Dum in the north to Kavi Subhash in the south from 0700-2145, Sun 1400-2145, every 7-15 mins; fare Rs 4-10. Note that Tollygunge has been renamed 'Mahanayak Uttam Kumar' on station signs, but is still commonly referred to as Tollygunge. There are women-only sections interspersed throughout the train.

Rickshaw Hand-pulled rickshaws are used by locals especially along the narrow congested lanes. Auto-rickshaws operate outside the city centre, especially as shuttle service to/from Metro stations along set routes. Auto-rickshaws from Sealdah station to Sudder St cost about Rs 70.

Taxi Car hire with driver: **Gainwell**, 8 Ho Chi Minh Sarani, T033-2454 5010; **Mercury**, 46 JL Nehru Rd, T033-2244 8377. Tourist taxis from **India Tourism** and **WBTDC** offices. Local taxis are yellow. Ambassadors: insist on the meter, then use conversion chart to calculate correct fare.

Train Kolkata is served by 2 railway stations, **Howrah** and **Sealdah**. Howrah station has a separate complex for platforms 18-21. Enquiries, Howrah, T033-2638 7412/3542, 'New' Complex, T033-2660 2217, Sealdah, T033-2350 3535. Reservation, T138 (computerized). Foreign tourist quota is sold at both stations until 1400, at which point tickets go on general sale. Railway reservations, Fairlie Place, BBD Bagh; 1000-1300, 1330-1700, Sun 1000-1400 (best to go early), tourists are automatically told to go to the Foreign Tourist Counter to get Foreign Tourist Quota. It takes 10-30 mins. You will need to show your passport and complete a reservation form. You can also pay in US dollars, sterling or euros, but expect a poor exchange rate.

Trains listed depart from Howrah (**H**), unless marked '(**S**)' for Sealdah. To **Allahabad**: see New Delhi. **Agra Fort**: *Jodhpur Exp 12307*, 2320, 20 hrs. **Bhubaneswar**: *Dhauli Exp 12821*, 0600, 7 hrs; *Falaknuma Exp 12703*, 0725, 6½ hrs; *Howrah Puri Exp 12837*, 2335, 7 hrs. **Chennai**: *Coromandel Exp 12841*, 1450, 26½ hrs; *Howrah Chennai Mail 12839*, 2345, 28 hrs. **Mumbai** (**CST**): *Gitanjali Exp 12860*, 1350, 31½ hrs (via **Nagpur**, 17½ hrs); *Howrah Mumbai Mail 12810*, 2015, 33 hrs (via **Nagpur**, 18 hrs); *Howrah Mumbai Mail 12321*, 2200, 37½ hrs (via **Gaya**, 7½ hrs). **Mumbai** (**Lokmanya Tilak**): *Jnaneswari SD Exp 12102*, 2255 (Mon, Wed, Thu, Sun), 31 hrs (via **Nagpur**, 17½ hrs). **Nagpur**: See Mumbai trains plus *Howrah Ahmedabad Exp 12834*, 2355, 19 hrs. **New Delhi** via **Gaya** and **Allahabad**: *Rajdhani Exp 12301*, 1655 (except Sun), 17 hrs; *Rajdhani Exp 12305*, 1405 (Sun), 20 hrs, via **Patna**; (**S**) *Rajdhani Exp 12313*, 1650 (daily), 17½ hrs. **New Jalpaiguri** (**NJP**): (**S**) *Kanchenjunga Exp 15657*, 0645, 11½ hrs; (**S**) *Darjeeling Mail 12343*, 2205, 10 hrs; *Kamrup Exp 15959*, 1735, 12½ hrs. **Puri**: *Jagannath Exp 18409*, 1900, 9½ hrs; *Howrah Puri Exp 12837*, 2235, 9 hrs. **Ranchi**: *Howrah Hatia Exp 18615*, 2220, 9 hrs; *Howrah Shatabdi Exp 12019*, 0605 (except Sun), 7 hrs.

To Bangladesh It is now possible to travel direct to **Dhaka** on the newly revived *Maitree Express*, Sat and Wed 0710, from **Kolkata (Chitpur) Terminal**, 12 hrs, stops only at the border for customs and immigration.

Tram Kolkata is the only Indian city to run a tram network. 0430-2300. 2nd-class carriage Rs 3.50-4, front '1st class' Rs 4-4.50, but no discernible difference. Many trams originate at **Esplanade depot** and it's a great way to see the city – ride route 1 to Belgachia through the heart of North Kolkata's heritage, or Route 26 from the **Gariahat depot** in the south all the way to Howrah, via Sealdah and College St. Services run from 0430-2230, with a restricted service at the weekends.

Directory

Kolkata *p601, maps p602, p605, p606, p608*

Banks There are 24-hr ATMs all over the city centre. Money changers proliferate on Sudder St. **Thomas Cook**, 4/A ground floor, Park Mansions, Park St. **Cultural centres and libraries** **British Council** Information Centre, L&T Chambers, 16 Camac St, T033-2282 5370. Good for UK newspapers, reference books. Mon-Sat 1100-1900. **French Association**, 217 AJC Bose Rd, T033-2281 5198. **Goethe Institut**, Max Mueller Bhavan, 8 Pramathesh Barua Sarani, T033-2486 6398, www.goethe.de/kolkata. Mon-Fri 0930-1730, Sat 1500-1700. **Embassies and consulates** **Bangladesh**, 9 Bangabandhu, Sheikh Mujib Sarani, T033-2290 5208/9, www.bdhckolkata.org. **Germany**, 1 Hastings Park Rd, T033-2479 1141-2, www.kalkutta.diplo.de. **Myanmar**, 4th floor, Block D, White House, 119 Park St, T033-2217 8273. **Nepal**, 1 National Library

Av, T033-2456 1224, nepalconsulate@ dataone.in. **Netherlands**, 5 Rameshwar Shaw Rd, T033-2289 7020, consulkolkata.netherlands@ gmail.com. **Norway**, 5B, Roudon St, T033-2287 9769. **Spain**, 1 Taratolla Rd, T033-2469 5954. **Sri Lanka**, 302A Centre Point, 28/2 Shakespeare Sarani, T9831-257401. **Thailand**, 18B Mandeville Gardens, T033-2440 7836, rtcgkkt@eth.net. **UK**, 1A Ho-Chi-Minh Sarani, T033-2288 5172-6, http://ukinindia.fco.gov.uk. **USA**, 5/1 Ho-Chi-Minh Sarani, T033-3984 2400. **Internet** You will need your passport to register the first time you visit an internet cafe. Many across the city; lots in Sudder St area with skype, printing, etc; standard charge is Rs 20 per hr. On Sudder St, very helpful and with good equipment are **Hotline Services**, daily 0830-2200. In the city centre, **E-Shan Digital Services**, 13B CR Ave, T033-2225 5716, fast connection but no skype, Rs 25 per hr, Mon-Sat 0900-2100. **Medical services** **Apollo Gleneagles Hospital**, 5B Canel Circular Rd, T033-2320 3040. **Wockhardt Medical Centre**, 2/7 Sarat Bose Rd, T033-2475 4320, www.wockhard hospitals.net, reliable diagnostic centre. **Woodlands Hospital**, 8B Alipore Rd, T033-2456 7076-9. There are many chemists around Lindsay St and Newmarket. **Angel**, 151 Park St (24-hr). **Dey's**, 6/2B Lindsay St. **Moonlight**, 180 SP Mukherjee Rd (24-hr). **Post** Poste Restante at GPO, 0800-2000, closed Sun and holidays. **Speed Post** At major post offices including airport and Park St. Book-post and packaging is convenient at Free School Post Office, Mon-Sat 1000-1730; parcel stitching service Mon-Fri 1000-1500, Sat 1000-1400. **DHL & Blue Dart**, Kanak Building, Middleton St, 24-hr counter T033-2288 1919.

South of Kolkata

To the south of Kolkata are the tidal estuary of the Hugli and the mangrove forests of the Sundarbans. Famous for their population of Bengal tigers, the Sundarbans reach into Bangladesh, but it's possible to take a day trip down to the mouth of the Hugli or boat trips into the Sundarbans themselves. ▸▸ *For listings, see pages 632-633.*

Sagardwip

Ganga Sagar Mela is held in mid-January, attracting over 500,000 pilgrims each year who come to bathe and then visit the **Kapil Muni Temple**. The island has been devastated many times by cyclones. To get there catch a bus from Esplanade or take a taxi to Kakdwip and then take a ferry across to Kochuberia Ghat (Sagardwip). From there it is a 30-minute bus ride across the island to where the Ganga meets the sea by the Kapil Muni Temple.

Sunderbans Tiger Reserve → *Colour map 4, C2.*

ⓘ *Permit required (maximum 5 days) from the WBTDC in Kolkata, T033-2248 8271, where you can book a package tour (take your passport). Or contact the Secretary, Department of Forests, G Block (top floor), Writers Building (top floor), T033-2221 5999. Avoid weekends.*

Sunderbans (pronounced Shunder-bon) is named after the Sunderi trees and literally means 'a beautiful forest'. The mangrove swamps are said to be the largest estuarine forests in the world. Improved management is battling to halt the loss of mangrove cover as it is exploited for fuel. Most villagers depend on fishing and forestry, while local honey gatherers who are active in April and May are said to wear masks on the backs of their heads to frighten away tigers, which they believe only attack from the rear! You will notice large areas of *bheries* for aquaculture. Prawn fisheries are the most lucrative and co-operative efforts are being encouraged by the government.

The reserve, a World Heritage Site, preserves the habitat of about 270 Bengal tigers (*Panthera tigris*). They are bigger and richer in colour than elsewhere in South Asia and are thought to be able to survive on salt water (rainwater is the only fresh water in the park). Tigers here are strong swimmers and known to attack fishermen. Methods of improved management include providing permanent sources of fresh water for tigers by digging deep, monsoon-fed ponds, installing solar-powered lighting to scare them away from villages and electrifying dummy woodcutters. Although you are unlikely to see a tiger, there are spotted deer, wild boar, monkeys, snakes, fishing cats, water monitors, Olive Ridley sea turtles and a few large estuarine crocodiles here, particularly on Lothian Island and Chamta block.

The best season is September-March. Heavy rains and occasional cyclones in April/May and November/December can make visiting difficult. Take water, torch, mosquito repellent and be prepared for cool nights. You must be accompanied by armed forest rangers. Motor launches can be hired from Canning and Sonakhali (Basanti), but it is better to go down the narrow creeks in human-powered boats. You may be able to go ashore on bamboo jetties to walk in the fenced-in areas of the forest which have watchtowers (dawn to dusk only).

Digha → *Colour map 4, C1. 185 km from Kolkata.*

Digha was described by Warren Hastings visiting in 1780 as the 'Brighton of the East', though there is not a pebble for at least 2000 km. The casuarina-lined, firm wide beach is popular with Bengalis and hotels are clustered around one main road. The small **Chandaneswar Temple**, 9 km away, actually in Orissa, is an important Siva temple which can be reached by bus.

South of Kolkata listings

For Sleeping and Eating price codes and other relevant information, see Essentials pages 38-42.

Sleeping

Sagardwip *p631*

WBTDC runs 2-day boat trips with lodging on board (**LL-A**) during **Ganga Sagar Mela** including a/c coach. You can also stay at the *dharamshala* for a donation.

F Youth Hostel. Book via the Youth Services office in Kolkata, T033-2248 0626, ext 27.

Sunderbans Tiger Reserve *p631*

A few basic lodges are found in Gosaba. There is also one in Pakhirala, the last village before Sajnekhali.

LL Vivada Cruises, T(0)9903-000268, www.sunderbancruises.com. The first luxury cruise boat to be launched on this route, eco-friendly with 32 rooms, internet, open-air gym, sauna, sunbathing deck and multicuisine restaurants. Package for 2 days/3 nights includes meals and excursions.

AL Sunderbans Jungle Camp, Bali village; book through **Help Tourism** in Kolkata (see page 627). Indigenous-style bungalows with modern bathrooms, in one of India's best community tourism ventures, set up by a group of ex-poachers. Local fishermen supply fish and offer trips into mangrove forests; it's also a chance to interact with villagers and experience authentic folk performances. Book as a package, all meals included, prices go down the more members in your group.

A Sunderban Tiger Camp, Sajnekhali, T033-3293 5749, www.sunderbantigercamp.com. 'Tents' with thatched roofs, huts, mud cottages and a/c cottages, in a peaceful location with nice gardens. Village walks and fishing trips available, as well as tours on comfortable boats. Restaurant serves range of cuisines and seafood, there's a bar and a library.

D Tourist Lodge, Sajnekhali, contact through **WBTDC**, T03218-214960, www.westbengal tourism.gov.in. Raised on pillars and fenced from wildlife, solar power, small basic rooms with mosquito nets, some Western toilets, hot water in buckets, 20-bed dorm, simple meals (price includes breakfast and 1 meal; if you buy fish, chef will cook it), no alcohol. Book ahead; carry your permit.

Digha *p631*

There is plenty of choice to suit all budgets.

C Sea Coast, T03220-266305. With some a/c rooms, this is the best 3-star option.

C-G Tourist Lodge, T03220-266255. Rooms on 3 floors, some a/c, 5-bed dorm (Rs 200), bar, restaurant. Breakfast included (not for dorm).

E-F Sea Hawk, T03220-266235. Comfortable rooms, on 3 floors, some a/c.

Activities and tours

Sunderbans Tiger Reserve *p631*

Help Tourism, Kolkata (see page 627). Excellent community-based tours and have a camp near the reserve (see Sleeping, opposite).

WBTDC Tours: 2-day and 3-day trips (infrequent during monsoon, Jul-Sep), by coach from Kolkata then 'luxury' launch with onboard accommodation. Prices vary between vessels and with standard of lodging: a 1-day/2-night tour costs Rs 2300 for 10-12 bed dorms to Rs 8600 for a double; 5% tax is added. The launch is the only way to visit the Sunderbans during monsoon.

Transport

Sunderbans Tiger Reserve *p631*

Road and boat From Kolkata: CSTC bus from Babu Ghat, Strand Rd, to **Sonakhali** (1st depart 0630 then hourly, 3½ hrs), then hire a **boat** to Sajnekhali (Rs 400-500, 3 hrs). Alternatively, from Basanti, take public ferry to **Gosaba** (1½ hrs, Rs 10), then travel across the island by flat-bed van rickshaw (5 km, 45 mins) which enables you to see interesting village life, and finally take a boat to Sajnekhali; recommended for at least one way. Lodge staff will arrange boat hire with park guide (about Rs 800 for 4 hrs, Rs 1500 for 8 hrs; boats can take 6-8 people). Since these are tidal waterways, boats are not always able to moor near the ghats, and during monsoons or bad weather they will not sail.

Train and boat Kolkata (Sealdah) to **Canning** (105 km) and then boat to Docghat where you can get a shared auto or bus to Sonakhali, where you get another boat. From Canning you can get a private boat direct to **Sajnekhali Lodge** (Rs 1000 per day), but the journey is long and dependent on the tide.

Digha *p631*
Bus A/c luxury buses leave from Esplanade, taking 4 hrs. Public buses leave from Esplanade and Howrah and take 4½-5 hrs (Rs 75).
Train Direct train from Howrah on Sun, 2867A, 0755, 3½ hrs. From Mon-Sat trains depart Salimar (on west bank of Hugli south of Howrah) at 0800.

North of Kolkata

The plains north of Kolkata are home to the peaceful university town of Santiniketan, home of Tagore, and the 300-year-old terracotta temples of Bishnupur. The legacy of the Muslim nawabs lives on in the impressive ruins of Gaur and Pandua, while atmospheric Murshidabad provides an accessible blend of Bengali history and relaxation. *For listings, see pages 638-640.*

Bishnupur

For listings, see pages 638-640. Colour map 4, C1. *Population: 61,900.*

The warrior Malla Kings of Bengal ruled this area from Bishnupur for nearly two centuries, until the East India Company sold it to the Maharajah of Burdwan in 1805, for arrears of land revenue. The Mallas were great patrons of the arts and built uniquely ornamental terracotta temples. It is also where the Dhrupad style of classical Indian singing originated, and the legendary Bishnupur Gharana (School of Music) still resonates from this ancient past. Local handicrafts include silk, tassar, conch-shell and bell-metalware and the famous terracotta Bankura horse, Dokhra, and also slate statues and artefacts. Bengali sweetmeats and flavoured tobacco are local specialities.

Ins and outs

Getting there Buses from Kolkata and Durgapur drop passengers on the edge of town. The train station is 3 km out of town, from where a cycle-rickshaw to the Tourist Lodge costs Rs 20.
Getting around The town is haphazardly clustered around the Pokabandh Lake; most visitors stay on College Road. It is possible to see all the temples listed by foot (and much more besides), but very easy to get lost in the intricate network of streets. Cycle rickshaws can be hired for Rs 100-150 for two hours.

Sights

There are more than two dozen temples in Bishnupur, mostly dedicated to Krishna and Radha. They are usually built of brick, but sometimes of laterite, and on a square plan with a gently curved roof imitating the Bengali thatched *chala* (hut). The terracotta tiles depict episodes from the *Ramayana* and *Mahabharata*, and also scenes from daily life. Inside, there is a *thakurbari* (sanctuary) and a *vedi* (platform) for the image, on one side. The upper storey has a gallery topped by one, five or even nine towers.

Most of the temples are concentrated within the fort, which was built later by Muslim rulers. Distances given are from the **Tourist Lodge**. The **Rasmancha** (500 m) is a unique Vishnu shrine with a pyramidal roof, built by Bir Hambir in 1600. It is illuminated at night by coloured floodlights. The well-preserved cannons, in particular the 4-m-long **Dalmadal** to the south of the Rasmancha, date back to the Mallas. Further south is **Jor Mandir** (1 km), a pair of hut-shaped temples with a single *sikhara* flanking a smaller diminutive temple with attractively ornamented panels, built in 1726 by Gopala Singha. The **Shyam Rai Temple** (1 km), perhaps the earliest example of the *pancharatna* (five towers), has a fine *sikhara* and dates from 1643. Each façade is triple arched and the terracotta panels show scenes from the *Ramayana*, the

Mahabharata and Krishna's life. The large **Madan Mohan Temple** (3 km), with a white façade, was built of brick with terracotta panels in 1694 by King Durjan, while the 17th-century **Lalji** and **Madan Gopal** are built of laterite. The **Mrinmoyee Mandir** (3 km) has a clay idol of Durga dating from AD 997, and in the courtyard a curiosity of nine trees growing together. Little remains of the Malla Kings' **Fort** (2.5 km). You can see the gate of laterite, with firing holes drilled in different directions and a 13th-century stone chariot. The water reservoirs are still there though the moat, once served by seven lakes, is partly dry.

Santiniketan → *For listings, see pages 638-640.* *Colour map 4, C1. Population: 65,700.*

Santiniketan, the 'Abode of Peace', is a welcome change from the hectic traffic, noise and dirt of Kolkata. Even a brief visit to the shady university campus, with its artistic heritage and its quiet, rural charm, makes a profound impression on most visitors, and is a must for aficionados of Bengal's greatest poet.

Ins and outs

Getting there The nearest railway station is Bolpur, which has trains from Kolkata's Haora and Sealdah stations. Cycle-rickshaws charge Rs 15-20 to Santiniketan, 3 km away. Local buses use a stand near the station. The road journey from Kolkata on the congested NH2 (213 km) can be very slow.

Getting around The Visva Bharati campus and Santiniketan's residential area are ideal for exploring on foot. The temples can be very difficult to find on foot in the maze of narrow streets. It is best to arrange a cycle-rickshaw for a tour, Rs 50 for 2½ hours.

Tourist information Public Relations Office (PRO) ⓘ *Vishva Bharati Office, T03463-252751, Thu-Tue 1000-1700.*

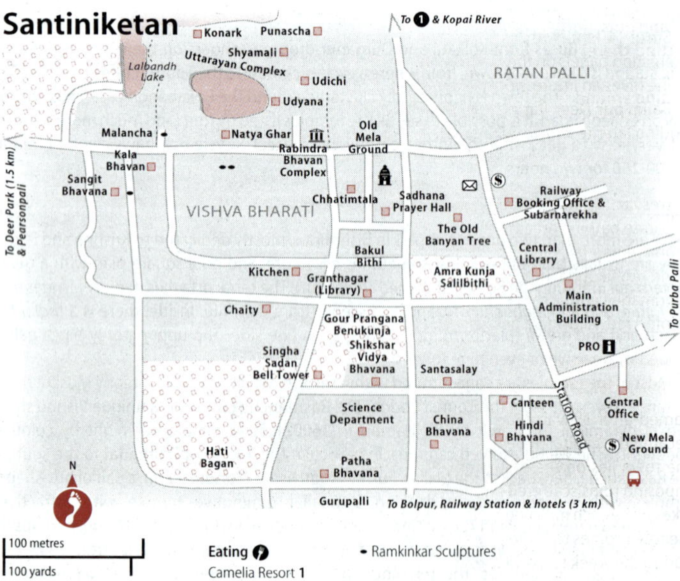

Sights

Vishva Bharati University ⓘ *closed Wed and Tue afternoon, sightseeing is permitted only after university hours: summer 1430-1700, winter 1415-1630 and during holidays 0700-1200, Rs 5, no photography, all compounds are subdivided by wire fences*, has an interesting history. The Maharishi Debendranath Tagore, father of Rabindranath Tagore, the Nobel Laureate, started an *ashram*, later named Santiniketan. In 1901 Rabindranath started an experimental place of learning with a classroom under the trees, and a group of five pupils. It went on to become the Vishva Bharati University in 1921. It now attracts students from all over the world and aspires to be a spiritual meeting ground in a serene, culturally rich and artistic environment. Open-air classes are still a feature of this unique university. Among the many *Bhavans* are those concentrating on fine art (Kala Bhavan) and music and dance (Sangit Bhavan). The **Uttarayan Complex** where the poet lived consists of several buildings in distinctive architectural styles. **Sadhana Prayer Hall**, where Brahmo prayers are held on Wednesday, was founded in 1863, see page 1419. The unusual hall enclosed by stained-glass panels has a polished marble floor which is usually decorated with fresh *alpana* designs. **Chhatimtala**, where Maharishi Debendranath sat and meditated, is the site of special prayers at Convocation time. In keeping with its simplicity, graduates are presented with a twig with five leaves from the locally widespread *Saptaparni* trees.

Rabindra Bhavan ⓘ *Uttarayan complex, Thu-Mon 1030-1330 and 1400-1630, Tue 1030-1330, no photography, bags may not be permitted, shoes must be removed before entering each building*, is a museum and research centre containing photographs, manuscripts and Tagore's personal belongings; the peripheral buildings also contain photos. The museum is well documented and very informative so allow at least an hour. The garden is delightful, particularly when the roses are blooming. **Kala Bhavan** ⓘ *Thu-Mon 1500-1700*, has a rich collection of 20th-century Indian art, particularly sculptures, murals and paintings by famous Bengali artists. **Nandan Museum** ⓘ *Thu-Mon 1000-1330 and 1400-1700, Tue 1000-1330*, has a collection of terracotta, paintings and original tracings of Ajanta murals.

Surul (4 km), with its evocative village atmosphere and small terracotta temples with interesting panels on their façades, makes a pleasant trip. The *zamindari* 'Rajbari' with its durga shrine gives an impression of times past.

Ballavpur Deer Park (3 km) ⓘ *Thu-Tue 1000-1600*, is a reclaimed wooded area of rapidly eroding laterite *khowai* with spotted deer and winter migratory birds.

Around Santiniketan

Bakresvar, 58 km northwest of Santiniketan, is known for its medicinal sulphurous hot springs (separate bathing areas for men and women, though you may not fancy the tepid pools full of people doing laundry). There are seven major *kunds* (springs) from 36°C to 67°C, the hottest being Agnikunda (fire spring). Temples to Siva, Sakti, Kali and Vishnu make it a Hindu pilgrimage centre. The temples are modern and white tiled though the Kali temple is old and painted red. Allow five hours for the trip.

Murshidabad → *For listings, see pages 638-640. Colour map 4, B1. Population: 36,900.*

Named after Nawab Murshid Kuli Khan, a Diwan under Emperor Aurangzeb, Murshidabad became the capital of Bengal in 1705 and remained so up to the time of the battle of Plassey. The town lies on the east bank of the Bhagirathi, a picturesque tributary of the Ganga, with imposing ruins scattered around and an enchanting time warp feel. A vibrant vegetable bazar takes place each morning beneath decaying columns left over from the days of the *nawabs*, and the town comes to life for the famed Muslim festival of **Muhurram** at the end of January. Come during the week to avoid the crowds.

Nizamat Kila on the river bank was the site of the old fort and encloses the Nawabs' Italianate **Hazarduari** ('1000 doors') **Palace** ⓘ *Sat-Thu 1000-1500, Rs 100, no photography*, built in 1837. It is now a splendid museum with a portrait gallery, library and circular durbar hall and contains a rare collection of old arms, curios, china and paintings. The large newer **Imambara** (1847) opposite, also Italianate in style, is under a continuous process of renovation and is worth exploring. The domed, square **Madina** (pavillion) with a veranda that stands nearby may be what remains of the original Imambara. There are numerous 18th-century monuments in the city which are best visited by cycle-rickshaw ⓘ *Rs 100-150 for 3 hrs*. Mir Jafar and his son Miran lived at **Jafaragunj Deorhi**, known as the traitor's gate. **Kat-gola** ⓘ *Rs 50*, the atmospheric garden palace of a rich Jain merchant, houses a collection of curios including Belgian glass mirror-balls and has an old Jain temple and boating 'lake' in the grounds. The **Palace of Jagat Sett**, one of the richest financiers of the 18th century, is 2 km from the Jafargung Cemetery to the north of the palace. The brick ruins of **Katra Masjid** (1723), modelled on the great mosque at Mecca and an important centre of learning, are outside the city to the east. It was built by Murshid Kuli Khan who lies buried under the staircase. **Moti Jheel** (Pearl Lake) and the ruins of **Begum Ghaseti's Palace** are 2 km south of the city. Only a mosque and a room remain. **Khosbagh** (Garden of Delight) ⓘ *across the river, easily accessible by bamboo ferries, Rs 1, 24-hr*, has three walled enclosures. It is recommended to hire a boat (Rs 250 from **Hotel Manjusha**) to journey upstream to Baranagar, three well-preserved terracotta temples in the Bangla style; drift back down and stop off at the Jain town of **Azimganj**.

Malda → *For listings, see pages 638-640.* *Colour map 4, B1.*

Malda is a convenient and comfortable base from which to visit the atmospheric ruins of Gaur and Pandua, with plenty of banks and other amenities in the town centre. Now famous mainly for its large juicy Fajli mangoes, Malda was established around 1680 by the English, who bought an entire village from a local landlord and built it into a market town. **Malda Museum** (1937) has a collection of stone images, coins and inscriptions from Gaur and Pandua. The **market** behind the **Tourist Lodge** is fascinating. Old Malda, which lies at a confluence of rivers 4 km away, has the **Jami Masjid**, built in 1596 out of decorated brick and stone with some good carving on the entrance pillars. The 17-m **Nimasarai Tower** across the river dates from the same period, and has strange stones embedded on the outer surface, which may once have been used to display beheaded criminals.

Gaur and Pandua → *Colour map 4, B1.*

Gaur's situation on the banks of the River Ganga, yet within easy reach of the Rajmahal Hills with their fine black basalt, made it possible for gifted stonemasons to construct beautiful religious and secular buildings. Muslim monuments of the sultanate period are strewn around the quiet, deserted city. Pandua alternated with Gaur as a capital of Bengal between 1338 and 1500, when it was abandoned. Some of the ruins here show clearly how the Muslims made free use of material from Hindu temples near Malda.

Gaur

On the ancient site of Lakshanavati, Gaur was the capital of King Sasanka in the seventh century, followed by the Buddhist Pala kings. The city became famous as a centre of education and culture during the reign of the Hindu Sena kings in the 12th century. In the early 13th century it was invaded by Bhaktiar Khalji and then captured by the Afghan Fakhr-ud-din Dynasty in the 14th century. They plundered the temples to construct their own mosques and tombs. Gaur was sacked by Sher Shah Suri in 1537 and the city's population was wiped out by plague in 1575.

The remains of the embankments of the fort are to the south on the bank of the Bhagirati. The great golden mosque, **Bari Sona Masjid** or Baroduari (12-door), was built in 1526 and is an enormous rectangular stone-faced brick structure with a large open square in front. Fine marble carving is still visible on the remains of the minarets. Note the small Kali temple at the entrance.

Bangladesh can be seen from the **Dakhil Darwaza** (early 15th century), the main fort gateway with its five-storeyed towers. It was built of small red bricks embossed with terracotta decorations. The turrets and circular bastions produce a striking contrast of light and shade with decorative motifs of suns, rosettes, lamps and fretted borders. During the 15th century, a number of mosques and mausoleums were built in the new architectural style.

The **Firuz Minar** (Victory Tower), built by Sultan Firuz Shah in 1486, has a spiral staircase. The lower storeys are 12 sided while the upper are circular, with striking blue and white glazed tiles, used in addition to the terracotta and brick. The builders of the **Chika Mosque** ('Bat Mosque', early 15th century), near the Kadam Rasul, made free use of Hindu idols in its construction. The **Chamkati Mosque** (circa 1475) shows the vaulted ceiling of the veranda. Inside the southeast corner of the fort is the massive **Baisgazi Wall**, which enclosed the Old Palace with its *darbar*, harem, etc. **Kadam Rasul** (1513) is a domed building with a Bengali *chala* roof, which housed the relic of the Prophet, a footprint in stone. The two-storeyed **Lukochuri Darwaza** (Hide-and-Seek Gate, circa 1655) is in the later Mughal style.

The **Tantipara Mosque** (circa 1475; *tanti*, weaver) has superbly decorated red brick with octagonal turrets and five entrance arches. The elegant **Lattan** (Painted) **Mosque** (1475), attributed to Yusuf Shah, was decorated with bands of blue, green, yellow and white glazed tiles. Some 2 km south, close to the Bangladeshi border, is the ruined **Chhoti Sona Masjid**, has a carved gate.

Ramkeli, not far from the Bari Sona Masjid, has the Madan Mohan Jiu Mandir and is of religious significance for followers of **Sri Chaitanya**, the 14th-century Bengali religious reformer. **Tamaltola** marks where he meditated under a tree and pilgrims come to see a footprint in stone.

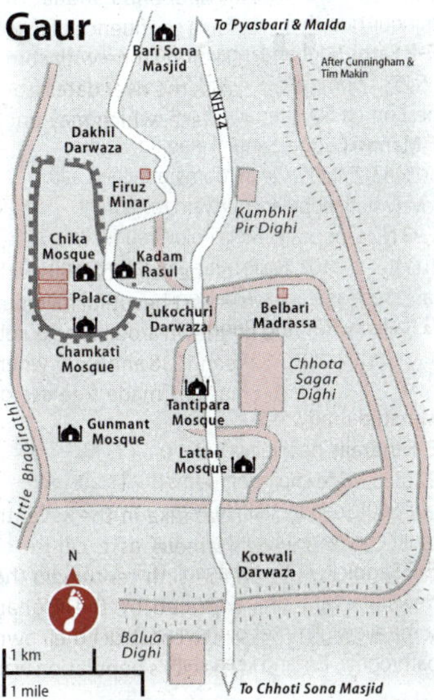

To get here, take a bus for Mohodipur from near the **Tourist Lodge** in Malda, and ask to be dropped at Pyasbari (tea and snacks available). Stay on the narrow tarmac road and you won't get lost. Turn right from the NH34 for the site, which you can wander around for free. To return to Malda, stop a bus or share a taxi. Or arrange a half-day taxi hire through the tourist office in Malda (Rs 600).

Pandua

The old brick-paved road, nearly 4 m wide and about 10 km long, passes through the town and most of the monuments stand close to it. The **Adina Masjid** (1364-1374) ⓘ *free*, exemplifies Muslim architecture in medieval Bengal. Built by Sultan Sikander Shah and once comparable to the great eighth-century mosque at Damascus, it is sadly in a poor state of repair. The vast space enclosed by pillared aisles has an 88-arch screen around a quadrangle with the mosque. Influence of 12th-century Sena architecture is evident in the tall, ornate, tiered *sikhara* and trefoil arches and the remarkable absence of a large entrance gateway. Most of the substructure, and some pillars, was of basalt plundered from existing Hindu temples and palaces. A small doorway in the western back wall of the mosque, clearly taken from an earlier Vishnu temple, exhibits the stonemasons' skill and the exceptional metalwork of the time. The **Eklakhi Mausoleum**, built of brick (circa 1412), has a Hindu idol carved on its front lintel. The **Qutb Shahi Mosque** (also *Sona* or Golden Mosque) was built in 1582. Further along are the ruins of the 17th-century **Chhoti** and **Bari Dargahs**.

To get to the site, take a Siliguri or Raiganj bus from the **Tourist Lodge** in Malda and ask to be dropped at Pandua Bus Stand. The narrow tarmac road to the site, off the NH34, is easy to follow and gives a fascinating behind-the-scenes view of Bengali village life. Buses from Adina return to Malda.

North of Kolkata listings

For Sleeping and Eating price codes and other relevant information, see Essentials pages 38-42.

Sleeping

Bishnupur *p633*

D-E Tourist Lodge, end of College Rd, T03244-252013. Lovely clean and spacious rooms are Rs 600, more expensive with a/c, Western toilets, balconies with view over garden, restaurant and bar, breakfast included. Run by WBTDC. Best option in town.

F Hotel Heritage, Chhinnamasta More, end of College Rd, T03244-254298. Range of rooms, some cleaner than others, a/c and non-a/c. Also dorms.

Other budget hotels in same area, though some can be quite seedy.

Santiniketan *p634, map p634*

There are a couple of cheap guesthouses within the campus; to arrange a stay (maximum 3 days) contact the Public Relations Office (PRO), T03463-252751.

C Camellia Resort, Prantik (3 km from campus), T03463-262043, www.welcomheritage hotels.com. Under renovation at the time of research, so should be a nice choice when finished. On 3 floors around a central courtyard, beautiful large garden, pool, well located in open countryside.

B-E Santiniketan Tourist Lodge (WBTDC), off main road, Bolpur, T03463-252398. Slightly faded standard rooms, some quite small, plusher with a/c, pleasant garden, breakfast included (but poor meals).

C-D Chhuti Holiday Resort, 241 Charupalli, Jamboni, T03463-252692, www.chhutiresort.com. Comfortable thatched rooms with bath, some a/c, good restaurant, innovative.

D-E Rangamati, Prabhat Sarani, Bhubandanga, Bolpur, T03463-252305. 22 decent rooms, some with balcony, dorm (Rs 170), restaurant (Indian and Chinese).

D-F Royal Bengal, Bhubandanga, Bolpur, T03463-257148. Clean and modern, all rooms with balcony and attached bath, dorm (Rs 200), soulless restaurant.

E Babli Farm, outside Santinikentan, T033-2441 3248, www.babli-farm.tripod.com. 12 acres of countryside devoted to encouraging agricultural employment among the community, with a tranquil guesthouse.

E-F Sathi, Bhubandanga Rd, Bolpur, T03463-254630. Some a/c, 3, 4 and 5-bedded rooms, best on 1st floor, terrace (front and back).

F Manasi Lodge, Santiniketan Rd, Bolpur, T03463-254200. Clean rooms, attached bath, lovely staff, popular courtyard restaurant.

F-G Nisa, opposite Mela Polo Ground, Bolpur, T03463-253101. Basic but clean rooms with fan, those at rear have balconies.

G Railway Retiring Rooms, Bolpur. 1 a/c, restaurant.

Murshidabad *p635*

E-F Indrajit, near railway station, T03482-271858. Wide choice of rooms of all standards (a/c 800), friendly staff, truly excellent multi-cuisine restaurant plus bar.

E-F Sagnick, 77 Omrahaganj, T03482-271492. New hotel with some a/c rooms, check a few, some allow glimpses of the river. Tiny tiled bathrooms, TVs and keen staff.

F Ashoke Mahal, Omrahaganj, T03482-320855. Clean and pleasant, rear room 202 is the best with a balcony overlooking the river.
F Manjusha, by Hazarduari Palace, T03482-270321. The best location in town, with serene riverside setting for spotting dolphins, lush garden of flowers and fruit trees, charming manager can help with bike, rickshaw and boat hire, food (by arrangement) is hit-and-miss. Rooms are simple but clean, with fans.
G Youth hostels at Lalbagh and Murshidabad, reserve through Youth Services, 32/1 BBD Bagh S, Kolkata, T03482-280626. Very cheap.

Malda *p636*

D-F Continental Lodge, 22 KJ Sanyal Rd, by State Bus Stand, T03512-252388. Reasonable rooms, restaurant, friendly, views over town from public balcony.
E-F Chanakya, NH34, town centre, T03512-266620. Some a/c in the 22 rooms, restaurant, bar, clean, modern.
E-F Tourist Lodge, NH34, T03512-220911, www.westbengaltourism.gov.in. 13 rooms around courtyard, non-a/c Rs 500, (4 a/c), a/c bar, restaurant.
G Railway Retiring Rooms. A/c rooms and dorm, modernized, helpful staff. (South Indian platform snacks recommended.)

Eating

Bishnupur *p633*

Sree Hotel, College Rd, beside Tagore statue, 0930-1500, 1800-2000. Bengali and South Indian food, excellent dosas, great value.

Santiniketan *p634, map p634*

Camelia Resort, Prantik. Should have a good restaurant, check to see if recent renovations are complete.
Chhuti (see Sleeping). Has restaurants but may require advance notice.
Kalor Dokan, an institution since the time of Tagore, open all hours.
Maduram, Santiniketan Rd, Bolpur. Highly recommended sweet shop.
Railway canteen. Cheap and reliable.

Festivals and events

Bishnupur *p633*

Aug Jhapan, in honour of the serpent goddess Manasa, dates from the 17th century. This regional harvest festival is linked with the fertility cult and is unique. Venomous snakes (cobras, pythons, vipers, kraits, flying snakes) are brought in baskets by snake-charmers who display amazing tricks.

Santiniketan *p634, map p634*

End Jan/early Feb Magh Mela, an agricultural and rural crafts fair at Sriniketan, marks the anniversary of the founding of Brahmo Samaj. **Vasanta Utsav** coincides with **Holi**. Programmes of dance, music and singing are held throughout the year, particularly good during festivals.
Late Dec (check with Bengal TIC) **Poush Mela**, an important fair, coinciding with the village's **Foundation Day**. Folk performances include Santals dances and Baul songs. Bauls are Bengal's wandering minstrels, who are worshippers of Vishnu. They travel from village to village singing their songs, accompanied by a single string instrument, *ektara*, and a tiny drum. Tribal silver and Dhokra metal crafts make attractive buys.

Murshidabad *p635*

Late Dec (check with Bengal TIC) **Muharram**, a fair lasting a few days, which culminates in a 6-hr procession through the village.

Shopping

Bishnupur *p633*

Cottage industries flourish in the different *paras* (quarters) each devoted to a specialized craft: pottery in Kamarpara, *sankha* (conch-shell); cutting in Sankharipara; and weaving, particularly Baluchari silk saris, in Tantipara. **Silk Khadi Seva Mandal**, Boltala, and **Terracotta Crafts**, 500 m from the Tourist Lodge, are recommended.

Santiniketan *p634, map p634*

The local embossed leather work is distinctive.
Smaranika Handicraft Centre, opposite Bolpur Station. Interesting embroidery, jewellery and saris at fixed prices.
Subarnarekha, next to railway booking office in Santiniketan. Sells rare books.

Suprabhat Women Handicrafts, Prabhat Sarani, Bhuban Nagar, opposite **Tourist Lodge**, Bolpur, 0930-1300, 1700-1900. Excellent, creative embroidery (including *kantha*), ready made or to order, crafted by local women.

Murshidabad *p635*

Woven and handblock-printed silk saris and bell-metal ware are the main local industries.

Transport

Bishnupur *p633*

Bus/rickshaw Cycle rickshaws are widely available. **WBSTC** buses from Esplanade to **Kolkata**, 5½ hrs on local roads. **STC Super Express** buses to **Durgapur** (1 hr).
Car hire Useful for exploring the surrounding area. Available from **Tourist Lodge**; **Kiron Homeo Hall**, Matukgunge.
Train Trains from Kolkata (**H**) to **Bankura**: *Rupasi Bangla Exp 12883*, 0600, 4 hrs, *Howrah-Purulia Exp 12827*, 1650, 3½ hrs.

Santiniketan *p634, map p634*

Taxi Mainly cycle-rickshaws; taxis available.
Train Trains from **Kolkata** (**H**): *Ganadevata Exp 13017*, 0605, 2¾ hrs; *Shantiniketan Exp 12337*, 1010, 2½ hrs. From **Bolpur**to **Kolkata** (**H**): *Shantiniketan Exp 12338*, 1310, 2½ hrs; *Kanchenjunga Exp 15658* (**S**), 1615, 3¼ hrs, booking recommended (avoid station counter as the better university booking office, 0800-1400, has a daily quota of 50 reserved seats). Also trains to New Jalpaiguri (for Darjeeling) via Malda.

Murshidabad *p635*

Bus/train The train *53181 Lalgola Passenger* from **Kolkata** (**S**) leaves 2305, 5½ hrs, daily; also *53173 Sealdah Lalgola Pass* at 0810. From Murshidabad, the *Bagirathi Mail 13104*, 0620, taking 4 hrs back to **Sealdah** is best. Arriving from northern destinations, trains stop at New Farakka from where it's a 2-bus to **Berhampur**. Buses between Berhampur and Kolkata are painful.
Jeep/rickshaw Jeeps from Berhampur local bus stand to **Lalbagh**, 40 mins, Rs 10; or shared auto-rickshaw, 30 mins, Rs 8. Then cycle-rickshaw to Hazarduari gate, Rs 10.

Malda *p636*

Bus/rickshaw Buses are cheap and rickshaws common. For **Gaur** and **Pandua**, buses, taxis (Rs 600 for half-day tour) and *tongas*. Bus to **Murshidabad**, 3-4 hrs, Rs 60. **Siliguri**, WBSTC Rocket buses 1700-2400, 6½ hrs. Buses to Kolkata not recommended.
Train To **New Jalpaiguri**: *Kanchenjunga Exp 15657*, 1355, 4½ hrs. **Kolkata** (**S**): *Kanchenjunga Exp 15658*, 1235, 7 hrs.

Directory

Bishnupur *p633*

Banks State Bank of India changes foreign cash, ATM next door. **Internet** Several along College Rd. **Hospitals** Sub-Division **Hospital**, near the Court.

Santiniketan *p634, map p634*

Banks State Bank of India, Bolpur and Santiniketan. **Hospitas** Pearson Memorial **Hospital**, Santiniketan.

Murshidabad *p635*

Banks Icici Bank, has ATM. **Internet** **Dolphin Service Centre**, T03482-270190. Only place with broadband, 1 computer, Rs 20 per hr, daily 1000-2330.

West Bengal Hills

The Himalayan foothills of northern West Bengal contain a wealth of trekking opportunities and hill stations in stunning locations including the region's prime tourist destination, Darjeeling. The old colonial summer retreat is surrounded by spectacular views and still draws plenty of visitors to enjoy cooler climes and a good cuppa. The area also holds one of the Indian one-horned rhino's last safe havens in the Jaldapara Wildlife Sanctuary.

In early 2008, tensions flared in the region over renewed demands for a separate Gorkha (ethnic Nepali) state to be carved out of West Bengal. Apparently galvanized by the success of Gorkha policeman Prashant Tamang in the Indian Idol TV talent contest, the protests resulted in strikes and road closures and occasional violence. Check on the situation before travelling. ▸▸ *For listings, see pages 652-663.*

Siliguri, Jaldapara and Gorumara → *For listings, see pages 652-663. Colour map 4, A1/A2.*

Surrounded by tea plantations, **Siliguri** is a largely unattractive transport hub with busy main roads lined with shops, a couple of good markets and one of the largest stupas in India (100 ft) at nearby Salugara Monastery, 5 km away. A narrow-gauge diesel train goes to Darjeeling each morning at 0900 (supposedly taking seven hours but in reality taking much longer) although at the time of writing, the service was suspended due to a landslide. Siliguri is an essential stepping-off point for travel into the hills and to a couple of national parks in the vicinity.

Tourist information Useful tourist information is available from **WBTDC** ⓘ *1st floor, 4 Hill Cart Rd, T0353-251 7561, www.westbengaltourism.gov.in, Mon-Fri 1000-1730, also at NJP Station and airport*, the Forest Development Corporation in the main office books the lodges in Jaldapara Wildlife Sanctuary. On the opposite side of Hill Cart Rd, the **Darjeeling Gorkha Hill Council (DGHC)** ⓘ *T0353-251 1974/9, Mon-Fri 0900-1700, Sat-Sun 0900-1300*, tourism office has little information but take bookings for their lodges in North Bengal.

The River Torsa flows through **Jaldapara Wildlife Sanctuary** ⓘ *Rs 50, still camera Rs 50, video Rs 500, jeeps Rs 200*. It covers an area of 116 sq km (only 30 sq km is open to tourists) and is situated close to Phuntsholing in Bhutan. The riverine forests of sal, khair and sheeshu harbour the one-horned rhino, elephants, leopards, gaur (Indian bison), wild boar, several species of deer, and sloth bears. Ornithologists come to see crested and fishing eagles, and the rare Bengal florican. Trained elephants and vehicle safaris are available to take visitors around, and there is good accommodation in the form of tourist lodges which are bookable in Siliguri (see above). The best time to visit is from November to April, when forest cover is thinner and animals are easier to sight. About a 1000-strong population of the Toto tribe still maintain their traditions and customs in the village of Totopara, 30 km to the north of the sanctuary.

Located in the Dooars (meaning 'door' in Bengali and Assamese) region, 90 km from Siliguri, the **Gorumara National Park** ⓘ *Rs 80/200 (sunset visit more expensive than at other times), still camera free, video Rs 300, car entrance Rs 60, guide Rs 60*, is an interesting diversion little visited by foreign tourists. Covering 85 sq km, the riverine grasslands and forests hide one-horned rhinos, gaur, leopard, elephants, deer and more than 200 species of bird. A few watchtowers give great views and the chance to spot elephants as they come to water. The park is closed from 15 June to 15 September.

Darjeeling → *For listings, see pages 652-663. Colour map 4, A1.*

For tens of thousands of visitors from Kolkata and the steamy plains, Darjeeling (*Dorje Ling* – Place of the Thunderbolt) is a place to escape the summer heat. Built on a crescent-shaped ridge the town is surrounded by hills, which are thickly covered with coniferous forests and terraced tea gardens. The idyllic setting, the exhilarating air outside town, and stunning views of the Kangchenjunga range (when you can see through the clouds) attract plenty of trekkers too. Nevertheless, Darjeeling's modern reality is a crowded, noisy and in places shockingly dirty and polluted town. Between June and September the monsoons bring heavy downpours, sometimes causing landslides, but the air clears after mid-September. Winter evenings are cold enough to demand log fires and lots of warm clothing.

Ins and outs → *Population: 107,500. Altitude: 2160 m at Chowrasta.*

Getting there Bagdogra, near Siliguri, is Darjeeling's nearest airport. Trains connect New Jalpaiguri (NJP) with Kolkata and other major cities. The diesel 'toy train' runs from Siliguri/NJP in season and is picturesque but very slow (the service was suspended at the time of research, due to a landslide). Most people reach Darjeeling by jeep and arrive at the motor stand in the lower town, though some go to Clubside on The Mall, which is more convenient for most accommodation.

Getting around Most of Darjeeling's roads slope quite gently so it is easy to walk around the town. The lower and upper roads are linked by a series of connecting roads and steep steps. For sights away from the centre you need to hire a taxi. Be prepared for seasonal water shortages and frequent power cuts. After dark a torch is essential. ▸▸ *See Transport, page 662.*

Tourist information WBTDC ⓘ *Bellevue Hotel, 1st floor, 1 Nehru Rd, T0354-225 4102, 1000-1700, off-season 1030-1600*, not much information available. DGHC ⓘ *Maple Tourist Lodge, Old Kutchery Rd (below Natural History Museum), T/F0354-225 5351, Mon-Sat 1030-1600 (closed 2nd and 4th Sat in month)*. Recently relocated, since the old office on the Mall was burnt down in Feb 2011. There's also a DGHC kiosk at **Clubside** ⓘ *daily 1000-1600.*

History

Darjeeling means region of the *dorje* (thunderbolt) and its official but rarely used spelling is Darjiling. The surrounding area once belonged to Sikkim, although parts were annexed from time to time by the Bhutanese and Nepalese. The East India Company returned the territory's sovereignty to the Rajas of Sikkim, which led to the British obtaining permission to gain the site of the hill station called Darjeeling in 1835, in return for an annual payment. It was practically uninhabited and thickly forested but soon grew into a popular health resort after a road and several houses were built and tea growing was introduced. The Bengal government escaped from the Kolkata heat to take up its official summer residence here. The upper reaches were originally occupied by the Europeans, who built houses with commanding views. Down the hillside on terraces sprawled the humbler huts and bazars of the Indian town.

Sights

In the pedestrianized centre of town, on the ridge, **Chowrasta** is the natural heart of Darjeeling and particularly atmospheric at dawn and dusk. The **Mahakal Mandir** atop **Observatory Hill**, sacred to Siva, is a pleasant walk though the views of the mountains are obscured by tall trees. Sacred to both Hindus and Buddhists, the temple is active and colourful, with prayer flags tied to every tree and pole in the vicinity. Beware of the monkeys as they bite. Further along Jawahar Road West is **Shrubbery (Nightingale) Park**, a pleasant detour if still too early to visit the zoo. Views to the north are excellent from the renovated park, and evening cultural shows take place here (information from the DGHC tourist office).

Padmaja Naidu Himalayan Zoological Park ⓘ *daily 0830-1630 (summer), 0830-1600 (winter) except Thu, Rs 100*, houses high-altitude wildlife including Himalayan black bears, Siberian tigers, Tibetan wolves and plenty of red pandas, as well as deer, a multitude of birds and the gorgeously marked rare clouded leopard. There are large enclosures over a section of the hillside, though at feeding time and during wet weather they retreat into their small cement enclosures giving the impression that they are restricted to their cells. There is a reasonably successful snow leopard breeding programme, with over 40 births since 1983, and it is the only Asian zoo to have successfully introduced red pandas into the wild. Entrance fees to the zoo also include the **Himalayan Mountaineering Institute** ⓘ *T0354-227 0158, no photography, entrance is through the zoo on Jawahar Rd West*. Previously headed by the late Tenzing Norgay who

Darjeeling

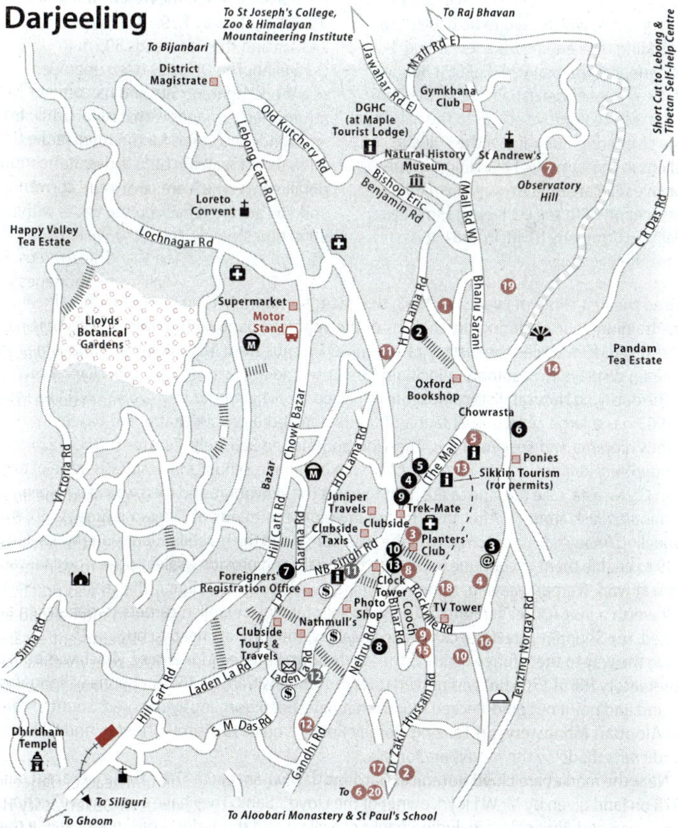

N

800 metres
800 yards

Sleeping
Alice Villa **1**
Aliment **2**
Andy's **4**
Bellvue & Main Old Bellevue **5**
Cedar Inn **6**
Classic **14**
Darjeeling Gymkhana Resort **7**
Dekeling **8**
Elgin **11**
Grace Inn **9**
Long Island **10**
Pagoda **12**
Planters' Club **3**
Shangrila **13**
Tower View **16**
Travellers Inn **15**
Triveni **17**
Valentino **18**
Windamere **19**
Youth Hostel **20**

Eating
Blind Date **1**
Café Coffee Day **6**
Cozy Bhutan **8**
Dekeva's **10**
Glenary's **5**
Hasty Tasty **4**
Hot Pizza Place **2**
Keventer's **9**
Kunga **10**
Lunar **13**
New Dish **7**
Sonam's Kitchen **3**

Bars & clubs
Dafey Mumal **11**
Joey's Pub **12**

Darjeeling Himalayan Railway – a mini miracle

For many people, the somewhat erratic narrow gauge Toy Train between New Jalpaiguri and Darjeeling, with its 0.6 m gauge track, which used to be hauled by sparkling tank engines, is a rewarding experience. The brainchild of East Bengal Railway agent Franklyn Prestage, the train promised to improve access to the hills from the sweltering humidity of the Kolkata plains in the summer. Following the line of an earlier steam tramway, the name was changed to the Darjeeling Himalayan Railway Company (DHR) in 1881. It is a stunning achievement, winding its way up the hillside, often with brilliant views over the plains covering the 82 km with gradients of up to 1:19. At Ghoom it reaches 2438 m and then descends 305 m to Darjeeling. The DHR has been upgraded to a World Heritage Site and has newly refurbished carriages with cushioned seats and window curtains for the tourist trains. It is a must for steam buffs – despite derailments which are "swiftly dealt with and you are lifted back on the tracks within 20 minutes".

shared the first climb of Everest in 1953, the Institute has trained up many a mountaineer and runs training courses during dry months of the year (see page 660). Within the complex, the Everest Museum traces the history of attempted climbs from 1857 and the Mountaineering Museum displays old equipment including that used on the historic Tenzing-Hillary climb.

The decaying **Natural History Museum** ⓘ *Bishop Eric Benjamin Rd, 0900-1630, Rs 10*, was set up in 1903 has a large collection of fauna of the region and a certain charm; the basement has a curious diorama and specimen jars. The **Tibetan Refugee Self-help Centre** ⓘ *T0354-225 5938, thondup@cal.vsnl.net.in, Mon-Sat 0800-1700*, with its temple, school and hospital is north of town. From Chowrasta, take the lane to the right towards the viewpoint, and then walk down for about 30 minutes (ask around). After the Chinese invasion, thousands of Tibetan refugees settled in Darjeeling (many having accompanied the Dalai Lama) and the rehabilitation centre was set up in 1959 to enable them to continue to practise their skills and provide a sales outlet. You can watch them at work (carpet weaving, spinning, dyeing, woodwork, etc) during the season, when it is well worth a visit (closes for lunch). The shop sells fabulous woollen carpets (orders taken and posted, see Shopping), textiles, curios and jewellery, though not cheap to buy.

On the way to the refugee centre is the lovely **Bhutia Bustee Monastery**, which was built on Observatory Hill in 1765 but was moved to its present position in 1861. Someone will show you around and point out gold-flecked murals that have been gorgeously restored. South of town, the **Aloobari Monastery**, on Tenzing Norgay Road, is open to visitors. Tibetan and Sikkimese handicrafts made by the monks are for sale.

Near the market are **Lloyd Botanical Gardens** ⓘ *Mon-Sat 0600-1700*. These were laid out in 1878 on land given by Mr W Lloyd, owner of the Lloyd's Bank. They have a modest collection of Himalayan and Alpine flora including banks of azaleas and rhododendrons, magnolias, a good hothouse (with over 50 species of orchid) and a herbarium. It is a pleasant and quiet spot. **Victoria Falls**, which is only impressive in the monsoons, provides added interest to a three-hour nature trail. There are several tea gardens close to Darjeeling, but not all welcome visitors. One that does is the **Pattabong Estate** on the road towards Sikkim.

Around Darjeeling

ⓘ *Roads can get washed away during the monsoon and may remain in poor condition till Oct.*

At **Ghoom (Ghum)**, altitude 2257 m, is the important Yiga Choeling Gompa, a Yellow-hat Buddhist Monastery. Built in 1875 by a Mongolian monk, it houses famous Buddhist scriptures (beautifully displayed) in an interior the colour of the surrounding forests. The austere monastery is a nice walk, at the end of Ghoom's main market street. Also worth visiting is the Sakyaguru

Darjeeling tea gardens

An ancient Chinese legend suggests that 'tay', or tea, originated in India, although tea was known to have been grown in China around 2700 BC. It is a species of Camellia, Camellia thea. After 1833, when its monopoly on importing tea from China was abolished, the East India Company made attempts to grow tea in Assam using wild chai plants found growing there and later introduced it in Darjeeling and in the Nilgiri hills in the South. Today India is the largest producer of tea in the world. Assam grows over half and Darjeeling about a quarter of the nation's output. Once drunk only by the tribal people, it has now become India's national drink.

The orthodox method of tea processing produces the aromatic lighter coloured liquor of the Golden Flowery Orange Pekoe in its most superior grade. The fresh leaves are dried by fans on withering troughs to reduce the moisture content and then rolled and pressed to express the juices which coat the leaves. These are left to ferment in a controlled environment to produce the desired aroma. Finally the leaves are dried by passing them through a heated drying chamber and then graded – the unbroken being the best quality, down to the fannings and dust. The more common crushing, tearing, curling (CTC) method produces tea which gives a much darker liquor.

Most of Darjeeling's tea is sold through auction houses, the largest centre being in Kolkata. Tea tasting and blending are skills which have developed over a long period of time and are highly prized. The industry provides vital employment in the hill areas and is an assured foreign exchange earner.

Monastery, closer to the Darjeeling road, which has 95 monks. It is well recommended to make the 11-km (45-minute) journey to Ghoom from Darjeeling by **steam train**, ending up at the highest railway station in India. The little **Railway Museum** ⓘ *Rs 20, daily 1000-1300 and 1400-1600, ticket from station and staff will unlock the gate*, outlines the history of the Darjeeling Himalayan Railway and has some interesting old photos. A few spruced up carriages offer a tourist-only ride in summer with a photo stop at Batasia (departing 1040, returning 1200, and again at 1320, returning 1440; but check times at the station or www.dhr.in, Rs 240); bookings must be made 90-days in advance, although it is possible to buy spare seats on the day from agents who have private counters set up at Darjeeling station. Alternatively, take the passenger steam train at 1015 (first class Rs 144; second class Rs 5), which goes to Kurseong via Ghoom, or the diesel train at 0915 (first class Rs 144; second class Rs 27), and return on foot or by jeep. (See also the *Toy Train*, page 661.) All pass through **Batasia Loop**, 5 km from Darjeeling on the way to Ghoom, which allows the narrow gauge rail to do a figure-of-eight loop. There's a war memorial here in a pleasant park with good mountain views.

The disused **Lebong Race Course**, 8 km from Darjeeling, was once the smallest and highest in the world and makes a pleasant walk, heading down from Chowrasta. It was started as a parade ground in 1885, and there is now talk of it becoming a race course once more.

If the weather is clear, it is worth rising at 0400 to make the hour's journey for a breathtaking view of the sunrise on Kangchenjunga at **Tiger Hill** ⓘ *shared jeep from Darjeeling Rs 80-100 return, just go to Clubside motor stand for 0430 to pick one up*. Mount Everest (8846 m), 225 km away, is visible on a good day. The mass of jeeps and the crowds at sunrise disappear by mid-morning; it's a nice walk back from Tiger Hill (about two hours, 11 km) via Ghoom and the Japanese Peace Pagoda, where drumming between 1630-1900 is worth seeing.

The trekking routes around Darjeeling are well established, having been popular for over 100 years. Walks lead in stages along safe tracks and through wooded hills up to altitudes of 3660 m. Trails pass through untouched nature filled with rhododendrons, magnolias, orchids and wild flowers, together with forests, meadows and small villages. All this to a backdrop of mountains stretching from Mount Everest to the Bhutan hills, including the third highest mountain in the world, **Kanchenjunga**. The best trekking seasons are April to May, when the magnolias and rhododendrons are in full bloom, and October to November when air clarity is best. In spring there may be the occasional shower. In autumn the air is dry and the visibility excellent. In winter the lower altitude trails that link Rimbick with Jhepi (18 km) can be very attractive for birdwatchers. There is an extensive network of varied trails that link the hillside towns and villages. Agents in Darjeeling can organize four- to seven-day treks, providing guide, equipment and accommodation (see page 660), though it is perfectly possible to go it alone.

In a bid to provide employment for local youth, the **West Bengal Forest and Wildlife Department** are strongly encouraging visitors to take a guide/porter when entering the Singalila National Park. If you haven't arranged a trek through an agent in Darjeeling, local guides can be hired in Manebhanjang for between Rs 300-500 per day (although paying more secures someone who speaks good English and has a better knowledge of local flora and fauna); porters are Rs 200-250. Entry fees for the park are also paid at the checkpoint in Manebhanjang (foreigners Rs 200, still camera Rs 50, video camera Rs 100). If you prefer to go alone, it is still possible (although some lodges may query as to where your guide is).

Darjeeling treks

Singalila trek

The 160-km Singalila trek starts from the small border town of **Manebhanjang**, 26 km from Darjeeling. The journey to and from Darjeeling can be done by shared or private jeep in one hour. Walking north to Sandakphu (rather than starting in Sandakphu and heading south) means you are always walking towards the most stunning views. Other possible starting points are **Dhotrey** (a further hour by jeep, north of Manebhanjang) which cuts out a large chunk of the steep ascent to Tonglu; or start at Rimbick, going via Gurdum, to Sandakphu. If you have not arranged for transport to meet you at a particular point then it is entirely possible to travel back to Darjeeling from any roadhead by jeep, with services at least once daily, often three to four times daily.

Note Singalila is not an easy trek, several parts are very steep and tough. Even up to May, temperatures at night are freezing and it is essential to take plenty of warm clothes.

There are plenty of government Trekkers' Huts and private lodges of varying standards and prices (on an organized trek these will have been booked for you) at Tonglu, Sandakphu, Phalut, Gorkhey, Molley, Rammam, Rimbick, Siri Khola and other villages. Although room is usually available, it's wise to book in advance during May/June and October when trails can be very busy. Any trekking agent in Darjeeling can arrange bookings for a small fee. Private lodges, such as **Sherpa Lodge** in Rimbick and Rammam, and other trailside lodges in Meghma, Jaubari and Kalpokhri, are generally friendly, flexible and provide reasonable basic accommodation. Some places can prepare yak curry on request, and be sure to sample hot *chhang*, the local millet brew, served in a wooden keg and sipped through a bamboo straw.

The entire area is a birdwatcher's paradise with over 600 species including orioles, minivets, flycatchers, finches, sunbirds, thrushes, piculets, falconets and Hoodson's Imperial pigeons. The mixed rhododendron, oak and conifer forests are particularly well preserved.

Day 1 To Tonglu (or Tumling) 1 km beyond Manebhanjang town you reach a rough stone paved track leading sharply up to the left. Tonglu (3030 m) is 11 km from this point if you follow the jeep track, slightly less if you take the frequent but very steep short cuts. Alternatively, head for Tumling, just the other side of the peak of the hill from Tonglu (you take the alternative road from Meghma and rejoin the main route 1 km after Tumling). There is a Trekkers' Hut at **Tonglu** with 24 beds and a fine view of the Kanchenjunga range. From here you can also see the plains of North Bengal and some valleys of Nepal in the distance. Closer to hand are the snow fed rivers, the Teesta in the east and Koshi in the west. You can also sleep in **Tumling** where **Shikhar Lodge** has simple basic and clean rooms, run by a local teacher's friendly family, "fabulous supper and breakfast" plus a lovely garden. There are tea shops at **Chitre** and at **Meghma**, which has an interesting monastery noted for its large collection of Buddhist statues; 108, according to locals. Ask at the tea house opposite to get in.

Day 2 To Jaubari and Gairibans A level walk along the ridge takes you past the long 'mani' wall to the Nepalese village of Jaubari; no visa is needed and good accommodation is available should you wish to spend a night in Nepal. After Jaubari the trail turns sharply to the right back into Indian territory and down through bamboo and rhododendron forests to the village of Gairibans in a forest clearing. You could carry on all the way to Sandakphu, a long day's hiking.

Day 3 To Sandakphu It is 14 km uphill to Sandakphu, with a lunch break in Kalpokhri with its attractive attractive 'black' lake surrounded by fir trees, about midway. Even in winter the lake never freezes. The last 3 km from Bhikebhanjang (tea shop) to Sandakphu are particularly steep; this section takes more than an hour but the views from the Singalila Ridge make it all worthwhile. **Sandakphu**, a small collection of lodges and government buildings located at 3636 m, is the highest point in West Bengal and the finest viewpoint on the trek (the prime destination for most visitors). Located 57 km from Darjeeling, it is accessible by jeep (the same narrow bumpy track used by trekkers), which is how many Indian tourists make the journey during the season. Sandakphu offers fantastic views, including the eastern face of Everest (8846 m, 140 km away as the crow flies), Kanchenjunga (8586 m), Chomolhari (the highest peak in Bhutan), Lluhe and Makchu (the fourth and fifth highest peaks in the world, respectively) and numerous peaks such as Pandim that lie in Sikkim. A five-minute walk past the towering Sherpa lodge brings you to three hillocks on the left side of the path; the middle one of these is the very highest point at 3636 m.

There is a Trekkers' Hut and several lodges, each with a dining area, toilets and cookhouse. These vary widely in standards and price, some costing up to Rs 500 per person with attached bathroom; it's worth seeing a few. The drive back to Manebhanjang by pre-arranged 4WD can take four hours along the very rough track, if you finish the trek here.

Day 4 **Sandakphu to Phalut** Phalut, 22 km from Sandakphu along an undulating jeepable track, is at the junction of Nepal, Sikkim and West Bengal. It offers even closer views of Kanchenjunga. It is best to avoid trekking here in May and June and mid-September to 25 October when large numbers of college trekking teams from West Bengal descend on the area. From Phalut it's possible to get a jeep back the way you came, via Sandakphu. Alternatively you can walk south for 4 km back towards **Bhikebhanjang** and then take a 16-km-long trail through fine forests of the Singalila National Park down to **Rimbick**.

Day 5 **Phalut to Rimbick** From Phalut, there is **Gorkhey**, with accommodation, and it's a further 3 km to the village of **Samanden**, hidden in a hanging valley. From Samanden, it is a 6-km walk to **Rammam** where there is a clean, comfortable **Sherpa Lodge** in a tiny garden, recommended for friendly service and good food. Alternatively, the **Trekkers' Hut** is 100 m climb (in the direction of Molley) before Rammam village. From Rammam it is a 1½-hour walk down to a couple of private lodges and a Trekkers Hut at **Siri Khola** and a further 1½ hours to Rimbick. Again, this area has a wealth of birdlife. From Rimbick there are around three jeeps a day to take you back to Darjeeling (Rs 100, four hours).

Although Gorkhey, Phalut, Rammam and Rimbick lie just south of the border with Sikkim, entering Sikkim is not permitted on this route, though agents say this may change in future; ask in Darjeeling about the current situation.

Sabarkum via Ramman to Molley or Bijanbari

An alternative quieter trail links Sabarkum (7 km before Phalut on the main Sandakphu– Phalut trail) with Rammam, with a possible overnight halting stay at the **Trekkers' Hut** in **Molley**. (Note: the manager of Molley Trekkers' Hut is often to be found at the Forest Office in Sabarkum; look for him on the way through in order to secure a room). Those with five days to spare can return by the **Rammam–Rimbick– Jhepi–Bijanbari** route (153 km). From Rammam you can cross by a suspension bridge over the Siri Khola River and follow the path up the valley, which leads to Dentam in Sikkim. This less well-trodden valley has rich birdlife (particularly kingfishers), and excellent views of undisturbed forest. From **Bijanbari** (762 m) it is possible to return to Darjeeling, 36 km away by jeep, or climb a further 2 km to Pulbazar and then return to Darjeeling, 16 km away. Those wishing only to go to Rimbick can get a jeep from there, or may return to Manebhanjang via Palmajua and Batasi (80 km).

Mirik → *For listings, see pages 652-663.*

The small low-key hill station of **Mirik**, at an altitude of 1600 m, has forests of japonica, orange orchards and tea gardens all within easy walking distance. Its restful ambience, dramatic views and homely accommodation make it an appealing stop for a couple of days relaxation or for good day-trekking. The focal point is **Sumendu Lake** encircled by a 3.5-km cobbled promenade that makes a pleasant stroll, and which offers boating and pony rides.

Krishannagar, south of the lake, is the main tourist centre while older **Mirik Bazar**, north of the lake, has a more local vibe. To orientate yourself and plan treks, pick up an excellent map from the Ratnagiri Hotel in Krishnanagar.

Towering **Bokar Gompa**, a 15-minute uphill walk from the main road in Krishnanagar, is definitely worth visiting (daily chanting at 0530 and 1500). If you continue walking from the monastery, past old Mirik Church and pretty houses, you reach **Rametay Dara** (Mirik's highest point at 1695 m) with a series of viewpoints across the hills to the plains. Equally impressive are the views to Nepal from the look-out tower at **Kawlay Dara** (east of Mirik), considered best at sunrise but worthwhile at any time. Near here, the tea gardens of the **Thurbo Tea Estate** roll over perfect hillocks and encompass the little Mahadev Tar temple where the mark of Siva's footprint and trident imprint the rocks. Visits to the Thurbo factory can be arranged, ask your hotel for help. Another excellent walk (four to five hours) goes from the Don Bosco church (open 0900-100, 1400-1600) down a new road and stone paths to the *bustee* (village) and tea gardens of Marma Tea Estate. From here forest trails and tracks can be followed up-and-down past orange orchards, squash canes and colourful houses to Mirik Bustee and on to Mirik Bazar. Jeeps ply this route should you become weary, from Marma to Mirik Bazar costs Rs 25. You can even trek to **Kurseong** (five to six hours) starting from Marma, going down to the Balasan River to cross a large bridge, and up the winding road on the other side. Or, less ambitiously, take a jeep 6 km up the Darjeeling road and walk back past the rolling Thurbo tea estates and little villages of flower-laden cottages.

Kurseong

Kurseong (1450 m) or 'Place of the White Orchid' east of Mirik, is a small town worthy of a couple of nights' pause on the way to/from Darjeeling. Surrounded by tea gardens and orange orchards (through which there is pleasant walking to be done), locals will sincerely tell you that they call Kurseong 'paradise'.

There are no grand sights in the town, but it is an interesting hike up to the ridge, via St Mary's hamlet (north of the market along Hill Cart Road). Shortcuts past quaint houses and the eerie Forestry College lead up to **St Mary's Well and Grotto**, which has fine views and a shrine with candles. Tracks through a young forest reach imposing Dow Hill School, established 1904, and either continue up and over the ridge to tiny Chetri Bustee, or bear right to the little **Forest Museum** at Dow Hill. Head back down via scenically located **Ani Gompa**, housing a small community of nuns belonging to the Red Hat sect, and past pretty cottages using footpaths. It's around a five-hour walk with stops; ask locals for directions, but double any time frame they give to destinations. Useful sketch maps can be provided by **Cochrane Place** (see listings, page 655), where it is also possible to arrange guided hikes tailored to match walkers' interests and stamina. In the town itself there's the narrow and crowded *chowk* market to explore, while a half-hour walk from the railway station brings you to **Eagle's Crag** (shadowed by the TV tower), an awesome vantage point in clear weather.

The **Makaibari Tea Estate**, 4 km from town, makes an interesting excursion. Dating from 1859 it is India's oldest tea garden, responsibly managed by charismatic Rajah Banerjee who has done much to support the community and initiate environmental and organic development on the estate. The highest price ever fetched at a tea auction was for Makaibari leaves when Rs 18,000 was paid for a kilogram in 2003. Nearby **Ambootia Tea Estate** also conduct factory visits, and from here there's a walk to an ancient Siva temple amid massive Rudraksh and Banyan trees. Kurseong is famed for its plethora of boarding schools. At **Tung** nearby, the St Alphonsus Social and Agricultural Centre, run by a Canadian Jesuit, is working with the local community through education, housing, agricultural, forestry and marketing projects. They welcome volunteers; contact ⓘ *SASAC, Tung, Darjeeling, West Bengal, T0354-234 2059, sasac@satyam.net.in*. The steam train to Darjeeling leaves every afternoon, supposedly at 1500.

Kalimpong → *For listings, see pages 652-663. Colour map 4, A2.*

Set in beautiful wooded mountain scenery with an unhurried air about it, Kalimpong was a meeting point of the once 'Three Closed Lands' on the trade route to Tibet, Bhutan and Nepal. Away from the crowded and scruffy centre near the motor stand, the town becomes more spaced out as mountain roads wind up the hillsides leading to monasteries, mission schools and orchid nurseries. Some say that the name is derived from *pong* (stronghold) of *kalon* (king's minister), or from *kalibong*, a plant fibre.

From Darjeeling, the 51-km journey (2½ hours) is through beautiful scenery. The road winds down through tea estates and then descends to 250 m at Tista where it crosses the river on a 'new' concrete bridge. 'Lovers' Meet' and 'View Point' give superb views of the Rangit and Tista rivers.

Kalimpong

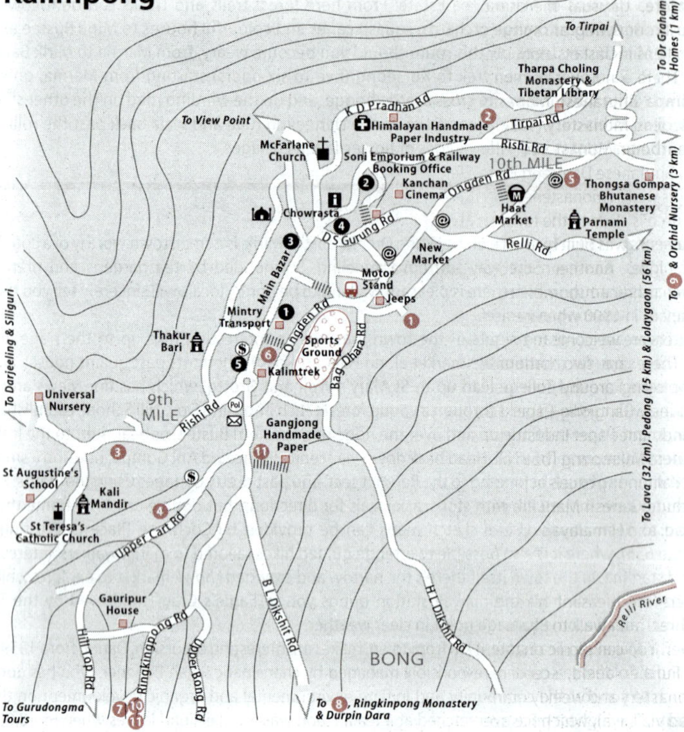

Sleeping
Cloud 9 **10**
Crown Lodge **1**
Deki Lodge **2**
Himalayan **4**
Holumba Haven **3**
JP Lodge **5**
Kalash & Vegetarian Snacketeria **6**
Kalimpong Park **7**
Morgan House **8**
Orchid Retreat **9**
Silver Oaks **11**

Eating
3 C's **1**
Balaji **4**
Cakes R Us/Shikhar & Lark's Provisions **2**
Gompus **3**
King Thai **5**

Ins and outs → *Population: 70,000. Altitude: 1250-1600 m.*

Getting there Bagdogra is the nearest airport and New Jalpaiguri the nearest railhead. Buses and shared jeeps arrive from there at the Bazar Motor Stand in about 2½ hours.

Getting around The centre is compact enough to be seen comfortably on foot. The surroundings are ideal for walking, though some may prefer transport to visit nearby sights. ▸▸ *See Transport, page 662.*

Tourist information DGHC ⓘ *DB Giri Rd, Mon-Sat 0930-1700, Sun-1230*, tourist office can advise on walking routes and rafting. Also see www.kalimpong.org.

Sights

The traditional **market** at 10th Mile has a great atmosphere. The *haat* here every Wednesday and Saturday draws villagers who come to sell fruit, unfamiliar vegetables, traditional medicines, woollen cloth, yarn and much more. It is remarkably clean and laid back, a delight to explore. Unusual merchandise includes: curly young fern tops, bamboo shoots, dried mushrooms, fragrant spices, musk, *chaang* paraphernalia, large chunks of brown soap, and tiny chickens in baskets alongside gaudy posters.

There a number of monasteries in and around Kalimpong; the oldest of which, **Thongsa Gompa Bhutanese Monastery** (1692), 10th Mile, has been renovated. The colourful **Tharpa Cheoling Monastery** (1922) has a library of Tibetan manuscripts and *thangkas*. Further north, is the **Tibetan Monastery** (Yellow Hat) at Tirpai. The **Pedong Bhutanese Monastery** (1837) near the old Bhutanese Damsang Fort at Algara (15 km away) holds ceremonial dances every February.

As well as monasteries, there are a couple of old churches worth popping into. The **Macfarlane Church** is close to the town centre, visible from the main street, and built in the Scottish style. **St Theresa's** was built by the Jesuits and resembles a Buddhist *gompa*, it is 2.5 km from the centre in 9th Mile. Another Scottish church is found at **Dr Graham's Home** on Deolo Hill, www.drgrahamshomes.org. The school was started by the missionary Doctor John Anderson Graham in 1900 when he admitted six Anglo-Indian children. Now there are about 1000 pupils; visitors are welcome to the school as well as the dairy, poultry and bakery projects.

There are two handmade paper factories in town, both are small-scale enterprises employing around four people. You can buy their products and watch the paper-making process. Gangjong Paper Factory is a short walk from the centre of town, while Himalayan Handmade Paper Industry is a good place to stop off if walking from Tharpa Chelong Monastery back to Kalimpong (both open Monday-Saturday 1000-1600).

Kalimpong excels in producing orchids, amaryllis, roses, cacti, dahlias and gladioli. **Nurseries** include **Ganesh Mani Pradhan** on 12th Mile; **Universal** on 8th Mile; **Shanti Kunj** on BL Dikshit Road; and **Himalayan** on East Main Road.

Walks

There are pleasant hikes along the Tista Road through rice fields to **Chitray Falls**, 9 km, a three-hour walk to **Bhalu Khop** and a 1½-hour downhill walk from the motor stand to the Relli River. You can picnic on the river beaches at Tista Bazar and Kalijhora.

Further afield, scenic two- to three-hour treks are possible from **Lava** (32 km east, monastery and weekly market on Tuesday), and **Kaffer (aka Lolaygaon)** (southeast, 56 km by road via Lava), which has spectacular views of Kangchendzonga. Lava especially is a popular destination for Bengali tourists in the school holidays. Rhododendrons flower in April around this region. Both villages are accessible by public jeep/bus from Kalimpong and have reasonably priced private and government accommodation (bookable at the Forest Dept at WBTDC office in Siliguri, see www.wbfdc.com); walking between the two is a lovely trek of about 10 km. There are other pleasant trails in the vicinity, and generally the walking is fairly level without too many ups-and-downs.

West Bengal Hills listings

For Sleeping and Eating price codes and other relevant information, see Essentials pages 38-42.

Sleeping

Siliguri *p641*

Hill Cart Rd is officially Tenzing Norgay Rd.

AL Cindrella, Sevoke Rd, '3rd mile' (out of town), T0353-254 7136, www.cindrellahotels.com. Comfortable a/c rooms, decent pool, competent vegetarian restaurant, internet, car hire, pick-up from airport, breakfast included. Drinks in the bar or on the roof terrace.

A Sinclairs, Pradhan Nagar, T0353-251 2440, www.sinclairshotels.com. Architecturally curious from the outside, a/c rooms are comfortable with flat-screen TVs although getting a bit worn. The restaurant and **O2** bar are stylish with good food, small pool is disappointing, attentive and warm service. Some **AL** suites. Breakfast included.

C-E Conclave, Hill Cart Rd (opposite SNT bus stand), T0353-251 6144, www.hotelconclave.com. A newish hotel with good-quality rooms starting at Rs 900 per double, a/c, satellite TV, licensed bar, eminent restaurant serving quality Indian/European food, intermittent internet, parking.

C-E Yatri Hotel, Hill Cart Rd (opposite main bus stand), T0353-251 4707, yatrihotel98@yahoo.com. Basic but clean rooms with bath (from Rs 600 per double), some a/c (Rs 1500), restaurant serves good food. The dim and cosy bar next door is a friendly place to have an icy beer (Rs 90-120) or watch some sport.

C-F Vinayak, Hill Cart Rd, T0353-243 1130. Clean rooms with bath, some a/c, good restaurant, look at a few rooms as some of the budget options are excellent value.

D-E Mainak Tourist Lodge (WBTDC), Hill Cart Rd (opposite main bus stand), T0353-251 2859, www.west bengaltourism.gov.in. Large and open 1970s-style hotel, 38 comfortable rooms (check a few, they vary), 14 a/c, and some **C** suites. Set back from the road in dusty gardens, with restaurant and bar, helpful staff. Be sure not to overlap with a wedding party; call ahead.

D-E The Tiara, Sevoke Rd (opposite the Gurudwara), T0353-243 6024, thetiarahotel@hotmail.com. A 'boutique' hotel where ethnic mixes with kitsch (particularly in the lobby which has a plastic grotto, trees and fish pond). Top-floor rooms each styled with traditional designs and decor of NE Indian States (Sikkim, Orissa, Bihar, etc). Public areas are clean and shiny, and the non-a/c rooms great value for a decent standard (doubles Rs 590). Good restaurant, see Eating, page 657.

E-F Anjali Lodge, Nabin Sen Rd (next to the Gurudwara), off Sevoke Rd, T0353-252 2964. Institutional building, bright white paint throughout, large rooms with concrete floors have clean sheets, towels, soap, TV, cheaper without a/c (doubles Rs 800/500), some have balcony or there is spacious public balcony. Suspicious staff soon warm up. A good choice.

F Hill View Hotel, Hill Cart Rd (opposite SNT bus stand), T0353-251 9951. Shabby old place, but about the only hotel in town with any character. Sadly, the wooden balcony only has views of the traffic on Hill Cart Rd. Manager is helpful and clean sheets are provided. Single rooms (Rs 170) share a common bath, doubles have private, little restaurant at rear.

F Siliguri Lodge, Hill Cart Rd (near SNT bus stand), T0353-251 5290. Grotty exterior but clean sheets and relatively quiet, being set back from the road. Kind staff.

G Railway Retiring Rooms, Siliguri Junction and New Jalpaiguri. 4 rooms and 6 dorm beds in each, good vegetarian snacks.

Jaldapara and Gorumara *p641*

AL Riverwood Forest Retreat, Gorumara, Dakshin Dhupjhora, www.riverwood retreat.com. This eco-friendly resort has lush surrounds, and some balconies have views of mountain peaks. Comfortable well-appointed rooms, attentive staff, no TVs or internet. Guided excursions into Gorumara, plus day treks, village visits and tea tourism (reasonably priced) can also be arranged.

B-F Madarihat Tourist Lodge, Madarihat. Outside the park boundaries, non-a/c double rooms are Rs 1600, a/c Rs 2200 or there's a dorm for Rs 400.

C Hollong Forest Tourist Lodge, Hollong, 6 km from Madarihat, T03563-262228, book well in advance (3 months) either directly, or via the Tourist Bureau, Siliguri, T0353-251 1974. Built of timber on stilts deep inside the park. 6 rooms (all meals), the lodge is very popular and is en route to Phuntsholing in Bhutan. The only place where you can organize elephants rides (Rs 200).

F Nilpara Forest Bungalow, Hasimara. 2 basic rooms, caretaker will prepare a simple meal if requested but take all provisions.

F Youth Hostel and Lodge, 4 km from Hasimara railway station, 18 km from Madarihat, at Baradabri. 3 rooms, 14 beds in 4 dorms, poor catering, reserve through DFO, Tourism Centre, Jalpaiguri, T03563-262239 or Kolkata, T033-2248 8271.

Darjeeling *p641, map p643*

Most hotels are within 2 km of the station and motor stand, a stiff walk uphill. Some top-end hotels include all meals and most offer discounts off season (Jul-Sep, Dec-Feb). Some charge extra for Christmas and New Year. Prices listed are for high season. There is a chronic water shortage, and you may find budget hotels ration their water supply.

LL Windamere, Observatory Hill, T0354-225 4041/2, www.windamerehotel.com. Enviable location, good views when clear, a true relic of the Raj. Spacious rooms and cottages (no phone or TV in some), beware those with dated bathrooms (limited hot water), terraces, chintzy and cluttered with memorabilia, coal fires (can be smoky), hotties in bed, pre-war piano favourites accompany tea. Lounge/bar is a characterful place for a drink, outside guests welcome for high tea (Rs 465) or beer (Rs 150). Full-board only.

LL-AL Cedar Inn, Dr Zakir Hussain Rd, T0354-225 4446, www.cedarinndarjeeling.com. Slightly out of town, but with great views and free shuttle service to town throughout the day. Family friendly, health club, sauna, lovely garden with wrought iron furniture. Wood panelled rooms are stylish and thoughtfully laid out (bathrooms a bit 1980s), fireplaces in some, public areas filled with enormous plants, bar and restaurant are welcoming and informal. Extension in same style as the original building, essential to book in advance.

L The Elgin, HD Lama Rd, T0354-225 7226, www.elginhotels.com. Beautifully renovated 120-year-old colonial hotel, rooms are full of atmosphere with polished floors, fireplaces, nooks and crannies while being plush and well-appointed, marble bathrooms. Photos, brass fittings and carpets give warmth to public spaces, lounge and bar area pleasantly like a country sitting room, tiered garden is small and flower-filled but looks onto a high fence. Annoyingly, there is no option but to take a package including all meals, and high tea is grossly overpriced for outside guests.

A-B Darjeeling Gymkhana Resort, next to Gymkhana Club, T0354-225 4391, www.sunflower-hotels.com. Wood panelled rooms (all with fireplaces) are large and modern yet warm and welcoming. Nice location on Observatory Hill, club on doorstep for sports/activities, location. Particularly suited to families (4-bed rooms Rs 3500). Indian restaurant good, but its position in the central foyer means staff chatter can be irritating when you're in your room.

B Shangrila, 5 Nehru Rd, T0354-225 4149. A small and characterful hotel in a good spot near Chowrasta. Large rooms have been tastefully renovated in 2009, subtly lit, flatscreen TVs, some with good views from the window seating. Swish new bathrooms, all double beds (no twins, 20% discount for single), 3 rooms have Victorian fireplaces. Excellent restaurant (see page 657).

B-C Planters' Club, The Mall, T0354-225 4348. Aka the 'Darjeeling Club', this wooden building dates from1868 and oozes history from the curved veranda and creaking balconies. New decor in VIP rooms is actually unattractive, a better choice are the 'super' doubles which are dated but have the Raj aura; huge fireplaces, white-painted furniture, bathrooms feel Victorian. Nice staff and a good place for an evening tipple (residents only).

B-D Main Olde Bellevue Hotel, Chowrasta, T0354-225 4178, www.darjeelinghotel.co.uk. Rooms with character in the Heritage bungalow on the hill are atmospheric although not high-spec, clear aspect from the picnic tables in the charming garden. Doubles in a newer front building are over-priced for shabby carpets and unrenovated bathrooms.

C Classic Guesthouse, CR Das Rd (below Chowrasta), T0354-225 7025, www.explore darjeeling.com. A small and quiet guesthouse with a cute lawn, stunning views from the private balcony of each of the 4 large rooms.

Plenty of furniture, heaters in winter, carpets, TV, decent big bathrooms. Rooms aren't stylish but they're very comfortable and the manager is nice.

C Travellers Inn, Dr Zakir Hussein Rd, T0354-225 8497. Very respectable rooms in a modern hotel, hot water, good views from the restaurant with booths, and a sweet indoor 'garden room' that catches any rays of sun.

C-E Bellevue, Chowrasta, T0354-225 4075, www.bellevuehotel-darjeeling.com. Wide range of rooms (Rs 800-2000) with bath and geysers, some large, bright and airy (eg rooms 35, 49), some with fireplaces or stoves, all have loads of character with old wooden fittings. Genuinely friendly management. Very centrally located, and the small rooftop has unparalleled K'junga view.

C-E Dekeling Resort, 51 Gandhi Rd (the Mall), T0354-225 4159, www.dekeling.com. Homely rooms are noticeably warm, most have private bath (24-hr hot water), delightful lounge areas with stoves. Range of room tariffs (average Rs 1200), some attic front rooms with views, 2 doubles with shared bath are a bargain (No 11 is best). Good restaurant, brilliant hosts, reserve ahead (1 month in advance in high season). Noisy when jeeps depart at 0400 for Tiger Hill with lots of hooting.

D Valentino, 6 Rockville Rd, T0354-225 2228, tashiphuntsok30@yahoo.com. Clean rooms with a green theme with good mountain views (especially from upper storeys), central heating and 24-hr hot water, good Chinese restaurant, bar, excellent sundeck.

D-E Alice Villa, 41 HD Lama Rd, below DGHC Tourist Office, Chowrasta, T0354-225 4181, hotelalicevilla@yahoo.com. Large clean rooms (fireplace in some, bucket of coal cost extra) in an old bungalow are simple, with colonial charm, and fairly priced at Rs 825 (high season). Bathrooms newly tiled in pastel shades and soft furnishings in the covered terrace are bad taste. The modern wing at the rear is not so appealing. Checkout 1200.

D-E Grace Inn, 8/B Cooch Bihar Rd, Nr TV Tower,T0354-225 8106, T(0)98326-15082, thegraceinn@sify.com. Some large, well-furnished rooms with hot water, much of the best at the back (with views), subtly lit restaurant with ambitious menu, cheerful staff. Worth stopping by on the way to backpacker places, as massive discounts are sometimes available.

E-F Aliment, 40 Zakir Hussain Rd, T0354-225 5068, alimentweb@sify.com. Clean rooms vary in size and cheerfulness, pay more for TV and 24-hr hot shower (otherwise hot water for 2 hrs each evening), cheap singles and triples (hot buckets Rs 10) average food in social restaurant (cheap beer Rs 90), internet (Rs 30 per hr), packed with travellers, good atmosphere, excellent library.

E-F Andy's, 102 Zakir Hussain Rd, T0354-225 3125, T(0)94341-66968, www.andysguesthouse.biz. Airy twin-bed rooms are notable for their cleanliness, some have hot shower (hot water on the night of arrival, and in the mornings) or hot buckets provided. Storage for trekkers, friendly and very honest atmosphere if slightly institutional. Rs 100 discount for single travellers. Often full, ring ahead. No food.

E-G Long Island, Rockville Dham, Dr Zakir Hussein Rd, near TV tower, T0354-225 2043, pritaya19@yahoo.com. Attractive exterior, clean basic rooms, some with private shower (hot water 0800-2000) or share communal bathroom. Appealingly quaint restaurant, quiet location, internet, great views from rooftop and upper rooms. Run by friendly Nepali family. Recommended, single room rates, try to book ahead.

F Tower View, Rockville Dham, down the back of TV Tower, T0354-225 4452. Pleasant, clean rooms, some with toilet but sharing bathrooms with hot bucket, more expensive with 24-hr hot water, wood stove and dusty book collection in the homely restaurant (which is a very popular place to eat, with a nice back terrace if the weather permits). Also a yoga-meditation retreat at Nagri Farm Tea Estate, 1 hr south from Darjeeling (www.artofliving.org).

G Pagoda, 1 Upper Beechwood Rd, T0354-225 3498. Clean but basic rooms with period furniture in a characterful building, some with bath (limited free bucket hot water), peaceful, good value. Rooms at front better, though not much view from shared balcony. Away from the main backpacker scene and an easier walk from transport links. Very friendly, small library.

G Triveni, 85 Dr Zakir Hussain Rd, T(0)9932-673511, T(0)9932-345607. Well-kept basic box rooms with bath and hot bucket (Rs 10).

Pleasant and low-key management, Triveni collects the overspill from the Aliment across the road. Good for solo travellers (Rs 150/120, with/without bath), 3-bed dorm (Rs 90), doubles Rs 260.

G Youth Hostel, Dr Zakir Hussain Rd, T0354-225 2290. Mainly cheap dorm beds, superb position on top of the ridge, no restaurant, trekking information available.

Trekking around Darjeeling *p646*

C Karmi Farm, Bijanbari, contact **Samsara Travel** in Darjeeling, T0354-225 6370, samsara@dte.vsnl.net.in. A haven of rural peace at Kolbong, which you may choose to use as a base, north of Bijanbari (access via Kaijali, 4WDs stop 20 mins' walk away, or it's 2-3 hrs by pony from Pulbazar). 7 doubles with bath, simple but spotless, superb food, US$20 includes food/porters.

F Teacher's Lodge, Jaubari. Excellent value. There is a large **Trekkers' Hut** at Gairibans with about 20 beds.

Mirik *p648*

The vast majority of accommodation is found in Krishnanagar on the south side of the lake, although there are also three hotels in Mirik Bazar on the north side.

B-D Jagjeet, Krishnanagar, T0354-224 3231, www.jagjeethotel.com. The cheapest rooms are comfortable but smell musty. Recommended to pay the extra for super deluxe (larger, wood-panelled, much more tasteful). Luxury rooms have contemporary fittings and decor. Very good restaurant and bar.

C-E Ratnagiri, Krishnanagar, T0354-224 3243, T(0)9641-041965. A range of bright spotless rooms, some with great views, and a cute garden for breakfast. Decent discounts negotiable for single travellers. The 2 split-level wooden cabins with working fireplaces are lovely (Rs 1500). Excellent choice.

E Tourist Lodge, 5 mins uphill from the lake, T0354-224 3371, (0)9775-900101. Huge wood-panelled rooms, slightly more expensive for suites with balconies (excellent views), standard rooms have carpets (Rs 550, Rm 102 is best), newly tiled bathrooms, no single room rates, ignore the faded exterior.

E-G Hotel Payal-cum-bar, Main Rd, Mirik Bazar, T(0)9734-977541. Should the Boudi be full, the Payal has cheap singles for Rs 250 with hot bucket, and more spacious rooms with geyser (Rs 300-700), all have TV. The restaurant-cum-bar is well stocked and staff sweet.

F Lodge Ashirvad, Krishnanagar, T0354-224 3272, (0)9832-439582. The best budget option with clean bright rooms, new paint and half-panelling, pay more for geyser or Rs 10 per hot bucket. Single Rs 200, doubles Rs 350/450. Rooftop with monastery views and run by a lovely family. Food available during high seasons. Recommended.

F Boudi, Main Rd, Mirik Bazar, T(0)9932-483476 (ask for Nitai). You could choose to stay in friendly bustling Mirik Bazar (and be the only tourist in the village). The back rooms at Boudi Hotel have stupendous balcony views to Kanchenjunga and are a bargain at Rs 300/350 single/double. Bright paint, laminate floors, TV, hot water in the morning only, restaurant downstairs. Ask for clean sheets if it's low season – as chances are dust will have collected. The informative owner plans to build 6 huts on the slope below, but these are a couple of years off.

Kurseong *p649*

B-E Cochrane Place, 132 Pankhabari Rd, Fatak, (2 km from Kurseong on the road to Mirik), T0354-233 0703, www.imperial chai.com. Rebuilt and recreated colonial home with de luxe rooms (all unique) crammed with antiques and atmosphere, the personal touch of the owner in evidence throughout. Passion fruits grow by balconies, the tiered garden is delightful (organic veg), spa/yoga/meditation and 'stick' massage are reasonably priced, superlative meals and tea menu (see page 658). Views of Kanchenjunga from some rooms. Newer annex is cheaper and simpler, still very comfortable with a chalet air. Dorm beds for backpackers Rs 700. Lovely walking through tea gardens and villages nearby. Management are informative and interesting. Wheelchair access. Highly recommended.

C-D Tourist Lodge, Hill Cart Rd (1 km from station), T0354-234 4409. Gloomy corridors but some lovely wooden rooms (check a couple), good views, 24-hr hot water, heaters in winter, snack bar, decent bar and restaurant. Car hire. Recommended.

D Makaibari Homestays, Makaibari, T033-2287 8560, www.makaibari.com. Villagers from the tea community provide all meals and a unique experience in their family homes, US$25 per day per couple, including all meals, Western toilets.
F Kurseong Palace, 11 Hill Cart Rd, T0354-234 5409, kurseong_palace@yahoo.com. Acceptable rooms with TV and carpets, hot water, nice staff.

Kalimpong *p650, map p650*
Hotels offer discounts during winter and monsoon.
AL Silver Oaks, Main Rd, T03552-255296, www.elginhotels.com. Beautiful rooms of a high standard have a Raj feel, some with fabulous views, buffet restaurant and rather formal bar, gorgeous terraced garden with views from the numerous seating areas.
B Himalayan Hotel, Upper Cart Rd, 10-min walk from town centre, T03552-255248, www.himalayanhotel.co.in. The original stone-built characterful family home of the McDonalds has 8 rooms with traditional furnishings, wooden floors, working fireplaces, no TV, lovely common verandas. 2 well-designed cottages to the rear both have 4 rooms with TV, more modern, trellises and flowers in abundance. Mountain views from the attractive lawn, the restaurant has atmosphere (set menu), comfortable bar with TV, helpful management. One of the oldest hotels in the area (since 1924). Charming.
B Kalimpong Park, Ringkingpong Rd, T03552-255304, www.kalimpongparkhotel.com. Raj atmosphere aplenty in the 4 good-sized, airy rooms in the Maharaja of Dinajpur's old 2-storeyed house, plus 20 rooms in newer building at rear. Both have new bathrooms and wooden floors; request a front room as back ones are decidedly gloomy. The **A** suites are not significantly better, soulless multi-cuisine restaurant but the pleasing bar (see Entertainment, page 659), large lawn and peaceful location are a big plus. It's a stiff walk from town. Car rental available, Wi-Fi.
B Orchid Retreat, Ganesh Villa, long walk from town (4 km from the market), T03552-274517, theorchidretreat.com. In interesting orchid nursery, 6 rooms in traditional thatched cottages (built with local materials) and 4 in a duplex building, hot water (no TV or phone), home-cooked meals (Rs 300), lovely terrace garden with special palm collection, personal attention, peaceful. No walk-ins, must book in advance. Bring your own alcohol.
B-D Morgan House (Kalimpong Tourist Lodge), Singamari, Durpin Dara Hill, T03552-255384, 3 km from centre. Beautiful location and a Raj-era building, 7 rooms with bath (good views from upstairs) but run-down and ill-managed, restaurant, bar, gardens.
C-D Holumba Haven, 1 km before the motor stand, 9th Mile, T03552-256936, T(0)9332-414999, www.holumba.com. This charming place has 8 cottages (you will struggle to choose between them) spread through a nursery garden, amongst trees and with spacious lawns. Rooms are delightfully decorated, spotless and comfortable (no TVs), with piping hot water and real character. The owners have created a homestay atmosphere and are really friendly and informative. Singles start from Rs 700, doubles are Rs 950-1800, there are also triple rooms. Highly recommended.
C-D JP Lodge, RC Mintry Rd, T03552-257457, www.jplodge.com. Clean and simple rooms, charming staff, designated meditation space in a wood-panelled garret (that's also just a good place to hang out). They have whacked their prices up too high though, and no single rates. See website for details of the homestay they operate 20 km away in Munsong village.
D Cloud 9, Ringkingpong Rd, T03552-259554, T(0)98332-039634. Clean respectable rooms though worn carpets, much better at front with balcony views, restaurant is average. Its proximity to the Kalimpong Park Hotel and the cosy Tibetan-styled TV lounge are the big plus points.
D-E Kalash, Main Rd, T03552-259564. Clean enough rooms over the good **Vegetarian Snacketeria** restaurant, but traffic noise can be a problem.
D-F Deki Lodge, Tirpai Rd, 10-mins uphill from Motor Stand, T03552-255095, www.dekilodge.ucoz.com. Very well-maintained rooms aimed at various budgets, nice terrace restaurant and outdoor seating area, kind and knowledgeable staff, a place with character. Recommended.
E Crown Lodge, off Bag Dhara Rd, near Motor Stand, T03552-255846, T(0)9832-334575. 21 clean well-maintained rooms with hot water (Indian toilets), TV, generator, friendly and helpful, old-style kind of place. Doubles at the back with much light are spacious.

Eating

Siguri *p641*

₹₹-₹ **Havelli**, SS Market Complex, Hill Cart Rd, T0353-253 5013. Open 1100-2230. Subtly lit, beige walls and wood sculptures prevail, more intimate than most. Multi-cuisine is high standard and the choices endless, including continental. Family atmosphere.

₹₹-₹ **Tera**, at **The Tiara Hotel**, 1st floor, Sevoke Rd, T0353-243 6024. An orderly restaurant with pleasing decor, tables with cloths and flowers, but a dominant TV screen. Mainly Indian cuisine, some Western breakfast choices, alcohol served.

₹ **Amit's Amardeep**, 7 Sevoke Rd. Open 0830-2230. Upstairs a/c, cheap youthful place with North Indian and Chinese, good biryani, friendly able staff.

₹ **Jain Jaika Bhojnalaya**, Shikha Deep Building (3rd floor), Sevoke Rd. Opens 0800-1530, 1830-2130. Look for their red and white sign down a tiny alley (there's a lift). Sunny orange walls and a chequered floor, pure veg food, best as a breakfast option (excellent paratha and veg – other items on menu generally unavailable).

₹ **Khana Khazana**, Hill Cart Rd. Open 0700-2230. Pleasant outdoor terrace plus indoor seating (fans), generous portions, South Indian is decent or there's tandoori, rolls, Chinese, veg/non, but lassis and shakes are average. Clean family atmosphere.

₹ **Rasoi**, Ganeshayan Building (2nd Fl), beside Sky Star Building, Sevoke Rd, T(0)97758-802071. Open 1030-2230. Pure veg food in a modern spacious environment, great for kebabs and South Indian (40 kinds of *dosa*), interesting *dhals*, plus some Chinese options.

Darjeeling *p641, map p643*

Hotels with restaurants will usually serve non-residents. Several have bars.

₹₹ **New Elgin**, see **The Elgin Hotel**. Formal dining room with some character, OK meals, very pleasant service. Come for a slice of history rather than the food. Afternoon tea is very overpriced, better to just have a drink and enjoy the surroundings.

₹₹ **Shangrila**, see Sleeping. Darjeeling's chicest dining experience, contemporary decor mixed with tasteful Tibetan artefacts, and a wide menu of delicious multi-cuisine food plus bar. Gracious service, open later than most; recommended.

₹₹-₹ **Glenary's**, Nehru Rd (the Mall), T0354-225 7554, glens_getaways@sancharnet.in. Tearoom with excellent confectionery and pastries, friendly, first class breakfast, Kalimpong cheese and wholemeal bread sold. Licensed restaurant upstairs is pricier but lively and with a good atmosphere, bar downstairs has local band on Sat (supposedly 1900-2200 but often finishes early). Speedy internet café (Rs 30 per hr).

₹ **Blind Date**, top floor, Fancy Market, NB Singh Rd, T0354-225 5404. Open 0930-1900. Warm and friendly place always packed with locals, cheap Tibetan and Chinese mains, divine soups and clean kitchen in open view, more limited choice for vegetarians.

₹ **Cafe Coffee Day**, Chowrasta. New addition to Darjeeling's 'scene', disappointing interior but a good spot to watch the world go by, plus great views from the terrace.

₹ **Cozy Bhutan**, Gandhi Rd. Open 0930-1930. Bhutanese cuisine consists of lots of beef and pork, plus a few interesting veg options, mix of mild or spicy. Friendly and charismatic elderly lady in charge. Lowest ceilings in Darjeeling, darkened cubby holes are rather seedy.

₹ **Dekeva's**, Dekling Hotel, 52 Gandhi Rd, Clubside. Nice little place with Tibetan specialities, plus Chinese and Continental, cosy, very popular.

₹ **Hasty Tasty**, Nehru Rd. Good pure vegetarian fast food, Indian, Chinese, pizzas and sandwiches, popular *thalis* aren't very spicy. Canteen-style service, cheap.

₹ **Hot Pizza Place**, HD Lama Rd. Genuinely great pizza plus other Western-friendly meals and snacks, one big table holds all-comers. Folks rave about it.

₹ **Keventer's**, Nehru Rd, Clubside. This Darjeeling classic has a rooftop, serving snacks, with fabulous views.

₹ **Kunga**, Gandhi Rd. Open 0830-2030. Cheerful unpretentious Tibetan joint, with great *momos*, also pizzas and huge backpacker-friendly breakfasts. But it's the range of fantastic soups that are most memorable. Has toilets.

₹ **Lunar**, 51 Gandhi Rd, T0354-225 4194. Open from 0730. Thoroughly delicious pure veg Indian dishes, and some decent sandwiches, pizzas and Chinese. Modern and informal, family environment, big windows for the view. Lassis are fragrant and creamy, service competent and kindly.

¥ **New Dish**, JP Sharma Rd. Open 0800-1930. Chinese. Adventurous menu, mainly Chinese (cheap), excellent chicken entrées, friendly staff. Scruffy aquamarine mirrored walls, serves beer (Rs 75).

¥ **Sonam's Kitchen**, Dr Zakir Hussein Rd. Open for breakfast, lunch and dinner (but not in between), Sonam has built up a loyal following for her home-cooking. Menu is limited, service can take a while, but the French toast is a must. Coffee will blow your head off.

Mirik *p648*

The restaurant at the Jagjeet hotel is excellent with a varied menu; there are extremely cheap *dhabas* near the bus stand offering passable noodle and other dishes. Meals in Mirik Bazar are half the price of Krishnanagar (Boudi Hotel has great veg momos).

¥ **Blue Lagoon**, behind PWD Rest House, near the lake, Krishnanagar. Open 0600-2130. Good Indian and Chinese veg and non-veg, served in a pleasant 'hut' with checked tablecloths and windows all around

¥ **Hills Restaurant**, near the jeep stand, Main Rd, Krishnanagar. Open from 0700 but closes early. Popular little place, with some Indian dishes alongside Tibetan and Chinese, delicious *thukpa*.

¥ **Lakeside Restaurant**, near the boat shed. Pure vegetarian food in a simple little eatery, with a couple of tables outside on the edge of the lake.

¥ **Samden**, next to Jagjeet Hotel, Main Rd, Krishnanagar. Open 0700-2030 (later than most). Great Tibetan food, spicy chai, monks for dining companions. At the time of writing the restaurant was being rebuilt, and was operating from a basement down a side alley.

Kurseong *p649*

¥¥-¥ **Chai Country**, at **Cochrane Place** (see Sleeping). A meal at Cochrane is not to be missed if in Kurseong. Food is gourmet and inventive, best are the Anglo-Indian dishes with a twist (*dhal* with mint, oyster mushrooms smoked with tea) otherwise African curry, veggie shepherd's pie and more; puddings are exquisite (baked mango). No liquor license.

¥ **Abhinandan Fast Food Corner**, Naya Bazar (on way to Eagle's Crag). Open 0900-2030. Cubby hole, with lampshades made of fishing basket traps and character, good veg rolls, thukpa, momos.

¥ **Gorkha Bhancha Ghar**, at the railway, opposite the platform. Open 0700-1900. This specialist *bhancha ghar* (kitchen) serves up cheap and excellent Nepali food in clean surroundings.

¥ **Hill Top**, 11 TN Rd, T(0)99331-29177. Good for Chinese and Tibetan in a cosy restaurant-cum-bar that makes a nod to Chinese decor. Cheap beer.

Kalimpong *p650, map p650*

Most restaurants shut at 2000. Little restaurants behind the jeep stand dish out delicious *momos* and noodle soups at rock-bottom prices. Be sure to try some Kalimpong cheese, which has been produced since the days of the Swiss Jesuits, available from Lark's Provisions (and very cheap).

¥¥-¥ **Gompus** (see Sleeping). Open 1000-2100. Largely meat-based menu, good for Tibetan and Chinese, very popular and a nice environment, alcohol served.

¥¥-¥ **King Thai**, 3rd floor, Maa Supermarket, T(0)8670-235007. Open from 0900-2130 (but sometimes till 0200 at weekends). Excellent food (more Chinese than Thai, despite the name) attracting a real mix of people. Warmly decorated and professional staff, alcohol served. Live music every night.

¥ **3C's** (formerly **Glenary's**), Main Rd. Hangout for local youth, with mainly Western food, breakfast items, great pastries and average coffee. Best for the buzzy vibe rather than the food.

¥ **Balaji Chowrasta**, great choice of vegetarian South/North Indian and Chinese dishes, cheap and good but definitely not glamorous.

¥ **Cakes R Us**, past DGTC on DB Giri Rd. Café-style offerings.

¥ **Shikhar**, next to Cakes R Us. Open 0700-1930. Dirt cheap and all vegetarian, limited menu of *momos*, chow, huge bowls of *thukpa* and lassis in a busy basement.

¥ **Vegetarian Snacketeria**, Main Rd, opposite Main Bazar. Tasty South and North Indian plus a wide choice of drinks.

Bars and entertainment

Darjeeling *p641, map p643*

English-language films show at the Inox cinema in Rink Mall, www.inoxmovies.com, T0354-225 7226. Seats from Rs 90-140.

There are several great options for a *chota peg* in Raj-era surroundings. Sadly the **Planters' Club** bar (see Sleeping, page 653), among the moth-eaten animal trophies inside or out on the terrace, is only open to residents, but the **Windamere** (see Sleeping, page 653) compensates with a cosy lounge-feel among knik-knaks, or the **Gymkhana Club** (see Activities, below) for billiards, worn leather seats, and bags of atmosphere. **Joey's Pub**, though housed in an unlikely looking heritage cottage, gathers a rowdy crowd every night for drinks in a true pub ambiance. Surprisingly good typical British bar snacks, very social, open 0930-2300, beers Rs 90-95. **Dafey Mumal**, Laden La Rd, has a decent bar upstairs (strong beer only); the restaurant downstairs is not up to much, though it has internet.

Kalimpong *p650, map p650*

The nicest place for a drink is the bar at the **Kalimpong Park Hotel**, which has a cosy lounge attached and green cane furniture on the small terrace, open until 2100 (beer Rs 130). Also pleasant, though not very pub-like, is the **Himalayan Hotel**.

Festivals and events

Darjeeling *p641, map p643*

Apr/May Buddha Purnima/Jayanti celebrates the birth of the Buddha in the monasteries.

Shopping

Darjeeling *p641, map p643*

The markets by the motor stand are colourful and worth visiting.

Books

Greenland, Laden La Rd, up some steps near entrance to Prestige Hotel. Book swap. **Oxford Bookshop**, Chowrasta. Good stock especially local interest, one of West Bengal's best bookshops.

Handicrafts

Local handicrafts sold widely include Buddhist *tankhas* (hand-painted scrolls surrounded by Chinese brocade), good wood carving, carpets, hand-woven cloth, jewellery, copper, brass and white metal religious curios such as prayer wheels, bowls and statues. Chowrasta shops are closed on Sun, Chowk Bazar and Middle Bazar on Thu. **Dorjee**, Laden La Rd. **Eastern Arts**, Chowrasta. **H Mullick**, curios from Chowrasta, a cut above the rest. **Nepal Curios**, Laden La Rd. **Tibetan Refugee Self-help Centre** (see page 644), hand-woven carpets in bold designs and colours (from US$360 including packaging, at least 6-month waiting list).

Photography

Das Studios, The Mall. Stationery, postcards, maps, interesting black-and-white prints from Raj days; order from album (1-2 days). Daily 0930-1900.

Tea

Nathmull's, Laden La Rd (above GPO) and at Rink Mall, nathmulls@goldentipstea.com. An institution, vast selection (Rs 140-10,000 per kg), avoid fancy packs, knowledgeable owner.

Kalimpong *p650, map p650*

Handicrafts

Tibetan and Nepalese handicrafts and woven fabrics are particularly good. There is an abundance of shops on RC Mintry Rd. **Gangjong**, Primtam Rd (ask at **Silver Oaks Hotel** for directions). Interesting paper factory. **Soni Emporium**, near Motor Stand, Mani Link Rd. Specializes in Himalayan handicrafts.

Activities and tours

Siliguri and Jaldapara *p641*

Tour operators

Help Tourism (Association of Conservation & Tourism), 143 Hill Cart Rd (1st floor), T0353-253 5893, www.helptourism.com. Recommended for eastern Himalaya and arranging homestays in villages around the tea gardens.
Shakul Pradan, T09749-391230. With 2-3 days advance notice, Shakul (who works for WBTDC) can arrange a package to Jaldapara, including elephant ride, jeep transport, private hotel in Madariat and all meals, for Rs1200 per person per day.

Darjeeling *p641, map p643*

Clubs

Gymkhana Club, T0354-225 2892, has good snooker tables, badminton, squash, tennis and roller skating (tie skates on with string). Temporary membership Rs 50 per day, up to Rs 55 for activities, excellent staff.
Planters' Club, The Mall, T0354-225 4348, the old Darjeeling Club, a relic of the Raj,

membership (Rs 50 per day for hotel residents only), allows use of pleasant colonial restaurant (buffet meals cost extra), bar, billiards, a bit run down but log fires, warm and friendly.

Mountaineering

Himalayan Mountaineering Institute, in the zoo compound, T0354-225 4087, www.himalayanmountaineeringinstitute.com. Office open Mon-Sat 1000-13000. Runs mountaineering training courses, from 'adventure' level (15-day, US$250, Nov-Dec and Apr-May), through basic (28-day, Mar-May and Sep-Nov) to advanced (28-day, Mar, May and Sep).

Riding

Pony rides are popular starting at Chowrasta (Rs 80-100 per hr); also possible to do a scenic half-day ride to Ghoom – agree price in writing.

River rafting

On the Tista, a range of trips from 1½ hrs to 2-day camps with fishing (Rs 2500 for 6 or more, transport extra), contact **DGHC** (see below).

Tour operators

Clubside Tours & Travels, JP Sharma Rd, T0354-225 5123. Hotel booking, tours, treks, good jeep hire, air tickets for all domestic carriers.
DGHC, runs a variety of tours leaving from the tourist office, including to Mirik, Tiger Hill, Darjeeling town and surrounding areas. Price lists are available at the office.
Darjeeling Transport Corp, 30 Laden La Rd. Maruti vans, jeeps, Land Rovers and a few *sumos* are available. Prices vary according to the season so negotiate rates.
Meghma Tours & Travels, 51 Gandhi Rd, T0354-228 9073, meghmatourstravels@yahoo.co.in. A variety of day tours as well as trips into Sikkim.

Trekking agents

Clubside Tours & Travels, see Tour operators, above.
Himalayan Adventures, Das Studios, Nehru Rd, T0354-225 4090, dastrek@aussiemail.com.au.
Himalayan Travels, 18 Gandhi Rd, T/F0354-225 2254, kkgurung@cal.vsnl.net.in. Long established, good for Sikkim and Singalila treks, tours to Bhutan (need 3-5 days' notice, US$180-240 per day depending on group size).
Trek-Mate, Singalila Arcade, Nehru Rd, T0354-225 6611, chagpori@satyam.net.in. Well-equipped, English-speaking guides, excellent service, recommended.

Kalimpong *p650, map p650*

Gurudongma Tours & Travels, T03552-225204, www.gurudongma.com. High-quality, personalized treks, priced accordingly. Recommended.
Kalimpong Village Tours, Mondo Challenge, Peepal Dhara, 8½ Mile, Rishi Rd, T0355-226 0026, T(0)9932-368974, http://kalimpongvillagetour.wordpress.com. Gentle trekking on 1- to 3-day tours, taking in local culture and village life in the Koshyem region.
Mintry Transport, Main Rd. Jet Airways and Air India agent.

Transport

Siliguri *p641*

Try to arrive at **Siliguri** or **NJP** in daylight (before 1900). Rickshaw drivers can be quite aggressive at NJP.
Air Bagdogra Airport, 13 km away, has daily flights to **Kolkata** and **Delhi** with **Kingfisher** and **Air India**, Hill Cart Rd (2nd floor, opposite Biswadeep Cinema), T0353-251 1495. Daily 1000-1700, closed Sun. **SpiceJet** and **Jet Airways**, Vinayak Building, Hill Cart Rd, T0353-243 5876, airport T0353-255 1675, have flights to **Delhi**, **Kolkata**, **Guwahati** and **Chennai**. Jet also connect to **Bombay** and **Dubai**, while **Drukair** have twice weekly flights to **Bangkok** and **Paro**. Helicopter daily in fine weather to **Sikkim** (see page 677), depending on demand. Taxis to Darjeeling (Rs 1300), Gangtok (Rs 1700), Kalimpong (Rs 1150), Siliguri (Rs 300) and NJP (Rs 400).
Bus Siliguri is on NH31, well connected with Darjeeling (80 km), Gangtok (114 km) and Kalimpong (54 km) and served by buses from WB, Assam, Bihar, Sikkim and Bhutan.

Tenzing Norgay Central Bus Terminus (CBT) is on Hill Cart Rd, next to Siliguri Junction Railway Station. There are also many private operators just outside the CBT offering similar services. Bus to **Madarihat** (for Jaldapara) leaves from the CBT at 0700, 3 hrs, Rs 60; **Malda**, frequent buses from 0430-2300, 6 hrs, Rs 120. The WBSTC's overnight Rocket bus to

Permits for Sikkim

Free Inner Line Permits (ILPs) for Sikkim are easiest to get at the Sikkim Tourist Office in Darjeeling (1st, floor, Main Old Bellevue Hotel, opposite Glenaries, Nehru Road, Monday-Saturday 1000-1600) where the processing time is 10 minutes; take one copy of your passport and visa, and one passport photo. An ILP allows foreigners to enter Sikkim for up to 30 days (request 30 days when applying, or you will be issued with the standard 15 days). The Foreigners' Regional Registration Office (FRRO) in Darjeeling also issue ILPs but the process is longer and more complicated. Here, you have to get a form from the FRRO (Laden La Road, T0354-225 4203, 0930-1800) then take your documents to the Office of the District Magistrate, Hill Cart Road (downhill from the motor stand, T0354-225 4233, Monday-Friday 1100-1300 and 1430-1600), which can take up to two hours. See also box, page 669.

Kolkata departs 1800, 1900 and 2000 from Hill Cart Rd, 12 hrs, Rs 215, but it's a tortuous journey on terrible roads. For greater comfort on a Volvo bus, try **Gupta Tour & Travels**, T0353-645 4077, departing at 2000. Ticket counter 13 in the CBT for buses to Assam: **Guwahati** at 1700, 12 hrs, Rs 250; **Tezpur** at 1400, 16 hrs, Rs 330. **SNT Bus Station**, is opposite CBT: **Gangtok**, buses leave regularly between 0730-1330, Rs 90-110, 5 hrs; de luxe private buses from CBT (separate ticket window), Rs 100.

To Bhutan **Bhutan Government** buses, tickets from Counter 14 at CBT, 0700-1200. To **Phuntsholing**: buses at 0720, 1200, 1400, 1500, Rs 75, 3-4 hrs. NBSTC buses run at 0700 and 1200, Rs 75.

To Nepal To **Kathmandu** buses (or more conveniently taxi or jeep, every 15 mins or so from opposite CBT) to **Panitanki** on the border (35 km, 1 hr); transfer to **Kakarbhitta** by cycle-rickshaw. See box, page 663. Also through tickets from private bus companies.

Jeep Shared jeeps are the best way to get to and around the hills, as they leave more frequently and are faster than buses, and only a little more expensive. **Kalimpong**, from Sevoke Rd stand, 2½ hrs Rs 90; Gangtok, Sevoke Rd or outside CBT on Hill Cart Rd, 3½-4 hrs Rs 140; **Darjeeling**, from Hill Cart Rd, 3 hrs, Rs 100; Kurseong, from Hill Cart Rd (near Conclave Hotel), 1½ hrs, Rs 60; **Mirik**, from Hill Cart Rd, opposite CBT, 2 hrs, Rs 60, and from the same place to **Jorethang**, 3½ hrs, Rs 120 (you need to get an ILP in advance to cross this border). Jeeps also leave from outside NJP direct for **Darjeeling**, **Kalimpong** and **Gangtok**, at a slightly higher price and with some waiting while drivers tout for customers.

Train Railway Enquiry at NJP, T0353-256 1555. **Siliguri Junction** and **NJP**, 5 km away, have tourist information. There are buses, tempos (Rs 15), cycle-rickshaws (Rs 60) and taxis (Rs 150) between the two. NJP has good connections to other major destinations in India. For long-distance rail journeys from NJP, first buy tickets at Siliguri (Computerized Reservations, Bidhan Rd near Stadium), 1000-1300, 1330-1700 (to avoid the queue go to Chief Reservations Officer at side of building), then go to NJP station for train.

To **Darjeeling**, the *Toy Train* leaves from NJP, calling at Siliguri Junction on its way.

Daily diesel service leaves at 0915, 7½ hrs (0930, 7hrs from Siliguri, though in reality the journey is usually 9 hrs). Services are often disrupted by landslides during the rains (at the time of writing the service was suspended while the track was being fixed), though the upper section from Kurseong (accessible by bus/jeep) continues to run; check beforehand.

Steam trains run daily from Siliguri to **Sukna**, 0855 (from Siliguri Town at 08:45, 35 mins, from Siliguri Jn at 08:55, 25 mins).

From NJP to **Kolkata** (**S**): *Darjeeling Mail, 12344*, 2000, 10 hrs. **Kolkata** (**H**): *Kamrup Exp, 15960*, 1645, 13¾ hrs; *Kanchenjunga Exp, 15658*, 0755, 11½ hrs. **Delhi** (**ANVT**) : *NE Exp, 12505*, 1705, 26 hrs; (New Delhi) *Rajdhani Exp* (Mon, Wed, Thu, Fri, Sun), 12423, 1305, 21 hrs. From Kolkata (**S**) to Siliguri: *Darjeeling Mail, 12343*, 2205, 10 hrs, connects with the Toy Train from NJP.

Jaldapara *p641*
Air The nearest airport is Bagdogra (see page 642).
Bus Buses from Siliguri to Madarihat, then change for Jaldapara Park. Forest Department transport to Hollong inside the sanctuary.
Train Hasimara station (18 km from park) has trains to **Siliguri Junction**: daily *Mahananda Exp 14083*, 0753, 2½ hrs.

Darjeeling *p641, map p643*
Air The nearest airport is Bagdogra (90 km), see Siliguri, above. Transfer by car takes 3 hrs. **Air India**, Bellevue Hotel, Chowrasta, T0354-225 4230. Mon-Sat 1000-1700, Sun 1000-1300.
Bus Minibuses go from the main transport stand to nearby villages including **Mirik** at 0825, 0900 and 0925 (Rs 40), via **Sukhia** and **Pashupati Fatak** (on the Nepalese border).
Jeep Shared jeep is the quickest and most convenient way of getting around the mountains. Jeeps leave regularly to local destinations, and if you pick a jeep that is already over half full, you won't be waiting long before you set off. During the high season it is well advised to book a day in advance (particularly to reserve seat No 1). To **Siliguri** from 0600-1630 (2-2½ hrs, Rs 100); to **Gangtok** from 0700-1500 (4-5 hrs, Rs 150); to **Mirik** (2 hrs, Rs 60); to **Kalimpong** from 0700-1600 (2½ hrs, Rs 80-90); to **Jorethang** from 0800-1500 (Sikkim permit not available at border, 2 hrs, Rs 90-100), change at Jorethang for **Pelling**. The journeys to Kalimpong and Mirik are particularly stunning, along narrow ridges planted with tea bushes and past wooden villages teetering on precipices.
Motorbike Enfields and other models can be rented from **Adventures Unlimited**, based in the internet café, 0830-2000, opposite Cyber Planet on Zakir Hussein Rd. Around Rs 350 per day.
Taxi Easily available in the lower part of town.
Train Diesel service to **New Jalpaiguri** (**NJP**) at 0915, 7½ hrs , 88 km away. However, at the time of research the train was not running due to a landslide between Mahanadi and Gayabari (that has taken over a year to fix, so far). A passenger train runs to Kurseong (Rs 27/144) via Ghoom (Rs 10/111) daily at 1015, taking 3 hrs and returning at 1500. Darjeeling station also has some old steam engines. A narrow-gauge steam tourist train to **Ghoom** (**Ghum**) with a photo stop at Batasia Loop, departs 1040, 1320 and 1600 taking 1¼ hrs (the morning train is always packed, but the 1600 only runs if there is enough demand), Rs 240 first-class only (see page 661). The ticket office at the station is open Mon-Sat 0800-1700, Sun -1400, lunch 1200-1230.

Mirik *p648*
From Krishnanagar, jeeps to Darjeeling between 0900-1430 (2 hrs, Rs 60); to Siliguri every 30 mins from 0700-1530 (2 hrs, Rs 60); to **Kurseong** at 1500 (2 hrs, Rs 60); to **Kalimpong** at 0600 (4-5 hrs, Rs 140). Also jeeps to the above destinations from Mirik Bazar, departing between 0600-1000. You can go to **Sandakphu** from Mirik, change jeep at **Sukhia**.
Train Mirik Out Agency, Main Rd, Krishnanagar, can book train tickets to/from NJP.

Kurseong *p649*
Jeep 51 km from Siliguri, off the main Darjeeling road, or via Pankhabari. Buses and jeeps to **Siliguri**, 1½ hrs and **Darjeeling**, 1 hr, leave from near the railway station; for **Mirik** jeeps leave from Pankhabari Rd.
Train A diesel service leaves for Darjeeling (see Siliguri, above), via Kurseong 3½ hrs.

Kalimpong *p650, map p650*
Air Nearest airport is at Bagdogra, 80 km, 2½-3 hrs, Rs 1300 private car (see Siliguri); seat in shared jeep Rs 110 to Bagdogra (then an auto for last couple of kms to airport). Flight bookings from **Mintry Transport**.
Bus Buses use the Motor Stand. Frequent to **Siliguri**, from 0530-1700 (2½ hrs, Rs 65); **Lava**, (2 hrs, Rs 35) and **Kaffer** (3, Rs 60) at 0800; to **Karkabitta** at 0530 and 1345 93 hrs, Rs 80); to **Gangtok** at 0730 (3½ hrs, Rs 70).
Jeep Shared jeeps depart 0630-1500, depending on demand; much quicker than buses. To **Darjeeling**, 2 hrs, Rs 80-90; **Siliguri** Rs 70/Rs 50; **Gangtok** Rs 120.
Train The nearest mainline railhead is New Jalpaiguri (NJP), 67 km. Tickets from **Rly Out Agency**, next to Soni Emporium, Motor Stand. Computerized bookings and a small tourist quota for trains departing to NJP.

Border essentials: India–Nepal

Kakarbhitta, the Nepalese border town, has only basic accommodation. Jeeps go from Siliguri frequently, as well as from Darjeeling. Single-entry 60-day visas cost US$30 to be paid in exact cash and you'll need two passport photos (multiple-entry 30-day US$40, multiple-entry 15-day US$25, multiple-entry 90-day US$100). From the border, buses depart 0300-2400, arriving in Kathmandu (595 km) 16-17 hours later; the journey can be very tiring. From Kakarbhitta it is also possible to fly (seasonal) from Bhadrapur (24 km, with free transfer to airstrip) to Kathmandu with Buddha Air (one hour). Alternatively, get a taxi to Biratnagar in Nepal (150 km) and fly from there to Kathmandu.

Directory

Siliguri *p641*

Banks Several ATMs on Hill Cart and Sevoke roads; there's a convenient Axis Bank cashpoint opposite the CBT by Hotel Heritage.
Internet **Moulik**, behind Vinayak, Hill Cart Rd, T0353-243 2312. **Net-N-Net**, 1st floor, off Hill Cart Rd opposite bus stand, handy and fast, requires photo ID, open 0930-2130 closed Sun. Rs 20 per hr. **Sai Raj**, Patel Rd, behind Khana Khazana, daily 1000-2230, Sun 1030-1400, Rs 20 per hr. **Hospital** **Hospital**, T0353-252 1920; **North Bengal Clinic**, T0353-242 0441.
Post GPO, Hospital Rd, Mon-Sat 0700-1900, Sun 1000-1400.

Darjeeling *p641, map p643*

Banks There are many ATMs and exchange houses all over town. **Couriers** FedEx at **Global Express**, Robertson Rd, T0354-225 8706. Open Mon-Fri 0900-1700, Sat 0900-1300.
Internet **Compuset Centre**, 14 Gandhi Rd, T0354-225 6415, compuset@yahoo.com. Fast connection, no skype, cheap printing, Rs 30 1 hr (min Rs 10), open 0800-2000 including Sun. **Glenary's**, the Mall, T0354-225 7554, speedy connection, Rs 30 per hr. **Hospitals** Planters' **Hospital**, Nehru Rd, T0354-225 4327. **Sadar Hospital**, T0354-225 4218. **Mariam Nursing Home**, below Gymkhana Club, T0354-225 4328, has been recommended for its medical facilities.
Post GPO, Laden La Rd.

Mirik *p648*

Banks Two ATMs on Main Rd, Krishnanagar.
Internet There are 3 internet cafes in Krishnanagar, best is **Prashant IT Solutions** with fast connection, new computers, skype and printing, Rs 30 per hr, daily 0930-2000. Internet in Mirik Bazar is much slower.

Kurseong *p649*

Banks **SBI**, has ATM, opposite station and another 500 m down Pankhabari Rd.
Internet **Cyber Planet**, in Unique Sweet Market, open 1000-2030, Rs 25 per hr.

Kalimpong *p650, map p650*

Banks Several ATMs in town. **Emporium**, Mani Link Rd, accepts Visa and Mastercard. **Medical services/post** There is a hospital and a post office near the police station.

Sikkim

Contents

Footprint features

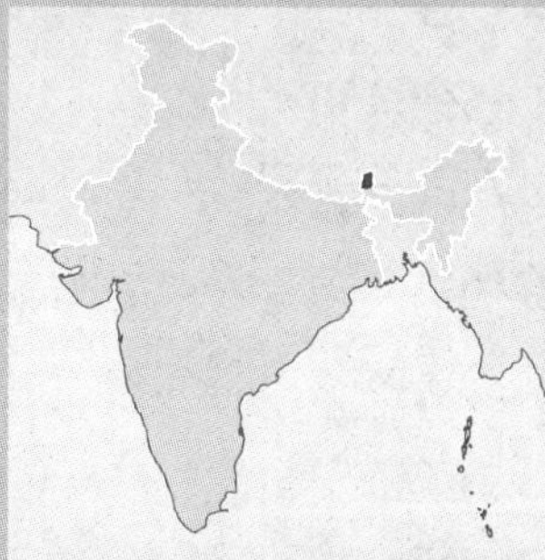

At a glance

Getting around Shared jeeps are cheap, fast and much more frequent than buses. Helicopter service from Bagdogra to Gangtok.

Time required 1-2 days in and around Gangtok, 2 days for Yumthang Valley, minimum 4-5 days for West Sikkim.

Weather Clear and warm in Sep, chilly Oct-Feb, warm and dry but often foggy from Mar until the start of the monsoon in late May/Jun. Best in Sep and Oct.

When not to go The monsoon can cause havoc with road transport.

★ **Don't miss ...**

1. **Tashi Viewpoint over the Kangchendzonga range**, page 672.
2. **Rumtek Monastery**, page 672.
3. **Saramsa Gardens**, page 673.
4. **An overnight stay and early-morning walk at Pemayangtse Monastery**, page 679.
5. **Trek to Khecheopalri Lake**, page 679.

Khangchendzonga, the third highest mountain in the world, dominates the skyline of Sikkim. The state is renowned as much for its wonderful wildlife and rich variety of plants and flowers as for its ethnically varied population. Sikkim's original inhabitants, the Lepchas, call the region Nye-mae-el, meaning 'Paradise'. To the later Bhutias it is Beymul Denjong, or the 'Hidden Valley of Rice'. The name Sikkim itself is commonly attributed to the Tsong word Su-khim, meaning 'New' or 'Happy House'. The monasteries of Rumtek and Pemayangtse are just two among a wealth of fascinating centres of Buddhism in the state.

Sikkim is an orchid-lovers' paradise, with 660 species found at altitudes as high as 3000 m. Organic farming and ecotourism are officially enshrined in government policy, and although trekking is less developed than in other parts of the Himalaya, the state is beginning to attract ramblers and trekkers in serious numbers.

You can stay a few days in Gangtok, making day trips to Rumtek and Phodong, then move on to Pelling or Yuksom, visiting Pemayangtse Monastery and Khecheopalri Lake, before continuing to Kalimpong or Darjeeling in West Bengal. Road journeys within Sikkim are very scenic, but numerous hairpin bends and unsealed sections can also make them extremely slow, so expect to travel at 10-40 kph. Conditions deteriorate considerably during the monsoon, which can sometimes make travel impossible.

Background → *Population: 607,000. Area: 7298 sq km.*

The land

Geography Sikkim nestles between the peaks of the eastern Himalaya, stretching only 112 km from south to north and 64 km from east to west. This small area contains a vast range of landscapes and habitats, from subtropical river valleys to snow-covered peaks. Despite comprising just 0.2% of India's landmass, Sikkim accounts for an astounding 26% of its biodiversity. The state encompasses the upper valley of the Tista River, a tributary of the Brahmaputra, the watershed of which forms the borders with Tibet and Nepal. In the east lies the Chumbi Valley, a tongue of Tibetan land separating Sikkim from Bhutan that gives the state its strategic and political sensitivity. The Sikkimese believe Khangchendzonga (known as Kanchenjunga in West Bengal, or the 'Five Treasures of the Great Snows'), at 8586 m, to be the repository of minerals, grains, salt, weapons and holy scriptures. On its west is the massive 31-km-long Zemu Glacier.

Climate In the lower valleys Sikkim's climate is subtropical. Above 1000 m, it is temperate, while the higher mountain tops are permanently under snow. Sikkim is one of the Himalaya's wettest regions, with most rain falling between mid-May and September.

History

From the 13th century Tibetans, like the Namgyal clan, immigrated to Sikkim. In 1642 Phuntsog Namgyal (1604-1670) became the Chogyal (king). With a social system based on Tibetan Lamaistic Buddhism, the land was split into 12 *dzongs* (fortified districts).

In the 18th century Sikkim lost land to Nepal, Bhutan and the British. When the Gurkhas of Nepal launched a campaign into Tibet and were defeated by the Chinese in 1791-1792, Sikkim won back its northern territories. The narrow Chumbi Valley, which separates Sikkim from Bhutan, remained with Tibet. When the British defeated Nepal in 1815, the southern part of the country was given back to Sikkim. However, in the next conflict with Nepal, Darjeeling was handed over to the British in return for their assistance. In 1848 the Terai region at the foot of the mountains was annexed by the British.

Nepalis migrated into Sikkim from the beginning of the 19th century, eventually becoming more numerous than the local inhabitants. This led to internal conflict also involving the British and the Tibetans. The British won the ensuing battles and declared Sikkim a Protectorate in 1890. The state was controlled by a British Political Officer who effectively stripped the *Gyalpos* of executive power. It was many years before the Sikkimese regained control.

Culture

Ethnic groups The Naong, Chang and Mon are believed to have inhabited Sikkim in prehistoric times. Each ethnic group has an impressive repertoire of folk songs and dances. The **Lepchas**, who call themselves Rongpas and claim to be the original inhabitants of Sikkim, may have come from Tibet well before the eighth century and brought Lamaistic Buddhism, which is still practised. They are now regarded as the indigenous peoples. They are deeply religious, peace loving and typically shy but cheerful. The government has reserved the Dzongu area in North and Central Sikkim for Lepchas, who now make up less than 10% of the population. For a long time, the Lepchas' main contact with the outside world was the market-place at Mangan, where they bartered oranges and cardamom. Their alphabet was only devised in the 18th century by the king.

The **Magar**, a minority group, are renowned as warriors and were involved in the coronation of Phuntsog Namgyal, the first Chogyal of Sikkim in 1642.

The **Bhotias** (meaning 'of Bhot/Tibet') or Bhutias entered Sikkim in the 13th century from Kham in Tibet. Many adapted to sedentary farming from pastoral nomadism and displaced the Lepchas. Some, however, retained their older lifestyle, and combined animal husbandry with

Permits

Free **Inner Line Permits** (**ILPs**) are issued to foreigners to enter Sikkim for up to 30 days. Make sure you request 30 days when applying, or you will be issued with the standard 15 days. Contact an Indian mission abroad when applying for an Indian visa (enclosing two extra photos), or apply at any FRO (Foreigners' Registration Office) or the Sikkim Tourism Office in New Delhi, Kolkata, Siliguri or Darjeeling (check www.sikkim.gov.in for office details). The easiest place to get an ILP is at the Sikkim Tourist Office in Darjeeling (Main Old Bellevue Hotel, opposite Glenaries, Nehru Road, Mon-Sat 1000-1600) where the processing time is 10 minutes; take one copy of your passport and visa, and one passport photo. The FRO in Darjeeling also issue ILPs but the process is longer and more complicated.

The checkpoint at Rangpo, on the border with West Bengal, issues a 15-day permit for foreigners on entering Sikkim; processing time is 10 minutes. If you wish to enter via Jorethang (for quicker access to West Sikkim) you need to arrange your ILP in advance. ILPs are extendable at the FRO in Gangtok (Yangthang Building, Kazi Rd, Gangtok, T03592-203041, open daily 1000-1600) or by the Superintendent of Police in Namchi (south) and Geyzing (west). ILPs are repeatedly renewable, allowing stays of up to three months. On exiting Sikkim, it is not permitted to return for three months.

Certain areas in north and west Sikkim (Chungthang, Yumthang, Lachen, Chhangu, Dzongri) have been opened to groups of two to 20 travellers, on condition that travel is with a registered agency. The required Protected Areas Permits (PAP) can be arranged by most local travel agents; apply with photocopies of your passport (Indian visa and personal details pages), ILP and two photos.

trading over the Trans-Himalayan passes: Nathula (4392 m), Jelepla (4388 m), Donkiala (5520 m) and Kongrala (4809 m). Over the years the Bhutias have come into increased contact with the Lepcha and intermarried with them. Nearly every Bhutia family has one member who becomes a monk. Monasteries remain the repositories of Bhutia culture and festivals here are the principal social events. However, those who have visited Ladakh or Zanskar may find them architecturally and artistically a little disappointing. The Bhutias are famous for their weaving and are also skilled woodcarvers.

The **Newars** entered Sikkim in large numbers from Nepal in the 19th century. Skilled in metal and woodwork, they were granted the right by the Chogyal to mine copper and mint the Sikkimese coinage. Other Nepali groups followed. With high-altitude farming skills, they settled new lands and built houses directly on the ground unlike the Lepcha custom of building on stilts. The Newars were followed by the Chettris and other Nepali clans who introduced Hinduism, which became more popular as their numbers swelled.

Religion In Sikkim, as in Nepal, Hinduism and Buddhism have interacted and amalgamated so Himalayan Hinduism includes a pantheon of Buddhist *bodhisattvas* as well as Hindu deities. The animist tradition also retains a belief in evil spirits.

Buddhist **prayer flags** flutter in the breeze everywhere. The different types, such as wind, luck and victory, are printed with texts and symbols on coloured pieces of cloth and are tied to bamboo poles or trees. **Prayer wheels** carrying inscriptions (which should be turned clockwise) vary in size from small hand-held ones to vast drums which are installed by a monastery or *stupa*. Whitewashed masonry **chortens** (*stupas*) usually commemorate the Buddha or Bodhisattva, the structure symbolizing the elements (earth, water, fire, air, ether). The eight **lucky signs** appear as parasol, pot or vase, conch shell, banner, two fishes, lotus, knot of eternity and the wheel of law (Dharma Chakra). Bowls of **water** (Thing Duen Tsar) are offered in prayer from left to right during Buddhist worship. The gift of water from one who is free from greed and meanness is offered to quench thirsty spirits and to wash the feet, and represents flower (or welcome), incense, lamp, perfume and food.

Festivals Since the 22 major festivals are dictated by the agricultural cycle and the Hindu-Buddhist calendar, it is best to check dates with the Gangtok tourist office.

Jan/Feb Bumchu meaning 'sacred pot' is a 1-day festival at the monastery in Tashiding. The sacred pot is opened once a year and the water level within forecasts the prosperity of Sikkim in the coming year.
Feb/Mar Losar (Tibetan New Year) is celebrated for about a week at Tashiding. It is preceded by Lama dances in Rumtek.
Apr/May Buddha Purnima/Jayanti is the most sacred day in the Buddhist calendar, falling on the full moon of the lunar month of Vaishaaka. 'Buddha's birthday' is also the day he gained enlightenment and attained Nirvana.
Jun Saga Dawn, a Buddhist festival with huge religious processions round Gangtok.
Rumtek Chaams Dance festival is held in commemoration of the 8 manifestations of Guru Padmasambhava, who established Buddhism in Tibet.
Aug/Sep Pang Lhabsol commemorates the consecration of Khangchendzonga as Sikkim's guardian deity; the Lepchas believe that the mountain is their birthplace. The masked warrior dance is especially spectacular; warriors wear traditional armour of helmets, swords and shields. Celebrations are held in Pemayangtse.
Sep/Oct Dasain is one of the most important Nepali festivals. It coincides with **Dasara** in North India, see page 44. On the 1st day barley seeds are planted in prayer rooms, invocations are made to Durga, and on the 8th day buffalo and goats are ritually sacrificed.
Dec Diwali (the Festival of Lights).
Kagyat Dances performed by monks (especially at Enchey), with religious music and chanting, enact themes from Buddhist mythology and end with the burning of effigies made of flour, wood and paper. This symbolizes the exorcism of evil spirits and the ushering in of prosperity for the coming year. **Losoog** (**Namsoong** for Lepchas at Gangtok) is the Sikkimese New Year, also called **Sonam Losar**. Farmers celebrate their harvest and beginning of their new cropping calendar.

Modern Sikkim

In 1950, Sikkim became a Protectorate of India. In 1973 there were growing demands for accession to India by the local population, consisting mainly of Nepalis, and Sikkim was formally made an associate state. The Gyalpos lost their power as a result of the new democratic constitution and Sikkim became the 22nd state in the Union in 1975. Although there is no separatist movement, India's takeover and the abolition of the monarchy, supported by many of Nepali origin, is still resented by many Sikkimese who don't regard themselves as Indians. The state enjoys special tax and other privileges, partly because of its highly sensitive geopolitical location on the disputed border with China. In the 2009 general election the Sikkim Democratic Front (SDF), a party confined to Sikkim, won all 32 seats in the State Assembly.

Gangtok and around

→ *Colour map 4, A2. Population: 98,658. Altitude: 1547 m.*

Gangtok ('High Hill'), the capital of Sikkim, sits on a ridge overlooking the Ranipul River. The setting is spectacular with fine views of the Khangchendzonga range, but the town has lost some of its quaint charm with the mushrooming of concrete buildings along the national highway and the main road. The crowded Mahatma Gandhi Marg and the colourful bazars below it are where all the town's commercial activity is concentrated. Away from here, there are many serene areas and quiet alleys that remain virtually untouched. ▸▸ *For listings, see pages 674-677.*

Ins and outs

Getting there There is a small airport near Gangtok linked to Bagdogra Airport (see page 660), 124 km away, by a regular helicopter service. Most visitors arrive from North Bengal by the attractive road following the Tista (NH31A), which is accessible all year except in very wet weather (mid-June to September) when there may be landslips. Permits and passports are checked at Rangpo where 15-day permits (extendable in Gangtok or district headquarters, see box, page 661) are available (passport and two photos required). SNT buses terminate at the Paljor Stadium Road stand, while jeeps from Siliguri/Bagdogra stop at Nam Nang jeep stand south of Gangtok, connected to the centre by a 10-minute ride in a shared minibus taxi. Jeeps for West Sikkim use the main jeep stand on NH31A just below the tourist office, while jeeps for destinations north leave from another stand near Vajra cinema (five-minute taxi ride north of centre). ▸▸ *See Transport, page 677.*

Getting around The busy hub around MG Marg, pedestrianized in the evening, is a 15-minute walk from end to end. Away from the bazars, the town is pleasant for walking around (see Rajesh Verma's *Sikkim: A Guide and Handbook*, Rs 140). For excursions further afield you'll need to hire a jeep or taxi; rates are fixed and displayed on the back window.

Tourist information Sikkim ⓘ *MG Marg, Gangtok Bazar, T03592-221634, www.sikkimtourism.com, daily 0800-2000.* Apply for permits here.

Sights

At the north end of town the **Government Institute of Cottage Industries** ⓘ *Mon-Sat 0900-1230 and 1330-1530, closed 2nd Sat of month*, produces a wide range of local handicrafts, including wool carpets, jackets, dolls, handmade paper, carved and painted wooden tables. Items are of high quality (and prices) but there's no parcel service for sending packages home.

Enchey Monastery is 3 km northeast of the main bazar. It's a pleasant walk that takes you past the small **flower garden** at Whitehall (orchids on show March-April). Originally built by the eighth Chogyal in the 1840s, the present building dates from 1909. Religious dances are held in August and December; see Festivals, page 670.

The **Palace of the Chogyal** is only open once a year in the last week of December for the Pang Lhabsol Festival. Below this is the **Tsuklakhang** or Royal Chapel, standing on a high ridge where royal marriages and coronations took place. This is the major place of worship and has a large and impressive collection of scriptures. The interior houses Buddha images and is lavishly decorated with woodcarving and murals. Visitors are welcome during Tibetan New Year but may not be permitted at other times; photography is prohibited.

Moving south along the road you pass the **Secretariat** complex on your left. Beyond this is the **Deer Park**, loosely modelled on the famous one at Sarnath, with a statue of the Buddha. From here a **ropeway** ⓘ *0930-1700, Rs 50 one way*, descends the hill to Deorali Bazar, near which is the unique **Namgyal Institute of Tibetology** ⓘ *Mon-Sat 1000-1600*, established in

1958 to promote research into Tibet and Mahayana Buddhism. The library maintains a large and important Buddhist collection with many fine *thangkas*, icons and art treasures on display. To the south, surrounded by 108 prayer wheels, the gold-topped **Do-drul** Chorten contains relics and a complete set of holy texts. Nearby is a monastery for young lamas with large statues of the Buddha and Guru Padmasambhava.

1 Gangtok

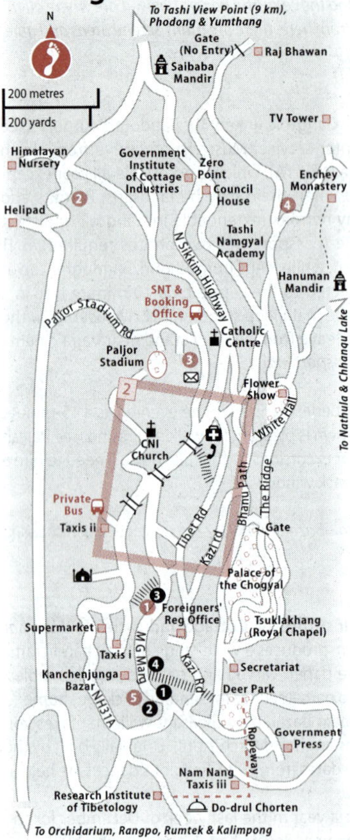

Gangtok maps
1 Gangtok, page 672
2 Gangtok centre, page 673

Sleeping
Denzong Inn **1**
Hidden Forest **2**
Norkhill **3**
Siniolchu Lodge **4**
Tashi Delek & Blue Poppy Restaurant **5**

Eating
China Pilot **1**
Oberoi's Barbique **2**
Ocean **3**
Taste of Tibet **4**

Tashi Viewpoint via Enchey Monastery is 9 km away. Go early to watch the sun rise over the Khangchendzonga range. **Hanuman Tok**, a hill with a small temple, 8 km away, is another viewpoint.

Around Gangtok

Rumtek Monastery → *Colour map 4, A2.*

24 km southwest of Gangtok. Altitude: 1550 m. www.rumtek.org.

Standing in one of the attractive lower valleys with fluttering prayer flags, the monastery is the headquarters of the Kagyu ('Black Hat') order of Tibetan Lamaistic Buddhism. The monks fled Tibet after the Chinese invasion, bringing with them whatever statues, *thangkas* and scriptures they could carry. At the invitation of the Chogyal they settled in Rumtek. The new monastery was built in the 1960s in the traditional style as a faithful copy of the Kagyu headquarters in Chhofuk, Tibet, with typical monastic paintings and intricate woodwork. The **Dharma Chakra Centre** houses the unique golden reliquary of the 16th Gyalwa Karmapa, who died in 1981.

Visitors are dropped at the gate at the bottom of a gentle uphill path; passports may be checked. A 20-minute walk past local houses and curio shops leads to the monastery. Outside, you may see pairs of monks chanting prayers in their quarters or catch some younger ones playing football in the field. The main hall is impressive but lacks Pemayangtse's atmosphere. Visitors are welcome but are asked not to disturb the monks during prayers (0400, 1800, except Sunday). In the adjacent building you can watch the wood-block printing of texts on handmade paper. The peace is broken when hordes of tourists arrive.

Fambong Lho Wildlife Reserve

ⓘ *25 km from Gangtok across the Ranipool Valley, Rs 5.*

A little beyond Rumtek, this reserve has serene jungle walks in the hills, with waterfalls, mountain views, orchids and wildlife (marten, fox, red panda, boar; even wolf and sloth bear). You are free to go on your own (though this is not advisable on some stretches) and can climb or walk for one to six days. There are log huts at Golitar and Tumin with cheap beds.

Saramsa Gardens → *14 km south of Gangtok.*

The gardens contain more than 500 indigenous species in what is more like a botanical garden with large orchidariums. The best season is March to early May; you may be disappointed at other times. The road to Saramsa forks east off the NH31A a few kilometres south of **Tadong**, which has a couple of places with rooms and refreshments including the fairly modern **Tashi Tadong** and the **Daragaon**.

Kyongnosla Alpine Sanctuary → *Altitude: 3200-4100 m. Permit required (see box, page 661).*

Located 31 km from Gangtok on the Nathula highway, which until 1962 was the main route for mule trains trading between Gangtok and Lhasa in Tibet, the sanctuary extends from the '15th Mile' check post to the ridges bordering Rongchu and Chhangu Lake. Among the junipers and silver firs the sanctuary harbours some rare ground orchids and rhododendrons and numerous medicinal plants including the *Panax pseudo-ginseng*. The best time to visit is April-August and October-November. The Himalayan marmot has been reintroduced here. Other mammals include goral, serow, red panda, Himalayan black bear, Tibetan fox and yellow-throated martens, together with very colourful pheasants.

Two easy treks lead to the Shiv Gufa (1 km from the road), where you can crawl into a tiny cave on your hands and knees to see a small Siva image and several tridents embedded in the soft floor, and to Kheding (4 km), while longer and more difficult ones to Simulakha, Namnang Lakha and Nakcho are very scenic. Trekkers with permits for Chhangu may return from Nakcho via the lake.

Chhangu (Tsomgo) Lake → *36 km from Gangtok. Altitude: 3774 m.*

The holy Chhangu Lake lies 5 km further along the precipitous Nathula road. Completely frozen in mid-winter, it's best to visit March-May and September to mid-December. There are excellent views of Khangchendzonga from the nearby ridge and superb sunsets, but the lake area is overcrowded and spoilt by snack kiosks and loud Hindi music. You can walk around the 1-km-long lake in about an hour. Permits are needed (apply with photo and passport a day ahead) or there are organized tours. If you go independently, allow six hours for the return trip; a jeep/minivan costs about Rs 800-1000.

2 Gangtok centre

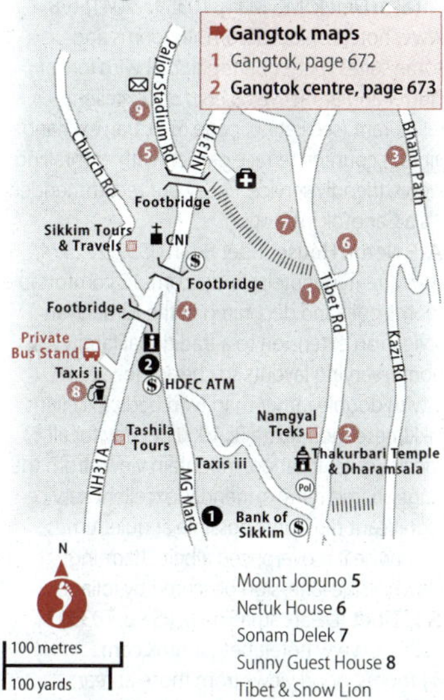

Sleeping
Chumbi Residency **1**
Lhakpa **2**
Mintokling Guest House **3**
Modern Central Lodge **4**
Mount Jopuno **5**
Netuk House **6**
Sonam Delek **7**
Sunny Guest House **8**
Tibet & Snow Lion Restaurant **9**

Eating
Masala **1**
Rasoi/Blue Sheep **2**

Gangtok and around listings

For Sleeping and Eating price codes and other relevant information, see Essentials pages 38-42.

Sleeping

Gangtok *p671, maps p672 and p673*

Heating is essential in winter. Some budget hotels charge extra for heaters. Dogs bark all night so take some ear plugs. Discounts are available Jul-Aug and Dec-Jan.

L Nor-khill, T03592-205637, www.elginhotels.com. Beautiful rooms in an old palace, meals included, spacious public rooms, good views and gardens, curio shop, once excellent but standards are slipping.

A Chumbi Residency, Tibet Rd, T03592-206618/9, www.thechumbiresidency.com. Modern hotel decked out with traditional Tibetan furniture, plenty of marble, good rooms with old fashioned but perfectly adequate bathrooms, clean and quiet, dynamic manager. Good restaurant (see Eating, page 675).

A Tashi Delek, MG Marg, T03592-204156-8, www.hoteltashidelek.com. 46 rooms and some suites (better on top floors) with lots of clutter and attractive *objets d'art*, excellent restaurant (see Eating, page 675), bar, exchange, airlines counter, terrace garden with enthralling views, friendly service. Pricey but recommended, it's a Gangtok institution.

A-B Netuk House, Tibet Rd, T03592-222374, www.heritagehotelsofindia.com. 12 comfortable rooms built and decorated in the Himalayan style in an extension to a traditional family home, varying layouts so check a few, only 2 with double rather than twin beds. Excellent Sikkimese food (extra Rs 1000 per day for all meals), quiet location, mountain views from the huge shared terrace, friendly, excellent service. Significant discounts possible at quiet times, otherwise it is overpriced albeit charming. Down a side lane, sign obscured by foliage.

B-C Tibet (Dalai Lama Trust), PS Rd, T03592-202523, www.hoteltibetgangtok.com. 34 rooms, good views from those at rear, restaurant, bar, exchange, Tibetan books and crafts for sale, very pleasant, peaceful and charming (but some critical reports).

B-D Sonam Delek, Tibet Rd, T03592-202566, www.hotelsonamdelek.com. Balconied rooms with bath, best choice for views of the mountains, pleasant restaurant (great local food), terrace garden, some **A** suites.

C Hidden Forest, 2 km from centre in Middle Sichey, T03592-205197, www.hiddenforestretreat.org. 12 spacious, timber-floored rooms in the home of a forest officer and his family, set in a 3-acre nursery full of orchids and medicinal plants, with paths leading into the surrounding forest, homegrown organic food served in cozy dining room, a unique choice. Recommended.

C Mintokling Guest House, Bhanu Path, T/F03592-204226, www.mintokling.com. Prettily decorated rooms with bath, timber-floored on 2nd storey or carpets on ground/1st, among working veg gardens, flowers, lawns and prayer flags, good restaurant, charming Sikkimese owner. Recommended, book in advance through the website as often full.

C-D Mount Jopuno (Sikkim Tourism), PS Rd, T03592-203502. Out of 12 rooms, 4 de luxe, good restaurant and service, eager young staff (at Institute of Hotel Management).

D-E Denzong Inn, near Kanchenjunga Bazar, T03592-202692, denzonginn@rediffmail.com. Set in an interesting complex with faint Chinese-mafia feel, 24 rooms and good if slightly threadbare suites (**C**). Some rooms on the terrace come with proper green baize card tables, and Chinese restaurant isn't bad.

D-E Sunny Guest House, by jeep stand on NH31A, T(0)8533-287109, www.sunnyguesthouse.com. Pleasantly old-school rooms with bath, TV, carpets, super K'dzonga views from top floor, forgettable room service. Handy location means now walking up hills with luggage.

D-F Travel Lodge, Tibet Rd, T03592-203858, travellodge.gangtok@gmail.com. Decent modern hotel, with rooms at the front that are spacious and light. Can get a good deal on smaller side rooms, a good step up from backpacker places but at budget prices.

All have reliable geysers and TV; affable staff.

E Modern Central Lodge, MG Marg, T03592-204670, www.modern-hospitality.com. Simple, clean and colourful rooms with bath, best in front on upper floors, a bit noisy, great lounge packed with books on Sikkim, basic but good restaurant, good jeep tours (long-established, using high standard accommodation), very friendly and helpful.

E-F Kanchen Residency, Tibet Rd, T(0)9232-513781, kanchenresidency@indiatimes.com. Great mountain views from front-facing large rooms, carpets, new bathrooms though some damp patches appearing. Cheaper side rooms, also older and shabbier, some rooms have squat toilets. Discounts possible.

E-F Siniolchu Lodge, near Enchey Monastery, T03592-202074. Good views, 24 rooms on 3 floors up a hillside, some with bath and heating, restaurant, bar, tours.

F-G Lhakpa, Tibet Rd, T03592-223002. Cheap rooms, some with bath, even cheaper dorm, restaurant (excellent Chinese), views.

Rumtek Monastery *p672*

A Bamboo Retreat, Sajong Village, T0353-220 2049, www.sikkim.ch. Gorgeous views of the mountains, set on the edge of paddy fields, with 10 large comfortable bedrooms in different colour themes. The Swiss owner has created a wonderful retreat, with meditation, massage, creative workshops, and a library to relax guests. Organic food is delicious, half-board. Recommended.

A Martam Village Resort, Gangkha, Upper Martam, 5 km from the monastery, T03592-203314. Overlooking the valley, 11 pleasant, traditional-style thatched cottages with large picture windows, good meals included in the price. Recommended.

F Sungay, near monastery gate. Basic rooms in old guest house, cleanish shared toilet, friendly.

Kyongnosla Alpine Sanctuary *p673*

F Log Huts, 2 rooms in each at Kyongnosla and Lamnang Lakha. You must apply for a permit (Rs 5) to Chief Wildlife Warden, Sikkim Forest Dept, Deorali, Sikkim 737102, to enter the sanctuary.

Eating

Gangtok *p671, maps p672 and p673*

Lightly spiced Sikkimese meat and vegetable dishes are usually eaten with noodles or rice. *Churpi* is a local yak milk curd cheese.

TT Blue Poppy, Tashi Delek (see Sleeping). International. Good meals at Rs 450 (Sikkimese recommended, order in advance) though the restaurant itself is soulless.

TT Snow Lion, in **Hotel Tibet** (see Sleeping). Good Tibetan and Sikkimese in elaborately decorated room, but service can be glacial and vegetarian meals may come with flecks of meat.

TT Tangerine, in **Chumbi Residency** (see Sleeping). Down in the bowels of the hotel, this appealing split-level restaurant has a mix of Thai cushions and standard seating, and a nice little terrace for drinks. Sikkim dishes are good (seasonal availability) and there is a diverse menu of Indian, Chinese, continental plus some Thai mains.

TT Taste of Tibet, MG Marg. The better of 2 similarly named places, serving excellent Tibetan soups and noodles to an accompaniment of whatever internet radio channel happens to be tuned in.

TT-T Masala, MG Marg under Karma Hotel, T03592-20484, www.masalatherestaurant.in. Open 0800-2230. Funkily decorated and fastidiously clean, serving pure vegetarian Indian (paneer is their strength) and Chinese. Intimate and cosy, serves alcohol.

T Baker's Cafe, branches dotted around town (including MG Marg). Reliable for pastries and authentic brown bread.

T China Palate, Star Cinema Building, MG Rd. Open 1030-2030. Excellent value Chinese in a laid-back place with a bar.

T Famous Roll Corner, New Market, Lal Bazar Bridge, T(0)97759-52175. Delicious, fast and famous rolls are spicy or not, depending on your choice of sauce.

T Hotel Paradise, National Highway (by footbridge near Sikkim Tourism). Open 0730-2130 for cheap and filling *thalis* in a functional canteen environment, veg/egg/fish start at Rs 35 with good variety of dishes.

T Marwari & Gujarati Thali (Jain Restaurant), Tibet Rd. Open 0700-2100. Utterly delicious thalis, that are endlessly refilled for Rs 50, a taste sensation. Plus great momos and competent staff.

T Rasoi (aka **Blue Sheep**), MG Marg (by the Tourist Office). Opens at 0830. Wonderful South Indian breakfast items and a broad spectrum of multi-cuisine items, served in an airy, clean, smart family restaurant. Creamy thick lassis and juices are particularly notable, gets very busy at night.

Bars and clubs

Gangtok *p671, maps p672 and p673*

Bars in most restaurants serve local spirits distilled at Rangpo: brandy, rum, whiskey and liqueurs. *Chhang* is the unofficial national drink. A bamboo mug (*thungba*) is filled with fermented millet through which boiled water is allowed to percolate; the drink is sipped through a bamboo straw. You can enjoy this mildly intoxicating pleasant drink for over an hour simply by adding hot water. More conventional alcoholic drinks are available at Gangtok's numerous Wine Shops.

Live & Loud, Sonam Gyatso Marg, Tibet Rd. Continental café-style ambiance on the balconies overlooking the street, and fun live music at weekends.

Pub 25, Naya Bazar, T03592-205324. Spacious with comfy leather seating, this smart but uninspired new bar has a large selection of cocktails/shooters etc and a good food menu (including Israeli and Italian dishes), music is inoffensive. Pricier than some. Smoking section upstairs.

The terrace at the hotel **Tashi Delek** has exceptional views and is recommended for a sunset beer (Rs 75).

Shopping

Gangtok *p671, maps p672 and p673*

Books

Good Books, down steps off MG Marg near Gandhi statue. Lots of choice including many local interest titles.

Handicrafts

Traditional crafts include carpets, *thangkas*, traditional jewellery, shirts, boots and fur caps and woodcarvings.

Charitrust Handicrafts, **Tibet Hotel**. Modest collection, good quality, books on Tibet.

Handcrafts Centre, Zero Point. Mon-Sat 0930-1230, 1300-1530. Artisans can be seen at work.

Markets

Lal Bazar (Haat on Sun, closed Thu) is an interesting walk down the steps off MG Marg. It winds up at Kanchenjunga Shopping Plaza, an uninspiring concrete edifice, but selling some unusual local fruit and vegetables and yak's milk cheese fresh and dried (skewered on string).

Festivals and events

Rumtek Monastery *p672*

Feb Special colourful **Losar** dances are held 2 days before the Tibetan New Year (check date). Arrive 3 days earlier to see rehearsals without masks, *pujas* and ceremonies are held during this period.

Jun The important **Rumtekchaam** is performed on the 10th day of the 5th month of the Tibetan calendar; masked dancers present 8 manifestations of the Guru Rimpoche. Tours in Jul-Aug from Gangtok.

Activities and tours

Gangtok *p671, maps p672 and p673*

Mountaineering

Himalayan Mountaineering Institute, based in Darjeeling, see page 660.

River rafting

Rafting trips are arranged by the **Department of Tourism**, and private travel agents, on the Tista River (from Dikchu or Singtam, 1-hr drive from Gangtok) and the Rangit River (from Melli Bazar, 4 km from Tista Bridge, which has a **Wayside Inn** for refreshments, or **Rishi**). 1-day trips cost US$45, 2-day US$70, some Grade II-III rapids. A 2-hr ride is ideal for the beginner; wonderful scenery.

Tour operators

Cheap tours of Gangtok are arranged from the Tourist Information Centre, T03592-221634, open daily 0800-2000. **Morning tour**: Government Institute of Cottage Industries, Deer Park, Chorten, Research Institute of Tibetology, Orchid Sanctuary and Enchey Monastery. In season daily 0930-1230. **Afternoon tour**: Orchidarium and Rumtek Monastery, 1400/1430-1700. **West Sikkim**: Requires a minimum 16. Fri at 1030 returning Sun 1600 (2 nights).

Some companies offer tours before the season opens, eg to North Sikkim in Jan/Feb when roads and trekking routes may be closed. To support ecologically responsible tourism, contact **Ecotourism Society of Sikkim (ECOSS)**, T03592-228211, www.sikkiminfo.net/ecoss/, for a list of approved tour operators. Most agents help to arrange Protected Area Permits for trekkers.

Adarsh Tours, Treks and Expeditions, 17 Tse-ka Commercial Complex, 31A National Highway Rd, near Old Private Taxi Stand, T03592-205053. Experienced in adventure travel for over 10 years, arranges trekking and mountaineering expeditions (to remote peeks), rafting, safaris plus travel-booking services and escorted tours in India and adjacent countries.

Modern Treks & Tours, MG Marg, T03592-204670, moderntreks@hotmail.com. Quality tour operator, good for North Sikkim where their accommodation is the best on offer.

Namgyal Treks and Tours, 75 Tibet Rd, T03592-223701, www.namgyaltreks.net. Experienced, well organized.

Singalila, NH31A, opposite petrol pump, T03592-221556, singalila@hotmail.com. Arranges coach tours and river rafting.

Yuksom Tours and Treks, Borong House (above Telephone Exchange), T03592-226822, www.yuksom-tours.com. Professional, well-equipped treks at the higher end of the market with great food, car hire Rs 1500-2500 per day.

Transport

Gangtok *p671, maps p672 and p673*

Air The nearest main airport is Bagdogra (124 km away), see page 660. **Air India**, above Green Hotel, MG Marg, T03592- 223354, www.airindia.com, 1000-1300, 1400-1600; **Jet Airways**, RNC, MG Marg, T03592-223556, www.jetairways.com.

To get to Gangtok: taxi Rs 1600, 4-5 hrs; or get bus/shared taxi to Siliguri and change to jeep for Gangtok (Rs 140, 4½ hrs). A daily government 5-seater helicopter (T03592-281372) runs between Bagdogra and Gangtok; unreliable since heavy cloud or rain prevents flights, but is an excellent option (Rs 2000 each way, 45 mins, 10 kg luggage) with mesmerizing views.

Bus SNT (Sikkim Nationalized Transport) Bus Stand, NH31A, 0900-1300, 1400-1600. Private buses from **West Point Taxi Stand**, NH31A, T03592-202858. Some only operate in the high season. Buy tickets 24 hrs in advance; hotels can help. Journeys cost between Rs 70-110. To **Rumtek**, 1600 1 hr; **Namchi**, 0730 (4½ hrs); **Namok**, **Phodong, Chungthang**, **Mangan**, 0700 (return 1500); **Pelling** via **Gezing**, 0700 (5 hrs); **Jorethang**, 0700. North Bengal service to **Kalimpong**, 75 km, 0715 (4-4½ hrs); to **Siliguri** (5 hrs), 0630-1330 (4½-5 hrs).

Taxi/jeep Shared taxis (Rs 10) run along NH31A, stopping at marked taxi stops. Charter taxis charge fixed, relatively high rates around town. Rates for sightseeing negotiable; around Rs 1600 per day for travel outside Sikkim, Rs 1300 within Sikkim; plus night halt Rs 200. Tourist office has a list of official rates.

There are several jeep stands in the city. Most useful to travellers is the main private bus and jeep stand on NH31A, office hours 0600-1800, T03592-2203 862. Advisable to book a day in advance. For South Sikkim: to **Ravangla**, 0700, 0745, 1230 and 1430, 3 hrs, Rs 80; several to **Namchi**, between 0700-1500, 3 hrs, Rs 90; and **Jorethang**, every 30 mins between 0630-1600, 3 hrs, Rs 100. To West Sikkim: **Gezing**, 0700, 1200, 1230 and 1300, 4 hrs, Rs 120; **Pelling**, 0700, 1230 and 1300, 4½ hrs, Rs 150; **Yuksom**, 0700 and 1300, 5½ hrs, Rs 150, via **Tashiding**, 4 hrs, Rs 130. Lal Bazar jeep stand is the hub for East Sikkim: **Rumtek**, Rs 35; Nam Nang Jeep Stand, Rs 10 taxi ride south from MG Marg (for North Bengal). North Jeep Stand: for Mangan, Rs 100. Share jeeps leave on a fixed schedule, most departing early morning; much quicker and more frequent than buses to most destinations.

Train Nearest mainline railhead is **NJP**. Computerized Bookings, SNT Compound, 0800-1400 (till 1100 on Sun).

Rumtek Monastery *p672*

Bus From **Gangtok** about 1600 (1 hr) along a steep narrow road, returns about 0800.

Jeep Shared jeep: Rs 35 each; last return to Gangtok 1300. **Rumtek** to **Pemayangtse**, 4 hrs.

Taxi Taxi from Gangtok, Rs 350 (return Rs 600, 1½-hr wait).

Directory

Gangtok *p671, maps p672 and p673*

Banks 1000-1400, Sat 1000-1200 (difficult to get exchange). **State Bank of India**, MG Marg. **State Bank of Sikkim**, Tibet Rd. Several ATMs on MG Marg, including UTI, HDFC.

Internet **Omni Cafe** (1st floor) above Panorama Photo Studio, T03592-220329. Open 0830-2000 daily, Rs 25 per hr, clean and pleasant with a café but only 3 pcs. Several others on Tibet Rd and MG Marg, Rs 30 per hr.

Medical services **STNM Hospital**, Stadium Rd, opposite Hotel Mayur, T03592-222944.

Post GPO, Stadium Rd, Mon-Fri 0900-1700, Sun 1000-1400, has reliable parcel service.

South and West Sikkim

This enchanting region contains the essence of Sikkim: plunging rice terraces, thundering rivers, Buddhist monasteries etched against the sky, and the ever-brooding presence of Mount Khangchendzonga. ▸▸ *For listings, see pages 680-683.*

Jorethang

For travellers, the market town of Jorethang on the Sikkimese border is chiefly a transport hub for destinations in south/west Sikkim and West Bengal. Darjeeling is just 30 km away, but to enter Sikkim via Jorethang (bypassing Gangtok altogether) it is necessary to obtain permission in advance as the border post does not issue permits. There is not much to see in the grid-pattern town itself; a stroll east along the riverbed from the suspension bridge brings you to a colourful hybrid temple with shady pagodas, and the market is a good place to stock up on food supplies. Near the bridge is the SNT bus station, opposite which is a **tourist information centre** ⓘ *daily 0830-2000*, where keen staff proffer a couple of brochures. The three jeep stands, plus hotels and bars, are in the street behind and beyond the tourist office. There's an ATM machine (State Bank of India) on Street 1, opposite the Walk In Hotel.

Ravangla and Maenam Sanctuary → *Altitude: 2155-3260 m.*

Ravangla (Rabongla), 65 km southwest of Gangtok, is a small village whose timber- fronted main street retains a strong frontier flavour and serves as the gateway to one of Sikkim's best day hikes. The 12-km trek through the sanctuary to **Maenam Peak** (3260 m), which dominates the town, takes about three hours. The sanctuary harbours red panda, civet, blood pheasant and black eagle, and is most beautiful when the magnolia and rhododendron are in bloom in April-May. **Bhaledunga**, another 30-minute hike along the ridge, on the steep cliff edge above the Tista, juts out in the shape of a cockerel's head.

Towering above it on the 'wish-fulfilling hill' of Samdruptse is a 45-m statue of Guru Padmasambhava, the patron saint of Sikkim who spread Buddhism to Tibet in the ninth century. Resplendent in copper and a coat of bronze paint, the **statue** ⓘ *0700-1700, free*, can be seen from Darjeeling, around 40 km away. A ropeway from Namchi is planned; otherwise take a taxi, Rs 250 return. Not to be outdone, a 33-m statue of Siva has risen on another hill at Solophok outside Namchi, which was completed in 2011.

The administrative headquarters of West Sikkim, **Gezing** (Gayzing, Gyalshing), 105 km west of Gangtok, is at the crossroads of bus routes and has a busy market with food stalls, shops, a few hotels (none recommended) but little else to detain visitors.

Tashiding

Forty kilometres north of Gezing is the gold-topped **Tashiding monastery**, built in 1716, which stands on a conical hill between the Rathong and Rangit rivers on a spot consecrated by Guru Rimpoche. The most sacred *chorten* in Sikkim is here, even the sight of it brings blessing and washes away sins. It contains relics of the Buddha, and stands in a field of many *stupas* surrounded by *mani* walls. You will see numerous stones with high-class carvings of *mantras* around the monastery, made on site by a prolific artisan. Following the track beyond the *stupa* field brings you to a small cemetery where cremations are performed, and continuing down (beware of leeches) is an area designated for 'burial of dissenters' who are left in wooden boxes while their clothes and possessions are thrown down the hillside.

The main *gompa* has been refurbished and all the frescos repainted; these particularly fine murals are intricate and expansive, with Tantric motifs. Pilgrims attend the **Bumchu Festival** in February/March to drink water from the sacred pot which has never run dry for over 300 years. Below the monastery is the small **Tshchu Phur Cave** where Guru Rinpoche meditated; follow the trail on the left of the main steps to the monastery until you see a small building, opposite which is a painting on the rocks. Carry a torch if you plan to crawl into the cave.

Pelling → *2 km from the monastery and 9 km by road from Gezing.*

Pelling sits on a ridge with good views of the mountains. The rather bleak little town has three areas linked by a winding road, Upper and Middle with views and hotels, and Lower Pelling with banks and other services. Upper Pelling is expanding rapidly with new hotels springing up to accommodate honeymooners from Kolkata, and makes the most convenient base for visits to Pemayangtse. You can also visit the **Sanga Choelling Monastery** (circa 1697), possibly the oldest in Sikkim, which has some colourful mural paintings. The hilltop monastery is about 3 km along a fairly steep track through thick woods (about 30 minutes). The area is excellent for walking. The **Sikkim Tourist Centre** ⓘ *Upper Pelling, near Garuda, T03595-250855*, is helpful.

Pemayangtse → *112 km west of Gangtok. Altitude: 2085 m.*

A full-day trip by car from Gangtok, along a very scenic road, Pemayangste (Perfect Sublime Lotus) was built during the reign of the third Chogyal Chador Namgyal in 1705. It is about 7 km from Gezing, above the main road to Pelling.

The awe-inspiring **monastery** ⓘ *0700-1600, Rs 10, good guided tours, 0700-1000 and 1400-1600 (if closed, ask for key), no photography inside*, Sikkim's second oldest, is near the start of the Dzongri trek. For many, the monastery is the highlight of their visit to Sikkim; it certainly has an aura about it. Take an early morning walk to the rear of the monastery to see a breathtaking sunrise in perfect peace. The walls and ceiling of the large *Dukhang* (prayer hall) have numerous *thangkas* and wall paintings, and there is an exceptional collection of religious artworks including an exquisite wooden sculpture on the top floor depicting the heavenly palace of Guru Rimpoche, the *Santhokpalri*, which was believed to have been revealed in a dream. The old stone and wood buildings to the side are the monks' quarters. According to tradition the monks have been recruited from Sikkim's leading families as this is the headquarters of the Nyingmapa sect. Annual *chaam* dances are held in late February and in September.

The **Denjong Padma Choeling Academy** (DPCA), set up to educate needy children, runs several projects, such as crafts and dairy, and welcomes volunteers, who can also learn about Buddhism and local culture. The meditation centre offers courses and can accommodate visitors for a small charge and volunteers for free at the new hostel (see below); a rewarding experience. Volunteers can spend up to six weeks during March-December. Contact Jules Stewart, London, T0207-229 4774, jjulesstewart@aol.com.

Rabdanste, the ruined palace of the 17th- to 18th-century capital of Sikkim, is along the Gezing-bound track from the monastery, 3 km from Pelling. From the main road, turn left just before the white sign 'Gezing 6 km', cross the archery field and turn right behind the hill (road branches off just below Pemanyangtse). Follow the narrow rocky track for 500 m to reach the palace.

Khecheopalri Lake and Yuksom

A road west of the Pelling–Yuksom road leads to this tranquil lake where the clear waters reflect the surrounding densely wooded slopes of the hills with a monastery above; Lepchas believe that birds remove any leaf that floats down. Prayer flags flutter around the lake and it is particularly moving when leaflamps are floated with special prayers at dusk. The sanctity of the lake may be attributed to its shape in the form of a foot (symbolizing the Buddha's footprint), which can be seen from the surrounding hills. The lake itself is not visually astonishing, but walks in the surrounding hills are rewarding and a night or two can easily be spent here. There are staggering views from the tiny hamlet by the *gompa* on the ridge (accessed by the footpath in the car park, just ask for the *gompa*) where homestays are available. You can trek from Pelling to Yuksom via the lake without a permit in two days, a beautiful journey.

Yuksom (Yuksam), 42 km north from Pelling by jeepable road, is where the first Chogyal was crowned in 1641, thus establishing the kingdom of Sikkim. The wooden altar and stone throne stand beside Nabrugang *chorten*, with lovely wall paintings and an enormous prayer wheel, in a beautifully peaceful pine forest. During **Buddha Purnima** (the Buddha's birthday) in late April and May, women from the local community gather mid-morning to sing and pray in a low-key yet moving ceremony. Below Nabrugang, past pretty houses, **Kathok Lake** is a small green pool though the reflection of the prayer flags that surround it are photogenic, and the monastery of the same name nearby is worth the short uphill walk.

Although most people are in Yuksom because it is the starting point for the Gocha La trek, the village makes a quiet and relaxing base for a few days' stay, with several day walks leading out from the centre. It's a 45-minute climb to the attractive **hermit's retreat** at **Dhubdi** (circa 1700) above the village. A rewarding three-hour hike leads to **Hongri Monastery**, about halfway to Tashiding, mainly following a stone trail. Descending the path between the Yangri Gang and Panathang hotels, it is 45 minutes to a wooden bridge over the Phamrong Khola which has deliciously icy pools (accessed from the other side). The trail continues to Tsong village, with a sweet homestay in the first cottage in Lower Tsong (Rs 100 per night, three beds, contact Tara Chetri T(0)9775-816745) and onwards up the steep hill to the plain stone-slab monastery. It's a perfect picnic spot, with stone tables among the mossy *chortens* and glorious views. From here, it is another three to four hours' walk to Tashiding.

South and West Sikkim listings

For Sleeping and Eating price codes and other relevant information, see Essentials pages 38-42.

Sleeping

Jorethang *p678*

F Hotel Namgyal, near SNT bus station, T03595-276852. Best choice in town with simple rooms (doubles only), typically slab-floored with walls painted split colours. Fans, TVs, hot water in garish bathrooms. Best at the back, where they have windows as well as balconies. Decent restaurant and cheap beer.

F-G Hotel Janta, near tourist information, T03595-276104. Basic place but fills up fast, only 7 rooms, dorm beds for Rs 120 and single-person discounts. Restaurant is cosy, with good *thukpa* and momos, well-stocked bar.

Ravangla *p678*

A Kewzing homestays, Kewzing village, 8 km towards Legship, T03595-260141, T094348-65154, ktdc@sikkimfoundation.org. A community-driven programme allows guests to stay in family homes in a quiet Bhutia village. Rooms vary widely, some better value than others, and there is a maximum 2-night stay in any house to ensure even distribution of income. A rare and fascinating insight into traditional rural life. Rates include all meals and guide; cultural programme extra Rs 1000.

C-E Mt Narsing Village Resort, 15th Mile (bookable through **Yuksom Tours & Treks**, see page 677). 2 rooms in a bungalow (**E**) situated in a delightfully flower-filled garden, with incredible views over the terraced valley slopes to a monastery. Plus an isolated annex, 1 km from the main road, which is more luxurious. Quaint rooms are carpeted, homely, with simple bamboo furniture and modern bathrooms (geysers). Good meals are served in the open-sided restaurant.

D-F Maenamla, Kewzing Rd, T03595-263861, maenamla@hotmail.com. Smartest choice in town, with carpeted rooms, clean baths, hot water from geyser, friendly and welcoming.

F Melody, Ralang Rd, T03595-260817. Basic but charming rooms with wooden floors, clean, friendly.

Tashiding *p678*

D-G Yatri Niwas, by monastery gate (250 m south of jeep stand), T(0)9832-623654. Brand new and with teething problems (running water not guaranteed) therefore generous discounts possible. 4 rooms are tasteful and comfortable (pay more for wood walls and parquet floors), or dorm beds for Rs 150. Pleasant gardens.

F Dhakkar Tashiding Lodge, 200 m down from jeep stand, T03595-243249. Large concrete rooms with great views from the back, 3 or 4 beds, best of the shared bathrooms in town.
F Mt Siniolchu, main market (50 m beyond Blue Bird), T03595-243211. Friendly, 5 clean rooms including 3 big and beautiful ones on the upper floor, shared bath, hot water.
F-G Blue Bird, main market, 50 m uphill from jeep stand, T03595-243248. Very basic old-school rooms, single/double/dorm, all share a bath (hot water if there is electricity), run by a kind Bengali family. Restaurant below is by far the best place to eat.

Pelling *p679*

Power and water cuts can last 4 hrs or more and dogs often bark all night. Several **F** in Upper Pelling, with excellent views if you can overlook the often dubious cleanliness. Best is **Kabur**, T03595-258504, with a terrace restaurant and internet. With over 30 places to choose from, and hotel building going on unchecked, the following are recommended.
D-E Sikkim Tourist Centre, Upper Pelling, near Jeep Stand, T03595-258556. Simple rooms, some with views, cheaper on roadside, rooftop restaurant (cooking excellent but service limited; only snacks after 1400), tours.
E Norbu Ghang, Main Rd, T03595-250566. Rooms with bath, better views from those away from road, views from the terrace are superb. Restaurant.
E-F Haven, Khecheopalri Rd, Middle Pelling, T03595-258238. Clean doubles with hot running water.
F-G Garuda, Upper Pelling, near bus stop, T03595-250614. Rooms in basic lodge with bath, hot water (heaters Rs 100-150), dorm, restaurant (breakfast on rooftop, mountain views), internet, backpackers' favourite.
F-G Sisters Family Guest House, near **Garuda**, T03595-250569. 8 simple clean rooms, shared bath (bucket hot water). Friendly, great food.

Pemayangtse *p679*

A Mount Pandim, 15-min walk below monastery, T03593-250756, www.elginhotels.com. Sparkling bright rooms with bath, some with beautiful mountain views, in freshly renovated and upmarket lodge.

Khecheopalri Lake *p679*

A couple of families take in guests at homestays in the small village on the ridge (25 mins' walk up the hill, left up the path by the car park near the lake). Highly recommended for a relaxing interlude with stunning mountain views.
F Pilgrims' Lodge, on the edge of the lake. Enterprising Mr Tenang provides Sikkimese porridge and millet bread (and much more), and leads short circular hikes around the lodge.
F Trekkers Hut, 400 m before the lake on the left. Simple rooms and friendly staff provide food, information and a bonfire at night.

Yuksom *p679*

A-B Yuksom Residency, Main Rd, T03595-241277. Huge new construction out of keeping with the village around, white marble predominates and terrace lit-up at night. Rooms are huge and well appointed (especially the **AL** suite with parquet flooring), furnishings high quality rather than rustic, flatscreen TVs, lots of light and some with good views. Giftshop has some nice jewellery, restaurant a bit stiff.
C Tashigang, T03595-241202, hoteltashigang@rediffmail.com. Intimate rooms with lovely views (some with balcony), wooden floors, striped bedspreads and simple tasteful furnishings. Aging in a good way. Marble and tile bathrooms, some **C** suites, everything clean and polished. Own vegetable patch and restaurant (see Eating, below), peaceful garden. Very welcoming and staff are on the ball.
E-F Hotel Pemathang, Main Rd, T03595-241221, T(0)9002-090180, kinzongbhutia@yahoo.com. Chic reception with lavish flowers, but most rooms big and blank, carpeted, paint already getting shabby. However, the 2 back doubles with balconies and view of Kabur peak are nice, others share a balcony.
E-F Hotel Yangrigang, Main Rd, T03595-241217, yan13jan@yahoo.com. The main backpacker hub, with an acceptable restaurant and internet facilities (Rs 60 per hr) as well as good standard rooms (doubles Rs 400-500) mostly with twin beds, bigger and better views upstairs (Rs 700-800), geysers and comfy beds. Manager is informative and pleasant. Treks easily arranged from here.
F Dragon, Main Rd, T03595-241290, T(0)9733-244759. Friendly and sociable guesthouse with

clean small rooms (shared bath, hot water unreliable). Nice outdoor area, and good for a snug beer/meal in the family kitchen.

F **Pemalingpa Cottage**, just below Tashigang Hotel. Lovely little homestay, basic, only 2 rooms one of which is delightfully rustic and sunny. Outside toilet, hot buckets provided, family make every effort to make guests welcome. Highly recommended.

Eating

Pelling *p679*

Don't miss local *chhang* brewed in the area.

† **Alpine**, Khecheopalri Rd (below **Garuda**, see Sleeping). Chinese, Kashmiri especially good. Yellow, wooden cottage run by friendly Ladakhi lady.

† **Mock-Too**, Upper Pelling opposite **Sikkim Tourist Centre** (see Activities and tours, below). Excellent fresh snacks including *momos*, paratha and samosas.

Yuksom *p679*

A 2000 curfew is imposed by the police in Yuksom, when all activities move indoors – get your food order in early.

††-† **Tashigang** (see Sleeping, above). Cheery hotel restaurant is unpretentious, with delicious Sikkimese specialities (seasonal) such as nettle soup and wild fern curry. Other more typically Indian dishes also available. Ingredients come from their vegetable garden or surrounding countryside. Recommended.

† **Gupta's**, on the main street, attracts travellers to its social outdoor seating area, and does surprisingly good quesadillas and pizza, as well as *thali* (no refills) and yak's cheese *momos*. Next door, **Yak** is of a similar ilk and with friendlier owners.

Activities and tours

Pelling *p679*

Help Tourism, **Sikkim Tourist Centre**, T03595-250855. Good information and tours.

Yuksom *p679*

Most people arrange their trek in Gangtok/ Darjeeling; US$30-40 per person per day, depending on service. There's a growing trend for agents to tag on extra group members (picked up in Yuksom) who get a greatly discounted price. While this works well for some parties, it can leave a sour taste for those who are funding the majority of the trip.

Transport

Buses can be crowded, especially during **Pujas** and **Diwali**. Quicker, more convenient jeeps run to/from Gangtok and between all main towns in the west, often leaving early morning; check locally for current times. If no jeep is going directly to your destination, it may be best to go to Gezing, Jorethang or Namchi, which have frequent services in all directions. Direct jeeps leave from all three towns for **Siliguri**, 4-5 hrs, and **Darjeeling**, 2-3 hrs.

Jorethang *p678*

The SNT bus stand has services to: **Siliguri**, 0930, Rs 71; **Gangtok**, 1230, Rs 72; **Rangpo**, 1230, Rs 45; **Namchi**, 0830, 1200 and 1600, Rs 20; **Soreng**, 1400, Rs 20; **Pelling**, 1500, Rs 50; **Ravangla**, 1200, Rs 45; **Teesta**, 0930, Rs 32.

There are 3 jeep stands in Jorethang, close together on the south side of town near the Tourism Office. The main stand serves: **Siliguri**, departures between 0700-1600, Rs 90, 2½ hrs; **Gangtok**, from 0700-1600, Rs 100, 3 hrs; **Karkabita** (for Nepal), 0730, 0830, 0930 and 1330, 4 hrs, Rs 130; **Kalimpong**, 0900-1430, Rs 60, 1½ hrs and **Gezing**, regular service, 2 hrs, Rs 55. The block slightly uphill behind the main stand has jeeps for: **Tashiding**, 1½ hrs, Rs 70 and **Yuksom**, 3 hrs, Rs 90, from 1200-1500. Closer to the Tourism Office, jeeps for: **Darjeeling**, from 0800-1530, 2 hrs, Rs 90 and **Namchi**, 0600-1100, 45 mins, Rs 25.

Tashiding *p678*

Several jeeps from **Gezing** via **Legship**, and from **Yuksom** (early morning). To **Jorethang**, 0700 & 0800, 1½ hrs, Rs 70; **Gangtok**, 0630 and 0700, 3½ hrs, via **Ravangla**, 1½ hrs, Rs 50; **Yuksom**, 1100 and 1300, 1 hr, Rs 50; **Gezing**, 1½ hrs, 0730, Rs 60. Tashiding is a day's trek from **Pemayangtse** or **Yuksom** (allow 7 hrs).

Pemayangtse *p679*

From **Gezing**: bus or shared jeep to monastery, 1000-1430, Rs 15-20. From **Pelling**, taxi Rs 50 one way, easy walk back.

Pelling *p679*

To **Gezing** reasonably frequent jeeps (Rs 20) or walk along steep downhill track, 1-2 hrs. To **Khecheopalri Lake**: last bus at 1400, or you can walk 5 hrs (part very steep; last 3 hrs follows road, with short cuts). Buses and shared jeeps to **Yuksom** (until 1500, 3 hrs), **Damthang**, **Gangtok** (4 hrs); **Darjeeling** via Jorethang, tickets from stand opposite **Hotel Garuda**, Rs 180. **Siliguri**: SNT bus 0700; tickets sold at provision store next to **Hotel Pelling** where bus starts, and stops uphill at jeep stand near **Garuda** hotel.

Khecheopalri Lake *p679*

From **Pelling**: jeep share, 1½ hrs; to **Tashiding** (3 options): **1)** 0700 bus to Gezing, then jeep. **2)** Bus to Yuksom 1500 (irregular) from 'junction', 10 km from lake, overnight in Yuksom, then bus at 0700 (or jeep) to Tashiding, 1 hr. **3)** Hitch a lift on the Pelling to Tashiding jeep, which passes the 'junction'at about 1400 (try sitting on top of jeep to enjoy the beautiful scenery).

Yuksom *p679*

Shared jeeps leave from near Gupta's restaurant, buy ticket a day ahead in season. To **Pelling**, 0630, 2½ hrs, Rs 60; **Gezing**, 0630, 3 hrs, Rs 60; **Jorethang**, 0630, 3½ hrs, Rs 90 via **Tashiding**, 1 hr, Rs 60; **Gangtok**, 0630 and 1300, 5 hrs, Rs 160; **Pelling**, 0630, 2½ hrs, Rs 60. To reach **Khecheopalri Lake**, private hire only.

North Sikkim

You'll need to join an organized tour to explore the outposts of the Yumthang and Tsopta valleys, where traditional Lepcha and Bhotia villages huddle beneath mountains that rear steeply towards Tibet. The scenery is spectacular, though the road well travelled – particularly by Indian tourists. Expect to be restricted in your movements and spend long days in a jeep. May to July is the best time to see primula and other alpine flowers in bloom in the high-altitude meadows.
▸▸ *For listings, see pages 685-686.*

Phodong → *Colour map 4, A2.*

The renovated early 18th-century monastery of Phodong is 1.5 km above the north Sikkim Highway, about 2 km before Phodong village. The track is accessible by jeep, and tours to North Sikkim usually include a visit to the monastery on the way backdown to Gangtok. Otherwise, it is a pleasant walk up to the *gompa* where friendly monks show you around; there are especially beautiful frescoes and wall paintings. A further hike of 2 km takes you to picturesque **Labrang** monastery of the Nyingmapa sect, unique in that it retains its original structure undamaged by time or fire. Below the track nearby is the ruined palace of **Tumlong**, the capital of Sikkim for most of the 19th century.

The Singhik Viewpoint is a worthwhile stop before Phodong, with an unusual aspect on the Kangchendzonga range if skies are clear.

Phodong to Chumthang

In addition to several police checkpoints, the road beyond Phodong passes through some mildly attractive villages, fluffy forested slopes, and past dramatic waterfalls on the way to bustling **Mangan**, the district headquarters, and then **Singhik**. In both places there are perfectly acceptable lodges with good views and a friendly welcome to the rare independent traveller who stops here (though Mangan has more opportunities for decent eating and transport connections). Beyond Singhik, permits are required for foreign tourists which travel agents arrange in Gangtok, along with vehicle, driver and accommodation, as part of a tour. The road and the Tista River part ways at Chumthang, dominated by a hydroelectric project, with one track leading northeast to the Yumthang Valley and the other northwest to Tsopta Valley.

Yumthang Valley → *Colour map 4, A2. 135 km north of Gangtok.*

Lachung sits among spectacular mountain scenery at 2400 m and acts as a gateway to the increasingly popular Yumthang Valley. Still run on the traditional democratic Dzomsa system, the village is a stronghold of Bhotia culture, though the daily influx of tourists from Gangtok and the rapid construction of lodges to accommodate them has begun to take its toll. Hotels, most over three storeys high, have started to dominate the series of small villages which make up Lachung. The central point is Faka Bazar by the suspension bridge, worth crossing to visit pretty **Lachung Monastery** (open mornings/evenings only) up the opposite hillside in Sharchog village; shortcuts past patches of cultivation and neat pastel-hued homes reach the monastery in about 30 minutes. The paintings of demons and the Wheel of Life in the porch are particularly dramatic, and a path behind the *gompa* climbs up for gorgeous views back down the valley.

The road north to Yumthang passes through the **Shingba Rhododendron Sanctuary**, which has 24 of the 40 rhododendron species found in Sikkim, along with attractive aconites, gentians, poppies, saxifrages, potentillas and primulas. May-July is the best time to see these and other high-altitude alpine flowers growing in the wild.

The valley slopes of **Yumthang**, the 'Valley of the Flowers', are surrounded by imposing snow-clad mountains. Glaciers flow down slopes forested with fir towards the milky turquoise water of Lachung River and, in summertime, the valley floor is indeed carpeted with purple primulas. This is the official end-point for foreigners, and a place where all jeep tours stop for a photo opportunity. A few minutes' walk from the refreshments stalls on the main road are unappealing sulphur hot springs; from here a stone path leads into a lovely hour's walk through the rhododendron forests. It is (unofficially) possible, and usually offered (for an additional charge), to continue for a further hour along the rough road to Samdong (Tibetan, meaning 'bridge'). It is a dramatic drive with views above the pink rocky riverbed and pale khaki-coloured valley walls, to a closer encounter with snowy peaks. Indians tourists can carry on further to Zero Point, but the final halting point for foreigners is signalled by impromptu noodle and liquor stands.

Tsopta Valley

The Bhotia village of **Lachen**, 122 km from Gangtok, is the chief overnight stop when visiting the stark landscape of the Tsopta (Chopta) Valley. Lachen straggles along one edge of the road along the steep river valley, surrounded by thick alpine forests. The 2000-strong population are known as Lachenpas, and traditionally were yak-herders. An unmetalled road follows the river from Lachen, up the mountainside past ponies, yaks and rhododendron cover to the more interesting village of Thangu 30 km north, where accommodation is also available. On the edge of **Thangu** (altitude 4260 m) potato, cabbage and spinach are cultivated from the arid land, men and women sharing the workload in the fields. Traditional sturdy wooden dwellings and dry stone walls demarcate the land and the scent of smouldering pine prevails. The wide river valley beyond the village has spectacular views towards the mountains and Tibet. It is a seasonal grazing ground for yaks, here grow Jatamasi plants which is used to make incense. Foreign tourists spend a couple of hours wandering the valley floor, covered in wild flowers in summer, while Indian tourists can continue up to Gurudongmar Lake (foreigners need a special permit from the Home Affairs Office in Delhi for this, which is not guaranteed).

Thangu is the starting point for the gruelling trek to **Green Lake** (altitude 5120 m) which takes around 14 days in total. Special permits are necessary that require at least six weeks to arrange – they are expensive, as is the entire venture as all supplies and equipment have be carried. The high cost means that tourist numbers are few. Much of the trek goes through thick spruce and fir forests, as well as the huge variety of rhododendron species for which the region is famed.

North Sikkim listings

For Sleeping and Eating price codes and other relevant information, see Essentials pages 38-42.

Sleeping

Phodong *p684*

F Yak and Yeti, T03595-260884. Quiet and clean. Some rooms with toilet, hot water in buckets, but meals are pricey. Recommended.

Yumthang Valley *p684*

Lachung

The tour agents determine where you stay in North Sikkim. Try to specify a certain hotel if you don't wish to leave it up to chance, and the cost will be built into the tour accordingly. Particularly nice options are listed below, in descending order of price and comfortableness, but all hotels are of a higher standard than budget travellers will be accustomed to.

Taagsing Retreat (aka **Modern Residency**), Singring, www.modernresidency.com. Lachung's most comfortable accommodation is a striking bottle-green pagoda on the southern edge of the village. The 22 Sikkimese-styled rooms are arranged on several levels, with balconies and great views. Pure veg restaurant serves buffet meals, plus there's a meditation hall, bar, library and little museum. Staff are lovely. Tours booked through **Modern Treks & Tours**, Gangtok (see page 677).

Golden Fish, Main Rd, Singring, T03592-214852, www.hotelgoldenfishitgo.com. This very clean and warm option has friendly, relaxed and efficient staff. Excellent food is prepared and high standards maintained. Some new suites with TVs. Can book a package through the website.

Season House, up the hill, Singring, T(0)9434-449042. Quaint rooms in the old log cabin or brand new ones in the chalet, excellent bathrooms. Quietly efficient staff and good food. At the highest point on the road, save for the Rimpoche's residence next door, so fabulous views from the terrace.

Sela Inn, Faka Bazar, T03592-214808. Older and shabbier, this well-established welcoming place has an atmospheric restaurant and is closer to any 'action' in town.

Sonam In Lodge, Main Rd, Singring, T03592-214830. Run by a charming family who speak little English, cosy simple rooms in an old-style wooden building are Rs 300, hot buckets provided.

Transport

Phodong *p684*

From Gangtok, take a bus to the start of the jeep track, 0800 (2 hrs), Rs 35; return bus, 1500. Jeeps travel up to **Labrang** monastery. Jeeps to **Mangan** leave in the early morning and it is advisable to book at least 2 days in advance.

Trekking in Sikkim

Trekking is the biggest draw of Sikkim for many foreign tourists, and no previous experience is necessary as most treks are at 2000-3800 m. The trail to Dzongri (three to four days) or on to Gocha La (8-9 days) is the most popular and climbs to nearly 5000 m, but there are plenty of day trails on clear paths that are less physically taxing. An added attraction is that dzos *(a cross between a cow and a yak) can carry your gear instead of porters, though they are slower. The trekking routes also pass through villages that give an insight into the tribal people's lifestyle. With this area coming under threat from pollution by rubbish left by trekkers, be sure to choose a trekking agency that enforces good environmental practices; ECOSS in Gangtok (see page 676) can point you in the right direction.* ▸▸ *For listings, see pages 674-677, 680-683 and 685-686.*

Ins and outs

Best time to visit March to late May and October to early December. April is best for flowers. **Leeches** can be a problem in the wet season below 2000 m.

Permits Foreigners must be in a group of at least two before applying for a trekking permit. Approved trekking agents can assist with applications. Areas open to foreigners include the Khangchendzonga Biosphere Reserve near Yuksom (permits can be arranged in a morning, from either Gangtok or Yuksom), the Lachung and Yumthang valleys in North Sikkim (very expensive, 6 weeks' processing time) and Chhangu in East Sikkim (one day).

Maps and guidebooks *Sikkim: A Guide and Handbook*, by **Rajesh Verma**, updated annually, introduces the state and has descriptions of treks, with trekking profiles. The **U 502** sheets for Sikkim are *NG 45-3* and *NG 45-4*. PP Karan published a map at the scale of 1:150,000 in 1969 (US$3, available from the Program Director of Geography, George Mason University, Fairfax, VA 22030, US). A very detailed map is *Sikkim Himalaya* (Swiss Alpine Club) – Huber 1:50,000, £16.

Khangchendzonga National Park

ⓘ *Rs 180 (5 days), Rs 50 for each extra day, camera Rs 10, porter Rs 5, pack animal Rs 5, camping Rs 25 per tent, trekkers' hut Rs 50 per person, Tsokha Hut Rs 75 per bed.*

The park offers trekking routes through picturesque terraced fields of barley, past fruit orchards to lush green forests of pines, oak, chestnut, rhododendrons, giant magnolias, then to high passes crossing fast mountain streams and rugged terrain. Animals in the park include Himalayan brown bear, black bear, the endangered musk deer, flying squirrel, Tibetan antelope, wild ass and Himalayan wild goat. The red panda lives mostly on treetops at 3000-4000 m. There are about 600 species of bird.

The Khangchendzonga trek falls within the newly designated national park, from which all forms of industry and agriculture have been officially banished. The park office in **Yuksom**, about 100 m below the trekkers' huts, has interesting exhibits and helpful staff.

The classic trekking route goes from **Yuksom to Gocha La** (variously spelt Goecha La and Gochela). This eight- to nine-day trek includes some magnificent scenery around Khangchendzonga, and there are excellent views as you travel up the Ratong Chu River to the amphitheatre of peaks at the head of the valley. These include Kokthang (6150 m), Ratong (6683 m), Kabru Dome (6604 m), Forked Peak (6116 m) and the pyramid of Pandim (6720 m) past which the trail runs.

Trekkers' huts (**F**), in picturesque places at Yuksom, Tsokha and Dzongri, are fairly clean with basic toilets. Bring sleeping bags; meals are cooked by a caretaker.

Day 1 Yuksom to Tsokha An eight-hour climb to the growing village of Tsokha, settled by Tibetan refugees. The first half of the climb passes through dense semi-tropical forests and across the Prek Chu on a suspension bridge. A steep climb of two hours leads first to **Bakhim** (2740 m), which has a tea stall, a forest bungalow and good views. The track goes through silver fir and magnolia to Tsokha (2950 m), the last village on the trek. Trekkers' hut and campsite at Tsokha.

Day 2 Tsokha to Dzongri Mixed temperate forests give way to rhododendron. **Phedang** is less than three hours up the track. Pandim, Narsingh and Joponu peaks are clearly visible, and a further hour's climb takes the track above the rhododendrons to a ridge. A gentle descent leads to Dzongri (4030 m, 8 km from Bakhim). There is a trekkers' hut and campsite. Dzongri attracts pilgrims to its *chortens* holding Buddhist relics. From exposed and windswept hillsides nearby are good panoramic views of the surrounding mountains and of spectacular sunrises or sunsets on Khangchendzonga.

Day 3 Dzongri to Thangshing A trail through dwarf rhododendron and juniper climbs the ridge for 5 km. Pandim is immediately ahead. A steep drop descends to the Prek Chu again, crossed by a bridge, followed by a gentle climb to Thangshing (3900 m). The southern ridge of Khangchendzonga is ahead. There is a trekkers' hut and campsite.

Day 4 Thangshing to Samity Lake The track leads through juniper scrub to a steeper section up a lateral moraine, followed by the drop down to the glacial and holy Samity Lake. The surrounding moraines give superb views of Khangchendzonga and other major peaks. You can't camp at the lake; a new campsite is 1 km away at Lammuney.

Day 5 To Zemathang and Gocha La and return The climb up to Zemathang (4800 m) and Gocha La (4900 m) gives views up to the sheer face of the eastern wall of Khangchendzonga. It is a vigorous walk to reach the pass, but equally impressive views can be gained from nearby slopes. Sometimes guides stop before the official 'Gocha La' viewpoint, be wary of this and ask the advice of other trekkers that you meet on the way. Much of the walk is on rough moraine.

Day 6 Samity Lake to Thangshing Return to Thangshing. This is only a two-hour walk, so it is possible to take it gently and make a diversion to the former yak grazing grounds of Lam Pokhari Lake (3900 m) above Thangshing. The area is rich in medicinal plants, and you may see some rare high-altitude birds and blue sheep.

Days 7 and 8 Thangshing to Tsokha The return route can be made by a lower track, avoiding Dzongri. Dense rhododendrons flank the right bank of the Prek Chu, rich in birdlife. Day 7 ends in Tsokha village. The next morning you retrace your steps to Yuksom.

Other treks in Sikkim

It's possible to trek from town to town, if you're prepared to do a lot of road walking and ask villagers to show you short cuts. One of the best circuits, for up to seven days but also enjoyable in smaller sections, begins from Pelling or Pemayangtse, descending through terraced fields to the Rimbi Khola river, then climbing up to Khecheopalri Lake. From here you can easily reach Yuksom in a day, then continue on to Tashiding, and either return to Pemayangtse or climb eastwards towards Kewzing and Ravangla.

Northeast States

Contents

Footprint features

At a glance

Getting around Flights are best to most of the state capitals; buses, jeeps or car hire elsewhere.

Time required 1-2 days for Kaziranga; 3 days for Shillong and Cherrapunji; a week each for central and western Arunachal; a week or more to explore tribal Nagaland.

Weather Wet and humid most of the year, especially in Jul which produces extraordinary downpours; Dec-Mar can be cold.

When not to go In the monsoon, unless you crave the sight of rain.

★ **Don't miss ...**

1 Kaziranga National Park (to see the Indian greater one-horned rhino), page 697.
2 Rafting and fishing in Nameri National Park, page 698.
3 Archery Stakes in Shillong, page 716.
4 Cherrapunji, the wettest place in the world, page 717.
5 Spectacular four-day journey to remote Tawang Monastery, page 726.
6 Khonoma 'green' village, page 737.

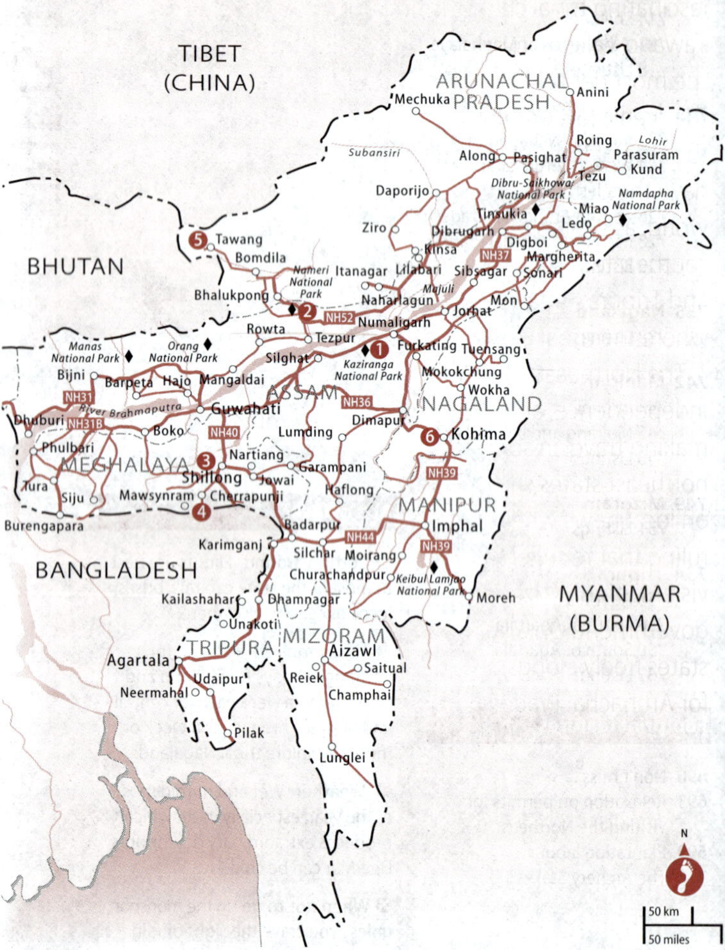

The Northeast is a true frontier region. It has more than 2000 km of border with Bhutan, China, Myanmar (Burma) and Bangladesh and is connected to the rest of India by a narrow 20-km-wide corridor of land – aptly coined the 'chicken neck' by locals. One of the most ethnically and linguistically diverse regions in Asia, each of the northeastern states has its distinct culture and tradition.

Arunachal Pradesh, only recently opened to visitors, is home to fascinating tribal cultures and the Buddhist enclave of the majestic Tawang Valley – more like Tibet than India. To its south, Assam, the most densely populated and largest of the states, occupies the scenic lowlands of the Brahmaputra Valley and attracts visitors to some of India's best national parks. Meghalaya's beautiful hills have the dubious distinction of being the wettest region in the world, as well as one of the friendliest. The little-visited four southeastern states of the region – Nagaland, Manipur, Mizoram and Tripura – make up a fascinating area, hilly, remote, and a zone where the tribal cultures of South and Southeast Asia intertwine.

The Northeast has been a politically sensitive region since Independence, and insurgency continues to surface occasionally making travel in some areas unsafe. Advice on travel to the northeast states should be sought before travel and keep an eye on local news when there. Since 1 January 2011, the 60-year-old ruling that required foreigners to obtain permits in advance to visit Manipur, Mizoram and Nagaland has been revoked by the government. On a year's trial basis, foreigners can enter these states freely alongside Assam and Tripura. Permits are still required for Arunachal Pradesh, as it is a sensitive border region.

Assam

→ *Population: 31.1 million. Area: 78,438 sq km.*

The lush valley of the Brahmaputra, one of the world's great rivers, provides the setting for Assam's culturally rich and diverse communities. Although it is tea that has put the state on the world map, the fertile river valley is home to generations of rice farmers, and tribal populations continue to have a significant presence. A highlight of any visit is Kaziranga National Park, where the population of Asian one-horned rhinos has been steadily increasing over recent years meaning that sightings are virtually guaranteed. ▸▸ *For listings, see pages 702-713.*

The land

Geography Assam stretches nearly 800 km from east to west, the length of the broad floor of the Brahmaputra Valley. The Himalaya to the north and the Shillong Plateau to the south can be clearly seen. The state is dominated by the unpredictable Brahmaputra, constantly changing course to create new sandbanks, and encasing Majuli, the largest riverine island on earth. Earthquakes are common; one in 1950 was estimated as the fifth biggest earthquake ever recorded.

Climate Unless you really want to see rain, avoid the monsoon. Assam is in one of the wettest monsoon belts in the world. Even the central Brahmaputra Valley, protected by the rain shadow of the Shillong Plateau, has over 1600 mm of annual rainfall. The rest of the Assam Valley has up to 3200 mm a year, mostly between May and September. Although summer temperatures are high, from December to February it can be cold, especially at night.

History

The Ahoms, a Shan ruling tribe, arrived in the area in the early 13th century, deposed the ruler and established the kingdom of Assam with its capital in Sibsagar. They later inter- mixed with Aryan stock and also with existing indigenous peoples (Morans, Chutiyas) and most converted to Hinduism. The Mughals made several attempts to invade without success, but the Burmese finally invaded Assam at the end of the 18th century and held it almost continuously until it was ceded to the East India Company in 1826. The British administered it in name until 1947 though many areas were beyond their effective control.

People

Nearly 90% of the people continue to live in rural areas. The ethnic origin of the Assamese varies from Mongoloid tribes to those of directly Indian stock. There has been a steady flow of Muslim settlers from Bengal since the late 19th century. The predominant language is Assamese, similar to Bengali although harder to pronounce. In Assamese, 'how are you?' is *'Apni kene koya?'* and 'good' is '*bahal*'.

Modern Assam

The Assam Valley is in a strategically sensitive corridor for India, lying close to the Chinese frontier. Its sensitivity has been increased by the tension between local Assamese and immigrant groups. The failure of the AGP (Assam Gana Parishad) to hold its alliance together and to control the violence that has become endemic through Assam contributed to its downfall. Congress returned to power in the 2006 elections under Chief Minister Tarun Gogoi, a lawyer and long serving member of the Lok Sabha, and won seven of the 14 Lok Sabha seats in 2009. The state has suffered a long-running low-intensity conflict and in late 2006 and early 2007 a number of bombings occurred in the capital Guwahati. The most troubled area is still the beautiful Cachar Hills in the south, and it is not recommended to visit this region in particular. Seek advice from your consulate and local tour agencies before travelling.

Relaxation on permits for visiting the Northeast

In a major change to the rules on 1 January 2011, the government has decided to withdraw the permit system for foreigners visiting Nagaland, Manipur and Mizoram on a year's trial basis. Foreigners visiting these states now only need register themselves at the Foreigners Registration Office (FRO) within 24 hours of arrival. However, a **Restricted Area Permit (RAP)** is still required for Arunachal Pradesh. Visitors to Assam, Meghalaya and Tripura do not need permits, but may need to register on arrival/departure at the airport.

Should the permit system be reinstated in 2012, you can apply for RAPs from the **Ministry of Home Affairs** (Foreigners Division, Lok Nayak Bhavan, Khan Market, New Delhi 110003, T011-2461 1430). Send two photos and allow up to six weeks. Groups of four and married couples stand a better chance. Indians still require **Inner Line Permits (ILPs)** from the Ministry of Home Affairs.

In **Kolkata** RAPs are issued at the **Foreigners Regional Registration Office (FRRO)**, 237A AJC Bose Road, T033-2283 7034, Monday-Friday 1100-1630 but come between 1100-1400; ask for the Officer in Charge. Bring one photo and a copy of your passport and visa. It takes a minimum of 24 hours for permits to be issued, which essentially means come in the morning and return the following afternoon to collect. The cost is at the discretion of the FRRO, which at the time of writing was Rs 1395 per person for each state. At the FRRO, it is necessary to apply as a group of four for each of the states; however, a married couple (with an original marriage certificate in English) can enter **Nagaland** as a pair. Permits are valid for a maximum of 10 days for Nagaland and Arunachal, four days for **Manipur**. It might be necessary to bring a copy of your confirmed return flight ticket to Manipur when applying for the RAP.

Local travel agents can help and save you some bureaucratic hassle. They can obtain permits within a few days, and even supply by fax or email, with a commission charge of around Rs 1000. This is especially worthwhile for **Arunachal Pradesh**, as agents can now obtain permits for individual travellers, at a cost of around US$100 plus commission, valid up to 30 days. **Mizoram** travel agents can arrange 10-day permits for individuals, Rs 500, the process takes about one week. See listings under each state for tour agents who can help.

Guwahati → *For listings, see pages 702-713. Colour map 4, B4.*

Despite its commanding position on the south bank of the mighty Brahmaputra, it is easy to forget that Guwahati is a riverside town, the waterside having little impact on people's lives. The main entrance point for visitors to the northeastern states, the city retains a relaxed and friendly atmosphere. Paltan Bazar, where most visitors arrive, is very busy and crowded as are the narrower streets and markets of Fancy Bazar to the west.

Ins and outs → *Population: over 1 million.*

Getting there LBG International Airport (23 km) has flights from Kolkata, Delhi, Bagdogra and airports throughout the Northeast, plus flights from Bangkok and Bhutan. Assam State Transport (ASTC) runs an air-conditioned coach to the city for Rs 100 (ticket office near Arrivals); pre-paid taxis cost Rs 400 or shared taxis Rs 120. Some 1150 km from Kolkata, Guwahati is at the junction of NH31, 37 and 40, and is well connected by road to all major centres of the northeast. The railway station is in the central Paltan Bazar, while long distance private buses arrive at the ISBT (Interstate Bus Terminal), 8 km from the centre, connected to the city centre by canter (Rs 10). ▸▸ *See Transport, page 710.*

Getting around It is easy to walk around the two main commercial areas of Paltan and Pan (pronounced *Paan*) Bazars, which have most of the hotels and restaurants. Citybuses or (red) canters are cheap and very efficient around the city (conductors call out the stops), whereas auto-rickshaws need hard bargaining. Political incidents in the city mean there is a visible military presence. Carry a torch when walking at night; large holes in the pavement lie in wait to plunge unwary travellers straight down into the sewers.

Tourist information Information booths for Assam, Nagaland and Meghalaya are at the airport, with useful maps; also a counter for Assam at the railway station. Assam Tourism ⓘ *Tourist Lodge, Station Rd, T0361-254 7102, www.assamtourism.org, daily 1000-1630.* Assam Tourism Development Corporation (ASTDC) ⓘ *AK Azad Rd, Paryatan Bhawan, T0361-263 3654.*

Guwahati

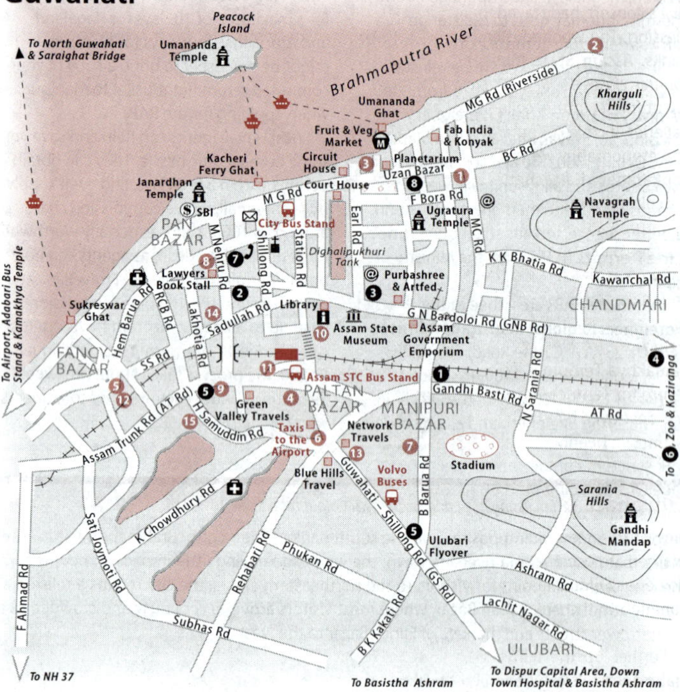

Sleeping
Baruah Bhavan 1
Bellevue 2
Brahmaputra Ashok 3
Broadview Lodge 14
Centre Point 13
City Palace 4
Dynasty & Tandoor 5
Nandan 6
Nova 12
Orchid & Magnolia Restaurant 7
Prag Continental 8
Railway Retiring Rooms 11
Rajmahal 9
Starline 15
Tourist Lodge 10

Eating
4 Seasons 8
Beatrix 1
Breeze & Sun Flower 7
Ming Room 6
New Zealand Natural 3
Paradise 4
US Pizza 2
Woodlands 5

N
300 metres
300 yards

History

Guwahati, on the site of the ancient capital of a succession of local chieftains, was once known as Pragjyotishpur ('City of Astrology'). The **Navagrah** ('nine planets') **Temple** on a hill here was the ancient centre of astronomy and astrology. It was also a centre of learning and a place of Hindu pilgrimage. In the seventh century, Hiuen Tsang described its beautiful mountains, forests and wildlife. Today it is the business capital while **Dispur**, the 'Capital Area', is just to the south.

Sights

The 10th-century **Janardhan Temple**, on the bank of the Brahmaputra, was rebuilt in the 17th century and has been modernised since. The Buddha image here uniquely blends Hindu and Buddhist features. The **Umananda** (Siva) **Temple** ⓘ *Peacock Island in the Brahmaputra, reached by 10-min ferry ride, Rs 10, 0930-1630*, was built by an Ahom king in 1594, in the belief that Uma, Siva's consort, had stayed there. Enter the candlelit rear shrine with other pilgrims to receive a blessing. The wooded island can be circled by the footpath and gives pleasant views of the banks. **Assam State Museum** ⓘ *Tue-Sun 1000-1630 (Mar-Sep), 1000-1545 (Oct-Feb), ticket counter closes 1300-1330, closed 2nd and 4th Sat of the month, Rs 5*, has an extensive and beautiful sculpture collection, and covers epigraphy and textiles in recently refurbished galleries. It is also informative on the neighbouring cultures, with sections on village life, crafts and ethnography – a reconstruction of a mud-brick thatched house can be explored. **Srimata Sankaradeva Kalakshetra** ⓘ *Panjabari, on road to Narangi, Tue-Sun 0800-2200, Rs 10, bus No 8*, is a cultural complex set up to serve as a centre for Assamese dance, drama, music, fine arts and literature ('a theme park of Assamese life'). It features a museum, theatre, artists' village and heritage park. **Assam State Zoo and Botanical Gardens** ⓘ *off Zoo Rd, 6 km southwest of the city, Rs 50, cameras Rs 70*, is a cheap way to get up close to one-horned rhinos, snow leopards, tigers and snakes for those who don't want to take their chances at Kaziranga or other national parks.

Excursions from Guwahati

Kamakhya Temple, 7 km west, is believed to be an old Khasi sacrificial site on Nilachal Hill. A centre for Tantric Hinduism and Sakti worship, rebuilt in 1665 after the 10th-century temple was destroyed by a Brahmin convert to Islam. It typifies Assamese temple architecture with its distinctive beehive-shape *sikhara* (spire), the nymph motifs and the long turtleback hall. The dark sanctum contains the creative part of the goddess which is said to have fallen here, see page 612, and pilgrims enter to touch the wet *yoni* of Kamakhya (Sakti). Apart from the carved stone symbol of Sakti's genitals, there are (unusually) no other images of the goddess inside the sanctum. Western visitors are allowed into the sanctum but should be prepared for the highly charged atmosphere and to walk barefoot on a floor awash with the sacrificial blood of a goat. No Bengali would leave Assam without visiting this temple, hence queues can be immense (a donation to the priests of Rs 500 will grant instant access, or go at dawn to be first in line).
▸▸ *See Festivals, page 708.*

Further up the hill is a smaller temple and a viewpoint with panoramic views of the Brahmaputra. It can be visited by bus from MG Road (towards Adabari Bus Stand); ask to be dropped near Kamakhya. From here take a canter (red minibus) from AT Road to the temple or walk up the steep and slippery rocky path at the back of the hill. An intense and memorable outing.

Basistha Ashram, 12 km south of Guwahati, is believed to be sage Basistha's (Vasistha) hermitage. It is a scenic spot with three mountain streams nearby.

North Guwahati is a sleepy town across Saraighat Bridge, which can be reached by public ferry from Sukreswar Ghat (Rs 5). The **Digheswari Temple** is worth a visit where the hazy little village is pleasant for a wander; ask the priests about the rare golden langurs that live here.

Around Guwahati

Hajo, a friendly and peaceful town, 34 km across the river, produces bell-metal work and is sacred to three religions. **Hayagriba Madhab Hindu temple** is said to contain a Buddhist relic. Some believe this is where the Buddha attained Nirvana. Its hilltop location is more spectacular than the temple itself. The main street behind the tank stocked with fish leads to an old **Ganesh temple** after 2 km; a friendly priest might allow you in. Hajo is also sacred to Muslims; the **Pao Mecca Mosque**, 3 km further, built by Pir Ghiasuddin Aulia is supposed to have a *pao* (quarter) of the sanctity of Mecca. Take a bus from Adabari Bus Stand, which drops you off at the Hindu temple (one hour, last return at 1600 but very crowded; you may have to travel on the roof).

The small village of **Sualkuchi**, on the north bank of the Brahmaputra, is famous for silk production from non mulberry leaf-fed worms, hence its unique natural colour. Every household is involved with weaving of *muga*, *endi* or *pat* silk; prices are 30% cheaper than in Guwahati. Take the ferry from Guwahati or a bus from Hajo (20 minutes).

Pabitora is a small wildlife sanctuary a two-hour drive from Guwahati (60 km), on the border of Nagaon and Kamrup districts; rhinos can be found here. **Madan Kamdev**, 45 km north of Guwahati, has been called Assam's Khajuraho due to the dozen or so erotic sculptures that adorn the walls. The temples which may date from the 11th to 12th centuries, possibly reconstructed in the 18th, are believed to be associated with tantric practices. The principal shrine to Uma-Mahesvara (Siva-Parvati) is still in use and the setting, surrounded by fields and nature, is picturesque. Buses from Guwahati go to Baihata on NH31, 4 km from the site; rickshaws transfer visitors from there.

Manas National Park → *For listings, see pages 702-713. Colour map 4, A3.*

A World Heritage Site and one of India's most beautiful sanctuaries, Manas lies in the Himalayan foothills, southeast of the river Manas, on the Assam–Bhutan border. Over half the area is covered with tall grass and patches of deciduous woodland. This changes to dense semi-evergreen forest in the upper reaches and to conifer on the hills towards Bhutan.

Ins and outs

Manas has two ranges; the main range is entered from Bansbari village and the eastern range from Koklabari village, both have offices which issue permits to the park. Charges for entry and camera are similar to Kaziranga (see below). Jeeps are available to rent for around Rs 1000 per day, you can walk or cycle, and sometimes elephant safaris are possible.

Pick up provisions beforehand. Use the Bansbari gate with a Forest Range Office to get to Mathanguri inside the park (20 km, 30 minutes). Book a car or taxi for the return trip. If you travel around dawn (0500) and before (1600) you may see some wildlife. Travel is not allowed after sunset. The maximum temperature in summer is 35°C, minimum 18°C; the winter maximum is 24°C, minimum 7°C. Annual rainfall is 4100 mm. The best season is November to March. Take something warm, a hat and shoes for wading through slippery streams.

Background

Manas, with a buffer zone of 2800 sq km (including two other far-flung sanctuaries) and a core area of 391 sq km, was demarcated in 1977-1978 when the preservation programme Project Tiger was launched. At the last count there were more than 80 tigers. Until 2005, Manas was the hideaway of Bodo rebels and poachers and generally deemed unsafe for visiting tourists and with the tiger population in steep decline, labelled as a UNESCO 'World Heritage Site in Danger'. This has been turned around since the creation of a separate 'Bodoland' in northwest Assam and the park is becoming a model for eco-tourism and community involvement, particularly in the Eastern Range which is managed by **Manas Maozigendri Ecotourism Society (MMES)**.

Sights

The forests are home to most of the larger animals found in Kaziranga, most common being wild buffalo, swamp deer, hog deer, sambar and elephant. Some 22 of the animal and bird species are on the endangered list of the **IUCN** including the rare capped and golden langur, which can be seen among the flowering trees, mostly on the Bhutan side. There are also pigmy hog, hispid hare, slow loris, clouded leopard, rhino and tiger. The sanctuary is rich in birdlife (over 400 species), and attracts migratory flocks of redstarts, forktails, mergansers and ruddy shelduck. The eastern range is famed for its huge population of Bengal floricans, which are best spotted December-March. Otters are frequently seen in the Manas River.

Kaziranga National Park → *For listings, see pages 702-713. Colour map 4, A5.*

Kaziranga was declared a game sanctuary in 1916 to save the Indian greater one-horned rhino and became a national park in 1974. It is now a World Heritage Site. In a beautiful setting on the banks of the Brahmaputra, and with the Karbi Anglong Hills to the south, the 430-sq-km park combines elephant grass mixed with thorny rattan cane, areas of semi-evergreen forest and shallow swamps.

Ins and outs

Guwahati is 215 km from Kohora, the main entry point to Kaziranga on the NH37. Park roads open 0800-1100, 1400-1630. Foreigners Rs 250. Camera fees change regularly: currently Rs 50, video, Rs 500. There's a 25% discount on fees after three consecutive days. Summer maximum 35°C, minimum 18°C; Winter maximum 24°C, minimum 7°C. Annual rainfall 2300 mm, heavy in summer. The best season is mid-November to the end of April (December and January are best for birds). The park is closed mid-April to mid-October during monsoons. Wear cotton clothing but take a jacket. ►► *See Transport, page 711.*

Entry into the park is by private vehicle, hired jeep or trained elephants. Although elephants cover less ground than motor vehicles, they can get a lot closer to the wildlife, particularly rhinos and buffalo. **Elephant rides** ⓘ *book the night before through the Forest Range Officer, foreigners Rs 1000, Indians Rs 120, plus jeep transfer from town, Rs 120*, carry four people and get mixed reports; the consensus seems to be that they are less enjoyable when demand is heavy. The viewing posts just inside the park may offer quieter viewing. **Jeeps** for five or six people can be hired from the **Department of Tourism** in Kaziranga or private agents. Government jeeps cost Rs 700 (Rs 120 per person in a shared vehicle) for three hours; private ones Rs 900-1000 for 50 km or 2½ hours. A car or jeep must be accompanied by a Forest Department Guard (Rs 50), who can give directions as well as spot wildlife. Cars and jeeps pay a road toll, Rs 150. Total price per jeep is Rs 920-1220.

Sights

The **rhino** population is over 2000 here and they are guaranteed to be seen in the marshes and grasslands. Despite Kaziranga's status as a national park, poachers still manage to kill the animal for its horn, which is used in Chinese and Tibetan medicine. The park also has over 1000 wild buffalo, sambar, swamp deer (over 500), hog deer, wild pig, hoolock gibbon, elephant (1246 in 2004), python and tiger (89 at last count in 2000), the only predator of the one-horned rhino. There is a rich variety of shallow-water fowl including egrets, pond herons, river terns, black-necked stork, fishing eagles and adjutant storks, pelicans and the rare Bengal florican. There are otters and dolphins in the river.

There are four road routes for visiting the park: the **Central Range** (Kohora, Daflang, Foliomari) is the the most visited as it is full of big mammals; the **Western Range** (Baguri, Monabeel, Bimoli, Kanchanjuri) has the highest rhinoceros density but tall elephant grass makes visibility difficult; the **Eastern Range** (Agortoli, Sohola, Rangamatia) has good possibilities for seeing wildlife, but at a distance; the **Burhapahar Range**, furthest west, has only recently become accessible. Keep receipts as fees are valid for several trips in one day.

Panbari Forest Reserve, 12 km from Kaziranga, has hoolock gibbons and a good variety of birdlife. Contact the Forest Office in Guwahati, for permission to visit.

Tezpur and around → *For listings, see pages 702-713. Colour map 4, A4.*

Tezpur, on the north bank of the Brahmaputra, 180 km northeast of Guwahati, is the site of Assam's first tea plantations. The **Tourist Lodge** ⓘ *Jenkins Rd, T03712-221016, Mon-Sat 1000-1615; closed every 2nd and 4th Sat of the month*, has a brochure and can sketch out a map of town. The town's ancient origins can be seen at **Da Parbatia**, 5 km west, which has the entrance gate of an early Gupta-style temple. In Tezpur's centre, **Chitralekha Udyan** (Cole Park) ⓘ *Rs 10, camera Rs 20, boat Rs 10, 0900-2000*, was created after an earthquake revealed ancient remains and is now a pleasant park around a lake that is lit up at night; some of the slabs of friezes and sculpture unearthed are on display outside the **museum** ⓘ *at the Dak Bungalow, near the Tourist Lodge*. The **Station Club**, opposite the District Commissioner's office, is one of Assam's oldest planters' clubs dating from 1875, with period furniture and a bar worthy of a drink if you can find a member to invite you. Otherwise they are happy to let you look around, although only the card tables, billards and tennis courts remain. A nice spot for sunset is **Agrigarh** ⓘ *Rs 10, 0800-1930*, a 1-km stroll past Ganesh Ghat, with hilltop views over the Brahmaputra and the town. Climb the lookout tower to catch the breeze and be on the same level as circling birds of prey. Possibly the largest Siva linga in India is found inside **Mahabhairab Mandir**, a Rs 10 rickshaw ride from the centre, which has a nightly *puja* at around 1830.

An interesting excursion is to take a Guwahati-bound bus, get off at the bridge over the Brahmaputra, then negotiate with a boatman to take you to the river's confluence with the Bhoreli for some river **dolphin watching**. Some hotels, **Luit**, for example, offer such trips. It involves a 30-minute rickshaw ride, Rs 150, followed by boat hire, around Rs 1000.

The 79-sq-km **Orang National Park** ⓘ *66 km northwest of Tezpur, foreigners Rs 250*, is often called a miniature Kaziranga. It has similar flora and fauna, though viewing is not as rewarding (rhinos appear only occasionally). This is compensated by the peaceful and intimate atmosphere, especially if staying inside the park. Elephants safaris cost Rs 750 for foreigners. Arriving by car is best from Tezpur, though buses between Guwahati and Tezpur go via Orang village. From the village, it is a 15-km dusty track to the park.

Nameri National Park ⓘ *35 km north of Tezpur, on the Arunachal border, entry and camera fees are similar to Kaziranga*, is on the river Jia Bhoroli and covers 210 sq km. It is home to tigers (26 in 2006), elephants, Indian bison, barking and hog deer, Himalayan black bears as well as 300 bird species, including the shy and endangered white-winged wood ducks. Flora includes evergreens, bamboo and some open grassland. Buses/*sumos* travelling between Tezpur and Tawang can drop travellers off at Hatigate on the main road. From here, it is 2.5 km down a track to the **Eco Camp** (see Sleeping, page 704), a recommended overnight stop and good place to arrange visits to the park. There are no roads; you can trek within the park with a forest guide after taking a boat across the river. The Eco-Camp can also organize catch-and-release angling and low-level rafting excursions. The best time (climatically) to visit is October-April, and the best chance of animal sightings are December-March.

Bhalukpong, 20 km west of Nameri, is on the Assam-Arunachal border en route to Tawang. This nondescript village is surrounded by the forests of **Pakhui Game Sanctuary**, a mass of ferns, moss and orchids, with a hot spring, orchid garden and good fishing. You can camp (take your own tent) on the picturesque bank of the River Jia Bhoreli or stay in the government tourist cottages overlooking the river. Jeeps and buses from Tezpur all pass through Bhalukpong en route to Tawang.

Plantation labour

Today Assam produces about 60% of India's tea, with small tea growers on the rise as well as traditional large plantations. Old colonial tea planters' bungalows surrounded by neat rows of emerald green tea bushes dominate the landscape, particularly in Upper Assam. After an early experiment using imported Chinese labourers ended in near mutiny, the British began the mass recruitment of Adivasis from the Chota Nagpur Plateau, Andhra Pradesh and Orissa. They have been assimilated into Assamese society but are recognized as a separate 'tea tribe' with a language, customs and dances that remain unique. One of the largest groups of organized labour in India today, they enjoy benefits undreamed of by other workers including free health care, education and subsidized food. The lifestyle of the plantation, hardly changed since the Raj, has been tarnished by the rise of insurgency, with isolated tea companies being targeted for extortion to fund militant groups.

Northeast Assam → *For listings, see pages 702-713.*

Jorhat → *Colour map 4, A5.*

Jorhat is one of Assam's major tea centres with a **Tea Festival** held in November. It's a relatively orderly town with good facilities but there are no historical sites nearby – most people only stop here because it is convenient for visiting Majuli Island to the north. The main commercial street, Gar-Ali, runs south for about 1 km from the railway station, down to AT Road where the bus stands are located to the west. Parallel to Gar-Ali (one block west) is MG Road, where you will find the helpful **Assam Tourism Office** ⓘ *T0376-232 1579, Mon-Sat 1000-1700 in summer, 1000-1615 in winter*, some cheap lodges and a miniature one-room **museum** ⓘ *inside the Post Graduate Training College, Mon-Sat 0930-1700, free*, displaying Ahom artefacts and curvaceous Krishnas minus his flute. During February (check dates with tourist office), horse races are held at the 1876 **Gymkhana Club** ⓘ *Club Rd North, T0376-221 1303, office open 0800-1600*, where there is also an 18-hole golf course, tennis, billiards and a bar with ancient staff, piano and pictures of England.

Majuli Island → *Colour map 4, A5.*

Majuli Island is one of the largest river islands in the world, though constantly changing, and currently around 650 sq km. The flooding of the Brahmaputra River means that at times Majuli is reduced to a cluster of islands, some as small as a hut top. Roads keep shifting but villagers adapt to re-routing by building cost-effective bamboo bridges. Cut off from the mainland to the south about 400 years ago, it is served by ferries from Jorhat, but it can still be accessed from North Lakhimpur by road (with two ferry crossings, six hours) during summer. The island is essentially a flat expanse of paddy fields and sky with very little motorized traffic, making it a peaceful place for cycling or exploring **Mishing villages** (where homes are built on stilts, not only to avoid flood-risk but also because it is believed to be more hygienic).

On the first Wednesday of the month **Gimnur Polo** (in February-March), the colourful Mishing festival of Ali-Ai-Lvigang is celebrated. See www.majulitourism.com, or contact Majuli's tourism officer (Jyoti Narayan Sarma, T(0)9435-657282) for festival dates. Majuli is also a birdwatchers' paradise.

At the forefront of Assamese Vaishnava culture, the island is an important centre for arts, crafts and science. Work is in progress to declare it a World Heritage Site. The *satras* (monasteries) here, inspired by the 15th-century saint Sankardeva and his disciple Madhavdeva, are worth visiting – particularly those to the east of Kamalabari. They are essentially small, self-sufficient villages where Vishnu is worshipped through regular performances of dance dramas at the temples. Out of 64 *satras*, 22 remain, the others have fallen victim to erosion by the Brahmaputra. A useful sketch map showing the location of the *satras* is available from La Masion de Ananda (see Sleeping, page 705).

Satras in and around **Kamalabari** and **Garamur** can be visited on foot, but others require a bicycle or rickshaw. **Auniati**, 5 km west of Kamalabari, is home to 450 monks and has a little museum with old manuscripts, utensils, jewellery and silver of the Ahom kings (entrance Rs 50). **Bengenatti**, east of Uttar Kamalabari, is a centre for performing arts and tribal dance forms. Others worth visiting are **Nauten Kamalabari** and **Dekhinpat**. Colourful traditional masks are still made at **Natun Chamaguri**, 12 km east of Kamalabari, and a visit is recommended.

Hollong Park Gibbon Sanctuary

ⓘ *16 km from Majuli Island, Rs 250 per person (4 hrs' viewing), includes an armed guide.*
The sanctuary at **Bhalowguri** was designated in 1998, but is scarcely visited by tourists. The low-key nature of the operation is a big part of the appeal, and few leave disappointed, although dense forest growth makes the gibbons hard to spot. Viewing the wild elephants requires an overnight stay in the specially constructed hut on stilts with two rooms, bring supplies (contact District Forest Officer in Jorhat, T0376-232 0008). To reach the park, 18 km south of Jorhat, catch a bus from the top of MG Road in Jorhat and go via Mariani by auto.

Sibsagar and around

District headquarters of the largest tea and oil producing area in the Northeast, **Sibsagar** was the Ahom capital for two centuries. The Ahoms arrived from southern China in 1228 and set up their first capital at Charaideo, 28 km from present-day Sibsagar, in 1253. Initially they were Buddhists, though Hinduism came to prevail. Daupadi (the Ahom King's wife) built the huge tank in the centre of town and the three temples on its bank in 1734. The central tower of the Siva Dol is one of the tallest in India, while the interior has an inverted lingum. It is a fascinating place to witness **Sivaratri** (celebrated in early March). On the east bank there is a small Buddhist Temple and a birdwatching tower, while on the west bank is the square red-brick **Tai Museum** ⓘ *Fri-Wed 1000-1600, Rs 5*. Ahom artefacts are displayed, including two wooden dragons found at Charaideo, brass pots and plates, silks, combs, basketry, ancient manuscripts and two *dolas* with wooden basins in which the women sat to be carried around.

All the sites around Sibsagar are open sunrise-sunset and charge foreigners a Rs 100 entrance fee. The **Joysagar Tank** at **Rangpur**, 5 km away, and the three temples on its bank date from 1697. The main Joydol (Vishnu temple) sits in pretty gardens; its exterior still has the original decorative terracotta tiles. The Shivadol and Devidol temples are less impressive, but free to enter. **Talatal Ghar**, 4 km from Sibsager, is a large two-storey palace which is being restored. Nearby, the two-storied oval **Rang Ghar** was the royal sports pavilion where elephant fights and games took place – said to be the oldest amphitheatre in Asia. Take a Tata Magic from AT or BG Rd (Rs 5-10, 20 minutes) to Joysagar, from where you can walk back in the direction of Sibsagar to visit Talatal Ghar and Rang Ghar (1.5 km away).

Gaurisagar, 12 km along the road to Jorhat, also has three temples and a tank dating from the time of Queen Phulesari (1722-1791). Striking **Karen Ghar**, 8 km east along the road to Sonari, was built in 1752 by King Rudra Singha and is a seven-storeyed palace, three floors of which are underground. Less impressive **Charaideo** 28 km east, was the original capital of the Ahoms and where the royals were buried in *maidams* (vaults covered by soil and bricks) along with their personal effects.

Dibrugarh, Tinsukia and Borajan Reserve Forest

Much of the town of **Dibrugarh** was destroyed during the 1950 earthquake, only a few old buildings remain on the main streets. The new town on the Brahmaputra is surrounded by tea estates, where a couple of delightful old tea-planters bungalows are available for guests to soak up some Raj nostalgia. Dibrugarh is a convenient stop when setting off for (or returning from) eastern and central Arunachal Pradesh as transport connections are good and hotels are comfortable. **Tinsukia**, a major transport junction in the Northeast, is convenient for visiting the nearby Dibru-Saikhowa National Park and the **Borajan Reserve Forest** ⓘ *5 km from Tinsukia.* The reserve consists of a small (500 sq m) patch of forest, which is home to five species of primate (Hoolock gibbon, capped langur, slow loris, stump tailed macaque and common macaque), though not all are easy to spot.

Dibru-Saikhowa National Park

ⓘ *Foreigners, Rs 250. Contact DFO, Rangagora Rd, Tinsukia, T0374-233 1472, for day visits.*
A national park since March 1999, on the southern flood plain of the Brahmaputra near Tinsukia, this is largely a semi-wet evergreen forest. The 340-sq-km core area is within a large biosphere reserve and provides a refuge for endangered species such as tiger, leopard, leopard cat, clouded leopard and elephant, though sightings are rare. The real draw is the rich birdlife, which includes the very rare white-winged wood duck (the state bird), best spotted during a dawn boat ride. Other attractions for ornithologists include the marsh babbler, the black-breasted parrotbill, and the Jerdon's bushchat. Silky brown dolphins are more commonly seen at sunset while wild horses congregate on the western edges of the park (allegedly the ancestors of these horses escaped from the World War II army camps). The best time to visit is November-March. Temperatures range from 6-36°C. Average annual rainfall is 2300-3600 mm.

Entry points are at **Guijan** on the southern edge of the park, and **Dhola** (near Saikhowa Ghat) in the north, both accessible by auto-rickshaw/jeep from Tinsukia. Arrival from Guijan is easier as a boat across the river takes you to the Range Office at the park entrance. If you cross from Dhola, the Range Office is 5 km into the park at Narbarmora; in either case it is best to notify your arrival beforehand. If stopping overnight to get an early start the only options are two simple eco-camps on the riverbank at Guijan.

Margherita ➔ *Colour map 4, A6.*

Margherita, the constituency of the present chief minister, is on the Dihing River at the foot of the Patkoi Range and was named by Italian railway engineers in the late 19th century after the Queen of Italy. The town is surrounded by tea estates and is the headquarters of Coal India Ltd. The last of the steam railway engines in Assam is still operating.

Ledo ➔ *Colour map 4, A6.*

The small coal mining town of Ledo, 6 km northwest of Margherita, was the headquarters of Northern Combat Area Command during the Second World War and is the start of the 470-km **Stilwell Road.** Named after General Joseph Stilwell, the road was the most ambitious and costly engineering project of the war, US$137 million at the time. Once a two-lane bitumen highway linking Ledo with Myitkyina in North Burma, through the Pangso Pass, and with Kunming in China, it is now closed beyond Nampong in Arunachal Pradesh. A sign, 6 km west of Ledo, commemorates the 'Road to Mandalay' but there is little else remaining.

Assam listings

For Sleeping and Eating price codes and other relevant information, see Essentials pages 38-42.

Sleeping

Guwahati *p693, map p694*

There are some budget hotels at Sadullah and M Nehru Rd crossing; those in Paltan Bazar are often full by the afternoon. Most medium-priced hotels have some a/c rooms and a restaurant.

L-AL Dynasty, SS Rd, T0361-251 6021, www.dynastyhotel.in. 76 comfortable rooms and suites, this is Guwahati's top hotel and even has a spa. Rooms are tastefully designed and modern, public areas quiet and refined, excellent restaurants serve Indian and Chinese food (see Eating, page 707). Gym, breakfast included, staff efficient.

AL-A Brahmaputra Ashok, MG Rd, T0361-260 2281, www.hotelbrahmaputraashok.com. Standard rooms are old style but with wooden floors and decent shower rooms (riverside ones with nice views), central a/c, TV, bamboo and cane furniture, restaurant, travel agency, Wi-Fi. The **Kaziranga** bar, with its zebra print furniture, is fun and there's Silver Streak disco on Sat nights.

AL-A Rajmahal, AT Rd, Paltan Bazar, T0361-254 9141-6, www.hotelrajmahal.in. 80 rooms conveniently located, good value, excellent restaurants, pool on 10th floor.

A-B Nandan, GS Rd, Paltan Bazar, T0361-254 0855, www.hotelnandan.com. The 55 clean rooms don't quite match up to the stylish frontage and feel a bit 1970s, some a/c, expensive suites, restaurants (including Thai, Mexican and Italian food), decent bar.

B-C Baruah Bhavan, T(0)9954-024165, www.heritagehomeassam.com. An Assamese mansion over 100 years old with 6 luxurious rooms, modern amenities and a charming roof terrace. Home-cooking, (Assamese, Indian, Chinese, reasonably priced), breakfast included, internet, transport can be arranged. A short walk from the riverside.

B-C Prag Continental, M Nehru Rd, Pan Bazar, T0361-254 0850, www.hotelpragcontinental.com. Range of rooms and suites (Rs 3000), regular rooms without a/c, multicuisine restaurant and eager staff.

C Bellevue, MG Rd, on river front opposite Raj Bhawan, T0361-254 0847. Being refurbished at the time of research, quiet location with elevated views over the river, restaurant, bit of a walk from the city centre.

C-D Nova, SS Rd, Fancy Bazar, T0361-251 1464, www.novahotel.in. Standard rooms are a bit fusty with dated bathrooms and no a/c (double **C** a/c, much brighter), but the vibe and public areas are nice. Delicious if utilitarian **Natraj** restaurant (Indian, Chinese) has slow service (room service quicker), yet pleasant, friendly and helpful. Location is spot on for the action in the bazar.

C-E City Palace, opposite ASTC bus stand, Paltan Bazar, T0361-263 5848/9. The lobby with white leather sofas and Astroturf on the walls sets the tone, the budget rooms are good, clean, and the location couldn't be handier for transport.

D-E Centre Point, opposite **Hotel Nandan**, GS Rd, Paltan Bazar, T0361-273 9632. Clean small rooms in a functional and respectable guest house, all with TV and decent bathrooms with hot water, some with a/c, helpful staff are a big plus point. Set back from the main road so not too noisy. Single room rates.

D-E Starline, Md Shah Rd, Paltan Bazar, T0361-251 8541. Of the 74 clean rooms, 12 have a/c with hot water 24 hrs. Chinese/Indian restaurant, polite and helpful staff.

E Broadview Lodge, Pan Bazar (by Overbridge Point), T0361-251 2811. Central location, rooms have clean bedding, powerful fans, TV and decent bathrooms (check a couple, layout varies), it's nothing special but suitably priced for what you get.

E Orchid, B Barua Rd, opposite stadium, Ulubari, T0361-252 3471. The best value single rooms in town, clean, well-furnished and bright (Rs 250-385), doubles start at Rs 550, pay more for a/c. Not right in the thick of things but 10-min walk to Paltan Bazar. The cheerfully decorated **Magnolia** restaurant is excellent, bar open till 2200.

E Prashaanti Tourist Lodge (Assam Tourism), Station Rd, close to railway station, T0361-254 4475, astdcorpn@sancarnet.in. Decent sized rooms with nets, bathroom and balcony, clean sheets and TV. Good restaurant and upstairs bar, tourist information (1000-1700).

Great value for non-a/c doubles (Rs 578) but single rooms cost almost as much. Book in advance, they are often full.

F-G Suradevi, MLN Rd, Panbazar, T0361-254 5050. Basic but totally bearable rooms are cheap and noisy, better at the rear, with attached bath, pay more for TV. Singles start at Rs 200, doubles Rs 305. Decent food in the restaurant. Dorm beds Rs 150.

F-G Railway Retiring Rooms. Some a/c rooms (Rs 600) or non (Rs 400) with worn attached bathrooms, large clean mixed sex dorm (Rs 60), book at Counter 14 (show a valid railway ticket).

Manas National Park *p696*

If you arrive late at Barpeta Rd you will need to spend the night there.

L Bansbari Lodge, at the park entrance, www.assambengalnavigation.com. Simple but comfy huts have tea gardens on one side and the jungle on the other. All 16 twin rooms have hot showers, plus attractive gardens, a library and delicious meals. The tariff includes all meals, park entrance fees, jeep/elephant rides, excursions (but not drinks).

B-D Manas Jungle Camp, Koklabari, T03666-268052, www.helptourism.com, www.manas100.com. 4 basic ethnic cottages at the boundary of the park, a chance to see the work of **MMES** and visit the handicraft workshop at a Bodo village nearby.

E-G Manas Guest House, Durgabari Rd, Barpeta Rd, T03666-260935. The best choice in town, clean, cheap and recommended for good service and helpful staff.

F Mathanguri Forest Lodges, on hill overlooking Manas River. Very simple but clean and well maintained, the lodges are within the park and enjoy staggering views. The erosion of land by the Beki River is threatening the upper bungalow, which is the nicer of the 2. Camping possible. Cook available but bring provisions (from Barpeta Rd). Book well in advance through the Field Director's Office, Main Rd, Barpeta Rd, T03666-261413.

Kaziranga National Park *p697*

New lodges are springing up around Kaziranga as quickly as the elephant grass. The government-run **Tourist Complex**, 1 km south of the main gate in Kohora village, has perfectly adequate options, while a few other places stand out for their eco-awareness and tastefulness. Good discounts are available off-season – but the park itself is closed.

LL Diphlu River Lodge, 15 km west of Kohora, T0361-260 2223, www.diphluriverlodge.com. Utterly chic luxury with a rustic slant, 12 Mishing-style huts, connected by bamboo walkway, surround rice paddies with a prime location on the edge of the national park. Rooms are furnished in a colonial theme from natural materials, bathrooms are inspired, 2 verandas for lounging, and the staff all faultless. Once inside the peaceful enclave everything is included in the price (apart from alcohol) – limitless visits to Kaziranga, walks with naturalists, picnics, meals, visits to Mishing villages. Come here for peace and serenity.

AL-A Iora, Bogorijuri, Kohora, T03776-262411/2, www.kazirangasafari.com. Stark white building out of keeping with the wildlife vibe, but the only place with a swimming pool. Rooms are contemporary, fitted out with stone, wood and woven cane and a sprinkling of southeast Asian aesthetics. Glass walk-in shower, elegant bar and restaurant.

C Jupuri Ghar, Kaziranga Tourist Complex, Kohora, T(0)9435-196377, jupuri@gmail.com. Peaceful setting on a slope above tea gardens and paddies, these new thatched cottages have cane furniture and woven walls, a/c and terraces onto the garden. Pleasant open restaurant, attractive tribal decorations, BYO until they get a license. Also bookable through **Network Travels**, see page 709.

C Wild Grass, 1.5 km from NH37, 5.5 km from Kohora, ask for Kaziranga IB Bus Stop, 400 m north of resort, T03776-262085, T(0)9954-416945, www.oldassam.com. Unpretentious and relaxing, with a lovely location, 18 spotless rooms in 2 lofty chalets, wooden floors, cane furniture, can get very cold in winter. Great meals (Rs 450 for 2 people) and service, beautiful walks through forests and tea plantations, excellent guided tours, pickup from Guwahati for groups, cultural shows in the evenings by the campfire of Assamese dancing. Half price May-Oct.

E Aranya Tourist Lodge, Tourist Complex, T03776-262429. White paint and marble predominate the 24 large rooms with bath (hot water) and good balcony. A/c is Rs 150 extra, simple garden, **Rhino Restaurant**, bar (slow service).

E Dhansree Resort, Kohora, T03776-262501. A variety of rooms and cottages with brick-red exteriors and thatch, fans and geysers. Incongruous water features and use of paint mar the pleasant garden, but nicely located among tea trees.

F Bonani, Tourist Complex, T03776-262423. 5 breezy white rooms with fans, nets, wicker furniture and large bathrooms (geysers) are good value. Much nicer on the upper level.

G Bonashree, Tourist Complex, T03776-262423. Cheaper still, 9 rooms, a large veranda lends some old-world charm, pleasant garden, but often full. Hot buckets available.

G Kunjaban Dormitory, Tourist Complex, T03776-262423. Linen optional (Rs 25), 12- or 3-bed rooms. Safe and secure, but no hot buckets.

Tezpur and around *p698*

LL Wild Mahseer, Addabarie Tea Estate, near Balipara, T(0)9435-197650, www.oldassam.com. In a world of its own, this pristine heritage bungalow sits among 9 ha of gardens and trees on the edge of a working tea garden. Rooms are luxurious yet homely with huge beds and bathrooms in modern colonial style, and every inch taken care of. Absorbing library, tea-tasting café and 3 (cheaper) bungalows in the grounds, Delicious Anglo-Indian food, warm and entertaining hosts.

C-E Centre Point, Main Rd (opposite the police station), Tezpur, T03712-232359, hotelcentre point.tezpur@gmail.com. Spanking new hotel with fresh linen and plumped up pillows, plain but pleasing decor and TVs. Cheaper rooms have hot water by the bucket, staff are eager to please and **Tiffin Restaurant** is good. Recommended, if you can deal with false windows and bad acoustics.

C-F Eco Camp, Nameri National Park, Sonitpur, T(0)9854-019932, or contact **Network Travels**, see page 709. 11 thatched-cottage tents with twin bamboo beds, bathrooms with hot water, brightly furnished with local fabrics, set among jungle trees around a grassy lawn. 6 bunk beds in the bamboo dorm, wash block, sunny little restaurant. A friendly and special place, worth spending a couple of nights.

D-F Luit, Ranu Singh Rd, 200 m from bus stand, Tezpur, T03712-222083, hotel_luit@rediffmail.com. Set back from the main road, this retro hotel has large but average rooms in new wing (Rs 700), some a/c (Rs 1200) and some bargain-basic rooms in the old wing (Rs 400), restaurant, bar.

E Durba, KK Rd, Tezpur, T03712-224276. Clean rooms with TV, **Appayam** restaurant.

E-F Basant, Main Rd, Tezpur, T03712-230831, T(0)9401-278499. Good, clean paintwork and sheets, well-maintained rooms all with TV (doubles Rs 350/400/780, cold water/hot water/ac), recommended to phone ahead. Singles are small but totally acceptable. Soulless restaurant on the top floor.

E-F Tourist Lodge, Jenkins Rd (opposite Chitralekha Udyan), Tezpur, T03712-221016. Budget non-a/c rooms for Rs 330, newly refurbed a/c Rs 550. All twin bed with attached bath. Book ahead, there are only 10 rooms. Cheap simple restaurant.

E-F Tourist Lodge, Bhalukpong, T03782-234037. 10 raised cottages with octagonal bedrooms, or 4 airy rooms sharing a terrace (good value) look out across the Jia Bhoroli River to Nameri and Pakhuya parks. Work is underway to turn the watch-tower into a restaurant. Can arrange local transport to visit Nameri. (The private guesthouse **Kunki Resort** next door is not nearly as appealing, but there if the lodge is full.)

F Forest Bungalows, Orang National Park. Reservations: District Forest Officer, Mangaldoi, T03713-230708, or Chief Conservator of Forests, Reharbari, Guwahati, T0361-251 7064. A newer lodge at the entrance to the park at Silbari, and another 1 km inside the park at Satsimulu, overlooking swampy grasslands where animal spotting is possible. Both are basic, bring your own sleeping bags and provisions; the cook/guide will prepare your food.

F Parajit, Main Rd, Tezpur, T03712-220565. Decent budget rooms have pink walls, clean furnishings and squat toilets in a bungalow with a bit of soul. Often full, ring ahead. Good restaurant has cheap *thalis*, 1100-1530 and 1930-2100.

Jorhat *p699*

A few hotels and the Tourist Lodge are on MG Rd and a more salubrious cluster (all pretty similar) is found on Solicitor Rd (off AT Rd) near the ASTC bus station. Some old planter's bungalows languish in the tea estates on the outskirts of town, far from the madding crowd.

A Thengal Manor, 15 km southeast of Jorhat, T0376-230 4673, www.welcomheritagehotels.com. Thengal feels regal with its white portico, marble-topped tables and antique furnishings. Rooms are elegant rather than luxurious, meals Anglo-Indian around the immense dining table, and staff incredibly kind. After bringing bed-tea, they throw open the shuttered windows to let in the morning sun. The immaculate grounds contain ponds, a swimming pool, vegetable gardens, and the family mausoleum. Excellent tea tours should be pre-arranged. Half-board.

B Burrah Sahib's Bungalow and **Mistry Sahib's Bungalow**, contact as for **Thengal Manor**, above. The joy of these 2 properties is in their location deep in the heart of tea country, in sweeping time-warp gardens, the air heavy with nostalgia. Recent refurbishment has mingled gloriously period furniture with ill-matched ceramics and artworks, but the wide verandas and strolls through the plantations compensate. Guests can use the golf course nearby, and swimming pools are planned.

C MD's Continental, MD House, Marwari Patty (off AT Rd), T0376-230 0430, mdscontinental@gmail.com. This hotel has tastefully furnished rooms, the theme Asian throughout with wooden floors, contemporary art and luxury bathrooms. Restaurant is slick and very reasonably priced, lounge-bar is more of a bistro (imported liquor), MD's sweets on the ground floor the best in town. Staff extremely professional.

D-F Paradise, Solicitor Rd, T0376-332 1521, www.fraindia.com/hotel/jorhat/paradise. Spacious 1970s rooms are clean with TV, hot water by bucket, most with balcony, some (overpriced) with a/c and heater, laundry, free internet/Wi-Fi. If you're lucky, your room might have alpine scenes or banana groves painted on the wall. Soulless restaurant and gloomy (but cheap) bar open till 2130. Air India office on the upper floors, see page 711.

E-F Dilip, Solicitor Rd, T0376-232 1610 www.hoteldilip.com. Modern rooms are good value (especially non-a/c at Rs 300/500 single/double) with clean towels and sheets, TV, decent bathrooms with reliable hot water. Very dark almost-funky bar opens 0900-2200, beer Rs 90.

E-F Prashaanti Tourist Lodge, MG Rd, T0376-232 1579. Spotless twin-bed rooms with essential mosquito nets have been recently refurbished (single Rs 473, double Rs 525, room 101 has best balcony), deluxe rooms cost about Rs 100 extra and have a/c. 24-hr hot water and TVs in all rooms. Men-only dorm (Rs 100) and nice new restaurant-cum-bar out the back is an unthreatening place for a quiet drink (beer Rs 75). Assam Tourism in the same building with helpful staff.

F Woodland Cottage, BG Rd (off MG Rd), T0376-232 2786. This Assamese-style bungalow has character, though rooms are faded, there's a patio out front with plants and murals which is good for morning tea. Hot running water, some rooms a/c, their nearby restaurant brings room service.

F-G Janata Paradise, Solicitor Rd, T0376-232 0610, T(0)943 5659461. Basic rooms are more cheerful than most with colourful walls, fans, free hot buckets, but no mossie nets and ask for a top sheet, pay extra for TV. Atmosphere is friendly, there's a decent cheap restaurant with Assamese thalis (Rs 60, open 1100-1600, 2000-2130) and the handy location makes this a good budget choice.

F-G Palace, MG Rd, T0376-232 3891. Small budget lodge, rooms have tiny attached bath, TV and plug-in mosquito deterrents. Charming owner will let you sample his home-made pickles. Cluttered rooftop but no balconies.

Majuli Island *p699*

C-E Mou Chapori, near Neematighat, Jorhat, contact Bibhuti Borah, T(0)9854-335242 or **Rhino Travels** (see page 709), www.mouchaporiresort.com. When the river is high (May-Sep) a boat leaves from Nimatighat to the island (Rs 50), during the dry season Mou Chapori is accessible by land. Cottages and huts are sadly heavier on painted plywood than bamboo but it's a good location and the price includes horse riding, boating, table tennis. Also a houseboat where guests can sleep (Rs 2000). Good place to spend the day (Rs 25), or camp on the sandy shores if you have a tent. Staff couldn't be nicer. Guided trips to Majuli arranged. Try local fish in the little restaurant.

F La Maison de Ananda and **Do:ni Po:lo**, Garamur, T03775-274768, T(0)9425-205539, danny002in@yahoo.com. A Mishing-style stilt house designed by a French architect who fell in love with Majuli, **La Maison** is quaint, made entirely of bamboo and yet very comfortable (sleeps 3 people). **Do:ni Po:lo** next door has a dorm with 2 doubles and 2 single beds, clean linen, blankets and nets, lit by pinpricks of light through the woven walls. A further 2 rooms have twin beds. Clean Indian-style toilet out the back and hot bucket on request. Bicycles/ motorbikes for rent. Both places have relaxing verandas and are managed by local fixer Danny Gam. Lovely family atmosphere.

G Circuit House, Garamur, T03775-274439. Twin-bed rooms, very basic but have mosquito nets and attached bath, decent food and bed tea. Foreigners should phone ahead, or write a letter of application on arrival at the SDO's office next door.

G Garamur Satra, Garamur, T(0)9435-466539. 4 rooms. Bedding and nets provided.

G Nautum Kamalabari Guest House, Kamalabari (8 km from Garmur), T03775-273302. Spartan and no hot water but incredibly cheap.

G Uttar Kamalabari Guest House, Kamalabari, Majuli Island, T(0)9435-823352. Very basic, bring own bedding and leave a donation, you may try to reserve by asking to call Dulal Saikia (the head priest) to the phone, then ring back after 10 mins.

Sibsagar *p700*

C-D Brahmaputra, BG Rd, T03772-222200, www.brahmaputrahotel.com. Endless corridors lead to pleasing deluxe double/single rooms with a/c, TV, hot water, new furniture and white paint. Also some better-value singles have fans and lots of space. Kaveri restaurant serves good food, the elevator works, staff are helpful. Gentle bargaining can achieve a significant reduction in price. An annoying 2 km from the centre of town, however.

C-E Shiva Palace, AT Rd, T03772-225204, hotel_shiva_palace@rediffmail.com. Best in town, with an excellent restaurant and 'trendy' bar, rooms are Western-style with mod cons. Cheaper rooms getting slightly scuffed, however. Less than 1 km from Shivadol.

C-E Siddhartha, BG Rd, T03772-222276, e7safari@rediffmail.com. 29 rooms, those with a/c homely and new, while non-a/c a bit faded with dirty paintwork, but both have TV and hot running water. Smart public areas and modern restaurant (open from 0630), pleasant bar. Nearly 2 km out of town centre.

D-E Raj Palace, AT Rd, T03772-222635/232951. Clean simple rooms with TV, fan, attached bath (hot water 0530-0900 or by the bucket). No windows, except in the very noisy rooms at the front. Not a bad deal, little English spoken.

E-F Tourist Lodge, near Siva Dol, T03772-222394. On the southwest corner of the tank, clean and newly tiled/painted rooms with attached bath are a real bargain (double with a/c and geyser Rs 575, non-a/c single/double Rs 300/400 with fan and hot bucket). Front garden, restaurant, quiet location. Only 9 rooms so often full, call in advance. Tourist office in same building (Mon-Sat 1000-1600, closed 2nd and 4th Sat in month).

Dibrugarh and Borajan Reserve Forest *p700*

B Chowkidinghee Chang Bungalow (aka Jalannagar South Bungalow), off Mancotta Rd, 1.5 km from Dibrugarh. A truly charming indulgence in colonial history, this managers' bungalow on the edge of a tea estate has gloriously period rooms opening out onto enormous screened verandas with white cane furniture. Built on stilts to avoid floods and wild animals. Shiny wood floors throughout, there's a Victorian fireplace in the sitting-cum-dining room, both bedrooms are en suite and have dressing rooms. An additional room downstairs is not nearly as attractive. The proximity of the road is the only thing to gripe about. Bring your own alcohol.

B Mancotta Chang Bungalow, off Mancotta Rd, Milan Nagar, 5 km from Dibrugarh. Another heritage planter's bungalow on stilts exudes the same ambiance but is larger, with 2 fabulous colonial bedrooms on the upper level, 2 modern rooms downstairs (walk through the patio doors in the morning to enjoy the garden) and a separate bungalow with a post-war feel that sleeps 2 singles. In the upstairs rooms chintzy curtains, brass fittings, Seypoy prints and plenty of tumblers and brandy glasses make drinks on the veranda more attractive than the satellite TV. Bathrooms have enamel claw-footed tubs. Horse riding, tea tours and more are arranged by **Purvi Discovery** who also take the bookings (see Activities and tours, page 710).

D Hotel Natraj, HS Rd, T0373-232 7275. Recently remodelled, this very modern hotel has tiled rooms with comfortable beds, tonal furnishings and excellent bathrooms. 24-hr hot water, a/c, TV. Zaffran restaurant is quite chic with Oriental/Indian food, Sonali restaurant is less formal and has delicious food, there's a soulless bar (with special deals, open till 2200). Breakfast included.

D-E Indsurya, RKB Path, Dibrugarh, T0373-232 6322. A short walk from the station, the grim frontage of the Indsurya hides good-value rooms which are clean and comfy. The attractive lobby sports an impressive wooden rhino and plenty of wicker furniture. It's often full so call ahead.

E-F Hotel Devika, Puja Ghat, off AT Rd, T0373-232 5956, www.hoteldevika.in. Rooms at the front are best with Western toilets and good light (others lack windows), TV, fans, very clean. Corridors are marble and the building has some character. Discounts available, staff obliging, food available. Hot water is by the bucket in cheaper rooms; a few downstairs rooms have shared baths and are Rs 450 per double (but they are reluctant to announce these). Also some **C-D** executive rooms.

G Asha Lodge, AT Rd (at intersection with HS Rd), T0373-232 0053. As basic as it gets, rooms are grim but the cheapest around. The dusty wooden veranda is good for watching the street-life below.

Tinsukia *p700*

D Banashree Eco-camp, Guijan, near Tinsukia, T(0)9954-594940. Owned by charismatic poacher-turned- ecologist, Benu, the **Banashree** provides good food and guiding in the national park. Simple stilt huts are a bit overpriced for plywood and grubby toilets however, and mosquitoes are nasty – insist on a net. Right on the banks of the Dibru River, erosion has caused the surrounding tea gardens to start sliding into the water in a most picturesque way. Adjacent **Wave Ecotourism** has wicker stilt huts.

E Highway, AT Rd, T0374-233 5383, 500 m from New Tinsukia station. Modern, 20 rooms, some a/c, vegetarian restaurant.

F President, Station Rd, T0374-233 8789, computer2@sancharnet.in. Basic, noisy rooms with attached bath, pay more for TV, average vegetarian restaurant, very handy for the station and kind staff.

G Retiring Rooms, New Tinsukia Station. Very basic vegetarian food, budget beds.

Eating

Guwahati *p693, map p694*

Assamese *thalis* including rice, fish and vegetable curry, often cooked with mustard, are milder than elsewhere in India. Try vegetarian *kharoli* (mashed mustard seeds) with *omita khar* (papaya cooked with burnt 'bark' of the banana plant). Larger hotels serve continental food and have bars.

TTT-TT Tandoor, Dynasty Hotel (see Sleeping). Daily 1130-1430, 1830-2230. Marvellous Indian veg and non-veg delicacies, served from traditional metalware, pleasing decor, perfect for a treat, alcohol served. Mains between Rs 300-650. The hotel also has continental and Chinese restaurants, and a rooftop bar/ restaurant open Oct-Mar from 1900-2300.

TT Ming Room, Rajgarh Rd, near Chandmari Flyover. Very good Chinese.

T 4 Seasons, Bhuban Rd, Uzan Bazar, T0361-263 9544. Open 1000-2130, Sun from 1600. Delicious Chinese, Indian, Tibetan and tandoor food, simple surrounds, good lassi.

T Beatrix, MC Rd, T0361-266 7563. Open Mon-Sat 1030-2200, Sun from 1600. Good quality family restaurant (a/c upstairs), cartoon decor and clean surrounds. Varied menu, with some interesting dishes, lone diners with appreciate the 'mini-meals' (which are still very generous). Recommended.

T Breeze, NCB Rd, Pan Bazar, T0361-273 1444. Open 1100-2130 daily. Huge chicken momos, good soups and other Chinese and Indian dishes. The coloured lanterns give a cosy feel and it's popular with couples. Next door is **Sun Flower** restaurant, which has more choice for vegetarians.

T New Zealand Natural, MC Rd. Open 1000-2300. Great ice creams and sorbets, and coffee is reasonably priced. Outdoor terrace or a/c inside.

T US Pizza, HB Path, near Donbosco School, Panbazar, T(0)970-600 0080. Open 1100-1800. Fairly authentic pizza joint with deals on pizza, plus salad and garlic bread Rs 120.

T Woodlands, AT Rd (older branch on GS Rd by Ulubari flyover). open from 0830. Indian vegetarian. Clean, a/c, specializes in lunch and dinner *thalis* (Rs 55-80), good *idly*.

Tezpur *p698*

Ỵ **Chinese Villa**, NC Rd, T03712-232726. Magnificent *momos* and a whole host of other delicacies in a high-rise block that also incorporates an Indian restaurant on the upper level and excellent south Indian snacks and *lassis* on the ground floor.

Ỵ **Madras Hotel**, off Main Rd. Decent *dosas*, *idli* and other south Indian delights provide welcome spice after the relative blandness of Assamese cooking. Basic, busy but under-staffed, and smoky from the kitchen fires.

Jorhat *p699*

On Majuli Island, food is available at simple eateries.

ỴỴ-Ỵ **Beijing Banquet**, MG Rd, near Tourist Lodge. Exciting variety for pork eaters and a usefully descriptive menu. The starkly square room is warmed by bright orange walls and passable Chinese *objets d'art*. Generous combo-meals are good value.

Ỵ **Food Hut**, MG Rd, next to **Beijing Banquet**. Simple eatery serving a delicious 8-dish Assamese *thali*; also pigeon and duck.

Ỵ **Woodlands**, BG Rd (between MG Rd and Gar-Ali), T0376-232 7653. Open 0930-2130. Veg and non-veg, good *thalis* and some welcome south Indian dishes. Small, popular and efficient.

Sibsagar *p700*

ỴỴ **Sky Chef**, at Shiva Palace hotel (see page 706). Open 1000-2200. The glitziest place in town has excellent tandoori dishes, as well as other Indian/Chinese dishes and a pleasing environment.

Ỵ **Hotel Priya**, AT Rd (on junction with Hospital Rd). Seriously cheap and good Assamese thalis, veg/fish/chicken, open from 0530.

Ỵ The little outdoor tea-shop under the bird-watching tower by the tank does excellent *chapatti/subji* throughout the day and is a good place to while away time.

Dibrugarh *p700*

Ỵ **Asha Refreshment Lodge**, AT Rd (by intersection with HS Rd). Very cheap food, *channa dal* is nourishing and salads fresh. The family room behind the curtains is much more pleasant than the murky main room.

Ỵ **Garden Treat**, beside the flyover, Mancotta Rd, T0373-232 4140. Open 1100-2100. Despite the proximity of the flyover this garden haven is lovely for eating great-value fish with mustard, under a sun umbrella. There are several continental dishes alongside the Indian and Chinese. Has an old-world charm though the building is actually modern.

Ỵ **H2O**, 1st floor, Amrit Mansion, RNC Path, T0373-232 1759. Closes 2200. More about having a drink than eating – it's hard to see your food in the almost pitch blackness. Modern and a bit trendy; disco lights.

Ỵ **Payash Sweets & Restaurant**, 1st floor, City Tower, HS Rd, T0373-232 4076. A good veg restaurant hidden up a flight of stairs in the shopping mall, popular with local youth. *Lassis* are cheap and frothy, huge *dosas*, plenty of great Chinese, interesting *paneer*dishes and fluffy pizzas. *Marwari thali* is delicious. Staff efficient and low-key.

Ỵ **Swagat Family Restaurant**, HS Rd (at the junction with AT Rd). Staggering numbers of staff milling around despite it always being busy. Rudimentary downstairs room is good for breakfast (opens at 0630), dosas and snacks while the yellow and blue restaurant upstairs is more sedate for lunch and dinner, serving Chinese and North Indian food which can take a while to prepare. Pure veg.

Tinsukia *p700*

Ỵ **Payash Sweets & Restaurant**, has 2 branches in Tinsukia, one of which is fortuitously close to the ASTC Bus Stand.

❂ Festivals and events

Guwahati *p693, map p694*

Jan Magh Bihu and;

Mid-Apr Rongali Bihu, are week-long festivities celebrated with singing, dancing and much enthusiasm.

Mid-Jun Ambubachi marks the end of Mother Earth's menstrual cycle with a fair at Kamakhya Temple.

Sep The **Manasa Festival** honours the Snake goddess. You can watch devotees dancing and entering into trances from galleries on the hillside.

26-28 Dec The **Assam Tea Festival** is celebrated with events in various places.

Shopping

Guwahati *p693, map p694*

Silk and handicrafts

Muga, pat and *endi* silks, hats, bamboo and cane baskets, flutes, drums and pipes are typical of the area. Guide prices: silk per metre: *muga* Rs 400+ (saris Rs 4000+), *pat* Rs 250 (saris Rs 2000+), *endi* Rs 150-300. *Pat mikhala* and *shador*, Rs 1500, *endi* shawls Rs 300+. Bargain in **Pan Bazar** and **Fancy Bazar**. Also try: **Assam Govt Emporium**, GNB Rd, Ambari, for silks, bamboo, wood, brass and ceramics; **Assam Co-op Silk House**, HB Rd, Pan Bazar, for pure silk items; **Artfed**, opp Emporium, for knick-knacks, bags, handloom, metalware and more, Mon-Sat 1000-2000; **Purbashree**, GNB Rd. Traditional crafts. For high-quality, tastefully selected goods go to **Konyak**, 47 MG Rd, Uzan Bazar Riverside, for silks, cushions, saris, and the adjacent franchise of **FabIndia** with clothing, home furnishings, etc (both are open daily 1000-2000).

Jorhat *p699*

People's Bookstore, Plaza Market, 37 Gar-Ali, T0376-232 1419. Daily 0830-2030, Sun lunchbreak 1300-1700. Surprisingly good selection of modern fiction, plus popular classics (Rs 60), magazines and newspapers.

Dibrugarh *p700*

Art Fed, just off Mancotta Rd, Thanachorali. Mon-Sat 1000-1900. Attractive *Muga* silks shawls, *Jhapi* wall decorations, and silk saris/ half saris with golden Assamese thread designs.

Activities and tours

Guwahati *p693, map p694*

Assam Bengal Navigation, 1st floor, Mandovi Apartments, GNB Rd, Ambari, Guwahati, T0361-260 2223, www.assambengalnavigation.com. Sister concern to **Jungle Travels** (see below) runs 7- or 10-day cruises along the Brahmaputra aboard the charming *RV Charaidew* and *RV Sukapha*, both with 12 en suite cabins, nostalgic saloon bar and quintessential sundeck; *Sukapha* also has a small Ayurvedic spa. Land excursions visit the national parks, villages, historical sites and provide opportunities to barbecue on the islands of the mighty river. From Jul-Sep, the *Charaidew* moves to the Hooghly for 7-day cruises between Kolkata and Jangipur. The company also runs **Bansbari Lodge** in Manas National Park and **Diphlu River Lodge**, a new luxurious resort in Kaziranga National Park (see Sleeping).

Assam Tourism, Tourist Lodge, Station Rd, T0361-254 7102. City: Basistha Ashram, Zoo, Museum, Kamakhya Temple, Govt Sales Emporium. Open 0900-1500. Rs 90. Tue, Sun (minimum 10). River cruises: from near Janardhan Temple, winter 1500, 1600; summer 1600, 1700, 1 hr, Rs 50. Kaziranga: Nov-Apr, departs 0900, arrives 1600, return 1600 on following day, Rs 600, foreigners Rs 1250 (inclusive) allows only from 1500 to 1000 (on next day) in the park.

Help Tourism, www.helptourism.com. Based in Kolkata/Siliguri, but with a field office in Guwahati. Award-winning eco-tours, maximizing the involvement of local people. Homestays and simple camps in rural areas, generally booked as part of a package. Good for trips to Namdapha, central and eastern Arunachal, as well as Assam.

Jungle Travels India, 1st floor, Mandovi Apartments, GNB Rd, Ambari, Guwahati, T0361-260 2223, www.jungletravels india.com. Wildlife, heritage, tribal, tea, and other tours around Assam, Arunachal and Sikkim. Top-notch service from experienced and friendly staff.

Network Travels, 17 Paltan Bazar, GS Rd, T0361-273 9630, www.north-east- tourism.com. Imaginative tours including river cruises, good for airline ticketing and buses, efficient and reliable.

Rhino Travels, M Nehru Rd, T0361-254 0061. For visiting game reserves and Shillong. Also recommended for permits to visit other northeast states.

Wild Grass, Krishna Nagar, Chandmari (near Assam Engineering Institute), T0361-213 2817, T(0)9435-048403, wildgrasskaziranga@ gmail.com, oldassam.com. Very helpful, knowledgeable, efficient. Highly recommended for good value wildlife, tribal tours and Arunachal (can get a permit in 5 days), free travel advice on phone (Nov-Apr).

Kaziranga National Park *p697*

Assam Tourism offers a 2-day tour, also see **Wild Grass**; both under Guwahati, above.

Tezpur and around *p698*

Adiytya Tours & Travels, SC Rd, Tezpur, T03712-232018, T(0)9854-000103, adiytyatours4731@rediffmail.com. Good for car hire up to Tawang (fleet of 12 vehicles) and do package tours to Arunachal.

Anand Air Travels, MC Rd, Tezpur, T03712-222109. For flight tickets, Mon-Sat 0900-1900, Sun until 1600.

Assam Anglers' Association, T03712-220004, assamangling@yahoo.com, operates a strict 'catch-record-release' system to conserve the golden mahseer.

Eco Camp, Potasali, T03714-244246. Organizes whitewater rafting, nature watching and mahseer fishing on the Bhoreli. Reasonable rates.

Jorhat *p699*

Assam Tourism, **Prashaati Tourist Lodge**, MG Rd, T0376-232 1579, www.assamtourism.org, www.assamtourismonline.com. Helpful staff provide advice on transport and accommodation, decent map and pamphlets.

Dibrugarh *p700*

Purvi Discovery, T0373-230 1120, www.purviweb.com, www.assamteatourism.com. Tours around the Northeast states with very professional service and attention to detail. Experienced in tours to Namdapha and around Arunachal. Managers of the Chowkidinghee and Mancotta Chang bunglows – a great base for the horse riding, kayaking, tea tours or cookery classes on offer. The un-signed office is located in the lane behind the Radha Krishna temple, Medical College area, Rs 30 in a cycle rickshaw from Dibrugarh centre.

Transport

Guwahati *p693, map p694*

Air **Air India**, Ganeshguri, T0361-226 4425; www.airindia.com. 2 daily to **Kolkata** and 1 to **Delhi**, **Agartala**, **Bagdogra**, **Imphal**, **Lilabari**. **Jet Airways**, Panchvati, GNB Rd, T0361-266 2202, airport T0361-284 0130, www.jetairways.com, to **Bagdogra**, **Delhi**, **Imphal**, **Kolkata**. Also flights with **Kingfisher**, T3300 8888, www.flykingfisher.com, **Indigo**, www.goindigo.com, and **Spicejet**, T1800-180 3333, www.spicejet.com, thrice daily to **Delhi**.

A helicopter service is run by **Meghalaya Transport Corp**, T0364-222 3129, T(0)9435-145033, to **Shillong**, Mon-Sat, Rs 945, on to **Tura** on Mon, Tue, Wed, Fri, Rs1985; tickets at airport. Pawan Hans helicopter to Tawang in Arunachal Pradesh, but the safety record is not great.

Bus Red minibus 'canters' cover the route from the ISBT, and buses link from Paltan Bazar with the ISBT.

Long distance Private coach tickets are sold by operators in Paltan Bazar, such as **Network Travels**, GS Rd, T0361-213 4819, reservations 0400-2100, **Blue Hill**, T0361-260 7145, and others, with morning and night buses to all the Northeast states. The buses leave from the ISBT, connected by shuttle buses run by the private operators. To: **Agartala** (15 hrs, Rs 660); **Aizawl** (22 hrs, Rs 650); **Imphal** (22 hrs, Rs 700); **Itanagar** (10 hrs, Rs 400); **Jorhat via Kohora (for Kaziranga)** (7 hrs, Rs 260); **Kaziranga** (3½ hrs, Rs 210) also via **Dibrugarh** (9 hrs, Rs 380); **Tinsukia** (11 hrs, Rs 380); **Kohima** via Dimapur (11 hrs, Rs 410); **North Lakimpur** (10 hrs, Rs 350); **Pasighat** (16 hrs, Rs 520); **Silchar** (12 hrs, Rs 390); **Siliguri** (12 hrs Rs 400); **Sonari** (10 hrs, Rs 350); **Tezpur** every 30 mins (3½ hrs).

ASTC bus stand, Paltan Bazar, T(0)9957-563033. Left luggage, Rs 10 per day. Ticket office open 0500-2000. ASTC buses are a bit slower and marginally less expensive than the private buses, but are modern. There are shuttle buses to the ISBT. ASTC also run a bus to **Along/Aalo** in Arunchal Pradesh at 1600 (Mon/Fri only, 14 hrs, Rs 500). **Meghalaya STC**, T0361-273 9557, in the ASTC compound, have frequent buses to **Shillong** between 0630-1700 (3½ hrs, Rs 89/120), to **Tura** at 0930 and 2000 (7 hrs, Rs 185).

City Bus Stand, Station Rd (north end): to **Hajo** (1½ hrs).

Adabari Bus Stand, AT Rd (4 km west of centre) reached by 'canters' from MG Rd, has buses to **Hajo**, **Orang** and **Nalbari**.

Sumo Jeeps go when full to Shillong (3½ hrs, Rs 140) from a rank next to the ASTC bus stand. Jeeps can be reserved (private) for long journeys (such as to Cherrapunji or Tawang) from a counter in the ASTC compound.

Train Station has tourist information, left luggage (Rs 10, trunks and suitcases only), on showing ticket. Enquiries: T1316133, T0361-254 0330. Reservations: 100 m north of the station on Station Rd, T0361-254 1799, 0800-1330, 1400-2000; Foreign Tourists, Counter 3, where patience is needed. To **Kolkata** (**H**): *Kamrup Exp 15960*, 0735, 23; *Saraighat Exp 12346*, 1245, 17 hrs (via **New Jalpaiguri**, 6½ hrs); *Kanchenjunga Exp 15658 (S)*, 2230, 21 hrs (via **New Jalpaiguri**, 9 hrs);. To **New Delhi** (**ND**): *Rajdhani Exp 12423/* 12435, 0705/0555, 27/32 hrs; *North East Exp 12505* (**ANVT**), 0945, 34 hrs. To **Dibrugarh** via Dimapur: *Rajdhani Exp 12436*, 1945 (Mon, Fri), 10¾ hrs; *Brahmaputra Mail 14056*, 1445, 13 hrs; *Kamrup Exp 15959*, 1600, 13½ hrs.

Manas National Park *p696*

Buses travel on a good fair weather road between Guwahati and Barpeta Rd but no further; taxis charge, Rs 600-800 per journey. The nearest train station is at Barpeta Rd (40 km) with trains to **Guwahati** and **Kolkata**.

Kaziranga National Park *p697*

Air Nearest airport is at Jorhat (88 km), see below. Foreign tourists must use Guwahati's **Borjhar Airport**, see page 693.
Bus/car Best to ask **Wild Grass** if they have a vehicle going from Guwahati, or confirm timings of private buses. **ASTC** buses between Guwahati and Jorhat via **Kohora** stopping at **Nagaon** (30 mins, where you can stop overnight); departs 0900, 1000, 1100, 1230, 5-6 hrs. Private buses: **Green Valley** (office behind bus station) coaches depart Guwahati for Tinsukia and Digboi, 0700 and 0730; lunch stop at **Wild Grass Resorts**, after 4 hrs. **Guwahati**: a/c bus from Dibrugarh stops at resort for lunch; leaves at 1330. **Kaziranga Forest Lodge** has 10 seats reserved on the Express coach between Golaghat and Guwahati. **Assam Tourism bus**, depart 0930 from **Bonashree Lodge**, arrive Guwahati 1600. From **Shillong** get a Jorhat bus and switch at **Jorabat** for Kaziranga.
Train **Furkating** (75 km) has the nearest station with trains from **Guwahati** and **Dibrugarh**; buses via **Golaghat**.

Tezpur and around *p698*

Air **Saloni Airport** is to the north of Tezpur: **Air India**, T03712-231657, www.airindia.com, flies to/from **Kolkata**.
Bus/taxi Frequent buses to/from **Guwahati** 0500-1330, Rs 80-90, luxury bus Rs 110-130 (4½-5 hrs); **Kaziranga** from 0600 until 1400 (2 hrs). Daily to **Dibrugarh**, 0615-1230, luxury at 0800 (7 hrs) via **Jorhat**; **Itanagar** at 1000 and 1215, Rs 130-150 (4½ hrs); **North Lakhimpur**, between 0545-1300, Rs 110 (5-6 hrs); **Tawang** (14 hrs). To **Nameri**, take a Bomdila-bound bus/*sumo* and get off at Hatigate, from where its 2.5 km to the Eco-camp. Taxi to **Orang/ Nameri**, Rs 600 plus petrol.
Sumos ASTC, T(0)9435-080318, T(0)9864-182449, and several private companies with offices near the bus stand run *sumos* to **Tawang** and destinations in between, leaving at 0530, 12-14 hrs, pickup from hotel.
Train The train station is 1 km past the main bus stand at Jhaj Ghat. Irregular services to **Guwahati** take 10 hrs, much better to take a bus. Trains also run from Rangapara to North Lakimpur, via Tezpur.

Jorhat *p699*

Air Jorhat has an airport 7 km from town with bus or autos for transfer. Private taxis Rs 100 to town or Rs 600 to Kaziranga. To **Kolkata** with **Air India**, Hotel Paradise, T0376-232 0011, airport, T0376-234 0294, www.airindia.com; **Jet Airlines**, airport, T0376-234 0881, www.jetairways.com; and **Kingfisher**, www.flykingfisher.com. **Air India**, to **Bangalore**, Thu and Sun, and **Guwahati**.
Bus **ASTC Stand** on AT Rd, T0376-230 1896, office open 0600-2130. Buses to **Guwahati**, 0615, 0700, 0740, 0900, 1245 (7 hrs, Rs 260); frequent services to **Tezpur** from 0600-1430 (3 hrs, Rs 75); **Sibsagar** from 0500-1600 (1½ hrs, Rs 40); **Dibrugarh** (5 hrs, Rs 80). Private buses leave from opposite ASTC, ticket booths are nearby and prices slightly higher, services to **Guwahati** and **Kaziranga** (2 hrs, Rs 60). Local services (to Nimatighat, Rs 10, and elsewhere) leave from the public bus stand at the north end of MG Rd.
Train Station (3 km southeast of bus stand) has no toilets. To **Guwahati**: *Jan Shatabdi Exp 12068*, Mon-Sat 1355, 7 hrs, via Lumding (from where narrow gauge goes to **Haflong**: 0615, 5 hrs – beautiful route but tourists are discouraged).

Majuli Island p699

Bus/rickshaw Bus from Jorhat (public bus stand, junction of MG and AT Rds) to **Nimatighat** (13 km north, Rs 10); allow 1 hr. Buses/shared buses meet incoming ferries at the *ghat*. To hire an auto- rickshaw Rs 150. During the dry months, North Lakhimpur is accessible by road; buses or shared taxis take about 6 hrs from Majuli.

Ferry Government ferry from **Nimatighat**, 0930, 1030, 1400, return 0730, 0830, 1330 and 1500. Confirm schedule, as they change seasonally, as does crossing time as boats have to circumnavigate sand bars, but going to Majuli about 1½ hrs, coming back is longer as it's upstream. The ferries can carry up to 2 cars. Buses run from the *ghat* in Majuli to **Kamalabari** (about 5 km) and **Garamur** (8.5 km, Rs 10).

Sibsagar p700

Nearest airport: Jorhat (60 km). Nearest railway station: Simaluguri (20 km), connected by frequent buses. Regular ASTC buses to **Guwahati** 5 in morning from 0700-0930, 5 in evening from 1830-2130 (9 hrs, Rs 310) plus private buses from AT Rd at 0715 and 1930. To **Dibrugarh** from 0530-1630 (2 hrs, Rs 40); to **Sonari** (for **Mon, Nagaland** from 0630-1530 (1½ hrs, Rs 30).

Dibrugarh p700

Air The airport is 16 km from town. **Air India**, T0373-230 0114, airport, T0373-238 2777, www.airindia.com, to **Kolkata**, Tue-Thu, Sun. **Jetlite** to **Kolkata** daily except Sun, and **Delhi** daily. Also flights to **Guwahati** with **Kingfisher**, **Jetlite** and **Air India**. **Pawan Hans** helicopters go to **Arunachal** daily, T(0)9435-734407, T(0)9436-051250.

Bus **Private Bus Stand** on AT Rd/RKB Path services to **Guwahati** at 1930, 2030 and 2130 (Rs 365), **Tezpur** at 2000 (6 hrs, Rs 260), **Itanagar/Naharlagun** at 1800 (12 hrs, Rs 460) via **North Lakimpur** (Rs 440), **Dimapur** at 2000 (Rs 280), and places in between.

ASTC Bus Stand is on Mancotta Rd, Chowkidinghee, with buses to **Guwahati**, **Jorhat**, **Tinsukia**. They often go and pick up more passengers from AT Rd (in front of the Asha Hotel) before leaving town.

Ferry To **Pasighat** in Arunachal Pradesh. Tickets for the jeep-ferry-jeep (Rs 180) can be bought in advance from the Kusum Hotel, Talkie House Rd, T0373-232 0143, and it is recommended to do so for ease of travel. Departure from the hotel at 0730, boat leaves at 0815. You land at Sonarighat (3 hrs) from where a jeep continues to Pasighat. There are later boats (1015, 1115, 1230 and 1330) if you wish to negotiate your own way to the ferry ghat.

Train To **Guwahati** (continuing to **New Delhi**): *Rajdhani Exp 12423/12435*, 2015/1900, 10 hrs *Kamrup Exp 15960*, 1825, 13 hrs (continues to **NJP** and **Kolkata (H)** in further 24 hrs). Local *BG Pass* to **Ledo** (via Tinsukia) 0705, 1615.

Tinsukia p700

Bus/train **ASTC Bus Stand** on AT Rd; private buses from top end of Rangagora Rd. To **Jorhat**, Rs 80. It's a Rs 5 rickshaw ride between the ASTC stand and the old train station, from where passenger trains run to **Jorhat** daily at 1415 (6 hrs, Rs 50). The 2 train stations are 3 km apart. New Tinsukia has most of the long-distance trains, to **Guwahati** (continuing to **New Delhi**) *Brahamaputra Mail 14055*, daily at 0025 (11 hrs), *Rajdhani Exp 12423/12435*, 2120/2005 (9 hrs) continues to **Delhi**, *Kamrup Exp 15960*, daily at 1940 (11½ hrs), continues to **NJP** and **Kolkata** (**H**).

Directory

Guwahati p693, map p694

Banks **United Bank of India**, HB Rd, Pan Bazar. ATM, plus many other ATMs around the centre. **Internet** There is a cluster internet cafes on Earl Rd, by the junction with GNB Rd, charging Rs 20 per hr. Nearby **Ice Net** has skype, Rs 15 per hr, Mon-Sat 1030-2100, Sun 1700-2000. **Medical services** **Ambulance**: T102. **Down Town Hospital**, GS Rd, Dispur, T0361-233 6906/233 1003, by far the best. **Post** GPO, Shillong Rd, with *Speed Post*.

Kaziranga National Park p697

Bank **State Bank of India**, ATM, 400 m east of the Tourist Complex gate. **Internet** Pharmacy to the right of the gate to the Tourist Complex has 1 computer, Rs 80 per hr. **Post** In the **Tourist Complex**. **Useful contacts** The **Wildlife Society** has a library of books and magazines and may show wildlife films to groups. **Range Officer**, T03776-226 2423. **Director**, Tourist Complex, Bokakhat, T03776-268095.

Tezpur p698

Banks **United Bank of India** and **Federal Bank**, Main Rd, both have ATMs. **Internet** **Animit Cyber Cafe**, Gopal Agarwalla Complex, Main Rd, T03712-230482, has new computers, daily 0930-2030. **Net Com**, Main Rd, Rs 20 per hr, daily 0930-2100.

Jorhat p699

Banks **State Bank of India**, AT Rd has ATM and exchanges TCs (show proof of purchase). **Internet** Several around town; handy for most hotels is **Trishool**, Solicitor Rd, good keyboards, Rs 20 per hr, Mon-Sat 1000-2100.

Majuli Island p699

Bank **United Bank of India**, Kamalabari, has ATM. **Internet** **Mice**, Garamur, has slow connection and only 1 computer, Rs 40 per hr, 0700-1900. Kamalabari has a couple of cybercafés.

Dibrugarh p700

Bank **State Bank of India**, ATM at the Railway Station. **Internet** **Cyber @ Generation Next**, HS Rd. Fast connection, Rs 20 per hr, staff speak English, printing, daily 0800-2200.

Meghalaya

➔ *Population: 2.9 million. Area: 22,500 sq km.*

Meghalaya ('abode of the clouds'), with its pine-clad hills, beautiful lakes, high waterfalls and huge caverns, has been tagged the 'Scotland of the East' because of the similarity of climate, terrain and scenery. The wettest region in the world, between May and September the rain comes down like waterfalls as the warm monsoon air is forced up over the hills. Home to the Garo, Khasi and Jaintia tribes, the hill state retains an untouched feel. There are traditional Khasi villages near Shillong with views into Bangladesh.

▸▸ *For listings, see pages 718-722.*

Background

The land Much of the plateau is made up of the same ancient granite as found in peninsular India; its south facing slope, overlooking Bangladesh, is dramatically steep. The hills rise to heights just under 2000 m, which makes it pleasantly cool and Cherrapunji is the wettest places on the earth. Much is still densely forested, although little wildlife remains. Shillong is the only important town; 80% of the people live in villages. Compact and isolated, Meghalaya's rolling plateau lies in a severe earthquake belt. In 1897, Shillong was entirely destroyed in an earthquake.

History The Khasi, Jaintia and Garo tribes each had their own small kingdoms until the 19th century when the British annexed them. The Garos, originally from Tibet, were animists. The Khasis are believed to be Austro-Asiatic. Jaintias are Mongolian and similar to the Shans of Burma. They believed in the universal presence of god and so built no temples. The dead were commemorated by erecting monoliths and groups of these can be seen in Khasi villages in central Meghalaya between Shillong and Cherrapunji. In the 19th century many Jaintias and Khasi were converted to Christianity by missionaries, although they continued many of their old traditions.

People Meghalaya is divided into three distinct areas, the Garo, Khasi and Jaintia Hills, each with its own language, culture and particular customs. All three tribes are matrilineal, passing down wealth and property through the female line, with the youngest daughter taking the responsibility of caring for the parents. The greeting '*kublei*' covers 'hello' and 'goodbye', while '*kublei shibun*' means 'thank you very much'.

Shillong

➔ *For listings, see pages 718-722. Colour map 4, B4.*

Situated among pine-clad hills and lakes, Shillong retains a measure of its colonial past particularly around Ward's Lake and in the quieter suburbs. Elsewhere in town, unattractive newer buildings have encroached upon open spaces and Shillong's trade-mark mists are being replaced by smog. Since the days of the British, Shillong has been an educational hub and school children (often boarders from other northeast states) are ever-present. A major attraction is the biggest market in the Northeast, while the daily betting on the archery competition (see box, page 716) is a unique feature.

Ins and outs ➔ *Population: 314,610. Altitude: 1491 m.*

Tourist information **India Tourism** ⓘ *GS Rd, Police Bazar, T0364-222 5632, Mon-Fri 0930-1730, Sat 0930-1400*, free map. **Meghalaya Tourism** ⓘ *opposite Meghalaya Bus Stand, Jail Rd, T0364-222 6220, www.meghalayatourism.com, daily 0700-1900*, have cheap day-tours around Shillong and further afield (see Activities and tours, page 721. **Directorate of Tourism** ⓘ *Nokrek Building, 3rd Meghalaya Secretariat, Lower Lachaumiere, T0364-250 0736, www.megtourism.gov.in, 0700-1800.*

Sights

The horseshoe-shaped **Ward's Lake** ⓘ *Rs 5, camera Rs 10, Wed-Mon 0830-1800 (winter 0830-1630)*, is pretty and popular for boating. Behind it is the **Botanical Garden** ⓘ *0900-1700*. Other colonial remnants include the immaculate little Presbyterian and All Saints churches.

Shillong

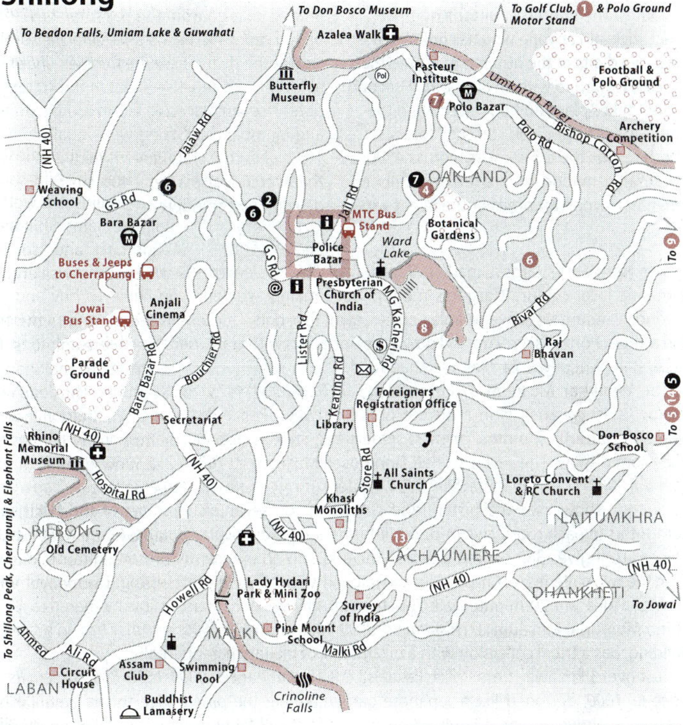

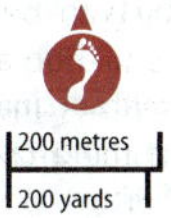

Lakkhotaa Lodge **1**
Pinewood **6**
Polo Towers **7**
Shillong Club **8**
White Orchid **13**
Yalana **14**

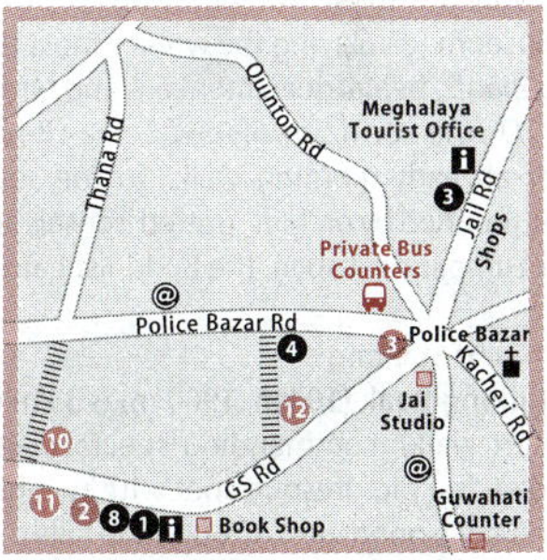

Sleeping
Ashutosh Inn **11**
Baba Tourist Lodge **2**
Broadway **12**
Centre Point & Le Galerie **3**
Earle Holiday Home **4**
Embassy **10**
Highway Inn **5**
Ken & Twill's **9**

Eating
Barbeque **1**
Bread Café **8**
City Hut Family Dhaba **7**
Eecee **3**
Jadoh Stall **4**
New World **6**
Regal **2**
TK's Dining Room **5**

The Archery Stakes

The Archery Stakes, unique to Shillong, take place Monday to Saturday. Members of different clubs shoot more than 500 arrows at a tiny cylindrical bamboo target for four minutes. The punters count the number that stick and anyone who has guessed the last two digits of the number of arrows that stick is rewarded with an 80:1 win. A second shoot takes place an hour later when the odds are 6:1 but if you correctly forecast both results the odds are as high as 4500:1. Naturally, the bookies are the best-dressed men in town. Start times of the event vary but it's usually around 1530-1600 (ask locally in the morning), and to find the inconspicuous field, go to Polo Bazar (just past the Polo Towers Hotel) and ask. Shared taxis go from the bazar for Rs 5, or you can walk the 1.5 km along the south side of the river. There are bookies' shops all over town and elsewhere in the state; bets are even placed as far off as Kolkata and Mumbai. The Stakes were legalized in 1983 when the state government realized that it could raise a hefty 40% tax on the daily money-spinner.

The Northeast's largest market, **Bara Bazar** ("BB" or *lewduh*) is well worth a visit to see authentic local colour. It attracts tribal people, mainly women, who come to buy and sell produce – mountains of vegetables, spices, giant fish, pots, chickens in baskets and even bows and arrows. Porters scurry up and down the tiny alleys with crazy loads on their backs; look out *jadoh* stalls where you can sample Khasi food.

The **Wankhar Museum of Entomology** ⓘ *T0364-254 4473, Rs 100, Mon-Sat 1100-1600, photos Rs 10 per shot*, is in a private house between Police Bazar and Wahingdoh, where beautiful butterflies, moths, beetles, spiders and stick insects are pinned out in a colourful one-room display. The seven-storied **Don Bosco Museum** ⓘ *T0364-255 0260, www.dbcic.org, Mon-Sat 0900-1730 (summer), 0900-1630 (winter), Rs 150, photos Rs 100 per shot, leave bags in the cloakroom*, showcases the history and culture of the seven sister states of the Northeast. Computers in each room give in-depth information, as do display boards. A 'sky-walk' up the pointed roof gives 360 degree views of Shillong. It is an excellently presented museum, and even the two galleries on Christianity and religion are surprisingly interesting. The museum is in Mawlai, a pleasant 20-minute walk from the Butterfly Museum or accessible by shared taxi. The **Rhino Memorial Museum** ⓘ *Hospital Rd, 0900-1300 and 1400-1800, entrance free*, in a striking building, has a tribal collection with a bizarre mix of military paraphernalia.

Just over 1 km away from Police Bazar is **Lady Hydari Park** ⓘ *0800-1630, Rs 5, camera Rs 10, video Rs 1000*, designed like a Japanese garden, where the pine native to the area – *Pinus khasiana* – thrive amongst English flowerbeds. It is well laid out with a tiny **Forest Wildlife Museum** (displaying the world's most threadbare clouded leopard) and a **Mini Zoo** with living leopards, bears, deer, monkeys and birds.

On the north side of town is the 18-hole golf course, amid pines, dating from 1898 and ideal for an early-morning walk. To the south, the **Crinoline Waterfalls** has a swimming pool surrounded by orchids, potted bonsais and a rock pool with reeds and water lilies. Further south at Lumparing, Laban, the Buddhist **Lamasery** is interesting but be prepared for a steep climb.

Around Shillong

Shillong Peak (10 km, 1960 m) is 3 km off the Cherrapunji Road (motorable, save for the last short walk), commanding spectacular views. **Elephant Falls** (12 km), off the Cherrapunji Road, is a picturesque spot with two high waterfalls. You can walk down to the lowest pool and get a good view, though the falls themselves are less impressive between November and May. The artificial **Umiam Lake** (Barapani), 16 km, offers fishing, boating and watersports from the Orchid Lake Resort.

Other areas of Meghalaya → *For listings, see pages 718-722.*

Mawsynram → *55 km from Shillong.*

Mawjymbuin Cave has water dripping from a breast-shaped stone on to what looks like a Siva lingam, and plenty of stalactites and stalagmites. Take a bus from Bara Bazar in Shillong at 1400 (three hours). **Mawphlang Sacred Forest**, 20 km from Shillong, is a revered ancient burial site and also a rare haven for flora and fauna, including orchids and ferns. Guided walks can be arranged with local guides.

Cherrapunji → *Colour map 4, B4. Altitude: 1482 m.*

The old administrative headquarters of the Khasis, picturesque Cherrapunji (also known as Shora, the official government name) is a pleasant, quiet town spread out along a ridge with gravestones dotting the surrounding hillocks. The best time to visit for spectacular views is during the drier months of November to February. The heat and humidity can be oppressive in the summer. By mid-March it is hazy most days and you should expect the odd torrential downpour. It holds the record as the wettest place on earth, with an average of 11,900 mm rainfall annually.

The colourful **Ka Iewbah Sohrarim** (market) is held every eight days in Cherra Bazar and attracts hordes of Khasi tribespeople. There is also a smaller Iewrit (market) every fourth day. Khasi women all wear a checked apron tied over one shoulder, and both sexes wrap up in Welsh plaid blankets against the cold. The local orange flower honey is sold during the winter season, along with sacks of betel nuts (*kwai*), gruesome chunks of meat, and anything else you care to imagine. Little food stalls are a good place to sample Khasi food. If possible, time your visit to Cherrapunji with to coincide with a market day (see www.cherrapunji.com for dates). If the market is due to fall on a Sunday, the date is moved to the preceding Saturday as most people observe the Christian day of rest.

Nohkalikai Falls, reputedly the world's fourth highest, is 5 km west of Cherrapunji, near Sohrarim. There is always a significant flow of water, while multiple torrents are seen during the rainy season. Limestone caves nearby include Krem Mawmluh (4503 m) with a five river passage and Krem Phyllut (1003 m) at **Mawsmai**, with a large fossil passage and two stream ways. Mawsmai also has high waterfalls in the wet season.

The most astonishing sight around Cherrapunji and a must-see of the Northeast are a series of **living root bridges** found near Mawshamok. Here, Khasi tribespeople have trained the roots of the *ficus elastica* rubber tree into robust bridges, spanning streams that become raging torrents in the monsoon. It takes 15-20 years for the bridges to become strong enough to support the crossing of people and goods between the villages, but they last for several centuries (possibly up to 800 years) – getting sturdier as they age. There is an excellent eco-friendly resort (see Sleeping, page 719) that can provide sketch maps for the challenging treks to the bridges. From the resort, a short trek entails a very steep 45-minute descent to the tangled mass of Ummunoi 'single' root-bridge, well worth the effort and pain of the ascent back up. Or it is possible to make a day-trek to the extraordinary Umshiang **'double-decker'** model ⓘ *camera Rs 10, video Rs 50*, in Nongriat village, from where it is a short walk to icy turquoise pools. This trek involves descending 3000 steps through the dense jungle, past pretty hamlets and several other root-bridges , with plenty of ups and well as downs. It is possible to stay overnight at **Nongriat**, and highly recommended to do so (see Sleeping, page 720).

Jainta Hills

The once beautiful scenery of the Jainta Hills has been spoilt somewhat in the last few decades by the coal mines that sustain the economy of the area. **Jowai**, 64 km southeast of Shillong on NH44, is the headquarters of the Jaintia Hills, circled by the Myntdu River. The market, full of tribal women, is especially colourful. From Shillong cars take 2½ hours, buses a little longer. **Nartiang**, 55 km from Shillong, is a scenic spot famed for its monoliths, which were raised in tribute to Jainta kings. It is only 12 km from Jowai and accessible by public transport, although vehicles are crammed way beyond capacity.

Syndai, 40 km south, has many caves used by ancient warriors as hide-outs, such as Krem Sweep with a vast chamber. India's longest (6381 m) and deepest (106.8 m) Eocene Age cave with cataracts and falls is **Krem Um-Lawan**, 60 km southeast of Jowai near **Lumshnong**.

Tura

The centre of the West Garo Hills District, Tura, 220 km southwest of Guwahati, sits at the foot of the jungle-clad 1457 m Nokrek Peak. It is a spread-out town with a slow pace of life. Tura Bazar is dominated by the supermarket, a red-and-white mini shopping mall, with an underground car park. The small fruit and vegetable market in the basement is well organized. The Tourist Office is 4 km out of town next to the **Orchid Lodge**, where you can arrange guides for excursions in the hills. Weekly tribal markets are held in surrounding villages and the **Wangala dance festival**, with great ceremonial drumming, occurs in November after the harvest.

Nokrek Peak can be reached by a 5-km trek, but involves rock climbing, so is best not attempted alone. **Nokrek National Park** is 45 km away. Jeeps from Tura Bazar cost Rs 1150-1500 for the round trip (daily rate). Ask the tourist office for a guide. **Naphak Lake**, 112 km, near the Simsang River is good for fishing and birdwatching.

Baghmara and Siju → *Colour map 4, B3.*

North of Baghmara by 35 km, with others nearby, is one of India's longest caves (4.8 km) with a fine river passage. Groups of at least four are needed for caving so look out on noticeboards. It is more enjoyable and cheaper to travel this way. Bus/jeep to Baghmara, 45 km, 1½ hours from Tura.

Meghalaya listings

For Sleeping and Eating price codes and other relevant information, see Essentials pages 38-42.

Sleeping

Shillong *p714, map p715*

LL-D Lakkhotaa Lodge, Mawpun, Polo Hills, T0364-259 0523/4, www.lakkhotaalodge.com. A modern palace with 9 hand-crafted rooms that are truly sumptuous. Run by a Jaintia-American couple who have paid every attention to guests comfort, melding Feng Shui elements with art from all over the world: Italian marble floors, a Gujarati marriage 'mandap', Moghul tiles, Uzebek tables and Cherokee designs. Each room is unique with marble bathroom and views over pine trees or the golf course. Excellent and varied cuisine, gift-shop, fitness room. Singles start from Rs 5000, doubles from Rs 7000, up to a presidential suite at Rs 15,000 (discounts if you forego breakfast/free Wi-Fi). A bunk-bed option, Rs 500 per person, gives budget travellers the chance to enjoy billiards, a glorious bar and luxurious seating areas (inside and out). Golf can be arranged.

AL-B Pinewood, Rita Rd, behind Ward's Lake, T0364-222 3146, www.meghalayatourism.org. An atmospheric Raj relic, however lurking behind the nostalgic colonial bungalow is a monstrous new plate-glass 'annex' with 75 rooms due to open in 2012. The 40 original rooms vary according to price, but standard ones are old-fashioned (needing a coat of paint) but charming in their way with working fireplaces (single/double Rs 1600/2200), also **L** cottages. Restaurant with good menu, nice bar, billiards, gym, free Wi-Fi.

AL-B Tripura Castle, Cleve Colony, T0364-250 1111, www.tripuraroyalheritage. The first heritage hotel in the northeast, with 9 art deco-style rooms with brass fireplaces, polished wood and heaps of class. The tea lounge, billiards and atmospheric bar all add to its charm. With 24 hrs notice they can prepare top-notch Khasi food. It was once the summer residence of the maharajahs of Tripura.

A Polo Towers, Oakland Rd, Polo Grounds, T0364-222 2341/2, www.hotelpolotowers.com. 50 well-appointed rooms (pay extra for classier more contemporary furnishings), modern and businesslike, most rooms have views over Polo Bazar, popular bar (see Entertainment, page 721) and Ginger restaurant is quite fancy.

A-C Centre Point, GS Rd, Police Bazar, T0364-222 5210, www.centrepointshillong.com. Comfortable no-nonsense rooms (standard ones quite small), most have views through huge windows (often over nearby construction work), contemporary furnishings in the club rooms, very good La Galerie restaurant, **Cloud 9** bar (see Listings, page 721), breakfast included, Wi-Fi in lobby.

A-D Shillong Club, MG Rd (near Ward's Lake), T0364-222 5497, shillongclubltdresi@hotmail.com. Best to book ahead, fading rooms in an annex behind the 'colonial' club, big bathrooms, balconies upstairs, but ratty carpets and the shabby sofas hanging around in the corridors don't appeal. However, guests still recommend it for the atmosphere. Also some expensive cottages; Indian restaurant, bar, tennis, billiards.

B Ken & Twill's, Law-U-Sib, Lumbatngen, Madanriting, T(0)9856-030474, www.saimikapark.com. Well away from the city centre in amongst pine trees, this homely house with 5 rooms is named after the lovely owner's parents. Plenty of character with wooden floors, Cherrapunji stone walls, open-plan lounge/dining room with fireplace, quilts in the bedrooms plus fridge and TV; it encourages a long stay. Mrs Phanbuh also has a place in Cherrapunji (see Sa-I-Mika, below).

B-F Earle Holiday Home, Oakland Rd, T0364-222 6614, T(0)9863-118214. Rooms in the old cottages are about the cheapest you'll find, spartan and faded but clean with squat loos and geysers (Rs 350/450), it's a good idea to book ahead. The original turreted bungalow has larger semi-delux rooms (Rs 650) while the annex (being extended) has more comfortable rooms in a range of categories (starting at Rs 750). The Dhaba restaurant is one of the nicest places to eat in Shillong.

C-D Broadway, GS Rd, T0364-222 6996. Well-maintained hotel with plants in the hallways and olde-worlde vibes from the old tourist posters and wood-panelled reception. Doubles are decent enough but it's best for single travellers, with simple rooms with TV sharing a clean bathroom (Rs 350) or private bath (Rs 600). Large front terrace looking down over the busy street.

D White Orchid, Upper Lachumiere, T(0)9206-315791, www.shillonghotel.com. Modern guesthouse with 8 rooms, clean, new mattresses and sheets, and some great views from the back rooms (Rm 103 especially). Out of the centre, though shared taxis connect with town.

D-E Ashutosh Inn, GS Rd, T0364-222 1276, www.ashutoshinn.com. Newly renovated rooms are small and (like so many hotels in Shillong) most of them lack outside windows, but they're comfortable and clean with wood panelling, TV, Wi-Fi and geysers.

D-E Highway Inn, near Taxi Stand, Laitumkhrah, T0364-250 4886. Decent hotel has rooms with newly laminated floors, fresh paint, white sheets, TV, squat toilets, hot buckets, but rather hard beds. Many don't have outside windows. Pay extra for spacious rooms with chairs and tables. Standard singles Rs 400, doubles Rs 700. Out of town (connected by shared taxi) but plenty of eateries, internet and cafes in the pleasant little centre of Laitumkhrah.

D-F Yalana, Main Rd, Laitumkrah (near Don Bosco), T0364-221 1240. Comfortable hotel of a good standard for the price, though dark carpets and horrid bedspreads detract. Cheaper rooms have geysers, but often not working when it's hot water by the bucket. Good restaurant, very friendly.

E Baba Tourist Lodge, GS Rd, T0364-221 1285. Basic, restaurant with Bengali/Assamese food, 27 rooms including some microscopic singles (Rs 500), popular with backpackers and doubles are still some of the cheapest in town, rude staff.

E Embassy, AC Lane, Police Bazar, T0364-222 3164. Clean rooms with TV, most have geysers, good management, the best of the budget choices in the town centre. The restaurant is good and cheap.

Cherrapunji *p717*

C Sa-I-Mika Park, 1 km before Cherrapunji, T0364-254 6501, www.saimikapark.com. Admirable Mrs JR Phanbuh (who also owns Ken & Twill's in Shillong) has created a park on the rocky moors outside Cherrapunji. A stream runs through with mini-waterfalls, and it's perfect for families (kid's swimming pool, volleyball, badminton). There are 6 comfortable stone walled rooms and slightly cheaper Khasi huts (hot water by bucket), the lack of TVs encourage guests to get back to nature. Khasi food is served, plus cooking huts. Hikes around Cherrapunji are easily arranged.

C-E Cherrapunji Holiday Resort, Laitkynsew village, T03637-244 218/9, T(0)9436-115925, www.cherrapunji.com. Lovely hosts and an idyllic setting make this resort particularly enchanting. Double tents are Rs 600 (only available in high season), or there are spacious rooms with comfy beds and nice bathrooms, plus an excellent restaurant. Plenty of help is given to lone trekkers, sketch maps of the area are provided, experienced guides lead river canyoning expeditions (best Oct-Feb), there's free Wi-Fi and good look-out points nearby. At a lower altitude than Cherrapunji town (920 m), it feels significantly warmer. Highly recommended.

E-F Shora Plaza, next to the sumo stand, Cherra Bazar, T03637-235762, T(0)9436-308007. 2 small, basic but cheerful rooms with adequate bedding, right next to the market, good restaurant and sweet people. Hot water by the bucket.

F Nongriat Rest House, 6 km from the village of Tyrna, T(0)9856-891520, T(0)9615-737690. 4 basic rooms for Rs 400, excellent cheap meals, idyllic location in the tiny village where the double-decker root bridge is located. "No extra charge for spider-killing"!

There are also 2 simple hotels on Ducant Rd in South Shora/Lower Cherra, near the main GPO, about 3 km downhill from Cherra Bazar: **Green Valley** (3 rooms) and the nearby **Halari** which has a good restaurant.

Tura *p718*

B-D Rikman Continental, Tura Bazar, T03651-220744, rikman_tura@hotmail.com. Clean rooms, larger and more expensive with a/c, ecomony non-a/c Rs 999 per double, good restaurant serves Garo dishes.

F Orchid Lodge (MTDC), New Tura (4 km from Tura Bazar), city bus to Dakopgre stops outside, or auto-rickshaw (Rs 50; Rs 70 at night), T03651-242394, T(0)9856-221160. Dorm (Rs 100), 7 rooms, TV (variable reception despite a giant satellite dish), dining hall meals at set times, tourist office next door (tours of Siju, Balpakram).

Baghmara and Siju *p718*

F-G Tourist Lodge (MTDC), Baghmara, T03639-222141. Take your own provisions, a chowkidar will cook for you. Great views.

Eating

Shillong *p714, map p715*

Try a local pork dish, *dohkhleh* (minced brains with onion and spices) with *jadoh* (rice flavoured with turmeric or pig's blood) and *saag* (greens) or *jhur khleh* (curried veg) with spicy *tung tap* (hot chutney made with dried fish) or *pudina* (mint chutney) at places in Bara Bazar.

₸₸-₸ Barbeque, GS Rd. Daily 1030-2030. This basement restaurant with a cosy red interior serves superlative Chinese dishes, plenty of chicken and pork, deservedly popular despite the high-ish prices.

₸₸-₸ City Hut Family Dhaba, Earle Holiday Home, T0364-222 0886. Open 1100-2130, closed every last Tue of the month. Probably the nicest restaurant in Shillong, with a huge choice including Mexican and Thai. Interesting Indian and Chinese dishes (paneer steak, tandoori duck, great thalis Rs 125-150), the cute gazebos are reserved for couples and families.

₸₸-₸ Le Galerie, 1st floor at **Center Point Hotel** (see Sleeping). Daily 1130-2130. Tempting Indian and Chinese food that is well-priced, good vegetarian selection, un-fussy decor with old pictures of Meghalaya, windows all around, efficient staff, very popular with families.

₸ Bread Cafe, 1st floor above Barbeque, GS Rd. Daily 1000-2000. Serves good pizzas and fast food, 'real' sandwiches on 'real' bread, pasta, good coffee, cheap and cheerful though the TV is sometimes rather loud. Recommended.

₸ Eee Cee, below **Eee Cee Hotel**, Police Bazar, T0364-222 0704. Daily 0930-2030. Good restaurant with lots of Western food as well as Chinese, great cakes, very reasonably priced, bright and unpretentious.

₸ New World, 2 branches, 1 on GS Rd in Bara Bazar and another in Police Bazar. Good Chinese, half-plates available, *hakka* chow very tasty, though the decor is rather gloomy and shabby.

₸ Regal Restaurant, Police Bazar, T0364-222 4527. Popular little place with locals and tourists, has some South Indian dishes as well as the usual Chinese and North Indian. Veg and non-veg.

TK's Dining Room, Main Rd, Laitumkhrah. Mon-Sat 1000-2000. Cheap Khasi meals (about Rs 45), veg and non-veg, simple canteen-style surrounds. They are happy to explain the menu.

Cherrapunji *p717*

Cherra Bazar has a few eateries.

Shora Plaza, see Sleeping, Mon-Sat 0700-2130. Serves good food, especially the meat momos and veg Indian (spice separate for Westerners), though their chow is uninspiring.

Bars and clubs

Shillong *p714, map p715*

Shillong is known for its retro music scene and weekend nights sometimes see rock bands performing in town, look for flyers. **Cloud 9** at Centre Point Hotel is a nice watering hole with great night-time views over the city, attracts a younger crowd, with DJs on Fri/Sat nights (2000-2300), open till 2130 weeknights (beer Rs 180). Hotel Polo Towers has popular **Platinum** bar with Happy Hours 1300-1600, Fri is Ladies Night, DJ on Sat, weekends open till 0100, sporting events shown; also **Piccadilly** British-style pub, beer Rs 150. The bars at the **Pinewood** (beer Rs 130) and **Shillong Club** have some atmosphere. *Kiad*, the local rice wine, is popular in roadside bars.

Festivals and events

Shillong *p714, map p715*

4-5 Feb Roots Festival Unlimited, a folk event at Orchid Lake Resort, Umiam, Barapani, 20-min drive from Shillong, www.rootfestival.co.in.

6 Feb Jammin' is a Bob Marley festival that attracts a few thousand, usually held at the Orchid Lake Resort, tickets Rs 50-100.

Apr Shad Suk Mynsiem is a 3-day Khasi dance festival during which fantastic costumes and jewellery are worn.

24 May Bob Dylan Festival, at the State Central Library Auditorium, Rs 100-1000.

Oct/Nov The 5-day Khasi **Nongkrem dance festival** is held in Smit, 11 km from Shillong.

Nov Wangala dance festival celebrates the harvest in the Garo Hills.

Shopping

Shillong *p714, map p715*

You can get handwoven shawls, canework, Khasi jewellery, handicrafts, orange flower honey. **Govt Emporia** are on Jail Rd and GS Rd. Look out in **Bara Bazar** for women selling attractive Khasi silver, gold and amber jewellery.

Activities and tours

Shillong *p714, map p715*

Tour operators

Cultural Pursuits, Hotel Pegasus Crown, T0364-2550753, www.culturalpursuits.com. Eco-adventure tours of Assam, Meghalaya.

Green Routes, T(0)986-349 5777, greenrouteshg@gmail.com. Eco-conscious tours and treks throughout Meghalaya and other Northeast states, reasonable rates; Ashley Lyngdoh is an experienced and helpful guy.

Meghalaya Tourism, Jail Rd, Police Bazar, T0364-222 6220, www.meghalayatourism.com. Tours around Shillong stopping a short time at sights, daily 0800-1430, Rs 170. Also to Cherrapunji (Rs 220), Nartiang (Rs 230) and Mawsynram (Rs 160). Tours only occur when there are sufficient numbers, so Sun is the safest bet. Good value for solo travellers.

Natural Ways, Hawakhana, Tura, T(0)9863-091278, somuingty@yahoo.co.in. Adventure tours in the Garo Hills.

Transport

Shillong *p714, map p715*

Air Shillong has a small airport with limited services to **Kolkata** with Air India. To **Guwahati Airport** (127 km). **Meghalaya Helicopter Service**, MTC Bus Stand, Jail Rd, T0364-222 3129, (0)9435-145033, 1000-1600, flies to/from **Guwahati**, on Mon-Sat and from Guwahati to **Tura** (Mon, Wed, Fri), maximum 10 kg baggage, but poor safety record.

Bus Meghalaya TC, Jail Rd, T0364-222 3129, booking office open 0600-1600. To **Guwahati** hourly from 0700-1600 (3½ hrs, Rs 90); **Silchar** 1 per day at 1900 (10 hrs, Rs 190, recommended to book in the morning); to **Tura** at 0715 and 1600 (9-10 hrs, Rs 255). Also from stands near Anjali Cinema, Bara Bazar to towns in Meghalaya, including **Cherrapunji** from Mawlong Hat bus stand at 1330 (1½ hrs), carrying on to **Laitkynsew**. Private bus companies (such as

Network Travels) have offices/booths around Police Bazar for long-distance connections in the Northeast: **Agartala** at 1830 (18 hrs, Rs 600); **Aizawl** at 1900 (17 hrs, Rs 540) via **Silchar** (Rs 350); **Imphal** at 1500 (18 hrs, Rs 750); **Kohima** at 1500 (12 hrs, Rs 600) via **Dimapur**; **Siliguri** at 1600 (14-15 hrs, Rs 450).
Sumo For **Guwahati** (3 ½ hrs, Rs 140) sumos leave from Police Bazar until 0800, after that from the Polo Grounds or move conveniently (but slower to fill up) from GS Rd. For **Cherrapunji (Sohra)** jeeps leave when full from Mowlang Hat bus stand (upper level), near Anjali Cinema in Bara Bazar (1 ½ hrs, Rs 50). If you are heading straight to the Cherrapunji Resort, there is one bus a day to the village close by (see buses, above). Jeeps to **Jowai** leave from the Jowai stand, also near Anjali Cinema.
Taxi Yellow-top taxis pick up passengers to share rides. Flag one down and hop in if it is going your way; short hops Rs 5, eg Police Bazar to Laitumkhrah, Rs 10. **Car hire** from the tourist office.

For long-distance: **Tourist Taxi Association**, Kacheri Rd, Police Bazar, T0364-222 3895, share taxi to **Guwahati**, Rs 200 or private hire Rs 800; to **Cherrapunji** private hire Rs 1600.
Train Guwahati (103 km) is the nearest railhead. Tickets from **MTC Bus Stand**, 0600-1100, 1300-1600.

Cherrapunji *p717*
Bus Infrequent to **Shillong** (Bara Bazar) (1½ hrs) you are better taking a sumo; bus to **Laitkynsew** village (for Cherrapunji Resort) 1 per day at 1530.
Sumo To **Shillong** from Cherra Bazar (leave when full) from 0700-1700 (1½ hrs, Rs 50). You might get a sumo to **Laitkynsew** (for Cherrapunji Resort) at around 1430; sumos leave from Laitkynsew for Shillong at 0600.
Taxi From Cherra Bazar for **Nohkalikai Falls**, **Krem Mawmluh** and views over the plains of Bangladesh, Rs 400; **Meghalaya Tourism** in Shillong also runs tours. To **Cherrapunji Resort** a taxi costs Rs 300.

Tura *p718*
Air Helicopter services to/from **Shillong** and **Guwahati**.
Bus To **Baghmara** 106 km (for Siju, none direct), 1300, 4-5 hrs, along the Bangladesh border. Buy tickets the day before from booth near **MTC Bus Stand**, Tura Bazar; ask your hotel to buy your ticket for a small fee. Private buses to **Guwahati** (8 hrs), **Shillong** (12 hrs, night bus arrives at 0400), **Siliguri** from Tura Bazar. Booking offices are easy to find.

❻ Directory

Shillong *p714, map p715*
Banks **State Bank of India**, MG Rd, 1st floor. Mon-Fri 1130-1400. **Indian Overseas Bank**, GS Rd (Police Bazar end). **Internet** Plenty of options in the centre of town; decent connection at **BK Technology**, basement of the Zara Arcade, GS Rd, Rs 20 per hr has skype, Mon-Sat 0830-2030. **Medical services** **Ambulance**, T0364-222 4100. **Civil Hospital**, GS Rd, T0364-222 3889. **Nazareth Hospital**, Laitumukhrah, T0364-222 4052. **Post** **GPO**, GS Rd, Police Bazar.

Arunachal Pradesh

→ *Population: 1.38 million. Area: 84,000 sq km.*

This is Northeast India's largest and most remote state. The Tawang Monastery, birthplace of the sixth Dalai Lama and surrounded by awesome mountainscapes, is a major attraction, along with the rich tribal heritage throughout the state. In the east, the forests canopies of Namdapha National Park shelter elephant, clouded leopard, snow leopard, tiger, Himalayan black bear, red panda and musk deer. ▸▸ *For listings, see pages 729-734.*

The land

On the Northeast frontier of India, Arunachal Pradesh is India's least densely populated state with just 13 people per sq km. It stretches from the foothills of the eastern Himalaya to their permanently snow-capped peaks to the north. The Brahmaputra, known here as the Siang River, enters the state from China and flows through a deeply cut valley. Stretching from the Himalaya to the steamy plains of the Brahmaputra valley, Arunachal Pradesh has an extraordinary range of forests from the Alpine to the subtropical – from rhododendrons to orchids, reeds and bamboo. It is an orchid lover's paradise with over 550 species identified.

Climate

Bomdila (2500 m) and Tawang (3500 m) are exceptionally cold between October and March with temperatures in Tawang dropping as low as -12°C. However, clear skies are most likely October to December, and it is also when many flowers are in bloom.

History

The entire region had remained isolated since 1873 when the British stopped free movement. After 1947 Arunachal became part of the North East Frontier Agency (NEFA). Its strategic significance was demonstrated by the Chinese invasion in 1962, and the Indian government subsequently broke up the Agency giving statehood to all the territories surrounding Assam. Arunachal became the 24th state in 1987, though China continues to argue that until the international border between it and India are agreed some of the territory remains disputed. At the same time the state is disputing its southern border with Assam, and in April 2001 the state government lodged a petition with India's Supreme Court against the government of Assam for 'large-scale encroachment' on its territory. Having long borders with China and Myanmar, it is a truly frontier State. The state was opened to tourists in 1995 with the first foreigners being given permission to trek only as recently as 1998. Congress won both Lok Sabha seats in 2009.

Culture

The Arunachali people are the state's greatest attraction, wth 26 different tribes residing here. In the capital Itanagar you see Nishi warriors wearing hornbill beaks on their woven caps, carrying bearskin bags and their knives in monkey-skin scabbards.

A great diversity of the tribal people speak over 60 different dialects. Most have an oral tradition of recording their historic and cultural past by memorizing verses handed down through generations. Some Buddhist tribes have, however, maintained written records, largely recording their religious history. Some tribes worship Donyi and Polo, the Sun and Moon gods.

Itanagar-Naharlagun

→ *For listings, see pages 729-734. Colour map 4, A5.*

Itanagar, the new capital, and Naharlagun, the old town 10 km away, together provide the capital's administrative offices. Itanagar, sited between two hills, has the governor's residence on one and a Buddhist temple on the other, with shops, bazars and hotels strung along the busy main road in between. The capital has been identified as Mayapur, the 11th-century capital of the Jitari Dynasty.

Ins and outs → *Population: 61,900.*

Getting there and around Visitors arriving at Lilabari or North Lakhimpur in Assam take two hours by bus (or a little less by jeep) to Itanagar, calling at Naharlagun before climbing up along a scenic road to the new capital. Regular buses run from Guwahati and Shillong. Frequent transport runs between Itanagar and Naharlagun from 0600 until 2000. Cycle-rickshaws only available in Naharlagun. » *See Transport, page 733.*

Tourist information Arunachal Pradesh Tourism ⓘ *Directorate of Tourism, H Sector, T0360-221 4745, www.arunachaltourism.com, 400 m along a steep side road starting by Nirvachan Bhavan, near Ganga Market, Mon-Fri 1000-1630,* has some colourful pamphlets but little practical advice.

Sights

The yellow-roofed and beautifully decorated **Buddhist temple** stands in well-kept gardens on a hilltop with good views. There is an evening puja at around 1630 each day. Below the Gompa, the **Jawaharlal Nehru State Museum** ⓘ *Sun-Thu 0930-1600, Rs 75,* has been undergoing renovation and displays dioramas of tribal people and related artefacts on the ground floor. Upstairs includes a spectacular jewellery collection (look for the Ido-Mishmi priest's belt decorated with fangs and cymbals), many carvings of figures (including animals), an impressive Thangka Gallery and archaeological finds from Malinthan, Ita Fort and Vijaynagar. Across the main road, the tiny **Archaeological Museum and Park** ⓘ *Mon-Fri, Rs 2* has scant brick remains of the **Ita Fort** western gate and is a five-minute visit. The Ita Fort (14th-15th century) is believed to have been built by King Ramachandra. The **Gyaker Sinyi** (Ganga Sekhi Lake), 6 km, is reached by a rough road through forests of bamboo and tree ferns. On reaching the foot of the hill, walk across a bamboo bridge, up steps cut on the hillside to reach a ridge overlooking the forest lake (water levels have been sinking in recent years). There is also a small zoo nearby.

Western Arunachal Pradesh → *For listings, see pages 729-734. Colour map 4, A4.*

The whole journey, from Tezpur in Assam (the nearest airport) to Tawang, is spectacular, passing waterfalls, terraced paddy fields, alpine forests and mountain streams. The road north crosses the border at **Bhalukpong** (see page 698), and continues towards Bomdila passing through low wooded slopes for about 60 km. On the bank of the Bhoreli River in the upper plains is **Tipi**, with the Orchid Research Centre and a glasshouse with 500 species of orchids. From there the road rises sharply to reach Bomdila.

Ins and outs

For those not travelling with a hired jeep, ASTC buses or *sumo* services ply between Tezpur and Tawang (in winter, buses only make it as far as Dirang). *Sumos* are far preferable, though more expensive: they are significantly quicker and can negotiate the narrow, terrifying roads far better. To take the journey in one go means a gruelling 12-14 hours, better to do this coming back rather than going up. When breaking the journey at Bomdila or Dirang, try to book onward *sumo* tickets in advance and ask for 'number 1 seat' for best views and comfort. Coming back down from Tawang, the best seats are reserved days in advance so again do some forward planning. Check travel conditions locally (Sela Pass is frequently closed by snow) and, if in a private vehicle, don't travel after dark as visibility on the narrow mountain roads can be very poor at night.

Bomdila → *Colour map 4, A4. Altitude: 2530 m.*

On a clear day, Bomdila has marvellous views of the snow-capped mountains. There's a craft centre, apple and cherry orchards, three Buddhist *gompas* and a museum. Transport links are good, there is internet connection and hotels are generally more comfortable than those in Dirang, but it is a sprawling rather unattractive place. Buses leave from the bus stand in the lower part of town and *sumos* from the main bazar, 2 km up the hill and therefore more convenient for hotels. **Himalayan Holiday** in the market has some basic tourist information.

Dirang → *Colour map 4, A4.*

About an hour's drive after Bomdila, the road cuts through the miniature village of Old Dirang and continues another 5 km to larger (newer) Dirang, which has a few guesthouses and simple places to eat. It is a more appealing stop than Bomdila when breaking the journey to Tawang, though make sure you book an onward ticket in advance. A day can easily be spent walking to tiny peaceful villages nearby. The obvious attraction is the old village, huddled around the confluence of two rivers, where a population of some 1200 Monpa tribespeople inhabit traditional stone dwellings with slatted wooden upper levels and woven roofs. One of the morning *sumos* to Bomdila can drop you off at the ancient three-storey **Khatsikpa Gompa** atop a small ridge, from where it's a steep walk past *stupas* and *mani* walls down to the village. Here, women walk along knitting, men carry woven *shingrong* baskets from head-straps and kids run around with babies tied on their backs. Across the main bridge, a sign points the way to the plain stacked stones of **Dirang Dzong** (generally locked), one of several *dzongs* in the district from where Tibetan officials collected taxes. An hour or so is sufficient to explore the pathways of the village, and then it's an easy walk back to New Dirang following the road along the river, criss-crossing a couple of bridges on the way.

From the central crossroads in New Dirang, the turning signed to the Yak Research Centre leads into a 2-km uphill tramp to lovely **Yewang** village. The track forks but both lead to the village: the new track to the right is quicker, but it's nice to turn left and walk through the first cluster of homes surrounded by terracing and agriculture before reaching the beautiful *gompa* at the highest point of Yewang. The forested foothills begin in earnest from here, while the village trickles down the hillside below among fields of yellow mustard flowers, pink peas, millet, cabbage or corn – depending on the season.

To Tawang → *Colour map 4, A4.*

After passing through the pretty Dirang Valley shrouded in pine woods, the route snakes past lonely army camps and teetering villages to the **Sela Pass** which at 4215 m presents a far starker view. The successor to Lama Guru Rimpoche has been found in a village nearby. Stop a while here above the clouds, along one of the highest motorable roads in the world, with views of a high-altitude lake and graphite peaks streaked with snow. **Jaswantpur**, 13 km from the pass, has the *samadhi* to the brave Jawan (soldier), Jaswant Singh, which commemorates how he, his fiancé and her friend valiantly held up the advancing Chinese army in 1962 for three days before laying down their lives. Drivers along this road, many of them ex-army personnel, stop to pay their respects at the poignant memorial.

The road then descends alongside a river before emerging on the edge of Tawang Valley, where the folded foothills are of an unimaginable scale, plunging and twisting towards Tibet. Numerous tiny hamlets and golden *gompas* speckle the near-vertical slopes opposite the improbably large village of **Jang**, 42 km before Tawang. Houses here are checkerboard Assamese-style or Monpa cubes, and many older Monpa wear a densely woven black yak-wool skullcap, the tentacles of which channel rainwater away from the wearer's face. After crossing the river, the old village of **Lhou** is especially atmospheric (worth a visit if using private transport) before the final 18 km to Tawang township.

Tawang → *Colour map 4, A4. Phone code: 03794. Population: 4600.*

Although set in breathtakingly dramatic scenery at 3500 m, the town of Tawang itself is not immediately attractive. The prayer wheels in the Old Market square, overlooked by a mini *gompa* and flower-laden balconies, have charm and two Tibetan-style gates are beautifully maintained. Most people are here to see the **monastery**, birthplace of the sixth Dalai Lama, and the second largest Buddhist monastery in the world (after Lhasa). Dating originally from 1681, it houses around 450 *lamas* belonging to the Gelugpa (Reformed) Sect of Mahayana Buddhist monks. Buddhism arrived in the area with Padmasambhava in the eighth century but the local Monpas were converted to the Tantric Buddhist cult only after the establishment of the monastery here by Merag Lama in the 17th century. During renovations in the 1990s, the main building was completely rebuilt. The lofty prayer hall, containing a 5.5-m-high golden Buddha heaped with silky prayer scarves, sees monks gather at 0500 and again at 0715 for worship (observers welcome) after which the young trainees go to the monastic school next door. It generally takes 15-20 years for the *lamas* to complete their doctorates in Buddhist philosophy, though the current Dalai Lama was just 25 when he finished. The **museum** ⓘ *opened on request, Rs 20, cameras Rs 20*, contains a wealth of treasures, including 700-year-old sculptures, numerous *thangkas* and priceless manuscripts. These, and other precious objects left in storage, are soon to be properly displayed in a new two-storey building.

Exiting via the south gate of the monastery complex takes you down a grassy ridge, strung with small *chortens* and *mani* walls, for some excellent views. Visible on a ridge northeast from the monastery is the **Gyangong Ani Gompa**, home to some three dozen nuns who are studying there, a 1½-hour (5 km) walk down and up a steep ravine (only advisable in dry weather).

Lake District

Just above Tawang beyond the monastery is the Lake District, an exceptionally beautiful area with many high-altitude lakes, including the tranquil Sangeshar Lake where a dance sequence from the film *Koyla* was shot. After a fork and an army outpost, the road continues towards **Klemta**, just a few kilometres from the border. There are a few scattered monasteries and a shrine to all faiths at the spot where Guru Nanak rested as he trekked into Tibet, 500 years ago. **Ptso**, 25 km from Tawang, has a small cabin by a lake which is used by the military. To explore this area you'll have to hire a jeep and guide, carry snacks and drinks, and be prepared for steep, treacherous mountain roads. It is all worth it for the breathtaking mountain scenery.

Gorsam Chorten

This immense 12th century *chorten* (*stupa*) is 100 km from Tawang, near Jimithang, where there are some simple places to stay. The setting is amazing, and the road little travelled by foreigners. A few public *sumos* run to the village each week, taking two to three hours; book ahead with an agent in Tawang or hire a vehicle.

Central Arunachal Pradesh → *For listings, see pages 729-734.*

Most visitors come to Central Arunachal to observe the fascinating tribal cultures that still predominate in the hills and valleys. It is also possible to do serious whitewater rafting on the Subansiri River, a journey of eight days, with the help of a specialist tour operator (see page 732). The Gerukamukh Dam at the southern point, due to be finished in 2013, threatens the eco-system upstream and will probably put an end to these rafting expeditions.

Ins and outs

Getting there and around A loop can be made through the main settlements, using public transport or as part of a tour. Starting from Itanagar, the loop takes you from Ziro to Pasighat, or coming from Assam (via Dibrugarh) from Pasighat to Ziro. Public transport connections work best when starting from Pasighat.

Ziro Valley → *Colour map 4, A5. Altitude: 1475 m. Population 25,000*

Ziro lies in a picturesque level valley of the Apatani plateau, surrounded by pine-covered hills. The settlement of Old Ziro has a small string of shops (closed on Mondays), the helipad and a government guesthouse scenically located on a hill; however, the majority of tourists stay in the commercial centre of Hapoli, 7 km to the southwest, where most jeeps arrive/depart. The **Apatani** tribals, who live in small densely populated villages clustered between the two towns, have evolved a sophisticated system of irrigated paddy cultivation which is interesting and picturesque to behold. The main tourist "attraction", however, are the Apatanis themselves. The older women wear curious bamboo nose-plugs and facial tattoos, whilst the men are more low-key with the occasional knot of hair above the forehead. Interaction with locals is problematic as the women are (unsurprisingly) shy and wary of camera-wielding foreigners and, unless you are with a sympathetic guide, it is invasive and inappropriate to attempt photographs. That said, you are welcome to wander around the villages and paddy fields on your own, and people are friendly.

Villages typically consist of rows of triangular-roofed houses surrounded by high bamboo-stake fences; often there is a wicker altar (*karung agyang*) adorned with eggs at the front, and pigs and chickens living beneath. Families live in nuclear groups, hence the small size and lack of space between the huts. About 80% of villagers still practice the **Donyi Polo** religion, although Christians from Mizoram, Nagaland and Kerala have made significant conversions in the last three years. Note the *Lapung* (raised platforms, used during the *Murung* festival in January/February) and *Babo* (huge bamboo poles erected during the Myoko festival, which rotates through the villages on a three-yearly cycle each March). To sample village life, a good day's walk starts in Old Ziro (autos run between Hapoli and Old Ziro, Rs 8) from where the village of **Hija** is signed on the western edge of town. From Hija, continue through **Dutta**, **Nenchalyang** and **Bamin**, which run into one another, before crossing the main road and following paddy-paths to **Hong**, the biggest tribal village in Asia. From Hong, tracks lead back (in the direction of Old Ziro, parallel to the main road) to **Biiri** (where there is a good restaurant) from where it is a short walk to **Hari**. From Hari, it is 1 km back to the main road to pick up an autorickshaw, or those with energy can continue on rural paths to Tajang, Kallung and Bulla villages.

Hapoli is where hotels, restaurants and transport are found; note that the bazar (where tribal women come to sell traditional foodstuffs) shuts on Sundays. The excellent **District Museum** ⓘ *Mon-Fri 0930-1600, T03788-224278, entrance free*, has an extensive collection of tribal artefacts from all over Arunachal in wonderful wooden cabinets. Of note among the jewellery collection are the biggest ear plugs imaginable; also intriguing are the penis covers crafted from brass and wood, range of pipes, and exquisite basketry. A small selection of books is for sale and interesting photos adorn the walls. The **Emporium Crafts Centre** ⓘ *T03783-224123, Mon-Fri 0900-1600 (closed lunch)*, is worth visiting; if you are lucky you will see items being made in the workshops, while the shop sells the products. An attraction for Hindu pilgrims is the **Siva Linga** near Sibe village, 4 km, signed off the road between Hapoli and Ziro on the left-hand side.

To get right off the beaten track, enquire about visiting **Talle Valley Wildlife Sanctuary**, about 30 km from Hapoli, accessed via Pange where there is a Forest Range Office and a camp.

Daporijo to Pasighat

Daporijo, a necessary overnight stop on the route from Ziro to Along/Aalo, is a rough-and-ready place of chiefly shanty-style buildings with a bustling centre. Lying in a river basin surrounded by wooded hills, with suspension bridges crossing the Subansiri, it has a scenic setting but travelling to surrounding villages is near impossible without your own transport.

The small town of **Along/Aalo** (altitude 700 m) is set in a picturesque landscape scattered with Adi villages that are much easier to access. In the town centre, the **District Museum** ⓘ *next to the Circuit House, Mon-Fri 0900-1200, 1300-1600, entrance free*, has several well-labelled rooms representing Arunachal's tribes. There are Buddhist items from the Monpa and Memba communities including painted masks, as well as woven hats (ornamented with hornbill skulls) and haversacks, clothing, statues and more.

A very enjoyable excursion from Along is to **Paya**; take an auto (Rs 150, 7 km) to Pobdi (itself a quaintly thatched village), then cross a wire bridge to unspoilt Paya, which is strung up the hillside and has a little shop for refreshments. Continue alongside the River Yomgo for 2 km, past bamboo boats, jhum (slash and burn) cultivation and friendly farmers to Ruyu where a new metal bridge spans the river to Kabu (the original bamboo bridge is now derelict, though picturesque). You can continue for a further 6 km on the same side and cross the river at the main bridge near Along, or cross here to Kabu from where it is a 4 km walk back to Along.

Visits to the Buddhist village of **Mechuka** near the border with Tibet, where there is a monastery and high altitude lake, are possible from Along. There is a Circuit House should you wish to make the intrepid journey.

Pasighat (altitude 155 m), the oldest town in Arunachal at 100 years, is home of the Adi tribe though tribal culture is fairly invisible. Lying on the banks of the Siang River, it is a low-level bustling market town. From here, it is relatively easy to reach Dibrugarh in Assam via jeep-ferry-jeep (see Transport, page 734).

Eastern Arunachal Pradesh → *For listings, see pages 729-734.*

One of the least explored regions of India, travel to many parts of Eastern Arunchal is permissible with the RAP. If you really want to strike off without a guidebook, this is the place to do so. There is accommodation in the form of Circuit Houses in the towns permitted on your permit.

Parasuram Kund → *Colour map 4, A6.*

This lake in Eastern Arunachal attracts thousands of pilgrims at **Makar Sankranti** (mid-January) who come to the fair to take a holy bath. It's possible to stay at the spartan **Government Tourist Lodge** (contact District Commissioner, Tezu, well in advance).

Namdapha National Park → *Colour map 4, A6.*

ⓘ *Permit required from the Field Director of Project Tiger Office, T03807-222253, in Miao where there is a simple government lodge. With the help of the Field Office, you can also hire porters and book Deban Guesthouse inside the park. Allow a couple of days in Miao for arrangements, and stock up on food and provisions. Entry to the park is in Deban, 25 km away. Most people visit on a pre-arranged tour (minimum of 2 people, Rs 1500-5 000 per day, depending which tour agent you choose). For independent transport, see page 734. Malaria is prevalent inside the park and leeches are voracious, take precautions. Waterproofs are essential year- round. The best season is Oct-Apr, as the monsoon rains make rivers and pathways impassable.*

Namdapha encompasses a range of altitudes from 200 m to 4500 m, from the low-lying flood plains to the snow-capped mountain of Daphabum. The sheer size and spread of the park is astonishing, its dense forest stretches over the Myanmar border in the far east and large tracts are unexplored except by the native Lisu people, whose settlements are a week's walk away from Miao. It is unique as it is home to four members of the cat family: tiger, leopard, snow leopard and clouded leopard, although it is extremely rare to see any of them. There are also elephants, Hoolock gibbons, butterflies, sambhar, deer, gaur, goral and wild hogs and a rich birdlife (especially hornbills). Expect to be on foot most of the time, in any case, as the 'road' is completely overgrown. The variety of vegetation is as fascinating as the fauna, and many people rate Namdapha as the best national park in India.

Arunachal Pradesh listings

For Sleeping and Eating price codes and other relevant information, see Essentials pages 38-42.

Sleeping

Itanagar-Naharlagun *p723*

Try to reserve rooms in advance. Some hotels seriously hike their prices Sep-Jan.

B DonyiPolo Ashok, Sector C, Itanagar, T0360-221 2626/7. Itanagar's most upmarket hotel, in a hilltop building with attractive gardens, all 20 rooms and 2 suites (Rs 3700 plus 5%) have views, a/c, heaters, fridge, hot water, and are appealing and homely despite being old-fashioned. The restaurant is OK and there is a bar. It's a 1 km uphill walk from the main road.

B-C Hotel Dawnland, Ganga Market, T0360-2299 1756. Modern new edifice, lit up at night, with plush rooms that suit the price, all mod cons. Cheapest is Rs 1700. Swanky restaurant and bar has appeal.

C-D Arun Subansiri, Zero Point, Itanagar, T0360-221 2806. A short walk from the State Museum, large and modest rooms have hot showers and other amenities you would expect for the price, a bit dated and the beds are hard.

E Blue Pine, Ganga Market, T0360-211 4196, www.traveldost.com/hotels.bluepine. Categorically the best value for money in Itanagar, rooms are newly refurbished, clean, marble floors, those at the front are best (bigger windows, though noisy), reliable hot water, and an excellent restaurant.

Bomdila *p725*

B-D Siphiyang Phong, T03782-222286, hotelsiphiyangphong@rediffmail.com. Pleasant but pricey, all rooms have hot water and TV. Restaurant is cheery with checked tablecloths and plenty of bamboo panelling. Travel desk T03782-223676.

F-G Tourist Lodge and **La**, are other options.

Dirang *p725*

B-D Heritage Pemaling, 1.5 km out of the village, T03780-242615, T(0)9436-877274. Standard/de luxe rooms are frumpy but clean with new tiled bathrooms, the only real difference being the valley views from the de luxe. Suites (Rs 3000 plus tax) are much more attractive in a chintz-and-wicker way, with large bathroom and balcony. Restaurant for residents only.

E Dirang Resort, IB Rd, T03780-242352, dirangresorts@yahoo.co.in. Modern Western bathrooms (geysers), separate sitting area, wooden floors and balcony, lace in the windows and cobwebbed pink walls – but you can hear something scratching about in the roof and the staff are dazed and vacant.

E Dirang Tourist Lodge, next to **Heritage Pemaling**, T03780-242175, www.himalayan-holidays.com. Spacious clean rooms, attached bath with geyser, and great views down over the river and Dirang. Only 4 rooms so booking necessary, Rs 750 per room (single or double). Meals provided, but give advance warning.

E Maa Laxmi, Leiky Complex, Main Market, T03780-242372, T(0)9435-083105. This basement hotel has 6 uninspiring rooms with attached (squat) toilets, bright blue paint and kitchen sinks. Beds are wide but you would expect clean sheets for the price.

E-F Moon, Main Rd, T03780-242438. Upstairs 4-bed room has a decent bathroom with geyser, but others share a smelly common bath (hot bucket available). Rooms have clean sheets and paintwork, hard beds, and nothing more.

F-G Dreamland, Main Rd, T03780-242296. 3 simple twin rooms in a family home (sharing their basic clean bathroom), potted plants aplenty, plenty of bedding provided although beds are hard. Beer in the little restaurant is appealing, but avoid the food. Hot buckets Rs 20.

Tawang *p726*

Apart from dormitory beds (men only), single travellers to Tawang will have to pay the price of a double room. There are plenty of lodges clustered around the Old Market area, where *sumos* terminate.

B-C Tenzin Guest House, 6 km from Tawang village by road, or a 45-min hike up footpaths (as is the monastery directly above), T03794-200095. A modern concrete house with 4 spotless rooms upstairs, bit overpriced, but certainly comfortable. The setting is peaceful and attractive.

C-D Tawang Inn, Nehru Market, T03794-224096. The highest-spec rooms in town, particularly in terms of bathrooms. Carpets, attractive furnishings, thick pillows, TV, heaters, lots of wood and cane. 6 **B** suites. Ask for a room with a view.

D-E Tourist Hut, Nehru Market, T03794-222739, T(0)9436-051291. The best value in Tawang, 7 rooms are new with heaters, towels, laminate floors, and plenty of colourfully clashing patterns and blankets – preferable on the 1st floor. A range of prices, pay more for TV or front-facing view, kind management willing to negotiate. Recommended.

F Tourist Lodge, 200 m (signed) from jeep stand in the Old Market, T03794-222359. A lodge with 20 well-furnished but poorly maintained rooms, but they do have heaters and hot water. The Tourist Office is in the same complex.

F-G Nefa, Nefa Complex, Nehru Market, T03794-222419. Double rooms are gloomy and old-fashioned while the staff are young and jolly. Men can stay in the 4-bed dorm.

Ziro *p727*

If you have your own transport, then there are some unique homestays on offer in the villages around the Ziro Valley.

C-E Ziro Valley Resort, Biiri village, 3 km from Old Ziro, T(0)985-691 0173, tagetabin@gmail.com. Very pleasing chalet rooms (Rs 1500) with modern if simple amenities, brand new and spacious, duvets, TV, best on the 1st floor with terraces. Also cheaper, simpler rooms (Rs 800) next to the restaurant, less stylish but also have geysers. A great choice if you don't have to depend on public transport (1 km off the main road, before Hari village, sign-posted) and the villages around Ziro are an easy walk away. Worth going for a meal even if you aren't staying (see Eating, page 732).

E Blue Pine, Pai Gate, Hapoli, T03788-224812. Most people's 1st choice for good reason, although other places are closer to town. Cosy rooms have wood panelling, TV, hot water, but dirty floors. Standard doubles (which they will be reluctant to tell you about, Rs 550), delux (Rs 880) are larger with more character. No single room rates, but room 304 is a 'dorm with 2 beds (Rs 200), sharing common bathroom. Pleasant restaurant area though food is merely OK; laundry service. They were extending at the time of research, with 10 more rooms being added.

E-F Hotel Valley View, Hapoli, T03788-225398. Institutional corridors lead to acceptable rooms with heaters and TV. Good choice for single travellers (Rs 400, attached bath, Rm 213 is best), also has doubles with shared bath for those on a budget (Rs 400), pay more for rooms with hot water. Extensive menu in the not unattractive restaurant.

E-F Pine Ridge, MG Rd, Hapoli, T03788-224725. You could get lost in this maze of a place, particularly as the lights never seem to be switched on in the corridors. It's good central location, but rooms are musty at the cheaper end. They come with TV and hot water. Restaurant is gloomy and deserted.

G Circuit House, Hapoli, reservations through Deputy Commissioner's Office, T03788-224255. Excellent value, on a hill with views, worth the effort of contacting the DC. 6 rooms in the new block have tiled floors, TV, fresh paint, heaters, hot water (request the VIP room, it is the same price as standard rooms, a steal at Rs 300). 3 rooms in the original bungalow. Food available.

G Government Guesthouse, Old Ziro, T(0)8575-202663. Perched on top of a hill, with amazing views of the valley and the villages enclosed within it; 6 double rooms with bath Rs 200, nets, cheerful patterns but musty smells. Essential to phone ahead for permission to stay.

Siiro

Two charming new homestays in the village of Siiro are involving the community in tourist development and are the perfect place to experience local culture. Contact them direct, or through **Future Generations NGO**, T(0)9436-059165, www.future.org. **C Ngunu Ziro**, T03788-225809, T(0)9436-047891, punyochada@gmail.com, about 5 km from Hapoli, has 3 cheerful rooms (2 share a bathroom) surrounded by a bamboo grove. Nicest on the upper floor among the eaves, hot water, meals available. Camping trips and treks to the Wildlife Sanctuary can be arranged.

To stay even deeper in the valley, next to paddies and streams (6 km from Hapoli), friendly **Hibu Tatu**, T03788-225808, T(0)9436-224834, has 2 chalets in his market garden of apple trees and veggies, simple concrete affairs with a front veranda, hot buckets, very clean, Rs 1000 per room (2 big beds), B&B, all meals can be provided.

Daporijo *p727*

E-F Hotel Sanatu, T03792-223531. 7 grim rooms with TV, fan, water by hot bucket in the scary bathrooms, dirty sheets. However, the very pleasant manager also has some decent rooms for Rs 650 in the **KK Palace Hotel**, but it's across the river.
G Circuit House, on hill above town, T03792-223250. It's a steal at Rs 300 for clean sheets, mossie nets, fans, plenty of space and excellent views. Food is good and bed-tea available, as are hot buckets. It is a 10-min uphill slog from town, however, and permission is required from the DCs office in order to stay; however, on our visit, a telephone call made by staff to the EAC sufficed.

Daporijio to Pasighat *p727*

Along/Aalo

D-E Hotel Aagaam, Yubo Complex, Nehru Chowk, T03783-223640/(0)940-2471774. More expensive than the **Holiday Cottage** for rooms with less appeal, but they do have geysers. Deluxe and suite rooms also available, newly renovated. There is a musty 3-bed dorm (Rs 150). On the main road.
E Holiday Cottage, near General Hospital, T03783-222463/(0)943-6090511. On a quiet street, rooms with a bit of character and it's good value. Standard rooms Rs 400 with nets and fans, 2 deluxe rooms have more light, space and sofas for Rs 600. Hot buckets for Rs 10, restaurant is good.
G Circuit House, opposite SBI, Main Rd, T03783-222232. An absolute bargain at Rs 300, 13 clean simple rooms, new block at the rear. On a small hill with views from the grounds. Often full, but try your luck.

The **Hotel Anachal Bhawan**, near the Police Station, is do-able if other places are full, though it costs more for worse rooms.

Pasighat *p727*

C Hotel Aane, MG Rd, T0368-222 7777/3333. The best hotel in town, all rooms are newly and bluely painted, with fans, shiny floors, balcony, geyser and clean furnishings. A couple can easily fit in the single rooms with double beds (Rs 1500), 2 suites are not worth the extra money. Restaurant pleasant, and roof terrace opens in the season.
D-E Hotel Oman, Oman Complex, Main Market, T0368-222 4464. Absolutely the best budget choice, rooms have attached bath, decent furniture, clean sheets, new mossie nets, towels, TV. Singles start at Rs 350, deluxe doubles are Rs 750 (but couples can squeeze into the single rooms with 'family bed' Rs 530). Food available.

The **Hotel Siang** close to the sumo counters is fine, should the Oman be full, though it is more costly for less appealing rooms.

Namdapha National Park *p728*

There is a simple **Circuit House** at Miao.
B Camp Namdapha, across the river from Deban Rest House. Picturesque location, offers 10 bamboo huts and log cabins as well as tented accommodation. Guides, porters and all meals are included in the price, booked as part of a tour.
G Deban Forest Rest House. Advance bookings through Field Director's office in Miao, T03807-223126. Basic clean rooms with mosquito nets and a dorm, bath, caretaker-cook. Ethnic bamboo huts overlooking the Noa Dihing River are more expensive.

Eating

Dirang *p725*

‡ Dipak Sweets & Snacks, Main Rd. Open 0600-1900. Excelllent *chola* with samosa or *puris* in the morning. One of few places open after noon on Thu.
‡ Hotel Raj, Main Rd. Open 0600-1800. Good *dal baht* (Rs 40) and *thukpa* (Rs 30).
‡ Hotel Samaroh, Main Rd. Cheap and busy, rice meals/chowmein/greasy rolls are tasty. Veg and non-veg.

Tawang *p726*

In Nehru Market, a small bakery sells substantial muffins and pastries.
‡‡-‡ Hotel Tawang View, Nehru Market, T03794-223009. Open 0830-2100. Probably the best restaurant in town, with a huge vegetarian and non-vegetarian menu, most of which is actually available (unlike other places). Indian dishes particularly recommended. Red

walls, coloured bulbs, plastic flowers, and the occasional drunk local.

Dragon Restaurant, Old Market, T03794-224475. Open 0700-2030. Delicious Chinese and Tibetan staples take a while to prepare, meat is rarely available, quite cosy surrounds with fairy lights. Look for the Chinese lanterns outside.

Ziro *p727*

Tribal Food Plaza, MG Rd, Hapoli, T03788-225322. Mon-Sat 0800-1830. Indigenous cuisine is meat-oriented, also some Chinese, Indian, soups, fish and Nagaland dishes. Colourful walls and lighting, view over the street as it is the 1st floor.

Ziro Valley Resort, Biiri village, T(0)985-691 0173. Open 0630-2130. A popular place with locals, excellent Indian/Chinese dishes, dining is either in the main restaurant or 3 little huts in the grounds. Alcohol available (beer Rs 60). It's well placed to take a break when walking around the valley villages. They also have lodgings (see page 730).

The restaurant at the **Hotel Valley View** has a varied menu, better for vegetarians than others. The **Blue Pine** hotel is a pleasant place to sit and relax, though the food is not outstanding. There are several cheap eateries on MG Rd.

Daporijo *p727*

The food at the Circuit House is good, for residents; nothing in town is outstanding though the **Sanatu** hotel is a safe bet and there are several other cheap options.

Daporijio to Pasighat *p727*

Along/Aalo

The restaurants at the **Aagaam**, T03783-222838, and **Holiday Cottage** hotels do good meals and are the best places in town to dine; both have a few tribal dishes in the menu.

CT Restaurant, below the **Aagaam**, does tasty Chinese/Tibetan fare (no menu).

Pasighat *p727*

Shangrila, opposite Main Market. Excellent and always busy, *thukpa*, chowmein, meat momos, all come with delicious soup. Half-plates are very generous and very cheap. Open 0730-1930.

Festivals and events

Feb Grand East Himalaya Festival comprises the Reh festival of the Ido-Mishmi (1-2 Feb) in lower Dibang Valley and the Namdapha Eco-Cultural festival (5-7 Feb) in Miao. See www.helptourism.com for details.

Feb/Mar Losar is celebrated for 8-15 days in western Arunachal.

Oct/Nov Buddha Mahatsova has cultural programmes, monastic and tribal dances, over 3 days in Tawang.

Shopping

Itanagar-Naharlagun *p723*

The cotton textiles available here are colourful and are beautifully patterned. You can also get wooden masks and figures, cane belts, haversacks and caps. **Government Sales Emporium** on MG Marg in Itanagar (opposite the Ashok Hotel) has a decent selection; Mon-Fri 0930-100, Sat -1200.

Activities and tours

Itanagar-Naharlagun *p723*

Arunachal Travels, Itanagar, agents for **Air India**.

Duyu Tamo, T(0)9436-044905, duyutours@yahoo.com. Tamo is from the Apatani tribe, and is hence a good choice for a tour from Ziro-Pasighat. He works in conjunction with Help Tourism (see below), and also efficiently arranges and dispatches permits for independent travellers in Arunachal.

Gibbon Travels, MLA Cottage Rd, E Sector, Itanagar, T0360-229 1181, T(0)9436-044069, www.gibbontravels.com. Helpful Komkar organizes tours throughout the northeast and can arrange permits for independent travellers to Arunachal quickly and efficiently (and at a significantly cheaper cost than other agents).

Help Tourism, www.helptourism.com. Known for their sustainable tourism development, Help have recently started weekend or week-long Elephant Safaris in the Mishmi Hills, Manas and Namdapha National Parks.

Himalayan Holidays, APST Rd, Ganga, Itanagar, T0360-221 8534, www.himalayan-holidays.com.

Nature Expeditions India, Gurgaon, T0124-236 8601, www.himalaya-india.com.

Bomdila *p725*

Dawa Tsering, based between Bomdila and Dirang, T(0)9436-676225, dawaap@yahoo.com.

Trustworthy and informative Dawa arranges treks and tours with a cultural slant, visiting villages, camping and homestays, and can swiftly arrange permits for Arunachal.

Himalayan Holidays, ABC Buildings, Main Market, T03782-222017, www.himalayan-holidays.com. Useful for booking *sumo* tickets in advance.

Tawang *p726*

Arunachal Tourism, at the **Tourist Lodge**, Old Market, T03794-222359. Has a couple of interesting pamphlets.

Himalayan Holidays, Old Market, T03794-223151, T(0)94362-48216, www.himalayan-holidays.com. Open 0500-1930. Organizes tours and jeep hire, good for booking advance *sumo* tickets back to Tezpur.

Tribal Discovery (same office as **Himalayan**), Old Market, T03794-223151, T(0)9436-045075, davidsongtom@yahoo.com. Reasonable prices on tours to tribal villages, the monastery, nunneries, etc. Vehicle hire (including petrol) for a day at the Lakes is Rs 2500.

Transport

Itanagar-Naharlagun *p723*

Air The nearest airport is **Lilabari**, North Lakimpur, in Assam, 57 km from Naharlagun, 67 km from Itanagar, which has daily flights to **Guwahati** and **Kolkata** . Transfer by bus. See **Air India**, www.airindia.com, and **Kingfisher**, www.flykingfisher.com.

There is a **helipad** at Naharlagun with Pawan Hans service, T0360-2245261, to Guwahati and Tawang (Mon-Sat), and bi-weekly connections to towns in Arunachal (Ziro) and **Dibrugarh**.

Bus APST from Itanagar, T0360-221 2338, to **Guwahati** at 1800 and 1930 (12 hrs, Rs 190); via **Shillong** (12 hrs, Rs 260); **Along (Aalo)** at 0530 and 1430 (12 hrs, Rs 230); **Bomdila** at 0600 exc Fri (11 hrs, Rs 200); **Daporijo** at 1330; **Pasighat** at 0530 and 0600 (9 hrs, Rs170); and **Tezpur** (5 hrs, Rs 110). Private buses leave from near the clocktower, several operators including **Blue Hills**, T0360-229 0931, overnight to **Guwahati** at 1815 (11½ hrs, Rs 390) and **Network**, T0360-229 2500, 3 buses at 1730, 1800 and 1830 (Rs 280, a/c Rs 450). Also to **Tinsukia**, **Dimapur** and **Tezpur**.

Taxi Naharlagun/Itanagar, Rs 170 plus fuel; Rs 25 (shared taxi).

Train The nearest railhead is North Lakhimpur in Assam, 50 km from Naharlagun and 60 km from Itanagar; **Harmoti station** is 23 km from Naharlagun. **Railway Out Agency**, Naharlagun bus station, T0360-224 4209. Nearest railheads for the bigger towns: **Along**: Silapathar; **Pasighat**: Mukakselek (however, at the time of research this section of the line was closed for security reasons); **Namdapha**: Margherita/Ledo.

Bomdila, Dirang and Tawang *p725 and 726*

Air There is a **helipad**, T(0)9435-734407, T(0)9436-051250, 40 km from Tawang, with flights to **Guwahati**, but the safety record is poor.

Bus ASTC buses run between Tezpur and Tawang when weather conditions permit; if there is too much snow they terminate at Dirang. The narrow and twisting road means *sumos* are recommended over the bus. **Tezpur–Tawang** (12-14 hrs, depart 0530, Rs 400); **Tezpur–Bomdila** (5½ hrs, Rs 180); **Bomdila–Dirang** (1½ hrs, Rs 80); **Bomdila–Tawang** (6-7 hrs, 0530, Rs 280); **Dirang–Tawang** (6½ hrs, 0830, Rs 280). *Sumos* pick up from hotels in all towns.

Use the contacts below to book seats in advance. In Tezpur: **ASTC Sumo Service**, T(0)9435-080318, T(0)9864-182449. In Bomdila: **Gourab**, T(0)9436-236055, or **Himalyan Holidays**, T03782-222017. In Dirang: **Dream Destination**, T03780-242737, **Dirang Valley Tours**, T03780-242560, or **Himalyan Holidays**, T03780-242464. In Tawang: **Himalyan Holidays**, T03794-223151, or **Pine Ridge**, T03794-222306.

Ziro *p727*

Bus APST bus to **Daporijo** on Mon (Rs 160), **Guwahati** on Sun & Thu at 1200 (Rs 300). Ticket counter opens at 0600.

Sumo Getting from Ziro to Daporijo by sumo is tricky, as you have to join a sumo coming from Itanagar, at around 1100, and take any free seats available (usually the rear seats; be warned, the road is particularly windy and bumpy on this stretch). To **Itanagar**, at 0530.

Daporijo p727

Bus APST bus (T03792-223107) to **Itanagar**, to **Ziro** on Tue at 0700, to **Along** except Mon (9 hrs, Rs 160).

Sumo Sumo counters/departures are in the bazar area, about 200 m from the **Sanatu** hotel. To **Ziro** at 0600 (5 hrs, Rs 300), to **Itanagar** at 0500 (12 hrs Rs 550). For reservations try Arunachal Yatayat, T03792-223679. **Note** There are no public sumos to Along, so it is the bus or a hired sumo for Rs 5000.

Daporijio to Pasighat p727

Along/Aalo

Bus APST (T03783-222475) bus to **Itanagar** at 0600 and 1600 (except Mon, 12 hrs, Rs 230), to **Guwahati** at 1000 (Mon/Thu only, 14 hrs, Rs 500), to **Daporijo** at 0700 (except Mon, 9 hrs, Rs 160). **Note** There are no public sumos along the route to Daporijo, so it is either the bus or a hired sumo (see below). To **Mechukha** at 0615 (except Fri, 12 hrs, Rs 160).

Sumo It is necessary to report to the sumo counter 30 mins before departure. To **Pasighat** at 1100 (4½-5 hrs, Rs 220); to **Itanagar** at 0530 (9 hrs, Rs 400). Sumos to **Daporijo** are by reserve only, Rs 5000.

Pasighat p727

Bus The APST bus stand is 1.5 km from the centre, Rs 40 in an auto.

Sumo It is necessary to report to the sumo counter 30 mins before departure. To **Along** at 0600 (4½-5 hrs, Rs 220); to **Itanagar** at 0600 (5 hrs, Rs 200). ASTC bus to **Guwahati** leaves from the sumo stand at 1130 (17-18 hrs, Rs 530).

Ferry Winger-ferry-sumo tickets to **Dibrugarh** (via Jonai) in Assam are sold by Otto Tours, T(0)986-209 3159 (at the sumo stand) departing 0600 (5 hrs, Rs 270).

Namdapha National Park p728

Air Dibrugarh (160 km) has the nearest airport (direct flights to/from **Kolkata**).

Bus/taxi State buses from Dibrugarh (irregular) and Tinsukia go to **Miao**, via **Margherita** (64 km). A taxi from Tinsukia costs Rs 3000 one-way, you can also hire taxis in Margherita.

Train The nearest local railhead is Margherita. The nearest mainline railhead is Dibrugarh.

Directory

Itanagar-Naharlagun p723

Banks/post There are banks and post offices.

Internet Numerous internet cafes on MG Marg, standard charge Rs 30 per hr. **Hospitals** RK Mission Hospital, T0360-221 2263.

Tawang p726

Banks SBI, near the Old Market has ATM.

Internet **Dofain Cyber Cafe**, Rs 50 per hr, new PCs, open winter 0930-1800, till 2000 summer. **Monyul Cyber Cafe**, Rs 50 per hr, efficient, winter 0830-1730, till 2000 summer.

Ziro p727

Banks SBI with ATM near the bazar.

Internet **Rivi's**, in the alley below the Pine Ridge hotel, Mon-Sat 0900-1900, Rs 40 per hr, unreliable connection.

Daporijo p727

Internet **B4U**, Rs 60 per hr, fast connection, new PCs, Tue-Sun 0700-1900.

Daporijio to Pasighat p727

Along/Aalo

Banks SBI with ATM on main road.

Internet **Internet Cafe**, opposite APST bus stand, Rs 40 per hr, slow connection.

Pasighat p727

Internet **Cyber Zone**, Banskota Rd, off MG Rd (near Hotel Aane), T0368-222 4132. Pricey at Rs 60 per hr, open till 1830.

Nagaland

➔ *Population: 1.98 million. Area: 16,579 sq km.*

Nagaland, the narrow strip of mountain territory, has a long border with Myanmar to the east. There are green valleys with meandering streams, high blue mountains with deep gorges and a rich variety of wildlife and flora. Most tourists come to experience the rich tribal culture for which the state is famed. Nagaland has a long wet season, from May to September. ▸▸ *For listings, see pages 738-741. For entry permits, see box, page 693.*

History

The British reached peace with the Nagas at the end of the 19th century and found them useful allies in the war against the Japanese, who advanced as far as Kohima before finally retreating from the region. After Indian Independence, Nagaland became a separate state on 1 December 1963. A separatist movement for full Independence continues, as the 1975 Shillong Accord was rejected. A series of month-to-month ceasefires in effect during the 1990s came to a drastic end in 2004, when insurgents attacked the railway station in Dimapur. As elsewhere in the Northeast, check with your consulate before travelling to Nagaland, and avoid travelling at night. The Nagaland People's Front won the single Lok Sabha seat in 2009.

Culture

Tribal groups Nagaland is almost entirely inhabited by 16 groups of the Tibeto-Burmese tribes – among them are the Angamis, Aos, Konyaks, Kukis, Lothas, Semas and Wanchus, collectively known as the **Nagas**. There are many tribal languages spoken: Angami, Ao, Chang are a few. The Nagas were once head hunters and were known for their fierceness and the regular raids they made on Assam and Burma. The warring tribes believed that since the enemy's animated soul (*yaha* in Wanchu dialect) was to be found at the nape of the neck, it could only be set free once beheaded. However, since the spiritual soul, *mio*, resided in the head and brought good fortune, enemy heads (and those of dead comrades) were prized as they could add to a community's own store of dead ancestors. The hilltop villages are protected by stone walls. The *morung*, a meeting house, acts as a boys' dormitory, and is used for storing weapons and once displayed the prizes of war (enemy heads). The huge sacred drum stands by each *morung* is a hollowed-out tree trunk resembling a buffalo head. Some believe that the Nagas' ancestors came from the seafaring nation of Sumatra and retain this link in legends, village drums and ceremonial jewellery, which uses shells.

Festivals When it comes to festivals Nagaland leads the party, with all 16 tribes enjoying their own ceremonies, feasts and dancing throughout the year. However, the big event is the five-day **Hornbill Festival** in the first week of December. Originally orchestrated by the government as a cultural *mêlée* to attract tourists from India and abroad, the festival has taken on a life of its own and many people plan a trip to Nagaland around it. Tribes rival with each other to put on the most memorable display, clad in fabulous traditional dress, and as well as the prevalent tribal music recent years have also seen a rock festival take place. Handicrafts and food stalls, distinctive to each tribe, give both locals and tourists a chance to sample different styles of home-cooking and local brews. The festival is held in Kisama village, 16 km from Kohima.

Religion Today 98% of the Nagas are Baptist Christians. Originally, although they revered natural spirits, the Nagas believed in a single overseeing superforce, and hence incorporated the Christian Gospel into their cosmology quite readily. The Bible was translated into many of the Naga dialects (written in a Roman script devised by missionaries, as the languages were previously unwritten), yet many old customs have been retained.

Crafts The ancient craft of weaving on portable looms is still practised by the women. The strips of colourful cloth are stitched together to produce shawls in different patterns which distinguish each tribe. Ao warriors wear the red and black striped shawl with a central white band embroidered with symbols.

Dimapur → *Colour map 4, B5. Population: 379,769.*

Dimapur, on the edge of the plains northwest of Kohima, is the railhead and has Nagaland's only airport. With numerous busy markets in the town centre, it is the state's main commercial and trading centre. For tourists, it serves merely as a transit point for onward travel into Nagaland.

One kilometre from the railway station are the remains of the old Hindu capital of the Kacharis (13th-16th century). The **Kachari relics** include a large brick-built arch and many mushroom-shaped carved megaliths believed to represent the fertility cult (these are behind railings, to prevent further vandalism and graffiti). The Kachari kingdom was destroyed by the Assamese Ahoms in the 16th century. You can also visit **Chumukedima** old village on a hill above town, or trek to the **Triple Falls** at Seithekima.

Kohima → *Colour map 4, B5. Population: 270,063. Altitude: 1495 m.*

Tourist information **Directorate of Tourism** ⓘ *opposite Indoor Stadium, Raj Bhavan Rd, Officers' Hill, T/F0370-224 3124, www.tourismnagaland.com, Mon-Fri 1100-1600.* Has a map of Kohima, arranges package tours (five to nine days, minimum four persons).

The British-built town of Kohima is spread over a series of ridges surrounded by higher peaks, with the original Angami Kohima village set on a hill overlooking the Main Bazar. Kohima attracted global attention during the Second World War because it was here that the Japanese advance was halted by the British and Indian forces. Most businesses and shops shut up as soon as it gets dark, and there may be a strong military presence in town.

Sights The **Second World War Cemetery** ⓘ *Mon-Sat 0830-1530 in winter, 0830-1630 in summer* is in a beautiful setting, with well-maintained lawns where rose bushes bloom. Two tall crosses stand out at the lowest and highest points. The stone markers each have a polished bronze plaque with epitaphs commemorating the men who fell here, to halt "the invasion of India by the forces of Japan in April 1944" by the British 14th Army under General William Slim. The cherry tree, which was used by Japanese soldiers as a snipers' post, was destroyed; what grew from the old stump marks the limit of the enemy advance. At the base of the Second Division lower cross, near the main entrance, are the lines: "When you go home/Tell them of us and say/For your tomorrow/We gave our today." The markings of the DC's tennis court still remain Three kilometres away by road, the striking red-roofed **Cathedral of Reconciliation** (1995) overlooks the cemetery from a hill. Part funded by the Japanese government, representatives from both sides of the conflict attended the inauguration.

The excellent **State Museum** ⓘ *Bayavu Hill Colony, Tue-Sun 0930-1530 winter, 1000-1600 in summer, Rs 5,* has a collection of anthropological exhibits including textiles, figurines, weaponry, skulls and carved totems. Dioramas effectively show the clothing and lifestyle of the different Naga tribes. The lower gallery displays some colourful jewellery including girdles, as well as the chunky armlets worn by men and, of course, their extraordinary headgear. Look out for the elaborate match boxes and a chair made of elephant bones. The museum is 3 km north of the main centre, shared taxis can drop you nearby.

The vast and appealing **Kohima Village** (aka T-Khel or Bara Basti, signed off the main road north of the centre) has a ceremonial gateway with two doors carved with motifs of guns, warriors and symbols of prosperity. Steps lead up, passing megaliths on the way, to the pinnacle of the village where a traditional Naga house remains. Though made of corrugated iron, there are crossed horns on the gables; the wooden doors are painted with tigers and *mithun* heads to signify the status of the family, and huge grain baskets stand in front.

The **local bazar** attracts colourful tribal women who come to buy and sell their produce, which includes snails, bags of frogs and the occasional dog.

The Heritage Village of **Kisama**, which hosts the Hornbill Festival, is 12 km from the capital.

Around Kohima

Kohnoma (population 6000) is an authentic Angami village, 20 km southwest of Kohima along a broken road. A night or two spent in the cute homestay here is a highlight of a trip to Nagaland. Surrounded by extensive rice terraces and high hills, the setting is dramatic and incredibly beautiful. Kohnoma is a 'green' village and numerous rubbish bins keep it spotlessly clean. There are 19 *morungs* spread throughout three *khels* (sub-villages); a gateway in the centre leads up to steep stone steps to a fort. For Kohnoma has a has a proud past, as it was here that the Naga warriors made their last stand against the British in 1879, commemorated by the pillar at the village's highest point. A one-hour walk through the rice terraces, where numerous monoliths are scattered around picturesque stone walls, brings you to little **Mezoma** village (population 2000). There are staggering views back to Kohnoma; call the Council Chairman, T(0)8014-56235, if you wish to stay in a homestay in Mezoma.

Another 20 km along the Kohmona road takes you to **Dzulekie**, at 2134 m, with attractive waterfalls and trout streams in a deep rocky gorge. There is a Tourist Rest House and Cottages. The trek to **Japfü Peak**, at 3043 m, 15 km south of Kohima, is tough going through forests and best between November and March for clear mountain views from the summit. **Dzükou Valley**, at 2438 m, 15 km further south, is best in Spring when orchids and lilies bloom, although from June to September you can see colourful rhododendrons and other meadow flowers. The main foliage, however, is bamboo. It is a good place to trek; Kohnoma can be used as a base to access western Dzükou.

Mokokchung

Mokokchung, 160 km from Kohima via Wokha, is the intellectual and cultural capital of Nagaland and home to the Ao tribe. The town itself is not much to look at, but neither is it unattractive with old wooden stores painted blue and good views from the hilltop location. An easy trip by bus is to nearby **Ungma** which has a ceremonial building dating from 1690 but rebuilt in 1985, the doorway decorated with tigers, mithun and hornbills, and a ceremonial drum. Further along the same road is **Longkhum** village, accessible by local bus although getting back is a problem as buses back to Mokokchung only run till 0800. Some ancient villagers still practise the Limapur animist religion, and a short walk down the hillside takes you to sacred stones marked by the feet of the old gods.

Mon

Mon (altitude 900 m) is a good place to get a taste of Nagaland as it is easily accessed via the Assamese town of Sonari (where the **Seven Sisters** hotel, Rs 200-400, is bearable; buses/sumos to Mon leave from outside). The hillside setting of Mon is spectacular, the township peters out into traditional thatch homes plus there are a couple of good places to stay. The region is home to the Konyak tribe who have long held a particular fascination for visitors as they were traditionally fierce head-hunters, and still appear war-like with facial tattoos and blackened teeth. To visit Konyak villages it is necessary to hire a vehicle, preferably with a driver who can act as a guide, as etiquette requires you to introduce yourself to the village Angh (king). The Angh typically lives at the summit of each village in a large hut adorned with mithun and buffalo skulls, and still has considerable power in deciding village affairs and settling disputes. Opium smoking is commonplace, introduced by the British to curb the Konyaks resistance to colonial rule, and photography is best facilitated by your guide. **Mon village** is only 10 km before the town of the same name; it is a pretty place to stroll around yet feels quite edgy. **Shangnyu** village (22 km) has a few monoliths and a tiny 'heritage museum' housing skulls, tusks and statues. Most intriguing is the wooden fertility shrine, carved from a single piece of banyan and decorated with a copulating couple and victorious warriors. A large entrance charge will be demanded from the Angh's family (up to Rs 500) which can be negotiated. There are several other traditional villages in the vicinity, including **Naganimora** (58 km), **Chui** (8 km) and **Longwa** (36 km) where a longhouse bisects the Indian and Myanmar border. The roads are terrible and you can only expect to see a couple of villages in a day.

The **Aoleong Festival** is celebrated in the first week of April to herald the coming of Spring. It is a chance to see the men in their warrior garb and women in traditional dress perform dances and songs.

Nagaland listings

For Sleeping and Eating price codes and other relevant information, see Essentials pages 38-42.

Sleeping

Dimapur *p736*

It is hard to find single room rates in Dimapur, but several hotels have dormitories. Next to the private bus stand on Golaghat Rd are some budget options that are much of a muchness.

B-C Hotel Trinity East, near SP Office, Nagarjan Jnt, T03862-224200. New hotel with Western-style rooms that are large and well-equipped, bathrooms are disappointing but still better than most in town.

C-E Hotel Kent, Golaghat Rd, T03862-234077, hotelkentnagaland@gmail.com. The executive rooms for Rs 800 are a good deal – clean, new, tiled, reliable hot water, TV and plenty of lights and plug sockets. Conveniently near the train station and private bus stand, without suffering too much road noise. Pleasant staff, restaurant, can arrange transport. There is a handy map of town on the back of their flyer.

D-E de Oriental Dream, Bank Colony, opposite Naga Shopping Arcade, T03862-231211, deorientaldream@yahoo.com. More attractive than other options, with stone floors and decent decor. All rooms have a/c, TV, hot water; a couple are cheaper as they are unrenovated. One of few hotels to offer a single room rate, some **C** delux rooms, multicusine restaurant, wireless internet Rs 100 per day. No lift, which is a killer for the 4th floor.

E-F Tourist Lodge, next to NST bus station. Closed for renovation at the time of research, but convenient location, budget prices, some dorm beds, call the government-run **Hotel Saramati** (T03862-234763) to check if lodge has reopened.

Kohima *p736*

A-B Hotel Cimorb, Old Minister Hill, near Telephone Exchange, T0370-2242 248, muzilo.cimorbhotel@hotmail.com. Kohima's newest and fanciest hotel, spotless double rooms have big windows, white linen and walls, red carpets/cushions, dark wood furniture, excellent bathrooms replete with thick towels (Rs 2500). There is an enormous suite for Rs 6000 and 3 singles for Rs 1500. The restaurant is good (see Eating, page 740).

B-C Hotel Japfü, PR Hill, T0370-224 0211-3, thehoteljapfu@yahoo.co.in. 26 heated rooms in a motel arrangement; standard have TV, balcony, carpets, rather drab furnishings and decent (if old-fashioned) bathrooms with geysers. Delux are larger, with brighter decor. Suites are huge, have new furniture, fridge, flatscreen, but are in the basement and overpriced. Shilloi restaurant is sunny and serves good multicuisine. Laundry and internet service.

B-D The Heritage, Old DC Bungalow, Officers' Hill, near Red Cross Building, T0370-2241 864, www.theheritage.in. Set atop a hill behind the War Cemetery, this colonial bungalow has 2 living rooms, verandas and gardens for guests to relax in. Rooms have polished wooden floors, TVs, original art and large bathrooms with tubs. There are 2 twins, 1 huge master bedroom and 1 smaller (new) annex with windows on both sides (which is cheapest and rather appealing). It is a charming place to stay, and well priced for a historic old place.

C Razhü Pru, Mission Compound, Kohima Village, T920-6198213, razhupru@yahoo.co.in. 9 rooms in an appealing bungalow, with a garden and lounge decked out with artefacts. Rooms have TV, heaters, tasteful furnishings, wooden floors and character, but only 2 have exterior windows (nos 1 and 7) and fireplaces aren't functioning. Suites Rs 4000. Food is available. Located on the lower slopes of old Kohima village, about 1 km from the main town.

C-D Hotel Grandeur, NH39, BOC area, T0370-2229 698/9, hotelgrandeur@yahoo.co.in, www.hotelgrandeur.net. Directly above the private bus stand (where overnight buses from Guwahati terminate), this hotel is clean and presentable if not 'grand'. Delux doubles are significantly larger and lighter than standard rooms (both have TV, hot water, towels) while the singles (Rs 800) at the rear have fantastic views from their balcony. Laundry service, parking, pleasant staff. (The **Holiday Inn** next door is inferior, though similarly priced).

D Explore Nagaland Guesthouse, Phool Bazar, T985-634 3037. A couple of rooms in a family apartment were being finished at the time of research but should be a good choice, Rs 500 per person B&B, with private bathrooms and welcoming atmosphere.

D-E Hotel Pine, Phool Bari, T0370-224 3129. Cosy little hotel, nothing fancy but 11 clean rooms have good views and cheery paintwork. Pay more for newer bathrooms and nicer decor in some rooms, but all have geysers and decent beds. Good choice.

F Capital Hotel, opposite NST bus stand. Bearable rooms with attached bath (no running water, buckets suffice), surfaces are clean if sheets aren't. The large back terrace enjoys a great vista of the slopes, and they are used to the occasional foreign tourist (which other budget hotels are not).

Around Kohima *p737*

Kohnoma

E Viu Meru's, T(0)9436-011266. A delightful little place with wooden floors, wonky stairs, lots of blankets and character. One room has a tiny balcony with views. Hot buckets, clean shared bathroom. Food is available (though breakfast isn't great and is pricey). Phone ahead; if full, they will advise on other homestays in the village. Single room rates available.

Mokokchung *p737*

B-G Metsüpen (Tourist Lodge), near Town Park, Mokokchung Village, T0369-2229 343, metsupen@yahoo.com. Perched on a hill in peaceful Mokokchung Village, a 5- to 10-min climb by foot, this hotel has a range of rooms all of which are clean and decent. Semi-standard rooms (Rs 400 single/double) are basic; standard rooms (Rs 750) more spacious, TV, fan (no heater), hot water by bucket (Rs 20). Deluxe rooms are newer and more attractive, with geysers, heaters; VIP rooms are overpriced. A 7-bed dorm costs Rs 200, and is male/female depending on which sex turns up first. Good restaurant (incl Naga dishes) and kind, professional staff. Internet/Wi-Fi available for a reasonable charge, laundry service.

D-E Whispering Winds, DC Hill, T0369-222 6935. A modern hotel with character on the highest point of the town with splendid views, a steep 10- to 15-min climb from the centre (not possible with bags) or Rs 80 in a taxi. The standard rooms need repainting but are tiled and clean, hot water is by bucket, choice of Western/Indian WCs. Deluxe and executive rooms very pleasant if in your budget (Rs 1000-1200). Food available, including local Ao dishes. Sunny living room to sit in, fires lit in the Naga-style huts outside in the evenings. Only 7 rooms, recommended to book ahead. Laundry and internet service.

Mon *p737*

D Helsa Cottage, NST Colony, T(0)9436-433782. Very pleasant rooms in a large family house, balconies, very comfortable. Phone ahead. Aunty can arrange guides and drivers. 500 m from the centre.

E Jah-poh-long Mountain View Resort, 5 km from Mon Town, T(0)9436-606212, www.interioradvanture.com. 4 tents and 3 cottages (preferable and the same price, Rs 700) with bathrooms (no running water), simply lovely views of Mon town and the surrounding hills. Circular Naga hut with a fireplace that is good for hanging out. The village of Mon is 4 km away. The owners also run Interior Adventures (see Tour operators, page 740), can arrange a car/guide and homestays in villages.

G Circuit House, DC District, T03869-221246.

Eating

Dimapur *p736*

There are numerous basic 'rice hotels' near the private bus stand, most serve meat thalis (look for a Hindu sign if you are veg), otherwise try a multicuisine restaurant in one of the better hotels; lassis in town are excellent.

Kohima *p736*

Note that in hotel restaurants, waiting time can be anything from 20-40 mins as food is freshly prepared. Local dishes are simple but may include water snails, eels, silkworm curry, hornet larvae or fermented fish. Alcohol is prohibited in Nagaland (but is available in *paan* shops for an inflated price).

Dimori Cove, 13 km on NH39 to Manipur. The eatery has a small swimming pool and good views from the foothills of Japfü Peak.

Dream Cafe, under UCO Bank, Phool Bari. Mon-Fri 0900-1730. Pleasant hangout attracting a lively young crowd, pizza and Chinese food.

The Heritage, see Sleeping page 738. Open from 1100. The verandas at the old DC's bungalow make pretty hilltop setting for lunch/dinner, food is Indian or Naga, long preparation time.

Hotel Cimorb, see Sleeping, page 738, is very reasonably priced for quality Indian/Chinese food, in a cosy green and wood interior, and has the benefit of opening later than most (till 2200, but phone ahead).

Mokokchung *p737*

The Restaurant, IM Rd, next to Supong Shopping Mall. Upstairs in an old building, this is the best and cosiest restaurant in town (outside of the 2 hotels). Huge menu covers Indian, Chinese and Tibetan dishes (veg and non) plus sandwiches, open Mon-Sat 0900-1730.

Grub Hub, Supong Shopping Mall, IM Rd. Limited menu of Indian and Chinese snacks, but music and youthful vibe are enjoyable. Mon-Sat 1000-1830.

Festivals and events

Kohima *p736*

The different tribes celebrate their special festivals when priests perform ceremonies followed by dancing, singing and drinking.

Feb Sekrenyi is celebrated by Angamis for 10 days when all work in the fields (by the men) ceases.

Mar/Apr Aoleong Monyu, a 6-day 'New Year' festival marking the beginning of spring, celebrated by the Konyak. **May Moatsu**, 6-day Ao festival marking the beginning of the growing season.

Dec Hornbill Festival, when all tribes gather in Kisama to display traditional sports and dance (see page 735).

Shopping

Dimapur *p736*

There are several small shops selling attractive Naga crafts, basketry, handloom, etc, in the Super Market complex less than 1 km from the railway. Prices are usually marked; closed on Sun.

Kohima *p736*

Warm, colourful Naga shawls are excellent (Rs 1300-2000). Also beads, shoulder bags, decorative spears, table mats, wood carvings and bamboo baskets. **Traditional Handicraft Centre**, opposite War Cemetery, has a good selection, open Mon-Sat 0830-1630. Also **Nagaland Handlooms and Handicrafts**, Main St, has a huge variety.

Activities and tours

Kohima *p736*

Explore Nagaland, T985-634 3037, www.explorenagaland.com. Custom-made tours which can include trekking, homestays, festivals: it's your choice. Nino is a warm and laid-back lady. Also has guest rooms in Kohima (see page 739).

Mon *p737*

Interior Adventures, T(0)9436-606212, www.interioradvanture.com. Packages including all transport, guide and accommodation in the Mon region (around US$ 140 per day). Also has a sister company, **Chain Reaction**, www.chainreactionindia.com which organizes excellent biking tours.

Transport

Dimapur *p736*

Air Airport is 3 km from town. **Air India**, www.airindia.com and **Kingfisher** to **Kolkata** and **Guwahati** daily.

Bus Note Transport in Nagaland grinds to a complete halt on Sun; it can be hard to find even a private taxi willing to take you, and prices are higher. Private buses from Golaghat Rd to **Guwahati** (11-12 hrs), **Imphal** (Rs 400, 9 hrs); from NST Bus Stand to **Kohima** hourly, 3 hrs.

Shared taxis To **Kohima** shared jeeps (2½ hrs, Rs 200) or shared taxis (Rs 300) leave from the taxi park next to the NST stand.
Train Enquiries: T131. To **Delhi**: *Brahmaputra Mail 14055*, daily 0535, 48½ hrs; *Rajdhani Exp 12435/12423*, 0025/0135, 37½/32½ hrs.
Dibrugarh: *Kamrup Exp 15959*, 2145, 8 hrs. *Brahmaputra Mail 14056*, 2020, 7½ hrs; *Rajdhani Exp 12424*, except Mon and Fri, 2240, 6½ hrs.
Guwahati: *Rajdhani 12435/12423*, 0025/0135, 4¾ hrs; *Jan Shatabdi Exp 12068*, except Sun 1615, 4½ hrs; *Brahmaputra Mail 14055*, 0535, 6 hrs; plus some slower trains.

Kohima *p736*

Air/train The nearest airport and railhead is 72 km away at Dimapur. For flight bookings, **Super Travels**, Hotel Japfü Complex, near Police HQ, PR Hill, T0370-224 4781, Mon-Sat 0900-1700.
Bus Private buses go to capitals in the Northeast, several companies including **Network Travels** leave from BOC area, 2 km south of the main town. **Nagaland State Transport (NST)**, in the main town, to **Dimapur** 7 per day from 0500-1500 (Rs 70, 2½ hrs); to **Khonoma** at 1330 (Rs 25, 1 hr); to **Mokokchung** at 0630 (Rs 150, 7 hrs); to **Zuheboto** at 0630 (Rs 150, 7 hrs); to **Tuensang** at 0630 (Rs 250/292, 10 hrs); to **Mon** go from Dimapur (there is a night-bus from Kohima only when demand is high, 1500, Rs 405); to **Imphal** at 0730 (Rs 155, 7 hrs).
Shared taxi To **Dimapur**, shared Rs 200 (private Rs 600), leaving from opposite NST, 2 hrs. Sumos to **Mokokchung** at 0600, 1000 (Rs 300, 5 hrs) and **Tuensang** at 0600 (Rs450, 10 hrs) leave from NSF Martyrs' Park, 1 km south of main town, at 0600.

Mokokchung *p737*

Bus NST buses go to **Kohima** (Rs 150) and **Dimapur** (Rs 250) at 0600; to **Mon** at 0600 (Rs 210); to **Mariani** at 1230 (Rs 95). **Local bus** to **Longkhum** at 0900, 0930, 1200, 1300 and 1500.
Sumo Bookings can be made from Lim, T0369-2226881 (and other agencies), for **Dimapur** departing 0600 (Rs 330); to **Kohima** at 0600 and 1000 (Rs 300); to **Jorhat** (4 hrs, Rs 170) via **Mariani** (Rs 150) at 0600 and 1200. Bookings from Link Transport, Hospital Rd, T0369-2228315, for **Mon** departing 0600 (Rs 530) and **Tuensang** at 0600 and 1200.

Mon *p737*

Bus NST bus to **Dimapur** at 1530 (12 hrs, Rs 340) via **Sonari** (3½ hrs, Rs 100).
Sumo First sumo to **Dimapur** at 0700; to **Mokokchung** at 0600, get very busy, try to book in advance.

Directory

Kohima *p736*

Banks There are ATMs in town. **Internet Kohima Computer Centre**, Khedi Market, opposite Capital Hotel, near NST bus stand, Main Town, T0370-229 1978, has fast connection, printing, Rs 30 per hr, Mon-Sat 0900-1700.

Manipur

→ *Population: 2.72 million. Area: 22,327 sq km.*

The former princely state of Manipur, the 'land of jewels', bordering Myanmar, has a low-lying basin in its centre surrounded by forested hills that rise to over 2000 m. The reedy Lake Loktak, the largest freshwater lake in the Northeast, and the flat-bottomed basin and river valleys that drain into it, add to the beauty of the land. It is the land of the graceful Ras Leela dance, of the famous women's market in Imphal, of rare orchids and the endangered Sangai, the brow-antlered deer. ▸▸ *For listings, see pages 746-748.*

Ins and outs

If you plan to travel out of Manipur overland, inform the FRO ⓘ *Jail Rd, Mon-Sat 0930-1700.*

History

Manipur has always been quite independent of its neighbouring tribal areas. It was often invaded from Burma but also enjoyed long periods of relatively stable government. At the end of the Indo-Burmese War in 1826 it was brought into India by the Treaty of Yandabo, British sovereignty being recognized in 1891. In 1939 a remarkable women's social revolt ('Nupilan' from '*nupi*', meaning women, and '*lan*', war) led to government action against monopolistic traders. The contemporary party Nisha Bandh consists of an all-women patrol that seeks to keep the streets safe at night. The role of women traders can be seen most colourfully in the women's market in Imphal. During the Second World War, Imphal was occupied by the Japanese. After Indian Independence Manipur became a Union Territory and achieved statehood in 1972. Congress won both Lok Sabha seats in 2009.

People

The majority of the population are Vaishnavite Hindus. They belong to the *Meitei* tribe and are related to the *Shans* of Burma, and live in the valleys. Twenty-nine hill tribes (mainly Naga and Kuki) constitute about a third of the population, most of whom are Christian. Like the Nagas, the Manipuris have a reputation for being great warriors, still practising their skills of wrestling, sword fighting and martial arts. Most wars were fought across the border in Burma. They are also keen on sport, and polo, which is said to have originated in Manipur, is the principal sport.

Dance, drama and music

The ancient musical forms of the valley dwellers are closely connected to the worship of Vishnu, expressed in Manipuri dancing. The *Ras Leela* dances performed at every ceremony are characterized by graceful and restrained movements and delicate hand gestures. The ornate costumes worn by the veiled women are glittering and colourful; the stiff, tubular skirts barely move. The *Sankirtana* dance is vigorous, rhythmic and athletic. It is usually performed by men, who play on the *pung* (drums) and cymbals while they dance. The tribal ritual dances, some of which are performed by priests and priestesses before deities, may end in a trance. Others can last several days, observing a strict form and accompanied by the drone of a bowed instrument, *pena*. *Thang-ta* is a skilful martial art performed to beating drums, and is practised by both sexes dressed in black.

Political developments

Troubled by a variety of internal conflicts since the late 1980s and with separatist movements voicing open dissent with rule from New Delhi, Manipur's State Assembly has had an unsettled recent history. One recent bone of contention is the Tipaimukh Dam, a 1500 mw hydro- and flood-protection project that has stirred up strong opposition from some quarters in Manipur and across the border in Bangladesh. The foundation stone for the project was laid in December 2006.

Democracy is very popular, with over 90% of the electorate turning out to vote in recent elections, but it has not produced stability. In the February 2007 elections the Indian National Congress under Chief Minister Okram Ibobi Singh won half the 60 seats, but it is too early to judge whether the long-running disturbances in the state will be resolved. Be sure to find out about the current situation before travelling to Manipur.

Imphal → *For listings, see pages 746-748. Colour map 4, B5.*

The capital Imphal (from *yumpham*, meaning homestead) lies in the heart of an oval- shaped valley cut through by narrow rivers and surrounded by forested hills. The old fort area of Kangla provides a large green central space, but otherwise the city is not particularly attractive. Due to its location it has become a principal export route for Myanmar's illegal drugs. The best time to visit is between December and May; temperatures range from 34°C to 0°C and annual rainfall is 1280 mm. Thank you in the Meitei language is *"thagatchari"*.

Ins and outs → *Population: 550,000. Altitude 720 m above sea level. Rainy season Jul-Aug*

Getting there and around Imphal's Tulihal airport is 8 km southwest of the city with taxi-vans and autos (Rs 150) available for hire . Outside is the main Airport Road, from where shared autos go into town. The dusty centre and the Ima Market are easy to cover on foot. Auto- and cycle-rickshaws can take you to places beyond the centre. ▸▸ *See Transport, page 748.*

Tourist information India Tourism ⓘ *Old Lambulane, Jail Rd, T0385-245 1131, Mon-Fri 0930-1630 in winter, 0930-1730 in summer,* helpful staff can advise on transport and other matters. Information desk at airport opens for flights and has a map of Imphal that is worth picking up. **Manipur Tourism** ⓘ *next to Hotel Imphal, T0385-245 1916, manipurtourismdept@gmail.com, Mon-Sat 0930-1600, closed 2nd Sat of the month.*

Sights

The ancient capital of **Kangla** ⓘ *open 0900-1600 (Nov-Feb) 0900-1700 (Mar-Oct), closed Wed, entrance Rs 2,* was the centre of Manipur's power until 1891. Since 2004, when the area was handed back to the people of Manipur by the Assam Rifles, the area has been undergoing renovation and beautification. In the southern area, the **Kangla Museum** ⓘ *1030-1600 winter, 1000-1600 summer,* has informative displays on the history and personalities of Manipur and so is worth visiting first. The brick-built Govindajee Temple, dating from 1842, and adjacent Beithab have been restored and nearby the Citadel walls are being rebuilt. Two dragons, *kangla-sha*, mark the spot where five British were beheaded during the Anglo- Manipur war, and their heads ritually buried. To the

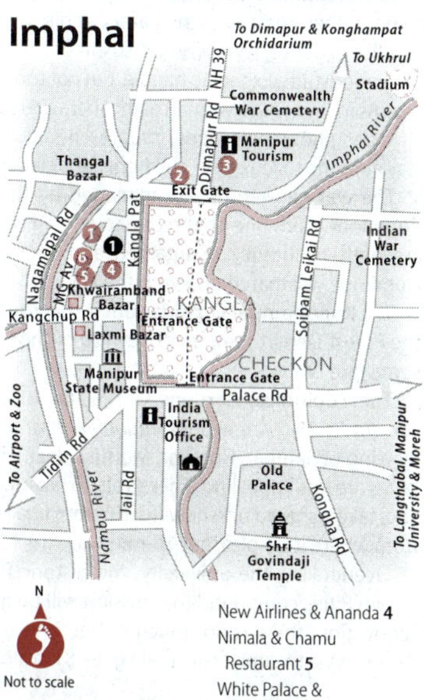

Sleeping
Anand Continental 1
Classic & Classic Café 2
Imphal & Emoinu Restaurant 3
New Airlines & Ananda 4
Nimala & Chamu Restaurant 5
White Palace & Chappan Bhog 6

Eating
Hotel Airlines 1

north are several bungalows built by the British, including that of Field Marshal General Slim, and is where rose gardens are being cultivated.

Near to Kangla Gate, inside the Bir Tikendrajit (BT) Park, stands the **Shaheed Minar** ⓘ *daily 1400-1700, but gate-keeper will unlock at other times*. This imposing structure commemorates the Manipuris who gave their lives fighting the British in 1891, two of their leaders were hanged here in front of 8,000 white-clad women.

The **Manipur State Museum** ⓘ *south side of BT Gardens, Tue-Sun 1030-1600 (closed every 2nd Sat and public holidays), entrance Rs 20*, is worth a visit. The Ethnology section has a collection of jewellery, headgear, smoking paraphernalia, arms and costumes belonging to Manipuri royalty and tribal groups. There is an Art Gallery (you may have to ask staff to unlock the door) with portraits of the Manipuri maharajahs as well as contemporary local art. Upstairs, the Natural History room includes geological and marine exhibits, dioramas with moth-eaten stuffed animals and birds, many specimen jars of pickled fish and a two-headed calf; a separate room displays costume dolls of the different states of India. Outside the museum's entrance is a huge royal boat, the *Hiyang Tannaba*, used in traditional rowing races.

The **Shri Govindajee Temple** ⓘ *Shrine open 0500-1030, 1430-1730*, dedicated to Krishna has two domes topped by tinkling bells, and in the temple forecourt one of the two bells was made in Croydon, England. This **Vaishnavite centre** with shrines to Vishnu, Balaram, Krishna and Jagannath has regular performances of ceremonial dancing; there is a peaceful *pooja* each afternoon (1530 in winter, 1630 in summer) which tourists are welcome to join. Adjacent to the temple is the royal palace, which was in the initial stages of being restored at the time of writing.

Khwairamband Bazar (Ima Market) ⓘ *0700-1900 in summer, till 1700 in winter*, in the town centre, is the largest women's bazar in India, some say in Asia. It is an excellent place for handicrafts, handloom goods, jewellery and cosmetics as well as fish, vegetables, pickles, orange honey and other foodstuffs. Expect to haggle, but not too hard – first price given is about 20% above the final cost. As many as 3000 women gather here every day, in three newly constructed buildings, making a vivid and photogenic scene. It represents a form of family work-sharing: while younger mothers stay at home to look after children, the older women and grandmothers come to the market.

The **war cemeteries** are managed by the Commonwealth War Graves Commission, the Commonwealth one on the Dimapur Road NH39 and the Indian one off the Ukhrul Road. They are both beautifully maintained and serenely peaceful sites, open during daylight hours (someone will materialise with the key).

The **Konghampat Orchidarium** ⓘ *12 km along the NH39, best time to visit Apr-May*, set up by the Forest Department, has over 120 of the 500 species of orchid found in Manipur including some rare ones.

The **Zoological Gardens** ⓘ *Tue-Sun 1000-1530, entrance Rs 10, Biological Museum Rs 5, camera Rs 25, 7 km west of Imphal in a rural setting*, are well maintained and allow close-up viewing of Sambar, Hog and Muntjac deer. The enclosures for the primates, birds, jackals and bears are less appealing. There's also a bizarre and dilapidated Biological Museum. To reach the zoo, take a shared rickshaw (Rs 10) from Ima Market to the Agricultural University in Iroisemba, from where it's a pleasant 10-min walk.

Overlooking the university, the historic **Palace of Langthabal** stands on a hill within an Assam Rifles compound (permission will be given for you to view the remains). Despite recent renovation, there is not much to detain you and a visit to the palace/temple is a short one. Access is via the university main gate, 8 km along the Indo-Burma road (Rs 10 in a shared auto).

Around Imphal

Situated at Andro village, 26 km from Imphal (less than one hour on public transport from Andro Parking), is a **Cultural Complex** ⓘ *daily 0830-1630*, seeking to preserve Manipuri and Northeastern culture. Run by the charming Mr Mutua, the Complex has replicas of various tribal dwellings and displays artefacts such as rare manuscripts, textiles, basketry, carving and jewellery.

Moirang and Loktak Lake → *For listings, see pages 746-748. Colour map 4, B5.*

Moirang, 45 km from Imphal, on Loktak Lake, is noted for its early Manipuri folk culture and traditional folk dance form. The temple to the forest god, known as Lord Thankjing, has robes of the 12th-century Moirang kings and holds the Lai Haraoba ritual dance festival each year. During the Second World War Moirang was the headquarters of the Indian National Army (INA) for a while, and their flag was raised as a symbol of national independence for the first time on 12 April 1944. There is an INA memorial and a **War Museum** ⓘ *Tue-Sun 1000-1600, entrance Rs 2*, displaying photos, letters and dusty war memorabilia relating to Subhas Chandra Bose, and which also has a gallery devoted to Manipur freedom fighters.

Loktak Lake is the largest freshwater lake in the Northeast, where fishermen live in huts on islands of floating weeds, using nets to farm fish and *singhara* (water chestnut). Perfectly circular floating pens made of weeds stretch as far as the eye can see, with enough room between each for the narrow wooden canoes to pass. About 1 km from Moirang Bazar, **Sendra Island** is currently home to a police post though in the future will have a tourist lodge; permission is given to walk to the top for views. Better is to continue on a shared auto/van for 20 minutes or so to the villages further on the lake. Tin-roofed huts are strung out along a series of hilly promontories which afford excellent views. The light is better for photographs in the afternoon.

Keibul Lamjao National Park

The park, covering 40 sq km, is the only floating sanctuary of its kind. It has a small population of thamin (Sangai), the endangered brow-antlered deer. The sanctuary was set up in 1977 on Loktak Lake when the swamps, the natural habitat of the Sangai, had been reclaimed for cultivation resulting in the near extinction of this 'dancing deer'. The Sangai feed on mats of floating humus covered with grass and *phumdi* reeds until the rainy season when they move to the hills. You can walk 20 minutes to a viewing tower on Babet Ching hillock and travel through the creeks on small wooden boats (when you are more likely to spot a Sangai). Other wildlife include hog deer, wild boar, panther, fishing cat and water birds. There is a forest resthouse in which you can stay with permission (see Sleeping, page 746).

Other areas of Manipur

Moreh, 110 km southeast of Imphal on the Indo-Myanmar border, has an interesting mix of cultures and is basically a giant market. A friendly police escort will accompany you during trips across the border (no phones or cameras allowed, but no visa/paperwork for Myanmar is necessary) where trading begins in earnest. After about 200 m, there are autos going to the larger market at **Tamu**, 5 km further into Myanmar. Both market areas are a good place to sample local cuisines, as well as shop for Chinese-made goods. There is transport back to Imphal in the afternoons, or plenty of basic hotels and restaurants should you wish to stay overnight (recommended, as the journey is tiring). Due to its location, Moreh has become a principal export route for heroin out of the Golden Triangle (as well as a main smuggling route for shoes, electronics, toys, and all else). Alcohol is plentiful in shops on both sides of the border.

Note It is a good idea to carry copies of your passport and visa to facilitate movement through several police and army check-posts along the road to Moreh.

Churachanpur (CC Pur), accessible by taxi from Moreh via Imphal, is a quiet market town with a good hotel. Apart from wandering its rural outskirts and exploring the market there is little to detain you.

Ukhrul, 83 km northeast of Imphal, is the domain of the Tanghul Nagas and the home of the Siroi Lily which grows on the Shirui-Kashong range at a height of 2591 m. The lily blooms in mid-May when trekking is possible from Shirui village, about 14 km from Ukhrul. The trek is not long (about 5 km, with a possible 10 km extension up Phungrei peak) through a mix of grassland and forest with rhododendrons. Volunteer guides are available from Shirui village and there are basic hotels in Ukhrul.

Manipur listings

For Sleeping and Eating price codes and other relevant information, see Essentials pages 38-42.

Sleeping

Imphal *p743, map p743*

Hotels in Imphal add 20% tax to the price of a room (the price brackets below include this). Check-out is usually 1200.

B-E The Classic Hotel, North AOC, T0385-244 3967/9, www.theclassichotel.in. Imphal's new 3-star hotel is by far the best in town, with spotless paintwork, shiny floors, flatscreens and quality furnishings. The cheapest room comes in at Rs 650/900 (single/double) without breakfast or a/c, other categories all include breakfast, and suites go all the way to Rs 5500. The **Classic Café** restaurant is stylish and has Indian/Chinese food and a chance to eat a Manipuri thali. Wi-Fi is Rs 25 per hr (non-guests can also pay and use), fitness centre, souvenir shop.

C Anand Continental, Khoyathong Rd, T0385-244 9422, hotel_anand@rediff.com. Good rooms with bath, TV, a/c, hot water and decent management.

C-E Hotel Nimala, MG Ave, T0385-245 9014. Popular choice, large rooms have flatscreens, geysers and clean furniture/paint. Central location close to Ima Market. Chamu restaurant has very good Indian/Chinese. Recommended to book ahead.

E Hotel New Airlines, MG Avenue, T0986-234 2968, hotelnewairlines@ymail.com. Clean and spacious rooms, with TV and colourful homely furnishings, the price isn't budget but the hotel is well maintained. Rooms at the back are pretty quiet. Xanadu Restaurant is open 0600-2100.

E Hotel Imphal, Dimapur Rd, North AOC, T0385-242 3372, hotelimphal@yahoo.in. Run by Manipur Tourism, this imposing white edifice was undergoing renovation at the time of research, with some rooms complete and many still to be finished. Rooms are large, with modern tiling, comfy beds, TV, fridge and reliable hot water. Suites range from Rs 1200-4000 and have a/c and new bathrooms. Pleasant gardens, restaurant is good (see Eating). Definitely the best value budget choice in town.

E-F White Palace, 113 MG Ave, T0385-245 2322. Rooms are weathered and could be cleaner, but they are a decent size, with plenty of furniture, TV and free hot buckets. Pleasant staff, food available in the room, hot buckets given. Singles start at Rs 252, doubles Rs 414, triples Rs 618 (plus 20%); suites are not worth the extra money.

Moirang *p745*

F Lake View, T03879-262242. On the junction, 2 km from Moirang Bazar, 4 km from Loktak Lake, by the bus stop for Imphal-CCPur. Rooms have seen better days, extremely hard beds, no fans or running water, but the owners are kindly and it is only hotel in Moirang,

The Dept of Tourism is planning to construct a lodge on **Sendra Island**, 2 km from Moirang Bazar, but this was far from finished at the time of research (when there was still an army post on the island!). Contact **Manipur Tourism** in Imphal for the current status, as is should be a peaceful spot with lake views.

Keibul Lamjao National Park *p745*

It is possible to sleep in the **Forest Lodge** on the edge of Keibul Lamjao National Park, but you need to get permission in advance from the Chief Wildlife Warden, Forestry Dept, Sanjenthong. Imphal. Set on a hillock with views of paddies and firs, the red-and-white lodge is pretty from the outside and very simple inside, with 2 single beds (nets), living room with chairs, fans, 2 bathrooms, and an outside kitchen (bring your own food). It's a short walk to a tiny village with a couple of dhabas/shops.

Other areas of Manipur *p745*

Moreh

There are several basic hotels in town, all of which lock up at 2100 and cost Rs 200-300 per room. The best of the bunch (with fans, nets, private/common bath) are the **River View**, **Neelraj** and **Luxmi**.

Churachanpur (CC Pur)

E Venus, Tiddim Rd, New Lamka, T920-631 6187/801-491 2932. Spotless rooms in a new hotel with comfy beds, clean sheets and paintwork, fans, long list of rules, doors locked at 2100, doubles Rs 500 (Rs 100 more for Western toilet). 2 beds available which share common bath (Rs 200). About 1 km from bus parking.

G Eden, Tiddim Rd, New Bazar, Basic shabby rooms with squat toilets, clean floors, nets and blankets, but 'not comfortable' (as staff are keen to emphasise). Close to bus stand.

Eating

Imphal *p743, map p743*

Manipur is a 'dry' state, though booze is available if you ask around. If you get a chance, try *iromba*, the Manipuri savoury dish of fish, vegetables and bamboo shoots and the sweet *kabok* made with molasses and rice. In the markets, women mix up snacks such as *kelichana* and *shingju*, a tasty mix of sprouts, raw veg, seasoning and split peas. The restaurants in the hotels are the safest bet for a decent meal; all serve veg and non-veg Indian and Chinese dishes.

TT Classic Café, at the **Classic Hotel**. Open 0600-2200. Does a Manipuri thali (veg Rs 300, non-veg Rs 350) in addition of other types of cuisine and is the smartest in town.

TT-T Emoinu, at the **Hotel Imphal**. Open 0630-2130. Serves up very tasty Indian food, as well as Chinese/some Western food, and interesting Manipuri feasts (veg Rs 230, non Rs 350), dishes take 15-30 mins to prepare.

T Chamu, at the **Nimala Hotel** has good mains, the muttar paneer is excellent. It's popular with locals, the gloomy lighting is brightened by pink walls and wood veneers.

T Chappan Bhog, MG Rd, opposite White Palace. Open 0600-2000. Serve decent puri/aloo in the mornings.

T Hotel Airlines, MG Ave (look for the sign for Sagar Pure Veg restaurant, go up the stairs), T0385-245 2177. Open 1030-2100. The usual Chinese and Indian dishes are OK and at a slightly cheaper price, but the main attraction here is alcohol (spirits available, strong beer Rs 150), expect Formica tables dimly lit by yellow lamps and the odd rat. Free delivery. Not to be confused with the Hotel New Airlines, nearby.

T Hotel Ananda, down an alley next to Hotel New Airlines. Open 0700-1900. Does a good cheap thali (veg Rs 35 or non-veg).

Moirang *p745*

Several small hotels serve tea, puri and curry; the food at the Lake View hotel is not recommended. In Moirang Bazar **T Loktak Fast Food**, open 0600-2000, has acceptable meat momos, chowmein, omelette, etc, while in the market hall itself, women make traditional Manipuri snacks.

Other areas of Manipur *p745*

Churachandpur (CC Pur)

T Sauliim in the New Bazaar and **Sauliim II** in Hebron Veng, New Lamka, open Mon-Sat 0800-1930, Sun from 1300, have decent food and snacks, lots of chicken, multicuisine, small portions. Otherwise there are cheap hotels serving simple food around New Bazar.

Entertainment

Imphal *p743, map p743*

Cultural shows with Manipuri dancing can be seen at **Rupmahal Theatre**, BT Rd, near Kangla Gate, and at **Kala Academy**.

Festivals and events

Imphal *p743, map p743*

Jan **Gang Ngai** celebrated by Kabui Nagas with dancing in ceremonial costumes in Imphal.

Feb/Mar **Yaosang** a Hindu festival on full moon night, boys and girls dance the Thabal Chongba and sing in a circle in the moonlight.

Apr-May Lai Haraoba is celebrated across the state with traditional dances and music.

Sep **Heikru Hitongba** is mainly non religious, when there are boat races along a 16-m-wide moat in narrow boats with large numbers of rowers.

Nov **Sangai Festival** runs for 7 days and showcases the culture, dance, food, sports and music of Manipur.

Shopping

Imphal *p743, map p743*

Silk thread embroidery in dark colours decorates the borders of the traditional *phaneks* worn by women. The best shopping experience is at the Khwairamband (see page 744). For woven wicker, handloom and souvenir items try **Eastern Handlooms Handicrafts**, Paona Bazar, open Mon-Sat 0900-1730.

Activities and tours

Imphal *p743, map p743*

Manipur Tourism, www.manipur.nic.in/tourism.htm. Tours to Sri Govindaji Temple, Bishnupur, INA Memorial, Moirang, KL National Park and the Loktak Lake, depart from **Hotel Imphal**, Sun 0800.

Seven Sisters, North AOC, T0385-244 3977, T(0)9957-171551, 7sistersholidays@gmail.com. For touring the region.

Transport

Imphal *p743, map p743*

Air Auto to town, Rs 150. **Air India**, MG Av, T0385-222 0999, www.airindia.com: **Kolkata**, daily (some via **Aizwal**); **Delhi**, **Guwahati**, **Jorhat**, 2-3 times weekly. **Jet Airways**, www.jetairways.com, to **Guwahati**, Tue, Wed; **Kolkata** (via Guwahati), Tue, Wed (via Jorhat), Thu, Sun. **Indigo**, www.goindigo.in, flies daily to **Delhi** and **Kolkata**.

Bus From North AOC, near Hotel Imphal, private buses connect with **Dimapur** (215 km) in Nagaland, the nearest railhead (8-9 hrs, Rs 400) via **Kohima** (6-7 hrs, Rs 300). Daily private buses (some a/c) for **Guwahati** (579 km, 24 hrs, Rs 700) via Silchar (198 km) and to **Shillong** (Rs 800). To **Moirang** (for Loktak Lake) transport leaves from Wahengban Leikai Parking. To **Moreh** sumos and Wngers from Moreh Parking near Kangla Gate, leaving when full between 0600-1100 (best to go early), Rs 200, 3-4 hrs. Fare is more expensive returning from Moreh, at least Rs 300.

Taxi Mini-vans can be taken as 'reservation'.

Other areas of Manipur *p745*

Churachandpur (CC Pur)

Bus/sumo Regular buses/wingers to **Imphal**, 2 hrs, Rs 60. It is possible to get sumos to **Moreh**, **Dimapur**, **Guwahati** and even **Aizawl** (24 hrs, Rs 750).

Directory

Imphal *p743, map p743*

Banks Banks in Thangal Bazar and MG Ave.

Hospitals Jenim's Hospital in Porompat and Shija Hospital in Langol (the best in town).

Post The GPO is near Jail Rd.

Other areas of Manipur *p745*

Churachandpur (CC Pur)

Internet Intermittent internet connection at **Sauliim Bookshop**, Hebron Veng, New Lamka, for Rs 30 per hr.

Moreh

Internet Good internet connection at **Anjali Computer**, on the main road opposite Hotel Neelraj, Rs 20 per hr, 0630-1930.

Mizoram

➔ *Population: 1,091,014. Area 21,000 sq km. Rainy season May-Sep.*

The southernmost of the Northeastern States, Mizoram lies between Myanmar (Burma) and Bangladesh. Until 1972 it was known as the Lushai Hills, a district of Assam, and it became the 23rd state of the Indian Union in 1987. The six or so parallel north–south ranges of hills, which rise to an altitude of over 2000 m, are covered in dense forests of bamboo and wild banana. At the bottom of the deep gorges the rivers run in narrow ribbons. Welsh missionaries made a great impact here, and it is perhaps India's most Westernised state with gender equality very much apparent. The tourist-tag of 'blue-hued hills' rings true, and the sparsely populated countryside is extremely beautiful. Monsoon occurs from May to September; winter is the best time for views. ▸▸ *For listings, see page 751-753.*

Culture

Tribal groups 'Mizo' is derived from *mi* (man) and *zo* (highland), a collective name given by their neighbours to a number of tribes that settled in the area. The different groups of tribal people are thought to have originally come from northwest China in the seventh century, gradually travelled southwards and reached this area less than 300 years ago. The Mizos were animists, believing in good and evil spirits of the woodland. Mizo villages perch on top of the ridges with the chief's house and the *zawlbuk* (bachelors' dormitory) in the centre. Built on steep slopes, houses often have front doors at street level while the backs stand precariously on stilts. Many homes proudly display bougainvillea, orchids and pots of geranium, begonia and balsam. More than 1000 varieties of medicinal plants grow wild. Every town and village has a Young Mizo Association (YMA) which aims to keep Mizo traditions and customs alive, and whose black, red and white colours adorn buildings and trees.

Religion The raiding of British tea plantations up until the end of the 19th century led to the introduction of Inner Line Permits, which restricted movement of people but gave free access to missionaries, who carried out their religious duties and introduced literacy (which is exceptionally high at 88%, the language having adopted the Roman script). Most Mizos are Christian converts following the Welsh Presbyterian faith and have a strong tradition of choral singing. The mainly nomadic Chakmas along the western border practise a religion which combines Hinduism, Buddhism and animism. Some even claim descent from one of the lost tribes of Israel. A few Kukis who were once headhunters, and Chins, have converted to Judaism.

Modern Mizoram

Rice and maize, supplemented by *jhum* (slash and burn) cultivation, supports 75% of the population. The government are attempting to encourage permanent cultivation and now grapes, ginger, passion fruit and oranges are being grown for export. There are no mineral resources exploited yet and no large-scale industries though the government has sponsored some light industrial development in Aizawl. Handicrafts and handwoven textiles predominate. The culture of hospitality (*tlawamngaihna*) is immediately noticeable and you will have trouble paying for a cup of tea; chewing *khuva* (paan) is endemic and both men and women smoke heartily. Mizoram is a dry state though rice wine is illegally brewed and sold, but (unlike Nagaland) drunkenness is not commonplace. Scooters and motorbikes buzz around (there are even Enfield gangs) and Western clothes are the norm – people joke that the Mizos would sooner spend money on fashion than food. 'Yes' in Mizo is *'Oh'*, which means everyone sounds permanently surprised.

Aizawl

➔ *Colour map 4, B5/C5. Population: 404,054. Altitude: 1200 m.*

Getting there Flights from Kolkata take 1½ hrs. Foreigners must register at the airport, and it is essential to sign in at the FRO in the CID Complex, Bungkawn (T0389-233 2982, daily

0900-1700) within 24 hours of arrival. The 37 km from Langpui Airport to Aizawl is by pre-paid taxi (Rs 600) or sumo (Rs 200 per person). Travellers from the rest of the Northeast usually arrive by bus via Silchar or Guwahati to the north.

Getting around City buses are useful and easy; cheap shared taxis connect to outer suburbs.

Tourist information **Directorate of Tourism** ⓘ *Bungkawn, near Khatla, T0389-233 3475, www.mizotourism.nic.in, a 10-min walk from the FRO, Mon-Fri 0900-1700*, has good brochures but no map of Aizawl, will help phoning tourist lodges around the state to book accommodation.

The road from Silchar comes upon the isolated capital Aizawl (pronounced Eye-zol), built along a central ridge and several surrounding spurs. The Tropic of Cancer runs through the heart of the city. White-painted churches stand out amongst the residential buildings that cling precariously to the hillsides. Navigating the sprawling city is surprisingly easy, and frequent buses ply the one-way system between the districts. From south to north, the order of districts is: Bawnkung, Khatla, Treasury Square, Zodin Square, Dawrpui (Bara Bazar), Zarkawt, Chanmari, Ramhlun, Chaltlang, Bawngkawn. A useful landmark is the Millennium Centre (multi-storey shopping mall), which is between Bara Bazar and Zarkawt.

Sights **Bara Bazar**, the main shopping centre, is on the east side of the central ridge. Steep Zion Street, lined with stalls selling garments and Mizo CDs, leads down to the **New Market** (0700-1800, closed Sun) where women gather in their traditional costumes to sell produce from farms and homesteads. The dingy multi-levelled complex is fascinating, with unrecognizable vegetables, heaps of tobacco, textiles, clothing and snails for sale; local eateries are found on the fourth floor.

Mizoram State Museum ⓘ *T0389-234 0936, McDonald's Hill, Zarkawt, Rs 5, Mon 1300-1600, Tue-Fri 1000-1600, Sat 1000-1400*, is well-maintained (most artefacts have been copiously varnished) and has an interesting collection of ethnographical relics and traditional implements. The textile gallery includes ancient costumes and basketry. There is a zoological section and an archaeological exhibition (although this was closed at the time of research). The museum lacks information panels, but items are labelled.

Around Aizawl

An attractive excursion about an hour from the city is **Reiek *tlang*** (peak), a forested area leading up to a grassy cliff with a fantastic viewpoint. It is recommended to stay (at the good value tourist lodge) for a truly peaceful experience. Caves beneath the overhang and a model Mizo village of furnished traditional huts are further attractions; the two-day annual Anthurium (flower) festival is held in April with dancing, music and games.

In Durtlang, 8 km from Aizawl, is **VK Paradise**, an unusual three-storey mausoleum built to honour a lady who died in a car accident in 2001. Known locally as the Mizo Taj Mahal, there are wonderful views from the terrace. From here, it is easy to continue to the Theological College from where all the photos of Aizawl at night-time are taken. The **Zoological Park**, 45-minutes north of the city on the airport road, has Hoolock gibbons, clouded leopards and other rare species; as Indian zoos go, this is one of the better ones.

Saitaul

A friendly sprawling village that has a couple of simple eateries and an excellent tourist lodge, Saitaul is an easy three-hour sumo ride from Aizawl. Nearby **Tamdil** (Lake of the Mustard Plant) is a large natural lake with boats for hire and some cottages where you can stay. It is possible to walk the 10 km from Saitual; downhill all the way, it takes about 2½ hours – but you will hope desperately that someone will give you a lift back up. Otherwise arrange a taxi/auto for the trip.

Champhai ➔ *Population: 125,370.*

Champhai (194 km from Aizawl, altitude 1680 m), on the Indo-Myanmar border and known as the fruit bowl of the Northeast, is worth a visit for its stunning location. The hilltop town looks onto a wide valley of rice plains dotted with fluffy hillocks and silver-roofed huts – the flattest part of the state – with the mountains of Myanmar looming beyond. There is little to do in the small town itself, except enjoy the spectacular views and walk to traditional villages nearby, such as Ruantlang. You can make the incredibly scenic journey to the border village of **Zokhawthar** (pronounced Zo-ko-ta, 27 km); if you do, sit on the left side going there and the right side coming back to get the views. In Zokhawthar, everyone will be keen to help you attempt to cross the river border to visit mythical **Rei Lake** in Myanmar. In theory it is possible if you manage to dodge the border guards (then take a motorbike taxi from the other side, Rs 150 return), but in all likelihood you will have to be content with a walk around the Burmese village accompanied by a police escort. The Myanmar police do not knowingly allow foreigners access. There is a tourist lodge at Zakhawthar, but little else. Attempts to make it a trading hub are ongoing (there's a huge customs building ready) but currently only 40 types of goods are allowed across, mostly vegetable items.

Phawngpui

Tucked in the southeast corner of Mizoram, Phawngpui, the state's highest peak at 2210 m, literally means 'Blue Mountain'. The taxing 300 km-journey from Aizawl means the national park's sub-tropical forests, orchids and rhododendron cover is little visited. Accommodation is available in Vawmbuk and Sangau villages. Trekking here is best arranged through a tour operator; **Jungle Travels** in Guwahati (see page 709) offers week-long trips.

Mizoram listings

For Sleeping and Eating price codes and other relevant information, see Essentials pages 38-42.

Sleeping

Aizawl *p749*

There is a cluster of hotels in Zarkawt (in addition to the ones listed below), each with a range of rooms of different categories, including the Chief, the Millennium and the Chawlhna. There are more attractive better value places to be had (listed below), but they are not in the centre of town.

C David's Hotel Clover, Chanmari, T0389-230 5736/7, www.davids-hotel-clover.com. All rooms have TV, hot water, fridge, colourful walls, fans, decent wood furniture and a cheerful feel (despite the lack of exterior windows). Cheapest single Rs 750, good sized doubles are Rs 1500, plus suites for Rs 2750. Free wireless, airport service Rs 600, car hire can be arranged. **David's Kitchen** is one of the best restaurants in town (see Eating, page 752).

D Arini, Upper Khatla, T0389-230 1557. Clean rooms that are spacious and have geysers (save for the small singles, Rs 600, hot bucket provided), nice TV lounge, restaurant, free Wi-Fi. Some balconies, good city views from the rear, attention has been given to colour schemes and decor. The best suites in town for Rs 2700. Good choice.

D-E Ritz, Bara Bazar, T0389-231 0409, www.ritzaizawl.com. Comfortable rooms in an old fashioned hotel, all with bath and TV, de luxe or standard (single/double Rs 650/800), good restaurant.

D-E Tourist Complex, Berawtlang, T0389-235 2067. An annoying 11 km east of the city (though buses go to Berawtlang village) with stunning views, cottages are good value and the cafeteria excellent.

D-E Tourist Lodge, Chaltlang, T0389-234 1083, www.mizotourism.nic.in. Large rooms are excellent value, newly painted, tiled bathrooms with geysers, TV, doubles have balconies, some 'suites'. Great views from the new wing that has just been added, while others (including all the singles, Rs 400) have consequently had their view obscured. Good restaurant (Mizo, Indian, Chinese, cheap), lovely staff, internet Rs 30 per hr. Unfortunately it is about 4 km from the main hub of Zarkawt and up a steep hill, although buses do run along the route.

E Tropicana, near Traffic Point, Zarkawt, T0389-234 6156. Walls are scuffed but sheets clean, more expensive on the upper levels though street noise is a problem at the front. TVs, attached baths, centrally controlled hot water.

F-G Imperial, Zarkawt, T0389-234 8168. Cheapest rooms in town are also the dirtiest (singles start at Rs 100 with common bath, doubles Rs 200), 3- and 4-bed rooms available.

F-G Sainik Rest House, Bungkawn, T0389-233 3129, Director T(0)9436-385287. The 2 VIP rooms here are the best deal in Aizawl at Rs 300 (single or double) for new furniture, clean bathrooms (squat toilets), double bed, side views of the ridge. Also 3-bed dorms with shared bath, mainly catering to Airforce personnel, not recommended. Good views from the back terraces. No food. Located between Khatla and the tourist office.

Around Aizawl *p750*

Reiek

F-G Tourist Lodge, T0389-256 7344. Cottages and rooms around a restaurant in the jungle make for a memorable stay, it is utterly peaceful and beautiful.

Saitual *p750*

F Tourist Lodge, T0389-256 2395, T(0)9862-775342. Quirky blue cottages with great balconies are large and clean, twin beds, nets, fans, modern bathrooms. Located 600 m uphill from the bazar, where there are a couple of simple eateries. Nice family. Food available in the empty dining hall, though it is average. A true bargain. (There are also tourist cottages at Tam Lake if you wish to really get away from things).

Champhai *p751*

E-F Tourist Lodge, T03831-234015. About 1.5 km downhill from the centre (shared taxi Rs 20 going down, auto back up Rs 10) set among pine trees on a promontory. Cottages are spacious and most have wonderful views from the terrace, with TV, geyser, seating. Rooms in the main building are clean and well-furnished, with mossie nets, hot water by the bucket, fan, some have balconies but no views. All have carpets which are getting a bit shabby. The restaurant serves up decent food (lacking spice) with an hour's notice.

The **Hotel Holiday**, T03831-234871, a short walk uphill from the centre of Champhai and commanding amazing views, was locked at the time of our visit.

Eating

Aizawl *p749*

There's cheap local Mizo food in New Market, Bara Bazar.

₮₮-₮ Curry Pot, Upper Khatla, T0389-232 4567. Open Mon-Sat 1100-2130. High standard Chinese, Mughal and Tandoor food in modern and subtly decorated surrounds; the hot and sour soup is delicious. Recommended.

₮₮-₮ David's Kitchen, Mon-Sat 1000-2130. You are bound to end up here at some point, the multicuisine food is good and the setting welcoming and well-lit. Plus there is Wi-Fi. Dolly, David's sister, also runs a cafe upstairs and Hotel Clover next door.

₮ Hot Pot, Main St, Zarkawt, T0389-230 6752. Open 0800-2100. A mix of North Indian, tandori, Chinese and Tibetan fare, clean bright surroundings, recommended.

₮ Puii, Treasury Sq. There's a cluster of restaurants here, all serving decent basic Chinese food, meat momos, rolls and good (if watery) lassis. Little Puii is always busy and had the best noodles and soups of the eateries we tried.

Festivals and events

Aizawl *p749*

Early Mar Chapchar Kut, a traditional 7-day spring festival marking the end of *jhumming* is celebrated with singing dancing and feasting. **Cheraw** is performed by nimble-footed girls who dance in and out of bamboo poles, clapped together by teams of young men. Similar dances are performed in Myanmar, Thailand and the Philippines.

Aug/Sep Mim Kut, Maize Festival, and **Dec/Jan Pawl Kut**, Harvest Festival, are celebrated with rice-wine and dancing.

Shopping

Aizawl *p749*

C Awmpuii Handloom, Solomon's Cave, Mission Veng. Good selection of textiles, bags and the typical bamboo peaked *khumbeu* ceremonial hat made using waterproof wild *hnahthial* leaves (Rs 250).

Zo-Dawr, Canteen Sq, Dawrpui. Textiles, hats, baskets and some great stools at a good price, Mon-Sat 0900-1730.

MAHCO, Treasury Sq. The government show rooms is disorganised but has a huge selection of textiles (including the original woven *puan* garment worn by men and women).

Activities and tours

Aizawl *p749*

Omega Travels, Zodin Sq, T0389-232 3548, T(0)9862-370544, omegatravels89@yahoo.co.in. Mon-Sat 1000-1700. Helpful agents, arrange trekking and other tours. Can efficiently sort out permits (should the RAP system be re-introduced) for 1-4 people. Email a scan of passport and visa; permits take 10 days. Open Mon-Sat 1000-1630.

Quality Travels, Chandmari, T0389-234 1265.

Transport

Aizawl *p749*

Air **Langpui Airport** (37 km north); **Air India**, T0389-234 1265, airport T0389-234 4733, www.airindia.com. The smaller Kingfisher planes are more reliable as they can land more easily, www.flykingfisher.com, fly to **Kolkata** and **Guwahati** daily, with some flights via Imphal.

Bus **Mizoram State Transport** (tickets can be bought 6 days in advance; at least 2 days in advance is advisable) run buses to **Silchar**, on Mon, Wed and Fri at 0600, (8 hrs, Rs 153), departing from Vanapa Hall next to Treasury Sq (T0389-232 2226, booking 0530-1500); same days to **Guwahati** (24 hrs, Rs 538/673) via Shillong (20 hrs, Rs 435/544) at 1200, departing from Chaltlang terminal (T0389-234 5024). To **Champhai** daily at 0600 (9 hrs, Rs 165) via Saitaul (Rs 48), depart from Vanapa Hall. Also private buses to **Silchar**, **Guwahati** (Rs 800) via **Shillong** (Rs 700) which are speedier and more comfortable but depart from Thuampui terminal which is 5 km from town, connected by bus/taxi.

Sumo The 4WD *sumos* are quicker if more pricey. **KT Travels**, amongst others, has sumos to **Silchar** at 0700, 1000, 1300, 1600 and 1800 (6 hrs, Rs 280), and to **Guwahati** (21 hrs, Rs 850) via Shillong, 0600 or night service at 1800. To **Champhai** daily at 0600, 0700, 0900, 1000 and 1100 (8 hrs, Rs 350) from Lower Zarkawt, opposite the Grace Nursing Home. For the **airport**, sumos leave from Lower Zarkawt at 0700, 0900 and 1000 (Rs 60, 1½ hrs).

Taxi Shared taxis run from hubs around the city (Rs 10) or are cheap to hire. Car hire is available from Hotel Clover.

Train The nearest railhead is at Silchar in Assam. Computerised rail office on the 2nd floor of Chaltlang bus terminal, open Mon-Fri 0930-1700.

Saitaul *p750*

Sumos To **Aizawl** at 0530, 0545, 0600, 0830, 1300 and 1330 (3 hrs, Rs 130), bookings and departure from the bazar.

Champhai *p751*

Sumos To **Aizawl** regular services until 1400 (7 hrs, Rs 250, or Rs 350 for No 1 seat) for **Saitaul** get down at Keifang (you will have to pay the full fare to Aizawl) from where a rickshaw is Rs 70 to the Tourist Lodge. To **Zokhawthar** services leave when full from Venglai Bazar (very close to centre of town), Rs 70, 1½ hrs.

Directory

Aizawl *p749*

Bank ATMs are plentiful, the main SBI is in Solomon's Cave, Zodin Sq. **Medical services** **Civil Hospital**, Upper Bazar, T0389-232 2318, **Presbyterian Hospital**, Durtland (7 km), T0389-236 1185. **Post** GPO, Treasury Sq.

Champhai *p751*

Internet GCI, by the main sumo counter. New computers, Rs 30 per hr, Mon-Fri 0700-1700; a couple of other internet cafes in town are open on Sat.

Tripura

→ Population: 3.76 million. Area: 10,492 sq km.

Still extensively forested, the tiny former Hindu Princely State of Tripura managed to retain a large degree of independence through much of the last millennium until it joined India in 1949. Partition and the 1971 creation of Bangladesh resulted in the influx of huge numbers of Bengali refugees, and although the tribal population still retain centuries-old practices they are now very much in the minority. For many years, travel here was deemed unsafe as tribal insurgents violently pursued their goals, but now successful government incentives and stricter border controls mean that this little-visited enclave is open for easy exploration. Impressive sights are few, but not far between, and the pretty villages and rolling scenery make for a relaxing if low-key few days. The tourist trail in Tripura is as yet virtually untrodden, and this is the chief pleasure in a visit to this unique and mellow state. *▸▸ For listings, see pages 757-760.*

The land

Covering just under 10,500 sq km, Tripura is almost surrounded on the north, west and south by Bangladesh. The north falls into four valleys, separated by hills rising to just under 1000 m. The more open land of the south is forested with hardwoods, including sal and teak, and 77% of the state is covered by trees. Parts of Tripura receive more than 4000 mm of annual rainfall.

History

Tripura is believed to have existed in the times of the epic *Mahabharata*. Historically, it was ruled by the Manikyas of Indo-Mongolian origin from the 14th century. Since Tripura was constantly feuding with her neighbours, particularly the Nawabs of Bengal, the British offered help to the maharaja and established a protectorate, separating the princely state from tribal lands outside the control of the Hindu rajas. The Manikyas ruled continuously right up to 15 October 1949 when Tripura acceded to India. It became a full state in 1972. In the 1930s, Maharaja Bir Bikram made his kingdom more accessible by opening an airport. Rabindranath Tagore based his play *Visarjan* and novel *Rajasri* on the legends of the Manikyas. The CPI(M) won both Lok Sabha seats in 2009.

Culture

The tribes of Tripura now make up just 31% of the population, and, although some distinctive customs have been retained, there has been much interchange between the predominant Bengali culture and indigenous traditions. A typical tribal welcome involves building a bamboo arch, garlanding the honoured guest while wafting incense, and this is now something seen in all Tripuri special occasions (such as marriages) regardless of peoples' ethnic roots. You may notice brightly coloured parasols in the village pond which are put there in honour of dead ancestors. An invitation into someone's home could be a chance to try *gudok*, a preparation of green and wild vegetables boiled without oil and very healthy.

There is a high degree of literacy in the state, estimated at 87% it is the fourth highest in the country, almost equal between the genders. And despite its small size it has no less than 100 daily newspapers (six in English) and numerous weekly and monthly publications.

Modern Tripura

Economy Rice is the main crop while rubber has gained importance (the state is now second only to Kerala in production). Tea, coffee beans, bamboo, pineapples and oranges are important cash crops. Sugar cane, mustard, potatoes and pulses are also grown. In recent years the Indian government has encouraged small industries and weaving, carpentry, pottery and basket making are common. Tripura suffers from the continuing failure of Bangladesh and India to agree a trade and travel treaty, which would allow goods to be taken in transit across

Bangladesh. This adds hugely to the time and cost of transport to Kolkata, still a major market for Tripura goods, and lorries can take two weeks to make a journey that could take two days by the direct route. This, coupled with the strength of the workers' and merchants' unions, means that the cost of living is high even in comparison to Delhi and Mumbai.

Government The state's democratic process operates under severe constraints. Politically motivated killings and kidnappings are becoming a thing of the past, as the government tries to control rebel factions. Of Tripura's 856-km border, 640 km has been fenced and this has had a great impact on movement of insurgents. The 60 member state assembly is controlled by the Left Front, and autonomous district councils operate in many areas.

Agartala → *For listings, see pages 757-760. Colour map 4, C4.*

A small and pleasant city, Agartala is noticeably green with many little backstreets of simple bungalows nurturing spindly betel-nut trees and banana plants in their gardens. The city centre is generally free from heavy traffic and comes to life with hundreds of cycle rickshaws during rush hours. The city's red brick official buildings contrast with the British preference for white paint, still obvious on some important structures, notably the maharaja's palace.

Ins and outs → *Population: 189,300. Altitude: 1280 m.*

Getting there The most convenient way to get to Agartala is by air, with connections to Kolkata and Guwahati taking under an hour. Foreigners must register their arrival at the airport. Transfer to the centre of town is by taxi (Rs 240) or auto (Rs 105). Buses from Guwahati take about 20 hours or the train involves a change at Lumding in Assam, then chair-car onward to Agartala. The border with Bangladesh, just 2 km from Agartala, is convenient for anyone with a visa to get to Dhaka, which is three hours by road and three hours by train.

Getting around The centre can be covered on foot, otherwise cycle-rickshaws are Rs 5 for short distances. There may be a strong military presence in town, although they show little interest in foreign tourists. ▸▸ *See Transport, page 759.*

Tourist information **Tourist office** ⓘ *Ujjayant Palace, East Wing, T0381-222 5930, www.tripura.nic.in*. **Bangladesh Visa Office** ⓘ *2 km north of the centre, Mon-Fri 1000-1200*, for applications. Six-month visas cost about US$46 for UK nationals; US$23 for nationals of USA and Australia.

Climate Summer maximum 35°C, minimum 24°C. Winter maximum 27°C, minimum 13°C. Annual rainfall: 2240 mm, June-August. Best time to visit: September-March.

Sights

The airport road from the north of town leads to the **Ujjayanta Palace** ⓘ *grounds open daily, 1700-1830, Rs 3, cameras free, no video allowed*. Built by Maharaja Radha Kishore Manikya in 1901, it stands amid large well-kept Mughal gardens with pools and floodlit musical fountains. Close up, the white paintwork is crumbling and water-stained but the grand marble staircase, imposing central dome and arched hallways still impress. The vast palace has magnificent tiled floors, a carved wooden ceiling in the Chinese room and beautifully crafted front doors. Now the State Legislature, it is normally closed to visitors, but you may ask to look around when the Assembly is not in session. The State Museum is destined to be re-homed here when the Assembly moves to a new building, but this is still some way off. Good views of the palace lit up at night can be had from the **Sri Laxminarayan temple** to the right of the main (south) entrance. The late 19th-century **Jagannath temple** across an artificial lake to the west of the palace, rises to a striking orange four-storeyed *sikhara*.

Tripura Government Museum ⓘ *HG Basak Rd, Mon-Sat 1000-1300 and 1400-1700, closed on public holidays, Rs 2, cameras free*, has a small but well-displayed collection of delicate stone images from the temples of Udaipur, eighth- to 10th-century Buddhist sculptures from Pilak (rather weathered), and ancient figurines (some dating from 2500 BC) which show the elaborate hairstyles of the Sunga Period. On the upper level, there are examples of Bengali *kantha* embroidery, tribal weaving and jewellery, and interesting portraits of the maharajahs – look for the last maharajah's coronation procession from the Ujjayanta Palace, in 1928.

The **Temple of Chaturdasa Devata**, 8 km east, near Old Agartala, is dedicated to 14 gods and goddesses, represented by their heads only. It combines the Bengali Bankura style with a Buddhist *stupa*-type structure. In July, **Kharchi Puja**, which has evolved from a tribal festival, attracts worshippers from all over Tripura.

North of Agartala → *For listings, see pages 757-760.*

Travelling outside Agartala is easy, with various one- to six-day tours organized by the tourism department and regular bus or jeep connections between towns. One section of the Agartala–Assam Highway is still heavily guarded by military forces and vehicles travel in convoy. Seek advice before travelling north through the state.

Unakoti and Kailashahar → *Colour map 4, B4.*

Ten kilometres from the friendly town of Kailashahar, **Unakoti** is the site of the largest bas-relief sculpture in India. Buses from Kailashahar drop off on the main road 1 km from the site but finding transport back can be difficult; auto-rickshaws will do a round trip. The seventh-century rock carvings are cut vertically into the hillside, the largest being an impressive 10-m-high depiction of Siva. The style is unusual, reminiscent of statues in South America more than representations of the Hindu pantheon. It is a quiet and peaceful place, unless you come during the mela (March/April). **Kailashahar** has a good market.

Jampui Hills

Some 220 km from Agartala, the Jampui Hills are a serene and forested area good for walking and tasting tribal culture. Between October and December the orange groves are heavy with fruit, while the famed orchids bloom between March and May. Very much off the foreign tourist trail, it's a worthy excursion if travelling into Tripura from the north.

South of Agartala → *For listings, see pages 757-760.*

Sepahijala Wildlife Sanctuary

ⓘ *24 km from Agartala, 0800-1600.*

The sanctuary has a botanical garden, small zoo and a boating lake and is a unique home to the spectacled monkey. The zoo is beautifully kept and new enclosures provide a more natural habitat. There are tigers, lions, cheetahs, bears and a rhino; the spectacle monkeys live in the trees above while the lake attracts migrating birds. Elephant rides are offered too. It may be possible to visit a rubber plantation and watch the processing on a trip. Buses and jeeps from Agartala take about 30 minutes, and a couple of tourist lodges have cottages bookable through the Wildlife Warden, T0381-236 1225/7.

Udaipur *Colour map 4, C4.*

The **Tripura Sundari Temple**, 57 km south from Agartala, near the ancient capital Udaipur, was built on Dhanisagar Hill in the mid-16th century. The Matabari is believed to be one of the 51 holy *pithasthans* mentioned in the *Tantras*, where the Mother Goddess is served by red-robed priests. The pond behind has huge turtles which are delighted to be fed. A large fair is held during **Diwali** in October/November. Other temples of interest, in various states of atmospheric decrepitude, are the Jagannath Mandir and the Bhubaneswari Mandir. There is a good lodge. Buses and jeeps from Agartala take about one hour.

Neermahal

Some 53 km southeast of Agartala, this water-palace in the middle of Rudrasagar Lake was built in 1930 by the late maharaja. The striking white and red fairytale castle with towers, kiosks, pavilions and bridges is fun to explore although the interiors are empty. Boats take passengers from the litter-strewn shore (Rs 15 for 10 people or Rs 150 to hire the whole boat) throughout the day. It is particularly beautiful illuminated at night, and on Saturdays and Sundays there is a **son et lumière show** ⓘ *1745-1845, Rs 35 includes boat ride and entrance, commentary in Bengali,* the highlight of which is witnessing the palace become floodlit, perfectly reflected in the still waters, as you journey across. The lake itself attracts migratory birds. Sunset across the water is marred somewhat by the chimney of a brick factory.

Pilak

The eighth- to ninth-century archaeological remains of Buddhist and Hindu statutory at Pilak are distinctly underwhelming. That said, the nearby village of **Jolaibari** has a pleasant tourist lodge and active nightmarket, and the walk through the paddies and villages to the sites is rewarding in itself. About 1.5 km beyond the village (signed off the main road) is the **Shyamsundar** *stupa*; the cross-shaped brick base is all that remains, lined with terracotta tiles of frolicking people and animals. Another 2 km brings you to weathered stone images of Avolokiteshwar and Narasimhha, where further excavations are still unearthing intricate metal and stone artefacts.

Tripura listings

For Sleeping and Eating price codes and other relevant information, see Essentials pages 38-42.

Sleeping

Agartala *p755*

Most **D** have some a/c rooms, book in advance if you have somewhere particular in mind as rooms fill up quickly. Checkout times are almost always 1200.

A-C Ginger, Airport Rd, T0381-230 3333, www.gingerhotels.com. Super new rooms are unquestionably the best in town and the standard far superior to others in this price range. Wi-Fi. The downside is being on the edge of town in a bit of a wilderness, though autos are cheap to the centre. Check online for last minute discounts.

A-E Welcome Palace, HGB Rd, T0381-238 4940, bantob@sancharnet.in. A very comfortable hotel with delightful staff and a range of a/c rooms, the cheapest (doubles Rs 900) get booked up fast so call ahead. Front desk can help with car hire and ticketing. The **Kurry Klub** restaurant is excellent.

D-E City Centre, Madhyapara Rd, off HGB Rd, T0381-238 5270/1, jaininn_pvtltd@hotmail.com. Well-equipped large a/c rooms are worth patient haggling over, as huge reductions are possible. Reasonably priced non-a/c are fine in any case. Marble floors are cooling, everything works and management are attentive without being overly so. The restaurant, however, disappoints.

D-E Rajdhani, BK Rd (northeast of Ujjayanta Palace), T0381-222 3387. 27 clean rooms with bath plus **C** suites, car hire, but no longer the "first lift in Tripura!" Alcohol allowed only in the rooms. Staff speak good English.

D-F Overseas Mansion, HGB Rd, T0381-238 2783, hotel_overseas@yahoo.co.in. Check a few rooms, as paintwork and condition is variable. It's not luxury but at Rs 350 for a non-a/c double (same room for a/c, but with the unit switched on) this is better value than most and usually has vacancies.

D-F Radha International, 54 Central Rd, T/F0381-238 4530. A good choice, non-a/c singles in particular are a real bargain although they are tiny. It's relatively new and hasn't had time to degenerate too much. All rooms have TV and private bath.

D-F Somraj Regency, HGB Rd, 2nd floor Swasti Bazaar, T0381-238 2069. Rooms (basic double Rs 450) are nothing special, but it's close at hand if the **Welcome Palace** is full.

F-G Hotel Sagarita, Sakuntala Rd, T0381-238 0838. Only 8 rooms, 2 doubles, 6 singles, this very Indian option is clean and cheerfully painted. Very little English spoken, but good collection of useful contact numbers for car hire and services. All rooms have bath (hot bucket), fans and nets.
F-G Minakshi, Hawkers Corner, Khushbagan (near Museum), T0381-238 5810. Basic old rooms have TV, mosquito nets and screens, attached bath, powerful fans and are cleaned daily. Staff are pleasantly eccentric. Simple fish and veg Indian meals prepared in the tiny 'restaurant'.

Kailashahar *p756*
F-G Unakoti Tourist Lodge, T03824-223635. Literally a stone's throw from the Bangladeshi border (fence-views from your window), this friendly and decent place has double rooms only (non-a/c Rs 220, a/c Rs 330).

Jampui Hills *p756*
G Eden Tourist Lodge, Vanghmun, T03824-238252. A simple place that's good value and clean, as is typical of Tripura's government accommodation.

Sepahijala Wildlife Sanctuary *p756*
G Forest Bungalow, contact Chief Conservator of Forests, Agartala, T0381-222 3779. In well-kept gardens above the lake, meals provided.

Udaipur *p756*
All of Udaipur's accommodation is found in the centre of town, 1 km from the bus/jeep stand.
E-G Gouri Hotel, Central Rd, T03821-222419. Clean and simple rooms plus a couple of pricier a/c doubles.
F-G Gomati Yatriniwas, T03821-223478. Government lodge with passable rooms should you decide to stop the night.

Neermahal *p757*
F-G Sagarmahal Tourist Lodge, on the lake, 1 km from Melagarh village, book through **Tripura Tourism**, T0381-222 5930, or just turn up. The majority of the comfortable rooms (a/c or non a/c) overlook the lake, as does the dorm. However, rooms in the new block have no views but are modern and superior. The restaurant serves generous and cheap meals (though salt-heavy), and staff are lovely.

Pilak *p757*
F-G Pilak Tourist Lodge, Jolaibari, T03823-263863. Newly decorated rooms are large (so are bathrooms) with wooden furniture, clean curtains, balconies, mosquito nets and old-style concrete floors. They are great value but directly on the road. The last room on the 1st floor is best, with lots of light coming through the many windows. Scary dorms. The manager will offer pricey trips to the sights on his motorbike. No meals, food available in the small village.

Eating

Agartala *p755*
Restaurants in Agartala (or anywhere else in Tripura) are not permitted to serve liquor. There is a lack of decent street food in town.
Bawarchi Kolkata, 4 Mantri Bari Rd, T0381-222 6892. Open 1300-2200. The a/c restaurant at the back serves Indian veg and non-veg staples, plus chowmeins, tandoori and prawn dishes. The roll counter at the front is very cheap with a fast turnover on delicious egg/*paneer* (and other) rolls.
Invitation Restaurant, off Sakuntala Rd (down a tiny alley, opposite **Sagarita Hotel**), T0381-238 1447. Open 0900-2130. Pure veg food, south and north Indian, this clean and simple sit-down place is good for *thalis* and *lassis*. Onion added on demand.
Kurry Klub, Welcome Palace (see Sleeping). Open 0630-2200. Offers welcome a/c and salubrious surroundings, with a hotch-potch of art on the walls and mellow lighting. Excellent Indian and Chinese food comes in generous portions, nicely presented, but takes time to prepare. *Lassis* are fluid but deliciously fragrant. Western breakfast available, and it's one of few places to open early.
Rajdharbar, Rajdhani Hotel (see Sleeping). The clean and shiny glass tables don't really gel with the cave-effect decor (fake rock walls, plastic flowers and bamboo bridges) but the view towards the palace from the 5th floor is awesome (go during daylight) and the multi-cuisine menu appetizing.

Shankar, NSCB Rd. Interesting Bengali dishes in a canteen environment. Completely dead by 2000 and in an area without streetlights, it's best to go during the day.

Neermahal *p757*

Superb Bengali snacks and sweets are sold along the road and simple clean restaurants serve good meals (Rs 25-40).

Shopping

Agartala *p755*

Most shops are closed on Sun and only work a half-day on Sat (1000-1400). **Craft-Ex** and nearby **Tripura Cottage Industries** (daily 0900-2000) on Akhaura Rd have some lovely woven basketwares, stools and attractive wooden carvings in among the twee religious portraits etched on bamboo. All are made in Tripura. Exquisitely woven rush mats (Rs 200-490) and baskets are on sale at the wholesale market on NS Rd.

Activities and tours

Agartala *p755*

Tripura Tourism, main office at Palace Compound, T0381-222 5930, Mon-Sat 1000-1700, Sun 1500-1700; also at airport, T0381-234 2393, 0730-1830. Active in promoting their tours, although the only actual activity tends to be during Bengali holidays. Tours are good value, ranging from 1-7 days. The palace branch can book any of the 27 tourist lodges throughout Tripura.

Transport

Agartala *p755*

Air Airport transfer, 13 km: taxi, Rs 225; auto-rickshaw, Rs 95. Flights to **Kolkata**, and **Guwahati** with **Air India**, Palace Compound, T0381-232 5470, airport, T0381-234 2020, www.airindia.com; **Jet Airways**, www.jetairways.com; **Indigo**, www.goindigo.in; and **Kingfisher**, www.flykingfisher.com.

Bus Travelling around Agartala is easy. North-bound buses within the state leave from the Motor Stand on Motor Stand Rd, along with *sumos*. The south-bound station has bus and jeep connections to **Neermahal**, **Udaipur** and all other southerly destinations, just turn up as departures are consistent from 0600 until around 1600. Jeeps are faster and a bit more expensive.

The new **International Bus Stand** is on HG Hospital Rd, where buses leave for **Bangladesh** daily at 1200 (booking counter opens at 1030, Rs 1000 through to Kolkata).

In the same building is the **TRTC** office (0530-1900) with daily buses to **Guwahati** (1130, 20 hrs, Rs 424/500 for non or a/c) via **Shillong** and **Silchar** (0600, 13 hrs, Rs 137). There are private buses, also from the International terminal, to **Guwahati** (2 leave at 0600, 7 leave at 1200, Rs 475-495) and **Silchar** (1 at 0600, 12 hrs, Rs 250).

Car/taxi Tourist taxi from Directorate of Information, about Rs 700 per day, T0381-222 2419. Car hire also possible from agents around town (clustered around Durga Bari Road). The **Welcome Palace** charge Rs 600 per day for an Indica car, plus Rs 6 per km.

Train Agartalans are proud of their gleaming new railway station (5 km south) completed in 2008 and modelled on the Ujjayanta Palace. Computerized bookings at the station or office opposite the International bus station, T0381-232 5533, Mon-Fri 0800-1945, Sun 0800-1345. 1 train per day link with **Lumding** (17 hrs), **Dharmanagar** and **Silchar** (16 hrs) but, as these are only chair-car, the bus might be the more comfortable option. If travelling north to **Kalaishahar**, it's much quicker to take the train than the bus. From Lumding, it's a sleeper car on to **Guwahati**. Construction is underway to complete the line, south to Sabroom, by 2011.

Kailashahar *p756*

To **Agartala** trains are quicker (3 per day, 3 hrs, Rs 36) than the bus (8 hrs, with army escort) and leave from Kumarghat. Frequent shared rickshaws cover the 20 km between Kailashahar and Kumarghat, Rs 20.

Udaipur *p756*

The bus and jeep stand are adjacent to each other, about 1 km from the town centre. Jeeps tend to run more frequently to **Jolaibari**, **Amarpur**, **Neermahal** and all nearby towns and villages. Autos are readily available to take you to the sights of **Udaipur**. If not staying overnight and in need of depositing luggage while you go sightseeing, the bus ticketing men have a safe room where they will store bags (till 1800).

Neermahal *p757*

Jeeps and buses drop off in the village of Melagarh. It's a Rs 10 rickshaw ride or 15-min walk to cover the 1.5 km to the lake.

Pilak *p757*

Between 0600-0800 5 buses leave Jolaibari (just north of the Tourist Lodge) for **Agartala**, others at 1200, 1300 and 1500 (Rs 48) stopping at **Udaipur** (2 hrs). Jeeps leave when full from the same place.

Directory

Agartala *p755*

Bank State Bank of India, HG Basak Rd.
Internet Netzone and **Tabbu**, 6 Sakuntala Rd, opposite each other and both with fast connections for Rs 20 per hr, daily 0700-2100.
Medical services GB Hospital, Kunjaban.
Post GPO: Chowmohani.

Orissa

Contents

Footprint features

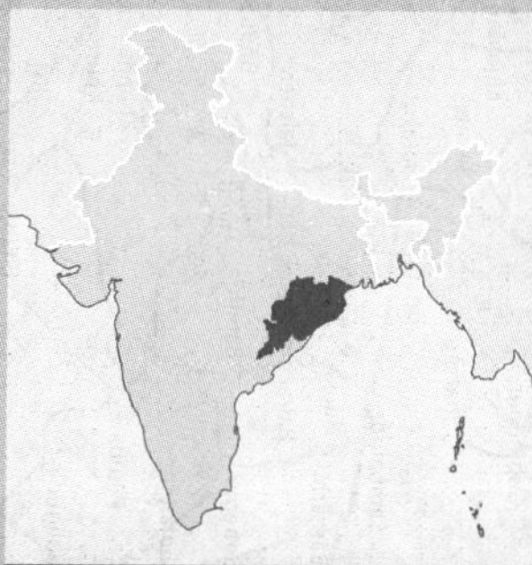

At a glance

Getting around Flights to Bhubaneshwar. Trains run up and down the coast; buses or car hire to explore the tribal lands.

Time required Minimum 3 days for the Mahanadi Delta; 2-3 days for Simlipal NP; 5 days for the south and a tribal safari.

Weather Hot year round; dry in Dec and Jan, heavy rain from Jun-Sep.

When not to go Avoid the Orissa monsoon (Jun-Sep), one of India's wettest.

★ **Don't miss ...**

1 Temples and a dance performance at Bhubaneswar, page 769.
2 Puri's car festival (Rath Yatra) at the end of June, page 780.
3 The temple porch at Konark, page 783.
4 A thousand olive ridley turtles laying their eggs on Rushikulya Beach, page 786.
5 Spotting estuarine crocdiles and a million migratory birds at Bhitarkanika, page 794.
6 The markets at Chatikona and Ankadeli, page 800.

Orissa played host to one of the richest periods in Indian temple construction, most strikingly preserved in the magnificent Sun Temple of Konark, which acted as a beacon for sailors for nearly a millennium. Its intricately carved, sensual sculptures continue to mesmerize modern-day travellers, while the great and architecturally astonishing temples of Bhubaneswar and Puri draw pilgrims in their millions from across India – climaxing each summer with the electrifying Rath Yatra festival. Meanwhile, holidaymakers from Kolkata have enjoyed Puri's broad and sandy beaches for years and backpackers find rest and respite in the shady cafés and mellow guesthouses.

More than 2000 years ago, the fertile delta on which the modern capital Bhubaneswar stands witnessed one of the most significant battles of India's history, when the Emperor Asoka, having massacred his Kalingan opponents, converted to Buddhism and laid the foundations for one of the great empires of world history.

Inland, Orissa's beautiful hills, home to the Adivasis (tribal peoples), are among the least densely populated and most densely forested regions of India. Beneath them lie rich resources of iron ore, coal, bauxite and other minerals, but despite some mining activity much of the interior retains its remote charm. Weekly *haats* (markets) draw tribal communities together in a medley of colour, ornamentation and palm wine, reinforcing a culture and tradition that predates most others of the subcontinent.

Orissa has been experiencing outbreaks of communal violence in recent years, with violent clashes between Hindus and Christians, particularly in western districts. For the time being, 'tribal tourism' is avoiding certain areas; check the situation with the tourist office before you travel.

Background → *Population: 41.9 million. Area: 156,000 sq km.*

The land

Geography Near the coast it is easy to get the impression that Orissa is nothing but a flat alluvial plain composed of mile after mile of paddy fields. The coastline has shifted significantly in the last 2000 years as the land has risen relative to sea level, leaving the shallow Chilika Lake, which with an area of 1100 sq km is Asia's largest brackish lake, cut off from the sea; the lake now maintains its salinity levels by means of a man-made channel.

Inland, the alluvial soils give way to the ancient rocks of peninsular India, some of which bear huge iron ore resources. Until recently the densely forested hills were made inhospitable both by the difficulty of clearing the forest and by the devastating prevalence of malaria. Dense deciduous *sal* forest, peopled only by tribal groups living in isolation, dominated the landscape, and shifting cultivation was widely practised. Much of the forest has now been severely thinned and cultivation has spread up many of the valleys, but there remain remote and sparsely populated areas and roads that rarely see traffic, and the scenic rewards for the slowness of parts of the journey are great. The lakes to the south of Koraput in the 3000-million-year-old hills are particularly striking.

Climate Lying just south of the Tropic of Cancer, Orissa is very warm throughout the year, though the hills are sufficiently high to bring a welcome coolness. January and February are dry, but showers increase through the spring and the monsoon from June to September is one of the wettest in India; travelling in this period is best avoided. Coastal districts are particularly at risk from cyclones in October and November. The most recent of these was the catastrophic cyclone of October 1999 which caused the death of over 8000 people, and an estimated three million cattle, as well as inflicting massive damage to villages, forests and agricultural land.

History

Coastal Orissa formed a part of the ancient kingdom of Kalinga, which grew wealthy through trading, extending its colonial influence as far afield as modern Indonesia from the port of Kalinganagar as early as the fourth century BC. The Mauryan Emperor Asoka crushed the Kalingan Kingdom at Dhauligiri in 262 BC, but after experiencing the horrors of war and the accompanying bloodshed he converted to Buddhism. He preached the philosophy of peace, and while Buddhism flowered, his tolerance allowed Jainism and Hinduism to continue. After Asoka, the first century BC King Kharavela, a fervent Jain, built up a vast empire, recorded in the remarkable Udayagiri caves near Bhubaneswar. After Kharavela, separate political territories emerged in the north and centre of the region. Maritime trade flourished and Buddhism became popular again.

The greatest period of temple building in Bhubaneswar coincided with the Kesaris (sixth-11th century), and then the Ganga Dynasty (11th-15th century), who were responsible for the Jagannath Temple in Puri (circa 1100) and the Sun Temple at Konark (circa 1250).

Orissa resisted the annexation of her territory by Muslims. After a short period of Afghan rule, the powerful Mughals arrived as conquerors in 1592 and during their reign destroyed many of the Bhubaneswar temples. It was their violent disruption of temple life in Puri and Bhubaneswar that later led the Brahmins to ban all non-Hindus from the precincts of the Lingaraj and Jagannath temples. The Mughals were followed by the Marathas in 1751.

In 1765 after Clive's win at Plassey, parts of Orissa, Bihar and Bengal were acquired by the East India Company with further gains in Cuttack and Puri at the beginning of the following century. Thus, by 1803, British rule extended over the whole region.

Culture

Tribal groups Orissa has the third highest concentration of tribals in India. The tribal population, nearly 25% of the total, live mainly in the Koraput, Kandhamal, Sundargarh and

Mayurbhanj districts. Some 62 **Adivasi** ('ancient inhabitants') or tribal groups live in remote hill regions of the state, some virtually untouched by modern civilization, and so have kept their tribal traditions alive. Each has a distinct language and pattern of social and religious customs. They are not economically advanced and literacy is low. However, the tribal groups have highly developed artistic ability, as seen in their body paintings, ornaments, weaving and wall paintings. Music and dance also form an integral part of life-cycle ceremonies and seasonal festivals. They are remarkable in having maintained their distinct identities in a hostile and exploitative environment. There has been a new interest in their rich heritage and the Tourism Department is keen to promote visits to tribal areas, see page 800. (Suggested reading: Norman Lewis, *A Goddess in the Stones*.)

The **Khonds**, the most numerous (about 100,000), live mainly in the west and speak Kuvi, a Dravidian language, and Kui. They used to practise human Meriah sacrifice (now replaced by animal sacrifice), offering the blood to their supreme goddess represented by a piece of wood or stone, to ensure fertility of the soil. They use bows and arrows to protect themselves against wild animals.

The **Santals**, the second most numerous group, come from the northern districts of Mayurbhanj and Balasore. In the northwestern industrial belt, they have abandoned their aboriginal lifestyle to work in the steel mills. They belong to 12 patrilineal clans (*paris* or *sibs*) and speak Santali, one of the oldest languages in India. Santals believe that evil spirits in trees, forests and rivers have to be appeased by magic. The women practice witchcraft while the *ojhas* are the medicine men. Music and dance are an integral part of their daily life, especially in festivals during October-November and March-April.

In the southern districts, especially in Koraput, there are about 6000 **Bondos** ('naked people') of Tibeto-Burmese origin. They live isolated on high hills, growing rice by shifting cultivation and keeping domesticated cows and goats, and can only be seen when they come to trade in local markets. Bondo women are noticeable for their striking bead, brass and silver necklaces, and their shaved heads, decorated with plaits of palmyra leaves.

The **Saoras**, another major tribe, mostly live in hilly areas of Parlakhemundi (Gajapati district) and Gunupur (Rayagada district). Saoras live in *birindas* (extended families), descended from a common ancestor, under a headman who is helped by a religious leader. The shamans are able to communicate with watchful deified ancestors. Village houses of mud and stone walls are raised on plinths with high wooden platforms inside to store grain. The walls are decorated with remarkable paintings; traditional designs now incorporate hunters on aeroplanes and bicycles.

The **Koya** who live in villages in clearings in the middle of dense forest are distinguished by their headgear made of bison horn.

Dance, drama and music The region's magnificent temple sculpture gave rise to a classical dance form, **Odissi**, which shadows the postures, expressions and lyrical qualities of the carved figures. The dance was a ritual offering performed in the *nata mandirs* by the *maharis* (temple dancers) resplendent in their costume and jewellery. The subject is often Jayadev's *Gita Govinda* (12th century), which explores the depths of Krishna's love for Radha, the dancer expressing the sensual and the devotional.

The **folk dances** usually performed during festivals take various forms: day-long *Danda Nata*, the traditional fishermen's dance; *Chaitighoda* which requires a horse dummy; the battle dance called *Paika Nritya*; and *Chhau*, the dance-drama reminiscent of Orissa's martial past. There are also tribal dances performed in colourful costumes with distinctive headgear made of animal horns and shells, to the accompaniment of string instruments, flutes and drums.

Food and drink Rice forms the staple food, wheat taking second place. Meals include lightly spiced side dishes of vegetables and pulses, chutneys and pickles. Fresh seafood, especially prawns and the flat *pomfret* fish, are common in coastal areas. Try *mahura* or *saga bhaja* (fried

Orissan temples

Orissan temples are graced by a tall, curvilinear tower, the *deul* (pronounced *day-ool*) or *rekha deul*, and a much lower, more open structure or porch in front of the entrance to the tower, the *jagamohana*. The dark interior of the sanctuary is designed to allow only a glimpse of the presiding deity and to enable priests to conduct ritual worship. A dancing hall (*nata mandir*) and a hall of offering (*bhoga mandir*) were often added in later temples.

The square plan of the sanctuary tower and the porch are broken vertically by the inward curving form of the main tower. Each exterior face of the sanctuary tower is divided by vertical, flat-faced projections (*rathas*).

Some Orissan architects likened the structure of the temple to that of the human body, and the names given to the vertical sections correspond to main parts of the body.

1 The platform (*pishta*) Early temples had no platform. In highly developed temples (eg Surya temple at Konark), the platform may be more than 3 m high.

2 The lower storey (*bada*) relates to the lower limbs. In early temples this was divided into three parts, the base (the foot), above which was a perpendicular section corresponding to the shin. This was topped by a set of mouldings. In some mature temples the scale of this section was greatly elongated and was itself then divided into five layers.

3 The upper storey (*gandi*, or human trunk) is a curvilinear spire in the case of the sanctuary, or a pyramidal roof in the case of the porch.

4 The head (*mastaka*) with crowning features. Divided into a series of elements, the 'head' or *mastaka* of the sanctuary developed over time. The 'neck' (*beki*) – a recessed cylindrical portion, is surmounted by the skull, *amla*. This is represented by a symbolic fruit, the *amalaka*. On the *amla* rests a 'water pot', an auspicious symbol, then on top of all comes the sacred weapon of the deity.

Orissan temple

After Brown

mustard or spinach leaves), *dahi baigono* (aubergines cooked with yoghurt) or the festive *besara* (vegetables cooked with mustard seed paste).

Orissa is particularly noted for its milk sweets – *rasamalai, khiramohan, rajbhoga, rabidi, chhenapodapitha* and *kalakanda. Khiri* is prepared with milk and rice, semolina or vermicelli while special *pithas* are often filled with sweetened coconut.

Art and architecture

The temples of Bhubaneswar, along with those of Puri and Konark, represent a remarkably full record of the development of Orissan architecture from the seventh to the 13th century. Although some of the temples have suffered structural damage many are virtually intact and some are still in everyday use; centres of active pilgrimage, worship and faith.

Crafts

Stone carving has been highly developed in Orissa for more than 2000 years. The artistry that can be seen in early sculptures and the superb carvings on Orissan temples in Bhubaneswar, Puri and Konark is kept alive by modern craftsmen. They produce beautiful figures, bowls or plates carved out of soft soapstone, hard *kochila* or multicoloured serpentine from Khiching. Orissa also has a tradition of **hornwork** in Parlakhemundi and Cuttack, buffalo horn being carved into the typical small flat figures of animals and birds.

Silver filigree is perhaps one of the most distinctive and exquisite works of the Cuttack jewellers who turn fine silver wire into beautiful, fragile objects with floral patterns. The metal used is close to sterling silver and is drawn through finer and finer holes to make the wire.

Metalwork is popular. Craftsmen use brass (alloy of copper and zinc) and bell-metal (alloy of copper and tin) to produce small figurines, vases and plates. The tribal metal casting in the *dhokra* style by the *cire perdue* (lost-wax) process is found in Dhenkanal and Mayurbhanj districts. A clay core of the basic shape is covered by fine wax 'threads' before the whole is enclosed in a shell of straw and clay and then baked in a tiny charcoal fire. At the firing, molten metal is poured in, to displace the melting wax. Similar casting is done by tribal peoples in Bihar, Madhya Pradesh, Manipur and West Bengal.

Brightly coloured **woodcarvings** of the deities in the Jagannath temple, and figures of animals and birds make attractive gifts. **Ivory** inlay (now replaced by plastic) was traditionally carried out for rich patrons of the Puri temple, and also for making illustrated wooden covers for palm leaf manuscripts. The tradition of using **papier-mâché** masks of deities and animal characters to tell stories from the epics also comes from Orissa.

The *chitrakars* (picture makers), particularly from the village of Raghurajpur, 12 km from Puri, **paint** the *pattachitras* on specially prepared cloth, coated with earth to stiffen it and finally finished with lacquer after painting, producing pictures and attractive playing cards. Old sets of *ganjapa* cards consisted of 96 discs. The vibrant colours traditionally came from earth, stone, leaves and flowers. The best *chitrakars* are those allowed the honour to paint the Puri temple deities and their 'cars' each year. They are also commissioned by the rich to produce fine temple murals and manuscripts on paper and palmleaf. However, what are usually available in the bazars are cruder examples for pilgrims to take home.

Finds of the 16th century reveal how illustrated manuscripts were produced by holding an iron stylus stationary while moving a **palm leaf** underneath. It was a technique that helped to give the Oriya script its rounded form. The leaves were first prepared by drying, boiling, drying again, and then flattening them before coating with powdered shell. After inscribing, the grooves were rubbed with soot or powdered charcoal, while colour was added with a brush. The leaves were then stacked and strung together and placed between decorative wooden covers. The *pattachitra* artists in Raghurajpur have also revived this art form.

Pipli, a small town about 20 km southwest of Bhubaneswar, is well known for its **appliqué** work using brightly coloured embroidered cloth, probably originally designed for use in the

Jagannath temple. The roadside stalls sell items for the house and garden – parasols, cushion covers, wall hangings – using striking animal, bird and flower patterns on a backcloth. Unfortunately, mass production has resulted in the loss of attention to detail of the original fine Pipli work, which picked out the motifs by cleverly stuffing sections of the pattern. Today, the best pieces of work are usually sent away to be sold in the government emporia in Bhubaneswar, Delhi and Kolkata.

Textile weaving has been a tradition throughout Orissa for generations and thousands are still employed in this cottage industry. It is one of the few regions in India producing **ikat**, the technique of resist-dyeing the warp or weft thread, or both, before weaving, so that the fabric that emerges from the loom has a delicate enmeshed pattern. The favourite designs include rows of flowers, birds and animals, using either *tussar* or cotton yarn. **Berhampur**, **Sambalpur**, **Mayurbhanj** and **Nuapatna** all produce silk and cotton *ikat* saris. Some also produce tapestry, bedspreads and embroidered fabric.

Crafts villages While some (for example, Raghurajpur and Pipli) are used to passing tourists, others are rarely visited by foreigners. It is worth visiting to see craftsmen at work and perhaps buy their goods. In **Raghurajpur** (reached via Chandapur, 10 km from Puri on the Bhubaneswar road), you can watch artists painting *pattachitras* in bright folk-art style or etching palm leaves (see *chitrakars* above). Sadly, the village has now been reduced to a sales exercise. **Pipli**, on the Bhubaneswar-Puri Road, specializes in appliqué work, **Balakati**, 10 km from Bhubaneswar, in bell-metal, while there is a community of Tibetan carpet weavers at **Chandragiri** near the Taptapani Hot Springs in tribal country. Adjacent to the Buddhist site of **Lalitgiri** is a stone-carvers' village. Master-weavers work at their looms in **Nuapatna** and **Maniabandha**, 100 km from Bhubaneswar, and in the narrow streets next to the temple at **Berhampur**. **Cuttack** remains famous for silver filigree work.

Modern Orissa

Political power in Orissa has alternated between the Congress and Opposition parties, most recently the BJD (the Biju Janata Dal, named after its former leader Biju Patnaik), which in alliance with the BJP won an overwhelming majority in the Assembly elections of February 2000. Chief Minister Naveen Patnaik, the son of Biju Patnaik, has held a range of ministerial posts in both state and central governments and has a strong reputation for integrity. In the 2009 State Assembly elections the BJD won 109 of the 147 seats. The BJP won seven, and the Congress 26. In the Lok Sabha elections the BJD won 14 of the 21 seats.

Bhubaneswar and around

Set on the edge of the lush green rice fields of the Mahanadi Delta, the pleasantly broad but increasingly crowded streets of the planned town of Bhubaneswar offer a striking contrast to the architectural legacy of its period of greatness over a thousand years ago. Named after 'The Lord of the Universe', Bhubaneswar still has some 500 of the original '7000' temples that once surrounded Bindusagar Tank. The graceful towers of those that remain, complemented by the extraordinary fineness of the stone carving, cluster by the lakeside away from the rushing traffic and often set among lovely gardens. ▸▸ *For listings, see pages 776-779.*

Bhubaneswar → *For listings, see pages 776-779. Colour map 6, A6.* *Population: 1.6 million.*

Ins and outs

Getting there The airport, served by direct flights from Delhi, Mumbai and Kolkata, is 4 km from the centre. Trains on the main Kolkata–Chennai line stop at Bhubaneswar station, from where many hotels are within walking distance. The New Bus Stand is 6 km northwest of town. Buses for Konark and Puri can be boarded by the State Museum.

Getting around The temples are a long walk from the modern centre and most hotels so it is best to hire a rickshaw to reach them. Once you're there it's easy enough to explore the old city on foot. ▸▸ *See Transport, page 778.*

Tourist information **Orissa Tourism** ⓘ *behind Panthanivas Hotel, Lewis Rd, T0674-243 2382, www.orissatourism.gov.in; also has a small office at the station (closes 2100)*, provides good information and can book hotels. In an adjacent building, **Orissa Tourism Development Corporation (OTDC)** ⓘ *T0674-243 1515*, runs daily tours. **Government of India Tourism** ⓘ *B-21, BJB Nagar, T0674-243 2203, itobbs@ori.nic.in*, is helpful but in an obscure location.

History

Several sites testify to the importance of the Bhubaneswar region far earlier than the seventh to 11th centuries, when the Kalinga kings ruled over the area. Both Jain and Buddhist shrines give clear evidence of important settlements around Bhubaneswar in the first two centuries BC. The remains of a ruined moated city, Sisupalgarh (opposite the Dhauligiri battlefield and Asokan edicts), show that it was occupied from the beginning of the third century BC to the middle of the fourth century AD and the pottery shows Roman influence. Bhubaneswar is the capital of Orissa, chosen in 1948 in place of Cuttack partly because it was the ancient capital of the Kalinga Empire.

Temples

Parsuramesvara Temple The seventh-century temple, though small, is highly decorated, and is the best preserved of the early Bhubaneswar temples. The rectangular porch and the stepped roof indicate an early date. Even so, the porch was probably built after the sanctuary itself, as suggested by the rather crude junction between the two. In the early period the masonry was kept in place by weight and balance alone. Other features include the carving of a goddess and two sea monsters on the lintel over the sanctuary door.

The temple marks an important stage in the development of Hindu power at the expense of Buddhism in seventh-century Orissa, illustrated by the frequent representation of **Lakulisa**, the priest responsible for Hindu proselytism. He is sculpted in Buddha-like form, and often surrounded by disciples. Note also, the distinctive *chaitya* windows developed earlier in Buddhist *chaitya* halls, as at Ajanta. There are two on the front of the sanctuary tower.

The sanctuary is divided horizontally and vertically into three sections. The carvings show motifs and styles that were to reach their full flowering in later temples. The base, for example, has a top moulding (close to the ground) decorated with scrolls, birds, humans and floral

Bhubaneswar

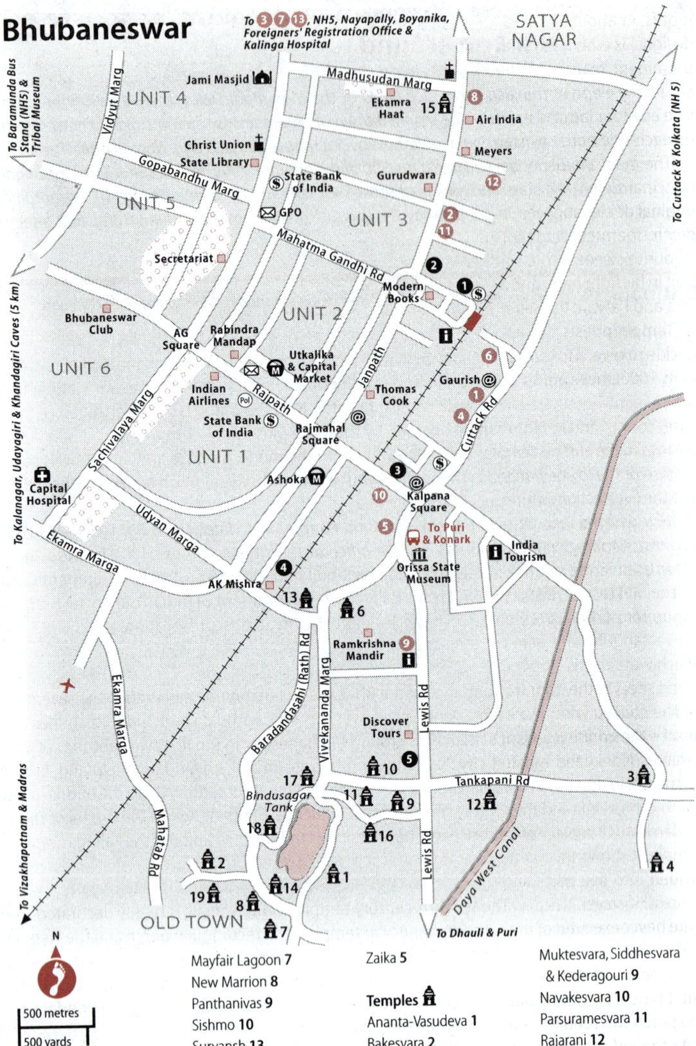

Sleeping
Bhubaneswar **1**
Bicky Inn **2**
Ekamra **4**
Ginger **3**
HHI **12**
Kalinga Ashok **5**
Lingaraj **6**
Mayfair Lagoon **7**
New Marrion **8**
Panthanivas **9**
Sishmo **10**
Suryansh **13**
Swosti **11**
Upasana **1**

Eating
Banjara **1**
Hare Krishna **2**
Park Inn **3**
Venus Inn **4**
Zaika **5**

Temples
Ananta-Vasudeva **1**
Bakesvara **2**
Bhaskaresvara **3**
Brahmesvara **4**
Lakshmanesvara, Bharatesvara & Satrughnesvara **6**
Lingaraja **7**
Makaresvara, Mitresvara & Chitrakarini **8**
Muktesvara, Siddhesvara & Kederagouri **9**
Navakesvara **10**
Parsuramesvara **11**
Rajarani **12**
Ramesvara **13**
Satrughnesvara Group **14**
Sri Ram Mandir **15**
Svarnajalesvara **16**
Uttaresvara **17**
Vaital & Sisiresvara **18**
Yamesvara **19**

motifs. At about eye level, the mouldings are distinctive. The recessed frieze (discarded in later designs) is embossed with early examples of the amorous couples that were to become such a prominent feature of the Konark temple, interspersed with *vyalas* (rampant lions) astride crouching elephants. In addition to the main entrance to the porch there is a door on the south side and four latticed windows. The vigorous and graceful sculptures of musicians and dancers on each side of the western doorway are outstanding, although some are badly weathered.

The main accessory deities are placed in niches on each side of the sanctuary housing the principal deity. The Parsuramesvara Temple was dedicated to Siva; only two of the three original deities survive. On the south of the sanctuary, at eye level in the middle of the tower, is the four-armed elephant-headed Ganesh, his trunk curled towards a bowl of *laddus,* his favourite sweet. In the southern niche is Karttikeya (Subrahmanya) with a peacock, carrying a fruit in his right hand and a spear in his left. The lintel above Karttikeya illustrates the marriage of Siva and Parvati; to their right are Agni (Fire), the kneeling Brahma, and Surya (Sun).

Temple priests will approach you for donations; these are not compulsory, but if you do decide to give, a token Rs 10 is sufficient. Visitor books may be proffered which show donations of Rs 1000; these are surely forged, don't feel pressured.

Muktesvara Temple Beautifully decorated with outstanding carvings, this late 10th-century temple belongs to the end of the first phase of temple building. Although it still has the three-fold horizontal division of the lower storey, a feature of the early period, the plan of the sanctuary is now divided into the five-sectioned form. Also, the platform here consists of five mouldings, as in later temples.

New designs include graceful female figures and pilasters carved with *nagas* and *naginis* (snakes). Strikingly, the porch has a new and more dramatic layered form. Ketu, too, is introduced as the ninth planet and Ganesh is joined by his mount, the mouse.

The Muktesvara displays the unique *torana* (gateway arch) dated at about AD 900; although the upper portion is restored, the original skill can still be seen in the graceful female figures. The rectangular tank at its east end, used by priests and devotees, and the well to the south, into which women still toss coins in the hope of curing infertility, symbolize the continued holiness of the site. On the door frame of the well is the figure of Lakulisa (see Parsuramesvara, above).

The *chaitya* windows carved on the sanctuary tower show the finest examples of the *bho* motif – the grinning face of a lion with beaded tassels emerging from its mouth, flanked by two dwarves. Notice the monkey scenes on the outer frame of the diamond-shaped lattice windows on the north and south walls.

Siddhesvara Temple Immediately to the northwest of the Muktesvara is the later Siddhesvara Temple. It shows the mature Orissan temple form almost complete. The vertical lower section is divided into five parts and the *amla* on top of the sanctuary is supported by four squatting figures. However, the overall effect is comparatively plain, as sculptures marked out on the rock were never executed.

Kederagouri Temple The Kederagouri Temple to the south is probably of the late 10th century but it is built in the *khakhara* form (see Vaital Deul, below), and has been substantially repaired. The porch was rebuilt in the early 20th century but still has a few original sculptures of real merit. Note the girl shown leaning against a post with a bird perched on it, on the south face of the eastern projection of the sanctuary. On the western projection is an equally beautiful sculpture of a girl removing her anklets.

Rajarani Temple ⓘ *0600-1800, foreigners Rs100, video camera Rs 25.* The entrance to the early 11th-century temple is 300 m east of the main road, set back from the road. It no longer has an image of the deity in the sanctuary and is out of use. The main tower is surrounded by four miniature copies, giving the sanctuary a near-circular appearance.

The *jagmohana* (porch) is plain although it has the mature style of a pyramidal roof. Many carvings are unfinished but give an insight into the method of cutting the stone into sections ('blocking out') followed by rough shaping ('boasted'), to be finished by the master sculptor. The finished work in the main sanctuary is impressive.

Perhaps the best-preserved features of the temple are the **Dikpalas** (Guardians of the eight cardinal directions) who protect the central shrine from every quarter. They are placed in pairs about 3 m above ground level, in the lower section of the main tower.

Starting from the left (south) of the porch they appear in the following order:

1 Facing east, **Indra**, the guardian of the east, holds a thunderbolt and an elephant goad, and his vehicle is the elephant.

2 At right angles to Indra, facing south, is the pot-bellied and bearded **Agni**, god of fire, riding a ram, guarding the southeast.

3 Moving a few metres along the wall, on the far side of the projection, is the south-facing **Yama**, holding a staff and a noose, with his vehicle the buffalo. The skull on his staff is a Tantric symbol.

4 Again at right angles to Yama is the west-facing **Nirritti**, guardian of the southwest. Nirritti, the god of misery, holds a severed head and a sword over the lying figure of a man.

5 Again facing west, but on the north side of the sanctuary's central projection, is the guardian of the west, **Varuna**. He holds the noose symbolizing fate in his left hand. His vehicle is the sea creature *makara*.

6 At right angles to Varuna, facing north, is **Vayu** (meaning 'wind'), guardian of the northwest. He holds a fluttering banner, and his vehicle is the deer.

7 The last pair of guardians are on the further side of the central projection, on the north and east facing sides respectively. First is **Kubera**, guardian of the north (pot-bellied to symbolize prosperity), placed above seven jars of precious stones. He has a horse.

8 **Ishana**, guardian of the northeast, symbolizing fecundity, is shown as was customary, with an erect phallus and accompanied by an emaciated figure.

Brahmesvara Temple The temple (built in 1060) is still in use today. Entering from the north you pass through the two enclosure walls, the inner forming a compact surround for the temple complex, raised on a platform. Facing you is a well-oiled image of Lakshmi, covered in cloth, with incense sticks burning in front. The sanctuary itself houses a Siva *linga*. There are minor shrines in each corner of the compound.

The sanctuary tower has a five-fold vertical division, typical of the later temples. The *pabhaga* (base) and the *varanda* (top of the wall) have rich carvings. The lower section of the wall is decorated alternately by miniature *khakhara* style 'temples', sculptures of rampant lions, while the central niches of the miniature temple carvings at the corners of the lower section have Dikpalas. In the corresponding spaces of the upper section are miniatures of the normal temple sanctuary towers, and graceful secular figures, including erotic couples.

Satrughnesvara Group The **Lakshmanesvara**, **Bharatesvara** and **Satrughnesvara** temples are almost certainly the oldest in Bhubaneswar, dating from the late sixth century. The southernmost temple in the group has been rebuilt by the Archaeological Department of Orissa. Only the cores of these three temple are now visible.

Vaital Temple A major feature of this small, late eighth-century temple is its form. Seen from the road the semi-cylindrical shape in

Dikpalas: the Directional Guardians

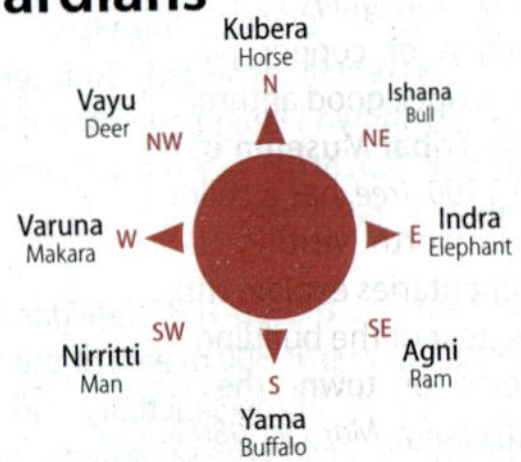

section of the *deul* is immediately obvious. Its *khakhara* style derives, as Percy Brown says, from the shape of the *gopurams* of Dravida temples in South India, taken originally from the Buddhist *chaitya* halls. Another striking feature is the temple's tantric associations, marked by its presiding deity, Chamunda (a terrible form of Durga). Durga herself appears on the north face of the *bada* as the eight- armed *Mahishasuramardini* (slayer of the buffalo demon) holding a snake, bow, shield, sword, trident, thunderbolt and an arrow, piercing the neck of the demon.

Outside, on the east face of the *deul*, the lower of the two *chaitya* windows has a beautifully carved figure of the sun god Surya, with Usha (Dawn) and Pratyusha shooting arrows on either side of him while Aruna (also Dawn) drives a chariot in front. It has a certain incongruity in view of the image within the sanctum itself. The upper *chaitya* window has a 10-armed Nataraja, or dancing Siva.

Further evidence of the tantric basis of the temple comes from the stone post to which sacrifices were tethered, just in front of the *jagamohana*. The figure of Chamunda in the central niche is extremely difficult to see without artificial light, though very early-morning sun penetrates the gloom of the interior. The most chilling of the other figures is that of a male on the north wall "rising from the ground after filling his skull-cup with the blood of a person whose severed head lies on the right; on the pedestal is an offering of two more heads".

Lingaraja Temple Along with the Jagannatha Temple at Puri, the Lingaraja Temple (AD 1000), built 100 years earlier, represents the peak of achievement of the Orissan middle period. Non-Hindus are not allowed inside but you can get a view from a special platform outside the north perimeter wall (donations sought), or from the roof of the hospital on the west side where no one will hassle for donations. Early morning and late afternoon are best for photography.

Even from a distance the sanctuary's 54-m-high *Sri Mandir* (tower) dominates the landscape. It is one of the four main buildings in the temple compound, with several subsidiary shrines. To the left of the tower is the *Jagamohana* (pillared porch), then the *Nata Mandir* (dancing hall) and finally the *Bhoga Mandir* (hall of offering). The latter two were added a century after the sanctuary and the porch.

The monumental tower, which rises in a distinctive curve, is 17 m sq in plan with projecting faces. The *amla* head with a pot-shaped pinnacle carrying the trident of Siva is supported by four mythical gryphons. The middle section has vertical lines of miniature towers sculpted in sharp relief on a background of horizontal mouldings. The massive protruding sculpture of a lion crushing an elephant on each side is a common symbol in Orissan architecture.

Ananta-Vasudeva Temple This is a hive of practical as well as spiritual activity in the mornings, when temple priests prepare kilos of rice, hoist pottery urns to-and-fro, chop mountains of vegetables and wash pots in time for the 1030 meal. It's a worthwhile halting point to absorb the charged smoky atmosphere as pilgrims amass.

Other sights

Orissa State Museum ⓘ *Gautam Nagar, Tue-Sun 1000-1700 (last entry 1630), closed government holidays, foreigners Rs 50, Indians Rs 5, camera Rs 100*, has archaelogical exhibits including a collection of copper plates, coins, sculptures, musical instruments and rare palm leaf manuscripts; good anthropological section. Allow an hour or two.

The **Tribal Museum of Man** ⓘ *CRP Sq, northwest of town, off NH5 on bus route, Tue-Sun 1000-1700, free*, has a collection of tribal dress, weapons, musical instruments and jewellery, and is worth visiting if you are planning to travel on to tribal regions. Five short documentaries explain tribal life and interesting reconstructions of typical houses are found to the rear of the building.

North of town, the Government Regional Plant Resource Centre, **Ekamra Kanan** ⓘ *Nayapally, Mar-Oct 0800-2000, Nov-Feb 0900-1900, Rs 5*, has a large rose garden, woods, flowerbeds and a large lake which attracts migratory birds. It also boasts a Cactus Garden with over 550 species of cacti and succulents, one of the largest collections in India.

Heading out on the subsidiary road from Bhubaneswar to Cuttack, the medieval regional capital, is **Nandan Kanan** ⓘ *20 km east, Tue-Sun 0800-1700, summer 0730-1730, foreigners Rs 100, Indians Rs 10, camera Rs 5, video Rs 500; cable car across the lake, Rs 22, last return 1600; safari Rs 15,* where the zoo and botanical garden are surrounded by dense forest. There are tigers, including rare white ones, lion and white tiger safaris, rhinos, panthers, leopards, wildfowl and reptiles in their natural surroundings. It has also succeeded in breeding black panthers and *gharials* in captivity. The botanical gardens with its cactus house and rosarium are across the lake; much of it is derelict. **Shradhanjali Restaurant** near the entrance serves good *thalis* and snacks.

Udayagiri and Khandagiri caves → *For listings, see pages 776-779. Colour map 6, A6.*

The caves, 6 km west of Bhubaneswar, on the two low hills of Udayagiri and Khandagiri, date from the time of Jain occupation of the region, at least the second century BC. A narrow valley winds between the hills, the route of an early Buddhist pilgrim track leading to a *stupa* which probably stood on the present site of Bhubaneswar. The coarse- grained sandstone which forms Khandagiri ('broken hill') and Udayagiri ('hill of the sunrise') rises nearly 40 m above the surrounding lateritic and infertile plain. The crumbling nature of the sandstone into which the caves were dug has exposed them to severe damage, moderately repaired by the Archaeological Survey of India.

Ins and outs

Getting there The caves are very easy to visit by car, bus, rickshaw (Rs 250 return, includes waiting) or bicycle from Bhubaneswar, but the area can get very crowded. Allow at least three hours for the round trip.

Getting around Heading straight up the ramp at Udayagiri will take you round the caves in reverse number order, better to head round the path to the right first. Some with sculptures are protected by wire-meshed gates. The most significant are described below.

Tourist information 0800-1800. Udayagiri costs Rs100, video Rs 25. Khandagiri is free.

History

The Jain caves are among the earliest in India. Furthermore, some of the rock inscriptions found above the Hati Gumpha (Elephant Cave, No 14) and elsewhere, speak of the Chedi Dynasty who ruled over Kalinga from their capital, probably at Sisupalgarh, 9 km southeast of Khandagiri.

Kharavela, according to his own record, extended his rule across a large part of North, Central and South India. At home he made great efforts to improve canals, rebuild his capital city of Kalinganagara, and also to excavate some of the caves at Udayagiri- Khandagiri. Probably all the caves now visible were constructed during the 150 years before Christ. Designed for the ascetic life of Jain monks, they simply provided dry shelter, with no concessions to any form of comfort. Too low to stand in, the cells are no more than cramped sleeping compartments.

Although the Jains did not enjoy royal patronage after the fall of Kharavela's Dynasty, Jain occupation was continuous throughout successive Buddhist and Hindu periods in the region. The Parsvanatha temple on top of Khandagiri was built in the early 19th century, while the Hindu temple dates from the 1970s.

Udayagiri

Cave 1 The **Rani Gumpha**, on the path to the right, is the largest and most impressive of the caves. It is a double-storeyed monastery cut on three sides of a quadrangle with fine wall friezes and some pillars that have been restored. The right wing of the lower storey has pilasters at the entrance to the cell and the arches are beautifully carved with religious and royal scenes while the main central wing celebrates the king's victory march. There are two small guard rooms with decorative outer walls. In the upper storey, the doorway arches to the cells are ornately carved; auspicious Jain symbols (snake and lotus) appear among vivid secular friezes of a woman's abduction, an elopement, and a duel between a man and a woman.

Cave 10 **Ganesh Gumpha**, about 50 m from the top of the hill, guarded by Ganesh statues, has friezes illustrating the Sanskrit love story of Udayan and Bassavadatta. From Cave 10 head up the path to the left, where an **apsidal structure** was unearthed in 1958. It is very similar to a Buddhist *chaitya* hall in plan and it was almost certainly a place of worship used by Jain monks. From here, there are stupendous views of Bhubaneswar and Khandagiri.

Cave 12 **Bagha Gumpha** is carved bizarrely into the shape of a tiger's open mouth, an inscription showing it to have been the cave of the town judge.

Cave 14 The last important cave on Udayagiri, the **Hati Gumpha** (Elephant Cave), has the most important inscription, that of King Kharavela. Protected by a masonry shelter since 1902, it is in the Magadhi script.

Udayagiri & Khandagiri Caves

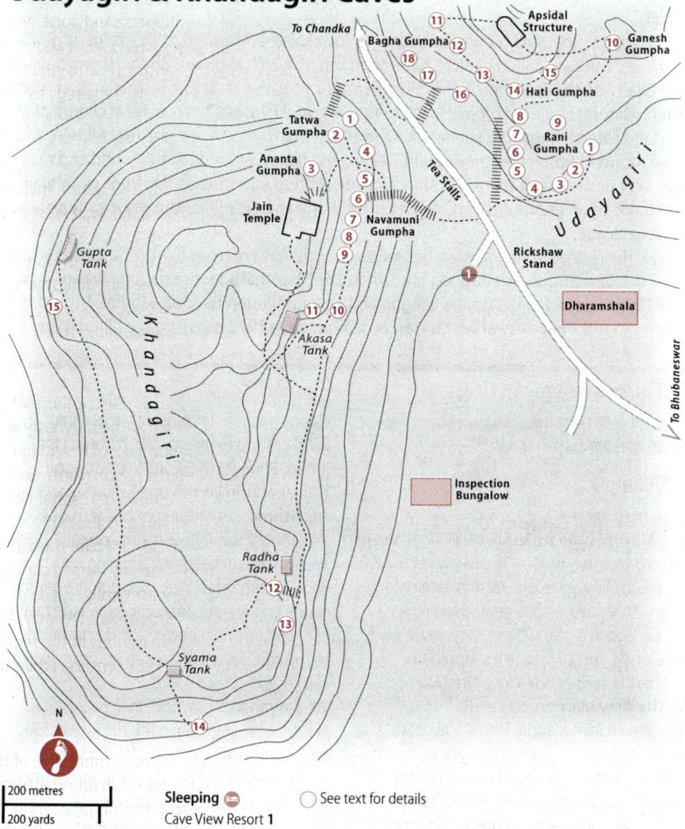

Khandagiri

Caves 1 and 2 Known as **Tatowa Gumpha** from the parrots carved above their door arches. Two sentries in *dhotis* guard Cave 1 which bears the name **Kusuma**. Modern steps lead up to the more elaborately carved Cave 2 on the left. On the back of the cell are Brahmi inscriptions in red pigment (first century BC to first century AD), obscured by modern Orissan graffiti.

Cave 3 **Ananta Gumpha**, at the top of the flight of steps, named after the two serpents on the door arches, has some very interesting reliefs using unique motifs, though the protective glass makes them hard to see. On the back wall of the cell, among the various symbols is the *svastika*, auspicious to the Jains.

Cave 7 **Navamuni Gumpha**, named after the nine Tirthankaras (*munis*) carved on the back and right walls, was originally a residential cell. On the back wall of the original right hand cell are seven Tirthankaras in high relief including Parsvanatha under a seven-hooded canopy, and Risabanatha with a halo, seated on a bull.

There are lovely carvings of Digambara Jains on the back wall of the shrine with a corrugated iron roof half way up to the Jain temple at the top, from where there are excellent views.

Dhauli

The horrors of the Kalinga war at Dhauli led Asoka to acknowledge the value of Buddhist teachings. The two 'Kalinga Edicts' differ from others which expound Buddhist principles. The rock edicts at the bottom of the hill (circa 260 BC) give detailed instructions to Asoka's administrators to rule his subjects with gentleness and fairness. "... You are in charge of many thousand living beings. You should gain the affection of men. All men are my children, and as I desire for my children that they obtain welfare and happiness both in this world and next, the same do I desire for all men ...". Above the inscription you can see the front of an elephant carved out of an enormous rock. Unfortunately, the edict is difficult to see clearly behind its protective cage.

Now the rock edicts are almost ignored by the bus loads of tourists who are taken on up the hill to the Buddhist **Peace Pagoda**. Known as the **Shanti Stupa**, the pagoda was built in the early 1970s by the Japan Buddha Sangha and Kalinga Nippon Buddha Sangha. The old Hindu temple of Lord Dhavaleswar which was reconstructed in 1972 is also on the hilltop here.

Bhubaneswar listings

For Sleeping and Eating price codes and other relevant information, see Essentials pages 38-42.

Sleeping

Bhubaneswar *p769, map p770*

LL-L Mayfair Lagoon, 8B Jaydev Vihar, Nayapalli, 5 km from centre, T0674-236 0101, www.mayfairhotels.com. Low-level expansive palace-style hotel with attractive cottages and rooms set around lagoon, 5-star facilities, very stylish yet quite kitsch. Friendly efficient staff, pickup included. Recommended for a fun splash-out.

AL The New Marrion, 6 Janpath, opposite Sri Ram Mandir, T0674-238 0850, www.hotelnewmarrion.com. Spacious rooms and overpriced suites boast peculiar decor, go for the cheaper rooms as the higher range merely have hot balconies overlooking the cloudy pool. Huge discounts negotiable. Food options excellent (**Mirch Masala** for Indian, **Bling** for Mexican/Western/good coffee), and an Irish-themed sports bar.

AL Sishmo, 86/A1 Gautam Nagar, T0674-243 3600/5, www.hotelsishmo.com. Well-run but in need of freshening up, with 72 comfortable a/c rooms, some getting musty and threadbare, facilities include health club and tiny pool that is supposedly being renovated, decent restaurant and bar is worn but cosy, checkout 1200.

AL Suryansh, P1 Jaydev Vihar, near Kalinga Hospital, Nandan Kanan Rd, T0674-230 3300, www.suryanshhotels.com. New and spruce rooms aren't huge but they're comfortable and well appointed, good restaurants (Rs 250 lunch buffet excellent, dinner à la carte) and a fresh and friendly bar (happy hour 1400-1900). Rooftop pool a bit disappointing, but gym is well equipped.

AL Swosti, 103 Janpath, T0674-253 5771, www.swosti.com. 60 a/c rooms (little difference between standard and de luxe), restaurant with some Orissan specialities, mall comfy bar, overpriced compared to those out of town but good discounts if you hint.

AL-A HHI, 112 Kharvel Nagar, Janpath, T0674-253 1465, www.hhihotels.com. With tastefully furnished rooms in cool mellow tones, the **HHI** fancies itself as boutique. The pool is tempting, restaurants chic, and the lounge bar has evening music. In the centre of town (unlike other high-end options), sizeable discounts available.

A Kalinga Ashok, Gautam Nagar, T0674-243 1055, www.hotelkalingaashok.com. 32 large clean rooms but getting jaded (especially the bathrooms), ones overlooking the lawn are preferable, all a/c, TV, restaurant and coffee shop. Sizeable discounts available.

A-C Ginger, Jayadev Nihar, Nayapali, T0674-230 3933, www.gingerhotels.com. By far the best value in this range, with sleek modern rooms and fantastic service. Amenities, TV and technology all state of the art; downsides are the barren surroundings, distance into town and buffet meals rather than à la carte. Great discounts if you book online last minute.

C Panthanivas Tourist Lodge, Lewis Rd, T0674-243 2515, www.panthanivas.com. Clean, spacious rooms but some getting a bit tatty (same price single or double), hot bath, all a/c, average restaurant, punitive 0800 check out, tourist office at the rear.

C-D Bicky Inn, 61 Janpath, T0674-253 6435. 26 small, but well-kept rooms, mostly a/c, Indian-style hotel, rooftop restaurant.

D-E Bhubaneswar, Cuttack Rd, T0674-231 3245. Generally clean and good value but staff could be more helpful. 42 rooms with bath, some a/c, some decrepit, always busy.

E Ekamra, Kalpana Sq, T0674-231 1732. Simple, grubby rooms, though clean linen, cheap singles, restaurant, internet café below. Mainly used by Indian workers.

E-F Lingaraj, Old Station Bazar, T0674-231 3565. Basic clean rooms, dorm.

E-F Upasana, Cuttack Rd, behind **Bhubaneswar**, T0674-231 4144. 20 fresh clean rooms, some a/c, with all-important mosquito mesh on windows, away from main road so quieter, decent room service, friendly, 24-hr checkout. Cheaper non-a/c rooms at back are a bargain for clean linens and TV. Recommended.

Udayagiri and Khandagiri caves

p774, map p 775

D-E Cave View Resort, T0674-247 2288. 5 rooms.

Eating

Bhubaneswar *p769, map p770*

TTT Deep Down South, **The New Marrion** (see Sleeping). An excellent, almost trendy choice for unusual South Indian: try tomato/chilly sponge *dosa*, or mint/*dhania*/gunpowder *dosa*, or safer ground is the delicious *rava masala dosa*. Good *lassis* too.

TTT Mayfair Lagoon (see Sleeping). Pleasant restaurants include outdoor truck stop-style. Great Western fast food and sweets.

TTT Swosti (see Sleeping). Varied menu. Dimly lit, generous, local specialities to advance order.

TT Banjara, Station Sq. Good lunch/dinner.

TT Hare Krishna, Lalchand Complex, Janpath, T0674-250 3188. Strict vegetarian. Upstairs, a/c, smart, tasty food.

TT Park Inn, Rajpath. Dim but unthreatening place for a beer (Rs 90-120) with a wide menu of Indian and Chinese veg/non dishes.

T New Ganguram Sweets, various locations around town. Delicious sweets and snacks.

T Venus Inn, 217 Bapuji Nagar (1st floor), T0674-253 1738. Clean and friendly, with decor that hints at temple architecture, subtle lighting and a/c. Best for South Indian vegetarian, *uttapams*, breakfasts and *dosas*. Recommended.

T The Zaika, Lewis Rd. Open 1100-1500 and 1900-2230. Hygienic and delicious food (Indian and Chinese), handy if you are staying in the Tourist Lodge.

Entertainment

Bhubaneswar *p769, map p770*

Programmes of Odissi and folk dances and folk drama are staged regularly and are worth seeking out. Schedules are irregular so call to see what's on. **Rabindra Mandap**, near GPO, T0674-251 7677, and **Jayadeva Bhavan** (State Information Centre) near bus stand, T0674-253 0794.

Festivals and events

Bhubaneswar *p769, map p770*

26 Jan-1 Feb Tribal Fair attended by groups from different regions – excellent performances and crafts exhibitions over 7 days.

Mar/Apr Asokashtami, the **Lingaraja Car Festival**. The image of Siva is drawn on a chariot from the Lingaraja Temple to visit the Ramesvara Temple for 4 days.

Shopping

Bhubaneswar *p769, map p770*

Some shops close on Thu and take a long lunch break. Market Building shops display prices but ask for a discount. The main street-market area is closed on Mon.

Boyanika, West Market. Recommended for saris and Orissan handloom fabrics.

Ekamra Haat, Madhusudan Marg. One-stop market for Orissan handicrafts and textiles.

Meyers, Janpath. The award-winning weavers have recently opened a fancy new store selling typical Orissan saris.

Utkalika, East Tower. Sells Orissa handloom and handicrafts.

Books

AK Mishra, 209 Bapuji Nagar, T0674-253 3349. Mon-Sat 1000-1400 and 1600-2100. Biggest and best bookshop in town, lots of fiction and not too jumbled.

Modern Book Co, Station Sq. Mon-Sat 0930-1400 and 1630-2100. Reasonable selection of novels.

Activities and tours

Bhubaneswar *p769, map p770*

Discover Tours, 463 Lewis Rd, T0674-2430477, T(0)9437-111230, www.orissa discover.com. For special interest tours (cultural, treks, wildlife parks and ethnological). Sarat Acharya and Bijaya Pattnaik are excellent guides and have won awards from the Regional Tourist Board. Tours organized even at short notice, though ask ahead for full service. Recommended.

OTDC, T0674-243 1515, runs various tours by 'luxury' coach from Transport Unit, behind **Panthanivas**. Ask about special tours to Chilika Lake. They will also pick up/drop off at hotels. To Nandankanan, Khandagiri, Udaigiri, Dhauli and museum with good guide (Tue-Sun 0900-1730, Rs 150, Rs 200 a/c). To Pipli, Konark and Puri (0900-1800, Rs 180/250, plus entry fee to Konark). To Puri and Satapada (0830-1800, Rs 175). To Barkul and Narayani (0830-1800, Rs 175). A new OTDC enterprise is the 'Hop On Hop Off' a/c bus which takes in city or heritage sights on a single ticket, 0830-2030, passing through designated stops at half-hourly intervals – pick up a route map from the OTDC office.

Transport

Bhubaneswar *p769, map p770*

Air

Airport 4 km. Taxi transfer, Rs 120 through **OTDC**. From airport Rs 130-160. **Air India**, Rajpath, T0674-253 0533, airport, T06274-534472, www.airindia.com, daily to **Delhi**, **Kolkata**, **Chennai**, **Bangalore** (**Bengaluru**), **Mumbai** and **Hyderabad**. **Indigo**, www.goindigo.in, **Kingfisher**, www.flykingfisher.com, and **Jetlite**, www.jetlite.com, also cover these routes. **Kingfisher** flies to **Raipur**.

Bus

Local City buses are cheap and cover major routes but avoid evening rush hour.

Long distance New Bus Stand is at Baramunda on the NH5 (6 km from centre) where there are auto-rickshaws for transfer. Enquiries T0674-235 4695, private bus enquiries T0674-235 4769. Some long-distance buses go through the city first, stopping at the Old Bus Stand, off Rajpath. Regular buses to **Puri** and **Konark** (both 1½-3 hrs) pick up passengers from outside the museum on Lewis Rd. Most are very full, but usually thin out at Pipli. Buses to **Cuttack** (1 hr) stop on the opposite side of the road.

Taxi

Tourist taxis, unmetered. **OTDC (Transport)** T0674-243 1515, and private operators have a/c and non a/c cars for full and half day sightseeing. Cars Rs 800, a/c, Rs 1000, for 8 hrs or 80 km. A round trip by car visiting Konark and Puri from Bhubaneswar takes 6-8 hrs. Allow at least 1 hr for Konark.

Train

Computerized booking hall is in separate building opposite the station. Auto- and cycle-rickshaws for transfer. **Chennai**: *Coromandal Exp 12841*, 2135, 20 hrs; *Howrah Chennai Mail 12839*, 0625, 21½ hrs. **Kolkata** (**H**): *Shatabdi 12074*, 0620, 6½ hrs, except Sun; *Dhauli Exp 12822*, 1320, 7 hrs; *Coromandal Exp 12842*, 0445, 7 hrs; *Falaknuma Exp 12704*, 1055, 6¾ hrs; *Howrah Mail 12840*, 2040, 7½ hrs; *Jagannath Exp 18410*, 0015, 8 hrs; *East Coast Exp 18646*, 0725, 8½ hrs, *Puri Howrah Exp 12838*, 2150, 7 hrs. **Mumbai** (**CST**): *Konark Exp 11020*, 1520, 36½ hrs. **Koraput**: *Hirakhand Exp 18447*, 1935, 14 hrs. **Secunderabad**: *Falaknuma Exp 12703*, 1400, 19½ hrs; *Konark Exp 11020*, 1520, 20 hrs; *East Coast Exp 18645*, 1955, 22 hrs; *Visakha Exp 17015*, 0835, 23 hrs. **New Delhi**: *Purushottam Exp 12801*, 2330, 30 hrs; *Utkal Exp 18477*, 2245, 40 hrs, both go via **Mughal Sarai** (**Varanasi**).

Directory

Bhubaneswar *p769, map p770*

Banks State Bank of India, Rajpath, by Police Station. ATM and exchange on 1st floor, sterling, US$ cash and TCs (closed Sun). **ICICI**, near Shree Raj Talkies, Janpath, and **Thomas Cook**, 130 Ashok Nagar, Janpath, for over the counter exchange. There are many ATMs on Janpath and around Kalpana Square, and also by the main entrance to the railway station. **Internet Gaurish Internet**, Cuttack Rd (opposite petrol station), daily 0900-2230, new and fast. Also at **Ekamra Hotel** and on Kalpana Sq (noisy location but quick). **Medical services Capital Hospital**, Unit 6, T0674-239 0688; **Kalinga Hospital**, Nandan Kanan Rd, T0674-230 0570/230 1227, private hospital. **Post GPO**, Sachivalaya Marg. **Useful contacts Foreigners' Registration Office**, Sahid Nagar, T0674-254 0555.

The Southeast

The Southeast encompasses Puri, one of the four holiest pilgrimage centres for Hindus, and Konark, which Mark Twain described as one of the wonders of the world. The Irrawady dolphins and flamingos of Chillika figure prominently in brochures, and the lake is an easy and rewarding excursion from Puri (particularly for birdwatchers) with some attractive places to stay overnight.

▸▸ *For listings, see pages 787-791.*

Puri

→ *For listings, see pages 787-791. Colour map 6, A6.*

Puri's tourist guesthouses cater to the flocks of Kolkata holidaymakers who take advantage of the highly revered Jagannath Temple and the long sandy beach to combine pilgrimage with relaxation. The massive curvilinear temple tower dominates the skyline, and the otherwise sleepy

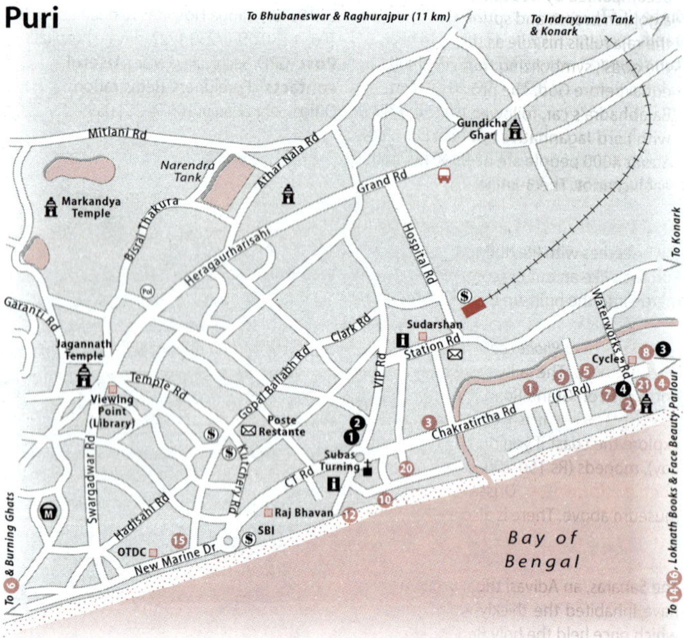

Sleeping
Arya Palace **1**
Baywatch Residency **2**
Chanakya BNR **3**
Derby **4**
Gandhara **5**
Hans Coco Palms **6**
Holiday House **7**
Kasi's Castle, Loknath Books & Tanuja Tribe Tour **7**
Lotus **8**
Love & Life **9**
Mayfair Beach Resort **10**
Panthanivas **12**
Pink House **14**
Puri **15**
Santana **16**
Sun Row Cottage & Internet **5**
Youth Hostel **20**
Z **21**

Eating
Chung Wah **1**
Harry's Café **3**
Honey Bee Bakery & Grass Routes Tours **4**
Peace **4**
Wild Grass **2**
Xanadu Garden **4**

Rath Yatra

Traditionally the only occasion on which non-Hindus and Hindus of low caste can set eyes on one of India's most beloved deities, Lord Jagannath's 'car festival' brings Puri's streets to life in an extraordinary frenzy of colour and noise. Shaped like a temple sanctuary and brightly decorated, Lord Jagannath's car is the largest; 13 m tall, it has 16 wheels each 2 m in diameter. Loud gongs announce the boarding of the deities onto the chariots with the arrival of the Raja of Puri accompanied by bedecked elephants. With a golden broom and sprinkling holy water, the raja fulfils his role as the 'sweeper of the gods', symbolizing that all castes are equal before God. The procession is led by Balabhadra's car, followed by Subhadra's with Lord Jagannath's bringing up the rear, about 4000 people are needed to draw each chariot. The 3-km journey to Gundicha Ghar, Lord Jagannath's birthplace, may take as much as 24 hours.

During the week away, the deities are daily dressed in new garments and treated to special *podapitha* (rice cakes) before they return with a similar procession nine days later. The ceremonies and the fairs attract more than 500,000 devotees to Puri each year. In the past some were said to have thrown themselves under the massive wheels to die a blessed death. Certainly accidental deaths often happened – Westerners who first saw the spectacle in the 18th century mistook such instances for human sacrifices. Fortunately, stricter security these days means that fewer devotees are crushed to death beneath the heavy wheels. After the festival, the *raths* are broken up and bits are sold to pilgrims as relics.

Rath Yatra is due to fall on 21 June 2012 and 10 July 2013 and 29 June 2014.

town seethes with life during the **Rath Yatra** (Car Festival) in June/July. Yet for most of the year Puri feels like an out of season backwater where quiet shady lanes and prettily painted houses merge into the built-up beach-front and animated market areas on the west side of town.

Ins and outs → *Phone code: 06752. Population: 157,600.*

Getting there The railway station is about 1 km from the main hotels and the bus stand, 500 m north of it, on Grand Road. Cycle-rickshaws tout for business all across town.

Getting around It is well worth renting a bike or motorbike to visit the temple, bazar and explore the coast if you don't wish to hire a rickshaw. Places on CT Road have bikes (Rs 40 per day), mopeds (Rs 150-200) or motorbikes (Rs 250-300) for hire. ▸▸ *See Transport, page 790.*

Tourist information **Orissa Tourism** ⓘ *Station Rd, T06752-222664, Mon-Sat 1000-1700*, with a museum above. There is also a tourist counter at the railway station, T06752-223536.

History

The Sabaras, an Adivasi tribal group who predated the Dravidians and Aryans, were believed to have inhabited the thickly wooded area around Puri. Some believe that this was Dantapura, which once held the holy Buddhist Tooth relic. According to Murray, in Japan and Sri Lanka, the **Tooth Festival** of Buddha was celebrated with three chariots and the similarity with the **Rath Yatra** at Puri further strengthens the theory that the deities here evolved from Buddhist symbols.

Sights

Jagannath Mandir This temple is the major attraction of Puri and, for Hindus, to remain here for three days and three nights is considered particularly rewarding. The temple attracts thousands on feast days and particularly during **Rath Yatra**. Non-Hindus are not allowed inside this temple. The fact that in the eyes of Jagannath (Lord of the Universe), there are no caste distinctions, has made Puri a very popular destination with the devout. The wooden figures of the three deities, **Jagannath, Balabhadra** and **Subhadra**, stand in the sanctuary garlanded and decorated by the priests. The extraordinary form that Jagannath takes is believed to be the unfinished work of the craftsman god Viswakarma, who in anger left this portrayal of Lord Vishnu incomplete. Small wooden replicas of the three images are available around the temple. There are vantage points for viewing the temple; for example, the roof of Raghunandan Library (closed Sundays) opposite the main entrance to the east or from the Jaga Balia Lodge nearby. A small donation is expected in return.

The temple is referred to by some as the white pagoda (the Konark Temple being the black pagoda) and was completed in the late 12th century. The original temple built in the Kalinga style consisted of the **deul** (sanctuary) and the **jagamohan** (audience hall) in front of it. It was only in the 14th or 15th century that the **nata mandir** (dance hall) and the **bhoga mandir** (hall of offerings) were added in alignment in the style of other Orissan temples. The *nata mandir* is unusual in that it has 16 pillars in four rows to support the large ceiling. The site is a virtual 200 m sq enclosed within an outer wall 6 m high. Within is another concentric wall which may have acted as fortification, inside which stands the tallest temple in Orissa, 65 m high, crowned by the wheel of Vishnu and a flag. On the higher ground in the enclosure are 30 small shrines, much in the Buddhist *stupa* tradition. Pilgrims are expected to visit at least three of these smaller temples before proceeding to the main temple. The outer wall has the main **Lion entrance.** On this east side there is an intricately carved 10-m-high free-standing stone pillar with a small figure of Aruna, the 'charioteer of the sun'. This once stood in front of the *nata mandira* at Konark, see page 784. To the left of the main entrance is the temple kitchen which daily prepares 56 varieties of food making up the *bhogas*, which are offered to the deities five times a day; the *mahaprasada* is then distributed from the Ananda Bazar to thousands. At festival times as many as 250,000 are served daily. The temple is supposed to be a self-sufficient community, served by 6000 priests and over 10,000 others who depend on it for their livelihood. The four sacred *tanks* in Puri provide thousands of pilgrims with the opportunity to take a holy dip. The **Narendra Tank** is particularly famous since the deities are taken there during the Snana Yatra.

Gundicha Ghar The terminus of the **Rath Yatra**, where the deities from the Jagannath Temple spend a week, is open to Hindus only. It shows the unique and ingenious way wrought-iron framework supported the laterite lintels of the massive temples.

The beach The long stretch of Puri's golden beach is shallow enough to walk out a long distance. Sunrise is particularly striking. The currents can be treacherous at times. Take great care and avoid swimming out too far. The best hotels have a stretch of fairly clean sand. The customary *nolia*, fisherman-turned-lifeguard in a distinctive conical hat, may be hired for either half or a full day, at a small price. The fishing villages along the coast east of CT Road are worth visiting particularly at sunrise or sunset when the fishing boats are coming and going, but be prepared to pick your way carefully.

Konark ➔ *For listings, see pages 787-791. Colour map 6, A6.*

Konark (Konarak) is one of the most vivid architectural treasures of Hindu India and is a World Heritage Site. It no longer stands as a landmark on the seashore since the land has risen and the sea is now 2 km away. Though much of it now lies in ruins, the porch is still magnificent. Be forewarned that the high volume of tourist traffic inevitably means that levels of 'hassle' increase proportionally.

Ins and outs ➔ *Phone code: 06758.*

Getting there and around The 35-km drive from Puri (small toll charged) through attractive scenery passes a Turtle Research Centre off the Marine Drive after 10 km and through coastal villages with beautifully decorated houses including Chaitan, a stone carvers' hamlet. The energetic can cycle to Konark and bring the bike back on the bus. The site itself is very compact and can only be seen on foot. ▸▸ *See Transport, page 791.*

Tourist information Archaeological Survey and government-approved **guides** conduct tours of less than an hour. Unofficial guides will press their services (about Rs 60), but can be unreliable.

History

The Sun Temple was built by King Langula Narasimha Deva in the 13th century, although there may have been an older ninth-century temple on the same site. Built of *khondalite*, it is said to have taken 1200 masons 16 years to complete. It was only in 1901 that the first tentative steps were taken to reclaim the ruins of the temple from the encroaching sand. By that stage not only had the sanctuary or *deul* collapsed but a number of the statues had been removed, many in the

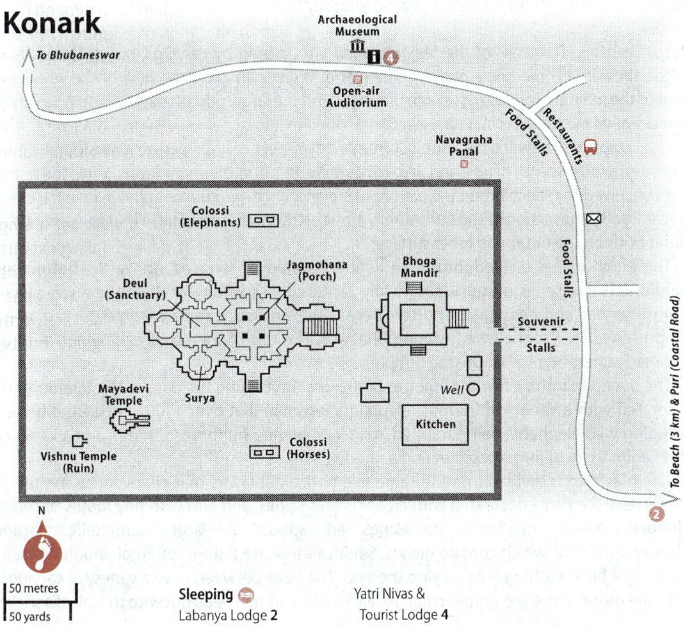

1830s by the Hindu Raja of Khurda, who wanted them to decorate temples he was building in his own fort, 100 km away, and at Puri. There has been substantial renovation, some of it protective and some replacing fallen stonework and sculptures.

The site

ⓘ *0600-1800, foreigners, Rs 250, video Rs 25. Official guides, Rs 100 per hr.*

The **Surya Temple** is set back 180 m from the road and is reached by a wide laterite path. The sanctuary has no deity for worship, so shoes may be worn. The exception is the small structure in the northeast corner of the site which houses the old *Navagraha* (nine planets) doorway arch, removed from the temple. The path to the temple is lined with beggars, as in major centres of Hindu pilgrimage.

Temple compound The temple presents its most imposing aspect from the steps of the *bhoga mandira* (refectory) at the eastern end of the complex, an isolated hall with pillars raised on a richly decorated platform guarded by a pair of stone lions; some believe this may have been a *nata mandira* (dancing hall). To its west is an open space leading to the porch (*jagamohana*) which rises magnificently to its original height of 39 m. The massive lower section of the original *deul* (sanctuary) was once over 60 m tall.

From the south wall you can see that the temple was built in the form of a war chariot. Twelve pairs of great wheels were sculpted on either side of the temple platform. In front of the eastern entrance a team of seven horses were shown straining to pull the chariot towards the dawn. In Hindu mythology the Sun god traverses the sky in a chariot drawn by seven horses, each representing a day of the week. The 12 pairs of wheels may have symbolized the 12 months of the year, and the eight spokes in each wheel, the divisions of the day into eight *prahars*. Each wheel also functions as a working sundial.

The sculptures The walls of the *bhoga mandir* are covered by carvings, but as Debala Mitra writes, they are of "mediocre quality". The platform gives an excellent view of the whole east front of the main temple with its porch doorway, and the large, remarkably vivid carvings on the terraces of its pyramidal roof, unique in Orissan architecture.

The sculptures draw for their subject from every aspect of life – dancers, musicians, figures from mythology, scenes of love and war, of court life, hunting, elephant fights. Since the temple was conceived to reflect a rounded picture of life and since *mithuna* or union in love is a part of that, a significant section of the sculpture is erotic art. Konark is unusual in that the carvings are found both on the outer and inner surfaces.

The porch roof is divided into three tiers, separated by terraces. Above the bottom and middle tiers is a series of musicians vividly captured in a variety of rhythmic poses playing drums, cymbals and *vinas*. On the bottom tier at either end of the central segments are dramatic sculptures of Siva as the awe-inspiring Bhairava. The top of the porch is crowned with the flattened spheres typical of Orissan temples.

The *upana* (plinth), a few centimetres high, runs right round the base of the temple, and is decorated with a variety of friezes – elephants (estimated at over 1700, and each different), including wild elephants being trapped, military marches, hunting, journeys, and a variety of other animals including crocodiles and a giraffe.

The platform is divided into the same five horizontal layers that characterize the temple itself. These are richly decorated with creepers and scrolls, and end with tiny motifs of *chaitya* windows. Along the lower mouldings are spaced miniature temple-like façades (*khakhara-mundis*) which contain niches. Set into these are figures, often of young women – caressing a bird, washing hair, playing the *vina*. The slabs between have a variety of carvings – some are erotic, some are *nagas* or *naginis*, each with a human head but with the tail of a snake.

The middle of the platform has three horizontal mouldings at about eye level. Above this, the *upper jangha* is richly sculpted, sometimes with religious scenes such as *Mahishasuramardini* (Durga as the goddess of destruction) and *Jagannatha*, enshrined in a temple. Other sculptures show royal courts or simple family scenes. Along the top of the platform is the veranda, consisting of two mouldings separated by a narrow recess. Though severely damaged, these are decorated with friezes.

From the platform you will see the intricately carved eight-spoked wheels, each shown with its axle, a decorated hub and an axle pin. Floral motifs, creepers and the widely shown *chaitya* windows cover the stonework. Medallions with gods such as Surya and Vishnu, erotic figures, nobles and animals all add life to the structure.

Sanctum sanctorum Although the *jagmohana* is now the dominant building of the complex, the scale of the sanctuary is still evident. The climb up the outer walls allows you to see at close quarters the remarkable chlorite statues of Surya, on the outer north, west and south walls. The large grey-green statues stand in sharp contrast with the surrounding yellowish-orange *khondalite* stone. Surya stands on a chariot drawn by his seven horses, lashed by Aruna, the charioteer, surrounded by two four-armed gods, a pot-bellied Brahma on the right and possibly Vishnu on the left. Below them are possibly four wives of Surya.

The sanctuary itself is currently inaccessible – a new stairway has been in the pipeline since at least 2003. The main feature inside is the chlorite platform at the western end of the 10-m-sq room intended for the presiding deity. This image from the pedestal was moved to the Jagannath Temple complex in Puri. The platform that remains is nonetheless outstanding; some carvings almost certainly show the king, the donor of the temple, accompanied by priests. The hollows on top of the platform's eastern edge resulted from the placing of pots over a long period.

The Colossi Originally each of the three staircases to the porch was guarded by a pair of colossi – rampant lions on top of a crouching elephant to the east, decorated elephants to the north, and war horses to the south. The last two pairs have been remounted a short distance from their original sites. The lions have been put in front of the eastern steps up to the *Bhoga mandira* near the entrance.

Archaeological Museum

ⓘ *Near Yatri Nivas, Sat-Thu 1000-1700, Rs 10.*

This museum has a small collection including many important pieces from the Sun Temple complex. Occasional lectures and films are shown. Archaeological Survey publications can be bought here.

Chilika Lake → *For listings, see pages 787-791. Colour map 6, A5.*

ⓘ *Boats from Barkul, Rambha and Satapada, 1 hr, around Rs 100. Nalabana birdwatching trip, Rs 200, 4 hrs. Book the night before, pay 0730 on the day and wait until the boat is full.*

Chilika is the largest brackish water lake in Asia (1100 sq km) stretching across the Khurdha, Puri and Ganjam districts, and forms an enormous lagoon as it is joined to the Bay of Bengal with a narrow mouth, a sandy ridge separating it from the sea.

The lake is the habitat of the rare Irrawaddy dolphin (particularly around Satapada), as well as being the winter home of migratory birds, some flying great distances from Iran, Central Asia and Siberia. During the winter months, from November to February, you can watch white-bellied sea eagles, ospreys, golden plovers, sandpipers, flamingos, shovellers, pelicans and gulls. The lake attracts fishermen who come in search of prawn, mackerel and crab. Some ornithologists blame the growth in prawn farming, as well as the increasing discharge from rivers, silting and salinity, for reduced bird numbers. The large **Nalabana Island** (Reed Island) sanctuary is at times below water. Human activity is also threatening the dolphins, currently numbering around 140, who meet their deaths in the propellers of motorized boats shockingly frequently.

The **Kalijai Temple** stands on one of the tiny rock islands. It gets very crowded at weekends. **Satapada**, on the other side of the lake, has a tourism complex.

Rushikulya

This is the only one of the three nesting sites in Orissa where it is currently possible and permitted to view the *arribada* (mass nesting) of olive ridley sea turtles. **Gahirmatha** in the north (at Bhitarkanika Wildlife Sanctuary) is a restricted area while the beach at Devi has become the 'lost arribada' with no turtles having appeared for several seasons. The beach at Rushikulya is found to the north of the river; the nearest place to stay is the government lodge in **Rambha** (20 km, book ahead), otherwise Gopalpur is conveniently close.

The phenomenon begins in November when the turtles, from as far away as South America and the Pacific, arrive in their *lakhs* to reproduce. Over the next few months they feed and mate (which takes place on the surface of the water, clearly visible) before coming ashore to nest around the middle of February. Peak nesting occurs at night, and it is an awesome sight to see the females traversing the beach in the early-morning mists. Six to eight weeks later, the eggs begin to hatch (around the first week of April) and the hatchlings make their way to the sea to take their chances with the fishing trawlers' nets and natural predators. Only about one in every 1000 will survive.

Gopalpur-on-Sea → *Phone code: 0680.*

Gopalpur was an ancient sea port from which early settlers from Kalinga sailed as far as Java, Bali and Sumatra. Then it was a port for the export of Aska sugar and 'coolie' labour to the Assam tea gardens. Later still it became a popular seaside resort for the British offering a beautiful sandy beach. Today, however, it has a rather faded feeling and appearance although tourists from West Bengal come in droves during the winter months. Sand dunes, groves of coconut and casuarinas separate the fringes of the small town from the beach, while the backwaters, creeks and lagoons give some variety. A red and white **lighthouse** ⓘ *1630-1730, Rs 10*, opens to visitors briefly each afternoon; there are good views but photography is not allowed. Gopalpur is a quiet retreat and a suitable base from which to visit Rushikulya, but sunbathing on the public beach is ill-advised and certainly not relaxing, making one or two days most people's limit.

The Southeast listings

For Sleeping and Eating price codes and other relevant information, see Essentials pages 38-42.

Sleeping

Puri *p780, map p780*

Avoid arriving at your hotel by rickshaw as commission will be added to the room rate. Instead, get down nearby and walk. Most backpackers stay in hotels on **CT Rd** towards the fishing village at the eastern end. Domestic visitors prefer the seaside resorts along **Marine Drive**. Most check out at 0800 and several have a 2200 curfew. Check before staying out late. Some hotels will arrange pickup from the station.

LL-L Mayfair Beach Resort, CT Rd, T06752-227800, mayfair1@sancharnet.in. Very well run, well-furnished a/c cottages and rooms, some with sea view, rampant tropical garden, good pool (residents only), clean private section of beach, decent restaurants, including breakfast, friendly staff.

L Hans Coco Palms, Swargdwar, off New Marine Dr, T06752-230038, www.hanshotels.com. 40 good sea-facing a/c rooms with balconies/terraces, palm- filled restaurant, pleasant garden, good pool, friendly staff, knowledgeable manager, book ahead in season, ask for the 25% discount, breakfast included.

B Chanakya BNR, CT Rd, T06752-222063, chanakyabnrpuri@hotmail.com. This slice of history has been extensively refurbished, fortunately in an appropriately old-world style. Spacious a/c rooms have dark wood furniture, cream trimmings and a colonial feel, with the bonus of trendy bathrooms. Best on the 1st floor with fabulous wide verandas overlooking sea, siestas encouraged (quiet hours 1400-1600), claim to serve the best continental food in town.

C Panthanivas (OTDC), CT Rd, T06752-222740, www.panthanivas.com. 48 rooms with a/c, rooms in old block run down, better in newer block, tour booking, pleasant garden with beach access.

C-D Arya Palace, CT Rd, T06752-232688, neeraj21jain@indiatimes.com. 32 rooms (some a/c) in new hotel, clean and airy, hot bath, TV, generous discounts when quiet.

C-E Baywatch Residency, CT Rd, T06752-226133. Close to the beach but out of 'the scene', most rooms have an extra seating area and TV. Ones at the front are preferable

C-E Puri, Marine Parade, T06752-222114, www.purihotel.in. Institutional hotel on seafront that is an institution in itself for Bengali family holidaymakers, thus quieter during the week. Wide choice (including 9- and 10-bed rooms!), clean, some a/c, vegetarian restaurant. In the 'Indian' part of Puri, killer views from the top floors. 24-hr checkout.

C-E Samudra, CT Rd, T06752-222705, hsamudra@yahoo.co.in. 52 decent clean rooms, all with breezy sea-facing balconies, pay more for a/c, better at front on higher floors with sea view, TV, restaurant, friendly staff.

C-F Z, CT Rd, T06752-222554, www.zhotelindia.com. 12 spacious rooms have minimal furniture, some with clean shared bath, some a/c. 2 rooms have wonderful balconies, but if you don't manage to reserve one of these it's not really worth the price. The women-only dorms are great value though at Rs 100, and very clean. In an old mansion, with a huge terrace and lots of sociable areas (movie/games room), solar-powered, popular.

D-E Gandhara, CT Rd, T06752-224117, www.hotelgandhara.com. Clean, comfortable rooms (some a/c) amid lovely gardens, quiet at the back, are good value and dorms are cheap. Friendly staff and impeccable service, but stringent security, restaurant, popular. Free pickup from the bus or railway station.

E-F Lotus, CT Rd, T06752-223852. Quite clean, 9 simple rooms (mostly **F**), good restaurant, **Harry's Café**.

E-G Pink House, CT Rd, T06752-222253. 15 basic rooms, some 3-5 bedded, only 1 with inside bath (hot buckets available). The only guesthouse directly on beach, very friendly, popular with long-stayers, beach shack restaurant will provide service to the room.

F Holiday House, CT Rd, T06752-223782, hhflourish@yahoo.co.in. The blank outside hides reasonable, good-sized rooms, better sea-facing (prices rise with altitude!), not a backpackers' hangout, restaurant has Orissan food and more.

F Kasi's Castle, CT Rd, T06752-224522. Only 7 spotless rooms (book ahead) with attached bath in friendly family house, good choice but not much light and lacking spaces to relax.

F Love & Life, CT Rd, T06752-224433, loveandlife@hotmail.com. Good-value rooms in 3-storey, airy building but much better are the cottages at rear, theoretical hot water, nets, the eccentric staff soon warm up. The kind of place people stay for a while.

F-G Derby, CT Rd, T06752-223961. Deservedly popular, 10 rooms with squat toilets, clean sheets and towels on request. Rooms onto the pretty garden are a bit pricier but better furnished and larger, the adjacent restaurant is good and the rooftops are relaxing.

G Santana, CT Rd, at the end of the fishing village, T06752-223491. Simple rooms in friendly, secure hotel, popular with Japanese visitors.

G Sun Row Cottage, CT Rd, T06752-223259, chitaranjan@hotmail.com. Set around small, colourful garden, 10 simple rooms in double cottages have little terraces, excellent restaurant, long-stay discounts. A true bargain.

G Youth Hostel, CT Rd, T06752-222424. Separate, though somewhat dishevelled male and female dorms, some 2-3 bedded, camping, good Indian meals.

Konark *p783, map p783*

E Yatri Nivas and **Tourist Lodge** (OTDC), T06758-236820. Good-value, clean rooms with nets, some 4-bedded, some a/c with geyser and TV, pleasant gardens, restaurant, free cultural programme on weekend evenings during season. Check-out 1200.

E-G Labanya Lodge, away from temple, T06758-236824, labanyalodge1@rediffmail.com. Most popular of the budget lodges. 13 musty rooms, mostly with attached bath, some with a/c, cycle hire, travel.

Chilika Lake *p786*

To stay in an attractive campsite by the lake, contact **Grass Routes** (see page 790).

C-E Panthanivas (OTDC), 1 km from road end, Barkul, T06756-220488, www.panthanivas.com. 35 small recently renovated rooms in a lovely lakeside setting, some a/c, bar, restaurant, tourist office, boating complex, 0800 checkout, busy during weekends and holidays.

D-F Yatri Nivas, Satapada, on the north side of the lake, closest to Puri, T06752-262077. Attractive location, decent rooms (non-a/c Rs 450). 1st floor rooms have balconies and the best views. Checkout 0900.

D-G Panthanivas (OTDC), Rambha, T06810-278346, www.panthanivas.com. 18 rooms or cottages, some a/c, dorm beds Rs 180, nice gardens, half rate for day visitors 0900-1700. Checkout 1200.

F-G Shree Khrishna Lodge, Barkul (500 m from **Panthanivas**), T06756-221195. Simple, clean rooms, some with bath.

Gopalpur-on-Sea *p786*

Discounts of 30% can often be negotiated, but during high season (Oct-Dec, and 20-30 Jan) hotels are busy with Bengali tourists.

A Swosti Palm Resort, southern end of the beach close to the lighthouse, T0680-234 3718, www.swosti.com. Renovated with 29 decent rooms around a small garden; the restaurant is a bit gloomy and there's no pool but the bar and atmosphere are relaxing. The most luxurious choice in Gopalpur.

D Song of the Sea, next to lighthouse, T0680-234 2347. Clean, light and airy rooms in family-run hotel, peaceful location, simple restaurant. The best rooms are at the front on 1st floor with sea view, pleasant though pricey.

D-E Sea Pearl, beachfront, T0680-234 2556. Cheaper non-a/c rooms are fairly basic (Rs 600) but some are sea facing (others face the building next door), it's better on the upper levels. All have baths and TV. Checkout 0900.

E-F Green Park, 1 block back from the beach, T0680-234 2016, greenpark016@yahoo.com. 17 clean rooms (some a/c), simple Indian-style hotel, best with sea view, 24-hr check out. No restaurant or bar.

E-F Hotel Kalinga, behind **Sea Pearl**, T0680-234 2067. Spotless rooms in a very well-maintained family-run hotel, some with TV, clean bath (hot bucket) and linen, simple but excellent food, nice terraces overlooking sea (though no private balconies). Posters adorn the highly colourful walls. Checkout 0900.

F Plaza Millennium, at the north end of the beach, T0680-234 2647, T(0)9853-921325.

Large breezy rooms have appalling murals and curtains, but clean bathrooms; there's a good 1st-floor option with a huge sea-facing balcony (Rs 400) that can sleep 4. Checkout 0900.

F Sea Side Breeze, T0680-234 3075. Right on the beach, 14 clean freshly painted rooms, 12 of which face the sea. Food on order and the bathrooms are decent (hot bucket), but some of the world's lumpiest pillows. Staff are accommodating without being ingratiating, it's ideal for backpackers.

F-G Heaven Spot, Rewu St, T0680-234 3274. 5 small, basic but clean rooms with attached bath, away from beach, serves as a base.

G Rosalin, beachfront, T0680-234 2367. Very basic rooms with attached bath around a scrubby littered garden. Strictly for those on a tight budget, it's friendly but prepare for mosquitoes. **Shining Dew** restaurant next door is hot and boxy.

Eating

Puri *p780, map p780*

Puri's signature dish is the *mahaprasad* of rice, dahl, vegetables and sweet prepared by 400 cooks at the Jagannath Temple. It can be bought at the Anand Bazar in the temple complex, or you can in theory have it delivered to your hotel. There is an abundance of fresh fish; ensure all is fresh and thoroughly cooked. Hotels expect advance notice from non-residents.

Fresh cheap local fish is grilled at numerous stalls along Marine Drive every evening, but the proximity of the burning ghats might be off-putting.

TT-T Chung Wah, Hotel Lee Garden, VIP Rd. Very good Chinese in a bustling environment, efficient and highly recommended, cooling a/c.

TT-T Peace, CT Rd. Friendly garden café, a pleasant place to relax. Outdoor seating is usually packed with Westerners, the muesli fruit curd is the biggest you'll ever see and this alone attracts a keen following. Interesting fish dishes and Japanese pretenders.

TT-T Wild Grass, VIP Rd, T06752-229293. Extremely pleasant open-air restaurant with rustic theme, lots of plants and wicker-work to relax among. Some Orissan specialities, the tomato *khata*, *tandoori* prawn and veg *jaikema* are particularly good. Friendly and not to be missed.

TT-T Xanadu Garden, CT Rd, T06752-227897. The vast breakfast menu covers any requirement, and for other times there's everything from burgers to *gado-gado*. Pretty at night with fairy lights and the obligatory Orissan mirrored lampshades, sand beneath your feet and painted palm trunks. Recommended for fish.

T Harry's Café, CT Rd. Pure vegetarian (no onion or garlic) South Indian. Good *thalis* and snacks.

T Honey Bee Bakery and Pizzeria, CT Rd, T06752-320479. Best for fresh bread, muffins and great coffee in a clean and chilled environment, no hint of staff resting on their laurels.

Konark *p783, map p783*

There are plenty of places serving *thalis* and snacks.

T Sun Temple Hotel. Good choice among the many basic eating places lining the road opposite the temple entrance. Friendly service, everything cooked fresh, and the breakfast *parathas* are fantastic.

Gopalpur-on-Sea *p786*

Super-cheap stalls opposite **Sea Shell** serve chow mein and *parathas*.

T Krishna, by **Sea Pearl Hotel** (see Sleeping). Opens at 0800, last food orders at 2200. Like much of Gopalpur, **Krishna** is painted Sprite-green. Clean and friendly with just a couple of tables, they do cheap Indian meals, Western breakfasts, and good fish, prawn and calamari.

T Naz restaurant, opposite **Krishna**. Similar in appearance and even cheaper, but with less variety.

T Sea Shell, beachfront. Umbrellas and stiff breezes enhance its air of a decaying British seaside snack stall, but the Chinese and Indian meals are reasonable and can be enjoyed with a beer.

Entertainment

Puri *p780, map p780*

Top hotels and resorts have bars. Classical *Odissi* dance, folk dances and drama which are always performed for festivals are also staged from time to time and are worth seeking out.

Festivals and events

Puri *p780, map p780*

Mid-Apr 21-day **Chandan Yatra** coincides with the **Hindu New Year** when images of Jagannath, his brother and sister are taken out in boats on the Narendra Tank. *Chandan* is the sandal paste used to anoint the deities. **Snana Yatra**, which follows, marks the ritual bathing of the deities on a special barge. For 15 days the gods are kept out of sight, when worshippers may only pray before *pattachitras* (paintings). Every few years new images of the deities are carved from specially selected trees and the old ones are secretly buried by the temple priests.
Jun **Rath Yatra**, see box, page 781.
Nov **Beach Festival**, a week of cultural shows, crafts and food stalls.

Konark *p783, map p783*

Feb Honouring the Sun god; pilgrims flock here from evening to sunrise.
19-21 Feb A dance festival is run by a private organization headed by Guru Ganga Dharpradhan.
1-5 Dec **Classical dance festival** at the open-air auditorium opposite Yatri Nivas.

Shopping

Puri *p780, map p780*

Visit the vast **bazar** around the Jagannath Temple, along Bada Danda and Swargadwara, but you have to bargain. **Pathuria Sahi** is the stone carvers' quarter and **Raghurajpur** (12 km) produces *pattachitras* and etchings on palm leaf, see page 767.

Books

Loknath, CT Rd. Second-hand books or sale/ exchange, library (Rs 7 per day), postcards.

Handicrafts

Stone carvings, papier-mâché masks, painted wood figures, paintings, appliqué and hornwork all make good buys.
Akbar, CT Rd. Cheap painted cards.
Odissi, Dolamandap Sahi. Handlooms.
Sudarshan, Station Rd. Stone carving, where you can also watch masons at work carving out images of deities.
Sun Crafts, Tinikonia Bagicha.
Utkalika and **Crafts Complex**, Mochi Sahi Sq.
Weavers' Co-op Society, Grand Rd.
For handlooms.

Activities and tours

Puri *p780, map p780*

The tourist office has a list of government-approved tour companies. Almost every hotel on CT Rd has a travel office, but for 'tribal tours' it's worth paying more to go with a conscientious agency.
Grass Routes, CT Rd, T(0)9437-029698/ T(0)9437-022663, www.grassroutes journeys.com. Offers a fascinating selection of outings in and around Puri, Claire and her husband are keenly promoting responsible tourism. Cooking classes go via the market to learning Orissan dishes in a family home, or excursions further afield visit tribal areas. Trips to Chilika Lake need 24 hrs' notice so the camping spot can be set up. Not cheap, but recommended.
Heritage Tours, **Mayfair Beach Resort**, T06752-223656. Expensive yet moral enterprise, offering a variety of tours. A good benchmark for comparing prices, but more importantly – 'tribal tourism' is taken seriously. Well-established and friendly.
OTDC, T06752-223526. Inexpensive full-day tours (except Mon, entry fees extra) to Konark, Dhauli, Bhubaneswar, Khandagiri, Udayagiri and Nandankanan Zoo. It is a long day, 0630-1830. Chilika Lake (Satapada), 0730-1730. Half-day tours also available.
Tanuja Tribe Tour, Tanuja Complex, CT Rd, T06752-220717, tanujatribetour@yahoo.com. Reputable agency with pleasant guides, not as pricey as some.

Gopalpur-on-Sea *p786*

Sagar Tours & Travels, Beach Rd, T0680-224 2963, T(0)9437-127548. Provides cheap car and driver hire, and can sort out train/bus tickets.

Transport

Puri *p780, map p780*

Air

Bhubaneswar, 60 km, is the nearest airport (see page 778). Prepaid taxi to Puri from the airport Rs 650, 1-1½ hrs.

Bicycle and motorcycle

Hiring a bike or a motorbike is a good option for exploring the coast. There are several outlets on CT Rd. Cycles costs around Rs 30 per day. Motorbikes around Rs 200-250 per day, moped Rs 120-150.

Bus

Enquiries, T06752-224461. The huge, open bus stand on Grand Rd runs regular buses to **Bhubaneswar** and **Konark**. Minibuses are faster. There are also services to **Cuttack**, **Visakhapatnam** and **Kolkata**.

Rickshaw

Cycle-rickshaws available all over town. From the bus stand to CT Rd costs Rs 30; from the railway station Rs 20. To avoid commission being added to room price, ask to be dropped off at the **BNR Hotel** and walk along CT Rd to your hotel.

Taxi

Tourist taxis from larger hotels, CT Rd agencies, and taxi stand, T06752-222161; Rs 800 per 8 hrs or 80 km. To **Bhubaneswar** around Rs 700.

Train

Enquiry, T131. **Kolkata** (**H**): *Jagannath Exp 18410*, 2250, 9 hrs; *Puri Howrah Exp 12838*, 2005, 9 hrs. **New Delhi**: *Purushottam Exp 12801*, 2150, 31 hrs; *Utkal Exp 18477*, 2110, 40½ hrs. **Guwahati** (**H**): *Guwahati Exp 15639*, 1405 (Tue only), 32 hrs via **New Jalpaiguri**, 22½ hrs.

Konark *p783, map p783*

Bus

OTDC 'luxury' coach or ordinary, very crowded bus from **Puri** (1½ hrs) and **Bhubaneswar** (up to 3 hrs).

Taxi

Prepaid taxi from Bhubaneswar airport costs Rs 650.

Chilika Lake *p786*

Chilika Lake is easiest to reach by road (NH5) from Barkul, 6 km south of Balugaon or Rambha at the south end of the lake.

Bus

Buses from **Bhubaneswar** and **Berhampur**. Satapada at the northern end can only be reached via **Puri**.

Ferry

OTDC motor launches are available from **Barkul**, **Rambha** and **Satapada** although during the week it may not be cost effective. Dolphin-watching is the main focus of boats from Satapada. Private country boats are also available at Barkul and Rambha.

Train

Slow passenger trains on the Chennai–Kolkata line stop at **Balugaon**, **Chilika**, **Khallikote** and **Rambha**.

Gopalpur-on-Sea *p786*

Bus

There are regular private buses from the **New Bus Stand**, **Berhampur** (Rs 10, 30 mins).

Directory

Puri *p780, map p780*

Banks Allahabad Bank, Temple Rd is best for changing cash. Other exchanges on CT Rd. Several ATMs on Grand Rd, CT Rd and at the railway station. **Internet** Nanako, near Sun Row Cottage on CT Rd. **Medical services** **District HQ Hospital**, T06752- 222062. **TB Hospital**, Red Cross Rd, T06752- 222094. **Post** **GPO** on Kutchery Rd. PCOs and internet on CT Rd.

Konark *p783, map p783*

Post **Sub Post Office**, near Panthanivas.

Chilika Lake *p786*

There is a post office, a government dispensary and a tourist office at **Barkul**, T06756-220855.

The Northeast

It is possible to visit several places of historic and religious interest in the north of Orissa in three to seven days, as well as to see outstandingly beautiful scenery and the Simlipal National Park. Some of the accommodation is excellent value (particularly at Chandipur), though in places it is very basic. *▸▸ For listings, see pages 797-799.*

Cuttack → *For listings, see pages 797-799. Colour map 6, A6.* *Population: 535,100.*

Cuttack occupies an important strategic position in relation to the network of canals in the region. Situated at the head of the Mahanadi delta and surrounded by the great river and its tributary the Kathjuri, the town is almost an island, its crowded streets and bazars clustered up towards its western end. **Orissa Tourism** ⓘ *Arunodaya Market Building, Link Rd, T0671-231 2225*, and **Railway Station Counter** ⓘ *T0671-261 0507*, both have helpful staff.

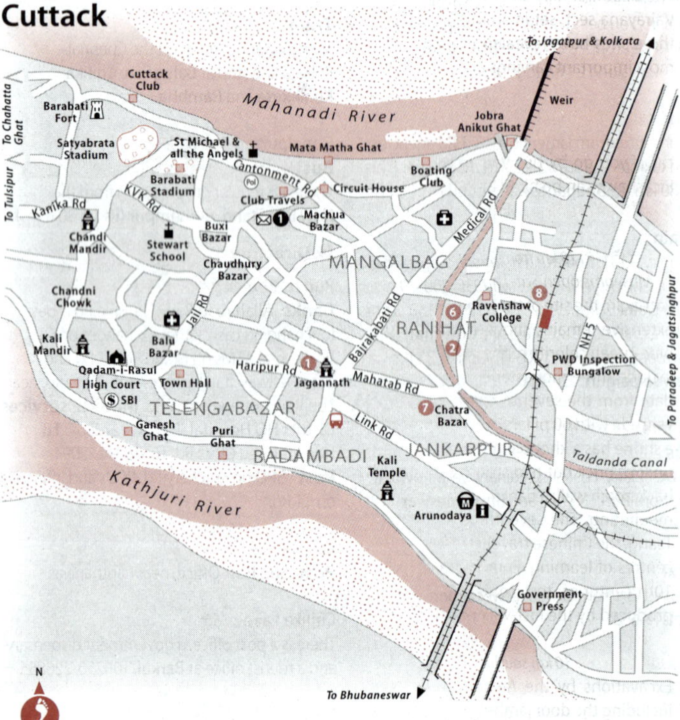

Sleeping
Akbari Continental 1
Ambica 2
Cuttack 6
Manorama Plaza 7
Railway Retiring Rooms 8

Eating
Temptations 1

Cuttack is one of Orissa's oldest cities and its medieval capital. It was founded by Nrupat Kesari (ruled 920-935). It remained the administrative centre until the end of the British Raj and was the state capital until 1956. The ancient **stone embankment** to the south was built in the 11th century by the Kesari ruler to protect the town from flooding by the Kathjuri River. It still stands as a reminder of the engineering skills practised over 900 years ago. The **Qadam-i-Rasul** (Kadam Rasul) in the centre of the old city, visited as a shrine by both Muslims and Hindus, has three 18th-century mosques with beautiful domes and a music gallery. The shrines contain relics of the Prophet Mohammad; the prophet's footprint is carved on a circular stone. The famous silver filigree shops are in Balu Bazar.

To the northwest, the blue granite 13th-century **Barabati Fort** retains its wide moat and gateway though the nine-storeyed palace has disappeared. Probably built by a Ganga ruler, it was in Marhatta hands when it was taken by the British in 1803. Close to the fort is the vast **Barabati Stadium** where major sporting and cultural events are held. The **Church of St Michael and all the Angels** (CNI) by the river, typical of Raj-style church buildings, is worth a visit.

Ratnagiri, Udayagiri and Lalitgiri → *For listings, see pages 797-799. Colour map 6, A6.*

The beautiful hills and rice-growing lands are home to remarkable Buddhist remains of the Vajrayana sect, set in an idyllic landscape surrounded by green fields. The excavations at the three sites have revealed Buddhist *stupas*, monasteries, sculptures and Buddha images. The most important carvings are on display in the State Museum in Patna, Bihar.

Ins and outs

Getting there and around The sites can all be visited in a day from Cuttack or Bhubaneswar by car. If you go by bus you will need to stay overnight (there is a government tourist lodge). Rickshaws can be hired at Patharajpur. ▸▸ *See Transport, page 798.*

Tourist information Entry to each site costs US$2 for foreigners.

Ratnagiri → *70 km from Cuttack, 115 km from Bhubaneswar.*

ⓘ *Museums open Sat-Thu 1000-1700.*

Ratnagiri, the site of the 'Jewel Hill', on the bank of River Keluo, has produced the best finds. The extensive remains show excellent sculptural skill combining different coloured stones, from blue-green chlorite to the purple-red garnets encrusted in brownish silver khondalite. The finds include three monasteries (two quadrangular), eight temples and several *stupas* believed to date from the seventh century. The largest monastery (No 1) is 55 m sq with a surrounding veranda with 60 pillars built around a courtyard entered through a carved gateway. At one end a shrine has a khondalite Buddha image and remnants of about 24 cells for monks which were built of brick but had stone door frames. Look for the intricate carving on the doorway of the back porch wall: a dancer stamping her feet; a royal lady with her arm around a maid; a woman meditating. The seventh-century University of Pushpagiri may have flourished here; Hiuen Tsang, the Chinese traveller, after his visit in AD 639 described it as one of Orissa's two Buddhist centres of learning. Four galleries display fine sculptural figures dating from the ninth to the 10th centuries, terracotta and ivory objects, inscribed copper plates and miniature bronzes produced by the lost-wax process.

Udayagiri → *10 km south of Ratnagiri.*

Excavations by the Archaeological Department have unearthed better preserved carvings including the door jambs to the sanctum. The monastery, within a large compound, has 18 cells with a veranda arranged around a courtyard. The 3-m Lokesvar Buddha image here has an eighth-century inscription on it. Further up the hill, fragments of sculpture have been excavated among the ruins.

Lalitgiri

The site about 3 km south of Bandareswar village was first excavated in 1985. Large architectural remains including a 20-m-high apsidal temple have been found together with sculptures and decorated door jambs. A stone platform with inscriptions dates this site closer to the second century although Kushana Brahmi inscriptions on an underlying brick *stupa* suggest Buddhist occupation around the first century BC. Three caskets were also found, two of which contained stone, silver and gold caskets with preserved relics inside. The caretaker will open the small museum. There is a stone-carvers' village at the base of Lalitgiri which traces its connections back to ancient times and produces excellent sculpture.

The coast → *For listings, see pages 797-799.*

Paradeep → *Colour map 6, A6. 94 km from Cuttack on the NH5A.*

Paradeep is a port at the mouth of the Mahanadi River. Some 2500 years ago Orissan sailors regularly set sail for Indonesia and mainland Southeast Asia from this point. The harbour is base to 1600 colourfully painted fishing trawlers, which are an amazing sight but it is largely these that are affecting the olive ridley turtles so adversely (see box, page 795). Visitors today find they can't escape industrial pollution here – "a layer of black dust settles on every surface in no time". There are a few overnight options and regular buses arrive from Cuttack and Bhubaneswar, should you decide to make the unusual choice of a detour to Paradeep.

Bhitarkanika Wildlife Sanctuary → *Colour map 6, A6.*

ⓘ *55 km from Bhadrak on NH5. Mail/express trains stop at Bhadrak. Foreigners Rs 1000 per day, plus boat transport of around Rs 2000. Entry is easiest from Chandbali, entry permits from the Assistant Conservator of Forests, T06786-220372, 0600-1800, though it is also possible from Rajnagar or Gupti. Tour operators in Puri or Bhubaneswar can make all the arrangements but need prior notice – otherwise try for a permit on the day with a local agent (try Sanjog Travels, Chandbali, T06786-220495). Best time to visit: Nov-Feb.*

Virtually every species of mangrove is found in the forests in the Bhitarkanika Sanctuary, but their swamps are better known for estuarine crocodiles, water monitors, cobras and the endangered olive ridley sea turtles (see box, page 795). The 10-km stretch of beach at **Gahirmatha** is a protected marine sanctuary that attracts thousands of nesting turtles each year, but for tourists it's off-limits due to the nearby missile-testing site on the **Wheeler Islands**. Onshore wildlife includes rhesus monkeys, wild boar and deer, plus many species of migratory and resident birds (storks, herons, kingfisher, ducks, eagles and more).

The creeks and waterways are negotiated by motorboat, with stop-offs at **Dangamar Island** to view immense estuarine crocodiles and **Bagagahana Island** to see the multitude of nesting storks. In any case, expect to see the various beasts in their natural environment on mud-banks and in trees when navigating the sanctuary. Tours usually finish up with a visit to an almost-too picture-perfect typical Orissan village. There is accommodation in the forest rest houses or a couple of comfortable lodges nearby (see Sleeping, page 797). Like all Orissa's national parks, Bhitarkanika is prohibitively expensive for many travellers but most visitors leave feeling satisfied with the wildlife sightings and overall experience.

Baleshwar → *Colour map 6, A6.*

Northeast from Bhubaneswar, this medieval maritime trading port was first established by the British in 1642 with subsequent competition from the French who called it *Farasidinga* and the Dutch *Dinamardinga*. Ruins of **Dutch tombs** can still be seen and traces of **canals**, up which ocean-going ships were hauled inland. The **Khirachora Gopinath Temple** is at Remuna (9 km) and **Panchalingesvar Temple**, 30 km away. **Orissa Tourism** ⓘ *Panthanivas Hotel, Police Line, T06782-262048.*

Turtles in peril

It is estimated that the coast of Orissa attracts 300,000-800,000 olive ridley turtles (*Lepidochelys olivacea*) to its beaches each year to lay their eggs. Sea turtles are believed to return to nest where they hatched so the mysterious cycle continues. They arrive at night, for a fortnight around the full moon from November to May, with a spectacular *arribadas* (from the Portuguese, meaning 'the coming') in February, when record numbers find their way from the Indian Ocean or from Australia, via the Pacific. They lay their eggs in nests excavated in the sand, a safe distance above the waterline and shed a salty 'tear' afterwards. The eggs hatch about two months later. Incubation temperature deciding the sex; clutches are male around 24-26°C and female around 30-32°C, mixed when temperatures are in between. The 10-km stretch of Gahirmatha beach attracts the vastest numbers, but Rushikulya further south is the only place where it is permitted to observe this natural phenomenon. The nesting beach at Paradeep is long gone, a consequence of the development of Damra Port with its inevitable ship canals and bright lights that disorientate the juvenile turtles. But the biggest threat is the nets of the trawler boats, which sweep up anything in their path. Legislation prohibiting trawlers from near-shore waters is almost never implemented, and hundreds of thousands of turtles have met their deaths in the last 10 years. Organizations working to improve the situation include www.greenpeaceindia.org and www.atree.org.

Chandipur → *Colour map 6, A6.*

On the coast 16 km from Balashwar, Chandipur has one of Orissa's finest beaches. The tide recedes 5 km daily and the dunes and casuarina groves make it particularly attractive and a pleasant, quiet stopping place. When the tide is in scores of fisherfolk trawl for small fish along the coast. About 3 km north of the **Panthanivas Hotel** is the fishing harbour at **Balarama Gadi** where fresh fish can be bought daily. The occasional explosions that can be heard come from the missile testing site nearby, which is on the road to Baleshwar.

Mayurbhanj District → *For listings, see pages 797-799.*

The district is thickly forested with hills, waterfalls and streams and is home to abundant wildlife, which can best be seen at Simlipal National Park. There are prehistoric sites at Kuchai and Kuliana. The historic sites are Khiching, Baripada and Haripur, where the Bhanja rulers have left their mark. The area produces excellent tussar silk, carvings in multi-coloured translucent serpentine stone (from Khiching) and tribal metal casting of toys and cult images. The tribal people have enriched the culture of the district particularly with their traditional dances. Accommodation throughout the district is very basic.

Haripur → *16 km southeast of Baripada.*

Haripur was founded by Maharaja Harihar in 1400 as the capital of the Bhanja Dynasty. A later king built the magnificent **Rasikaraya Temple** which, though now in ruins, is a unique example of a brick-built Orissan temple. The area is still fascinating as it has several more historic buildings nearby. The ruins of Ranihamsapur, the inner apartment of the queen, is to the north of the courtyard while the remains of the Durbar Hall with its beautiful sculptured stone columns and arches is to the east. The brick **Radhamohan Temple** and 14th-century **Jagannath Temple** are interesting architecturally although the deities were moved and are now worshipped nearby in **Pratapapur**.

Baripada → *Colour map 6, A6.*

The district headquarters has a **museum** ⓘ *Tue-Sun 0700-1200 summer, 1000-1700 winter, closed holidays*, to the east of town with a small collection of stone sculpture, coins and inscriptions. **Chhau dance festival**, known as **Chaitra Parba**, is held in mid-April; the **Rath Yatra** in July is unique because the chariot carrying *Subhadra* is drawn by women. **Tourist office** ⓘ *Baghra Rd, near the bus stand, T06792-252710.* **Tiger Reserve Office** ⓘ *Bhanjpur (2 km), T06792-252593, simitig@dte.vsnl.net.in.*

Simlipal National Park → *Colour map 6, A6.*

ⓘ *320 km from Bhubaneswar, entry for day visitors 0600-1200; those with reservations 0600-1400. All must leave before sunset. Foreigners Rs 1000 per day, plus vehicle and trekking charge; camera Rs 100 for 3 days, video camera Rs 10,000 per day. Malaria prophylaxis is strongly recommended. Entry is from Pithabata, near Baripada (NH5), or Jashipur (NH6). Entry permits from the Range Officer, Pithabata Check Gate or the Assistant Conservator of Forests, Khairi, Jashipur, T06797-232474. Some tour operators in Bhubaneswar can make all the arrangements (eg Discover Tours) but need 4 weeks' notice – otherwise try for a permit on the day with a local agent (eg Ambika in Baripada). Best time to visit: Nov to Feb (park open 1 Nov-15 Jun); May to Jun can be very hot. Temperature, 45-50°C. Rainfall, 2000 mm.*

Simlipal is Orissa's principal wildlife sanctuary covering 2750 sq km at the heart of which is one of the country's earliest tiger reserves. The area has majestic sal forests interspersed with rosewood and flowering trees, as well as broad expanses of grassland, waterfalls, gorges and river valleys. The landscape is actually the main draw these days, as the core area to which visitors are permitted access is very small and consequently much trampled. Sightings of big beasts are rare, and many recent visitors have been disappointed.

The 42 species of animals include tiger (101), elephant (565), leopard (119), wolf, chital, sambar, deer, gaur and flying squirrel. There are over 230 species of birds including mynahs, parakeet and peacocks. Visitors are allowed to go to the waterfalls, the **Chahala woodland** and **Nawana Valley**, in the core area, on the dedicated forest road. The **Barehipani waterfall**, with a drop of 400 m, and the **Joranda Falls**, 150 m, are both very impressive as are the **Bachhurichara grassland** where you might see a herd of elephants and the 1158 m peak of Meghasani. However, most of the larger wildlife prefer to remain further inside the core area which does not allow visitors.

Open jeeps or Tata *sumos* (more comfortable, though enclosed) are the usual choice of vehicle inside the park (Rs 1200-1500 for up to five passengers). Jeep hire can be arranged through the Forest Office in Jashipur, **Baripada Tourist Office**, or **Ambika** in Baripada (see Sleeping, page 797) which can also arrange accommodation. Logging disturbance and dense vegetation make viewing difficult and is further hindered by visitors who ignore the signs asking for silence, and there is an increasing problem of litter in the park.

Khiching → *Colour map 6, A6. 20 km west of Joshipur along the NH6.*

The capital of the Bhanja rulers in the 10th to the 11th century, a visit to Khiching can be combined with an excursion to Simlipal from Chandipur. The local deity Kichakesvari, once the family goddess of the Mayurbhanj royal family, has a temple built entirely of chlorite slabs. The reconstructed 20th-century temple, which has fine carvings, is believed to have used the traditional temple building skills which date back to the eighth century. Nearby there are a number of other temples built in the Kalinga style, some of which are still in use.

The Northeast listings

For Sleeping and Eating price codes and other relevant information, see Essentials pages 38-42.

Sleeping

Cuttack *p792, map p792*

B Akbari Continental, Haripur Rd, Dolmundai, T0671-242 3251. 60 rooms, central a/c, hot bath with tubs, balconies view of garden obscured by ugly extension, inefficient reception, all a bit tatty for the price.

D-E Manorama Plaza, Mahatab Rd, T0671-233 1681. Most of the 54 clean and reasonable (standard doubles Rs 650), though small, some rooms have a/c. Restaurant, travel desk, bizarre birdsong doorbells.

E-G Ambica, Pilgrim Rd, College Sq, T0671-261 0137. Range of rooms from a/c to cheap singles with shared bath, clean and simple, friendly manager, vegetarian restaurant, close to railway. Breakfast and bed-tea included.

F-G Cuttack, College Rd, T0671-261 0766. Basic, but serviceable, some with bath.

G Railway Retiring Rooms. 4 rooms (1 a/c), cheap dorm.

Bhitarkanika Wildlife Sanctuary *p794*

D-E Aranyanivas, Chandbali, T06786-220397. Handy location for arranging visits to the sanctuary, this small and pleasant lodge (7 rooms) has garden surrounds and a decent cheap restaurant.

F Forest Lodges, Ekakula, Gupti and Dangamala. Reserve and pay in advance through the Divisional Forest Officer in Rajnagar, T06729-272460. Bring your own food supplies.

Baleshwar *p794*

C-D Torrento, Januganj, 4 km from centre near NH5, T06782-263482. 28 rooms, some a/c, good restaurant, exchange, health club.

E-F Swarnachuda, Sahadev Khunta (close to bus stand), T06782-262657. Range of rooms with bath, some a/c, all have TV, restaurant/bar.

G Railway Retiring Rooms. A/c and non a/c rooms, dorm.

Chandipur *p795*

Some hotels are reluctant to accept foreigners.

C-E Panthanivas (OTDC), on beach, T06782-270051, www.panthanivas.com. 41 rooms, some a/c, deluxe and some suites, nets, internet, decent food, helpful staff, newer block better, ample mosquitoes in old block nearer beach. Tours including Simlipal (minimum 10 people). Checkout 0800.

E-F Chandipur, T06782-270030. Small, simple rooms with attached bath, clean linen, nets.

Baripada *p796*

D-F Ambika, Roxy Rd, T06792-252557. 10 reasonable rooms, a/c Rs 1000, non a/c Rs 400, helpful staff, decent restaurant, tours of Simlipal, good value.

D-F Sibapriya, Traffic Sq, T06792-255138. 20 rooms, "best in town" but non a/c rooms grubby (Rs 400), a/c better, restaurant.

E-F Mahapatra, opposite bus stand, T06792-255226. Bit grubby, 8 simple rooms, some a/c, balconies overlook the bus stand.

F Ganesh Bhavan, Main Market, T06792-252784. 32 basic rooms, some with bath.

Simlipal National Park *p796*

E-D Aranyanivas (OTDC), at Lulung (3 km from Pithabata Gate), reserve at Baripada Tourist Office, T06792-252710, or www.panthanivas.com. 8 non-a/c double rooms, 2 dorms with 12 beds each (Rs 200), only restaurant inside park, completely run on solar power.

D-F Panthasala, outside the park area, 35 km from Baripada towards Jashipur, has 4 doubles. Reservations as for **Aranyanivas**.

E Forest Rest Houses, the booking process is complicated and all food should be taken with you. Most rooms have several beds and cost Rs 200-400 per head if full, otherwise it can work out to be expensive. Maximum stay is 3 nights. Those at **Chahala** (an old hunting lodge, 35 km from Jashipur), **Nomana** (60 km), **Joranda** (72 km) and **Barẹhpani** (with view of waterfall, 52 km) must be booked through Field Director, Simlipal Tiger Reserve Office, PO Bhanjpur, Baripada, 757002 Orissa, T06792-252593. Write enclosing an SAE (minimum 30 days, maximum 60 days before date of stay) and include names of group members, sex, age, nationality, visa/passport details. You will hear about method of advance payment. Rest houses at **Badampahar** (16 km from Jashipur), **Gudgudia** (25 km) and **Jamuani** (25 km), though not in the core area can be reserved in person up to 10 days in advance from DFO, Karanjia, Jashipur, T06796-220226. Reservation counter open daily 1000-1330.

Khiching *p796*

E-F Inspection Bungalow, contact Executive Engineer, PO Baripada.
E-F Revenue Rest Shed, PO Khiching, contact District Magistrate, PO Baripada.

Eating

Cuttack *p792, map p792*

Outside the better hotels there are few decent eateries. In the evenings street stalls set up around Buxi Bazar for cheap bites.
Temptations, near Buxi Bazar. Best ice creams in town, also reasonable pizzas.

Entertainment

Cuttack *p792, map p792*

You can try a makeshift pedalo on the Mahanadi River. **Mahanadi Boating Club** (2 men, a few chairs and an umbrella), on the Ring Rd, charges Rs 15 per person per 30 mins. Power boats cost Rs 550 per hr.

Shopping

Cuttack *p792, map p792*

Utkalika, Jail Rd. Very good selection of textiles and handicrafts including horn and brass objects and jewellery. The famous silver filigree shops are in **Nayasarak** and **Balu Bazar**.

Activities and tours

Cuttack *p792, map p792*

Club Travels, Mani Sahu Chowk, Buxi Bazar, T0671-230 4999.

Transport

Cuttack *p792, map p792*

Bus Long-distance buses stop at the bus stand in Link Rd. Services to all points in Orissa from the main bus stand in Badambari. Regular services to **Bhubaneswar**. Also state transport to major towns in **Andhra Pradesh**, **Chhattisgarh**, **Madhya Pradesh** and **West Bengal** (including Kolkata).

Taxi At the railway station and some hotels. Full-day trip to **Lalitgiri**, **Ratnagiri** and **Udayagiri** (excluding entrance fees), Rs 600-800, depending on bargaining skills.
Train East of town, Enquiries T131. **Bhubaneswar** and **Puri**: Several express and passenger trains, but timings can be unreliable, so quicker to take bus. **Chennai**: *Coromandal Exp 12841*, 2045, 20½ hrs; *Howrah Madras Mail 12839*, 0537, 22 hrs. **Kolkata (H)**: *Shatabdi 12074*, 0700, 6 hrs, except Sun; *Dhauli Exp 12822*, 1355, 6 hrs; *Coromandal Exp 12842*, 0530, 6½ hrs; *Falaknuma Exp 12704*, 1130, 6 hrs; *Jagannath Exp 18410*, 0050, 7½ hrs; *East Coast Exp 18646*, 0805, 8 hrs. **New Delhi**: *Purushottam Exp 12801*, 0010, 29 hrs. **Secunderabad**: *Falaknuma Exp 12703*, 1310, 20½ hrs; *East Coast Exp 18645*, 1900, 23 hrs.

Ratnagiri, Udayagiri and Lalitgiri *p793*

A day excursion from Cuttack or Bhubaneswar is possible by car (Rs 800). Get to Chandikhol on NH5 (43 km), with some roadside eating places, and turn right on NH5A (towards Paradeep) and then take the first turn left (at '12 km', before Patharajpur). Udayagiri is 1.5 km west of the road (8 km from NH5A) and Ratnagiri, 10 km further north. Return to the NH5A and continue towards Paradeep passing the Patharajpur **Panthasala** (Rest House) on the right. Turn right (south) at 20 km for Lalitgiri, 5 km away. Alternatively, buses from Cuttack stop at Chandikhol where you can hire a car for a 85-km return journey. Or take another bus to Patharajpur, hire a rickshaw and visit the first 2 sites.

Baleshwar *p794*

Bus The stand at Sahadevkhunta Rd has services to major towns, but few to **Chandipur**.
Train Written '**Balasore**' in timetables, the railway station is 500 m from bus stand, on the main Chennai–Kolkata line. There are frequent trains to **Bhubaneswar**: best is *Dhauli Exp 12821*, 0930, 3¼ hrs. **Chennai**: *Coromandel Exp 12841*, 1800, 23 hrs; *Howrah Madras Mail 12839*, 0300, 25 hrs. **Kolkata (H)**: *Shatabdi 12074*, 0915, 3½ hrs, except Sun; *Coromandel Exp 12842*, 0805, 4 hrs; *Falaknuma Exp 12704*, 1355, 4 hrs; *East Coast Exp 18646*, 1130, 4½ hrs. **New Delhi**: *Rajdhani Exp 12421*, 1410 (Wed, Sat, Sun), 20½ hrs; *Rajdhani Exp 12443*, 1217 (Mon, Tue,

Thu, Fri), 22½ hrs; *Purushottam Exp 12801*, 0235, 26 hrs. **Puri**: *Jagannath Exp 18409*, 2305, 5½ hrs; *Purushottam Exp 12802*, 0010, 5 hrs. **Secunderabad**: *Falaknuma Exp 2703*, 1035, 23 hrs; *East Coast Exp 18645*, 1605, 26 hrs.

Chandipur *p795*

There are only 4-5 buses per day to/from **Baleshwar** (20 km, with the nearest railhead). Ask at Panthanivas for approximate timings. Ask for Rs 250 for a taxi to/from **Baleshwar**.

Baripada *p796*

Private and government buses serve the region's main towns. You can hire a jeep to visit Simlipal. Ask at **Ambica** (see page 797) or tourist office. The nearest train stations are at Baleshwar (Balasore) and Tata Nagar.

Simlipal National Park *p796*

The road from Baripada is via Lulung, 30 km west, which has a regular bus service. The nearest train stations on the Southeastern Railways are at Tatanagar and Balasore.

Khiching *p796*

Regular buses from Baripada, 150 km. Nearest train station is 96 km away, but it is better to get down at Balasore, 210 km, which has a fast service on the Southeast Railway.

Directory

Cuttack *p792, map p792*

Banks State Bank of India, near High Court, with ATM. Forex on 1st floor. **Internet** Jail Rd next to cinema. Good connection, Rs 25 per hr. **Medical services** Christian Mission Hospital, recommended. Private clinics on Medical Rd.

Baleshwar *p794*

Banks State Bank of India, Branch, near ITT, 3 km from railway station; the only bank authorized to deal in foreign exchange between Cuttack and Kolkata.

Baripada *p796*

There is a district hospital, post office and shops selling local handicrafts and handloom. **Banks** Nearest is at Baleshwar. The Central Co-op Bank paints a list of its top 10 defaulters on the wall outside!

Western Orissa

Settled in ancient times, Ptolemy's text of the second century refers to this area as a diamond trading centre. In the eighth century King Indrabhuti became a Buddhist and a preacher of the Vajrayana sect.
▸▸ *For listings, see pages 803-806.*

Tribal areas → *For listings, see pages 803-806. Colour map 6, B3/4.*

Orissa's rich tribal heritage has survived among the hills and forests across the districts of Koraput, Kandhamal, Kalahandi, Ganjam, Keonjhar, Dhenkanal and Mayurbhanj (see page 764). The state government is actively promoting tourism in some of these areas, however, at the time of writing, only the southwestern areas were accessible due to disturbances between Hindus and Christians in northwest and central regions.

It is best to book a tour at least a month ahead to allow time to get permits to visit tribal territories. Without permits, tours are restricted to roadside villages where development programmes are already changing traditional values and in some cases the influx of tourism has created a disappointing 'circus' effect, with demands of money for photos, dances and sweets for the children. With permits and a guide, it is possible to visit the more isolated villages, do some trekking and spend nights camping in picturesque locations. Individual visitors face difficulties from the local police, so it is best to take a guide in any instance. Always seek out the village chief for permission to enter a village.

Photography is prohibited in Bondo and Dongariya territories. Permission should always be asked before taking photographs of tribal people. Respect their privacy should they decline. Walking around settlements with a video camera is not appreciated.

Transport is usually by car (a/c ups the tour price but is necessary during the hotter months) or jeep. Foreign exchange is only available in Sunubeda so it's best to change money in advance, although there are ATMs in larger towns.

Tribal markets

Typical 'social interest' tours offered by travel agents include a number of tribal villages with a chance to attend fascinating markets and witness 'cultural' dances. Some of the tribes seen in these areas include Dongariya Kondhs, Dhurubas, Parajas, Koyas, Bondos and Gadabas. In Koraput District, **Ramgiri**, 70 km southwest of Jeypore, has a picturesque Tuesday market where Kondh people come to sell fresh vegetables and baskets and to buy salt. **Chatikona** brings Kondh women to the colourful Wednesday market where they sell beedi leaves and large almond-flavoured seeds. **Ankadeli**, 70 km southwest of Jeypore, has a tourist-heavy Thursday market where Bondo women, clad entirely in bead, sell handloom fabric (Rs 200), lengths of coloured beads, metal jewellery (don't be tempted to purchase one of their antique neck-rings) and exquisite woven grass bracelets. The later you stay, the busier it gets. **Nandapur**, 44 km south of Koraput, has a huge Thursday *haat* where trading in livestock, saris, vegetables and the local alcohol takes place on either side of the National Highway. Jeypore (see page 801) in particular has some good accommodation. Sleeping and eating are also available at **Laxmipur**, **Rayagada** and **Baliguda** (see page 803).

Ganjam District → *For listings, see pages 803-806. Colour map 6, B5.*

Ganjam District, south of Chilika Lake, takes its name from the Persian *'Ganj – Am'*, meaning 'granary of the world' – a testimony to its agricultural fertility. Still largely covered in dense forest, it was settled in prehistoric times and came under the influence of Emperor Asoka's rule. The handicrafts of the region include brass and bell-metal ware, hornwork, wood carvings, silks and carpets.

Ganjam

Ganjam used to be the District Headquarters, but the administration was moved to Chatrapur because of its unhealthy location. Its chief interest is the small East India Company **fort** and a Christian **cemetery** at the north end of town, near a large factory between the main road and the sea. An interesting excursion inland takes you to **Aska** (52 km) and **Bhanjanagar** (85 km).

Berhampur

A trading centre for silk fabric, Berhampur is the district's major commercial town. The **Thakurani**, **Jagannath** and **Nilakanthesvar Siva temples** ⓘ *near DIG Residence, Tue-Sun 0700-1400 (summer), 1000-1700 (winter), closed government holidays*, are all worth visiting. Berhampur is also a good place to shop for silks. The **museum** has a collection of sculpture, anthropological and natural history specimens; no photos are permitted. **Tourist office** ⓘ *New Bus Stand, 1st floor, T0680-228 0226*. **Railway station counter** ⓘ *T0680-220 3870*.

Taptapani

Water from the very hot sulphur springs discovered at Taptapani in a forest setting, 50 km from Berhampur, is channelled to a pool for bathing. There is a shrine to goddess Kandhi inside the original *kund* (pool) as it is believed to cure infertility – tribal women come to the hot water pool near the **Panthanivas** hotel to try to pick up a seed pod from the mud at the bottom. Direct buses leave from Berhampur, 50 km away, and Bhubaneswar, 240 km away.

Chandragiri

In the tribal hills, 32 km south of Taptapani, Tibetan carpet weavers have settled in a refugee colony at Chandragiri. The temple and Buddhist prayer flags lend a distinctive atmosphere. You can watch weavers and craftsmen at work; good prices.

Jaugada → *35 km north of Berhampur.*

Jaugada in the Malati Hills is famous for one of Asoka's '**Kalinga Edicts**' (see Dhauli, page 776), which was discovered at the beginning of the 19th century, but the shelter was built only in 1975. Emperor Asoka's doctrine of conquest through love instead of the sword and his declaration "All men are my children" appears here. Sadly, some parts of the inscriptions have now disappeared. The old fort (circa sixth century) contains stone images of the five *Pandavas*, which are worshipped in the Guptesvar Temple. Jaugada is reached by a jeep road from Purusottampur which has buses from Berhampur.

Buguda, a few kilometres away, has the Viranchinarayan Temple with its beautifully carved wooden *Jagamohan* and murals depicting stories from the epic *Ramayana*. Also, close by, **Buddhakhol** has Buddhist sculptures as well as shrines to Siva.

Koraput District → *For listings, see pages 803-806. Colour map 6, B3/4.*

Jeypore

Jeypore itself is unspoilt by tourism and is surrounded by incredibly beautiful scenery. There is a derelict fort and palace, to which entrance is sadly forbidden, and an interesting market that is bustling until 2200. A good range of accommodation and friendly locals make it an excellent base for a few days. It is possible to organize your own tour from Jeypore and reportedly easier to get permits to visit tribal areas in Koraput rather than in Bhubaneswar. Most people stay in Jeypore on Wednesdays in order to visit **Ankadeli market** the next morning; it's a glorious 75-km drive through the rolling hills, past brown rivers and glassy reservoirs. One of the world's oldest terracing systems creeps up the shallow valleys between hills wooded with cashew and mango trees, the undergrowth thick with coffee and black pepper plants. Tribal women working in the paddies add splashes of colour to a landscape already made vibrant by emerald and gold crops against the tangerine earth.

Koraput

Koraput is another useful base for visiting the tribal areas. **Orissa Tourism** ⓘ *Raipur-Visakhapatnam Rd, T06852-250318, Mon-Sat 1000-1700*, can help arrange car hire. The elevated **Jagannath Temple** admits non-Hindus (unlike the temple in Puri) and is an interesting place to lunch (see Eating, page 805). Note the painting ceilings inside the main building. Further up the hill, there is a worthwhile **Tribal Museum** ⓘ *daily 1000-2130, donation*, where you can purchase the *Tribes of Koraput* booklet (Rs 90), which is a valuable introduction to the region. Displays include tribal jewellery, weaving, cultivation methods and some illuminating maps of the area. The **Orissa Coffee Planters' Association**, around 20 km from Koraput, is happy to show visitors around the plantation which has fruits and spices as well as coffee.

Kotapad → *46 km northwest of Jeypore on N43.*

The clean area of weavers' houses in Kotapad has large pots of cotton and tussore silk soaking in natural dyes, while skeins hang drying. Weavers are happy to show you work in progress. The Co-op ensures even pricing; a 3-m shawl costs Rs 350-600. It is worth seeking out award winner Jagabandhu Samarth. As the word gets around that there are visitors in town, weavers will find you to show their pieces but there is no pressure to buy.

Sambalpur and around → *Colour map 6, A5.*

Sambalpur is a pleasant, small town with a number of decent hotels and a few restaurants grouped in the centre. The presiding deity Samalesvari, to whom a temple was built here by the Chauhans in the mid-16th century, probably accounts for the town's name. The district is famous for its textiles, particularly its tie-dye ikat work. **Orissa Tourism** ⓘ *Panthanivas, T0663-241 1118*, has helpful staff and can help plan excursions. **Railway counter** ⓘ *Khetrajpur, T0663-252 1661*. Tours are often cancelled due to lack of passengers.

The villages and the countryside are pleasant in themselves and you might consider visiting **Baragarh**, 1½ hours, and **Barpali**, three hours' drive, with a guide, if you are interested in weaving. **Sonepur**, a lively small town with a colourful market square and temple, is particularly rewarding. A scenic road from Sambalpur along the Mahanadi River ends in a footpath down across the wide sandbank over half the river in the dry season. Small boats ferry passengers across the remainder.

Debjharan Sanctuary has been recently created and developed as a picnic spot in forest situated 35 km south of Sambalpur, 5 km east of the NH6. There is a small waterfall and a dam with waterhole at Chaura Asi Mal and a Forest Rest House. Taxis from Sambalpur cost Rs 800 for a return day trip.

Ushakothi Wildlife Sanctuary → *Colour map 6, A5. 48 km east of Sambalpur on the NH6.*

Ushakothi is densely forested and covers 130 sq km. The sanctuary has wild elephant, leopard, tiger, bison, wild boar and chital (barking deer). The best time to visit is from November to June, at night. Take a guide with search lights and see the wildlife from the watchtowers sited near watering points to which the animals come. Open hooded jeeps are recommended. Permits to visit, and guides, can be obtained from the Forest Range Officer, PO Badrama. The **Forest Rest House**, Badrama, 3 km away, is very basic with no electricity.

Hirakud Dam → *Colour map 6, A4.*

The Mahanadi created enormous problems every year through devastating floods of the delta region and in order to combat these the Hirakud Dam was built about 20 km northwest of Sambalpur. The key section is a 1100-m-long masonry dam, with a further earth dam of over

3500 m. One of the longest mainstream dams in the world, it is over 60 m high and drains an area twice the size of Sri Lanka. Since its completion in 1957 there have been no serious floods in the Mahanadi delta and it allows the irrigation of vast areas of high-quality land. You get an excellent view from the revolving tower, Gandhi Minar, at one end of the dam. Contact the Deputy Superintendent of Police, Security Force, Hirakud before visiting. There are regular buses from Sambalpur.

Debrigarh Wildlife Sanctuary

This sanctuary adjoins Hirakud Lake, around 50 km from Sambalpur. With an area of 347 sq km, the dry deciduous forest is home to tiger, leopard, sloth bear, chital, sambar, nilgai and a number of resident and migratory birds. Muggar crocodiles and freshwater turtles are among the reptiles present. Entry to the sanctuary is at Dhodrokusum, with a watchtower at Pathedurga. There are basic **Forest Rest Houses** at Dhodrokusum and Dechua, or a **Tourist Cottage** at Chaurasimal. The best season to visit is from October to May. For permission and guides, contact DFO (Wildlife), Motijharan, T0663-240 2741. For information contact Chief Wildlife Warden (Orissa), Bhubaneswar, cwlwob@hotmail.com.

Huma → *About 32 km south of Sambalpur.*

Huma has a famous **Leaning Temple**, on the bank of the Mahanadi, dedicated to Lord Siva. The temple leans southwards but the pinnacle is vertical. The colourful Kudo fish, which are easily seen from January to June, are believed to belong to Siva so are never caught by fishermen; visitors may feed them grain. Country boats are available for hire. There are regular buses from Sambalpur to Huma Chowk, then walk 2 km to the temple.

Sundargarh District

To the north of Sambalpur is Sundargarh District. In the tribal heartland, it is an area of undulating hills with the richest deposits of mineral wealth in the state. Cave paintings are evidence of the existence of early man. Once relatively untouched by modern civilization, the district was chosen for the siting of the first public sector steel plant at Rourkela. The route from Sambalpur to Rourkela runs north, 192 km, passing through some glorious scenery. The Brahmani flows along a wide rocky and sandy bed, a torrent in the monsoon, with forested hills on either side. A large industrial town girdled by a range of hills and encircled by rivers, **Rourkela** has a major steel plant and fertilizer complex, both of which may be visited with permission from the PRO. There are banks, post offices, shops and hospitals.

Western Orissa listings

For Sleeping and Eating price codes and other relevant information, see Essentials pages 38-42.

Sleeping

Tribal areas *p800*

Laxmipur

F Hotel Konark, green building by Ambedkar Chowk. Good *thalis*, friendly young English-speaking owner. Decent lunch stop.

Rayagada

D-E Hotel Sai International, JK Rd, T06856-225554/5. The best rooms around, but on a limb on the edge of town. Multi-cuisine restaurant is nothing special, but there's a bar and travel desk that can help with car rental. Non-a/c rooms are Rs 700 and have hot water by the bucket, or Rs 1200 for a room with geyser and a/c. Staff are well meaning but a little confused.

E-F Jyoti Mahal, Convent Rd, T06856-223015. Decent and friendly, 25 reasonably sized rooms with bath, good restaurant, non-a/c rooms are great value.

F Swagath, New Colony, T06856-222208. 44 clean rooms, good local-style restaurant.

Baliguda

Baliguda is basically a one-street town, a quiet, friendly place with a slow pace of life.

F-G Santosh, off Main Rd. 16 rooms, best on the 1st floor with attached bath.

Berhampur *p801*

Few visitors stay overnight. However, if arriving late, the following are adequate:

D-F Kameswari, close to railway station on Station Rd, T0680-221 1283, radhahotelbam@rediffmail.com. 28 rooms, 7 a/c.

E-F Hotel Radha, near the Old Bus Stand, T0680-222 2341. Some a/c in the 45 rooms (Rs 650) or non-a/c Rs 350 per double.

F Udipi, near the Old Bus Stand, T0680-222 2196. Little English spoken.

G Puspa, Gatekeeper's Sq, 1.5 km from the New Bus Stand, T0680-222 1117. Very basic (as the Rs 140 per double price tag indicates).

Taptapani *p801*

B-E Tourist Lodge, Padamari, T06816-255031. For breaking the journey in a place where there's literally nothing to do but relax, this is ideal. Variety of simple accommodation – 12 rooms, 5 tents, log cabins and a treehouse furnished entirely from woven reeds. The 2 de luxe suites in the main cottage have gigantic wet rooms and, although the Roman baths aren't that appealing, the low-lit barn-like rooms are tastefully so. **Hillview Restaurant** is OK, breakfast included. Irritating 0800 checkout.

Jeypore *p801*

B-E Hello Jeypore, East Octroi Check Post, NH43, 2 km from centre, T06854-231127, www.hotelhellojeypore.com. Comfortable, well-furnished a/c rooms some overlooking garden (roadside is noisy) starting from Rs 995 per double. Hot power shower, TV, efficient service, restaurant or dinner in the garden (try *alu raita*, veg much better than non-veg, plenty of Chinese). Smoky blue-lit bar gets busy or drinks on the lawn at reasonable prices. Of the mid-range options it has the best atmosphere in town. They also have some **A** suites.

D-E Mani Krishna, MG Rd, T/F06854-231139, www.hotelmanikrishna.com. Modern a/c rooms are spacious and nicely fitted-out, also non-a/c, all with balconies some of which see the sunset over the ramshackle roofs of Jeypore. Bathrooms are the best in town, good management, but lacking any character or space to relax. Restaurant and alcohol via room service.

D-E Sai Krishna, MG Rd, T06854-230253/5, www.hotelsaikrishna.com. Next door to the Mani, in the same tall mirrored edifice, and not much to choose between the 2 although non-a/c here are cheaper, starting from Rs 595. There's a bar and restaurant, underground car park, and eager staff. Central location is good for exploring town.

F-G Madhumati, NKT Rd, T06854-241377, hotelmadhumati@yahoo.com. 30 large rooms (being renovated), some a/c but non-a/c are a bargain, TV, mosquitoes, hot water, good restaurant, bar only has strong beer, very helpful manager. Attractive location next to the palace. Definitely the best budget choice in town.

G Shankar Hotel, Main Rd, T06854-233150. Basic grim doubles, the de luxe ones get booked out quickly, some cheap rooms (Rs 100) with common bath (but "not for ladies"), noisy yet friendly.

Koraput *p802*

F-G Athithi Bhavan, Gundicha Chowk, T06852-250610. At the base of the temple and managed by the Jagannath Temple Trust, non-a/c and a/c rooms with bath have TV and are clean and attractively painted with faux chalk designs on terracotta. The whole building is light and airy and characterful. Temple *thalis* available in the restaurant.

G Ambica Heavens, T06852-251136. Bearable rooms with bath, TV, quieter at back.

Sambalpur *p802*

D Sheela Towers, VSS Marg, T0663-240 3111. The 41 smallish rooms are clean and comfortable, all have a/c and TV, 2 restaurants.

D-F Panthanivas (OTDC), Brook's Hill, end of VSS Marg, T0663-241 1282, www.panthanivas.com. Despite all having balconies, few of the 34 rooms (clean linen, 12 a/c with TV) have decent views. Restaurant, bar. Checkout 0800.

D-F Saket, T0663-240 2345. Some a/c in 30 decent, clean rooms with hot bath, TV, restaurant.

D-F Uphar Palace, T0663-240 0519. 29 good clean rooms with bath, some a/c, TV, 2 restaurants (good South Indian).
E-G Uphar, T0663-240 3078. Slightly cheaper sister concern of **Uphar Palace**.
F-G Rani Lodge, next to **Uphar Palace**, T0663-252 2173. Clean, simple rooms with bath, nets, early-morning mosque noise.

Hirakud Dam *p802*
E Ashok Nivas. Good guesthouse.

Sundagarh District *p803*
B Radhika, Bisra Rd, opposite railway station, Rourkela, T0661-251 0300. Clean, a/c, 60 large rooms, helpful staff.
D-F Panthanivas (OTDC), Sector 5, 2 km from Rourkela, T0661-264 3280, www.panthanivas.com. 31 rooms, some a/c or good value non-a/c for Rs 450, restaurant/bar. Checkout 0800.

Eating

Jeypore *p801*
There are also restaurants in the hotels listed, as well as plenty as pure veg eateries close to the bus station on Main Rd.
Aroma, Hello Jeypore Hotel (see Sleeping). The restaurant is quiet and a/c but shame about the huge projector screen dominating the otherwise lovely lawn.
Bhagwan Restaurant, MG Rd, T06854-232616, above Lokesh Parlour. Open 1030-1500 and 1800-2230. Standard veg (Rs 30-70) and non-veg (Rs 70-120) Indian meals, conveniently located in the centre of town near the main market.

Koraput *p802*
Jagannath Temple. Serves a filling and tasty *thali* and is popular with families. Make a donation of Rs 25 on entering the temple then join the queues. Meals eaten off leaves with the hands cross-legged on the stone floor.
Jungle Restaurant, at the Tribal Museum. Open till 2200. Has cheap offerings on a shady patio surrounded by foliage.

Activities and tours

Jeypore *p801*
Discover Tours (see page 778) and **Grass Routes** (see page 790) are recommended.
Perfect Travels, Rajmahal Chowk, T06854-242 1856. Car and driver, Rs 1200 per day.
Travel Care, Sardar Patel Marg, T06854-2422291. For tours write to Mr Pujari 4-6 weeks in advance with a photocopy of the relevant passport pages.

Sambalpur *p802*
Providing jeeps and taxis for sightseeing: **Nalini Travels**, Buddharaja, near flyover; **Swati Travels**, near Ashoka Talkies.

Transport

Berhampur *p801*
Bus The Old and New Bus Stands are about 3 km from the railway station, 2 km from each other. Government buses use the **Old Bus Stand**, private buses (which are more regular and reliable) the **New Bus Stand** and cover major towns in Orissa and neighbouring states. Several buses to **Bhubaneswar** a day, Rs 80, 4 hrs on a good road.

Train Berhampur, sometimes referred to as **Brahmapur** in timetables, is on the main Chennai–Kolkata line, enquiries T131. **Chennai**: *Coromandel Exp 12841*, 0005, 17 hrs; *Howrah Madras Mail 12839*, 0905, 19 hrs. **Kolkata (H)** via **Bhubaneswar**: *Coromandel Exp 12842*, 0200, 10 hrs; *Falaknuma Exp 12704*, 0755, 10 hrs; *East Coast Exp 18646*,, 0430, 11½ hrs. **Secunderabad**: *Falaknuma Exp 12703*, 1635, 17 hrs; *Konark Exp 11020*, 1755, 18 hrs; *East Coast Exp 18645*, 2250, 19 hrs; *Visakha Exp 17015*, 1105, 20½ hrs.

Jeypore *p801*
Bus Government buses, T06854-233181, 0700-2200, run to nearby cities, you can book tickets in advance (a good idea if wanting to travel by more comfortable high-tech rather than ordinary service). Frequent bus service to **Koraput** between 0400-2300 (1 hr, Rs 15). Also 5 buses per day to **Sambalpur** (15 hrs, Rs 300), **Bhubaneswar** (20 hrs, a/c Rs 410, non-a/c Rs 300) and **Visakhapatanam** (6 hrs, a/c Rs 140). Buses leave from next to the government stand, T(0)9437-373180, and go to neighbouring villages, enquire about times. For **Ankedelli market** a bus leaves at 0700, returning 1400. Private buses also to **Bhubaneswar** (1800,

Rs 330), **Raipur** (1900, 2000, 2100, Rs 280) and **Berhampur** (1830, 1930, Rs 170-200).

Car If travelling by car from the coast, make sure the car can manage the hill roads and the driver isn't worried about entering tribal areas.

Train The train station is 7 km away. A daily train connects with **Vishakhapatnam**. From **Vizag**, *Kirandol Exp*, 0745, 8 hrs. Superb views for first 3 hrs uphill then down to Araku Valley; 2nd class is full of firewood and farm produce and best avoided. From the north, travel to Vizianagaram station, and then by bus or taxi.

Koraput *p802*

Koraput has more passenger trains connecting it than Jeypore, which is mainly used for goods and mineral transportation. Trains to **Bhubaneswar**: *Hirakhand Exp 18448*, 1825, 14 hrs. From Bhubaneswar, *Hirakhand Exp 18447*, 1935, 14 hrs. **Kolkata (H)**: *Koraput Howrah Exp 18006*, 0645, 24 hrs, via **Sambalpur**, 11 hrs.

Sambalpur *p802*

Bus Sambalpur has 2 bus stands, one for government buses, the other for private buses near Laxmi Talkies. Both are within a short cycle-rickshaw ride from VSS Marg, though the latter has more regular services to major towns in the area.

Jeep/taxi Jeep/taxi hire is the easiest way to visit wildlife sanctuaries. Contact the tourist office for tours. Return jeeps to **Debjharan**, Rs 300-400; to **Ushakothi** (1600-0400), Rs 500.

Train There are 2 stations: Sambalpur and Sambalpur Rd, both 2-3 km from hotels on VSS Marg. **Kolkata (H)**: *Koraput Howrah Exp 18006*, 1815, 12 hrs. **Puri** (via **Bhubaneswar**): *Tapaswini Exp 18451*, 2240, 8½ hrs (6½ hrs).

Sundagarh District *p803*

Bus Rourkela's **New Bus Stand** is in walking distance of Bisra Rd hotels; turn right and right again. Buses to all major destinations.

Train Rourkela's train station is a minute's walk from Bisra Rd and hotels. **Kolkata (H)**: *Howrah Maiil 12809*, 2310, 7 hrs; *Azad Hind Exp 12129*, 2125, 6½ hrs. **Mumbai (CST)**: *Gitanjali Exp 12860*, 2010, 25 hrs. **Patna**: *South Bihar Link Exp 13287*, 1530, 15 hrs. **Puri** via **Bhubaneswar** (all stop at Balasore and Cuttack): *Tapaswini Exp 18451*, 1920, 12 hrs (9½ hrs).

Directory

Berhampur *p801*

There is a **Christian Mission Hospital**, post offices and shops. **Bank** **State Bank of India**, Main Branch, State Bank Rd, has ATM.

Jeypore *p801*

Bank **State Bank of India**, has ATM at Main Road branch, and behind the Private Bus Stand. **Internet** **SJRM**, Main Rd (opposite the government hospital), daily 0900-1400 and 1500-2200, speedy connection and new computers, Rs 15 per hr. Other internet places are dotted around town, including opposite the Hotel Madhumati. **Post** Main Rd.

Koraput *p802*

Bank **State Bank of India**, has ATMs by the bus and railway stations.

Sambalpur *p802*

Bank **State Bank of India**, near Collectorate, for foreign exchange. **Post** **Main post office**, near Collectorate. Several internet cafés on VSS Marg, Rs 20-25 per hr.

Bihar & Jharkhand

Contents

Footprint features

Border crossings

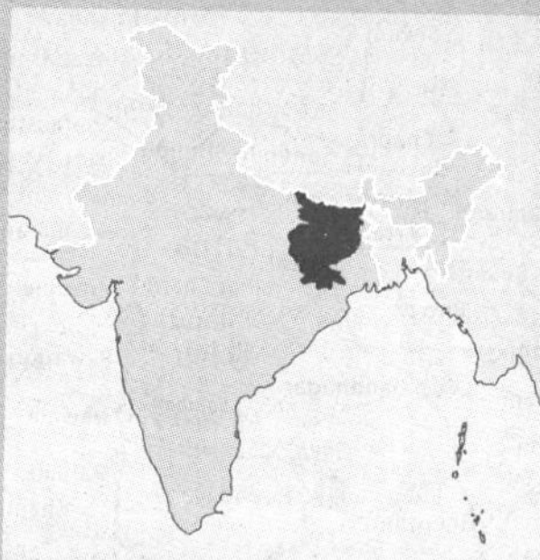

At a glance

Getting around Be ultra-aware of your personal safety: kidnappings, robberies and highway hold-ups are by no means rare. Book a/c accommodation on trains, and restrict road travel to daylight hours.

Time required Allow 4-5 days to see Bodhgaya, Nalanda and Rajgir.

Weather Hot and sticky during summer. Best between Oct and Mar, with warm days and cool nights.

When not to go The height of summer can be punishingly hot.

★ **Don't miss ...**

1. Quila House in Patna where time stands still, page 815.
2. Sonepur Cattle Fair in November, page 815.
3. The ruins at Nalanda, page 819.
4. Bodhgaya, one of the holiest Buddhist pilgrimage centres, page 823.
5. Sher Shah's mausoleum, page 825.
6. Sunrise from Parsnath Hill, page 830.

Bihar, which takes its name from the word *vihara* (monastery), was the early home of Buddhism and the birthplace of one of India's most revered emperors, Asoka. His Buddhist legacy has left its imprint in some of the state's most visited pilgrimage sites, for while it may be on the outskirts of modern Patna, Kumrahar still has fragmentary remains of the early Mauryan capital; in Bodhgaya and Nalanda, Buddhism's tradition is powerfully visible.

After the creation of the new state of Jharkhand, modern Bihar is confined to the densely populated, and desperately poor, Ganges plains. The state has a chequered recent political history. Separated from Bengal in 1912, in 1936 another partition led to the creation of Orissa. After Independence the reorganization of Indian states saw the transfer of territory from Bihar to West Bengal, while the tribal groups had already begun to campaign for a separate state for the tribal areas of the Chota Nagpur Plateau in South Bihar. On 15 November 2000 this dream was finally achieved with the division of Bihar into two: the mineral-rich Chota Nagpur plateau becoming the new state of Jharkhand.

In recent years Bihar in particular has acquired an unfortunate, now almost proverbial, reputation for crime and banditry. Travellers intending to visit or travel through should be aware that this is one of India's poorest regions, and should strictly avoid travelling by night on rural roads. Nevertheless, most travellers who adopt the necessary precautions emerge unscathed.

Background → *Population: Bihar 90 million, Jharkhand 26.9 million. Area: Bihar 174,000 sq km, Jharkhand 80,000 sq km.*

The land

Bihar and Jharkhand form a region of transition. The wet lowlands to the east give way to the much drier and now more prosperous alluvial plains to the west. From north to south, the two states stretch 600 km from the foothills of the Himalaya across the flat plains to the forested and mineral-rich hills of Chota Nagpur. The River Ganga runs through the heart of the plains, joined by its tributaries from the Nepalese Himalaya to the north and from the Vindhyan Hills to the south. North of the Ganga are the scars of old river beds, which often form chains of lakes during the monsoon and provide a vital source of fish. North Bihar is India's biggest producer of freshwater fish, over half of which is sold in Kolkata. Torrential rain in the Himalayan foothills and the flatness of the Ganga valley floor cause some of the rivers, like the Kosi, to flood catastrophically. Over a period of 130 years the Kosi has moved over 110 km westwards.

History

The name Bihar is derived from *vihara* (monastery), suggesting its wealth of religious monuments. All the major religions of India have left a mark, most notably Buddhism and Jainism. The world's first university of Buddhist learning was founded at Nalanda. Bihar was settled from the west as Aryan tribes moved down the Ganga valley, clearing the forest and developing cultivation. Agriculture provided the base for the Magadhan kings who ruled from the sixth to the fourth centuries BC. The early Magadhan kings had their capital at **Rajgir**, 100 km southeast of modern Patna. It was surrounded by 40 km of stone walls which can still be seen. Later they moved their capital to **Pataliputra**, the site of modern Patna.

The Guptas, who played a central role in the flowering of Hindu culture of the classical period, rescued Magadha in the fourth to fifth centuries AD from more than 600 years of obscurity. They were followed by the Palas of Bengal who ruled until defeated by the Muslims in 1197. The Delhi sultans and a succession of independent Muslim rulers controlled the region until the arrival of the Mughals who retained it until the British won the Battle of Buxar in 1764. Subsequently Bihar was separated from Bengal and became a province under British rule until India's Independence in 1947.

Culture

There is a sharp division between the agricultural plains of north Bihar, with three-quarters of the combined population total, and the Chota Nagpur plateau to the south. The plains are peopled largely by Hindus but five centuries of Muslim political dominance have resulted in a significant Muslim population (16% today). Aboriginal **tribal peoples** dominate Jharkhand, including Santal, Oraon, Munda, Kharia and Ho tribes. Some groups, notably the Munda, have converted to Christianity in large numbers; however, the majority still follow tribal religions such as Sarna or have adopted Hinduism. Hindi is dominant throughout the plains, with related dialects spoken elsewhere (eg Maithili, Bhojpuri, Magahi). Urdu is spoken by many Muslims, and tribal languages by nearly 10% of the population (eg Austro-Asiatic Santali and Dravidian Oraon).

Festivals

In **March Holi**, is celebrated with much fervour with festivities lasting two days, during which a public holiday is observed by businesses. **April/May** is **Buddha Jayanti**, celebrating the Buddha's birth, when Bodhgaya and Rajgir attract Buddhists from all over the world, while **Mahavira Jayanti** brings Jains to the sacred Parsnath Hill. In **June** a 14-day **marriage market** takes place in a mango grove in Saurath where the nation's Mithila Brahmins gather. **October/November** has **Pataliputra Festival** starting with **Dasara** in October and ends with the **Sonepur Fair** in November, one of Asia's most remarkable cattle fairs. **Durga puja, Dasara** and

Bihar's plains: gift of the Himalaya?

Severe flooding of Bihar's rivers has prompted some environmentalists to blame deforestation in Nepal. A rising population, commercial logging and bad agricultural practices have been held responsible for widespread damage on Bihar's plains. But recent research sheds doubt on this simple cause and effect. The River Kosi has been shifting its course for decades, and floods have for centuries washed down Himalayan silt, without which the plains would not exist. A protective embankment along the southern flank of the Himalaya was built in 1960 to limit the flooding and westward movement of the river, and to protect agricultural land. Attempts to control the Kosi by building dams in Nepal are still under consideration, but the huge amounts of silt, plus the fact that the Himalayan foothills are a zone of major earthquakes, makes projects extremely difficult to implement effectively. To add to the problem, when the Ganga is in full flow it rises higher than the tributaries which join it from the south, so it is also subject to severe floods between July and October.

Diwali are celebrated. **Chhath** or **Surya Puja** takes place six days after Diwali. To mark the harvest, fresh paddy, sweets and fruit are offered by devotees in procession; women, waist deep in the Ganga, offer homage at sunrise and sunset.

Food and drink

The typical Bihari meal consists of rice, unleavened bread, lentils and vegetables cooked with hot spices. *Sattoo*, a grain mix, is made into a dough and eaten as a savoury, or sweetened with sugar or jaggery. The mixture can also be taken as a drink with milk or water and flavoured with cardamoms and cloves. *Puri-aloo*, deep fried Indian bread with potatoes cooked with onions and garlic, and *kachoris*, made with wheat and lentil flour and then served with *kala chana* (black gram), are delicious snacks. Unfortunately, the average roadside *dhaba* serves up very disappointing food, so make the most of sit-down restaurants in the larger towns.

Modern Bihar

From its pre-eminent position in the culture and politics of early and classical India, Bihar has declined to one of India's poorest and most badly administered states. There are periodic outbreaks of violence in the countryside and it has had one of the most troubled political administrations of modern India. Successive governments have been charged with corruption and it is still widely regarded across India as the most lawless state in the country.

For 15 years, since the mid-1990s, the state government was run by ex-railways minister Laloo Prasad Yadav and his wife Rabri Devi, at the head of their Rabri Janata Dal (RJD) Party. They have been accused by some of stripping the state of its wealth and promoting caste-based leadership. Despite a strong core of support, the RJD lost the re-run November 2005 election, being ousted by the Janata Dal (United)-BJP coalition. Nitish Kumar, who is seen as promoting development ahead of caste, was sworn in as chief minister. The 2009 Lok Sabha elections confirmed the dominance of the JDU-BJP coalition, the JDU winning 20 and the BJP 12 of Bihar's 40 seats, with Nitish Kumar being re-elected.

Patna

→ *Colour map 3, B5. Population: 1.4 million.*

Bihar's straggling capital, Patna, has the air of a semi-rural provincial town in its more attractive areas, despite its size. It is one of India's poorest cities, stretching along the south bank of the Ganga for about 15 km. Divided in two by the large open Maidan, to the west are many administrative buildings of the British and to the east lies the chaotic old Chowk area. The central city is crowded and dusty; scant evidence remains of its earlier wealth and political supremacy. However, the new Buddha Smriti Park by the station, illuminated at night, is a sign of regeneration in the city. It is be interesting to take a cycle-rickshaw round by day or night. Many tribal people come into the town, often working on roads or building sites. ▸▸ *For listings, see pages 817-818.*

Ins and outs

Getting there and around Patna airport, 7 km west of the centre, has coaches and taxis for the transfer into town. State buses arrive at Gandhi Maidan Bus Stand, 15-25 minutes' walk from most budget hotels. These are strung out along Fraser Road towards Patna Junction railway station. Chaotic Mithapur Bus Stand (with private buses serving Gaya, Bodhgaya, Varanasi and Nepal) is located 2.5 km from Junction station; autos (Rs 5) run between the two. The centre is compact enough to walk around, though shared rickshaws are available along all routes. Hire an unmetered taxi from major hotels for longer trips. ▸▸ *See Transport, page 818.*

Patna City

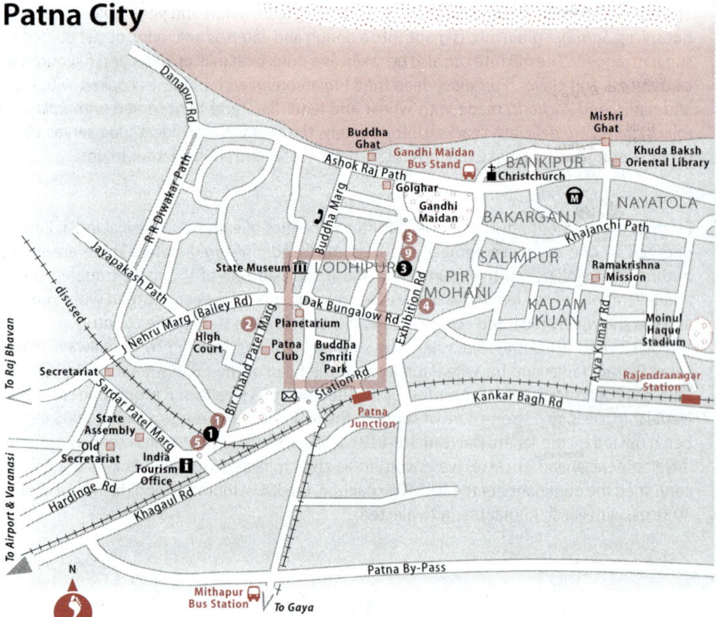

1 km
1 mile

Sleeping
Chanyaka **5**
Kautiliya Vihar & Tourist Office **1**
Maurya & Spice Court Restaurant **3**
Mayur **6**
Patliputra Ashok **2**
Rajasthan **7**

Tourist information India Tourism ⓘ *Kranti Marg (near PNT Club), R Block, T0612-250 6032. Mon-Fri 0930-1800*, provides excellent service from their brand new office on the first floor. Nearby BSTDC ⓘ *Hotel Kautilya Vihar, Bir Chand Patel Marg, T0612-250 6219, Mon-Sat 1000-1700* can help with car hire for day trips (minimum Rs 1300, 200 km, Rs 6.5 per km thereafter), also has counters at the airport and Patna Junction Railway Station. ITDC ⓘ *Pataliputra Ashok, T0612-222 6270*, can also help with car hire. Tourism Department ⓘ *Government of Bihar, 9D Hutment, Secretariat, T/F0612-222 4531.*

History

At the confluence of the rivers Son, Punpun, Gandak and Ganga, Patna's history can be traced back 2500 years. Ajatasatru, the second Magadha king who ruled from Rajgir, built a small fort at Pataligrama. Later Chandragupta Maurya founded the Mauryan Empire with Pataliputra as its capital. Buddhist histories suggest that it was here that Asoka usurped the throne of his father, Bindusara, murdering all his rivals and starting a reign of terror, before a conversion eight years later. It marked the beginning of perhaps the greatest reforming kingship the world has known. The Greek ambassador Megasthenes was deeply impressed by the efficiency of the Chandragupta administration and the splendour of the city. Ruins can be seen at Kumrahar, Bhiknapahari and Bulandhi Bagh with its 75 m wooden passage. Excavations date the site back to the pre-Mauryan times of 600 BC. In the 16th century the Pathan Sher Shah Suri established the foundations of a new Patna, building a majestic mosque in 1540 which dominates the skyline.

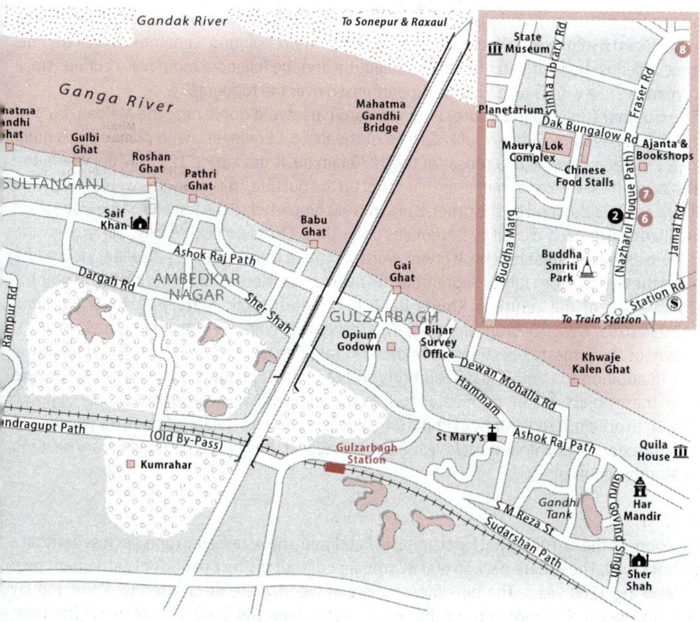

Republic **4**
Sheodar **8**
Youth Hostel **9**

Eating
Armpali Café **1**
Bansi Vihar **2**
Garden Court Club **3**

Sights

Patna's buildings reflect its administrative and educational functions. The Collectorate, Court and educational institutions are all in the western part of the city, along with the Raj Bhavan, the High Court and the better residential areas (Sinha Library Rd, near the State Musuem, has a fine collection of old bungalows). To the east is Old Patna with its bazars, godowns, old mosques, Har Mandir and St Mary's Church.

The central area

The restful **Buddha Smriti Park** ⓘ *Fraser Rd, Tue-Sun 0900-1300 and 1600-1900, Rs 10, leave bags at the entrance*, opened in March 2011. The central *stupa* and surrounding buildings are fashioned from modernist slabs of grey stone; water features, grass, a meditation hall and Bo trees planted by the Buddhist countries of the world make it one of the city's most peaceful spots.

The glorious facade of the **State Museum** ⓘ *Buddha Marg, Tue-Sun 1030-1600, entrance a shocking Rs 250, or Rs 500 to also see the relics of the Buddha*, houses a collection of exquisite stone sculptures, including the famous (and very voluptuous) life-size Didarganj Yakshi (Mauryan period) and the oldest known Jain image, a smoothed torso dating from the 3rd century BC). Noteworthy is a carving showing the birth of Buddha and a realistic image of a turbaned Buddha from Afghanistan (first century AD). Also on the ground floor is a gallery of moth-eaten stuffed animals and 'freaks of nature'. The first floor galleries are better lit with one of the most extensive collections *thangkas* outside of Tibet. Some random tribal artefacts (from throughout India) are worth a look, and a gallery displays a wealth of bronze statuary including some ancient naked Jain figurines. The miniature paintings include works on ivory and Patna Kalam paintings, which were commissioned by Company officials at the time when court-painting went into its final decline. Further galleries show artefacts found at Pataliputra and the Rajendra room has a curious small ivory map of India with Queen Victoria superimposed over the topography.

The **Golghar** (*Gola*, round house) is an extraordinary ovoid dome near the Maidan, built of stone slabs in 1786 by Captain John Garstin of the Bengal Engineers, who planned this grain store for the army in case of a repeat of the 1770 famine. It has a base 125 m wide, where the wall is 3.6 m thick, with two staircases that spiral up the outside; the workforce were to carry the grain up one and descend by the other. It was never completed so the last line of the inscription "First filled and publicly closed by ..." remains unfinished. Occasionally, it is possible to go inside and listen to the remarkable echo. It is well worth climbing the steps for an excellent view of the city and the Ganga. From July to September the river can be more than 5 km wide at this point.

To the east of the centre is **Khuda Bakhsh Oriental Public Library** ⓘ *Ashok Raj Path, T0612-230 0209, www.kblibrary.nic.in, Sat-Thu 0930-1700, entrance free*, inaugurated in 1891, with one of the largest collections of books and rare Persian and Arabic manuscripts in the world, in addition to Patna Qalam paintings and Moghul miniatures on ivory. The value and rarity of these objects means permission to view the originals (which are under double custody) is difficult to obtain. A slide-show of important pieces is offered instead; otherwise a selection of the manuscripts are exhibited each year from 1-5 August. It is now a national library bustling with Muslim scholars.

Kumrahar

Excavations at the site of the ancient capital of Pataliputra have revealed ruins enclosed within a high brick wall. These date back to 600 BC, the first of four distinct periods of settlement over the following 1200 years. The buildings, mainly of wood, were devastated by a fire and lay hidden in the silt. The more recent fifth phase dates from the early 17th century. The most important finds are rare wooden ramparts and a large Mauryan three-storeyed assembly hall, with 15 rows of five highly polished sandstone pillars dating back to 400-300 BC. The garden has little to show today other than the single 6 m intact pillar. The tiny museum has its small collection of valuable finds almost invisibly shut away in a dark room. Shared autos leave from Junction Station and pass by the site.

Gulzarbagh

Some 8 km east the centre (near the ASP's bungalow and Old City Court) are the former East India Company's main opium *godowns* (warehouses), now home to a government printing press. The three long buildings with porticoes on each side were strategically placed by the river for boats to carry the opium to Kolkata. The old *godowns*, ballroom and hall are open to visitors.

Har Mandir and around

Har Mandir is in the Chowk area of old Patna, accessible by shared auto from Gandhi Maidan (Rs 15). The *gurudwara* built by Maharaja Ranjit Singh is the second of the four great *takhts* (thrones) of the Sikhs and consecrates the birthplace of the 10th Guru, Gobind Singh, in 1660. The shrine of white marble has kiosks on the terrace. Singers and musicians add to the beauty of the interior (heads must be covered before entering). There is a museum on the second floor of the gatehouse, which consists of panels telling the Sikh history.

Quila House (Jalan Museum) ⓘ *advance permission required from the family; contact Mr Aditya Jalan, Hira Place, Dak Bungalow Rd, Patna 1, T0612-265 5479/264 1121, visit@quilahouse.com;. advisable to arrange 48 hrs in advance, preferred timings for visits Mon-Sat 0900-1100, Sun 100-1600; take a copy of your passport and visa pages*, is about 400 m from Har Mandir (locals will direct you). The private mansion was built over the ruins of Sher Shah's fort, and its setting by the Ganga is most tranquil and atmospheric. The diverse collection is particularly noteworthy for its Chinese porcelain and valuable jade pieces. Other highlights include Napoleon's bed and Tipu Sultan's palanquin , while panels in the hallway open up to reveal a set of George III Crown Derby. There are also beautiful ivory pieces, Toby jugs, French tapestries, Chinese paintings and a collection of silver filigree work of the Mughal period.

Saif Khan's Mosque (Pathar-ki-Masjid), on the river bank, was built in 1621 by Parwez Shah, the son of the Mughal Emperor Jahangir.

Around Patna

Sonepur → *Colour map 6, A4.*

ⓘ *Sonepur and Vaishali can be visited comfortably in a day. You can hire a taxi or take a tour.*

Sonepur is situated at the confluence of the Ganga and the Gandak and has a station on the Northeast Railway. Sonepur has Asia's biggest cattle market, beginning on the full moon of the Hindu month of **Kartik Purnima** (October/November). The fair lasts for two weeks to one month and draws thousands to the magic shows, folk dances, contests, handicrafts stalls and handlooms. Mark Shand's *Travels on my Elephant* gives a colourful account of the fair. Not just cattle but camels, horses, chimpanzees, birds and more are bought and sold (though numbers are dwindling); however, it is the large number of elephants, decorated for sale, which are the main attraction.

Vaishali → *Colour map 3, B5.*

Vaishali – derived from King Visala, from the *Ramayana* – dates back to the sixth century BC when it was a flourishing city of the Lichchavis, reputedly one of the first cities in the world to adopt a republican form of government. This is where the Buddha preached his last sermon and announced his approaching Nirvana. In 383 BC, 100 years later, it was the venue of the second Buddhist Council, when two *stupas* were erected. Jains of the Svetambara sect believe that Mahavir was born in Vaishali in 599 BC. Today, the district is part of the Mithila region, famous for Madhubani paintings on village houses.

Border essentials: India–Nepal

To Nepal Private buses run daily from Mithapur Bus Stand and state buses go from Gandhi Maidan to Raxaul (six to seven hours). However, timings are difficult and the buses packed and uncomfortable. Night buses reach the border early in the morning. Morning buses from Patna connect with the night bus to Kathmandu. Either way you have an overnight bus journey, unless you stay at Birganj - an unenviable option, though there are a couple of modest hotels. **Raxaul** has little to offer; Ajanta, Ashram Road, has rooms with bath. You can cross the border to **Birganj** by rickshaw/*tempo* (15-20 minutes). In Birganj the *tempo* stand and Bus Park are in Adarsh Nagar, to the south of town. In the morning, buses depart from the bus stand east of the clock tower. To **Tandi Bazar** (four hours, for **Chitwan**), **Pokhara** (11-12 hours) and **Kathmandu** (11-12 hours). Even Express buses are slow and packed. Tourist minibuses are the only moderately comfortable option. You need an exit stamp in Raxaul from the Indian Immigration office (round the corner, and across the road from the Customs office), which is a great hassle. After crossing the border you need to get an entry stamp from the Nepalese Immigration counter (open early morning to late evening). Occasionally an unjustified additional fee is demanded for 'extras', eg registration card, or a 'visa' fee in US dollars.

From Nepal When travelling to India via Patna it is best to stay overnight in **Hetauda** and catch the 0530 bus to Birganj (three hours); go to the bus stand at 0500 to get a seat. At **Birganj**, walk or get a rickshaw to the *auto-tempo* stand at the second crossroads. From there travel to Raxaul. Remember to get an exit stamp from Nepalese Immigration before crossing the border and an entry stamp from Indian Immigration in Raxaul.

The **Asoka Pillar** at **Kolhua**, also known as *Bhimsen-ki-Lathi* (stick), is a single 18 m piece of highly polished red sandstone with a bell-shaped inverted lotus capital and a life-sized lion carved on top. Asoka *stambhas* (pillars) were unornamented, with a circular section tapered like a palm tree trunk. They may have been forerunners of temples developed from the ancient form of worshipping in the forest. This is one of two Asoka pillars that remain in situ. The Wheel of Law on top of many pillars, which appears on the Indian flag, is the mark of the social and political order laid down by the emperor.

Ramkund is also known as Monkey Tank since it was thought to have been dug by monkeys who offered the Buddha a bowl of honey. The two Buddhist *stupas* are said to hold urns containing the Buddha's ashes; the second was only excavated in 1958. The ancient **Coronation Tank** (*Kharauna Pokhar*) contains holy water which was used for anointing the ruler of Vaishali at his coronation. The **Lotus Tank** nearby is thought to be a picnic spot of the sixth century BC.

A pleasant, easy 5-km walk from the **Tourist Bungalow** to the Asoka Pillar goes through pretty villages, passing the Japanese *stupa*, museum and an old small *stupa*.

Patna listings

For Sleeping and Eating price codes and other relevant information, see Essentials pages 38-42.

Sleeping

Patna *p812, map p812*

Some streets have been renamed: Bir Chand Patel Path (or Marg) has replaced Gardiner Rd. Some old names continue to be used, eg Bailey Rd (J Nehru Marg), Fraser Rd (Nazharul Huque Path), Exhibition Rd (Braj Kishore Path). Avoid the **Railway Retiring Rooms**.

LL Maurya, South Gandhi Maidan, T0612-220 3040, www.maurya.com. 80 a/c rooms and very expensive suites (up to Rs 25,000). Swankiest in town geared towards business people, modern rooms have polished stone surfaces and a luxurious feel. Excellent restaurant, cafe and bar (see Eating).

L-AL Chanakya, Bir Chand Patel Marg, T0612-222 0590, www.chanakyapatna.com. Inviting rooms feel fresh and well-lit, with flatscreen TV, walk-in showers, good views from the higher levels, nice restaurants/bar.

AL Patliputra Ashok (ITDC), Bir Chand Patel Path, T0612-250 5270-6, www.ashokpatna.com. 46 modern rooms, freshly decorated in muted colour schemes, fridge, bathrooms are better (walk-in showers) in the slightly pricier 'club' rooms, good restaurant, travel desk and tourist office, Wi-Fi. Bar 1000-2200 (beer Rs 205). Pool (Rs 150 non residents). Breakfast and airport transfer included.

B Republic, Lauriya Bagh, Exhibition Rd, T0612-232 0021, lawlysen@sancharnet.in. 35 rooms, a/c, good veg meals, roof garden, safe middle-range choice.

D Rajasthan, Fraser Rd, T0612-222 5102. 20 rooms some a/c, good vegetarian meals, very welcoming, gets full so book ahead, not much to look at from the outside.

D-E Kautilya Vihar (Bihar Tourism), Bir Chand Patel Path, T0612-222 5411, http://bstdc.nic.in. 44 rooms of different categories, all clean and acceptable (cheapest double Rs 600), some a/c, dorm beds (Rs 100), multi-cuisine restaurant, tourist information on site. Book ahead.

D-E Sheodar, Fraser Rd, T0612-222 7210. Clean rooms and nice staff, starts at Rs 565 (double), some with a/c, gets busy, definitely book ahead.

D-F Mayur, Fraser Rd, T0612-222 4149. Large rooms recently painted with clean sheets and towels, though bathrooms could be better maintained, it is still good value for the standard rooms. Quite pricey with a/c, good restaurant and a dark bar that is somehow funky (beer a reasonable Rs 100, open 0700-2200).

G Youth Hostel, Fraser Rd, T0612-221 1486. T(0)9973-174837. A cheap bed and acceptable enough, dorms Rs 120, doubles Rs 250, restaurant.

Eating

Patna *p812, map p812*

Hotels on Fraser Rd usually have a restaurant. There is a row of stalls selling excellent and cheap Chinese food (seating) next to the Maurya Lok Complex.

TTT-TT Spice Court, Hotel Maurya (see Sleeping). Open 1230-1530 and 1930-2330. Pan Asian cuisine (Vietnamese, Malaysian satay, etc), alcohol available, mains Rs 250-500, lovely staff. Adjacent Vaishali Cafe is also very pleasant.

TT-T Amrpali Cafe, Bir Chand Patel Path (next to **Kautilya Vihar**), T0612-222 9272. Open 0900-2300. Indian, Chinese, international veg and non-veg dishes. Bright and modern, tablecloths and TV, with a/c.

TT-T Garden Court Club, Fraser Rd, T0612-320 2279. Open 24 hrs, but best to go 1500-2300. Though there is not much of view from this rooftop restaurant, the plants and open air make it a pleasant escape and the menu is varied.

T Bansi Vihar, Fraser Rd. Daily 0800-2230. Fantastic South Indian menu, plus some Chinese, served by white-clad efficient waiters, has a/c. Highly recommended.

Shopping

Patna *p812, map p812*

Patna and its surrounding villages are known for wooden toys, inlay work, *tussar* silk, lacquerware, leather shoes and *Madhubani* paintings. The run-down **Bihar State Export**, Udyog Bhawan, East Gandhi Maidan, near the Mona Cinema Hall, has cheap *Madhubani* paintings, textiles and handicrafts, as do **Khadi Gramudyog**, **Bihar Emporium** and **Sonali State Emporium** at Maurya Lok Complex (items are priced though 30% discount is customary, shops open Mon-Sat 1100-2000). Better quality *Madhubani* paintings are found at **Ajanta**, Fraser Rd, Mon-Sat 1030-2030.

There are 2 good bookshops in the Hotel Satkar Arcade on Fraser Rd, **Readers Library** and **Tricel**, both closed on Sun.

Activities and tours

Patna *p812, map p812*

Ashok Travels & Tours, Hotel Pataliputra Ashok, T0612-222 6270-9. Reasonably priced car hire for half- or full-day tours.

Bihar Tourism (**BSTDC**), runs city sightseeing Oct-Mar, Rajgir, Nalanda and Pawapuri, usually 0800-2200. Also to Vaishali, Bodhgaya, Buxar and Sasaram.

Transport

Patna *p812, map p812*

Air Transport to town is by taxi, auto-rickshaw or **Indian Airlines** coach to their City Office via some hotels. **Indian Airlines**, East Gandhi Maidan, T0612- 222 2554, www.indianairlines.nic.in. Daily to **Delhi**, **Lucknow**, **Mumbai** and **Ranchi**. **Jet Airways**, www.jetairways.com, also flies to **Delhi**.

Bus **Bihar SRTC**, Gandhi Maidan, has state services to **Ranchi** and **Raxaul**. Mithapur private bus stand is 2.5 km from Junction railway station, with Luxury and Express services between Patna and regional centres including **Kolkata**, **Siliguri**, **Bodhgaya** and **Ranchi**.

Taxi Private unmetered taxis available from the airport, some hotels and important tourist sites. Fix rates beforehand.

Train

Patna Junction railway Station, enquiries, T131/0612-242 7812, reservations, T0612-222 2197. **Delhi** (**ND**): *Vikramshila Exp 12367*, 1710, 14½ hrs; *Rajdhani Exp 12423*, 2150, not Tue or Sat, 12½ hrs. **Delhi** (**OD**): *Brahmaputra Mail 14055*, 1310, 17 hrs. **Gaya**: *Patna Hatia Exp 18625*, 1140, 2 hrs; *Palamau Exp 13348*, 2155, 2½ hrs. **Guwahati**: *NE Exp 12506*, 2220, 18½ hrs; *Rajdhani Exp 12424/22424*, 0210, not Mon, 15 hrs. **Kolkata**: *Toofan Exp 13008*, 0630, 13 hrs; *Rajdhani Exp 12306*, 0500, Sat, 7½ hrs; *Poorva Exp 12304*, 0805, Mon, Thu, Fri, Sun, 8½ hrs. **Mumbai** (**Lokmanya Tilak**): *Rajendranagar Lokmanya Tilak Exp 12142*, 1110, 28½ hrs. **Varanasi**: *Farraka Exp 13413/13483*, 0530, 4½ hrs; *Shramjeevi Exp 12391*, 1050, 3½ hrs.

Directory

Patna *p812, map p812*

Banks **State Bank of India** have an ATM at the station and on Gandhi Maidan; there are many other ATMs in the central area.

Internet Plenty of cafes in the centre, Rs 20 per hr; on the 1st floor of Maurya Lok Complex are 2 cafes, open Mon-Sat 0830-2030, Sun 1000-2000. **Hospitals** **Patna Medical College Hospital**, Ashok Raj Path E, T0612-267 0132. **Nalanda Medical College Hospital**, T0612-263 1159, By-Pass Rd. **Post** **GPO**: Station Rd, in a splendid Raj-era building.

Patna to Bodhgaya

→ *Colour map 3, B5/6.*

The area to the south of Patna has many major Buddhist sites, and also some Muslim, Jain and Hindu places of pilgrimage. A route to the southwest of Patna visits the ruins of Nalanda, one of the world's oldest universities, Rajgir, royal capital of the Magadh Empire, the Barabar Caves and Bodhgaya. Between Bodhgaya and Varanasi, you can visit the immense tombs of Sher Shah at Sasaram. Once out of Patna the countryside is often very attractive, early morning being particularly crisp and inviting. From March to the monsoon it gets extremely hot during the day. ▸▸ *For listings, see pages 825-828.*

Biharsharif and Pawapuri

On the NH31, these two towns can be visited prior to arriving at Nalanda. **Bihar Sharif**, 13 km from Rajgir, remained an Islamic cultural centre up to the 16th century. The *dargahs* (tombs) of Mukhdoom Shah, a 13th-century saint and Malik Ibrahim Baya, draw large numbers of Muslims, particularly during the annual **Urs fair**.

Pawapuri, also Apapuri which means 'sinless town', is particularly sacred to the Jains since Mahavir, the founder of Jainism, gained enlightenment here. The lotus pond where he bathed, and on whose bank he was cremated, has a white marble temple, the *Jalamandir*, in its centre and a Samosharan Temple.

Nalanda → *For listings, see pages 825-828. Colour map 3, B6.*

Nalanda has the ruins of one of the world's oldest universities, founded in the fifth century AD on an ancient site of pilgrimage and teaching which had been visited by the Buddha and Mahavir (who spent '14 rainy seasons' in the area). Hiuen Tsang ascribed its name, which means 'charity without intermission', to the Buddha's liberality in an earlier birth. From the bus stand, *tongas* take passengers to the site 2.5 km away for Rs 50. There is a tourist information centre and good government cafeteria near the entrance, as well as numerous stalls selling food and souvenirs.

History

Nalanda was hidden under a vast mound for centuries. Its archaeological importance was only established in the 1860s with most of the excavation taking place over about 20 years from 1916. The monasteries went through varying periods of occupation, and in one case nine different levels of building have been discovered. The Buddhist monastic movement resulted in large communities withdrawing into retreats. Even in the seventh century, according to Hiuen-Tsang, Buddhism was declining except in Bihar and Bengal where it enjoyed royal patronage and the support of the laity. The sanctuaries were often vast, as is the one here (500 m by 250 m).

The site

ⓘ *Ticket office open 0900-1600 (Oct-Feb), 0900-1700 (Mar-Sep), site open until sunset, entrance Rs 100. Note: Museums are closed on Fri.*

The remains of 11 monasteries and several *chaityas* (temples) built mainly in red brick have been found, as well as a large stairway, a library, lecture halls, dormitories, cells, ovens and wells. The buildings are in several storeys and tiers on massive terraces of solid brick, with stucco decorations of the Buddha as well as Hindu deities, and secular figures. Several of the monasteries have a guarded entrance on the western wall; the monks' cells are around a central courtyard with a wide veranda

The monasteries are numbered one to 11, from south to north. The path from the gate enters the complex between monasteries one and five and leads across an open space to **Temple**

No 3, the largest here and the focal point for pilgrims' worship. Almost certainly this was originally built by Asoka. The earliest temples were small structures, completely incorporated into the successively larger mounds you see today. The north facing shrine chamber on top may have once contained an enormous Buddha image. Staircases lead up, but access is not allowed.

Returning east, **monasteries 1, 1A** and **1B** are the best restored and most important of the monastery group. It is possible to walk around all three of these southern monasteries and get a true sense of the scale of Nalanda past.

There are several interesting features in the other monasteries: double rows of cells in **monastery 5**, brick courtyards and two sets of double ovens in the upper courtyard of **6**, and evidence of three successive monasteries built on the same site at **7**. There are the remains of arched doorways in **10** and the fragments of the 25 stone pillars that lined the veranda were found in the ruins of **11**, which stood 1 m apart and 2 m high.

In addition to the monasteries and the main temple, four other temples have been excavated. **Temples 12, 13** and **14** are in a line stretching north from the main temple. They all have a square outline and originally had large Buddha images, now destroyed. **Temple 2** (signed) is worth the short detour to see the sculpted dado with over 200 panels showing a huge variety of Hindu deities.

The **Archaeological Museum** ⓘ Sat-Thu 0900-1645, Rs 5i displays some fabulous stone and bronze statues, some of which are perfectly preserved, found at Nalanda and nearby sites. Jain and Hindu figures feature prominently alongside the Buddha, but look for the the legs of a Buddhist deity crushing Siva and Gauri that illustrate the triumph over the Hindu pantheon.

Nava Nalanda Mahavihar

About 2 km from the principal site is a postgraduate Institute for Research into Buddhism and Pali literature set up by the Bihar government, which has many rare manuscripts; it is now the site of the Indira Gandhi Open University. There is a colourful **Thai Temple** built in the 1980s. **Kundalpur**, 1.5 km north of Nalanda, is believed by the Digambara sect of Jains to be the birthplace of Mahavir.

Nalanda

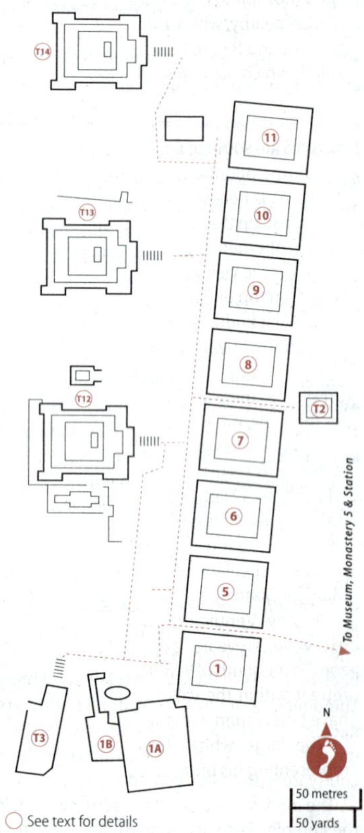

Rajgir

For listings, see pages 825-828.

Colour map 3, B6. Population: 33,700.

Encircled by low ranges of rugged hills, Rajgir is held sacred by Buddhists who have built several temples in the area. **Mahavir** spent "14 rainy seasons" teaching in Rajgir and the 20th Tirthankara was born here, so it is also a major Jain pilgrimage centre, with temples on most of the hilltops. You can still see parts of the 40 km cyclopean dry stone wall that once enclosed the ancient city and fort. Today, the

Monastic University for the Buddhist world

It is assumed that the Gupta emperors were responsible for Nalanda's first monasteries. In the seventh century Hiuen-Tsang spent 12 years, both as a student and a teacher, at Nalanda which once had over 3000 teachers and philosophers. The monks were supported by 200 villages, and a library of nine million manuscripts attracted men from countries as far flung as Java, Sumatra, Korea, Japan and China. Great honour was attached to a Nalanda student and admission was restricted with seven or eight out of 10 applicants failing to gain a place.

I-Tsing, another Chinese scholar, arrived here in AD 673 and also kept detailed records, describing the severe lifestyle of the monks. The divisions of the day were measured by a water clock, and the syllabus involved the study of Buddhist and Brahmanical scriptures, logic, meta-physics, medicine and Sanskrit grammar.

The university flourished until 1199 when the Afghan Bhaktiar Khalji sacked it, burning, pillaging and driving the surviving residents into hiding. It was the end of living Buddhism in India until the modern revival.

kund (hot springs) with large open-air baths are a special attraction for local tourists. The Kund Market nearby, where buses stop, has shops, stalls and basic rooms. For an idea of the layout of sites around Rajgir, visit the Gautam Vihar Tourist Bungalow (a five-minute walk from the bus stand) which has a map outside and a tourist information office.

The site

About 5 km south of Kund (take a *tonga*, Rs 100 one way) the **Gridhrakuta** ('Hill of Vultures') was one of the Buddha's favourite places where he delivered many important sermons, and was where he is believed to have converted the Magadhan King Bimbisara, who had built the old stone road up the hill. It was used by Hiuen-Tsang in the seventh century and still provides good access. Alternatively, you can take the 600-m **cable car** ⓘ *usually 0900-1300, 1500-1700, Rs 40 (good for the views)*, to the **Visva Santi Stupa** built by the Japanese and dedicated to world peace, on top of Ratnagiri. From here it is an easy walk to Gridhrakuta.

The first Buddhist Council was held in the **Saptaparni Cave** on Vaibhara Hill, six months after the Buddha's death, and his teachings were written down for the first time. On the way to the cave is the large, 7-m-high **tone house**, an extraordinary 'watchtower' built of blocks of stone. On all sides there are small cells for guards which were later used by monks. Allow plenty of time for this walk, it takes about 40 minutes to reach Saptaparni Cave from the drop-off point.

Little survives of the fifth century BC **Ajatasatru Fort**. The outer wall was built with blocks of stone up to 1.5 m long, with smaller boulders in its core. In places it was 4 m high and over 5 m wide. Of the 32 large gates (and 64 small ones) mentioned in ancient texts, only one to the north has survived. Of the inner city wall, which was about 5 km long and roughly pentagonal, only a section to the south remains, with three gaps through which the old roads ran. In the valley, a 6-m-high circular brick structure, decorated with stucco figures, had an old Jain shrine called **Maniyar Math**.

Nearby **Venuvana**, the bamboo grove where the Buddha spent some time, where excavations revealed a room, some *stupas* and the Karanda Tank, is now a deer park with a small zoo. To the south of Venuvana there are Jain and Hindu temples. The ruins of Buddha's favourite retreat within the valley, called the **Jivakamarvana Monastery** (fourth to third century BC), have been found with four halls and several rooms.

The large white Nipponzan Myohoji *stupa* has four golden statues of the Buddha representing his birth, enlightenment, preaching and death.

Gaya → *For listings, see pages 825-828. Colour map 3, B5. Population: 383,200.*

Gaya, on slightly raised ground in the valley between two hills, was blessed by Vishnu with the power to absolve all temporal sins. Its many sacred shrines attract Hindus at Pitrapaksh Tarpan (September-October), when prayers are offered for the dead before pilgrims take a dip in the holy River Phalgu. Cremations take place on funeral pyres in the ghats along the river. **Bihar Tourism** ⓘ *Gaya Junction Railway Station Main Hall, Mon-Sat 1000-1700*, do their best to assist and have a brochure on Bihar.

Sights

There are several old Buddhist temples and monastery remains around Gaya. Three kilometres south of the town centre is the **Vishnupad Temple**, which is supposed to have been built over Vishnu's footprint, imprinted on a rock set in a silver basin. The 30-m-high temple has eight rows of beautifully carved pillars supporting the *mandapa* (pavilion), which were refurbished in 1787. Only Hindus are permitted into the sanctum and temple grounds which has the *Akshayabat* (the immortal banyan tree under which the Buddha is believed to have meditated for six years), where the final *puja* for the dead takes place. Non-Hindus can visit the ghats on the River Phalgu (a dry riverbed from November-June, when pilgrims have to collect holy water from wells) and the old alleyways spreading north of the temple, which are reminiscent of Varanasi. Brahmayoni Hill, 1 km southwest, has 500 stone steps, which lead to a vantage point for viewing both Gaya and Bodhgaya.

The **Surya Temple** at **Deo**, 20 km away, dedicated to the Sun God, attracts large crowds in November when **Chhatt Puja** is celebrated.

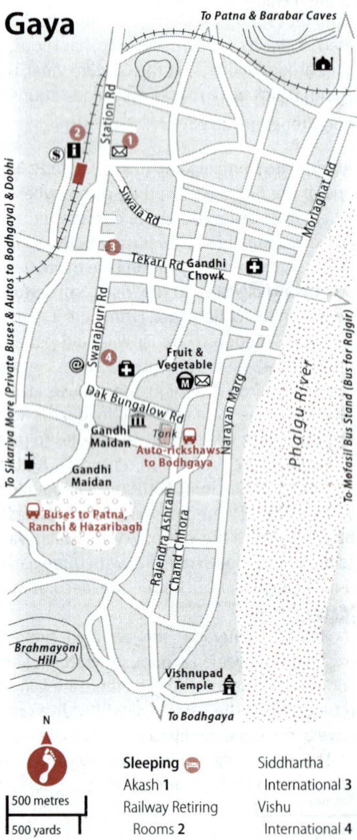

Around Gaya

Barabar Caves are 35 km north or Gaya. The 22-km rough track leading to the caves in the impressive granite hill turns east off the main road to Patna at **Belagunj** (30 minutes from Gaya, two hours from Patna) where buses stop. From here allow four hours to walk up ("a real challenge" by 4WD). It is only safe to go in daylight and certainly not alone (a *sadhu* is inclined to jump out at you from nowhere!) Enquire about safety at Belagunj police station.

The whale-backed quartzite gneiss hill stands in wild and rugged country. Inscriptions reveal that, on instructions from Asoka, four chambers were excavated, cut and chiselled to a high polish by the stonemasons, as retreats for ascetics who belonged to a sect related to Jainism. Percy Brown pointed out that the extraordinary caves, particularly the *Lomas Rishi* and the *Sudama*, are exact copies of ordinary beehive-shaped huts built with bamboo, wood and thatch. The barrel-vaulted chamber inside the *Sudama* is 10 m long, 6 m wide and 3.5 m high, which through a doorway leads to a circular cell. The most impressive craftsmanship is seen on the façade of the *Lomas Rishi* which replicates the horseshoe shaped gable end of a wooden structure with two lunettes which have very fine carvings of lattice-work and rows of elephants paying homage to Buddhist *stupas*. There is also a Siva temple on the Siddheshwar peak.

The caves inspired the setting of EM Forster's A Passage to India. They date from the third century BC and are the earliest examples of rock-cut sanctuaries.

At **Nagarjuna Hill** there are three further rock-cut sanctuaries, 1 km northeast from Barabar. The *gopi* (milkmaid's) cave having the largest chamber. Inscriptions date these to about 50 years after the excavations at Barabar.

Bodhgaya → *For listings, see pages 825-828. Colour map 3, B5. Phone code: 0631. Population: 30,900.*

Bodhgaya, a quiet sprawling village near the River Niranjana (Phalgu), is one of the holiest Buddhist pilgrimage centres in India. It was under the Bo tree here that Gautama, the prince, attained Enlightenment to become the Buddha.

Ins and outs

Getting there and around Travel in daylight only, for your own safety. Buses run from Patna, Nalanda and Rajgir. Most people arrive by auto-rickshaw from Gaya. Most hotels and monasteries are an easy walk the bus/auto stands. ▸▸ *See Transport, page 827.*

Tourist information Bihar Tourism ⓘ *in the BSTCD complex on Dumahan Rd, T0631-220 0445, Mon-Fri 1000-1700.* Not very useful.

Bodhgaya

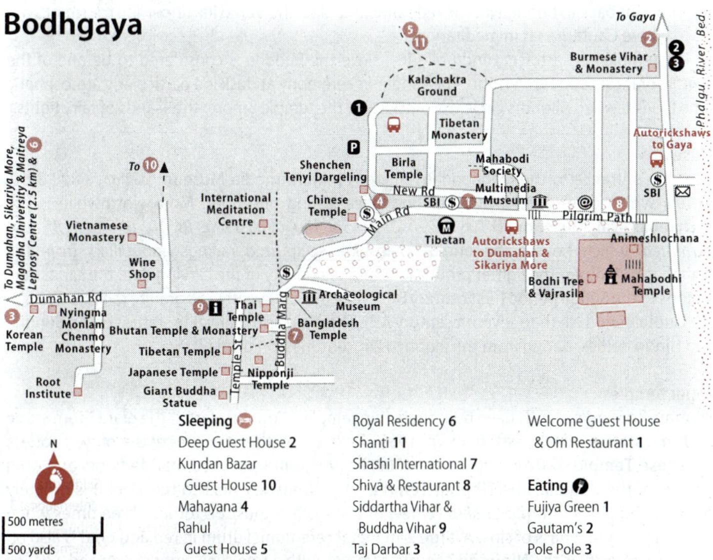

Sleeping
Deep Guest House 2
Kundan Bazar Guest House 10
Mahayana 4
Rahul Guest House 5
Royal Residency 6
Shanti 11
Shashi International 7
Shiva & Restaurant 8
Siddartha Vihar & Buddha Vihar 9
Taj Darbar 3
Welcome Guest House & Om Restaurant 1

Eating
Fujiya Green 1
Gautam's 2
Pole Pole 3

The site

Declared a World Heritage Site in 2002, Bodhgaya was 'lost' for centuries until rediscovered by Burmese Buddhists in 1877, which led to restoration work by the British. Lamas, Rimpoches and Buddhists from all over the world assemble here during the week-long *monlam* (December-January) when the area north of the bus station resembles a medieval encampment with tents serving as informal restaurants and accommodation. The food is smoky and there are long waits, but it is atmospheric and full of colour. The 'tourist season' draws to a close at the end of February when many restaurants close and most meditation courses stop running.

Mahabodhi Temple

ⓘ *0400-2100, entrance free.*

Asoka's original shrine near the Bodhi tree was replaced a temple in the second century, which in turn has been through several alterations. The temple on a high and broad plinth, with a soaring 52-m-high pyramidal spire with a square cross-section and four smaller spires, houses a gilded image of the Enlightened Buddha. The smaller spires may have been added when Burmese Buddhists attempted extensive rebuilding in the 14th century. An ornately carved stone railing in bas relief surrounds the temple on three sides and several carved Buddhist *stupas* depict tales from the Buddha's early life. The lotus pond where the Buddha may have bathed is to the south, with a seated Buddha statue at its centre. Adjacent to the north side of the temple is the *Chankramana*, a raised platform (first century) with lotus flowers carved on it, which marks the consecrated promenade used by the Buddha while meditating. Further north, the **Animeshlochana** is another sacred spot where the Buddha stood to gaze in gratitude at the Bodhi tree for a week, after his Enlightenment.

The original Bodhi tree (pipal or *Ficus religiosa*) was supposedly destroyed by Asoka before he was converted, and others which replaced it also died. The present tree behind the temple is believed to come from the original stock - Prince Mahinda carried a sapling from the sacred Bo tree to Sri Lanka when he went to spread Buddhism there. This in turn produced a sapling which was brought back to Bodhgaya. The red sandstone slab, the **Vajrasila**, under the tree marks the place where Gautama sat in meditation.

The temple also attracts Hindu pilgrims since the Buddha is considered to be one of the *avatars* or incarnations of Vishnu. The candle-lit ceremony at dusk is a particularly atmospheric time to visit, when pilgrims circle the outskirts of the temple among thousands of fairy lights.

Museums

Near the entrance to the Mahabodhi Temple is a **Multi-media Museum** ⓘ *daily 0800-2000, Rs 100*, which gives a 3D history of Bodhgaya lasting one hour. More worthwhile is the **Archaeological Museum** ⓘ *T0631-220 0739, Sat-Thu 0900-1700, Rs 10, photography not permitted*, which houses the original 2-m-high sculptured railings and pillars from the Mahabodhi Temple. The lighter proportions and the quality of the carving date the sandstone railings to the Sunga period (first century BC), while the less-weathered granite railings are from the Gupta period (sixth to seventh century AD). There are also many fine statues of the Buddha and Hindu deities, dating from the eighth-12th centuries, on display.

Other temples

Pilgrims from many lands have built their own temples. You can start at the giant 20-m stone **Buddha statue** which was built in 1989. Next door, the modern two-storey, spotless **Japanese Temple** ⓘ *0700-1200, 1400-1800*, has beautiful polished marble floors and gold images of the Buddha. The **Tibetan Temple** and **Monastery** next to this (1938) is ornately painted and has a *Dharma Chakra* (Wheel of Law) which must be turned three times when praying for forgiveness of sins. A large 2-m metal ceremonial drum in red and gold is also on display. Opposite is the **Nipponji Temple** complex with a free clinic, monastery and a Peace

Bell (rung from 0600-1200 and at 1700). Returning to the Mahabodhi Temple you will pass the colourful **Bhutan Temple** protected by carved Himalayan deities, a glittering pagoda-style **Thai Temple** and a **Bangladesh Temple**. The **Chinese Temple** houses an enormous, revolving ceremonial prayer drum.

Teaching centres

Meditation courses varying from a week to a month are available (most only during the Oct-Mar season), following both the Mahayana and Hinanyana traditions; enquire at the Burmese, Tibetan and Thai monasteries. The **Root Institute** ⓘ *off Dumahan Rd, office hrs 0830-1130 and 1330-1630, T0631-220 0714, www.rootinstitute.com*, offers popular Vipassana courses from Oct-March (dates listed on the website, usually bi-monthly), rooms for personal retreats (year round) and is involved in community self-help schemes; the accommodation and setting is lovely and payment is by donation. **Insight Meditation** ⓘ *www.insightmeditation.org*, has been running 10-day retreats since 1975, during January and February in the Thai monastery. The **International Meditation Centre** ⓘ *T0631-220 0707*, holds a variety of informal courses throughout the year.

Sasaram → *Colour map 3, B5.*

ⓘ *This Muslim site, between Gaya and Varanasi, is well worth a visit. The tombs are a short rickshaw ride from the railway station, which has left luggage (Rs 10).*

Sher Shah Suri, who was responsible for the tombs, asked the master-builder Aliwal Khan to build a tomb for his father Hasan Khan around 1535. This later inspired the building of the impressive second tomb for Sher Shah himself. The first imitated the octagonal structure and walled enclosure of the earlier Lodi tombs but was rather plain. What followed, however, was extraordinary not only in scale, but also in its conception. **Sher Shah's mausoleum** ⓘ *Mar-Jul 0700-1800, Aug-Feb 0800-1700, Rs 100*, was set in a large artificial lake so it appears to float. A modern redbrick gateway opposite the Dak Bungalow leads down to the tombs. You enter it by a causeway after going through a guard room on the north bank (originally visitors approached by barge from the ghat on the east side). The grounds and lake provide a relaxing break, though travellers report a certain amount of hassle from local youth.

Patna to Bodhgaya listings

For Sleeping and Eating price codes and other relevant information, see Essentials pages 38-42.

Sleeping

Nalanda *p819*

Nalanda is small and accommodation is available in the Chinese monastery, though it is recommended to stay in Rajgir.

Rajgir *p820*

There are several Jain *dharamshalas* near the bazar plus a host of unpleasant cheapies by the bus stand (many will not accept foreigners).

L-AL Indo Hokke, 3 km from Kund Market, T06112-255245, centaur@bani.in. The best hotel in town, 44 attractive rooms in an austere brick edifice, with lots of space, wide beds and East Asian influences, primarily catering to Japanese pilgrims, excellent restaurant with Indian, Thai and Japanese food, reserve well ahead in high season, or get significant discounts in low season. Located 3 km from the centre of town.

E-F Siddharth, near Kund Market, T06112-255616. Good rooms with bath (Western toilets), TV and decent food.

E-F Tathagat Vihar, near Viragtan, T/F06112-225176, http://bstdc.bih.nic.in. 32 rooms that are a standard government offering in that they are simple but clean, with TV, tiled floors and bathrooms (Rs 578). Slightly smaller rooms with Indian toilets are a bit cheaper, or pay more for a/c, plus some suites for Rs 2200, Indian restaurant. Nice location at the foot of the hills.

F-G Mahalaxmi, Kund Market, T(0)9431-487646. Of the cheap options near the bus stand, this is the best choice with clean sheets provided and airy terraces. Not much English spoken.

Gaya *p822, map p822*

It is only worth staying in Gaya if you have an early train to catch; accommodation is much better value in Bodhgaya.

B-E Siddhartha International, just off Station Rd, T0631-222 0958, hotelsiddhartha1@rediffmail.com. A few cheaper rooms (Rs 650-950), pricier with a/c, rather drab furnishings and scuffed surfaces, some rooms have balconies, decent Kapila restaurant and bar.

D-F Vishnu International, Swarajpuri Rd, T0631-222 4422. Clean and bright, doubles start at Rs 495, with a/c Rs 900, large public balcony and an all-important generator. Pleasant management.

G Akash, Laxman Sahay Rd (the alley opposite the station), T0631-222 2205. Rooms around a dark courtyard, renovations being done at the time of research with improved tiled bathrooms, bucket hot water, pay Rs 150 extra for air cooler, the best bottom-rung option in town.

G Railway Retiring Rooms. 6 rooms, 2 a/c, dorm Rs 70 (men only).

Bodhgaya *p823, map p823*

Budget hotels often quote higher rates so bargain; good off-season (Mar-Oct) discounts are available.

AL-A The Royal Residency, Dumahan Rd, T0631-220 0181, www.theroyalresidency.net. The most attractive rooms of the higher end hotels, though the exterior is typically blank and it's at least 1 km from the centre. Flatscreen TVs, a/c, quality furniture, wide inviting beds and large marble bathrooms with walk-in showers and tubs. Restaurant is featureless, as is the bar (1000-2200, beer Rs 250). Some suites.

A Taj Darbar, Dumahan Rd, T0631-220 0053, T(0)97739-320524, www.hoteltajdarbar.com. A popular place with Thai pilgrims, white-walled rooms are modern and quite trendy, with flatscreens TVs, duvets, a/c, hair dryers. There's a multi-cuisine restaurant, no bar but staff will send out for alcohol.

B-C Mahayana, Main Rd, T0631-220 0756, mahayanagt@yahoo.com. Huge bright rooms, a/c and TV, in an airy building with courtyards, peaceful vibe and charming staff, a good choice. Worth haggling over the price.

D Shashi International, Buddha Marg, T0631-220 0459, www.hotelshashi.com. Small rooms are starting to fade, but if you want a/c and flat-screen TV then it is one of the cheaper options.

D-G Siddartha Vihar, Bodhgaya Rd, T0631-220 0445. The state tourism department runs 3 adjacent lodgings, by far the best is the Siddartha with decent and reasonably priced a/c and non-a/c rooms with balconies and TVs in a quirky circular building; next door **Buddha Vihar** and **Sujata Vihar** have dorm beds (Rs 75-150).

E-F Shivan, opposite temple, T0631-220 0425. Clean rooms, some with bath, hot water, friendly, restaurant downstairs.

E-G Welcome Guest House, above **Café Om** (see Eating), T0631-220 0377, T(0)9934-221943, welcomeguest_house@yahoo.co.in. Caters to backpackers, cheaper rooms share bathrooms (hot water), some have TV, also 5-bed mixed dorm (Rs 50), good central location. A string of similar guesthouses surround.

F Deep Guest House, next to Burmese Monastery, near Sujata Bridge, T0631-220 0463. Clean rooms, friendly staff, roof terrace in high season, peaceful atmosphere.

F Kundan Bazar Guest House, Bhagalpur village, T0631-220 0049, www.kundanbazar.com. This little guesthouse with bright clean rooms fulfils all travellers' needs, with free Wi-Fi in the rooms, a community kitchen, bicycles for rent, free use of the washing machine, bookshop, clothes for sale and rooftop café with amazing views. Great value.

F Rahul Guest House, behind Kalachakra Ground, T0631-220 0709, T(0)9934-463849, rahul_bodhgaya@yahoo.com. Bright and cheery rooms (some with attached bath), spotless sheets, fans, clean paintwork, towels, plus great front terraces with views to paddies. Although new buildings are fast encroaching, it remains a more peaceful location and is the best value choice among the small cluster of guesthouses here.

F Shanti Guest House, behind Kalachakra Ground, T0631-220 0129, T(0)9934-153387, www.shanti-guesthouse.com. Very clean rooms, white linens, attached or shared baths, some with a/c, communal front balconies; only downside might be the children running around.

Monasteries

Some monasteries provide spartan accommodation primarily for pilgrims; contact the monk in charge. They expect guests to conform to certain rules of conduct.

G **Bhutan Monastery**, Buddha Rd. 18 rooms in guesthouses, shared facilities.

G **Burmese Vihar**, Gaya Rd. Simple rooms (some newer) with nets, dorm, no fan, garden (eat at **Pole Pole** opposite).

Eating

Rajgir *p820*

Food is not brilliant in the dhabas near the bus stop, for a decent meal you will have to try one of the higher-end hotels.

Bodhgaya *p823, map p823*

Most tent restaurants operate in winter only.

Café Om, Main Rd. Decent Western fare draws in most backpackers in town.

Fujiya Green, near Kalachakra Ground. Extensive vegetarian/non-vegetarian menu, specializes in Tibetan but it has every continent covered. Attractive interior lives up to the name, recently refurbished, friendly service.

Gautam's, opposite Burmese Vihar. Apple strudel and cinnamon rolls.

Pole Pole, tent opposite Burmese Vihar. Clean, excellent management, good though not exceptional food. Open during the season.

Shiva, diagonally opposite entrance to Mahabodi temple. Japanese and simple Western food.

Transport

Nalanda *p819*

Regular buses from **Patna** to **Bihar Sharif** where you change to **Rajgir** (15 km) with the nearest railway station or **Nalanda**. Cycle-rickshaw and *tonga* (Rs 50) between the bus stop to the site.

Rajgir *p820*

Bus to **Bihar Sharif** then change for **Patna** (105 km), 3½ hrs total journey time; to **Gaya** (78 km) 2 hrs.

Gaya *p822, map p822*

Bus

From Mofasil bus stand across the river to **Rajgir** (78 km, 2 hrs); state buses from Gandhi Maidan Bus Stand to Patna, Ranchi and Hazaribagh. More frequent private buses leave from Sikariya More (Rs 8 in a shared auto from the station). To **Bodhgaya** a private auto-rickshaw should cost Rs 100 but you may have to pay Rs 150; shared autos leave from main auto stand opposite the market (Rs 8-10), or from Sikariya More (Rs 10). After 1800 only private auto-rickshaws are available: bargain hard, Rs 100-150. A cycle-rickshaw from the station to main auto stand is Rs 10-15.

Rickshaw

Auto- and cycle-rickshaws are readily available.

Train

Gaya is on the Grand Chord line of the Delhi-Kolkata section of Eastern Railway. **Delhi**: *Rajdhani Exp 12301*, 2239, except Sun, 11½ hrs; *Rajdhani Exp 12421*, 2313, Wed, Sat, Sun, 11½ hrs; *Purushottam Exp 12801*, 1415, 15 hrs; **Kolkata (H)**: *Howrah Exp 12308*, 2018, 7½ hrs; *Kalka-Howrah Mail 12312*, 2328, 8 hrs; *Rajdhani Exp 12302*, 0404, except Sat, 6 hrs; plus others. **Patna**: *Palamau Exp 13347*, *Hatia Patna Exp 18626*, 1310, 2½ hrs. **Varanasi**: *Doon Exp 13009*, 0510, 5 hrs; *Poorva Exp 12381*, 1455, Wed, Thu, Sun, 3½ hrs; plus lots that arrive/depart in middle of night, and others that go to **Mughal Sarai**, with transfer by auto-rickshaw to Varanasi.

Bodhgaya *p823, map p823*

Air

There is an international airport 8 km away (T0631-221 0129), with daily flights from Bangkok during the high season (Thai Airways office, Royal Residency hotel, T0631-220 0368, Mon-Sat, 1000-1300, 1500-1800), Yangon (Indian Airlines, T0631-221 0688) and Sri Lanka.

Bus

There are daily buses to **Patna** run by BSTDC at 0700 and 1400 (Rs 60) leaving from outside the Hotel Buddha Vihar.

Rickshaw

Auto-rickshaws take 30 mins to Gaya; the last shared one leaves 1800, then private hire (Rs 100-150) until 2100.

Train
Gaya (16 km) has the nearest train station.

Sasaram *p825*
Train to **Gaya**, *Doon Exp 13010*, 1914, 2 hrs. To **Varanasi**, *Doon Exp 13009*, 0705, 2 hrs.

Directory

Gaya *p822, map p822*
Banks State Bank of India ATM at station.
Post Station Rd and GB Rd. Warning from travellers whose mail/parcels were pilfered here.

Bodhgaya *p823, map p823*
Banks State Bank of India has an ATM.
Internet There are many internet cafes all over Bodhgaya, Rs 30 per hr, decent connection.
Post Close to the entrance to Mahabodhi Temple, Mon-Fri 1000-1530, Sat 1000-1230.

Jharkhand

Jharkhand's enigmatic blend of forests, tribes and fuming industrial belts has yet to find favour with the majority of visitors to India. Exploring the state is not for the faint-hearted - Naxalite bandits are active in many areas - but if you crave a taste of life far beyond the tourist trail, this remote corner of central India provides it in spades. ▸▸ *For listings, see pages 831-832.*

Background

The land Jharkhand lies on the once densely forested northern edge of the Indian Peninsula. The rolling plateau, at 300-400 m with occasional outcrops rising to nearly 1000 m, is mostly granite and gneiss of ancient Gondwanaland. On the north it drops quite sharply to the plains of the Ganga, while a great fault has created the valley of the mineral rich Damodar. The plateau still has an open feel, with forest interspersed by agricultural land, except where coal and iron ore mining have created a scarred industrial landscape of mines and soil tips. To the south of the Damodar Valley are the Ranchi plateaux, broken up by remarkable looking flat-topped hillocks or *mesas*. Up to 20% is still forested, though exploitation of this continues. The soils are often poor, sometimes lateritic, and easily eroded if conservation measures are not adopted.

Politics The inauguration of the state in the early hours of 15 November 2000 was timed symbolically to take place on the birth anniversary of Birsa Munda, leader of the Santhal rebellion in 1831-1832. The origins of the present state can be traced to the formation of the Chota Nagpur Unnati Samaj in 1921, which proposed the creation of a separate Jharkhand state in 1928. Jharkhand's future is heavily dependent upon the exploitation of its mineral wealth. Many of the tribal peoples have been under pressure from agricultural settlers from the plains, and increasingly from both state and national governments keen to exploit the mineral wealth that lies beneath their lands. By way of resistance, some tribal people have joined Maoist militias, the so-called Naxalites, while many others have been conscripted into a government-backed opposing force, the ironically named Salva Judum (Peace March). In 2006 battles between the rival groups resulted in a number of deaths and violence continues to flare up, especially around election times. Often in desperation the poor have moved to cities like Kolkata and Mumbai, or to work on tea estates.

Ranchi → *For listings, see pages 831-832. Colour map 3, C6. Population: 846,500.*

Once the summer capital of Bihar state, Ranchi still attracts holiday-makers for its location on higher ground in the heart of the Chota Nagpur tribal country. An industrial town and a major educational centre, Ranchi is also known for its mental asylum at Kanke, 9 km north. The town is surrounded by rolling forests with waterfalls and lakes in the heart of one of India's great tribal belts. The Ranchi district has been the recent scene of violently suppressed demonstrations, opposed to Koel-Karo dam project. **Birsa Vihar Tourist Complex** ⓘ *5 Main Rd, T0651-233 08522, jharkhandtourism@yahoo.co.in, also at the train station, T0651-220 8815.*

Ranchi Lake is popular for local people to relax, while the adjacent **Ranchi Hill** offers good views of the town and surrounding countryside. **Tagore Hill**, 3 km away, is named after Rabindranath Tagore who wrote several books and poems here. **Ranchi University** ⓘ *Shaheed Chowk, T0651-220 8553, 1100-1700*, has ethnographic collections of central Indian states and Andaman and Nicobar Islands. **Ranchi Museum** ⓘ *Tribal Research Institute Building, Morabadi Rd, Mon-Sat 1030-1700, free*, 4 km away, has a collection of stone sculpture, terracottas and arms.

The 17th-century **Jagannath Temple** on a hillock at Jagannathpur, 10 km southwest, is in the style of the great temple in Puri. The annual **Ratha Yatra** takes place in June/July.

Around Ranchi

The Subhanarekha River, which rises southeast of the town, is interrupted by several impressive waterfalls, within easy range of Ranchi. **Hundru Falls**, 45 km east, are formed by the 100 m drop of the river, particularly impressive just after the monsoons. You can picnic and bathe in the pools at the bottom. Others in the area include **Johna**, 40 km east on the Purulia Road, and **Dassamghagh Falls** (34 km) which has a tea house. It is dangerous to bathe at Dassamghagh; several people have drowned. Mundas believe that the god of the Falls demands sacrifices.

Chota Nagpur Plateau → *For listings, see pages 831-832. Colour map 3, B5/C5.*

There are game reserves set in often stunningly beautiful and remote scenery on the Chota Nagpur Plateau, which can be easily reached from Ranchi. This is one of the poorest areas of India, with extensive missionary activity, though efforts are in place to conserve traditional tribal culture, which the government sees as a strong tourist draw.

Palamau (Betla) National Park was once the home of the extinct Indian cheetah and the world's first tiger census was taken in this **Project Tiger Reserve** in 1932. Recent developments in the park have not been encouraging: a survey taken by forest rangers reported that in 2006 visitors sighted a grand total of two tigers, although elephant sightings are much more commen. The wildlife also includes leopard, gaur, sambar, muntjac and nilgai, Indian wolf and many species of birds. The North Koel River and its tributary run through the park but in the summer animals become dependent on waterholes. The wooden towers at **Hathibajwa** and **Kamaladah**, and the hide at **Madhuchuhan**, are good vantage points. Elephants can be seen from the end of the monsoon until the waterholes begin to dry up in March. The Flame of the Forest (*Butea monosperma*) and *mahua* flowers attract birdlife: over 200 species of water and woodland birds have been recorded, while hot springs and the remains of two 16th-century **forts** of Chero kings who once ruled from here add to the interest. Palamau's vegetation is mainly sal and bamboo, though it is now considerably degraded. Jeeps for viewing the animals can be hired from the Forest Department. The park is open throughout the year, though the best time to visit is from October to April.

Also a Project Tiger Reserve, **Hazaribagh Wildlife Sanctuary** ⓘ *Evening park tour from Divisional Forest Office, Hazaribagh, 1700-2200, Rs 150,* is part of the Chota Nagpur plateau in forested tribal territory, interspersed with grass meadows and some deep waterways. Hazaribagh ('thousand gardens') town is close to the wildlife sanctuary, waterfalls at **Tilaiya**

Dam (55 km) and **Konar Dam** (51 km). The sanctuary is set in hilly terrain but is slightly lower than the town at 550 m. The park supports sambar, nilgai, deer, chital, leopard, tiger, wild boar and wild cat, though here too animal numbers are dwindling. There are 10 watchtowers and hides for viewing. Roads allow easy access; the NH33 takes you to the Pokharia gate, 16 km from Hazaribagh. The best time to visit is from February to April.

The Hazaribagh area also has some Mesolithic shelters where rock art can be seen and several Neolithic monuments including dolmens similar to those found in Celtic Europe. For more details contact Bulu Imam at **Sanskriti Crafts Store** ⓘ *Hazaribagh, T06546-264820, www.sanskritihazaribagh.com*, who sells authentic tribal artworks and has founded a Tribal Women's Artists' Cooperative for traditional arts.

Eastern Jharkhand → *For listings, see pages 831-832.*

Jamshedpur → *Population: 570,300.*

This flourishing steel town lies 130 km southeast of Ranchi, established as a planned township by the Parsi industrialist Jamshedji Tata in 1908. Located close to rich iron and coal deposits, there are also limestone quarries and some magnesite. The town has retained much of its natural attraction, with its lakes and rivers enclosed by the Dolma hills, in spite of the pollution from its heavy plants. The town is split in two by the steel plant and rail sidings. **Keenan Stadium** ⓘ *Bistupur, north of town*, is the venue for international cricket matches. **Dalma Wildlife Sanctuary** ⓘ *a few kilometres out of Jamshedpur, on the Ranchi road, free*, is noted for its elephant population. For information contact **Jharkhand Tourism** ⓘ *near Air India office, Bistupur, T0657-243 2892.*

Other centres have emerged along the **Damodar Valley**, which cuts through a rocky, thickly wooded section of the Chota Nagpur plateau, the home of the many aboriginal tribal people of Jharkhand. The Santals, Bedia, Khond, Munda and Oraon were the original inhabitants of this land, and though a few still live in isolated villages, most have joined the workforce in the industrial townships. The river valley has a number of hydroelectric power stations and large dams. Industrial activities in the valley include coal in Dhanbad, and locomotives in Chittaranjan and Bokaro.

Parsnath Hill → *Colour map 3, B6. Altitude: 1366 m.*

The holy hill of Parsnath is about 150 km along the Kolkata Road from Bodhgaya, near Dumri and Madhuban; note that Madhuban's *dharamshalas* and lodges may be full during holidays and festivals. Particularly sacred to the Jains, a track winds up through Parsnath's forested slopes to the 24 shrines which crown the hilly northern outcrops of the Indian peninsula. The shrines are rarely visited by foreigners but are a regular pilgrimage site for thousands of devout Jains and Hindus. The highest shrine is dedicated to the last forerunner of Mahavir himself, Lord Parsvanatha, see page 1425, who is believed to have achieved enlightenment while meditating in the cave, now enshrined in the temple.

Most pilgrims start climbing at 0400, the best time to catch superb views of sunrise and the countryside. It is a three-hour climb but *dhoolis* are available; allow eight hours in all. The super-fit can manage a climb in just over two hours and run down much faster. A visit is highly recommended. Leather items are not allowed on the hill.

Jharkhand listings

For Sleeping and Eating price codes and other relevant information, see Essentials pages 38-42.

Sleeping

Ranchi *p828*

Most hotels in Ranchi are generally full. Book in advance if possible.

AL-A Capitol Hill, Main Rd, T0651-233 1330, www.hotelcapitolhill.com. Smart rooms with minibar and internet, good central location, multi-cuisine restaurant, 24-hr room service.

A Yuvraj Palace, Doranda, T0651-248 0326/7, www.hotelyuvrajpalace.com. Best in town, 25 central a/c rooms and elegant suites, multi-cuisine restaurant, bar, 24-hr café.

B-C Hindustan, Main Rd, T0651-220 6039. 32 reasonable rooms with TV, some a/c, decent restaurant, overpriced but likely to have vacancies.

B-C Kwality Inns, Station Rd, T0651-246 0128. 36 rooms, mostly a/c, reasonable, clean, restaurant, though lacklustre staff.

B-D BNR, Station Rd, T0651-220 8044. 22 rooms in cottages in station building, some a/c, restaurant, lawns, tennis, old-world feel.

C-D Yuvraj, Doranda, T0651-248 2423. 35 rooms, some a/c, restaurant/bar.

E-F Birsa Vihar (JTDC), Main Rd, T0651-233 1828. Dorm, 30 simple rooms, tourist office.

Chota Nagpur Plateau *p829*

Palamau (Betla) National Park

D Tree House, Betla, Palamau National Park, book through Conservator of Forests, T06562-222650, fdptrpalamau@yahoo.co.in. Rickety little shack perched in a tree amid forest, lots of deer and other wildlife, the most atmospheric choice by far.

D Tree House, Maromar, bookings as above. Another Robinson Crusoe affair, built entirely of wood but it has modern facilities.

D-F Van Vihar, inside the reserve, Betla, T06567-226513. Reports of no electricity or food, 25 rooms, fairly comfortable a/c, good deer viewing, tourist information.

E Debjani, near the forest gate at Palamau. Food available.

E Forest Rest Houses, Kehr and Kechki. Reservations: Field Director, Project Tiger, Palamau, Daltonganj, T06562-222650.

E Rest Houses at Mundu, Garu, Chhipadohar and Baresand, contact Div Forest Officer, S Forest Div, Daltonganj, T06562-222427.

E Tourist Lodge, near the reserve. 10 rooms.

Hazaribagh Wildlife Sanctuary

D-E Tourist Lodge, T06546-224337. 9 rooms, some a/c, tourist information.

F Govt Guest House, 12 rooms, near the bus stand.

G Canary Hill Rest House, on hill overlooking lake, get permission from Forest Officer, T06546-222339. Very simple and basic but great views, wake up to birdsong.

Eastern Jharkhand *p830*

Budget hotels in Jamshedpur are close to Tata Nagar railway station. Mid-range hotels are 2-3 km from bus and train stations in Bistupur.

A Fortune Hotel Centrepoint, 2 Inner Circle Rd, Bistupur, T0657-222 4200, www.fortuneparkhotels.com. 42 rooms, central a/c, health club, good business facilities.

C-E Boulevard, Main Rd, Bistupur, T0657-242 5321, www.theboulevardhotel.org. Stately old place, large, sparse non-a/c rooms and range of a/c options. TV, hot bath, clean, friendly, well located, complimentary bed-tea. Recommended.

C-E South Park, Q Rd, Bistupur, T0657-243 5001. Inviting rooms, some a/c, clean hot bath, good restaurant, helpful. Recommended.

Transport

Ranchi *p828*

Air

The airport is 13 km away. **Indian Airlines**, Main Rd, T0651-220 6160, airport, T141, T0651-250 1554, www.indian-airlines.nic.in. Daily to **Delhi**, **Mumbai** and **Patna**. 4 flights a week to **Kolkata** and **Lucknow**.

Bus

Private Bus Stand at Kantatoli, 2 km from Main Rd, T0651-230 8907; serves major towns in Jharkhand and surrounding states.

Government Bus Stand, Station Rd, T0651-230 4328. Also **Ratu Rd Bus Stand** (4 km) for buses to Madhya Pradesh (eg **Daltonganj**).

Train

Enquiries, T131. Reservations, T135. Computerized Reservation Centre, G-41 Sainak Market, Main Rd, T0651-230 1097. **Dhanbad**: *Maurya Exp 15027*, 1720, 4½ hrs. **Gaya**: *Hatia Patna Exp 18626*, 0625, 6½ hrs; *Hatia Patna Exp 18624*, 1930, 8 hrs. Both continue to **Patna**, 9½ hrs and 11 hrs. **Kolkata** (**H**): *Hatia Howrah Exp 18616*, 2140, 9 hrs. **New Delhi**: *Rajdhani Exp 12439*, 1750 (Wed and Sun), 17 hrs; *Jammu Tawi Exp 18601*, 1530, 29 hrs.

Chota Nagpur Plateau *p829*

The nearest airport to Palamau is at Ranchi, 140 km away. If in a car, take the road west-north west out of Ranchi for **Kuru** (57 km), in Kuru fork right to Tori, then towards Daltonganj. The closest stations are **Daltonganj** (25 km) and **Barwadih** (15 km).

Hazaribagh Wildlife Sanctuary

If in a car, go north from Ranchi on the NH33 through Ramgarh to Hazaribagh (91 km) and to the main gate at Pokharia. The nearest train station is Koderma (60 km).

Jamshedpur *p830*

Bus

Jamshedpur Bus Stand is at Mango, 4 km from Bistupur; services to the main centres.

Rickshaw

Shared auto-rickshaws (unmetered) run along main routes, or you have to take a 'reserved rickshaw'; expect to bargain. Don't pay more than Rs 30 for Tata Nagar to Bistupur.

Train

Tata Nagar station is on the SE railway on Kolkata (Howrah)-Mumbai line. Enquiries, T131. To **New Delhi**: *Purushottam Exp 12801*, 0645, 22 hrs. **Kolkata** (**H**): *Jan Shatabdi Exp 12022*, 1710, 3½ hrs; *Steel Exp 12814*, 0615, 4 hrs; *Gitanjali Exp 12859*, 0830, 4 hrs. **Puri** via **Bhubaneswar**: *Purushottam 12802*, 2020, 9 hrs (7½ hrs); *Neelachal Exp 12876*, 0745 Mon. Wed. And Sun, 9½ hrs. **Ranchi**: *Howrah Hatia Exp 18615*, 2220, 8½ hrs.

Parsnath Hill *p830*

Dhanbad is the nearest large town with hotels (see Damodar Valley, page 830). Train from **Dhanbad** to Parsanath station, 1 convenient train for those staying overnight in Madhuban: *Poorva Exp 12381*, 1205, 30 mins; then minibus from Parsnath station to **Madhuban**, Rs 15, 40 mins, or taxi, Rs 200. Buses also from Dhanbad, 0545, to **Isri**; then taxi (for return that day) or another bus to **Madhuban** at 1000, and stay overnight in a *dharamshala*. Return bus from Madhuban at 1530.

❶ Directory

Jamshedpur *p830*

Banks Bank of Baroda, Main Rd, Bistupur, cash on credit cards. **ICICI**, K Rd, Bistupur; ATM Visa withdrawals.

Andaman & Nicobar Islands

Contents

Footprint features

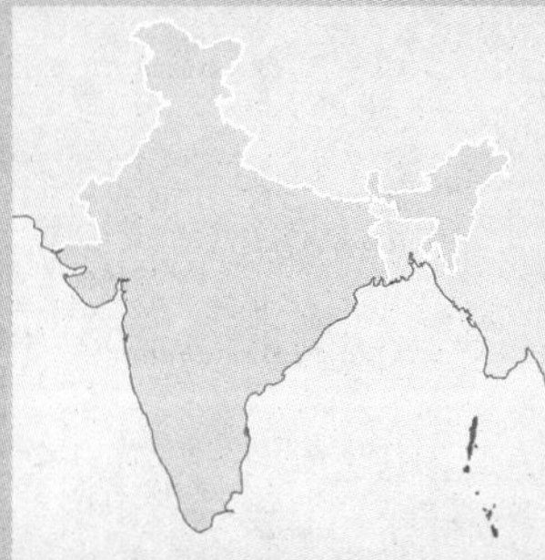

At a glance

Getting around Slow government ferries run to an erratic timetable from Port Blair; private charters preferable. Bikes and motorbikes, auto-rickshaws and taxis for hire on the larger islands.

Time required At least 2 weeks (most people stay as long as possible).

Weather Tropical, with temperatures never higher than 32°C.

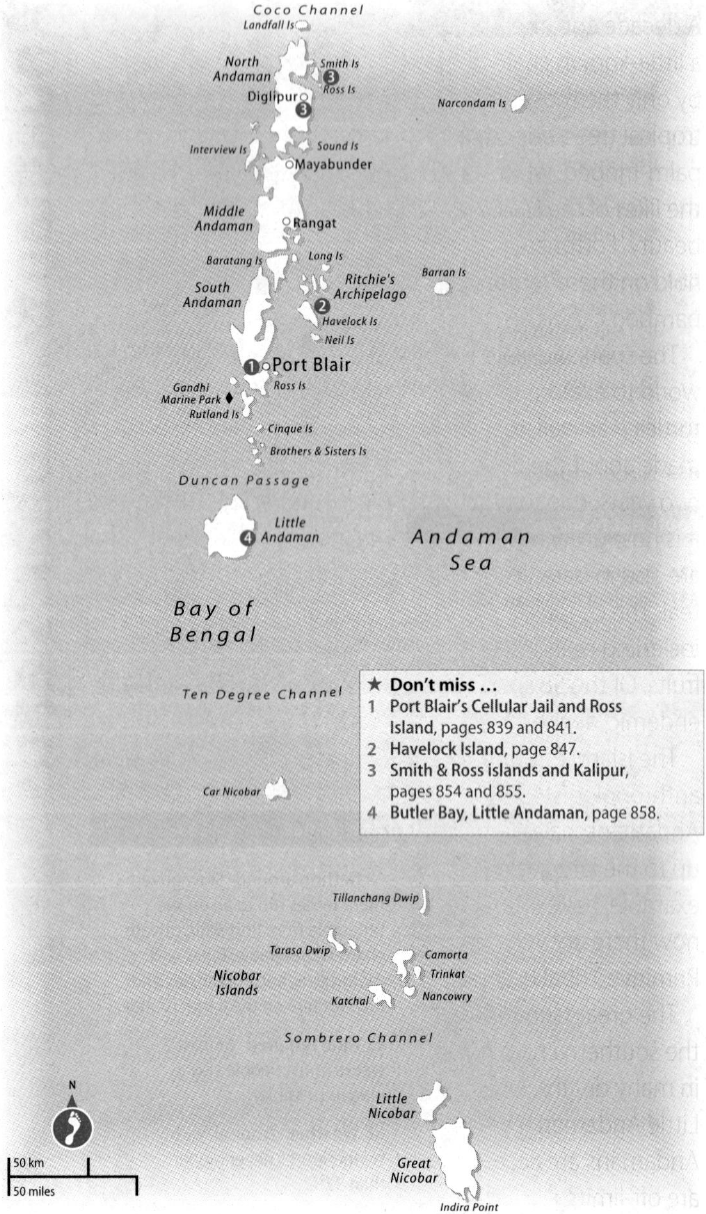

★ Don't miss ...

1. **Port Blair's Cellular Jail and Ross Island**, pages 839 and 841.
2. **Havelock Island**, page 847.
3. **Smith & Ross islands and Kalipur**, pages 854 and 855.
4. **Butler Bay, Little Andaman**, page 858.

A decade ago, the Andaman and Nicobar Islands were a little-known chain of tropical islands in the Bay of Bengal visited by only the most intrepid. Thickly wooded with rainforest and tropical trees, edged by mangrove swamps and pristine palm-fringed, white-sand beaches and coral reefs, they easily rival the likes of the Maldives or the Caribbean in terms of natural beauty. Fortunately, five-star all-inclusive resorts have not taken hold on these remote islands, although joining the backpacker bamboo cabins are some resorts with all the creature comforts.

The sparkling clear water makes it one of the best places in the world to explore the seabed; rare species – dugong and marine turtles – as well as tropical fish are a big attraction. Much has been made about the death of coral reefs near the surface over the last two years, due to high water temperatures, but there is evidence it is now growing back (to the delight of snorkellers). Birdwatchers are also in paradise with 242 species recorded, including the grey teal. The canopied rainforests harbour 3000 species of plant including mangroves, ferns, orchids, palms, climbers and tropical fruits. Of the 58 species of mammal and 83 reptiles, many are endemic, as the islands are so isolated.

The islands' aboriginal tribal people are of special interest to anthropologists. Some, such as the Jarawas and Sentinalese in the Andamans, have remained isolated and hostile to outsiders even up to the late 20th century. Others, the Great Andamanese for example, have interacted with non-tribal settlers for decades and now there are very few left. The Indian government keeps the Primitive Tribal Reserve Areas out of bounds.

The great tsunami in 2004 damaged parts of this paradise; the southern chain of islands, the Nicobars, was badly hit resulting in many deaths. Only the southernmost island in the Andamans – Little Andaman – was substantially affected. Much of the Andamans are accessible to foreigners, while the Nicobars are off-limits.

Background → *Population: 380,00. Area: 8249 sq km.*

The land

Geography The Andaman and Nicobar group comprises about 330 islands formed by a submarine mountain range which divides the Bay of Bengal from the Andaman Sea. The islands lie between latitudes 6° to 14° north (about level with Chennai) and longitudes 92-94° east, a span of 725 km. The land rises to 730 m (Saddle Peak), formed mainly of limestones, sandstones and clays. The Andamans are separated from the Nicobars by a 90-m-deep 150-km strait. The Andamans group has 204 islands (26 inhabited) with its three main islands of North, Middle and South, which are separated by mangrove-fringed islets, together called Great Andaman. The Nicobar Islands comprise 12 inhabited and seven uninhabited islands including three groups: Car Nicobar in the north, Camorta and Nancowry in the middle and the largest, Great Nicobar, in the south.

Climate Tropical, with temperatures of 20-32°C. Annual rainfall is 2540 mm. Monsoon seasons are usually early-May to mid-September, and November to mid-December (though the first may arrive as early as mid-April, bringing heavy rain on most days). The best time to visit is end November to mid-April. The climate has no extremes, the main contrasts coming with the arrival of the monsoons and tropical storms.

History

Lying on the trade route between Burma and India the islands appeared on Ptolemy's second-century map and were also recorded by the Chinese traveller I-Tsing in the seventh century. At the end of the 17th century the Marathas established a base here to attack the trading British, Dutch and Portuguese ships. Dutch pirates and French Jesuits had made contact with the islands before the Danish East India Company made attempts to evangelize the islands in the mid-18th century. The reputation of ferocity attributed to the Nicobarese may have been partly due to Malay pirates who attacked and killed sailors of any trading vessel that came ashore (some anthropologists believe that, despite common belief, the aboriginals themselves were not cannibals). The first British attempt to occupy the islands was made in 1788 when the governor general of India sent Lieutenant Blair (whose name was given to the first port) and, although the first convicts were sent there in 1794, it was abandoned within a couple of years.

After the 'First War of Independence' (the 'Mutiny') in 1857, the British gained control of most of the islands and used them as a penal colony for its prisoners (who until then had been sent to Sumatra) right up to Indian Independence, with a short break from 1942-1945 when the Japanese occupied Port Blair, Ross Island and the Nicobar Islands. However, political prisoners were sent in large numbers only after the completion of the Cellular Jail in 1906. Each revolt on the mainland resulted in the transportation of people from various parts of India, hence the presence of Bengalis, Malayans and Burmese among others. Subhas Chandra Bose, the Indian Nationalist, first raised the Indian tricolour here in 1943.

Culture

Sir Arthur Conan Doyle in 1890 described the islanders as "perhaps ... the smallest race upon this earth ... fierce, morose and intractable". In the mid-19th century, the British guessed the tribal population was around 5000 but the number has been steadily dwindling. Today most of the inhabitants are Indians, Burmese and Malays – some being descendants of the criminals who were taken there. Since the 1950s, refugees from East Pakistan (Bangladesh), Burma and Indian emigrants from Guyana have settled on the main islands to be followed more recently by Tamils from Sri Lanka. The largest concentration is around the capital, Port Blair, with the majority of tribal people (about 15% of the population) living in the Nicobars.

Tribals of Andaman and Nicobar

The islands have been inhabited by Aboriginal tribes (some Negrito) for thousands of years but long remained unexplored because anyone attempting to land would be attacked. Today there are only a few **Andamanese** (who once inhabited the Great Andamans), less than 100 **Onges** who live in Dugong Creek in Little Andaman (and traditionally painted their naked bodies), the fierce **Jarawas** on South and Middle Andaman and the **Sentinelese** on North Sentinel. Car Nicobar (Carnic) is inhabited by mongoloid **Nicobarese. Shompens**, who may have been of pre-Dravidian stock, live on Great Nicobar.

The islanders hunted wild pigs, fished with nets and caught turtles with harpoons from dug-out canoes, they used iron for arrowheads and metal from wrecks for harpoons. Some tribes made pottery but the **Andamanese** particularly were exceptional since they had not discovered the art of fire-making.

The Anthropological Survey of India and the Andaman Administration have been jointly trying to establish friendly contact with the Jarawas and Sentinelese since the 1960s. They consistently repelled groups of explorers with poisoned arrows. In 1991, Indian anthropologists succeeded in landing on North Sentinel and a few Sentinelese boarded a lifeboat to accept gifts of coconuts (which do not grow on their island). Study groups have made regular visits, removing most of their clothes in order to be accepted. The 400 or so Sentinelese do not appear to have a hierarchical social structure; they are naked, painting their bodies with chalk and ochre and wearing bead and bone ornaments.

The 250 or so **Jarawas** remain within the Tribal Reserve set aside to the west of the Andaman Trunk Road. However, since contact was made in 1997, some now visit the hospital and markets in Port Blair and groups are frequently seen by the roadside as the daily convoys pass through. It is forbidden to photograph them, and efforts are now being made to protect them from voyeurs. The road is due to be re-routed and the plans of Barefoot to build an eco-resort in Collipur, close to the Reserve, have caused much controversy.

Hindi, Bengali, Tamil, Malayalam and English are spoken. The Andamanese language does not resemble any other; it uses prefixes and suffixes to indicate the function of a word and is extraordinary in using simply two concepts of number, 'one' and 'greater than one'.

Modern Andaman and Nicobar

Economy Tourism is rapidly becoming the islands' most important industry, although forests still represent an important resource. The government has divided 40% of the forests into Primitive Tribal Reserve areas which are only open to Indian visitors with permits, and the remaining 60% as Protected Areas set aside for timber for export as plywoods, hardwoods and matchwoods (a Swedish multinational owns extensive logging rights). Rubber and mahogany have been planted in addition to teak and rosewood which are commercially in demand. Fishing – lobsters, prawns and sea fish – and agriculture are also important, with rice a staple food crop.

Tsunami

In December 2004, following the powerful earthquake off the coast of Indonesia, devastating tidal waves hit many countries. In this region, the aboriginal tribals living on the Nicobar Islands bore the brunt of the casualties. Of the 572 islands (38 inhabited), Car Nicobar was the worst affected. Elsewhere, Little Andaman's two resorts were razed, though Port Blair, the Andaman capital, was unscathed. Havelock Island, the government's prime focus for tourism, was not badly damaged, The official human fatalities are daunting: 8000 died in the Nicobars alone, and 80 died on Little Andaman.

Ins and outs

Getting there

Foreigners with tourist visas for India are issued with a Restricted Area Permit (RAP) valid for 30 days on arrival at Port Blair by air or sea. This can then be extended for a further 15 days at the Office of the Superintendent of Police/FRO in Port Blair, T03192-233077, or at local police stations (in Havelock they are familiar with the procedure). It is necessary to wait until your RAP is due to expire before you can extend it, and you need to produce proof of an outward flight ticket. Permits are checked when embarking and disembarking ferries, and by guesthouses, so keep them safe. Foreigners are permitted to visit and stay overnight in Port Blair, Havelock, Long Island, Neil Island, Kadamtala (excluding tribal reserve), Baratang, Rangat, Mayabunder, Kalighat, Diglipur, and Little Andaman (excluding tribal reserve). You can also visit Jolly Buoy/Red Skin, South Cinque, Ross Island, Interview, Brother, Sister and Barren Island during the daytime. In practice, requests to visit remote islands such as North Passage and Narcondam, which have been opened to tourists, are often refused. It is not permitted to visit tribal reserve areas or restricted islands including Nicobar. See also www.tourism.andaman.nic.in. ▸▸ *For Transport, see page 845.*

Getting around

If you can find someone willing to hire you a scooter it is the most enjoyable and practical way to visit places around Port Blair (recommended particularly for trips to Wandoor, Chiriya Tapu, Mount Harriet and Corbyn's Cove). Buses cover sights and towns on the limited road network. Inter-island ferries sail to coastal towns and islands, and bicycles and scooters/motorbikes are available for rent on Havelock.

Port Blair and around

→ *Colour map 6, C6. Population: 100,200.*

Port Blair, the capital, about 1200 km from Kolkata and Chennai, has only a handful of sights. The small town has changed in the last 40 years from one that received a ship from the mainland once a month if the weather permitted to a place connected by several daily flights from Chennai and Kolkata. It has a hospital, shops, schools and colleges and a few museums, in addition to hotels and water sports facilities. ▸▸ *For listings, see pages 843-846. See also South Andaman map, page 848.*

Ins and outs

Getting there **Veer Savarkar Airport**, 3 km south of Port Blair, has flights from Kolkata and Chennai. You can get an auto-rickshaw into town for Rs 50 if you bargain, or a pre-paid taxi for Rs 100, or leave the airport compound and take a bus from the opposite side of the road (Rs 4-5). Ships from the mainland dock at Haddo Jetty where you can get taxis, but they invariably overcharge.

Getting around As Port Blair is very small, you can easily see the sights in a couple of days. Aberdeen Bazar in the town centre has most of the budget hotels, the bus station, shops and offices and is easily walkable although it's hilly.

Tourist information **Directorate of Tourism** ⓘ *opposite Air India office, T03192-232694, www.tourism.andaman.nic.in, Mon-Fri 0830-1300, 1400-1430, Sat 0830-1300.* Books boat tours, and has up-to-date ferry schedules. An essential stop if you want to book accommodation in the government hotels around the islands (T03192-232747, www.accommodation@and.nic.in, bookings taken between 0845-1130 and 1415-1515, 25% deposit required). **Government of India Tourism** ⓘ *2nd floor (above Super Shoppe), 189 Junglighat Main Rd (VIP Rd), T03192-233006.*

Sights

North of Aberdeen Jetty, the **Cellular Jail** (1886-1906) ⓘ *Tue-Sun 0900-1230, 1330-1615, Rs 10, camera Rs 25, video camera Rs 100, allow 1 hr,* was originally built by the British to house dangerous criminals and could hold 698 solitary prisoners in small narrow cells. Subsequently, until 1938, it was used to incarcerate Indian freedom fighters. The Japanese used it to hold their prisoners of war during their occupation from 1942 to 1945. Three of the original seven wings, which extended from the central guard tower in a star-shape, survive. The jail was renovated in 1998 and is well maintained and the gardens flower-filled. The **galleries** display photographs and lists of 'convicts' held. There is a 'death house' with gallows and implements used in torture. Entering the cells gives an impression of the conditions within the prison in the early 1900s. There is a **son et lumière show** ⓘ *Mon, Wed and Fri at 1845, Rs 20, 45 mins, in English,* (more sound than light) on prison life under the British.

The **Zonal Anthropological Museum** ⓘ *Fri-Wed 0900-1300, 1330-1630, Rs 10,* is worth a visit; it has a small but interesting collection of photographs of 'exploratory expeditions' to visit the islanders and their dwellings. Woven baskets, pottery, bows and arrows, and other beautifully crafted artefacts are on display.

Chatham Saw Mill ⓘ *Mon-Sat 0830-1430, entrance Rs 2, allow 1½ hrs, no photography,* is one of the oldest in Asia, employing 1000 workers. Tours take you through the different processes of turning logs into 'seasoned' planks. For tours, report to the Security Office just outside the main gate. The **Forest Museum** ⓘ *0800-1200, 1430-1700,* here has unusual local woods including red paduk, satin and marble woods. It shows how different wood is used in the timber industry and methods of lumbering/finishing.

The **Mini Zoo** ⓘ *Tue-Sun 0800-1700,* has a small, uninspiring collection in some very old wooden cages with a few specimens of unusual island fauna including a sea crocodile farm. The saltwater crocodile that killed a tourist on Havelock in 2010 has been re-homed here. **Marine Museum** ⓘ *opposite Andaman Teal House, Tue-Sun 0830-1200, 1400-1700, Rs 10, camera Rs 20,*

Port Blair

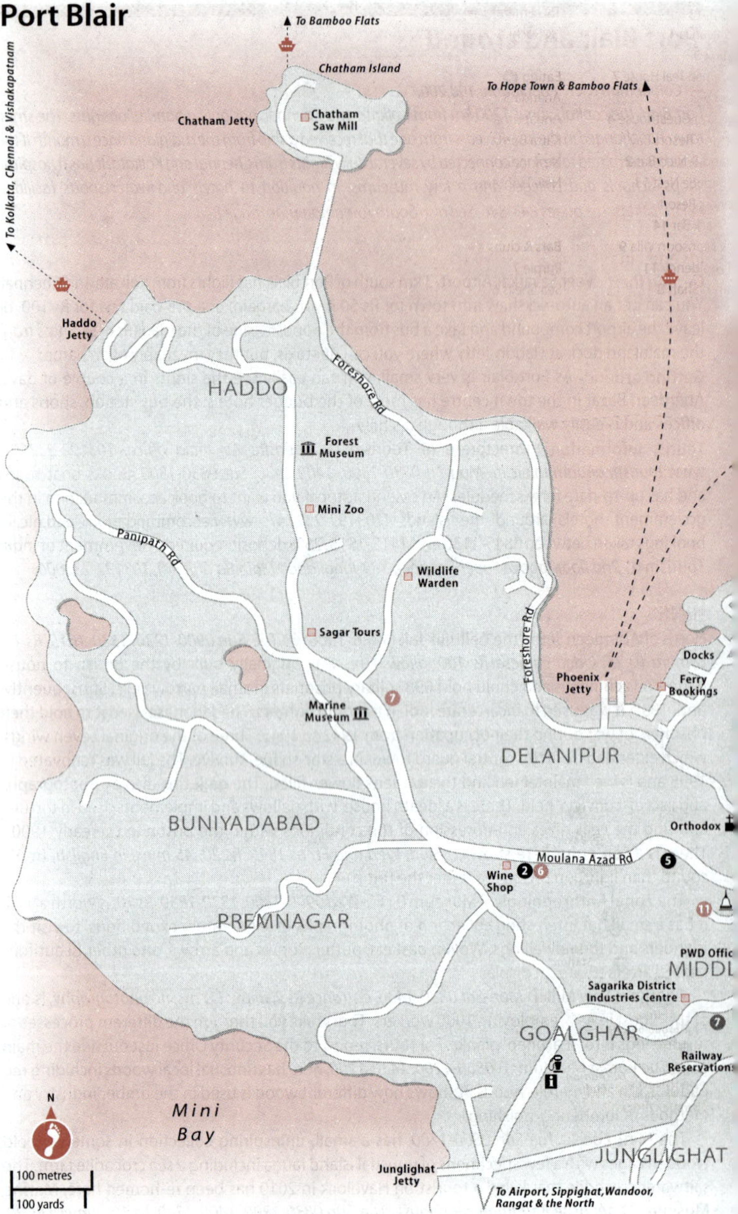
To Bamboo Flats
Chatham Island
Chatham Jetty
Chatham Saw Mill
To Hope Town & Bamboo Flats
To Kolkata, Chennai & Vishakapatnam
Haddo Jetty
HADDO
Foreshore Rd
Forest Museum
Mini Zoo
Panipath Rd
Wildlife Warden
Sagar Tours
Foreshore Rd
Phoenix Jetty
Docks
Ferry Bookings
Marine Museum
DELANIPUR
BUNIYADABAD
Orthodox
Moulana Azad Rd
Wine Shop
PREMNAGAR
PWD Offic
MIDDL
Sagarika District Industries Centre
GOALGHAR
Railway Reservations
Mini Bay
N
JUNGLIGHAT
100 metres
100 yards
Junglighat Jetty
To Airport, Sippighat, Wandoor, Rangat & the North

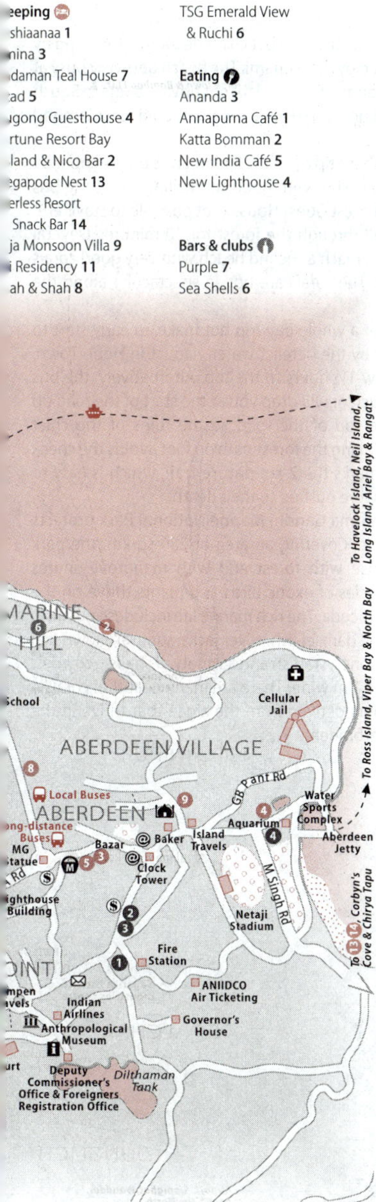

video camera Rs 40, allow 30 mins, has a collection of corals and shells and a display of 350 species of marine life. There is also an **Aquarium** ⓘ *Tue-Sun (closed on 2nd Sat in the month) 0900-1300 1400-1645, Rs 5* near the Watersports Complex.

Ross Island ⓘ *boats leave Thu-Mon 0830, 1030, 1230 and 1400, from Aberdeen jetty, buy tickets (Rs 75) at the Watersports Centre before the jetty; entrance to the island is Rs 20, boats return 2 hrs later*, was originally developed under the British as the Residence of the Chief Commissioner and administrative headquarters. The **Farzand Ali store** near the jetty has a few interesting old photos of the island as it looked under the British. During the Second World War, it was occupied by the Japanese whose legacy is a complex of concrete bunkers, mostly still intact. Almost all the other buildings on the island are ruins with spotted deer living peacefully among them. In many cases the walls are only still standing because of the climbing trees – the best example being the AC's house at the summit. The remains of the Anglican church (the spire of which has turned into a tree) and the Subalterns' club are evocative, and when wandering off down any path you will find yourself spookily alone. The tiny Ross Restaurant near the jetty is pricey but surprisingly good.

Viper Island, near Haddo Wharf at the mouth of the harbour, is where convicts were interned before the Cellular Jail was built. Boats go at 1500 (Rs 90) or you can visit as part of a three-island tour (including Ross and Northbay) at 1500 (Rs 300) from Aberdeen jetty daily.

Although the only beach close to Port Blair (5 km away), **Corbyn's Cove** is only busy at weekends. The water is warm with gentle surf but the palm-fringed white sand beach is not as clean as others.

South Andaman

An easy bus ride away from Port Blair is **Wandoor**, an attractive beach made more interesting by the vast hulks of skeleton trees that were deposited by the tsunami. The beach gets very busy at weekends, particularly Sundays. The jetty at Wandoor is the place to rent private boats to **South Cinque Island** which has spectacular snorkelling and diving; boats should cost around Rs 500-1000 (plus permission from the DC's Office).

Chiriya Tapu, 28 km from Port Blair at the southern tip of South Andaman, is only an hour by road. Popular for birdwatching, it has excellent beaches with good snorkelling. From the bus stop, which has some tea shops, a track past the **Forest Guest House** (not possible to stay here) leads to the first beach. Continue along the trail through the forest for 20 minutes (several smaller trails are ideal for birdwatching), until you reach a second beach with very good corals 50 m out; at low tide you can walk a long way. The corals are not so spectacular along the coastline, but there is a large range of fish.

Mount Harriet is good for either a morning or a whole day trip but make an early start to avoid the heat. A path through the forest starts by the derelict water viaduct in Hope Town, which joins the surfaced road near the top. Allow 1½ hours to the top. Alternatively, the bus from the jetty stops in Hope Town near the viaduct, or will drop you at the start of the road up the hill with a 4-km walk from here. Near the top of the road lie the ruins of the chief commissioner's bungalow, abandoned in 1942. Taking the forest path on foot avoids the check post and fees. From Mount Harriet, a signpost marks the 2-km **nature trail**, which is easy to follow to **Black Rocks**, the spot where prisoners were pushed to their death.

About 30 km southwest of Port Blair, the **Mahatma Gandhi Marine National Park** protects some exceptional coral beds and underwater life. Covering an area of 280 sq km, the park comprises 15 uninhabited tropical islands dense with forest and with mangrove shores interrupting the aquamarine waters. Several species of exotic birds and plants thrive on the land while underwater lurk turtles, sharks and barracuda. The rich marine life includes angelfish, green parrot, yellow butterfly, black surgeon, blue damsel fish, silver jacks, squirrel, clown fish and sweetlips as well as sea cucumbers, sea anemones, starfish and a variety of shells – cowries, turbots, conches and the rarer giant clam, up to a 1 m wide. There are many beautiful corals – brain, finger, mushroom and antler – their colours derived from the algae that thrive in the living coral. Coral and shell collecting is strictly forbidden.

Port Blair and around listings

For Sleeping and Eating price codes and other relevant information, see Essentials pages 38-42.

Sleeping

Port Blair and around *p839, map p840*

Most hotels offer significant discounts Apr-Sep, while prices rise significantly during peak times (Dec-Jan). The prices listed here reflect standard prices during the Oct to end-Mar season. Many hotels have terribly early check-out times.

AL Fortune Resort Bay Island, Marine Hill, 2 km, T03192-234101, www.fortunehotels.in. Colonial-style hotel with 48 spacious a/c rooms (not all have sea view, which costs more), some small replica local huts, cool open bar and restaurant, good gardens but poor tennis court, unappealing sea water pool, far from any beach but excellent view across harbour entrance. B&B, half or full board.

AL-A Peerless Resort, Corbyn's Cove (4 km), set back from beach, T03192-229311/3, ppbeachin@sancharnet.in. 48 rooms, 4 cottages, pleasant and airy, well-kept mature gardens, tennis, beach nearby (take own snorkelling equipment), dive centre, excellent service, warm atmosphere, free airport transfer but need taxis to town (by day, wait on the beach for one to pass).

A-B Megapode Nest, Haddo Hill, T03192-232380/232207, www.aniidco.nic.in. 19 good a/c rooms, 4 deluxe and 10 thatched Nicobari cottages, restaurant, bar, large terrace, very peaceful and gardens have superb views. Includes breakfast.

A-C TSG Emerald View, 25 Moulana Azad Rd, Phoenix Bay, T03192-246488, www.andamantsg hotels.com. Recently refitted, 50 rooms are modern and comfortable, plus some suites (Rs 6000). Gym, excellent restaurant (see Eating, page 844) and nautical-themed bar. Check-out 0700.

D-E Dugong Guesthouse, near the Watersports Complex, T03192-243237. Clean rooms in a slightly institutional building are suitably priced at Rs 800 per a/c double, suites are Rs 1200. Cheap breakfast available.

E-F Aashiaanaa Guesthouse, near Marine Dockyard, Marine Hill, T03192-242858, T(0)9474-217008. Competent and friendly operation, with a range of rooms, all clean and cheerful with fans, nets and TVs, some have private bathrooms, front rooms (more expensive) have balcony and a/c. Can pick up from airport (Rs 150), laundry service. Close to the ferry dock.

E-F Andaman Teal House, Delanipur, book through **Director of Tourism**, T03192-232694. Good views, 27 clean rooms with bath, non-a/c doubles good value, comfortable wicker furniture, spacious lounge-restaurant.

E-F Azad, Aberdeen Bazar, T03192-242646. The choice of many budget tourists despite the lackadaisical staff and curious smell in cheaper rooms. Newer rooms are clean, large, tiled and newly painted, some with attached baths, some with a/c, all with TV. Single rooms rates available. Set back slightly from the main road.

E-F Hornbill Nest, 10 mins' walk from Corbyn's Cove, T03192-211939, hornbillresort@ rediffmail.com. Clean rooms, some on hillside overlooking sea, central open-air lounge and restaurant, transport difficult (stop a returning empty taxi) although they have bikes for rent.

E-F Raja Monsoon Villa, 9 RP Rd, opposite Jama Masjid, T(0)9474-226394. Clean spacious rooms, good bathrooms and furniture, TVs, in a new building. Best on the top floor, which has a huge breezy terrace. Recommended. Significant discounts possible with a bit of patience.

E-F Sai Residency, near Lighthouse Building, T(0)9434-262965. Small clean rooms with TV, fresh sheets, some with a/c, 1 has a balcony, cheap singles. Handy for the jetty. Look for the sign for **Sagarika Guesthouse**, it's immediately before.

F Amina Lodge, Aberdeen Bazar (opposite Ganesh Temple), T(0)9933-258703, aminaloege@ymail.com. Run by a really lovely couple with good English, 5 spotless rooms are excellent value if rather small and cramped, as are bathrooms. Colourfully decorated, with clean furniture and satellite TV. Recommended.

F Shah-N-Shah, near the bus stand, Aberdeen Bazar, T03192-233696, shahnshahrediff@ mail.com. 23 large rooms are a little shabby but clean; benefits are the huge 1st-floor balcony, helpful owner, and proximity to bus station and ferry. Cheap singles for Rs 250, or doubles with TV for Rs 500, plus triple or 4-bed rooms.

Eating

Port Blair and around *p839, map p840*

South Indian cuisine is prevalent and seafood is excellent. Recommended is local fish fry (spiced tuna or mackerel chunks). Larger hotels have a wide selection, but meals (most ingredients are imported from the mainland) can be expensive. There are several juice bars between the bus stand and clock tower.

₹₹-₹ **Annapurna**, Aberdeen Bazar. Open 0730-2200. Clean and a/c, always busy with families, modern fittings. Wide selection of vegetarian Indian, good Chinese dishes, but *lassis* disappointing and locals feel the standard of food is slipping.

₹₹-₹ **New Lighthouse**, by Aberdeen Jetty. Wide choice of Indian and Chinese dishes in an open-air café, but the reason to come is for the fish – which almost everyone does at some point when in Port Blair. The evening barbecue has excellent tandoori fish, and lobster and crab come recommended. Sadly, the upstairs seating area no longer serves up beer.

₹₹-₹ **Ruchi**, at **TSG Emerald View** (see Sleeping). Wide menu of Indian, Chinese and some continental dishes, some of which are quite inventive, try the Akhbari kofta, alcohol available. A modern place that is nice for a treat and not too formal or pricey.

₹ **Ananda**, Aberdeen Bazar, T03192-244041. Mon-Fri 1000-1830, Sat 1000-1400. Western breakfasts, soups, huge choice of veg and non-veg Indian food; the a/c section is preferable.

₹ **Hotel Katta Bomman**, Aberdeen Bazar, T03192-221394. 0630-2130, Sun 0630-0930. Excellent *dosas*, *idli*, etc, from a plastic tray in a small cheerful café. Food is fiery. The lunchtime, 1100-1530, Rs 60 *thali* is a winner.

₹ **New India Café**, next to **Hotel Jaimathi**. Good South Indian breakfasts, in a slightly shabby environment. Great food and prices.

Bars and clubs

Port Blair and around *p839, map p840*

A nice place for a drink is the airy terrace of the Nico Bar at **Fortune Bay Island**, under the soaring roof, with great views (during the day) and larger- than-life ancestor statues as decoration (beer Rs 135). Also particularly nice is the rooftop bar at **Hotel Sea Shells**. **Peerless Beach Resort** and **TSG Emerald View** have decent bars, and Purple Bar at the **Sun Sea Resort** has a back room with some atmosphere and cheap beer. There are several cheap local bars around Aberdeen Bazar.

Festivals and events

Port Blair and around *p839, map p840*

Dec/Jan Island Tourism Festival for 15 days, with music and dancing from all over India and focusing on local crafts, culture and food.

Shopping

Port Blair and around *p839, map p840*

Local curio shops are by the clock tower and opposite the post office. Tailors sell hammocks.

Sagarika District Industries Centre, Middle Point, near tourist office, Mon-Sat 0900-2000. Selection of souvenirs in wood and shell (the government limit collection of shells), good for jewellery.

Activities and tours

Port Blair and around *p839, map p840*

Boat trips

The **Directorate of Tourism** runs 1-day boat trips to Jolly Buoy or Red Skin (open alternately to tourists, for 6 months at a time) and Baratang, as well as selling tickets for Ross Island (Rs 75) and the Harbour Cruise (Rs 75, at 1500).

Diving

Foreign tourists generally head to Havelock for diving trips and courses (see page 851).

Swimming

Swimming is excellent off the uninhabited islands that tourists may visit for the day in Mahatma Gandhi National Park. The sea at Corbyn's Cove is not as clean as it should be.

Tour operators

ANIIDCO Air Ticketing Unit, Vikas Bhawan, T03192-244312. Good for flights, Mon-Fri 0900-1300 and 1400-1800.

Island Travel, Aberdeen Bazar, T03192-233358. Flight agents. Offers a variety of excursions and car hire.

Shompen Travels, 2 Middle Pt, T03192-232360. Mon-Sat 0830-2100. Tours of Port Blair and the islands, can book tickets to Havelock, etc (heavy commission, take your permit).

⊖ Transport

Port Blair and around *p839, map p840*

Air Air India and JetLite fly daily from **Kolkata** and **Chennai**, plus **Kingfisher** and **Indigo** fly from **Chennai**. Transport to town: frequent buses pass the airport entrance (Rs 4-5). Autos should charge Rs 50 per person but will demand more, agree fare first. Pre-paid taxis are Rs 100 for the first 5 km, which will take you into the centre. Flights are best booked a few weeks in advance (earlier for Apr-May) to get the cheapest prices. You can also request your international carrier to get Andamans' tickets, preferably months ahead. **Air India**, G55 Middle Pt, behind PO, T03192-233108, Mon-Sat 1000-1300, 1400-1600. **Jet Airways**, 189 Main Rd, Junglighat, T03192-236922.

There is now a **seaplane** service between **Port Blair** and **Havelock**, the views are incredible, costing Rs 4100. Also to **Diglipur** and flights over **Barren Island**, contact ANIIDCO, T03192-244312, T(0)9933-280141, andamanseaplane@gmail.com.

Bus Local State buses leave from the bus station in Aberdeen Bazar. Computerized tickets are issued 0345-1800. There is a regular service to villages and districts. From Port Blair, buses go to **Wandoor Jetty** at 0450, 0600, 0745, 0900, 1200, 1340, 1500 and 1640, last returning at 1745 (1 hr, Rs 10-12). To **Corbyn Junction** buses hour from 0450-2000 (45 mins, Rs 5), change to an auto (Rs 30) for the last 2 km to the cove, last back at 2030. To **Chiriya Tapu** buses leave at 0500, 0630, 0800, 0900, 1000, 1200, 1340, 1500, 1700 (1 hr, Rs 10-12), returns 10 mins after arrival, last at 1800. **Private buses** go to **Chatham** regularly from the adjacent bus stand.

Long distance Bus is quickest to the north (which involves crossing 2 wide creeks by ferry transfer), tickets can be bought in advance at the bus station. To **Diglipur** at 0400 and 0430 (10 hrs, Rs 170), via **Baratang**; to **Mayabunder** at 0500 and 0945 (8 hrs, Rs 130); to **Rangat** at 0545 and 1145 (7 hrs, Rs 95). **Private buses**, to **Rangat** daily at 1100 (6-7 hrs, Rs1 30-180), **Mayabunder** and **Diglipur** are also available, buy tickets a day ahead from agents around the bus stand.

Ferry Inter-island ferries operate from Phoenix Bay Jetty. The office is open for advance reservations Mon-Fri 0900-1600 (lunch break 1300-1400), Sat 0900-1200, closed Sun, T03192-245555/231794. Sailings appear in the *Daily Telegrams* newspaper (or ring Shipping Corporation of India to check times, T03192-233347/233590). Daily to **Havelock**, at 0620, 1130 (via Neil) and 1400 (Rs 195/250, or Rs 260/350 depending on vessel); journey time is 2½ hrs if direct, or 4½ hrs if the boat goes via **Neil**. There is a faster new catamaran service, the **MS Makruzz**, T03192-212355/236677, www.makruzz.com, which leaves daily at 0845 and 1330 (1½ hrs, Rs 650, a/c). To **Neil** daily at 0630 and 1130, also at 0615 on Mon, Wed and Sat. The Line Ferry leaves Port Blair 3-4 times per week at 0615 (usually on Mon, Wed, Fri and Sat but check the weekly schedule at Port Blair booking office); the service always calls at **Havelock**, **Long Island** (Rs 50/55) and **Rangat** (Rs 50/85, 7-8 hrs) but alternating services also stop at **Neil** and **Strait Island** (a tribal reserve, disembarking is forbidden). Direct ferries to **Diglipur** (Aerial Bay Jetty), Tue evening and Fri morning, 9 hrs. **Little Andaman** (Hut Bay), daily at either 0615 (fast boat, Rs 25, 6 hrs) or, on alternating days, at 0700 (slow boat, Rs 55, 8 hrs). Boats to **Ross Island** daily except Wed, 0830, 1000,1230, 1400, Rs 75, buy tickets at the Watersports Centre, by Aberdeen Jetty from where the boats depart. From Chatham Jetty to Bamboo Flats and Dundas Pt, hourly, 0600-2025 (20 mins).

Mainland ferries Operated by the Shipping Corporation of India, these sail between Haddo Jetty in Port Blair (T03192-233590) and **Kolkata** (T033-2248 2354, 66 hrs) and **Chennai** (T044-2522 0841, 60 hrs) running to a schedule of sorts 3 to 4 times a month. Also **Vishakapatnam** (56 hrs) once a month. For immigration formalities, see page 838. Tentative schedules for the month are usually available at the end of the previous month; times of departure and arrival appear about a week before in the local papers. Also see www.shipindia.com. Last-minute changes are made depending on weather conditions and tides. Tickets are issued 7 days ahead but are not sold on the day of sailing. They can be difficult to get. Foreigners often stand a better chance than Indians, as there is a separate foreign quota available from booking office at Phoenix Jetty. Apply with 3 photos. **Note** End Apr/start May, 50% of tickets are reserved for the 'teachers' sailings' and finding a ticket out becomes almost impossible.

Ships vary, but prices per person are: De luxe Cabin (2 beds, shower), Rs 7640; 1st/A Class (4 bunks, shower), Rs 6320; 2nd Class (for 6), Rs 5030/3890; Bunk Class, Rs 1960. The ships are 25 to 65 years old. Meals are available but they are not appealing after the first day, so it's a good idea to carry some snacks. A kiosk sells biscuits, cigarettes, mineral water, soft drinks. Disembarkation can be chaotic and a free-for-all.

Rickshaw Autos should charge Rs 20 for central areas of town, Rs 40 if it's a bit further; to the airport should be Rs 50 but you will have to haggle.

Train **Railway Reservations Office**, near Secretariat, 0800-1230, 1300-1400. Supposedly separate queues for **Kolkata** and **Chennai**, but a total free-for-all in a small building – best avoided. Buy tickets in advance on the mainland if possible.

Directory

Port Blair and around *p839, map p840*

Banks Credit cards are not accepted at most places in the Andamans. Make sure you have plenty of cash before leaving Port Blair – there are ATMs on Havelock but the machines sometimes run out of money. **State Bank of India**, opposite bus station, open 0900-1300, Sat 0900-1100, has ATM. **Canara Bank** ATM by the clocktower is reliable. TCs and currency can be changed at **Island Travels**, Aberdeen Bazar, and at larger resorts. **Forest Department** Haddo Wharf, T03192-233549, can help book Forest Guesthouses. **Internet** Port Blair has a few internet cafes in Aberdeen Bazar which have skype, CD burning, wireless and decent connection speed for Rs 30 per hr. **Networld**, near the clock tower, Aberdeen Bazar, T03192-242459, open 0900-2100, closed during Fri prayers (1130-1400) and on Sun. On the opposite side of the road **Net City**, T03192-239938, theoretically has a/c, open 0830-2100, Sun 1500-2100. **Medical services** Hospital, T03192-232102. **Post** GPO, Mon-Fri 0900-1700. **Useful contacts** Police, T03192-230100. **Chief Conservator of Forests**, T03192-233321; **Deputy**, T03192-232816.

Ritchie's Archipelago

→ *Colour map 6, C6.*

The archipelago lies 20-40 km off the east coast of South Andaman and Baratang. Most of the islands are inhabited, but only three are open to foreign visitors: Havelock, Neil and Long Island. They are the focus of the government's tourist effort and can be reached by regular ferry service between Port Blair (Phoenix Jetty) and Rangat Bay (Nimbutala Jetty). ▸▸ *For listings, see pages 849-852.*

Havelock Island

This beautiful island with pristine white beaches is the government's principal centre for tourist development outside Port Blair. The **tourist office** ⓘ *a short walk from the jetty, daily 0900-1630,* is not very useful. Havelock is the island most visited by foreigners and for good reason – the long stretch of beach from the jetty at Village No 1 down to No 5 beach is unquestionably one of the most beautiful in the whole archipelago and has incredibly soft white sand. New hotels, restaurants and amenities are appearing at a rapid rate, some of which are insensitively landscaped and of an inappropriate scale for the small island. Yet, despite its popularity, you can easily – as anywhere in the Andamans – escape from other visitors and find your own private strip of sand for the day.

It is a fairly tough cycle ride, otherwise there are infrequent buses, or hire a scooter (Rs 200-250 per day, or an auto (Rs 200 to drop) along the road to **Radhanagar Beach** (No 7), a dramatic curved bay with a beautiful lagoon at the far end. Near the lagoon, a tourist was killed by a saltwater crocodile in 2009 and you will no doubt hear rumours of further croc sightings during your stay in the Andamans. Beach No 7 has been acclaimed as Asia's best beach in recent years and is absolutely worth visiting. Narrow **Elephant Beach** can be reached by a jungle trek (not possible in wet conditions) and is a popular choice for snorkellers and novice divers who come by boat; note that mornings can be quite crowded. The **lighthouse** and **Turtle Beach**, both near to Elephant Beach, are also good spots for snorkelling. Sand flies can be a real nuisance on some of the beaches, notably No 7.

A week-long **Mela**, marking the birth of Subhas Chandra Bose, is held in January with special Bengali cultural programmes.

Neil Island

Neil is a small and lushly forested island that is very relaxed and attracts far fewer visitors than Havelock (those who do come tend to spend weeks here). **Bharatpur** (No 4) is the best beach for swimming although parts look onto the jetty. Snorkelling is easily accessible from the shore, along a reef that begins at the jetty and stretches west along the coast to Beach No 1, although here as elsewhere corals have died due to the increased water temperatures in 2009-2011. Bicycles are for hire from resorts or in the village, and interesting half-day trips include the **Natural Bridge** on the southwest tip of the island (a pleasant spot to watch the sunset) and **Sitapur** in the east (Beach No 5). At Sitapur a beautiful curve of bay finishes at limestones caves where Hawabill birds (unique to the Andamans) construct their 'edible' nests. The tiny island of **Chota Neil** is visible from the beach; it is possible to arrange snorkelling trips through resorts or Green Heaven restaurant. Shops sell decent provisions but not tents or hammocks (camping is not permitted on the beaches).

Long Island → *Population 2082.*

Another beautiful island, much less touristed than others due to the lack of facilities, yet most visitors fall in love with the place. Ferries from Havelock stop at Strait Island (population 42) en route, which is a protected tribal area where Onge people from Little Island have been resettled post-tsunami (no photos permitted). There are currently only a couple of places to

South Andaman & Ritchie's Archipelago

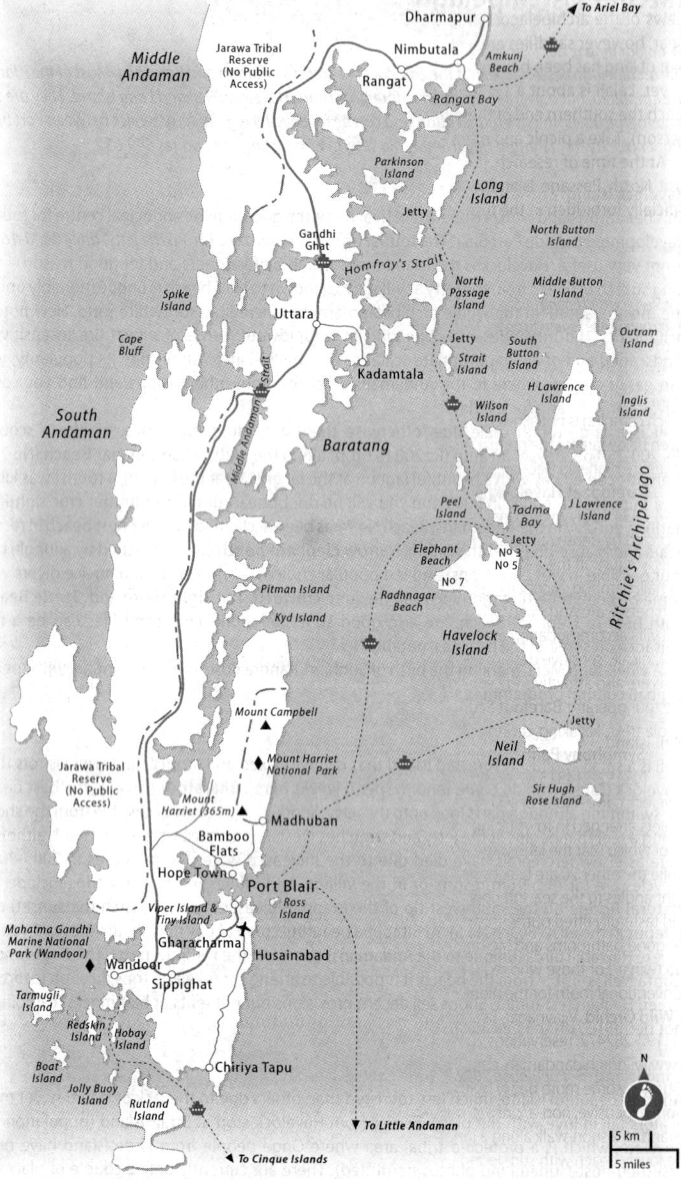

stay on Long (both under the same management) and getting around is by foot as there are no proper roads. The market area has some simple eateries, and the nearby beach has wonderful views of the archipelago. Long Island's main beach, **Lalaji**, is pristine and the waters crystal clear, however sandflies are a real issue. The far end of the beach is lined with coconut trees; a plot of land has been bought here by a five-star hotel chain, but there is no evidence of building as yet. Lalaji is about a 1½-hour walk through woods, fields and then along a jungle track to reach the southern end of the beach. It is possible to return by boat, a beautiful ride (Rs 100 per person). Take a picnic and plenty of water if you are spending the day.

At the time of research, it was possible to charter a boat for the day from local fishermen to visit North Passage Island, with its stunning Merk Bay (Rs 600); this trip, however, may be officially forbidden in the future.

Ritchie's Archipelago listings

For Sleeping and Eating price codes and other relevant information, see Essentials pages 38-42.

Sleeping

Havelock Island *p847, map p848*

Beach camping is not allowed on the island. Prices given below are for the normal Oct-Mar season; prices are higher in Dec-Jan, lower in Apr-Sep.

LL-L Barefoot at Havelock, Beach No 7, T044-2434 1001, www.barefootindia.com. Encircled by dense rainforest and tall mahua trees, yet just off the 2-km white-sand beach. 9 small, bamboo, Nicobari cottages on stilts with nets, 8 a/c Andaman villas, duplex cottages and villa accommodation available, all of an ecologically sensitive design. The restaurant/bar areas are also attractive. Price includes breakfast. The tour operator **Barefoot Scuba** organizes jungle treks, kayaking, diving and snorkelling.

AL-A Symphony Palms, Govindanagar, Beach No 3, T03192-214315, www.symphonypalms havelock.com. A total of 100 wood/concrete chalets arranged in rows facing each other, 80 of which scar the landscape across the road while the other 20 are beach- side although at right angles to the sea. Interiors are comfortable and tastefully fitted out, with stone floors, a/c, TV, good bathrooms and big double beds (no twins). For those who require a more conventional room for the night.

A Wild Orchid, Vijaynagar, Beach No 5, T03192-282472, reservations T03192-233358, www.wildorchidandaman. com. Thai-style cottages, some more newly built which are more expensive, non-a/c or a/c, delightful verandas, a short walk along a jungle path to the lovely beach with sun- loungers (Rs 200 for non-residents, includes towel, coconut and mineral water), luxuriant gardens, **Red Snapper** restaurant and bar. Breakfast included. Sometimes 'parties' are organized at either **Wild Orchid** or **Emerald Gecko**.

B-E Emerald Gecko, Vijaynagar, Beach No 5, T03192-282170, www.emerald-gecko.com. Same management as **Wild Orchid** and same high standards but a more rustic vibe. Good-value huts are bamboo-chic, with white sheets, box mosquito nets, shared washrooms. bungalows have sand-floored bathrooms open to the elements, while 5 split-level lodges have reed blinds and great upstairs verandas.

C-G Barefoot Scuba, Beach No 3, www.dive andamans.com. Comfortable palm and bamboo bungalows, some duplex with terraces onto the sea, are attractive with rush walls, towelling dressing gowns and soft mattresses. Clientele mainly divers on packages, but some budget 'chicken huts' (Rs 150, just a mattress) are cute and clean and a good budget choice. **Café del Mar** restaurant is average and un-atmospheric, though the proportions generous.

C-G Ocean Pearl, Beach No 2, T(0)947-6071998, www.diveandaman.com. Well-designed and attractively placed huts in a pleasing garden. Small and simple ones with common bath are good value (Rs 200) and clean, a couple of which are ideally placed by the sea. Larger available with attached bath, or duplex (much more costly). Sedate atmosphere. Not known for their diving, which caters mainly to Indian tourists doing intro-dives.

E-F Sea View Beach Resort, Beach No 3, T03192-282442/(0)943-4298979. Simple bamboo huts, all with baths and front terraces, wicker-weave walls and clean interiors. Pay more for the more spacious ones, but none are pokey. Arranged in a pretty little garden, quiet atmosphere and nice thatched restaurant on the beach. Deservedly popular.

E-G Green Valley, Village No 5, T(0)9933-213802, gourangahl@yahoo.co.in. A range of accommodation, from new concrete/wood chalets with attached bath to basic thatched-roofed huts near the beach (however, this area is quite scruffy). Across the road, they have blue wicker huts nicely spaced out among a grove of betel trees, with clean shared baths. Staff have a relaxed attitude.

F Green Imperial, Beach No 5, T(0)9474-206301. Raised *chetal* huts (wicker walls and floors) with decent bathrooms, have front terraces looking onto banana and betel trees. Lovely owner, quiet atmosphere, simple and fairly priced at Rs 500. Across the road from the beach. Guests sing its praises.

G Smile Garden, Beach No 2. About the cheapest of budget options with a slight hippyish vibe, very simple huts are arranged around a scruffy garden, with raised beds, mosquito nets, and nothing else (not even fans). It's 20 m past a local fishing family's home to the beach. Nice staff and only Rs 150 (high season) or Rs 80 (low). Arrival is marred by the mirror-glass monstrosity of The Kingdom hotel across the road.

Neil Island *p847, map p848*

At the time of research, **Dive India** (see Activities, page 851) were soon to finish construction of a new resort near the jetty, which will be the most comfortable option by far.

E-G Hawabill Nest, T03192-82630, T(0)9434-291002. Government accommodation, in the village rather than next to the beach. Simple, spotless rooms with a/c (Rs 800) with hot shower although only has running water 0600-0700 and 1800-1900. Clean 4-bed dorms (Rs 150), TV room and dining room. Reservations, Secretariat, Director of Tourism, Port Blair, T03192-232694.

E-G Pearl Park, Laxmanpur Beach, T03192-282510/233880, pearlpark_2002@yahoo.co.in. The furthest camp to the west, basic huts share an unpleasant common toilet, more expensive and spacious ones have private baths, plus some (unappealing) concrete chalets. Nevertheless, it is a lovely setting among lush gardens, close to the beach with sunset views and good snorkelling (a dugong is often spotted here). Food, however, is average and staff lacklustre.

E-G Coco-N-Huts Beach Resort, Neil Kendra, T03192-282528, srikudvt@yahoo.com. Decent, mostly tiny huts (wicker, no unsightly concrete), some 2-storey, set out among palm trees, next to a nice patch of mangrove/beach although the end of the jetty is visible in distance. Central circular restaurant.

E-G Tango Beach Resort, Laxmanpur Beach (No 1), T(0)9434-270454, www.tangobeachresort.in. Rather grotty huts have nets but no fans, and concrete chalets are rather blank (though clean). 2 Nicobari-style huts are large and lack furnishings, with squat toilets. Jungle atmosphere among the towering trees, direct access to the beach with good snorkelling. Decent meals.

F-G A-N-D Beach Resort, Bharatpur, T(0)9474-238770. Well-managed and relatively new, these are the nicest huts on Neil with clean sheets, nets, little terraces, some with private bath otherwise the common bathroom is very acceptable. Cheaper rooms have no fans. Handy for the village and owner is delightful. Adjacent Bharatpur beach is the best on Neil for swimming, the downside is that it's adjacent to the jetty.

Long Island *p847, map p848*

C-E Blue Planet, T03192-215923, T(0)9474-212180, www.blueplanetandamans.com. Adjoining raised wicker huts, variety of prices and amenities, cheapest share a clean bath, encircling a shady restaurant. Front terraces are too small to sit on and walls anything but soundproof, but sheets are clean, nets provided and some furniture, 5 mins from a lovely beach. The owners put overspill guests in the newer 'Blue Cottage', 4 decent large rooms (2 with private bath, Rs 300 per person) which is quieter and, some might say, preferable. If they are really stuck for space, there are 2 tents.

F Vanashree Forest Guest House, take steps uphill to the left from jetty. 3 comfortable tiled rooms, with TV and private bath, very clean, 1 room has a/c. You are supposed to get permission from the DFO in Rangat, but you could try you luck asking at the Range Office on arrival at Long Island.

Eating

Havelock Island *p847, map p848*

Near Jetty in Village No 1 and at Village No 3 there are several basic places serving excellent grilled fish, vegetable and rice dishes.

₹₹ **B3 Barefoot Bar & Brasserie**, by the jetty. Italian and Indian menu in the upstairs restaurant, rated chiefly for its pizzas, terrace is pleasant place to be, was not permitted to serve alcohol at the time of research.

₹₹ **Blackbeard's Bistro**, **Emerald Gecko** (see Sleeping). Authentic Bengali and delicious continental dishes, good standard but not too highly priced, alcohol available and excellent breakfasts (get there by 1000).

₹₹ **Eco Villa**, Beach No 2. German bakery and Western-orientated menu, lovely beach-side setting, recommended for authentic pizzas and chicken burgers.

₹₹-₹ **Full Moon Cafe**, **Island Vinnie's/Dive India**, Beach No 3. Categorically the best food on the Andamans, with a creative fusion menu of Indian and international dishes. Suitably priced for the generous potions: daily fish specials, delicious *dhal*, inventive wraps, thoughtful breakfasts and the only real coffee on the islands. Mellow atmosphere and excellent management have attracted a loyal following.

₹ **Gita's**, Govindanagar, Village No 3. Good for cheap generous *thalis*, including *puri* and *channa* (but not spicy, ask for pickle), plenty to cater for Israeli tourists.

₹ **World Class Restaurant**, Beach No 3. A good roadside eatery, reliable breakfasts, excellent cheap juice, usual wide menu, always busy.

Neil Island *p847, map p848*

It is hoped that **Full Moon Café** will open up at the new Dive India resort for the 2011-2012 season.

₹₹-₹ **Green Heaven**, on the road to Tango. Open from 0800 till folks leave. Currently most people's top choice, it's a bit pricier but excellent food in generous portions. Grilled fish (try coconut), seafood, pasta, Western breakfasts.

₹ **Blue Sea**, Ramnagar No 3, east of the market. Open till 2230. A simple thatched gazebo in a grassy garden, seafood, chilled out staff, a good place to rest on a bike ride though not the greatest (nor speediest) food.

₹ **Chand**, by the market in the village, does great chickpea *dhal*, egg rolls and *vada*, plus a whole host of items aimed at tourist palates.

Shopping

Havelock Island *p847, map p848*

Village No 3 has a good fruit and vegetable market. Memento t-shirts are a popular purchase (Rs 50), plus there's an (un-named) clothes shop just south of village No 3 with a good selection of women's clothes, bags and accessories. Coconut and shell jewellery is crafted by **Anupam Eco Arts World**, Village No 3. Waxing/threading and other hair treatments are available at **Sneha Beauty Parlour**, Village No 3, near Big Bazar on the road to Radhanagar. Open 0930-1230 and 1530-1830.

Activities and tours

Havelock Island *p847, map p848*

Dive operators

Almost all foreign tourists choose to do diving from Havelock, which is closer to the best dive sites, and has competitive prices and experienced instructors. Most operations shut during monsoon (31 May-1 Aug).

Andaman Bubbles, T03192-282140 www.andamanbubbles.com.

Barefoot Scuba, Beach No 3 and Beach No 7, www.diveandamans.com. Promotes 'eco-friendly tourism'. Digital equipment, PADI courses, high standards and the only dive shop in the world to employ an elephant. However, swimming with Rajan the rescue- elephant, who's become something of a celebrity, is costly at around Rs 10,000 per person.

Dive India, **Island Vinnie's**, Beach No 3, www.islandvinnie.com. Excellent standards and great staff, they also visit dive sites that other operators haven't discovered yet. Customers are always happy.

Havelock Tourist Services, Village No 3. Helpful Nafisa organizes snorkelling and fishing trips, and is a good source of information about ferries and buses.

Transport

Havelock Island *p847, map p848*

Air There is now a **seaplane** service between **Havelock** and **Port Blair** costing Rs 4100. Contact ANIIDCO, T(0)9531-828333.

Auto-rickshaws Autos for hire from the jetty should cost Rs 40-50 to Beach No 3 and 5 but you will be very lucky to get this; to No 7 around Rs 200.

Bicycle hire Bikes and scooters available from Jetty, No 3, and from most hotels/ camps. Bikes Rs 50-75 per day; scooters, Rs 200; motorbikes, Rs 250 (significantly less in the low season).

Bus Service from Jetty (No 1) all the way to **Radhanagar Beach** (No 7), via Village No 3; hourly, 0730-1130, 1330-1630; from No 7, 0830-1200, 1430-1730 (Rs 10-15, 20 mins). Avoid being swamped by school children at 0800 and 1500.

Ferry Getting a ticket out of Havelock can be traumatic, with long queues and only last-minute availability at the office (which opens at 0900). Paying an agent Rs 50-100 commission to obtain your ticket for you is recommended. There are a few boats to **Port Blair** daily, the fastest being the Makruzz at 1100 and 1600 (1½ hrs, Rs 650, a/c; the 1600 tends not to run in low season); others leave at 1400, 1500 and 1630 taking about 2½ hrs (Rs 250). Boats to **Neil Island** Sun and Thu at 1000 and 1500, Mon, Wed and Sat at 1500, Tue at 0900 and 1500, Fri at 1500 (1½ hrs, Rs 195), carry on to Port Blair (4 hrs). **Line Ferry** on Mon, Wed, Fri, Sat to **Long Island** (3 hrs, Rs 195) and **Rangat** at 1000 (4 hrs, Rs 195). Check all timings – internet cafés have copies of latest schedules.

Neil Island *p847, map p848*

Ferry Boats leave to **Port Blair** daily at 0845 and 1630 (2 hrs, Rs 195). To **Havelock Island** daily at 0830 and 1330 (1½-2 hrs, Rs 195). The **Line Ferry** connects with **Long Island** and **Rangat** Mon, Wed, Fri, Sat at 0900. There are no problems with purchasing tickets at Neil, just pay on board the ferry.

Long Island *p847, map p848*

Ferry Usually 4 boats a week from **Port Blair**, Phoenix Bay Jetty, via **Havelock Island** which carry on to **Rangat**. Daily local ferry to **Rangat** at 0700 (1 hr, Rs 8) – a beautiful journey past mangrove islands – returns to Long Island around 1300.

Directory

Havelock Island *p847, map p848*

Bank 3 ATMs in Village 3, though they sometimes run out of money. **Internet** Several places offer internet, including **Havelock Tourist Services**, Village No 3 (open 0830-1300 and 1600-2000) and **Lord Corner**, near Island Vinnie's, Beach No 5 (open 0830-2230), wjth slow unreliable connections, Rs 80 per hr, CD/DVD burning; **Ocean Pearl** near No 5 has satellite internet for Rs 300 per hr, fast connection. **Medical services** Medical centre at Village No 3.

Middle and North Andamans

→ *Colour map 6, C6.*

The Andaman Trunk Road is the only road to the north from Port Blair. Since it passes through the restricted Jarawa tribal reserve, vehicles travel in convoy in those areas; there are daily buses to Rangat, Mayabunder and Diglipur. The bumpy journey takes you past beautiful landscape and involves two ferry crossings. Occasionally the more adventurous Jarawas hitch a lift on the bus to the edge of the reserve. The route runs through some spectacular forest but sadly, despite controls, there has already been a lot of selective clearance of hardwoods. ▸▸ *For listings, see pages 855-857.*

Middle Andaman → *For listings, see pages 855-857.*

Rangat

Rangat is a small transit town with a few acceptable lodges. The main reason travellers spend a night here is in order to catch the Line Ferry to other islands, which leaves four times per week. **Amkunj Beach**, 8 km away, has little shade left but there is good snorkelling off the rocks at the top end of the beach. From Rangat, take any bus heading for Nimbutala or Mayabunder up to the fork for Rangat Bay, then walk 1 km along track to right just after the helipad.

There is a good sandy beach, ideal for swimming, across the road from **Hawksbill Nest** on Cuthbert Bay. However, the beach is a wildlife sanctuary where turtles nest between November to April and permission is needed from the Forest Department at Rangat or Mayabunder, or from the Beat Officer at Betapur, 4 km north of **Hawksbill Nest**.

Mayabunder → *157 km by sea from Port Blair.*

Mayabunder is the administrative centre for the Middle and North Andamans. All amenities are situated along a single road which runs along the brow of a ridge sticking out into the bay; the port is at the north end. A nice guesthouse (see page 855) and great value local fish and prawns add to the appeal of Mayabunder as a place to relax for a couple of days. You can visit the dark sand **Karmatang Beach**, 20-30 minutes away by bus or jeep. A shallow sandy slope over 1 km long, with a few rocks at the north end, it good for swimming but not snorkelling as it is exposed and the sea is choppy. Sandflies can be a real problem. There are several islands in the bay opposite the jetty which can be reached by *dunghy*; you can ask fishermen to take you and expect to pay Rs 700-1000 for a boat charter for several hours, or arrange through a guesthouse. All offer safe beaches for swimming but there is no good coral.

Avis Island

This tiny island is just east of Mayabunder but its ownership is disputed between the Forestry Department and The Coconut Society of Mayabunder. To visit, permission is required from Forest Office in Mayabunder, you need to charter a *dunghy* from fishermen (or **Sea N Sand** hotel, see page 855, can arrange a boat, standard price is Rs 1000 to spend the day; they drop you and come back to pick up; Anmol Guesthouse can arrange a similar trip, or a shorter option costing Rs 700 for a couple of hours with waiting time). There is a lovely coral sand beach; it makes a great day trip (take a packed lunch) with good snorkelling – and no sandflies. Also enquire about permission to visit **Curlew Island, Rayhill Island, Sound Island, Interview Island** and **Mohanpur** on the eastern coast of North Andaman. Tourists are encouraged to destroy any illegal deer traps they find.

Interview Island

Interview Island is home to wild elephants, crocodiles and other wildlife and has a protected forest. Day visits can be organized from Mayabunder (**Sea N Sand** hotel can arrange and help with permits, which cost Rs 500 per person).The island can only be visited in a private boat (three hours, Rs 3500 for up to eight passengers).

Barren Island

Across to the east from Middle Andaman, Barren has India's only active volcano, which erupted in 1991 causing widespread destruction of the island's ecosystem. Smoky fire belches from the side of the crater. It is only possible to visit on a day trip with no landings permitted; the tourist office in Port Blair runs excursions or the seaplane makes flights over the island.

North Andaman → *For listings, see pages 855-857.*

Kalighat

A small settlement on a creek where ferries once called, but now a sleepy village that can be visited as a day-trip between Mayabunder and Diglipur (you have to sign in at the police station, T03192-278149, on arrival; there is no accommodation, shops in the market will look after luggage). You can cross the river by the mangrove footbridge and follow the path up into the forest (good for birdwatching) that leads 3 km to Nischintapur village; it's a lovely jungle path, although the village itself is not particularly pretty. A new road is being built to the village, but avoid this and stick to the jungle route. You can (with some effort; little English is spoken) take a bus to a beautiful beach near Ramnagar Bazar (11 km) from where you will have to walk the last 2 km to **Ramnagar beach**, or hire a rickshaw (Rs 600 with waiting time).

Diglipur

Previously known as Port Cornwallis, Diglipur has a good market and shops; a special Mela is held January/February, which attracts many traders.

Aerial Bay

This small fishing village is handy for getting supplies if you are staying in Kalipur (as almost everyone does) and is the departure point for the line ferry back to Port Blair. Buses between Kalipur and Diglipur stop at Ariel Bay.

Smith and Ross islands

From Aerial Bay, you can visit Smith and Ross islands to the north, connected to one another by a white sandbar. You need permission (Rs 500 per person for foreigners) from the

North Andaman

Range Officer, opposite the jetty entrance. This permit plus hire of a *dunghy* (Rs 800-2000 depending on number of passengers, 40 minutes crossing) make it an expensive day-trip, but it is well worth doing. Smith Island, the larger of the two, has sun-loungers and wicker huts providing a bit of shade. Seventeen families live on the island. There is good snorkelling. Take your own food and water.

Kalipur, Lamiya Bay and Saddle Peak National Park

Kalipur, a few kilometres south of Aerial Bay, has appealing accommodation and is where most travellers are heading. There is a beach with good snorkelling off its northern side, Saddle Peak gives an impressive backdrop, and two small islands in the bay have even better snorkelling. The sand is volcanic, however, and sandflies are a problem.

Lamiya Bay, 3.5 km south of Kalipur, has a pebble beach which you can walk to (from the bus stop the road leads straight on for 30 minutes). To the north, there are small bays strewn with large eroded boulders along which it is possible to clamber your way back to Kalipur beach (not recommended for lone women), while the beaches to the south stretch towards Saddle Peak.

Theoretically, permits (Rs 500) for **Saddle Peak** are required; however, the path is clearly signed from Lamiya Bay on to Saddle Peak (8.5 km). Despite the relatively short ascent to the peak (730 m), the initial walk on flat ground for 4.5 km, followed by the steep climb, the thick forest and the heat, mean that you need a whole day for the trek, starting very early in the morning. It is essential to take at least 4 litres of water per person, plus food, and expect the excursion to take around 8-9 hours.

Narcondam Island

East of North Andaman, this is the most remote island in the group. An extinct craterless volcano, it is covered in luxuriant forest (home to the Narcondam hornbill) and was declared a sanctuary in 1977. It is a birdwatchers' paradise though permission to visit is very hard to get and only 24-hour stops are allowed.

Middle and North Andamans listings

For Sleeping and Eating price codes and other relevant information, see Essentials pages 38-42.

Sleeping

Rangat *p853*

E-F Hawksbill Nest, Cuthbert Bay, 18 km from Rangat (buses to Mayabunder go past, ask for Yatri Niwas). Book ahead at Directorate of Tourism, Port Blair, T03192-282630. 8 clean sea-facing rooms (Rs 400, better views on 1st floor), 2 a/c (Rs 800) 4-bed dorms (Rs 150).

E-G RG Lodge, 300 m north of town centre, T03192-274340. Cheap non-a/c rooms, 1-4 beds, some a/c, off the main road therefore quieter.

F-G Hotel Avis, town centre. Simple rooms with (Rs 600) or without (Rs 300) a/c, no food available.

F-G RK Lodge, centre of town by bus stop, T03192-274060. Bearable rooms are just about clean, same price for single or double, some with common bath, not much Eng spoken.

Mayabunder *p853*

E-F APWD Guesthouse, near the jetty. Stay by application to the AC's office nearby, T03192-273208 (Mon-Fri). Nice rooms in an old bungalow building, a/c, for Rs 800, or in the newer building, non-a/c, Rs 400, with balconies on the upper level enjoying staggering sea views. Gardens. Often full with government officials, but the views could be worth the hassle of a visit to the AC.

E-F Sea N Sand, 2 km before town, T03192-273454, T(0)9434-287040. Run by a delightful Burmese lady, this friendly guesthouse has a cosy restaurant with cold beer or they will put a table outdoors for you, however the meals are no great shakes. Newer rooms are pink-painted and clean with views of the mangroves and the ocean, best from the upstairs rooms (though these are sun-traps)., with TV, shower and Western toilets (Rs 500-700, bargaining is possible). Shabby older rooms go for Rs 350 (often full). It's on the road about 1.5 km before town.

E-F Swiftlet Nest, 13 km from Mayabunder, near Karmatang beach, contact Port Blair Directorate of Tourism, T03192-232694/273211, overlooking paddy fields (forest not cleared at the beach). 10 good rooms, 4 a/c, dorm, 'manager absent' but good food, helpful staff.

F Anmol Guesthouse, MKS Complex, Bazaar, T03192-262695/(0)9474-540064. Very helpful manager, right in the heart of the town, rooms are clean and OK, the problem is many don't have outside windows. Most have TV and attached bath, some are spacious, a couple of **C** rooms. Good choice for single travellers on a budget (Rs 250).

Diglipur *p854*

Most travellers are heading straight to Kalipur, but should you get stuck or want to take the early bus, try:

F-G Drua, T03192-272313, T(0)9933-257995. The 15 rooms are about the best in town, some with private bathrooms, respectable families keep it busy, unhelpful manager.

G JN Bepari Lodge, T03192-272326. Modest rooms, little light, powerful fans, own bathroom, nice owner, Rs 300.

G MV Lodge, T03192-320197, T(0)9434-297998. Surprisingly (judging from the outside) the best of the ultra-cheap options, front rooms (with clean common bath, Rs 200/250, single/double) are bright if basic, and the manager is friendly and speaks some Eng. Back rooms have private bath (Rs 300). Very close to the bus stop.

Aerial Bay *p854*

G There is a nameless lodge in the bazar, with bare basic rooms sharing a primitive bathroom, Rs 100 per bed, handy if you are catching the early morning Geetanjali bus to Port Blair and don't mind meeting rats in the passageways. Very pleasant manager.

Kalipur

B-G Pristine Beach Resort, Kalipur, T03192-271792, T(0)9474-286787, www.andamanpristineresorts.com. Nestled in the jungle a short walk from the beach, 13 rooms (and more to come) ranging from simple huts (outside bathroom, Rs 250) to chalets with stylish interiors (Rs 2000, air-con costs extra), though perhaps nicest are the split-level huts with lovely bamboo balconies (Rs 800). Rather posh multicuisine restaurant, beer usually available. Can provide snorkelling equipment and help arrange interesting trips. Currently the only place kitted out for travellers, best to phone ahead if you want a cheap hut. Most travellers love it here, and end up spending much longer than they intended.

E-F Turtle Resort, Kalipur, book through Directorate of Tourism in Port Blair T03192-232747/232369. Comfortable rooms, some a/c, dorm (Rs 150), food available only for guests. Very peaceful, on a hillock directly opposite Pristine Beach Resort, the views are magnificent. Essential to book ahead in Port Blair, however.

Eating

Rangat *p853*

Annapurna, on corner of vegetable market (from bus stand, turn left opposite **Krishna Hotel**, the right and left again). Good food.

Nisha dhaba next to the bus stand, OK *dosas* good and *parathas/subji*.

There are also a few *dhabas* at Nimbutala Jetty (from where the Line Ferry departs) which serves up a better omelette than you find in town.

Kalighat *p854*

There are a couple of cheap and very basic dhabas in the village, and shops with cold drinks.

Diglipur *p854*

Plenty of little restaurants; fresh fruit in the big market.

Aerial Bay *p854*

A few shops sell provisions and there is a small veg market, plus some little *dhabas* near the bus stop.

Mohan, on the edge of the village towards the jetty (no sign). The owner speaks English and is helpful, good *thalis*, *dosas*, etc, it's the only 'restaurant' in town. There's a dodgy bar next door.

Transport

Rangat p853

Bus Infrequent to **Mayabunder**, between 0530-1600 (2½-3 hrs, Rs 30) or join a Diglipur bus and get off at Mayabunder Jct and wait for a local jeep to take you the last 8 km (Rs 10); to **Port Blair**, daily, 0800, 0900; 2 ferry crossings (at Nilambur and Gandhi Ghat), takes up to 7 hrs. Expect the experience to be very bumpy.
Ferry The main jetty is Nimbutala, 7 km from town. The Line Ferry goes to **Port Blair** on Mon, Wed, Sat at 2000 and on Fri at 1300 (Rs 80, 8 hrs), via Long Island, Strait Island, Havelock and Neil Island. To **Havelock** daily at 0600, except Fri at 1300. Tickets can be bought on board same day if there is space, but better to buy day before at the ticket office in Rangat. Boats from Yeratta Jetty (connected by a 20-min bus ride) to **Long Island** daily at about 0700 and 1300 (1 hr, Rs 8); **Mayabunder**, 3 per week, 3 hrs.

Mayabunder p853

Bus Government bus to **Port Blair** at 0430 and 0800, departing from the bazar (9 hrs, Rs 130); private Anand bus daily at 0600 (Rs 200) has push-back seats (can book through Anmol Hotel). To **Rangat** infrequent local bus, 0830-1700 (2½-3 hrs, Rs 30). To **Karmatang** beach, every hr or so from the bazar between 0700-1700 (30-40 mins, Rs 20, return bus approximately 35 mins after these times, last one at 1930); jeeps also go to/from Karmatang (Rs 20). To **Diglipur** at 0530, 0730, 0930, 1230 (very busy on weekdays), 1715, (2½ hrs); or you can join the private Anand bus coming from Port Blair which passes through around 1300-1430.
Ferry For **Diglipur** there is a local ferry to Aerial Bay at 0800 on Tue (3½ hrs, Rs 40), or inter-island ferry from Port Blair calls en route to Aerial Bay. To **Port Blair** on Wed at 0900 and Fri at 2200 (Rs 71), but check at the ticket office by the ferry for schedules and bookings (opens 0900).

Kalighat p854

Bus To **Diglipur**: regular local service between 0500-2000 (45 mins, Rs 10) and faster jeeps. For **Mayabunder** and **Rangat** change at Kalara Jct and wait for a bus south..

Diglipur p854

Air There is now a **seaplane** service to **Port Blair**, Rs 10,500. Contact ANIIDCO, T(0)9531-828444.
Bus Local bus to **Kalipur** (40 mins, Rs 10), via **Aerial Bay** (20 mins, Rs 7), at least 1 per hr, returning from Kalipur on the hr. Regular service to **Kalighat**, 45 mins (last at 1900).
Long-distance buses 2 state buses to **Port Blair** at 0500 and 0700 (Rs 170) via Rangat (Rs 70); the Geetanjali private bus starts in **Aerial Bay**, via Diglipur, at 0425 (booking office in Aerial Bay, Rs 240) or the private Anand bus starts in Diglipur at 0430. Recommended to book in advance. To **Mayabunder** at 0615, 1100 and 1400 (2½ hrs, Rs 40).
Ferry To **Port Blair** from Aerial Bay jetty on Tue at 0600, Wed and Sat at 2100 (direct, 9 hrs, bunk and chair class available, Rs 91) Tickets from Diglipur; to avoid a long wait there, buy on the boat, though you may sometimes have to pay more, and only get a deck ticket.
Helicopter To **Port Blair** on Tue and Fri, 45 mins, a steal at Rs 800, book through the AC's office, but preference given to government officials.

Directory

Rangat p853

Bank **State Bank of India**, by the bus stand, has an ATM, plus 2 others in town.
Post Opposite the police station.

Mayabunder p853

Bank There is an ATM in the bazar.

Diglipur p854

Bank **State Bank of India** has an ATM.
Internet **Sudeep Enterprises**, next to Drua hotel, T(0)9933-243625, Rs 40 per hr, daily 0830-2200, connection unreliable.

Little Andaman

→ *Colour map 6, C6.*

This large island lies 120 km south of Port Blair across the Duncan Passage, six or more hours on a boat. The main village, **Hut Bay** to the southeast, is 1 km away from the jetty. Heavily deforested during the 1960s and 1970s, much of the island is dominated by betel, red palm and banana plantations which are scenic enough. The tsunami pretty much destroyed tourism on Little Andaman for a few years. Now, a small string of guesthouses (Rs 150 per night) has grown up 500 m away from the jetty in Hut Bay although they are not on most foreign tourists' agenda. The attraction, particularly for surfers, is the large and beautiful beach at **Butler Bay**, around 20 km from the jetty, where it is possible (although not officially permitted) to camp or put up hammocks. If you do make the trip, take plenty of water; food is available in the village a half hour's walk away. Bicycles, but not motorbikes, are available for touring the island to visit an attractive waterfall. There are no facilities for hiring snorkelling equipment, so bring your own. Be aware that the area is notorious for mosquitoes and sandflies, and malaria is a genuine problem.

A boat leaves daily from Port Blair for Little Andaman; on alternate days a fast boat leaves at 0615, returning at 1300 (six hours, Rs 25), or the slow boat leaves at 0700 returning at 2000 (at least nine hours, inexplicably more expensive, Rs55).

Nicobar Islands

→ *Colour map 6, C5.*

The names given by travellers and sailors from the east and the west all referred to these islands as the 'Land of the Naked' (Nicobar is derived from the Tamil word *nakkavaram*). The islands, which lay on the trade route to the Far East, were visited in the 11th century by the seafaring Cholas during the rule of King Rajendra I who attempted to extend his rule here. Before the British used the Nicobars as a penal territory in the late 19th century, European missionaries (particularly the Danish) made converts during the 17th and 18th centuries but few survived the difficulties of the climate and most died of fever within a year.

The islands, including **Katchal** with a large rubber plantation, **Nancowry** harbour, **Indira Point**, India's southernmost tip and **Campbell Bay** (Great Nicobar), are closed to foreign visitors; **Car Nicobar** to the north can be visited by Indians with a permit. The significant tribal population live in distinctive huts, which look like large thatched domes that are raised on stilts about 2 m high and are entered through the floor. The Nicobarese enjoy wrestling, fishing, swimming and canoeing but are best known for their love of music. Villages still participate in competitions of traditional unaccompanied singing and dancing which mark every festivity.

Tamil Nadu

Contents

Footprint features

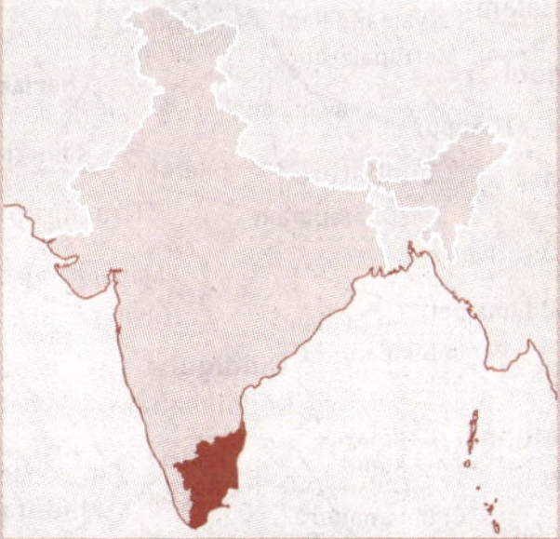

At a glance

Getting around Frequent buses between the temple towns, otherwise hire a cab or join a tour group. The rack-and-pinion train to Ooty is a treat. City bus tours from the tourism office recommended for Chennai.

Time required A week for the temples, 4 days for the hills, as little as possible in Chennai, 3 days in Pondicherry; 2 days for Mahabalipuram, allow more for beach R&R. Optional 2-day detour to Chettinad.

Weather Monsoon Oct-Dec. Warm year round but oppressively hot from the end of Mar. Hill stations are cool all year but wet from Jun.

When not to go Cyclones Nov and Dec. Avoid the hottest months between Apr and Jul.

★ **Don't miss ...**

1. *Descent of the Ganga* in seaside Mahabalipuram, page 892.
2. Pondicherry, page 899.
3. The fortnightly bathing of the beautiful Brihadisvara Temple's Nandi at Thanjavur, page 917.
4. The unique temple society of the Brahmins at Chidambaram, page 920.
5. The Blue Mountain Railway to Ooty, page 931.
6. Temple of the fish-eyed goddess, Madurai, page 948.
7. Chettinad: gaudy palaces in arid ghost towns, and India's hottest cuisine, page 954.

Tamil Nadu smells of sacrificial burning camphor and the perfume from jasmine garlands piled up before its beautifully carved granite gods, well oiled with gingelly smeared from the palms of centuries of devotees, then reddened with sandal powder and washed with devotional milk baths.

About 90% of the 60-million-strong Tamil population is Hindu and religious ritual here is lived and breathed: men's entire foreheads are daubed with potash, huge horizontal sweeps or fingernail-thin red edges drawn from the hair's centre-parting sideways, while women sprinkle intricate geometric designs of ground rice powder on their hearths every dawn. It's rare to find a temple that has outlived its religious purpose – seldom the shrine that is mere monument. But nor is worship confined to the feats of architecture that dot Tamil Nadu. Banyan trees are festooned with dangling sacred talismen; tridents are slammed into the ground to create makeshift mounds of worship; village gods in life-size stucco renderings bare their teeth and brandish knives at every roadside, and files of pilgrims pick their way along baked dirt tracks.

Here, then, is the heady temple trail: Kanchipuram, Mahabalipuram, Chidambaram, Thanjavur, Madurai, the second Varanasi of Rameswaram, and the holy toe-tip of India in Kanniyakumari. Here too, for serious seekers and dilettante yogis, the contrasting ashram atmospheres of introspective Tiruvannamalai, futuristic utopian Auroville, and the industrious urban campus of Sri Aurobindo in Pondicherry.

Welcome antidotes to temple fatigue come in the form of Pondicherry's charming French domestic architecture and the crumbling palatial homes of Chettinad, or in big breaths of nature in the blue Nilgiri mountains around the celebrated hill stations of Ooty and Kodaikkanal.

Background → *Population: 62.1 million. Area: 130,000 sq km.*

The land

Geography Tamil Nadu rises from the flat coastal plains in the east to the Western Ghats – the Nilgiris in the north and the Palani, Cardamom and Anamalai hills in the south. The Nilgiris ('blue mountains') rise like a wall above the haze of the plains to heights of over 2500 m. The plains are hot, dry and dusty, with isolated blocks of granite forming bizarre shapes on the ancient eroded surface. The coast itself is a flat alluvial plain, with deltas at the mouths of major rivers. The occasional medieval water tanks add beauty to the landscape.

Tamil Nadu's coast bore the brunt of India's casualties of the 2004 tsunami. Along 1000 km of shoreline, at least 8000 people died, and 470,000 were displaced. As well as loved ones, the wave washed away infrastructure: communities, homes, livelihoods, schools, and health clinics. See box, opposite.

Climate Most rain falls between October and December, making this the worst time to travel. The best time to visit is from mid-December to early March when the dry sunny weather sets in and before the heat gets too crushing, although the hills can still be very cold, especially at night. In the rain shadow of the Western Ghats, temperatures never fall much below 21°C, except in the hills, but although humidity is often high maximum temperatures rarely exceed 42°C.

History

Tamil Nadu's cultural identity has been shaped by the Dravidians, who have inhabited the south since at least the fourth millennium BC. Tamil, India's oldest living language, developed from the earlier languages of people who were probably displaced from the north by Aryan-based culture from 2000 BC to 1500 BC.

By the fourth century BC Tamil Nadu was under the rule of three dynasties: the **Cholas**, the **Pandiyas** and the **Cheras**. The **Pallavas** of Kanchi came to power in the fourth century AD and were dominant between AD 550 and AD 869. Possibly of northern origin, under their control Mahabalipuram (Mamallapuram) became an important port in the seventh century. The **Cholas** returned to power in AD 850 and were a dominant political force until 1173 before the resumption of Pandiya power for a further century. The defeat of the great Vijayanagar Empire by a confederacy of Muslim states in 1565 forced their leaders south. As the Nayaka kings they continued to rule from as far south as Madurai well into the 17th century. When Muslim political control finally reached Tamil Nadu it was as brief as it was tenuous.

It was more than 150 years after their founding of Fort St George at Madras in 1639 before the **East India Company** could claim political supremacy in South India. Haidar Ali, who mounted the throne of Mysore in 1761, and his son Tipu Sultan, allied with the French, won many battles against the English. When the Treaty of Versailles brought the French and English together in 1783 Tipu was forced to make peace. The English took Malabar (in Kerala) in 1792, and in 1801 Lord Wellesley brought together most of the south under the Madras Presidency. The **French** acquired land at Pondicherry in 1673. In 1742, Dupleix was named governor of the French India Company and took up residence there. He seized Madras within a few years but in 1751 Clive attacked Arcot. His victory was the beginning of the end of French ambitions in India. The Treaty of Paris brought their empire to a close in 1763, although they retained five counting houses.

Culture

The majority of Tamilians are Dravidians with Mediterranean ethnic origins, settled in Tamil Nadu for several thousand years. Tamil is spoken by over 85% of the population, which is 90% Hindu. Five per cent are Christian, a group especially strong in the south where Roman Catholic and Protestant missions have been active for over 500 years. There are small but significant minorities of Muslims, Jains and Parsis. There are isolated groups of as many as 18 different

The effect of the tsunami

The tsunami waves triggered by the Bay of Bengal earthquakes on 26 December 2004 killed nearly 11,000 people on the Indian subcontinent, nearly 8000 of them in Tamil Nadu. The death toll was highest in Nagapattinam, but tourist centres of Chennai, Mahabalipuram, Kanniyukumari and Pondicherry were all badly affected.

The waves touched all areas of Tamil life: 54,620 homes were hit, 68,000 boats destroyed and 252 schools wiped out. Where seawater washed inland over farmland it left a thick layer of saline deposits.

Relief was swift, and the government response in particular praised, but with a reconstruction effort of this scale (the total cost to India is put at US$1.2 billion), involving the rebuilding of homes, schools, health centres, roads and power lines, the work goes on: of the 53,000 houses being constructed by the Tamil Nadu government under the 'build back better' mantra, just under three quarters had been completed by the middle of 2009.

It hasn't all been good news, however. The relief effort broke against society already fragmented by caste and gender inequality, and efforts to help dalits, for example, were in some cases fiercely opposed by village *panchayats*. Human trafficking among women and children was already relatively high in Tamil Nadu, and the chaos and economic problems following the tsunami provided an extra window of opportunity for exploitation; rates of organ harvesting, for example, have increased. In other areas the relief effort has been a victim of its own success, diminishing the self-sufficiency of fishing communities. Oversupply of resources such as boats has led some boys to skip school to go fishing, and handouts have allowed others to turn to the bottle. The stampede of relief agencies to the Andaman and the Nicobar islands has damaged the delicate social fabric of these formerly isolated communities.

Of the natural attractions, while the Point Calimere Sanctuary is saltier than before, and the flamingos have flown inland, ecologists believe the tsunami's effects to be glancing. The Gulf of Mannar Marine National Park was sheltered by Sri Lanka. Only 2% of India's coral reef appears to have been damaged.

types of **tribal people** in the Nilgiri Hills. Some of them are of aboriginal stock although local archaeological discoveries suggest that an extinct race preceded them. The **Todas**' life and religion revolve around their long-horned buffalo which are a measure of wealth. Their small villages are called *munds* with around six igloo-like windowless bamboo and dried grass huts. Their chief goddess Tiekirzi, the creator of the indispensable buffalo, and her brother On rule the world of the dead and the living. There are only about 1000 Todas left. The **Badagas** are the main tribal group and probably came from Karnataka. They speak a mixture of Kannada and Tamil and their oral tradition is rich in folk tales, poetry, songs and chants. As agriculturalists their villages are mainly in the upper plateau, with rows of three-roomed houses. They worship Siva and observe special tribal festivals. Progressive and adaptable, they are being absorbed into the local community faster than others.

Cuisine Many Tamilians are vegetarian and the strict Brahmins among them avoid the use of garlic and onion and in some cases even tomatoes. Favourites for breakfast or *tiffin* (snacks) include *dosa* (thin crisp pancakes, plain or stuffed with mildly spiced potato and onion as *masala dosa*), *iddli* (steamed, fermented rice cakes), delicious rice-based *pongal* (worth searching out) and *vadai* (savoury lentil doughnuts), all served with coconut chutney and *sambar* (a spicy lentil and vegetable broth). A *thali* here comes in the form of boiled rice with small steel containers of a variety of vegetables, pickles, *papadum*, *rasam* (a clear, peppery lentil 'soup') and plain curd. The most prized Tamil cuisine is that of the Chettinad region, which draws on unusual spices (including one derived from a tree- growing lichen) to create subtle blends of flavour; its reputation for relentless spiciness has come about only recently, and is the result of a crossover

The new organ grinders

While Karnataka, with its glut of world-class cardiac surgeons, pitches itself as the hot new 'health tourism' destination, neighbouring Tamil Nadu has drummed up its own less enviable reputation on the operating table. The state is at the centre of the Indian organs racket as its poor harvest their own kidneys as a lucrative cash crop. Around 60 to 70 transplants take place in the state each month.

A *Journal of the American Medical Association* investigation revealed that in 96% of cases those going under the knife did so to pay off debts. The fee? Not steep, by international standards: Indian donors typically receive around US$1070 (although most are initially promised more than double). Still, not bad for a state where the poverty line is US$538 a year per family.

Transplant tourism began in the subcontinent in the 1980s, but has since boomed, even though the success rate is pitifully low; as many as half of those kidneys bought abroad fail, and a third of patients die. But with almost a third of the 40,000 awaiting transplant in Europe dying in the queue for a legal donor, it's clearly a risk many feel is worth taking.

India outlawed the trade in 1995, when individual states set up medical authorization committees to determine the authenticity of relationships between donor and recipient – or to uncover evidence of financial inducements – but name changes and speedy weddings between Gulf men and Indian women (followed by equally swift post-operative divorces), make these committees easy to hoodwink.

Nor has South India's burgeoning medical industry done much to impede the trade; transplant operations bring in cash and confer prestige on institutions and surgeons.

And while the lure of short-term cash prizes will replenish the numbers in the donor queues, evidence shows that most quickly sink back to earlier levels of indebtedness, only now with the added handicap of one less kidney.

There has been little political will to end the trade, except for the storm triggered in early 2007 when a local NGO unearthed a high number of kidney donations among a small fishing community devastated by the 2004 tsunami (see box, page 863). In one village just north of Chennai 150 women had sold a kidney. But Tamil Nadu's vulnerable are desperate to fight their common enemy, poverty, even at the cost of their health, with the only tool they have: their own organs.

with Andhra cuisine. Dessert is usually the creamy rice pudding *payasam*. The drink of choice is coffee, which comes freshly ground, filtered and frothy, with hot milk and sugar.

Literature As the oldest living Indian language, Tamil has a literature stretching back to the early centuries before Christ. A second century AD poets' academy, the **Sangam** in Madurai, suggests that sages sat at the top of the Tamil social order, followed by peasants, hunters, artisans, soldiers, fishermen and scavengers – in marked contrast to the rest of the subcontinent's caste system. From the beginning of the Christian era Tamil religious thinkers began to transform the image of Krishna from the remote and heroic figure of the epics into the focus of a new and passionate devotional worship – *bhakti*. From the seventh to the 10th century there was a surge of writing new hymns of praise, sometimes referred to as the Tamil *Veda*.

Music Changes constantly occurred in different schools of music within the basic structure of **raga-tala-prabandha** which was well established by the seventh century. Differences between the *Hindustani* or the northern system (which included the western and eastern regions) and the *Carnatic* or the southern system became noticable in the 13th century. The southern school has a more scale-based structure of *raga* whereas the northern school has greater flexibility and thus continued to develop through the centuries. The *tala* too is much more precise. It is nearly always devotional or didactic whereas the northern system also includes non-religious, every day themes and is occasionally sensuous. Telugu naturally lends itself to the southern system.

Screen gods

Tamil Nadu's lively temple society also keeps aflame sculpture and the arts, and makes for a people singularly receptive to iconography. Tamil film-making is every bit as prolific and profitable as its closest rival, Hindi-language Bollywood. The state's industry is famous for its dancing and choreography and the super-saturated colour of its film stock. Film stars too, are massive here; worshipped like demigods, their careers often offering them a fast track into politics, where they are singularly well placed to establish personality cults. Two such figures who have hopped from the screen into the state's political driving seat as chief minister are the cherished MGR – MG Ramachandran, the film star and charismatic chief minister during the 1980s – and Jayalalitha, his one-time girlfriend and contentious successor, three times chief minister since 1991 despite being the figure of multiple corruption scandals.

The violin accompanies the vocal music – imported from the West but played rather differently.

Dance and drama **Bharata Natyam** may be India's oldest classical dance form: a highly stylized solo for a woman of movement, music, mime, *nritta* (pure dance) and *nritya* (expression). Its theme is usually spiritual love.

Modern Tamil Nadu

Tamil Nadu took its present form as a result of the States Reorganization Act of 1956. Until 1967 the Assembly was dominated by the Indian National Congress, but after an attempt by the central government to impose Hindi as the national language the Congress Party was routed in 1967 by a regional party, the Dravida Munnetra Kazhagam (DMK) under its leader CN Annadurai. After his death the party split and since then either the DMK, or the splinter party, the All India Anna DMK (AIADMK), has been in power in the state. Neither party has any constituency beyond Tamil Nadu and thus at the all India level each has been forced to seek alliances with national parties. From the late 1960s the AIADMK, which controlled the State Assembly for most of the time, has been led by two film stars. The first, MG Ramachandran, remained the chief minister until his death (even after suffering a stroke which left him paralysed). The record of Jayalalitha, his successor, one-time lover and fellow film star, has been less consistent, and her rule dogged by scandal. She and her party were ousted by the DMK in the May 1996 elections and she was temporarily jailed until, cleared of a wide range of criminal charges, she re-entered the Legislative Assembly in March 2002, taking over once more as chief minister after winning the state elections with an 80% margin (her administration then arrested the previous chief minister, senescent 83-year-old Karunanidhi, in a corruption case that some say was motivated by revenge). In the May 2004 national elections, though, the party, allied to the BJP and vocal in its opposition to Sonia Gandhi's foreign origin, failed to win a single seat. A coalition of opposition parties, arguing that she had lost her political mandate, demanded Jayalalitha's resignation, but she hung on to office, albeit swiftly reversing a raft of controversial policies – such as scrapping free electricity schemes, reducing rice rations, banning animal sacrifices – introduced during the earlier years of power. Karunanidhi, though, DMK co-founder in 1949, got the last laugh and became chief minister for the fifth time in the elections of May 2006. In the 2009 Lok Sabha elections the DMK and Congress won 18 and eight respectively of the 39 seats.

The civil war in Sri Lanka caused tremendous stresses in Tamil politics on the mainland, neither the AIADMK nor the DML wanting wither to alienate Tamil sentiment, nor wishing to back Sri Lanka's LTTE. Whether the ending of that conflict brings much needed relief will depend crucially on the political approach adopted by the Sri Lankan government to the Tamil populations in the island.

Tamil stats in words

Tamil Nadu's state's wealth and literacy rates are far lower here than in neighbouring Kerala: Tamil Nadu's infant mortality rate is more than double Kerala's and its literacy levels is 20% less. Tamil is deeply agricultural: Keralites, whose higher level of education have made them tire of tending fields, import most of their vegetables from here. The bullock cart continues to square up against the goods truck on the state's roads and housing is often basic: mud thatch with woven banana roofs. Migrant workers in the steel industry, cotton, or road building cross the countryside for jobs, while for those at the higher end of society, the metro lifestyles of Chennai and preferably Bengaluru (Bangalore) beckon.

Economy Since India gained Independence in 1947, Tamil Nadu has become the country's second largest industrial state. With a quarter of India's spinning capacity, textiles are tremendously important and the state is famous both for handloom cottons and silks and for factory-made textiles. Leather and fabrics have also long been a vital export industry, but new industries exploiting abundant raw materials like iron ore, bauxite and magnesite have also developed. Chennai, home to the Ford and Hyundai car factories and manufacturer of lorries, buses and trains, has been dubbed India's Detroit. Software is strong too, thanks to the creation of Special Economic Zones of guaranteed 'flexibility' and autonomy in working hours. Tamil Nadu is the fifth largest economy and the seventh most populous state in India, but remains deeply agricultural.

Chennai (Madras)

→ Colour map 7, A6. Phone code: 044. Population: 5.36 million.

Chennai (Madras), South India's sprawling chief metropolis and India's fourth largest city, is dubbed 'India's Detroit' thanks to its chiefly automotive industrial revolution. The analogy is apt in more ways than one. Chennai's beautiful Indo-Saracenic buildings now stand like islands of elegance in a sea of concrete sprawl, and seen from the back of a taxi crawling along Anna Salai in the rush hour, the city can seem to be little more than a huge, sweltering traffic jam.

Nevertheless, modern Chennai remains the de facto capital of Indian high culture – complex dances such as Bharatnatyam are still widely taught and practised here – and the city retains an air of gentility that's missing from the other Indian metros. Despite attempts to carpet-bomb the southern suburbs with IT parks and malls, you'll find little here of the boom of Mumbai or the overheated dynamism of Bengaluru. Chennai's urban elite of textile magnates, artists and web entrepreneurs still maintain their networks around the bars and walking tracks of the city's Raj-era clubs, where chinos and loafers rule and churidars and lungis are checked at the door.

Outside the gates of these green refuges, Chennai can be a hard city to love. It's polluted, congested, tricky to negotiate and lacks anything resembling a centre. Nevertheless, there are reasons to stick around for more than the customary pre- or post-flight overnight stay, particularly if you base yourself near the old Brahmin suburb of Mylapore, which with its beautiful temple towers, old-time silk emporia and dingy cafes, makes a worthy introduction or postscript to the Tamil temple circuit. ▸▸ *For listings, see pages 877-888.*

Ins and outs

Getting there Chennai's international and domestic air terminals are next to each other about 15 km from the city: allow 50 minutes, although it may take as little as half an hour. Airport buses run the circuit of the main hotels, and include Egmore station; otherwise it's best to get a pre-paid taxi: either yellow-topped government taxis or the more comfortable and expensive private cabs (note the number written on your charge slip). Trains from the north and west come into the Central Station behind the port, while lines from the south terminate at Egmore; both stations have abundant hotels nearby. State-owned buses terminate at the Koyembedu Moffusil terminus, 10 km west of the centre, and private buses at the nearby Omni terminus; it's worth asking whether the driver can drop you closer to your destination.

Getting around Chennai is very spread out and walking is usually uncomfortably hot so it's best to find an auto-rickshaw. Most refuse to run their meter, so ask your hotel for an approximate rate to your destination. Taxis are comparatively rare and a bit more expensive, but there's an efficient system of radio taxis which can be yours for as little as Rs 100 per hour. The bus network is extensive with frequent services, but it's often very crowded. ▸▸ *See Transport, page 884.*

Orientation Chennai is far from an 'organized' city. The main harbour near the old British military zone of **George Town** is marked by cranes for the cargo business. Nearby is the **fort**, the former headquarters of the British and now the Secretariat of the Tamil Nadu Government, and the High Court. The **Burma bazar**, a long line of pokey shops, runs between the two near Parry's Corner, while the two main rail stations lie to the west of George Town. From the fort, **Anna Salai** (Mount Road of old) cuts a southwest-ward swathe through the city, passing through or near to most areas of interest to visitors: **Triplicane**, where most of Chennai's cheap accommodation can be found; **Thousand Lights** and **Teynampet**, where ritzier hotels and malls dominate; and the commercial free-for-all of **T Nagar**. Just south of the central area between Anna Salai and the long sweep of Marina Beach lies **Mylapore**, older than Chennai itself and the cultural heart of the city. Further south still, industrial and high-tech sprawl stretches down the coast almost as far as **Mahabalipuram**.

Tourist information Most tourist offices are located in the the new **Tourism Complex** ⓘ *2 Wallajah Rd, near Kalaivanar Arangam*. **Tamil Nadu Tourism (TN)** ⓘ *T044-2536 8358,* *www.tamilnadutourism.org*, also has offices opposite Central station (T044-2535 3331), in Egmore (T044-2819 2165), and at the Domestic and International airports. **Tamil Tourist Development Corporation** (TTDC) ⓘ *T044-2538 9857, www.ttdconline.com*. **Kerala Tourism** ⓘ *T044-2538 2639*; **Andhra Pradesh Tourism** ⓘ *T044-6543 9987*; **Andaman and Nicobar Islands Tourism** ⓘ *T044-2654 9295*.

Possibly the best organized office is **Government of India Tourism** ⓘ *154 Anna Salai, T044-2846 0285, Mon-Fri 0915-1745, Sat until 1300*. **India Tourism Development Corporation** (ITDC) ⓘ *29 Ethiraj Salai, T044-2821 1782, Mon-Sat 0600-2000, Sun 0600-1400*. For city information see also www.chennaionline.com.

History

Armenian and Portuguese traders had settled the San Thome area before the arrival of the British. In 1639, **Francis Day**, a trader with the East India Company, negotiated the grant of a tiny plot of sandy land to the north of the Cooum River as the base for a warehouse or factory. The building was completed on 23 April 1640, St George's Day. The site was chosen partly because of local politics – Francis Day's friendship with Ayyappa Nayak, brother of the local ruler of the coast country from Pulicat to the Portuguese settlement of San Thome – but more importantly by the favourable local price of cotton goods.

By 1654 the patch of sand had grown into Fort St George, complete with a church and English residences – the 'White Town'. To its north was 'Black Town', referred to locally as Chennaipatnam, after Chennappa Nayak, Dharmala Ayyappa Nayak's father. The two towns merged and Madraspatnam grew with the acquisition of neighbouring villages of Tiru-alli-keni (meaning Lily Tank, and Anglicised as Triplicane), in 1676. In 1693, Governor Yale (founder of Yale University in the USA) acquired Egmore, Purasawalkam and Tondiarpet from Emperor Aurangzeb, who had by then extended Mughal power to the far south. In 1746 Madras was captured by the French, to be returned to British control as a result of the Treaty of Aix-la-Chapelle in 1748. Villages like Nungambakkam, Ennore, Perambur, San Thome and Mylapore (the 'city of the peacock') were absorbed by the mid-18th century with the help of friendly Nawabs. In 1793, the British colonial administration moved to Calcutta, but Madras remained the centre of the East India Company's expanding power in South India.

It was more than 150 years after they had founded Fort St George at Madras (in 1639) before the East India Company could claim political supremacy in South India. Haidar Ali, who mounted the throne of Mysore in 1761, and his son Tipu Sultan, allied with the French, won many battles against the English. The 1783 Treaty of Versailles forced peace. The English took Malabar in 1792, and in 1801 Lord Wellesley brought together most of the south under the Madras Presidency.

The city continues to grow, although many services, including water and housing, are stretched to breaking point. Since Independence an increasing range of heavy and light goods industries, particularly automotive, has joined the long-established cotton textiles and leather industries.

Sights

Apart from anomalous little pockets of expats, such as Chetpet's Jamaican and South African communities, life in Chennai continues much as it always has done: brahminical neighbourhoods still demand strict vegetarianism of all tenants; and flat sharing, a commonly accepted practice among the young in Bengaluru (Bangalore), is taboo. Superstition is important here too: rents are decided according to vasthu, India's equivalent of feng shui, and a wrong-facing front door can slash your payments.

You have to squint hard today to picture the half-empty grandeur that was the Madras of the East India Presidency. Triplicane has some of the finest architectural remains but the derelict district is better known today as 'bachelors' neighbourhood' due to its popularity with young men who come to make their fortune in the city.

The long expanse of Marina Beach, just seaward of Triplicane, made Chennai's residents tragically vulnerable to the 2004 tsunami, which devastated this public land – the city's cricket pitch, picnic ground and fishing shore. There's no trace of the ferocity of the waves today, but here alone it took about 200 lives.

1 Chennai city

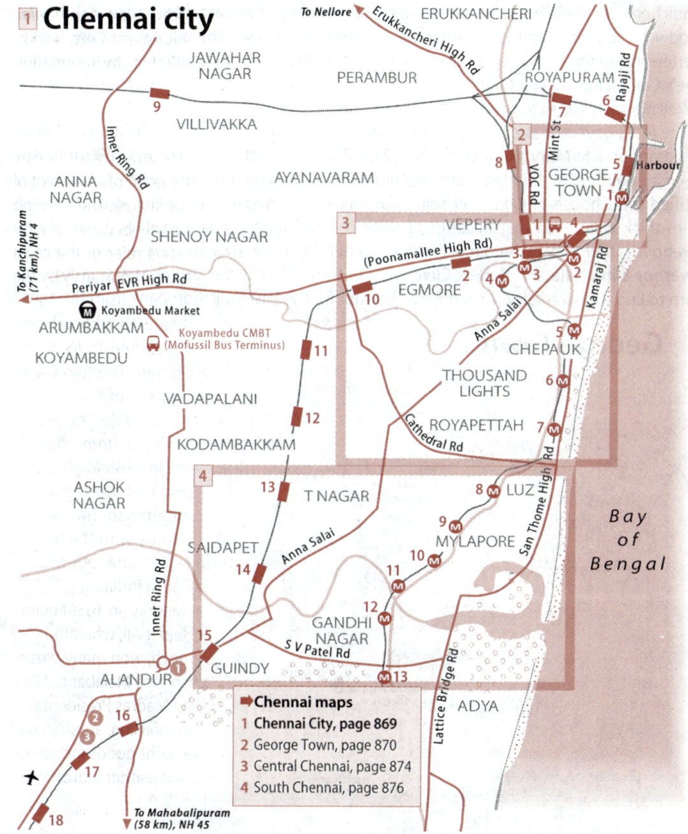

Sleeping
Le Royal Meridien 1
Mount Manor 2
Trident 3

Suburban railway
Madras Central 1
Egmore 2
Park 3
Fort 4
Beach 5
Roypuram 6
Washermanpet 7
Basin Bridge 8
Perambur 9
Chetput 10
Nungambakkam 11
Kodambakkam 12
Mambalam 13
Saidapet 14
Guindy 15
St Thomas Mount 16
Meenambakkam 17
Trisoolam 18

MRTS
Beach Junction 1
Fort 2
Park 3
Chintadripet 4
Chepauk 5
Tiruvellikeni 6
Lighthouse 7
Luz 8
Tirumailai 9
Mandaveli 10
Greenways Rd 11
Kotturpuram 12
Kasturba Nagar 13

The fort and port: St George and George Town

Madras began as nothing more than a huddle of fishing villages on the Bay of Bengal, re-christened Madras by British 17th-century traders after they built the Factory House fortifications on the beach. The present fort dates from 1666. The 24 black **Charnockite pillars**, see page 1430, were reclaimed by the British in 1762 after the French had carried them off to Pondicherry in 1746. Now the site of state government, the **State Legislative Hall** has fine woodwork and black and white stone paving. You can also see the old barracks and officers' quarters including Lord Clive's house, which he rented from an Armenian merchant. One room, Clive's Corner, has small exhibits. The house once occupied by Arthur Wellesley, the future Duke of Wellington, is 100 m further along.

The fort's governor Streynsham Master was responsible for the most interesting building in the compound, **St Mary's Church** ⓘ *T044-2538 2023*. Built between 1678 and 1680, it ranks as the first English church in India and the oldest British building to survive. It's unusually well fortified for a house of God – all solid masonry with semi-circular cannon-proof roofs and 1.3-m-thick walls – so that in times of siege it could function as a military dormitory and storehouse, and had to be almost entirely rebuilt in 1759 after military action in a siege. **Governor Elihu Yale** and **Robert Clive** were both married in the church. Yale, an American (born to English parents), who worked as a writer for the East India Company from the ages of

2 George Town

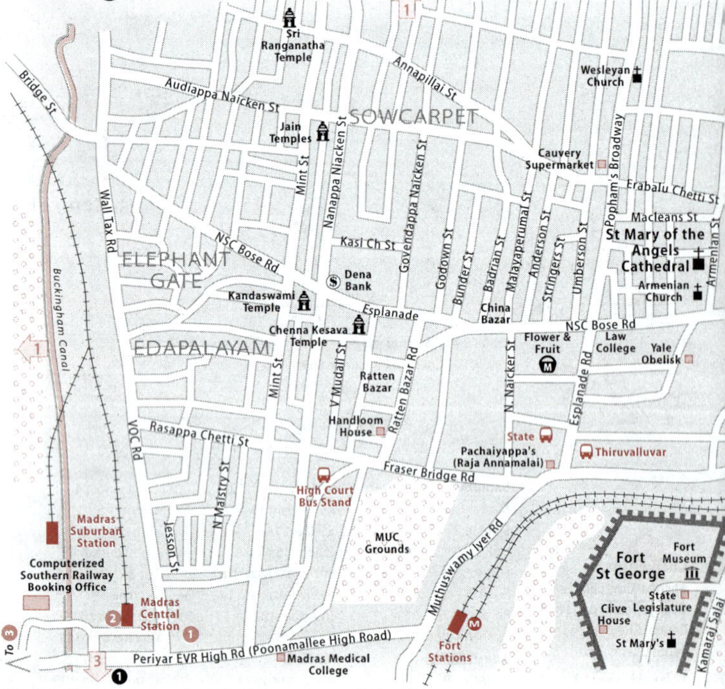

Sleeping
Railway Retiring Rooms **2**
Sonata Park **3**
Sornam International **1**

Eating
Buhari's **1**

24 to 39, rose to become governor; his son David is buried under the Hynmers Obelisk in the old burial ground. The famous missionary **Schwartz**, at one time the intermediary between the British and Haidar Ali, is also celebrated here for his role just "going about doing good". Job Charnock is commemorated for carrying a Hindu widow from the funeral pyre she was about to burn herself on and whereupon he took her as his wife. You can also learn the unhappy end of poor Malcolm McNeill, a colonel of the Madras Light Cavalry, who died at Rangoon in 1852 from neither battle nor disease but from a case of sunstroke. Nor is he alone: many Britishers appear to have fallen "a martyr to an ungenial climate".

The original black font, made from 3000-million-year-old Charnockite from Pallavaram, has been in continuous use since the church was consecrated. Outside the west entrance lies one of the oldest British inscriptions in India: the tombstone of Elizabeth Baker.

Also in the compound is an 18th-century building housing the **Fort Museum** ⓘ *Sat-Thu 1000-1700, US$2, photography prohibited*, with exhibits from 300 years of British Indian history including brilliant portraits of Madras governors. It includes prints, documents, paintings, sculpture, arms (medieval weapons with instructions on their use) and uniforms. The Indo-French gallery has some Louis XIV furniture and clocks. Clive Corner, which includes letters and photographs, is particularly interesting. The building itself was once an exchange for East India Company merchants, becoming an officers' mess later.

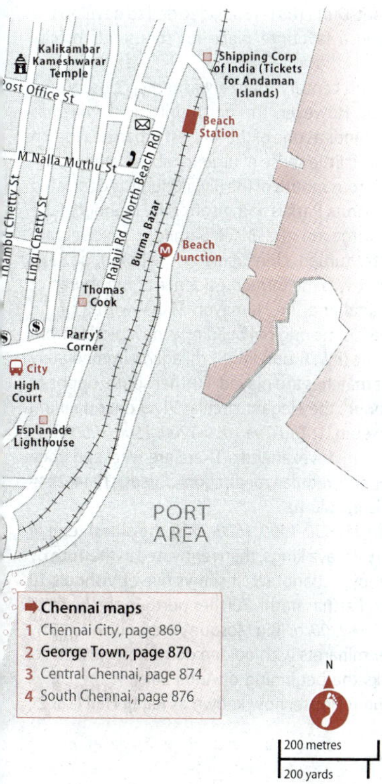

Chennai maps
1 Chennai City, page 869
2 **George Town, page 870**
3 Central Chennai, page 874
4 South Chennai, page 876

Within walking distance of the compound, to the north, is the city's long-standing commercial centre, **George Town**. The area was renamed after the future King George V when he visited India in 1905. You first reach the grand Indo-Saracenic complex of the **High Court** ⓘ *Mon-Sat 1045-1345, 1430-1630, contact registrar for visit and guide, Rs 10*, developed in the style of the late 19th-century architects like **Henry Irwin**, who was also responsible for the National Art Gallery. You are allowed to visit the courtrooms by using the entrance on the left. A fine example is Court No 13 which has stained glass, fretted woodwork, carved furniture, silvered panels and a painted ceiling. The huge red central tower, nearly 50 m tall (you can climb to the top), built like a domed minaret to serve as a lighthouse, can be seen 30 km out at sea. It was in use from 1894 until 1977. The original **Esplanade Lighthouse**, southeast of the High Court, is in the form of a large Doric pillar and took over from the Fort lighthouse in 1841.

Cross NSC Bose Road from the High Court's north gate to walk up Armenian Street for the beautiful Armenian **Church of the Holy Virgin Mary** (1772) ⓘ *0930-1430, bells rung on Sun at 0930*. Solid walls and massive 3-m-high wooden doors conceal the pleasant open courtyard inside, which contains a pretty belltower and many Armenian tombstones, the oldest dating from 1663. The East India Company praised the Armenian community for their 'sober, frugal and wise' lifestyle and they were given the same rights as English settlers in 1688. Immediately north again is the Roman Catholic Cathedral, **St Mary of the Angels** (1675). The inscription above the entrance – 1642 – celebrates the date when the Capuchin monks built their first church in Madras.

Popham's Broadway, west from the St Mary cathedral, takes its name from a lawyer called Stephen (in Madras 1778-1795) who was keen to improve the city's sanitation, laying out what was to become Madras's main commercial street. Just off Popham's Broadway in Prakasham Road is the **Wesleyan Church** (1820).

In the 18th century there was major expansion between what is now First Line Beach (North Beach Road) and **Mint Street** to the west of George Town. The Mint was first opened in 1640, and from the late 17th century minted gold coins under licence for the Mughals, but did not move to Mint Street until 1841-1842.

The 19th-century growth of Madras can be traced north from **Parry's Corner**. **First Line Beach**, built on reclaimed land in 1814 fronted the beach itself. The **GPO** (1844- 1884) was designed by Chisholm. The completion of the harbour (1896), transformed the economy of the city.

Central Chennai and the Marina

Triplicane and **Chepauk** contain some of the finest examples of late 19th-century Indo-Saracenic architecture in India, concentrated in the area around the University of Madras. The Governor of Madras, Mountstuart Elphinstone Grant-Duff (1881-1886), decided to develop the Marina as a promenade, since when it has been a favourite place for thousands of city inhabitants to walk on a Sunday evening.

Until the harbour was built at the end of the 19th century the sea washed up close to the present line of Kamaraj Salai (South Beach Road). However, the north-drifting current has progressively widened **Marina Beach**, which now stands as one of the longest urban beaches in the world – a fact that fills Chennai with great pride, if little sense of urgency about keeping the beach itself clean. The area just south of the malodorous mouth of the River Cooum is dedicated to a series of memorials to former state governors: **Anna Park** is named after the founder of the DMK party, CN Annadurai, while pilgrims converge on the **MGR Samadhi** to celebrate **MG Ramachandran** – the charismatic 1980s filmstar-turned- chief minister (see box, page 865). **Chepauk Palace**, 400 m away on South Beach Road, was the former residence of the Nawab of the Carnatic. The original four-domed Khalsa Mahal and the Humayun Mahal with a grand *durbar* hall had a tower added between them in 1855. The original building is now hidden from the road by the modern Public Works Department (PWD) building, Ezhilagam. Immediately behind is the Chepauk **cricket ground** where test matches are played. Further south, opposite the clunky sculpture entitled 'the Triumph of Labour', the elegant circular **Vivekenanda Illam** was Madras' first ice house, and now hosts a **museum** ⓘ *Thu-Tue 1000-1200, 1500-1900, Rs 2*, devoted to the wandering 20th-century saint, Swami Vivekananda. There are weekend yoga classes at the ice house (weekends, 0630-0830) and regular meditation classes (T044-2844 6188, Wednesday at 1900) run by the Sri Ramakrishna Math.

Inland from here lies the **Parthasarathi Temple** ⓘ *0630-1300, 1500-2000*, the oldest temple structure in Chennai. It was built by eighth-century Pallava kings, then renovated in the 16th by Vijayanagara rulers. Dedicated to Krishna as the royal charioteer, it shows five of Vishnu's 10 incarnations, and is the only temple dedicated to Parthasarathi. Further north in the heart of Triplicane, the **Wallajah Mosque** ⓘ *0600-1200, 1600-2200*, or 'Big Mosque', was built in 1795 by the Nawab of the Carnatic. There are two slender minarets with golden domes on either side. North again, near the Round Thana which marks the beginning of Anna Salai, is the Greek temple style banqueting hall of the old Government House, now known as **Rajaji Hall** (1802), built to mark the British victory over Tipu Sultan.

Egmore

A bridge across the Cooum at Egmore was opened in 1700, and by the late 18th century, the area around Pantheon Road became the fulcrum of Madras's social and cultural life, a 'place of public entertainment and balls'. Egmore's development, which continued for a century, started with the building of Horden's garden house in 1715. The original pantheon (public assembly rooms) was completely replaced by one of India's National Libraries. The **Connemara Library** (built 1896) began in 1662, when residents exchanged a bale of Madras calico for books from London. At the southwest corner of the site stands Irwin's Victoria Memorial Hall, now the **Government Museum and Art Gallery** ⓘ *486 Pantheon Rd, T044-2819 3238, Sat-Thu 0930-1630, closed Fri, foreigners Rs 250, Indians Rs 15, camera Rs 500*. The red brick rotunda surrounded by an Italianate arcade was described by Tillotson as one of "the proudest expressions of the Indo-Saracenic movement". There are locally excavated Stone and Iron Age implements and striking bronzes including a 11th-century Nataraja from Tiruvengadu, seated images of Siva and Parvati from Kilaiyur, and large figures of Rama, Lakshmana and Sita from Vadak-kuppanaiyur. Buddhist bronzes from Nagapattinam have been assigned to Chola and later periods. The beautiful Ardhanariswara statue here is one of the most prized of all Chola bronzes: Siva in his rare incarnation as a hermaphrodite. There are also good old paintings including Tanjore glass paintings, Rajput and Mughal miniatures and 17th-century Deccan paintings. Contemporary art is displayed at the **Gallery of Modern Art** ⓘ *Government Museum, T044-2819 3035.*

Egmore has other reminders of the Indo-Saracenic period of the 19th and early 20th centuries, the station itself being one of the last to be built, in the 1930s. Northeast of the station is the splendid **St Andrew's Church** ⓘ *Poonamalle High Rd, T044-2538 3508*. With a façade like London's St Martin-in-the-Fields, it has a magnificent shallow-domed ceiling. Consecrated in 1821, it has an active congregation.

Mylapore and South Chennai

Mylapore, which is technically older than Chennai and is the seat of city's urban elite, is more charming than the city centre. The present **Basilica of San Thomas** (1898) ⓘ *24 San Thome High Rd, T044-2498 5455*, surrounded now by the tenement rehousing scheme of a fishermen's colony, is claimed as one of the very few churches to be built over an apostle's tomb. St Thomas Didymus (Doubting Thomas) is believed to have come to India in AD 52. According to one legend, he crossed the peninsula from his landing on the west coast to reach Mylapore (the 'town of peacocks') where he proceeded to live and preach, taking shelter from persecution in Little Mount (see below). An alternative story argues King Gondophernes invited him to Taxila, where he converted the king and his court before moving to South India. Some claim that his body was ultimately buried in the Italian town of Ortona. Marco Polo in his travels in 1293 recorded the chapel on the seashore and a Nestorian monastery on a hill to the west where the apostle was put to death. In 1523, when the Portuguese started to rebuild the church they discovered the tomb containing the relics consisting of a few bones, a lance head and an earthenware pot containing bloodstained earth. The church was replaced by the neo-Gothic structure which has two spires and was granted the status of a basilica in 1956. The relics are kept in the sacristy and can be seen on request. There are 13th-century wall plaques, a modern stained glass window, a 450-year-old Madonna brought from Portugal and a 16th-century stone sundial. The basilica is now subject to an ambitious US$164,400 restoration project. To stop the Mangalore tile roof leaking, concrete reparations are being peeled back and replaced with original lime mortar.

Kapaleeswarar Temple ⓘ *0600-1300, 1600-2200*, to the west, is a 16th-century Siva temple with a 40-m *gopuram* (gateway), built after the original was destroyed by the Portuguese in 1566. Sacred to Tamil Shaivites, non-Hindus are only allowed in the outer courtyard, but it's absolutely worth a visit, especially at sunset when worshippers gather for the evening *puja*, conducted amidst ropes of incense smoke and swirling pipe music.

3 Central Chennai

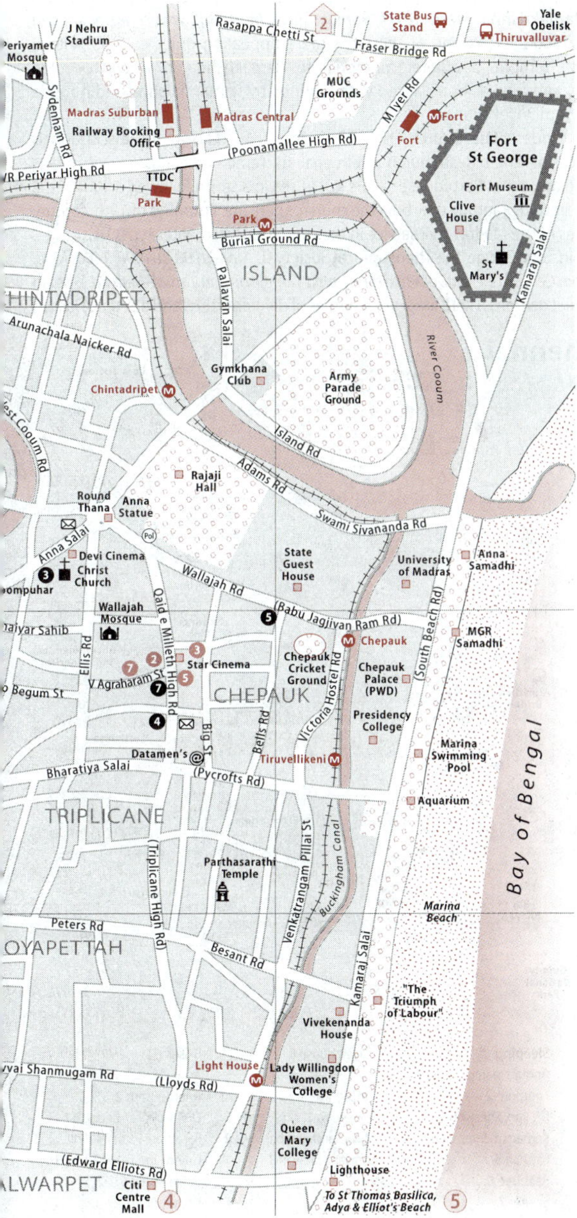

Sleeping

Ambassador Pallava **1** *B3*
Ashoka **14** *B3*
Blue Diamond **15** *A2*
Comfort **2** *C4*
Cristal **3** *C4*
Harrisons **4** *C1*
Himalaya International **5** *C4*
Impala Continental **16** *A3*
Imperial Plaza **17** *A3*
New Laxmi Lodge **18** *B3*
New Victoria **20** *A3*
Oriental Inn **6** *D3*
Pandian **21** *B3*
Paradise **7** *C4*
Railway Retiring Rooms **22** *A3*
Ranjith **9** *C2*
Regent **21** *B3*
Residency **10** *D1*
Satkar **25** *A2*
Taj Connemara **11** *C3*
Taj Coromandel **12** *C2*
The Park **8** *D2*
Udipi Home **26** *B3*
World University Service **27** *B2*
YWCA **19** *A3*
YWCA International Guest House **28** *A3*

Eating

Amaravathi **1** *D3*
Annalakshmi **2** *B3*
Buhari's **3** *B4*
Fisherman's Fare **9** *B2*
Gem **4** *C4*
Hotel Savera **6** *D3*
Nair Mess **5** *C4*
Rangi's **8** *C2*
Suriya's **7** *C4*
Vasantha Bhavan **11** *A3*

The nearby **Sri Ramakrishna Math** ⓘ *31 Ramakrishna Mutt Rd, www.sriramakrishnamath.org, 0500-1145, 1500-2100*, is one of the city's more appealing quiet corners, with a spectacular multi-faith temple, a quieter memorial to Ramakrishna in a prettily tiled Chettinad-style house, and a bookshop packed with writings by Ramamkrishna and notable devotees, including Swami Vivekananda.

The diminutive Portuguese **Luz Church**, 1547-1582 (the 1516 date in the inscription is probably wrong), is possibly the oldest church in Chennai. Its Tamil name, *Kattu Kovil*, means 'jungle temple'. Legend has it that Portuguese sailors lost at sea in a storm followed a light to the shore, where it disappeared. In gratitude they built the church. There are a number of 19th-century marble plaques to wives of the Madras civil service in the church and an ornate crypt.

To the south of Elphinstone Bridge, the **Theosophical Society** ⓘ *Mon-Fri 0830-1000, 1400-1600, Sat 0830-1000, bus 5 from Central Chennai, ask taxi for Ayappa Temple on San Thome High Rd*, is set in large and beautifully quiet gardens. There are several shrines of different faiths and a Serene Garden

4 South Chennai

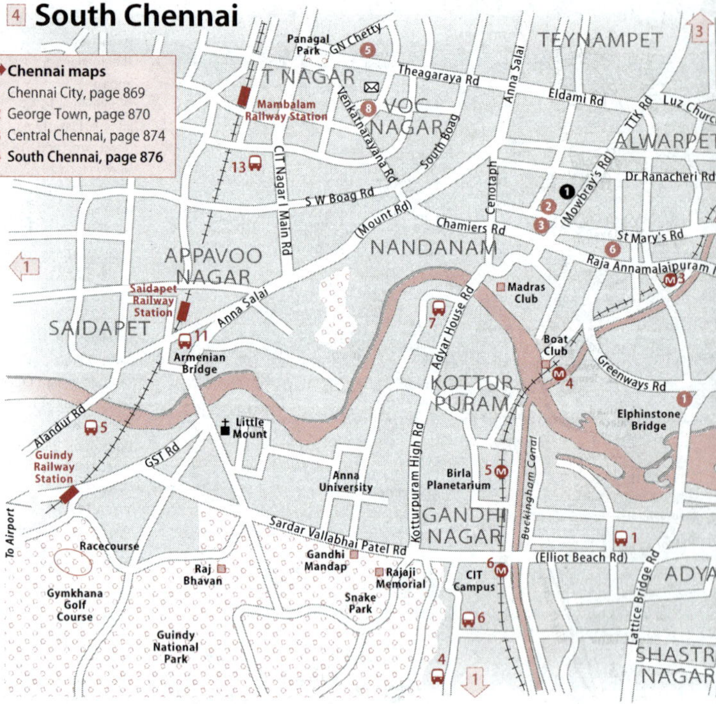

Sleeping
Andhra Mahila Sabha **1**
Footprint **2**
ITC Park Sheraton **3**
Karpagam International **4**
Parthan **5**
Rain Tree **6**
Shelter **7**
Transit House **8**

Eating
Benjarong **1**
Mylai Karpagambal Mess **2**
Saravana Bhavan **3**

Buses
Adyar **1**
Anakaputhur **2**
Dr Ambedkar Bridge **3**
Foreshore Estate **4**
Guindy Industrial Estate **5**
Indira Nagar **6**
Kotturpuram **7**

of Remembrance for Madame Blavatsky and Colonel Olcott who founded the society in New York in 1875 and moved its headquarters to Madras in 1882. There's a huge 400-year-old banyan past the kitchen garden, a library and a meditation hall. The brackish river attracts waders and seabirds.

Tucked away near Saidapet is the **Little Mount** area. The older of the two churches (1551), with its small vaulted chapel, was built by the Portuguese. The modern circular church was built in 1971. St Thomas is believed to have been martyred and bled to death in AD 52 on the **Great Mount**, though others believe he was accidentally killed by a hunter's arrow. On top of the 90-m-high 'mount' is the **Church of Our Lady of Expectation**. The altar marks the spot where, according to legend, Thomas fell. Some legends suggest that after St Thomas had been martyred on the Little Mount, near Saidapet Bridge, his body was brought back to the beach which had been his home and was buried there.

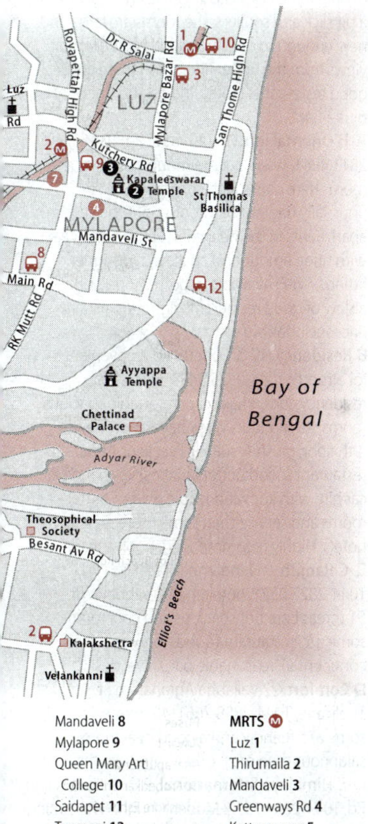

Mandaveli **8**	MRTS Ⓜ
Mylapore **9**	Luz **1**
Queen Mary Art College **10**	Thirumaila **2**
Saidapet **11**	Mandaveli **3**
Taramani **12**	Greenways Rd **4**
T Nagar **13**	Kotturpuram **5**
	Kasturba Nagar **6**

Chennai (Madras) listings

Hotel prices

LL over US$200 **L** US$151-200 **AL** US$101-150
A US$66-100 **B** US$46-65 **C** US$31-45
D US$21-30 **E** US$12-20 **F** US$7-11
G US$6 and under

Restaurant prices

over US$12 US$6-12 under US$6

Sleeping

Chennai has a wealth of accommodation options, many of them pitched at the city's ever-growing business sector. Those at the top end, with notable exceptions including the **Raintree**, the **Park** and the 2 **Taj** properties, tend to be characterless concrete boxes. However, there are some excellent mid-range options, including a slew of serviced apartments and one solitary but wonderful B&B. Cheap hotels congregate around Central and Egmore stations and on hectic Triplicane High Rd, but even here you'll tramp a long way to find an acceptably clean room for under Rs 400. For more atmosphere, up your budget a little and stay near the temple in Mylapore.

Chennai airport

These hotels offer free airport transfers. Other hotels are 12-15 km from the airport.

L Trident, 1/24 GST Rd, T044-2234 4747. 166 rooms in characterless but functional hotel. Pleasant swimming pool in the garden.

AL Le Royal Meridien, 1 GST Rd, St Thomas Mount, T044-2231 4343, www.leroyal meridien-chennai.com. Plush hotel with all facilities including good restaurants and bars.

B-C Mount Manor, GST Rd, St Thomas Mount, T044-2231 0975. New business-style hotel with modern facilities and free airport transfers, but guests warn drivers may try to take you to inferior nearby hotels (eg Mount Heera) for commission.

George Town *p870, map p870*

Good location for Central Station and State bus stands. Many cheap hotels are along VOC (Walltax) Rd, while slightly more salubrious accommodations jostle for space with cheap restaurants and travel agencies along EVR Periyar (Poonamallee) High Rd.

E Sornam International, 7 Stringer St, T044-2535 3060. Pleasant, 50 rooms with TV and balcony, hot water, rooftop vegetarian restaurant.

E-F Sonata Park, 41 Sydenhams Rd, T044-4215 2272. Simple but well-looked-after rooms and excellent-value suites, within walking distance of the station, but away from the usual budget hotel belt.

F-G Railway Retiring Rooms, Central Station, T044-2535 3337. Some a/c rooms, dorms.

G Youth Hostel (TTDC), EVR Park (near Central Railway Station), T044-2538 9132. Reasonably quiet.

Central Chennai *p872, map p874*

Many accommodation options are within 1 km of Anna Salai (Mount Rd). **A-E** hotels charge an extra 12.5% tax.

LL The Park, 601 Anna Salai, T044-4267 6000, www.theparkhotels.com. Converted from the site of the Gemini Film Studios, this is a quintessentially film hotel. Conran interiors, original film posters on the walls, world-class business facilities and restaurants and lovely rooftop pool with magnificent views over Chennai.

L Taj Connemara, Binny Rd (off Anna Salai), T044-6600 0000, www.tajhotels.com. Supremely comfortable hotel with 148 renovated rooms that retain splendid art deco features. Excellent restaurants, bar and good **Giggles** bookshop – so heavily stocked you can't get in the door. Heavily booked Dec-Mar.

L Taj Coromandel, 37 Mahatma Gandhi Rd, Nungambakkam, T044-6600 2827, www.tajhotels.com. 201 rooms, fine restaurants, good pool. Recommended but Western tours dominate.

AL Ambassador Pallava, 53 Montieth Rd, T044-2855 4476, www.ambassadorindia.com. Enormous, frumpy wedding cake of a hotel, with 120 rooms split between 'Heritage' (red carpet, quirky old furniture, antique bathroom fittings) and slightly cheaper, tile-floored 'Executive'. Neither are brilliant value, but good restaurants (especially Chinese), a pool and health club make it a viable choice if you want a taste of retro Indian high-end hospitality.

AL Harrisons, 315 Valluvar Kottam High Rd, T044-4222 2777, www.harrisonshotels.com. A new 4-star tower bock stands on the site of one of the city's classic hotels. Though it's all a bit slick and soulless, the rooms are large and new enough to qualify as spotless, with great views from the upper floors, and there are 2 good restaurants (South Indian and Chinese) plus a bar.

A-B Oriental Inn, 71 Cathedral Rd, T044-2811 4941, www.orientalgroup.in. The older rooms here come with crisp sheets and unusually fragrant bathrooms, but the studio apartments in the new wing are the real steal, with huge amounts of space and designer fittings. Wi-Fi available in both wings, and a slew of good restaurants right downstairs. Price includes breakfast.

B Residency, 49 GN Chetty Rd (convenient for airport), T044-2825 3434, www.theresidency.com. 112 very comfortable spacious rooms, 4th floor upwards have good views (9th floor, plush **A** suites). Excellent **Ahaar** restaurant (good buffet lunches), exchange, car hire with knowledgeable drivers. Better rooms and service than some more expensive hotels. Highly recommended, book ahead.

B-C Ranjith, 9 Nungambakkam High Rd, T044-2827 0521, hotelranjith@yahoo.com. 51 threadbare but spacious and cool rooms, some a/c, restaurant (good non-vegetarian continental), reasonable bar, travel desk.

D Comfort, 22 Vallabha Agraharam St, Triplicane, T044-2858 7661. 40 rooms, some a/c, friendly and a good deal more salubrious than most other options in the area.

D-E Himalaya International, 91 Triplicane High Rd, T044-2854 7522. Modern, bright, welcoming, 45 rooms with nice bath, some a/c, clean. No food but available from **Hotel Gandhi** next door.

E Paradise, 17/1 Vallabha Agraharam St, Triplicane, T044-2859 4252, paradisegh@hotmail.com. Spacious clean rooms with fans (some with 2), shower, good value, very friendly and helpful owners. A firm budget-traveller favourite.

F-G Cristal, 34 CNK Rd, Triplicane, T044-2857 2721. Clean basic rooms with tiled bath, very helpful service, better and cheaper than some others in the area.

Egmore *p873, map p874*

Many hotels (including several good budget options) are around the station and along EVR Periyar (Poonamallee) High Rd, an auto-rickshaw ride away to the north of the railway line. Try to book ahead as budget hotels opposite the station and down Kennet Lane often fill up by midday.

A-B New Victoria, 3 Kennet Lane (200 m from station), T044-2819 3638. 51 a/c rooms, restaurant (excellent breakfast), bar, spacious, quiet, ideal business hotel. Recommended.

B-C Ashoka, 47 Pantheon Rd, T044-2855 3377, www.ballalgrouphotels.com. The funky 1950s flavour and encouraging whiff of disinfectant run out of steam before they make it to the rooms, but this is one of Egmore's more appealing mid-range options, set back from the street and right opposite the museum, with an in-house restaurant and 'Ice Cream Park'. Popular wedding venue, so ring ahead.

B-C Pandian, 15 Kennet Lane, T044-2819 1010, www.hotelpandian.com. A decent budget choice that's cornered the foreign- traveller market, with a host of handy facilities including travel desk, multiple internet cafés and an a/c restaurant and bar. But the 90 rooms are small and poky for what you're paying, and the whole place could do with a lick of paint.

B-E Udipi Home, Udipi Junction (corner of Hall's Rd and Police Commissioner's Rd), T044-6454 6555, uhome@redifmail.com. Some excellent business-class 'Deluxe' rooms with colourful glass dividers separating sleeping and meeting areas, plus more basic doubles, some windowless, at the cheaper end. There's an internet café and a superb restaurant downstairs. Book ahead – walk-ins rarely get a room.

D Blue Diamond, 934 EVR Periyar High Rd, T044-2641 2244. 33 rooms, some a/c, quieter at rear, good a/c restaurant (busy at peak times), exchange.

D YWCA International Guest House, 1086 EVR Periyar High Rd, T044-2532 4234. Restaurant (rate includes breakfast), 60 rooms with bath and a/c, available to both men and women, popular so book early, excellent value, also campsite and plenty of parking – good for bikers.

D-F Imperial Plaza, 6 Gandhi Irwin Rd, T044-4214 7362. A friendly mid-priced option, set back from the street in a complex of 5 'Imperial' hotels, each owned by a different member of the same family. Rooms are average for the area – clean enough, but don't expect sparkling value, and there's a huge markup if you want the a/c switched on.

E Satkar, 65 Ormes Rd (junction of Flowers Rd and Miillers Rd), T044-2642 5179. Spotless rooms with bath, some a/c, good vegetarian **Suryaprakash** restaurant, helpful staff, good value but very noisy.

E Silver Star, 5 Purasawalkam High Rd, T044-2642 4414. Set back from the road, 38 simple clean rooms, open-air restaurant in courtyard, helpful and friendly staff.

E-F YMCA, 74 Ritherdon Rd, T044-2532 2628. Good rooms and an extensive range of sports facilities including badminton, snooker, table tennis.

F Impala Continental, opposite station, T044-2819 1778. Near **Vasanta Bhavan** restaurant, 50 excellent clean rooms with TV, good service.

F New Laxmi Lodge, 16 Kennet Lane, T044-2819 4576. Old building, set back in garden, with 50 rooms around courtyard.

F Railway Retiring Rooms, Egmore Station, T044-2819 2527.

F Regent, 11 Kennet Lane, T044-2819 1801. 45 renovated clean rooms set motel-style around a leafy courtyard/car park. The friendly owner makes this the pick of the Egmore cheapies.

F World University Service, East Spur Tank Rd, T044-2836 4422. Some rooms with bath, dorm, International student cards needed, couples not allowed to share a room, cheap canteen for Indian snacks, good value, well situated for Egmore and south central Chennai.

South Chennai *p873, map p876*

L-AL ITC Park Sheraton, 132 TTK Rd, T044-2499 4101. Good pool, 160 rooms, **Dakshin Chettinad** restaurant.

L-AL Rain Tree, 120 St Mary's Rd, T044-4225 2525, www.raintreehotels.com. Beautiful luxury hotel, and Chennai's first to be run on an environmentally sustainable basis.

A Footprint Bed and Breakfast, behind **Park Sheraton**, off TTK Rd, T044-3255 7720, T(0)9840-037383, www.footprint.in. Beautifully cool, peaceful and intimate retreat from the city, with 9 stylish but unfussy rooms, decorated with handmade paper from Auroville, spread over 2 floors of a residential apartment block. Indian and continental breakfasts come with fresh newspapers, and there's a small library, free internet and Wi-Fi. Owner, Rucha, pops in every day to check on things, and will negotiate weekly and monthly rates if you want to stay longer. Highly recommended.

C Parthan, 75 GN Chetty Rd (near Panagal Park), T044-2815 8792. Restaurant (Chinese), 29 clean, large, comfortable and quiet rooms, exchange. Recommended.

C Shelter, 19-21 Venkatesa Agraharam St, T0411-2495 1919, T(0)9840-037483, www.hotelshelter.com. Business hotel located in Mylapore. Clean rooms with hot water, central a/c, very helpful staff, internet café, exchange, restaurant.

D-E Karpagam International, 41 South Mada St, Mylapore, T044-2495 9984. Basic but clean rooms amid the Mylapore temple madness; the best ones face straight across the lake. Book 2 weeks in advance.

E Andhra Mahila Sabha, 12 D Deshmukh Rd, T044-2493 8311. Some **D** a/c rooms, vegetarian restaurant.

Eating

Central Chennai *p872, map p874*

Most restaurants are in Central Chennai and are open 1200-1500, 1900-2400. Those serving non-vegetarian dishes are often more expensive.

TTT 601, The Park (see Sleeping). Possibly the best choice in town for a night out, with fantastic fusion food in a super elegant setting. Also at The Park, **Aqua**, serves excellent Mediterranean dishes and cocktails in poolside cabanas, and lays on a barbeques with live music on Wed nights.

TTT Copper Chimney, Oriental Inn (see Sleeping). Rich Mughlai and tandoori offerings in very clean setting. In the same building you can eat Chinese at **Chinatown** and good Spanish tapas at **Zara** (see Bars and clubs).

TTT Hotel Savera, 146 Dr Radhakrishnan Rd, T044-2811 4700. Atmospheric rooftop restaurant with superb views, excellent Indian food, friendly service and live Indian music in the evenings. The hotel pool is open to non-residents, Rs 150.

TTT Raintree, Taj Connemara (see Sleeping). Romantic outdoor restaurant with good food, atmosphere and ethnic entertainment but cavalier service. Very good buffet dinner on Sat night.

TTT Southern Spice, Taj Coromandel (see Sleeping). Very good South Indian, along with evening dance recitals and freezing a/c.

TT Annalakshmi, Anna Salai (near **Higginbotham's** bookshop). Wholesome, health-restoring offerings, Southeast Asian specialities (profits to charity, run by volunteers). Closed Mon. Recommended.

TT Buhari's, 83 Anna Salai, and EVR Periyar Rd opposite Central Station. Good Indian. Dimly lit a/c restaurant, with terrace and unusual decor. Try crab curry, egg *rotis* and Muslim dishes; also in Park Town near Central Station.

TT Cedars, 29 Gandhi Mandapam Rd, Kotturpuram, T044-2447 5073. Closed Mon. Great Lebanese place serving a mean squid batter fry.

TT Dynasty, Harrisons (see Sleeping). Highly regarded Chinese, a popular venue for business lunchers.

TT Rangi's, Continental Chambers, 142 Nungambakkam High Rd. Tiny but excellent hole-in-the-wall Chinese bistro.

T Amaravathi, corner of TTK Rd and Cathedral (Dr Radhakrishan) Rd. Great value for spicy Andhra food, but relatively little joy for vegetarians.

T Gem, Triplicane High Rd. Tiny non-veg Muslim place.

T Nair Mess, 22 Mohammed Abdullah 2nd St, Chepauk. Fast and furious Kerala 'meals' joint, dishing out rice and *sambhar* in mountain-sized portions until 2100 sharp.

T Saravana Bhavan, branches all over the city including Cathedral Rd opposite **Savera Hotel**, both railway stations, **Spencer Plaza Mall** and

Pondy Bazar. Spotlessly clean Chennai-based chain restaurant, serving excellent snacks and 'mini tiffin', fruit juices (try pomegranate), sweetmeats, all freshly made.
Suriyas, 307 Triplicane High Rd. Shiny and clean vegetarian restaurant, with North and South Indian options.

Egmore *p873, map p874*
Jewel Box, Blue Diamond (see Sleeping). Cool a/c, good for breakfasts, snacks and main courses.
Fisherman's Fare, 21 Spur Tank Rd. Outstanding value fish and seafood cooked in Indian, Chinese and Western styles.
Mathsya, Udipi Home, 1 Hall's Rd (corner of Police Commissioner's Rd). Chennai's night-owl haunt par excellence has been burning the oil (the kitchen stays open until 0200) by government order since the Indo-Chinese war. It also happens to serve some of the city's best pure veg food; their Mathsya *thali* comes with tamarind and sweetened coconut *dosas* and will keep you going all day. Recommended.
Vasanta Bhavan, 1st floor, 10 Gandhi Irwin Rd, opposite Egmore station. Very clean and super cheap, excellent food, friendly staff, downstairs bakery does delicious sweets.

South Chennai *p873, map p876*
Dakshin, ICT Park Sheraton Hotel (see Sleeping). High on the list of the best South Indian restaurants in the city, with Kanchipuram silk draped everywhere and a huge range of veg and non-veg choices. Book ahead.
Benjarong, 537 TTK Rd, Alwarpet, T044-2432 2640. Upscale Thai restaurant, doing very passable renditions of *tom kha* and *pad thai* amid a collection of Buddhas in glass cases. Plenty of veg options.
Mylai Karpagambal Mess, 80 East Mada St, Mylapore. If you can handle the all-round dinginess, this place serves superb, simple food – *vada*, *dosas* and a sweet *pongal* to die for – to an avid Tamil Brahmin crowd.
Saravana Bhavan, north of the temple tank, Mylapore. Similarly excellent food in a more salubrious if less interesting environment.

Bars and clubs

Chennai *p867, maps p869, p870, p874, p876*
You can buy booze without difficulty despite local restrictions. Regulations change periodically, however, and All India Liquor Permits are available from either an Indian mission or a Government of India tourist office abroad or in one of the regional capitals.
10 Downing, Kences Inn, BN Rd, T Nagar, T044-2815 2152. Noisy and popular bolthole, with live jazz and classic rock bands, but not a place for a quiet conversation.
Bike and Barrel, Residency Towers, Sri Thyagaraya Rd, T044-2815 6363. Split-level restaurant and bar, playing rock, trance and house.
Dublin, ICT Park Sheraton (see Sleeping). A notionally Irish pub by day, at night Dublin turns into a pulsating nightclub, pumping out the tunes until the early hours.
Havana, Rain Tree (see Sleeping). Lounge bar with dance floor, hosts various theme nights.
Leather Bar, The Park (see Sleeping). Not as kinky as the name suggests, but this dark womb of a bar, with black leather floors and olive suede walls, is still one of the city's sexiest.
Oakshott Bar, Taj Connemara (see Sleeping). A large, bright bar, offering huge tankards of beer, great snacks and a huge TV.
Pasha, The Park (see Sleeping). The city's sleekest dance club.
Zara, Oriental Inn (see Sleeping). Cocktails and Indian-style Spanish classics are the order of the day at this buzzing tapas bar, where you can lounge on leather banquettes with the trendies of Chennai.

Entertainment

Chennai *p867, maps p869, p870, p874, p876*
Although Chennai is revered for its strong cultural roots, much of it is difficult for tourists to access. Events are often publicized only after they have passed. Check the free *Cityinfo* guide, published fortnightly, and www.explocity.com, for upcoming events.

Cinemas
Cinemas showing foreign (usually English-language) films are mostly in the centre of town on Anna Salai.

Sathyam, 8 Thiru-vi-ka Rd, Royapettah, T044-4392 0200. Chennai's first multiplex is also India's highest grossing cinema, with 6 screens and a mix of new-release Hollywood, Bollywood and Tamil films. Worth visiting if only to overload on chocolate and caffeine at Michael Besse's **Ecstasy** bakery.

Music, dance and art galleries

Sabhas are membership societies that offer cultural programmes 4 times a month to their members, but occasionally tickets are available at the door.

Chennai Music Academy, TTK Rd, T044-2811 2231, www.musicacademymadras.in. The scene of many performances of Indian music, dance and theatre, not only during the prestigious 3-week music festival from mid-Dec but right through the year.

Kalakshetra, Tiruvanmiyur, T044-2446 1943. Daily 0900-1700, entry Rs 50. A temple of arts founded by Rukmani Devi Arundale in 1936 to train young artists to revive the dance form *Bharatnatyam*. The foremost exponents of the art are now trained here, and you can have a peek at lessons in progress between 0930 and 1130.

Madras Terrace House, 16 Sri Puram 2nd St, Royapettah. Photographic and art exhibitions, talks, and a boutique selling swish embroidered clothing.

Shree Bharatalaya, Mylapore. One of the key dance fine arts institutes run by respected guru Sudharani Raghupathy, Sura Siddha, 119 Luz Church Rd, T044-2499 4460.

Festivals and events

Chennai *p867, maps p869, p870, p874, p876*

Jan 14 Pongal Makara Sankranti, the harvest thanksgiving, is celebrated all over Tamil Nadu for 3 days (public holiday). After ritually discarding old clothes and clay pots, festivities begin with cooking the first harvest rice in a special way symbolizing good fortune, and offering it to the Sun god. The 2nd day is devoted to honouring the valuable cattle; cows and bulls are offered special 'new rice' dishes prepared with jaggery or nuts and green lentils. You will see them decorated with garlands, bells and balloons, their long horns painted in bright colours, before being taken out in procession around villages. Often they will pull carts decorated with foliage and flowers and carrying children, accompanied by noisy bands of musicians. On the final day of feasting, it is the turn of the 'workers' to receive thanks (and bonuses) from their employers.

Shopping

Chennai *p867, maps p869, p870, p874, p876*

The main shopping areas are **Parry's Corner** in George Town and **Anna Salai**. **Khader Nawaz Khan Rd** is a very pleasant and (for a change) walkable street, with several elegant boutiques.

Note that many drivers – even those from reputable agents and companies – see little wrong in collecting a sweetening kickback from Kashmiris staffing huge shopping emporia, in exchange for dumping you on their doorstep. These are expert salesmen and although they do have some beautiful items, will ask at least double. The commission comes out of whatever you buy, so exercise restraint.

Most shops open Mon-Sat 0900-2000, some close for lunch 1300-1500. Weekly holidays may differ for shops in the same locality. There are often discount sales during the festival seasons of Pongal, Diwali and Christmas. The weekly *Free Ads* (Rs 5, Thu) has listings for second-hand cameras, binoculars, etc, which travellers might want to buy or sell.

Books

Most bookshops open 0900-1900; many upmarket hotels also have a selection of books for sale.

Higginbotham's, 814 Anna Salai and F39 Anna Nagar East, near Chintamani Market.

Landmark, Apex Plaza, 3 Nungambakkam High Rd, T044-2822 1000.

Clothes and crafts

Amethyst, next to Corporation Bank, Whites Rd, Royapettah, T044-6499 3634. Open 1100-2000. Elegant Indian couture and jewellery, plus a lovely café shaded by raintrees, in the restored bungalow of the Maharaja of Jeypore.

Atmosphere, K Nawaz Khan Rd. Beautiful modern furniture, fabrics and curtains – mostly silks – which can be shipped anywhere within India within 72 hrs.

Central Cottage Industries, 118 Nungambakkam High Rd, opposite

Taj Coromandel. Wide variety of handicrafts, fixed prices.
Chamiers, 85 Chamiers Rd. Home to the beloved Anokhi store, for tribal-style block print fabrics and jewellery, plus a nice-looking but terrible-value outdoor café.
Evoluzione, 30 Khader Nawaz Khan Rd. High-end brands and cutting-edge Indian designers.
Habitat, K Nawaz Khan Rd nearby. Good for special, unusual gifts.
Kalakshetra at Thiruvanmiyur (see Entertainment). Excels in *kalamkari* and traditional weaving, good household linen.
Kalpa Druma, 61 Cathedral Rd (opposite **Chola Sheraton**). Attractive selection of wooden toys and panels.
Khazana, **Taj Coromandel** (see Sleeping). Good for special, unusual gifts.
Naturally Auroville, Khader Nawaz Khan Rd. Products from the new-age colony of Auroville, including incense, hand-made papers, clothing and delicious breads and cheeses.
New Kashmir Arts, 111 Anna Salai. Good carpets.
Poompuhar, 818 Anna Salai. Tamil Nadu crafts store, specializes in first-class bronzes.
Tiffany's, 2nd floor, Spencer's Plaza. Antiques and bric-a-brac.
Vatika, 5 Spur Tank Rd. Good for special, unusual gifts.
Victoria Technical Institute, Anna Salai near **Taj Connemara** hotel and opposite the Life Insurance Corporation of India. This fixed-rate, government-backed operation is the best for South Indian handicrafts (wood carving, inlaid work, sandalwood). Other government emporia are along Anna Salai.

Department stores and malls

Most open 1000-2000.
Burma Bazar, Rajaji Salai, George Town. For imports, especially electronic. Bargain hard.
Citi Centre, 10-11 Dr Radhakrishnan Salai, Mylapore. Huge new mall packed with international names, plus **Lifestyle** department store, bookshop, food court.
Ispahani Centre, 123/4 Nungambakkam High Rd. Where the hip Madrasis hang out. Very snazzy designer 'ethnic' clothes shops.
Spencer's Plaza, Anna Salai near **Taj Connemara**, is a dizzyingly huge mall with excellent choice for shopping in comfort. **Westside** department store on the ground floor, good for general clothing.
Supermarket, 112 Davidson St and TNHB Building, Annanagar (closed Fri).

Fabrics

Chennai was founded because of the excellence of the local cotton.
Co-optex (government run) shops, 350 Pantheon Rd. These stock handloom silks and cottons. The alleyway directly to the north is Cotton St, where piles of export surplus fabrics are sold at less than half the normal shop prices.
Khadi, 44 Anna Salai. Stores specialize in handspun and handwoven cotton.
Shilpi or **Urvashi**, TTK Rd. Good for cottons.

Jewellery

Radha Gold Jewellers, 43 North Mada St, Mylapore, T044-249 1923. Open 0930-1300 and 1600-2100. 'Antique'-finished items and dance jewels.
Sri Sukra Jewels, 42 North Mada St, Mylapore, T044-2464 0699, www.sukra.com. Brilliant temple and costume jewellery. Fixed price.

Silk and saris

Look out for excellent Kanchipuram silk and saris. Recommended for quality and value:
Handloom House, 7 Rattan Bazar.
Nalli, opposite Panagal Park, with excellent selection, both in T Nagar.
Radha, 1 Sannadhi St, Mylapore (near east gate of temple). 4 floors of silk and cotton saris, *salwar kameez* sets, men's *kurtas* and children's clothes. Great old-fashioned department store atmosphere.
Rupkala, 191 Anna Salai. Good prices, helpful.

Activities and tours

Chennai *p867, maps p869, p870, p874, p876*

Body and soul

Krishnamacharya Yoga Mandiram, New No 31 (Old No13), Fourth Cross St, R K Nagar (near Tirumailai MRT station), T044-2493 7998, www.kym.org. Runs 2- and 4-week intensive courses in yoga, plus an extended Diploma course, and a very well-regarded yoga therapy program.

Golf

Cosmopolitan Club, 334 Anna Salai, T044-2432 2759. The best course in town, though you may need an invitation to play. Also offers tennis, billiards, library and bar.

There's another, less exclusive golf course at **Guindy Race Course**.

Sports clubs and associations

Most clubs are members-only domains, though temporary membership may be available for sports facilities. The **Chennai Cricket Club** in Chepauk and the **Gymkhana Club** at the racecourse on Anna Salai both offer tennis, swimming, cricket, billiards, library and a bar – definitely worth experiencing if you can make friends with a member.

Chennai Riders' Club, Race View, Race Course, Velachery Rd. Riding (including lessons) throughout the year except Jun.

Tamil Nadu Sailing Association, 83 East Mada Church Rd, Royapuram, T044-2538 2253. Open to the public.

Wildertrails Adventure Club, T044-2644 2729. Camping and hiking trips.

Swimming

The pool at the **Savera** hotel is open to non-residents. Others open to the public are at Marina Beach and the YMCA pool at Saidapet. Sea bathing is safe at Elliot's Beach, though no longer attractive.

Tennis

Clubs allowing members' guests and temporary members to use courts are: **Chennai Club, Gymkhana Club, Cricket Club, Cosmopolitan Club, Presidency Club** and **Lady Willingdon Club**. YMCA at Saidapet also has courts.

Tours and tour operators

Cox & Kings, 10 Karuna Corner, Spur Tank Rd, T044-3091 9500.

Mercury, 191 Anna Salai, T044-2852 2993.

Milesworth Holidays, RM Towers, 108 Chamiers Rd, T044-2432 0522, www.milesworth.com. Andamans specialists, but can book interesting accommodation throughout India.

Sita, 26 C-in-C Rd, T044-28278861.

STIC, 672 Anna Salai, T044-2433 0211

Surya, 1st fl, Spencer's Plaza, Anna Salai, T044-2849 3934. Very efficient, friendly, personal service.

Thomas Cook, 45 Monteith Rd, opposite Ambassador Pallava hotel, T044-2855 4600.

Tamil Nadu Tourism, sales counters at: Tourism Complex, 2 Wallajah Rd, T044-2536 8358; 4 EVR Periyar High Rd (opposite Central Station), T044-2536 0294; and Express Bus Stand near High Ct compound, T044-2534 1982 (0600-2100). You can book the some tours online, www.ttdconline.com.

The following tours are on deluxe coaches and accompanied by a guide.

City sightseeing half-day, daily 0800-1300, 1330-1830. Fort St George, Government Museum (closed Fri), Valluvar Kottam, Snake Park, Kapaleeswarar Temple, Elliot's Beach, Marina Beach. Rs 120, a/c Rs 170.

Mahabalipuram and Kanchipuram, 0730-1900, Rs 200 (a/c Rs 350) and Tirupati, 0630-2200, Rs 375 (a/c Rs 600).

Hop-On Mahabalipuram tours leave hourly 0900-1600, returning 1040-1740; the ticket (Rs 250) lets you stop at several points along the way, eg at Dakshinachitra and the Crocodile Bank, and catch a later bus.

Welcome, 150 Anna Salai, near India Tourist Office, T044-2846 0614. Open 24 hrs.

Walking tours

Story Trails, T(0)9940-04 0215, www.storytrails.in. Themed walking tours that allow the city to unfold through its stories, including Spice Trail, Mystic Trail and Bazar Trail.

⊖ Transport

Chennai *p867, maps p869, p870, p874, p876*

Air

The **Aringar Anna International Airport** (named after CN Annadurai) with 2 terminals and the **Kamaraj Domestic Airport**, T044-2256 0501, are on one site at Trisulam in Meenambakkam, 12 km from the centre. Enquiries, T140, arrivals and departures, T142.

Pre-paid taxis from both; to Chennai Central or Egmore, Rs 250-300 (yellow taxis are cheaper than private), 30 mins; Rs 900 to Mahabalipuram. Buses to centre Rs 75 (day), Rs 100 (night).

Airport, T044-2234 6013. **Auto-rickshaws** to Chennai Central, Rs 200, but you have to walk to the main road to catch one. **Suburban railway** the cheapest way into town, from Trisulam suburban line station to Egmore and Fort, but trains are often packed. Free Fone in the main concourse, after collecting baggage in the international airport, to ring hotels. Railway bookings 1000-1700.

Domestic Flights to **Bengaluru (Bangalore)**, **Bhubaneswar**, **Coimbatore**, **Delhi**, **Goa**, **Hyderabad**, **Kochi**, **Kolkata**, **Madurai**, via **Tiruchirappalli**; **Mumbai**, **Port Blair** and **Pune**, **Puttaparthy**, **Thiruvananthapuram**, **Visakhapatnam**.

Indian Airlines (Marshalls Rd, Egmore, T044-2345 3301 (daily 0800-2000). Reservations, all 24 hrs: T044-2855 5209, airport T044-2256 1065.

International Connections with: **Abu Dhabi**, **Bangkok**, **Brussels**, **Colombo**, **Doha**, **Dubai**, **Frankfurt**, **Kuala Lumpur**, **Kuwait**, **London**, **Muscat**, **New York**, **Paris**, **Singapore** and **Toronto**.

Air France, 42 Kubers, Pantheon Rd, T1800-180 0044. **Air India**, 19 Rukmani Lakshmipathy Rd (Marshalls Rd), T044-2855 4747 (0930-1730, avoid 1300-1400), airport T044-2256 1065. **British Airways**, 10/11 Dr Radha Krishnan Salai, T98-4037 7470. **Cathay Pacific**, 47 Spur Tank Rd, T044-4298 8400; airport, T044-2256 1229. **Emirates**, 12 Nungambakkam High Rd, T044-6683 4444. **Gulf Air**, 52 Montieth Rd, T044-2855 4417. **Jet Airways**, 43 Montieth Rd, Egmore, T044-3959 3333, airport T044-2256 1818. **Kuwait Airways**, 476, Anna Salai, Nandanam, T044-2431 5162. **Malaysian Airlines**, 90 Dr Radha Krishnan Salai, T044-4219 1919. **Singapore Airlines**, 108 Dr Radhakrishna Rd, T044-3297 7771; airport, T044-2256 0409. **Sri Lankan**, 4 Vijaya Towers, Kodambakkam High Rd, T044-4392 1100. **Thai**, at ITC Park Sheraton, TTK Rd, T044-4206 3311.

General Sales Agents (GSA): **Air Kenya**, **Garuda Airways**, **Japan Airlines**, Global Travels, 703 Anna Salai, T044-285 23957. **Air Canada**, **Bangladesh Biman** and **Royal Jordanian**, Thapar House, 43 Montieth Rd, T044-2856 9232. **Delta**, at Interglobe, 1, 4th St, Dr. Radhakrishnan Salai, T044-2847 2070. Continental, **Iberian** and **Royal Nepal Airlines**, at STIC Travels, 672 Anna Salai, T044-24330211.

Bus

Local The cheap and convenient local bus service is not overcrowded and offers a realistic alternative to auto-rickshaws and taxis outside the rush hour (0800-1000, 1700-1900). Make sure you know route numbers as most bus signs are in Tamil (timetables from major bookshops).

Metropolitan Transport Corp (PTC), Anna Salai, runs an excellent network of buses from 0500-2300 and a skeleton service through the night. '**M**' service on mini-buses are good for the route between Central and Egmore stations and journeys to the suburban railway stations. The 'V' service operates fast buses with fewer stops and have a yellow board with the route number and LSS (Limited Stop Service). PTC has a half-hourly 'luxury' mini-bus service between **Egmore Station**, **Indian Airlines**' Marshall's Rd office and the airports at **Meenambakkam** picking up passengers from certain hotels (inform time keeper at Egmore in advance, T044-2536 1284). The fare is about Rs 20.

Long-distance For long-distance journeys, the state highways are reasonably well maintained but the condition of other roads varies. The fast new highways leading north and south of Chennai and the East Coast Rd (ECR) have helped to cut some journey times. Fast long-distance a/c buses now run on some routes, giving a comfortable ride on air-cushioned suspension.

Chennai is amazingly proud of its bus station – Asia's biggest, with 30 arrival and 150 departure terminals. Officially titled the **Chennai Mofussil Bus Terminus** (**CMBT**) it is known to rickshaw drivers as Koyambedu CMBT, Jawaharlal Nehru Rd near Koyambedu Market, T044-2479 4705.

Tamil Nadu Govt Express, T044-2534 1835, offers good connections within the whole region and the service is efficient and inexpensive. Best to take a/c coaches or super deluxe a/c. Bookings 0700-2100. Other state and private companies cover the region but you may wish to avoid their video coaches which make listening, if not viewing, compulsory as there are no headphones.

Beware of children who 'help' you to find your bus in the expectation of a tip; they may not have a clue. There have also been reports of men in company uniforms selling tickets, which turn out to be invalid; it is best to buy on the bus. The listings given are for route number, distance. **Coimbatore** *No 460*, 500 km; **Chidambaram** and **Nagapattinam** *326*; **Kanchipuram** *76B*; **Kanniyakumari** *282 and 284*, 700 km; **Kumbakonum** *303F*, 289 km, 6½ hrs; **Madurai** *137*, 447 km, 10 hrs; **Mahabalipuram** *109*, Rs 19, 1½ hrs (*108B* goes via Meenambakkam airport, 2½ hrs) can be very crowded; **Nagercoil** *198*, 682 km, 14 hrs; **Ooty** *468*, 565 km, 13 hrs; **Pondicherry** *803*, 106 km, 3 hrs; **Thanjavur** *323*, 320 km, 8 hrs; Tiruchirappalli *123*, 320 km and Route *124*, 7 hrs; **Tiruvannamalai** 180 km, 5 hrs; **Yercaud** *434*, 360 km, 8 hrs; **Bengaluru (Bangalore)** via **Vellore** and **Krishnagiri** *831*, 360 km, 8 hrs; **Bengaluru (via Kolar)** 350 km, 7½ hrs; **Mysore via Bengaluru** *863*, 497 km, 11 hrs; **Tirupati via Kalahasti** *802*, 150 km, 3½ hrs. Also several **Andhra Pradesh STC** buses to Tirupati daily. **APSTC** runs daily buses to many other towns in the state, as does **Karnataka State Express Bus Service** to Karnataka.

Car

A/c or ordinary cars with drivers are good value and convenient for sightseeing, especially for short journeys out of the city when shared between 3 and 5 people. Large hotels can arrange, eg **Regency** (Rs 600 per 8 hrs; Rs 750 for Mahabalipuram). **Ganesh Travels**, 35/1 Police Commisioner Office Rd, T044-2819 0202; **TTDC**, 2 Wallajah Rd, T044-2536 8358.

Ferry

Passenger ships leave every 7-10 days to the Andaman and Nicobar Islands, taking 3 days, and as visas are now issued on arrival at Port Blair the process of getting a ticket is less convoluted than it used to be. Ships are operated by the **Shipping Corporation of India**, Jawahar Building, Rajaji Salai, T044-2523 1401, and the **Deputy Directorate of Shipping Services**, 6 Rajaji Salai, T044-2522 6873. Check sailing schedules, then take 4-5 passport photos, originals plus 3 copies of your passport and visa, and queue up for a ticket, 1000-1300. Women have an advantage when queuing.

Motorbike hire or purchase

Southern Motors, 995A Koleth Court, 11th Main Rd, 2nd Ave, Anna Nagar, T044-2616 4666, T044-2499 0784, is a good modern garage with efficient service. The **YWCA**, EVR Periyar Rd, is a good hotel for bikers and has a big shaded garden to park bikes securely.

MRTS

The **Mass Rapid Transit System** (raised, above-ground railway) runs from Chennai Beach south to Velacheri in the IT belt, passing through Chepauk, Triplicane (Thiruvallikeni) and Mylapore on the way. Station facilities are minimal, and there's little information about when the next train might depart.

Rickshaws

Three-wheeler scooter taxis are the most common form of transport around the city. Drivers demand high fares compared with other cities, but it's easier to negotiate a rate than try to insist on using the meter. Rs 40-70 gets you between most neighbourhoods. As always, drivers get kickbacks from emporium owners to encourage detours via shops.

Taxi

Taxis are better than rickshaws for extended trips and sightseeing. Many companies offer 'packages' of fixed times and distances – Rs 400 for 40 km and 4 hrs, Rs 800 for 80 km and 8 hrs, plus Rs 100 for each extra hour. Expect to pay more for a/c. **Bharati Call Taxi**, T044-2814 2233. **Chennai Call Taxi**, T044-2598 4455. **Fast Track**, T044-2473 2020. **Thiruvalluvar Travels**, T044-2474 5807.

Train

Suburban railway Inexpensive and handy, but very crowded at peak times. Stops between Beach Railway Station and Tambaram (every 5 mins in rush hour) include Fort, Park, Egmore, Chetpet, Nungambakkam, Kodambakkam, Mambalam, Saidapet, Guindy, St Thomas Mt. Also serves suburbs of Perambur and Villivakkam. Convenient stop at Trisoolam for the airports, 500-m walk from the terminals.
Long distance Chennai has 2 main stations, **Chennai Central (MC)** for broad gauge trains to all parts of India and **Egmore (ME)** for trains to

the south; a few significant trains also start from Tambaram, in the southern suburbs. Egmore and Central are linked by minibus; taxis take 5 mins. There is a reservations counter at the domestic airport, as well as at the stations. **Chennai Central** enquiry, T131, reservations, T132, arrivals and departures, T133, then dial train no. Advance Reservations Centre, Mon-Sat 0800-1400, 1415-2000, Sun 0800-1400, is in a separate building in front of the suburban station, to the left of the main station. Indrail Passes and booking facilities for foreigners and NRIs on the 1st floor. From Chennai Central to **Bengaluru** (**Bangalore**) *Shatabdi Exp 12007*, 0600, not Tue, 7 hrs; *Lalbagh Exp 12607*, 1545, 5¾ hrs; *Brindavan Exp 12639*, 0715, 6 hrs. **Coimbatore** *Kovai Exp 12675*, 0615, 7¾ hrs; *West Coast Exp 16627*, 1100, 8¾ hrs; *Cheran Exp 12673*, 2145, 8½ hrs. **Delhi** (**ND**) *Tamil Nadu Exp 12621*, 2200, 33½ hrs; *GT Exp 12615*, 1630, 37½ hrs. **Delhi** (**HN**) *Rajdhani Exp 12431*, 1915, Tue, Thu, 29½ hrs. **Guntakal** (for Hospet): *Chennai Dadar Exp 11064*, 0650, 8 hrs; *Chennai-Mumbai Mail 6010*, 2220, 10 hrs. **Hyderabad** *Charminar Exp 12759*, 1810, 14½ hrs; *Chennai-Hyderabad Exp 17053*, 1600, 15 hrs. **Kochi** (**Cochin**) *Chennai-Aleppey Exp* 16041, 1945, 13¾ hrs; *Guwahati Cochin Exp 15624*, 1210, Fri, 14¾ hrs. **Kolkata** (**H**) *Coromandel Exp 12842*, 0905, 29 hrs; *Howrah Mail 6004*, 2230, 32½ hrs. **Mettupalayam** *Nilgiri Exp 16605*, 2015, 10 hrs. **Mumbai** (**CST**) *Chennai-Mumbai Mail 16010*, 2155, 30 hrs; *Chennai-Mumbai Exp 16012*, 1145, 27 hrs. **Mysore** *Shatabdi Exp 12007*, 0600, daily not Tue, 7 hrs; *Chennai Mysore Exp 16222*, 2245, 9¼ hrs. **Thiruvananthapuram** *Guwahati Trivandrum Exp 15628*, 1210, Wed, 19¼ hrs; *Howrah Trivandrum Exp 16324*, 0440, Tue, Sun, 18½ hrs.

Egmore enquiry, T135, arrivals and departures, T134. No counter for foreign tourist quota bookings. To **Kanniyakumari** *Chennai-Kanniyakumari Exp 16121*, 1900, 15 hrs. **Madurai** *Chennai-Kanniyakumari Exp 16121*, 1815, 10 hrs; *Vaigai Exp 12635*, 1225, 8 hrs; *Pandyan Exp 16717*, 2100, 9½ hrs via Kodai Rd (this connects with the bus service at **Kodaikkanal** arriving at midday). **Tiruchirappalli** *Vaigai Exp 12635*, 1225, 5½ hrs; *Pallavan Exp 12606*, 1530, 5½ hrs.

Directory

Chennai *p867, maps p869, p870, p874, p876*

Banks ATMs accepting foreign cards are now on virtually every street corner in Chennai, particularly in shopping areas like Anna Salai, Nungambakkam High Rd and T Nagar, as well as in and around the railway stations. Many of them are in 24-hr a/c booths; you may have to insert a card to get inside. For changing money, most banks open either 0830-1230 or 1000-1400 on weekdays; morning only on Sat, closed Sun and national holidays (foreign exchange dealing may close an hour early). A few big hotels have 24-hr banks. At airport: **State Bank of India**, **Thomas Cook**, **TT Travels**, 24 hrs. In the city: **American Express**, G17, Spencer Plaza, Anna Salai, T044-2849 3592, 0930-1930, offers all foreign exchange and TC services. **Thomas Cook** branches at: 45 Montieth Rd, Egmore. 112 NH Rd, Mon-Fri 0930-1830 (closed 1300-1400), Sat 0930-1200. Both recommended. **Madura Travels**, Kennet Lane (near corner of Gandhi Irwin Rd), Egmore, good rate for TCs. **Cultural centres** These often have libraries, daily newspapers from home and cultural programs including film shows and photo exhibitions. **Alliance Française**, 24 College Rd, Nungambakkam, T044-2827 9803. **American Center**, 561 Anna Salai, library 0930-1800, closed Sun, T044-2827 7825. **British Council**, 737 Anna Salai, 1000-1900, closed Mon, T044-4205 0600. **InKo**, 51 6th Main Rd, Raja Annamalaipuram, T044-2436 1224, runs workshops in traditional Korean arts e.g calligraphy. **Max Müeller Bhawan**, Mon-Sat 0900-1900, 4, 5th St, Rutland Gate, T044-2833 1314. **Russian**, 74 Kasturi Rangan Rd, Alwarpet, T044-2499 0050. **Embassies and consulates** Most open 0830-1330, Mon-Fri. For Indian visa extensions go to **Foreigners' Registration Office**, Shastri Bhavan Annexe, 26 Haddows Rd. T044-2345 4970, Mon-Fri 0930-1800. **Austria**, Kothari Bldg, MG Rd, Nungambakkam, T044-2833 4513. **Belgium**, 88 Anna Salai, Guindy, T044-2235 2336. **Canada**, YAFA Tower, Khader Nawaz Khan Road, Nungambakkam, T044-2833 0888. **Denmark**, 9 Cathedral Rd, T044-2811 8140. **Finland**, 202 Anna Salai, T044-2852 4141. **France**, 40 College Rd, T044-2826 6561. **Germany**, 9 Boat Club Rd, T044-2430 1600. **Greece**, 9 Cathedral Rd, T044-2811 8000.

Italy 9 Rajaji Salai, T044-2534 1110. **Japan**, 60 Spur Tank Rd, Chetpet, T044-2826 5594. **Malaysia**, 6 Sriram Nagar, North St, Alwarpet, T044-2434 3048. **Netherlands**, A Block, Raheja Towers, 177 Anna Salai, T044-5215 8388. **New Zealand**, 132 Cathedral Rd, T044-2811 2473. **Norway**, 44-45 Rajaji Salai, T044-2524 5314. **Singapore**, 17A North Boag Rd, T Nagar, T044-2827 3795. **Spain**, 8/2 Nimmo Rd, San Thome, T044-2827 6036. **Sri Lanka**, 196 TTK Rd, T044-2498 7896. **Sweden**, 6 Cathedral Rd, T044-2811 2232. **Switzerland**, 224 TTK Rd, T044-2433 2701. **Thailand**, 21/22 Arunachalam Rd, Kotturpuram, T044-4230 0730. **UK**, Deputy High Commission, 20 Anderson Rd, Nungambakkam, T044-5219 2308. **USA** 220 Anna Salai, T044-2857 4242. **Internet** Internet places are ubiquitous, especially in Triplicane and Egmore. Rates range from Rs 20-30 per hr. Most hotels in the mid range and above have data sockets, and a few (see Sleeping) offer free Wi-Fi. **Info Cafe**, Eldorado complex, Nungambakkam High Rd. **Sify I-way**, 32 Dr Radhakrishnan Salai, Mylapore. **SRIS**, 1st floor, F22-A, Spencer Plaza, 769 Anna Salai. **Language schools** Bharatiya Vidya Bhavan, 38/39 R E Mada St, T044-2494 3450, for Sanskrit. **Hindi Prachar Sabha**, T Nagar, T044-2434 1824. **International Institute of Tamil Studies**, Central Polytechnic, T044-2254 2992. **Medical services** Ambulance (Government), T102; **St John's Ambulance**, T044-2819 4630, 24-hr. **Dental hospital (Government)**, T044-2534 0441; **All-in-One**, 34 Nowroji Rd, T044-2641 1911, 0400-2000, 0900-1200 Sun. **Chemists** Apollo Pharmacy, many branches including 320 Anna Salai, Teynampet; 52 Usman Rd South, T Nagar. **SS Day & Night Chemists**, 106D, 1st Main Rd, Anna Nagar. **Hospitals** **Apollo Hospital**, 21 Greams Rd, T044-2829 3333. **CSI Rainey**, GA Rd, RA Puram, T044-2595 3322, with 24-hr pharmacy. **Deviki Hospital**, 148 Luz Church Rd, Mylapore, T044-2499 2607. **National Hospital**, 2nd Line Beach Rd, T044-2524 0131. **Post** Poste restante at the GPO, Rajaji Salai, George Town; other major post offices which accept Speed Post Mail are in Anna Salai, Pondy Bazar, T Nagar, Meenambakkam, NH Rd, Flower Bazar and Adyar. CTO, Rajaji Salai (near Parry's Corner). Opening times vary, the first 3 are open 0800-2030. Computerized ISTD booths all over town, some open 24 hrs. **Telephone** Directory enquiries, T183, only from Chennai city itself. **Mobile Store**, Ispahani Centre, Numgambakkam High Rd, T044-6459 8788. Chain store, reliable for mobile connections.

Around Chennai

South of the capital, easily reached in a day but worthy of at least a weekend, lies Mahabalipuram, an intriguing little beachside town given over entirely to sculpture, both ancient and modern. Part open-air museum and part contemporary workshop, its seventh-century bas-reliefs are some of the world's largest and most intricate, telling the Indian flood myth, the Descent of the Ganga. Within earshot of the old shore temples you can find modern-day masons industriously piling their shacks and yards high with freshly and beautifully chiselled deities. Inland from Chennai, the former Pallava capital of Kanchipuram is one of India's seven sacred cities, chock-full of temples and overflowing with silks spun straight from the loom.

▸▸ *For listings, see pages 896-898.*

Mahabalipuram (Mamallapuram) → *For listings, see pages 896-898. Colour map 7, B6.*

Mahabalipuram's mix of magnificent historic rock temples, exquisite alfresco bas reliefs and inviting sandy beach bestows a formidable magnetism, and it has matured into a buzzing backpacker hamlet, complete with all the high-power Kashmiri salesmanship and insistent begging that such a role implies. Though the beach and ocean are dirty enough to make you think twice about swimming, the craftsmanship that built the temples continues today and the whole place echoes with the sound of chisels tapping industriously on stone.

If travelling from Chennai, there are three good stop-off points before Mahabalipuram. The first is 19 km from Chennai at **Cholamandal Artists' Village** ⓘ *East Coast Rd, Enjampakkam, T044-2449 0092, 0900-1900, free.* The artists' community, started in 1969, gives living, working and exhibition space for artists creating sculptures, pottery and batik. They sometimes hold dance performances in a small open-air theatre, and there are some simple cottages for hire if you want to stick around for a workshop or residency.

The second stop is the **Madras Craft Foundation**'s model village, **Dakshinchitra** ⓘ *East Coast Rd, T044-2747 2603, www.dakshinachitra.net, Wed-Mon 1000-1800, foreigners Rs 175, Indians Rs 50,* which showcases the rich cultural heritage of the four southern states against a backdrop of 17 authentic buildings, each relocated piece by piece from their original homes around South India. There's a regular programme of folk performances, including puppet shows, plus a small textile museum, a restaurant and a fortune-telling parrot.

Finally, 14 km before Mahabalipuram, is Romulus Whitaker's **Madras Crocodile Bank** ⓘ *Tue-Sun 0830-1730, Rs 20, camera Rs 10, video Rs 75,* established by the American-born herpetologist (known as the Snake Man of India) as a captive breeding centre for Indian crocodilians. You can now see several rare species from India and beyond, including Siamese and African dwarf crocodiles, basking around the open pools. There's a small extra charge to visit the snake venom bank, where snakes donate small quantities of poison for use in antivenins before being released back to the wild.

Ins and outs → *Phone code: 04114. Population: 12,050.*

Getting there Buses from Chennai take around 1½ hours to the bus stand in the centre of the small village. They may stop at hotels north of Mahabalipuram, on the way, otherwise autos from anywhere in the village will ferry you there for Rs 50. Arriving by car, you may have to pay a Rs 20 toll at the booth near the post office on Kovalam Road.

Getting around The town is small enough to explore on foot, but hiring a bike can get you further afield. ▸▸ *See Transport, page 898.*

Tourist information **Tamil Nadu Tourist Office** ⓘ *Kovalam Rd, 300 m north of Othavadai St, T044-2744 2232, Mon-Fri 0945-1745,* can arrange guides, car and cycle hire. The best time to visit is early morning, for the best light on Bhagiratha's Penance. Allow two hours for a circuit. It's hard to get lost but the paths on the top of the rock are not always clear.

Background

The coastal temple town Mahabalipuram is officially known as Mamallapuram after 'Mamalla' ('great wrestler'), the name given to Narasimhavarman I Pallavamalla (ruled AD 630-668). The Pallava ruler made the port famous in the seventh century and was largely responsible for the temples. There are 14 cave temples and nine monolithic *rathas* (shrines in the shape of temple chariots), three stone temples and four relief sculptured rock panels.

The **Dravida** or Dravidian style underwent several changes over the course of the different dynasties that ruled for about 1000 years from the time of the Pallavas who laid its foundations. In Mahabalipuram, rock-cut cave temples, *mandapas* (small excavated columned halls), and *rathas* were carved out by the early Pallavas. These were followed by structural temples and bas relief sculptures on giant rocks. The Ekambaresvara Temple in Kanchipuram (see page 894) shows the evolution of the Dravidian style – the shrine with its pyramidal tower and the separate *mandapa* (pillared portico) all within the courtyard with its

Mahabalipuram

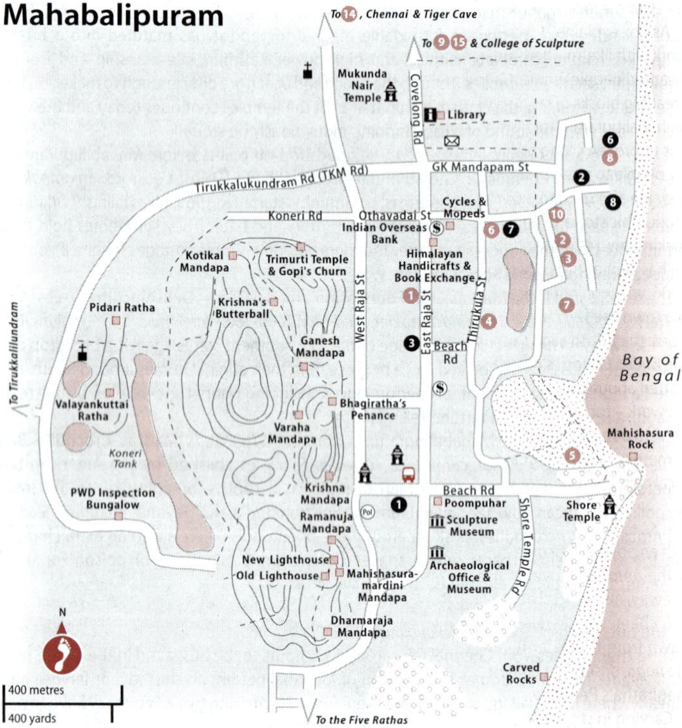

Sleeping
Fisherman's Cove 9
Greenwoods Resort 3
Ideal Beach Resort 14
La Vie en Rose 5
Lakshmi Lodge & Siva Guesthouse 2
Mamallaa Heritage 1
Ramakrishna Lodge 6
Sea Breeze 7
Siva Guest House 4
Sri Harul 8
Tamil Nadu Beach Resort 15
Tina Blue View Lodge 10

Eating
Dreamland 2
Gazebo 3
Luna Magica 6
Mamalla Bhavan 1
Moonrakers 7
Sea Rock 8

Stone temple pilot

When the British Council sponsored Bristol-born artist Stephen Cox to scout India for a place to make his huge-scale stone works for the national art prize, the Indian Triennale, he chose not the country's best art schools, but a little fishing village on the Coromandel coast of Tamil Nadu. It may sound bloody minded, until you arrive in Mahabalipuram, where the whole air clatters with the sound of chisel on rock. It must be the most industrious seat of Hindu idol-making the world over; everywhere you look masons sit on their haunches hammering away at the local dolerite rock.

As Cox explains: "I didn't go to India to work with like-minded contemporary artists, I wanted people who could work with great big blocks of stone without fear. Mahabalipuram is totally unique in having this unbroken, living tradition of making idols for people to pray to, and that means that they are also used to working with huge monolithic stone so no-one's daunted by making my 14-tonne sculptures." Although he has kept a studio there from that first year, 1986, you won't find any of his sculpture in the town itself – these are mainly kept for cities: the British High Commission at Delhi, the British Council's office in Chennai and dotted about London's Square Mile. Indeed his work – too minimalist for Hindu temple carving purists – has been received with something less than gusto by some of the local craftsman, and journalist Mark Tully, branded Cox's use of Indian labour a form of 'neo-colonialism'. One sculpture alone can take up to a year to make and will have passed through, on average, 20 pairs of Indian hands before being shipped for exhibition. "At the end of the day of course, I wouldn't be working in India over Carrara in Italy if it wasn't economically viable," Cox concedes, but he also says "my raison d'être for working in India is because, in working amongst and with the temple carvers, I can immerse myself in a living antique tradition. It is not just the cost factor. The hand skills of the silpies have been lost to the rest of the world."

The town has changed dramatically since he arrived in 1986, but Cox spares the burgeoning tourist industry infrastructure to reserve his criticism for the Architectural Survey of India's maintenance of the monuments themselves. "Since it was declared a World Heritage Site, they've buggered the Shore Temple up; it's not a shore temple anymore, instead it sits in a bijou plot of grassland, while the five *rathas* are fenced off, destroying the whole beauty of these wonderful monuments in a natural environment."

And his favourite piece of sculpture in a town teeming with them? It's the Pallava's flair for observation that still gets him: "the naturalism that Giotto was supposed to have invented you find in a ninth-century relief carving here. It is amazing. I only hope fewer and fewer people come."

high enclosure wall made up of cells. Six centuries later the two separate structures were joined by the *antarala* (covered hall). A large subsidiary shrine, which took the place of an entrance gateway, also hinted at the later *gopuram*.

A characteristic feature of the temples here was the system of water channels and tanks, drawn from the **Palar River**, which made it particularly suitable as a site of religious worship. The *naga*, or serpent cult associated with water worship, can be seen to be given prominence at Bhagiratha's Penance.

Carving in stone is still a living art; stone masons can be heard chipping away from dawn to dusk along the dusty roadsides, while students at the **Government School of Sculpture** ⓘ *near the bus stand, Wed-Mon 0900-1300, 1400-1830,* continue to practise the skills which flourished centuries ago.

Temple cars or rathas *are tall and often elaborately carved and painted temple-shaped chariots which carry temple deities through the streets during celebratory processions. Between festivals, they're often parked in makeshift, corrugated-iron garages at the side of temples.*

Sights

Bhagiratha's Penance *Descent of the Ganga*, also called **Arjuna's Penance**, is a bas relief sculpted on the face of two enormous adjacent rocks, 29 m long and 7 m high. It shows realistic life-size figures of animals, gods and saints watching the descent of the river from the Himalaya. Bhagiratha, Rama's ancestor, is seen praying to Ganga. A man-made waterfall, fed from a collecting chamber above, issues from the natural crack between the two rocks. Some see the figure of an ascetic (to the top left-hand side of the rock, near the cleft) as representing Arjuna's penance when praying for powers from Siva, though this is disputed. There are scenes from the fables in the *Panchatantra* and a small shrine to Vishnu.

A path north goes to the double-decker rectangular **Ganesh** *ratha* with a highly decorative roof and two pillars with lions at their base – an architectural feature which was to become significant. The Ganesh image inside is mid-20th century. To the west are the **Valayankuttai** and twin **Pidari** *rathas*. The path continues past the precariously balanced **Krishna's Butterball** through some huge boulders at the north end of the hillock to the **Trimurti Temple** caves that hold three shrines to Brahma, Vishnu and Siva, the last with a lingam.

Mandapas The 10 *mandapas* are shallow, pillared halls or porticos in the rocky hillside which hold superb sculptures from mythological tales, and illustrate the development of the Dravidian (South Indian) temple style.

On the south is a **Durga niche** (AD 630-660), while next door is the **Gopi's Churn**, a Pallava cistern. Walk back along the ridge, passing Krishna's Butterball on your left and boulders with evidence of incomplete work. The **Varaha Mandapa** (AD 640-674) on the left of the ridge shows two incarnations of Vishnu – Varaha (boar) and Vamana (dwarf) – among scenes with kings and queens. The base forms a narrow water pool for pilgrims to use before entering the temple. From here you can walk to the top of Bhagiratha's Penance.

Krishna Mandapa (mid-seventh century) has a bas relief scene of Krishna lifting Mount Govardhana to protect a crowd of his kinsmen from the anger of the Rain God, Indra. The cow licking its calf during milking is remarkably realistic.

Kotikal Mandapa (early seventh century) may be the earliest of the *mandapas*, roughly carved with a small shrine with no image inside. **Ramanuja Mandapa** was originally a triple-cell Siva temple, converted later into a Vaishnava temple.

South of the new lighthouse the simple **Dharmaraja cave** (early seventh century) contains three empty shrines. To its west is **Isvara Temple** (or Old Lighthouse), a truncated Siva temple still standing like a beacon on the highest summit, with a view for miles around. (To the south, across the Five Rathas, is the nuclear power station of Kalpakkam; to the west is the flat lagoon and the original port of Mahabalipuram.)

Mahishasuramardini Mandapa (mid-seventh century) is immediately below. It has fine bas relief and carved columns with lion bases. The main sculpture shows the goddess Durga slaying the buffalo demon Mahishasura while another relief shows Vishnu lying under Adishesha, the seven-hooded serpent.

Pancha Rathas ⓘ *Rs 250, Indians Rs 10.* These mid-seventh-century monolithic temples, 1.5 km south of the Old Lighthouse, were influenced by Buddhist architecture as they resemble the *vihara* (monastery) and *chaitya* (temple hall). They imitate in granite temple structures that were originally built of wood and are among the oldest examples of their type.

The five *rathas* to the south of the hill are named after the Pancha Pandava (five Pandava brothers) in the epic *Mahabharata* and their wife Draupadi. The largest is the domed **Dharmaraja** with many images including an interesting Ardhanarishvara (Siva-Parvati) at the rear. The barrel-vaulted **Bhima** nearby has a roof suggestive of a thatched hut, while next to it the dome-shaped ratha **Arjuna** imitates the Dharmaraja. **Draupadi ratha** is the smallest and simplest and is again in the form of a thatched hut. The base, now covered by sand, conceals a lion in front which appears to carry it, which suggests that it may be a replica of a portable shrine. Immediately east is a large unfinished *Nandi*. To its west is the apsidal **Nakula-Sahadeva ratha** with a freestanding elephant nearby. The Bhima and Nakula- Sahadeva follow the oblong plan of the Buddhist *chaitya* hall and are built to two or more storeys, a precursor to the *gopuram*, the elaborate entrance gateway of the Dravidian temple.

Shore Temple ⓘ *0900-1730, foreigners Rs 250, Indians Rs 10, video Rs 25, includes Panch Rathas if visited on same day*. This beautiful sandstone World Heritage Site, built in the seventh century by King Rajasimha, is unusual for holding shrines to both Siva and Vishnu. Its gardens have been laid out to ape their ancient antecedents. Its base is granite and it has a basalt *kalasha* at its top. Its position on the water's edge, with an east-facing altar designed to catch the rising sun and a stone pillar to hold the beacon for sailors at night, meant that there was no space for a forecourt or entrance gateway, but two additional shrines were built to the west. The second smaller spire adds to the temple's unusual structure. The outer parapet wall has lines of *Nandi* (Siva's sacred bull) and lion pilasters.

Saluvankuppam Five kilometres north of Mahabalipuram, on the coast, is the temple at Saluvankuppam. It holds the **Tiger Cave** *mandapa* with carvings of tiger heads. The cave, not signposted from the beach, is secluded and peaceful – perfect for a picnic. On the way you will see the **Mukunda Nayar Temple**.

Beaches Mahabalipuram's beach is far from pristine, particularly north of the temples towards the Ashok and in the rocky area behind the Descent of the Ganga where it serves as an open latrine. To sunbathe undisturbed by hawkers pay Rs 200 to use the small pools at **Crystal Shore Palace** or **Sea Breeze**, or the bigger pool, 1 km north at **Tamil Nadu Beach Resort**.

Around Mahabalipuram

Tirukkalukundram is a small Siva temple dedicated to Vedagirishvara on top of the 3000-million-year-old rock 14 km west of Mahabalipuram. About 400 steps take you to the top of the 160-m hill which has good views, plus money-conscious priests and 'guides'. Be prepared for a hot barefoot climb, 'donations' at several shrines and Rs 10 for your shoes. At midday, two Neophran vultures (Pharaoh's chickens) sometimes fly down to be fed by the priests. The Bhaktavatsleesvara in town with its *gopuram* (gateway) stands out like a beacon. The tank is considered holy and believed to produce a conch every 12 years. Small shops in the village sell cold drinks. Buses from Mahabalipuram take 30 minutes or you can hire a bike.

Sriperumbudur, 44 km from Chennai on National Highway 4, is the birthplace of the 11th-century Hindu philosopher Ramanuja, and is where Rajiv Gandhi was assassinated on 21 May 1991. There is a memorial at the site in a well-kept garden.

Kanchipuram → *For listings, see pages 896-898. Colour map 7, A5.*

What Darjeeling is to tea, and Cheddar is to cheese, so Kanchipuram is to silk. One of Hinduism's seven most sacred cities (see page 1409), 'the Golden City of a Thousand Temples', dates from the early Cholas in the second century. The main temple complexes are very spacious and only a few of the scattered 70 or so can be seen in a day's visit. The town itself is relatively quiet except for crowds of pilgrims. **Tourist information** ⓘ *Hotel Tamil Nadu, T044-2722 2553, 1000-1700*.

History

The **Pallavas** of Kanchi came to power in the fourth century AD and were dominant from AD 550 to 869. Possibly of northern origin, under their control Mahabalipuram became an important port in the seventh century. Buddhism is believed to have reached the Kanchipuram area in the third century BC. Successive dynasties made it their capital and built over 100 temples, the first as early as the fourth century. As well as being a pilgrimage site, it was a centre of learning, culture and philosophy. Sankaracharya and the Buddhist monk Bodhidharma lived and worked here.

Sights → *Phone code: 044. Population: 153,000.*
ⓘ *Temples are usually open from 0600 and closed 1200-1600, but very few allow non-Hindus into the inner sanctum. Have change ready for 'donations' to each temple you visit.*
Ekambaresvara Temple ⓘ *Small entry fee, cameras Rs 3, only Hindus are allowed into the inner sanctuary.* The temple has five enclosures and a 'Thousand-pillared Hall' (if you're

Kanchipuram

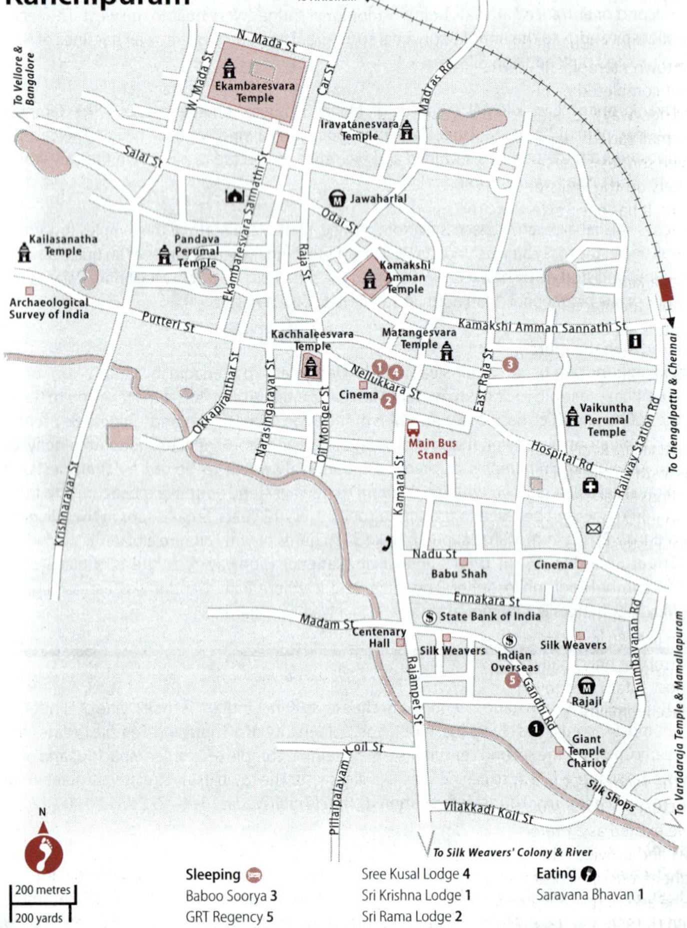

pedantically inclined, the number is actually 540). Dedicated to Siva in his ascetic form it was begun by the Pallavas and developed by the Cholas. In the early 16th century the Vijayanagara king Krishna Deva Raya built the high stone wall which surrounds the temple and the 59-m-tall *rajagopuram* (main tower) on which are sculpted several figures of him and his consort.

The main sanctuary has a *lingam* made of earth (Siva as one of the elements) and the story of its origin is told on a carved panel. The teasing Parvati is believed to have unthinkingly covered her husband Siva's eyes for a moment with her hands which resulted in the earth being enveloped in darkness for years. The enraged Siva ordered Parvati to do severe penance during which time she worshipped her husband in the form of an earth *lingam* which she created. When Siva sent a flood to test her, she clung to the *lingam* with her hands until the waters subsided. Some believe they can see her finger- prints on the *lingam* here. On 18 April each year the sun's rays enter the sanctum through a small square hole.

Kailasanatha Built in the early seventh century, this is considered to be the most beautiful of the town's temples. It was built of sandstone by the Pallava king Narasimha Varman II with the front completed by his son Mahendra III. The outer structure has a dividing wall with a shrine and doorways, separating a large courtyard from a smaller one. The unusual enclosure wall has 58 small raised shrines with a *Nandi* in most pavilions and some frescoes have survived. The seven shrines in the temple complex have images of different Siva forms. The intricately carved panels on the walls depict legends about Siva with accompanying text in ancient Grantha script. It has been extensively restored. The festival **Mahashivaratri** is held here in February.

Vaikuntha Perumal Eighth century and dedicated to Vishnu, this temple was built by the Pallava king Nandivarman just after the Kailasanatha and illustrates the progress of Dravidian temple architecture. The sanctuary is separated from the *mandapa* by an open space. The cloisters are built from rows of lion pillars. Panels of bas relief accompanied by lines in old Tamil trace the history of the wars between the Pallavas and Chalukyas. There is an unusual *vimana* (tower) with shrines in three tiers with figures of Vishnu in each.

Varadaraja (Devarajasvami) ⓘ *0630-1200, 1530-2000, Rs 5, camera Rs 5, video Rs 100.* Built by the Vijayanagara kings (circa 16th century), 3 km southeast of town, it has superb sculpture in its marriage hall (with 96 pillars). Figures on horseback wear half North Indian/ half South Indian costumes. Note the rings at each corner and the massive flexible chain supposedly carved out of one piece of granite, although it is no longer in one piece. The main shrine is on an elephant-shaped rock, Hastagiri. The **Float Festival** is in February and November, **Brahmotsavam** in May and **Garuda Sevai** in June.

Chengalpattu (Chingleput) The fort here was built by the Vijayanagar king Thimmu Raya after his defeat at the Battle of Talikotta in 1565. After 1687 it was absorbed into the Mughal Empire. Then in 1750 it was taken by the French, who held it until it was captured by Clive in 1752; British control was only finally established after the defeat of Haidar Ali in 1781. Although the fort is now almost totally destroyed (the railway runs through the middle of it), the Raja Mahal ('King's Palace') remains.

Around Kanchipuram

On the Trichy Road, 87 km from Chennai and 60 km from Mahabalipuram, the **Vedanthangal Bird Sanctuary** ⓘ *0530-1800, Rs 5, camera Rs 50, see Transport, page 898,* and Karikili Tank are thought to have existed as a protected area for about 250 years. The marshy site attracts numerous water fowl and provides their main nesting place. Visitors and residents include crested cormorants, night herons, grey pelicans, sand pipers, grey wagtails, open-billed storks, white ibis, egrets, little grebe and purple moorhens. The best time to visit is November to February, at dawn and from 1500 to 1800; avoid weekends and holidays.

Marakkanam, mentioned in Roman records as an important port in the first century AD, has an ancient Siva temple with many inscriptions. Immediately inland is the Kaliveli Tank, an extremely important staging post and wintering area for about 40,000 migratory water fowl, including over 200 pelicans.

Around Chennai listings

For Sleeping and Eating price codes and other relevant information, see Essentials pages 38-42.

Sleeping

Mahabalipuram *p889, map p890*

Even modest hotels charge 20% luxury tax. Several new places in the Othavadai St area. It's busy during the Jan dance festival.

LL Fisherman's Cove (Taj), Kovalam Rd, 8 km north, T044-6741 3333, www.tajhotels.com. A beautiful resort, recently expanded and given a sleek and thoroughly modern fitout. Pick of the rooms are the beachfront cottages with private sit-outs and open-air showers.

LL-AL Ideal Beach Resort, Kovalam Rd (3.5 km north), T044-2744 2240, www.idealresort.com. 30 rooms in cottages, some a/c (limited hours), good restaurant, exchange, spa with Ayurvedic massage, pool and gardens, clean, comfortable.

AL-C Sea Breeze, Othavadai Cross, T044-2744 3035, www.hotelseabreeze.in. Clean, spacious, well-furnished rooms (some a/c with fridge, Rs 700), direct beach access, pool (non-residents Rs 200), good food. Iffy 'hot water', mediocre upkeep. Next door annexe is cheaper.

D Mamalla Heritage, 104 East Raja St, T044-2744 2060. Spotless, friendly and reasonable value, 43 clean spacious rooms, 17 a/c, nice balconies, pool, excellent vegetarian restaurant, exchange, travel, 24-hr hot water, and complimentary toiletries. Recommended.

D Sea Breeze Annexe, see above. Clean doubles with fan and deck, but rates don't include access to the **Sea Breeze** hotel pool.

D Tamil Nadu Beach Resort, north of town on Covelong Rd, T044-2744 2361. Beautiful setting, 48 cottages, some a/c but neglected, damp, restaurants, bar (limited hours), exchange, good pool (non-residents Rs 75).

D-F Greenwoods Beach Resort, 7 Othavadai Cross St, T044-2744 2212, greenwoods_resort@yahoo.com. Basic but good and clean rooms with mosquito nets in a rambling building lushly shaded by banana and mango trees. The family owners are genuinely welcoming, and there's a well-regarded Ayurvedic clinic on-site.

C-E Lakshmi Lodge, Othavadai St, T044-2744 2463. Friendly, popular with backpackers, 26 clean rooms in main building, upstairs small but light, downstairs dark and poor, plus an annexe out the back with larger, brighter a/c rooms and a pool (which you pay extra to use if you stay in the cheap rooms). Restaurant with beach view.

E Sri Harul Guest House, 181 Bajanai Koil St, T(0)93846-20173, lings6@rediffmail.com. Friendly little guesthouse right on the beach, with interesting views over the fishermen's colony. Rooms on the ground floor have private balconies.

E-F Siva Guest House, 2 Othavadai Cross St, T044-2744 3534, www.sivaguesthouse.com. 11 very clean rooms, taxi hire, internet, friendly. Highly recommended.

F La Vie en Rose, 9 Old College Rd, near bus stand, T(0)94448-77544. Small, quiet hotel slowly going to rack and ruin, but it's a genuine cheapie and the manager is friendly

F Ramakrishna Lodge, 8A Othavadai St, T044-2744 2431. Friendly, good value, 31 well-kept, clean rooms with fan, shower, Western toilets, no nets, courtyard, good rooftop restaurant with travellers' menu and music; contact Vijay for informal yoga classes. Possibly the best cheap deal in town.

F-G Tina Blue View Lodge, 1 Othavadai St, T044-2744 2319. Very friendly, 25 rooms with bath and balcony (Room 9 best), cottages for long-term stays, garden and rooftop restaurant, massage. Recommended.

Kanchipuram *p893, map p894*

B-D GRT Regency, Gandhi Rd, T044-2722 5250, www.grthotels.com. The best in town by a long chalk, with smart, spotless rooms and all the facilities of a luxury business hotel.

C-D Baboo Soorya, 85 East Raja St, T044-2722 2555. Set back off main road down palm-fringed lane. 38 clean, spacious rooms, some a/c, restaurant, snack bar, glass 'bubble' lift, friendly staff, quiet.
E Sri Rama Lodge, 20 Nellukkara St, near Bus Stand, T044-2722 2435. Fairly basic rooms, some a/c and TV, a/c restaurant, relatively quiet, helpful staff.
F Sree Kusal Lodge, 68C Nellukkara St, T044-2722 3356. 25 clean and good-value rooms, TV, vegetarian restaurant.
F Sri Krishna Lodge, 68A Nellukkara St, T044-2722 2831. Helpful, friendly manager, 28 good, clean rooms, some with bath.

Around Kanchipuram *p895*

F Forest Rest House, 1 km from Vedanthangal Sanctuary gates, contact Wildlife Warden, T044-2432 1471. Rest house with 4 well-kept rooms (2 with a/c), meals available on request.

Eating

Mahabalipuram *p889, map p890*

Beachside cafés are pleasant for a drink: Sea Rock and Luna Magica in particular. In top hotels waterfront cafés are especially attractive in the evening.
TT Curiosity, Othavadai St. Wide range, excellent food, very willing to please.
TT Gazebo, East Raja St. Charcoal-grilled fish, pleasant seating.
TT Moonrakers, Othavadai St, www.moonrakersrestaurant.com. Long-established backpacker favourite. Pleasant and friendly vibe during the week, but very rushed at weekends – you may be ordered out of your seat to make way for incoming diners.
TT Temple View, GRT Temple Bay Kovalam Rd, T044-2744 3636. Multi-cuisine restaurant overlooking shore temple, breakfast lunch and dinner, plus less formal, open-air **Beach Comber** and **High Tide** bars (1000-2200).
T Dreamland, Othavadai St. Western favourites, very friendly, relaxed.
T Mamalla Bhavan, opposite bus stand. Classic high-ceilinged South Indian restaurant, excellent for cheap breakfasts.

Kanchipuram *p893, map p894*

Baboo Soorya (see Sleeping). A/c, cheap Indian vegetarian restaurant, good *thalis*.
Bakery Park Place, Odai St. Cakes and sweets.
Saravana Bhavan, next to Jaybala International 504 Gandhi Rd (50 m off the road). "Best in town".
Sri Rama Lodge, a/c, and **Sri Vela**, Station Rd. Good breakfasts.

Festivals and events

Mahabalipuram *p889, map p890*

Dec-early Feb 6-week **Dance Festival** starting on 25 Dec; at Bhagiratha's (Arjuna's) Penance, classical 1800-2030, folk 2030-2100, every Sat, Sun and holidays. Long speeches in Tamil on opening (full moon) night.
Mar **Masi Magam** attracts large crowds of pilgrims.
Apr-May **Brahmotsava** lasts for 10 days.
Oct-Nov the **Palanquin Festival** is held at the Stalasayana Perumal Temple.

Kanchipuram *p893, map p894*

Mar-Apr The **Panguni Uthiram Festival** is the largest of Kanchipuram's festivals, very atmospheric. Celebrated all over Tamil Nadu.

Shopping

Mahabalipuram *p889, map p890*

Hidesign, 138 East Raja St. Excellent Western-style leather goods, very reasonable. Recommended.
Himalayan Handicrafts, 21 East Raja St, also has 900 books for exchange.
JK Books, off the beach on Othavadai St. Books and newspapers.
Silver Star, 51 East Raja St, good tailor.

Kanchipuram *p893, map p894*

Silk and cotton fabrics with designs of birds, animals and temples or in plain beautiful colours, sometimes 'shot', are sold by the metre in addition to saris. It's best to buy from govern- ment shops or Co-operative Society stores.
AS Babu Shah, along Gandhi Rd. High-quality silks.
BM Silks, 23G Yadothagari, Sannathi St. Worth a look.
Murugan Silk Weavers' Co-operative, 79 Gandhi Rd.
Sreenivas, 135 Thirukatchi Nambi St (Gandhi Rd).

Activities and tours

Mahabalipuram *p889, map p890*

Tour operators

Hi Tours, 123 East Raja St, T044-2744 3360, www.hi-tours.com. Train/air tickets, tours, foreign exchange, Kerala house boats.

Tamil Nadu Tourism runs a hop-on-hop-off bus service from Chennai, departing the Tourism Complex (2 Wallajah Rd) at 0900, 0930, 1000, 1100, returning from Mahabali- puram at 1600, 1700, 1730 and 1800; stops include the Crocodile Bank and Dakshina Chitra; tickets Rs 250. Also day tours to Kanchipuram and Mahabalipuram. 0630-1900. Tiring, but good value if you don't mind being rushed. It also includes a stop at the appallingly garish Indian kitsch, VGP Beach Resort.

Transport

Mahabalipuram *p889, map p890*

Bicycle/car hire Bicycle hire from tourist office and shops in East Raja St and hotels, Rs 40-50 per day. Recommended for **Tirukkalukundram** – from Dec to Feb a comfortable and very attractive ride. The same shops also hire out mopeds and motorbikes at around Rs 200-300. Car hire from the tourist office.

Bus The bus stand in the centre has buses to **Tirukkalukundram**, and further afield to **Chennai**, **Pondicherry** and **Tiruvannamalai**.

Taxi Taxis charge Rs 1000-1200 for a 1-day excursion from Chennai, around Rs 1000 from Mahabalipuram to the airport.

Train The nearest train station is Chengalpattu, 29 km away, which has express trains to **Chennai** and south Tamil Nadu; buses from here to Mahabalipuram take an hour.

Kanchipuram *p893, map p894*

Auto-rickshaws Available for visiting temples. Also cycle rickshaws.

Bicycle hire The town is flat and easy to negotiate so the best and cheapest way to get about is by hiring a bike from near the bus stand or off East Raja St.

Bus The bus station in the middle of town with direct Govt Express to **Chennai** (*No 828*) 2½ hrs, **Bengaluru** (**Bangalore**) (*No 828*), **Kaniyakumari** (*No 193*), **Pondicherry** (*No 804*, 109 km) 3½ hrs, and **Tiruchirappalli** (*No 122*). For **Mahabalipuram** (65 km) 2 hrs, direct bus or take a bus to Chengalpattu (35 km) and catch one from there. Frequent buses to **Vellore**, other buses go to **Tirupati**, **Tiruttani** and **Tiruvannamalai**.

Train The train station, on a branch line, is under 1 km to the northeast of the bus stand. There are 3 direct passenger trains to **Chennai** (**Egmore**), at 0715, 1750 and 1900, 2 hrs; for long-distance trains, it's better to go by bus to **Arakkonam**, 28 km to the north, which is on the main Chennai–Bengaluru line.

Around Kanchipuram *p895*

Vedanthangal Bird Sanctuary is best accessed by car; an overnight taxi from Chennai will cost around Rs 2500, less from Mahabalipuram. The closest major town and railway station is Chengalpattu, which has several daily buses to the sanctuary and frequent connections to Chennai and Mahabalipuram.

Directory

Mahabalipuram *p889, map p890*

Banks **Cherry**, Beach St, for exchange. **LKP**, 130 East Raja St. Good rate, speedy. **Prithvi Securities**, opposite **Mamalla Heritage**, no commission, transfers money. **Libraries** English-language dailies. Book exchange at **Himalayan Handicrafts**. **Post** Post office on a back street off Kovalam Rd.

Kanchipuram *p893, map p894*

Banks **State Bank of India**, Gandhi Rd, with ATM. Amex TCs not accepted; **Indian Overseas Bank**, Gandhi Rd. **Post** Head Post Office, 27 Gandhi Rd.

Pondicherry and Auroville

Pretty little Pondicherry has all the lazy charm of a former French colony: its stately whitewashed 18th-century homes froth with bright pink bougainvillea and its kitchens still smack gloriously of Gaul – excellent French breads, hard cheese and ratatouilles that run with olive oil, accompanied by real French wines. The primly residential French quarter contrasts wonderfully with the dog-eared heritage houses of the Tamil districts, whose streets were built to tilt towards Mecca, while the scores of pristine grey mansions indicate the offices of the Sri Aurobindo Ashram, headquarters of one of India's liveliest spiritual schools of thought. Up the road is the 1960s Westernized branch of Sri Aurobindo's legacy, Auroville, the 'City of Dawn', which was conceived as "a place where human beings could live freely as citizens obeying one single authority, that of the supreme Truth". This is the industrious fulcrum of people seeking an alternative lifestyle – a place of spirulina, incense, and white cotton weeds. ▸▸ *For listings, see pages 903-907.*

Pondicherry (Puducherry) → *For listings, see pages 903-907. Colour map 7, B5.*

Pondicherry is the archetypal ambling town: cleaved in two with the **French quarter** along the beach, boasting pretty high-ceilinged wood-slatted residential houses with walled gardens and bougainvillea, and with the markets, mess, businesses and 'talking streets' of the **Tamil** ('black') town to its west. While the French area, with 300 heritage buildings, is well maintained (the majority owned by the ashram), the Tamil area, despite its 1000 homes now classified as heritage, is dangerously dilapidated. The European Commission has funded the restoration of Calve Subraya Chettiar (Vysial) street (between Mission and Gandhi streets), while Muslim domestic architecture is clearly visible in the streets of Kazy, Mulla and Tippu Sultan, in the southern part of the Tamil quarter.

Many people come to Pondicherry to visit the campus-like ashram of **Sri Aurobindo Ghosh** and his chief disciple Mirra Alfassa ('The Mother'). Ghosh was an early 20th- century Bengali nationalist and philosopher who struggled for freedom from British colonial power (see page 1418) and wrote prodigiously on a huge variety of subjects, particularly Integral Yoga and education. In his aim to create an ashram utopia he found a lifelong *compadre* in the charismatic Frenchwoman Alfassa, who continued as his spiritual successor after his death in 1950. It was Alfassa who pushed into practice Sri Aurobindo's ideas on integral schooling, the aim of which is to develop all aspects of the student's being – "mind, life, body, soul and spirit". In the ashram school, class sizes are limited to eight students, and both pupils and teachers enjoy an extraordinary freedom to alter classes according to individual needs. Alfassa died in 1973 at the age of 93. Both Sri Aurobindo and Alfassa live on as icons, their images gazing down from the walls of almost every building in Pondicherry.

Ins and outs → *Phone code: 0413. Population: 220,700.*

Getting there Buses take under four hours from Chennai on the East Coast Road. The well-organized bus stand is just west of the town, within walking distance, or a short auto-ride from the centre (expect the usual hassle from rickshaw-wallahs). The train station, on a branch line from Villupuram which has trains to major destinations, is a few minutes' walk south of the centre.

Getting around Pondicherry is lovely to explore on foot, but hiring a bike or moped will give you the freedom to venture further along the coast. ▸▸ *See Transport, page 906.*

Tourist information **Pondicherry Tourism** ⓘ *40 Goubert Salai, T0413-233 9497, http://tourism.pondicherry.gov.in, 0845-1300, 1400-1700.* Well run with maps, brochures, and tours. The **Indian National Trust for Art and Cultural Heritage (INTACH)** ⓘ *62 rue Aurobindo St, T0413-222 5991, http://intach pondicherry.org,* is particularly active in Pondicherry and runs heritage walks from its offices. **La Boutique d'Auroville** ⓘ *38 JL Nehru St, T0413-233 7264.* Provides information on visiting Auroville.

Pondicherry

Sleeping

Ajantha Sea View **1** *F5*
Aurodhan **5** *A5*
Balan Guest House **2** *C2*
De l'Orient **3** *E4*
De Pondicherry and Le Club **4** *F4*
Executive Inn **6** *B4*
Family Guest House **7** *E2*
International Guest House **9** *C4*
Mother Guest House **10** *C4*
Mother Sea View Residency **15** *F5*
Park Guest House **11** *F5*
Ram Guest House **12** *D2*
Sea Side Guest House **13** *C5*
Suguru **14** *A3*
Villa Helena **16** *E4*
Youth Hostel **19** *A2*

Eating

Ananda Bhavan **7** *C4*
Ashram Dining Hall **1** *C4*
Au Feu de Bois **2** *E4*
Baker Street **8** *E3*
Blue Dragon **3** *F5*
Café des Artes **16** *D5*
Hot Breads **4** *C4*
Indian Coffee House **5** *C3*
La Terrasse **6** *F4*
Le Café **9** *D5*
Le Club **7** *F5*
Lighthouse **10** *D5*
Rendezvous **13** *E4*
Satsanga **14** *F4*

Bars & clubs

Asian House **11** *F4*
Le Space **12** *E4*
Seagulls **15** *F5*

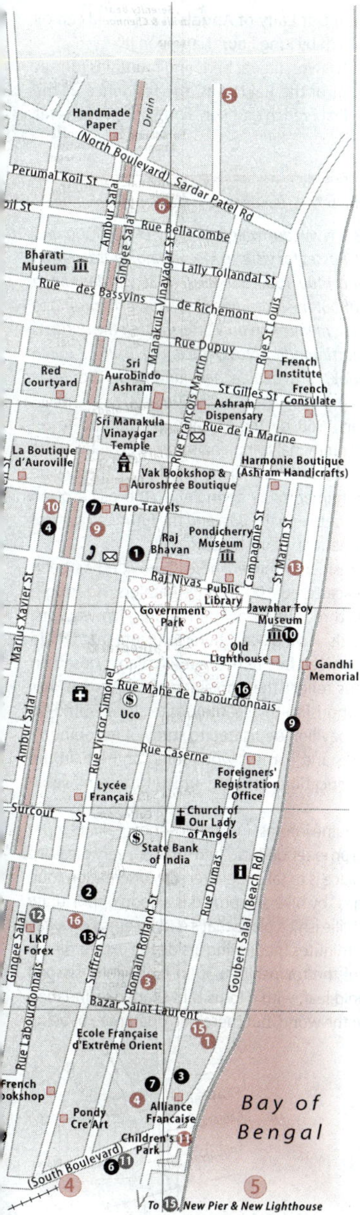

History

Ancient Vedapuri was where the sage **Agastya Muni** had his hermitage in 1500 BC and in the first century AD Romans traded from nearby Arikamedu. The French renamed the area Puducherry in 1673. In 1742, Dupleix, newly named Governor of the French India Company, took up residence. In 1746 the British lost Fort St George in Madras to Dupleix but in 1751 Clive counter-attacked by capturing Pondicherry in 1761. Puducherry was voluntarily handed over to the Indian government in 1954 and became the Union Territory of Pondicherry.

Sights

The **French Quarter**, which extends from the seafront promenade inland to the canal, contains most of Pondicherry's sights, and wandering the quiet streets, stopping into antique shops and colonial mansions, is a pleasure in itself.

The **Sri Aurobindo Ashram** ⓘ *rue de la Marine, 800-1200, 1400-1800, free, meditation Mon-Wed, Fri 1925-1950*, has its main centre in Rue de la Marine. Painted in neat grey and white like most of the ashram's buildings, it contains the flower-bedecked marble Samadhi (resting place and memorial) of both Sri Aurobindo and the Mother.

The **French Institute** ⓘ *rue St Louis*, was set up in 1955 for the study of Indian culture and the 'Scientific and Technical Section' for ecological studies. There's a French and English library looking over the sea, and the colonial building is an architectural treat in its own right.

Pondicherry Museum ⓘ *next to the library, rue St Louis, Tue-Sun 0940-1300 and 1400-1720, closed public holidays, free*, has a good sculpture gallery and an archaeological section with finds discovered at the Roman settlement at Arikamedu. The French gallery charts the history of the colony and includes Dupleix's four-poster bed. Another place worth seeking out is the grand whitewashed **Lycée Français** ⓘ *rue Victor Simonel*, with its lovely shady courtyard and balconies.

The French Catholic influence is evident in a number of churches, notably the **Jesuit Cathedral** (Notre Dame de la Conception,

1691-1765). The attractive amber and pink **Church of Our Lady of Angels** (1855) holds an oil painting of Our Lady of Assumption given to the church by King Louis Napoleon III.

The **Government (Pondicherry) Park**, laid out with lawns, flower beds and fountains (one at the centre is of the Napoleon III period), lies in front of the Raj Niwas, the residence of the lieutenant governor. This was the original site of the first French garrison, Fort Louis, which was destroyed in Clive's raid of 1761.

Auroville → *For listings, see pages 903-907.* *Colour map 7, B5. Phone code: 0413. Population 1700.*

ⓘ *Visitor centre, International Zone, T0413-262 2239, www.auroville.org, daily 0900- 1300 and 1330-1730. All visitors are expected to report here first. Passes for visits to Matrimandir gardens and Amphitheatre are issued here (Mon-Sat 0930-1230 and 1400-1600, Sun 0930-1230; gardens open daily 1000-1250 and 1400-1630), and a 5-min video about the Matrimandir is shown according to demand. Visitors may enter the Inner Chamber for silent meditation only after visiting the gardens and watching the video; to arrange a time call the Matrimandir Access Office, T0413-262 2268. A useful information booklet,* The Auroville Handbook, *is available here and at La Boutique d'Auroville, 38 JL Nehru St, Pondicherry.*

Futuristic Auroville, 'City of Dawn', was founded in 1968 by the Mother as a tribute to Sri Aurobindo, and remains a fascinating experiment in communal living and spiritual evolution. The founding charter reads: "To live in Auroville one must be a willing servitor of the Divine Consciousness," and describes it as belonging "to humanity as a whole ... the place of an unending education, of constant progress ... a bridge between the past and the future ... a site of material and spiritual researches for a living embodiment of actual human unity".

A baked and desolate plateau when the first residents moved here, Auroville has been transformed into a lush forest, among which are scattered 100 distinct hamlets, housing a permanent population of 2200 people plus a regular throughflow of international eco-warriors, holistic therapists and spiritually-inclined intellectuals. It's a place where concepts that would be deemed too flakey to fly in the outside world are given free rein: the town plan is based on the shape of a spiralling galaxy, the main buildings reflect the principles of Sri Aurobindo's philosophy, and a town that can't provide enough housing to accommodate all its would-be residents has found the money to build a gleaming pavilion dedicated to study of Aurobindo's epic poem Savitri. Yet there's a great deal of serious and earnest work going on here, in the fields of sustainable architecture, reforestation, education, organic agriculture, renewable energy and self-development.

The community welcomes visitors who have a genuine interest in its philosophy – all the more so if you can find a project you'd like to work on – and an extended stay here makes a very pleasant retreat from India. An ideal way to get to know the place is to take the three-day orientation tour, which guides you around many of Auroville's "villages" by bike and provides a good opportunity to interact with Aurovilians. On the other hand, Auroville isn't a place that's easy to enjoy on a day trip. With some forward planning you can spend 10 minutes meditating inside the extraordinary Matrimandir, the spiritual and geographic centre of the township, a 30-m-high globe-shaped meditation chamber clad in shimmering discs of gold leaf, with a lotus bud shaped foundation urn and a centrepiece crystal said to be the largest in the world, but there's no guarantee of being able to get in on the day you visit.

Pondicherry and Auroville listings

For Sleeping and Eating price codes and other relevant information, see Essentials pages 38-42.

Sleeping

Pondicherry *p899, map p900*

L-AL The Dune, 15 km from Pondicherry, T0413-265 5751, www.thedunehotel.com. Funky beachside eco-hotel with 36 themed villas and 15 colourful, clean and comfortable rooms spread amongst 12 ha of landscaped grounds. Yoga, reflexology, Ayurvedic massage, organic food and optional detox programmes are on offer, along with a pool, tennis and free bike hire.

AL-A Aurodhan, 33 rue François Martin, T0413-222 2795, www.aurodhan.com. 16 superb rooms stuffed with top-quality art and quirky antique furniture in an otherwise undistinguished building, with art galleries on the lower floors, Wi-Fi, a kitchen for home cooking and great views from the rooftop.

AL-B Hotel de l'Orient, 17 Romain Rolland St, T0413-234 3067, www.neemranahotels.com. Beautifully renovated 19th-century school now a small exclusive hotel, with 16 tastefully decorated rooms in colonial style with objets d'art. Mixed reviews of the restaurant (French/Creole) and service, but achingly beautiful location. Recommended.

A Ajantha Sea View, 1C 50 Goubert Salai, T0413-234 9032, www.ajanthaseaview hotel.com. The best-value sea views in town (other than the ashram guesthouses, see below). Not the most modern rooms, but they're clean, bright and have huge balconies gazing straight out into the Bay of Bengal.

B Hotel de Pondichery, 38 rue Dumas, T0413-222 7409, www.hoteldepondichery.com. Simple, clean, tastefully decorated 10 rooms (some with no windows but private courtyard), in the same colonial-style building as the popular French bistro **Le Club** (so can get noisy). Very friendly and efficient staff. A/c. Babysitting service available.

B Villa Helena, 14 Suffren St, T0413-222 6789, galleryhotels@hotelstamilnadu.com. 5 comfortable rooms with antique furniture set around large shady courtyard, suite on the 1st floor, includes breakfast.

B-C Mother Sea View Residency, 1-C rue Bazar St Laurent, T0413-222 5999, mother_residency@yahoo.co.in. A handful of spacious, airy, marble-floored rooms with balconies pointing seawards.

C-D Executive Inn, 1a Perumal Koil St, T0413-233 0929, www.executiveinn.biz. 11 a/c suites, TV, restaurant, internet, no smoking, no alcohol, quiet yet short walk from the beachfront and bazar, good value. Recommended.

C-D Surguru, 104 Sardar Patel Rd, T0413-233 9022. Good, clean rooms, some a/c, excellent South Indian restaurant, bit noisy.

D-E Ram Guest House, 546 MG Rd, 278 Avvai Shanmugham (Lloyds) Rd, T0413-222 0072, ramguest@hotmail.com. 20 excellent rooms set back from the main road, maintained to European standards, spotless, good breakfast from clean kitchen. Recommended.

E-F Balan Guest House, 20 Vellaja St, T0413-233 0634. 17 immaculate rooms with bath, clean linen.

E-F Family Guest House, 526 MG Rd, T0413-222 8346, fghpondy@yahoo.co.in. 4 rooms, TV, hot water, bit cramped but very clean, roof terrace, hall, dining area, friendly.

E-F Mother Guest House, 36 Ambur Salai, T0413-233 7165. Well-located cheap dive just off the JL Nehru shopping strip, with dark but clean enough rooms squirrelled away along labyrinthine corridors above a clothes shop.

F Youth Hostel, Solaithandavan Kuppam, T0413-222 3495, north of town. Dorm beds (Rs 30), close to the sea among fishermen's huts. Bicycle or transport essential.

Ashram guesthouses

Though these are mainly for official visitors and guests associated with the ashram, they are open to the public. Gates close by 2230 (late-comers may be locked out) and alcohol and smoking are prohibited. Book well in advance.

D Park Guest House, near Children's Park, T0413-223 7495, parkgh@auroville.org.in. 93 excellent sea-facing rooms, breakfasts, clean, quiet, great garden, reading room, ideal for long stays. Recommended.

D Sea Side Guest House, 14 Goubert Salai, T0413-233 1713, seaside@sriaurobindo society.org.in. 25 excellent, large rooms, hot showers, breakfast, spotless, sea views. Recommended.

E-F International Guest House, Gingee Salai, T0413-233 6699. 57 very clean and airy rooms, some a/c, huge for the price, very popular so often full.

Auroville *p902*

For details of the 20-odd guesthouses scattered around Auroville, see www.aurovilleguesthouses.com. Accommodation ranges from basic thatched huts with shared toilets to self contained studios, with rooms available in 4 distinct zones: Centre (close to the Matrimandir, theatres and cafes), Residential, Forest and Beach. The **Auroville Guest Service**, T0413-262 2704, can also help with finding a room. Costs vary from **B-F**, though some operate a kibbutz-type arrangement.

D-E Centre Guest House, T0413-262 2155. Most short-stay visitors are accommodated here ("welcomes those who wish to see and be in Auroville, but not to work there"), lovely setting under a huge banyan treee. Bikes and scooters for rent, famous weekly pizza.

Eating

Pondicherry *p899, map p900*

TTT Le Club, 38 rue Dumas, T0413-233 9745. Tue-Sun 0830-1830. French and Continental. Smart, excellent cuisine (Rs 400 for a splurge), French wine (Rs 1000). Mixed reviews: "we could have been in a French Bistro!" to "dearest but not the best".

TTT Lighthouse, on the roof of Promenade Hotel, 23 Goubert Salai, T0413-222 7750. Superb barbecue fare, including some quite adventurous veg options alongside the expected seafood and meat options, served on a glassed-in terrace with front-row sea views. Good cocktails, too.

TT Blue Dragon, 30 rue Dumas near New Pier (south end of Goubert Salai). Chinese. Excellent food, antique furniture.

TT Cafe des Arts, 1 rue Labourdonnais. Very pleasant courtyard cafe serving good coffees and sandwiches, attached to an art gallery. Also has free wifi and clean toilets.

TT La Terrasse, 5 Subbaiyah Salai. Thu-Tue 0830-2000. Excellent Continental. Good value, huge salads, no alcohol.

TT Rendezvous, 30 Suffren St. French and Continental. Attractive, modern, reasonable food but overpriced wine, nice roof terrace, pleasant atmosphere: the owner worked for a wealthy American family for 20 years and so his continental grub is first rate.

TT Satsanga, 32 rue Mahe de Labourdonnais, T0413-222 5867. Closed Thu. Continental (quite expensive wine), friendly, French atmosphere with art 'gallery'. Garden setting and staff make up for mediocre food.

T Ananda Bhavan, 15 Nehru St. Big, buzzy and modern pure veg place, excellent for sweets and *thalis*, and good fun if you don't mind elbowing your way to the front of the queue.

T Ashram Dining Hall, north of Govt Pl. Indian vegetarian. Simple, filling, meals (Rs 30 per day) in an unusual setting, seating on cushions at low tables, farm- grown produce, non-spicy and non-greasy. Buy a ticket (from Ashram guesthouses or Central Bureau), then turn up at 0640, 1115, 1745 or 2000. Recommended, though non-ashramites can expect a grilling before being sold a ticket.

T Au Feu de Bois, rue Bussy. Pizzas, salads, crêpes at lunchtime.

T Baker Street , 123 rue Bussy. Closed Mon. Excellent new French sandwich shop and patisserie, with good but pricey coffee and handmade chocolates.

T Hot Breads, Ambur Salai. 0700-2100. Good burgers, chicken puffs, pizzas, pastries, sandwiches and shakes.

T Indian Coffee House, 41 Nehru St. Real local vegetarian fare from 0700.

T Le Café, Goubert Salai, by Gandhi statue. Cute beachside pavilion in a grassy garden, great for hanging out with a milkshake or ice cream, though service is stretched and you'll be in for a long wait if it's busy.

Bars and clubs

Pondicherry *p899, map p900*

Asian House, 7 Beach Blvd. Slick Bali-themed disco-pub, with a Buddha presiding over the bartenders and a DJ playing Euro house until the lights come on at 2300.

Le Space, 2 rue de la Bourdonnais. Sociable hippy-chic roof terrace hideaway strung with lanterns, with cheap drinks and music that's not too loud to talk over. Draws a mixed crowd of backpackers, Chennai hipsters and Pondy's young and beautiful.
Seagulls, near Children's Park. Recently renovated, but the old formula of cheap beer and sea views remains unchanged.

Festivals and events

Pondicherry *p899, map p900*

4-7 Jan International Yoga Festival held at Kamban Kalairangam, contact Pondicherry Tourism for full details.
Jan Pongal is a 3-day harvest, earth and sun festival, popular in rural areas.
Feb/Mar Masi Magam on the full moon day of the Tamil month of Masi, pilgrims bathe in the sea when deities from about 40 temples from the surrounding area are taken in colourful procession for a ceremonial immersion. 'Fire walking' sometimes accompanies the festival.
14 Jul Bastille Day.
Aug Fete de Pondicherry cultural programme.

Shopping

Pondicherry *p899, map p900*

The shopping areas are along Nehru St and Mahatma Gandhi Rd. *Experience! Pondicherry* booklet has a good shopping guide.

Dolls of papier mâché, terracotta and plaster are made and sold at Kosapalayam. Local grass is woven into *Korai* mats. Craftsmen at the Ashram produce marbled silk, hand dyed cloths, rugs, perfumes and incense sticks.

Antiques Geethanjali, 20 rue Bussy. Pricey but well selected and restored pieces. **Heritage Art Gallery**, rue Romain Rolland.

Books Focus, 204 Mission St. Good selection of Indian writing in English, cards, stationery, CDs, very helpful. **Kailash French Bookshop**, 87 Lal Bahadur Shastri St. Large stock.

Clothes and crafts Several Ashram outlets on Nehru St. **Aurosarjan**, rue Bussy. Auroville clothes and crafts. **Cluny Centre**, 46 Romain Rolland St, T/F0413-233 5668. This is run by a French order in a lovely colonial house where nuns both design and oversee high quality embroidery. **Curio Centre**, 40 Romain Rolland St. Some fine antiques and good reproduction colonial furniture. **Kalki**, 134 Mission St, T0413-233 9166. Produces exceptional printed and painted silk scarves, hangings, etc. **Pondy Cre'Art**, 53B Suffren St. Intriguing variety of locally handmade products, from pencil cases and notebooks to pottery, cushion covers and bespoke bamboo fountains. Also some fantastic clothes. Highly recommended. **Red Courtyard**, 4 Chetty St. Floaty, feminine, boho clothing in silks, linens and cottons by local designer Virginie Malé, plus artworks, bags and jewellery by other local creators. **Sri Aurobindo Handmade Paper Factory**, 44 Sardar Patel Rd. Shop sells attractive products.

Auroville *p902*

Shops at the visitor centre sell products made in the hive of industry that is Auroville, including handmade paper, incense, wind chimes and the like. **La Boutique d'Auroville** has excellent clothes and accessories, cut to suit Western tastes.

Activities and tours

Pondicherry *p899, map p900*

Swimming
Pools in **Hotel Blue Star** and **Calve Bungalow**, Kamaraj Salai open to non-residents for a fee.

Tours and tour operators
Auro Travels, Karikar Building, Nehru St, T0413-233 5560. Efficient, quick service.
PTDC, T0413-233 9497. Full day sightseeing, 0930-1730, Rs 200 inc lunch: Ashram, Govt Museum, Botanic Gardens, Sacred Heart church, Auroville and Matrimandir. Half day covers ashram, museum and Auroville, 1430-1730, Rs 100. Departs from tourist office on Goubert Salai.

Yoga
Ananda Ashram, on Yoga Sadhana Beach, 16 Mettu St, Chinna Mudaliarchavadi, Kottakuppam, T0413-224 1561. It runs 1-, 3- and 6-month courses starting in Jan, Apr, Jul and Oct; or book through Pondicherry Tourism, Rs 1500 for 10 lecture modules.

Auroville *p902*

Body and soul
With a guest pass to Auroville you can participate in retreat activities from Indian dance to ashtanga yoga. There's also a Quiet Healing Centre on the nearby beach, well known for its underwater body treatments. The hydrotherapy treatment tank is a little public so it may be best to stick to the good Ayurvedic massages.

Tours
Available 0830-1100 from **Ashram**, Pondicherry, autocare@auroville.org.in; 1430-1745 from **Cottage Complex**, Ambur Salai, includes Auroville Visitor Centre and Matrimandir. Visitors recommend going independently. A 5-day residential introduction to Auroville is available through the **Guest Service**, T0413-262 2704, www.aurovilleguestservice.org.

⊖ Transport

Pondicherry *p899, map p900*

Bicycle/scooter hire Bike hire is well worthwhile as the streets are broad, flat and quiet. The best choice of mopeds and bikes is on Mission St between Amballattadavar Madam St and Caltisvaran Koil St. Day rates start from Rs 30 for a bike, Rs 100 for a scooter, Rs 200 for a motorbike, plus photo ID (some places ask to keep it) and Rs 500 deposit.

Bus **Local bus stand**: T0413-233 6919. 0430-1230, 1330-2130. **Main bus stand** a few hundred metres west of the junction of Anna Salai and Lal Bahadur Shastri, T0413-233 7464, serves all State bus companies. Computerized Reservations: 0700-2100 (helpful staff). **Pondicherry Tourism Corporation (PTC)**, T0413-233 7008, 0600- 2200, also runs long-distance services. Left luggage, Rs 20 per 24 hrs, at cloakroom on Platform 5. Auto-rickshaw to town Rs 30-40.

Bengaluru (Bangalore): 7½ hrs, overnight Volvo service with PTC; **Chennai**: frequent Express buses via East Coast Rd, 3 hrs; **Chidambaram**: frequent, 1½ hrs; **Coimbatore** via **Salem** and **Erode**: 8½-9½ hrs; **Kanniyakumari**: overnight service; **Kannur** and **Mahé**: 15 hrs; **Karaikal**: 4 hrs; **Madurai** via **Tiruchirappalli**: 6½-8 hrs overnight; **Mahabalipuram**: several, 4 hrs; **Tirupati**: 6½-7 hrs; **Tiruvannamalai** (via **Villupuram** or **Tindivanam**, 1 hr, and **Gingee**, 2 hrs): regular buses between 0600-2000, 3½-4 hrs; **Kottakarai**, frequent service from **Town Bus Stand**.

Car hire One-way and round trips to many destinations can be arranged at roughly Rs 10 per kilometre, eg **Bengaluru (Bangalore)** (310 km) Rs 3250; **Chidambaram** (74 km), Rs 1000 return; **Chennai** (166 km), Rs 1700; **Mahabalipuram** (130 km), Rs 1300; **Tiruvannamalai**, Rs 1200. Also available for multi-day trips, eg **Madurai**, 2 days, Rs 3500; **Ooty**, 3 days, Rs 5300; **Cochin**, 4 days, Rs 6000. Add 20% for a/c, plus extra charges for driver (Rs 200 per day), hill driving (Rs 350), tolls and parking.

Companies include: **Siva Sakthi**, 66 Perumal Koil St, T0413-222 1992, www.sivasakthitravels.com, helpful but with limited English. **Praveen Cabs**, 63 Laporte St, T0413-222 9955.

Taxi Easiest to find along the canal. For local sightseeing, expect to pay around Rs 400 for 4 hrs (40 km), Rs 800 for 8 hrs (80 km).

Train Reservations: T0413-233 6684, Mon-Sat 0800-1400 and 1500-1900, Sun 0800- 1400. Pondy has virtually no direct express trains, but is connected by branch line to Villupuram, which has good connections towards Chennai and Madurai. If booking online, search for trains to/from 'Puducherry'.

Direct express trains: to **Chennai**, *Chennai Egmore Exp 16116*, 0535; *Chennai Pass 56038*, 1435, 5 hrs. To **Villapuram**: 6 trains daily at 0535, 0805, 1340 (continues to Tirupati, 9 hrs), 1435, 1705 and 1935. Also frequent buses, which drop off at the bus stop 100 m from Villlupuram station.

Express trains from Villupuram: **Chennai** several daily; **Madurai**: *Vaigai Exp 12635*, 1505, 6 hrs, via **Trichy**, 3 hrs, and **Kodaikanal Rd**, 5½ hrs. It's possible to make computerized reservations from Pondy station to any other station, and there is a quota on major trains leaving from Chennai Central.

Auroville *p902*

Bicycle hire Rent a bicycle (Rs 25 per day, though at some guesthouses they are free) and take advantage of the many cycle paths. **Centre Guest House** is one of several places renting bikes/mopeds.

Rickshaw/taxi Either of the 2 roads north from Pondicherry towards Chennai leads to Auroville. A rickshaw from **Pondicherry** will cost around Rs 200, a taxi costs around Rs 500 return.

Directory

Pondicherry *p899, map p900*
Banks Many ATMS along Nehru St, Mission St and MG Rd**Andhra Bank**, 105 Easwaran Koil St, offers cash against Visa. **State Bank of India**, 5 Suffren St, changes cash and TCs (Amex, Thomas Cook), 24-hr ATM. **LKP**, 185 Mission St. No commission. **Cultural centres** French Institute, rue St Louis, close to the north end of Goubert Salai. **Alliance Française**, southern end of Goubert Salai for cultural programmes, Mon-Fri 0800-1230, 1500-1900, Sat 0830-1200. **Embassies and consulates** French Consulate, 2 Marine St. **Internet Coffee.com**, 236 Mission St, plays DVDs, great coffee and real Italian pasta, but service and connection are equally slow. **Shreenet**, 54 Mission St. High speed, good computers, scanning. **Medical services** General Hospital, rue Victor Simone, T0413-233 6050; **JIPMER**, T0413-227 2381. **Ashram Dispensary**, Depuis St, near seaside. **Post** Head Post Office, northwest corner of Govt Place, T0413-233 3051. **CTO**, Rangapillai St. **Useful contacts** Foreigners' Regional Registration Office, Goubert Salai.

Palar Valley

Running between the steep-sided northern Tamilnad hill range is the broad, flat bed of the River Palar, an intensively irrigated, fertile and densely populated valley cutting through the much poorer and sometimes wooded high land on either side. The whole valley became the scene of an Anglo-French- Indian contest at the end of the 18th century. Today it is the centre of South India's vitally important leather industry and intensive agricultural development. ▸▸ *For listings, see pages 911-912.*

Vellore → *Colour map 7, A5. Phone code: 0416. Population: 177,400.*
The once strategically important centre of Vellore, pleasantly ringed by hills, is in the process of converting itself from the dusty market town of old into an unmissable stop on the Tamil Nadu temple circuit, complete with its own airport. The reason for this transformation is the glittering new **Sripuram temple** ⓘ *12 km south of town at the base of the Thirumalaikodi hills, www.sripuram.org, 0700-2000, free entry*, which opened in late 2007 with funding from the local Sri Narayani Peedam trust, headed by Sri Sakthi Amma. The central temple building is covered in 1.5 tonnes of gold leaf – more than adorns the Golden Temple in Amritsar – which is laid over sheets of copper embossed with figures of gods. The temple has attracted no small measure of controversy, largely because of the huge sum of money ploughed into its construction – an estimated 600 million rupees – which some feel would have been better spent on poverty alleviation programs. Sri Sakthi Amma has defended the temple on the basis that it will serve as an attraction to people from all over the world, with lasting financial benefits to the area's people – from increased tourism spending as well as from donations to the trust's various beneficent activities – and spiritual benefits to visitors. To reach the temple you have to negotiate a 2-km-long covered walkway, modelled after the star-shaped Sri Chakra and festooned with quotes from the Vedas, Bible and Koran. The inner sanctum contains a granite idol of Mahalaxmi, the goddess of wealth, draped in golden adornments.

Before Sripuram, Vellore was best known for its **Christian Medical College Hospital**, founded by the American missionary Ida Scudder in 1900. Started as a one-room dispensary, it extended to a small hospital through American support. Today it is one of the country's largest hospitals with over 1200 beds and large outpatients' department which caters for over 2000 patients daily. The college has built a reputation for research in a wide range of tropical diseases. One of its earliest and most lasting programmes has been concerned with leprosy and there is a rehabilitation centre attached. In recent years it has undertaken a wide-ranging programme of social and development work in villages outside the town to back up its medical programmes.

Vijayanagar architecture is beautifully illustrated in the temple at **Vellore Fort**, a perfect example of military architecture and a *jala durga* (water fort). Believed to have been built by the Vijayanagara kings and dating from the 14th century, the fort has round towers and huge gateways along its double wall. The moat, still filled with water by a subterranean drain, followed ancient principles of defence: it was home to a colony of crocodiles. A wooden drawbridge crosses the moat to the southeast. In 1768 Vellore came under the control of the British, who defended it against Haidar Ali. After the victory in Seringapatnam in 1799, Tipu Sultan's family was imprisoned here and a mutiny of 1806, in which many British and Indian mutineers were killed, left many scars. In the fort is a parade ground, the CSI church, the temple and two-storeyed mahals, which are used as government offices.

Vellore

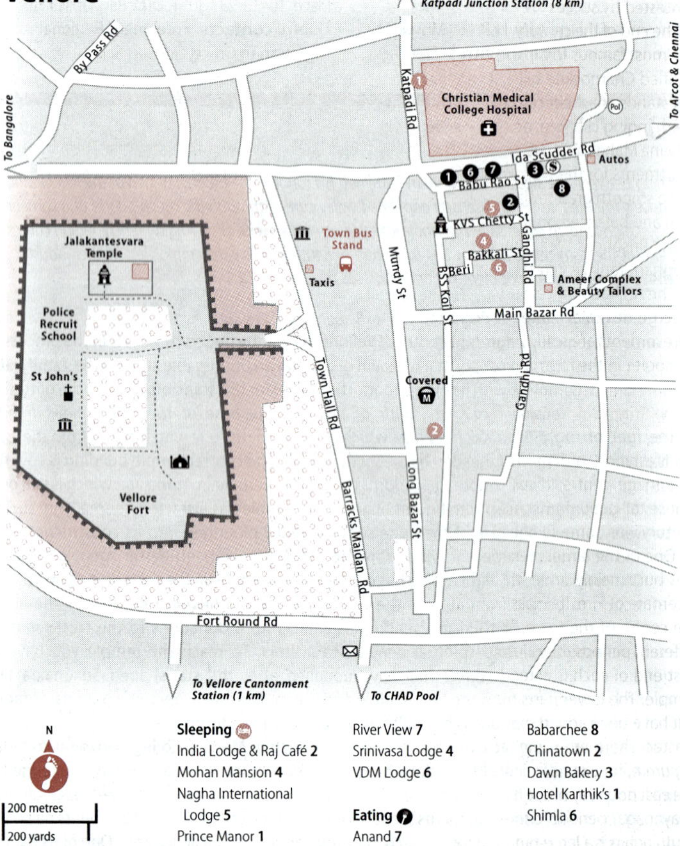

Sleeping
India Lodge & Raj Café **2**
Mohan Mansion **4**
Nagha International Lodge **5**
Prince Manor **1**
River View **7**
Srinivasa Lodge **4**
VDM Lodge **6**

Eating
Anand **7**
Babarchee **8**
Chinatown **2**
Dawn Bakery **3**
Hotel Karthik's **1**
Shimla **6**

Jalakantesvara Temple ⓘ *bathing Rs 2*, with a 30-m high seven-storeyed granite *gopuram*, has undergone considerable restoration. Enter from the south and inside on the left, the *kalyana mandapa* (wedding hall), one of the most beautiful structures of its kind, has vivid sculptures of dragons and 'hippogryphs' on its pillars. The temple consists of a shrine to Nataraja in the north and a lingam shrine in the west.

Gingee ➔ *Colour map 7, B5. Phone code: 04145.*

Gingee (pronounced *Senjee*), just off the NH45, situated between Chennai and Tiruvannamalai, has a remarkable 15th-century Vijayanagar fort with much to explore. It is well off the beaten track, very peaceful and in beautiful surroundings. Spend the night here if you can. Lovers come here at the weekends; it's on the domestic tourist map because it is often used as a film location. The landscape is made up of man-sized boulders, like Hampi, piled on top of each other to make mounds the texture of cottage cheese.

The fort ⓘ *0900-1700, allow 2½ hrs for Rajagiri, and 2 hrs for Krishnagiri (if you have time), foreigners Rs 100, Indians Rs 20, camera Rs 50, video Rs 250, includes both forts,* was intensely contested by successive powers before being captured by an East India Company force in 1762, by the end of the century, however, it had lost its importance. Although it had Chola foundations, the 'most famous fort in the Carnatic' was almost entirely rebuilt in 1442. It is set on three strongly fortified Charnockite hills: Krishnagiri, Chakklidrug and Rajagiri. In places the hills on which the fort stands are sheer cliffs over 150 m high. The highest, Rajagiri ('King's Hill'), has a south-facing overhanging cliff face, on top of which is the citadel. The inner fort contains two temples and the Kalyana Mahal, a square court with a 27-m breezy tower topped by pyramidal roof, surrounded by apartments for the women of the governor's household. On top of the citadel is a huge cannon and a smooth granite slab known as the Raja's bathing stone. An extraordinary stone about 7 m high and balanced precariously on a rock, surrounded by a low circular brick wall, it is referred to as the Prisoner's Well. There are fine Vijaynagara temples, granary, barracks and stables and an 'elephant tank'. A caretaker may unlock a temple and then expect a tip.

The Archaeological Survey of India Office is just off the main road towards the fort. They may have guides to accompany you to the fort. Carry provisions, especially plenty of drinks; a few refreshments are sold, but only at the bottom of the hill. The climb is only for the fit and healthy; it's cooler in the morning and the views are less hazy.

Tiruvannamalai ➔ *Colour map 7, B5. Phone code: 04175. Population: 130,300.*

At the foot of rocky Arunachala Hill, revered by Hindus across South India as the physical manifestation of Siva, Tiruvannamalai is one of Tamil Nadu's holiest towns. It is a major pilgrimage centre, focused around the enormous and fascinating Arunachaleshwar Temple whose tall *gopurams* stand dazzling white against the blue sky, and for the first half of the 20th century was home to one of India's most beloved saints, the clear-eyed Sri Ramana Maharishi.

One of the largest temples in South India, the 16th- and 17th-century **Arunachala Temple** was built mainly under the patronage of the Vijayanagar kings and is dedicated to Siva as God incarnate of Fire. Its massive bright white *gopurams*, the tallest of which is 66 m high, dominate the centre of the town. The temple has three sets of walls forming nested rectangles. Built at different periods they illustrate the way in which many Dravidian temples grew by accretion. The east end of each is extended to make a court, and the main entrance is at the east end of the temple. The lower parts of the *gopurams*, built of granite, date from the late Vijayanagar period but have been added to subsequently. The upper 10 storeys and the decoration are of brick and plaster. There are some remarkable carvings on the *gopurams*. On the outer wall of the east *gopuram*, for example, Siva is shown in the south corner dancing, with an elephant's skin. Inside the east doorway of the first courtyard is the 1000-pillared *mandapa* (hall, portico) built in the late Vijayanagar period. To the south of the court is a small shrine dedicated to Subrahmanya. To the south again is a large tank. The pillars in the *mandapa* are typically carved vigorous horses, riders and lion-like *yalis*. The middle court has four much earlier *gopurams* (mid-14th century), a large columned *mandapa* and a tank. The innermost court may date from as early as the 11th century and the main sanctuary with carvings of deities is certainly of Chola origin. In the south is Dakshinamurti, the west shows Siva appearing out of a lingam and the north has Brahma. The outer porch has small shrines to Ganesh and Subrahmanya. In front of the main shrine are a brass column lamp and the *Nandi* bull.

Two kilometres southwest of the centre, the **Sri Ramanasramam** ⓘ *T04175-237292, www.sriramanamaharshi.org*, was founded by Sri Ramana Maharishi, the Sage of Arunachala (1879-1950). Aged 16, he achieved spontaneous self-realization and left his family to immerse himself in *samadhi* at the foot of the holy mountain. He spent 20 years in caves, steadily accumulating followers, one of whom was his own mother, who died at the base of the mountain in 1922. Recognized as a saint herself, Sri Ramana chose his mother's shrine as the site for his ashram.

The peacock-filled ashram grounds, which attract a sizeable community of Westerners between December and April, contain a library with 30,000 spiritual books and many photos of Maharishi, the last of which were taken by Henri Cartier-Bresson, who photographed him when he was alive and also the morning after his death in April 1950. Apart from the two daily *pujas* (1000 and 1815) the ashram organizes few daily programs; the focus here is on quiet self-enquiry and meditation. Foreigners wishing to stay need to write to the ashram president with proposed dates.

A gate at the back of the ashram gives access to the hillside, from where you can begin the 14-km *pradakshina* (circuit) of Arunachala. The hike is done barefoot – no shoes should be worn on the holy mountain – and takes four to five hours; on full moon nights, particularly during the annual Karthikai Deepam festival (November-December), the trail fills with crowds of pilgrims who chant the name of Siva and make offerings at the many small temples along the way. Another track, branching off to the right shortly after the ashram gate, climbs to Skandasramam, a shady hermitage dug into the rock at which Sri Ramana lived from 1916 to 1922. From here there's a wonderful view over the town, best at sunrise when the temples rise out of the haze like a lost Mayan city. The challenging trek to the summit of Arunachala continues beyond Skandasramam (allow six hours up and down).

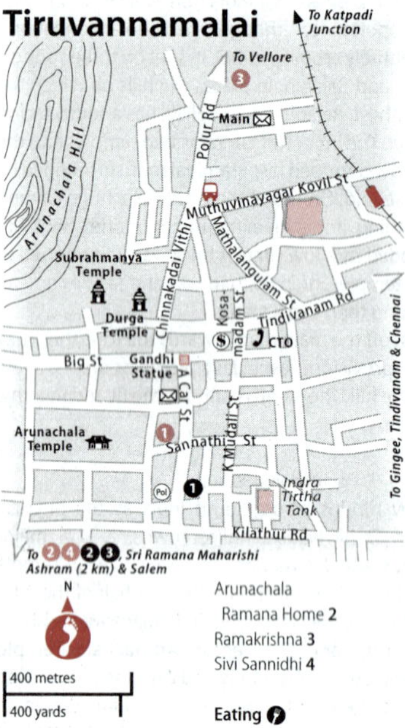

Sleeping
Arunachala **1**
Arunachala Ramana Home **2**
Ramakrishna **3**
Sivi Sannidhi **4**

Eating
Brindavan **1**
Manna **2**
Pumpernickel Bakery **3**

Palar Valley listings

For Sleeping and Eating price codes and other relevant information, see Essentials pages 38-42.

Sleeping

Vellore *p907, map p908*

D Prince Manor, 41 Katpadi Rd, T0416-222 7106. Comfortable rooms, excellent restaurant.

D River View, New Katpadi Rd, T0416-222 5251, 1 km north of town. 31 rooms, some a/c (best on tank side), modern, pleasant courtyard with mature palms, 3 good restaurants.

F India Lodge. Cheap. **Raj Café** downstairs.

F Mohan Mansion, 12 Beri Bakkali St, T0416-222 7083, 15 mins' walk from bus stand. Small, basic and clean, quieter than others.

F Nagha International Lodge, 13/A KVS Chetty St, T0416-222 6338. Some **E** a/c rooms.

F Srinivasa Lodge, Beri Bakkali St, T0416-222 6389. Simple and clean.

G VDM Lodge, T0416-222 4008. Very cheap, pleasant, helpful staff.

Gingee *p909*

Avoid **Aruna Lodge**, near bus stand.

E Shivasand, M Gandhi Rd, opposite bus stand, T04145-222218. Good views of fort from roof, 21 clean rooms with bath, some a/c, veg restaurant, a/c bar, helpful manager.

Tiruvannamalai *p909, map p910*

The best areas to stay are around the temple and in the streets opposite the ashram; hotels opposite the bus stand are uniformly grim. At full moon pilgrims arrive to walk around Arunachala Hill and hotels are overbooked.

E-F Arunachala, 5 Vadasannathi St, T04175-228300. 32 clean, rooms, 16 a/c, TV, hot water, best away from temple, can get noisy during festivals, great vegetarian food downstairs.

E-F Ramakrishna, 34F Polur Rd, T04175- 250005, info@hotelramakrishna.com. Modern, 42 rooms, 21 a/c, TV, hot water, excellent vegetarian tandoori restaurant, parking, helpful and friendly staff. Recommended.

F Arunachala Ramana Home, 70 Ramana Nagar, off Chengam Rd near ashram, T04175-236120. Friendly place with clean, good-value rooms. The owners can arrange bike hire and taxis, and also hand out a home-made map of the ashram area and mountain circuit.

F Siva Sannidhi, Siva Sannidhi St, opposite ashram, T04175-236972. Spacious, simple and clean rooms, some with balconies overlooking Arunachala, slightly institutional feel of this large complex. Free veg meals.

Eating

Vellore *p907, map p908*

Anand, Ida Scudder Rd. Excellent breakfasts.

Babarchee, Babu Rao St. Good fast food and pizzas.

Best, Ida Scudder Rd. Some meals very spicy, nice parathas, 0600 for excellent breakfast.

Chinatown, Gandhi Rd. Small, friendly, a/c. Good food and service.

Dawn Bakery, Gandhi Rd. Fresh bread and biscuits, cakes, also sardines, fruit juices.

Geetha and **Susil**, Ida Scudder Rd. Rooftop or inside, good service and food.

Shimla, Ida Scudder Rd. Tandoori, naan very good.

Tiruvannamalai *p909, map p910*

This town is a *thali* lover's paradise with plenty of 'meals' restaurants.

Brindavan, 57 A Car St. Great *thali*.

Pumpernickel Bakery, Agni Nilam St near ashram. Western-orientated place split between 2 neighbouring rooftops, serving good breakfasts, soups and fantastic fresh pastries.

Manna, next to **Arunachala Ramana Home** (see Sleeping). Super-relaxed place for salads and snacks, with free Wi-Fi and a noticeboard listing upcoming events.

Festivals and events

Tiruvannamalai *p909, map p910*

Nov-Dec Karthikai Deepam, full moon day. A huge beacon is lit on top of the hill behind the temple. The flames, which can be seen for miles around, are thought of as Siva's lingam of fire, joining the immeasurable depths to the limitless skies. A cattle market is also held.

Shopping

Vellore *p907, map p908*

Most shops are along Main Bazar Rd and Long Bazar St. Vellore specializes in making 'Karigari' glazed pottery in a range of traditional and modern designs. Vases, water jugs, ashtrays and dishes are usually coloured blue, green and yellow.

Beauty, Ameer Complex, Gandhi Rd. Cheapest good-quality tailoring.

Mr Kanappan, Gandhi Rd. Very friendly, good-quality tailors, bit pricier.

Activities and tours

Vellore *p907, map p908*

Hillside Resort, CHAD (Community Health and Development), south of town. Open early morning to late evening, closed Mon and 1200-1500. Excellent pool, Rs 250 per day.

Transport

Vellore *p907, map p908*

Bus The new long-distance bus stand is 2 km north of the town centre, which can be reached by local buses 1 and 2 or auto-rickshaw. Buses to **Tiruchirappalli**, **Tiruvannamalai**, **Bengaluru** (**Bangalore**), **Chennai**, **Ooty**, **Thanjavur** and **Tirupathi**. The regional state bus company **PATC** runs frequent services to **Kanchipuram** and **Bengaluru** from 0500 (2½ hrs) and **Chennai**. From the **Town Bus Stand**, off Long Bazar Rd near the Fort, buses 8 and 8A go to the Sripuram temple.

Train Vellore Town station has daily passenger trains to **Tirupati** at 1015 and 1800. The main station, Katpadi Junction, 8 km north of town, is on the broad gauge line between **Chennai** and **Bengaluru**. Buses and rickshaws (Rs 35) into **Vellore**. **Chennai** (**C**): dozens of trains a day; *West Coast Exp 16628*, 1245, 2½ hrs. **Bengaluru** (**C**): *Brindavan Exp 12639*, 0903, 4¼ hrs; *Lalbagh Exp 12607*, 1745, 4 hrs. **Tirupati**: *Seshadri Exp 17209*, 1755, 2 hrs; also unreserved passenger trains at 0610, 1030, 1415, 1820 and 2100. It is also on the metre gauge line to **Villupuram** to the south, with 1 or 2 trains per week to **Pondicherry**, **Trichy** and **Madurai**.

Gingee *p909*

Bus Buses to/from **Pondicherry**, infrequent direct buses (2 hrs); better via Tindivanam (45 mins). To/from **Tiruvannamalai**, 39 km: several buses (1 hr), Rs 13; Express buses will not stop at the fort. TPTC bus 122 to/from **Chennai**.

Rickshaw To visit the fort take a cycle- rickshaw from the bus stand to the hills; Rs 30 for the round trip, including a 2-hr wait. There are bicycles for hire next to the bus station.

Tiruvannamalai *p909, map p910*

Bicycle Cycling can be hazardous in this very busy small town, but it's a practical way to get around the ashram area. Bikes for hire from a stand just east of the **Amman Rooftop Café**, Rs 20 per day.

Bus Buses to major cities in **Tamil Nadu**, **Kerala** and **Karnataka**. Local people will point out your bus at the bus stand; you can usually get a seat although they do get crowded. To **Gingee**, frequent, 1 hr; **Chennai**, 5 hrs, Rs 30, including 4 non-stop a/c buses per day; **Pondicherry**, 3-3½ hrs.

Train At present there are no trains to Tiruvannamalai. The closest useful stations are Tindivanam, on the Chennai–Trichy line, and Katpadi on the Chennai–Bengaluru line. Frequent buses to both.

Directory

Vellore *p907, map p908*

Banks **Central Bank**, Ida Scudder Rd, east of hospital exit, is at least 10 mins faster at changing TCs than the **State Bank of India**. **Internet** **Net Paradise**, north of bus stand. **Medical services** **CMC Hospital**, Ida Scudder Rd, T0416-228 2066. **Post** CMC Hospital has PO, stamps, takes parcels.

Tiruvannamalai *p909, map p910*

Bank ATM on South Sannadhi St. **Vysya Bank**, Sannathi St. Quick for cash and TCs. **Internet** **Sri Bhagavan Net Park**, 18/7 Manakkula Vinayagar St (near ashram), good connection, Wi-Fi, cold drinks. **Post** A Car St.

Chola Heartland and the Kaveri Delta

Chidambaram, Trichy and Tanjore together represent the apotheosis of Tamilian temple architecture: the great temples here act as thirthas, *or gateways, linking the profane to the sacred. This pilgrim's road boasts the bare granite Big Temple in the charming agricultural town of Tanjore, which was for 300 years the capital of the Cholas; Trichy's 21-gopuram, seven-walled island city of Srirangam, a patchwork quilt of a temple built by successive dynastic waves of Cholas, Cheras, Pandyas, Hoysalas, Vijayanagars and Madurai Nayaks; and the beautiful Nataraja Temple at Chidambaram, with its two towers given over to bas reliefs of the 108* mudras, *or gestures, of classical dance.* ▸▸ *For listings, see pages 923-927.*

Tiruchirappalli (Trichy) → *For listings, see pages 923-927. Colour map 7, B5.*

Trichy, at the head of the fertile Kaveri delta, is an industrial city that is more spread out than Madurai although its population is smaller. Land prices are high here, and houses, as you'll see if you climb up to its 84-m-high rock fort, are densely packed, outside the elegant doctors' suburbs. If you are taking public transport you will want to break here to visit the sacred Srirangam temple but if you have your own wheels you may prefer to bypass the city, which has little else to offer by way of easily accessed charms. Allow at least half a day to tour Srirangam, then stay in the more laid-back agricultural centre of Tanjore to the north or the more atmospheric temple madness of Madurai further south.

Ins and outs → *Phone code: 0431.*

Getting there Trichy airport, 8 km from the centre, has flights to Madurai and Chennai. Well connected by train to major towns, the Junction Railway Station and the two bus stations are in the centre of the main hotel area, all within walking distance.

Getting around Much of Trichy is quite easy to see on foot, but plenty of autos and local buses run to the Rock Fort and Srirangam. ▸▸ *See Transport, page 926.*

Tourist information Tourist office ⓘ *New Central Bus Stand, T0431-246 0136.* Also counters at the railway station and airport.

Background

Trichy was mentioned by Ptolemy in the second century BC. A Chola fortification from the second century, it came to prominence under the Nayakas from Madurai who built the fort and the town, capitalizing on its strategic position. In legend its name is traced to a three-headed demon, Trisiras, who terrorized both men and the gods until Siva overpowered him in the place called Tiruchi. Cigar making became important between the two world wars, while the indigenous *bidis* continue to be made, following a tradition started in the 18th century. Trichy is the country's largest artificial diamond manufacturing centre. Jaffersha Street is known as Diamond Bazar. The town is also noted for its high-quality string instruments, especially veenas and violins.

Sights

Rock Fort, 1660, stands on an 84-m-high rock. **Ucchi Pillayar Koil** (**Vinayaka Temple**) ⓘ *Tue-Sun 0600-1200, 1600-2100, camera Rs 10, video Rs 50*, approached from Chinna Bazar, is worth climbing for the stunning panoramas but don't expect much from the temple. At the top of the first flight of steps lies the main 11th-century defence line and the remains of a thousand-pillared hall, destroyed in 1772. Further up is a hundred-pillared hall where civic receptions are held. At the end of the last flight is the **Tayumanasvami Temple**, dedicated to Siva, which has a golden *vimana* and a lingam carved from the rock itself. There are further seventh-century Pallava cave temples of beautiful carved pillars and panels.

Try to make time to explore the atmospheric old city, particularly **Big Bazar Street** and **Chinna Bazar**. The Gandhi Market is a colourful vegetable and fruit market.

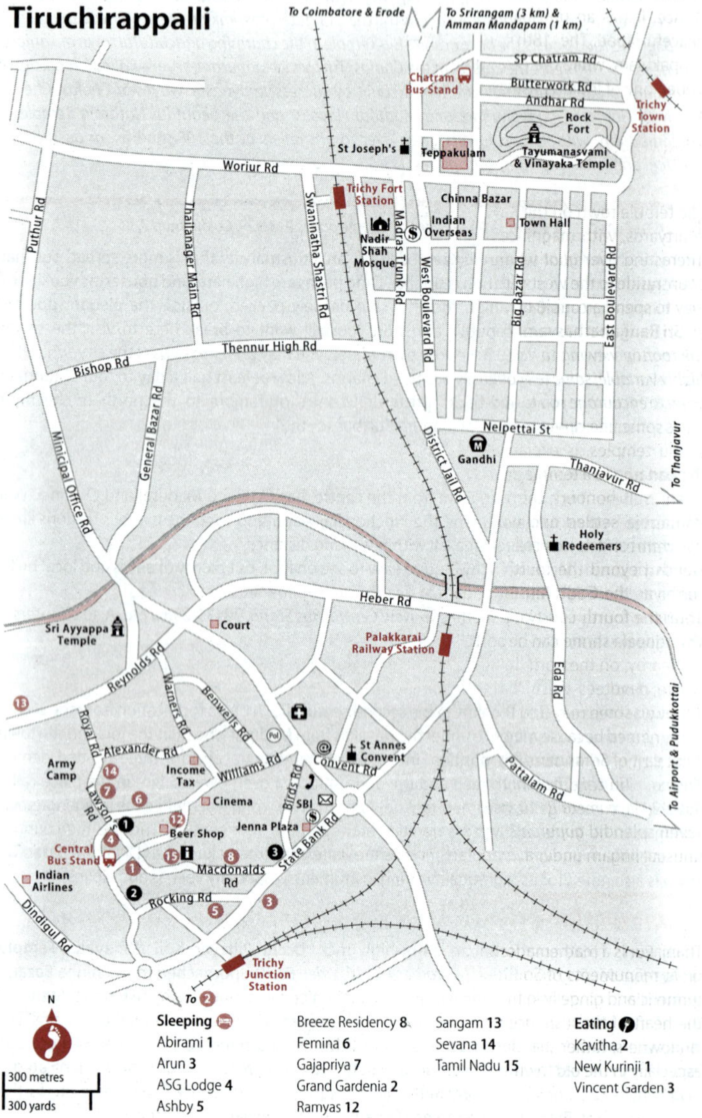

Among the dozen or so mosques in the town, the **Nadir Shah Mosque** near the city railway station stands out with its white dome and metal steeple, said to have been built with material taken from a Hindu temple. **St Joseph's College Church** (Church of our Lady of Lourdes), one of several Catholic churches here, was designed as a smaller version of the Basilica at Lourdes in France. It has an unusual sandalwood altar but is rather garish inside. The grounds are a peaceful spot. The 18th-century **Christ Church**, the first English church, is north of the Teppakulam, while the early 19th-century **St John's Church** has a memorial plaque to Bishop Heber, one of India's best known missionary bishops, who died in Trichy in 1826.

Around Tiruchirappalli → *For listings, see pages 923-927.*

Srirangam

The temple town on the Kaveri, just north of Trichy, is surrounded by seven concentric walled courtyards, with magnificent gateways and several shrines. On the way to Srirangam is an interesting river *ghat* where pilgrims take their ritual bath before entering the temple. The countryside to the west of the temple is an excellent place to sample rural Indian life and a good way to spend a couple of hours.

Sri Ranganathasvami Temple ⓘ *0700-1300, 1400-1800, camera Rs 50, video Rs 100 (Rs 10 for the rooftop viewing tower), allow about 2 hrs, guides will greet you on arrival (their abilities are highly variable; some tell you that the staircase to the viewpoint will close shortly, which is usually a scam to encourage you to use their services)*, is one of the largest in India and dedicated to Vishnu. It has some fine carvings and a good atmosphere. The fact that it faces south, unlike most other Hindu temples, is explained by the legend that Rama intended to present the image of Ranganatha to a temple in Sri Lanka but this was impossible since the deity became fixed here, but it still honours the original destination. The temple, where the Vaishnava reformer **Ramanuja** settled and worshipped, is famous for its superb sculpture, the 21 impressive *gopurams* and its rich collection of temple jewellery. The 'thousand' pillared hall (904 columns) stands beyond the fourth wall, and fifth enclosure there is the unusual shrine to Tulukka Nachiyar, the God's Muslim consort. Non-Hindus are not allowed into the sanctuary but can enter the fourth courtyard where the famous sculptures of *gopis* (*Radha's* milk maids) in the Venugopala shrine can be seen.

Nearby, on the north bank of the Kaveri, **Amma Mandapam** is a hive of activity. The *ghats*, where devotees wash, bathe, commit cremated ashes and pray, are interesting to visit, although some may find the dirt and smell overpowering.

So named because a legendary elephant worshipped the lingam, **Tiruvanaikkaval** is located 3 km east of Srirangam. It has the architecturally finer **Jambukesvara Temple** ⓘ *200 m east off the main Tiruchi–Chennai road, a short stroll from Srirangam or easily reached by bus, officially 0600-2045, camera Rs 10, non-Hindus are not allowed into the sanctuary*, with its five walls and seven splendid *gopurams* and one of the oldest and largest Siva temples in Tamil Nadu. The unusual lingam under a *jambu* tree always remains under water.

Thanjavur (Tanjore) → *For listings, see pages 923-927. Colour map 7, B5.*

Thanjavur is a mathematically perfect Brihadisvara Temple. A World Heritage Site, it is one of the great monuments of South India, its huge Nandi bull washed each fortnight with water, milk, turmeric and gingelly in front of a rapt audience that packs out the whole temple compound. In the heart of the lush, rice-growing delta of the Kaveri, the upper echelons of Tanjore life are landowners, rather than industrialists, and the city itself is mellow in comparison with Trichy, especially in the old town surrounding the Royal Palace.

Ins and outs → *Phone code: 04362. Population: 215,700.*

Getting there Most long-distance buses stop at the New Bus Stand 4 km southwest of the centre, from where there are frequent buses and autos (Rs 60) to town. There's a second, more central bus stand off South Rampart Street, close to several budget hotels, which has some direct buses to Chennai. The train station is at the south end of the town centre, about a 20-minute walk from the Brihadisvara Temple, with connections to Tiruchirappalli, Chennai and Bangalore.

Getting around Most hotels are within a 15-minute walk of the temple. Auto-rickshaws charge Rs 20-30 for trips around town. ▸▸ *See Transport, page 926.*

Tourist information ⓘ *In the grounds of Hotel Tamil Nadu, Railway Station Rd (aka Gandhiji Rd), T04362-230984.*

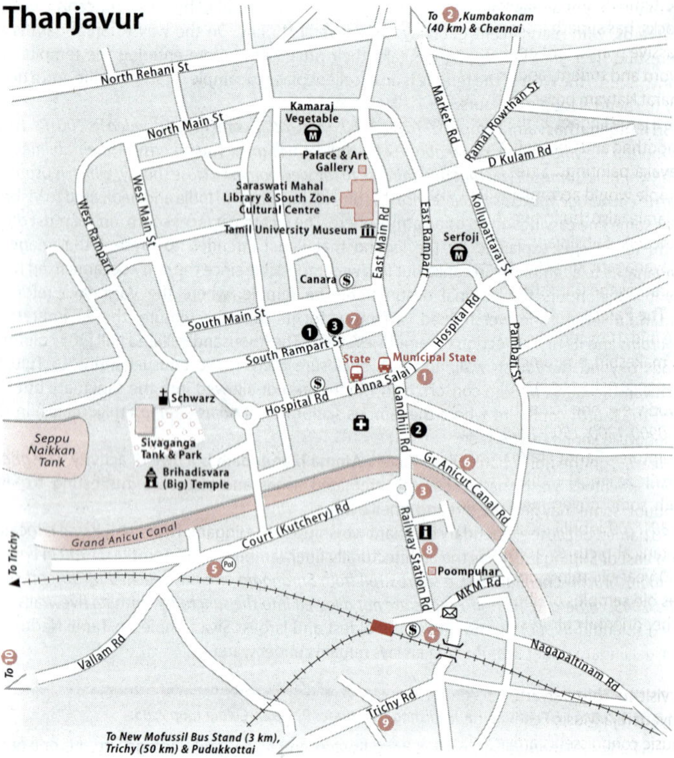

Sleeping
Gnanam **1**
Ideal River View Resort **2**
Lion City & Sri Dhevar's Café **3**
Manees Residency **4**
Pandyar Residency **5**
Parisutham **6**
Ramnath **7**
Tamil Nadu **8**
Yagappa **9**
Youth Hostel **10**

Eating
New Bombay Sweets **1**
Sathars **2**
Vasantha Bhavan **3**

Sights

Brihadisvara Temple ⓘ *0600-2030, inner sanctum closed 1230-1600*, known as the Big Temple, was the achievement of the Chola king Rajaraja I (ruled AD 985-1012). The magnificent main temple has a 62-m-high *vimana* (the tallest in India), topped by a dome carved from an 80-tonne block of granite, which needed a 6.5-km-long ramp to raise it to the top. The attractive gardens, the clean surroundings and well-lit sanctuaries make a visit doubly rewarding, especially in the evening. The entrance is from the east. After crossing the moat you enter through two *gopurams*, the second guarded by two *dvarapalas* typical of the early Chola period, when the *gopurams* on the outer enclosure walls were dwarfed by the scale of the *vimana* over the main shrine. An enormous Nandi, carved out of a single block of granite 6 m long, guards the entrance to the sanctuary. According to one of the many myths that revolve around the image of a wounded Nandi, the Thanjavur Nandi was growing larger and larger, threatening the temple, until a nail was driven into its back. The temple, built mainly with large granite blocks, has superb inscriptions and sculptures of Siva, Vishnu and Durga on three sides of the massive plinth. Siva appears in three forms, the dancer with 10 arms, the seated figure with a sword and trident, and Siva bearing a spear. The carvings of dancers showing the 81 different Bharat Natyam poses are the first to record classical dance form in this manner. The main shrine has a large lingam. In the inner courtyard are Chola frescoes on walls prepared with lime plaster, smoothed and polished, then painted while the surface was wet. These were hidden under later Nayaka paintings. Since music and dance were a vital part of temple life and dancing in the temple would accompany the chanting of the holy scriptures which the community attended, Rajaraja also built two housing colonies nearby to accommodate 400 *devadasis* (temple dancers). Subsidiary shrines were added to the main temple at different periods. The Vijayanagara kings built the Amman shrine, the Nayakas the Subrahmanya shrine and the Marathas the Ganesh shrine.

The Palace ⓘ *1000-1700, foreigners Rs 50, Indians Rs 5, camera Rs 30*, built by the Nayakas in the mid-16th century and later completed by the Marathas, is now partly in ruins, its walls used as makeshift hoardings for the latest Tamil movie release or political campaign. Still, there's evidence of its original splendour in the ornate Durbar Hall. The towers are worth climbing for a good view; one tower has a whale skeleton which was washed up in Chennai. The **art gallery** ⓘ *0900-1300, 1500-1800, foreigners Rs 20, Indians Rs 5, camera Rs 30*, with bronze and granite sculptures, **Sangeeta Mahal** (the Hall of Music, where musicians and dancers performed before the Chola kings) with excellent acoustics, and the **Tamil University Museum** are here, together with some government offices. The pokey **Saraswati Mahal Library** ⓘ *Thu-Tue 1000-1300, 1330-1700*, is brilliant: among its 40,000 rare books are texts from the medieval period, beautiful botanical pictures from the 18th century, palm leaf manuscripts of the Ramayana, intricate 250-year-old miniatures, and splendid examples of the gaudy Tanjore style of painting. It also has old samples of dhoti cloth design, and 22 engravings illustrating methods of torture from other oriental cultures in the 'Punishments of China'.

Around Thanjavur

A visit to **Thiruvaiyaru**, 13 km away, with the Panchanatheswara Siva temple, known for its **Thyagaraja Music Festival**, gives a glimpse of South Indian rural life. Hardly visited by tourists, music connoisseurs arrive in large numbers in January. Performances vary and the often subtle music is marred by loud amplification. There is a **Car Festival** in March. Catch one of the frequent, crowded buses from the old bus station in Thanjavur, taking 30 minutes.

Point Calimere (Kodikkarai) Wildlife and Bird Sanctuary ⓘ *open throughout the year, best season mid-Dec to Feb, Rs 5, camera Rs 5, video Rs 50*, is 90 km southeast of Thanjavur. The coastal sanctuary, half of which is tidal swamp, is famous for its migratory water birds. The Great Vedaranayam Salt Swamp (or 'Great Swamp') attracts one of the largest colonies of flamingos in Asia (5000-10,000) especially in December and January. Some 243 different bird species have been spotted here. In the spring green pigeons, rosy pastors, koels, mynahs and barbets can be seen. In the winter vegetables and insects attract paradise flycatchers, Indian pittas, shrikes, swallows, drongos, minivets, blue jays, woodpeckers and robins among others. Spotted deer, black buck, feral horses and wild boar are also found, as well as reptiles. The swamp supports a major commercial fishing industry. Jeeps can be booked at reception. Exploring on foot is a pleasant alternative to being 'bussed'; ask at reception for a guide.

Kumbakonam

→ *For listings, see pages 923-927.* *Colour map 7, B5. Phone code: 0435. Population: 140,000.*

This very pleasant town, 54 km from Thanjavur, was named after the legend where Siva was said to have broken a *kumbh* (water pot) after it was brought here by a great flood. The water from the pot is reputed to have filled the Mahamakam Tank. High-quality betel vines, used for chewing paan, are grown here.

Sights

The temples in this region contain some exceptional pieces of jewellery – seen on payment of a small fee. There are 18 **temples** ⓘ *closed 1200-1630, no photography,* in the town centre and a monastery of the Kanchipuram Sankaracharya. The oldest is the **Nagesvara Swami Temple**, a Shaivite temple begun in AD 886. The small Nataraja shrine on the right before you reach the main sanctum is designed to look like a chariot being pulled by horses and elephants. Superb statues decorate the outside walls of the inner shrine; Dakshinamurti (exterior south wall), Ardinarisvara (west facing) and Brahma (north) are in the central panels, and described as being among the best works of sculpture of the Chola period. The temple has a special atmosphere and is definitely worth a visit.

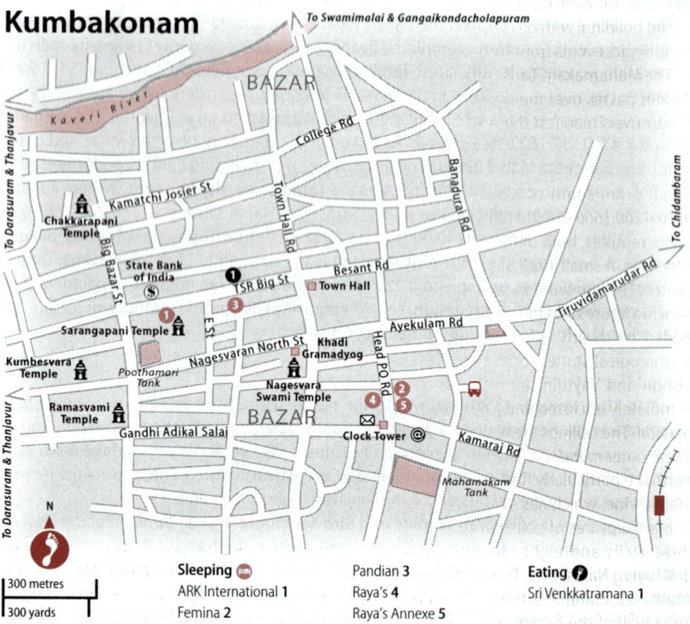

The terrifying guardian deities

Many Hindu villagers in Tamil Nadu believe in guardian deities of the village – Ayyanar, Muneeswaram, Kaliamman, Mariamman and many more. Groups of larger-than-life images built of brick, wood or stone and covered in *chunam* (brightly painted lime plaster) guard the outskirts of several villages. They are deliberately terrifying, designed to frighten away evil spirits from village homes, but villagers themselves are also very frightened of these gods and try to keep away from them. The deities are supposed to prevent epidemics, but if an epidemic does strike, special sacrifices are offered, mainly of rice. Firewalking, often undertaken in fulfilment of a vow, is a feature of the special festivals at these shrines. Disease is also believed to be held at bay by other ceremonies, including piercing the cheeks and tongue with wire and the carrying of *kavadis* (special carriages or boxes, sometimes designed like a coffin).

Sarangapani is the largest of Kumbakonam's shrines. Dedicated to Vishnu (one of whose avatars is Krishna the cowherd), it is also one of the few temples in Tamil Nadu where you will see devotees actively paying reverence to cows. Beyond the 11-storey main *gopuram* that towers above the entrance lies a cattle shed, where visitors can offer gifts of leaves before tiptoeing in (barefoot, naturally) to touch the hindquarters of the closest cow. The Nayaka *mandapa*, with huge beams of beautifully carved stone, leads through a second, smaller *gopuram* to a further *mandapa* carved in the form of a chariot, towed by horses and elephants.

The **Kumbesvara Temple** dates mainly from the 17th century and is the largest Siva temple in the town. It has a long colonnaded *mandapa* and a magnificent collection of silver *vahanas* (vehicles) for carrying the deities during festivals. The **Ramasvami Temple** is another Nayaka period building, with beautiful carved rearing horses in its pillared *mandapa*. The frescoes on the walls depict events from the *Ramayana*. The Navaratri Festival is observed with great colour.

The **Mahamakam Tank** is visited for a bathe by huge numbers of pilgrims every 12 years, when 'Jupiter passes over the sign of Leo'. It is believed that on the day of the festival nine of India's holiest rivers manifest themselves in the tank, including the Ganga, Yamuna and Narmada.

Darasuram

About 5 km south of Kumbakonam is Darasuram with the **Airavatesvara Temple** ⓘ *open 0600-1200,1600-2000*, after Thanjavur and Gangaikondacholapuram, the third of the great Chola temples, built during the reign of **Rajaraja II** (1146-1172). The entrance is through two gateways. A small inner gateway leads to a court where the mainly granite temple stands in the centre. The *gopuram* is supported by beautifully carved *apsaras*. Inside, there are friezes of dancing figures and musicians. The *mandapa* is best entered from the south. Note the elephant, ridden by dwarfs, whose trunk is lost down the jaws of a crocodile. The pillars illustrate mythological stories for example 'the penance of Parvati'. The five gods Agni, Indra, Brahma, Vishnu and Vayu in the niches are all shown paying homage to Siva. The **main mandapa**, completely enclosed and joined to the central shrine, has figures carved in black basalt on the outside. The ceilings are also richly decorated and the pillars have the same flower emblems as in the outer *mandapa*. The main shrine has some outstanding sculptures; the guardians on the north are particularly fine. Sculpted doorkeepers with massive clubs guard the entrance to the main shrine, which has a *Nandi* at the entrance. Some of the niches inside contain superb early Chola sculptures of polished black basalt, including a unique sculpture of Ardhanarisvara with three faces and eight arms, a four-armed Nagaraja and a very unusual sculpture of Siva destroying Narasimha. The **outer walls** are also highly decorative. Siva as Dakshinamurti on the south wall, Brahma on the north wall and Siva appearing out of the lingam on the west wall. The inner wall of the *prakara* (encircling walkway) is divided into cells, each originally to house a deity. The corners of the courtyard have been enlarged to make four *mandapas*, again with beautiful decoration.

Gangaikondacholapuram → *For listings, see pages 923-927. Colour map 7, B5.*

Once the capital of the Chola king Rajendra (1012-1044), this town (whose name means 'The city of the Chola who conquered the Ganga') has now all but disappeared. The temple and the 5-km-long 11th-century reservoir embankment survive.

The **temple** ⓘ *0700-1200, 1600-2100,* that Rajendra built was designed to rival the Brihadisvara temple built by Rajendra's father Rajaraja in Thanjavur. Unlike the *Nandi* in Thanjavur, the huge *Nandi* facing the *mandapa* and sanctuary inside the compound by the ruined east *gopuram* is not carved out of one block of stone. As in Thanjavur, the *mandapa* and sanctuary are raised on a high platform, orientated from west to east and climbed by steps. The whole building is over 100 m long and over 40 m wide. Two massive *dvarapalas* (doorkeepers) stand guard at the entrance to the long closed *mandapa* (the first of the many subsequent *mandapas* which expanded to 'halls of 1000 pillars'); the plinth is original. A *mukha-mandapa* (narrow colonnaded hall) links this hall to the shrine. On the east side of this hall are various carvings of Siva for example bestowing grace on Vishnu, who worships him with his lotus-eye. On the northeast is a large panel, a masterpiece of Chola art, showing Siva blessing Chandikesvara, the steward. At the centre of the shrine is a huge *lingam* on a round stand. As in Thanjavur there is a magnificent eight-tiered, pyramidal *vimana* (tower) above the sanctuary, nearly 55 m high. Unlike the austere straight line of the Thanjavur Temple, however, here gentle curves are introduced. Ask the custodian to allow you to look inside (best for light in the morning). Immediately to the north of the *mandapa* is an excellently carved shrine dedicated to Chandikesvara. To north and south are two shrines dedicated to Kailasanatha with excellent wall sculptures. The small shrine in the southwest corner is to Ganesh.

Ancient Hindu bronzes continue to be unearthed in India every year because so many were buried by priests to protect them from Muslim invaders.

Chidambaram → *For listings, see pages 923-927. Colour map 7, B5. Phone code: 04144.*

The capital of the Cholas from AD 907 to 1310, the temple town of Chidambaram is one of Tamil Nadu's most important holy towns. The town (population 59,000) has lots of character and is rarely visited by foreigners. Its main attraction is the temple, one of the only ones to have Siva in the cosmic dance position. It is an enormously holy temple with a feeling all its own.

The **Nataraja Temple** ⓘ *0400-1200, 1630-2200, visitors may be asked for donations, entrance into the inner sanctum Rs 50, men must remove their shirts,* was the subject of a supreme court battle that ended in Delhi, where it was decided that it should remain as a private enterprise. All others fall under the state, with the Archeological Survey of India's sometimes questionable mandate to restore and maintain them. The unique brahmin community, with their right forehead shaved to indicate Siva, the left grown long and tied in a front top knot to denote his wife Parvati, will no doubt trot this out to you. As a private temple, it is unique in allowing non-Hindus to enter the sanctum (for a fee); however, the brahmins at other shrines will ask you to sign a book with other foreign names in it, supposedly having donated Rs 400. The lack of state support does make this temple poorer than its neighbours, but if you want to give a token rupee coinage instead then do so. The atmosphere of this temple more than compensates for any money-grabbing tactics, however. Temple lamps still hang from the hallways, the temple music is rousing and the *puja* has the statues coming alive in sudden illumination. The brahmins themselves have a unique, stately presence too. The evening *puja* at 1800 is particularly interesting. At each shrine the visitor will be daubed with *vibhuti* (sacred ash) and paste. It is not easy to see some of the sculptures in the interior gloom. You may need patience and persuasive powers if you want to take your own time but it is worth the effort.

There are records of the temple's existence before the 10th century and inscriptions from the 11th century. One legend surrounding its construction suggests that it was built by 'the golden-coloured emperor', Hiranya Varna Chakravarti, who suffered from leprosy. He came to Chidambaram on a pilgrimage from Kashmir in about AD 500. After bathing in the temple tank he was reputed to have recovered from the disease and in gratitude offered to rebuild and enlarge the temple.

On each side are four enormous *gopurams*, those on the north and south being about 45 m high. The east *gopuram* (AD 1250), through which you enter the temple, is the oldest. The north *gopuram* was built by the great Vijayanagar king **Krishna Deva Raya** (1509- 1530). Immediately on entering the East Gate is the large **Sivaganga** tank, and the **Raja Sabha**, a 1000-columned *mandapa* (1595-1685). In the northwest of the compound are temples dedicated to Subrahmanya (late 13th century), and to its south the 12th century shrine to Sivakumasundari or Parvati (circa 14th century). The ceiling paintings are 17th century. At the southern end of this outer compound is what is said to be the largest shrine to **Ganesh** in India. The next inner compound has been filled with colonnades and passageways. In the innermost shrine are two images of Siva, the Nataraja and the lingam. A later Vishnu shrine to Govindaraja was added by the Vijayanagar kings. The **inner enclosure**, the most sacred, contains four important *Sabhas* (halls), the **deva sabha**, where the temple managers hold their meetings; the **chit sabha** or *chit ambalam* (from which the temple and the town get their names), meaning the hall of wisdom; the **kanakha**

1 Chidambaram

Chidambaram maps
1 Chidambaram, page 921
2 Nataraja Temple, page 922

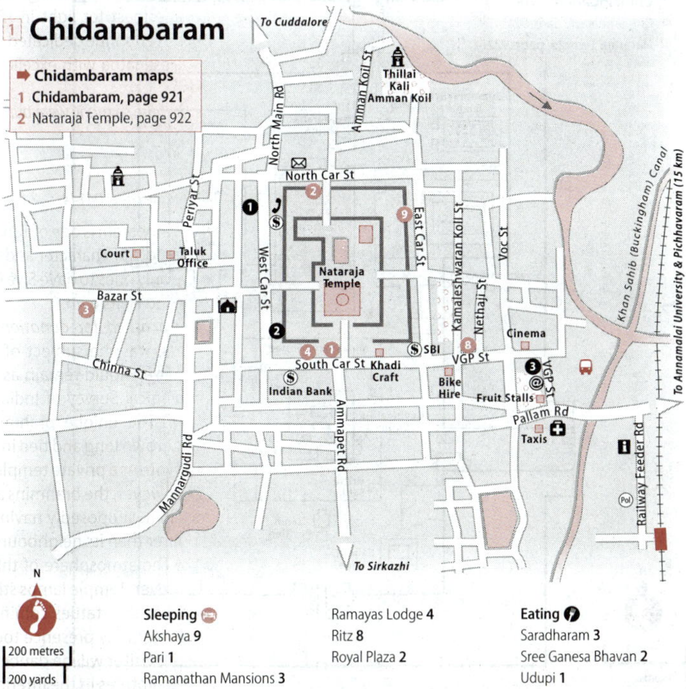

Sleeping
Akshaya **9**
Pari **1**
Ramanathan Mansions **3**
Ramayas Lodge **4**
Ritz **8**
Royal Plaza **2**

Eating
Saradharam **3**
Sree Ganesa Bhavan **2**
Udupi **1**

sabha, or golden hall; and the **nritta sabha**, or hall of dancing. Siva is worshipped in the *chit ambalam*, a plain wooden building standing on a stone base, in his form as Lord of the Dance, Nataraja. The area immediately over the deity's head is gold plated. Immediately behind the idol is the focus of the temple's power, the Akasa Lingam, representing the invisible element, 'space', and hence is itself invisible. It is known as the Chidambaram secret.

Around Chidambaram

The Danish king Christian IV received permission from Raghunath Nayak of Thanjavur to build a fort here at **Tranquebar** (Tharangampadi) in 1620. The Danish Tranquebar Mission was founded in 1706 and the Danesborg **fort** and the old **church** still survive. The Danes set up the first Tamil printing press, altering the script to make the casting of type easier and the Danish connection resulted in the National Museum of Copenhagen today possessing a remarkable collection of 17th-century Thanjavur paintings and Chola bronzes. There is a **museum** and a good beach, plus the evocatively ruined 14th-century Masilamani Nathar temple on the seashore. From Chidambaram most transport requires a change at Sirkazhi. From Thanjavur there are some direct buses; other buses involve a change at Mayiladuthurai (24 km).

2 Nataraja Temple, Chidambaram

➡ Chidambaram maps
1 Chidambaram, page 921
2 **Nataraja Temple, page 922**

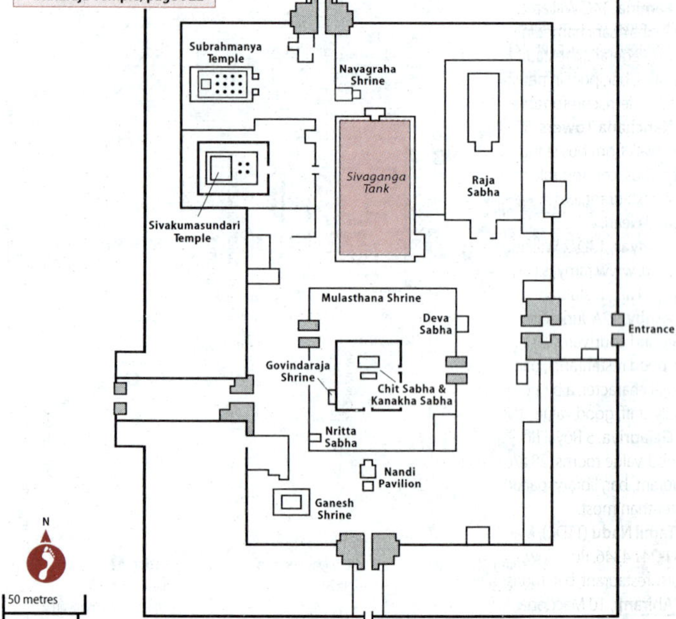

Chola Heartland and the Kaveri Delta listings

For Sleeping and Eating price codes and other relevant information, see Essentials pages 38-42.

Sleeping

Tiruchirappalli *p913, map p914*

L-AL Sangam, Collector's Office Rd, T0431-241 4480. Very friendly, 58 comfortable a/c rooms, restaurants (great tandoori), good breakfast in coffee shop, pleasant bar, exchange, pool, spacious lawns.

AL-A Grand Gardenia, Mannarpuram Junction (1 km south of station), T0431-404 5000, www.grandgardenia.com. Excellent new business hotel with spacious, sparkling clean rooms and good Chettinadu restaurant. Currently the best upscale deal in town.

A Breeze Residency, 3/14 Macdonalds Rd, T0431-241 4414, www.breezehotel.com. Pool (non-residents Rs 100), 93 a/c rooms, those in newer wing smaller but in better condition, good restaurants, excellent travel desk, exchange, beauty salon.

A-C Femina, 14C Williams Rd, T0431-241 4501, try_femina@sancharnet.in. 157 clean rooms, 140 a/c, vegetarian restaurants for great breakfasts, bar, pool in new block, good value, modern, comfortable 4-storey hotel.

C-D Kanchana Towers, 50 Williams Rd, 2-min walk from bus stand, T0431-420 0002. 90 spacious, comfortable rooms with bath, 26 a/c, restaurant, bar, travel agent, very quiet, new and clean.

C-D Ramyas, 13D/2 Williams Rd, T0431-400 0400, www.ramyas.com. 78 spotless rooms, 24 a/c, restaurants, bar.

D-E Ashby, 17A Junction Rd, T0431-246 0652. Set around courtyard, 20 large a/c rooms with bath, good restaurants, bar, oldest hotel in town, with Raj character, a bit noisy but excellent friendly staff, good value.

D-E Gajapriya, 5 Royal Rd, T0431-241 4411. 66 good-value rooms, 28 a/c (no twin beds), restaurant, bar, library, parking, spacious hotel, quieter than most.

C-E Tamil Nadu (TTDC), Macdonalds Rd, Cantt, T0431-241 4346. Run-down, 36 rooms, some a/c or bath, restaurant, bar, tourist office.

D-E Abirami, 10 Macdonalds Rd, T0431-241 5001. Old fashioned, noisy location, 55 rooms, some a/c with bath, good busy a/c restaurant (vegetarian), exchange.

E-F Sevana, 5 Royal Rd, Cantt, T0431-241 5201. Quiet, friendly, 44 rooms, some a/c with bath, a/c restaurant (Indian), bar.

F Arun, 24 State Bank, Rd T0431-241 5021. 40 rooms in garden setting, restaurant, bar, TV, excellent value. Recommended.

G ASG Lodge, opposite **Arun**. Very noisy but quite clean (from Rs 100).

Thanjavur *p915, map p916*

Even modest hotels charge 20% Luxury Tax. Cheapies congregate near the railway station and opposite the Central Bus Stand on South Rampart Rd, but cleanliness standards are, with the odd notable exception, awful.

LL Parisutham, 55 GA Canal Rd, T04362-231801, www.hotelparisutham.com. The poshest place in town, with 52 well-kept but wildly overpriced a/c rooms in a 1980s building. Passable restaurants, massages in cabin by pretty coconut-shaded pool, free internet (and claims of free Wi-Fi in rooms), relatively peaceful location, but derives most of its custom from package tours.

AL Ideal River View Resort, Vennar Bank, Palli Agraharam, 6 km north of centre, T04362-250533, www.idealresort.com. Clean, comfortable cottages (some a/c) in large grounds, restaurant, boating, peaceful, big pool, shuttle to town. Recommended.

B-C Gnanam, Anna Salai (Market Rd), T04362-278501, www.hotelgnanam.com. The mid-range sister hotel to **Parisutham** lacks the pool and top-end facilities, but offers much better value. 30 sparkling clean a/c rooms, some with balcony, vegetarian multi-cuisine restaurant, safety deposit lockers and travel desk, free Wi-Fi in lobby. Recommended.

D-E Yagappa, off Trichy Rd, south of station, T04362-230421. Good size, comfortable rooms with bath, restaurant, bar, good value.

E Lion City, 130 Gandhiji Rd, T04362-275650, hotellioncity@hotmail.com. 25 well-appointed but unremarkable rooms in a fairly convenient but noisy location. TV, hot water, acceptably clean, spacious, good service.

E-F Manees Residency, 2905 Srinivasam Pillai Rd (next to train station), T04362- 271574, www.maneesresidency.com. The cleanest, newest and most pleasant in a row of similarly priced places on this street, with a veg restaurant downstairs.
E-F Ramnath, 1335 South Rampart St, T04362-272567. Modern and friendly choice in the hectic bus stand area, with bright artworks adorning the corridors and pleasant, spacious, well-scrubbed rooms, plus a clean and popular restaurant downstairs.
E-F Tamil Nadu I (TTDC), Gandhiji Rd, 5-min walk from railway station, T04362-231325. Pleasant setting around a cool inner courtyard, 32 moderately clean rooms with bath, some a/c, a bit mosquito-ridden, simple restaurant, bar, tourist office.
G Youth Hostel, Medical College Rd, T04362-235097. Dorm Rs 40.

Around Thanjavur *p917*

Nov-Dec are busy at Point Calimere (Kodik- karai) Wildlife Sanctuary, 3 Main St, Thanjavur.
F PV Thevar Lodge, 40 North Main St, Vedaranyam, 50 m from bus station (English sign high up only visible in daylight), T04369-250330. Good value, 37 basic rooms with bath and fan, can be mosquito-proofed, fairly clean, very friendly owners. Indian vegetarian meals in the bazar near bus stand.
G Poonarai Ilam, Point Calimere Sanctuary reservations via the Wildlife Warden, Collectorate, Nagapattinam, T04365-253092. 14 simple rooms with bath and balcony, caretaker may be able to arrange a meal with advance notice, intended for foreign visitors, rooms are often available.

Kumbakonam *p918, map p918*

Luxury Tax of 10-12.5% is always added. Most places offer 24-hr checkout
C-D Raya's Annexe, 19 Head PO Rd, near Mahamaham tank, T0435-242 3270, www.hotelrayas.com. The shiny exterior conceals the best and cleanest rooms in town: 'Standard' rooms are a/c, light and spacious with good bathrooms; 'Elite' and 'Studio' rooms offer extra space and dining/ sitting areas. Interesting views across temple roofs from upper floor lobbies.
D-E ARK International, 21 TSR Big St, T0435-242 1234, www.hotelark.in. 50 good-size a/c rooms, some cleaner and brighter than others (some barely clean at all), all with bathroom and TV. Pure veg restaurant, room service meals.
D-E Raya's, 18 Head PO Rd, T0435-242 2545. Older and dingier than the annexe opposite, but OK at the price, and the otherwise uninspiring 'garden villas' come family-friendly with 1 double and 1 single bedroom. A/c restaurant downstairs, exchanges cash.
G Femina, 15/8 Head PO Rd, T0435-242 0369. Typically grim budget choice, with dank, grimy and musty rooms, but tolerable if you can snare one of the end rooms with outward-facing windows.
G Pandian, 52 Sarangapani East Sannathi St, T0435-243 0397. The very cheap rooms here come with bath and TV, but little in the way of light and air. Chiefly popular with Tamil men, whose conversations echo along the corridor.

Chidambaram *p920, map p921*

The overall quality of hotels partly explains why most people visit the town on day trips, but there are plenty of lower-bracket choices around the temple, particularly on East Car St (also known as East Sannithi).
D-E Akshaya, 17-18 East Car St, T04144-220192, www.hotelakshaya.com. Comfortable small hotel right in the centre (can be noisy) with 24 well-swept rooms and a rooftop overlooking the temple grounds.
D-E Ritz, 2 VGP (Venugopal Pillai) St, T04144-223312, alritzhotel@gmail.com. Drab and decrepit-looking from the outside, but the all-a/c rooms and suites are cleaner than most in town, and service is enthusiastic – especially when tips might be in the offing.
F-G Pari, 1 South Car St, T04144-220733. With a great atmospheric location near the temple's south gate and relatively grime-free rooms, this is the pick of the rock-bottom options. A/c available in 3- and 4-bed rooms.
G Ramanathan Mansions, 127 Bazar St, T04144-222411. Away from busy temple area, quieter than most, 28 rooms with bath, spacious and airy (no power sockets), friendly.
G Royal Plaza, North Car St, T04144-222179. Good and friendly cheapie, with most rooms boasting Indian toilets and no pretence of

hot water, on the rarely tourist-trod northern edge of the temple.

Eating

Tiruchirappalli *p913, map p914*

Good Indian vegetarian places in Chinna Bazar are **New Kurinji**, below Hotel Guru Lawson's Rd. A/c vegetarian. **Ragunath** and **Vasantha Bhawan**, *thalis*, good service.

Abirami's, T0431-246 0001. A/c, Vasantha Bhawan at the back, serves excellent vegetarian; front part is a meals-type eatery.

Breeze Residency, see Sleeping. Good Chinese, extensive menu, attentive service but freezing a/c. Also Wild West bar.

Kavitha, Lawson's Rd. A/c. Excellent breakfasts and generous vegetarian *thalis*.

Sangam's, T0431-246 4480. Indian and continental.

Vincent Garden, Dindigul Rd. Pleasant garden restaurant and pastry shop, lots of coloured lights but on a busy road.

Thanjavur *p915, map p916*

Parisutham (see Sleeping). Good North Indian meat dishes, excellent vegetarian *thalis* ("best of 72 curries"), service can be slow.

New Bombay Sweets, South Rampart St. Tasty Indian snacks including pakora and kachori, and good sweets.

Sathars, Gandhiji Road. Tandoori. Recommended.

Sri Dhevar's Café, Gandhiji Rd below Lion City Hotel. Widely recommended for pure veg meals.

Vasantha Bhavan 1338 South Rampart Rd near Hotel Ramnath. Wide range of South and North Indian and Chinese dishes, good juices bursting with sugar, very popular.

Kumbakonam *p918, map p918*

Sri Venkkatramana Hotel, 40 Gandhi Park North St. Excellent vegetarian restaurant, with pure veg *thali*-style meals (complete with digestive *paan* package to finish) served in Brahmnical cleanliness in a/c hall, and the usual gamut of snacks in the somewhat fly-blown main room.

Chidambaram *p920, map p921*

Hotel Saradharam, 10 VGP St. Popular, a/c. Excellent range of meals, pizzas and European dishes. Good variety and value.

Sree Ganesa Bhavan, West Car St. South Indian vegetarian. Friendly, helpful staff.

Udupi, West Car St. Good vegetarian, clean.

Entertainment

Thanjavur *p915, map p916*

Bharat Natyam, 1/2378 Krishanayar Lane, Ellaiyamman Koil St, T04362-233759. Performances by Guru Herambanathan from a family of dancers.

South Zone Cultural Centre Palace, T04362-231272. Organizes programmes in the Big Temple, 2nd and 4th Sat; free.

Festivals and events

Tiruchirappalli *p913, map p914*

Mar Festival of Floats on the Teppakulam when the temple deities are taken out onto the sacred lake on rafts.

Around Tiruchirappalli *p915*

Srirangam

Dec/Jan Vaikunta Ekadasi (bus No 1 (C or D) from Trichy or hire a rickshaw), and associated temple car festival, draws thousands of pilgrims who witness the transfer of the image of the deity from the inner sanctum under the golden *vimana* to the *mandapa*.

Tiruvanaikkaval

Special festivals in Jan and the spring.

Aug Pancha Piraharam is celebrated and in the month of **Panguni** the images of Siva and his consort Akhilandesvari exchange their dress.

Chidambaram *p920, map p921*

Feb/Mar Natyanjali dance festival for 5 days starting with **Maha Sivaratri**.

Jun/Jul Ani Tirumanjanam Festival.

Dec/Jan Markazhi Tiruvathirai Festival.

Shopping

Thanjavur *p915, map p916*

You may not export any object over 100 years old. Thanjavur is known for its decorative copper plates with silver and brass relief (*repoussé*) work, raised-glass painting, wood carving and bronze/brass casting. Granite carving is being revived through centres that produce superb sculpted images. Craft shops abound in Gandhiji Rd Bazar.

Govindarajan's, 31 Kuthirai Katti St, Karandhai (a few kilometres from town), T04362-230282. A treasure house of pricey old, and affordable new, pieces; artists and craftspeople at work.

Activities and tours

Tiruchirappalli *p913, map p914*

Indian Panorama, 5 Anna Av, Srirangam, T0431-422 6122, www.indianpanorama.in. Tours from Chennai, Bengaluru (Bangalore), Kochi, Madurai and Thiruvananthapuram. Recommended for tours (good cars with drivers), ticketing, general advice.

Thanjavur *p915, map p916*

TTDC, enquire at tourist office. Temple tour of Thanjavur and surroundings by a/c coach. Mon-Fri, 1000-1745.

Transport

Tiruchirappalli *p913, map p914*

Air

The airport, T0431-234 0551, is 8 km from the centre (taxi Rs 100-150). **Indian Airlines**, Dindigul Rd, 2 km from Express Bus Stand, T0431-248 3800, airport T0431-234 1601; flies to **Chennai** daily except Mon and Fri. **Sri Lankan**, 14 Williams Rd, T0431-246 0844, (0900-1730) to **Colombo**. **Air Asia**, www.airasia.com, no-frills flights to **Kuala Lumpur.**

Bus

Local Good City Bus service. From airport, Nos 7, 63, 122, 128, take 30 mins. The Central State Bus Stand is across from the tourist office (No 1 Bus passes all the sights); 20 mins to Chatram Bus Stand.

Long distance The bus stands are 1 km from the railway station and are chaotic; TN Govt Express, T0431-246 0992, Central, T0431-246 0425. Frequent buses to **Chennai** (6 hrs), **Coimbatore** 205 km (5½ hrs), **Kumbakonam** 92 km, **Madurai** 161 km (3 hrs), **Palani** 152 km (3½ hrs), **Thanjavur** (1½ hrs). Also 2 to **Kanniyakumari** (9 hrs), **Kodai** (5½ hrs) and **Tirupati** (9½ hrs).

Taxi

Unmetered taxis, and tourist taxis from **Kavria Travels**, Hotel Sangam, Collector's Office Rd, T0431-246 4480. Cycle-rickshaws and auto-rickshaws are best avoided.

Train

Enquiries, T131. **Bengaluru (Bangalore)**: *Mayiladuturai Mysore Exp 16232*, 2040, 9½ hrs, continues to **Mysore**, 3¼ hrs. **Chennai**: several throughout the day, including *Pallavan Exp 12606*, 0630, 5½ hrs; *Vaigai Exp 12636*, 0850, 5¼ hrs; all go via Villupuram (for Pondicherry), 3 hrs. **Kollam**: *Nagore-Quilon Exp 16361*, 1615, 12½ hrs. **Madurai**: *Vaigai Exp 12635*, 1745, 2¾ hrs.

Thanjavur *p915, map p916*

Bus

Most long-distance buses use the **New Bus Stand**, T04362-230950, 4 km south of town off Trichy Rd. Daily services to **Chennai** (8 hrs), **Chidambaram** (4 hrs), **Kumbakonam** (1 hr), **Madurai** (3½ hrs), **Pondicherry** (6 hrs), **Tirupathi**, **Tiruchirappalli** (1½ hrs). Also to **Vedaranyam** (100 km) for Point Calimere, about hourly, 4-4½ hrs. Buses to Kumbakonam, and the odd one to Chennai and Pondicherry, also leave from the **State Bus Stand** on South Rampart St.

Taxi

Taxis wait at the railway station and along South Rampart St, but drivers quote high rates, eg Pondicherry Rs 3500, Madurai Rs 2500, Chidambaram Rs 2000.

Train

Reservations, T04362-231131, Mon-Sat 0800-1400, 1500-1700; Sun 0800-1400. **Bengaluru (Bangalore)**: *Mayiladuturai Mysore Exp 16231*, 1915, 11½ hrs, continues to **Mysore**, 3¼ hrs. **Chennai (ME)**: *Rockfort Exp 16878*, 2030, 9 hrs. **Tiruchirappalli**: several fast passenger trains throughout the day.

Around Thanjavur *p917*

Point Calimere (Kodikkarai)

Bus Buses via Vedaranyam, which has services to/from **Thanjavur**, **Tiruchirappalli**, **Nagapattinam**, **Chennai**, etc. From Thanjavur buses leave the **New Bus Stand**

for **Vedaranyam** (100 km) hourly (4-4½ hrs); buses and vans from there to **Kodikkarai** (11 km) which take about 30 mins. Avoid being dropped at 'Sri Rama's Feet' on the way, near a shrine that is of no special interest.

Kumbakonam *p918, map p918*

Car hire Half day for excursions, Rs 400.

Bus TN Govt Express buses to **Chennai**, *No 305*, several daily (7½ hrs); half hourly to **Thanjavur**. The railway station is 2 km from town centre. Trains to **Chennai** (**Egmore**), 1010-2110, change at Tambaram (8½-9 hrs), **Chidambaram** (2 hrs), **Thanjavur** (50 mins) and **Tiruchirappalli**, 0600-1555 (2½ hrs).

Gangaikondacholapuram *p920*

Bus Frequent buses shuttle back and forth from Kumbakonam, and a few buses between **Trichy** and **Chidambaram** also stop here.

Chidambaram *p920, map p921*

Bus The bus station is chaotic with daily services to **Chennai**, **Madurai**, **Thanjavur**, and to **Karaikal** (2 hrs), **Nagapattinam** and **Pondicherry** (2 hrs).

Train Reservations T04144-222298, Mon-Sat 0800-1200, 1400-1700; Sun 0800-1400. **Chennai** (**E**) *Cholan Exp 16854*, 1200, 6 hrs. **Rameswaram**: *Rameshwaram Exp 16701*, 0130, 10½ hrs, via **Chettinad** (6 hrs). **Tiruchirappali**: *Cholan Exp 16853*, 1255, 3½ hrs, via **Kumbakonam**, 1½ hrs, and **Thanjavur**, 2 hrs.

Directory

Tiruchirappalli *p913, map p914*

Banks Lots of ATMs around the bus stands. Exchange is available at Western Union money transfer in Jenne Plaza, Cantonment. Mon-Sat 0900-1730. Quick; good rates. **Internet** **Mas Media**, Main Rd, 6 terminals; **Central Telegraph Office**, Permanent Rd.

Thanjavur *p915, map p916*

Banks ATMs at the station, along South Rampart St, and opposite the tourist office on Gandhiji Rd. Canara Bank, South Main St, changes TCs. **Medical services** **Govt Hospital**, Hospital Rd, south of the old town. **Post** Head Post and Telegraph Office are off the Railway Station Rd. **Useful contacts** **Police**, south of the Big Temple between the canal and the railway, T04362-232 200.

Kumbakonam *p918, map p918*

Banks Changing money is difficult. **State Bank of India**, TSR Big St. **Internet** End of Kamaraj Rd, close to clock tower. **Post** Near Mahamakam Tank.

Chidambaram *p920, map p921*

Banks Changing money can be difficult. **City Union Bank**, West Car St has exchange facilities. **Indian Bank**, 64 South Car St. **Post** Head Post Office, North Car St.

Tamil's hill stations

The Tamil ghats were once shared between shola forest and tribal peoples. But the British, limp from the heat of the plains, invested in expeditions up the mountains and before long had planted eucalyptus, established elite members' clubs and substituted jackals for foxes in their pursuit of the hunt. Don't expect to find the sheer awe-inspiring grandeur of the Himalaya, but there is a charm to these hills where neatly pleated, green tea plantations run like contour lines about the ghats' girth, bringing the promise of a restorative chill and walking tracks where the air comes cut with the smell of eucalyptus. ▸▸ *For listings, see pages 936-945.*

Ins and outs

The northern Nilgiris or the more southerly Palani hills offer rival opportunities for high-altitude stopovers on the route between Tamil Nadu, Karnataka and Kerala. The most visited towns of Ooty and Kodai both have their staunch fan bases – Ooty tends to attract nostalgic British and rail enthusiasts, while Kody gets the American vote, thanks in part to its international schools. Both are well connected by road: Kody is best approached from Madurai; Ooty makes a good bridge to Kerala from Mysore or Tamil's more northern temple towns. The famous narrow-gauge rack-and-pinion railway is most dramatic between Coonoor and Mettupalayam, which in turn has trains from Coimbatore and Chennai. The roads worsen dramatically when you cross the Tamil border from Kerala, reflecting the different levels of affluence between the two states. ▸▸ *See Transport, page 942.*

Udhagamandalam (Ooty) → *For listings, see pages 936-945. Colour map 7, B3.*

Ooty has been celebrated for rolling hills covered in pine and eucalyptus forests and coffee and tea plantations since the first British planters arrived in 1818. A Government House was built, and the British lifestyle developed with cottages and clubs – tennis, golf, riding – and tea on the lawn. But the town is no longer the haven it once was; the centre is heavily built up and can be downright unpleasant in the holiday months of April to June, and again around October. It's best to stay either in the grand ruins of colonial quarters on the quiet outskirts where it's still possible to steal some serenity or opt instead for the far smaller tea garden town of Coonoor (see page 930), 19 km down mountain. **Tamil Nadu Tourism** ⓘ *Wenlock Rd, T0423-244 3977*, is not very efficient.

Sights → *Phone code: 0423. Population 93,900. Altitude: 2286 m.*

The **Botanical Gardens** ⓘ *0800-1800, Rs 25, camera, Rs 50, video Rs 500, 3 km northeast of railway station*, house more than 1000 varieties of plant, shrub and tree including orchids, ferns, alpines and medicinal plants, but is most fun for watching giant family groups picnicking and gambolling together among beautiful lawns and glass houses. To the east of the garden in a Toda *mund* is the Wood House made of logs. The **Annual Flower Show** is held in the third week of May. The **Rose Garden** ⓘ *750 m from Charing Cross, 0830-1830*, has over 1500 varieties of roses.

Ooty Lake was built in 1825 as a vast irrigation tank and is now more than half overgrown with water hyacinth, though it is still used enthusiastically for boating and **pedalo hire** ⓘ *0900-1800, Rs 60-110 per hr.*

Kandal Cross ⓘ *3 km west of the railway station*, is a Roman Catholic shrine considered the 'Jerusalem of the East'. During the clearing of the area to make way for a graveyard in 1927, an enormous 4-m-high boulder was found and a cross was erected. Now a relic of the True Cross brought to India by an Apostolic delegate is shown to pilgrims every day. The annual feast is in May.

St Stephen's Church was Ooty's first church, built in the 1820s. Much of the wood is said to be from Tipu Sultan's Lal Bagh Palace in Srirangapatnam. The inside of the church and the graveyard at the rear are worth seeing.

Dodabetta ⓘ *1000-1500, buses from Ooty, autos and taxis (Rs 200 round trip) go to the summit,* is 10 km east of the railway station off the Kotagiri road. Reaching 2638 m, the 'big mountain' is the second highest in the Western Ghats, sheltering Coonoor from the southwest monsoons when Ooty gets heavy rains. The top is often shrouded in mist. There is a viewing platform at the summit. The telescope isn't worth even the nominal Rs 2 fee.

Walks and hikes around Ooty

Hiking or simply walking is excellent in the Nilgiris. It is undisturbed, quiet and interesting. Climbing Dodabetta or Mukurti is hardly a challenge but the longer walks through the *sholas* are best undertaken with a guide. It is possible to see characteristic features of Toda settlements such as *munds* and *boas*, see page 863.

Dodabetta-Snowdon-Ooty walk starts at Dodabetta Junction directly opposite the 3 km road to the summit. It is a pleasant path that curves gently downhill through a variety of woodland

Udhagamandalam (Ooty)

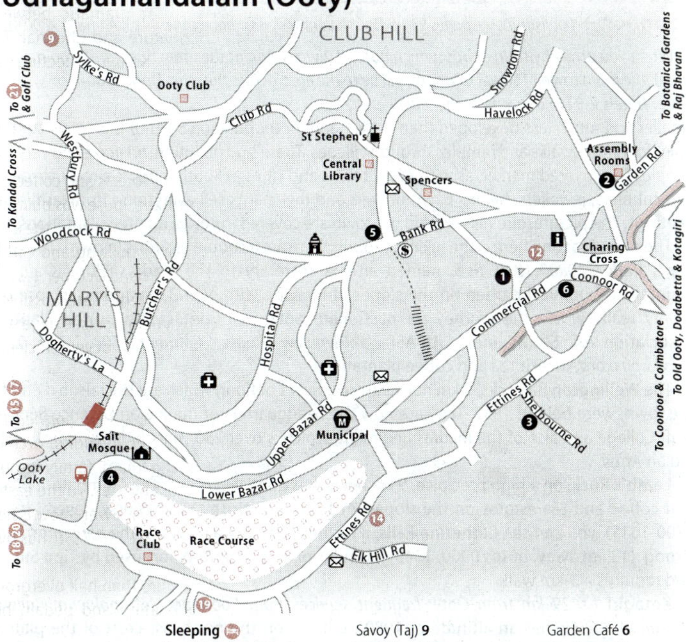

Sleeping
Fernhills Palace **20**
Glyngarth Heritage **21**
Lakeview **17**
Nilgiri Woodlands **19**
Reflections Guest House **15**
Regency Villa **18**
Savoy (Taj) **9**
Tamil Nadu **12**
YWCA Anandagiri **14**

Eating
Blue Hills **1**
Chandan Vegetarian **6**
Garden Café **6**
Hot Breads **2**
Sharma Bhojanalaya **4**
Shinkow's **5**
Pavilion **3**

N
300 metres
300 yards

(mainly eucalyptus and conifers) back to Ooty and doesn't take more than a couple of hours. For longer treks, contact **Nilgiris Trekking Association** ⓘ *Kavitha Nilayam, 31-D Bank Rd, or R Seniappan, 137 Upper Bazar, T0423-244 4449, sehi appan@yahoo.com.*

Mukurti Peak ⓘ *buses from Ooty every 30 mins from 0630 or you can take a tour (see page 941), book early as they are popular,* is 36 km away, off the Gudalur road. After 26 km you reach the 6-km-long Mukurti Lake. Mukurti Peak (the name suggests that someone thought it resembled a severed nose), not an easy climb, is to the west. The Todas believe that the souls of the dead and the sacrificed buffaloes leap to the next world from this sacred peak. It is an excellent place to escape for walking, to view the occasional wildlife, to go fishing at the lake or to go boating.

Avalanche ⓘ *24 km from town, buses from Ooty, 1110,* a valley, is a beautiful part of the *shola*, with plenty of rhododendrons, magnolias and orchids and a trout stream running through it, and is excellent for walking. The **Forestry Department Guest House** is clean and has good food. Contact the **Wildlife Warden** ⓘ *1st floor, Mahalingam Building, Ooty T0423-244098.*

The **River Pykara** ⓘ *19 km from Ooty, several buses 0630-2030, or take a car or bicycle,* has a dam and power plant. There is breathtaking scenery. The **waterfalls**, about 6 km from the bridge on the main road, are best in July though it is very wet then, but they are also worth visiting from August to December.

Coonoor

→ *For listings, see pages 936-945. Colour map 7, B3.* *Phone code: 0423. Altitude: 1800 m.*

ⓘ *When you arrive by train or bus (which doesn't always stop at the main bus stand if going on to Ooty), the main town of Lower Coonoor will be to the east, across the river. Upper Coonoor, with the better hotels 2-3 km away, is further east.*

Smaller and much less developed than Ooty, Coonoor (population 50,100) is an ideal starting point for nature walks and rambles through villages. There's no pollution, no noise and very few people. The covered market, as with many towns and cities in South India, is almost medieval and cobblers, jewellers, tailors, pawn brokers and merchants sell everything from jasmine to beetroot. The picturesque hills around the town are covered in coffee and tea plantations.

The real attraction here is the hiking, though there are a couple of sights in town. The large **Sim's Park** ⓘ *0800-1830, Rs 5,* named after a secretary to the Madras Club, is a well-maintained botanical garden on the slopes of a ravine with over 330 varieties of rose but is only really worth the journey for passionate botanists. Contact the **United Planters' Association of South India (UPASI)** ⓘ *Glenview House, Coonoor, T0423-223 0270, www.upasi.org,* to visit tea and coffee plantations.

The **Wellington Barracks**, 3 km northeast of Lower Coonoor, which are the raison d'être for the town, were built in 1852. They are now the headquarters of the Indian Defence Services Staff College and also of the Madras Regiment, which is over 250 years old, the oldest in the Indian Army.

Lamb's Rock, on a high precipice, 9 km away, has good views over the Coimbatore plains and coffee and tea estates on the slopes. At **Dolphin's Nose** (12 km away, several buses 0700-1615), you can see **Catherine Falls**, a further 10 km away (best in the early morning). **Droog** (13 km away, buses 0900, 1345) has ruins of a 16th-century fort used by Tipu Sultan, and requires a 3-km walk.

Kotagiri (ⓘ *29 km from Ooty, frequent services from Coonoor, Mettupalayam Railway Station and Ooty,* has an altitude of 1980 m. It sits on the northeast crest of the plateau overlooking the plains. It has a milder climate than Ooty. The name comes from Kotar–Keri, the street of the *Kotas* who were one of the original hill tribes and who have a village to the west of the town. You can visit some scenic spots from here: **St Catherine Falls** (8 km) and **Elk Falls** (7 km), or one of the peaks, **Kodanad Viewpoint** (16 km) – reached through the tea estates or by taking one of the several buses that run from 0610 onwards – or **Rangaswamy Pillar**, an isolated rock, and the conical Rangaswamy Peak.

The Blue Mountain Railway

Ever since 15 June 1899, the narrow gauge steam *Mountain Railway*, in its blue and cream livery, has chugged from Mettupalayam to Ooty via Coonoor, negotiating 16 tunnels and 31 major bridges and climbing from 326 m to 2193 m. This was the location for the railway scenes of the *Marabar Express* in the film *A Passage to India*.

It's a charming 4½-hour (46 km) journey through tea plantations and forest, but – outside first class – be prepared for an amiable Indian holiday- makers' scrum. There are rest stops at Hillgrove (17 km) and Coonoor (27 km).

For enthusiasts, the pricier and more spacious *Heritage Steam Chariot* runs between Ooty and Runneymede picnic area, 23 km away, at weekends (more often in high season). The drawback is that you can be stranded for hours when the engine breaks down; some decide to scramble to the nearest road to flag down a bus.

Mettupalayam and the Nilgiri Ghat Road → *For listings, see pages 936-945.*

The journey up to Coonoor from Mettupalayam is one of the most scenic in South India, affording superb views over the plains below. Between Mettupalayam and the start of the Ghat road, there are magnificent groves of tall, slender areca nut palms. Mettupalayam has become the centre for the areca nut trade as well as producing synthetic gems. The palms are immensely valuable trees: the nut is used across India wrapped in betel vine leaves – two of the essential ingredients of India's universal after-meal digestive, *paan*.

The town is the starting point of the ghat railway line up to Ooty, see box, page 931. If you take the early-morning train you can continue to Mysore by bus from Ooty on the same day, making a very pleasant trip.

Mudumalai Wildlife Sanctuary → *For listings, see pages 936-945. Colour map 7, B3.*

ⓘ *Minibus safaris 0630-0900, 1530-1800, Rs 45, still camera Rs 25, video Rs 150; Reception Range Office, Theppakadu, T0423-252 6235, open 0630-1800, is where buses between Mysore and Ooty stop. There is a Ranger Office at Kargudi. The best time to visit is Sep-Dec and Mar-May when the undergrowth dies down and it's easier to see animals, especially at dawn when they're on the move. Forest fires can close the park temporarily during Feb-Apr.*

The sanctuary adjoins Bandipur National Park (see page 1067) beyond the Moyar River, its hills (885-1000 m), ravines, flats and valleys being an extension of the same environment. The park is one of the more popular and is now trying to limit numbers of visitors to reduce disturbance to the elephants.

There are large herds of elephant, gaur, sambar, barking deer, wild dog, Nilgiri langur, bonnet monkey, wild boar, four-horned antelope and the rarer tiger and leopard, as well as smaller mammals and many birds and reptiles. **Elephant Camp**, south of Theppakadu, open 0700-0800 and 1600-1700, tames wild elephants. Some are bred in captivity and trained to work for the timber industry. You can watch the elephants being fed in the late afternoon, learn about each individual elephant's diet and the specially prepared 'cakes' of food.

You can hire a jeep for about Rs 10 per km but must be accompanied by a guide. Most night safaris are best avoided. Elephant rides from 0700-0830 and 1530-1700 (Rs 50 per person for 30 minutes); check timing and book in advance in Theppakadu or with the Wildlife Warden, Mount Stuart Hill, Ooty, T0423-244 4098. They can be fun even though you may not see much wildlife. There are *machans* near waterholes and salt licks and along the Moyar River. With patience you can see a lot, especially rare and beautiful birds. Treks and jeep rides in the remoter parts of the forest with guides can be arranged from some lodges, including **Jungle**

Retreat (see page 937). You can spend a day climbing the hill and bathe at the impressive waterfalls. The core area is not open to visitors.

Coimbatore and the Nilgiri Hills → *For listings, see pages 936-945. Colour map 7, B3.*

Coimbatore → *Phone code: 0422. Population: 923,000.*

As one of South India's most important industrial cities since the 1930s development of hydroelectricity from the Pykara Falls, Coimbatore holds scant charm to warrant more than a pit stop. It was once the fulcrum of tussles between Tamilian, Mysorean and Keralite coastal rulers (the word *palayam* crops up tellingly often in Coimbatore – its translation being 'encampment') and sadly violence continues today. You are likely to stay here only if fascinated by the cotton trade or stuck for an onward bus or train.

Coimbatore's nickname is 'India's Manchester', because it is the subcontinent's capital of cotton weaving – skyscrapers called things like 'Viscose Towers' aren't uncommon.

Salem → *Colour map 7, B4. Phone code: 0427. Population: 693,200.*

Salem, an important transport junction, is surrounded by hills: the Shevaroy and Nagaramalai Hills to the north and the Jarugumalai Hills to the southeast. It is a busy, rapidly growing industrial town – particularly for textiles and metal-based industries – with modern shopping centres. The old town is on the east bank of the River Manimutheru. Each evening around Bazar Street you can see cotton carpets being made. The **cemetery**, next to the Collector's office, has some interesting tombstones. To the southeast of the town on a ridge of the Jarugumalai Hills is a highly visible *Naman* painted in *chunam* and ochre. On the nearby hill the temple (1919) is particularly sacred to the weavers' community. Some 600 steps lead up to excellent views over the town.

Yercaud and the Shevaroy Hills → *Phone code: 04281. Altitude: 1515 m.*

The beautiful drive up the steep and sharply winding ghat road from Salem quickly brings a sharp freshness to the air as it climbs to over 1500 m. The minor resort has a small artificial lake and Anna Park nearby. Some attractive though unmarked walks start here. In May there is a special festival focused on the **Shevaroyan Temple**, on top of the third highest peak in the hill range. Many tribal people take part but access is only possible on foot. Ask for details in the **Tamil Nadu Tourist Office** in Chennai, see page 867. There's also a tourist information office in the Tamil Nadu hotel in town.

Just outside town is **Lady's Seat**, overlooking the ghat road, which has wonderful views across the Salem plains. Near the old Norton Bungalow on the Shevaroyan Temple Road is another well-known local spot, **Bear's Cave**. Formed by two huge boulders, it is occupied by huge colonies of bats. The whole area is full of botanical interest. There is an orchidarium-cum-nursery and a horticultural research station.

Kodaikkanal and the Palani Hills → *For listings, see pages 936-945. Colour map 7, C4.*

The climb up the Palanis starts 47 km before Kodaikkanal (Kodai) and is one of the most rapid ascents anywhere across the ghats. The views are stunning. In the lower reaches of the climb you look down over the Kambam Valley, the Vaigai Lake and across to the Varushanad Hills beyond, while higher up the scene is dominated by the sawn-off pyramid of Perumal Malai. Set around a small artificial lake, the town has crisply fresh air, even at the height of summer, and the beautiful scent of pine and eucalyptus make it a popular retreat from the southern plains. Today Kodai is a fast growing resort, yet it retains a relatively low-key air that many feel gives it an edge over Ooty.

Ins and outs → *Phone code: 04542. Population: 32,900. Altitude: 2343 m.*
Buses make the long climb from Madurai and other cities to the Central Bus Stand, which is within easy walking distance from most hotels. The nearest train station is Kodai Road. Kodai is small enough to walk around, though for some of the sights it is worth getting an unmetered taxi. There's a **Tamil Nadu tourist office** ⓘ *Hospital Rd next to Bus Stand, T04542-241675, 1000-1745 except holidays*, with helpful staff and maps available. ▸▸ *See Transport, page 944.*

Background
The **Palani Hills** were first surveyed by British administrators in 1821, but the surveyor's report was not published until 1837, 10 years after Ooty had become the official sanatorium for the British in South India. A proposal to build a sanatorium was made in 1861-1862 by Colonel Hamilton, who noted the extremely healthy climate and the lack of disease, but the sanatorium

Kodaikkanal

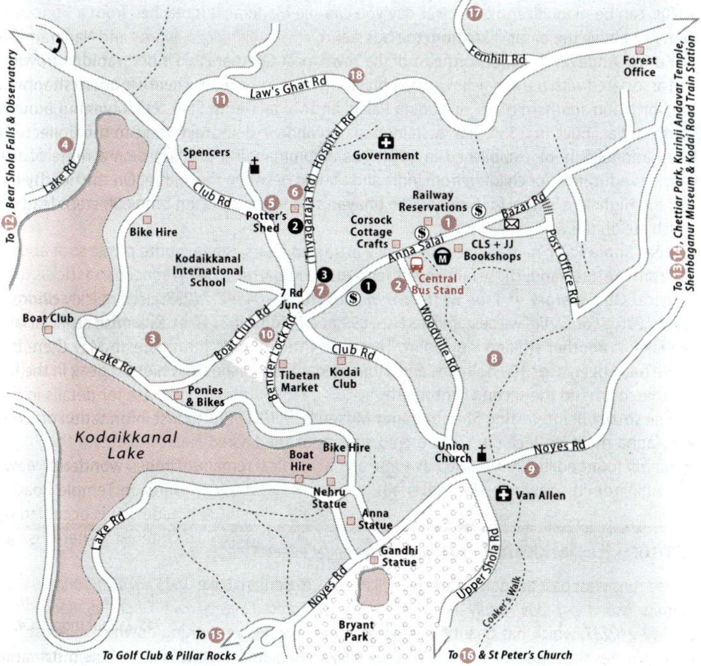

N

100 metres
100 yards

Sleeping
Anjay 1
Bala 2
Bison Wells 12
Carlton 3
Elephant Valley 13
Ferncroft 14
Garden Manor 4
Green Acres 15
Greenlands 16
Hilltop Towers 5
J's Heritage 6
Jewel 7
Kodai Plaza 8
Kodai Resort 9
Paradise Inn 18
RR Residency 10
Vignesh 11
Villa Retreat 9
Youth Hostel 17

Eating
Pastry Corner 1
Silver Inn 2
Tava 3

was never built because the site was so inaccessible. So it was that Kodaikkanal became the first hill station in India to be set up not by heat-sick Britons but by American missionaries.

The American Mission in Madurai, established in 1834, had lost six of their early missionaries within a decade. The missionaries had been eyeing a site in the Sirumalai Hills, at around 1300 m, but while these were high enough to offer respite from the heat of the plains they were still prone to malaria. Isolated Kodai, almost 1000 m higher, proved to be the ticket, and the first two bungalows were built by June 1845. Kodai's big transformation came at the turn of the 20th century with the arrival of the car and the bus. In 1905 it was possible to do the whole journey from Kodai Road station to Kodai within the hours of daylight. The present road, up Law's Ghat, was opened to traffic in 1916.

Sights

Kodaikkanal Lake covers 24 ha in a star shape surrounded by wooded slopes. The walk around the lake takes about one hour, boating is popular and you can fish (with permission), although the water is polluted. The view over the plains from **Coaker's Walk**, built by Lieutenant Coaker in the 1870s, can be magnificent; on a clear day you can see Madurai. It is reached from a signposted path just above the bazar, 1 km from the bus stand.

Kurinji Andavar Temple, northeast of the town, past Chettiar Park, is dedicated to Murugan and associated with the *kurinji* flower that blossoms once in 12 years. There are excellent views of the north and southern plains, including Palani and Vaigai Dams. **St Peter's Church** (Church of South India), built in 1884, has a stained-glass window dedicated to Bishop Caldwell. The **International School**, established in 1901, has a commanding position on the lakeside, and provides education for children from India and abroad between the ages of five and 18. There is also the **Highclere School for Girls** and the **Bhavan's Gandhi Vidyasram School**, founded in 1983, which are on the way to Pillar Rocks.

Bear Shola Falls, named because it once attracted bears, is a favourite picnic spot about 2 km from the bus stand. These falls and others around Kodai have been reduced to a trickle. **Solar Physical Observatory** ⓘ *4 km west from the bus stand, T04542-240588, during the season, Fri 1000-1230, 1900-2100*, was established in 1899 at a height of 2347 m. **Pillar Rocks**, 7 km from the lake, is another striking viewpoint. There are three granite formations over 120 m high. There have been over 100 dolmens and other megalithic remains discovered in the Palanis, all datable to around the second century AD.

The small but interesting **Shenbaganur Museum** ⓘ *1000-1130, 1500-1700*, is the local flora and fauna museum including 300 orchid species at the Sacred Heart College, a theological seminary founded in 1895. It also has some archaeological remains. There is an attractive walk downhill from the town passing waterfalls.

Around Kodaikkanal

→ *For listings, see pages 936-945.*

A road runs west past the golf course and Pillar Rocks to **Berijam Lake** ⓘ *15 km away, only 10 visitor permits issued per day, apply at 1000 to District Forest Office, Law's Ghat Rd, Kodaikkanal, T04542-240287*, which has beautiful views over the lake before running down to it. Apart from timber lorries the road is little used. You can walk to Berijam in about four hours and stay at the adequate **Forest Rest House**, Rs 50. There is a restaurant but no shop here.

You can continue the next day, by a short cut to **Top Station** in Kerala in five to six hours, where there is a **Forest Hut** and shops and tea stalls selling snacks. There are then buses to **Munnar**, 41 km away.

The ghat road to **Palani** passes through smallholdings of coffee, oranges and bananas. Inter-planting of crops such as pepper is further increasing the yields from what can be highly productive land, even on steep slopes. The shrine to **Murugan** (Subrahmanya) on top of Palani (or Sivagiri) Hill is a very important site of pilgrimage. At full moon in January to

February pilgrims walk from as far afield as Chettinad and Munnar to climb the 659 steps to the shrine. Many carry shoulder poles with elaborate bamboo or wooden structures on each end, living out the myth of Idumban, who carried the twin hills of Sivagiri and Shaktigiri from Mount Kailash to their present locations on either end of a bamboo *kavadi* . Around the temple, Palani presents a chaotic but compelling pastiche of pilgrim fervour, religious souvenir shopping and decaying flower garlands.

Pollachi, in a key strategic position on the east to west crossing of the Ghats through the Palakkad Gap, has been an important trading centre for over 2000 years, as witnessed by the finds of Roman silver coins bearing the heads of the emperors Augustus and Tiberias. Today its main appeal is as the gateway to the small but very attractive Anamalai (Indira Gandhi) National Park (see below).

Anamalai (Indira Gandhi) Wildlife Sanctuary

ⓘ *0600-1800, Rs 15, camera Rs 25, video Rs 150; best time to visit Dec-Jun, closed mid Feb to mid Apr, avoid Sun. Reception and Information Centre at Top Slip organizes bus rides, elephant safaris and trekking guides. Day permits from entrance gate at Sethumadai; for overnight stays advance written permission is needed from Wildlife Warden, 1176 Meenakalai Salai, Pollachi, T04259-225356 (1.5 km out of town on road towards Top Slip).*

This beautiful, unspoilt park covering 960 sq km of grassland, rainforest and mountain shola forest, is rarely visited except by Indian day trippers. Wildlife includes Nilgiri langur, lion-tailed macaque, elephant, *gaur*, tiger, panther, sloth, wild boar, birds – including pied hornbill, drongo, red whiskered bulbul, black-headed oriole – and a large number of crocodiles in the Amaravathi reservoir. There is an elephant camp, claimed to be the largest in Asia, reached by a two- to three-hour minibus ride through the forest (0615, 1130 and 1515, Rs 25), and short elephant rides can be arranged. Birdwatching is good from Kariam Shola watchtower, 2 km from Topslip.

There are some **trekking** routes that vary from easy treks to Pandaravara (8 km), Kozhikamuthi (12 km) and Perunkundru peak (32 km), which is demanding. Permits can be obtained from the Range Officer at Top Slip, Rs 150-300 per person. Private guides charge upwards of Rs 100 for a three-hour trek.

Dindigul

→ *For listings, see pages 936-945.*

Now a large market town, Dindigul, north of Madurai, commands a strategic gap between the **Sirumalai Hills** to its east and the **Palani Hills** to the west. The market handles the produce of the Sirumalai Hills, including a renowned local variety of banana. Dindigul is particularly known for its cheroots.

The massive granite rock and **fort** ⓘ *2 km west of the bus stand, 0730-1730, foreigners Rs 100, Indians Rs 5, autos Rs 20*, towers over 90 m above the plain. The Mysore army captured it in 1745 and Haidar Ali was appointed governor in 1755. It was ceded to the British under the Treaty of Seringapatam. There are magnificent views of the town, valley and hills on either side from the top of the rock fort. **Our Lady of Dolours Church**, one of several churches in the town, is over 250 years old and was rebuilt in 1970. The Old City is interesting to walk around; you can walk up to the fort from there. The station is 2 km south of the bus stand that has cheap lodges nearby.

Tamil's hill stations listings

For Sleeping and Eating price codes and other relevant information, see Essentials pages 38-42.

Sleeping

Udhagamandalam (Ooty) *p928, map p929*

Rates quoted are for the high season. Good discounts Jul-Mar except during Puja and Christmas (add 30% tax in upper categories). Winter nights can be bitterly cold and hotel fireplaces are often inadequate. Avoid the budget accommodation round Commercial Rd and Ettines Rd, particularly if you are a woman travelling alone.

LL-L Fernhills Palace, Fernhill Post, T0423-244 3910, www.fernhillspalace.com. After years of stop-start renovation, Wadiyar, the current Mysore Maharaja has opened his ancestral palace as a luxury heritage hotel. It offers 30 suites, with teak furniture, wooden panelling, fireplaces and jacuzzis. Spa, gym, plus correspondingly high price tags.

LL-L Savoy (Taj), 77 Sylkes Rd, T0423-244 4142, www.tajhotels.com. Worth visiting for its interesting history and lovely gardens. 40 well-maintained rooms with huge wooden doors and separate dressing areas.

B-C Hotel Regency Villa, Fernhill Post, T0423-244 2555, regency@sancharnet.in. The Maharaja of Mysore's staff had some of the best sunset views of the blue hills from their bungalows. Today carpets are mismatched, paint is peeling, and the cheaper rooms are small and musty, but despite that the **Regency**, with its rows of colonial photographs, reeks of character too. Log fire fuel costs extra.

C Glyngarth Villa, Golf Club Rd, Fingerpost (2 km from centre), T0423-244 5754, www.glyngarthvilla.com. Just 5 huge double rooms with period furniture plus original fittings including all-teak floors and fireplaces in a Raj building – complete with metal roof – dating from 1853. Modern bathrooms, meals made from fresh garden produce, large grounds, clean, excellent service, tremendously characterful (too much for some) good value. Walking distance to golf course. Recommended.

C-D Hotel Lakeview, West Lake Rd, T0423-244 3580, www.lakeview.com. An Indian hill station version of Butlins, with 115 big rooms in rows of pinkish bungalows boasting fireplaces, TV and matching furniture. Lawns to sit out on with bus loads of domestic tourists.

C-D The Nilgiri Woodlands, Race Course Rd, T0423-244 2551, nilgiris_woodlands@yahoo.com. 22 rooms ranging from paint-peeling doubles to spacious cottages. Shared veranda outside racecourse-facing rooms that give onto a garden and the pink/green/blue bungalows of Ooty central. Quiet and spacious rooms tucked round the back (without views) are best value.

D Tamil Nadu (TTDC), Charing Cross, up the steps by the tourist office, T0423-244 4378. Spotless rooms and penthouse with good views, restaurant, bar, exchange, pleasant hotel tucked away. Avoid the food.

D YWCA Anandagiri, Ettines Rd, T0423-244 2218, www.ywcaagooty.com. Basic, a little institutional, 32 rooms set around large complex screened from town by pine trees, with nice sitting rooms and dining hall, potted geraniums dotted around. Pleasant, large cottages, dorm beds from Rs 90.

D-E Reflections Guest House, North Lake Rd, T0423-244 3834. Clean, homely, quiet, with good views of the lake, 9 rooms (cheaper dorm beds), pleasant dining and sitting room serving good food, friendly owners. Rs 50 for wood for the fire or to use the stove for your own cooking, dodgy plumbing, can get chilly, restricted hot water.

Coonoor *p930*

Most hotels are 3-5 km from the station and bus stand.

L-AL Gateway Hotel, Church Rd, Upper Coonoor, T0423-223 0021, www.tajhotels.com. 32 rooms, spacious cottage style and homely (**A** off season), many with open fires, very well kept, good dining room though service can be slow, beautiful gardens, yoga studio, treadmill, table tennis, tennis, Ayurvedic centre, but no pool. Wood-panelled high-ceilinged bar, **The Hampton**, 1130-1500, 1830-2200. Lunch 1230-1500, dinner 1930-2230.

A The Tryst, Carolina Tea Estate, Coonoor, T0423-220 7057, www.trystindia.com. The shelves at this homestay groan under years of hoarding. 5 double rooms with well-stocked library, snooker table, games galore and gym, plus a huge cottage that sleeps 10. Unexpected and in an outstanding location away from all other accommodation cradled in the nape of a rolling tea estate. Excellent walking. Book in advance.

E Tamil Nadu (TTDC), Ooty Rd, Mt Pleasant (1 km north of station), T0423-223 2813. Simple rooms, TV, restaurant, bar and dorm.

E 'Wyoming' Holiday Home (YWCA), near Hospital, Upper Coonoor (auto from bus stand Rs 25), T0423-223 4426. Set in a house with character and idyllic views, 8 large rooms and 2 dorms (8-bedded), excellent food (no alcohol) but some warn you should check bill and watch out for the neurotic labrador who is known to bark through the night. Garden, friendly, helpful, popular. Manager qualified in alternative therapies (runs clinic and courses). Book ahead.

F Blue Star, Kotagiri, next to bus station. Rooms with shower and toilet in modern building.

Mettupalayam *p931*

D Saravana Bhavan, out of town on Ooty road near gates to Black Thunder Water theme park, T04254-221728. Newish and finding its feet.

E-F Bharath Bharan, 200 m from railway station, T04254-222126. Very basic, some with bath and a/c, could be cleaner, quiet surroundings.

F Surya International, 345 Ooty Main Rd, T04254-223502, fairly clean rooms (Rs 150), rooftop restaurant, often empty, quiet, but characterless.

Mudumalai Wildlife Sanctuary *p931*

Advance booking is essential especially during the season and at weekends. Accommodation is better near Masinagudi which also has restaurants and shops but there is some in Bokkapuram, 3 km further south. Ask private lodges for pickup if arriving by bus at Theppakadu.

AL-E Jungle Retreat, Bokkapuram, T0423-252 6469, www.jungleretreat.com. 5 large rooms and 7 cottages with modern baths, private terrace, superb views, plus dorm (Rs 525), "wonderful quiet place", friendly relaxed owners (Mr and Mrs Mathias), high standards, TV, hot water, etc, good treks with local guides, elephant rides, excellent swimming pool, somewhat pricey food (choice of Indian and Western). TCs accepted. Highly recommended.

A Bamboo Banks Farm Guest House, Masinagudi, T0423-252 6211, www.bamboobanks.in. 6 clean rooms, 4 in cottages in a fine setting, attractive garden, good food, birdwatching, riding, jeep.

A-B Jungle Hut, near Bokkapuram, T0423-252 6463, www.junglehut.in. In valley, 12 clean, simple rooms with bath in 3 stone cottages plus a few small tents (**C**), good food ("lovely home cooking"), pool, jeep hire, game viewing and treks, very friendly welcome. Recommended.

B Blue Valley Resorts, Bokkapuram, T0423-252 6244, www.bluevalleyjungleresorts.com. Scenic location, 8 comfortable huts (**C** suites), restaurants, wildlife tours, good value 2-night packages.

B New Mountania, Masinagudi, T0423-252 6267, www.newmountania.com. Rooms in cottages (prices vary), "nice but a bit overpriced", restaurant, jeep tour to waterfalls, easy animal spotting (evening better than morning).

C-D Monarch Safari Park, Bokkapuram, on a hill side, T0423-252 6250. Large grounds, with 14 rooms in twin *machan* huts on stilts with bath (but rats may enter at night), open-sided restaurant, cycles, birdwatching, good riding (Rs 150 per hr), some sports facilities, meditation centre, "lovely spot", management a bit slack but friendly, if slow, service.

D Forest Hills Farm, 300 m from **Jungle Hut**, T0423-252 6216, www.foresthillsindia.com. Friendly, 6 modern rooms with bath. Good views, good food, game viewing. Recommended.

E Tamil Nadu (TTDC hostel), Theppakadu, T0423-252 6249. 3 rooms, 24 beds in dorm (Rs 45), restaurant, van for viewing.

F-G Forest Department Huts, reserve in advance through Wildlife Warden, Mudumalai WLS, Mt Stuart Hill, Ooty, T0423-244 4098 or Reception Range Officer, Theppakadu, T0423-252 6235. Most have caretakers who can arrange food.

Abhayaranyam Rest House, Kargudi. 2 rooms.

Abhayaranyam Annexe, Kargudi. 2 rooms. Recommended.

Minivet and **Morgan**, Kargudi. Dorm, 8 and 12 beds.

Peacock, Kargudi. 50-bed dorm, excellent food.

Rest House and **Annexe**, Kargudi. Ask for deluxe rooms.

Log House, Masinagudi, 5 rooms.
Rest House, Masinagudi, 3 rooms.

Coimbatore *p932*

A Heritage Inn, 38 Sivaswamy Rd, T0422- 223 1451, www.hotelheritageinn.in. Standard hotel with good restaurants, internet, excellent service, 63 modern, a/c rooms, good value.
B Sabari Nest, 739-A Avanashi Rd, 2 km from railway, T0422-450 5500, www.sabarihotels.com. 38 a/c rooms, some small, restaurant, bar, amazing supermarket downstairs (for Western snacks and last stop for supplies), business facilities, roof garden. Recommended.
B-C City Tower, Sivaswamy Rd (just off Dr Nanjappa Rd), Gandhipuram, near bus stand, T0422-223 0641, www.hotelcitytower.com. 91 excellent redecorated rooms, some a/c, small balconies, 2 restaurants (rooftop tandoori), no alcohol, superb service. Recommended.
D-F Channma International, 18/109 Big Bazar St, T0422-239 6631. Oldish art deco-style hotel, 36 spacious clean rooms, tiny windows, restaurant, internet, health club and pool next door.
E-F KK Residency, 7 Shastri Rd, by Central Bus Stand, Ramnagar, T0422-223 2433. 42 smallish but clean rooms, 6 a/c, good condition, restaurant, friendly service. Recommended.
E-F Meena, 109 Kalingarayar St, T0422-223 5420. Small family hotel with 30 clean and pleasant rooms, vegetarian restaurant.

Salem *p932*

Choose a room away from the road if possible.
C Salem Castle, A-4 Bharati St, Swarnapuri, 4 km from railway station, T0427-244 8702. Rather brash modern hotel with 64 comfortable, very clean a/c rooms. Restaurants (good Chinese but expensive, the rest are Indian-style), coffee shop, bar, exchange, pool.
D-E City View, Omalur Main Rd, T0427-233 4232. Rooms with bath, some clean, strong a/c, meals, travel. **Shree Saravanabhavan** in the same block does good south Indian veg.
D-E Ganesh Mahal, 323 Omalur Rd, T0427-233 2820, www.ganeshmahal.com. Modern and comfortable, 45 pleasant rooms, TV, good restaurant, bar.
D-E Raj Castle, 320 Omalur Rd, T0427-233 3532. 21 nicely fitted rooms, 4 a/c, some with balcony, TV, hot water mornings, tourist car.
D-E Selvam, T0427-233 4491. Clean rooms with bath, some a/c, good restaurant.
F Railway Retiring Rooms. Battered but with olde-worlde feel.

Yercaud *p932*

Most hotels offer off-season discounts Jan-Mar, Aug-Dec.
C Sterling Resort, near Lady's Seat, T04281-222700. 59 rooms (few **B** suites), modern, excellent views.
D Shevaroys, Main (Hospital) Rd, near lake, T04281-222288. 32 rooms, 11 **C** cottages with baths, restaurant, bar, good views.
D Tamil Nadu (TTDC), Salem-Yercaud Ghat Rd, near lake, behind Panchayat Office, T04281 - 222273. 12 rooms, restaurant, garden.

Kodaikkanal *p932, map p933*

Room rates are high in Kody compared to the rest of Tamil Nadu, but so are standards of cleanliness, in every price category. Off-season rates are given here: prices rise by 30-100% Apr-Jun and 12.5% tax is charged everywhere. On Anna Salai cheap basic lodges, mostly with shared bathroom, can charge Rs 800 in season
AL Carlton, Boat Club Rd, T04542-240056, carlton@krahejahospitality.com. Fully modernized but colonial-style hotel with 91 excellent rooms, many with private terraces overlooking the lake. Excellent restaurant, billiards, tennis, golf and boating, often full in season. Recommended.
AL-A Elephant Valley, Ganesh Puram village (20 km from Kodai off Palani road), T0413-265 5751, www.elephantvalleyhotel.com. This tranquil eco-resort comprises 13 cute rustic stone cottages (some in converted village houses) dotted across a 30-ha organic farm on either side of a rocky river, visited by wild boar, gaur and elephants (best sightings Apr-Jun). Restaurant serves good food based on home-grown veg and herbs, fantastic salads, plus superb coffee which is grown, roasted and ground entirely on-site. Highly recommended.

AL-D Green Acres, 11/213 Lake Rd, T04542-242384, www.greenacresresort.biz. Well-appointed, clean rooms in pleasant colonial-style home, quiet, peaceful.

B-C Kodai Resort, north end of Coaker's Walk, T04542-240632, www.kodairesort hotel.com. 50 well-furnished 'cottages' with balcony, great views, restaurant. Clean, spacious, quiet setting.

B-D Villa Retreat, Coaker's Walk, T04542-240940, www.villaretreat.com. 8 deluxe rooms in an old house, 3 cottages (open fireplace), rustic, good service. Garden setting, excellent views, clean but overpriced.

C Bison Wells Jungle Lodge, Camp George Observatory, T04542-240566, www.wilderness-explorer.in. A cottage for the nature purist, with no electricity and space for only 3, a whole mountain range away from the rest of the hill station. Jeep transport from Kody arranged on request at extra cost.

C Ferncroft, 17 km from town on Palani Rd, T04542-230242, jfmfernando33@yahoo.com. Simple, rustic lodgings on the ground floor of Tamil-Scots couple Jo and Maureen Fernando's stone built house, set among trees heavy with peaches, passion fruit and avocado. There's a small but comfortable bedroom, a kitchenette and living room with wicker chairs, plus a parcel of lush lawn with beautiful views down the valley. Far from town, but hard to beat for peace and quiet.

C RR Residency, Boathouse Rd, T04542- 244300, residency@rediffmail.com. 7 well- furnished, top-quality rooms in newish hotel, though views are lacking and there's potential olfactory disturbance from adjacent petrol pump. Vegetarian restaurant next door.

C-D Garden Manor, Lake Rd (10-min walk from bus station), T04542-240461. Good location in pleasant gardens overlooking lake, with 7 rooms (including a 4-bed), restaurant with outdoor tables.

C-D J's Heritage, PT Rd, T04542-241323, www.jsheritage.com. 14 clean, comfortably furnished rooms in a quiet spot, friendly and helpful management and a wealth of dining choices nearby.

D Hilltop Towers, Club Rd, T04542-240413, www.hilltopgroup.in. 26 modern, properly cleaned and comfortable rooms, some noise from passing buses and limited hours for hot water, but the management are very obliging and the complex contains a slew of good restaurants. Recommended.

E Bala, 11/49 Woodville Rd, opposite the bus station (entrance tucked away in private courtyard), T04542-241214, www.bala cares.com. Friendly and well-kept hotel, with 57 rooms (ask for one on 2nd or 3rd floor as lower rooms look out on neighbouring walls), good vegetarian restaurant, friendly staff.

E Jewel, 7 Rd Junction, T04542-240518. 9 clean, adequate rooms, 24-hr hot water, friendly, good value.

E Paradise Inn, Laws Ghat Rd, T04542-241075. Now rather faded, but good views, 40 comfortable spacious rooms, restaurant.

E Vignesh, Laws Ghat Rd, near lake, T04542-244348. Old period-style house, 6 spacious rooms (can interconnect), good views, garden setting. Recommended.

E-F Anjay, Anna Salai, T04542-241080, www.hotelanjay.com. 24 adequate rooms with balcony, popular restaurant and ice cream shop downstairs.

F Kodai Plaza, St Anthoia Koil St (walk uphill from bus stand and turn left down steep narrow lane), T04542-240423. The cheapest choice around the bus stand, rooms not the cleanest but survivable, and some have good views of distant peaks framed by fluttering prayer flags.

F Youth Hostel (TTDC), Fernhill Rd, T04542-241336. **D** rooms, dorm beds.

F-G Greenlands, St Mary's Rd, Coaker's Walk end, T04542-240899. Clean, small and friendly budget traveller choice. 15 very basic, clean rooms (jug and bucket of hot water 0700-0900), amazing views. A few newish rooms are less atmospheric but have hot water on tap. Pleasant gardens, 62-bed dorm (Rs 55-65).

Anamalai (Indira Gandhi) Wildlife Sanctuary

p935

There are several Forest Department rest houses scattered around Top Slip and other parts of the sanctuary including Mt Stuart, Varagaliar, Sethumadai and Amaravathinagar. May allow only 1 night's stay. Reservations: District Forest Officer, Coimbatore S Div, 176 Meeanakalai Salai, Pollachi, T04259-225356. The friendly canteen in Top Slip serves good *dosa* and *thalis* for lunch.

E Sakti, 144 Coimbatore Main Rd, T04259-223050, Pollachi. Newish, large and smart, rooms, vegetarian restaurant.

Dindigul *p935*

B Cardamom House, Athoor village, Kamarajar Lakeside, T0451-255 6765, www.cardamomhouse.com. This pretty home of a retired British doctor from Southsea introduces you to Tamil village life in Athoor and is a good bridge for journeys between either Kerala and Tamil Nadu or Trichy and Madurai. Tucked out of the way at the foothills of the Palani hills overlooking the lake, which is rich in birdlife, 7 rooms spread across 3 buildings all with lake views.

B-D Maha Jyothi, Spencer Compound, T0451-243 4313, hotelmahajyothi@rediffmail.com. Range of rooms, a/c, clean, modern, 24-hr check out.

E-G Sukanya Lodge, 43 Thiruvallur Salai (by bus stand), T0451-242 8436. Small, rather dark a/c rooms, but very clean, friendly staff, good value.

F Prakash, 9 Thiruvalluvar Salai, T0451-242 3577. 42 clean, spacious rooms. Recommended.

G Venkateshwar Lodge, near bus stand, T0451-242 5881. Very cheap, 50 rooms, basic, clean, vegetarian restaurant next door.

Eating

Udhagamandalam (Ooty) *p928, map p929*

There are usually bars in larger hotels. **Southern Star** is recommended, but pricey.

TTT Savoy (see Sleeping). Old-world wood-panelled dining hall serving up and good food. Also has bar, café, snooker and table tennis halls.

TT Chandan Vegetarian, Nahar Nilgiris, Charing Cross, T0423-244 2173. 1230-1530, 1900-2230. Roomy restaurant inside the **Nahar** hotel complex serving up vegetarian North Indian and Chinese food.

TT The Pavilion, Fortune Hotel, 500 m from town, Sullivan Court, 123 Shelbourne Rd, T0423-244 1415. In modern hotel, good multi-cuisine plus separate bar.

T Blue Hills, Charing Cross. Good-value Indian and continental, non-vegetarian.

T Garden Café, Nahar Nilgiris, Charing Cross. 0730-2130. Lawn-side coffee shop and snack bar with South Indian menu: *iddli*, *dosa* and *chats* from Rs 30.

T Hot Breads, Charing Cross. Tasty hot dogs, pizzas, etc.

T Hotel Ooty Saravanaa's, 302 Commercial Rd. 0730-1000, 1130-2230. The place for super-cheap south Indian breakfast: large mint green place that does a fast trade in *iddli*, *dosa* and meals.

T Sharma Bhojanalaya 12C Lower Bazar Rd. Gujarati and North Indian food served upstairs in comfortable (padded banquettes) but not aesthetically pleasing venue, overlooks race course, good vegetarian lunch *thali* (Rs 40).

T Shinkow's, 38/83 Commissioner's Rd (near Collector's Office) T0423-244 2811. 1200-1545, 1830-2145. Authentic Chinese, popular, especially late evening. Chicken chilli Rs 120. Tartan tablecloths and fish tank. Highly recommended.

Cafés

Try local institutions **Sugar Daddy** and **King Star** (established in 1942), 1130-2030, for brilliant home-made chocolates such as fruit'n'nut and fudges.

Coonoor *p930*

TT Velan Hotel Ritz, Bedford, T0423-223 0632. 0730-1030, 1230-1530, 1930-2230. Good multi-cuisine restaurant overlooking the Ritz's lawns – don't expect speedy service, though.

T The Only Place, Sim's Park Rd. Simple, homely, good food.

T Sri Lakshmi, next to bus station. Freshly cooked, quality vegetarian; try paneer butter masala and Kashmiri naan.

Mettupalayam *p931*

Karna Hotel in the bus station is good for *dosas*.

Coimbatore *p932*

TTT Cloud Nine, City Tower Hotel (see Sleeping). Excellent views from rooftop of one of city's tallest buildings, good international food (try asparagus soup), buzzing atmosphere especially when it's full of families on Sun evening, pleasant service but slightly puzzling menu.

TT Dakshin, Shree Annapoorna Hotel Complex, 47 East Arokiasamy Rd, RS Puram. International. Very smart, serving good food.

Solai Drive-in, Nehru Stadium, near VOC Park. Chinese, Indian food and good ice creams.
Indian Coffee House, Ramar Koil St. South Indian snacks.
Royal Hindu, opposite Junction station. Indian vegetarian.

Kodaikkanal *p932, map p933*
Carlton Hotel, set in very pleasant grounds overlooking lake and Garden Manor, good for tea and snacks.
Royal Tibet Hotel, J's Heritage Complex, for noodle soup and momos.
Silver Inn, Hospital Rd. Travellers' breakfasts and Indian choices. Popular but slow service.
Tava, Hospital Rd, very good Indian.
Tibetan Brothers Hotel, J's Heritage Complex. 1200-2200 (closed 1600-1730) serves excellent Tibetan, homely atmosphere, good value. Highly recommended.

Bakeries and snacks
Eco-Nut, J's Heritage Complex. Good wholefoods, brown bread, jams, peanut butter, etc (cheese, yoghurts, better and cheaper in dairy across the road).
Hot Breads, J's Heritage Complex. For very good pastries.
Pastry Corner, Anna Salai Bazar. Brown bread, pastries and chocolate brownies, plus a couple of tables out the front.
Philco's Cold Storage, opposite Kodai International School. For home-made chocolate, cakes, frozen foods, delicatessen. Also internet.
Spencer's Supermarket, Club Rd. Wide range of local and foreign products (cheeses).

Dindigul *p935*
Cascade Roof Garden, at Sree Arya Bhavan, 19 KHF Building, near the bus stand. Serves very good vegetarian.
Janakikarm, near new Roman Catholic Church. Don't miss their pizzas, sweets and snacks, surprisingly good value, "*channa samosa* to die for".

Festivals and events

Udhagamandalam (Ooty) *p928, map p929*
Jan **Pongal**.
May The **Annual Flower and Dog Shows** in the Botanical Gardens. **Summer Festival** of cultural with stars from all over India.

Kodaikkanal *p932, map p933*
May **Summer Tourist Festival**: boat race, flower show, dog show, etc.

Shopping

Udhagamandalam (Ooty) *p928, map p929*
Most shops open 0900-1200, 1500-2000. The smaller shops keep longer hours.
Higginbotham's, Commercial Rd, Ooty, T0423-244 3736. 0930-1300, 1550-1930, closed Wed. Bookseller.
Toda Showroom, Charing Cross. Sells silver and tribal shawls.
Variety Hall, Silver Market. Old family firm (1890s) for good range of silk, helpful, accepts credit cards.

Kodaikkanal *p932, map p933*
Belgian Convent shop, east of town. Hand-embroidered linen.
Cottage Crafts Shop, Anna Salai (Council for Social Concerns in Kodai). Mon-Sat 0900-1230, 1400-1830. Volunteer-run.
Govt Sales Emporium, near Township Bus Stand. Only open in season.
Kashmir Handicrafts Centre, 2 North Shopping Complex, Anna Salai. Jewellery, brass, shawls, walnut wood crafts and Numdah rugs.
Potter's Shack, PT Rd. Lovely earthy cups and vases made by local potters Subramaniam and Prabhu under tutelage of Ray and Deborah Meeker of Pondicherry. Visits to the workshop can be arranged, and proceeds go to help disadvantaged children.

Activities and tours

Udhagamandalam (Ooty) *p928, map p929*
Horse riding
Gymkhana Club, T0423-244 2254. Big bar open 1130-1530 or 1830-2300. Temporary membership; beautifully situated amidst superbly maintained 18-hole golf course. Riding from Regency Villa: Rs 500 for 2 hrs with 'guide'; good fun but no helmets.

Tour operators

Tours can be booked through the **TTDC**, at Hotel Tamil Nadu, T0423-244 4370. Ooty and Mudumalai: Ooty Lake, Dodabetta Peak, Botanical Gardens, Mudumalai Wildlife Sanctuary. 0830-2000. Rs 150. Kotagiri and Coonoor: Kotagiri, Kodanad View Point, Lamb's Rock, Dolphin's Nose, Sim's Park. 0830-1830. Rs 130.

Blue Mountain, Nahar Complex, Charing Cross, T0423-244 3650. Luxury coach bookings to neighbouring states.

George Hawkes, 52C Nahar Complex, T0423-244 2756. For tourist taxis.

Sangeetha Travels, 13 Bharathiyar Complex, Charing Cross, T0432-244 4782. Steam train.

Woodlands Tourism, Race Course Rd, T0423-244 2551. Ooty and Coonoor. 0930-1730. Rs 130. Stunning views.

Yoga

Rajayoga Meditation Centre, 88 Victoria Hall, Ettines Rd.

Coonoor *p930*

TTDC from Ooty (reserve in Ooty Tourist Office). Coonoor-Kotagiri Rs 120, 6 hrs; visiting Valley View, Sim's Park, Lamb's Rock, Dolphin's Nose, Kodadu viewpoint.

Coimbatore *p932*

Alooha, corner near **Heritage Inn**. Helpful travel agency.

Kodaikkanal *p932, map p933*

Boating

Boat Club, T04542-241315. Rents out pedal boats, 6-seater row boats and romantic Kashmir-style *shikaras*, Rs 40-160 per 30 mins plus boatman fees. The boatmen here are friendly and speak good English. 0900-1730.

TTDC Boathouse, next door. Similar services and prices. 0900-1730.

Golf

Golf club, T04542-240323. Kodai's forest-swathed course is one of the most beautiful and (out of season) peaceful in the world, and the greens and fairways are maintained with minimal watering and no chemical pesticides. A round costs Rs 200-250, club hire Rs 200.

Horse riding

Ponies for hire near the Boat House, Rs 300 per hr.

Tour operators

Several tour operators around town book similar sightseeing tours, at around Rs 85 for a half day, Rs 150 full day.

Vijay Tours, Anna Salai, T04542-241137.

Trekking

A reputable local guide is Vijay Kumar, T(0)9994-277373, www.nature-trails.net.

Transport

Udhagamandalam (Ooty) *p928, map p929*

Arrive early for buses to ensure a seat. They often leave early if full. Ghat roads have numerous hairpin bends which can have fairly heavy traffic and very bad surfaces at times. The Gudalur road passes through Mudumalai and Bandipur sanctuaries. You might see an elephant herd and other wildlife, especially at night.

Air The nearest airport is at Coimbatore, 105 km away. Taxis available.

Bus State government and private Cheran buses (T0423-244 3970) pull in to the bus stand, just south of the railway station and a 10-min walk from the town centre. Frequent buses to **Coimbatore** (every 20 mins, 0530-2000, 3½ hrs), **Coonoor** (every 10 mins, 0530-2045), and **Mettupalayam** (0530-2100, 2 hrs). Daily buses to **Bengaluru (Bangalore)** (0630-2000), **Mysore** (0800-1530, 3½-5 hrs), **Kozhikode** (0630-1515), **Chennai** (1630- 1830), **Palakkad** (0715-1515), **Palani** (0800- 1800), **Hassan** (1130, 1500), **Kannur** (0915, 2000), **Kanniyakumari** (1745), **Kodaikkanal** (0630, 9½ hrs via magnificent route through Palani); **Madikeri** (0700, 1100); **Pondicherry** (1700); **Salem** (1300). Check timings. Several on the short route (36 km) to **Masinagudi** in Mudumalai, 1½ hrs on a steep and bendy but interesting road.

Train Railway station, T0423-244 2246. From **Mettupalayam** *Blue Mountain* (steam to **Coonoor**; then diesel to Ooty), 1 return train daily, see Mettupalayam transport, below. The *Heritage Steam Chariot* to **Runneymede** runs at weekends (more frequent in season). It departs Ooty 1000, returns 1600 (delayed when engine runs out of steam!). Highly recommended. Tickets include Indian packed lunch: Rs 280, or Rs 550 in Maharaja coach, from *Sangeetha* (listed above) or Ooty railway station.

Coonoor *p930*

Bus Frequent buses to **Ooty** (every 10 mins from 0530) some via Sim's Park and many via Wellington. Also regular services to **Kotagiri** and **Coimbatore** (every 30 mins) through **Mettupalayam**. Direct bus to **Mysore** (or change at Ooty).

Train The *Blue Mountain Railway* runs from **Mettupalayam** to Coonoor (steam), 3 hrs; continues to **Ooty** (diesel), 1½ hrs. See Mettupalayam transport, below. The *Heritage Steam Chariot* runs from Ooty to **Runneymede** beyond Coonoor. See Ooty transport, above (and box, page 931).

Mettupalayam *p931*

Train The *Nilgiri Exp* from Chennai via Coimbatore, connects with the *Blue Mountain Railway* (see box, page 931). This line is subject to landslides and washouts that can close the route for some months. Check before travelling. From **Chennai** *Nilgiri Exp 12671*, 2100, 2015, 10 hrs; to Chennai, *Nilgiri Exp 12672*, 1945, 10½ hrs. For those coming from Coimbatore, it is better to arrive in advance at Mettupalayam by bus; this avoids a mad dash at the station from Platform 2 to 1 to catch the connecting train. If you have time to spare the engine sheds are interesting to look around.

To **Coonoor** and **Ooty** 1 return train daily; *56136* (**S**), 0710, arrive Coonoor, 1030, Ooty, 1200 (5½ hrs); return from Ooty, *56137*, (**S**), 1400, arrive Coonoor, 1505, Mettupalayam 1735, 3½ hrs.

Mudumalai Wildlife Sanctuary *p931*

Bus Theppakadu is on themain Mysore– Ooty bus route. From **Mysore**, services from 0615 (1½-2 hrs); last bus to Mysore around 2000. From **Ooty** via **Gudalur** on a very winding road (about 2½ hrs); direct 20 km steep road used by buses, under 1 hr. Few buses between Theppakadu and Masinagudi.

Jeeps are available at bus stands and from lodges.

Coimbatore *p932*

Air **Peelamedu Airport**, 12 km centre, runs airport coach into town, Rs 25; taxis Rs 150-200; auto-rickshaw Rs 85. On Trichy Rd: **Indian Airlines**, T0422-239 9833, airport T0422-257 4623, 1000-1300, 1345-1730, to **Bengaluru** (**Bangalore**), **Chennai**, **Delhi**, **Kochi**, **Kozhikode**, **Mumbai**. **Jet Airways**: 1055/1 Gowtham Centre, Avinashi Rd, T0422-221 2034, airport T0422-257 5375, to **Bengaluru** (**Bangalore**), **Chennai**, **Mumbai**.

Bus City buses run a good service: several connect the bus stations in Gandhipuram with the Junction Railway Station 2 km south. No 20 goes to the airport (Rs 20).

There are 4 long-distance bus stations, off Dr Nanjappa Rd.

City or **'Town' Bus Stand** in Gandhipuram. **Thiruvallur Bus Stand**, Cross Cut Rd. Computerized reservations T0422-226700, 0700-2100. Frequent Government Express buses to **Madurai** (5 hrs), **Chennai** (12 hrs), **Mysore** (6 hrs), **Ooty** (3 hrs), **Tiruchirappalli** (5½ hrs).

'Central' Bus Stand is further south, on corner of Shastri Rd. State buses to **Bengaluru** (**Bangalore**) and **Mysore**; **Ooty** via **Mettupalayam** (see below for train connection) and **Coonoor** every 20 mins, 0400-2400, 5 hrs.

Ukkadam Bus Stand, south of the city, serves towns within the state (**Pollachi**, **Madurai**) and in north Kerala (**Pallakad**, **Thrissur**, **Munnar**).

Taxi Tourist taxis and yellow top taxis are available at the bus stations, railway station and taxi stands. Rs 2.5 per km; for out-station hill journeys, Rs 3 per km; minimum Rs 30.

Train Junction Station, enquiries, T132, reservations, T131, 0700-1300, 1400-2030. **Bengaluru** (**Bangalore**): *Tilak Exp 11014*, 0800, 7¼ hrs; *Bangalore Exp 12678*, 1245, 7 hrs; **Kanniyakumari**: *Kanyakumari Exp 16381*, 0010, 9 hrs. **Chennai**: *West Coast Exp 16628*, 0630, 9 hrs; *Kovai Exp 12676*, 1420, 7½ hrs. **Kochi** (**HT**):

Ernakulam Exp 12677, 1310, 4hrs; *Hyderabad-Kochi Exp 7030*, 0935, daily, 5½ hrs.

For **Ooty** best to take the bus to Mettupalayam (see above).

Salem *p932*

Bus The **New Bus Stand**, north of the hospital, off Omalur Rd, T0427-226 5917, has buses to all major towns in Tamil Nadu, Kerala and South Karnataka.

Train Salem Junction is the main train station. Enquiries, T132. Reservations, T131, 0700-1300, 1400-2030. **Bengaluru** (**Bangalore**): *Tilak Exp 1014*, 1040, 4½ hrs; *Bangalore Exp 12678*, 1535, 4 hrs. **Chennai** (**C**): *Coimbatore–Chennai Exp 12680*, 0835, 5 hrs. **Kochi** (**Cochin**): *Ernakulam Exp 12677*, 1005, 7 hrs. *Trivandrum Mail 12623*, 0010, 6 hrs, (continues to Trivandrum, 11 hrs). **Madurai**: *Tuticorin Exp 16732*, not Tue, Wed, Sun, 0200, 5 hrs. For **Ooty**, *Nilgiri Exp 12671*, 0135, connects with narrow-gauge steam train from Mettupalayam.

Yercaud *p932*

Bus There are no local buses but some from **Salem** (1 hr) continue to nearby villages.

Kodaikkanal *p932, map p933*

Bicycle hire There are several bike hire stands around the lake, charging Rs 10 per hr, Rs 100 per day for good new bikes.

Bus Check timings; reservations possible. To **Bengaluru** (**Bangalore**), overnight, 12 hrs; **Chennai** (497 km) 12 hrs, **Coimbatore** (171 km) 6 hrs; **Dindigul** (90 km) 3½ hrs, via Kodai Rd, **Madurai** (120 km), 0730-1830, 4 hrs; **Kumily** (for Periyar NP), 5½ hrs, change buses at Vatigundu; **Palani** (65 km) 3 hrs; **Tiruchirappalli** (197 km) 6 hrs. To **Munnar** by bus takes 8 hrs, changing at Palani and Udhamalpet.

Taxi Unmetered taxis available for sight-seeing. Tourist taxis from agencies including **Raja's**, near Pastry Corner on Anna Salai, T04542-242422. Taxi transfer to **Munnar** around Rs 2200, or Rs 450 for a seat in a shared taxi.

Train Reservations counter off Anna Salai behind **Anjay** hotel, 0800-1200, 1430-1700, Sun 0800-1200. No Foreign Tourist Quota bookings. The nearest station is Kodai Rd, 80 km away. Taxi drivers at the station quote Rs 1000 to drop you in Kodai, but this price drops if you cross the road and look determined to catch a bus. **Hotel Tamil Nadu**, just south of the station, has rooms if you get stuck.

Anamalai (Indira Gandhi) Wildlife Sanctuary *p935*

Bus 3 daily buses connect **Top Slip** with Pollachi, which has connections to **Coimbatore** and **Palani**. To Top Slip: 0600, 1100, 1500 (but check timings); From Top Slip: 0930, 1300, 1830.

Dindigul *p935*

Bus Good and frequent bus service to **Tiruchirappalli**, **Chennai**, **Salem** and **Coimbatore** and long-distance connections.

Train Train to **Chennai** (**ME**) *Vaigai Exp 12636 (AC/CC)*, 0730, 6¾ hrs via **Tiruchirappalli** 1½ hrs. **Madurai** *Vaigai Exp 12635 (AC/CC)*, 1905, 1¼ hrs.

Directory

Udhagamandalam (Ooty) *p928, map p929*

Banks ATMs congregate along Bank Rd and Commercial Rd. **State Bank of India**, on Bank Rd, deals in foreign exchange. **Internet Gateways**, 8/9 Moosa Sait Complex, Commercial Rd. Excellent, fast, ISDN lines, Rs 30 per hr. **Medical services** **Govt Hospital**, Hospital Rd, T0423-244 2212. **Post** **Head Post Office**, Collectorate and Telegraph Office, Town W Circle. **Useful contacts** **Police**, T100. **Wildlife Warden**, 1st floor, Mahalingam Building, T0423- 244098, 1000-1730. Closed 1300-1400.

Coonoor *p930*

Banks **Travancore Bank**, Upper Coonoor (Bedford Circle) changes cash. **South Indian Bank**, Mount Rd, 1000-1400 changes cash and TCs. **Medical services** **Lawley Hospital**, Mt Rd, T0423-223 1050.

Coimbatore *p932*

Banks Several on Oppankara St. **State Bank of India** (exchange upstairs), and **Bank of Baroda** are on Bank Rd. **Medical services** **Government Hospital**, Trichy Rd. **Post** Near flyover, Railway

Feeder Rd. **Useful contacts** Automobile Association, 42 Trichy Rd, T0422-222 2994.

Yercaud *p932*

Banks Banks with foreign exchange are on Main Rd. **Medical services** Govt Hospital, 1 km from bus stand; **Providence Hospital**, on road to Lady's Seat. **Post** On Main Rd.

Kodaikkanal *p932, map p933*

Banks Several branches with ATMs on Anna Salai. **Indian Bank** does foreign exchange **Hotel Tamil Nadu**, has a counter for foreign exchange counter. **Medical services** **Van Allan Hospital**, T04542-241273, is recommended. Consultations (non-emergency): Mon-Fri 0930-1200, 1530-1630. Sat 1000-1200. Clean and efficient, good doctors. **Government Hospital**, T04542-241292. **Post** Head Post Office on Post Office Rd.

Madurai and around

→ Colour map 7, C4. Phone code: 0452. Population: 922,900.

Madurai is a maddening whirl of a temple town: the red-and-white striped sanctuary of the 'fish-eyed goddess' is a towering edifice crested by elaborate gaudy stucco-work gopurams, soundtracked by tinny religious songs, peopled by 10,000 devoted pilgrims prostrating themselves at shrines, lighting candles and presenting flower garlands to idols, seeking blessings from the temple elephant or palmistry on the shores of the Golden Lotus tank. Even the city's town planning reflects the sanctity of the spot: surrounding streets radiate like bicycle spokes from the temple in the mandala architectural style, a sacred form of geometry. There is the usual combination of messy crumbling buildings harking back to times of greater architectural aspirations, modern glass-and-chrome palaces, internet cafés, flower sellers, tailors and tinkers and Kashmiri antique and shawl dealers. The centre seems all dust and cycle-rickshaws, but Madurai, as the second biggest city in Tamil Nadu, is also a modern industrial place that never sleeps. Around the city the area of fertile agricultural land is dotted with exotically shaped granite mountain ranges such as Nagamalai (snake hills) and Yanaimalai (elephant hills). ▸▸ *For listings, see pages 955-960.*

Madurai → *For listings, see pages 955-960.*

Ins and outs

Getting there The airport is 12 km from town and is linked by buses, taxis and autos to the city centre. The railway station is within easy walking distance of many budget hotels (predatory rickshaw drivers/hotel touts may tell you otherwise). Hire an auto to reach the few north of the river. Most intercity buses arrive at the Mattuthavani Bus Stand 6 km northeast of the centre; those from Kodaikkanal and destinations to the northwest use the Arapalayam stand, 3 km northwest. Both are linked to the centre by bus and auto. ▸▸ *See Transport, page 959.*

Getting around The city centre is compact and the temple is within easy walking distance of most hotels. Prepare for hordes of touts, To visit the sights around the city, buses and taxis are available.

Tourist information ⓘ *W Veli St, T0452-233 4757, Mon-Fri 1000-1745*, has useful maps, tours (arranged through agents), guides for hire. Also at **Madurai Junction Railway Station** ⓘ *Main Hall, 0630-2030*, and the airport counter during flight times.

History

According to legend, drops of nectar fell from Siva's locks on this site, so it was named Madhuram or Madurai, 'the Nectar City'. The city's history goes back to the sixth century BC. Ancient Madurai, which traded with Greece and Rome, was a centre of Tamil culture, famous for its writers and poets during the last period of the three *Sangam* (Tamil 'Academies') nearly 2000 years ago.

By the fourth century, Madurai, Tirunelveli and a part of southern Kerala were under the **Pandiyas**, a major power from the sixth to the early 10th century. The Pandiyas made Madurai their capital and remained here for 300 years, staying on even during the rule of the **Cholas**; after Chola power declined in the late 12th century the Pandiyas regained control of Madurai, and they presided over a period of flourishing international trade until Malik Kafur destroyed the city in 1310.

For a period Madurai became a sultanate, but Muslim rule in Tamil Nadu proved as short-lived as it was tenuous. In 1364 the city was recaptured by the Hindu Vijayanagar kings (see Hampi, page 1093), who remained until 1565, when the defeat of the Vijayanagar Empire by a confederacy of Muslim states forced their leaders to take refuge in Madurai. As the **Nayaka** kings, they continued to rule well into the 17th century. The Nayakas have been seen essentially as warriors, given an official position by the Vijayanagar rulers, but in Sanskrit the term applied to someone of prominence and leadership. Burton Stein comments, "the history of the Vijayanagara is essentially the history of the great Telugu Nayakas" from Madurai.

The Vijayanagar had been great builders, preserving and enriching the architectural heritage of the town, and the Nayakas held true to their legacy. They laid out the old town in the pattern of a lotus, with narrow streets surrounding the Meenakshi Temple at the centre, and took up the Vijayanagar predilection for building temple complexes with tall *gopurams*. These increased in height to become dominating structures covered profusely with plaster decorations. The tall *gopurams* of Madurai were built by Thirumalai (ruled 1623-1655), the greatest of the Nayaka rulers, and may have served a strategic purpose as they moved away from the earlier Chola practice of giving the central shrine the tallest tower. The *kalyana mandapa* or marriage hall with a 'hundred' or 'thousand' pillars, and the temple tank with steps on all four sides, were introduced in some southern temples, along with the *Nandi* bull, Siva's vehicle, which occupies a prominent position at the entrance to the main Shaivite shrine.

1 Madurai

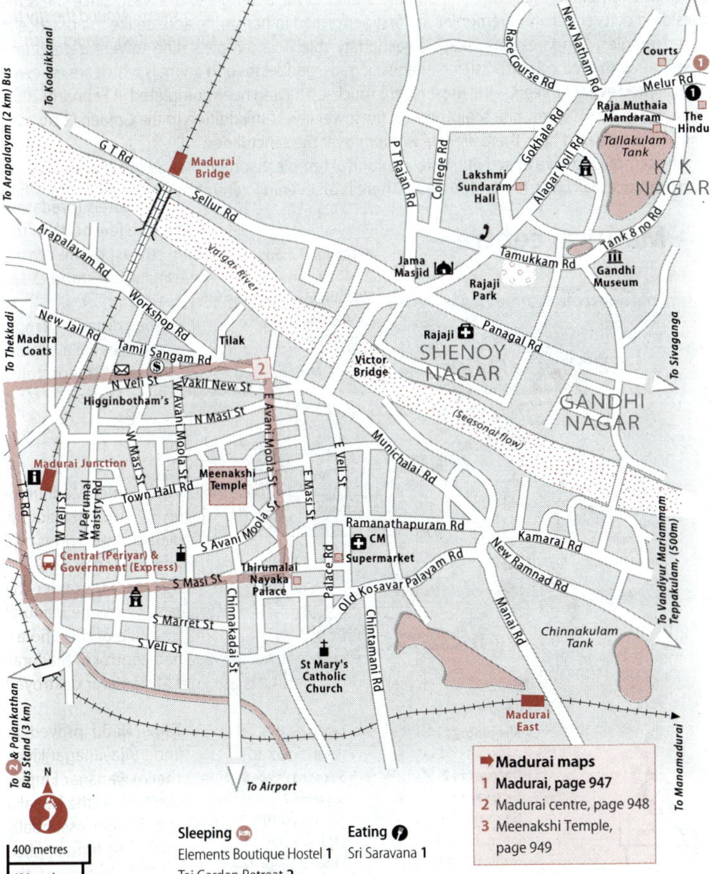

In 1840, after the Carnatic Wars, the British destroyed the fort, filling in the surrounding moat; its original course is now followed by the four Veli streets. The inner streets encircling the central temple are named after the festivals which take place in them and give their relative direction: South 'Chitrai Street, East 'Avani Moola' Street and West 'Masi Street'.

Sights

Meenakshi Temple ① *Inner Temple 0500-1230, 1600-2130, foreigners Rs 50, camera Rs 50, tickets from counters near South Entrance and Thousand-Pillared Hall (valid for multiple entries on same day); art museum 0600-2030, Rs 5, camera fee Rs 50. Metal detectors and body searches at entrance gates. Sanctuaries of Meenakshi and Sundareswarar are open only to Hindus. Offers of good viewpoints made by helpful bystanders will invariably turn out to be from the roofs of nearby shops.* This is an outstanding example of Vijayanagar temple architecture and an exact contemporary of the Taj Mahal in Agra. Meenakshi, the 'fish-eyed goddess' and the consort of Siva, has a temple to the south, and Sundareswarar (Siva), a temple to the west. Since she is the presiding deity the daily ceremonies are first performed in her shrine and, unlike the practice at other temples, Sundareswarar plays a secondary role. The temple's nine towering *gopurams* stand out with their colourful stucco images of gods, goddesses and animals which are renewed and painted every 12 years – the most recent touch-up having been completed in February 2009. There are about 4000 granite sculptures on the lower levels. In addition to the Golden Lotus tank and various pillared halls there are five *vimanas* over the sanctuaries.

The temple is a hive of activity, with a colourful temple elephant, flower sellers and **musical performances** ① *1800-1930, 2100-2130*. There is an evening ceremony (arrive by 2100), when

2 **Madurai centre**

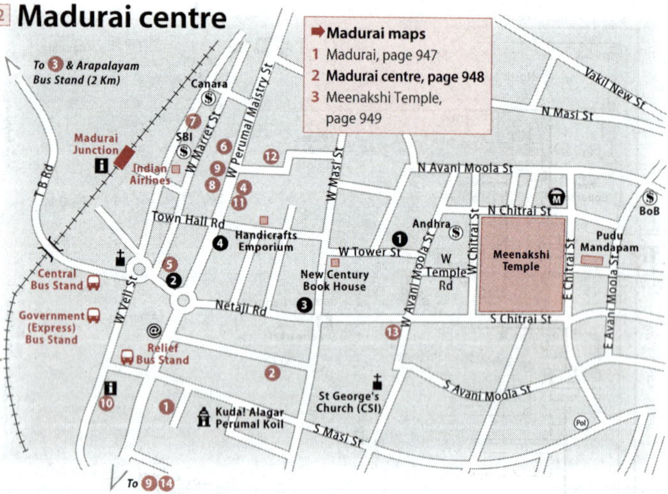

Sleeping
Aarathy 1
Dhanamani 2
Gateway 14
Germanus 3
International 4
Madurai Residency 5
Park Plaza 6
Royal Court 7
Sulochna Palace 8
Supreme 9
Tamil Nadu 10
TM Lodge 11
Visakam Lodge 12
YMCA 13

Eating
Delhiwala Sweets 1
Jayaram Sweets 2
New Arya Bhavan 3
Sri Sabarees 4

an image of Sundareswarar is carried in procession, to a heady accompaniment of whirling pipe and drum music and clouds of incense, from the shrine near the east *gopuram* to Meenakshi, to 'sleep' by her side; he is returned first thing the next morning. The procession around the temple is occasionally led by the elephant and a cow. During the day the elephant is on continual duty, 'blessing' visitors with its trunk and then collecting a small offering.

The main entrance is through a small door of the **Ashta Sakthi Mandapa (1)** (Porch of the Eight Goddesses) which projects from the wall, south of the eastern *gopuram*. Inside to the left is the sacred **Tank of the Golden Lotus (2)**, with a lamp in the centre, surrounded by pillared cloisters and steps down to the waters. The Sangam legend speaks of the test that ancient manuscripts had to undergo: they were thrown into the sacred tank, and only if they floated were they considered worthy of further study. The north gallery has murals (under restoration at the time of writing) relating 64 miracles said to have been performed by Siva, and the southern has marble inscriptions of the 1330 couplets of the *Tamil Book of Ethics*. To the west of the tank is the **Oonjal Mandapa (3)**, the pavilion leading to the Meenakshi shrine. Here the pillars are carved in the form of the mythical beast *yali* which recurs in temples throughout the region. Golden images of Meenakshi and Sundareswarar are brought to the *oonjal* or swing each Friday evening where they are worshipped. Cages with parrots, Meenakshi's green bird that brings luck, hang from the ceiling of the neighbouring **Kilikootu Mandapam (4)**, which is

3 Meenakshi Temple

➡ Madurai maps
1 Madurai, page 947
2 Madurai centre, page 948
3 **Meenakshi Temple, page 949**

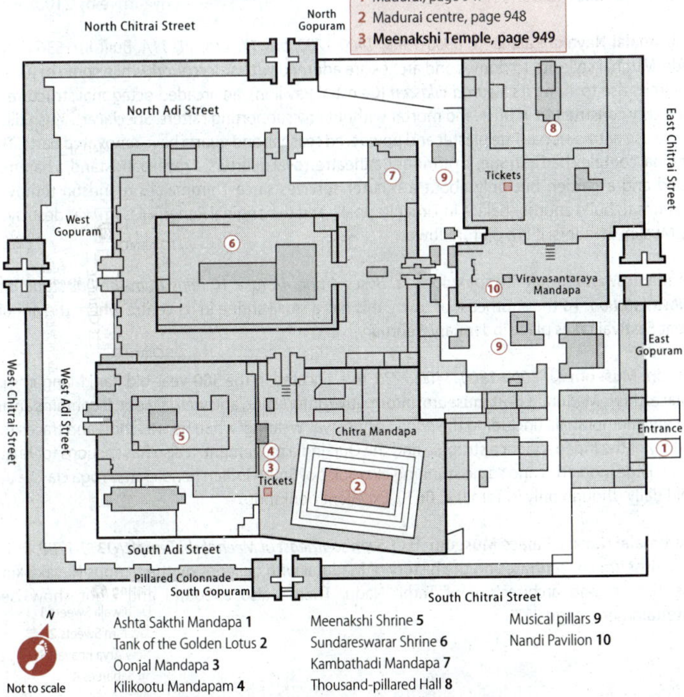

Ashta Sakthi Mandapa **1**
Tank of the Golden Lotus **2**
Oonjal Mandapa **3**
Kilikootu Mandapam **4**
Meenakshi Shrine **5**
Sundareswarar Shrine **6**
Kambathadi Mandapa **7**
Thousand-pillared Hall **8**
Musical pillars **9**
Nandi Pavilion **10**

flanked by finely carved columns. The **Meenakshi shrine (5)** with the principal image of the goddess, stands in its own enclosure with smaller shrines around it.

To the north of the tank is another enclosure with smaller *gopurams* on four sides within which is the **Sundareswarar shrine (6)** guarded by two tall *dwarapalas*. In the northeast corner, the superb sculptures of the divine marriage of Meenakshi and Sundareswarar being blessed by Vishnu and Brahma, and Siva in his 24 forms are in the 19th-century **Kambathadi Mandapa (7)**, around the golden flagstaff.

The mid-16th century **Thousand-pillared Hall (8)** is in the northeast corner of the complex. The 985 exquisitely carved columns include a lady playing the *vina*, a dancing Ganesh, and a gypsy leading a monkey. The art museum here exhibits temple art and architecture, fine brass and stone images, friezes and photos (the labelling could be improved). Just inside the museum to the right is a cluster of five **musical pillars (9)** carved out of a single stone. Each pillar produces a different note which vibrates when tapped. Nayaka musicians could play these as an instrument.

The **Nandi pavilion (10)** is to the east and is often packed with market stalls peddling flowers, trinkets and coconuts. The long *Pudu Mandapa* (New Mandapa), across the road from the East Tower, is lined with yet more beautiful sculptures of *yalis*, Nayaka rulers and elephants, and during the day Beyond lies the base of the unfinished *Raya Gopuram* which was planned to be the tallest in the country.

Northeast of the Meenakshi Temple, off N Avani Moola Street, is the **flower market**, a profusion of colour and activity at its best 0500-0730. It is a two-storey hall with piles of jasmine of all colours, lotuses, and huge jumbles of floral prettiness amid a sea of decomposing mulch of flowers trampled underfoot.

Thirumalai Nayaka Palace ⓘ *0900-1300, 1400-1700, bus 17, 17A, 11, 11A*. Built in 1636 in the Indo-Mughal style, its 15 domes and arches are adorned with stucco work while some of its 240 columns rise to 12 m. Its *Swarga Vilasam* (Celestial Pavilion), an arcaded octagonal structure, is curiously constructed in brick and mortar without any supporting rafters. Special artisans skilled in the use of traditional lime plaster and powdered seashell and quartz have renovated parts. The original complex had a shrine, an armoury, a theatre, royal quarters, a royal bandstand, a harem, a pond and a garden but only about a quarter survives since Thirumalai's grandson removed sections to build another palace in Tiruchirappalli, and the original *Ranga* Vilasam was destroyed by Muslim invaders. It is a bit run down.

Vandiyur Mariammam Teppakulam ⓘ *Buses 4 and 4A take 10 mins from the bus stand and railway station*. To the southeast of town, this has a small shrine in its centre where the annual **Float Festival** takes place in January/February.

Gandhi Museum ⓘ *1000-1300, 1400-1730, free*. Located in the 300-year-old Rani Mangammal Palace, this is Madurai's best museum: informative, interesting and well laid out. It contains an art gallery, memorabilia (including the *dhoti* Gandhi was wearing when he was shot) and traces the history of the Independence struggle and the Quit India movement. It also has sections for Khadi and Village Industries and some stunning examples of South Indian handicrafts. Yoga classes are held daily (though only in Tamil) at 0630. Excellent bookshop.

Thirumalai Nayaka Palace Museum ⓘ *1.5 km southeast of Meenakshi Temple, 0900-1700, Rs 10*. This museum concentrates on the history of Madurai with galleries on the famous Nayaka king and the art and architecture of Tamil Nadu. There's also a Sound and Light show, see Entertainment, page 957.

Ramesvaram and around → *For listings, see pages 955-960. Colour map 7, C5.*

The conch-shaped island of Ramesvaram is normally lapped by the limpid blue waters of the Gulf of Mannar, but cyclones can whip the sea here into ferocious stormy waves. This is where Rama is believed to have worshipped Siva, making it sacred to both Shaivites and Vaishnavites, and so a pilgrim to Varanasi is expected to visit Ramesvaram next if he is to reach salvation. The great Ramalingesvara temple, which forms the core of the scrappy town, is one of India's most memorable, as much for the sight of priests spattering pilgrims with holy water from each of 22 sacred wells as for its cavernous, echoing corridors.

Ins and outs → *Phone code: 04573. Population: 38,000.*

Getting there Ramesvaram is connected to Madurai and other centres by regular bus and train services. The bus stand is 2 km from the centre, the railway station 1 km southwest of the great temple. There are also daily tours from Madurai.

Getting around Local buses and auto- rickshaws link the bus and train stations to the temple, where there are a few places to stay. ▸▸ *See Transport, page 959.*

Tourist information Tourist office ⓘ *14 East Car St, T04573-221371, 1000-1700.* Also at the Railway Station ⓘ *T04573-221373, open (with some breaks) 0700-2030.* The Temple Information is on the east side of the temple.

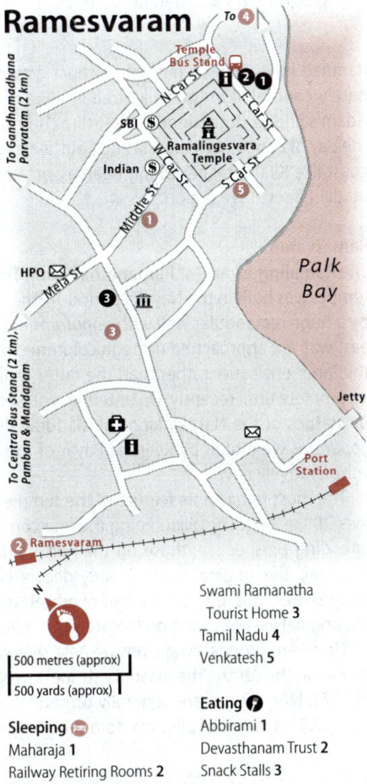

History

The *Ramayana* tells how the monkey king Hanuman built the bridges linking Ramnad to Pamban and Danushkodi (a spot where Rama is believed to have bathed) to help Rama rescue Sita from the demon king Ravana. When Rama returned he was told by the *rishis* that he must purify himself after committing the sin of murdering a Brahmin, for *Ravana* was the son of a Brahmin. To do this he was advised to set up a *lingam* and worship Siva. The red image of Hanuman north of the main East Gate illustrates this story.

The original shrine long predates the present great Ramesvaram temple. It is one of India's most sacred shrines and is visited by pilgrims from all over India. The temple benefited from huge donations from the 17th-century *Setupatis* (the so-called guardians of the causeway), who derived their wealth from the right to levy taxes on crossings to the island. The temple stands on slightly higher ground, surrounded by a freshwater lake.

To Ramesvaram and Adam's Bridge

Seen from the air the plains of the Vaigai River form one of the most remarkable landscapes in India, for there are over 5000 tanks, and irrigation has been so developed that barely a drop of water is wasted. The coastal districts of

Holy dips

Having bathed in the Ganga at Varanasi, Hindu pilgrims head straight for Rameswaram, where a bath in the 22 *theertham* (holy wells) dotted within and around the Ramalingesvara temple promise a final release from the chains of *karma*.

The *theertham* circuit is a festive event for the pilgrims, complete with much cheering and song as buckets are emptied over heads, and as a visitor it can offer one of the most atmospheric and memorable temple experiences in Tamil Nadu, especially if you can get yourself adopted by a group of Indian visitors. The locals tend to bring along a change of clothes and submit to a thorough drenching, but if you come overdressed it is possible to request a light sprinkle. It's also traditional, but not obligatory, to taste of the waters; each apparently has a distinct flavour.

Brahmin priests wait at the train and bus stations and along the shoreline east of the temple to greet new arrivals, but he haggling of old has now been replaced by a standard charge of Rs 51 per person, which includes a dunking in each of the wells and access to the inner sanctum. Non-Hindus are traditionally prevented from entering the sanctum, but if you dress appropriately and arrive with a group (day tours from Madurai are an all-but-guaranteed way to join one) there's a good chance the priests will allow you in. If you do the circuit alone, it's best to leave valuables outside the temple: bystanders who offer to watch your bags are not all trustworthy.

Ramnad have their own highly distinct economy and society. For the Hindus the sandbanks barely concealed in the Palk Strait are like giant stepping stones linking India and Sri Lanka: Adam's Bridge. Both Hindu and Muslim communities have long-established trading links across the Bay of Bengal, to Malaysia and Southeast Asia and to Sri Lanka. Small settlements along the coast like Kilakkarai have long been associated with smuggling. The civil war in Sri Lanka has made it a sensitive region.

Ramesvaram

The **Ramalingesvara** (or **Ramanathasvami) Temple** was founded by the Cholas but most of the temple was built in the Nayaka period (16th-17th centuries). It is a massive structure, enclosed by a huge rectangular wall with *gopurams* in the middle of three sides. Entrances through the east wall are approached through columned *mandapas* and the east *gopuram* is on the wall of the inner enclosure rather than the outer wall. Over 45 m high, it was begun in 1640 but left incomplete until recently. On entering, you see the statue of Hanuman, then the *Nandi* flanked by statues of the Nayaka kings of Madurai, Visvanatha and Krishnama. The north and south *gopurams* were built by Keerana Rayar of the Deccan in about AD 1420; the west *gopuram* is comparatively new.

The most remarkable feature of the temple is its pillared *mandapas*, the longest of which is over 200 m long. The pillars lining the four corridors, nearly 4 m tall, give an impression of almost unending perspective: those on the north and south sides are particularly striking. Tragically, however, the original stone pillars, decorated with scrollwork and lotus motifs, are being progressively phased out in favour of graceless grey concrete facsimiles. You're only likely to see the original versions lying on the ground in piles.

There are two gateways on the east side which give access to the Parvati and Ramalinga shrines at the centre; the masonry shrine is probably the oldest building on the site, going back to 1173. Non-Hindus are generally turned away, but you might be able to enter if you can tag along with a group of pilgrims doing the holy well circuit (see box, above).

Gandhamadana Parvatam

Gandhamadana Parvatam, 2 km north of Ramesvaram, takes its name from the Sanskrit words *gandha* (fragrance) and *mad* (intoxicate), 'highly fragrant hill'. Dedicated to Rama's feet, this is the spot from which Hanuman is believed to have surveyed the area before taking his leap across the narrow Palk strait to Sri Lanka. You can get an excellent view from the top of the *mandapa*.

Dhanuskodi

Dhanuskodi ('the end of the bow') is the island's toe-tip where the Bay of Bengal meets the Indian Ocean, so named because Rama, at the request of Vibishana, his friend, destroyed the bridge to Sri Lanka with the end of his bow. Some 20 km to the east of Ramesvaram island, it is considered particularly holy. There is a good beach, on which pilgrims will be making *puja*, and beautiful flat turquoise waters in which they take their holy bath, not to mention excellent views. A trip across the scrappy sand dunes is only recommended for the really hardy – get a local person to go with you. Travel by bus, and then join a pilgrim group on a jeep or lorry for the last desolate few miles (this should cost Rs 50 for a round trip but establish the price up front). Alternatively, take an auto to Adam's Bridge; insist on going as far as the radio mast for beach and fishing shack photos.

Cardamom Hills → *See pages 955-960. Colour map 7, C3/4.*

To the south of Madurai is a series of modest towns situated in the lee of the southern ranges of the Western Ghats. From Madurai to Thiruvanathapuram is a comfortable day's drive either via Tirunelveli or over the ghats, but there are several interesting places on the way if you wish to take your time.

Rajapalayam

ⓘ *To Sankaracoil, Rs 12, 30 mins; from there to Kalugumalai, Rs 8, 30 mins, buses to and from Tenkasi, Rs 30, 2 hrs.*

The town originated on the dispersal of the Vijayanagar families after 1565, see page 1046. The Sankarankovil temple is worth visiting. The Western Ghats rise to heights of over 1200 m immediately behind the town. Wild elephants still come down through the forests, devastating farmland.

Tenkasi

ⓘ *To Courtallam Falls frequent buses, Rs 8, to Courtallam Bus Stand, then walk through the grey arch to the 'Main Falls'. See Rajapalayam, above, for transport to Tenkasi.*

Literally the 'Kashi (Varanasi) of the South', Tenkasi is the nearest town to the Kuttalam (Courtallam) Falls, 6 km away. The impressive 16th-century Visvanatha temple dedicated to Siva has some fine carvings inside. The temple flagstaff is believed to be 400 years old. From Tenkasi the road goes through a low pass into the densely forested hills of Kerala.

Courtallam (Kuttalam)

With average temperatures of 22-23°C, Courtallam is a very popular health resort, especially during the monsoon. The impressive **Main Falls** is in town where the river Chittar cascades over 92 m. The approach is lined with spice, banana chips and knick- knack stalls and at the falls you'll find pilgrims washing themselves and their clothes. The waters, widely believed to have great curative powers, draw big crowds at the **Saral Festival** in July. The **Thirukutralanathar Temple** contains old inscriptions while the small **Chitra Sabha Temple** nearby contains religious murals.

Virudhunagar

The name Virudhupatti (Hamlet of Banners) was changed to Virudhunagar (City of Banners) in 1915, and was upgraded to a full municipality in 1957, reflecting the upwardly mobile social status of the town's dominant local caste, the Nadars. Originally low caste toddy tappers, they have established a wide reputation as a dynamic and enterprising group. The powerful Congress leader, Kamaraj Nadar, was chiefly responsible for Indira Gandhi's selection as prime minister.

Kalugumalai

Some 6 km south of Kovilpatti, Kalugumalai (Kazhugumalai) has a profusion of magnificent fifth-century bas-relief Jain figures on a huge rock which are well worth the detour. The Jain temple is to the north of the rock and is easily missed. There is also an unfinished monolithic cave temple to Siva (circa AD 950).

Chettinad

→ *For listings, see pages 955-960. Colour map 7, B5/C5.*

The magnificent palaces of South India's old merchant and banking classes rise from the hot and dusty plains to stand as strong as fortresses and as gaudy as a packet of French Fancies. As the merchants, bankers and money-lenders of the British Empire, the Nattukottai Chettiars raked in enormous riches on their postings to places such as Burma, Sri Lanka, Indochina and South Africa, wealth they ploughed into these glorious architectural pastiches that explode in a profusion of colour in the arid desert-scape.

Now their monumental arches and long processional corridors open onto empty halls, the bats are more at home here than princes and shafts of light break on empty, cob- webbed dining rooms. The Nattukottai Chettiars saw their riches contract with the Second World War and the wanton palaces they built turned into tombstones, the series of south Indian villages they stand in left as virtual ghost towns. Architectural salvage merchants in the main town of Karaikkudi now sell off the portraits and granite pillars this proud caste have been forced to surrender to stave off financial hardship, while Bollywood crews make regular pilgrimages to the old mansions, propping up the owners with *lakhs* of studio rupees in return for the right to daub their chosen colour scheme across the walls.

Karaikkudi is in the heart of Chettinad, and has several typical mansions, particularly along the back lanes leading off busy Sekkalai Road (ask for the Thousand Window House, a well-known landmark). From here you can walk south to the local *santhai* (market), where you can find gold and silversmiths in their workshops, as well as antique and textile shops and several colourful temples.

Devakottai, 18 km south of Karaikkudi, is Chettinad's second largest town and offers similarly rich pickings in the way of old mansions and palaces: look out for the particularly grand Periya Minor's *veedu*.

Kanadukathan, 12 km north of Karaikkudi, has a number of magnificent mansions, – some still inhabited by friendly owners (who'll let you have a look around for a Rs 100 donation), others are empty except for bats, monkeys and antique dealers. It has been estimated that the Burma teak and satinwood pillars in a single Chettiar house weighs 300 tonnes, often superbly carved. The plaster on the walls is made from a mixture of lime, egg white, powdered shells and myrobalan fruit (the astringent fruit of the tree *Phyllantles emblica*), mixed into a paste which, when dried, gives a gleaming finish. Most houses have the goddess of wealth, Lakshmi, made of stucco over the main arch.

The **Raja of Chettinad's Palace** ⓘ *0930-1630, free, caretakers provide brief free tours*, is an amazing place overlooking the town's pond and full of sepia, larger-than-life-size portraits of stern family members, the frames garlanded with heavy yellow flowers. Next door is **Visalakshi Ramaswamy's house**, with a museum of local crafts, artefacts and handlooms upstairs. The raja's waiting room at the railway station is also pretty special.

Athangudi, 9 km away, is renowned for its tiles, which grace the floors of most Chettiar mansions; ask locally if you want to visit one of the 30-40 workshops in town. Nearby is Pillaiyarpatti, one of the most important temples in Chettinad, dedicated to Ganesh (known as Pillaiyaru in Tamil Nadu) and with an inner sanctum carved into a natural boulder.

At **Avudayarkoil**, 30 km northeast of Karaikkudi, the **Athmanathar Temple** has one of the most renowned sites in Tamil history. A legend tells that Manickavaskar, a Pandyan prime minister, redirected money intended for the purchase of horses to build the temple. However, his real fame lies as author of the *Thiruvasakam* ('Holy Outpourings'), one of the most revered Tamil poetic texts. Completely off the beaten track, the temple has superb sculptures, and is noted for the absence of any images of Siva or Parvati, the main deities, whose empty pedestals are worshipped. The woodcarvings on the temple car are notable too.

Even the roofs of Chettiar buildings are symbols of their owners' wealth; look up to see the wanton use of tiles, layered many times over, on top of each other

Pudukkottai and around

Pudukkottai, on the northern edge of Chettinad, 50 km south of Trichy, was the capital of the former princely state ruled by the Tondaiman Rajas, founded by Raghunatha Raya Tondaiman in 1686. At one entrance to the town is a ceremonial arch raised by the raja in honour of Queen Victoria's jubilee celebrations. The town's broad streets suggest a planned history; the temple is at the centre, with the old palace and a tank. The new palace is now the District Collector's office.

Thirukokarnam, 5 km north of the railway station, is the site of the rock-cut **Sri Kokarnesvarar Temple** ⓘ *closed 1200-1600,* dates from the Pallava period. The natural rock shelters, caves, stone circles, dolmens and Neolithic burial sites show that there was very early human occupation. The local **museum** ⓘ *Big St, open daily except except Fri, 2nd Sat of the month, public holidays, 0930-1700, free, allow 40 mins, recommended,* has a wide range of exhibits including sections on geology, zoology and the economy as well as sculptures and the arts. The archaeology section has some excellent sculptures from nearby temples. There is a notable carving of Siva as *Dakshinamurti* and some fine bronzes from Pudukkottai itself.

Sittannavasal, 13 km away, has a Jain cave temple (circa eighth century) with sculptures, where monks took shelter when they fled from persecution in North India. In a shrine and veranda there are some fine frescoes in the Ajanta-style and bas-relief carvings. You can also see rock-hewn beds of the monks. The *Brahmi* inscriptions date from the second century BC.

Madurai and around listings

For Sleeping and Eating price codes and other relevant information, see Essentials pages 38-42.

Sleeping

Madurai *p946, maps p947 and p948*

Tax of up to 20% is added even by modest hotels. Cheap hotels line up along and around West Peramul Maistry St, 2 blocks east of the railway station, but rooms can be hard to find by late afternoon. Most offer 24-hr checkout. Although there are slick hotels across the Vaigai these are not good value as they lack character and are away from the town's atmosphere. It's best to visit Madurai either from the charming remove of the hilltop **Taj**, or abandon yourself to the throng and take a room near the temple.

AL Gateway (Taj), Pasumalai Hills, 7 TPK Rd, 5 km southwest of centre on NH7, T0452-237 1601, www.thegatewayhotels.com. A real oasis, great views over surrounding country, 30 rooms (some in old colonial house) sheltered by the shade of trees, gardens full of peacocks, outdoor dining, good bookshop, lovely pool.

A-B Germanus, 28 By-Pass Rd, T0452-238 2001, www.hotelgermanus.com. Quiet, bright rooms, functional, fridge, bath, take rooms at the rear to save you from the busy roundabout in front, excellent food and service. Rooftop restaurant 1900-2300 for Chettinad specials.

A-B Royal Court, 4 West Veli St, T0452-435 6666, www.royalcourtindia.com. 70 extremely clean a/c rooms with bath, satellite TV and great views from rooftop (open 1900-2300), good value.

A-B Park Plaza, 114 W Perumal Maistry St, T0452-234 2112. Some of the 56 smart, 60s-print, stylish a/c rooms offer temple views, breakfast included, excellent rooftop restaurant (1700-2300), bar, all facilities. Free pickup from airport/railway station.

B-C Supreme, 110 W Perumal Maistry St, T0452-234 3151, www.supremehotels.com. 69 slightly tatty but adequately clean rooms with marble and plastic furniture, 31 a/c, good rooftop restaurant, **Surya**, with temple views, bar, 24-hr travel desk, exchange, Sify internet booths in the basement, a bit noisy and a mite overpriced. Security and service both wanting.

C-D The Madurai Residency, 14-15 West Marret St, T0452-234 3140, www.madurai residency.com. Rather grand for Madurai: 75 rooms over 7 floors, glass lift. Economy rooms better than a/c due to musty smell.

D Aarathy, 9 Perumalkoil, west of Kundalalagar Temple, T0452-233 1571. Decently appointed though dingy rooms, some a/c with balcony, vegetarian restaurant, quiet, very friendly.

D YMCA International Guest House, Main Guard Sq, near temple, T0452-234 0861, www.ymcamadurai.com. A great option within spitting distance of the temple. The double rooms here are simple but spacious and clean, the staff are friendly, and profits go to worthwhile projects.

E Hotel Tamil Nadu, West Veli St, T0452-233 7471. Mint-coloured guesthouse dating from 1968 set around courtyard attached to the friendly TN tourist office. In bad need of a new lick of paint – it's pretty grubby – but there are TVs, huge rooms and the staff are charming.

E-F Dhanamani, 20-22 Sunnamukara St, T0452-234 2703. Nice rooms with bath, fan, TV, roof terrace on 8th floor with temple views.

E-F Sulochna Palace, 96 W Perumal Maistry St, T0452-234 1071. Good-value, clean rooms, and slightly more salubrious than the nearby bottom-bracket options. Avoid lower floors where generator noise is obtrusive.

F International, 46 W Perumal Maistry St, T0452-437 7463. Friendly, 34 clean and tidy rooms with TV and views from upper floors. Tends to have rooms when others are full.

F TM Lodge, 50 W Perumal Maistry St, T0452-234 1651. 57 rooms (hot water), some a/c, some with TV, balcony, very clean, bookings for rail/bus journeys. Glowing reports.

F Visakam Lodge, 9 Kakathope St, T0452-274 1241. Good value place with 18 clean rooms, very popular with Indian tourists.

Ramesvaram *p951, map p951*

D-E Hotel Tamil Nadu (TTDC), 14 East Car St, T04573-221064. Sea-facing balconies, 53 rooms (2-6 beds), some a/c, clean, grubby restaurant (breakfast from 0700), bar, sea bathing nearby, exchange. Very popular; book well in advance.

D-E Maharaja, 7 Middle St, west of the Temple, T04573-221271. 30 rooms, some a/c with bath, exchange, temple music broadcast on loudspeakers, otherwise recommended.

D-E Venkatesh, West Car St, T04573-221296. Some a/c rooms in a modern, 4-storey concrete block.

F Railway Retiring Rooms, T04573-221226. 9 rooms and dorm.

F Swami Ramanatha Tourist Home, opposite museum, T04573-221217. Good clean rooms with bath, best budget option.

Chettinad *p954*

Chettinad is still largely uncharted territory, and the few really good places to stay are priced towards the higher end. A handful of cheaper options exist in Karaikkudi and other towns, but they do not have the guides on hand to gain access to the old private homes (without whose help the Raja of Chettinad's Palace may be the only house you look inside).

L Visalam, Kanadukathan, T04565-273302, www.cghearth.com. Romantic and supremely comfortable high-celinged rooms, sparely furnished with Chettiar writing desks and 4-posters, in a beautifully restored art deco mansion – the only one in Chettinad built for a girl. The chef serves banana leaf lunches and does cooking demonstrations, good local guides are available for walking and bike tours, plus there's a huge pool and lawns.

AL The Bangala, Senjai, T04565-220221, www.thebangala.com. 8 bright and spacious a/c rooms with period colonial furniture, in restored 1916 bungalow, a heritage guest- house of character set amidst orchards and palms, serves full-on, totally authentic Chettinad feasts for a fair whack at Rs 800 per meal (must be booked in advance, rest stop facilities for day visitors and a full-board option. The family here wrote the (coffee table) book on Chettinad architecture.

AL Chettinadu Mansion, behind the Raja's Palace, Kanadukathan, T04565-273080; book through **Deshadan Tours and Travels**, T0484-232 1518, www.chettinadumansion.com. Dating back to 1902, this stunning house takes up half the block, with courtyard after courtyard stretching back from the street. Huge rooms, with a quirky green-brown colour scheme, heavy painted shutters and private rooftop sit-outs, encircle the upper floor. Downstairs is still used for family *pujas* and storing the wedding dowry. Simple Chettinad- style meals, served in the colonnaded dining room or under stars in the courtyard, cost Rs 450, and the charming Mr Chandramouli, who was born in the house, is often on hand to share stories or sharp business advice.

D-F Golden Singar, 100 Feet Rd, Karaikuddi, T04565-235521. Remarkably clean and good-value marble-floored rooms (fan-cooled half the price of a/c), handy for bus stand though a bit distant from the market and temples. Clean restaurant downstairs and cheap internet cafés nearby.

E-F Hotel Udhayam, A-333 Sekkalai Rd, Karaikuddi, T04565-233142. Another decent cheap option, similar to the Golden Singar but closer to the action.

F Nivaas, Devakottai, 1st left from bus station coming from the north (no sign in English). Basic (no electric sockets), no English spoken.

Eating

Madurai *p946, maps p947 and p948*

TT Surya, Hotel Supreme (see Sleeping). 1600-2400. 7th-floor rooftop restaurant with international as well as Indian menu. Excellent Andhra *thalis*, very busy Sun evenings.

TT Temple View, Park Plaza Hotel (see Sleeping). Excellent rooftop venue.

T Delhiwala Sweets, W Tower St. Delicious Indian sweets and snacks.

T Jayaram Sweets, 6-7 Netaji Rd. Good salty namkeens and fantastic coconut buns.

T New Arya Bhavan, North and South Indian choices, ice cream.

T Sri Sabarees, corner of W Perumal Maistry St and Town Hall Rd. Serves simple South Indian fare – *thalis* (lunchtime only), *pongal*, *iddli* and *dosai* – but the 2 dining halls are perpetually packed, as is the coffee stall out front.

T Sri Saravana, 7 Melur Rd, opposite Court. Delicious sweets (try the spectacular milk *peda*) and decent meals, across the river from town. Worth a diversion if you're at the Gandhi Museum.

Ramesvaram *p951, map p951*

Don't expect anything other than *thalis* here. There are several popular snack stands, with signs only in Tamil, on the road between Mela St and the museum.

Abbirami Hotels, off East Car St on road towards beach. Neat place churning out lunchtime meals and tiffin (*dosas*, *vada* and the like) after 1500.

Devasthanam Trust, has a canteen opposite the east gate of the temple.

Entertainment

Madurai *p946, maps p947 and p948*

Folk performances, in the 4 'Chitrai' streets by the temple, every Sat 1700-1800, free.

Meenakshi Temple: 'Bedtime of the God' 2100, is not to be missed (see page 948).

Thirumalai Nayaka Palace: Sound and Light show: English 1845-1930; Rs 5 (take mosquito repellent), sadly, "poor, faded tape". During the day, dance drama and concerts are held in the courtyard.

Festivals and events

Madurai *p946, maps p947 and p948*

Jan **Jallikattu Festival** (Taming the Bull).

Jan/Feb The annual **Float Festival** marks the birth anniversary of Thirumalai Nayaka. Many temple deities in silks and jewels, including Meenakshi and Sundareswarar, are taken out on a full moon night on floats decorated with hundreds of oil lamps and flowers. The floats carry them to the central shrine to the accompaniment of music and chanting.

Apr/May The 10-day **Chitrai Festival** is the most important at the Meenakshi Temple, celebrating the marriage of Siva and Meenakshi.

Aug/Sep The **Avanimoolam** is the Coronation Festival of Siva when the image of Lord Sundareswarar is taken out to the river bank dressed as a worker.

Pudukkottai *p955*

Jan/Feb Bullock races (*manju virattu*) are held in the area.

O Shopping

Madurai *p946, maps p947 and p948*

Kashmiri emporia pay 40-50% commission to touts who lure you into their shops with spurious promises of views into the temple. Best buys are textiles, wood and stone carvings, brass images, jewellery and appliqué work for temple chariots. Most shops are on South Avani Moola St (for jewellery), Town Hall Rd, Masi St and around the temple.

Books

Higginbotham's Book Exchange, near the temple.
New Century Book House, 79-80 West Tower St. Recommended.

Handicrafts

Handicrafts Emporium, 39-41 Town Hall Rd. Also try: **Khadi Gramodyog Bhandar** and **Surabhi** on W Veli St.

Textiles and tailors

The market near Pudu Mandapam, next to Meenakshi East Gate. Sells fabric and is a brilliant place to get clothes made.
Femina, 10 W Chitrai St. Similar to the market (you can take photos of the Meenakshi Temple from their rooftop).
Hajee Moosa, 18 E Chitrai St. Tailoring in 8 hrs; 'ready-mades' at **Shabnam**, at No 17.

Chettinad *p954*

Antiques

Muneesvaran Kovil St in Karaikkudi is lined with antiques shops selling old sepia photographs, temple lamps, old advertising posters, scrap book matter, religious paintings and Czech pewter jars.
Kattu Raja's, Palaniappa Chettiar St.
Old Chettinad Crafters, Murugen Complex, 37/6 Muneesvaran Kovil St, Karaikkudi, T(0)98428-223060, chettinaduantiques@yahoo.co.in. One of the best.
VJ Murugesan, sells old wooden furniture, household articles, wooden pillars, glass.
Venkateswara Furniture and Timber Merchant, No 8 Keela Oorani West, Karaikkudi, T(0)98424-232112. If you're in the market for bigger objects and weight is no object, this architectural salvage yard is a good starting point. Bargain hard: a granite pillar shouldn't cost more than Rs 1500.

Cotton and fabrics

MM Street and The Weavers' Lane beside the Bangala have Chettinad cotton for sale straight off the loom. Ask locally for the next *sandais*, the colourful local weekly markets.

Activities and tours

Madurai *p946, maps p947 and p948*

Body and soul

Yoga classes at **Gandhi Museum**, T0452-248 1060. Daily at 0630.

Swimming

Rs 300 gets you unlimited use of the pool at the **Taj Garden Retreat** (see Sleeping), a brilliant antidote to the craziness of the temple.

Tour operators

Tours can be arranged with **TTDC**, via Hotel Tamil Nadu, West Veli St, T0452-233 7471, or through most hotel desks. **Temple tour** of Madurai and attractive surroundings by a/c coach; half day, 0700-1200, 1500-2000. Rs 125. Recommended for an overview. Apr-Jun: **Courtallam** Rs 300. **Kodaikkanal** 0700-2100, Rs 300. **Rameswaram** Rs 275.
Ex-Serviceman Travels, 1 Koodalalagar, Perumal Kovil St, T0452-273 0571, City tour, half day, 0700, 1500, Rs 140; Kodaikkanal or Ramesvaram 0700-1900, Rs 275; overnight to Kanniyakumari, Rs 350.
Indian Panorama (Trichy), T0431-243 3372, www.indianpanorama.in. Tours from Madurai (and other towns). The Pandians are very helpful, efficient, South India tours, car with excellent driver. Highly recommended.

Pleasant Tours and Travels, Mr Ian Fernandez, Plot No 6, St Joseph St (opposite Ellis Nagar Telephone Exchange T0452-261 0614, www.pleasanttours.org.
Siraj, 19A TPK Rd, opposite Malai Murasu, T0452-273 9666, mshersha@md4.vsnl.net.in. Ticketing, good multilingual guides, cars.

Transport

Madurai *p946, maps p947 and p948*

Air

Airport to city centre (12 km) by Pandiyan coach (calls at top hotels); taxi (Rs 375) or auto-rickshaw (Rs 80). **Indian Airlines**, 7A W Veli St, T0452-234 1234. 1000-1300, 1400-1700; Airport, T0452-269 0433. Flights to **Chennai** and **Mumbai**. **Air India**, opposite train station, W Veli St. **Jet Airways**, T0452-252 6969; airport T0452-269 0771.

Bus

Local There is a good network within the city and the suburbs. **Central (Periyar) Bus Stands**, near W Veli St, are now used for buses around town and destinations nearby. Approaching on a bus from the south, to get to the centre, change to a city bus at Tirumangalam (15 km south).
Long distance Most intercity buses use the well-organized **New Central Bus Stand** (Mattuthavani Bus Terminal), 6 km northeast of town (continuation of Alagar Koil Rd), T0452-258 0680; Rs 100 by rickshaw, or catch city buses 3, 48 or 700. Buses for **Bengaluru (Bangalore)** (11 hrs), **Ernakulam (Kochi)**, **Chennai** (10 hrs), **Pondicherry** (9 hrs), **Thiruvananthapuram** (8 hrs), **Kumbakonum**, **Ramesvaram** (under 4 hrs, every 15 mins), **Thanjavur** (4 hrs), **Tiruchirappalli** (2½ hrs), **Tirunelveli** (4 hrs, Rs 40). **Arapalayam Bus Stand**, 3 km northwest of centre (Bus route No 7A, auto-rickshaws Rs 40), T0452-236 1740, for destinations to the west and northwest, including **Kodaikkanal**, buses (crowded in peak season, Apr-Jul); 3½ hrs (longer via Palani), Rs 150. Also buses to **Coimbatore** (5 hrs, change there for Mysore or Ooty), **Periyar/ Kumili** (4 hrs), **Salem** (5½ hrs), **Dindigul**.

Rickshaw

Autos Rs 25-40, cycle Rs 20 for trips in town.

Taxi/car hire

Unmetered; 12 hrs/100 km, Rs 700-1000; 3 hrs/30km, Rs 400-800; 6 hrs sightseeing, Rs 490 (Rs 750 a/c); 1 hr/10 km, Rs 65, Rs 100 (a/c). **Janakiraman**, 184 North Veli St; **Supreme**, 110 Perumal Maistry St, T0452-274 3151.

Train

Madurai Junction is the main station: enquiries, T131. 0700-1300, 1330-2000. New Computer Reservation Centre to south of main entrance. Left-luggage facilities. Pre-paid auto-rickshaw kiosk outside. **Chennai** (**ME**) via Villupuram for **Pondicherry**: *Vaigai Exp 12636*, 0630, 8 hrs; *Pandiyan Exp 12638*, 2045, 10 hrs. **Coimbatore**: *Coimbatore Exp 16609*, 0040, 7 hrs. **Kanniyakumari**: *Chennai-Guruvayoor Exp 16127*, 1640, 5 hrs. **Ramesvaram**: 3 unreserved passenger trains a day, at 0010, 0615 and 1815, 3-4 hrs. **Tiruchirappalli**: several, *Vaigai Exp 12636*, 0630, 2½ hrs (beautiful countryside); *Pandiyan Exp 12638*, 2045, 3½ hrs.

Ramesvaram *p951, map p951*

Bicycle hire

Bike hire from West Car or East Car St.

Bus

Local Marudhu Pandiyan Transport Corporation (MPTC) covers the town and area around. Bus station is 2 km west of town. Take a bus from the train station to the Ramalingesvara Temple, to Pamban or to Dhanuskodi. From the temple's east gate to Dhanuskodi roadhead and to Gandhamadana Parvatam, both every 2 hrs.
Long distance State, MPTC and private bus companies run regular services via **Mandapam** to several towns nearby. The **Central Bus Stand** is 2 km from the main temple gate. **Govt Express Bus Reservations**, North Car St, 0700-2100. Frequent buses to **Madurai**, 173 km (4½ hrs); tourist coaches (hotel-to-hotel) are better.

Taxi

A few cars and jeeps are available from the train station and hotels.

Train
Ramesvaram Railway Station, enquiries and reservations, T226. 0800-1300, 1330-1730. **Chennai**: *Sethu Exp 16714*, 2000, 12½ hrs, via **Karaikkudi**, 4 hrs, and **Villupuram** (for Pondicherry), 9 hrs. **Madurai**: 3 unreserved passenger trains a day, at 0005, 0525, 1735. **Tiruchirappalli**: *Chennai Egmore Exp 16702*, 1700, 5½ hrs.

Virudhunagar *p954*

Bus Leave Madurai early morning to catch the Kollam train; get off at police station and go to the end of the road opposite and turn left; the railway station is about 1 km on the right (take a rickshaw if carrying heavy luggage).
Train To **Kollam** and **Thiruvananthapuram**, Platform 3 across the bridge.

Chettinad *p954*

Bus Bus routes link **Karaikkudi** with every part of the state. Auto-rickshaws provide slow but relatively cheap transport between towns – Karaikkudi to Kanadukathan should cost around Rs 150.

Train **Chennai**: *Sethu Exp 16714*, 2345, 9 hrs; **Rameswaram**: *Rameswaram Exp 16701*, 0720, 4½ hrs. **Tiruchirappalli**: passenger trains at 0635, 0910, 0940, 1830, 2½ hrs.

Pudukkottai *p955*

Bus to **Tiruchirappalli, Thanjavur, Karaikkudi** via **Kanadukathan** (for Chettinad), **Madurai, Ramnad, Ramesvaram**, and to **Sittanavasal**.

Train Pudukkottai is 1 hr north of Karaikkudi on the Chennai-Rameswaram line. All trains listed for Karaikkudi stop here.

Directory

Madurai *p946, maps p947 and p948*

Banks Several on East Avani Moola St. **Alagendran Finance**, 182D N Veli St, good rate for cash US$ but not for TCs. **Andhra Bank**, W Chitrai St, accepts credit cards; **Canara Bank**, W Veli St, cashes Amex and sterling TCs. **Internet** Many west of the temple and in the budget hotel area charge Rs 20 per hr. **Medical services** **Christian Mission Hospital**, East Veli St; **Grace Kennet Hospital**, 34 Kennet Rd. **Post** The town GPO is at the north end of W Veli St (Scott Rd). In Tallakulam: Head Post Office and Central Telegraph Office, on Gokhale Rd.

Pudukkottai *p955*

Banks **State Bank of India**, East Main St.

Far South

India's southernmost point is a focus of pilgrimage that captures the imagination of millions of Hindus on a daily basis. Kanniyakumari occupies a beautiful headland site where the waters of the Bay of Bengal, the Indian Ocean and the Arabian Sea mingle together and crash upon the rocks. An hour further towards Kerala is Padmanabhapuram Palace, the painstakingly maintained ancient seat of the Travancore rulers. Tirunelveli, one-time capital of the Pandyas, is now a market and educational centre that is often passed over on the trail towards Madurai. ▸▸ *For listings, see pages 964-966.*

Tirunelveli and Palayamkottai → *For listings, see pages 964-966. Colour map 7, C4.*

Phone code: 0462. Population: 411,300.

On the banks of the Tamraparni, the only perennial river of the south, **Tirunelveli** is an attractive town surrounded by a belt of rice fields (*nelveli* means 'paddy-hedge') irrigated from the river's waters. Rising only 60 km to the east, at an altitude of over 1700 m, the river benefits from both the southwest and southeast monsoons; it tumbles down to the plains where it is bordered by a narrow strip of rich paddy land. Tirunelveli is now joined with the twin settlement of Palayamkottai. It is a market town and one of the oldest Christian centres in Tamil Nadu. St Francis Xavier settled here to begin his ministry in India in the early 16th century, but it has also been a centre of Protestant missionary activity. In 1896 it became the head of an Anglican diocese, now Church of South India.

Kanthimathi Nellaiyappar Temple ⓘ *closed 1230-1600, no photography*, is worth visiting; it is a twin temple, with the north dedicated to Siva (Nellaiyappar) and the south to Parvati (Kanthi). Each section has an enclosure over 150 m by 120 m. The temples have sculptures, musical pillars, valuable jewels, a golden lily tank and a 1000-pillared *mandapa*. There is a large white Nandi at the entrance. There is a **car festival** in June/July. The old town area around the temple is well worth a few hours of anyone's time, with the blue-painted houses reminiscent of Jodhpur (but without the tourist crowds). **Palayamkottai** has **St John's Church** (Church Missionary Society) with a spire 35 m high, a landmark for miles around. The town produces palm-leaf items.

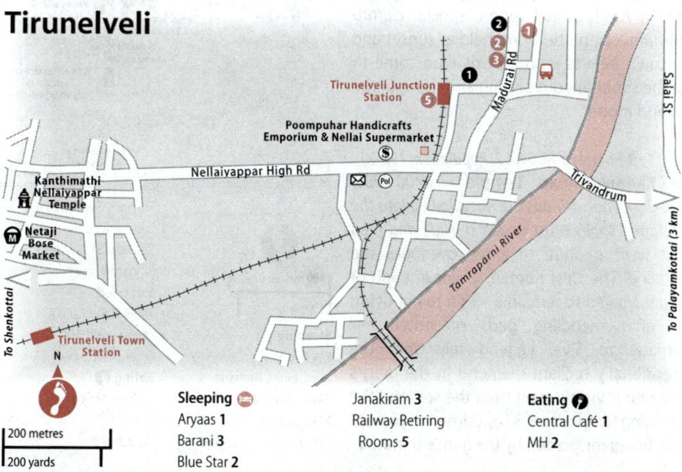

Sleeping
Aryaas 1
Barani 3
Blue Star 2
Janakiram 3
Railway Retiring Rooms 5

Eating
Central Café 1
MH 2

Around Tirunelveli

Tiruchendur, 50 km east of Tirunelveli, has a famous **shore temple** ⓘ *Rs 50 for 'fast darshan', men must remove shirts*, dedicated to Subrahmanya, and considered to be one of his six 'abodes'. See page 1086. It is a hive of activity during festivals. There are caves with rock-cut sculptures along the shore.

Manapad, the predominantly Roman Catholic coastal village 18 km south of Tiruchendur, is where St Francis Xavier is said to have landed and lived in a cave near the headland. The Holy Cross Church (1581) close to the sea is believed to house a fragment of the True Cross from Jerusalem.

Kanniyakumari → *For listings, see pages 964-966. Colour map 7, C4.*

Kanniyakumari's grubby streets come alive in the hour before dawn, as thousands throng the shoreline to witness the sunrise over the southern tip of India. This important pilgrimage site is centred on worship of the Goddess Kumari, 'the protector of India's shores'. The new day is heralded in by the scent of jasmine garlands, the wail of temple music and the whoops and applause of excited children as the sun finally crawls its way over the sea. It's an early-morning party that everyone is invited to join. The view offshore is dominated by India's answer to the Statue of Liberty: a 133-ft sculpture of the Tamil poet Thiruvalluvar. Just behind is a memorial to the philosopher Swami Vivekananda, a spiritual leader inspired by the Devi . Both can be reached by a quick ferry ride. In April, at full moon, special *chithra pournami* celebrations are held at sunset and the town heaves with crowds who come to see the simultaneous setting and rising of the sun and moon.

Sights → *Phone code: 04652. Population: 19,700.*

The **Kanniyakumari Temple** ⓘ *0400-1200, 1600-2000, non-Hindus are not allowed into the sanctuary, shoes must be left outside and men must wear a* dhoti *to enter*, overlooks the shoreline. The Devi Kumari, an incarnation of Parvati, vowed to remain a virgin to her dying day after meddling gods prevented her marriage to Siva. Legend tells that the exceptionally brilliant diamond in the deity's nose ring is visible even from the sea, and the sea-facing temple door is kept closed to prevent ships being misguided by the gem's shimmer.

Kanniyakumari

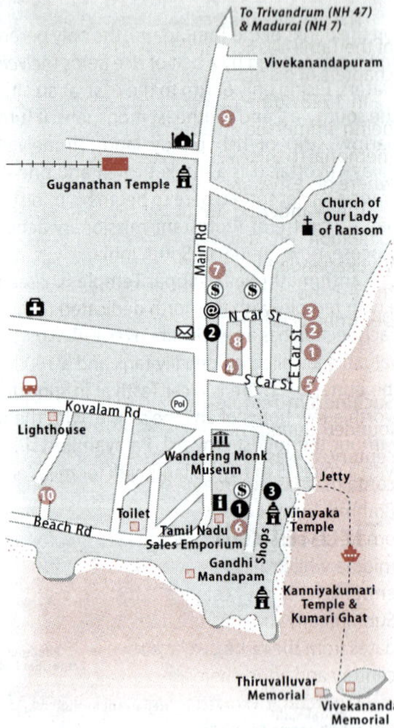

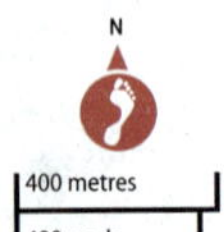

Sleeping
Lakshmi **1**
Maadhini & Archana Restaurant **2**
Manickam **3**
Parvathi Nivas Lodge **4**
Sankar's Guest House **7**
Saravana Lodge **6**
Seaview **5**
Singaar **9**
Sunrock **8**
Tamil Nadu & TTDC Restaurant **10**

Eating
Annapoorna **1**
Sangam **2**
Sravanas **3**

The **Vivekananda Memorial** ⓘ *0800-1600, Rs 10, ferry Rs 20, 15 mins (see page 965), allow 1 hr for the visit, smoking and eating prohibited, take off shoes before entering*, stands on one of two rocks, about 500 m from the mainland. The Bengali religious leader and philosopher Swami Vivekananda swam out here when a simple monk and devotee of the Devi, to sit in long meditation on this rock in 1892. He left convinced that religion could be a powerful instrument of social regeneration and individual development and was inspired to speak on Hinduism at the Parliament of Religions in Chicago, preaching that "the Lord is one, but the sages describe Him differently". On his return, he founded the Ramakrishna Mission in Chennai, which now has spread across the world. The rock was renamed Vivekananda Rock and a memorial was built in 1970. The design of the *mandapa* incorporates different styles of temple architecture from all over India and houses a statue of Vivekananda. People also come to see Sri Pada Parai, where the 'footprint' of the Devi has been enshrined on the rock.

The massive **Thiruvalluvar Statue** ⓘ *0800-1600, free, ferry Rs 20, 15 mins*, immortalizes the writer of the Tamil classic, *Thirukkural*. The statue is exactly 133 ft (40 m) tall, to correspond with the 133 chapters of his most famous work. Stairs allow visitors to stand at his giant feet.

In 1948 some of Mahatma Gandhi's ashes were brought here for public display before being immersed in the sea. The **Ghandi Mandapam** ⓘ *0700-1900, free*, was built as a memorial to this event. At midday on Gandhi's birthday, 2 October, the sun shines on the spot where his ashes were placed.

The **Wandering Monk Museum** ⓘ *Main Rd, 0830-1200, 1600-2000, Rs 5*, has an informative exhibition on the life and work of Vivekananda. There is also a photo exhibition, in **Vivekanandapuram**, 1 km north, which can be reached by an easy walk along the beach though there is no access from the north side. The **Yoga Kendra** there runs courses from June to December. Further north there is a pleasant sandy beach, 3.5 km along Kovalam Road.

Around Kanniyakumari

Suchindram Temple ⓘ *open to non- Hindus, priests acting as guides may expect donations*, was founded during the Pandiyan period but was expanded under Thirumalai Nayaka in the 17th century. It was also used later as a sanctuary for the rulers of Travancore to the west and so contains treasures from many kingdoms. One of the few temples dedicated to the Hindu Trinity, Brahma, Vishnu and Siva, it is in a rectangular enclosure that you enter through the massive ornate seven-storeyed *gopuram*. North of the temple is a large tank with a small shelter in the middle while round the walls is the typically broad street used for car festivals. Leading to the entrance is a long colonnade with musical pillars and sculptures of Siva, Parvati, Ganesh and Subrahmanya on the front and a huge Hanuman statue inside. The main sanctuary, with a *lingam*, dates from the ninth century but many of the other structures and sculptures date from the 13th century and after. There are special temple ceremonies at sunset on Friday.

Nagercoil, 19 km from Kanniyakumari, is set with a stunning backcloth of the Western Ghats, reflected from place to place in the broad tanks dotted with lotuses. The landscape begins to feel more like Kerala than Tamil Nadu. It is an important railway junction and bus terminal. It is often a bottleneck filled with lorries so be prepared for delays. The old town of **Kottar**, now a suburb, was a centre of art, culture and pilgrimage. The **temple** ⓘ *0630-0900, 1730-2000*, to Nagaraja, after which the town is named, is unique in that although the presiding deity is the Serpent God Naga, there are also shrines to Siva and Vishnu as well as images of Jain *Tirthankaras*, Mahavira and Parsvanatha on the pillars. The temple is alive with snakes during some festivals. Christian missionaries played an important part in the town's development and left their mark in schools, colleges, hospitals and churches of different denominations. There is also a prominent Muslim community in Kottar, reflected in the shops closing on Fridays and remaining open on Sunday.

Padmanabhapuram → *For listings, see pages 964-966.*

ⓘ *Tue-Sun 0900-1300, 1400-1630 (last tickets 1600), Rs 200, child Rs 50 (accredited guide included, but expects a 'donation' after the tour), camera Rs 25, video Rs 1500. Best at 0900 before coach parties arrive.*

Padmanabhapuram, the old palace of the Rajas of Travancore, contains some fascinating architecture and paintings but some of the methods employed during its restoration have been criticized. Although decaying somewhat, the Kuthiramalika Palace in Trivandrum – if you are venturing into Kerala – might be better worth looking round. The name Padmanabhapuram (*Padma*, lotus; *nabha*, navel; *puram*, town) refers to the lotus emerging from the navel of Vishnu. From the ninth century this part of Tamil Nadu and neighbouring Kerala were governed by the Ay Dynasty, patrons both of Jainism and Hinduism. However, the land was always contested by the Cholas, the Pandiyas and the Cheras. By the late 11th century the new Venadu Dynasty emerged from the Chera rulers of Kerala and took control of Kanniyakumari District in AD 1125 under Raja Kodai Kerala Varman. Never a stable kingdom, and with varying degrees of territorial control, Travancore State was governed from Padmanabhapuram between 1590-1790, when the capital was shifted to Thiruvananthapuram. Although the Rajas of Travancore were Vaishnavite kings, they did not neglect Siva, as can be seen from various sculptures and paintings in the palace. The King never officially married and the heir to the throne was his eldest sister's oldest son. This form of matrilineal descent was characteristic of the earlier Chera Empire (who ruled for 200 years from the early 12th century). The palace shows the fine craftsmanship, especially in woodworking, characteristic of Kerala's art and architecture. There are also some superb frescoes and excellent stone-sculpted figures. The outer cyclopean stone wall is fitted together without mortar. It encloses a total area of 75 ha and the palace buildings 2 ha.

Far South listings

For Sleeping and Eating price codes and other relevant information, see Essentials pages 38-42.

Sleeping

Tirunelveli *p961, map p961*

Hotels are often full during the wedding season (Apr-Jun). Book ahead or arrive early. Several budget hotels are clustered near Junction Railway Station, most with Western toilet and shower.

B-D Janakiram, 30 Madurai Rd, near bus stand, T0462-233 1941. 70 clean rooms, with hot shower, some a/c, lift, smart, brightly lit, outstanding vegetarian rooftop restaurant. Highly recommended.

C-E Aryaas, 67 Madurai Rd, T0462-233 9001. 69 rooms, 25 a/c, in dark bordello-style, non a/c better value, restaurants (separate vegetarian one, but it's also a mosquito's heaven), bar. Excellent internet café opposite.

C-E Bharani, 29 Madurai Rd, T0462-233 3234. 43 rooms, with hot shower, 10 a/c, clean, well maintained, vegetarian restaurant, in large modern block, lift, ample parking.

F Blue Star, 36 Madurai Rd, T0462-233 4495. 50 rooms with cold shower, 10 a/c, good veg restaurant, Indian style, modern. Good value.

F Railway Retiring Rooms. Clean, secure rooms and dorm. Excellent value.

Kanniyakumari *p962, map p962*

Hotels are in heavy demand; book well ahead. Cheaper places may only offer squat toilets.

AL-A Seaview, East Car St, T04652-247841, www.hotelseaview.in. Plush, central hotel with spotlessly clean, a/c rooms. Helpful staff, restaurant, bar. Recommended.

B Hotel Singaar, Main Rd, 2 km from attractions, T04652-247992. Smart, popular hotel with comfortable rooms, many with balcony. Nice pool, decent restaurant. Breakfast included.

C-E Hotel Tamil Nadu (TTDC), Beach Rd, T04652-246257, www.ttdconline.com. Quiet location away from the busy centre. Pleasant rooms with terraces looking out to sea. Nice garden setting. Popular with Indian families. Also has dorm accom for Rs 50.

C-E Maadhini, East Car St, T04652-246787. Wide variety of good value rooms. A/c rooms have balconies with sea views. Restaurant, bar, central location.

D-E Manickam, North Car St, T04652-246387. Under same management as **Maadhini**, this cheaper option has good-sized rooms but unfriendly staff. Overpriced a/c rooms.

E-F Lakshmi, East Car St, T04652-247203. Friendly, family-run hotel with clean rooms, some a/c. Can be noisy as guests arrive at 0500 to see sunrise from the roof. Excellent value.

E-F Sunrock, Pillyarkoil St, T04652-246167. Newish hotel tucked away down a back alley. Clean rooms, some a/c, all with terraces, but no views.

F Sankar's Guest House, Main Rd, T04652-246260. Best of the cheapies. Quiet and clean rooms all with TV and balcony. Very friendly management. Recommended.

F-G Saravana Lodge, Sannathi St, T04652-246007. Moderately clean, basic rooms. Upstairs rooms open onto wide veranda with good sea view. The temple next door provides alarm clock services at 0500. Cheerful, helpful staff.

G Parvathi Nivas Lodge, West Car St, T04652-246351. Very basic, dark, cell-like rooms with bucket showers, in an old-style, decrepit lodge.

Around Kanniyakumari *p963*

D Parvathi, Nagercoil, T04652-233020. Clean good-sized rooms, some a/c.

D Rajam, MS Rd, Vadasery, Nagercoil, T04652-276581. Good-value rooms, restaurant, roof garden.

Eating

Tirunelveli *p961, map p961*

Central Café, near station, good vegetarian.

MH Restaurant, opposite **Aryaas**. Western fast food, pizzas. Modern.

Kanniyakumari *p962, map p962*

You'll find a dozen tiny restaurants serving cheap and tasty snacks of *dosai, vadai, bhaji* and *pakora* on Main Rd between Sth Car St and the Text MediumSangam Hotel.

Archana, Hotel Maadhini (see Sleeping). Good mixed menu of Indian, Chinese and International options.

Annapoonna, Sannathi St. Excellent vegetarian food in clean, bright surroundings. Very popular with families.

Sangam, Sangam Hotel, Main Rd. Good *thalis*.

Sravanas, Sannathi St. Cheap and cheerful vegetarian meals. Recommended.

TTDC Restaurant, Hotel Tamil Nadu (see Sleeping). Looks like a barracks, but excellent non-vegetarian Indian meals.

Festivals and events

Kanniyakumari *p962, map p962*

Apr **Chithra Pournami** is a special full moon celebration at the temple usually held in the 2nd week of Apr.

Oct Special **Navarathri** celebrations in 1st week of Oct.

Transport

Tirunelveli *p961, map p961*

Bus Good bus connections to **Kanniyakumari**, **Thiruvananthapuram**, and to **Madurai** (faster to change buses at Tirumangalam), **Tiruchirappalli** and **Chennai**. For **Courtallam**, go to Tenkasi (Rs 12, 1½ hrs) and take bus to Courtallam (Rs 2, 20 mins).

Train Train to **Chennai** (**ME**): *Nellai Exp 12632*, 1845, 12 hrs, via **Madurai** (2½ hrs). **Kanniyakumari**: *Kanyakumari Exp 12633*, 0450, 2 hrs.

Kanniyakumari *p962, map p962*

Bus Long-distance buses leave from the station west of town on Kovalam Rd, 15 mins' walk from centre, T04652-271285. There are frequent services to **Nagercoil** (½ hr, Rs 10) and **Thiruvananthapuram** (2½ hrs, Rs 45). For **Kovalam** and **Varkala** change at **Thiruvananthapuram**. There are 4 daily departures to **Chennai** (16 hrs, Rs 390), via **Madurai** (6 hrs, Rs 145), at 0930, 1345, 1445 and 1630.

Ferry The ferry to **Vivekananda Rock** runs every 30 mins, 0700-1100, 1400-1700, Rs 20). Expect long queues during festivals.

Train The station is to the north, on Main Rd. There are 2 trains a day to **Nagercoil**, at 0720 and 2040 (¼ hr). Daily services to **Mumbai**, *Kanniyakumari Mumbai Exp 16382*, 0530, 48 hrs, via **Thiruvananthapuram** (2¼ hrs) and **Ernakulam** (7½ hrs); **Bengaluru**, *Island Exp 16525*, 1030 (21 hrs), via **Thiruvananthapuram** (2¼ hrs) and **Varkala** (3½ hrs); **Chennai**, *Kanyakumari Exp 12634*, 1720, 15 hrs, via **Madurai** (5 hrs). Once a week you have the opportunity to take the longest train journey in India. The *Him Sagar Exp 16317*, departs every Fri at 1405, to **Jammu** (3 days).

Around Kanniyakumari *p963*

Bus From **Nagercoil** there are frequent buses to **Thiruvananthapuram** (2 hrs); **Kanniyakumari** (30 mins); and **Madurai** (6½ hrs).

Train At **Nagercoil** the railway station is 3 km from the bus station. The daily *Kanniyakumari Mumbai Exp 16382*, and *Kanniyakumari Bengaluru Exp 16525* both stop here on their way to, and from **Kanniyakumari**. Frequent bus connections to **Thiruvananthapuram**, **Kanniyakumari** and **Madurai**.

Padmanabhapuram *p964*

Bus Regular buses to **Thiruvananthapuram** and **Kanniyakumari**. Less frequent buses to and from **Kovalam**. From Kovalam, depart approximately 0940 to **Thuckalai**. Return buses from Thuckalai depart 1445, 1530.

Taxi A taxi from Kovalam or Thiruvananthapuram costs Rs 800.

Directory

Tirunelveli *p961, map p961*

Banks On Trivandrum High Rd. **Medical services** Hospital in High Ground, Palayamkottai. **Post** GPO, Trivandrum High Rd.

Kanniyakumari *p962, map p962*

Banks Canara Bank, State Bank of India and State Bank of Travancore, are all on Main Rd. All have ATMs. **Internet** There are several internet cafés on Main Rd. All charge around Rs 20 per hr. **Medical services** General Hospital, off Main Rd, T04652-248505. **Post** Head Post Office, Main Rd, 0800-1600, 1000-1400.

Kerala

Contents

Footprint features

At a glance

Getting around Famous for its converted rice boat backwaters tours; take the ferry for a more local route around. Bus/car journeys in the backwaters are picturesque too. Trains from Malabar to Ernakulum and on to Trivantharapuram.

Time required 2 days is enough for a backwaters cruise. Leave a couple of days for Fort Kochi and a few in Varkala. A week will make Malabar a worthwhile detour. Add 3 days for inland or Ghat nature – like the Wayanad.

Weather Hot year round. Monsoon in Jun, Jul and Aug.

When not to go Mar and Apr are stiflingly hot.

★ **Don't miss …**

1. Ayurvedic medicine at Kovalam and Varkala, pages 987 and 988.
2. Backwaters, page 991.
3. Snake boat races at Alappuzha in August, page 998.
4. Dusk at Fort Kochi, page 1001.
5. Periyar National Park, page 1014.
6. Monsoon rafting and folk culture along the River Nila, pages 1025 and 1030.
7. Pooram festival at the end of April in Thrissur, page 1029.
8. Theyyam dances in Kerala's northern villages, page 1038.

Kerala ebbs by at snail's pace, most picturesquely in the slow-flowing networks of lagoons and rivers that make up its backwaters, where nature grows in such overwhelming profusion that canals sit choked with pretty water-lily thickets and dragonflies bunch in clouds over lotus leaves. Dawn mists drift through canopies made by antique mango and teak trees, as farmers slip their oars into the silent waters, and women's dresses glare extra bright in the reflections of the still glass waters.

In the ramshackle port city of Fort Kochi, it's as if the clocks stopped a few centuries back: wizened traders sift spice in the shadows of derelict go-downs, the churches glow lime white, at the harbour's edge lines of cantilevered Chinese fishing nets swoop for their next catch of silvery sprats, and medieval streets and antique shops thread the route between the tiny blue-tiled synagogue and grand Dutch wooden palace of Mattancherry.

Unwind with Ayurvedic massages on the southern beaches of Kovalam and Varkala, but Malabar, in the north, is the real unsung jewel of the state, an outpost of staunch Hindu religiosity and capital of the Muslim Moplah community. Here, hushed families gather at dawn in leafy temple gardens to watch spectacles of the unique, hypnotic temple dance-form *Theyyam* and, come nightfall, the precision athletes of the swashbuckling martial art *Kalarippayattu* draw their swords.

Switchback turns bear you from the lush green paddy fields of the plains through spindly rubber plantations and blooming coffee-tree forests up to the thick tea-shrub territory of the high mountain villages of Thekaddy and Munnar, whose nature reserves hide tigers and herds of elephant.

Background → *Population: 32 million. Area: 39,000 sq km.*

The land

Geography Stretching from some of the highest mountains of the Western Ghats to the lush coastal plain, Kerala encapsulates the rich diversity of western India's coastal landscapes. Its narrow coastal fringe has been raised from the sea in the last million years. Inland are rolling hills of laterite, succeeded by the ancient rocks that form the backbone of the Western Ghats.

Climate Kerala does not have an extended totally dry season characteristic of the rest of India, but is particularly wet from June to September. Maximum temperatures seldom rise above 32°C while minimum temperatures at sea level never drop below 20°C.

History

The **Cheras**, who established themselves in the Kuttanad region around Alappuzha as the first Kerala power, developed a wide network of trade links in which both the long-established Christian community and the Jewish community participated fully. However, the neighbouring Cholas launched several successful attacks against Chera power from AD 985. When Chola power disintegrated at the end of the 11th century, Calicut gradually became dominant under the **Zamorin** (literally 'Lord of the Sea'), who had well-established contacts with the Arab world. By some accounts the Zamorins were the wealthiest rulers in contemporary India, but were never able to use these advantages to unite Kerala, and during the 16th century the Portuguese exploited the rivalry of the Raja of Kolattiri with the Zamorin of Calicut, being granted permission to trade from Kochi in 1499. Over the following century there was fierce competition and sometimes open warfare between the Portuguese, bent on eliminating Arab trading competition, and the Zamorin, whose prosperity depended on that Arab trade. After a century of hostility, the Dutch arrived on the west coast. The Zamorin seized the opportunity of gaining external support, and on 11 November 1614 concluded a treaty giving the Dutch full trading rights. In 1615 the British East India Company was also given the right to trade by the Zamorin. By 1633 the Dutch had captured Portuguese forts. The ruler of Kochi rapidly made friends with the Dutch, in exchange for having the new Mattancherry Palace built for him. In the decade after 1740 Raja Marthanda Varma succeeded in uniting a number of petty states around Thiruvananthapuram and led them to a crushing victory over the Dutch in the Battle of Kolachel in 1741. By 1758 the Zamorin of Calicut was forced to withdraw from Kochi, but the **Travancore** ruler's reign was brief. In 1766 Haidar Ali had led his cavalry troops down onto the western coastal plain, and he and his son Tipu Sultan pushed further and further south with a violence that is still bitterly remembered. In 1789, as Tipu was preparing to launch a final assault on the south of Travancore, the British attacked him from the east. He withdrew his army from Kerala and the Zamorin and other Kerala leaders looked to the British to take control of the forts held by Tipu's officers. Tipu Sultan's first defeat at the hands of Lord Cornwallis led to the Treaty of Seringapatam in 1792, under which Tipu surrendered all his captured territory in northern Kerala, to direct British rule. Travancore and Kochi then became Princely states under ultimate British authority.

Culture

The distinctiveness of Kerala's cultural identity is reflected in the Brahmin myths of its origin. As Robin Jeffrey explains, Parasurama, the sixth incarnation of Vishnu, having been banished from India, was given permission by Varuna, the Lord of the Sea, to reclaim all the land within the throw of his axe. When Parasaruma threw the axe it fell from Kanniyakumari to Gokarna, and as the sea withdrew Kerala was formed.

Matriarchy This may have originated in the 10th-century conflict with the Cholas. Krishna Chaitanya suggests that as many men were slaughtered there was a surplus of women,

Kerala's social underbelly

Although you'll get the sense of living under one long coconut palm thicket, locals have good reason to call Kerala the city state; the ratio of people per square metre outstrips that of anywhere else in India. And don't let the socialist rhetoric of their political parties fool you – in the main, Keralites are a prosperous bunch and money and status certainly matters. Kerala is where the marketing people come to test their advertising campaigns, and the state boasts of how highly it scores in all quality of life indicators. But relative affluence brings with it social problems: Kerala also has both the highest suicide rate and one of the highest rates of alcohol consumption per capita on the subcontinent, and huge swathes of agricultural land go uncultivated as high literacy creates a class with loftier ambitions than tilling the soil.

encouraging the development of a matrilineal system in which women controlled family property. Kerala is the first state in India to claim 100% literacy in some districts and women enjoy a high social status. The 2001 Census shows that overall literacy has reached 91%, and uniquely in India there are more women than men in the population.

Religion The majority of the population is Hindu, but as much as a quarter is Christian and there is also a large Muslim population. Religious communities have often lived amicably together. There is no conflict between the varying Hindu sects, and most temples have shrines to each of the major Hindu divinities. Christianity, which is thought to have been brought by St Thomas the Apostle to the coast of Kerala at Kodungallur in AD 52, has its own very long tradition. The equally large Muslim community traces its origins back to the spread of Islam across the Indian Ocean with Arab traders from the seventh century.

Cuisine Kerala's cuisine reflects its diverse religious traditions, its location on the seaboard and the ubiquitous presence of the coconut. Uniquely in India, beef is widely eaten, although seafood is far more common. Fish *moilee* is prepared with coconut milk and spices while for *pollichathu* the fish is baked with chilli paste, curry leaves and spices. Coconut-based dishes such as *thoran*, a dry dish of mixed vegetables chopped very small, herbs and curry leaves, and *avial*, similar to *thoran* but cooked in a sauce, are widely eaten. *Erisseri* is a thick curry of banana or yam and *kichadi* is beetroot or cucumber in coconut-curd paste. You can try these with the soft centred, lacy pancake *appam* or the soft noodle rice cakes *iddiappam*. Jack fruit, pineapples, custard apples and an endless variety of bananas also play a vital part in many dishes. For dessert, you might get milk *payasam,* made with rice or vermicelli.

Language Malayalam, the state language, is the most recent of the Dravidian languages, developing from the 13th century with its origin in Sanskrit.

Dance The special dance form of Kerala, *Kathakali*, has its origins in the *Theyyam*, a ritual tribal dance of North Kerala, and *kalaripayattu*, the martial arts practised by the high-caste Nayars, going back 1000 years. In its present form of dance-drama, *Kathakali* has evolved over the last 400 years. The performance is usually outdoors, the stage bare but for a large bronze oil lamp, with the drummers on one side and the singers with cymbal and gong, who act as narrators, on the other. The art of mime reaches its peak in these highly stylized performances which used to last through the night; now they often take just three to four hours. The costume is comprised of a large billowing skirt, a padded jacket, some heavy ornaments and headgear. The make-up is all-important: *Pacha* (green) characterizing the Good and *Kathi* (knife, shape of a painted 'moustache'), the Villain; *Thadi* (bearded), white for superhuman *hanumans*, black for the hunter

Body language

Ayurveda, a Sanskrit word meaning 'the knowledge (*veda*) of life (*ayur*)', is an Indian holistic system of health dating back over 5000 years. Indians see it as a divine gift from Lord Brahma, their Hindu creator God, which has been developed by sages and holy men over the centuries. In contrast to the Western system of medicine, which is geared to treating an already diseased body or mind, Ayurveda seeks to help the individual strengthen and control both mind and body in order to prolong life and prevent illness. In today's world, it's a brilliant complement to Western medicine and, as well as detoxing the body and mind and relieving stress, has been used to treat ME, high blood pressure, allergies, asthma, back pain, rheumatism, skin diseases, migraines and insomnia, and is used as an effective follow-up treatment to chemotherapy.

How it works In essence, Ayurveda combines body treatments and detoxification therapies with a balanced diet, gentle exercise and meditation to promote wellbeing. The type of treatments and therapies are dictated by an individual's constitution, defined by a balance of three bodily energies or *doshas*: *vata*, *pitta* and *kapha*. Composed of the five elements – earth, water, fire, air and ether (or space) – these *doshas* govern our bodily processes: *vata* controls circulation and the nervous system; *pitta* the metabolism and digestion; *kapha* bodily strength and energy. When we feel out of kilter, our *doshas* are likely to be out of balance, which a course of Ayurvedic treatments will seek to remedy. If we're uptight and prone to multi-task, it will calm us down and help us focus. If we're sluggish and suffer from bad digestion, it will energize us and get our bowels moving again.

An experienced Ayurvedic doctor will diagnose your *dosha* type by taking your pulse, and observing such things as how quickly you speak and move, your build, the colour of your eyes and the quality of your skin. You'll also be asked lots of questions about your preferences – on anything from climate to the spiciness of food. The more open and honest you are, the more accurate a judgement will be, though it's uncanny how the best doctors will read you just right, whatever you tell them.

What you do Any programme of Ayurveda will include preparation treatments and elimination (or detox) therapies. The former include soothing, synchronized oil applications and massages, and *swedana* (purifying steam and herbal baths), while the latter involve ingesting or retaining herbal medicines, medicated oils and ghee (or clarified butter), inhalations, *bastis* (or oil enemas), therapeutic vomiting and bloodletting. Preparation treatments often include sleep-inducing *shirodara*, when a wonderful continuous stream of warm oil is poured across your forehead; *choornaswedana*, where hot herbal or lemon poultices are massaged all over you to induce sweating; and the supremely nourishing four-handed *abhyanga* and *marma* massage. *Pizhichil* is often regarded as the 'Marmite' of Ayurveda. Gallons of cleansing sesame oil are poured continuously over your body and massaged in by two therapists as the oil increases in heat. You'll slip about like a sardine in a tin, but this treatment is very effective. Look at the oil afterwards, and you'll be shocked at just how dirty you were. If you're a smoker, it's likely to be black.

Any hotel or retreat venue that offers only Ayurvedic massages is offering only a part of what Ayurveda is all about. You need time for Ayurveda treatments to have any real effect. A proper course of Ayurveda needs at least two weeks to be effective and offer any real lasting benefit, and rest between treatments is vital. Most people who undertake a course of Ayurveda have a '*panchakarma*' – which literally translates as five therapies, and which also refers to a general Ayurveda detox lasting two weeks or more.

and red for evil and fierce demons; *Kari* (black) signifying demonesses; *Minukku* (shining) 'simple' make-up representing the Gentle and Spiritual. The paints are natural pigments while the stiff 'mask' is created with rice paste and lime. The final application of a flower seed in the lower eyelid results in the red eyes you will see on stage. This classical dance requires lengthy, hard training to make the body supple, the eyes expressive. The 24 *mudras* express the nine emotions of serenity, wonder, kindness, love, valour, fear, contempt, loathing and anger. The gods and mortals play out their roles amid the chaos brought about by human ambition, but the dance ends in peace and harmony restored by the gods.

Modern Kerala

Government Kerala politics have often been unstable – even turbulent – since the first elections were held in March 1957, when Kerala became the first state in the world to democratically elect a Communist government. The debate has always been dominated by the struggle between the Marxist Communist Party, the Congress and various minor parties; and the state government has often been formed by coalitions. Politics here have traditionally been secular, as the BJP's failure to gain a single seat in the 2009 Lok Sabha elections suggests, though Muslim sentiment has found voice in the election of two members of the Kerala Muslim League. The Congress party returned to dominance in the 2009 elections.

Economy Traditionally Kerala's economy has depended heavily on agriculture. Estate crops, especially tea and rubber, make a major contribution to exports, while coconut and coconut products like coir (the coarse fibre used for matting and string and rope production), or copra (the oil-rich flesh of the coconut), continue to be vital to the state. Recent decades have seen the rise of Kerala as a remittance economy, with large flows of money being repatriated by Malayali workers in the Gulf to invest in land, housing and small-scale industries. Highly educated and increasingly middle class, Keralites have been abandoning old-fashioned and 'menial' industries such as agriculture. Rice production has been in long-term decline, as farmers converted paddy land to other more profitable uses, and where farm fields still exist, they are largely run by Tamils or other migrant workers – who in turn earn more in Kerala than in their home states. However, the collapse of Dubai's building boom looks set to trigger a reverse exodus, with hundreds of thousands of workers expected to return to Kerala in the next few years. The challenge this poses to the state is enormous, not only in supporting the families affected, but in managing a population whose aspirations and debts have been built around Gulf salaries. Business leaders bemoan the leftist culture of the state and the stranglehold the trade unions have on its workforce, which makes for a working week dominated by strikes, thus barring the way for the high levels of foreign investment that characterize Bengaluru (Bangalore), Hyderabad and Chennai's urban economies.

Thiruvananthapuram and the far south

The state capital, a pleasant city built over gently rolling coastal land, is very much a village as soon as you step away from the crowded centre. There's none of the throb, bustle and boom-time of Ernakulam, its opposite city up north, and no one could accuse it of being cosmopolitan; you'll be pushed to find a club, or bar, or even any traffic on the roads after midnight. It is, however, a stone's throw from here to the white sands of Kovalam, still a working fishing village, albeit one that survives under the lengthening shadow cast by unchecked tourist development. The backpackers who first populated Kovalam have left it to the package holidaymakers and luxury resorts and head instead to Varkala, a pilgrimage village and beach marked out by its sheer red rock face. Inland are the little- visited forests of Ponmudi and just over the southern border lies Kanniyakumari, the sacred toe-tip of India where three seas converge.
▸▸ *For listings, see pages 981-990.*

Ins and outs

Getting there The international airport is 6 km from the centre, a 15-minute drive outside rush hour, and half an hour from Kovalam. It has direct flights from Colombo, the Maldives, Kuala Lumpur, Singapore and the Middle East, as well as most major Indian cities. You can hire a pre-paid taxi (Rs 85) or auto (about Rs 30) into town or wait for a local bus. At the southern end of town are the central (long-distance) bus station, with services throughout Kerala and into neighbouring Tamil Nadu, and the railway station from where trains run up and down the coast. Local buses, including those bound for Kovalam, leave from the East Fort City stand opposite the fort entrance, southwest of the station. Buses to Kovalam can drop you at Waller Junction, five minutes' walk from the Samudra Beach hotels. A further 1.5 km on they turn off for the main Kovalam Bus Stand at the Ashok Hotel gate, five minutes from most southern hotels and cafés. Lighthouse Road is steep and narrow, but autos and taxis are able to drive up it. ▸▸ *See Transport, page 988.*

Getting around Thiruvanathapuram is relatively strung out, though the centre is compact. Autos or taxis are more convenient than the packed buses but bargain hard: businesses have fast acclimatized to the price naivety that goes hand in hand with package tourism. Minimum charges start at Rs 75 for taxis, Rs 15 for autos; thereafter the rate per running kilometre for cars is Rs 4.50 (non a/c), Rs 6.50 (a/c), rickshaws Rs 3. Drivers may be reluctant to accept the going rate.

Tourist information Tourist offices have plenty of leaflets and information sheets and are very helpful. Thiruvananthapuram's main tourist office is at the **Kerala Tourism** ⓘ *Park View, T0471-232 1132, www.keralatourism.org, Mon-Sat 1000-1700*, where you can book day and half-day tours around the city (Rs 110 and Rs 70 respectively). There are also offices at Thampanoor Central Bus Station, the railway station and the airport.

Thiruvananthapuram (Trivandrum) → *For listings, see pages 981-990. Colour map 7, C3. Phone code: 0471. Population: 744,739 of 3,234,356 in the Trivandrum District.*

According to legend, the **Sri Padmanabhaswamy Temple** ⓘ *East Fort, T0471-245 0233, 0415-0515, 0645-0715, 0830-1115, 1145-1200, 1700-1815 and 1845-1930*, was built in stages to house the statue of Vishnu reclining on the sacred serpent *Ananta*, which was found in the forest. It was rebuilt in 1733 by Raja Marthanda Varma who dedicated the whole kingdom, including his rights and possessions, to the deity. Unusually for Kerala, it is in the Dravidian style with beautiful murals, sculptures and 368 carved granite pillars which support the main pavilion or *Kulashekhara Mandapa*. You can see the seven-storeyed *gopuram* with its sacred pool from outside; otherwise to get a closer look you first have to persuade the famously strict Kerala Brahmins to waive the Hindus-only entry restriction. It becomes easier to do so if men have donned a crisp white *dhoti*, women a sari and blouse.

Thiruvananthapuram (Trivandrum)

The Travancore king, Maharajah Swathi Thirunal Balarama Varma, was a musician, poet and social reformer, and his palace, just next door to the temple, **Kuthiramalika (Puthenmalika) Palace** ⓘ *Temple Rd, East Fort, T0471-247 3952, Tue-Sun 0830-1230 and 1530-1730, Rs 20, camera Rs 15*, is a fine reflection of his patronage of the arts. On the upper level a window gives an angle on scores of fine wood-carved horses that look like a huge cavalry charge, and among the portraits painted in the slightly unsettling Indian/ European classical hybrid style is one from an artist who trumped his rivals by painting not just eyes that follow you around the room, but also feet. Sadly, it is ill maintained, but a gem nonetheless.

Napier Museum ⓘ *North Park Grounds, city north, T0471-231 8294, Tue-Sun 1000-1645, Wed morning only, closed public holidays*, is a spectacular landmark. The structure designed by RF Chisholm in traditional-Kerala-meets-Indo-Saracenic style, was completed in 1872. Today, it houses a famous collection of eighth to 18th-century South Indian bronzes, mostly from Chola, Vijayanagar and Nayaka periods, a few Jain and Buddhist sculptures and excellent woodcarvings. **Sri Chitra Art Gallery** ⓘ *just north of the museum, 1000-1645, closed Mon and Wed mornings, Rs 5*, has a fine catalogue of Indian art from early to modern schools: works by Raja Ravi Varma, 20th-century pioneer of the radical post-colonial school of painting, sit among paintings from Java, Bali, China and Japan, Mughal and Rajput miniatures. The Tanjore paintings are studded with semi-precious stones. The **Zoological Park** ⓘ *entrance at southwest corner of park, Tue-Sun 0900-1815, Rs 5, cameras Rs 15*, is a hilly woodland of frangipani and jacaranda with a wide collection of animals and a well-labelled botanical garden.

The name Thiruvananthapuram is derived from Tiru Ananta Puram, the abode of the sacred serpent Ananta upon whose coils Vishnu lies in the main temple.

Kovalam and nearby resorts

→ *For listings, see pages 981-990. Colour map 7, C3.*

Phone code: 0471. Population: 25,400.

Local fishermen's boats still sit on Kovalam's narrow strip of sand right next to sunbathing tourists, but the sleepy Lakshadweep seaside village of old has now been almost completely swallowed up by package tourist infrastructure: Ayurveda, trinkets, tailoring shops and tour operators line every inch of the narrow walkways behind the shore. In peak season it's something of an exotic god's waiting room, popular with pensioners, and it's safe and sedate enough for families. Backpackers tend to return off season.

North and south of Kovalam are four main stretches of beach, about 400 m long, divided by a rocky promontory on which sits the Charles Correa-designed **Leela**. The area to the north of the promontory, known as **Samudra Beach** and **Pozhikara Beach**, 5 km away offers the most sheltered bathing and the clearest water. The southern beaches, **Lighthouse Beach** and **Eve's Beach**, are more crowded and lively. Lighthouse Beach is far and away the most happening and has a long line of bars screening pirated Hollywood films, cafés selling muesli and pastries and hawkers peddling crafts or drugs; but it is still low-key compared to the costas. Further south still is where the classy resorts are clustered. **Pulinkudi Beach** and **Chowara Beach**, respectively 8 km and 10 km to the south, is where to go for hand-and-foot attentiveness, isolation, heritage-style villas and Ayurveda in luxurious surrounds. Chowara Beach has security staff but some sunbathers still feel plagued by hawkers. **Poovar Island**, 20 km south, is accessible only by boat (Rs 200). There are now lifeguard patrols but you still need to be careful when swimming. The sea can get rough, particularly between April and October with swells of up to 6 m. From May the sea level rises, removing the beach completely in places, and swimming becomes very dangerous.

Within easy walking distance of Kovalam, sandwiched in between Lighthouse and Poovar beaches but scarcely visited by tourists, is **Vizhinjam**, a scruffy town with a low-rise string of bangle shops, banana stalls, beauticians and seamstresses sewing jasmine buds onto strings for garlands. It's hard to believe it today but Vizhinjam was once the capital of the Ay rulers who

Kovalam

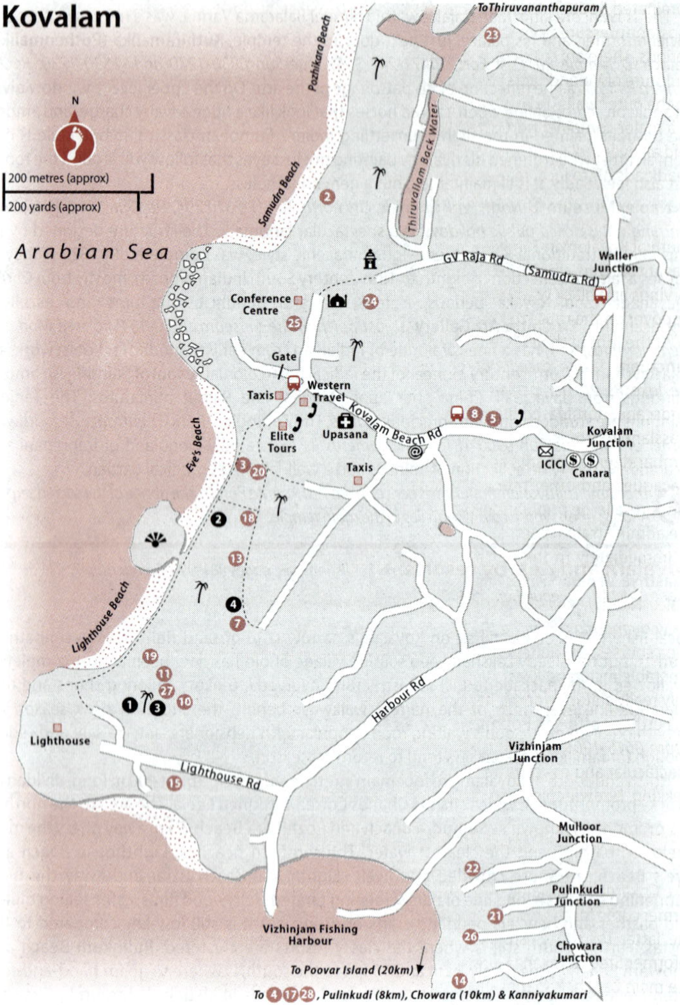

Sleeping

Bethsaida Hermitage **26**
Coco Land **13**
Coconut Bay Beach Resort **22**
Friday's Place Poovar **4**
Greenland **11**
Green Valley Cottages **7**
Holiday Home Resort **8**
Karikkathi Beach House **28**
Lagoona Davina **23**
Leela **25**
Maharaju Palace **10**
Molly's **24**
Neelakanta & Fusion Restaurant **3**
Poovar Island Resort **17**
Rani & Indian Residency **27**
Rockholm **15**
Sea Flower Beach Resort **11**
Somatheeram Ayurvedic Beach Resort **14**
Surya Samudra Beach Garden **21**
Taj Green Cove **2**
Usha's **19**
White House **18**
Wilson Tourist Home **20**

Eating

Karuna **3**
Lonely Planet **4**
Sea Face **2**
Suprabhatan **1**

dominated South Travancore in the ninth century AD. In the seventh century they had faced constant pressure from the Pandiyans who kept the Ay chieftains under firm control for long periods. There are rock-cut sculptures in the 18th-century cave temple here, including a rough sculpture of Vinandhara Dakshinamurthi in the shrine and unfinished reliefs of Siva and Parvati on the outer wall. Today Vizhinjam is the centre of the fishing industry and is being developed as a major container port. The traditional boats are rapidly being modernized and the catch is sold all over India, but you can still see the keen interest in the sale of fish, and women taking headloads off to local markets.

Around Kovalam

South of Kovalam in Tamil Nadu, is **Padmanabhapuram**, the old wooden palace of the Rajas of Travancore. It is a beautiful example of the Kerala school of architecture and has murals, floral carvings and black granite floors. It makes a great day trip from town or Kovalam, and is a neat stopover on the route to **Kanniyakumari**, see page 962.

At the foot of the Western Ghats, 30 km east of Thiruvananthapuram, the **Neyyar Wildlife Sanctuary** ⓘ *free, speedboat for 2 people Rs 100/150, larger boats to view the forests enclosing the lake Rs 20 per person, minibus safari Rs 10*, occupies a beautiful wooded and hilly landscape, dominated by the peak of Agasthya Malai (1868 m). The vegetation ranges from grassland to tropical, wet evergreen. Wildlife includes gaur, sloth bear, Nilgiri tahr, jungle cat, sambar deer, elephants and Nilgiri langur; the most commonly seen animals are lion-tailed macaques and other monkeys. Tigers and leopards have also been reported. **Neyyar Dam** supports a large population of crocodiles and otters; a crocodile farm was set up in 1977 near the administrative complex.

Immediately to the northeast of the Neyyar Wildlife Sanctuary a section of dense forest, **Agasthya Vanam**, was set aside as a biological park in 1992 to recreate biodiversity on a wide scale. Nearby, the **Sivananda Yoga Vedanta Dhanwantari Ashram** ⓘ *T0471-227 3093, www.sivananda.org/neyyardam, minimum stay 3 days*, runs highly regarded meditation and yoga courses. It is quite an intensive schedule, with classes that start just after dawn and a strict timetable including karma yoga (meditation or devotion to God through physical labour). It is only really suitable for the hardy; others may find it heavy on Hinduism and Indian diet.

Further north sits **Ponmudi** ⓘ *buses from Trivandrum, Thampanoor Bus Stand 0530-1630; return 0615-1905, 2½ hrs*, the nearest hill station to Thiruvananthapuram, 65 km away. In a spectacular and peaceful setting, the tourist complex, though basic, serves as a good base for trekking, birdwatching and visiting the nearby minimalist deer park.

Varkala → *For listings, see pages 981-990. Colour map 7, C3. Phone code: 0472. Population: 42,300.*

Like Gokarna in Karnataka, Varkala is a pilgrimage centre for both backpackers and Hindus. The former come for the ruddy beach which lies at the bottom of the dramatic drop of a laterite cliff, the latter for the Vaishnavite **Janardhanaswamy Temple** and the Sivagiri Mutt of social reformer Sree Narayana Guru. The sea is far from calm (it has lifeguards for good reason), and the main beach, **Papanasam**, accessed by steep steps hacked in the cliffs, is shared between holidaymakers and fishermen. Along the cliff path, particularly along the **North Cliff**, is the tourist village high street; sizeable concrete hotels, travel agents, internet cafés, tailors stitching out endless pairs of fisherman's trousers and a huge preponderance of Kashmiri and Tibetan salespeople pushing their customary turquoise, silverware and carpets. Further north, the tourist shacks bleed into fishing village life around the **Alimood Mosque** (dress modestly). Watch your step around the cliff, particularly at night; carry a torch after dark.

The south, bordered by a golden beach, has a lovely village feel, with traditional houses built around the 13th-century temple dedicated to Vishnu. The **Arratu festival** in March-April draws thousands of visitors.

Opposite is the **Sri Rama Hanuman Temple**, whose large temple tank three wheeler drivers splash through in the morning, while women thwack their *lungis* clean on its steps. The main 'town' area (including the train station) is a further 2 km inland from Temple Junction.

A two-hour excursion takes you to **Golden Island** for a glimpse of local backwaters; there's a small temple here but it's the type of visit you'd make for the atmosphere more than anything else. A boat round the island should cost Rs 50 for the hour.

Lullaby@Varkala, www.lullabyatvarkala.in, runs tours to introduce tourists to *anganwadis*, childcare centres for underprivileged families. The project helps feed, clothe and educate its beneficiaries.

Varkala

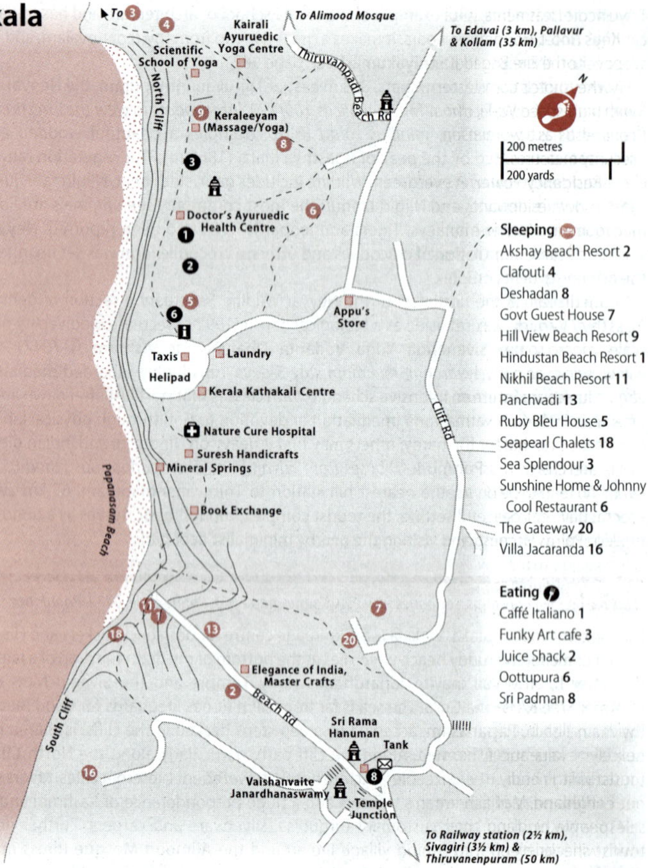

Thiruvananthapuram and the far south listings

For Sleeping and Eating price codes and other relevant information, see Essentials pages 38-42.

Sleeping

Thiruvananthapuram *p975, map p976*

L-A Thapovan Heritage Home, Nellikunnu, T0471-248 0453, www.thapovan.com. 18 km south of town with rooms in beautiful gardens or overlooking Nellikunu beach. Ayurvedic treatments, yoga centre, restaurant.

A Keys Hotel, Housing Board Junction (opposite the Fire Brigade), T0471-394 4100, www.keyshotels.com. Ultra-modern hotel with high-speed Wi-Fi, gym and all mod-cons. Also has a women's-only floor with extra security measures.

A-C Residency Tower, Press Rd, T0471-233 1661, www.residencytower.com. Top-quality a/c rooms in a business hotel, with full facilities. Highly efficient, good restaurants, bar, rooftop pool (non-residents Rs 350). A bit swish.

B-C Chaithram (KTDC), Station Rd, T0471-233 0977, www.ktdc.com. Very clean decent-sized rooms, some a/c. Next to railway and bus stand so can be noisy. Restaurant, bar.

B-D Thamburu International, Aristo Junction, T0471-232 1974 www.thamburu.com. Quiet, well-run hotel with wood-panelled walls and cheesy music in foyer. Rooms (all with TV) tend to be on small side. Some a/c rooms have balcony.

C Wild Palms Homestay, Mathrubhoomi Rd, Vanchiyoor, 10 mins' walk from Statue Junction or ask for pickup, T0471-247 1175, wildpalm@md3.vsnl.net.in. Modern welcoming guesthouse set in pretty tropical garden in the leafy suburbs. Spacious rooms, some a/c. Price includes breakfast.

C-D Geeth, off MG Rd, near GPO, Pulimudu, T0471-247 1987. Renovated business hotel, with smallish but clean rooms and some large, excellent value suites. Excellent rooftop restaurant. Friendly.

C-E Highland, Manjalikulam Rd, T0471-233 3416, www.highland-hotels.com. Busy hotel with wide variety of clean rooms. Budget rooms good value.

D-E Manjalikulam Tourist Home, Manjalikulam Rd, T0471-233 0776, www.manjalikulam.com. Quiet yet central hotel with large, spotlessly clean rooms. Very friendly staff. Good value, recommended.

E Asha, 200 m from airport, T0471-250 1050. Very handy for early departures. Decent rooms with bath.

F Greenland, Aristo Junction, T0471-232 3485. Great value rooms in quiet, immaculate, freshly renovated hotel, perfectly located within a couple of mins of both bus and railway stations. Best budget choice in town.

F Youth Hostel (YHAI), Veli (10 km from centre), T0471-250 1230. Rooms and a dorm surrounded by coconut groves, with a pretty lagoon and clean beach. Very cheap vegetarian lunches, boating, watersports, good views.

Kovalam and nearby resorts *p977, map p978*

Long power cuts are common here, so a/c often doesn't work. Look for rooms with windows on 2 walls to get a good through-breeze. There are numerous budget cottages and rooms to let with a range of rooms from Rs 150-1000. The alleys behind **Lighthouse Beach** tend to have the cheapest accommodation. Scouts greet arrivals at the bus stand but you may pay considerably more if you use their services. You will find rooms to let, behind bars and restaurants, by walking from the Sea Rock hotel towards the lighthouse, and on the **Samudra Beach** and **GV Raja Rd** (Samudra Rd). Be aware that management of the cheaper hotels often changes hands and hotel names can change from year to year. Rates shown here are for the high season. Prices skyrocket in all hotels for the 3-week peak period (23 Dec-7 Jan), though it still pays to bargain. High season is 1-19 Dec, 11 Jan-28 Feb; in the low season, especially May-Jul, expect 40-75% discounts.

LL Karikkathi Beach House, near Nagar Bhagavathy Temple at Mulloor Thottam, Pulinkudi, T0471-240 0956, www.karikkathi beachhouse.com. 2 doubles with linked lounge, palm thatch roof, no a/c or TV, perfect for honeymooners or those used to being kept; the house comes with private beach, chef, waiter and servants. There's a cottage should families or groups need extra beds.

LL The Leela, Samudra Beach, Kovalam, T0471-305 1234, www.theleela.com. Uber-snazzy chain hotel amid brilliant grounds on a hill above Kovalam. 2 huge infinity pools boast some of the world's best coastal views, and the Ayurvedic spa has one of the prettiest yoga *shalas* ever built; down-to-earth American teacher Bridget Shields (www.bridgetshields.com) runs retreats here. And if this isn't luxurious enough for you, splash out on a stay at **The Club**, the hotel's discreet and deluxe clubhouse: each suite has beautiful views over the Arabian Sea, there's a 24-hr butler service, your own spa and living room.

LL Poovar Island Resort, Poovar Island, T0471-221 2068, www.poovarislandresort.com. Award-winning boutique hotel with 'floating' cottages where the backwaters meet the sea. Pool, handicrafts, Ayurveda, watersports.

LL Vivanta by Taj, GV Raja Vattapara Rd, Kovalam, T0471-661 3000, www.vivantabytaj.com. Appealing and luxurious Balinese-flavoured complex set in 4 ha of tropical grounds with superb views of the sea, infinity pool, excellent spa, gym and Wi-Fi.

LL-AL Somatheeram Ayurvedic Beach Resort, Chowara Beach, south of Kovalam, T0471-226 8101, www.somatheeram.in. Kerala's first Ayurvedic resort and also the repeat winner of the state's competition to find the best. Its cottages and traditional Keralite houses set in coconut groves are dotted over a steep hill above the beach. If you want more peace, and the use of an oyster-shaped pool with whirlpool, stay at sister resort, **Manaltheeram**. 15 doctors and 90 therapists work in 48 treatment rooms at the shared Ayurvedic facilities. British-based holistic health and beauty therapist, **Bharti Vyas**, T+44(0)20-7935 5312 (UK), www.bharti-vyas.com, leads 10-day retreats here, or join a yoga retreat with uplifting American vinyasa flow teacher, **Shiva Rea**, www.yogaadventures.com.

LL-A Bethsaida Hermitage, Pulinkudi, T0471-226 7554, www.bethsaidahermitage.com. Eco-friendly stone and bamboo beach *cabanas* surrounded by coconut groves. Profits support a variety of charitable projects. Family-friendly, informal and unpretentious.

L Friday's Place Poovar, Poover Island, TT097-4416 1636, www.fridaysplacekerala.com. Remote, watery eco-hideaway with 3 solar-powered teak and mahogany cottages and a spectacular Ark-like 'Tsunami House', set on an isolated sandbank amid rows of palms and hibiscus, frangipani and bougainvillea, run by British couple Mark and Sujeewa, the latter a Sivananda yoga teacher and reiki healer. Food is fresh, with fruit for breakfast, *thali* lunches, fish and chicken suppers. Kayaking and temple tours.

L Surya Samudra Beach Garden, Pulinkudi, near Kovalam, T0471-226 7333, www.suryasamudra.com. Sitting high on a rocky bluff between Kovalam and Kannyukamari, this elite resort boasts a world-class spa and offers Ayurveda treatments from its beautifully designed complex. There are just 21 traditional Keralite cottages, with 4-posters, big plantation chairs and open-air bathrooms, spread over 9 ha of jackfruit, bamboo, cinnamon, mango, frangipani, palm and hibiscus trees. The **Octopus** restaurant serves great North and South Indian specials and Western food. Excellent Sivananda yoga on a one-on-one basis at an open-air pavilion overlooking the sea.

L-A Coconut Bay Beach Resort, Mulloor, T0471-2480 566, www.coconutbay.com. Spacious stone villas on beach, good restaurant, friendly. Secluded location in traditional fishing village. Recommended.

AL-A Lagoona Davina, Pozhikkara Beach, near Trivandrum, T0471-238 0049, www.lagoonadavina.com. Modest but chic place on the backwaters between Trivandrum and Kovalam run by the chic and idiosyncratic Davina. An island of sand separates the river bank from the wider sea. Small library, plenty of cushion-strewn seats cut into the seawall to read the books in, and a small shop selling hybrid Indian-Western clothes; part-sari, part-Kings Rd. Tasty and healthy food, orthopaedic beds, your own 'houseboy', excellent yoga and massage and jasmine piles fragrance your room at night. But the water pressure is iffy, the internet doesn't work, lights fail, rooms are modest (fan only) and the pool's a bit small. Popular with independent female travellers.

AL-E Holiday Home Resort, Beach Rd, T0471-248 0497, www.holidayhomeresort.net. Cute cottages amid a tree-filled, shady garden with hammocks to laze in. Serene location 10 mins' walk from beach. Excellent, friendly service from the helpful manager, Shar. Camping,with own tent, is possible (Rs 150). Recommended.

A Molly's, Samudra Beach Rd, Kovalam, T0471-326 2099, www.mollyskovalam.com. 2-storey hotel set around a pool. Each room has a terrace overlooking a jungly thicket of coconuts. The restaurant, which serves Mexican, European, Indian and tandoor food, is very popular.

A-B Maharaju Palace, Lighthouse Beach, T0471-248 5320, martinweber@hotmail.com. Beautiful, shady garden setting, quiet and set back from beach. 6 very clean rooms inside and outside cottages complete with chandeliers and frou-frou interiors. Genial staff, very popular.

A-C Hotel Neelakanta, Lighthouse Beach, T0471-248 0321, www.hotelneelakanta kovalam.com. Large airy rooms with big bathrooms facing the beach, TV, balcony. The hotel owns **Fusion Restaurant** next door.

B Kailasam Yoga and Ayurveda Holidays, Kovalam, T0471-248 4018, book through **Free Spirit Travel**, T+44 (0)127-356 4230 (UK), www.yogaindia.co.uk. Peaceful oasis set up by a yoga teacher and Ayurvedic physician. Yoga classes held in tiled areas under coconut-leaf roofs, surrounded by trees and open-sided to catch the sea breezes. Price includes all yoga classes.

B Rockholm, Lighthouse Rd, T0471-248 0406, www.rockholm.com. Very pleasant hotel owned by an Anglo-Indian family with cheerful staff. Good-sized rooms, with balcony, in a wonderful position just above the lighthouse. Direct access to beach. Good terrace restaurant.

B-D Sea Flower Beach Resort, Lighthouse Rd, T0471-248 0554, www.seaflowerkovalam.com. Great location right on the shore. Good-sized rooms with decent bath and balcony. Helpful staff, good value, big discounts for long stays.

B-E Coco Land, between Lighthouse Beach and Eve's Beach, T0471-653 3591, cocoheritage@yahoo.com. Bamboo huts and 'luxury' wood cottages in a little garden set back from the beach. Cottages boast TVs, a/c and hot water. Friendly management. Recommended.

C-F Hotel Greenland, Lighthouse Beach, T0471-248 6442, hotelgreenland@yahoo.com. Friendly female manger has a variety of spotlessly clean rooms set amongst her flowery garden. All have porch, fly- screens, 4 have kitchenettes and TV. Cheaper rooms are excellent value. Recommended.

D-E Shirley's Beach White House, between Lighthouse Beach and Eve's Beach, T(0)9447-224902, www.shirleysbeach.com. The sea-facing rooms here are a cut-above other hotels in this price range. All are breezy and painted a cheerful blue, some with balcony. The owner is a wealth of knowledge. Quiet location, very good value. Recommended.

E Green Valley Cottages, between Lighthouse Beach and Eve's Beach, T0471-248 0636, indira_ravi@hotmail.com. Spick and span simple rooms with fly-screens and sit-outs. Good value.

E Wilson Tourist Home, up path behind Neelkantha, T0471-248 0052. Clean, quiet rooms with bath, balcony, fan, some with a/c. Open-air restaurant, pretty garden, helpful service. Recommended.

F Hotel Rani, Lighthouse Beach, T(0)9995-566039, www.hotelrani.com. Basic, well-maintained rooms that open out onto a communal veranda. Friendly owner.

F-G Usha's, Lighthouse Beach, T0471-279 0563. Good little cheapie in the winding alleys behind the beach. Basic rooms, all with bath and fly-screens. Run by the genial Usha and her family.

Around Kovalam *p979*

L Duke's Forest Lodge, Anappara, near Ponmudi, T0471-226 8822, www.dukesforest.com. 5 luxury villas, each with its own plunge pool, set on organic estate. Great trekking.

F Government Guest House, Ponmudi, T0471-289 0211. 24 rooms and 10 cottages, in attractive gardens surrounded by wooded hills, spartan facilities but spacious rooms, restaurant serves limited but reasonable vegetarian meals, beer available, also a post office and general store.

Varkala *p979, map p980*

There are at least 50 guesthouses, plus rooms in private houses. The **North Cliff** area is compact, so look around until you find what you want: the northernmost area is where the most laid-back, budget options are and has the most character, while the far south side has a few fancier places. None, however, is actually on the beach. Outside the high season of Nov-Mar, prices drop by up to 50%. During the monsoon (Jun-Jul) many close.

AL Hindustan Beach Resort, Papanasam Beach, Janardhanapuram, T0470-260 4254 www.hindustanbeachretreat.com. Not much to look at from outside, but inside are well-appointed rooms with amazing sea views. Plunge pool set in small lawn and rooftop restaurant. Executive rooms have balconies, suites have chaise lounges. All a/c. Easily the smartest place to stay in Varkala if you need all mod cons.

AL-A Villa Jacaranda, Temple Rd West, South Cliff, T0470-261 0296, www.villa- jacaranda.biz. A delightful guesthouse, home with 5 huge rooms elegantly but sparely decorated. Jasmine, birds of paradise and magnolia blossoms are tucked into alcoves, there's a lotus-filled pond and tropical garden and everything is immaculately maintained. Guests have their own keys and entrance. Really special.

AL-D Marine Palace, Papanasam Beach, T0471-260 3204, www.varkalamarine.com. 12 rooms in total with 3 lovely old-style wooden rooms with balconies and a sea view. The honeymoon suite has a truly gigantic bed. Good service and nice *tandoori* restaurant on the beach. Recommended.

A Varkala Deshadan, Kurakkanni Cliff, T0470-320 4242, www.deshadan.com. Scrupulously clean Chettinadu-style a/c bungalows set around a large pool. Price includes breakfast.

B-C Clafouti, North Cliff, T0470-260 1414, www.clafoutiresort.com. Efficiently run if overpriced resort with spotlessly clean bamboo and wood cottages set around a manicured lawn. Cheaper, non a/c rooms are inside house. All have modern baths. French-run bakery for excellent pastries. Internet, restaurant, cooking classes.

B-D Akshay Beach Resort, Beach Rd (about 200 m from beach), T0470-260 2668. Wide variety of bright, clean rooms. Quiet location away from the cliff. Restaurant, TV lounge, good value.

C-D Nikhil Beach Resort, Beach Rd, T0470-260 5191, www.nikhil-resort.com. Friendly little complex with good-sized rooms, some with a/c.

C-D Sea Pearl Chalets, Beach Rd, T0470-260 0105, www.seapearlchalets.com. Circular thatched huts perched scarily near the cliff edge. Great views, breakfast included. Recommended.

C-E Hill View Beach Resort, North Cliff, T0470-260 5744, www.varkalahillview.neehaarika.org Self-contained cottages and budget rooms in a smart resort. Internet, airport pickup, hot water.

D-E Panchavadi, Beach Rd, T0470-260 0200, www.panchavadi.com. Excellent location close to beach. Very clean and secure with simple rooms. Budget rooms very good value. Restaurant, helpful staff. Recommended.

E-G Sunshine Home/Johnny Cool & Soulfood Café, North Cliff, Varkala Beach, T(0)9341-201295. Colourful, chilled-out Rasta house set back off the cliff. Bongo drums and Marley posters abound. There's a variety of rooms, some with balcony, plus a little standalone thatched cottage out the back. The café does pastas, noodles, fish and chips – but in its own sweet time.

F Government Guest House, towards **The Gateway** (see Eating), T0470-260 2227. Immense, high-ceilinged rooms with marble floors and big baths, in the leafy former summer residence of the maharaja. Isolated, idyllic and quiet. Book in advance, recommended.

F Sea Splendour, North Cliff end, Odayam Beach, T0470-266 2120, www.seasplendour.com. Homely choice with simple rooms in retired teacher's guesthouse. Excellent home cooking (unlimited and spoilt for choice), very peaceful.

Eating

Thiruvananthapuram *p975, map p976*

🍴 Kalavara, Kalavara Hotel, Press Rd, T0471-232 2195. Indian, Continental, Chinese, fast food (burgers, shakes), takeaway. Food average, slow service but good value buffets in upstairs thatched section with a patch of garden – good ambience, limited views.

🍴 Kalpakavadi, Hotel Kalpakavadi, Press Rd. Mixed menu. Modern and smart. Recommended.

🍴 Kerala House, near Statue Junction, T0471-247 6144. Keralite cuisine in the basement of shopping complex. Slow for breakfast but newspapers available, outside seating in the evening in roadside car park area is cheaper. Colourful and fun place to pass some time, even if the food arrives cold. Try *neem, kappa* and rice (delicious fish with tapioca), or inexpensive chicken dishes with coconut; bakery in the complex does excellent samosas and puffs.

Mascot, Mascot Hotel, Museum Rd. Excellent lunchtime buffet, pleasant, 24-hr coffee shop for all types of snacks, good value, a cool haven at midday.

Queen's, Aristo Junction. Indian non-vegetarian. Chilli chicken recommended.

Arul Jyoti, MG Rd, opposite Secretariat. South Indian vegetarian. With a/c family room, clean, wide choice of good value dishes, try jumbo *dosas*. Great Tamil Nadu *thalis*.

Indian Coffee House, 2 on MG Rd, with others near YWCA, north of the Secretariat, and near KSRTC Bus Stand (the latter designed by the English architect Laurie Baker). Worth seeing, excellent value coffee and snacks.

Kovalam and nearby resorts *p977, map p978*

There are hundreds of restaurants here. Service can be slow, and quality hit-and-miss since management often changes hands. Below is a very short list of those that have proved consistent. The restaurants at the **The Leela** and the **Taj** are good, if predictable; **The Leela's** Sun brunch has a giant salad counter and loud live music. Avoid 'catch of the day' on Sun – it's unlikely to be fresh. Some restaurants will screen pirated DVDs, sometimes to compensate for underwhelming cuisine.

Fusion, Eve's Beach, T0471-248 4153. Kovalam's take on fusion food doesn't really pull it off but the cold coffees are exceptional and the menu has a nice varied mix of international and Indian food.

Rockholm Hotel, Lighthouse Rd. Very good international food and *tandooris* served on a pleasant terrace with beautiful views, especially early morning.

Sea Face, Eve's Beach. Breezy raised terrace on the beach by a pleasant pool. Varied choice including versatile fish and seafood. Friendly and attentive.

Karuna, Lighthouse Beach. Excellent Keralite breakfasts, home-made brown bread, decent coffee.

Lonely Planet, between Lighthouse Beach and Eve's Beach. Wholesome, mildly spiced Ayurvedic vegetarian food. Set around a pond with ducks – and mosquitoes. Sells recipe books and runs cookery courses.

Suprabhatan, Lighthouse Beach, opposite **Hotel Greenland**. South and North Indian vegetarian meals.

Varkala *p979, map p980*

There are numerous restaurants along North Cliff, most with facsimile menus, slow service and questionable kitchens; take extra care with drinking water here. 'Catch of the day' splayed out for you to inspect, usually costs Rs 100-150 depending upon the type/size of fish, but make sure you don't get 'catch of yesterday' (fresh fish keep their glassy eyes and bright silvery scales). Many restaurants close out of season.

The Gateway, Gateway Hotel, near **Government Guest House**. Every Sun 1230-1530 (Rs 300, includes pool use). Good-value eat-all-you-want buffet, delicious rich vegetarian cuisine.

Caffé Italiano, North Cliff, T(0)9846-053194. Good Italian and seafood, but quite pricey.

Sri Padman, near Hanuman Temple, T0472-260 5422. Sri Padman's terrace overlooking the temple tank offers the best non-beachfront position in town. Come here for South Indian vegetarian breakfasts served in big stainless steel *thali* trays, and oily *parathas* to sop up spicy curries and coconut chutneys.

Clafouti, Clafouti Hotel, North Cliff (see Sleeping). Fresh pastries and cakes, but standards seem to drop when the French-Keralite owners are away.

Funky Art Café, North Cliff. Eclectic multi-cuisine menu. Sometimes hosts local bands playing Varkala versions of Western rock songs, which can be an amusing diversion while waiting for the incredibly slow service.

The Juice Shack, cliffside Varkala, turn off at Tibetan market. Shady little spot with healthy juice, good coffee and excellent toasted sandwiches. Brilliant for breakfast – they even have Marmite.

Oottupura, cliffside Varkala, near helipad, T0472-260 6994. A Varkala institution. Excellent 100% vegetarian with 60 vegetarian curries and everything from Chinese to macaroni cheese. Breakfast can be *iddlies* or toasted sandwiches, all served under a giant pistachio tree covered in fairy lights.

Entertainment

Thiruvananthapuram *p975, map p976*
Performances of *Kalarippayattu*, Kerala's martial art, can be seen through: **CVN Kalari**, East Fort, T0471-247 4182 (0430-0830); and **Balachandran Nair Kalari Martial Arts Gymnasium**, Parasuvaikal, T0471-223 2686, www.kalari.in.

Kovalam and nearby resorts *p977, map p978*
Kalakeli Kathakali Troupe, T0471-248 1818. Daily at hotels including **Ashok** and **Neptune**, Rs 100.

Varkala *p979, map p980*
Varkala is a good place to hang out, chill and do yoga but there's no organized nightlife to speak of, only impromptu campfire parties.
Kerala Kathakali Centre, by the helipad, holds a daily *Kathakali* demonstration (Rs 150, make-up 1700-1800, performance 1830-2000). The participants are generally students of the art rather than masters.

Festivals and events

Thiruvananthapuram *p975, map p976*
In Nov 2010 the city hosted an outlier of the **Hay Festival**, featuring authors including Vikram Seth and William Dalrymple and gigs by the likes of Bob Geldof. It's hoped it will become an annual event. Check out www.hayfestival.com/kerala.
Mar Chandanakuda, at Beemapalli, a shrine on Beach Rd 5 km southwest of the railway station. 10-day festival when local Muslims go to the mosque, holding incense sticks and pots. Marked by sword play, singing, dancing, elephant procession and fireworks.
Mar-Apr (Meenam) and Oct-Nov (Thulam) **Arattu** is the closing festival of the 10-day celebrations of the Padmanabhaswamy Temple, in which the deity is paraded around the temple inside the fort and then down to the sea.
Sep/Oct Navaratri at the special *mandapa* in Padmanabhaswamy Temple. Several concerts are held which draw famous musicians. **Thiruvonam week** in Sep.
1-10 Oct Soorya Dance Festival.
Nov-Mar A similar **Nishangandhi Dance Festival** is held at weekends when all-important classical Indian dance forms are performed by leading artistes at Nishagandhi open-air auditorium, Kanakakkunnu Palace.

Shopping

If shopping, bear in mind that prices are relatively high here: traders seldom honour the standard rates for 92.5 silver, charging by piece not weight.

Thiruvananthapuram *p975, map p976*
Shopping areas include the **Chalai Bazar**, the **Connemara Market** and the main road from Palayam to the East Fort. Usually open 0900-2000 (some take a long lunch break). Although ivory goods have now been banned, inlay on woodcarving and marquetry using other materials (bone, plastic) continue to flourish. *Kathakali* masks and traditional fabrics can be bought at a number of shops.

The shopping centre opposite East Fort Bus Stand has a large a/c shop with a good selection of silks and saris but is not cheap. *Khadi* recommended from shops on both sides of MG Rd, south of Pulimudu Junction.
Co-optex, Temple Rd. Good for fabrics and *lungis*.
Handloom House, diagonally across from **Partha's**. Has an excellent range of fabrics, clothes and export quality dhurries;
Partha's, towards East Fort. Recommended.
Premier Stationers, MG Rd, opposite Post Office Rd. The best best in town.
Raymonds, Karal Kada, East Fort. Good selection of men's clothing.

Handicrafts

Gift Corner and **Natesan Antique Arts**, MG Rd. High-quality goods including old dowry boxes, carved wooden panels from old temple 'cars', miniature paintings and bronzes.
Gram Sree, MG Rd. Excellent village crafts.
Kairali, MG Rd. Items of banana fibre, coconut, screw pine, mainly utilitarian, also excellent sandalwood carvings and bell-metal lamps, utensils.
Kalanjali, Palace Garden, across from the museum. Recommended.
SMSM Handicrafts Emporium, behind the Secretariat. Government-run, heaps of items reasonably priced.

Kovalam and nearby resorts *p977, map p978*
Numerous craft shops, including Kashmiri and Tibetan shops, sell a wide range of goods. Most are clustered around the bus stand at the gate of

the Ashok with another group to the south around the lighthouse. Good-quality paintings, metalwork, woodwork and carpets at reasonable prices. Gems and jewellery are widely available but it is notoriously difficult to be sure of quality.

Tailoring is available at short notice and is very good value with the fabrics available. Charges vary, about Rs 50-80 per piece.

Brother Tailors, 2nd Beach Rd.

Raja, near hotel **Surya**.

Suresh, next to **Garzia** restaurant.

Zangsty Gems, Lighthouse Rd. Sells jewellery and silver and has a good reputation for helpfulness and reliability.

Varkala *p979, map p980*

Most of the handicraft shops are run by Kashmiris, who will tell you that everything (including the tie-dye T-shirts) is an antique from Ladakh.

Elegance of India and **Mushtaq**, Beach Rd. Sell Kashmiri handicrafts, carpets, jewellery, etc, reported as honest, will safely air-freight carpets and other goods.

Satori, T(0)9387-653261. Cliff-top boutique, selling pretty Western clothes made with local fabric and jewelled Rajasthani slippers.

Suresh, on path south from helipad. Handicrafts from Karnataka.

▲ Activities and tours

Thiruvananthapuram *p975, map p976*

Body and soul

Institute of Yogic Culture, Vazhuthacaud, T0471-304 9349, www.pillaisyogicculture.com. Yoga therapy, research, Ayurvedic massage.

Sivananda Ashram, Neyyar Dam, T0471-227 3093, www.sivananda.org/ndam. One of India's most highly regarded yoga teacher training programs.

Swimming

Mascot Hotel, small rooftop pool at the Residency Tower (0700-1900, Rs 250), with great views.

Waterworks, pool near museum, T0471-231 8990.

Tour operators

IATA-approved agencies include:

Aries Travel, Press Rd, T0471-233 0964, www.ariestravel.net.

Great India Tour Co, Mullassery Towers, Vanross Sq, T0471-301 1500, www.gitctour.com. Offers afternoon city tours, among others. Reliable but pricey.

Jayasree, PO Box 5236, Pettah, T0471-247 6603, www.jayasreetravels.com. One-stop travel service, good coaches.

KTDC, **Hotel Chaithram**, Station Rd, T0471-233 0031, www.ktdc.com. Can arrange 2- to 3-day tours to Munnar and Thekkady and also runs the following local tours:

City tour: daily 0730 and 1300, 5½ hrs including Padmanabhapuram, Puthenmalika Palace, Shangumugham beach and Napier Museum, Rs 250 (Padmanabhapuram is closed on Mon).

Kanniyakumari: daily 0730-2100, including Kovalam, Padmanabhapuram and Kanniyakumari, Rs 550. Tours can feel quite rushed with little time spent at sights.

TourIndia, MG Rd, T0471-233 0437, www.tourindiakerala.com. The pioneers of backwater tourism and Periyar's Tiger Trails trekking program, highly recommended for innovative and unusual experiences, eg tree-house holidays or sport fishing off Fort Kochi.

Trekking and birdwatching

Trekking is best Dec-Apr. Obtain permission first from the Chief Conservator of Forests (Wildlife), Forest HQ, Thiruvananthapuram, T0471-232 2217, or the Assistant Wildlife Warden at Neyyar Dam, T0471-227 2182.

Kovalam and nearby resorts *p977, map p978*

Body and soul

Ayurvedic treatments are also offered by most upmarket resorts (a massage will set you back about Rs 700).

Dr Franklin's Panchakarma Institute and Research Centre, Chowara, T0471-248 0870, www.dr-franklin.com. The good doctor's family have been in Ayurveda for 4 centuries, and he himself is the former district medical officer of Kerala Government. Programmes include treatment for infertility, sluggishness, paralysis and obesity. 15-day body purification therapy (*panchakarma* and *swetakarma*) costs US$714. 21-day *Born To Win* programme US$968. Others include *You and your spine*, *Body Mind Soul*, and there are age-reducing treatments including body immunization and longevity treatments

(28 days, US$1290). The slimming programme takes 28 days, US$1200. 51-day *panchakarma*, US$2390. Cheaper treatments include: face pack US$7, 1-hr massage US$17. Also training courses in massage, Ayurveda and *panchakarma*.

Medicus, Lighthouse Rd, T0471-248 0596, where Mrs Babu has a loyal clientele, many of whom return year after year.

Padma Nair, Pink Flowers, Lighthouse Beach, T098-9588 2915, www.yogashala.in. One of *kalaripayattu* master Balachandran Nair's students, Padma Nair has 10-day massage programmes at her village home from US$180.

Vasudeva, T0471-222 2510, in the Rohith Hotel (near Green Land). Simple but with experienced professionals.

Fishing

Can readily be arranged through the hotels, as can excursions on traditional catamarans or motor boats. You may be promised corals and beautiful fish just offshore but don't expect to see very much.

Indian martial arts

Guru Balachandran Nair, is the master of the **Indian School of Martial Arts**, Parasuvykal, 20 km from Trivandrum, T0471-272 5140, www.kalari.in. This is a college teaching *kalaripayattu*, India's traditional martial art, as well as *kalarichikitsa*, an ancient Indian healing tradition combining Ayurveda with *marma* therapy, which manipulates the vital pressure points of the body to ease pain. A fighter would have had an intimate knowledge of these points to know what to harm or how to heal. A fascinating place to stay.

Tour operators

There are dozens of tour operators on the roads leading down to the beach and on the beach-front. Nearly all of them offer money exchange, onward travel booking and backwater tours.

East India Premier Tours, behind **Neelkantha Hotel**, between Lighthouse and Eve's Beach, T0471-248 3246. Can suggest unusual hotels.

Great Indian Travel, Lighthouse Rd, T0471-248 1110, www.keralatours.com. Wide range of tours, exchange, eco-friendly beach resorts.

Visit India, Lighthouse Rd, T0471-248 1069. Friendly and helpful, exchange, short backwater tours from Thiruvallam.

Varkala *p979, map p980*

Body and soul

Keraleeyam, North Cliff. One of the best of the many yoga/Ayurvedic massage centres.

Lakshmi Herbal Beauty Parlour, Clafouti Hotel (see Sleeping). Individual attention, amazing massages plus waxing, henna, etc.

Nature Cure Hospital, North Cliff. Opened in 1983, treats patients entirely by diet and natural cures including hydrotherapy, chromotherapy (natural sunbath with different filters) and mud therapy, each treatment normally lasting 30 mins.

Naturomission Yoga Ashram, near the helipad. Runs 1-, 2- and 7-day courses in yoga, massage, meditation, and healing techniques. Payment by donation.

Scientific School of Yoga, Naturopathy and Massage, Diana Inn, North Cliff, T0470-320 6294. 10-day yoga and massage course (2 classes daily), Rs 500, professionally run by English-speaking doctor. Also has a shop selling Ayurvedic oils, soaps, etc.

Tour operators

Most hotels offer tours, air tickets, backwater trips, houseboats, etc, as do the many agents along North Cliff.

JK Tours & Travels, Temple Junction Varkala, T0802-668 3334. Money exchange, daily 0900-2100.

⊖ Transport

Thiruvananthapuram *p975, map p976*

Air The airport, T0471-250 1426, is 6 km away from the beach. **Transport to town**: by local bus no 14, pre-paid taxi (Rs 85) or auto (about Rs 30, 20 mins). Confirm international bookings and arrive in good time. Expect inflated prices at refreshments counter, though you can get cheap tea and coffee in the final lounge after security check. Banks at the airport are outside arrivals. **Johnson & Co** travel agent opposite domestic terminal, T0471-250 3555. Note that the teminal is closed at night.

Airlines **Sri Lankan Airlines**, Spencer Building, MG Rd, T0471-247 1810; **Kuwait**

Airways, airport, T0471-250 1401; **Indian Airlines**, Mascot Sq, T0471-231 6870 (airport T0471-250 1537) and **Air India**, Museum Rd, Velayambalam, T0471-231 0310 (airport T0471-250 1426).

Domestic departures include: **Indian Airlines** to **Bengaluru** (**Bangalore**), **Chennai**, **Delhi** and **Mumbai**. **Air India** to **Mumbai**. **Jet Airways** to **Chennai** and **Mumbai**.

International departures include: **Air India Express** to several **Gulf** destinations; **Emirates** to **Dubai**; **Etihad** to **Abu Dhabi**. **Maldivian** to **Malé**; **Silk Air** to **Singapore**; **Sri Lankan** to **Colombo**.

Local bus City Bus Stand, T0471-246 3029. Green buses have limited stops; yellow/red buses continue through town up to museum. Blue/white bus (No 888) to **Kovalam** goes from **East Fort Bus Station** (30 mins, Rs 9).

Long distance bus Buses leave from **KSRTC Bus Station**, Station Rd, near railway station, T0471-232 3886. Buses to **Kanniyakumari** via **Nagercoil** or direct, 0530, 0930, 1000, 1200, 1500, 1600 and 1830 (2½ hrs, Rs 40) and frequent departures to **Kozhikode**, (10 hrs, Rs 200) via **Kollam** (2½ hrs, Rs 44), **Alappuzha** (4 hrs, Rs 96), **Ernakulam/Kochi** (5½ hrs, Rs 129), and **Thrissur** (7 hrs, Rs 173). You can include a section of the backwaters on the way to Kochi by getting a boat from Kollam (shared taxis there cost Rs 60 each, see below). **TNSTC** to **Chennai**, **Coimbatore**, **Cuddalore**, **Erode**, **Kanniyakumari**, **Madurai** from opposite the Central Railway station.

Rickshaw Rickshaws to the Kovalam beach area should cost around Rs 70-100. You will need to bargain. Tell auto-rickshaw drivers which beaches you want to get to in advance, otherwise they will charge much more when you get there.

Taxi Prepaid taxis from the airport charge around Rs350 to Kovalam. From outside **Mascot Hotel** taxis charge about Rs 7 per km; to **Kovalam**, Rs 175, return Rs 225 (waiting: extra Rs 50 per hr). From outside train station, Rs 5 per km. To **Kanniyakumari** with a stop at Padmanabhapuram costs about Rs 900/1100.

Train **Central Station**, T132. Reservations in building adjoining station. Advance, upstairs, open 0700-1300, 1330-1930, Sun 0900-1700; ask to see Chief Reservations Supervisor, Counter 8. **Kochi** (**Ernakulam**) (5¼ hrs), via **Varkala** and the backwater towns: around 20 trains daily 0500-2145 including: *Kerala Exp 12625*, 1115 (continues to **Delhi**, 48 hrs); and *Trivandrum Ernakulam Exp 16342*, 1710. **Bengaluru** (**Bangalore**): *Island Exp 16525*, 1255, 18 hrs. **Mangalore**; *Parasuram Exp 16650*, 0630, 14 hrs; and *Malabar Exp 16629*, 1830. **Chennai**: *TVC Chennai Exp 12696*, 1710, 15 hrs. **Kanniyakumari**: *Kanyakumari Jayanti Exp 16381*, 1020, 2½ hrs; *Island Exp 16526*, 1515, 4 hrs.

Kovalam and nearby resorts *p977, map p978*

There are 3 main points of access to Kovalam's beaches. Remember to specify which when hiring an auto or taxi.

Local bus Frequent buses depart 0540-2100 to East Fort, **Thiruvananthapuram**, from bus stand outside **Ashok Hotel** gate on Kovalam Beach (30 mins, Rs 9). From **East Fort bus station**, walk or catch an auto-rickshaw to town centre (Rs 20).

Long distance bus To **Kanniyakumari**, **Kochi** via **Kollam** (**Quilon**) and **Kottayam**, **Nagercoil**, **Padmanabhapuram**, **Varkala** and **Thodopuzha** via **Kottayam**.

Rickshaw Auto-rickshaw to **Thiruvananthapuram**, Rs 70-80, but you need to bargain hard.

Taxi From taxi stand or through **Ashok** or **Samudra** hotels. One-way to **Thiruvananthapuram** or airport, Rs 200; station Rs 175; city sights Rs 600; **Kanniyakumari**, **Padmanabhapuram** Rs 1750 (8 hrs); **Kochi** Rs 2250 (5 hrs); **Kollam** Rs 1100; **Thekkady** Rs 2650 (6 hrs).

Varkala *p979, map p980*

Bus To/from **Temple Junction** (not beach) for **Alappuzha** and **Kollam**, but often quicker to go to Paripally on NH47 and catch onward buses from there.

Motorcycle Kovalam Motorcycle hire, Voyager Travels, Eye's Beach Rd, T0471-248 1993. Next door to **JA Tourist Home**, Temple Junction; and **Mamma Chompo**, Beach Rd.

Rickshaw/taxi Autos and taxis can be found on Beach Rd and near the helipad. Both charge about Rs 50 to train station. Taxi to **Thiruvananthapuram**, Rs 800 (1¼ hrs).

Train Varkala sits on the Kochi–Trivandrum line, with at least 20 trains a day in each direction. All northbound trains call at **Kollam**, while many of the southbound trains continue to **Kanniyakumari**.

Directory

Thiruvananthapuram *p975, map p976*

Banks Mon-Fri 1000-1400, Sat 1000-1200. Most banks can be found on MG Rd including **Andhra Bank**, **Canara Bank** and **State Bank of India**. All have ATMs. The airport has banks and money exchange facilities including **Thomas Cook**, T0471-250 2470. **Internet Central Telegraph office**: Statue Rd, 200 m to its north; open 24 hrs, best value internet. **Megabyte**, CSI Building, 3rd and 4th floors, MG Rd, Rs 10 per hr. **Tandem Communications**, Statue Rd (MG Rd end), good telephone and fax centre; colour photocopying, laser printing. **Medical services** Many chemists, near hospitals; a few near Statue Junction. **Opticians**: **Lens & Frames**, Pulimudu Junction, T0471-247 1354. **General Hospital**, Vanchiyoor, T0471-230 7874, **Ramakrishna Ashrama Hospital**, Sasthamangalam, T0471-272 2125, **Cosmopolitan Hospital**, T0471-244 8182 and **Vrindavan Ayurvedic Health Centre**, Kumarapuram, T0471-244 0376. **Post General Post Office**, Pulimudu Junction, T0471-247 3071, 0830-1800. **Post Office**, north of Secretariat, off MG Rd, is better. **DHL**, at Thampanoor, opposite Manjalikulam Rd, T0471-232 7161. **Useful contacts Foreigners' Regional Registration Office**, City Police Commissioner, Residency Rd, Thycaud, T0471-232 0579; allow up to a week for visas, though it can take less. Mon-Sat 1000-1700. **Wildlife Warden**, PTP Nagar, Vattiyoorkavu, T0471-236 0762.

Kovalam and nearby resorts *p977, map p978*

Banks **Canara Bank**, **ICICI Bank**, both at Kovalam Junction; ATMs. **Catholic Syria Bank**, Kovalam Beach Rd, has an ATM. **Central Bank**, branch in Kovalam Hotel (around the corner near the bookshop) changes money and TCs for non-residents after 1045, T0471-248 0101. Nearly all tour operators and many hotels offer money exchange. Best rates, however, are at the airport. **Wilson's**, T0471-248 1647, changes money, any time, no hassle. Or try **Phroze Framroze & Co** near Kovalam Bus Station T0471-248 7450. **Internet** Several on Lighthouse Beach. **Medical services** Emergency assistance either through your hotel or from **Government Hospital** in Thiruvananthapuram. **Upasana Hospital**, near *Le Meridien* gate, T0471-248 0632, has experienced English-speaking doctor. **Post** Inside **Le Meridien** gate. **Telephone** Check printed prices before paying for calls. Some ISD booths near the bus stand. **Western Travel**, opposite bus stand, until 2200. **Elite Tours**, T0471-248 1405, 2nd Beach Rd (30 m below bus stand). 24-hr ISD from the **Batik House**, Lighthouse Beach.

Varkala *p979, map p980*

Banks **State Bank of India**, Temple Junction has an ATM. There are several money changers: along the north cliff and around Temple Junction (lower than US$/£ rate at Trivandrum airport), and most will give cash advances on credit cards (at a hefty 5% commission). **Internet** Dozens of places along Varkala cliff. Most charging approx Rs 40 per hr. **Post** Next to Sree Padman, Temple Junction, Mon-Sat 1000-1400; ISD phones opposite; also at Maithalam and on North Cliff.

Backwaters

Kerala is synonymous with its lyrical backwaters: a watery cat's cradle of endlessly intersecting rivers, streams, lagoons and tanks that flood the alluvial plain between the Indian Ocean and Western Ghats. They run all the way from Kollam via Alappuzha and Kottayam to Kochi to open up a charming slow-tempo window onto Keralite waterfront life: this is the state's lush and fertile Christian belt, Arundhati Roy country, with lakes fringed by bird sanctuaries, idyllic little hamlets, beside huge paddy ponds rustling in the breeze.

The silent daybreak is best, as boats cut through mists, geese and ducks start to stir along banks, plumes from breakfast fires drift out across the lagoons. As the hamlets and villages wake, Kerala's domestic scene comes to life: clothes are pounded clean, teeth brushed, and smartly turned out primary school children swing their ways to class.

Luxury houseboats are the quintessential way of seeing the waterfront, but they can be shocking polluters, and if your budget or attention span won't stretch that far the state-operated ferries will give you much the same access for a fraction of the fee. Alternatively, borrow a bicycle or move around by car; the roads and canals are interchangeable. Both thread their way through flood plains the size of football pitches, brown lakes with new shoots prodding out and netted fields that protect prawns and fish from snooping white egrets. At dusk the young men sit about on bridges or congregate by teashops made of corrugated iron, as men shimmy up coconut palms to tap a fresh supply of sour moonshine toddy, and kids catch fish with poles. ▸▸ *For listings, see pages 995-1000.*

Ins and outs

Getting there and around Kollam is 70 km north of Trivandrum and linked to Alappuzha, Kottayam and Kochi by road and rail. Alappuzha is 64 km south of Kochi. The largest backwater body is the Vembanad Lake, which flows through Alappuzha and Kottayam districts to open into the sea at Kochi Port. This has made Alappuzha the principal departure point for houseboat operators. Kollam sits on Ashtamudi Lake, the second largest after Vembanad. Starting here gives you the longest ride (eight hours); the ferry for Alappuzha leaves at 1030. ▸▸ *See Transport, page 999.*

Tourist information In Kollam: **District Tourism Promotion Council (DTPC)** ⓘ *Govt Guest House Complex, T0474-275 0170; also at DTPC bus station, T0474-274 5625, train station and ferry jetty, www.dtpckollam.com*, offers cruises, coach tours, and details of *Kathakali* performances. In Alappuzha: **KTDC** ⓘ *Motel Araam, T0477-224 4460;* **ATDC**, *Komala Rd, T0477-226 4462, info@atdcalleppey.com;* **DTPC** ⓘ *KSRTC bus station near jetty, T0477-225 3308, 0830-2000*, is helpful and offers good backwaters trips. In Kottayam: **tourist office** ⓘ *Government Guest House, Nattakom, T0481-256 2219.*

Kollam (Quilon) → *For listings, see pages 995-1000. Colour map 7, C3. Phone code: 0474.*

Kollam (population 361,400) is a busy shaded market town on the side of the Ashtamudi Lake and the headquarters of India's cashew nut trading and processing industry. It is congested and there's little reason to linger, but its position at the south end of Kerala's backwaters, where the waterways are less crowded than those further north, make it a good alternative starting point for boat trips up the canals. ▸▸ *See Activities and tours, page 999.*

Known to Marco Polo as *Koilum*, the port saw trading between Phoenicians, Persians, Greeks, Romans and Arabs as well as the Chinese. Kollam became the capital of the Venad Kingdom in the ninth century. The educated king Raja Udaya Marthanda Varma convened a special council at Kollam to introduce a new era. After extensive astronomical calculations the new era was established to start on 15 August AD 825. The town was associated with the early history of Christianity.

Kerala backwaters

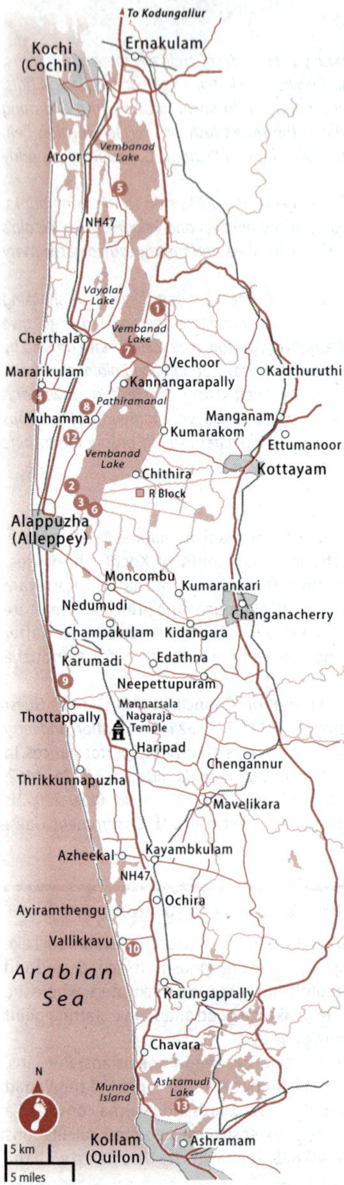

Roughly a third of the town is covered in the waters of the **Ashtamudi Lake** ⓘ *boats for hire from the Kollam Boat Club or DTPC, for 2 or 4, Rs 200 per hr each*. The lake, with coconut palms on its banks and picturesque promontories, extends north from the town. You might see some 'Chinese' fishing nets and in wider sections large-sailed dugouts carrying the local coir, copra and cashew.

Kollam to Alappuzha → *Backwater tours: A ferry leaves for Alappuzha at 1030 (8 hrs).*
Mata Amritanandamayi Ashram ⓘ *10 km north of Kollam at Vallikkavua, accessible by boat or road (through Kayambkulam or Karungappally), www.amritapuri.org, Rs 150 per day*, a giant, pink skyscraper sandwiched on the backwaters between the sea and the river, is the ashram of 'Amma' (the hugging 'Mother'). Thousands, Western and Indian alike, attend *Darshan* in hope of a hug. The ashram feels a bit lacklustre when Amma is on tour. She has hugged three million people so far. In the early days, these used to last for minutes; now she averages one hug every 1½ seconds, so she can happily hug 30,000 in a day. The ashram has shops, a bank, library and internet. Smoking, sex and alcohol are forbidden.

Mannarsala, 32 km before Alappuzha, has a tremendously atmospheric **Nagaraja Temple** buried deep in a dense jungle forest. Traditionally *naga* (serpent) worshippers had temples in serpent groves. Mannarsala is the largest of these in Kerala with '30,000 images' of snake gods lined up along the path and among the trees, and many snakes living around the temple. Childless women come for special blessing and also return for a 'thanksgiving' ceremony afterwards when the child born to the couple is placed on special scales and gifts in kind equalling the weight are donated. The temple is unusual for its chief priestess.

Sleeping
Anthraper Home Stay **1**
Cambay Palm Lagoon **13**
Casa Del Fauno **12**
Coconut Palms **9**
Kayaloram Lake Resort **2**
Keraleeyan Lakeside Ayurvedic Resort **3**
Marari Beach & Marari Beach Home **4**
Mata Amritanandamayi Ashram **10**
Olavipe **5**
Pooppally's Heritage Homestay **6**
Thaneermukkom Ayurvedic Lake Resort **7**
Vembanad Homestay **8**

The village of **Haripad** has one of Kerala's oldest and most important **Subrahmanya temples.** The four-armed idol is believed to have been found in a river, and in August the three-day Snake Boat Race at Payipad, 3 km by bus, commemorates its rescue and subsequent building of the temple. There are boat processions on the first two days followed by competitive races on the third day. There is a guesthouse on **Mankotta Island** on the backwaters; the large comfortable rooms with bath are well kept.

Squeezed between the backwaters and the sea, and 12 km from Haripad station, **Thottapally** makes a good stop on a backwaters trip, two hours from Alappuzha.

About 10 km from Chengannur, **Aranmula** has the Parthasarathi Temple and is known for its unique metal mirrors. The **Vallamkali** (or **Utthrittathi**) **festival** on the last day of Onam (August-September) is celebrated with a boat race. The festival celebrates the crossing of the river by Krishna, who is believed to be in all the boats simultaneously, so the challenge is to arrive at the same time, rather than race.

Alappuzha (Alleppey) and around

→ *For listings, see pages 995-1000. Colour map 7, C3.*
Phone code: 0477. Population: 177,100.

Alappuzha (pronounced *Alappoorra*) has a large network of canals, choked with the blue flowers of water hyacinth, passing through the town. It's the chief departure point for cruises into the

Alappuzha (Alleppey)

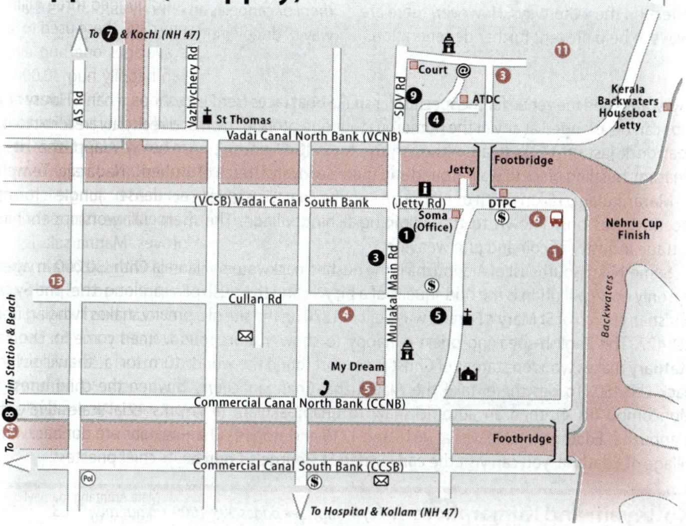

Sleeping
Cherukara Nest 1
Govt (KTC) Guest House 6
Johnson's The Nest 13
Kayaloram Lake Resort 8
Keraleeyam Lake Side Ayurvedic Health Resort 9
Motty's Homestay 11
Neo Narasimhapuram Lodge 4
Palmy's Residency 3
Raheem Residency & Chakara Restaurant 14
St George Lodge 5

Eating
Alleppey Prince 7
Harbour 8
Himalaya Bakery 9
Hot Kitchen 1
Indian Coffee House 3
Komala 4
Saurashtra 5

Preserving the backwaters for the future

The backwaters are lagoons fed by a network of perennial rivers with only two permanent outlets to the sea. The salts are flushed out between May and September, but sea waters rush inland by up to 20 km at the end of the monsoon and the waters become increasingly brackish through the dry season. This alternation between fresh and salt water has been essential to the backwaters' aquatic life. However, as land value has rocketed and reclamation for agriculture has reduced the surface water area, the backwaters' fragile ecology has been put at risk. Many of the original swamps have been destroyed and the waters are becoming increasingly saline.

Tourism, too, is taking its toll. Exploring the backwaters in a traditional *kettuvallam* is the ultimate Kerala experience but the popularity of these trips is having an adverse effect on the waterways. However, there are ways to help prevent further degeneration.

The trend so far has been for houseboat operators to offer larger, more luxurious boats (some even equipped with plunge pools) to meet the demands of tourists. The powerful outboard motors contribute heavily to pollution levels in the canals. Opting for a smaller boat not only helps ease environmental damage but also allows you to venture into the many narrower and less visited lagoons that the larger boats are unable to access.

Some operators are becoming aware of the damage being caused and are putting responsible travel practices in place. Support these efforts by checking that your houseboat is equipped with a chemical toilet (to prevent your waste being dumped into the canals) and if possible, opting for a solar-powered boat. Alternatively consider hiring a hand-propelled *thoni* or canoe as an entirely carbon-neutral way of discovering this unique region.

backwaters and the venue for the spectacular **snake boat races** (see Festivals, page 999). **Houseboat** trips can be arranged at any of the numerous tour operators in town or directly, by heading to the boat dock just off VCNB Road. Although the town itself doesn't have many tourist sites, it's a pleasant, bustling place to walk around and there's a lovely stretch of undeveloped beach as well.

Mararikulam, 15 km north of Alappuzha on the coast, is a quiet, secluded beach which, until recently, was only known to the adjoining fishing village. The main village has a thriving cottage industry of coir and jute weaving.

Some 16 km southeast of Alappuzha is the hushed backwaters village of **Champakulam** where the only noise pollution is the odd squeak of a bicycle and the slush of a canoe paddle. The Syrian Christian church of **St Mary's Forane** was built in 1870 on the site of a previous church dating from AD 427. The English-speaking priest is happy to show visitors round. Nearby the **St Thomas Statuary** makes wooden statues of Christ for export round the world: a 2-m-tall Jesus will set you back US$450. To get there, take the Alappuzha–Changanacherry bus (every 30 minutes) to Moncombu (Rs 4), then an auto-rickshaw to Champakulam (4 km, Rs 12). Alternatively the Alappuzha–Edathna ferry leaves at 0615 and 1715 and stops at Champakulam. In the backwater village of **Edathna**, you can visit the early Syrian **St George's Church**.

Kottayam and Kumarakom → *For listings, see pages 995-1000. Colour map 7, C3.*

Phone code: 0481. Population: 60,700.

Around Kottayam lies some of the lushest and most beautiful scenery in the state, with hills to its east and backwaters to its west. Kottayam itself is the capital of Kerala's Christian community, which belonged to the Orthodox Syrian tradition up till the Portuguese arrival. Two churches of the era survive 2 km north of town, in the 450-year-old **Cheria Palli** ('Small' St Mary's Church), which has beautiful vegetable dye mural paintings over its altar, and the **Valia Palli** ('Big' St Mary's Church), from 1550, with two Nestorian crosses carved on plaques behind two side altars. One has a Pallavi inscription on it, the other a Syriac. The cross on the left of the altar is the original and may be the oldest Christian artefact in India; the one to the right is a copy. By the altar there is an unusual small triptych of an Indian St George slaying a dragon. Note the interesting Visitors' Book (1898-1935); a paper cutting reports that "the church has attracted many European and native gentlemen of high position". Mass at Valia Palli at 0900 on Sunday, and Cheria Palli at 0730 on Sunday and Wednesday. The Malankara Syrian Church has its headquarters at Devalokam.

Ettumanoor, just north of Kottayam, has possibly the wealthiest temple in Kerala. The present Mahadeva temple was constructed in 1542, and is famous for its murals depicting scenes from the *Ramayana* and the Krishna legends, both inside and outside the *gopuram*. The typical circular shrine with a copper-covered conical roof encloses a square sanctuary. The Arattu festival in March draws thousands of pilgrims when gold elephant statues are displayed. They weigh 13 kg each.

Tucked among the waterways of Vembanad Lake, in mangrove, paddy and coconut groves with lily-studded shores, is **Kumarakom**, 16 km from Kottayam. Here are stacks of exclusive hotels where you can be buffed and Ayurvedically preened, bent into yoga postures, peacefully sunbathe or take to the water: perfect honeymoon territory.

The tourism department has developed an old rubber plantation set around the Vembanad Lake into a **bird sanctuary** ⓘ *1000-1800.* A path goes through the swamp to the main bird nesting area. **Pathiramanal** ('midnight sands') **Island** in the middle of the lake can be reached by boat. The best season for birdlife is June to August; try to visit early in the morning.

Backwaters listings

For Sleeping and Eating price codes and other relevant information, see Essentials pages 38-42.

Sleeping

Kollam *p991, map p992*

LL-L Fragrant Nature Retreat and Resorts, Paravur, T0474-251 4000, www.fragrantnature.com. A 4-star luxury lakeside resort with spa, swimming pool and jacuzzi. Accommodation in lakeside rooms or villas.

L-A Cambay Palm Lagoon, Vellimon West, T0474-254 7214, www.thecambay.com. Delightful setting 18 km from town centre on north side of Ashtamudi Lake, can be reached from backwater cruise. Attractive thatched cottages, includes full board.

AL-A Aquasserenne, Paravoor, 15 mins from town by road or boat, T0474-2512410, www.aquasereneindia.com. Splendid backwaters location, well-furnished chalets (some reassembled Kerala houses) with TV, restaurant, Ayurvedic massage/treatment, boat rides.

AL-C Valiyavila Family Estate, Panamukkam Jetty, Kureepuzha, access by ferry (frequent, Rs 3) from Kollam boat jetty, T0474-270 1546, www.kollamlakeviewresort.com. 6 bright, breezy rooms in large house right on the lakeside. Peaceful location, lovely garden with hammocks, great views. Friendly, attentive staff. Wide selection of meals available. Eccentric 55-ft statue of 'Goddess of Light' in garden means you can't miss this place. Good discounts off-season. Canoe trips. Recommended.

C Tamarind (KTDC), Ashramam, T0474-274 5538, www.ktdc.com/tamarind. Newly renovated rooms in a bland block building. All rooms with a/c, TV. Nice views of the waterway. Quiet location, restaurant, boat hire.

C-E Sudarsan, Hospital Rd, Parameswar Nagar, 5 mins from jetty, T0474-274 0480, www.hotelsudarsan.com. Busy Indian business hotel. Rooms all with TV and decent bath, some a/c. Cheaper rooms are good value. Restaurant, coffee shop.

F-G Government Guest House, Ashramam, T0474-274 3620. Live like the British Raj on a pauper's budget. 12 simply-furnished rooms, all with attached bath, in the sprawling former residence of the British governor. More expensive rooms have bathrooms large enough to throw a party in. High ceilings, shady veranda, huge garden, bags of character, friendly staff. Some cheaper rooms are in bland modern building at the back. Meals on request. Recommended.

F-G Mahalaxmi Lodge, opposite bus station, T0474-276 3823. Smallish, moderately clean, basic rooms, some with attached bath and TV.

Kollam to Alappuzha *p992, map p992*

C-D Coconut Palms, Kumarakodi, book through **Aries Travel**, Trivandrum, T0471-233 1165, www.ariestravel.net. Idyllic 200-year-old traditional house in shaded compound, on backwaters and 100 m from sea. Yoga, Ayurveda and package deals available.

G Mata Amritanandamayi Ashram, Vallikkavu, T0476-289 6399, www.amrita puri.org. Amma's ashram offers spartan but spacious accommodation in a multi-storey block, with hugs and South Indian meals included in the price. Western canteen (at extra cost) serves American-style meals.

Alappuzha (Alleppey) and around *p993, maps p992 and p993*

Book ahead to avoid the scramble off the ferry. Hotels north of Vadai Canal are quieter.

LL Marari Beach, Mararikulam, Alappuzha, T0484-301 1711, www.cghearth.com. Well-furnished, comfortable, local-style cottages (garden villas, garden pool villas and 3 deluxe pool villas) in palm groves – some with private pool. Good seafood, pool, Ayurvedic treatment, yoga in the morning, *pranayama* in the evening, shop, bikes, badminton, beach volleyball, boat cruises (including overnight houseboat), farm tours, friendly staff, discounts Apr-Sep. Recommended.

LL Olavipe, Thekanatt Parayil, Olavipe, 25 km from Cochin, T0478-252 2255, www.olavipe.com. Century-old mansion belonging to family of Syrian Christan notables, on a 16-ha organic farm on the lush island of Olavipe. 5 rooms: 3 in the main house and 2 in a cottage.

LL Purity, Muhamma, Aryakkara, (8 km from Alappuzha town), T0484-221 6666, www.malabarhouse.com. The former Casa del Fauno has a new name and a new owner (the folks from Malabar House in Fort Kochi), but this beautiful Italianate villa on an acre of tropical grounds overlooking Lake Vembanad remains the most elegant lodging for miles around, with coolly minimalist decor and a smattering of rare antiques. There's a pool, a private beach, Ayurvedic treatments and yoga classes.

LL Raheem Residency, Beach Rd, Alappuzha, T0477-223 9767, www.raheemresidency.com. Special luxury heritage hotel housed in a beautifully restored colonial 19th-century bungalow, on a pristine piece of Kerala's coast. 10 immaculate rooms, all with a/c and lovely antique furnishings. Palatial living room, jasmine-scented garden, excellent restaurant and a lovely pool under a velvet apple tree. The Irish journalist owner also offers the property as a writers' retreat (contact for prices). Easily the best address in Alappuzha. Recommended.

L-AL Anthraper Home Stay, Cherthala, T0478-2813211, www.anthrapergardens.com. Charming country house on the backwaters. Sprawling garden, cooking demonstrations, yoga, canoeing, fishing and river walks.

L-AL Emerald Isle Heritage Villa, Kanjooparambil-Manimalathan, T0477-270 3899, www.emeraldislekerala.com. 4 rooms on the shores of an island of lush jungle, surrounded by sunken paddy field. Toddy on tap, cookery courses, boat trips, Ayurveda. The magic of the place begins on the 10-km journey from Alappuzha.

AL Kayaloram Lake Resort, Punmamada, Vembanad Lake, T0477-223 2040, www.kayaloram.com. Kerala-style wood and tile cottages around small inner courtyard with 'open-to-sky' showers. Comfortable, very quiet and peaceful. Pool, restaurant, Ayurveda. Backwaters or lake trips. Recommended.

L Motty's Homestay, Kidangamparambu Rd, Alappuzha, T(0)98470 32836, motty@alleppeybeach.com. Just 2 double rooms, with old furniture and 4-poster beds, in a private house on Alappuzha's outskirts. Excellent home-cooked breakfast and dinner included.

AL Vembanad House Home Stay, Puthankayal, Alappuzha, T0478-286 8696, www.vembanadhouse.com. 4 spacious rooms in stately heritage house surrounded by a lake in the pretty Muhamma area. Fresh food from the family farm cooked to Kerala recipes. Traditional architecture with modern bathrooms (no a/c). The house is managed by the delightful Balakrishnan family.

A Pooppally's Heritage Homestay, Pooppally Junction, Nedumudy, T0477-276 2034, www.pooppallys.com. Traditional wooden cottage (water bungalow) and rooms, with open-air bathrooms, in 19th-century family farmhouse, shaded by a mango tree, set in a garden stretching down to the River Pampa. Great home- cooked food. Catch the ferry to Alappuzha for 90 mins of free houseboat.

B Keraleeyam Lake Side Ayurvedic Health Resort, off Thathampally main road, Alappuzha, T0477-223 1468, www.keraleeyam.com. Keraleeyam sits on one of the prettiest nubs of the backwaters and is one of the most reasonable places to embark on a proper Ayurvedic programme. Doctors attend daily, there's no alcohol, and the menu is tailored according to your Ayurvedic body type. Cottages on the lake are better than the drab rooms in the main house.

C-E Cherukara Nest, just around the corner from KSRTC bus station, Alappuzha, T0477-225 1509, www.cherukaranest.com. Airy, cool, spotlessly clean rooms in a peaceful traditional family home. Rattan furniture on large shady porches. Pigeon house in the back garden. Very helpful and friendly. Meals available on request.

D-G Johnson's The Nest, Lal Bagh Factory Ward (West of Convent Sq), Alappuzha, T0477-224 5825, www.johnsonskerala.com. Friendly family-run guesthouse in a quiet street away from the town centre. 6 rooms, each with balcony. Free pickup from bus station, internet, houseboat facility, popular.

E-F Palmy's Residency, north of new Matha footbridge, Alappuzha, T0477-223 5938, www.palmyresort.com. Large, clean rooms with fly-screens and fans. Quiet but central location. More expensive rooms have big balconies to lounge in. Local waterway canoe trips (4-5 hrs, Rs 200 per hr). Free bike hire. Recommended.

E-G Government Guest House (KTDC), Jetty Rd, Alappuzha, T0477-224 4460. Bright yellow building next door to the KSRTC bus station. More expensive rooms are large but have tired-looking bathrooms. Cheaper bamboo-walled rooms on 3rd floor. Be careful not to trip over the staff members fast asleep on the veranda. Free bike hire, internet.

G Narasimhapuram Lodge, Cullen Rd, Alappuzha, T0477-226 2662. Basic, dark, but clean rooms with rock-hard beds and squat toilets. Some rooms slightly smelly so ask to see a few. Occasional weight-lifting competition with live commentary over loudspeakers!

G St George Lodge, CCNB Rd, Alappuzha, T0477-225 1620. Don't let the dilapidated façade put you off – this is an excellent cheapie. 80 very basic but clean rooms, some with attached bath. Friendly staff.

Kottayam and Kumarakom *p994*

In Kumarakom 26% taxes are added to bills.

LL Coconut Lagoon, Vembanad Lake Kumarakom (CGH Earth), T0484-301 1711, www.cghearth.com. Comfortable heritage *tharavads* (traditional Keralite wooden cottages), heritage mansions and pool villas. Outdoor restaurant facing lagoon, good dinner buffet, pool, yoga, very friendly, Ayurvedic treatments, attractive waterside location, spectacular approach by boat (10 mins from road). Vechoor cows mow the lawns. Recommended. Discounts Apr-Sep.

LL Philipkutty's Farm, Pallivathukal, Ambika Market, Vechoor, Kottayam, T0482-927 6529, www.philipkuttysfarm.com. 5 immaculate waterfront villas sharing an island on Vembanad Lake. The delightful working farm boasts coconut, banana, nutmeg, coca and vanilla groves. Delicious home cooking and personal attention from all the family. No a/c or TV. Cooking and painting holidays.

LL Privacy at Sanctuary Bay, Kannamkara, opposite Kumarakom, T0484-221 6666, www.malabarhouse.com. Beautiful lakeside isolation in 3-bedroom bungalow. Old Keralite facade with stunning verandas. Modern, opulent interior. Fully staffed, ultimate luxury.

LL Vivanta by Taj, Kumarakom, T0481- 252 5711, www.vivantabytaj.com. 19 a/c rooms, in sensitively renovated 120-year-old 'Bakers' House', as featured in *The God of Small Things*. Also newer cottages and a moored houseboat, good meals. An intimate hotel but packed.

LL-L Waterscapes (KTDC), Kumarakom, T0481-252 5861. Idyllic cottage experience on the backwaters. All chalets have a/c and cable TV. Pool, bar, restaurant.

B-D Anjali Park, KK Rd, 4 km from railway, Kottayam, T0481-256 3661. Decent rooms with bath and a/c. Good restaurants.

C-D Aida, MC Rd, 2 km from railway, Kottayam, T0481-256 8391, www.hotelaidakerala.com. Clean, pleasant rooms with bath, some with a/c. Front rooms can be noisy. Restaurant, bar, helpful staff.

D-E Kaycee's Residency, off YMCA Rd, Kottayam, T0481-256 3440. Good value, clean, decent-sized rooms.

D-F Green Park, Kurian Uthup Rd, Nagampadam, T0481-256 3331, greenparkhotel@yahoo.co.in. Adequate rooms with bath. A/c rooms noisy, non-a/c at back too hot. Restaurant.

E Vembanad Lake Resort, near Kodimatha Jetty, 2 km from bus stand, T0481-236 0866, ktm_vembanad@sancharnet.in. Simple rooms in 10 cottages, waterside garden, good houseboat restaurant.

E-F Ambassador Hotel, KK Rd (set back), T0481-256 3293. Friendly Indian-style hotel with good restaurant and bar. Very good value.

F PWD Rest House, on hill 2 km south of Kottayam, T0481-256 8147. Remarkable late 19th-century building with superb furniture, overlooking vista of paddy fields.

F Venad Tourist Complex, Ancheril Building, near State Bus Stand, Kottayam, T0481-258 1383. Modern building with clean rooms. Restaurant. Recommended.

Eating

Kollam *p991, map p992*

Eat N Pack, near Taluk Office, Main St. Excellent value, clean, good choice of dishes, friendly. Recommended.

Indian Coffee House, Main Rd. For good coffee and vegetarian and non-vegetarian South Indian food. Nice waiter service and good atmosphere.

Suprabhatam, opposite clock tower, Main St. Adequate vegetarian.

Alappuzha (Alleppey) *p993, map p993*

Chakara, Raheem Residency, Beach Rd. Rooftop dining with attentive service and excellent multi-cuisine food. The 4-course set dinner menu (pegged at rupee equivalent to €11) is unbeatable value. Alcohol available.

Alleppey Prince Hotel, AS Rd (NH47), 2 km from town. International, comfortable a/c restaurant, reasonable food, alcohol in bar only.

Harbour, Beach Rd. Specializes in seafood but also has Indian and European dishes. Excellent value. Alcohol available. Recommended.

Himalaya Bakery, SDV Rd. Large range of sweet and savoury pastries, and other snacks, to take out or eat in at the tiny seating area.

Hot Kitchen, Mullakal Main Rd. Good for *iddli*, *dosa*, *vadai*, etc.

Indian Coffee House, Mullakal Main Rd. Good value, tasty non-vegetarian snacks.

Komala, Komala Hotel, Zilla Court Ward. Excellent South Indian *thalis* and Chinese.

SAS, Jetty Rd. Good South Indian vegetarian and Chinese.

Saurashtra, Cullan Rd. Vegetarian, ample helpings on banana leaf, locally popular.

Kottayam and Kumarakom *p994*

The below are situated in Kottayam. For options in Kumarakom, see hotels listed above.

Aida, MC Rd. Large, uninspired menu. Pleasantly cool 'chilled' drinks may arrive slightly warm.

Green Park, Kurian Uthup Rd. International menu. Reasonable but slow service. Dinner in mosquito-ridden garden (or in own room for guests). Alcohol available.

Near the state bus station

Black Stone, T B Rd. Good vegetarian.

Milkshake Bar, T B Rd, opposite Blackstone Hotel. 20 flavours.

Festivals and events

Kollam *p991, map p992*

Jan **Kerala Tourism boat race** on 19 Jan.

Apr Colourful 10-day **Vishnu festival** in Asram Temple with procession and fireworks.

Aug-Sep Avadayattukotta Temple celebrates a 5-day **Ashtami Rohani** festival. **Muharram** too is observed with processions at the town mosque.

Alappuzha and around *p993, map p993*

For more details see www.keralatourism.org.

9-12 Jan **Cheruppu** is celebrated in the Mullakkal Devi Temple with a procession of elephants, music and fireworks.

17-19 Jan **Tourism Boat Race**.

Jul/Aug **DTPC Boat Race** (3rd Sat) in the backwaters. **Champakulam Boat Race**, Kerala's oldest, takes place 16-km ferry ride away on 'Moolam' day. The Nehru Trophy, inaugurated in 1952, is the largest **Snake Boat Race** in the state. As many as 40 highly decorated 'snake boats' are rowed by several dozen oarsmen before huge crowds. Naval helicopters do mock rescue operations and stunt flying. Entry by ticket;

Rs 125 (Rs 60/75 tickets allow access in to overcrowded and dangerous areas). There are other snake boat races held throughout the year.

Activities and tours

Kollam *p991, map p992*

Tour operators

You will be spoilt for choice where backwater trips are concerned. As well as houseboat trips on traditional *kettuvallams*, there are also the much cheaper options of Kollam-to-Alappuzha cruises and shorter canal journeys to Munroe Island. The gentle pace and tranquil waterways make these tours very worthwhile, but the heat and humidity may sometimes make overnight stays on houseboats uncomfortable.

DTPC, boat jetty, T0474-275 0170, www.dtpckollam.com. Daily 8-hr backwater cruise from Kollam to Alappuzha; depart 1030 (Rs 400). You can be dropped off halfway at Alumkadavu (Rs 200) or at Vallikkavu for the Ashram (Rs 150). The only stops are for meals; some travellers find the trip a little too long and samey. A good alternative is a canal trip to Munroe Island village; depart 0900,1300 (6 hrs return, Rs 300).

A more expensive option is to hire a *kettuvallam*. For a 1-bed houseboat prices start at Rs 5000 for 8 hrs day trip, Rs 6500 for overnight, to Rs 12300 for 2 days and 1 night, inclusive of all meals. There are also cruise packages which combine a day cruise with an overnight stay at a backwater resort (Rs 3500).

Independent operators include:

Southern Backwaters Tour Operators, opposite KRSTC Bus Station, Jetty Rd, Kollam, T(0)94959 76037, www.southernbackwaters.com. A/c deluxe and standard houseboats for 1- to 3-night packages. Also motorboat cruises and Munroe Island tours.

Alappuzha and around *p993, map p993*

Tour operators

Alappuzha is the starting point of backwater boat trips to Kollam, Changanacherry, Kottayam and Kochi, and everybody you meet seems to have a houseboat to rent. Trips and boat standards vary widely. Always ask to check your boat before handing over the full payment to make sure you are getting what you agree to pay for. For information ask at the **DTPC**.

CGHEarth, T0484-301 1711, Kochi, www.cghearth.com. Runs 'spice boat' cruises in modified *kettuvallams*, which are idyllic if not luxurious: shaded sit-outs, modern facilities including solar panels for electricity, 2 double rooms, limited menu. US$325.

Discovery 1, Malabar House, Fort Kochi, see page 1007. Malabar Escapes' take on the houseboat is silent and pollutant free. Because it's nimble and trips are for a minimum of 3 nights, it's guaranteed to take you far from the wider watery motorways bigger rice boats ply. 1 bedroom, large bathroom and sitting room plus sun deck. Food is to the Malabar House's high standard.

DTPC, Jetty Rd, T0477-225 1796, www.dtpcalappuzha.com. Runs the same 8-hr backwater cruises as its sister office in Kollam, except going the other way. Departs 1030 from Alappuzha ferry jetty (Rs 400). There is also a shorter round-trip to Kumarakom (4 hrs, Rs 200), and canoe trips through local waterways (Rs 200 per hr).

Lakes and Lagoons Tour Co, Punnamada, T0477-2266842, www.lakeslagoons.com. Solar-powered 2-bed boats. Consistently recommended operator.

Rainbow Cruises, VCNB Rd, opposite jetty, Alappuzha, T0477-226 1375, www.rainbowcruises.in. Solar powered with high safety standards and emergency speedboat support (houseboats have been known to sink).

Transport

Kollam *p991, map p992*

Local auto-rickshaws are plentiful and bikes are available for hire.

Bus **Local** buses are plentiful. **Long distance** buses run from the KSRTC station, T0474-275 2008. Buses every 30 mins from 0600 to **Kochi** (3½ hrs, Rs 87) via **Alappuzha** (2 hrs, Rs 55) and other towns on the coast. Buses run 24 hrs to **Thiruvananthapuram**, leaving every 10 mins in the day and every 30 mins during the night (2 hrs, Rs 44). Change at Thiruvananthapuram for **Kovalam**. It is difficult to get to **Varkala** by bus; take the train.

Car To **Alappuzha**, Rs 750, from bus station.

Ferry Public ferries sail to **Ghuhandapuram** at 0730, 1100, 1330, 1545 and 1745 (1 hr, Rs 5) and then return to Kollam. It's an interesting journey with views of village life and Chinese fishing nets on the way. The 1745 departure lets you enjoy sunset over the waterways.

Train Junction railway station, T131, is about 3 km east of the boat jetty and bus station. There are several trains a day south to **Thiruvananthapuram** including: *Malabar Exp 6630*, 0715 (1½ hrs); *Vanchinad Exp 16303*, 0815 (1½ hrs); and the *Island Exp 16526*, 1335 (1¾ hrs), which continues to **Kanniyakumari** (4¼ hrs). All these trains stop at **Varkala** (½ hr). Going north: to **Chennai**, *TVC Chennai Exp 12696*, 1815 (15 hrs). The *Cape Mumbai Exp 16382* heads to **Mumbai** at 0925 (44 hrs). To **Bangalore** (**Bengaluru**), *Island Exp 16525*, 1415 (16 hrs). All these trains stop at **Ernakulam**.

Alappuzha and around *p993, map p993*

It is only a 5-min walk between the ferry jetty and the KSRTC bus station despite what many local rickshaw drivers will tell you.

Bus From the **KSRTC Bus Station**, T0477-225 2501, there are frequent long-distance buses to **Kochi**, 0630-2330 (1½ hrs, Rs 37); **Thiruvananthapuram**, 0600-2000, (4 hrs, Rs 96) via **Kollam** (2 hrs, Rs 55); **Champakulam**, 0515-2000 (45 mins, Rs 10) and **Kottayam**, 0730-1800 (1½ hrs, Rs 30). There are several buses daily to **Coimbatore**, from 0600 (7 hrs, Rs 96).

Car A car with driver from Alappuzha to **Fort Kochi** (65 km) costs Rs 500-600.

Ferry Public ferries, T0477-225 2015, sail to **Kottayam**, 0730, 1000, 1130, 1300, 1430 and 1730 (3 hrs) and **Changanassery**, 1000, 1300 and 1730 (3 hrs). Also frequent services to **Nedumudi** (1 hr).

Train The train station, T0477-225 3965, is on the coastal route from **Trivandrum-Varkala-Kollam-Ernakulam**, 3 km from the jetty. There are frequent trains in both directions.

Kottayam and Kumarakom *p994*

Bus The new **Private Bus Station** is near the railway station. Buses to Alappuzha only leave from the **KSRTC Bus Station**, 2 km away; local buses to to **Kumarakom Tourist Village** also run frequently from here. There are fast and frequent long-distance buses to **Alappuzha**, every 45 mins (2 hrs, Rs 30); **Thiruvananthapuram**, every 30 mins (4 hrs, Rs 90); **Kochi**, every 30 mins (1½ hrs, Rs 45) and **Kumily**, every hour (4½ hrs, Rs 68). There are 2 evening departures to **Madurai**, 2045 and 2145 (7 hrs, Rs 120) and 5 buses daily head to **Munnar**, 0600-1600 (5 hrs, Rs 100).

Car Car with driver to **Thekkady**, Rs 850, 4 hrs.

Ferry Ferries leave from the **Kodimatha Jetty** except during the monsoons, when you should head to the **Town Jetty** 3 km south- west of the train station. Ferries to **Alappuzha**, 0730, 0930, 1130, 1430,1730 (3 hrs). This is an interesting trip but gets very busy in peak season. Other departures include **Champa- kulam**, 1530 (4 hrs) and **Mannar**, 1430 (3 hrs).

Train Trains run throughout the day, south to **Trivandrum** via **Kollam** and **Varkala**, and north to Ernakulam and beyond. No trains to Alappuzha, which is on the parallel coastal line.

Directory

Kollam *p991, map p992*

Medical services District Hospital, T0474-279 3409. **Post** Head Post Office, Parameswara Nagar. Mon-Sat until 2000, Sun until 1800.

Alappuzha and around *p993, map p993*

Banks Catholic Syria Bank, Jetty Rd, and **State Bank of India**, Cullan Rd. Both have ATMs. **Internet** Several places on Mullakal Rd. **Net Café**, opposite Kidangamparampu Temple, charges Rs 20 per hr. **Medical services** District Hospital, T0477-225 3324. **Post** Off Mullakal Rd.

Kottayam and Kumarakom *p994*

Banks In Kottayam: Banks are clustered around Ghandi Sq on TB and MC Rds including **Bank of India**, MC Rd and **Ing Bank**, TB Rd. Both have ATMs. **Internet** Many places around Ghandi Sq. **Medical services** District Hospital, T0481-256 3651. **Post** MC Rd, 0800-2000, 1400-1730 on holidays.

Fort Kochi and Ernakulam

→ *Colour map 7, C2. Phone code: 0484. Population: 1.15 million (Kochi 596,500, Ernakulam 558,000).*

Charming Fort Kochi (Cochin) is a true one-off in modern Kerala: a layer cake of colonial India, where British parade grounds overlay Portugese forts, where Dutch palaces slowly crumble into the soil alongside synagogues, where every turn takes you down some romantically fossilized narrow winding street. Despite a tourist invasion that's flooded the lanes with antique shops, internet cafés and shops flogging fisherman trousers, parts of the ramshackle island still feel frozen back in the 15th and 16th centuries, and the huge trees here are so old that their parasitic aphids are as tall as trees themselves. In the southern quarter of Mattancherry, row upon row of wood-fronted doors give glimpses of rice and spice merchants sitting sifting their produce into small 'tasting' bowls. The iconic batwing Chinese fishing nets, first used in the 14th century, stand on the shores of the north fort area, silhouetted against the lapping waters of one of the world's finest natural harbours: a wide bay interrupted by narrow spits of land and coconut-covered islands.

All of which does little to prepare you for arriving into Kochi via the city's modern centre of gravity – grubby, dynamic Ernakulam, a Rs 5 ferry ride and half a world away across the harbour. While Fort Kochi languishes dreamily in the past, its ambitious sibling is expanding outwards and upwards at breakneck pace, propelled by the vast new container terminal on Vallarpadam Island. The first port in India capable of handling the huge container ships that until now have had to berth in Colombo or Singapore, Kochi stands poised to transform India's logistical landscape, and over the next decade this hitherto sleepy southern city will undoubtedly assume a front-and-centre seat in the future of the Indian economy. ▸▸ *For listings, see pages 1007-1012.*

Ins and outs

Getting there Kochi International Airport is at Nedumbassery, 36 km northeast. Both the main railway station, Ernakulam Junction, and the main long-distance bus station are in Ernakulam. A rickshaw from either to the main jetty, for Fort Kochi, is approx Rs 25. ▸▸ *See Transport, page 1011.*

Getting around There are three main places to stay, but everything to see is in Fort Kochi, on the southern promontory. Willingdon Island has precious few tourist charms to draw you across the causeway from Ernakulam and is awkwardly placed without your own transport. Immediately opposite the jetty at Ernakulam is Bolghatty Island, and beyond it Vypeen Island. During the day, a fun, quick ferry service stops at major points around the bay. Once in Fort Kochi, the palace and the synagogue in Jew Town are close to a jetty but you'll need to rent a rickshaw or bicycle to get to St Francis' Church. After 2130 public transport begins to grind to a halt and you'll need to take a rickshaw or taxi to get around.

Tourist information **Kerala Tourism Development Corporation** (KTDC) ⓘ *Shanmugham Rd, Ernakulam, T0484-235 3234, 0800-1800.* **Tourist Desk** ⓘ *Main Boat Jetty, Ernakulam, T0484-237 1761, and on Tower Rd in Fort Kochi, T0484-221 6129, www.touristdesk.in, 0900-1800.* This travel agent, with good maps and local information, runs daily backwater tours, has information on more than 2000 temple festivals in Kerala, and runs **Costa Malabari** guesthouse (see Sleeping, page 1036).

Background

"If China is where you make your money," declared Italian traveller Nicolas Conti in the Middle Ages, "then Kochi surely is the place to spend it." Kochi has acted as a trading port since at least Roman times, and was a link in the main trade route between Europe and China. From 1795 until India's Independence the long outer sand spit, with its narrow beach leading to the wide bay inland, was under British political control. The inner harbour was in Kochi State, while most of the hinterland was in the separate state of Travancore. The division of political authority delayed development of the harbour facilities until 1920-1923, when the approach channel was dredged so ships that could get through the Suez Canal could dock here, opening the harbour to modern shipping.

Sights

If you land at the Customs Jetty, a plaque in nearby Vasco da Gama Square commemorates the landing of Vasco da Gama in 1500. Next to it is the **Stromberg Bastion**, "one of the seven bastions of Fort Emanuel built in 1767", named after the Portuguese king. Little is left of the 1503 Portuguese fort except ruins. Along the seafront, between the Fort Kochi Bus Stand, the boat jetty and the Dutch cemetery, run the cantilevered Chinese fishing nets. These are not unique to Kochi, but are perhaps uniquely accessible to the short-stay visitor.

Mattancherry Palace and **Parikshith Thampuran Museum** ⓘ *Mattancherry, daily 1000-1700 except Fri and national holidays, Rs 2, photography not allowed*, was first built by the Portuguese around 1557 as a sweetener for the Raja Veera Kerala Varma of Kochi bestowing them trading rights. In 1663, it was largely rebuilt by the new trading power, the Dutch. The layout follows the traditional Kerala pattern known as *nalukettus*, meaning four buildings, which are set around a quadrangle with a temple. There are display cases of the Rajas of Kochi's clothes, palanquins, etc, but these are no match for the amazing murals. The royal bedroom's low wooden walls squeezes the whole narrative of the *Ramayana* into about 45 late 16th-century panels. Every inch is covered with rich red, yellow, black and white. To the south of the Coronation Hall, the *kovinithilam* (staircase room) has six large 18th-century murals including the coronation of Rama. Vishnu is in a room to the north. Two of the women's bedrooms downstairs have 19th-century murals with greater detail. They relate Kalidasa's *Kumarasambava* and themes from the *Puranas*. This stuff is triple x-rated. If you are of a sensitive disposition avert your eyes from panel 27 and 29, whose deer, birds and other animals are captioned as giving themselves up to 'merry enjoyment', a coy way of describing the furious copulation and multiple penetration in plain view. Krishna, meanwhile, finally works out why he was given so many limbs, much to the evident satisfaction of the gopis who are looking on.

The **synagogue** ⓘ *Mattancherry, Sun-Fri 1000-1200, 1500-1700, no video cameras, shoes must be removed*, dating from 1568 (rebuilt in 1662), is near Mattancherry Palace at the heart of what is known as Jew Town, which is a fascinating mixture of shops (some selling antiques), warehouses and spice auction rooms. Stepping inside the synagogue is an extraordinary experience of light and airiness, partly due to the 18th-century blue Cantonese ceramic tiles, hand painted and each one different, covering the floor. There are original glass oil lamps. For several centuries there were two Jewish communities. The earlier group (often referred to as 'black' Jews), according to one source, settled here as early as 587 BC. The earliest evidence of their presence is a copper inscription dated AD 388 by the Prince of Malabar. Those referred to as 'white' Jews came much later, when, with Dutch and then British patronage, they played a major role as trading agents. Speaking fluent Malayalam, they made excellent go-betweens for foreigners seeking to establish contacts. The community has shrunk to six families, with many now settled at Moshav Nevatim in Israel's Negev desert. The second Jewish synagogue (in Ernakulam) is deserted.

St Francis' Church ⓘ *Fort Kochi, Mon-Sat 0930-1730, Sun afternoon, Sun services in English 0800 (except for the 3rd Sun of each month)*, was originally dedicated to Santo Antonio, the patron saint of Portugal and is the first church to reflect the new and European- influenced tradition. The original wooden structure (circa 1510) was replaced by the present stone building (there is no authority for the widely quoted date of 1546). Vasco da Gama died on the site in 1524 and was originally buried in the cemetery. Fourteen years later his body was removed to Portugal. The church was renamed St Francis in 1663, and the Dutch both converted it to a Protestant church and substantially modified it. They retained control until 1795, adding the impressive gable façade at the entrance. In 1804, it became an Anglican church. In 1949 the congregation joined the Church of South India. Note the old string-pulled *punkahs* (fans) and the Dutch and Portuguese gravestones that now line the walls.

Santa Cruz Cathedral, near St Francis' Church, originally built in 1557 by the Portuguese, and used as a warehouse by the British in the 18th century, was rebuilt in the early 20th century. It has lovely carved wooden panels and pulpit, and an interesting graveyard.

Museum of Kerala History ⓘ *Ernakulam, 1000-1200 and 1400-1600 except Mon and national holidays*, starts with Neolithic man through St Thomas and Vasco da Gama. Historical personalities of Kerala are represented with sound and light.

Around Fort Kochi and Ernakulam

Bolghatty Island has the 'palace' (circa 1745), set in large gardens and converted into a hotel. It was originally built by the Dutch and then became the home of the British Resident at the court of the Raja of Kochi after 1799. There is still some atmosphere of colonial decay which haunted the old building in its pre-modernized form and gave it much of its charm.

Vypeen Island lies on the northwestern fringe of the harbour. There are quiet beaches here, along with the Portuguese Azhikotta Fort, built around 1503. You can see cannon holes on the

1 Fort Kochi detail

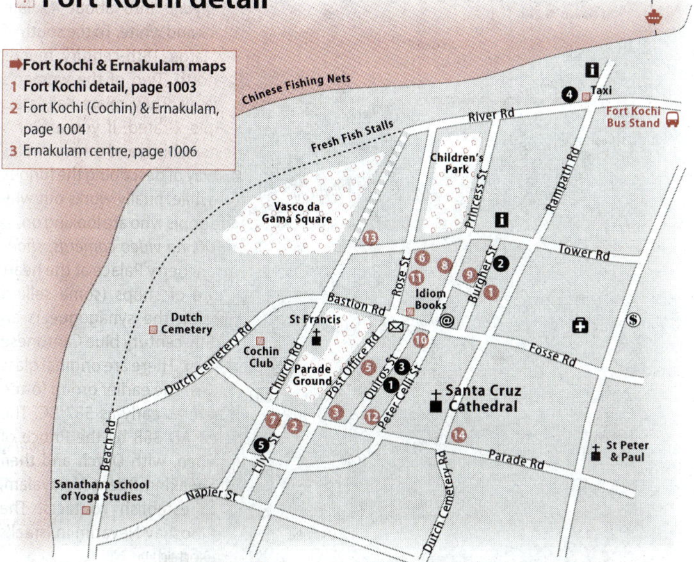

➡Fort Kochi & Ernakulam maps
1 Fort Kochi detail, page 1003
2 Fort Kochi (Cochin) & Ernakulam, page 1004
3 Ernakulam centre, page 1006

Sleeping
Adam's Old Inn **1**
Chiramel Residency **2**
Delight Homestay **3**
Koder House **6**
Malabar House & Restaurant **7**
Old Courtyard **8**
Old Harbour **13**
Oys Tourist Home **9**
Park Avenue **10**
Raintree Lodge **12**
Rossitta Wood Castle **11**
Trinity **5**
Vintage Inn **14**

Eating
Dal & Roti **5**
Feast **3**
Kashi **2**
Marina **4**
Teapot **1**

2 Fort Kochi (Cochin) & Ernakulam

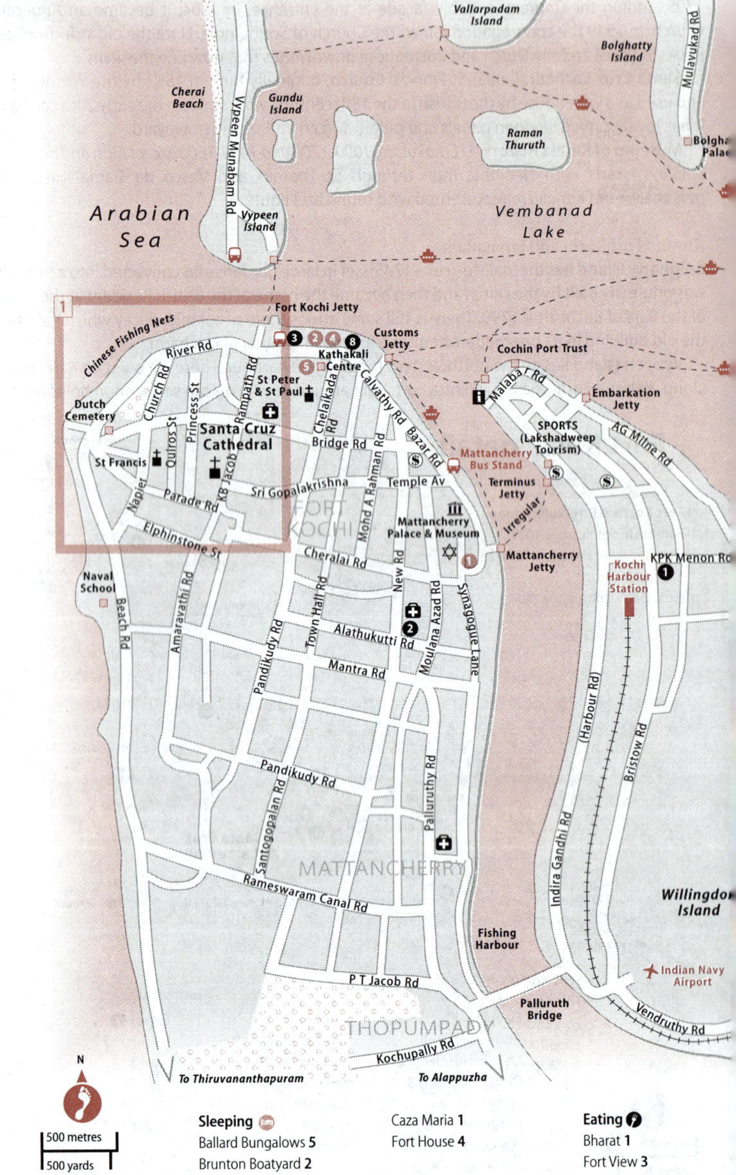

Sleeping
Ballard Bungalows **5**
Brunton Boatyard **2**
Caza Maria **1**
Fort House **4**

Eating
Bharat **1**
Fort View **3**

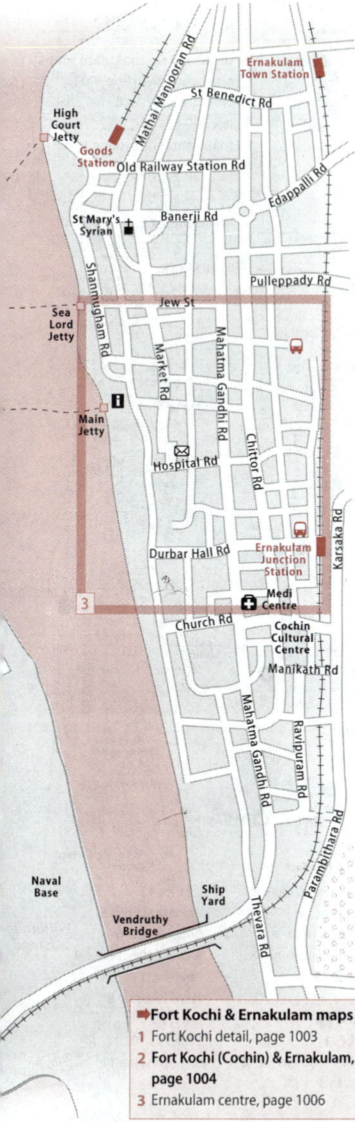

Kayikkas **2**
Seagull **8**

walls of the octagonal fort, which was garrisoned by 20 soldiers when it guarded the entrance to the backwaters. Vehicle ferries make the crossing from Fort Kochi.

Our Lady's Convent ⓘ *Palluruthy, Thoppampady, 14 km south, by appointment, T0484-223 0508,* specializes in high-quality needlework lace and embroidery. The sisters are very welcoming and it is an interesting tour with items for sale.

Raksha ⓘ *Yasmin Manzil, VII/370 Darragh-es-Salaam Rd, Kochangadi, T0484-222 7707,* works with children with physical and mental disabilities. Interested volunteers should contact the principal.

Hill Palace Archaeological Museum ⓘ *Thirpunithura, 12 km east of Ernakulam, Tue-Sun 0900-1230, 1400-1700, Rs 11,* has a huge number of historical records and artefacts of the old royal state of Cochin, with portraits, ornaments, porcelain, palm leaf records and ancient musical instruments.

Some 45 km northeast of Kochi is the town of **Kalady**, on the bank of the Periyar River. This popular pilgrimage site was the birthplace of one of India's most influential philosophers, **Sankaracharya**, who lived in the eighth century. He founded the school of *advaita* philosophy, see page 1408, which spread widely across South India. The **Adi Sankara Kirti Stambha Mandapam** ⓘ *0700-1900, small entry fee,* is a nine-storied octagonal tower, 46 m high, and details Sri Sankara's life and works and the Shan Maths, or six ways to worship. Inside the **Shankara Temple** (Hindus only), are two shrines, one dedicated to Sankaracharya and the other to the goddess Sarada. The management of the shrines is in the hands of the Math at Sringeri in Karnataka, see page 1086. Kalady can easily be visited in an afternoon from Kochi.

3 Ernakulam centre

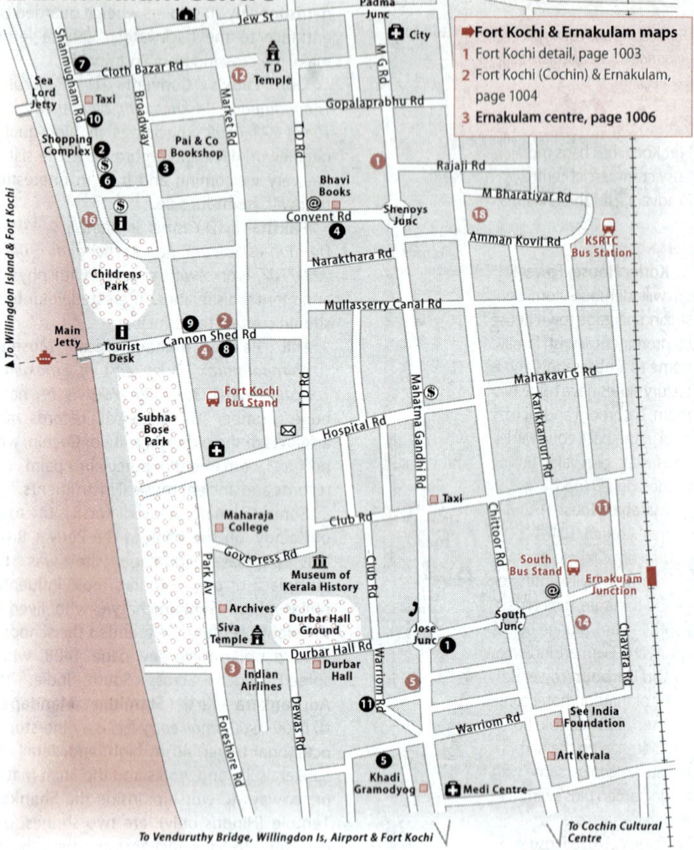

➡Fort Kochi & Ernakulam maps
1 Fort Kochi detail, page 1003
2 Fort Kochi (Cochin) & Ernakulam, page 1004
3 Ernakulam centre, page 1006

Sleeping

Abad Plaza & Canopy Restaurant **1**
Bharat & Subhiksha Restaurant **3**
Dwaraka **5**
Maple Regency **4**
Metropolitan **11**
Modern Guest House **12**
Piazza Residency **14**
SAAS Tower & City Park Restaurant **2**
Taj Gateway **16**
YMCA International House **18**

Eating

Bimbi's **1**
Bimbi's Southern Star **2**
Caravan **3**
Chariot **4**
Chinese Garden **5**
Coffee Beanz **6**
Indian Coffee House **9**
Khyber **1**
New Colombo **8**
Oven **7**
Sealord's **10**
Sri Krishna Inn **11**

Fort Kochi and Ernakulam listings

For Sleeping and Eating price codes and other relevant information, see Essentials pages 38-42.

Sleeping

Fort Kochi has bags more character than the busy commercial centre of Ernakulam; book well in advance for the Christmas period.

Fort Kochi *p1001, maps p1003 and p1004*

LL Koder House, Tower Rd, T0484-221 8485, www.koderhouse.com. Boutique hotel in a striking heritage town house formerly owned by prominent Jewish family, and sometime home to ambassadors and heads of state. Luxury suites have huge bedrooms, sitting room, bathroom and jacuzzi. Tiny plunge pool in the back courtyard, spa with massage and facials, plus valet, business centre, superb home-cooked food.

LL Malabar House, 1/268 Parade Rd, near St Francis' Church, T0484-221 6666, www.malabar house.com. Old meets new, with comfortable, a/c rooms in stylish 18th-century colonial house. Period furniture, dining pavilion (good Italian, South Indian), plunge pool in shaded grassy courtyard. German/Indian owners.

LL Old Harbour, Tower Rd, T0484-221 8006, www.oldharbourhotel.com. Impeccably restored, 300-year-old Portuguese and Dutch building slap on the harbour front. Rooms have private balconies, some with harbour views. Large garden plus swimming pool, Wi-Fi, Ayurveda, jacuzzi.

LL Trinity, 1/658 Ridsdale Rd, Parade Ground, T0484-221 6669, www.malabarhouse.com. Ultra-modern, minimalist and modish 3-bedroom apartment with airy bathrooms, spacious sitting/dining room, mezzanine, tiny swimming pool. Service is immaculate, food is at **Malabar House** on the other side of the parade ground.

LL-L Vivanta by Taj, Willingdon Island, T0484-664 3000, www.vivantabytaj.com. Large, swish hotel overlooking the harbour, with beautifully renovated rooms, the usual superb Taj service. Pool, spa, gym and 5 bars and restaurants.

L Casino Hotel, Willingdon Island, T0484-301 1711, www.cghearth.com. Pool, Ayurveda centre, great seafood restaurant.

L-AL Brunton Boatyard, Calvathy Rd, T0484-301 1711, www.cghearth.com. Easily the best address in Fort Kochi, adjacent to the Chinese fishing nets on the edge of the Arabian Sea. 18 characterful rooms and 4 deluxe suites, each of which overlooks the harbour in an elegantly restored original boatyard and merchant's house built around a courtyard with a giant rain-tree. Charming details include air perfumed with lemongrass and jasmine on pillows. Generous swimming pool. Discounts Apr-Sep.

AL Fort House, 2/6A Calvathy Rd, T0484-221 7103, www.hotelforthouse.com. Tidy bungalows set in a quiet walled courtyard with its own little jetty. Some rooms charmingly old fashioned, others made from bamboo. Newer, more expensive rooms have modern baths, but they're pretty spartan for the price. Good restaurant overlooking the water.

AL-A Old Courtyard, 1/371 Princess St, T0484-221 6302, www.oldcourtyard.com. Beautiful, comfortable rooms, superbly styled with old wooden furniture, overlooking large, breezy courtyard of pretty pot plants and sit-outs. The suite is easily the most romantic with a 4-poster bed and white cotton. Attentive liveried staff, breakfast included, average food but excellent cakes and Turkish coffee, and lovely calm atmosphere. Recommended.

AL-C Rossitta Wood Castle, Rose St, T0484-221 5671, www.rossittawoodcastle.com. 300-year-old Dutch mansion. Rooms, with quirky features and lots of wood-panelling, set around an open-air restaurant courtyard. Breakfast included. Art gallery, library internet café, spa, hot water, yoga.

A Ballard Bungalows, Ballard Rd, T0484-221 5854, www.cochinballard.com. Adequate a/c rooms in the charming former residence to the British collector of Cochin, Mr Ballard, with restaurant, satellite TV, foreign exchange and travel desk.

B Caza Maria Hotel, 6/125 Jew Town Rd, Mattancherry, T0484-395 8837, cazamaria@ rediffmail.com. Just 2 huge and wonderful rooms in beautiful converted house, with tiled floors, wooden furniture and antiques: isolated (the only hotel in Jew Town), romantic and shabbily elegant. Fan only. Breakfast is included, at French/Indian restaurant of same name (on the opposite side of the street). Highly recommended.

B Raintree Lodge, Petercelli St, T0484-325 1489, www.fortcochin.com. Friendly little lodge in quiet location. Large clean rooms all with hot water and a/c. Pretty roof terrace to relax on.

B-C Chiramel Residency, 1/296 Lily St, opposite Parade Ground, T0484-221 7310, www.chiramelhomestay.com. Airy old family home. Non a/c rooms with lots of wood floors, high ceilings, and period furnishings. A/c rooms in modern annex are disappointingly plain and overpriced.

B-E Delight Homestay, Parade Ground, Ridsdale Rd, T0484-221 7658. This lovingly restored Portuguese provides a welcoming peaceful haven. Airy, spotlessly clean rooms open onto a wide terrace, budget rooms are great value. The garden is a riot of colourful blooms. Breakfast is served at the family table. A home away from home. Highly recommended.

C-E Park Avenue, Princess St, T0484-221 6671, hotelparkavenue@rediffmail.com. Large, rather bland rooms, some with balcony and a/c. Good value but little charm.

D-E Vintage Inn, Ridsdale Branch Rd, near Jaliparambu Junction, T0484-221 5064, www.vintageresorts.in. Wonderful, homely guesthouse with a cheerful owner. Airy modern rooms with huge baths in a quiet corner of town. Excellent value. Recommended.

E Oy's Tourist Home, Burgher St, T099-4759 4903. Decent rooms in lovely lamp-lit old building, with lots of plants. Can be noisy.

F Adam's Old Inn, CC1/430 Burgher St, T0484-221 7595. Popular budget-traveller haunt in restored old building. Dorm beds are available for Rs 150. Helpful manager.

Ernakulam *p1001, maps p1004 and p1006*

L Taj Gateway, Marine Dr, T0484-667 3300, www.thegatewayhotels.com. Immaculate rooms with commanding views over bay. Good restaurants, gym, bar, all business facilities and friendly service.

AL-A Abad Plaza, MG Rd, T0484-238 1122, www.abadhotels.com. A veteran of many monsoons, with large but slightly moth-eaten rooms all with a/c, fridge and cable TV. Rooms on street side can be noisy, quieter rooms on 5th floor. Breakfast included. Restaurants, gym, Ayurveda clinic, rooftop pool.

B Metropolitan, Chavara Rd, near Junction Station, T0484-237 6931, www.metropolitancochin.com. Bright, spotlessly clean modern a/c rooms, excellent restaurants and service, superb value. "Best railway station hotel in South India". Recommended.

B-D Bharat, Gandhi Sq, Durbar Hall Rd, T0484-235 3501, www.bharathotel.com. Popular Indian business hotel. Clean spacious rooms, some a/c, best sea-facing. Restaurant with excellent lunch *thalis* (South Indian and North Indian). Great service, good value.

C-E Dwaraka, MG Rd, T0484-238 3236, dwaraka_hotel@rediffmail.com. Centrally located, family-run hotel. Good-sized, rather noisy rooms with TV, some with balcony. Only moderately clean. Adequate.

C-E SAAS Tower, Canon Shed Rd, T0484-236 5319, www.saastower.com. Friendly but noisy hotel, very popular with Indian families. The decaying rooms are sorely in need of a makeover, but the location is good, and renovation work on the excellent restaurant may bode well for the hotel. Worth a look.

C-E YMCA International House, Chittoor Rd, 100 m from Central Bus Station, T0484-235 3479, www.ymcaernakulam.org. Simple rooms (some a/c), restaurant, welcoming.

D-F Piazza Residency, Kalathiparambu Rd, near south railway station, T0484-237 6408. Slightly dank and musty rooms in quiet location. Good value singles. Friendly staff.

F Maple Regency, Cannon Shed Rd, T0484-235 5156. Large clean rooms, all with TV, in a great location right beside the boat jetty.

F Modern Guest House, Market Rd, T0848-235 2130. Busy, clean hotel with helpful staff. Well-maintained rooms with bath.

Eating

Fort Kochi *p1001, maps p1003 and p1004*

For a really fresh seafood meal, buy your own fish from the fishmonger stalls along the shorefront and take it to one of the nearby 'you buy, we cook' stalls, such as **Marina** or **Fort View**, where they'll be grilled or masala-fried with chips.

Malabar House Residency, Parade Rd. Excellent seafood platter and chef's salad, the latter of huge dimensions. Authentic Mediterranean and local dishes.

Caza Maria, Jew Town Rd (opposite hotel). 1200-2130. 2 large rooms with wooden chairs, frescoes and old framed prints on the wall. Small menu includes fish *moilee* and lime rice, *palak paneer* and *chapatti* and apple pie and ice cream. Great atmosphere.

Feast, Peter Celli St. 1700-2100. With a menu focused on Keralite specialities, lovely staff that are passionate about their food and an ambient dining room, this place is a great for trying out autehntic local dishes.

Dal Roti, 1/293 Lilly St, T0484-221 7655. Firmly established favourite for pukka North Indian food – delicious khati rolls, huge stuffed parathas – served up by the affable Ramesh and his family. Don't arrive starving as queues often stretch out the door.

Kashi, Burgher St, Kochi, T0484-221 5769, www.kashiartgallery.com. If you've been away a while, Kashi is the type of place you'll fall on in wonder. The first 2 rooms are the art gallery, the rest is a restaurant where you can drink coffee fresh from your own cafetière, or indulge in a perfect cappuccino. There's a handful of excellently made sweets and 1-2 dishes they make for breakfast or lunch.

Kayikka's, Rahmathulla Hotel, Kayees, New Rd, near Aanavaadal, Fort Kochi, T0484-222 6080, kayees@sify.com. 1200-1430, 1830-2030. This family concern is the busiest biryani restaurant in Kochi and a local institution. Great mutton and chicken biryanis all week with fish biryanis on Fri and prawn on Tue. Arrive early to avoid disappointment.

Seagull, Calvathy Rd. Good value (Rs 80 buffet lunch), pleasant veranda for drinks and dining overlooking harbour.

Teapot Café , Peter Celli St, T0484-221 8035, tpleaz@hotmail.com. Bare terracotta roof tiles dangle with teapots and fans, tables are tea crates and walls are hung with antique tea-related paraphernalia. Stop in for a brew of Darjeeling, Assam, Nilgiris or mint-flavoured teas, an iced coffee, or milkshake. There's a delicious selection of cakes and desserts, tasty toasted sandwiches and more substantial meals like prawn *moilee*, and mustard fish. With loads of newspapers and magazines left out for customers to read, it's a lovely place to while away a couple of hours.

Ernakulam *p1001, maps p1004 and p1006*

Bimbi's Southern Star, Shanmugam Rd. Generous portions of tasty Indian food.

Khyber, Durbar Hall Rd. North Indian meals upstairs.

Sealord's, Shanmugam Rd. Rooftop setting with good fish and Chinese dishes.

Sri Krishna Inn, Warriom Rd, next to Chinmaya Vidya Peeth, T0484-236 6664. One of the best pure-veg places in a city of seafood, with great North and South Indian options.

Subhiksha, Bharat Hotel, Durbar Hall Rd. Excellent value buffet lunch.

Bharat, Willingdon Island. Very good vegetarian *thalis* and Indian specialities in clean surroundings.

Chinese Garden, Warriom Rd. Good variety of decent Chinese meals. Alcohol available.

City Park, SAAS Tower, Cannon Shed Rd. Has a loyal following for its great Keralite meals. Under renovation as of mid-2011.

Indian Coffee House, Cannon Shed Rd. Tasty North and South Indian dishes.

New Colombo, Canon Shed Rd. Good snacks, fruit juices.

Cafés

Bimbi's, Durbar Hall Rd. Good fast food.

Caravan, Broadway (south). For ice creams and shakes.

Chariot, Convent Rd. Good café-style meals.

Coffee Beanz, Shanmugan Rd. Daily 0900-2300. Cold coffees, *appam*, *dosa*, popular, poky a/c coffee bar with just 6 tables.

Oven, Shanmugham Rd. Good pizzas and snacks (savoury and sweet).

Entertainment

Fort Kochi and Ernakulam
p1001, maps p1003, p1004 and p1006

There are daily *Kathakali* performances. Arrive early to watch the extraordinary make-up being applied.

Cochin Cultural Centre, Manikath Rd, off Ravipuram Rd, Ernakulam, T0484-235 7153. A/c 'theatre', authentic performance with English explanations; 1830-1930, make-up 1730, Rs 125.

ENS Kalari, Nettoor, Fort Kochi, T0484-280 9810. *Kalarippayattu* performances, 0400-0700 and 1700-2000.

Kerala Kathakali Centre, River Rd, Fort Kochi, T0484-222 1827. Rustic surroundings but lively performance, enjoyable; 1830-1930 (make-up 1700) but check timing, Rs 100.

See India Foundation, Kalathil Parampil Lane (enter Chittoor Rd south) near Junction station, Ernakulam, T0484-236 9471. Dr Devan's 'interpreted' taste of *Kathakali* with esoteric English commentary; 1845-2000 (make-up from 1800), Rs 125.

Festivals and events

Fort Kochi and Ernakulam

p1001, maps p1003, p1004 and p1006

Jan/Feb Ulsavam at the Siva Temple in Ernakulam for 8 days and at Tripunithura Temple in **Nov/Dec**. Elephant processions each day, folk dance and music performances.

Aug/Sep Onam.

Shopping

Fort Kochi and Ernakulam

p1001, maps p1003, p1004 and p1006

Coir products (eg mats), carvings on rose- wood and buffalo horn and antiques may catch your eye here. Several narrow streets in **Jew Town**, towards the synagogue, have become popular for 'antique' hunters in the last 25 years. All these shops sport a similar range of old (some faux) and new curios.

There are several government emporia on MG Rd, Ernakulam, including **National Textiles** (another in Banerji Rd). Other shopping areas are in Broadway, Super Bazar, Anand Bazar, Prince St and New Rd.

Cinnamon, Stuba Hall, 1/658 Ridsdale Rd, Parade Ground, Fort Kochi, T0484-221 7124. Posh clothing, fabrics and interiors shop.

Dhamdhere, Pandithan Temple Rd, Mattanchery, T0484-222 4481. Interesting perfume manufacturers who confess many are synthetic (Rs 12), but the sandalwood oil is the real McCoy (Rs 100).

Idiom Books, branches on VI/183 Synagogue Lane, Jew Town and Bastion Rd, Fort Kochi, T0484-224028. Very good range on India, travel, fiction, religion, philosophy, etc.

Indian Industries, Princess St, Fort Kochi, T0484-221 6448. One of Fort Kochi's oldest antique dealers. Lovely family-run store with fixed prices and no-hassle browsing.

Activities and tours

Fort Kochi and Ernakulam

p1001, maps p1003, p1004 and p1006

Body and soul

Be Beautiful, Princess St, Fort Kochi, T0484-221 5398. Open 0900-2030. Good, cheap beauty salon with massage, hairdressers, pedicure and manicure in new premises.

Sanathana School of Yoga Studies, XV/2188-D Beach Rd Junction, T0484-229 4155, www.sanathanayoga.com. Daily classes 0730-0930 and 1630-1830 *pranayama*, and *asanas* plus 28-day teacher training programmes in a pretty residence in downtown Fort Cochi.

Tour operators

Hi! Tours, Jomer Arcade, South Junction, Chittoor Road, Ernakulam, T0484-237 7415. Efficient and well-connected inbound travel agent, who can hook you up with homestays, authentic Ayurveda retreats and responsible tour operators throughout Kerala. Helpful and highly recommended.

KTDC, Shanmugham Rd, Ernakulam, T0484-235 3234. Full- and half-day backwater tours on *kettuvallams*. Full-day tour 0830-1830 (includes lunch), half-day tour 0830-1300 and 1400-1830. Tours include visits to coir factory, spice garden, canoe ride and toddy tapping demonstration. Also daily half-day Kochi sightseeing boat cruises, 0900-1230 and 1400-1730, which cover Bolgatty Island, Chinese fishing nets, St Francis Church and Mattancherry Palace. Tour departs from Sealord Jetty.

Olympus, south end of MG Rd, Ernakulam, T0484-236 9544. Very competent and helpful.

Pepper Tours, House No 127, Subash Chandra Bose Rd, Jawahar Nagar, Kadavanthara, PO Cochin 682020, T0484-405 8886, www.peppertours.com. Memorable journeys in Kerala, Rajasthan and Goa.

Pioneer Personalized Holidays, Pioneer House, 5th Cross, Willingdon Island, T0484-266 6148, www.pioneertravels.com. Fleet of cars with tailor-made tour packages from a well-

established and highly competent tour company. Efficient and knowledgeable, with unusual homestay and guesthouse options.
Sundale Vacations, 39/5955 Atlantis Junction, MG Rd, Ernakulam, T0484-235 9127, www.sundale.com. Surface and hotel arrangements in Kerala, specializes in homestays catering to 'foreign independent tourists', promoting insight into Kerala's customs. Programmes from US$467.
Tourist Desk, Main Boat Jetty, Ernakulam, T0484-237 1761, www.touristdesk.in. One of the best budget tour operators. Daily backwater tours, 0800-1700, Rs 550, using both *kettuvalloms* and canoe. Tour includes visits to see coir making, spice garden, local village and lunch. Also 2- to 3-day tours to Wayanad and Kannur. Highly recommended.
Visit India North Janatha Rd, T0484-233 9045, www.visitindiatravel.com. Half-day backwater tours in a dugout, punted and engineless, through very peaceful shady waterways passing unspoilt villages with toddy tappers, coir making, fishing, etc; led by an excellent guide. Rs 450 for 4 hrs, depart 0830, 1430. Highly recommended. Also offers trips in traditional *kettuvallams*; Rs 5000 (for couple) or Rs 8000 (2 bedroom); for 24 hrs, includes all meals.
Viceregal Travels and Resorts, S17/18 GCDA Shopping Complex, Marine Dr, Ernakulam, T0484-237 2644, www.viceregal travels.com. Runs a 9-day homestay package to charming properties, including a/c Ambassador cab, from Cochin to Peermade, Cherthala for the backwaters and Kovalam for Kanniyakumari. Rs 21,000 per person.

Transport

Fort Kochi and Ernakulam

p1001, maps p1003, p1004 and p1006

Air New international airport, 36 km northeast, T0484-261 0115. Pre-paid taxis to Ernakulam, around Rs 500; to Fort Kochi, Rs 700. A/c buses leave from outside the International Terminal for Fort Kochi (Rs 80) via Vytilla Junction (Rs 60), 3 km west of Ernakulam centre.

Daily domestic flights to: **Bangalore** (**Bengaluru**), **Chennai**, **Mumbai**, **Delhi** via **Goa**, **Thiruvananthapuram**; and several flights per week to **Coimbatore**, **Hyderabad**, **Kozhikode** and **Tiruchirapalli**.

International flights to: **Doha** (Qatar), **Dubai**, **Kuala Lumpur**, **Kuwait**, **Muscat** (Oman), **Sharjah** (UAE) and **Singapore**.

Airline offices All are on MG Rd unless stated otherwise. **Air India**: T0484-237 1141. **Cathay Pacific** and **KLM**, c/o Spencer Travel Services, Kurisupally Rd, T0484-238 0517. **Go Air** , Airport, T0484-261 0697. **Indian Airlines**, Durbar Hall Rd, T0484-237 1141, and airport T0484-261 0041 (domestic), T0484-238 1874 (international). **Jet Airways**, Elmar Sq Bldg, MG Rd, T0484-235 9212, airport T0484-261 0037. **Kingfisher**, T0484-235 1144. **Emirates**, opposite Wyte Fort Hotel, NH47, T0484-408 4444. **Singapore Airlines** and **Swissair**, c/o Aviation Travels, T0484-236 7911. **Spice Jet** , Airport, T0484-261 1750. **Sri Lankan Airlines**, T0484-236 1666.
Local bus Buses journey between Ernakulam, Willingdon and Fort Kochi frequently during the day. There are no local buses after 2100.
Long distance bus Buses run from the **KSRTC Bus Station**, Chavara Rd, T0484-237 2033. There are frequent services to **Alappuzha**, every 20 mins (1½ hrs, Rs 38); **Kottayam**, every 30 mins (1½ hrs, Rs 38); **Kozhikode**, every 30 mins (5 hrs, Rs 128) and **Thiruvananthapuram**, every 30 mins (5 hrs Rs 128). There are 7 departures daily to **Kumily** (6 hrs, Rs 130) or take a bus to Kottayam and change there. There is an 0630 departure to **Munnar** (4 hrs, Rs 97), and departures to **Kannur** at 1445 and 2345 (7 hrs, Rs 156). Interstate services include: 9 daily to **Bangalore** (**Bengaluru**) (14 hrs, Rs 304) via **Kozhikode** (5 hrs, Rs 128) and **Mysore** (10 hrs, Rs 256); **Kanniyakumari**, at 1430 (7½ hrs, Rs 159); and **Chennai** at 1400 (15 hrs, Rs 328) via **Coimbatore** (5 hrs, Rs 123).

Private operators from **Kalloor** and **Ernakulam South bus stands** including **Indira Travels**, DH Rd, T0484-236 0693 and **SB Travels**, String Dew Bldg, Tripunithura, T0484-277 7949, **Princy Tours**, opposite Sealord Hotel, T0484-237 3109. Overnight coaches to **Bengaluru** (**Bangalore**) (12 hrs), and **Mysore** (10 hrs). Departures every 30 mins to **Kottayam** (2 hrs), and **Munnar**, (4 hrs). Also to **Chennai** and **Coimbatore**.
Ferry Regular ferry services connect Ernakulam with Fort Kochi and are the fastest and easiest form of transport. Ferry tickets cost Rs 2.50. Most

ferries take bikes and motorbikes. It's also possible to hire a motor boat for up to 20, from Sea Lord jetty in Ernakulam through the **KTDC** office.

Ernakulam Main Boat Jetty, Cannon Shed Rd. Ferries depart approx every 30 mins to Fort Kochi 'Customs' jetty between 0555-2130. There are also regular ferries to the Fort Kochi Mattancherry jetty (last departure to Mattencherry is 1845), and to Willingdon Island's 'Embarkation' Jetty from here. Ferries to Bolghatty depart from the High Court Jetty off Shanmugham Rd approx every 20 mins between 0600-2100 Mon-Sat.

Fort Kochi The main 'Customs' jetty links Fort Kochi with Ernakulam with regular departures between 0620-2150. The last ferry leaves for Ernakulam from the Mattencherry jetty at 1930. From the northern Vypeen Jetty there are services every 30 mins to Vypeen Island between 0600-2130.

Willingdon Island There are 2 jetties: 'Embarkation' (north) and 'Terminus' (west). Ferries run every 30 mins to Ernakulam from 'Embarkation' from 0600-2110. From the 'Terminus' jetty there are irregular services to Mattencherry on Fort Kochi.

Rickshaw Auto-rickshaw drivers have a reasonably good reputation here. But, if you are likely to arrive late at night, insist on being taken directly to your hotel. A rickshaw between Fort Kochi and Ernakulam should cost around Rs 120. Fares within Fort Kochi or Ernakulam: Rs 20-40.

Taxi Ernakulam Junction to Fort Kochi, Rs 170. To airport, Rs 350-400. On MG Rd, Ernakulam: **Corp Taxi Stand**, T0484-236 1444.

Train Ernakulam/Kochi is on the broad gauge line joining Thiruvananthapuram to Mangalore, Bengaluru (Bangalore) and Chennai. Most trains from major cities stop at Ernakulam Junction (the main station, booking code: ERS) although a few stop at Ernakulam Town (ERN), T0484-239 0920. Enquiries: Ernakulam Junction, T131 or T0484-237 5131.

Bengaluru (**Bangalore**): *Bangalore Intercity Exp 12678*, 0910 (from ERS), 11 hrs; *Island Exp 16525*, 1755 (from ERN), 13 hrs; both via Thrissur, Palakka and Coimbatore. **Chennai**: *Chennai Mail 12624*, 1915 (from ERN), 12 hrs. **Mangalore**: *Parasuram Exp 16650*, 1110 (from ERN), 9½ hrs); *Malabar Exp 16629*, 2350 (ERN), 10 hrs; both via Thrissur, Kozhikode and Kannur. **Mumbai** (**LT**): *Netravati Exp 16346*, 1400 (from ERS), 27 hrs, via Madgaon (16 hrs). **Thiruvananthapuram**: more than 20 trains a day, all via Kollam and Varkala. **Trivandrum**: *Jan Shatabdi Exp 12075*, 1725 (from ERS), 3½ hrs, via Alappuzha. *Parasuram Exp 16649*, 1330 (from ERN), via Kottayam.

Directory

Fort Kochi and Ernakulam

p1001, maps p1003, p1004 and p1006

Banks In Ernakulam most banks congregate on MG Rd, including **ING Bank** and **Federal Bank**, and on Shanmugham Rd, including **State Bank of India**. All have ATM's. Most banks open till 1500. There are also several banks with ATMs in Fort Kochi including **ICICI** and **Federal Bank**, both on Chelaikada Rd. **Thomas Cook**, Palal Towers, 1st floor, MG Rd, T0484-236 8164 (Mon-Sat 0930-1800), changes TCs and currency. In Fort Kochi there are several foreign exchange offices on Princess St and Bastion St. **Internet** In Ernakulam **Net Point**, on Durbar Hall Rd, near Junction station, has very fast connections. **Net Park**, Convent Rd, charges Rs 20 per hr and also has a scanner and printing facilities. In Fort Kochi there are several small internet cafés clustered around Princess St and Bastion Rd; **Brisbane Internet** and **New Arcade** have fast connections. **Medical services General Hospital**, Hospital Rd, Ernakulam, T0484-238 1768. **Govt Hospital**, Fort Kochi, T0484-222 4444. On MG Rd: **City**, T0484-236 1809, and **Medical Trust Hospital**, T0484-235 8001, have 24-hr pharmacies. **City Dental Clinic**, T0484-236 8164. **Post Ernakulam Head PO**, Hospital Rd, 0830-2000, Sat 0930-1430, Sun 1000-1600, other holidays 1400-1700. **Kochi Main PO**, Mattancherry (for **Poste Restante**), 0800- 2000, Sun 0930-1700; often empty. **North End PO**, Willingdon Island. **Useful contacts Tourist Police**: T0484-266 6076, help with information of all kinds. **Visa extension:** City Police Commissioner, High Court Ferry Station, Ernakulam, T0484-236 0700. **Foreigners' Regional Registration Office**, T0484-235 2454.

Munnar and Idukki's high ranges

Inland from the plains around Kottayam and Kochi lie the foothills of the Western Ghats, swathed in tropical evergreen forests and an ever-creeping tide of monoculture rubber plantations. As you climb higher these give way to pepper and cardamom, until finally you reach the rolling tea plantations and rarefied air of landlocked Idukki District. To the south sits Thekkady and the unmissable Periyar National Park, home to tiger, wild elephant, and an innovative project that is steadily turning yesterday's poachers into tomorrow's tour guides. Overnight treks into the park's hinterland offer an unmatched opportunity to see big animals up close and on foot, but even on a day visit Periyar can show you some impressive nature: wild boar foraging along the lakeside, butterflies as big as bats bouncing beneath the canopies of prehistoric jack trees, and the thud-thwack-holler as unruly gangs of Nilgiri Langur swoop through the high branches of giant figs.

Munnar, meanwhile, five hours uphill from Kochi, is chai central: a surreal rippling mosaic of yellow-green tea bushes and red dust roads stretching from valley deep to mountain high, with dark granite peaks pointing like fingers toward the bald grassy dome of South India's highest mountain, Anaimudi. At 1600 m, Munnar is much higher than Thekkady and gets genuinely cold, a fact that made it a favourite summer bolthole for the raj. Wildlife tourists flock to the nearby Eravikulam National Park for a glimpse of the endangered but semi-tame Nilgiri thar, a variety of ibex, while further to the north are the forests and deeply etched ravines of magnificent, rarely visited Chinnar Wildlife Sanctuary.
▸▸ *For listings, see pages 1019-1023.*

Ins and outs

Getting there and around The nearest transport hub for Munnar is Kochi-Ernakulam; Thekkady (Periyar Reserve/Kumily town) is best accessed from Kottayam. There are no train links to the high ranges; buses take a minimum of four hours to climb the hills to both hill stations, and roads linking the two take the same length of time. ▸▸ *See Transport page 1022.*
Tourist information District tourism offices are at **Kumily** ⓘ *T0486-922 2620*, and **Old Munnar** ⓘ *T04865-253 1516.*

The Midlands (Kottayam to Thekkady)

An interesting drive to the hills, this route follows the Ghat road, which has superb views down the east side of the Ghats onto the Tamil Nadu plains. You may meet herds of Zebu cattle, buffalo and donkeys being driven from Tamil Nadu to market in Kerala. Above 1000 m the air freshens and it can be cold. Be prepared for a rapid change in temperature.

Pala, off the Kottayam–Thekkady road, is a town famous for its learned citizens – graduates of the European-style Gothic university, which was built, along with the Gothic church, by one of its affluent sons. Nehru visited in the 1950s and said that Pala was full of "people of vision". The town was the most literate place in India long before Kerala achieved 100% literacy, and Meenachil *Taluka* has the highest proportion of educated women in the country. It is also famous for its tamarind and pepper as well as the rubber estates belonging to the Dominic family, who serve hot Syrian-Catholic lunches in their 100-year-old plantation bungalow and 50-year-old estate mansion. Plantation tours to watch latex collection and packing can be arranged through **CGH Earth**, see page 999.

Further east lies **Erattupetta**, whose grey St George's Church holds naïve wood-painted doves and disembodied cherubims, and which hosts the **High Range Festival** every April. Carry on for **Vagamon**, a village set on a chain of three hills: Thangal, Murugal and Kurisumala. A dairy farm here is managed by Kurisumala monks.

Some 25 km south from Vagamon is **Peermade**, named after Peer Mohammed, a Sufi saint and crony of the royal family of Travancore. It is surrounded by tea, rubber and cardamom plantations, including **Abraham's Spice Garden**, where a member of the family gives excellent spice tours for Rs 50. Buses between Kottayam and Kumily can drop you here.

A modern mass pilgrimage

Sabarimala pilgrims are readily visible in many parts of South India as they wear black *dhotis* as a symbol of the penance they must undergo for 41 days before they make the pilgrimage. In addition to the black dress, pilgrims must take two baths daily and only eat food at home during this period. The pilgrimage, which begins at Deepavali, is only for males and prepubescent and post-menstrual females, to avoid the defilement believed to be associated with menstruation.

The pilgrimage in January is deliberately hard, writes Vaidyanathan, because "the pilgrimage to the shrine symbolizes the struggle of the individual soul in its onward journey to the abode of bliss and beatitude. The path of the spiritual aspirant is always long, arduous and hazardous. And so is the pilgrimage to Sabarimala, what with the observance of severe austerities and trekking up forested mountains, risking attacks from wild animals".

Many Hindu pilgrims make the journey to the forest shrine dedicated to Sri Aiyappan at **Sabarimala**, 191 km north of Thiruvananthapuram (see box, above). Aiyappan is a particularly favoured deity in Kerala and there are growing numbers of devotees. The shrine is only open on specific occasions: **Mandalam**, mid-November to the end of December; **Makaravilakku**, mid-January; **Vishu**, mid-April; **Prathistha** one day in May-June; and during the **Onam** festival in August-September.

The first rubber plantation was cultivated in 1902. India is now among the top three rubber producers worldwide, and most of that comes from Kerala. Crops in Kerala are determined by height: tea grows above 1500 m, cardamom, coffee and other spices between 1500 m and 600 m, coconut and rubber below 600 m.

Thekkady (Periyar National Park, Kumily Town) → *For listings, see pages 1019-1023. Colour map 7, C3.*

Covering 930 sq km of montane forest and grassland and centred on an attractive lake, the **Periyar National Park** ⓘ *115 km east of Kottayam, T0486-922 4571, www.periyartigerreserve.org, Rs 300 per day, video camera fee Rs 200, for more information visit the Eco Tourism Information Centre, Ambady Junction, Kumily, 0800-1800*, may not throw up many tiger sightings nowadays, but still attracts more than 300,000 visitors a year for its beautiful setting and unique range of soft adventure activities. Elephants, *gaur* and wild boar, though by no means guaranteed, are regularly spotted from the lake cruise boats, while sloth bear, porcupine and Malabar giant squirrel also haunt the woods.

The sanctuary was established by the old Travancore State government in 1934 and brought under the umbrella of Project Tiger in 1973, but Periyar's finest hour came in 1998 when the Kerala Forest Department, in partnership with the World Bank and the Thekkady Wildlife Society (a local NGO), set up a project to deploy a band of reformed cinnamon poachers from the surrounding villages as tour leaders and forest rangers in remote parts of the park. The camo-clad members of the **Ex-Vayana Bark Collectors Eco Development Committee** now earn a steady income from tourism, not to mention new-found respect within their communities, and their hard-won knowledge of the terrain and sharp instincts for animal behaviour makes them skilled, if not exactly chatty, forest guides. Trekking with them for a day represents your best chance of getting up close with elephants.

The centre of activities in the park is the boat jetty on pretty **Lake Periyar**, 3 km down a beautiful forest road from the tourist village of **Kumily**, which was created in 1895 by a dam that inundated 55 sq km of rich forest. A 180-m-long tunnel now leads the water eastward into the Suruli and Vaigai rivers, irrigating extensive areas of Ramanathapuram and Madurai districts in Tamil Nadu.

Ins and outs

Getting there and around Long-distance buses from Kottayam and Kochi reach Thekkady lakeside via Kumily town. Buses run between Kumily and the lake jetty, or you can hire a bike or rickshaw, share a jeep, or take the pleasant walk. ▸▸ *See Transport, page 1022.*

Tourist information Eco Tourism Office ⓘ *Ambady Junction, Kumily, T0486-922 4571, www.periyartigerreserve.org*, has information and books tickets for all treks and tours in the park. District Tourism Information Office ⓘ *T0486-922 2620*, runs plantation tours to Abraham's Spice Garden (4 km) and Vandiperiyer (18 km). The best time to visit is December-April, when dry weather brings animals closer to the lake. Dawn and dusk are best for wildlife, so stay overnight (winter nights can get quite cold). Avoid weekends and holidays.

Activities

The classic way to see Periyar is to take a **motor launch trip** ⓘ *depart 0700, 0930, 1100, 1400 and 1600, Rs 40-150; no advance reservation required,* on the lake, which provides good opportunities for spotting animals, particularly early or late in the day. Herds of elephants are regularly seen bathing in the water or grazing on the lakeside pastures, most commonly before March/April. The majority of Periyar's bull elephants are tuskless (*makhnas*). Bison, sambar, wild boar and barking deer are also fairly common.

From the Forest Information Office at the boat jetty you can also book a three-hour **trek** ⓘ *maximum 5 people, depart 0700, 1000, 1400, Rs 100, no advance reservations so get to office early to queue.* Much depends on your guide and your luck, and not everybody comes face to face with a herd of elephants; some return very disappointed. Carry water and beware of leeches. Guides may also offer to arrange unofficial private walking tours in the park periphery in the afternoon (not the best time for spotting wildlife); try to assess the guide before signing up.

The following activities, run by the Ex-Vayana Bark Collectors Eco Development Committee, all need to be booked in advance at the Eco Tourism Office: **tiger trails** for two or three days, one or two nights, depart 0900 twice a week (Rs 3000/5000, including food and tent,

Periyar National Park

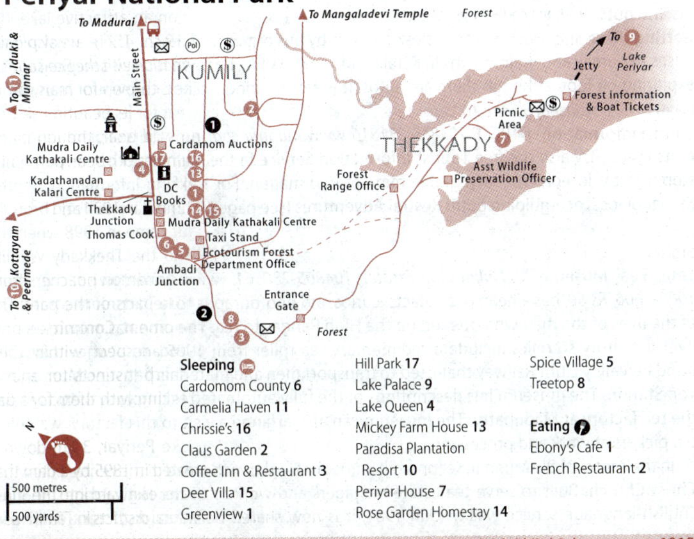

Sleeping
Cardomom County 6
Carmelia Haven 11
Chrissie's 16
Claus Garden 2
Coffee Inn & Restaurant 3
Deer Villa 15
Greenview 1
Hill Park 17
Lake Palace 9
Lake Queen 4
Mickey Farm House 13
Paradisa Plantation Resort 10
Periyar House 7
Rose Garden Homestay 14
Spice Village 5
Treetop 8

Eating
Ebony's Cafe 1
French Restaurant 2

up to five people); **border hiking**, 0800-1700 (Rs 750, including food, up to five people); **bamboo rafting**, 0800 (Rs 1000, up to 10 people); **coracle and bullock cart rides**, 0600 and 1430 (Rs 750, up to five people); '**clouds walk**' to tribal village and heritage museum 0800 (Rs 200, up to five people); and '**jungle patrol**' night trekking with powerful spotlights, 1900-2200, 2200-0100, 0100-0400 (Rs 500, up to five people). You can also stay in a cottage overnight (Rs 1500-2000) at the **Jungle Inn**; the price includes dinner and trekking.

Around Thekkady

There are a number of attractions within easy reach of Thekkady. These include the traditional Keralite-style **Mangaladevi Temple**, set amongst dense woodland on the peak of a 1337 m hill, 15 km northeast of Thekkady. Permission to visit the area must be obtained from the Wildlife Warden in Thekkady, though the temple itself is only open during the **Chithra Pounami** holiday. Other picturesque spots around Thekkady include **Pandikuzhi** (5 km) and **Chellarkovil** (15 km).

Munnar → *For listings, see pages 1019-1023. Colour map 7, C3.*

A major centre of Kerala's tea industry, Munnar sits in the lee of Anaimudi, South India's highest peak at 2695m, and is the nearest Kerala comes to a genuine hill station. The landscape is European Alpine, minus the snow, plus tea bushes – inestimable millions of them. The town is surrounded by about 30 tea estates, among them the highest in the world at Kolukkumalai, yet despite the increasingly commercial use of the hills you can still find forests that are rich in wildlife, including the endangered Nilgiri tahr. The workers on the tea estates are mostly Tamilians who moved here eight or nine generations ago. The surrounding hills are also home to the rare Neelakurunji orchid (*Strobilanthes*), which covers the hills in colour for a month once every 12 years (next due 2018). During the monsoon cotton wool swabs of cloud shift and eddy across hillsides sodden as a sponge with fresh rains, and springs burst their banks and surge across the pathways where villagers, dark-skinned tribals in ski jackets and woollen noddy hats, swing past on Enfields on their way home from a day on the tea plantations.

Ins and outs → *Phone code: 04865. Altitude: 1520 m.*

Getting there and around The easiest access is by bus or taxi from Kochi. There are also daily buses to Kumily and major towns in Kerala and Tamil Nadu. The town is small and pleasant for exploring on foot, although there are autos. It is worth hiring a bike or a jeep for trips out of town. ▸▸ *See Transport, page 1023.*

Tourist information DTPC ⓘ *T04865-231516, www.munnar.com*, runs tours of plantations and rents cycles. Try also the free **Tourist Information Service** in the Main Bazar opposite the bus stop, run by Joseph Iype, a veritable mine of information. For trekking information, Senthil Kumar of local eco-guiding outfit **Kestrel Adventures** (see page 1022) is hard to beat .

Sights

Tata Tea Museum ⓘ *Nullatanni Estate, T04865-230561, www.keralatourism.org, open 1000-1600, Rs 50*, has a heap of artefacts, curios and photographs to help conjure something of the lives of the men who opened up the High Ranges to tea. The crop has grown here for over a century so relics include a rudimentary tea roller from 1905 and a wheel from the Kundale Valley Light Railway that used to transport men and materials between Munnar and Top Station. The museum has descriptions of the fully automated technology of today from the tea factory at Madupatty. The museum can also arrange a visit to this factory, watching tea pickers at work and processing.

In the centre of Old Munnar, set on a hill immediately above the road in the centre of town, is **Christ Church**. Built to serve tea estate managers and workers of the High Ranges, the last English-language service was held in 1981; it is now shared between protestant Tamil and

Malayalam worshippers. The exterior is unprepossessing: rather squat and now blackened by weathering, but inside it is a charming small church, and still contains its original 14 rows of wooden pews. Ask to see the diminutive record of births and deaths of the town's founders, the British planters. Immediately behind the church a zigzag path up the hill leads to the small pioneer cemetery that was established long before the church itself as the chosen burial ground of Mrs Eleanor Knight, General Manager Knight's 24-year-old bride who caught cholera after arriving in the High Range in 1894.

Mount Carmel Roman Catholic Church, the first Catholic church in the High Ranges, is in Old Munnar on the road up to the Tata General Hospital. The first chapel on the site was founded in 1898 by Friar Alphonse who arrived in Munnar from Spain in 1854. The present church was built by the then Bishop of Vijayapuram in 1938.

High Range Club ⓘ *T04865-230253*, is a private members' club more relaxed than the famously 'Snooty' Ooty Club (see page 928). A tradition allowed members to hang their hats on the wall of the bar after 30 years of belonging to the club – the last was hung in 1989 to make 51 hats in all. Saturday is strictly jacket and tie only and backpackers will need to scrub up well to get in any day of the week. "We like scholars and researchers, professionals and club people," says the club secretary, "they know how to move in a club." It's a wonderful place with teak floors, squash courts, library and fascinating planters to chat to if you're interested in the planters' social history.

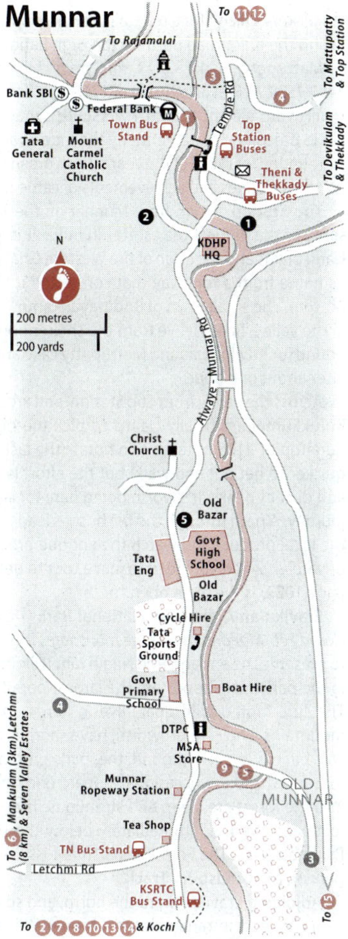

Sleeping
Arafa Tourist Home **1**
Copper Castle **2**
East End **3**
Isaac's Residency **4**
John's Cottage **5**
Nature Zone **6**
Olive Brook **7**
Royal retreat **8**
Sisiram Cottages **9**
Tall Trees **10**
Tea County **11**
Tea Sanctuary **15**
Theresian Cottages **12**
Windermere Estate **13**
Zeena Cottages **14**

Eating
Bamboo Hut **1**
Silver Spoon **2**
Vegetarian **5**

Bars & clubs
High Range Club **3**
KDH Club **4**

Around Munnar

There are some excellent **cycle rides** around Munnar, not all of them steep. One ride goes up a gentle slope through a beautiful valley 8 km to the Letchmi Estate. There is a *chai* stall at the estate and the road continues to the head of the valley for views down to the forest. A second ride (or walk) leaves Munnar by the south road for 3 km, turning left at the Head Works Dam, then takes a right turn past Copper Castle, then left to a tea stall, viewpoint, tea and cardamom plantations, again with superb views. Continue to the next tea pickers' village for a tea stall. A shorter option for this route is to cross the dam and turn left, taking the quiet road north to the High Range Club and Munnar.

Mattupetty Lake ⓘ *13 km from Munnar, T04865-230389, visits between 0900-1100, 1400-1530, Rs 5*, at an altitude of 1700 m, is flanked by steep hills and woods. It was created by the small hydro-electricity dam. To its south is the Kerala Livestock Development Board's research and cattle breeding centre, formerly the Indo-Swiss dairy project. In a beautiful semi-Alpine setting surrounded for much of the year by lush green fields, the centre offers interesting insights into the practical realities and achievements of cattle breeding in India today.

Top Station, 34 km from Munnar on the Tamil Nadu border, at an altitude of 2100 m, has some of the highest tea estates in India. It is an idyllic spot, with superb views over the Tamil Nadu plains and the edge of the Western Ghats. Stalls serve tea and soft drinks. Top Station took its name from a ropeway that connected it via Middle Station to Lower Station at the valley bottom. The small town of **Bodinayakkanur**, which can be reached on the Devikulam road, lies in the valley. Buses leave from the shelter north of Munnar post office at 0715, 0915 and 1115 bound for Kovilor, passing Mattupetty Lake and Kundala Dam. Get off at Top Station, return bus after about one hour.

Across the valley from Top Station, and around 40 km east of Munnar, the small plantation of **Kolukkumalai** officially claims to pick the highest tea leaves in the world. The drive to the ridgetop at 2175 m takes two hours (the last section on a plantation road so bad it might be quicker to get out and walk) but the effort is repaid by astonishing views across misty valleys and distant peaks. It's worth being here for sunrise; set off by 0400 and wrap up warm for the journey. A path through the tea bushes leads down to the 1930s factory, where you can sample the local product and watch the antique processing equipment in action. As the plantation is privately owned you need to join a tour to get in; **Kestrel Adventures** (see Activities and tours, page 1022) is the main operator.

Eravikulam/Rajamalai National Park ⓘ *21 km northeast of Munnar, www.eravikulam.org, closed Feb-Mar and during the monsoons, Rs 200, camera Rs 25, video Rs 200,* was set up in 1978 to preserve the endangered Nilgiri tahr (Nilgiri ibex). The conservation programme has resulted in the park now supporting the largest population of the species in the world, of nearly 2000. The sure-footed wild goats live in herds on the steep black rocky slopes of the Anaimudi mountains. They are brownish, have short, flat horns with the male carrying a thick mane, and can be easily seen around the park entrance. There are also elephants, sambars, gaurs, macaques and the occasional leopard and tiger. The scenery is magnificent, though the walks into the forest are steep and strenuous. There is an easier paved path from the park entrance following the road immediately below the bare granite outcrop of the Naikundi Hill to the Rajamalai Gap. The Forest Department issues a limited number of permits to trek through the park on the **Goldsbury Track**.

Adjoining Eravikulam to the north, and spreading down the eastern slope of the ghats into Tamil Nadu, the rarely-visited **Chinnar Wildlife Sanctuary** ⓘ *contact the Forest Information Office in Munnar, T04865-231587*, offers near-guaranteed sightings of elephant and bison, and has tree houses and log huts to stay in.

The road to Kochi

The route from Kochi to Munnar is one of South India's most attractive ghat roads. The one sight of note is the is the 25-sq-km **Salim Ali Bird Sanctuary** ⓘ *Thattekad, 70 km east of Kochi on a side road heading north out of Kothamangalam; contact Assistant Wildlife Warden, Thattekad, T0485-258 8302*. A tropical evergreen and semi-evergreen forest with teak and rosewood plantations, the sanctuary is surrounded by the Periyar River, which remains shallow most of the year. It attracts water birds and the indigenous Malabar grey hornbill, rose and blue-winged parakeet, egret, heron and mynah, while rarer birds like the Ceylon frog-mouth and rose-billed rollers are also sometimes seen here.

Munnar and Idukki's high ranges listings

For Sleeping and Eating price codes and other relevant information, see Essentials pages 38-42.

Sleeping

The Midlands (Kottayam to Thekkady) *p1013*

LL Kottukapally Nazarani Tharavad, Palai, T04822-212438, www.nazaranitharavad.com. An opportunity to stay with the Kottukapally family (Kerala political royalty). There are grand Byzantine icons, Persian carpets and Travancore brass lamps. The roomy 250-year-old Kerala/Dutch/Spanish- style house of teak, rosewood and Basel tiles has 3 roomy doubles. Book in advance.

AL Heron's Pool, Kallivayalil House, Mundakayam East, Idukki, T0486-928 0982, homestay@heronspool.com. Traditional planter family throw open the doors of their laid-back home, set in groves of rubber, vanilla, cardamom, coffee, pepper, cocoa and banana. Rosewood and teak furniture, private sit-outs overlooking the plantation, gardens, bar and library. Classic Kerala cuisine is served under the stars in the cobbled courtyard (*naalu kettu*). Plantation visits, swimming, tennis, badminton, billiards, golf.

AL The Pimenta, Haritha Farms, The Pimenta, Kadalikad Post, T0485-226 0216, www.harithafarms.com. An eco-tourism concern in a pepper-growing region. Guest numbers are limited to minimize impact on the village. 4 newly built simple cottages close to the family farmhouse. The family are advocates of the return to traditional methods of agriculture, Haritha grows bio-organic spices, medicinal herbs and tropical fruit and re-plants crops lost to monoculture tea and rubber plantations. All meals included.

AL Vanilla County, Mavady Estate, Teekoy, Vagamon, T0482-228 1225, www.vanilla county.in. At the source of the Meenachil River. A charming, family-friendly place with 3 rooms within 60-year-old estate house that you share with your hosts. Coffee is from the plantation around you and you can swim in nearby natural ponds. Internet access. Price includes all meals.

B Grandma's Mansion, Plassnal, near Palai, T0482-227 2080, www.ghstay.com. 3 rooms in a charming homestay built in the traditional Christian style with a genteel, elderly hostess. An immaculately maintained house with fans, narrow beds and swinging daybeds, set in a garden with pond. Excellent home-cooked meals included. Advance booking essential.

Thekkady *p1014, map p1015*

Check www.thekkady.com for information.

LL Cardomom County, Thekkady Rd, T0486-922 4501, www.cardamomcounty.com. Spacious, comfortable cottages, good restaurant, nice pool, friendly (request off-season discount). Recommended.

LL Lake Palace, Lake Periyar, T0486-922 3887, www.lakepalacethekkady.com. 6 rooms in interesting building inside the reserve. Idyllic island setting with superb views and wildlife spotting. Access by free ferry (20 mins) from jetty (last trip 1600). Relaxed and informal.

LL Paradisa Plantation Retreat, Murinjapuzha, Kottayam–Kumily Rd, T0469-270 1311, www.paradisaretreat.com. 10 traditionally built new cottages with beautiful antique granite pillars and room furnishings, on an organic plantation estate with stunning valley views and a pool. Yoga recommended but booking essential.

LL Spice Village (CGH Earth), Thekkady–Kumily Rd, T0486-922 2314, www.cghearth.com. Cottages with elephant grass thatch (cool and dark with wide eaves), spice garden, badminton, tennis, good pool, yoga centre. Excellent restaurant, lunch and dinner buffets (Rs 500), chilled beer. Good cookery demonstrations, great Ayurvedic massage and forest walks to see smaller wildlife. Luxurious, quiet, restful, friendly, with superb service. Discounts Apr-Sep.

L-A Carmelia Haven, Vandanmedu (20 km north on Puliyanmala Rd), on a tea, spice and coconut plantation, T0486-827 0272, www.carmeliahaven.com. Exclusive and private, with a tree house 6 m above ground, a cave house 3 m below, and a few discreetly spaced cottages in a local style using lots of thatch. An excellent open-air restaurant serves delicious Malabari food. Tours of tea factory, cardamom plantations, treks and boating. Tea and cardamom for sale.

L-A Hotel Treetop, Thekkady Rd, T0486-922 3286, www.hoteltreetop.com. Clean and efficient resort of gabled cottages with all mod cons and private balconies, just on the fringes of the Periyar National Park. Family bungalow has a kitchen and living area. Library, restaurant, Ayurveda massages available.

A-B Chrissie's, Thekkady Bypass Rd, T0486-922 4155, www.chrissies.in. Modern minimalist rooms all with balcony. Lush, peaceful garden with shady seating areas to relax in. Restaurant, yoga studio.

A-B Periyar House (KTDC), 5 mins' walk from the lake, T0486-222 2026, www.periyarhousethekkady.com. Pleasant, clean and comfortable rooms. Buffet meals and strong Goan beer available. Good service.

B-C Lake Queen, Thekkady Junction, T0486-922 2084, www.lakequeen.com. Large clean and rather bland rooms, all with a/c and cable TV. Good restaurant.

B-D Claus Garden, Rosapukandam, 10 mins' uphill from bus stand behind PO, 3rd turn right, T0486-922 2320, claus.hoppe@web.de. Spacious rooms in a peaceful house surrounded by jungle. Funky communal area, book exchange, friendly chilled-out vibe.

D-E Deer Villa, Thekkady Bypass Rd, T0486-922 3568, www.deervilla.com. Friendly family home boasting clean, airy rooms with balcony, fan and hot water. Breakfast included. Internet café downstairs.

D-G Coffee Inn, Thekkady Rd, 5-mins' walk from entrance gate, T0486-922 2763, coffeeinn@satyam.net.in. Wide variety of rooms, cheaper huts in quiet garden annex 100 m down the road. Popular budget traveller hang-out. Restaurant, book exchange, friendly. No reservations – rooms are allocated on a first come first served basis.

D-G Green View, Hotel Ambadi Junction, Thekkady Bypass Rd, T0486-922 4617, www.sureshgreenview.com. Suresh and Sulekha run a welcoming 'home away from home' in a rambling house surrounded by mango trees. Hammocks are slung out in the garden. All 16 spotlessly clean rooms have large bathrooms (towels, loo roll and soap provided). Standard and deluxe rooms have cable TV and balcony. Suresh is an ex-tour guide and can provide maps for mountain treks and walks in the area. Meals available on request, cookery classes, breakfast included. Friendly and helpful. Recommended.

E Micky Farm House, Thekkady Bypass Rd, T0486-922 3196, www.mickeyhomestay.com. Pleasant airy rooms in pretty garden, all with balcony. Cheaper rooms with outside bath. Micky runs 4- to 7-day treks to Kottayam/Alappuzha (advance notice required). Friendly family, excellent value. Recommended.

E-F Rose Garden Homestay, Hotel Ambadi Junction, Thekkady Bypass Rd, T0486-922 3146, rosegardenhomestay@yahoo.co.in. Sathi has 6 simply furnished rooms, all with TV, in the back garden of her flowered house. Lots of hanging wicker chairs on porches, Lovely family provide traditional Keralite breakfasts and suppers. Discounts for long stays.

F-G Hill Park, Main St, T0486-268 5509, hillpark@aol.in. 17 moderately clean and basic rooms all with bath and fan. Friendly staff.

Munnar *p1016, map p1017*

Hotel prices are on the rise. Cheaper places can be found around the bazar and bus stand, where touts will greet you brandishing the cards of 25-room concrete block 'cottages'.

LL Tall Trees, Bison Valley Rd (3 km south of town), T04865-230641, www.ttr.in. A drastic price hike means the rather musty cottages here offer dubious value, but the location, beneath a canopy of ancient rainforest, is undeniably magic.

LL-AL Windermere Estate, Pothamedu, T04865-230512, www.windermeremunnar.com. Standalone cottages, an alpine farmhouse with 5 rooms and an elegant and utterly comfortable planters' bungalow with 3 rooms. The whole complex is set around an enormous granite boulder, with sweeping across the tops of clouds from the top, and there's a fantastically light and airy reading room done out with rustic timber furniture and vaulted ceilings. Pricey but recommended.

AL NatureZone, Pullipara, 5 km up dirt track off Letchmi Rd, west of TN Bus Stand, bookings on T0484-649 3301, www.thenaturezone.org. Arriving here is like stepping into Jurassic Park – you have to get out of the car and unhook the elephant-repelling electric fence. A leading outward-bound training centre with stunning valley views, the drawcards here are the jungly remoteness and the 2 rustic-chic treehouses, with branches growing right through the room. The safari tents down at ground level are OK but get pretty musty. On-site canteen serves good food.

AL Tea County (KTDC), 1 km north of town, T04865-230460, www.ktdc.com. 43 immaculately kept rooms set in 3 ha of neat garden, good facilities, beautiful views, great walking, own transport essential.

AL The Tea Sanctuary, KDHP House, T04865-230141, www.theteasanctuary.com. 6 quaint old-fashioned bungalows on the working Kanan Devan tea estate, pukka colonial-style atmosphere plus activities like mountain biking, trekking, horse riding, golf and angling, and everything clubbable at the **High Range** and **Kundale** clubs.

A Olive Brook, Bison Valley Rd, Pothamedu, 3 km south of Munnar, T04865-230588, www.olivebrookmunnar.com. 5 well-appointed double rooms in beautiful lush location on a cardamom farm, excellent alfresco barbecues on request. Price includes meals, trekking and cookery classes.

A-B Copper Castle, Kannan Devan Hills (out of town), T04865-230633, coppercastle@vsnl.com. Perched on hillside with beautiful views, good-sized comfortable rooms with baths (hot showers) and restaurant (good sizzlers). Friendly staff but slow service.

A-C Royal Retreat, 500 m south of KSRTC Bus Stand, T04865-230240, www.royalretreat.co.in. Agreeable standard doubles with TV and hot water, plus excellent newly renovated garden rooms and suites with fluffy quilts and DVD players.

B East End, Temple Rd, T04865-230452. 18 pleasant rooms and some cottages (solar heated water), good but pricey restaurant, attractively designed, quiet garden location.

B-C Isaac's Residency, Top Station Rd, T04865-230501. Excellent quality, 32 lovely rooms with contemporary furnishings, Executive rooms with great views, 2 restaurants, bar. Recommended.

D John's Cottage, MSA Rd, near Munnar Supply Association, T04865-231823. Small bungalow home in a well-tended lawn running down to the river, with 8 clean rooms. Indian/Chinese food or use of kitchen.

D Sisiram Cottage Homestay, IX/18A MSA Rd, T04865-231908, www.sisiram.com. 2-storey cottage on the riverbank, with large, nicely furnished rooms upstairs and a 3-bed apartment (**A**) downstairs.

E Arafa Tourist Home, Upper Bazar, T04865-230302. 14 rooms with TV, phone in riverside lodge, handy for late-night bus arrivals. Noise travels, but the rooms are clean and good value.

E Theresian Cottages, north of town before Tea County, T04865-230351. For once, a cottage that's actually a cottage. Three rooms open off the shared living room of this sweet little 1930s house, and though sizes vary, each has a fireplace, chaise longue and clean bathroom.

E Zeena Cottages, near **Hill View Hotel** in Tata tea plantation, T04865-230560, www.hillviewhotel.com. Rooms in colonial house, good views, friendly people. Ask at the **Tourist Information Service** in the bazar (see page 1016).

The road to Kochi *p1018*

AL Plantation Homestay, Mundackal Estate, Pindimana, Kothamangalam Junction, T0485-257 0717, nestholidays@hotmail.com. 3 rooms in a homestay that lies deep inside a rubber, pepper and coconut plantations. Daisy is a mean cook and offers lessons (US$20), while George arranges boat trips to the bird sanctuary.

A Periyar River Lodge, Anakkayam, Kothamanagalam, T0485-258 8315, www.periyarriverlodge.com. 2-bedroom cottage in a rubber plantation on the banks of Periyar River right next to Thattekad Bird Sanctuary. Bamboo rafting, fishing, forest treks, jeep safaris to 30-m-high waterfalls for swimming, boat and bike tours. Lounge, en suite, river views. Keralite food.

Eating

Thekkady *p1014, map p1015*

TTT Spice Village, Thekkady Rd. International, excellent food and service, rustic decor, fresh garden vegetables and chef's cooking show nightly.

TT Coffee Inn, Thekkady Rd, 0700-2200. International dishes served at tables outside under the palms, bonfire in the evening, relaxed and peaceful. Friendly but very slow service.

T Ebony's Café, Thekkady Bypass Rd. Rooftop restaurant with huge range of Indian and international dishes.

Ⲯ **Edassery's Farm Yard**, NH 49 Chattupara Adimali Idukki, T04864-224210. 0600-2200. Makes a good break on the Kottayam–Kumily road with tasty soups and meals, *dosa* and vegetable stews.

Ⲯ **French Restaurant** , Thekkady Rd. Good bread, muesli, snacks and coffee.

Munnar *p1016, map p1017*

ⲮⲮ **The Greens**, **East End** (see Sleeping). Pleasant, glassed-in veranda serving good food, or go for the cheap simple meals in the eatery below.

ⲮⲮ **Royal Retreat** (see Sleeping). International. Very pleasant, wide choice.

Ⲯ **Bamboo Hut**, overlooking river opposite the Tea Museum. About to move at the time of research, but worth asking around for as cook-owner Isaac makes some of the best food in town, from traveller-friendly fare like muesli with fruit salad and curd to Keralite curries.

Ⲯ **Silver Spoon**, near **Munnar Inn**. For good breakfast choices.

Ⲯ **Vegetarian Restaurant** (next to Misha), Old Bazar. Serves very good meals.

Bars and clubs

Munnar *p1016, map p1017*

High Range Club, T04865-230253. Charming colonial-style planters' club, members only (or with reciprocal arrangements), visit by asking a planter to introduce you.

KDH Club, on side road opposite DTPC office. For Tata staff, old-world, visit with permission, excellent pool table.

Entertainment

Thekkady *p1014, map p1015*

Kadathanadan Kalari Centre, Thekkady Rd, Kumily, T0486-922 2988, www.thekkady tours.in. One hour demonstration of Kerala's traditional martial art, *kalarippayattu*. Show time 1800, Rs 200, video charge Rs 250.

Mudra Daily Kathakali Centre, Thekkady Rd, Kumily, T(0)9447-15 7636, www.mudra kathakali.com. Classical dance theatre show by performers from Kalamandalam school of dance. Make-up 1600 and 1830, show times 1630 and 1900. Rs125, video charge Rs 200.

Shopping

Munnar *p1016, map p1017*

Good for tea, cardamom and pepper.

Munnar Supply Assoc (**MSA**), next to tourist information. Established 1900, a bit of the old world, where you can get everything. Tailors in the bazar can copy your garments in 24 hrs. The newer Main Bazar is to the north.

Uravu, near Ambady Junction, Idukki, T(0)9387-469369, www.uravu.org. Fair trade outfit supporting local producers of agrihorticultural products, bamboo products, processed foods, handicrafts, forest honey, spices tea and coffee.

Activities and tours

Thekkady *p1014, map p1015*

Eco Tourism Information Centre, Hotel Ambadi Junction, Thekkady Bypass Rd, Kumily, T0486-922 4571, www.periyartiger reserve.com. Organizes a full range of tours within the park: bamboo rafting, tiger trails with 1 or 2 nights camping, evening jungle patrols, border hiking and treks to tribal settlements.

Forest Information Centre, near boat jetty, Thekkady. Sells tickets for 2-hr boat trips on Lake Periyar 0700, 0930, 1100, 1400 and 1600 (Rs 40) and 3-hr nature treks 0700, 1000, 1400 (Rs 100). No advance bookings, arrive early and queue at office.

Munnar *p1016, map p1017*

DTPC, Old Munnar Bazar. Runs tours to: Tea Valley, 1000-1800, Rs 250; Sandal Valley and Wildlife, 0900-1900, Rs 300.

Kestrel Adventures, PB No 44, KTDC Rd, T094-4703 1040, www.kestreladventures.com. Senthil Kumar leads a team of 9 specialist guides, some expert in birds, others in tea growing and history. Highly recommended for camping and trekking, wildlife spotting in Chinnar Wildlife Sanctuary, and the only company in town that can get you into Kolukkumalai for sunrise. Also offers rock climbing, mountain bike tours/hire and jeep safaris.

Transport

Thekkady *p1014, map p1015*

Beware of 3-wheelers and guides at the bus station, who are working on commission from guesthouses. Nearly all hotels in Kumily are within a 10-min walk of the bus station.

Local bus Minibuses hourly from Kumily go down to **Aranya Nivas** on the lakeside, Rs 2. At Kumily jeep drivers will tell you there is no bus to Thekkady and charge Rs 50 for the trip; autos charge Rs 25 plus.
Long distance bus From Kumily: frequent services to **Kottayam** every 20 mins from 0600, 4½ hrs, Rs 68. Regular buses to **Kochi/ Ernakulam** 6 per day, first at 0600, 6½ hrs, Rs 107; **lappuzha** 6 per day, first at 0600, 6 hrs, Rs 87; **Thiruvananthapuram**, 3 per day, first at 0830, 8 hrs, Rs 150; **Munnar**, 5 per day, first at 0600, 4½ hrs, Rs 68. Daily bus to **Kodaikkanal** (cancelled occasionally), 0630, 5½ hrs, Rs 78, or go to **Vathalakundu** and change;. Buses also go from Thekkady itself (behind *Aranya Nivas*): frequent departures to **Madurai**; every 20 mins, from 0600, 4 hrs, Rs 55.

Munnar *p1016, map p1017*
Bike hire From tourist information office, Rs 50 per day. **Kestrel Adventures** (see Activities and tours) has 18-speed mountain bikes.
Bus State buses start and terminate at 2 separate stands south of town, but also call at the **Town Bus Stand** near the market. Enquiries, T04865-230201. Frequent services to **Mattupetty** (30 mins), **Devikulam** (30 mins), **Adimali** (1 hr) and **Top Station** (1 hr). Daily to **Coimbatore** (6 hrs); **Ernakulam/ Kochi** (4½ hrs); **Kodaikkanal** 0700 via Udumalpettai, change for Palani and Kodai. If the Palani–Kodai Rd is closed a further bus goes to Vatalakundu and then Kodai; **Kottayam** (5 hrs); **Madurai** via Theni (5 hrs); **Palani** (4½ hrs); **Thekkady** (4½ hrs), leaves from stop next to the post office; **Thiruvanantha puram** (9 hrs), **Thrissur** via **Perumbavoor** (5 hrs).
Jeeps/taxis Shared jeeps and minibus taxis for **Eravikulam** and **Mattupetty Lake** wait around the post office. For

Directory

Thekkady *p1014, map p1015*
Banks **Federal Bank**, Thekkady Junction, **State Bank of India**, Main St. Both have ATM. **Thomas Cook**, Thekkady Rd. **Internet** **Periyar Net Café**, Thekkady Bypass Rd. Rs 30 per hr. **Medical services** **Kumily Central Hospital**, Open 0900-1300 and 1630-2000, 24 hrs call out for emergencies. **Post** Main St, next to bus station.

Munnar *p1016, map p1017*
Banks **State Bank of Travancore** ATM, in the centre near KDHP headquarters. **Federal Bank**, near Tata Hospital Rd, very helpful; **State Bank of India**, 1000-1400, Sat 1000-1200. **Internet** **Olivia**, next to footbridge in the bazar, Rs 30, good connection and free sweets. **Medical services** Excellent **Tata General Hospital**, T04865-230270, on the north edge of town on the Rajamalai Rd. **Post** New Town centre.

Thrissur, Palakkad and the River Nila

The blue thread of the River Nila, Kerala's equivalent of the Ganges and the crucible of much of the state's rich cultural heritage, stitches together a collection of fascinating sights and experiences in the rarely explored central belt of Kerala between Kochi and Kozhikode. Busy Thrissur, the state's cultural capital, is unmissable in April and May when it holds its annual Pooram festival and millions pack into the city's central square, sardine-style, to watch the elephant procession and fireworks display. Coastal Guruvayur, meanwhile, is among Kerala's most sacred Hindu pilgrimage spots; it is home to one of India's wealthiest temples as well as an elephant yard where huge tuskers and their mahouts relax before they hit the road for the next festival. Inland, the Palakkad Gap cuts a broad trench through the Western Ghats, the only natural break in the mountain chain, providing a ready conduit for roads, railway lines, innumerable waves of historical migrants, and blasts of scorching air from the roasted plains of Tamil Nadu. Palakkad itself is now known as Kerala's granary, and makes a good stopover point on the route to or from Tamil Nadu. ▸▸ *For listings, see pages 1028-1031.*

Ins and outs

Getting there Trains on the main north–south line stop in Thrissur and Shoranur Junction, a handy jumping-off point for the River Nila. Trains from Kerala to Coimbatrore and Chennai call at Palakkad. There are bus connections from these towns to the smaller centres. ▸▸ *See Transport, page 1030.*

Tourist Information **Thrissur** ⓘ *Palace Rd, T0487 2320800, www.dtpcthrissur.com*. **Guruvayur** ⓘ *Vyjayanti Building, East Nada, Guruvayur, T0487-255 0400.* **Palakkad DTPC** ⓘ *West Fort Rd, Palakkad, T0491-253 8996, www.dtpcpalakkad.com.*

Thrissur (Trichur) and around → *Colour map 7, B2. Phone code: 0487. Population: 317,500.*

Thrissur sits at the west end of the Palakkad gap, which runs through the low pass between the Nilgiri and the Palani hills. The route through the ghats is not scenic but it has been the most important link to the peninsula interior since Roman times. Thrissur is built round a hill on which stand the Vadakkunnathan Temple and an open green, which form the centre of the earth-shaking festivities. The town's bearings are given in cardinal directions from this raised 'Round'.

The **Vadakkunnathan Temple** ⓘ *0400-1030, 1700-2030, non-Hindus not permitted inside except during the Pooram festival*, a predominantly Siva temple, is also known as the Rishabhadri or Thenkailasam ('Kailash of the South'). At the shrine to the Jain Tirthankara Vrishabha, worshippers offer a thread from their clothing, symbolically to cover the saint's nakedness. The shrine to Sankara Narayana has superb murals depicting stories from the *Mahabharata*. It is a classic example of the Kerala style of architecture with its special pagoda-like roof richly decorated with fine wood carving. The temple plays a pivotal role in the **Pooram** celebrations, see page 1029. In September and October, there are live performances of Chakyarkothu, a classical art form. There is a small elephant compound attached to the temple.

The **Town Hall** is a striking building housing an art gallery with murals from other parts of the state. In the **Archaeological Museum** ⓘ *Town Hall Rd, Tue-Sun 0900-1500*, ask to see the royal chariot. Next door, the **Art Museum** has woodcarvings, sculptures, an excellent collection of traditional lamps and old jewellery. Nearby, **Thrissur Zoo** ⓘ *Tue-Sun 1000-1700, small fee*, is known for its snake collection. The impressive **Lourdes Church** has an interesting underground shrine.

Guruvayur

As one of the holiest sites in Kerala, Guruvayur, 29 km west of Trichur, is a heaving pilgrimage centre, filled with stalls and thronged from 0300 to 2200 with people wanting to take *darshan* of Guruvayurappan.

It is one of the richest temples in India: there is a waiting list for the auspicious duty of lighting its oil lamps that stretches to 2025. On well-augured marriage days there is a scrum in which couples are literally shunted from the podium by new pairs urgently pressing behind them in the queue, and the whole town is geared towards the wedding industry; most hotels here have huge marriage halls and expect guests to stay a maximum of two nights. The ceremony of children's first rice feed falls on the first of every *Malayali* month. The **Sri Krishna Temple**, which probably dates from at least the 16th century has an outer enclosure where there is a tall gold-plated flagpost and a pillar of lamps. The sanctum sanctorum is in the two-storeyed *srikoil*, with the image of the four-armed Krishna garlanded with pearls and marigolds. Photography of the tank is not allowed. Non-Hindus are not allowed inside and are not made to feel welcome.

On the left as you walk towards the temple is the **Guruvayur Devaswom Institute of Mural Painting** ⓘ *Mon-Fri 1000-1600*, a tiny educational institute where you can see the training of, and buy finished works from, the next generation of mural painters. In a similar vein to *Kathakali*, with the weakening structure of feudalism and opposition to the caste system, the age-old decorative arts of temple culture steadily declined during the 20th century. When Guruvayur lost three walls to a fire in 1970 there were hardly any artists left to carry out renovation, prompting authorities to build the school in 1989. Today the small institute runs a five-year course on a scholarship basis for just 10 students. Paintings sell for Rs 500-15,000 depending on size, canvas, wood, etc. Humans are stylized (facial expressions and gestures can be traced back to *Kathakali* and *Koodiyattom*) and have wide-open eyes, elongated lips, over-ornamentation and exaggerated eyebrows and hand gestures.

Devotees to Guruvayur's Sri Krishna temple aren't afraid to put their money where their mouths are: in one month alone the temple can earn as much as Rs 11 million, along with just short of 4 kg of gold and almost 14 kg of silver.

Punnathur Kotta Elephant Yard ⓘ *0900-1700, bathing 0900-0930, Rs 25, take care as elephants can be dangerous, buses from Thrissur (45 mins)*, is situated within a fort 4 km out of town. Temple elephants (68 at the last count) are looked after here and wild ones are trained. There are some interesting insights into traditional animal training but this is not everyone's cup of tea. Though captive, the elephants are dedicated to Krishna and appear to be well cared for by their attendants. The elephants are donated by pious Hindus but religious virtue doesn't come cheap: the elephants cost Rs 500,000 each.

Kodungallur

At one time Kodungallur, 50 km southwest of Trichur on the border of Ernakulam District, was the west coast's major port, and the capital of the Chera king Cheraman Perumal. Nearby **Kottapuram** is where St Thomas is believed to have landed in AD 52. The commemorative shrine was built in 1952. Kodungallur is also associated by tradition with the arrival of the first Muslims to reach India by sea. Malik-ibn-Dinar is reputed to have built India's first **Juma Masjid**, 2 km from town. **Tiruvanchikulam Temple** and the **Portuguese fort** are worth visiting. The Syrian orthodox church in **Azikode** blends early Christian architecture in Kerala with surrounding Hindu traditions. Thus the images of Peter and Paul are placed where the *dvarapalas* (doorkeepers) of Hindu temples would be found, and the portico in front of the church is for pilgrims.

Along the River Nila

North of Thrissur the road and railway cut through lush countryside of paddy fields, quiet villages and craggy red hills mantled with coconut and rubber plantations, before crossing the wide sandy bed of the Bharatapuzha River at Shoranur. Known to the people who populate its banks as Nila, this is Kerala's longest river, rising on the eastern side of the Palakkad Gap and winding lazily through 209 km to spill into the Arabian Sea at the bustling fishing port of

Ponnani. Though its flow is severely depleted by irrigation dams and its bed gouged by sand miners, the importance of the river to Kerala's cultural development is hard to overstate: Ayurveda, *kathakali* and the martial art *kalaripayattu* were all nurtured along the banks of the Nila, not to mention the cacophonous classical music that soundtracks festive blow-outs like the Thrissur **Pooram**. Folk tradition too is vibrantly represented: elaborately adorned devotees carry colourful effigies to temple festivals, snake worshippers roam house to house performing ancient rituals to seek blessing from the serpent gods, and village musicians sing songs of the paddy field mother goddess, passed down from generation to generation.

Despite all this, the Nila thus far remains refreshingly untouched by Kerala's tourism boom, and few travellers see more of it than the glimpses afforded by the beautiful train ride between Shoranur and Kozhikode. This is in part because there's little tourist infra- structure, few genuine 'sights', and no easy way for a travellers to hook into the cultural scene. Traditional potters and brass-smiths labour in humble workshops behind unmarked houses, while performers (singers and dancers by night, coolies, plumbers and snack sellers by day) only get together for certain events. With your own transport you can search out any number of beautiful riverside temples, but unless you join one of the superb storytelling tours run by local guiding outfit **The Blue Yonder** (see page 1030), **Kerala Kalamandalam** (see below) might be the only direct contact you have with the Nila's rich heritage.

The residential school of **Kerala Kalamandalam** ⓘ *3 km south of river, Cheruthuruthy, south of Shoranur Junction, T04884-262305, www.kalamandalam.org, Mon-Fri 0930-1300, closed public holidays and Apr-May*, is dedicated to preserving the state's unique forms of performance art. Founded in 1930, after the provincial rulers' patronage for the arts dwindled in line with their plummeting wealth and influence, the Kalamandalam spear- headed a revival of *Kathakali* dancing, along with *Ottam Thullal* and the all-female drama *Mohiniyattam*. The school and the state tourism department run a fascinating three-hour tour of the campus, 'A Day With the Masters' (US$25), with in-depth explanations of the significance and background of the art forms, the academy and its architecture, taking you through the various open air *kalaris* (classrooms) to watch training sessions. There are all-night *Kathakali* performances on 26 January, 15 August, and 9 November. *Koodiyattam*, the oldest surviving form of Sanskrit theatre, is enshrined by UNESCO as an 'oral and intangible heritage of humanity'. Frequent private buses from Thrissur's northern bus stand (ask for Vadakkancheri Bus Stand) go straight to Kalamandalam, taking about one hour.

In the bustling port town of **Ponnani** at the mouth of the Nila, the **Ponnani Juma Masjid** ⓘ *42 km northwest of Thrissur, nearest train station 21 km away at Kuttipuram; admission to non-Muslims not assured, dress conservatively, women should wear a headscarf*, was built in the mid-15th century by the spiritual leader Zainudhin Ibn Ali Ibn Ahmed Ma'bari, who employed a Hindu carpenter to design the exterior. Ignorant of traditional Islamic architecture, the carpenter carved the elaborate teak-wood facade to resemble a Hindu temple incorporating many intricate Hindu designs. The carpenter was killed by a fall from the roof as he finished construction and lies buried inside inside the mosque. The nearby fishing docks are a hive of activity, but prepare for plenty of attention from local boys.

Palakkad (Palghat) → *Colour map 7, B3. Phone code: 0491. Population: 130,700.*

Kerala's rice cellar, prosperous Palakkad has long been of strategic importance for its gap – the only break in the mountain ranges that otherwise block the state from Tamil Nadu and the rest of India. Whereas once this brought military incursions, today the gap bears tourist buses from Chennai and tractors for the rich agricultural fields here that few educated modern Keralites care to plough using the old bullock carts (although the tradition is kept alive through *kaalapoottu*, a series of races between yoked oxen held in mud-churned paddy fields every January). The whole of Palakkad is like a thick paddy forest, its iridescent old blue mansions, many ruined by the Land Reform Act, crumbling into paddy ponds. There are village idylls like a

Constable painting. Harvest hands loll idly on pillows of straw during lunch hours, chewing ruminatively on chapattis.

The annual festival of **Chinakathoor Pooram** (late February to early March) held at the Sri Chinakathoor Bhagavathy Temple, Palappuram, features a 33-tusker procession, plus remarkable evening puppet shows. Bejewelled tuskers can also be seen at the 20-day **Nenmara-Vallangi Vela**, held at the Sri Nellikulangara Bhagavathy Temple in Kodakara (early April): an amazing festival with grander firework displays than Trichur's **Pooram** but set in fields rather than across the city.

The region is filled with old architecture of *illams* and *tharavadus* belonging to wealthy landowners making a visit worthwhile in itself – but chief among the actual sights is **Palakkad Fort**, a granite structure in Palakkad town itself, built by Haider Ali in 1766, and taken over by the British in 1790. It now has a Hanuman temple inside. Ask directions locally to the 500-year-old Jain temple of **Jainimedu** in the town's western suburbs, a 10-m-long granite temple with Jain *Thirthankaras* and *Yakshinis* built for the Jain sage Chandranathaswami. Only one Jain family is left in the region, but the area around this temple is one of the only places in Kerala where remnants of the religion have survived.

Also well worth visiting in the region are the many traditional Brahmin villages: **Kalpathy**, 10 km outside Palakkad, holds the oldest Siva temple in Malabar, dating from AD 1425 and built by Kombi Achan, then Raja of Palakkad. But the village itself, an 800-year-old settlement by a self-contained Tamil community, is full of beautiful houses with wooden shutters and metal grills and is now a World Heritage Site that gives you a glimpse of village life that has been held half-frozen in time for nearly 1000 years. The temple here is called **Kasiyil Pakuthi Kalpathy** meaning Half Banares because its situation on the river is reminiscent of the Banares temple on the Ganges. A 10-day **car festival** in November centres on this temple and features teak chariots tugged by people and pushed by elephants.

Another unique feature of Palakkad is the *Ramassery Iddli* made at the **Sarswathy tea stall** ⓘ *daily 0500-1830, iddli Rs 1.50, chai Rs 2.50.* If you spend any time on the street in South India, your morning meal will inevitably feature many of these tasty steamed fermented rice cakes. Palakkad is home to a peculiar take on the dumpling, one that has been developed to last for days rather than having to be cooked from fresh. The four families in this poky teashop churn out 5000 *iddlis* a day. Originally settlers from somewhere near Coimbatore, in Tamil Nadu, over 100 years ago, they turned to making this variety of *iddli* when there wasn't enough weaving work to sustain their families. They started out selling them door to door, but pretty soon started to get orders for weddings. The *iddlis* are known to have travelled as far afield as Delhi, by plane in a shipment of 300. Manufacturers have started to arrive in order to buy the secret recipe.

The name Palakkad comes from pala, *a type of tree, and* kadu, *which means forest; the area was once thickly covered in forests of this tree.*

Nelliyampathy, 56 km from Palakkad town, is a hill station with a tiny community of planters. It is famous for its oranges, but there are also orchids, bison, elephant and butterflies in abundance. The view across the Keralite plains from Seethakundu stunning; a third of the district lies spread out under you. The area has good trekking, too.

Megalith trail: Guruvayur to Kunnamkulam

The Palakkad Gap has been one of the few relatively easy routes through the ghats for 3000 years and this area is noted for its megalithic monuments. Megalithic cultures spread from the Tamil Nadu plains down into Kerala, but developed local forms. The small villages of Eyyal, Chovvanur, Kakkad, Porkalam, Kattakampala and Kadamsseri, between Guruvayur and Kunnamkulam, have hoodstones, hatstones, dolmens, burial urns and *menhirs.*

Thrissur, Palakkad and the River Nila listings

For Sleeping and Eating price codes and other relevant information, see Essentials pages 38-42.

Sleeping

Thrissur *p1024*

Reserve ahead for **Pooram**, when prices rocket.

L-A Kadappuram Beach Resort, Nattika Beach, southwest of Thrissur, T0487-239 4988, www.kadappurambeachresorts.com. Self- contained complex of bungalows and cottages in traditional Kerala design, but the emphasis here is on the Ayurveda and most come for the 14-day *panchakarma* (€560). The Ayurveda centre is functional and not luxurious, but massage and medical attention are excellent. After treatments, cross the pretty river to a huge garden of coconut trees and hammocks that separates the hotel from the sea.

B Surya Ayurvedics, Kaipily Rd, Arimpur, T0487-231 2240, www.ayurvedaresorts.com. 10 rooms (some a/c) in impressive old buildings, vegetarian meals, Ayurvedic treatments, yoga, exchange.

C-F Luciya Palace, Marar Rd, T0487-242 4731, luciyapalace@hotmail.com. 35 rooms, 15 a/c, 2 suites, Large, clean and quiet rooms, TV, garden restaurant, internet next door, good service, very pleasant hotel.

E-F Bini Tourist Home, Round North, T0487-233 5703. 24 rooms, TV, shower, 10 a/c, basic but clean and spacious rooms, restaurant, bar.

F Railway Retiring Rooms. Well looked after and very good value.

Guruvayur *p1024*

A-C Krishna Inn, East Nada, T0487-255 0777, www.krishnainn.com. Glossy hotel with white marble floors and spacious. 24-hr coffee shop, vegetarian, multi-cuisine **Thulasi** restaurant.

B-E Mayura Residency, West Nada, T0487-255 7174, www.mayuraresidency.com. 65 good-value, well-appointed rooms in high-rise hotel with excellent views from its rooftop. 24-hr coffee shop, **Amrutham** vegetarian (continental, South or North Indian) restaurant.

C-D Sree Hari Guest House, Samuham Rd, West Nada, T0487-255 6837. 8 big rooms, some a/c, with hot water, draped with purple crushed velvet in guesthouse stuffed with Krishnas and 1960s-style curtains.

D-E Hotel Vanamala, Kusumam South Nada, T0487-255 5213. Popular with domestic tourists, 2-star hotel, very clean rooms with big beds and TV, telephone and hot water. A/c, vegetarian restaurant (Keralite food, 0600-2300), laundry.

Along the River Nila *p1025*

L-A River Retreat, Palace Rd, Cheruthuruthy, T0488-426 2244, www.riverreatreat.in. Heritage hotel and Ayurvedic resort in the former (and much-extended) home of the maharajas of Kochi. Spacious rooms have a/c, TV and modern baths, great views onto large tree-filled garden that backs onto the Nila. Period furniture adds a nice touch to the airy communal areas. Tours of the local area, restaurant, bar, pool, Wi-Fi.

AL Ayurveda Mana, Peringode, via Kootanadu, T0466-237 0660, www.ayurvedamana.com. Authentic Ayurveda centre set in a fascinating 600-year-old *illam*, with treatments following the traditional methods of Poomully Aram Thampuran, a renowned expert in the discipline. Quiet airy rooms (all with TV, and some with unique) open onto shady veranda and peaceful manicured grounds. Full range of general health care treatments available and specialized therapies for arthritis, sports injuries, infertility, etc. All treatments include individually assessed diet, massage and medicine.

A Maranat Mana, Old Ooty-Mysore Rd, Pandikkad (an hour's drive north of Pattambi), T0493-128 6252, www.maranatmana.com. Special homestay in a traditional *namboodhiri* (Kerala Brahmin) household. Hosts Praveen and Vidya have sensitively converted the 160-year-old guesthouse attached to their ancestral home into 3 cool and airy rooms, all with fans and modern baths. You can visit the sprawling main family residence, one of the last surviving examples of Keralite *pathinaru kettu* ('four courtyards') architecture, which contains a Ganesh shrine to which devotees flock from far and wide. Delicious vegetarian meals included, and local tours, Ayurvedic treatments, yoga classes, cultural activities can be arranged. Fascinating and highly recommended, reservations essential.

Palakkad *p1026*

LL Kalari Kovilakom, Kollengode, T0492-326 3155, www.kalarikovilakom.com. Ayurveda for purists. Far from the Ayurveda tourist traps, the Maharani of Palakkad's 1890 palace has been restored to make this very elite retreat. It's extremely disciplined yet very luxurious: the indulgence of a palace meets the austerity of an ashram. Treatments include anti-ageing, weight loss, stress management and ailment healing. Lessons include yoga, meditation, Ayurvedic cookery. Strictly no exertion (no sunbathing or swimming). No mod cons (TV, etc), bar, internet. US$414 per day all-inclusive. Minimum stay of 14, 21 or 28 days.

AL Kandath Tharavad, Thenkurussi, T0492-228 4124, www.tharavad.info. A magical place tucked away in Palakkad's fields, 6 rooms in a 200-year-old mud and teak ancestral home with natural dyed floor tiles of ochre, terracotta and blue. Nadumuttams open out onto the stars and doors are thick wedges of teak and brass. Bagwaldas, your gracious host, will guide you through local customs and culture as engagingly as he steers you through the physical landscape.

AL-A Olappamanna Mana, Vellinezhi, T0466-228 5797, www.olappamannamana.com. Majestic manor house, in rosewood, teak and jackfruit trees, to the highest Keralite Hindu caste of *namboodris*, parts of which date back 3 centuries. Pure vegetarian cuisine, no alcohol, 6 bedrooms, with bathroom and fan, no a/c.

A Kairali Ayurvedic Health Resort, Kodumbu, T0492-322 2553, www.kairali.com. Excellent resort, beautifully landscaped grounds, own dairy and farm, pool, tennis, extensive choice of treatments (packages of Ayurveda, trekking, astrology, golf, pilgrimage), competent and helpful staff. Recommended.

B-D Fort Palace, West Fort Rd, T0491-253 4621. 19 rooms, groovy old-style hotel some good a/c, restaurant, brash mock turrets. Satellite TV and hot water. Continental/ Indian food in restaurant, and bar, both gloomy and packed (lawn service). Nice shared sit-out on 1st floor, spotless, large double beds. Chandeliers, wood panelling.

B-D Indraprastha, English Church Rd, T0491-253 4641, www.hotelindraprastha.com. Kitsch and cool: 30 rooms in 1960s block, dark wood, leather banquettes and bronze lettering. Dark bar permanently packed, lawn service, 24-hr vegetarian coffee shop, exchange, internet, bookshop. Multi-cuisine restaurant.

C Garden House (KTDC), Malampuzha, T0491-281 5217. 17 somewhat chintzy rooms in a 1-star government restaurant on hilltop overlooking popular domestic picnic spot (Malampuzha gardens with lotus pond). Mostly non a/c rooms, pleasant.

Eating

Thrissur *p1024*

Most **D** hotels have good restaurants, particularly **Siddhartha Regency's Golden Fork**, on Veliyannur Rd near the station. In general, though, eating out is still somewhat frowned on by the traditional Brahmin families of Kerala, so most eating options are down-at-heel *dhabas*.

City Centre, next to **Priya Tourist Home**. Western snacks, bakery and good supermarket.

Navaratna, Naduvilal, Round West, T0487-242 1994. 1000-2300. Pure vegetarian North Indian restaurant divided into booths.

Elite Bharat, Chembottil Lane. For good South Indian breakfast and lunch.

Sapphire, Railway Station Rd. 0630-2200. Excellent lime green and stone eatery dishing up *thalis* and the best chicken biryanis in town.

Palakkad *p1026*

Ashok Bhavan, GB Rd. Modest vegetarian South Indian snacks.

Hotel Noor Jehan, GB Rd, T0491-252 2717. Non-vegetarian a/c restaurant that specializes in *moplah biryani* and *pathiri*, rice chappatis.

KR Bakes. 0900-2300. Puffs, ice creams, *halva* plus juice bar and savoury meals after 1600.

Festivals and events

Thrissur *p1024*

Jan-Feb Several temple festivals involving elephants are held in the surrounding villages which can be as rewarding as **Pooram** (eg **Koorkancherry Thaippoya Mahotsavam**, or **Thaipooya Kavadiyattam**, held at Sri Maheswara Temple, Koorkancherry, 2 km from Thrissur). Also held at the end of Feb is the **Uthralikavu Pooram**, at its most colourful at the Sri Ruthura Mahakalikavu Temple, Parithipra, Vodakancherry, en route to Shornur Junction.

End Mar 7-day **Arratupuzha Festival** at the Ayappa Temple, 14 km from Thrissur. On the 5th day the deity parades with 9 decorated elephants, while on the 6th day **Pooram** is celebrated on a grand scale with 61 elephants in the temple grounds.

Apr-May The magnificent 8-day **Pooram**, a grand festival with elephants, parasols, drums and fireworks, should not be missed. Several temples in town participate but particularly the Thiruvambady and Paramekkavu. It is marked by very noisy, colourful processions, joined by people from all religious groups, irrespective of caste. The festivities are held 1300-1700 and again at night from around 2000. Elaborately bedecked elephants (each temple allowed up to 15) specially decorated with lamps and palm leaves, march to the Vadakkunnathan Temple carrying priests and deities to the accompaniment of extraordinary drumming. On the final day temple teams meet on the Tekkinkadu *maidan* for the drumming and *Kudumattam* competition; the festival terminates with a huge display of fireworks.

Aug/Sep Kamdassamkadavu Boat Races at *Onam*. Also performances of **Pulikali**, unique to Thrissur, when mimers dressed as tigers dance to drumbeats.

Guruvayur *p1024*

Punnathur Kotta

Feb/Mar Utsavam, 10 days of festivities start with an elephant race and continue with colourful elephant processions and performances of *Krishnanattom* dances. Details from Kerala tourist offices.

Nov-Dec 5-day **Ekadasi** with performances of *Krishnanattom*, a forerunner of *Kathakali* – an 8-day drama cycle.

Activities and tours

Along the River Nila *p1025*

Body and soul

Arya Vaidya Sala, Kottakal town, T0483-274 2216, www.aryavaidyasala.com. One of the biggest and best Ayurvedic centres in India, with a fully equipped hospital offering 4-week *panchkarma* treatments as well as on-site medicine factory and research department.

The Blue Yonder, 23-24 Sri Guru Nivas, Bengaluru, Karnataka, T080-4115 2218, www.theblueyonder.com. Award-winning responsible travel tour operator, focused on conserving local culture and traditions. Tours are carried out in a way that allows travellers to become fully immersed in the region's way of life, and travelling here can feel like being in an episode of the Arabian Nights, as the knowledgeable guides unfold local folk tales and fables. Flexible, individual itineraries can include homestays, cultural performances, monsoon rafting in self-built bamboo-and-inner-tube rafts, backwater *thoni* (country boat) cruises, legend and heritage trails and wildlife safaris. Unique in India, and heartily recommended.

Transport

Thrissur *p1024*

Bus There are yellow-top local buses available. For long distance, there are 3 bus stands. **KSRTC**, near railway station, T0487-242 1842, south-west of 'Round' including several to **Alappuzha** (3½ hrs), **Bengaluru** (**Bangalore**) (10 hrs), **Coimbatore** (3 hrs), **Guruvayur** (1 hr), **Kochi** (2 hrs), **Kozhikode**, **Chennai** (13 hrs), **Palakkad**, **Thiruvananthapuram** (7 hrs). **North (Priyadarshini)**, just north of 'Round', buses to **Cheruthuruthy**, **Ottapalam**, **Palakkad**. **Sakthan Thampuran**, 2 km south of 'Round', for frequent private buses to **Guruvayur**, **Kannur**, **Kozhikode**.

Train Enquiries, T0487-242 3150. All trains connecting Kochi with points north stop in Thrissur. **Ernakulam**: more than 20 trains a day; *Kannur Ernakulam Intercity Exp 16306*, 1843, 1¼ hrs. **Chennai (MC)**: *Chennai Mail 12624*, 2040, 10½ hrs. **Bengaluru** (**Bangalore**): *Bangalore Intercity Exp 12678*, 1020, 9½ hrs. **Mangalore**: *Parasuram Exp 16650*, 1240, 7½ hrs (via Kozhikode, 3 hrs).

Palakkad *p1026*

Bus KSRTC, buses run from the **Municipal Bus Stand**, T0491-252 7298, to **Coimbatore**, **Kozhikode**, **Mannarghat** (Silent Valley), **Pollachi**.

Train The main **Junction station**, T0491-255 5231, is 5 km northeast of town. Some passenger trains also stop at the more central **Town station**. **Coimbatore**: frequent trains all day, 1-1½ hrs, including *Bangalore Intercity Exp 12678*, 1145, continues to **Bengaluru** (8 hrs), and *Mangalore Chennai Exp 16108*, 1435, continues to **Chennai** (15 hrs). **Ernakulam (Kochi)**: many trains, including *Ernakulam Intercity Exp 12677*,

1420, 2½ hrs; all go via Thrissur, 1-2 hrs. **Mangalore**: *Chennai Mangalore Exp 16107*, 1300, 9 hrs, via Kozhikode, 4 hrs.

Directory

Thrissur *p1024*

Banks ATMs are everywhere, including at the railway station. **State Bank of India**, Town Hall Rd, Round East, near Paramekkavu Temple; **State Bank of Travancore** (upstairs), opposite. **Internet** **Sruthy**, north of temple ring. Good connections, Rs 30 per hr. **Medical services** **Amala Cancer Hospital**, Amalanagar (9 km, along the Guruvayur Rd), T0487-221 1950. Recommended for medicine, surgery.

Malabar coast

The Malabar region is the unsung jewel of Kerala: the combination of the state's political administration in the south plus the pious Muslim community and orthodoxy of the Hindu population have made it more resistant to tourist development than the more easy-going Catholic-influenced stretch south from Kochi. Any cohesion between north and south Kerala is political, not cultural: Malabar was under the Madras Presidency before Independence, lumped together with the Travancore south only in 1956. The atmosphere couldn't be more different. The coastal towns of Kozhikode (formerly Calicut), Thalassery and Kannur are strongholds of the Muslim Moplah community, whose long-standing trading links with the Middle East have bred a deep cultural affinity that's reflected in the lime-green houses lining the roads and the increasing number of women seen in purdah. At the same time, Malabar is one of the best places to see Kerala's Hindu religious and cultural traditions in their proper context: Theyyam (the ritual temple dance that spawned Kathakali*) and* Kalaripayattu *(the stunning martial art), are both practised here. Inland from Kozhikode, the glorious hilltop district of Wayanad experiences some of the heaviest levels of rainfall in the world, and its familiar stubble of tea plantations is interspersed with some of the most stunning and accessible rainforest in the state.* ▸▸ *For listings, see pages 1036-1039.*

Kozhikode (Calicut) → *See listings, page 1036-1039. Colour map 7, B2.*

Kozhikode is a major commercial centre for northern Kerala and the centre for Kerala's timber industry; it is also dependent on the petro-dollar, as testified by the scores of direct flights to the Gulf each day. Around 1.2 million Keralites work in the Gulf, generating revenue of about US$12 billion for Kerala. The city itself is engaged in mostly small-scale retail. Off the brash and crowded main boulevard, tiny lanes thread between high laterite walls with everything happening on the street. Remnants of the spice trade remain and the markets are great – Court Road is home to pepper, the black gold that lured Vasco, as well as copra and coconut oil. There are beautiful wooden mosques built like Hindu temples, and in nearby Beypore, where the Chaliyar river meets the Arabian Sea, you still have half a chance of watching the birth of an *uru* – the massive deep-sea hauler-sized wooden boats that have been built by Muslim Khalasi shipbuilders without many technological changes since Cheraman Perumal ordered one for a trip to Arabia in the sixth century.

Ins and outs → *Phone code: 0495. Population: 436,500.*

Getting there and around Karipur airport, 25 km south, has connections with the Middle East as well as several major Indian cities. The station and main bus stand are on opposite sides of the town centre, both within easy reach of several hotels. Autos are widely available and surprisingly cheap. ▸▸ *See Transport, page 1038.*

Tourist information Kerala Tourism ⓘ *Malabar Mansion hotel, SM Rd, T0495-272 1395*, has limited information about the town. The branch at the railway station hands out brochures on North Kerala and can help with hotel bookings.

Sights

The Sunni Muslim quarter of **Kuttichera**, behind the railway station to the west of town, holds several fascinating multi-tiered wooden mosques, set around a huge green pond to which flocks of white-capped elders range up in the late afternoon. Legend has it that a ghost within the pond seizes a human sacrifice each year, releasing the body only after three days. The mosques date from the 15th century and bear a puzzlingly close resemblance to Hindu temple structures. **Mishkal Masjid** is one of the oldest, and was named for the wealthy trader who built it, but also look for **Jami Masjid** and **Munchunthi Palli**. The latter has a 13th-century *vattezhuthu* (inscribed slab of stone) that proclaims the donation of the land to the mosque by a Zamorin. Women should cover their head, shoulders and limbs in this area of town.

Note the size of the houses around here, which are known to accommodate more than 150 family members each. The *puyappala* tradition (literally translates as 'fresh husband') means that each marrying daughter takes the husband back into her parents' home. One house is supposed to have 300 people living under the same roof: each building has an average of three kitchens. From here you can walk along Beach Road, where crumbling old buildings that were

Kozhikode (Calicut)

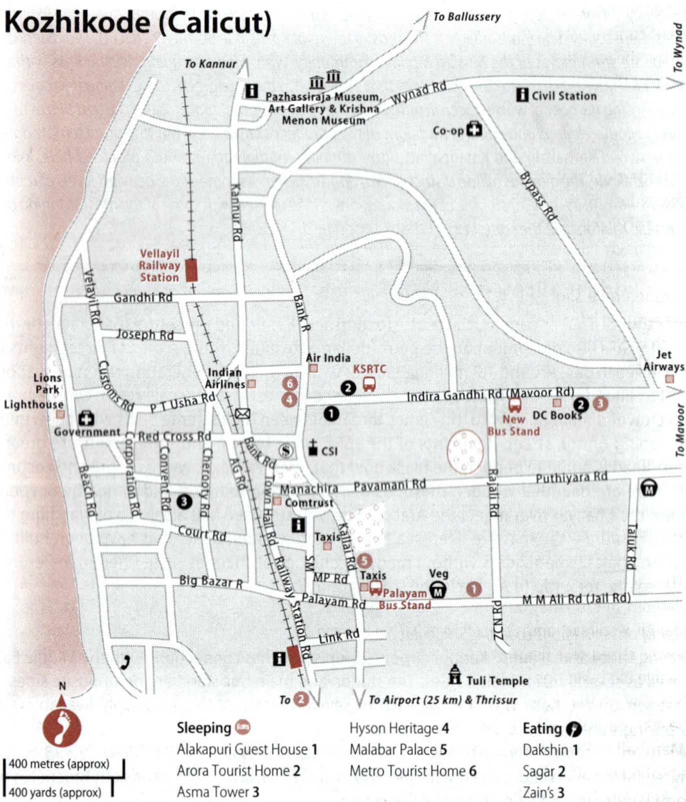

Sleeping
Alakapuri Guest House **1**
Arora Tourist Home **2**
Asma Tower **3**
Hyson Heritage **4**
Malabar Palace **5**
Metro Tourist Home **6**

Eating
Dakshin **1**
Sagar **2**
Zain's **3**

once trading centres are now being busily demolished. The beach itself is more of a town latrine than a place for swimming.

Pazhassiraja Museum ⓘ *5 km north of the centre on East Hill, Tue-Sun 0900-1630, Rs 10*, has copies of original murals plus bronzes, old coins and models of the some of the area's megalithic monuments. Next door are the **art gallery**, with an excellent collection of paintings by Indian artists as well as wood and ivory carvings, and the **Krishna Menon Museum** ⓘ *Mon, Wed only, 1000-1230, 1430-1700, free*, dedicated to the Keralite politician who became a leading left-wing figure in India's post-Independence Congress government.

Around Kozhikode

Kappad, 16 km north, and now the site of a poor, mainly Muslim fishing village, is where Vasco da Gama and his 170 sailors landed on 27th May 1498. There is an old plaque by the approach road to the beach commemorating the event. Although it is a pleasant spot, the sea is unsuitable for swimming since pollution from Kozhikode filters down this far and the beach itself is used as a toilet by the fishermen.

Beypore, half an hour south of Calicut, was once a significant port, but is now famous only for its boatyard, where families of Khalasis have used traditional methods to make *urus* (huge wooden vessels) for 1500 years. The wiry Khalasis craft the ships using memorized plans and ancient construction techniques, and until fairly recently would have been busy 365 days of the year, but the *uru's* popularity among the Arab clients who have kept the industry afloat is dwindling; locals fear that the boat under construction in 2009 may be the last to sail out of Beypore.

Mahé → *Colour map 7, B2.*

The borders of the 9 sq km that make up French Kerala are marked not by baguette bakeries or pavement cafés, but by shops screaming 'Foreign Liquor'. By night, the 35,000 residents of this outpost of Pondicherry disappear to make way for the truckers who rush through to stock up on half-price whiskies and brandies, taking advantage of the colony's special tax status. By day, however, Mahé is pretty enough: policemen wear French hats and the town is beautifully positioned on a slight hill overlooking the river. It was named after Mahé de Labourdonnais, who captured it for the French in 1725. Many people here still speak French and the very French **Church of St Theresa** celebrates its feast day on 14-15 October. The beaches to the south and north of town are dirty and are not safe for swimming due to undercurrents.

Thalassery (Tellicherry) → *For listings, see pages 1036-1039. Colour map 7, B2.* *Phone code: 0490.*

Like everywhere along the Malabar's increasingly gold coast, banks here have queues for gold loans where your branch manager doubles as a pawnbroker. Despite an obsession with wealth, at the wide, tree-covered street level you'll find a town that's friendly, brilliantly walkable and lined with 19th-century shops complete with original wooden cupboards and cobwebs. Author Herman Hesse's mother was born here.

Thalassery was set up by the British East India Company in 1683 to export pepper and cardamom. In 1708 they obtained permission to build a **fort** which, having survived a siege laid by Haidar Ali, is still standing today on a rocky promontory about 15 m above sea level. Its proud little gateway, raised on a flight of steps, is flanked by colourful mustachioed figures. There are some attractive old buildings. The Armenian church is rather shabby now but the Catholic church still thrives though the population is largely *Moplah* (Kerala Muslims). The **Odathil Mosque**, believed to be 400 years old, is in the traditional Kerala style with a gabled roof and copper sheeting.

Mambally's Royal Biscuit Factory ⓘ *near the Old Police Station, T0490-232 1207, 0900-2030*, established in 1880, claims to be where cake was first baked in Kerala. Nowadays you'll find jam rolls, ketchup, Nestlé milky bars and lime pickle along with the fresh bakes. The downstairs of the double-decker shops is crowded with hessian sacks full of cinnamon from China, cloves from Madagascar, raisins from Afghanistan and star anise from China and Vietnam. Some of the owners are third generation traders.

The **fish market** ⓘ *0600-1800*, is one of the liveliest in Kerala. Men with cleavers stand tall over barracudas and manta, while stacks of clams, mussels, shrimp and mackerel are constantly replenished with new loads. Fish are then sped along the state highway to reach markets in Cochin and Mangalore.

Thalassery is also a centre for training in gymnastics and circus acts, so street performers and acrobats are not uncommon; 90% of India's circus companies originate here. You can see martial arts in local *kalaris*: one of the best being the tricky-to-find *kalari* of **K Viswanathan Gurukkal** ⓘ *MKG Kalari Sangham, Kuzhippangad, PO Chirakkara, T0490-237110, call in advance.*

Muzhapilangad Beach, 8 km from Thalassery, is nicknamed 'Drive In Beach'. It is an unspoilt, beautifully picturesque 4-km-long stretch of golden sand edged by palm trees at the northern end. Amazingly empty most of the time, it earned its nickname from the local custom of ragging trucks and Ambassadors up and down its firm sands.

Kannur (Cannanore) → *For listings, see pages 1036-1039. Colour map 7, B2. Phone code: 0497.*

Standing on raised ground with cliffs at the sea face, this town boasts a coconut-fringed coastline with some attractive beaches. Weavers' co-operatives and *beedi* factories provide employment but this is also a good place to watch *Theyyam* dances. DTPC ⓘ *at the railway station, T0497-270 3121, www.dtpckannur.com.*

The centre of the Moplah community (a group of Arab descent), Kannur was also the capital of the North Kolathiri Rajas for several hundred years. **Fort St Angelo** ⓘ *0900-1800* was built out of laterite blocks by the Portuguese in 1505 and taken over by the British in 1790 as their most important military base in the south. The picturesque **Moplah town** is round the bay to the south of the fort. The attractive **Payyambalam Beach** is 2 km away.

Handloom weavers produce silk and cotton saris, shirts, *lungis* and soft furnishings sold through local cooperatives. **Kanhirode Weavers' Cooperative Society** ⓘ *Koodali Kannur, T0497-285 7259, 0900-1700, free*, was founded in 1952 on Gandhian principle, has a yearly turnover of Rs 150 million (US$3.7 million) and exports 95% of its pure handloom fabric to the UK for the Futon Bed Company. Spun cotton is shipped in from Coimbatore, and dyed in huge vats after which the cooperative's 450 staff are expected to feed bobbins through the high wooden looms fast enough to make 42 m within 3½ days for women, or three for men. While some weave, others feed the raw heaps of cotton from wire frames onto wheels to make thread – in the silk section they use bicycle wheels. The daily wage is Rs 100 (US$2.45), and apparently the co-op is having trouble recruiting more of the caste, who, as caste rules relax, are going for higher paid jobs elsewhere. A visit here is well worth the journey.

Bekal and Kasaragod → *For listings, see pages 1036-1039. Phone code: 04994.*

Bekal, 16 km south of Kasaragod, has an ancient **fort** on the sea, the largest and best preserved in Kerala, which gives superb views of the coastline. Originally built by the Kadamba kings, the fort passed under the control of Vijayanagar and of Tipu Sultan before being brought into the hands of the East India Company. Excavations have exposed some interesting structures. Just outside the fort is the **Sri Mukhyaprana Temple**. Bekal also has a beautiful and undeveloped beach that **Kerala Tourism** talks of turning into a major resort. En route to Bekal the road passes **Ezhimala**, with a beach and a hill famous for its Ayurvedic herbs.

Kasaragod is the northernmost town in Kerala. From the bus stand, the walk to the sea through a sprawling residential area – mainly Moplah – takes about 30 minutes. The beach is magnificent and deserted. You can walk a long way before scrambling back to the main road, crossing paddy fields, backwaters, and the Konkan railway line. For *Theyyam* and *Yakshagana* performances contact the **Kasaragod DTPC** ⓘ *Vidya Nagar, T04994-256450, www.dtpckasaragod.com.*

Not catering to the tourist rupee means that beaches on the Malabar coast are often strewn with litter. Also, swimming togs can cause alarming levels of attention, even outright hostility.

Wayanad → *For listings, see pages 1036-1039. Colour map 7, B2.*

The forest-shrouded shoulders of Chembra Peak stand guard over Wayanad ('land of paddy fields'), a beguiling highland district of spice farms, tea plantations, waterfalls and weird upwellings of volcanic rock, inland from Kozhikode on the picturesque road to Mysore. An easy weekend break from either city, Wayanad so far remains delightfully unspoiled, and its cool misty mornings make a refreshing contrast with the sultry coastal plains. It's also prime wildlife spotting territory: elephants patrol the woodlands of Muthanga and Tholpetty sanctuaries, while the dense *shola* forests around Vythiri are home to whistling thrushes, leaping frogs and giant squirrels. Many of the plantation bungalows have thrown open their doors as luxurious, atmospheric homestays, and the vogue for building treehouses makes this the best place in India if you want to wake up among the branches of a fig tree looking out over virgin forest.

Ins and outs → *Phone code: 04936.*

Getting there and around The main transport hubs are Kalpetta and Sultan Bathery, with buses from both to Kozhikode and Mysore, and from Sultan Bathery south to Ooty. Local buses connect these towns to the smaller villages, with jeeps and auto-rickshaws available for local transfers. However, hiring a car can save a lot of time and hassle.

Tourist information DTPC ⓘ *north Kalpetta, T04936-202134, www.dtpcwayanad.com*, is run by the efficient and knowledgeable Dinesh, who is a good source of information on trekking and wildlife.

Sights

The road from Kozhikode to Wayanad corkscrews steeply up the Western Ghats, topping out after 65 km at **Vythiri**, a popular but low-key weekend getaway set amid stunning forests, with kayaking and nature walks available at **Pookot Lake**. At Chundale (5 km from Vythiri) the road divides: the main route continues to busy **Kalpetta**, which offers plenty of hotels and banks but little in the way of charm, while the more appealing Ooty road leads east to **Meppadi**, the starting point for treks up wild and rugged **Chembra Peak** (2100 m) ⓘ *Forest Range Office, Kalpetta Rd, Meppadi, T04936-282001, trekking Rs 1000 per group including guide; call ahead to check the track is open*, on whose summit lies a heart-shaped lake. Beyond Meppadi the road continues through the rolling teascapes of Ripon Estate, then through cardamom, coffee, pepper tree and vanilla plantations to reach **Vaduvanchal** (18 km). Six kilometres south of here, **Meenmutty Falls** ⓘ *Rs 600 per group including guide (ask for Anoop, who speaks English and knows the forest intimately)*, are Wayanad's most spectacular waterfalls, tumbling almost 300 m in three stages. An adventurous forest track leads down to a pool at the base of the second fall; take your swimming things.

Sulthan Bathery (Sultan's Battery), the main town of western Wayanad, was formerly known as Ganapathivattom, or 'the fields of Ganapathi'. In the 18th century Tipu Sultan built a fort here, but not much of it remains. Some 12 km southwest of the town are the **Edakkal Caves**, a natural deep crevice set high on a granite hill on which engravings dating back to the Neolithic era have been discovered. Around 30 km to the east is **Muthanga Wildlife Sanctuary** ⓘ *0700-0900 and 1500-1830 (last entry 1700), Rs 100, Indians Rs 10, guide fee Rs 100 per group, jeep entry Rs 50; jeeps can be hired for Rs 300 per safari*, the least developed section of a giant reserve that also includes Karnataka's Bandipur and Tamil Nadu's Mudumalai National Parks. Jeep rides in the sanctuary, noted for its elephants, leave from the entrance gate.

Malabar coast listings

For Sleeping and Eating price codes and other relevant information, see Essentials pages 38-42.

Sleeping

Kozhikode *p1031, map p1032*

AL Harivihar Ayurvedic Heritage Home, Bilathikulam, T0495-276 5865, www.harivihar.com. In Calicut's pretty Brahminical suburbs, this immaculate former royal home is surrounded by lawns with giant mango and jackfruit trees and a beautiful green water tank where you can undertake pukka Ayurveda or study Indian philosophy, Sanskrit, vasthu and yoga in a small guesthouse setting run by conventional medics. You can also stay on a B&B basis, in one of 5 doubles and 3 singles. Gentle Sivananda yoga, Ayurveda from Coimbatore Arya Vaidya Pharmacy, no alcohol.

AL Tasara, Calicut–Beypore Rd, Beypore, T0495-241 4832, www.tasaraindia.com. A weaving centre amid a garden of mango and jackfruit trees. Rooms with fan and basic bath. Vasudevan, Balakrishnan and their sisters have been running textile workshops here since 1979, and guests come to take courses in weaving, block-printing, batik, silkscreen and natural dyeing. Price includes all meals, tuition and activities. Good discounts for monthly stays, reservations essential.

B Malabar Palace, GH Rd, Manuelsons' Junction, T0495-272 1511, www.malabarpalacecalicut.com. 52 a/c rooms, excellent a/c restaurant, bar, very helpful reception.

B-C Hotel Asma Tower, Mavoor Rd, T0495-272 3560, www.asmatower.com. 44 a/c and non a/c rooms in gleaming new tower. Inside, expect 2-tone mint green decor, frosty a/c system, perfumed air, muzak and TV and telephone in every room. Good value.

B-E Hyson Heritage, 114 Bank Rd, T0495-276 6423, www.hysonheritage.com. A breezy, efficient and well-maintained business hotel, with 89 spotless, smallish rooms with phone, cable TV, bath, 47 a/c, set around a large courtyard. Ayurvedic treatments available.

D-E Alakapuri Guest House, Moulana Mohammed Ali Rd, T0495-272 3451. 40 rooms set around a charming garden brimming with plants and trees and lotus pond. Simple, spacious, with old furniture, phone, tubs and TV. Dates from 1958, and easily Calicut's most characterful mid-range option. Bar 1000-2200, dining hall 0700-2200.

D-F Metro Tourist Home, Mavoor Rd Junction, T0495-276 6029. 42 pleasing rooms in bustling hotel, some with TV, a bit noisy, South Indian restaurant. Gloomy with grubby paintwork but clean sheets, big mirrors and good fans.

E-F Arora Tourist Home, Railway Station Rd, T0495-230 6889. Not as ship-shape as the outside and ground floor suggest, but the huge rooms here are clean enough if you just want to dump your bags after a train ride. Street noise dies down overnight, but mosquitoes don't rest.

F Railway Retiring Rooms. Very spacious, clean, good service.

Thalassery *p1033*

LL Ayisha Manzil, Court Rd, T0490-234 1590, www.ayishamanzil.uniquehomestays.com. A delightful mid-19th century, colonial-style heritage home overlooking the sea. 6 huge a/c rooms with carved teak and rosewood furniture, massive baths, lots of British and Malabari memorabilia, amazing fresh seafood and cookery courses, temple pond pool, superb panoramic views, excursions.

C-E Hotel Pranam, AVK Nair Rd, Narangapuram, T0490-222 0634. 14 cleanish rooms with bath – 4 with a/c, a little grubby. The a/c deluxe room has an extraordinary green carpeted sitting room attached.

D-G Paris Presidency, New Paris Complex, Logan's Rd, T0490-234 2666, www.parispresidency.com. 24 clean and comfortable rooms with baths, TV, phone, restaurant, wood furniture, bright white walls in busy shopping area. Multi-cuisine restaurant.

Kannur *p1034*

C Costa Malabari, near Adykadalaya Temple, 6 km south of town (by bus, ask to get out at Thazhe Chowwa), T0484-237 1761, www.costamalabari.com. An unpretentious guesthouse converted from a warehouse with 5 rooms off a main hall. The owners have authored a book on Kerala's festivals and have encyclopaedic knowledge of the local *Theyyam* scene. Difficult to get to and far from the centre, but there are 5 idyllic, wholly empty beaches within walking distance. Meals included.

C-D Royal Omars Thavakkara Kannur, very close to the railway station and colourful market area T0497-276 9091. Spanking new, with spacious standard non a/c doubles at bargain rates. 65 rooms, TV, credit cards.

C-E Mascot Beach Resort, near Baby Beach, Burnassery, 2 km from centre, T0497-270 8445, www.mascotresort.com. Good rooms in high-rise business hotel overlooking the sea, residents-only pool, located in the quiet cantonment area (Ayurvedic centre attached).

D-E Hotel Savoy, Beach Rd, T0497-276 0074. Bags of character in this super-clean, old-fashioned complex of bungalow cottages set around a lawn. A/c cottages are wonderfully spacious and cool. Bar attached.

Wayanad *p1035*

Wayanad is Kerala's treehouse capital, and has superb homestay options, but offers relatively little joy at the budget end. Cheaper places are generally restricted to Kalpetta and Sulthan Bathery.

LL-AL Vythiri Resort, 6 km up dirt road east of highway, T04936-255366, www.vythiriresort.com. Beautiful resort hidden beside a tumbling forest stream, with a choice of cute *paadi* rooms (low beds and secluded courtyards with outdoor shower), high- ceilinged cottages, or a pair of superb new treehouses in the branches of fig trees, one of which involves being hand-winched up and down. Leisure facilities include spa, pool (swimming and 8-ball), badminton and yoga, and there's a good outdoor restaurant (buffet meals included in price) where you can watch monkeys trying to make away with the leftovers.

AL-A Aranyakam, Valathur (south of Ripon off Meppadi–Vaduvanchal Rd), T04936-280261, T(0)9388-388203, www.aranyakam.com. Atmospheric homestay in Rajesh and Nima's 70-year-old bungalow, set amid a sea of coffee bushes and avocado trees. Huge rooms in the elegant main house come with raked bare-tile ceilings and balconies, or opt for the valley- facing treehouses where you can look out for deer and sloth bear while watching sunset over Chembra Peak. Nima serves genuine home-style Kerala food in the thatched, open sided dining room.

AL-B Green Gates, TB Rd, North Kalpetta, T04936-202001, www.greengateshotel.com. Modern if slightly scuffed and musty rooms with a/c, TV and hot showers, within walking distance of Kalpetta's shops. There's a pool and Ayurvedic spa, and a helpful travel desk arranges trips to caves, wildlife sanctuaries and tribal colonies of Wayanad.

A Edakkal Hermitage, on road before Edakkal Caves, T04936-260123, www.edakkal. com. A sustainable tourism initiative with 5 comfortable cottages and a sweet, simple treehouse, built in, around and on top of a series of huge boulders. Tree frogs inhabit the bamboo-fringed pond, and the sunset views over paddy fields and mountain ranges are magic. The highlight, though, is dinner, served in a natural grotto that's lit with hundreds of candles. Price includes meals.

A-F Haritagiri, Padmaprabha Rd, T04936-203145, www.hotelharitagiri.com. A modern building in the heart of Kalpetta just off the highway, some a/c rooms, clean and comfortable, restaurant 'reasonable', good value but rather noisy.

C-F Regency, on the main road in Sulthan Bathery, T04936-220512. A good range of neat and tidy rooms, better value at the cheaper end.

D-F PPS Tourist Home, just off highway at south end of Kalpetta, T04936-203431. Has a range of reasonable rooms, good cheap restaurant.

E-F Dwaraka, on the main road in Sulthan Bathery, T04936-220512. Far from sparkling, but offers the cheapest rooms in town.

G YMCA Camp, off the highway in Vythiri, T(0)9895-544609. There's just one simple room in this peaceful encampment, but it's big, cool and exceptional value.

Eating

Kozhikode *p1031, map p1032*

TT Malabar Palace (see Sleeping). International, a/c, excellent food and service.

T Dakshin, 17/43 Mavoor Rd, T0495-272 2648. 0630-2230. Dead cheap place for *dosa*, pizza, cutlet and curd rice (meals from Rs 15).

T Hotel Sagar, 5/3305 Mavoor Rd, T0495-272 5058. 0530 onwards. So popular they've launched their own hotel, and another restaurant (the original is already multistorey).

Sagar is famous for its biriyanis, and also does superb breakfasts of *dahl* and *parotta*. Upstairs is for families and a/c rooms; downstairs is the cheaper scrum of cattle class.

Zain's Hotel, Convent Cross Rd, T0495-276 1482. A simple place run by a Muslim husband and wife. Mussels, biriyanis for Rs 30 and fish curries for Rs 15.

Thalassery p1033

Ayisha Manzil, Court Rd, T0490-234 1590. Peerless homestay, serving food unlike you'll get anywhere outside a home. Phone for meals in advance.

Royal Visitors' Family Restaurant, Pranam Tourist Home, T0490-234 4292. 0630-2300. Grilled mussels, etc.

Kannur p1034

Chakara Drive in Restaurant, Cliff Exotel International, Payyabalam, T0497-271 2197. Specials are sizzlers plus spicy fried *kallumakais* mussels and Malabar biriyani.

Indian Coffee House, Fort Rd. For snacks.

Mascot Beach Resort's Restaurants, near Baby Beach, Burnasseri, T0497-270 8445, www.mascotresort.com. Some of the best top-end eating in town.

MVK Restaurant, SM Rd, T0497-276 7192. 1000-2200. A local institution which has been packed from its opening 50 years ago, thanks to its commitment to fresh, home- ground spice mixes for its biriyanis, their rice grains steeped in ghee. Serves beautiful, potent lime tea too.

Regency Snacks and Fast Food, opposite Sangeetha Theatre, SN Park Rd, T0497-276 8676. Popular café with locals.

Your Choice Restaurant, Fort Rd. Authentic Malabari food.

Entertainment

Kannur p1034

Theyyam dance

At **Parssinikadavu Temple**, 20 km north of Kannur, reached by bus. Performances (Dec-Mar) of ritual dance theatre at dawn (taxi essential) and often late afternoon to dusk. Pilgrims sometimes seek blessing from the principal dancer who may go into a trance after taking on the role of Mutthapan, a manifestation of Siva as Hunter.

Activities and tours

Kannur p1034

PVA Ayurvedic Multi Speciality Nursing Home, Onden Rd, T0497-276 0609, www.pvaayurvedic.com. The down-at-heel PVA provides training courses in Ayurveda as well as rejuvenation, purification packages and direct treatments for ailments like disc prolapse, psoriasis and obesity. The 3 doctors here are highly regarded.

Bekal p1034

Bekal Resorts Development Corporation, T0467-227 2007, www.bekal.org. The tourism-starved north wants a piece of the houseboat action. Happily it has amazingly pristine mangroves.

Wayanad p1035

The Blue Yonder (see page 1030) can arrange excellent, forest-savvy guides for trekking in the area.

Transport

Kozhikode p1031, map p1032

Air Airport, T0495-271 1314 (Domestic), T0495-271 0517 (International). Transport to town: pre-paid taxi Rs 300. **Indian Airlines**, Eroth Centre, Bank Rd, T0495-276 6243; airport, T0495-271 3700, flies to **Mumbai**, **Coimbatore**, **Goa**, **Chennai**, **Tiruchirapalli**. **Jet Airways**, Arayedathupalam, near BM Hospital, T0495-274 0052, to **Mumbai**.

International flights to **Abu Dhabi** (UAE), **Bahrain**, **Doha** (Qatar), **Jeddah** (Saudi Arabia), **Kuwait**, **Muscat** (Oman), **Ras-Al-Khaimah** (UAE) and **Sharjah** (UAE).

Bus KSRTC, T0495-272 2771, from bus stand Mavoor Rd (near Bank Rd junction) to **Bengaluru (Bangalore)**, **Thiruvanantha puram** (via Thrissur, Ernakulam, Alappuzha, Kollam), 0630-2200 (10 hrs), **Ooty** (see Wayanad, below). The **New Bus Stand**, T0495-272 2823, is further east on Mavoor Rd for private buses to the north including **Kannur**. Local buses operate from the **Palayam Bus Stand** on Kallai Rd, T0495-272 0397.

Train Enquiries, T0495-270 1234. Trains to **Chennai**, **Coimbatore**, **Ernakulam** (4½ hrs) via Shoranur and Thrissur, Goa, **Mangalore** (5 hrs), Mumbai, **Thiruvananthapuram** (9½-10 hrs).

Kannur *p1034*

Bus Enquiries: T0497-2707777. To **Kozhikode** (2½ hrs), **Mangalore** (4½ hrs), **Mercara** (6 hrs), **Mysore** (6 hrs).

Train Enquiries: T0497-2705555. To **Mangalore**: *Chennai Mangalore Mail 12601*, 0940, 2¾ hrs; *Parasuram Exp 16650*, 1740, 2½ hrs. **Palakkad**: *Kannur Yesvantpur Exp 16528*, 1745, 5 hrs, continues to **Bengaluru** (YPR), add 9 hrs; *Mangalore Chennai Mail 12602*, 1550, 5 hrs, continues to **Chennai**, add 10 hrs. **Ernakulam (Kochi)**: *Kannur Ernakulam Intercity Exp 16306*, 1430, 5½ hrs.

Wayanad *p1035*

Bus From **Kalpetta Bus Stand**, T04936-203040, to **Kozhikode**, 3½ hrs, via Vythiri; **Mysore** via Sulthan Bathery. From **Sulthan Bathery**, T04936-220217, to **Ambalavayal** (for Edakkal Caves), **Vaduvanchal** and **Ooty**.

Directory

Kozhikode *p1031, map p1032*

Banks ATMs on Kallai Rd and at station. Exchange at **SBI**, Bank Rd. Good rates, no commission, friendly. Also **Thomas Cook**. **Internet** Nidhi, near New Bus Stand or behind **Malabar Mansion**, SM St. Fast, Rs 30 per hr. **Sreeram Travels**, shop 3, opposite district hospital, T0495-253 4807. **Medical services Government Hospital**, T0495-236 5367. **Medical College Hospital**, T0495-235 6531. **Post** Near Mananchira Park.

Thalassery *p1033*

Banks Federal Bank, MM Rd, 1000-1530 (Sat 1000-1230 Sun closed) for speedy transactions. **Internet Telynet Internet Café**, Masjid Building near Municipal Office, MG Rd, T0490-234 4390, telynet@rediffmail.com. 0900-2100.

Kannur *p1034*

Internet Search World, near Railway Station, MA Rd, T0497-270 4735. Very fast connection, Rs 30 per hr.

Wayanad *p1035*

Banks ATMS in Kalpetta and Sulthan Bathery. For exchange, try **UAExchange**, on the main road in Kalpetta. **Internet** Several places in Kalpetta and Sulthan Bathery.

Lakshadweep, Minicoy and Amindivi Islands

→ Population: 60,600. 225-450 km west of Kerala. Area: 39,000 sq km. Total land area: 32 sq km. The islands, which make up the Lakshadweep ('100,000 islands'), have superb beaches and beautiful lagoons. There are, despite the name, only 11 inhabited and 11 uninhabited islands making up the group. Minicoy, the southernmost island, is 183 km from Kalpeni, its nearest neighbour. Geologically they are the northernmost extensions of the chain of coral islands that extends from the far south of the Maldives. The atolls are formed of belts of coral rocks almost surrounding semi-circular lagoons, with none more than 4 m above sea level. They are rich in guano, deposits of centuries of bird droppings. The wealth of coral formations (including black coral) attracts a variety of tropical fish – angel, clown, butterfly, surgeon, sweetlip, snappers and groupers. There are also manta and sting rays, harmless sharks and green and hawksbill turtles. At the right time of the year you may be able to watch them laying eggs, arriving on the beach at night, each laying 100-200 eggs in the holes they make in the sand.
►► For listings, see pages 1041-1042.

Ins and outs

You can only visit the islands on a package tour – individuals may not book independently. Lakshadweep Tourism's **Society for Promotion of Recreational Tourism and Sports (SPORTS)** and other tour operators organize package tours. Everyone needs a permit, for which you need to provide details of the place and date of birth, passport number, date and place of issue, expiry date and four photos; apply two months ahead. If you plan to dive, get a doctor's certificate. Foreign tourists may only visit Bangaram and Kadmat Islands; Indians can also visit Kadmat, Kavaratti, Kalpeni and Minicoy. Thinakkara and Cheriyam are being developed.
►► See Activities and tours, and Transport, page 1042.

The islands

Kavaratti, the administrative capital, is in the centre of the archipelago. The Ajjara and Jamath mosques have the best woodcarvings and the former has a particularly good ceiling carved out of driftwood; a well nearby is believed to have medicinal water. The aquarium with tropical fish and corals, the lake nearby and the tombs are the other sights. The woodcarving in the Ajjara is by superb local craftsmen and masons. Kayaks and windsurfers are available for rent, there's a dive centre, plus a bank and a few *dhabas* selling local food.

Some of the other islands in the group are **Andratti**, one of the largest which was first to be converted to Islam, and **Agatti**, which has Lakshadweep's only airport, a beautiful lagoon and a palm-shaded resort.

Barren, desolate and tiny, **Pitti Island** comprises a square reef and sand bank at its south end. It is a crucially important nesting place for terns and has now been listed as a wildlife sanctuary. Conservation groups are pressing for a ban on the planting of trees and the mining of coral, but the main risk to the birds is from local fishermen who collect shells and the terns' eggs for food. Nearby **Cheriam** and **Kalpeni** have suffered most from storm damage.

Bangaram is an uninhabited island where **CGH Earth** runs the **Bangaram Island Resort** (see Sleeping, below).

Kalpeni, with its group of three smaller uninhabited satellite islands, is surrounded by a lagoon rich in corals, which offers excellent snorkelling and diving. The raised coral banks on the southeast and eastern shores are remains of a violent storm in 1847; the Moidin Mosque to the south has walls made of coral. The islands are reputedly free from crime; the women dress in wrap-around *lungis* (sarongs), wearing heavy gold ornaments here without any fear. Villagers entertain tourists with traditional dances, *Kolkali* and *Parichakkali*, illustrating themes drawn from folk and religious legends and accompanied by music and singing.

Minicoy (Maliku), the southernmost and largest, is interesting because of its unique Maldivian character, having become a part of the archipelago more recently. Most people speak *Mahl* (similar to *Dhivehi*; the script is written right to left) and follow many of their customs. The ancient seafaring people have been sailing long distances for centuries and the consequential dominance by women may have led Marco Polo to call this a 'female island'. Each of the nine closely knit matrilineal communities lives in an *athir* (village) and is headed by a *Moopan*. The village houses are colourfully furnished with carved wooden furniture. Tuna fishing is a major activity and the island has a cannery and ice storage. The superb lagoon of the palm-fringed crescent-shaped island is enclosed by coral reefs. Good views from the top of the 50-m lighthouse built by the British. You can stay at the **Tourist Huts**.

The **Amindivi** group consists of the northern islands of **Chetlat**, **Bitra** (the smallest, heavily populated by birds, for a long time a rich source of birds' eggs), **Kiltan** where ships from Aden called en route to Colombo, **Kadmat** and the densely populated **Amini**, rich in coconut palms, which was occupied by the Portuguese. **Kadmat**, an inhabited island 9 km long and only 200 m wide, has a beach and lagoon to the east and west, ideal for swimming and diving. The **Tourist Huts** shaded by palms are away from the local village. The Water Sports Institute has experienced, qualified instructors. There are 10 executive and **Tourist Cottages** and a **Youth Hostel** with a dorm for 40.

Lakshadweep, Minicoy and Amindivi Islands listings

For Sleeping and Eating price codes and other relevant information, see Essentials pages 38-42.

Sleeping

Lakshadweep, Minicoy and Amindivi Islands *p1040*

Kavaratti and **Kadmat** have basic tourist cottages resembling local huts. Each hut has 1-2 bedrooms, mosquito nets, fans and attached baths; electricity is wind or diesel. Meals are served on the beach and are similar to Keralite cuisine, with plenty of coconut. Breakfast might be *iddlis* or *puris* with vegetables. Lunch and dinner might be rice and vegetable curry, *sambhar*, meat or fish curry. Vegetarian meals available on request. Alcohol is available on board ship and on **Bangaram Island** (tourists requested not to carry it though).

L Bangaram Island Resort, T0484-301 1711, www.cghearth.com. 26 standard huts on the beach with fan, fridge and bathrooms or 3 deluxe beach huts which sleep 4. Scuba-diving, snorkelling, deep-sea fishing, kayaking. International cuisine served.

Activites and tours

Lakshadweep, Minicoy and Amindivi Islands *p1040*

Tourism is still in its infancy and facilities on the islands are limited. Package tours (the only way to visit) are relatively expensive. Tours operate Oct-May; most are late Jan to mid-May. Schedules may change, so allow for extra days when booking onward travel.

CGH Earth, Kochi, see page 999. For the resort only, US$250-350 (for 2), US$500-700 for 4, US$70 extra person (discounts Apr-Sep).

Bangaram Kayaks, catamarans and sailing boats are free. For an extra charge each time: scuba diving for beginners and the experienced (equipment for hire); deep-sea big-game fishing 1 Oct-15 May – only minimal fishing equipment and boat crew; excursion to 3 neighbouring islands or snorkelling at shipwreck (for 8); glass-bottomed boat. Snorkelling in the lagoon can be disappointing due to poor visibility and dead corals. **Kadmat Island scuba-diving** US$800, 1-star CMAS Certificate US$30, Certified diver US$25 per dive; accompanying adult US$350, child (under 10) US$165. Travel by ship from Kochi (deck class) included; return air from Kochi or Goa to Agatti, US$300; return helicopter (Agatti-Kadmat), 15 mins, US$60, or local *pablo* boat.

SPORTS (Lakshadweep Tourism), Indira Gandhi Rd, Willingdon Island, Kochi T0484-266 8387, T0484-266 6789. 3 packages costing Rs 6000-10,000 per person (student discounts), including transport from Kochi. **Coral Reef**: 5 days to Kavaratti, Kalpeni and Minicoy Islands.

Kadmat Water Sports: 6 days (including 2-day sailing, stay in **Kadmat Cottages** or hostel). **Paradise Island Huts**: 6 days to Kavaratti.

Tour operators

For a list of authorized tour operators, see www.lakshadweeptourism.com/agents.html.

Watersports

Activities include windsurfing, scuba-diving (**Poseidon Neptune School**), parasailing, waterskiing and snorkelling. Deep-sea fishing (barracuda, sailfish, yellow-fin, travelly) is possible on local boats with crew; serious anglers should bring their own equipment; no diving or deep-sea fishing Apr-Sep.

Transport

Lakshadweep, Minicoy and Amindivi Islands

p1040

Air Agatti has a basic airport. **Indian Airlines** and **Kingfisher** fly to/from **Kochi**, daily except Tue and Sun.

Ferry *MV Tipu Sultan* sails from **Kochi**. 26 passengers in 1st and executive class have 2- and 4-berth a/c cabins with washbasins, shared toilets, Rs 5000; 120 passengers in 2nd class in reclining seats in a/c halls, Rs 3500. Ship anchors 30-45 mins away from each island; passengers are ferried from there. Total travel time from Kochi can take up to 30 hrs.

Inter-island transfers are by helicopter (when available) during monsoons, 15 May-15 Sep (return US$60), or by *pablo* boats for 8.

Directory

Lakshadweep, Minicoy and Amindivi Islands

p1040

Agatti has a medical centre; emergencies on the islands have helicopter back-up.

Karnataka

Contents

Footprint features

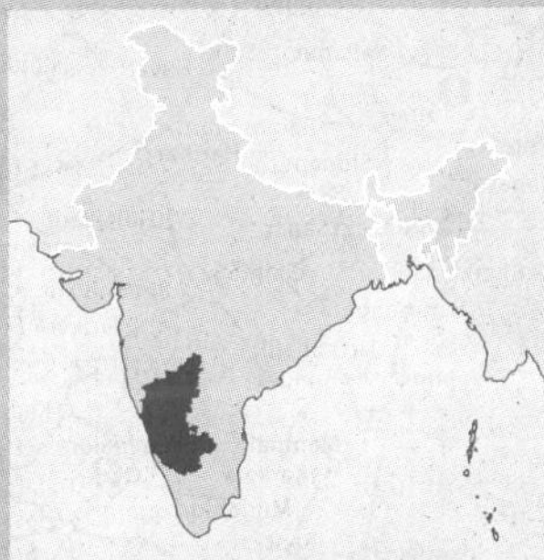

At a glance

Getting around The Konkan railway, local buses or chartered taxi, especially for the more remote ruins around the Deccan.

Time required A weekend in Bangalore, 2 days in Mysore, minimum 4 days to see Hampi and its environs justice, 2-3 days for the Western Plateau temples, a week to walk in Coorg.

Weather Hot all year round.

When not to go It's oppressively hot in Apr and May.

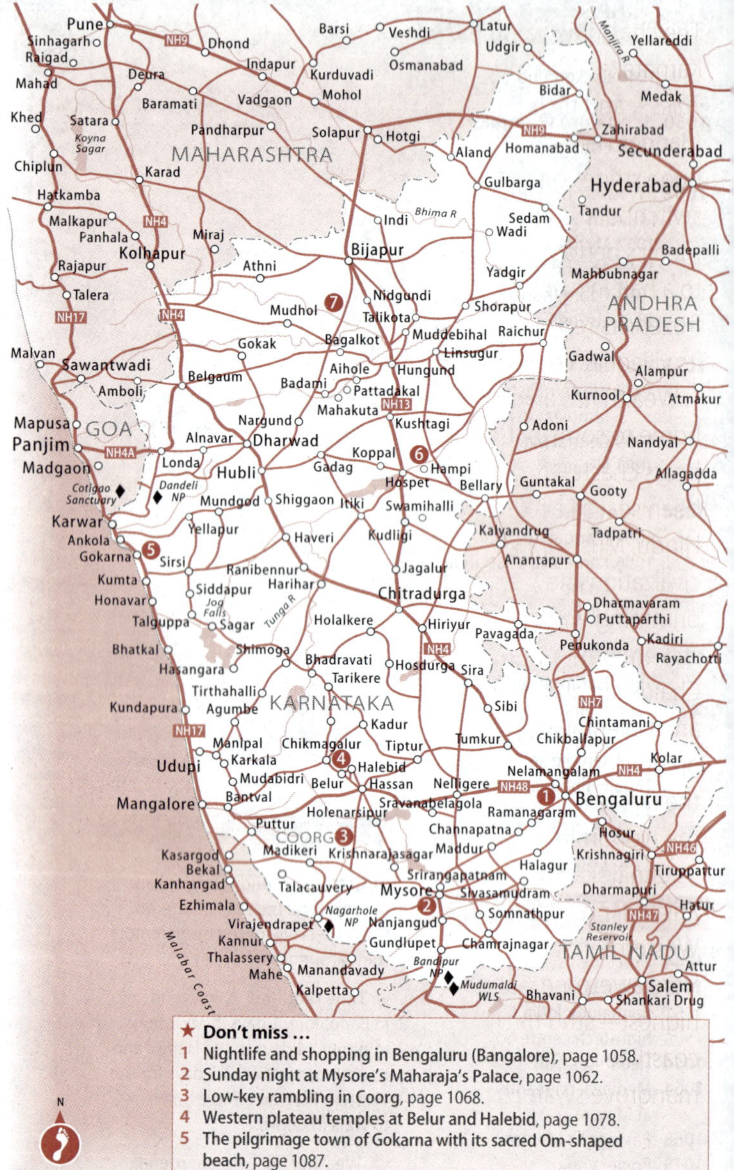

★ Don't miss …

1. Nightlife and shopping in Bengaluru (Bangalore), page 1058.
2. Sunday night at Mysore's Maharaja's Palace, page 1062.
3. Low-key rambling in Coorg, page 1068.
4. Western plateau temples at Belur and Halebid, page 1078.
5. The pilgrimage town of Gokarna with its sacred Om-shaped beach, page 1087.
6. The ancient Vijayanagar empire of Hampi, page 1093.
7. Bijapur to Badami, pages 1096-1101.

The chasm between the values, outlook and prosperity of rural Karnataka – the source matter for novelist R K Narayan's *Malgudi Tales* – and the cosmopolitan high-tech metropolis of Bengaluru (Bangalore), is at times shockingly wide. While the city takes huge strides on the global software and biotechnology stages, switchboards hum with outsourced call centre traffic, world-class medics perform miracle heart and brain surgeries, and roads grind to a halt in rush-hour traffic, much of Karnataka remains as if frozen: its red and black earth rocky and covered with scrub, its villagers' concerns wholly agrarian.

Wealth has always come and gone here: the state's interior, home to some of the earliest settlements in peninsular India, bears chastening witness to the ravages of time. The state has been seat to a roll-call of dynasties, both alien and homegrown – Hindu, Muslim, Jain, British – whose once-great cities and civilizations now stand largely in dusty ruins. As a result, it is brimming with architectural and archaeological riches: the still-emerging Vijayanagara kingdom capital of Hampi in the north; Chalukyan and Hoysala temples throughout Pattadakal, Belur and Halebid; the Islamic palaces of Tipu Sultan in the south; the onion-dome tombs of his Turkish and Persian antecedents in the far northeast; the British boulevards of Bengaluru; and the wondrous palaces of the Hindu maharajas at Mysore.

Karnataka's three great rivers, the Kaveri, Tungabhadra and Krishna, originate in the beautiful, forested hill country of the Western Ghats, the state's natural and hugely biodiverse border. Here awesome waterfalls – Jog Falls being one of the world's highest – stud the Malnad's wildlife parks. The little-visited coastline is emerald lush with river estuaries feeding unique mangrove swamps that rival Kerala's famous backwaters.

Background → *Population: 52.7 million. Area: 192,000 sq km.*

The land

Geography The Western Ghats, called the Malnad or hill country, have beautiful forests with waterfalls and wildlife parks. To the east stretches the Mysore Plateau. Parts of northern Karnataka are barren, rocky and covered with scrub, but the state in other places is richly fertile (particularly around the 'sugar bowl' region of Mandya) and it has a lush coastline. From Coondapur to Karwar, the estuaries of the short fast-running rivers flowing west from the ghats still have mangroves, some in uniquely good condition, although commercial exploitation seriously threatens their survival.

Climate The whole of the west coast is extremely wet from June to September, with 1500 mm falling in June and July alone. However, immediately to the east of the Western Ghats rainfall decreases dramatically. Temperatures rise to the low 30°C between February and June but fall slightly during and after the monsoon. On the plateaux of the south, especially around Bengaluru (Bangalore) and Mysore, temperatures are moderated somewhat by the altitude (generally around 1000 m), and nights are pleasantly cool most of the year. The central and northern parts of the state get considerably hotter in April and May, often exceeding 40°C for days at a time.

History

The region between the Tungabhadra and the Krishna rivers was home to some of the earliest settlements in peninsular India, dating back more than 500,000 years. By the Middle Stone Age there was already a regional division appearing between the black cotton soil area of the north and the granite-quartzite plateau of the south. In the north hunters used pebbles of jasper taken from riverbeds while quartz tools were developed to the south. The first agricultural communities of the peninsula have been identified from what is now northern Karnataka. Radiocarbon dating puts the earliest of these settlements at about 3000 BC; millets and gram were already widely grown by the first millennium BC. They have remained staple crops ever since.

Karnataka has borne witness to an alarming array of dynasties, and their ruins. Legend has it that India's first emperor, Chandragupta Maurya, became a Jain and renounced all worldly possessions, retiring to Sravanabelagola to meditate. The Western Gangas, from the third to 11th centuries, and the Banas, from fourth to ninth centuries, controlled large parts of the region. The Chalukyas of central Karnataka took some of the lands between the Tungabhadra and Krishna rivers in the sixth century and built great temples in Badami. They and the Rashtrakutas tried to unite the plateau and the coastal areas while there were Tamil incursions in the south and east. The break-up of the Tamil Chola Empire created a power vacuum in their former fiefdoms. In Karnataka the Hoysalas (11th-14th centuries) seized their chance, and left magnificent temples at their old capitals at Belur, Halebid and Somnathpur, exquisite symbols of their power and their religious authority. Then came the Sangama and Tuluva kings of the Vijayanagar Empire, which reached its peak in the mid-16th century with Hampi as its capital.

Karnataka was repeatedly in the frontline in the power struggle between Hindu and Muslim rulers. **Muhammad bin Tughlaq** attacked northern Karnataka in the 13th century, and during the Vijayanagar period the **Muslim sultanates** to the north continued to extend their influence. The Bidar period (1422-1526) of Bahmani rule was marked by wars with Gujarat and Malwa, continued campaigns against Vijayanagar, and expeditions against Orissa. **Mahmud Gawan**, the Wazir of the Bahmani sultanate, seized Karnataka between 1466 and 1481, and also took Goa, formerly guarded by Vijayanagar kings. By 1530 the kingdom had split into five independent sultanates. At times they came together to defend common interests, and in 1565 they co-operated to oust the Vijayanagar Raja. But two of the sultanates, Bijapur and Golconda, gathered the lion's share of the spoils until the Mughals and British supplanted them.

South Karnataka saw a different succession of powers. While the Mughals were preoccupied fighting off the Marathas, the Hindu **Wodeyar** rulers of Mysore took Srirangapatnam and then Bengaluru (Bangalore). They lost control to **Haidar Ali** in 1761, the opportunist commander-in-chief who joined forces with the French to extend his control west to make Srirangapatnam his capital. The fierce Mysore Wars followed and with Haidar Ali's and then his son Tipu Sultan's death, the **British** restored the Wodeyars' rule in 1799. The Hindu royal family was still administering Mysore up to the reorganization of the states in the 1950s when the maharaja was appointed state governor.

Kannadigas argue that the unanimous benevolence of successive waves of rulers has bred in them a deep-rooted tolerance; the communal tensions so endemic in post-partition India are near unheard of here and people of all faiths charge into celebration of each other's festive days with shared gusto.

Culture

A fault line runs through mainstream Kannada culture and politics, cleaving society into the northern Karantaka peasant caste, the **Lingayats** and the **Vokkaligas**, of the south. Lingayats follow the egalitarian and keen educationalist 12th-century saint Basavanna. The name Vokkaligas comes from 'okkalu', meaning to thresh, and these people are mostly farmers. The Kodavas from the southwest are a culture apart, physically fair and tall, worshippers of the goddess Cauvery and Lord Iguthappa. Karnataka has its share of tribal people. The nomadic Lambanis in the north and west are among several tribal peoples in the hill regions. The Siddis are of African origin, Navayats Arab. The state has a significant Muslim minority of nearly seven million, and Mangalore particularly has a notable Catholic community.

Cuisine The Kannada temple town of Udupi has spawned its own fabled brand of pure vegetarian meal such as *iddli* and *dosa* – traditionally served on a plantain leaf or stainless steel plate – variations of which you can taste all over the state and South India.

Language Most people speak the Dravidian language *Kannada* (Kanarese), although this has fused to form Indo-Aryan dialects in the north. Kannada has the second oldest Dravidian literary tradition. The earliest known classic is the ninth-century *Kavirajamarga*.

Art and architecture Karnataka's role as a border territory was illustrated in the magnificent architecture of the Chalukyan Dynasty from AD 450 to 650. Here, notably in Aihole, were the first stirrings of *Brahman* temple design. Relics show the parallel development of Dravidian and North Indian temple architecture: in Pattadakal alone there are four temples built on North Indian *Nagari* principles and six built on South Indian *Dravida* lines. Belur, Halebid and Somnathpur's star-shaped bases, bell-towered shrines and exquisite carvings represent a distinctive combination of both traditions. The Vijayanagara kings advanced temple architecture to blend in with the rocky, boulder-ridden landscape at Hampi. Bijapur has some of the finest Muslim monuments on the Deccan from the austere style of the Turkish rulers to the refinement in some of the pavilions and the world's second largest dome at the Gol Gumbaz.

Dance, drama and music Open-air folk theatre or *Bayalata* grew from religious ritual and is performed in honour of the local deity. Actors improvise their plays on an informal stage. Performances usually start at night and often last into the early hours. The famous *Yakshagana* or *Parijata* tends to have just one narrator while other forms have four or five, assisted by a jester. The plots of the *Dasarata* which enacts several stories and *Sannata* which elaborates one theme, are drawn from mythology but sometimes highlight real- life incidents. The *Doddata* is less refined than the *Yakshagana* but they have much in common, beginning with a prayer to the god Ganesh, using verse, and drawing from the stories of the epics *Ramayana* and *Mahabharata*. The costumes are elaborate with fantastic stage effects, loud noises and war cries and vigorous dances.

Indian tiger

The economic transformation of India has been one of the greatest business stories of modern times. Now acknowledged as major player in the fields of information technology and pharmaceuticals, in the past five years the economy has been growing at close to 9% a year, largely thanks to an investment boom, and as stifling regulations have been lifted entrepreneurship has flourished. Mukesh Ambani, director of petrochemicals and retail giant Reliance Industries, is currently rated by Forbes as the seventh richest man in the world, and Lakshmi Mittal, head of the world's biggest steel company Arcelor Mittal, is only one place behind him.

So powerful has the economy become that, 60 years after independence, the colonized have turned colonizers. The global ambitions of 'India Inc' have become evident in a series of high-profile buyouts, none more symbolic than the Tata Corporation's US$13.2 billion acquisition of Anglo-Dutch steel giant Corus, a company whose ancestry can be traced to many of the companies that once symbolized Britain's industrial pre-eminence. Chairman Ratan Tata proudly boasted that the takeover was "the first step in showing that Indian industry can step outside its shores into an international market place as a global player". Tata has also snapped up such emblems of Englishness as Jaguar and Tetley Tea and, not content with taking over the world, has set itself to cultivating the ambitions of India's rapidly growing middle class. The Nano car, launched in 2009 with a price tag of less than US$1000, together with the Shubh Griha project in suburban Mumbai which sells new apartments for just US$10,000, has made the house-and-car lifestyle a realistic aspiration for millions of Indians.

How big a dent the global recession might put in India's plans for growth remains to be seen. The IT industry, dependent on outsourcing dollars from the hard-hit US market, has suffered a profit slowdown and been forced to send workers on year-long sabbaticals. However, with most of the major banks being publicly owned, the country has been shielded from the worst excesses of the credit crunch, and the relatively low importance of exports – 22% of the economy, compared to China's 37% – puts India in a good position to survive comparatively unscathed.

A bigger issue for India is how to reduce poverty. Arundhati Roy, a notorious fly in the ointment of Indian triumphalism, wrote (in the days before Tata takeovers) that India, having nowhere else to colonize, has made its fortune by colonizing itself. Rich Indians, disconnected from the reality of where their money comes from, pay little regard to the plight of eight-year-old workers hammering fist-sized lumps of rock into powder in Karnataka's iron ore mines, or the villagers whose lands are repossessed so companies can build cars on the cheap. While the media trumpets the nation's new-found power to put men into space, Infosys executives into mansions and millions of rupees into cricketers' pockets, government reports suggest that 75% of people in India survive on less than Rs 20 per day. As much as 40% of the country still exists below the official poverty line, and statistics on child malnourishment (India has the third highest rate in the world, after Timor-L'Este and Yemen), infant mortality (2.1 million children die every year) and corruption (bribes worth Rs 9 billion a year are hoovered up from below-poverty-line households for basic public services such as policing and schooling) show that for all its progress, the economy still has an awful lot of growing up to do.

Modern Karnataka

Government The 19 districts are grouped into four divisions – Bengaluru (Bangalore), Mysore, Belgaum and Gulbarga. Caste rivalry between Vokkaligas and Lingayats remains a powerful factor and faction fighting within parties is a recurrent theme. In 2004, Congress suffered a swingeing backlash against its liberal economic policies that had fuelled Bengaluru's rise to become the darling of the IT and biotechnology industries. The BJP became the largest single party in the Assembly with 79 seats, the Congress's 65 and the Janata Dal's 58, producing a coalition government, first with Dharam Singh of the BJP as chief minister, followed by HD Kumaraswamy of the Janata Dal (Secular). The apparent opportunism of a party with 'secular' in its title joining forces with the avowedly Hindu nationalist BJP was underlined when the coalition splintered in November 2007, but despite the JD(S) realigning with the Congress party, caste- and religion-based voting saw the BJP retain power with a solid majority in the 2009 Lok Sabha elections.

Economy Karnataka is one of India's most rapidly modernizing states, and an undisputed leader in IT skills, biotech and industrial activity. Based on its early development of aeronautics and high precision machine tools, Bengaluru has become a world centre for the computer industry, receiving a much-quoted seal of approval from Bill Gates. Outside the cities agriculture and forestry remain important. Demand for irrigation is growing rapidly against a backdrop of frequent droughts. The water issue is the cause of escalating tension with neighbouring Tamil Nadu, a conflict that plays out at the top political level, with a verdict reached by the Indian Supreme Court to allocate resources in 2007, and as a trigger for mass demonstrations, rallies have led to violent clashes against Tamilian interests, property and people within Karnataka's borders.

Karnataka is the origin of 70% of India's raw silk, 70% of its flower exports and is also by far India's largest coffee producer. The first beans were supposed to have been smuggled back to the subcontinent by a Haj pilgrim, Baba Budan, in the 17th century.

Bengaluru (Bangalore)

→ *Colour map 7, A4. Phone code: 080. Population: 6.2 million.*

IT capital Bengaluru (Bangalore), the subcontinent's fastest-growing city, is the poster boy of India's economic ascendance. Its buoyant economy has cost the so-called 'garden city' and 'pensioner's paradise' its famously cool climate and sedate pace, while its wealthy retirees are long gone. In their place are streets throttled with gridlocked traffic, a cosmopolitan café culture, a lively music scene and dynamic, liberal-minded people, which combine to make the city a vibrant and forward- thinking metropolis, one whose view of the world is as much attuned to San Francisco as to the red baked earth of the surrounding state of Karnataka.

And there's more to Bengaluru than Wipro, Infosys and call centres: Bengaluru rivals Kancheepuram for silk; it's the site of India's aeronautical defence industry's headquarters; it boasts a mammoth monolithic Nandi Bull temple; has boulevards shaded by rain and flame trees and the great green lungs of Lal Bagh Gardens and Cubbon Park; and holds a number of fine administrative buildings left over from the British. For all its outward-looking globalism, if you walk around the jumbles of rope and silk shops, tailors, temples and mosques in the ramshackle and unruly bazars of Gandhi Nagar, Sivaji Nagar, Chickpet and City Market, you can almost forget the computer chip had ever been invented. ▸▸ *For listings, see pages 1055-1061.*

Ins and outs

Getting there The new **Bengaluru International Airport** (BLR), 25 km north of the city in Devanahalli, has direct flights from London, Frankfurt, the Middle and Far East, Sri Lanka and Nepal, as well as all major Indian cities. There are metered taxis (generally better value than the overpriced prepaid taxi booths in the Arrivals terminal), and fast airport buses serve a range of destinations in the city including **Kempegowda Bus Station** (the main long-distance bus station, also handy for the City railway station and the seedy 'Majestic' area, home to many cheap hotels) and the MG Road/Brigade Road area, where more upscale hotels are located. Trains arrive at one of three main stations: **City**, in Gandhi Nagar next to the main bus stand; **Cantonment**, a few kilometres to the northwest, most convenient for MG Road; and **Yeswantpur** in the inner northern suburbs. Virtually all long-distance buses, both state-run and private, will leave you at or near the bus stand. ▸▸ *See Transport, page 1060.*

Getting around Bengaluru is very spread out and you need transport to get around. City buses run a frequent and inexpensive service throughout the city. Taxis and auto-rickshaws are available for trips around town, and should readily use their meters; they charge 50% extra after 2200. There are prepaid rickshaw booths at each of the stations. If you're planning on covering a lot of sights in a day it can work out cheaper to hire a car and driver. Despite a subway under construction and flyovers already in place, infrastructure has failed to keep pace with the transport explosion. City traffic is so bad that weekdays are best avoided, and even weekends can see the streets descend into something approaching gridlock.

Tourist information **Karnataka State Tourism Development Corporation** (KSTDC) ⓘ *head office, No 49, Khanija Bhavan, West Entrance, Race Course Rd, T080-2235 2901, www.karnatakaholidays.net, Mon-Sat 1000-1730, closed every 2nd Sat; booking counter for tours and hotels at Badami House, NR Sq, T080-2227 5869*, has counters at the airport and City railway station. **India Tourism** ⓘ *KSFC Building, 48 Church St, T080-2558 5417; Mon-Fri 0930-1800, Sat 0900-1300*, is very helpful. For events, pick up the fortnightly *Time Out* magazine (www.timeoutbengaluru.net), and the bimonthly *City Info* (www.explocity.com). An excellent online resource is http://bangalore.burrp.com/events.

History

The 16th-century Magadi chieftain Kempe Gowda built a mud fort and four watchtowers in 1537 and named it Bengalaru (you can see his statue in front of the City Corporation buildings). Muslim king Haidar Ali strengthened those fortifications before his death at the hands of the British,

Bengaluru: India's high-tech centre

The contemporary high-tech and biotech blossoming in Bengaluru (Bangalore) has deep roots: the city was consciously developed into India's research capital after Independence, with public sector units in electronics, aeronautical industry and telecoms established in the city, and educational institutions to match. National programmes of space research and aircraft design continue to be concentrated here, and it is home to the Indian Institute of Science.

leaving his son Tipu Sultan to pick up where he left off. When the British gained control after 1799 they installed the Wodeyar of Mysore as the ruler and the rajas developed it into a major city. In 1831 the British took over the administration for a period of 50 years, making it a spacious garrison town, planting impressive avenues and creating parks, building comfortable bungalows surrounded by beautiful lawns with tennis courts, as well as churches and museums.

In 2006 Bangalore became the fourth metro, after Mumbai (Bombay), Kolkata (Calcutta) and Chennai (Madras), to ditch its anglicized moniker. It reverted to Bengaluru, a name possibly derived from the phrase 'benda kalu', or 'boiling bean' in reference to the meal fed to a lost Prince Hoysala by an old peasant woman who took him in.

Sights

The 1200 ha of **Cubbon Park** in the Cantonment area was named after the 19th-century British representative in Bangalore. The leafy grounds with bandstand, fountains and statues are also home to the Greco-Colonial High Court, State Library and museums, now overshadowed by the post-Independence granite of Vidhana Soudha, the state's legislature and secretariat buildings across the street.

Government Museum ⓘ *Kasturba Rd, Cubbon Park, T080-2286 4563, Tue-Sun 1000- 1700, Rs 4*, is idiosyncratic and slightly dog eared; opened in 1886, it is one of the oldest in the country. There are 18 galleries: downstairs teems with sculptures, huge-breasted Durga and a 12th-century figure of Ganesh from Halebid sit alongside intricate relief carvings of Rama giving his ring to Hanuman, and there are Buddhas from as far afield as Bihar. An upstairs gallery holds beautiful miniatures in both Mysore and Deccan styles, including a painting of Krishnaraj Wodeyar looking wonderfully surly. There are also Neolithic finds from the Chandravalli excavations, and from the Indus Valley, especially Mohenjo Daro antiquities. In the same complex, the **K Venkatappa Art Gallery** ⓘ *Kasturba Rd, Cubbon Park, T080-2286 4483, Tue-Sun 1000-1700, Rs 4*, shows a small cross-section of work by the late painter (born 1887). His paintings of the southern hill stations give an insight into the Indian fetishization of all things pastoral, woody and above all cold. There is also the story and blueprints of his truncated design for the Amba Vilas Durbar Hall in Mysore and miniatures by revered painter Abanindranath Tajore (1871-1951), alongside a second portrait of Krishnaraj Wodeyar.

Visveswaraya Industrial and Technological Museum ⓘ *Kasturba Rd, next to the Government Museum, Tue-Sun 1000-1800, Rs 15*, will please engineering enthusiasts, especially the basement, which includes a 1917 steam wagon and India's oldest compact aircraft. Others might be left cold by exhibits on the 'hydrostatic paradox' or 'the invention of the hook and eye and zip fastener technology'. Upstairs is a wing devoted to educating the inhabitants of Bengaluru on genetic engineering. You might find the debate a little one-sided: "agricultural biotechnology is a process … for the benefit of mankind," it states in capital letters. A small corner (next to the placard thanking AstraZeneca, Novo Nordisk Education Foundation, Novozymes and Glaxo-SmithKline), is dubbed 'Concerns', but you can see how cloning and genetically strengthened 'golden' rice might seem more attractive when put in the context of the growling Indian belly.

Bengaluru

Sleeping

Ajantha **1**
Brindavan **17**
Green Path Apartments **3**
Ivory Tower **18**
Kamat Yatrinivas **2**
Mahaveer **4**
New Central Lodge **5**
Oberoi **6**
Park **10**
Railway Retiring Rooms **7**
Sri Lakshmi Comforts **16**
St Mark's **8**
Taj West End **9**
Vellara **11**
Villa Pottipati **12**
Vybhab **13**
Woodlands **14**
YMCA Guest House **15**

N

600 metres
600 yards

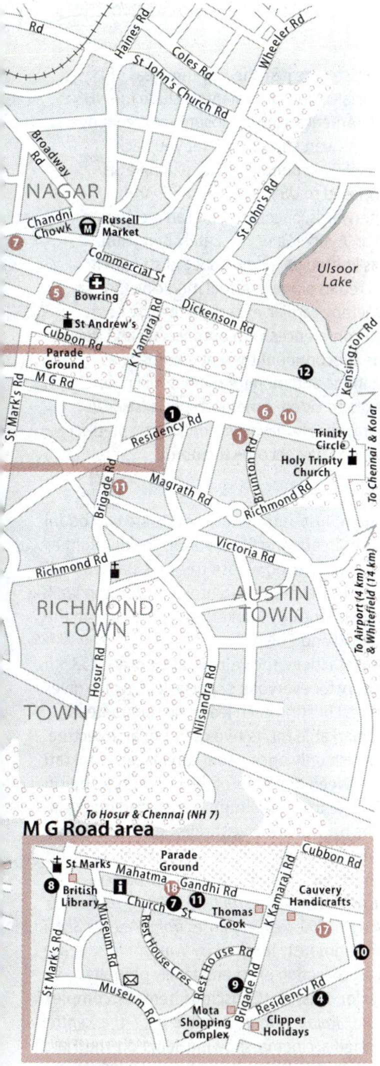

Eating
Amaravathi **1**
Benjarong **12**
Chalukya **2**
Coconut Grove **7**
Halli Mane **3**
Indian Coffee House **11**
Karavalli **4**
Koshy's **8**
MTR **5**
Nilgiri's Upper Crust **9**
Palmgrove **10**
Sukh Sagar **6**

To the southwest lies the summer palace that Tipu Sultan, the perennial thorn in the side of the British, boasted was "the envy of heaven". **Tipu's Summer Palace** ⓘ *City Fort, 0800-1730, foreigners Rs 100, Indians Rs , video camera Rs 25*, was begun by his father Haidar Ali and was completed by Tipu in 1789. Based on the Daria Daulat Bagh in Srirangapatnam, the understated two-storey structure is largely made of teak with walls and ceilings painted in brilliant colours with beautiful carvings. A room downstairs is given over to documenting Haidar and Tipu's reigns and struggles against the British.

Lal Bagh Gardens ⓘ *southeast of the Summer Palace, 0600-1900, Rs 10*, were laid out across 97 ha by Haidar Ali in 1760 and are second only to Kolkatta's in size. Tipu added a wealth of plants and trees from many countries (there are over 1800 species of tropical, subtropical and medicinal plants) and the British brought a bandstand. Sadly, the Indian affection for botanical beauty means that the rose gardens are kept behind bars. At dusk, Lal Bagh is popular with businessmen speed-walking off their paunches, and courting couples and newlyweds who sit on the banks of the lotus pond eating ice cream. The rocky knoll around the Kempe Gowda tower has great city views, and is popular at sunset. There are fortnightly Sunday evening performances of Kannada folk theatre, song and dance; go on for supper at **MTR** (see Eating, page 1057) for a pukka Bengaluru evening. The **Glass House**, with echoes of London's Crystal Palace and Kew Gardens, holds flower shows in January and August to mark Republic and Independence days.

Further south, the hefty **Nandi Bull at Bull Temple** ⓘ *Bull Temple Rd, Basavanagudi, 0600-1300, 1600-2100*, was carved at the behest of Kempe Gowda, making it one of the city's oldest temples. The monolithic Nandi was believed to be growing unstoppably until a trident was slammed into his forehead: he now towers nearly 5 m high and is 6 m in length. His huge proportions, draped imperiously in jasmine garlands, are made of grey granite polished with a mixture of groundnut oil and charcoal. Under his hooves you can make out the *veena* or south Indian

Health tourism

For decades, Western travel to India was synonymous with emaciated hippies, and backpackers' conversations invariably veered towards the scatological as everyone, at some stage, was sure to catch the dread 'Delhi belly'. It's a sign of the times that, although the British National Health Service failed to award India its whole back-up project in 2004, the country has become a very real alternative to private health care, representing huge cost reductions on surgery.

The centrepiece for this emerging industry is arguably Bengaluru, which has the largest number of systems of medicine approved by the World Health Organization in a single city: cardiac, neurology, cancer care and dentistry are just a few of the areas of specialization, and clients include the NHS and America's largest insurance company. Open-heart surgery will set you back US$4500 in Bengaluru, for example, as opposed to US$18,000 abroad. And afterwards, of course, you can recuperate at an Ayurveda resort. Lately Bengaluru has knitted its medical specialists with its IT cred to pioneer virtual medicine too, whereby cardiac experts in the city hold teleconferences with outposts up and down the subcontinent to treat emergencies, examine and monitor patients via phone, text and video, a method specialists at Narayana Hrudayalaya confidently predict will one day become the norm.

sitar on which he's resting. Behind him is a yonilingam. Just outside the temple are two bodhi trees, with serpent statues draped with sacred strands in offering for children. To your right as you exit the temple lies Bugle Park, a pretty little patch of wood whose trees are packed with fruit bats. It also holds one of Kempe Gowda's four 16th-century watchtowers. You can walk past the old fort under the subway to reach the atmospheric City Market, and from there to the busy market area of the Old Town around Avenue Road and Chikpet.

For those interested in ancient Indian astrological practices, the **Palm Leaf Library** ⓘ *33 5th Main Rd, Chamarajpet*, is supposed to be the repository for everyone's special leaf, which gives accurate details of character, past, present and future. Locating each leaf is not guaranteed.

Sri Gavi Gangadhareshwara Temple is most remarkable for its two quirks of architecture. First, the 'open window' to the left of the temple, which only once a year (on **Makara Sankrati Day**, 14/15 January) allows a shaft of light to shine between the horns of the stone Nandi bull in the courtyard and to then fall on the Siva lingam in the inner sanctum. The second quirk can only be seen by bending double to crouch around the back of the cave shrine. The Dravida-style **Venkataramanasvami Temple** is where the Wodeyar Maharaja chose to worship first, when his dynasty's rule was reinstated at the end of the 18th century, before entering the palace.

The grand, Tudor-style **Bangalore Palace** ⓘ *north of Cubbon Park, T080-2336 0818, 1000-1800, foreigners Rs 200, Indians Rs 100, camera Rs 500, video Rs 1000; frequent buses from Majestic/Sivaji Nagar*, built by Chamaraja Wodeyar in 1887, was incongruously inspired by Windsor Castle. The entry price buys you a tour of the Mysore mahahrajas' collection of art and family portraits.

The sprawling modern **International Society for Krishna Conscious temple complex (ISKCON)** ⓘ *Hare Krishna Hill, 1R Block, Chord Rd, Rajaji Nagar, northwest of the centre, 0700-1300, 1615-2030*, holds five shrines, a multimedia cinema showing films on the Hare Krishna movement, lofty *gopurams* and the world's tallest *kalash shikara*. Around 9000 visitors make the pilgrimage every day; *bhajans* (religious songs) are sung daily.

Around Bengaluru

Whitefield, 16 km east of Bengaluru, is known for the **Sai Baba Ashram** at Brindavan. It also has the International Technical Park, a modern self-contained community of high tech workers.

Nandidurg, Tipu's fortified summer retreat in the Nandi Hills, lies on top of a granite hil with sheer cliffs on three sides 10 km from Chikballapur, to the north of Bengaluru. Literally 'the fort of Nandi', the place, today a minor hill resort with great views from the 60-m-high 'Tipu's drop', was named after Siva's bull. The ninth-century **Bhoganandisvara Temple** at the foot of the hill is a good example of the Nolamba style; its walls are quite plain but the stone windows feature carvings of Nataraja and Durga. The 16th century brought typical Vijayanagar period extensions such as the *gopuram* at the entrance. To get there, take a bus from the Central Bus Stand (ask for the Nandi Hill bus, not Nandidurga); they leave at 0730, 0830, 0930, returning at 1400, 1630, 1830.

Nrityagram ⓘ *30 km north of Bengaluru, T080-2846 6313, Tue-Sat 1000-1400*, is a dance village where young dancers learn all disciplines of traditional Indian dance. It was founded by the late Odissi dancer Protima Gauri. Guided tours include lunch, dance demonstrations and a short lecture.

Bannerghatta Bio Park ⓘ *22 km south of the city, T080-2782 8540, www.bannerghattabiopark.org, 0900-1300, 1400-1700, entry has become absurdly overpriced at Rs 1000 (Indians Rs 200), plus Rs 100 for a seat in the government safari bus, or Rs 1000 for your own car or jeep and a further Rs 500 for a guide; video camera Rs 1000*, covers more than 100 sq km of dry deciduous forest, and is home to wild populations of elephant, bison, boar, deer and the occasional leopard. A portion has been fenced, and the Forest Department run a range of minibus safaris to see tigers, bears and Asiatic lions at close range in quasi-natural surroundings; many of the animals here have been rescued from circuses. The park also contains a butterfly garden and an unappealing zoo.

Bengaluru (Bangalore) listings

For Sleeping and Eating price codes and other relevant information, see Essentials pages 38-42.

Sleeping

Bengaluru *p1050, map p1052*

Cheap hotels share the streets of the ill-named Majestic district, northeast of the bus stand around SC (Subedar Chatram) Rd, with seedy bars and cinemas – a daunting prospect at night. **MG Rd** offers a more sanitized environment, and has rooms for every budget from backpacker to super-luxury. Top end hotels can add 25% in taxes.

LL Oberoi, 39 MG Rd, T080-2558 5858, www.oberoihotels.com. 160 superb rooms and suites with private sit-outs, all of which have views across the lush tropical gardens. Decent-sized swimming pool. Good restaurants, bar, spa and fitness centre, beauty salon.

LL The Park, 14/7 MG Rd, T080-2559 4666, www.theparkhotels.com. Global minimalist c hic, 109 plush rooms in an achingly hip business hotel. Each room has a balcony, there's a lovely long pool surrounded by gazebos. Cool black and white photographs on the walls, DVDs, library, Wi-Fi and 24-hr room service. Some suites have jacuzzi.

LL Taj West End, 23 Race Course Rd, near railway, T080-6660 5660, www.tajhotels.com. Charming 1887 colonial property set in beautiful gardens; much more than a business hotel. 117 immaculately appointed suites and rooms with balconies and verandas, Wi-Fi, flat screen TV. There's also a splendidly restored Heritage Wing, dating from 1907. George Soros, Gordon Brown and Sting are some of its former guests. Pool, good restaurant and **Blue Bar**, with house/lounge music (until 2330).

LL-AL St Mark's Hotel, 4/1 St Mark's Rd, T080-4001 9000, www.stmarkshotel.com. Nice carpeted rooms in very quiet and capable business hotel. All rooms have Wi-Fi and bath. Good views, questionable decorative taste. Price includes breakfast.

L-AL Villa Pottipati, 142 8th Cross, 4th Main Rd, Mallesaram, T080-2336 0777, www.neemranahotels.com. 8 rooms in historic townhouse furnished with rosewood 4-posters and sepia Indian portrait photography. Set in garden in the charming quiet tree-lined avenues of Bengaluru's Brahminical suburbs. A/c and internet facilities, small plunge pool. Atmospheric, but a bit lacklustre. Thin mattresses.

AL-A Ivory Tower, Penthouse (12th) floor of Barton Centre, 84 MG Rd, T080-4178 3333, www.hotelivorytower.com. 22 comfortable, spacious rooms (huge beds) in slightly ragged venue, stunning views over city, old fashioned but spotless, good value, friendly. Wi-Fi, a/c, fridge, phone. Good terrace bar and restaurant onsite.

AL-B Woodlands Hotel, 5 Raja Ram Mohan Roy Rd, T080-2222 5111, info@woodlands.in. Large but charming old-fashioned hotel with 240 rooms, some a/c and cottages, with attached baths and fridge, good a/c restaurant, bar, coffee shop, exchange, safe, good location but calm, good value. Phone, satellite TV, lockers.

A Keys Hotel, Hosur Main Rd (opposite the Volkswagen showroom), T080-3944 1000, www.keyshotels.com. Ultra-modern hotel near Electronic City with free Wi-Fi, swimming pool and all mod cons. Also opening soon is **Keys Hotel and Apartments**, Plot 6 Kundalahalli Main Rd, Whitefield, 16 km east of Bengaluru.

A-B Green Path Serviced Apartments, 32/2 New BEL Rd, Seenappa Layout (north of centre near Hebbal flyover), T080-4266 4777, www.thegreenpath.in. Comfortable and spacious if slightly anonymous 1- to 3- bedroom (**L**) apartments, built and run on eco principles – rainwater harvesting, solar hot water, renewable materials. There's the obligatory Wi-Fi lifeline, plus bikes to ride to the local shops, and the price includes an organic breakfast spread.

B-C Sri Lakshmi Comforts, 117 MG Rd, next to LIC, T080-2555 9388, www.slcomforts.com. Good lower-range choice right amongst the MG Rd action, with spartan but clean rooms, friendly staff and a good thali restaurant.

C-D Kamat Yatrinivas, 1st Cross, Gandhinagar, T080-2226 0088, www.kamat yatri.in. 57 decent rooms set around a central courtyard. Thin mattress spring beds, but it's clean and well maintained. 2 dining rooms, North Karnatakan and South Indian meals. Satellite TV, direct dial phone, lockers.

C-E Ajantha, 22A MG Rd, T080-2558 4321. 62 basic 'deluxe' rooms and much better value cottages with sitting areas and campbed-style beds, set in a calm compound filled with bougainvillea and pot plants. South Indian veg restaurant, helpful management.

C-E Vellara, 126 Brigade Rd, T080-2536 9116. A grim exterior conceals one of the MG Rd area's best deals. 36 spacious and well-kept rooms, which get better the higher up you go. TV and phone in each room, and the value and location are excellent. Recommended.

D YMCA Guest House (City), Nrupathunga Rd, near Cubbon Park, T080-2221 1848, www.ymca blr.net. One of the best budget deals in the city. The location is wonderfully peaceful, just across the fence from Cubbon Park, and many of the rooms open on to an indoor sports hall where you can sit like Caesar watching badminton or karate championships. Afternoon cricket matches, excellent café.

D-F Brindavan, 108 MG Rd, T080-2558 4000. Giant old-fashioned budget hotel in an excellent location, with good views from the upper floors. 113 slightly gritty and strictly no-frills rooms with shower, some a/c, and some quite nice suites. Dingy but good *thali* restaurant. Recommended.

E New Central Lodge, 56 Infantry Rd, at the Central St end, T080-2559 2395. 35 simple, rooms, clean enough, some with bath, hot water (0500-1000).

E Railway Retiring Rooms, City Station. 23 rooms and cheaper dorm for passengers in transit.

E-F Mahaveer, 8/9 Tank Bund Rd, opposite bus station, near City railway station, T080-3061 0384. Basic and decaying place on a noisy road, but just about OK if you want to drop your bags after a long bus ride. Larger (**D**) deluxe rooms at back quieter.

F Vybhav, 60 SC Rd down passageway opposite Movieland Talkies, T080-2287 3997. As basic as they come, and pretty grimy, but the rooms are relatively big and airy and some open on to a shared terrace where pot-bellied Brahmins hang out and chat to each other. Good value.

F YHA Guest House and Programme Centre. Contact Mr Sridhara, KFC Building, 48 Church St, T080-2558 5417.

Around Bengaluru *p1054*

LL Shreyas Bangalore, 335 km northwest of town in Nelamangala, T080-2773 7183 www.shreyasretreat.com. The place for peace and yoga in 5-star luxury, with twice-daily classes and silent meditations, Vedanta consultants, life coaching. Pampering includes Balinese massage and exotic fruit body scrubs, and the vegetarian cuisine is exceptional. Alcohol is forbidden, but there's a gym, book and DVD library, and in case you forgot you were in Bangalore, Wi-Fi throughout the property. 3- to 6-night packages start at around US$1500.

LL Soukya International Holistic Health Centre, Whitefield, 17 km east of Bengaluru,

T080-2531 8405, www.soukya.com. This healing centre offers restorative, personalized programmes: detox, de-stress and weight loss, or relax with naturopathy and Ayurveda suited to asthma, diabetes, hypertension and addictions. Accommodation is in individual cottages around lawns, flowers and trees. Programmes cost from US$160-350 a day.

Eating

Look out for Grover wine, which is the product of the first French grape grown in Indian soil, sown 40 km from Bengaluru at the foot of the Nandi hills. Veuve Clicquot has a stake in the company, which is now exporting to France.

Bengaluru *p1050, map p1052*

For excellent fresh, cheap, South Indian staples like *iddli*, *dosa* and *vada* look for branches of **Darshini**, **Shiv Sagar**, **Shanthi Sagar**, **Sukh Sagar** and **Kamat** all of which are hygienic and efficient. At the other end of the price scale, the Taj West End hotel has the Vietnamese restaurant **Blue Ginger** and The Park has the Italian **i-t.ALIA**, both of which are pricey but excellent if you yearn for non-Indian fare. The Sunday all you-can-eat brunch at the Leela is popular with expats and the city's business elite. If you're missing international fast food head for Brigade and MG Rd and the food court at the Forum shopping mall. Chains of **Barista** and **Cafe Coffee Day** are ubiquitous.

TTT **Ebony Restaurant**, **Ivory Tower** (see Sleeping), T080-4178 3344. 1230-1500 and 1930-2300. Parsee dishes like mutton *dhansak* and curry *chawal*, along with Muglai, Tandoori and French food, but come for the views from this penthouse terrace restaurant, which are the best in Bengaluru.

TTT **Karavalli**, at the Taj Gateway, 166 Residency Rd, T080-6660 4519. The best high-end Indian restaurant in the city.

TT **Amaravathi**, 45/3 Residency Rd. T080-2591 3718. Excellent traditional spicy South Indian, Andhra and Chettinad dishes. A local favourite.

TT **Benjarong**, 1/3 Ulsoor Rd, T080-4206 6166. If you're craving Thai, this is the place. Expect charming service and authentic red curry, dished dished up with lots of free extras.

TT **Coconut Grove**, 86 Spencer Building, Church St, T080-2559 6149. Good varied Southern Indian menu, beers, buzzing place with sit-outs under shades.

TT **Koshy's**, 39 St Mark's Rd, T080-2221 3793. 0900-2330. Pleasant, old fashioned, atmospheric, licensed. Good grills and roasts, Syrian Christian fish curries and Sunday South Indian brunch. Also does Western breakfasts like baked beans on toast, cutlets, eggy bread or eggs any way you like. A local institution.

TT **Tandoor**, MG Rd, T080-2558 4620. 1230-1500 and 1900-2330. Possibly the city's best non-vegetarian restaurant serving North Indian food: Punjabi, Muglai and Tandoori.

T **Chalukya**, Race Course Rd, by the **Taj West End Hotel**. Excellent vegetarian.

T **Halli Mane**, 12 Sampige Rd, Malleswaram. Fun and buzzing vegetarian canteen decked out like a village house: order at the counter, present your ticket at the relevant counter and elbow yourself a bit of table space. A good place to try Karnataka specials like *ragi roti*.

T **Indian Coffee House**, 78 MG Rd. 0800-2030. The South Indian filter coffee is some of the best in the city, but it's worth coming just to sample one of the last vestiges of old Bangalore: waiters in turbans, old men at formica tables arguing about politics.

T **MTR** (**Mavalli Tiffin Rooms**), 11 Lalbagh Rd, T080-2222 0022. Tiffin 0630-1100 and 1530-1930, lunch 1230-1400 and 2000-2100. Closed Mon lunch. The quintessential Bengaluru restaurant: a classic Kannadiga Brahmin vegetarian oozing 1920s atmosphere, full of Bengaluru elders, at the edge of Lalbagh gardens. A 14-course lunch lasts 2 hrs, but you'll be lucky to get a table – If you're in a hurry it does parcels. The simple vegetarian food is superb, the interiors and people watching is half the fun.

T **Palmgrove**, **Ballal Residence Hotel**, 74/3 III Cross, Residency Rd, T080-2559 7277. Atmospheric place for Kannada Brahmin food, a/c, serves excellent giant lunch *thalis* Rs 75.

T **Vidyarthi Bhavan**, 32 Gandhi Bazar, T080-2667 7588. Sat-Thu 0630-1130 and 1400-2000. Unassuming vegetarian joint in the Basavanagudi district (near Nandi Bull and Gandhi Bazar) whose 'Mysore Masala Dosa' is justly famous, served with a side order of butter, coconut chutney and potato and onion curry. Open since 1938.

Cafés, bakeries and ice cream

Nilgiri's Upper Crust Café, Brigade Rd. Primarily a supermarket.

Sweet Chariot Bakery, 15/2 Residency Rd and branches all across the city. Open 1030-2030. Excellent cakes and pastries.

Bars and clubs

Bengaluru *p1050, map p1052*

Bengaluru has what is possibly India's coolest party scene, with the bars that crowd along Brigade Rd, Residency Rd and Church St playing everything from hip hop and house to rock until the unholy hour of 2330 – the government-imposed curfew that was introduced to stamp out a rise in crime. Hotel bars are exempt from the law, and tend to offer a more refined atmosphere: those at the **Taj West End** have a particular raj-esque elegance, while the Park Hotel's **i-bar** is sleek and pared down. New venues spring up all the time, while others fall out of fashion or change names, so ask around for the latest hotspot. Note that most of the better places have a couples-only policy to prevent an oversupply of slavering stags.

13th Floor, **Hotel Ivory Tower**, 84 MG Rd, T080-2558 9333. The least pretentious bar, with the best view of the city.

F-Bar and Lounge and **Insomnia**, at **Le Meridien**, Sankey Rd, T080-2226 2233. Co-owned by Fashion TV, and correspondingly upscale and precious.

Fuga, 1 Castle St, Ashok Nagar, T080-4141 1180. World-class club/absinthe bar hosting big-name DJs.

Hard Rock Cafe, St Mark's Rd, T080-4124 2222. Brand-phobics beware: this spanking-new venue is one of the hottest tickets in town, with a variety of drinking and dining spaces carved out of a lovely old library building.

Pecos, Rest House Rd, off Brigade Rd. Connoisseurs of dinge should head directly here for cheap beer and hard-rockin' tunes.

Taika, the Pavilion, 62 MG Rd, entry in Church St. Would-be slick rooftop place with lounges and a huge dancefloor, popular with students.

Shopping

Bengaluru *p1050, map p1052*

Bengaluru is a byword for shopping in India. **Commercial St, MG Rd** and **Brigade Rd** remain favourite hangouts for the city's youth.

Unless you want Western goods, though, the best shopping is to be had at the **City Market** (officially known as the KR Market) in Chickpet, where you can get silver, gold and silk saris; it's supposed to be the country's biggest silk wholesale/retail district and makes for some seriously fun people watching when it comes alive at dusk. **Russel Market**, in Shivajinagar, is stuffed with vegetables, meat and antiques.

Shops and markets open early and close late (about 2000) but close 1300-1600.

Books

Gangarams, 72 MG Rd. Has a wide-ranging and expanding collection.

Premier, 46/1 Church St (and Museum Rd). Small, with a good selection of specialist and academic books (as well as an impressive PG Wodehouse collection), helpful owner.

Sankar's, 394 First D Main Rd, Domlur Layout (east of town towards old HAL airport, T080-25357899. A bit of a trip from the centre, but worth it for one of the best selections in the city.

Crafts and gifts

Karnataka is best known for silks, especially saris, and sandalwood products, from oils and incense to intricate carvings. Other local products include Mysore paintings (characterized by gold leaf and bright colours from vegetable and mineral dyes), *dhurries* (carpets incorporating floral and natural motifs, traditionally made from wool though cotton is now more widely used), inlaid woodwork and wooden toys and Channaptna dolls. Bidriware, a form of metalwork whereby silver and gold is inlaid or engraved onto copper and polished with zinc, originates from Bidar in the state's far northeast, but is produced throughout the state.

Cauvery Crafts Emporium, 49 MG Rd.

Central Cottage Industries Emporium, 144 MG Rd.

Desi, 27 Patalamma St, near South End Circle.

Kala Madhyam, 77/8 Nandidurg Rd (Benson Cross Rd Corner), Benson Town, T080-2353 7358, www.kalamadhyam.org. NGO-run store showcasing metalwork, pottery, clothing and jewellery made by folk artists and tribal craftspeople throughout India. High quality.

Khadi Gramudyog, Silver Jubilee Park Rd, near City Market. For homespun cotton.

Mota Shopping Complex, Brigade Rd.

Raga, A-13, Devatha Plaza, 131 Residency Rd. Attractive gifts.
UP Handlooms, 8 Mahaveer Shopping Complex, Kempe Gowda Rd.

Jewellery

Most gold and jewellery is, logically enough, on Jewellers St, but also look along MG Rd, Brigade Rd, Residency Rd and Commercial St.

Silk and saris

Silk is, to many, what shopping in Bengaluru is really all about. There's a vast range at:
Deepam, MG Rd. Fixed prices, excellent service, 24 hrs from placing an order to making up your designs.
Janardhana, Unity Building, JC Rd.
Karnataka Silks Industries, Jubilee Showroom, 44/45 Leo Complex, MG Rd. Specializing in traditional Mysore Crepe designs.
Vijayalakshmi, 20/61 Blumoon Complex, Residency Rd. Will also make shirts.

Activities and tours

Bengaluru *p1050, map p1052*

Golf

Bangalore Golf Club, Sankey Rd, T080-2228 7980. Foreign visitors pay US$30.
KGA Golf Club, Golf Av, Kodihalli, Airport Rd. Rs 2000, T080-4009 0000.

Horse racing

Bengaluru is famous for racing and stud farms.
Bangalore Turf Club, Race Course Rd, T080-2226 2391, www.bangaloreraces.com. Season May-Jul and Nov-Mar.

Swimming

Of late, the top hotels have become reluctant to let non-residents use their pools. However, there are great municipal pools, with swimming times segregated by gender. Try **Kensington Park Rd**, near Ulsoor Lake, or **Sankey Tank**, Sadhiv Nagar, Jayanagar 3rd Block. Rs 40, closes at 1600.

Tour operators

The Blue Yonder, 23-24 Sri Guru Nivas, Amarjyoti Layout, Sanjay Nagar, T080-4115 2218, www.theblueyonder.com. Superb responsible tourism packages in Kerala, Karnataka and elsewhere, and also offer reliable ticketing and hotel bookings.
Clipper Holidays, 4 Magrath Rd, T080-2559 9032, www.clipperholidays.com. Tours, treks (everything provided), Kerala backwaters, etc. Very helpful and efficient.
Hammock Leisure Holidays, Indranagar, T080-4202 3333, www.hammockholidays.com.
Karnataka State Tourism Development Corporation (KSTDC) runs tours from Badami House, opposite Corporation Office, NR Sq, T080-4334 4334, www.kstdc.net. **Bangalore city sightseeing**: half-day tours, covering Tipu's Palace, Bull Temple, Lal Bagh, Ulsoor Lake, Vidhan Soudha, Gava Gangadhareshwara Temple, Museums, runs 0730-1400 and 1400-1930. Rs 170, recommended; full-day tour, to Rajarajeshwari Temple, HAL Museum, Bennerghatta Bio Park, ISKCON temple and more, 0715-2000, Rs 290, long and exhausting.
India Tourism tour, departing from Swiss Complex, No 33 Race Course Rd, T080-2256 0001, same schedule as half-day tour but lasts from 0900-1700 and includes ISKCON, Rs 190. **1-day Sravanabelagola, Belur and Halebid**, Fri, Sun (except monsoons), 0715-2200, Rs 340; **Mysore** daily, 0715-2300, Rs 240-300 including meals.
Skyway, Tourism House, Papanna St, 8 St Marks Rd, T080-2211 1401, www.skyway tour.com. Booking agents for **Jungle Lodges** resorts and the *Golden Chariot* luxury train. Also ayurveda packages and excellent car and driver hire.
Sita, 507 Prestige Centre Point, Cunnigham Rd, T080-4112 2651.
Thomas Cook, 55 MG Rd, T080-2558 1337 (foreign exchange and TCs), and 70 MG Rd (all services), T080-2558 8028.

Trekking and adventure sports

Chalukyas, info@chalukyas.com. A club of outdoor enthusiasts who welcome visitors to join them on hiking weekends around Bengaluru and elsewhere in India.
Getoff Ur Ass, 858 1D Main Rd, T080-2672 2750, www.getoffurass.com. The shop has camping and outdoor gear for sale and hire, while the owner organizes a variety of trekking and rafting trips in the Nilgiris and Western Ghats, plus kayaking and paragliding courses, photography workshops and camping weekends in private forest areas.

Walking tours
Bangalore Walks, T(0)9845-523660, www.bangalorewalks.com. Excellent guided tours of the city's cultural and historic landmarks, Rs 495 including brunch.

Transport

Bengaluru *p1050, map p1052*

Air Opened in 2008, **Bengaluru International Airport** (BLR), T080-6678 2251, www.bengaluruairport.com, is the bold new face of Indian airports: it's gleaming, expensive, and the taxi touts in Arrivals greet you in suits. The domestic and international terminals are in the same building, around 35 km northeast of the city by a fast new road. Prepaid taxis in the terminal quote upwards of Rs 1000 to deliver you to the city centre, but metered taxis queue outside Arrivals and work out at roughly half the price. Airport buses run every 20-30 mins on 9 fixed routes to and from various parts of the city: Route 9 to Kempegowda Bus Station (Majestic) and Route 4 to Jeevan Bhima Nagar (via Cubbon Rd, parallel to MG Rd) are the most useful for hotels. **Note** Departing domestic passengers must pay a Rs 260 'User Development Fee' at a counter outside the terminal; allow 10 mins to queue, and show the receipt to gain entry.

Bengaluru is becoming an increaingly important international hub, with direct flights to London, Frankfurt and Paris, as well as Singapore, Kuala Lumpur and many Gulf cities.

Daily domestic flights serve **Chennai**, **Coimbatore**, **Delhi**, **Goa**, **Guwahati**, **Hubli**, **Hyderabad**, **Jaipur**, **Kochi**, **Kolkata**, **Mangalore**, **Mumbai**, **Pune** and **Thiruvananthapuram**. The best network is with **Air India (Indian Airlines)**, Cauvery Bhavan, Kempe Gowda Rd, T080-2297 8427, airport T080-6678 5168, Reservations T141. **Indigo**, T080-2221 9810. **Jet Airways**, 1-4 M Block, Unity Bldg, JC Rd, T080-3989 9999. **Kingfisher**, T080-4114 8190. **Spicejet**, T080-2522 9792.

International Airline offices Air India, Unity Building, JC Rd, T080-2227 7747. **Air France** and **KLM/Northwest**, Sunrise Chambers, 22 Ulsoor Rd, T080-2558 9358, airport T080-6678 3109. **British Airways**, airport T080-6678 3150. **Cathay Pacific**, 21 Wood St, T1800-209 1616. **Emirates**, 3 Vittal Mallya Rd, T080-6629 4444. **Interglobe Air Tansport** (**Air Mauritius**, **China Eastern**, **Delta**, **SAS**, **United Airlines**, 17-20 Richmond Towers, 12 Richmond Rd, T080-2229 1377. **Kuwait**, T080-2558 9841. **Lufthansa**, 44/42 Dickenson Rd, 080-2506 0800. **Singapore Airlines**, T080-2286 7999. **Sri Lankan**, Cears Plaza, Residency Rd, T080-4112 5204.

Bus **City Bus Station**, opposite the City Railway Station, is the very busy but well-organized departure point for services within the city.

Just to the south, the **Central Bus Station** handles long-distance buses run by the governments of **Karnataka (KSRTC)**, T080-2287 3377; **Andhra Pradesh (APSRTC)**, T080-2287 3915; **Kerala**, T080-2226 9508; and **Tamil Nadu (SETC)**, T080-2287 6975.

Computerized reservations are available on many services, from the booking counter. There are efficient, frequent and inexpensive services to all major cities in Southern and Central India. Frequent service to **Mysore** (3 hrs); several to **Hassan** (4 hrs), **Hyderabad**, **Madikeri** (6 hrs), **Madurai** (9 hrs), **Mangalore** (9 hrs), **Ooty** (7 hrs), **Puttaparthi** (4-5 hrs, Rs 65), **Tirupati** (6½ hrs). 'Deluxe' or 'ordinary' coaches run by private operators are usually more comfortable though a bit more expensive. They operate from opposite the **Central**and **Kalasipalyam** bus stations.

Car Firms for city and out-of-town sightseeing include: **Classic City Cabs**, T080-2238 6999; **KSTDC** (see page 1050); **Safe Wheels**, T080-2343 1333; and **Skyway**, T080-2211 1401. Rs 1000-2000 for 8 hrs or 80 km; extra km Rs 10-25 depending on the type of car. Rates for overnight or extended sightseeing will be higher, with additions for driver overnight charges and hill driving.

Metro The 1st phase of Bengaluru's brand new Namma Metro has been substantially delayed and is now due to be fully operational by 2013. There are 2 lines: **purple**, running east–west from Baiyappanahalli to Mysore Rd via MG Rd and City Railway Station; and **green**, running north–south from Nagasandra to Puttenahalli via Lal Bagh and Yesvantpur station. The lines intersect at Kempegowda. Trains are expected to run every 4 mins, with fares costing Rs 7-15. Check www.bmrc.co.in for exact times.

Taxi and autorickshaw There are prepaid taxi booths at the airport and all 3 railway stations; prices should be clearly marked, and will be a little higher than the meter fare. Minimum charge in a meter taxi is Rs 125, which covers up to 5 km; Rs 10 per extra kilometre. There are severable reputable radio taxi companies with clean a/c vehicles and digital meters, including **EasyCabs**, T080-4343 4343, callcenter@ easycabs.com.

Autorickshaws should also operate on a meter system: Rs 14 for the first kilometre, Rs 7 per extra kilometre. In practice it can be hard to persuade drivers to use the meter, especially during rush hour.

Both taxi and rickshaw fares increase by half between 2200 and 0600.

Train **Bangalore City Junction** (still known by the old spelling; code SBC) is the main departure point; enquiries T131, reservations T139. Computerized advance reservations are in the newer building on left of the entrance; No 14 is the 'Foreigners' Counter'. The Chief Reservations Officer is on the ground floor. Many trains also stop at **Cantonment Station**, T135. A few begin at **Yesvantpur Junction**, 10 km north of the city. Unless stated departure times are from City.

Bhopal: *Karnataka Exp 12627*, 1920, 29 hrs. **Delhi** (**HN**): *Rajdhani Exp 12429/12493*, 2020, 33½ hrs (AC only), via Secunderabad (11 hrs), Nagpur (19 hrs) and Bhopal (25 hrs); *Karnataka Exp 12627*, 1920, 39 hrs. **Chennai**: *Shatabdi Exp, 2008*, daily except Wed, 1625, 5 hrs; *Lalbagh Exp 12608*, 0630, 5½ hrs; *Brindavan Exp 12640*, 1430, 5¼ hrs; *Sanghamitra Exp 12295*, 0900, 6 hrs. **Goa** (**Madgaon**): *Vasco da Gama Exp 17309*, 1515, 14 hrs (Sun and Tue only); better to go to **Londa** on *Rani Channama Exp 16859*, 2115, 10½ hrs. **Hospet**: *Hampi Exp 16592*, 2100, 10 hrs. **Hyderabad** (**Kacheguda**): *Kacheguda Exp 12786*, 1820, 11½ hrs. **Kolkata (H)**: *Howrah Exp 12864*, 1935 (from YPR), 35 hrs. **Madurai**: *Tuticorin Exp 16732*, 2120, 10 hrs. **Mumbai** (**CST**): *Udyan Exp 16530*, 2010, 24 hrs; *Chalukya Exp 11018*, 0630 (from YPR), 26 hrs, via **Londa** (for Goa), 10½ hrs. **Maddur** and **Mysore**: *Chamundi Exp 16216*,1815, 2½ hrs; *Tipu Express 12614*, 1500, 2½ hrs; *Shatabdi Exp 12007*, daily except Wed, 1100, 2 hrs. **Thiruvananthapuram**: *Island Exp 16526*, 2140, 17½ hrs, via Coimbatore (8 hrs) and Kochi (12 hrs).

Directory

Bengaluru *p1050, map p1052*

Banks Usually open 1000-1400, Mon-Fri. There are hundreds of 24-hr ATMs that are compatible with cards bearing the MasterCard, Visa, Maestro, Cirrus or Plus logos. **Citibank**, **Canara Bank**, **HSBC**, **HDFC** are reliable. For counter services: **Citibank**, MG Rd, T080-2559 6363, **HDFC**, Kasturba Rd, T080-2227 4600, **Standard Chartered**, MG Rd, T080-3940 4444, **State Bank of India**, St Mark's Rd, T080-2594 3120. For foreign exchange, **Thomas Cook**, 55 MG Rd, T080-2558 1337, and **Weizmann Forex**, Residency Rd, T080-2559 5379, are quicker than banks for TCs. **Cultural centres** **Alliance Française**, Millers Tank Bund Rd, off Thimmaiah Rd, opposite station, T080-4123 1340. **British Library**, St Mark's Rd/Church St corner (Koshy's Bldg), 1030-1830, Tue-Sat. **Goethe Institut**, 716 CMH RD, Indranagar, T080-2520 5305. **Internet** **Computer Planet**, 1st floor, 5th Av shopping plaza, Brigade Rd, T080-2559 7116, super-fast with USB ports and software/hardware retailer. **Cyber Café** on Brigade Rd (near Church St); very good, safe cold coffee. **Cyber Q**, Brigade Rd, near Vellara, with pool tables; **St Mark's Business Centre**, 8 St Mark's Plaza, 14 St Mark's Rd T080-5112 1032. Mon-Sat 0830- 1930. Internet plus facilities for scanning, lamination, colour xerox and CD writing. **Trans World**, 2 Magrath Rd, with coffee shop. **Medical services** **Ambulance**: T102. **Bowring and Lady Curzon Hospital**, Hospital Rd, T080-2559 1362, north of Cubbon Park. **Mallya Hospital**, Vittal Mallya Rd, south of Cubbon Park, T080-2227 7997, one of the best. There ae chemists at hospitals and **Cure**, 137 GF2, Business Point, Brigade Rd T080-2227 4246. For dentists contact **Grace**, 1 Dinnur Main Rd, RT Nagar, T080-2333 4638; excellent. **Post** **GPO**, Cubbon Rd near Raj Bhawan, 1000-1800. Poste Restante, Mon-Sat, 1030-1600, T080-2286 6772. **DHL**, Jubilee Building, 43 Museum Rd, T080-2558 8855. **UPS**, 4 1st Cross 10th Main Indiranagar, T080-2525 3445. **Telephone** **Mobile Store**, Devatha Plaza, 131/14 Residency Rd, and branches all over town, www.mobilestore.in. For reliable mobile connections and handsets. **Useful contacts** **Visa extensions**: Commissioner of Police, Infantry Rd. **Police** T100. **Fire** T101. **Chief Wildlife Warden**, Aranya Bhavan, 18th Cross, Malleswaram, T080-2334 1993.

Mysore and Southern Maidan

The charming, unruly city of Mysore, the former capital of the princely state, does a brisk trade in its eponymous shimmering silks, sandalwood and jasmine against a backdrop of its stunning, borderline gaudy Indo-Saracenic palace. On the outskirts of the city is the empty ruin of Srirangapatnam, the island fortress of Britain's nemesis Tipu Sultan, and the bird-crammed Ranganathittu Sanctuary.

Further on is the Chennakesava Temple of Somnathpur, a spellbinding example of Hoysala architecture. Leopards and tigers stalk the two parklands, Bandipur and Nagarhole, that spill over Karnataka's borders with neighbouring Tamil Nadu and Kerala, and closer to the coast you can climb the Ghats to the tiny Kodagu district for forests of wild elephants and coffee plantations nursed by a warrior people. Also in Kodagu lies Sera, the university at the centre of one of India's biggest Tibetan Buddhist refugee settlements. ▸▸ *For listings, see pages 1071-1077.*

Mysore → *For listings, see pages 1071-1077. Colour map 7, B3.*

Mysore centre is a crowded jumble presided over by the gaudy, wondrous kitsch of the Maharaja's Palace, a profusion of turquoise-pink and layered with mirrors. But for some Mysore's world renown is centred less on the palace, its silk production or sandalwood than on the person of Sri Pattabhi Jois and his Mysore-style ashtanga yoga practice (see box, page 1075). This all happens outside the chaotic centre, in the city's beautiful Brahmin suburbs, where wide boulevard-like streets are overhung with bougainvillea.

Ins and outs → *Phone code: 0821. Population: 742,300.*

Getting there The railway station is about 1 km to the northwest of the town centre while the three bus stands are all in the centre, within easy reach of the hotels. ▸▸ *See Transport, page 1076.*

Getting around Karnataka's second biggest town, Mysore is still comfortably compact enough to walk around, though there are plenty of autos and buses.

Tourist information **Department of Tourism** ⓘ *Old Exhibition Building, Irwin Rd, T0821-242 2096, www.mysore.nic.in, 1000-1730.* See also www.karnataka.com/tourism/mysore. There are information counters at the train station and bus stand. **Karnataka State Tourism Development Corporation (KSTDC)** ⓘ *Yatri Nivas, 2 JLB Rd, T0821-242 3652*, is efficient.

Sights

The **Maharaja's Palace** ⓘ *enter by south gate, T0821-243 4425, 1000-1730, Rs 200 includes audio guide, cameras must be left in lockers (free, you take the key), allow 2 hrs if you wish to see everything, guidebook Rs 10; go early to avoid the crowds; downstairs is fairly accessible for the disabled*, or 'City Palace' (Amba Vilas) was designed by Henry Irwin and built in 1897 after a fire burnt down the old wooden incarnation. It is in the Indo-Saracenic style in grand proportions, with domes, arches and colonnades of carved pillars and shiny marble floors. The stained glass, wall paintings, ivory inlaid doors and the ornate golden throne (now displayed during Dasara) are remarkable. The fabulous collection of jewels is seldom displayed. Try to visit on a Sunday night, public holiday or festival when the palace is lit up with 50,000 fairy lights.

On the ground floor, visitors are led through the 'Car Passage' with cannons and carriages to the *Gombe thotti* (Dolls' pavilion). This originally displayed dolls during Dasara and today houses a model of the old palace, European marble statues and the golden *howdah* (the maharaja used the battery-operated red and green bulbs on top of the canopy as stop and go signals to the *mahout*). The last is still used during Dasara but goddess Chamundeshwari rides on the elephant. The octagonal *Kalyana Mandap* (marriage hall), or Peacock Pavilion, south of the courtyard, has a beautiful stained glass ceiling and excellent paintings of scenes from Dasara and other festivities on 26 canvas panels. Note the exquisite details, especially of No 19. The Portrait Gallery and the Period Furniture Room lead off this pavilion.

On the first floor, a marble staircase leads to the magnificent Durbar Hall, a grand colonnaded hall measuring 47 m by 13 m with lavishly framed paintings by famous Indian artists. The asbestos-lined ceiling has paintings of Vishnu incarnations. A passage takes you past the beautifully ivory-on-wood inlaid door of the Ganesh Temple, to the Amba Vilas where private audiences (*Diwan-i-Khas*) were held. This exquisitely decorated hall has three doors. The central silver door depicts Vishnu's 10 incarnations and the eight *dikpalas* (directional guardians), with Krishna figures on the reverse (see the tiny Krishna on a leaf, kissing his toes), all done in *repoussé* on teak and rosewood. The room sports art nouveau style, possibly Belgian stained glass, cast iron pillars from Glasgow, carved wood ceiling, chandeliers, etched glass windows and the *pietra dura* on the floors.

Mysore

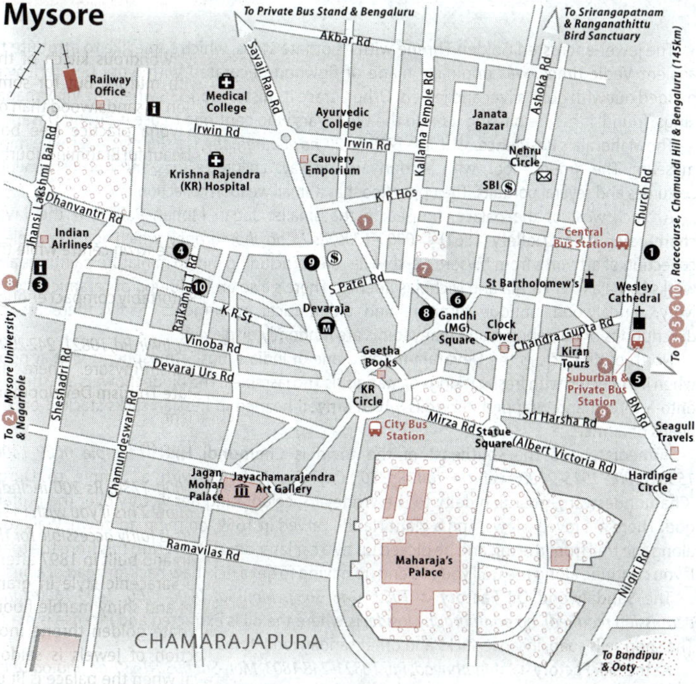

N

200 metres
200 yards

Sleeping
Bombay Tiffany's **1**
Greens' Boarding & Lodging **2**
Indus Valley **5**
Lalith Mahal Palace **6**
Mysore Dasaprakash **7**
Park Lane **9**
Ritz **4**
Royal Orchid Metropole **8**
Siddharta **3**
Windflower **10**

Eating
Ganesh **1**
King's Kourt Hotel **3**
Penguin Ice-cream Parlour **4**
Raghu Niwas **5**
RRR **6**
Shilpashri **8**
Sri Rama Veg & Ashok Books **9**

Medieval pageantry at Mysore

The brilliantly colourful festival of Dasara is celebrated with medieval pageantry for 10 days. Although the Dasara festival can be traced back to the Puranas and is widely observed across India, in the south it achieved its special prominence under the Vijayanagar kings. As the Mahanavami festival, it has been celebrated every year since it was sponsored by Raja Wodeyar in September 1610 at Srirangapatnam. It symbolizes the victory of goddess Chamundeswari (Durga) over the demon Mahishasura. On the last day a bedecked elephant with a golden howdah carrying the statue of the goddess processes from the palace through the city to Banni Mantap, about 5 km away, where the Banni tree is worshipped. The temple float festival takes place at a tank at the foot of Chamundi Hill and a car festival on top. In the evening there is a torchlight parade by the mounted guards who demonstrate their keen horsemanship and the night ends with a display of fireworks and all the public buildings are ablaze with fairy lights.

The jewel-encrusted Golden Throne with its ornate steps, which some like to attribute to ancient Vedic times, was originally made of figwood decorated with ivory before it was padded out with gold, silver and jewels. Others trace its history to 1336 when the Vijayanagar kings 'found' it before passing it on to the Wodeyars who continue to use it during **Dasara**.

The **Maharaja's Residence** ⓘ *1000-1730, Rs 20, no photography*, is a slightly under-whelming museum. The ground floor, with a courtyard, displays children's toys, musical instruments, costumes and several portraits. The upper floor has a small weapon collection.

A block west of the palace, housed in the smaller Jagan Mohan Palace, is the **Jayachamarajendra Art Gallery** (1861) ⓘ *0800-1700, Rs 25, no photography*, which holds a priceless collection of artworks from Mysore's erstwhile rulers, including Indian miniature paintings and works by Raja Ravi Varma and Nicholas Roerich. There's also an exhibition of ceramics, stone, ivory, sandalwood, antique furniture and old musical instruments. Sadly, there are no descriptions or guidebooks and many items are randomly displayed.

North of KR Circle is the **Devaraja market**, one of India's most atmospheric: visit at noon when it's injected with fresh pickings of marigolds and jasmines. The bigger flowers are stitched onto a thread and wrapped into rolls which arrived heaped in hessian sacks stacked on the heads of farmers.

Immediately to the southeast of the town is **Chamundi Hill** ⓘ *temple 0600-1400, 1530-1800, 1915-2100; vehicle toll Rs 30, City Bus No 185*, with a temple to Durga (Chamundeswari), guardian deity to the Wodeyars, celebrating her victory over the buffalo god. There are lovely views, and a giant Nandi, carved in 1659, on the road down. Walk to it along the trail from the top and be picked up by a car later or catch a return bus from the road. If you continue along the trail you will end up having to get a rickshaw back, instead of a bus.

The **Sandalwood Oil Factory** ⓘ *T0821-248 3651, Mon-Sat 0900-1100, 1400-1600 (prior permission required), no photography inside*, is where the oil is extracted and incense is made. The shop sells soap, incense sticks and other sandalwood items.

At the **Silk Factory** ⓘ *Manathavadi Rd, T0821-248 1803, Mon-Sat 0930-1630, no photography*, weavers produce Mysore silk saris, often with gold *zari* work. Staff will often show you the process from thread winding to jacquard weaving, but they speak little English. The shop sells saris from Rs 3000. Good walks are possible in the Government House if the guard at the gate allows you in.

Sri Mahalingeshwara Temple ⓘ *12 km from Mysore, 1 km off the Bhogadi road (right turn after K Hemmanahalli, beyond Mysore University Campus), taxi or auto-rickshaw*, is an 800-year-old Hoysala Temple that has been carefully restored by local villagers under the supervision of the Archaeological Survey of India. The structure is an authentic replica of the old temple: here, too, the low ceiling encourages humility by forcing the worshipper to bow before the shrine. The surrounding garden has been planted with herbs and saplings, including some rare medicinal trees, and provides a tranquil spot away from the city.

Around Mysore → *For listings, see pages 1071-1077.*

Srirangapatnam → *Colour map 7, B3. Phone code: 08236. Population: 21,900.*

ⓘ *The island is over 3 km long and 1 km wide so it's best to hire a cycle from a shop on the main road to get around.*

Srirangapatnam, 12 km from Mysore, has played a crucial role in the region since its origins in the 10th century. Occupying an easily fortified island site in the Kaveri River, it has been home to religious reformers and military conquerors. It makes a fascinating day trip from Mysore; Daria Daulat Bagh and the Gumbaz are wonderful.

The name Srirangapatnam comes from the **temple of Sri Ranganathaswamy** ⓘ *0600-1400, 1600-2030, Rs 10 for shoe stand*, which stands aloof at the heart of the fortress, containing a highly humanistic idol of Lord Vishnu reclining on the back of a serpent. Dating from AD 894, it is far older than the fort and town, and was subsequently added to by the Hoysala and Vijayanagar kings. The latter built the fort in 1454, and occupied the site for some 150 years until the last Vijayanagar ruler handed over authority to the Hindu Wodeyars of Mysore, who made it their capital. In the second half of the 18th century it became the capital of Haidar Ali, who defended it against the Marathas in 1759, laying the foundations of his expanding power. He was succeeded by his son Tipu Sultan, who also used the town as his headquarters until Colonel Wellesley, the future Duke of Wellington, established his military reputation by defeating the Tiger of Mysore in battle on 4 May 1799 (see page 1392). Tipu died in exceptionally fierce fighting near the north gate of the fort; the place is marked by a simple monument.

The fort had triple fortifications, but the British destroyed most of it. The **Jama Masjid** ⓘ *0800-1700*, which Tipu had built, has delicate minarets, and there are two Hindu **temples**, to Narasimha (17th century) and Gangadharesvara (16th century). The **Daria Daulat Bagh** (Splendour of the Sea) ⓘ *1 km east of the fort, Sat-Thu 0830-1730, foreigners Rs 100, Indians Rs 5*, is Tipu's beautiful summer palace, built in 1784 and set in a lovely garden. This social historical jewel has colourful frescoes of battle scenes between the French, British and Mysore armies, ornamental arches and gilded paintings on the teak walls and ceilings crammed with interesting detail. The west wall shows Haidar Ali and Tipu Sultan leading their elephant forces at the battle of Polilur (1780), inflicting a massive defeat on the British. As a result of the battle Colonel Baillie, the defeated British commander, was held prisoner in Srirangapatnam for many years. The murals on the east walls show Tipu offering hospitality to neighbouring princes at various palace durbars. The small museum upstairs has 19th-century European paintings and Tipu's belongings.

Three kilometres east, the **Gumbaz** ⓘ *Sat-Thu 1000-1700, donation collected*, is the family mausoleum, approached through an avenue of cypresses. Built by Tipu in memory of his father, the ornate white dome protects beautiful ivory-on-wood inlay and Tipu's tiger-stripe emblem, some swords and shields. Haider Ali's tomb is in the centre, his wife to the east and Tipu's own to the west.

On the banks of the Cauvery just north of the Lal Bagh Palace is a jetty where six-seater *coracles* are available for river rides.

Ranganathittu Bird Sanctuary

ⓘ *5 km upstream of Srirangapatnam, 0700-1800, foreigners Rs 300, Indians Rs 50, camera Rs 25, video Rs 250. Boats (0830-1330, 1430-1830), foreigners Rs 300, Indians Rs 50. Jun-Oct best. Mysore City Bus 126, or auto-rickshaw from Srirangapatnam.*

The riverine site of this sanctuary was established in 1975. Several islands, some bare and rocky, others larger and well wooded, provide excellent habitat for waterbirds, including the black-crowned night heron, Eurasian spoonbill and cormorants. Fourteen species of waterbirds use the sanctuary as a breeding ground from June onwards. There is a large colony of fruit bats in trees on the edge of the river and a number of marsh crocodiles between the small islands. Guided boat trips from the jetty last 15-20 minutes.

Somnathpur → *Phone code: 08227.*

This tiny village boasts the only complete Hoysala temple in the Mysore region. The drive east from Srirangapatnam via Bannur is particularly lovely, passing a couple of lakes through beautiful country and pretty, clean villages. The small but exquisite **Kesava Temple** (1268) ⓘ *0900-1700, foreigners Rs 100, Indians Rs 5, allow 1 hr, canteen, buses from Mysore take 1-1½ hrs; via Bannur (25 km, 45 mins) then to Somnathpur (3 km, 15 mins by bus, or lovely walk or bike ride through countryside)*, is one of the best preserved of 80 Hoysala temples in this area. Excellent ceilings show the distinctive features of the late Hoysala style, and here the roof is intact where other famous temples have lost theirs. The temple has three sanctuaries with the *trikutachala* (triple roof) and stands in the middle of its rectangular courtyard (70 m long, 55 m wide) with cloisters containing 64 cells around it. From the east gateway is a superb view of the temple with an ambulatory standing on its raised platform, in the form of a 16-pointed star. The pillared

Srirangapatnam

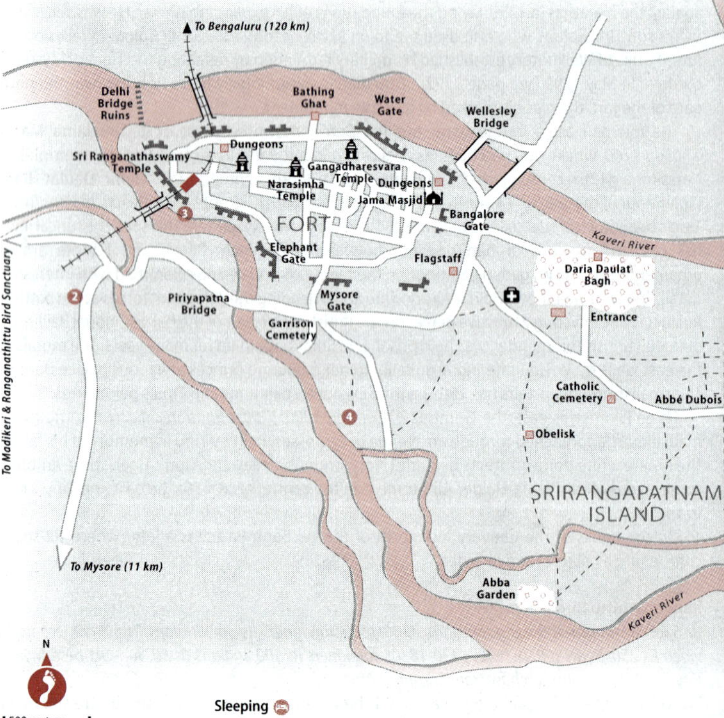

Sleeping

Balaji Garden Resort **2**
Fort View Resort **3**
Mayura River View **4**
PWD Rest House **4**

hall in the centre with the three shrines to the west give it the form of a cross in plan. Walk around the temple to see the fine bands of sculptured figures. The lowest of the six shows a line of elephants, symbolizing strength and stability, then horsemen for speed, followed by a floral scroll. The next band of beautifully carved figures (at eye level) is the most fascinating and tells stories from the epics. Above is the *yali* frieze, the monsters and foliage possibly depicting the river Ganga and uppermost is a line of *hamsa*, the legendary geese.

Sivasamudram

Here, the Kaveri plunges over 100 m into a series of wild and inaccessible gorges. At the top of the falls the river divides around the island of Sivasamudram, the Barachukki channel on the east and the Gaganchukki on the west. The hydro- electricity project was completed in 1902, the first HEP scheme of any size in India. It's best visited during the wet season, when the falls are an impressive sight, as water cascades over a wide area in a series of leaps.

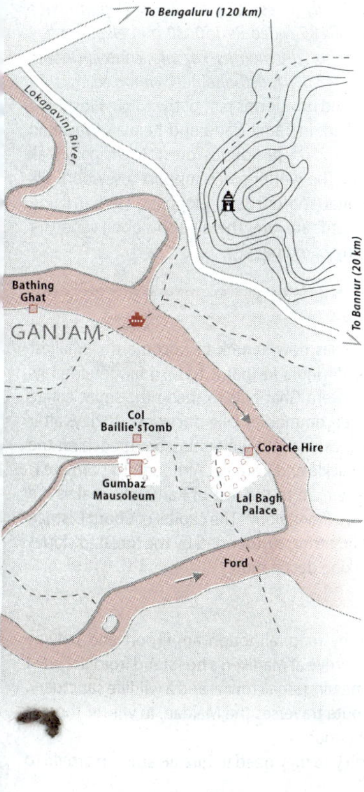

Biligiri Rangaswamy Wildlife Sanctuary

➔ *Altitude: 1000-1600 m.*

ⓘ *80 km south of Mysore, 0600-0900, 1600-1830, foreigners Rs 1000, Indians Rs 200, car safari Rs 300, guide fee Rs 250. From Mysore, access is via Nanjangud (23 km) and Chamarajanagar, where there's a Forest Check Post. For information, contact Deputy Conservator of Forests, Sultan Sheriff Circle, Chamarajanagar, T08226-222059.*

A hilly area with moist deciduous and semi-evergreen forests interspersed with grassland, the Biligiri Rangaswamy hills represent a biodiversity crossroads between the eastern and western sides of the Ghats. Some of the largest elephant populations east of the divide occur here, along with sloth bear (better sightings here than at other southern sanctuaries), panther, elephant, deer, gaur and the occasional tiger, as well as 270 species of bird. The local Forest Department has recently begun offering treks through the sanctuary, guided by members of the tribal community; see www.mysterytrails.com for details. The best time for wildlife sighting is November to May. The local Soliga hill tribes pay special respect to an ancient champak tree (*Doddasampige mara*) believed to be 1000 years old and the abode of Vishnu.

Bandipur National Park ➔ *Colour map 7, B3.*

Altitude: 780-1455 m. Area: 874 sq km.

ⓘ *96 km southwest of Mysore. 0600-0900, 1530-1830, reception centre 0900-1630; Mysore–Ooty buses stop at the main entrance. Entry fees have increased stratospherically: Rs 1000 per entry for foreigners, Rs 300 for*

Passage to Mysore

The southern route to Mysore through Kanakapura and Malvalli is longer than the more northerly rail and road route. This way crosses the open parkland of the Maidan, rising to over 1200 m. The ancient rocks of some of the oldest granites in India which give reddish or brown soils, often with extraordinary hilly outcrops and boulders, provided David Lean and Richard Goodwin with the ideal filming location to capture the atmosphere of E M Forster's Barabar Cave for their film of *A Passage to India* without the hazards of working in Bihar.

The lower cave sequences were filmed at **Savandurga**. To get there, take the BTS bus from Bengaluru City Bus Stand 0700, 0900, or take a bus to Magadi, then an auto-rickshaw, Rs 50, ask at the Lakshmi store for directions or a guide. It's a stunning climb up Kempi Gowda hill.

There is also a small Forest Park and the upper caves at **Rama Dhavara**, 2 km from Ramanagaram. The caves are visible from the road and easy to find, though only false entrances were made for the film, with interior shots filmed in a studio.

Indians. Except for jeep safaris run by local lodges, the only access is by the Forest Department's uninspiring 1-hr bus safari: foreigners Rs 200, Indians Rs 85, video Rs 150. 30-min elephant 'joy rides', Rs 65. Best times to visit are Nov-Feb to avoid the hot, dry months. For info, contact Deputy Conservator of Forests, T08229-236043, Mysore T0821-248 0901, dcfbandipur@yahoo.co.in.
Bandipur was set up by the Mysore maharaja in 1931, and now forms part of the Nilgiri Biosphere Reserve, sharing borders with Mudumalai National Park in Tamil Nadu and Kerala's Wayanad Wildlife Sanctuary. It has a mixture of subtropical moist and dry deciduous forests (principally teak and anogeissus) and scrubland in the Nilgiri foothills. The wetter areas support rosewood, silk cotton, sandalwood and *jamun*. You may spot gaur, chital (spotted deer), elephant, sambar, flying squirrel and four-horned antelope, but tigers and leopards are rare. There's also a good variety of birdlife including crested hawk, serpent eagles and tiny-eared owls.

Coorg (Kodagu) → *For listings, see pages 1071-1077.*

Coorg, once a proud warrior kingdom, then a state, has now shrunk to become the smallest district in Karnataka. It is a beautiful anomaly in South India in that it has, so far, retained its original forests. Ancient rosewoods jut out of the Western Ghat hills to shade the squat coffee shrubs which the British introduced as the region's chief commodity. Like clockwork, 10 days after the rains come, these trees across whole valleys burst as one into white blossom drenching the moist air with their thick perfume, a hybrid of honeysuckle and jasmine. Although the climate is not as cool as other hill stations, Coorg's proximity by road to the rest of Karnataka makes it a popular weekend bolt hole for inhabitants of Bengaluru (Bangalore). The capital of Coorg District, Madikeri, is an attractive small town in a beautiful hilly setting surrounded by the forested slopes of the Western Ghats and has become a popular trekking destination.

Ins and outs

Getting there At present Coorg is only accessible by road, although an airport and railway station are planned. Frequent local and express buses arrive at Madikeri's bus stand from the west coast after a journey through beautiful wooded hills passing small towns and a wildlife sanctuary. From Mysore and Coimbatore an equally pleasant route traverses the Maidan. In winter there is often hill fog at night, making driving after dark dangerous.
Getting around Madikeri is ideal for walking though you may need to hire an auto on arrival to reach the better hotels. ▸▸ *See Transport, page 1077.*

Tourist information There's a small **tourist office** ⓘ *Mysore Rd south of the Thinmaya statue, T08272-228580*. **Coorg Wildlife Society** ⓘ *2 km further out on Mysore Rd, T08272- 223505, www.cws.in*, can help with trekking advice and permits for catch-and-release mahseer fishing on the Kaveri River.

Background

Although there were references to the Kodaga people in the Tamil Sangam literature of the second century AD, the earliest Kodaga inscriptions date from the eighth century. After the Vjiayanagar Empire was defeated in 1565, many of their courtiers moved south, establishing regional kingdoms. One of these groups were the Haleri Rajas, members of the Lingayat caste whose leader Virarajendra set up the first Kodaga dynasty at Haleri, 10 km from the present district capital of Madikeri.

The later Kodagu rajas were noted for some bizarre behaviour. Dodda Vira (1780- 1809) was reputed to have put most of his relatives to death, a pattern followed by the last king, Vira Raja, before he was forced to abdicate by the British in 1834. In 1852 the last Lingayat ruler of Kodagu, Chikkavirarajendra Wodeyar, became the first Indian prince to sail to England, and the economic character of the state was quickly transformed. Coffee was introduced, becoming the staple crop of the region.

The forests of Kodagu are still home to wild elephants, who often crash into plantations on jackfruit raids, and other wildlife. The Kodaga, a tall, fair and proud landowning people who flourished under the British, are renowned for their martial prowess; almost every family has one member in the military. They also make incredibly warm and generous hosts – a characteristic you can discover thanks to the number of plantation homestays in inaccessible estates of dramatic beauty pioneered here following the crash in coffee prices. Kodagu also has a highly distinctive cuisine, in which *pandi* curry (pork curry) and *kadumbuttu* (rice dumplings) are particular favourites.

Madikeri (Mercara) ➔ *Colour map 7, B2. Phone code: 08272. Population: 32,300. Altitude: 1150 m.*

The **Omkareshwara Temple**, dedicated to both Vishnu and Siva, was built in 1820. The tiled roofs are typical of Kerala Hindu architecture, while the domes show Muslim influence. On high ground dominating the town is the **fort** with its three stone gateways, built between 1812-1814 by Lingarajendra Wodeyar II. It has a small **museum** ⓘ *Tue-Sun 0900-1700, closed holidays*, in St Mark's Church as well as the town prison, a temple and a chapel while the palace houses government offices. The **Rajas' Tombs** (*Gaddige*), built in 1820 to the north of the town, are the memorials of Virarajendra and his wife and of

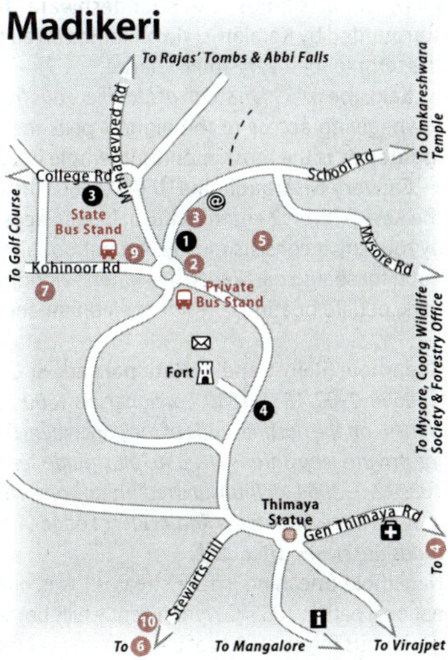

Not to scale

Sleeping
Cauvery **2**
Chitra **3**
East End **4**
Hilltown **5**
Mayura Valley View **6**
Popular Residency **7**
Rajdarshan **10**
Vinayaka Lodge **9**

Eating
Choice **1**
Taj **3**
Udupi Veglands **4**

Lingarajendra. Although the rajas were Hindu, their commemorative monuments are Muslim in style; Kodagas both bury and cremate their dead. The **friday market** near the bus stand is very colourful as all the local tribal people come to town to sell their produce. It is known locally as shandy, a British bastardization of the Coorg word *shante*, meaning market. On Mahadevped Road, which leads to the Rajas' tombs, is a 250-year-old **Siva temple** which has an interesting stone façade. Madikeri also has an attractive nine-hole golf course.

Around Madikeri

Madikeri and the surrounding area makes for beautiful walking but if you want to venture further you'll need to take a guide as paths can soon become indistinct and confusing. **Abbi Falls** is a 30-minute rickshaw ride (9 km, Rs 150 round-trip) through forests and coffee plantations. It is also an enjoyable walk along a fairly quiet road. The falls themselves are beautiful and well worth the visit. You can do a beautiful short trek down the valley and then up and around above the falls before rejoining the main road. Do not attempt it alone since there are no trails and you must depend on your sense of direction along forest paths. **Honey Valley Estate** (see page 1073) has a book of walks around the guesthouse.

At **Bhagamandala** ⓘ *36 km southwest, half-hourly service from Madikeri's private bus stand from 0630-2000, Rama Motors tour bus departs 0830, with 30-min stop*, the Triveni bathing ghat can be visited at the confluence of the three rivers: Kaveri, Kanike and Suiyothi. Among many small shrines the **Bhandeshwara Temple**, standing in a large stone courtyard surrounded by Keralan-style buildings on all four sides, is particularly striking. You can stay at the temple for a very small charge.

Kakkabe ⓘ *35 km south of Madikeri, bus from Madikeri to Kakkabe at 0630, jeep 1 hr*, is a small town, giving access to the highest peak in Coorg, **Thandiandamole** (1800 m). Nearby, **Padi Iggutappa** is the most important temple in Coorg.

Cauvery Nisargadhama ⓘ *0900-1800, Rs 150, still camera Rs 10*, is a small island reserve in the Kaveri River, 2 km from Kushalnagar, accessed over a hanging bridge. Virtually untouched by tourism, it consists mostly of bamboo thickets and trees, including sandalwood, and is very good for seeing parakeets, bee eaters, woodpeckers and a variety of butterflies. There is a deer park, pedalo boating, a resident elephant and tall bamboo tree houses for wildlife viewing.

Nagarhole (Rajiv Gandhi) National Park ➔ *Colour map 7, B2.*

ⓘ *0600-0900, 1530-1830. Foreigners Rs 1000, Indians Rs 200, video Rs 1000. Main entrance is near Hunsur on the northern side of the park where Deputy Conservator of Forests may grant permission for private jeep safaris (Rs 550, plus guide fee of Rs 50) and forest treks; enquire in advance on T08222-252064, dcfhunsur@rediffmail.com. The southern entrance, with better accommodation, is at Karapur, 5 km from Kabini River Lodge. Arrive during daylight as elephant activity means the roads are closed after dusk.*

Nagarhole (meaning 'snake streams') was once the maharajas' reserved forest and became a national park in 1955. Covering gentle hills bordering Kerala, it includes swampland, streams, moist deciduous forest, stands of bamboo and valuable timber in teak and rosewood trees. The Kabini River, which is a tributary of the Kaveri, flows through the forest where the upper canopy reaches 30 m. The park is accessible both by road and river. A number of tribesmen, particularly Kurumbas (honey gatherers) who still practise ancient skills, live amongst, and care for, the elephants.

In addition to elephants, the park also has gaur (Indian bison), dhole (Indian wild dogs), wild cats, four-horned antelopes, flying squirrels, sloth bears, monkeys and sambar deer ("better sightings than at Mudumalai"). Tigers and leopards are sighted very rarely. Many varieties of birds include the rare Malabar trogon, great black woodpecker, Indian pitta, pied hornbill, whistling thrush, green imperial pigeon and also waterfowl and reptiles.

The edge of the dam is the best place to view wildlife, particularly during the dry period from March to June. The Forest Department runs 45-minute bus tours during the morning and evening opening hours; there's a one-hour tour at 1715 with viewing from *machans* near the waterholes. You can also visit the government's Elephant Training Camp at Haballa, and take a 30-minute ride (Rs 75).

Mysore and Southern Maidan listings

For Sleeping and Eating price codes and other relevant information, see Essentials pages 38-42.

Sleeping

Mysore *p1062, map p1063*

May is the most important wedding month and so hotels get booked in advance. In the expensive hotels sales tax on food, luxury tax on rooms and a service charge can increase the bill significantly. The **Gandhi Square** area has some Indian-style hotels which are clean and good value. Note that JLB Rd is Jhansi Lakshmi Bai Rd, B-N Rd is Bengaluru-Nilgiri Rd.

LL-AL Lalith Mahal Palace (ITDC), Narasipur Rd, Siddartha Nagar T0821-257 1265. 54 rooms (**A**) and suites in the palace built in 1931 for the maharaja's non-vegetarian, foreign guests. Regal setting near Chamundi Hill, old fashioned (some original baths with extraordinary spraying system), for nostalgia stay in the old wing, attractive pool, but avoid the below par restaurant.

L-AL Royal Orchid Metropole, 5 JLB Rd, T0821-425 5566, www.royalorchidhotels.com. After languishing in disrepair for years, the Karnataka government has resuscitated the glorious colonial Metropole building. Airy, high-ceilinged rooms, massage and yoga classes plus a small pool and excellent restaurant.

L-AL Windflower Resort, Maharanpratap Rd, T0821-252 2500, www.thewind flower.com. Good, newish resort in a peaceful location on the outskirts, with large rooms and suites arranged around a monumental (but strictly ornamental) pool. Ground floor apartments come with sit-outs and outdoor showers, and huge fluffy beds perched on plinths that all but guarantee a midnight toe-stubbing. There's a spa, a proper swimming pool, and bikes for rent.

L-B Green Hotel, Chittaranjan Palace, 2270 Vinoba Rd, Jayalakshmipuram (near Mysore University), T0821-251 2536, www.green hotelindia.com. Princess's beautiful palace lovingly converted with strong sustainable tourism ethos: hot water from solar panels, profits to charity and staff recruited from less advantaged groups. The best of the 31 rooms are in the palace but if you stay in the cheaper, newer block you can still loll about in the huge upper lounges: excellent library, chess tables and day beds. Unique, but beyond walking distance from Mysore centre.

AL-C Indus Valley, near **Lalith Mahal** (see above), T0821-247 3437, www.ayurindus. com. Health resort in a splendid location, halfway up a hill, 22 rooms (in main building or in cottage), hot showers and Western toilets, TV in lounge, Ayurvedic massages, pleasant walks, vegetarian Ayurvedic restaurant, herbal wines, friendly staff, family run.

A-D Mayura Hoysala (KSTDC), 2 JLB Rd, T0821-242 5349. 20 rooms in lovely, ochre-painted, ramshackle raj-style hotel: full of chintzy soft furnishings, overspilling with plant pots, en suite bathrooms have both Western and squat loos, tiny whitewashed cane stools are propped up on terracing along with mismatched 1970s furniture. 3 restaurants, bar, tourist desk.

A-D Siddharta, 73/1 Guest House Rd, Nazarabad, T0821-528 0999, www.siddharta group.com. 105 rooms, some a/c, huge with baths, good restaurant (Indian vegetarian), exchange, immaculate, well run.

B Kaynes Hotel, off Hunsur Rd, T0821-240 2931. 22 rooms with bath, reasonable restaurant, pool, tennis, gym.

C-E Bombay Tiffany's, 313 Sayyaji Rao Rd, T0821-243 5255, bombaytiffanys@yahoo.com. Affable owner in hotel with 60 rooms (12 a/c in new hotel), clean and in mint condition, if a little plasticky and gilt. The regular rooms are spartan, but the deluxe and a/c ones are very good value.

C-G Mysore Dasaprakash, Gandhi Sq, T0821-244 2444, www.mysoredasaprakashgroup.com. 144 rooms in this labyrinthine blue-white complex set around an attractive, large courtyard. Milk coffee-coloured rooms are stocked with wood furniture and scrupulously clean white sheets. Peaceful and quiet despite being slap bang in the centre.

D Park Lane, 2720 Sri Harsha Rd, T0821-243 0400, parklanemysore@yahoo.com. Freshly renovated, with a price hike to match, but the folk-art-rustic rooms are clean and good value. The noise, including nightly classical Indian performances, from popular downstairs restaurant does travel (open 1030-2330).
E-F Hotel Ritz, Bengaluru–Nilgiri Rd near Central Bus Station, T0821-242 9082, hotelritz@rediffmail.com. Bags of character in this 60-year-old house and garden set back from the busy road. 4 rooms with wooden furniture off cool communal area with TV, dining table and chairs. Pleasant open shaded courtyard. Legendary amongst backpackers so book ahead.
F Greens' Boarding and Lodging, 2722/2 Curzon Park Rd, T0821-242 2415. Dark hallways give onto these green gloss-painted rooms with dark wood furniture. Cool, spacious, central and darn cheap, but bathrooms are not the best.

Srirangapatnam *p1065, map p1066*

B-E Fort View Resort, T08236-252777. 12 upmarket rooms (4 with corner tub), Rajasthani architecture, huge beds, shady landscaped gardens, gloomy and pricey restaurant, organic kitchen garden, pool, boating, fishing, efficient.
C Mayura River View, Mysore Rd, T08236-217454. Beautifully situated on the croc-filled river with 8 comfortable rooms, sit-outs, 2 a/c, good vegetarian restaurant (Indian, Chinese), most relaxing, really quiet.
C-E Balaji Garden Resort, Mysore Rd (1 km from Piriyapatna Bridge), T08236-217355. 12 good-value cottages and 28 smallish rooms built with some style around a central courtyard, well furnished, tiled and comfy, cottages are good value, pool, restaurant.
F PWD Rest House. Book ahead at PWD office near Ranganathaswami Temple, T08236-252051. Charming former residence of George Harris. Basic rooms (Rs 50), but clean and quiet.

Biligiri Rangaswamy Wildlife Sanctuary *p1067*

As in most Karnataka wildlife parks, the lodges and forest rest houses here charge foreigners as much as double the rate Indians pay.
LL-L K Gudi Camp, Kyathadevara, book via **Jungle Lodges**, T080-4055 4055, www.junglelodges.com. 8 twin-bedded quality tents with modern toilets, simple meals in the open air or 4 rooms with 4 beds at royal hunting lodge, elephant rides, birding, trekking, comfortable experience despite remoteness.

Bandipur National Park *p1067*

Reserve rooms in advance; avoid weekends.
LL-L Bandipur Safari Lodge, at Melkamanahalli nearby, T080-4055 4055, www.junglelodges.com. Simple rooms in cottages and restaurant under shady trees; rates include nature walks, park safaris and entry fees.
L Dhole's Den, Kaniyanapura village, T08229-236062, www.dholesden.com. Lovely small resort, with 2 rooms, a spacious suite and 2 large cottages, done out in modern minimalist style with a minimal-impact ethic: there's no TV or a/c, most electricity comes from wind turbines and solar, and you can pick your own veggies from the organic garden for dinner.
AL Tusker Trails, Mangla Village, 3 km from Bandipur campus, T08229-236055, www.tuskertrails.in. 6 rustic cottages with verandas around pool with good views, bamboo hut on stilts, nearby dam attracts wildlife, includes meals, entry and park rides.
D Venu Vihar Lodge, 20 km from park reception. Book in advance through Forest Department, Woodyard, Mysore, T0821-248 0110. Set in the beautiful Gopalaswamy Hills. Meals available but take provisions.

Madikeri *p1069, map p1069*

Power cuts are common. Carry a torch, keep candles handy. Book early during holidays.
LL Orange County, Karadigodu Post, Siddapur, T08274-258481, www.orange county.in. The poshest place for miles around, with beautiful red-brick cottages set among 300 acres of coffee plantation. Good bird guides, coracle rides on the river and great food.
B-C Capitol Village, 5 km southeast of town on Siddapur Rd, T08272-225975. 13 large, airy rooms, dorm (Rs 150), traditional Keralan building (tiled roof, wooden beams) set in a coffee, cardamom and pepper estate, very quiet, outdoor eating under shady trees (Rs 75-150), rickshaw from centre Rs 40.
C Mayura Valley View (KSTDC), Raja's Seat, T08272-228387, or book at Karnataka Tourism, Bengaluru (Bangalore), T080-2221 2901. Perched

on a cliff-top with stunning views especially at sunset. 25 rooms but sadly very run down and half deserted.

C-D Rajdarshan, 116/2 MG Rd, T08272-229142, hotelrajdarshan.net. 25 well laid-out, clean rooms (need renovating), excellent restaurant, friendly staff, modern, with views over town.

C-E Chitra, School Rd, near bus stand, T08272-225372, www.hotelchitra.com. 54 nondescript rooms with Western toilets, hot shower, simple but clean, North Indian vegetarian restaurant, bar, helpful and knowledgeable English-speaking trekking guide (Mr Muktar).

C-E East End, Gen Thimaya Rd, T08272-229996. Darkish rooms but good restaurant, serves excellent *dosas*.

E Hilltown, Daswal Rd, T08272-223801, hilltown@rediffmail.com. 38 modern, pleasant and airy rooms with TV in new hotel, marble-floored throughout, restaurant, great value. Highly recommended.

E Popular Residency, Kohinoor Rd, T08272-221644. 10 clean and pleasant rooms in new hotel, well fitted out, North Indian vegetarian restaurant, good value.

E-G Cauvery, School Rd, T08272-225492. 26 clean, pleasant but basic rooms with fans, Indian meals, bar, away from main road. Helpful management, information on trekking (stores luggage).

F-G Vinayaka Lodge, 25 m from bus stand, T08272-229830. Good value 50 rooms with bath, hot water buckets, friendly staff, clean, quiet (bus stand can be noisy early morning).

Around Madikeri *p1070*

D-E Forest Rest House, Cauvery Nisar- gadhama, contact Forestry Office, Madikeri, T08272-228305, dfo_madikeri@ yahoo.com. 11 simple cottages built largely of bamboo and teak, some with balconies on stilts over the water, electricity (no fan), hot water, peaceful (despite nocturnal rats), but poor food.

D-E Palace Estate, 2 km south of Kakkabe (Rs 35 in a rickshaw) along Palace Rd, T08272-238446, www.palaceestate.co.in. A small, traditional farm growing coffee, pepper, cardamom and bananas lying just above the late 18th-century Nalnad Palace, a summer hunting lodge of the kings of Coorg. 6 basic rooms with shared veranda looking across 180° of forested hills all the way to Madikeri. Isolated and an excellent base for walking; Coorg's highest peak is 6 km from the homestay. Home-cooked local food, English-speaking guide Rs 150.

D-F Honey Valley Estate, Yavakapadi, Kakkabe, 3 km up a track only a jeep can manage, T08272-238339, www.honeyvalley india.in. This place has less stunning views than **Palace Estate** (the house is screened by tall trees) but equally good access by foot to trekking trails. Facilities are mostly better and it can fit over 30 guests, charming host family too. Also has a hut 2 km into the forest for those wanting more isolation.

Nagarhole *p1070*

A 2-tier pricing structure operates in Nagarhole. Prices quoted are for foreigners.

LL Kabini River Lodge, at Karapur on reservoir bank, T082-2826 4402, www.junglelodges.com. 14 rooms in Mysore Maharajas' 18th-century hunting lodge and bungalow, 6 newer cabins overlooking lake, 5 tents, simple but acceptable, good restaurant, bar, exchange, package includes meals, sailing, rides in buffalo-hide coracles on the Kaveri, jeep/minibus at Nagarhole and Murkal complex, park tour with naturalist, very friendly and well run.

AL Jungle Inn, Veerana Hosahalli (near Hunsur gate), T08222-246160, www.jungleinn.in. Colonial-style lodge, 20 well-appointed rooms and a handful of tents, 3 dorms, meals, boating, elephant rides.

AL Waterwoods, 500 m from Kabini River Lodge, surrounded by the Kabini river, T08228-264421. Exquisitely furnished ranch-style house, 6 luxury rooms with sit-outs, beautiful gardens on water's edge, delicious home cooking, solar power, friendly staff, boating, jeep, Ayurvedic massage, gym, swimming, walking, charming, informal atmosphere, peaceful, secluded. Highly recommended.

B-G Forest Department Rest Houses, at various locations within the park, book at least 15 days in advance via Deputy Conservator of Forests, Hunsur, T08222- 252401. Facilities range from **G** dorm beds to simple cottages with attached bath and hot water.

❷ Eating

Mysore *p1062, map p1063*

ŸŸŸ Green, atmospheric, with food served in the palace itself, on a veranda, or under the stars in the hotel's immaculate garden. But not the best food.

₹₹₹ **Om Shanti, Siddharta** (see Sleeping). Pure vegetarian either with/without a/c, thronged with domestic tourists, which is a fair reflection of its culinary prowess.

₹₹ **King's Kourt hotel**, Metropole Circle, JLB Rd. **Mysore Memories** and outdoor **Raintree** barbecue restaurants are popular.

₹₹ **Park Lane** (see Sleeping). Red lights hang from the creeper-covered trellis over this courtyard restaurant: turn them on for service. Superb classical music played every evening 1900-2130, good food, including barbecue nights. Popular, lively and idiosyncratic.

₹₹ **Shanghai**, Vinoba Rd. 1100-1500, 1830-2300. Superb Chinese despite shabby interior.

₹₹ **Shilpashri**, Gandhi Sq. Comfortable rooftop, reasonably priced, tourist orientated, chilled beers, friendly but service can be slow.

₹₹ **Siddharta** (see Sleeping). Great South Indian but in crowded non-a/c room facing car park.

₹ **Amaravathi** (Roopa's), Hardinge Circle. Excellent, spicy hot Andhra meals served on banana leaves.

₹ **Ganesh**, opposite Central Bus Stand. Great *dosas*, sweets.

₹ **Jewel Rock, Maurya Residency**, Sri Harsha Rd. Dark interior, great chicken tikka, spicy cashew nut chicken, go early to avoid queues.

₹ **Mylari, Hotel Mahadeshwara**, Nazarbad Main Rd (ask rickshaw driver). The best *dosas* in town served on a banana leaf, mornings until 1100, basic surroundings, may have to queue. Biriyanis also legendary.

₹ **Mysore Dasaprakash** (see Sleeping). Good breakfast, huge southern *thali* (Rs 25).

₹ **RRR**, Gandhi Sq. Part a/c, tasty non- vegetarian on plantain leaves, good for lunch.

₹ **Samrat**, next to Indra Bhavan, Dhanvantri Rd. Range of tasty North Indian vegetarian.

₹ **Santosh**, near bus station. Excellent value *thalis* (Rs 16).

₹ **SR Plantain Leaf** (Chalukya's), Rajkamal Talkies Rd. Decent vegetarian *thalis* on banana leaf; also tandoori chicken.

Cafés and snacks

Bombay Tiffany's, Devraja Market Building. Try the 'Mysore pak', a ghee-laden sweet.

Indra Café, Sayaji Rd, on fringes of market. Excellent *bhel puri, sev puri, channa puri*.

Penguin Ice-cream Parlour. Sofas shared with local teens listening to Hindi pop.

Raghu Niwas, B-N Rd, opposite **Ritz**. Does very good breakfasts.

Sri Rama Veg, 397 Dhanvantri Rd. Serves fast food, good juices.

Madikeri *p1069, map p1069*

Capitol, near Private Bus Stand. Despite its exterior, serves excellent vegetarian fare.

Choice, School Rd. Wide menu, very good food, choice of ground floor or rooftop.

Taj, College Rd. 'Cheap and best', clean and friendly.

Udupi Veglands, opposite fort. Lovely, clean, spacious wooden eatery, delicious and cheap vegetarian *thalis*.

Bars and clubs

Mysore *p1062, map p1063*

The best bars are in hotels: try the expensive but elegant **Lalitha Mahal Palace**, or the funky lounge at the **Adhi Manor**, Chandragupta Rd.

Festivals and events

Mysore *p1062, map p1063*

Mar-Apr Temple car festival with a 15-day fair, at the picturesque town of Nanjangud, 23 km south (Erode road); **Vairamudi** festival which lasts 6 days when deities are adorned with 3 diamond crowns, at Melkote Temple, 52 km.

11 Aug Feast of St Philomena, 0800-1800, the statue of the saint is taken out in procession through the city streets ending with a service at the Gothic, stained-glass-laden cathedral.

End Sep to early-Oct Dasara, see box, page 1064.

Shopping

Mysore *p1062, map p1063*

Books

Ashok, Dhanvantri Rd, T0821-243 5533. Excellent selection.

Clothing

For silks at good prices, try Sayaji Rao Rd.

Badshah's, 20 Devraj Urs Rd, T0821-242 9799. Beautifully finished *salwar kameez*. Mr Yasin speaks good English.

Power yoga

If you know the primary series, speak fluent *ujayyi* breath and know about the *mulla bandha* odds are that you have heard the name of Sri Pattabhi Jois, too. His is the version of yoga that has most percolated contemporary Western practice (it's competitive enough for the type-A modern societies we live in, some argue), and although for most of the years of his teaching he had just a handful of students, things have certainly changed.

Though the Guru left his body in May 2009, a steady flow of international students still make the pilgrimage to his Ashtanga Yoga Nilayam in Mysore, where his daughter Saraswathi and grandson Sharath Rangaswamy continue the lineage.

Saraswathi's classes are deemed suitable for Ashtanga novices, but studying with Sharath is not for dilettante yogis; the Westerners here are extremely ardent about their practice – mostly teachers themselves – and there is a strict pecking order which first-timers could find alienating. Classes start from first light at 0400, and the day's teaching is over by 0700, leaving you free for the rest of the day. The schooling costs US$500 a month.

There's no rule that says you must know the series, but it might be better, and cheaper, to dip a toe in somewhere a bit less hardcore and far-flung, such as Purple Valley in Goa (see page 1258).

In a curious side note, the prevalence of foreigners running under-the-table yoga businesses in Mysore has led the local police to institute what may be the world's only city-specific visa. Prospective students heading for Mysore must now apply for a Yoga Visa, essentially a student visa which requires admission papers from a recognized yoga school. Teachers risk a fine if they so much as demonstrate a Surya Namaskar without checking your papers.

Kerala police have been pushing for a similar rule, but as yet, yoga centres outside Mysore seem unaffected by the new rule.

For details and Sharath's teaching schedule, see www.kpjayi.com.

Craft Emporium, middle part of Vinoba Rd. Good selection and quality but beware those pretending to be government emporia. Also sells cloth.
Karnataka Silk Industry, Mananthody Rd, T0821-248 1803. Mon-Sat 1030-1200, 1500-1630. Watch machine weaving at the factory shop.

Handicrafts

Superb carved figures, sandalwood and rosewood items, silks, incense sticks, handicrafts. The main shopping area is Sayaji Rao Rd.
Cauvery Arts & Crafts Emporium, for sandalwood and rosewood items, closed Thu (non-receipt of parcel reported by traveller).
Devaraja Market, lanes of stalls selling spices, perfumes and much more; good 'antique' shop (fixed price) has excellent sandalwood and rosewood items. Worth visiting.
Ganesh, 532 Dhanvantri Rd.
Shankar, 12 Dhanvantri Rd.
Sri Lakshmi Fine Arts & Crafts (opposite the zoo); also has a factory shop at 2226 Sawday Rd, Mandi Mohalla.

Activities and tours

Mysore *p1062, map p1063*

Body and soul

Jois Ashtanga Yoga Research Institute, www.kpjayi.org. Not for dilettante yogis at Rs 8000 a month, the minimum period offered.
Sri Patanjali Yogashala, Parakala Mutt, next to Jaganmohan Palace. Ashtanga Vinyasa yoga; daily instruction in English from BNS Iyengar, 0600-0900, 1600-1900, US$100 per month: some say the conditions here are slapdash, although teaching is good.

Swimming

Mysore University, Olympic-sized pool, hourly sessions 0630-0830 then 1500-1600, women only 1600-1700.
Southern Star Mysore, 13-14 Vinoba Rd, T0821-242 1689, www.ushalexushotels.com. More of a pool to relax by and sunbathe.

Tour operators

KSTDC, Yatri Nivas hotel, 2 JLB Rd, T0821-242 3492. **Mysore**, daily 0715-2030, Rs 155, tours of local sights and Chamundi Hill, Kukkara Halli Lake, Somanathapura, Srirangapatnam and Brindavan Gardens. Tours also run to **Belur**, **Halebid**, and **Sravanabelagola** if there are 10 or more guests: a long and tiring day, but worth it if you are not travelling to Hassan.

Seagull Travels, 8 Hotel Ramanashree Complex, BN Rd, T0821-426 0054. Good for cars, drivers, flights, wildlife tours, etc, helpful.

Skyway International Travels, No 370/4, Jansi Laxmibai Rd, T0821-244 4444, www.skywaytour.com. Official booking agent for government-run **Jungle Lodges**, plus excellent car hire service.

TCI, Gandhi Sq, T0821-526 0294. Very pleasant and helpful.

Madikeri *p1069, map p1069*

Fishing

Coorg Wildlife Society (see page 1069). Arranges licences for fishing on the Kaveri river (Rs 500 per day, Rs 1000 weekend). The highlight is the prospect of pulling in a *mahseer*, up to 45 kg in weight; all fish must be returned to the river. Fishing takes place at Trust Land Estate, Valnoor, near Kushalnagar, where there is a lodge; you'll need to bring your own food.

Trekking

Friends' Tours and Travel, below **Bank of India**, College Rd, T08272-229974. Recommended for their knowledge and enthusiasm. Tailor-made treks Rs 275 per person per day including guide, food and accommodation in temples, schools, etc. A base camp is at Thalathmane, 4 km from Madikeri, which people can also stay at even if not trekking. Basic huts and blankets for Rs 50 each, home cooking nearby at little extra cost.

Hotel Cauvery (see page 1073). Also arranges treks.

Transport

Mysore *p1062, map p1063*

Air Mysore's tiny-but-shiny new airport on the southern edge of town has flights with **Kingfisher** to **Bengaluru** and **Chennai**.

Local bus **City bus station**, southeast of KR Circle, T0821-242 5819. To **Silk Weaving Centre**, Nos 1, 2, 4 and 8; **Brindavan Gardens**, No 303; **Chamundi Hill**, No 201; **Srirangapatnam**, No 313. **Central Bus Station**, T0821-2529853. **Bandipur**, Platform 9, **Ooty** etc, Platform 11.

Long distance but There are 2 bus stations. The confusingly-named **Suburban** (or **Central**) bus stand, T0821-252 0853, is mainly used by long-distance **SRTC** companies of Karnataka, Tamil Nadu and Kerala, all of which run regular daily services between Mysore and other major cities. The bus station has a list of buses with reserved places. To **Bengaluru** (**Bangalore**): every 15 mins from non-stop platform. Also frequent services to **Hassan**, 3 hrs; **Mangalore** (7 hrs); and **Ooty** (5 hrs) via **Bandipur** (2 hrs). Daily services to **Coimbatore**; **Gokarna** (12 hrs); **Hospet**: 1930 (10 hrs), very tiring; **Kochi**, 10 hrs; **Kozhikode** via **Wayanad**; **Salem** (7 hrs); **Thiruvananthapuram** (Super deluxe, 14 hrs). Several to **Satyamangalam** where you can connect with buses to Tamil Nadu. The journey is through wilderness and forests with spectacular scenery as the road finally plunges from the plateau down to the plains.

Private companies operate from the **Private Bus Stand**, next to the railway station on Sayyaji Rao Rd. Services to **Somnathpur** leave from here, around 1 hr direct, as well as overnight sleeper services to popular destinations (eg Panaji), but these often fill up in advance.

Car Travel companies and **KSTDC** charge from Rs 500 (4 hrs/40 km) for city sightseeing; Rs 850 to include Srirangapatnam and Brindavan Gardens.

Train Advance Computerized Reservations in separate section; ask for 'foreigners' counter'. Enquiries T131, 0800-2000 (closed 1330-1400); Sun 0800-1400. Left luggage 0600-2200, Rs 3-6 per day. Tourist information, telephone and toilets on Platform 1. Taxi counter at entrance. To **Bengaluru** (**Bangalore**) (non-stop): *Tipu Exp, 16205*, 1120, 2½ hrs; *Shatabdi Exp,12008*, daily except Tue, 1410, 2 hrs. **Bengaluru** via **Srirangapatnam**, **Mandya** and **Maddur**: *Chamundi Exp 16215*, 0645, 3 hrs; *Kaveri Chennai Exp 16221*, 2015, 2¾ hrs. **Chennai**: *Chennai Exp 16221*, 2015, 10½ hrs; *Shatabdi Exp 12008*, Wed, 1415, 7 hrs. **Madurai**: *Tuticorin Exp 16732*, 1800, 13 hrs. **Mumbai**: *Sharavathi Exp, 11036*, Thu only, 0615, 26 hrs.

Srirangapatnam *p1065, map p1066*
Trains and buses between **Bengaluru (Bangalore)** and **Mysore** stop here but arrival can be tiresome with hassle from rickshaw drivers, traders and beggars. Buses 313 and 316 from Mysore **City Bus Stand** (half-hourly) take 50 mins.

Bandipur National Park *p1067*
Bus Bandipur and the neighbouring Mudumalai NP in Tamil Nadu are both on the Mysore to Ooty bus route, about 2½ hrs south from Mysore and 2½ hrs from Ooty. Buses go to and from **Mysore** (80 km) between 0615-1530.

Madikeri *p1069, map p1069*
Auto-rickshaw From **Hotel Chitra** to **Abbi Falls**, Rs 150 including 1-hr wait there.
Bus From **KSRTC Bus Stand**, T08272-229134, frequent express buses to **Bengaluru (Bangalore)**, Plat 4, from 0615 (6 hrs); **Chikmagalur**; **Hassan** (3½ hrs); **Kannur**; **Mangalore**, Plat 2, 0530-2400 (3½ hrs); **Mysore** Plat 3, half-hourly 0600-2300 (3 hrs) via **Kushalnagar** (for Tibetan settlements), very crowded during the rush hour; **Thalassery**. Daily to **Coimbatore**, **Madurai**, **Mumbai**, **Ooty**, **Virajpet**.

Private Bus Stand: **Kamadenu Travels**, above bus stand, T08272-225524, for **Purnima Travels** bus to **Bengaluru**. **Shakti Motor Service** to **Nagarhole** (4½ hrs).
Train The closest stations are Mysore (120 km), Hassan (130 km) and Mangalore (135 km). Computerized reservations office on Main Rd, T08272-225002, Mon-Sat 1000-1700, Sun 1000-1400.

Around Madikeri *p1070*
The bus from Madikeri to **Nisargadhama** passes park gates 2 km before Kushalnagar. A rickshaw from Kushalnagar Rs 10.

Nagarhole *p1070*
Bus From **Mysore**, *Exp*, 3 hrs, Rs 35; **Madikeri**, 4½ hrs. **Bengaluru (Bangalore)**, 6 hrs. For **Kabini River Lodge** and **Water Woods**, be sure to get the **KSRTC** bus to **Karapur**, not Nagarhole. **Jungle Lodges**, T080-2559 7021, www.junglelodges.com, buses leave Bengaluru at 0730, stop in Mysore (around 0930), reaching Kabini around 1230; return bus departs 1315.
Train The nearest station is Mysore (96 km).

❶ Directory

Mysore *p1062, map p1063*
Banks Many ATMs accepting international cards on Ashoka Rd and DD Urs Rd. **State Bank of Mysore**, corner of Sayaji Rao Rd and Sardar Patel Rd and opposite GPO in city centre. **LKP Forex**, near clock tower. **Thomas Cook**, Ashoka Rd, T0821-242 6157. **Internet Coca Cola Cyber Space**, 2 Madvesha Complex, Nazarabad, near Sri Harsha Rd. **Cyber Net Corner**, 2/3B Indira Bhavan, Dhanvantri Rd. **Sify I-Way**, has a branch near Green Hotel and the Jois yoga shala at 2996/1A 1st floor, Kalidasa Rd, VV Mohalla, T0821-251 0467. **Pal Net**, Nehru Circle. Avoid **Internet World** near Ritz. **Medical services KR Hospital**, T0821-242 3300; **Medical College**, corner of Irwin and Sayaji Rao Rd; **Mission Hospital** (Mary Holdsworth), Tilaknagar, T0821-244 6644, in a striking building dating from 1906. **Post GPO**, on corner of Ashoka and Irwin roads. T0821-241 7326, has Poste Restante. **Useful contacts Deputy Conservator of Forests**, T0821-248 3853.

Madikeri *p1069, map p1069*
Banks Canara Bank, Main Rd, has an ATM and accepts some TCs. **Internet Cyber Zone**, next to Chitra Hotel. Rs 30 per hr, excellent. **Post** Behind Private Bus Stand. **Useful contacts Community Centre**, south of Fort, Main Rd, holds occasional shows. **Forestry Office**, Aranya Bhavan, Mysore Rd, 3 km from town, T08272-225708.

Western Plateau

The world's tallest monolith – that of the Jain saint Gommateshwara – has stood majestic, 'skyclad' and lost in meditation high on Sravanabelagola's Indragiri hill since the 10th century. It is a profoundly spiritual spot, encircled by long sweeps of paddy and sugar cane plains, and is one of the most popular pilgrimage points for practitioners of the austere Jain religion. Some male Jain followers of the Digambar or skyclad sect of the faith climb the rock naked to denote their freedom from material bonds. Nearby lie the 11th- and 12th-century capital cities of Halebid and Belur, the apex of Hoysala temple architecture whose walls are cut into friezes of the most intricate soapstone. These villages of the Central Maiden sit in the path of one of the main routes for trade and military movement for centuries. ▸▸ *For listings, see pages 1081-1083.*

Western Plateau temples → *For listings, see pages 1081-1083.*

Sravanabelagola, Belur and Halebid can all be seen in a very long day from Bengaluru (Bangalore), but it's far better to stay overnight near the sights themselves or in **Hassan**, a pleasant, busy and fast-developing little town with plenty of hotels a short walk from the bus stand. There are direct buses from Mysore and Bengaluru. The railway station is 2 km to the east.

Belur → *Colour map 7, A2. Phone code: 08177.*

ⓘ *Open daily 0600-2000, but some temples close 1300-1600; free; carry a torch, ASI- trained guides on-site (often excellent), Rs 200 for 4 visitors, though official rate is higher.*

Belur, on the banks of the Yagachi River, was the Hoysala dynasty's first capital and continues to be a significant town that is fascinating to explore. The gloriously elaborate Krishna Chennakesavara temple was built over the course of a century from 1116 as a fitting celebration of the victory over the Cholas at Talakad.

At first glance **Chennakesava Temple** (see also Somnathpur, page 1066) appears unimpressive because the super-structure has been lost. However, the walls are covered with exquisite friezes. A line of 644 elephants (each different) surrounds the base, with rows of figures and foliage above. The detail of the 38 female figures is perfect. Look at the young musicians and dancers on either side of the main door and the unusual perforated screens between the columns. Ten have typical bold geometrical patterns while the other 10 depict scenes from the *Puranas* in their tracery. Inside superb carving decorates the hand lathe-turned pillars and the bracket-figures on the ceiling. Each stunning filigree pillar is startlingly different in design, a symptom of the intensely competitive climate the sculptors of the day were working in. The **Narasimha pillar** at the centre of the hall is particularly fine and originally could be rotated. The detail is astounding. The jewellery on the figures is hollow and movable and the droplets of water seem to hang at the ends of the dancer's wet hair on a bracket above you. On the platform in front of the shrine is Santalesvara dancing in homage to Lord Krishna. The shrine holds a 3-m-high black polished deity, occasionally opened for *darshan*. The annual **Car Festival** is held in March-April. To the west is the **Viranarayana Temple** with some fine sculpture and smaller shrines around it. The complex is walled with an ambulatory. The entrance is guarded by the winged figure of Garuda, Vishnu's carrier, who faces the temple with joined palms.

Halebid

ⓘ *Open daily 0700-1730, free.*

The ancient capital of the Hoysala Empire was founded in the early 11th century. It was destroyed by the armies of the Delhi sultanate in 1311 and 1327. The great Hoysalesvara Temple, still incomplete after the best part of a century's toil, survived but the capital lay deserted and came to be called Halebid (ruined village), a name it continues to live up to.

Temples of Belur and Halebid

The Hoysalas, whose kingdom stretched between the Krishna and Kaveri rivers, encouraged competition among their artisans; their works even bear 12th-century autographs. Steatite meant that sculptors could fashion doily-like detail from solid rock since it is relatively soft when fresh from the quarry but hardens on exposure to air. The temples, built as prayers for victory in battle, are small but superb.

Detour 1 km south to walk around the Basthalli garden filled with remarkably simple 12th-century Jain Bastis. These have lathe-turned and multi-faceted columns, dark interiors and carved ceilings. The smaller **Kedaresvara Temple** with some highly polished columns is on a road going south. There are cycles for hourly hire to visit these quieter sites.

The **Hoysalesvara Temple** set in lawns has two shrines dedicated to Siva with a Nandi bull facing each. The largest of the Hoysala temples, it was started in 1121 but remains unfinished. It is similar in structure to Belur's, but its superstructure was never completed. Belur's real treats are in its interiors, while Halebid's are found on the outside reliefs. Six bands circle the star-shaped temple, elephants, lions, horsemen, a floral scroll and stories from the epics and the Bhagavata Purana. This frieze relates incidents from the *Ramayana* and *Mahabharata*; among them Krishna lifting Mount Govardhana and Rama defeating the demon god Ravana. The friezes above show *yalis* and *hamsa* or geese. There are exceptional half life-size deities with minute details at intervals. Of the original 84 female figures (like the ones at Belur) only 14 remain; thieves have made off with 70 down the centuries.

The **Archaeological Museum** ⓘ *Sat-Thu 0800-1700, Rs 5, no photography*, is on the lawn near the south entrance, with a gallery of 12th- to 13th-century sculptures, wood carvings, idols, coins and inscriptions. Some sculptures are displayed outside. To the west is a small lake.

Sravanabelagola (Shravanabelgola) → *Phone code: 08176*

The ancient Jain statue of Gommateshwara stands on Vindhyagiri Hill (sometimes known as Indrabetta or Indragiri), 150 m above the plain; Chandragiri to the north (also known as Chikka Betta) is just under half that height. The 17-m-high Gommateshwara statue, erected somewhere between AD 980 and 983, is of the enlightened prince Bahubali, son of the first Tirthankara (or holy Jain teacher). The prince won a fierce war of succession over his brother, Bharata, only to surrender his rights to the kingdom to take up a life of meditation.

You'll have to clamber barefoot up over 700 hot steep granite steps that carve up the hill to reach the statue from the village tank (socks, sold on-site, offer protection from the hot stone; take water), or charter a *dhooli* (a cane chair tied between two poles and carried), to let four bearers do the work for you. The small, intricately carved shrines you pass on the way up are the **Odeagal Basti**, the **Brahmadeva Mandapa**, the **Akhanda Bagilu** and the **Siddhara Basti**, all 12th-century except the Brahmadeva Mandapa which is 200 years older.

The carved statue is nude (possibly as he is a *Digambara* or 'sky-clad' Jain) and captures the tranquillity typical of Buddhist and Jain art. The depth of the saint's meditation and withdrawal from the world is suggested by the spiralling creepers shown growing up his legs and arms, and by the ant hills and snakes at his feet. Although the features are finely carved, the overall proportions are odd: he has huge shoulders and elongated arms but stumpy legs.

The 'magnificent anointment' (or *Mastakabhisheka*) falls every 12th year when Jain pilgrims flock from across India to bid for 1008 *kalashas* (pots) of holy water that are left overnight at the saint's feet. The next morning their contents, followed with ghee, milk, coconut water, turmeric paste, honey, vermilion powder and a dusting of gold, are poured over the saint's head from specially erected scaffolding. Unusually for India, the thousands of devotees watching the event do so in complete silence. The next celebration is in 2017.

In the town itself is the **Bhandari basti** (1159, with later additions), about 200 m to the left from the path leading up to the Gommateshwara statue. Inside are 24 images of Tirthankaras in a spacious sanctuary. There are 500 rock-cut steps to the top of the hill that take half an hour to climb. It is safe to leave luggage at the tourist office branch at the entrance, which closes 1300-1415. The main **tourist office** ⓘ *Vartha Bhavan, BM Rd, T08172-268862,* is very helpful. There are 14 shrines on Chandragiri and the Mauryan emperor Chandragupta, who is believed by some to have become a Jain and left his empire to fast and meditate, is buried here. The temples are all in the Dravidian style, the **Chamundaraya Basti**, built in AD 982 being one of the most remarkable. There is a good example of a free-standing pillar or *mana-stambha* in front of the Parsvanathasvami Basti. These pillars, sometimes as high as 15 m, were placed at the temple entrance. Here, the stepped base with a square cross section transforms to a circular section and the column is then topped by a capital.

Chikmagalur

Situated northeast of Belur, Chikmagalur sits at the centre of one of the country's most important coffee growing areas. Coffee was first smuggled from Mocha to India in 1670 by the Sufi saint Baba Budan, after whom the surrounding Baba Budangiri Hills are named, and the Central Coffee Research Institute was set up here in 1925. Chikmagalur is now a popular weekend destination from Bengaluru, with scores of plantation 'homestays'. There are excellent views from the top of Mulayanagiri (1930 m), reached by a motorable road. Chikmagalur town has the Hoysala-style Kodandarama Temple, a number of mosques and a moated fort.

Jog Falls → *Colour map 7, A2.*

These falls, the highest in India, are not the untamed spectacle they once were, but still make a stunning sight if you visit at the end of the wet season; the best times are from late November to early January. Come any earlier and you'll be grappling with leeches and thick mist; any later, and the falls will be more a trickle than a roar, thanks to the 50-km-long **Hirebhasgar Reservoir**, which regulates the flow of the Sharavati River in order to generate hydroelectricity. The Mysore Power Corporation releases water to the falls every second Sunday from 1000 to 1800, but even on a low-flow day the scenery and the rugged walk to the base of the falls make a visit worthwhile.

There are four falls. The highest is the **Raja**, with a fall of 250 m and a pool below 40 m deep. Next is the **Roarer**, while a short distance to the south is the **Rocket**, which shoots great gouts of water into the air. Finally comes the **Rani** (once called the White Lady), which froths elegantly over rocks. A walk to the top (not possible in the monsoons) offers breathtaking views of the cascading river and the valley. Less ambitiously, you can get another excellent view from the Inspection Bungalow on the north side of the river gorge.

Central Maidan → *For listings, see pages 1081-1083.* *Colour map 7, A3.*

Chitradurga → *Colour map 7, A3.*

At the foot of a group of granite hills rising to 1175 m in the south, is Chitradurga, 202 km northwest of Bengaluru (Bangalore). The **Fort of Seven Rounds** ⓘ *2 km from the bus stand, 4 km from the railway station, open sunrise to sunset, closed public holidays, Rs 100, allow 2 hrs,* was built in the 17th century by Nayak Poligars, semi-independent landlords who fled south after the collapse of the Vijayanagar Empire in 1565. They were crushed by Haidar Ali in 1779 who replaced the Nayaka's mud fort with stone and Tipu Sultan built a palace, mosque, granaries and oil pits in it. There are four secret entrances in addition to the 19 gateways and ingenious water tanks which collected rainwater. There are also 14 temples, including a cave temple to the west of the wall. They are placed in an extraordinary jumble of granite outcrops, a similar setting to that of Hampi 300 km to the north. The Hidimbeshwara temple is the oldest temple on the site.

Belgaum → *Colour map 5, C4. Phone code: 0831. Population: 399,600.*

An important border town, Belgaum makes an interesting stop on the Mumbai–Bengaluru (Bangalore) road or as a trip from Goa. The crowded market in the centre gives a glimpse of India untouched by tourism. With its strategic position in the Deccan plateau, the town had been ruled by many dynasties including the Chalukyas, Rattas, Vijaynagaras, Bahmanis and the Marathas. Most of the monuments date from the early 13th century. The **fort**, immediately east of the town centre, though originally pre-Muslim, was rebuilt by Yusuf Adil Shah, the Sultan of Bijapur, in 1481. Inside the **Masjid-i-Sata** (1519), the best of the numerous mosques in Belgaum, was built by a captain in the Bijapur army, Azad Khan. Belgaum is also noted for its Jain architecture and sculpture. The late Chalukyan **Kamala Basti**, with typical beautifully lathe-turned pillars and a black stone Neminatha sculpture, stands within the fort walls. To the south of the fort and about 800 m north of the Hotel Sanman on the Mumbai-Bengaluru bypass, is a beautifully sculpted Jain temple which, according to an inscription, was built by Malikaryuna.

Western Plateau listings

For Sleeping and Eating price codes and other relevant information, see Essentials pages 38-42.

Sleeping

Hotels in Belur, Halebid and Sravanabelagola have only basic facilities, but allow you to see these rural towns and villages before or after the tour groups. Due to the climb, Sravanabelagola particularly benefits from an early start. Hassan and Chikmagalur are more comfortable.

Western Plateau temples *p1078*

Hassan

L Hoysala Village Resort, Belur Rd, 6 km from Hassan T08172-256764, www.hoysalavillageresorts.in. 33 big cottage rooms with hot water, TV, tea and coffee maker and fan spread out across the landscaped, bird-filled resort. Rustic, with small handicraft shops, good restaurant, very attentive service, good swimming pool.

AL Hotel Southern Star, BM Rd, T08172- 251816, www.ushalexushotels.com. Large modern hotel with 48 excellent a/c rooms, hot water, phone, satellite TV, great views across town and countryside, excellent service.

AL-A The Ashhok Hassan (ITDC), BM Rd, 500 m from bus stand, T08172-268731, www.hassanashok.com. Dramatic renovation creating 37 lovely rooms in immaculate, soundproofed central Hassan hotel. It's all been done on clean lines, with modern art and all mod cons from a/c to Wi-Fi. Charming suites have big rattan armchairs, and the Presidential suite has its own dining room, bar and steam bath (**LL**). Excellent service and tidy garden grounds with pool.

C-E Hotel Sri Krishna, BM Rd, T08172-263240. 40 basic rooms with hot water and TV, the best of which are in the main building above the busy South Indian restaurant.

C-E Hotel Suvarna Regency, 97 BM Rd, 500 m south of bus stand, T08172-264006. 70 clean, big rooms, some with bath, a/c a bit musty but deluxe and suite rooms are nice, good vegetarian restaurant, car hire. Also has 6 bed, 4 bed and triples.

Belur *p1078*

D-E Mayura Velapuri (KSTDC), Temple Rd, T08177-222209. Reasonably clean and spacious 6 doubles, 4 triples and 2 dorms sleeping 20 (Rs 75 per person), hot water, with fan, TV and sitting areas. Friendly staff. Good South Indian meals in restaurant.

D-E Vishnu Regency, Main Rd, T08177- 223011, vishnuregency_belur@yahoo.co.in. 20 clean rooms opening onto a courtyard, some with TV, fan, hot water in the morning. Welcoming hotel with shop and good veg restaurant serving tandoor, curries and *thalis*.

Halebid *p1078*

D-E Mayura Shantala (KSTDC), T08177- 273224. Inspection Bungalow compound in nice garden overlooking temple. 4 twin-bed tiled rooms with fan, nets and bath, kitchen.

Sravanabelagola *p1079*
The temple Management Committee (SDJMI), T08176-257258, can help organize basic but clean accommodation, often with attached bath, in pilgrim hostels. Check in the **SP Guest House** by the bus stand.
G Vidyananda Nilaya Dharamshala, closest to the bus stand, reserve through SDJMI. Rooms with toilet and fan, bucket baths, blanket but no sheets, courtyard, good value.
G Raghu, near base of stairs up to Indragiri, T08176-257238. Small and utterly basic but clean rooms above a decent veg restaurant.

Chikmagalur *p1080*
LL The Serai, 7 km from town on Kadur-Mangalore Rd, T08262-224903, www.theserai.in. Fabulously luxe new resort owned by the Coffee Day café chain, with beautiful and very private villas cascading down the hill among coffee and pepper bushes. Everything's designed on clean lines, the villas come with private pools, and service is discreet and efficient. There's a spa, billiard room, and daily plantation tours. Popular with visiting cricketers and movie stars.
AL Gateway, outside town, on a hillside, T08262-660660, www.thegateway hotels.com. 29 luxury a/c rooms lined along the pool, superb staff and food, a good base for visiting Belur and Halebid (40 km).

Jog Falls *p1080*
Hotels are very basic and there are very limited eating facilities at night. Local families take in guests. Stalls near the falls serve reasonable breakfast and meals during the day.
F-G Mayura Gerusoppa (KSTDC), Sagar Taluk, T08186-244732. Decaying concrete hotel overlooking the falls; 22 rooms and a 10-bed dorm.
F-G PWD Inspection Bungalow, west of the falls, T08186-244333. Just a handful of neat a/c rooms, preferable to the various KSTDC options, but a challenge to book.
G Youth Hostel, Shimoga Rd, T08186-244251. Utterly basic dorms with mattresses on the floor.

Chitradurga *p1080*
C-D Amogha International, Santhe Honda Rd, T08194-220763. Clean, spacious, modern rooms, some a/c suites, 2 restaurants, good vegetarian but service slow. Best in town.
F Maurya, Santhe Bagilu (within city walls), T08194-224448. 26 acceptable rooms, some with a/c and TV, bit noisy.

Belgaum *p1081*
Hotels are mostly on College and PB roads.
C-E Adarsha Palace, College Rd, T0831-243 5777, adarshapalace@yahoo.co.in. Small, modern and personal, some a/c rooms, excellent **Angaan** vegetarian restaurant (rooftop non-vegetarian), good value, pleasant atmosphere, friendly staff. Recommended.
C-E Sanman Deluxe, College St, T0831-243 0777, www.hotelsanman.org. Similar to **Adarsha Palace**, in a new building (much cheaper in old Sanman), 2 restaurants.
D-F Milan, Club Rd (4 km railway), T0831-242 5555. 45 rooms with bath (hot shower), some a/c, vegetarian restaurant, good value.
E-F Keerthi, Pune–Bengaluru Rd, short walk from Central Bus Stand, T0831-246 6999. Large modern hotel, some a/c rooms, restaurant.
E-F Sheetal, Khade Bazar near bus station, T0831-242 9222. Clean-ish rooms with bath, vegetarian restaurant, Indian style, noisy hotel in busy and quite entertaining bazar street.
F Mayura Malaprabha (KSTDC), Ashok Nagar, T0831-247 0781. 6 simple clean rooms in modern cottages, dorm (Rs 40), restaurant, bar, tourist office.

Eating

Western Plateau temples *p1078*
Hassan
The veg restaurant and multi-cuisine **Suvarna Gate** at **Hotel Suvarna Regency** are the best in town, but the restaurant at **Hotel Sri Krisha** is popular, while the restaurants attached to **Hassan Ashhok**, **Hoysala Village** and **Southern Star** are best for those worried about hygiene.
GRR, opposite bus stand. For non-veg food and friendly staff.

Belur *p1078*
This sizeable town has numerous tea shops and vegetarian stands. **Vishnu Hotel** has the best tourist restaurant.

Belgaum *p1081*
Gangaprabha, Kirloskar Rd. Recommended for pure-veg food.

Zuber Biryaniwala, Kaktives Rd. For creamy biryanis and good non-veg curries.

Transport

Western Plateau temples p1078

Hassan

Bus For local buses, T08172-268418. Long-distance buses at least hourly to **Belur** from about 0700 (35 km, 1 hr) and **Halebid** from about 0800 (31 km, 1 hr); very crowded. Few direct to **Sravanabelagola** in the morning (1 hr); alternatively, travel to **Channarayapatna** and change to bus for Sravanabelagola. Also to **Bengaluru** about every 30 mins (4½ hrs), **Goa** (14 hrs), **Mangalore** (5 hrs), **Mysore** hourly (3 hrs). If heading for Hampi, you can reserve seats for the 0730 bus to **Hospet** (9 hrs).

Taxi Taxis charge around Rs 1000 for a day-tour to **Halebid** and **Belur**, and the same for a trip to **Sravanabelagola**. Drivers park up along AVK College Rd near the bus stand.

Train The railway station is 2 km east of centre, T08172-268222, with several daily passenger trains to **Mysore** and 1-2 services to **Bengaluru** and **Mangalore**.

Arsikere Jn, 45 km north of Hassan and 31 km from Halebid, has much more frequent trains to Bengaluru. Passenger trains link Arsikere to Hassan.

Belur p1078

Bus Bus stand is about 1 km from the temples. Half-hourly to **Hassan** (1 hr; last at 2030) and **Halebid** (30 mins). Also to **Shimoga**, where you can change for **Hampi** and **Jog Falls** (4 hrs); and to **Mysore** (1½ hrs).

Halebid p1078

Bus The bus stand, where you can get good meals, is near the temples. KSRTC buses run half-hourly to **Hassan** (45 mins) and from there to **Bengaluru** (**Bangalore**), **Mangalore**, **Mysore**. Also direct to **Belur** (12 km, 30 mins).

Sravanabelagola p1079

Bus Direct buses to/from **Mysore** and **Bengaluru** run in the morning; in the afternoon, change at **Channarayapatna**. The morning express buses to/from Mysore serve small villages travelling over dusty but interesting roads up to Krishnarajapet, then very few stops between there and Mysore.

Chikmagalur p1080

Bus Frequent buses to **Hassan** via **Belur**. Buses to **Bengaluru** every hour; a/c Volvo buses at 0500, 1200 and 1330. For Mangalore, go to Dharmastala and change.

Jog Falls p1080

Bus Daily buses connect Jog Falls with **Honnavar** (2½ hrs) and **Karwar**, both on the Konkan railway line; some Honnavar buses continue to **Kumta** (3 hrs), which has frequent services to **Gokarna**. Direct buses also go daily to **Mangalore** (7 hrs), **Bengaluru** (9 hrs), and **Panaji**. Hourly buses to **Shimoga** (4 hrs) for connections to **Belur**, **Hassan** and **Hospet** (7 hrs from Shimoga). For a wider choice of departures get a local bus to **Sagar**. 30 km southeast on NH-206.

Taxi To **Panaji**, Rs 1500 (6 hrs).

Train Jog Falls is 16 km from the railway at **Talguppa**. Trains from **Bengaluru** (**Bangalore**) involve a change in **Shimoga** town.

Chitradurga p1080

Bus Buses to/from **Bengaluru**, **Davangere**, **Hospet**, **Hubli** and **Mysore**. Train from **Arsikere**, **Bengaluru**, **Guntakal**, **Hubli**.

Belgaum p1081

Bus Long-distance buses leave from the **Central Bus Stand**, T0831-246 7932, to **Panaji** (0600-1715), **Margao** (0545-1500), **Mapusa** (0715-1715). The train station is near the bus stand, 4 km south of the centre; autos available **Bengaluru**: *Ranichennamma Exp 16590*, 1810, 13 hrs. **Mumbai** (**DR**) and **Pune**: *Chalukya/Sharavathi Exp, 11018/11036*, 1800, 14 hrs. **Goa via Londa**: 7 trains daily, 0135-2030, 1 hr.

Directory

Western Plateau temples p1078

Hassan

Banks **State Bank of Mysore** and **State Bank of India**, Narasimharaja Circle, have ATMs and change currency and TCs. **Medical services** **General Hospital**, Hospital Rd. **Mission Hospital**, Race Course Rd. **Internet** Next to Suvarna and Vaishnavi hotels. **Post** 100 m from bus stand.

West coast

Despite being sandwiched between the holiday honeypots of Goa and south Kerala, and despite having been given a glittering new name by the tourist board, Karnataka's 'Sapphire Coast' has thus far been slow to attract tourists. Yet the landscapes here are dreamy, riven by broad mangrove-lined creeks and carpeted with neon green paddy fields, and the beaches retain a wild beauty, almost entirely innocent of the joys and perils of banana pancakes, necklace hawkers and satellite TV.

The hilly port town of Mangalore makes a pleasant, relaxing stop between Goa and Kerala, but the jewel in the Sapphire Coast's crown thus far is undoubtedly Gokarna: a hippy stronghold, mass pilgrimage site and tremendously sacred Hindu centre. It's little more than one narrow street lined with traditional wooden houses and temples, but it is packed with pilgrims and has been adopted, along with Hampi, by the Goa overspill: people lured by spirituality and the beautiful, auspiciously shaped Om beach. The no-frills hammock and beach hut joints of yore have now been joined by the snazzy, eco-conscious CGH Earth's well-regarded boutique yoga hotel, SwaSwara, based on the Bihar school.

▸▸ *For listings, see pages 1089-1092.*

Mangalore

→ *See listings, pages 1089-1092. Colour map 7, A2.*

Set on the banks of the Netravathi and Gurupur Rivers, the friendly capital of South Kanara District is rarely explored by Western tourists, but Mangalore offers some interesting churches and temples and makes a worthy stopping point on your way between beaches. An important shipbuilding centre during Haider Ali's time, it is now a major port exporting coffee, spices and cashew nuts.

Ins and outs

→ *Phone code: 0824. Population: 328,700.*

Getting there Bajpe airport is 22 km north of town,with flights from Mumbai, Bengaluru, Chennai and Dubai. The Konkan railway carries trains from Goa and Mumbai while the broad gauge line goes down the coast to Kozhikode and then inland to Coimbatore.

The old Mangalore City railway station is just south of the busy Hampankatta junction which marks the town centre, but only trains that start and finish in Mangalore use it; trains on the Mumbai–Kerala line stop at the newer Kankanadi station, 10 km east of the city.

The KSRTC bus station is 3 km north of the centre. To get to the town centre and railway, leave the bus station, turn left for 50 m to the private bus shelter and take bus Nos 19 or 33. Long-distance private buses use a more convenient stand a few minutes southwest of Hampankatta.

Getting around The centre is compact enough to be covered on foot but auto-rickshaws are handy for longer journeys. Most refuse to use their meters. Local buses roar around town from the City Bus Stand, opposite the Private Bus Stand. ▸▸ *See Transport, page 1091.*

Tourist information Main **tourist office** ⓘ *City Corporation Building, Lalbagh, just west of the State Bus Stand, T0824-245 3926, 1000-1730.*

Sights

St Aloysius College Chapel ⓘ *Lighthouse Hill, 0830-1300, 1600-2000,* has remarkable 19th-century frescoes painted by the Italian-trained Jesuit priest Moscheni, which cover the walls and ceilings in a profusion of scenes. The town has a sizeable Roman Catholic population (about 20%). The nearby **Old Lighthouse** in Tagore Park was built by Haider Ali.

The tile-roofed low structure of the 10th-century **Mangaladevi Temple** ⓘ *south of the train station, bus 27 or 27A, 1600-1200, 1600-2000,* is named after a Malabar Princess, Mangala Devi, who may have given her name to Mangalore. The 11th-century **Sri Manjunatha Temple** ⓘ *4 km northeast of the centre in the Kadri hills, 0600-1300, 1600-2000, Rs 30-40 by auto*, has a rough lingam; its central image is a superb bronze Lokeshwara made in AD 968, said to be one of the finest in South India. **Sreemanthi Bai Memorial Museum** ⓘ *just north of the KSRTC Bus Station, 0900-1700, free*, has a collection including archaeology, ethnology, porcelain and woodcarvings.

South of the Netravathi River lies **Ullal**, which has a pleasant beach and the *dargah* of **Sayyed Mohammed Shareefulla Madani**, a Sufi saint who sailed here from Medina in the 16th century. The *dargah* itself was built in the 19th century, and is credited with healing powers: You can

Mangalore

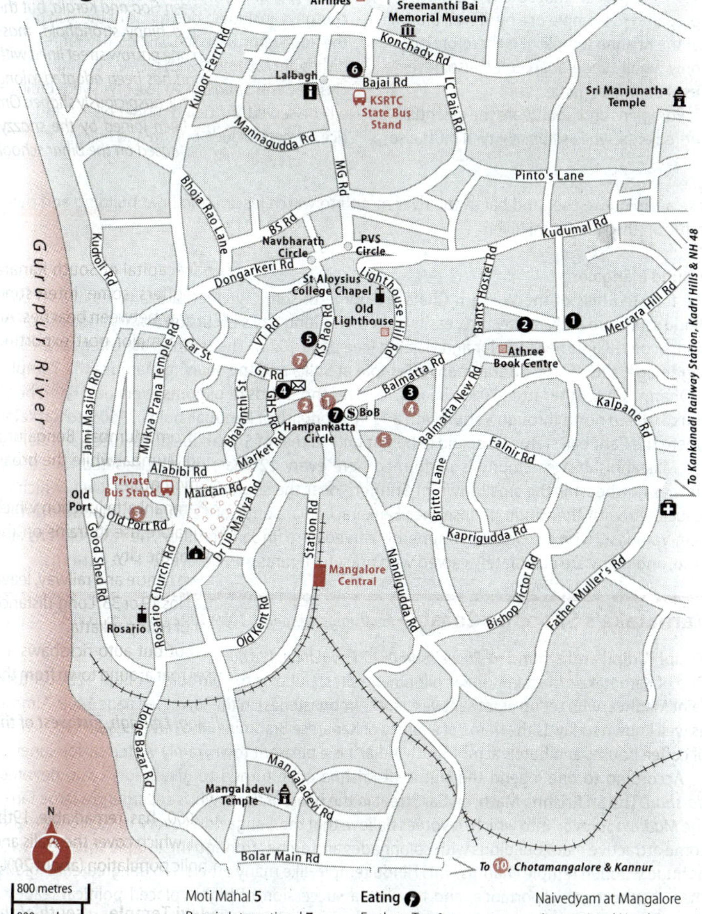

Sleeping
Adarsh Lodge 2
Dhanyawad 1
Moti Mahal 5
Poonja International 7
Summer Sands Beach Resort 10
Surya 4
Taj Manjarun 3

Eating
Froth on Top 1
Hao Hao 2
Lalith 3
Maya Darshini 4
Naivedyam at Mangalore International Hotel 5
Surabhi 6
Taj Mahal 7

Vegetarian victuals

The name of Udupi is associated across South India with authentic Brahmin cooking, which means vegetarian food at its best. But what is authentic Udupi cuisine? Pamela Philipose, writing in the *Indian Express*, suggests that strictly it is food prepared for temple use by Shivali Brahmins at the Krishna temple. It is therefore not only wholly vegetarian, but it also never uses onions or garlic.

Pumpkins and gourds are the essential ingredients, while *sambar*, which must also contain ground coconut and coconut oil, is its base. The spicy pepper water, *rasam*, is compulsory, as are the ingredients jackfruit, heart-shaped colocasia leaves, raw green bananas, mango pickle, red chilli and salt. *Adyes* (dumplings), *ajadinas* (dry curries) and chutneys, including one made of the skin of the ridge gourd, are specialities. Favourite dishes are *kosambiri* with pickle, coconut chutney and *appalam*. At least two vegetables will be served, including runner beans, and rice. Sweets include *payasa* and *holige*.

take a trip out to the sand bar at the river mouth to watch fascinating boat building and river traffic on the Netravathi River.

Around Mangalore

The forested hills of the Western Ghats are home to some wonderful examples of Jain and Hindu sculpture and architecture, easily visited on a long day's excursion from Mangalore or as a break on the journey to Belur and Halebid (see page 1078). The temples are often centres of pilgrimage, such as the **Subrahmanya Temple** at Sullia and the Shaivite **Manjunatha Temple** at Dharmasthala; the latter, 70 km inland, receives thousands of pilgrims every day. From here you can head north through **Venur**, with a 12-m monolith of Bahubali built in 1605, to **Karkala**, where the Bahubali statue is second in height only to that of Sravanabelagola (see page 1079); the Mastabhisheka ceremony is performed here every 12 years (next scheduled for 2014). Further northeast is the small town of **Sringeri**, near the source of the Tunga River, which is associated with the Hindu philosopher Sankaracharya. South of Karkala lies **Mudabidri**, the 'Jain Varanasi', with a collection of superbly carved *basti*. In Jain tradition, no two columns are alike, and many are elaborately carved with graceful figures and floral and knot patterns.

Karnataka's Sapphire Coast → *For listings, see pages 1089-1092. Colour map 7, A2.*

Udupi (Udipi) and around → *Phone code: 0820. Population: 113,000.*

One of Karnataka's most important pilgrimage sites, Udupi is the birthplace of the 12th-century saint Madhva, who set up eight sannyasi *maths* (monasteries) in the town, see page 1409. Almost as well known today as the home of a family of Kanarese Brahmins who have established a chain of coffee houses and hotels across South India, it is a pleasant town, rarely visited by foreigners.

According to one legend the statue of Krishna once turned to give a low caste devotee *darshan*. The **Sri Krishna Math**, on Car Street in the heart of the town, is set around a large tank, the *Madhva Sarovar*, into which devotees believe that the Ganga flows every 10 years. There are some attractive *math* buildings with colonnades and arches fronting the temple square, as well as huge wooden temple chariots. This Hindu temple, like many others, is of far greater religious than architectural importance, and receives a succession of highly placed political leaders. Visitors are 'blessed' by the temple elephant. In the biennial **Paraya Mahotsava**, on 17/18 January of even-numbered years, the temple management changes hands (the priest-in-charge heads each of the eight *maths* in turn). The **Seven-Day Festival**, 9-15 January, is marked by an extravagant opening ceremony complete with firecrackers, dancing elephants, brass band and eccentric re-enactments of mythical scenes, while towering wooden temple cars, illuminated by strip lights followed by noisy portable generators, totter around the square, pulled by dozens of pilgrims. **Sri Ananthasana Temple**, where Madhva is believed to have dematerialized while teaching his followers, is in the centre of the temple square. The eight important *maths* are around Car Street: Sode, Puthige and Adamar (south); Pejawar and Palamar (west); Krishna and Shirur (north); and Kaniyur (east).

Some 5 km inland from Udupi, **Manipal** is a university town famous throughout Karnataka as the centre of *Yakshagana* dance drama, which like *Kathakali* in Kerala is an all-night spectacle. **Rashtrakavi Govind Pai Museum** ⓘ *MGM College*, has a collection of sculpture, bronze, inscriptions and coins.

There are good beaches north and south of Udupi, so far with little in the way of accommodation or infrastructure. The closest is at **Malpe**, 5 km west of Udupi, but it's none too appealing: the fishing village at one end of the beach and the fish market on the docks are very smelly, and the beach itself is used as a public toilet in places. If you are prepared for a walk or cycle ride you can reach a deserted sandy beach. Across the bay is the island of Darya Bahadurgarh and 5 km to the southwest is tiny **St Mary's Isle**, which is composed of dramatic hexagonal basalt; Vasco da Gama landed here in 1498 and set up a cross. Boats leave Malpe for the island from 1030; the last one returns at 1700, Rs 70 return.

One of the many bullock cart tracks that used to be the chief means of access over the Western Ghats started from **Bhatkal**, a stop on the Konkan Railway. Now only a small town with a mainly Muslim population, in the 16th century it was the main port of the *Vijayanagar* Empire. It also has two interesting small temples. From the north, the 17th-century Jain *Chandranatha Basti* with two buildings linked by a porch, is approached first. The use of stone tiling is a particularly striking reflection of local climatic conditions, and is a feature of the Hindu temple to its south, a 17th-century Vijayanagar temple with typical animal carvings. In the old cemetery of the church is the tomb of George Wye (1637), possibly the oldest British memorial in India.

Gokarna → *Colour map 7, A1. Phone code: 08386.*

Shaivite pilgrims have long been drawn to Gokarna by its temples and the prospect of a holy dip in the Arabian Sea, but it's the latter half of the equation that lures backpackers. The long, broad expanses of beach stretching along the coast, of which the graceful double curve of **Om Beach** is the most famous, provide an appealing alternative hideaway to Goa, and the busy little town centre plays host to some fascinating cultural inversions: pilgrims wade in the surf in full *salwar kameez* while hippy castaways in bikinis sashay past the temple. And whilst the unspoiled beaches south of town remain the preserve of bodysurfers, *djembe* players and frisbee throwers, the recent rise in incidences of rape (by outsiders, the locals hasten to point out) should serve to remind that travellers would do well to respect local sensitivities.

Gokarna's name, meaning 'cow's ear', possibly comes from the legend in which Siva emerged from the ear of a cow – but also perhaps from the ear-shaped confluence of the two rivers here. Ganesh is believed to have tricked Ravana into putting down the famous Atmalinga on the spot now sanctified in the **Mahabalesvara Temple**. As Ravana was unable to lift the lingam up again, it is called *Mahabala* ('the strong one'). The **Tambraparni Teertha** stream is considered a particularly sacred spot for casting the ashes of the dead.

Most travellers head for the beaches to the south. The path from town passing **Kudle Beach** (pronounced *Koodlee*) is easy enough to follow but quite rugged, especially south of **Om Beach** (about 3 km), and should not be attempted with a full backpack during the middle of the day. Stretches of the track are also quite isolated, and even during the day it's advisable for single women to walk with a companion, especially on weekends when large groups of Indian men descend on the beaches with bottles of rum. Both Om and Kudle beaches can get extremely busy in season, when the combination of too many people, a shortage of fresh water and poor hygiene can result in dirty beaches. **Half Moon** and **Paradise Beaches**, popular with long-stayers, can be reached by continuing to walk over the headlands and are another 2 km or so apart.

Project Seabird, Karwar and Anjedives → *Colour map 7, A1.*

Karwar, on the banks of the Kalinadi River, is the administrative headquarters of North Kanara District. **Devbagh Beach**, off the coast, has a deep-water naval port protected by five islands. One of these was 'Anjedive' of old, known to seafarers centuries before Vasco da Gama called at the island in 1498, and the Portuguese built a fort there. It was later used as a Goan penal colony. From 1638 to 1752 there was an English settlement here, surviving on the pepper trade. The Portuguese held it for the next 50 years until the old town was destroyed in 1801. Today Karwar, strung out between the port and the estuary, has an unpleasant beach. However, the beaches a little to the south rival those of Goa but are still deserted. Of interest is the hill fort, an octagonal church, and a 300-year-old temple.

India's Western Naval Command, which controls the 'sword arm' of the subcontinent's powerful Western fleet, has since the 1960s planned to move here from Mumbai – a principally commercial port and one that is worryingly close to Pakistani missiles – but work on the immense **Project Seabird** only began in October 1999. When complete it will become the largest naval base this side of the Suez Canal and will hold 140 plus warships, aircraft and repair dockyards, while the hillsides will be put to use concealing submarines. Karwar, crucially, is 900 nautical miles from Karachi versus Mumbai's 580. Since the area is under the control of the Navy it is off-limits to foreigners but driving past it gives a striking portrait of the subcontinent's military might and ambition.

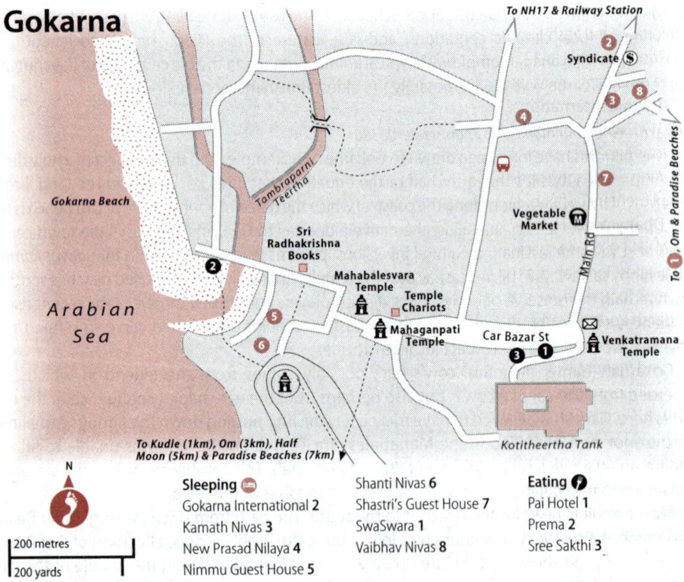

West coast listings

For Sleeping and Eating price codes and other relevant information, see Essentials pages 38-42.

Sleeping

Mangalore *p1084, map p1085*

AL-A Taj Manjarun, Old Port Rd, T0824-242 0420, www.tajhotels.com. 101 excellent rooms with tubs ('budget' rooms perfectly adequate), some with sea/river view, restaurant, all facilities, pool (non-residents half-day Rs 200), friendly service.

A Summer Sands Beach Resort, Ullal Beach, 10 km south of town, T0824-246 7690, www.summer-sands.com. 85 rooms, 30 a/c, in simple but comfortable local-style bungalows, superb Konkani meals, bar, good pool, Ayurvedic treatments, yoga, local trips.

B-D Moti Mahal, Falnir Rd, T0824-244 1411, www.motimahalmangalore.com. Tired- looking on the outside, but the 90 rooms and suites are comfortable and fresh. Excellent pool and health club (non-residents Rs 120), decent Chinese and Indian restaurants and a poolside BBQ.

C-D Poonja International, KS Rao Rd, T0824-244 0171, www.hotelpoonjainternational.com. 154 rooms, central a/c, wide range of facilities including exchange, spotlessly clean, excellent complimentary buffet breakfast, great value.

D-E Dhanyawad, Hampankatta Circle, T0824-244 0066. 44 spacious rooms, not the quietest location but the non-a/c doubles are huge for the price.

F Adarsh Lodge, Market Rd, T0824-244 0878. 60 basic rooms with bath, some with TV, well kept and friendly, excellent service, good value especially for singles.

F Surya, Greens Compound, Balmatta Rd, T0824-242 5736. 3 floors of uninspiring but adequate rooms with bath in a popular backpacker hotel, set back from road in a tranquil tree-shaded compound. Friendly and helpful management.

Udupi and around *p1086*

B Valley View International, on campus, Manipal, T0820-257 1101. Has 70 good a/c rooms with upmarket facilities, pool. Recommended.

C-E Swadesh Heritage, MV Rd, Udupi, T0820-252 9605, www.hotelswadesh.com. 34 spotlessly clean rooms, 14 a/c, in newish hotel (even basic rooms very good value), bar, 2 restaurants. Highly recommended.

C-F Srirama Residency, opposite post office, Udupi, T0820-253 0761. Top-quality new hotel with 30 excellent rooms, bar, 2 restaurants, travel desk, good service.

D-E Silver Sands, Thottam Beach, 1 km north of Malpe, T0820-253 7223, www.freewebs.com/silversands. 8 pleasant cottages, limited menu restaurant, friendly. Recommended.

D-F Green Park, Manipal, T0820-257 0562. 38 rooms, some a/c, has a restaurant.

D-F Udupi Residency, near Service Bus Stand, Udupi, T0820-253 0005. New hotel with 33 excellent rooms, 11 a/c, clean, well maintained, restaurant. Highly recommended.

E Tourist Home, halfway to Thotham Beach, Malpe. 4 pleasant, seaside rooms. Indian breakfast at the top of the road.

Gokarna *p1087, map p1088*

D-E Gokarna International, Main Rd, T08386-256848. From the outside this looks like Gokarna's smartest hotel, but the decaying lift and gritty, musty rooms are a huge letdown. OK in a pinch.

E-F Kamath Nivas, Main Rd, T08386-256035. Newish, plain and simple rooms, some with TVs and balconies overlooking the road.

E-F New Prasad Nilaya, behind **Om Hotel** near bus stand, T08386-257133. Spacious but dusty and fairly run-down rooms with shower, some with balconies, friendly staff.

E-F Nimmu Guest House, near Temple, Mani Bhadra Rd, T08386-256730, nimmuhouse@yahoo.com. Small but decent rooms spread over 2 separate wings, the 5 newest rooms are better value as they are big, bright and catch the breeze, limited roof space for overspill, garden, laid-back and friendly, safe luggage storage. Recommended.

E-F Shanti Nivas, Gayatri Rd (behind **Nimmu**'s), T08386-256983. Set in a coconut grove just inland from the south end of Gokarna Beach. Choose from clean simple rooms in the main house, apartments in the annexe, or a couple of solid hexagonal huts with mosquito nets and mattresses.

F Shastri's Guest House, Main Rd near the bus stand, T08386-256220. 24 rooms with bath, some have up to 4 beds, set back from road, a bit gritty but quiet and decent value. Luggage storage.

F Vaibhav Nivas, Ganjigadde off Main Rd (5 mins' walk from bazar), T08386-256714. Family-run guesthouse with small rooms, annexe with 10 rooms, some with bath (Indian and Western WC), meals, luggage storage.

Beaches

The cafés along **Gokarna**, **Kudle**, **Om** and **Paradise** beaches let out mud and palm leaf huts with shared facilities (often just one squat toilet and a palm-screened shower) for Rs 50-150 a night during season; many are closed from Apr-Oct. The more expensive huts come with thin mattresses, fans and mosquito nets, but little in the way of security. The guesthouses in town offer to store luggage for a small charge. The options listed below are secure.

LL SwaSwara, Om Beach, 15 mins from town, T08386-257131, www.swaswara.com. Elite retreat with 'yoga for the soul' on 12-ha complex on the curve of gorgeous Om Beach. Classes taught by Indian *swamis*: ashtanga, hasya, kundalini, yoga nidra (psychic sleep) and meditation. From the hilltop the thatched Konkan stone villas look like an Ewok village, with private gardens and a pool; beds are strewn with flowers in the day and philosophical quotes in the evening. But despite its size and expense the resort has virtually no visual impact on the beach, and fishermen can still shelter under the mangroves out front. Also offers Ayurveda, archery, kayaking, trekking, butterfly and birdwatching, and jungle walks.

D Gokarna International Resort, Kudle Beach, T08386-257843. The smartest rooms on Kudle beach, some with sea-facing balconies. Ayurvedic massages on site.

E-F Namaste Café, Om Beach, T08386- 257141. Open all year. The hub of Om's traveller scene has adequate rooms with en suite, some with beach views, and a cute but not mosquito-proof bamboo cottage up in the woods. Travel agent, internet, OK food.

E-G Nirvana Café, Om Beach, T08386-329851. Pleasant complex under coconut trees, with a choice of basic huts and solid concrete-and-tile cottages.

Eating

Mangalore *p1084, map p1085*

TTT Embers, **Taj Manjarun Hotel** (see Sleeping). For open-air dinners by the pool .

TT Froth on Top, Balmatta Rd. Convivial pub, serving a good range of beers and beer-friendly snacks.

T Hao Hao, Bridge Rd, Balmatta. Fun old-school Chinese restaurant dishing out mountain-sized bowls of fried noodles.

T Lalith, Balmatta Rd. Basement restaurant with excellent non-veg and seafood, cold beer and friendly service.

T Maya Darshini, GHS Rd. Succulent veg biryanis and great north Indian fare, plus interesting local breakfasts – rice balls and *goli baje* (fried dough balls with chutney).

T Naivedyam, **Mangalore International** (see Sleeping), KS Rao Rd. Smart, superb value place for pure veg cooking, with a/c and non-a/c sections.

T Surabhi, opposite State Bus Stand, Lalbagh. Tandoori and cold beer, handy if waiting for a night bus.

T Taj Mahal, Hampankatta Circle. Dingy ancient joint serving superb chilly-laden *upma*, crispy *dosa* and good cheap juices.

Udupi and around *p1086*

Dwarike, Car St, facing Temple Sq, Udupi. Immaculately clean, modern, good service, comfortable, Western and South Indian food, excellent snacks, ice creams.

Gokul, opposite **Swadesh Heritage** (see Sleeping), Udupi. Excellent vegetarian, good value.

JJ's Fast Food, **Hotel Bhavani**, Parkala Rd, Manipal. For Western snacks.

Gokarna *p1087, map p1088*

Cheap vegetarian *thalis* are available near the bus stand and along Main St while places towards the town beach serve up the usual array of pancakes, falafel, spaghetti and burgers. Standards are improving on the southern beaches, with Nepali-run kitchens dishing out traveller food, often of excellent quality. If you don't want to add to the mounds of plastic bottles littering the beaches, ask around for cafés that will let you fill your bottle from their cooler – it should cost a little less than the price of a new bottle.

Dragon Café, Kudle Beach. Good *thalis* and *pakora*, excellent pizza and, perhaps, the best mashed potatoes in Gokarna.

Old La Pizzeria, Kudle. Popular hangout joint, with laundry and internet facilities as well as good Western food.

Pai Hotel, near Venkatramana Temple in Main St. Good *masala dosa*.

Prema, by the car park at Gokarna Beach. Serves great fruit salads, the best *gudbad* in town and its own delicious soft garlic cheese, but popularity has resulted in slow and surly service.

Sree Sakthi, near Venkatramana Temple. Superb ice cream and Indian food, comfort snacks (try the home-made oil-free peanut butter on toast). Basic but clean and well run.

Karwar *p1088*

Fish Restaurant, in the **Sidvha Hotel**. Excellent bistro-type place.

Shopping

Mangalore *p1084, map p1085*

Athree Book Centre, Sharavasthi Bldg (below **Quality Hotel**), Balmatta Rd, T0824-242 5161. Excellent selection of English-language novels and non-fiction.

Gokarna *p1087, map p1088*

Sri Radhakrishna Books, on main road near beach. Tiny bookshop with an astonishingly good range of beach reads.

Activities and tours

Mangalore *p1084, map p1085*

The swimming pool at **Moti Mahal hotel** (see Sleeping) is open to non-residents for Rs 120 per hr.

Gokarna *p1087, map p1088*

You can hire canoes from a small office on the northern part of Om Beach: Rs 200 per hr.

Transport

Mangalore *p1084, map p1085*

Air Bajpe Airport is 22 km out of town. Transport from town: taxi, Rs 400; shared Rs 100 each; coach from **Indian Airlines**, Hathill Complex, Lalbag, T0824-245 1045, airport, T0824-225 4253 to **Chennai** via Bengaluru (Bangalore), **Mumbai**. **Jet Airways**: Ram Bhavan Complex, Kodaibail, T0824-244 0794, airport, T0824-225 2709 to **Bengaluru** (**Bangalore**) and **Mumbai**. **Kingfisher**, T080-4197 9797, airport T0824-225 4433, to **Bengaluru** (**Bangalore**), **Chennai** and **Mumbai**.

Bus Numerous private long-distance bus companies around Taj Mahal Restaurant, Falnir Rd (and a few opposite KSRTC) serve **Bengaluru** (**Bangalore**), **Bijapur**, **Goa**, **Ernakulam**, **Hampi**, **Gokarna**, **Kochi**, **Mumbai**, **Udupi**, etc.

KSRTC State Bus Stand, Bajjai Rd, is well-organized. Booking hall at entrance has a computer printout of timetable in English; main indicator board shows different bus categories: **red** – ordinary; **blue** – semi-deluxe; **green** – super-deluxe. (*Exp* buses may be reserved 7 days ahead). **Mysore** and **Bengaluru (Bangalore)**: 296 km, 7 hrs and 405 km, 9 hrs, every 30 mins from 0600 (route via Madikeri is the best); trains take 20 hrs. **Chennai** 717 km; **Madurai** 691 km, 16 hrs. **Panaji**, 10 hrs.

Rickshaw Minimum charge Rs 10, though arriving at the train station or bus stand at night you'll be charged extra. Rs 100 to **Kankanadi** station from centre.

Train **Central Station** has a computerized booking office, T0824-242 3137. **Chennai**: *Mangalore Mail 12602* (AC/II), 1315, 19 hrs; *West Coast Exp 16628*, 2130, 19 hrs. Both via **Kozhikode**, 4 hrs, and **Palakkad**, 8 hrs. **Gokarna Rd**: *Matsyagandha Exp 12620*, 1440, 4 hrs; *Mangalore Verna Pass 56640*, 0620, 4 hrs. **Madgaon (Margao)**: *Matsyagandha Exp 12620*, 1440, 6 hrs (on to Thane and Lokmanya Tilak for Mumbai). **Thiruvananthapuram** (17 hrs) via **Kochi** (9 hrs) and **Kollam** (15 hrs): *Malabar Express 16330*, 1800; *Parasuram Exp 6350*, 0415.

From **Mangalore Junction (Kankanadi) Station**, T0824-243 7824: **Mumbai** (Lokmanya Tilak) via Madgaon: *Nethravati Exp 16346*, 0015, 17½ hrs. **Madgaon**: *Lakshadweep Exp 12617*, 2215, 5 hrs.

Udupi and around *p1086*

Bus Udupi's **State** and **Private bus stands** are next to each other in the central square. From Udupi, frequent service to **Mangalore** (1½ hrs). Mornings and evenings to **Bengaluru** (**Bangalore**) and **Mysore** from 0600; **Hubli** from 0900; **Dharmashala**, from 0600-0945, 1400-1830; **Mumbai** at 1120, 1520, 1700, 1920.

Train The station is 5 km from the town centre; auto, Rs 60. **Madgaon**: *Matsyagandha Exp 12620*, 1600, 4 hrs, via **Gokarna Rd**, 3 hrs, and on to **Mumbai** (**LT**) (14½ hrs).

Gokarna *p1087, map p1088*

Boat Boatmen on Om Beach quote Rs 300-500 for a dropoff to either **Gokarna** or **Paradise Beach**, or Rs 50-100 per person if there's a group. Return trips to Paradise Beach may only give you 30 mins on land.

Bus KSRTC buses provide a good service: **Chaudi** 2 hrs; **Karwar** (via Ankola) frequent (1 hr); **Hospet** 1430 (10 hrs); **Margao**, 0815 (4 hrs); **Mangalore** via **Udipi** 0645 (7 hrs); **Panaji** 0800 (5 hrs). Private sleeper buses to **Bengaluru** (**Bangalore**) and **Hampi** can be booked from agents in the bazar; most depart from Kumta or Ankola.

Taxi Most hotels and lodges offer to organize taxis, but often quote excessive prices; no destination seems to be less than 100 km away. To **Gokarna Rd**, bargain for Rs 120; to Ankola, around Rs 550.

Train **Gokarna Road Station** is 10 km from town, 2 km from the NH17; most trains are met by auto-rickshaws and minibus taxis: Rs 125 to Gokarna Bus Stand, Rs 200 to Om Beach. State buses to/from Kumta pass the end of the station road, a 1-km walk from the station. **Madgaon** (**Margao**): *Matsyagandha Exp 12620*, 1840, 2 hrs; *Mangalore Verna Pass 56640*, 1020, 2¼ hrs. **Mangalore** (**Central**): *Verna-Mangalore Pass 56641*, 1620, 5 hrs.

Karwar *p1088*

Bus To **Jog Falls**, 0730 and 1500 (6 hrs). Frequent buses to **Palolem**, **Margao** (Madgaon) and **Panaji**, also direct buses to **Colva**. Buses often full; you may have to fight to get on. The road crosses the Kali River (car toll Rs 5) then reaches the Goa border and check post (8 km north).

Directory

Mangalore *p1084, map p1085*

Banks Several ATMs on Balmatta Rd and near Hampankatta Circle. **Canara Bank**, Balmatta Rd, cash against credit cards. **Trade Wings**, Lighthouse Hill Rd, T0824-242 6225, good service for TCs, plus flight bookings. **Internet Frontline**, Ayesha Towers, KS Rao Rd, T0824-244 1537, charges Rs 40 per hr. **Internet World**, City Light Building, Falnir Rd. Cheap, helpful.

Post Panje Mangesh Rd (1st left after Poonja Arcade, by petrol station) has Speed Post.

Gokarna *p1087, map p1088*

Banks Foreign exchange at: **Pai STD**, opposite **Ramdev Lodge**, and **Kiran's Internet**, change money. The Karnataka Bank ATM on Bus Stand Rd accepts Visa cards. **Internet** Several in town and on Kudle and Om beaches. **Sriram**, near post office. **Ganga**, fastest on Kudle Beach. **Namaste**, Om Beach.

Northern Karnataka

Down the centuries, northeast Karnataka has been host to a profusion of Deccani rulers. Hampi, site of the capital city of the Vijayanagar Hindu empire that rose to conquer the entire south in the 14th century, is the region's most famous, and is an extraordinary site of desolate temples, compounds, stables and pleasure baths, surrounded by a stunning boulder-strewn landscape. The cluster of temple relics in the villages of Aihole, Pattadakal and Badami dates from the sixth century, when the Chalukyans first started experimenting with what went on to become the distinct Indian temple design. Nearby are the Islamic relics of Bijapur and Bidar, sudden plots of calm tomb domes with their Persian inscriptions ghosted into lime, and archways into empty harems; all the more striking for being less visited. ▸▸ *For listings, see pages 1108-1112.*

Hampi-Vijayanagar

→ *For listings, see pages 1108-1112. Colour map 5, C5.*

Climb any boulder-toppled mountain around the ruins of the Vijayanagar Empire and you can see the dizzying scale of the Hindu conquerors' glory; Hampi was the capital of a kingdom that covered the whole of southern India. Little of the kingdom's riches remain; now the mud huts of gypsies squat under the boulders where noblemen once stood, and the double decker shopfronts of the bazar where diamonds were once traded by the kilo is now geared solely towards profiting from Western tourists and domestic pilgrims. Away from the hubbub and hassle of the bazar, Hampi possesses a romantic, hypnotic desolation. You'll need at least a full day to get a flavour of the place, but for many visitors the chilled-out vibe has a magnetic attraction, and some end up staying for weeks.

Ins and outs → *Phone code: 08394.*

Getting there and around Apart from the hugely expensive five-seater aircraft, buses and trains arrive in Hospet, from where it is a 30-minute rickshaw (around Rs 200) or bus ride to Hampi. The site is spread out, so hiring a bicycle is a good idea though some paths are too rough to ride on. You enter the area from the west at Hampi Bazar or from the south at Kamalapuram. ▸▸ *See Transport, page 1111.*

Tourist information **Tourist office** ⓘ *on the approach to Virupaksha Temple, T08394-241339, 0800-1230, 1500-1830.* A four-hour guided tour of the site (without going into the few temples that charge admission) costs around Rs 400. As well as filling in the usual hotel forms, all international tourists are required to personally register at the police station in Hampi Bazar on arrival.

History

Hampi was founded on the banks of the Tungabhadra River in 1336 by two brothers, Harihara and Bukka, and rose to become the seat of the mighty Vijayanagar Empire and a major centre of Hindu rule and civilization for 200 years. The city, which held a monopoly on the trade of spices and cotton, was enormously wealthy – some say greater than Rome – and the now-sorry bazar was packed with diamonds and pearls, the crumbled palaces plated with gold. Although it was well fortified and defended by a large army, the city fell to a coalition of northern Muslim rulers, the Deccan Sultans, at Talikota in 1565. The invading armies didn't crave the city for themselves, and instead sacked it, smiting symbolic blows to Hindu deities and taking huge chunks out of many of the remaining white granite carvings. Today, the craggy 26-sq-km site holds the ghost of a capital complete with aqueducts, elephant stables and baths as big as palaces. The dry arable land is slowly being peeled back by archaeologists to expose more and more of the kingdom's ruins.

The site for the capital was chosen for strategic reasons, but the craftsmen adopted an ingenious style to blend in their architectural masterpieces with the barren and rocky landscape. Most of the site is early 16th century, built during the 20-year reign of Krishna Deva

Raya (1509-1529) with the citadel standing on the bank of the river. Today Hampi has a population of 3000 across its 62 sq km. Once that figure was closer to 1.5 million.

Sacred Centre

The road from the west comes over Hemakuta Hill, overlooking the sacred centre of Vijayanagar (the 'Town of Victory'), with the Virupaksha Temple and the Tungabhadra River to its north. On

the hill are two large monolithic Ganesh sculptures and some small temples. The road runs down to the village and the once world-famous market place. You can now only see the wide pathway running east from the towering **Virupaksha** (*Pampapati*) **Temple** with its nine-storey *gopuram*, to where the bazar once hummed with activity. The temple is still in use; note the interesting paintings on the *mandapam* ceiling.

Riverside

You can walk along the river bank (1500 m) to the famous Vitthala Temple. The path is easy and passes several interesting ruins including small 'cave' temples – worthwhile with a guide. Alternatively, a road skirts the Royal Enclosure to the south and goes all the way to the Vitthala Temple. On the way back (especially if it's at sunset) it's worth stopping to see **Raghunatha Temple**, on a hilltop, with its Dravidian style, quiet atmosphere and excellent view of the countryside from the rocks above.

After passing **Achyuta Bazar**, which leads to the Tiruvengalanatha Temple 400 m to the south, the riverside path goes near **Sugriva's Cave**, where it is said that Sita's jewels, dropped as she was abducted by the demon Ravana, were hidden by Sugriva. There are good views of the ancient ruined bridge to the east, and nearby the path continues past the only early period Vaishnavite shrine, the 14th-century **Narasimha Temple**. The **King's Balance** is at the end of the path as it approaches the Vitthala Temple. It is said that the rulers were weighed against gold, jewels and food, which were then distributed to Brahmins.

Vitthala Temple ⓘ *0830-1700, US$5/Rs 250, allows entry to Lotus Mahal on the same day*, a World Heritage Monument, is dedicated to Vishnu. It stands in a rectangular courtyard enclosed within high walls. Probably built in the mid-15th century, it is one of the oldest and most intricately carved temples, with its *gopurams* and *mandapas*. The *Dolotsava mandapa* has 56 superbly sculpted slender pillars which can be struck to produce different musical notes. It has elephants on the balustrades and horses at the entrance. The other two ceremonial *mandapas*, though less finely carved, nonetheless depict some interesting scenes, such as Krishna hiding in a tree from the *gopis* and a woman using a serpent twisted around a stick to churn a pot of buttermilk. In the courtyard is a superb chariot carved out of granite, the wheels raised off the ground so that they could be revolved!

Krishnapura

On the road between the Virupaksha Bazar and the Citadel you pass Krishnapura, Hampi's earliest Vaishnava township with a Chariot Street 50 m wide and 600 m long, which is now a cultivated field. **Krishna temple** has a very impressive gateway to the east. Just southwest of the Krishna temple is the colossal monolithic **statue of Lakshmi Narasimha** in the form of a four-armed man-lion with fearsome bulging eyes sheltered under a seven-headed serpent, Ananta. It is over 6 m high but sadly damaged.

The road south, from the Sacred Centre towards the Royal Enclosure, passes the excavated **Prasanna Virupaksha** (misleadingly named 'underground') **Temple** and interesting watchtowers.

Royal Enclosure

At the heart of the metropolis is the small **Hazara Rama Temple**, the Vaishanava 'chapel royal'. The outer enclosure wall to the north has five rows of carved friezes while the outer walls of the *mandapa* has three. The episodes from the epic *Ramayana* are told in great detail, starting with the bottom row of the north end of the west *mandapa* wall. The two-storey **Lotus Mahal** ⓘ *0600-1800, US$5/Rs250, allows entry to Vitthala Temple on the same day*, is in the **Zenana** or ladies' quarter, screened off by its high walls. The watchtower is in ruins but you can see the domed **stables** for 10 elephants with a pavilion in the centre and the guardhouse. Each stable had a wooden beamed ceiling from which chains were attached to the elephants' backs and necks. In the **Durbar Enclosure** is the specially built decorated platform of the **Mahanavami**

Dibba, from which the royal family watched the pageants and tournaments during the nine nights of *navaratri* festivities. The 8-m-high square platform originally had a covering of bricks, timber and metal but what remains still shows superb carvings of hunting and battle scenes, as well as dancers and musicians.

The exceptional skill of water engineering is displayed in the excavated system of aqueducts, tanks, sluices and canals, which could function today. The attractive **Pushkarini** is the 22-sq-m stepped tank at the centre of the enclosure. The road towards Kamalapuram passes the **Queen's Bath**, in the open air, surrounded by a narrow moat, where scented water filled the bath from lotus-shaped fountains. It measures about 15 m by 2 m and has interesting stucco work around it.

Daroji Bear Sanctuary

ⓘ *15 km from Hampi Bazar, daily 0600-1800.*

The relatively new Daroji sanctuary protects 55 sq km of boulder-strewn scrubland, which is home to around 120 sloth bears. The bears have become accustomed to regular treats of honey, courtesy of the park rangers, and a handful of them come regularly to a particular rock to feed. A watchtower placed high above the spot makes this perhaps the best place in India to observe the species in the wild. The sanctuary also has leopard, wolf, jackal, Eurasian horned owl, and good populations of the beautiful painted sandgrouse.

Hospet ➔ *Colour map 5, C5. Phone code: 08394. Population: 163,300.*

The transport hub for Hampi, Hospet is famous for its sugar cane; the town exports sugar across India, villagers boil the milk to make *jaggery* and a frothing freshly wrung cup costs you just Rs 4. Other industries include iron ore, biscuit making and the brewing of Royal Standard rum. The main bazar, with its characterful old houses, is interesting to walk around. **Tungabhadra Dam** ⓘ *6 km west, Rs 5, local bus takes 15 mins,* is 49 m high and offers panoramic views. One of the largest masonry dams in the country, it was completed in 1953 to provide electricity for irrigation in the surrounding districts.

Muharram, the Muslim festival that marks the death of Mohammed's grandson Imam Hussein, is celebrated with a violent vigour both here and in the surrounding villages and with equal enthusiasm by both the area's significant Muslim population and Hindus. Ten days of fasting is broken with fierce drum pounding, drink and frequent arguments, sometimes accompanied by physical violence. Each village clusters around icons of Hussein, whose decapitation is represented by a golden crown on top of a face covered with long strings of jasmine flowers held aloft on wooden sticks. Come evening, fires are lit. When the embers are dying villagers race through the ashes, a custom that may predate Islam's arrival. The beginnings or ends of livestock migrations to seasonal feeding grounds are marked with huge bonfires. Cattle are driven through the fires to protect them from disease. Some archaeologists suggest that Neolithic ash mounds around Hospet were the result of similar celebrations over 5000 years ago.

Bijapur ➔ *For listings, see pages 1108-1112.* *Colour map 5, C5.*

Mohammed Adil Shah was not a man to be ignored; the tomb he built from the first day of his rule in anticipation of his own death hovers with dark magnificence over Bijapur and is so large it can be seen from over 20 km away. His brooding macabre legacy threw down the gauntlet to his immediate successor. Ali Adil Shah II, who took over from Mohammed in 1656, began his own tomb, which would surely have been double in size and architectural wonder had he not died too soon, 26 years into his reign, with only archways complete. His Bara Kamaan is nearby, while to the north of the city lies Begum's equally thwarted attempt to match Mohammed's strength in death. Bijapur has the air of a northern Muslim city with its mausoleums, mosques and palaces. It has some of the finest mosques in the Deccan and retains real character. The *chowk* between the bus station and MG Road is quite atmospheric in the evening. Overall it is a provincial, grubby but unhurried town.

Ins and outs → *Phone code: 08352. Population: 245,900.*

Getting there Bijapur is connected by train with Bangalore (Bengaluru), Hyderabad and Mumbai. The railway station is just outside the east wall of the fort less than 1 km from the Gol Gumbaz. Long-distance buses draw in just west of the citadel. Both arrival points are close enough to several hotels.

Getting around It is easy to walk or cycle round the town. There are also autos and *tongas*; negotiate for the 'eight-sight tour price'. ▸▸ *See Transport, page 1111.*

Tourist information There's a tourist office ⓘ *opposite the stadium, T08352-250359, Mon-Sat 1030-1330 and 1415-1730*, but it's not very useful.

History

The Chalukyas who ruled over Bijapur were overthrown in the late 12th century. In the early years of the 14th century the Delhi Sultans took it for a time until the Bahmanis, with their capital in Gulbarga, ruled through a governor in Bijapur who declared Independence in 1489 and founded the Adil Shahi Dynasty. Of Turkish origin, they held power until 1686.

The 55-ton canon was employed against Vijayanagar. Ali Adil Shah I, whose war it was, was somewhat chastened at the destruction his marauding Muslim armies had wreaked on the Hindu empire at Hampi. By way of atonement, and in a show of the inordinate riches that had fallen into his lap by supplanting Vijayanagar, he did his communal civic duty and built the

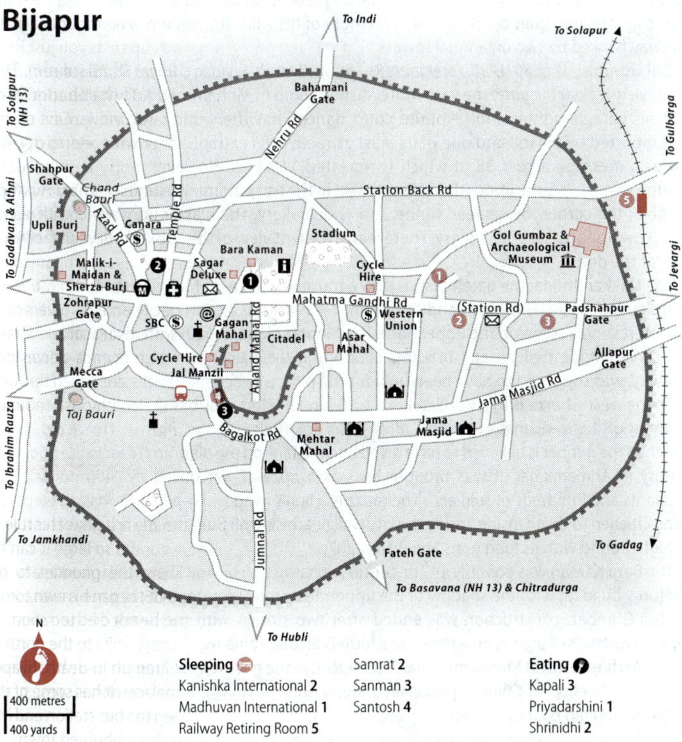

exquisite Jama Masjid. It was his nephew Mohammed, he of the giant Gol Gumbaz, who later commissioned the Quaranic calligraphy that so sumptuously gilds the western wall.

Sights

The **Jama Masjid**, one of the finest in the Deccan, has a large shallow, onion-shaped dome and arcaded court. Built by Ali Adil Shah I (ruled 1557-1579) during Bijapur's rise to power it displays a classic restraint. The Emperor Aurangzeb added a grand entrance to the mosque and also had a square painted for each of the 2250 worshippers that it can accommodate. The **Citadel** with its own wall has few of its grand buildings intact. One is the Durbar Hall, **Gagan Mahal** (Sky Palace), open to the north so that the citizens outside were not excluded. It had royal residential quarters on either side with screened balconies for the women to remain unseen while they watched the court below. Another worth visiting is the **Jal Manzil,** or the water pavilion, a cool sanctuary.

Ibrahim Rauza ⓘ *0600-1800, foreigners Rs 100, Indians Rs 5, video camera Rs 25, visit early morning to avoid crowds*, the palatial 17th-century tomb west of the city wall, is well proportioned. It has slender minarets and carved decorative panels with lotus, wheel and cross patterns as well as bold Arabic calligraphy, bearing witness to the tolerance of the Adil Shahi Dynasty towards other religions. Built during the dynasty's most prosperous period (after the sacking of Vijayanagar) when the arts and culture flourished, it also holds the tomb of Ibrahim Adil Shah II (ruled 1580-1626) who had it built for his wife but died first. Near the Rauza is a huge tank, the Taj Bauri, built by Ibrahim II in memory of his wife. The approach is through a giant gateway flanked by two octagonal towers.

Gol Gumbaz ⓘ *0630-1730, foreigners Rs 100, Indians Rs 5, video camera Rs 25, some choose to just view it from the gate*, the vast whitewashed tomb of Mohammad Adil Shah buried here with his wife, daughter and favourite court dancer, has the world's second largest dome (unsupported by pillars) and one of its least attractive. Its extraordinary **whispering gallery** carries a message across 38 m which is repeated 11 times. However, noisy crowds make hearing a whisper quite impossible; it's quietest in the early morning. Numerous narrow steps in one of the corner towers lead to the 3-m-wide gallery. The plaster here was made out of eggs, cow dung, grass and jaggery. There is an excellent view of the city with its walls from the base of the dome.

The **Nakkar Khana**, the gatehouse, is now a museum. The **Asar Mahal** (circa 1646) was built with a tank watered by the old conduit system. It was used as a court house and has teak pillars and interesting frescoes in the upper floor. The **Mehtar Mahal** (1620) with its delicate minarets and carved stone trellises and brackets supporting the balconies which form a decorative gateway, was supposed to have been built for the palace sweepers.

To the west, **Sherza Burj** (Lion Gate) in the 10-km-long fort wall, has the enormous 55-tonne, 4.3-m-long, 1.5-m-diameter cannon *Malik-i-Maidan* (Ruler of the Plains). (To avoid being deafened the gunner is believed to have dived into the tank off the platform!) Cast in the mid-16th century in Ahmadnagar, it was brought back as a prize of war pulled by "400 bullocks, 10 elephants and hundreds of soldiers". The muzzle, a lion's head with open jaws, has an elephant being crushed to death inside. Inside the city wall nearby is **Upli Burj**, the 24-m-high watchtower on high ground with its long guns and water tanks.

The **Bara Kaman** was possibly a 17th-century construction by Adil Shah III. Planned as a huge 12-storey building with the shadow of the uppermost storey designed to fall onto the tomb of the Gol Gumbaz, construction was ended after two storeys with the death of the ruler. An impressive series of arches on a raised platform is all that remains.

The **Archaeological Museum** ⓘ *1000-1700, Rs 2*, in the gatehouse of the Gol Gumbaz has an excellent collection of Chinese porcelain, parchments, paintings, armoury, miniatures, stone sculpture and old Bijapur carpets.

Cradle of Hindu temple architecture → *For listings, see pages 1108-1112.*

Although Bijapur became an important Muslim regional capital, its surrounding region has several villages which, nearly 1500 years ago, were centres of Chalukyan power and the heart of new traditions in Indian temple building. At a major Indian crossroads, the temples at Aihole represent the first finely worked experiments in what were to become distinct North and South Indian temple styles.

Ins and outs

Getting there Trains from Bijapur to Gadag stop at Badami, which makes a useful hub for visiting other sights. Buses from Hubli, Hospet and Kolhapur.

Getting around If you're travelling by bus it's best to visit Badami first, then Pattadakal and Aihole, but since it takes half a day to see Badami, visiting the sites by bus doesn't allow time for Mahakuta. If you want to see all the sights comfortably in a day it is well worth hiring a car in Bijapur, going to Aihole first and ending at Badami. ▸▸ *See Transport, page 1111.*

Tourist information Tourist office ⓘ *next to Mayura Chalukya, Badami, T08357-220414.*

Aihole → *Colour map 5, C5. Phone code: 0831.*

ⓘ *The main temples are now enclosed in a park, open sunrise to sunset, foreigners Rs 100, Indians Rs 5, flash photography prohibited.*

Aihole was the first Chalukyan capital, but the site was developed over a period of more than 600 years from the sixth century AD and includes important Rashtrakuta and late Chalukyan temples, some dedicated to Jain divinities. It is regarded as the birthplace of Indian temple architectural styles and the site of the first built temples, as distinct from those carved out of solid rock. Most of the temples were dedicated to Vishnu, though a number were subsequently converted into Shaivite shrines.

There are about 140 temples – half within the fort walls – illustrating a range of developing styles from Hoysala, Dravida, Jain, Buddhist, Nagara and Rekhanagara. There is little else. All the roads entering Aihole pass numerous temple ruins, but the road into the village from Pattadakal and Bagalkot passes the most important group of temples which would be the normal starting point for a visit. Some prefer to wander around the dozens of deserted (free) temples around town instead of joining the crowds in the park.

Durgigudi Temple is named not after the Goddess Durga but because it is close to the *durga* (fort). Dating from the late seventh century, it has an early *gopuram* structure and semi-circular apse which imitates early Buddhist *chaitya* halls. It has numerous superb sculptures, a series contained in niches around the ambulatory: walking clockwise they represent Siva and Nandi, Narasimha, Vishnu with Garuda, Varaha, Durga and Harihara.

According to recent research **Lad Khan Temple** has been dated from around AD 700, not from AD 450 as suggested by the first Archaeological Survey of India reports in 1907. This is indicated by the similarity of some of its sculptures to those of the Jambulinga Temple at Badami, which has been dated precisely at AD 699. Originally an assembly hall and *kalyana mandapa* (marriage hall), it was named after Lad Khan, a pious Muslim who stayed in the temple at the end of the 19th century. A stone ladder through the roof leads to a shrine with damaged images of Surya, Vishnu and Siva carved on its walls. It bears a striking resemblance to the megalithic caves that were still being excavated in this part of the Deccan at the beginning of the period. The roof gives an excellent view of the village.

Gaudar Gudi Temple, near the Lad Khan temple, is a small, rectangular Hindu temple, probably dating from the seventh century. It has a rectangular columned *mandapa*, surrounded on three sides by a corridor for circumambulation. Its roof of stone slabs is an excellent example of North Indian architecture. Beyond the Gaudar Gudi Temple is a small temple decorated with a frieze of pots, followed by a deep well. There are others in various states of repair. To see the most important of the remaining temples you leave the main park. Excavations are in progress, and the boundaries of the park may sometimes be fenced. Turning right out of the main park, the Bagalkot road leads to the **Chikki Temple**. Similar in plan to the Gaudar Gudi, this temple has particularly fine carved pillars. The beams which support the platform are also well worth seeing.

Ravan Phadi Cave Temple is reached from the main park entrance on the left, about 300 m from the village. The cave itself (formerly known as the Brahman) is artificial, and the sixth-century temple has a variety of carvings of Siva both outside and inside. One is in the *Ardhanarisvara* form (half Siva, half Parvati), another depicts Parvati and Ganesh dancing. There is a huge lotus carved in the centre of the hall platform; and two small eighth-century temples at the entrance, the one to the northwest dedicated to Vishnu and that to the south, badly weathered, may have been based on an older Dravidian-style temple.

The **Buddhist Temple** is a plain two-storey Buddhist temple on a hill beyond the end of the village on the way to the Meguti Temple. It has a serene smiling Buddha with the Bodhi Tree emerging from his head, on the ceiling of the upper floor. Further uphill is the **Jain temple**, a plain structure lacking the decorations on the plinth, columns and *gopuram* of many Hindu temples. It has a statue of Mahavira in the shrine within. Climb up through the roof for a good view of Aihole.

The **Meguti Temple** (AD 634) is reached from the Buddhist Temple down a path leading to a terrace. A left-hand route takes you to the foot of some stairs leading to the top of a hill which overlooks the town. This is the site of what is almost certainly the oldest building in Aihole and one of the oldest dated temples in India. Its 634 date is indicated by an inscription by the court poet to the king Ravikirtti. A Dravidian-style temple, it is richly decorated on the outside, and although it has elements which suggest Shaivite origins, it has an extremely impressive seated Jain figure, possibly Neminath, in the sanctuary which comprises a hall of 16 pillars.

The **Kunti Group** is a group of four Hindu temples (dating from seventh to ninth centuries). To find them you have to return down to the village. The oldest is in the southeast. The external columns of its *mandapa* are decorated with *mithuna*, or erotic couples. The temple to the northwest has beautifully carved ceiling panels of Siva and Parvati, Vishnu and Brahma. The other two date from the Rashtrakuta period.

Beyond these temples is the **Hucchappayya Math**, seventh century, which has sculptures of amorous couples and their servants, while the beams inside are beautifully decorated. There is a tourist resthouse close to the temples should you wish to stay.

Pattadakal

On the banks of the Malaprabha River, Pattadakal, a World Heritage Site, was the second capital of the Chalukyan kings between the seventh and eighth centuries and the city where the kings were crowned. Ptolemy referred to it as 'Petrigal' in the first century AD. Two of their queens imported sculptors from Kanchipuram. Most of the temples ⓘ *sunrise to sunset, foreigners Rs 250, Indians Rs 10*, cluster at the foot of a hill, built out of the pink-tinged gold sandstone, and display a succession of styles of the southern Dravida temple architecture of the Pallavas (even miniature scaled-down models) as well as the North Indian Nagara style, vividly illustrating the region's position at the crossroads of North and South Indian traditions. With one exception the temples are dedicated to Siva. Most of the site is included in the archaeological park. Megalithic monuments dating from the third to fourth centuries BC have also been found in the area.

Immediately inside the entrance are the small eighth-century **Jambulinga** and **Kadasiddheshvara Temples**. Now partly ruined, the curved towers survive and the shrine of the Jambulinga Temple houses a figure of the dancing Siva next to Parvati. The gateways are guarded by *dvarapalas*.

Just to the east is the eighth-century **Galaganatha Temple**, again partly damaged, though its curved tower characteristic of North Indian temples is well preserved, including its *amalaka* on top. A relief of Siva killing the demon Andhaka is on the south wall in one of three original porches.

The **Sangamesvara Temple** dating from the reign of Vijayaditya (AD 696-733) is the earliest temple. Although it was never completed it has all the hallmarks of a purely Dravidian style. Beautifully proportioned, the mouldings on the basement and pilasters divide the wall. The main shrine, into which barely any light is allowed to pass, has a corridor for circumambulation and a *lingam* inside. Above the sanctuary is a superbly proportioned tower of several storeys.

To the southwest is the late-eighth century North Indian-style **Kashi Vishveshvara Temple**, readily distinguishable by the *Nandi* in front of the porch. The interior of the pillared hall is richly sculpted, particularly with scenes of Krishna.

The largest temples, the **Virupaksha** (AD 740-744) with its three-storey *vimana* and the **Mallikarjuna** (745), typify the Dravida style, and were built in celebration of the victory of the Chalukyan king Vikramaditya II over the Pallavas at Kanchipuram by his wife, Queen Trailokyamahadevi. The king's death probably accounted for the fact that the Mallikarjuna temple was unfinished, and you can only mark out some of the sculptures. However, the king's victory over the Pallavas enabled him to express his admiration for Pallava architecture by bringing back to Pattadakal one of the chief Pallava architects. The Virupaksha, a Shaivite temple, has a sanctuary surrounded by passageways and houses a black polished stone Siva *lingam*. A further Shaivite symbol is the huge 2.6-m-high chlorite stone *Nandi* at the entrance, contrasting with the pinkish sandstone surrounding it. The three-storey tower rises strikingly above the shrine, the outside walls of which, particularly those on the south side, are richly carved. Many show different forms of Vishnu and Siva, including some particularly striking panels which show Siva appearing out of a *lingam*. Note also the beautifully carved columns inside. They are very delicate, depicting episodes from the *Ramayana*, *Mahabharata* and the *Puranas*, as well as giving an insight into the social life of the Chalukyas. Note the ingenuity of the sculptor in making an elephant appear as a buffalo when viewed from a different side.

In the ninth century the Rashtrakutas arrived and built a Jain temple with its two stone elephants a short distance from the centre. The carvings on the temples, particularly on the **Papanatha** near the village which has interesting sculpture on the ceiling and pillars, synthesizes North and South Indian architectural styles.

Mahakuta

Once reached by early pilgrims over rocky hills from Badami, 5 km away, Mahakuta is a beautiful complex of Chalukyan temples dating from the late seventh century and worth a detour. The superstructures reflect influences from both North and South India and one has an Orissan *deul*.

The restored temple complex of two dozen shrines dedicated to Siva is built around a large spring-fed tank within an enclosure wall. The old gateway to the southeast has fasting figures of Bhairava and Chamunda. On entering the complex, you pass the *Nandi* in front of the older **Mahakutesvara Temple** which has fine scrollwork and figures from the epics carved on the base. Larger Siva figures appear in wall niches, including an *Ardhanarisvara*. The temple is significant in tracing the development of the super-structure which began to externally identify the position of the shrine in Dravidian temples. Here the tower is dome-like and octagonal, the tiers supported by tiny 'shrines'. The **Mallikarjuna Temple** on the other side of the tank is similar in structure with fine carvings at the entrance and on the ceiling of the columned *mandapa* inside, depicting Hindu deities and *mithuna* couples. The enclosure has many smaller shrines, some carrying fine wall carvings. Also worth visiting is the **Naganatha Temple**, 2 km away.

Badami → *Colour map 5, C5. Phone code: 08357. Population: 25,900.*

Badami occupies a dramatic site squeezed in a gorge between two high red sandstone hills. Once called Vatapi, after a demon, Badami was the Chalukyan capital from AD 543-757. The ancient city has several Hindu and Jain temples and a Buddhist cave and remains peaceful and charming. The transcendent beauty of the Hindu cave temples in their spectacular setting warrants a visit. The village with its busy bazar and a large lake has whitewashed houses clustered together along narrow winding lanes up the hillside. There are also scattered remains of 18 stone inscriptions (dating from the sixth to the 16th century). The sites are best visited early in the morning. They are very popular with monkeys, which can be aggressive, especially if they see food. End the day by watching the sun set from the eastern end of the tank. The area is well worth exploring by bicycle.

The **South Fort** ⓘ *foreigners Rs 100, Indians Rs 5*, is famous for its cave temples, four of which were cut out of the hillside in the second half of the sixth century. There are 40 steps to **Cave 1**, the oldest. There are several sculpted figures, including Harihara, Siva and Parvati, and Siva as Nataraja with 18 arms seen in 81 dancing poses. **Cave 2**, a little higher than Cave 1, is guarded by *dvarapalas* (door keepers). Reliefs of Varaha and Vamana decorate the porch. **Cave 3**, higher still, is dedicated to Vishnu. According to a Kannada inscription (unique in Badami) it was excavated in AD 578. It has numerous sculptures including Narasimha (man-lion), Hari-Hara (Siva-Vishnu), a huge seated Vishnu and interesting friezes. Frescoes executed in the tempera technique are similar to that used in the Ajanta paintings, and so are the carved ceilings and brackets. **Cave 4**, probably about 100 years later than the three earlier caves, is the only Jain cave. It has a statue of the seated Parsvanatha with two *dvarapalas* at the entrance. The fort itself above the caves is closed to the public.

The **Buddhist Temple** is in the natural cave close to the ancient artificial Bhutanatha Lake (Agasthya Lake), where the mossy green water is considered to cure illnesses. The Yellamma

Badami

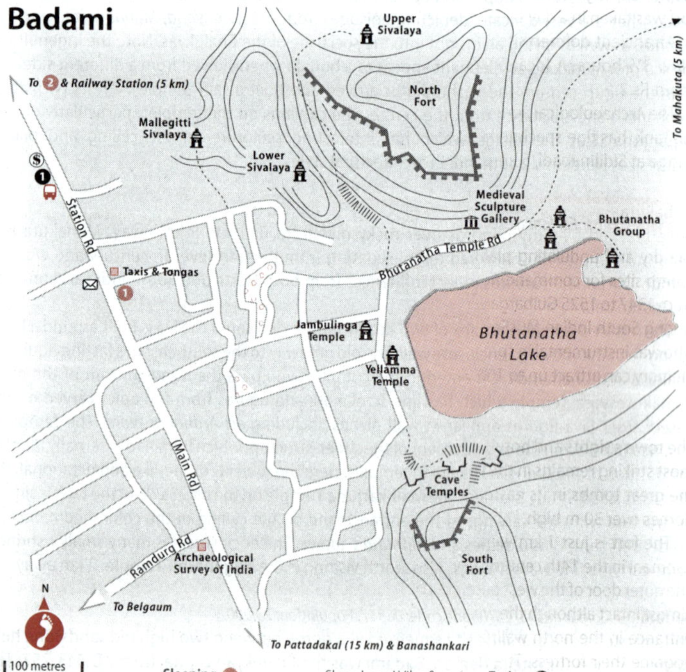

Sleeping Badami Court 2 · Shree Laxmi Vilas & Restaurant 1

Eating Sanman 1

Temple has a female deity, while one of the two Shaivite temples is to Bhutanatha (God of souls); in this form, Siva appears angry in the dark inner sanctuary.

The seventh-century **Mallegitti Sivalaya Temple**, which is one of the finest examples of the early Southern style, has a small porch, a *mandapa* (hall) and a narrower *vimana* (shrine), which Harle points out is typical of all early Western Chalukya temples. The slim pilasters on the outer walls are reminders of the period when wooden pillars were essential features of the construction. Statues of Vishnu and Siva decorate the outer walls, while animal friezes appear along the plinth and above the eaves. These are marked by a moulding with a series of ornamental small solid pavilions.

Jambulinga Temple is an early temple in the centre of the town near the rickshaw stand. Dating from AD 699 as attested by an inscription and now almost hidden by houses, the visible brick tower is a late addition from the Vijayanagar period. Its three chapels, dedicated to Brahma, Vishnu and Siva, contain some fine carving, although the deities are missing and according to Harle the ceiling decoration already shows signs of deteriorating style. The carvings here, especially that of the Nagaraja in the outside porch, have helped to accurately date the Lad Khan Temple in Aihole (see page 1099). Opposite the Jambulinga temple is the 10th-century Virupaksha Temple.

The mainly seventh-century **North Fort temples** ⓘ *Rs 2, carry water*, provide an insight into Badami's history. Steep steps, almost 1 m high, take you to 'gun point' at the top of the fort which has remains of large granaries, a treasury and a watchtower. The **Upper Sivalaya Temple**, though damaged, still has some friezes and sculptures depicting Krishna legends. The North Fort was taken in a day by Colonel Munro in 1918, when he broke in through the east side.

An ancient **dolmen** site can be reached by an easy hike through interesting country- side; allow 3½ hours. A local English-speaking guide, Dilawar Badesha, at Tipu Nagar, charges about Rs 2.

The Archaeological Survey's **Medieval Sculpture Gallery** ⓘ *Sat-Thu 1000-1700, free*, north of the tank, has fine specimens from Badami, Aihole and Pattadakal and a model of the natural bridge at Sidilinapadi, 5 km away.

Gulbarga

→ *For listings, see pages 1108-1112. Colour map 5, B5. Phone code: 08472. Population: 427,900.*

The dry and undulating plains from Hospet to Bidar are broken by rocky outcrops providing superb sites for commanding fortresses, such as the one that sits in ruins overlooking Gulbarga. From 1347 to 1525 Gulbarga served as the first capital of the Bahmanis, but it is also widely known among South Indian Muslims as the home of Saiyid Muhammad Gesu Daraz Chisti (1320-1422) who was instrumental in spreading pious Islamic faith in the Deccan. The annual **Urs festival** in his memory can attract up to 100,000 people.

Sights

The town's sights and hotels are quite spread out so it is worth hiring an auto for half a day. The most striking remains in the town are the fort, with its citadel and mosque, the Jami Masjid, and the great tombs in its eastern quarter – massive, fortress-like buildings with their distinctive domes over 30 m high.

The **fort** is just 1 km west of the centre of the present town. Originally built by Ala-ud-din Bahmani in the 14th century, most of the outer structures and many of the buildings are in ruins. The outer door of the west gate and the *bala hissar* (citadel), a massive structure, however, remain almost intact although the whole place is very overgrown. A flight of ruined steps leads up to the entrance in the north wall; beware of dogs. It's easy to see why the Bahamis were so keen to upgrade their fortress. The fat fort walls at Gulbarga – romantically named as the 'bouquet of lovers' – may sit proud above the more modern artificial lake, and the *bala hissar* itself stands high with its plump rotund columns, but the whole is all too pregnable and modest. And there's no commanding hilltop to provide the impenetrability that the plateaux around Bidar bequeathed the dynasty's subsequent rulers.

All that remains of the palace structures are solitary walls stamped with arches, but the **Jami Masjid**, with its incongruous, uncanny likeness to the mosque at Córdoba in southern Spain, is both active and well maintained (similarities with the mosque at Córdoba have contributed to the legend that it was designed by a North African architect from the Moorish court). Beautiful geometrical angles of archways form as you walk under the 75 small roof domes zagging between the four corner domes. The whole area of 3500 sq m is covered by a dome over the *mihrab*, four corner domes and 75 minor domes, making it unique among Indian mosques. It was built by Firoz Shah Bahmani (1397-1432).

The **tombs** of the Bahmani sultans are in two groups. One lies 600 m to the west of the fort, the other on the east of the town. The latter have no remaining exterior decoration though the interiors show some evidence of ornamentation. The Dargah of the Chisti saint, **Hazrat Gesu Nawaz** – also known as Khwaja Bande Nawaz – who came to Gulbarga in 1413 during the reign of Firoz Shah Tughlaq, is open to visitors. The two-storey tomb with a highly decorated painted dome had a mother-of-pearl canopy added over the grave. Note that women are not allowed to enter the tombs. The **Dargah library**, which has 10,000 books in Urdu, Persian and Arabic, is open to visitors.

The most striking of all the tombs near **Haft Gumbaz**, the eastern group, is that of **Taj-ud-Din Firuz** (1422). Unlike the other tombs it is highly ornate, with geometrical patterns developed in the masonry.

Bidar

→ *For listings, see pages 1108-1112. Colour map 5, B6.* *Phone code: 08357. Population: 172,300.*

The scruffy bungalow town that is modern day Bidar spreads out in a thin layer of buildings both within and without the imposing rust-red walls of the 15th-century fort that once played capital to two Deccan-ruling Muslim dynasties. The buildings may be new but there's still something of a medieval undercurrent to life here. Islam still grows sturdily: apart from the storehouses of government-subsidized industries to counter 'backwardness', the outskirts are littered with long white prayer walls to mop up the overspill from over-burdened mosques during Id. A few lone tiles, tucked into high corners, still cling to the laterite brick structures that stand in for the succession of immaculately made palaces which must once have glowed incandescent with bright blue, green and yellow designs. Elsewhere you can only see the outline of the designs. The old fort commands grand vistas across the empty cultivated land below. Each successive palace was ruined by invasions then built anew a little further east.

History

The walled fort town, on a red laterite plateau in North Karnataka, once the capital of the **Bahmanis** and the **Barid Shahis**, remained an important centre until it fell to Aurangzeb in 1656. The Bahmani Empire fragmented into four kingdoms, and the ninth Bahmani ruler, **Ahmad Shah I**, shifted his capital from Gulbarga to Bidar in 1424, rebuilding the old Hindu fort to withstand cannon attacks, and enriching the town with beautiful palaces and gardens. With the decline of the Bahmanis, the Barid Shahi Dynasty founded here ruled from 1487 until Bidar was annexed to Bijapur in 1619.

Sights

The intermingling of Hindu and Islamic architectural styles in the town has been ascribed to the use of Hindu craftsmen, skilled in temple carving in stone (particularly hornblende), who would have been employed by the succeeding Muslim rulers. They transferred their skill to Muslim monuments, no longer carving human figures, forbidden by Islam, but using the same technique to decorate with geometric patterns, arabesques and calligraphy, wall friezes, niches and borders.

The pillars, often of wood, were intricately carved and then painted and burnished with gold to harmonize with the encaustic tiles.

The **Inner Fort** built by Muhammad Shah out of the red laterite and dark trapstone was later embellished by Ali Barid. The steep hill to the north and east provided natural defence. It was protected to the south and west by a triple moat (now filled in). A series of gates and a drawbridge over the moat to the south formed the main entrance from the town. The second gate, the **Sharaza Darwaza** (1503) has tigers carved in bas relief on either side (Shia symbols of Ali as protector), the tile decorations on the walls and the *Nakkar Khana* (Drum gallery) above.

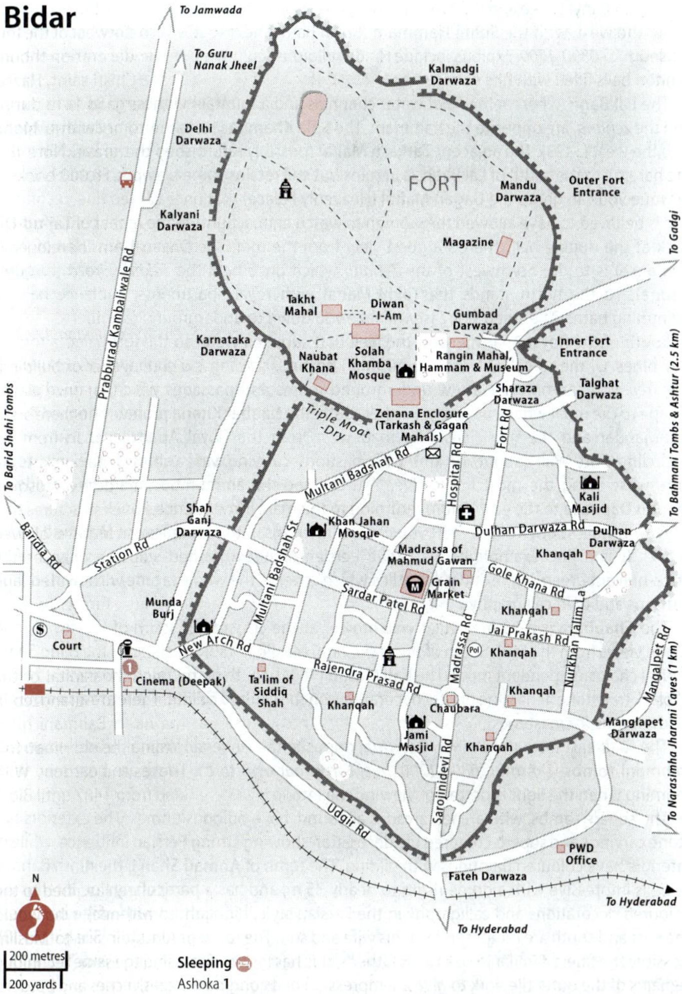

Beyond this is a large fortified area which brings you to the third gate, the huge **Gumbad Darwaza**, probably built by Ahmad Shah Wali in the 1420s, which shows Persian influence. Note the decorated *gumbad* (dome).

You will see the triple moat to the right and after passing through the gateway, to your left are steps leading to the **Rangin Mahal** (Coloured Palace) where Muhammad Shah moved to, after finding the nearby Shah Burj a safe refuge in 1487 when the Abyssinians attacked. This small palace (an indication of the Bahmanis' declining years) was built by him, elaborately decorated with coloured tiles, later enhanced by Ali Barid with mother- of-pearl inlay on polished black granite walls as well as intricate wood carvings. If locked, ask at the museum (see below) for a key.

The old banyan tree and the **Shahi Matbak** (once a palace, but served as the Royal Kitchens) are to the west, with the **Shahi Hammam** (Royal Baths) next to it, which now houses a small **museum** ⓘ *0800-1700*. Exhibits include Hindu religious sculptures, Stone Age implements and cannon balls filled with bits of iron.

The **Lal Bagh**, where remains of water channels and a fountain witness to its former glory, and the *zenana*, are opposite the hammam. The **Sola Khamba** (16 columns) or **Zanani Mosque** is to the west (1423). The adjacent **Tarkash Mahal** (possibly refurbished by the Barid Shahis for the harem), to the south of Lal Bagh, is in ruins but still retains some tilework. From behind the mosque you can get to the **Gagan Mahal** (Heavenly Palace) that once carried fine decorations and is believed to have allowed the women to watch animal fights in the moat below from the back of the double hall. There's a good view from the roof. The **Diwan-i-Am** (Hall of Public Audience) is to the northwest of the *Zenana* which once held the *Takht-i-Firoza* (turquoise throne). To the north stands the **Takht Mahal** with royal apartments, audience hall and swimming baths. The steep staircase will take you down to underground chambers.

South of the Royal Apartments is the well that supplied water to the fort palaces through clay pipes. Of the so-called **Hazar** ('thousand') **Kothri** ⓘ *cycling is a good way of exploring the site, free,* you can only see a few underground rooms and passages which enabled a quick escape to the moat when necessary. Further south, the **Naubat Khana** probably housed the fort commander and the musicians. The road west from the Royal Apartments leads to the encircling Fort Wall (about 10 km) with bastions carrying vast cannons, the one to the northwest being the most impressive. You can see the ammunition magazine inside the **Mandu Darwaza** to the east before returning to the main fort entrance.

As you walk south from the fort you can see the ruins of the **Madrassa of Mahmud Gawan** (1472). It is a fine example of his native Persian architecture and still bears signs of the once-brilliant green, white and yellow tiles which covered the whole façade with swirls of floral patterns and bold calligraphy.

The **Chaubara** is a 23-m circular watchtower at the crossroads, south of the town centre (good views from the top). South of this is the **Jami Masjid** (1430) which bears the Barid Shahis' typical chain and pendant motif. The **Kali Masjid** (1694), south of the Talghat Darwaza, is made of black trapstone. It has fine plaster decorations on the vaulted ceiling. There are also a number of **khanqahs** (monasteries).

The road east from the Dulhan Darwaza, opposite the General Hospital, leads to the eight **Bahmani tombs** ⓘ *Ashtur, 0800-1700, free, carry your own torch*. These are best seen in the morning when the light is better for viewing the interiors.

The square tombs, with arched arcades all round, have bulbous domes. The exteriors have stone carvings and superb coloured tile decoration showing strong Persian influence, while the interiors have coloured paintings with gilding. The tomb of **Ahmad Shah I**, the ninth Bahmani ruler, is impressive with a dome rising to nearly 35 m, and has a particularly fine interior with coloured decorations and calligraphy in the Persian style, highlighted with white borders. To the east and south are minor tombs of his wife and son. The tomb of **Alauddin Shah II** (1458) is possibly the finest. Similar in size to his father's, this has lost its fine painting inside but enough remains of the outer tilework to give an impression of its original magnificence.

On the way back is the **Chaukhandi of Hazrat Khalil-Ullah** which is approached by a flight of steps. Most of the tilework has disappeared but you can see the fine carvings at the entrance and on the granite pillars.

The **Barid Shahi tombs**, each of which once stood in its own garden, are on the Nanded Road to the west of the old town. That of **Ali Barid** is the most impressive, with the dome rising to over 25 m, with granite carvings, decorative plasterwork and calligraphy and floral patterns on the coloured tiles, which sadly can no longer be seen on the exterior. Here, abandoning the customary *mihrab* on the west wall, Ali Barid chose to have his tomb left open to the elements. It includes a prayer hall, music rooms, a combined tomb for his concubines and a pool fed by an aqueduct are nearby. There are fine carvings on the incomplete tomb to his son **Ibrahim Barid**, to the west. You can also see two sets of granite *ranakhambas* (lit battleposts) which may have been boundary markers. Other tombs show the typical arched niches employed to lighten the heavy walls which have decorative parapets.

The road north from Ali Barid's tomb descends to **Nanak Jhera**, where a *gurdwara* marks the holy place where Sikhs believe a miracle was performed by Guru Nanak (see page 1426) and the *jhera* (spring) rose.

Childless couples voluntarily transfer to the nearby Indian Air Force base in the hope that the famous virility-enhancing waters of Bidar will help solve their problem.

Raichur → *For listings, see pages 1108-1112. Colour map 5, C6. Phone code: 08532. Population: 205,600.*

The main road from Hospet to Hyderabad passes through the important medieval centre of Raichur, once dominant in the Tungabhadra-Krishna *doab*, now an important but dusty market town, in the middle of a cotton-growing area.

The site of the fort's **citadel** at Raichur gives magnificent views over the vast open spaces of the Deccan plateau nearly 100 m below. Built in the mid-14th century Raichur became the first capital of the Bijapur Kingdom when it broke away from the Bahmani Sultans in 1489. Much of the fort itself is now in ruins, but there are some interesting remains. The north gate is flanked by towers, a carved elephant standing about 40 m away. On the inner walls are some carvings, and a tunnel reputedly built to enable soldiers access to barricade the gate in emergency. Near the west gate is the old palace. The climb to the citadel begins from near the north gate. In the citadel is a shrine with a row of cells with the Jami Masjid in the east. Its eastern gateway has three domes. The top of the citadel is barely 20 sq m.

There are some other interesting buildings in the fort below the hill, including the **Daftar ki Masjid** (Office Mosque), built around 1510 out of masonry removed from Hindu temples. It is one of the earliest mosques in the Deccan to be built in this way, with the bizarre result of producing flat ceilings with pillars carved for Chalukyan temples. The **Ek Minar ki Masjid** ('one-minaret mosque') is in the southeast corner of the courtyard. It has a distinctively Bahmani-style dome.

Northern Karnataka listings

For Sleeping and Eating price codes and other relevant information, see Essentials pages 38-42.

Sleeping

Hampi-Vijayanagar *p1093, map p1094*

Some use Hospet as a base for visiting Hampi; it has plusher accommodation and the nearest railway station. However, it means a 30-min commute to Hampi, which is quieter and vastly more atmospheric. A throng of cheap guesthouses, all with similarly basic rooms and rooftop cafes serving the same international menus, line the lanes between Hampi Bazar and the river. Most are **E-F** (Nov-Jan), but prices rise 30% at the height of season, and can easily triple during festivals. Across the river (by *coracle*, Rs 15) you can reach the hamlet of **Virupapur Gaddi**, a beautiful paddy planted village with budget guesthouses, coco-huts and cottages to stay in. Only a small selection are listed here. Power cuts are common; a supply of candles and a torch are essential. Mosquitoes can be a real problem.

LL Sloth Bear Resort, near Kannada University, Kamalapur, bookings T080-4055 4055, www.junglelodges.com. Excellent new nature resort, with tribal-style stone-and- thatch cottages set amid scrub a 20-min drive from Hampi Bazar. Good birding safaris, visits to Daroji bear sanctuary and a sunrise trip to Hampi are included. Good food and attentive service.

A-B Mayura Bhuvaneswari, 2 km from site, Kamalapuram, T08394-241574. Government-run place that feels by turns weird and worn out; the budget rooms are overpriced, grimy and falling apart, while the newer suites have bizarre ultraviolet tube lights that lend the feel of sleeping in an abandoned nightclub. Decent food and chilled beer, but service is stretched.

D Ranjana Guest House, down lane opposite Bus Stand, T08394-241696. A friendly guesthouse with 5 rooms, plus hot water, cheaper rooms have a cooler, rather than a/c.

D-E Gopi, Janata Plot (in lane behind **Shanti Guest House**), T08394-241695, kirangopi2002@yahoo.com. Clean rooms, hot water, those in older wing have Indian toilets.

D-F Mowgli Guest House, 1.5 km from ferry in Virupapur Gaddi, T08533-287033, www.mowglihampi.com. A wide selection of rooms, from basic cells with shared bath to cute circular huts and lovely bright a/c rooms on the second floor with expansive views over stunningly green paddy fields terracing down to the river. Hot water a few hours a day, international restaurant and pool table. Mellow without being too mellow.

D-F Shanthi Guest House, next to Mowgli, Virupapur Gaddi, T08394-325352, shanthi.hampi@gmail.com. More chilled-out than its neighbour, with atmospheric mud huts and a lovely covered lounge gazing out over the swaying rice. Great for absorbing the sunset, good service, hot water by the bucket.

E Archana, Janata Plot (in lane behind **Shanti Guest House**), T08394-241547, addihampi@yahoo.com. The pick of the Hampi Bazar hotels, with 9 clean, quiet rooms (some a/c), good atmosphere and great views from the roof.

E Raju, behind **Shanti Guest House**, T08394-241349. 2 old characterful buildings on either side of the river, with 2 and 14 rooms respectively. Clean, with a rooftop restaurant.

E Shanti Guest House, River Rd, near Virupaksha Temple, T08394-241568. Not to be confused with **Shanthi** (see above). 23 rooms with fans around pleasant courtyard, common shower, clean, well run, friendly, cycle hire, good coffee and cakes.

E Vicky, 200 m north of main road (turn off at tourist office), T08394-241694, vickyhampi@yahoo.co.in. 7 rooms (4 with bath), bucket hot water, Indian toilet, good rooftop restaurant, internet.

Hospet *p1096*

Several acceptable **F** hotels are clustered around the bus stand and along Station Rd.

L-AL Malligi, 6/143 Jambunatha Rd, T08394-228101, www.malligihotels.com. 188 a/c rooms and large **L** suites, restaurant and bar by pool (non-residents pay Rs 25 per hr), health club, exchange, travel (good Hampi tour), creakingly slow internet and overpriced STD/ISD service, but generally pleasant. 2-tier pricing in place: Indians pay Rs2-3000 less.

C-D Karthik, 252 Sardar Patel Rd, T08394-220038. 40 good-sized, clean rooms, 10 a/c in quiet, modern hotel, garden dining, friendly and good value.

C-E Shanbhag Towers, College Rd, T08394-225910, shanbhagtowers@yahoo.com. 64 spacious rooms, 32 a/c with tub, TV, fridge, in brand new hotel, breathtaking Hampi theme, restaurants (one rooftop with great views), bar.
D The Shine, near Bus Stand, Station Rd, T08394-694233, www.sainakshatra.com. Sparkly new business hotel, with functional but pleasant and clean rooms, hot water and lift. Excellent value.
D-E Nagarjuna Residency, Sardar Patel Rd, opposite **Karthik**, T08394-229009. Spotless, modern, excellent value rooms, some a/c, extra bed Rs 30-50, very helpful. Recommended.
E-F SLV Yatri Nivas, Station Rd, T08394-221525. 15 bright, airy rooms and dormitory in clean, well-run hotel. Good vegetarian restaurant and bar.
F-G Viswa, MG Rd, opposite bus station, away from the road, T08394-227171. 42 basic rooms (some 4-bed) with bath, adjacent **Shanthi** restaurant. No frills but good value.

Bijapur *p1096, map p1097*

There has been a sudden spurt in decent hotels and restaurants.
B-C Madhuvan International, off Station Rd, T08352-255571. 35 rooms, 10 a/c, very pleasant, good vegetarian garden restaurant and rooftop terrace, beer in rooms only, travel desk, but a bit overpriced. Quite noisy till 2330 because of restaurant.
B-E Hotel Kanishka International, Station Rd, T08352-223788, www.kanishkabijapur.com. 24 rooms (10 a/c) with decidedly garish decor (giant mirrors) also has cable TV, telephone, en suite, laundry, and excellent **Kamat Restaurant** downstairs.
D-E Hotel Pearl, opposite Gol Gumbaz, Station Rd, T08352-256002. 32 rooms (17 a/c) in a modern, 3-storey, scrupulously clean, modest, mint pastel-coloured hotel set round a central courtyard with vegetarian basement restaurant (booze and non-vegetarian food through room service). Telephones, cable TV in all rooms, laundry and parking.
D-F Godavari, Athni Rd, T08352-270828. 48 good rooms, friendly staff, good vegetarian and non-vegetarian food.
E-F Hotel Navaratna International, Station Rd, T08352-222771. The grand colonnaded drive belies the modest price tag of the 34 rooms here (12 a/c). Communal areas scream with huge modernist paintings and rooms are done up with colour-coded care. TV, phone and smaller rooms have sit-outs. Very popular non-vegetarian courtyard restaurant, bar and pure vegetarian restaurant. They also have rooms and baths for drivers – a giant leap in the humane direction for an Indian hotel.
E-G Samrat, Station Rd, T08352-250512. 30 basic rooms, 6 with a/c are passable, but the rest are battered. Good vegetarian garden restaurant but beware of the mosquitoes.
E-G Sanman, opposite Gol Gumbaz, Station Rd, T08352-251866. 24 clean, pleasant rooms with shower, nets, 6 a/c. Very good value. Separate vegetarian and non-vegetarian restaurant with bar. Recommended.
F-G Santosh, T08352-252179. 70 good, clean rooms including some **D** a/c, quieter at back, convenient, good value.
G Railway Retiring Room and dorm. Very clean, contact ticket collector on duty.

Badami *p1101, map p1102*

There is no formal money exchange but the **Mookambika** hotel, opposite the bus stand, may change small denominations of TCs.
A-B Badami Court, Station Rd, 2 km from town, T08357-720207. Pleasant stroll or frequent buses. 26 clean, modern, though cramped rooms (with bath), some a/c, good restaurant, pool (but small and only knee-deep; non-residents Rs 80 per hr), gym, garden. Rates sometimes negotiable, only accepts rupees, has a near monopoly on accommodation and service; maintenance reflects the absence of competition.
F-G Shree Laxmi Vilas, Main Rd, T08357-220077. Simple rooms, 3 with balconies with great views back to the temples. Right in the thick of it, so it's interesting but noisy.

Gulbarga *p1103*

D Santosh, University Rd (east of town), T08472-265338. Some a/c rooms, good non-vegetarian restaurant (beer). Best in town.
D-E Aditya, Humnabad Rd, T08472-224040. Reasonable rooms, some a/c with bath, clean vegetarian restaurant, very good value.

D-E Pariwar, Humnabad Rd, near station, T08472-221421, hotelpariwar@yahoo.com. Some a/c rooms, some cleaner and better value than others. Old but tidy, friendly staff and tasty vegetarian meals (no beer).

Bidar *p1104, map p1105*

D-F Sapna International, Udgir Rd, T08482-220991. An unexpected gem in Bidar, with well-maintained rooms, welcoming staff and Wi-Fi. No restaurant, but room service available.
F Mayura Barid Shahi (KSTDC), opposite New Bus Stand, T08482-228142. Several very basic hotels near Old Bus Station. A roadside Punjabi *dhaba* near the junction of NH9 and the Bidar Rd serves very good meals, clean (including toilet at back).

Raichur *p1107*

D-E Nrupatunga, Station Rd, T(0)94486 90341, www.nrupatunga.com. 70 plain but pleasant rooms, veg restaurant.
F Railway Retiring Rooms and dorm.

Eating

Hampi-Vijayanagar *p1093, map p1094*

All restaurants are vegetarian, eggs are sometimes available.
Boomshankar, on path to Vittahla Temple. Well-prepared, fresh river fish.
Gopi (see Sleeping). Good cheap *thalis*.
Mango Tree, on the river bank, 500 m west of the temple. Relaxed and pleasant, slightly expensive riverside restaurant that's popular with backpackers.
Manju. Family-run, simple but enticing food (apple *parathas*), takeaways for tiffin boxes (will even lend boxes).
Mayura Bhuvaneswari, Kamalapuram. Cheap adequate meals.
New Shanti, opposite **Shanti Guest House**, between Virupaksha Temple and the river. Good carrot/apple/banana/chocolate cakes to order.
Shambhu, near **Shanti Guest House**. For fresh pasta/noodles and espresso plus all the usual; also bus/train tickets for small commission.
Suresh Guest House, T08394-241606, 30 m from **New Shanti** on path towards river. Very friendly family, made to order so takes a while, but worth the wait. Also has simple ensuite rooms (**E-F**).

Hospet *p1096*

The hotels serve chilled beer.
Waves, Malligi. By pool. Multi-cuisine. Good food, bar.
Iceland, Station Rd, behind the bus station. Good South Indian meals.
Shanbhag, near bus station. Good South Indian cuisine.

Bijapur *p1096, map p1097*

Most good places to eat are north of Sation Rd.
Kapali, opposite bus stand. Decent South Indian food.
Priyadarshini, MG Rd, opposite Gagan Mahal. Vegetarian snacks.
Shrinidhi, Gandhi Chowk. Quality vegetarian meals.

Badami *p1101, map p1102*

Dhabas near the Tonga Stand sells snacks.
Laxmi Vilas, near taxi stand. Veg meals.
Parimala and **Geeta Darshini**. South Indian.
Sanman, near bus stand. Non vegetarian.

Festivals and events

Hampi-Vijayanagar *p1093, map p1094*

Jan-Feb Virupaksha Temple Car festival.
3-5 Nov Hampi Music festival at Vitthala Temple when hotels get packed.

Bijapur *p1096, map p1097*

Jan Siddhesvara Temple festival. Music festival accompanied by Craft Mela.

Pattadakal *p1100*

Jan Nrutytsava draws many famous dancers and is accompanied by a Craft Mela.
Mar-Apr Temple car festivals at Virupaksha and Mallikarjuna temples.

Shopping

Bidar *p1104, map p1105*

Shops sell excellent *bidriwork* (see page 1117), particularly near the Ta'lim of Siddiq Shah. Craftsmen can be seen in the narrow lanes.

Activities and tours

Hampi-Vijayanagar *p1093, map p1094*

Licensed tour guides hang out around the entrance to the main sights. Expect to pay Rs 250-400 for 2-3 hrs, or up to Rs 1000 for a

group for a full day. Good guides include Venkatesh, T(0)94487 95104, and Krishna, T(0)94499 81479, who also leads 4-hr bike tours (Rs 250 per person plus bike hire).
New Shanti Tours and Travels, River Rd, T(0)94481 46258. Reliable for car hire and train/bus/air tickets.

Hospet *p1096*

Tour operators

Tours from **KSTDC**, T08394-221008; **KSRTC**, T08394-228537; and **SRK Tours and Travels** at Malligi Hotel, T08394-224188. All run day-tours to Hampi, some also including Tungabhadra Dam; Rs 100-150 per person. Day trips also go to Aihole, Badami and Pattadakal, 0830-1930, Rs 350 per person, but it's a very long day. Local sightseeing by taxi Rs 800 per day. Bijapur 1-day trip by bus Rs 175, taxi Rs 2100. English-speaking guide but rather rushed.

Transport

Hampi-Vijayanagar *p1093, map p1094*

Bicycle hire From Hampi Bazar (try the stall behind the temple, Rs 30-40 per day; scooters Rs 150), and Kamalapuram.
Bus Buses to/from Hospet run every 30 mins from the bazar. A few KSRTC long-distance buses also go to **Bengaluru** (**Bangalore**) and **Goa**. Agents in the bazar sell train tickets and seats on overnight sleeper buses to Goa and **Gokarna**, most of which leave from Hospet.
Ferry Motor boats cross the river from the jetty west of Virupaksha Temple every few mins until 1800.

Hospet *p1096*

Bus Frequent buses to **Hampi**'s 2 entry points (Kamalapuram and Hampi Bazar, both taking around 30 mins), from 0530; last return around 2000. The Kamalapuram road is better, especially in the rainy season when the slower road to Hampi Bazar is barely passable.

From the busy bus stand, T08394-228802, express buses run to/from **Bengaluru** (**Bangalore**) (10 hrs) and **Mysore** (10½ hrs). Several daily services to other sites, eg **Badami** (6 hrs), **Bijapur** (6 hrs), **Chitradurga** (3 hrs). More comfortable **Karnataka Tourism** luxury coaches run overnight to various towns. A few buses go direct to **Panaji** (**Goa**) – *Luxury*, 0630 (10½ hrs), State bus, 0830 (reserve a seat in advance); others involve a change in **Hubli** (4½ hrs).
Paulo Travels Luxury Sleeper coach from Hotel Priyadarshini, at 1845, Rs 350, daily; **West Coast Sleeper**, from Hotel Shanbhag, 1830, Rs 350; daily (Oct-Mar only); strangers may be expected to share a bunk. It's better to take a train to **Londa** (under 5 hrs) and get a bus to **Madgaon** or **Panaji** (3 hrs).
Rickshaw From train station to bus stand should cost about Rs 30. To **Hampi**, Rs 150-200.
Taxi KSTDC, T08394-21008, T08394-28537 or from Malligi Hotel; about Rs 700-1000 per day.
Train **Bengaluru** (**Bangalore**), *Hampi Exp 16591*, 2025 (via Guntakal, 2½ hrs) 10½ hrs. For **Belur/ Halebid**: *Arsikere* (for Belur/Halebid): *Bangalore Pass 56910*, 1330, 12 hrs; more trains from **Hubli** (for main line connections to **Mumbai** and **Pune**): 6-8 daily, 0630-0300. **Hyderabad** (via **Guntakal**): *Amaravathi Exp 18048/17226*, 1450, 14 hrs. **Madgaon**, *Amaravathi Exp 18047*, Mon, Wed, Thu, Sat, 0630, 7½ hrs.

From nearby **Gadag**, train to **Bijapur**: *Gadag Solapur Exp 11424*, 1340, 4 hrs.

Bijapur *p1096, map p1097*

Bus A service runs between the station and the west end of town. Horse-drawn carriages ply up and down MG Rd; bargain hard.

From the bus stand, T08352-251344, frequent services to **Bidar**, **Hubli**, **Belgaum** and **Solapur** (2-2½ hrs). Buses to **Badami** 3½ hrs. For **Hospet**, travel via Gadag or Ikal. Reservations can be made on the following daily services to **Aurangabad**: 0600, 1830, **Hospet**, **Bengaluru** (**Bangalore**): 1700, 1800, 1930, 2130 (12 hrs), Ultra fast at 1900, 2000; **Belgaum**: 0630, **Hubli**: 0900, 1400, 1600, **Hyderabad**: 0600, 1800; Deluxe at 2130, **Mumbai** (**CT**): 0800, 1600, 1700, 2030, **Mumbai** (**Kurla**): 1900, 2000, 2100, **Mysore**: 1700, **Panaji**: 1900 and **Vasco de Gama**: 0715. Several private agents also run services to **Bengaluru** (**Bangalore**), **Mangalore**, **Mumbai** and **Pune** (7 hrs).
Train Computerized Reservation Office open 0800-2000, Sun 0800-1400. **Solapur**: 7 trains daily, 0700-0050, 2½-3 hrs. **Gadag**: 5 trains daily for connections to **Hospet**. Buses more convenient.

Badami *p1101, map p1102*

Bicycle Bike hire from stalls along the main road, Rs 5 per hr; pleasant to visit Banashankari, Mahakuta and Pattadakal.
Bus Few daily to **Hospet** (6 hrs), very slow and crowded but quite a pleasant journey with lots of stops; **Belgaum** via **Bagalkot**, 4 hrs; **Bijapur**, 0645-0930 (4 hrs). Several to **Pattadakal** and **Aihole** from 0730. **Aihole** (2 hrs), from there to **Pattadakal** (1600). Last return bus from Aihole 1715, via Pattadakal.
Car Hire from Badami with driver for Mahakuta, Aihole and Pattadakal, about Rs 650.
Train The station is 5 km north on the **Bijapur– Gadag** line, with 6 trains daily in each direction (enquire about schedules); frequent buses to town.

Gulbarga *p1103*

Bus There are bus connections to **Hyderabad** (190 km) and **Solapur**.
Train **Mumbai (CST)**: 8 trains daily, 13 hrs. **Bengaluru**: *Udayan Exp 16529*, 1845, 13½ hrs; *Coimbatore Exp 11013*, 0835, 13 hrs. **Chennai (MC)**: *Dadar Chennai Exp 12163*, 0610, 14 hrs. **Hyderabad**: *Mumbai-Hyderabad Exp 17031* (AC/II), 0030, 5¾ hrs; *Hussainsagar Exp 12701*, 0720, 5 hrs.

Bidar *p1104, map p1105*

Auto-rickshaw Easily available, Rs 15 being the going rate for most short hops across town.
Bicycle Cycling is the best way to get around and see the sights. 'Cycle taxis' can be hired for Rs 20 per day from several outlets all over town and near the **New Bus Station**. You may have to ask a few before you find a shop that will rent to you, but persevere. Don't waste time with Ganesh Cycle Taxi near the New Bus Station.
Bus Services from **New Bus Station**, 1 km west of centre, to most regional destinations, but check timings since the last bus is often quite early. From **Hyderabad** or **Gulbarga** (under 4 hrs), or **Bijapur** (8 hrs). Private buses to **Mumbai**: 1700, 5 hrs, Rs 260. **Pune**: 1530, 3½ hrs, Rs 220. Taxi to **Gulbarga** Rs 800.
Train Bidar is on a branch line from Vikarabad to Parbhani Junction. Too slow to be of much use. **Aurangabad**: *Bilaspur-Manmad Exp 17481*, 2015, 8½ hrs. **Bengaluru**: *Nanded-Bangalore Exp 16593*, 1230, 18 hrs. **Secunderabad**: *Sainagar Shirdi Exp 17001/17205/17207*, 0510, 4 hrs.

Directory

Hampi-Vijayanagar *p1093, map p1094*

Banks Several money changers on main street. **Modi Enterprises**, main road, near tourist office, changes TCs and cash. Also **Neha Travels**.
Internet Some lodges (eg **Shanti**, **Sree Rama**), also offer money exchange and internet, Rs 60 per hr (frequent power cuts).

Hospet *p1096*

Banks **State Bank of India**, next to tourist office, with ATM; only changes cash (US$ and £). **Monica Travel**, near bus station, changes TCs (3% charge). **Internet** **Cybernet**, College Rd, next to Shivananda. **Post** Opposite veg market.

Bijapur *p1096, map p1097*

Banks **State Bank of India** in the citadel, **Canara Bank**, north of market, best for exchange.
Internet **Cyber Park**, 1st floor, Royal Complex, opposite GPO, 0930-2300 fast connection.

Andhra Pradesh

Contents

Footprint features

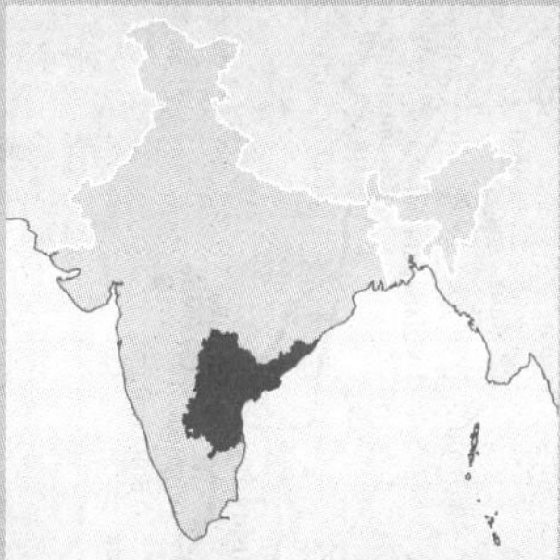

At a glance

Getting around Andhra's sites are spread out: local bus, Ambassador cabs or internal flights advised: reach Tirumalai from Chennai.

Time required Allow 3 days for Hyderabad.

Weather Either bakingly hot or hit by NW monsoon (with cyclones in Nov and Dec) for much of the year, the window for Andhra is Jan-Mar.

When not to go Apr and May, when temperatures of up to 45°C make travel intolerable. In Hyderabad, aim for a weekend to avoid city congestion.

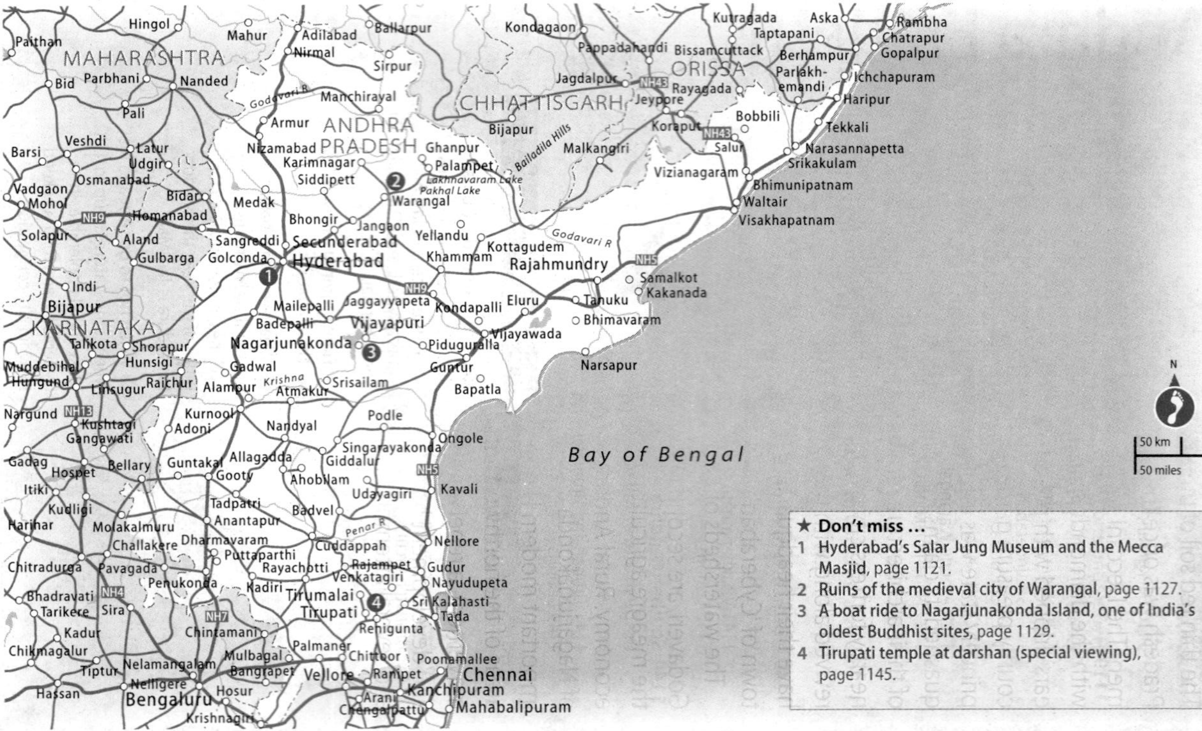

★ **Don't miss ...**

1 Hyderabad's Salar Jung Museum and the Mecca Masjid, page 1121.
2 Ruins of the medieval city of Warangal, page 1127.
3 A boat ride to Nagarjunakonda Island, one of India's oldest Buddhist sites, page 1129.
4 Tirupati temple at darshan (special viewing), page 1145.

The thin red soil of the hot and desolate interior of Andhra Pradesh was once the stage for some of the world's wealthiest men. The Deccani sultans – whose fetish for jewels was sated with the diamonds quarried from rich local seams and whose ears dripped with pearls – left a landscape dotted with their courtly pleasure gardens and palaces. India's largest Muslim-ruled princely state was integrated into the Indian union when the army quashed its claims for independence, but much of the splendour of their architecture remains, particularly in Hyderabad and its nearby fortress city of Golconda. And the city's fortunes have revived along with the success of the software industries who have their headquarters at the glass-and-chrome satellite town of 'Cyberabad'.

The watersheds of Andhra Pradesh's rivers, the Krishna and Godaveri, are second only to the Ganga and are vital in supporting the meagre agricultural subsistence of the bullock-and-cart paddy economy. Rural Andhra holds the ancient Buddhist centres of Nagarjunakonda and Amaravati and one of India's most important modern Hindu pilgrimage centres, Tirumala. Large areas of the northwest also hide the secretive Maoist Naxalite movement, a rebel army whose often violent opposition to aid and development has lead to the blocking of road-building efforts and several attempts on the state's former chief minister's life.

Background → *Population: 75.7 million. Area: 275,000 sq km.*

The land

Geography For much of the year the interior looks dry and desolate although the great delta of the Krishna and Godavari rivers retains its lush greenness by virtue of their irrigation water. Water is the state's lifeblood, and the great peninsular rivers have a sanctity that reflects their importance. The Godavari, rising less than 200 km north of Mumbai, is the largest of the peninsular rivers. The Krishna rises near Mahabaleshwar at an altitude of 1360 m. After the Ganga these two rivers have the largest watersheds in India, and between them irrigate nearly six million ha of farmland.

Climate Andhra Pradesh is hot throughout the year, and getting hotter: the record- breaking heatwave in 2010 saw temperatures in Hyderabad climb above 45°C. The interior is in the rain shadow of the Western Ghats and receives less rainfall than much of the coast. The heaviest rainfall is between June and October, but the south gets the benefit of the retreating monsoon between October and December. Cyclones sweeping across the Bay of Bengal can wreak havoc in the flat coastal districts in November and December.

History

The first evidence of a people called the Andhras came from Emperor Asoka. The first known Andhra power, the **Satavahanas** encouraged various religious groups including Buddhists. Their capital at Amaravati shows evidence of the great skill of early Andhra artists and builders. Around AD 150 there was also a fine university at Nagarjunakonda. In 1323 Warangal, to the northeast of the present city of Hyderabad, was captured by the armies of Muhammad bin Tughlaq. Muslim expansion further south was prevented for two centuries by the rise of the **Vijayanagar Empire**, itself crushed at the Battle of Talikota in 1565 by a short-lived federation of Muslim States; the cultural life it supported had to seek fresh soil.

From then on Muslim rulers dominated the politics of central Andhra, Telangana. The Bahmani kingdoms in the region around modern Hyderabad controlled central Telangana in the 16th century. They were even able to keep the Mughals at bay until Aurangzeb finally forced them into submission in the late 17th century. Hyderabad was the most important centre of Muslim power in Central and South India from the 17th to the 19th centuries. It was founded by the fifth in line of an earlier Muslim dynasty, **Mohammad Quli Qutb Shah**, in 1591. Through his successors Hyderabad became the capital of a Princely State the size of France, ruled by a succession of Muslim Nizams from 1724 till after India's Independence in 1947.

During the 18th century British and French traders spread their influence up the coast. Increasingly they came into conflict and looked for alliances with regional powers. At the end of the 18th century the British reached an agreement with the **Nizam of Hyderabad** in which he accepted British support in exchange for recognition of British rights to trade and political control of the coastal districts. Thus Hyderabad retained a measure of independence until 1947 while accepting British suzerainty.

There was doubt as to whether the Princely State would accede to India after Partition. The Nizam of Hyderabad would have liked to join fellow Muslims in the newly created Muslim State of Pakistan. However, political disturbances in 1949 gave the Indian Government the pretext to take direct control, and the state was incorporated into the Indian Union.

Culture

Most of Andhra Pradesh's 78 million people are Dravidians. Over 85% of the population speak Telugu. However, there are important minorities. Tamil is widely spoken in the extreme south, and on the border of Karnataka there are pockets of Kannada speakers. In Hyderabad there are large numbers of Urdu speakers who make up 7% of the state's population.

Attacks on mosques

A crude bomb detonated near the marble *wuzukhana* (ablution tank) in Mecca Masjid during Friday afternoon prayers on 18 May 2007, killed 11 people, with six more killed by police. The circumstances were similar to the bombing of Delhi's Jama Masjid in April 2006 and Malegaon in Maharashtra in September of the same year, both of which also targeted Sunni mosques, fuelling speculation that the bombs were designed to fan communal tensions. Investigators have linked two Islamic terrorist groups, Bangladesh's Harkat ul-Jihad Islami and Pakistan's Jaish-e-Mohammed, to the Hyderabadi attack, although there has been no proof of culpability.

Hyderabad, the capital of modern Andhra Pradesh, was the seat of government of the Muslim Nizams. Under their rule many Muslims came to work in the court, from North India and abroad. The Nizam's capital was a highly cosmopolitan centre, drawing extensively on Islamic contacts in North India and in west Asia, notably Persia.

Andhra **food** stands out as distinct because of its northern influence and large number of non-vegetarians. The rule of the Muslim Nawabs for centuries is reflected in the rich, spicy local dishes, especially in the area around the capital. Try *haleem* (spiced pounded wheat with mutton), *paya* (soup) or *baghara baigan* (stuffed aubergines). Rice and meat *biryani*, *nahari*, *kulcha*, egg *paratha*, and *kababs* have a lot in common with the northern Mughlai cuisine. The abundance of locally grown hot chillies has led to a fiery traditional cuisine, for which 'Andhra-style' is a byword. Also grown locally, good quality grapes (especially *anab- e-shahi*) or *khobani* (puréed apricots) provide a welcome neutralizing effect.

Craft industries

Andhra's **bidriware** uses dark matte gunmetal (a zinc and copper alloy) with silver damascening in beautiful flowing floral and arabesque patterns and illustrates the Persian influence on Indian motifs. The articles vary from large vases and boxes, jewellery and plates to tiny buttons and cuff links. The name is derived from Bidar in Karnataka and dates back to the Bahmani rulers.

Miniature wooden figures, animals, fruit, vegetables and birds are common subjects of *Kondapalli* **toys** which are known for their bright colours. *Nirmal* toys look more natural and are finished with a herbal extract which gives them a golden sheen, *Tirupati* toys are in a red wood while *Ethikoppaka* toys are finished in coloured lacquer. Andhra also produces fine figurines of deities in sandalwood.

Hyderabadi **jewellers** work in gold and precious stones which are often uncut. The craftspeople can often be seen working in the lanes around the Char Minar – shops selling the typical local bangles set with glass lie to the west. Hyderabadi cultured pearls and silver filigree ware from Karimnagar are another speciality.

The state is famous for **himru shawls** and **fabrics** produced in cotton/silk mixes with rich woven patterns on a special handloom. Silver or gold threads produce an even richer brocade cloth. A boy often sits with the weavers 'calling out' the intricate pattern.

The All India Handicrafts Board has revived the art of weaving special **ikat** fabrics. Pochampally, a village about 60 km east of Hyderabad, is synonymous for its *ikat* fabric in cotton and silk. The world-famous textile has been awarded IPR (Intellectual Property Rights) protection to safeguard it from imitation and competition. Interestingly, oil is used in the process of dyeing the warp and weft threads before weaving in to produce a pattern, hence the fabric's name *teli rumal* (literally oil kerchief).

Kalahasti, in Andhra's south, and Pedana, in coastal Andhra, produce distinctive **Kalamkari cloth paintings** (*kalam* refers to the pen used); the dyes come from indigo, turmeric and pomegranate. The blues stand out from the otherwise dullish ochre colours. Designed from mythology tales (*Mahabharata* and *Ramayana*), they make excellent wall hangings.

Modern Andhra Pradesh

Government In 1953 Andhra Pradesh was created on the basis of the Telugu-speaking districts of Madras Presidency. This was not enough for those who were demanding statehood for a united Telugu-speaking region. One political leader, Potti Sreeramulu, starved himself to death in protest at the government's refusal to grant the demand. In 1956, Andhra Pradesh took its present form; all Telugu-speaking areas were grouped together in the new state of Andhra Pradesh.

Andhra Pradesh was regarded as a stronghold of the Congress Party until 1983 when a regional party, the Telugu Desam Party (TDP), founded by the film star NT Rama Rao, won a crushing victory in the State Assembly elections. The Assembly elections on 5 October 1999 saw a repeat performance, with the highly-regarded modernizing Chief Minister N Chandrababu Naidu being swept back to power with nearly a two-thirds majority. Allied with the BJP in the governing coalition in New Delhi, the Telugu Desam had a reputation for pushing ahead with rapid economic modernization, particularly visible in Hyderabad, but Naidu, who borrowed heavily from the World Bank and took China, Singapore and Malaysia as his business models, won only 47 of the 295 seats in the State Assembly elections in 2004. The Congress and its newly formed regional party ally, the Telangana Rashtra Samiti, with 226 seats, reclaimed power.

The Congress Chief Minister YS Rajasekhara Reddy (known as YSR) took charge of a state with high debts to the World Bank, where rural poverty was endemic and where suicide had become a major problem among poor farmers. YSR charmed the rural poor with a series of social welfare initiatives, including low-interest loans to women entrepreneurs and free medical treatments for people living below the poverty line. He became one of the most popular leaders in recent Indian history, making serious inroads into Andhra's hitherto-intractable Naxalite problem, and he led the Congress Party to a rare absolute majority victory in the May 2009 elections. His death in a helicopter crash over Naxalite-controlled jungle in September 2009 has left a power vacuum in the state that has yet to be convincingly filled.

Current politics revolve around the movement to create a new state in the region of Telangana, which would see Andhra Pradesh carved into two with Hyderabad becoming the capital of the new state. Outside of the wealthy technology hub, Telangana is an overwhelmingly rural region which contains nine of the 34 districts of India identified as facing acute farm distress. Several of these districts are also strongholds for Naxalite forces, who have campaigned stridently for separation, and critics point out that an independent Telangana would be a ripe target for Maoist political parties. The current Congress government's vacillation on the subject – one day declaring support, the next day backtracking – only serves to improve the rebels' prospects.

Hyderabad and North Central Andhra Pradesh

Hyderabad, one of the poster boys for India's biotech and software boom, has emerged as a great place to soak up the atmosphere of the New India. It's also a city that heaves with history: splendid markets, mosques, architecture and museums and pearl bazars. On the outskirts of the city are film-set theme parks, the grand medieval fortress of Golconda, and a collection of 17th-century tombs of old rulers lying in gardens of frilly bougainvillea. A day's drive to the southeast lies Nagarjunakonda, where the relocated ruins of one of India's richest Buddhist civilizations rise from the middle of an artificial lake. ▸▸ *For listings, see pages 1131-1135.*

Hyderabad and Secunderabad → *For listings, see pages 1131-1135. Colour map 6, B1.*

The Twin Cities of Hyderabad and Secunderabad, founded by the rulers of two separate Muslim dynasties, have long since bled into one conglomerate metropolis. The southern half, **Hyderabad**, holds the dusty and congested Old City; here you will find the beautiful but faded palaces of Islamic architecture, while the atmospheric lanes around the Char Minar throb with a contemporary Muslim mania. **Secunderabad**, which served as a prominent British army base prior to independence and remains the biggest military cantonment in the country, is separated from Hyderabad by the Hussain Sagar lake.

N Chandrababu Naidu, Andhra's chief minister from the late 1990s until 2004, had development dreams as lofty as the legendarily eccentric Nizam. The result is a city with town planning unequalled in India, including huge theme resorts where you can stand at minus temperatures (a tribute to the famous heat of Andhra), and Hitech City (brilliantly named 'Cyberabad'; a rival to Silicon Valley and home to Microsoft's first overseas base). The success of these high-tech and biotech industries has spawned a new elite to keep the old pearl peddlers in business since trade from the jewel-draped Nizams dried up.

Ins and outs → *Phone code: 040. Population: 5.5 million.*

Getting there The old Begumpet airport has been replaced by the **Rajiv Gandhi International Airport**, 25 km south of the city. The new facility, equipped with world-class amenities, has ambitions to take over as India's aviation hub. Meter taxis from outside Arrivals charge Rs 15 per kilometre, while Aeroexpress shuttle buses run a round-the-clock service to various locations in the twin cities for Rs 150 per person. **Secunderabad station**, with trains to major cities, is in the Cantonment area, while the **Hyderabad City station** at Nampally is close to the Abids shopping district, with the majority of budget accommodation. The large **Imbli-Ban Bus terminal** for long-distance buses is south of Abids on an island in the Musi River. The **Jubilee Bus Terminal** is in Secunderabad.

Getting around Autos (or taxis) are the best means of getting about the city north of the Musi and in Secunderabad, but in the congested old quarter you are best off walking, though there are cycle-rickshaws. ▸▸ *See Transport, page 1134.*

Tourist information **Government of Andhra Pradesh** ⓘ *Yatri Nivas, SP Road, Secunderabad, T040-2789 3100, www.tourisminap.com; Tank Bund Rd, near Secretariat, T040-2345 3036.* **Andhra Pradesh Tourism Development Corporation** (APTDC) ⓘ *Tourism House, Himayatnagar, T040-2326 2151.* **India Tourism** ⓘ *Netaji Bhavan, Himayatnagar, T040-2326 1360.*

Old City and Char Minar

To celebrate the founding of Hyderabad, Sultan Mohammed Quli Qutb Shah built the lofty archway of **Char Minar** ⓘ *0900-1730, Rs 5,* at the entrance to his palace complex. Capped with four soaring minarets (*char minar* means 'four towers') and holding the city's original mosque on its roof, it has been the showpiece of the city since construction was finished in 1612. Today

1 Hyderabad-Secunderabad

Sleeping
Baseraa 3
Dwaraka Heritage 4
Fortune Select Manohar 2
Golkonda Hyderabad 14
ITC Kakatiya 1
Taj Banjara 6
Taj Krishna 7
Taj Mahal 8
Yatri Nivas 11
YMCA 13
Youth Hostel 12

Eating
Paradise Food Court 3

it stands at the centre of a busy crossroads, surrounded by the Old City's sprawling bazar of pearl, perfume and jewellery shops. The monument is lit up every evening from 1900-2100.

Immediately to the southwest is the vast **Mecca Masjid**, so named because of the red clay bricks from Mecca embedded in its impressive outer walls. The second largest mosque in India and among the seven biggest in the world, construction of the building began in 1614 under the sixth Sultan Abdulla Qutb Shah and was completed by Aurangzeb when he annexed Golconda in 1692. Comprising huge slabs of black granite quarried nearby, the mosque was designed to hold 10,000 people at prayer times. The tombs of the Asaf Jahi rulers, the Nizams of Hyderabad, are in an enclosure with a roof, to the left of the courtyard.

Towards the river is the **Jama Masjid**, the second mosque built in the old city at the end of the 16th century, beyond which on Sadar Patel Road are the four arches of **Charkaman**. The eastern Black Arch was for the drums, the western arch led to the palaces, the northern was the Fish Arch, and the southern arch was for the Char Minar.

Lad Bazar area The heart of the Muslim part of the city, the area around the Mecca Masjid and the Char Minar is a fascinating hive of bazars, made up of beautiful wooden buildings with stone carvings and pink elephant gates, packed with people. You arrive at the **chowk** which has a mosque and a Victorian clock tower.

Southeast of the Lad Bazar is the enormous complex of palaces which were built by the different Nizams, including the grand **Chowmahalla Palace** ⓘ *1100-1700, closed holidays, Rs 150; T040-2452 2032*, a facsimile of the Shah's Palace in Tehran. The stuccoed, domed Durbar Hall, courtyards and gardens have been carefully restored at the behest of Princess Esra, the eighth Nizam's wife. In the Durbar Hall is a platform of pure marble on which the *Takht-e-Nishan* (royal seat) was placed. Nizam Salabhat Jung began the splendid palace complex in 1750, but it was only completed more than a century later by Nizam Afzar-ud- Dawla Bahadur. The *Khilwat*, or Durbar Hall, *Afzal Mahal*, *Mahtab Mahal*, *Tahniyat Mahal* and *Aftab Mahal* – the four ('chow') palaces ('mahal') of the complex's name – are still under restoration. *Aftab Mahal* has a European façade of Corinthian columns and a parapet.

Salar Jung Museum and the banks of the Musi

The modern **Salar Jung Museum** ⓘ *Salar Jung Marg, T040-2452 3211, Sat-Thu 1030-1700, closed public holidays, allow 1½ hrs, Rs 150, cameras and bags must be left at counter, tape recorded guides at ticket office*, houses the collection of Sir Yusuf Ali Salar Jung III, the *wazir* (prime minister) to the Nizam between 1899-1949. The fact that it is one of only three national museums in India is a telling indication of the extant of the riches he amassed. Originally housed on the edge of the city in one of the palaces, it was rehoused in this purpose-built museum in 1968. Exhibits are described in English, Urdu, Hindi and Telugu. The collection includes Indian textiles, bronzes, paintings and fine ivory art pieces, armoury, Far Eastern porcelain and entertaining curiosities. The Indian miniatures are stunning.

The **High Court**, built on the new roads laid out along the Musi's embankments after the great flood, is a splendid Mughal-style building in the old Qutb Shahi gardens **Amin Bagh**, near Afzal Ganj Bridge. This was Vincent Esch's most striking work. It was built in 1916 from local pink granite, with red sandstone carved panels and columns, a large archway and domes. These days it is painted pink. A further change is the enclosure of the verandas. The detail is Mughal, but some argue that the structure and internal form are Western.

Next door to the High Court is Esch's **City College** (1917-1920), originally the City High School for boys. Built largely of undressed granite, there are some distinctive Indian decorative features including some marble *jalis*. Esch deliberately incorporated Gothic features, calling his style Perpendicular Mogul Saracenic.

In the opposite direction along the riverbank from the Salar Jung Museum is one of the oldest *imambaras* in the country, the **Badshahi Ashurkhana** (house of mourning), built in the

Qutb Shahi style in the late 16th century. It has excellent tile mosaics and wooden columns in the outer chamber, both later additions.

Over the river is the **Osmania Women's College**, the former British residency built by James Achilles Kirkpatrick – the central character of William Dalrymple's history, *White Mughals* – in 1803. This imposing colonial structure, whose grounds run down to the river bank, was the first symbol of British presence in the city. It was deliberately built to the same proportions as the Char Minar in order to be the only equal to its minarets on the city skyline. After decades of decline, the World Monuments Fund is carrying out structural conservation as well as fundraising for further restoration, while it continues to function as an educational institute for 4000 girl students (whose modesty visitors are urged to respect). The ornate palace Kirkpatrick built for his Muslim bride was razed in 1861 as a symbol of his perceived immorality. Dalrymple's book was launched from the stately, ochre-painted stately building's Durbar Hall. This is a room of giant chandeliers, French windows, mirrors shipped in from Brighton palaces, tatty fans and glorious floral tracings on its ceiling. The Palladian-villa style central complex, the entrance porch with Corinthian columns, the Durbar Hall, oval offices, billiard rooms and bedrooms were initially independent of the flanking wings, separated by drawbridges, whose pulleys are still in place. Outlying buildings hold printing presses dating from the 1900s. Turn out of the King's Gate then left down a pathway towards the pigeon rookery to see the model of the Residency that Kirkpatrick had made so his Hyderabadi princess Khairunnissa could see the main house without breaking her *purda*.

Hyderabad Centre: New City

The **Osmania General Hospital** (1918-1921) is the third of Vincent Esch's impressive buildings in Hyderabad. It stands across the river, opposite the High Court. The 200-m-long building was one of the largest and best equipped hospitals in the world when it opened. To its east, also on the river, is the imposing **Asafia State Central Library** (1929-1934) with its priceless collection of Arabic, Persian and Urdu books and manuscripts.

The **Public Gardens** ⓘ *closed public holidays,* in Nampally, north of Hyderabad Station, contain some important buildings including the Archaeological Museum and Art Galleries and the State Legislative Assembly (Vidhan Sabha).

Andhra Pradesh State Museum ⓘ *near the Lal Bahadur Shastri Stadium, 10 mins by car from Banjara Hills area, 1030-1700, closed public holidays, nominal entrance fee, photography Rs 10, guidebook Rs 15*, is a small museum with a crowd-drawing 4000- year-old Egyptian mummy. Behind the museum in Ajanta Pavilion are life-size copies of frescoes from the Ajanta Caves while the Nizam's collection of rare artefacts is housed in the Jubilee Hall.

The **City Railway Station** (1914) was intended by Esch to be pure Mughal in style but built entirely of the most modern material then available: pre-cast, reinforced concrete. It has a wide range of distinctively Indian features including the *chhattris* of royalty, wide *chajjas* (eaves) and onion domes.

Naubat Pahad (Kala Pahad or Neeladri) are two hills situated north of the Public Gardens. The Qutb Shahis are believed to have had their proclamations read from the hill tops accompanied by drums. In 1940 pavilions were built and a hanging garden was laid out on top of one; it's now occupied by the **Birla Planetarium** ⓘ *Fri-Wed at 1130, 1600 and 1800, Rs 20,* and **Science Centre** ⓘ *1030-2000, Rs 20.*

The nearby **Venkatesvara Temple** (Birla Mandir) ⓘ *reached by a stall-lined path opposite Thomas Cook on Secretariat Rd, 0700-1200, 1400-2100, photography of inner sanctum prohibited,* is a modern, stunning white marble temple with an intricately carved ceiling which overlooks Husain Sagar. It was built by the Birlas, the Marwari business family who were responsible for building important new Hindu temples in several major cities, including Laxmi Narayan Temple in New Delhi. Completed in 1976, the images of the deities are South Indian, although the building itself drew craftsmen from the north as well, among them some who claimed to have ancestors who built the Taj Mahal.

Hyderabad centre

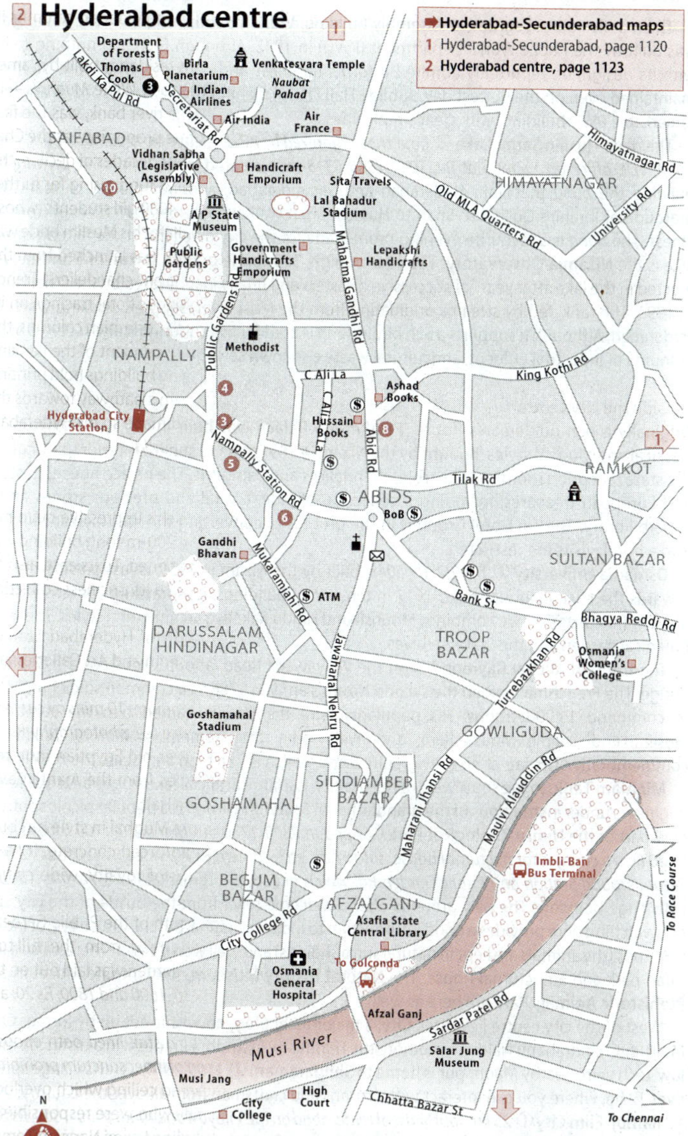

Sleeping
Comfort Inn City Park **10**
Imperial & Kamat Restaurant **3**
Residency **4**
Sai Prakash **5**
Saptagiri Deluxe **6**
Taj Mahal **8**

Eating
Kamat **3**

The massive State Legislative Assembly building, **Vidhan Sabha**, originally the Town Hall, was built by the Public Works Department (PWD) in 1922. Although Esch had nothing to do with its design, he reportedly admired it for its lightness and coolness, which the building maintained even on the hottest day. **Jubilee Hall** (1936), behind the Vidhan Sabha, is another remarkable PWD building, with clear simple lines.

The deep **Husain Sagar Lake** ⓘ *boat trips organized by APTDC leave from Lumbini Park, near the APTDC office on Secretariat Rd, T040-2345 5315*, was created in the mid-16th century by building the *bund* that links Hyderabad and Secunderabad, and was named to mark the gratitude of Ibrahim Quli Qutb Shah to Hussain Shah Wali, who helped him recover from an illness. The *bund* is a favourite evening promenade for the city dwellers. At the far end of the lake is the **Nizamia Observatory**. The 17.5-m-high, 350-tonne granite **statue of Buddha** was erected in the lake after years of successive disasters and finally inaugurated by the Dalai Lama in 1993. The tank, fed by streams originating from the Musi River, supplies drinking water to Hyderabad. Although it supports a rich birdlife and is used for fish culturing it also receives huge amounts of industrial effluent, agricultural waste and town sewage.

Outside the city centre

Originally a rich nobleman's house, **Falaknuma Palace** was built in 1873 in a mixture of classical and Mughal styles. Bought by the Nizam in 1897, it has a superb interior (particularly the state reception room) with marble, chandeliers and paintings. The palace houses Eastern and European treasures, including a collection of jade, crystal and precious stones and a superb library. The Taj Hotel Group is in the process of converting the spectacular building into a hotel; visits are restricted.

Osmania University ⓘ *T040-2709 6048*, built by the Nizam in 1939, is just outside the city towards the east. Inaugurated in 1917 in temporary buildings, its sprawling campus with its black granite Arts College combines Moorish and Hindu Kakatiya architectural styles. There is a botanical garden and the State Archives.

The **tomb of Michel Raymond** is off the Vijayawada Road, about 3 km from the Oliphant Bridge. The Frenchman joined the second Nizam's army in 1786 as a common soldier and rose to command 15,000 troops. His popularity with the people earned him the combined Muslim-Hindu name Moosa Ram, and even today they remember him by holding a commemorative **Urs fair** at his grey granite tomb, which is 7 m high and bears the initials JR.

Mir Alam Tank, to the southwest of the old city, is a large artificial lake. It was built by French engineers under instructions of the grandfather of Salar Jung III and is a popular picnic spot. It is now part of the **Nehru Zoological Park** ⓘ *Apr-Jun 0800-1730, Jul-Mar 0830-1700, closed Mon, Rs 20 (extra charges for nocturnal house, safari ride, etc), camera Rs 20, video Rs 100, bus 7Z from Secunderabad Station and Public Garden Rd*, which occupies a remarkable 13-ha site studded with huge boulders. The hilly grounds offer a welcome relief from the bustle of the city, and birdwatching here provides a good introduction to Indian avifauna, but this is also one of India's best zoos (the animals are kept in natural surroundings) and well worth a visit. There's also a lion safari park and a nocturnal house. The **Natural History Museum**, **Ancient Life Museum** and **Prehistoric Animals Park** are here as well.

West of the city centre lies **Hitec City**, a major technology township set up by former Chief Minister Chandrababu Naidu to promote the IT industry in Andhra Pradesh. In a distinctly more low-tech vein, nearby Madhapur is home to **Shilparamam** ⓘ *1100-2300*, a crafts village spread over 12 ha, where you can interact with artisans and craftsman from all over the country.

Ramoji Film City ⓘ *25 km southeast of Hyderabad on the Vijayawada road, 0900-1800, Rs 300, children under 12 Rs 250, T08415-246555, www.ramojifilmcity.com, take bus 204, 205, 206 or 207 from Hyderabad (Women's College stop, Koti), or 290 from Secunderabad's Uppal bus stop*, is a sherbet-dipped shrine to the many uses of plaster of Paris. Bus tours take visitors around the 'city', and though they're conducted mainly in Hindi, you'll still gather that everywhere from

Mumbai's Chor Bazar to Mysore's Brindavan Gardens have been re-created since media baron Ramoji Rao founded his film lot in 1991. Over 3000 films have been shot here since then. It's oddly compelling to see an audience sit in rapt thrall to a show of aspiring film dancers gyrating in spandex hot pants, while their male opposite numbers inexplicably morris dance; this is only for the committed Indian film buff. It doesn't have the diversionary value of Universal Studios, but there is a theme park, **Fundustan**, for kids. **AP Tourism**, T040-6674 6370, conducts 'regular bus tours' rather than 'services, from Hyderabad.

Golconda → *Colour map 5, B6.*

Golconda, one of the most accessible of great medieval fortresses in India, was the capital of the Qutb Shahi kings who ruled over the area from 1507 to 1687. Nizam-ul-Mulk repossessed it in 1724 and restored it to its former glory for a time. Modern day restorations are being carried out by the Archaeological Survey of India.

Ins and outs

Golconda is 11 km west of Hyderabad, Buses 119 or 142M from Nampally or 66G from Char Minar take one hour to the fort. Buses 123 and 142S go direct from Char Minar to the Qutb Shahi Tombs, Rs 10. Autos take 30 minutes, Rs 150. Cycling in the early morning is a good option as it's an easy journey. Both the fort and the tombs are popular sites and get crowded and very noisy after 1000; if you arrive early it's worth asking to be allowed in.

The fort

ⓘ *T040-2351 2401, 0700-2000, Rs 100, Indians Rs 10. Official guides wait at the entrance (Rs 250), unofficial ones greet you under the Fateh Darwaza. Allow 2-3 hrs. There is an excellent 1-hr son et lumière show in English (Mar-Oct 1830, Nov-Feb 1900; Rs 50/100); tickets go on sale at Golconda 1 hr before the start, Rs 25. Some people buy buy their 'sound and light' ticket as soon as the office opens and take a quick tour (45 minutes) of the fort before sunset in time for the show.*

Originally built of mud in the 12th century by the Hindu Kakatiyas, the fort was reinforced by masonry by the Bahmanis who occupied it from 1363. The massive fort, built on a granite hill, was surrounded by three walls. One encircled the town, another the hill on which the citadel stood and the last joined huge boulders on the high ridge with parts of masonry wall. The citadel's 5-km double wall had 87 bastions with cannons and eight huge gates with outer and inner doors and guardrooms between. Some of the guns of the Qutb Shahis are still there with fortifications at various levels on the way up. Another of India's supposed underground tunnels is believed by some to run for about 8 km from a corner of the summit to Gosha Mahal. The fort had an ingenious system of laminated clay pipes and huge Persian Wheels to carry water to cool the palace chambers up to the height of 61 m where there were hanging gardens. The famous diamond vault once held the *Koh-i-noor* and *Hope* diamonds. The fort fell to Emperor Aurangzeb after two attempts, an eight-month siege and the help of a Qutb general-turned-traitor. English traveller Walter Hamilton described it as being almost deserted in 1820: "the dungeons being used by the Nizam of Hyderabad as a prison for his worst enemies, among whom were several of his sons and two of his wives".

The Fateh Darwaza or Victory Gate at the **Grand Portico (1)** entrance, made of teak, with a Hindu deity engraved, is studded with iron spikes as a defence against war elephants. The superb acoustics enabled a drum beat, bugle call or even a clap under the canopy of this gate to be heard by someone at the very top of the palace; it is put to the test by the visiting crowds today. A couple of glass cases display a map and some excavated finds.

Beyond the gate the **Mortuary Bath (2)** on the right has beautiful arches and a crypt-like ceiling; you see the remains of the three-storey **armoury (3)** and the women's palaces on the left. About halfway up is a large water tank or well and to the north is what was once the most densely populated part of the city. Nearby, the domed storehouse turned into the **Ramdas Jail (4)** and has steps inside that lead up to a platform where there are relief sculptures of deities on the wall, dominated by Hanuman. The **Ambar Khana (5)** (granary) has a Persian inscription on black basalt stating that it was built between 1626 and 1672. The steps turn around an enormous boulder with a bastion and lead to the top passing the Hindu **Mahakali Temple (6)** on the way. The breezy **Durbar Hall (7)** is on the summit. It is well worth climbing the stairs to the roof here for good views. The path down is clearly signposted to take you on a circular route through the **harem (8)** and **Rani Mahal (9)** with its royal baths, back to the main gate. **AP Tourism** conducts regular bus tours from Hyderabad.

Qutb Shahi tombs

ⓘ *Sat-Thu 0930-1830, Rs 100, Indians Rs 10, camera Rs 10, car Rs 20, bicycle Rs 5. Allow 2 hrs, or half a day for a leisurely exploration. Inexpensive guidebook available.*

About 800 m north-northwest of Golconda fort on a low plateau (a road leaves the fort through the Banjara Gate) are the Qutb Shahi Tombs. Each tomb of black granite or greenstone with plaster decoration is built on a square or octagonal base with a large onion dome and arches with fine sculptures, inscriptions and remains of glazed decoration. The larger tombs have their own mosque attached which usually comprises an eastward opening hall with a *mihrab* to the west. The sides have inscriptions in beautiful Naksh script, and

Golconda fort

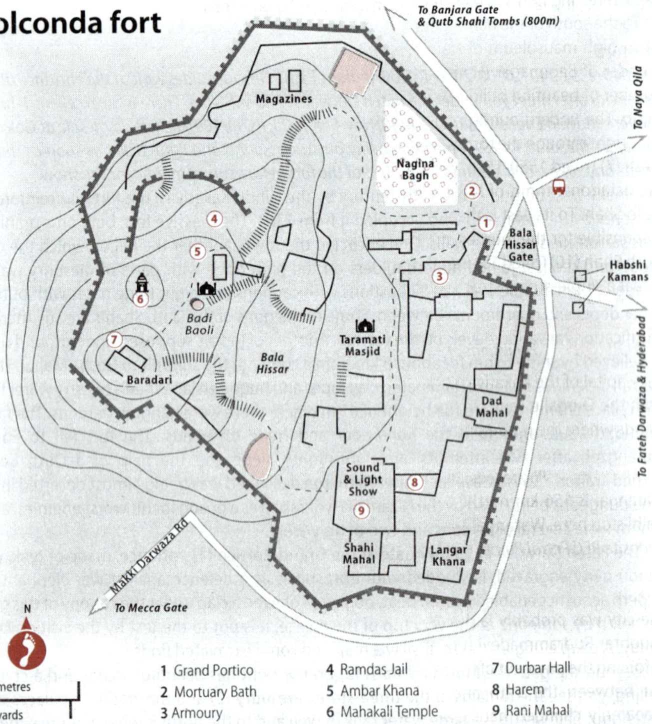

remnants of the glazed tiles that used to cover them can still be seen in places. The tombs of the rulers were built under their own supervision but fell into disrepair and the gardens ran wild until the end of the 19th century when Sir Salar Jang restored them and replanted the gardens. It is now managed and kept in an excellent state of repair by the Archaeological Survey of India. The gardens are being further improved.

The road north from Golconda fort passes the tomb of **Abdullah Qutb Shah (1)** (1626- 1672) as it approaches the entrance to the tombs, which is at the east gate of the compound. On the left side of the road just outside the compound is the tomb of **Abul Hasan Tana Qutb Shahi (2)** (ruled 1672-1687). He was the last of the kings to be buried here as the final king in the line of the Qutb Shahi Dynasty, Abul Hasan, died in the fort at Daulatabad in 1704. To the right of the entrance are the tomb of Princess **Hayat Baksh Begum (3)** (died 1677), the daughter of Ibrahim Qutb Shah, and a smaller mosque, while about 100 m directly ahead is the granite tomb of **Muhammad Qutb Shah (4)** (ruled 1612-1626). Tucked away due north of this tomb is that of **Pemamati (5)**, one of the mistresses of Muhammad Qutb Shah, dating from 1663. The path turns south and west around the tomb of Muhammad Qutb Shah. About 100 m to the south is a tank which is still open. The **Badshahi Hammam (11)**, the oldest structure in the compound, is the bath where the body of the king was washed before burial. You can still see the channels for the water and the special platforms for washing the body. The Badshahi kings were Shi'a Muslims, and the 12 small baths in the Hammam stand symbolically for the two *imams* revered by the Shi'a community. Next door, a small **Archaeological Museum** ⓘ *1000-1300, 1400-1630,* has interesting items in glass cases.

To the south of the hammam is a series of major tombs. The most striking lies due south, the 54-m-high mausoleum of **Muhammad Quli Qutb Shah (6)** (ruled 1581-1612), the poet king founder of Baghnagar (Hyderabad). It is appropriate that the man responsible for creating a number of beautiful buildings in Hyderabad should be commemorated by such a remarkable tomb. The underground excavations here have been turned into a Summer House. You can walk right through the tomb and on to the tomb of the fourth king of the dynasty, **Ibrahim Qutb Shah (7)** (ruled 1550-1580), another 100 m to the south. At the west edge of the compound is the octagonal tomb of **Kulsum Begum (8)** (died 1608), granddaughter of Mohammad Quli Qutb Shah. To its east is the tomb of **Jamshid Quli Qutb Shah (9)** (ruled 1543-1550), who was responsible for the murder of his 90-year-old father and founder of the dynasty, **Sultan Quli Qutb Shah (10)** (ruled 1518-1543). This has the appearance of a two-storey building though it is in fact a single-storey structure with no inscription. There are some other small tombs here.

Warangal → *For listings, see pages 1131-1135. Colour map 6, B1.*

The capital of the Kakatiya Empire in the 12th and 13th centuries, Warangal's name is derived from the Orugallu (one stone) Hill, a massive boulder with ancient religious significance that stands where the modern town is situated.

Ins and outs → *Phone code: 0870. Population: 528,600.*

Warangal is 156 km northeast of Hyderabad and most express trains between Chennai and Delhi stop here. **Warangal Tourist Office** ⓘ *1st floor, Talwar Hyndai Show Room, Chaitanyapuri, opposite REC Petrol Pump, Kazipet, T0870-244 6606.*

History

The city was probably laid out during the reigns of King Ganapatideva (1199-1262) and his daughter Rudrammadevi (until 1294). Warangal was captured by armies from Delhi in 1323, enforcing the payment of tribute. Control of Warangal fluctuated between Hindus and Muslims but between the 14th and 15th centuries it remained in Bahmani hands. Thereafter it repeatedly changed hands, and some argue that although the military fortifications were repeatedly strengthened, the religious buildings were largely destroyed, including the great Siva temple in the middle of the city. Marco Polo was highly impressed by Warangal's riches, and it is still famous for the remains of its temples, its lakes and wildlife, and for its three circuits of fortifications. The modern town itself, however, is not very interesting.

Sights

At the centre of the **'fort'** ⓘ *0600-1800, Rs 100, Indians Rs 5*, is a circular area about 1.2 km in diameter. Most of it is now farmland with houses along the road. Near the centre are the ruins of the original Siva temple. Remains include the large beautifully carved stone entrance gateways, replicas of which adorn many of the government offices, hotels and even private residences in the city. The gateways lead to the almost square enclosure, aligned along the cardinal directions and beyond are overturned slabs, smashed columns, brackets and ceiling panels.

Nearby Siva temples are still in use, and to the west is the **Khush Mahal**, a massive royal hall used by the Muslim Shitab Khan in the early 16th century for state functions. It may well have been built on the site of earlier palaces, near its geometric centre, while some structures in the central area may have been granaries.

From the centre, four routes radiate along the cardinal directions, passing through gateways in the three successive rings of fortification. The innermost ring is made of massive granite blocks, and is up to 6 m high with bastions regularly spaced along the wall. The middle wall is of unfaced packed earth, now eroded, while the outermost circuit, up to 5 m high, is also of earth. The four main roads pass through massive gateways in the inner wall, and there are also incomplete gateways in the second ring of fortifications. Some of the original roads that crossed the city have disappeared.

Some suggest that the plan of Warangal conforms to early Hindu principles of town planning. **'Swastika towns'**, especially suited to royalty, followed the pattern of concentric circles and swastika of the *yantras* and *mandalas*. They were a miniature representation of the universe, the power of god and king recognized symbolically, and in reality, at the centre.

The Chalukya-style '1000-pillar' **Siva Rudresvar temple** ⓘ *0500-1200, 1600-2000*, on the slopes of the Hanamakonda Hill, 4 km to the north, has beautiful carvings. It is a low, compact temple, built on several stepped platforms with subsidiary shrines to Vishnu and Surya, rock-cut elephants, a large superbly carved *Nandi* in the courtyard and an ancient well where villagers have drawn water for 800 years.

Around Warangal → *Colour map 6, B1.*

Pakhal, Ethurnagaram and Lakhnavaram

ⓘ *Warangal Bus Station to Narsampet. Regular bus service from Narsampet to Pakhal Lake or take a taxi.*

The great artificial lakes 40 km northeast of Warangal – from the south, Pakhal, Lakhnavaram, Ramappa and Ghanpur – were created as part of the Kakatiya rulers' water management and irrigation schemes in the 12th and 13th centuries and are still in use. The lakes are fringed with an emerging marsh vegetation and surrounded by extensive grasslands, tropical deciduous forests and evergreens. The park was set up in 1952 and has problems of the grazing of domestic livestock and illegal burning.

This is the richest area for wildlife in the state, with tiger, panther, hyena, wild dogs, wild boars, gaur, foxes, spotted deer, jackals, sloth bears and pythons. There are also otters and alligators and a variety of waterbirds and fish in the lakes. Pakhal Lake is especially important as an undisturbed site well within the sanctuary; Laknavaram Lake is 20 km to the north. They are superb for birdwatching (numerous migratory birds in winter) and occasional crocodile spottings. Tigers and panthers live deep in the forest but are rarely seen. Forest rangers might show you plaster casts of tiger pug marks.

Palampet → *Colour map 6, B2.*

Palampet lies close to the Ramappa Lake. The **Ramappa Temple**, dedicated to Siva as Rudreswara, was built in 1234 and is one of the finest medieval Deccan temples. The black basalt sculpture is excellent (even richer than that at the 1000-pillar temple) with famous Mandakini figures of female dancers which appear on brackets at the four entrances. The base of the temple has the typical bands of sculpture, the lowest of elephants, the second, a lotus scroll, the third which is the most interesting depicting figures opening a window on the life of the times and finally another floral scroll. There are more fine sculptures inside, some displaying a subtle sense of humour in common with some of the figures outside, and paintings of scenes from the epics on the ceiling. Note that no bottled water is available.

Nagarjunakonda → *For listings, see pages 1131-1135.* *Colour map 6, C1.*

Some 150 km southeast of Hyderabad is one of India's richest Buddhist sites, now almost entirely under the lake created by the Nagarjunasagar Dam, completed in 1960. The remains of a highly cultured Buddhist civilization had remained almost undisturbed for 1600 years until their discovery by AR Saraswati in March 1926. The reconstructed buildings are on a comparatively small scale, in a peaceful setting on top of the hilltop fort, now an island planted with low trees.

Ins and outs → *Phone code: 08680.*

The island is 11 km from Vijayapuri. There are three ferries daily from the jetty, 0930, 1030 and 1330. The last ferry leaves the island at 1600. Enquiries T08642-243457. Other ferries are reserved for APTDC tours, which can be organized locally or from Hyderabad. **AP State Tourist Office** ⓘ *Project House, Hill Colony, T08680-277364/276540.* A guide is available through this office; others can be arranged from the APTDC in Hyderabad.

History

Rising from the middle of the artificial lake is the Nagarjuna Hill which was once nearly 200 m above the floor of the secluded valley in the northern ranges of the Nallamalais (black hills) which surround the lake on three sides. On the fourth side was the great river Krishna, superimposed on the hills as it flows towards the Bay of Bengal.

Early archaeological work showed the remnants of Buddhist monasteries, many limestone sculptures and other remains. The Archaeological Survey carried out a full excavation of the sites before they were covered by the rising waters of the lake. More than 100 distinct sites ranging from the prehistoric early Stone Age period to the late medieval were discovered. Some of the most important remains have been moved and reconstructed on the hilltop fort. These include nine monuments, rebuilt in their original form, and 14 large replicas of the ruins.

The Ikshvakus made Nagarjunakonda the centre of extraordinary artistic activity from the third century AD. In the mid-fourth century AD the Pallavas pushed north from Tamil Nadu and eclipsed the Ikshvaku Kingdom, reducing Nagarjunakonda to a deserted village. However, during the Chalukya period a Saiva centre was built at Yellaswaram, on the other bank of the Krishna. In the 15th and 16th centuries the hill became a fortress in the contest for supremacy between the Vijayanagar, Bahmani and Gajapati kings. After the fall of the Vijayanagar Empire both the hill and the valley below lost all importance.

Sights

The Ikshvaku's capital was a planned city on the right bank of the Krishna – **Vijayapuri** (city of victory). The citadel had rampart walls on three sides with the river on the fourth. The buildings inside including houses, barracks, baths and wells were probably destroyed by a great fire. The nine **temples** show the earliest developments of Brahmanical temple architecture in South

India. The Vishnu temple (AD 278) had two beautifully carved pillars which were recovered from its site. Five temples were dedicated to Siva or Karttikeya. The river bank was dotted with Brahmanical shrines.

Nagarjunakonda excavations also revealed some of India's finest early sculptures and memorial pillars. Over 20 pillars were raised in the memory not just of rulers and nobles but also of artisans and religious leaders. The sculptures represent the final phase of artistic development begun at Amaravati in the second century BC.

The **hill fort** (early 14th-century) has remnants of the Vijayanagar culture though the present layout of the fort probably dates from as recently as 1565. The main entrance was from the northeast, near where the ferry now lands on the island. In places the walls are still over 6 m high, with regular bastions and six gateways. There are two temples in the east, where the museum now stands.

The **museum** ⓘ *Sat-Thu 0900-1600*, has a collection of coins and ornaments, but most importantly sculptures (including a 3-m-high standing Buddha). There are also prehistoric and protohistoric remains and several panels and friezes depicting Buddhist scenes.

Srisailam Wildlife Sanctuary ➔ *Colour map 6, C1.* *Altitude: 200-900 m.*

ⓘ *Information from AP Dept of Forests (see Useful contacts, page 1135). Cars are not permitted in the reserve 2100-0600. Temperature: 12-42°C. Rainfall: 1500 mm. Best to visit Oct-Mar.*

The largest of the state's wildlife sanctuaries is at Srisailam, a popular pilgrimage town on the banks of the Krishna near Nagarjunasagar. The park is India's largest tiger reserve, covering 3560 sq km of the Nallamalai Hills in an area deeply incised by gorges, has deciduous and bamboo forest and semi-desert scrubland. Besides tigers, there are leopards, Indian pangolins, panthers, wild dogs, civets, hyenas, jackals, wolves, giant squirrels, crocodiles, lizards, pythons, vipers, kraits and over 150 species of bird. There is a nature trail signposted 1 km short of Srisailam, or you can walk the access road and explore from there; a guide is available. Unfortunately the sanctuary is frequently disturbed by Naxalite activity and can be very difficult to get permission to visit. Check the latest position with the Forest Officer.

Srisailam also attracts Shaivite pilgrims, who come for the 14th century **Mallikarjuna Temple**, containing one of India's 12 *jyotirlingas*. Some 300 m long, the outer face has often been attacked and damaged, but is richly decorated with carved scenes from the Hindu epics and a portrait of Krishna Deva Raya, the Vijayanagar Emperor who visited the site in 1514. Non-Hindus are allowed into the inner sanctuary to witness the daily *puja*. Arrive early to avoid queuing in the middle of the day – first prayers at 0545. The **Mahasivaratri festival** draws large crowds. The ancient **Mahakali Temple** on a hill in the Nallamalai forest contains a rare *lingam* attracting large crowds of pilgrims, especially during **Sivaratri**.

Hyderabad and North Central Andhra listings

For Sleeping and Eating price codes and other relevant information, see Essentials pages 38-42.

Sleeping

Secundarabad is closer to the interstate train station and business district, but Hyderabad is better placed for sightseeing. High demand from business travellers has meant soaring room rates at middle and top end. Power cuts are routine. Larger hotels have generators, but a/c, lifts, etc in smaller hotels can fail.

Hyderabad *p1119, maps p1120 and p1123*

LL ITC Kakatiya, Begumpet, T040-2340 0132, www.itcwelcomegroup.in. 188 exquisitely furnished guest rooms and suites suit business and leisure travellers. There's a 24-hr coffee shop and speciality Indian restaurants, and an unusual pool built around a natural rock.

LL Taj Falaknuma, Engine Bowli, Falaknuma, T040 -6629 8585, www.tajhotels.com. The most opulent palace ever built by the Hyderabadi Nizams has been restored to its original condition and now plays host to one of India's most extraordinary hotels. The pick of the 60 rooms are the Historical and Royal suites, fitted out with Edwardian antiques and Italian marble floors, with sweeping views over the city or carefully-tended lawns. Public areas are similarly exquisite, with cavernous ballrooms and dining tables that stretch for miles, and the overall feeling is akin to being a private guest in a stately home.

LL Taj Krishna, Road No 1, Banjara Hills, T040-6666 2323, www.tajhotels.com. The flagship luxury Taj hotel in the city's elite district has 2 restaurants (Indian, Chinese), 260 rooms, 24-hr gym, the city's best pool and nightclub, **Ahala**, beautiful gardens, immaculate service. The Presidential suite has its own private pool.

L The Golkonda Hyderabad, Masab Tank, Mahavir Marg, T040-6611 0101, www.the golkondahyderabad.com. Completely renovated with minimalist decor and 5-star status, the **Golkonda** has 150 rooms, a/c, phone, TV, excellent showers. Breakfast included. Complimentary airport transfers.

AL-A Minerva Grand Banjara, Road No 11, Banjara Hills, T040-6612 7373, www.minerva grand.com. A boutique hotel with 44 designer rooms and suites in the upmarket Banjara Hills, close to the main commercial, retail and entertainment centres. Breakfast included.

AL-A Residency (Quality Inn), Public Garden Rd, T040-3061 6161, www.qualityinnresidency.com. Efficient business hotel, 95 a/c rooms, polite service, popular with Indians, good vegetarian restaurant and basement pub, **One Flight Down**.

C City Park, Chirag Ali Rd, T040-6610 5510, www.cityparkhyd.com. 54 bright prefab rooms with phone, en suite and writing tables, car park, internet, but stale a/c smell. Well placed just at the edge of Abid shopping district. Breakfast included. Rooftop multi-cuisine restaurant **Degh** has panoramic views over city.

C-D Taj Mahal, 4-1-999 Abid Rd, T040-2475 8250, sundartaj@satyam.net.in. 20 good-sized simple a/c rooms in 1940s building. Busy South Indian vegetarian restaurant, meals, laundry, good value, friendly and the most characterful of the budget options. Recommended.

E Sai Prakash, Nampally Station Rd, T040-2460 5239, www.hotelsaiprakash.com. Business hotel with 102 clean, comfortable a/c rooms and a good restaurant.

E-F Hotel Saptagiri Deluxe, off Nampally Station Rd, T040-2461 0333. Peaceful hotel in interesting area with 36 scrupulously clean rooms. Choice of a/c and non-a/c. Western toilet, shower. Gets busy so book in advance.

E-F Hotel Sri Brindavan, Nampally Station Rd, near the Circle, T040-2320 3970. 70 clean rooms in custard-colour compound set back from road. Mostly male guests; unsuitable for lone female travellers. Otherwise decent value, good restaurants, good budget choice.

E-F Imperial, corner of Nampally Station and Public Gardens roads (5 mins from Hyderabad station), T040-6682 7777. Large hotel with 48 clean rooms, some with bath, avoid roadside rooms, bucket hot water, helpful, excellent service. Not recommended for lone women travellers.

Secunderabad *p1119, map p1120*

LL Fortune Select Manohar, adjacent to old airport in Begumpet, T040-6654 3456, www.fortunehotels.in. A full-service business-class hotel with 132 well-appointed rooms and suites, club lounge overlooking pool, health club. Check for discounts.

LL-L Marriott, Tank Bund Rd, T040-2752 2999, www.marriott.com. Plush business hotel with charming pool and spa, set on the shores of Hussain Sagar Lake. Rates fluctuate according to city conference schedule; it's worth phoning. Low categories exclude breakfast.

AL Green Park, Begumpet, T040-6651 5151, www.hotelgreenpark.com. A sedate and large Indian business and family hotel with 146 rooms. Rooms come with bath, a/c and TV. Free Wi-Fi.

B Hotel Baseraa, 9-1, 167/168 SD Rd, T040-2770 3200, www.baseraa.com. 75 tatty but comfortable a/c rooms in busy friendly, family hotel with great service and good restaurants.

B-C Yatri Nivas (Joint management by AP Tourism and Amogh Hotels Ltd), SP Rd, T040-2346 1840. Clean, airy, well kept, 32 rooms, mostly a/c, 3 restaurants, bar.

D-E Dwaraka Heritage, Chenoy Trade Centre, Parklane, SD Road, T040-2789 5111. 40 clean and comfortable rooms in the heart of the city's business district. Breakfast included.

D-F Taj Mahal, 88 SD Rd, T040-2781 2171. 40-year-old characterful building with 20 faded but good rooms (a/c suite, a/c double, non-a/c double and non-a/c single). Popular South Indian vegetarian restaurant.

F Retiring Rooms, at railway station.

F YMCA, SD Rd, T040-2780 5408. This place has 15 rooms (mostly singles, but big enough to take an extra bed), shared bath, clean, roomy, friendly, 'treated as family', Extra charge for temporary membership.

F Youth Hostel, near Sailing Club, T040-2754 0763 . Total of 90 beds in dorms. Women preferred over men during room allocation. Extra charge for temporary membership.

Warangal *p1127*

Though it is possible to visit Warangal in a long day from Hyderabad, it's worth staying a night to soak in the old-world atmosphere.

C Ashoka, Hanamkonda, near Chowrashta city bus station, T0870-6692220. One of the oldest hotels in the city, with spacious but poorly maintained rooms. Safe for women travellers.

C Suprabha, Nakkalagutta, Hanamkonda, T0870-2573888. New hotel near railway station, 52 clean airy rooms (a/c and non a/c), excellent service, internet, breakfast included.

Nagarjunakonda *p1129*

C Vijay Vihar (APTDC), Nagarjuna Sagar, T08680-277362. The most luxurious and picturesque accommodation, with lake-facing rooms and suites (all a/c), bar and restaurant.

D-E Nagarjuna Resort, near the jetty, T08642-242471. Clean comfortable rooms (a/c and non a/c) and garden, but no views.

Srisailam Wildlife Sanctuary *p1130*

At the time of writing, the Forest Rest Houses in Srisailam Sanctuary were not accepting bookings. Most accommodation in town is managed by the Temple Management Committee, T08524-288883.

C Haritha Hotel (APTDC), 1 km south of Mallikarjuna Temple, T08524-288311. Clean a/c and non a/c rooms, garden, veg restaurant.

E-F Ganga Sadan, 1 km south of temple, T08524-288888. Clean spacious rooms and excellent view. Recommended.

Eating

Hyderabad *p1119, maps p1120 and p1123*

Subway, KFC, Pizza Hut, McDonalds and Domino's are in the city, as well as the pure vegetarian chain **Kamat**. The shopping malls **Lifestyle** and **Hyderabad Central** have good food courts. **Madina** crossroad in Char Minar has good authentic Hyderabadi street food.

TTT **The Water Front**, Eat St, Necklace Rd, T040-2330 8899. Lunch and dinner. When Hyderabadi's need to impress, they go to this open-air restaurant right on Hussain Sagar Lake. The food is coastal Indian and Asian, the bill hefty, the atmosphere stylish and romantic.

TTT-TT **Firdaus**, Taj Krishna hotel (see Sleeping), T040-6666 2323. Excellent Mughlai cuisine and one of the only places in the city where you can get the special Hyderabadi treat, *haleem*. Meaning 'patience', this meat, wholewheat and gram dish is slow-cooked and is traditionally made to break the Ramadan fast.

TT **Hyderabad House**, opposite JNTU College, Masab Tank, T040-2332 7861; also opposite Mosque Rd, No 3, Banjara Hills, T040-2355

4747. Very good biryanis and *lukhmis*. Parcel service available.

₸₸ **Southern Spice**, 8-2-350/3/2, Road No 3, Banjara Hills, T040-2335 3802. Breakfast, lunch and dinner. Good Andhra, Chettinad, tandoori and Chinese cuisine.

₸₸-₸ **Paradise Food Court**, 38 Sarojini Devi Rd/MG Rd. T040-6631 3721. 1100-2400. Utterly synonymous with biryani, and such an institution that the surrounding area is now named 'Paradise'. You can get parcels from downstairs, eat standing up at the fast- food section, or go upmarket at **Persis Gold**.

Bars and clubs

Hyderabad-Secunderabad

p1119, maps p1120 and p1123

Mostly in the top-end hotels; night life doesn't compare to Bengaluru. **Ahala**, Taj Krishna hotel, is the most modish; **One Flight Down**, opposite Hyderabad Railway Station, Public Garden Rd (1100-2300) is a modern, British-style pub, snooker tables and TV. Dark but popular.

Entertainment

Hyderabad-Secunderabad

p1119, maps p1120 and p1123

Cinema

Some cinemas show English-language films.

Lalit Kala Thoranam, Public Gardens. Hosts art exhibitions and free film shows daily.

Ravindra Bharati, Public Garden Rd, Saifabad, T040-2323 1245. Regularly stages dance, theatre and music programmes, a/c.

Sound and light show

Golconda fort (page 1125). Spectacularly voiced over by Bollywood legend Amitabh Bhachan.

Shopping

Hyderabad-Secunderabad

p1119, maps p1120 and p1123

Most shops open 1000-1900. Some close on Fri. Every other shop sells pearls; look for shape, smoothness and shine to determine quality. Size is the last criteria in deciding a pearl's price. Bargain for at least 10% off asking prices. Also look out for *bidri* ware, crochetwork, Kalamkari paintings, *himroo* and silk saris. **Lad Bazar**, around the Char Minar, is great for bangles. For more on Andhra Pradesh's craft tradition, see page 1117.

Antiques

Govind Mukandas, Bank St.

Humayana, **Taj Banjara** hotel.

Books

Akshara, 8-2-273 Pavani Estates, Road No 2, Banjara Hills, T040-2354 3906. Excellent collection on all aspects of India in English.

Haziq and Mohi, Lal Chowk. Good antiquarian bookshop, especially for Arabic and Persian.

Handicrafts

Government emporia include: **Nirmal Industries**, Raj Bhavan Rd; **Lepakshi**, and **Coircraft**, Mayur Complex, Gun Foundry; and **Co-optex**. There are several others in Abids. Non-government shops may charge a bit more but may have more attractive items.

Bidri Crafts, Abids.

Fancy Cloth Store, 21-2-28 Pathergatti, Hyderabad, T040-2452 3983. For silk. Exports cloth to Selfridges in the UK.

Khadi, Sultan Bazar and Municipal Complex, Rashtrapati Rd, Secunderabad.

Kalanjali, Hill Fort Rd, opposite Public Gardens. Large selection of regional crafts.

In Secunderabad try: **Baba Handicrafts**, MG Rd; and **Jewelbox**, SD Rd.

Pearls

Mangatrai Pearl and Jewellers, 6-3-883 Punjagutta, T040-2341 1816, www.mangatrai.com. For quality pearls. Jewellers to Indian nobility, with everything from Basra pearls to black Tahitian pearls.

Activities and tours

Hyderabad-Secunderabad

p1119, maps p1120 and p1123

Swimming

BV Gurumoorthy Pool, Sardar Patel Rd.

Tour operators

APTDC, T040-2326 2151, offers the following tours: **City sightseeing**: full day, 0915-1745, from offices at Yatri Nivas and Secretariat Rd, Rs 270; unsatisfactory as it allows only 1 hr at the fort and includes unimportant sights. **Golconda**: sound and light show, 1600-2100, Rs 200. **Nagarjunasagar**: daily to Dam, Nagarjunakonda Museum, Right Canal and

Ethipothala Falls, 0700-2130, Rs 450. **Ramoji Film City**: 0745-1800, Rs 500 (entry fee included). Allows 4-5 hrs at the studios, plus Sanghi Temple and shopping time.

Mercury, 1st floor, Paradise, Jaya Mansion 126 (opposite Hotel Kamath), Sarojini Devi Rd, Secunderabad, T040-2781 2712.

Sita, 3-5-874, Sita House, Hyderguda, T040-4009 4444.

TCI, 102 Regency House, Greenland Rd, Somajiguda, T040-2340 2722.

Thomas Cook, 5-9-100, Doyen Trade House, Public Garden Rd, T(0)9849-258491; also at Cyber Tower, Madhapur, T040-6666 1100.

Nagarjunakonda *p1129*

Tour operators

APTDC, runs a day trip from Hyderabad; tiring (with 4 hrs on a coach each way) but convenient and cheap. 0645-2145, Rs 450 including lunch. Nagarjunasagar is the village beside the dam from which boats ferry visitors to the temples and museum on the island (at 0800, 1200, 1500, trip takes 1 hr). If you take the 2nd boat you still have time to visit the sights and return on the next boat. You can leave your luggage for a few hours at this pier provided someone is on duty.

Transport

Hyderabad-Secunderabad

p1119, maps p1120 and p1123

Air Rajiv Gandhi International Airport is 25 km south of the city, T040-6676 4000, www.hyderabad.aero. Transport to town: pre-paid taxis cost Rs 450-500; there are no auto-rickshaws. **Aeroexpress shuttles**, T1800-419 2008, run on fixed routes to various parts of the city, including Charminar.

Daily domestic flights to **Ahmedabad**, **Bengaluru**, **Chennai**, **Delhi**, **Goa**, **Kolkata**, **Mumbai**, **Pune**, **Tirupati**, **Visakhapatnam**.

International connections with: **Abu Dhabi**, **Doha**, **Dubai**, **Frankfurt**, **Kuala Lumpur**, **London**, **Muscat**, **Sharjah** and **Singapore**.

Airline offices Air India/Indian Airlines, 5-10-193, HACA Bhavan, opposite Public Gardens Rd, T040-2338 9747, airport T040-2338 9723; domestic, T1800-180407. **British Airways**, T1800-1023 5922. **Etihad**, Regus Business Centre, Midtown Rd No 1, Banjara Hills, T1800-209 0808. **Emirates**, Reliance Classic Bldg, Rd No 1, Banjara Hills, T040-6623 4444. **Jet Airways**, 5-10-197 ABC, Hill Fort Rd, T040-3989 3333. **Saudi Arabian**, ground floor, Krishna Residency, Hill Fort Rd, Adarsh Nagar, T040-2324 0315. **Singapore Airlines**, White House, Begumpet Rd, Begumpet, T040-2340 2873. **Thai**, 1st floor, 6-3-249/6, Road No 1, Banjara Hills, T040-2333 3030.

Bicycle Hire is readily available (ask for the 'bicycle taxi' shop near Nampally Railway station), Rs 50 per day, but may ask for a large deposit. Good for visiting Golconda, but the city is only for cyclists who are experienced with heavy, fast-flowing traffic.

Local bus City buses are crowded in rush hour. Useful routes: No 119 (Nampally to Golconda); 87 (Nampally to Char Minar); 2/2V (Charminar to Secunderabad Station).

Long distance bus The vast **Imliban Bus Station**, T040-2461 3955, has long-distance state-run buses to all destinations in Andhra Pradesh and neighbouring states. Also **APSRTC**, T040-2343 4268, www.apsrtc.gov.in. Advance reservations available. Private deluxe coaches depart from opposite Hyderabad Railway Station to **Aurangabad**, **Bengaluru** (**Bangalore**), **Mumbai**, **Chennai** and **Tirupati**; reservations from **Royal Lodge**, at the entrance to the station.

Secunderabad has the **Jubilee Bus Station**, T040-2780 2203, with services to major destinations. From Nampally: buses to **Golconda**. **Venus Travel**, opposite Residency Hotel, runs a bus to **Gulbarga**, 0730, 5 hrs.

Car Tourist taxis and luxury cars from **AP Tourism**, Tank Bund Rd, T040-2345 3036, **Ashok Travels**, ground floor, Mukhram Jha Rd T040-2326 1360. **Travel Express**, 58 Nagarjuna Hills, Punjagutta, T040-2335 8855. Rs 800 per 8 hrs or 80 km, Rs 400 per 4 hrs.

Rickshaw and taxis Auto-rickshaws charge Rs 12 for 2 km; will use meter after mild insistence. Cycle rickshaws are cheaper. Local taxis charge Rs 15 per km; reliable radio taxi companies include **Easy Cabs**, T040-4343 4343, and **Meru Cabs**, T040-4422 4422.

Train Trains listed below arrive and depart at 3 main stations: **Hyderabad** (**H**), also known as Hampally, **Secunderabad** (**S**), and **Kacheguda** (**K**). South-Central Enquiries: T139. Reservations: T134. Buses 20V and 49 link the 3 stations, Rs 10.

Trains to: **Aurangabad**: *Devagiri Exp 17058*, 1330, 9½ hrs. **Bengaluru** (**Bangalore**): *Bangalore Exp 12785*, 1905, 11½ hrs (**K**); *Rajdhani Exp 12430*, 1910 (Tue, Wed, Thu, Sun) (**S**), 12 hrs. **Chennai** (**MC**): *Charminar Exp 12760 (AC/II)*, 1830 (**H**), 1930 (**S**), 14½ hrs; *Hyderabad Chennai Exp 12604*, 1655 (**S**), 14½ hrs. **Delhi** (**HN**): *Rajdhani Exp 12429*, 0750 (Mon, Tue, Thu, Fri) (**S**), 22½ hrs. **Delhi** (**ND**): *New Delhi AP Exp 12723*, 0625 (**H**), 0700 (**S**), 26 hrs. All Delhi trains go via Nagpur and Bhopal. **Guntakal**: (for Hospet and Hampi), *KCG-YPR Exp 17603*, 2100, 6½ hrs (**K**). **Kolkata** (**Howrah**): *E Coast Exp 18646*, 1000, 32½ hrs (**H**). **Mumbai** (**CST**): *Hyderabad-Mumbai Exp 17032*, 2040, 17 hrs; *Hussainsagar Exp 12702*, 1445 (**H**), 15¾ hrs; *Konark Exp 11020*, 1145 (**S**), 17½ hrs. **Tirupati**: *Krishna Exp 17406*, 0600 (**S**), *Venkatadri Exp 12797*, 2005, 11½ hrs (**K**); *Narayanadri Exp 12734*, 1805 (**S**), 13½ hrs.

Warangal *p1127*

Bus Frequent buses to **Hyderabad** (3½ hrs) and **Vijayawada** (7 hrs).
Train Many Express trains stop here. **Chennai** (**MC**): *Tamil Nadu Exp 12622*, 2101, 10 hrs. **Delhi** (**ND**): *Tamil Nadu Exp 12621*, 0724, 24 hrs; **Nagpur**: Several daily 7½-8½ hrs. **Secunderabad**: *Konark Exp 11020*, 0735, 3½ hrs; *Golconda Exp 17201*, 1012, 3½ hrs; *Krishna Exp 17405*, 1704, 3½ hrs. **Vijayawada**: *Secunderabad-Guntur Exp 12706*, 1000, 3½ hrs.

Nagarjunakonda *p1129*

Buses from Hyderabad to Macherla stop at Nagarjuna Sagar (4 hrs), and buses also go to Vijayawada. It's easier, if rushed, to visit on an **APTDC** day tour (see Activities and tours).

Srisailam Wildlife Sanctuary *p1130*

Srisailam can be reached from Kurnool, 170 km away on the Hyderabad–Bengaluru highway and railway line. From Hyderabad it's a 200-km drive across the wide open Telangana Plateau; buses take about 6 hrs. The nearest train station is Macherla (13 km).

Directory

Hyderabad-Secunderabad *p1119, maps p1120 and p1123*

Banks Mon-Fri 1000-1400, Sat 1000-1200. In Hyderabad, several banks with ATMs on Bank St, Mahipatram Rd and Mukaramjahi Market; in Secunderabad look on Rashtrapati Rd. **Amex**, Samrat Complex, 5-9-12, Saifabad, T040-2323 4591. **Thomas Cook**, Nasir Arcade, 6-1-57, Saifabad, T040-259 6521. **Travel Club Forex**, next door, carries Western Union transfers. **Cultural centres and libraries Alliance Française**, near Planetrium, Naubat Pahad, T040-2770 0731. **British Library**, Secretariat Rd, T040-2323 0774, Tue-Sat 1100-1900. **Goethe Centre**, Hill Fort Rd, T040-2324 1791. **Bharatiya Vidya Bhavan**, King Kothi Rd, T040-223 7825. **Internet** Several in Abids and Charag Ali Lane (Rs 30-40 per hr). Good coverage throughout the twin cities. **Medical services** Outpatients usually from 0900-1400. Casualty 24 hrs. **Newcity** (Secunderabad), T040-2780 5961. **Post** In Hyderabad: **GPO** (with Poste Restante) and **CTO**, Abids. In Secunderabad: **Head PO** in RP Rd and **CTO** on MG Rd. **Useful contacts AP Dept of Forests**, Public Garden Rd, near Secretariat (opposite **Reserve Bank**), T040-040-23231404. Excellent advice, may help with arrangements to visit wildlife reserves. The Chief Conservator of Forests T(0)9440-810001 is very helpful. **Foreigners' Regional Registration Office**: Commissioner of Police, Purani Haveli, Hyderabad, T040-2452 1041, www.hyderabadpolice.gov.in.

Krishna-Godavari Delta

The rice-growing delta of the Krishna and Godavari rivers is one of Andhra Pradesh's most prosperous and densely populated regions, and the core region of Andhra culture. The flat coastal plains are fringed with palmyra palms and occasional coconut palms, rice and tobacco. Inland, barely 40% of the land is cultivated. About 120 km to the west of the road south to Chennai run the Vellikonda Ranges, only visible in very clear weather. To the north the ranges of the Eastern Ghats can often be clearly seen. ▸▸ *For listings, see pages 1137-1139.*

Vijayawada ➔ *Colour map 6, C2. Phone code: 0866. Population: 825,400.*

At the head of the Krishna delta, 70 km from the sea, the city of Vijayawada has been in existence for over 2000 years, and derives its name from the goddess Kanakdurga or Vijaya, the presiding deity of the city; there is an important temple to her on a hill beside the river. The city is surrounded by bare granite hills, which radiate heat during the searing summer: temperatures of over 45°C are not uncommon in April and May, though in winter they drop to a positively fresh 20°C. The Qutb Shahi rulers made Vijayawada an important inland port. It is still a major commercial town and has capitalized on its position as the link between the interior and the main north-south route between Chennai and Kolkata. It is also the operational centre of the Krishna delta canal scheme, one of the earliest major irrigation developments in South India (completed in 1855), which irrigates nearly one million hectares of land, banishing famine from the delta and converting it into one of the richest granaries in the country. The **Prakasam Barrage**, over 1 km long, carries the road and railway lines across the water.

There are several sites with caves and temples with inscriptions from the first century AD. The **Kanakdurga Temple**, on a hill to the east of town, is the most atmospheric of the temples. **Mogalarajapuram Temple** has an Ardhanarisvara statue which is thought to be the earliest in South India. There are two 1000-year-old Jain temples and the **Hazratbal Mosque**, which has a relic of the Prophet Mohammed. **Victoria Jubilee Museum** ⓘ *MG Rd, Sat-Thu 1030-1700, free, camera Rs 5*, has sculpture and paintings.

AP Tourist Office ⓘ *MG Rd, T0886-257 1393, 0600-2000*, also has counters at the bus stand on Machilipatnam Road, and the train station.

Amaravati

Located 30 km west of Vijaywada, Amaravati was the capital of the medieval Reddi kings of Andhra, but some 1500 years before they wielded power Amaravati was a great Mahayana Buddhist centre (see page 1423). Initially built in the third and second centuries BC, the shrine was dedicated to the Hinayana sect, but under Nagarjuna was changed into a Mahayana sanctuary where the Buddha was revered as Amareswara. Very little remains *in situ*, most of the magnificent sculpted friezes, medallions and railings having been removed to museums in Chennai, Kolkata and London's British Museum. The onsite **Archaeological Museum** ⓘ *Sat-Thu 0900-1700, free, buses via Guntur or by ferry from Krishneveni Hotel*, contains some exquisitely carved sculptures of the Bodhi Tree alongside a collection of broken panels, *chakras* and caskets holding relics.

Guntur ➔ *Colour map 6, C2.*

From Vijayawada the NH5 southwest crosses the barrage (giving magnificent views over the Krishna at sunset) to Guntur, a major town dealing in rice, cotton and tobacco where the ancient charnockite rocks of the peninsula meet the alluvium of the coastal plain. In the 18th century it was capital of the region Northern Circars and was under Muslim rule from 1766 under the Nizam of Hyderabad. The Archaeological Museum in Amaravati exhibits local finds including fourth-century Buddhist stone sculptures. Some 40 km to the south, the unspoiled golden sands of **Suryalanka Beach** see very little tourist traffic; there is a newly built **AP Tourism** resort right on the beach.

Machilipatnam and around

The once-flourishing sea port of Machilipatnam ('fish town'), 60 km southeast of Vijayawada, derived its name from the old city gateways, one of which still stands, decorated with painted fish eyes. A one-time port of the kingdom of Golconda, it was one of the earliest British settlements in India, existent as early as 1611. It is also well known for its Kalamkari painting (see page 1117) widely prevalent in the neighbouring village of Pedana, the art having been fostered by the Qutub Shahis. The beach at Manginapudi, 10 km from Machilipatnam, has black clay sand. This area is battered by frequent cyclones; one in 1864 is said to have taken 30,000 lives.

Rajahmundry and the Konaseema Backwaters ➔ *Colour map 6, C3. Phone code: 0883.*

Set on the banks of the Godavari, Rajahmundry was the scene of a bitter 300-year tug-of-war between the Chalukya, Vengi and Orissan kingdoms and the Deccan Muslims, until the French annexed the city in 1753. It is remembered for the poet Nannayya who wrote the first Telugu classic *Andhra Mahabharathamu*, and is also noted for its carpets and sandalwood products. Every 12 years the **Pushkaram** celebration (next in 2015) draws thousands of pilgrims to the river banks.

Rajahmundry makes a convenient base from which to visit both the Eastern Ghats and the coastal districts. Some 80 km northwest of the town, the Godavari cuts through a gorge in the Papi hills, creating a succession of stunningly beautiful lakes, reminiscent of Scottish lochs, where you can take boat trips. Another appealing side trip is to the **Konaseema Delta**, 70 km south of Rajahmundry, a verdant cocktail of coconut groves, mango orchards and paddy fields encircled by the waters of the Godavari and the Bay of Bengal. **AP Tourism** operates **houseboat trips** on the Godavari, and a 24-hour trip from Dindi (departs 1000 from the Coconut County resort, bookings T08862-227993, T(0)9848- 780524), sailing up past quaint little villages and islands, offers the kind of peace and solitude that have long been missing from the Kerala backwaters. Houseboats have two well-furnished air-conditioned bedrooms; meals and drinks are served on board.

Krishna-Godavari Delta listings

For Sleeping and Eating price codes and other relevant information, see Essentials pages 38-42.

Sleeping

Vijayawada *p1136*

There are some **F** hotels on MG Rd near the bus stand and around the railway station.

A Fortune Murali Park, MG Rd, Labbipet, T0866-398 8008. The smartest rooms in town by a long chalk, plus a host of extra services including babysitting.

B Ilapuram, Besant Rd, T0866-257 1282. 81 large clean rooms, some a/c, restaurants.

C-E Berm Park (AP Tourism), on the banks of Krishna river T0866-241 8057. 30 clean rooms (most a/c), restaurant, tourist office, car hire, boat trips to nearby Bhavani Island.

D-E Santhi, Near Apsara Theatre Governorpet, T0866-257 7355. Clean rooms with bath (hot water), good vegetarian restaurant.

E Kandhari International, MG Rd, Labbipet, T0866-249 7797. Some a/c in the 73 rooms, some a/c, also restaurants with a/c.

E Mamata, Eluru Rd, 1 km from centre, T0866-257 1251. Good a/c restaurants (1 rooftop), bar, 59 rooms, most a/c with bath.

F Railway Retiring Rooms. Large and well-maintained rooms, an excellent budget option.

Guntur *p1136*

D Haritha Beach Resort, Suryalanka, Bapatla Mandal, Guntur, T08643-224616. 13 beach-facing a/c cottages, garden, multi-cuisine restaurant.

D Vijayakrishna International, Collectorate Rd, Nagarampalem, T0863-222 2221. The best place in town and often frequented by Telugu cinestars, several of whom hail from Guntur. 42 good rooms, some a/c, and a popular restaurant.

E Annapurna Lodge, opposite APSRTC Bus Stand, T0866-222 2979. A/c and non-a/c rooms, quality meals, helpful and obliging.
F Sudarsan, Kothapet, Main Rd, T0863-222 2681. 28 rooms, some a/c, good vegetarian restaurant.

Machilipatnam and around *p1137*

E Swarnandhra Resort, Manginapudi Beach, T08672-242070. Sea-facing cottages (a/c and non a/c) set in landscaped gardens, food available.

Rajahmundry *p1137*

A-B Anand Regency, 26-3-7, Jampet, T0883-246 1201, www.hotelanandregency.co.in. Business hotel but with great ambience, good service, 3 restaurants , arranges sightseeing and boating trips.
B River Bay Hotel, Near Gowthami Ghat, T0883-244 7000, www.riverbay.co.in. Decent rooms with excellent river views, complimentary breakfast.
C Coconut Country Resort, Dindi (starting point of houseboat cruise), T08862-227991. 32 well-furnished a/c rooms overlooking the river, swimming pool, garden.
E Dwaraka Hotel, Kandakam Rd, Fort Gate, T(0)9848-484349. Budget hotel in city centre, decent rooms, good service.

Eating

Vijayawada *p1136*

The restaurants in the **Kandhari** and **Mamata** hotel are recommended.
Greenlands, Bhavani Gardens, Labbipet. Food served in 7 huts on the garden lawns.

Shopping

Vijayawada *p1136*

Some shops close 1300-1600. Local Kondapalli toys and Machilipatnam Kalamkari paintings are popular.

The emporia are in MG Rd, Eluru Rd, and Governorpet. Recommended are: **Apco**, Besant Rd; **Ashok**, opposite Maris Stella College, T0866-247 6966; **Handicrafts Shop**, Krishnaveni Motel; **Lepakshi**, Gandhi Nagar.

Activities and tours

Vijayawada *p1136*

KL Rao Vihara Kendram, Bhavani Island on Prakasham Barrage Lake. Offers rowing, canoeing, water scooters, pedal boats.

Rajahmundry *p1137*

Maruthi Mini Travels, T0883-242 4577. Booking agent for Konaseema backwater cruises, and also conducts daily boat trips to Papi Hills from Rajahmundry, 0630-2100, Rs 500 per person.

Transport

Vijayawada *p1136*

Bus Good local network in city but buses get very crowded. Long-distance buses to destinations in AP and neighbouring states including **Chennai** (9 hrs) operate from the **New Bus Stand** on MG Rd near the river; enquiries T0866-247 3333.
Car hire From **AP Tourist Office**, see page 1136.
Ferry To **Bhavani Islands**, 0930-1730. Also services between Krishnaveni Hotel and **Amaravati**. Daily 0800. Rs 50 return. Book at hotel or at bus station.
Rickshaw and taxi Very few metered yellow-top taxis. *Tongas*, auto- and cycle-rickshaws are available.
Train Vijayawada is an important junction, with trains to **Chennai** (**MC**): *Pinakini Exp 12711*, 0600, 7 hrs; *Coromandel Exp 12841* (AC/II), 1045, 6¾ hrs. **Delhi** (**HN**): *GT Exp 12615*, 0205, 30 hrs; *Link Daksin Exp 12861*, 2130, 31 hrs. **Hyderabad**: *Godavari Exp 12727*, 2355, 7 hrs. **Hospet**: *Amaravati Exp 18047*, 1855 hrs, 13 hrs. **Kolkata** (**H**): *Coromandel Exp 12842* (AC/II), 1525, 22 hrs, via **Bhubaneswar**, 11½ hrs. **Secunderabad**: *Satavahana Exp 12713*, 0610, 5½ hrs; *Krishna Exp 17405*, 1330, 7 hrs.

Guntur *p1136*

Bus The **APSRTC Bus Stand** is well organized and clean. Buses every 30 mins to **Vijayawada** (0600-2300) and **Bapatla** (0600-2000), from where shared autro-rickshaws can get you to **Surylanka**.
Train **Kolkata**: *Faluknama Exp 12704*, 2035, 21 hrs. **Chennai**: *Hyderabad Chennai Exp 17054*, 2200, 8 hrs. **Hospet**: *Amravati Exp 12604*, 2225, 12 hrs. **Secunderabad**: *Palnadu Exp 12747*, 0545, 5 hrs; *Golconda Exp 17201*, 0530, 8 hrs.

Rajahmundry *p1137*

Trains to **Kolkata** (**H**): *Coromandel Exp 12842 (AC/II)*, 1830, 19½ hrs. **Vijayawada**: *Coromandel Exp 12841*, 0733, 2¾ hrs; *Chennai Mail 12839*, 1730, 3½ hrs; *Ratnachal Exp 12717*, 1530, 3 hrs. **Visakhapatnam**: *Coromandel Exp 12842*, 1830, 3¾ hrs; *Chennai Howrah Mail 12840*, 0909, 4 hrs; *Ratnachal Exp 12718*, 0829, 3½ hrs.

Directory

Vijayawada *p1136*

Banks **State Bank of India**, Babu Rajendra Prasad Rd. ATMs at the bus stand and on Atchutaramaiah St. **Post** Kaleswara Rao Rd.

Northeastern Andhra Pradesh

From Rajahmundry the NH5 travels north over the narrowing coastal plain, the beautiful hills of the Eastern Ghats rising sharply inland. The pattern of life here contrasts sharply with that further south. Higher rainfall and a longer wet season, alongside the greater fertility of the alluvial soils, contribute to an air of prosperity; they also mean you should check weather forecasts before setting out on a journey. Village houses, with their thatched roofed cottages and white painted walls, are quite different and distinctive, as are the bullock carts. ▸▸ *For listings, see pages 1142-1144.*

History

The area was brought under Muslim rule by the Golconda kings of the Bahmani Dynasty in 1575 and ceded to the French in 1753. In 1765 the Mughal emperor granted the whole area to the East

Visakhapatnam

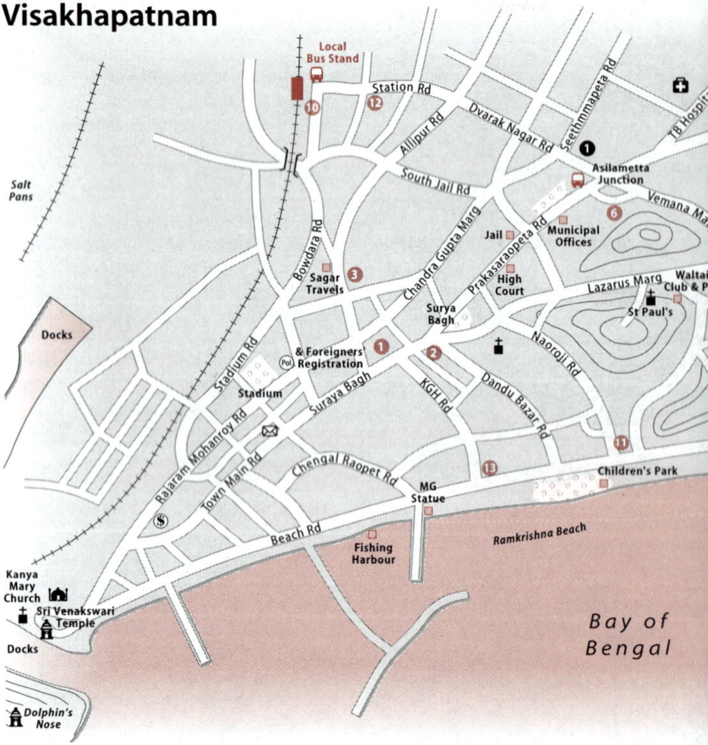

Sleeping
Apsara **1**
Daspalla **2**
Dolphin **3**
Gateway **11**
Meghalaya **6**
Palm Beach **8**
Park **9**
Punnami Beach Resort **7**
Railway Retiring Rooms **10**
Simhagiri **12**
Supreme **13**

Eating
Blue Diamond **1**

India Company, its first major territorial acquisition in India. The region is also the most urbanized part of Andhra Pradesh, with a dozen towns of more than 100,000 people. Most are commercial and administrative centres with neither the functions nor the appearance of industrial cities, but they serve as important regional centres for trade, especially in agricultural commodities, and they are the homes of some of Andhra's wealthiest and most powerful families.

Although the building of dams on both the Krishna and the Godavari rivers has eliminated the catastrophic flooding common until the mid-19th century, the totally flat delta, lying virtually at sea level, is still prone to cyclones; in 1864 one claimed over 34,000 lives. The area was completely engulfed by a tidal wave in 1883 when the volcano of Mount Krakatoa blew up 5000 km away, and further catastrophic cyclones in 1977 and 1996, not to mention the 2004 tsunami, caused massive damage and loss of life. You may notice the increasing number of small concrete buildings on raised platforms along the roadside designed to provide temporary shelter to villagers during cyclones.

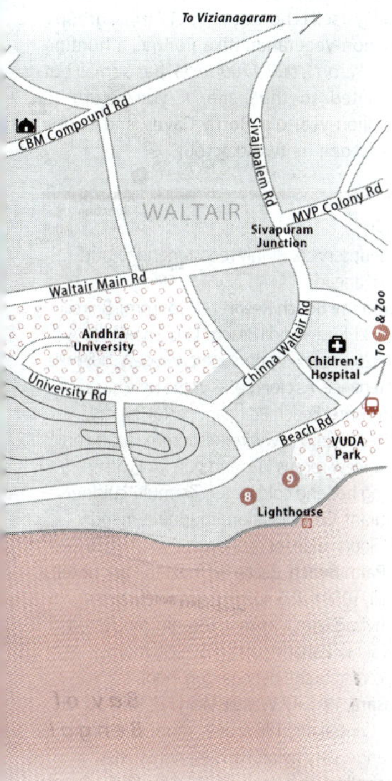

Visakhapatnam

→ *For listings, see pages 1142-1144. Colour map 6, B4.*

Set in a bay with rocky promontories, Visakhapatnam (Vizag) commands a spectacular position between the thickly wooded Eastern Ghats and the sea. It has become one of the country's most rapidly growing cities. Already India's fourth largest port, it has developed ship building, oil refining, fertilizer, petrochemical, sugar refinery and jute industries, as well as one of India's newest and largest steel mills. This is also the Navy's Eastern Fleet's home base. On the Dolphin's Nose, a cliff rising 174 m from the sea, is a lighthouse whose beam can be seen 64 km out to sea.

Its twin town of **Waltair** to the north used to be thought of as a health resort with fine beaches, though increasing atmospheric pollution is a problem. **Ramakrishna Beach**, along the 8 km Lawson's Bay and below the 300 m Mount Kailasa, 6 km away, is best. Don't swim at the harbour end of the beach.

Ins and outs

→ *Phone code: 0891. Population: 969,600.*

AP Tourism ⓘ *Vuda Building, Siripuram, T0891-275 4716, 1000-1700, closed Sun and 2nd Sat of the month.* Also at the railway station.

Sights

Andhra University was founded in 1926 in the Uplands area of Waltair. The red stone buildings are built like a fortress and sit on a large campus. The country's major **Ship Building Yard** at Gandhigram makes all types of ocean-going vessels: passenger liners, cargo vessels as well as naval ships. The **zoo** to the northeast is large and attempts to avoid cages, keeping its animals in enclosures which are close to their natural habitat.

The **Venkateswara Temple** on the Venkateswa Konda was built in 1866 by the European Captain Blackmoor. The Muslims have a **mausoleum** of the saint Baba Ishaq Madina on the Darga Konda, while the highest Ross Hill has a **Roman Catholic Church**. A Buddhist relic was discovered at Dhanipura nearby.

Simhachalam, 16 km northwest, is noted for its 13th-century Varaha Narasimha Temple, set in the Kailasa Hills, which has some well-known hot springs.

Araku Valley

The Araku Valley, nestling amid the Anantagiri Hills 110 km inland from Vishakhapatnam, lies at the end of one of India's most scenic train rides. The four-hour journey through dense forests is liberally spiced with waterfalls, lush green paddy fields, views of distant blue hills and no less than 48 tunnels, the longest measuring 1.2 km. The valley itself is home to over 17 tribal groups, and in April plays host to the fascinating but strictly non-vegetarian **Itika Pongal**, a hunting festival. The **Tribal Museum** ⓘ *near AP Tourism's Mayuri Resort1, 000-1700, Rs 15*, has a small but worthwhile collection of artefacts and exhibits related to tribal life. If you return to Visakhapatnam by road you can stop off at the million-year-old **Borra Caves** and coffee plantations in Ananthagiri; **AP Tourism** runs this trip as a one- or two-day tour.

Northeastern Andhra Pradesh listings

For Sleeping and Eating price codes and other relevant information, see Essentials pages 38-42.

Sleeping

Visakhapatnam *p1141, map p1140*

Late night arrivals are quoted high prices by auto-rickshaws to go to the beach. Stay overnight at a simple hotel near the bus station (walk right from railway station) and move next morning.

AL Park, Beach Rd, T0891-275 4488, www.theparkhotels.com. 64 rooms, pricey suites, spa with gym, clean pool, well-kept gardens, slick management, best for direct beach access (beware of rocks when swimming), popular with German and Czech expats.

AL-A Gateway Hotel, Beach Rd (2 km from centre), T0891-662 3670, www.thegateway hotels.com. 93 narrow sea-facing rooms, restaurant (pricey but generous), best in town, access to an unremarkable public beach across road.

B-C Dolphin, Daba Gardens, T0891-256 7000, www.dolphinhotelsvizag.com. Family-run hotel with 147 rooms, popular restaurants, rooftop has good views, live band, health club, exchange and pool (but quite a distance from the beach). Excellent service. Highly recommended but reserve ahead.

D Punnami Beach Resort (AP Tourism), Bhimili Beach Rd, Rushikonda Beach (15 km north), T0891-278 8826. Great location, superb sea view, but poor maintenance. Ask for rooms in the new block.

D Supreme, Beach Rd near Coastal Battery, T0891-278 2472 www.hotelsupremevizag.com. 54 sea-view rooms (a/c and non a/c) with running hot and cold water, TV, multi-cuisine restaurant. Great location, courteous friendly staff. Good value for money.

D-E Palm Beach, Beach Rd (next to **Park hotel**), Waltair, T0891-255 4026, www.hotelpalm beachvizag.com. Pleasant, recently renovated hotel set in a shady palm grove. 55 rooms, 30 a/c, restaurant, beer garden, pool.

E Apsara, 12-1-17 Waltair Main Rd, T0891-276 4861. Central a/c, 130 rooms, restaurants, bar, exchange, very helpful and friendly staff.

E Daspalla, Surya Bagh, T0891-256 4825. 102 rooms, **C** suites, central a/c, 2 good restaurants (continental and *thalis*), exchange bar, set back from road, no late-night check-in.

E Simhagiri, Main Rd 500 m from railway station, T0891-250 5795, www.hotelsim hagiri.com. 35 clean, spacious rooms (a/c and non a/c), a budget traveller favourite.

F Meghalaya, Asilametta Junction (5-min walk from bus, short rickshaw ride from station), T0891-255 5141. Popular with Indian tourists, good value, dull vegetarian restaurant (non-veg available from room service), pleasant roof garden, friendly and helpful.
F Railway Retiring Rooms. Decent rooms (a/c and non a/c), men's dorm.

Araku Valley *p1142*
C-D Mayuri and Valley Resort (AP Tourism), next to Tribal Museum, T08936-249201. 115 rooms and suites, swimming pool, barbeque area, playground, bar, restaurant. Spacious and well maintained. Prior reservation mandatory.
E Krishnatara Comforts, Padmapuram junction, T08936-249330. Rooms are good value for money and have great view, friendly staff. Recommended.
E Rajadhani, Padmapuram junction, T08936-249745. Clean rooms, restaurant serves great Indian and Chinese food.

Eating

Visakhapatnam *p1141, map p1140*
Most eateries serve alcohol. Apart from hotels, there are restaurants on Station Rd.
Black Dog, Surya Bagh, near Jagdamba Theatre.
Blue Diamond, opposite RTC, Dabagardens.
Delight, 7-1-43 Kirlampudi, Beach Rd.
Winy's, roadside eatery on Beach Rd and **Spudds** (multi-cuisine restaurant) next to it serves good succulent *kababs*.

Festivals and events

Visakhapatnam *p1141, map p1140*
Dec Navy Mela and **Navy Day Parade**, along Beach Rd.

Activities and tours

Visakhapatnam *p1141, map p1140*

Swimming
Pools at **Park** and **Palm Beach** hotels are open to non-residents. **Waltair Club** has a pool.

Tour operators
Boat rides from Rushikonda, T(0)9848-235793, 0900-1700, run for 30 mins and go 2-3 km out to sea where there's a good chance of seeing dolphins. Rs 150 per person.
AP Tourism, RTC Complex, T0891-278 8820. Local sightseeing day trip, 0830-1700, Rs 300. Araku Valley rail/road tour, departs 0700: 1 day Rs 650, 2 days Rs 1500-2200 including accommodation.

Transport

Visakhapatnam *p1141, map p1140*
Air Airport is 16 km from city centre; taxi (Rs 350) or auto-rickshaw. **Indian Airlines**, T0891-279 6501; airport, T0891-257 2521. Flights to **Hyderabad**; **Bhubaneswar**, **Kolkata**, **Chennai**, **Mumbai**. **Jet Airways**, VIP Rd, T0891-276 2180, airport T0891-262 2795, to **Hyderabad**.
Bus Aseelmetta Junction Bus Station is well organized. APSRTC run services to main towns in the state. Enquiries, T0891-256 5038, reservations 0600-2000. **Araku Valley**, **Guntur** (0930, 1545, 2045), **Hyderabad** (638 km, 1630), **Kakinda**, **Puri** (0700), **Rajahmundry**, **Srikakulam**, **Vijayawada** (1945, 2015), **Vizianagram** (57 km, 0610-2130).
Ferry Operates 0800-1700 between the Harbour and **Yarada Hills**.
Rickshaw Auto-rickshaws are common. Minimum fare Rs 15; night fares exorbitant. Only cycle rickshaws in the centre.
Taxi At airport, train station or from hotels: 5 hrs/50 km, Rs 500; 10 hrs/100 km, Rs 1000.
Train Enquiries, T0891-256 9421. Reservations T0891-254 6234. 0900-1700. Advance Reservations, left of building (facing it). Computer bookings close 2100, Sun 1400. Counter system avoids crush at ticket window. City Railway Extension Counter at Turner's Chowltry for Reservations. Taxi from centre, Rs 50.

Chennai: *Howrah-Chennai Mail 12839*, 1355, 16 hrs. **Kolkata (H)**: *Coromandel Exp 12842*, 2210, 15 hrs; *Chennai Howrah Mail 12840*, 1320, 17¼ hrs; **Secunderabad**: *Godavari Exp 12727*, 1725, 13¾ hrs; *VSKP Garib Rath 12739*, 2030, 12 hrs; *East Coast Exp 18645*, 0410, 14 hrs; *Falaknuma Exp 12703*, Tue 2135, 12 hrs. **Tirupati**: *Tirumala Exp 17488*, 1350, 16 hrs. For **Araku Valley**, take *Kirandul Pass 58501*, 0650, 5 hrs. Sit on the right for the best views.

Directory

Visakhapatnam *p1141, map p1140*

Banks Several on Surya Bagh, with ATMs. **State Bank of India** is at Old Post Office. **Hospital** **King George**, Hospital Rd, Maharani Peta, T0891-256 4891. **Post** **Head Post Office**, Vellum Peta; also at Waltair Railway Station. **Useful contacts** **Foreigners' Regional Registration Office**, SP Police, T0891-256 2709.

Southern Andhra Pradesh and Tamil borders

Southern Andhra plays host to one of India's most astounding religious spectacles, the 10th-century Sri Venkatesvara Temple of Tirupati, to which devotees flock in their tens of thousands for a second's glimpse of the bejewelled deity of Lord Vishnu. *▸▸ See listings, pages 1149-1150.*

Tirupati and Tirumala → *For listings, see pages 1149-1150. Colour map 7, A5.*

The Tirumala Hills provide a picture-book setting for the Sri Venkatesvara Temple, possibly the most famous and most revered temple in all India. So important is the shrine that Bollywood royal Amitabh Bachchan made a special journey here to seek Lord Venkateshwara's blessings prior to his son Abhishek's wedding to Aishwarya Rai. Thankfully for the wedding snaps, but no doubt to the regret of the temple's accountants, Aishwarya didn't actually take part in the ritual for which Tirupati is renowned: a ceremonial head-shave, with the fallen locks being sold off to the wig-making trade (see box, page 1145). The main town of Tirupati lies at the bottom of the hill where there are several other temples, some pilgrimage centres in their own right. The seven hills are compared to the seven-headed Serpent God Adisesha who protects the sleeping Vishnu under his hood.

Tirupati

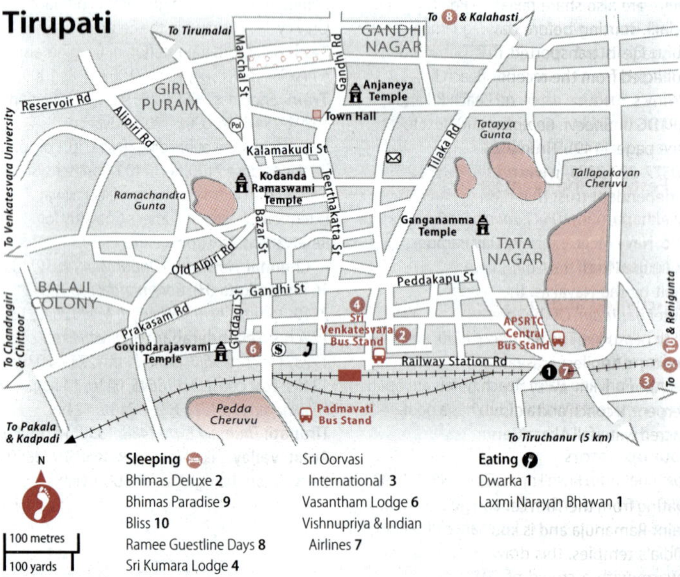

Sleeping
Bhimas Deluxe **2**
Bhimas Paradise **9**
Bliss **10**
Ramee Guestline Days **8**
Sri Kumara Lodge **4**
Sri Oorvasi International **3**
Vasantham Lodge **6**
Vishnupriya & Indian Airlines **7**

Eating
Dwarka **1**
Laxmi Narayan Bhawan **1**

Tirupati haircuts

Sri Venkatesvara Temple, architecturally unremarkable, is probably the wealthiest in India, and the *devasthanam* (or temple trust) now sponsors a huge range of activities, from the Sri Venkatesvara University in Tirupati to hospitals, orphanages and schools. Its wealth comes largely from its pilgrims, numbering on average over 10,000 a day. All pilgrims make gifts, and the *hundi* (offering) box in front of the shrine is stuffed full with notes, gold ornaments and other offerings.

Another important source of income is the hair-cutting service. Many pilgrims come to Tirupati to seek a special favour (eg to seek a suitable wife or husband, to have a child or to recover from illness) and it is regarded as auspicious to grow the hair long and then cut it as a sacrifice. You may see many pilgrims fully shaven at the temple when appearing before the deity. Lines of barbers await the arriving pilgrims. Free numbered ticket and a razor blade can be collected from the public bath hall, which pilgrims take to the barber with the same number to claim a free haircut. The hair is collected, washed and softened before being exported to the American and Japanese markets for wig making.

Ins and outs → *Phone code: 0877. Population: 245,500.*

Getting there Flights from Chennai and Hyderabad arrive at the airport 15 km from Tirupati. The railway station in the town centre has several fast trains from Chennai and other southern towns while the main (central) bus stand is 500 m east of it, with frequent express buses to Chennai, Bengaluru (Bangalore) and Hyderabad. Private buses arrive from an incredible array of destinations all across India. To save time and hassle on arrival, try to buy a through Link ticket to Tirumala. ▸▸ *See Transport, page 1150.*

Getting around Buses for Tirumala leave from stands near the station every half hour, but there are also share taxis available. Some choose to join pilgrims for a four- to five-hour walk uphill, starting before dawn to avoid the heat, though the path is shaded most of the way. Luggage is transported free from the toll gate at the start of the 15-km path and may be collected from the reception office at Tirumala.

Tourist information AP State tourist office ⓘ *Srinivasam Complex, T0877-2289129.* APTDC ⓘ *Sridevi Complex, Tilak Rd, T0877-225 5385* . **Karnataka Tourism** ⓘ *Hotel Mayura* (see page 1149). **Tirumala Tirupati Devasthanam (TTD)** ⓘ *TTD Administrative Building, KT Rd, T0877-223 3333, www.tirumala.org; also has counters at the airport and railway station*, is an independent trust that manages the Tirumala Venkateswara Temple.

Sights

In Tirupati itself the **Govindarajasvami Temple** (16th to 17th centuries), is the most widely visited. Built by the Nayakas, the successors to the Vijayanagar Empire, the temple has an impressive outer *gopuram*. Of the three *gopurams* the innermost is also the earliest, dating from the 14th to 15th centuries. The main sanctuaries are dedicated to Vishnu and Krishna. Another temple worth seeing is **Kapilesvarasvami**, in a beautiful setting with a sacred waterfall, **Kapila Theertham**.

About 1 km away are strange **rock formations** in a natural arch, resembling a hood of a serpent, a conch and a discus, thought to have been the source of the idol in the temple. There is a sacred waterfall **Akasa Ganga**, 3 km south of the temple. The **Papa Vinasanam Dam** is 5 km north.

Sri Venkatesvara Temple

Dating from the 10th century, this temple is believed to have been dedicated by the Vaishnava saint Ramanuja and is known as *Balaji* in the north and *Srinivasa Perumalai* in the south. Of all India's temples, this draws the largest number of pilgrims: even on a slow day the grounds swarm with a crowd of 10,000 people, while on festival days the number can be closer to

150,000. The town of Tirupati at the base of the hill was established in approximately AD 1131 under the orders of Ramanuja that the temple functionaries who served in the sacred shrines must live nearby. Although a road runs all the way up the hill to a bus stand at the top, most pilgrims choose to walk up the wooded slope through mango groves and sandalwood forest, chanting "*Om namo Venkatesaya*" or "*Govinda, Govinda*" as they walk. Order is maintained by providing 'Q sheds' under which pilgrims assemble.

Theoretically the inner shrines of the Tirumala temple are open only to Hindus. However, foreigners are usually welcome. They are sometimes invited to sign a form to show they sympathize with Hindu beliefs. According to the tourist information leaflet: "The only criterion for admission is faith in God and respect for the temple's conventions and rituals".

The atmosphere inside is unlike any other temple in India. Turnstiles control the never-ending flow of pilgrims into the main **temple complex**, which is through an intricately carved *gopuram* on the east wall. There are three enclosures. The first, where there are portrait sculptures of the Vijayanagar patrons, include Krishnadeva Raya and his queen and a gold-covered pillar. The outer colonnades are in the Vijayanagar style; the gateway leading to the inner enclosure may be of Chola origin. The second enclosure has more shrines, a sacred well, and the temple kitchen, where cooks prepare the holy *prasadam* (consecrated sweet) given to pilgrims after their *darshan*; the kitchen gets through an estimated 4.5 tons of ghee a day, supplied direct by pipeline from the dairy. The main temple and shrine is on the west side of the inner enclosure. The **sanctuary** (ninth to 10th centuries), known as *Ananda Nilayam*, has a domed *vimana* entirely covered with gold plate, and gold covered gates. Inside, dimly lit by oil lamps, stands the image for which people queue for hours to see: a 2-m-high statue of Vishnu (Sri Venkatesvara) carved of black stone, standing on a lotus and richly ornamented with gold and jewels. Two of his four arms carry a conch shell and a *chakra* or discus and he wears a diamond crown which is said to be the most precious single ornament in the world. The idol is flanked by *Sridevi* and *Bhudevi*, Vishnu's consorts.

There is a small **museum** ⓘ *0800-2000*, of temple art in the temple compound, with a collection of stone, metal and wooden images.

Every day is festival day with shops selling holy souvenirs remaining open 24 hours. The image of Sri Venkatesvara is widely seen across South India, in private homes, cars, taxis and in

Sri Venkatesvara Temple

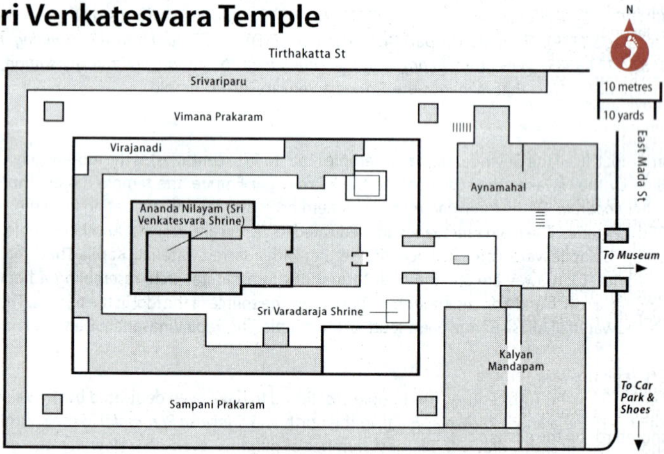

public places, and is instantly recognizable from his black face and covered eyes, shielded so that the deity's piercing gaze may not blind any who look directly at him. In the temple the deity's body is anointed with camphor, saffron and musk.

Visiting the temple ⓘ *The temple is at Tirumala, 22 km by road or a tough 4-hr climb on foot from central Tirupati.* No electronic items are allowed in the temple. There are two types of queue: for *darshan*, or viewing. Sarvadarsan is open to all, and it can take between two and five claustrophobic hours to reach the idol (Mondays and Tuesdays tend to be quieter). Those who pay for 'special' *darshan* (Rs 40 and up) enter by a separate entrance and join a shorter queue. The actual *darshan* (0600-1100) itself lasts a precious 1½ seconds, even though the 'day' at the temple may last 21 hours: from *Suprabhatham* (awakening of the deity) at 0330 to *Ekantha seva* at 2330.

The Sudarsanam token system has been introduced to minimize the waiting time for Sarvadarsanam, 'special' *darshan* and other paid *darshan/sevas*; pilgrims can enter the Vaikuntam Queue Complex at Tirumala at the time indicated on the tokens. The tokens are available free of cost at the First Choultry (opposite the Tirupati Railway Station), Second Choultry (behind the Railway Station), Alipiri Bus Stand, Vaikuntam Queue Complex, Pilgrim Amenities Centre (Near CRO) and near the Rambagicha Guest House in Tirumala. TTD has also started the E-Darshan, which makes it possible to book special *darshans* and accommodation at Tirumala in advance through www.ttdonline.com.

Around Tirupati

Chandragiri, 11 km southwest, became the capital of the Vijayanagaras in 1600, after their defeat at the battle of Talikota 35 years earlier. The **fort** ⓘ *1930-2015, Rs 30, children Rs 20,* was built on a 180-m-high rock. You can still see the well-preserved defences and some of the palaces and temples, including the Rani Mahal and Raja Mahal with a pretty lily pond and a small museum (closed Friday) containing Chola and Vijayanagar bronzes. A visit to the fort would be incomplete without witnessing the **sound and light show** organized everyday by the APTDC. The Palace of Sri Ranga Raya, built in 1639, witnessed the signing by Sri Ranga Raya of the original land grant entitling the East India Company to build Fort St George, the starting point of modern-day Chennai.

Srikalahasti (Kalahasti) ⓘ *state buses run the 36 km northeast from Tirupati*, is sited on the banks of the Svarnamukhi River at the foot of the Kailasa Hills, the southernmost limit of the Vellikonda Ranges. The town and temple, built in the 16th and 17th centuries, developed largely as a result of the patronage of the Vijayanagar kings and their successors, the Nayakas. The **Kalahastisvara Temple** dominates the town and, like the temple at Tirumala, is built in the Dravida style, set within high walls with a single entrance to the south, with a strong Nayaka influence typified by the columns carved into the shape of rearing animals. The temple is particularly revered for the white stone Siva *lingam* in the western shrine, believed to be worshipped by *sri* (spider), *kala* (king cobra) and *hasti* (elephant). The detached *gopuram* facing the river was built by the Vijayanagar emperor Krishnadeva Raya. The bathing ghats of the Swarnamukhi (golden) River and the temple attract a steady flow of pilgrims.

In addition to its function as a pilgrim centre, the town is known for its *kalamkaris*, colourful **hand-painted textiles** used as temple decoration. You can find pieces for sale in the BP Agraharam area, 1 km west of the temple, but they may come as a disappointment if you've seen the fine examples in Hyderabad's Salar Jung Museum (see page 1121).

South Andhra Coast

Pulicat Lake, on the coast 48 km east of Srikalahasti and 50 km north of Chennai, is the second largest saltwater lagoon in India and one of the most important wetlands for migratory shorebirds on the eastern seaboard of India. The northern area near the islands of Vendadu and Irukkam has large concentrations of greater flamingos. There are also many birds of prey. About

20 km north of Suluru is the **Neelapattu Lake**, which was given protected status in 1976 to conserve a large breeding colony of spotbilled pelicans.

Some 80 km north of Pulicat Lake, the town of **Nellore** derives its name from the sweet-smelling nelli rice, grown in abundance in the area. It is also reputed to produce the best shrimp on the east coast. **Mypadu Beach**, 20 km away, offers golden sands, surf and, outside the weekend rush, a slice of solitude. AP Tourism runs a guesthouse on the beach.

Horsley Hills

Popularly known as 'the Ooty of Andhra', this small hill station is located about 114 km west of Tirupati in the Nallamala Range. Nestling at an elevation of 1265 m, the resort is named after WD Horsley, the Collector of Cuddapah District, who chose the spot for his summer residence. It remains more popular with weekending public servants than anybody else, but the hills are thickly forested and home to a wide variety of wildlife, and can make a relaxing break from the roasting Andhra plains. **Madanapalle**, the nearest town 30 km to the south, is the birthplace of the famous 20th-century philosopher J Krishnamurti.

Lepakshi

This tiny village, close to the Karnataka border and 130 km from Bengaluru (Bangalore), houses a massive sculpture of Siva's bull *Nandi*, 5 m high and 8 m long, carved out of a single red granite boulder. Nearby, set on an outcrop of gneiss, is the remarkable **Virabhadra Temple**, built in 1538 under the Vijayanagar emperor Achutyadeva Raya. It has well- preserved sculptures, including a towering 6-m-high *nagalingam* and a life-size Virabhadra, decked with skulls and carrying weapons and apparently bent on revenge, while the roof of the shrine is decorated with what is claimed to be the largest mural in Asia.

Rural Development Trust FVF ⓘ *Bangalore Highway, T08554-31503, fvfatp@hd2.dot. net.in*, an NGO working in over 1500 villages, was started by a former Spanish Jesuit, Vincente Ferrer, more than 30 years ago. The project covers health, education, housing, etc. Visitors interested in seeing the work can be accommodated for up to four days.

Puttaparthi → *Colour map 7, A4.*

Puttaparthi, a remote village 150 km from Bengaluru, is now famous as the birthplace of **Bhagawan Sri Sathya Sai Baba**, a tremendously popular figure revered by millions as a reincarnation of the Maharashtrian saint Sai Baba of Shirdi. The current Sai Baba's predilection for spectacle (celebrations at his imposing **Prasanthi Nilayam** ashram typically involve stunt shows with massed ranks of motorcycle riders) have led some to dismiss him as a charlatan, and there have been allegations of sexual misconduct by a handful of former devotees. Nevertheless, the ashram provides free schooling and medical care to all comers, and fosters a peaceful atmosphere that attracts people from all around the world.

Southern Andhra and the Tamil borders listings

For Sleeping and Eating price codes and other relevant information, see Essentials pages 38-42.

Sleeping

Tirupati and Tirumala *p1144, map p1144*

The Temple Trust's *choultries* in Tirumala can accommodate about 20,000 pilgrims. They vary from luxury suites and well-furnished cottages to dorms and unfurnished rooms (some free). Contact **PRO**, T0877-226 4501. Accommodation can also be booked at www.ttdsevaonline.com. If you arrive without a reservation, go to the Central Reception Office in Tirumala, T0877-226 3883. The places listed below are in Tirupati.

C Bliss, Renigunta Rd, T0877-223 7773. 72 modern clean a/c rooms, restaurants.

C Ramee Guestline Days, 14-37 Karakambadi Rd, 3 km from town, T0877-228 0800. 140 rooms, central a/c, restaurants (including non-veg), bar, pool.

C-D Bhimas Deluxe, 34-38 Govindaraja Car St, T0877-222 5521, www.thirupathibhimas hotels.com. 60 rooms, 40 a/c, restaurant (Indian, a/c), exchange.

D-E Bhimas Paradise, 33-37 Renigunta Rd, T0877-222 5744, www.hotelbhimas.com. 90 rooms, some a/c, pool, garden, good restaurant.

D-E Sri Oorvasi International, Renigunta Rd, 1 km from railway station, T0877-222 0202. 78 rooms, some a/c, veg restaurant.

E Mayura, 209 TP Area, T0877-222 5925. 65 rooms, half a/c, veg restaurant, exchange. More expensive than others in this price category.

F Vishnupriya, T0877-225 8401. 134 rooms, some a/c, restaurants, exchange, **Air India** office.

G Sri Kumara Lodge, near railway station. Decent rooms.

G Vasantham Lodge, 141 G Car St, T0877-222 0460. Reasonable rooms with bath.

South Andhra Coast *p1147*

C DR Uthama, near Madras Bus Stand, Nellore, T0861-231 7777. Best hotel in town, with 51 rooms, swimming pool, health club.

E Murali Krishna, beside Leela Mahal, Nellore, T0861-230 9030. Well-reputed hotel with 22 spacious, clean rooms and a restaurant serving authentic Andhra fare.

F Beach Resort, Mypadu, T0861-234 1877. 6 rooms, right on the beach, restaurant.

Horsley Hills *p1148*

All accommodation here (except Forest Rest House which can be booked from Madanapalle, T08571-222436) is owned by **AP Tourism**.

C Haritha Resort, T08571-279324. Cottages and rooms (a/c and non a/c) on hill top, Governor's Bungalow recommended.

Puttaparthi *p1148*

Good **F-G** accommodation in rooms and dormitories at the ashram, T08555-287164, www.srisathyasai.org.in. No advance bookings.

Eating

Tirupati and Tirumala *p1144, map p1144*

Tirupathi-Tirumala Devasthanam Trust (TTD) provides free veg meals at its guesthouses. Outside hotels, veg restaurants include: **Laxmi Narayan Bhawan** (ƚƚ) and **Dwarka**, opposite APSRTC Bus Stand; **Indian Coffee House**, TTD Canteen and the APSRTC Bus Stand. **Konark**, Railway Station Rd; **New Triveni**, 139 TP Area; **Woodlands**, TP Area. **Tea Board Restaurant**, near the Indian Coffee House (all ƚ).

South Andhra Coast *p1147*

ƚƚ **Komala Vilas Hotel**, Trunk Rd, Nellore. Andhra lunch (prawn curry and *chepala pulusu* (murrel fish cooked in tamarind gravy), eaten with aromatic *nelli* rice. Highly recommended.

Festivals and events

Tirupati and Tirumala *p1144, map p1144*

May/Jun Govind Brahmotsavam.

Sep-Oct Brahmotsavam is the most important festival, especially grand every 3rd year when it is called **Navarathri Brahmotsavam**. On the 3rd day the Temple Car Festival **Rathotsavam** is particularly popular. **Rayalseema Food and Dance** follows later in the month.

Shopping

Tirupati and Tirumala *p1144, map p1144*

Copper and brass idols, produced at Perumallapalli village, 8 km away, and wooden toys are sold locally. Try **Poompuhar** on Gandhi Rd and **Lepakshi** in the TP Area.

Activities and tours

Tirupati and Tirumala *p1144, map p1144*

AP Tourism, Room 15, Srinivasa Choultry, T0877-2289219. Local sightseeing tour starts at the **APSRTC** Central Bus Stand, 0915-1730. Rs 300. Tirupati (not Venkatesvara), Kalahasti, Tiruchanur, Chandragiri and Srinivasamangapuram. From Chennai to Tirumala, Rs 300.

Transport

Tirupati and Tirumala *p1144, map p1144*

Air Transport to town by APSRTC coach to **Tirupati** (Rs 50) and **Tirumala** (Rs 80); taxis Rs 250. **Indian Airlines**, 20-5-746F, Thirumala Bypass Rd, Konagunta Jn, T0877-228 3992, airport T0877-227 5336. To **Chennai**: Tue, Thu, Sun and **Hyderabad**: Tue, Thu, Sat. **Jet Airways**, T0877-2256916, Renigunta airport T0877-2271471, to **Hyderabad**.

Bus Local service between Tirupati and Tirumala every 3 mins, 0330-2200.

In Tirupati: **Sri Venkatesvara Bus Stand**, opposite railway station for passengers with through tickets to Tirumala; Enquiries: 3rd Choultry, T0877-222 5203. **Padmavati Bus Stand** in TP Area, T0877-220203; queues for buses but buying a return ticket from Tirupati (past the railway footbridge) saves queuing.

In Tirumala: **Kesavanagar Bus Stand**, 500 m southeast of temple; walk past canteen and shop. Depart from **Rose Garden Bus Stand**, east of the temple.

Long distance to **Chennai**, 4 hrs, **Kanchipuram**, 3 hrs, **Vellore**, 2½ hrs. Enquiries, T0877-228 9900. 24-hr left luggage.

Taxi Tourist taxis through **AP Tourism** from the bus stand and railway station to **Tirumala**, Rs 800 return, for 5½ hrs. Share taxi between Tirupati and Tirumala, about Rs 75 per person. **Balaji Travels**, 149 TP Area, T0877-2224894.

Train Trains are often delayed. Phone the station, T0877-227 5227, in advance if catching a night train as it could be delayed until next morning. **Chennai** (**C**): *Intercity Exp 16204*, 0620, 3¼ hrs; *Saptagiri Exp 16058*, 1720, 3¼ hrs. **Mumbai** (**CST**): bus to Renigunta (10 km) for *Chennai-Mumbai Exp 11042*, 1445, 24 hrs; or direct: *Cape Mumbai Exp 16382*, 0345, 25 hrs. **Guntakal**: *Rayalaseema Exp 17430 (AC/II)*, 1600, 6½ hrs. **Hyderabad**: *Narayanadri Exp 12733*, 1825, 13¾ hrs (for Secunderabad).

South Andhra Coast *p1147*

Train Tirupati–Hyderabad trains stop at Nellore.

Horsley Hills *p1148*

Bus A direct bus leaves the **Central Bus Station** in Tirupati at 1300. Easier to go via **Madanapalle**, from where buses for the hills leave every 2 hrs till 1700.

Directory

Tirupati and Tirumala *p1144, map p1144*

Banks Most are on Gandhi St. **State Bank of India**, opposite APSRTC. **Useful contacts** **Foreigners' Regional Registration Office**: 499 Reddy Colony, T0877-222 0503

Maharashtra

Contents

Footprint features

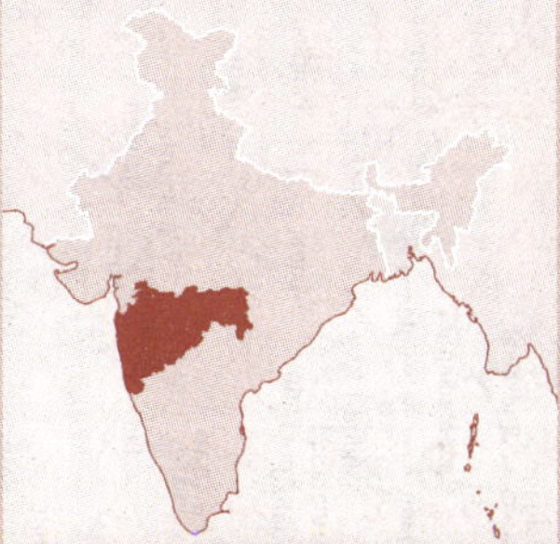

At a glance

Getting around Ride the suburban railway network in Mumbai, the narrow gauge up to Matheran and the Konkan railway out of state. In Mumbai cabs and motor rickshaws are plentiful.

Time required Allow 48 hrs for Mumbai, 2 days for Ajanta and Ellora.

Weather Hot all year, with a heavy monsoon.

When not to go Jun and Jul when rainfall is torrential.

★ **Don't miss ...**

1 **Mumbai**, page 1157.
2 **Deogiri fortifications** in the late afternoon, page 1192.
3 **Kailasanatha Temple at Ellora**, page 1194.
4 **The murals at Ajanta Caves**, page 1197.
5 **A meditation course at Osho Commune**, page 1210.
6 **Raigad in the evening**, page 1214.

There are some beautiful and fascinating sites in Maharashtra. The earliest of the world-famous frescoes and carvings at Ajanta and Ellora caves date from the second century BC. Wonderful ruined forts built by the Marathas and the Portuguese are scattered along the 500 km of coastline while others are perched precariously on the hilltops of the Western Ghats. From these fastnesses, the 17th-century Marathas, masters in the art of guerrilla warfare, carved out a territory that stretched the width of India. Today Maharashtra boasts not only India's most vibrant city, Mumbai, and a diverse and rapidly growing industrial economy, but also a rich agricultural hinterland.

Small beaches offer an escape from the busy city while train buffs can enjoy a ride up the scenic narrow-gauge railway to Matheran in the hills. The thriving 'modern' city of Pune, across the Ghats, attracts the visitors to the lavish Osho Commune, which has drawn large numbers of Westerners in search of an alternative spiritual answer.

Background → *Population: 96.8 million. Area: 308,000 sq km.*

The land

Geography Hills and plateaux give Maharashtra a distinctive topography. In the west the state is guarded by the Sahyadri Range of the Western Ghats, which rise as an abrupt and almost impenetrable wall reaching over 1400 m in places, while the Satpura Range to the north forms a natural border with Madhya Pradesh. The volcanic lavas of the Deccan Trap, which poured out over 65 million years ago as the Indian peninsula broke away from the African coast, gave the plateau that stretches away towards the east both its name and its very distinctive black soils. East of Nagpur the lava gives way to gently rolling granite hills 250-350 m above sea level, an extraordinary landscape of huge open spaces and sweeping views. A number of important rivers rise in the Western Ghats. Most follow the trend of the Godavari and the Krishna, rising within 100 km of the Arabian Sea and then flowing east- wards across the Deccan plateau to the Bay of Bengal. The annual rains also send a number of streams and rivers westward across the undulating Konkan coastal lowlands, which reach their widest near Mumbai, tapering off to a narrow belt towards the border of Goa.

Climate Most of Maharashtra is hot during the daytime throughout the year, the coast being very humid as well. Daily maximum temperatures are between 28°C in January and 33°C in May, although night-time temperatures fall considerably from November to March. Only the hill stations of the Western Ghats experience much cooler weather, a particular relief in April and May. The southwest monsoon normally breaks on the coast in the second week of June and finishes in September, bringing most of the region's rain in often prolonged and violent storms. The Ghats give rise to a strong rain-shadow effect, which makes the coastal Konkan strip much wetter than the interior upland.

History

The name Maharashtra was first used in a seventh century AD inscription, but its origins are unclear. One view is that it is derived from the word *rath* (chariot) whose drivers formed an army (*maharathis*). They are thought to have migrated south and settled in the upland area where they mingled with aboriginal tribes.

The dry western margins of the plateau have sites from the earliest **prehistoric** settlements in India, and Nevasa and Chirki in the Godavari Valley, have palaeolithic remains. The relatively open lands in the lee of the Ghats were one of the major routes from North to South India but lacked the resources to become the centre of a major political power. In the early period from the eighth to the 14th century there were a number of Hindu kingdoms, followed by the first Muslim dynasty in 1307. The Muslim use of Persian as a court language left its mark on the development of the Marathi language.

The Marathas divided the country into *Swarajya* (homeland – a concept that re-emerged as one of the watchwords of the Independence struggle in the 20th century), and *Mughlai* (territory controlled by foreigners), and set about reclaiming the latter by means of a series of daring raids. The *nonpareil* hero of this process was Maharashtra's late 17th-century leader **Shivaji**, whose name still generates a passion enjoyed by very few figures in Indian history. The state's modern political life resonates with the myths of his military abilities, political cunning and Hindu revivalism. Matching the political skills of a Machiavelli to the military ambitions of a Napoleon, within four years of his coronation Shivaji had begun to retake the forts ceded under the treaty with the Mughal Emperor Aurangzeb. By the time of his death from dysentery in 1680 he had re-established a powerful base around Pune and an expanding Maratha Empire.

On Aurangzeb's death in 1707, Shivaji's former kingdom became a confederacy under the charge of a hereditary minister called the Peshwa and four main Maratha chiefs – Holkar, Scindia, Gaekwad and Bhonsla. By 1750 their power reached across India to Orissa, which they occupied, and Bengal, which they attacked. Maratha power was only decisively curbed when they were defeated at Panipat by the Afghan Ahmad Shah Abdali. On the death of the young Peshwa, Madhao Rao I, in 1772, the five Maratha powers became increasingly independent of one another. Weakened and divided, they were unable to resist the advance of British power.

Culture

Ethnically, Maharashtra contains a variety of **peoples**. The Bhil, Warli, Gond, Korku and Gowari tribal groups living in the Satpura and Sahyadri ranges in the north are Australoid aboriginals. The Kunbi Marathas found all over the state are believed to be the descendants of immigrants from the north at the beginning of the Christian era. Parsis first arrived in the region in the eighth century from Persia. Just over 80% of the population is Hindu, with Islam and Buddhism the most numerous minority religions. The Buddhists are recent converts from among formerly outcaste Hindus.

Marathi is the main regional **language** (spoken by 90% of the population), and has undergone a very political revival recently. Both Hindi and English are widely understood, especially in the major cities. Konkani on the west coast and Gondi in the north are important regional languages. Gujarati and its variants are also widely spoken.

The main regional **dishes** reflect Maharashtra's transition position between the wheat-growing regions of the north and the rice-growing coastal lands, while millets are grown in the interior. Lightly spiced vegetables and sweet and sour dishes are popular, with a distinctive emphasis on dried and salted fish such as Bombay duck cooked with lentils. There are also recipes that use sprouted lentils. Konkan cuisine has more in common with the coastal food of Goa and Kerala, revolving around fish and vegetable curries flavoured with coconut. If you're adventurous, try *sol kadhi* – a purple tangy and salty drink made with the sour fruit of the kokum plant mixed in coconut milk and flavoured with spices. Mumbai has the heaviest concentration of Parsis in the country, so try their cuisine here: *dhansak*, a special lentil curry with lamb or chicken cooked with five varieties of spice, or *patrani machli*, fish (often pomfret) stuffed with coconut chutney and coriander, steamed in banana leaves.

Festivals

The majority of Hindu festivals are observed in the state. The highly colourful **Ranga Panchami** and **Holi**, marking the beginning of spring, are very popular. **Janmashtami** (July/August) celebrates the birth of Lord Krishna. Men and boys in local teams form human pyramids to break pots of curds that have been hung from high places. The winners usually take home a 'matka' of money as well. On **Ganesh Chaturthi** in Mumbai (August/September) massive figures of the ever-popular elephant god Ganesh (the god of overcoming obstacles and the city's guardian diety) are towed through the streets and immersed in the sea; Pune has special celebrations that last 10 loud days. **Dussehra** (October), the last day of the nationally celebrated **Navratri** festival, is significant because it was the day on which the Marathas usually began their military campaigns. The Muslim festival of **Mohurram**, which commemorates the martyrs of Islam, is often observed by Hindus as well.

Modern Maharashtra

The old British administrative region of the Bombay Presidency had never coincided with the area in which Marathi was the dominant language, and the present state did not take shape until 1960, when Gujarati areas in the north and Kannada-speaking areas in the south were allocated to Gujarat and Karnataka respectively.

Maharashtra's legislature has two houses; the Vidhan Parishad (legislative council) and Vidhan Sabha (legislative assembly). Except for an annual meeting at Nagpur, the old Maratha capital, these meet in Mumbai. The state is represented by 48 members in the Lok Sabha (Lower House) and 19 members in the Rajya Sabha (Upper House) of the national parliament in New Delhi. The Hindu-Maratha chauvinist party, the Shiv Sena, under the leadership of the former satirical cartoonist Bal Thackeray, has been a force in Maharashtra's politics for over 30 years. Its imprint is evident in several events, from the mass renaming of Mumbai's streets after Marathi heroes (and significant party donors) to the communalist riots against Muslims following the demolition of the Babri Mosque in Ayodhya in 1992 (see page 140) and, more recently, attacks against hand-holding couples, shops selling Valentine's Day cards, and other supposed threats to Hindu purity. His estranged nephew Raj Thackeray heads the Maharashtra Navnirman Sena (Renaissance Army) an increasingly jingoistic regional party that was responsible for widespread violence against immigrant workers in 2007.

Following the terrorist attacks on Mumbai in November 2008 that targeted elite destinations such as the Taj and Oberoi hotels along with the busiest local railway station, Chief Minister Vilasrao Deshmukh was forced to resign and the state's Minister for Industry Ashok Chavan took his place. In the 2009 Lok Sabha elections the Congress and its allies won a surprise victory, gaining 25 of the 48 seats. The right-wing Hindu parties, the BJP and the Shiv Sena, won 20, leaving the field wide open for the Assembly elections to be held in October 2009.

Maharashtra has been described as India's industrial and commercial backbone. The nerve centre of India's stock market, the headquarters of a large number of Indian and multinational companies' operations in India and a major manufacturing state in its own right, Maharashtra has not only India's largest city, Mumbai, but a large number of rapidly industrializing smaller cities. These have been encouraged to develop through government policies aimed at stimulating decentralized industrial growth. With only 10% of India's population Maharashtra accounts for nearly 25% of India's total industrial output, with textiles, petrochemicals, pharmaceuticals, electronics and a wide range of other products. However, agriculture remains important, cash crops like sugar cane accounting for 30% of the country's total sugar production. Alongside sugar, rice, sorghum, millets and gram are all important, while horticultural crops and fruit like banana, oranges, grapes and the almost-legendary Alphonso mango have rapidly grown in importance.

Mumbai (Bombay)

➔ *Colour map 5, B3. Phone code: 022.*

Maximum City, the City of Dreams, India's economic capital and melting pot. You can throw epithets and superlatives at Mumbai until the cows come home, but it refuses to be understood on a merely intellectual level. Like London and New York, it's a restless human tapestry of cultures, religions, races, ways of surviving and thriving, and one that evokes palpable emotion; whether you love it or hate it, you can't stay unaffected.

From the cluster of fishing villages first linked together by the British East India Company in 1668, Mumbai has swelled to sprawl across seven islands, which now groan under the needs of 19 million stomachs, souls and egos. Its problems – creaking infrastructure, endemic corruption coupled with bureaucratic incompetence, and an ever-expanding population of whom more than two thirds live in slums – are only matched by the enormous drive that makes it the centre of business, fashion and film-making in modern India, and both a magnet and icon for the country's dreams, and nightmares.

The taxi ride from the airport shows you both sides of the city: slum dwellers selling balloons under billboards of fair-skinned models dripping in gold and reclining on the roof of a Mercedes; the septic stench as you cross Mahim Creek, where bikers park on the soaring bridge to shoot the breeze amid fumes that could drop an elephant; the feeling of diesel permeating your bloodstream and the manically reverberating mantra of Horn OK Please *as you ooze through traffic past Worli's glitzy shopping malls and the fairytale island mosque of Haji Ali. And finally the magic moment as you swing out on to Chowpatty Beach and the city throws off her cloak of chaos to reveal a neon-painted skyscape that makes you feel like you've arrived at the centre of all things.*

Gothic clocktowers and glass skyscrapers, mill chimneys and minarets, vibrant temples and tarpaulin-roofed shacks mingle below the smog. Stitching them together are streets aswarm with panel-beaten double-decker buses, yellow and black taxis, long wooden carts stacked with hessian-stitched parcels being towed by teams of grimacing Bihari migrant workers, and white-hatted dabbawalas weaving their way through the chaos carrying stacks of metal tins – the guardians of a hundred thousand office lunches.

Hundreds of fresh migrants arrive in the city daily, and whether they come by plane, sweeping in over the crescent bays and the smog-wrapped slums bound for South Mumbai, where real estate is more expensive than Manhattan, or by packed train carriage through the endless sprawl of apartment blocks to eke out a space among the poorest of the poor in Dharavi, Mumbai, somehow, finds a way to absorb them all. ▸▸ *For listings, see page 1168-1180.*

Ins and outs

Getting there **Chhatrapati Shivaji International Airport** is 30 km from Nariman Point, the business heart of the city. The domestic terminals at Santa Cruz are 5 km closer. Pre-paid taxis to the city centre are good value and take 40-90 minutes; buses are cheaper but significantly slower. If you arrive at night without a hotel booking it is best to stay at one of the hotels near the airports. Long-distance trains arrive and depart from several distinct stations in the centre and suburbs: **Chhatrapati Shivaji Terminus (CST)**, close to the hotels of Colaba, and **Mumbai Central**, a few kilometres north, are the most convenient, while **Dadar, Bandra** and **Lokmanya Tilak** all involve a lengthy trip into town by taxi or local train (the latter only feasible outside rush hour). State-run MSRTC buses terminate at **Mumbai Central Bus Stand**, opposite the railway station. Private interstate buses might drop you on the road outside, but those from Pune and other parts of Maharashtra tend to stop out in the suburbs, at Dadar, Bandra, Andheri or Borivali ▸▸ *See Transport, page 1177.*

Getting around The sights are spread out and you need transport. Taxis are metered and good value. Ask for the rate card for conversions. There are frequent buses on major routes, and the two suburban railway lines are useful out of peak hours, but get horrendously crowded. Auto-rickshaws are only allowed in the suburbs north of Mahim Creek.

Tourist information **Government of India** ⓘ *123 M Karve Rd, opposite Churchgate, T022-2207 4333, Mon-Sat 0830-1730 (closed 2nd Sat of month from 1230); counters open 24 hrs at both airports; Taj Mahal Hotel, Mon-Sat 0830-1530 (closed 2nd Sat from 1230)*. Helpful staff who can also issue liquor permits (essential for Gujarat). **Maharashtra Tourist Development Corporation (MTDC)** ⓘ *CDO Hutments, Madam Cama Rd, T022-2204 4040, www.maharashtratourism.gov.in; Koh-i-Noor Rd, near Pritam Hotel, Dadar T022-2414 3200; CST Railway Station, T022-2262 2859*. Information and booking counters at international and domestic terminals and online.

Background

Hinduism made its mark on Mumbai long before the Portuguese and British transformed it into one of India's great cities. The caves on the island of Elephanta were excavated under the Kalachuris (AD 500-600). Yet, only 350 years ago, the area occupied by this great metropolis comprised seven islands inhabited by Koli fishermen. The British acquired these marshy and malarial islands as part of the marriage dowry paid by the Portuguese when Catherine of Braganza married Charles II in 1661. Four years later, they took possession of the remaining islands and neighbouring mainland area and in 1668 the East India Company leased the whole area from the crown for £10 a year, which was paid for nearly 50 years. The East India Company shifted its headquarters to Mumbai in 1672.

Isolated by the sharp face of the Western Ghats and the constantly hostile Marathas, Mumbai's early fortunes rested on the shipbuilding yards established by progressive Parsis. It thrived entirely on overseas trade and, in the cosmopolitan city this created, Parsis, Sephardic Jews and the British shared common interests and responded to the same incentives.

After a devastating fire on 17 February 1803, a new town with wider streets was built. Then, with the abolition of the Company's trade monopoly, the doors to rapid expansion were flung open and Mumbai flourished. Trade with England boomed, and under the governorship of Sir Bartle Frere (1862-1869) the city acquired a number of extravagant Indo-Gothic landmarks, most notably the station formerly known as the Victoria Terminus. The opening of the Suez Canal in 1870 gave Mumbai greater proximity to European markets and a decisive advantage over its eastern rival Kolkata. It has since become the headquarters for many national and international companies, and was a natural choice as home to India's stock exchange (BSE). With the sponsorship of the Tata family, Mumbai has also become the primary home of India's nuclear research programme, with its first plutonium extraction plant at Trombay in 1961 and the establishment of the Tata Institute for Fundamental Research, the most prestigious science research institute in the country.

Mumbai is still growing fast, and heavy demand for building space means property value is some of the highest on earth. As in Manhattan, buildings are going upward: residential skyscrapers have mushroomed in the upscale enclaves around Malabar Hill. Meanwhile, the old mill complexes of Lower Parel have been rapidly revived as shopping and luxury apartment complexes. An even more ambitious attempt to ease pressure on the isthmus is the newly minted city of Navi Mumbai, 90 minutes east of the city, which has malls, apartments and industrial parks, but little of the glamour that makes Mumbai such a magnet.

The latest project is the controversial redevelopment of Dharavi, a huge chunk of prime real estate that's currently occupied by Asia's biggest slum – home to one third of Mumbai's population, in desperately squalid makeshift hovels originally designed to house migrant mill workers. In addition, an uncounted number live precariously in unauthorized, hastily rigged and frequently demolished corrugated iron or bamboo-and-tarpaulin shacks beside railways and roads, while yet more sleep in doorways and on sheets across the pavement.

In recent decades, the pressure of supporting so many people has begun to tell on Mumbai. Communal riots between Hindus and Muslims have flared up several times since the destruction by militant Hindus of the Babri Masjid in 1992, and the disastrous 2005 monsoon, which dumped almost a metre of rainfall on the city overnight and left trains stranded with

1 Central Mumbai

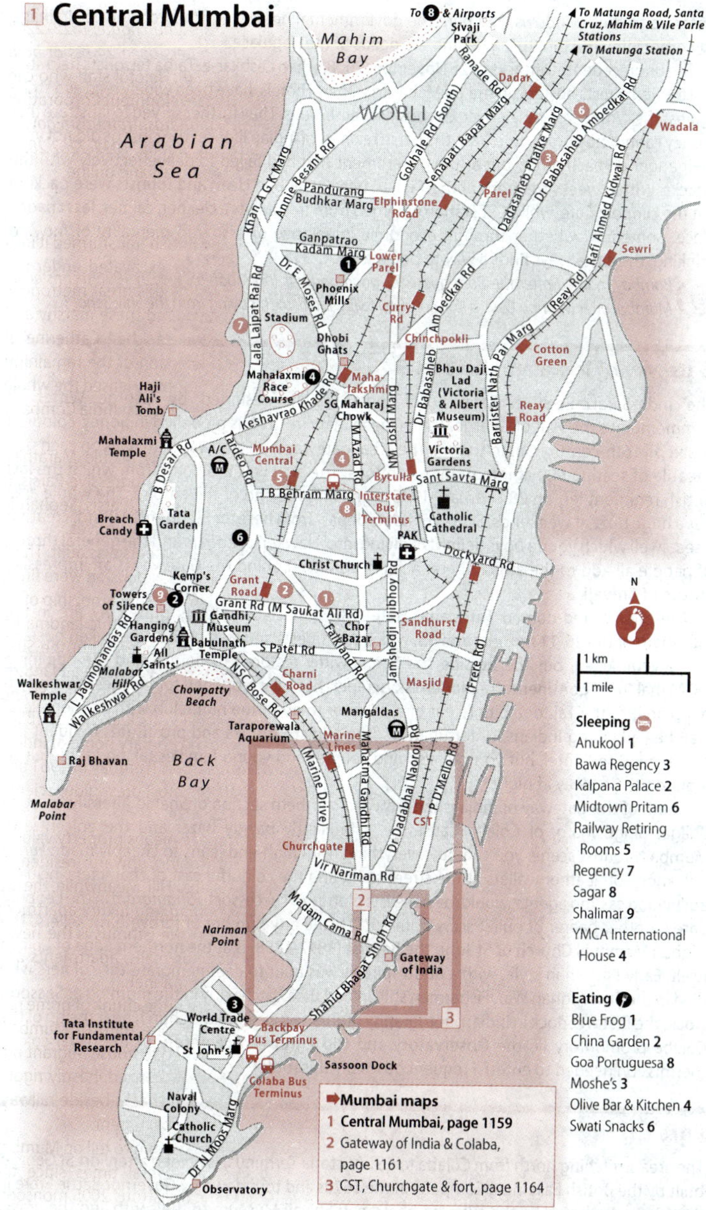

Sleeping
- Anukool 1
- Bawa Regency 3
- Kalpana Palace 2
- Midtown Pritam 6
- Railway Retiring Rooms 5
- Regency 7
- Sagar 8
- Shalimar 9
- YMCA International House 4

Eating
- Blue Frog 1
- China Garden 2
- Goa Portuguesa 8
- Moshe's 3
- Olive Bar & Kitchen 4
- Swati Snacks 6

Mumbai maps
1 Central Mumbai, page 1159
2 Gateway of India & Colaba, page 1161
3 CST, Churchgate & fort, page 1164

water up to their windows, laid bare the governmental neglect which had allowed drainage and other infrastructure to lag behind the needs of the populace.

The unprecedented attacks of 26 November 2008, when Lashkar-e-Taiba terrorists held staff and foreign guests hostage in the Taj Mahal and Oberoi hotels, have been widely read as a strike against the symbols of India's overseas business ambitions. They further served to illustrate that money cannot buy protection from the harsh realities of Indian life. Yet the citizens did not vent their anger on each other, but at the government that had failed to deal effectively with the attacks. Within weeks the front of the Taj had been scrubbed clean and tourists were packing out the Leopold Café, while CST station emerged from the bullets a cleaner, calmer, less chaotic place. Somehow, whether through economic imperative or a shared mentality of forward thinking, the city always finds a way to bounce back.

Bombay, named after the Portuguese for good harbour (bom bahia), was in 1996 rechristened Mumbai after Mumba Devi, a Koli goddess, following fierce lobbying from the Shiv Sena.

Gateway of India and Colaba

The Indo-Saracenic-style Gateway of India (1927), designed by George Wittet to commemorate the visit of George V and Queen Mary in 1911, is modelled in honey-coloured basalt on 16th-century Gujarati work. The great gateway is an archway with halls on each side capable of seating 600 at important receptions. The arch was the point from which the last British regiment left on 28 February 1948, signalling the end of the empire. The whole area has a huge buzz at weekends. Scores of boats depart from here for **Elephanta Island,** creating a sea-swell which young boys delight in diving into. Hawkers, beggars and the general throng of people all add to the atmosphere. A short distance behind the Gateway is an impressive **statue of Shivaji**.

The original red-domed **Taj Mahal Hotel** was almost completely gutted by fire in the aftermath of the 26/11 terrorist attacks, which saw guests and staff of the hotel taken hostage and several killed, but the outside has been swiftly restored to normal and the adjoining **Taj Mahal Inter-Continental**, a modern skyscraper, has fully reopened for business. It is worth popping into the Taj for a bite to eat or a drink, or to go to the nightclub with its clientele of well-heeled young Indians. Unfortunately, drug addicts, drunks and prostitutes frequent the area behind the hotel, but you can also find couples and young families taking in the sea air around the Gateway at night.

South of the Gateway of India is the crowded southern section of Shahid (literally 'martyr') Bhagat Singh Marg, or Colaba Causeway, a brilliantly bawdy bazar and the epicentre of Mumbai's tourist scene; you can buy everything from high-end jeans to cheaply made *kurtas* and knock-off leather wallets at the street stalls, and the colourful cast of characters includes Bollywood casting agents, would-be novelists plotting a successor to *Shantaram* in the **Leopold Café** (another bearer of bullet scars from 26/11), and any number of furtive hash sellers. The Afghan Memorial **Church of St John the Baptist** (1847-1858) is at the northern edge of Colaba itself. Early English in style, with a 58-m spire, it was built to commemorate the soldiers who died in the First Afghan War. Fishermen still unload their catch early in the morning at **Sassoon Dock**, the first wet dock in India; photography prohibited. Beyond the church near the tip of the Colaba promontory lie the **Observatory** and **Old European cemetery** in the naval colony (permission needed to enter). Frequent buses ply this route.

Fort

The area stretching north from Colaba to CST (Victoria Terminus) is named after Fort St George, built by the British East India Company in the 1670s and torn down by Governor Bartle Frere in the 1860s. Anchored by the superb Chhatrapati Shivaji Museum to the south and the grassy parkland of Oval Maidan to the west, this area blossomed after 1862, when Sir Bartle Frere became governor (1862-1867). Under his enthusiastic guidance Mumbai became a great civic centre and an extravaganza of Victorian Gothic architecture, modified by Indo-Saracenic influences. This area is worth exploring at night, when many of the old buildings are floodlit.

2 Gateway of India & Colaba

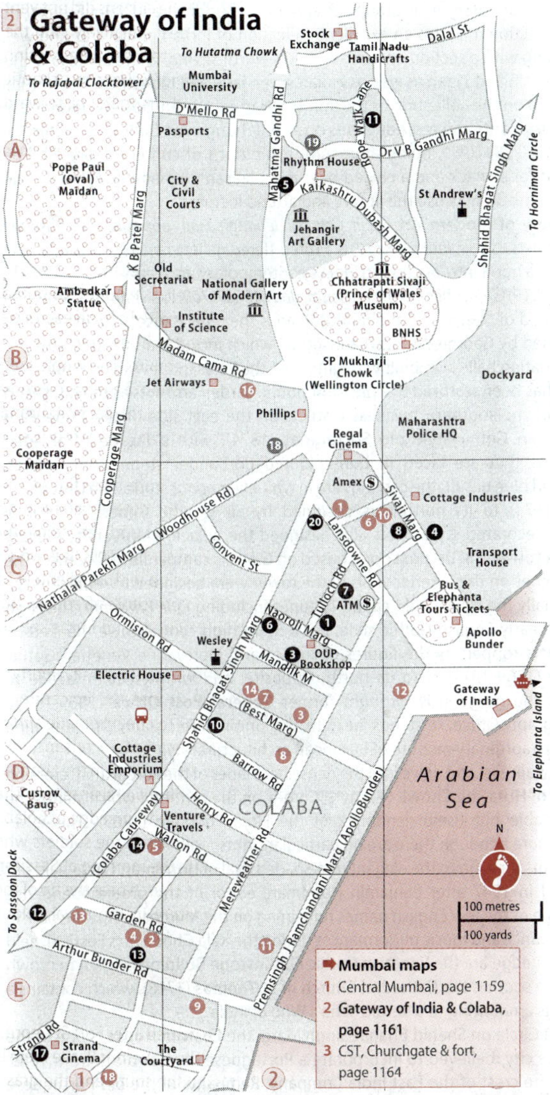

Mumbai maps
1 Central Mumbai, page 1159
2 Gateway of India & Colaba, page 1161
3 CST, Churchgate & fort, page 1164

Sleeping
Apollo **1** *C2*
Ascot **13** *E1*
Cowie's **5** *D1*
Diplomat **3** *D2*
Fariyas **18** *E1*
Garden **2** *E1*
Godwin **4** *E1*
Gordon House, All Star Fry & Polly Esther **6** *C2*
India Guest House & Sea Shore **9** *E2*
Moti **14** *D2*
Regent **7** *D2*
Salvation Army **8** *D2*
Suba Palace **10** *C3*
Strand **11** *E2*
Taj Mahal & Souk **12** *D3*
YWCA International Centre **16** *B2*

Eating
Bade Miyan **7** *C2*
Bagdadi **1** *C2*
Café Basilico **13** *E1*
Café Churchill **14** *D1*
Food-Inn **6** *C2*
Indigo **3** *C2*
Indigo Deli **8** *C3*
Kamat Samarambh **10** *D2*
Khyber **5** *A2*
Le Pain Quotidien **4** *C3*
Leopold's **6** *C2*
Ling's Pavilion **7** *C2*
Mondegar **20** *C2*
Shubh Sagar **17** *E1*
Theobroma **12** *E1*
Trishna **11** *A2*

Bars & clubs
Red Light **19**
Woodside Inn **18**

Chhatrapati Shivaji (Prince of Wales) Museum ⓘ *Oct-Feb Tue-Sun 1015-1800, last tickets 1645; foreigners Rs 300 (includes audio guide), Indians Rs 15, camera Rs 15 (no flash or tripods), students Rs 10, children Rs 5, avoid Tue as it is busy with school visits*, is housed in an impressive building designed by George Wittet to commemorate the visit of the Prince of Wales to India in 1905. The dome of glazed tiles has a very Persian and Central Asian flavour. The archaeological section has three main groups: Brahminical; Buddhist and Jain; Prehistoric and Foreign. The art section includes an excellent collection of Indian miniatures and well displayed *tankhas* along with a section on armour that is worth seeing. There are also works by Gainsborough, Poussin and Titian as well as Indian silver, jade and tapestries. The Natural History section is based on the collection of the Bombay Natural History Society, founded in 1833. Good guidebooks, cards and reproductions on sale. **Jehangir Art Gallery** ⓘ *within the museum complex, T022-2284 3989*, holds short-term exhibitions of contemporary art. The Samovar café is good for a snack and a chilled beer in a pleasant, if cramped, garden-side setting. Temporary members may use the library and attend lectures.

The **National Gallery of Modern Art** ⓘ *Sir Cowasji Jehangir Hall, opposite the museum, T022-2285 2457, foreigners Rs 150, Indians Rs 10*, is a three-tiered gallery converted from an old public hall which gives a good introduction to India's contemporary art scene.

St Andrew's Kirk (1819) ⓘ *just behind the museum, daily 1000-1700*, is a simple neoclassical church. At the south end of Mahatma Gandhi (MG) Road is the renaissance-style **Institute of Science** (1911) designed by George Wittet. The Institute, which includes a scientific library, a public hall and examination halls, was built with gifts from the Parsi and Jewish communities.

The **Oval Maidan** has been restored to a pleasant public garden and acts as the lungs and public cricket pitch of the southern business district. On the east side of the **Pope Paul Maidan** is the Venetian Gothic-style **old Secretariat** (1874), with a façade of arcaded verandas and porticos that are faced in buff-coloured porbander stone from Gujarat. Decorated with red and blue basalt, the carvings are in white *hemnagar* stone. The **University Convocation Hall** (1874) to its north was designed by Sir George Gilbert Scott in a 15th-century French decorated style. Scott also designed the adjacent **University Library** and the **Rajabai clock tower** (1870s) next door, based on Giotto's campanile in Florence. The sculpted figures in niches on the exterior walls of the tower were designed to represent the castes of India. Originally the clock could chime 12 tunes including *Rule Britannia*. The **High Court** (1871-1879), in early English Gothic style, has a 57-m-high central tower flanked by lower octagonal towers topped by the figures of Justice and Mercy. The Venetian Gothic **Public Works Office** (1869-1872) is to its north. Opposite, and with its main façade to Vir Nariman Road, is the gorgeously wrought former **General Post Office** (1869-1872). Now called the Telegraph Office, it stands next to the original Telegraph Office adding romanesque to the extraordinary mixture of European architectural styles.

From here you can walk east and delve into the dense back lanes of the Fort district, crossing the five-way junction of **Hutatma Chowk** ('Martyrs' Corner', in the centre of which stands the architecturally forgettable but useful landmark of the Flora Fountain (1869). This is an interesting area to explore although there are no particular sights

Vir Nariman Road cuts through to the elegant tree-shaded oval of **Horniman Circle** , laid out in 1860 and renamed in 1947 after Benjamin Horniman, editor of the pro-independence *Bombay Chronicle* – one of the few English names remaining on the Mumbai map. The park in the middle is used for dance and music performances during the **Kala Ghoda Arts Festival**, held in January. On the west edge are the Venetian Gothic **Elphinstone Buildings** (1870) in brown sandstone, while to the south is the **Cathedral Church of St Thomas** (1718), which contains a number of monuments amounting to a heroic 'Who's Who of India'.

South of Horniman Circle on Shahid Bhagat Singh Marg, the **Custom House** is one of the oldest buildings in the city, believed to incorporate a Portuguese barrack block from 1665. Over the entrance is the crest of the East India Company. Remnants of the old Portuguese fort's walls can be seen and many Malabar teak 'East Indiamen' ships were built here. Walk north from here and you'll reach the **Town Hall** (1820-1823), widely admired and much photographed as one of the best neoclassical buildings in India. The Corinthian interior houses the **Assembly Rooms** and the **Bombay Asiatic Society**. Immediately north again is the **Mint** (1824-1829) ⓘ *visit by prior permission from the Mint Master, T022-2270 3184, www.mumbaimint.org*, built on the Fort rubbish dump, with Ionic columns and a water tank in front of it. The nearby **Ballard Estate** is also worth a poke around while you're in the area, with some good hotels and restaurants, as well as Hamilton Studios, the swanky offices of *Vogue* magazine, and the Mumbai Port Authority.

Around the CST (VT)

Chhatrapati Shivaji Terminus (1878-1887), formerly Victoria Terminus and still known to many elder taxi drivers as 'VT', is far and away the most remarkable example of Victorian Gothic architecture in India. Opened during Queen Victoria's Golden Jubilee year (1887), over three million commuters now swarm through the station daily, though the bustling chaos of old has been reined in somewhat since November 2008's terror attacks, when at least 50 people were shot dead here. Several scenes from *Slumdog Millionaire* were filmed on the suburban platforms at the west end of the station.

The station was built at a time when fierce debate was taking place among British architects working in India as to the most appropriate style to develop to meet the demands of the late 19th-century boom. One view held that the British should restrict themselves to models derived from the best in Western tradition. Others argued that architects should draw on Indian models, trying to bring out the best of Indian tradition and encourage its development. By and large, the former were dominant, but the introduction of Gothic elements allowed a blending of Western traditions with Indian (largely Islamic) motifs, which became known as the Indo-Saracenic style. The station that resulted, designed by FW Stevens, is its crowning glory: a huge, symmetrical, gargoyle-studded frontage capped by a large central dome and a 4-m-high statue of Progress, with arcaded booking halls, stained glass and glazed tiles inspired by St Pancras. The giant caterpillar-like walkway with perspex awnings looks truly incongruous against the huge Gothic structure.

There are many more Victorian buildings in the area around CST, particularly along Mahapalika Marg (Cruickshank Road), which runs northwest of the station past the grand **Municipal Buildings** (also by Stevens, 1893), and Lokmanya Tilak Marg (Camac Road), which joins Mahapalika Marg at the Metro Cinema traffic circle – a landmark known to every Mumbai cabbie.

Immediately to the north of CST lies **Crawford Market** (1865-1871), now renamed **Mahatma Jyotiba Phule Market** after a Maharashtran social reformer, designed by Emerson in 12th-century French Gothic style, with paving stones imported from Caithness and fountains carved by Lockwood Kipling. The market is divided into bustling sections for fruit, vegetables, fish, mutton and poultry, with a large central hall and clock tower.

Running northwest of Crawford Market towards Mumbai Central Railway Station is **Falkland Road**, the centre of Mumbai's red-light district. Prostitutes stand behind barred windows, giving the area its other name, 'The Cages' – many of the girls are sold or abducted from various parts of India and Nepal. AIDS is very widespread, and a lot of NGOs are at work in the area educating the women about prevention.

North of Crawford Market is **Masjid Station**, the heart of the Muslim quarter, where agate minarets mingle with the pollution-streaked upper storeys of 1960s residential towers. The atmosphere here is totally different from the crumbling colonial architectural glory of the Colaba and Fort area: balconies on faded apartment blocks are bedecked with fairy lights, laundry dries on the window grilles, and at sunset the ramshackle roads hum with taxis, boys wielding wooden carts through traffic and Muslim women at a stroll. One of the city's most

3 CST, Churchgate & Fort

N

300 metres

300 yards

Sleeping

Chateau Windsor & Kamling **2** *B1*

City Palace **1** *B3*

Grand **8** *B3*

Intercontinental Marine Drive **10** *B1*

Manama **3** *A3*

Oberoi & Trident **4** *C1*

Popular Palace **9** *B3*

Sea Green **11** *B1*

Travellers Inn **12** *B3*

West End **7** *A2*

Eating

210 Degrees **6** *C2*

Apoorva **15** *B3*

Badshah Cold Drinks **1** *A3*

Berry's **2** *B1*

Britannia **13** *B3*

Chopsticks **2** *B1*

Croissants Etc **4** *B2*

Excellensea & Bharat Lunch Home **9** *B3*

Gaylord **5** *B2*

Kailash Parbat **3** *D2*

Lalit **8** *B3*

Paradise **10** *D2*

Pearl of the Orient **11** *B1*

Satkar **18** *B2*

Tea Centre **16** *B2*

Bars & clubs

Geoffreys **19** *B1*

Not Just Jazz by the Bay **20** *B1*

interesting markets, the **Chor Bazar** (Thieves' Market) ⓘ *Sat to Thu 1100-1900*, spreads through the streets between the station and Falkland Road. The bazar is a great place to poke around in with tonnes of dealers in old watches, film posters, Belgian- or Indian-made temple lamps, enamel tiles and door knobs. The area around Mutton Street is popular with film prop-buyers and foreign and domestic bric-a-brac hunters.

Marine Drive to Malabar Hill

When the hustle of the city becomes too much, do as the Mumbaikars do and head for the water. The 3-km sweep of **Marine Drive** (known as the 'Queen's Necklace' for the lines of streetlights that run its length) skirts alongside the grey waters of the Arabian Sea from Nariman Point in the south to exclusive Malabar Hill in the north. This is where you'll see Mumbai at its most egalitarian: servants and *babus* alike take the air on the esplanades in the evening. For an interesting half-day trip, start downtown at Churchgate Station and follow the curving course of the Queen's Necklace to the Walkeshwar Temple out on the end of Malabar Hill; start at lunchtime and you can be strolling back down Marine Drive, ice cream in hand, among the atmospheric sunset crush of power-walking executives and festive families.

Churchgate Station (1894-1896), on Vir Nariman Road at the north end of the Oval Maidan, was the second great railway building designed by FW Stevens. With its domes and gables, Churchgate has an air of Byzantine simplicity that contrasts with CST's full-tilt Gothic overload, but the rush hour spectacle is no less striking: Sebastiao Salgado's famous photograph of commuters pouring out of suburban trains was taken here.

A block to the west is Netaji Subhash Road, better known as **Marine Drive**, which bends northwest past Wankhede cricket stadium, several luxury hotels and the run-down Taraporewala Aquarium. At the north end in the crook of Malabar Hill is **Chowpatty Beach**, a long stretch of grey-white sand that looks attractive from a distance, but is polluted. Swimming here is not recommended but there is a lot of interesting beach activity in the evening. Chowpatty was the scene of a number of important 'Quit India' rallies during the Independence Movement. During important festivals, like **Ganesh Chaturthi** and **Dussehra** (see Festivals, page 1174), it is thronged with jubilant Hindu devotees.

Mahatma Gandhi Museum (**Mani Bhavan**) ⓘ *west of Grant Rd station at 19 Laburnum Rd, www.gandhi-manibhavan.org, 0930-1800, Rs 10, allow 1 hr*, is north of Chowpatty on the road to Nana Chowk. This private house, where Mahatma Gandhi used to stay on visits to Mumbai, is now a memorial museum and research library with 20,000 volumes. There is a diorama depicting important scenes from Gandhi's life, but the display of photos and letters on the first floor is more interesting, and includes letters Gandhi wrote to Hitler in 1939 asking him not to go to war, and those to Roosevelt, Einstein and Tolstoy.

At the end of Chowpatty, Marine Drive becomes Walkeshwar Road and bends southwest to pass the **Jain Temple** (1904), built of marble and dedicated to the first Jain Tirthankar. Much of the colourful decoration depicts the lives of the Tirthankars. Visitors can watch various rituals being performed. Jains play a prominent part in Mumbai's banking and commerce and are one of the city's wealthiest communities. Beyond, on the tip of Malabar Point, is **Raj Bhavan**, now home to the Governor of Maharashtra.

Behind the Jain Temple, Gangadhar Kher Rd (Ridge Road) runs up Malabar Hill to the **Hanging Gardens** (**Pherozeshah Mehta Gardens**) so named since they are located on top of a series of tanks that supply water to Mumbai. The gardens are well kept with lots of topiary animals and offer an opportunity to hang out with Mumbai's elite, whose penthouse apartments peer down on the park from all sides; there are good views over the city and Marine Drive from the **Kamala Nehru Park** across the road. It's worth a visit after 1700 when it's a bit cooler, but it's reputed to be unsafe after nightfall. Immediately to the north are the Parsi **Towers of Silence**, set in secluded gardens donated by Parsi industrialist Sir Jamshetji

Dabbawallahs

If you go inside Churchgate station at mid-morning or after lunch, you will see the *dabbawallahs*, members of the Bombay Union of Tiffin Box Carriers. Each morning, the 2500 *dabbawallahs* call on suburban housewives who pack freshly cooked lunch into small circular stainless steel containers – *dabbas*. Three or four are stacked one on the other and held together by a clip with a handle. Typically the *dabbawallah* will collect 30-40 tiffin boxes, range them out on a long pole and cycle to the nearest station. Here he will hand them over to a fellow *dabbawallah* who will transport them into the city for delivery.

Over 100,000 lunches of maybe sabze (vegetable curry), chappattis, dahl and pickle make their way daily across town to the breadwinner. The service, which costs a few rupees a day, is a good example of the fine division of labour in India, reliable and efficient, for the dabbawallahs pride themselves on never losing a lunch. He makes sure that the carefully prepared pukka (proper) food has not in any way been defiled.

Jeejeebhoy. This very private place is not accessible to tourists but it can be glimpsed from the road. Parsis believe that the elements of water, fire and earth must not be polluted by the dead, so they lay their 'vestments of flesh and bone' out on the top of the towers to be picked clean by vultures. The depletion in the number of vultures is a cause for concern, and more and more agiarys now opt for solar panels to speed up the process of decay.

At the end of the headland behind Raj Bhavan stands the **Walkeshwar Temple** ('Lord of Sand'), built about AD 1000 and one of the oldest buildings in Mumbai. In legend this was a resting point for Lord Rama (see page 1402) on his journey from Ayodhya to Lanka to free Sita from the demon king Ravana. One day Rama's brother failed to return from Varanasi at the usual time with a *lingam* that he fetched daily for Rama's worship. Rama then made a *lingam* from the beach sand to worship Siva. You'd also do well to visit **Banganga**, a freshwater tank that's part of an 12th-century temple complex. Legend has it that when Rama got thirsty Lakshman raised his bow and shot a *baan* (arrow) into the ground, bringing forth fresh water from the Ganga in this ocean locked island. The site is being renovated and is regularly used as a venue for concerts, festivals and pilgrimages alike.

Central Mumbai

Other than to catch a train from Mumbai Central Station, relatively few visitors venture into the area north of Marine Drive, yet it contains some fascinating only-in-Mumbai sights which, with judicious use of taxis and the odd suburban train, can easily be combined into a day trip with the coastal sights described above.

On the coast, 1 km north of the Ghandi Museum on Bhulabhai Desai (Warden Road), are the **Mahalakshmi temples**, the oldest in Mumbai, dedicated to three goddesses whose images were found in the sea. Lakshmi, goddess of wealth, is the unofficial presiding deity of the city, and the temple is host to frenzied activity – pressing a coin into the wall of the main shrine is supposed to be a sign of riches to come. Just to the north, **Haji Ali's Mosque** sits on an islet 500 m offshore. The mosque, built in 1431, contains the tomb of Muslim saint Haji Ali, who drowned here while on pilgrimage to Mecca, and as a last request demanded that he be buried neither on land nor at sea. A long causeway, usable only at low tide, links the mosque and tomb to the land, and is lined by Muslim supplicants. The money changers are willing to exchange one-rupee coins into smaller coins, enabling pilgrims to make several individual gifts to beggars rather than one larger one, thereby reputedly increasing the merit of the gift.

From Haji Ali's Tomb go east along Keshavrao Khade Road, passing the **Mahalakshmi Race Course** ⓘ *racing season Nov-Apr, www.rwitc.com*, to SG Maharaj Chowk (**Jacob's Circle**), and turn north to Mahalakshmi Bridge, reachable by local trains from Churchgate. From the bridge there is a view across the astonishing Municipal **dhobi ghats**, where Mumbai's dirty laundry is soaked, smacked in concrete tubs and aired in public by the *dhobis* (washerfolk); vistas unfold in blocks of primary colours, though you may have to fend off junior touts to enjoy them in peace. A short distance further north are the disused Victorian cotton mills of **Lower Parel**. Closed in 1980 after an all-out strike, some remain standing in a state of picturesque ruin (local residents may offer to show you round for Rs 50-100) while others, notably the Phoenix, Mathuradas and Bombay Dyeing mill compounds, have been converted into slick new malls, nightclubs and studio spaces popular with publishers and advertising agencies.

Southeast of Mahalakshmi station in Byculla are the **Veermata Jijibai Bhonsle Udyan** gardens, formerly Victoria Gardens. The attractive 48-acre park is home to Mumbai's **zoo** ⓘ *Thu-Tue 0900-1800, Rs 5*, be warned though, the signboards are missing and while the birds are gorgeous – they have birds of paradise, white peacocks and pink pelicans among others – there's no indication of what you're looking at. The gardens share space with the newly renovated **Bhau Daji Lad Museum** (**Victoria and Albert Museum**) ⓘ *www.bdl museum.org, Thu-Tue, 1000-1730, foreigners Rs 100, Indians Rs 10, children half price*. Inspired by the V&A in London and financed by public subscription, it was built in 1872 in a palladian style and is the second oldest museum in India. The collection covers the history of Mumbai and contains prints, maps and models that show how the seven disjointed islands came to form Mumbai.

Bandra, Juhu Beach and Andheri

If you really want to get under the skin of the city, a jaunt into the far-flung northern suburbs is essential. Close to the airports and relatively relaxed compared to living in the city centre, Bandra and Juhu are popular with Mumbai's upper crust, and most Bollywood A-listers have at least one of their homes here. **Bandra** is a lively suburb, full of the young and wealthy, with some exciting places to eat and some of the coolest bars, coffee shops, gyms and lounges in the city. Linking Road is home to a long open-air shoe bazar where you can find cheap, colourful sandals and knock-offs of every brand of clothing. Bandra's two seaside promenades, one at Bandra Bandstand by the Taj Lands End Hotel and one at Carter Road, the next bay northwards, feature sea-facing coffee shops with spectacular sunset views.

Juhu Beach, 20 km north of the centre, used to be an attractive and relaxed seaside area, but one sniff of the toxic water oozing out of Mahim Creek is enough to dissuade anyone from dipping so much as a toe in the ocean. Hordes of people still visit every day to walk on the beach, eat *bhel puri* and other spicy street food that delicate stomachs had best avoid, while kids buy balloons and take rides on horse-driven chariots. Beyond the beach Juhu is primarily a residential area, full of luxurious apartments, elegant old bungalows (Bollywood megastar Amitabh Bachchan has a place here) and day spas.

Andheri, spreading north of the airports, is the biggest suburb in Mumbai: it covers 50 sq km, is home to between 1.5 million and four million people depending on who's counting, and has sprung up from villages and mangrove swamps in a mere 30 years. There are few sights of note, but as a city within a city, with its own social subdivisions (mega- trendy residential enclaves and malls to the west, business parks and down-at-heel slums to the east, and even a suburban monorail system in construction), Andheri may well come to represent Mumbai's second city centre. If you want to explore, the areas to know about are Lokhandwala, New Link Road and Seven Bungalows/Versova; all are in Andheri West.

Mumbai (Bombay) listings

Hotel prices
LL over US$200 **L** US$151-200 **AL** US$101-150
A US$66-100 **B** US$46-65 **C** US$31-45
D US$21-30 **E** US$12-20 **F** US$7-11
G US$6 and under
Restaurant prices
ΨΨΨ over US$12 ΨΨ US$6-12 Ψ under US$6

Sleeping

Room prices in Mumbai are stratospheric by Indian standards, and there's no such thing as low-season: if possible make reservations in advance or arrive as early in the day as you can. Most hotels are concentrated in the downtown area, between **Colaba** and **Marine Dr**, and around the airport in the suburbs of **Santa Cruz**, **Juhu**, **Bandra** and **Andheri**. There are also several options around Mumbai Central and Dadar stations – handy for a quick getaway or an un-touristy view of the city.

Backpackers usually head for the **Colaba** area, which has the only acceptable cheap rooms in the city. **Arthur Bunder Rd** is a hotspot, with several places hidden away on upper floors of apartment blocks, usually with shared facilities, cold water and windowless rooms; arrive early and inspect room first. For guest accommodation contact **India Tourism**, 123 M Karve Rd, Churchgate, T022-2203 3144. You can also look on www.ndtvclassifieds.com.

Gateway of India and Colaba *p1160, map p1161*

Rooms with a sea view are more expensive. There are few budget hotels left in the area charging under Rs 800, though you can still find a dormitory bed for Rs 200.

LL Gordon House Hotel, 5 Battery St, Apollo Bunder, Colaba, T022-2289 4400, www.ghhotel.com. A spruce boutique hotel in the edgy Colaba district. 3 themed floors that really do leave India outside: yellow Med-style walls, quilts in the country cottage rooms and blonde wood on the Scandinavian floor.

LL Taj Mahal, Apollo Bunder, T022-6665 3366, www.tajhotels.com. The grand dame of Mumbai lodging, over a century old. The glorious old wing has been fully restored and updated after the 26/11/08 attacks, joining the 306 rooms in the **Taj Mahal Intercontinental** tower. Several top-class restaurants and bars, plus fitness centre, superb pool and even a yacht on call.

L Ascot, 38 Garden Rd, T022-6638 5566, www.ascothotel.com. The tan-wood rooms, shoehorned into a graceful 1930s building, veer dangerously close to IKEA anonymity, but they're generously proportioned and new, with safe deposit boxes, work desks and granite shower stalls. Great views from the upper floors. Breakfast included.

AL Apollo, 22 Lansdowne Rd, Colaba, behind **Taj**, T022-2287 3312, hotelapollogh@hotmail.com. 39 rooms, some a/c, some amazing sea views. Tatty linen and walls, but friendly staff.

AL Diplomat, 24-26 BK Boman Behram Marg, behind **Taj**, T022-2202 1661, www.hoteldiplomat-bombay.com. 52 a/c rooms, restaurant, quiet, friendly, relaxed atmosphere, good value. Very simple furnishings, small beds. Recommended.

AL Godwin, 41 Garden Rd, T022-2287 2050, www.hotelgodwin@mail.com. 48 large, clean, renovated, a/c rooms with superb views from upper floors, mostly helpful management and a good rooftop restaurant – full of wealthy Mumbaikars on Fri and Sat night.

AL-A YWCA International Centre, 2nd floor, 18 Madam Cama Rd, T022-2202 0598, www.ywcaic.info. For both sexes, 34 clean, pleasant rooms with bath, breakfast and dinner included, essential to write in advance with Rs 1300 deposit. Recommended.

A Strand, 25 PJ Ramchandani Marg, T022-2288 2222, www.hotelstrand.com. Friendly. Clean rooms, some with bath and sea view.

A Suba Palace, Apollo Bunder, T022-2220 2063, hotelsubapalace.com. Clean, modern, well run. Recommended.

B Cowie's, 15 Walton Rd, near Electric House, Colaba T022-2284 0232. 20 rooms with central a/c, bathroom en suite, TV and phone, in old-world hotel on one of the tree-lined residential streets off Colaba Causeway. Excellent value.

D India Guest House, 1/49 Kamal Mansion, Arthur Bunder Rd, T022-2283 3769. 20 rooms along long corridor, white partitions that you could, at a push, jump over. Fan, no toilet or shower. The corner room has a neat panorama over the bay. Sound will travel.

D Sea Shore, top floor, 1/49 Kamal Mansion, Arthur Bunder Rd, T022-2287 4238. Kitsch as you like, 15 bright gloss-pink rooms and purple corridors with plastic flowers, shower in room but no sink, 7 with window and TV and fan, 8 without. Sea view room has 4 beds. 2 rooms come with toilet, TV and hot water.

E-G The Salvation Army, Red Shield House, 30 Mereweather Rd, T022-2284 1824, redshield@vsnl.net. The only remotely backpacker-orientated place in Mumbai, with dorms (Rs 200 including breakfast) and some doubles and triples, a few with a/c. Rooms have high ceilings and there's a sociable canteen, but the internet is slow, shared bathrooms are dilapidated, and the mattresses can be something of a bedbug fest. Checkout 0900, lockers obligatory for dorm guests. Book in advance or arrive early.

Fort *p1160, map p1164*

A Grand, 17 Sprott Rd, Ballard Estate, T022-6658 0500, www.grandhotelbombay.com. Old-fashioned, built around a central courtyard, 73 a/c rooms, exchange, book counter, helpful service, very relaxing.

C-E Traveller's Inn, 26 Adi Murzban Path, Ballard Estate, T022-2264 4685, www.hoteltravellersinn.co.in. A relatively new addition to Mumbai's backpacker repertoire, with simple, clean rooms, a 3-bed dormitory, internet and Wi-Fi, and friendly staff.

D-E Popular Palace, 104-106 Mint Rd, near GPO, Fort Market, T022-2269 5506. Small but clean rooms with bath (hot water), some a/c, helpful staff, good value.

Around the CST (VT) *p1163, map p1164*

B City Palace, 121 City Terrace (Nagar Chowk), opposite CST Main Gate, T022-2261 5515. Tiny though clean, functional rooms (some no windows), with bath (Indian WC), some a/c, helpful staff, convenient location.

B-C Manama, 221 P D'Mello Rd, T022-2261 3412. Decent rooms, some with bath and a/c.

Marine Drive to Malabar Hill *p1165, map p1164*

LL Intercontinental Marine Drive, 135 Marine Dr, T022-3987 9999, www.mumbai.intercontinental.com. 59 rooms in luxury hotel overlooking Marine Drive. Bose stereo, plasma TV screens, Bulgari toiletries, personal butler service and beautiful rooftop pool.

LL The Oberoi, Nariman Pt, T022-6632 5757, www.oberoimumbai.com. Newly renovated and reopened, with beautiful sea-view rooms, glass-walled bathrooms, and 3 top-class restaurants.

LL Trident, Nariman Pt, T022-6632 4343, www.tridenthotels.com. Attached to the **Oberoi**, this 550-room tower is worth splashing out on if you can snag one of the renovated sea-view rooms on the upper floors. Good pool, spa and gym, great restaurant, but beefed-up security can make check-in slow.

AL West End, 45 New Marine Lines, T022-4083 9121, www.westendhotelmumbai.com. 80 small, pleasant suites but in need of refurbishment. Good restaurant, excellent service, efficient front desk, well located, good value. Recommended.

A Chateau Windsor Guest House, 86 Vir Nariman Rd, T022-6622 4455, www.cwh.in. Friendly and helpful place in a great location. The rooms on the 1st and 3rd floors are the best, newly renovated with large spotless bathrooms, marble tiles and balconies. Some of the older rooms are small, poky and dark. Recommended.

A Shalimar, August Kranti Marg, Kemps Corner (at east end of Malabar Hill), T022-6664 1000, www.shalimarhotel.com. 80 small, pleasant suites, good restaurant but plays the same 1980s muzak on repeat, efficient front desk, well located, Wi-Fi.

B Sea Green, 145 Marine Dr, T022-2282 2294, www.seagreenhotel.com. 34 rooms, 22 a/c, pleasant breezy informal sitting area.

Central Mumbai *p1166, maps p1159 and p1164*

L-AL Regency, Worli, T022-6657 1234, www.regencymumbai.com. 80 clean rooms, internet, good location, personable, friendly staff, some sea-facing rooms. Good value. Recommended.

A Bawa Regency, Gokuldas Pasta Rd, Dadar East, T022-4049 8383. Some a/c in the 31 rooms, mostly shared but clean baths. Flexible checkout, friendly. Recommended.

B Sagar, Nagpada Junction (Bellasin Rd/JB Behram Marg corner), Byculla, T022-2308 1441. Very clean rooms, good restaurant, friendly.

B-C YMCA International House, 18 YMCA Rd, near Mumbai Central, T022-6154 0100. Decent rooms, shared bath, meals included, temp membership Rs 120, deposit Rs 1300, good value, book 3 months ahead.
D Anukool, 292-8 Maulana Saukat Ali Rd, T022-2308 0201, hotelanukool@hotmail.com. 23 rooms, some a/c, friendly, helpful, good value, but inspect room first.

Bandra, Juhu Beach and Andheri *p1167*

Most hotels near the airport offer free transfer. Tourist information at the airport can book.
LL Citizen, 960 Juhu Tara Rd, T022-6693 2525, www.citizenhotelmumbai.com. Despite unexciting appearance, 45 small but very well-appointed rooms, suites, efficient airport transfer.
LL Leela, near International Terminal, T022-6000 2233, www.theleela.com. 460 modern rooms, excellent restaurants, pricey but excellent bar (residents only after 2300), all-night coffee shop, happening night club.
LL Novotel (formerly Holiday Inn), Balraj Sahani Marg, Juhu Beach, T022-6693 4444. Brand new, featuring 203 rooms, 1 lounge, 4 restaurants, health club and swimming pool.
LL Sun-n-Sand, 39 Juhu Beach, T022-6693 8888, www.sunnsandhotelcom. 118 rooms, best refurbished, comfortable, though cramped poolside, good restaurant.
LL-L Orchid, 70C Nehru Rd, Vile Parle (east), 5 mins' walk from domestic terminal, T022-2616 4040, www.orchidhotelcom. Refurbished, attractive rooms, eco-friendly. Boulevard restaurant boasts a good midnight buffet and '15-min lightning' buffet. Recommended.
L-AL Metro Palace, 355 Ramdas Nayak Rd (Hill Rd), near Bandra station (W), T022-2642 7311. Convenient, close to domestic airport and shops, good restaurant.
AL Juhu Plaza, 39/2 Juhu Beach, T022-6695 9600, www.hoteljuhuplaza.com. 40 rooms, excellent restaurant. Recommended.
AL Juhu Residency, 148B Juhu Tara Rd, T022-6783 4949, www.juhuresidency.com. Across the road from the Marriott, with just 28 attractive refurbished rooms, free Wi-Fi, friendly efficient staff and 2 excellent restaurants. A great deal by Mumbai standards.
AL Pali Hills, 14 Union Park, Pali Hill, Bandra, T022-2649 2995. Quiet location, near market, continental restaurant.
AL Residency, Suren Rd, T022-2692 3000, www.residencymumbai.com. New hotel 3 km from the airport, request free pickup. 72 a/c smallish rooms, good restaurant, quiet back street, friendly staff. Recommended.
AL Transit, off Nehru Rd, Vile Parle (east), T022-6693 0761, www.hoteltransit.in. Modern, 54 rooms, reasonable overnight halt for airport, excellent restaurant (draught beer), airport transfer. Special rates for day use (0800-1800).
B-C Atithi, 77A Nehru Rd, 7 mins' walk from domestic terminal, T022-2618 7941, www.atithihotel.net. 47 rooms, functional, clean, 3 star, set meals included, good value, efficient desk, popular.

Eating

Gateway of India and Colaba *p1160, map p1161*

Most restaurants in the area, including the cheaper ones, provide filtered drinking water.
TTT All Stir Fry, Gordon House Hotel, T022-2287 1122. Oriental nosh served up in *Wagamama*-style at long shared benches. DIY food too. Don't experiment too much with the drinks though, stick to standards.
TTT Indigo, 4 Mandlik Rd, behind **Taj Hotel**, T022-2218 2829. Excellent Mediterranean in smart restaurant, good atmosphere, additional seating on rooftop.
TTT Indigo Deli, Chhatrapati Shivaji Maharaj Marg, T022-565 51010. Café and deli with fresh cold cuts, sandwiches and burgers. Other meals are pricey for the quantity and quality.
TTT Le Pain Quotidien, Dhanraj Mahal, CSM Rd, T022-6615 0202. Belgian bakery chain serving some of Mumbai's best breads and pastries, as well as light meals, salads and delectably crumbly apple pie.
TTT Ling's Pavilion, 19/21 KC College Hostel Building, off Colaba Causeway (behind **Taj** and Regal Cinema), T022-2285 0023. Stylish decor, good atmosphere and delightful service, colourful menu, seafood specials, generous helpings. Recommended.
TTT Souk, Taj Mahal Apollo Bunder, T022-6665 3366, www.tajhotels.com. Taj's top floor is home to a North African themed restaurant. Open from 1900, great views. A glass of imported red wine

(excellent though it may be) costs Rs 900 before tax.

Café Basilico, Sentinel House, Arthur Bunder Rd, T022-6634 5670. Bistro with all-day breakfast and a decent Sun brunch. Excellent *rawas*, sandwiches, desserts and coffee, but no alcohol.

Moshe's, 7 Minoo Manor, next To Euphoria Gym, Bhadwar Park, Cuffe Parade, T022-2216 1226. Cosy bistro-café with great risottos and Turkish chicken. Save room for dessert.

Bade Miyan, Tullock Rd behind Ling's Pavilion. Streetside Kebab corner, but very clean. Try *baida roti*, *shammi* and *boti* kebabs. The potato *kathi* rolls are excellent veg options.

Bagdadi, Tullock Rd (behind **Taj Hotel**). One of the cheapest, with first-class food, fragrant biryani, delicious chicken, crowded and utterly basic but clean. Recommended.

Café Churchill, 103-8, East West Court Building, opposite Cusrow Baug, Colaba Causeway, T022-2284 4689, 1000-2330. A tiny little café with 7 tables crammed with people basking in a/c, towered over by a cake counter and a Winston Churchill portrait. Great breakfasts, club sandwiches, seafood, fish and chips, lasagne and Irish stew.

Kamat Samarambh, opposite Electric House, Colaba Causeway. Very good and authentic South Indian food, *thalis* and snacks. Try the moist, fluffy *uttapam* and *upma*. Clean drinking water.

Paradise, Sindh Chambers, Colaba Causeway. Tue-Sun. Spotless Parsi place, serving excellent dhansak; try *sali boti* (mutton and 'chips').

Shubh Sagar, mouth of Colaba Market, Mistry Chambers, opposite Telephone Bhawan, Colaba, T022-2281 1550. 0900-2400. Excellent hygienic and clean vegetarian restaurant, great biryanis and South Indian snacks outside normal restaurant mealtimes.

Cafés and snacks

Many serve chilled beer and waiters care too much for large tips from tourist groups:

Kailash Parbat, 1st Pasta La, Colaba. Excellent snacks and chats, in an old-style eatery also serving Punjabi *thalis*. The tooth-rotting *pedas* from the counter are a Mumbai institution.

Leopold's, Colaba, T022-2283 0585. An institution among Colaba backpackers and Mumbai shoppers. The food, predominantly Western with a limited choice of Indian vegetarian, is average and pricey (similar cafés nearby are far better value) but Leo's gained cachet from its cameo role in the novel *Shantaram*, and was the first target of the terror attacks in Nov 2008.

Mondegar, near Regal Cinema. Similar to Leopold in spirit, but a little cheaper on the pitchers, and with a loud rock soundtrack.

Theobroma, Colaba Causeway, next to Cusrow Baug. Decent coffee and terrific egg breakfasts. The brownies here are to die for – try the millionaire brownie or the rum-and- raisin with coffee. Egg-less cakes available.

Fort *p1160, map p1164*

Khyber, 145 MG Rd, Kala Ghoda, T022-2267 3227. North Indian. For an enjoyable evening in beautiful surroundings, out-standing food, especially lobster and *reshmi* chicken kebabs, try *paya* soup (goats' trotters).

Trishna, Sai Baba Marg, next to Commerce House, T022-2261 4991. Good coastal cuisine, seafood, excellent butter garlic crab. Recommended.

Apoorva, near Horniman Circle, Fort, T022-2287 0335. Very good seafood, especially crabs and prawns (downstairs is a cheaper).

Britannia, Wakefield House, Sprott Rd, opposite New Custom House, Ballard Estate, T022-22615264. Mon-Sat 1200-1600. Incredible Parsi/Iranian fare with a delicious berry *pullav* made from specially imported Bol berries (cranberries from Iran). Try the *dhansak* and the egg curry. Recommended.

The Excellensea & Bharat Lunch Home, 317 Bharat House, Fort Market, Mint Rd, T022-2261 8991. Excellent seafood and crab as well as *naans* and *rotis*: or try Bombay duck.

Lalit, Rustom Sidhwa Rd opposite **Residency Hotel**. Simple but friendly and hygienic pure-veg café, good for South Indian breakfasts, *pav bhaji* in the afternoon, and chai served in dainty china cups. There's a cramped a/c section upstairs.

Around the CST (VT) *p1163, map p1164*

Badshah Cold Drinks & Snacks, opposite Crawford Market. Famous for its *kulfi* (hand-churned ice cream) and fresh fruit juices (drink without ice), it's a default stop for everyone shopping at Crawford Market. Good and fast *pav-bhaji* (mixed veggies with buttered rolls).

Sadananda, opposite Crawford Market. Excellent south Indian and Gujarati *thalis* and vegetarian food, popular with Indian families.

Marine Drive to Malabar Hill *p1165, map p1164*

China Garden, Om Chambers, Kemps Corner (at east end of Malabar Hill), T022-3242 3802. Chinese with an Indian hangover. Good food, generous portions, decent alcohol, tables inside and out, no children under 10 allowed inside.

Gaylord, Vir Nariman Rd, opposite Churchgate. Indian. Good food (huge portions) and service, tables inside and out, barbecue, pleasant, good bar, tempting pastry counter.

Pearl of the Orient, Ambassador Hotel, T022-2204 1131. This revolving restaurant offers stunning views, especially at night, and very ordinary Chinese food.

Berry's, Vir Nariman Rd, near Churchgate Station, T022-2204 8954. North Indian. Tandoori specialities, good *kulfi*.

Chopsticks, 90A Vir Nariman Rd, Churchgate, T022-2204 9284. Chinese, good, hot and spicy. Offering unusual dishes (*taro* nest, date pancakes, toffee bananas).

Kamling, 82 Vir Nariman Rd, T022-2204 2618. Genuine Cantonese. Simple surroundings, but excellent preparations, try seafood, often busy, even at lunchtime.

Satkar, Indian Express Building, opposite Churchgate station, T022-2204 3259. Indian. Delicious vegetarian, fruit juices and shakes; a/c section more expensive.

Purohit's, Vir Nariman Rd, near Churchgate. Indian. Excellent vegetarian *thalis*.

Cafés and snacks

210 Degrees, in Samrat Restaurant complex, Jamshjedji Tata Rd, T022-4213 5407. Superb selection of pure-vegetarian (ie eggless but not vegan) cakes and pastries. Come for afternoon tea as the best stuff is gone by evening.

Tea Centre, 78 Vir Nariman Rd, near Churchgate. Old-fashioned white table cloths and patrons talking in hushed tones make this a throwback to the Colonial period, but they do have dozens of light and refreshing tea options, along with a menu of heavy Indian food. Good value and a/c.

Central Mumbai *p1166, maps p1159 and p1164*

Goa Portuguesa, THK Rd, Mahim (8 km north of Mumbai Central on way to airport). Authentic dishes, taverna-style with guitarist, try *sungto* (prawn) served between *papads*, *kalwa* (oyster), lobsters cooked with tomatoes, onions and spices and *bebinca* to end the meal.

Swati Snacks, Tardeo Rd, opposite Bhatia Hospital, T022-2352 6411. Gujarati and Parsi snacks along with street foods made in a hygienic fashion: try *khichdi, sev puri, pav bhaji, dahi puri* here. Be prepared for a 20- to 40-min wait, but it's worth it.

Viva Paschim, City View, Dr AB Rd, Worli, T022-2498 3636. Quality coastal Maharashtrian. Sunday lunch buffet great value (Rs 225), folk dances at dinner often.

Bandra, Juhu Beach and Andheri *p1167*

Olive, Union Park, Pali Hill, Bandra, T022-2605 8228. The original **Olive** features wicker furniture in an upscale environment, catering to a cast of characters from Bollywood. Free entry, great pizza and a chic clientele.

Pali Village Cafe, Ambedkar Rd, Bandra (W), T022-2605 0401. Super-trendy new restaurant done out in shabby-chic industrial style, cascading across different rooms and levels. Good desserts and tapas-style starters, though the wine list and general vibe outweigh the quality of food and service.

Da Vinci, 8 Fatima Villa, 29th Rd, Pali Naka Lane, Bandra West, T022-3248 6033. Italian, one of few sit-down places in Bandra that also serves alcohol. Try the pasta Arabiatta and their version of jalapeno peppers. Leave room for dessert.

Gajalee, Kadambari Complex, Hanuman Rd, Vile Parle (E), T022-6692 9592, www.gajalee.com; also in Phoenix Mills. Fine coastal cuisine, try fish tikka, stuffed Bombay Duck and shellfish with the traditional breads *ghawne* and *amboli*.

Just Around the Corner, 24th-30th road junction, TPS III, Bandra (W). Bright casual American-style diner with all-day salad bar, extensive breakfast menu (0800-1100), and thin crust pizza. Good soup, salad and sandwich combinations.

Out of the Blue, at Union Park, Pali Hill. Steak and fondue, great sizzlers, unusual combinations, flavoured ice teas, flambéed desserts, UV lit inside or outside smoke-free.

Zenzi, Waterfield Rd, Bandra (W). Pan-Asian fusion food, small servings but tasty pork and vegetables. Always packed with a hip media crowd for after-work drinks.

Bars and clubs

All major hotels and restaurants have bars, others may only serve beer. Most clubs expect couples Fri-Sun, and lone males ('stags' in local parlance) may find it hard to get in. Most pubs charge Rs 350-400 for a 3-litre 'pitcher'; cocktails Rs 400-700. Ask for domestic liquor if you're having vodka or rum cocktails, both Smirnoff and Bacardi are made locally and are half the price. Pick up *Time Out Mumbai*, published every fortnight, for listings and the latest openings, or check http://mumbai.burrp.com.

Gateway of India and Colaba *p1160, map p1161*

Privé, 41/44 Minoo Desai Marg, Colaba, T022-2202 8700. 2130-0130 (weekends until 0230). Rs1000 per couple (Rs 500 for ladies). Slick lounge with hard party music. Serious party-goers with a serious see-and-be-seen scene.
Polly Esther, **Gordon House Hotel**. A reggae, pop, rock disco, retro-themed club, where anything goes. Open late, most people come here after they finish partying elsewhere.
Woodside Inn, opposite **Regal Cinema** Colaba. Cramped pub carved out of stone Gothic building, with decent retro music, good dining upstairs (pizzas and sandwiches are surprisingly decent) and good selection of whiskies. Free Wi-Fi, too.

Fort *p1160, map p1164*

Red Light, above **Khyber** (see Eating). Popular with a slightly younger party set, slightly sleazy, always a crowd to get in, 'stags' will find it hard to get in after 2300. Couple entry Rs 1500. DJs rotate, spinning *bhangra*, Top 40, hip hop and Hindi.

Marine Drive to Malabar Hill *p1165, map p1164*

Dome, **Intercontinental Hotel**, Marine Dr, T022-6639 9999. Rooftop restaurant and lounge bar with a stunning view of the Queen's Necklace. Try the grilled prawns with your cocktails.
Pizza by the Bay, 143 Marine Dr, T022-2285 1876. Fun place near Churchgate, with live music, karaoke, good food menu (great starters and desserts), generous portions, wide selection of drinks. Loud and lively.

Bandra, Juhu Beach and Andheri *p1167*

Aurus, Juhu Tara Rd, Juhu. Trendy seaside patio bar where Bollywood stars rub shoulders with the glitterati. No dance floor, but avant-garde DJs, some international, spin inside. Expensive appetizers, good signature drinks and ocean views. Free entry, easier for couples.
Bling, **Leela Hotel** (see Sleeping). Club that lives up to its name, stays open late so attracts the spillover from the other clubs. Entry Rs 700-2500 depending on the time, the night, and the bouncers.
China House, **Grand Hyatt Hotel**, Santa Cruz (E), near domestic airport, T022-6676 1086. High-end Chinese restaurant turns into a happening party after other clubs close around 0130. DJs and music vary. Excellent martinis. Entry Rs 1500 a couple on Fri-Sat.
Hawaiian Shack, 16th Rd, Bandra (W). 1980s bar downstairs, hip hop and dance floor upstairs. Ladies get in free, always crowded.
Toto's, 30th Rd, off Pali Naka, Bandra (W). Retro music, regular clients, and no attitude amid funky automotive decor.
Vie Lounge, Juhu Tara Rd, Juhu. Slightly less attitude than **Aurus** makes this sea-view lounge bar an attractive, but just as pricey, hotspot. Attracts a marginally older crowd.

Entertainment

Mumbai *p1157, maps p1159, p1161 and p1164*

Check *TimeOut Mumbai* for upcoming events.

Cinema

Bollywood and international films are screened in dozens of cinemas, most of which are in multi plexes and malls; timings are listed in local newspapers. Multiplexes in South Mumbai include **INOX**, Nariman Point, **Big Cinemas Metro**, southwest corner of Azad Maidan Few independent theatres remain: Try **Eros** opposite Churchgate station, **Regal**, Colaba, or **Sterling**, near CST.

Theatre and classical music

Multilingual Mumbai puts on plays in English, Hindi, Marathi and Gujarati, usually beginning at 1815-1900.

National Centre for Performing Arts, next to Hilton Towers, Nariman Point, T022-6622 3737, www.ncpamumbai.com. Has regular classical music concerts and an Experimental Theatre, which is predictably hit-and-miss.

Festivals and events

Mumbai *p1157, maps p1159, p1161 and p1164*
In addition to the national Hindu and Muslim festivals there are the following:
Feb Elephanta Cultural Festival at the caves. Great ambience. Contact MTDC, T022-2202 6713, for tickets Rs 150-200 including launch at 1800. **Kala Ghoda Arts Festival.** Showcase of all forms of fine arts held in various locations around Colaba and Fort. T022-2284 2520.
Mar Jamshed Navroz. This is New Year's Day for the Parsi followers of the Fasli calendar. The celebrations which include offering prayers at temples, exchanging greetings, alms-giving and feasting at home, date back to Jamshed, the legendary King of Persia.
Jul-Aug Janmashtami celebrates the birth of Lord Krishna. Boys and young men form human pyramids and break pots of curd hung up high between buildings.
Aug Coconut Day. The angry monsoon seas are propitiated by devotees throwing coconuts into the ocean.
Aug-Sep Ganesh Chaturthi. Massive figures of Ganesh are towed through the streets to loud techno and storms of coloured powder, before a final *puja* at Chowpatty Beach where they're finally dragged out into the sea. The crowds making their way on foot to the beach cause immense traffic pileups, and the scene at Chowpatty is chaotic, with priests giving *puja* to Ganesh and roaring crowds of men psyching themselves up for the final push into the ocean. A similar celebration happens shortly after at **Durga Pooja** time, when the goddess Durga is worshipped and immersed.
Sep-Oct Dussehra. Group dances by Gujarati women in all the auditoria and residents have their own *garba* and *dandiya* dance nights in the courtyards of their apartment buildings. There are also **Ram leela** celebrations at Chowpatty Beach, where the story of the *Ramayana* is enacted in a dance drama. **Diwali** (The Festival of Lights) is particularly popular in mercantile Mumbai when the business community celebrate their New Year and open new account books. **Eid ul-Fitr**, the celebration when Ramzan with its 40 days of fasting is also observed. Since both the Hindu and Islamic calendar are lunar, there is often overlap between the holidays.
25 Dec Christmas. Christians across Mumbai celebrate the birth of Christ. A pontifical High Mass is held at midnight in the open air at the Cooperage Grounds, Colaba.

Shopping

Mumbai *p1157, maps p1159, p1161 and p1164*
Most shops are open Mon-Sat 1000-1900, the bazars sometimes staying open as late as 2100. Mumbai prices are often higher than in other Indian cities, and hotel arcades tend to be very pricey but carry good-quality select items. Best buys are textiles, particularly tie-dye from Gujarat, hand-block printed cottons, Aurangabad and 'Patola' silks, gold-bordered saris from Surat and Khambat, handicrafts, jewellery and leather goods.

It is illegal to take anything over 100 years old out of the country. CDs of contemporary Indian music in various genres make good souvenirs as well as gifts.

Bazars

Crawford Market, Ambedkar Rd (fun for bargain hunting) and **Mangaldas Market**. Other shopping streets are South Bhagat Singh Marg, M Karve Rd and Linking Rd, Bandra. For a different experience try **Chor (Thieves') Bazar**, on Maulana Shaukat Ali Rd in central Mumbai, full of finds from raj leftovers to precious jewellery. Make time to stop at the **Mini Market**, 33-31 Mutton St, T022-2347 2425, minimarket@rediffmail.com (closed Fri), nose through the Bollywood posters, lobby cards, and photo-stills. On Fri, 'junk' carts sell less expensive 'antiques' and fakes.

Books

There are lines of second-hand stalls along Churchgate St and near the University. An annual book fair takes place at the Cross Maidan near Churchgate each Dec. **Crossword**, under the flyover at Kemps Corner bridge (east of Malabar Hill). Smart, spacious, good selection.

Nalanda, Taj Mahal Hotel. Excellent art books, Western newspapers/magazines.
Strand Books, off Sir PM Rd near HMV, T022-2206 1994. Excellent selection, best deals, reliable shipping.

Clothes

Benzer, B Desai Rd, Breach Candy. Open daily. Good saris and Indian garments.
The Courtyard, 41/44 Minoo Desai Marg, Colaba. Very elite and fashionable mini-mall includes boutiques full of stunning heavy deluxe designs (Swarovski crystal-studded saris, anyone?) by **Rohit Bal**. **Rabani & Rakha** (Rs 17,000 for a sari) but probably most suitable to the Western eye is textile designer Neeru Kumar's **Tulsi** label, a cotton textiles designer from Delhi. Beautiful linen/silk stoles and fine *kantha* thread work. There's also a store from top menswear designer Rajesh Pratap Singh.
Ensemble, 130-132 South Bhagat Singh Marg, T022-2287 2882. Superb craftsmanship and service for women's clothes – Indian and 'East meets West'.
Fabindia, Jeroo Building, 137 M G Rd, Kala Ghoda, and 66 Pali Hill, Bandra, www.fabindia.com. Fair-trade handloom Western and Indian wear including *kurtas*, pants, etc, for men, women, children, bamboo, earthenware and jute home furnishings, *khadi* and *mulmul* cloth.
Melange, 33 Altamount Rd, Kemps Corner, T022-2385 4492. Western-tailored, Indian embroidery clothes. Stocks designs from great labels.

Crafts and textiles

Government emporia from many states sell good handicrafts and textiles; several at **World Trade Centre**, Cuffe Parade. In Colaba, a street **Craft Market** is held on Sun (Nov-Jan) in K Dubash Marg.
Anokhi, 4B August Kranti Marg, opposite Kumbala Hill Hospital. Gifts and handicrafts.
Bombay Electric, 1 Reay House, BEST Marg, Colaba, T022-2287 6276, www.bombayelectric.in. Pricey, chic, trendsetter art and couture.
Bombay Store, Western India House, 1st floor, PM Rd, Fort, www.bombaystore.com. Open daily. Ethnic lifestyle supplies, from home decor and fancy paper to clothing, gifts, best one-stop shop, value for money. Recommended.
Cottage Industries Emporium, Apollo Bunder, Colaba. A nationwide selection, especially Kashmiri embroidery, South Indian handicrafts and Rajasthani textiles. Colaba Causeway, next to **BEST**, for ethnic ware, handicrafts and fabrics.
Curio Cottage, 19 Mahakavi Bhushan Rd, near the Regal Cinema, Colaba, T022-2202 2607. Silver jewellery and antiques.
Good Earth, 104 Kemp's Corner and Raghuvanshi Mills, Lower Parel. Smart, trendy, pottery, glass homewares.
Natesan in Jehangir Gallery basement; also in **Taj Hotel**. For fine antiques and copies.
Phillips, Madame Cama Rd, Colaba. An Aladdin's cave of bric-a-brac and curios. Pricey.
Sadak Ali, behind **Taj Hotel**, Colaba. Good range of carpets, but bargain hard.
Yamini, President House, Wodehouse Rd, Colaba, especially for vibrant textiles.

Electronics

DN Rd between Flora Fountain and CST has mobile and camera shops every few steps, but prices for genuine goods are not particularly low. There are a few second-hand camera shops towards CST. If buying new equipment, ask for a bill and international warranty.
Croma, Horniman Circle; also at Phoenix Mills, Lower Parel. Electronics store for cameras, phones and USB drives.
Heera Panna Shopping Arcade, Haji Ali. Formerly the grey-market for smuggled electical goods, now mostly above board.

Jewellery

In Bandra, Turner Rd has about 10 jewellery stores in a row to cater to every price range and taste – from traditional Indian styles to contemporary updates in gold, diamonds, and other precious and semi-precious stones. The **Cottage Industries Emporium**, near Radio Club, Colaba Causeway, has affordable silver and antique jewellery from across India.
Popli Suleman Chambers, Battery St, Apollo Bunder, Colaba, T022-2285 4757. Semi- precious stones, gems, garnets and pearls.

Music

Musical instruments on VB Patel Rd, **RS Mayeka** at No 386, **Haribhai Vishwanath** at No 419 and Ram Singh at Bharati Sadan.

Bright lights of Bollywood

Mumbai produces around 860 films a year, making Bollywood the world's second largest film-maker after Hong Kong. The stars live in sumptuous dwellings, many of which are on Malabar Hill, Mumbai's Beverley Hills, and despite the spread of foreign videos, their popularity seems to be undiminished.

It is difficult to get permission to visit a studio during filming but you might try **Film City**, Goregaon East, T022-2840 1533 or **Mehboob Studios**, Hill Road, Bandra West, T022-2642 8045. Alternatively, the staff at the Salvation Army Hostel (see Sleeping) may be able to help foreigners get on as 'extras'; Rs 500 per day.

Hiro, Hill Rd, Bandra. Good Indian classical CDs.
Planet M, opposite CST station; smaller branches in most malls. Also has book/poetry readings, gigs.
Rhythm House, next to Jehangir Gallery. Excellent selection of jazz and classical CDs. Also sells tickets for classical concerts.

Silks and saris

Many places including **Kala Niketan**, MG Rd and **Juhu Reclamation**.
Biba, next to Crossword, Kemp's Corner, Phoenix Mills, Lower Parel, Bandra (W). Affordable designer wear for ladies, alterations possible.
Nalli, Shop No 7, Thirupathi Apartments, Bhulabhai Desai Rd, T022-23535577. Something for every budget.
Ritu Kumar, Turner Rd, Bandra (W), Phoenix Mills, Lower Parel, Bandra (W), Ethnic and Western designer wear for ladies, including very contemporary silk T-shirts.
Sheetal, Tirupati Apartments, B Desai Rd. Saris from all over India; fair prices.

Activities and tours

Mumbai *p1157, maps p1159, p1161 and p1164*

Adventure tourism

Maharashtra Tourism, www.maharashtratourism.gov.in. Actively encourages adventure tourism (including jungle safaris and water sports) by introducing 'rent-a-tent' and hiring out trekking gear, and organizing overnight trips; some accommodation comes with. Prices range from US$35-150 per day/weekend depending on season and activity. It has also set up 27 holiday resorts around the state providing cheap accommodation at hill stations, beaches, archaeological sites and scenic spots. Details from tourist offices.

Odati Adventures, T(0)9820-079802, www.odati.com. Camping, weekend hiking, bike rides, rock climbing and waterfall rappelling around the Mumbai area. If you go rappelling in Maljesh Ghat during the monsoon, you'll glimpse thousands of flamingos. Bikes can be hired. Call or book online. Weekend cycle tours are Rs 2000-3000.

Body and soul

Iyengar Yogashraya, Elmac House, 126 Senapati Bapat Marg (off Tulsi Pipe road opposite Kamla Mills), Lower Parel, T022-2494 8416, www.bksiyengar.com. Iyengar drop-in centre. Call before dropping in.
Kaivalyadahama, next to Taraporewala Aquarium, Marine Dr.
Kerala Ayurvedic Health Spa, Prabhadevi, next to Subway and Birdy's, T022-6520 7445. Very reasonable rates for massage, Rs 900 for 45 mins. Call for an appointment.
Yoga Institute, Praghat Colony, Santa Cruz (E). T022-2611 0506.
Yoga Training Centre, 51 Jai Hind Club, Juhu Scheme, T022-2649 9020.
Yoga Vidhya Niketan, Sane Guruji Marg, Dadar, T022-2430 6258.

Horse racing

Mahalaxmi Race Course, opposite Haji Ali. Season Nov-Mar, Sun and holidays, 1400-1700. Many of India's top races are held at the delightful course (1878), including the Derby in Feb/Mar. Check newspapers for listings.

Tour operators

If you wish to sightsee independently with a guide, ask at the tourist office. See page 1158.

Be the Local, T(0)9930-027370, www.bethelocaltoursandtravels.com. Fascinating walking tours of Dharavi, which take you through some of the cottage industries – from traditional Gujarati pottery to plastic – which sustain Mumbai from within Asia's largest slum. Owned and run by local students, the tours are neither voyeuristic nor intrusive, and photography is prohibited. Rs 400 per person includes transport from Colaba; private tours Rs 3500 for up to 5 people.
Bombay Heritage Walks, T022-2369 0992, www.bombayheritagewalks.com. Informative walking tours specialising in Mumbai's built history, founded by a pair of local architects.
City sightseeing Approved guides from the **India tourist office**, T022-2203 6854. City tour usually includes visits to The Gateway of India, the Chhatrapati Shivaji (Prince of Wales) Museum, Jain temple, Hanging Gardens, Kamla Nehru Park and Mani Bhavan (Gandhi Museum). Suburban tour includes Juhu Beach, Kanheri Caves and Lion Safari Park.
MTDC, Madam Cama Rd, opposite LIC Building, T022-2202 6713. City tour Tue-Sun 0900-1300 and 1400-1800, Rs 100. Suburban tour 0915 (from Dadar 1015-1815. Fort walk is a heritage walk around CST and Fort area with the Kala Ghoda Association, Army & Navy Building, T022-2285 2520, www.art india.co.in. Elephanta tours from Gateway of India. Boat, 0900-1415, Rs 70 return; reserve at Apollo Bunder, T022-2202 6364.
Mumbai Magic, T(0)98677-07414, www.mumbaimagic.com. Deepa Krishnan and her army of erudite guides offer a vast range of tours covering every inch of the city from Colaba to Bandra and beyond. Highlights include South Indian cuisine tours of Matunga, a walk through the Chor Bazaar, and the Mumbai Local tour which hops you around the city by taxi, local train and bus. Personalised itineraries available. Professional and highly recommended.

Travel agents **Cox and Kings**, 16 Bank St, Fort, T022-2270 9100; **Everett**, 1 Regent Chambers, Nariman Pt, T022-2204 8141; **Mercury**, 70VB Gandhi Rd, T022-6615 3477; **Space Travels**, 4th floor, Sir PM Rd, T022-2266 2481, for discounted flights and special student offers, Mon-Fri, 1000-1700, Sat 1030-1500; **TCI**, 324 Dr DN Rd, Fort, T022-6160 3333; **Thomas Cook**, Cooks Building, Dr DN Rd, T1800-209 9100; **Venture**, ground floor, Abubakar Mansion, Shahid Bhagat Singh Marg, T022-2287 6666, efficient, helpful.

Transport

Mumbai *p1157, maps p1159, p1161 and p1164*

Air

Mumbai is one of the 2 main entry points to India, with daily international flights from Europe, North America, the Middle East, Asia, Australia and Africa, and frequent domestic connections with every major city in India, and most minor ones. All touch down at **Chhatrapati Shivaji International Airport**, enquiries T022-6685 0222, www.csia.in. The recently smartened-up international terminal is 30 km north of the city. There are exchange counters, ATMs, tourist offices, domestic airline and railway reservation counters, and a cloakroom for left luggage.

Domestic, recently renovated with 2 separate terminals - 1A for **Air India** and **Kingfisher** (enquiries T022-6685 1351), 1B for **Jet Airways** and all budget airlines (enquiries T022-2626 1149), is 4 km closer to the city in Santa Cruz and has most of the same facilities. Free shuttle buses link the domestic and international terminals every few mins.

Transport to and from the airport
Pre-paid taxis, from counters at the exits, are the simplest way of getting downtown. Give the exact area or hotel and the number of pieces of luggage, and pay at the booth. On the receipt will be scribbled the number of your taxi: ask the drivers outside to help you find it, and hand the receipt to the driver at the end of the journey. There is no need to tip, though drivers will certainly drop heavy hints. To **Nariman Point** or **Gateway of India**, about Rs 430, 1-2 hrs depending on traffic. To **Juhu Beach** Rs 290. Metered taxis picked up outside the terminal should be marginally cheaper than a prepaid, but make sure the driver starts the meter when you get in. The cheaper alternatives – crowded and slow **BEST** buses that connect both terminals with the city, and even more crowded local **trains** – have only economy in their favour. The closest railway stations are **Vile Parle** (for International) and **Santa Cruz** (Domestic), both on the Western line to Mumbai Central and Churchgate.

Airline offices

Domestic The easiest way to comparison shop for domestic fares is online, though not all sites accept international credit cards. One that does is www.cleartrip.com.

Air India (Indian Airlines), **Jet Airways** and **Kingfisher** are full-service airlines and have the most comprehensive networks; budget carriers such as **Go Air**, **Indigo** and **Spicejet** serve major routes and charge for extras. During the winter, prepare for a 'congestion charge' on certain domestic routes, including Mumbai–Delhi.

Air India, Nariman Pt, T022-2202 3031, www.airindia.com, to all major cities. **Go Air**, T(0)9223-222111, T1800-222 111, www.goair.in. **Indigo**, T(0)9910-383838, T1800-180 3838, www.goindigo.in. **Jet Airways**, T022-3989 3333, www.jetairways.com. **Kingfisher**, T(0)9910-383838, www.flykingfisher.com. **Spicejet**, T1800-180 3333, T(0)9871-803333, www.spicejet.com.

International **Air India**, 1st floor, Nariman Pt (Counters also at Taj Mahal Hotel and airports), T022-2758 0777, airport T022-2615 6633. **Air Canada**, Amarchand Mansions, Madam Cama Rd, T022-2202 0597. **Air France**, Sarjan Plaza, 100 Annie Besant Rd, Worli, T022-2202 4818, airport T022-2682 8072. **British Airways**, 202-B Vulcan Ins Building, Vir Nariman Rd, T1800-1023 5922, Mon-Fri 0800-1300, 1345-1800. Sat 0900-1300. **Emirates**, Mittal Chamber, Nariman Pt, T022-4097 4097. **Gulf Air**, Maker Chambers, 5 Nariman Pt, T022-2202 1626. **Interglobe**, ground floor, Podar House, Sitaram D Marg, Marine Dr, T022 6137 0808, handles enquiries for China Eastern, Delta, SAS, South African, and United. **Japan**, Raheja Centre, Nariman Pt, T022-2283 3215. **KLM**, Sarjan Plaza, 100 Annie Besant Rd, Worli, T022-6685 9174. **Kuwait**, 9th floor, Nariman Bhavan, Nariman Point, T022-6655 5655. **Lufthansa**, Express Towers, Nariman Pt, T022-2682 9898. **PIA**, Mittal Towers, Nariman Pt, T022-2202 1598. **Qantas**, 4th floor, Sunteck Centre, 37-40 Subhash Rd, Vile Parle (East), T022-6111 1818. **Royal Jordanian**, Dalamal Tower, Nariman Point, T022-2202 2779. **Singapore Airlines**, Taj Intercontinental, T022-2202 2747. **Sri Lankan**, Raheja Centre, Nariman Pt, T022-2284 4148, airport T022-2832 7050. **Thai Airways**, 15 World Trade Centre, Cuffe Parade, T022-6637 3737.

Bus

Local Red **BEST** (Brihanmumbai Electrical Supply Co) buses are available in most parts of Greater Mumbai. There's a handy route finder at http://bestundertaking.com/transport/index.htm. Fares are cheap, but finding the correct bus is tricky as the numbers and destinations on the front are only in Marathi. English signs are displayed beside the back doors. Ask locals to help point out a bus going your way.

Long distance Maharashtra SRTC operates from the Mumbai Central Bus Stand, T022-2307 4272, http://msrtconline.in/timetable.aspx, to most major centres in the state as well as interstate destinations including **Ahmedabad**, **Bengaluru** (**Bangalore**), **Goa**, **Mangalore**, **Indore**, **Vadodara** and **Hyderabad**. Buses to **Nashik** and **Pune** leave from the more inconvenient stand on Senapati Bapat Marg, north of the centre in Dadar, T022-2430 2667.

Private buses also serve long-distance destinations: most leave from the streets surrounding Mumbai Central, where there are ticket agents, while others leave from Dadar; information and tickets from **Dadar Tourist Centre**, outside Dadar station, T022-2411 3398. The most popular company is **Neeta Volvo**, T022-2411 6114. Some private buses can be booked in advance on www.redbus.in.

Car

Costs for hiring a car are (for 8 hrs or 80 km): luxury a/c cars Rs 1500; Maruti/Ambassador, a/c Rs 1000, non-a/c Rs 800. Companies include: **Auto Hirers**, 7 Commerce Centre, Tardeo, T022-2494 2006. **Blaze**, Colaba, T022-2202 0073. **Budget**, T022-2494 2644, and **Sai**, Phoenix Mill Compound, Senapati Bapat Marg, Lower Parel, T022-2494 2644. Recommended. **NRI Services**, Chowpatty, T(0)98212-52287, www.nriservicesindia.com. **Wheels**, T022-2282 2874.

Auto-rickshaw

Not available in central Mumbai (south of Mahim). Metered; about Rs 9 per km, revised tariff card held by the driver, 25% extra at night (2400-0500). Some rickshaw drivers show the revised tariff card for taxis!

Taxi

Metered yellow-top cabs and more expensive a/c Cool Cabs are easily available. Meter rates are Rs 16 for the 1st kilometre and Rs 10 for each extra kilometre. Drivers should carry tariff cards that convert the meter fee into current prices; a new fleet of yellow-top Indica cars have digital meters that show the correct price. Always get a prepaid taxi at the airport.

A/c radio taxis can be pre-booked. They charge Rs 15 per km and provide metered receipts at the end of your journey. Tip the driver about 10 percent if you feel they had to do a lot of waiting. Megacab T022-4242 4242. **Meru Cab**, T022-4422 4422.

Train

Local Suburban electric trains are economical. They start from Churchgate for the western suburbs and **CST (VT)** for the east but are often desperately crowded; stay near the door or you may miss your stop. There are 'ladies' cars' in the middle and ends. Avoid peak hours (south-bound 0700-1100, northbound 1700-2000), and keep a tight hold on valuables. The difference between 1st and 2nd class is not always obvious although 1st class is 10 times as expensive. Inspectors fine people for travelling in the wrong class or without a ticket. If you're travelling frequently, invest in a smart card that lets you avoid queues at the ticket counter by printing tickets from a machine.

Long distance Times for trains are published each Sat in the *Indian Express* paper. Mumbai is the HQ of the **Central and Western Railways**, CST, enquiries, T134/135; reservations, T022-2265 9512, 0800-1230, 1300-1630 (Foreigners' Counter opens 0900; best time to go). **Western Railway**, at Churchgate and Mumbai Central, 0800-1345, 1445-2000. All stations have a Foreign Tourist counter for Indrail Passes and Foreign Tourist Quota bookings; bring your passport and an ATM receipt or encashment certificate.

The following depart from **CST** unless specified by these abbreviations: **Bandra** (**B**), **Central** (**C**), **Dadar** (**D**), **Lokmanya Tilak** (**LT**): **Ahmedabad** (all from Mumbai Central): *Shatabdi Exp 12009*, 0625, except Fri, 7 hrs; *Karnavati Exp 12933*,1340, except Wed, 7¾ hrs; *Saurashtra Mail 19005*, 2025, 9 hrs; *Gujarat Mail 12901*, 2150, 9 hrs. **Allahabad**: *Kolkata Mail 12322*, 2125, 23½ hrs; *Mahanagari Exp 11093*, 2355, 24¼ hrs. **Agra Cantonment**: *Punjab Mail 12137*, 1910, 21½ hrs. **Aurangabad** (for **Ajanta** and **Ellora**): *Tapovan Exp 17617*, 0610, 7½ hrs; *Devgiri Exp 17057*, 1205, 7½ hrs. **Bengaluru** (**Bangalore**): *Udyan Exp 16529*, 0755, 24¾ hrs; *Coimbatore Exp 11013*, 2220 (**LT**), 23¾ hrs. **Bhopal**: *Pushpak Exp 12133*, 0810, 14 hrs; *Punjab Mail, 12137*, 1910, 14 hrs. **Chennai**: *Dadar Chennai Exp 11063*, 2020 (**D**), 23¾ hrs; *Chennai Exp 11041*, 1400, 26¾ hrs. **Ernakulam** (**Kochi**): *Netravati Exp 16345*, 2300 (**LT**), 29½ hrs. **Guntakal** (for **Hospet/Hampi**): *Dadar Chennai Exp 11063*, 2020 (**D**), 15 hrs; *Udyan Exp 16529*, 0755, 16¾ hrs; *Coimbatore Exp 11013*, 2220 (**LT**), 16¼ hrs; *Kanniyakumari Exp 11081*, 1535, 17¾ hrs. **Gwalior**: *Punjab Mail 12137*, 1910, 19¾ hrs. **Hyderabad**: *Hussainsagar Exp 17001*, 2155, 15¼ hrs; *Hyderabad Exp 17031*, 1235, 17½ hrs. **Kolkata** (**Howrah**): *Gitanjali Exp 12859*, 0600, 33 hrs; *Howrah Mail 18001*, 2015, 35½ hrs. **Lucknow**: *Pushpak Exp 12133*, 0810, 25½ hrs.

Madgaon (for **Goa**): The day train is a good option, the night service is heavily booked. Special trains during the winter high season. *Mandavi Exp 10103*, 0515, 11 hrs; *Konkan Kanya Exp 10111*, 2240, 12 hrs; *Netravati Exp 16345*, 1140, 13½ hrs (**LT**). **New Delhi**: *Rajdhani Exp 12951*, 1655 (**C**), 17 hrs; *Golden Temple Mail 12903*, 2130 (**C**), 21½ hrs; *August Kranti Rajdhani Exp 12953*, 1740 (**C**), 17¼ hrs (to Hazrat Nizamuddin). **Pune**: deluxe trains *Shatabdi Exp 12027*, 0640, 3½ hrs; *Deccan Queen Exp 12123*, 1710, 3½ hrs, among many. **Thiruvananthapuram**: *Netravati Exp 16345*, 1140 (**LT**), 35 hrs. **Ujjain**: *Avantika Exp 12961*, 1925 (**C**), 12½ hrs. **Varanasi**: *Lokmanya Tilak Varanasi Exp 12165*, 0520 (**LT**), Mon, Thu, Sat, 26 hrs; *Muzaffarpur/ Darbanga Exp 11061*, 1215 (**LT**), 27¼ hrs.

Directory

Mumbai *p1157, maps p1159, p1161 and p1164*

Banks ATMS are now ubiquitous in all parts of the city, including at the airports and stations, and most take foreign cards. For other services, branches open Mon-Fri 1000-1400, Sat 1000-1200. It's more efficient to change money at the airport, or at specialist agents, eg **Bureau de Change**, upstairs in Air

India Building, Nariman Pt; **Thomas Cook**, 324 Dr DN Rd, T022-2204 8556; also at 102B Maker Tower, 10th floor, F Block, Cuffe Pde, Colaba. **Credit cards American Express**, Oriental Bldg, 364 Dr DN Rd; **Diners Club**, Raheja Chambers, 213 Nariman Pt; **MasterCard**, C Wing, Mittal Tower, Nariman Pt; **Visa**, Standard Chartered Grindlays Bank, 90 MG Rd, Fort. **Embassies and consulates Australia**, 36 Maker Chambers VI, Nariman Point, T022-6116 7100. **Austria**, Maker Chambers VI, Nariman Pt, T022-2285 1066. **France**, Datta Prasad, NG Cross Rd, T022-2495 0918. **Canada**, 6th floor, 221 Dr DN Rd, T022-6749 4444. **Germany**, 10th floor, Hoechst House, Nariman Pt, T022-2283 2422. **Indonesia**, 19 Altamount Rd, T022-2386 8678. **Israel**, 50 Deshmukh Marg, Kailas, T022-2386 2794. **Italy**, Kanchenjunga, 72G Deshmukh Marg, T022-2380 4071. **Japan**, 1 ML Dahanukar Marg, T022-2493 4310. **Malaysia**, Rahimtoola House, Homji St, T022-2266 0056. **Netherlands**, 1 Marine Lines Cross Rd, Churchgate, T022-2201 6750. **Philippines** , Sekhar Bhavan, Nariman Pt, T022-2281 4103. **Spain**, 6 K Dubash Marg, T022-2287 4797. **Sri Lanka**, 34 Homi Modi St, T022-2204 5861. **Sweden**, 85 Sayani Rd, Prabhadevi, T022- 2421 2681. **Thailand**, 43 B Desai Rd, T022- 2363 1404. **UK**, Naman Chambers, C/32 G Block, Bandra Kurla Complex, Bandra (E), T022-6650 2222. **USA**, Lincoln House, B Desai Rd, T022-2363 3611 (24 hrs). **Emergencies** **Ambulance** T102. **Fire** T101. **Police** T100. **Internet** Internet cafés are increasingly strict about demanding photo ID. There are several on the back streets of Colaba near Leopold Café: **I-way**, corner of Colaba Causeway and Barrow Rd (near Kamat restaurant), has many terminals and fast access; you must first register as a member but it's well worth it, and there are branches throughout India. **Infotek**, Express Towers, ground floor, Nariman Pt. **British Council**, A Wing, 1st floor, Mittal Tower, Nariman Pt, T022-2282 3560, 1000-1745, Tue-Sat. **Cybercafé**, Waterfield, Bandra, enjoy coffee and cake while you surf, take government- issued ID to access free Wi-Fi; a number of bars and cafés now offer Wi-Fi access free or by prepaid voucher, including **Woodside Inn**, opposite Regal Cinema, Colaba, and **Banyan Tree Café and Bakery**, opposite Podar Hospital, Worli (north of Haji Ali), T022-6452 7222. **Medical services** The larger hotels usually have a house doctor, the others invariably have a doctor on call. Ask hotel staff for prompt action. The telephone directory lists hospitals and GPs. Admission to private hospitals may not be allowed without a large cash advance (eg Rs 50,000). Insurers' guarantees may not be sufficient. **Prince Aly Khan Hospital**, Nesbit Rd near the harbour, T022-2377 7800/900, Jaslok Hospital on Peddar Rd, T022-6657 3333; Hinduja Hospital T022-2444-0431; Lilavati Hospital in Bandra (W), T022-2642 1111 are recommended. Chemists: several open day/ night especially opposite Bombay Hospital. **Wordell**, Stadium House, Churchgate; **New Royal Chemist**, New Marine Lines. **Post** Nagar Chowk, Mon-Sat 0900-2000 (Poste Restante facilities 0900-1800) and Sun 1000-1730; parcels from 1st floor, rear of building, Mon-Sat 1000-1700; cheap 'parcelling' service on pavement outside; Colaba PO, Henry Rd, 2 blocks south of Taj Mahal. Counter at Domestic airport. **Useful contacts Commissioner's Office**, Dr DN Rd, near Phule Market. **Foreigners' Regional Registration Office**, 3rd floor, Special Branch Building, Badruddin Tayabji Lane, Behind St Xaviers College, T022-2262 1169. **Passport office**, T022-2493 1731.

Chaul, Kihim and Alibag beaches → *For listings, see pages 1185-1186.*

A group of Moorish and Portuguese forts lie to the south at the mouth of Mumbai harbour. **Chaul** was taken in 1522 by the Portuguese. Similar to Bassein with a very attractive fort, it never equalled it in importance. The Marathas took it in 1739 and in 1818 it passed into British hands. Little remains of the settlement apart from ruined churches and broken walls. If you look across the creek you will see the hilltop Muslim fort of Korlai. The clean beach, safe waters and very pleasant surroundings make **Kihim** very attractive but the summer sun can be murderously hot. The beach is muddy at **Alibag** and it is possible to walk across to the fort at low tide but it is not worth the Rs 100 entrance fee. If you decide to stay, there are a few places on Kihim Beach.

Kanheri Caves → *For listings, see pages 1185-1186.*

Sanjay Gandhi National Park, north of the city at Goregaon, is worth a visit in itself for its dense deciduous and semi-evergreen forest providing a beautiful habitat for several varieties of deer, antelope, butterflies, birds and the occasional leopard. However, the main reason for visiting is for the **Kanheri Caves** situated in the heart of the park.

Some 42 km north of Mumbai, the caves (also known as Mahakali Caves) are on a low hill midway between Borivli and Thane. The hills used to form the central part of Salsette Island, but the surrounding land has long since been extensively built on. Further up the ravine from the caves there are some fine views across the Bassein Fort and out to sea. Still shaded by trees, the entrance is from the south. There are 109 Buddhist caves, dating from the end of the second to the ninth century AD with flights of steps joining them. The most significant is the **Chaitya Cave** (cave 3) circa sixth century. The last Hinayana chaitya hall to be excavated is entered through a forecourt and veranda. The pillared entrance has well carved illustrations of the donors, and the cave itself comprises a 28 m x 13 m colonnaded hall of 34 pillars. At one end these encircle the 5-m-high *dagoba*. Some of the pillars have carvings of elephants and trees. Fifty metres up the ravine is **Darbar of the Maharajah Cave** (Cave 10). This was a *dharamshala* (resthouse) and has two stone benches running down the sides and some cells leading off the left and back walls. Above Cave 10 is **Cave 35** which was a *vihara* (monastery), which has reliefs of a Buddha seated on a lotus and of a disciple spreading his cloak for him to walk on. All the caves have an elaborate drainage and water storage system, fresh rainwater being led into underground storage tanks.

Above the cave complex is **Ashok Van**, a sacred grove of ancient trees, streams and springs. From there, a three-hour trek leads to 'View Point', the highest in Mumbai. There are breathtaking views. Photography is prohibited from the radar station on top of the hill; there are excellent opportunities just below it.

The park is also home to hyena and panther, though rarely seen, while three lakes have ducks, herons and crocodiles. Nature trails lead from Film City (reached by bus from Goregaon station). A lion safari leaves from **Hotel Sanjay** near Borivli station.

North Konkan → *For listings, see pages 1185-1186. Colour map 5, B2/3.*

The undulating lowland of the North Konkan coast forms a narrow strip between the Arabian Sea and the often daunting west facing slopes of the Ghats. There are occasional good beaches, scattered mangrove swamps, and rice growing valleys, interspersed with poor laterite covered hills. The beaches to the north, a two-hour journey away, make them a popular getaway from Mumbai, although foreign tourists are virtually unheard of. The beaches can't compare to those of Goa or Kerala and litter and other debris is all too evident.

Bassein (Vasai)

Bassein, at the mouth of the Ulhas River on the mainland, is 60 km north of central Mumbai. Due to silting, the fort on the Bassein Creek is now some distance from the sea. The structure is in ruins, but it is well worth walking round the sea face. Originally built by Bahadur Shah, Sultan of Gujarat, it was one of a chain of forts against the Portuguese. However, the chain was breached, and the Portuguese remodelled the city along their own lines, renaming it **Vasai**. From 1534 to 1739 it became so prosperous as a centre of shipbuilding and the export of Bassein stone that it was called the Court of the North. As a walled city it contained a cathedral, five convents, 13 churches and the splendid houses and palaces of the aristocracy, or Hidalgos, who with members of the religious orders, alone were allowed to live within the walls. The Marathas took Vasai in February 1739 after a long and desperate siege. Almost the whole Portuguese garrison, 800 strong, was killed in the battle; the Marathas are thought to have lost 5000 men. In 1780 the British evicted the Marathas, only to return it to them three years later under the Treaty of Salbai.

Approached from the north, the fort in the town contains the ruins of St Joseph's Cathedral (1536), St Anthony's, the Jesuit church and the convents, all belonging to Franciscans, Dominicans, Jesuits or Augustinians. **Nalasopara**, 10 km northwest, is the ancient Konkan capital where Buddhist relics have been found.

The Ghats → *For listings, see pages 1185-1186.* *Colour map 5, B3.*

The Ghats represent an historic divide between the outward looking coastal lowlands with the trading centre of Mumbai at their hub, and the much drier interior, a battle ground of successive Indian dynasties. Today the hilltops are littered with fortified sites, while hill stations offer weekend breaks to Mumbai's elite. The routes through the Western Ghats from Mumbai climb to nearly 1600 m through the forested slopes, particularly beautiful before the end of the rains in September when wild flowers are everywhere, and rivers and waterfalls are full. Road travel is often disrupted in the rains, but the railways through the Ghats are spectacular. On the Nashik route alone the line passes through 10 tunnels, over five viaducts and 11 bridges, while the line between Neral and Lonavla passes through stunning countryside of ravines countryside, the line has gradients of one in 37 to overcome problems posed by 'the big step' the hills presented.

Matheran → *Colour map 5, B3. Phone code: 021483. Population: 6000. Altitude: 785 m.*

Mumbai's nearest hill station, in an extension of the Sahyadri Range, Matheran (meaning 'Mother Forest' or 'Wooded Head') has stunning views, refreshingly cool air and pleasant walks. Though very much geared towards the Mumbai weekend crowd, it maintains its unique sense of quiet by banning all forms of motor vehicles within the town. A visit is recommended, but stay a night as it is too strenuous to do in a day from Mumbai. Check road conditions before planning a trip in the monsoons. Limited tourist information is available from the MTDC Resort ⓘ *3 km uphill from the centre in Dasturi Naka, T02148-230540.*

The town sprawls out along a north-south ridge and there are splendid views down the almost sheer hillsides to the valleys below. The best views are from Little Chouk, Louisa and Porcupine, which is also known as **Sunset Point**. Allow one hour to walk and see the stunning sunsets. From the northernmost vantage points you can see the lights of Mumbai on a clear night. The layout of the town conforms with standard British Hill Station planning with central civic buildings and dispersed bungalows. You can sightsee on horseback here.

The most scenic route for this diversion is by the spectacular light railway through the ghats from Neral, which is closed during the monsoon. You will appreciate the problems facing the early railway engineers here (see box, above). The steam engines are no longer used after working the route for 77 years but you will see one proudly displayed at the station.

India's first railway line

The opening of India's first railway line from Mumbai to Thane in 1853 prepared the route through the Ghats to the Deccan Plateau. Mumbai became the hub of regional and international trade. Victoria Terminus (CST now) was the product of a magnificent era of railway building at the end of the 19th century when the British Raj was striding confidently towards the 20th century.

With the disappearance of the East India Company after the Mutiny, the Government of India took over the responsibility for running the railways. On 16 April 1853 the first train made its run from Mumbai along 32 km of line to Thane. Subsequent advances were rapid but often incredible natural obstacles presented great challenges to the railway builders. The 263-km line to Surat encountered 18 rivers and some of the foundations for the bridges had to be driven 45 m in to the ground to cope with the monsoon floodwaters.

Vajreshwari, Akloli and Ganeshpuri

Some 81 km northeast of Mumbai, **Vajreshwari** is renowned for its temple, built by the Maratha warrior Chamiji Appa after hammering the Portuguese at Bassein, but even more so for the **Akloli hot springs**, which pour into an unattractive collection of concrete tanks beside the river Tansa. There are more springs, quieter than those at Akloli, 2 km away in **Ganeshpuri** – locals claim to be able to boil rice in one of the tanks. The village is full of temples, including one to the 20th-century sage Nityanand, who established the nearby **Shri Gurudev Ashram**, a popular destination for foreign seekers.

Around Mumbai listings

For Sleeping and Eating price codes and other relevant information, see Essentials pages 38-42.

Sleeping

Matheran *p1184*

Budget hotels near the station can be very noisy. Prices often include meals and rise considerably during holidays (eg **Diwali**) but most offer good off-season discounts.

LL-L Usha Ascot, MG Rd, T02148-230360, www.ushaascot.com. 64 rooms, most a/c, pool, sauna, tennis courts, health club, disco.

LL-AL The Byke, T02148-230365, www.thebyke.com. Good pool, 46 comfortable rooms, 5 a/c, great restaurants (pure vegetarian only).

AL-A Lord's Central, MG Marg, T02148-230228, www.matheranhotels.com. Perched on a ridge with excellent views, 23 colonial-style rooms in 4 bungalows ('Valley' room best), restaurant (meals included), bar, pool, park, riding, friendly. Recommended.

C Royal, Kasturba Bhavan, T02148-230247. Health club, 61 rooms, 5 a/c, restaurant, bar.

C-D Alexander, Alexander Pt, T02148-230069. In unspoilt woodland, 24 rooms, 3 a/c, good restaurant.

C-D Holiday Camp (MTDC), 30 mins uphill from centre 1 km before Matheran (train stops at camp), T02148-230540. 39 rooms cottages, for 2-4, and dorm, limited catering.

E Girivihar, Shivaji Rd, T02148-230231. Quiet, spacious gardens, some rooms with balconies.

E Hope Hall, MG Marg (opposite Lord's Central), T02148-230253. Good-sized, clean rooms with bath (bucket hot water), friendly family, pleasant location.

E Prasanna, opposite railway station, T02148-230258. Restaurant, 10 small, clean rooms.

Eating

Matheran *p1184*

Kwality Fruit Juice House, MG Rd, south of the train station among many. Excellent honey and *chikki* (a sweet peanut brittle).

Woodlands, Chinoy Rd. Indian.

Activities and tours

Elephanta Caves *p1181*

MTDC, T022-2284 5678, launches with good guides leave the Gateway of India every 30 mins 0900-1500 (last one leaves Elephanta at 1730) except during the monsoon (Jun- Sep). The pleasant journey takes 1-1½ hrs Rs 80-100 return). The higher fare is for 'deluxe' boats with an open upper deck. However, the boat boys demand extra payment to sit on top! Small private boats without guides continue during the monsoon when the seas can be very rough.

Kanheri Caves *p1183*

MTDC tours from Mumbai; or by train to Borivli station (from Mumbai Central, 30 mins). From there, by taxi or auto-rickshaw (10 km), or by bus on Sun and public holidays.

Transport

Chaul, Kihim and Alibag beaches *p1183*

From the **New Ferry Wharf** at the Gateway of India in Mumbai, it is a 90-min trip to **Mandwa** (Rs 60-110) then a 6-km bus or auto ride to **Kihim**; or 30-km bus ride to **Chaul**.

Bassein (Vasai) *p1184*

Trains go from **Mumbai Central** to Vasai Rd station, then hire a taxi for 11 km.

Matheran *p1184*

From Neral, south of Kalyan, the narrow gauge train takes 2 hrs to cover the 21 km to Matheran. The station is in the town centre. A tax (Rs 25) is charged on arrival (pay before leaving the station). It's best to book in advance; essential on weekends. Sit on the right on the way up for the best views; 1st class window seats are Nos 1, 4, 5, 8. From **Neral**, trains depart daily at 0730, 0850, 1015, 1135 and 1705 (also 1410 on weekends). From **Matheran**, depart 0700, 0945, 1340, 1445, 1625 (also 1740 on weekends). To reach Neral from Mumbai CST, take a Pune-bound express train to **Karjat**, and backtrack on one of the regular local trains, or a 'fast' local train direct to Neral. The *Deccan Exp 11007* at 0710; *Koyna Exp 17307* at 0845; From **Pune** *Sahyadri Exp* at 0730. Taxis to Matheran can go no further than the MTDC Resort in Dasturi Naka, from where you can walk (porters available for luggage) or take a hand-pulled rickshaw.

Directory

Matheran *p1184*

Post office and tourist office opposite railway station. **Union Bank of India**, MG Rd, changes TCs and cash, poor rate; also **Hotel Prasanna**.

Northwest Maharashtra

The holy site of Nashik lies at the head of the Godavari River and is one of the locations of the 12-yearly Kumbh Mela. But the 'Ganges of the Deccan' has also watered a fast-growing city, as well as the vineyard of popular Indian winemaker Sula. Caves of ancient Buddhist relics lie just outside town. The town that was host to wartime British transfer camps, Deolali, from whose sanatoria we've gained the expression 'doolally', is nearby. ▸▸ *For listings, see pages 1189-1189.*

Nashik (Nasik)

→ *For listings, see page 1189.* *Colour map 5, A3. Phone code: 0253. Population: 1.08 million.*

Nashik, an unprepossessing mixture of featureless market town, pilgrim centre and sprawling modern industrial estates, nonetheless has an old city area near the ghats with characteristic traditional buildings. It is one of Hinduism's most holy sites, taking its sanctity from its position on the headwaters of the Godavari River. It commands the strategic route from northwestern India to the southern Deccan.

Ins and outs

Getting there and around Trains arrive at Nasik Road Station, 7 km south of town. City buses run to town (Rs 5), stopping at Shalimar Circle, three minutes' walk from the Central Bus Stand (CBS) at the town centre; otherwise auto-rickshaws and taxis are around. Buses arrive from Aurangabad at the CBS, close to the budget hotels. Mumbai buses use the Mahamarga Bus Stand, a few kilometres from the centre, where you can get an auto; trains from Mumbai are a faster and better option. Buses to local places of interest use the CBS but a few people speak English in case you need to ask the way. ▸▸ *See Transport, page 1189.*

Tourist information MTDC ⓘ *T/1 Golf Club, Old Agra Rd, T0253-257 0059. Sightseeing 0730-1500, Rs 80.*

Sights

Nashik shares the **Kumbh Mela** with Ujjain, Haridwar and Allahabad (see page 182) and every 12 years millions of pilgrims converge on the Godavari River (sometimes referred to as the 'Ganga of the Deccan'), to bathe; Nashik will next host the event in 2015. The Godavari, which rises 30 km away at Trimbak, is believed to have a common underground source with the Ganga itself. In the last 10 years Nashik has been one of India's fastest growing cities, but the town itself is undoubtedly ancient, and Ghose suggests that it has an unbroken history of over 2500 years. At Pandu Lena (see below), within a few kilometres of the town centre, palaeolithic settlements have been discovered. Chalcolithic pottery has been found at Gangawadi, 15 km northwest of Nashik. Other finds date from the fifth century BC up to the first century AD and Roman pottery has been found in the third period level. However, none of Nashik's temples are very old. The Vaishnavite **Sundar Narayana Temple** (1756) on the west bank has three black Vishnu images. The **Ramesvara Temple** (18th century) is where Rama is believed to have carried out the funeral rites for his father and to have bathed in the **Rama Kund** nearby. It is a popular place to throw ashes of the dead into the river. The banyan-shaded **Sita Gupha** cave on the east side of town is where Rama's wife hid from Ravana the demon. Nearby is the **Kala** (black) **Rama Temple** (1782) which has a 25-m-high *shikhara*.

In recent years Nashik has emerged as the centre of India's burgeoning wine industry, with locally produced Shiraz and Sauvignon Blanc from vineyards such as Chateau Indage and Sula are becoming a fixture on wine lists both in Indian metros and internationally, and the vineyards are attempting to capitalise by promoting Napa-esque wine tourism, with architect-designed tasting rooms, vineyard tours, and ever-more indulgent resorts and restaurants. The pick of the tasting tours is at Sula, an eco-sensitive vineyard a 40-minute drive west of the city centre (Govardhan Village, off Gangapur-Savargaon road, T0253-223 1663, www.sulawines.com; tours and tasting sessions every hour 1130-1730, Rs 150).

Around Nashik

Pandu Lena

Some 8 km southwest of Nashik there is a group of 24 rock cut Buddhist monuments on a hillock, the earliest dating from the first century BC. They include over 20 caves. Some have excellent carving, particularly on the exterior doorways. **Cave 3** has 19 monastic cells, a carved Buddha decorates the rear of **Cave 10**, while the exterior of the early **Cave 18**, a *chaitya* (chapel), is finely decorated.

Deolali, 7 km southeast, was the transfer camp for British soldiers going home during the two world wars. To go 'Doolally Tap' was to go crazy with boredom waiting there. A mental hospital accommodated these casualties.

Trimbak

The town of Trimbak, 30 km west of Nashik, is centred around the beautiful **Gangasagar Tank**. About 690 steps lead up the hill behind Trimbak to the source of the Godavari itself where you get good views. The town is partly surrounded by a fantastic semi-circle of hills, topped by a near vertical scarp. **Trimbakeshwar Temple**, an 18th-century Siva sanctuary with a *jyotirlinga*, is a pilgrimage site. In February/March a large fair is held; the important **Sinhastha Fair** takes place every 12 years. There is a simple hotel here. **Prayag Tirth**, on the road to Trimbak, has a beautiful stone-lined tank with two temples. Further on near **Anjaneri**, two 300-m-high conical hills are on either side of the road, sweeping round in a broad arc behind the town of Trimbak. Hourly buses from Nashik take about 45 minutes.

Igatpuri

The 'Town of Difficulties' is on top of the plateau at the end of the ghat section of railway. **Kalsubai** (1540 m), the highest mountain in Maharashtra, is visible to the south. About 1 km beyond the town the road passes the end of the beautiful **Beale Lake**. The town is now best known as home to the **Vipassana International Academy** ⓘ *PO Box 6, Dhammagiri, T02553-244076*, which offers austere, deeply challenging but highly regarded 10-day silent meditation retreats.

Jawhar

The former capital of a tribal kingdom, Jawhar is noted for its *warli* paintings. Rice paste or poster colours are used to decorate the hut walls. **Jai Vilas**, the palace (ask locally to visit) and **Bhupatgad**, the fort, still show evidence of the tribal kingdom, while there are attractive waterfalls at Dadar Kopra.

Northwest Maharashtra listings

For Sleeping and Eating price codes and other relevant information, see Essentials pages 38-42.

Sleeping

Nashik *p1187*

Cheap rooms are hard to come by.

LL-L Gateway (Taj), P-17 MIDC Ambad, Mumbai-Agra Rd (14 km from Nasik Rd station, 6 km from city), T0253-660 4499, www.tajhotels.com. Well-equipped business hotel in large grounds, with stylishly light and airy rooms, Wi-Fi and pool.

LL Beyond, Sula Vineyards, T0253-223 0141, www.sulawines.com. Smart and elegant rooms set around a large pool, with great views across the vines to a lake. Kayaking and cycling tours available, and buffet meals included.

C-D Panchavati Elite, Trimbak Rd, near Vinod Auto, T0253-257 9031. 26 rooms, some a/c, restaurants (**Kwality, Coffee House**) and a cheaper guesthouse.

C-D Rama Heritage, next to Kalika Mandir, Mumbai Naka, T0253-258 2887, www.hotelramaheritage.com. Small and efficient business hotel, with plain but very clean rooms, Wi-Fi and good restaurant. Good value.

D Panchavati Yatri, 430 Vakil Wadi, T0253-257 2290. Well run and efficient, 41 rooms, 30 a/c rooms (cold showers), good Gujarati *thali* restaurant, bar, coffee shop, Recommended.

D-F Green View, 1363 Trimbak Rd, T0253-2572231. Quiet, garden, 24 rooms, 14 a/c, restaurant.

E Siddharth, Nashik Pune Rd, 2 km towards airport, T0253-257 3288. Pleasant garden, 32 rooms, some **D** a/c. Good veg restaurant.

E-F Pushkaraj, near Shalimar City Bus Stop, T0253-250 2598. Restaurant, 30 rooms, helpful.

E-F Rajmahal, opposite the bus stand, T0253-258 0501. Friendly, clean, 28 roooms.

F Mazda, Old Agra Rd, 5-min walk from CBS, T0253-259 5009. Basic rooms with bath, café.

Eating

Nashik *p1187*

The best restaurants are in hotels, especially the **Taj Residency** and **Panchavati** hotels, for Indian vegetarian.

Anand, MG Rd. Fast food.

Annapoorna Lunch House, MG Rd. Breakfast and South Indian dishes.

Dairy Don, MG Rd. Ice creams.

Nindinee Woodlands, Nashik Pune Rd (opposite **Siddhartha hotel**). Recommended for South Indian vegetarian and coffee.

Shilpa Hotel, MG Rd. Excellent Gujarati *thalis*.

Activities and tours

Nashik *p1187*

Best to book tours in advance the evening before at CBS. Nashik Darshan tours start from the Central Bus Stand (CBS) 0730-1700, Rs 90 (includes Hindi guide). Visits Pandu Lena, Bhaktidham, Kala Ram Mandir/Sita Gupha, Tapovan, Muktidham (lunch), Ved Mandir, Somneshwar, Trimbak; good value, well-timed, although the hour's stop at Trimbak is too short to see the source of the Godavari, and non-Hindus are not allowed inside the temple. Possible to leave the tour at this point and return to Nashik by bus or share taxi.

Transport

Nashik *p1187*

Bus/taxi

Regular buses to **Mumbai** (Dadar), 6 hrs, from the **Mahamarg Bus Stand** south of the centre; share taxis are available as far as Thane, from where local trains run into central Mumbai. For **Aurangabad** and **Pune**, buses depart from the **New Central Stand**, 5 hrs.

Train

Nasik Rd station is 8 km southeast of the centre. Local buses and shared taxis for transfer to town. City booking counter off MG Rd, Mon-Fri 1000-1700. **Mumbai (CST)**: *Tapovan Exp 17618*, 1800, 4 hrs; *Panchavati Exp 12110*, 0700, 4 hrs; many others scheduled throughout the day. **Delhi (ND)**: *Punjab Mail 12137*, 2325, 24 hrs, via **Bhopal**, 10 hrs, and **Agra**, 19 hrs/ **Jalgaon** (for Ajanta Caves), *Sewagram Exp 12139*, 1835, 3½ hrs.

Directory

Nashik *p1187*

Banks **State Bank of India**, Old Agra Rd, has an ATM and can change currency.

Central Maharashtra

The splendid carved volcanic caves (Hindu, Jain and Buddhist) at Ellora and Ajanta, dating from the sixth and second centuries AD respectively, are among India's finest sights, including monasteries, meditation chambers, cloisters, chapels and colonnaded halls gouged from rock, graced with friezes and shrines. The triumphant Kailasanatha Temple is the star of Ellora. Ajanta's exquisite craftsmanship – Buddha's story etched into a sheer cliff face – was nearly lost to the world, lying hidden under dense jungle from the seventh to the 19th century. Aurangabad, Mughal ruler Aurangzeb's military headquarters during his Deccan campaign, is a spacious town to base yourself en route to the caves. ▸▸ *For listings, see pages 1203-1206.*

Aurangabad →

For listings, see pages 1203-1206. *Colour map 5, A5. Phone code: 0240. Population: 872,700.*

A pleasantly spacious town, Aurangabad is the most common starting point for visiting the superb caves at Ellora and Ajanta. The gates are all that is left of the old city walls. There is a university, medical and engineering colleges and an airport to complement the town's industrial and commercial activities.

Ins and outs

Getting there and around Chikalthana airport is 10 km east of the town with taxis (Rs 250, a/c Rs 350) or hotel transport into the town centre. The railway station is on the southern edge of town, within walking distance of most hotels and the Central Bus Stand just under 2 km north on Dr Ambedkar Road. The city is easy to navigate. There are plenty of autos to see the sights, most of which are too scattered to see on foot. ▸▸ *See Transport, page 1205.*

Tourist information **India Tourism** ⓘ *Krishna Vilas, Station Rd, T0240-236 4999, Mon-Fri 0830-1830, Sat 0830-1330; airport counter open at flight times.* **MTDC** ⓘ *TRC Bldg, Station Rd, T0240-233 4259; also at railway station, 0430-0830, 1100-1600, Tue-Sun 0900-1600.*

History

Originally known as Khadke, the town was founded in 1610 by Malik Ambar, an Abyssinian slave who became the *wazir* (prime minister) to the King of Ahmadnagar. It was later changed to Aurangabad in honour of the last great Mughal, Aurangzeb. His wife is buried in the Bibi ka Maqbara and he is buried in a simple grave at Rauza. It acted as the centre of operations for his Deccan campaign which occupied him for the second half of his 49-year reign.

Sights

The British **cantonment** area is in the southwest quadrant, along the Kham River and can be seen on the way to Ellora. The old Holy Trinity church is in very poor condition. To the northwest is the **Begampura** district in which there is the attractive Pan23 Chakki water mill and the Bibi ka Maqbara, both worth visiting.

Aurangzeb built the 4.5-m-high crenellated city walls in 1682 as defence against the Marathas. **Killa Arrak** (1692), his citadel, lay between the Delhi and Mecca Gates. Little remains, though when it was Aurangzeb's capital over 50 maharajahs and princes attended the court. With Aurangzeb gone, the city's significance faded. At the centre in a grove of trees lies the **Jama Masjid**, a low building with minarets and a broad band carved with Koranic inscriptions running the length of the façade.

Other interesting monuments include: **Kali Masjid** (1600), a six-pillared stone mosque built by Malik Ambar; **Shahganj Masjid** (circa 1720) in the market square with shops on three sides; **Chauk Masjid** (1665), built by Shayista Khan, Aurangzeb's uncle, with five domes; and **Lal Masjid** (1655) in red-painted basalt. The **City Chowk** is worth visiting.

Aurangabad

Sleeping
Ajinkya **1**
Bagga International **2**
Devpriya **3**
Holiday Camp (MTDC) **4**
Khemi's Inn **15**
Lemon Tree **5**
Panchavati **11**
Printravel **6**
Residency (Taj) **8**
Shree Maya **7**
The Meadows **10**
Tourist Home **9**

Eating
Angeethi **6**
Bhoj **1**
Chanakya **5**
Foodwalla's Tandoori **2**
Mingling **3**
Palace **4**

Bibi ka Maqbara ⓘ *sunrise to 2000, foreigners Rs100, Indians Rs 5, floodlit at night*, beyond the Mecca Gate, is the mausoleum of Aurangzeb's wife, Rabia Daurani (1678). The classic lines of a garden tomb give it an impressive setting. However, it is less impressive close up. Modelled on the Taj Mahal, which was completed 25 years earlier, it is about half its size. Far less money was spent (one three hundredth by some estimates) and the comparative poverty of the finish is immediately obvious. It uses marble on the bottom 2 m of the mausoleum and four of the *jali* screens, but plaster elsewhere. The proportions are cramped and the minarets are too heavy in relation to the main mausoleum. Despite its failings it is one of the finest buildings of its period. The brass door carries an inscription which says Ata Ullah was the chief architect and Haibat Rai the maker of the door. On the tomb itself, in place of a marble slab, there is bare earth covered with a decorated cloth, a sign of humility. Light enters through a precisely angled shaft, allowing the early morning sun's rays to light the tomb for three minutes. The second tomb in the corner is said to be that of Rabia Daurani's nurse.

On the same side of the river is the **Pan Chakki** (1696) ⓘ *sunrise to 2000, Rs 5, refreshments*, which has a white marble shrine to Baba Shah Muzaffar, the devout Aurangzeb's spiritual adviser. The pre-Mughal 17th-century water mill for turning large grinding stones was powered by water channelled from a spring some distance away and released through a dam.

Aurangabad Caves

ⓘ *3 km north of Aurangabad, sunrise to sunset, foreigners Rs100, Indians Rs 5.*

The Aurangabad Caves are very interesting though not a substitute for Ajanta and Ellora. Overlooking the town they fall into two groups of five each, about 1.5 km apart. They date from the Vakataka (fourth and fifth centuries AD) and Kalachuri dynasties (sixth to eighth centuries), though the older Hinayana Cave 4 is believed to be at least first century, if not earlier. Waiting charges for auto-rickshaws can be high – bargain. Or, if it is cool and you are fit, you can walk back to the edge of town and get an auto-rickshaw back.

The **Western Group** are all *viharas* except for the earlier Cave 4 which is a *chaitya*. Cave 1 (incomplete) has finely carved pillars with ornamentation around doorways and walls and figures on brackets. Cave 2 has a shrine and columned hallways, a large Buddha and intricately carved panels. The larger Cave 3 has a plain exterior but superb carvings on 12 pillars of the hallway; the sanctuary has panels illustrating *jataka* stories and a fine large Buddha figure on his throne with attendant devotees illustrating contemporary dress and style. Cave 4, the *chaitya* has a rib-vaulted ceiling with a *stupa* containing relics and a Buddha figure outside. Cave 5 is damaged and retains little of its original carvings.

The **Eastern Group** has more sculptures of women and Bodhisattvas. Cave 6 has a large Buddha supporting Ganesh, indicating a later period when Hinduism was gaining in importance over Buddhism. Note the paintings on the ceiling of the balcony. Cave 7 is regarded as the most interesting of both groups. Columned shrines at each end of the veranda house images of Hariti (right) and six goddesses, including Padmini (left). The central shrine has an ambulatory passage around it and a large preaching Buddha at the back. The wall carvings depict deliverance and numerous female dancers and musicians. The importance of Tara and of Tantric Buddhism is evident here. There is little to see in the unfinished Cave 9; the carvings of pre-Nirvana figures suggest Buddhism was waning. The incomplete Cave 10 illustrates the first stages of cave excavation.

Daulatabad → *For listings, see pages 1203-1206. Colour map 5, A4.*

Thirteen kilometres from Aurangabad is the fort of Deogiri on a volcanic lava rock towering 250 m above the surrounding countryside. The fort dates from the Yadava period of the 11th-14th centuries although the first fort had probably been built in the ninth century. Before that it had been a Buddhist monastery. It is an extraordinary site, particularly attractive in the late

Deogiri fortifications

The hillside around Deogiri was made steeper to make scaling the fort extremely difficult. The three concentric walls had strong gates, surrounded by a deep moat and the path climbed through the gates then up the steep slope towards the citadel. Today a new path has been cut to avoid the obstacles that were designed to prevent attackers from gaining entry. There is an L-shaped keep, a long, tortuous tunnel which could be sealed by an iron cover at the top after firing with hot coals, and a chamber which could be filled with noxious fumes. At one point the tunnel divides and meets, to fool attackers to kill each other in the dark. The only genuine access was narrowed so that an invader would have to crawl through the last few metres, making it possible for defenders to kill them on sight. The bodies were disposed of by chutes down into the crocodile infested moat 75 m below. A guide will take you through. Take a torch and allow two hours to get the most out of the extraordinary site.

afternoon when the crowds have gone. If you are lucky you may get the resident guide who takes visitors through the dark tunnels with a flaming torch.

Deogiri fort

ⓘ *Sunrise to sunset, Rs100 foreigners, Rs 5 Indians, allow 3 hrs.*

From Ala-ud-din Khalji's capture of Deogiri in 1296 until Independence in 1947, by which time it was under the control of the Nizam of Hyderabad, the fort remained in Muslim hands. Muhammad bin Tughluq (see page 98) determined to extend his power south, seized Daulatabad, deciding to make it his capital and populate it with the residents from Delhi. Thousands died as a result of his misconceived experiment. The outermost of the three main ring walls and the bastion gates were probably built by the Muslims. For snacks there are numerous dhabas opposite the entrance.

The Persian style **Chand Minar** (1435) stands at the bottom of the fort, towering as a celebration of victory like the Qutb Minar in Delhi. Its original covering of Persian blue tiles must have made it even more striking. Opposite is the **Jama Masjid** (1318), with 106 pillars taken from a Hindu temple, and a large tank. The 31 m high victory tower built by Ala-ud-din Bahmani to celebrate his capture of the fort has at its base 24 chambers and a small mosque. The path passes bastions, studded gates, a drawbridge and the **Chini Mahal** where Abdul Hasan Tana Shah, the last King of Golconda, was imprisoned in 1687 for 13 years. The 6.6-m long Kila Shikan (Fort Breaker) iron cannon is on the bastion nearby. At the end of the tunnel (see box, above) inside the citadel is a flight of steps leading up to the **Baradari** (Pavilion), said to be the palace of the Yadavi Queen and later Shah Jahan. The **citadel** is reached by climbing 100 more steps and passing through two more gateways. At the top is another cannon with a ram's head on the butt; the Persian inscription around the muzzle reads 'Creator of Storms'.

Rauza

Rauza (or **Khuldabad**) ('Heavenly Abode') is 22 km from Aurangabad and was once an important town around which Aurangzeb built a wall with seven gates. He died at the age of 89 on Friday (the day of his choice), 20 February 1707. There is a simple tomb to him and over 20 others of Muslim rulers of the Deccan. Since Aurangzeb wanted a simple grave as a sign of humility, open to the sky, his grave has no canopy. The marble screen around it was erected later by Lord Curzon and the Nizam of Hyderabad. Close to Aurangzeb's tomb are those of various saints, going back to the 14th century. Some are decorated with silver. There are several relics – hairs of the Prophet's beard said to multiply every year, the Prophet's robe, and the supposed remnants of trees miraculously converted to silver by the saint Saiyed Burhan-ud-Din (died 1344).

Ellora

→ *For listings, see pages 1203-1206. Colour map 5, A4.*

The Hindu, Jain and Buddhist caves carved in the volcanic rocks at Ellora are among the finest in India. Lying near an important ancient trade route between Ujjain in Madhya Pradesh and the west coast, the caves are thought to be the work of priests and pilgrims who used the route.

Ins and outs

Ellora, 26 km from Aurangabad, takes about 45 minutes. Hiring a taxi (Rs 650-1050) gives you flexibility to stop at other sites on the way, auto rickshaws around Rs 350. Alternatively, join a tour group (Rs 150 per person). Car and driver hired through a travel agent will cost around Rs 1800 return (non a/c). Tour buses usually arrive at the car park, directly in front of the Kailasnatha temple itself. Arrive early and see the Kailasnatha first to avoid the very large crowds. For visiting Ellora and Ajanta, take lunch and drinks as decent options are limited. Also wear a hat and comfy shoes and take a strong torch.

The site

ⓘ *Wed-Mon 0900-1730, Kailashnatha entry Rs 250 foreigners (other caves remain free), Rs 10 Indians. Cameras may be used outside, flash photography and tripods are not allowed inside. Guides available (some European languages and Japanese spoken). 'Light passes' for groups wishing to see darker caves illuminated are available (best to join a group if on your own). Painted caves open at 1000, others at 0900 – light is better in the afternoon. For the elderly and infirm, dhoolies (chairs carried by men) are available.*

Like the caves at Ajanta, Ellora's caves were also abandoned and forgotten. Twelve of the 34 caves are Buddhist (created from circa AD 600-800), 17 Hindu (AD 600-900) and five Jain (AD 800-1100). Most have courtyards in front. They face west and are best seen in the afternoon. To see the caves in chronological order, start at the east end and visit the Buddhist *viharas* first. In this way the magnificent Hindu Kailasnatha temple is seen towards the end.

Buddhist Caves (Nos 1-12) These belong to the **Vajrayana** sect of the Mahayana (Greater Vehicle) School. The caves include *viharas* (monasteries) and *chaityas* (chapels) where the monks worshipped. It has been suggested that the stone-cut structures were ideally suited to the climate which experienced monsoons, and rapidly became the preferred medium over more flimsy and less durable wood.

Cave 1 A simple *vihara*.

Cave 2 Adjoining is reached by a flight of steps. At the door of the cave are *dwarapala* (guardians) flanked by windows. The interior (14.5 sq m) comprises a hall supported by 12 pillars, some decorated with the pot and foliage motif. In the centre of the back wall is a 3-m-high seated Buddha and two standing Buddhas while along each of the side walls are five Buddhas accompanied by Bodhisattvas and *apsaras* (celestial nymphs).

Cave 3 Similar to Cave 2, having a square central chamber with a Buddha image, this time seated on a lotus. Around the walls are 12 meditation cells.

Cave 4 Two-storeyed and contains a Buddha sitting under the Bo (pipal) tree.

Cave 5 The **Maharwada**, is the largest of the single storeyed caves in this group (17.6 m by 36 m). Two rows of 10 columns each run the length of the cave, as do two raised platforms which were probably tables, suggesting that this cave was a dining hall. There are attractive carvings on the first pillar on the left. The Buddha at the back is guarded on the left by Padmapani, a symbol of purity. On the right is Vajrapani holding a thunderbolt, the symbol of esoteric knowledge and the popular deity of the sect responsible for creating the caves. The Buddha is seated, not cross-legged on the floor as is usual, but on a chair or stool. He demonstrates some of the 32 distinctive marks: three folds in the neck, long ear lobes and the third eye. The *mudra* here signifies the Buddha's first sermon at the Deer Park, see page 177, and is a teaching pose.

The next four caves can be bypassed as they contain nothing new.

Cave 10 Viswakarma, or 'Carpenter's Cave', is the only *chaitya* (chapel) cave in the group. It used to be a monastery. This is on the ground floor and above are what are presumed to have been the monks' living quarters. In front is a large courtyard approached by a flight of steps. The galleries around it have square-based pillars at the foot of which was a lion facing outwards. At the back of these galleries are two elaborately carved chapels. The exterior decoration gives the impression that instead of stone, wood was the building material, hence 'Viswakarma'. The façade has a trefoil window with *apsara* groups for ornamentation. The main hall is large (26 m by 13 m, 10 m high). The curved fluted 'beams' suggest to some the upturned hull of a ship. The chamber has 28 columns, each with a vase and foliage capital, dividing it up into a nave and aisles. The aisle runs round the decorated *stupa* (*dagoba*) with a colossal 4.5-m 'Preaching Buddha' carved in front of it. The upper gallery, reached by an internal flight of steps, was supposed to have subsidiary shrines at either end but the left hand one was not finished. Decorating the walls are loving couples, indicating how much Buddhism had changed from its early ascetic days. You can get a view of the friezes above the pillars which show Naga queens, symbolic precursors of the monsoon, and dwarfs as entertainers, dancing and playing musical instruments. Sunlight pouring through the circular window at the entrance to the cave gives the cave a truly ethereal quality.

Cave 11 (*Do Thal* – two-storeyed) was found to have a third storey in 1876 when the basement was discovered. The lowest level is a veranda with a shrine and two cells at the back of it. The middle level has eight front pillars and five rear cells of which only the central three are completed and decorated. The upper level has a porch opening into a long colonnaded hall with a Buddha shrine at the rear. Images of Durga and Ganesh suggest that the cave was later used by Hindus. Cave 11 and 12 illustrate the use of the upper levels of these caves as a residence for monks and pilgrim hostels.

Cave 12 (*Tin Thal* – three-storeyed) has cells for sleeping (note the stone benches) on the lower floors but it is the figures of the Buddha which are of particular interest. The rows of seven Buddhas are symbolic of the belief that he appears on earth every 5000 years and has already visited it seven times.

Ellora caves

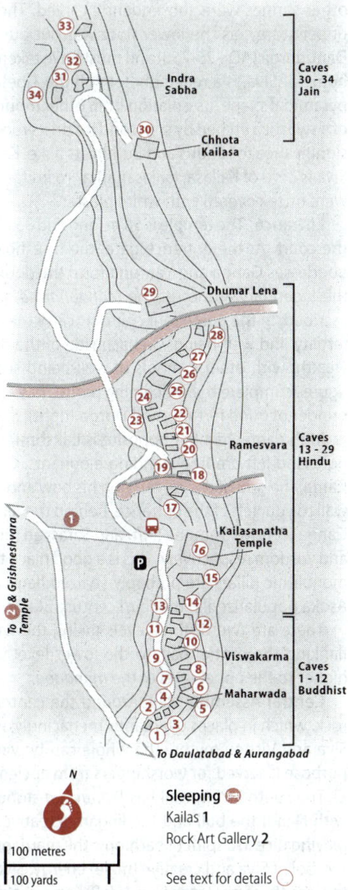

Hindu Caves (Nos 13-29) These caves lie in the centre of the group and are the most numerous. **Cave 13** is a plain room while **Cave 14** (**Ravana ki** khai, seventh century), is single storeyed and the last of the collection from the early period. River goddesses and guardians stand at the doorway while inside is a broken image of Durga and figurative panels on the walls of the principle deities, Vishnu, Siva, Lakshmi and Parvati. **Cave 15** (*Das Avatara*, mid- eighth century), reached by a flight of steps, has a large courtyard and is two-storeyed.

Kailasanatha Temple (mid-eighth century onwards) This is the most magnificent of all the rock-cut structures at Ellora, and is completely open to the elements. It is the only building that was begun from the top. Carved out of 85,000 cu m of rock, the design and execution of the full temple plan is an extraordinary triumph of imagination and craftsmanship. Excavating three deep trenches into the rock, carving started from the top of the cliff and worked down to the base. Enormous blocks were left intact from which the porch, the free standing pillars and other shrines were subsequently carved. The main shrine was carved on what became the upper storey, as the lower floor was cut out below. It is attributed to the Rashtrakuta king Dantidurga (AD 725-755) and must have taken years to complete. **Mount Kailasa** (6700 m), the home of Siva, is a real mountain on the Tibetan plateau beyond the Himalaya. Its distinctive pyramidal shape, its isolation from other mountains, and the appearance to the discerning eye of a swastika etched by snow and ice on its rock face, imbued the mountain with great religious significance to Hindus and Buddhists alike. Kailasa was seen as the centre of the universe, and Siva is Lord of Kailasa, Kailasanatha. To imitate the real snow-covered peaks, the *sikharas* here were once covered with white plaster.

Entrance The temple is 50 m long and 33 m wide and the tower rises 29 m above the level of the court. At the entrance gate, the threshold between the profane and sacred worlds, the goddesses **Ganga** and **Yamuna** form the door jambs. Just inside are two seated sages: **Vyasa**, the legendary author of the *Mahabharata*, and **Valmiki** to whom the *Ramayana* has been ascribed. In the porch four columns carry the North Indian vase and foliage motif, a symbol of fertility and well-being. On each side of the doorway there are images of **Kubera**, the god of wealth, with other symbols of well-being such as the conch shell and the lotus. Two more figures complete the welcoming party. They are **Ganesh** (left), the elephant headed son of Siva, bringer of good fortune, and **Durga** (right), Siva's wife who fought the demons.

In the antechamber opposite is **Lakshmi**, the goddess of wealth. In the courtyard, to your right and left are free-standing elephants. On the left round the corner is a panel depicting **Kama**, the god of desire, carrying his bow and five arrows, one for each of the senses. On the far wall to your left of the entrance, behind the pillars, is the shrine of the **Three River Goddesses** – Ganga (centre), Yamuna (left) and Sarasvati (right). Symbolically they stand for purity, devotion and wisdom respectively. This is a good place to photograph the central shrine. The two carved monolithic pillars are probably stylized flagstaffs indicating royal patronage – a practice that Asoka popularized in the third century BC.

There are two distinct levels taking the worshipper from the courtyard by two staircases flanking the central hall, to the lower level with its processional path and then rising even higher to the upper level of the *mandapa*.

Central Assembly Hall Around the central shrine is a colonnaded hall gouged from the rock, which in places overhangs menacingly. Inside this cloister is a series of panels portraying Siva and Vishnu myths. The whole can be viewed as a sort of instructional picture gallery, a purpose it served for worshippers from ancient times who could not read.

The south facing wall has *Ramayana* stories – **Ravana** offering his heads; Siva and Parvati with Nandi the bull and the lingam (creative power); Siva playing the vina; Siva and Parvati playing dice in a spirit of harmony; the marriage of Siva and Parvati; the origin of the lingam, the symbol of Siva and creative (male) energy; Siva dancing and Siva tricking Parvati. The panel on the south of the mandapa of Ravana shaking Mount Kailasa, attempting to carry it off, disturbing Parvati and her attendants, one of whom is seen frightened and fleeing, and Siva restoring order with the movement of his toe.

Along the north-facing wall are stories from the *Mahabharata* above and Krishna legends below. The panels include **Krishna** stealing buttermilk; Vishnu as **Narasimha**, half man, half lion; Vishnu reclining on **Ananda** the serpent inbetween incarnations; Vishnu the **Preserver**. Finally there is **Annapurna**, Goddess of Plenty.

The inner porch contains two panels, Siva as **Lord of Knowledge** and Siva as **Bhairava** killing the Elephant Demon.

Main Shrine Steps lead to the upper floor which contains a *mandapa* (central hall, 17 m by 16 m) of 16 stout pillars arranged in groups of four, with aisles that correspond to the cardinal points leading to an open central area. At the far end is the *garbhagriha* (shrine) with **Ganga** and **Yamuna** as door guardians. Inside is the *yoni lingam*, symbol of Siva's creative power. Running around the back is a passageway with five small shrine rooms off it, each with a replica of the main temple. The Nataraja painting on the *mandapa* ceiling. There are remnants of paintings on the porch ceilings (particularly to the west) where you will see *apsaras*, dwarfs and animals. The temple rises in a pyramid, heavier and more squat looking than later towers in the north. The shape suggests enormous strength. As you leave, the path to the left leads up and around the temple, giving an interesting bird's-eye view of the magnificent complex.

Cave 21 (**Ramesvara**, late sixth century) has a court with a stone Nandi bull in the middle and side shrines. A *linga* sanctuary leads off the veranda. This cave is celebrated for its fine sculptures of amorous couples and the gods. **Cave 29** (**Dhumar Lena**, late sixth century) is very similar to Elephanta (see page 1181) in concept. Access is from three sides, there is a spacious hall with a separate small sanctuary with a *lingam* at the end. Wall panels depict Siva legends especially as Destroyer.

Jain Caves (Nos 30-34) These caves are an anticlimax after the Hindu ones, but they have an aura of peace and simplicity. **Cave 30** (**Chhota Kailasa**, early ninth century) was intended as a smaller scale replica of the Kailasanatha Temple but never completed. The columned shrine has 22 *tirthankaras* with *Mahavira* in the sanctuary. **Cave 32** (**Indra Sabha**, early ninth century) is the finest of the Jain series and is dedicated to Mahavir. A simple gateway leads into an open court in the middle of which stands the shrine. The walls have carvings of elephants, lions and *tirthankaras*. The lower of the two is incomplete but the upper has carvings of Ambika and also Mahavir flanked by guardians of earlier *tirthankaras*. The ceiling is richly carved with a massive lotus at the centre and you can see signs of painted figures among clouds.

Ajanta → *For listings, see pages 1203-1206. Colour map 5, A5.*

Older than those at Ellora, the caves date from about 200 BC to AD 650. They are cut from the volcanic lavas of the Deccan Trap in a steep crescent-shaped hillside in a forested ravine of the Sahyadri Hills. After the late seventh century, the jungle took over and they lay unnoticed for centuries.

Ins and outs

Getting there The bus or taxi drive from Aurangabad (106 km) takes 2½ to three hours. Good tours are available from Aurangabad for Rs 200 per person (though a hired non air-conditioned car and driver will cost around Rs 2000-3000). Taxis Rs 1200-1500. Shilod (Silod) is a popular halting place and has a number of restaurants. About 10 km from Ajanta, the road descends from the plateau; then there are dramatic views of the Waghora Valley, where the caves are located. Coming from the north, the closest railhead is Jalgaon, with many main line services to Mumbai, Madhya Pradesh and the northeast. ▸▸ *See Transport, page 1206.*

The challenge of preservation

Preservation of the murals poses enormous challenges. Repeated attempts to reproduce and to restore them have faced major problems. After all but five of Robert Gill's paintings were destroyed by fire, the Bombay School of Arts sent out a team to copy the wall paintings under the guidance of the principal John Griffiths in the 1870s. The copies were stored in the Victoria and Albert Museum in London but this also had a fire in 1885, when 87 were destroyed.

In 1918 a team from Kyoto University Oriental Arts Faculty arrived at Ajanta to copy the sculptures. This they did by pressing wet rice paper against the surface to make casts which were then shipped back to Japan. In the early 1920s they were all destroyed by an earthquake.

In 1920 the Ajanta paintings were cleaned by the former Hyderabad Government under whose jurisdiction the caves lay. Two Italian restorers were commissioned and they set about fixing the peeling paintings to the walls of the caves. They first injected casein between the paintings and the plastered wall, then applied shellac as a fixative. The Griffiths team from Bombay had also applied a coat of varnish to bring out the colours of the paintings.

However, these varnishes darkened over the years, rendering the murals less visible. They also cracked, aiding the peeling process and the accumulation of moisture between the wall and the outer membrane. The Archaeological Survey of India is now responsible for all restoration at the site.

Getting around There's a small settlement with a restaurant, curio market and aggressive salesmen at the approach to the caves. The entrance is a short uphill walk along a stepped concrete path. *Dhoolis* are available for hire if you wish to be carried. You can approach the caves from the river bed in the bottom of the valley, where the bus stops; the View Point, is worth getting to. You have to buy your ticket from the kiosk first, and if there is water in the stream you have to wade through, but it is much shadier than the path cut out of the cliff.

History

In 1819, a party of British army officers from Madras noticed the top of the façade of Cave 10 while tiger hunting. They investigated and discovered some caves, describing seeing 'figures with curled wigs'. Others made exploratory trips to the fascinating caves. In 1843, James Fergusson, horrified by the ravages of the elements, requested that the East India Company do something to preserve and protect the deteriorating caves.

In 1844 **Captain Robert Gill**, an artist, was sent to copy the paintings on the cave walls. He spent 27 years living in a small encampment outside, sending each new batch of paintings to Bombay and London. After nearly 20 years his work was almost complete and displayed in the Crystal Palace in London. In December 1866 all but a few of the paintings were destroyed in a fire. Gill soldiered on for another five years before giving up, and died from illness soon afterwards. He is buried in the small European cemetery at **Bhusawal**, 60 km to the north, 27 km from Jalgaon.

The site

ⓘ *Tue-Sun 0900-1730, foreigners US$10, Indians Rs 10. No flash photography. Some caves have electric lights for illuminating the paintings; hawkers sell cheap postcards and slides (Rs 100). In the Mahayana caves with paintings there is a restriction on the number of visitors allowed in at any one time. Computer kiosks are planned, designed to show a 'virtual' history of the caves.*

Hiuen-Tsang, recorded in the seventh century (although he did not visit it), a description of the "monastery in a deep defile ... large temple with a huge stone image of the Buddha with a tier of seven canopies".

The terrain in which the caves were excavated was a sheer cliff facing a deeply incised river meander. At the height of Ajanta's importance the caves are thought to have housed about 200 monks and numerous craftsmen and labourers. The masterpieces retell the life story of the Buddha and reveal the life and culture of the people of the times, royal court settings, family life, street scenes and superb studies of animals and birds. The *Jatakas* relate the Buddha's previous births – showing the progress of the soul.

Originally the entrance to the caves was along the river bed and most had a flight of stairs leading up to them. The first to be excavated was Cave 10, followed by the first Hinayana caves (in which the Buddha is not depicted in human form), on either side. Later Mahayana caves were discovered, completing the spectrum of Buddhist development in India.

There is a round trip walk, up the side of the valley where all the caves are located then down to the river to cross to the other side. An attractive low level walk through forest brings you back to the roadhead. **Caves 1, 2, 10, 16** and **17** have lights. **11, 19** and **26** are also particularly worth visiting.

Mahayana group **Cave 1** (late fifth century) is one of the finest *viharas* (monasteries), remarkable for the number and quality of its murals. A veranda with cells and porches either side has three entrances leading into a pillared hall. Above the veranda are friezes depicting the sick man, old man, corpse and saint encountered by the Buddha, who is shown above the left porch. The hall has 20 ornamented pillars, a feature of the late period caves. Five small monks' cells lead off three sides, and in the centre of the back wall is a large shrine of the Buddha supported by Indra, the rain god. At the entrance are the river goddesses Yamuna and Ganga and two snake-hooded guardians at the base.

The **murals** are among the finest at Ajanta. In the four corners are panels representing groups of foreigners. The Mahajanaka jataka (where the Buddha took the form of an able and just ruler) covers much of the left-hand wall including Renunciation, and the scenes where he is enticed by beautiful dancing girls.

On either side of the entrance to the antechamber of the shrine room are two of the best known murals at Ajanta. On the left is the **Bodhisattva Padmapani** (here holding a blue lotus), in a pose of spiritual detachment, whilst on the right is the **Bodhisattva Avalokitesvara**. Together compassion and knowledge, the basis of Mahayana Buddhism, complement one another. Their size dwarfs the attendants to enhance the godlike stature of the bodhisattva. The Buddha inside the shrine is seated in the teaching position, flanked by the two carved bodhisattvas. Under the throne appears the **Wheel of Life**, with deer representing Sarnath where he preached his first sermon, see page 177.

One of the sculptural tricks that a guide will display is that when the statue is lit from the left side (as you face it), the facial expression is solemn, suggesting contemplation. Yet from the other side, there is a smile of joy, while from below it suggests tranquillity and peace. Note the paintings on the ceiling, particularly the elephant scattering the lotus as it rushes out of the pond, and the charging bull. Also look for the 'black princess' and the row of the dancer with musicians. On the way out is a pillar that has four deer sculpted skilfully, sharing the same head.

Cave 2 (sixth century) is also a *vihara* hall, 14.6 sq m with 12 pillars, with five cells on each side of the left and right hand walls and two chapels on each side of the ante- chamber and shrine room. The veranda in front has a side chapel at each end. The doorway is richly carved. On the left hand wall is the mural depicting **The Birth of The Buddha**. Next to this is the **'Thousand' Buddhas**, which illustrates the miracle when the Buddha multiplied himself to confuse a heretic. On the right are dancing girls before the king, shown with striking three-dimensional effect.

The cave is remarkable for its painted ceiling, giving the effect of the draped cloth canopy of a tent. The *mandala* (circular diagram of the cosmos) is supported by demon- like figures. The Greek key designs on the border are possibly influenced by Gandharan art, first to third centuries AD. The ceiling decorations portray a number of figures of Persian appearance apparent from the style of beard and whiskers and their clothing.

The Yaksha (nature spirits) Shrine in the left chapel is associated with fertility and wealth. The main shrine is that of Buddha in the teaching position, again flanked by the two bodhisattvas, both holding the royal fly whisk. The **Hariti** Shrine on the right is to the ogress who liked eating children! The panel on your left as you leave the hall is a *jataka* telling the story of the Bodhisattva's life as the Pandit Vidhura.

Caves 3-7 are late fifth century. **Cave 3** has no veranda and **Cave 4** is the largest *vihara* at Ajanta, planned on an ambitious scale and not completed. The hall is 27 sq m and supported on 28 pillars. Along the walls are cells whilst at the rear is a large shrine. **Cave 5** is unfinished.

Hinayana group A Hinayana group comes next (**Caves 6-10** and **12**, **13** and **15**) dating from the second century BC. **Cave 6** is on two levels with only seven of the 16 octagonal pillars standing. A shrine contains a seated Buddha. **Cave 7** has no hall. The veranda has two porches each supported by heavy octagonal Elephanta-type columns. These lead to four cells. These and the antechamber are profusely carved. The shrine is that of Buddha, his hand raised in blessing. **Cave 8** (first century BC) is a small *vihara*. **Cave 9** (circa 100 BC), a *chaitya*, is 14 m long, 14 columns run the length of each side and 11 continue round the *stupa*. The vaulted roof was once wooden ribbed and leads back from a huge arched *chaitya sun* window which throws light on the *stupa* at the rear. Two phases of wall painting have been identified. The earlier ones dating from the construction of the cave can be seen at the far left side and consist of a procession to a *stupa* as well as a thin band above the left colonnade. Above this are later Buddha figures from the Mahayana period when the figures of the Buddha on either side of the entrance were painted.

Cave 10 (circa 150 BC) is much larger. Like the previous cave the roof was once fitted with wooden ribs which subsequently collapsed. The long hall with an apse housing the *stupa* was one of the first excavated and also the first rediscovered by army officers. An inscription above the façade, now destroyed, dated the excavation to the second century BC through a generous donation by the king. The *dagoba* or *stupa* resembles that of Cave 9 and is a double storey drum. There are also paintings dating from the Hinayana and Mahayana periods. The early ones depict figures in costumes resembling those seen at Sanchi, see page 260. Traces of later paintings survive on the pillars and aisle ceilings and later Buddha figures are often superimposed on earlier works. The main subjects of the Hinayana paintings are *jataka* stories. On the rear wall are the King (in a ceremonial headdress) and Queen approaching the Sacred Bodhi Tree, one of the earliest Ajanta paintings.

Cave 11 (originally second century BC, with sixth century alterations), has a veranda and roof painted with birds and flowers, a hall supported by four heavy pillars and a stone bench running along the right side. There are five cells and a shrine of a seated Buddha. **Cave 12** (with glauconite rock wall) and **Cave 13** (second century BC) are small *viharas*. **Cave 14** (fifth century AD) was planned on a grand scale but not completed and can be missed along with **Cave 15** (fifth century) which is a long hall with a Buddha carved out of the rock.

Later Mahayana period The remaining caves all belong to the Later Mahayana period and date from the fifth century. **Cave 16**, with kneeling elephants at the entrance and the Cobra King, has a 20 m long and 3.5 m deep veranda that carries six plain octagonal pillars. There is a good view of the ravine from here. The magnificent columned hall inside has six cells on each side and a beamed ceiling. The Teaching Buddha is seated on a lion throne. On the left the 'Dying Princess' portrays Nanda's new bride being told that he has been ordained a monk and renounced the world. Her misery is shared by all and everything around her. On the right wall are the remains of a picture of Prince Siddhartha, later the Buddha, using a bow.

Cave 17 (late fifth century) is similar to No 16 in layout and has the greatest number of murals. On the left of the veranda is a painted Wheel of Life. Over the entrance door is a row of

Tempera techniques in cave painting

To prepare the rock for painting it was chiselled to leave a rough surface. Two layers of mud-plaster containing fibrous material (grain-husk, vegetable fibres and rock grit) was applied, the first coarse, the second fine. Metal mirrors must have been used by the artists, to reflect sunlight into the dark caves. It is thought that the tempera technique was used. On a dry surface, a red cinnabar outline defined the picture, filled in, possibly initially with grey and then numerous colour pigments usually mixed with glue; the completed painting was burnished to give a lustrous finish. The pigments were mainly taken from the land around, the principal ones being red and yellow ochre, white from lime and kaoline, green from glauconite, black from lamp-black and blue from imported lapis lazuli. The shellac used in restoration after 1819 was found to be cracking. Since 1951 this has been removed by the Archaeological Survey of India, with UNESCO's help. PVA is now used.

seven Past Buddhas and the eighth, the Maitreya or Future Buddha, above a row of amorous Yaksha couples. Sculpted deities are carved on either side.

Murals show scenes from 17 *jatakas*: the worship of the Buddha, the Buddha preaching; Hansa *jataka*, with paintings of geese; Vessantara *jataka*, where the greedy Brahmin is portrayed, grinning; the miraculous 'Subjugation of the rogue elephant', sent to kill the Buddha; and the ogress who turns into a beautiful maiden by day! There are also panels showing royal processions, warriors, an assembled congregation from which you can get an accurate and detailed picture of the times. **Cave 18** (late fifth century) has little of merit and can be missed.

Cave 19 (late fifth century) is a Mahayana *chaitya* hall and was painted throughout. The façade is considered to be one of the most elegant in terms of execution and elaborate ornamentation, and has the arched *chaitya* window set into it. The interior is in the layout seen before, two rows of richly decorated columns leading up to and around the back of the standing Buddha, which here is in front of the slender *stupa*. This tall shrine has a triple stone umbrella above it. Note the seated Nagaraja with attendants.

Cave 20 is comparatively small and has imitation beams carved into the ceiling.

Later caves The final few caves belong to the seventh century and are a separate and distinct group at the farthest end of the horseshoe near the waterfall. Only one, **Cave 26**, need be visited. **Cave 21** (early seventh century) has a fallen veranda with flanking chapels. **Cave 24** was intended to be the largest *vihara* but was not completed.

Cave 26 is a large *chaitya hall*. A partly damaged columned façade stretches across the front with the customary side chambers at each end. The 3-m-high window is flanked by sculptured Buddha reliefs. Inside, 26 pillars run in an elongated semi circle around the cylindrical *stupa* which is decorated with Buddhas. The walls are decorated with sculpture, including the temptations by Mara's daughters, but the most striking being a 9-m reclining image of the Parinirvana Buddha, about to enter Nirvana, his death mourned by his followers.

The walk back along the promenade connecting the shrines is pleasant enough but the return via the river, waterfall and forest walkway is delightful. Steps lead down from Cave 16 (with the carved elephants). The hilltop opposite the caves offers a fine view of the horseshoe shaped gorge.

Jalgaon

Jalgaon, 64 km from Ajanta on the NH6, is the rail junction for the Ajanta Caves. It was once at the centre of a savannah forest region, the habitat of tigers, leopards and other game. Now it has become an important cotton growing area and is interesting to walk around.

Eastern Deccan → *For listings, see pages 1203-1206. Colour map 5, A5, B4 and B5.*

To the east of Aurangabad the road and railway go down the gentle slope of the great basin of the Godavari. Ancient erosion surfaces covered in some of India's richest black lava soils dominate the landscape. Rainfall gradually increases eastwards, and on the lower land the soils are some of the best in the peninsula – rich black soils derived from the lava, though on the higher land the much poorer red soils surface. Given the relative dryness an extraordinarily high percentage is cultivated. Sorghum (*jowar*) and short stapled cotton dominate. In the west, pearl millet.

Jalna

Jalna is the town to which **Abul Fazl**, who wrote the *Ain i Akbari*, was exiled and ultimately murdered by Bir Singh Deo of Orchha, see page 285, at the instigation of Jahangir. The area is dotted with forts. There is a **Dak Bungalow** and a **Rest House** in the town.

Lonar

Lonar, 145 km east of Aurangabad, is famous for its remarkable 2-km-wide **meteor crater**, believed to have formed 50,000 years ago. It contains a pool of green water around which are dotted the ruins of several temples. Wildlife including chinkara and gazelles can be spotted in the woods surrounding the lake, along with peacocks, storks and numerous other species of birds.

Nanded

Guru Gobind Singh, the 10th Sikh guru, was assassinated here in 1708, see page 1426. There is an important *gurudwara* 1.5 km from the station, which is rumoured to be covered in gold in the near future. Today Nanded (Nander), which stands on the river Godavari, is an important administrative and commercial town. It is also on the main railway line between Hyderabad/ Secunderabad and Aurangabad/Nashik.

Paithan

One of the oldest cities of the Deccan, Paithan is 55 km south of Aurangabad on the north bank of the Godavari River as it leaves the Nath Sagar reservoir. The **Jayakwadi Project** at Nath Sagar is a large earthen dam and reservoir. The Left Bank scheme is already providing irrigation all the way down the Godavari to Nanded 140 km to the east, and the equivalent Right Bank scheme is in progress.

Paithan is famous for a special kind of silk sari with brocaded gold borders and *pallu* (end-piece). Motifs of geese, parrots, peacocks and stylized leaves, flowers and creepers in dark greens, red and blue are brocaded against the golden background.

Ahmadnagar → *Colour map 5, B4. Phone code: 0241. Population: 307,500.*

Ahmadnagar, an historic Muslim town, has several Islamic monuments to visit. The town was founded in 1490 by Ahmad Nizam Shah Bahri, the son of a Brahmin from Vijayanagar who converted to Islam. His dynasty ruled the territory stretching from Aurangabad to Bassein until 1636. Its Islamic history reflects strong Persian influence, both architecturally in the Persian style Husaini Mosque, and theologically in the presence of Shi'a Muslims from Persia in the court.

Alamgir's Dargah is a small enclosure near the cantonment. Aurangzeb, who had begun his long Deccan campaign 24 years earlier, died here on 3 March 1707. The *dargah* marks his temporary resting place before his body was moved to Aurangabad. To the east is a white marble **Darbar Hall**, well worth visiting for the view from the roof. The fort (1599) is 1 km to the east of the city, 4 km northeast of the railway station. Circular, it has an 18-m-high wall reinforced with 22 bastions. The fort is now occupied by the army, but entry is possible (sign in at gate), to see the 'Leaders' Room' where Nehru and 11 colleagues spent 1942-1945, now a small museum. No photography. Among the numerous **mosques** in the city are the small but attractive Qasim (1500-1508), the Husaini, with its Persian style dome, and the Damadi (1567) with its splendid carved stonework. The Malik-i-Maidan cannon now standing on the Lion Bastion at Bijapur (see page 1096), was cast here. The well-preserved **Tomb of Nizam Shah** is in a large garden on the left bank of the Sina River.

Junnar

The **birthplace of Shivaji** in 1627, Junnar is another rock-cut cave temple site. The hill fort contains a monument commemorating Shivaji and a temple. On the east side of the hill there are more than 50 **Buddhist caves**. Most are *viharas* (monasteries) and date from the second century BC to the third century AD. They comprise the **Tulja Lena Group**, 2 km west of the town, which includes an unusual circular *chaitya* (chapel, Cave 3) with a dome ceiling. The **Bhuta Lena Group** is on the side of Manmodi Hill, 1500 m south of the town. The unfinished *chaitya* hall (Cave 40) has a well preserved façade containing reliefs of Laxmi. The **Ganesh Lena Group** is 4 km south of Junnar on the Lenyadri Hill. Cave 7 is a *vihara* with 19 cells leading off the main congregational hall and a colonnaded veranda. The octagonal columns are repeated in the *chaitya* hall next door (Cave 6).

Shivner Fort rises over 300 m above the plain and is approached from the south by a track that passes over the moat, through four gates, then dog-legs up the final stretch to the plateau. Shivaji's birthplace is to the north and not far from it is a ruined mosque. There are four tanks running down the centre. In the third century the site was a Buddhist *vihara* and on the east face there are about 50 rock cells. Maloji Bhonsla, Shivaji's grandfather, was granted the fort in 1599. Shivaji did not remain in it long as it was captured by the Mughals from the early 1630s. Several attempts to win it back failed.

Bhimashankar

Completely off the beaten track, the pilgrim site of Bhimashankar can be reached by road from Shivner or from the NH50 at Narayangaon. However, even buses are infrequent. The site is important to Hindus for the **Siva temple** built by the Peshwa Nana Phadnavis to house one of Maharashtra's five *jyotirlingas*.

Central Maharashtra listings

For Sleeping and Eating price codes and other relevant information, see Essentials pages 38-42.

Sleeping

Aurangabad *p1190, map p1191*

Some hotels offer discounts between Apr and Sep. Most will provide packed lunch for trip to the caves. Most are 24-hr checkout.

LL-L Residency (Taj), Ajanta Rd, 8 km from railway station, 9 km from the airport, T0240-661 3737, www.tajhotels.com. 40 large rooms, quiet swimming, excellent service, imposing building in lovely gardens, on outskirts, beautiful gardens, difficult for the disabled (no lift, some rooms on 1st floor, reception and restaurant on ground floor).

L-AL The Meadows, Gat 135-136, Mitmita village, Ellora Rd, T0240-267 7412, www.themeadowsresort.com. A pleasant change from Aurangabad's corporate offerings, with 40 comfortable cottages set among 11 acres of bird-filled gardens. Quiet and relaxing.

AL Lemon Tree, R 7/2, Chikalthana, Airport Rd, T0240-660 3030, www.lemontree hotels.com. Excellent new hotel with 102 sleek and spacious rooms arranged around a large pool. Spa and fitness centre, good food, helpful management.

B-C Bagga International, opposite Akashwani, Jalna Rd, T0240-235 4000, www.hotelbagga.com. Clean and modern if slightly anonymous rooms in a newish business hotel. Good room service, helpful and attentive staff, good value.

B Khemi's Inn, 11 Town Centre, CIDCO (4 km from town, first left after **Ambassador Ajanta**, then first right), T0240-248 4868, khemis@vsnl.com. 10 spotless a/c rooms with hot bath, good home cooking, quiet, pleasant garden, has the feel of an English B&B, very hospitable.

C-D Holiday Camp (MTDC), Station Rd, T0240-233 1513. 48 rooms (22 a/c) with bath and mosquito net, pleasant, busy, but poor restaurant, bar, tourist office, checkout 0900. Bedbug problems reported.

D-E Ajinkya, east of Central Bus Stand, T0240-232 1981. Decent rooms, some a/c.

D-E Panchavati, off Station Rd, Padampura, T0240-232 8755. Good value, 25 clean simple rooms with bath, good restaurant, friendly.

E Devpriya, Circular building near Central Bus Stand Rd, Dr Ambedkar Rd, T0240-233 2344. Family hotel, 62 decent rooms (hot water in morning), restaurant, bar, good value.

E Shree Maya, Bharuka Complex, behind tourist office, Padampura Rd, T0240-233 3093. 23 rooms with hot shower, 8 a/c, restaurant, arranges bus tickets, 24-hr checkout, mixed reports about management.

E-F Railway Retiring Rooms, T0240-233 5650. 3 rooms (1 a/c), 4-bedded dorm.

E-G Printravel, Dr Ambedkar Rd, T0240-232 9707. Old-fashioned but large clean rooms with bath, good **Patang** restaurant, very well run. Recommended.

F Tourist Home, Station Rd, T0240-233 7212. 26 rooms with bath, friendly, meals.

Ellora *p1194*

A-C Kailas, near the bus stand, T02437-244543, www.hotelkailas.com. 25 decent rooms in group of 'cottages', best a/c face the caves, dorm in annexe, restaurant, very pleasant garden, good service.

E-F Rock Art Gallery, T02437-244552. 9 very simple rooms, 'art' including copies of murals.

Ajanta *p1197*

D Travellers' Lodge (MTDC), T02438-244 226. 4 clean rooms , chilled beer.

D-E Holiday Resort (MTDC), Fardapur, 5 km from Ajanta caves, T02438-244230. 12 basic rooms with bath (mosquito net vital, not provided), 16 a/c rooms in gardens are better value, dorm (mattress only), restaurant.

D-E Murli Manohar, in Fardapur, T02438-244 289. 12 clean and pleasant rooms, plus dorm.

Jalgaon *p1201*

C-F Tourist Resort, Nehru Chowk, Station Rd, T0257-222 5192. 26 clean spacious rooms with bath, 4 a/c, some have TV.

E Plaza, 241 Navi Peth, Station Rd, T0257-222 7354. Very clean, 10 air-cooled rooms with bath and TV, hot water in bucket, very helpful and friendly manager. Highly recommended.

Lonar *p1202*

E-F MTDC Holiday Resort, near crater, T07260-221602. Simple self-contained rooms in a shadeless clump of new cottages, some with crater views. Check whether food is available when booking.

Nanded *p1202*

D-E Ashiana Park, opposite Kala Mandir, off Doctor's Lane, near bus stand, T02462-236412. Good value for a night halt, 21 good rooms, young enthusiastic manager, friendly.

Paithan *p1202*

C-D Goradia, off Pimpalwadi Rd, T02766-255257. Indian restaurant, 80 a/c rooms.

D Sai Leela, 9/5 Pimpalwadi Rd, near temple, T02766-255139. 72 rooms, some a/c, restaurant, pool.

D-E Pilgrim's Inn (MTDC), near Sai Baba Shrine, T02766-255194. 50 rooms (10 a/c), Indian restaurant.

Ahmadnagar *p1202*

D Sanket, Tilak Path, Station Rd, T/F0241-358701. 30 rooms, some a/c, restaurant.

E-F Swastik, Station Rd, 1 km from station, T0241-357575. Has 25 rooms.

Eating

Aurangabad *p1190, map p1191*

Angeethi, next to **Jet Airways**, Jalna Rd, T0240-244 1988. Excellent Marathi specialities, book ahead.

Chanakya, Station Rd. North Indian. Part outdoors, fashionable, a/c, well prepared, bar.

Foodwalla's Tandoori, 500 m from **Holiday Camp**. Indian. A/c, tender chicken preparations, popular, good value, bar.

Mastercook, Hotel Mayur, Jalna Rd. Popular locally.

🍴🍴 **Mingling**, **Hotel Rajdoot**, JL Nehru Marg. For Chinese.

🍴🍴 **Palace**, Shahgunj. Indian (Mughlai).

🍴 **Bhoj**, Ambedkar Marg (above **Manas Hotel**) near Central Bus Stand. Excellent Gujarati and Rajasthani *thalis*. Arrive at 1845 to listen to *puja* in the kitchen with chanting and cymbals.

🍴 **Guru**, Station Rd. Punjabi.

Jalgaon *p1201*

🍴🍴 **Bombay**, opposite **Anjali**. Excellent food, well-stocked bar.

🍴 **Anjali**, by the station. Great spicy *thalis*.

🍴 **Shreyas**, 201 Navi Peth. Inexpensive South Indian vegetarian. Good bakery and ice cream shop on Station Rd.

Nanded *p1202*

🍴 **Gujarati Bhoj Nalya** (sign in Hindi – look for **High Class Veg Lunch Home**), near bus stand. Excellent food in unlikely looking *dhaba*.

Ahmadnagar *p1202*

🍴 **Panchratna**, Shivaji Chowk, T02438-235 9202. Cheap Indian and continental cuisine.

Festivals and events

Aurangabad *p1190, map p1191*

Feb/Mar **Mahashivratri**, large fair at Ghrishneshwara Temple, near Ellora and **Ellora Yatra**.

Shopping

Aurangabad *p1190, map p1191*

Shops open Mon-Sat 1000-2000. The city is known for its handwoven Himroo shawls (brocades occasionally with Ajanta motifs), and special textile weaves – *Mashru*, *Patihani silk* and *Kinkhab* – as well as artificial silk. You can also get good decorative lacquer work, Bidriware and agate articles. Main shopping areas are City Chowk, Gulmandi, Nawabpura, Station Rd, Shahganj, Sarafa, Mondha.

In Shahganj, **Cottage Industries**. On Station Rd, **Silk Loom Fabrics** and **Government Emporium**, opposite Holiday Resort. At Zaffar Gate, Mondha Rd is **Aurangabad Himroo Industry**, a factory showroom producing beautiful Ajanta patterns in silk, the young English speaking owner is very informative. Recommended.

Activities and tours

Aurangabad *p1190, map p1191*

Swimming

Some top hotels open their pools to non-residents for a fee, eg **Ambassador Ajanta**, Rs 250 (includes other sporting facilities), **Aurangabad Ashok**, Rs 125; **President Park**, Rs 125; and **Vedant** (Quality Inn), Station Rd, T0240-235 0701, Rs 150.

Tours

Ashoka Travels, Station Rd, T0240-232 0816. Mr Karolkar arranges hotels, cars and excursions, charges fairly and is reliable.

Classic, TRC Building, Station Rd, T0240-233 7788, and at **Ambassador Ajanta**. Helpful and efficient; car hire, ticketing, hotels, Ajanta/Ellora and city tour, Rs 300/250 per person.

ITDC, Ashok Tours and Travels counter, near Goldie Cinema, Station Rd, T0240-233 1143.

MTDC see page 1190. Good sightseeing tours to Ajanta, Ellora and the City. Ajanta tour highly recommended, but Ellora and City tour visits too many places in too little time. Tours start from **MTDC Holiday Camp**, Station Rd, T0240-233 1513, and pickup from major hotels and the **Central Bus Stand**: Ellora and City Wed-Mon 0930-1800, Rs 200; Ajanta Tue-Sun 0830-1730, Rs 200; book at Window 1 (behind book stall) at bus stand; check times.

Transport

Aurangabad *p1190, map p1191*

Air The airport is 10 km from the centre and has regular flights to **Delhi**, **Mumbai**, **Jaipur** and **Udaipur**. Transport to town: Taxi, Rs 200 (Rs 300 through travel agents).

Indian Airlines, near Rama International, Airport Rd, T0240-248 5421, Mon-Sat 1000-1700; airport, T0240-248 2111. **Jet Airways**, 4 Vidya Nagar, Jalna Rd, T0240-244 1770. 0900-1800; airport T0240-248 4269.

Bicycle hire 'Cycle taxi' from shops near railway station north of the bus stand (CBS). Rs 5 per hr.

Local bus Services to **Daulatabad**, and **Ellora** (45 mins) from platform 7 of the Central Bus Stand, Ambedkar Rd.

Long distance bus MSRTC operates a/c luxury coaches to **Mumbai Central** (388 km), 10 hrs. Also services to **Ajanta** (3 hrs), **Jalgaon** (4½ hrs), **Nagpur**, **Nashik** and **Pune**. State and

private buses run to destinations in other states, including **Ahmedabad**, **Bengaluru** (**Bangalore**), **Bijapur**, **Hubli**, **Hyderabad**, **Indore** and **Udaipur**. Book through agents on Station Rd West, near the bus stand.
Car hire Rs 1200 per day (Rs 1500, a/c) from **Aurangabad Transport Syndicate**, Hotel Rama International, T0240-248 6766.
Rickshaw For auto-rickshaws, insist on using the meter, about Rs 10 per km. Day hire to visit Ellora and Daulatabad, Rs 500-600 from bus station.
Taxi Rates Rs 600 for 4 hrs, 40 km. Rs 1000 for 8 hrs, 80 km.
Train Beware of touts at the station offering package tours to Ellora and Ajanta. Easier by local bus. **Mumbai**: *Devgiri Exp 17058*, 2325, 8½ hrs; *Tapovan Exp 17618*, 1435, 8¼ hrs. **Secunderabad** (**Hyderabad**): *Ajanta Exp 17063*, 2240, 10 hrs. **Delhi** (**ND**): *Sachkhand Exp 12715*, 1335, 23 hrs, via **Agra** (19 hrs)

Daulatabad *p1192*

Bus Buses from Aurangabad's Central Bus Stand (platform 8), not all Ellora buses stop here.

Ajanta *p1197*

Bus Regular buses from Fardapur (5 km from Ajanta Caves) to **Ellora** and **Aurangabad** (3 hrs), and **Jalgaon** (1½ hrs). Some buses also go direct from the caves to Aurangabad.
Taxi Taxis and auto-rickshaws can be hired for the day for visiting the sights. Expect to pay Rs 2000 for round trip from Aurangabad.
Train The caves can also be visited from **Jalgaon**, 59 km, which has the nearest railway station. *Gitanjali Exp* (convenient from Kolkata) does not stop at Jalgaon so best to get off at Bhusawal.

Jalgaon *p1201*

Bus The **local bus stand** is about 1 km from the railway; auto-rickshaws Rs 10-15 for transfer. Direct buses to **Ajanta** from bus stand, 0815, 1030. Private buses from Station Rd for **Aurangabad**, **Indore**, **Hyderabad**, **Nagpur**, **Pune**, most between 2100-2200. Some via **Fardapur** (1½ hrs), go to Ajanta before going to Aurangabad (first departure 0700, 4 hrs, Rs 50); pleasant, interesting journey.
Train To **Mumbai** (**CST**): *Punjab Mail*, 2138, 0010, 7¾ hrs. **Delhi** via **Bhopal** and **Agra**: *Punjab Mail*, 2137, 0215, 18 hrs.

Jalna *p1202*

Bus Regular buses from **Lonar** (2 hrs), **Aurangabad** (2 hrs) and **Nanded** (5 hrs)
Train **Aurangabad**: several trains between 0800 and 1500 1 -1½ hrs. **Mumbai**: *Devgiri Exp, 17058, 2205, 9½ hrs; Tapovan Exp 17618, 1325, 10 hrs. Secunderabad: Ajanta Exp 17063, 2340, 9½ hrs.*

Lonar *p1202*

Bus By bus from **Jalna** (75 km, 2 hrs), **Jintur** (50 km, 1½ hrs); **Ajanta**/**Fardapur** (137 km) via **Buldana** and **Mehkar** (total 5 hrs).

Nanded *p1202*

Bus Connections to many destinations. Several agents by bus stand for private buses.
Train **Aurangabad**: Mumbai trains and *Mudkhed Manmad Exp 17688*, 0510, 5 hrs. **Bengaluru** (**Bangalore**): *Bangalore Exp 16593*, 0600, 24½ hrs. **Mumbai** (**CST**) : *Tapovan Exp 17618*, 1030, 12½ hrs; *Devgiri Exp 11004*, 1850, 12½ hrs. **New Delhi**: *Sachkhand Exp 12715*, 0930, 29 hrs (onto **Amritsar**, 37¼ hrs).

Ahmadnagar *p1202*

Bus Regular buses to **Mumbai**, **Pune** and other towns in the state.

Train
Bengaluru (**Bangalore**): *Karnataka Exp 12628*, 1820, 19½ hrs. **Bhopal**: *Goa Exp 12779*, 0703, 12 ½ hrs; *Jhelum Exp 11077*, 2025, 12½ hrs (on to **New Delhi**, 24¾ hrs). **Pune**: *Jhelum Exp 11078*, 1110, 4 hrs; *Goa Exp 12780*, 1250, 4½ hrs (on to **Vasco de Gama** (**Goa**), 18¾ hrs).

Directory

Aurangabad *p1190, map p1191*

Banks **State Bank of India**, Kranti Chowk, Rajendra Prasad Marg (Adalat Rd), junction of Paithan Darwaza Rd, set back from Rd, deals in foreign currency. **Medical services** **Medical College Hospital**, T0240 240 2412, northwest of town; **Govt Hospital**, Shahganj. **Post** GPO: Juna Bazar Chowk. Cantt Post Office.

Southern Maharashtra

Pune vies with Mumbai in terms of Maharashtran metropoles. Its reputation as an IT and industrial hub has now firmly eclipsed its reputation for the ashram utopianism – and free-sex and fast AIDS tests – associated with the red-robed Osho commune. Southwest is the hilltop fort of Raigad, and nearby is Maharashtra's wine-producing region, Kolhapur, and the cotton trade capital, Solapur.
▸▸ *For listings, see pages 1218-1226.*

Pune →

For listings, see pages 1218-1226. *Colour map 5, B3. Phone code: 020. Population: 2.54 million.*

After the small towns and seemingly endless spaces of the Deccan Plateau, Pune comes as a vibrant surprise. Touched by the élan of Mumbai, which is within commuting distance, the town comes to life in the early evening with open-air cafés and pavements crowded with young people out to enjoy themselves in a modern, cosmopolitan atmosphere, a place to see and be seen. It is an important and respected university town and one of the fastest growing IT centres of India, whilst the Osho Meditation Resort continues to attract large numbers of Westerners desperately seeking something.

Ins and outs

Getting there The airport, 10 km to the northeast, has flights from major cities. There are airport buses, taxis and rickshaws to the centre. Pune Junction Station is on the main railway line south from Mumbai and has daily direct trains south to Goa, Bengaluru and Kerala, and north towards Delhi and Gujarat. The main station is in the thick of the action: 1 km north of MG Road, the main shopping street, and 2 km west of Koregaon Park and the Osho resort. The other station, Shivaji Nagar, is five minutes further west and handy for the hotels and shops of Deccan Gymkhana. Most buses from the north terminate at the nearby Shivaji Nagar Bus Stand, and those from the south at Swargate, 3 km to the south. The Railway Bus Stand, next to Pune Junction, serves the city and Mumbai.

Getting around Pune is very spread out so it is best to hire an auto-rickshaw. Shared rickshaws run on popular routes, such as Pune Station to Swargate Bus Stand, and are more frequent but a bit more expensive than the red city buses. ▸▸ *See Transport, page 1224.*

Tourist information MTDC ⓘ *I-Block, Central Building, at corner of Sassoon and BJ Rds (enter from BJ Rd), T020-2612 6867*, is only useful if you want to book MTDC accommodation or buy a state map. There are counters at Pune Station, T020-2611 1720, and the airport.

Best time to visit The climatic contrast between Pune and the ghats just 70 km away is astonishing. The monsoon winds of June to September drop most of their rain on the ghats, over 3500 mm a year to Pune's 715 mm.

Background

The early home of Shivaji, Pune became the Maratha capital in 1750. After a period under the **Nizam of Hyderabad**'s rule it came under British control in 1817, who then developed it as a summer capital for Mumbai and as a military cantonment. It is now a major growth centre with a booming computer software industry. For all its connections with the Marathas there are few physical reminders of their power. The Campsite has wide streets with a British colonial feel while old Pune still has narrow streets, old shops and brick and mud houses. The town is renowned for its military cantonment and educational and scientific institutions.

Sights

The city stands on the right bank of the Mutha River before its confluence with the Mula and was divided up into 19 *peths* (wards). Some were named after the days of their weekly market, others after well-known people.

Pune

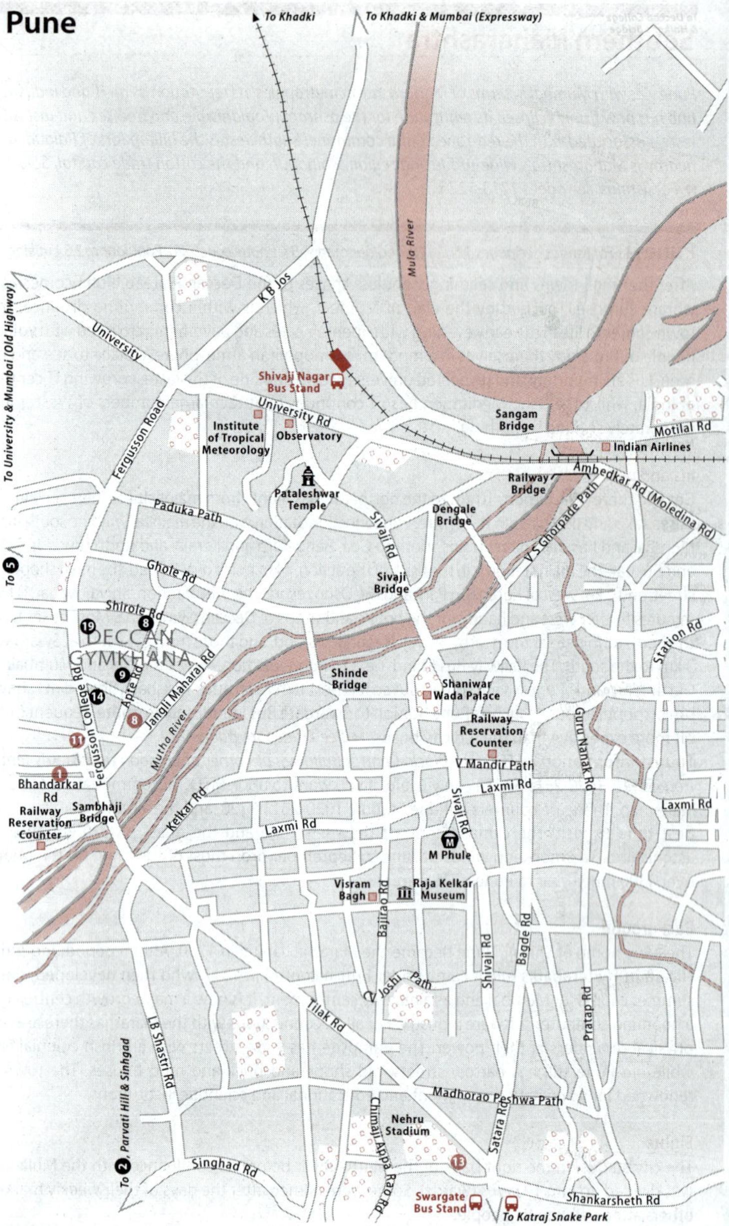
To Khadki
To Khadki & Mumbai (Expressway)
To University & Mumbai (Old Highway)
Mula River
K B Jos
University
Shivaji Nagar Bus Stand
University Rd
Fergusson Road
Institute of Tropical Meteorology
Observatory
Sangam Bridge
Motilal Rd
Indian Airlines
Railway Bridge
Ambedkar Rd (Moledina Rd)
Pataleshwar Temple
Paduka Path
Dengale Bridge
V S Ghorpade Path
Sivaji Rd
Ghole Rd
Sivaji Bridge
To 5
Shirole Rd
19
8
DECCAN GYMKHANA
9
Apte Rd
14
Jangli Maharaj Rd
Fergusson College Rd
Station Rd
Shinde Bridge
Shaniwar Wada Palace
Railway Reservation Counter
Guru Nanak Rd
Mutha River
8
11
1
Bhandarkar Rd
V Mandir Path
Laxmi Rd
Sivaji Rd
Laxmi Rd
Railway Reservation Counter
Sambhaji Bridge
Kelkar Rd
Laxmi Rd
M Phule
Visram Bagh
Bajirao Rd
Raja Kelkar Museum
Shivaji Rd
Bagde Rd
Joshi Path
Tilak Rd
Pratap Rd
LB Shastri Rd
To 2, Parvati Hill & Sinhgad
Madhorao Peshwa Path
Chimaji Appa Rao Rd
Nehru Stadium
Satara Rd
Singhad Rd
13
Swargate Bus Stand
To Katraj Snake Park
Shankarsheth Rd

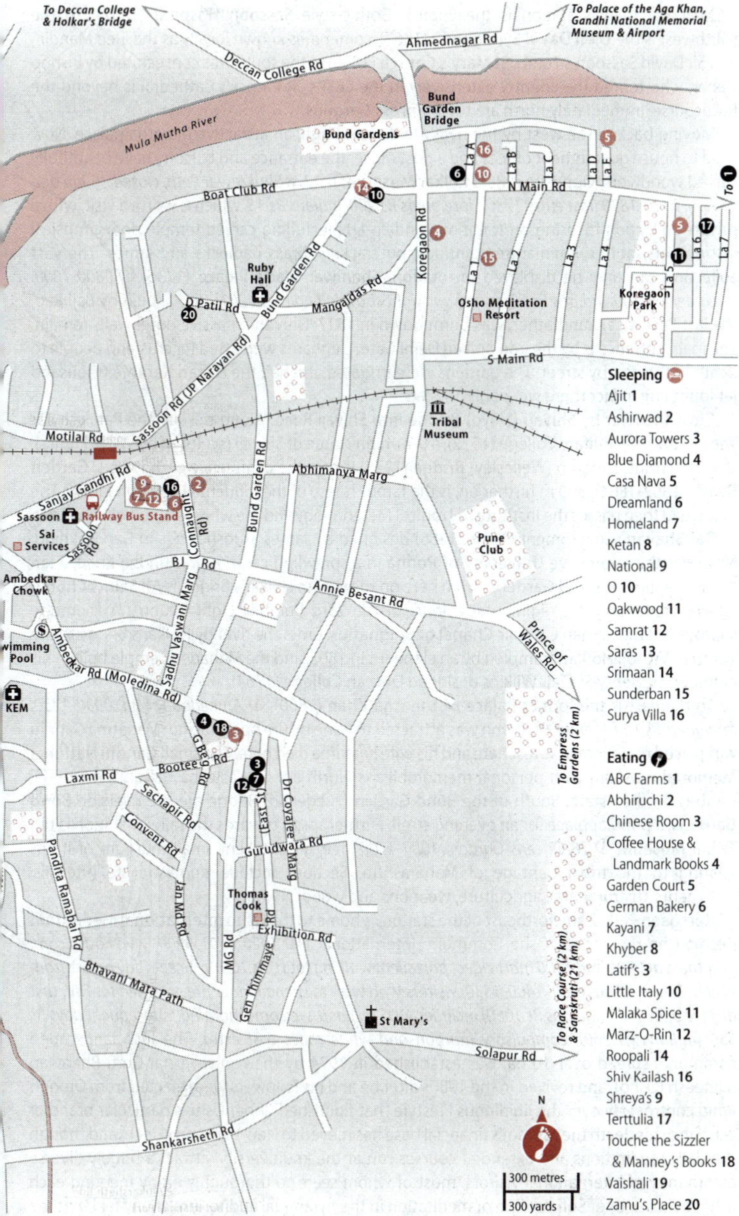

To Deccan College & Holkar's Bridge
To Palace of the Aga Khan, Gandhi National Memorial Museum & Airport
Ahmednagar Rd
Deccan College Rd
Mula Mutha River
Bund Garden Bridge
Bund Gardens
Boat Club Rd
N Main Rd
La A
La B
La C
La D
La E
To 1
Koregaon Rd
La 1
La 2
La 3
La 4
La 5
La 6
La 7
Koregaon Park
Osho Meditation Resort
S Main Rd
Ruby Hall
Bund Garden Rd
Mangaldas Rd
D Patil Rd
Sassoon Rd (JP Narayan Rd)
Motilal Rd
Tribal Museum
Sanjay Gandhi Rd
Sassoon
Railway Bus Stand
Sai Services
Sassoon Rd
Abhimanya Marg
Bund Garden Rd
(Connaught Rd)
Pune Club
BJ Rd
Ambedkar Chowk
Annie Besant Rd
Prince of Wales Rd
wimming Pool
Ambedkar Rd (Moledina Rd)
Sadhu Vaswani Marg
KEM
To Empress Gardens (2 km)
G Beg Rd
Bootee Rd
Laxmi Rd
Sachapir Rd
Convent Rd
(East St)
Dr Coyajee Marg
Gurudwara Rd
Pandita Ramabai Rd
Jan Md Rd
Thomas Cook
MG Rd
Gen Thimmaye Rd
Exhibition Rd
Bhavani Mata Path
St Mary's
To Race Course (2 km) & Sanskruti (21 km)
Solapur Rd
Shankarsheth Rd
N
300 metres
300 yards
Sleeping
Ajit 1
Ashirwad 2
Aurora Towers 3
Blue Diamond 4
Casa Nava 5
Dreamland 6
Homeland 7
Ketan 8
National 9
O 10
Oakwood 11
Samrat 12
Saras 13
Srimaan 14
Sunderban 15
Surya Villa 16
Eating
ABC Farms 1
Abhiruchi 2
Chinese Room 3
Coffee House & Landmark Books 4
Garden Court 5
German Bakery 6
Kayani 7
Khyber 8
Latif's 3
Little Italy 10
Malaka Spice 11
Marz-O-Rin 12
Roopali 14
Shiv Kailash 16
Shreya's 9
Terttulia 17
Touche the Sizzler & Manney's Books 18
Vaishali 19
Zamu's Place 20

Near the railway station is the English Gothic-style **Sassoon Hospital** (1867). To the southwest is the **Oleh David Synagogue** (1867), sometimes known locally as the 'Red Mandir', and Sir David Sassoon's Tomb. **St Mary's Church** (1825) to the south was consecrated by Bishop Heber, who toured the country extensively in the 1830s. St Patrick's Cathedral is beyond the Racecourse. Immediately north are the **Empress Gardens**.

Moving back to the west by the river are **Visram Bagh**, an attractive Maratha palace. Now used to house government offices and a post office, the entrance and balcony have beautifully carved woodwork. Opposite is **Raja Kelkar Museum** ⓘ *1378 Shukrawar Peth, closed 26 Jan and 15 Aug, 0930-1830 (last entry 1730), foreigners Rs 200, Indians Rs 15,* which is worth a visit, with a private collection focusing on traditional Indian arts including carved temple doors, musical instruments, pottery, miniature paintings, nutcrackers, brass padlocks and lamps. The vast collection can only be displayed in rotation. **Shaniwar Wada Palace** (1736) ⓘ *0800-1800, foreigners Rs 100, Indians Rs 50; sound and light show in English at 2015, Rs 25*, built by Baji Rao, the last Peshwa's grandfather, was burnt down in 1827. Only the massive outer walls remain. The main entrance is by the iron-spiked Delhi Gate. Elephants were used for crushing people to death in the nearby street. The gardens were irrigated and had the **Hazari Karanje** (thousand jet fountain); in fact there were only 197 jets.

Cross the river by **Shivaji** (Lloyd) **Bridge** into Shivaji Road. Along this are the Pataleshwar Temple and the Military College (1922), a 9-m-high statue of Shivaji (sculpted by VP Karkomar), stands in front. **Sangam** (Wellesley) **Bridge** (1875) is near the confluence of the rivers. **Garden Reach** (1862-1864), 300 m further on, is the family house of the influential Sassoon family. The main road then passes the Institute of Tropical Meteorology and the white-domed observatory.

Raj Bhavan (Government House, 1866) designed by James Trubshawe is in Ganeshkhind. Nearby is the impressive **University of Poona** in a sprawling campus. In Aundha Road, 3 km north, are the **Botanical Gardens**. From here on the way to Holkar's Bridge is **All Saints Church** (1841), containing the regimental colours of the 23rd Bombay Light Infantry. A kilometre southeast is the Roman Catholic **Chapel of St Ignatius.** Cross the river by Holkar's Bridge to the **Tomb of Vithoji Holkar**, trampled by an elephant in 1802, and the Mahadeo Temple built in his memory. Sir Henry St Clair Wilkins designed **Deccan College** (1864).

To the east is the former **Palace of the Aga Khan** (1860) ⓘ *Ahmednagar Rd, 0930-1730, foreigners Rs 100, Indians Rs 5*, who was attracted to Pune by the horse racing. Mahatma Gandhi was placed under house arrest here and his wife Kasturba died here. The small **Gandhi National Memorial** museum with personal memorabilia is worth a visit. Kasturba Gandhi's memorial tomb is on the estate. South of the Bund Garden (Fitzgerald) Bridge are the riverside **Bund Gardens**, a popular place for an evening stroll. Further south towards the railway station is the **Tribal Museum** ⓘ *28 Queens Garden, 1000-1700, free*, an excellent small museum of items relating to the tribal heritage of Maharashtra. Sections include domestic life (utensils, ornaments, instruments), agriculture, weapons and woodcarving.

Koregaon Park, 2 km northeast of the station, is home to the **Osho International Meditation Resort** (the rebranded "Osho Commune International") ⓘ *T020-6601 9900, www.osho.com, 1-hr tours at 0900 and 1400 (part video, part silent walking tour), Rs 10, buy tickets day before from Visitor Centre, 0900-1200, 1400-1530; visitors who wish to spend longer are screened for HIV; first day fee of Rs 1410 (Indians Rs 1060) includes AIDS test and 'welcome morning'; subsequent days Rs 550 (Indians Rs 200); compulsory maroon and white robes cost extra.* The lush landscaped commune, spread over 10 ha, was established in 1974 by the controversial Guru Bhagwan Rajneesh (Osho), and revived in the 1980s after he and his followers were ejected from Oregon amid controversy over the libidinous lifestyle that flourished under Osho's particular brand of zen. Since his death the ashram's financial base has moved to New York and Zurich, and though the daily meditations and extended courses run at the 'multiversity' attract a hugely diverse community of international visitors, most of whom seem to thoroughly enjoy meeting each other over a spot of Sufi twirling or meditation in the pyramidal auditorium, many feel that the essence of the guru's teachings has been compromised. Described by the *Wall Street Journal* as the "spiritual Disneyland for disaffected First World yuppies" (there's an Olympic-size pool, frequent parties and a serene guesthouse with rooms from Rs 3500 a night), the ashram has nevertheless done a superb job of greening the suburb of Koregaon Park; the gardens of **Osho Teerth** ⓘ *0600-0900, 1500-1800, free*, a block east of the main ashram entrance, make a beautiful place for a stroll or some meditation.

Parvati Hill, just south of the Mutha Right Bank Canal, has Hindu temples and commands excellent views over the town and surrounding countryside. Pune also has the **National Defence Academy** which trains cadets for the three defence services. There are parks and gardens dotted around the city.

Around Pune

The Maratha forts south of Pune are best visited by hiring a car since bus journeys can be slow and tiring. **Sinhagarh** is 24 km southwest of Pune. The 'Lion Fort', situated in the Bhuleshwar range, was a small hill station during the British period. The ruined, roughly triangular **fort** stands in a beautiful setting on a hill 700 m above the land below. The ascent is steep. To the north and south are cliffs topped with 12-m high basalt walls. There were two entrances, the Pune Gate (northeast) and Kalyan Gate (southwest), both protected by three successive gates. On the west side of the hill the wall was continued across a gorge, creating a dam. Muhammad Tughluq, see page 98, captured the fort in 1328, and in 1486 Malik Ahmad, founder of Ahmadnagar took it. Nearly 200 years later the Marathas captured it in what has become a legendary feat of bravery and skill by the commander scaling the cliffs at night and taking the garrison by surprise. To the western end is a small, covered, natural spring (known as 'Dev Taki' or 'God's Tank'), which yields cool, fresh sweet water throughout the year. Sinhagarh is a popular day out for people from Pune. Try the locally produced curd served in black clay pots with jeera seeds, salt and sugar.

On the way to Sinhagarh from Pune you pass the **Khadakwasla reservoir** on the Mutha River. The dam was constructed in 1879, the first large dam in the Deccan.

35 km southeast of Pune at an altitude of 1220 m, the hill fort of **Purandhar** commands a high point on the Western Ghats. It is a double fort, the lower one, **Vajragad** to the east and Purandhar itself. Together they command a narrow passage through the hills. Like other hill forts, Purandhar was defended by curtain walls, in this case 42 km in extent, relieved by three gateways and six bastions. The earliest fortifications date from 1350.

Purandhar Fort

Some 35 km southeast of Pune, at an altitude of 1220 m, this fort commands a high point on the Western Ghats. It is a double fort, the lower one, **Vajragad** to the east and **Purandhar** itself. Together they command a narrow passage through the hills. Like other hill forts, Purandhar was defended by curtain walls, in this case 42 km in extent, relieved by three gateways and six bastions. The earliest fortifications date from 1350.

Lonavla → *For listings, see pages 1218-1226.* *Colour map 5, B3. Phone code: 02114. Population: 55,700.*

Lonavla's reputation as a hill station for Mumbai is scarcely a preparation for the narrow, densely packed street astride the National Highway. The expressway from Mumbai to Bengaluru (Bangalore) now shadows the town. Trinket and knick-knack shops and *chikki* stalls piled high with the famous peanut brittle type sweet, is the strung out reality of the town. Yet it has a reasonable range of hotels and pleasant walks and is a good base for the Karla and Bhaja Caves and the Rajmachi, Lohagon and Visapur Forts nearby. The railway journey to Kalyan is interesting for rail enthusiasts. MTDC ⓘ *near Lonavla Railway Station.*

Sights

The town has some lovely walks around and about. **Ryewood Park** is within a few minutes' reach along Ryewood Road. Further along the same road, 1.5 km from the bazar, the scenic **Monsoon Lake** with a small island and its temple has a kilometre long dam which gives a good bird's eye view. A further 2 km along INS Shivaji Road leads to **Bushy Dam** which attracts crowds who come to soak themselves on monsoon weekends. **Old Khandala Road** which joins the highway near **Fariyas Hotel** was once the main approach to Lonavla. Now it is pleasantly quiet, lined with stately bungalows and is good for an evening stroll. **Tungarli Dam**, a disused water reservoir on a hill, is near **Lion's Den Hotel** and can be reached by taking the left turn from the highway petrol pump near **Jewel Resort**. Clean public toilets are at the start of Ryewood Road (market end). Pleasant circuits around town start at **Lonavla Bazar**.

Karla and Bhaja caves → *For listings, see pages 1218-1226.*

Karla Caves

ⓘ *11km east of Lonavla, north side of the valley, Rs100 foreigners, Rs 5 Indians.*

This is the largest and best preserved Buddhist *chaitya* (chapel) cave in India, dating from the second to first century BC. Here, as at Bhaja, the stone mason imitated the earlier wooden structures; the main *chaitya* shows evidence of stone supporting a wooden gallery. Unlike Ajanta and Ellora it is off the beaten tourist track for foreigners, though it can be crowded with local tourists at weekends.

The approach is across an excavated court. At the massive entrance stands a stone column topped with *sinha stambha* (four lions). The Hindu temple just outside the entrance may have been built over the remains of a second pillar. The façade contains a large horseshoe shaped window above the three doorways (one for the priest and the other two for pilgrims). In front of the side doors were shallow water-filled troughs through which the pilgrims walked to cleanse their feet. The remarkable sun window diffused the light into the hall, falling gently onto the *stupa* at the end. Buddha images (circa fifth century) partly decorate the exterior. There are also panels between the doorways depicting six pairs of donors.

The main chamber (38 m by 14 m), entered through a large outer porch, is supported by 37 pillars. It is 8 m from floor to ceiling which is barrel vaulted and ribbed with teak beams. There are 15 octagonal columns along either side, each capital having kneeling elephants carrying an embracing couple carved on it. The *stupa* is similar to that in Cave 10 at Ellora but here is topped by a wooden umbrella which is carved with delicate patterns. The other caves to the right of the entrance are of little interest.

Bhaja Caves → *Phone code: 02114.*

ⓘ *11 km east of Lonalva, south side of the valley; 5 km from Karla Caves.*

There are 18 caves dating from the second century BC. You will need to climb about 170 steps. **Cave 12** is the best and possibly the first apsidal *chaitya* (a long hall with a semi-circular end) in India. The apse contains a *dagoba*. The vaulted roof of the chapel is supported by 27 columns. The exterior was once covered in a bas-relief, much of this has now been defaced. On either side of the main cave are others which were probably nuns' cells and working quarters. The inner sanctum of the last cave to the south has very fine sculptures, including the 'Dancing Couple'; you will need to tip the caretaker to open the door (surprisingly only the central cell echoes). To the south are 14 *stupas*, five of which are inside the cave.

The ruined **Lohagen Fort** is about 4 km beyond Bhaja and was twice taken and lost by Shivaji. **Visapur Fort**, which stands 600 m from the foot of the hill, is nearby. You can see them from the Bhaja Caves.

Mahabaleshwar and around → *For listings, see pages 1218-1226.*

→ *Colour map 5, B3. Phone code: 02168. Population 13,000. Altitude: 1370 m.*

Situated in one of the wettest parts of the Western Ghats, Mahabaleshwar is in a pleasantly wooded setting at the head of the Krishna River. It is the main hill station for Pune, and almost as popular as Matheran among Mumbai weekenders. Cool and relaxed with some good walking trails and excellent views, it's a good place for an overnight stop. The altitude makes the climate pleasant during the dry season. It is, however, becoming increasingly touristy with crowds of Mumbai holidaymakers descending upon it, especially during school holidays. Tourist information is available from **MTDC Resort** ⓘ *T02168-260318*.

'Discovered' in 1824 by General Lodwick, to whom there is still a monument on the Elephant's Head Point, Mahabaleshwar was declared an official British sanatorium in 1828 and was once the summer capital of the Bombay Presidency. These days there are pleasant walks and waterfalls to visit. **Arthur's Seat** (12 km) looks out over a 600-m precipice to the Konkan. The nine-hole Golf Course is built on a cliff side. **Venna Lake** has boating and fishing. From **Mumbai Point** and the hills around the town you can see the sea on a clear day.

There are several typical British hill station buildings: **Christchurch** (1842, enlarged 1867); the cemetery; **Frere Hall** (1864) with its mullioned windows and the Club, founded in 1882; **Government House** (1829) on Mount Malcolm; The **Lodwick Monument** (1874) in honour of the town's founder, and the **Beckwith Monument**.

The old town contains three temples (Krishnabai, Ram and Hanuman) which you can walk to from a turn off Elphinstone Road. **Krishnabai** or Panchganga with a self-formed *linga* resembling a piece of volcanic lava, is said to have five streams, including the Krishna, flowing from it. The 13th-century Yadav King Singhan built a small tank at the Krishna's source which starts its 1400-km journey across the Deccan to the sea. This part of the 'Deccan Trap' has underground caverns which hold water and give rise to springs.

Panchgani

Settled as a hill station before Mahabaleshwar, Panchgani is set among casuarinas and silver oak at an altitude of 1334 m, surrounded by the five hills from which it takes its name. It has a compact centre with lovely walks, stunning views and friendly people, which makes it well worth a visit. MTDC can arrange for you to visit some of the old British and Parsi bungalows. The drive to Mahabaleshwar offers beautiful views; sit on the left travelling from Panchgani.

Wai

Wai stands on the left bank of the Krishna River, 14 km east of Panchgani, where the riverside, lined with shady temples, is very attractive, particularly the finely carved *mandapam* in front of the Mahadev temple. Hills rise sharply around the town. On a hilltop **Pandavgad** fort, which according to local tradition was visited by the Pandava brothers of the *Mahabharata*. The town's sanctity is enhanced by its proximity to the source of the Krishna.

Satara

Satara, south of Wai on the NH-4 and 42 km southeast of Mahabaleshwar lies in a hollow near the confluence of the Krishna and Venna rivers. It is considered a place of great sanctity and there are several temples on the banks at **Mahuli**. The cantonment contains Sir Bartle Frere's **Residency** (1820). A 'New Palace' (1838-1844) was built by the engineer responsible for the bridges over the two rivers.

The ruling house of Satara was descended from Sahu, Shivaji's grandson, who was brought up at the Mughal court. Their **mansion**, 200 m from the New Palace, contains a number of Shivaji's weapons. These include the notorious 'tigers' *waghnakh* (claws) with which Shivaji is reputed to have disembowelled Afzal Khan. Other weapons include *Jai Bhavani*, his favourite sword (made in Genoa), and his rhinoceros hide shield. There is an **Historical Museum** (1930) which contains a fine collection of archival material on the Marathas. Satara Road railway station is 6 km from the city and bus stand.

Wasota Fort on the south side of the town can be reached by both road and footpath. Reputedly built by the Raja of Panhala in the 12th century, it's 14-m-high walls (which remain only at the gateway) and buttresses contain the remains of the rajah's palace, a small temple and a bungalow. It passed to the Mughals under Aurangzeb, for a time, after he besieged the fort in 1699, but returned to the Marathas in 1705 with the help of a Brahmin agent who tricked the Mughals.

Pratapgarh

To the west of Mahabaleshwar, the setting for this **Maratha fort** is spectacular. From the summit (1080 m) on which it is sited there is a splendid view down the forested hillside. A road leads to the foot of the hill, then 500 steps run up to the top.

The fort comprises a double wall with corner bastions. The gates are studded with iron spikes. Inside, the Bhavani temple in the lower fort has two *dipmal* (lantern towers); their exteriors are covered with regularly placed projections like giant coat hooks. Presumably lanterns were placed on these or hung from them, the towers then acting as beacons. The upper fort has a Siva temple. Its ramparts can be seen nearly all of the way down the very scenic (but slow) road to Poladpur.

Raigad (Raigarh) → *Colour map 5, B3.*

ⓘ 63 km northwest of Pratapgarh, foreigners Rs 100, Indians Rs 5, cable car (Rs 150) avoids the 6-km walk up but power failures can cause delays, look for signs for 'Ropeway' leading to a right turn before reaching the end of the paved road and be prepared for a scary ride in a cage.

The views from this three-pronged hilltop fort are magnificent, especially the stunningly beautiful panorama across the lakes to the north. Difficult to reach, the fort is rarely visited by foreigners, though there are plenty of Indian tourists since Shivaji, the greatest hero in Maratha history, once ruled his kingdom from here. Raigad dates from around the 12th century. Known as 'Rairi' it was the seat of a Maratha chief. Later it passed in turn to the Vijayanagaras, the Nizam of Ahmadnagar, the Bijapuri Adil Shahis until Shivaji regained it in 1648 and made it the home of his much-revered mother, Jiji Bai. In 1674 he chose it for his coronation at the hands of Brahmin priests but died here in 1680. Aurangzeb acquired it in 1690 but it soon reverted back to the Marathas who surrendered it to the British in 1818.

The path to the fort climbs 1400 steps from its start at **Wadi**, and makes for a tough hike at any time of year. The flat hilltop is about 2500 m long and 1500 m across at the widest. A bastioned wall encloses it while two outer curtain walls contour round the hillsides. Heavily fortified in each corner of the irregular triangle, in Shivaji's day the fort was one of the strongest in India. The main gate (Maha Darwaza) is flanked by two large bastions, both 21 m high, one concave, the other convex. Inside the fort, the extensive **Palace** and **Queen's Chamber** are placed between two tanks. In the courtyard is a low platform where the throne stood and after the coronation the title Chhatrapati ('Lord of the Umbrella') was bestowed on Shivaji. In the centre of the town was a market which had more than 40 shops in two parallel rows for the 2000 people housed in the fort. To the northeast is Shivaji's **Samadhi** (memorial), as well as a *chhattri* for his dog. If you go up in the evening when the heat has died down, it is extremely atmospheric.

Kolhapur and around → *For listings, see pages 1218-1226. Colour map 5, C4. Phone code: 0231. Population: 485,200.*

Set in the wide open plains of the southern Deccan, Kolhapur, founded under the 10th- century Yadavas, was once one of the most important Maratha states. Shivaji's younger son, inherited the southern regions of his father's kingdom, but after a history of bitter factional dispute it became an important Princely State under the British. Today it has the unlikely distinction of being at the heart of India's small wine producing region, and is also witnessing a flow of foreign investment, making it one of the major industrial centres of Maharashtra. The area has rich bauxite deposits and the damming of the Koyna, a tributary of the Krishna, is providing electricity for aluminium smelting. For tourist information contact **MTDC** ⓘ *Kedar Complex, Station Rd, T0231-265 2935*; or **Goa Tourism** ⓘ *Mohan Travels, 517E Pune–Bangalore Rd, T0231-265 0911*.

At the core of the old city is the hugely atmospheric **Amba Bai** (Mahalaxmi) **Temple**, dedicated to the mother goddess, which buzzes with devotional activity throughout the day. It has 10th-century foundations, a tall pyramidal tower added in the 18th century and an impressive carved ceiling to the pillared hall. Note Vishnu with the eight *Dikpalas*, see page 772. Immediately to its east, the **Juna Rajwada** (Old Palace), which was badly damaged by fire in 1810, contains a temple to Tuljabhawani, the favourite goddess of Shivaji, and is entered through a traditional drum gallery or *nakkar khana* (music hall). Upstairs in the palace is the Durbar Hall and armoury which contains one of Aurangzeb's swords and other interesting memorabilia.

Much of Kolhapur's architecture can be attributed to the British army engineer Major Charles Mant, whose connection to the city began when he designed a cenotaph for Maharajah Rajaram, who died in Florence in 1871. His **New Palace** (1881), 2 km north of the centre, belongs to the period when all the succession disputes had been resolved and Kolhapur was being governed as a model state. Built out of grey stone around a central courtyard, it's a bizarre blend of Jain temple and Rajasthani palace with a Victorian clock tower perched on top, and is home to the **Shahu Museum** ⓘ *Tue-Sun 1100-1300, 1600- 1800*, packed to the ceiling with stuffed animals, jewellery, weapons and other royal paraphenalia collected by the maharaja, who still resides in the palace, and his forefathers.

Among Mant's other buildings in the town are the Town Hall (1873), halfway between the new and old palaces with a small **museum of antiquities** ⓘ *1030-1300, 1330-1730*, the General Library (1875), Albert Edward Hospital (1878) and High School (1879).

The sacred Panchganga River skirts the north of the city, and ghats and temples line its banks. **Brahmapuri Hill**, the Brahmin cremation ground, overlooks the river to the west of town. Nearby is the **Rani's Garden** where the royal family have memorial *chhattris*.

Panhala

Panhala (977 m), 19 km northwest of Kolhapur, is where Rajah Bhoj II, whose territory extended to the Mahadeo Hills north of Satara, had his **fort**. However, it is particularly associated with Shivaji, who often stayed here. The Marathas and Mughals occupied it in turn until the British took it in 1844. The fort is triangular with a 7 km wall with three gates around it, in places rising to 9 m. The Tin Darwaza (three gates) leads to a central courtyard or 'killing chamber'; the inner gate leads to the Guard Room. The Wagh Gate (partly ruined) adopts similar principles of defence. Inside are vast granaries, the largest of which covers 950 sq m, has 11 m high walls and enabled Shivaji to withstand a five-month siege. By the ruins is a temple to Maruti, the Wind god. To the north is the two-storey palace.

Solapur and east of Pune

→ *For listings, see pages 1218-1226. Colour map 5, B5.*
Phone code: 0217.

In the heart of the cotton growing area, **Solapur** (Sholapur) has been a focus of the cotton trade for over a century. Almost entirely an industrial city, it still has an atmospheric area with traditional old buildings along Navee Peth and Rajvadee Chowk.

From Solapur the main road to Pune follows the Bhima River northwest across the vast open fields and scattered settlements of the plateau. It is a region rich in archaeological sites, as it was a major centre of prehistoric settlement.

Pandharpur, on the south bank of the Bhima River, is regarded by many as the spiritual capital of Maharashtra. It has a shrine to Vithoba, an incarnation of Vishnu, dating from 1228. Although some tourist literature puts its origins as early as AD 83 there is no evidence for this early date. There are 12 bathing ghats on the river bank, and during the main pilgrimage times (Ashadhi Ekadashi in July and Kartik Ekadashi in Oct), tens of thousands of pilgrims converge on the town. *Rath Yatra*, or temple car procession, dates back to 1810.

South Konkan coast → *For listings, see pages 1218-1226. Colour map 5, B3, C3 and C4.*

The 593-km coast route from Mumbai to Goa, now followed by the Konkan Railway and the NH17, runs through the economically backward but scenically attractive South Konkan region. It passes a string of small towns which developed at the heads of estuaries – transshipment points for cargo brought in by sea, then hauled by pack animals over the Ghats. Although lowland, it is far from flat. Many of the densely wooded slopes have been cleared, leaving bare and unproductive laterites, alternating with patches of intensive rice cultivation and coconut groves. The coastal estuaries support mangrove swamps, while scattered along the beaches are a series of domestic-focused holiday resorts. Outside holiday weekends this is a quiet, beautiful coast, with serious rewards for explorers who aren't dependent on public transport or a daily dose of banana porridge.

Murud-Janjira

Some 160 km south of Mumbai, the old town of **Murud** contains a number of interesting painted buildings built by the Siddis, a warrior tribe of Abyssinian origin whose descendants still live in the area. An empty palace belonging to the nawab, south the town centre, is clearly visible from the road to Rajpuri jetty. Signs warn trespassers away, but the caretaker may allow you to look at the ghost of the once opulent lifestyle of the nawabs, Rs 50 tip expected. Some decaying Muslim tombs stand among baobab trees, 1 km south of the jetty.

From here, boats sail to **Janjira Fort** ⓘ *0700-1800, Rs 10, closed Fri 1200-1400*, built by the Siddis and reputedly one of the strongest coastal forts in India: even the fearsome Marathas never captured it. The fort retains a number of remarkable buildings, including mosques, the *topkhana* guarded by canons and a five-storeyed crumbling **palace**. Across the bay is the fort of Padmadurg, built by the Maratha leader Sambhaji to combat the Siddis.

Just north of Murud centre is the temple to the triple-headed **Dattatraya** representing Brahma, Vishnu and Siva. It is worth climbing the 250 steps, not least for the commanding views. **Kashid**, 15 km further north, has an excellent 3-km-long silver-sand beach, which is a popular weekend resort but deserted on weekdays. The sea is polluted and swimming is not advised. A good beach, 2 km away, is suitable for camping and the hills are good for walking.

Chiplun

The NH17 runs south through Khed to Chiplun on the banks of the Vashishti River, fed from the **Koyna Lake**, one of the largest artificial lakes in the Western Ghats. There are spectacular views across the flat valley bottom, criss-crossed by the several courses of the meandering river. After Khed and 10 km before Chiplun, near an attractive small village and temple (difficult to find when travelling north) there is accommodation.

Ratnagiri

Now a rapidly growing and unprepossessing port town with a lot of road works, Ratnagiri ('Jewel hill'), 13 km west off the NH17 at Hathkamba, was the birthplace of two leaders of the Independence Movement, Gangadhar Tilak and GK Gokhale. It was also the internment home for the last king of Burma, King Thibaw, who was held here from 1886 until his death in 1916. His 'palace' is now part of the polytechnic.

Ganpatipule

Revered and much visited by Hindus for its *swayambhu* ('naturally occurring' or 'self- created') Ganesh, Ganpatipule, north of Ratnagiri, has a beautifully white deserted beach which gets busy at weekends. The sea is clean but beware of strong currents. **Jaigad Fort**, 35 km, makes a pleasant excursion.

Vijayadurg (Viziadurg)

A minor road west off the NH17 at Talera leads to the formidable fort guarding the river which was built on an ancient site. The Sultans of Bijapur enlarged it and Sivaji further strengthened it by adding the three outer walls. It has 27 bastions, an inner moat, good water supply and carried 278 guns in 1682. The Maratha pirate Kanhoji Angria made it his base in 1698, plundered European shipping and withstood assaults by the Portuguese and the British.

Malvan and around

A coastal road leads south from Vijayadurg, passing through Devgad, renowned for producing India's sweetest mangoes, to Malvan. The old town runs the length of a crowded little street that leads to a port, from where boats can take you to Sivaji's coastal fort of **Sindhudurg** ⓘ *boatmen charge around Rs 25 per person*, now deserted, which sits atop a low-lying island just off the coast. There are several shrines within the fort – to Maruti, Bhavani, Mahadeo and uniquely to Sivaji. There is an unconventional statue of Sivaji and two well-known temples to Sri Devi Sateri and Rameshwar.

South of Malvan, a narrow road runs down to the peninsula of **Tarkarli**, where casuarina trees straggle along the back of a largely deserted beach. There are a few low-key resorts and guesthouses here, almost exclusively geared towards domestic tourists (signs are in Marathi only). At Karli Creek boatmen offer **dolphin-watching cruises** (best early in the morning), and MTDC runs **houseboat trips** ⓘ *Rs 6050-7100 per room per night, bookings from MTDC offices statewide, www.maharashtratourism.gov.in, or locally on T02362-228785.*

Vengurla

The former trading settlement on an island is now joined to the land. On the NH17, close to the Goa border, the coast here is lined with beautiful white-sand beaches. Salt pans provide an important product for export from the region.

Sawantwadi

Sawantwadi was the capital of the Bhonsle kings of southern Maharashtra who were constantly trying to extend their territory into Goa. Today it is a large and ramshackle but friendly market town, centred around the large Moti Talav ('Pearl Lake') with an out-of- town station on the Konkan Railway. It was once noted for the production of fine hand-painted *ganjifa* (playing cards), which the Sawantwadi royal family is keeping alive by allowing a few artists/craftsmen to work in the once-impressive darbar hall of the **palace** ⓘ *0930-1230, Rs 50.*

The brightly coloured *ganjifa* were originally produced by pasting layers of cloth together, using tamarind seed gum then coating the 'card' with chalk before polishing it with a stone to provide a smooth white base for decorating the face with natural pigments while the back was stiffened with lacquer. The packs of circular cards come in various sizes and suits. The 10 suits of the *Dasavatara* (featuring Vishnu's 10 incarnations), for example, forms a pack of 120 cards while the *Navagraha* (nine planets) has nine suits. The miniature paintings with patterns drawn from mythology, history and nature, often reflect folk traditions. Prices range from Rs 800 to Rs 3000, but the best-decorated cards make their way straight to shops in Mumbai. Local craftsmen also produce painted lacquered furniture, chessmen, board games and candle sticks.

Amboli

From Sawantwadi, a state road goes up the ghats to the minor hill station of Amboli, at an altitude of 690 m. The road continues on to **Belgaum**. Set on the flat-topped heights of the Western Ghats overlooking the coastal plain below, Amboli is a quiet and little-visited resort. There are attractive walks and several waterfalls. **Bauxite mines**, 10 km away, can also be visited.

Redi Beach

Just 3 km north of the Goa border and Tiracol, a turn off from NH17, south of Shiroda, leads to Redi Village and beach. An old **Maratha Fort**, now in ruins but interesting to wander round, dominates the view over a stunning and, for now, rarely visited bay, though plans for wider roads and a large resort are on the table.

Southern Maharashtra listings

For Sleeping and Eating price codes and other relevant information, see Essentials pages 38-42.

Sleeping

Pune *p1207, map p1208*

Room rates have soared along with Pune's credentials as a business city, but the recession has bitten and many middle and upper-bracket hotels have been humbled into giving discounts. Genuinely cheap rooms are hard to find; the best bet is to trawl the lanes of **Koregaon Park**, where auto-rickshaw drivers promise rooms in guest-houses for Rs 300-500. There are also excellent deals to be had in the lower-middle range (Rs1200-3000). Discounts often available Apr-Sep.

LL Aurora Towers, 9 Moledina Rd, T020-2613 1818, www.hotelauroratowers.com. 68 large rooms with views, good restaurants, friendly service, 24-hr exchange, terraced pool (non-residents Rs 100), good value and location near the top of MG Rd.

LL Blue Diamond (Taj), 11 Koregaon Rd, T020-6602 5555, www.tajhotels.com. 110 rooms, stylish, comfortable and classy, special discounts for business guests with partners.

LL O Hotel, North Main Rd, Koregaon Park, T020-4001 1000, www.ohotelsindia.com. Pune's first design hotel, decked out in dark woods and granite, with huge white bathtubs overlapping between bed and bathroom. The 9th-floor spa offers massage and haircuts with a view, and the adjoining resto-bar has Pune's coolest rooftop site, with circular day beds set on granite islands in a shallow pond. Wi-Fi in rooms.

L-AL Ashirwad, 16 Connaught Rd, T020-2612 8687. 44 neat and modern but overpriced rooms, and good, spacious business-ready suites with separate dining/meeting room (but Wi-Fi is charged extra). Good *thali* restaurant downstairs, exchange, helpful. Ask for discount rates.

L-AL Oakwood, Good Luck Sq, off FC Rd, T020-2567 0011, www.tghotels.com. 41 comfortable rooms in plush business hotel, good service, airport transfer, internet.

L-E Sunderban, 19 Koregaon Park, next to **Osho Resort**, T020-2612 4949, www.tghotels.com. The 58 rooms here vary hugely, from grey and dingy little economy doubles out the back to lovely suites and studios in the art deco main building. Deluxe rooms are good value, with well-worn leather lounges and lots of space. Set around pleasant lawns, and serenaded by Osho meditations from the ashram next door. Wi-Fi available, breakfast included.

AL-B Casa Nava, various locations in Koregaon Park, T(0)9823-169507, www.casa nava.com. Superb, individually decorated apartments run by expat interior designer Nava. Some have a boho-chic feel, with colourful day-beds and painted desks overlooking the river, others go for a minimalist white look. Each comes with fully equipped kitchen and internet. Popular with the Osho crowd, and excellent for long stays.

A-B Samrat, 17 Wilson Garden, near Pune Station, T020-2613 7964, thesamrathotel@vsnl.net. The doubles here represent one of the best deals in town, spotless and modern, set around a soaring lobby, but the suites are bizarre, with 2 TVs placed back to back in the wide open hatch between bedroom and living room. Wi-Fi is extra, buffet breakfast is included.

B-C Ketan, 917/19A Shivajinagar, FC Rd, T020-2565 5081. Very clean, 28 rooms with bath, some spacious a/c, helpful.

B-C Surya Villa, Lane A, behind **O Hotel**, Koregaon Park, T020-2612 4501, www.hotelsuryavilla.com. An Osho favourite, with light, clean and spacious rooms, internet downstairs and the popular **Yogi Tree** café serving a pan-global menu from tofu steaks to pasta.
C Srimaan, 361/5 Bund Garden Rd, T020-2613 3535. 30 pleasant rooms, clean, Italian restaurant.
C-D Ajit, 766/3 Deccan Gymkhana, T020- 2567 1212. 16 rooms, some a/c, restaurant, small, dark but functional, peaceful location.
C-D Dreamland, 2/12 Connaught Rd, T020-2612 2121. 43 rooms, some a/c, above the excellent Sagar restaurant (good vegetarian *thalis*), well kept and often full.
C-D Homeland, 18 Wilson Garden, T020-2612 3203, www.hotelhomeland.net. 22 small but reasonably clean rooms in an appealing art deco building. The attached 'theatre restaurant' is more "bar with big TV screen".
D-E National, 14 Sassoon Rd, T020-2612 7780. Surprisingly quiet for its location opposite the station, this decaying old timber mansion offers decent value en suite doubles and cheaper, mildly grimy cottages with shaded sit-outs in the back yard. The cheapest rooms, gloomy little cells with no windows, share unpleasant toilets. Room service chai and snacks and filtered drinking water available.
E Saras, Nehru Stadium, Swargate, T020-2443 0499, near bus station. Good value, 20 pleasant rooms, 1 a/c, restaurant.

Lonavla *p1211*

Mumbai–Pune Rd is the NH4.
LL Fariyas Holiday Resort, Tungarli, Frichley Hills, T02114-273852. 103 luxurious rooms, some newer, solar heated pool, health club.
AL Biji's Hill Retreat, New Tungarli Rd, T02114-279654. Has 32 spacious rooms (round glass house with round bed), restaurant, bar, pool.
A Duke's Retreat, Mumbai–Pune Rd, 4 km from Lonavla Railway in Khandala, T02114- 269201. 62 rooms, restaurant, bar, pool, superb views.
A Lakeview Resort, 4 Ryewood, T02114-272755. 22 airy, breezy rooms, very clean, excellent location overlooking lake.
A Rainbow Retreat, NH4, opposite Valvan Dam (away from town), T02114-272128. Modern, 46 rooms, pricey bar, poolside disco at weekends, pleasant garden.
B-C Adarsh, near bus stand, T02114-272353. Efficiently run hotel in a relatively tranquil location, between bus and train stations but away from the main road, with a good pure vegetarian restaurant.
C-D Chandralok, Shivaji Rd, opposite bus stand entrance, T02114-272294. Large, clean, comfortable airy rooms, some a/c, excellent unlimited *thalis* (Rs 80-100).
D-E Shamiana, 66 Mumbai Pune Rd, opposite Bajrang Baug, T02114-272356. Set in charming unkempt garden off highway, 7 cottage suites (2-4 beds), nice but noisy, simple but comfortable (no mosquito nets).
E DT Shahani Health Home, DT Shahani Rd, behind bus stand, T02114-272784. Very clean triples in quiet locality, varied menu in canteen.

Karla Caves *p1212*

A-E Holiday Resort (MTDC), off Mumbai- Pune Rd (NH4), T02114-282230. Vast sylvan surroundings, 64 clean rooms in cottages for 2-4 (some comfortable a/c), canteen, bar.

Mahabaleshwar *p1213*

Many hotels here; several family-run. The bazar sells local honey which is justly famous, as are jams from locally grown fruit.
L-AL Brightland Holiday Village, Nakhinda Village (4 km from centre), Kates Pt Rd, T02168-260707, www.brightlandholiday.com. 30 rooms, restaurants, bar, pool, gardens.
A Fountain, opposite Koyna Valley, T02168-260227. In Mahabaleshwar's oldest resort, 98 rooms air cooled with TV, vegetarian restaurant with a good choice.
A Valley View Resort, Valley View Rd, off James Murray Peth Rd, T02168-260066, www.valleyview-resort.com. 80 very clean rooms, 40 a/c, real grass to balconies, pure vegetarian restaurant (no beer), great views from garden. Recommended.
B-D Holiday Resort (MTDC), 2 km from centre (taxi Rs 40), T02168-260318. Large complex with 100 cottages, rooms and garden suites, dorm (no beds) Rs 100, restaurant, permit room, pleasant setting and atmosphere, tourist office near gate, popular.
C-D Dreamland, off MG Rd, behind ST Stand, T02168-260227, www.hoteldreamland.com. 80 rooms with view, old cottages and newer a/c

suites with cable TV and phone by the pool, restaurant (vegetarian) in large garden.

D-E Grand, Woodlawn Rd, away from centre, T02168-260322. Modest rooms with veranda, gardens.

E Sai Niwas, 338 Koli Alley, T02168-260549. Good value, clean rooms.

Panchgani *p1213*

B-E Five Hills (MTDC), opposite Dr Ambedkar Nagar, Rajpuri Rd, T02168-240301. 64 doubles and suites, good restaurant.

D-E Amer, 188 Chesson Rd, T02168-240211. Some a/c rooms with bath.

Kolhapur *p1214*

AL-B Shalini Palace, by Rankala Lake, T0231-263 0401, hotelshalinipalace@rediffmail.com. This dusty old 1930s pile set amid green lawns lets you sleep like a royal, albeit a minor one sent broke by the credit crunch. The big suites are excellent, with timber-screened sitting areas and new showers. Older royal rooms are fine too, with high ceilings and plenty of space, but check the bathtubs before you agree to stay. Upstairs rooms share a long wraparound veranda with lake views, and the frumpy old restaurant and bar offer plenty of atmosphere.

A Victor Palace, Rukmini Nagar, Old Pune-Bangalore Rd, T0231-253 7001, info@hotelvictorpalace.com. The swinging metal doors in the corridors could have come from an emergency ward, but the newly renovated rooms are modishly fitted out in black and chrome with swish bathrooms. There's an excellent pool and gym plus a bar and good barbeque restaurant. Breakfast included.

B-C Woodland, 204 E Ward, Tarabai Park (5 mins by rickshaw north of bus stand), T0231-265 0941, www.hotelwoodland.net. One of the most pleasant in town, bright clean rooms, free in-room broadband hookup and a great Gujarati *thali* restaurant upstairs, all wrapped in a peaceful garden with burbling fountains.

D-E Opal, Pune–Bangalore Rd, T0231-253 6767, www.hotelopal.co.in. Appealing 1960s hotel, with just a handful of a/c and non-a/c rooms, a popular non-veg Maharashtran restaurant, and a ready supply of city maps and info. Undergoing renovation at the time of update, so prices may rise.

D-E Vrindavan Deluxe, Shivaji Park, T0231-266 4343. A great budget deal, with super-comfortable and clean rooms in a new, airy and attractive hotel a 1-min walk from the bus stand. Veg restaurant.

E-F Maharaja, 514E Station Rd, opposite bus stand, T0231-265 0829. Budget favourite right by the bus stand, the undergoing renovation at time of research.

F Pathik, immediately behind **Maharaja**, T0231-265 0606. Small but quite clean rooms with attached Indian-style toilets, set down a side street and relatively quiet for its location.

Panhala *p1215*

C-D Valley View Grand, Tabak Baug, Panhala, T02328-235036, has fabulous views from rooms and open-air restaurant (very good food), pretty gardens.

D Mahalaxmi Resort (MTDC/private), near Bajiprabhu Statue, Panhala, T02328-235048. 21 good rooms and an outdoor restaurant. Dorm.

Solapur and east of Pune *p1215*

C Pratham, 560/61 South Sadar Bazar, T0231-231 2581. 30 clean, modern, pleasant rooms, half a/c with bath, excellent open-air restaurant, friendly and helpful staff.

C Surya Executive, 3/3/2 Murarji Peth, T0231-272 9880. Next door to **Surya International**. Good, clean excellent value, air-cooled rooms, restaurant.

E Srikamal, 77 Railway Lines, T0231-272 2964. Clean rooms, hot shower, good terrace restaurant, run by helpful, friendly family.

F Railway Retiring Rooms and dorm.

Murud-Janjira *p1216*

A Kashid Beach Resort, 500 m from beach across main road, T02144-278501, www.nivalink.com/kashid. 25 split-level clean rooms, some with good sea views, bathrooms a bit run down, restaurant (beer appears as 'snacks' on the bill), in large grounds, bike hire.

B Golden Swan Beach Resort, Darbar Rd, T02144-274078, www.goldenswan.com. Comfortable rooms in cottages near beach, adequate restaurant serving coastal cuisine.

E Seashore Resort (no sign), south of Golden Swan Resort, T02144-274223. 3 rooms, bath, friendly family, lovely garden on beach.

E-F Aman Palace, Darbar Rd, T02144-274297. Simple rooms with bath, hammocks in garden.

Chiplun *p1216*

There are several very cheap lodges around the town centre and bus stand.

AL The Riverview, Dhamandivi, near Parshuram Temple, T02355-259081, www.chiplunhotels.com. With 37 comfortable rooms, most a/c, excellent restaurant, pool to indulge in, helipad, attractive garden setting, peaceful.

Ganpatipule *p1217*

A-F Holiday Resort (MTDC), on the beach, T02357-235248, on the beach, among palm trees. 68 clean, comfortable a/c suites to 4-bed rooms (11 and 12 best) and some musty old tents, poor restaurant (serves beer), onsite bank changes TCs, poor service and 0900 checkout, but great location, relaxing.

B-D Landmark, on hillside going down to village, T02357-235284. Good rooms, excellent Chinese/Indian restaurant, beer.

C-E Abishek, 500 m down dirt track opposite **Landmark**, T022-2437 0801 (Mumbai). Typical Indian hotel, restaurant with sea views.

Malvan *p1217*

B-D MTDC Resort, 5 km south of Malvan on Tarkarli Beach, T02365-252390. Simple self-contained cottages set in a casuarina grove on a quiet stretch of beach. The restaurant here has the best variety of food for miles.

D-F Manali Resort, 3 km beyond **MTDC Resort** on Tarkarli Creek, T02365-248550, T(0)9423-304384. Glass-fronted cabins on top of a dune facing the fishing boats on the beach, and small and super-basic rooms with no views set around the kitchen. Basic fish or veg *thalis* available, or buy supplies in town and the family that runs the place will cook them.

Sawantwadi *p1217*

C-D Mango, Pateshwar Complex, Main Rd, T02363-271041, www.hotelmango.co.in. Smart new business hotel in the heart of the bazar, with large, sparkling a/c rooms and a deserted restaurant.

E-F Tara, Gandhi Chowk, 5 mins' walk south of bus stand, T02363-272644. Slightly more dog-eared, but the rooms are clean and bright enough, the staff are friendly, and there's a dingy little restaurant.

Amboli *p1218*

C-E Green Valley Resort (MTDC/private), T02363-240239. A reasonably comfortable base with a choice of 21 rooms including some suites.

C-E JRD International, Vengurla–Belgaon Rd, 1 km from bus stand, T02363-240223. 30 pleasant, clean rooms, better in 'cottages', reasonable Indian restaurant, bar.

Eating

Pune *p1207, map p1208*

Pune has a variety of dining options to rival Mumbai. In Deccan Gymkhana, Jangli Maharaj (JM) Rd claims to have the highest concentration of eateries of any street in India. MG Rd and East St in Camp have juice shops and cafes to keep the shoppers happy, while Koregaon Park and nearby Kalyani Nagar are where expats, ashramites and local cool kids fill up on expensive international fare. Many of the top hotels lay on a Sun brunch; the one at **Le Meridien**, north side of Pune Station, is among the best.

ABC Farms, North Main Rd, Koregaon Park. A complex of upscale restaurants and pubs, including Swiss Cheese Garden (for fondues), Shisha Café (Persian food and the best atmosphere, with hookahs and low-slung day beds), and the popular Curve Bar. No longer the trendiest in town and a bit tired- looking, but still packed on weekends.

TT Abhiruchi, at junction of Singhad Rd and Mumbai-Pune bypass, 8 km southwest of centre. Rustic village-style restaurant in 16 ha. Unlimited Maharashtrian *thali* (Rs 100) including 6 types of bread. More a day out than a lunch break. Recommended.

TT Chinese Room, Gen Thimmaya Rd. One of Pune's oldest Chinese joints. High standards and a loyal fan base. Bar and good ice creams.

TT Garden Court, 76/2 Pashan–NDA Rd, Pashan Hills 5 km west of Gymkhana, T020-2528 3502. Excellent food and ambience, especially at night when the city lights spread out below. Recommended.

TT Khyber, 1258/2 JM Rd. Indian, some continental, beer bar and ice creams.

TT Latif's, Gen Thimmaya Rd. Good for North Indian, chicken dishes. Recommended.

₹₹ Little Italy, **Srimaan** hotel (see Sleeping). Italian. Recommended for tomato and mozzarella salad, great pizza, pasta, fresh bread, pleasant candlelit atmosphere and.

₹₹ Malaka Spice, Lane 5, Koregaon Park, T(0)9923-329299. Indoor-outdoor place surrounded by pot plants, with an interesting menu of pan-Southeast Asian with an Indian twist: the *laksa* is tasty, but not for purists. Wi-Fi.

₹₹ The Place, Touché the Sizzler, Clover Centre, 7 Moledina Rd. 1130-1530, 1900-2100. Best sizzlers in town (the sizzler reputedly was invented by the present owner's father). Also chicken platters, super ice creams and spotless toilets. Recommended.

₹₹ Terttulia, north end of Lane 6, Koregaon Park. Pune's first effort at a gastro-pub, with specials chalked up on a blackboard (risottos, pizza, etc), and outside tables where the hip young things in wraparound shades and cigarettes glued to their lips enjoy the chilled-out vibe.

₹₹ Zamu's Place, Dhole Patil Rd. Western. Good sizzlers and Parsi dishes.

₹ Poona Coffee House, 1256/2 Deccan Gymkhana. Local landmark, good for sandwiches, snacks and sweets.

₹ Roopali, FC Rd. An old favourite for cheap South Indian *thalis* and *dosas*.

₹ Shabree, **Hotel Parichay**, FC Rd. Unlimited Maharashtrian *thalis*, and traditional vegetarian snacks.

₹ Shreya's, 1242-B Apte Rd, Deccan Gymkhana. Superb Maharashtran thalis.

₹ Vaishali, FC Rd. South Indian. Starts early for breakfast, mainly snacks, their special SPDP (Sev Potato Dahi Puri) is a Pune institution, no one should leave town without trying it, very popular meeting place (queues in evenings for lovely rear garden), spotless. Highly recommended.

Cafés and snacks

Coffee House, 2 Moledina Rd. Good coffee and South Indian snacks.

Shiv Kailash, Sassoon Rd opposite Pune Station. The best *lassis* in the city, always crowded.

Bakeries

German Bakery, North Main Rd. This 2-decade old magnet for travellers and Osho ashramites, destroyed by a bomb in Feb 2010, was due to reopen at the time of writing. Expect the same great coffee and pastries, with added CCTV cameras.

Kayani, East St. Irani bakery with a long pedigree, specializing in Mawa cakes and Shrewsbury biscuits.

Marz-O-Rin, MG Rd. One of the few cafes in Pune to make it onto INTACH's heritage walk, serving good sandwiches, cakes and ice cream since 1965.

Lonavla *p1211*

₹₹ Lonavla Hotel, 1st floor, NH-4 near bus stand. Excellent Indian, pleasant ambience (try chicken kebabs), generous helpings, bar (affordable drinks), very clean, a/c.

₹₹ Shivam Garden Restaurant is cheaper but equally good and strictly pure vegetarian.

₹ Zeus Bakery, MG Rd, near National Chikki. Burger, sandwiches, snacks, etc, from Rs 25.

Mahabaleshwar *p1213*

₹₹₹-₹₹ Grapevine Restaurant, Masjid Rd. Small eclectic restaurant with Thai, Italian and other non-Indian specials. Try lobster, fresh strawberries washed down with Indian 'Chardonnay'. Excellent though pricey.

Kolhapur *p1214*

The restaurants in the **Victor Palace** and **Woodland** hotels (see Sleeping) are among the best in town.

₹ Subraya, opposite bus stand. Friendly place serving excellent *thalis* and milkshakes.

Murud-Janjira *p1216*

₹ Nest, Darbar Rd. Indian including *thalis*.

₹ Patil Khanaval, on the seafront. The best fish in Murud, dusted with turmeric and tamarind and fried.

Ganpatipule *p1217*

Cheap *thalis* are served in 2 eateries outside the Ganesh Temple on the shopping street. Look out for the local delicacy of *poli* -thin pancakes with *amba poli* (dried and crushed mango) or *phanas poli* (jackfruit).

Malvan *p1217*

₹₹ Arun Bhojnalaya, Malvan town. One of the best places to try Malvan's heavily sea-focused cuisine: prawns, crabs, and pomfret in tangy masala.

Abhishek, Malvan . Offers Malvani vegetarian alongside seafood.

Sawantwadi *p1217*

Visava, Gandhi Chowk. Good South Indian fare and snacks, excellent thick *lassis*.

Bars and clubs

Pune *p1207, map p1208*

Check *Pune Times* supplement in *The Times of India* for listings. FC Rd, MG Rd, Kalyani Nagar and ABC Farms (see Eating) are popular student hangouts in the evenings, while the Osho Meditation Resort hosts what devotees claim are the best parties in town. Most clubs open 2130-0200.

1000 Oaks, 2417 East St. Intimate pub with outdoor seating area, live music, family atmosphere, good for a quiet night out.

Club Polaris, at **Taj Blue Diamond**. Exclusive feel, reserved for members and hotel guests.

Fire and Ice/Soho's, next to Bishop's School, Kalyani Nagar. Literally an old barn, Soho's has pleasant outdoor seating and good food, while Fire and Ice offers a shockingly loud Indian disco.

Scream, **Le Meridien** hotel. Huge dancefloor, happening parties.

TDS (**10 Downing Street**), Boat Club Rd. Done out in imitation of an English pub, with disco upstairs.

Festivals and events

Pune *p1207, map p1208*

Aug/Sep Ganesh Chaturthi 11 day MTDC festival with concerts, food fairs, bullock-cart races, folk shows.

Dec/Jan Pune Marathon.

Lonavla *p1211*

Feb/Mar Sivaratri is celebrated at Mahadev Temple with great ceremony and a fair.

Shopping

Pune *p1207, map p1208*

The main shopping centres in Pune are in **MG Rd** (Camp area), **Deccan Gymkhana**, **Karve Rd**, **Laxmi Rd** (for clothing and textiles) and **Hanuman Mandir** (for silver jewellery and leather *chappals*).

Books and music

Alurkar Music House, 4 Swapna Nagri, Karve Rd, T020-2544 0662. Family-run shop, specialists in Indian classical music.

Crossword Books, junction of RBM Rd and Connaught Rd, northeast of Pune Station. Wide range of books, magazines and stationery.

Landmark, Moledina Rd. Big new shop on 2 levels, with CDs and DVDs downstairs and a huge selection of books upstairs.

Manney's, Clover Centre, Moledina Rd. Comfortable a/c, excellent stock, bargains.

Modern Book Store, Gen Thimmaya Rd. Good selection. Recommended.

Crafts and gifts

Either/Or, same complex as **Crossword Books**, T020-2605 02225, www.eitheror.in. Funky, ethnic and eco-sensible handmade crafts, textiles, board games, jewellery and homewares. Highly recommended.

Malls

Nirman Shopping Complex, opposite Shivaji Market, Convent St, is a modern mall.

Markets

Juna Bazaar, in Vir Santaji Ghorpade Rd, near Maldhaka Chowk. Every Wed and Sun 0900-1500. Excellent flea market, with everything from second-hand saris to antique coins.

Textiles

Look out for Pune saris (cotton-silk weave).

Kalaniketan, opposite Sancheti Hospital, JM Rd, for premium silkwear. Wholesale sari market at **Raviwarpeth** ('Sunday Lane').

Lonavla *p1211*

Chikki, the candy mix of jaggery and dried fruit and nuts, is the local favourite, with endless variety in the shops in the market along MG Rd. About Rs 40 per kilo; dried fruit chikki, Rs 200 or more.

Cooper's, in market near railway station. Famous for fudge; try coconut or choco walnut.

Shakti, Shivaji Rd/ Flyover junction. Excellent, unusual concoctions for health seekers; vitamin C-rich Indian gooseberry (*awala*), black sesame (*til*), sugar-free cashew and dried fruit is delicious.

Activities and tours

Pune *p1207, map p1208*

Apple Travels, Amir Hotel Building, Connaught Rd, T020-2612 8185. Agent for **Indian Airlines**, efficient service.

Pune Municipal Transport (**PMT**), T020-2444 0417. Runs daily 'Pune Darshan' Tours, 0900-1700, Rs 140. Booking at Swargate and Deccan bus depots.
Sundar, 19 MG Rd, T020-2613 1848.
TCI, Dhole Patil Rd, T020-2612 2126.
Thomas Cook, Thakkar House, 2418 Gen Thimaya Rd, Camp, T020-2633 0978.

Lonavla *p1211*

Kaivalyadhama Yogic Health Care Centre, Valvan Dam approach road, T02114-273039, www.kdham.com. The 76-year-old institute founded by Swami Kuvalyananda, a spiritual adviser to Gandhi, tries to demystify yoga and offers a range of options from 1-week 'nature cure' packages (a holistic approach to curing everything from a bad back to diabetes, using yoga, massages, diet and very retro hydro-therapy) to a 1-year diploma in yoga and 6-week teacher training courses. There's also an Ayurvedic clinic on site, run under the guidance of respected Pune-based Dr Jagadish Bhutada.
Vedanta Academy, Malavali Station Rd, T02114-282278, satva@vsnl.com). A lush haven off the Mumbai Pune Highway offers a free 3-year (or shorter) course for 50 students from around the world. Swami Parthasarathy lectures regularly in London and New York, and insists on a well-integrated mixture of serious study and physical exercise. Phone in advance if you want to visit.

Mahabaleshwar *p1213*

MTDC deluxe buses for sightseeing, 1400, Pratapgarh, 0930, 1000, and Panchgani, 1100. Reservations at **Holiday Resort**, www.maharashtratourism.gov.in.

Transport

Pune *p1207, map p1208*

Bengaluru (**Bangalore**) (840 km); **Belgaum** (336 km); **Mumbai** (184 km); **Delhi** (1424 km); **Mahabaleshwar** (120 km); **Nashik** (184 km).
Air Transport to town: Ex-Servicemen's coach for 8-km city transfer or airlines bus; taxi Rs 220. Daily flights to **Ahmedabad**, **Bengaluru** (**Bangalore**), **Chennai**, **Delhi**, **Hyderabad**, **Indore**, **Jaipur**, **Kolkata** and **Mumbai** and **Nagpur**. **Indian Airlines**, T020-2605 2147, enquiries T140; airport, T020-2668 3211. **Jet Airways**, 243 Century Arcade, B/2 Narangi Bagh Rd, T020-2616 7524; airport, T020-2668 5591. **Kingfisher**, T020-2605 9351; airport, T020-2661 4040. **Go Air**, T(0)9223-222111. **Indigo**, T020-2612 5410; airport, T020-2661 0557. **Spicejet**, T020-2661 5603; airport, T020-26615525.
Auto-rickshaw The best mode for getting around town. Drivers should use meter and carry a rate card; Pune Station to Koregaon Park costs Rs 30-40. Swargate to Railway Station Bus Stand Rs 40- 50. Extra charges out-of-town and 2400-0500. Shared rickshaws from next to the Town Bus Stand run on key routes, eg to Swargate; drivers call out their destination, Rs 15 per seat.
Local bus Pune Municipal Transport (PMT) buses run throughout the city and suburbs from the **City Bus Stand** next to Pune Station, T020-2444 0417. Routes 2, 3, 4 between Pune Station and **Swargate Bus Stand**; Route 74 Pune Station to Deccan Gymkhana
Long distance bus MSRTC buses connect Pune with all major towns within the state from three different bus stands.

City (Railway) Bus Stand, T020-2612 6218, for Mumbai and the south: **Belgaum**; **Chiplun**; **Ganpatipule**; **Hubli**; **Kolhapur**; **Mumbai**; **Mahabaleshwar**; ASIAD deluxe buses every 15 mins; **Panaji**; **Ratnagiri**; **Solapur**.

Shivaji Nagar Bus Stand, T020-2553 6970, for the east/northeast: **Ahmedabad**; **Alibag**; **Amravati**; **Aurangabad**; **Indore**; **Nagpur**; **Hyderabad**; **Nashik**; **Shirdi**; **Vadodara**.

Swargate Bus Stand, T020-2444 1591, for south/southeast. **Belgaum**; **Kolhapur**; **Solapur**; **Mahabaleshwar**; **Mangalore**; **Ratnagiri**.

Kadamba Transport Corporation, operates the **Panaji** route at 0630, 1800 and 1900, via **Mapusa**; buses poor and often dirty; Booking office open 0900-1200, 1500-1800. *Asiad* and *Express* buses run regular services.

Private companies run more comfortable buses to many of these destinations, and to **Sahar International Airport**, 4 hrs; agents have offices opposite Pune Station.
Car hire About Rs 900-1250 per day, or from Rs 9000 per week with driver from **Sai Services**, Ashoka Pavillion, Dr Ambedkar Rd, T020-2605 5603. **Budget**, T020-2544 4118. **Wheels**, Pride Executive Hotel, T020-2325 5345; airport T020-2668 3615.

Taxi Ordinary local taxis are not metered, but some companies offer point-to-point billing and time/distance packages, eg **Cel Cabs**, T020-6060 9090. Taxis to/from **Mumbai** (Dadar station), Rs 1000-1500, or shared Rs 260-320 per seat; enquiries, T020-2614 5365, T020-2416 0737.
Train The main booking counter is at Pune Junction Station, which has a counter for foreigners on Platform 1. Other booking offices in Deccan Gymkhana (Karve Rd) and Raviwar Peth (NC Kelkar Rd). Enquiries T131, Reservations T132. **Bengaluru** (**Bangalore**) via **Guntakal** (for connections to **Hospet/ Hampi**): *Udyan Exp 16529*, 1145, 20½ hrs; *Coimbatore Exp 11013*, 0200, 20 hrs. **Mumbai** (**CST**): 17 trains daily, best are *Deccan Queen 12124*, 0715, 3½ hrs; *Indrayani Exp 11022*, 1835, 3¾ hrs; *Pragati Exp 11026*, 0750, 3¾ hrs; *Sinhagad Exp 11010*, 0605, 4 hrs; *Deccan Exp 11008*, 1530, 4½ hrs, all via **Lonavla**, 1-1½ hrs. **Delhi**: *Jhelum Exp 11077*, 1720, 27¾ hrs; **(ND)** *Goa Exp 12779*, 0415, 26½ hrs (**HN**). **Hyderabad**: *Mumbai-Hyderabad Exp 17031*, 1635, 13¼ hrs; *Hussainsagar Exp 17001*, 0125, 11½ hrs. **Secunderabad**: *Konark Exp 11019*, 1925, 12¼ hrs. **Jammu Tawi**: *Jhelum Exp 11077*, 1720, 42½ hrs. **Chennai** via **Solapur** and **Guntakal**: *Dadar Chennai Exp 12163*, 0010, 20 hrs; *Chennai Exp 11041*, 1810, 22½ hrs. **Vasco de Gama** (**Goa**): *Goa Exp 12780*, 1630, 14½ hrs.

Lonavla *p1211*

Bus ST buses to the **caves**: couple of buses to Karla in the morning from 0600, last return about 1900. To **Rajmachi Fort** ,buses are unpredictable; **Pune** (62 km) and **Mumbai** (101 km); special a/c every 30 mins, last dep 1630, Rs 81. **Lucky Travels**, Hotel Gulistan, Bombay Pune Rd, near Flyover, T02114-270332, runs fast a/c buses to **Mumbai**, Rs 200.
Rickshaw Auto-rickshaw from Lonavla to the **Karla** and **Bhaja Caves**, Rs 250, more for **Bedsa**. From station to **Kaivalyadhama**, Rs 40.
Taxi Tourist taxis from near ST Bus Stand, **JK Travels**, T(0)9870-779000, kkuku28@hotmail.com, friendly, reliable for Mumbai/Pune airport pickups; **Parekh**, in line with Adarsh Hotel, T02114-273886. **Karla** and **Bhaja** Rs 400. One way to **Mumbai** Rs 1550-1750 (under 4 hrs), **Pune** Rs 900-1100.
Train Enquiries, T02114-272215. Lonavla is on the **Mumbai** (**CST**)–**Pune** line with at least 16 trains daily in each direction. To **Mumbai**, 2½-3 hrs; **Pune**, 1-1½ hrs.

Karla and Bhaja caves *p1212*

Tourist taxis from Lonavla charge Rs 400 for 3 hrs, allowing a brief visit to both caves. For Karla Caves: from the Karla/Bhaja crossroads on the NH4 at Karla village, turn left (north). The car park is at the bottom of the ridge with a steps up to the caves (20 mins). Buses from Lonavla: a couple from 0600; last return 1900.

For Bhaja Caves: from Karla village on the NH4, a road to the south goes to Bhaja, crossing the railway at Malavli. Vehicles stop at the car park in new Bhaja 'town', from there follow a path and then climb uphill for about 20 mins to the caves. Heavy rain can close part of the Bhaja Rd to vehicles. Local passenger trains stop at Malavli.

Mahabaleshwar *p1213*

Bus For the best views, sit on the right of the bus travelling from Pune to Mahabaleshhwar. Regular services to/from **Pune**, Rs 30 (4 hrs). **MTDC** several deluxe buses daily (except monsoons) to **Mumbai** 1500 (6½ hrs) and from Mumbai (7 hrs), Rs 145. The semi-luxury and luxury buses to Pune stop at **Swargate**, a Rs 45 auto ride away from the railway station.

Panchgani *p1213*

Bus Buses run from **Mumbai** (via Mahad) and **Pune** ('Luxury' to Swargate stand only).
Train The nearest railway station is **Satara** (28 km).

Pratapgarh *p1214*

Bus Buses to **Pratapgarh** from **Mahabaleshwar** (22 km), taking 50 mins.

Raigad *p1214*

Bus Buses go from **Mumbai** (via Mahad, 210 km) and **Pune** (126 km).

Kolhapur *p1214*

Bus State buses pull into the **Central Bus Stand** on Station Rd. Half-hourly services to **Panhala** (30 mins) and **Pune** (via **Satara**), and several a day to **Belgaum** (2½ hrs), **Bijapur** (4 hrs), **Mahabaleshwar** (4 hrs), **Mumbai Central** (8 hrs), **Panaji** (6 hrs) and **Ratnagiri**

(4 hrs). Agents for private buses at the bus stand, including several in the Royal Plaza building on Dabholkar Corner. Check departure/arrival points, particularly for Mumbai.
Train Trains to **Kolhapur** arrive via a branch line from Miraj. If booking online, Kolhapur station is known as 'C Shahumharaj T' Enquiry, T131. To **Mumbai** (**CST**): *Koyna Exp 11030*, 0755, 12½ hrs; *Sahyadri Exp 11024*, 2250, 13 hrs; both go via **Pune**, 8 hrs .**Bengaluru** (**Bangalore**): *Ranichannama Exp 16590*, 1420, 17½ hrs . **Hyderabad**: *Hyderabad Exp 17004*, 0730, 21 hrs.

Solapur and east of Pune *p1215*
Bus Excellent connections to **Mumbai**, **Hyderabad**, **Aurangabad** to the north and **Bijapur** (3 hrs) to the south.
Train To **Bengaluru** (**Bangalore**): *Udyan Exp 16529*, 1620, 16 hrs. **Bijapur**, *Bagalkot Exp 11423*, 0620, 2 hrs; *Mumbai-Bijapur Fast Pass 51029*, 0930, 3 hrs. **Mumbai** (**Dadar**): *Chennai Dadar Exp 11064*, 2115, 9 hrs. **Mumbai** (**CST**): *Chennai-Mumbai Mail 11028*, 1820, 9½ hrs; *Chennai Mumbai Exp 11042*, 0440, 9 hrs; *Siddheswar Exp 12116*, 2245, 8½ hrs. **Hyderabad**: *Mumbai Hyderabad Exp 17031*, 2225, 8 hrs; *Hussainsagar Exp 12701*, 0540, 6½ hrs. **Chennai**: *Chennai Exp 12163*, 0405, 15 ¾ hrs; *Mumbai Chennai Exp 11041*, 2325, 17 hrs.

Murud-Janjira *p1216*
Bus/ferry From **Mumbai Central**, ASIAD buses cover the 165 km in less than 6 hrs but it may be quicker to get a ferry from the **New Ferry Wharf** (Bhaucha Dhakka) at the Gateway of India to **Mandwa**, and from there catch a bus or taxi to **Murud** (72 km) or **Kashid** via **Alibaug**. There can be a long wait for buses.

Ganpatipule *p1217*
Bus Direct State Transport buses run from **Mumbai**, **Pune** and **Ratnagiri**.

Malvan *p1217*
Bus Local buses to **Devgad** up the coast road, **Kankauli** (on NH-17, for connections to **Kolhapur**, **Mumbai** and **Pune**), **Kudal** (for connections to Goa), **Sawantwadi**, **Vengurla**. Auto-rickshaw to Tarkarli, Rs 60-70.

Sawantwadi *p1217*
Bus The bus stand is close to the centre. Buses to **Mapusa** (2 hrs), **Malvan** (2 hrs), and destinations in southern Maharashtra.

Amboli *p1218*
Bus/train From the coastal towns of **Ratnagiri** (210 km) and **Vengurla** (50 km) there are buses. Or you can get the train to **Kolhapur** or **Belgaum**, then by local bus.

❶ Directory

Pune *p1207, map p1208*
Banks ATMs accepting foreign cards are now everywhere, including the railway station. **Amex**, 19 MG Rd. **Central Bank**, MG Rd, accepts MasterCard and Visa. **Thomas Cook**, 13 Thakkar House, Gen Thimaya Rd, T020-2633 0978 (Mon-Sat 1000-1700) is best for TCs. **Cultural centres** **British Library**,917/1 FC Rd, Shivaji Nagar, T020-2565 4351. **Internet** Many outlets across the city, Rs 20-30 per hr. **Medical services** **Ambulance**: T102. **Ruby Hall Clinic**, T020-2612 3391. **Sassoon** (Govt), JP Narayan Rd, T020-2612 8000. **Post** **Head Post Office** (city): Laxmi Rd. **Useful contacts** **Fire**: T101. **Police**: T100. **Foreigners' Registration Office**, ground floor, Main Building, Police Commissioner's Office, Sadhu Waswani Rd, T020-2612 8977.

Lonavla *p1211*
Banks **HDFC**, on Mumba–Pune Rd towards Kaivalyadham, is most reliable ATM for foreign cards. **State Bank of India**, Tilak Rd.
Internet **Cybercafé** Basement of *Kumar Resort*, near road bridge over railway line, 1000-2300, Rs 30 for 30 mins. **Medical services** **Dahanukar Hospital**, T02114- 272673; **Favourite Medical**, Tilak Rd. **Post** Shivaji Rd. **Useful contacts** **Fire**: T101. **Police**: T100.

Mahabaleshwar *p1213*
Banks Banks are on Dr Sabbana Rd.

Kolhapur *p1214*
Banks **HDFC ATM** opposite bus stand takes foreign cards. Only **State Bank of India**, Main Branch, Dasara Chowk Bridge (near railway station), changes cash, TCs from 1130.

Vidharba

Maharashtra's winter capital, Nagpur, is the capital of Maharashtrian district Vidharba, a large political and industrial city. Sevagram, Gandhi's 'village of service' from 1933 to 1942, is now a shrine to the man's principles. The nearby hill station of Chikhaldara, peopled by tribals, marks the southern limits of the Hindi tongue. ▸▸ *For listings, see pages 1229-1230.*

Nagpur → *Colour map 6, A1. Phone code: 0712. Population: 2 million.*

Nagpur, the former capital of the Central Provinces, is one of the older towns of Central India. Today, although an important commercial centre attracting new businesses and multinationals, most of the industrial units are thankfully located on the outskirts so Nagpur retains a pleasant relaxed feel with friendly inhabitants and signs of fast growing affluence. Sometimes known as the winter capital of Maharashtra, the area is famous for its oranges, giving it the nickname 'The Orange City'. More recently strawberry farms have grown in importance while the surrounding countryside is a major cotton producing area. Contact the MTDC ⓘ *Sanskruti Bachat Bhavan, opposite Hardeo Hotel, near Lakshmie Theatre, Sitabuldi, T0712-253 3325*, for information and MTDC accommodation.

The city stands on the Nag River and is centred on the **Sitabuldi Fort** ⓘ *only open to the public on 26 Jan and 15 Aug*, which is surrounded by cliffs and a moat. At the highest point there is a memorial to those who fell in the Battle of Sitabuldi between the Marathas and the British. Today the fort is headquarters of the Territorial Army. Among the British buildings scattered around the western half of the city are the red brick Council Hall (1912-1913); the Anglican Cathedral of All Saints (1851), and the High Court (1937-1942), suggestive of Rashtrapati Bhavan in New Delhi.

On the other high hill in the town is the **Raj Bhavan** (Government House). The **Bhonsla Chhattris** are in the Sukrawari area south of the old city. Around town there are also a number of 'tanks' (lakes) and parks; **Maharaj Bagh**, west of the flyover is an attractive park/zoo.

Ramtek

About 40 km northeast of Nagpur, Ramtek has a **fort** with several Hindu **temples** at its western end, some dating back to the fifth century AD. The fort walls on the well-wooded 'Hill of Rama' were built in 1740 by Raghoji I, the first Bhonsla of Nagpur. The citadel is older and the principal temples are those to Rama and Sita. The fort is approached by a flight of steps from the village of Ambala. The poet Kalidasa wrote his epic *Meghdoot* here. Nearby is **Khindsey Lake**, 8 km, a popular picnic spot with boating facilities. Ramsagar is another lake closer to town. The 15-day **Ramnavami** fair is held in November.

Wardha and around → *Colour map 6, A1. Phone code: 07152. 62 km southwest.*

After vowing not to return to Sabarmati Ashram in Ahmedabad until India gained its independence, Mahatma Gandhi established his **Sevagram Ashram** (Gandhian Village of Service) in 1933. Jamnalal Bajaj, a dedicated follower of Gandhi, provided the land, 8 km outside of Wardha, and the resources to set up the ashram in which Gandhi remained until 1942 and visited regularly until his death in 1948. It is now a national institution where you can visit the residences **Nivases** and **Kutirs**, see the Mahatma's personal belongings, watch hand-spinning (*khadi* cloth is sold through shops) and attend prayers at the open-air multi-faith Prayer Ground (0430 and 1800). Mahatma Gandhi Research Institute of Medical Sciences and Kasturba Hospital with 325 beds to provide affordable health care for local villagers, is on the bus route. A path from here leads to the Ashram.

The **Magan Sanghralaya** (Centre of Science for Villages) is an alternative technology museum, on the Nagpur Road at **Duttapur**. Visitors are welcome to see papermaking, pottery, latrine making and other crafts. The **Chetna Organic Farm**, nearby, develops sustainable farming techniques. The **Laxmi Narayan Temple** claims to have been the first in India to have allowed Harijans to enter in 1928. The **Viswa Shanti Stupa** (1993), for 'World Peace', with four golden statues of Buddha, is a more recent attraction. Prayers are held each evening in the small prayer hall.

At **Paunar**, 10 km north of Wardha, **Vinoba Bhave**, one of Gandhi's keenest disciples, set up his Ashram. He championed the 'land gift' or **Bhoodan Movement**, seeking with remarkable success to persuade large landowners to give away land to the poor. The self-help concept is kept alive by his followers (mostly women) dressed in blue, unlike other ashramites elsewhere in India who conventionally adopt white or saffron. It is possible to hike across from the Sevagram hospital along a village track for about 45 minutes to get there.

Tadoba National Park

ⓘ *Open Wed-Mon 0600-1100 (last entry 0930) and 1400-1800 (last entry 1630); Rs 20 per person per safari drive, plus Rs 50-75 for vehicle and Rs 100 for guide; jeep hire with driver costs Rs1500-2500 per trip. There are 3 zones, of which Moharli and Tadoba offer best wildlife sightings; entry to each zone is limited to 20 vehicles per safari. Weekends are very busy. It's often easiest to arrange safaris through a hotel or a local naturalist guide; one with a good reputation is Manish Varma, T(0)98606-92422 or T08055920303, manish.varma96@gmail.com.*

Approximately 100 km south of Nagpur, the area around Tadoba was once in the possession of the Gond tribals. The compact 120-sq-km park has rich deciduous forest – mainly teak with bamboo, gardenia and satinwood. There are several troops of langur monkeys, palm civets, gaur, jackal, wild boar, chital, bison, sambar and a few tigers (although you are more likely to see a leopard in the evening). Waterbirds attracted by the perennial circular lake include cattle egrets, purple moorhens and jacanas. It also has quite a number of marsh crocodiles with a breeding farm for the *palustris* species. There are minibuses for viewing, which is best in the evening around lake in the dry season. A road runs around the lake, while other roads radiate to the park perimeter. The best season to visit is between November and June. The nearest transport connections are at Chandrapur, 45 km away.

Achalpur

Until 1853 this important market town was the capital of Berar Kingdom, established in 1484 by Imad Shah. The old cantonment, which had been occupied by a regiment of the Hyderabad infantry, was abandoned in 1903.

To the north, and just before reaching Chikhaldara, is the fort of **Gawilgarh** (Gavilgarh). An important fortress of the 15th-century Shahi Dynasty, it was taken over when the kingdom of Ahmednagar expanded in 1574. Arthur Wellesley, subsequently the Duke of Wellington, who had defeated Tipu Sultan of Mysore at Srirangapatnam just four years previously, captured the fort in 1803 during the second Maratha War. The defences were destroyed after the 'Indian Mutiny' in 1858. Today it is a deserted ruin.

Chikhaldara

Known as the only hill station in the Vidharba region and as the northernmost coffee growing region in India, Chikhaldara is high in the Gavilgarh Hills, at an altitude of 1200 m, a branch of the Satpura Mountains. Established as a hill station by the British in 1839, historically the hills marked the southern limits of the core region within which the epics of Hinduism were played out. It remains a tribal region, peopled largely by the Korkus, an Austric tribal group. The settlement is reputed to have taken its name from Kichaka, a prince who was killed by Bhima, one of the Pandava brothers, for having insulted Draupadi. Today, the Satpura Range in which Chikhaldara lies mark the southern boundary of Hindi speech.

The **Melghat Sanctuary** surrounding Chikaldara was one of the earliest to be designated a Project Tiger reserve. Its altitude makes it pleasantly cool during January-June, the best months to visit. The latest count suggests it has 45 tigers, occasionally seen in the dense and dry deciduous teak forest which also supports panther, gaur, chital, sambar and nilgai.

Vidharba listings

For Sleeping and Eating price codes and other relevant information, see Essentials pages 38-42.

Sleeping

Nagpur *p1227*

C and **D** hotels don't have all usual facilities of the grade but all have restaurants, bars and free transfer for airport

AL Pride, Wardha Rd, 500 m from airport, T0712-229 1102, www.pridehotel.com. 70 tired rooms, 30 new better, decent restaurant but inefficient reception, unappealing pool next to busy NH7.

A-B Tuli International, Residency Rd, Sadar, T0712-253 4784, www.tuligroup.com. Once the best in town, the tired rooms now provide poor value for the price, and service tends to be chaotic. Worth considering for location and the good restaurants.

B Jagsons, 30 Back Central Av, T0712-272 8611. 28 clean carpeted rooms, some a/c, TV, bar/restaurant.

B-C Radhika, Panchsheel Sq, Wardha Rd, T0712-252 2011. 60 clean rooms, some larger a/c with hot bath, dark corridors, unreliable TV, restaurant, bar.

C-D Darshan Towers, 60 Central Av, T0712-272 6845. Well-furnished rooms, central a/c, hot baths (some tubs), double-glazed so quieter than others, good restaurant/bar, friendly and efficient. Recommended.

D Skylark (*Tuli* group), 119 Central Av, T0712-272 4654. Good value but suffers some noise from road and nightly disco. 48 rooms in need of a makeover, most a/c, efficient and friendly service, restaurant/bar.

D-E Blue Moon, Central Av, T0712-272 6061, micron@bom3.vsnl.net.in. 30 clean rooms, some a/c, TV, room service, quieter rooms at rear.

Ramtek *p1227*

D-E Tourist Resort (MTDC/private), Ramtek, T07114-255620. Dorm and 17 rooms.

Wardha and around *p1227*

E Holiday Resort (MTDC/private), near bus stand, T07152-243872. Cheap singles, 18 rooms with bath, restaurant. Also some cheap hotels near railway station.

F Ashram Guest House and **Yatri Niwas**, Sevagram, T0715-222 2172. Some doubles and dorm, serves cheap vegetarian meals, checkout 0800, friendly, small bookshop of Gandhi's works. Highly recommended (donations welcome), reserve on arrival (or ahead if possible). Alcohol, smoking and non-vegetarian food are prohibited.

F Yatri Niwas, Paunar. Similar to the one in Sevagram but more female oriented.

Tadoba National Park *p1228*

C MTDC Rest House, at Moharli Gate, T07172-251654. One of the better deals around, with acceptably clean rooms and a pleasant lakeside setting. Often full so book well ahead.

E-G Forest rest houses, in various areas of the park can be booked at the Forest Dept, Mul Rd, Chandrapur, T07172-256339

Chikhaldara *p1228*

B-C Convention Complex (MTDC), T07220-230234. Simple though adequate, 10 rooms with 4 beds, and dorm with mattresses but no beds (Rs 100), restaurant nearby. Improved accommodation planned.

C-E Green Vallies Resort (MTDC), Chikhaldara, T07220-230215. Wide choice, 20 suites, some a/c.

Eating

Nagpur *p1227*

Hotel restaurants at **Darshan Towers** and **Tuli International** are recommended. Several others are along Residency Rd and Wardha Rd near the junction with Central Bazar Rd.

Wardha and around *p1227*

Annapurna, Wardha near station, Paunar; couple in Saraf Lines.

Festivals and events

Nagpur p1227

Apr/May Ram Naumi, colourful procession in various parts of the city.

Aug/Sep Janmashtami, Krishna's birthday is celebrated with the distinctive tradition of stringing clay pots full of curd high above the streets. Young men try to pull them down by forming human pyramids. **Pola**, the cattle and monsoon harvest festival. **Ganesh Chaturthi**, when idols of Ganesh are immersed in streams and tanks.

Shopping

Nagpur p1227

Main areas are Sitabuldi, Dharampeth, Sadar and Itwari, Mahatma Phule Market. Also try: **Gangotri UP Handicrafts**, in Sadar; and **Khadi Gramudyog**, in Mahal.

Transport

Nagpur p1227

Air The airport is 10 km south of the city centre with taxis for transfer. **Indian Airlines**, Amravati Rd, T0712-252 3069; airport T0712-226 0348, flight information T140/141: to **Delhi**, **Mumbai**, **Hyderabad** and **Kolkata**. **Jet Airways**, Shree Mohini Complex, 345 Kingsway, Sitabuldi, T0712-255 9875, airport T0712-227 3384: to **Mumbai**.

Bus **New Maharashtra ST Bus Stand**, Ganesh Peth, southeast of the railway station, T0712-272 6221, to towns in Maharashtra plus **Hyderabad**, **Allahabad** and **Varanasi**.

MP Bus Stand, T0712-253 3695, buses to **Bhopal**, **Indore** and **Raipur**.

Madhya Pradesh buses use the stand just south of the train station.

Car **Pigale**, Dharampeth, T0712-252 2291; **Saibaba**, near Pancsheel Cinema, T0712-252 2416; Rs 600 per 5 hrs.

Train Nagpur is an important railway junction. The station is in the centre of town. Enquiry T131, Reservations T135. **Chennai**: *Tamil Nadu Exp 12622*, 1410, 16½ hrs; *Grand Trunk Exp 12616*, 1220, 18 hrs. **New Delhi**: *Andhra Pradesh Exp 12723*, 1555, 16½ hrs; *Tamil Nadu Exp 12621*, 1415, 17½ hrs; *Grand Trunk Exp 12615*, 1225, 18½ hrs. **Kolkata (H)**: *Gitanjali Exp 12859*, 1905, 18½ hrs; *Mumbai Howrah Mail 12809*, 1130, 20½ hrs. **Mumbai (CST)**: *Vidarbha Exp 12106*, 1715, 14¾ hrs; *Howrah Mumbai Mail 12810*, 1420, 15½ hrs. **Mumbai (Dadar)**: *Sewagram Exp 11440*, 2100, 16 hrs. **Pune**: *Maharashtra Exp 11040*, 1055, 19½ hrs. **Secunderabad**: *Andhra Pradesh Exp 12724*, 0955, 10½ hrs; *Dakshin Exp 12722*, 1745, 13½ hrs.

Ramtek p1227

Bus Buses from ST Bus Stand, Nagpur, 70 mins. Buses run from Ramtek to **Khindsey Lake**. **Ramsagar** can be reached by auto-rickshaw.

Wardha and around p1227

Bus Several to/from Wardha from **Nagpur**, 77 km, Express 2½ hrs; ask to be dropped off at **Paunar**. Local bus to **Sevagram** (8 km).

Train Share auto-rickshaws from the station to Sevagram (25 mins). **Ahmedabad**: *Howrah Ahmedabad Exp 12834*, 2030, 19½ hrs. **Chennai**: *Navjivan Exp 12655*, 2235, 18 hrs. **Kolkata (H)** via **Nagpur** and **Raipur**: *Gitanjali Exp 12859*, 1730, 19 hrs. **Mumbai (CST)**: *Vidarbha Exp 12106*, 1820, 13½ hrs; *Howrah Mumbai Mail 12810*, 1530 (1520 from Sevagram), 14½ hrs. **Nagpur**: Several fast trains daily; slow passenger trains stop at Sevagram, though the bus is quicker and more convenient. **Pune**: *Maharashtra Exp 17384*, 1220, 18 hrs.

Chikhaldara p1228

Bus State buses from Amaravati, Nagpur, Wardha and Akola. Also, taxis from Amravati (100 km). **Badnera** is on the Mumbai–Kolkata train line, so is a convenient station. Amaravati is on a short spur (10 km) from Badnera.

Directory

Nagpur p1227

Banks Kingsway; Sitabuldi and Central Av. **Internet** Rs 20 per hr. **Medical services** Private. **CIIMS**, T0712-223 6441, **Jasleen**, T0712-252 3779, **Orange City**, T0712-223 8431. **Post** GPO, Palm Rd.

Goa

Contents

Footprint features

At a glance

Getting around Goa is rickshaw free. Local buses, chartered mini-buses, taxis and motorbike taxis are all the norm. Hiring your own Honda or Enfield is a popular option.

Time required Allow 1 day for Old Goa, 1 day for the palaces of the south: and 3 days' round-trip for Hampi (in Karnataka). Then factor in beach time: some tire of Goa's beaches after 1-2 days, some spend a fortnight, some never leave.

Weather Chilly evenings in Dec and Jan, best Oct-Feb. Humidity rises from Mar.

When not to go Avoid monsoon and peak season (Christmas and New Year) when prices sky rocket as the state opens up for the domestic Indian tourist's equivalent of 'Spring Break'.

★ **Don't miss ...**

1 Panjim's Latin quarters, San Thome and Fontainhas, page 1240.
2 Old Goa: a ghost town in dense jungle, page 1242.
3 Anjuna's Flea Market and Saturday Night Bazar, pages 1257 and 1257.
4 Cabo da Rama, page 1287.
5 Charter a fishing boat at Palolem, page 1297.
6 Inland Goa on a bike or motorcycle, page 1301.
7 Spice plantations, page 1304.

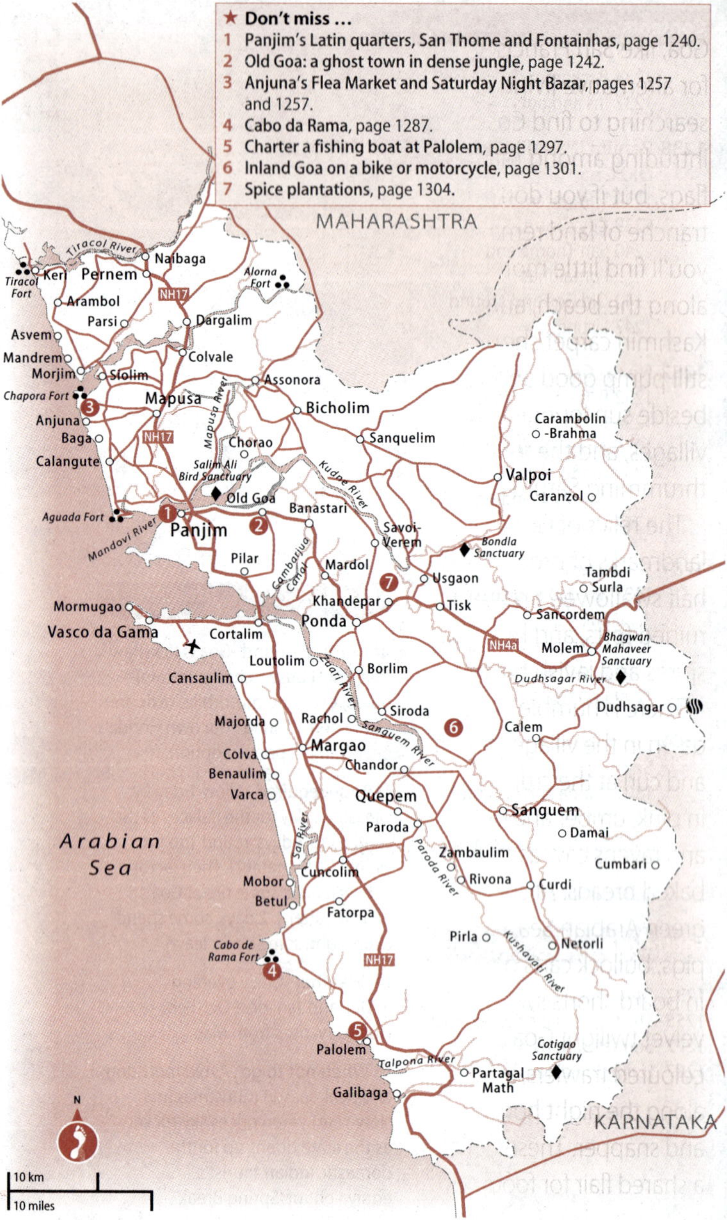

Goa, like San Francisco, Kathmandu and Spain, became a mecca for alternative living in the 1960s. Nowadays, it doesn't take much searching to find Costa Brava beer bellies and big-screen soccer intruding among the California tie-dye and palm-hung prayer flags, but if you don't need your sand Mr Whippy-white this tiny tranche of land remains, in pockets, unmatched. In most places you'll find little more than drowsy one-storey guesthouses strung along the beach, and away from the St George crosses and Kashmiri carpet shops the heartbeats of Goa's multilayered culture still pump good and strong: fishermen's boats rest on the sand beside sun loungers, Portuguese *fados* drift on the air in colonial villages, and the feral trance crew still hold their own at Anjuna's thrumming Saturday night market.

The relics of Goa's colonial past, though no match for the giant landmarks of broader India, are still rococo and baroque gems, half swallowed up by nature. Lush jungles twist their way around ruined forts, and huge banyans shelter centuries-old church spires and lavish basilicas.

There is humble everyday beauty to be had elsewhere too. At dawn in the villages, blue mists lie low and hazy across paddy fields and curl at the crumbling fronts of 18th-century Portuguese manors in pink, umber and blue. Exotic birds dive about sprawling raintrees and ravens caw as delivery boys push bicycles stacked with freshly baked breads. At sunset, the amber hues blaze against the mottled green Arabian Sea, fire embers smoke at the feet of chickens and pigs, bullock carts dredge through muddy fields of paddy and boys in board shorts swing their cricket bats in the straw stubble. Then at velvet twilight Goa's fisherfolk steal out of quiet harbours in brightly coloured trawlers, whose torches twinkle like a thread of fairy lights along the night horizon as they fill their nets with silvery pomfret and snapper. These gentle-paced and easy-living people also enjoy a shared flair for food, wine and song.

Background → *Population: 1.3 million. Area: 3800 sq km.*

The land

Geography By Indian standards Goa is a tiny state. The coastline on which much of its fame depends is only 97 km long. The north and south are separated by the broad estuaries of the Zuari and Mandovi rivers. Joined at high tide to create an island on which Panaji stands, these short rivers emerge from the high ranges of the Western Ghats less than 50 km from the coast. In the 16th century, Alfonso de Albuquerque quickly grasped the advantages of this island site: large enough to give a secure food-producing base but with a defensible moat, and well placed with respect to the important northwestern sector of the Arabian Sea.

Climate Goa is always warm, but its coastal position means it never becomes unbearably hot. Nonetheless, from mid-April until the beginning of the monsoon in mid-June, both the temperature and humidity rise sharply, making for steamy hot days and balmy nights. The six weeks of the monsoon in June/July often come as torrential storms, while the warm dry weather of its tropical winter (October-March) is the best time to visit. Weather patterns are fluctuating: 2007 had the coldest January in 40 years; 2008 the hottest February for 40 years.

History

Some identify Goa in the *Mahabharata* (the Sanskrit epic) as Gomant, where Vishnu, reincarnated as Parasurama, shot an arrow from the Western Ghats into the Arabian Sea and with the help of the god of the sea reclaimed the beautiful land of Gomant.

Arab geographers knew Goa as Sindabur. Ruled by the Kadamba Dynasty from the second century AD to 1312 and by Muslim invaders from 1312 to 1367, it was then annexed by the Hindu Kingdom of Vijayanagar and later conquered by the Bahmani Dynasty of Bidar in North Karnataka, who founded Old Goa in 1440. When the Portuguese arrived, Yusuf Adil Shah, the Muslim King of Bijapur, was the ruler. At this time Goa was an important starting point for Mecca-bound pilgrims, as well as continuing to be a centre importing Arab horses.

The **Portuguese** were intent on setting up a string of coastal stations to the Far East in order to control the lucrative spice trade. Goa was the first Portuguese possession in Asia and was taken by **Alfonso de Albuquerque** in March 1510. Three months later Yusuf Adil Shah blockaded it with 60,000 men. In November Albuquerque returned with reinforcements, recaptured the city after a bloody struggle, massacred all the Muslims and appointed a Hindu as governor. Mutual hostility towards Muslims encouraged links between Goa and the Hindu kingdom of Vijayanagar. A Christian-Hindu fault-line only appeared when missionary activity in India increased. Franciscans, Dominicans and Jesuits arrived, carrying with them religious zeal and intolerance. The Inquisition was introduced in 1540 and all evidence of earlier Hindu temples and worship was eradicated from the territories of the 'Old Conquests'. Goa became the capital of the Portuguese Empire in the east. It reached its greatest splendour between 1575 and 1600, the age of 'Golden Goa', but when the Dutch began to control trade in the Indian Ocean it declined. The fall of the Vijayanagar Empire in 1565 caused the lucrative trade between Goa and the Hindu state to dry up. Between 1695 and 1775 the population of Old Goa fell from 20,000 to 1600; by the 1850s only a few priests and nuns remained.

Albuquerque's original conquest was of the island of Tiswadi, where Old Goa is situated, plus the neighbouring areas – Bardez, Ponda, Mormugao and Salcete. These formed the heart of the Portuguese territory, known today as the **Old Conquests**. The **New Conquests** cover the remaining areas and which came into Portuguese possession considerably later. By the time they were absorbed, the intolerant force of the Inquisition had passed. As a result, the New Conquests did not suffer as much cultural and spiritual devastation.

The Portuguese came under increasing pressure in 1948-1949 to cede Goa to India. The problem festered until 1961 when the Indian Army, supported by a naval blockade, marched in

and brought to an end 450 years of Portuguese rule. Goa became a Union Territory together with the enclaves of Daman and Diu. On 30 May 1987 it became a full state of the Indian Union.

When British explorer Richard Burton arrived in Goa in 1850, he described Old Goa, once the oriental capital of Portuguese empire-building ambition and rival to Lisbon in grandeur, as a place of "utter desolation" and its people "as sepulchral-looking as the spectacle around them."

Culture

Religion While in the area of the Old Conquests tens of thousands of people were converted to Christianity, the Zuari River represents a great divide between Christian and predominantly Hindu Goa. Today about 70% of the state's population is Hindu, and there is also a small but significant Muslim minority.

Language Portuguese used to be much more widely spoken in Goa than English was in the rest of India, but local languages remained important. The two most significant were Marathi, the language of the politically dominant majority of the neighbouring state to the north, and Konkani, the language commonly spoken on the coastal districts further south and now the state's official language. English and Hindi are understood in parts visited by travellers.

Local cuisine The large expat community has brought regional kitchens with them to make for an amazingly cosmopolitan food scene. You can get excellent, authentic Thai spring rolls, Italian wood-baked pizza, German schnitzel, Russian borscht, California wheatgrass shots and everything in between. Local food is a treat, too, sharing much with the Portuguese palate, and building on the state's bounty in fresh fish and fruit. Unlike wider India, Christianity's heritage means beef is firmly on the menu here, too. Generally, food is hot, making full use of the local bird's-eye chillies. Common ingredients include rice, coconut and cashew nuts. Spicy pork or beef *vindalho* marinated in garlic, vinegar and chillies is very popular, quite unlike the vindaloo you'll taste elsewhere. *Chourisso* is Goan sausage of pork pieces stuffed in tripe, boiled or fried with onions and chillies, eaten in bread. *Sorpotel*, a fiery dish of pickled pig's liver and heart seasoned with vinegar and tamarind, is the most famous of Goan meat dishes. *Xacutti* is a hot chicken or meat dish made with coconut, pepper and star anise. For *chicken cafrial,* the meat is marinated in pepper and garlic and braised over a fire.

'Fish curry rice', is the Goan staple (the equivalent of England's fish'n'chips or ham and eggs). Most beach shacks offer a choice of fish depending on the day's catch. *Apa de camarao* is a spicy prawn pie and *reichado* is usually a whole fish, cut in half, and served with a hot *masala* sauce. *Bangra* is mackerel and *pomfret* a flat fish; fish *balchao* is a preparation of red masala and onions used as a sauce for prawns or kingfish. *Seet corri* (fish curry) uses coconut. Spicy pickles and chutneys add to the rich variety of flavours.

Goan bread is good. *Undo* is a hard-crust round bread. *Kankonn*, hard and crispy and shaped like a bangle, may be dunked in tea. *Pole* is like chapatti, often stuffed with vegetables. The Goan version of the South Indian *iddli* is the *sanaan*. The favourite dessert is *bebinca*, a layered coconut and jaggery treat of egg yolks and nutmeg. Other sweets include *dodol*, a mix of jaggery and coconut with rice flour and nuts, *doce*, which looks like the North Indian *barfi*, *mangada*, a mango jam, and *bolinhas*, small round semolina cakes. There are also delicious fruits: *alfonso* mangos in season, the rich jackfruit, papaya, watermelons and cashew nuts.

Drinks in Goa remain relatively cheap compared to elsewhere in India thanks to the state's low taxes. The fermented juice of cashew apples is distilled for the local brew *caju feni* (*fen*, froth) which is strong and potent. Coconut or *palm feni* is made from the sap of the coconut palm. *Feni* is an acquired taste; it is often mixed with soda, salt and lime juice.

Modern Goa

The Goa Legislative Assembly has 40 elected members while the state elects three members to the Lok Sabha, India's central government. Political life is strongly influenced by the regional issue of the relationship with neighbouring Maharashtra. Communal identity also plays a part in elections, with the Congress largely securing the Catholic vote and the BJP winning the support of much of the Hindu population. There is also a strong environmental lobby, in which the Catholic Church plays a role. Goa has had a series of unstable governments with periods of governors imposed by the central government to try and override failures of the democratic process. The state assembly elections in 2007 saw the Congress win 16 and the BJP 14 of the total of 40 seats, and a Congress administration resumed office under the Chief Ministership of Digambar Kamat, who took office on 8 June 2007. The state elects two, not three, members to the Lok Sabha. In the 2009 elections, these were split evenly between the Congress and the BJP.

In common with much of India's west coast, Goa's rural economy depends on rice as the main food crop, cash crops being dominated by coconut, cashew and areca. Mangos, pineapples and bananas are also important. Seasonal water shortages have prompted the development of irrigation projects, the latest of which was the interstate Tillari Project in Pernem *taluka*. Iron ore and bauxite have been two of the state's major exports but heavy industrial development has remained limited to pockets in the east. Tourism (domestic and international) remains one of the state's biggest earners, and money also comes in the form of remittance cheques from overseas workers stationed in the Gulf or working on cruise ships.

Ins and outs → *For arrivals by train, see Panjim, page 1238.*

Vasco da Gama is the passenger railway terminus of the Central Goa branch line, and is the capital of the industrial heart of modern Goa. Dabolim Airport is 3 km away and was developed by the Navy. It is currently shared between the needs of the military and the escalating demands of tourism. Vasco is 30 km from Panjim, the main arrival point for long- distance buses. Trains via Londa bring visitors from the north and east – Delhi and Agra, Hospet and Bengaluru (Bangalore) – while trains from Mumbai, Kerala and coastal points in between arrive via the Konkan Railway, which offers several jumping-off points in Goa besides the main station at Margao (Madgaon). For rail reservations, call T0832-251 2833.

Charter companies fly direct to Dabolim Airport between October and April from the UK, the Netherlands, Switzerland and Russia. There are several flights daily from various cities in India – including Mumbai, Thiruvananthapuram, Bengaluru, Delhi and Chennai -with Air India, Indian Airlines, Kingfisher and Jet Airways. Package tour companies and luxury hotels usually arrange courtesy buses for hotel transfer, but even if you're coming independently the Arrivals terminal is relatively relaxed. A pre-paid taxi counter immediately outside has rates clearly displayed (such as Panjim Rs 450, 40 minutes; north Goa beaches from Rs 700; Tiracol Rs 1400; Arambol Rs 1200; south Goa beaches from Rs 500; Palolem Rs 900). State your destination at the counter, pay and obtain a receipt that will give the registration number of your taxi. Keep hold of this receipt until you reach your destination. The public bus stop on the far side of the roundabout outside the airport gates has buses to Vasco da Gama, from where there are connections to all the major destinations in Goa.

A popular way to get around is by hiring a scooter, available in all towns and villages. However, make sure the bike has yellow and black number plates, which signal that the vehicle is for hire; plain black-and-white plates could result in a fine from the police.

Panjim (Panaji) and Old Goa

→ *Colour map 5a, B1.*

Sleepy, dusty Panjim was adopted as the Portuguese capital when the European empire was already on the wane, and the colonizers left little in the way of lofty architecture. A tiny city with a Riviera-style promenade along the Mandovi, it's also splendidly uncommercial: the biggest business seems to be in the sale of kaju (cashews), gentlemen-shaves in the barbieris and feni-quaffing in the booths of pokey bars – and city folk still insist on sloping off for a siesta at lunch. The 18th- and 19th-century bungalows clustered in the neighbouring quarters of San Thome and Fontainhas stand as the victims of elegant architectural neglect. Further upriver, a thick swathe of jungle – wide fanning raintrees, the twists of banyan branches and coconut palms – has drawn a heavy, dusty blanket over the relics of the doomed Portuguese capital of Old Goa, a ghost town of splendid rococo and baroque ecclesiastical edifices. ▸▸ *For listings, see pages 1247-1251.*

Ins and outs

Getting there Prepaid taxis or buses run the short distance from Dabolim airport across Mormugao Bay to Panjim. The closest station on the Konkan Railway is at Karmali, 10 km east, with trains from Mumbai to the north and coastal Karnataka and Kerala to the south; taxis and buses run from Karmali to Panjim. The state-run Kadamba buses and private coach terminals are in Patto to the east of town. From there it is a 10-minute walk across the footbridge over the Ourem Creek to reach the city's guesthouses. ▸▸ *See Transport, page 1250.*

Getting around Panjim holds the archbishop's palace, a modern port and government buildings and shops set around a number of plazas. It is laid out on a grid and the main roads run parallel with the seafront. The area is very easy to negotiate on foot, but autos are readily available. Motorcycle rickshaws are cheaper but slightly more risky. Local buses run along the waterfront from the City Bus Stand past the market and on to Miramar.

Tourist information Goa Tourism Development Corporation (GTDC) ⓘ *east bank of the Ourem Creek, beside the bus stand at Patto, T0832-243 8750, www.goa-tourism.com, Mon-Sat 0900-1130, 1330-1700, Sun 0930-1400.* Also has an information counter at Dabolim airport, and runs a moderately helpful info line, T0832-241 2121. India Tourism ⓘ *Church Sq, T0832-222 3412, www.incredibleindia.com.*

Panaji is the official spelling of the capital city, replacing the older Portuguese spelling Panjim. It is still most commonly referred to as Panjim, so we have followed usage.

History

The Portuguese first settled Panjim as a suburb of Old Goa, the original Indian capital of the sea-faring *conquistadores*, but its position on the left bank of the Mandovi River had already attracted Bijapur's Muslim king Yusuf Adil Shah in 1500, shortly before the Europeans arrived. He built and fortified what the Portuguese later renamed the Idalcao Palace, now the oldest and most impressive of downtown Panjim's official buildings. The palace's service to the sultan was short-lived: Alfonso de Albuquerque seized it, and Old Goa upstream – which the Islamic rulers had been using as both a trading port and their main starting point for pilgrimages to Mecca – in March 1510. Albuquerque, like his Muslim predecessors, built his headquarters in Old Goa, and proceeded to station a garrison at Panjim and made it the customs clearing point for all traffic entering the Mandovi.

The town remained little more than a military outpost and a staging post for incoming and outgoing viceroys on their way to Old Goa. The first Portuguese buildings, after the construction of a church on the site of the present Church of Our Lady of Immaculate Conception in 1541, were noblemen's houses built on the flat land bordering the sea. Panjim had to wait over two centuries – when the Portuguese Viceroy decided to move from Old Goa in 1759 – for settlement to begin in earnest. It then took the best part of a century for enough numbers to relocate from Old Goa to make Panjim the biggest settlement in the colony and to warrant its status as official capital in 1833.

The waterfront

The leafy boulevard of Devanand Bandodkar (DB) Marg runs along the Mandovi from near the New Patto Bridge in the east to the Campal to the southwest. When Panjim's transport and communication system depended on boats, this was its busiest highway and it still holds the city's main administrative buildings and its colourful market.

Walking from the east, you first hit **Idalcao Palace** ⓘ *behind the main boat terminal, DB Marg*. Once the castle of the Adil Shahs, the palace was seized by the Portuguese when they first toppled the Muslim kings in 1510 and was rebuilt in 1615 to serve as the Europeans' Viceregal Palace. It was the official residence to Viceroys from 1759 right up until 1918 when the governor-general (the viceroy's 20th-century title) decided to move to the Cabo headland to the southwest – today's Cabo Raj Niwas – leaving the old palace to become government offices. After Independence it became Goa's secretariat building (the seat of the then Union Territory's parliament) until that in turn shifted across the river to Porvorim. It now houses the bureaucracy of the state passport office. Next to it is a striking dark statue of the **Abbé Faria** (1756-1819) looming over the prone figure of a woman. José Custodio de Faria, who went on to become a celebrated worldwide authority on hypnotism, was born into a Colvale Brahmin family in Candolim. The character in Dumas' Count of Monte Cristo may have been based on this Abbé.

Further west, on Malacca Road, almost opposite the wharf, are the central library and public rooms of the **Braganza Institute** ⓘ *Mon-Fri 0930-1300, 1400-1745*. It was established as the Instituto Vasco da Gama in 1871 (the anniversary of the date that the Portuguese explorer da Gama sailed round the Cape of Good Hope), to stimulate an interest in culture, science and the arts. It was renamed for Luis Menezes de Braganza (1878-1938), an outstanding figure of social and political reform in early 20th-century Goa. The blue tile frieze in the entrance, hand painted by Jorge Colaco in 1935, is a mythical representation of the Portuguese colonization of Goa. An art gallery upstairs has paintings by European artists of the late 19th and early 20th centuries and Goan artists of the 20th century. The **central library** ⓘ *0930-1300, 1200-1700*, dating from 1832, has a rare collection of religious and other texts.

City centre

The giant whitewashed 16th-century **Church of the Immaculate Conception** ⓘ *Church Sq, Emidio Gracia Rd, Mon-Sat 0900-1230, 1530-1730, Sun 1100-1230, 1530-1700, free, English Mass Mon-Fri 0800, Sun 0830*, looms pristine and large up a broad sweep of steps off the main square, Largo Da Igreja, blue and white flags fluttering at its fringes. Its dimensions were unwarranted for the population of what was at the time of its construction in 1541, in Panjim, little more than a marshy fishing village; its tall, Portuguese baroque twin towers were instead built both to act as a landmark for and to tend to the spiritual needs of arriving Portuguese sailors, for whom the customs post just below the hill at Panjim marked their first step on Indian soil. The church was enlarged in 1600 to reflect its status as parish church of the capital and in 1619 was rebuilt to its present design. Inside is an ornate jewel in Goan Catholicism's trademark blue, white and gold, wood carved into gilt corkscrews, heavy chandeliers and chintz. The classic baroque main altar *reredos* (screens) are sandwiched between altars to Jesus the Crucified and to Our Lady of the Rosary, in turn flanked by marble statues of St Peter and St Paul. The panels in the Chapel of St Francis, in the south transept, came from the chapel in the Idalcao Palace in 1918. Parishioners bought the statue of Our Lady of Fatima her crown of gold and diamonds in 1950 (candlelight procession every 13 October). The church's feast day is on 8 December.

The Hindu **Mahalaxmi Temple** ⓘ *Dr Dada Vaidya Rd, free,* (originally 1818, but rebuilt and enlarged in 1983) is now hidden behind a newer building. It was the first Hindu place of worship to be allowed in the Old Conquests after the close of the Inquisition. The **Boca de Vaca** ('Cow's Mouth') spring, is nearby.

San Thome and Fontainhas

On Panjim's eastern promontory, at the foot of the Altinho and on the left bank of the Ourem Creek, sit first the San Thome and then, further south, Fontainhas districts filled with modest 18th- and 19th-century houses. The cumulative prettiness of the well- preserved buildings' colour-washed walls, trimmed with white borders, sloping tiled roofs and decorative wrought-iron balconies make it an ideal area to explore on foot. You can reach the area via any of the narrow lanes that riddle San Thome or take the footbridge across the Ourem Creek from

Panjim

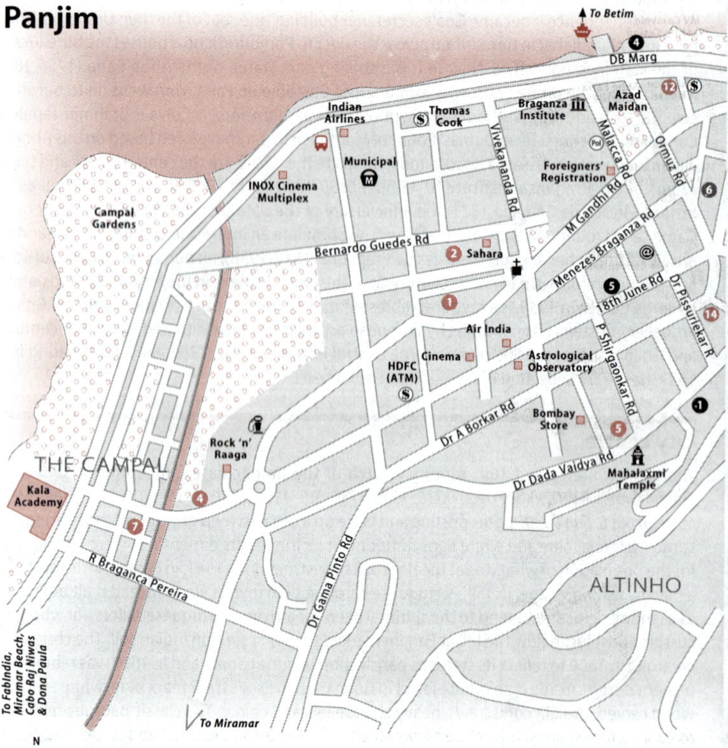

Sleeping
Afonso **6**
Blessings **1**
Campal **7**
Comfort Guest House **8**
Delmon **2**
Mandovi & Riorico Restaurant **12**
Manvin's **13**
Panjim Inn **9**
Panjim Peoples **3**
Panjim Residency **10**
Pousada Guest House **15**
Rajdhani **14**
Virashree **5**

the New Bus Stand and tourist office that feeds you straight into the heart of the district. A narrow road that runs east past the Church of the Immaculate Conception and main town square also ends up here. But probably the best way in is over the Altinho from the Mahalaxmi Temple: this route gives great views over the estuary from the steep eastern flank of the hill, a vantage point that was once used for defensive purposes. A footpath drops down between the Altinho's 19th- and 20th-century buildings just south of San Sebastian Chapel to leave you slap bang in middle of Fontainhas.

The chief landmark here is the small **San Sebastian Chapel** ⓘ *St Sebastian Rd, open only during Mass held in Konkani Mon-Tue, Thu-Sat 0715-0800, Wed 1800-1900, Sun 0645-0730, English Mass Sun 0830-0930, free,* (built 1818, rebuilt 1888) which houses the large wooden crucifix that until 1812 stood in the Palace of the Inquisition in Old Goa where the eyes of Christ watched over the proceedings of the tribunal. Before being moved here, it was in Idalcao Palace's chapel in Panjim for 100 years.

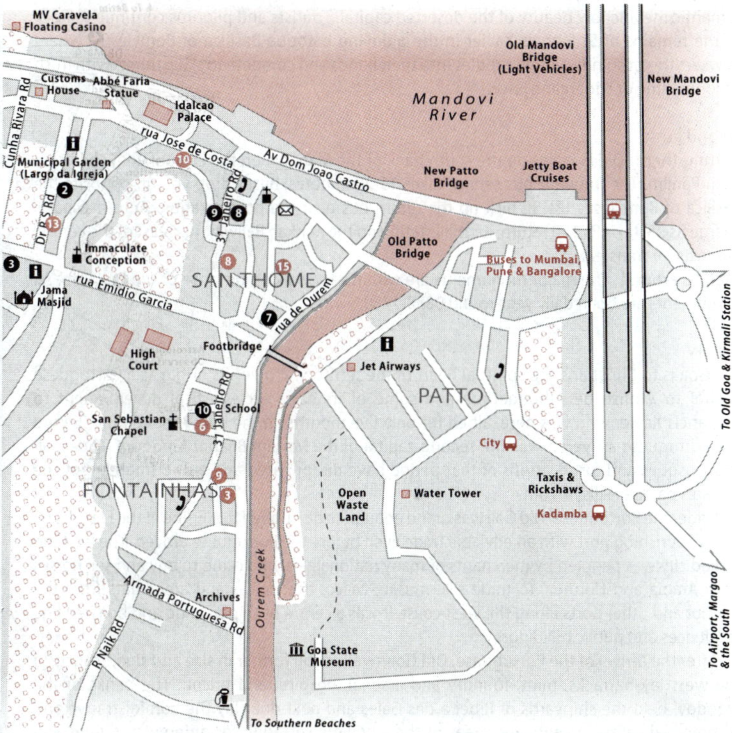

Vivanta by Taj **4**

Eating
A Pastelaria **1**
Anandarhram **9**
Café Tato **2**
Horseshoe **7**
Kamat **3**
Quarterdeck **4**
Satkar **5**
Venite **8**
Viva Panjim **10**

Bars & clubs
Moderna **6**

The **Goa State Museum** ⓘ *Patto, 0930-1730, free, head south of Kadamba Bus Stand, across the Ourem Creek footbridge, right across the waste ground and past the State Bank staff training building,* is an impressive building that contains a disappointingly small collection of religious art and antiquities. Most interesting are the original Provedoria lottery machines built in Lisbon that are on the first floor landing. A few old photos show how the machines were used.

Portuguese law decreed that owners colour-wash the outsides of their homes after each year's monsoon; the only buildings painted all white were churches, while secular buildings came in ochre with windows and door frames picked out in other colours.

Old Goa and around

The white spires of Old Goa's glorious ecclesiastical buildings burst into the Indian sky from the depths of overgrown jungle that has sprawled where admirals and administrators of the Portuguese Empire once tended the oriental interests of their 16th-century King Manuel. The canopies of a hundred raintrees cast their shade across the desolate streets, adding to the romantic melancholy beauty of the deserted capital. Tourists and pilgrims continue to flock to the remains of St Francis Xavier in the giddying baroque Basilica of Bom Jesus, where hawkers thrust spindly votive candles into their hands and compete to slake thirsts with fresh coconut, lime or sugarcane juice.

Ins and outs

Getting there Old Goa lies on the south bank of the Mandovi on the crest of a low hill 8 km from Panjim. The frequent bus service takes 15-20 minutes. Buses drop you off opposite the Basilica of Bom Jesus (Rs 5); pick up the return bus near the police station. Auto-rickshaws charge Rs 25, taxis Rs 150 return. Karmali station on the Konkan Railway, just east of the centre, has taxis for transfers.

Getting around The major monuments are within easy walking distance of the bus stop. All monuments are open daily year-round 0830-1730.

History

Old Goa is to Christians the spiritual heart of the territory. It owes its origin as a Portuguese capital to Afonso de Albuquerque and some of its early ecclesiastical development to St Francis Xavier who was here, albeit for only five months, in the mid-16th century. Before the Portuguese arrived it was the second capital of the Muslim Bijapur Kingdom. Today, all the mosques and fortifications of that period have disappeared and only a fragment of the Sultan's palace walls remain.

Under the Portuguese, Old Goa was grand enough to be dubbed the 'Rome of the East', but it was a flourishing port with an enviable trade even before the Portuguese arrived. The bustling walled city was peopled by merchants of many nationalities who came to buy and sell horses from Arabia and Hormuz, to trade silk, muslin, calico, rice, spices and areca nuts from the interior and other ports along the west coast. It was a centre of shipbuilding and boasted fine residences and public buildings.

After the arrival of the Portuguese, Old Goa swelled still further in size and significance. In the west lay barracks, mint, foundry and arsenal, hospital and prison. The banks of the Mandovi held the shipyards of Ribeira des Gales and next door lay the administrative and commercial centre. Streets and areas of the city were set aside for different activities and merchandise, each with its own character. The most important, Rua Direita ou dos Leiloes (Straight Street), was lined with jewellers, bankers and artisans. It was also the venue for auctions of precious goods, held every morning except Sunday. To the east was the market and the old fortress of Adil Shah, while the true centre of the town was filled with magnificent churches built by the Franciscans, themselves joined by waves of successive religious orders:

first the Dominicans in 1548, the Augustinians from 1572, the Carmelites from 1612 and finally the Theatines from 1655. By the mid-17th century, the city, plagued by cholera and malaria and crippled economically, was abandoned for Panjim.

Basilica of Bom Jesus

The Renaissance façade of Goa's most famous church, the Basilica of Bom (the Good) Jesus, a UNESCO World Heritage Site, reflects the architectural transition to baroque then taking place in Europe. Apart from the elaborate gilded altars, wooden pulpit and the candy-twist Bernini columns, the interior is very simple.

The church has held the treasured remains of **St Francis Xavier**, a former pupil of soldier-turned-saint Ignatius Loyola, the founder of the Order of Jesuits since the 17th century. Francis's canonization was in 1622.

The tomb, which lies to the right of the main chancel (1698), was the gift of one of the last of the Medicis, Cosimo III, Grand Duke of Tuscany, and took the Florentine sculptor Giovanni Batista Foggini 10 years to complete. It is made of three tiers of marble and jasper; the upper tier holds scenes from the saint's life. The casket is silver and has three locks, the keys being held by the Governor, the Archbishop and the Convent Administrator. You can look down on to the tomb from a small window in the art gallery next to the church.

After his canonization, St Francis's body was shown on each anniversary of his death until 1707, when it was restricted to a few special private expositions. In 1752, the cadaver was again paraded to quash rumours that the Jesuits had removed it. The exhibition now happens every 10 to 12 years (the last exposition was in 2005), when the relics are taken to the Sé Cathedral. Feast Day is 3 December.

The Basilica of Bom Jesus is on the World Monuments Fund's list of the world's 100 most endangered sites.

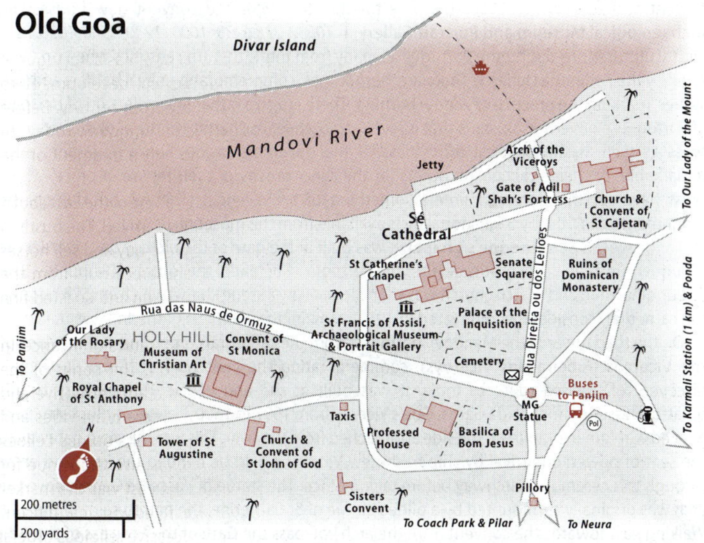

Sé Cathedral

Across the square sits the Sé Cathedral, dedicated to St Catherine on whose day (25 November) Goa was recaptured by Albuquerque. Certainly the largest church in Old Goa, it could even be the biggest in Asia and was built on the ruins of a mosque by the Dominicans between 1562 and 1623. The building is Tuscan outside and Corinthian inside, with a barrel-vaulted ceiling and east-facing main façade. One of the characteristic twin towers collapsed in 1776 when it was struck by lightning. The remaining tower holds five bells including the Golden Bell (cast in Cuncolim in 1652). The vast interior, divided into the barrel-vaulted nave with clerestory and two side aisles, has a granite baptismal font. On each side of the church are four chapels along the aisles; on the right, these are dedicated to St Anthony, St Bernard, the Cross of Miracles and the Holy Spirit, and on the left, starting at the entrance, to Our Lady of Virtues, St Sebastian, the Blessed Sacrament and Our Lady of Life. The clerestory windows are protected by a shield crowned by a balustrade to keep out the sun. The main altar is superbly gilded and painted, with six further altars in the transept. The marble-top table in front of the main altar is where, since 1955, St Francis Xavier's remains have been held during their exposition. The main *reredos* has four panels illustrating the life of St Catherine. There is also an **art gallery** ⓘ *Mon-Thu, Sat 0900-1230, Sun 0900-1030, closed during services, Rs 5.*

Around the cathedral

Southwest of the cathedral's front door are the ruins of the **Palace of the Inquisition**, where over 16,000 cases were heard between 1561 and 1774. The Inquisition was finally suppressed in 1814. Beneath the hall were dungeons. In Old Goa's heyday this was the town centre.

There are two churches and a museum in the same complex as the Cathedral. The **Church and Convent of St Francis of Assisi** is a broad vault of a church with two octagonal towers. The floor is paved with tombstones and on either side of the baroque high altar are paintings on wood depicting scenes from St Francis' life while the walls above have frescoes with floral designs. The original **Holy Spirit Church** in the Portuguese Gothic (manueline) style was begun by Franciscan friars in 1517; everything except the old doorway was replaced by the larger present structure in the 1660s (itself restored 1762-1765). The convent now houses the **Archaeological Museum and Portrait Gallery** ⓘ *T0832-228 6133, 1000- 1230, 1500-1830, Rs 5*, with sculptures pre-dating the Portuguese, many from the 12th-13th centuries when Goa was ruled by the Kadamba Dynasty. There are 'hero stones' commemorating naval battles, and 'sati stones' marking the practice of widow burning. There is also a rather fine collection of portraits of Portuguese governors upstairs that is revealing both for its charting of the evolution of court dress as well as the physical robustness of the governors inside. Some governors were remarkable for their sickly pallor, others for the sheer brevity of their tenure of office, which must have set the portrait painters something of a challenge. (The ASI booklet on the monuments, *Old Goa*, by S Rajagopalan, is available from the museum, Rs 10.)

To the west is **St Catherine's Chapel**. It was built at the gate of the old city on the orders of Albuquerque as an act of gratitude after the Portuguese defeat of the forces of Bijapur in 1510. The original mud and thatch church was soon replaced by a stone chapel which in 1534 became the cathedral (considerably renovated in 1952), remaining so until Sé Cathedral was built.

On the road towards the Mandovi, northeast from the cathedral compound, lies the **Arch of the Viceroys** (**Ribeira dos Viceroys**), commemorating the centenary of Vasco da Gama's discovery of the sea route to India. It was built at the end of the 16th century by his great-grandson, Francisco da Gama, Goa's Viceroy from 1597 to 1600. Its laterite block structure is faced with green granite on the side approached from the river. This was the main gateway to the seat of power: on arrival by ship each new Viceroy would be handed the keys and enter through this ceremonial archway before taking office. The statue of Vasco da Gama above the arch was originally surmounted by a gilded statue of St Catherine, the patron saint of the city. Walking east towards the convent from the arch you pass the **Gate of the Fortress of the Adil**

Shahs, probably built by Sabaji, the Maratha ruler of Goa before the Muslim conquest of 1471. The now-ruined palace was home to the Adil Shahi sultans of Bijapur who occupied Goa before the arrival of the Portuguese. It was the Palace of the Viceroys until 1554 after which it served as both the hall of trials for the Inquisition and to house prisoners.

A little further still stands the splendid, domed baroque **Convent and Church of St Cajetan (Caetano)**. Pope Urban III dispatched a band of Italian friars of the Theatine order to spread the Gospel to the Deccani Muslim city of Golconda near Hyderabad but they got a frosty reception so headed back west to settle in Goa. They acquired land around 1661 to build this church, which is shaped like a Greek cross and is partly modelled on St Peter's in Rome. It is the last domed church in Goa.

The crypt below the main altar, where the Italian friars were buried, has some sealed lead caskets that are supposed to contain the embalmed bodies of senior Portuguese officials who never returned home. Next door is the beautiful former convent building which is now a pastoral foundation (closed to the public).

On a hill a good way further east is the modest **Chapel of Our Lady of the Mount**, dating from 1510, which gives you a good idea of how the other churches here must originally have looked. It is a peaceful spot with excellent panoramic views across Old Goa, evocative of the turbulent past when Albuquerque and Adil Shah vied for control of the surrounding area. The altar gilding inside has been beautifully restored. In front of the main altar lies the body of architect Antonio Pereira whose burial slab requests the visitor to say an Ave Maria for his soul.

Holy Hill

Between the domineering central monuments of Old Goa's broad tree-lined centre and Panjim stand the cluster of churches of Holy Hill. The first building you reach (on your left) as you leave the central plaza is the **Church and Convent of St John of God**, built in 1685 and abandoned in 1835. The **Museum of Christian Art** ⓘ *Sun-Thu 1000-1700, Rs 5*, is to the right, with 150 items gathered from Goa's churches, convents and Christian homes to give a rich cross section of Indo-Portuguese sacred craft in wood, ivory, silver and gold.

Next door sits the **Convent of St Monica** (1607-1627), the first nunnery in India and the largest in Asia. A huge three-storey square building, with the church in the southern part, it was built around a sunken central courtyard containing a formal garden. At one time it was a royal monastery, but in 1964 it became a theological institute, the Mater Dei Institute for Nuns. It was here in 1936 that Bishop Dom Frei Miguel Rangel is believed to have had a vision of the Christ figure on the Miraculous Cross opening his eyes, his stigmata bleeding and his lips quivering as if to speak. The vision was repeated later that year in the presence of the Bishop, the Viceroy Dom Pedro de Silva and a large congregation.

It is well worth the effort of the hike, taking the left fork of the road, to reach the **Royal Chapel of St Anthony** (1543) – dedicated to Portugal's national saint and restored by its government in 1961 – and, opposite, the **Tower of St Augustine**. The Augustinians came to Goa in 1572; the church they immediately began, bar the belfry, now lies in ruins. It once boasted eight chapels, a convent and an excellent library and was enlarged to become one of the finest in the kingdom. It was finally abandoned in 1835 because of religious persecution. The vault collapsed in 1842, burying the image; the façade and main tower followed in 1931 and 1938. Only one of the original four towers survives. The large bell now hangs in Panjim's Church of the Immaculate Conception. The Archaeological Survey of India is spearheading extensive repairs.

Behind is the **Chapel of Our Lady of the Rosary** (1526). Belonging to the earliest period of church building, it is called Manueline after Manuel I, the Portuguese king who oversaw a period of great prosperity that coincided with the country's conquest of Goa. The use of Hindu and Muslim craftsmen in building the chapel led to an architectural style that borrowed from Iberian decoration but also absorbed both local naturalistic motifs and Islamic elements (seen on the marble cenotaph). The church here has a two-storey entrance, a single tower and low flanking turrets. It was from here that Albuquerque directed the battle against the Adil Shahi forces in 1510.

Around Panjim

Gaspar Dias Fortress was finished around 1606. The Panjim-Ribandar causeway, built in 1634, gave it direct land access to the capital at Old Goa and its significance grew accordingly. The walls, likely laterite blocks 1.5 m thick and 5 m high, made space for 16 cannons. These saw repeated action against the Dutch until the middle of the 17th century, but the fortress' importance waned after the Maratha onslaught and it fell into disrepair under 15 years of occupation by a British garrison in the early 19th century. It was made new but the Portuguese army finally abandoned it in 1870 as a result of further damage sustained during the mutiny against the Prefect of 1835. For a while the military still stationed soldiers here to convalesce but by the 20th century it had crumbled beyond recognition. All that is left is one cannon at the Miramar circle that marks the possible site of the fort. **Miramar Beach** is a bit grubby but it's a pleasant drive with good views over the sea and, if you've got a little time to kill, it offers the best quick escape from the city.

The nearby fort **Cabo Raj Niwas** has fared little better: six cannons and some bits of wall crumbling in the gardens of Raj Bhavan, or the State Governor's House, are all that remain. It is closed to the public but you can get passes for Sunday Mass at 0930 on the gate. The first small **Our Lady of Cabo shrine** was built in 1541. Documents from 1633 refer to both the chapel and a fort with four guns. A British troops garrison stationed here from 1799 during the Napoleonic Wars explains the overgrown graves in the nearby **British Cemetery**. Around 1844, after the religious orders were abolished, the Archbishop of Goa was given the convent, which he converted into an impressive residence. It was the official address of the governor-general of Goa in 1918. Its grand interior was left intact after the Portuguese left in 1961. The viewing platform near the entrance gives superb views over the sweep of the coastline across the Mandovi estuary to Fort Aguada.

Panjim (Panaji) and Old Goa listings

For Sleeping and Eating price codes and other relevant information, see Essentials pages 38-42.

Sleeping

Panjim has a wide choice of accommodation, Old Goa none. There are upmarket options south of Panjim in the beach resorts of Miramar and Dona Paula, but for character it's best to book into one of the guesthouses in the atmospheric Fontainhas district. If you don't want to stay overnight you can pack the best of Panjim and Old Goa into a day. Guesthouses have early checkout to make way for new arrivals coming off the trains and buses.

Panjim *p1238, map p1240*

LL-AL Taj Vivanta, www.vivantabytaj.com. The Taj Vivanta opened in Panjim in 2009 and is a smart upmarket option centrally located. Common areas and restaurants are beautiful. Rooms are a little on the boutique-side, ie small and have this new trend of glass-walled bathrooms where you have to shut the blinds each time if you are sharing the room. Very odd. Overall everything you would expect from the Taj group.

AL-B Mandovi, D B Marg, T0832-242 6270, www.hotelmandovigoa.com. Old building with hints of art deco, relaxing but lacks great character. 66 large a/c rooms (river facing more expensive); rates include breakfast. 1st floor **Riorico** restaurant, popular pastry shop, terrace bar, exchange.

B-C Delmon, C de Albuquerque Rd, T0832-222 6846, www.alcongoa.com. 50 clean rooms, TV, desk, some a/c, breakfast included. Modern, comfortable hotel, popular restaurant.

B-C Manvins, 4th floor (accessed by lifts), Souza Towers, Muncipal Gardens/Church Sq, T0832-222 4412, www.goamanvins.com. 45 acceptable rooms with TV, some sleep 4, stunning views over Municipal Gardens and Mandovi River, hot water. Terrace has great views of Panjim. Unusual approach to interior design. Disco and pub.

D Hotel Campal, opposite Kala Academy, Campal, T0832-222 4533. Clean rooms with TV and a/c possible, hidden in beautiful location in Campal area, near Kala Academy, Inox cinemas and the river.

D Rajdhani, Dr Atmaram Borkar Rd, T0832-222 5362. Modern business hotel with 35 smallish clean rooms with bath, some a/c (Rs 100 extra), pure vegetarian restaurant.

D-E Blessings, MG Rd, behind Bhatkar House, T0832-222 4770, hotelblessings@yahoo.com. 18 ordinary rooms, TV (extra Rs 50), 2 have huge terraces instead of balconies, restaurant, quiet tree-filled backyard.

D-E Panjim Residency (GTDC), overlooking the river, T0832-242 4001. Best views from top floor, 40 good-sized rooms with balcony, some a/c (overpriced), good open-air restaurant, often full, can organize tours and boat trips.

D-E Virashree, opposite Mahalaxmi Temple, Dr Dada Vaidya Rd, T0832-222 6656, virashree@hotmail.com. 12 large, comfortable rooms with TV but lacking quality finish.

Fontainhas *p1240, map p1240*

A The Panjim Peoples, opposite **Panjim Inn**, www.panjiminn.com. The latest heritage project from the Sukhija family, this one is genuinely top end with just 4 rooms, antique 4-poster beds and bathtubs, plus internet access. Changing art exhibitions on the ground floor.

B-C Panjim Inn, E212, 31 January Rd, T0832-222 6523, www.panjiminn.com. Goa's first heritage hotel is idiosyncratic, even in the context of the historic Fontainhas district. 14 rooms of varying size all fitted with 4-poster beds, a/c for an extra Rs 250.

B-C Panjim Pousada, up the road from **Panjim Inn**. Slightly cheaper sister hotel to the **Panjim Inn** with double rooms set around a permanent art gallery in a courtyard. It is an evocative, attractive renovation. Best rooms at the back overlook another courtyard. Recommended.

E Afonso, near San Sebastian Chapel, Fontainhas, T0832-222 2359. Atmospheric family-run guesthouse, obliging and friendly, 8 clean rooms with bath, shaded roof terrace for breakfast. It's first come first served, though, as the owners don't take advance bookings. Recommended.

E Pousada Guest House, Luis de Menezes Rd, T0832-561 8308. Pousada's basic rooms are higgledy-piggledy but have a/c, TV and fridge and attached bath. Will take advance bookings.

F Comfort Guest House, 31 January Rd, T0832-222 8145. Good location, some rooms with TV, but often full and you can't book ahead. The cheaper of its 12 basic rooms have shared bath.

Around Panjim *p1246*

Miramar Beach

AL-A Goa Marriott Resort, Mandovi River, T0832-246 3333, www.marriott.com. 153 large rooms, good facilities, pool, close to public beach, best hotel in area. Weekend buffet lunches popular with Panjim locals.

B Swimsea Beach Resort, T0832-246 4481, swimsea@satyam.net.in. 28 a/c rooms with small balconies, pretty underwhelming, sea facing best, pool, close to black if you want a quality beach experience better to stay elsewhere.

Eating

Panjim *p1238, map p1240*

Horseshoe, Rua de Ourem, T0832-243 1788, Mon-Sat 1200-1430, 1900-1030. Portuguese/Goan restaurant set in 2 high-ceilinged rooms with exceptionally good service. Most meals excellent value (Rs 60-80) but daily fish specials are far more costly (from Rs 300). The house pudding, a cashew cake, *Bolo San Rival* (Rs 50), trumps all the great main courses.

Quarterdeck, next to Betim ferry jetty, T0832-243 2905. Goan, Indian, Chinese. Riverside location is the best in Panjim, very pleasant in the evening when brightly lit cruise boats glide gaudily by. Live music.

Venite, 31 Janeiro Rd, T0832-222 5537, Mon-Sat 0800-2200, closes in the afternoon. The most charming of Panjim's eateries has 1st-floor balconies overlooking the Sao Thome street life and good music. Specializing in fish, this place has a great atmosphere.

Viva Panjim, house no 178, signposted from 31 Janeiro Rd, T0832-242 2405. This family-run joint in the atmospheric Fontainhas quarter spills out of the restaurant and out into a courtyard, and dishes up Goan specials like *xacuti* and *cafreal* along with seafood, plus takeaway parcels of Indian, Chinese and continental.

Anandashram, opposite **Venite** 31 Janeiro Rd. Serving up platters of fish and veg thali, this is a great place to break *pao* (local bread) with the locals. Recommended.

Café Tato, off east side of Church Sq. Closed evenings. Something of a local institution, tiny little **Tato** is packed at lunchtime when office workers descend for its limited range of Goan vegetarian food. Expect tiny platters of chickpea, tomato or mushroom bhaji served with fresh puffed *puris* or soft bread rolls, or vegetarian cutlets and *thalis*. Upstairs is a/c.

Kamat, south end of Municipal Gardens. Pure vegetarian canteen, huge servings of *thalis*, excellent paper *dosas* and *puri bhajis*. Very popular large central dining hall.

Satkar, 18 June Rd, oppsote Bombay Bazaar. **Satkar** serves up fantastic pure veg food that runs the gamut from South Indian *idlis* and *thalis* to north Indian *sabzi* and tandoor dishes, and the best Punjabi samosas in India. Recommended.

Bakeries, cafés and snacks

A Pastelaria, Dr Dada Vaidya Rd. Good choice of cakes, pastries and breads. **Mandovi Hotel** has a branch too (side entrance).

Bars and clubs

Panjim *p1238, map p1240*

You can't go 20 paces in Panjim without finding a bar: pokey little rooms with a handful of formica tables and chairs and some snacks being fried up in the corner. Many are clustered around Fontainhas. The *feni* (Goa's cashew- or coconut-extracted moonshine) comes delivered in jerry cans, making it cheaper than restaurants. Try **Café Moderna**, near Cine National, food none too good, claustrophobic upstairs dining area, quality atmosphere.

Entertainment

Panjim *p1238, map p1240*

Read the 'today's events' columns in the local papers for concerts and performances.

Astronomical Observatory, 7th floor, Junta House, 18th June Rd (entrance in Vivekananda Rd). Open 14 Nov-31 May, 1900-2100, in clear weather. Rooftop 6-inch Newtonian reflector telescope and binoculars. Worth a visit on a moonless night, and for views over Panjim at sunset.

Inox, Campal, near Kala Academy, www.inoxmovies.com. Fantastic state-of-the-art glass-fronted cinema – like going to the movies in

California. You can catch the latest Bolly- and Hollywood blockbusters here, and they try to show the Oscar-nominated Best Movies every year.

Kala Academy, D B Marg, Campal, T0832-222 3288. This modern and architecturally impressive centre designed by Charles Correa was set up to preserve and promote the cultural heritage of Goa. There are exhibition galleries, a library and comfortable indoor and outdoor auditoria. Art exhibitions, theatre and music programmes (from contemporary pop and jazz to Indian classical) are held, mostly during the winter months. There are also courses on music and dance.

MV Caravela, Fisheries dept building, D B Marg, Panjim, www.casinocity.com/in/panjim/caravela. India's first floating casino is docked on the Mandovi, 66 m of high-rupee-rolling catamaran casino, all plush wall-to-wall carpets, chandeliers and sari-bedecked croupiers. The boat accommodates 300 people, has a sun deck, swimming pool and restaurant and the Rs 1200 entrance includes short eats and dinner and booze from 1730 till the morning.

Festivals and events

Panjim *p1238, map p1240*

Feb/Mar In addition to the major festivals in Feb, the **Mardi Gras Carnival** (3 days preceding Lent in Feb/Mar) is a Mediterranean-style riot of merrymaking, marked by feasting, colourful processions and floats down streets: it kicks off near the Secretariat at midday. One of the best bits is the red-and-black dance held in the cordoned-off square outside the old world Clube Nacional on the evening of the last day: everyone dresses up (some cross- dressing), almost everyone knows each other, and there's lots of old-fashioned slow-dancing to curiously country and Western-infused live music. The red and black theme is strictly enforced.

Mar-Apr **Shigmotsav** is a spring festival held at full moon (celebrated as **Holi** elsewhere in India); colourful float processions through the streets often display mythological scenes accompanied by plenty of music on drums and cymbals.

1st Sun after Easter **Feast of Jesus of Nazareth.** Procession of All Saints in Goa Velha, on the Mon of Holy Week.

Dec/Jan **Fontainhas Festival of Arts**. Timed to coincide with the film festival (see below), 30 heritage homes open up as temporary art and artefact galleries in an event organized by Fundacao Oriente, Goa Heritage Action Group and the Entertainment Society of Goa.

International Film Festival of India, www.iffigoa.org. India's answer to Cannes: a 10-day film mart packed with screenings for the industry and general public alike, with its headquarters based around the Kala Academy and the Inox building on the banks of the Mandovi. Held in Goa since 2004.

Food and Culture Festival at Miramar Beach.

8 Dec **Feast of Our Lady of the Immaculate Conception**. A big fair is held in the streets around Church Sq and a firework display is put on in front of the church each night of the week before the feast (at 1930). After morning Mass on the Sun, the Virgin is carried in a procession through the town centre.

24 Dec **Christmas Eve**. This is celebrated with midnight Mass at 140 churches in the state, but some of the best attended are the Church of the Immaculate Conception and Dom Bosco Church in Panjim and the Basilica of Bom Jesus in Old Goa.

Shopping

Panjim *p1238, map p1240*

Books and Music

Broadway Books, next to Rock and Raaga off 18th June Rd, T0832-6647038. Largest bookshop in Goa with good range.

Mandovi Hotel (see Sleeping). The hotel bookshop has a small range of books and magazines, including American news magazines.

Pedro Fernandes & Co, Rua Jose de Costa, near Head Post Office, T0832-2226642. If you have a hankering to pick up a sitar or learn to play tabla, this small store has a great selection of musical instruments.

Varsha, near Azad Maidan. Holds a large stock in tiny premises, and is especially good for books on Goa. Obscure titles are not displayed but ask the knowledgeable staff.

Clothes and textiles

Government handicrafts shops are at the tourist hotels and the Interstate Terminus. There are other emporia on RS Rd.

Bombay Store, Casa Mendes, SV Rd, opposite Old Passport Office. A new branch of the lifestyle retail store has arrived in Goa close to the main shopping road 18th June Rd , with good selection of fabrics and clothes, as well as cards, stationery and homewares.

Fab India, Braganza Bungalow, opposite Indoor Stadium, Campal, T0832-246 3096. This is a particularly lovely branch of this great chain which sells handblock print clothes, textiles home furnishings and furniture. They have an extensive collection.

Government Emporia, RS Rd. Good value for fixed-rate clothes, fabric and handicrafts.

Khadi Showroom, Municipal (Communidade) Building, Church Sq, good value for fixed-rate clothes, fabric and handicrafts. Nehru jackets, Rs 250, plus perishables like honey and pickles.

Sacha's Shop, Casa Mendes, next to **Bombay Store**, T0832-222 2035. Dubbed a 'curious little space' by the owner, the eponymous Sacha, it is a collection of clothes, flea market finds, designer frocks, organic soaps and textiles.

Velha Goa Galeria, 4/191 Rua De Ourem, Fontainhas, T0832-242 6628. Hand-painted ceramics, wall hangings and tabletops of tiles.

Wendell Rodricks Design Space, 158 Luis Gomes Garden, Altinho, T0832-223 8177. Rodricks is probably Goa's most famous fashion designer who built his name making minimalist clothing. Here you'll find his luxury clothes and footwear.

Activities and tours

Panjim *p1238, map p1240*

Cruises

Lots of evening cruises go along the Mandovi River, but as all boats seem to sport loud sound systems it's hardly a peaceful cruise.

Music lessons

Manab Das plays regularly at the **Kala Academy** and the **Kerkar** in Calangute (see page 1253). He and his wife, Dr Rupasree Das, offer sitar and singing lessons to more long-term visitors. To arrange lessons T0832-242 1086 or email manabrupasreegoa@yahoo.in.

Tour operators

Alpha Holidays, 407-409 Dempo Tower, 4th floor, 16 EDC Patto Plaza, T0832-243 7450, www.alphagoa.com.

Pepper Tours, 127 Subash Chandra Bose Rd, Jawahar Nagar, Kadavanthara, PO Cochin 682020, T484-405 8886, Mob 98473 22802, www.peppertours.com.

Transport

Panjim *p1238, map p1240*

Air The airport is at Dabolim. From Dabolim airport, 29 km via the Zuari Bridge from Panjim, internal flights can be taken through **Air India** to **Mumbai** and **Thiruvananthapuram**. For pre-paid taxis, see Ins and outs, page 1237.

Airline offices **Air India**, 18th June Rd, T0832-243 1101. **Indian Airlines and Alliance Air**, Dempo House, D B Marg, T0832-223 7821, reservations 1000-1300, 1400-1600, airport T0832-254 0788, flights to **Bengaluru** (**Bangalore**), **Delhi** and **Mumbai** daily (US$95), and **Chennai**. **British Airways**, 2 Excelsior Chambers, opposite Mangaldeep, MG Rd, T0832-222 4573. **Jet Airways**, Sesa Ghor, 7-9 Patto Plaza, T0832-243 1472, airport T0832-251 0354. Flights to **Mumbai** (US$103), and **Bengaluru** (**Bangalore**). **Kuwait Airways**, 2 Jesuit House, Dr DR de Souza Rd, Municipal Garden Sq, T0832-222 4612. **Sahara**, Live-In Appt, Gen Bernard Guedes Rd, airport office, T0832-254 0043. To **Mumbai**, US$95, daily, and **Delhi**.

Auto-rickshaw Easily available but agree a price beforehand (Rs 20-35), more after dark. Motorcycle taxis and private taxis are a little cheaper.

Local bus Crowded **Kadamba** (**KTC**) buses and private buses operate from the bus stand in Patto to the east of town, across the Ourem Creek, T0832-222 2634. Booking 0800-1100, 1400-1630. The timetable is not strictly observed: buses leave when full. Frequent service to **Calangute** 35 mins, Rs 7; **Mapusa** 15 mins, Rs 8 (try to catch a direct one). Via Cortalim (Zuari bridge) to **Margao** 1 hr, Rs 10; **Vasco** 1 hr, Rs 8. To **Old Goa** (every 10 mins) 20 mins, Rs 5, continues to **Ponda** 1 hr, Rs 8.

Long distance bus 'Luxury' buses and 'Sleepers' (bunks are shared). Prices double at Diwali, Christmas and New Year, and during the May school holidays. Private operators: include **Laxmi Motors**, near Customs House, T0832-222 5745; company at Cardozo Building near KTC Bus Stand; **Paulo Tours**, Hotel Fidalgo, T0832-222 6291.

State buses are run by **Kadamba TC**, **Karnataka RTC**, **Maharashtra RTC**. Check times and book in advance at Kadamba Bus Stand. Unlicensed operators use poorly maintained, overcrowded buses; check out beforehand.

Buses to **Bengaluru** (**Bangalore**): 1530-1800 (13 hrs), Rs 300; **Belgaum**: 0630-1300 (5 hrs); **Gokarna** and **Hospet** (**Hampi**): 0915-1030 (10 hrs), Rs 150 (Rs 350 sleeper); **Hubli**: many; **Londa**: 4 hrs, Rs 60; **Mangalore**: 0615-2030 (10 hrs), Rs 180; **Miraj**: 1030 (10 hrs); **Mumbai**: 1530- 1700 (15 hrs+), Rs 550 (sleeper), others (some a/c) Rs 300-450; **Pune**: 0615-1900 (12 hrs), Rs 200, sleeper Rs 400.

Car hire **Hertz**, T0832-222 3998; **Joey's**, town centre opposite the Mandovi Hotel, T0832-242 2050. **Sai Service**, 36/1 Alto Porvorim, north of the Mandovi Bridge, T0832-241 7063, or at airport. **Wheels**, T0832-222 4304, airport, T0832-251 2138.

Ferry Flat-bottomed ferries charge a nominal fee to take passengers (and usually vehicles) when rivers are not bridged. **Panjim-Betim** (the Nehru bridge over the Mandovi supplements the ferry); **Old Goa-Diwar Island**; **Ribandar-Chorao** for Salim Ali Bird Sanctuary.

Taxi Tourist taxis are white; hire from **Goa Tourism**, Trionora Apts, T0832-222 3396, about Rs 700 per day (80 km). Share-taxis run on certain routes; available near the the ferry wharves, main hotels and market places (up to 5). **Mapusa** from Panjim, around Rs 10 each. **Airport**, about 40 mins; Rs 380.

Train Some **Konkan Railway** trains stop at **Karmali**, T0832-228 6398, near Old Goa (20 mins taxi). **Rail Bookings**, Kadamba Bus Station, 1st floor, T0832-243 5054, 0930-1300 and 1430-1700. **South Central Railway** serves the Vasco-Londa/Belgaum line; for details see page 1237, and Margao (Madgaon), page 1298.

Directory

Panjim *p1238, map p1240*

Banks Many private agencies change TCs and cash. **Thomas Cook**, 8 Alcon Chambers, D B Marg, T0832-243 1732, Mon-Sat. Also for Thomas Cook drafts, money transfers; **Amex**, at Menezes Air Travel, Rua de Ourem, but does not cash TCs. Cash against certain credit cards from **Central Bank**, Nizari Bhavan; **Andhra Bank**, Dr Atmaram Borkar Rd, opposite EDC House, T0832-222 3513; **Bank of Baroda**, Azad Maidan; **HDFC**, 18 June Rd, T0832-242 1922, 24-hr ATM, most convenient way to obtain cash in Panjim. **Embassies and consulates** **Germany**, Hon Consul, c/o Cosme Matias Menezes Group, Rua de Ourem, T0832-222 3261; **Portugal**, LIC Bldg, Patto, T0832-222 4233; **UK**, room 302, 3rd floor, Manguirish Bldg, 18th June Rd, T0832-222 8571, bcagoa@goa1.dot.net. **Internet** Among many charging Rs 35-40 per hr: **little.dot.com cyber café**, 1st floor, Padmavati Towers, 18th June Rd, 0930-2300. Best in town: **Suraj Business Centre**, 5 terminals upstairs, excellent fast connection (128 kbps ISDN line), 0900-2300. **Medical services** **Goa Medical College**, Av PC Lopez, west end of town, T0832-222 3026, is very busy; newer College at Bambolim; **CMM Poly Clinic**, Altinho, T0832-222 5918. **Post** Old Tobacco Exchange, St Thome, towards Old Patto Bridge, with Poste Restante on left as you enter, Mon-Sat 0930-1730, closed 1300-1400.

North Goa

While Baga and Calangute, the fishing villages first settled by the 'freaks', now stand as cautionary tales to all that's worse in mass tourism, Anjuna, a place synonymous with psychedelia, drugs and Goa trance parties, has managed to retain a village feel despite the existence of its unquestionably shady underbelly. It's a more tranquil place to be now that a 2200 music curfew has put a stop to outdoor parties. The weekly flea market is a brilliant bazar – like Camden or Portobello but with sacred cows, sadhus, fakirs and snake charmers – and makes it onto every holidaymaker's itinerary. But if you stick around you'll find that the little stretch of shoreline from the northern end of Anjuna Beach to the Chapora River is beautifully desolate: rust-coloured rugged cliffs covered with scrub interrupt scrappy bays strewn with laterite boulders. Pretty cliff-backed Vagator stands just south of the romantic ruins of Chapora Fort, with its busy fishing jetty, where trawler landings are met by a welcoming committee of kites, gulls and herons wheeling hungrily on high, while further upstream around the pretty village of Siolim young men wade through mangrove swamps to sift the muds for clams, mussels and oysters. Over the Chapora lies Arambol, a warm, hippy backpacker hamlet, and its beach satellites of Mandrem, Asvem and Keri and the wonderful little Catholic enclave clustered around the ancient Tiracol Fort. ▸▸ *For listings, see pages 1262-1280.*

Baga to Candolim → *For listings, see pages 1262-1280.*

The faultless fawn shoreline of Bardez *taluka*, particularly Calangute, until 40 years ago was a string of fishing villages. Now it acts as sandpit to the bulk of Goa's travel trade. Chock full of accommodation, eateries, travel agents, money changers, beggars and under-dressed, over-sunned charter tourists, the roads snarl up with minivans, buses and bikes, and unchecked development has made for a largely concrete conurbation of breezeblock hotels and mini markets. For all that, if you squint hard or come in monsoon you can still see what once made it such a hippy magnet: wonderful coconut-fringed sands backed by plump dunes occasionally broken by rocky headlands and coves. The main reason to head this way is for business, banks, or posh food and nightlife. To get out again, you can paddle in the waters of the Arabian Sea all the way between the forts of Aguada and Vagator.

Ins and outs

Getting there The NH17 acts as the main arterial road between all of Goa's coastal belt. From Panjim, the highway crosses the Mandovi Bridge to the area's main hub, Calangute (16 km from Panjim, 10 km from Mapusa). Buses from Mapusa (20 minutes) and Panjim (35 minutes) arrive at Calangute Bus Stand near the market; a few continue to Baga to the north from the crossroads. You can charter tourist minivans from places such as Panjim and Dabolim. The closest stop on the Konkan Railway route between Mumbai and Mangalore is Tivim near Mapusa. On market days there are boats between Baga and Anjuna. There are buses from Mapusa and Panjim to Calangute, Anjuna, Chapora and Arambol.

Getting around There are 9 km of uninterrupted beach between Fort Aguada and the bridge over Baga river in the north, which takes you to Anjuna. These are split into four beaches, south to north: Sinquerim, Candolim, Calangute and Baga. Each has its own stab at a high street, Calangute's being the most built up. There are taxis, motorcycle taxis, tourist vans and old Ambassador cabs, or cheap but slow public buses. Roads are fairly good for motorbikes and scooters; watch out for speed bumps. Accidents happen with grim regularity, but bikes give you the independence to zip between beaches.

Background

The name Bardez may have come from the term *bara desh* (12 'divisions of land'), which refers to the 12 Brahmin villages that once dominated the region. Another explanation is that it refers to 12 *zagors* celebrated to ward off evil. Or it could be *bahir des*, meaning 'outside land' – ie, the land beyond the Mandovi River. It was occupied by the Portuguese as part of their original conquest, and bears the greatest direct imprint of their Christianizing influence.

Calangute → *Colour map 5a, A1.*

More than 25 years of package tourism has guaranteed that there is little left to draw you to Calangute apart from ATMs, some decent restaurants and a quirky hexagonal *barbeiria* (barber's shop) at the northern roundabout. In the 1960s, the village was short-hand for the alternative life, but the main feature of the streets today is their messy Indian take on beach commercialism. Shops peddle everything from cheap ethnic tat to extravagant precious gemstones. The shacks on the beach serve good food and cheap beer and most fly the St George's Cross in tribute to Calangute's charter coin. Between the busy beachfront and the grubby main road, coconut trees give shade to village houses, some of which rent out private rooms.

Away from the town centre, the striking gold and white **Church of St Alex** is a good example of rococo decoration in Goa, while the false dome of the central façade is an 18th-century architectural development. The pulpit and the *reredos* are particularly fine. **Kerkar Art Complex** ⓘ *Gaurawaddo, T0832-227 6017, www.subodhkerkar.com*, is a beautiful art space showcasing Subodh Kerkar's paintings and installation work. Inspired by the ocean, nature is both the theme and medium of his work, using shells, light and water to create static waves or, in his recent installations, using fishermen standing on the beach to create the shapes and forms of fishing boats – all captured in stunning black and white photography.

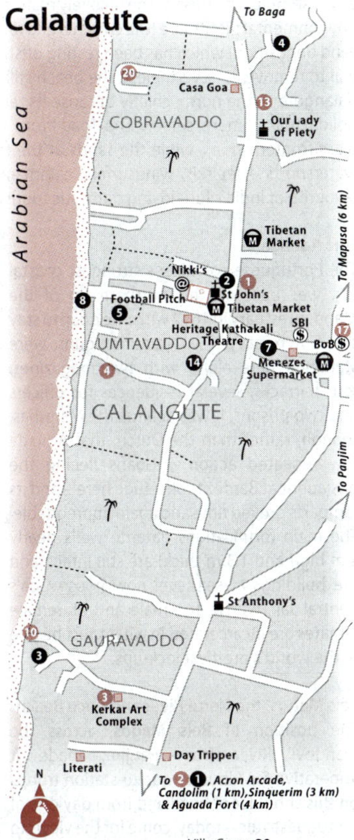

200 metres
200 yards

Sleeping
Aashyana Lakhanpal **2**
Coco Banana **4**
Golden Eye **10**
Kerkar Retreat **3**
Martin's Guest Rooms **13**
Pousada Tauma **17**
Saahil **1**
Villa Goesa **20**

Eating
A Reverie **3**
Bomras **1**
Infanteria **2**
Le Restaurant Français **4**
Oriental at Hotel Mira **14**
Plantain Leaf **7**
Souza Lobo **8**
Tibetan Kitchen **5**

Baga

Baga is basically Calangute North: there's continuity in congestion, shops, shacks and sun loungers. Here though, there are also paddy marshes, water tanks and salt pans, the beach is still clean, and the river that divides this commercial strip of sand from Anjuna in the north also brings fishermen pulling in their catch at dawn, and casting their nets at dusk. The north bank, or **Baga River**, is all thick woods, mangroves and birdlife; it has quite a different, more villagey feel, with a few classy European restaurants looking out across the river. You can take an hour to wade across the river at low tide, then walk over the crest of the hill and down into Anjuna South, or detour inland to reach the bridge.

Candolim and Sinquerim beaches

The wide unsheltered stretch of beach here, backed by scrub-covered dunes, offers unusual visual stimulus courtesy of the unlovely rusting wreck of the *Sea Princess* tanker, an eyesore and environmental nightmare (the currents eddying around its bows are playing havoc with coastal sand deposition) which has been resting offshore for years waiting for someone to muster the will to remove it. Nevertheless, the beach still attracts a fair crowd: more staid than Baga and Calangute to the north, chiefly because its restaurants and hotels are pricier and the average holidaymaker more senior. The road from Calangute to Fort Aguada is lined with shiny glass-fronted shops, while the sands at the foot of the Taj complex offers the full gamut of watersports – jet skis, windsurfers, catamaran and dinghies are all for hire – making it a favourite of India's fun- loving domestic tourists.

Fort Aguada

The Portuguese colonizer's strongest coastal fort was built on this northern tip of the Mandovi estuary in 1612 with one goal: to stay the Dutch navy. Two hundred guns were stationed here along with two magazines, four barracks, several residences for officers and two prisons. It was against the Marathas, though, rather than the Dutch, that Aguada saw repeated action – Goans fleeing the onslaught at Bardez took refuge here – and its ramparts proved time and again impregnable. The main fortifications (laterite walls nearly 5 m high and 1.3 m thick) are still intact, and the buildings at sea level now house Goa's Central Jail, whose 142 male and 25 female inmates are incarcerated in what must be one of the world's prettiest lock-ups.

Reis Magos, the Nerul River and Coco Beach

The position of **Reis Magos**, across the Mandovi River from Panjim, made it imperative for Albuquerque to station troops on this shoulder of headland from day one of Portuguese rule – today, come for the views to the capital, and for the crumbling **Royal Fort** whose angular 16th-century architecture is now overrun with jungle. Its canons served as the second line of defence against the Dutch after Aguada. The next door **church** is where the village gets its name – this was where the first Mass on Goan soil was celebrated in 1550, and the Hindu temple was promptly turned over into a church to the three Magi Kings – Gaspar, Melchior and Balthazar – whose

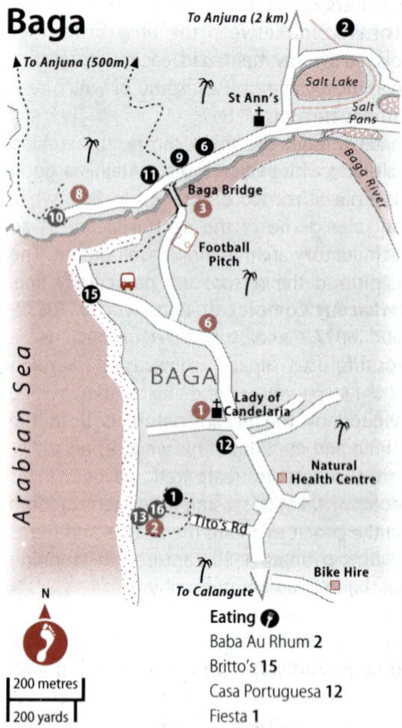

Sleeping
Alidia Beach Cottages **1**
Baga Queen Beach Resort **2**
Cavala **6**
Nani's & Rani's **8**
Riverside **3**

Eating
Baba Au Rhum **2**
Britto's **15**
Casa Portuguesa **12**
Fiesta **1**
J&A's Italiano House **6**
Le Poisson Rouge **11**
Lila's Café **9**

Bars & clubs
Mambo's **13**
Sunset **10**
Tito's **16**

The trance dance experience

The 'freaks' (beatniks with super-nomadic genes, giant drug habits and names like Eight Finger Eddie) first shipped into Goa shortly after the Portuguese left. Some brought guitars on which, after soaking up a bit of Hindu spirituality on the way, they were charged with playing devotional songs at beach campfire parties.

By the end of the 1960s, thousands of freaks were swarming into Goa, often spilling down from Kathmandu, and word got back to proper paid-up acid rock musicians about the scene. Some more substantial entertainment was called for.

The first music to run through the speakers was rock and reggae. Led Zeppelin, The Who and George Harrison rocked up and played live, but the freaks' entertainment was mostly recorded: Santana, Rolling Stones and Bob Marley. Kraftwerk and synth had filtered in by the late 1970s but the shift to electronica only really came in the early 1980s when musicians got bored of the lyrics and blanked out all the words on albums of industrial noise, rock and disco, using the fully lo-fi production method of taping between two cassette decks. Depeche Mode and New Order albums were stripped down for their drum and synth layers. Some of the rock faithful were angry with the change in the soundtrack to their lives; at those early 1980s parties, when the psychedelic-meets-machine-drum sound that still defines Goa trance was first being pumped out, legend has it that the decks had to be flanked by bouncers.

The music, developing in tandem to German nosebleed techno and UK acid house, locked into a worldwide tapestry of druggy drumscapes, but the Goan climate created its own sound. As records would warp in India's high temperatures, music had to be put down on DATS rather than vinyl which in turn meant tracks were played out in full, unmixed. A track had to be interesting enough then, self-contained, so it could be played uninterrupted in full; producers had to pay more attention to intros, middles and outros – in short, the music had to have a story. It also meant there was less art to a set by a trance DJ in Goa than DJs in Manchester, Detroit and Paris, who could splice records together to make their own new hybrid sounds.

Many of the original makers of this music had absorbed a fair whack of psychedelia and had added the inevitable layer of sadhu thinking to this – superficially measured in incense, *oms*, dreads and the swirling dayglo mandalas that unmistakeably mark out a Goa trance party. The music reflected this: sitars noodled alongside sequencer music to make the Goan signature sound.

By the 1990s, though, Ecstasy had arrived in Goa. The whole party scene opened right up, peopled by Spiral Tribe crusties as well as middle-class gap year lovelies and global party scenesters who came looking for an alternative to the more mainstream fare in Ibiza. Paul Oakenfold's Perfecto was a key label in fuelling the sound's popularity but there were more: Dragonfly, The Infinity Project, Return to the Source. Today the music comes from labels like Electrojump, Hux Flux, Errorhead, Color Drop, Wizzy Noise, Psycho+ Trolls, Droidsect, Parasense, Peace Data, In-R-Voice. Although much of it is from European or Japanese studios, there's the odd label that's more homegrown, like the resolutely Goan label Made In Chapora.

stories are told on the inside *reredos*. Fort Aguada and Fort Reis Magos are divided by the Nerul River: stop off at Nerul's **Coco Beach** for lunch and a swim. The temple in the village dates from 1910 and the Church of Our Lady of Remedies from 1569.

Mapusa → *For listings, see pages 1262-1280. Colour map 5a, A1.*

Standing in the nape of one of Goa's east-west ridges lies Bardez's administrative headquarters: a buzzy, unruly market town filled with 1960s low-rise buildings set on former marshland on the banks of the Mapusa River; 'Maha apsa' means 'great swamps', a reference to Mapusa's watery past. Mapusa town won't find its way onto many tourist postcards, but it's friendly, small and messy, is an important transport hub and has an excellent daily **municipal market**, worth journeying inland for, especially on its busiest day, Friday. Open from early morning Monday to Saturday, it peters out 1200-1500, then gathers steam again till night, and has giant rings of *chourica* sausage, tumbles of spices and rows of squatting fruit and vegetable hawkers.

Walk east for the small 16th-century **St Jerome's Church**, or 'Milagres', Our Lady of Miracles (1594), rebuilt first in 1674 then again in 1839 after a candle sparked a devastating fire. In 1961 the roof was badly damaged when the Portuguese blew up a nearby bridge in their struggle with the liberating Indian army. The church has a scrolled gable, balconied windows in the façade, a belfry at the rear and an interesting slatted wood ceiling. The main altar is to Our Lady, and on either side are St John and St Jerome: the *retables* (shelves behind the altar) were brought from Daugim. The church is sacred to Hindus as well as Catholics, not only because it stands near the site of the Shanteri Temple but also because 'Our Lady of Miracles' was one of seven Hindu sisters converted to Christianity. Her lotus pattern gold necklace (kept under lock and key) may also have been taken from a Hindu deity who preceded her.

The **Maruti Temple** ⓘ *west of the market opposite taxi stand*, was built on the site of a firecracker shop where Rama followers in the 1840s would gather in clandestine worship of first a picture, then a silver image, of monkey god Hanuman after the Portuguese destroyed the local Hindu temples.

Barely 5 km east of Mapusa lies **Moira**, deep in the belly of a rich agricultural district that was once the scene of Portuguese mass baptisms. The town is ancient – some say it was the site of a sixth or seventh century AD Mauryan settlement – and until the arrival of the Portuguese it must have been a Brahmin village. A total of seven important temples were destroyed during the Inquisition and six idols moved to Mulgaon in Bicholim district (immediately east).

Today the village is dominated by the unusual **Church of Our Lady of the Immaculate Conception**. Originally built of mud and thatch in 1619, it was rebuilt during the 19th century with square towers close to the false dome. The balustrades at the top of the first and second floors run the length of the building and the central doorways of the ground and first floors have Islamic-looking trefoil arches that contrast with the Romanesque flanking arches. There is an interesting exterior pulpit. Inside, the image of the crucifixion is unusual in having its feet nailed apart instead of together. A Siva *lingam* recycled here as the base of the font after its temple was razed is now in the Archaeological Museum at Old Goa. Moira's famous long red bananas (grown nearby) are not eaten raw but come cooked with sugar and coconuts as the cavity-speeding sweet *figada*.

Anjuna and around → *For listings, see pages 1262-1280. Colour map 5a, A1.*

When the freaks waded across the Baga River after the squares got hip to Calangute, Anjuna was where they washed up. The village still plays host to a large alternative community: some from that first generation of hippies, but the latest influx of spiritual Westerners has brought both an enterprising spirit and often young families, meaning there's fresh pasta, gnocci, marinated tofu or chocolate brownies to be had, cool homespun threads to buy, great, creative childcare, amazing tattoo artists, alternative therapists and world-class yoga teachers. For the beautiful life lived cheap Anjuna is still hard to beat; the countryside here is hilly and lush and jungly, the beaches good for swimming and seldom crowded. A state crackdown has made for a hiatus in the parties for which Anjuna was once synonymous, but as you head south along the shore the beach shack soundtracks get progressively more hardcore, until Curlies, where you'll still find arm-pumping techno and trance.

The **Flea Market** ⓘ *Dandovaddo, south Anjuna, Oct-Apr Wed 0800 till sunset, water taxis or shared taxis from anywhere in Goa*, is a brilliant hullabaloo with 2000 stalls hawking everything from Gujarati wooden printing blocks to Bhutanese silver and even Burberry- check pashminas. The trade is so lucrative by the subcontinent's standards that for six months a year several thousand Rajasthani, Gujaratis, Karnatakans and Tibetans decamp from their home states to tout their wares. The flea had very different origins, and was once an intra-community car boot-style bric-a-brac sale for the freaks. Anjuna's links with trade pre-date the hippies though – the port was an important Arab trading post in the 10th and 12th centuries.

Saturday Night Bazar ⓘ *Arpora Hill, 1630-2400*, is a more sanitized and less headlong version of the flea. There's no shortage of dazzling stall fronts draped with glittering saris and the beautiful Rajasthani fare, but while there are fewer stalls there's more variety here; expats who've crafted everything from baby maharaja outfits and designer mosquito nets to handmade leather goods are more likely to pitch up here than at the Wednesday event. But

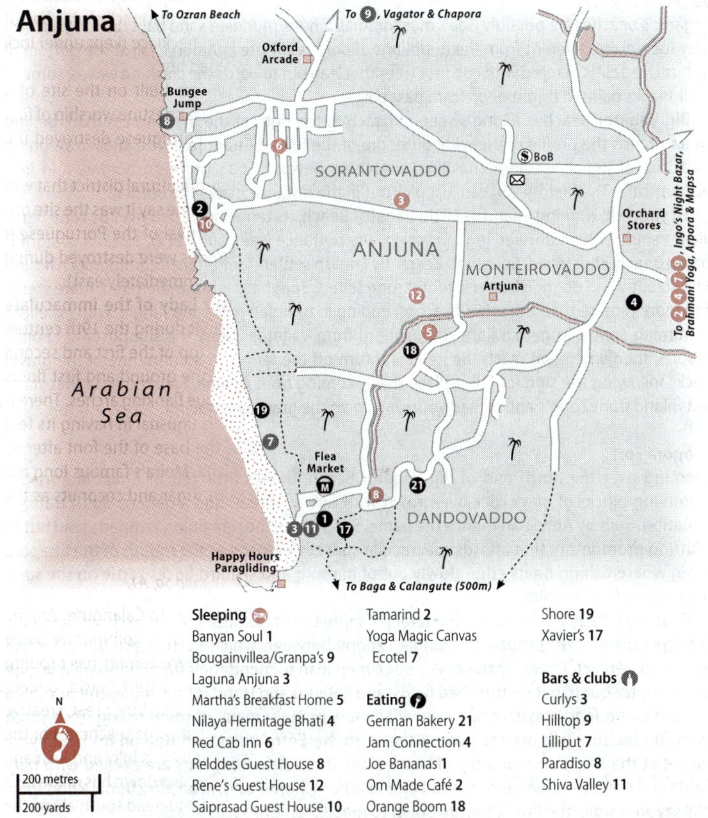

Sleeping
Banyan Soul **1**
Bougainvillea/Granpa's **9**
Laguna Anjuna **3**
Martha's Breakfast Home **5**
Nilaya Hermitage Bhati **4**
Red Cab Inn **6**
Relddes Guest House **8**
Rene's Guest House **12**
Saiprasad Guest House **10**
Tamarind **2**
Yoga Magic Canvas Ecotel **7**

Eating
German Bakery **21**
Jam Connection **4**
Joe Bananas **1**
Om Made Café **2**
Orange Boom **18**
Shore **19**
Xavier's **17**

Bars & clubs
Curlys **3**
Hilltop **9**
Lilliput **7**
Paradiso **8**
Shiva Valley **11**

there's no need to shop at all – the live music and huge range of food stalls make the Night Bazaar the weekly social event for tourist and long-stayer alike. You'll find most of North Goa out for the evening, and many businesses shut up shop for the night as a result of the bazar's magnetic appeal. Bring cash and an appetite.

The Anjuna area is also home to two of Goa's best contemporary yoga schools. **Brahmani** ⓘ *www.brahmaniyoga.com*, housed in two airy *shalas* in the gardens of **Hotel Bougainvillea**, runs workshops and drop-in classes, from excellent *ashtanga*, Mysore-style, to more experimental forms of yoga, like *Kundalini*, dance yoga, and *Scaravelli*. Packages with unlimited yoga are offered, but accommodation is not onsite or specifically for yoga students. Ten minutes away in the neighbouring village of **Assagao**, the **Purple Valley Yoga Retreat** ⓘ *T0832-226 8364, www.yogagoa.com, US$600 per room per week including yoga and meals (see box, page 1277)*, runs two-week *ashtanga* retreats with leading teachers like Sharath Rangaswamy, grandson of Sri K Pattabhi Jois, David Swenson and Nancy Gilgoff, two of the first to introduce *ashtanga* to the West in the 1970s. Lessons are held in a lovely *shala* in delightful gardens, food is vegetarian and the atmosphere collegiate.

Vagator

Vagator's beaches are possibly Goa's most dramatic: here, muddied sand bays upset by slabs of gray rock, quite different from the bubblings of porous laterite in Anjuna, fall at the bottom of terraced red cliffs planted with coconut trees that lean out towards the crashing waves, some of their trunks painted bright neon from past parties.

Big Vagator Beach is a long sweep of beach to the right of the main access road, behind which stands the profile of the wide outer rim of the ruined **Chapora Fort** against a stunning backdrop of India's western coastline, stretching beyond Goa's northern borders and into Maharashtra. The factory you can just pick out in the distance marks the border.

To your left, running inland, is **Little Vagator Beach**, its terracing lorded over by **Nine Bar**, a giant venue with an unswerving musical loyalty to trance (see page 1272). Just out of sight is **Ozran Beach**, christened 'Spaghetti Beach' by English settlers for its Italian community. Though a bit scrappy and dogged by persistent sarong sellers, **Spaghetti** is more sheltered, more scenic and more remote than the other beaches, ending in tumbled rocks and jungle, with excellent swimming spots. To get straight to Spaghetti from Vagator follow the signposts to Leoney Resorts, then when you reach the headland turn off the tarmac road onto one of the gravel tracks following the sign for Shiva Place shack; coming from Anjuna, take the path that starts just inland from Zoori's and thread your way down the gravelly terracing.

Chapora Fort

Looming over the north end of Big Vagator Beach, there's little left of Chapora Fort but crumbling blocks of black rock overgrown with tawny grasses and a general air of tranquil ruination. Built by Adil Shah (hence the name, Shah pura), the remaining ramparts lead out to a jutting promontory that affords spectacular sunset views across the mouth of the Chapora River, where fishing boats edge slowly out of harbour and seabird flocks settle on the sand spits across from Morjim.

Chapora village itself may be too feral for some tastes. At dusk the smoke from domestic fires spreads a haze through the jungle canopy between which Portuguese houses stand worn and derelict. Down by the river's edge men lean to mend their fuzzy nets while village boys saunter out to bat on threshed fields, and Enfields and Hondas hum along the potholed roads bearing long-stayers and Goan village folk home – many of them toting fresh catch from the buzzing fish market (ignore the stern 'No Entry' signs and ride on in) held every sunset at the harbour. Along the village's main street the shady bars are decked with fairy lights and the internationals (who call Chapora both 'home' and, in an affectionate nod to its less savoury side, 'the Bronx') settle down to nurse their drinks.

The flat arc of the estuary here is perfect for cycling: the rim-side road will take you all the way out to the bridge at **Siolim** where you can loop back to take a look at the **Church of St Anthony**. Built in 1606, it replaced an earlier Franciscan church dating from 1568. Both Goa's Hindu and Catholic communities pray to St Anthony, Portugal's patron saint, in the hope of good fishing catches. The high, flat-ceilinged church has a narrow balustraded gallery and Belgian glass chandeliers, with statues of Jesus and St Anthony in the gabled west end.

Splendid Portuguese houses stand scattered about the village's shadows in varying degrees of disrepair; it's worth walking around to take in some of the facades. You can even stay in one which has been refurbished, the lovely Siolim House, see page 1265. The ferry that once crossed the Chapora River at the northern end of the village no longer runs (there's a bridge instead) but it's worth heading up this way for the little daily fish market and the handful of food stalls selling fresh grilled catch. The village also has a basic bar, **Mandola**, on the coast road heading back towards Chapora, selling European snacks and cold beer.

Arambol, Keri, Morjim, Asvem, Mandrem → *For listings, see pages 1262-1280.*

Colour map 5a, A1.

The long bridge that spans the Chapora River joins Bardez to the last – and thus most heavily Hindu – of the new conquests, hilly Pernem *taluka*. This is the gateway to a series of pretty and quiet beaches that hug the coastal road in a nearly unbroken strip up to the Maharashtra border, where a tiny pocket of Catholicism squats in the shadow of the pretty pride of the district, Tiracol Church and Fort. Haphazard and hippy Arambol has a warm community feel and is rightly popular with open-minded travellers of all ages, who are drawn to its vibey scene, its live music, the dolphins that fin along its beaches and its famous saltwater lake. Sunset takes on the magnitude of a ritual in Arambol: people gather to sing, dance, juggle, do *capoeira* or find a silent spot for meditation and contemplation. To the south, Mandrem and Asvem are more chic and less busy, and will suit those less prepared to compromise on their accommodation. With construction of a new airport near Pernem and a large road bridge over the Tiracol to Maharashtra in the offing, Northern Goa will become more accessible, and there will be increased development no doubt.

Ins and outs

All of Pernem *taluka* is within easy reach of the hotels in Panjim or Calangute, but you'd be doing yourself a disservice to visit what are arguably North Goa's loveliest beaches just on a day trip. Better to set up camp in one and make it your base to explore the rest. If you are crossing the bridge at Siolim on a motorbike turn left off the new main road immediately after the bridge to use the smaller, more scenic coastal roads. There also regular buses to the villages from Mapusa and from Chopdem. Each beach is about 10 minutes apart.

History

The Bhonsles of Sawantwadi in modern Maharashtra were the last to rule Pernem before being ousted by the Portuguese in 1788, and Maratha influences here remain strong.

Arambol (Harmal) → *Colour map 5a, A1.*

Arambol, which you reach when the plateau road noses down through paddy fields and cashew trees, is a beautiful long stretch of sand at the bottom of a bumpy dirt track that's fringed with stalls selling brightly coloured, heavily embroidered clothes and pretty *lungis*. This is the creative and holistic hub of Goa – many Western designers, artists, performers, yogis and healers have been inspired to make the area home, and because people have put down roots here, the village is abuzz with industriousness. Flyers advertise *satsang* with smiling Western gurus: there's also *tabla* classes and drumming circles, yoga teacher training, reiki and belly dancing. Arrive at the right time of year and you might catch the **International Juggling**

Convention in full swing, or stumble across a phenomenal fire- dancing show by performers who work their magic on the stages of Vegas. Arambol is also synonymous with live music, with everything from Indian classical to open mike, Sufi musicians and psychedelic metal bands playing in rotation at the beach bars. Inevitably, though, Arambol's ever-growing popularity means both long and short-term accommodation get more expensive by the year.

You have to skirt the beach's northern cliff and tiny basalt rocky bays by foot to reach the real lure: a second bay cut off from the roads and a **natural 'sweet water' lake** that collects at the base of a jungle spring. The lagoon collects just metres from the high tide line where the lush forest crawls down to the water's edge. You can walk up the spring's path to reach a belt of natural mineral clay: an idyllic spot for self-service **mud baths**. Further into the jungle is the famous **banyan tree**, its branches straddling 50 m, which has long been a point of Hindu and hippy pilgrimage. Or clamber over the boulders at the north to join the scrappy dirt track over the headland for the half-hour walk it takes to reach the achingly lovely and reliably empty **Keri Beach**.

Keri (Querim) and Tiracol Fort → *Colour map 5a, A1.*

Goa's northernmost beach is uniquely untouched. The drive towards Keri (Querim) along the banks of the Tiracol River from Pernem passes through some stunning rural areas untouched by any tourist development.

Arambol Beach

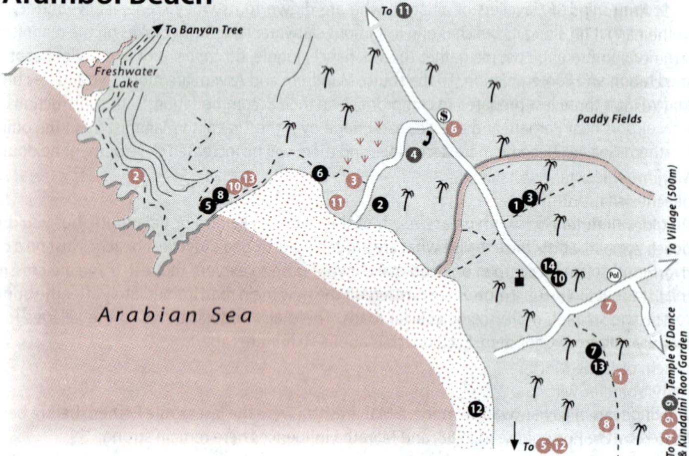

N

200 metres
200 yards

Sleeping
Arambol Plaza **7**
Atman **5**
Ave Maria **1**
Famafa Beach Resort **3**
God's Gift **4**
Ivon's Guesthouse **9**
Lamuella **6**
Oceanic **8**
Om Ganesh **2**
Residensea Beach Huts **10**
Sky Blue **13**
Welcome **11**
Whispering Lakes **12**

Eating
Bee's Knee's **10**
Coco Loco **12**
Double Dutch **1**
Dreamland **3**
Dylans **7**
Eyes of Buddha **5**
Fellini's **2**
Relax Inn **6**
Rice Bowl **8**
Rutik's Coconuts **13**
Sai Deep **14**

Bars & clubs
Arkan **9**
Loekie's Café **4**
Psybar **11**

Walk across deep dunes to a casuarina thicket and out onto empty sand that stretches all the way from the mouth of the Tiracol river to the highland that splits it from Arambol. There's just one solitary shack at either end of the beach, both of which can arrange rooms with villagers from Rs 100. **Querim** gets busy on weekends and is now host to the parties that have been forced on from Anjuna, but remains a lovely spot of sand. You can reach the beach from the north on foot from the Tiracol ferry terminal, or from the south by walking round the headland from Arambol. The Tiracol ferry runs every 30 minutes 0600-2130 taking 15 minutes, depending on the tides. If you arrive outside these times you can charter a fishing boat for Rs 55.

Tiracol (Terekhol), at the northernmost tip of Goa, is a tiny enclave of just 350 Catholics on the Maharashtra border just 3.5 km across where *feni* production is the biggest business. Its name probably comes from *tir-khol* ('steep river bank') and it's a jungly little patch of land full of cashew trees, banyans, orange blossoms, black-faced monkeys and squirrels.

The small but strategic **fort** ⓘ *0900-1800, cross Tiracol river by ferry (every 30 mins 0600-2130) and walk the remaining 2 km; ferries take cars and motorbikes*, stands above the village on the north side of the Tiracol River estuary on a rugged promontory with amazing views across the water. Its high battlement walls are clearly visible from the Arambol headland. Built by the Maharaja Khem Sawant Bhonsle in the 17th century, it is protected from attacks from the sea, while the walls on the land side rise from a dry moat. It was captured in 1746 by the Portuguese Viceroy Dom Pedro Miguel de Almeida (Marques de Alorna), who renamed it Holy Trinity and had a chapel built inside (now St Anthony's). You can explore the fort's battlements and tiny circular turrets that scarcely seem fit for slaying the enemy. The views south are magnificent. Steps lead down to a terrace on the south side while the north has an open plateau.

St Anthony's Church ⓘ *open on Wed and Sun for Mass at 1730*, inside the tiny fort, was built in the early 1750s soon after the Portuguese takeover. It has a classic Goan façade and is just large enough to cater for the small village. In the small courtyard, paved with laterite blocks, stands a modern statue of Christ. The **Festival of St Anthony** is held here at the beginning of May (usually on the second Tuesday) instead of on the conventional festival day of 13 June.

Morjim (Morji) to Asvem

Morjim, which stands on the opposite side of the estuary from Chapora, has two wide sweeping beaches that both sit at the bottom of separate dead end streets. This inaccessibility means that, development-wise, it has got away relatively unscathed. The southern, protected, turtle beach appears at the end of the narrow track that winds along the north bank of the Chapora rivermouth. Loungers, which are mostly empty, are strewn haphazardly north of the official-looking **Turtle Nesting Control Room**.

The wide shoreline with its gentle incline (the water is hip height for about 100 m) is washed by easy rolling breakers, making it one of North Goa's best swimming beaches. The northern beach, or **Little Morjim**, a left turn off the main coast road is, by comparison, an established tourist hamlet with guesthouses and beach huts. Plans for an upmarket hotel complex here with a private beach, which would deny local people free access to a section of the waterfront, have been dropped, so this fine stretch of beach should be safe.

The road from Morjim cuts inland over the low wooded hills running parallel to the coast. After a few kilometres the road drops down to the coast and runs along the edge of northeast tilting **Asvem Beach**. (Morjim faces Chapora to the south and west.) The northern end of this peaceful palm-fringed beach is divided by a small river.

Mandrem

Mandrem creek forces the road to feed inland where it passes through a small commercial centre with a few shops and a bank. Mandrem village has the **Shri Bhumika Temple** housing an ancient image. In the **Shri Purchevo Ravalnatha Temple** there is a particularly striking medieval image of the half-eagle, half-human Garuda, who acts as the *vahana* (carrier) of Vishnu.

A little further on, a lane off to the left leads down towards the main beach and a secluded hamlet in a beautifully shaded setting. The **beach** is one of the least developed along this stretch of coast; for the moment it is managing to tread that fine line between having enough facilities for comfort and enough isolation to guarantee idyllic peace. Further north there is a lagoon fringed by palm trees and some simple rooms, virtually all with sea view.

North Goa listings

For Sleeping and Eating price codes and other relevant information, see Essentials pages 38-42.

Sleeping

For more on places to stay in this area, see www.goatourism.org/accomodation/north.

Calangute *p1253, map p1253*

LL Pousada Tauma, Porba Vaddo Calangute T0832-227 9061, www.pousada-tauma.com. A shady little complex built of Goa's trademark laterite rock set around a beautiful pool. It's discreet but full of character, with old-fashioned but understated service. Suites are spacious, but come with shower not bath. Classy without a modern 5-star swagger.

AL-B Villa Goesa, Cobravaddo, off Baga Rd, T0832-227 7535, www.nivalink.com/vilagoesa. 57 clean rooms, some a/c, some very shaded, excellent restaurant, lovely gardens, pool, quiet, relaxing, very friendly owners, 300-m walk from the beach. Recommended.

A Kerkar Retreat, Gauravaddo, T0832-227 6017, www.subodhkerkar.com/retreat. Get inspired by staying above this beautiful art gallery (see page 1253). Subodh Kerkar is a visionary artist and has created a beautiful oasis in the midst of Calangute. Just 5 doubles with an overflowing library and naturally an array of stunning artwork. A guesthouse feel that's ideal for families since it also has a kitchen you can use. Somewhat sedate by Calangute's standards – but that's a compliment. Highly recommended.

A-D Golden Eye, Philip's Cottages, Gauravaddo, T0832-329 0549, www.hotelgoldeneye.com. 25 roomy suites and clean rooms, all with balcony, a/c or non a/c, half-price singles, right on the beach (built before restrictions) with genuine sea views.

C-E Coco Banana, 5/139A Umtavaddo, back from Calangute Beach, T/F0832-227 6478, www.cocobananagoa.com. In a nice neighbourhood in the backlanes of Calangute, this is one of the best local guesthouses and has 6 spotless en suite bungalows set in a leafy garden. All rooms come with nets and fridges, some have TV and a/c, and the place is airy, light and comfortable. The Swiss-German owners are caring and helpful. They also rent out 2 apartments in **Casa Leyla**, and have a whole house, **Soledad**, with all mod cons and maid service.

D Martin's Guest Rooms, Baga Rd, T0832-227 7306, martins@goatelecom.com. 5 rooms in family house, attractive verandas, use of kitchen but on the busy main road and could do with a lick of paint.

D-E Saahil, Khobra Vaddo, Baga Rd, T0832-227 6647. Lots of big, clean rooms within walking distance of all the action. Good value.

Baga *p1253, map p1254*

Of the family guesthouses on the northern side of Baga River up towards Arpora, those to the left of the bridge (west or seaward) are quieter. You might be able to get a room in houses/ cottages with good weekly or monthly rates. Standards vary so check room and security first. Try Wilson Fernandes at **Nani's & Rani's** or ask at **Four Seasons Restaurant** at Jack's Corner.

A-D Cavala, Sauntavaddo, top end of Baga village, T0832-227 6090, www.cavala.com. Sandwiched between Baga Rd and a big field stretching towards the mountains, **Cavala** is traditional but very well maintained, with friendly and attentive management, and set in lovely gardens. The 30 rooms are big, with giant fridges and huge bathrooms, although only shower. Some have TV. Recommended.

B-C Alidia Beach Cottages, behind the Church, Sauntavaddo, T0832-227 9014, alidia@ rediffmail.com. Weave around the pot-plant covered yards to reach this charming hotel in a series of 2-storey cottages, run professionally but with the warmth of a guesthouse. Rooms are spotless and old fashioned, with features including handmade fitted wardrobes, and offer lots of privacy around the well-tended garden. New pool. One of the best of its kind so book ahead.

C-D Riverside, Baga River by the bridge, T0832-227 7337, www.hotelriversidegoa.com. Nice location overlooking the river. Clean modern rooms with good balconies. Some cottages with kitchens available near the pool. Has a tour group feel about the place, but lovely location.

E-F Nani's & Rani's, T0832-227 7014, www.naniranigoa.com. 8 spartan rooms (shared or own bath), budget meals served in pleasant garden, bar, email, STD/ISD. One of the few local budget options with a sea view and a relaxing quiet location – attractive main building. Renowned healer Dr Patrick hosts sessions and workshops here on occasion. Short walk across Baga Bridge for nightlife.

E-G Baga Queen Beach Resort, T0832-227 6880. Close to beach, better value than others nearby, 15 good-sized, clean rooms with bath.

Candolim and Sinquerim beaches *p1254*

LL-AL Aashyana Lakhanpal, Escrivao Vaddo, Candolim, T0832-248 9225, www.aashyana lakhalpal.com. One of the most stunning places in Goa – beautiful gardens with great swathes of green lead right down to the beach. If you don't fancy the beach, there's a lovely pool. And the rooms and villas are beautifully decorated. This is a great place to hide away.

LL-AL Lemon Tree Amarante Beach Resort, Vadi, Candolim, T0832-398 8188, www.lemon treehotels.com. Try to get one of the 6 heritage rooms here, housed inside a grand century-old Portuguese mansion but restored now, as the rest of the hotel, in mock 15th-century Portuguese style. The complex has Wi-Fi, a kids' centre, pool, 2 restaurants, a spa and all mod cons.

LL-AL The Sol, road opposite Bank of India, Nerul (directly inland 2 km from Calangute/ Sinquerim), T0832-671 4141, www.thesol.in. Designed by fashion designer Tarun Tahiliani this is a nouveau heritage-style property where they strive to create an atmosphere that honours Goa as it once was. Tucked in lush foliage with views of Sinquerim river, the rooms are big, the beds are 4-postered, but it does seem a bit new and not quite as polished as it should.

L Fort Aguada Beach Resort, Sinquerim, T0832-664 5858, www.tajhotels.com. The self-confessed sprawling Taj complex spreads over 36 ha. In descending order of cost, these are 17 hilltop family villas that make up the Aguada Hermitage, 130 rooms with sea views at the Fort Aguada Beach Resort, built in the fort's ruins, and scores of cottages for up to 8 on the beach in the **Taj Holiday Village**. The complex has many 5-star facilities including 2 freshwater pools, 9 restaurants, Ayurvedic and other spa treatments, plus golf, tennis and a creche. The Thai restaurant on site is recommended.

A Marbella Tourist Home, left off the road to Taj Fort Aguada Beach Resort, T0832-247 9551, www.marbellagoa.com. Splendid mock-Portuguese period mansion with 6 lovingly decorated rooms. Its owners have scavenged bona fide antiques and furnishings like mosaic tiles from old villas to create this elegant and unpretentious homestay in a forest at the end of a dirt track. Lovely garden sit-out for meals. All rooms have a/c and cable TV.

G Ludovici Tourist Home, Dando, Sinquerim, T0832-237 9684. Pretty family home set back off the main road with 4 modest en suite doubles, all with fan. It very much feels that you are one of the family. There's a bar and restaurant and a lovely porch with chairs that gives onto a spacious garden. Sedate and modest guesthouse with traditional charm.

Mapusa and inland *p1256*

LL Panchavatti Corjuem, on the island of Corjuem, 9 km east of Mapusa, T(0)9822-580632, www.islaingoa.com. Just 4 elegant rooms in this stunning secluded house overlooking the Mapusa River, potentially by time of reading there will be more rooms available in neighbouring properties. Not much to do here except laze in bliss with Ayurvedic massages and facials, amazing food and mesmerizing views.

AL-A Presa di Goa, near Sublime, Arais Wado, Nagoa-Saligao, T0832-240 9067, www.presa digoa.com. Dubbed as a country house retreat, **Presa di Goa** is a beautifully decorated place with antique furniture, some with four-poster beds.There's a relaxed vibe and a lovely swimming pool. And even though it's not close to the sea and there's not much going on around there, it's perfect for getting away from it all and it's walking distance to one of Goa's best restaurants **Sublime**.

AL-A Wildernest, www.wildernestgoa.com. Amazing eco resort tucked into the border of Goa with Maharashtra and Karnataka – it's 1½ hrs from Mapusa. This eco hotel sprung up as a protest – the land was to be sold to a big mining company and in order to save it **Wildernest** was created. So this place is the real deal, they are concerned with the local wildlife and there is a research centre on-site and for guests there are birdwatching tours and waterfall treks. The luxe log cabins hug the valley with amazing views of the ghats and there is an infinity swimming pool hanging just above the horizon. Working closely with six local villages from all three states, they offer up delicious home-cooked food. This is a totally alternative view of Goa. Whole-heartedly recommended.

Anjuna and around *p1256, map p1257*

At the budget end, the best options in Anjuna, Vagator and Chapora tend to be unofficial, privately owned residences.

LL Nilaya Hermitage Bhati, T0832-227 6793, www.nilayahermitage.com. A luxury retreat in topaz on a hilltop in Arpora overlooking Anjuna. Elite accommodation in 10 unique bungalows and 4 tents in lush gardens set around a beautiful plunge pool. Tennis, badminton, gym, yoga, jogging trail, DVD library and excellent restaurant, highly prized music room, but some have found fault with the warmth of service and food.

AL-A Laguna Anjuna, Sorantovaddo, T(0)9822-162111, www.lagunaanjuna.com. Atmospheric cottages spiralling off behind stunning swimming pool and lush gardens, some with amazing domed ceilings and divan daybeds. Beautiful bathrooms and comfy beds. This is a vibey place serving up great food from the popular restaurant by the frangipani-fringed pool. The only drawback is the terracotta-tiled Goan roofs, they look pretty but you will hear your neighbours and it is a romantic place. You can come and use the lovely pool for Rs 150.

A-D Hotel Bougainvillea/Granpa's, Gaumwadi, T0832-227 3270, www.goacom.org/hotels/granpas. Popular but pricey for what you get – better value elsewhere. Lovely pool though More likely to attract yogis than the party crowd.

B Yogamagic Canvas Ecotel, 2 km from Anjuna beach, T0832-652 3796, www.yogamagic.net. A luxury campsite in a field of paddy and palms featuring 7 Rajasthani hunting tents, a naturally filtered pool, immaculate gardens of bougainvillea, lilies and lotus flowers, yoga and holistic therapies, delicious vegetarian South Indian food and environmentalism. There are also eco-lodges, teepees and the Maharani suite, a wing of the main house with its own veranda. Solar panels, compost loos, 5 mins' walk from Brahmani yoga centre (page 1258).

B-C The Banyan Soul, behind German Bakery, off Flea Market Road, T(0)9820-707283, sumityardi@thebanyansoul.com. Chic complex of rooms nestled under giant banyan tree. Funky modern rooms with beautiful artistic lighting and all mod cons, sexy showers, TVs and compact verandas. The only drawback is the rooms take up the whole site; there are smart gardens bordering the hotel, but it is a bit boxed in.

C The Tamarind, 3 km inland from Anjuna, behind St Michael's Church, Kumar Vaddo, Mapusa Rd, T0832-227 4319, www.the tamarind.com. Great value. 22 rooms with flagstone floors and balconies in stone-built Portuguese-style house set in landscaped gardens with pool, which some complain fails to catch sunlight. Courtesy bus service to beaches.

C-F Martha's Breakfast Home, House No 907, Monteiro Vaddo Anjuna, T0832-227 3365, mpd8650@hotmail.com. Set in the gardens of a house that give onto an orchard where pigs roam in the shade. 8 spic-and-span rooms, twin beds, small shower rooms (cold water) with nice little balconies. Better though are the 2 villas with 2 doubles, little lounges with telly, and kitchenettes with gas stove, sink and fridge. Ask for the Sunset Villa, which has incredible views. Basic but perfect.

D-E Saiprasad, north beach, T(0)9890-394839, saiprasadguesthouse@gmail.com. Uninspiring rooms some with a/c, but great location – right on the beach which is unusual for Anjuna. Pretty little gardens and beachside restaurant.

E Pebbles, Piqueno Peddem, Flea Market Rd, T(0)9923-649993, www.anjunapebbles.com. Well-located for market and beach – you could almost get away without getting your own transport which is a rarity for Anjuna. Basic rooms but great value, friendly owner. You might want to hide on Wed when the road will be busy outside.

E Rene's Guest House, Monterio Waddo, opposite Artjuna, T0832-227 3405, renesguesthousegoa@yahoo.co.in. A gem: 14 rooms around a colourful garden run by a friendly family. Best are the 3 self-contained cottages, with 4-poster beds, good kitchens with gas stove, sinks and big fridges; these are meant for long lets (2 are designed for couples, the other sleeps 3). Individual rooms are decent too.

Vagator *p1258*

A Casa Vagator, Cliffside, T0832-227 4931, www.casaboutiquehotels.com. Chic branch of these boutique hotels with modern rooms, some of the deluxe ones are a bit over the top with beds on plinths. Beautiful pool area. Also owns **Casa Colvale** a stunning property on the River Chapora 15 mins' drive from Mapusa, T(0)9373-081973, www.casacolvale.com.

A Living Room, T(0)966-545729, www.livingroomhotel.in. Brand new shiny hotel in stark contrast to the rest of the Vagator abodes. Definitely a sign of the changing face of Goa, chic rooms with all the mod cons, nice courtyard pool, Arabian themed restaurant.

B Leoney Resort, 10-min walk from beach, T0832-227 3634, www.leoneyresort.com. 13 rooms, 3 cottages, a/c extra Rs 400. Clean, modern, family run, low-key, quiet, pool.

B Ocean Bliss, Ozran Beach, T0832-645 4563, oceanbliss_24@hotmail.com. Selection of bamboo cottages hanging on the cliffside, bit pricey but all with TV/fridges and great views.

C-F Julie Jolly, **Jolly Jolly Lester**, **Jolly Jolly Roma**, T0832-227 3357, www.hoteljollygoa.com. With 3 different properties offering a whole range of a/c and non a/c rooms with hot showers, TV and a pool.

D Thalassa Huts, T(0)9850-033537. Tucked behind popular atmospheric restaurant, nice huts with attached bathrooms. Short walk down the cliff to the beach. Although staying here might affect your waistline.

E-F Garden Villa, Main Beach Rd, near **Abu John's**, T0832-652 9454. 8 clean rooms, some with bath, restaurant with a decent choice.

E-F Paradise Huts, Small Vagator, Ozran, T(0)9922-230041. Good selection of huts on the cliff, some with views, shared bathroom.

Chapora Fort *p1258*

Chapora Fort and Siolim caters mainly for long-term budget travellers.

A Siolim House, opposite Vaddy Chapel, Siolim, T0832-227 2138, www.siolimhouse.com. Lovingly restored 300-year-old house. This is a stunning property once owned by the governor of Macau. 4-poster beds, epic bathrooms and fantastic large windows. Restored in 1999, it recently had a further facelift in 2009 and the pool is one of the most beautiful places you could find yourself. Great food, chilled atmosphere. There is a sister property with just 3 rooms away in another beautifully crafted house – **Little Siolim**. And further up on the Arpora Hill there is a new development for rent aimed at yoga groups. Highly recommended.

F Noble Nest, opposite the Holy Cross Chapel, Chapora, T0832-227 4335. Basic but popular, 21 rooms, 2 with bath but ample facilities for sharing, exchange and internet.

Arambol *p1259, map p1260*

Arambol is low budget. Pack a sleepsheet and a lock (few rooms are secure but many have lockers).

D Atman, Palm Grove Girkar waddo, next to Surf Club, T(0)9881-311643, www.atmangoa.com. A lovely collection of palm-fringed coco huts with good use of sari drapes and chic decor, all surrounding a pretty restaurant. There is also a yoga space and it's all just steps from the beach.

D Whispering Lakes, Girkar Waddo, follow signs to Surf Club and Wooden Heritage, T(0)9272-462656, rajanbhai@gmail.com. Simple huts hugging lake, each with it's own cushioned sit-out hanging over the lake. A bit pricey for what you get and noise can carry from the Surf Club, but very pretty and unique location – catch special sunsets from your lakeside podium.

D-E Arambol Plaza, Beach Rd. Very different to the usual Arambol fare but lacking any design aesthetic, basic modern rooms with swimming pool.

D-E Lamuella, 292 Beach Rd, T0832-651 4563, lamuella@gmail.com. 1 floor of spotless and brilliantly maintained rooms sandwiched between the fantastic garden café and therapy treatment rooftop of **Lamuella**, Rooms are sweet and clean and have hot water. Great vibe here and good place to meet people.

D-E Om Ganesh, Cliffside on way to Sweet Lake, T0832-224 2957. Lots of rooms clustered on the cliffside – great views and lots of places to hang a hammock. Rooms are basic, but with attached bathroom. Ask at Om Ganesh restaurant on cliff or in town at Om Ganesh General Store. Now have rooms on high street above general store too. Recommended.

D-F Famafa Beach Resort, Beach Rd, Khalchawada, T0832-224 2516, famafa_in@yahoo.com. 25 rooms in an unimaginative development on the right of the stall-studded road down to the beach. No a/c, but many pitch up for the hot showers.

E Ave Maria, inland, down track opposite police post, Modhlowado, T0832-224 7674, avemaria@satyam.net.in. One of the originals, offering some of the best accommodation. Simple but nevertheless recommended. Very popular.

E Ivon's Guest House, Girkarwada, near **Kundalini Yoga Roof Garden**, www.goarambol.com. Popular rooms looking out on to the coconut grove, from the top floor you can just about see the sea. Basic clean rooms with attached bathrooms.

E Luciano Guest Rooms, Cliffside, T(0)9822-180215. Family house with toilet and shower. Cliffside rooms get heavily booked up.

E Oceanic, inland at south end, T0832-224 2296. Secluded guesthouse with simple rooms, all hidden behind wall in mature gardens, popular. Recommended.

E Residensea Beach Huts, north end of Arambol Beach, T0832-224 2413. Basic bamboo shacks set back from the beach in pretty location, all have fans and secure locker facilities (outside toilets). German Shepherd keeps watch.

F Sky Blue, north end of beach, near Eyes of Buddha. 4 small rooms in a cottage, shared veranda, great beach view, usually taken by long-term visitors.

F-G God's Gift, House No 411, Girkar Waddo, T0832-224 2391. Budget-friendly family guesthouse a little way from village, but a nice walk through palm grove, with hammocks hanging about its balconies. Western loos, balconies and kitchenettes. Still plenty of restaurants around and close to Kundalini Yoga Roof Garden and Temple of Dance.

Keri and Tiracol Fort *p1260*

Keri is pretty out of the way and it helps to have your own transport. The beaches around here are dotted with typical budget beach shacks.

L Fort Tiracol Heritage Hotel, Tiracol, T0236-622 7631, www.forttiracol.com. In 2003 the owners of **Nilaya** in Arpora, took over Fort Tiracol to create an outpost of isolated, personalized luxury with unbroken views of the Arabian Sea. Just 7 exquisite rooms, all with giant en suite, set in the fort walls that surround the Catholic Church which is still used by the 350 villagers of the wholly Christian Tiracol for their Mass. Goa's most romantic hotel. Prices include breakfast and delicious dinners. Highly recommended.

E-F Dream House, Keri, off main road on way to beach, T(0)9604-800553. Large rooms with attached bathroom sandwiched between family house and **Coconut Inn** rooftop restaurant.

E-F Raj Star, Keri, near New English High School, T(0)9881-654718, raj-star@hotmail.co.uk. Pretty rooms in attractive guest house. Nice communal sitting areas.

Morjim to Asvem *p1261*

This pretty stretch of coastline is dominated by hotels and restaurants catering to Russian package tourists, with a few notable exceptions.

AL-A Ku, Asvem Beach, www.kugoamorjim.webs.com. In stark contrast to its new naff neighbour in Aswem, **Marbella Beach Resort**, Ku is quite possibly one of the most beautiful places you can stay in India. Dubbed a 'zen hotel in mother india' there are stunning handbuilt Japanese style wooden bungalows with sliding doors and true rustic elegance. And sitting on the upper deck looking out at rice fields and palm trees or gazing down at the water feature that runs through Ku like an aorta, is pretty close to Nirvana. Problem is you just won't want to move out. Exceptional food too.

AL-A Sur La Mer, above Asvem Beach, T(0)985-005 6742, www.surlamergoa.com. Beautiful rooms with 4-poster beds and super-stylish bathrooms around lovely pool. All have good views of the neighbouring fields and the beach; with special mention going to the stunning penthouse with almost 360-degree views of paradise. The food is also highly-praised.

AL-A Yab Yum Eco Resort, Asvem Beach, T0832-651 0392, www.yabyumresorts.com. 10 deluxe 'eco-domes' made of local materials – blue painted lava rocks make up the bases, woven palm leaves and mango wood the roofs, spread across a huge shady expanse of coconut and banana grove tucked behind a row of trees from the sand dunes. The pods come in 2 sizes – family or single – but both have living areas, and en suite bathrooms. It's classy, discreet and bohemian. There's a reading room over the sea, a yoga *shala*, and a children's teepee crammed with toys. The price includes breakfast and papers. Also now new chic accommodation available at sister property in the hills, **Jivana Plantation**, which is absolutely stunning.

A-B Leela Cottages, Asvem Beach, T(0)982-340 0055, www.leelacottage.com. Close to the beach, these are posh wooden huts with antique doors from a palace in Andhra Pradesh and decorated with beautiful furniture. Very stylish but with relaxed vibe and on-site yoga too.

A-D Arabian Sea, Aswem Beach, past Aswem village, T0832-329 0703, www.meemsbeach resort.com. Range of accommodation, simple huts to pretty luxe wooden bungalows. Bit pricey but very popular.

B-C Aquatica, Asvem Beach, T(0)9096-620023, www.aquaticagoa.com. Cute cottages nestled at the bottom of the hill with beautiful restaurant and on-site pilates and yoga studio. Prices reflect the vibe of the area.

B-C Yoga Gypsys Asvem, close to Yab Yum, T(0)9326-130115, yogagypsys@yahoo.com. 5 terracotta bungalows, tree huts and tipis in a peaceful palm grove close to a Hindu temple the base for group yoga retreats but can also be rented independently. Teachers such as Katy Appleton and Scaravelli teachers Marc Woolford and Sophy Hoare have all flexed their toned bodies here. Check the website for coming attractions.

B-D Montego Bay Beach Village, Vithaldas Wado, Morjim, T(0)9822-150847, www.montegobaygoa.com. Rajasthani-style luxury tents pitched in the shade past beach shrubs at the southern end of the beach, plus log cabins, a/c rooms and a beach villa.

D-F Palm Grove, Asvem towards Morjim, T(0)9657-063046, www.palmgroveingoa.com. Quirky place with cottages and huts named 'Happy Hippie' and 'Rosie Slow' there are comfy beds and a sweet beach restaurant.

Mandrem *p1261*

LL Elsewhere's Beach House, T(0)9326-020701, www.aseascape.com. 3 lovely bedrooms in the understated luxury of a redecorated 19th-century house on a sandy spit with the sea on one side and a saltwater creek the other. Living room, dining room and kitchen are sea facing; facilities include maid service, day and nightwatchman, stereo, extra for cook. Minimum rental period 1 week at US$2000-4000. Also runs the **Priest's Houses**, 3 similarly carefully restored villas nearby.

L Elsewhere Otter Creek Tents. Under same ownership as above, 3 luxury Rajasthani tents each with 4-poster beds, en suite hot showers, private jetties and sit-outs.

AL-A Mandala, next to **Ashiyana**, access from Aswem–Mandrem road, T(0)9657-898350, www.themandalagoa.com. The highlights at Mandala are the chic 2-storey hut extravaganzas – downstairs you will find a swing seat, up the stairs a tented bedroom with 2 loungers on the front deck. There are murals by a Danish artist Ulrik Schiodt. There are also stylish rooms in the main house and smaller huts.

A-B Ashiyana, Mandrem River, opposite **Villa River Cat** by footbridge, www.ashiyana-yoga-goa.com. Spacious resort catering mainly to yoga fellows borrows from Bali and Morocco – dark wooden treehouses, beautiful rooms painted in aubergine, draping saris and magnificent handcrafted mosquito nets. The vibe is chilled and yogic, with a range of focused yoga retreats and holidays inviting people to dip in to yoga, dance and meditation. Beautiful restaurant on site and a chic café shack on the beach across the footbridge. Also a great spa with massages and treatments, and a pool on the way. Prices are per person and often rooms are shared.

C-D Villa River Cat, Junasvaddo, T0832-224 7928, www.villarivercat.com. 13 rooms in a 3-tiered roundhouse overlooking the river and a wade over deep sand dunes from the beach. The whole place is ringed with a belt of shared balconies and comes with big central courtyards stuffed with swings, sofas, plantation chairs and daybeds. There's a mosaic spiral staircase and a cavalier approach to colour: it's downbeat creative and popular with musicians and actors – in the best possible way. Cat lovers preferred.

D-E Dunes, Junasvaddo, T0832-224 7219, www.dunesgoa.com. **Dunes** is just set back off the beach with lots of nice-sized coconut huts and a few bungalows, most with attached bathroom. A peaceful place to stay with a good restaurant that has occasional live music.

D-E O'Saiba, Junasvaddo, T(0)9420-897906, sunnymehara@yahoo.com. **O'Saiba** offers a range of coco huts, bungalows and 2 small blocks of typical guest house rooms. Also has a good restaurant by the beach.

Eating

Even Calangute's most ardent detractors will brave a trip for its restaurants, some of which are world class. While costly by Indian standards a slap-up meal will cost you a fraction of its equivalent at European prices.

Calangute *p1253, map p1253*

TTT **A Reverie**, next to **Hotel Goan Heritage**, Holiday St, T0832-317 4927, areverie@rediff mail.com. After a recent facelift, this chic restaurant is a great place to splash out.

TTT **Bomras**, Candolim towards Sinquerim, T982-210 6236, bawmra@yahoo.com. Mouth-watering Burmese and Asian fusion food, such as seared rare tuna, mussel curry and Nobu-esque blackened miso cod. Fantastic vegetarian dishes and curries too. Washed down with quite possibly the best cocktail in the world spiced with lemongrass and ginger. Beautiful chic setting – amidst the bright lights of Candolim, you could almost blink and miss it.

TTT **Souza Lobo**, on the beach. Somewhat of an institution, this place serves up excellent fresh seafood, lobster (Rs 550) and sizzlers served on a shaded terrace, well-known restaurant that has managed to retain a good reputation for years.

TTT **Sublime**, H No 1/9-A, Grande Morod, Saligao, inland from Candolim, T(0)9822-484051. Worth driving inland, this is one of the best restaurants in Goa. Chris Saleem offers up fantastic fusion food using as much organic and locally sourced products as possible – ginger battered calamari with apricot chutney, fish in banana leaf, asian-style beef and delicious desserts. It's a beautiful restaurant tucked away – it would be a secret if it wasn't so deservedly popular and now he has his own TV show too. Booking essential.

TT **Oriental**, The Royal Thai Cuisine, **Hotel Mira**, Umtawaddo, T0832-329 2809, T(0)9822-121549. Impeccable Thai food in pretty courtyard in odd looking hotel. Home-made tofu daily, plus pasta, steaks, schnitzel, goulash, cakes and excellent espresso. Cookery courses Mon 1400-1700.

T **Café Ciocolatti**, main road Candolim, T(0)9326-112006. Fantastic range of all things chocolate. Lovely daytime café.

T **Infanteria**, Baga Rd, near beach roundabout. 'The breakfast place' to locals, Rs 125 set breakfast, eggs, coffee, juice, toast. Bakery and confectionery. Very atmospheric.

T **Plantain Leaf,** near petrol pump, Almita III. T0832-227 6861. Mean *dosas*, jumbo *thalis*, sizzlers and a range of curries; unbeatable for your pukka pure vegetarian Indian.

T **The Tibetan Kitchen**, at the bottom of a track leading off Calangute Beach Rd. 0900-1500, 1800-2230. This airy garden restaurant is part tent, part wicker awning, part open to the skies. Tibet's answer to ravioli – *momos* – are good here, but more adventurous starters like prawns, mushrooms and tomatoes seeping onto wilting lettuce leaves are exceptional.

Baga *p1253, map p1254*

TTT **Casa Portuguesa**, Baga Rd. An institution of a restaurant run by German/Goan couple with live music in the gloriously overgrown jungle of a garden. Strongly recommended.

TTT **Fiesta**, Tito's Lane, T0832-227 9894. Open for dinner Wed-Mon. One of Baga's destination eateries serving Mediterranean nosh in stylish surroundings, unusual Portuguese and Italian dishes , and great desserts. Even though it's a big restaurant, the tables seem spread out and hidden – there is even one table inside an old fishing boat. Good for romantic dinners.

TTT **J&A's Ristorante Italiano House**, 560 Baga River, T0832-228 2364, www.littleitalygoa. com. Open for dinner Oct-Apr. Jamshed and

Ayesha Madon's operation – along with their pizzas and pastas – has earned them an evangelical following.

TTT **Le Poisson Rouge**, next to Baga Bridge, Baga River, T0832-324 5800, www.lepoisson rouge-goa.com. Gregory Bazire is turning things French in Goa with this restaurant in Baga and Aquatica in Asvem. This is French fusion with a little Goa thrown in – fish, filet de boeuf and veggie options all served up in a myriad of sauces, correction 'emulsions' and who can refuse a sweet samosa and ice cream for dessert.

TT **Britto's Bar and Restaurant**, Baga Beach, T0832-227 7331. Cajie Britto's puddings are an institution and his staff (of 50) boast that in high season you'll be pushed to find an inch of table space from the restaurant's inside right out to the seashore. Great range of traditional Goan dishes like vindaloo and *cafreal*.

T **Baba au Rhum**, off the main road between Arpora and Baga. Serving up fantastic cappuccino, breads, croissants and salads in a laid-back vibe. Extraordinarily good desserts, coffee éclair or chocolate and passion fruit pie anyone?

T **Lila's Café**, north bank of Baga River, T0832-227 9843, lilacafe@sify.com. Closed evenings. Slick German-run restaurant, good selection of European dishes, check blackboard for specials, smoked kingfish. Home-made cheeses and jams, Also serves beers. Shaded terrace overlooking the river.

Mapusa *p1256*

T **Ashok**, opposite the market's entrance. Serves genuine South Indian breakfasts like *uttapam* and *dosa*.

T **Hotel Vilena**, near Municipality building. Has 2 restaurants, 1 on the rooftop and 1 a/c indoors, best food in town.

T **Mahalaxmi**, Anjuna Rd. A/c, South Indian vegetarian.

T **Navtara**, on Calangute Rd. Excellent range of Goan, South and North Indian fare – great dosas and yummy mushroom xacuti with puris for breakfast.

Anjuna and around *p1256, map p1257*

TTT **Xavier's**, Praias de San Miguel (follow signs from behind small chapel near flea market site, bring a torch at night), T0832-227 3402. One of the very first restaurants for foreigners has grown into a smart restaurant with 3 separate kitchens (Indian/Chinese/ continental), excellent fresh seafood, tucked away under palm trees.

TT **Blue Tao**, Anjuna main road. Good range of salads, pizzas, tofu dishes and juices (including wheatgrass), also has a kids' area and puts on belly dancing and live music evenings.

TT **Joe Bananas**, through the Flea Market behind Curlies, family-run place offering up amazing fish thalis – the fish is seasoned to perfection or there is a great array of bhaji like pumpkin.

TT **Shore Bar**, 400 m north of flea market. Lovely raised beach bar and restaurant offering a prime spot for sunset. It used to be party central here back in the day, now the focus is on the food and the view. Great menu with lots of traditional Indian and Goan food, as well as some of the best salads in Goa – paneer and toasted cashews on a bed of greens, or an amazingly generous prawn version. Extensive wine list and creative cocktails.

T **German Bakery**, south Anjuna, towards the Flea Market and Curlies. A little fiefdom of bohemian perfection: the bakery's sign is hung over a huge garden with an awning of thick tropical trees, where comfortable mattresses pad out the sides of low-slung booths. The atmosphere alone is habit- forming, but the food is the real thing too: huge salads with every healthy thing under the sun (including sprouts and avocado) plus good veggie burgers, Indian food and extreme juices. There is massage available on site and a small health food counter.

T **The Jam Connection**, just off Baga shortcut road, South Anjuna. Thu-Tue 1100-1900. A family favourite for lazy lunches, or skip straight to dessert – there are 21 types of home-made ice creams, chocolate fondue, eclairs and profiteroles, while mains are mostly Mediterranean and Middle Eastern like quiches, salads, gazpacho, humous and tahini plates. Proper coffee.

T **Om Made Café**, north beach Anjuna cliff, T(0)9823-850276. Another serving from the owner of Le Poisson Rouge, this chic little café has great coffee, tasty sandwiches, wraps and salads and great ice cream from amore. A welcome addition to the neighbourhood.

T **Orange Boom**, south Anjuna, Flea Market Rd. Daytime only. Efficient and spotlessly clean canteen. Food is hyper-hygienic and meticulously made, with a menu offering the usual breakfast fare plus 100 ways with eggs (like poached eggs and French toast), most served with mushrooms and grilled tomatoes. Baked beans can be masala or Heinz (proper ketchup on the tables), also croque madame and sautéed avocado on toast.

Vagator *p1258*

Several restaurants line the streets to the beach. Some serve good fresh fish including **Mahalaxmi**. **Primrose Café** serves tasty health foods and also hosts spontaneous parties.

TTT **Le Bluebird**, T0832-227 3695. A short and excellent menu matched by an amazing wine list (Chablis, Sauterne, Sancerre) and fine cheeses in the garden restaurant of a long-standing reputation run by Goan/French couple. Entrecôte and fillet are cooked in a variety of ways and sauces, and there's ratatouille and bouillabaisse, king and tiger prawns and lobster

TT **The Alcove**, on the cliff above Little Vagator. Smartish, ideal position, excellent food, pleasant ambience in the evening, sometimes live music.

TT **Bean Me Up**, near the petrol pump, Vagator, T0832-227 3479. Closed all day Sat and daily 1600-1900. You can choose from salad plates and delicious tempeh and tofu platters. There's massage offered onsite, a useful noticeboard for mind-body-spirit stuff, kids' area and a few simple, clean rooms for rent. Under new management, so maybe in for a revamp.

TT **Mango Tree**, in the village. Wide choice of continental favourites.

TT **Thalassa**, on the clifftop overlooking Ozran Beach, T(0)9850-033537. Beautiful restaurant perched on the cliff, amazing sunset views and great Greek food from dolmades and souvlaki to salads and moussaka. Booking essential. Great boutique on-site too.

T **Fusion**, on the clifftop above Ozran Beach. A sprawling tent strewn with cushions and low tables, offering beautiful sunset views through silhouettes of coconuts. Try spit-roasted chicken, humous, baba ghanoush, vegetable quiche, roast tatties or one of the dozens of salads (including beetroot, Caprese and carrot). More substantial stuff is mostly Italian: spaghetti, lasagne, meatballs, a great pizza list and for pudding, pannacotta, tiramisu and profiteroles. Lemonade recommended.

Chapora Fort *p1258*

TT **Da Felice & Zeon**, above Babba's. Open 1800-2400. Just a handful of tables dancing with fairy lights and psychedelic art at this rooftop restaurant run by the Italian brothers Felice and Zeon. Felice is an Italian chef in London over monsoon, Zeon makes trance music and trance art. Carbonara, lasagna, prosciutto, spaghetti alla vongole all feature, but meat is recommended.

TT **La Befa**, Chapora Market road. Some people drive an hour for the roast beef sandwich here. Or there's parma ham or marinated aubergine – all on freshly baked French bread.

T **Jai Ganesh Juice Bar** the hub of Chapora. This is the only place to be seen in Chapora for every juice under the sun.

Arambol *p1259, map p1260*

There are beach cafés all along the main beach and around the headland to the north. The 2 German bakeries fall short of the lovely restaurant in Anjuna.

TT **Double Dutch**, Beach Rd, T0832-652 5973, doubledutchgoa@yahoo.co.uk. 0700-2300. Lovely laid-back garden restaurant with sand underfoot and lots of leafy foliage and sculptures created by the owner around. Breakfasts are tip top here with home-made breads like carrot or watermelon seed and also home-made jams – you can also get a full 'English' Goa style. Candle-lit in the evening, there are lots of great salads as well as Dutch dishes, Indonesian, Thai, pastas and the steaks come with the best recommendation. There is a Sun morning second-hand market and a bit of live music too. Recommended.

TT **Fellini's**, Beach Rd, T0832-229 2278, arambolfellini95@yahoo.com. Thu-Tue 1000-2300, Wed 1800-2300. Fellini's is an institution serving up pizzas and calzone to the hungry masses.

TT **Lamuella**, Main Rd, T0832-651 4563. Atmospheric restaurant in the heart of Arambol under the watchful eye of chef Gome. Home-made mushroom or pak choi raviolis, great fish, tagines, salads and huge breakfast platters. This is a great spot to meet and greet. There's also a great shop specializing in clothes crafted by Westerners in Arambol. If you can't face the night market, see what Westerners get up to creatively here. Recommended.

Ŧ **Bee's Knees**, Main Rd, nearish to Double Dutch. Great value with range of Mexican dishes, Indian and salads. Deservedly popular.

Ŧ **Dreamland Crepes**, main road, near **Double Dutch**. Blink-and-you-miss-it 2-tier coffee house serving up fabulous cappuccinos and healthy juices, as well as a wide range of crêpes and sandwiches. And Wi-Fi.

Ŧ **Dylans**, coconut grove near **Rutik's Coconuts** and behind **Coco Loco**. Coffee houses have sprung up in Arambol to fuel the creative types and designers that make Arambol their home. If you like your coffee strong, this Manali institution delivers, along with hot melty chocolate cookies and soups and sandwiches. Film nights and occasional live music.

Ŧ **Eyes Of Buddha**, north end of Arambol Beach. Long on Arambol's catering scene, this place has you well looked after with scrupulously clean avocado salads, a great range of fish and the best Indian food in town, all topped off with a great view of the beach. Highly recommended.

Ŧ **Relax Inn**, north end of beach. The only beach shack with a good reputation, this is a firm favourite with the expats. Slow service but worth the wait for Spaghetti a la vongole, grilled kingfish with ratatouille and a range of fresh pasta dishes.

Ŧ **Rice Bowl**, next door to **Eyes of Buddha**. Great views south across Arambol Beach, with a billiard table. Simple restaurant that has been serving reliably good Chinese for years. All the usual chop suey, wontons, noodles and sweet and sours of calamari, pork, beef or fish, plus Japanese dishes like *gyoza*, *sukiyaki*, tempura and Tibetan *momos*.

Ŧ **Rutik's Coconuts**, entrance to beach behind **Coco Loco**. Serving up thalis all day, this place is best visited for coconuts. It's a great place to hang-out, see and be seen.

Ŧ **Sai Deep**, Beach Rd. A family-run *dhaba* offering amazing veg and fish plates at lunchtime, mountainous fruit plates and a good range of Indian and continental food.

Morjim to Asvem *p1261*

Join the masses as they descend on La Plage every Sun. Restaurants in Morjim central cater mainly to Russians.

There are plenty of shacks catering to Asvem and Mandrem beaches. Some have free loungers, others charge up to Rs 100.

ŦŦŦ **Ku**, Asvem, T(0)9326123570, www.kugoamorjim.webs.com. Serving up fresh food that she fancies cooking each day, Maria runs a chic little ship here with tastes from the Mediterranean and from Asia. This is a special place – shhh don't tell everyone!

ŦŦŦ **La Plage**, Asvem, T(0)9822-121712. Hidden slightly from the beach, you can still feel the breeze in this lovely laidback restaurant. The food is excellent and ambitious; tapas include beef carpaccio, chicken liver and fish ceviche, there's fish soup with aioli and *ile flottante* or everyone's favourite chocolat fondant for pudding. There are specials every day, as well as renowned rare tuna and wasabi mash and a giant hamburger. Vegetarians well catered for too, try the sage butter ravioli and the breakfasts are legendary. Nice wines, fabulous peppery Bloody Marys with mustard seeds and curry leaf. Also has rooms and an excellent shop featuring jewellery from expat designer Simona Bassi.

Ŧ **Arabian Sea**, Asvem Beach. Tasty *thalis*, both Indian and Mediterranean and range of salads, fish and tofu dishes. Also has a good range of rooms and huts.

Ŧ **Change Your Mind**, Asvem Beach. This typical beach shack serves up great Indian food, tasty fried calamari and monumental fruit plates. This is where the expats come to enjoy their day off.

Ŧ **Pink Orange**, Asvem Beach. Low-level seating overlooking the beach with chilled out trance vibe. Menu serves up a great range of salads, sweet and savoury crêpes, juices, coffees and great choc brownies. Recommended.

Mandrem *p1261*

ŦŦ **Café Nu**, Junnaswaddo, Mandrem Beach. T(0)9850-658568. Another helping from Sublime guru Chris Saleem Agha Bee – great food in laidback locale. Mustard encrusted fish, Asian beef and the mega salad is monumental. Good food to linger over. Highly recommended.

Ŧ **Dunes**, Mandrem Beach. Great restaurant with the typical extensive and eclectic menu, but all done well. Very good Indian and fish dishes. Regular high-quality live music, great sound system.

Ŧ **Oasis**, south end Mandrem Beach. Perched above Mandrem Beach, with good Indian food, pizzas and sunset views.

🍴 **Well Garden Pizzeria**, near O'Saiba, off main road. Sweet garden restaurant with great range of pizzas, broccoli and pesto pastas and an almost infamous warm chickoo cake. Service can be a bit hit or miss though.

Bars and clubs

Calangute *p1253, map p1253*

Saligao

Club WestEnd, near Porvorim, 3 km out of Calangute towards Panjim. Miles out of the way, this club gets away with hosting 3-day parties by being too remote to disturb anyone.

Baga *p1253, map p1254*

Locals know which way their bread is buttered, and in this neighbourhood, it's beer up. Many bars here have a happy hour from 1700 to 1930 and show live Premier League football, in a bit of a home-from-home for many visitors. Along the beach, shacks also serve a wide range of drinks and cocktails to sip while watching the sunset.
Cavala, Sauntavaddo, top end of Baga village. A genuine bar, with friendly atmosphere, attentive staff, great cocktails, and occasional live music evenings.
Sunset, north of Baga River. A great place to watch the goings-on of Baga Beach as dusk falls. Prime location but less hectic as it's north of the river bridge.
Tito's, Tito's Lane, T0832-227 5028, www.titosgoa.com. Tito's is an institution in Goa, and has adapted down the decades to reflect the state's changing tourist reality by going from a down-at-heel hippie playground in the 1960s to a swish international dance club and now the focus seems to be more on food – are the dancing days of Goa really over? Further along Tito's Lane towards the beach is the Tito's spin-off, **Mambo's**. It's more laid back than the club and free to get in.

Anjuna *p1256, map p1257*

The days of all-night parties in North Goa are long gone, and politicians imposed a ban on loud music after 2200 for several seasons – they keep changing the rules so sometimes you might be lucky and find yourself dancing until dawn . Indoor venues like **Liquid Sky** in Aswem and **West End** in Saligao stay open later. Wed and Fri tend to be the big nights especially at places like Curlies, but there is usually something going on each night over the Christmas and New Year period; just ask around (taxi drivers invariably know where). Venues are often recognizable by illuminated trees and luminous wall hangings.
Curlies, at the very far south of Anjuna. A kind of unofficial headquarters of the scene, playing techno and ambient music, although **Shiva Valley** next door has taken over in recent years.
Lilliput, a few hundred metres north of **Curlies**, www.cafelilliput.com. Lots of live music and fire-dancing performances at this beach shack – usually after the flea market on Wed and sometimes on Fri. Also has an a/c internet booth.
Paradiso, on clifftop next to **Zoori's**. Looking like a wild Fred Flintstone flight of fancy, Paradiso advertises itself as a performance art space, but it's dyed-in-the-wool techno.

Vagator *p1258*

Hilltop, Little Vagator Hill, above Vagator. Although it has suffered from the 2200 curfew, Hilltop has been inventive with day parties Sun 1600-2200 and Funky Friday markets with DJs and live music.
Nine Bar, Ozran Beach. A booming mud-packed bar with huge gargoyle adornments and a manic neon man carved out of the fountain. Majestic sunset views.

Arambol *p1259, map p1260*

Live music and performances are the highlight of being in Arambol. **Ash**, **Surf Club**, **Coco Loco** and **Psybar** offer up both live music and DJ nights. **Arkan Bar** and **Loekie's** have open mic nights. Special mention goes to **Ash**, a stunning performance space with beautiful artwork hosting nights as diverse as mesmerizing bellydancing performances, Siberian shamanic singing or fantastic fire dancing. At dusk there's normally drumming, dancing and high spirits outside **Full Moon** on the beach to celebrate the sun going down on another day.

Morjim to Asvem *p1261*

With pricey drinks and sometimes entry fees, the venues in Morjim and Aswem are mostly Russian affairs, but **Shanti** is a fun and welcoming place. Check www.sashanti.com for listings – it has a chic seafront locale and great music know-how as they also run a renowned club in Moscow and the fun boutique house bar at the Saturday Night Market. Guest DJs from Russia and Europe feature highly on the playlist, but great coups have been Talvin Singh and DJ Cheb i Sabbah, as well as great resident DJs like Phabi-D and her all-woman show Fatale Beats. Special mention also goes to **Liquid Sky** the brainchild of DJ Axailles, high on the hill above Asvem beach and with an inside dancefloor for post 2200 high jinx, this has been extremely popular since opening in 2009. Serving up minimal techno and the occasional trance beat.

Mandrem *p1261*

The Prawn Factory, North Beach, Junas Waddo. Literally an old prawn factory set in the palm grove, it has been turned into a dance venue with varying success. One season it's on, the next it's off, but keep your eyes peeled for flyers.

Entertainment

Calangute *p1253, map p1253*

Heritage Kathakali Theatre, **Hotel Sunflower**, opposite the football ground, Calangute Beach Rd, T0832-258 8059. Daily in season, 1800-2000. The breathtakingly elaborate mimes of 17th-century Keralan mime dance drama take over 12 hrs to perform in the southern state. Here, however, it comes abbreviated for tourist attention spans: watch the players apply their make-up, brief background of the dance, then a snatch of a classic dance-drama.

Kerkar Art Complex, Holiday St, Calangute. Chic restaurant hosts traditional Indian dance and classical music, Tue 1830. Under new management, there is a combined dinner/music price.

Festivals and events

Calangute *p1253, map p1253*

Mar Carnival is best celebrated in villages or in the main district towns but Calangute has brought the party to the tourists.

May (2nd week) **The Youth Fête** attracts Goa's leading musicians and dancers.

Mapusa *p1256*

Mon of the 3rd week after Easter Feast of Our Lady of Miracles The *Nossa Senhora de Milagres* image is venerated by Christians as well as Hindus who join together to celebrate the feast day of the Saibin. Holy oil is carried from the church to Shanteri temple and a huge fair and a market are held.

Mandrem *p1261*

Jan International Juggling Convention Gala performances, juggling workshops, firedancing, creative movement of a phenomenally high standard. Hosted in 2011 at **Galaxy** in Asvem, this is an event not to be missed – check out www.injuco.org.

Shopping

Do your homework before you buy: prices in tourist shops are massively inflated, and goods are often worth less than a 3rd of the asking price. 92.5 silver should be sold by weight; check the current value online, but be ready to pay a little more for elaborate workmanship. The bigger Kashmiri shops, particularly, are notorious both for refusing to sell by weight, instead quoting by the 'piece', and for their commission tactic whereby rickshaw and taxi drivers get Rs 100 per tourist delivered to shops plus 10% commission on anything sold. However, if you are buying jewellery be aware that prices for silver and gold have skyrocketed over the last couple of years, so maybe the shopkeeper isn't trying to take you for a ride! Gold prices have doubled in 3 years, while silver went up 40% in just 3 months early 2011.

Calangute *p1253, map p1253*

Mini markets like **Menezes** on Calangute Beach Rd or **Lawande** on Fort Aguada Rd for staples, plus adaptor plugs, water heating filaments, quince jam, wine, cashew *feni* in plastic bottles to take home, full range of sun lotion factors and brands, tampons, etc and money change.

For silver, head for either of the Tibetan covered handicraft markets where the Tibetan community in exile gently sell silver, which you can buy by weight.

Casa Goa, Cobravado, Baga Rd, T0832-228 1048, cezarpinto@hotmail.com. Cezar Pinto's shop is quite a razzy lifestyle store: beautifully restored reclining plantation chairs next to plates brought over by the Portuguese from Macau plus modern-day dress from local fashion designer Wendell Rodricks. Cool modern twists on old Goan shoes by local Edwin Pinto too.

PlayClan, Shop No S-3, Ida Maria Resort, next to HDFC bank, Calangute, T(0)9372280862, www.theplayclan.com. Fantastic shop selling all manner of clothes, notebooks, lighters and pictures with great colourful cartoon designs created by a collective of animators and designers – giving a more animated view of India's gods, goddesses, gurus and the faces of India.

Candolim and Sinquerim beaches *p1254*

Acron Arcade, 283 Fort Aguada Rd, Candolim, T0832-564 3671, www.acron arcade.com. A posh mini-mall with well-stocked bookstore (yoga, Ayurveda, Indian cookery, Indian flora and fauna, guidebooks, plus fiction and business books) and swish Indian lifestyle products (modestly ethnic cushions and throws and bedspreads, good stainless steel items) and fancy clothes.

Fabindia, Sea Shell Arcade, opposite Canara Bank, Candolim. Branch of this great shop selling textiles, homewares and funky traditional Indian *kurtas* and clothes.

Literati, off main road, Calangute, parallel to Holiday Street, T0832-227 7740, www.literati-goa.com. Wonderful bookshop in beautiful old house – it's like stumbling into someone's library. The best selection of books, novels, non-fiction and poetry you'll find in Goa. There are sometimes readings here, including an inaugural reading by William Dalrymple.

Rust, 409A Fort, Aguada Rd, Candolim, T0832-247 9340. Everything from wrought-iron furniture to clothes.

Sangolda, Chogm Rd, opposite Mac de Deus Chapel, Sangolda, T0832-240 9309, sangolda@sancharnet.in. Mon-Sat 1000-1930. Lifestyle gallery and café run by the owners of **Nilaya Hermitage** selling handcrafted metalware, glass, ethnic furniture, bed and table linen, lacquerware, wooden objects.

Mapusa *p1256*

Municipal Mapusa Bazaar, on south edge of the fruit and veg market. Fixed-price basic food supplies like rice, spice, lentils and cereals: useful if you're here long term.

Other India Bookstore, 1st floor, St Britto's Apartment, above Mapusa clinic, T0832-226 3306. Unconventional and excellent. Heavily eco conscious. Has a large catalogue and will post worldwide.

Union Ayurveda, 1st floor, opposite the taxi and bus stand. Great one-stop shop for all things Ayurvedic, herbal and homeopathic – phenomenal range of products to keep you travelling healthy.

Anjuna *p1256, map p1257*

Artjuna, House no 972, Monteiro Vaddo, T0832-321 8468, www.artjuna.com. Beautiful collection of mainly jewellery and clothes, but with a few nice bits of home décor too. Stunning collection of gold jewellery, but also cheaper tribal trinkets from Nagaland. Owners Moshe and Anastasia showcase quite a few local designers here as well as offering up their own wares. There's also art on sale and a great art fair every Feb. Recommended.

Flea Market, Wed, attracts hordes of tourists from all over Goa. By mid-morning all approach roads are blocked with taxis, so arrive early.

Natural Health Food Store, Monteirovaddo.

Orchard Stores, Monteirovaddo. Amazing selection catering for Western cravings. Olive oil, pasta, fresh cheese, frozen meats, etc. Locally made soaps and organic supplements.

Oxford Arcade, De Mellovaddo, next to **Munche's**. Good general store close to beach.

Oxford Stores, Monteirovaddo. For groceries, foreign exchange and photo processing.

Chapora Fort *p1258*

Narayan, Chapora. Book stall, local newspapers.

Arambol *p1259, map p1260*

Arambol Hammocks, north end of Arambol Beach, near **Eyes of Buddha**, www.arambol.com. The original and the best place for hammocks and their flying chair designs and now even baby hammocks.

Lamuella. Serving up the best of the Western designers who make Arambol their home, as well as imported clothes and bikinis from Thailand and Europe. Stunning jewellery for little magpies too.

Morjim to Asvem *p1261*

As well as having a great little boutique on-site with lovely clothes and jewellery from Simona Bassi, La Plage has competition on its hands from a cluster of neighbouring chic beach shack boutiques including one little black number from Jade Jagger. The local ex-pats are laying bets on whether it will be there again next season. But special mention goes to **Dust** which sells beautifully designed clothes in raw silk and hand-block prints from JonnyJade and also a handful of one-off pieces crafted by local Westerners – www.jonnyjade.com.

Activities and tours

Calangute *p1253, map p1253*

Body and soul

Holystamina Yoga Ashram, Naikavaddo, T0832-249 7400, www.cyrilyoga.com. 4 classes daily, 0830, 1000, 1530 and 1630, Rs 300 a class. All abilities. Inner healing yoga meditation, juice bar, yoga camps and good karma-promoting volunteer activities.

River cruises

Floating Palace, book through **Kennedy's Adventure Tours and Travels**, T0832-227 6493, T(0)9823-276520, kennedy@goatelecom.com, opposite **Milky Way** in Khobravaddo. Try a Kerala-style backwater cruise by staying overnight in this 4-cabin bamboo, straw and coir houseboat. You sail from Mandovi in late afternoon, are fed a high tea then a continental dinner as you drift past the Chorao Island bird sanctuary. International standards of safety. Much pricier than a similar boat trip in Kerala.

Tour operators

Day Tripper, Gauravaddo, T0832-227 6726, www.daytrippergoa.com. Offers tours all over Goa, best deals in the region. Also runs trips to spice plantations, or short tours out of state, for birdwatching or empty beaches in Karnataka. Recommended.

Baga *p1253, map p1254*

Boat trips and wildlife

Mikes Marine, **Fortune Travels**, Sauntavaddo, by the bus stand at the top end of Baga, T0832-227 9782. Covered boat, dolphin trips, river cruises and birdwatching.

Rahul Alvares, all over Goa, based in Parra, T(0)9881961071, www.rahulalvares.com. Fancy getting eye-to-eye with a cobra? For an alternative day-out in Goa, maybe you want to handle or at least see a wild snake. For the less wild at heart or snake-aphobic, there are also amazing bird watching trips and jungle camping expeditions. You will be in expert hands with Rahul. He organizes trips all over Goa.

Body and soul

Ayurvedic Natural Health Centre (ANHC), Baga-Calangute Rd, Villa 2, Beira Mar Complex, www.healthandayurveda.com; also in Saligao. The **ANHC** is not for the faint-hearted; the centre was originally built for the local community that it continues to serve and hasn't made many concessions to Western sensibilities. Those checking into the 2-week *panchakarma* can expect almost every cavity to be flushed. They do offer smaller, less daunting packages, like 2½-hr rejuvenations (Rs 300), and have a herb garden where you can taste first-hand leaves that tingle your tongue (used to stop stuttering) or others that eliminate your sense of sweet taste.

Ayurclinic Goa, Baga Creek, T(0)9637473366, www.ayurvedagoa.com. Under the watchful eye of fantastic Dr Rohit Borkar, you can get a whole host of treatments, massages and panchakarma processes here. Has another branch in Mandrem.

Diving and snorkelling

Goa Dive Center, Tito's Lane, T0832-215 7094. Goa isn't really on the diving map, chiefly because it has only 2 dive sites, both of which have what's known as variable, ie less than great, visibility. However, this outfit offers inexpensive PADI courses. Options range from the half-day Discover Scuba programme (from aged 10 years, Rs 2700) to the 4-day Open Water Diver programme, Rs 14,500. Snorkelling tours also available.

Candolim and Sinquerim beaches *p1254*

Body and soul

Amrita Kerala Ayurvedic, next to Lawande supermarket, Annavaddo, T0832-312 5668, 0730-2000. Set inside an old Goan villa, this massage centre is geared up for the foreign tourist. Westerners are on hand to explain the philosophy behind Indian life science. The centre also teaches. A basic course takes 7 days. Courses in *panchakarma* last 6 months (Rs 7500). Rs 750 for 75-min massage.

Dolphin watching

John's Boats, T0832-227 7780. Promises 'guaranteed' dolphin watching, morning trips start around 0900, Rs 550 (includes meal and hotel pickup). Also crocodile-spotting river trips with lunch.

Parasailing

Occasionally offered independently on Candolim Beach, Rs 600-850 for a 5-min flight.

Fort Aguada *p1254*

Taj Sports Complex, **Fort Aguada Beach Resort**. Excellent facilities that are open to non-residents at the **Taj Holiday Village**, and a separate access between Aguada Beach Resort and the Holiday Village. Rs 450 per day for the complex, Rs 350 for the pool. Tennis (Rs 450 per hr); squash and badminton (Rs 150 for 30 mins); mini golf (Rs 200). Yoga classes, scuba diving, sailing/ water skiing/windsurfing/ rod fishing Rs 450-500 per hr; parasailing/jet ski Rs 900-950 per hr.

Anjuna *p1256, map p1257*

Body and soul

Some excellent yoga teachers teach in Goa during the season, many of whom gravitate towards Anjuna: check the noticeboards at the **German Bakery**, **The Jam Connection** and **Bean Me Up** (see page 1270). You'll also stumble on practitioners of all sorts of alternative therapies: reiki healers, acupuncturists, chakra and even vortex cleansing can all be bought.

Brahmani Yoga, next to **Hotel Bourgainvillea**, Anjuna, www.brahmaniyoga.com. Drop-in centre for all things yogic – flex your limbs Mysore style, or try *vinyasa* flow, hatha, *kundalini*, *pranayama*. There are also 1-day workshops and regular *bhajans*. They also promote beach cleaning Karma Yoga. Deservedly popular.

Healing Here And Now, The Health Center, St Michael's Vaddo, T0832-227 3487, www.healinghereandnow.com. If you want an 'ultimate cleanse', sign up for a 5-day detox: fasting, detoxifying drinks and twice-daily enemas. Also offers parasite cleansing, kidney cleanse and wheat grass therapy.

Purple Valley Yoga Retreat (see page 1258). 2-week retreats with celebrities of the *ashtanga vinyasa* yoga circuit. Beautiful backdrop for downward dog.

Watsu, Assagao-Mapusa road, T(0)9326-127020, www.watsugoa.com. Utterly amazing treatment. Working one-on-one, you are in a heated pool and the practitioner takes you through a range of movements both above and below the water. Using the art of shiatsu, this is an underwater massage which takes relaxation to a whole new level. The underwater dance makes you feel that you are flying and can give you a total release – a bit like being reborn. Highly recommended.

Bungee jumping

Offered by a Mumbai-based firm with US-trained staff, at Rs 500 a go. Safety is a priority, with harnesses, carabinas and air bags employed. There are pool tables, a bar, an auditorium for slide/film shows and beach volleyball. 1000-1230 and 1730 until late.

Paragliding

Happy Hours Café, south Anjuna Beach. 1230-1400. Rs 500 (children welcome), or at the hill-top between Anjuna/Baga, or Arambol.

Arambol *p1259, map p1260*

Boat trips and dolphin watching

21 Coconuts Inn, 2nd restaurant on left after stepping on to the beach. Dolphin watching trips or boats to Anjuna, Rs 150 for each.

Body and soul

You can practice every form of yoga here including *Kundalini* – a rarity in India – as well as learn massage of all styles, have your *chakras* balanced, receive Tibetan singing bowl healing, participate in *satsang*, capoeira on the beach at sunset, do firewalking and learn all styles of dance. There are an amazing group of internationally trained therapists here, along with lots of practitioners with zero qualifications, so ask around.

Balanced View, in the rice fields behind Double Dutch, www.balancedview.com. Arambol has become one of the hubs for Balanced View – guidance to living life in clarity and awareness. Has a great following – definitely worth checking out.

Sun salutations

It's one of those funny ironies that yoga, now at the zenith of its international popularity, is given a resounding thumbs down by your average metropolitan Indian, who's much more likely to pull on Lycra and go jogging or pump iron down the gym than pursue the perfect *trikonasana*. They look with curiosity at the swarms of foreign yogis yearning to pick up extreme postures from the various *guru-jis* scattered about the subcontinent. "For them, it's the equivalent of having hoards of middle-class Indians rocking up in Yorkshire to study something we see as outmoded as morris dancing," admits Phil Dane, who runs Yogamagic Canvas Ecotel.

While some Indians look askance at the vast numbers of *firangi* yogis, others are making the most of it. Yoga is a good line of work on the subcontinent. In some places, there are certainly a fair few yoga teachers to choose from. Some are put off by the commercialization by those who see *ashtanga* yoga for example as the lowliest building block towards the greater endeavour of advanced Hindu consciousness. Asana CDs, featuring cameos from students such as Sting, only serve to irk these traditionalists. Similarly yoga teacher Lalit Kumar who runs Himalaya Yoga Valley in Goa, was often told that he should grow his hair, ditch his western garb and grab a white kurta - live up to the image - He said, 'Why? I'm just a yoga teacher.' Many don the spiritual uniform and aim for the pedestal, both the teachers and the students reinforce their spiritual ego by telling everyone just how fit/spiritual/holistic they are.

India remains, nevertheless, one of the best places to study the ancient art, and many people who have embarked on yoga courses purely for its physical benefits also end up reaping some mental and emotional rewards. Yoga done with awareness can give you a taste of the bigger picture. Just keep asking around to find the right teacher. As Viriam Kaur, who runs the Kundalini Yoga Roof Garden in Arambol says "Maybe even more than finding the yoga that you most resonate with, it is essential that you find a teacher that you resonate with. You want a teacher that inspires you. But you also want a teacher that pushes your limits and makes you grow into your potential. The mantra for the Kundalini Yoga teacher as decried by Yogi Bhajan, is 'to poke, provoke, confront and elevate'!"

The large alternative communities settled around Arambol and Anjuna make good starting points if you are looking for some ad hoc teaching, but if you are travelling to India specifically to practice it's worth doing your homework first. Brahmani Yoga in Anjuna offer a great range of classes and Purple Valley offer retreats (see page 1258). Purple Valley particularly attracts internationally acclaimed yoga teachers, such as Sharath Jois, John Scott and Gingi Lee; for these, you need to book far in advance, both for courses and flights. Some might baulk at seeking out a Western teacher in India, but often Western teachers have a better understanding of the needs of their students.

Good books include: BKS Iyengar's *Light On Yoga*, *Light On Life*, *Light on the Yogasutras of Patanjali*, *Practice Manual* by David Swenson and *Yoga Darshan*.

Seek out different schools in the four corners of India in Pune (BKS Iyengar), Mysore (Pattabhi Jois), Neyyar Dam (Sivananda), Anandapur Sahib (Yogi Bhajan - Kundalini Yoga) and Bihar (Paramahamsa Satyananda). There is also the International Yoga Festival in Rishikesh every year in February or March.

Himalaya Iyengar Yoga Centre, follow the many signs, T01892-221312, www.hiyoga centre.com. Established Iyengar centre in town, 5-day courses and teacher training.

Kundalini Yoga Rooftop Garden and Healing Centre, Girka Waddo, near Temple of Dance, www.organickarma.co.uk. One of the few places in India where you can study

Kundalini yoga as taught by Yogi Bhajan. Beautiful space for yoga, meditation, in-depth courses, healing sessions, Ayuryogic massage and therapeutic bodywork. Massage trainings also possible. Highly recommended.

T'ai Chi Garden, near **Piya's Guest House**. Panda has been teaching T'ai Chi and chakra healing in Arambol for many years and has a great reputation. Most courses are 3 weeks.

Temple of Dance, off shortcut road towards God's Gift and Villa Pedro, Girko Waddo. Beautiful location offering dance classes from Bollywood to Gypsy, Balinese to tribal fusion belly dance, as well as fire dancing, hula hooping and *poi*. Recommended.

Bronze casting and sculpting

One-off classes and a 3-week course in bronze casting, held every Jan with Lucie from **Double Dutch** (see Eating), a woman of many talents. Ask at **Double Dutch** for details.

Jewellery making and silversmithing

Several places on Arambol high street offer jewellery making courses; one of the best is with Krishna at **Golden Hand Designs**, on the Kinara junction before Arambol main road.

Paragliding and kitesurfing.

Paragliding is synonymous with the hill between Arambol and Keri – ask for Andy at **Arambol Hammocks** on the cliff near **Eyes of Buddha** for tandem flights and the paragliding lowdown. Check boards in **Double Dutch** or **Lamuella** for kitesurfing lessons.

Tour operators

SS Travels, Main Rd Arambol, near Om Ganesh General Store. Quality service on tours, tickets and money exchange. Also for Western Union. This is the place where all the local ex-pats go. Tried and trusted.

Morjim to Asvem *p1261*

Body and soul

Raso Vai, S No 162/2-A, Morjim–Aswem road (towards Mandrem from Morjim), Mardi Wada, Morjim, T(0)9850-973458 and T(0)9623-556828, www.rasovai.com. Runs training courses in their signature treatments (Ayuryogic massage and Ayurbalancing), fusion massages encompassing traditional Ayurvedic techniques and yoga stretches (10 days, US$270, 4 days US$180), as well as offering more traditional treatments such as *panchakarma*, *swedan*, *pizhichil*, *shirodhara* and *snehapanam*, from a community oriented centre with meditation. Ayurvedic doctor on site. Highly recommended.

Tour operators

Speedy, near post office, Mazalvaddo, T0832-227 3208. 0900-1830. Very helpful for all your onward travel arrangements; also changes money. Very helpful, comprehensive service.

Windsurfing

Boards are sometimes available for hire at the south end of the beach for Rs 100 per hr.

Mandrem *p1261*

Body and soul

Ashiyana (see Sleeping). Stunning yoga *shalas* in Balinese style complex. There is drop-in yoga, meditation and dance here as well as courses and retreats and a range of massage and healing options in their new spa.

Himalaya Yoga Valley www.yogagoaindia.com. Great morning drop-in classes at pretty *shala* but the main focus here is exceptional Yoga Teacher Training with talented team headed up by Lalit Kumar. They run regular trainings throughout the season and then head to Europe and Thailand for the summer months. If you want to take your practice to the next level, this place is inspirational. Highly recommended.

Transport

Baga *p1253, map p1254*

Bicycle/scooter hire The only place in Baga to hire bikes is 200 m down a small lane past the Hacienda, on the left. Rs 40 per day, a little extra to keep it overnight. Almost every guesthouse owner or hotelier can rustle up a scooter at short notice – expect to pay Rs 150-350 for 1 day discounts for longer periods. Those recycled water bottles of lurid orange liquid displayed at the side of the road are not tizer but petrol often mixed with kerosene and therefore not good for the engine. Better to find a proper petrol station – dotted around in Baga, Vagator and Arambol. Although alas it's not a guarantee that the petrol from the stations is pure either! Petrol is Rs 55 per litre or 65/70 at the side of the road.

Mapusa *p1256*

Bus To **Calangute** (every 20-30 mins), some continue on to **Aguada** and **Baga**, some go towards **Candolim**; check before boarding or change at Calangute. Non-stop minibuses to **Panjim**; buy tickets from booth at market entrance. Buses also go to **Vagator** and **Chapora** via **Anjuna** and towns near by. Buses to **Tivim** for Konkan Railway and trains to **Mumbai**, Rs 8 (allow 25 mins).

Long-distance buses line up opposite the taxi stand and offer near-identical routes and rates. To **Bengaluru** (**Bangalore**): 1830, 12 hrs, Rs 250 (luxury), Rs 450 (sleeper). **Hospet** (for Hampi): 1800, 10 hrs, Rs 350 (sleeper). **Mumbai** 1600, 14 hrs, Rs 300 (luxury), Rs 500 (sleeper).

Car hire Pink Panther, T0832-226 3180.

Motorcycle hire **Peter & Friends Classic Adventures**, Casa Tres Amigos, Socol Vado 425, Parra, Assagao, 5 km east (off the Anjuna Rd), T0832-225 4467, www.classic-bike-india.com. To really get off the beaten track and see India in the raw, go on an enfield bike tour with Peter and Friends. Recommended for reliable bikes and tours of Southern India, Himachal and Nepal. Also has quality rooms and a lush swimming pool at his Casa.

Taxis Maximum capacity 4 people. To **Panjim**, Rs 100; **Calangute/Baga**, Rs 150; **Arambol** Rs 300; **Chapora/Siolim**, Rs 80. Auto to **Calangute**, Rs 50. Motorcycle taxi to **Anjuna** or **Calangute**, Rs 70, but open to bargaining.

Train **Tivim station**, on the Konkan Railway, is convenient if you want to head straight to the **northern beaches** (Calangute, Baga, Anjuna and Vagator), avoiding Panjim and Margao. A local bus meets each train and usually runs as far as the Kadamba Bus Stand in Mapusa. From here you either continue on a local bus to the beach or share a tourist taxi (rates above). Enquiries and computerized tickets: T0832-229 8682.

To **Ernakulam** (for junction): *Mangalore Exp 12618*, 1952 (arr 1345), 18 hrs. To **Jaipur** (from Ernakulam): *Exp 12977*, 1138, Mon. To **Margao**: *Mandovi Exp 10103*, 1650, 90 mins; *Konkan Kanya Exp 10111*, 0924, 90 mins. To **Mumbai** (**CST**): *Mandovi Exp 10104*, 1038, 10 hrs; *Konkan Kanya Exp 10112*, 1846, 11 hrs (via Pernem). To **Mumbai Kurla** (**Tilak**) (from Trivandrum): *Netravati Exp 16346*, 0648, 11 hrs. To **Thiruvananthapuram** (**Trivandrum**): *Netravati Exp 16345*, 2152, 19 hrs (via Margao and Canacona for Palolem beach).

Arambol *p1259, map p1260*

Bus There are regular buses from **Mapusa** and a frequent service from **Chopdem**, 12 km along the main road (1 hr); the attractive coastal detour via **Morjim** being slightly longer. It's a 2-hr-walk north through Morjim and Mandrem by the coast. **SS Travels** and **Tara**, in the village, exchange cash and TCs, good for train tickets (Rs 100 service charge); also sells bus tickets.

Keri and Tiracol Fort *p1260*

Bus Regular buses from **Mapusa** to Keri, then catch ferry to Tiracol Fort.

Mandrem *p1261*

Bus Buses towards **Siolem** pass along the main road at about 0930 and 1345. Direct services also to **Mapusa** and **Panjim**.

Directory

Calangute *p1253, map p1253*

Banks Many tour operators double as money changers, but there are **State Bank of India** and **ICICI** ATM on either sides of Beach Rd. Also **Bank of Baroda**, Baga. **Internet** **I way**, **NetXcess Cyber Café**, Shop No 1, Sunshine Complex, Baga Rd, T0832-228 1516, netxcess@mail.com. Broadband internet chain I way's branch is faster than most. **Nikki's Internet Café**, Calangute Tourist Resort Annexe, T0832-228 1950, 0900-2400, Rs 40 per hr, 8 terminals, café, forex, pool table. Useful during frequent power cuts. **Police** T0832-227 8284. **Telephone** Look for the yellow STD ISD signs.

Candolim and Sinquerim beaches *p1254*

Medical services **Health Centre**, Main Rd; **Bosto Hospital**, Panjim Rd.

Mapusa *p1256*

Banks **Bank of India**, opposite Municipal Gardens, changes TCs, cash against Visa and MasterCcard. Mon-Fri 1000-1400, Sat 1000-1200. **Pink Panther Agency** changes Visa and MasterCard, Mon-Fri 0900-1700, Sat 0900-1300.

State Bank of India, exchanges cash and TCs, 15-20 mins. Foreign exchange on 1st floor, Mon-Fri 1000-1600, Sat 1000-1200.
Internet Several across town, well signposted. Most charge Rs 90 per hr. Best at **LCC** 3rd floor, Bhavani Apartments, daily 0700-2130, Rs 15 per 15 mins, 6 terminals. **Medical services** **Ambulance**: T0832-226 2372. **Asilo Hospital**, T0832-226 2211. Pharmacies: including **Bardez Bazar**; **Drogaria**, near the Swiss Chapel, open 24 hrs; **Mapusa Clinic**, T0832-226 2350. **Police** T0832-226 2231. **Post** Opposite the police station.

Anjuna *p1256, map p1257*

Banks **Bank of Baroda**, Sorranto Vaddo, Mon-Wed, Fri 0930-1330, Sat 0930-1130, accepts most TCs, Visa/MasterCard, 1% commission (minimum Rs 50); also provides Safe Custody Packets. Thomas Cook agent at **Oxford Stores**, central, quicker and more efficient. **Internet** **Raju**'s, near Blue Tao restaurant, gives you computers on proper desks, notepads for scribbling and a good connection. Rs 40 per hr, 0900-2100. **Medical services** **St Michael's Pharmacy**, Main Rd, Sorranto, open 24 hrs. **Police** T0832-227 3233. **Post** Poste Restante at post office, Mon-Sat 1000-1600; efficient, parcels are also accepted without a fuss.

Chapora Fort *p1258*

Internet **Sonya Travels**, near Holy Cross. Offers foreign exchange, money transfers, ticketing and internet.

Arambol *p1259, map p1260*

Banks Nearest ATM is in Mandrem. **Medical services** Pharmacy on the main road opposite post office. **Health centre**, T0832-229 1249. **Police** T0832-229 7614. **Post** The small village post office is at the T junction, 1500 m from the beach.

Mandrem *p1261*

Banks **Canara Bank**, on the main road accepts TCs. **Medical services** **Hospital**, T0832-223 0081.

South Goa

The prosperous south is poster-paint green: lush coconut thickets that stretch along the coastline blend with broad swathes of iridescent paddy, broken by the piercingly bright white spears of splendid church steeples. Beneath the coastal coconut fronds sit the pretty villages of fishermen and agriculturalists: Salcete taluka is where the Portuguese were most deeply entrenched, and in the district's interior lie the beautiful fossilized remnants of centuries-old mansion estates built by the Goan colonial elite. Sprawling drawing rooms and ballrooms are stuffed with chandeliers and antiques and paved with splendid marble, every inch the fairytale doll's house. ▸▸ *For listings, see pages 1290-1300.*

Margao and coastal Salcete → *For listings, see pages 1290-1300. Colour map 5a, B2.*

A wide belt of golden sand runs the length Salcete's coast in one glorious long lazy sweep, hemmed on the landward side by a ribbon of low-key beach shacks; tucked inland lie Goa's most imposing and deluxe hotels. The thrumming nightlife of North Goa is generally absent here, but some beaches, Cavelossim in particular, have been on the receiving end of a building boom kept afloat by Russian package tourists, while Colva has gone all out and built itself a line of Baywatch-style lifeguard shacks – buxom blonde lifesavers not included. Inland, in various states of decline, lie the stately mansions of Goa's landowning classes: worn-out cases of homes once fit for princes.

Ins and outs

Getting there and around The Konkan Railway connects Margao directly with Mumbai, Mangalore and Kerala. Madgaon/Margao station is 1.5 km southeast of the bus stands, municipal gardens and market area (where you'll find most of the hotels and restaurants). Rickshaws charge Rs 15 to transfer or walk the 800 m along the railway line. Interstate buses and those running between here and North Goa use the New Kadamba (State) Bus Stand 2 km north of town. City buses take you to the town bus stands for destinations south of Margao. Colva and Benaulim buses leave from the local bus stand east of the gardens. There are plenty of auto-rickshaws and eight-seater taxis for hire. ▸▸ *See Transport, page 1298.*
Tourist information Goa Tourism Development Corporation (GTDC) ⓘ *Margao Residency, south of the plaza, T0832-271 5204.* Also has a counter at the railway station, T0832-270 2298.

Margao (Madgaon) → *Colour map 5a, B2.*

Margao is a fetching, bustling market town which, as the capital of the state's historically richest and most fertile fertile *taluka*, Salcete, is a shop window for fans of grand old Portuguese domestic architecture and churches. Sadly, in their haste to get to the nearby beaches, few tourists take the time to explore this charming, busy provincial town.

The impressive baroque **Church of the Holy Spirit** with its classic Goan façade dominates the Old Market square, the Largo de Igreja. Originally built in 1564, it was sacked by Muslims in 1589 and rebuilt in 1675. A remarkable pulpit on the north wall has carvings of the Apostles. There are also some glass cabinets in the north aisle containing statues of St Anthony and of the Blessed Joseph Vaz. Vaz was a homegrown Catholic missionary who smuggled himself to Sri Lanka dressed as a porter when the Dutch occupation challenged the island's faith. The church's feast day is in June.

The real gem of Margao is the glut of run-down 18th-century houses especially in and around Abade Faria Road, of which **da Silva House** ⓘ *visits arranged via the GTDC*, is a splendid example. Built around 1790 when Inacio da Silva stepped up to become Secretary to the Viceroy, it has a long façade whose roof was once divided into seven separate cropped 'towers', hence its other name, 'Seven Shoulders'; only three of these have survived. The house's grandeur is also evident in its interiors, featuring lavishly carved dark rosewood furniture, gilded mirrors and fine chandeliers. Da Silva's descendants still live in a small wing of the house.

The **municipal market** (Mercado de Afonso de Albuquerque) is a labyrinthine treat of flower garlands, silks and agricultural yield.

Chandor → *Colour map 5a, B2.*

By the late 18th century, an educated middle-class elite had emerged in the villages of the Old Conquests. With newly established rights to property, well-to-do Goans began to invest in large

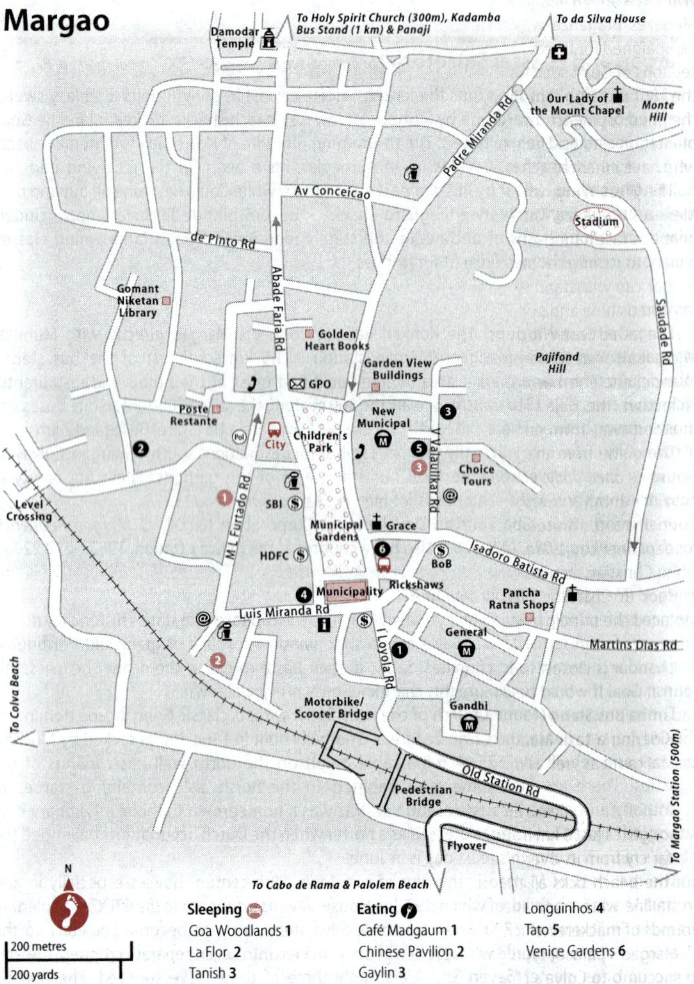

homes and very fine living. West of the Zuari River, the villages of Lutolim and Chandor are two of a number that saw the distinct development of estates and houses built on this grand scale. Their houses were stuffed with tokens of their Europeanization and affluence, mixed with traditions appropriated from their native ancestry, installing personal chapels instead of *devachem kuds*, or Hindu prayer rooms.

Despite being something of a backwater today, the once-grand village of Chandor nonetheless boasts several fine Portuguese mansions. Foremost among them is the enormous **Menezes Braganza family house** ⓘ *13 km east of Margao, both wings usually open 1000-1730 but confirm by telephone. West Wing: T0832-278 4201, 1300-1400 or early evening after 1830; East Wing: T0832-278 4227; a donation of Rs 100 at the end of the tour is greatly appreciated.* Luis de Menezes Braganza was an influential journalist and politician (1878-1938) who not only campaigned for freedom from colonial rule but also became a champion of the less privileged sections of Goan society. The late 16th-century two-storey mansion he inherited (extended in the 18th and 19th centuries), still complete with much of the family furniture and effects, shows the sheer opulence of the life enjoyed by those old Goan families who established great plantation estates. The two wings are occupied separately by members of the Braganza family who have inherited the property.

The **West Wing**, which is better maintained and has finer antiques, is owned by Aida de Menezes Braganza. The guided tour by this elderly member of the family – when she resides here – is fascinating. She has managed to restore the teak ceiling of the 250-year-old library gallery to its original state; the old *mareta* wood floor survived better since this native Goan timber can withstand water. There is much carved and inlaid antique furniture and very fine imported china and porcelain, some specially ordered, and bearing the family crest.

The faded **East Wing**, occupied by Sr Alvaro de Perreira-Braganza, partly mirrors the West Wing. It also has some excellent carved and inlaid furniture and a similar large salon with fine chandeliers. The baroque family chapel at the back now has a prized relic added to its collection, the bejewelled nail of St Francis Xavier, which had, until recently, been kept guarded away from public view.

The guide from the East Wing of the Braganza House can also show you the **Fernandes House** ⓘ *open daily, phone ahead T0832-278 4245, suggested donation Rs 100,* if he's not too busy. It's another example of a once-fine mansion just to the southeast of the village, on the Quepem road. This too has an impressive grand salon occupying the front of the house and a hidden inner courtyard. Recent excavations have unearthed an underground hiding place for when Christian families were under attack from Hindu raiders.

Back in Chandor village itself, the **Church of Our Lady of Bethlehem,** built in 1645, replaced the principal **Sapta Matrika** (Seven Mothers) **temple**, which was demolished in the previous century.

Chandor is closest to Margao but can also easily be visited from Panjim or the beaches in central Goa. It would be an arduous day trip from the northern beaches. Buses from Margao Kadamba Bus Stand (45 minutes) take you within walking distance of the sights but it is worth considering a taxi. Madgaon Railway Station, with connections to Mumbai and the Konkan coastal route as well as direct trains to Hospet, is close by.

Colva (Colwa) → *Colour map 5a, B2.*

Although it's just 6 km from the city and is the tourist hub of the southern beaches, sleepy Colva is a far cry from its overgrown northern equivalent Calangute. The village itself is a bit scruffy, but the beach ticks all the right boxes: powdery white sand, gently swaying palms, shallow crystalline waters and lines of local fishermen drawing their nets in hand over fist, dumping pounds of mackerel which are left to dry out in glistening silver heaps.

Margao's parasol-twirling elite, in their search for *mudanca* or a change of air, were the first to succumb to Colva's charms. They would commandeer the homes of local fisher- folk, who had decamped to their shacks for months leading up to the monsoon. The shacks have now traded up for gaudy pink and turquoise guesthouses and the odd chi-chi resort, but Colva's holiday scene remains a mostly domestic affair, beloved by Indian fun-seekers who'll willingly shell out the cash to go parasailing for 90 seconds.

Out on the eastern edge of town, the large **Church of Our Lady of Mercy** (Nossa Senhora das Merces), dating from 1630 and rebuilt in the 18th century, has a relatively simple façade and a single tower on the south side that is so short as to be scarcely noticeable, and the strong horizontal lines normally given to Goan churches by three of four full storeys is broken by a narrow band of shallow semi-circular arches above the second floor. But the church is much less famous for its architecture than for the huge fair it hosts, thanks to its association with the miraculous **Menino Jesus**. Jesuit Father Bento Ferreira found the original image in the river Sena, Mozambique, en route to Goa, and brought it to Colva where he took up his position as rector in 1648. The image's miraculous healing powers secured it special veneration.

The **Fama of Menino Jesus festival** (Monday of 12-18 October) sees thousands of frantic devotees flock to kiss the statue in hope of a miracle. Near the church, specially blessed lengths of string are sold, as well as replicas of limbs, offered to the image in thanks for cures.

Betalbatim to Velsao

A short walk from Colva, **Betalbatim** is named after the main Hindu temple to Betall that stood here before the deity was moved to Queula in Ponda for safety. This is a pleasant stretch with a mix of coconut palms and casuarinas on the low dunes. At low tide, when the firm sand is exposed, you can cycle for miles along the beach in either direction.

The broad, flat open beaches to the north – **Velsao**, **Arossim**, **Utorda** and **Majorda** – are the emptiest: the odd fishing village or deluxe resort shelters under coconut thicket canopy.

Bogmalo is a small, palm-fringed and attractive beach that's exceptionally handy for the airport (only 4 km, and a 10-minute drive away). **Hollant Beach**, 2 km further on, is a small rocky cove that is fringed with coconut palms. From Bogmalo village you can get to **Santra Beach**, where fishermen will ferry you to two small islands for about Rs 350 per boat.

The quiet back lanes snaking between these drowsy villages make perfect bicycle terrain and Velsao boasts some particularly grand examples of old mansions.

Verna

The church at Verna (the 'place of fresh air'), inland from the northern Salcete beaches on the NH17, was initially built on the site of the Mahalsa Temple, which had housed the deity now in Mardol (see page 1302) and featured exquisite carvings, but was destroyed and marked by the cross to prevent it being re-used for Hindu worship. As a sanctuary for widows who did not commit *sati*, it was dubbed the Temple of Nuns.

Verna was also picked to house the fifth century BC, 2.5-m-high **Mother Goddess figure** from Curdi in Sanguem, which was under threat of being submerged by the Selaulim Dam project in 1988. Two megalithic sites were found in the area. It is surrounded by seven healing springs. Just north towards Cortalim are the popular medicinal **Kersarval springs**.

Benaulim to Mobor → *Colour map 5a, B2.*

At Colva Beach's southern end lies tranquil **Benaulim**, which, according to the myth of Parasurama, is 'where the arrow fell' to make Goa. It is now a relaxed village set under palms, where business centres around toddy tapping and fishing. The hub of village activity is Maria Hall crossing, just over 1 km from the beach.

On a hill beyond the village is the diminutive **Church of St John the Baptist**, a fine piece of Goan Christian architecture rebuilt in 1596. Although the gable façade, with twin balustraded towers, is striking, the real treat is inside, in its sumptuous altar *reredos* and wonderful rococo pulpit with its depiction of the Lamb of the Apocalypse from the Book of Revelation.

The picturesque lane south from Benaulim runs through small villages and past white-painted churches. Paddy gives way to palm, and tracks empty onto small seaside settlements and deserted beaches. Benaulim beach runs into **Varca**, and then Fatrade, before the main road finally hits the shoreline amid a sprouting of resorts and restaurants at **Cavelossim**. Farthest south, **Mobor**, about 6 km from Cavelossim, lies on the narrow peninsula where the river Sal joins the sea. The Sal is a busy fishing route, but doubles as a lovely spot for boat rides.

Betul

Idyllic Betul, which overlooks Mobor from the opposite bank of the Sal in Quepem *taluka*, is an important fishing and coir village shaded by coconut palms and jackfruit, papaya and banana trees. A sand bar traps the estuary into a wide and protected lagoon and the cool breezes from the sea temper even the hottest Goan high noon. Just after the bridge, which crosses the mouth of a small river, a narrow road off to the right by the shops zigzags through the village along the south side of the Sal.

From Cavelossim the shortest route to Betul is by taking the ferry across the Sal (a signposted road leads southeast from a junction just north of Cavelossim) to Assolna; turn left off the ferry, then turn right in the village to join the main road towards Betul. From Margao, the NH17 forks right (6 km) towards Assolna at Chinchinim. After a further 6 km,

Benaulim

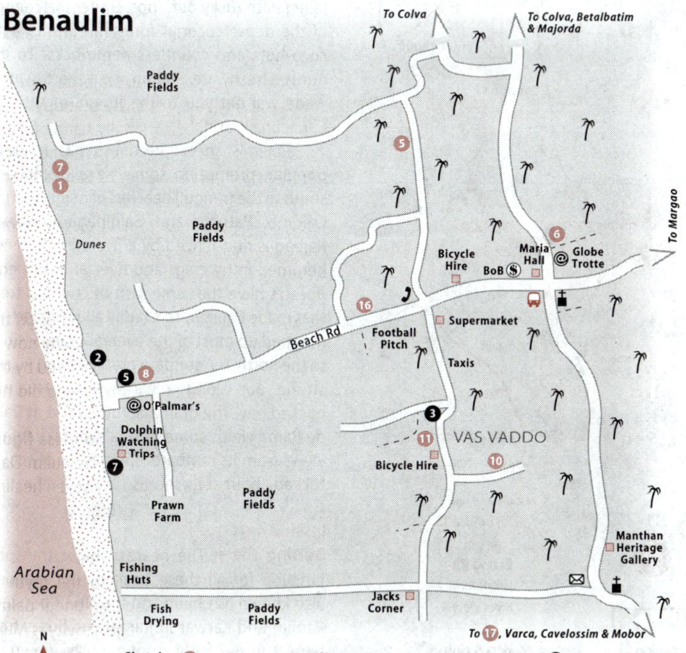

Sleeping
Anthy's **1**
D'Souza Guest House **5**
Failaka **6**
Furtado's **7**
L'Amour **8**
Oshin Holiday Care **10**
Palm Grove Cottages **11**
Taj Exotica **17**
Tansy Cottages **16**

Eating
Johncy's **2**
Malibu **3**
Pedro's **5**
Tito's **7**

there is a second turning in Cuncolim for Assolna. Buses from Margao to Betul can be very slow, but there is a fairly regular service stopping in all the settlements along the way (a couple of them continue as far as Cabo de Rama).

Cuncolim

The Jesuits razed Cuncolim's three principal Hindu temples (including the Shantadurga) and built churches and chapels in their stead.

Hindu 'rebels' killed five Jesuits and several converts in reprisal, triggering a manhunt which saw 15 men killed by the captain of Rachol Fort's soldiers. The relics of the Christian 'martyrs of Cuncolim' now lie in the Sé Cathedral in Old Goa (see page 1244). The cathedral's golden bell, Goa's largest, was cast here in 1652.

Varca to Betul

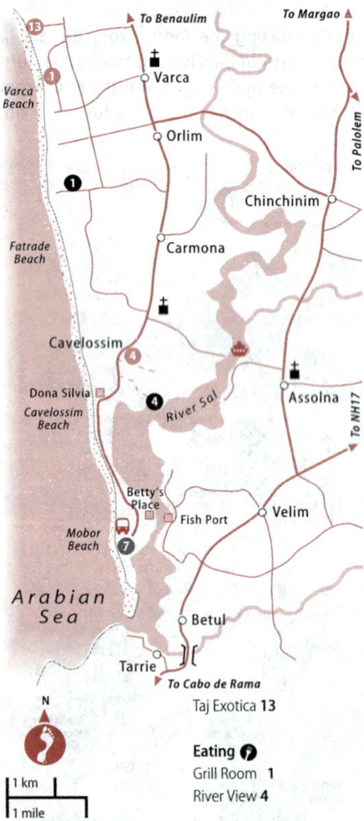

Sleeping
Club Mahindra **1**
Hippo Cool **4**
Taj Exotica **13**

Eating
Grill Room **1**
River View **4**

Bars & clubs
Aqua at Leela Palace Hotel **7**

Cabo de Rama, Palolem and the far south → *For listings, see pages 1291-1300. Colour map 5a, C2.*

Palolem is the closest Goa gets to a picture-postcard perfect bay: a beautiful arc of palm-fringed golden sand that's topped and tailed with rocky outcrops. Under the canopy of the dense coconut forests lie restaurants, coco-huts and countless hammocks. To the north, a freshwater stream and a short swim or wade will get you to the jungle of the tiny Canacona Island.

Palolem's sheer prettiness has made it popular, prompting some travellers to drift south to the tranquil beaches of neighbouring Colomb, Patnem and Galgibaga (beautiful Rajbag is ring-fenced by a five-star). Patnem, hemmed in by crags and river at either end, doesn't have the same rash of coconut trees that made Palolem so shadily alluring and has mopped up most of the overspill. Less visited, to the north, is Agonda, a pretty fishing village strung out along a windswept casuarina-backed bay. The dramatic ruined fort at Cabo de Rama yields some of Goa's most dramatic views from its ramparts and has empty coves tucked about at its shores.

Ins and outs

Getting there The nearest major transport junction for all these beaches is Canacona, also known as Chaudi, on the NH17 between Panjim and Karwar in Karnataka. Buses from here shuttle fairly continuously down to Palolem, and less frequently to Agonda, while there's a less frequent service from the beaches direct to Margao (37 km) which take about an hour. Canacona station on the

Living the dream?

The happy combination of easy living, tropical sun, cheap flights and the innumerable beautiful Portuguese-style houses – big porches, bright white lime walls, window panes of oyster shell and red tile roofs crumbling into disrepair – all across Goa has triggered many a foreigner's fantasy of getting their own tattered toehold in the state.

Renting is commonplace, and for US$300-$500 a month you can snare yourself a six-bedroom place so romantically derelict you'd swoon.

For longer term, there are plenty of modern condos set around swimming pools, simplifying the whole process, but setting yourself up in your own 100-year-old house takes graft. Goan houses for rent are likely to be vacant because children, emigrant or living elsewhere in the state, are bickering about how best to divest themselves of the brick and mortar inheritance of their parents' ancestral homes.

This means they are unlikely to be in good decorative order. One missing roof tile opens these old houses to a violent monsoon beating. Mud and lime walls dissolve quickly, wood rots and takes in termites, and shortly the wildlife (animal and vegetable) starts moving in. Initial set up costs as most places are unfurnished could easily set you back US$2000.

Agents are springing up to act as intermediaries in what is still a largely amateurish and deregulated industry, but you will pay pretty high charges to avoid the headache of having to handle things yourself. The best representative is probably the slick **Homes & Estates**, head ofice: Parra-Tinto, Bardez, T0832-247 2338, www.homesgoa.com, which also publishes a quarterly magazine.

Making a longer-term commitment to the Goan property market used to be a breeze, but beware. In 2006, the state government launched a retrospective investigation into some 445 property deals brokered for foreign nationals, on the basis that many foreigners had taken advantage of Goa's decidedly lax enforcement of India's Foreign Exchange Management Act, which dictates that foreigners must be resident in the country for six months before purchases are legal.

Nor are Goan des reses quite the steal they once were: New-build 2-bed condos can cost as little as US$34,000 but rise to US400,000.

One thing's for sure: if you are intent on joining the 5000 foreigners with homes in Goa, 3000 of them Brits, it's more important than ever to seek professional legal advice.

Konkan railway is only 2 km from Palolem. Canacona's main square has the bus and autorickshaw stands; rickshaws cost Rs 50-150 to any of these bays.

Getting around The area between the beaches is small and wandering between them becomes a leisure pursuit in itself. The drive to Cabo de Rama, although riddled with hairpin bends, is particularly lovely, and going under your own steam means you can hunt out tucked away beaches nearby and stop over at the fishing dock at the estuary north of Agonda. Buses run along this route between the bays roughly hourly.

Cabo de Rama (Cape Rama)

➔ *Colour map 5a, C2.*

Legend has it that the hero of the Hindu epic *Ramayana* lived in this desolate spot with his wife Sita during their exile from Ayodhya, and the fort predated the arrival of the Portuguese who seized it from its Hindu rulers in 1763. Its western edge, with its sheer drop to the Arabian Sea, gives you a stunning vista onto a secluded stretch of South Goa's coastline.

The main entrance to the **fort** seems far from impregnable, but the outer ramparts are excellently preserved with several cannons still scattered along their length. The gatehouse is only 20 m or so above the sea, and is also the source of the fort's water supply. A huge tank was excavated to a depth of about 10 m, which even today contains water right through the dry season. If a local herdsman is about ask him to direct you to the two springs, one of which gives out water through two spouts at different temperatures.

Agonda

Snake through forests and bright paddy south from Cabo De Rama towards Palolem to uncover artless Agonda, a windswept village backed by mountains of forestry full of acrobatic black-faced monkeys. Local political agitators thwarted plans for a five-star hotel and so have, temporarily at least, arrested the speed of their home's development as a tourist destination. However year on year, more restaurants and coco-huts open up along the length of the beach. There's no house music, little throttling of Enfield engines and you need to be happy to make your own entertainment to stay here for any serious length of time. Less photogenic than Palolem, Agonda Bay has pine-like casuarina trees lining the beach instead of coconuts and palms. The swimming is safe and the sea wonderfully calm. The northern end of the beach, close to the school and bus stop, has a small block of shops including the brilliantly chaotic and original **Fatima stores & restaurant** (Fatima Rodrigues, not one to be a jack of all trades, has limited her menu to just spaghetti and *thali*) and **St Annes bookstore**, a video library.

Palolem → *Colour map 5a, C2.*

For a short spell, when the police cracked down most severely on parties up north, Palolem looked like it might act as the Anjuna overflow. Today, **Neptune's Point** has permission to hold parties once every two weeks, but so far, Palolem's villagers are resisting the move to make the beach a mini-party destination and authorities are even stumping up the cash to pay for litter pickers. The demographic here is chiefly late-20s and 30-something couples, travellers and students. The large church and high school of **St Tereza of Jesus** (1962) are on the northern edge of town.

Beaches further south

Over the rocky outcrops to the south you come to the sandy cove of **Colomb**. Wholly uncommercial, its trees are pocked with long-stayers' little picket fences and stabs at growing banana plants, their earthy homesteads cheek by jowl with fishermen's huts. The locals are currently holding firm against a controversial development planned by a Russian group, and for now the only sounds here are the rattle of coconut fronds and bird song. Although just a bay away, you could almost be on a different planet to Palolem.

At the end of the track through Colomb, a collection of huts marks the start of the fine sweep of **Patnem Beach**. The 500 villagers here have both put a limit on the number of shacks and stopped outsiders from trading, and as a result the beach has conserved much of its unhurried charm. The deep sandbanks cushion volleyball players' falls and winds whip through kite flyers' sails: but fishing boats far outnumber sun loungers. A hit with old rockers, Israelis and long-stayers, there is no nightlife, no parties and, no coincidence, a healthy relationship between villagers and tourism. Hindu temples in Patnem have music most Fridays and Saturdays, with tabla, cymbals and harmonica.

Further south, wade across a stream (possible before the monsoon) to reach the dune- and casuarina-fringed **Rajbag Beach**, its southern waters a-bob with fishing boats. Although it's virtually unvisited and has perfect swimming, the luxury five-star that opened here in 2004 has provoked a storm of protest; allegations against the hotel include the limited access to the sea, the failure to meet local employment quotas, and the rebuilding of the ancient Shree Vita Rukmayee Temple, which villagers argue was tantamount to the hotel 'swallowing our God'. The isolated **Kindlebaga Beach** is east of Rajbag, 2 km from Canacona.

Galgibaga

Nip across the Talpona River by the ferry to reach a short strip of land jutting out to sea, where well-built houses lie among lucrative casuarina plantations. Like Morjim, **Galgibaga Beach** is a favourite stopover for Olive Ridley **turtles**, which travel vast distances to lay their eggs here each November. Shacks are mushrooming, to environmentalists' concern.

Partagali and Cotigao Wildlife Sanctuary → *Colour map 5a, C3.*

At a left turn-off the NH17, 7 km south of Canacona, to Partagali, a massive concrete gateway marks the way to the temple. If you go a little further, you reach a 2-km-long road that leads to the Cotigao Wildlife Sanctuary. Partagali's **Shri Sausthan Gokarn Partagali Jeevotam Math** is a centre for culture and learning on the banks of the river Kushavati. The *math* (religious establishment) was set up in AD 1475 at Margao when the followers, originally Saivites, were converted and became a Vaishnav sect. During the period of Portuguese Christianization (1560-1568), the foundation was moved south to Bhatkal (in northern Karnataka). The sixth Swami returned the *math* to Partagali, and built its Rama, Lakshman, Sita and Hunuman temple. An ancient *Vatavriksha* (banyan tree) 65 m by 75 m, which represents this Vaishnav spiritual movement, is a sacred meditation site known as *Bramhasthan*. The tree and its *Ishwarlinga* (the *lingam* of the Lord, ie Siva) have drawn pilgrims for more than a millennium. The temple, which also has a typical tall Garuda pillar, celebrates its festival in March/April.

Cotigao Wildlife Sanctuary ⓘ *60 km south of Panjim, www.goaforest.com/wildlife mgmt/body_cotigao.htm, year-round 0730-1730 (but may not be worthwhile during the monsoon), Rs 5, 2-wheelers Rs 10, cars Rs 50, camera Rs 25, video Rs 100,* lies in one of the most densely forested areas of the state. The 86-sq-km sanctuary is hilly to the south and east and has the Talpona River flowing through it. There is a nature interpretation centre with a small reference library and map of the park roads at the entrance. The vegetation is mostly moist deciduous with some semi-evergreen and evergreen forest cover. You may be very lucky and spot gazelles, panther, sloth bear, porcupine and hyena, and several reptiles, but only really expect wild boar, the odd deer and gaur and many monkeys. Bird-spotting is more rewarding; rare birds include rufous woodpecker, Malabar crested lark and white-eyed eagle. You need your own vehicle to reach the treetop watchtowers and waterholes that are signposted, 3 km and 7 km off the main metalled road on a variable rough track. There are no guides available, but the forest paths are easy to follow - just make sure you have drinking water and petrol. The chances of seeing much wildlife, apart from monkeys, are slim, since by the opening time of 0730 animal activity has already died down to its daytime minimum.

The first tower by a waterhole is known as **Machan Vhutpal**, 400 m off the road, with great views of the forest canopy. The second tower is sturdier and the best place to spend a night (permission required).

Most visitors come for a day trip, but if you are keen on walking in the forest this is a great place to spend a day or two. You can either stay near the sanctuary office or spend a night in a watchtower deep in the forest. A short way beyond the sanctuary entrance the metalled road passes through a small hamlet where there is a kiosk for the villagers living within the reserve, which sells the usual array of basic provisions. If you are planning to spend a few days in the park it is best to bring your own fresh provisions and then let the staff prepare meals. Rudimentary facilities like snake proof campsites, with canvas tents available from the forest office. You'll also need written permission to stay in the forest rest house or watchtower from the Deputy Conservator Of Forests, 3rd floor, Junta House, Panaji, as far in advance of a visit as possible.

The cheapest way to visit the park is to get a group together from Palolem. If you leave the beach just before 0700 you will be at the park gates when they open. Motorbikes are also allowed in the sanctuary.

South Goa listings

For Sleeping and Eating price codes and other relevant information, see Essentials pages 38-42.

Sleeping

Margao *p1281, map p1282*

With Colva and other beaches little over 15 mins away, there is not much point staying in Margao itself.

B Goa Woodlands, ML Furtado Rd, opposite City Bus Stand, T0832-271 5522, goawoodland@yahoo.co.in. Recently tarted up into a swish business hotel, the 35 rooms here are clean, spacious and anonymous. Restaurant, bar, good value, but mixed reports.

D-E La Flor, E Carvalho St, T0832-273 1402, laflorgoa@gmail.com. 35 rooms with bath, some a/c, restaurant, clean, away from bustle of town and very pleasant for the price.

D-E Tanish, Reliance Trade Centre, V V Rd, T0832-273 5656. New place with smart, good value rooms, sharing a business complex with cybercafés and mobile phone dealers. It's an OK for one night kind of place. Several good restaurants nearby.

Chandor *p1282*

AL The Big House, T0832-264 3477, www.ciarans.com. This is the stone-walled, terracotta-tiled ancestral Portuguese/Goan home of John Coutinho, owner of **Ciaran's Camp** in Palolem (see page 1292). 2 bedrooms (the master with a 4-poster, the other a twin) plus high-beamed ceilings, large sitting room, fully fitted kitchen, hot water, maid service, cable TV, DVD, phone and cooking available. Great for families, couples or groups of friends.

Colva *p1283*

Most hotels are 6-8 km from Margao Railway Station. Prices rise on 1 Dec. Discounts are possible for stays of a week or more.

AL Soul Vacation Resort, 4th Ward, T0832-278 8144, www.soulvacation.in. Everything is uber-white here and attempting to look chic in white in Goa is very challenging as most things look a little shabby around the edges. Nice pool area and rooms with all the mod cons.

C C A Guest House, 470/2 4th Ward (turn right on side street north of Soul Vacation), T0832-278 0047. Cool and pleasant 2-bed apartments with balconies and basic kitchen in a huge, pastel pink house.

E Tourist Nest, 2 km from the sea, T0832-278 8624, touristnest@indiatimes.com. Crumbling old Portuguese house, 12 rooms in secure new block, fan, Rs 200 with bathroom, 2 small self-contained cottages, good restaurant. Old part of house recommended for long stay (Rs 8000 per month for 2 bedrooms), spacious dining area, large lounge, antique furniture, balcony, bathroom and cooking facilities.

F-G Sea Pearl, 476/4 South Ward (opposite Soul Vacation), T0832-278 0176. Not particularly well maintained, but the big high-ceilinged rooms upstairs with private bath and balcony offer the best cheap deal in town. Good seafood restaurant downstairs.

Betalbatim to Velsao *p1284*

LL-L Alila Diwa Goa, Adao Waddo, Majorda, T0832- 274 6800, www.aliladiwagoa.com. The latest of the lush hotels to open its doors in the Majorda area, it has already racked up a host of awards. Stunning lobby and beautiful infinity pool – beyond that the rooms are stylish and have lovely balconies. In the exclusive Diwa wing there is another swimming pool, personalized menus and bespoke packages.

L-AL Vivenda Dos Palhacos, Costa Vaddo, Majorda, T0832-322 1119, www.vivendagoa.com. One of the most charming places you can lay your hat in Goa. Stunning renovation of old Portuguese mansion – all rooms are different; Madras has a beautiful outdoor bathroom so you can shower under the stars, The Chummery is a lovely cottage with its own veranda and you can stay in a huge luxe tent beyond the pretty swimming pool. Dinners are a fantastic communal affair although obviously you can opt out, but you never know who you might meet. Run by the hosts with the most Simon and Charlotte Hayward who come from the lineage of Haywards 5000 and their bar is dedicated to the tipple. Whole-heartedly recommended.

D-E Manuelina Tourist House, Thonvaddo, behind **Ray's**, T0832-880 1154. 5 spacious, clean rooms with bath, TV lounge, some food available, pleasant, secure, quiet with a lovely communal veranda next to the banyan tree.

E Baptista, Beach Rd, Thonvaddo, Betalbatim, T0832-288 0048. 2 simple rooms with fan, 2 self-catering flats with gas stove, use of fridge and utensils (Rs 350), good for long stays – discounts, short walk from beach. Friendly family and friendly dog once he gets to know you.

Benaulim to Mobor *p1284, map p1285*

Budget hotels and rooms in private houses can be found along Benaulim Beach Rd, in the coconut groves on either side, and along the beach south of **Johncy's**, but the rock bottom deals are drying up fast. Even simple beach guesthouses don't mind charging Rs 1000 a night for a room with bath.

LL Taj Exotica, Calvaddo, towards Varca, T0832-658 3333, exoticabc.goa@tajhotels.com. 23 ha of greenery and views of virgin beaches from each of its 138 luxurious rooms. Good restaurants, including Mediterranean, coffee shop, nightclub, excellent pool, golf course, floodlit tennis, kids' activities, jacuzzi, water-sports, gym, jogging track, library and bike hire. Spa offers treatments like Balinese massage, acupuncture and aromatherapy.

C Palm Grove Cottages, Vas Vaddo, Benaulim, T0832-277 0059, www.palmgrove goa.com. 20 clean spacious but not stylish rooms. The newer blocks at rear with showers and balconies are better. Pleasant palm-shaded garden, good food, Ayurvedic treatments. Not on the beach but plenty of places to hire a bicycle just outside. Welcoming. Recommended.

C-D L'Amour, end of Beach Rd, Benaulim, T0832-277 0404, www.lamourbeachresort. com. Close to the sea, 20 cottage-style rooms amid pleasant gardens, in a well-established hotel run by same team as **Johncy's** beach shack. Good terrace restaurant, handy for exchange and booking rail and bus tickets.

C-E Furtado's, north of Benaulim, Sernabatim Beach, T0832-277 0396. Tired-looking cottages that are better inside than out; only the cheaper, nicer non-a/c versions are worth staying in.

D Anthy's, Sernabatim Beach (2-min walk south of **Furtado's**), T(0)9922-854566, www.goaguest homes.com. A tiny collection of simple white cottages with bed, bathroom, mosquito net and not much more, set behind a popular beach café. Simple but nicely done and on a pleasant bit of beach.

D Failaka, Adsulim Nagar, near Maria Hall crossing, Benaulim, T0832-277 1270, hotelfailaka@hotmail.com. 16 spotless, comfortable rooms, 4 with TV, quieter at rear, excellent restaurant, friendly-family set-up.

D-E Heaven, north of Benaulim, Sernabatim Beach, T0832-324 6325, www.heavengoa.in. Absolutely stunning views of palm trees and green foliage, but it's 500 m from the beach. Great value rooms and deservedly popular – book ahead. Also ayurvedic massage available on-site. Recommended.

E L'Amour, end of Beach Rd, Benaulim, T0832-277 0404, www.lamourbeachresort.com. Close to the sea, 20 cottage-style rooms amid pleasant gardens, in a well-established hotel run by same team as **Johncy's** beach shack. Good terrace restaurant, handy for exchange and booking rail and bus tickets.

E Tansy Cottages, Beach Rd, Benaulim, T0832-277 0574, tansytouristcottages@ yahoo.co.in. The simple, boxy rooms with balconies in this pair of lime-and-lilac blocks offer decent value if you can cope with oil-stained sheets and a faint odour of must. Good restaurant (super breakfast), internet, friendly.

F Oshin Holiday Care, House no 126, Vas Vaddo, Benaulim, T0832-277 0069, www.oshin-guesthouse.com. You'll need a bicycle to get to the beach but the peaceful location overlooking egret and buffalo ponds is well worth it. 14 good large rooms with bath on 3 floors (room 11 best, **D**), breakfast, dinner on request, friendly manager, superb well-kept grounds. Recommended.

Agonda *p1288*

A-C H20, towards south end of the beach, T(0)9423-836994, www.h2oagonda.com. Black is the new color for chic boho beachhuts in south Goa. H20 is the new kid on the beach, offering up a smarter alternative, but feels a little out of place here in Goa. Great sunloungers for sundowners, a spa on site and the food hits the spot too.

A-E Shanti Village, towards south end of the beach, T(0)9823-962154, www.shantiagonda. com. With lovely views and chic huts (again in the colour of the season – black), Shanti is giving **H2O** a run for its money – being smaller than its watery neighbour, it has a more intimate vibe. Also at another location towards the north end of the beach near **Simrose**, they have some cheaper huts, although still very nice with tribal masks and textiles to decorate.

B Blue Lagoon Resort, 4 km north of Agonda at Khola beach, T0832-264 7842, www.bluelagoongoa.com. Rajasthani tents set up on this secluded beach north of Agonda – blissful. There are also lovely huts, a restaurant and amazing views.

C-D Common Home, south end of the beach, T0832-264 7890. Innovatively designed a/c rooms with Rajasthani wooden doors, and beach huts with sleek slate bathrooms and cow dung walls – all with interesting furniture and draped fabrics.

C-E Monsoon, north end of the beach, T(0)9823-198025, monsoongoa@hotmail.com. Assortment of rice grass huts and some sweet rooms at the back. Looking a little shabby round the edges.

C-E Simrose, towards north end of the beach, T(0)9420-162474, www.simrose-goa.com. Stylish beach shacks and nice rooms at the back dotted around pretty restaurant. Restaurant has plenty of little nooks for romantic suppers or shady spots for daytime lounging. Good value – recommended.

D-E White Sand, north end of the beach, T0832-264 7831, whitesandbb@yahoo.co.in. Bungalows and 2-tiered huts dotted around great circular restaurant, also nice spacious rooms in converted family house at back. 2-tier rooms are blessed with great views. Recommended.

D-F Dersy Beach Resort, south end of the beach, T0832-264 7503. 50-year-old family house developed to fit 12 clean rooms with bathrooms. Over the road on the beach are 12 basic bamboo huts with spotless shared wash block. Good value generally, but in high season the huts are not worth the price.

F Sun Set, up the cliff, south end of the beach, T0832-264 7381. Simple cottages on the cliff with great views, most with shared facilities, some with attached bathrooms and kitchen. The restaurant perched high on the rocks has prime views of Agonda.

F-G Nana's Nook, extreme south end of the the beach, T(0)9421-244672. Simple beach huts dotted around a central café with shared bath. The best huts at the front offer ideal views. Recommended.

Palolem *p1288*

Palolem's popularity has soared inordinately and in high season prices go off the scale. Off season, bargain hard and ask around for rooms inside family houses. There is a wide range of accommodation.

A-B Art Resort, close to **Bhakti Kutir**, T(0)966-598 2344, www.art-resort-goa.com. Colourful seafront cottages with interesting interior design from Riki Hinteregger using khadi natural cotton.

A-B Ciaran's Camp, beach, T0832-264 3477, www.ciarans10.com. Primo glass-fronted wooden huts are spaced wide apart in palm-covered landscaped gardens; many have their own roof terrace with loungers. A library, lovely shop, table tennis and great restaurant plus promises of live jazz all make it the leader in Palolem cool.

A-B Village Guesthouse, beach, off the main road, T0832-264 5767, www.villageguesthousegoa.com. Stylish renovation of an old house, which, although only 5 mins' walk from beach feels a million miles away. Beautiful rooms with a/c, TV and chic decor and quite possibly the most luxe bathrooms in Goa. Great views across rice fields from the communal veranda, and a courtyard garden in the back.

B-C Bhakti Kutir, cliffside, south end of the beach, T0832-264 3469, www.bhaktikutir.com. This original eco-friendly abode perched on the hilltop above Palolem beach has a relaxed charm. 2-tier huts with antique furniture, compost toilets and bucket baths. There is a popular super-healthy restaurant on-site offering up a selection of every grain you can think of. Renowned yoga teacher Swami Yogananda is based here and has a dedicated following.

B-D Dreamcatcher, riverbank, North Palolem, T0832-647 0344, www.dreamcatcher.in. Thirty-nine colourful plywood cottages in the coconut grove running along the pretty estuary. Cottages are quite close together. Yoga, reiki courses and ayurvedicmassage centre on site.

C-E Cozy Nook, at northern end, T0832-264 3550. Plastered bamboo huts, fans, nets, shared toilets, in a good location between the sea and river, Ayurvedic centre, art and crafts, friendly. Very popular. Getting a bit pricey. Goa Sailing is based here.

C-E Ordo Sounsar extreme north end of the beach, over a small bridge, T(0)9822-488769, www.ordosansour.com. Simple beach huts nestling north of the estuary away from the business and busy-ness of Palolem Beach. Exceptional location, amazing restaurant serving up traditional Goan tastes. Highly recommended.

D Green Inn on the Agonda road, near Spiral Ark, T(0)7588-444937, www.palolemgreen inn.com. Exceptional location, this 2-storey guest house juts out into the vibrant green rice fields offering up almost a 360-degree view of nature. Nice clean rooms with flatscreen TVs and modern bathrooms, alas no individual balconies, but amazing views from rooftop restaurant.

D-E Chattai set back from the beach, behind Bhakti Kutir and Neptune's Point, T(0)9822-481360, www.chattai.com. Fantastic coco huts, most with loungey roof terraces. Lovely chilled atmosphere.

D-F Papillon south end of beach, T(0)9890-507490, www.papillonpalolem.com. Good-value chic beach huts with laidback vibe, a cut above the rest.

E-F Fernandes, next to **Banyan Tree**, T0832-264 3743. 2 branches of this family-run guesthouse and restaurant on the beach. Lovely wooden cottages with attached bathrooms, good value.

F Om Ganesha, next to **Dream Catcher**, T(0)9923-171298. Clean, basic rooms with bathrooms, set behind the beach. Secure.

Beaches further south *p1288*

Patnem

The following places are all in Patnem. Demand and room rates rocket over Christmas and New Year.

A-B The Hill, the hill above Colomb beach, T(0)9823-257709, free2b_bfree2b@yahoo.com. Tucked away on a jungle hill with great views of all four of the local beaches Patnem, Rajbag, Palolem and Colomb, you will find large luxury tents with en-suite bathrooms. You get a great sense of privacy here as you are surrounded by jungle and yet are only a stone's throw away from the beaches, restaurants and nightlife. There's a deli-style restaurant too with spectacular sunset views, showcasing a range of locally produced foods, including amazing cheeses (price includes breakfast). There is also a workshop space for yoga, dance and chi kung. Highly recommended.

B-C April 20, next to **Home**, T(0)996-091 6989,vickygoan@gmail.com. Smart 1- and 2-tiered beach bungalows with nice balconies and great views, formerly called **Goyam & Goyam**.

B-C Bodhi Eco Resort, north end Patnem, T(0)954-533 7387, www.oasisecoresort.com. Uniquely designed white canvas rooms – one is even 2-storey, all ensuite. Laidback vibe with a nod to the environment. Beautiful bamboo restaurant on stilts hovers above the beach.

B-C Hidden Gourmet, Colomb, T(0)992-368 6185, www.gourmetpatnem.com. As the name suggests this place is off the beaten track, or at least thru the village and tucked away on the promontory overlooking Patnem beach. Beautifully decorated stone rooms all with a stunning ocean view and 2 mango wood and bamboo huts with stylish open-roofed bathrooms. Recommended.

B-D Home Guesthouse, Patnem, T0832-264 3916, homeispatnem@yahoo.com. Vibey rooms with nice décor make these a cut above the rest – deservedly popular. Quality linen and fairy lights make for good ambience, although opt for a room set back from the kitchen and very popular restaurant.

B-D Papayas, Patnem, T(0)9923-079447, www.papayasgoa.com. Eco-friendly huts running on solar power with beautifully kept gardens. Chilled atmosphere set behind small beachfront restaurant.

D-E Bonkers, south end Patnem beach, T(0)982-266 4026, rocking.bonkers@gmail.com. Floppy fringed palm huts borrowing their design from neighbours **Lotus Yoga**, laid back vibe at the quieter end of the beach.

D-E Secret Garden, Patnem Rd, T(0)9850-925668, smartsheikh@redirrmail.com. Set behind Patnem beach on the little strip leading to the main road, these rooms are tucked away in a very pretty garden.

D-F Solitude Dream Woods, Patnem, T0832-327 7081, solitudedreamwoods@yahoo.com. Basic plywood structures, but good value and all with attached bathroom. There is a yoga space here and swinging chairs dotted around.

E-G Namaste, Patnem, T(0)9850-477189, namaste_patnem@yahoo.in. Variety of wooden huts and bamboo bungalows – good value. Nice vibe and lively restaurant.

Eating

Margao *p1281, map p1282*

TT Chinese Pavilion, M Menezes Rd (400 m west of Municipal Gardens). Chinese. Smart, a/c, good choice.

TT Gaylin, 1 V Valaulikar Rd. Chinese. Tasty hot Szechuan, comfortable a/c.

TT Longuinhos, near the Municipality. Goan, North Indian. Open all day for meals and snacks, bar drinks and baked goodies.

TT Tato, G-5 Apna Bazaar, Complex, V Valaulikar Rd. Superb vegetarian, a/c upstairs.

TT Venice Gardens, near Our Lady of Grace Church, opposite Lohia Maidan, T0832-271 0505. Little garden oasis in the middle of Margao offering up the usual fare.

T Café Madgaum, near Railway Gate. Good South Indian snacks.

Colva *p1283*

T Joe Con's, 4th Ward. Excellent fresh fish and Goan dishes, good value.

T Sagar Kinara, 2 mins back from beach overlooking the main road junction. Rare pure-veg restaurant, offering good value *thalis* and biryanis on a breezy terrace.

T Viva Goa, 200 m south of roundabout at east end of town. Local favourite, serving proper Goan food on red checked tablecloths. Recommended.

Betalbatim to Velsao *p1284*

It's worth coming to Majorda for the food, there are a range of great restaurants.

TTTT Fusion, Majorda Beach Rd, Pacheco Vaddo, T0832-288 1694. Winning a Times Food Award in 2011, this place offers up a lot of meat. Steaks and carpaccio are their specialities, but naturally there are some fish and veg options too. And leave room for their chocolate fondant.

TTT Martin's Corner, Betalbatim (coming from the south, look for sign on left after village), T0832-648 1518. Huge place in front of an old house, serving great seafood including lobster, tiger prawns and crab. As cricket superstar Sachin Tendulkar has bought a house here, it's become the hangout of choice for holidaying cricket stars and media types.

TTT Miyabi, Majorda Beach Rd, T(0)9767-704244. Serving up for-real Japanese food – fresh sushi, tasty tempura and all sorts of fish dishes. Beautiful restaurant run by Japanese/Russian couple. Recommended.

TTT Yum Yum Tom Yum, opposite Alila Diwa Goa, T(0)9049-775449. Recently moved from Palolem, offers up great Thai food under the watchful eye on one careful Thai lady owner.

TTT Zeebop, Utorda Beach, follow signs to Kenilworth resort, www.zeebopbythesea.com. Lovely beach front restaurant offering up a delicious range of seafood, try the crab papads and great goan specialities. Recommended.

TT Roytanzil Garden Pub, set back from the beach at the end of Majorda beach road past **Martin's Corner** (no sea views). Neat grounds, alfresco and small covered area. Seafood and Indian. One of the best restaurants on the south coast.

Benaulim to Mobor *p1284, map p1285*

Beach shacks all down the coast offer Goan dishes and seafood at reasonable prices.

TT La Afra, Tamborin, Fatrade. Excellent steaks and fresh fish, sensibly priced. Boatmen ferry holidaymakers to **River Sal**, Betul.

TT Pedro's, by the car park above the beach, Benaulim. Good seafood and tandoori. Imaginative menu, friendly.

TT River View, Cavelossim. Tranquil, open-air location, overlooking the river. Wide choice, international menu, good ambience despite being surrounded by ugly hotels. Cocktails Rs 100, sizzlers Rs 150-200, tiger prawns Rs 500.

T D'Souza's (see Sleeping). Good juices, *lassis* and fast food.

T Goan Village, lane opposite Dona Sylvia, Cavelossim. The best in the area for all cuisines.

T Johncy's, Benaulim. Varied menu, good seafood, big portions, tandoori recommended (after 1830) but service can be erratic. Pleasant atmosphere though; backgammon, scrabble.

T Malibu, Benaulim. Lush garden setting for spicy fish/meat kebabs.

Cabo de Rama *p1286*

Pinto's Bar, near the fort entrance. Offers meals and cool drinks on a sandy shaded terrace, may also have rooms available. If there are few visitors about (most likely) ask here for a meal before exploring the fort to save time waiting later.

Agonda *p1288*

Most of the places recommended for accommodation also have good food, especially H20 and Monsoon.

Blue Planet, Palolem–Agonda Rd, 5 km before Agonda, T0832-264 7448, www.blueplanet-cafe.com. This Palolem institution has taken a risk and moved into the countryside just outside Agonda – but it's a beautiful risk to take. Great drive and lovely view from their new abode. On the menu, you will find an array of vegetarian and organic healthy treats.

White Sand, north end of beach. Comfortable laid-back circular restaurant offering up great salads, lots of fresh fish and delicious desserts.

Greek Place, opposite **H2O**. This hardy perennial of the Agonda scene has moved from the crossroads, but serves up memorable souvlaki and greek treats.

Madhu, north end of beach, T(0)9423-813140, www.madhuhuts.com. Always packed, this beach shack serves up a great range of traditional spicy Goan food as well as a range of Indian, Chinese and continental food. Also has nice huts available.

Palolem *p1288*

Bhakti Kutir (see Sleeping). Excellent fresh fish dishes, homegrown organic produce and fresh juices. Name any number of obscure nutritious grains and they'll be here.

Café Inn, at the beach road junction. Funky courtyard cafe serving up quality cappuccinos, a huge array of juices, tortilla wraps and unusual pancakes like strawberry and meringue.

The Cheeky Chapatti, Main Rd. Tasty fusion food like Kingfish wraps and feta burgers with chilli jam, topped off with legendary lemon tart. Sun dinners are a great event.

Dropadi Beach Restaurant and Bar. Routinely packed out. Lobster and lasagne and North Indian food are the specials – the ex-pat community do rave about the quality of the fish here.

Ordo Sansour, over bridge at far north end of beach. Simple menu focusing on Goan food – strangely a rarity in these parts. Fantastic stuffed mackerel, calamari masala, Goan-style fishcakes, unique papaya curry, fried plantain chips – exceptional stuff. Highly recommended.

Spiral Ark, on the Palolem-Agonda road, T0832-264 3870, spiralark@gmail.com. Great food in this vibey courtyard café – tasty thalis, organic salads, and great desserts – and a shop with beautiful textiles, clothes and deli.

Banyan Tree, near **Dreamcatcher** (see Sleeping). Sitting in the shade of a lovely banyan tree, the menu here focuses on Thai food and mostly gets it just right – good *pad thai* and green curries. Open mic night on Fri.

Shiva Sai, off main road. Great cheap *thalis*.

Tibet Bar and Restaurant, Main Rd, T(0)9822-142775. Super-fresh ingredients in these excellent Himalayan dishes. Small restaurant that's worth stepping back from the beach for.

Beaches further south *p1288*

Nestled between Palolem and Patnem is Colomb Bay with a few huts, restaurants and the main venue **Neptune's Point**. Most of the places mentioned for accommodation in Patnem also serve up great food.

Hidden Gourmet, Colomb, T(0)9923-686185, www.gourmetpatnem.com. Passionate about their food, the team here serves up a great range of fish and steaks, crisp salads and delicious desserts – all with a stunning view of Patnem beach.

Home, Patnem. Great range of salads, pastas, and veggie specials like beetroot and vodka risotto – make sure you leave room for their legendary desserts like chocolate brownie and sharp lemon tart – with a very chilled chic beachfront vibe.

Magic View, Colomb, in front of **Hidden Gourmet**, T(0)9960-917287. Remarkably popular Italian restaurant delivering fantastic pizzas served up on tree trunks, deliciously decadent pastas like gorgonzola and fish specials – choose from 2 views, one over-looking the rocks at Colomb and the other gazing over Patnem.

Boom Shankar, Colomb, T(0)9822-644035. The latest 'in' place for sundowners, this place also offers a great range of food and rooms to rent; all have great views over the rocks.

Mamoos, set back from beach, T0832-264 4261. Recently moved from downtown Palolem, Mamoos has served up excellent North Indian food at great prices for years.

Bars and clubs

Colva *p1283*

Boomerang, on the beach a few shacks north of **Pasta Hut** (see Eating). Appealing sea-view drinking hole with pool table, sociable circular bar, dancefloor (music veers wildly from cool to cheesy), and daytime massages courtesy of Gupta.

Johnny Cool's, halfway up busy Beach Rd. Scruffy surroundings but popular for chilled beer and late-night drinks.

Splash, on beach, 500 m south of main car park. *The* place for music, dancing and late drinking, open all night, trendy, very busy on Sat (full after 2300 Mon-Fri in season), good cocktails, poor bar snacks. May not appeal to all, especially unaccompanied girls.

Benaulim to Mobor *p1284, map p1285*

Aqua, **Leela Palace**, Mobor. A gaming room and cigar lounge which turns into a late-night disco after 2000.

Palolem *p1288*

Cuba Beach Cafe, Palolem road, behind Syndicate Bank, T0832-264 3449. Cool, upbeat bar for a sundowner with regular sunset DJ sessions.

Hare Krishna Hare Ram, Patnem. Latest place for sunsets and dancing run by old schoolmates, local boys done good.

Laguna Vista, Colomb. Come here on Fri nights for French singer Axailles accompanied by Indian classical musicians – great vibe.

Neptune's Point Bar and Restaurant, T(0)9822-584968. Wide dancefloor nestled between the rocks for a mellow daily chill-out from 1700-2200 with a proper party on a weekly basis. This is also the venue for Silent Noise headphone parties (www.silent noise.com) – an ingenious way to defy the 2200 curfew. Plugged in via wireless 'phones, you can dance your heart out to a choice of 2 DJs and there's no noise pollution. A giant screen plays movies on Wed nights.

Festivals and events

Chandor *p1282*

6 Jan Three Kings Festival Crowds gather on each year at Epiphany for the Three Kings Festival, which is similarly celebrated at Reis Magos, with a big fair, and at Cansaulim (Quelim) in southern Goa. The 3 villages of Chandor (Cavorim, Guirdolim and Chandor) come together to put on a grand show. Boys chosen from the villages dress up as the 3 kings and appear on horseback carrying gifts of gold, frankincense and myrrh. They process through the village before arriving at the church where a large congregation gathers.

Colva *p1283*

12-18 Oct (Mon that falls between these dates) **Fama of Menino Jesus** when thousands of pilgrims flock to see the statue in the Church of our Lady of Mercy in the hope of witnessing a miracle.

Benaulim to Mobor *p1284, map p1285*

24 Jun Feast of St John the Baptist (Sao Joao) in Bernaulim gives thanks for the arrival of the monsoon. Young men wearing crowns of leaves and fruits tour the area singing for gifts. They jump into wells (which are usually full) to commemorate the movement of St John in his mother's womb when she was visited by Mary, the mother of Jesus.

Palolem *p1288*

Feb Rathasaptami The Shri Malikarjuna Temple 'car' festival attracts large crowds.

Apr Shigmo, also at the Shri Malikarjuna Temple, also very popular.

Shopping

Margao *p1281, map p1282*

The Old Market was rehoused in the 'New' (Municipal) Market in town. The **covered market** (Mon-Sat 0800-1300, 1600-2000) is fun to wander around. It is not at all touristy but holidaymakers come on their shopping trip to avoid paying inflated prices in the beach resorts. To catch a glimpse of the early morning arrivals at the **fish market** head south from the Municipal Building.

Books and CDs

Golden Heart, off Abbé Faria Rd, behind the GPO. Closed 1300-1500. Bookshop.
Nanutel Hotel. Small bookshop.
Trevor's, 5 Luis Miranda Rd. Sells CDs.

Clothes

J Vaz, Martires Dias Rd, near Hari Mandir, T0832-272 0086. Good-quality men's tailor.
MS Caro, Caro Corner. An extensive range including 'suiting', and will advise on tailors.

Benaulim to Mobor *p1284, map p1285*

Khazana, Taj Exotica, Benaulim. A veritable treasure chest (books, crafts, clothes) culled from across India. Pricey.
Manthan Heritage Gallery, main road. Quality collection of art items.

Palolem *p1288*

Chim, main Palolem Beach road. Good collection of funky Indian-inspired clothes and *kurtas*, as well as bikinis and accessories.
Spiral Ark, on Palolem-Agonda road. Great range of mainly organic fabrics from across India. Also lots of beautiful wooden toys and trinkets, delicious food stuffs from the deli and everything from organic turmeric to local frankincense from Karnataka.

Activities and tours

Colva *p1283*

Tour operators

Meeting Point, Beach Rd opposite William Resort, T0832-278 8003. Mon-Sat 0830-1900 (opens later if busy). Very efficient, reliable flight, bus and train booking service,

Betalbatim to Velsao *p1284*

Watersports

Goa Diving, Bogmalo; also at **Joet's**, and based Chapel Bhat, Chicalim, T0832-255 5117, goadiving@sancharnet.in. PADI certification from Open Water to Assistant Instructor.
Splash Watersports, Bogmalo, T0832-240 9886. Run by Derek, a famous Indian champion windsurfer. Operates from a shack on the beach just below **Joet's**, providing parasailing, windsurfing, waterskiing, trips to nearby islands; during the high season only.

Benaulim to Mobor *p1284, map p1285*

Body and soul

At **Taj Exotica**, Benaulim, yoga indoors or on the lawn. Also aromatherapy, reflexology.

Dolphin watching

The trips are scenic and chances of seeing dolphin are high, but it gets very hot (take a hat, water and something comfy to sit on). Groups of dolphins here are usually seen swimming near the surface. Most hotels and cafes offer boat trips, including **Café Dominick** in Benaulim (signs on the beach). Expect to pay Rs 250-300 per person.
Betty's Place, in a road opposite the Holiday Inn in Mobor, T0832-287 1456. Offers dolphin viewing (0800-1000, Rs 300), birdwatching (1600, Rs 250) and sunset cruises up the river Sal River (1700, Rs 200). Recommended.

Agonda *p1288*

Boat hire and cruises

Monsoon, **Madhu** and **Om Sai** hotels organize trips to the spice plantations and boat trips to Butterfly and Cola beaches.
Aquamer rents kayaks.

Palolem *p1288*

Boat hire and cruises

You can hire boats to spend a night under the stars on the secluded Butterfly or Honeymoon beaches, and many offer dolphin-watching and fishing trips. You can see the dolphins from dry land around Neptune's Point, or ask for rowing boats instead of motorboats if you want to reduce pollution. Mornings 0830-1230 are best. Arrange through **Palolem Beach Resort**, travel agents or a fisherman. About Rs 600 for a 1-hr trip for 4 people, Rs 1500 for 3 hrs. Take sunscreen, shirt, hat and water.
Ciaran's Camp, T0832-264 3477. Runs 2-hr mountain bike tours or charter a yacht over-night through Ciaran's bar for Rs 8000.
Goa Sailing, moored at **Cozy Nook** in Palolem, T(0)985-045 8865, www.goasailing.com. With 3 catamarans for hire with Matthew Taylor at the helm, a qualified Royal Yachting Association instructor, Palolem makes for a great experience in sailing or learning the ropes.

Body and soul

Harmonic Healing Centre, Patnem, T(0)9822-512814, www.harmonicingoa.com. With an enviable location high above the north end of Patnem beach, you can perform your *asanas* while looking out to sea. You can have massage with just the sky and the cliffs as a backdrop. Drop-in yoga, Bollywood and Indian classical dance classes and a full range of alternative treatments are on offer. The owner Natalie Mathos also runs 2-week non-residential reiki courses and yoga retreats from Nov-Mar.

Lotus Yoga Retreats, south end Patnem beach, T(0)960-429 0688, www.lotus-yoga-retreat.com. Offering up a range of yoga holidays and retreats with guest teachers from Europe, Lotus has an enviable location at the relaxed end of Patnem beach. Beautiful yogashala and stylish accommodation made from local materials.

Language and cooking courses

Sea Shells Guest House, on the main road. Hindi and Indian cookery classes.

Tour operators

Rainbow Travels, T0832-264 3912. Efficient flight and train bookings, exchange, Western Union money transfer, safe deposit lockers (Rs 10 per day), good internet connection.

⊖ Transport

Margao *p1281, map p1282*

Bus All state-run local and long-distance buses originate from the **Kadamba Bus Stand** 2 km to the north of town, T0832-271 4699. Those from the south also call at the **local bus stand** west of the municipal gardens, and buses for Colva and Benaulim can be boarded near the Kamat Hotel southeast of the gardens. From the Kadamba stand, city buses motorcycle taxis (Rs 15) can get you to central **Margao**.

Frequent services to **Benaulim**, **Colva** and non-stop to **Panjim** (1 hr, buy tickets from booth at Platform 1. Several a day to Betul, **Cabo da Rama**, **Canacona** and Palolem. Daily to **Gokarna** (1500), but trains are much quicker.

Private buses (eg **Paulo Travels**, Cardozo Building opposite bus stand, T0832-243 8531), to **Bengaluru** (**Bangalore**) (15 hrs); **Mangalore** (8-10 hrs); **Mumbai** (**Dadar**/ **CST**) (16 hrs), Rs 600 (sleeper); **Pune** (13 hrs).

Car hire **Sai Service**, T0832-241 7063. Rs 1000-2000 per day with driver.

Rickshaw Most trips in town should cost Rs 30-40; main bus stand to railway Rs 50. The prepaid rickshaw booth outside the station main entrance has high rates but probably better than bartering on the street. Motorcycle taxi drivers hang around quoting cheaper (but still overpriced) fares. Avoid tourist taxis: they can be 5 times the price.

Train Enquiries, T0832-271 2790. The new station on the broad gauge network is 1 km southwest of central Margao. The reservation office on the 1st floor, T0832-271 2940, is usually quick and efficient, with short queues. Mon-Sat 0800-1400, 1415-2000, Sun 0800-1400. Tickets for **Mumbai**, **Delhi** and **Hospet** (for **Hampi**) should be booked well ahead.

Konkan Kanya Express (night train) and **Mandovi Express** (day train) from **Mumbai** also stop at **Tivim** (for northern beaches; take the local bus into Mapusa and from there catch another bus or take a taxi) and **Karmali** (for Panjim and Dabolim airport) before terminating at **Margao**. Both are very slow and take nearly 12 hrs. From **Mumbai** (**CST**): *Mandovi Exp 10103*, 0515 (arr 1815; 13 hrs), doesn't stop at Pernem; *Konkan Kanya Exp 10111*, 2250 (arr 1045).

To **Delhi** (**Nizamuddin**): *Goa Exp 12779*, 1549, 35 hrs. *Rajdhani Exp 12431*, 1020, Wed, Fri, Sat, 26 hrs; *Goa Sampark Kranti Exp 12449*, 1120, Tue, Wed, 30 hrs. **Ernakulam** (**Jn**): *Mangala Lakshaweep Exp 12618*, 1935, 16 hrs. **Hospet** (for **Hampi**): *Amaravati Express 18048*, 0800, Tue, Thu, Fri, Sun, 7 hrs. **Mumbai** (**CST**): *Mandovi Exp 10104*, 0940, 11½ hrs (via Karmali, Tivim); *Konkan Kanya Exp 10112*, 1800, 12 hrs (via Karmali, Tivim, Pernem). **Mumbai** (**Lokmanya Tilak**): *Netravati Exp 16346*, 0555, 11 hrs (via Karmali, Tivim). **Thiruvanant- hapuram** (**Trivandrum**): *Rajdhani Exp 12432*, 1235, Mon, Wed, Thu, 18 hrs (via Mangalore, 5 hrs, and Ernakulam, 13 hrs). *Netravati Exp 16345*, 2250, 18 hrs (via Canacona for Palolem beach).

The broad gauge line between **Vasco da Gama** and **Londa** in Karnataka runs through Margao and Dudhsagar Falls and connects stations on the line with **Belgaum**. There are services to **Bengaluru** (**Bangalore**) *Vasco Bangalore Exp 17310*, 2059, Mon, Thu.

Colva *p1283*

Air From the airport, taxis charge about Rs 500. If arriving by train at Margao, 6 km away, opt for a bus or auto-rickshaw for transfer. Buses pull in at the main crossroads and then proceed down to the beach about 1 km away. Auto-rickshaws claim to have a Rs 30 'minimum charge' around Colva itself.

Scooter hire is available on every street corner, for Rs 200-250 a day; motorbikes for Rs 300 per day, less for long-term rental, more for Enfields. Bicycles are hard to come by – ask at your hotel.

Bus/taxi Bus tours to **Anjuna**, every Wed for the Flea Market, tickets through travel agents, depart 0930, return 1730, Rs 200; to **Margao** half-hourly, take 30 mins, Rs 8 (last bus 1915, last return, 2000). Also to **Margao**, motorcycle taxi, Rs 40-50 (bargain hard); auto-rickshaw, Rs 70-100.

Betalbatim to Velsao *p1284*

Bus Buses from Margao (12 km). The **Margao-Vasco** bus service passes through the centre of Cansaulim.

Taxi To/from **airport**, 20 mins (Rs 300); **Margao** 15 mins (Rs 200). From **Nanu Resort**, **Panjim** Rs 500, **Anjuna** Rs 750, or Rs 1000 for 8 hrs, 80 km.

Train **Cansaulim station** on the **Vasco-Margao** line is handy for **Velsao** and **Arossim** beaches, and **Majorda station** for **Utorda** and **Majorda** beaches. Auto-rickshaws meet trains.

From Cansaulim and Majorda there are 3 trains a day to **Vasco** via **Dabolim** for the airport. Westbound trains head to **Kulem** (for Dudhsagar Falls) via **Margao**.

Benaulim to Mobor *p1284, map p1285*

Bus Buses from all directions arrive at Maria Hall crossing, Benaulim. Taxis and autos from the beach esplanade near Pedro's and at Maria Hall crossing. To/from **Margao**: taxis Rs 130; autos Rs 100; bus Rs 7. **Anjuna** Wed flea market bus 0930, return 1530, Rs 200; you can take it one-way, but still have to buy a return ticket.

From Margao to **Cavelossim**, the bus is slow (18 km); auto-rickshaws transfer from bus stand to resorts. From **Margao** taxis charge around Rs 300.

Bicycle/scooter hire Cycle hire from **Rocks**, outside Dona Sylvia in Cavelossim, cycles Rs 10 per hr, Rs 150 a day; scooters Rs 300 a day without petrol, Rs 500 with 7 litres of fuel. In Benaulim, bikes and scooters for hire, Rs 100 and Rs 200 per day.

Agonda *p1288*

Bus/rickshaw First direct bus for **Margao** leaves between 0600-0630, last at 1000, takes about 1 hr. Alternatively, arrange a lift to the main road and flag down the next bus (last bus for Margao passes by at around 2000, but it is advisable to complete your journey before dark). Hourly buses between **Betul** and **Palolem** call at Agonda (and Cabo de Rama). Easy to visit for the day by taxi, motorbike or bicycle from Palolem Beach.

From Palolem/Chaudi Junction, auto-rickshaws charge Rs 120-150; turn off the road by the Niki bar and restaurant.

Car/scooter hire **Madhu** and **White Sands** in Agonda, hire out scooters, motorbikes and cars.

Palolem *p1288*

Bus Many daily direct buses run between **Margao** and **Canacona** (40 km via Cuncolim), Rs 20, on their way to **Karwar**. From Canacona, taxis and auto-rickshaws charge Rs 40-60 to **Palolem** beach only 2 km away. From Palolem, direct buses for Margao leave at around 0615, 0730, 0930, 1415, 1515, 1630 and take 1 hr. At other times of the day take a taxi or rickshaw to the main road, and flag down the next private bus. Frequent private services run to Palolem and Margao as well as south into **Karnataka**.

Train From **Canacona Junction station**, 2 km away from Palolem beach. The booking office opens 1 hr before trains depart. Inside the station there is a phone booth and a small chai stall. A few auto-rickshaws and taxis meet all trains. If none is available walk down the approach road and turn left under the railway bridge. At the next corner, known locally as Chaurasta, you will find an auto-rickshaw to take you to **Palolem** beach (Rs 50) or **Agonda Beach**; expect to pay double for a taxi.

To **Ernakulam Junction**, *Netravati Exp 16345*, 2325, 15 hrs, sleeper Rs 280, 3 tier a/c Rs 790, and on to **Thiruvananthapuram** (20 hrs); **Mangalore**, *Matsyagandha Exp 12619*,

0020, 6 hrs, Rs 49; **Margao**, 2 passenger trains a day, *KAM 2up*, 0630, *KAR 2up*, 1237, 45 mins, Rs 11; **Mumbai (Tilak)**, *Netravati Exp 16346*, 0548, 13 hrs, 2nd class sleeper Rs 300, 3 tier a/c Rs 800; via Margao 45 mins; **Mumbai (Thane)**, *Matsyagandha Exp 12620*, 2010, 12 hrs; via Margao 45 mins.

Beaches further south *p1288*

Bus/taxi For **Canacona**, buses run to Palolem and Margao and also to Karnataka. You can hire a bicycle for Rs 4 per hr or Rs 35 per day. Direct buses for Margao leave at around 0615, 0730, 0930, 1415, 1515, 1630 and take an hour. Alternatively, take a taxi or rickshaw to the main road and flag down the next private bus. Palolem is 3 km from **Canacona Junction train station**, which is now on the Konkan line (*Netravati Express*).

Directory

Margao *p1281, map p1282*

Banks ATMs on Station Rd, in market, and on both sides of the municipal gardens. **State Bank of India**, west of the Municipal Gardens. Get exchange before visiting beaches to the south where it is more difficult. International money transfer is possible through **Weizmann**, Miguel Miranda Building, near Mohidin Petrol Pump (Mon-Sat 1000-1800). There is also a branch in Colva. **Internet Cyber Inn**, 105 Karnika Chambers, V Valauliker Rd, 0900-2000, Rs 30 per hr; **Cyber Link**, Shop 9, Rangavi Complex. **Medical services** Ambulance T102; **Hospicio**, T0832-270 5664; **Holy Spirit Pharmacy**, 24 hrs. **Police** T0832-272 2175; emergency T100. **Post** North of children's park; **Poste Restante**, near the telegraph office, down lane west of park, Mon-Sat 0830-1030 and 1500-1700.

Benaulim *p1284, map p1285*

Bank Bank of Baroda, near Maria Hall, has ATM and best rates for exchange. **Bank of Baroda**, near the church in Cavelossim, Mon-Wed, Fri, Sat 0930-1330, accepts Visa, MasterCard, TCs; helpful staff. **Internet GK Communications**, Beach Rd. 24-hr phone, money exchange and internet with 4 terminals, book ahead when very busy, Rs 100 per hr. **Medical services** Late night pharmacy near the main crossroads.

Palolem *p1288*

Banks Several exchanges along the beach approach road issue cash against credit cards, usual commission, 3-5%. **Internet** Widely available throughout the village, rates approximately Rs 60 per hr. **Post** Nearest in Canacona. **Useful contacts Petrol Aryadurga** HP station 1 km north of the Palolem turning, towards Margao.

Ponda and interior Sanguem

There is enough spirituality and architecture in the neighbouring districts of Ponda and Salcete to reverse even the most cynical notions of Goa as a state rich in beach but weak on culture. Once you've had your fill of basking on the sand you'll find that delving into this geographically small area will open a window on a whole new, and richly rewarding, Goa.

Just over the water lies Salcete and the villages of Goa's most sophisticated and urbane elite, steeped in the very staunchest Catholicism. Here you can see the most eloquent symbols of the graceful living enjoyed by this aristocracy in the shape of palatial private homes, the fruits of their collusion with the colonizers in faith. Ironically, one of the finest – Braganza House in Chandor – is also the ancestral home of one of the state's most vaunted freedom fighters, Luis de Menezes-Braganza. ▸▸ *For listings, see pages 1307-1308.*

Ponda and around → *For listings, see pages 1307-1308. Colour map 5a, B2.*

Ponda, once a centre of culture, music, drama and poetry, is Goa's smallest *taluka*. It is also the richest in Goan Hindu religious architecture. A stone's throw from the Portuguese capital of Old Goa and within 5 km of the district's traffic-snarled and fume-filled town centre are some of Goa's most important temples including the Shri Shantadurga at Queula and the Nagesh Temple near Bandora. Ponda is also a pastoral haven full of spice gardens and wonderfully scenic views from low hills over sweeping rivers. The Bondla Sanctuary in the east of the *taluka*, though small and underwhelming in terms of wildlife, is a vestige of the forest-rich environment that once cloaked the entire foothills of the Western Ghats.

Ins and outs

Getting there and around Ponda town is an important transport intersection where the main road from Margao via Borlim meets the east–west National Highway, NH4A. Buses to Panjim and Bondla via Tisk run along the NH4A, which passes through the centre of town. The temples are spread out so it's best to have your own transport: take a bike or charter an auto-rickshaw or taxi; you'll find these around the bus stand. ▸▸ *See Transport, page 1308.*

History

The Zuari River represented the stormy boundary between the Christianized Old Conquests and the Hindu east for two centuries. St Francis Xavier found a dissolute band of European degenerates in the first settlers when he arrived in the headquarters of Luso-India and recommended the formation of an Inquisition. Founded in 1560 to redress the failings within their own community, the Portuguese panel's remit quickly broadened as they found that their earliest Goan converts were also clinging clandestinely to their former faith. So the inquisitors set about weeding out these 'furtive Hindus', too, seeking to impose a Catholic orthodoxy and holding great show trials every few years with the public executions of infidels. Outside those dates set aside for putting people to death, intimidation was slightly more subtle: shrines were desecrated, temple tanks polluted and landowners threatened with confiscation of their holdings to encourage defection. Those unwilling to switch religion instead had to look for places to flee, carrying their idols in their hands.

When the conquistadors (or *descubridores*) took to sacking shrines and desecrating temples, building churches in their place, the keepers of the Hindu faith fled for the broad river banks and the Cumbarjua creek to its west, to build new homes for their gods.

Ponda

Ponda wasn't always the poster-boy for Goa's Hindu identity that it is today. The **Safa Mosque** (Shahouri Masjid), the largest of 26 mosques in Goa, was built by Ibrahim 'Ali' Adil Shah in 1560.

It has a simple rectangular chamber on a low plinth, with a pointed pitched roof, very much in the local architectural style, but the arches are distinctly Bijapuri. Because it was built of laterite the lower tier has been quite badly eroded. On the south side is a tank with *meherab* designs for ritual cleansing. The gardens and fountains were destroyed under the Portuguese, today the mosque's backdrop is set off by low rising forest-covered hills.

Khandepar

Meanwhile, for a picture of Goa's Buddhist history, travel 4 km east from Ponda on the NH4A to Khandepar to visit Goa's best-preserved cave site. Believed to be Buddhist, it dates from the 10th or 11th century. The first three of the four laterite caves have an outer and an inner cell, possibly used as monks' living quarters. Much more refined than others discovered in Goa, they show clear evidence of schist frames for doors to the inner cells, sockets on which wooden doors would have been hung, pegs carved out of the walls for hanging clothing, and niches for storage and for placing lamps. The site is hidden on the edge of a wooded area near a tributary of the Mandovi: turn left off the main road from Ponda, look for the green and red archaeological survey sign, just before the bridge over the river. Turn right after the football pitch then walk down the track off to the right by the electric substation.

Farmagudi

On the left as you approach Farmagudi from Ponda is a **Ganesh temple** built by Goa's first chief minister, Shri D Bandodkar, back in the 1960s. It is an amalgam of ancient and modern styles. Opposite is a statue of Sivaji commemorating the Maratha leader's association with **Ponda's Fort**. The fort was built by the Adil Shahis of Bijapur and destroyed by the Portuguese in 1549. It lay in ruins for over a century before Sivaji conquered the town in 1675 and rebuilt it. The Portuguese viceroy attempted to re-take it in October 1683 but quickly withdrew, afraid to take on the Maratha King Sambhaji, who suddenly appeared with his vast army.

Velinga

Lakshmi-Narasimha Temple ⓘ *just north of Farmagudi at Velinga, from the north take a right immediately after crossing a small river bridge*, is Goa's only temple to Vishnu's fourth avatar. The small half-man, half-lion image at this 18th-century temple was whisked away from the torches of Captain Diogo Rodrigues in 1567 Salcete. Its tower and dome over the sanctuary are markedly Islamic. Inside there are well-carved wooden pillars in the *mandapa* and elaborate silverwork on the screen and shrine.

Priol

Shri Mangesh Temple ⓘ *Priol, northwest of Ponda on a wooded hill, on the NH4A leading to Old Goa*, is an 18th-century temple to Siva's incarnation as the benevolent Mangesh is one of the most important temples in Goa. Its Mangesh *lingam* originally belonged to an ancient temple in Kushatali (Cortalim) across the river. The complex is typical of Goan Hindu temple architecture and the surrounding estate provides a beautiful setting. Note the attractive tank on the left as you approach, which is one of the oldest parts of the site. The complex, with its *agrashalas* (pilgrims' hostel), administrative offices and other rooms set aside for religious ceremonies, is a good representative of Goan Hindu temple worship: the temple is supported by a large community who serve its various functions. February 25 is **Jatra**.

Mardol

Two kilometres on from Shri Mangesh, the early 16th-century **Mahalsa Narayani Temple** is dedicated to Mahalsa, a Goan form of Vishnu's consort Lakshmi or, according to some, the god himself in female form *Mohini* (from the story of the battle between the *devas* and *asuras*). The deity was rescued from what was once a fabulous temple in Verna at around the same time as the Mangesh Sivalinga was brought to Priol. The entrance to the temple complex is through the arch under the *nagarkhana* (drum room). There is a seven- storeyed *deepstambha* and a tall brass Garuda pillar which rests on the back of a turtle, acting as an impressive second lamp tower. The half-human half-eagle *Garuda*, Vishnu's vehicle, sits on top. A stone 'cosmic pillar' with rings, next to it, signifies the axis along which the temple is aligned. The new *mandapa* (columned assembly hall) is made of concrete, but is hidden somewhat under the red tiling, finely carved columns and a series of brightly painted carvings of the 10 *avatars*, or incarnations, of Vishnu. The unusual dome above the sanctuary is particularly elegant. A decorative arched gate at the back leads to the peace and cool of the palm-fringed temple tank. A palanquin procession with the deity marks the February **Mardol Jatra**, **Mahasivaratri** is observed in February/March and **Kojagiri Purnima** celebrated at the August/September full moon.

Bandora

A narrow winding lane dips down to this tiny hamlet and its **temple** ⓘ *head 4 km west from Ponda towards Farmagudi on the NH4A, looking for a fork signposted to Bandora*, to Siva as Nagesh (God of Serpents). The temple's origin is put at 1413 by an inscribed tablet here, though the temple was refurbished in the 18th century. The temple tank, which is well stocked with carp, is enclosed by a white-outlined laterite block wall and surrounded by shady palms. The five-storey lamp tower near the temple has brightly coloured deities painted in niches just above the base, the main *mandapa* (assembly hall) has interesting painted woodcarvings illustrating stories from the epics *Ramayana* and *Mahabharata* below the ceiling line, as well as the *Ashtadikpalas*, the eight Directional Guardians (Indra, Agni, Yama, Nirritti, Varuna, Vayu, Kubera and Ishana). The principal deity has the usual *Nandi* and in addition there are shrines to Ganesh and Lakshmi-Narayan and subsidiary shrines with *lingams*, in the courtyard. The **Nagesh Jatra**, normally in November, is celebrated at full moon to commemorate Siva's victory.

In a valley south of the Nagesh Temple lies the **Mahalakshmi Temple**, thought to be the original form of the deity of the Shakti cult. Mahalakshmi was worshipped by the Silaharas (chieftains of the Rashtrakutas, AD 750-1030) and the early Kadamba kings. The sanctuary has an octagonal tower and dome, while the side entrances have shallow domes. The stone slab with the Marathi inscription dating from 1413 on the front of the Nagesh Temple refers to a temple to Mahalakshmi at Bandora. The *sabhamandap* has an impressive gallery of 18 wooden images of Vishnu. Mahalakshmi is special in that she wears a *lingam* in her headdress and is believed to be a peaceful, 'Satvik', form of Devi; the first temple the Portuguese allowed at Panjim is also dedicated to her.

Queula (Kavale)

Just 3 km southwest from Ponda's Central Bus Stand is one of the largest and most famous of Goa's temples; dedicated to Shantadurga (1738), the wife of Siva as the Goddess of Peace. She earns the Shanti (Sanskrit for peace) prefix here because, at the request of Brahma, she mediated in a great quarrel between her husband and Vishnu, and restored peace in the universe. In the sanctuary here she stands symbolically between the two bickering gods. The temple, which stands in a forest clearing, was built by Shahu, the grandson of the mighty Maratha ruler Sivaji, but the deity was taken from Quelossim well before then, back in the 16th century. It is neoclassical in design: the two-storey octagonal drum, topped by a dome with a lantern, is a classic example of the strong impact church architecture made on Goan temple design. The interior of polished marble is lit by several chandeliers. Steps lead up to the temple complex which has a large tank cut into the hillside and a spacious courtyard surrounded by the usual pilgrim hostels and administration offices.

Shri Sausthan Goud Padacharya Kavale Math, named after the historic seer and exponent of the Advaita system of Vedanta, was founded between Cortalim and Quelossim. This Hindu seminary was destroyed during the Inquisition in the 1560s and was temporarily transferred to

Golvan and Chinar outside Goa. After 77 years, in the early 17th century, the Math regrouped here in Queula, the village where the Shantadurga deity (which had also originated in Quelossim) had been reinstalled. There is a temple to Vittala at the Math. The foundation has another Math at Sanquelim.

North of Ponda → *For listings, see pages 1307-1308. Colour map 5a, B2.*

Spice Hills

There are a number of spice plantations in the foothills around northeast Ponda that have thrown open their gates to offer in-depth tours that detail medicinal and food uses of plants during a walk through these cultivated forests. These are surprisingly informative and fun. Of these, Savoi Spice Plantation is probably the most popular and the guide is excellent. Taxis from the coastal resorts cost around Rs 700 return from Candolim, but it's better value to ask a travel agent as many offer competitive rates including entrance fees.

Savoi Spice Plantation ⓘ *6 km from Savoi, T0832-234 0272, www.savoiplantation.com, 1030-1730, tour Rs 350, 1 hr, awkward to reach by public transport, ask buses from Ponda or Banastari heading for Volvoi for the plantation*, now over 200 years old, covers 40 ha around a large irrigation tank. Half the area is wetland and the other half on a hillside, making it possible for a large variety of plants and trees to grow. The plantation was founded by Mr Shetye and is now in the hands of the fourth generation of his family, who regularly donate funds to local community projects such as the school and temple. All plants are grown according to traditional Goan methods of organic farming. The tour includes drinks and snacks on arrival, and concludes with the chance to buy packets of spices (good gifts to take home) and a tot of *feni* to 'give strength' for the return journey to your resort. You will even be offered several cheap, natural alternatives to Viagra, whether you need them or not.

Pascoal Spice Plantation ⓘ *signposted 1.5 km off the NH4A, near Khandepar between Ponda and Tisk, T0832-234 4268, 0800-1800, tours Rs 300*, is pleasantly located by a river and grows a wide variety of spices and exotic fruit. A guided tour takes you through a beautiful and fascinating setting. Spices can be bought directly from the plantation.

Sahakari Spice Farm ⓘ *on the Ponda–Khandepar road, Curti, T0832-231 1394*, is also open to the public. The spice tour includes an authentic banana-leaf lunch.

Tropical Spice Plantation ⓘ *Keri, clearly signposted off the NH4A (just south of the Sri Mangesh Temple), T0832-234 0625, tours Rs 300, boats for hire Rs 100*, is a very pleasant plantation situated in a picturesque valley. Guides are well informed and staff are friendly. It specializes in medicinal uses for the spices, the majority of which seem to be good for the skin. At the end of the tour an areca nut picker will demonstrate the art of harvesting by shinning up a tall palm with his feet tied together in a circle of rope. The demonstration ends with the equally impressive art of descent, a rapid slide down the trunk like a fireman. After the tour a delicious lunch is served in the shade overlooking a lake where there are a couple of boats for hire. Visitors arriving in the early morning will find the boats an excellent opportunity for viewing the varied birdlife around the lake.

Bondla Wildlife Sanctuary

ⓘ *20 km northeast of Ponda, mid-Sep to mid-Jun, Fri-Wed 0930-1730. Rs 5, camera Rs 25, video Rs 100, 2-wheelers Rs 10, cars Rs 50. Buses from Ponda via Tisk and Usgaon stop near the sanctuary where you can get taxis and motorcycle taxis. KTC buses sometimes run weekends from Panjim. During the season the Forest Department minibus runs twice daily (except Thu) between Bondla and Tisk: from Bondla, 0815, 1745; from Tisk, 1100 (Sun 1030) and 1900. Check at the tourist office. If you are on a motorbike make sure you fill up with petrol; the nearest pumps are at Ponda and Tisk. Bondla is well signposted from the NH4A east of Ponda (5 km beyond Usgaon, a fork to the right leads to the park up a winding steep road).*

Bondla is the most popular of Goa's three sanctuaries because it is relatively easily accessible. The 8-sq-km sanctuary is situated in the foothills of the Western Ghats; sambar, wild boar, gaur (Indian bison) and monkeys live alongside a few migratory elephants that wander in from Karnataka during the summer. The mini-zoo here guarantees sightings of 'Goa's wildlife in natural surroundings', although whether the porcupine and African lion are examples of indigenous species is another matter. Thankfully, the number of animals in the zoo has decreased in recent years and those that remain seem to have adequate space compared to other zoos in India. The small **Nature Education Centre** has the facility to show wildlife videos, but is rarely used. Five-minute elephant rides are available 1100-1200 and 1600-1700. A deer safari (minimum eight people), 1600-1730, costs Rs 10. The park also has an attractive picnic area in a botanical garden setting and a 2.4-km nature trail with waterholes, lake and treetop observation tower.

Central and southern interior → *For listings, see pages 1307-1308. Colour map 5a, B2/3.*

Sanguem, Goa's largest *taluka*, covers the state's eastern hill borderland with the South Indian state of Karnataka. The still-forested hills, populated until recently by tribal peoples practising shifting cultivation, rise to Goa's highest points. Just on the Goan side of the border with Karnataka are the Dudhsagar Falls, some of India's highest waterfalls, where the river, which ultimately flows into the Mandovi, cascades dramatically down the hillside. Both the Bhagwan Mahaveer Sanctuary and the beautiful, small Tambdi Surla Temple can be reached in a day from the coast (about two hours from Panaji).

Ins and outs

Getting there Buses running along the NH4A between Panjim, Ponda or Margao and Belgaum or Bengaluru (Bangalore) in Karnataka stop at Molem, in the north of the *taluka*. Much of the southeastern part of Sanguem remains inaccessible. Trains towards Karnataka stop at Kulem (Colem) and Dudhsagar stations. Jeeps wait at Kulem to transfer tourists to the waterfalls. If you are travelling to Tambdi Surla or the falls from north or central Goa, then the best and most direct route is the NH4A via Ponda. By going to or from the southern beaches of Salcete or Canacona you can travel through an interesting cluster of villages, only really accessible if you have your own transport, to see the sites of rock-cut caves and prehistoric cave art. ▸▸ *See Transport, page 1308.*

Getting around There is no direct public transport between Molem and the sites, but the town is the start of hikes and treks in December and January.

Bhagwan Mahaveer Sanctuary → *Colour map 5a, B3.*

ⓘ *29 km east of Pondon on NH4A, T0832-260 0231, or contact Forest Dept in Canacona, T0832-296 5601. Open 0700-1730 except public holidays. Rs 5, 2-wheelers Rs 10, cars Rs 250. Entrance to Molem National Park, within the sanctuary, 100 m east of the Tourist Complex, is clearly signed but the 14 km of tracks in the park are not mapped. Tickets at the Nature Interpretation Centre, 100 m from the police check post in Molem.*

Goa's largest wildlife sanctuary holds 240 sq km of lush moist deciduous to evergreen forest types and a herd of gaur (*bos gaurus*, aka Indian bison). The **Molem National Park**, in the central section of the sanctuary, occupies about half the area with the **Dudhsagar Falls** located in its southeast corner; the remote **Tambdi Surla Temple** is hidden in the dense forest at the northern end of the sanctuary. Forest department jeeps are available for viewing within the sanctuary; contact the Range Forest Officer (Wildlife), Molem. Motorbikes, but not scooters, can manage the rough track outside the monsoon period. In theory it is possible to reach Devil's Canyon and Dudhsagar Falls via the road next to the Nature Interpretation Centre, although the road is very rough and it may require a guide. Make sure you have a full tank of petrol if attempting a long journey into the forest.

Sambar, barking deer, monkeys and rich birdlife are occasionally joined by elephants that wander in from neighbouring Karnataka during the summer months, but these are rarely spotted. Birds include the striking golden oriole, emerald dove, paradise flycatcher, malabar hornbill and trogon and crested serpent eagle.

Dudhsagar Falls

ⓘ *The 2779 Goa Express leaves Margao daily at 1549, and reaches the falls late in the afternoon. It's a spectacular journey worth taking in its own right, as the railway tracks climb right across the cascades, but trains no longer stop at the falls themselves; to get to the pools at the bottom you can take a road from Kulem, where jeep owners offer 'safaris' through the jungle to the base of the falls. If taking the train simply for the view, it's best to travel through to Belgaum in Karnataka, from where there are good bus and train services back to Goa.*

The Dudhsagar Falls on the border between Goa and Karnataka are the highest in India and measure a total drop of about 600 m. The name, meaning 'the sea of milk', is derived from the white foam that the force of the water creates as it drops in stages, forming pools along the way. They are best seen just after the monsoon, between October and December, but right up to April there is enough water to make a visit worthwhile. You need to be fit and athletic to visit the falls. It's no longer possible to visit Dudhsagar by train, but we have retained the following description in case the station re-opens in the near future.

From the train station, a rough, steep path takes you down to a viewing area which allows you a better appreciation of the falls' grandeur, and to a beautifully fresh pool which is lovely for a swim (take your costume and towel). There are further pools below but you need to be sure-footed. The final section of the journey is a scramble on foot across stream beds with boulders; it is a difficult task for anyone but the most athletic. For the really fit and adventurous the arduous climb up to the head of the falls with a guide, is well worth the effort. Allow three hours, plus some time to rest at the top.

By road, motorbikes, but not scooters, can get to the start of the trail to the falls from Molem crossroads by taking the road south towards Kulem. From there it is 17 km of rough track with at least two river crossings, so is not recommended after a long period of heavy rain. The ride through the forest is very attractive and the reward at the end spectacular, even in the dry season. A swim in the pool at the falls is particularly refreshing after a hot and dusty ride. Guides are available but the track is easy to follow even without one.

Tambdi Surla

ⓘ *A taxi from Panjim takes about 2½ hrs for the 69-km journey. There is no public transport to Tambdi Surla but it is possible to hike from Molem. From the crossroads at Molem on the NH4A, the road north goes through dense forest to Tambdi Surla. 4 km from the crossroads you reach a fork. Take the right fork and after a further 3 km take a right turn at Barabhumi village (there is a sign). The temple is a further 8 km, just after Shanti Nature Resort. Make sure you have enough petrol before leaving Molem. It is also possible to reach the site along minor roads from Valpoi. The entrance to the temple is a short walk from the car park.*

This Mahadeva (Siva) Temple is a beautifully preserved miniature example of early Hindu temple architecture from the Kadamba-Yadava period. Tucked into the forested foothills, the place is often deserted, although the compound is well maintained by the Archaeology Department. The temple is the only major remaining example of pre-Portuguese Hindu architecture in Goa; it may well have been saved from destruction by its very remoteness.

Ponda and interior Sanguem listings

For Sleeping and Eating price codes and other relevant information, see Essentials pages 38-42.

Sleeping

Ponda *p1301*

Ponda is within easy reach of any of Goa's beach resorts and Panjim.

C-D Menino, 100 m east of bus stand junction, 1st floor, T0832-231 4147. 20 rooms, some a/c, pleasant, comfortable, good restaurant serves generous main courses, impressive modern hotel, good value.

E Padmavi, Gaunekar House, 100 m north of bus stand on NH4A, T0832-231 2144. Some of the 20 large clean rooms, have bath and TV.

E President, 1 km east of bus stand, supermarket complex, T0832-231 2803. 11 rooms, basic but clean and reasonable.

Farmagudi *p1302*

C-D Atish, just below Ganesh Temple on NH4A, T0832-233 5124, www.hotelatish.com. 40 comfortable rooms, some a/c, restaurant, large pool in open surrounds, gym, modern hotel, many pilgrim groups, friendly staff.

D-E Farmagudi Residency (GTDC), attractively located though too close to NH4A, T0832-233 5125. 39 clean rooms, some a/c, dorm (Rs 150), adequate restaurant (eat at **Atish**, above).

Spice Hills *p1304*

B Savoi Farmhouse, Savoi Plantation, T0832-234 0243, www.savoiplantations.com. An idyllic traditional Goan-style farmhouse built from mud with 2 adjoining en suite double rooms each with private veranda. Electricity and hot water; rates are for full board and include plantation tour. A night in the forest is memorable, highly recommended. Ideally, stay 2 nights exploring deep into the forested hills, good for birdwatching.

Bondla Wildlife Sanctuary *p1304*

F Eco-Cottages, reserve ahead at Deputy Conservator of Forests, Wildlife Division, 4th floor, Junta House, 18th June Rd, Panjim, T0832-222 9701 (although beds are often available to anyone turning up). 8 basic rooms with attached bath, newer ones better. Also 1 km inside park entrance (which may be better for seeing wildlife at night) are 2 dorms of 12 beds each (Rs 30).

Bhagwan Mahaveer Sanctuary *p1305*

There is nowhere to stay inside the sanctuary; take provisions. GTDC accommodation is at the Tourist Complex in Molem, east along the NH4A from the Molem National Park entrance.

E Tourist Resort (GTDC), 300 m east of police check post, about 500 m from the temple, Molem, T0832-260 0238. 3 simple but well-maintained, clean rooms, some a/c, dorm, check-out 1200, giving time for a morning visit to Tambdi Surla, restaurant has limited menu serving north Indian food and beer.

F Molem Forest Resthouse. Book via the Conservator's Office, 3rd floor, Junta House, 18th June Rd, Panjim, T0832-222 4747.

Tambdi Surla *p1306*

C Shanti Nature Resort, 500 m from temple, T0832-261 0012. Emphasis on rest, Ayurvedic treatment and meditation, 9 large mud huts with palm-thatched roofs, electricity and running water in natural forest setting. Restaurant, spice garden visits, birdwatching, hikes, trips to Dudhsagar, etc, arranged (2 nights, US$120). Highly recommended for location and eco-friendly approach.

Eating

Ponda *p1301*

¶ **Amigos**, 2 km east of centre on Belgaum Rd.

¶ **Spoon Age**, Upper Bazaar, T0832-2316191. Garden restaurant serving Goan meals for locals, friendly new set-up. Occasional live music at weekends.

Spice Hills *p1304*

Tropical Spice Plantation offers tasty lunches.

¶¶ **Glade Bar and Restaurant**, Pascoal Spice Plantation. 1130-1800. Good but pricey.

Bondla Wildlife Sanctuary *p1304*

¶ **The Den Bar and Restaurant**, near the entrance. Serves chicken, vegetables or fish with rice. A small cafeteria, inside the park near the mini-zoo, sells snacks and cold drinks.

Activities and tours

Bhagwan Mahaveer Sanctuary *p1305*

Popular hiking routes lead to **Dudhsagar** (17 km), the sanctuary and **Atoll Gad** (12 km), **Matkonda Hill** (10 km) and **Tambdi Surla** (12 km). Contact the **Hiking Association**, 6 Anand Niwas, Swami Vivekananda Rd, Panjim.

Transport

Ponda *p1301*

Bus Buses to **Panjim** and **Bondla** via Tisk (enquiries, T0832-231 1050), but it is best to have your own transport.

Bhagwan Mahaveer Sanctuary *p1305*

If coming from the south, travel via Sanguem. The road from Sanvordem to the NH17 passes through mining country and is therefore badly pot-holed and has heavy lorry traffic. From Kulem, jeeps do the rough trip to **Dudhsagar** (Rs 300 per head, Rs 1800 per jeep). This is a very tough and tiring journey at the best of times. From Molem, a road to the south off the NH4A leads through the forested hills of Sanguem *taluka* to **Kulem** and **Calem** railway stations and then south to **Sanguem**. From there, a minor road northwest goes to **Sanvordem** and then turns west to **Chandor**.

Bus Buses between **Panjim**, **Ponda** or **Margao**, and **Belgaum/Bengaluru** (**Bangalore**), stop at Molem for visiting the Bhagwan Mahaveer Sanctuary and Dudhsagar Falls.

Train From the southern beaches, you can get the Vasco-Colem Passenger from Vasco at 0710, or more conveniently Margao (Madgaon) at 0800, arriving at **Kulem** (**Colem**) at 0930. Return trains at 1640, arriving **Margao** at 1810; leave plenty of time to enjoy the falls. Jeep hire is available from Kulem Station.

Directory

Ponda *p1301*

Banks UTI ATM accepts foreign cards. **Internet** **Fun World.Com**, Viradh Building, T0832-231 6717. **Useful contacts** Deputy Conservator of Forests (North) T0832-231 2095. **Community Health Centre,** T0832-231 2115.

Gujarat

Contents

Footprint features

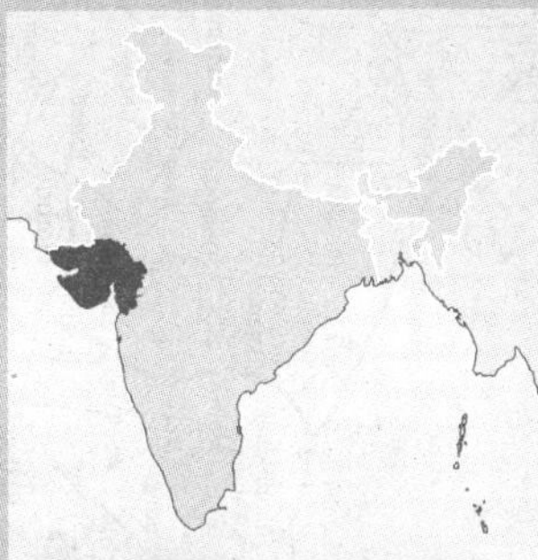

At a glance

Getting around Ahmedabad is the hub for the state, with flights from most big cities. Good train or bus links to all of Gujarat.

Time required 3-4 days for Ahmedabad and nearby sights, minimum 1 week for Saurashtra, 3-4 days for Kachchh.

Weather Dry for most of the year and very cool at night in winter. Best between Oct and Feb.

When not to go Jun and Jul, when even the locals try to escape the crippling heat.

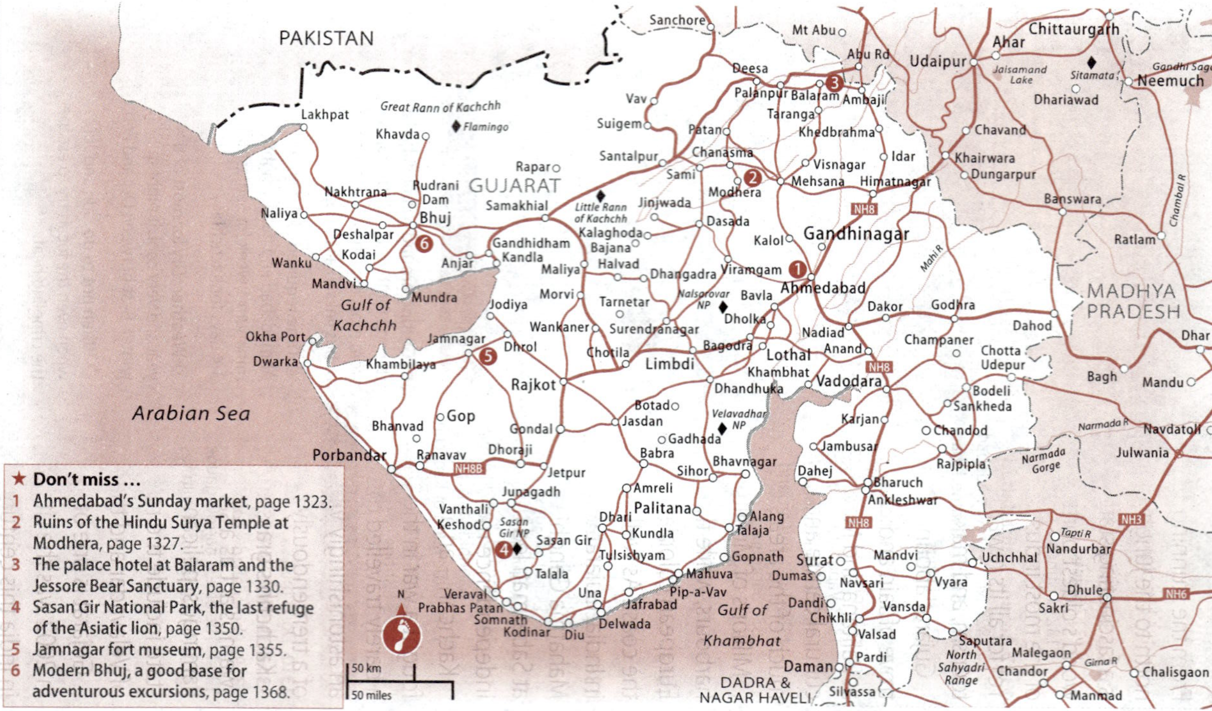

★ **Don't miss …**

1 Ahmedabad's Sunday market, page 1323.
2 Ruins of the Hindu Surya Temple at Modhera, page 1327.
3 The palace hotel at Balaram and the Jessore Bear Sanctuary, page 1330.
4 Sasan Gir National Park, the last refuge of the Asiatic lion, page 1350.
5 Jamnagar fort museum, page 1355.
6 Modern Bhuj, a good base for adventurous excursions, page 1368.

From the stunning salt plains of the Great Rann of Kachcch in the north to the jungle of Sasan Gir National Park in the South, Gujarat is a fascinating state with picturesque landscapes and some of the world's oldest ports. It has the fastest growing economy and is one of the most industrial states – mills and factories dot the horizon. Yet for all its rewards, it remains squarely off the radar of mainstream tourism, and makes a challenging place for independent travel.

Gujarat abounds in anthropological interest, with a treasure trove of Jain and Hindu buildings, including the superb temples at Palitana and Modhera. Ahmedabad, the state's industrial and cultural centre and until recently its capital, is a showcase for much of the area's distinctive regional architecture.

Millions of Muslim pilgrims have set sail for Mecca from Gujarat's harbours, while the 15th-century scramble for supremacy saw European colonial powers set up factories and trading bases along the coast. As well as being the East India Company's first toehold in India, Gujarat was also a key site in the British Empire's decline: Mahatma Gandhi was born at Porbandar and from his ashram at Sabarmati led the Salt March that galvanized India's independence movement.

Kachchh – an arid peninsula over which Pakistan and India fought a war in the 1960s – is India's answer to the Wild West: a barely travelled desert region whose people have developed an astonishingly vibrant cultural identity against the backdrop of a tremendously harsh terrain.

Kachchh's grasslands, salt marshes, mudflats and mangrove swamps act as a sanctuary for wildlife including migratory flamingos, pelicans and wild ass. Other rare species native to the state include the rare swift-footed blackbuck, found on the plains of Velavadar and the Asiatic lions which inhabit Gir National Park.

Gujarat is one of India's most rapidly modernizing states and in 2002 was the site of the worst communal violence to happen in India this century – in riots which cost 1000 lives.

Background → *Population: 50.6 million. Area: 196,000 sq km.*

The land

Geography Gujarat has nearly 1600 km of coastline and nowhere is more than 160 km from the sea. **Kachchh** (Kutch), on the northwest border of the peninsula, rises to heights of around 300 m and, like the plains of the Indus into which it drops almost imperceptibly, it is almost desert. It has a central ridge of Jurassic sandstone with underlying basalts breaking through from place to place. To the north is the Great Rann of Kachchh, a 20,700-sq-km salt marsh. To the south is the Little Rann. During the monsoon the Rann floods, virtually making Kachchh an island, while during the hot dry summer months it is a dusty plain. Earthquakes have had dramatic effects on the landscape. A particularly large quake in 1819 formed a new scarp up to 6 m high and 80 km long, diverting the old channels of the Indus. It has become known as Allah's Bund, or 'God's embankment'. Another severe earthquake hit Gujarat in January 2001 and claimed around 20,000 lives. With its epicentre near Bhuj, the tremors which hit 7.7 on the Richter scale virtually flattened the town and several nearby villages. Limbdi, Halvad and Morvi in Saurashtra were also badly damaged.

The Kathiawad Peninsula, also known as **Saurashtra**, lies to the southeast of the Gulf of Kachchh, bulging southward into the Gulf of Khambhat (Cambay). Rarely rising to more than 180 m, it is flanked by sandstones in the north. Over most of Kathiawad are great sheets of Deccan lavas, cut across by lava dykes. Around the ancient and holy city of Dwarka in the west and Bhavnagar in the east are limestone and clays, separated by a 50-km belt of alluvium, whose creamy-coloured soft stone is widely known as Porbandar stone. **Northeast Gujarat** is a continuation of central Kachchh and is characterized by small plains and low hills. The railway line from Mumbai to Delhi runs through these hills that surround Ahmedabad. The **Western Ghats** extend into southeast Gujarat, the wettest region of the state.

Climate In Ahmedabad the maximum winter temperature is 27°C, although nights are cold and sub-zero cold spells have been recorded. In summer it is extremely hot and maximum temperatures can reach 48°C. Further south the winter temperatures never fall as far, and the summer temperatures are slightly more moderate. In the far south, around Daman, rainfall is still strongly affected by the southwest monsoon and often exceeds 1500 mm, nearly all between June and October. However, because Gujarat is marginal to the main rain-bearing winds the total amounts are highly variable, decreasing rapidly northwards. Ahmedabad normally receives about 900 mm a year while Kachchh, on the borders of the true desert, has recorded less than 25 mm.

History

Some of India's earliest Stone Age settlements developed in these marginal areas; for example, at Rojadi near Rajkot and Adamgarh near the border with Madhya Pradesh. Other Stone Age settlements have been found around the Sabarmati and Mahi rivers in the south and east of the state.

There are a number of **Indus Valley** and **Harappan** centres such as Lothal, Dhoravira, Rangpur, Amri, Lakhabaval and Rozdi. The discovery of a copper ring with a spiral motif, similar to those found in artefacts of ancient Crete, points to the significance of Kuntasi, a Harappan port with a 'factory'. The unusual double fortifications seem to date from two periods (circa 2200 BC and 1900-1700 BC).

Rock edicts in the Girnar Hills indicate that Asoka extended his domain into Gujarat. The Sakas (Scythians; AD 130-390) controlled it after the fall of the Mauryan Empire. During the fourth and fifth centuries it formed part of the Gupta Empire. Gujarat attained its greatest territorial extent under the Solanki Dynasty, from the ninth century. The Vaghela Dynasty that followed was defeated by the Muslim Ala-ud-din Khalji, the King of Delhi. There was then a

The Wild West

A visit to Gujarat can be rewarding but you must be prepared for slow and arduous journeys on public transport and be aware that English is only sporadically spoken outside the larger cities and tourist towns.

A good option is to hire a car with driver or splash out on the *Royal Orient*, Gujarat's answer to the famous 'Palace on Wheels'. It uses the metre-gauge railway carriages no longer needed in Rajasthan and runs a somewhat whirlwind eight-night tour from Delhi visiting Chittaurgarh, Udaipur, Junagadh, Somnath, Sasan Gir, Diu, Palitana, Ahmedabad and Jaipur. Contact the **Royal Orient**, A/6 Emporia Building, Baba Kharak Singh Marg, Delhi, T011-2336 4724, www.royalorienttrain.com.

Hotels in atmospheric old palaces and converted forts offer the chance to stay off-the-beaten track, but should be booked in advance. Contact a tour operator such as **North West Safaries**, see page 1325.

long period of Muslim rule. Ahmad Shah I, the first independent Muslim ruler of Gujarat, founded Ahmadabad in 1411.

The Mughal ruler Humayun fought a brilliant campaign in 1534-1535 to take Malwa and Gujarat, but soon lost them. His son, Akbar, reclaimed both areas in a similarly daring and inspired military operation; this saw the start of two centuries of Mughal rule, only terminated by the Marathas in the mid-18th century.

In the 17th-century scramble for trading bases the Dutch, English, French and Portuguese all established coastal ports here: the British East India Company's first headquarters in India was at Surat, before moving to Bombay. As the British established maritime supremacy all but the Portuguese at Daman and Diu withdrew. The state came under first the control of East India Company in 1818 and, after the 1857 Mutiny (Rebellion), the Crown. The state was then divided into Gujarat province (25,900 sq km), with the rest composed of princely states.

Art and architecture

Gujarati provincial architecture flowered between 1300 and 1550, so on conquering the state its new Muslim rulers inherited highly skilled Hindu and Jain craftsmen who built mosques and tombs that marry Islamic architectural principles with Hindu and Jain motifs.

Culture

About 15% of the **population** is tribal, including the Bhil, Bhangi, Koli, Dhubla, Naikda and Macchi-Kharwa. Mahatma Gandhi was strongly influenced by Jainism, which remains strong in Gujarat today. Gandhi also rejected the deep divisions between high and low caste Hindus, renamed the 'untouchables' as Harijans (God's people), and fought for their rights and dignity. Caste division remains a potent political force in Gujarat today. Most people speak Gujarati, an Indo-Aryan **language** of Sanskrit origin but with some Persian, Arabic, Portuguese and English vocabulary deriving from maritime contacts. In the 19th century many Gujaratis went first to East Africa and thence to England, North America and New Zealand. Within India, Gujaratis are prominent in the business community, and have gained a reputation for philanthropy and spiritual endeavour; even today it is not uncommon for businessmen in the later stages of life to renounce their material possessions and strike out, sometimes with their family in tow, on the ascetic path of the wandering sanyasin.

Despite an abundance of fish and shellfish, Jain and Hindu orthodoxy has encouraged vegetarianism. The Gujarati diet is chiefly rice, wholemeal *chapati*, a variety of beans and pulses rich in protein, and coconut and pickles; a *thali* would include all these, the meal ending with sweetened yoghurt. The dishes themselves are mild, though somewhat sweeter than those of neighbouring states. Popular dishes include: *kadhi*, a savoury yoghurt curry with chopped vegetables and a variety of spices; *undhyoo*, a combination of potatoes, sweet potatoes, aubergines (eggplants) and beans cooked in an earthenware pot in the fire; Surat *paunk* made with tender kernels of millet, sugar balls, savoury twists and garlic chutney. *Ganthia* or *farsan* (light savoury snacks prepared from chickpea and wheat flour), is a regional speciality. Desserts are very sweet. Surat specializes in *gharis* of butter, dried fruit and thickened milk and rich *halwa*. *Srikhand* is saffron-flavoured yoghurt with fruit and nuts.

Modern Gujarat

At Independence in 1947, Gujarat proper was incorporated into Bombay state. In 1956 Saurashtra and Kachchh were added; on 1 May 1960 Bombay state was split into present day Maharashtra and Gujarat states. in 1961 India forcibly annexed the Portuguese possessions of Daman and Diu (along with Goa). After Partition, India and Pakistan disputed the Rann of Kachchh and fought a war over it in 1965. Following the ceasefire on 1 July, an international tribunal recommended that 90% should remain with India and 10% pass to Pakistan.

Gujarat remained one of the Congress Party's chief strongholds for almost the entire first 40 years after Independence. It produced a number of national leaders after Mahatma Gandhi, including the first prime minister of the Janata government in 1977, Morarji Desai. However, since the State Assembly elections of March 1995 the BJP has held control. In the Assembly elections of 2007 the BJP won 117 of the 182 seats, the Congress claiming 59. A landmark piece of investigative journalism by Indian news weekly *Tehelka* exposed the complicit role of chief minister Narendrar Modi in sanctioning three days of bitter communal violence that saw close to 800 Muslims killed in a reprisal for a Muslim fire attack on a train returning from disputed holy site Ayodhya, in which 58 Hindu pilgrims died. These claims have still not been proved in court. Despite his reputation as the economic moderniser, the BJP only narrowly managed to win majority of the seats in Gujarat during the 2009 Lok Sabha Polls, losing the Rajkot seat after almost 20 years of control. In 2010-2011, the hopes of a resurgent Congress were defeated when the Modi-led BJP swept the civic polls almost everywhere in Gujarat, winning even the Muslim-dominated constituencies.

Gujarat is one of India's leading industrial states. Building on the cotton textile industry established in the 19th century, chemicals and petrochemicals, fertilizers and cement and engineering industries all have a major role. The state also has huge petrochemical complexes, Reliance's new factory at Jamnagar being one of the biggest oil-refining and petrochemical complexes in the world. Agriculture remains important, with cotton, tobacco and groundnut important cash crops, and wheat and millet important cereals. Perhaps Gujarat's most striking agricultural development has been its dairy industry. India, now the world's largest milk producer, experienced a revolution in the dairy industry originating in Gujarat's dairy co-operatives'; their milk, butter and cheese now have India-wide markets.

Ahmedabad

→ *Colour map 2, C3. Phone code: 079. Population: 3.5 million.*

The congested former capital Ahmedabad spreads out chaotically along both banks of the Sabarmati River. While the modernized west bank holds busy boulevards lined by shopping malls, the Old City remains a maze of narrow winding alleys with carved wooden house fronts and thriving bazars. The outstanding Calico Museum and Mahatma Gandhi's Sabarmati Ashram, as well as the culinary delights, attract visitors to stop for a day or two, though some find the city's noise and pollution off-putting.
▸▸ *For listings, see pages 1321-1326.*

Ins and outs

Getting there The airport is 13 km northeast of town. Regular city buses collect passengers from the airport and arrive at Lal Darwaza, close to many budget hotels. Taxis charge Rs 200-250 from the airport, autos about Rs 100. Train travellers arrive at the Junction Station to the east of the Old City. Rickety old government buses use the Rajpur Gate Terminus to the south, while private buses depart from an array of informal locations around the city. There are plenty of metered taxis and auto-rickshaws to take you to a hotel. ▸▸ *See Transport, page 1325.*

Getting around Ahmedabad is far too sprawling to cover all the sights on foot so you will need to struggle with local buses or hire an auto or taxi.

Tourist information Gujarat Tourist Office (TCGL) ⓘ *HK House, opposite Bata, Ashram Rd, T079-2658 9172, www.gujarattourism.com; Mon-Sat, closed Sun and 2nd and 4th Sat each month. Also at airport and railway station.* MP Tourist Office ⓘ *T079-2646 2977.* Rajasthan Tourist Office ⓘ *Divya Aptmt, near Mithakali Underbridge, off Ashram Rd, T079-2646 9580.* Prohibition is in force. Ask for a liquor permit on arrival in India at the airport tourist counter; getting one in the city is tortuous. Larger hotels may issue 'spot' permits.

History

Ahmedabad retains a highly distinctive feel born out of a long and continuously evolving social history. It was founded in 1411 by Ahmad Shah I, then king of Gujarat. He made Asaval, an old Hindu town in the south, his seat of power, then expanded it to make it his capital. Almost constantly at war with the neighbouring Rajputs, fortifications were essential. The **Bhadra** towers and the square bastions of the royal citadel were among the first to be built. The city walls had 12 gates, 139 towers and nearly 6000 battlements.

Although most of the **Old City** walls have gone, many monuments remain, some of them striking examples of Indian Islamic architecture. The provincial Gujarati style flourished from the mid-15th century, and in addition to the religious buildings many of the houses have façades beautifully decorated with woodcarving. The Swami Narayan Temple, Kalipur, Rajani Vaishnav Temple and Harkore Haveli, near Manek Chowk as well as *havelis* on Doshiwadani Pol, illustrate traditional carving skills. Unfortunately, much of the old carving has been dismantled to be sold off to collectors.

The **'new' city**, on the west bank, has the site of Mahatma Gandhi's famous Sabarmati Ashram from where he began his historic Salt March in protest against the Salt Law in 1915. Recent developments in urban design have contributed to the city's architectural tradition. Modern Ahmedabad has several showpieces designed by famous architects, among them Le Corbusier, Louis Kahn, Doshi and Correa. The School of Architecture, the National Institute of Design and the Indian Institute of Management (IIM) are national centres of learning.

With a long tradition in craftsmanship under Gujarati Sultans and Mughal Viceroys, Ahmedabad was one of the most brilliant Indian cities. Its jewellers and goldsmiths are still renowned today; its copper and brassworkers craft very fine screens; and carpenters produce fine *shisham* wood articles. There are skilled stone masons, lacquer artists, ivory

1 Ahmedabad

Ahmedabad maps
1 Ahmedabad, page 1316
2 Ahmedabad centre, page 1318

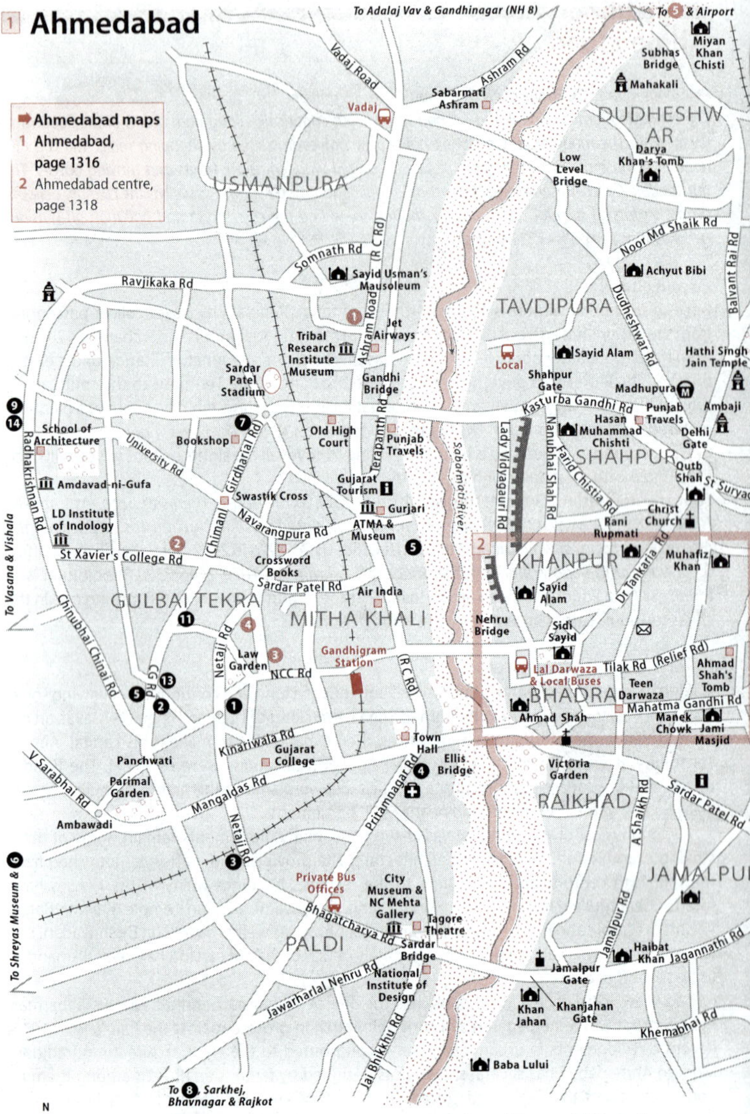

Sleeping
Fortune Landmark **1**
Klassic Gold **2**
Lemontree **4**
Nalanda **3**
Taj Residency Ummed **5**

Eating
Black Knight **2**
Gopi **4**
Jai Siyaram **3**
Mehta **4**
Mirch Masala **7**
New Honest Corner **5**
Rajwadu **6**

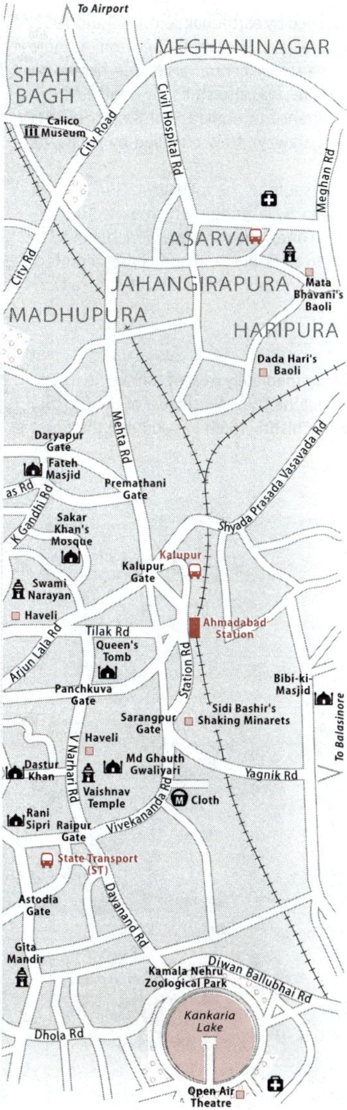

Rasrajan **9**
Sankalp **10**
Sheeba **11**
Swati Snacks **1**
Tomato **13**
Upper Crust **14**
Vallabha **10**
Vishala **8**

and bone carvers, hand-block printers and embroiderers producing exquisite pieces with beads and mirrors.

Sights

In the Jami Masjid, Ahmedabad has one of the best examples of the second period of Gujarat's provincial architectural development. In 1411, Ahmad Shah I, the founder of a new dynasty, laid the foundations of the city that was to be his new capital. By 1423 the Jami Masjid, regarded by many as one of the finest mosques in India, was finished. He encouraged others to construct monumental buildings as well. Mahmud I Begarha (ruled 1459-1511) established the third phase of Gujarati provincial architecture, building some of India's most magnificent Islamic monuments.

The central city

The citadel of the planned city formed a rectangle facing the river. A broad street was designed to run from Ahmad Shah's fortified palace in the citadel to the centre of the city, lying due east. The ancient citadel built by Ahmad Shah I in 1411, now known as the **Bhadra** (see above), lies between the Nehru and Ellis bridges. In the east face is the **Palace**, now the post office. **Sidi Sayid's Mosque** (circa 1570) formed part of the wall on the northeast corner but now stands isolated in a square. Ten windows of wonderful stone tracery depicting a branching tree are famous here, and have become the symbol of the city. Those on the west wall are particularly worthy of note.

Jami Masjid The essential orientation of the Qibla wall to Mecca meant that the main entrance to the mosque itself had to be in its east wall. The mosque was aligned so that the present Mahatma Gandhi Road passed its north entrance. This is still the point at which you enter by a flight of steps. It is pleasantly quiet and peaceful inside. The vegetable and fruit market near the south entrance is worth visiting for the artistic display of stallholders' wares.

The beauty of the sanctuary is emphasized by the spacious courtyard paved in marble, with a tank in the middle. The façade has a screen of arches flanked by a pillared portico.

The two 'shaking minarets', once 26 m high, were destroyed by earthquakes in 1819 and 1957. More than 300 graceful pillars are organized in 15 square bays. The whole rises from a single storey through the two-storey side aisles to the three-storey central aisle. The octagonal lantern, rising through both storeys and covered by a dome, was also strikingly original.

Teen Darwaza is immediately to the east of the entrance to Ahmad Shah's mosque, the triumphal archway also known as the Tripolia (Triple gateway). Now crowded by shops, its effect is considerably diminished.

Northeast of the Astodia Gate and a short distance south of the railway station are **Sidi Bashir's Shaking Minarets**, two tall towers connected by a bridge which was once the entrance to the old mosque (now replaced by a modern one). The minarets were believed to shake or vibrate in sympathy as they are cleverly built on a flexible sandstone base to protect against earthquake damage. **Bibi-ki-Masjid** (1454), Gomtipur, southeast of the railway station, also has a shaking minaret.

The north

Sayid Usman's mausoleum is across the Gandhi bridge, immediately west of Ashram Road. The *rauza* (circa 1460) is one of the first examples of the Begarha style. Northwest of the Old City near Shahpur Gate, the **Mosque of Hasan Muhammad Chishti** (1565) has some of the finest tracery work in Ahmedabad.

2 Ahmedabad centre

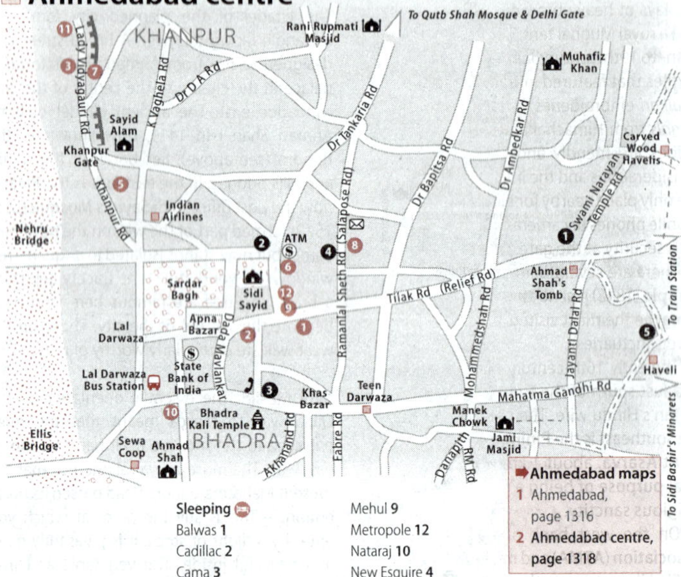

➡ Ahmedabad maps
1 Ahmedabad, page 1316
2 Ahmedabad centre, page 1318

N

200 metres
200 yards

Sleeping
Balwas **1**
Cadillac **2**
Cama **3**
Centra **7**
Host Inn **5**
House of MG, Agashiye, Green House & HBM Restaurants **6**
Kingsway **8**
Mehul **9**
Metropole **12**
Nataraj **10**
New Esquire **4**
Sarovar Portico **11**

Eating
Bhagyodaya **4**
Chetna **1**
Mangaldas Ni Haveli **5**
New Lucky **2**
Paramount **3**

- - - Heritage Walk

Ahmedabad's *pols*

The old parts of the city are divided into unique, self-contained *pols*, or quarters, fascinating to wander round. Huge wooden doors lead off from narrow lanes into a section of houses with decorative wooden screens and brackets where small communities of people practising a craft or skill once lived. Merchants, weavers, woodworkers, printers and jewellers each had their *pol*, their houses strung along winding alleys that met in common courtyards and squares. Today, these old quarters are being developed rapidly, with tower blocks rising up from just inside the Old City walls. The guided Heritage Walk (see page 1325) is an excellent way to see some of those that have survived.

The **Calico Museum** ⓘ *3 km north of Delhi Gate, www.calicomuseum.com, closed Wed and holidays, free, entry only by somewhat rushed guided tour (minimum group size 15, you may have to wait for others to arrive), tours from 1030-1230 (secular textiles), 1445-1645 (religious textiles, plus superb collection of Chola bronzes), last entry 1515; report at least 15 mins before – only 10 are allowed first come first serve and 15 by organized groups; children under 10 are not permitted, guided tour of the garden is by appointment only*, a part of the Sarabhai Trust, is superbly set in an attractive *haveli* in the botanically interesting Shahi Bagh gardens. It is one of the finest museums of its kind in the world. Some exhibits date from the 17th century and include rich displays of heavy brocades, fine embroideries, saris, carpets, turbans, maharajahs' costumes and a royal Mughal tent. The religious section exhibits outstanding medieval Jain manuscripts, 14th- to 19th-century Jain icons, *pichhwais* and *pattachitras*. The secular section contains Indian textiles that featured in trade, historic pieces of tie-dye and embroidery from Gujarat, Punjabi *phulkari* embroideries, *patola* silk saris from Patan, Pashmina shawls from Kashmir, Chamba *rumals* from Himachal and silks from Orissa and South India. It is also open for research. The guides are friendly and charming. Numbers and times are restricted because of lighting considerations and the impact it has on this amazing collection of textiles. **Moti Manor Hotel** is the only place nearby for lunch. Alas, you are not allowed to take any bags, including handbags, mobile phones or cameras into the museum and there is only a haphazard system to leave them with security at the gate. Only take essentials.

There are several Jain temples in the city. The highly decorated white marble **Hathi Singh Temple** (1848) just north of the Delhi Gate, dedicated to Dharamanath, the 15th Jain *Tirthankar*, is maybe the most visited. Along the streets of Ahmedabad, it is common to see Jain *parabdis* (bird sanctuaries).

The early 16th-century **Rani Rupmati Masjid** in Mirzapur district, southwest of Delhi Gate and just south of the **Grand Hotel**, incorporates Hindu and Islamic design. Rupmati was the Sultan's Hindu wife. The carvings in the gallery and the *mihrabs* are particularly attractive. To the southeast is the **Pinjrapol**, or Asylum for Animals.

At **Asarva**, about 1 km northeast of Daryapur Gate, are the *baolis*, which often serve a dual purpose of being a cool, secluded source of water during the summer and a place of religious sanctity.

On the west bank of the Sabarmati there is the **Ahmedabad Textile Mill Owners' Association (ATMA)** and **museum**, both of which were designed by Le Corbusier, see page 459.

Six kilometres north of the centre is Gandhi's Ashram, **Sabarmati Ashram** ⓘ *0830-1800, last admission 30 mins before closing, free, Son et Lumière Sun, Wed, Fri (English 2100), closed during monsoons, Rs 5, donations for upkeep gratefully received*, which was founded in March 1930. It was the starting point for Gandhi's celebrated 385-km Salt March to Dandi in March 1930. He vowed not to return to the ashram until India gained independence. Gandhi and 81 supporters began the march and by the end of it there were 90,000 protesters marching against the unpopular British Salt Tax Laws. Salt manufacture, a government monopoly, was chosen for the protest as it was a commodity every peasant used and could understand. At Dandi beach on 6 April Gandhi went down to the sea and made a small amount of salt, for which he was promptly arrested. In the following months, thousands of Indians followed his example and were arrested by the British. The **Sangrahalaya** includes a library, archives and a picture gallery depicting Gandhi's life in photographs and paintings. Some of the original ashram's work, such as a school for Harijan girls, continues. **Hridaya Kunj**, Gandhi's home for 15 years, containing simple mats, desk, spinning wheel and some personal belongings, overlooks the central prayer corner and the river and remains undisturbed, as does the unfurnished room of his wife, Kasturba.

To the west

LD Institute of Indology Museum ⓘ *Gujarat University Campus*, contains over 3300 pieces of medieval sculpture, many dating from the 11th to 13th centuries, an outstanding Jain section and archaeological finds. The 'caves' of **Amdavad-ni-Gufa** here were an inspirational venture by the architect Doshi and the artist MF Hussain to display their work. Tribal paintings and other works of art are being added.

Shreyas Museum ⓘ *near Shreyas Railway Crossing, winter Tue-Sun 1030-1730, summer Tue-Sun 0830-1300, closed Diwali, Christmas and school summer holidays, Rs 35 (foreigners)*, has a comprehensive collection of contemporary rural textiles from all over Gujarat: excellent beadwork, embroideries, utensils, religious objects and bullock cart accessories. The children's section upstairs exhibits folk art items, including dance costumes, masks and puppets.

The **City Museum** ⓘ *Tue-Sun 1000-1700, free*, an award-winning design by Le Corbusier with ramps of steps leading up from a pool and its fountains, houses interesting exhibits related to Ahmedabad's history and culture, plus an excellent collection of old and contemporary art, which are superbly exhibited. The **NC Mehta Gallery** here has a vast collection of miniatures from the Rajasthan, Mewar, Mughal, and Kangra schools, among others. The series of 150 paintings on the Gita Govinda theme and a set from the Gujarat Sultanate period are rare exhibits.

The **Tribal Research Institute Museum** ⓘ *Gujarat Vidyapith, Ashram Rd, Mon-Fri 1100-1430 and 1500-1800, Sat 1130-1430*, has recreations of tribal hamlets of Gujarat, as well as weapons, implements, wall art, terracotta figurines and textiles. It makes a good first point of contact for anyone keen to visit tribal areas in the state.

To the south

Kamala Nehru Zoological Park ⓘ *Satellite Rd, off M Dayanand Rd, Kankaria, Sat-Thu 1000-1800*, was masterminded by the late Reuben David, a 'captive breeding' genius – note the albino porcupine, squirrel and deer here.

Excursions from Ahmedabad

Vishala, 5 km away, is a purpose-built collection of traditional Gujarati village huts serving *thalis* at lunch and dinner, accompanied by music and traditional dancing. It's especially appealing in the evening when it's lit entirely by lanterns.

Indroda Village Deer Park, next to Sarita Udyan by Sabarmati River, has an interesting reptile collection and well-marked nature trails through forests where you may spot nilgai, porcupine, jackal, crested honey buzzard and paradise fly-catcher, among others. There is also a campsite here.

Adalaj is the hamlet where, in a garden setting, one of the finest step wells in India can be found. The Vav (or *baoli*) shows a combination of Hindu, Muslim and Buddhist styles. A flight of steps descends over 30 m to the water. It has four floors, each cooler than the one above. Ornately carved pillars, niches and cross beams create large octagonal landings (now inaccessible) that served as resting places. Remains of the bullock ramp used for drawing water are still visible. Queen Rupabai is believed to have had it built to provide the traveller with a cool and pleasant refuge from the summer heat. A visit is highly recommended. It is 17 km north of Ahmedabad near the Gandhinagar crossroads; autos charge Rs 125-150 return or take the No 85 city bus from Lal Darwaza to the end, then a shared rickshaw to Adalaj, Rs 5, from where the Vav is a 1-km walk.

Ahmedabad listings

For Sleeping and Eating price codes and other relevant information, see Essentials pages 38-42.

Sleeping

Ahmedabad *p1315, maps p1316 and p1318*

Most hotels are within a few mins' walk of Sidi Sayid Mosque, 3 km from railway station. The **D-E** hotels on Tilak (Relief) Rd between **Chetna Restaurant** and Sidi Sayid Mosque are similar in standard and facilities; most rooms have phone and bath with hot water, some a/c. Some quote a cheaper rate for those arriving on foot rather than by auto- rickshaw, so ask if such a discount is available.

L-A House of MG, opposite Sidi Sayid Mosque, Lal Darwaza, T079-2550 6946, www.houseofmg.com. One of the most atmospheric places you can lay your hat in India. 12 vast, beautifully decorated rooms in a centrally located heritage hotel, surrounded by familial memorabilia it is like stepping into another time, superb indoor pool, 2 excellent restaurants (see Eating, below), friendly, professional staff, best top-bracket choice in the city. Also offers great audio-based and guided walking tours of the Old City – check out the Night Heritage Walk in particular. Far too-tempting shop in the lobby. Highly recommended.

AL-A Cama, Khanpur Rd, T079-2560 1234, www.camahotelsindia.com. Best with river view, 50 a/c rooms, totally renovated and upgraded on 1st and 2nd floors with long bathrooms, communal areas are a little tired, pool (not spotless), garden, good coffee shop, friendly management.

AL-A Fortune Landmark, Ashram Rd, T079-3988 4444, www.fortunelandmark.com. One of the best but on busy main road, massive, 96 varied rooms, worth upgrading to a suite from a standard – more for your buck, good restaurants (buffet breakfast to set you up for the day), health club, jacuzzi pool.

AL-A Lemontree, Mithakali Six Cross Roads, T079-4423 2323, www.lemontreehotels.com. Funky, upmarket chain of hotels offering up boutique style rooms with all the mod cons. Great buffet breakfast and comfortable rooms, could do without the citrus aromatherapy and the "cool" pop tunes playing everywhere though.

A-B Sarovar Portico, Khanpur Rd, T079-2560 1111, www.sarovarhotels.com. Quiet, 69 clean, comfortable rooms (some overlook river), restaurant, free airport transfer, lawn. Discounts available online.

B Klassic Gold, CG Rd, T079-2656 5194, www.klassicgold.com. Good value, 35 rooms on the modern west bank of the river, superb restaurant, efficient management.

B Nalanda, Mithakhali 6 Rd, T079-2646 8899, www.hotelnalanda.in. 44 clean but run-of-the-mill rooms (standard rooms tiny; bath tubs and fridge in the best), good location, excellent restaurant. Free airport transfer.

C Centra, opposite **Cama** (see above), T/F079-2550 0275. Good value but a bit on the shabby side, some a/c, decent restaurant, friendly.

C Host Inn, opposite **Le Meridien**, Khanpur, T079-3022 6555, www.hotelhostinn.com. Clean a/c rooms in well-run hotel, unusual some deluxe rooms have beds on floor, hot water can be problematic, smart restaurant, friendly and obliging manager, staff a little less so. Better value than Centra.

D-E Kingsway, near GPO, T079-2550 1215. 33 large rooms with fan, bath (hot water), modern, small breakfast menu and snacks. Maybe bring your own incense.

D-E Mehul, Hanuman Lane, off Relief Rd opposite Electricity House, T079-2550 6525. Good value clean rooms (small singles) some a/c, good room service. Quieter than nearby hotels thanks to alleyway location and slightly better than its older brother hotel 'Metropole' next door (Metropole T029-2550 7988).

E Balwas, 6751 Relief Rd, near Electricity House, T079-2550 7135. After a facelift, this is the best value of the budgets. 26 clean rooms, 6 small at rear (side entrance), decent restaurant attached but crowded, noisy area, 24-hr checkout.
E-F New Esquire, near **House of MG**, T079-3298 4711. At the time of writing, the whole place was being redecorated, which was transforming the former grunge of this hotel – cheaper than other budgets in the area.
F Nataraj, Dada Mavlankar Rd, near Ahmad Shah Mosque. With a "Do Not Spit" sign to welcome you, this is as simple as it gets, hostel-like.
G Cadilac, opposite Electricity House, Lal Darwaza, T079-2550 7558. Characterful, but dilapidated building with small and basic rooms. Cheap as chapatti with and without bath, helpful travel desk, noisy but cleanish.

Eating

Ahmedabad *p1315, maps p1316 and p1318*
Thalis are around Rs 50; Kathiawadi has more chilly and garlic, while Gujarati is sweetened with sugar and jaggery.

Very cheap (under Rs 30) Indian meals and snacks are available from street stands including Bhatiar Gali, Law Garden, Raipur Gate and IIM Rd. Try *khakhra*, a delicious snack roughly similar to a flaky poppadom, flavoured with fenugreek leaves.

TTT Fortune Landmark (see Sleeping). Pleasant rooftop restaurant, city views, open after dark. Great atmosphere, live music, specializes in kebabs, tandoori, roasts and grills.
TT Agashiye, **House of MG** (see Sleeping). Attractive Gujarati *thali* restaurant on the terrace of a 1920s heritage building. Unique atmosphere, local music, Gujarati *thalis* topped off with hand-churned ice cream flavoured by the fruits of the season. Beautiful decor and setting, although the street noise does bubble up. Recommended.
TT Bhagyodaya, GPO Rd, opposite **Kingsway** (see Sleeping). Good food, varied choice, pleasant outlook.
TT Barbecue Nation, Shivalik III, Drive-In Rd. Chain restaurant popular for kebabs and a "live grill" at your table.
TT Black Knight, Lal Darwaza. Good Indian, Chinese, continental, medieval European theme decor.
TT Green House, **House of MG** (see Sleeping). Even if you don't get to stay at House of MG, both restaurants are exceptional. The downstairs courtyard café serves up a delicious range of traditional Gujarati snacks like patra leaves, potato patties wth coconut or try some spicier *Parsi dhansak*. Their saffron anise *kulfi* is one of the best-selling ice-creams on the menu and their house *sharbat* of coconut water and ginger is delicious. Take a minute to browse the lobby for all the memorabilia and photographs before winding up in their beautiful shop. Highly recommended.
TT Ikobo, next to Doordarshan Kendra, Drive-in Rd. Popular with the well-heeled of Ahmedabad and sating their taste for kebabs, Ikobo serves up a wide range of meat and veg sizzlers and *shashlik* dishes.
TT Mangaldas Ni Haveli, Lakha Patel ni Pol, contact **House of MG** (see Sleeping) for more details. Stunningly restored wooden *haveli* in the heart of the labyrinthine old city boasts a rooftop café which serves up great breakfasts and afternoon teas albeit at the top of a pretty rickety staircase. Lots of character. Guided walks start off here, including the acclaimed Night Heritage Walk.
TT Mirch Masala, Swastik Crossroads, CG Rd. Very spicy North Indian Juhu beach-shack. Bollywood theme with film and posters and music to match. Tempting and hygienic street snacks.
TT Paramount, Teen Darwaja. Indian. Famous for mutton and chicken biryanis, tikkas, a/c.
TT Rajwadu, Jivraj Park. Rural theme restaurant. Rajasthani/Gujarati dinner, delightful open-air garden setting, water courses, folk entertainment, large meals in brass/copper vessels, refills galore, like a Bollywood film set; not as authentic as **Vishalla** but more comfortable and accessible.
TT Sheeba, opposite telephone exchange, Navrangpura. International, a/c, excellent North Indian (try fish, paneer or chicken *tikkas*), friendly. Continental and Chinese fast-food counter (to avoid excess spices, request when ordering). Highly recommended.
TT Swati Snacks, Thakorbhai Hall, Law Garden. Specializing in Gujarati snacks, this slick diner offers up great dishes like *panaki* a rice pancake cooked between banana leaf and *nariyal kothir tikki* stuffed potato patties. Recommended.

Tomato, CG Rd. Western, a/c, 1950s American diner-theme, rock'n'roll-era decor and music, good atmosphere, young crowd; also Mexican and Italian. Coffee shop serves great coffee, nachos, tacos, sandwiches.

Vishala, 5 km southwest of centre. Village theme restaurant, where you sit cross-legged at low tables (low stools also provided), eat proper Gujarati food off green leaves or metal *thalis*, and drink from clay tumblers. Hospitable, friendly staff, interesting traditional dancing after dinner, touristy in an Indian way and good fun. Meals around Rs 200 with deluxe dinners at Rs 450.

Chetna, Krishna Cinema, Relief Rd. Unlimited Gujarati *thalis*.

Gopi, Ashram Rd. A/c, mildly spiced *thalis* for foreigners, good service, family-run.

Jai Siyaram, near Paldi Railway Crossing. Delicious *kesar pedas* (saffron-flavoured milk sweets).

Kamal, Revdi Bazar, near the station. For excellent Indian sweets.

Mehta, Ellis Bridge, *thalis* and snacks.

New Honest Corner, White House, CG Rd. Clean café serving good pan-Indian vegetarian fast food and fresh juices.

New Lucky, Lal Darwaza. Cheap and cheerful chai and snacks counter, popular for early morning 'bun-butter', with a slightly more elaborate South Indian restaurant attached. The best cheap option in the area.

Rasrajan, Vijay Crossroads (a/c). Self service, a/c upstairs. good vegetarian salad bar, Indian and Chinese vegetarian meals.

Sankalp, CG Rd. South Indian, rooftop terrace garden with fountain, good *dosas*. and exceptional range of chutneys. Delicious.

Tulsi, near Gujarat University. North Indian *thalis* and à la carte, a/c.

Upper Crust, Vijay Crossroads. Good breads, cakes and desserts, *kathi kabab* rolls, sizzlers, Sun breakfast (Rs 50).

Vallabha, 1 Jeet Complex, around corner from **Mom's Kitchen** off C G Rd. Excellent Gujarati *thalis*.

Excursions from Ahmedabad *p1320*

Bageshree, on Gandhinagar Highway towards Adalaj. Gujarati *thalis* in lovely garden setting.

Gokul, Gandhinagar Highway. Similar concept to **Vishalla** (see above), Gujarati *thalis* served in huts, folk concerts.

Kathiawadi, near Adalaj crossroads. Highly spiced *thalis*.

Festivals and events

Ahmedabad *p1315, maps p1316 and p1318*

14-15 Jan Makar Sankranti marks the end of winter. It is celebrated with kite flying by people of all ages, accompanied by colourful street markets and festivities. Kites come in all colours, shapes and sizes, the best varieties reputedly being available in Manek Chowk and Tankshala, Kalupur. The flying continues after sunset, when the kites are lit with candles.

Sep/Oct Navratri, honouring Goddess Amba (*Shakti*), has special significance here and at Vadodara. 9 days of music and traditional *Garba Ras* dancing. The custom of women balancing clay pots while they dance is still practised.

Shopping

Ahmedabad *p1315, maps p1316 and p1318*

Shops usually open from 0900-1900, most close on Sun. **Manek Chowk** is the main bazar, while **CG Rd** is the centre for malls, brand outlets and upmarket clothing shops. Other centres are **Relief Rd**, **Ashram Rd**, **Lal Darwaza** and **Kapasia Bazar**. Go to the huge **Sunday Market**, on the river bank at Ellis Bridge, in the morning to pick up 'antiques', handicrafts and second-hand books.

Books

Art Book Centre, Madalpur, near **Inder Residency**.

Crossword, B6 Sri Krishna Centre, Mithakhali 6 Rds, T079-2643 0238. A/c, extensive selection of books, magazines CDs, art supplies and accessories. There is also a branch of **Café Coffee Day** on-site.

Mapin, Darpana Academy, Usmanpura, Ashram Rd. Specializes in Indian arts. Beautiful selection of greetings cards.

Natraj, Ashram Rd, with branches all over the city. Books and CDs.

Handicrafts

Good bargains at **Satellite Rd** and Law Garden (after 1600), where Kachchhi and Saurashtrian artisans sell embroideries, block prints and handicrafts: appliqué bedspreads, wall hangings, etc, but bargain hard.

Garvi and **Gurjari**, Ashram Rd. Govt. Open 1030-1400, 1500-1900. Embroidered dresses, block-printed bedspreads, lacquered furniture, etc, well displayed.

Kamdhenu Complex opposite Polytechnic, Ambawadi. State Handicraft Co-ops.

Shringar, near **Honeycomb**. Sells upmarket 'antiques'.

Treasure, near Judge's bungalow, Satellite Rd. Art and handicrafts gallery. Brassware and woodcarvings are sold at Manek Chowk.

Textiles

Gujarat's famous embroideries, *bandhani* and block prints are sold at **Rani-no-Haziro** and **Dalgarwad** near Manek Chowk in the walled city. There are *Khadi Bhandars'* and Handloom Houses for textiles on Ashram Rd, between Gandhi Ashram and Natraj Theatre. **Revdi Bazar** and **Sindhi Market** have semi-wholesale textile shops. CG Rd is the upmarket shopping area.

Bhandej, next to **Crossword Bookshop**, T079-2642 2181. Upmarket salon selling stunning fabrics and beautiful locally made clothes.

Bhujodi, Mithakhali Rd, T079-2640 0967. Good ethnic-styled clothing and handicrafts.

Sewa, above **Mirch Masala** (see Eating). A commendable women's co-op producing very fine shadow embroidery and clothes.

Activities and tours

Ahmedabad *p1315, maps p1316 and p1318*

Ahmedabad Municipal Transport Service, Lal Darwaza, T079-2550 7739, where you can reserve the following: **Tour 1**, 0830-1830, Rs 160 a/c coach, to Sidi Sayid mosque, Shaking minarets, Huteehsinh Jain temples, Gandhi Ashram, Gujarat Vidyapit, ISKCON temple, Sundarvan, Shreyas museum, Gandhinagar (also Akshardham) and Adalaj step well. **Tour 2**, 0900-1700, slightly different, Rs 125 (non-a/c). **Tours 3,4**, 0900-1300, 1330-1730, Rs 75, Rs 85 a/c, split the sights.

Florican Tours, opposite Electricity House, Lal Darwaza, T079-2550 6590. Bookings for Poshina.

Heritage Walking Tours, 0800-1030, Rs 50. Excellent tour with qualified architects/ conservationists; starts at Swaminarayan temple, Relief Rd, Kalupur, of *havelis*, *pols*, artisans' workshops, etc. Check ahead at CRUTA, at the temple complex, T079-2539 1811, extension 509. Highly recommended.
House of MG Heritage Walks, House of MG hotel (www.houseofmg.com) has created fantastic D* Tours audio guided walks around the city armed with an MP3 player. They also run an amazing Night Heritage Walk which is guided by a local and offers fantastic insight into the city. It's like being let into a secret.
North West Safaries, 91/92 Kamdhenu Complex, opposite Sahajanand College, Ambawati, T079-2630 8031, www.northwest safaries.com. Experienced local company, highly recommended for hotel booking, car hire and a great insight into Gujarat.
Sita, Suflam Building, Mithakhali, Ashram Rd, T079-2656 1551.
TCI, Usha Deep Building, opposite Navrangpura Police Station, Ashram Rd, T079-2642 1981.

Transport

Ahmedabad *p1315, maps p1316 and p1318*

Air Air India, 2nd floor, GCCI Complex, Ashram Rd, TT079-2550 5198/99. **Air France**, T1800-180 0055 (toll free). **British Airways**, T1800-102 1213 (toll free). **Lufthansa**, T1800-102 5838 (toll free). **Emirates**, T079-6607 4444. **Singapore Airlines**, T079-3001 2828. **Swissair**, T079-2656 8143. . International flights to **Abu Dhabi**, **Bangkok**, **Dubai**, **Geneva**, **Hong Kong**, **Kuwait**, **Muscat** and **Sharjah**.

Domestic flights to **Bengaluru (Bangalore)**, **Chennai**, **Coimbatore**, **Delhi**, **Goa**, **Hyderabad**, **Jaipur**, **Jammu**, **Kolkata**, **Mumbai**, **Nagpur** and **Pune**. The following airlines serve the city, but check a third-party website such as www.flightraja.com or www.makemytrip.com for the latest fares and schedules. **Indian**, Lal Darwaza, near Roopalee Cinema, T079-2550 5198. 1000-1315, 1415-1715, airport Intl T079-2286 7237, Domestic T079-2286 9233, www.airindia.com **Indigo**, Empire Tower, CG Rd, T079-6450 5921. **Jet Airways**, Income Tax Char Rasta, Ashram Rd, T079-2754 3304, airport T079-2286 6540, www.jetairways.com. **Kingfisher**, T079-2844 2234, www.flykingfisher.com. **Spicejet**, T1800-1803333.

Local bus City service available from main bus station, Lal Darwaza, railway station and all major points in the city.

Long distance bus Central Bus Station, Geeta Mandir, T079-2546 3396; reservations 0700- 1900. Advance booking for night services 1500-2300, luxury coach services 1030-1800. Arrive early to find your bus. **ST buses** to **Bhavnagar** 4-5 hrs, **Mehsana** (2 hrs on good new road), **Mumbai** (492 km, 11 hrs), **Palitana** 217 km, **Porbandar** 394 km, **Rajkot** 216 km, **Sasan Gir** 385 km, **Surat** 120 km, and **Vadodara** 113 km. **Udaipur** 287 km. Private coaches offering sleeper seating to major towns in Gujarat and Rajasthan leave from around the **ST Bus Stand** and various suburban stands, often leaving at night. Ticket offices and departure points are usually close together. Agencies around ST stand may overcharge for a seat 'booking' then simply flag down the first bus that comes past; cheaper to wait outside stand (ask **Punjab Travels**, from K Gandhi Rd, Delhi Darwaza, and Embassy Market, Ashram Rd, T079-2658 9200. **Pawan**, Pritamnagar 1st Dhal, Ellis Bridge, T079-2657 5214, many places in Gujarat and Rajasthan. **Shrinath**, Shahibaug Rd, T079-2562 5351, for **Udaipur**. **Tanna**, Paldi Crossing, T079-2657 6351, for **Bhavnagar**. **Shajanand**, Shefali Complex, Paldi, for **Diu**; **Mt Abu**, 7 hrs (via Khed Brahma).

Rickshaw Drivers readily use meters, which for now give an accurate reading. Station to Khanpur Rd/ Sidi Sayid area around Rs 30.

Taxi Cars and 4WDs for hire from **North West Safaries**, see above; **Green Channel**, T079-2656 0489. Rs 6-12 per km, minimum Rs 250-350; around Rs 750-1200 per day.

Train Always confirm from which station train departs. Ahmedabad Junction is on a broad gauge line to Mumbai (Platforms 1-4, near the main entrance) and a metre gauge line to Delhi (Platforms 7-12). Platforms 5 and 6 serve both, according to demand. A small number of trains use Gandhigram station on west bank. Computerized reservations at both stations: 1st class 0800-1530, 2nd class 0800-1430, 1500-2000, T135, enquiry T131. Last-minute berths can also be booked for some trains at a temporary counter on the platform;

premium charged. The following leave from Junction unless stated.

Agra Cantt: *Ahmedabad Gorakhpur Exp 15045*, 0515, Tue, 25 hrs. **Ajmer**: *Ahmedabad Haridwar Mail 19105*, 0950, 10½ hrs (to Jaipur); *Ashram Exp 12915*, 1745, 7 hrs. **Bengaluru (Bangalore)**: *Ahmedabad Bangalore Exp 16501*, 1800, Tue, 13¾ hrs. **Bhavnagar**: *Bhavnagar Exp 12971*, 0600, 5½ hrs. **Bhopal**: *Rajkot-Bhopal Jabalpur Exp 11465/11463*, 1845, 14 hrs. **Chennai**: *Navjivan Exp 12655*, 0630, 22¾ hrs. **Delhi (OD)**: *Ashram Exp 12915*, 1745, 16½ hrs. **Jaipur**: *Aravali Exp 19707*, 0645, 13¾ hrs; *Ashram Exp 12915*, 1745, 11 hrs. **Kolkata (H)**: *Howrah Exp 12833*, 2355, 20 hrs. **Jamnagar**: *Saurashtra Exp 19215*, 2015, 7½ hrs; *Mumbai Okha Saurashtra Mail 19005*, 0530, 7½ hrs (all stop at **Rajkot**, 2 hrs before Jamnagar). **Jodhpur**: *Ranakpur Exp 14708*, 0030, 10 hrs (continues to **Bikaner**, 6 hrs). **Junagadh**: *Veraval Exp 11464*, 0815, 8 hrs; *Somnath Exp 19221*, 2145, 10 hrs (both continue to **Veraval**, 2 hrs). **Mehsana**: *Aravali Exp 19707*, 0645, 1¾ hrs; *Haridwar Mail 19105*, 0950, 2 hrs; *Ashram Exp 12915*, 1745, 1½ hrs. **Mumbai Central**: *Shatabdi Exp 12010*, 1430, not Sun, 7¼ hrs; *Gujarat Mail 12902*, 2205, 8¾ hrs. **Porbandar**: *Mumbai Porbandar Saurashtra Exp 19215*, 2015, 10½ hrs. **Udaipur City**: *DSR Express 19944*, 2315, 9 hrs. **Vadodara**: see Mumbai, journey time 2-2½ hrs.

Directory

Ahmedabad *p1315, maps p1316 and p1318*
For Talking Yellow Pages T079-2777 7777.
Banks Many ATMS on CG Rd, Ashram Rd and in Lal Darwaza, give cash on Cirrus/Maestro and credit cards. **Amex, Foreign Exchange Bureau**, all on CG Rd; **Thomas Cook**, Super Mall, CG Rd, less paperwork and open till late. **Cultural centres** West of Ellis Bridge, **Alliance Française**, behind Gujarat College. **British Library**, near Law Garden, T079-2646 4693, a/c, clean toilets. **Internet Cyber Café**, Shri Krishna Centre, Mithakhali. **Log-In**, 92 Kamdhenu Complex, Polytechnic Rd, Ambawadi, T079-2630 2019, also printouts. **Random Access**, Ambawadi, 10 terminals. **Medical services** Ambulance: T102. **Civil Hospital**, Asarwa, T079-2268 3721; Rajasthan T079-2286 6311; VS T079-2657 7621; Heart Foundation, T079-2657 5555. **Post** GPO: off Relief Rd. Others at Navrangpura, Ellis Bridge, Gandhi Ashram, Gandhi Rd, Gujarat University, IIM, Madhavpura market, Polytechnic and Ambawadi, all with Speed Post. **Useful contacts** Fire: T101. **Police**: T100. **Foreigners' Regional Registration Office**: Police Commissioner's Office, Shahi Bagh.

Around Ahmedabad

Architecture buffs will find much to occupy them around the capital, from Modhera's ancient Sun Temple and the fabulous step well in Patan to the more modern, esoteric charms of Le Corbusier's Gandhinagar. The hills that rise up toward the Rajasthan border hide a number of wildlife sanctuaries and small palace hotels, while a side trip to the south could take in the Nalsarovar Bird Sanctuary and the desolate remains of Lothal, one of the world's oldest ports. ▸▸ *For listings, see pages 1331-1332.*

North of Ahmedabad → *For listings, see pages 1331-1332.*

The fertile irrigated land immediately north of Ahmedabad becomes increasingly arid towards Rajasthan. When approaching Mehsana there are signs of the growing economy, including natural gas, fertilizers, milk products and rapeseed oil processing. There are some worthy trips in this area.

Gandhinagar → *Colour map 2, C3. Phone code: 02712 or 082 from Ahmedabad. Population: 195,900.*

When Bombay state was divided along linguistic lines into Maharashtra and Gujarat in 1960, a new capital city was planned for Gujarat named after Mahatma Gandhi. As with Chandigarh, Le Corbusier was instrumental in the design. The 30 residential sectors around the central government complex are similarly impersonal. Construction began in 1965 and the Secretariat was completed in 1970. Located 23 km north of Ahmedabad, Gandhinagar – with multiplex theatre complexes and parks – has become a popular place for day trippers from Ahmedabad.

Akshardham ⓘ *Sector 20, Nov-Feb 0900-1830, Mar-Oct 1000-2000, part closed on Mon, Rs 25, no cameras or electronic devices*, is a temple with a cultural complex and entertainment park and is run by volunteers. Though not on the same scale as its counterpart in Delhi, the pink sandstone main building, floodlit at dusk, exhibits similar architectural influences. It houses a 2-m-high gold leaf idol and some relics of Sri Swaminarayan, who established the headquarters of his 19th-century Vedic revivalist movement in the Gujarati town of Loj. The three exhibition halls feature a variety of informative sound and light presentations relating to Sri Swaminarayan, the *Vedas* and the Hindu epics. Sahajanabad Vun, the garden for meditation, is impressive and has 'singing fountains' and a restaurant.

Mehsana (Mahesana)

Mehsana, 80 km north of Ahmedabad, has an impressive Jain temple, built in the 1980s in traditional architectural style. Mehsana is used by visitors to Modhera and Patan for an overnight stop. Women travellers have reported being hassled by men near the bus station.

Modhera → *Colour map 2, C2.*

ⓘ *Sunrise-sunset, foreigners Rs 100, video camera Rs 25. A Classical Dance Festival is held on the 3rd weekend in Jan.*

Virtually a deserted hamlet 25 km west of Mehsana, Modhera has the remains of one of the finest Hindu temples in Gujarat. Quite off the beaten track, it retains a great deal of its atmosphere and charm. Visit early in the day as it get busy. The partially ruined **Surya** (Sun) **Temple** (1026), built during the reign of Bhimdev I and consecrated in 1026-1027, two centuries before the Sun Temple at Konark, is a product of the great Solanki period (eighth-13th centuries). Despite the temple's partial destruction by subsequent earthquakes that may have accounted for the collapse of its tower, it remains an outstanding monument, set against the backdrop of a barren landscape. Superb carvings of goddesses, birds, beasts and blossoms decorate the remaining pillars. Over the last 20 years the complex has undergone major restoration by the Archaeological Survey of India that is continuing as funds permit. Unlike the temple at Konark, the main temple stands well above the surrounding land, raised by a high brick terrace faced with stone.

A rectangular *kund* (pool), now dry, over 50 m long and 20 m wide, with flights of steps and subsidiary shrines, faces the front of the temple. A remarkable structure, despite the damage caused by weathering, it is still possible to gain an impression of the excellence of the carving. On the west side of the tank a steep flight of steps leads up to the main entrance of the east *mandapa* through a beautifully carved *torana*, of which only the pillars now remain. The **sabha mandapa**, a pillared hall, is 15 sq m. Note the cusped arches which became such a striking feature of Mughal buildings 600 years later. The corbelled roof of this entry hall, which has been reconstructed, is a low stepped pyramid. Beautiful columns and magnificent carvings decorate the hall. The western part of the oblong temple contains the raised **inner sanctuary.** The upper storeys have been completely destroyed, though it clearly consisted of a low pyramidal roof in front of the tall *sikhara* (tower) over the sanctuary itself. Surya's image in the sanctuary (now missing) was once illuminated by the first rays of the rising sun at each solar equinox (proof of the mathematical and astronomical knowledge of the designers). Images of Surya and Agni are among the more well-preserved carvings on the external walls which also contain some erotic scenes. The interior walls were plain other than for niches to house images of Surya.

Patan

Little visited, Patan has more than 100 beautifully carved Jain temples and many attractive traditionally carved wooden houses. It remains a centre for fine textiles, particularly silk *patola* saris produced by the characteristic *ikat* technique which involves tie-dyeing the warp threads before weaving to create designs on the finished fabrics. Only three extended families (at Salvivad and Fatipal Gate) can be seen at work on the highly prized double *ikat* weaving where both the warp and the weft threads are tie-dyed before being set on traditional looms – only to be found in Indonesia and Japan outside India. It takes three to six months to weave a sari, hence each piece sells for at least Rs 120,000; samples are Rs 2000. You can see them in production at the Salvi brothers' **workshop** ⓘ *Patolawala St, T02766-232274, www.patanpatola.com.* Patan is 35 km northwest of Mehsana and can be reached either by bus or train. Buses also run from Modhera.

The spectacular **Rani ki Vav** (11th century) ⓘ *sunrise-sunset, Rs 100 foreigners; video camera Rs 25, 4 km from Patan Bus Stand*, named after a Solanki queen, is one of the largest step wells in India with superb carvings on seven storeys. Flights of steps lead down to the water, lined by string courses of sculptured voluptuous women, Vishnu avatars and goddesses. The **Sahasralinga Talao**, 4.5 km from Patan Bus Stand, is a cluster of Solanki period (11th-12th century) shrines facing a small lake. Excavations are in progress.

Vadnagar

The town, 40 km northeast of Mehsana, has the finest example of the *torana* arches that characterize North Gujarat. Beautiful sculptures decorate two of the original four 12th- century arched gateways on *kirti stambha* pillars. The Solanki period city gates are beautifully sculpted, the best being near the lake. The impressive 17th-century **Haktesvar temple**, the most important Siva temple in Gujarat, has fine carvings, erotic sculpture and a silver shrine. Tana-Riri, two poetess-singers from Vadnagar, are said to have saved Tansen from the burning effects of the *Deepak Raga* (Song of Fire) by singing the *Maldaar Raga* (Song of Rain). Akbar invited the sisters to sing in his court, but rather than refuse to sing for a Muslim emperor (which was against their custom) they immolated themselves. Their shrine can be seen at Vadnagar.

Taranga

Named after Tara Devi, Taranga, 55 km northeast of Mehsana by bus, has a wonderful complex of well-preserved, if somewhat over-restored, 12th-century Jain temples surrounded by spectacular hills. The large central sandstone temple to Adinatha is beautifully carved with sensual dancing figures, Hindu deities and Jain *Tirthankaras*. Inside is a bejewelled central statue carved out of a single piece of alabaster. There is a scenic trek from the main Adinath temple, passing some dramatic rock formations, to the hilltop Shilp Temple where one of the Jain saints meditated. Panthers have been sighted near the temple complex.

Ambaji

Close to the Rajasthan border, en route to Mount Abu, Ambaji is known for its marble mines. You can see marble artisans at work at this temple town (and at Khedbrahma nearby) where **Bhadra Purnima fair** is held, with processions of flag bearing pilgrims followed by musicians and dancers. A picturesque ropeway goes to Gabbar hill, a holy pilgrimage for Hindus (Rs 40). Ahmedabad-Mount Abu buses stop at Ambaji.

The five 11th- and 12th-century Jain temples just east of Ambaji at **Kumbhariya** ⓘ *0630-1930, Aarti worship 0900-0930 and 1900, tea canteen, very cheap thalis*, are worth visiting for their exquisite marble carvings. Be sure to see the second temple; the main one has been largely rebuilt. Catch a jeep from Ambaji Bus Stand.

Danta

En route from Taranga to Ambaji, the princely state of Danta was known for its cavalry. It is dominated by the medieval **Parmara Rajput fort**. The jungles and rocky hills harbour panther, nilgai and four-horned antelope, and there is extensive birdlife. To explore, bicycles can be hired from in the village.

Poshina

The small 15th-century Poshina fort, 45 km south of Abu Road, stands at the confluence of two holy rivers (Sai and Panhari) with views over the hills. It was the capital of the North Gujarat branch of Vaghela Rajputs. There are ancient Jain and Siva temples nearby as well as tribal villages where you can watch arrow making, potters, basketwork and silversmiths. You will find collections of up to 2000 terracotta horses here – the story goes that you make a wish and then if that wish comes true, you make an offering of one or many horses (depending on the size of the wish) and a *puja*. It's quite magical. The area is home to Bhils, colourful Garasias and Rabaris who herd camels, cattle and goats. The busy and interesting **market** centre is well worth stopping at; the last stretch of the approach road is very poor. Ahmedabad-Ambaji buses stop at Kheroj from where it is possible to get shared jeeps to Poshina (12 km).

Chitra Vichitra Fair is held a fortnight after *Holi* at **Gunbakhari**, 8 km away. It is attended by Bhils, Garasias and Rabaris (some of whom are now abandoning their traditional *dhotis* and turbans). The fair is very colourful with much revelry, dancing and singing, food stalls etc. Matchmaking is often followed by elopements. **Florican Tours** ⓘ *T079-2550 6590*, can arrange visits to the fair. Try staying in a tent (contact **Gujarat Tourism**) during the fair. Delicious flavoured *lassi* is available near the village entrance but ask for it be prepared with your own filtered or mineral water.

Vijaynagar

Stunning ruined Hindu and Jain temples hide away in an enchanting forest in Vijaynagar. Once part of a kingdom ruled by the Rathod Rajputs of Marwar, Vijaynagar is home to beautiful groups of temples. In some places, it feels as if the forest has won as it grows through the temples, but a lot of work has gone into clearing the areas around the temples and there are even paved pathways and signboards. It's incredibly atmospheric, especially late afternoon. There is one Shiva temple still active within the forest which is quite magical.

Palanpur and Balaram

The *maqbara* with fine mausolea in the old Nawabi capital of Palanpur stands rather neglected. The palace is now the court; look in to see the fabulous ceiling paintings and sandalwood carvings. The 1915 Kirti Stambha has the 700-year-long history of the Nawabs of Palanpur inscribed on it. Nearby Balaram has one of the best-kept palace hotels in Gujarat, 3 km off the highway and 14 km north of Palanpur. About 20 km from there, the **Jessore Bear Sanctuary** in the Aravallis has sloth bear (occasionally spotted), panther, nilgai, sambhar, four-horned antelope etc, but these are best seen by climbing Jessore hill.

South of Ahmedabad → *For listings, see pages 1331-1332.*

Vautha

The **Vautha Mela**, starting at Kartik Purnima (November), is held at the confluence of the Sabarmati and Vatrak rivers, some 46 km south of Ahmedabad. Less colourful than Pushkar fair it is also far less touristy. About 4000 donkeys, painted in vivid colours, and over 2000 camels are traded. There is a great atmosphere on the river banks early in the morning, with haggling over animals and craft sales. **Gujarat Tourism** provides tents and catering.

Nalsarovar Bird Sanctuary

The sanctuary, 65 km southwest of Ahmedabad, is noted for waterbirds including migratory ducks, flamingos and geese. The lake and the Surendranagar Reservoirs were declared a bird sanctuary in 1969. Uniquely in Saurashtra, Nalsarovar is surrounded by reed beds and marshes though the lake often dries out before the rains. Bharwad and Jat herdsmen and their water buffaloes live on the reed islands; you can get hot buttered millet chapatis and chutney with sweet tea or *lassi* from some shacks. Padhar fisherfolk who live around the lake are good artisans. **Forest Dept Bungalows** have two or three simple rooms and views of lake. The best time to visit is between November and February.

Lothal 'Mound of the dead'

ⓘ *Sat-Thu 1000-1700, Rs 100 for foreigners. There's no shade or proper drinks outlet so carry bottled water.*

Southeast of Moenjodaro, 720 km as the crow flies, Lothal has some of the most substantial remains of the Harappan culture in India dating from circa 2500-1700 BC. Once a port sandwiched between the Sabarmati River and the Bhogavo River, it is now 10 km inland from the Gulf of Khambhat on a flat, often desolate-looking plain. Thorn scrub and parched soils surround the site and even in February a hot desiccating wind picks up flurries of dust. Lothal's location and function as a port have led most authorities to argue that it was settled by Harappan trading communities who came by sea from the mouths of the Indus. Others suggest that the traders came by an overland route. The site is surrounded by a mud-brick embankment 300 m north-south and 400 m east-west. Unlike the defensive walls at Harappa and Moenjodaro, the wall at Lothal enclosed the workers' area as well as the citadel. The presence of a dry dock and a warehouse further distinguish it from other major Harappan sites. Some visitors find that the recent restoration work has made the walls look too modern.

The massive excavated **dry dock** runs along the east wall of the city. A 12-m-wide gap in the north side is believed to have been the entrance by which boats came into the dock, while a spillway over the south wall allowed excess water to overflow. The city wall at this point may have been a wharf for unloading. Excavations of the warehouse suggest that trade was the basis of Lothal's existence. The building at the southwest corner of the wharf had a high platform made of cubical mud-brick blocks, the gaps between them allowing ventilation. Over 65 Indus Valley seals discovered here show pictures of packing material, bamboo or rope, suggestive of trade; one from Bahrain is evidence of overseas trade. Excavations show a

planned city in a grid pattern, with an underground drainage system, wells and brick houses with baths and fireplaces. The raised brick platform to the southeast may have been a kiln where seals and plaques were baked. Objects found include painted pottery, terracotta toys, ivory, shell, semi-precious stone items, bangles and necklaces made of tiny gold beads. Rice and millet were clearly in use, and there is evidence that horses had been domesticated. The nearby cemetery had large funerary vessels indicating pit burials.

Wadhwan

Northwest of Limbdi, Wadhwan was a princely state of the Jhalas, a Rajput clan. The fortified old township has plenty of interesting architecture including two old step wells with attractive carvings and some fine 11th- to 16th-century temples. It is an ideal place to watch and shop for *bandhani*, wood and stone carving, silverwork and textiles.

The opulent 19th-century **Raj Mahal** (*Bal Vilas*) occupied by the royal family has a grand Durbar hall with chandeliers, frescoes, carved furniture, crystal and velvet curtains, Sheesh Mahal library and billiard room. The vast landscaped gardens contain lily ponds and fountains. Maharajah Chaitanya Dev is a keen restorer of classic cars and has a vintage car collection.

Around Ahmedabad listings

For Sleeping and Eating price codes and other relevant information, see Essentials pages 38-42.

Sleeping

Gandhinagar *p1327*

A-C Fortune Inn Haveli, Sector 11, opposite Sachivalaya, T079-3988 4422, www.fortune hotels.in. 84 below-par rooms, restaurants, exchange, car hire, free airport transfer, Wi-Fi.

F Youth Hostel, Sector 16, T079-2322 2364. 2 rooms, 42 beds in 6-bed and 8-bed dorms, very good, no reservations.

Mehsana *p1327*

A-C Water World Resort, 25 mins' drive out of town, T02762-282351, www.waterworld resort.com. A/c cottages, modern, Mughal garden with a/c 'royal tents', vegetarian restaurant, wave pool, sports complex, lake.

D-E Natraj, 1 km from bus stand. 12 rooms (dorms to a/c with bath), good veggie restaurant.

F Railway Retiring Rooms. (Rs 70) with bath.

Patan *p1328*

D-F Surya Palace, University Rd, near railway crossing, T02766-329872. Cheap and cheerful, not very inspiring, but quieter than Yuvraj.

D-G Yuvraj, opposite bus stand, T02766-281397. Wide range of rooms, some a/c, convenient but noisy location, restaurant serves very cheap unlimited *thalis*.

F Toran Tourist Bungalow, **Gujarat Tourism**. 2 simple rooms, café, convenient for step well.

Danta *p1329*

B Bhavani Villa, on a hilltop, T02749-278705, www.bhavanivilladanta.com. Very welcoming. 4 modern a/c rooms facing the hills, 1 non-a/c in colonial period mansion, delicious Rajput meals, friendly hosts – it's like staying with family, great for nature lovers, game drives, riding (Rs 400 per hr), very good horse safaris (Rs 5000 per person). Get a tour of their farm – lovely scenery. Recommended.

Poshina *p1329*

A Darbargadh (Heritage Hotel), fort complex, www.poshina.com. Reservations: **Florican Tours**, T079-2550 6590. In 17th-century wing of the fort. Pleasant with open courtyards and hill views, old world charm, now renovated with antiques, Rajasthani miniatures and rare Tanjore paintings, 15 comfortable, air-cooled rooms , spicy Indian meals, camel rides, friendly owner is knowledgeable about local tribes and crafts, good village safaris, folk entertainment. Your host is the Secretary of the Heritage Hotels Association Gujarat. Recommended.

Vijaynagar *p1329*

A Vijay Villas (Heritage Hotel), T07926 747690, www.vijayvilasvijaynagar.com. Home away from home in this heritage style property. Nice rooms around little courtyard and great family food on offer. Beautifully located near polo forest.

Balaram *p1330*

B Balaram Palace Resort, Chitrasani, T079-2657 6388, www.balarampalace.com. Splendid riverside location surrounded by hills but little bit soulless. Well restored 1930s palace, 17 a/c rooms (interiors too modern and characterless for some), 4 colonial rooms with old fireplaces (some windowless) and rooms upstairs with views, Nawab Suite has huge arched windows. Excellent terrace restaurants, lovely formal Nawabi garden, pool fed by natural cascading spring, good gym, bike hire.

South of Ahmedabad *p1330*

A-B Balasinore Garden Palace, 45 km from Kheda, T02690-262786. Early 20th-century building with 6 refurbished rooms, delicious Mughlai meals, one of few Nawab-family-run heritage hotels, pleasant orchard garden, tours of dinosaur site and tribal villages.

Eating

Gandhinagar *p1327*

Sector 21 has street vendors offering good snacks. Ask for the Bhatiar couple who make *bajra ka rotla* (millet *chapatis*) and chicken curry, meat samosas and dahl in a little shack, not too far from Akshardham.

Chills, Thrills & Spills, Sector-21 Shopping Centre. Pizzas, sandwiches, vegetarian *thalis*.

Premawati, Akshardham Complex. Gujarati vegetarian food, lime tea, delicious ice cream.

Relief, excellent Indian and Continental.

Torana, Sector-28. Punjabi, South Indian snacks, in a garden.

Mehsana *p1327*

Kudarat, near **Vijay** (Hindi sign with a tree symbol). South Indian and Punjabi. Open air, so you may have a monkey for company.

Sher-e-Punjab, by a petrol station, east of NH8. Good omelettes.

Ambaji *p1329*

Hotel Ambaji International. Highly recommended vegetarian *thalis*.

Transport

Gandhinagar *p1327*

Train and buses to **Ahmedabad** take 1 hr. ST Bus Station, Sector 11.

Mehsana *p1327*

Buses from **ST Bus Stand** to **Ahmedabad** on a good new road (2 hrs); **Modhera**, 45 mins, Rs 8, last return from Modhera 1730; **Patan**, 1¼ hrs. Trains bound for Rajasthan and Delhi from Ahmedabad stop at Mehsana.

Patan *p1328*

Hourly to Ahmedabad, 3 hrs, Rs 60-70, and every 30 mins to Modhera, 1 hr, Rs 15.

Palanpur *p1330*

Ahmedabad and Delhi trains stop here. Direct buses go to **Mount Abu**; **Ambaji** (also share jeeps, Rs 20); **Poshina** through attractive countryside and tribal areas, 1200 (1 hr), Rs 7.

Nalsarovar Bird Sanctuary *p1330*

Direct bus from Ahmedabad (0700, 1500) 2 hrs.

Lothal *p1330*

Trains from Ahmedabad and Bhavnagar go to Lothal-Burkhi, close to Lothal. Luxury and state buses can drop you at **Gundi** railway crossing; from there *chhakras* (motorbike-rickshaw) charge Rs 5 for the drop to Lothal. Get back on the highway to get a bus to **Ahmedabad** or **Bhavnagar**. It can be a long hard day, with little to see. Taxis (Rs 1000-1200) or motorbikes make it easier: travelling from Ahmedabad, Lothal is 7 km (awful road) from a level crossing on the SH1 near **Bagodra**, at the junction with NH8A. Coming from Bhavnagar, follow the SH1 for 127 km via Vallabhipur and Barwala.

Vadodara and the old forts

The route south from Ahmedabad crosses the fertile alluvial plains of the Sabarmati and Mahi rivers before entering the Konkan region. The plains gradually give way south to broken hills while inland, parallel ridges reach 500-600 m where strategically placed atmospheric old forts are sited. Rice dominates agriculture further south, but ragi (finger millet) and pulses are also common. A pleasant day trip by car from Vadodara could include the forts of Champaner in the foothills, Pawagadh on a hilltop and Dabhoi Fort. ▸▸ *For listings, see pages 1339-1342.*

Vadodara →

For listings, see pages 1339-1342. Colour map 2, C3. *Phone code: 0265. Population: 1.3 million.*

Formerly Baroda, Vadodara was the capital of one of the most powerful princely states. It is now a rapidly expanding industrial town, yet the older part is pleasant and interesting to wander through. The Gaekwad stood high in the order of precedence among rulers, being one of only five to receive a 21-gun salute. He was reputedly so rich that he had a carpet woven of diamonds and pearls, and cannons cast in gold.

Ins and outs

Getting there The airport is 9 km away with taxis and auto-rickshaws to town. Better hotels offer free airport transfer. The railway and long-distance bus stations are northwest of town, near hotels. ▸▸ *See Transport, page 1342.*

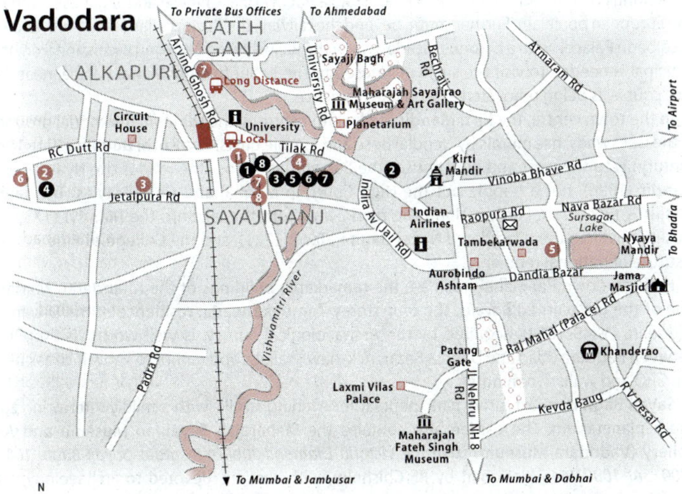

500 metres
500 yards

Sleeping
Apex Intenational 4
Express 2
Neelam 3
Surya 1
Surya Palace 7
Utsav 5
Vadodara 6
Yuvraj 8

Eating
Café Coffee Day 3
Gokul 2
Kansar 1
Kwality 5
Pizza King 8
Sahayog 4
Vanity 6
Volga 7

The oldest narrow gauge

The Vadodara–Dabhoi–Chandod line is the world's oldest surviving narrow-gauge railway. The 19th-century line was commissioned for bullock-drawn locomotives in 1863. Later turned to steam, it is now run by a diesel engine. There are some vintage locomotives including steam engines in the Dabhoi station yard dating back to 1902. Take a ride on this line from Vadodara to Chandod via Dabhoi for the experience.

Getting around The local bus station is just opposite the railway station. There are taxis and autos to take you to the town centre and the sights.

Tourist information Gujarat Tourism ⓘ *opposite railway station, T0265-279 4456, www.gujarattourism.com.*

Sights

Many of the city's treasures, which can be seen in the palaces and museums, reflect the wealth of the Gaekwads, a dynasty established by the powerful 18th-century Maratha General, Damaji. See page 1154.

The **Laxmi Vilas Palace** (1880-1890) ⓘ *Rs 100 (no photography)*, was built by RH Chisholm. The magnificent palace is somewhat neglected but the interiors are decorated with Venetian mosaic, Italian marble, porcelain, antique furniture, European stained glass, sculptures, a royal armoury, etc. Nearby is the **Naulakhi Well**, a well- preserved *baoli* which has galleried levels.

Just to the south of the palace, the **Maharajah Fateh Singh Museum** ⓘ *Nehru Rd, Laxmi Vilas Palace, Tue-Sun 1000-1730 (Apr-Jun 1600-1900), Rs 100,* has a good display of royal state collection of European art (copies of some Murillo, Titian, Raphael, Rubens), a prized collection of paintings by the 19th-century Indian artist Raja Ravi Verma, Chinese and Japanese statuary and European porcelain. Further south, beyond the railway, the **Pratap Vilas** (circa 1910, known as Lalbagh Palace), with a baroque façade, is now the Railway Staff College; permission from the principal is needed to visit the small rail museum. The beautiful **Shiv Mahal Palace**, near the race course, is being renovated as a private residence.

In the town centre, the **Kirti Mandir** (early 20th century), the *samadhi* (memorial ground) of the Gaekwads, has murals by Nandlal Bose and marble busts. The **Kothi Building** (late 19th century) is to the west and now houses the Secretariat. Across the road is the **Nyaya** (Law) **Mandir** (1896), not a temple but the High Court, in Mughal and Gothic styles. The **Jama Masjid** is next door. Further along the road away from the lake are the **Mandvi** (1736), a Muslim pavilion, the dilapidated **Nazar Bagh Palace** (1721), and the **College of Fine Art**, an institute of national renown.

Halfway down Raj Mahal Road are the remarkable buildings of the **Khanderao Market**. One of the old painted *havelis*, the four-storey **Tambekarwada**, residence of the Diwan of Vadodara (1849-1854), acquired by the Archaeological Survey, is well worth visiting. It is between Raopura Road and Dandia Bazar; rickshaw-wallahs appear not to know it so ask near the GPO and walk two minutes.

Sayaji Bagh is an extensive park, popular for evening strolls, with a mildly interesting zoo and a planetarium. The garden also contains the **Maharajah Sayajirao Museum and Art Gallery** (**Vadodara Museum**) ⓘ *in the Victoria Diamond Jubilee Institute, Sayaji Bagh, 1000-1700, Sat 1000-1645*, designed by RF Chisholm, with sections devoted to archaeology, art, ethnology and ancient Jain sculptures, as well as industrial arts, Mughal miniatures and European paintings. Nearby is the **Archaeology and Ancient History Museum** ⓘ *MS University, Mon-Sat 1400-1700, closed public holidays.* It contains Buddhist antiquities, archaeological finds from North Gujarat and good pre-history exhibits of Gujarat.

Around Vadodara → *For listings, see pages 1339-1342.*

Champaner

ⓘ *47 km northeast of Vadodara, 0900-1800, Rs 250.*

Champaner, stands at 880 m in the Girnar Hills. Now a World Heritage Site, the fortress was the old capital of the local Rajputs, but was lost in 1484 to Mahmud Beghara, who renamed it Muhammadabad and took 23 years to build his new city. In his campaign in Gujarat, the Mughal Emperor Humayun personally led a small team that scaled the walls of the city using iron spikes and then let the rest of the army in through the main gate. With the collapse of the empire, Champaner passed to the Marathas.

In the **old city**, the remains of many 15th- and 16th-century mosques and palaces show a blend of Islamic and Jain traditions, a unique style encouraged by Champaner's relative isolation. The **Jami Masjid** (1523), a large, richly ornamented mosque, is exemplary of the Gujarati style with interesting features such as oriel windows. Few older structures of the Chauhan Rajputs remain: **Patai Rawal palace**, the domed granary **Makai Kota**, the 11th- and 12th-century **Lakulisha Temple** and some old wells.

Some 4 km southwest of Champaner, **Pawagadh Fort** ⓘ *US$2/Rs 100* or included in entry price of Champaner, dominates the skyline and is visible for miles around. According to legend, Pavagadh was believed to have been part of the Himalaya carried off by the monkey god Hanuman. Occupying a large area, it rises in three stages: the ruined fort, the palace and middle fort, and finally the upper fort with Jain and Hindu temples, which are important places of pilgrimage. Parts of the massive walls still stand. The ascent is steep and passes several ruins including the Budhia Darwaza (Gate), and the Champavati Mahal, a three-storey summer pavilion. The temple at the summit had its spire replaced by a shrine to the Muslim saint Sadan Shah.

Dabhoi Fort

Dabhoi, 29 km southwest of Vadodara, was fortified by the Solanki Rajputs from 1100 and the fort was built by a King of Patan in the 13th century. Dabhoi is regarded as the birthplace of the Hindu Gujarati architectural style. The fort is a particularly fine example of military architecture with its four gates, a reservoir fed by an aqueduct and farms to provide food at times of siege. The **Vadodara Gate** (northwest) is 9 m high with pilasters on each side and carved with images depicting the reincarnation of Vishnu. The **Nandod Gate** (south) is similarly massive. The **Hira Gate** (east) with carvings, is thought to have the builder buried beneath it. **Mori Gate** (north) lies next to the old palace and on the left of this is the **Ma Kali Temple** (1225), shaped like a cross, with profuse carvings.

Chandod

South of Dabhoi, this is the meeting place of the Narmada's two tributaries with picturesque bathing ghats and several temples. Take a mechanized country-style river boat to visit temples, passing spectacular ravines and water-sculpted rocks.

Chhota Udepur

Around 100 km east of Vadodara, picturesque Chhota Udepur (Chotta Udaipur), centred around a lake, was once the capital of a Chauhan Rajput princely state. The town has palaces and many colonial period buildings. It is the capital of a tribal district where Bhils and Ratwas live in secluded hamlets of a handful of mud huts each. The huts are decorated with wall paintings or *pithoras* (tigers and other animals are favourite subjects) and protected from evil spirits by small terracotta devotional figures. If you stay at Jambugodha Palace (25km from Chhota Udepur), you can arrange to visit the *pithoras* in a nearby village and get a little insight into village life.

There are colourful weekly *haats* or **markets** in nearby villages which offer an insight into tribal arts, crafts and culture. (The one in town is held by the lake on Saturday – it's quite charming and not touristy at all.) The government-run tribal **museum** in Diwan Bungalow has interesting examples of *pithoras*, folk costumes, artefacts, aboriginal weapons and handicrafts, but the labelling is in Gujarati and the attendant knows little English. There is a better museum 15km from Chhota Udepur – see below.

Despite its Mughal architectural style, the imposing Rajput **Kusum Vilas** palace, set in 16 ha, has impressive European decorative features inside. The large Mughal-style gardens have fountains, ponds, European marble statuary, a colonnaded art deco pool and tennis courts, while the garages have old cars and interesting carriages.

Dasara Fair here is famous. Other fairs held around **Holi** (March/April) in nearby villages like Kawant, with dancing, music and craft stalls, offer a glimpse of tribal life.

Fifteen kilometres west of Chhota Udepur is the Tribal Academy at Tejgadh, which is working to document aboriginal languages and culture in the entire country. Great collection of photographs. There is a good library, mainly covering the local Bhil, Bhilala and Ratwa tribes, and the staff can offer practical advice on visiting local tribes. The canteen offers local food for a nominal fee, and *tadi*, a potent palm liquor, is available in season.

Surat and around

→ *For listings, see pages 1339-1342. Colour map 5, A3.* *Phone code: 0261. Population: 2.4 million.*

Situated on the banks of the Tapti River, Surat was an important trading centre by 1600 but went into decline in the 19th century. Today it is again a rapidly growing industrial and commercial city, but despite its historic significance there is little to attract tourists.

The **museum** ⓘ *Wed-Sat 1045-1345, 1445-1745, Tue, Sun 1445-1745, photography prohibited*, near the castle, has an interesting collection of textiles, furniture, paintings, stamps, coins and ceramics. A strong Muslim influence is evident in several 16th- and 17th-century mosques. There are two Parsi **fire temples** (1823) and the triple-domed **Swami Narayan Temple**. The **Chintamani Jain Temple**, dating from the 15th century, has some fine woodcarvings.

Navsari, 39 km from Surat, has a historic Parsi fire temple which is one of the most important Zoroastrian pilgrim places in India. You cannot enter the temple but the building and garden are worth seeing from outside. **Dandi**, 13 km from Navsari, is where Gandhiji ended his Salt March from Ahmedabad to the south Gujarat coast, and picked up a handful of salt, see box, page 1319. A monument marks the spot and a photo gallery depicts events in Gandhi's life. **Karadi**, nearby, is where Gandhi was arrested after the Dandi March; his hut is still preserved. There is a small **Gandhi Museum**. You can sleep at the guesthouse, which is very peaceful and friendly; contact *'Om Shanti'*, Matwad (English spoken).

Saputara

→ *For listings, see pages 1339-1342. Colour map 5, A3.* *Phone code: 02631. Altitude: 50-1083 m.*

Saputara, a pleasant hill resort created after Independence in the Sahayadri hills, is Gujarat's only hill station. Set in a tribal region, there is an attractive lake and forests nearby. It is a relaxing place to enjoy walks, scenic places and folklore but gets very crowded during weekends and holidays.

Ins and outs

Getting there State buses run from Surat (135 km) and Nashik (Maharashtra, 80 km). Trains on the Mumbai-Ahmedabad line get you as far as Billimora (110 km), with buses to Saputara. ▸▸ *See Transport, page 1342.*

Getting around The resort is ideal for walking. The best time to visit is November to May.

Sights

The name Saputara is derived from the snake deity, which is worshipped here by the tribal people. The hub of activity at Saputara is the **lake** which has boating facilities and lake view eating places. The plateau is rather barren and not particularly appealing but there are some lovely walks around the hill resort. You could find attractive quartzite rocks, orchids and wild flowers on the trails.

There are good views of the valley from **Sunset Point**, with a 10-minute ropeway service, and from **Valley View Point**, which involves a strenuous climb of 1.5 km. There are also some old Maratha hill forts that involve steep climbs and are recommended only for serious trekkers. The Hatgadh fort offers superb views and a chance to see rock chats, martens and wolf snakes in cracks on the fort walls. Carry water.

The **Dangs** district comprises more than 300 villages with a population of over 150,000, more than 94% of them belonging to tribal communities. The Bhils, Kunbis, Warlis and Gamits depend on the forest for their livelihood, obtaining timber, honey and lac. They are known for their traditional musical instruments and vigorous dances wearing wooden masks. Most villages have a shrine to Wagha-Deva, the tiger god, sculpted on stone. The **Dangs Cultural and Ecological Museum**, with a stone serpent at the entrance, offers an insight into the tribal area and the Dangs's natural history. There are interesting dioramas, folk costumes, tribal weaponry and musical instruments. The **Artists' Village** holds workshops of bamboo crafts, papier mâché and pottery.

Around Saputara

Dangs Darbar held at Ahwa, 32 km north, is celebrated with a **tribal fair** around March and April. Tribal chieftains called Bhil Rajas and Kunbi Rajas, who still receive privy purses from the government, are honoured during this festival. For **Nag Panchami** tribal huts are decorated with paintings.

Daman

→ *For listings, see pages 1339-1342.* *Colour map 5, A3. Phone code: 02636. Population: 35,700.*

Daman, on the coast, retains something of the atmosphere of its distinctive Portuguese inheritance which linked it both with Mediterranean Europe and Africa. A few people still use Portuguese in everyday speech, but visitors expecting a colonial coastal idyll may be disappointed by the scrappy beaches.

Ins and outs

Getting there and around The nearest railway station is at Vapi, 13 km southeast, on the Mumbai- Ahmedabad line. From there you can get taxis for transfer (visitors arriving by car pay Rs 20 entry fee) or walk about 600 m for a bus. Long-distance buses run from the major centres. They arrive at the main bus stand in Nani Daman. The settlement north of the river, known as *Nani* (small) Daman, has most of the accommodation. To the south, *Moti* (large) Daman has a few colonial remains. Bicycle hire is available from Nani Daman Bazar. Avoid the Indian holiday periods. ▸▸ *See Transport, page 1342.*

History

The 380-sq-km enclave of Daman, along with Diu and Goa, was a Portuguese possession until taken over by the Indian government in 1961. Its association with Goa ceased when the latter became a state in 1987. It is now a Union Territory with its own Pradesh council. Daman developed at the mouth of the tidal estuary of the Daman Ganga River as a trading centre in 1531. Much of its early commerce was with the Portuguese territories in East Africa. Later (1817-1837), it was a link in the opium trade chain until this was broken by the British.

Sights

Moti Daman retains something of the Portuguese atmosphere. The landward (east) side has a moat and drawbridge. The shaded main street inside the **fort** wall runs north-south between attractive arched gateways which have Portuguese arms carved on them. One shows a saint carrying a sword but the sculpted giants on the doorways are modelled on the guardian *dwarpalas* at entrances to Hindu temples.

The former **Governor's Palace** and other administrative buildings are along the main road while towards the south end is the old **Cathedral Church of Bom Jesus**, started in 1559 but consecrated in 1603. Large and airy when the main south door is open, the chief feature is its painted and gilt wooden altar reredos and pulpit. Much of the ornamentation, notably the gold crowns of the saints, have been stolen. On the west side of the small square is the old **jail**, still in

Daman town

Sleeping
China Town 3
Cidade de Daman 8
Gurukripa 1
Miramar 4
Rahee Guest House 5
Sandy Resort 6
Silver Sands 7
Sovereign 2

Eating
Damanganga Lake Garden 2
Duke 3
Jampore Beach Resort 4
Samrat 1

use. To the south, against the fort wall, is the **Rosario Chapel**, formerly the Church of the Madre Jesus, with a unique feature in Indian churches of carved and gilded wooden panels illustrating stories from the life of Christ. These include the adoration of the Magi, Jesus teaching in the synagogue as a child, and Mary's ascension. The carved ceiling features charming cherubs.

Jampore Beach, 3 km south of Moti Daman, is planted with casuarina groves and has a sandy beach with safe swimming but is otherwise not very appealing. **Nani Daman**, north of the river, is reached by a bridge across Daman Ganga which gives attractive views of Moti Daman's walls and the country fishing boats on either bank. The smaller **fort** here encloses a church, now used as a school, and a cemetery. Some of the old houses retain beautifully carved wooden doors and lintels. The crowded town is thick with bars trading on Daman's exemption from Gujarati prohibition.

Vadodara and the old forts listings

For Sleeping and Eating price codes and other relevant information, see Essentials pages 38-42.

Sleeping

Vadodara *p1333, map p1333*

L-AL Vadodara (Welcomgroup), RC Dutt Rd (west from station), T0265-233 0033, www.itcwelcomgroup.com. 134 rooms, some cramped, pool and gardens, golf arranged.

AL-A Surya Palace, opposite Parsi Agiari, Sayajiganj, T0265-222 6000, www.surya palace.com. 150 a/c rooms, smart but small rooms, extensive buffet lunch in a/c restaurant, business services.

AL-A Taj Residency, Akota Gardens, T0265-235 4545, www.tajhotels.com. 84 luxurious rooms overlooking palace, gardens, pool, health club.

A-B Surya, Sayajiganj, T0265-222 6161, www.hotelsurya.com. 82 rooms (most a/c), restaurant (wide choice, good *thalis*), friendly.

A-C Express, RC Dutt Rd, T0265-305 5000, www.expressworld.com. Central a/c, 65 rooms, restaurants (excellent *thalis* at the beautiful **Mandap** restaurant), cake/sweet shop, helpful staff, unimpressive exterior but pleasant atmosphere.

B-C Sayaji, opposite Rajshree Cinema, Sayajiganj, T0265-222 6363, www.sayajihotels.com. All the usual mod cons including wi-fi, restaurants, pleasant rooftop dining (good *thalis*), 53 a/c rooms, business centre.

C-D Apex International, near Sardar Patel Statue, Sayajigunj, T0265-236 2551, www.hotelapex.com. Including breakfast, this centrally located hotel offers up clean rooms with all the usual mod cons and friendly service.

C-D Utsav, Prof Manekrao Rd, T0265-243 5859. Under renovation at time of writing, was looking good but probably the prices will inch up, 28 a/c rooms, restaurants, exchange, courtesy coach.

D Kaviraj, RC Dutt Rd, T0265-232 3401. Recently refurbished with 30 rooms, some a/c, some with hot water, restaurant, mostly well known for it's wine shop which issues permits till 1830.

D Yuvraj, near ST stand, T0265-279 5252, www.yuvrajhotel.net. 45 a/c rooms, restaurant, pool, gym, business centre.

F-G Neelam, 27 Viswas Colony, Alkapuri, T0265-231 1490. 34 simple rooms on quiet side street, best with balcony, bathrooms tiny and dark, bucket hot water, but clean enough and good value for budget travellers. Many similar **F-G** places on the same street.

Champaner *p1335*

D-E Hotel Champaner, on a plateau reached by cable car, run by Gujarati Tourism, T02676-245641. 32 clean rooms and dorm, pleasant garden, lively monkeys.

Chandod *p1335*

D-E Sarita Mandvi Mahal, Juna Mandwa, T02663-233371, www.heritagehotelsof india.com. 10 mins' walk from the river. 19th-century, simple rooms, some a/c, dorm beds (Rs 150), library, period furniture, home-cooked Indian food in courtyard, bullock cart tours of the village, walking tours in the ravines, friendly, a bit shabby but good value.

Chhota Udepur *p1335*

A-B Kusum Vilas Palace undergoing refurbishment, this is a huge project which is unlikely to open any time soon.

B Kali Niketan T(0)9825-556413, http://chhotaudepur.com. One of the most eccentric palace homestays you can come across, one guestroom has 2 leopards presiding over the bed. It has a ramshackle charm.

C-D Jambughoda Palace, Jambughoda (25 km from Champaner and 50 km from Chhota Udepur), T02676-241 258, www.jambughoda.com. Billed as a 'home for nature lovers', this heritage property is close to the Jambughoda Wildlife Sanctuary and you can also check out *pithora* tribal paintings in nearby villages. Simple rooms with great home-cooked food with locally-grown organic vegetables.

Surat and around *p1336*

AL Gateway, Athwa Lines, T0261-222 6565, www.tajhotels.com. 140 rooms, good restaurant (breakfast included), modern, attractive location, riverside pool, health club, efficient, polite staff, smartest in town.

B-C Embassy, Sufi Baug, near station, T0261-244 3170, www.embassyhotelsurat.com. Modern, but bare rooms, pleasant, 60 a/c rooms, popular restaurant (North Indian, Gujarati *thalis*).

C Yuvraj, opposite railway station, T0261-241 3001, yuvraj_surat@hotmail.com. Modern, 55 rooms, central a/c, good restaurant, rooftop garden café, business services.

C-D Everyday Inn, near New Civil Court, by the main road, T0261-266 5154. 8 a/c doubles with bath (hot water) and TV.

G Vihar, opposite the railway station. Rooftop views of the city, friendly and safe.

Saputara *p1336*

A-B Shilpi, opposite Govt Shopping Centre, T02631-237231, www.shilpihillresort.com. Clean and comfortable, 10 rooms, attached baths, set back from main road towards the hills, restaurant (meals included). The restaurant **Vaity**, offers the widest choice including non-vegetarian, and good views and outdoor seating.

A-C Vaity, Chimney Ropeway near Sunset Point, T02631-237210. Superbly situated on a hill with a panoramic views, clean, comfortable rooms, lawn, friendly staff but 'unsophisticated' management, guides for surrounding excursions on weekdays.

A-E Toran Hill Resort (Gujarat Tourism), near the bus stand, T02631-237226. Huge variety of styles and standard of room, from deluxe a/c cottages and log huts to dorms (Rs 100), restaurant (*thalis* Rs 25-35). Book at any tourism office.

B-D Patang, opposite the Boat Club, T02631-237251, www.hotelpatang.com. Comfortable a/c rooms, plushest in town.

C Savshanti Lake Resort, Nageshwar Mahadev Rd, T02631-237292, www.savshantihotels.com. 40 rooms, some a/c and overlooking lake, modern facilities.

D-E Anando, Nageshwar Mahadev Rd, T02631-237204. Facing the lake, 23 rooms with bath, vegetarian restaurant, good views.

E Chitrakut, Nasik-Saputara Rd, T02631-237221. Well situated with view of hills, average rooms with bath.

Daman *p1337, map p1338*

Plenty of cheap places on the seafront.

B-C Cidade de Daman, Devka Beach, T0260-225 0590, www.cidadededaman.com. Impressive hotel, 72 breezy, a/c rooms, pool, tennis and badminton, candlelit beach dinners popular for conferences.

B-C Silver Sands, Devka Beach, T0260-225 4376, www.silverresorts.co.in. 32 rooms, modern facilities, pool, bar, disco, across the road from the beach.

C Miramar, Devka Beach, T0260-225 4971. One of the oldest in town, rooms with pleasant balcony plus some cottages, pool, beachside restaurant plays loud Indian film music till late on weekend nights. They have also opened a new water park resort in the area, bit more expensive.

C-D Gurukripa, Nani Daman, T0260-645 2494, www.hotelgurukripa.com. 25 large a/c rooms with bath, good restaurant (wide choice of Punjabi, Gujarati, some Chinese), roof garden, car hire.

C-D Sandy Resort, Devka Beach, T0260-225 4644, www.sandyresort.com. Bills itself as a 'class hotel for class people'. Quietest and most pleasant, across the road from the beach, 46 rooms, some a/c (best upstairs), restaurant, disco, pool.

D China Town, Jampore Beach, T0260-225 4416. Few of the 20 rooms have sea views, some a/c but short beds, shower and toilets could improve, friendly helpful staff, good restaurant serves Chinese/Indian food, bar does piña coladas with fresh coconuts.

D Sovereign, T0260-225 0236. Friendly, 24 a/c rooms, clean, secure, vegetarian restaurant (good Gujarati *thali*), chilled beer, travel desk.

E Rahee Guest House (PWD), Marwad Rd, between Nani Daman and Devka Beach, T0260-225 4614. Neglected old building with

15 rooms, some with bath and hot water, cheaper with Indian toilets.

Eating

Vadodara *p1333, map p1333*

Vadodara (see Sleeping). Extensive menu, polished service, plush, pricey, but try lunch buffet; alcohol against passport or permit.

Goodies, Race Course Rd. Parsee couple offer great baked goods.

Kansar, Sayajiganj. Gujarati and Rajasthani *thalis*. Traditional decor, turbaned waiters.

Kwality, Sayajiganj. Wide choice, good Italian and Peshwari dishes, garden seating.

Pizza King, Alkapuri. Italian, justly popular.

Surya Palace (see Sleeping). Serves sumptuous buffets. International, range of desserts, Rs 30-400.

Vanity, near Sardar Patel statue, Sayajiganj. Fluorescent-lit basement serving a range of vegetarian and non- vegetarian Indian meals.

Volga, Alankar Cinema, Sayajiganj. Good Mughlai kebabs and Chinese.

Café Coffee Day, opp Hotel Apex. Caffeine boosts and good range of snacks and sandwiches.

Gokul, Kothi Charrasta. Indian. Good Gujarati *thalis*, small place, large local clientele.

Sahayog, 1st left past **Express** hotel (see Sleeping). Good South Indian *thalis* (Rs 45) and Punjabi.

Chhota Udepur *p1335*

Neelam, near highway, Chokadi. Variable Punjabi food, decent pulao, English spoken.

Neera, near goverment offices, Alirajpur Rd. Rather approximate place where Punjabi dishes are served "depending on availability".

Surat and around *p1336*

Bhathvari, Vadodara Rd, T(0)9898-011022. Excellent Kathiawadi and Marwari *thalis* served on low tables in thatched pavilions in a pleasant garden environment.

Yuvraj (see Sleeping). Rooftop garden café.

Dotivala, Makkai Bridge, Nanpura. Surat's best bakery is a good place to try *naan khatai*, a delicious butter biscuit.

Saatvik, opposite railway station. Excellent, unlimited Gujarati *thalis*, Rs 45.

Daman *p1337, map p1338*

You can get fresh fish lunches and dinners at most hotels, also fish snacks at the bars.

Damanganga Lake Garden, Daman-Vapi Rd. Popular lake-facing restaurant, with gardens and fountains. Unusual, though garish, bar has a Mughal theme with miniature paintings of royal drinking parties. Good atmosphere, decent food.

Duke, Devka Beach. Parsi and *tandoori* food outdoors (also rooms to let in the old Parsi bungalow next door, Rs 400).

Kadliya Lake Resort, is an island restaurant created by **Daman Tourism**, with lawns, gardens, cascades, fountains and boating facilities. The food upstairs is not bad and there is a bar and snacks downstairs by the lake. Service is slow and suffers an occasional scourge of flies and mosquitoes. Entry fee Rs 10, camera Rs 10, parking Rs 10.

Jampore Beach Resort. Cafeteria, bar, meals/snacks upstairs with view of sea, outdoor dining area, hammocks for relaxing.

Samrat, Seaface Rd. Simple and clean, excellent *thalis*.

Festivals and events

Vadodara *p1333, map p1333*

Mar Navratri is very colourful when local Garba, Dandia and Raas performances are held, and pilgrims head for Pawagadh.

Aug Ganesh Chaturthi is celebrated by the large Maharashtrian population here.

Shopping

Vadodara *p1333, map p1333*

Vadodara is a centre for silver jewellery. Shopping areas are Raopura, Mandvi, Teen Darwaza, National Plaza, Leheripura Mandir Bazar and Alkapuri Arcade.

Crossword, 2/1 Arunodaya Society, Alkapuri. Wide selection of new books and CDs.

Khadi Bhandar, Kothi Rd. For handlooms and local handicrafts.

Activities and tours

Vadodara *p1333, map p1333*

Swimming

Lal Bagh and Sardar Bagh pools, Alkapuri; also at **Vadodara** and **Surya Palace** hotels.

Tour operators

Prominent, 7/12 Race Course Circle, T0265-230 0120. Recommended for ticketing.

Tradewings, Sayajiganj, T0265-232 7127. Changes money (even on Sat).

Transport

Vadodara *p1333, map p1333*

Air Indian, Fatehgunj, T0265-279 4747, 1000-1330, 1415-1700; airport, T0265-244 3262, www.indianairlines.nic.in. **Jet Airways**, 11 Panorama Complex, Alkapuri, T0265-233 7051, airport T0265-248 3938. Flights to **Mumbai** and **Delhi**.

Local bus From opposite the railway station.

Long distance bus State Transport (ST) stand is a 5-min walk north of the railway station, T0265-232 7000. Reservations 0700-2200. Advance booking 0900-1300, 1330-1700. Buses to **Ahmedabad** every 30 mins, 2 hrs; also to **Diu via Bhavnagar**, **Mumbai** (425 km), **Pune**, **Udaipur** and **Mount Abu** and **Ujjain** (403 km), among others.

Taxi Tourist taxis from tourist office and travel agents. Non a/c Ambassador, Rs 7 per km, airport drop Rs 200, airport pickup Rs 250. A day's sightseeing (80 km, 8 hrs) Rs 900-1200.

Train Vadodara is on the Western Railways' Delhi-Mumbai broad-gauge line. Enquiries, T131. Reservations T135. 0800-2000 (2nd class) and 0800-1800 (1st class). **Ahmedabad**: any northbound train, including *Gujarat Queen 19109*, 0808, 2¼ hrs; *Gujarat Exp 19011*, 1303, 2¼ hrs. **Mumbai Central**: *Gujarat Mail 12902*, 0006, 6¼ hrs; *Kutch Exp 19032*, 0455, 6½ hrs; *Paschim Exp 12926*, 0852, 6¼ hrs. **New Delhi**: *Paschim Exp 12925*, 1803, 16¾ hrs; *Rajdhani Exp 12951*, 2127, 11 hrs. **Porbandar** via Rajkot and Jamnagar: *Saurashtra Exp 19215*, 1642, 14 hrs.

Champaner *p1335*

Shared jeeps and ST buses from Vadodara and Ahmedabad go to **Machi** where the cable cars start for the ascent to the monuments on the hill; Rs 45 return (only hand baggage of 5 kg allowed), 0900-1300, 1400-1700.

Surat and around *p1336*

Train Ahmedabad: *Shatabdi Exp 2009*, 0954, not Sun, 3½ hrs; *Gujarat Exp 19011*, 1041, 4¾ hrs; **Mumbai Central**: *Kranti Rajdhani 12954*, 0615, 3¾ hrs; *Paschim Exp 12926*, 1045, 4¼ hrs. **New Delhi**: *Janata Exp 19023*, 1349, 24 hrs; *Paschim Exp 12925*, 1547, 19 hrs. **Porbandar**: *Saurashtra Exp 19215*, 1405, 16½ hrs. **Rajkot** and **Jamnagar**: *Janata Exp 19017*, 2205, 10½ hrs (Rajkot), 12½ hrs (Jamnagar).

Saputara *p1336*

From the NH8, the turn off is at Chikhli to the west. Petrol is only available at Waghai (51 km northwest), and at a pump 40 km from Saputara, on the Nashik road.

Bus From **Mumbai**, there are private luxury buses (**Modern Travels**) on alternate days during the season.

Train Train from **Ahmedabad** (400 km) or **Mumbai** (255 km) to **Billimora** and then local bus or taxi; or a narrow gauge train to **Waghai**.

Daman *p1337, map p1338*

Bus For the bus stand: turn right out of Vapi station, walk 500 m along main road to a T-junction; the stand is nearby, on the left.

Taxi Shared taxis go to Daman but with 8 others can be a squeeze (Rs 20 each); Rs 160 per taxi. By car, turn off the NH8 at Karmbeli between Bhilad and Vapi.

Train Not all trains stop at **Vapi** from Mumbai. *Gujarat Exp 19011*, 0851, 3 hrs; *Saurashtra Exp 19215*, 0745, 3½ hrs. From **Ahmedabad**: *Karnavati Exp 12934*, 0500, 5¼ hrs; *Shatabdi Exp 12010*, , 1435 (except Wed) 4¾ hrs.

Directory

Vadodara *p1333, map p1333*

Banks There are convenient ATMs opposite railway station and around Sayajiganj. For exchange, **Trade Wings** in Sayajiganj, and **Thomas Cook**, Landmark Building, Race Course Circle, are fast and efficient. **Medical services Sayaji Hospital**, Sayajiganj; **Maharani Jamunabai Hospital**, Mandvi. **Post** GPO: Raopura. **Useful contacts** Forest office: T0265-242 9748. **Foreigners' Regional Registration Office**: Collector's Office, Kothi Kacheri.

Surat and around *p1336*

Banks Exchange at **State Bank of India**, Chowk Rd. **Internet Cyber Cafés**, at Belgian Sq, Athwa Lines, Ambaji Rd and **Bellevue Hotel**, near the station.

Daman *p1337, map p1338*

Banks State Bank of India, Kabi Kabarda Rd. **Post** GPO: near bridge to Moti Daman.

Saurashtra

Around the coastal region of the Saurashtra Peninsula are some of India's most remarkable religious sites, from Dwarka in the west to Palitana in the east, while the coastline itself is fringed with some attractive beaches and the former Portuguese territory of Diu. The historic town of Junagadh and wildlife parks also draw visitors. Northern Saurashtra, with Rajkot at its centre, is one of the major groundnut growing regions of India. ▸▸ *For listings, see pages 1358-1367.*

Rajkot → *Colour map 2, C2. Phone code: 0281. Population: 966,600.*

Rajkot is a bustling commercial city with a large number of shopping complexes and heavy traffic, but there are also some fine late 19th-century colonial buildings and institutions since the British Resident for the Western Indian States lived here. There has been rapid industrialization recently, based especially in the processing of agricultural products.

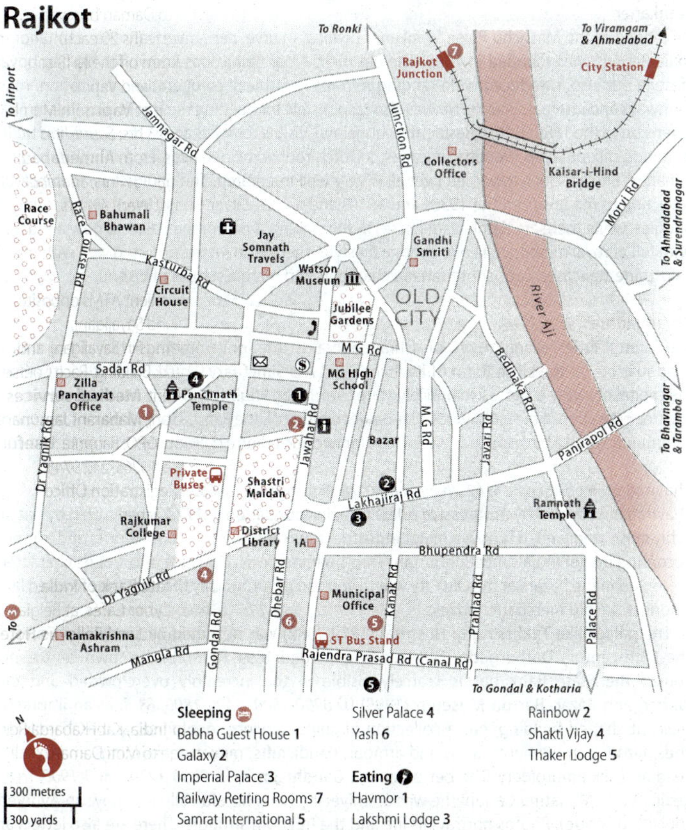

Sleeping
Babha Guest House 1
Galaxy 2
Imperial Palace 3
Railway Retiring Rooms 7
Samrat International 5
Silver Palace 4
Yash 6

Eating
Havmor 1
Lakshmi Lodge 3
Rainbow 2
Shakti Vijay 4
Thaker Lodge 5

Although there is an early Palaeolithic site at Rajkot, there is very little evidence of the settlement. Rajkot was the capital of the Jadejas, who ruled earlier from a place named Sardhar on the Rajkot-Bhavnagar road, and later set up this new city which became the headquarters of the British representatives in Saurashtra. The British impact can be seen in the impressive **Rajkumar College**, a famous public school founded in 1870 set in vast grounds, and the richly endowed **Watson Museum** ⓘ *Jubilee Gardens, Thu-Tue 0900-1230, 1430-1800, closed 2nd and 4th Sat each month, Rs 5, Rs 2 per photo,* with exhibits from the Indus Valley civilization, medieval sculpture, pottery and crafts, and colonial memorabilia. The gardens also contain the **Memorial Institute** and its crumbling Lang Library. **Gandhi Smriti** (Kaba Gandhino Delo), the early home of Mohandas K Gandhi, is in Ghee Kanta Road, between MG Road and Lakahjiraj Road (rickshaw-wallahs know the way). The **Gandhi Museum** ⓘ *Dharmandra Rd, Mon-Sat 0900-1200, 1500-1800,* in the Gandhi family home (1880), contains photographs and personal effects. Descriptions are mainly in Hindi and Gujarati; guides speak no English. **Rashtriya Shala** is where Mahatma Gandhi went to school and promotes one of his greatest ideals: handloom and handicrafts. Among the textiles being promoted is Patola-style *ikat* silk weaving.

Wankaner

On a bend of the Machchu River, Wankaner (*wanka* – curve, *ner* – river), another capital of the Jhala Rajputs, was founded in 1605. The old ruler, Amar Sinhji, was known for his flamboyant lifestyle but also introduced wide-ranging reforms in farmers' co-operatives, education, roads, tramways and internal security. He was also responsible for building the **Ranjitvilas Palace** (1907 extension to the 1880s British Residents' bungalow), visible for miles across the plains. It is built in a strange mix of styles (Venetian façades, a Dutch roof, *jarokha* balconies, a 'Mughal' pavilion, minarets, English clock tower, etc) yet all is very well integrated. The garage has an interesting collection of models from the 1930s and 1940s and a 1921 Silver Ghost, jeeps, wagons and old buggies, while there are Kathiawadi horses in the stables. A part of the palace is now a **museum** brim full of royal memorabilia of a bygone lifestyle. There is an interesting step well with marble balustrade staircases, cool, subterranean chambers and marble statues of Vishnu.

Dhrangadhra

The pretty little village town of Dhrangadhra is the government Forest Department's headquarters for the **Little Rann of Kachchh Wild Ass Sanctuary** ⓘ *T02754-223016*. It was also the capital of a very progressive princely state, which had English and vernacular schools in 1855 and free education in the early 1900s. Full-day jeep tours of Little Rann, to see wild asses, salt mining communities and a bird sanctuary, is Rs 2000 for two, including a delicious home-cooked lunch.

Bhavnagar → *Colour map 5, A2. Phone code: 0278. Population: 511,000.*

Bhavnagar was ruled by progressive rulers from its foundation in 1723. Surrounded by flat and richly cultivated land, it is now a major industrial town and cotton export centre, and is rapidly becoming one of India's most important ship-building ports. However, most of its character is preserved in the bazars of the Old City where you can pick your way through the crowded lanes amongst the old merchants' *havelis*.

The palace-like **Takhtsinghji Hospital** (1879-1883) was designed by Sir William Emerson. The 18th-century **Darbargadh** (Old Palace, extended 1894-1895), in the town centre, now houses the State Bank but is scarcely visible in the incredibly overcrowded and dirty Darbargadh Bazar. **Barton Museum** (1895) ⓘ *0900-1300, 1400-1800, Rs 5,* in an impressive crescent-shaped building, has a collection of coins, carvings, geological and archaeological finds, farming implements, arms and armour, handicrafts, miniature paintings and excellent bead and silk embroidery. The better known **Gandhi Smriti** ⓘ *0830-1230, 1500-1900, free,* is dedicated to Mahatma Gandhi (he was at university here; his old college is now an Ayurvedic education centre). Photos portray his life and the freedom struggle. There are also letters and mark sheets showing his scores at university. The unremarkable marble **Takhteshwar Temple** on a hillock has good views over the city and the distant coastline.

Victoria Park, 2 km from the centre, is a former royal hunting preserve. Far removed from the image conveyed by its name of a manicured British city park, it has rolling scrub forests and marshes rich in birdlife. Nilgai, hyena, jackal, jungle cat and monitor lizard can all be seen. A pleasant stroll from the Nilambagh Palace, it is a great place for walks. **Gaurishankar Lake**, a popular escape from the city with parks and steps along the embankments, is good for winter birdwatching when cranes, pelicans and ducks arrive. Plovers, terns and other birds nest on the islands.

Velavadar National Park

ⓘ *Some 10 km off the Bhavnagar–Vadodara Highway, 0630-0830 and 1630-1830, closed mid-Jun to mid-Oct, US$5, camera US$5; guide (some don't speak English), US$10 per trip, jeep US$25 per drive. Pay at Forest Range Office at park entrance.*

The compact 36 sq km of flat grassland broken by dry open scrubland and patches of thorn forest was set up to protect the Indian blackbuck, of which it has the largest population in the country – about 1000 permanent residents and another 1000 that wander in from the surrounding area. The Bhavnagar royal family came here for cheetah coursing, falconry and hunting and also harvested grass for fodder for their cattle and horses.

Bhavnagar

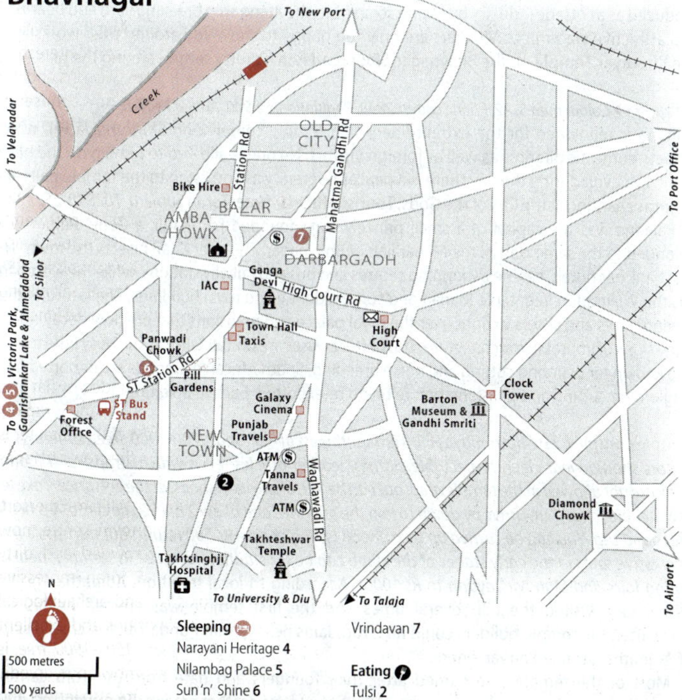

Sleeping
Narayani Heritage **4**
Nilambag Palace **5**
Sun 'n' Shine **6**
Vrindavan **7**

Eating
Tulsi **2**

The blackbuck is the second largest of the antelopes and the fastest long-distance runner of all animals. It can keep going at a steady 90 kph. The black-and-white dominant males sport spiral horns; the juvenile males are brown and white while the hornless females are brownish, with lighter parts. It is one of the most hunted animals in India, and so is an endangered species. Impressive males clash horns to establish territory and court females. Wolves, their prime predator, have been reduced to only two families, but they can still be seen. The park also contains a few sounders of wild boar in addition to 50-60 nilgai, usually seen near waterholes, jungle cat, which can be seen at dawn and dusk, and jackal. Birdlife is rich with numerous birds of prey including the largest harrier roost in the world; some 1500 to 2000 of these light-bodied hawks gather here at sunset in November and December. During the monsoon the park is the best place in India to spot the lesser florican. In addition to the two rivers that border the park, there are three waterholes and three small pools that attract animals at midday.

Sihor

Midway between Bhavnagar (27 km) and Palitana, the former Gohil Rajput capital has the 17th-century hilltop **Darbargadh Palace** (now government offices). Though rather dilapidated, you can still see some intricate carved wooden balconies and pillars outside and 19th-century wall paintings inside. The Brahm **Kund** (11th-12th century), about 2 km west of Sihor centre and 500 m south of the main road, is a deeply set stepped tank (now empty). It has around 100 sculpted images of deities in small niches, a few of which are still actively worshipped. There are also pillared galleries with rich carvings of musicians. In the village nearby brass utensils are produced as a cottage industry by rolling scrap from the Alang ship breaking yard and beating it into attractive water pots. Villagers are only too happy to show you around their workshops. The **Khodiyar Temple** on the Bhavnagar-Sihor road is in a pretty setting among the hills.

Palitana → *Colour map 5, A2. Phone code: 02848. Population: 51,900. Area: 13 sq km.*

Palitana is renowned for the extraordinary Jain temple complex on Shatrunjaya Hill which attracts domestic pilgrims as well as foreign visitors. No one is allowed to remain on the hill at night, but even during the day there is a peaceful serenity as you listen to the temple bells and pilgrims chanting in the City of the Gods. **Tourist office** ⓘ *Hotel Toran Sumeru, T02848-252327.*

Palitana was the capital of a small princely state founded by Shahji, a Gohel Rajput who belonged to the same clan as the Maharajah of Bhavnagar. The river Khari bisects the town. The east bank has hotels, eateries, shopping centres and bus and railway stations, while the west bank has the Willingdon Vegetable Market and some older raj and royal buildings. The last ruler died leaving wives and sisters to fight over the royal palace and mansions that are now decaying but show signs of impressive architecture. The better houses are on Taleti Road. The busy little town is also known for diamond cutting and horse breeding. South African diamonds are imported from Belgium for cutting and polishing before being re-exported back to Belgium.

Temple complex ⓘ *Shatrunjaya Hill, 3 km southwest of Palitana, 0700-1900, free, camera Rs 40, visitors should wear clean respectable clothes, leather articles (even watch straps) and food or drink are not allowed in the temple area, but can be left, along with shoes, at the entrance. Take lots of water and a sun hat, arrive by dawn to join the pilgrims, and allow 2 hrs for the climb, 4-5 hrs for the round trip. You can be carried up by a dhooli (string chair – Rs 500 return) but the hassle from aggressive touts in the early stages of the climb can be substantial (rates rise in summer, peaking during fairs and Mahavir Jayanti to Rs 1000).* According to local tradition, Adinatha, the first Tirthankara, visited the hill several times and the first temple was erected by his son. Thereafter, the temple builders could not stop. Jains believe that Pundarika, the chief disciple of Adinatha, attained nirvana here.

Most of the temples are named after their founders and date from the 16th century, although the earliest may date from the 11th. It would appear that many others were destroyed by the Muslims in the 14th and 15th centuries, but later, when Jains obtained religious toleration, they began rebuilding.

The 863 temples are strung along the two ridges of the hill, with further temples in the hollow between, linking them. There are nine enclosures of *tuks* (fortifications) which provided defence. There are lovely views over the flat, cultivated black soils of the coastal plain, and on a clear day after the rains it is sometimes possible to see the Gulf of Khambat away to the east, and the Chamardi peak and the granite range of Sihor to the north.

There are two routes up the 600 m climb. The main route starts in the town of Palitana to the east of the hill, while a shorter and steeper route climbs up from the village of Adpur to the west. Both are excellently made stepped paths. The main pilgrim route starts in Palitana. Over 3500 steps – you will be told more by the *dhoolie* carriers at the bottom – lead up to the temples. There are two long flat stretches, but since some of the path is unshaded, even in winter it can get very hot.

Temples in this southern group include one of **Ramaji Gandharia** (16th century), and the **Bhulavani** (labyrinth, 18th century) which is a series of crypt-like chambers each surmounted with a dome. The **Hathiapol** (Elephant Gate, 19th century) faces southeast. The **Vimalavasi Tuk** occupies the west end of the south ridge. In it is the **Adishvara Temple** (16th century) which dominates the site. It has a double-storey *mandapa* inside which is a large image of Rishabhanatha with crystal eyes and a gold crown of jewels. The **Vallabhai Temple** (19th century) with its finely clustered spires and the large **Motisah Temple** (1836) occupy the middle ground between the ridges.

The **Khartaravasi Tuk** is the largest and highest temple complex, stretched out along the northern Ridge and includes the **Adinatha Temple** (16th century). There are quadruple *Tirthankara* images inside the sanctuary.

A comprehensive restoration project is being carried out on some of the temples, with many of the old stone carvings being 'refreshed' using a butterscotch-coloured mortar. It is interesting to watch the craftsmen in action, but some may feel that the new decorations lack the sculptural finesse and timeworn appeal of the originals.

If you wish to take the track down to Adpur turn left out of the complex entrance courtyard where you leave your shoes. Follow the sign to Gheti Pag Gate.

Alang

The beach at Alang has turned into the world's largest scrapyard for redundant ships, the industry yielding rich pickings from the sale of salvaged metal (bronze, copper) and the complete range of ship's fittings from portholes to furniture, diesel engines and lifeboats. Alang village, which is 50 km south of Bhavnagar, has developed this surprising specialization because of the unusual nature of its tides. The twice-monthly high tides are exceptional, reputedly the second highest in the world, lifting ships so that they can be beached well on shore, out of reach of the sea for the next two weeks. During this period the breakers move in unhindered. Labourers' 'huts' line the coast road though many workers commute from Bhavnagar.

Even though entry to Alang port may not be available, the last few kilometres to the port are lined with the yards of dealers specializing in every item of ships' furniture. Valuable items are creamed off before the 'breaking' begins, but if you want 3-cm-thick porthole glass, a spare fridge-freezer or a life jacket, this is the place to browse. However, customs officers always get first choice of valuables as they have to give permission for vessels to be beached, so don't expect too much. Some have found the journey not worth the trouble since they couldn't enter the fenced-off 'lots'.

Alang is only open to tourists with **special permission**, obtained from the **Gujarat Maritime Board** ⓘ *Sector 10A, opposite Air Force Station, Gandhinagar, T02842-235222, the Port Officer, New Port, Bhavnagar 5, T0278-229 3090*, or in Alang itself. Foreigners report finding it difficult to get permission to enter the beach/port area. Hotels in Bhavnagar may be able to help individuals gain entry but permits for groups are virtually impossible. Photography is not allowed. Strong shoes and modest dress are recommended.

Mahuva and Gopnath

The picturesque town of **Mahuva** (pronounced Mow-va), south of Palitana, was known for its historic port. Beautiful handcrafted furniture with lacquer work and intricate hand painting is made here.

About 30 km northeast of Mahuva, **Gopnath** is where the 16th-century mystic poet Narsinh Mehta is said to have attained enlightenment. Near the lighthouse is the 1940s summer home of late Maharajah Krishna Kumar Singhji of Bhavnagar, part of which is now a hotel. There are pleasant rocky, white-sand beaches – dangerous for swimming but good for walking – and a 700-year-old temple, 1 km away.

Gondal → *Colour map 5, A1. Phone code: 02825.*

The fascinating old town of Gondal, 38 km south of Rajkot, was the capital of one of the most progressive, affluent and efficient princely states of the British period. The exemplary state, ruled by Jadeja Rajputs, had an excellent road network, free compulsory education for all children including girls, sewage systems and accessible irrigation for farmers. The rulers rejected *purdah*, their palaces have no *zenanas*, and imposed no taxes on their subjects, instead earning revenue from rail connections between the port towns of Porbandar and Veraval with Rajkot and cities inland. The **Naulakha Palace** (1748) ⓘ *0900-1200, 1500-1800, Rs 100,* with a sculpted façade, pretty jharoka windows and carved stone pillars, has an impressive Darbar Hall and a museum of paintings, furniture, brass and silver. Silver items include caskets, models of buildings and scales used for weighing the Maharajah (he was weighed against silver and gold on his 25th and 50th birthday; the precious metals were then distributed to the poor). A gallery has toys from the 1930s and 1940s. The **Vintage and Classic Car Museum** ⓘ *open same hours, Rs 100,* is one of the finest in the country. Exhibits include 1910 New Engine, 1920s Delage and Daimler, 1935-1955 models, horse-drawn carriages, etc. Boating is possible on **Veri Lake** nearby, which attracts large numbers of rosy pelicans, flamingos, demoiselle and common eastern cranes and many others, particularly in January and February. You can visit the **Bhuvaneshwari Ayurvedic Pharmacy**, founded in 1910, which still prepares herbal medicines according to ancient principles and runs a hospital offering massages and treatment. The early 20th-century **Swaminarayan Temple** has painted interiors on the upper floors.

Junagadh → *Colour map 5, A1. Phone code: 0285. Population: 168,700.*

ⓘ *You can tackle the town on foot allowing plenty of time for Uparkot. However, it's best to get an early start on Girnar Hill with the help of a rickshaw (around Rs 50 return).*

The narrow winding lanes and colourful bazars of this small town, entered by imposing gateways, are evocative of earlier centuries. A large rock with 14 Asokan edicts, dating from 250 BC, stands on the way to the temple-studded Girnar Hill, believed to be a pre-Harappan site. But the modern town is marred by ugly new buildings and dirty slums.

Established by the Mauryans in the fourth century BC, from the second to fourth centuries Junagadh was the capital of Gujarat under the Kshattrapa rulers. It is also associated with the Chudasama Rajputs who ruled from Junagadh from AD 875. The fort was expanded in 1472 by Mahmud Beghada and again in 1683 and 1880. Sher Khan Babi, who took on the title of Nawab Bahadur Khan Babi, declared Junagadh an independent state in the 1700s. At the time of Partition the Nawab exercised his legal right to accede to Pakistan but his subjects were predominantly Hindu and after Indian intervention and an imposed plebiscite their will prevailed. The Nawab was exiled along with his 100 dogs.

The old **Uparkot citadel** ⓘ *0700-1900, Rs 5, plus Rs 100 to visit the Buddhist caves,* on a small plateau east of the town, was a stronghold in the Mauryan and Gupta empires. The present walls are said to date from the time of the Chudasama Rajputs (ninth-15th century). The deep moat inside the walls is believed to have once held crocodiles. The Ottoman canons of Suleman Pasha, an ally of the sultans, were moved here after the Muslim forces were unable to save Diu from Portuguese naval forces. The town was repeatedly under attack so there was a huge granary to withstand a long siege. The **Jama Masjid** was built from the remains of a Hindu palace. The 11th-century **Adi Chadi Vav**, a *baoli* with 172 steps and an impressive spiral staircase, is believed to commemorate two slave girls who were bricked up as sacrifice to ensure the supply of water. The 52-m-deep Naghan Kuva is a huge 11th-century well, which has steps down to the water level through the rocks, with openings to ventilate the path. The **Buddhist cave monastery** in this fort complex dates from Asoka's time. Two of the three levels are open to visitors. The drainage system was very advanced, as shown by the rainwater reservoir. The ventilation cleverly achieved a balance of light and cool breezes. Other Buddhist caves are hewn into the hillsides near the fort.

Junagadh

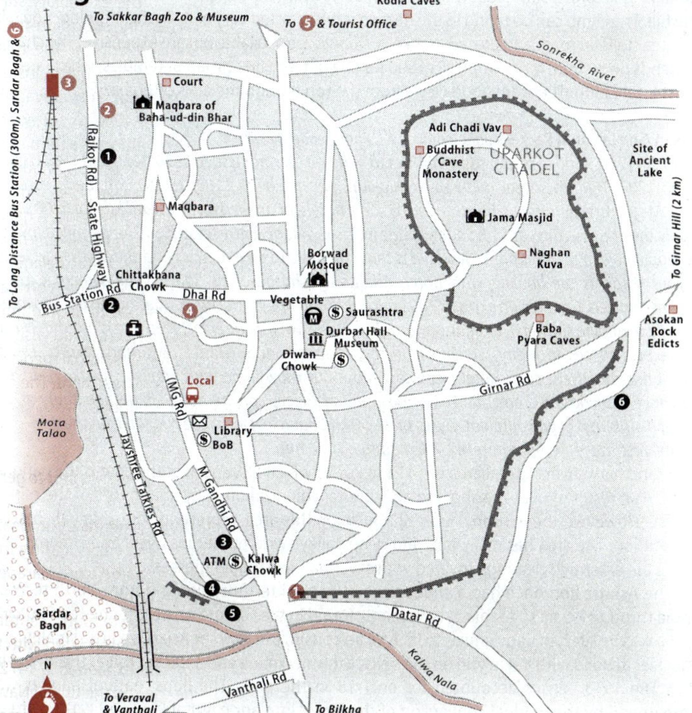

300 metres
300 yards

Sleeping
Girnar 5
Lotus 2
Madhuwati 1
Railway Retiring Rooms 3
Relief 4
Vishala 6

Eating
Garden Café 6
Geeta & Sharda 1
Poonam 2
Sagar 5
Santoor 3
Swati 4

In the town, the late 19th-century mausolea of the Junagadh rulers, not far from the railway station, are impressive. The **Maqbara** of Baha-ud-din Bhar with its silver doors and intricate, elaborate decoration, has an almost fairground flamboyance. The **Old Mausolea** at Chittakhana Chowk (opposite **Relief Hotel**, which has views of them from the roof), which were once impressive, are now crumbling and overgrown.

The **Durbar Hall Museum** ⓘ *Nawab's Palace, circa 1870, Janta Chowk, Thu-Tue 0900-1215, 1500-1800, Rs 5, plus Rs 2 per photo, small but recommended*, houses royal memorabilia, including portraits, palanquins, gem-studded carpets and costumes.

Further east, **Asokan rock edicts** ⓘ *at the foot of the Girnar Hill, 0830-1800, closed Wed and holidays, Rs 100*, are carved in the Brahmi script on a large boulder. The emperor instructed his people to be gentle with women, be kind to animals, give alms freely and to plant medicinal herbs. The 13 edicts are summed up in the 14th.

Girnar Hill, rising 900 m above the surrounding plain, 3 km east of town, has been an important religious centre for the Jains from the third century BC. The climb up this worn volcanic cone by 10,000 stone steps takes at least two hours. You start just beyond Damodar Kund in teak forest; at the foot is the Asokan Edict while a group of 16 Jain temples surmounts the hill. The climb can be trying in the heat so is best started very early in the morning. You will find tea stalls en route and brazen monkeys. *Dhoolis* are available but are expensive. The charge depends on weight; for example, Rs 1500 for 60 kg to the first group of temples, which are the most interesting. There are good views from the top though the air is often hazy.

Sasan Gir National Park → *Colour map 5, A1. Phone code: 02877.*

ⓘ *0700-1200, 1500 to sunset from mid-Oct to mid-Feb (permits issued 0630-1030 and 1500-1700); 0700-1200, 1600 to sunset mid-Feb to mid-Jun (permits 0630-1100, 1600-1730); best season is Mar-May. Entry permits can be arranged by some hotels, or applied for in advance (ie for 0700 safari apply the previous day) at Sinh Sadan Lodge in Sasan village. Entry fees: US$40 for permit, allowing 6 people in jeep to enter park. New rule is that you have to go in person and show passport, even if your safari is pre-booked with hotel. Additional charge of Rs 500 if your camera exceeds 7.1 megapixels. Count in an extra Rs 100 for a guide and tips (some have little English but can make excellent wildlife spotters). Indians pay roughly 10-25% of foreigner fee. Jeep hire is around Rs 750, but expect all fees, including jeep hire to increase 25% on Sat-Sun and 50% during Navratri, Diwali and Christmas/New Year. Hotel jeeps cost more but may come with English- speaking drivers. Advance bookings recommended as a maximum of 35 jeeps are permitted in the sanctuary at one time, distributed over 6 different routes of 22-50 km. But a few jeeps are available on the day – first come, first shove. Temperature: 42-7°C. Rainfall: 1000 mm.*

The sanctuary covers a total area of 1412 sq km, of which 258 sq km at the core is the national park. As a result of over-grazing and agricultural colonization, only about 10% of the park is forest. However, the scrubby look of much of the area represents the original, natural vegetation. The area has rocky hills and deep valleys with numerous rivers and streams, and there are extensive clearings covered with savannah-like fodder grasses.

The **Asiatic lion** once had a wide range of natural territory running from North to West India through Persia to Arabia. It is now only found in the Gir forest; the last one seen outside India was in 1942, in Iran. Similar to its African cousin, the tawnier Asian is a little smaller and stockier in build with a skin fold on the belly, a thinner mane and a thicker tuft at the end of its tail. The 1913 census accounted for only 18 in the park. The lions' natural habitat was threatened by the gradual conversion of the forest into agricultural land and cattle herders grazing their livestock here. The conservation programme has been remarkably successful. There are now reckoned to be around 350 animals in the park; too many, some say, for the territory to support. These, and 300-plus **panthers**, make Gir arguably India's best big cat sanctuary, while the existence of a handful of Sudanese villages in the park add to the slightly surreal African-safari feel of the place.

Though there have been attacks on villagers by park lions, these are thought likely to have been provoked as there are few reported man-eaters. Nevertheless, relations between the lions and the human settlements within and around the boundaries are becoming increasingly strained, with several reports of revenge killings of lions (principally for hunting livestock) being reported in the last couple of years. Deaths by poaching are also beginning to occur with disturbing regularity.

During the course of three to four jeep safaris you have a reasonably good chance of spotting lions. They are more likely to be seen with the help of a good tracker and guide, but the government system for apportioning guides to a different group each session means it is impossible to guarantee the quality of your tracker from one drive to the next; inevitably, some visitors return disappointed. If you don't see one, the Interpretation Zone's safari park has a few lions (see below).

A **watch tower** camouflaged in the tree canopy at Kamleshwar overlooks an artificial reservoir harbouring wild crocodiles but it is poorly located and overcrowded with bus loads of noisy visitors at weekends. Other towers are at Janwadla and Gola. For birdwatching, Adhodiya, Valadara, Ratnaghuna and Pataliyala, are good spots. A walk along Hiran River is also rewarding.

The Tulsishyam **hot springs** in the heart of the forest (Tulsishyam is also a Krishna pilgrimage centre), and Kankai Mata **temple** dedicated to Bhim, the *Mahabharata* hero, and his mother Kunti, add interest.

Gir Interpretation Zone ⓘ *Devaliya, 12 km west of Sasan, foreigners US$20, Indians Rs 75 for 45-min tour by electric minibus; a taxi will charge around Rs 200-300 return including wait*, is 16 sq km of Gir habitat fenced in as a safari park to show a cross section of wildlife; the four or five lions can be easily seen in open scrubland in the area. The lions here are less shy than those in the sanctuary, but you may be frustrated by the briefness of the encounter. Other Gir wildlife include spotted deer, sambar, nilgai, peafowl. Permits are available at the reception.

Crocodile Rearing Centre ⓘ *near entrance to Sinh Sadan, and road leading to Lion Safari Lodge, 0800-1200, 1500-1800, free*, is full of marsh crocodiles, varying in size from a few centimetres to 1 m, for restocking the population in the sanctuary. Eggs are collected in the park and taken to Junagadh for hatching under controlled conditions. Unfortunately, keepers prod the crocodiles to make them move.

Veraval

Veraval is a noisy, unbearably smelly and unattractive town which provides a base for visiting the Hindu pilgrimage centre of Somnath at Prabhas Patan. Its importance now is as a fishing port – hence the stench. Seagoing *dhows* and fishing boats are still being built by the sea without the use of any modern instruments, traditional skills being passed down from father to son.

Prabhas Patan (Somnath)

Somnath Temple ⓘ *6 km east of Veraval, puja at 0700, 1200 and 1900*, a major Hindu pilgrimage centre, is said to have been built out of gold by Somraj, the Moon God (and subsequently in silver, wood and stone). In keeping with the legend, the stone façade appears golden at sunset. Mahmud of Ghazni plundered it and removed the gates in 1024. Destroyed by successive Muslim invaders, it was rebuilt on the same spot. The final reconstruction did not take place until 1950 and is still going on. Unfortunately, it lacks character but it has been built to traditional patterns with a soaring 50-m-high tower that rises in clusters. Dedicated to Siva, it has one of the 12 sacred *jyotirlingas*, see page 271. You cannot take bags of any kind, cameras or mobiles into the temple.

Nearby is the ruined **Rudreshvara Temple**, which dates from the same time as the Somnath Temple and was laid out in a similar fashion. The sculptures on the walls and doorways give an indication of what the original Somnath Temple was like. There is a really old Shiva Linga here – very atmospheric temple.

Krishna was believed to have been hit by an arrow, shot by the Bhil, Jara, when he was mistaken for a deer at Bhalka Teerth, and was cremated at Triveni Ghat, east of Somnath.

Diu → *Colour map 5, A1. Phone code: 02875. Population: 21,600.*
The island of Diu has a fascinating history and a relaxed atmosphere with little traffic. The north side of the island has salt pans and marshes which attract wading birds, the south coast has some limestone cliffs and pleasant, sandy beaches. Although often compared to Goa, it is nowhere near as picturesque. The island is still visited by relatively few foreign travellers though its tavernas attract those deprived of alcohol from neighbouring Gujarat and the bars can get noisy especially at the weekend. It can be quite intimidating for women. It's no paradise island, but if you're in the area it offers a welcome break from the rigours of travelling around Gujarat. Most hotels cater for Gujarati families and so can be noisy. Diu town however has a relaxed vibe, crumbling charm and friendly locals.

Information is available from the **Tourist Complex** ⓘ *Ghogla, Mon-Fri 0930-1315, 1400-1745*, or the **Information Assistant** ⓘ *Diu jetty north of Bunder Chowk, T02875-252653, www.diuindia.com.*

Background Like Daman across the gulf, Diu was a Portuguese colony until 1961. In 1987 its administration was separated from Goa (some 1600 km away), which then became a State – Diu remains a Union Territory. From the 14th to 16th centuries the sultans of Oman held the reins of maritime power here. The Portuguese failed to take Diu at their first attempt in 1531 but succeeded three years later. Like Daman, it was once a port for the export of opium from Malwa (Madhya Pradesh) but with the decline of Portugal as a naval power it became little more than a backwater.

About 5000 of the elders here (out of a population of 40,000) still speak fluent Portuguese. There are around 200 Catholic families and the local convent school teaches English, Gujarati, Portuguese and French. The Divechi people remain eligible for Portuguese passports and a few apply daily. Many families have a member working in Lisbon or former Portuguese Africa.

Diu town The small town is squeezed between the fort on the east and a large city wall to the west. With its attractively ornamented buildings and its narrow streets and squares, it has more of a Portuguese flavour than Daman. While some visitors find it quite dirty and decaying, and are disappointed by the number of liquor shops, others find Diu an enjoyable little place. The night market is a great place to have a drink and to wander around.

St Paul's Church (1601-1610), on Travessa dos Hospital, the road running from the fort, has a fine baroque façade, impressive wood panelling and an attractive courtyard. At this

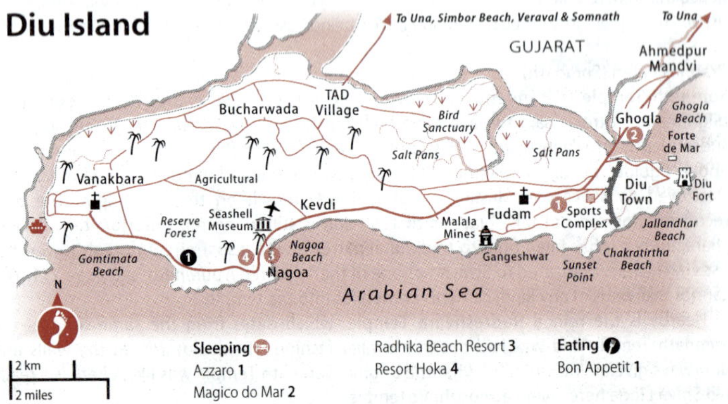

church, take the left-hand turning on to Rua de Isabel Fernandes for the **Church of St Francis of Assisi** (1593), part of which is a hospital (a doctor is available at 0930 for a free consultation). On Rua de Torres Novas is **St Thomas's Church** ⓘ *0800-2000*, housing the museum with an interesting local collection. It has been renovated and now houses stone sculptures, woodcarvings and shadow clocks, as well as a café and pleasant rooms to let. These, and the fort, are floodlit at night.

Diu Fort (1535-1541) ⓘ *0700-1800*, considered to be one of Asia's foremost Portuguese forts, was built after the Mughal Emperor Humayun attacked the Sultan of Gujarat with the help of the Portuguese. Until 1960 it garrisoned 350 Portuguese soldiers. Skirted by the sea on three sides and a rock-cut canal on the fourth, it had two moats, one of which was tidal. The lighthouse stands at one end and parts of the central keep are still used as a jail but has few occupants. Despite being damaged, some of the structures – walls, gateways, arches, ramps, bastions – still give us an idea of the formidable nature of the defences. It's worth allowing an hour for a visit.

Makata Lane or **Panchwati**, near the Zampa gate, has some impressive old mansions of rich Portuguese and Indian merchants ranging from Venetian Gothic-style bungalows to traditional carved wooden or stone *havelis*.

Forte de Mar Forte de Mar (Fortress of Panikot), built in 1535, was strategically important as an easily defended base for controlling the shipping lanes on the northeast part of the Arabian Sea. It has a lighthouse and a chapel to Our Lady of the Sea. It can be approached from Diu jetty when canoes or motor boats are available although landing is not permitted at present. The other fort at the eastern end of the island guarded the mint, while two others once guarded the west at Vanakbara and the bay to the south at Nagoa.

Bird sanctuary The creeks to the north of Diu island have been declared a bird sanctuary. There are watchtowers to spot flocks of shore birds including oyster-catchers, sanderlings and plovers. Lots of herons and ibises, flamingos, pelicans, etc, visit seasonally. Jackals, jungle cats and porcupines are seen in the evening.

Beaches Several beaches on the south side of Diu Island are easy to get to from Diu town by cycle or auto-rickshaw. Beaches between Nagoa and Vanakbara are safe all year except between May and July and are often empty, as is the beach along Ghogla. However, beware of the giant thorns that are hazardous to cycle tyres.

Jallandhar Beach, to the south, is pleasant and the nearest to Diu. There have been several reports of groups of teenage boys, who not only come to watch and pester tourists but aggressively offer sex.

Chakratirtha Beach, just southwest, has a sunset view point, an open auditorium and a small beach which has been spoiled by the glut of beachside cabins.

Just east of Diu Town **Fudam** (or Fofrara) has the air of a Portuguese village with the crumbling Church of Our Lady of the Remedies. **Malala Mines** are limestone quarries off the Nagoa road. **Gangeshwar Temple** nearby has an attractive *Nandi* and Siva *linga* washed by the sea at high tide.

About 7 km from town, facing the Arabian Sea, **Nagoa** offers the best location for a quiet stay away from Diu town. Its semi-circular palm-fringed beach suitable for swimming is popular with foreigners but also large numbers of Indian tourists who come to watch. There are quieter beaches nearby and the forests are pleasant for walks although the entire stretch from Nagoa is being landscaped for development. A **sea shell museum** ⓘ *Rs 10*, has opened on the road from the airport to Nagoa. It displays a large number of mollusc and crustacean shells, corals and marine life from all over the world, collected by a retired merchant navy captain.

The fishing village of **Ghogla-Ahmedpur Mandvi** on the mainland is also part of Diu. Its name changes to Ahmedpur Mandvi on crossing to the Gujarat side of the border. The beach is good for swimming and it has splendid views of fishing villages and the fort and churches on Diu island. **Jyoti Watersports** and **Magico Do Mar** offer a variety of watersports here including parasailing, speed boating and waterskiing. Beware of the rip tide just a few metres out to sea, which has claimed several lives.

Bucharwada, to the north, lacks attractive beaches but has cheap spartan rooms in **Viswas Hotel**. **Gomtimata**, a secluded white sand beach to the west, is where a **Tourist Hostel** is expected to open – but no evidence at time of writing. **Vanakbara**, the fishing village on the western tip of the island, has the Church of Our Lady of Mercy. Get to the early-morning fish market and watch the colourful trawlers unload catches of shark, octopus and every kind of fish imaginable. The drying fish on 'washing lines' and waterside activities provide photo opportunities. You can also watch traditional *dhow* building.

There is a ferry service across to Gomtimata. **Simbor Beach** is a pleasant and little- known beach. It is 27 km from Diu town, off the Una road, and can be reached in 45 minutes from Diu by hiring a moped or scooter. Take food and water.

Diu Town

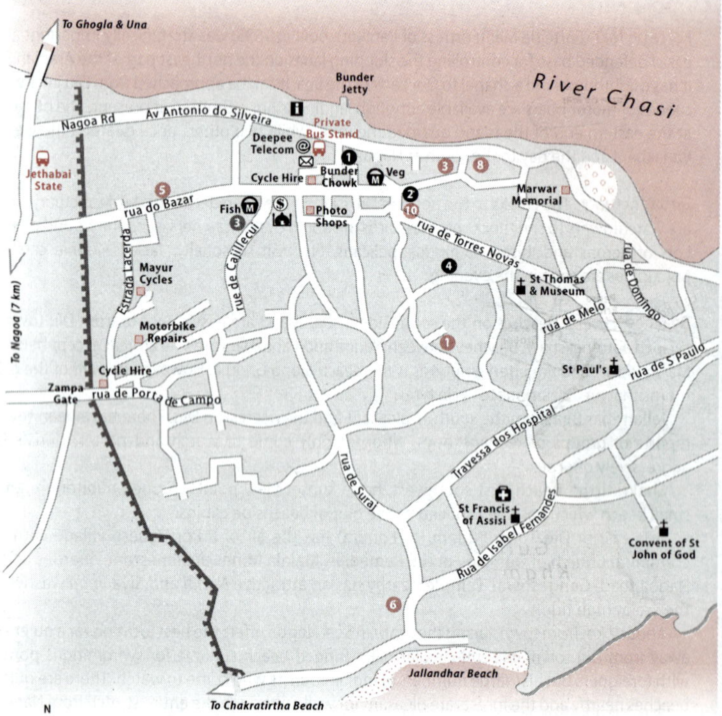

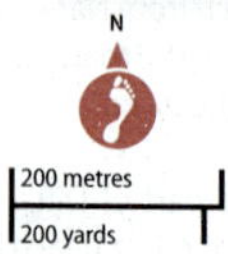

Sleeping
Apana Guest House **3**
Hare Krishna **5**
Hermenca de Goesa **1**
Jay Shankar Guest House **6**
Samrat & Super Silver **10**
Sanmaan Palace **8**

Eating
O'Coqueiro **4**
Ram Vijay **1**
Uma Shakti **2**

Bars & clubs
Nilesh Hotel **3**

Porbandar → *Colour map 5, A1. Phone code: 0286. Population 133,000.*

The former capital of the Jethwa Rajput petty princely state, Porbandar was previously named Sudamapuri, after Krishna's devoted friend, and has a temple dedicated to her. The *dhow*-building tradition that continues on the seashore to the present day reflects a history of maritime trade with North Africa and Arabia. Today, Porbandar is closely associated with Mahatma Gandhi and is also known for its production of gold and silver trinkets, fine-quality silk and cotton manufacture and chemical and cement factories.

Mahatma Gandhi was born in Porbandar in 1869. Next to the family home with its carved balconies is **Kirti Mandir** ⓘ *sunrise-sunset, but the guide takes a lunch break from 1300-1400*, a small museum that traces his life and contains memorabilia and a library. **Darbargadh**, a short walk from Kirti Mandir, the old palace of the Maharanas of Porbandar, was built in the 1780s but is now deserted. It has some intricate carvings and carved balconies; the rooms inside (if you can get in) have interesting paintings. **Sartanji** (or Rana-no) **Choro** (1785), near the ST stand, is the beautiful pleasure pavilion of Maharajah Sartanji, a great poet, writer and music lover. The pavilion has domes, pillars and carved arches and its four sides represent the four seasons. The Maharana's deserted sprawling **Hazur Palace** is near the seafront. Ask for permission to visit the rooms inside at the office. **Daria Rajmahal**, the splendid turn-of-the-century palace of the Maharana of Porbandar, now a college, has intricate carvings, courtyards, fountains, carved arches and heavily embellished façades. The tower has excellent views of the seashore. **Chaya**, 2 km from Chowpatty sea face, is the old capital of the Jetwas. The **Darbargadh Palace** with a beautiful carved balcony, is believed to have secret tunnels and passages to temples and places of safety.

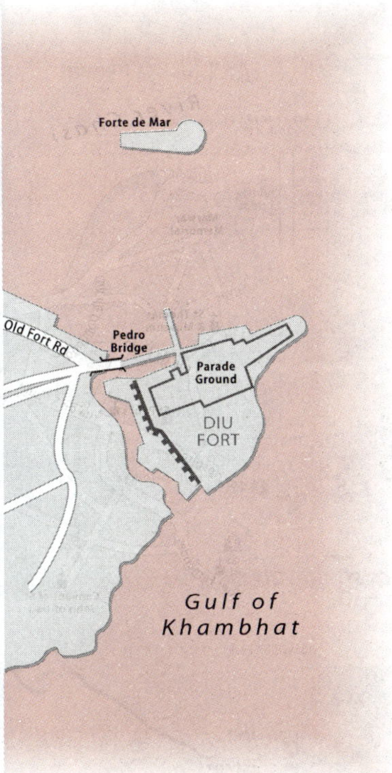

The **Bharat Mandir Hall** in Dayananda Vatika garden is across the Jubilee (Jyubeeli) Bridge. It has a large marble relief map of India on the floor and bas reliefs of heroes from Hindu legends on the pillars. Nearby **Arya Kanya Gurukul** is an experiment in education for girls based on ancient Indian tradition. The dated **planetarium** has shows in Gujarati only. The architecture incorporates different religious styles illustrating Gandhi's open mind.

Jhavar Creek attracts scores of waterbirds. Flamingos, pelicans, storks and heron can be seen from the road in the mangrove marshes. Fisheries have appeared around the creek where the fish put out to dry attract thousands of terns and gulls.

Jamnagar and around → *Colour map 2, C1. Phone code: 0288. Population: 447,700.*

Jamnagar, now an expanding town, was a 16th-century pearl fishing centre with one of the biggest pearl fisheries in the world until the early 20th century. The famous cricketer Ranjitsinghji was its ruler from 1907-1933.

The walled city is famous for its embroidery, silverware and *bandhani* (tie-dye) fabrics produced in workshops in the narrow lanes. **Pirotan Island** in the middle of the Ranmal lake in the Old City, reached by a stone bridge, has the **Lakhota Fort** and **Kotha Bastion** ⓘ *Thu-Tue 1030-1300, 1500-1730, closed 2nd and 4th Sun*, with its arsenal. The **fort museum** has a collection of sculpture and pottery found in ruined medieval villages nearby. It is also a pleasant, cool and quiet spot just to relax while listening to the strains of *Shri Ram, Jai Ram, Jai Jai Ram* wafting across the lake from the **Bala Hanuman Temple**. The temple is worth a visit, especially early evening. The bastion has an old well from which water can be drawn by blowing into a small hole in the floor. The **solarium** uses solar radiation to cure diseases. A group of **Jain temples** in the Old City are profusely decorated with glass, gilding and mirrors.

Northwest of the town centre is the **Ayurvedic University** ⓘ *T0288-266 4866, www.ayurveduniversity.com*, at present the only one in India, which teaches courses to bachelor and postgraduate level in Ayurvedic medicine and yoga. A limited number of places are available for suitably qualified foreign students.

Porbandar

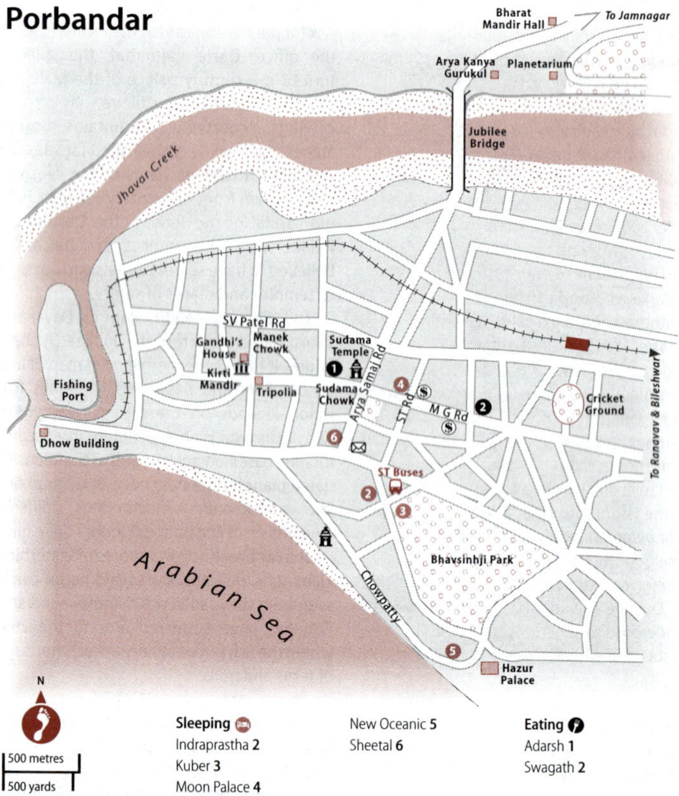

Sleeping
Indraprastha **2**
Kuber **3**
Moon Palace **4**
New Oceanic **5**
Sheetal **6**

Eating
Adarsh **1**
Swagath **2**

Khijadia Lakes ⓘ *10 km northeast of Jamnagar, US$5, car with up to 6 passengers US$20; camera US$5, professional still camera US$10, video US$500; guide US$5*, are three freshwater lakes surrounded by salt pans and salt marshes. Entirely flooded in the wet season, the lakes remain fresh throughout the dry season, though they occasionally dry out completely. The lakes, a bird sanctuary, are an important staging post for migratory birds, including swallows, martins and wagtails, and many waterfowl.

Marine National Park ⓘ *30 km away, same price as Khijadia Lakes*, offshore from the southern coast of the Gulf of Kachchh, comprises an archipelago of 42 islands noted for their coral reefs and mangroves. It is possible to see dolphins, finless porpoise and sea turtles and a variety of colourful tropical fish. The area also attracts a host of waterbirds. The best island to visit is 1.5-sq-km **Pirotan**. To get there hire motor boats for 15-45 people from Jamnagar jetty (or from Okha) and take a guide. Permits are needed and are available from the Director, Marine National Park, Rajdarshan Ground, Jamnagar. Pirotan is uninhabited except for lighthouse staff.

Bala Hanuman temple is in the Guinness Book of Records for continuous chanting – 13,892 days, over 38 years.

Dwarka → *Colour map 2, C1. Phone code: 02892. Population: 33,600.*

A small coastal town on the tip of the Kathiawad Peninsula, Dwarka is one of the most sacred sites for Vaishnavite Hindus. It has the unique distinction of being one of Hinduism's four 'Holy Abodes' as well as one of its seven 'Holy Places'. Heavily geared up to receive pilgrims, the people are easy going, friendly and welcoming, even to the rarely seen tourist. The beach is good but without any palms for shade.

Archaeological excavations indicate that present-day Dwarka is built on the sites of four former cities. Work in 1990 by the marine archaeologist SR Rao discovered triangular anchors weighing 250 kg similar to those used in Cyprus and Syria during the Bronze Age, suggesting that ships of up to 120 tonnes had used the port around the 14th century BC. Marine research in early 2002 revealed evidence of a substantial city off the coast more than 100 m below current sea level, reviving the debate about the origins of Dwarka's offshore archaeological sites.

The present town mostly dates from the 19th century when Gaekwad princes developed Dwarka as a popular pilgrimage centre. Celebrated as Krishna's capital after his flight from Mathura, thousands come for Krishna's birthday and at Holi and Diwali.

The 12th-century **Rukmini Temple** has beautifully carved *mandapa* columns and a fine sanctuary doorway, but much else is badly weathered. The mainly 16th-century **Dwarkadisha Temple** ⓘ *0600-1200, 1700-2100*, was supposedly built in one night, and some believe that the inner sanctum is 2500 years old. The sanctuary walls probably date from the 12th century. The exterior is more interesting. The soaring five-storey tower is supported by 60 columns. Non-Hindus may enter after completing a form to show some level of commitment to Hinduism and to Krishna, but no photography is allowed inside and cameras must be left at the entrance. Some visitors are approached for a minimum donation of Rs 100. A **lighthouse** ⓘ *1600-1800 or 1 hr before sunset, whichever is earlier, Rs 1, no photography*, stands to the west of the temples. The good-humoured keepers may treat you to a free private guided tour in exchange for any foreign coin (they all 'collect'). The views are beautiful; it's a very peaceful place to rest a while.

Outside Dwarka, the **Nageshwar Mandir** contains one of the 12 *jyotirlingas* in an underground sanctum. It helps to be agile if you wish to catch a glimpse. **Gopi Talav Teerth** is associated with Krishna (and Arjun) and has several shrines in the complex.

Okha

A small port at the head of the Gulf of Kachchh, Okha is 32 km north of Dwarka. You can visit the Marine National Park by hiring a motor boat from the jetty (see Jamnagar, page 1355). A pilgrimage to Dwarka is not complete without a visit to the island of **Beyt Dwarka** off the coast from Okha. This is where Krishna is believed to have resided while Dwarka was his capital. The

19th-century temple complex contains several shrines and images of Krishna and his 56 consorts. Archaeological excavations have revealed Harappan artefacts which date from the second millennium BC.

Saurashtra listings

For Sleeping and Eating price codes and other relevant information, see Essentials pages 38-42.

Sleeping

Rajkot *p1343, map p1343*

Like many towns in Saurashtra, Rajkot suffers from critical water shortages; limit water use as much as possible. Cleanliness standards in virtually all **C** hotels and below are poor.

AL-A Imperial Palace, Dr Yagnik Rd, T0281-248 0000, www.theimperialpalace.biz. Smartest business hotel in town, with elaborate lobby, in-room internet ports, indoor and outdoor pools, gym, swish restaurant and well-stocked wine shop (alcohol permit required).

B-C Silver Palace, Gondal Rd, T0281-248 0008, www.hotelsilverpalace.com. Smart and modern rooms, deluxe with bathtub, quieter 'executive' rooms face away from street, good **Flavours** restaurant.

C-E Galaxy, Jawahar Rd, T0281-222 2905, www.thegalaxyhotelrajkot.com. Great value modern hotel with 37 very well furnished, clean rooms, most a/c, pleasant roof garden, exchange (including TCs, credit cards), well run, courteous and efficient, no restaurant but room service to bring in food, access by lift only. Does not look promising from the street, but a pleasant surprise once you get upstairs. Courtesy pick-up and drop off from airport.

E-F Babha Guest House, Panchnath Rd, T0281-222 0861, hotelbabha@rajkot.com. Small, cleanish rooms, some a/c, excellent vegetarian *thalis*.

E-F Samrat International, 37 Karanpura, T0281-222 2269. Promising lobby belies adequate but unloved rooms, some a/c, vegetarian restaurant, genial staff, exchange, the best-kept option near bus stand.

F-G Railway Retiring Rooms, 1st floor. 3 rooms (1 a/c), 4-bed dorm, reasonable vegetarian restaurant, good value.

G Hotel Yash, Dhebar Rd near bus stand, T0281-222 3574. Cheap as chapatti options in this area, not much going for them. Hotel Yash is cleanish.

Wankaner *p1344*

A-B Royal Oasis, T02828-220000, www.heritagehotelsofindia.com. Stepping back in time, this guesthouse of the Ranjitvilas is set in large fruit orchards with original 1930s art deco features. There is a stunning *vaav* (step well) onsite with three intricately carved levels, as well as a beautiful art deco pool, although probably empty most of the time. The rooms are a little past their prime and you can eat dinner in the gardens, although mosquitoes can be a problem.

Bhavnagar *p1344, map p1345*

A-B Nilambag Palace, Ahmedabad Rd, T0278-242 9323, www.nilambagpalace.com. A little faded 1850s palace stuffed with the usual array of hunting trophies, 27 upmarket a/c rooms, long bathrooms with tubs (main palace better than cottage annexe, and twice the price), lobby with intricate woodcarving, chandeliers, royal portraits, grand banquet hall now restaurant, vast gardens with peacocks, beautiful stepped pool.

B Narayani Heritage, in grounds of Nilambag Palace, T0278-251 3535, narayaniheritage@gmail.com. Plain but spacious rooms in converted boys' school, rooms open on to paved courtyard. Shares facilities of Nilambag Palace, eg pool, tennis court. Odd atmosphere definitely feels like an old school.

C Sun 'n' Shine, ST Rd, Panwadi, T0278-251 6131. Decaying exterior but incredibly grandiose lobby. Average a/c rooms; those with marble floors are better, reasonably clean throughout, smart and popular vegetarian restaurant, gym, sauna, travel desk, internet.

F-G Vrindavan, Darbargadh, T0278-251 9149. Sprawling buildings, part of the old Darbargadh complex (18th-19th century) converted to a budget hotel, 100 rooms, some with baths, a few have Western toilets, some **D** a/c, also Rs 50 dorm beds, a/c Gujarati restaurant (*thali* Rs 50), rather noisy surroundings.

Velavadar National Park *p1345*

D Kaliyar Bhuvan Forest Lodge, reserve at Forest Office in Bhavnagar, T0278-242 6425. Simple but adequate, 5 small rooms, reasonably furnished, but prohibitively priced for foreigners. Similarly here food is priced different for foreigners.

Palitana *p1346*

Difficult to find cheap rooms but dorm beds are Rs 20-50.

A Vijay Vilas Palace (Heritage Hotel), in Adpur, a cattle herders' village ringed by hills, book ahead through **North West Safaries**, T079-263 08031, www.northwestsafaries.com. 6 rooms in lovely 1906 lodge (Italian country house feel), surrounded by greenery. Delicious home-cooked Indian meals (non-residents Rs 250 with advance notice). The shorter but steeper route to the Palitana temple complex starts about 200 m away at the temple in Adpur village (follow the milkmaids carrying curd!). 7 km from town (rickshaws Rs 75, shared motorbike-rickshaws Rs 6), tricky to find after dark.

E Shravak, opposite Central bus station, T02848-252428. 18 rooms with baths (Western toilets, hot shower), cheaper with Indian toilet. Better than expected.

E-G Sumeru (Gujarat Tourism), Station Rd, near bus stand, T02848-252327. Typical Gujarat Tourism vibe – lacklustre, 16 rooms, 4 a/c, 16 dorm beds (Rs 75) with cold water only, limited menu restaurant, tourist office, checkout 0900.

G Patel House, Station Rd, T02848-242441. Run by private farmer's trust, rather basic and impersonal but set around an open courtyard that shuts off some of the traffic noise, double rooms (cold taps, hot water in buckets, Indian toilet), some 4- and 6-bedded.

Gondal *p1348*

Heritage hotels are worth the experience.

AL Orchard Palace, Palace Rd, near ST Bus Stand, T02825-220002, www.gondalpalaces.com. Overlooking mango and lime groves, 6 a/c rooms in one wing of palace, with old-fashioned baths, attractive gardens, 35 vintage cars, pool (but little water to fill it), excellent dance shows, mosquito nuisance so burn rings, good food ("bland European dishes; order Indian in advance" or sometimes a bit of both on the same plate!). Price includes meals; **A** without meals. Atmospheric. You can also book through **Northwest Safaries**, www.northwestsafaries.com.

A Riverside Palace, by river Gondali, T02825-220002, www.gondalpalaces.com. 19th-century, with a glassed-in terrace, 11 large, attractive non a/c rooms, 4-poster beds. Similar vibe to Orchard, but a little more lacklustre.

A Royal Saloon, in garden near **Orchard Palace**, T02825-220002. Beautifully renovated suite in Maharaja's old train, with drawing and dining rooms and sit-outs on the platform, meals from the **Orchard Palace**. Sheer nostalgia. Highly recommended.

C-E Bhuvaneswari Rest House, at Shri Bhuvaneswari Pith Temple, T02825-220968. Atmospheric part of town with 2 resthouse options. The newer build is good and clean but a bit pricey at 1800rs a night. In the older building, it's looking pretty run down and in need of an overhaul. *Thali* meals available and the temple and ayurvedic factory close by is fascinating.

Junagadh *p1348, map p1349*

Rates double during Diwali (Oct-Nov) when large number of Indians visit Girnar.

C-D The Lotus Hotel, Station Rd, T0285-265 8500, www.thelotushotel.com. Almost chic, this very white hotel has a nice vibe, Wi-Fi and 24-hr room service.

C-F Vishala, 3rd floor, Dhara Complex, opposite ST Bus Stand, T0285-263 1599. Bright and modern rooms, some veering towards contemporary, some with quite eccentric bamboo decor in good new hotel, uncrowded dorm, quite clean, friendly staff, internet, high enough above street to avoid worst of traffic noise. Good rooftop restaurant. Recommended.

E-F Madhuwati, Kalwa Chowk, T0285-262 0087. Noisy location above a shopping complex, 27 spacious rooms, some a/c, attached bath (hot showers in winter only), clean, comfortable, courteous staff. Rooms are OK but the entrance feels unsafe.

E-G Girnar, Majwadi Darwaja, 2 km north, T0285-262 1201 (**Gujarat Tourism**). 24 decent rooms, some a/c with bath, best with balcony, dorm (Rs 75), unattractive building but in good location, poor management.

F-G Relief, Dhal Rd, T0285-262 0280. 14 rooms (some share bath), hot water, 2 a/c, snacks available, untrained but friendly staff, polite owner can help with excursions.

G Railway Retiring Rooms. Clean and well maintained.

Sasan Gir National Park *p1350*

AL-A Vassavo, Sangodra Village, T02877-285 971, www.vibranthotels.net. Innovative design, cottages dotted around central lawn. Cottages are airy with gardens behind glass as your headboard. Bathrooms have private outdoor shower. Lovely decor throughout. Some with river view. Price includes breakfast, lunch, dinner and 1 safari.

AL-B Lion Safari Camp, near Hirenshwar Temple, Chitrod, T02877-296 507, www.campsofindia.com. Characterful tents with a/c and stylish bathrooms. Nice atmosphere.

AL-B Maneland Jungle Lodge, 2 km north of Sasan, T02877-285555, www.maneland.com. Well-appointed suites in bungalow (VIP faces jungle), and rooms in cottages resembling royal hunting lodges, restaurant with limited menu, delightfully designed but needs a bit of a facelift, jungle ambience, lions and panthers heard and occasionally spotted nearby, rich birdlife, wildlife videos.

A Gir Birding Lodge, 1.5 km north of Sasan down dirt track, T02877-295514, www.girbirdinglodge.com, or reserve with **North West Safaries**, see page 1324. Clean and comfortable cottages and a 2-bedroom suite downstairs in the main lodge, set in a mango orchard over the wall from the national park. Good naturalist guides available, good buffet breakfast served on veranda looking over wall into forest, lots of langurs, leopards occasionally seen. Beautiful views as you sit on your balcony in the orchard. Highly recommended.

B Sinh Sadan Forest Lodge (Govt), T02877-285540. Ridiculously overpriced and run-down rooms (foreigners US$50), with Indian toilets, better a/c chalets (US$75), tents with shared bath, 30-bed dorm (US$5). Food is equally over-priced for foreigners. You can find much better value.

C-D Gir Jungle Lodge (Govt), T02877-285 600, www.girjungle.com. New build with basic rooms, still a bit rough around edges needs some finishing touches and maybe the prices will increase when they are done. Bonus is a good ayurvedic centre with full range of treatments at good prices on-site.

E Umang, near Sasan bus stop, T02877-285728. Has a backdrop of the sanctuary but a crowded village on one side (calls from the mosque disturb the peace). 9 basic rooms in varying states of decay with mediocre baths, rooftop dining room (order meal well ahead), jeep safaris, knowledgeable owner can help with visits to the sanctuary.

G Nitin Ratangayra Family Rooms, near Sasan bus stop and Umang, T02877- 285686. Just 5 basic rooms but cleaner than most and friendly.

Somnath and Veraval *p1351*

Mostly you would stay in Veraval to visit temple at Somnath but now there are some new build hotels on the Somnath by-pass road.

C-D Hotel Ambar, Somnath by-pass, T02876-231 358, www.hotelambar.in. Charmless modern block with comfortable standard and 'elegance' rooms.

D-E Shubh Suvidha, Kamal Park, Somnath by-pass, T02876- 231695. Modern block with comfortable a/c and non a/c rooms available. Best value of the slew of identikit hotels in the area.

D-E Madhuram, Junagadh Rd, Veraval, T02876-221938. Comfortable rooms, some a/c, taxis, travel desk, small cafeteria (limited menu), dorms, run down.

Prabhas Patan *p1351*

E Mayuram, Triveni Rd, T02876-231286. Acceptable rooms, good restaurant, clean.

G Shri Somnath Guest House, near temple, T02876-220212. Has 20 very basic rooms.

Diu *p1352, maps p1352 and p1354*

Most places are basic. Some have a/c rooms with TV and charge double for these, but offer good discounts in low season. High season: Diwali, Christmas/New Year and Apr-May.

AL-A Azzaro, Fofrara, Diu-Nagoa Rd, Fudam, T02875-255 421, www.azzarodiu.com. Stylish lobby and smart looking rooms with chic fabrics and flatscreen TVs – all a/c. Pool is nice, although doesn't quite fit with the decor of the rest of the place.

A-B Radhika Beach Resort, Nagoa, close to the beach, T02875-252555, www.radhikaresort.com. 24 comfortable a/c rooms in modern villas, a/c restaurant, good pool in well-tended garden, prompt service, small provisions store handy for beach.

A-B Magico do Mar, Ghogla-Ahmedpur Mandvi, T02875-252116, www.magicodomar.com. Lovely a/c huts with traditional vibe, Saurashtrian decor and mirrorwork, around a 1930s mansion of a Junagadh Nawab (best Nos 510-513), cheaper non-a/c rooms in unimpressive bungalow, fantastic views, good access to beach, some water sports. Recommended.

B-C Sugati Beach, Ghogla-Ahmedpur Mandvi, T02875-252212, www.sugatibeach resort.com. Cluster of attractive good-sized bungalows, well-appointed, clean a/c rooms, restaurant, bar, terrace opens onto beach and sea, lacks atmosphere.

C The Resort Hoka, 100 m from the beach among Hoka palms and trees at Nagoa, T02875-253036, www.resorthoka.com. 10 decent rooms with bath, 3 with shared facilities, clean, pleasant garden, restaurant serves excellent fresh fish, bar, laundry, travel, environment-conscious and friendly management, discounts for long stays, not luxurious but pleasant and good value.

C Sanmaan Palace , Pensao Beira Mar Building, Fort Rd, T02875-253031. Pleasant colonial house, sea-facing balcony, 6 rooms and suites, rooftop restaurant. With so many modern places, nice to see some old world charm.

C-D Apana Guest House, Old Fort Rd, T02875-253650. Has 29 clean rooms, 4 a/c, some with bath (best with TV, hot water, sea view and balcony) and dorm, can be noisy (mainly from Hindi films) especially at weekends, roadside terrace with restaurant and bar.

C-D Samrat, Collectorate Rd, T02875-252354. 12 clean rooms, 3 a/c, balconies, good restaurant, helpful manager.

E-F Heranca Goesa, behind Diu Museum, T02875-253851. Very popular relaxed place with local family. Serving leisurely breakfasts and slap-up fish suppers with Goan and Portuguese influences – step in even if you don't score a room here.

E-F Super Silver, near Samrat and Foreign Market, T02875-252020, hotel_supersilverdiu@yahoo.com. Clean basic rooms, no frills but good value, some with a/c. Internet café and shops in complex downstairs.

F-G Jay Shankar Guest House, 1 min from Jallandhar Beach, T02875-252424. Small dorm (Rs 50), backpacker abode with some cleanish rooms – look around to pick the best of the bunch. There's alcohol on sale downstairs which might help with some of the dingier rooms.

G Church Hostel, in the old Fudam church. Simple rooms (Rs 100), use of kitchen, very quiet and pleasant.

Porbandar *p1355, map p1356*

C-E Kuber, Bhavsinhji Park, near ST station, T0286-224 1024. Most of the 19 rooms have a/c, suites with fridge, friendly and helpful manager, free airport transfer. Recommended.

C-E Sheetal, Arya Samaj Rd, opposite GPO, T/F0286-224 8341. Some a/c rooms with shower or tub, 24-hr "homely" food service. They pride themselves on home comforts.

D-E New Oceanic, 8 Chowpatty, T0286-224 2917. Sea views, modern, 17 rooms, some a/c, good garden restaurant (Western, Indian) but rather expensive. Downstairs rooms bit dingier, so aim for second floor.

D-F Indraprastha, near ST Station, T0286-224 2681. Large modern hotel, comfortable, all the usual features, some a/c.

E-F Moon Palace, ST Rd, near Bhavsinhji Park, ST Rd, T0286-224 1172, moonpalace@mail.com. Clean, cosy rooms with bath.

Jamnagar *p1355*

A Express Hotel, Motikhavdi, Sikka, 21 km down Dwarka Rd, T0288-234 4416, www.express world.com. 117 centrally a/c rooms in modern hotel with good business facilities .

A-C Aram (Heritage Hotel), Pandit Nehru Rd, 3 km northwest of centre, T0288-255 1701. Good a/c rooms in 1940s character mansion (bit garish), Raj memorabilia, pleasant vegetarian garden restaurant, friendly, good service. At time of writing, under renovation so maybe prices will go up.

D-E Aashiana, New Supermarket, Bedi Gate, 3rd floor, T0288-255 9110, www.ashiana hotel.com. 34 rooms, 14 clean a/c rooms with TV, better than the competition, simple restaurant serving inexpensive Indian vegetarian, good value.

D-F President, Teen Batti, T0288-255 7491, www.hotelpresident.in. 48 bright, spacious rooms, most a/c, some with balcony, relaxing a/c restaurant (efficient service), internet.

E-F Relax, opposite Town Hall, T0288-255 6115. Good clean rooms – great value. And for boys, very nice dorms (they are mixed dorms but cannot imagine ladies wanting to stay in a dorm). Dorms just Rs 250.

Dwarka *p1357*

C-E Dwarka Residency, near ISKCON gate, T02892-235032, www.dwarkaresidency.com. Smart, modern business hotel hiding behind quirky 'robotic' façade, with comfortable a/c rooms and a salubrious restaurant. Website is quite cosmic too.

E-F Toran (Gujarat Tourism), near Govt Guest House, T02892-234013. 12 clean, well-maintained rooms with nets, dorm (Rs 75), courteous service, checkout 0900, "dedicated and friendly manager". Recommended.

F Meera, near railway station, T02892-234031. Friendly, excellent *thalis*.

F Satnam Wadi, near the beach. Rooms with bath and sea view.

Eating

Rajkot *p1343, map p1343*

Havmor, Jawahar Rd, near **Galaxy Hotel** (see Sleeping). Good non-vegetarian food (varied menu, mainly Chinese), a/c but a bit fly-ridden.

Lakshmi Lodge in road opposite **Rainbow**, see below. Good *thalis*.

Rainbow Lakhajiraj Rd. Good South Indian, also very busy in the evenings.

Shakti Vijay, various locations including Dheba Rd and Sadar Rd. Delicious home-made ice creams, recommended.

Thaker Lodge, Kanta Sree Vikas Gruh Rd, T222 1836. Highly regarded place for local food, often queues to get in at night.

Bhavnagar *p1344, map p1345*

Sweet shops around Piramal Chowk and Waghawadi Rd sell melt-in-the mouth *pedas* and *sangam*, a cashew nut candy, as well as savoury snacks like Bhavnagar *ganthias*.

Greenland, Krishnanagar, near Barton Museum. North Indian and ice creams in a pleasant garden setting.

Murli, Panwadi Chowk, T431037. Excellent *thalis*.

Nilambag Palace (see Sleeping). Banquet Hall (chandeliers, Belgian mirrors, Burma teak furniture). Wide choice of mainly non-vegetarian tandoori food. Garden restaurant at night is pleasant, except for loud Hindi film music.

Tulsi, Kalanala Chowk. An attractive little restaurant, with subtle lighting and good, mainly North Indian food.

Palitana *p1346*

Many eateries in Taleti Rd offer Gujarati *thali* as well as *pau-bhaji* and ice cream. Along Station Rd, *thalis* are Rs 10-15.

Mansi Park, Bhavnagar Rd. North Indian, Chinese. Pleasant open-air restaurant, tables on the lawn and in kiosks, hill views (main dishes Rs 35-50), also tea-time treats (cheese toast, finger chips, *iddli*, *dosa*).

Gondal *p1348*

Bhajiya shop, near railway station. Sells a variety of delicious vegetarian *pakoras* (*bhajiya*) with dips, pickles and chutneys.

Dreamland, Kailash Complex, ST Rd. First-class unlimited Gujarati and Punjabi *thalis*, served in separate rooms, delightfully cool a/c.

Junagadh *p1348, map p1349*

Near **Kalwa Chowk**, try *Dal-Pakwana* (a Sindhi brunch), stuffed parathas, fruit juices (*kesar* mango Apr-Jun). In **Azad Chowk**, try milk sweets, snacks and curds.

Garden Café, Girnar Rd. Attractive outdoor restaurant with view of hills, flowering plants and lawns, average food, good atmosphere and service; handy for visitors to the hill.

Geeta and **Sharda**, both near railway station. Good *thalis*.

Poonam, Dhal Rd, Chittakhana Chowk, 1st floor. Unlimited Gujarati *thalis* (Rs 35-60). Excellent food and service.

Sagar, Jayshree Talkies Rd. Good Punjabi and Gujarati, vegetarian, Indian breakfast (*puri-sabzi*), *idly*, *lassi*.

Santoor, off MG Rd, near Kalwa Chowk, upstairs. 0945-1500, 1700-2300. Very good Indian and Chinese vegetarian dishes, a/c, excellent value.

¥ **Swati**, Jayshree Talkies Rd. Mainly Punjabi, some South Indian and Chinese, all vegetarian. Good food and *lassi*, courteous, enthusiastic staff, clean and comfortable, a/c, one of the town's most popular restaurants.

Veraval *p1351*

¥ **Ali Baba**, near **Park Hotel** (see Sleeping). Recommended for seafood.

¥ **Sagar**, Riddhi-Siddhi Complex, 1st floor, between bus stand and clock tower. A/c, excellent service, vegetarian Punjabi and South Indian.

Diu *p1352, maps p1352 and p1354*

Some Catholic homes serve traditional Portuguese food to Western travellers with an hour's notice (ask directions in the Christian locality near St Paul's Church).

¥¥ **Apana**, Old Fort Rd. Large seafood platters (shark, lobster, kingfish, crab and vegetarian), Rs 300, easily shared by 4-6. Recommended.

¥¥ **Bon Appetite**, Nagoa–Gomti road, 1 km from Nagoa Beach, T09879593713. Chilled out place with floor seating, offering up a range of fresh fish and a small selection of other fare. Phone to order pizzas from the wood-oven or a barbecue.

¥¥ **Martha's Place**, opposite the museum. Excellent home-cooking, good views.

¥¥-¥ **O'Coqueiro**, Firangiwada Road, near Diu Museum, T09824681565. Serving up a range of great fish curries or try grilled fish and coriander potatoes. There's a great selection of veg and chicken dishes too, but seafood is where it's at. Chilled out vibe and super friendly family. Recommended.

¥¥-¥ **Radhika Beach Resort**, Nagoa. Wide choice of Indian, Chinese, some continental. Well-prepared meals from spotless kitchen, a/c and attentive service. Not much of a vibe though.

¥ **Ram Vijay**, Bundi Chowk, near State Bank of Saurashtra. Excellent 'home-made' ice creams – coconut and date 'n' almond are particularly good, milk shakes and sodas, friendly.

¥ **Uma Shakti**, near Samrat. Good food and service (try toasted cheese sandwiches).

Porbandar *p1355, map p1356*

Sudama Chowk near the ST Stand is where locals gather for samosas, *pakodas, bhel, kachori, pau bhaji*, etc, in the evening.

¥ **Adarsh**, MG Rd. A/c, Indian vegetarian and ice creams.

¥ **Khana Khazana**, MG Rd. Open sunset to past midnight. Recommended for cheese and chutney sandwiches, cheese toasts, burgers and coffee; South Indian snacks (hot *idlis*) on Sun. Also takeaway.

¥ **Swagath**, MG Rd. Excellent *thalis*, pleasant. The bazar sells *khajli* (fried dough snack), *thabdi* and *peda* (milk sweets).

Jamnagar *p1355*

¥¥ **Rangoli**, near Anupam Talkies, near Bedi Gate. Open lunchtime and evening (except Wed). A/c, good but pricier vegetarian Punjabi and South Indian, friendly.

¥ **Kalpana**, near Teen Batti. Vegetarian dishes.

¥ **Urvee**, Supermarket, Town Hall Rd. Good Gujarati *thalis* at lunch time.

Dwarka *p1357*

Poor choice of rather dirty eating places, best to eat in one of the hotels. **Dwarkeshwar** is best for tasty, hygienic *thalis* but slow service.

Bars and clubs

Diu *p1352, maps p1352 and p1354*

The night market, near post office, is very popular. Kingfisher, Turbo, London Pilsner, Rs 20-30 per bottle; tasty snacks from stalls too. Most bars close around 2130. **Nilesh**, stays open until 2300.

Festivals and events

Palitana *p1346*

Mar Teras Fair at Gheti (Adpur-Palitana, 4 km from town) 3 days before **Holi**. Thousands of Jain pilgrims attend, joined by villagers who come for free lunches.

Junagadh *p1348, map p1349*

Feb-Mar Bhavnath Fair at **Sivaratri** at Damodar Kund near the Girnar foothills is very spectacular. Attended by *Naga Bawas* (naked sages), who often arrive on decorated elephants to demonstrate strange powers (including the strength of their penis), and colourful tribal people who come to worship and perform *Bhavai* folk theatre.

Nov-Dec A popular 10-day **fair** is held at the Jain temples starting at Kartik Purnima.

Dwarka *p1357*
Aug/Sep Janmashtami. Special worship and **fair** (Aug).

Shopping

Bhavnagar *p1344, map p1345*
Textiles, locally embroidered cushion covers, shawls, *bandhni* and mock-silver jewellery are good buys. Try **Vora Bazar**, **Radhanpuri Market**, **Amba Chowk**, **Darbargadh Lane** and **Talao** fruit and veg market. Handlooms and handicrafts are best at **Khadi stores** in the Barton Museum building.

Palitana *p1346*
Local handicrafts include embroidery (saris, dresses, purses, bags, wall hangings, etc) and metal engraving. You can watch the craftsmen making harmonium reeds.

Diu *p1352, maps p1352 and p1354*
The night market is very lively in the evenings. Govt **Cottage Emporia** near the jetty sell local crafts of stone, metal and shell; **Jaysukh**, Sangaria Lane, has good shell crafts. Don't be tempted by star tortoise and turtle shell bangles and souvenirs; they are illegal under the Wildlife Protection Act, severe penalties attached. There is a fine second-hand bookshop in **Super Silver Hotel**.

Activities and tours

Diu *p1352, maps p1352 and p1354*

Cruises
Evening cruises from Bunder Chowk jetty to Nagoa Beach, with music, Rs 100 per person; enquire at the tourist office.

Tour operators
Oceanic, Bunder Chowk, T02875-252 1800.
Reshma, facing **Nilesh Hotel**, T02875-252241.

Watersports
At Nagoa and Ahmedpur-Mandvi have parasailing, windsurfing, 8-seater speed boats and jet skiing. A pool/water slide complex is next to Kohinoor on the Diu–Nagoa road.

Dwarka *p1357*
Dwarka Darshan. A tour of 4 local pilgrimage sites (Nageshwar Mandir, Gopi Talav Teerth, Beyt Dwarka, Rukmini Temple) by minibus, departs 0800, 1400, 5 hrs (can take 7). Tickets Rs 30; book a day in advance for morning tour. Or visit only Beyt Dwarka for a worthwhile day spent with pilgrims.

Transport

Rajkot *p1343, map p1343*
Air Some 4 km northwest, airline buses run transfers to town. **Indian**, Angel's Hotel, Dhebar Chowk, T0281-222 2295, airport T0281-245 3313, www.indian-airlines.nic.in. **Jet Airways**, 7 Bilkha Plaza, Kasturba Rd, T0281-247 9623, airport T0281-245 4533, www.jetairways.com, flies to **Mumbai** daily.
Bus The ST bus station is just south of the busy Dhebar Chowk at the centre, with buses to **Junagadh** (2 hrs), **Veraval** (5 hrs), **Jamnagar** (2 hrs), **Dwarka** and **Ahna**. More comfortable private long-distance coaches leave from locations around the city, especially around Shastri Maidan. **Eagle Travels**, 107-108 Yagnik Rd, T0281-304 8611, www.eaglecorporate.com, runs several luxury buses daily to **Ahmedabad**, as well as to **Mount Abu**, **Mumbai**, **Porbandar**, Udaipur and Vadodara. **Jay Somnath Travels**, Umesh Complex, near Chaudhari High School, T0281-243 3315, have 3-4 buses a day to **Bhuj**.
Train Junction Station **Ahmedabad**: *Rajkot Ahmedabad Exp 19154*, 0630, 4¼ hrs; *Saurashtra Exp 19216*, 0045, 6½ hrs (continues to **Vadodara**, 2¾ hrs); *Sau Janta Exp 19018*, 1520, 5¼ hrs (continues to **Vadodara**, 2½ hrs). **Mumbai (Central)**: *Okha Mumbai Saurashtra Mail 19006*, 1735, 14½ hrs; *Saurashtra Exp 19216*, 0050, 18½ hrs. **Porbandar**: *Saurashtra Exp 19215*, 0135, 4¾ hrs; *Porbandar Exp 19264*, 0825, Mon, Thu, 5 hrs. **Vadodara**: same as Mumbai, 7¼-9 hrs. **Veraval**: *Jabalpur-Veraval Exp 11464*, 1310, 4 hrs.

Bhavnagar *p1344, map p1345*
Air The airport is 5 km southeast of town; auto-rickshaws to town insist on Rs 65-75. **Indian**, T0278-249 3445, airport T0278-249 3130, www.indian-airlines.nic.in, **Jet Airways**, Surat House, Waghawadi Rd, T0278-243 3371, airport

T0278-220 2004, www.jetairways.com, flies to **Mumbai**.

Bus Frequent rickety buses from the ST stand in the New Town. Routes include: **Palitana** (1¾ hrs); several to **Una for Diu** (6 hrs); **Velavadar** (1 hr). Private operators: **Tanna Travels**, Waghawadi Rd, T0278-242 0477, has luxury coaches (reclining seats) to/from **Ahmedabad**, almost hourly from 0600, 4½ hrs plus short tea break, recommended; to **Vadodara**, 5½ hrs, 3 daily. **Punjab Travels**, Kalanala, T0278-242 4582.

Train The station is in the Old City, about 3 km north of the ST Bus Stand. **Ahmedabad**: a slow journey as the line takes a circuitous route to skirt the marshes; buses are generally preferable. *Bandra Exp 12972*, 12045, 5½ hrs; continues to **Mumbai** (Bandra). Also several local trains.

Velavadar National Park *p1345*

A few buses from Bhavnagar; better to hire a car. Alternatively hire a Jeep/*chhakra* (motorbike trailer) from Vallabhipur on the Ahmedabad-Bhavnagar highway. A new bridge being built near Bhavnagar port to Adhelai near the park will make access faster and easier.

Palitana *p1346*

Bus ST Bus (0800-1200, 1400-1800) to **Ahmedabad** (often with a change at Dhandhuka), deluxe from Ahmedabad (0700, 0800, 0900); to Bhavnagar (1½ hrs), **Jamnagar**, **Rajkot**, **Surat**, **Una**, **Vadodara** and Veraval (for Sasan Gir). Private de luxe coaches to **Surat** and **Mumbai** via **Vadodara**. Operators: **Paras**, Owen Bridge, T02848- 252370. Opposite ST depot: **Khodiar**, T02848- 252586 (to Surat) and **Shah**, T02848-252396.

Taxi For up to 7, run between **Bhavnagar** (57 km by State Highway) and Palitana, Rs 35 per seat.

Train To **Bhavnagar** a few times a day.

Alang *p1347*

Buses from ST Bus Stand in Bhavnagar, through the day from 0600 (last return 1800), 1¾ hrs, Rs 25. Taxis take 1½ hrs, Rs 500-600 return, and auto-rickshaws Rs 300-400 with bargaining. At Alang, *tongas* go up and down the beachfront past the shipyards for Rs 7.

Junagadh *p1348, map p1349*

Bicycle Hire from shops on Dhal Rd, near Relief Hotel; Rs 25-30 per day.

Bus Regular buses to **Ahmedabad**, **Rajkot** (2 hrs), **Veraval**, **Porbandar** and **Sasan Gir** (2½ hrs). One direct bus to **Palitana**, 0500, 6 hrs; otherwise change at **Songadh** (4 hrs)

Train **Ahmedabad**: *Somnath Exp 19222*, 2105, 7¼ hrs; *Jabalpur Exp 11463/11465*, 1130, 9 hrs; *Veraval Ahmedabad Exp 19129*, 0843, 7½ hrs; all via **Rajkot**, 2½-3¼ hrs. **Veraval**: *Veraval Exp 11464/11466*, 1536, 1¾ hrs. For **Sasan Gir**: take *Fast Pass 352* to **Delwada**, 0605.

Sasan Gir National Park *p1350*

Air Nearest convenient airport is Rajkot.

Bus Service to/from **Junagadh** (54 km), 2½ hrs, and **Veraval** (40 km), 2 hrs. Service to **Una** for **Diu** is unpredictable, morning depart 1100. Occasional buses to **Ahmedabad**.

Train From **Junagadh** to Sasan Gir, *352*, 0650, 3 hrs, continues to **Delwada** near Diu; return to Junagadh, *351*, 1827, so possible to visit for the day. The route is very attractive. **Talala** is the last major station, 15 km before Sasan, so stock up with fruit, biscuits, liquids there. From **Veraval**, take *359* at 1039, or *353* at 1409, both bound for Khijadiya; return to **Veraval**, by *354* at 1138 or *360* at 1535.

Veraval *p1351*

Somnath Travels, Satta Bazar, will obtain tickets for long-distance journeys.

Bicycle Hire from opposite bus station or railway station, some in poor condition (road between Veraval and Somnath is appalling).

Bus Buses to **Diu**, **Porbandar** (2 hrs), **Bhavnagar** (9 hrs). **Deepak Ramchand Taxis**, T02876-222591 has non-a/c Ambassador taxis. To **Ahmedpur Mandvi** (via docks) and **Somnath** Rs 550, **Diu** Rs 600, tour of docks and Somnath Rs 250.

Taxi Taxis from **Tower Rd** and **ST bus stands** are cheaper than those at the railway station.

Train Train to **Ahmedabad**: *Somnath Exp 19222*, 1900, 11¼ hrs; *Veraval Ahmedabad Exp 19120*, 0630, 10¾ hrs.

Prabhas Patan *p1351*

From **Veraval**, auto-rickshaw (bargain to Rs 30 return) or frequent bus.

Diu *p1352, maps p1352 and p1354*
Most visitors arrive by long-distance buses either via Una or direct to the island, easiest from Ahmedabad via Bhavnagar. A road bridge connects Diu Town with Ghogla which has more frequent buses.
Air The airport is 6 km west of the town; auto-rickshaws charge around Rs 50 to transfer. **Jet Airways**, at the airport, Nagoa Rd, T02875-253542, www.jetairways.com, accepts credit card payment. **Mumbai**, daily except Sat.
Bicycle Hire about Rs 50 per day. **A to Z**, near Veg Market, Panchwati Rd; **Shilpa**, Bunder Chowk; **Mayur**, past Ankur Hotel (across rough ground, then 20 m along alley to left), excellent bikes; **Daud**, Zampa Gate, well-maintained, new bikes; **Krishna Cycles** at Ghogla.
Local bus Bus stand: to **Nagoa** 3 daily; frequent service to **Bucharwada-Vanakbara** and **Una**, Rs 4 (minibus Rs 6).
Long-distance bus Most long-distance buses operate from the **Jethabai Bus Stand** just south of the bridge to Ghogla. ST services to **Ahmedabad** via Bhavnagar, 0700 (10 hrs); **Bhavnagar**, ask for 1035 'direct bus' as some go through Mahuva and are packed; **Jamnagar** via Junagadh, 0600; **Porbandar**, 1300; **Rajkot**, several 0445-1725 (7 hrs); **Vadodara**, 1730; **Veraval**, several 0400-1300 (2½ hrs). Buses often leave 15-20 mins early.

A wider choice of buses serve Una, 8 km from Diu on the mainland, connected by local buses and auto-rickshaws.

Private agents in the Main Sq offer buses from the private bus stand to **Mumbai** (1000), **Ahmedabad** (1900) and major towns in Gujarat; often more reliable than ST buses. **Goa Travels** serve Bhavnagar, Junagadh (5 hrs) and Palitana.

Shiv Shakti, **Sahajan and** and **Gayatri Travels** run from the main bus station to **Ahmedabad**, **Bhavnagar**, **Mumbai**, **Vadodara**, etc.

Vanakbara, at the west end of the island, has buses to **Okha** via **Veraval**, **Porbandar** and **Dwarka** at 0700 and 0800.
Motorbike Hire in the market area; mopeds, scooters and motorbikes cost from about Rs 140-300 a day plus fuel and deposit. **Kismet**, T252971, has good new scooters, friendly service. Repairs off Estrada Lacerda.
Rickshaw Auto-rickshaw: Rs 30 to **Nagoa**, Rs 25 to **Ghogla**. Demand Rs 100 to **Una** or **Delwada**
Train Delvada, 8 km north between Diu and Una, is the nearest railhead just south of Una; auto-rickshaws demand Rs 100 from Diu to Una or Delwada. The station is a short walk from the centre of town – follow the locals. Slow, crowded trains with hard wooden benches go to **Junagadh** via **Sasan Gir**.

Porbandar *p1355, map p1356*
Air **Jet Airways**, T0286-222 0974, www.jetairways.com, flies daily to **Mumbai**.
Bus ST buses serve most centres of Gujarat. **Bharat** and **Eagle Travels** run regular private luxury buses to **Ahmedabad**, **Jamnagar**, **Junagadh**, **Rajkot** etc.
Train Trains are as follows: **Mumbai** (**Central**): *Saurashtra Exp 19216*, 2000, 23½ hrs, calls at **Rajkot** and **Ahmedabad**.

Jamnagar *p1355*
Air Airport, 10 km west. **Indian**, T0288-255 2911, www.indian-airlines.nic.in, to **Mumbai**.
Bus STC bus services to **Rajkot** (frequent), **Ahmedabad**, **Dwarka** and **Porbandar**.
Train Railway station 6 km northwest of town. **Mumbai** (**Central**): *Saurashtra Exp 19216*, 2305, 20¾ hrs; *Saurashtra Mail 19006*, 11535, 17½ hrs; both via **Rajkot**, 1¾-2¼ hrs, **Ahmedabad**, 7¼ hrs, and **Vadodara**, 10-11½ hrs.

Dwarka *p1357*
Bus Bus to **Jamnagar**, **Porbandar** and **Somnath**. Private operators run to most major towns.
Train Trains to **Ahmedabad** and **Vadodara**: *Saurashtra Mail 19006*, 1308, 10 hrs, and **Mumbai** (**Central**): 20 hrs. Also *Okha-Puri Exp*, 0835.

Okha *p1357*
Boats to Beyt Dwarka take 10-15 mins each way. Local buses to **Dwarka**, 1 hr. Buses to all main towns, including a direct morning service to **Bhuj**. Train to **Ahmedabad**: *Saurashtra Mail 19006*, 1230, 10 hrs.

Directory

Bhavnagar *p1344, map p1345*

Banks State Bank of Saurashtra, Darbargadh, changes currency and TCs. ATMs for foreign cards on Waghiwada Rd.
Useful contacts Forest office, near Nilambag Palace, T0278-242 8644.

Palitana *p1346*

Medical services Mansinhji Govt Hospital, Main Rd; **Shatrunjaya Hospital**, Taleti Rd.
Post GPO: Main Rd, with Poste Restante; PO, Bhairavnath Rd.

Junagadh *p1348, map p1349*

Banks Bank of Baroda, near the town post office is very efficient and changes TCs; **Bank of Saurashtra**, changes currency.
Internet MagicNet, MG Rd.

Sasan Gir National Park *p1350*

Health Centre, Post Office and **Bank** at Sasan. **Market** at Talala. The post office in the village has an excellent 'frank' for postcards/letters.

Diu *p1352, maps p1352 and p1354*

Banks State Bank of Saurashtra, near Fish Market opposite *Nilesh* hotel, has an ATM. Authorised foreign exchange dealers next to **Reshma Travels** and **Alishan Hotel** are more efficient for exchange (sterling, euro and US dollar TCs and currency). **Internet** Deepee Telecom and Cyber café, Bunder Chowk.
Medical services Manesh Medical Store is a pharmacy with a doctor in the building.
Post The main Post Office is on Bunder Chowk, the other is at Ghogla.

Porbandar *p1355, map p1356*

Banks Bank of India, Kedareshwar Rd, and **State Bank of India**, MG Rd (and sometimes **Bank of Baroda**) change TCs of reputed companies. After frauds and fake notes, they are wary of currency.

Jamnagar *p1355*

Banks and internet Money exchange and internet are around Teen Batti in the New Town Centre. **Post** Head Post Office at Chandni Chowk. Forestry Office, T0288-255 2077.

Kachchh (Kutch)

The scenic Maliya Miyana bridge, across salt marshes often filled with birds, gives a beguilingly attractive impression of the gateway to Kachchh. Yet this region is climatically perhaps the least appealing of Gujarat, and it is certainly the most sparsely populated. It is well and truly off the tourist trail. The various communities such as Rabaris, Ahirs and Meghwals each have a distinct dress that is still an integral part of daily life, and each practise a particular craft, a fact that is being fostered and promoted by a number of co-operatives and NGOs. For the adventurous traveller willing to forego such luxuries as hot showers and reliable bus timetables, Kachchh offers some fascinating opportunities for adventurous, life-affirming travel. ▸▸ *For listings, see pages 1375-1377.*

Background

The central peninsula of Kachchh is surrounded by the seasonally flooded Great and Little Ranns. The Gulf of Kachchh to the south, a large inlet of the Arabian Sea, has a marine national park and sanctuary with 42 islands and a whole range of reefs, mudflats, coastal salt marsh and India's largest area of mangrove swamps. The **Kachchh Peninsula** is relatively high, covered with sheets of volcanic lava but with often saline soil. When you drive out to the Great Rann of Kachchh it's like driving to the end of the world. You look out onto a white horizon and stand on a bed of salt. Dry and rocky, there is little natural surface water though there are many artificial tanks and reservoirs. Intensive grazing has inhibited the development of the rich vegetation around the tanks characteristic of neighbouring Sindh in Pakistan, and there is only sparse woodland along the often dry river beds. The wetlands are severely over-exploited, but some of the lakes are important seasonal homes for migratory birds including pelicans and cormorants. The **Rann of Kachchh** in the north runs imperceptibly into the Thar Desert. A hard smooth bed of dried mud in the dry season, some vegetation survives, concentrated on little grassy islands called *bets*, which remain above water level when the monsoons flood the mudflats.

With the arrival of the southwest monsoon in June the saltwater of the Gulf of Kachchh invades the Rann and the Rajasthan rivers pour freshwater into it. It then becomes an inland sea and Kachchh virtually becomes an island. From December to February, the Great Rann is the winter home of migratory **flamingos** when they arrive near **Khavda**. There are also sand grouse, Imperial grouse, pelicans and avocets.

Local traditional **embroidery** and **weaving** is particularly prized. Kachchh is an extraordinary place for tribal peoples and their crafts. When the monsoons flooded vast areas of Kachchh, farming had to be abandoned and handicrafts flourished which not only gave expression to artistic skills but also provided a means of earning a living. Mirrorwork, Kachchh appliqué and embroidery with beads, *bandhani* (tie-dye), embroidery on leather, gold and silver jewellery, gilding and enamelling and colourful wool-felt *namda* rugs are available.

Bhuj

→ *For listings, see pages 1375-1377.* *Colour map 2, C1. Phone code: 02832. Population: 120,000.*

The devastating earthquake in January 2001, which hit 7.7 on the Richter scale and claimed around 20,000 lives, had its epicentre a few kilometres from this old walled town with its tightly packed maze of narrow winding streets. Much was destroyed, and most of the town's picturesque heritage buildings suffered extensive damage. Some of the structures described below are being restored by experts, but a number of treasures have been lost permanently. Walking through the old palaces like Rao Lakha and the Aina Mahal, where debris of stone pillars and carved wooden screens still lies scattered in piles on the ground, can be a haunting experience. The old part of Bhuj still retains its magic though.

Vast amounts of money and manpower have been poured into Bhuj for the recovery effort, and the rapidly transforming town has gained prosperous-looking new suburbs, a university and a new broad-gauge railway line – perhaps at the cost of some of its cultural uniqueness. Nevertheless, it still forms a hub of trade for scores of tribal villages, and visitors can expect a genuine warm welcome from a town still getting back on its feet.

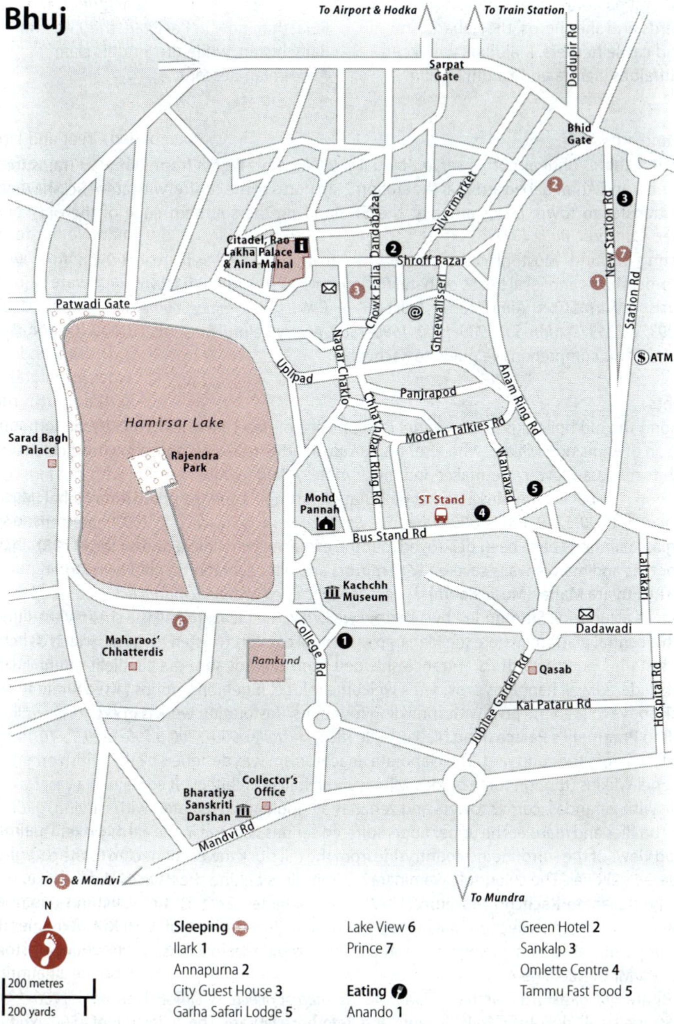

Sleeping
Ilark **1**
Annapurna **2**
City Guest House **3**
Garha Safari Lodge **5**
Lake View **6**
Prince **7**

Eating
Anando **1**
Green Hotel **2**
Sankalp **3**
Omlette Centre **4**
Tammu Fast Food **5**

A melting pot of cultures

Kachchh is a meeting point of Sindhi, Gujarati, Muslim and Rajasthani cultures; the local language is more Sindhi than Gujarati. The arid grasslands to the north, south and west of Bhuj are home to several pastoral tribes: the Bharwad goat herds and shepherds, the Rabari camel and cattle herders, Maldhars who keep buffaloes, Samra and Sindhi Muslim cameleers and others. The communities have Lohan merchants, Langa musicians of the Indian desert and Kanbi Patel agriculturalists among them. They came from near and far; the Sodha Rajputs originated from the area neighbouring Rajasthan now in Pakistan, the Jats from Baluchistan, while the Sindhis claim Abyssinian descent.

Ins and outs

Getting there Bhuj airport is served by daily **Jet Airways** flights from Mumbai. Trains from Mumbai and Ahmedabad arrive at the station 2 km north of the centre, with auto- rickshaws for the transfer to town. Buses arrive at the ST stand on the southern edge of the old town. ▸▸ *See Transport, page 1377.*

Getting around Most places of interest in town can be easily reached on foot, with auto-rickshaws and local buses on hand for journeys to surrounding towns.

Tourist Information **Aina Mahal Trust** ⓘ *in Rao Lakha Palace complex, T02832-220004, T(0)9374-235379, Mon-Sat 0900-1200, 1500-1800*. A very helpful Mr Jethi, T02832-220004, sells copies of his comprehensive guide to Kachchh.

Sights

Among the old buildings in the citadel is the palace of **Rao Lakha** (circa 1752), the fortunate patron of Ramsingh Malam, who after his European adventures became a master clockmaker, architect, glass-blower, tile-maker and much more. A large white mansion with carvings and fretwork, the palace contains a Darbar Hall, State Apartments and the noted **Aina Mahal** (Mirror Palace) ⓘ *0900-1200, 1500-1800, closed Sat, Rs 10, camera Rs 30, video Rs 100*. Some items such as glass paintings have been destroyed, but the exquisite ivory inlaid doors (circa 1708), china floor tiles and marble walls covered with mirrors and gilt decorations could be restored.

The **Fuvara Mahal** (Music Room) ⓘ *next door, included with Aina Mahal ticket, same opening times*, is a curiosity. Surrounded by a narrow walkway, the pleasure hall is a shallow tiled pool with a central platform where the Maharao sat in cool comfort to listen to music, watch dancers or recite his poetry. With its entrance shielded from the hot sun, the candlelit interior with embroidered wall hangings provided a welcome refuge. Ingenious pumps raised water to the tank above to feed the pool with sprinkling fountains. Restoration work is in progress.

Rao Pragmalji's Palace (Prag Mahal; built 1865) ⓘ *daily 0900-1200, 1500-1800, Rs 10*, in red brick, is across the courtyard. The elaborate anachronism was designed by the British engineer Colonel Wilkins (though some guides will say by an Italian architect). It contained a vast Darbar Hall, with verandas, corner towers and zenanas all opulently decorated with carving, gilding, Minton tiles and marble. The upper floors suffered serious damage in the earthquake. There are good views of the surrounding countryside from the tall clock tower connected to the palace by covered galleries. The colourful Swaminarayan Temple is behind the Palace near the lake.

The Italianate **Kachchh Museum** (1877), near Mahadev Gate, is the oldest in Gujarat. It exhibits the largest collection of Kshatrap inscriptions (the earliest, of AD 89), textiles and an anthropological section. Anyone interested in local traditional folk music and instruments may contact Mr UP Jadia here.

Bharatiya Sanskriti Darshan ⓘ *Mandvi Rd, near Collector's Office, Wed-Mon 1100-1700, Rs 50*, is a small, delightful Folk Museum and Reference Library. The collection of 4500 exhibits includes traditional handicrafts, textiles, weaponry and other historic and artistic artefacts, as well as a recreated village of typical Kachchhi *bhungas* (huts) of different communities. *Kutch – People and their handicrafts*, by PJ Jethi (Rs 100), and postcards are for sale.

Sarad Bagh Palace ⓘ *Sat-Thu 0900-1200, 1500-1800, Rs 10, camera Rs 30, video Rs 100,* west of Hamirsar, the last residence of the Maharao (died 1991) is set in lovely gardens. Exhibits include furniture and exotic ornaments. Further south, the Maharaos' *chhatterdis* (memorial tombs), built of red sandstone, were severely damaged in the 1819 earthquake and again in 2001. Some are beyond repair. Ramkund, nearby, has a stone-lined tank with carvings of Hindu deities.

Qasab ⓘ *11 Nootan Colony, behind Santoshi Mata Mandir, south of town centre,* is an outlet for **KMVS** (**Kutch Mahila Vikas Sangathan**), a collective of 1200 craftswomen from 130 local villages who are practising and refining their traditional skills to produce high- quality Indian and Western clothes, home furnishings and leather goods. The women market the products themselves, bypassing an intermediary, thus controlling the speed and quality of production and achieving a fairer deal for themselves and their producer group. Their collection and craftsmanship is outstanding. ▸▸ *See Shopping, page 1376.*

Around Bhuj

Rudrani Dam ⓘ *14 km north, 30-min drive from Bhuj on the Sumrasar road,* has the colourful **Rudramata Temple**, originally 17th-century, nearby. The goddess Sati's 'rudra' (frightening) aspect is believed to have fallen on this spot and is hence a place of pilgrimage, see page 1412.

Craft villages → *For listings, see pages 1375-1377. Colour map 2, C1. Population: 37,000.*

Handicrafts are a living tradition of Kachchh and the girls of various communities make beautifully embroidered garments for their own trousseaus while women produce attractive fabrics for a second income. Some men too are working on handblock prints like the Khatri family in Ajrakhpur. Some visitors to villages near Bhuj are disappointed to find that the previously nomadic tribes are being housed in whitewashed urban housing in expanded older villages that are losing their traditional architecture. Cement and modern materials are replacing mud walls and cow dung. However, the handicrafts of these villages are still of a high standard.

North of Bhuj

ⓘ *Permits are required for visits to many communities. Apply with passport and visa plus photocopies to the District Superintendent's Office near Kachchh Museum. Closed on Sun. Buses from the ST stand in Bhuj go to the main villages, often just once a day (check time). For more flexibility arrange a taxi or hire a motorbike. There is little official accommodation, but villagers will readily find you a bed somewhere. The visitor book at the Annapurna Hotel (see page 1375) is full of practical tips on travel in this region.*

The vast grasslands of **Banni** meet the Great Rann in the Khavda region, north of Bhuj. They are home to numerous pastoral nomadic, semi-nomadic and resident people who keep sheep, goats, camels, buffaloes and other livestock. The 40 or so hamlets here are best known for the minute detail of their embroidery. More recently, these villages have started focusing on selling handicrafts as their main source of income and there are signs of modernization and commercialization. The traditional *bhungas* (circular huts with sloping thatched roofs) are made from mud plastered with cow dung which are often decorated with hand-painted floral patterns and inlaid with mirrors during festivals. Traditional utensils are still used for cooking, eating and storage in the houses. The area is known for its raptors – eagles, vultures and other birds of prey.

Dhorodo, 80 km north, is the centre for Mutua embroidery, using chain stitches inset with small mirrors, leather embroidery as well as silver jewellery.

Sumrasar, 25 km northeast, is famous for its Ahir embroidery and Soof embroidery of the Sodhas, done without a plan but by counting the warp and weft of the material. **Kala Raksha**

ⓘ *Parkar Vas, Sumrasar Sheikh, near Collector's Office, T02832-277237, www.kala-raksha.org*, is a grassroots organization that maintains a small but fascinating **museum** of heirloom textiles – it's an amazing collection and really interesting to be able to compare the styles of the different tribal embroideries. It works with and trains 180 artisans to create contemporary pieces inspired by their own traditions. It is now run by Judy Frater, the American author of *Threads of Identity*. **Tunda Vandh** is a good place to see typical *bhungas* of Kachchh. Architecture students come to see, study and photograph the traditional architecture adapted to this hostile climate. The interiors have beautiful Rabari cupboards, chests, inlaid mirrors and paintings.

Loria (Ludia), 60 km away, has huts with painted and mirror inlaid walls, and is famed for its wood crafts.

Khavda, Further north than Ludia, in Khavda, you can visit the home of Ibrahim Kaka, where the men make traditional pots and the womenfolk paint them – it is good luck for marriage to have them in your home. There is also a small branch of KMVS (Qasab) here. **Zura**, 30 km, produces embroidered footwear and other leather crafts. Copper bells are also made in this village. **Nirona**, 40 km northwest, has embroidery, lacquered wood crafts, wood carving and is the only home of highly skilful rogan-painting (fabrics painted using iron rods). Buses from Bhuj take about 1½ hours.

Hodka, 63 km north, is the site of an indigenous tourism project, with a resort comprising tents and traditional *bhungas* built in traditional style, owned and run by the village in cooperation with hospitality professionals and **KMVS** (see page 1371). Local guides show visitors around the village, providing ample opportunity to interact with the residents, and to buy embroidery direct from the artisans.

Nakhtarana, northwest in the heart of the craft village belt, produces some tie-dye work. There is a Chinkara Sanctuary at **Narayan Sarovar**, 110 km further west, and **Lakhpat**, close to the Pakistan border, the remains of a port left stranded when the Indus shifted course following the 1890 earthquake.

Charri Dund Lake, a reservoir near Charri village, offers splendid birdwatching opportunities. Flamingos, pelicans, cranes, storks, ducks and other water birds gather in large numbers, especially in winter, while nearby grasslands are filled with passerine and ground dwelling birds. The Banni grasslands are known for their huge eagle and vulture congregations. **The Bombay Natural History Society** ⓘ *www.bnhs.org*, and other organizations monitor bird migrations in the Banni region, and bird-banding camps are set up around Charri Lake. The grasslands are home to wolf, hyena, jackal, Indian and desert foxes and lesser wild cats but are imperilled by the government's decision to convert Banni into pastureland.

Dholavira ⓘ *250 km northeast of Bhuj, daily 0900-1800*, is the site of excavation of a Harappan town (pre-2500 BC) which some estimate to be larger than Moenjodaro, in Pakistan. It was only discovered in 1967 and excavation began in 1990. The drive to Khadir beyt, an oasis in the Great Rann, through dazzling salt flats is very scenic. Excavations reveal interesting new finds on a regular basis and show the complex to be on three levels (Citadel, Middle and Lower Towns) with pottery, stone cutting, coppersmithing, drainage systems and town planning at an advanced level. The fortifications with walls, bastions and double ramparts reflect danger from invasions or enemies. An inscribed tablet found here bears 10 letters in the Harappan script, claimed to be the oldest signboard in the world. The bus from Bhuj (via Rapar) takes seven hours. Gujarat Tourism's **Toran Bungalow** provides good accommodation.

South of Bhuj

ⓘ *Buses to Rajkot or Ahmedabad can drop you off at most of the villages.*

There are a number of interesting villages south of Bhuj en route to Gandhidham, including the craft honeypots of Bhujodi and Mandvi on the coast.

Bhujodi, 10 km southeast, off the main road and a 10-minute walk from the bus stand, is the centre for pitloom weaving. The weavers have now been organized into a co-operative. They produce colourful *galichas* (carpets), *durries* (rugs), *dhablos* (blankets), and other items from wool, camel and goat hair, cotton and even synthetic fibres. Some embroidery and tie-dye can be seen here as well. Mr Vanka Kana Rabari has reasonably priced local embroidery and other items but not the most select quality. **Shrujan** ⓘ *T02832-240272, www.shrujan.org*, run by the astute Daya Nathani, is another pioneer behind the revival in high-quality Kachchhi handicrafts; the shop sells upmarket embroideries and home furnishings. There is also a nice crafts park near Shrujan at Ashapura if you do not have time to travel into the villages north of Bhuj.

Padhdhar, 22 km southeast of Bhujodi, produces Ahir embroidery using round mirrors with floral and geometrical patterns. **Dhaneti** is also a centre for Ahir and Rabari embroidery. Meet Govindbhai, a local entrepreneur, and his friendly family who will show you the embroidered and mirror inlaid fabrics made for their own use. There are some intricate *pallias* (hero stones) by the village lake.

Dhamanka, 50 km east of Bhuj, is famous for its Ajrakh hand-block printed fabrics, using primarily vegetable dyes – you can watch them boiling up natural indigo and making orange colours from old iron horseshoes and pomegranate skin. Used blocks can be bought here as well as an array of garments and bed linen. You can meet Dr Ismail Khatri who is keeping the tradition alive and supplying big stores like Fab India and Anokhi. He says "True Ajrakh is like stars in the night sky – In Arabic, 'Aj' is the universe and 'Ajrakh' means blue. Clear shining stars show the Ajrakh is good quality." You can also visit Ajrakhpur closer to Bhuj – part of the family relocated here after the earthquake.

Anjar, 22 km southeast, was an early Jadeja Rajput capital of Kachchh, founded 450 years ago. The Jesal-Toral shrine has a romantic tale of the reform of an outlaw prince through the love of a village girl. Anjar is also known for its metalcrafts, especially betel nut crackers and ornaments, *bandhni* and block printing. The 1818 Bungalow of Captain McMurdoch, the first European to settle in Kachchh, now government offices, has some Kamangari paintings on the ground floor.

Mandvi → *For listings, see pages 1375-1377.*

Mandvi, 54 km southwest of Bhuj, is a pretty little seaside town, with a reservoir in the centre and a river beyond. During the 18th century the town outclassed Bhuj in importance, the sea-faring people dominating the sea trade, taking cotton, rice, spices, etc, to the Persian gulf, Arabia and Zanzibar. The skill of building *dhows* and boats using simple tools is being revived along the river – worth having a look.

The town is now a centre for handicrafts like *bandhani* tie-dyed fabrics, jewellery and shell toys. It is a desert town but important agricultural research for the Kachchh region is being carried out here in the Gujarat Agricultural University and the Vivekenand Research Institute, to improve farming in the often hostile environment. There is an 18th-century **palace** with an Aina Mahal (Mirror Hall) and music rooms which have remains of intricate stone carvings of Dutchmen, tigers and dancing girls and woodcarvings in the courtyard. The magnificent 1940s **Vijay Vilas Palace** ⓘ *Rs 5, camera Rs 20, plus vehicle charge*, with huge domes, combines Indian and European styles. You can see the drawing room with royal memorabilia, and the attractive *jali* windows of the *zenana*. The terrace, reached by a spiral staircase, with excellent sea views, especially at sunset, is ideal for a picnic. The beaches on the town side are good for swimming and even camel or horse riding. A wind farm next to the beach is working hard to produce an alternative energy source. The Maharao's pleasant **private beach** ⓘ *Rs 30*, is open to visitors and worthwhile for women, to escape hassle from male onlookers. Out of town, you can visit a magnificent new Jain temple.

Bhuvad, Kandla and Gandhidham → *For listings, see pages 1375-1377.*

On the Mundra Road, 19 km southwest of Anjar, Bhuvad has the ruined 13th-century **Bhuvaneshwar Mahadev Temple**. The *mandapa* (1289-1290) is supported by 34 unusual pillars (square base, octagonal middle and circular upper section). A local legend describes how the headless body of the chieftain Bhuvad, killed in battle in 1320, fought its way to the village. The *District Gazetteer* records that a shrine with a red headless figure is dedicated to him.

Further east along the coast is the port of **Kandla**, built to replace declining Mandvi. After Independence, Kandla was further developed by the Indian government to service the states in northwest India.

Gandhidham, 27 km north of Kandla, was founded by the Maharaos of Kachchh to accommodate refugees from Sindh in Pakistan after Partition in 1947. The enterprising community made a promising start and now the town is a prosperous business centre, though the old handloom and embroidery co-operatives for refugees still exist. The town has developed with the increasing importance of Kandla as a port having lost Karachi sea port to Pakistan. The Institute of Sindhology is researching on various aspects of Sindhi culture.

Little Rann of Kachchh Sanctuary → *For listings, see pages 1375-1377. Colour map 2, C2.*

ⓘ *The southern part of the sanctuary is accessible all year, 0600-1800. Forest Department fees US$5, still camera US$5, at Bajana and Dhrangadhra. Temperature: maximum 42°C, minimum 7°C; Annual rainfall: 1000 mm. Best season to visit is late-Oct to mid-Mar.*

The 4950-sq-km wild ass sanctuary of the Little Rann of Kachchh (created in 1973) and the 7850-sq-km desert wildlife sanctuary of the Great Rann together would comprise the largest contiguous tract of protected wildlife territory in India were it not divided by a road. The Little Rann is mostly a saline wilderness, broken by *beyts* (islands during the monsoon) covered with grass, bushes, acacia and thorn scrub. The area is under severe threat from the salt works, which clear the vegetation, release toxic effluents into the wetlands and pollute the air. A fast-growing thorn scrub – *Prosopis juliflora* – is destroying most other vegetation.

Sights

This is the last home of the **Asiatic wild ass** (locally called *khacchar* or *ghorker*), a handsome pale chestnut brown member of the wild horse family with a dark stripe down the back. Wild asses are usually seen as lone stallions, small groups of mares or harems of a male with mares. Large herds of 40-60 are sometimes seen but they are loosely knit. Males fight viciously, biting and kicking, for their females. Nilgai, antelope and chinkara (Indian gazelle) are other mammals seen, but the chinkara numbers have dwindled due to poaching. Blackbucks have become almost extinct in the Little Rann of Kachchh but are seen in villages nearby. Wolf is the primary predator, though not common. You might spot jackal, desert fox, jungle and desert cat on a drive. Birdlife is abundant. Houbara bustard, spotted and common Indian sand grouse, nine species of larks, desert warbler, desert wheatear, Indian and cream coloured courser, grey francolin and five species of quails are spotted at the *beyts*. The salt marshes teem with flamingos, pelicans, storks, ducks, herons and wading birds. Thousands of demoiselle and common eastern cranes spend the winter here. Wear strong footwear when walking in this area as prosopsis thorns can pierce through thin-soled shoes.

Around Little Rann of Kachchh Sanctuary

The 13th-century **Jhinjwada fort**, on the edge of Little Rann west of Dasada, has majestic gateways. At the southeast corner of the Rann, **Kharaghoda**, southwest of Dasada on the way to Bajana Lake, is particularly interesting. The principal British salt trading post with an old village-pony express, it retains plenty of colonial architecture including Raj bungalows, a cricket pavilion and a bandstand. **Dasada** is a convenient base for visits to the Little Rann. The interesting village has an old fort with wood carvings, 15th-century tombs, potters, a shepherd's colony and nomadic settlements. The Malik Dynasty, who received the 56 km estate in return for military services to the sultan of Ahmedabad, now live in a 1940s mansion, **Fatima Manzil.**

Kachchh (Kutch) listings

For Sleeping and Eating price codes and other relevant information, see Essentials pages 38-42.

Sleeping

Bhuj *p1368, map p1369*

A-C Garha Safari Lodge, at Rudrani Dam, T937-433 5853. An option for an out-of- town stay. 14 whitewashed *bhungas* (local style huts), tribal furniture, hot water, 7 air-cooled, exchange, pool, atmospheric, beautiful views of lake, jeep tours, mixed reports about food, cleanliness and service.

A-C Hotel Ilark, Station Rd, www.hotelilark.com, T02832-258 999. Hotel with all the mod cons, smart with nice use of traditional textiles. Good food and small branch of Kala Raksha in the lobby.

B-D Prince, Station Rd, T02832-220370, www.hotelprinceonline.com. Rooms with bath, not spotless but double glazed against traffic noise, restaurant (varied menu), shops (there is a small Qasab handicrafts outlet in the lobby), free airport transfer, guided tours of local villages Rs 1500 per car, crowded area, no credit cards, 'spot' liquor permits.

D-F Lake View, Rajendra Park, T02832-220 622. Classic faded Indian hotel, grubby but comfortable non-a/c to de luxe a/c rooms with bath, some with fridge, garden restaurant, *thalis* indoors, attractive location facing Hamirsar lake (birds in winter).

F-G Annapurna, Bhid Gate, T02832-220831. Clean rooms but noisy, friendly owners, great Kachchhi cuisine.

G City Guest House, Langa St, near Bazar, T02832-221067. Well run, excellent value, 32 clean, quiet rooms, some with own shower, quiet garden for relaxing, cycle hire, helpful, used by foreign backpackers.

Craft villages *p1371*

AL Infinity, 60 km northwest of Bhuj, T02835-273 433, www.infinityresorts.com. With a nod to conservation, Infinity is one of 3 beautiful resorts in India (another is in Corbett National Park). Expect luxury tents and a beautiful swimming pool right in the heart of the Kachcch wildlife.

A-B Shaam-e-Sarhad, Hodka, 63 km north of Bhuj, T02832-574124, www.hodka.in. Award-winning, genuine village tourism project, very comfortable and unique accommodation in circular adobe huts or tents, both with attached bath and running water, although a few older ladies reported a little too much insect life for their liking. Beautifully decorated, amazing food and music under an endless sky – magical. Village visits free of commercial pressure, a chance to contact local culture. Whole-heartedly recommended.

Mandvi *p1373*

AL The Beach at Mandvi Palace, on private beach of **Vijay Vilas Palace**, T02834-295725, www.mandvibeach.com. A handful of safari-style tents with private bath on an isolated stretch of beach, seafood barbecues on the sand, walks in palace grounds, interesting views of wind farm.

E-G Rukmavati Guest House, near Bridge Gate, T02834-223 558. Characterful place with clean rooms and kitchen access near the shipbuilding.

Little Rann of Kachchh Sanctuary *p1374*

B Camp Zainabad, 9 km from Dasada, contact **Desert Coursers** in Ahmedabad, T079-2675 2883. A cluster of 16 self-contained *kooba* huts in a eucalyptus grove, Rs 2000 each includes meals and safaris, recreating a local village, well located, atmospheric but small cots, hard mattresses and sometimes insipid food, a bit shabby around the edges – enthusiastic owner former ruling family of Zainabad, well-organized jeep safaris in the Little Rann, recommended by birders, also camel/horse/village safaris, boating at nearby lake.

B Rann Riders, Dasada. Beautiful air-cooled rooms in 22 spacious Kachchhi *bhungas* and Kathiawadi *koobas* (huts) all with unique features amid plantation and farms, tiled hot showers, lovely swimming pool, great atmosphere at night often with live music and tribal dancingdelicious home cooking (specially meat dishes) with home grown organic vegetables, fresh fish and poultry, enthusiastic owner, good jeeps for tours, whole-heartedly recommended, contact **North West Safaries**, see page 1324.

E-F Guest Houses, Govt, closer to the Rann at Bajana and Dhrangadhra, where a jeep can be hired for visiting the Little Rann.

Eating

Bhuj *p1368, map p1369*

Typical local *dhabelis* (spicy burger of peanuts and potatoes, in a roll), and *bhal* (nuts, gram, vegetables in a spicy sauce), can be sampled on Vaniyawad and Station Rd.

Sankalp, **Oasis Hotel**, Mews Complex, New Station Rd, behind Hotel Prince. Branch of this South Indian chain serving up mammoth dosas and a mind-boggling array of chutneys.

Toral, **Prince Hotel**. Good Gujarati food, vegetarian *thalis*; bit more expensive than elsewhere, but in a more comfortable setting.

Anando. Excellent for Indian (including Gujarati) snacks. Friendly staff, a/c.

Annapurna Guest House (see Sleeping). Very cheap, authentic dishes, homely, allow you to sample each dish.

Green Hotel, Shroff Bazar. South Indian vegetarian. Well-prepared food, friendly staff.

Noor, behind the bus station. Good, reasonably priced *biryani* and chicken masala.

Omlette Centre, near bus station. Popular for breakfast and snacks, excellent filled omelettes, sandwiches and 'English tea'.

Tammu Fast Food, between Abha (see Sleeping) and **Janataghar**. Good hot samosas, South Indian snacks and *batakawadas*.

Mandvi *p1373*

Zorba the Buddha (Rajneesh Hotel), near Azad Chowk. Best- value *thalis* in simple dining area. The bazar has fresh coconuts, biscuits and excellent local corn-on-the-cob. In the evening, handcarts emerge with popular snacks.

Festivals and events

Bhuj *p1368, map p1369*

Feb/Mar 4-day **Rann Utsav (Kachchh Festival)** organized by Gujarat Tourism during **Sivaratri** – tribal crafts, folk dances and music, and tours of nearby sights. **Fairs** in many villages (*Nag Panchami*).

Aug-Sep **Fairs** in the Janmashtami area.

Shopping

Bhuj *p1368, map p1369*

Excellent folk embroidery, leather shoes, appliqué, mirrorwork, block-printed fabrics, painted pottery and local weaving are available. The **market** area stretches from Station Rd to the Darbargadh Palace complex, a maze of alleys specializing in handicrafts. Most shops are closed 1200-1500.

Danda Bazar **Al Md Isha** for outstanding tie-dye; **Khatri Daod** for block-prints, embroideries.

Kansara Bazar For silver jewellery. **Bandhini Ghar**, for tie-dye. **AA Wazir**, opposite General Hospital, near High School, selection of old pieces of embroideries; some for sale.

Shroff Bazar Has craft shops for hassle-free browsing, lots of silver shops, and clothes: **Uday**, T02832-224660, a talented designer (Rs 600 for trousers and top), interesting block prints, excellent tailoring (made-to-measure in a few hours).

A number of NGOs have organized craft co-operatives for the benefit of artisans.

Qasab, 11 Nootan Colony, T02832-222124 (also has a small shop in **Prince** hotel). Exquisite embroidered goods such as bags, cushion covers, wall hangings, etc, run by informative staff who can explain the process and stories behind the pieces. You can watch as they select and sew. But the real juice of this area is to get out into the villages and visit the craftswomen themselves, for example at Sumrasar or Ludia.

Activities and tours

Bhuj *p1368, map p1369*

Arpit Deomurari, deomurari@gmail.com. An enthusiastic and capable young guide for wildlife and birding trips in Kachchh, he has also extended his reach into the rest of Gujarat.

Kutch Ecological Foundation in the village of Tera, 100 km from Bhuj, kerc@sancharnet.in. Recommended as a contact for birdwatching and wildlife trips; they can help put you in touch with Mohammed Daddu, reported to be a passionate and skilled birding guide. Contact in advance.

Little Rann of Kachchh Sanctuary *p1374*

Check with Rann Riders (see Sleeping) or Northwest Safaris for information and guides.

Transport

Bhuj *p1368, map p1369*

Air **Indian Airlines**, T02832-222433, www.Indian-airlines.nic.in, and **Jet Airways**, Station Rd, T02832-253671, www.jetairways.com, flies to **Mumbai**. Security is tight. **Sagar Travels**, opposite Prince hotel, T02832-226393, books tickets for flights and trains for a negligible fee.
Bus Frequent service to **Ahmedabad**, 411 km;. **Bhjujodi**; **Mandvi** and **Rapar**; **Rajkot**, 5 hrs. 1-2 daily to **Bhavnagar**; **Jaisalmer**, 8 hrs; **Jamnagar**, **Junagadh**, **Palitana**; **Porbandar**, **Veraval** and **Somnath**. Most long-distance buses are scheduled to arrive at sunrise or sunset, so times change seasonally. 'Luxury buses' with reclining seats, more leg room, comfort stops etc are strongly recommended. Many private operators cluster around the bus station, and run to major towns in Gujarat.
Train To **Mumbai**: *Bandra Terminus Exp 19116*, 2030, 17½ hrs; *Kutch Exp 19032*, 2000, 16 hrs. Both via **Ahmedabad**, 7-7½ hrs, and **Vadodara**, 9½-10 hrs. For **Rajasthan**, easiest but to go via Ahmedabad.

Mandvi *p1373*

Bus Express bus from **Bhuj**, 1 hr; others very slow. From bus station, auto-rickshaws, Rs 50 for return trip to palace (bargain). Possible to visit **Mundra**, further along the coast from Mandvi, on same day, and return direct to Bhuj.

Bhuvad, Kandla and Gandhidham *p1374*

Bus The bus station is a 3-min walk: turn right from the railway station. Frequent buses to **Bhuj**, but very crowded.
Train All trains to and from **Bhuj** stop at Gandhidham. **Mumbai** (**Central**), *Kachchh Exp 19032*, 2110, 17 hrs via Ahmedabad and Vadodara. **Trivandrum**: *Nagercoil Exp 16335*, 48 hrs, via **Madgaon** (Goa) (27 hrs) and **Kochi** (42 hrs). Several local passenger trains to **Kandla Port**.

Little Rann of Kachchh Sanctuary *p1374*

Bus Dhrangadhra is the main transport base, with ST (Govt) buses from main towns in Gujarat (frequent from **Ahmedabad**, 93 km, 2½ hrs); some continue to **Zainabad**, which has local buses to **Dasada**.
Train Trains between Mumbai/Ahmedabad and Bhuj stop in Dhrangadhra and at **Viramgam**, 33 km southeast of Dasada, but at inconvenient hours of the night. Hotels/resorts can arrange transfer on prior notice, at extra cost.

Directory

Bhuj *p1368, map p1369*

Banks **State Bank of India**, Station Rd changes Thomas Cook TCs, 1100-1500 weekdays, till 1300 Sat. **Bank of Baroda**, almost opposite changes Amex TCs (photocopy of passport needed). ICICI nearby has an ATM. **Internet** **NDS Cybercafe**, Chhathibari Ring Rd. Good connection, Rs 30 per hr. **Post** **Head PO**: Lal Takri, Mon-Sat 0700-1300, 1500-1800. **Sub-PO** in the chowk at entrance to Aina Mahal. **Useful contacts** **Fire**: T02832-221490. **Police**: T02832-220892. **Forestry Office**: T02832-250600.

Background

Contents

Footprint features

History

The first village communities in South Asia grew up on the arid western fringes of the Indus Plains 10,000 years ago. Over the following generations successive waves of settlers – sometimes bringing goods for trade, sometimes armies to conquer territory and sometimes nothing more than domesticated animals and families in search of land and peace – moved across the Indus and into India. They left an indelible mark on the landscape and culture of all the countries of modern South Asia.

The first settlers

A site at Mehrgarh, where the Indus Plains meet the dry Baluchistan Hills in modern Pakistan, has revealed evidence of settlement as early as 8500 BC. By 3500 BC agriculture had spread throughout the Indus Plains and in the thousand years following there were independent settled villages well to the east of the Indus. Between 3000 and 2500 BC many new settlements sprang up in the heartland of what became the Indus Valley civilization.

Most cultural, religious and political developments during that period owed more to local development than to external influence, although India had extensive contacts with other regions, notably with Mesopotamia. At its height the Indus Valley civilization covered as great an area as Egypt or Mesopotamia. However, the culture that developed was distinctively South Asian. Speculation continues to surround the nature of the language, which is still untranslated.

India from 2000 BC to the Mauryas

In about 2000 BC Moenjo Daro, widely presumed to be the capital of the Indus Valley Civilization, became deserted and within the next 250 years the entire Indus Valley civilization disintegrated. The causes remain uncertain: the violent arrival of new waves of Aryan immigrants (a theory no one now accepts), increasing desertification of the already semi-arid landscape, a shift in the course of the Indus and internal political decay have each been suggested as instrumental in its downfall. Whatever the causes, some features of Indus Valley culture were carried on by succeeding generations.

BC	Northern South Asia	Peninsular India	External events	BC
900,000			Earliest hominids in West Asia.	450,000
500,000	Lower Palaeolithic sites from NW to the Peninsula; Pre-Soan stone industries in NW.	Earliest Palaeolithic sites – Narmada Valley; Karnataka; Tamil Nadu and Andhra.	First occupation of North China. Origin of *homo sapiens* in Africa.	150,000
			Homo sapiens in East Asia.	100,000
			First human settlement in Americas (Brazil).	30,000
10,000	Beginning of Mesolithic period.	Continuous occupation of caves and riverside sites.	Earliest known pottery – Kukui, Japan.	10,500
			Ice Age retreats – Hunter gatherers in Europe.	8300
8000	First wheat and barley grown in Indus plains.	Mesolithic.	First domesticated wheat, barley in fertile crescent; first burials in North America.	8000
7500	Pottery at Mehrgarh; development of villages.	Increase in range of cereals in Rajasthan.	Agriculture begins in New Guinea.	7000
6500	Humped Indian cattle domesticated, farming develops.	Cultivation extends south.	Britain separated from Continental Europe by sea level.	6500

Probably from about 1500 BC northern India entered the Vedic period. Aryan settlers moved southeast towards the Ganga valley. Classes of rulers *(rajas)* and priests *(brahmins)* began to emerge. Conflict was common. In one battle of this period a confederacy of tribes known as the Bharatas defeated another grouping of 10 tribes. They gave their name to the east of the Indus which is the official name for India today – Bharat.

The centre of population and of culture shifted east from the banks of the Indus to the land between the rivers Yamuna and Ganga, the doab (pronounced *doe-ahb*, literally 'two waters'). This region became the heart of emerging Aryan culture, which, from 1500 BC onwards, laid the literary and religious foundations of what ultimately became Hinduism, spreading to embrace the whole of India.

The Vedas The first fruit of this development was the Rig Veda, the first of four Vedas, composed, collected and passed on orally by Brahmin priests. While some scholars date the oral originsas early as the beginning of the second millennium BC, the date of 1300 BC to about 1000 BC still seems more probable. In the later Vedic period, from about 1000 BC to 600 BC, the Sama, Yajur and Artha Vedas show that the Indo-Aryans developed a clear sense of the Ganga-Yamuna *doab* as 'their' territory.

From the sixth to the third centuries BC the region from the foothills of the Himalaya across the Ganga plains to the edge of the Peninsula was governed under a variety of kingdoms or Mahajanapadhas – 'great states'. Trade gave rise to the birth of towns in the Ganga plains themselves, many of which have remained occupied to the present. Varanasi (Benaras) is perhaps the most famous example, but a trade route was established that ran from Taxila (20 km from modern Islamabad in Pakistan) to Rajgir 1500 km away in what is now Bihar. It was into these kingdoms of the Himalayan foothills and north plains that both Mahavir, founder of Jainism and the Buddha, were born.

The Mauryas

Within a year of the retreat of Alexander the Great from the Indus in 326 BC, **Chandragupta Maurya** established the first indigenous empire to exercise control over much of the subcontinent. Under his successors, that control was extended to all but the extreme south of peninsular India.

BC	Northern South Asia	Peninsular India	External events	BC
3500	Potter's wheel in use. Long distance trade.		Sumeria, Mesopotamia: first urban civilization.	3500
3000	Incipient urbanization in the Indus plains.	First neolithic settlements in south Deccan (Karnataka). Ash mounds, cattle herding.	First Egyptian state; Egyptian hieroglyphics; walled citadels in Mediterranean Europe.	3100
2500	Indus valley civilization cities of Moenjo Daro, Harappa and many others.	Chalcolithic ('copper' age) in Rajasthan; Neolithic continues in south.	Great Pyramid of Khufu China: walled settlements; European Bronze Age begins: hybridization of maize in South America.	2530 2500
2000	Occupation of Moenjo Daro ends.	Chalcolithic in Malwa Plateau, Neolithic ends in south; in Karnataka and Andhra – rock paintings.	Earliest ceramics in Peru. Collapse of Old Kingdom in Egypt. Stonehenge in Britain. Minoan Crete.	2300 2150
1750	Indus Valley civilization ends.	Hill-top sites in south India.	Joseph sold into Egypt – Genesis.	1750

The centre of political power had shifted steadily east into wetter, more densely forested but also more fertile regions. The Mauryans had their base in the region known as Magadh (now Bihar) and their capital at Pataliputra, near modern Patna. Their power was based on massive military force and a highly efficient, centralized administration.

The greatest of the Mauryan emperors, **Asoka** took power in 272 BC. He inherited a full-blown empire, but extended it by defeating the Kalingans in modern Orissa, before turning his back on war and preaching the virtues of Buddhist pacifism. Asoka's empire stretched from Afghanistan to Assam and from the Himalaya to Mysore.

The state maintained itself by raising revenue from taxation – on everything, from agriculture, to gambling and prostitution. He decreed that 'no waste land should be occupied and not a tree cut down' without permission because all were potential sources of revenue for the state. The *sudras* (lowest of Hindu castes) were used as free labour for clearing forest and cultivating new land.

Asoka (described on the edicts as 'the Beloved of the Gods, of Gracious Countenance') left inscriptions on pillars and rocks across the subcontinent. Over most of India these inscriptions were written in *Prakrit*, using the *Brahmi* script, although in the northwest they were in Greek using the *Kharoshti* script. They were unintelligible for over 2000 years after the decline of the empire until James Prinsep deciphered the Brahmi script in 1837.

Through the edicts Asoka urged all people to follow the code of **dhamma** or dharma – translated by Indian historian Romila Thapar as 'morality, piety, virtue and social order'. He established a special force of *dhamma* officers to try to enforce the code, which encouraged toleration, non-violence, respect for priests and those in authority and for human dignity.

However, Romila Thapar suggests that the failure to develop any sense of national consciousness, coupled with the massive demands of a highly paid bureaucracy and army, proved beyond the abilities of Asoka's successors to sustain. Within 50 years of Asoka's death in 232 BC the Mauryan Empire had disintegrated and with it the whole structure and spirit of its government.

A period of fragmentation: 185 BC to AD 300

Beyond the Mauryan Empire other kingdoms had survived in South India. The Satavahanas dominated the central Deccan for over 300 years from about 50 BC. Further south in what is now Tamil Nadu, the early kingdoms of the Cholas and the Pandiyas gave a glimpse of both power and cultural development that was to flower over 1000 years later. In the centuries following the break up of the Mauryan Empire these kingdoms were in the forefront of developing

BC	Northern South Asia	Peninsular India	External events	BC
1750 1500	Successors to Indus Valley. Aryans invade in successive waves. Development of Indo-Aryan language.	Copper Age spreads, Neolithic continues. Gram and millet cultivation. Hill terracing. Cattle, goats and sheep.	Anatolia: Hittite Empire. New Kingdom in Egypt. First metal working in Peru. First inscriptions in China; Linear B script in Greece, 1650.	1650 1570 1500 1400
1400	Indo-Aryan spread east and south to Ganga – Yamuna doab.	Horses introduced into south. Cave paintings, burials.	Tutankhamun buried in Valley of Kings.	1337
1200	Composition of Rig Veda begins?	Iron age sites at Hallur, Karnataka.	Middle America: first urban civilization in Olmec; collapse of Hittite Empire, 1200.	1200
1000	Earliest Painted Grey Ware in Upper Ganga Valley; Brahmanas begin to be written.	Iron Age becomes more widespread across Peninsula.	Australia: large stone-built villages; David King of Israel, Kingdom of Kush in Africa.	

overseas trade, especially with Greece and Rome. Internal trade also flourished and Indian traders carried goods to China and Southeast Asia.

The classical period – the Gupta Empire: AD 319-467

Although the political power of Chandra Gupta and his successors never approached that of his unrelated namesake nearly 650 years before him, the Gupta Empire which was established with his coronation in AD 319 produced developments in every field of Indian culture. Their influence has been felt profoundly across South Asia to the present.

Geographically the Guptas originated in the same Magadhan region that had given rise to the Mauryan Empire. Extending their power by strategic marriage alliances, Chandra Gupta's empire of Magadh was extended by his son, Samudra Gupta, who took power in AD 335, across North India. He also marched as far south as Kanchipuram in modern Tamil Nadu, but the heartland of the Gupta Empire remained the plains of the Ganga.

Chandra Gupta II reigned for 39 years from AD 376 and was a great patron of the arts. Political power was much less centralized than under the Mauryans and as Thapar points out, collection of land revenue was deputed to officers who were entitled to keep a share of the revenue, rather than to highly paid bureaucrats. Trade with Southeast Asia, Arabia and China all added to royal wealth. That wealth was distributed to the arts on a previously unheard of scale. Some went to religious foundations, such as the Buddhist monastery at Ajanta, which produced some of its finest murals during the Gupta period. But Hindu institutions also benefited and some of the most important features of modern Hinduism date from this time. The sacrifices of Vedic worship were given up in favour of personal devotional worship, known as *bhakti*. Tantrism, both in its Buddhist and Hindu forms, with its emphasis on the female life force and worship of the Mother Goddess, developed. The focus of worship was increasingly towards a personalized and monotheistic deity, in the form of either Siva or Vishnu. The myths of Vishnu's incarnations also arose at this period.

The Brahmins The priestly caste who were in the key position to mediate change, refocused earlier literature to give shape to the emerging religious philosophy. In their hands the *Mahabharata* and the *Ramayana* were transformed from secular epics to religious stories. The excellence of contemporary sculpture both reflected and contributed to an increase in image worship and the growing role of temples as centres of devotion.

BC	Northern South Asia	Peninsular India	External events	BC
800	Mahabharata war – Bhagavad Gita; Aryan invaders reach Bengal. Rise of city states in Ganga plains, based on rice cultivation.		First settlement at Rome. Celtic Iron Age begins in north and east of Alps.	850 800
750		Megalithic grave sites.	Greek city states.	750
700	Upanishads begin to be written; concept of transmigration of souls develops; Panini's Sanskrit grammar.		Iliad composed.	700

Regional kingdoms and cultures

The collapse of Gupta power opened the way for smaller kingdoms to assert themselves. After the brief reign of **Harsha** in the mid-seventh century, which recaptured something both of the territory and the glory of the Guptas, the Gangetic plains were constantly fought over by rival groups, none of whom were able to establish unchallenged authority. Regional kingdoms developed, often around comparatively small natural regions.

The Deccan The Rashtrakutas controlled much of the central Peninsula between AD 700-950. However, the southern Deccan was dominated by the Chalukyas from the sixth century up to AD 750 and again in the 11th and 12th centuries. To their south the Pandiyas, Cholas and Pallavas controlled the Dravidian lands of what is now Kerala, Tamil Nadu and coastal Andhra Pradesh. The Pallavas, responsible for building the temples at Mamallapuram, just south of modern Madras (Chennai), flourished in the seventh century.

In the eighth century Kerala began to develop its own regional identity with the rise of the **Kulashekharas** in the Periyar Valley. Caste was a dominating feature of the kingdom's social organization, but with the distinctive twist that the **Nayars**, the most aristocratic of castes, developed a matrilineal system of descent.

It was the **Cholas** who came to dominate the south from the eighth century. Overthrowing the Pallavas, they controlled most of Tamil Nadu, south Karnataka and southern Andhra Pradesh from AD 850 to AD 1278. They often held the Kerala kings under their control. Under their kings **Rajaraja I** (984-1014) and **Rajendra** (1014-1044) the Cholas also controlled north Sri Lanka, sent naval expeditions to Southeast Asia and successful military campaigns north to the Ganga plains. They lavished endowments on temples and also extended the gifts of land to Brahmins instituted by the Pallavas and Pandiyas. Many thousands of Brahmin priests were brought south to serve in major temples such as those in Chidambaram, and Rajendra wished to be remembered above all as the king who brought water from the holy Ganga all the way to his kingdom.

The Rajputs The political instability and rivalry that resulted from the ending of Gupta power in the north opened the way for waves of immigrants from the northwest and for new groups and clans to seize power. Among these were the Rajputs (meaning '*sons of kings*') who claimed descent from a mythical figure who rose out of a pit near Mount Abu. From the seventh century AD Rajputs were always a force to be reckoned with in the northwest, albeit at a comparatively local level. The temples at Khajuraho in Central India, one of contemporary India's most remarkable sites, were built during the Rajput dynasty of the Chandelas (AD 916-1203). However, the Rajputs never succeeded in forging a united front strong enough to establish either effective central government, control internally or protection from external attack.

BC	Northern South Asia	Peninsular India	External events	BC
600	Northern Black Pottery.		First Latin script; first Greek coins.	600
599	Mahavir born – founder of Jainism.		First iron production in China; Zoroastrianism becomes official religion in Persia.	550
563	Gautama Buddha born.			
500	Upanishads finished; Taxila and Charsadda become important towns and trade centres.	Aryans colonize Sri Lanka. Irrigation practised in Sri Lanka.	Wet rice cultivation introduced to Japan.	50
326	Alexander at Indus.	Megalithic cultures.	Crossbow invented in China.	3[illegible]
321	Chandragupta establishes Mauryan Dynasty.			

The spread of Islamic power – the Delhi Sultanate

From about AD 1000 the external attacks which inflicted most damage on Rajput wealth and power came increasingly from the Arabs and Turks. Mahmud of Ghazni raided the Punjab virtually every year between 1000 and 1026, attracted both by the agricultural surpluses and the enormous wealth in cash, golden images and jewellery of North India's temples which drew him back every year. He sacked the wealthy centres of Mathura (UP) in 1017, Thanesar (Haryana) in 1011, Somnath (Gujarat) in 1024 and Kannauj (UP). He died in 1030, to the Hindus just another *mlechchha* ('impure' or sullied one), as had been the Huns and the Sakas before him, soon to be forgotten. Such raids were never taken seriously as a long-term threat by kings further east and as the Rajputs often feuded among themselves the northwest plains became an attractive prey.

Muslim political power was heralded by the raids of Mu'izzu'd Din and his defeat of massive Rajput forces at the Second Battle of Tarain in 1192. Mu'izzu'd Din left his deputy, Qutb u'd Din Aibak, to hold the territorial gains from his base at Indraprastha. Mu'izzu'd Din made further successful raids in the 1190s, inflicting crushing defeats on Hindu opponents from Gwalior to Benaras. The foundations were then laid for the first extended period of such power, which came under the Delhi sultans.

Qutb u'd Din Aibak took Lahore in 1206, although it was his lieutenant **Iltutmish** who really established control from Delhi in 1211. Qutb u'd Din Aibak consolidated Muslim dominion by an even-handed policy of conciliation and patronage. In Delhi he converted the old Hindu stronghold of Qila Rai Pithora into his Muslim capital and began several magnificent building projects, including the Quwwat-ul-Islam mosque and the Qutb Minar, a victory tower. Iltutmish was a Turkish slave – a *Mamluk* - and the Sultanate continued to look west for its leadership and inspiration. However, the possibility of continuing control from outside India was destroyed by the crushing raids of **Genghis Khan** through Central Asia and from 1222 Iltutmish ruled from Delhi completely independently of outside authority. He annexed Sind in 1228 and all the territory east to Bengal by 1230.

A succession of dynasties followed, drawing on refugees from Genghis Khan's raids and from still further to the west to strengthen the leadership. In 1290 the first dynasty was succeeded by the Khaljis, which in turn gave way to the Tughluqs in 1320. **Mohammad bin Tughluq** (ruled 1324-1351) was described by the Moorish traveller Ibn Batuta as 'a man who above all others is fond of making presents and shedding blood'. Despite its periodic brutality, this period marked a turning point in Muslim government in India, as Turkish Mamluks gave way to government by Indian Muslims and their Hindu allies. The Delhi sultans were open to local influences and employed Hindus in their administration. In the mid-14th century their capital, Delhi, was one of the leading cities of the contemporary world but in 1398 their control came to an abrupt end with the arrival of the Mongol Timur.

BC	Northern South Asia	Peninsular India	External events	BC
300 297	Sarnath and Sanchi stupas. Mauryan power extends to Mysore.	First Ajanta caves in original form.	Mayan writing and ceremonial centres established.	300
272- 250 232	Asoka's Empire. Brahmi script. Death of Asoka.	Chola Pandiya, Chera kingdoms: earliest Tamil inscriptions.	Ptolemy. First towns in Southeast Asia. Rome captures Spain.	285 250 206
185	Shunga Dynasty, centred on Ujjain.	Megalithic cultures in hills of south.	Romans destroy Greek states.	146
100	Kharavela King of Kalingans in Orissa. Final composition of Ramayana.	South Indian trade with Indonesia and Rome. Roman pottery and coins in South India.	Indian religions spread to Southeast Asia. Discovery of monsoon winds Introduction of Julian calendar.	100

Timur's limp caused him to be called Timur-i-leng (Timur the Lame, known to the west as Tamburlaine). This self-styled 'Scourge of God' was illiterate, a devout Muslim, an outstanding chess player and a patron of the arts. Five years before his arrival in India he had taken Baghdad and three years before that he had ravaged Russia, devastating land and pillaging villages. India had not been in such danger from Mongols since Genghis Khan had arrived on the same stretch of the Indus 200 years before.

After Timur, it took nearly 50 years for the Delhi Kingdom to become more than a local headquarters. Even then the revival was slow and fitful. The last Tughluqs were succeeded by an undistinguished line of Sayyids, who began as Timur's deputies who were essentially Afghan soldier/administrators. They later called themselves sultans and Lodi kings (1451-1526) and moved their capital to Agra. Nominally they controlled an area from Punjab to Bihar but they were, in fact, in the hands of a group of factious nobles.

The Deccan Kingdoms

The Delhi Sultanate never achieved the dominating power of earlier empires or of its successor, the Mughal Empire. It exercised political control through crushing military raids and the exaction of tribute from defeated kings, but there was no real attempt to impose central administration. Power depended on maintaining vital lines of communication and trade routes, keeping fortified strongholds and making regional alliances. In the Peninsula to the south, the Deccan, regional powers contested for survival, power and expansion. The Bahmanis were the forerunners of a succession of Muslim dynasties, who sometimes competed with each other and sometimes collaborated against a joint external enemy.

Across West and South India today are the remains of the only major medieval Hindu empire, the Vijayanagar Empire, to resist effectively the Muslim advance. The ruins at Hampi demonstrate the power of a Hindu coalition that rose to power in the south Deccan in the first half of the 14th century, only to be defeated by its Muslim neighbours in 1565.

For over 200 years Vijayanagar ('*city of victory*') kings fought to establish supremacy. It was an empire that, in the words of one Indian historian, made it 'the nearest approach to a war state ever made by a Hindu kingdom'. At times its power reached from Orissa in the northeast to Sri Lanka. In 1390 King Harihara II claimed to have planted a victory pillar in Sri Lanka. Much of modern Tamil Nadu and Andhra Pradesh were added to the core region of Karnataka in the area under Vijayanagar control.

AD	North India	Peninsular India	External events	AD
		Satavahanas control much of Peninsula up to 300 AD. Thomas brings Christianity to South India. *Tamil Sangram*.	Rome population of 1 million. Pyramid of the sun at City of Teotihuacan, Mexico.	50
78	Kushan rulers in Northwest followed by Scythians.			
		Arikamedu – trade with Rome.	Buddhism reaches China.	68
100	Vaishnavism spreads to north and northwest.		Paper introduced in China; first metal work in Southeast Asia.	100
	Lawbook of Manu Gandharan art.	Mahayana Buddhism spreads. Nagarjunakonda major centre in Andhra Pradesh. First cities on Deccan plateau.	Hadrian's wall in Britain.	125
200	Hinayana/Mahayana Buddhist split.			

The Mughal Empire

In North India it is the impact of the Mughal rule that is most evident today. The descendants of conquerors, with the blood of both Tamburlaine and Genghis Khan in their veins, they came to dominate Indian politics from Babur's victory near Delhi in 1526 to Aurangzeb's death in 1707. Their legacy was some of the most magnificent architecture in the world, and a profound impact on the culture, society and future politics of South Asia.

Babur (the tiger) Founder of the Mughal Dynasty, Babur was born in Russian Turkestan on 15 February 1483, the fifth direct descendant on the male side of Timur and 13th on the female side from Genghis Khan. He established the Mughal Empire by leading his cavalry and artillery forces to a victory over the combined armies of Ibrahim Lodi, last ruler of the Delhi Sultanate and the Hindu Raja of Gwalior, at **Panipat**, 80 km north of Delhi, in 1526. When he died four years later, the Empire was far from secured, but he had laid the foundations of political and military power and also begun to establish courtly traditions of poetry, literature and art which became the hallmark of subsequent Mughal rulers. Babur, used to the delights of Persian gardens and the cool of the Afghan hills, was unimpressed by India. In his autobiography he wrote: "Hindustan is a country that has few pleasures to recommend it. The people are not handsome. They have no idea of the charms of friendly society, of frankly mixing together, or of familiar intercourse. They have no genius, no comprehension of mind, no politeness of manner, no kindness or fellow-feeling, no ingenuity or mechanical invention in planning or executing their handicraft works, no skill or knowledge in design or architecture". Babur's depressing catalogue was the view of a disenchanted outsider. Within two generations the Mughals had become fully at home and brought some radical changes. Babur was charismatic. He ruled by keeping the loyalty of his military chiefs, giving them control of large areas of territory.

Humayun However, their strength posed a problem for Humayun, his successor. Almost immediately after Babur's death Humayun was forced to retreat from Delhi through Sind with his pregnant wife. His son Akbar, who was to become the greatest of the Mughal emperors, was born at Umarkot in Sindh, modern Pakistan, during this period of exile, on 23 November 1542.

Akbar Akbar was only 13 when he took the throne in 1556. The next 44 years were one of the most remarkable periods of South Asian history, paralleled by the Elizabethan period in England, where Queen Elizabeth I ruled from 1558 to 1603. Although Akbar inherited the throne, it was he who really created the empire and gave it many of its distinguishing features. Through his marriage to a Hindu princess he ensured that Hindus were given honoured positions in government, as well as respect for their religious beliefs and practices. He sustained

AD	North India	Peninsular India	External events	AD
300		Rise of Pallavas.	Classic period of Mayan civilization.	300
319	Chandra Gupta founds Gupta Dynasty (Samudra 335, Chandra II 376, Kumara 415).		Constantinople founded.	330
454	Skanda Gupta, the last imperial Gupta, takes power. Dies 467.		End of Roman Empire.	476
			Teotihuacan, Mexico, population 200,000.	500
540	Gupta rule ends.		Saint Sophia, Constantinople.	532
550		First Chalukya Dynasty,	Buddhism arrives in Japan.	550
578		Badami cave temple; last Ajanta paintings.		
600	Period of small Indian states.	Bhakti movement. Chalukyan Dynasty in		
629	Hiuen Tsang travels India.	west and central Deccan.	Death of Mohammad.	632
630		Pallavas in Tamil Nadu.		

a passionate interest in art and literature, matched by a determination to create monuments to his empire's political power and he laid the foundations for an artistic and architectural tradition which developed a totally distinctive Indian style. This emerged from the separate elements of Iranian and Indian traditions by a constant process of blending and originality of which he was the chief patron.

But these achievements were only possible because of his political and military gifts. From 1556 until his 18th birthday in 1560, Akbar was served by a prince regent, Bairam Khan. However, already at the age of 15 he had conquered Ajmer and large areas of Central India. Chittor and Ranthambore fell to him in 1567-1568, bringing most of what is now Rajasthan under his control. This opened the door south to Gujarat.

Afghans continued to cause his empire difficulties, including Daud Karrani, who declared independence in East India in 1574. That threat to Mughal power was finally crushed with Karrani's death in 1576. Bengal was far from the last of his conquests. He brought Kabul back under Mughal control in the 1580s and established a presence from Kashmir, Sind and Baluchistan in the north and west, to the Godavari River on the border of modern Andhra Pradesh in the south. Akbar deliberately widened his power base by incorporating Rajput princes into the administrative structure and giving them extensive rights in the revenue from land. He abolished the hated tax on non-Muslims *(jizya)* - ultimately reinstated by his strictly orthodox great grandson Aurangzeb – and ceased levying taxes on Hindus who went on pilgrimage. He also ended the practice of forcible conversion to Islam. **Artistic treasures** abound from Akbar's court, often bringing together material and skills from across the known world. Akbar's eclecticism had a political purpose; he was trying to build a focus of loyalty beyond that of caste, social group, region or religion. Like Roman emperors before him, he deliberately cultivated a new religion in which the emperor attained divinity, hoping to give the empire a legitimacy which would last. While his religion disappeared with his death, the legitimacy of the Mughals survived another 200 years, long after their real power had almost disappeared.

Jahangir Akbar died of a stomach illness in 1605. He was succeeded by his son, Prince Salim, who inherited the throne as Emperor Jahangir ('*world seizer*'). He added little to the territory of the empire, consolidating the Mughals' hold on the Himalayan foothills and parts of central India and restricting his energies to pushing frontiers of art. He commissioned works of art and literature, many of which recorded life in the Mughal court. Hunting scenes conveyed the real dangers of hunting lions or tigers; implements, furniture, tools and weapons were made with lavish care and often exquisite design.

From early youth Jahangir had shown an artistic temperament, but he also became addicted to alcohol and then to opium. In his autobiography, he wrote: "I had not drunk until I was 18 ...

AD	North India	Peninsular India	External events	AD
			Buddhism reaches Tibet.	645
670	Rajputs become powerful force in northwest.	Mahabalipuram shore temples.		
712	Arabs arrive in Sind.	Nandivarman II in Tamil Nadu. Pandiyas in Madurai.	Muslim invasions of Spain.	711
757		Rashtrakutas dominate central Peninsula.		
775		Kailasanath Temple, Ellora. Rise of Cholas.	Charlemagne crowned.	800
			Settlement of New Zealand.	850
			Cyrillic script developed.	863
950	Khajuraho temples started.	Rajendra Chola.	Sung Dynasty in China.	979
984		Rajaraja 1st.		

a gunner said that if I would take a glass of wine it would drive away the feeling of being tired and heavy ... After that I took to drinking wine ... until wine made from grapes ceased to intoxicate me and I took to drinking arrack (local spirits). By degrees my potions rose to 20 cups of doubly distilled spirits".

Nur Jahan Jahangir's favourite wife, Nur Jahan, brought her own artistic gifts. Born the daughter of an Iranian nobleman, she had been brought to the Mughal court along with her family as a child and moved to Bengal as the wife of Sher Afgan, see page 156. She made rapid progress after her first husband's accidental death in 1607, which caused her to move from Bengal to be a lady in waiting for one of Akbar's widows.

At the Mughal court in 1611, she met Jahangir. Mutually enraptured, they were married in May. Jahangir gave her the title Nur Mahal (Light of the Palace), soon increased to Nur Jahan (Light of the World). Aged 34, she was strikingly beautiful and had an astonishing reputation for physical skill and intellectual wit. She was a crack shot with a gun, highly artistic, determined yet philanthropic. Throughout her life Jahangir was captivated by her, so much so that he flouted Muslim convention by minting coins bearing her image.

By 1622 Nur Jahan effectively controlled the empire. She commissioned and supervised the building in Agra of one of the Mughal world's most beautiful buildings, the **I'timad ud-Daula** ('Pillar of government'), as a tomb for her father and mother. Her father, **Ghiyas Beg**, had risen to become one of Jahangir's most trusted advisers and Nur Jahan was determined to ensure that their memory was honoured. She was less successful in her wish to deny the succession after Jahangir's death at the age of 58 to Prince Khurram. Acceding to the throne in 1628, he took the title of Shah Jahan (*Ruler of the World*) and in the next 30 years his reign represented the height of Mughal power.

Shah Jahan The Mughal Empire was under attack in the Deccan and the northwest when Shah Jahan became Emperor. He tried to re-establish and extend Mughal authority in both regions by a combination of military campaigns and skilled diplomacy. Akbar's craftsmen had already carved outstandingly beautiful *jalis* for the tomb of Salim Chishti in Fatehpur Sikri, but Shah Jahan developed the form further. Undoubtedly the finest tribute to these skills is found in the Taj Mahal, the tribute to his beloved wife Mumtaz Mahal, who died giving birth to her 14th child in 1631.

Aurangzeb The need to expand the area under Mughal control was felt even more strongly by Aurangzeb ('*The jewel in the throne*'), than by his predecessors, see page 1190. He had shown his intellectual gifts in his grandfather Jahangir's court when held hostage to guarantee Shah Jahan's good behaviour, learning Arabic, Persian, Turkish and Hindi. When he seized power at the age of 40, he needed all his political and military skills to hold on to an unwieldy empire that was in permanent danger of collapse from its own size. Aurangzeb realized that the resources of

AD	North India	Peninsular India	External events	AD
1001	Mahmud of Ghazni raids Indus plains. Rajput dynasties grow.	Chola kings – navies sent to Southeast Asia: Chola bronzes.	Easter Island stone carvings.	1000
1050	Sufism in North India. Rajput dynasties in northwest.		Norman conquest of England.	1066
			First European universities.	1100
1110		Rise of Hoysalas.		
1118	Senas in Bengal.			
			Angkor Wat, Cambodia; paper making spreads from Muslim world.	1150
1192	Rajputs defeated by Mu'izzu'd Din.		Srivijaya Kingdom at its height in Java; Angkor Empire at greatest.	1170

the territory he inherited from Shah Jahan were not enough. One response was to push south, while maintaining his hold on the east and north. Initially he maintained his alliances with the Rajputs in the west, which had been a crucial element in Mughal strategy. In 1678 he claimed absolute rights over Jodhpur and went to war with the Rajput clans at the same time embarking on a policy of outright Islamization. However, for the remaining 39 years of his reign he struggled to sustain his power.

The East India Company and the rise of British power

The British were unique among the foreign rulers of India in coming by sea rather than through the northwest and in coming first for trade rather than for military conquest. The ports that they established – Madras, Bombay and Calcutta – became completely new centres of political, economic and social activity. Before them Indian empires had controlled their territories from the land. The British dictated the economy by controlling sea-borne trade. From the middle of the 19th century railways transformed the economic and political structure of South Asia and it was those three centres of British control, along with the late addition of Delhi, which became the foci of economic development and political change.

The East India Company in Madras and Bengal

In its first 90 years of contact with South Asia after the Company set up its first trading post at **Masulipatnam**, on the east coast of India, it had depended almost entirely on trade for its profits. However, in 1701, only 11 years after a British settlement was first established at Calcutta, the Company was given rights to land revenue in Bengal.

The Company was accepted and sometimes welcomed, partly because it offered to bolster the inadequate revenues of the Mughals by exchanging silver bullion for the cloth it bought. However, in the south the Company moved further towards consolidating its political base. Wars between South India's regional factions gave the Company the chance to extend their influence by making alliances and offering support to some of these factions in their struggles, which were complicated by the extension to Indian soil of the European contest for power between the French and the British.

Robert Clive The British established control over both Bengal and Southeast India in the middle of the 17th century. Robert Clive, in alliance with a collection of disaffected Hindu landowners and Muslim soldiers, defeated the new Nawab of Bengal, the 20-year-old Siraj-ud-Daula, in June 1757. At Plassey (Palashi), about 100 km north of Calcutta.

AD	North India	Peninsular India	External events	AD
1198	First mosque built in Delhi; Qutb Minar Delhi.		Rise of Hausa city states in West Africa.	1200
1206	Delhi Sultanate established.		Mongols begin conquest of Asia under Genghis Khan.	1206
1206	Turkish 'slave dynasty'.	Pandiyas rise.		
			First Thai kingdom.	1220
1222	Iltutmish Sultan of Delhi.			
1230		Konark, Sun Temple, Orissa		
			Marco Polo reaches China.	1275
1290	Khaljis in Delhi; Jalal ud Din Khalji.			
1320-24	Ghiyas ud Din Tughluq.		Black Death spreads from Asia to Europe.	1348
1324-51	Mohammad bin Tughluq.			

Hastings and Cornwallis The essential features of British control were mapped out in the next quarter of a century through the work of **Warren Hastings**, Governor-General from 1774 until 1785 and **Lord Cornwallis** who succeeded and remained in charge until 1793. Cornwallis was responsible for putting Europeans in charge of all the higher levels of revenue collection and administration and for introducing government by the rule of law, making even government officers subject to the courts.

The decline of Muslim power

The extension of East India Company power in the Mughal periphery of India's south and east took place against a background of the rising power of Sivaji and his Marathas.

Sivaji and the Marathas Sivaji was the son of a Hindu who had served as a small-scale chief in the Muslim-ruled state of Bijapur. The weakness of Bijapur encouraged Sivaji to extend his father's area of control and he led a rebellion. The Bijapur general Afzal Khan, sent to put it down, agreed to meet Sivaji in private to reach a settlement. In an act which is still remembered by both Muslims and Marathas, Sivaji embraced him with steel claws attached to his fingers and tore him apart. It was the start of a campaign which took Maratha power as far south as Madurai and to the doors of Delhi and Calcutta.

Although Sivaji himself died in 1680, Aurangzeb never fully came to terms with the rising power of the Marathas, though he did end their ambitions to form an empire of their own. While the Maratha confederacy was able to threaten Delhi within 50 years of Aurangzeb's death, by the early 19th century it had dissolved into five independent states, with whom the British ultimately dealt separately.

Nor was Aurangzeb able to create any wide sense of identity with the Mughals as a legitimate popular power. Instead, under the influence of Sunni Muslim theologians, he retreated into insistence on Islamic purity. He imposed Islamic law, the *sharia*, promoted only Muslims to positions of authority, tried to replace Hindu administrators and revenue collectors with Muslims and reimposed the *jizya* tax on all non-Muslims. By his death in 1707 the empire had neither the broadness of spirit nor the physical means to survive.

Bahadur Shah The decline was postponed by the reign of Aurangzeb's son. Sixty-three when he acceded to the throne, Bahadur Shah restored some of its fortunes. He made agreements with the Marathas and the Rajputs and defeated the Sikhs in Punjab before taking the last Sikh guru into his service. Nine emperors succeeded Aurangzeb between his death and the exile of the last Mughal ruler in 1858. It was no accident that it was in that year the British ended the rule of its East India Company and decreed India to be its Indian empire.

AD	North India	Peninsular India	External events	AD
1336		Vijayanagar Empire established, Harihara I.		
1347		Ala-ud-Din sets up Bahmani dynasty, independent of Delhi, in Gulbarga.		
1351-88	Firoz Shah Tughluq.		Ming dynasty in China established.	1368
			Peking the largest city in the world.	1400
1398	Timur sacks Delhi.		Ming sea-going expeditions to Africa.	1405
1412	End of Tughlaq Dynasty.			
1414	Sayyid Dynasty.	Bidar/Bahmani Kingdom in Deccan.		1428
1440	Mystic Kabir born in Benaras.		Aztecs defeat Atzcapatzalco. Incas centralize power.	1438
1451	Afghan Lodi Dynasty established under Bahlul.		Byzantine Empire falls to Ottomans.	1453
1469	Guru Nanak born in Punjab.			
1482		Fall of Bahmanis.	Columbus reaches the Americas; Arabs and Jews expelled from Spain.	1492

Mohammad Shah remained in his capital of Delhi, resigning himself to enjoying what Carey Welch has called "the conventional triad of joys: the wine was excellent, as were the women and for him the song was especially rewarding". The idyll was rudely shattered by the invasion of **Nadir Shah** in 1739, an Iranian marauder who slaughtered thousands in Delhi and carried off priceless Mughal treasures, including the Peacock Throne, see page 79.

The East India Company's push for power

Alliances In the century and a half that followed the death of Aurangzeb, the British East India Company extended its economic and political influence into the heart of India. As the Mughal Empire lost its power India fell into many smaller states. The Company undertook to protect the rulers of several of these states from external attack by stationing British troops in their territory. In exchange for this service the rulers paid subsidies to the Company. The British extended their territory through the 18th century as successive regional powers were annexed and brought under direct Company rule.

Progress to direct British control was uneven and often opposed. The Sikhs in Punjab, the Marathas in the west and the Mysore sultans in the south, fiercely contested British advances. **Haidar Ali** and **Tipu Sultan**, who had built a wealthy kingdom in the Mysore region, resisted attempts to incorporate them. Tipu was finally killed in 1799 at the battle of Srirangapatnam, an island fort in the Kaveri River just north of Mysore, where Arthur Wellesley, later the Duke of Wellington, began to make his military reputation.

The Marathas were not defeated until the 1816-18 war. Even then the defeat owed as much to internal fighting as to the power of the British-led army. Only the northwest of the subcontinent remained beyond British control until well into the 19th century. Thus in 1799 **Ranjit Singh** was able to set up a Sikh state in Punjab, surviving until the late 1830s despite the extension of British control over much of the rest of India.

In 1818 India's economy was in ruins and its political structures destroyed. Irrigation and road systems had fallen into decay and gangs terrorized the countryside. Thugs and dacoits controlled much of rural areas in Central India and often robbed and murdered even on town outskirts. The stability of the Mughal period had long since passed. From 1818 to 1857 there was a succession of local and uncoordinated revolts in different parts of India. Some were bought off, some put down by military force.

AD	North India	Peninsular India	External events	AD
1500		Vasco da Gama reaches India.	Inca Empire at its height.	1498
		Vijayanagar dominates South India; Krishnadevraya rules 1509-30.	Spanish claim Brazil; Safavid Empire founded in Persia.	1500
1506	Sikander Lodi founds Agra.			
		Albuquerque seizes Goa;		1510
		Nizamshahis establish independent Ahmadnagar sultanate.	Ottomans capture Syria, Egypt and Arabia.	1516
1526	Babur defeats Ibrahim Lodi to establish Mughal power in Delhi.	Dutch, French, Portuguese and Danish traders.	Spaniards overthrow Aztecs in Mexico.	1519
			Potato introduced to Europe from South America.	1525
1540	Sher Shah forces Humayun into exile.			

A monument to grief?

The grief that Mumtaz's death caused may have been the chief motivating force behind Shah Jahan's determination to build the Taj Mahal, a monument not just to his love for her, but also to the supremacy of Mughal refinement and power. However, that power had to be paid for and the costs were escalating. Shah Jahan himself had inherited an almost bankrupt state from his father. Expenditure on the army had outstripped the revenue collected by tribute from kings and from the chiefs given the rights and responsibility over territories often larger than European countries. Financial deficits forced Shah Jahan onto the offensive in order to guarantee greater and more reliable revenue.

Major reforms helped to reduce the costs of his standing army. However, maintaining the force necessary to control the huge territories owing allegiance to the emperor continued to stretch his resources to the full. By 1648, when he moved his capital to Delhi, the empire was already in financial difficulties and in 1657 the rumour that Shah Jahan was terminally ill immediately caused a series of battles for the succession between his four sons.

Aurangzeb, the second son and sixth child of Shah Jahan and Mumtaz Mahal – tough, intriguing and sometimes cruel, but also a highly intelligent strategist – emerged the winner, to find that Shah Jahan had recovered. Rather than run the risk of being deposed, Aurangzeb kept his father imprisoned in Agra Fort, where he had been taken ill, from June 1658 until his death in February 1666.

A period of reforms

While existing political systems were collapsing, the first half of the 1800s was also a time of radical social change in territories governed by the East India Company. **Lord William Bentinck** became governor-general at a time when England was undergoing major reform. In 1828 he banned the burning of widows on the funeral pyres of their husbands (**sati**) and then moved to suppress **thuggee** (ritual murder and robbery carried out in the name of the goddess Kali). His most far reaching change was to introduce education in English.

From the late 1830s massive new engineering projects began to be taken up; first canals, then railways. The innovations stimulated change and change contributed to the growing unease with the British presence. The development of the telegraph, railways and new roads, three universities and the extension of massive new canal irrigation projects in North India

AD	North India	Peninsular India	External events	AD
1542		St Francis Xavier reaches Goa.		
1555	Humayun re-conquers Delhi.			
1556	Akbar Emperor.			
1565		Vijayanagar defeated.	William Shakespeare born.	1564
		First printing press in Goa.		1566
			Dutch East India Co set up.	1602
1603	Guru Granth Sahib compiled.		Tokugawa Shogunate in Japan.	1603
1605	Jahangir Emperor.		First permanent English settlement in America.	1607
1608		East India Co base at Surat.		
			Telescope invented in Holland.	1609

seemed to threaten traditional society, a risk increased by the annexation of Indian states to bring them under direct British rule. The most important of these was Oudh.

The Rebellion

Out of the growing discontent and widespread economic difficulties came the Rebellion or 'Mutiny' of 1857. On 10 May 1857 troops in Meerut, 70 km northeast of Delhi, mutinied. They reached Delhi the next day, where **Bahadur Shah**, the last Mughal Emperor, took sides with the mutineers. Troops in Lucknow joined the rebellion and for three months Lucknow and other cities in the north were under siege. Appalling scenes of butchery and reprisals marked the struggle, only put down by troops from outside.

The period of Empire

The 1857 rebellion marked the end not only of the Mughal Empire but also of the East India Company, for the British government in London took overall control in 1858. Yet within 30 years a movement for self government had begun and there were the first signs of a demand among the new Western-educated elite that political rights be awarded to match the sense of Indian national identity.

Indian National Congress Established in 1885, this was the first all-India political institution and was to become the key vehicle of demands for independence. However, the educated Muslim élite of what is now Uttar Pradesh saw a threat to Muslim rights, power and identity in the emergence of democratic institutions which gave Hindus, with their built-in natural majority, significant advantages. Sir Sayyid Ahmad Khan, who had founded a Muslim University at Aligarh in 1877, advised Muslims against joining the Congress, seeing it as a vehicle for Hindu and especially Bengali, nationalism.

The Muslim League The educated Muslim community of North India remained deeply suspicious of the Congress, making up less than 8% of those attending its conferences between 1900-1920. Muslims from UP created the All-India Muslim League in 1906. However, the demands of the Muslim League were not always opposed to those of the Congress. In 1916 it concluded the Lucknow Pact with the Congress, in which the Congress won Muslim support for self-government, in exchange for the recognition that there would be separate constituencies for Muslims. The nature of the future independent India was still far from clear, however. The British conceded the principle of self-government in 1918, but the reforms already fell far short of heightened Indian expectations.

Mahatma Gandhi Into a tense atmosphere Mohandas Karamchand Gandhi returned to India in 1915 after 20 years practising as a lawyer in South Africa. He arrived as the government

AD	North India	Peninsular India	External events	AD
1628	Shah Jahan Emperor.		Masjid-i-Shah Mosque in Isfahan.	1616
1632-53	Taj Mahal built.			
		Fort St George, Madras, founded by East India Co.		1639
			Manchus found Ch'ing Dynasty.	1644
			Tasman 'discovers' New Zealand.	1645
1658	Aurangzeb Emperor.			
			Louis XIV of France – the 'Sun King'.	1653-1715

Mahatma Gandhi

Mohandas Karamchand Ghandi, a westernized, English-educated lawyer, had lived outside India from his youth to middle age. He preached the general acceptance of some of the doctrines he had grown to respect in his childhood, which stemmed from deep Indian traditions – notably *ahimsa*, or non- violence. On his return the Bengali Nobel Laureate poet, Rabindranath Tagore, had dubbed him 'Mahatma' – Great Soul. From 1921 he gave up his Western style of dress and adopted the hand spun dhoti worn by poor Indian villagers. Yet, he was also fiercely critical of many aspects of traditional Hindu society. He preached against the discrimination of the caste system which still dominated life for the overwhelming majority of Hindus. Often despised by the British in India, his death at the hands of an extreme Hindu chauvinist in January 1948 was a final testimony to the ambiguity of his achievements: successful in contributing so much to achieving India's Independence, yet failing to resolve some of the bitter communal legacies which he gave his life to overcome.

of India was being given new powers by the British parliament to try political cases without a jury and to give provincial governments the right to imprison politicians without trial. In opposition to this legislation Gandhi proposed to call a *hartal*, when all activity would cease for a day, a form of protest still in widespread use. Such protests took place across India, often accompanied by riots.

On 13 April 1919 a huge gathering took place in the enclosed space of Jallianwala Bagh in Amritsar, see page 473. It had been prohibited by the government and General Dyer ordered troops to fire on the people without warning, killing 379 and injuring at least a further 1200. It marked the turning point in relations with Britain and the rise of Gandhi to the key position of leadership in the struggle for complete independence.

The thrust for Independence Through the 1920s Gandhi developed concepts and political programmes that were to become the hallmark of India's Independence struggle. Ultimately political Independence was to be achieved not by violent rebellion but by *satyagraha* – a "truth force" which implied a willingness to suffer through non-violent resistance to injustice. In 1930 the Congress declared that 26 January would be Independence Day – still celebrated as Republic Day in India today. Mohammad Iqbal, the Leader of the Muslim League, took the opportunity of his address to the League in the same year to suggest the formation of a Muslim state within an Indian Federation. Also in 1930 a Muslim student in Cambridge, **Chaudhuri Rahmat Ali**, coined a

AD	North India	Peninsular India	External events	AD
1677		**Shivaji** and Marathas.	Pennsylvania founded.	1681
1690	Calcutta founded.			
1699	Guru Gobind Singh forms Sikh Khalsa.	Regional powers dominate through 18th century:	Chinese occupy Outer Mongolia.	1697
1703	Nawabs of Bengal.	Nawabs of Arcot (1707);	Foundation of St Petersburg, capital of Russian Empire.	1703
1707	Death of Aurangzeb; Mughal rulers continue to rule from Delhi until 1858 Nawabs of Avadh.	Maratha Peshwas (1714); Nizams of Hyderabad (1724).		
1739	The Persian Nadir Shah captures Delhi and massacres thousands.			
1757	Battle of Plassey; British power extended from East India.	East India Co strengthens trade and political power through 18th century.	US War of Independence.	1775-8

name for the new Muslim state **PAKISTAN**. The letters were to stand 'P' for Punjab, 'A' for Afghania, 'K' for Kashmir, 'S' for Sind with the suffix '*stan*', Persian for country. The idea still had little real shape however and waited on developments of the late 1930s and 1940s to bear fruit.

By the end of the Second World War the positions of the Muslim League, now under the leadership of **Mohammad Ali Jinnah** and the Congress led by **Jawaharlal Nehru**, were irreconcilable. While major questions of the definition of separate territories for a Muslim and non-Muslim state remained to be answered, it was clear to General Wavell, the British Viceroy through the last years of the war, that there was no alternative but to accept that independence would have to be given on the basis of separate states.

Independence and Partition

One of the main difficulties for the Muslims was that they made up only a fifth of the total population were scattered throughout India. It was therefore impossible to define a simple territorial division which would provide a state to match Jinnah's claim of a '*two-nation theory*'. On 20 February 1947, the British Labour Government announced its decision to replace Lord Wavell as Viceroy with Lord Mountbatten, who was to oversee the transfer of power to new independent governments. It set a deadline of June 1948 for British withdrawal. The announcement of a firm date made the Indian politicians even less willing to compromise and the resulting division satisfied no one.

Independence arrived on 15 August for India and the 14 August for Pakistan because Indian astrologers deemed the 15th to be the most auspicious moment. Several key Princely States had still not decided firmly to which country they would accede. Kashmir was the most important of these, with results that have lasted to the present day.

Modern India

India, with an estimated 1.21 billion people in 2011, is the second most populated country in the world after China. That population size reflects the long history of human occupation and the fact that an astonishingly high proportion of India's land is relatively fertile. About 60% of India's surface area is cultivated, compared with 10% in China and 20% in the US.

Although the birth rate has fallen steadily over the last 40 years, initially death rates fell faster and the rate of population increase in 2011 was 17.6%. Today over 320 million people live in towns and cities.

Politics and institutions

When India became independent on 15 August 1947 it faced three immediate crises. Partition left it with a bitter struggle between Muslims on one side and Hindus and Sikhs on the other which threatened to tear the new country into pieces. An estimated 13 million people migrated between the two new countries of India and Pakistan.

In the years since Independence, striking political achievements have been made. With the two year exception of 1975-1977, when Mrs Gandhi imposed a state of emergency in which all political activity was banned, India has sustained a democratic system in the face of tremendous pressures. The general elections of May 2004 saw the Congress Party return as the largest single party, with 220 of the 540 Lok Sabha seats. They managed to forge alliances with some of the smaller parties and thus formed the new United Progressive Alliance government under the prime ministership not of the Congress Party's leader, Sonia Gandhi, but of ex-finance minister, Manmohan Singh.

The constitution

Establishing itself as a sovereign democratic republic, the Indian parliament accepted Nehru's advocacy of a secular constitution. The president is formally vested with all executive powers exercised under the authority of the prime minister.

Parliament has a lower house (*Lok Sabha* – House of the people) and an upper house (*Rajya Sabha* – Council of States). The former is made up of directly elected representatives from the 543 parliamentary constituencies (plus two nominated members from the Anglo-Indian community), the latter of members elected by an electoral college and nominated members.

India's federal constitution devolves certain powers to elected state assemblies. Each state has a governor who acts as its official head. Many states also have two chambers, the upper generally called the Rajya Sabha and the lower (often called the Vidhan Sabha) being of directly elected representatives. In practice many of the state assemblies have had a totally different political complexion from that of the Lok Sabha. Regional parties have played a far more prominent role, though in many states central government has effectively dictated both the leadership and policy of state assemblies.

States and Union Territories Union territories are administered by the president "acting to such an extent as he thinks fit". In practice Union territories have varying forms of self-government. Pondicherry has a legislative Assembly and Council of Ministers. The 69th Amendment to the Constitution in 1991 provided for a legislative assembly and council of ministers for Delhi, elections for which were held in December 1993. The Assemblies of Union Territories have more restricted powers of legislation than full states. Some Union Territories – Dadra and Nagar Haveli, Daman and Diu, all of which separated from Goa in 1987 when Goa achieved full statehood – Andaman and Nicobar Islands and Lakshadweep, have elected bodies known as Pradesh Councils.

Secularism One of the key features of India's constitution is its secular principle. Some see the commitment to a secular constitution as having been under challenge from the Hindu nationalism of the Bharatiya Janata Party, the BJP.

Judiciary India's Supreme Court has similar but somewhat weaker powers to those of the United States. The judiciary has remained effectively independent of the government except under the Emergency between 1975-1977.

Civil service India continued to use the small but highly professional administrative service inherited from the British period. Renamed the Indian Administrative Service (IAS), it continues to exercise remarkable influence across the country. The administration of many aspects of central and regional government is in the hands of this elite body, who act largely by the constitutional rules which bind them as servants of the state. Many Indians accept the continuing efficiency and high calibre of the top ranking officers in the administration while believing that the bureaucratic system as a whole has been overtaken by widespread corruption.

Police India's police service is divided into a series of groups, numbering nearly one million. While the top ranks of the Indian Police Service are comparable to the IAS, lower levels are extremely poorly trained and very low paid. In addition to the domestic police force there are special groups: the Border Security Force, Central Reserve Police and others. They may be armed with modern weapons and are called in for special duties.

Armed forces Unlike its immediate neighbours Pakistan and Bangladesh, India has never had military rule. It has around one million men in the army, one of the largest armed forces in the world. Although they have remained out of politics the army has been used increasingly frequently to put down civil unrest especially in Kashmir.

Congress Party The Congress won overall majorities in seven of the 10 general elections held before the 1996 election, although in no election did they obtain more than 50% of the popular vote. In 1998 its popular support completely disappeared in some regions and fell below 30% nationally and in the 1999 elections Sonia Gandhi, Rajiv Gandhi's Italian-born widow, failed to achieve the much vaunted revival in the Party's fortunes. Through 2001 into

2002 a change began with the BJP losing power in state assemblies in the north and becoming increasingly unpopular nationally, and the Congress picking up a wide measure of support, culminating in their victory in the 2004 general election, when Sonia Gandhi nominated Manmohan Singh as prime minister. In the 2009 elections, the Congress Party won again and Singh continued at the helm.

Non-Congress parties Political activity outside the Congress can seem bewilderingly complex. There are no genuinely national parties. The only alternative governments to the Congress have been formed by coalitions of regional and ideologically based parties. Parties of the left – Communist and Socialist – have never broken out of their narrow regional bases. The **Communist Party of India** split into two factions in 1964, with the Communist Party of India Marxist (CPM) ultimately taking power in West Bengal and Kerala. In the 1960s the **Swatantra Party** (a liberal party) made some ground nationally, opposing the economic centralization and state control supported by the Congress.

At the right of the political spectrum, the **Jan Sangh** was seen as a party of right wing Hindu nationalism with a concentrated but significant base in parts of the north, especially among higher castes and merchant communities. The most organized political force outside the Congress, the Jan Sangh merged with the **Janata Party** for the elections of 1977. After the collapse of that government it re-formed itself as the **Bharatiya Janata Party** (BJP) and developed a powerful campaign focusing on reviving Hindu identity against the minorities. The elections of 1991 showed it to be the foremost challenger to the Congress in North India. In the decade that followed it became the most powerful single party across northern India and established a series of footholds and alliances in the South. Elsewhere a succession of regional parties dominated politics in several key states, including Tamil Nadu and Andhra Pradesh in the south and West Bengal and Bihar in the east. By mid-2001 the gloss had worn off the popularity of the BJP and it had suffered scandals, but the prime minister had kept the core of the government together.

Recent developments The attacks on New York and Washington on 11 September and the US-led 'War on Terror' has had major repercussions in India and Pakistan. Both India and Pakistan sought political advantage from the war on terror, and when a terrorist attack was launched on the Indian parliament in December 2001 the Indian government pushed massive reinforcements to the Pakistan border from Gujarat and Rajasthan to Kashmir. Cross-border firing intensified along the Line of Control in Kashmir and attacks in Kashmir continued. After the change of government in May 2004, however, things improved but the rising strike power of terrorist groups in Pakistan led to increasing fears in India of a collapse of political control in its western neighbour. The Mumbai terror attacks on 26-29 November 2008 that killed 164 people proved this fear to be correct. Carried out by the banned *Lashkar e Taiba* Islamic group, co-ordinated from illegal camps within Pakistan, the attacks greatly strained relations between the two countries. Talks to resolve the Kashmir situation were suspended and only in February 2011 have moves been made to resume the peace process. However, the positive emotions generated by the 2011 Cricket World Cup prompted Prime Minister Manmohan Singh to invite President Asif Ali Zardari to India to watch the India-Pakistan semi-final. It is hoped that peace talks will be resumed in the near future.

Economy

Agriculture

Although agriculture now accounts for less than 20% of India's GDP, it remains the most important single economic activity. Over half of India's people depend directly on agriculture and its success has a crucial effect on the remainder of the economy.

Indian agriculture is enormously varied due to different climate, soil and relief. Cereal farming dominates, but wheat, grown as a winter crop, is most important in western Uttar Pradesh through Haryana to Punjab. Rice, the most important single foodgrain, is concentrated in the wetter regions of the east and south. Production of both crops has more than doubled in the last 20 years.

Other cereal crops – sorghum and the millets – predominate in central India and unirrigated parts of the north. In addition to its cereals and a range of pulses, India produces important crops of tea, cotton and sugar cane. All have seen significant growth, tea and cotton manufacturers making major contributions to export earnings.

Between Independence and the late 1960s most of the increase in India's agricultural output came from extending the cultivated area. In the last 20 years increasingly intensive use of land through greater irrigation and use of fertilizer, pesticides and high-yielding varieties of seeds (HYVs) has allowed growth to continue. Indian agriculture is dominated by small holdings. While the Green Revolution – the package of practices designed to increase farm output – has had its opponents, it has now transformed the agricultural productivity of many regions of India, allowing a population twice the size of that thirty years ago to be fed without recourse to imports or aid. Much of this has been achieved as the result of seed breeding and agricultural research in India's own agricultural research institutions.

Resources and industry

India has extensive resources of iron ore, coal, bauxite and some other minerals. Reserves of coal at likely rates of use are estimated at well over 100 years (at least 30 billion tonnes, plus six billion tonnes of coking coal). Medium and high grade iron ore reserves (five billion tonnes) will last over 200 years at present extraction rates. Although iron ore is found widely across peninsular India, coal is largely restricted to West Bengal, Bihar, Orissa and Meghalaya.

An intensified search for oil has proved India to have reserves of 4.7 billion barrels in 2011. Development of the Bombay High, off the coast of Gujarat, has contributed to the total output of over 26 million tonnes, about a third of total consumption in 2009. Oil, coal and gas provide the energy for just over half of India's 100 million kw electric generation capacity, 20 million kw being hydro and two million mw nuclear. Following the nuclear deal with the USA nuclear capacity is planned to rise to 40,000 mw by 2020, a doubling of the pre-agreement target.

By 2002 India's power production had grown to over 470 billion kwh, rising by 2006 to 703 bn kwh. However, demand has risen so fast that many states continue to have power blackouts or 'loadshedding'. Firewood is estimated to provide nearly 30% of the total energy requirement, agricultural waste 9% and cow dung, a universal fuel in some poorer areas, 7%. Sustainable alternatives such as solar and wind continue to contribute under 1%.

India's Five Year Plans

In the early 1950s India embarked on a programme of planned industrial development. Borrowing planning concepts from the Soviet Union, the government tried to stimulate development through massive investment in the public sector, imposing a system of tight controls on foreign ownership of capital in India and playing a highly interventionist role in all aspects of economic policy. The private sector was allowed to continue to operate in agriculture and in a wide range of 'non-essential' industrial sectors.

Although significant achievements were made in the first two Five Year Plans (1951-1956, 1956-1961), the Third Five Year Plan failed catastrophically. Agriculture was particularly hard hit by three poor monsoons. After a period of dependence on foreign aid at the end of the 1960s, the economy started moving forward again. The Green Revolution enabled Indian agriculture to increase production faster than demand and through the 1980s it was producing surplus foodgrains, enabling it to build up reserves.

Achievements and problems

India today has a far more diversified industrial base than seemed imaginable at Independence. It produces goods, from aeroplanes and rockets to watches and computers, from industrial and transport machinery to textiles and consumer goods. The influence of India's manufacturing industry reaches every village. The most striking modern development is in the IT sector. According to the London *Financial Times* since the early 1990s India has become one of the world's leading centres for software development and India is rapidly trans- forming itself into a computer-based society. Yet despite economic successes, many claim that the weaknesses remain profound. Perhaps half of the population continues to live in absolute poverty and despite surplus grain production many still lack an adequate diet.

Culture

Language

The graffiti written on the walls of any Indian city bear witness to the number of major languages spoken across the country, many with their own distinct scripts. In all the states of North and West India an Indo-Aryan language – the easternmost group of the Indo-European family – is predominant. Sir William Jones, the great 19th-century scholar, discovered the close links between Sanskrit (the basis of nearly all North Indian languages) German and Greek. He showed that they all must have originated in the common heartland of Central Asia, being carried west, south and east by the nomadic tribes who shaped so much of the following history of both Europe and Asia.

Sanskrit As the pastoralists from Central Asia moved into South Asia from 2000 BC onwards, the Indo-Aryan languages they spoke were modified. Sanskrit developed from this process, emerging as the dominant classical language of India by the sixth century BC, when it was classified in the grammar of Panini. It remained the language of the educated until about AD 1000, though it had ceased to be in common use several centuries earlier.

Hindi and Urdu The Muslims brought Persian into South Asia as the language of the rulers, where it became the language of the politically powerful élite. The most striking example of Muslim influence on the earlier Indo-European languages is that of the two most important languages of India and Pakistan, Hindi and Urdu respectively. Most of the other modern North Indian languages were not written until the 16th century or after. Hindi developed into the language of the heartland of Hindu culture, stretching from Punjab to Bihar and from the foothills of the Himalaya to the marchlands of central India.

Bengali At the east end of the Ganga plains Hindi gives way to Bengali (Bangla), the language today of over 50 million people in India, as well as more than 115 million in Bangladesh. Linguistically it is close to both Assamese and Oriya.

Gujarati and Marathi South of the main Hindi and Urdu belt of India and Pakistan is a series of quite different Indo-Aryan languages. Panjabi in both Pakistan and India (on the Indian side of the border written in the Gurumukhi script) and Gujarati and Marathi, all have common features with Urdu or Hindi, but are major languages in their own right.

Dravidian languages The other major language family of South Asia today, Dravidian, has been in India since before the arrival of the Indo-Aryans. Four of South Asia's major living languages belong to this family group – Tamil, Telugu, Kannada and Malayalam, spoken in Tamil Nadu (and northern Sri Lanka), Andhra Pradesh, Karnataka and Kerala respectively.

Each has its own script. All the Dravidian languages were influenced by the prevalence of Sanskrit as the language of the ruling and educated elite. There have been recent attempts to rid Tamil of its Sanskrit elements and to recapture the supposed purity of a literature that stretches back to the early centuries BC. Kannada and Telugu were clearly established by AD 1000, while Malayalam, which started as a dialect of Tamil, did not develop fully until the 13th century. Today the four main Dravidian languages are spoken by 180 million people.

Scripts

It is impossible to spend even a short time in India or the other countries of South Asia without coming across several of the different scripts that are used. The earliest ancestor of scripts in use today was **Brahmi**, in which Asoka's famous inscriptions were written in the third century BC. Written from left to right, a separate symbol represented each different sound.

Devanagari For around 1000 years the major script of northern India has been the Nagari or Devanagari, which means literally the script of the 'city of the gods'. Hindi, Nepali and Marathi join Sanskrit in their use of Devanagari. The Muslim rulers developed a right to left script based on Persian and Arabic.

Dravidian scripts The Dravidian languages were written originally on leaves of the palmyra palm. Cutting the letters on the hard palm leaf made particular demands which had their impact on the forms of the letters adopted. The letters became rounded because they were carved with a stylus. This was held stationary while the leaf was turned. The southern scripts were carried overseas, contributing to the form of the non-Dravidian languages of Thai, Burmese and Cambodian.

Numerals Many of the Indian alphabets have their own notation for numerals. This is not without irony, for what in the western world are called 'Arabic' numerals are in fact of Indian origin. In some parts of South Asia local numerical symbols are still in use, but you will find that the Arabic number symbols familiar in Europe and the West are common.

Literature

Sanskrit was the first all-India language. Its literature has had a fundamental influence on the region's religious, social and political life. Early literature was memorized and recited. The hymns of the Rig Veda did not reach their final form until about the sixth century BC.

The Vedas

The Rig Veda is a collection of 1028 hymns, not all religious. Its main function was to provide orders of worship for priests responsible for the sacrifices that were central to the religion of Indo-Aryans. Two later texts, the Yajurveda and the Samaveda, served the same purpose. A fourth, the Atharvaveda, is largely a collection of magic spells.

The Brahmanas Central to the Vedic literature was a belief in the importance of sacrifice. At some time after 1000 BC a second category of Vedic literature, the Brahmanas, began to take shape. Story telling developed as a means to interpret the significance of sacrifice. The most famous and the most important of these were the Upanishads, probably written at some time between the seventh and fifth centuries BC.

The Mahabharata The Brahmanas gave their name to the religion emerging between the eighth and sixth centuries BC, Brahmanism, the ancestor of Hinduism. Two of its texts remain the best known and most widely revered epic compositions in South Asia, the *Mahabharata* and the *Ramayana*.

Dating the Mahabharata

Tradition puts the date of the great battle described in the *Mahabharata* at precisely 3102 BC, the start of the present era, and names the author of the poem as a sage, Vyasa. Evidence suggests however that the battle was fought around 800 BC, at **Kurukshetra**. It was another 400 years before priests began to write the stories down, a process which was not complete until AD 400. The *Mahabharata* was probably an attempt by the warrior class, the Kshatriyas, to merge their brand of popular religion with Brahmanism ideas. The original version was 3000 stanzas long, but it now has over 100,000; eight times as long as Homer's Iliad and the Odyssey put together.

Good and evil The battle was seen as a war of good and evil, the **Pandavas** being interpreted as gods and the **Kauravas** as devils. The arguments were elaborated and expanded until the fourth century AD by which time, as Shackle says, "Brahmanism had absorbed and set

The story of Rama

Under Brahmin influence, Rama was transformed from the human prince of the early versions into the divine figure of the final story. Rama, the 'jewel of the solar kings', became deified as an incarnation of Vishnu. The story tells how Rama was banished from his father's kingdom. In a journey with his wife, Sita, and helper and friend, Hanuman (the monkey-faced God depicted in many Indian temples, shrines and posters), Rama fought the king **Ravana**, changed in late versions into a demon. Rama's rescue of Sita was interpreted as the Aryan triumph over the barbarians. The epic is seen as South Asia's first literary poem and is recited in all Hindu communities.

Ravana, demon king of Lanka

its own mark on the religious ideas of the epic and Hinduism had come into being". A comparatively late addition to the *Mahabharata*, the *Bhagavad-Gita* is the most widely read and revered text among Hindus in South Asia today.

The Ramayana

Valmiki is thought of in India as the author of the second great Indian epic, the *Ramayana*, though no more is known of his identity than is known of Homer's. Like the *Mahabharata*, it underwent several stages of development before it reached its final version of 48,000 lines.

Sanskrit literature

Sanskrit was the language of the elite. Other languages replaced it in common speech by the third century BC, but it remained in restricted use for over 1000 years after that period. The remarkable Sanskrit grammar of Panini (see page 795) helped to establish grammar as one of the six disciplines essential to understanding the Vedas properly and to conducting Vedic rituals. The other five were phonetics, etymology, meter, ritual practice and astronomy. Sanskrit literature continued to be written in the courts until the Muslims replaced it with Persian, long after it had ceased to be a language of spoken communication.

Literally 'stories of ancient times', the Puranas are about Brahma, Vishnu and Siva. They were not compiled until the fifth century AD. The stories are often the only source of information about the period immediately after the early Vedas. Each Purana dealt with five themes: "the creation of the world (sarga); its destruction and recreation (pratisarga); the genealogy of gods and patriarchs (vamsa); the reigns and periods of the Manus (manvantaras); and the history of the solar and lunar dynasties".

The Muslim influence

Persian In the first three decades of the 10th century AD Mahmud of Ghazni carried Muslim power into India. For considerable periods until the 18th century, Persian became the language of the courts. Classical Persian was the dominant influence, with Iran as its country of origin and Shiraz its main cultural centre, but India developed its own Persian-based style. Two poets stood out at the end of the 13th century AD, when Muslim rulers had established a sultanate in Delhi, Amir Khusrau, who lived from 1253 to 1325 and the mystic Amir Hasan, who died about AD 1328.

Turki The most notable of the Mughal sponsors of literature, Akbar (1556-1605) was illiterate. Babur left one of the most remarkable political autobiographies of any generation, the Babur-nama, written in Turki and translated into Persian. His grandson Akbar commissioned a biography, the Akbar-nama, which reflected his interest in the world's religions. His son Jahangir left his memoirs, the Tuzuk-i Jahangiri, in Persian. They have been described as intimate and showing an insatiable interest in things, events and people.

The Colonial Period

Persian was already in decline during the reign of the last great Muslim Emperor, **Aurangzeb** and as the British extended their political power so the role of English grew. There is now a very wide Indian literature accessible in English, which has thus become the latest of the languages to be used across the whole of South Asia.

In the 19th century English became a vehicle for developing nationalist ideals. However, notably in the work of **Rabindranath Tagore**, it became a medium for religious and philosophical prose and for a developing poetry. Tagore himself won the Nobel Prize for Literature in 1913 for his translation into English of his own work, Gitanjali. Leading South Asian philosophers and thinkers of the 20th century have written major works in English, including not only MK Gandhi and Jawaharlal Nehru, the two leading figures in India's Independence movement, but S Radhakrishnan, Aurobindo Ghose and Sarojini Naidu, who all added to the depth of Indian literature in English.

Several South Asian regional languages have their own long traditions of both religious and secular literature which are discussed in the relevant sections of this book.

Science

Views of the universe Early Indian views of the universe were based on the square and the cube. The earth was seen as a square, one corner pointing south, rising like a pyramid in a series of square terraces with its peak, the mythical Mount Meru. The sun moved round the top of Mount Meru in a square orbit and the square orbits of the planets were at successive planes above the orbit of the sun. These were seen therefore as forming a second pyramid of planetary movement. Mount Meru was central to all early Indian schools of thought, Hindu, Buddhist and Jain.

However, about 200 BC the Jains transformed the view of the universe based on squares by replacing the idea of square orbits with that of the circle. The earth was shown as a circular disc, with Mount Meru rising from its centre and the Pole Star above it.

The science of early India By about 500 BC Indian texts illustrated the calculation of the **calendar**, although the system itself almost certainly goes back to the eighth or ninth century BC. The year was divided into 27 *nakshatras*, or fortnights, years being calculated on a mixture of lunar and solar counting.

Technology The only copy of Kautiliya's treatise on government (which was only discovered in 1909) dates from about 100 BC. It describes the **weapons** technology of catapults, incendiary missiles and the use of elephants, but it is also evident that gunpowder was unknown. Large-scale **irrigation** works were developed, though the earliest examples of large tanks may be those of the Sri Lankan King Panduwasa at Anuradhapura, built in 504 BC. During the Gupta period dramatic progress was made in **metallurgy**, shown in the pure iron pillar which can be seen in the Qutb Minar in Delhi.

Mathematics Conceptions of the universe and the mathematical and geometrical ideas that accompanied them were comparatively advanced in South Asia by the time of the Mauryan Empire and were put to use in the rules developed for building temple altars. Indians were using the concept of zero and decimal points in the Gupta period. Furthermore in AD 499, just after the demise of the Gupta Empire, the astronomer Aryabhatta calculated Pi as 3.1416 and the length of the solar year as 365.358 days. He also postulated that the earth was a sphere rotating on its own axis and revolving around the sun and that the shadow of the earth falling on the moon caused lunar eclipses. The development of science in India was not restricted to the Gupta court. In South India, Tamil kings developed extensive contact with Roman and Greek thinkers during the first four centuries of the Christian era. Babylonian methods used for astronomy in Greece remained current in Tamil Nadu until very recent times. The basic texts of astronomy (the Surya Siddhanta) were completed by AD 400.

Architecture

Over the 4000 years since the Indus Valley civiiization flourished, art and architecture have developed with a remarkable continuity through successive regional and religious influences and styles. The Buddhist art and architecture of the third century BC left few remains, but the stylistic influence on early Hindu architecture was profound. From the sixth century AD the first Hindu religious buildings to have survived into the modern period were constructed in South and East India.

Hindu temple buildings

The principles of religious building were laid down by priests in the *Sastras*. Every aspect of Hindu, Jain and Buddhist religious building is identified with conceptions of the structure of the universe. This applies as much to the process of building – the timing of which must be undertaken at astrologically propitious times – as to the formal layout of the buildings. The cardinal directions of north, south, east and west are the basic fix on which buildings are planned. George Michell suggests that in addition to the cardinal directions, number is also critical to the design of the religious building. The key to the ultimate scale of the building is derived from the measurements of the sanctuary at its heart. Indian temples were nearly always built according to philosophical understandings of the universe. This cosmology, of an infinite number of universes, isolated from each other in space, proceeds by imagining various possibilities as to its nature. Its centre is seen as dominated by **Mount Meru** which keeps earth and heaven apart. The concept of *separation* is crucial to Hindu thought and social practice. Continents, rivers and oceans occupy concentric rings around the mountain, while the stars encircle the mountain in another plane. Humans live on the continent of **Jambudvipa**, characterized by the rose apple tree (*jambu*). For more information on temple architecture specific to the South, see Footprint's *South India*.

Mandalas The Sastras show plans of this continent, organized in concentric rings and entered at the cardinal points. This type of diagram was known as a **mandala**. Such a geometric scheme could be subdivided into almost limitless small compartments, each of which could be designated as having special properties or be devoted to a particular deity. The centre of the mandala would be the seat of the major god; they provided the ground rules for the building of *stupas* and temples across India and gave the key to the symbolic meaning attached to every aspect of religious buildings.

Temple design The focal point of the temple, its sanctuary, was the home of the presiding deity, the 'womb-chamber' (*garbhagriha*). A series of doorways, in large temples leading through a succession of buildings, allowed the worshipper to move towards the final encounter with the deity to obtain *darshan* – a sight of the god. Both Buddhist and Hindu worship encourage the worshipper to walk clockwise around the shrine, performing *pradakshina*. The elevations are symbolic representations of the home of the gods. Mountain peaks such as Kailasa are common names for the most prominent of the towers. In North and East Indian temples the tallest of these towers rises above the *garbagriha* itself, symbolizing the meeting of earth and heaven in the person of the enshrined deity. In later South Indian temples the gateways to the temple come to overpower the central tower. In both, the basic structure is usually richly embellished with sculpture. When first built this would usually have been plastered and painted and often covered in gems. In contrast to the extraordinary profusion of colour and life on the outside, the interior is dark and cramped but here it is believed, lies the true centre of divine power.

Muslim religious architecture

Although the Muslims adapted many Hindu features, they also brought totally new forms. Their most outstanding contribution, dominating the architecture of many North Indian cities, are the mosques and tomb complexes (*dargah*). The use of brickwork was widespread and they brought with them from Persia the principle of constructing the true arch. Muslim architects succeeded in producing a variety of domed structures, often incorporating distinctively Hindu features such as the surmounting finial. By the end of the great period of Muslim building in 1707, the Muslims had added magnificent forts and palaces to their religious structures, a statement of power as well as of aesthetic taste.

European buildings

Nearly two centuries of architectural stagnation and decline followed the demise of Mughal power. The Portuguese built a series of remarkable churches in Goa that owed everything to Baroque developments in Europe. Not until the end of the Victorian period, when British imperial ambitions were at their height, did the British colonial impact on public rather than domestic architecture begin to be felt. Fierce arguments divided British architects as to the merits of indigenous design. The ultimate plan for New Delhi was carried out by men who had little time for Hindu architecture and believed themselves to be on a civilizing mission, see page 76. Others at the end of the 19th century wanted to recapture and enhance a tradition for which they had great respect. They have left a series of buildings, both in formerly British ruled territory and in the Princely States, which illustrate this concern through the development of what became known as the Indo-Saracenic style.

In the immediate aftermath of the colonial period, Independent India set about trying to establish a break from the immediately imperial past, but was uncertain how to achieve it. In the event foreign architects were commissioned for major developments, such as Le Corbusier's design for Chandigarh and Louis Kahn's buildings in Dhaka and Ahmadabad. The latter, a centre for training and experiment, contains a number of new buildings such as those of the Indian architect Charles Correa.

Music and dance

Music Indian music can trace its origins to the metrical hymns and chants of the Vedas, in which the production of sound according to strict rules was understood to be vital to the continuing order of the Universe. Through more than 3000 years of development and a range of regional schools, India's musical tradition has been handed on almost entirely by ear. The chants of the **Rig Veda** developed into songs in the **Sama Veda** and music found expression in every sphere of life, reflecting the cycle of seasons and the rhythm of work.

Over the centuries the original three notes, which were sung strictly in descending order, were extended to five and then seven and developed to allow freedom to move up and down the scale. The scale increased to 12 with the addition of flats and sharps and finally to 22 with the further subdivision of semitones. Books of musical rules go back at least as far as the third century AD. Classical music was totally intertwined with dance and drama, an interweaving reflected in the term *sangita*.

At some point after the Muslim influence made itself felt in the north, North and South Indian styles diverged, to become Carnatic (Karnatak) music in the south and Hindustani music in the north. However, they still share important common features: *svara* (pitch), *raga* (the melodic structure) and *tala* or *talam* (metre).

Hindustani music probably originated in the Delhi Sultanate during the 13th century, when the most widely known of North Indian musical instruments, the *sitar*, was believed to have been invented. Amir Khusrau is also believed to have invented the small drums, the *tabla*. Hindustani music is held to have reached its peak under *Tansen*, a court musician of Akbar. The other important northern instruments are the stringed *sarod*, the reed instrument *shahnai* and the wooden flute. Most Hindustani compositions have devotional texts, though they encompass a great emotional and thematic range. A common classical form of vocal performance is the *dhrupad*, a four-part composition.

The essential structure of a melody is known as a raga which usually has five to seven notes and can have as many as nine (or even 12 in mixed ragas). The music is improvised by the performer within certain rules and although theoretically thousands of ragas are possible, only around a 100 are commonly performed. Ragas have become associated with particular moods and specific times of the day. Music festivals often include all night sessions to allow performers a wider choice of repertoire.

Carnatic (Karnatak) music, contemporary South Indian music, is traced back to Tyagaraja (1759-1847), Svami Shastri (1763-1827) and Dikshitar (1775-1835), three musicians who lived and worked in Thanjavur. They are still referred to as the Trinity. Their music placed more emphasis on extended compositions than Hindustani music. Perhaps the best known South Indian instrument is the stringed *vina*, the flute being used for accompaniment with the violin (played rather differently to the European original), an oboe-like instrument called the *nagasvaram* and the drums, *tavil*.

Dance The rules for classical dance were laid down in the Natya shastra in the second century BC, which is still one of the bases for modern dance forms. The most common sources for Indian dance are the epics, but there are three essential aspects of the dance itself, Nritta (pure dance), Nrittya (emotional expression) and Natya (drama). The religious influence in dance was exemplified by the tradition of temple dancers, *devadasis*, girls and women who were dedicated to the deity in major temples. In South and East India there were thousands of *devadasis* associated with temple worship, though the practice fell into widespread disrepute and was banned in independent India. Various dance forms (for example Odissi, Manipuri, Bharat Natyam, Kathakali, Mohinyattam) developed in different parts of the country. India is also rich in folk dance traditions.

Cinema Film goers around the world are taking greater note of Indian cinema, both home-grown and that produced and directed by Indians abroad. Not all fall into the category of a Bollywood '*masala* movie' or 'curry western' churned out by the Mumbai (Bombay) film industry but many offer an insight into what draws millions to watch diverse versions of Indian life on the silver screen. A few titles, both all time favourites as well as new releases are listed here. Viewing: *3 Idiots; Bombay; Dhobi Ghat; Dil Chahta Hai; Kuch Kuch Hota Hai; Lagaan; Luck By Chance; Monsoon Wedding; Mother India; My Name is Khan; Pather Panchali; Peepli Live; Rang De Basanti; Sholay; Titash Ekti Nadir Naam.*

Religion

It is impossible to write briefly about religion in India without oversimplifying. Over 80% of Indians are Hindu, but there are many minorities. Muslims number about 125 million and there are over 23 million Christians, 19 million Sikhs, six million Buddhists and a number of other religious groups. One of the most persistent features of religious and social life is the caste system. This has undergone substantial changes since Independence, especially in towns and cities, but most people in India are still clearly identified as a member of a particular caste group. The government has introduced measures to help the backward, or 'scheduled' castes, though in recent years this has produced a major political backlash.

The four stages of life

Popular Hindu belief holds that an ideal life has four stages: the student, the householder, the forest dweller and the wandering dependent/beggar (*sannyasi*). These stages represent the phases through which an individual learns of life's goals and of the means of achieving them.

One of the most striking sights today is that of the saffron-clad *sannyasi* (sadhu) seeking gifts of food and money to support himself in the final stage of his life. There may have been sadhus even before the Aryans arrived. Today, most of these have given up material possessions, carrying only a strip of cloth, a *danda* (staff), a crutch to support the chin during *achal* (meditation), prayer beads, a fan to ward off evil spirits, a water pot, a drinking vessel, which may be a human skull and a begging bowl.

Hinduism

It has always been easier to define Hinduism by what it is not than by what it is. Indeed, the name 'Hindu' was given by foreigners to the peoples of the subcontinent who did not profess the other major faiths, such as Muslims or Christians. While some aspects of modern Hinduism can be traced back more than 4000 years before that, other features are recent.

Key ideas

According to the Indian philosopher and former president of India, S Radhakrishnan, religion for the Hindu "is not an idea but a power, not an intellectual proposition but a life conviction. Religion is consciousness of ultimate reality, not a theory about God". There is no Hindu organization, like a church, with the authority to define belief or establish official practice. Not all Hindu groups believe in a single supreme God. In view of these characteristics, many authorities argue that it is misleading to think of Hinduism as a religion. Be that as it may, the evidence of the living importance of Hinduism is visible across India. Hindu philosophy and practice has also touched many of those who belong to other religious traditions, particularly in terms of social institutions such as caste, and in post- Independence India religious identity has become an increasingly politicized feature of life.

Darshan One of Hinduism's recurring themes is 'vision', 'sight' or 'view' – **darshan**. Applied to the different philosophical systems themselves, such as *yoga* or *vedanta*, 'darshan' is also used to describe the sight of the deity that worshippers hope to gain when they visit a temple or shrine hoping for the sight of a 'guru' (teacher). Equally it may apply to the religious insight gained through meditation or prayer.

The four human goals Many Hindus also accept that there are four major human goals; material prosperity (*artha*), the satisfaction of desires (*kama*) and performing the duties laid down according to your position in life (*dharma*). Beyond those is the goal of achieving liberation from the endless cycle of rebirths into which everyone is locked (*moksha*). It is to the search for liberation that the major schools of Indian philosophy have devoted most attention. Together with dharma, it is basic to Hindu thought.

The *Mahabharata* lists 10 embodiments of **dharma**: good name, truth, self-control, cleanness of mind and body, simplicity, endurance, resoluteness of character, giving and sharing, austerities and continence. In *dharmic* thinking these are inseparable from five patterns of behaviour: non-violence, an attitude of equality, peace and tranquillity, lack of aggression and cruelty and absence of envy. Dharma, an essentially secular concept, represents the order inherent in human life.

Karma The idea of *karma*, 'the effect of former actions', is central to achieving liberation. As C Rajagopalachari put it: "Every act has its appointed effect, whether the act be thought, word

Karma – an eye to the future

According to the doctrine of karma, every person, animal or god has a being or 'self' which has existed without beginning. Every action, except those that are done without any consideration of the results, leaves an indelible mark on that Self, carried forward into the next life.

The overall character of the imprint on each person's Self determines three features of the next life: the nature of his next birth (animal, human or god), the kind of family he will be born into if human and the length of the next life. Finally, it controls the good or bad experiences that the self will experience. However, it does not imply a fatalistic belief that the nature of action in this life is unimportant. Rather, it suggests that the path followed by the individual in the present life is vital to the nature of its next life and ultimately to the chance of gaining release from this world.

or deed. The cause holds the effect, so to say, in its womb. If we reflect deeply and objectively, the entire world will be found to obey unalterable laws. That is the doctrine of karma". See also box, above.

Rebirth The belief in the transmigration of souls (*samsara*) in a neverending cycle of rebirth has been Hinduism's most distinctive and important contribution to Indian culture. The earliest reference is in one of the *Upanishads*, around the seventh century BC, at about the same time as the doctrine of *karma* made its first appearance.

Ahimsa AL Basham pointed out that belief in transmigration must have encouraged a further distinctive doctrine, that of non-violence or non-injury – *ahimsa*. The belief in rebirth meant that all living things and creatures of the spirit possessed the same essential soul. One inscription threatens that anyone who interferes with the rights of Brahmins to land given to them by the king will 'suffer rebirth for 80,000 years as a worm in dung'. Belief in the cycle of rebirth was essential to give such a threat any weight!

Schools of philosophy

It is common now to talk of six major schools of Hindu philosophy. *Nyaya*, *Vaisheshika*, *Sankhya*, *Yoga*, *Purvamimansa* and *Vedanta*.

Yoga Yoga, can be traced back to at least the third century AD. It seeks a synthesis of the spirit, the soul and the flesh and is concerned with systems of meditation and self denial that lead to the realization of the Divine within oneself and can ultimately release one from the cycle of rebirth.

Vedanta These are literally the final parts of the Vedic literature, the *Upanishads*. The basic texts also include the Brahmasutra of Badrayana, written about the first century AD and the most important of all, the *Bhagavad-Gita*, which is a part of the epic the *Mahabharata*. There are many interpretations of these basic texts. Three are given here.

Advaita Vedanta holds that there is no division between the cosmic force or principle, *Brahman* and the individual Self, *atman* (also referred to as 'soul'). The fact that we appear to see different and separate individuals is simply a result of ignorance. This is termed *maya* (illusion), but Vedanta philosophy does not suggest that the world in which we live is an illusion. *Jnana* (knowledge) is held as the key to understanding the full and real unity of Self and Brahman. **Shankaracharya**, born at Kalady in modern Kerala, in AD 6, is the best known Advaitin Hindu philosopher. He argued that there was no individual Self or soul separate from the creative force of the universe, or Brahman and that it was impossible to achieve liberation (*moksha*), through meditation and devotional worship, which he saw as signs of remaining on a lower level and of being unprepared for true liberation.

The 11th- to 12th-century philosopher, **Ramanuja**, repudiated ideas of **Vishishtadvaita**. He transformed the idea of God from an impersonal force to a personal God and viewed both the

Self and the World as real but only as part of the whole. In contrast to Shankaracharya's view, Ramanuja saw *bhakti* (devotion) as of central importance to achieving liberation and service to the Lord as the highest goal of life. **Dvaita Vedanta** was developed by the 14th-century philosopher, Madhva. He believed that Brahman, the Self and the World are completely distinct. Worship of God is a key means of achieving liberation.

Worship

Puja For most Hindus today, worship ('performing puja') is an integral part of their faith. The great majority of Hindu homes will have a shrine to one of the gods of the Hindu pantheon. Individuals and families will often visit shrines or temples and on special occasions will travel long distances to particularly holy places such as Benaras or Puri. Such sites may have temples dedicated to a major deity but may also have numerous other shrines in the vicinity dedicated to other favourite gods.

Acts of devotion are often aimed at the granting of favours and the meeting of urgent needs for this life – good health, finding a suitable wife or husband, the birth of a son, prosperity and good fortune. Puja involves making an offering to God and *darshan* (having a view of the deity). Hindu worship is generally, though not always, an act performed by individuals. Thus Hindu temples may be little more than a shrine on a river bank or in the middle of the street, tended by a priest and visited at special times when a darshan of the resident God can be obtained. When it has been consecrated, the image, if exactly made, becomes the channel for the godhead to work.

Holy places Certain rivers and towns are particularly sacred to Hindus. Thus there are seven holy rivers – the Ganga, Yamuna, Indus and mythical Sarasvati in the north and the Narmada, Godavari and Kaveri in the Peninsula. There are also seven holy places – Haridwar, Mathura, Ayodhya and Varanasi, again in the north, Ujjain, Dwarka and Kanchipuram to the south. In addition to these seven holy places there are four holy abodes: Badrinath, Puri and Ramesvaram, with Dwarka in modern Gujarat having the unique distinction of being both a holy abode and a holy place.

Rituals and festivals The temple rituals often follow through the cycle of day and night, as well as yearly lifecycles. The priests may wake the deity from sleep, bathe, clothe and feed it. Worshippers will be invited to share by bringing offerings of clothes and food. Gifts of money will usually be made and in some temples there is a charge levied for taking up positions in front of the deity in order to obtain a darshan at the appropriate times.

Every temple has its special festivals. At festival times you can see villagers walking in small groups, brightly dressed and often high spirited, sometimes as far as 80-100 km.

Hindu deities

Today three Gods are widely seen as all-powerful: Brahma, Vishnu and Siva. While Brahma is regarded as the ultimate source of creation, Siva also has a creative role alongside his function as destroyer. Vishnu in contrast is seen as the preserver or protector of the universe. Vishnu and Siva are widely represented have come to be seen as the most powerful and important. Their followers are referred to as Vaishnavite and Shaivites respectively and numerically they form the two largest sects in India.

Brahma Popularly Brahma is interpreted as the Creator in a trinity, alongside Vishnu as Preserver and Siva as Destroyer. In the literal sense the name Brahma is the masculine and personalized form of the neuter word Brahman.

In the early Vedic writing, *Brahman* represented the universal and impersonal principle which governed the Universe. Gradually, as Vedic philosophy moved towards a monotheistic interpretation of the universe and its origins, this impersonal power was increasingly personalized. In the *Upanishads*, Brahman was seen as a universal and elemental creative spirit. Brahma, described in early myths as having been born from a golden egg and then to have

How Sarasvati turned Brahma's head

Masson-Oursel recounts one myth that explains how Brahma came to have five heads. "Brahma first formed woman from his own immaculate substance and she was known as Sarasvati, Savitri, Gayatri or Brahmani. When he saw this lovely girl emerge from his own body Brahma fell in love with her. Sarasvati moved to his right to avoid his gaze, but a head immediately sprang up from the god. And when Sarasvati turned to the left and then behind him, two new heads emerged. She darted towards heaven and a fifth head was formed. Brahma then said to his daughter, 'Let us beget all kinds of living things, men, Suras and Asuras'. Hearing these words Sarasvati returned to earth, Brahma wedded her and they retired to a secret place where they remained together for a hundred (divine) years".

created the Earth, assumed the identity of the earlier Vedic deity Prajapati and became identified as the creator.

By the fourth and fifth centuries AD, the height of the classical period of Hinduism, Brahma was seen as one of the trinity of Gods – *Trimurti* – in which Vishnu, Siva and Brahma represented three forms of the unmanifested supreme being. It is from Brahma that Hindu cosmology takes its structure. The basic cycle through which the whole cosmos passes is described as one day in the life of Brahma – the *kalpa*. It equals 4320 million years, with an equally long night. One year of Brahma's life – a cosmic year – lasts 360 days and nights. The universe is expected to last for 100 years of Brahma's life, who is currently believed to be 51 years old.

By the sixth century AD Brahma worship had effectively ceased (before the great period of temple building), which accounts for the fact that there are remarkably few temples dedicated to Brahma. Nonetheless images of Brahma are found in most temples. Characteristically he is shown with four faces, a fifth having been destroyed by the fire from Siva's third eye. In his four arms he usually holds a copy of the Vedas, a sceptre and a water jug or a bow. He is accompanied by the goose, symbolizing knowledge.

Sarasvati Seen by some Hindus as the 'active power' of Brahma, popularly thought of as his consort, Sarasvati has survived into the modern Hindu world as a far more important figure than Brahma himself. In popular worship Sarasvati represents the goddess of education and learning, worshipped in schools and colleges with gifts of fruit, flowers and incense. She represents 'the word' itself, which began to be deified as part of the process of the writing of the Vedas, which ascribed magical power to words. The development of her identity represented the rebirth of the concept of a mother goddess, which had been strong in the Indus Valley Civilization over 1000 years before and may have been continued in popular ideas through the worship of female spirits.

In addition to her role as Brahma's wife, Sarasvati is also variously seen as the wife of Vishnu and Manu or as Daksha's daughter, among other interpretations. Normally white coloured, riding on a swan and carrying a book, she is often shown playing a vina. She may have many arms and heads, representing her role as patron of all the sciences and arts.

Vishnu Vishnu is seen as the God with the human face. From the second century a new and passionate devotional worship of Vishnu's incarnation as Krishna developed in the South. By 1000 AD Vaishnavism had spread across South India and it became closely associated with the devotional form of Hinduism preached by **Ramanuja**, whose followers spread the worship of Vishnu and his 10 successive incarnations in animal and human form. For Vaishnavites, God took these different forms in order to save the world from impending disaster. AL Basham has summarized the 10 incarnations (see table opposite).

Rama and Krishna By far the most influential incarnations of Vishnu are those in which he was believed to take recognizable human form, especially as Rama (twice) and Krishna. As the

Vishnu's 10 incarnations

Name	Form	Story
1 *Matsya*	Fish	Vishnu took the form of a fish to rescue Manu (the first man), his family and the Vedas from a flood.
2 *Kurma*	Tortoise	Vishnu became a tortoise to rescue all the treasures lost in the flood, including the divine nectar (Amrita) with which the gods preserved their youth. The gods put Mount Kailasa on the tortoise's back and when he reached the bottom of the ocean they twisted the divine snake round the mountain. They then churned the ocean with the mountain by pulling the snake.
3 *Varaha*	Boar	Vishnu appeared again to raise the earth from the ocean's floor where it had been thrown by a demon, Hiranyaksa. The story probably developed from a non-Aryan cult of a sacred pig.
4 *Narasimha*	Half-man, half lion	Having persuaded Brahma to promise that he could not be killed either by day or night, by god, man or beast, the demon Hiranyakasipu then terrorized everybody. When the gods pleaded for help, Vishnu appeared at sunset, when it was neither day nor night, in the form of a half man and half lion and killed the demon.
5 *Vamana*	A dwarf	Bali, a demon, achieved supernatural power by asceticism. To protect the world Vishnu appeared before him in the form of a dwarf and asked him a favour. Bali granted Vishnu as much land as he could cover in three strides. Vishnu then became a giant, covering the earth in three strides. He left only hell to the demon.
6 *Parasurama*	Rama with the axe	Vishnu was incarnated as the son of a Brahmin, Jamadagni as Parasurama and killed the wicked king for robbing his father. The king's sons then killed Jamadagni and in revenge Parasurama destroyed all male kshatriyas, 21 times in succession.
7 *Rama*	The Prince of Ayodhya	As told in the Ramayana, Vishnu came in the form of Rama to rescue the world from the dark demon, Ravana. His wife Sita is the model of patient faithfulness while Hanuman, is the monkey-faced god and Rama's helper.
8 *Krishna*	Charioteer of Arjuma Many forms	Krishna meets almost every human need, from the mischievous child, the playful boy, the amorous youth to the Divine.
9 The *Buddha*		Probably incorporated into the Hindu pantheon in order to discredit the Buddhists, dominant in some parts of India until the 6th century AD. An early Hindu interpretation suggests that Vishnu took incarnation as Buddha to show compassion for animals and to end sacrifice.
10 *Kalki*	Riding on a horse	Vishnu's arrival will accompany the final destruction of this present age, Kaliyuga, judging the wicked and rewarding the good.

Prince of Ayodhya, history and myth blend, for Rama was probably a chief who lived in the eighth or seventh century BC. Although Rama is now seen as an earlier incarnation of Vishnu than Krishna, he came to be regarded as divine very late, probably after the Muslim invasions of the 12th century AD. Rama (or Ram, pronounced to rhyme with *calm*) is a powerful figure in contemporary India. His supposed birthplace at Ayodhya became the focus of fierce disputes

Worship of Siva's linga

Worship of Siva's linga – the phallic symbol of fertility, power and creativeness – is universal across India. Its origins lie in the creation myths of the Hindu trinity and in the struggle for supremacy between Hindu sects. Saivite myths illustrate the supreme power of Siva and the variety of ways in which Brahma and Vishnu were compelled to acknowledge his supreme power.

One such story tells how Siva, Vishnu and Brahma emerged from the ocean, whereupon Vishnu and Brahma begged him to perform creation. Siva agreed – but then to their consternation disappeared for 1000 celestial years. They became so worried by the lack of creation that Vishnu told Brahma to create, so he produced everything that could lead to happiness. However, no sooner had Brahma filled the universe with beings than Siva reappeared. Incensed by the usurping of his power by Brahma, Siva decided to destroy everything with a flame from his mouth so that he could create afresh.

As the fire threatened everything, Brahma acknowledged Siva's total power and pleaded with him to spare the creation that Brahma had brought forth. "But what shall I do with all my excess power?" "Send it to the sun", replied Brahma, "for as you are the lord of the sun we may all live together in the sun's energy."

Siva agreed, but said to Brahma "What use is this linga if I cannot use it to create?" So he broke off his linga and threw it to the ground. The linga broke through the earth and went right into the sky. Vishnu looked for the end of it below and Brahma for the top, but neither could find the end. Then a voice from the sky said "If the linga of the god with braided hair is worshipped, it will grant all desires that are longed for in the heart." When Brahma and Vishnu heard this, they and all the divinities worshipped the linga with devotion."

between Hindus and Muslims in the early 1990s which continue today. Krishna is worshipped extremely widely as perhaps the most human of the gods. His advice on the battlefield of the *Mahabharata* is one of the major sources of guidance for the rules of daily living for many Hindus today.

Lakshmi Commonly represented as Vishnu's wife, Lakshmi is widely worshipped as the goddess of wealth. Earlier representations of Vishnu's consorts portrayed her as Sridevi, often shown in statues on Vishnu's right, while Bhudevi, also known as Prithvi, who represented the earth, was on his left. Lakshmi is popularly shown in her own right as standing on a lotus flower, although eight forms of Lakshmi are recognized.

Hanuman The *Ramayana* tells how Hanuman, Rama's faithful servant, went across India and finally into the demon Ravana's forest home of Lanka at the head of his monkey army in search of the abducted Sita. He used his powers to jump the sea separating India from Sri Lanka and managed after a series of heroic and magical feats to find and rescue his master's wife. Whatever form he is shown in, he remains almost instantly recognizable.

Siva Professor Wendy Doniger O'Flaherty argues that the key to the myths through which Siva's character is understood, lies in the explicit ambiguity of Siva as the great ascetic and at the same time as the erotic force of the universe.

Siva is interpreted as both creator and destroyer, the power through whom the universe evolves. He lives on Mount Kailasa with his wife **Parvati** (also known as **Uma**, **Sati**, **Kali** and **Durga**) and two sons, the elephant-headed Ganesh and the six-headed Karttikeya, known in South India as Subrahmanya. In sculptural representations Siva is normally accompanied by his 'vehicle', the bull (*Nandi* or *Nandin*).

Siva is also represented in Shaivite temples throughout India by the *linga*, literally meaning 'sign' or 'mark', but referring in this context to the sign of gender or phallus and *yoni*. On the one hand a symbol of energy, fertility and potency, as Siva's symbol it also represents the yogic power of sexual abstinence and penance. The *linga* is now the most important symbol of the cult of Siva. O'Flaherty suggests that the worship of the *linga* of Siva can be traced back to the pre-Vedic societies of the Indus Valley civilization (circa 2000 BC), but that it first appears in Hindu iconography in the second century BC. From that time a wide variety of myths appeared to explain the origin of *linga* worship. The myths surrounding the 12 **jyotirlinga** (*linga* of light) found at centres like Ujjain go back to the second century BC and were developed to explain and justify *linga* worship.

Siva's alternative names Although Siva is not seen as having a series of rebirths, like Vishnu, he none the less appears in very many forms representing different aspects of his varied powers. Some of the more common are: **Chandrasekhara** – the moon (*chandra*) symbolizes the powers of creation and destruction. **Mahadeva** – the representation of Siva as the god of supreme power, which came relatively late into Hindu thought, shown as the *linga* in combination with the *yoni*, or female genitalia. **Nataraja** – the Lord of the Cosmic Dance. The story is based on a legend in which Siva and Vishnu went to the forest to overcome 10,000 heretics. In their anger the heretics attacked Siva first by sending a tiger, then a snake and thirdly a fierce black dwarf with a club. Siva killed the tiger, tamed the snake and wore it like a garland and then put his foot on the dwarf and performed a dance of such power that the dwarf and the heretics acknowledged Siva as the Lord. **Rudra** – Siva's early prototype, who may date back to the Indus Valley Civilization. **Virabhadra** – Siva created Virabhadra to avenge himself on his wife Sati's father, Daksha, who had insulted Siva by not inviting him to a special sacrifice. Sati attended the ceremony against Siva's wishes and when she heard her father grossly abusing Siva she committed suicide by jumping into the sacrificial fire. This act gave rise to the term *sati* (*suttee*, a word which simply means a good or virtuous woman). Recorded in the *Vedas*, the self immolation of a woman on her husband's funeral pyre probably did not become accepted practice until the early centuries BC. Even then it was mainly restricted to those of the Kshatriya caste. **Nandi** – Siva's vehicle, the bull, is one of the most widespread of sacred symbols of the ancient world and may represent a link with Rudra, who was sometimes represented as a bull in pre-Hindu India. Strength and virility are key attributes and pilgrims to Siva temples will often touch the Nandi's testicles on their way into the shrine.

Ganesh One of Hinduism's most popular gods, Ganesh is seen as the great clearer of obstacles. Shown at gateways and on door lintels with his elephant head and pot belly, his image is revered across India. Meetings, functions and special family gatherings will often start with prayers to Ganesh and any new venture, from the opening of a building to inaugurating a company, will not be deemed complete without a Ganesh puja.

Shakti, the Mother Goddess Shakti is a female divinity often worshipped in the form of Siva's wife Durga or Kali. As Durga she agreed to do battle with Mahish, an *asura* (demon) who threatened to dethrone the gods. Many sculptures and paintings illustrate the story in which, during the terrifying struggle which ensued, the demon changed into a buffalo, an elephant and a giant with 1000 arms. Durga, clutching weapons in each of her 10 hands, eventually emerges victorious. As Kali ('black') the mother goddess takes on her most fearsome form and character. Fighting with the chief of the demons, she was forced to use every weapon in her armoury, but every drop of blood that she drew became 1000 new giants just as strong as he. The only way she could win was by drinking the blood of all her enemies. Having succeeded she was so elated that her dance of triumph threatened the earth. Ignoring the pleas of the gods to stop, she even threw her husband Siva to the ground and trampled over him, until she realized to her shame what she had done. She is always shown with a sword in one hand, the severed head of the giant in another, two corpses for earrings and a necklace of human skulls. She is often shown standing with one foot on the body and the other on the leg of Siva.

The worship of female goddesses developed into the widely practised form of devotional worship called Tantrism. Goddesses such as Kali became the focus of worship which often involved practices that flew in the face of wider Hindu moral and legal codes. Animal and even

Hindu deities

Deity	Association	Relationship
Brahma	Creator	One of Trinity
Sarasvati	Education and culture, "the word"	Wife of Brahma
Siva	Creator/destroyer	One of Trinity
Bhairava	Fierce aspect of Siva	
Parvati (Uma)	Benevolent aspect of female divine power	Consort of Siva, mother of Ganesh
Kali	The energy that destroys evil	Consort of Siva
Durga	In fighting attitude	Consort of Siva
Ganesh/ Ganapati	God of good beginnings, clearer of obstacles	Son of Siva
Skanda	God of War/bringer of disease (Karttikkeya, Murugan, Subrahmanya)	Son of Siva and Ganga
Vishnu	Preserver	One of Trinity
Prithvi/ Bhudevi	Goddess of Earth	Wife of Vishnu
Lakshmi	Goddess of Wealth	Wife of Vishnu
Agni	God of Fire	
Indra	Rain, lightning and thunder	
Ravana	King of the demons	

Siva as Nataraj

Kali, the "black" Mother-goddess

Ganesh, bringer of prosperity

Parvati, wife of Siva

Attributes	Vehicle
4 heads, 4 arms, upper left holds water pot and rosary or sacrificial spoon, sacred thread across left shoulder	Hamsa (goose/swan)
Two or more arms, vina, lotus, plam leaves, rosary	Hamsa
Linga; Rudra, matted hair, 3 eyes, drum, fire, deer, trident; Nataraja, Lord of the Dance	Bull – Nandi
Trident, sword, noose, naked, snakes, garland of skulls, dishevelled hair, carrying destructive weapons	Dog
2 arms when shown with Siva, 4 when on her own, blue lily in right hand, left hand hangs down	Lion
Trident, noose, human skulls, sword, shield, black colour	Lion
4 arms, conch, disc, bow, arrow, bell, sword, shield	Lion or tiger
Goad, noose, broken tusk, fruits	Rat/ mouse/ shrew
6 heads, 12 arms, spear, arrow, sword, discus, noose cock, bow, shield, conch and plough	Peacock
4 arms, high crown, discus and conch in upper arms, club and sword (or lotus) in lower	Garuda – mythical eagle
Right hand in abhaya gesture, left holds pomegranate, left leg on treasure pot	
Seated/standing on red lotus, 4 hands, lotuses, vessel, fruit	Lotus
Sacred thread, axe, wood, bellows, torch, sacrificial spoon	2-headed ram
Bow, thunderbolt, lances	
10 heads, 20 arms, bow and arrow	

Ardhanarisvara, the male/female form of Siva

Vishnu, Preserver of the Universe

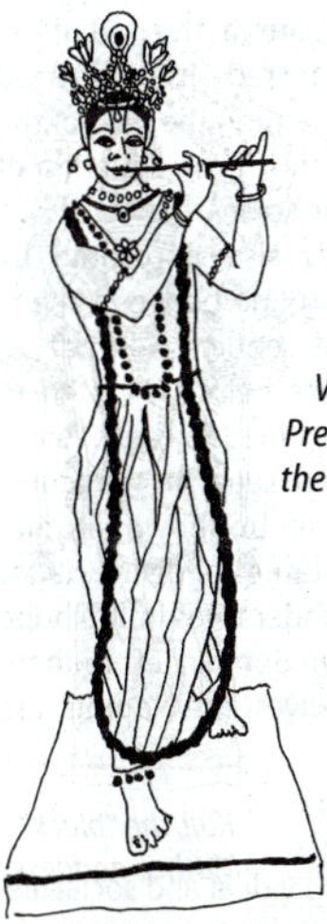

Krishna, eighth incarnation of Vishnu

Durga, Mother-goddess, destroyer of demons

human sacrifices and ritual sexual intercourse were part of Tantric belief and practice, the evidence for which may still be seen in the art and sculpture of some major temples. Tantric practice affected both Hinduism and Buddhism from the eighth century AD; its influence is shown vividly in the sculptures of Khajuraho and Konark and in the distinctive Hindu and Buddhist practices of the Kathmandu Valley in Nepal.

Skanda The God of War, Skanda (known as Murugan in Tamil Nadu and by other regional names) became known as the son of Siva and Parvati. One legend suggests that he was conceived by the Goddess Ganga from Siva's seed.

Gods of the warrior caste Modern Hinduism has brought into its pantheon over many generations gods who were worshipped by the earlier pre-Hindu Aryan civilizations. The most important is **Indra**, often shown as the god of rain, thunder and lightning. To the early Aryans, Indra destroyed demons in battle, the most important being his victory over Vritra, 'the Obstructor'. By this victory Indra released waters from the clouds, allowing the earth to become fertile. To the early Vedic writers the clouds of the southwest monsoon were seen as hostile, determined to keep their precious treasure of water to themselves and only releasing it when forced to by a greater power. Indra, carrying a bow in one hand, a thunderbolt in another and lances in the others and riding on his vehicle Airavata, the elephant, is thus the Lord of Heaven. His wife is the relatively insignificant **Indrani**. **Mitra** and **Varuna** have the power both of gods and demons. Their role is to sustain order, Mitra taking responsibility for friendship and Varuna for oaths and as they have to keep watch for 24 hours a day Mitra has become the god of the day or the sun, Varuna the god of the moon. **Agni**, the god of fire, is a god whose origins lie with the priestly caste rather than with the Kshatriyas, or warriors. He was seen in the Vedas as being born from the rubbing together of two pieces of dead wood and as Masson-Oursel writes "the poets marvel at the sight of a being so alive leaping from dry dead wood. His very growth is miraculous". Riding on a ram, wearing a sacred thread, he is often shown with flames leaping from his mouth and he carries an axe, wood, bellows or a fan, a torch and a sacrificial spoon, for he is the god of ritual fire. The juice of the soma plant, the nectar of the gods guaranteeing eternal life, **Soma** is also a deity taking many forms. Born from the churning of the ocean of milk in later stories Soma was identified with the moon. The golden haired and golden skinned god **Savitri** is an intermediary with the great power to forgive sin and as king of heaven he gives the gods their immortality. **Surya**, the god of the sun, fittingly of overpowering splendour is often described as being dark red, sitting on a red lotus or riding a chariot pulled by the seven horses of the dawn (representing the days of the week). **Usha**, sometimes referred to as Surya's wife, is the goddess of the dawn, daughter of Heaven and sister of the night. She rides in a chariot drawn by cows or horses.

Devas and Asuras In Hindu popular mythology the world is also populated by innumerable gods and demons, with a somewhat uncertain dividing line between them. Both have great power and moral character and there are frequent conflicts and battles between them. The **Rakshasas** form another category of semi-divine beings devoted to performing magic. Although they are not themselves evil, they are destined to cause havoc and evil in the real world. The multiple-hooded cobra head often seen in sculptures represents the fabulous snake gods the **Nagas**, though they may often be shown in other forms, even human. In South India it is particularly common to find statues of divine Nagas being worshipped. They are usually placed on uncultivated ground under trees in the hope and belief, as Masson-Oursel puts it, that "if the snakes have their own domain left to them they are more likely to spare human beings". The Nagas and their wives, the **Naginis**, are often the agents of death in mythical stories.

Hindu society

Dharma Dharma is seen as the most important of the objectives of individual and social life. But what were the obligations imposed by dharma? Hindu law givers, such as those who compiled the code of Manu (AD 100-300), laid down rules of family conduct and social obligations related to the institutions of caste and jati which were beginning to take shape at the same time.

Caste Although the word caste was given by the Portuguese in the 15th century AD, the main feature of the system emerged at the end of the Vedic period. Two terms – varna and jati – are used in India itself and have come to be used interchangeably and confusingly with the word caste.

Varna, which literally means colour, had a fourfold division. By 600 BC this had become a standard means of classifying the population. The fair-skinned Aryans distinguished themselves from the darker skinned earlier inhabitants. The priestly varna, the Brahmins, were seen as coming from the mouth of Brahma; the Kshatriyas (or Rajputs as they are commonly called in northwest India) were warriors, coming from Brahma's arms; the Vaishyas, a trading community, came from Brahma's thighs and the Sudras, classified as agriculturalists, from his feet. Relegated beyond civilized Hindu society were the untouchables or outcastes, who were left with the jobs which were regarded as impure, usually associated with dealing with the dead (human or animal) or with excrement.

Many Brahmins and Rajputs are conscious of their varna status, but the great majority of Indians do not put themselves into one of the four varna categories, but into a **jati** group. There are thousands of different jatis across the country. None of the groups regard themselves as equal in status to any other, but all are part of local or regional hierarchies. These are not organized in any institutional sense and traditionally there was no formal record of caste status. While individuals found it impossible to change caste or to move up the social scale, groups would sometimes try to gain recognition as higher caste by adopting practices of the Brahmins such as becoming vegetarians. Many used to be identified with particular activities and occupations used to be hereditary. Caste membership is decided by birth. Although you can be evicted from your caste by your fellow members, usually for disobedience to caste rules such as over marriage, you cannot join another caste and technically you become an outcaste.

Right up until Independence in 1947 such punishment was a drastic penalty for disobeying one's dharmic duty. In many areas all avenues into normal life could be blocked, families would disregard outcaste members and it could even be impossible for the outcaste to continue to work within the locality.

Gandhi spearheaded his campaign for independence from British colonial rule with a powerful campaign to abolish the disabilities imposed by the caste system. Coining the term *Harijan* (meaning 'person of God'), which he gave to all former outcastes, Gandhi demanded that discrimination on the grounds of caste be outlawed. Lists – or 'schedules' – of backward castes were drawn up during the early part of this century in order to provide positive help to such groups. The term itself has now been widely rejected by many former outcastes as paternalistic and as implying an adherence to Hindu beliefs (Hari being a Hindu deity) which some explicitly reject and today the use of the secular term **'dalits'** – the 'oppressed' has been adopted in its place. There are several websites devoted to dalit issues, including www.dalits.org.

Marriage, which is still generally arranged by members of all religious communities, continues to be dictated almost entirely by caste and clan rules. Even in cities, where traditional means of arranging marriages have often broken down and where many people resort to advertising for marriage partners in the columns of the Sunday newspapers, caste is frequently stated as a requirement. Marriage is mainly seen as an alliance between two families. Great efforts are made to match caste, social status and economic position, although rules governing eligibility vary from region to region. In some groups marriage between first cousins is common, while among others marriage between any branch of the same clan is strictly prohibited.

Hindu reform movements

In the 19th-century English education and European literature and modern scientific thought, alongside the religious ideas of Christian missionaries, all became powerful influences on the

Auspicious signs

Some of Hinduism's sacred symbols are thought to have originated in the Aryan religion of the Vedic period.

Om The Primordial sound of the universe, 'Om' (or more correctly the three-in-one 'Aum') is the Supreme syllable. It is the opening and sometimes closing, chant for Hindu prayers. Some attribute the three constituents to the Hindu triad of Brahma, Vishnu and Siva. It is believed to be the cosmic sound of Creation which encompasses all states from wakefulness to deep sleep and though it is the essence of all sound, it is outside our hearing.

Svastika Representing the Sun and it's energy, the svastika usually appears on doors or walls of temples, in red, the colour associated with good fortune and luck. The term, derived from the Sanskrit 'svasti', is repeated in Hindu chants. The arms of the symbol point in the cardinal directions which may reflect the ancient practice of lighting fire sticks in the four directions. When the svastika appears to rotate clockwise it symbolizes the positive creative energy of the sun; the anti- clockwise svastika, symbolizing the autumn/ winter sun, is considered to be unlucky.

Six-pointed star The intersecting triangles in the 'Star of David' symbol represents Spirit and Matter held in balance. A central dot signifies a particle of Divinity. The star is incorporated as a decorative element in some Muslim buildings such as Humayun's Tomb in Delhi.

Lotus The 'padma' or 'kamal' flower with it's many petals appears not only in art and architecture but also in association with gods and godesses. Some deities are seen holding one, others are portrayed seated or standing on the flower, or as with Padmanabha it appears from Vishnu's navel. The lotus represents purity, peace and beauty, a symbol also shared by Buddhists and Jains and as in nature stands away and above the impure, murky water from which it emerges. In architecture, the lotus motif occurs frequently.

Om

Svastika

Six-pointed star

Lotus

newly emerging western educated Hindu opinion. That opinion was challenged to re-examine inherited Hindu beliefs and practice.

Some reform movements have had regional importance. Two of these originated, like the **Brahmo Samaj**, in Bengal, see box, page 1419. The **Ramakrishna Mission** was named after a temple priest in the Kali temple in Calcutta, Ramakrishna (1834-1886), who was a great mystic, preaching the basic doctrine that 'all religions are true'. He believed that the best religion for any individual was that into which he or she was born. One of his followers, **Vivekananda**, became the founder of the Ramakrishna Mission, which has been an important vehicle of social and religious reform, notably in Bengal, see page 612.

Aurobindo Ghose (1872-1950) links the great reformers from the 19th century with the post-Independence period. Educated in English – and for 14 years in England itself – he developed the idea of India as 'the Mother', a concept linked with the pre-Hindu idea of Shakti, or the Mother Goddess. For him 'nationalism was religion'. After imprisonment in 1908 he retired to Pondicherry, where his ashram became a focus of an Indian and international movement, see page 899.

The Hindu calendar While for its secular life India follows the Gregorian calendar, for Hindus, much of religious and personal life follows the Hindu calendar (see also Festivals,

From liberal reform to a new fundamentalism

The first major reform movement was launched by the Bengali Brahmin, Ram Mohan Roy (1772-1833). He founded the Brahmo Samaj, the Society of God, in 1828, "to teach and to practise the worship of the one God". Services were modelled closely on those of the Unitarian Church, but he never broke with orthodox Hinduism. The Brahmo Samaj became very influential, particularly in Bengal, even though it divided and its numbers remained tiny.

In North India reform was carried out under the leadership of what one writer has called "the Luther of modern Hinduism", Dayananda Saraswati (1824-1883). Rejecting idolatry and many of the social evils associated with mid-19th century Hinduism, Dayananda Saraswati established the Arya Samaj (the Aryan Society). In the early 19th century the Arya Samaj launched a major attack on the caste system, through recruiting low caste Hindus and investing them with high caste status. At the same time they encouraged a movement for the reconversion of Christians and Muslims (the suddhi movement). By 1931 the Arya Samaj claimed about one million members. With a strongly Hindu nationalist political line, its programme underlay the rise in post-Independence India of the Jana Sangh Party and the present day BJP.

page 43). This is based on the lunar cycle of 29 days, but the clever bit comes in the way it is synchronized with the 365-day Gregorian solar calendar of the west by the addition of an 'extra month' (*adhik maas*), every 2½ to three years.

Hindus follow two distinct eras. The *Vikrama Samvat* which began in 57 BC (and is followed in Goa), and the *Salivahan Saka* which dates from AD 78 and has been the official Indian calendar since 1957. The *Saka* new year starts on 22 March and has the same length as the Gregorian calendar. In most of South India (except Tamil Nadu) the New Year is celebrated in the first month, *Chaitra* (corresponding to March-April). In North India (and Tamil Nadu) it is celebrated in the second month of *Vaisakh*.

The year itself is divided into two, the first six solar months being when the sun 'moves' north, known as the *Makar Sankranti* (which is marked by special festivals), and the second half when it moves south, the *Karka Sankranti*. The first begins in January and the second in June. The 29-day lunar month with its 'dark' (*Krishna*) and 'bright' (*Shukla*) halves based on the new (*Amavasya*) and full moons (*Purnima*), are named after the 12 constellations, and total a 354-day year. The day itself is divided into eight *praharas* of three hours each and the year into six seasons: *Vasant* (spring), *Grishha* (summer), *Varsha* (rains), *Sharat* (early autumn), *Hemanta* (late autumn), *Shishir* (winter).

Hindu and corresponding Gregorian calendar months:

Chaitra	March-April	*Ashwin*	September-October
Vaishakh	April-May	*Kartik*	October-November
Jyeshtha	May-June	*Margashirsh*	November-December
Aashadh	June-July	*Poush*	December-January
Shravan	July-August	*Magh*	January-February
Bhadra	August-September	*Phalgun*	February-March

Islam

Even after partition in 1947 over 40 million Muslims remained in India and today there are around 120 million. Islamic contact with India was first made around AD 636 and then by the navies of the Arab Mohammad al Qasim in AD 710-712. These conquerors of Sindh made very

The sacred thread

The highest three *varnas* were classified as 'twice born' and could wear the sacred thread symbolizing their status. The age at which the initiation ceremony (*upanayana*) for the upper caste child was carried out, varied according to class – 8 for a Brahmin, 11 for a Kshatriya and 12 for a Vaishya.

The boy, dressed like an ascetic and holding a staff in his hand, would have the sacred thread (*yajnopavita*) placed over his right shoulder and under his left arm. A cord of three threads, each of nine twisted strands, it was made of cotton for Brahmans, hemp for Kshatriyas or wool for Vaishyas. It was – and is – regarded as a great sin to remove it.

The Brahmin who officiated would whisper a verse from the Rig Veda in the boy's ear, the Gayatri mantra. Addressed to the old solar god Savitr, the holiest of holy passages, the Gayatri can only be spoken by the three higher classes. AL Basham translated it as: "Let us think on the lovely splendour of the god Savitr, that he may inspire our minds".

few converts, although they did have to develop a legal recognition for the status of non-Muslims in a Muslim-ruled state. From the creation of the Delhi Sultanate in 1206, by Turkish rather than Arab power, Islam became a permanent living religion in India.

The victory of the Turkish ruler of Ghazni over the Rajputs in AD 1192 established a 500-year period of Muslim power in India. By AD 1200 the Turkish sultans had annexed Bihar in the east, in the process wiping out the last traces of Buddhism with the massacre of a Buddhist monastic order, sacked Varanasi and captured Gwalior. Within 30 years Bengal had been added to the Turkish empire and by AD 1311 a new Turkish dynasty, the Khaljis, had extended the power of the Delhi Sultanate to the doors of Madurai.

The early Muslim rulers looked to the Turkish ruling class and to the Arab caliphs for their legitimacy and to the Turkish elite for their cultural authority. From the middle of the 13th century, when the Mongols crushed the Arab caliphate, the Delhi sultans were left on their own to exercise Islamic authority in India. From then onwards the main external influences were from Persia. Small numbers of migrants, mainly the skilled and the educated, continued to flow into the Indian courts. Periodically their numbers were augmented by refugees from Mongol repression in the regions to India's northwest as the Delhi Sultanate provided a refuge for craftsmen and artists from the territories the Mongols had conquered from Lahore westwards.

Muslim populations Muslims only became a majority of the South Asian population in the plains of the Indus and west Punjab and in parts of Bengal. Elsewhere they formed important minorities, notably in the towns of the central heartland such as Lucknow. The concentration at the east and west ends of the Ganga valley reflected the policies pursued by successive Muslim rulers of colonizing forested and previously uncultivated land. In the central plains there was already a densely populated, Hindu region, where little attempt was made to achieve converts.

The Mughals wanted to expand their territory and their economic base. To pursue this they made enormous grants of land to those who had served the empire and particularly in Bengal, new land was brought into cultivation. At the same time, shrines were established to Sufi saints who attracted peasant farmers. The mosques built in East Bengal were the centres of devotional worship where saints were venerated. By the 18th century many Muslims had joined the **Sunni** sect of Islam. The characteristics of Islamic practice in both these regions continues to reflect this background.

In some areas Muslim society shared many of the characteristic features of the Hindu society from which the majority of them came. Many of the Muslim migrants from Iran or Turkey, the élite **Ashraf** communities, continued to identify with the Islamic elites from which they traced their descent. They held high military and civil posts in imperial service. In sharp contrast, many of the non-Ashraf Muslim communities in the towns and cities were organized in social groups

Islamic patronage

The spread of Islam across India was achieved less by force than by patronage offered by the new rulers to Muslim saints and teachers. These were particularly influential in achieving conversions among the lower Hindu castes.

Islam underwent important modifications in India. From the outset the Muslim invaders had to come to terms with the Hindu majority population. If they had treated them as idolators they would have been forced to give them the choice of conversion or death. The impossibility of governing as a tiny minority on those terms encouraged them to give Indian subjects the status of 'protected peoples'.

very much like the *jatis* of their neighbouring Hindu communities. While the elites followed Islamic practices close to those based on the Qur'an as interpreted by scholars, the poorer, less literate communities followed devotional and pietistic forms of Islam.

Muslim beliefs The beliefs of Islam (which means 'submission to God') could apparently scarcely be more different from those of Hinduism. Islam, often described as having 'five pillars' of faith (see box, page 1422) has a fundamental creed: 'There is no God but God; and Mohammad is the Prophet of God' (*La Illaha illa 'llah Mohammad Rasulu 'llah*). One book, the *Qur'an*, is the supreme authority on Islamic teaching and faith. Islam preaches the belief in bodily resurrection after death and in the reality of heaven and hell.

The idea of heaven as paradise is pre-Islamic. Alexander the Great is believed to have brought the word into Greek from Persia, where he used it to describe the walled Persian gardens that were found even three centuries before the birth of Christ. For Muslims, Paradise is believed to be filled with sensuous delights and pleasures, while hell is a place of eternal terror and torture, which is the certain fate of all who deny the unity of God.

Islam has no priesthood. The authority of Imams derives from social custom and from their authority to interpret the scriptures, rather than from a defined status within the Islamic community. Islam also prohibits any distinction on the basis of race or colour and most Muslims believe it is wrong to represent the human figure. It is often thought, inaccurately, that this ban stems from the Qur'an itself. In fact it probably has its origins in the belief of Mohammad that images were likely to be turned into idols.

Muslim sects During the first century after Mohammad's death Islam split in to two sects which were divided on political and religious grounds, the Shi'is and Sunni's. The religious basis for the division lay in the interpretation of verses in the Qur'an and of traditional sayings of Mohammad, the Hadis. Both sects venerate the Qur'an but have different *Hadis*. They also have different views as to Mohammad's successor.

The **Sunnis** believe that Mohammad did not appoint a successor and that Abu Bak'r, Omar and Othman were the first three caliphs (or vice-regents) after Mohammad's death. Ali, whom the Sunni's count as the fourth caliph, is regarded as the first legitimate caliph by the Shi'is, who consider Abu Bak'r and Omar to be usurpers. While the Sunni's believe in the principle of election of caliphs, Shi'is believe that although Mohammad is the last prophet there is a continuing need for intermediaries between God and man. Such intermediaries are termed Imams and they base both their law and religious practice on the teaching of the Imams.

Akbar, the most eclectic of Mughal emperors, went as far as banning activities like cow slaughter which were offensive to Hindus and celebrated Hindu festivals in court. In contrast, the later Mughal Emperor, Aurangzeb, pursued a far more hostile approach to Hindus and Hinduism, trying to point up the distinctiveness of Islam and denying the validity of Hindu religious beliefs. That attitude generally became stronger in the 20th century, related to the growing sense of the Muslim's minority position within South Asia and the fear of being subjected to Hindu rule.

The five pillars of Islam

In addition to the belief that there is one God and that Mohammed is his prophet, there are four requirements imposed on Muslims. Daily prayers are prescribed at daybreak, noon, afternoon, sunset and nightfall. Muslims must give alms to the poor. They must observe a strict fast during Ramadan (no eating or drinking from sunrise to sunset). Lastly, they should attempt the pilgrimage to the Ka'aba in Mecca, known as the Hajj. Those who have done so are entitled to the prefix Hajji before their name.

Islamic rules differ from Hindu practice in several other aspects of daily life. Muslims are strictly forbidden to drink alcohol (though some suggest that this prohibition is restricted to the use of fermented grape juice, that is wine, it is commonly accepted to apply to all alcohol). Eating pork, or any meat from an animal not killed by draining its blood while alive, is also prohibited. Meat prepared in the appropriate way is called *halal*. Finally, usury (charging interest on loans) and games of chance are forbidden.

The Islamic calendar The calendar begins on AD 16 July 622, the date of the Prophet's migration from Mecca to Medina, the Hijra, hence AH (Anno Hejirae). *Murray's Handbook for travellers in India* gave a wonderfully precise method of calculating the current date in the Christian year from the AH date: "To correlate the Hijra year with the Christian year, express the former in years and decimals of a year, multiply by .970225, add 621.54 and the total will correspond exactly with the Christian year".The Muslim year is divided into 12 lunar months, totalling 354 or 355 days, hence Islamic festivals usually move 11 days earlier each year according to the solar (Gregorian) calendar. The first month of the year is *Moharram,* followed by *Safar, Rabi-ul-Awwal, Rabi-ul-Sani, Jumada-ul-Awwal, Jumada-ul- Sani, Rajab, Shaban, Ramadan, Shawwal, Ziquad* and *Zilhaj*.

Buddhism

India was the home of Buddhism, which had its roots in the early Hinduism, or Brahmanism, of its time. Today it is practised only on the margins of the subcontinent, from Ladakh, Nepal and Bhutan in the north to Sri Lanka in the south, where it is the religion of the majority Sinhalese community. Most are very recent converts, the last adherents of the early schools of Buddhism having been killed or converted by the Muslim invaders of the 13th century. However, India's Buddhist significance is now mainly as the home for the extraordinarily beautiful artistic and architectural remnants of what was for several centuries the region's dominant religion.

India has sites of great significance for Buddhists. Some say that the Buddha himself spoke of the four places his followers should visit. **Lumbini**, the Buddha's birthplace, is in the Nepali foothills, near the present border with India. **Bodh Gaya**, where he attained what Buddhists term his 'supreme enlightenment', is about 80 km south of the modern Indian city of Patna; the deer park at **Sarnath**, where he preached his first sermon and set in motion the Wheel of the Law, is just outside Varanasi; and **Kushinagara**, where he died at the age of 80, is 50 km east of Gorakhpur. There were four other sacred places of pilgrimage – **Rajgir**, where he tamed a wild elephant; **Vaishali**, where a monkey offered him honey; **Sravasti**, associated with his great miracle; and **Sankasya**, where he descended from heaven. The eight significant events associated with the holy places are repeatedly represented in Buddhist art.

In addition there are remarkable monuments, sculptures and works of art, from Gandhara in modern Pakistan to Sanchi and Ajanta in central India, where it is still possible to see the vivid evidence of the flowering of Buddhist culture in South Asia. In Sri Lanka, Bhutan and Nepal the traditions remain alive.

The Buddha's Four Noble Truths

The Buddha preached Four Noble Truths: that life is painful; that suffering is caused by ignorance and desire; that beyond the suffering of life there is a state which cannot be described but which he termed nirvana; and that nirvana can be reached by following an eightfold path.

The concept of nirvana is often understood in the west in an entirely negative sense – that of 'non-being'. The word has the rough meaning of 'blow out', meaning to blow out the fires of greed, lust and desire. In a more positive sense it has been described by one Buddhist scholar as "the state of absolute illumination, supreme bliss, infinite love and compassion, unshakeable serenity and unrestricted spiritual freedom". The essential elements of the eightfold path are the perfection of wisdom, morality and meditation.

The Buddha's Life Siddharta Gautama, who came to be given the title of the Buddha – the Enlightened One – was born a prince into the warrior caste in about 563 BC. He was married at the age of 16 and his wife had a son. When he reached the age of 29 he left home and wandered as a beggar and ascetic. After about six years he spent some time in Bodh Gaya. Sitting under the Bo tree, meditating, he was tempted by the demon Mara, with all the desires of the world. Resisting these temptations, he received enlightenment. These scenes are common motifs of Buddhist art. The next landmark was the preaching of his first sermon on 'The Foundation of Righteousness' in the deer park near Benaras. By the time he died the Buddha had established a small band of monks and nuns known as the *Sangha* and had followers across North India. His body was cremated and the ashes, regarded as precious relics, were divided among the peoples to whom he had preached. Some have been discovered as far west as Peshawar, in Pakistan and at Piprawa, close to his birthplace. From the Buddha's death, or *parinirvana*, to the destruction of Nalanda (the last Buddhist stronghold in India) in AD 1197, Buddhism in India went through three phases. These are often referred to as Hinayana, Mahayana and Vajrayana, though they were not mutually exclusive, being followed simultaneously in different regions.

Hinayana The Hinayana or Lesser Way insists on a monastic way of life as the only path to the personal goal of *nirvana*, see box, above, achieved through an austere life. Divided into many schools, the only surviving Hinayana tradition is the **Theravada Buddhism**, which was taken to Sri Lanka by the Emperor Asoka's son Mahinda, where it became the state religion, and spread to southeast Asia as practised in Thailand, Myanmar, Cambodia and Laos today. Suffering, sorrow and dissatisfaction are the nature of ordinary life and can only be eliminated by giving up desire. In turn, desire is a result of the misplaced belief in the reality of individual existence. Theravada Buddhism taught that there is no soul and ultimately no God. *Nirvana* is a state of rest beyond the universe, once found never lost.

Mahayana In contrast to the Hinayana schools, the followers of the Mahayana school (the Great Way) believed in the possibility of salvation for all. They practised a far more devotional form of meditation and new figures came to play a prominent part in their beliefs and their worship – the **Bodhisattvas**, saints who were predestined to reach the state of enlightenment through thousands of rebirths. They aspired to Buddhahood not for their own sake but for the sake of all living things. The Buddha is believed to have passed through numerous existences in preparation for his final mission. Mahayana Buddhism became dominant over most of South Asia and its influence is evidenced in Buddhist art from Gandhara in north Pakistan to Ajanta in Central India and Sigiriya in Sri Lanka.

Vajrayana A new branch of Buddhism, Vajrayana, or the Vehicle of the Thunder bold, appeared which began to lay stress on secret magical rituals and cults of female divinities. This new 'Diamond Way' adopted the practice of magic, yoga and meditation. It became associated with secret ceremonies, chanting of mystical 'mantras' and taking part in orgiastic rituals in the cause of spiritual gain in order to help others. The ideal of Vajrayana Buddhists is to be 'so fully in harmony with the cosmos as to be able to manipulate the cosmic forces within and outside himself'. It had developed in the north of India by the seventh century AD, matching the parallel growth of Hindu Tantrism. The magical power associated with Vajrayana requires instruction from a teacher or *lama*, hence the Tibetan form is sometimes referred to as 'Lamaistic'. See also page 559.

Buddhist beliefs Buddhism is based on the Buddha's own preaching. However, when he died none of those teachings had been written down. He developed his beliefs in reaction to the Brahmanism of his time, rejecting several of the doctrines of Vedic religion which were widely held in his lifetime: the Vedic gods, scriptures and priesthood and all social distinctions based on caste. However, he did accept the belief in the cyclical nature of life and that the nature of an individual's existence is determined by a natural process of reward and punishment for deeds in previous lives – the Hindu doctrine of karma, see page 1407. In the Buddha's view, though, there is no eternal soul. He denied the identification of the Self with the everchanging Mind-Body (here, some see parallels in the Advaita Vedanta philosophy of Self-*Brahman* in Hinduism). In Buddhism, *Anatta* (no-Self), overcame the egoistical Self, given to attachment and selfishness. Following the Buddha's death a succession of councils was called to try and reach agreement on doctrine. The first three were held within 140 years of the Buddha's death, the fourth being held at Pataliputra (modern Patna) during the reign of the Emperor Asoka (272-232 BC), who had recently been converted to Buddhism. Under his reign Buddhism spread throughout South Asia and opened the routes through Northwest India for Buddhism to travel into China, where it had become a force by the first century AD.

Buddhism's decline The decline of Buddhism in India probably stemmed as much from the growing similarity in the practice of Hinduism and Buddhism as from direct attacks. Mahayana Buddhism, with its reverence for Bodhisattvas and its devotional character, was increasingly difficult to distinguish from the revivalist Hinduism characteristic of several parts of North India from the seventh to the 12th centuries AD. The Muslim conquest dealt the final blow, as it was also accompanied by the large scale slaughter of monks as well as the destruction of monasteries. Without their institutional support Buddhism faded away.

Jainism

Like Buddhism, Jainism started as a reform movement of the Brahmanic religious beliefs of the sixth century BC. Its founder was a widely revered saint and ascetic, Vardhamma, who became known as **Mahavir** – 'great hero'. Mahavir was born in the same border region of India and Nepal as the Buddha, just 50 km north of modern Patna, probably in 599 BC. Thus he was about 35 years older than the Buddha. His family, also royal, were followers of an ascetic saint, Parsvanatha, who according to Jain tradition had lived 200 years previously.

Mahavir's life story is embellished with legends, but there is no doubt that he left his royal home for a life of the strict ascetic. He is believed to have received enlightenment after 12 years of rigorous hardship, penance and meditation. Afterwards he travelled and preached for 30 years, stopping only in the rainy season. He died aged 72 in 527 BC. His death was commemorated by a special lamp festival in the region of Bihar, which Jains claim is the basis of the now-common Hindu festival of lights, Diwali.

Unlike Buddhism, Jainism never spread beyond India, but it has survived continuously into modern India, claiming four million adherents. In part this may be because Jain beliefs have much in common with puritanical forms of Hinduism and are greatly respected and admired. Some Jain ideas, such as vegetarianism and reverence for all life, are widely recognized by Hindus as highly commendable, even by those who do not share other Jain beliefs. The value Jains place on non-violence has contributed to their importance in business and commerce, as they regard nearly all occupations except banking and commerce as violent. The 18-m- high

The Jain spiritual journey

The two Jain sects differ chiefly on the nature of proper ascetic practices. The Svetambara monks wear white robes and carry a staff, some wooden pots and a woollen mop for sweeping the path in front of them, wool being the softest material available and the least likely to hurt any living thing swept away. The highest level of Digambara monks will go completely naked, although the lower levels will wear a covering over their genitalia. They carry a waterpot made of a gourd and peacock feathers to sweep the ground before they sit.

Jains believe that the spiritual journey of the soul is divided into 14 stages, moving from bondage and ignorance to the final destruction of all karma and the complete fulfilment of the soul. The object throughout is to prevent the addition of new karma to the soul, which comes mainly through passion and attachment to the world. Bearing the pains of the world cheerfully contributes to the destruction of karma.

free-standing statue of Gommateshvara at Sravana Belgola near Mysore (built about AD 983) is just one outstanding example of the contribution of Jain art to India's heritage.

Jain beliefs Jains (from the word Jina, literally meaning 'descendants of conquerors') believe that there are two fundamental principles, the living (*jiva*) and the non-living (*ajiva*). The essence of Jain belief is that all life is sacred and that every living entity, even the smallest insect, has within it an indestructible and immortal soul. Jains developed the view of ahimsa – often translated as 'non-violence', but better perhaps as 'non-harming'. Ahimsa was the basis for the entire scheme of Jain values and ethics and alternative codes of practice were defined for householders and for ascetics.

The five vows may be taken both by monks and by lay people: not to harm any living beings (Jains must practise strict vegetarianism-and even some vegetables, such as potatoes and onions, are believed to have microscopic souls); to speak the truth; not to steal; to give up sexual relations and practice complete chastity; to give up all possessions-for the *Digambara* sect that includes clothes. Celibacy is necessary to combat physical desire. Jains also regard the manner of dying as extremely important. Although suicide is deeply opposed, vows of fasting to death voluntarily may be regarded as earning merit in the proper context. Mahavir himself is believed to have died of self-starvation. The essence of all the rules is to avoid intentional injury, which is the worst of all sins. Like Hindus, the Jains believe in *karma*.

Jains have two main **sects**, whose origins can be traced back to the fourth century BC. The more numerous **Svetambaras** – the 'white clad' – concentrated more in eastern and western India, separated from the **Digambaras** – or 'sky-clad'- who often go naked. The Digambaras may well have been forced to move south by drought and famine in the northern region of the Deccan and they are now concentrated in the south of India.

Unlike Buddhists, Jains accept the idea of God, but not as a creator of the universe. They see him in the lives of the 24 **Tirthankaras** (prophets, or 'makers of fords' – a reference to their role in building crossing points for the spiritual journey over the river of life), or leaders of Jainism, whose lives are recounted in the Kalpsutra – the third century BC book of ritual for the Svetambaras. Mahavir is regarded as the last of these great spiritual leaders. Much Jain art details stories from these accounts and the Tirthankaras play a similar role for Jains as the Bodhisattvas do for Mahayana Buddhists. The first and most revered of the Tirthankaras, Adinatha, also known as Rishabnath, is widely represented in Jain temples.

Sikhism

Guru Nanak, the founder of the religion was born just west of Lahore and grew up in what is now the Pakistani town of Sultanpur. His followers, the Sikhs (derived from the Sanskrit word for 'disciples') form perhaps one of India's most recognizable groups. Beards and turbans give them a very distinctive presence and although they represent less than 2% of the population they are both politically and economically significant.

Sikh beliefs The first Guru, accepted the ideas of *samsara* – the cycle of rebirths – and *karma*, see page 1407, from Hinduism. However, Sikhism is unequivocal in its belief in the oneness of God, rejecting idolatry and any worship of objects or images. Guru Nanak believed that God is One, formless, eternal and beyond description.

Guru Nanak also fiercely opposed discrimination on the grounds of caste. He saw God as present everywhere, visible to anyone who cared to look and as essentially full of grace and compassion. Some of Guru Nanak's teachings are close to the ideas of the Benaras mystic **Kabir**, who, in common with the Muslim mystic sufis, believed in mystical union with God. Kabir's belief in the nature of God was matched by his view that man was deliberately blind and unwilling to recognize God's nature. He transformed the Hindu concept of *maya* into the belief that the values commonly held by the world were an illusion.

Guru Nanak preached that salvation depended on accepting the nature of God. If people recognized the true harmony of the divine order (*hookam*) they would be saved. Rejecting the prevailing Hindu belief that such harmony could be achieved by ascetic practices, he emphasized three actions: meditating on and repeating God's name (*naam*), 'giving', or charity (*daan*) and bathing (*isnaan*).

Many of the features now associated with Sikhism can be attributed to **Guru Gobind Singh**, who on 15 April 1699, started the new brotherhood called the *Khalsa* (meaning 'the pure', from the Persian word *khales*), an inner core of the faithful, accepted by baptism (*amrit*). The 'five ks' date from this period: *kesh* (uncut hair), the most important, followed by *kangha* (comb, usually of wood), *kirpan* (dagger or short sword), *kara* (steel bangle) and *kachh* (similar to 'boxer' shorts). The dagger and the shorts reflect military influence.

In addition to the compulsory 'five ks', the new code prohibited smoking, eating *halal* meat and sexual intercourse with Muslim women. These date from the 18th century, when the Sikhs were often in conflict with the Muslims. Other strict prohibitions include: idolatry, caste discrimination, hypocrisy and pilgrimage to Hindu sacred places. The Khalsa also explicitly forbade the seclusion of women, one of the common practices of Islam. It was only under the warrior king Ranjit Singh (1799-1838) that the idea of the Guru's presence in meetings of the Sikh community (the *Panth*) gave way to the now universally held belief in the total authority of the **Guru Granth**, the recorded words of the Guru in the scripture.

Sikh worship The meditative worship Guru Nanak commended is a part of the life of every devout Sikh today, who starts each day with private meditation and a recitation of the verses of Guru Nanak himself, the *Japji*. However, from the time of the third Guru, Sikhs have also worshipped as congregations in Gurudwaras ('gateways to the Guru'). The Golden Temple in Amritsar, built at the end of the 16th century, is the holiest site of Sikhism.

The present institutions of Sikhism owe their origins to 19th-century reform movements. Under the Sikh Gurudwaras Act of 1925 all temples were restored to the management of a Central Gurudwara Management Committee, thereby removing them from the administrative control of the Hindus under which many had come. This body has acted as the religion's controlling body ever since. See also Amritsar, page 469.

Sikhism's Gurus

Guru	Teachings and practice	Developments and events	External powers
1 *Nanak* 1469-1539	The life stories (**janam-sakhis**) of Guru Nanak, written 50-80 years after his death, recorded wide travels, including Bengal and Mecca, studying different faiths.	Devotional and mystic tradition established by Guru Nanak, similar to that of Kabir.	Delhi sultanates
2 *Angad* 1504-1538	Special ceremonies and festivals began to augment individual devotions.		
3 *Amar Das* 1509-1574	Introduction of worship in Gurudwaras.		Portuguese make contact with India.
4 *Ram Das* 1534-1581	Built first lake temple in Amritsar; the first hereditary guru. Widening of congregational worship.	Tolerance for religious experiment.	Akbar
5 *Arjan Dev* 1563-1606	In 1603-4 collected hymns and sayings of the first 3 Gurus, of Sikh mystics and of his father's and his own in a single volume the Adi Granth (Guru Granth Sahib). Started Amritsar's Golden Temple.	The Adi Granth comprises nearly 6000 hymns, 974 attributed to Guru Nanak. Written in Gurumukhi script, developed from Punjabi by the second Guru.	Akbar and Jahangir. Arjan Dev executed by Jahangir at Lahore
6 *Har Gobind* 1595-1645	Jat caste becomes dominant influence. Sikhs began to take up arms, largely to protect themselves against Mughal attacks. Har Gobind decided to withdraw to the Siwalik Hills.	The next 4 Gurus all spent much of their time outside Punjab in the Siwalik Hills, where they developed new martial traditions.	Jahangir and Shah Jahan
7 *Har Rai* 1630-1661			Shah Jahan
8 *Har Krishna* 1656-1664		Died at Delhi.	Aurangzeb
9 *Tegh Bahadur* 1622-1675		Executed by Aurangzeb.	Aurangzeb
10 *Gobind Singh* 1666-1708	Reformed Sikh government introduced the features now universally associated with Sikhism today. Assassinated at Nanded in Maharashtra.	The Khalsa was open to both men and women, who replaced their caste names with Singh (lion) and Kaur ('lioness' or 'princess') respectively.	Aurangzeb

Christianity

There are about 23 million Christians in India. Christianity ranks third in terms of religious affiliation after Hinduism and Islam.

The great majority of the Protestant Christians in India are now members of the Church of South India, formed from the major Protestant denominations in 1947, or the Church of North India, which followed suit in 1970. Together they account for approximately half the total number of Christians. Roman Catholics make up the majority of the rest. Many of the church congregations, both in towns and villages, are active centres of Christian worship.

Origins Some of the churches owe their origin either to the modern missionary movement of the late 18th century onwards, or to the colonial presence of the European powers. However, Christians probably arrived in India during the first century after the birth of Christ. There is evidence that one of Christ's Apostles, **Thomas**, reached India in AD 52, only 20 years after Christ was crucified. He settled in Malabar and then expanded his missionary work to China. It is widely believed that he was martyred in Tamil Nadu on his return to India in AD 72 and is buried in Mylapore, in the suburbs of modern Chennai. St Thomas' Mount, a small rocky hill just north of Chennai airport, takes its name from him. Today there is still a church of Thomas Christians in Kerala.

The Syrian church Kerala was linked directly with the Middle East when Syrian Christians embarked on a major missionary movement in the sixth century AD. The Thomas Christians have forms of worship that show very strong influence of the Syrian church and they still retain a Syriac order of service. They remained a close-knit community, who have come to terms with the prevailing caste system by maintaining strict social rules very similar to those of the surrounding upper caste Hindus. They lived in an area restricted to what is now Kerala, where trade with the Middle East, which some centuries later was to bring Muslims to the same region, remained active.

Roman Catholicism The third major development took place with the arrival of the Portuguese. The Jesuit St Francis Xavier landed in Goa in 1542 and in 1557 Goa was made an Archbishopric, see page 1243. Goa today bears testimony to the Portuguese influence on community life and church building. They set up the first printing press in India in 1566 and began to print books by the end of the 16th century.

Northern missions Protestant missions in Bengal from the end of the 18th century had a profound influence on cultural and religious development. On 9 November 1793 the Baptist missionary **William Carey** reached the Hugli River. Although he went to India to preach, he had wide-ranging interests, notably in languages and education and the work of 19th-century missions rapidly widened to cover educational and medical work as well. See page 613. Converts were made most readily among the backward castes and in the tribal areas. The Christian populations of the tribal hill areas of Nagaland and Assam stem from such late 19th-century and 20th-century movements. But the influence of Christian missions in education and medical work was greater than as a proselytizing force. Education in Christian schools stimulated reformist movements in Hinduism itself and mission hospitals supplemented government-run hospitals, particularly in remote rural areas. Some of these Christian-run hospitals, such as that at Vellore, continue to provide high class medical care.

Christian beliefs Christian theology had its roots in Judaism, with its belief in one God, the eternal Creator of the universe. Judaism saw the Jewish people as the vehicle for God's salvation, the 'chosen people of God' and pointed to a time when God would send his Saviour, or Messiah. Jesus, whom Christians believe was 'the Christ' or Messiah, was born in the village of Bethlehem, some 20 km south of Jerusalem. Very little is known of his early life except that he was brought up in a devout Jewish family. At the age of 29 or 30 he gathered a small group of followers and began to preach in the region between the Dead Sea and the Sea of Galilee. Two years later he was crucified in Jerusalem by the authorities on the charge of blasphemy – that he claimed to be the son of God.

Christians believe that all people live in a state of sin, in the sense that they are separated from God and fail to do his will. They believe that God is personal, 'like a father'. As God's son, Jesus accepted the cost of that separation and sinfulness himself through his death on the cross. Christians believe that Jesus was raised from the dead on the third day after he was crucified and that he appeared to his closest followers. They believe that his spirit continues to live today and that he makes it possible for people to come back to God.

The New Testament of the Bible, which, alongside the Old Testament, is the text to which Christians refer as the ultimate scriptural authority, consists of four 'Gospels' (meaning 'good news') and a series of letters by several early Christians referring to the nature of the Christian life.

Christian worship Although Christians are encouraged to worship individually as well as together, most forms of Christian worship centre on the gathering of the church congregation. Different denominations place varying emphases on the main elements of worship, but in most church services today the congregation will take part in singing hymns (songs of praise), prayers will be led by the minister, priest or a member of the congregation, readings from the Bible will be given and a sermon preached. For many Christians the most important service is the act of Holy Communion (Protestant) or Mass (Catholic) which celebrates the death and resurrection of Jesus in sharing bread and wine, which are held to represent Christ's body and blood given to save people from their sin.

Zoroastrianism

The first Zoroastrians arrived on the west coast of India in the mid-eighth century AD, forced out from their native Iran by persecution of the invading Islamic Arabs. Until 1477 they lost all contact with Iran and then for nearly 300 years maintained contact with Persian Zoroastrians through a continuous exchange of letters. They became known by their now much more familiar name, the **Parsis** (or Persians).

Although they are a tiny minority (approximately 100,000), even in the cities where they are concentrated, they have been a prominent economic and social influence, especially in West India. Parsis adopted westernized customs and dress and took to the new economic opportunities that came with colonial industrialization. Families in West India such as the Tatas continue to be among India's leading industrialists, just part of a community that in recent generations has spread to Europe and north America.

Origins Zoroastrians trace their beliefs to the prophet Zarathustra, who lived in Northeast Iran around the seventh or sixth century BC. His place and even date of birth are uncertain, but he almost certainly enjoyed the patronage of the father of Darius the Great. The passage of Alexander the Great through Iran severely weakened support for Zoroastrianism, but between the sixth century BC and the seventh century AD it was the major religion of peoples living from North India to central Turkey. The spread of Islam reduced the number of Zoroastrians dramatically and forced those who did not retreat to the desert to emigrate.

Parsi beliefs The early development of Zoroastrianism marked a movement towards belief in a single God. **Ahura Mazda**, the Good Religion of God, was shown in rejecting evil and in purifying thought, word and action. Fire plays a central and symbolic part in Zoroastrian worship, representing the presence of God. There are eight Atash Bahram – major fire temples – in India; four are in Mumbai, two in Surat and one each in Navsari and Udwada. There are many more minor temples, where the rituals are less complex.

Earth, fire and air are all regarded as sacred, while death is the result of evil. Dead matter pollutes all it touches. Where there is a suitable space therefore, dead bodies are simply placed in the open to be consumed by vultures, as at the Towers of Silence in Mumbai. However, burial and cremation are also common.

Land and environment

Geography

India falls into three major geological regions. The north is enclosed by the great arc of the Himalaya. Along their southern flank lie the alluvial plains of the Ganga and to the south again is the Peninsula. The island chains of the Lakshadweep and Minicoy off the west coast of India are coral atolls, formed on submarine ridges under the Arabian Sea.

The origins of India's landscapes

Only 100 million years ago the Indian Peninsula was still attached to the great land mass of what geologists call 'Pangaea' alongside South Africa, Australia and Antarctica. Then as the great plates on which the earth's southern continents stood broke up, the Indian Plate started its dramatic shift northwards, eventually colliding with the Asian plate. As the Indian Plate continues to get pushed under the Tibetan Plateau so the Himalaya continue to rise.

The Himalaya The Himalaya dominate the northern borders of India, stretching 2500 km from northwest to southeast. They are unparalleled anywhere in the world. Of the 94 mountains in Asia above 7300 m, all but two are in the Himalaya. Nowhere else in the world are there mountains as high. The Himalaya proper, stretching from the Pamirs in Pakistan to the easternmost bend of the Brahmaputra in Assam, can be divided into three broad zones. On the southern flank are the Shiwaliks, or Outer Ranges. To their immediate north run the parallel Middle Ranges of Pir Panjal and Dhauladhar and to the north again is the third zone, the Inner Himalaya, which has the highest peaks, many of them in Nepal. The central core of the Himalayan ranges did not begin to rise until about 35 million years ago. The latest mountain building period, responsible for the Shiwaliks, began less than five million years ago and is still continuing, raising some of the high peaks by as much as 5 mm a year. Such movement comes at a price and the boundary between the plains and the Himalayan ranges is a zone of continuing violent earthquakes and massive erosion.

The Gangetic Plains As the Himalaya began their dramatic uplift, the trough which formed to the south of the newly emerging mountains was steadily filled with the debris washed down from the hills, creating the Indo-Gangetic plains. Today the alluvium reaches depths of over 3000 m in places (and over 22 km at the mouth of the Ganga in Bangladesh), and contains some of the largest reserves of underground water in the world. These have made possible extensive well irrigation, especially in Northwest India, contributing to the rapid agricultural changes which have taken place. The Indo-Gangetic plains are still being modified. The southern part of Bengal only emerged from the sea during the last 5000 years. The Ganga and the Indus have each been estimated to carry over one million tonnes of silt every year. The silts washed down from the Himalaya have made it possible for intensive rice cultivation to be practised continuously for hundreds of years, though they cause problems for modern irrigation development. Dams in the Himalayan region are being rapidly filled by silt, over 33 million tonnes being deposited behind the Bhakra Dam on the Sutlej River alone.

The Peninsula The crystalline rocks of the Peninsula are some of the oldest in the world, the **Charnockites** – named after the founder of Kolkata an enthusiastic amateur geologist, Job Charnock (see page 601) being over 3100 million years old. Over 60 million years ago, when India split from Madagascar, a mass of volcanic lava welled up through cracks in the earth's surface and covered some 500,000 sq km of northern Karnataka, Maharashtra, southern Gujarat and Madhya Pradesh. The fault line which severed India from Africa was marked by a north-south ridge of mountains, known today as the Western Ghats, set back from the sea by a coastal plain which is never more than 80 km wide. In the south, the Nilgiris and Palanis are over 2500 m high. From the crest line of the **Western Ghats**, the Peninsula slopes generally eastwards, interrupted on its eastern edge by the much more broken groups of hills sometimes referred to as the **Eastern Ghats**. The east flowing rivers have created flat alluvial deltas which have been the basis of successive peninsular kingdoms.

Climate

India is divided almost exactly by the Tropic of Cancer, stretching from the near- equatorial Kanniyakumari to the Mediterranean latitudes of Kashmir – roughly the same span as from the Amazon to San Francisco, or from Melbourne to Darwin. Not surprisingly, climate varies considerably and high altitudes further modify local climates.

The monsoon The term monsoon refers to the wind reversal which replaces the dry northeasterlies, characteristic of winter and spring, with the very warm and wet southwesterlies of the summer. The arrival of the monsoon is as variable as is the amount of rain which it brings. What makes the Indian monsoon quite exceptional is not its regularity but the depth of moist air which passes over the subcontinent. Over India, the highly unstable moist airflow is over 6000 m thick compared with only 2000 m over Japan, giving rise to the bursts of torrential rain which mark out the wet season.

Winter High pressure builds up over Central Asia. Most of India is protected from the cold northeast monsoon winds that result by the massive bulk of the Himalaya and daytime temperatures rise sharply in the sun. Right across the Ganga plains night temperatures fall to below 5°C in January and February. To the south the winter temperatures increase having a minimum temperature of around 20°C. Although much of North India often has beautiful weather from November through to March, there are periods when it is cool and overcast. Elsewhere, however, the winter is a dry season through nearly all of India. The low winter night temperatures coupled with increasing pollution in the larger cities such as Delhi and Kolkata, contribute to the growing problem of morning fog in December- January, a major health hazard as well as causing periodic travel chaos.

Summer From April onwards much of India becomes almost unbearably hot. Temperatures of over 50°C are not unknown. It is a time of year to get up to the hills. At the end of May very moist southwesterlies sweep across South India and the Bay of Bengal. They then double back northwestwards, bringing tremendously heavy rain first to the eastern Himalaya then gradually spreading northwestwards.

The wet season The monsoon season lasts from between three and five months depending on the region. Many parts of the west coast get a three-month soaking and the Shillong plateau has received as much as 26 m in one year! If you are travelling in the wetter parts of India during the monsoon you need to be prepared for extended periods of torrential rain and major disruption to travel. However, many parts of India receive a total of under 1000 mm a year. Rainfall decreases towards the Northwest, Rajasthan and northern Gujarat merging imperceptibly into desert. Tamil Nadu has an exceptional rainfall pattern, receiving most of its rain during the retreating monsoon, October-December.

Storms Some regions suffer major storms. Cyclones may hit the east coast causing enormous damage and loss of life, the risk being greatest between the end of October and early December. In Northwest India, '*the Loo*', between April and June, brings dust storms and very hot winds. In Bengal Nor'westers can cause enormous damage in April-May

Humidity The coastal regions have humidity levels above 70% for most of the year which can be very uncomfortable. However, sea breezes often bring some relief on the coast itself. Moving north and inland, between December-May humidity drops sharply, often falling as low as 20% during the daytime.

Vegetation

India's location ensured that 16 different forest types were represented. The most widespread was tropical dry deciduous forest. However, today forest cover has been reduced to about 13% of the surface area, mainly the result of demand for wood as a fuel.

Deciduous forest Two types of deciduous tree remain particularly important, **Sal** (*Shorea robusta*), now found mainly in eastern India and **Teak** (*Tectona grandis*). Most teak today has been planted. Both are resistant to burning, which helped to protect them where people used fire as a means of clearing the forest.

Tropical rainforest In wetter areas, particularly along the Western Ghats, you can still find tropical wet evergreen forest, but even these are now extensively managed. Across the drier areas of the peninsula heavy grazing has reduced the forest cover to little more than thorn scrub.

Mountain forests and grassland At between 1000-2000 m in the eastern hill ranges of India and in Bhutan, for example, wet hill forest includes evergreen oaks and chestnuts. Further west in the foothills of the Himalaya are belts of subtropical pine at roughly the same altitudes. Deodars (*Cedrus deodarus*) form large stands and moist temperate forest, with pines, cedars, firs and spruce, is dominant, giving many of the valleys a beautifully fresh, alpine feel. Between 3000-4000 m alpine forest predominates. Rhododendron are often mixed with other forest types. Birch, juniper, poplars and pine are widespread. There are several varieties of coarse grassland along the southern edge of the Terai and alpine grasses are important for grazing above altitudes of 2000 m. A totally distinctive grassland is the bamboo (*Dendo calamus*) region of the eastern Himalaya.

Trees

Flowering trees Many Indian trees are planted along roadsides to provide shade and they often also produce beautiful flowers. The **Silk Cotton Tree** (*Bombax ceiba*), up to 25 m in height, is one of the most dramatic. The pale greyish bark of this buttressed tree usually bears conical spines. It has wide spreading branches and keeps its leaves for most of the year. The flowers, which appear when the tree is leafless, are cup-shaped, with curling, rather fleshy red petals up to 12 cm long while the fruit produce the fine, silky cotton which gives it its name. Other common trees with red or orange flowers include the Dhak (also called 'Flame of the forest' or *Palas*), the Gulmohur, the Indian coral tree and the Tulip tree. The smallish (6 m) deciduous **Dhak** (*Butea monosperma*), has light grey bark and a gnarled, twisted trunk and thick, leathery leaves. The large, bright orange and sweet pea-shaped flowers appear on leafless branches. The 8-9 m high umbrella-shaped **Gulmohur** (*Delonix regia*), a native of Madagascar, is grown as a shade tree in towns. The fiery coloured flowers make a magnificent display after the tree has shed its feathery leaves. The scarlet flowers of the **Indian Coral Tree** (*Erythrina indica*) appear when its branches with thorny bark are leafless. The tall **Tulip Tree** (*Spathodea campanulata*) (not to be confused with the North American one) has a straight, darkish brown, slender trunk. It is usually evergreen except in the drier parts of India. The scarlet bell-shaped, tulip-like, flowers grow in profusion at the ends of the branches from November to March.

Often seen along roadsides the **Jacaranda** (*Jacaranda mimosaefolia*), has attractive feathery foliage and purple-blue thimble-shaped flowers up to 40 mm long. When not in flower it resembles a Gulmohur, but differs in its general shape. The valuable **Tamarind** (*Tamarindus indica*), with a short straight trunk and a spreading crown, often grows along the roadside. An evergreen with feathery leaves, it bears small clusters of yellow and red flowers. The noticeable fruit pods are long, curved and swollen at intervals. In parts of India, the rights to the fruit are auctioned off annually for up to Rs 4000 (US$100) per tree.

Of these trees the Silk cotton, the Dhak and the Indian coral are native to India. Others were introduced mostly during the last century: the Tulip tree from East Africa, the Jacaranda from Brazil and the Tamarind, possibly from Africa.

Fruit trees The familiar apple, plum, apricot and cherry grow in the cool upland areas of India. In the warmer plains tropical fruits flourish. The large, spreading **Mango** (*Mangifera indica*) bears the delicious, distinctively shaped fruit that comes in hundreds of varieties. The evergreen **Jackfruit** (*Artocarpus heterophyllus*) has dark green leathery leaves. The huge fruit (up to 90 cm long and 40 cm thick), growing from a short stem directly off the trunk and branches, has a rough, almost prickly skin and is almost sickly sweet. The **Banana** plant (*Musa*), actually a gigantic herb (up to 5 m high) arising from an underground stem, has very large leaves which grow directly off the trunk. Each large purplish flower produces bunches of up to 100 bananas. The **Papaya** (*Carica papaya*) grows to about 4 m with the large hand-shaped leaves clustered near the top. Only the female tree bears the fruit, which hang down close to the trunk just below the leaves.

Palm trees **Coconut Palms** (*Cocos nucifera*) are common all round the coast of India. It has tall (15-25 m), slender, unbranched trunks, feathery leaves and large green or golden fruit with soft white flesh filled with milky water, so different from the brown fibre-covered inner nut which makes its way to Europe. The 10-15 m high **Palmyra palms** (*Borassus flabellifer*), indigenous to South and East India, have distinctive fan-like leaves, as much as 150 cm across. The fruit, which is smaller than a coconut, is round, almost black and very shiny. The **Betel Nut Palm** (*Areca catechu*) resembles the coconut palm, its slender trunk bearing ring marks left by fallen leaf stems. The smooth, round nuts, only about 3 cm across, grow in large hanging bunches. **Wild Date Palms** (*Phoenix sylvestris*), originally came from North Africa. About 20-25 m tall, the trunks are also marked with the ring bases of the leaves which drop off. The distinctive leaflets which stick out from the central vein give the leaf a spiky appearance. Bunches of dates are only borne by the female tree.

All these palm trees are of considerable **commercial importance**. From the fruit alone the coconut palm produces coir from the outer husk, copra from the fleshy kernel from which coconut oil or coconut butter is extracted, in addition to the desiccated coconut and coconut milk. The sap is fermented to a drink called toddy. A similar drink is produced from the sap of the wild date and the palmyra palms which are also important for sugar production. The fruit of the betel nut palm is wrapped in a special leaf and chewed. The trunks and leaves of all the palms are widely used in building and thatching.

Other trees Of all Indian trees the **Banyan** (*Ficus benghalensis*) is probably the best known. It is planted by temples, in villages and along roads. If it grows in the bark of another tree, it sends down roots towards the ground. As it grows, more roots appear from the branches, until the original host tree is surrounded by a 'cage' which eventually strangles it. The famous one in Kolkata's Botanical Gardens is more than 400 m in circumference. Related to the banyan, the **Pipal** or Peepul (*Ficus religiosa*), also cracks open walls and strangles other trees with its roots. With a smooth grey bark, it too is commonly found near temples and shrines. You can distinguish it from the banyan by the absence of aerial roots and its large, heart-shaped leaf with a point tapering into a pronounced 'tail'. It bears abundant 'figs' of a purplish tinge which are about 1 cm across. The **Ashok** or **Mast** (*Polyalthia longifolia*) is a tall evergreen which can reach 15 m or more in height. One variety, often seen in avenues, is trimmed and tapers towards the top. The leaves are long, slender and shiny and narrow to a long point. **Acacia** trees with their feathery leaves are fairly common in the drier parts of India. The best known is the **Babul** (*Acacia arabica*) with a rough, dark bark. The leaves have long silvery white thorns at the base and consist of many leaflets while the flowers grow in golden balls about 1 cm across. The **Eucalyptus** or **Gum Tree** (*Eucalyptus grandis*), introduced from Australia in the 19th century, is now widespread and is planted near villages to provide both shade and firewood. There are various forms but all may be readily recognized by their height, their characteristic long, thin leaves which have a pleasant fresh smell and the colourful peeling bark. The wispy **Casuarina** (*Casuarina*) grows in poor sandy soil, especially on the coast and on village waste land. It has the typical leaves of a pine tree and the cones are small and prickly to walk on. It is said to attract lightning during a thunder storm.

Bamboo (*Bambusa*) strictly speaking is a grass which can vary in size from small ornamental clumps to the enormous wild plant whose stems are so strong and thick that they are used for construction and for scaffolding and as pipes in rural irrigation schemes.

Flowering plants

Common in the Himalaya is the beautiful flowering shrub or tree, which can be as tall as 12 m, the **Rhododendron** which is indigenous to this region. In the wild the commonest colour of the flowers is crimson, but other colours, such as pale purple occur too. From March to May the flowers are very noticeable on the hill sides. Another common wild flowering shrub is **Lantana**. This is a fairly small untidy looking bush with rough, toothed oval leaves, which grow in pairs on the square and prickly stem. The flowers grow together in a flattened head, the ones near the middle being usually yellowish, while those at the rim are pink, pale purple or orange. The fruit is a shiny black berry.

Many other flowering plants are cultivated in parks, gardens and roadside verges. The attractive **Frangipani** (*Plumeria acutifolia*) has a rather crooked trunk and stubby branches, which if broken give out a white milky juice which can be irritating to the skin. The big, leathery leaves taper to a point at each end and have noticeable parallel veins. The sweetly scented waxy flowers are white, pale yellow or pink. The **Bougainvillea** grows as a dense bush or climber with small oval leaves and rather long thorns. The brightly coloured part (which can be pinkish-purple, crimson, orange, yellow, etc) which appears like a flower is not formed of petals, which are quite small and undistinguished, but by large papery bracts.

The unusual shape of the **Hibiscus**. The trumpet shaped flower, as much as 7 or 8 cm across, has a very long 'tongue' growing out from the centre and varies in colour from scarlet to yellow or white. The leaves are somewhat oval or heart-shaped with jagged edges. In municipal flowerbeds the commonest planted flower is probably the **Canna Lily**. It has large leaves which are either green or bronzed and lots of large bright red or yellow flowers. The plant can be more than 1 m high. On many ponds and tanks the floating plants of the **Lotus** (*Nelumbo nucifera*) and the **Water Hyacinth** (*Eichornia crassipes*) are seen. Lotus flowers which rise on stalks above the water can be white, pink or a deep red and up to 25 cm across. The very large leaves either float on the surface or rise above the water. Many dwarf varieties are cultivated. The rather fleshy leaves and lilac flowers of the water hyacinth float to form a dense carpet, often clogging the waterways.

Crops

Of India's enormous variety, the single most widespread crop is **rice** (commonly *Orysa indica*). This forms the most important staple in South and East India, though other cereals and some root crops are also important elsewhere. The rice plant grows in flooded fields called *paddies* and virtually all planting or harvesting is done by hand. Millets are favoured in drier areas inland, while wheat is the most important crop in the northwest. There are many different sorts of millet, but the ones most often seen are finger millet, pearl millet (bajra) and sorghum (jowar). **Finger millet**, commonly known as ragi (*Eleusine corocana*), is so-called because the ear has several spikes which radiate out, like fingers. Usually less than 1 m high, it is grown extensively in the south. Both **pearl millet** (*Pennisetum typhoideum*, known as *bajra* in the north and *cumbu* in Tamil Nadu) and **sorghum** (*Sorghum vulgare*, known as *jowar* in the north and *cholam* in the south) look similar to the more familiar maize though each can be easily distinguished when the seed heads appear. Pearl millet, mainly grown in the north, has a tall single spike which gives it its other name of bulrush millet. Sorghum bears an open ear at the top of the plant. **Tea** (*Camellia sinensis*) is grown on a commercial scale in tea gardens in areas of high rainfall, often in highland regions. Over 90% comes from Assam and West Bengal in the Northeast and Tamil Nadu and Kerala in the South. Left to itself tea grows into a tree 10 m tall. In the tea gardens it is pruned to waist height for the convenience of the tea pluckers and forms flat topped bushes, with shiny bright green oval leaves. **Coffee** (*Coffea*) is not as widely grown as tea, but high-quality arabica is an important crop in parts of South India. Coffee is also a bush, with fairly long, shiny dark green leaves. The white, sweet smelling flowers, which yield the coffee berry, grow in groups along the stems. The coffee berries start off green and turn red when ripe. **Sugar cane** (*Saccharum*) is another commercially important crop. This looks like a large grass, up to 3 m tall. The crude brown sugar is sold as jaggery and has a flavour of molasses. Of the many spices grown in India, the two climbers pepper and vanilla and the grass-like cardamom are the ones most often seen. The **pepper** vine (*Piper nigrum*) is indigenous to India where it grows in the warm moist regions. As it is a vine it needs support such as a trellis or a tree. It is frequently planted up against the betel nut palm and appears as a leafy vine with almost heart-shaped leaves. The peppercorns cluster along hanging spikes and are red when ripe. Both black and white pepper is produced from the same plant, the difference being in the processing. **Vanilla** (*Vanilla planifolium*), which belongs to the orchid family, also grows up trees for support and attaches itself to the bark by small roots. It is native to South America, but grows well in India in areas of high rainfall. It is a rather fleshy looking plant, with white flowers and long slender pods. **Cardamom** (*Elettaria cardomomum*) is another spice native to India and is planted usually under shade. It grows well in highland areas such as Sikkim and the Western Ghats. It is a herbaceous plant looking rather like a big clump of grass, with long leafy shoots springing out of the ground as much as 2-3 m in height. The white flowers grow on separate shoots which can be upright, but usually sprawl on the ground. It is from these flowers that the seed bearing capsules grow. The **cashew nut** tree (*Anacardium occidentale*) was introduced into India, but now grows wild as well as being cultivated. It is a medium-sized tree with bright green, shiny, rounded leaves. The nut grows on a fleshy fruit called a cashew apple and hangs down below this. **Cotton** (*Gossypium*) is important in parts of the west and south. The cotton bush is a small knee-high bush and the cotton boll appears after the flower has withered. This splits when ripe to show the white cotton lint inside. The **castor oil** plant (*Ricinus communis*) is cultivated as a cash crop and is planted in small holdings among other crops and along roads and paths. It is a handsome plant up to about 2 m in height, with very large leaves which are divided into some 12 'fingers'. The young stems are reddish and shiny. The well-known castor oil is extracted from the bean which is a mottled brown in colour.

Wildlife

India has an extremely rich and varied wildlife, though many species only survive in very restricted environments. Alarmed by the rapid loss of wildlife habitat the Indian government established the first conservation measures in 1972, followed by the setting up of national parks and reserves. Some 25,000 sq km were set aside in 1973 for Project Tiger. Tigers are reported to be increasing steadily in several game reserves but threats to their survival continue, mainly due to poaching. The same is true of other less well-known species. Their natural habitat has been destroyed both by people and by domesticated animals (there are some 250 million cattle and 50 million sheep and goats). There are now nearly 70 national parks and 330 sanctuaries, as well as programmes of afforestation and coastline preservation. Most sanctuaries and parks are open October-March; in the northeast they are closed April-September, while many in Madhya Pradesh and Uttar Pradesh close July-September.

The animals

The big cats Of the three Indian big cats the Asiatic lion is virtually confined to a single reserve. The other two, the tiger and leopard, occasionally occur outside. The **tiger** (*Panthera tigris*), which prefers to live in fairly dense cover, is most likely to be glimpsed as it lies in long grass or in dappled shadow; see also box, above. The **asiatic lion** (*Panthera leo*) is now found only in the Gir National Park. Less sleek than the African lion, it has a more shaggy coat and a smaller, often black mane. The **leopard** or **panther** as it is often called in India (*Panthera pardus*), is far more numerous than the tiger, but is even more elusive. The all black form is not uncommon in areas of higher rainfall such as the Western Ghats and Northeast India, though the typical form is seen more often.

Elephant and rhino The **Indian elephant** (*Elephas maximus*) has been domesticated for centuries and today it is still used as a beast of burden. In the wild it inhabits hilly country with forest and bamboo, where it lives in herds which can number as many as 50 or more individuals. They are adaptable animals and can live in all sorts of forest, except in dry areas. Wild elephants are mainly confined to reserves, but occasionally move out into cultivation, where they cause great damage. The **great Indian one-horned rhinoceros** (*Rhinoceros unicornis*) has folds of skin which look like rivet covered armour plating. It stands at up to 170 cm at the shoulder.

Deer, antelope, oxen and their relatives Once widespread, these animals are now largely confined to the reserves. The male deer (stags) carry antlers which are branched, each 'spike' on the antler being called a tine. Antelopes and oxen, on the other hand, have horns which are not branched. There are several deer species in India, mainly confined to very restricted ranges. Three species are quite common. The largest and one of the most widespread, is the magnificent **sambar** (*Cervus unicolor*) which can be up to 150 cm at the shoulder. It has a noticeably shaggy coat, which varies in colour from brown with a yellowish or grey tinge through to dark, almost black, in the older stags. The sambar is often found on wooded hillsides and lives in groups of up to 10 or so, though solitary individuals are also seen. The **barasingha** or **swamp deer** (*Cervus duvauceli*), standing about 130 cm at the shoulder, is also quite common. The females are usually lighter and some are spotted, as are the young. The antlers are much more complex than those of the sambar, having as many as 20 tines, but 12 is more usual. Barasingha prefer swampy habitat, but are also seen in grassy areas, often in large herds. The small **chital** or **spotted deer** (*Axis axis*), only about 90 cm tall, are seen in herds of 20 or so, in grassy areas. The bright rufous coat spotted with white is unmistakable; the stags carry antlers with three tines. These animals live in open grasslands, never too far from water. The beautiful **blackbuck** or **Indian antelope** (*Antilope cervicapra*), up to 80 cm at the shoulder, occurs in large herds. The distinctive colouring and the long spiral horns make the stag easy to identify. The coat is chocolate brown above, very sharply demarcated from the white of the underparts. The females do not usually bear horns and like the young, have yellowish brown coats. The larger and heavier **nilgai** or **blue bull** (*Boselaphus tragocamelus*) is about 140 cm at the shoulder and is rather horse-like, with a sloping back. The male has a dark grey coat, while the female is sandy coloured. Both sexes have two white marks on the cheek, white throats and a white ring just above each hoof. The male carries short, forward-curving horns and has a tuft of long black hairs on the front of the neck. They occur in small herds on grassy plains and scrub land.

The very graceful **chinkara** or **Indian gazelle** (*Gazella gazella*) is only 65 cm at the shoulder. The light russet colour of the body has a distinct line along the side where the paler underparts start. Both sexes carry slightly S-shaped horns. Chinkara live in small groups in rather broken hilly countryside. The commonest member of the oxen group is the **Asiatic wild buffalo** or water buffalo (*Bubalus bubalis*). About 170 cm at the shoulder, the wild buffalo, which can be aggressive, occurs in herds on grassy plains and swamps near rivers and lakes. The black coat and wide-spreading curved horns, carried by both sexes, are distinctive. In the high Himalaya, the **yak** (*Bos grunniens*) is domesticated. The wild yak, found on bleak Himalayan hillsides has a shaggy, blackish brown coat and large horns; the domesticated animals are often piebald and the horns much smaller. The **Indian bison** or **gaur** (*Bos gaurus*) can be up to 200 cm at the shoulder with a heavy muscular ridge across it. Both sexes carry curved horns. The young gaur is a light sandy colour, which darkens with age, the old bulls being nearly black with pale sandy coloured 'socks' and a pale forehead. Basically hill animals, they live in forests and bamboo clumps and emerge from the trees to graze. The **bharal** or **blue sheep** (*Pseudois nayaur*) are found on the open slopes around Ladakh. About 90 cm at the shoulder, it has a grey-blue body and horns that curve backwards over the neck. The rare **asiatic wild ass** (*Equus hemionus*) is confined to the deserts of the Little Rann of Kachchh. The fawn body has a distinctive dark stripe along the back. The dark mane is short and erect. The **wild boar** (*Sus scrofa*) has a mainly black body and a pig-like head; the hairs thicken down the spine to form a sort of mane. A mature male stands 90 cm at the shoulder and, unlike the female, bears tusks. The young are striped. Quite widespread, they can often cause great destruction among crops. One of the most important scavengers of the open countryside, the **striped hyena** (*Hyena hyena*) usually comes out at night. It is about 90 cm at the shoulder with a large head with a noticeable crest of hairs along its sloping back. The **common giant flying squirrel** are common in the larger forests of India, except in the northeast (*Petaurista petaurista*). The body can be 45 cm long and the tail another 50 cm. They glide from tree to tree using a membrane stretching from front leg to back leg which acts like a parachute.

In towns and villages The **common langur** (*Presbytis entellus*), 75 cm, is a long-tailed monkey with a distinctive black face, hands and feet. Usually a forest dweller, it is found almost throughout India. The **rhesus macaque** (*Macaca mulatta*), 60 cm, is more solid looking with shorter limbs and a shorter tail. It can be distinguished by the orange-red fur on its rump and flanks. **Palm squirrels** are very common. The **five-striped** (*Funambulus pennanti*) and the **three-striped palm squirrel** (*Funambulus palmarum*), are both about the same size (30 cm long, about half of which is tail). The five-striped is usually seen in towns. The two bats most commonly seen in towns differ enormously in size. The larger so-called **flying fox** (*Pteropus giganteus*) has a wing span of 120 cm. These fruit eating bats, found throughout, except in the driest areas, roost in large noisy colonies where they look like folded umbrellas hanging from the trees. In the evening they can be seen leaving the roost with slow measured wing beats. The much smaller **Indian pipistrelle** *(Pipistrellus coromandra)*, with a wing span of about 15 cm, is an insect eater. It comes into houses at dusk, roosting under eaves and has a fast, erratic flight. The **jackal** (*Canis aureus*), a lone scavenger in towns and villages, looks like a cross between a dog and a fox and varies in colour from shades of brown through to black. The bushy tail has a dark tip. The **common mongoose** (*Herpestes edwardsi*) lives in scrub and open jungle. It kills snakes, but will also take rats, mice and chicken. Tawny coloured with a grey grizzled tinge, it is about 90 cm in length, of which half is pale-tipped tail. The **sloth bear** (*Melursus ursinus*), about 75 cm at the shoulder, lives in broken forest, but may be seen on a lead accompanying a street entertainer who makes it 'dance' to music as a part of an act. They have a long snout, a pendulous lower lip and a shaggy black coat with a yellowish V-shaped mark on the chest. If you take a boat trip on the Ganga or the Brahmaputra rivers, look out for the fresh water **gangetic dolphin** (*Platanista gangetica*) as it comes to the surface to breathe.

Birds

Town and village birds Some birds perform a useful function scavenging and clearing refuse. One of the most widespread is the brown **pariah kite** (*Milvus migrans*, 65 cm). The more handsome chestnut and white **brahminy kite** (*Haliastur indus*, 48 cm) is largely confined to the waterside. The common brown **white-backed vulture** (*Gyps bengalensis*, 90 cm) looks ungainly and has a bare and scrawny head and neck. The smaller **scavenger vulture** (*Neophron percnopterus*, 65 cm) is mainly white, but often has dirty looking plumage and the bare head and neck of all vultures. In flight its wedge-shaped tail and black and white colouring are characteristic. The **house crow** (*Corvus splendens*, 45 cm) on the other hand is a very smart looking bird with a grey body and black tail, wings, face and throat. It occurs in almost every town and village in India. The **jungle crow** (*Corvus macrorhynchos*, 50 cm) originally a bird of the countryside has started to move into populated areas and in the hill stations tends to replace the house crow. Unlike the house crow it is a glossy black all over and has a much deeper, hoarser caw. The **feral pigeon**, or **blue rock dove** (*Columba livia*, 32 cm), found throughout the world, is generally a slaty grey in colour. It invariably has two dark bars on the wing and a white rump. The **little brown dove** (*Streptopelia senegalensis*, 25 cm) is bluey grey and brown above, with a pink head and underparts and a speckled pattern on the neck. The **collared dove** (*Streptopelia decaocto*, 30 cm) with a distinct half collar on the back of its neck, is common, especially in the drier parts of India. Bulbuls are common in gardens and parks. The **red-vented bulbul** (*Pycnonotus cafer*, 20 cm), a mainly brown bird, can be identified by the slight crest and a bright red patch under the tail. The **house sparrow** (*Passer domesticus*, 15 cm) can be seen in towns. The ubiquitous **common myna** (*Acridotheres tristis*, 22 cm), feeds on lawns, especially after rain or watering. Look for the white under the tail and the bare yellow skin around the eye, yellow bill and legs and in flight the large white wing patch. A less common, but more striking bird also seen feeding in open spaces, is the **hoopoe** (*Upupa epops*, 30 cm), easily identified by its sandy plumage with black and white stripes and long thin curved bill. The marvellous fan-shaped crest is sometimes raised. Finally there is a member of the cuckoo family which is heard more often than seen. The **koel** (*Eudynamys scolopacea*, 42 cm), is commonly heard during the hot weather – kuoo-kuoo-kuoo, the double note starts off low and flute-like, rises in pitch and intensity, then suddenly stops, only to start all over again. The male is all black with a greenish bill and a red eye; the female streaked and barred.

Water and waterside birds The *jheels* (marshes or swamps) of India form one of the richest bird habitats in the world. Cormorants abound; the commonest, the **little cormorant** (*Phalacrocorax niger*, 50 cm) is found on most inland waters. An almost entirely black bird with just a little white on the throat, it has a long tail and a hooked bill. The **coot** (*Fulica atra*, 40 cm), another common black bird, seen especially in winter has a noticeable white shield on the forehead. The magnificent **sarus crane** (*Grus antigone*, 150 cm) is one of India's tallest birds. It is widespread all year round across northern India, almost invariably in pairs. The bare red head and long red legs combined with its height and grey plumage make it easy to identify. The commonest migrant crane is probably the **common crane** (*Grus grus*, 120 cm), present only in winter, often in large flocks. It has mainly grey plumage with a black head and neck. There is a white streak running down the side of the neck and above the eye is a tuft of red feathers. The **openbill stork** (*Anastomus oscitans*, 80 cm) and the **painted stork** (*Ibis leucocephalus*, 100 cm) are common too and are spotted breeding in large colonies. The former is white with black wing feathers and a curiously shaped bill. The latter, mainly white, has a pinkish tinge on the back and dark marks on the wings and a broken black band on the lower chest. The bare yellow face and yellow down-curved bill are conspicuous. By almost every swamp, ditch or rice paddy up to about 1200 m you will see the **paddy bird** (*Ardeola grayii*, 45 cm). An inconspicuous, buff-coloured bird, it is easily overlooked as it stands hunched up by the waterside. As soon as it takes off, its white wings and rump make it very noticeable. The **bronze-winged jacana** (*Metopidius indicus*, 27 cm) has very long toes which enable it to walk on the floating leaves of water-lilies and there is a noticeable white streak over and above the eye. Village ponds often have their resident bird. The commonest and most widespread of the Indian kingfishers is the jewel-like **common kingfisher** (*Alcedo atthis*, 18 cm). With its brilliant blue upperparts and orange breast it is usually seen perched on a twig or a reed beside the water.

Open grassland, light woodland and cultivated land The **cattle egret** (*Bubulcus ibis*, 50 cm), a small white heron, is usually seen near herds of cattle, frequently perched on the backs of the animals. Equal in height to the sarus crane is the impressive, but ugly **adjutant stork** (*Leptopilos dubius*, 150 cm). This often dishevelled bird is a scavenger and is thus seen near rubbish dumps and carcasses. It has a naked red head and neck, a huge bill and a large fleshy pouch which hangs down the front of the neck. The **rose-ringed parakeet** (*Psittacula krameri*, 40 cm) is found throughout India up to about 1500 m while the **pied myna** (*Sturnus contra*, 23 cm) is restricted to northern and central India. The rose-ringed parakeet often forms huge flocks, an impressive sight coming in to roost. The long tail is noticeable both in flight and when the bird is perched. They can be very destructive to crops, but are attractive birds which are frequently kept as pets. The pied myna, with its smart black and white plumage is conspicuous, usually in small flocks in grazing land or cultivation. It feeds on the ground and on village rubbish dumps. The all black **drongo** (*Dicrurus adsimilis*, 30 cm) is almost invariably seen perched on telegraph wires or bare branches. Its distinctively forked tail makes it easy to identify. Weaver birds are a family of mainly yellow birds, all remarkable for the intricate nests they build. The most widespread is the **baya weaver** (*Ploceus philippinus*, 15 cm) which nest in large colonies, often near villages. The male in the breeding season combines a black face and throat with a contrasting yellow top of the head and the yellow breast band. In the non-breeding season both sexes are brownish sparrow-like birds.

Hill birds Land above about 1500 m supports a distinct range of species, although some birds, such as the ubiquitous **common myna**, are found in the highlands as well as in the lower lying terrain. The highland equivalent of the red-vented bulbul is the **white-cheeked bulbul** (*Pycnonotus leucogenys*, 20 cm) which is found in gardens and woodland in the Himalaya up to about 2500 m and as far south as Mumbai. It has white underparts with a yellow patch under the tail. The black head and white cheek patches are distinctive. The crest varies in length and is most prominent in birds found in Kashmir, where it is very common in gardens. The **red-whiskered bulbul** (*Pycnonotus jocosus*, 20 cm) is widespread in the Himalaya and the hills of South India up to about 2500 m. Its pronounced pointed crest, which is sometimes so long that it flops forward towards the bill, white underparts and red and white 'whiskers' serve to distinguish it. It has a red patch under the tail. In the summer the delightful **verditer flycatcher** (*Muscicapa thalassina*, 15 cm) is a common breeding bird in the Himalaya up to about 3000 m. It is tame and confiding, often builds its nest on verandas and is seen perching on telegraph wires. In winter it is more widely distributed throughout the country. It is an active little bird which flicks its tail up and down in a characteristic manner. The male is all bright blue green with somewhat darker wings and a black patch in front of the eyes. The female is similar, but duller. Another species associated with man is the **white wagtail** (*Motacilla alba*, 21 cm), very common in the Himalayan summer up to about 3000 m. It is found near water, by streams and lakes, on floating vegetation and among the house boats in Kashmir. Its black and white plumage and constantly wagging tail make it easy to identify. Yet another species common in Kashmir and in other Himalayan hill stations is the **red-billed blue magpie** (*Urocissa erythrorhyncha*, 65 cm). With a long tail and pale blue plumage, contrasting with its black head, it is usually seen in small flocks. This is not so much a garden bird, but prefers tea gardens, open woodland and cultivation. The highlands of India, especially the Himalaya, are the home of the ancestors of **domestic hens** and also of numerous beautiful **pheasants**. These are mainly forest dwellers and are not easy to see as they tend to be shy and wary of man. Last but not least, mention must be made of India's national bird, the magnificent and well-known **Peafowl** (*Pavo cristatus*, male 210 cm, female 100 cm), which is more commonly known as the peacock. Semi-domesticated birds are commonly seen and heard around towns and villages, especially in the northwest of India. In the wild it favours hilly jungles and dense scrub.

Reptiles and amphibians

India is famous for its reptiles, especially its snakes which feature in many stories and legends. In reality, snakes keep out of the way of people. One of the most common is the **Indian rock python** (*Python molurus*) a 'constrictor' which kills it's prey by suffocation. Usually about 4 m in length, they can be much longer. Their docile nature make them favourites of snake handlers. The other large snakes favoured by street entertainers are cobras. The various species all have a hood which is spread when the snake draws itself up to strike. They are all highly venomous and the snake charmers prudently de-fang them to render them harmless. The best known is probably the **spectacled cobra** (*Naja naja*), which has a mark like a pair of spectacles on the back of its hood. The largest venomous snake in the world is the **king cobra** (*Ophiophagus hannah*) which is 5 m in length. It is usually brown, but can vary from cream to black and lacks the spectacle marks of the other. In their natural state cobras are generally inhabitants of forest regions. Equally venomous, but much smaller, the **common krait** *(Bungarus caeruleus)* is just over 1 m in length. The slender, shiny, blue-black snake has thin white bands which can sometimes be almost indiscernible. They are found all over the country except in the northeast where the canniballistic **banded krait** with bold yellowish and black bands have virtually eradicated them. In houses everywhere you cannot fail to see the **gecko** (*Hemidactylus*). This small harmless, primitive lizard is active after dark. It lives in houses behind pictures and curtain rails and at night emerges to run across the walls and ceilings to hunt the night flying insects which form its main prey. It is not usually more than about 14 cm long, with a curiously transparent, pale yellowish brown body. At the other end of the scale is the **monitor lizard** (*Varanus*), which can grow to 2 m in length. They can vary from a colourful black and yellow, to plain or speckled brown. They live in different habitats from cultivation and scrub to waterside places and desert. The most widespread crocodile is the freshwater **mugger** or Marsh crocodile (*Crocodilus palustrus*) which grows to 3-4 m in length. The only similar fresh water species is the **gharial** (*Gavialis gangeticus*) which lives in large, fast flowing rivers. Twice the length of the mugger, it is a fish-eating crocodile with a long thin snout and, in the case of the male, an extraordinary bulbous growth on the end of the snout. The enormous, aggressive **estuarine** or **saltwater crocodile** (*Crocodilus porosus*) is now restricted to the brackish waters of the Sundarbans, on the east coast and in the Andaman and Nicobar Islands. It grows to 7 m long and is sleeker looking than the rather docile mugger.

Books

The literature on India is as huge and varied as the subcontinent itself. India is a good place to buy English language books as foreign books are often much cheaper than the published price. There are also cheap Indian editions and occasionally reprints of out-of-print books. There are excellent bookshops in all the major Indian cities. Below are a few suggestions.

Art and architecture

Burton, TR *Hindu Art*, British Museum P. Well illustrated; broad view of art and religion.
Cooper, I and Dawson, B *Traditional Buildings of India*, Thames & Hudson.
Michell, G *The Hindu Temple*, Univ of Chicago Press, 1988. An authoritative account of Hindu architectural development.
Ramaswami, NS *Temples of South India*, Chennai, Maps and Agencies, 1996, and **KR Srinivasan**'s *Temples of South India*, 3rd ed, New Delhi, National Book Trust, 1985, good background information.
Sterlin, H *Hindu India*. Köln, Taschen, 1998. Traces the development from early rock-cut shrines, detailing famous examples; clearly written, well illustrated.
Tillotson, G *The Rajput Palaces*, Yale, 1987; *Mughal architecture*, London, Viking, 1990; *The tradition of Indian architecture*, Yale 1989. Superbly clear writing on Indian architecture under Rajputs, Mughals and the British.

Cities, sites and places

Aurangabad

C Berkson *The caves of Aurangabad*, Mapin, Ahmadabad, 1986.

Delhi

Barton, G, and Malone, L *Old Delhi: 10 easy walks*. Delhi, Rupa, 1988. Interesting companion for exploring the old city, helpful maps.
Kaul, H, Ed *Historic Delhi: an anthology*. Delhi, OUP, 1985.
Miller, S *Delhi Adventures in a Megacity*. Penguin 2008. A non-fiction bestseller.
Sainty, S *Lost monuments of Delhi*. Delhi, Harper Collins, 1997. A booklet covering Islamic architecture in brief.
Sengupta, R *Delhi Metropolitan*. Penguin 2008.
Sharma, YD *Delhi and its neighbourhood*. Delhi, ASI, 1972. History, architecture and site details.

Dharamshala

Avedon *In exile from the land of the snows*.
Dalai Lama *My land and my people* and *Freedom in Exile*.

Norbu and Turnbull *Tibet: Its history, religion and people.*
Sogyal Rinpoche *The Tibetan Book of Living and Dying.*

Goa

Hutt, A *Goa: A Traveller's Historical and Architectural Guide.* Extensive and richly illustrated.
Rajagopalan, S, ASI's *Old Goa.*

Gujarat

Royal Families and Palaces of Gujarat. Scorpion Cavendish,1998. Beautifully produced.
Desai, SH *Junagadh and Girnar.*
Soundara Rajan, KV *Junagadh*, ASI booklet, 1985. Details the edicts and Buddhist caves on Uparkot.
Yagnik, A and Sheth, S *The Shaping of Modern Gujarat.* Penguin 2005.

Hampi

Longhurst's *Hampi Ruins.* Recommended.
Settar's *Hampi* (both at *Aspirations Bookshop*, Hampi Bazar).

Kanpur

Malgaonkar, M *The Devil's Wind: Nana Saheb's story*, 1988, New Delhi. Largely factual.
Trevelyan, GO *Cawnpore*, 1992, Delhi.

Khajuraho

Desai, D *Religious Imagery of Khajuraho.* Good ASI booklet by Krishna Deva, Rs 5. Detailed edition with colour plates, Rs 400. Mar 2000.
Punja *A Divine Ecstasy*, Viking (Penguin, India), 1992. Carries an original interpretation.

Kullu

Chetwode, P *Kulu, to the end of the habitable world*, John Murray, 1972. Chronicles her travels from Narkanda to Ani and over the Jalori Pass to Banjar and Aut in the Tirthan valley. Penelope passed away near Khanag in the 1990s.

Ladakh

Harres, H *Ladakh*, Innsbruck, 1980.
Harvey, A *A Journey in Ladakh*, London, 1983.
Norberg-Hodge, H *Ancient Futures: Learning from Ladakh*, Rider, London, 1992.
Paldang *Monasteries of Ladakh.*
Rizvi, J *Ladakh, Crossroads of High Asia*, OUP 1983.
Shipton, E *That Untravelled World.*
Singh, M *Himalayan art*, UNESCO, 1971.
Snellgrove, DL and Skorupski, T *The Cultural Heritage of Ladakh*, Aris & Phillips, Delhi, 1980.

Lucknow

Llewellyn-Jones, R *A fatal friendship: the Nawab, the British and the city of Lucknow*, 1992, OUP, Delhi. A lively guide to the city and its history. Her *A Very Ingenious Man* (1992, Delhi) follows the fortunes of Claude Martin.
Taylor, PJO *A Companion to the Indian Mutiny of 1857*, 1996, OUP, Delhi.

Recommended books about the 'Uprising':
Farrell, JG *The Siege of Krishnapur*, a funny and cynical novel.
Hibbert, C *The Great Mutiny: India 1857*, Penguin. A factual history.

Mahabalipuram

Lockwood, M *Mahabalipuram and the Pandavas* Madras, Christian Literature Soc, 1982.
Sivaramamurti, C *Mahabalipuram* 5th ed, New Delhi, Archaeological Survey of India, 1992.

Sanchi

Mitra, D, *Sanchi*, Archaeological Survey of India.

Shekhawati

Cooper, I, *The painted towns of Shekhawati*, Mapin, Allahabad, 1994. Photos and maps.
Rakesh, P and Lewis, K *Shekhawati: Rajasthan's painted houses.* Also well illustrated.

Shimla

Farrell, JG, *The Hill Station.* This last, unfinished novel describes colonial Shimla of 1871.
Kanwar, P *Imperial Simla: the political culture of the Raj*, OUP, New Delhi, 1990.
Scott, P *Staying On*, Booker Prize-winning novel set in post-Independence Shimla.

Varanasi

Gol *A Pilgrimage to Kashi*, Indica, 1999. An accessible cartoon strip; the city's history and culture as seen by modern-day visitors.
Rai, R *Varanasi: Portrait of a Civilization*, Harper Collins. Raghu Rai captures the heart and soul of life by the Ganga in his stunning photographs

West Bengal

Humphrey, K *Walking Calcutta*, Grosvenor House, 2009. A good way to discover the city, off the tourist trail.
Moorhouse, G *Calcutta*, 1971.
Winchester, S *Calcutta*, 2004.

Zanskar

Peissel, M *Zanskar, the Hidden Kingdom.*
Folloni, O *Zanskar, a Himalayan Kingdom.* Features superb photos.

Current affairs and politics

French, P *India: A Portrait*, Allen Lane. An intimate biography of 1.2 billion people.
Granta 57 *India: the Golden Jubilee*. Superb edition devoted to India's 50th anniversary of Independence, 22 international writers give brilliant snapshot accounts of India today.
Khilnani, S *The idea of India*, Penguin, 1997. Excellent introduction to contemporary India.
Naipaul, VS *A Million Mutinies Now*, Penguin, 1992. 'Revisionist' account of India turns away from the despondency of his earlier books (*An Area of darkness* and *India: a wounded civilisation*).
Silver, RB and Epstein, B *India: a mosaic.* New York, NYRB, 2000. Distinguished essays on history, politics and literature. Amartya Sen on Tagore, Pankaj Mishra on nuclear India.
Tharur, S *India: from midnight to the millennium.* Viking, 1997.
Tully, M *No full stops in India*, Viking, 1991. An often superbly observed but controversially interpreted view of contemporary India.

History: medieval and modern

Beames, J *Memoirs of a Bengal Civilian.* A readable insight into the British Raj in the post-Mutiny period, London, Eland, 1991.
Dalrymple, W *White Mughals*, Harper Collins, 2002. The early days of the East India Company (his later book *The Last Mughal* is not quite as readable).
Edwardes, M *The Myth of the Mahatma.* Presents Gandhi in a whole new light.
Gandhi, R *The Good Boatman* Viking/Penguin 1995. An excellent biography by one of Gandhi's noted grandson's.
Gascoigne, B *The Great Moghuls*, London, Cape, 1987.
Giridharadas, A *India Calling* Harper Collins, 2011. Highly readable account of the rapid changes occurring in Indian society.
Keay, J *India: a History*, Harper Collins, 2000. A major new popular history of the subcontinent.
Nehru, J *The discovery of India*, New Delhi, ICCR, 1976.
Robinson, F (ed) *Cambridge Encyclopaedia of India*, Cambridge, 1989. An introduction to many aspects of South Asian society.
Spear, P and Thapar, R *A history of India*, 2 vols, Penguin, 1978.
Wolpert, S *A new history of India*, OUP 1990.

History: pre- and early history

Allchin, B and R *Origins of a civilisation*, Viking, Penguin Books, 1997. The most authoritative up-to-date survey of the origins of Indian civilizations.
Basham, AL *The Wonder that was India*, London, Sidgwick & Jackson, 1985. One of the most comprehensive and readable accounts of the development of India's culture.

Language

Snell, R and Weightman, S *Teach Yourself Hindi.* An excellent, accessible teaching guides with cassette tapes.
Yule, H and Burnell, AC (eds) *Hobson-Jobson*, 1886. New paperback edition, 1986. A delightful insight into Anglo-Indian words and phrases.

Literature

Adiga, A *White Tiger.* HarperCollins India, 2008. Controversial take on the complexities of modern Indian society.
Anand, MJ *Untouchable.* Penguin Classics, 1935. A day in the life of a casteless toilet-sweeper.
Chatterjee, U *English August.* London, Faber, 1988. A wry modern account of an Indian civil servant's year in a rural posting.
Chaudhuri, N Vivid, witty and often sharply critical accounts of India across the 20th century. *The autobiography of an unknown Indian*, Macmillan, London; *Thy Hand, Great Anarch!*, London, Chatto & Windus, 1987.
Desai, K *The Inheritance of Loss.* Hamish Hamilton, 2006. Set in Kalimpong in the 1980s during the Gorkha uprising.
Ghosh, A *The Hungry Tide.* HarperCollins, 2005. A sweet novel set in the Sunderbans.

Kanga, F *Trying to Grow*, Bloomsbury, 1989. Mumbai life seen through the experiences of a Parsi family.

Mistry, R *A Fine Balance*. Faber, 1995. A tale of the struggle to survive in the modern Indian city.

Narayan, RK Gentle and humorous novels and stories of South India: *The Man-eater of Malgudi* and *Under the Banyan Tree and Other Stories*, *Grandmother's Stories*, London, Penguin, 1985.

Ramanuja, AK: *The collected essays*. Ed by V Dhawadker. New Delhi, OUP, 1999. Brilliant essays on Indian culture and literature.

Roberts, GD *Shantaram*. Scribe Publications, 2003. A compelling, apparently true and often beautifully written account of an escaped convict's life in the Mumbai underworld. A real page-turner.

Roy, A *The God of Small Things*. Indian Ink/Harper Collins, 1997. Excellent first novel about family turmoil in a Syrian Christian household in Kerala.

Rushdie, S *Midnight's Children*, London, Picador, 1981. India since Independence, with funny and sharp critiques of South Asian life in the 1980s. *The Moor's Last Sigh*, Viking, 1996, is of particular interest to those travelling to Kochi and Mumbai.

Scott, P *The Raj Quartet*, London, Panther, 1973; *Staying on*, Longmans, 1985. Outstand- ingly perceptive novels of the end of the Raj.

Seth, V *A Suitable Boy*, Phoenix House London, 1993. Prize-winning novel of modern Indian life.

Theroux, Paul. *A Dead Hand. A Crime in Calcutta*. Hamish Hamilton 2009. A murder-mystery set in Calcutta that will interest volunteers and cynics alike.

Weightman, S (ed) *Travellers Literary Companion: the Indian Sub-continent*. Invaluable introduction to the diversity of Indian writing.

Music and cinema

Menon, RR *Penguin Dictionary of Indian Classical Music*, Penguin New Delhi 1995.

Mohan, L *Bollywood, Popular Indian Cinema*, Joshi (Dakini).

People

Bumiller, E *May you be the mother of one hundred sons*, Penguin, 1991. An American woman journalists' account of coming to understand the issues that face India's women.

Dalrymple, W *Nine Lives*, Bloomsbury. Insight into the spirited and spiritual lives of 9 individuals in modern India.

Holmstrom, L *The Inner Courtyard*. A series of short stories by Indian women, translated into English, Rupa, 1992.

Lewis, N *A goddess in the stones*. An insight into tribal life in Orissa and Bihar.

Lloyd, S *An Indian Attachment*, London, Eland, 1992. A very personal and engaging account of time spent in an Indian village.

Varma, PK *Being Indian*. Penguin 2004.

Religion

Doniger O'Flaherty, W *Hindu Myths*, London, Penguin, 1974. A sourcebook translated from the Sanskrit.

Jain, JP *Religion and Culture of the Jains*, 3rd ed. New Delhi, Bharatiya Jnanapith, 1981.

Qureshi, IH *The Muslim Community of the Indo-Pakistan Sub-Continent 610-1947*, OUP, Karachi, 1977.

Rahula, W *What the Buddha Taught*.

Singh, H *The heritage of the Sikhs*, 2nd ed, New Delhi, 1983.

Waterstone, R *India, the cultural companion*, Duncan Baird, Winchester, 2002. India's spiritual traditions brought up to date, well illustrated.

Zaehner, RC *Hinduism*, OUP.

Travel

Dalrymple, W *City of Djinns*, Indus/Harper Collins, 1993, paperback. Superb account of Delhi, based on a year living in the city. *The Age of Kali*, published in edited form in India as *In the court of the fish-eyed Goddess*, is his second anecdotal but insightful account.

Fishlock, T *Cobra Road.*,London, John Murray, 1991. Impressions of a news journalist.

Frater, A *Chasing the monsoon*, London, Viking, 1990. Prize-winning account of the human impact of the monsoon's sweep across India.

Hatt, J *The tropical traveller: the essential guide to travel in hot countries*, Penguin, 3rd ed, 1992. Wide ranging and clearly written, based on extensive experience and research.

Keay, J *Into India*, London, John Murray, 1999. Seasoned traveller's introduction to under- standing and enjoying India.

Parkes, F *Begums, Thugs and White Mughals.* Eland, 2001. Journals of an intrepid lady traveller during the early days of the Raj.

Trekking

Aitken, B *The Nanda Devi Affair*, Penguin India, 1994.
Bonnington, C *Annapurna South Face*, London, Cassell, 1971; Everest the hard way, London, Hodder & Stoughton, 1979.
P Chabloz N Cremieu *Hiking in Zanskar and Ladakh*, Geneva, Olizane, 1986.
Hardy, J *The Ochre Border*, 1995, Constable, London. An account of crossing the Puri Parvati Pass from Kullu to Spiti.
Hillary, E *High Adventure*, New York, Dutton, 1955. Classic account of Himalayan climbs.
Kapadia, H *Spiti: Adventures in the Trans-Himalaya*, 1996, Indus.
Khosla, GD *Himalayan Circuit*, 1989, OUP. An early account of travel into this then virtually unknown region of Kinnaur and Spiti.
Loram, C *Leh & Trekking in Ladakh*, 1996, Trailblazer, Hindhead, Surrey.
Salkeld, A *The History of Great Climbs*, 1995, The Royal Geographical Society. A magnificently illustrated and written account of historic climbs.
Sax, W *Mountain Goddess*, OUP, 1991. About Nanda Devi.
Swadi, D and Sanan, D *Exploring Kinnaur and Spiti in the Trans-Himalaya*, 1998, Indus.

More practical publications include:
Chand, G and Puri, M *Explore Himachal*, New Delhi, International Publishers, 1991. Descriptions of 110 routes and 27 detailed trekking maps.
Iozawa, T *Trekking in the Himalayas*, Delhi, Allied Publishers, 1980. *Nest & Wings*, Post Box 4531, New Delhi 110016, T011-644 2245: 'Trekking', 'Holiday & Trekking' and 'Trekking Map' titles (Rs 40-140) cover most trekking destinations in the Indian Himalaya; trekking itineraries are listed in brief but some booklets give additional insight into the history and culture of the area.
Swift, H *Trekking in Pakistan and India*, London, Hodder & Stoughton, 1990. Detailed practical guide, based on first hand experience.

Also useful are:
Himalayan Club's *Himalayan Journal* (annual) from PO Box 1905, Mumbai 400001.
Indian Mountaineering Foundation's Indian Mountaineer from Benito Juarez Rd, New Delhi 110021. *Peaks and passes of the Garhwal Himalaya* published by Alpinists Club, 1990.

Wildlife and vegetation

Ali, S *Indian hill birds*, OUP.
Ali, Sand Dillon Ripley, S *Handbook of the birds of India & Pakistan* (compact ed).
Cowen, DV *Flowering Trees and Shrubs in India.*
Ewans, M *Bharatpur: Bird Paradise*, Lustre Press, Delhi.
Grimmet, R, and Inskipp, C and T *Pocket guide to Birds of the Indian Sub-Continent.* 1999.
Ives, R *Of tigers and men*, Doubleday, 1995.
Kazmierczak, K and Singh, R *A birdwatcher's guide to India*. Prion, 1998, Sandy, Beds, UK. Well researched and carrying lots of practical information for all birders.
Nair, SM *Endangered animals of India*, New Delhi, NBT, 1992.
Polunin, O and Stainton, A *Flowers of the Himalaya*, OUP, 1984.
Prater, SH *The Book of Indian Animals.*
Sippy, S and Kapoor, S *The Ultimate Ranthambhore Guide*, 2001. Informative, practical guide stressing conservation.
Thapar and Rathore *Wild tigers of Ranthambhore* OUP, 2000.

Footnotes

Contents

Language

Hindi words and phrases

Pronunciation

a as in *ah* i as in *bee*
nasalized vowels are shown as an *un*
o as in *oh* u as *oo* in book

Basics

Hello, good morning, goodbye *namaste*
Thank you/no thank you *dhanyavad* or *shukriya/ nahin shukriya*
Excuse me, sorry *maf kijiye*
Yes/no *ji han/ji nahin*
Never mind/that's all right *koi bat nahin*

Questions

What is your name? *apka nam kya hai?*
My name is ... *mera nam... Hai*
Pardon? *phir bataiye?*
How are you? *kya hal hai?*
I am well, thanks, and you? *main thik hun, aur ap?*
Not very well *main thik nahin hun*
Where is the...? *kahan hai...?*
Who is? *kaun hai?*
What is this? *yeh kya hai?*

Shopping

How much? *Kitna?*
That makes (20) rupees *(bis) rupaye*
That is very expensive! *bahut mahanga hai!*
Make it a bit cheaper! *thora kam kijiye!*

The hotel

What is the room charge? *kiraya kitna hai?*
Please show the room *kamra dikhaiye*
Is there an air-conditioned room? *kya a/c kamra hai?*
Is there hot water? *garam pani hai?*
... a bathroom/fan/ mosquito net *... bathroom/pankha/ machhar dani*
Is there a large room? *bara kamra hai?*
Please clean it *saf karwa dijiye*
Are there clean sheets/ blanket? *saf chadaren/ kambal hain?*
Bill please *bill dijiye*

Travel

Where's the railway station? *railway station kahan hai?*
How much is the ticket to Agra? *Agra ka ticket kitne ka hai?*
When does the Agra bus leave? *Agra bus kab jaegi?*
How much? *Kitna?*
Left/right *baien/dahina*
Go straight on *sidha chaliye*
Nearby *nazdik*
Please wait here *yahan thahariye*
Please come at 8 *ath bajai ana*
Quickly *jaldi*
Stop *rukiye*

Restaurants

Please show the menu *menu dikhaiye*
No chillies please *mirch nahin dalna*
...sugar/milk/ice *...chini/ doodh/baraf*
A bottle of water please *ek botal pani dijiye*
Sweet/savoury *mitha/ namkin*
Spoon, fork, knife *chamach, kanta, chhuri*

Time and days

right now *abhi*
month *mahina*
morning *suba*
year *sal*
afternoon *dopahar*
evening *sham*
night *rat*
today *aj*
tomorrow/yesterday *kal/kal*
day *din*
week *hafta*
Sunday *ravivar*
Monday *somvar*
Tuesday *mangalvar*
Wednesday *budhvar*
Thursday *virvar*
Friday *shukravar*
Saturday *shanivar*

Numbers

1	*ek*	2	*do*
3	*tin*	4	*char*
5	*panch*	6	*chhai*
7	*sat*	8	*ath*
9	*nau*	10	*das*
11	*gyara*	12	*barah*
13	*terah*	14	*chaudah*
15	*pandrah*	16	*solah*
17	*satrah*	18	*atharah*
19	*unnis*	20	*bis*
100/200		*sau/do sau*	
1000/2000		*hazar/ do hazar*	
100,000		*lakh*	

Basic vocabulary

Words such as airport, bank, bathroom, bus, doctor, embassy, ferry, hotel, hospital, juice, police, restaurant, station, stamp, taxi, ticket, train are used locally though often pronounced differently eg *daktar, haspatal.*
and *aur*
big *bara*
café/food stall *dhaba/hotel*
chemist *dawai ki dukan*
clean *saf*

closed *band*
cold *thanda*
day *din*
dirty *ganda*
English *angrezi*
excellent *bahut achha*
food/ to eat *khana*
hot (spicy) *jhal, masaledar*
hot (temp) *garam*
luggage *saman*
medicine *dawai*
newspaper *akhbar*
of course, sure *zaroor*
open *khula*
police station *thana*
road *rasta*
room *kamra*
shop *dukan*
sick (ill) *bimar*
silk *reshmi/silk*
small *chhota*
that *who*
this *yeh*
town *shahar*
water *pani*
what *kya*
when *kab*
where *kahan/kidhar*
which/who *kaun*
why *kiun*
with *ke sathh*

Food and drink

Eating out is normally cheap and safe but menus can often be dauntingly long and full of unfamiliar names. Here are some Hindi words to help you.

Meat and fish

chicken *murgh*
fish *macchli*
meat *gosht, mas*
prawns *jhinga*

Vegetables (sabzi)

aubergine *baingan*
cabbage *band gobi*
carrots *gajar*
cauliflower *phool gobi*
mushroom *khumbhi*
onion *piaz*
okra, ladies' fingers *bhindi*
peas *matar*
potato *aloo*
spinach *sag*

Styles of cooking

Many items on restaurant menus are named according to methods of preparation, roughly equivalent to terms such as 'Provençal' or 'sauté'.

bhoona in a thick, fairly spicy sauce
chops minced meat, fish or vegetables, covered with mashed potato, crumbed and fried
cutlet minced meat, fish, vegetables formed into flat rounds or ovals, crumbed and fried (eg prawn cutlet, flattened king prawn)
do piaza with onions (added twice during cooking)
dum pukht steam baked
jhal frazi spicy, hot sauce with tomatoes and chillies
jhol thin gravy (Bengali)
Kashmiri cooked with mild spices, ground almonds and yoghurt, often with fruit
kebab skewered (or minced and shaped) meat or fish; a dry spicy dish cooked on a fire
kima minced meat (usually 'mutton')
kofta minced meat or vegetable balls
korma in fairly mild rich sauce using cream/yoghurt
masala marinated in spices (fairly hot)
Madras hot
makhani in butter rich sauce
moli South Indian dishes cooked in coconut milk and green chilli sauce
Mughlai rich North Indian style
Nargisi dish using boiled eggs
navratan curry ('9 jewels') colourful mixed vegetables and fruit in mild sauce
Peshwari rich with dried fruit and nuts (northwest Indian)
tandoori baked in a tandoor (special clay oven) or one imitating it
tikka marinated meat pieces, baked quite dry
vindaloo hot and sour Goan meat dish using vinegar

Typical dishes

aloo gosht potato and mutton stew
aloo gobi dry potato and cauliflower with cumin
aloo, matar, kumbhi potato, peas, mushrooms in a dryish mildly spicy sauce
bhindi bhaji okra fried with onions and mild spices
boti kebab marinated pieces of meat, skewered and cooked over a fire
dhal makhani lentils cooked with butter
dum aloo potato curry with a spicy yoghurt, tomato and onion sauce
matar panir curd cheese cubes with peas and spices (and often tomatoes)
murgh massallam chicken in creamy marinade of yoghurt, spices and herbs with nuts

nargisi kofta boiled eggs covered in minced lamb, cooked in a thick sauce
rogan josh rich, mutton/beef pieces in creamy, red sauce
sag panir drained curd (panir) sautéd with chopped spinach in mild spices
sarson-ke-sag and makkai-ki-roti mustard leaf cooked dry with spices served with maize four roti from Punjab
shabdeg a special Mughlai mutton dish with vegetables
yakhni lamb stew

Rice

bhat/sada chawal plain boiled rice
biriyani partially cooked rice layered over meat and baked with saffron
khichari rice and lentils cooked with turmeric and other spices
pulao/pilau fried rice cooked with spices (cloves, cardamom, cinnamon) with dried fruit, nuts or vegetables. Sometimes cooked with meat, like a biriyani

Roti – breads

chapati (roti) thin, plain, wholemeal unleavened bread cooked on a tawa (griddle), usually made from ata (wheat flour). Makkaikiroti is with maize flour.
nan oven baked (traditionally in a tandoor) white flour leavened bread often large and triangular; sometimes stuffed with almonds and dried fruit
paratha fried bread layered with ghi (sometimes cooked with egg or with potatoes)
poori thin deep-fried, puffed rounds of flour

Sweets

These are often made with reduced/thickened milk, drained curd cheese or powdered lentils and nuts. They are sometimes covered with a flimsy sheet of decorative, edible silver leaf.
barfi fudge-like rectangles/diamonds
gulab jamun dark fried spongy balls, soaked in syrup
halwa rich sweet made from cereal, fruit, vegetable, nuts and sugar
khir, payasam, paesh thickened milk rice/ vermicelli pudding
kulfi cone-shaped Indian ice cream with pistachios/ almonds, uneven in texture
jalebi spirals of fried batter soaked in syrup
laddoo lentil based batter 'grains' shaped into rounds
rasgulla (roshgulla) balls of curd in clear syrup
sandesh dry sweet made of curd cheese

Snacks

bhaji, pakora vegetable fritters (onions, potatoes, cauliflower, etc) deep-fried in batter
chat sweet and sour fruit and vegetables flavoured with tama rind paste and chillies
chana choor, chioora ('Bombay mix') lentil and flattened rice snacks mixed with nuts and dried fruit
dosai South Indian pancake made with rice and lentil flour; served with a mild potato and onion filling (masala dosai) or without (ravai or plain dosai)
iddli steamed South Indian rice cakes, a bland breakfast given flavour by spiced accompaniments
kachori fried pastry rounds stuffed with spiced lentil/ peas/potato filling
samosa cooked vegetable or meat wrapped in pastry triangles and deep fried
utthappam thick South Indian rice and lentil flour pancake cooked with spices/onions/ tomatoes
vadai deep fried, small savoury lentil 'doughnut' rings. Dahi vada are similar rounds in yoghurt

Glossary

Words in italics are common elements of words, often making up part of a place name

A

aarti (arati) Hindu worship with lamps
abacus square or rectangular table resting on top of a pillar
abad peopled
acanthus thick-leaved plant, common decoration on pillars, esp Greek
achalam hill (Tamil)
acharya religious teacher
Adi Granth Guru Granth Sahib, holy book of the Sikhs
Adinatha first of the 24 Tirthankaras, distinguished by his bull mount
agarbathi incense
Agastya legendary sage who brought the Vedas to South India
Agni Vedic fire divinity, intermediary between gods and men; guardian of the Southeast
ahimsa non-harming, non-violence
akhand path unbroken reading of the Guru Granth Sahib
alinda veranda
ambulatory processional path
amla/amalaka circular ribbed pattern (based on a gourd) at the top of a temple tower
amrita ambrosia; drink of immortality
ananda joy
Ananda the Buddha's chief disciple
Ananta a huge snake on whose coils Vishnu rests
anda literally 'egg', spherical part of the stupa
Andhaka demon killed by Siva
anicut irrigation channel (Tamil)
anna (ana) one 16th of a rupee (still occasionally referred to)
Annapurna Goddess of abundance; one aspect of Devi
antarala vestibule, chamber in front of shrine or cella
antechamber chamber in front of the sanctuary
apsara celestial nymph
apse semi-circular plan
arabesque ornamental decoration with intertwining lines
aram pleasure garden
architrave horizontal beam across posts or gateways
ardha mandapam chamber in front of main hall of temple
Ardhanarisvara Siva represented as half-male and half-female
Arjuna hero of the Mahabharata, to whom Krishna delivered the Bhagavad Gita
arrack alcoholic spirit fermented from potatoes or grain
aru river (Tamil)
Aruna charioteer of Surya, Sun God; Red
Aryans literally 'noble' (Sanskrit); prehistoric peoples who settled in Persia and North India
asana a seat or throne (Buddha's) pose
ashram hermitage or retreat
Ashta Matrikas The eight mother goddesses who attended on Siva or Skanda
astanah threshold
atman philosophical concept of universal soul or spirit
atrium court open to the sky in the centre In modern architecture, enclosed in glass
aus summer rice crop (Apr-Aug) Bengal
Avalokiteshwara Lord who looks down; Bodhisattva, the Compassionate
avatara 'descent'; incarnation of a divinity
ayacut irrigation command area (Tamil)
ayah nursemaid, especially for children

B

babu clerk
bada cubical portion of a temple up to the roof or spire
badgir rooftop structure to channel cool breeze into the house (mainly North and West India)
badlands eroded landscape
bagh garden
bahadur title, meaning 'the brave'
baksheesh tip 'bribe'
Balabhadra Balarama, elder brother of Krishna
baluster (balustrade) a small column supporting a handrail
bandh a strike
bandhani tie dyeing (West India)
Bangla (Bangaldar) curved roof, based on thatched roofs in Bengal
bania merchant caste
banian vest
baoli or vav rectangular well surrounded by steps
baradari literally 'twelve pillared', a pavilion with columns
barrel-vault semi-cylindrical shaped roof or ceiling
bas-relief carving of low projection
basement lower part of walls, usually with decorated mouldings
basti Jain temple
batter slope of a wall, especially in a fort
bazar market
bedi (vedi) altar/platform for reading holy texts
begum Muslim princess/ woman's courtesy title
beki circular stone below the amla in the finial of a roof
belvedere summer house; small room on a house roof
bhabar coarse alluvium at foot of Himalayas

bhadra flat face of the sikhara (tower)
Bhadrakali Tantric goddess and consort of Bhairav
Bhagavad-Gita Song of the Lord; section of the Mahabharata
Bhagiratha the king who prayed to Ganga to descend to earth
bhai brother
Bhairava Siva, the Fearful
bhakti adoration of a deity
bhang Indian hemp
bharal Himalayan blue sheep
Bharata half-brother of Rama
bhavan building or house
bhikku Buddhist monk
Bhima Pandava hero of the Mahabharata, famous for his strength
Bhimsen Deity worshipped for his strength and courage
bhisti a water-carrier
bhogamandapa the refectory hall of a temple
bhumi literally earth; a horizontal moulding of a sikhara
bidi (beedi) Indian cigarette, tobacco wrapped in tendu leaves
bigha measure of land – normally about one-third of an acre
bo-tree (or Bodhi) *Ficus religiosa*, pipal tree associated with the Buddha
Bodhisattva Enlightened One, destined to become Buddha
bodi tuft of hair on back of the shaven head (also *tikki*)
Brahma Universal self-existing power; Creator in the Hindu Triad.
Brahmachari religious student, accepting rigorous discipline (eg chastity)
Brahman (Brahmin) highest Hindu (and Jain) caste of priests
Brahmanism ancient Indian religion, precursor of modern Hinduism
Buddha The Enlightened One; founder of Buddhism
bund an embankment
bundh (literally closed) a strike
burj tower or bastion
burqa (burkha) over-dress worn by Muslim women observing purdah
bustee slum

C

cantonment planned military or civil area in town
capital upper part of a column
caryatid sculptured human female figure used as a support for columns
catamaran log raft, logs (*maram*) tied (*kattu*) together (Tamil)
cave temple rock-cut shrine or monastery
cella small chamber, compartment for the image of a deity
cenotaph commemorative monument, usually an open domed pavilion
chaam Himalayan Buddhist masked dance
chadar sheet worn as clothing
chai tea
chaitya large arched opening in the façade of a hall or Buddhist temple
chajja overhanging cornice or eaves
chakra sacred Buddhist wheel of the law; also Vishnu's discus
chala Bengali curved roof
Chamunda terrifying form of the goddess Durga
Chandra Moon; a planetary deity
chankramana place of the promenade of the Buddha at Bodh Gaya
chapati unleavened Indian bread cooked on a griddle
chaprassi messenger or orderly usually wearing a badge
char sand-bank or island in a river
char bagh formal Mughal garden, divided into quarters
char bangla (char-chala) 'four temples' in Bengal, built like huts
charan footprint
charka spinning wheel
charpai 'four legs' – wooden frame string bed
chatt(r)a ceremonial umbrella on stupa (Buddhist)
chauki recessed space between pillars: entrance
chaukidar (chowkidar) night-watchman; guard
chaultri (choultry) travellers' rest house (Telugu)
chaumukha Jain sanctuary with a quadruple image, approached through four doorways
chauri fly-whisk, symbol for royalty
chauth 25% tax raised for revenue by Marathas
cheri outcaste settlement; slum (Tamil Nadu)
chhang strong mountain beer of fermented barley maize rye or millet or rice
chhatri umbrella shaped dome or pavilion
chhetri (kshatriya) Hindu warrior caste
chikan shadow embroidery on fine cotton (especially in Lucknow)
chikki nut crunch, a speciality of Lonavla
chit sabha hall of wisdom (Tamil)
chitrakar picture maker
chlorite soft greenish stone that hardens on exposure
chogyal heavenly king (Sikkim)
choli blouse
chorten Himalayan Buddhist relic shrine or a memorial stupa
chowk (chauk) a block; open place in a city where the market is held
chunam lime plaster or stucco made from burnt seashells
circumambulation clockwise movement around a shrine
clerestory upper section of the walls of a building which allows light in
cloister passage usually around an open square
coir fibre from coconut husk

corbel horizontal block supporting a vertical structure or covering an opening
cornice horizontal band at the top of a wall
crenellated having battlements
crewel work chain stitching
crore 10 million
cupola small dome
curvilinear gently curving shape, generally of a tower
cusp, cusped projecting point between small sections of an arch

D

dacoit bandit
dada (dadu) grandfather; elder brother
dado part of a pedestal between its base and cornice
dahi yoghurt
dais raised platform
dak bungalow resthouse for officials
dak post
dakini sorceress
Dakshineshvara Lord of the South; name of Siva
dan gift
dandi wooden 'seat' carried by bearers
darbar (durbar) a royal gathering
dargah a Muslim tomb complex
darshan (darshana) viewing of a deity or spiritual leader
darwaza gateway, door
Dasara (dassara/dussehra/dassehra) 10-day festival (Sep-Oct)
Dasaratha King of Ayodhya and father of Rama
Dattatraya syncretistic deity; an incarnation of Vishnu, a teacher of Siva, or a cousin of the Buddha
daulat khana treasury
dentil small block used as part of a cornice
deodar Himalayan cedar; from deva-daru, the 'wood of the gods'
dervish member of Muslim brotherhood, committed to poverty
deul in Bengal and Orissa, generic name for temple; the sanctuary
deval memorial pavilion built to mark royal funeral pyre
devala temple or shrine (Buddhist or Hindu)
devasthanam temple trust
Devi Goddess; later, the Supreme Goddess
dhaba roadside restaurant (mainly North India) truck drivers' stop
dhal lentils, pulses
dhansak Parsi dish made with lentils
dharamshala (dharamsala) pilgrims' rest house
dharma moral and religious duty
dharmachakra wheel of 'moral' law (Buddhist)
dhobi washerman
dhol drums
dhooli (dhooli) swinging chair on a pole, carried by bearers
dhoti loose loincloth worn by Indian men
dhyana meditation
digambara literally 'sky-clad' Jain sect in which the monks go naked
dighi village pond (Bengal)
dikka raised platform around ablution tank
dikpala guardian of one of the cardinal directions mostly appearing in a group of eight
dikshitar person who makes oblations or offerings
dipdan lamp pillar
distributary river that flows away from main channel
divan (diwan) smoking-room; also a chief minister
Diwali festival of lights (Oct-Nov)
diwan chief financial minister
diwan-i-am hall of public audience
diwan-i-khas hall of private audience
do-chala rectangular Bengali style roof
doab interfluve, land between two rivers
dokra tribal name for lost wax metal casting (cire perdu)
dosai (dosa) thin pancake
double dome composed of an inner and outer shell of masonry
Draupadi wife-in-common of the five Pandava brothers in the Mahabharata
drug (durg) fort (Tamil, Telugu)
dry masonry stones laid without mortar
duar (dwar) door, gateway
dun valley
dupatta long scarf worn by Punjabi women
Durga principal goddess of the Shakti cult
durrie (dhurrie) thick handloom rug
durwan watchman
dvarpala doorkeeper
dvipa lamp-column, generally of stone or brass-covered wood

E

eave overhang that shelters a porch or veranda
ek the number 1, a symbol of unity
ekka one horse carriage
epigraph carved inscription
eri tank (Tamil)

F

faience coloured tilework, earthenware or porcelain
fakir Muslim religious mendicant
fan-light fan-shaped window over door
fenestration with windows or openings
filigree ornamental work or delicate tracery
finial emblem at the summit of a stupa, tower, dome, or at the end of a parapet
firman edict or grant issued by a sovereign
foliation ornamental design derived from foliage
frieze horizontal band of figures or decorative designs

G

gable end of an angled roof
gadba woollen blanket (Kashmir)
gaddi throne
gadi/gari car, cart, train
gali (galli) lane; an alley
gana child figures in art
Gandharva semi-divine flying figure; celestial musician
Ganesh (Ganapati) elephant-headed son of Siva and Parvati
Ganga goddess personifying the Ganges
ganj market
ganja Indian hemp
gaon village
garbhagriha literally 'womb-chamber'; a temple sanctuary
garh fort
Garuda Mythical eagle, half-human Vishnu's vehicle
Gauri 'Fair One'; Parvati
Gaurishankara Siva with Parvati
ghagra (ghongra) long flared skirt
ghanta bell
ghat hill range, hill road; landing place; steps on the river bank
ghazal Urdu lyric poetry/love songs, often erotic
ghee clarified butter for cooking
gherao industrial action, surrounding home or office of politician or industrial manager
giri hill
Gita Govinda Jayadeva's poem of the Krishnalila
godown warehouse
gola conical-shaped storehouse
gompa Tibetan Buddhist monastery
goncha loose woollen robe, tied at waist with wide coloured band (Ladakh)
Gopala (Govinda) cowherd; a name of Krishna
Gopis cowherd girls; milk maids who played with Krishna
gopuram towered gateway in South Indian temples
Gorakhnath historically, an 11th-century yogi who founded a Saivite cult; an incarnation of Siva
gosain monk or devotee (Hindi)
gram chick pea, pulse
gram village; gramadan, gift of village
gudi temple (Karnataka)
gumbaz (gumbad) dome
gumpha monastery, cave temple
gur gur salted butter tea (Ladakh)
gur palm sugar
guru teacher; spiritual leader, Sikh religious leader
gurudwara (literally 'entrance to the house of God'); Sikh religious complex

H

Haj (Hajj) annual Muslim pilgrimage to Mecca
hakim judge; a physician (usually Muslim)
halwa a special sweetmeat
hammam Turkish bath
handi Punjabi dish cooked in a pot
Hanuman Monkey devotee of Rama; bringer of success to armies
Hara (Hara Siddhi) Siva
harem women's quarters (Muslim), from 'haram', Arabic for 'forbidden by law'
Hari Vishnu Harihara, Vishnu-Siva as a single divinity
Hariti goddess of prosperity and patroness of children, consort of Kubera
harmika the finial of a stupa in the form of a pedestal where the shaft of the honorific umbrella was set
hartal general strike
Hasan the murdered eldest son of Ali, commemorated at Muharram
hat (haat) market
hathi (hati) elephant
hathi pol elephant gate
hauz tank or reservoir
haveli a merchant's house usually in Rajasthan
havildar army sergeant
hawa mahal palace of the winds
Hidimba Devi Durga worshipped at Manali
hindola swing
hippogryph fabulous griffin-like creature with body of a horse
Hiranyakashipu Demon king killed by Narasimha
hiti a water channel; a bath or tank with water spouts
Holi spring festival (Feb-Mar)
hookah 'hubble bubble' or smoking vase
howdah seat on elephant's back, sometimes canopied
hundi temple offering
Hussain the second murdered son of Ali, commemorated at Muharram
huzra a Muslim tomb chamber
hypostyle hall with pillars

I

Iat pillar, column
icon statue or image of worship
Id principal Muslim festivals
iddli steamed rice cake (Tamil)
Idgah open space for the Id prayers
ikat 'resist-dyed' woven fabric
imam Muslim religious leader
imambara tomb of a Shiite Muslim holy man; focus of Muharram procession
Indra King of the gods; God of rain; guardian of the East
Ishana Guardian of the Northeast
Ishvara Lord; Siva
iwan main arch in mosque

J

jadu magic
jaga mohan audience hall or ante-chamber of an Orissan temple
Jagadambi literally Mother of the World; Parvati
Jagannath literally Lord of the World; particularly, Krishna worshipped at Puri

jagati railed parapet
jaggery brown sugar, made from palm sap
jahaz ship: building in form of ship
jali literally 'net'; any lattice or perforated pattern
jamb vertical side slab of doorway
Jambudvipa Continent of the Rose-Apple Tree; the earth
Jami masjid (Jama, Jumma) Friday mosque, for congregational worship
Jamuna Hindu goddess who rides a tortoise; river
Janaka Father of Sita
jangha broad band of sculpture on the outside of the temple wall
jarokha balcony
jataka stories accounts of the previous lives of the Buddha
jatra Bengali folk theatre
jauhar (jauhar) mass suicide by fire of women, particularly in Rajasthan, to avoid capture
jawab literally 'answer,' a building which duplicates another to provide symmetry
jawan army recruit, soldier
jaya stambha victory tower
jheel (jhil) lake; a marsh; a swamp
jhilmil projecting canopy over a window or door opening
-ji (jee) honorific suffix added to names out of reverence and/or politeness; also abbreviated 'yes' (Hindi/Urdu)
jihad striving in the way of god; holy war by Muslims against non-believers
Jina literally 'victor'; spiritual conqueror or Tirthankara, after whom Jainism is named
Jogini mystical goddess
jorbangla double hut-like temple in Bengal
Jyotirlinga luminous energy of Siva manifested at 12 holy places, miraculously formed lingams

K

kabalai (kavalai) well irrigation using bullock power (Tamil Nadu)
kabigan folk debate in verse
kachcha man's 'under-shorts' (one of five Sikh symbols)
kacheri (kutchery) a court; an office for public business
kadal wooden bridge (Kashmir)
kadhi savoury yoghurt curry (Gujarat/North India)
kadu forest (Tamil)
Kailasa mountain home of Siva
kalamkari special painted cotton hanging from Andhra
kalasha pot-like finial of a tower
Kali literally 'black'; terrifying form of the goddess Durga, wearing a necklace of skulls/heads
Kalki future incarnation of Vishnu on horseback
kalyanamandapa marriage hall
kameez women's shirt
kanga comb (one of five Sikh symbols)
kankar limestone pieces, used for road making
kantha Bengali quilting
kapok the silk cotton tree
kara steel bracelet (one of five Sikh symbols)
karma impurity resulting from past misdeeds
Kartikkeya (Kartik) Son of Siva, God of war
kashi-work special kind of glazed tiling, probably derived from Kashan in Persia
kati-roll Muslim snack of meat rolled in a 'paratha' bread
kattakat mixed brain, liver and kidney (Gujarat)
keep tower of a fort, stronghold
kere tank (Kanarese)
keystone central wedge-shaped block in a masonry arch
khadi woven cotton cloth made from home-spun cotton (or silk) yarn
khal creek; a canal
khana suffix for room/office/ place; also food or meal
khanqah Muslim (Sufi) hospice
kharif monsoon season crop
khave khana tea shop
kheda enclosure in which wild elephants are caught; elephant depot
khet field
khola river or stream in Nepal
khondalite crudely grained basalt
khukri traditional curved Gurkha weapon
kirpan sabre, dagger (one of five Sikh symbols)
kirti-stambha 'pillar of fame,' free standing pillar in front of temple
kohl antimony, used as eye shadow
konda hill (Telugu)
kos minars Mughal 'mile' stones
kot (kota/kottai/kotte) fort
kothi house
kotla citadel
kovil (koil) temple (Tamil)
Krishna Eighth incarnation of Vishnu
kritis South Indian devotional music
Kubera Chief yaksha; keeper of the treasures of the earth, Guardian of the North
kulam tank or pond (Tamil)
kumar a young man
Kumari Virgin; Durga
kumbha a vase-like motif, pot
Kumbhayog auspicious time for bathing to wash away sins
kumhar (kumar) potter
kund lake, well or pool
kundan jewellery setting of uncut gems (Rajasthan)
kuppam hamlet (Tamil)
kurta Punjabi shirt
kurti-kanchali small blouse
kutcha (cutcha/kacha) raw; crude; unpaved; built with sun-dried bricks
kwabgah bedroom; literally 'palace of dreams'

L

la Himalayan mountain pass
lakh 100,000
Lakshmana younger brother of Rama
Lakshmi Goddess of wealth and good fortune, consort of Vishnu
Lakulisha founder of the Pashupata sect, believed to be an incarnation of Siva
lama Buddhist priest in Tibet
lassi iced yoghurt drink
lath monolithic pillar
lathi bamboo stick with metal bindings, used by police
lena cave, usually a rock-cut sanctuary
lingam (linga) Siva as the phallic emblem
Lingaraja Siva worshipped at Bhubaneswar
lintel horizontal beam over doorway
liwan cloisters of a mosque
Lokeshwar 'Lord of the World', Avalokiteshwara to Buddhists and form of Siva to Hindus
lunette semi-circular window opening
lungi wrapped-around loin cloth, normally checked

M

madrassa Islamic theological school or college
maha great
Mahabharata Sanskrit epic about the battle between the Pandavas and Kauravas
Mahabodhi Great Enlightenment of Buddha
Mahadeva literally 'Great Lord'; Siva
mahal palace, grand building
mahalla (mohulla) division of a town; a quarter; a ward
mahamandapam large enclosed hall in front of main shrine
mahant head of a monastery
maharaja great king
maharana Rajput clan head
maharani great queen
maharishi (Maharshi) literally 'great teacher'
Mahavira literally 'Great Hero'; last of the 24 Tirthankaras, founder of Jainism
Mahayana The Greater Vehicle; form of Buddhism practised in East Asia, Tibet and Nepal
Mahesha (Maheshvara) Great Lord; Siva
Mahisha Buffalo demon killed by Durga
mahout elephant driver/keeper
mahseer large freshwater fish found especially in Himalayan rivers
maidan large open grassy area in a town
Maitreya the future Buddha
makara crocodile-shaped mythical creature symbolizing the river Ganga
makhan butter
malai hill (Tamil)
mali gardener
Manasa Snake goddess; Sakti
manastambha free-standing pillar in front of temple
mandala geometric diagram symbolizing the structure of the Universe
mandalam region, tract of country (Tamil)
mandapa columned hall preceding the temple sanctuary
mandi market
mandir temple
mani (mani wall) stones with sacred inscriptions at Buddhist sites
mantra chant for meditation by Hindus and Buddhists
maqbara chamber of a Muslim tomb
Mara Tempter, who sent his daughters (and soldiers) to disturb the Buddha's meditation
marg wide roadway
masjid literally 'place of prostration'; mosque
mata mother
math Hindu or Jain monastery
maulana scholar (Muslim)
maulvi religious teacher (Muslim)
maund measure of weight about 20 kg
mausoleum large tomb building
maya illusion
medallion circle or part-circle framing a figure or decorative motif
meena enamel work
mela festival or fair, usually Hindu
memsahib married European woman, term used mainly before Independence
Meru mountain supporting the heavens
mihrab niche in the western wall of a mosque
mimbar pulpit in mosque
Minakshi literally 'fish-eyed'; Parvati
minar (minaret) slender tower of a mosque
mitthai Indian sweets
mithuna couple in sexual embrace
mofussil the country as distinct from the town
Mohammad 'the praised'; The Prophet; founder of Islam
moksha salvation, enlightenment; literally 'release'
momos Tibetan stuffed pastas
monolith single block of stone shaped into a pillar
moonstone the semi-circular stone step before a shrine (also chandrasila)
mouza (mowza) village; a parcel of land having a separate name in the revenue records
mridangam barrel-shaped drum (musical)
muballigh second prayer leader
mudra symbolic hand gesture
muezzin mosque official who calls the faithful to prayer
Muharram period of mourning in remembrance of Hasan and Hussain, two murdered sons of Ali
mukha mandapa, hall for shrine
mullah religious teacher (Muslim)
mund Toda village

muqarna Muslim stalactite design
mural wall decoration
musalla prayer mat
muta limited duration marriage (Leh)
muthi measure equal to 'a handful'

N

nadi river
nadu region, country (Tamil)
Naga (nagi/nagini) Snake deity; associated with fertility and protection
nagara city, sometimes capital
nakkar khana (naggar or naubat khana) drum house; arched structure or gateway for musicians
nal mandapa porch over a staircase
nallah (nullah) ditch, channel
namaaz Muslim prayers, worship
namaste common Hindu greeting (with joined palms) translated as: 'I salute all divine qualities in you'
namda rug
Nandi a bull, Siva's vehicle and a symbol of fertility
nara durg large fort built on a flat plain
Narayana Vishnu as the creator of life
nata mandapa (nat-mandir; nritya sala) dancing hall in a temple
Nataraja Siva, Lord of the cosmic dance
nath literally 'place' eg Amarnath
natya the art of dance
nautch display by dancing girls
navagraha nine planets, represented usually on the lintel or architrave of the front door of a temple
navaranga central hall of temple
navaratri literally '9 nights'; name of the Dasara festival
nawab prince, wealthy Muslim, sometimes used as a title
niche wall recess containing a sculpted image or emblem, mostly framed by a pair of pilasters
Nihang literally 'crocodile': followers of Guru Gobind Singh (Sikh)
nirvana enlightenment; literally 'extinguished'
niwas small palace
nritya pure dance

O

obelisk tapering and usually monolithic stone shaft
oriel projecting window

P

pada foot or base
padam dance which tells a story
padma lotus flower, Padmasana, lotus seat; posture of meditating figures
paga projecting pilaster-like surface of an Orissan temple
pagoda tall structure in several stories
pahar hill
paisa (poisa) one hundredth of a rupee
palanquin covered litter for one, carried on poles
palayam minor kingdom (Tamil)
pali language of Buddhist scriptures
palli village
pan leaf of the betel vine; sliced areca nut, lime and other ingredients wrapped in leaf for chewing
panchayat a 'council of five'; a government system of elected councils
pandal marquee made of bamboo and cloth
pandas temple priests
pandit teacher or wise man; a Sanskrit scholar
pankah (punkha) fan, formerly pulled by a cord
parabdis special feeding place for birds
parapet wall extending above the roof
pargana subdivision of a district usually comprising many villages; a fiscal unit
Parinirvana the Buddha's state prior to nirvana, shown usually as a reclining figure
parishads political division of group of villages
Parsi (Parsee) Zoroastrians who fled from Iran to West India in the 8th century to avoid persecution
parterre level space in a garden occupied by flowerbeds
Parvati daughter of the Mountain; Siva's consort
pashmina fine wool from a mountain goat
Pashupati literally Lord of the Beasts; Siva
pata painted hanging scroll
patan town or city (Sanskrit)
patel village headman
patina green film that covers materials exposed to the air
pattachitra specially painted cloth (especially Orissan)
pau measure for vegetables and fruit equal to 250 g
paya soup
pediment mouldings, often in a triangular formation above an opening or niche
pendant hanging, a motif depicted upside down
peon servant, messenger (from Portuguese *peao*)
perak black hat, studded with turquoise and lapis lazuli (Ladakh)
peristyle range of columns surrounding a court or temple
Persian wheel well irrigation system using a bucket lift
pettah suburbs, outskirts of town (Tamil: *pettai*)
pice (old form) 1/100th of a rupee
picottah water lift using horizontal pole pivoted on vertical pole (Tamil Nadu)
pida (pitha) basement
pida deul hall with a pyramidal roof in an Orissan temple

pietra dura inlaid mosaic of hard, semi-precious stones
pilaster ornamental small column, with capital and bracket
pinjra lattice work
pinjrapol animal hospital (Jain)
pipal Ficus religiosa, the Bodhi tree
pir Muslim holy man
pitha base, pedestal
pithasthana place of pilgrimage
podium stone bench; low pedestal wall
pokana bathing tank (Sri Lanka)
pol fortified gateway
porch covered entrance to a shrine or hall, generally open and with columns
portico space enclosed between columns
pradakshina patha processional passage
prakaram open courtyard
pralaya the end of the world
prasadam consecrated temple food
prayag confluence considered sacred by Hindus
puja ritual offerings to the gods; worship (Hindu)
pujari worshipper; one who performs puja (Hindu)
pukka literally 'ripe' or 'finished'; reliable; solidly built
punya merit earned through actions and religious devotion (Buddhist)
Puranas literally 'the old' Sanskrit sacred poems
purdah seclusion of Muslim women from public view (literally curtains)
pushkarani sacred pool or tank

Q

qabr Muslim grave
qibla direction for Muslim prayer
qila fort
Quran holy Muslim scriptures
qutb axis or pivot

R

rabi winter/spring season crop
Radha Krishna's favourite consort
raj rule or government
raja king, ruler (variations include rao, rawal)
rajbari palaces of a small kingdom
Rajput dynasties of western and central India
Rakshakas Earth spirits
Rama Seventh incarnation of Vishnu
Ramayana Sanskrit epic – the story of Rama
Ramazan (Ramadan) Muslim month of fasting
rana warrior (Nepal)
rangamandapa painted hall or theatre
rani queen
rath chariot or temple car
Ravana Demon king of Lanka; kidnapper of Sita
rawal head priest
rekha curvilinear portion of a spire or sikhara (rekha deul, sanctuary, curved tower of an Orissan temple)
reredos screen behind an altar
rickshaw three-wheeled bicycle-powered (or two-wheeled hand-powered) vehicle
Rig (Rg) Veda oldest and most sacred of the Vedas
Rimpoche blessed incarnation; abbot of a Tibetan Buddhist monastery (gompa)
rishi 'seer'; inspired poet, philosopher
rumal handkerchief, specially painted in Chamba (Himachal Pradesh)
rupee unit of currency in India
ryot (rayat/raiyat) a subject; a cultivator; a farmer

S

sabha columned hall (sabha mandapa, assembly hall)
sabzi vegetables, vegetable curry
sadar (sadr/saddar) chief, main especially Sikh
sadhu ascetic; religious mendicant, holy man
safa turban (Rajasthan)
sagar lake; reservoir
sahib title of address, like 'sir'
sahn open courtyard of a mosque
Saiva (Shaiva) the cult of Siva
sal a hall
sal hardwood tree of the lower slopes of the Himalayan foothills
salaam literally 'peace'; greeting (Muslim)
salwar (shalwar) loose trousers (Punjab)
samadh(i) literally concentrated thought, meditation; a funerary memorial
sambar lentil and vegetable soup dish, accompanying main meal (Tamil)
samsara transmigration of the soul
samudra large tank or inland sea
sangam junction of rivers
sangarama monastery
sangha ascetic order founded by Buddha
sangrahalaya rest house for Jain pilgrims
sankha (shankha) the conch shell (symbolically held by Vishnu); the shell bangle worn by Bengali women
sanyasi wandering ascetic; final stage in the ideal life of a man
sarai caravansarai, halting place
saranghi small four-stringed viola shaped from a single piece of wood
Saraswati wife of Brahma and goddess of knowledge
sarkar the government; the state; a writer; an accountant
sarod Indian stringed musical instrument
sarvodaya uplift, improvement of all
sati (suttee) a virtuous woman; act of self-immolation on a husband's funeral pyre

Sati wife of Siva who destroyed herself by fire
satyagraha 'truth force'; passive resistance
sayid title (Muslim)
schist grey or green finely grained stone
seer (ser) weight (about 1 kg)
sepoy (sepai) Indian soldier, private
serow a wild Himalayan antelope
seth merchant, businessman
seva voluntary service
shahtush very fine wool from the Tibetan antelope
Shakti Energy; female divinity often associated with Siva
shala barrel-vaulted roof
shalagrama stone containing fossils worshipped as a form of Vishnu
shaman doctor/priest, using magic, exorcist
shamiana cloth canopy
Shankara Siva
sharia corpus of Muslim theological law
shastras ancient texts defining temple architecture
shastri religious title (Hindu)
sheesh mahal palace apartment with mirror work
shehnai (shahnai) Indian wind instrument like an oboe
sherwani knee-length coat for men
Shesha (Sesha) serpent who supports Vishnu
shikar hunting
shikara boat (Kashmir)
shisham a valuable building timber
sikhara curved temple tower or spire
shloka (sloka) Sanskrit sacred verse
shola patch of forest or wood (Tamil)
sileh khana armoury
sindur vermilion powder used in temple ritual; married women mark their hair parting with it (East India)
singh (sinha) lion; Rajput caste name adopted by Sikhs
sinha stambha lion pillar
sirdar a guide who leads trekking groups
Sita Rama's wife, heroine of the Ramayana epic
sitar classical stringed musical instrument with a gourd for soundbox
Siva (Shiva) The Destroyer in the Hindu triad of Gods
Sivaratri literally 'Siva's night'; a festival (Feb-Mar)
Skanda the Hindu god of war; Kartikkeya
soma sacred drink mentioned in the Vedas
spandrel triangular space between the curve of an arch and the square enclosing it
squinch arch across an interior angle
sri (shri) honorific title, often used for 'Mr'; repeated as sign of great respect
sridhara pillar with octagonal shaft and square base
stalactite system of vaulting, remotely resembling stalactite formations in a cave
stambha free-standing column or pillar, often for a lamp or figure
steatite finely grained grey mineral
stele upright, inscribed slab used as a gravestone
step well (vav) vertical shaft leading down to a well, with elaborately carved walls
sthan place (suffix)
stucco plasterwork
stupa hemispheric Buddhist funerary mound
stylobate base on which a colonnade is placed
subahdar (subedar) the governor of a province; viceroy under the Mughals
Subrahmanya Skanda, one of Siva's sons; Kartikkeya in South India
sudra lowest of the Hindu castes
sufi Muslim mystic; sufism, Muslim mystic worship
sultan Muslim prince (sultana, wife of sultan)
Surya Sun; Sun God
svami (swami) holy man; a suffix for temple deities
svastika (swastika) auspicious Hindu/ Buddhist cross-like sign
swadeshi home-made goods
swaraj home rule
swatantra freedom

T

tabla a pair of drums
tahr wild goat
tahsildar revenue collector
taikhana underground apartments
takht throne
talao (*tal*, talar) water tank
taluk administrative subdivision of a district
tamasha spectacle; festive celebration
tandava (dance) of Siva
tank lake dug for irrigation; a masonry-lined temple pool with stepped sides
tapas (tapasya) ascetic meditative self-denial
Tara literally 'star'; a goddess
tarkashi Orissan silver filigree
tatties cane or grass screens used for shade
Teej Hindu festival
tehsil subdivision of a district (North India)
tempera distemper; method of mural painting by means of a 'body,' such as white pigment
tempo three-wheeler vehicle
terai narrow strip of land along Himalayan foothills
teri soil formed from wind blown sand (Tamil Nadu)
terracotta burnt clay used as building material

thakur high Hindu caste; deity (Bengal)
thakur bari temple sanctuary (Bengal)
thali South and West Indian vegetarian meal
thana a police jurisdiction; police station
thangka (thankha) cloth (often silk) painted with a Tibetan Mahayana deity
thug professional robber/murderer (Central India)
tiffin snack, light meal
tika (tilak) vermilion powder, auspicious mark on the forehead; often decorative
tikka tender pieces of meat that have been marinated and barbecued
tillana abstract dance
tirtha ford, bathing place, holy spot (Sanskrit)
Tirthankara literally 'ford-maker'; title given to 24 religious 'teachers', worshipped by Jains
tonga two-wheeled horse carriage
topi (topee) pith helmet
torana gateway; two posts with an architrave
tottam garden (Tamil)
tribhanga triple-bended pose for standing figures
Trimurti the Hindu Triad, Brahma, Vishnu and Siva
tripolia triple gateway
trisul the trident chief symbol of the god Siva
triveni triple-braided
tsampa ground, roasted barley, eaten dry or mixed with milk, tea or water (Himalayan)
tso lake (Ladakh)
tuk fortified enclosure containing Jain shrines
tulsi sacred basil plant
tykhana underground room for use in hot weather (North India)
tympanum triangular space within cornices

U

Uma Siva's consort in one of her many forms
untouchable 'outcastes', with whom contact of any kind was believed by high caste Hindus to be defiling
Upanishads ancient Sanskrit philosophical texts, part of the Vedas
ur village (Tamil)
usta painted camel leather goods
ustad master
uttarayana northwards

V

vahana 'vehicle' of the deity
vaisya the 'middle-class' caste of merchants and farmers
Valmiki sage, author of the Ramayana epic
Vamana dwarf incarnation of Vishnu
vana grove, forest
Varaha boar incarnation of Vishnu
varam village (Tamil)
varna 'colour'; social division of Hindus into Brahmin, Kshatriya, Vaishya and Sudra
Varuna Guardian of the West, accompanied by Makara (see above)
Vayu Wind god; Guardian of the Northwest
Veda (Vedic) oldest known Hindu religious texts
vedi (bedi) altar, also a wall or screen
veranda enlarged porch in front of a hall
vihara Buddhist or Jain monastery with cells around a courtyard
vilas house or pleasure palace
vimana towered sanctuary containing the cell in which the deity is enshrined
vina plucked stringed instrument, relative of sitar
Vishnu a principal Hindu deity; the Preserver (and Creator)
vyala (yali) leogryph, mythical lion-like sculpture

W

-wallah suffix often used with a occupational name, eg rickshaw-wallah
wav (vav) step well, particularly in Gujarat and western India (baoli)
wazir chief minister of a raja (from Turkish 'vizier')
wazwan ceremonial meal (Kashmir)

Y

yagya (yajna) major ceremonial sacrifice
Yaksha (Yakshi) a demi-god, associated with nature
yali see vyala
Yama God of death, judge of the living
yantra magical diagram used in meditation; instrument
yatra pilgrimage
Yellow Hat Gelugpa Sect of Tibetan Buddhism – monks wear yellow headdress
yeti mythical Himalayan animal often referred to as 'the abominable snowman'
yoga school of philosophy stressing mental and physical disciplines; yogi
yoni a hole symbolising female sexuality; vagina
yura water channel (Ladakh)

Z

zamindar a landlord granted income under the Mughals
zari silver and gold thread used in weaving or embroidery
zarih cenotaph in a Muslim tomb
zenana segregated women's apartments
ziarat holy Muslim tomb
zilla (zillah) district

Index → *Entries in bold refer to maps*

Abbreviations used for state references: **A&N** = Andaman & Nicobar Islands; **AP** = Andhra Pradesh; **Ar** = Arunachal Pradesh; **As** = Assam; **Bi** = Bihar; **Chh** = Chhattisgarh; **Goa** = Goa; **Guj** = Gujarat; **HP** = Himachal Pradesh; **J&K** = Jammu & Kashmir; **Jh** = Jharkhand; **Kar** = Karnataka; **Ke** = Kerala; **Mah** = Maharashtra; **Meg** = Meghalaya; **Miz** = Mizoram; **MP** = Madhya Pradesh; **Man** = Manipur; **Nag** = Nagaland; **Or** = Orissa; **P&H** = Punjab & Haryana; **Raj** = Rajasthan; **Sik** = Sikkim; **TN** = Tamil Nadu; **Tri** = Tripura; **UP** = Uttar Pradesh; **Utt** = Uttarakhand; **WB** = West Bengal.

A

B

K

O

P

Q

R

Advertisers' index

Acknowledgements

Vanessa Betts

Thanks for your time, help and company to Asit Biswas, Sanjoy Biswas and Sandip Samaddar in Kolkata; to Bibhuti Borah, Hemanta Das (Network Travels) and Dudu in Assam; to David and Rahul (Travel the Unknown) in the UK; to Mr Aditya Jalan in Patna; to Dr Tage Kanno (Future Generations) and Mr JK Riba (Gibbon Travels) in Arunachal Pradesh; to Lorraine Close, Adil Khan and Niamh Moran in the Andaman Islands; to Denis P Rayen and his charming family in Meghalaya; and to Nino Zhasa in Nagaland. Thanks also to my family – Jane and Mike Betts, Katharine Bowerman and Eran Shaham. Special thanks are due to Wil Lee-Wright for his research in West Bengal, and to David Stott and Victoria McCulloch for their comradeship. And, of course, my thanks to Nicola Gibbs and Alan Murphy at Footprint.

Victoria McCulloch

Many thanks to scribes Leona Stephens-Ofner, Joanna Lester-George, Kaushal Desai from Above 14000 ft and Vishwas Raj and Alka at Rimo Expeditions. Thanks for the all the top tips and lush lowdowns – Victoria and Bertie Dyer and Indiabeat team, Peter Dos Santos, Raj Dylan Nalwa, Lucy and Axel, Surekha Narain, Darren Odell, Ayesha Sood, Fiona Smith, Simona Bassi, Chris Saleem Agha Bee, Sunny Travels and Joanne Smallwood. For always making me feel at home - Satinder Singh and the Pearl Palace team, Ashwani Bazaz, Guru Dharm Kaur, Josie Knight and the Tree of Life family, Jora and the Shahi Palace boys, Poonam and Dicky Singh, Anoop Mehrotra en famille, Ilan and Shiran, Farrokh Maneckshaw, Cipriano Rodrigues and family and Tarun Bhaskar. Eternal thanks to Anil Bhagia at Northwest Safaris, Rajnish Kaistha at Paradise Travels, and Srinivasa Varadan. For not getting me lost, thanks to Shiv Singh, Ripan Kumar and for excellent driving, all the jokes and the dodgy Hindi lessons many thanks to Akhtar Khan. Thanks to Annie Dare for passing the baton and for moral support from Vanessa Betts, David Stott and the Footprint team in the UK Nicola Gibbs and Alan Murphy. Whole-hearted thanks to the Arambol tribe, all my students and their feedback and most of all Adam for keeping me company whether together or apart.

David Stott

Thanks to everyone who offered support, advice, stories, company, hospitality or encouragement along the way, especially to: Ashish and Rucha Gupta, Nipin Bharathan and C. Venkatesh in Chennai; Thomas Lilly in Auroville; Binu Philip, Gopi Parayil, Sandeep Sinha and Vinod Cherakkode in Bengaluru; Manu at Skyway Tours in Mysore; Venkatesh in Hampi; Praveen and Vidya at Maranat Mana and Pradeep and the Vayali team; Deepa Krishnan, Sean and Pervin Mahoney and Yatin Desai in Mumbai; Dr Jagdish Bhutada and everyone at Kaivalyadhama; Ashwani and Suruchi Bazaz at Tree of Life; Saurabh Kapur, Vishal Sadharwal, Surekha Narain and editor extraordinaire Pranav Capila in Delhi; Ratnamala Kapoor, Sonal, Sher Singh and all at Village Ways for a glimpse of the most phenomenal Himalayan scenery; Swami Yatidharmananda for scooter rides, coffee and cricket; Daniel Jalba, Ma Radha Bharati and Karin Fiedler at SRSG in Rishikesh; Yogi Choudhary in Rudraprayag; and Shivang Mehta at Corbett.

Thanks as always to Dr David Snashall, Dr Martin Taylor and Dr Anthony Bryceson for keeping the Health section up to date. A special mention to editor-in-chief Nicola Gibbs for rallying to the cause and changing every train number in the book, not to mention for the precious gift of two weeks off to welcome my son into the world. And finally, profound thanks to Helen and Benjamin for the companionship and inspiration that keeps me going through countless hotel reviews, overnight bus rides and wading through train timetables.

First published in 2012

OM
Om Books International

Corporate & Editorial Office
A-12, Sector 64, Noida – 201 301
Uttar Pradesh, India
Phone: +91-120-477 4100
Email: editorial@ombooks.com
Website: www.ombooksinternational.com

Sales Office
4379/4B, Prakash House, Ansari Road
Darya Ganj, New Delhi – 110 002, India
Phone: +91 11 2326 3363, 2326 5303
Fax: +91 11 2327 8091
Email: sales@ombooks.com
Website: www.ombooks.com

Photography credits Front cover: Leslie West/Photononstop/Photolibrary.com. Back cover: Bruno Morandi/hemis.fr. Colour section photograhy credits: P1: Luciano Mortula/Shutterstock. P2-3 Christophe Boisvieux/hemis.fr. P6-7: jean-Leo Dugast/Photolibrary.P8: regien Paasen/Shutterstock.

Originally published by Footprint Handbooks Ltd, Bath, UK 2011

Printed in India by Nutech Photolithographers, New Delhi

CIP DATA: A catalogue record for this book is available from the British Library
ISBN: 978-93-80070-24-7

Footprint Mini Atlas
India

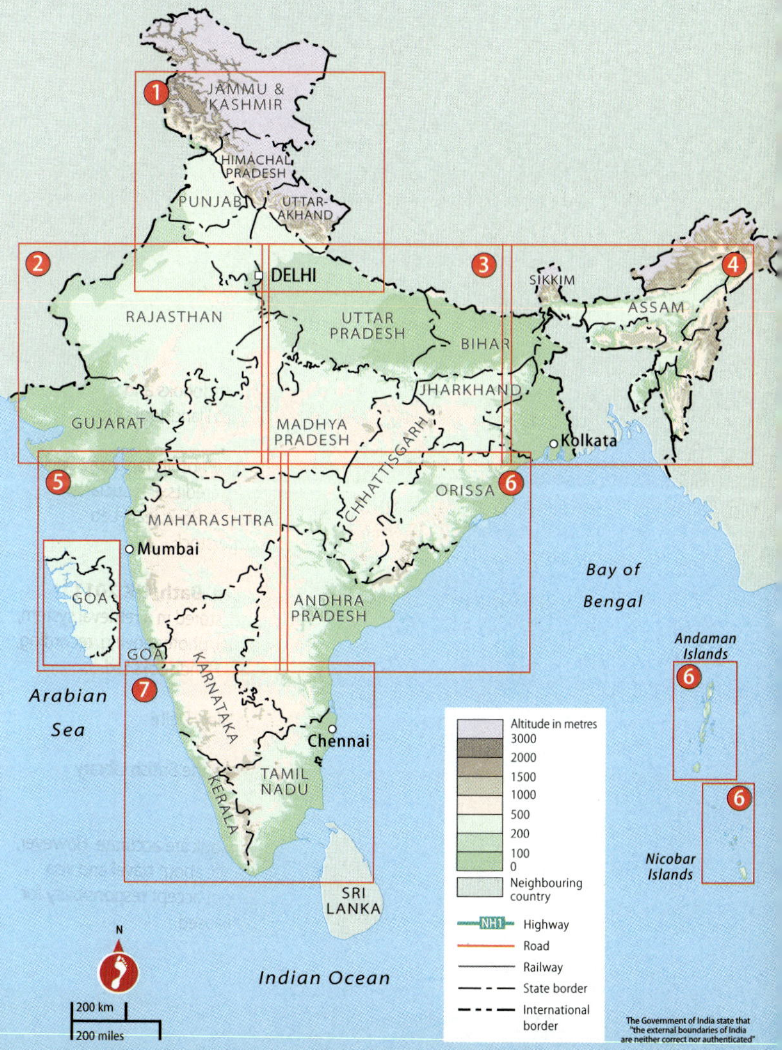

Map 1

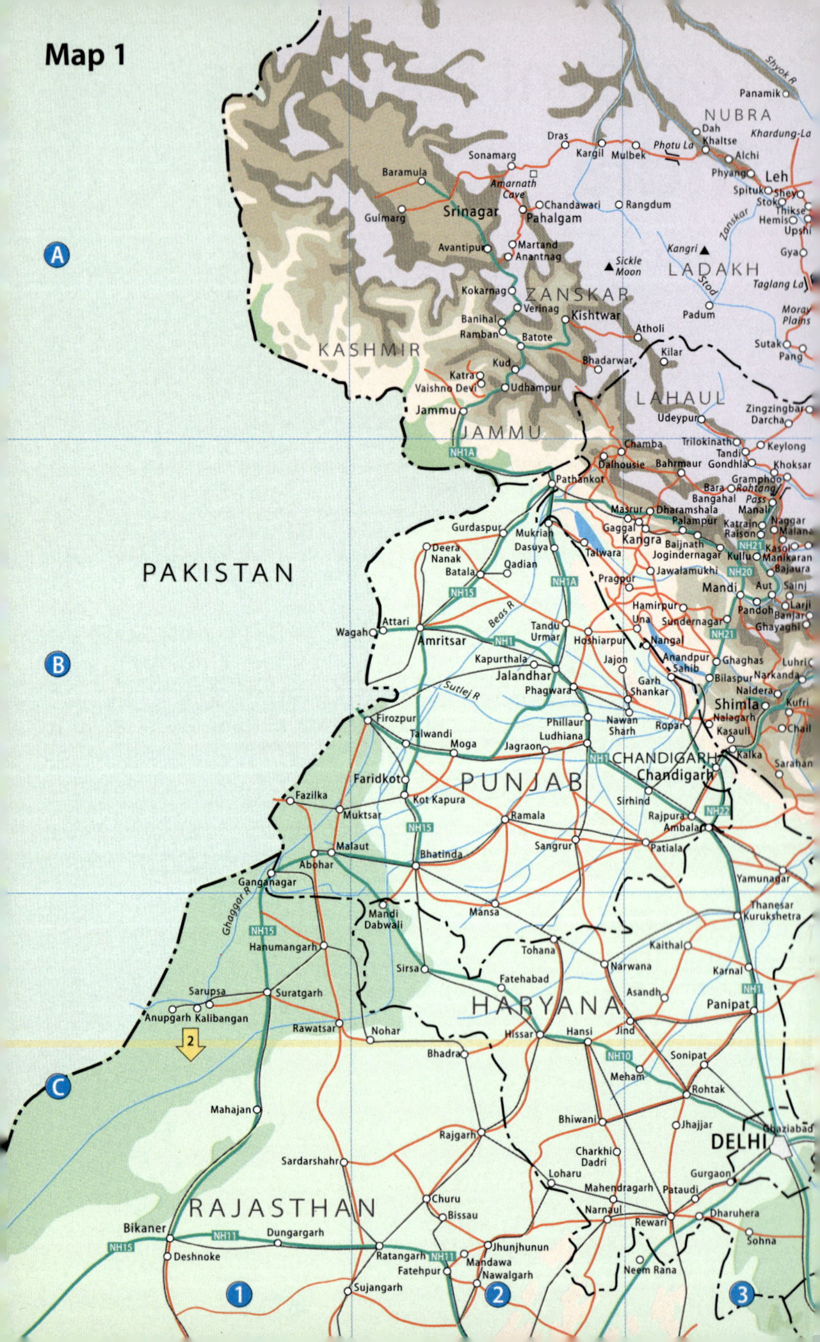
PAKISTAN
KASHMIR
JAMMU
ZANSKAR
LADAKH
NUBRA
LAHAUL
PUNJAB
HARYANA
RAJASTHAN
CHANDIGARH
DELHI
A
B
C
1
2
3
Shyok R
Panamik
Dah
Khaltse
Khardung-La
Dras
Kargil
Mulbek
Photu La
Alchi
Phyang
Leh
Spituk
Shey
Stok
Thikse
Hemis
Upshi
Gya
Sonamarg
Amarnath Cave
Baramula
Gulmarg
Srinagar
Chandawari
Pahalgam
Rangdum
Zanskar
Kangri
Sickle Moon
Stod
Taglang La
Avantipur
Martand
Anantnag
Kokarnag
Verinag
Kishtwar
Padum
Moray Plains
Banihal
Ramban
Batote
Atholi
Sutak
Pang
Kud
Bhadarwar
Kilar
Katra
Vaishno Devi
Udhampur
Jammu
Udeypur
Zingzingbar
Darcha
NH1A
Chamba
Trilokinath
Tandi
Keylong
Dalhousie
Bahrmaur
Gondhla
Khoksar
Pathankot
Gramphoo
Bara
Rohtang Pass
Bangahal
Manali
Masrur
Dharamshala
Gaggal
Palampur
Katrain
Raison
Naggar
Malana
Kangra
Baijnath
Jogindernagar
Kullu
Kasol
Manikaran
Gurdaspur
Mukrian
Dasuya
Talwara
Deera Nanak
Batala
Qadian
NH15
NH1A
Pragpur
Jawalamukhi
NH20
NH21
Bajaura
Mandi
Aut
Sainj
Pandoh
Larji
Banjar
Ghayaghi
Hamirpur
Una
Sundernagar
Beas R
Attari
Wagah
Amritsar
NH1
Tandu Urmar
Hoshiarpur
Nangal
Jajon
Anandpur Sahib
Ghaghas
Luhri
Kapurthala
Jalandhar
Phagwara
Garh Shankar
Bilaspur
Narkanda
Naldera
Sutlej R
Shimla
Kufri
Nawan Shahr
Nalagarh
Kasauli
Chail
Firozpur
Phillaur
Ludhiana
Ropar
Talwandi
Moga
Jagraon
Kalka
Sarahan
Chandigarh
Faridkot
Sirhind
Fazilka
Kot Kapura
Muktsar
NH15
Ramala
Rajpura
NH22
Ambala
Sangrur
Patiala
Malaut
Abohar
Bhatinda
Yamunagar
Ganganagar
Ghaggar R
Mandi Dabwali
Mansa
Thanesar Kurukshetra
NH15
Hanumangarh
Tohana
Kaithal
Sirsa
Narwana
Karnal
Fatehabad
Asandh
NH1
Panipat
Sarupsa
Suratgarh
Anupgarh
Kalibangan
Rawatsar
Nohar
Hissar
Hansi
Jind
Bhadra
NH10
Sonipat
Meham
Rohtak
Mahajan
Bhiwani
Jhajjar
Ghaziabad
Rajgarh
Charkhi Dadri
Sardarshahr
Loharu
Gurgaon
Mahendragarh
Pataudi
Churu
Bissau
Narnaul
Dharuhera
Bikaner
Rewari
Sohna
NH11
Dungargarh
NH15
Deshnoke
Ratangarh
Jhunjhunun
Mandawa
Fatehpur
Nawalgarh
Neem Rana
Sujangarh

TIBET
(CHINA)
NEPAL
RUPSHU
SPITI
HIMACHAL PRADESH
UTTARAKHAND
UTTAR PRADESH
Shyok
Tangtse
Lukung
Spangmik
Pangong Tso
Indus R
Tashigong
Gardzong
Tso-Moriri
Kibber
Kaza
Lalung
Dankar
Tabo
Kungri Gompa
Pin Valley NP
Gulling
Sumdo
Mudh
Sangam
NH22
Khab
Puh
Kalpa
Wangtu
Recong Peo
Sarahan
Sangla
Rampur Bushahr
Chitkul
Kailash
Yamunotri
Gangotri
Meru
Kedarnath
Badrinath
Hemkund
Barkot
Uttarkashi
Joshimath
Auli
Mussoorie
Tehri
Dehra Dun
Nanda Devi
Srinagar
Rishikesh
Deoprayag
Byasi
Rudraprayag
Karnaprayag
Trisul
Rajaji NP
Haridwar
Larsho
Gwaldam
Baijnath
Kausani
Saharanpur
Roorkee
Kotdwara
Ranikhet
Pithorgarh
Muzaffarnagar
Nathjabad
Corbett NP
Almora
Khatauli
Nagina
Ramnagar
Nainital
Bhowali
Kashipur
Kathgodam
Haldwani
Bijnor
3
Meerut
Lalkuan
Mahendranagar
Bilaspur
Banbassa
Kichha
Rampur
Pilibhit
Moradabad
Ramganga R
Dudwa NP
Hapur
NH24
Sambhal
Chandausi
Puranpur
Bulandshahr
Bareilly
Bisalpur
Mailani
Ghaghara R
Nepalganj Road
Khurja
Nanpara
Ganga R
Lakhimpur
Aligarh
Kasganj
Shahjahanpur
Vrindavan
Sravasti
Sitapur
Bahraich
Balrampur
A
B
C
4
5
6
N
50 km
50 miles
The Government of India state that "the external boundaries of India are neither correct nor authenticated"

Map 2

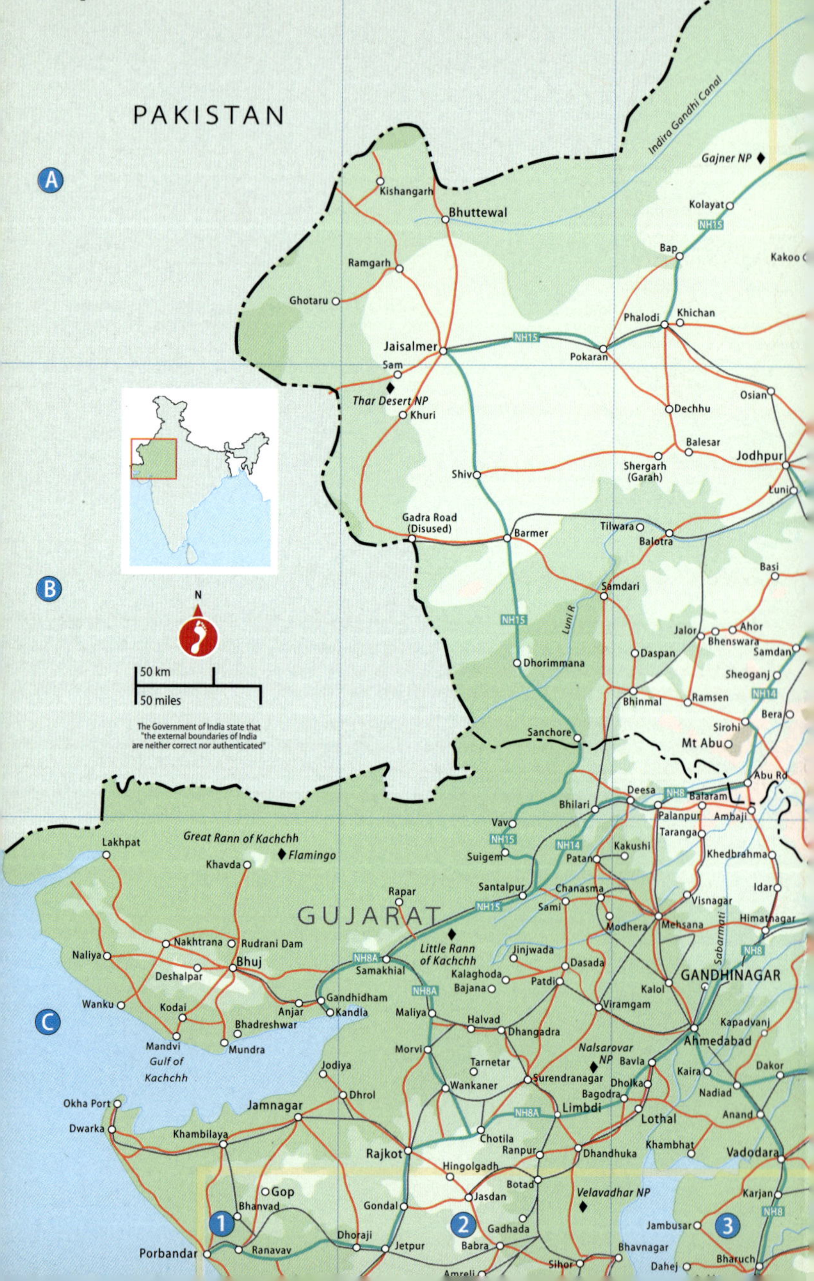
PAKISTAN
A
B
C
1
2
3
N
50 km
50 miles
The Government of India state that "the external boundaries of India are neither correct nor authenticated"
Indira Gandhi Canal
Gajner NP
Kolayat
NH15
Bap
Kakoo
Kishangarh
Bhuttewal
Ramgarh
Ghotaru
Jaisalmer
NH15
Phalodi
Khichan
Pokaran
Sam
Thar Desert NP
Khuri
Osian
Dechhu
Balesar
Jodhpur
Shergarh (Garah)
Shiv
Luni
Gadra Road (Disused)
Barmer
Tilwara
Balotra
Basi
Samdari
Luni R
NH15
Jalor
Ahor
Bhenswara
Samdan
Daspan
Dhorimmana
Sheoganj
Bhinmal
Ramsen
NH14
Bera
Sirohi
Sanchore
Mt Abu
Abu Rd
Deesa
NH8
Balaram
Bhilari
Palanpur
Ambaji
Vav
Taranga
NH15
Suigem
NH14
Kakushi
Patan
Khedbrahma
Lakhpat
Great Rann of Kachchh
Flamingo
Khavda
Santalpur
Chanasma
Idar
Rapar
Sami
Visnagar
GUJARAT
NH15
Modhera
Mehsana
Himatnagar
Sabarmati
Nakhtrana
Rudrani Dam
Little Rann of Kachchh
NH8
Naliya
Bhuj
NH8A
Samakhial
Jinjwada
Dasada
Deshalpar
Kalaghoda
Patdi
GANDHINAGAR
Bajana
Kalol
NH8A
Wanku
Kodai
Anjar
Gandhidham
Kandla
Maliya
Viramgam
Bhadreshwar
Halvad
Dhangadra
Kapadvanj
Mandvi
Mundra
Ahmedabad
Gulf of Kachchh
Morvi
Nalsarovar NP
Bavla
Jodiya
Tarnetar
Surendranagar
Dholka
Kaira
Dakor
Wankaner
Dhrol
Bagodra
Nadiad
Okha Port
Jamnagar
NH8A
Limbdi
Dwarka
Lothal
Anand
Khambilaya
Chotila
Khambhat
Rajkot
Ranpur
Dhandhuka
Vadodara
Hingolgadh
Gop
Botad
Velavadhar NP
Karjan
Bhanvad
Jasdan
Gondal
NH8
Jambusar
Gadhada
Dhoraji
Porbandar
Ranavav
Jetpur
Babra
Bhavnagar
Bharuch
Amreli
Sihor
Dahej

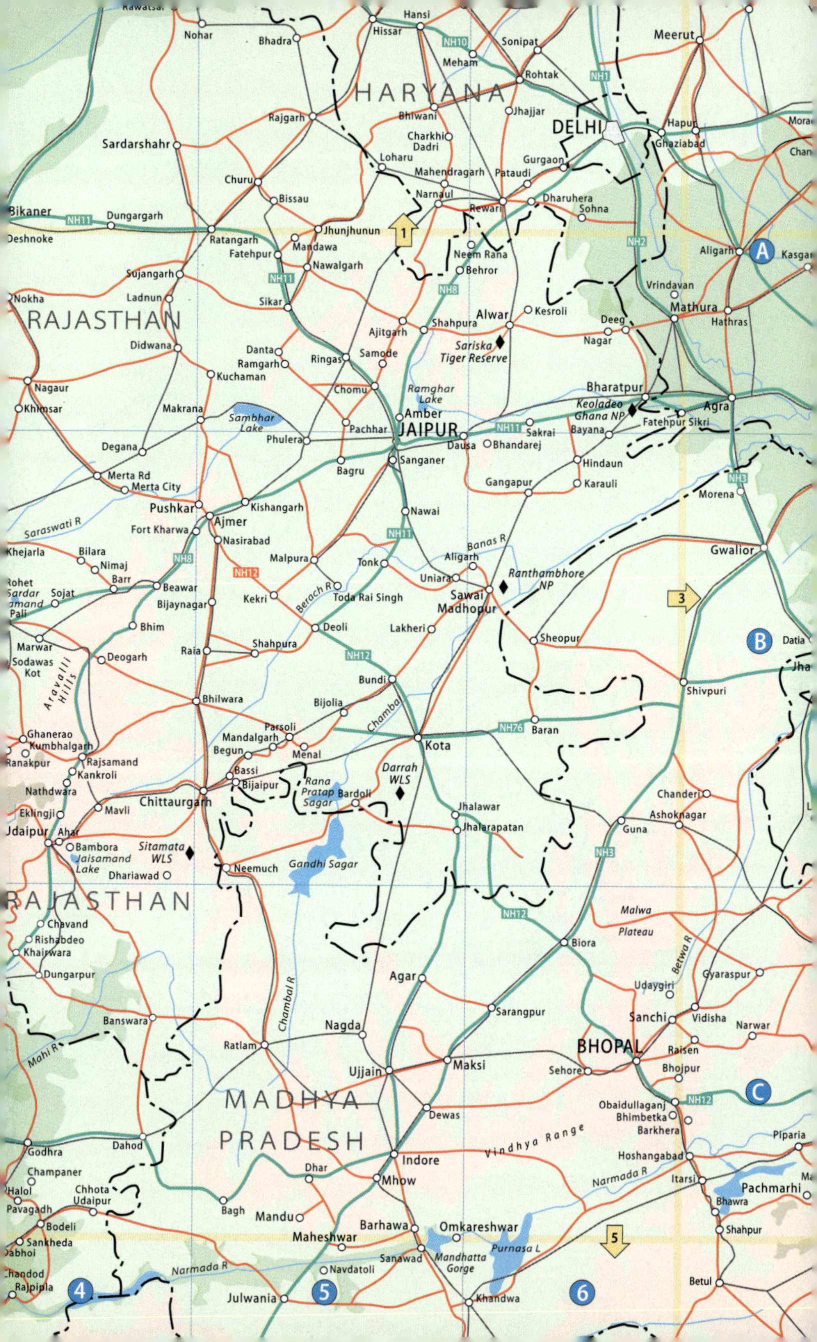

Hansi
Hissar
Nohar
Bhadra
NH10
Sonipat
Meerut
Meham
Rohtak
NH1
HARYANA
Jhajjar
Bhiwani
Rajgarh
DELHI
Hapur
Ghaziabad
Sardarshahr
Charkhi Dadri
Loharu
Gurgaon
Mahendragarh
Pataudi
Churu
Narnaul
Rewari
Dharuhera
Sohna
Bissau
Bikaner
NH11
Dungargarh
Jhunjhunun
Deshnoke
Ratangarh
Mandawa
Fatehpur
Neem Rana
Aligarh
Kasgar
Nawalgarh
Behror
NH2
Sujangarh
NH11
Vrindavan
Nokha
Ladnun
NH8
Sikar
Mathura
Hathras
Kesroli
Alwar
RAJASTHAN
Shahpura
Deeg
Ajitgarh
Nagar
Didwana
Danta
Samode
Sariska Tiger Reserve
Ramgarh
Ringas
Kuchaman
Nagaur
Chomu
Ramghar Lake
Bharatpur
Khimsar
Amber
Keoladeo Ghana NP
Agra
Makrana
Sambhar Lake
Pachhar
JAIPUR
NH11
Sakrai
Fatehpur Sikri
Phulera
Dausa
Bhandarej
Bayana
Degana
Bagru
Sanganer
Hindaun
Merta Rd
Merta City
Gangapur
Karauli
NH3
Morena
Pushkar
Kishangarh
Saraswati R
Ajmer
Nawai
Fort Kharwa
NH11
Nasirabad
Banas R
Gwalior
Khejarla
Bilara
NH8
Malpura
Aligarh
Nimaj
Tonk
Ranthambhore NP
NH12
Uniara
Barr
Beawar
Rohet
Sardar Samand
Sojat
Pali
Kekri
Berach R
Toda Rai Singh
Sawai Madhopur
Bijaynagar
Bhim
Deoli
Lakheri
Sheopur
Datia
Marwar
NH12
Shahpura
Sodawas
Kot
Raia
Deogarh
Aravalli Hills
Bundi
Shivpuri
Bhilwara
Bijolia
Chambal
Parsoli
NH76
Baran
Ghanerao
Mandalgarh
Kumbhalgarh
Begun
Menal
Kota
Ranakpur
Rajsamand
Kankroli
Darrah WLS
Bassi
Rana Pratap Sagar
Nathdwara
Bijaipur
Bardoli
Chanderi
Chittaurgarh
Eklingji
Mavli
Jhalawar
Ashoknagar
Udaipur
Ahar
Jhalarapatan
Guna
Bambora
Sitamata WLS
Jaisamand Lake
NH3
Neemuch
Gandhi Sagar
Dhariawad
RAJASTHAN
Malwa Plateau
NH12
Chavand
Rishabdeo
Biora
Khairwara
Betwa R
Dungarpur
Agar
Gyaraspur
Udaygiri
Chambal R
Sarangpur
Sanchi
Vidisha
Banswara
Narwar
Nagda
BHOPAL
Raisen
Ratlam
Mahi R
Maksi
Sehore
Bhojpur
Ujjain
MADHYA PRADESH
NH12
Obaidullaganj
Dewas
Bhimbetka
Barkhera
Vindhya Range
Pipharia
Godhra
Dahod
Indore
Hoshangabad
Champaner
Dhar
Narmada R
Itarsi
Halol
Chhota Udaipur
Mhow
Pachmarhi
Pavagadh
Bhawra
Bagh
Mandu
Bodeli
Barhawa
Omkareshwar
Shahpur
Sankheda
Maheshwar
Dabhoi
Purnasa L
Sanawad
Mandhatta Gorge
Chandod
Narmada R
Navdatoli
Rajpipla
Betul
Julwania
Khandwa

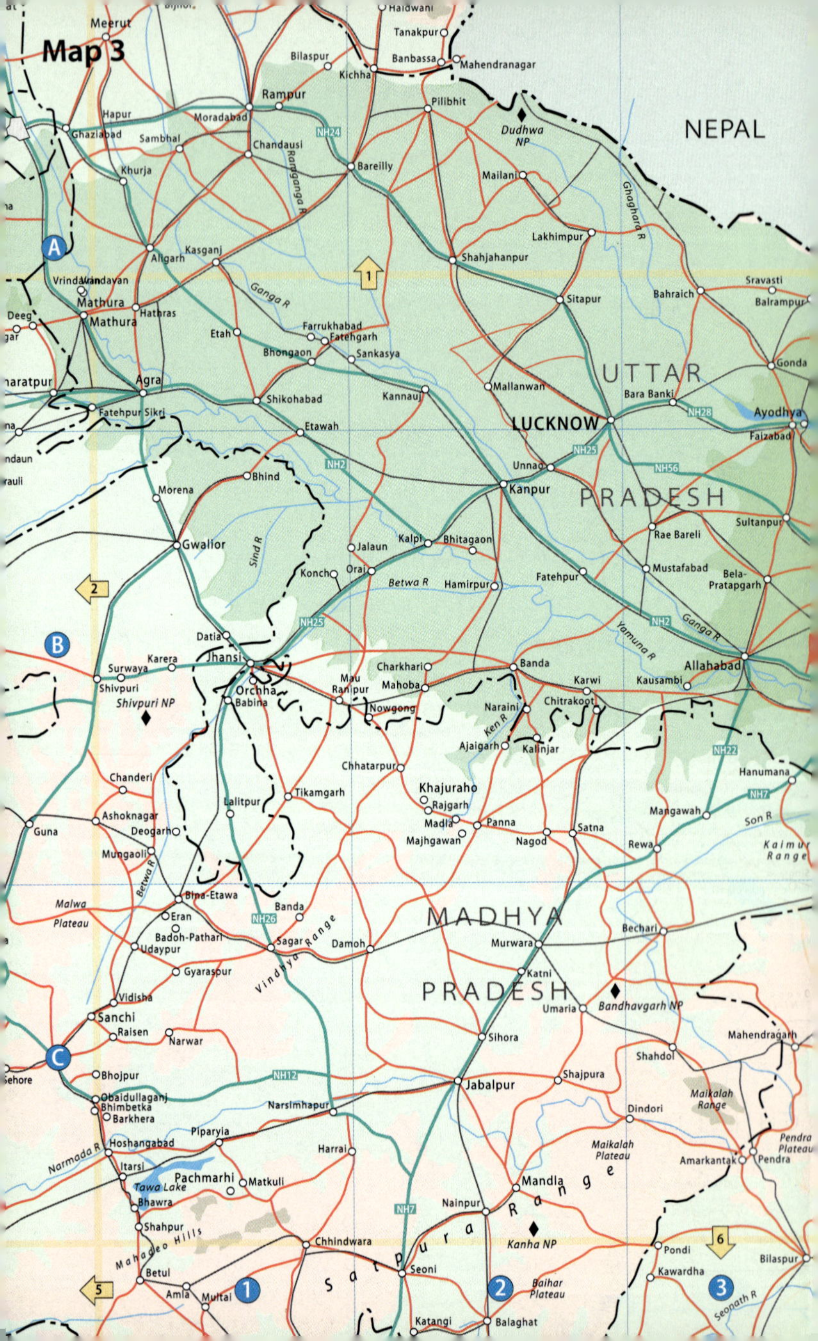

Map 3
NEPAL
UTTAR
PRADESH
MADHYA
PRADESH
LUCKNOW
Meerut
Haldwani
Tanakpur
Bilaspur
Kichha
Banbassa
Mahendranagar
Rampur
Pilibhit
Dudhwa NP
Hapur
Moradabad
Ghaziabad
Sambhal
NH24
Chandausi
Ramganga R
Bareilly
Khurja
Mailani
Ghaghara R
Lakhimpur
Aligarh
Kasganj
Shahjahanpur
Vrindavan
Mathura
Hathras
Ganga R
Sitapur
Bahraich
Sravasti
Balrampur
Deeg
Etah
Farrukhabad
Fatehgarh
Bhongaon
Sankasya
Gonda
Agra
Fatehpur Sikri
Shikohabad
Kannauj
Mallanwan
Bara Banki
NH28
Ayodhya
Faizabad
Etawah
NH25
NH56
Unnao
NH2
Bhind
Morena
Kanpur
Sultanpur
Rae Bareli
Gwalior
Sind R
Jalaun
Kalpi
Bhitagaon
Mustafabad
Bela-Pratapgarh
Konch
Orai
Betwa R
Hamirpur
Fatehpur
Datia
Yamuna R
Jhansi
Karera
Surwaya
Shivpuri
Shivpuri NP
Orchha
Babina
Mau Ranipur
Charkhari
Mahoba
Nowgong
Banda
Karwi
Kausambi
Allahabad
Naraini
Chitrakoot
Ken R
Ajaigarh
Kalinjar
Chhatarpur
NH22
Hanumana
Chanderi
Khajuraho
Rajgarh
Tikamgarh
Lalitpur
NH7
Mangawah
Son R
Ashoknagar
Guna
Deogarh
Madla
Panna
Majhgawan
Nagod
Satna
Rewa
Kaimur Range
Mungaoli
Betwa R
Bina-Etawa
Malwa Plateau
Eran
Banda
NH26
Badoh-Pathari
Udaypur
Sagar
Vindhya Range
Damoh
Murwara
Bechari
Katni
Gyaraspur
Vidisha
Sanchi
Raisen
Narwar
Umaria
Bandhavgarh NP
Sihora
Mahendragarh
Shahdol
Sehore
Bhojpur
NH12
Jabalpur
Shajpura
Obaidullaganj
Bhimbetka
Barkhera
Narsimhapur
Maikalah Range
Dindori
Piparya
Hoshangabad
Narmada R
Harrai
Maikalah Plateau
Pendra Plateau
Itarsi
Pachmarhi
Matkuli
Tawa Lake
Amarkantak
Pendra
Mandla
Bhawra
NH7
Nainpur
Shahpur
Mahadeo Hills
Chhindwara
Satpura Range
Kanha NP
Pondi
Bilaspur
Kawardha
Betul
Amla
Multai
Seoni
Baihar Plateau
Seonath R
Katangi
Balaghat

N
50 km
50 miles
The Government of India state that "the external boundaries of India are neither correct nor authenticated"
A
B
C
4
5
6
BIHAR
JHARKHAND
CHHATTISGARH
ORISSA
PATNA
Sonauli 'crossing'
Nautanwa
Bagaha
Pharenda
Gorakhpur
Basti
Kasia
Kushinagar
Birganj
Raxaul
Sonbasa
Basopatti
Jaynagar
Laukaha
Dakha
Sitamarhi
Lauriya
Gopalganj
Dumra
Madhubani
Nimali
Jogbani
Forbesganj
Akbarpur
Ghaghara R
Deoria
Siwan
Gandak R
Darbhanga
Kishanpur
Supaul
Raniganj
Basa
Kanti
Muzaffarpur
Vaishali
Pusa
Samastipur
Saharsa
Madhepura
Sarsi
Kosi R
Azamgarh
Mau
Shahganj
Chapra
Sonepur
Hajipur
Ghugri R
Purnia
Jaunpur
Maner
Ganga R
Barauni
Khagarja
Katihar
Damraon
Arrah
Buxar
Saidpur
Ghazipur
Sarnath
Varanasi
Mughal Sarai
Arwal
Bihar Sharif
Jahanabad
Nalanda
Mokameh
Monghyr
Bhagalpur
Colgong
Luckaseeri
Bhimandh
Piro
Bikramganj
Ramnagar
Rajgir
Pawapuri
Belagunj
Sikandra
Mirzapur
Chunar
Sasaram
Bhabua Road
Son R
Daudnagar
Barabar Caves
Nawala
Barahat
Bausi
Gaya
Jha Jha
Katuria
Hausdiha
Rajuali
Rohtasgarh
Bodhgaya
Sherghati
Khajuri
Deoghar
Robertsganj
Dhanwar
Madhupur
Giridi
Tilaiya Reservoir
Barhi
Hazaribagh Road
Parsnath
Hazaribagh NP
Topchanchi Lake
Singrauli
Pipri
Rihand (Pant Sagar)
Daltonganj
Manika
Maithon Reservoir
Suri
Chipadohar
Hazaribagh
Dumri
Dhanbad
Kulti
Asanol
Raniganj
Durgapur
Palamau Betla NP
Bokaro
Lodh Falls
Tori
Hundru Falls
Ramgarh
Damoda
Kuru
Deogarh Hills
Ghagri Falls
Netarhat
Lohardaga
Ranchi
Bero
Jonha Falls
Purulia
Bankura
Bundu
Baikuntapur
Sisai
Khunti
Dasam Falls
Balarampur
Surajpur
Ambikapur
Jashpur Hills
Gumla
Raipur
Tatanagar
Chandil
Jamshedpur
Sitapur
Subarnarekha R
Chaisbasa
Birmitrapur
Pathalgaon
Gua
Rourkela
Jamda
Naomundi
Badampahar
Baripada
Bada Barabil
Joshipur
Talbandh
Jaleswar
Sundargarh
Gobindpur
Bonai Hills
Barsua
Khiching
Brahmani R
Similipal NP
Rawgarh
Hirakud Dam
Jharsugada
Baleshwar
Chandipur
Mahanadi R
Keonjhargarh
Deogarh
Barakot
NH29
NH28
NH30
NH31
NH2
NH33
NH32
NH23
NH6

Map 4

A
B
C
1
2
3
SIKKIM
Yumthang
Kangchendzonga NP
Lachung
Chemathang
Thangshing
Mangan
Phodong
Dzongri
Rumtek
Gangtok
Legship
Singtam
Naya Bazar
Rangpo
Sandakphu
Darjeeling
Kalimpong
Siliguri
Mirik
Bagdogra
New Jalpaiguri
Jalpaiguri
Coochbehar
Jaldapara WLP
Alipur Duar
BHUTAN
Manas NP
Nalbari
Bijni
Bongaigon
Saptagram
Barpeta Rd
Barpeta
Goalpara
River Brahmaputra
Krishnai
Dhuburi
Boko
NH31
NH31B
NH51
Phulbari
MEGHALAYA
Songsak
Darugiri
Singrimapi
Tura
Jadukata R
Jakrem
Siju
Burengapara
Laukaha
Jogbani
Nimali
Forbesganj
Kishanpur
Supaul
Raniganj
Kishanganj
Basantpur
Islampur
Dalkola
Madhepura
Saharsa
Sarsi
Purnia
Ghugri R
Mahanada R
NH34
Katihar
Khagarja
Monghyr
Colgong
WEST BENGAL
Bhagalpur
BIHAR
Bhimandh
Pandua
Malda
Ingraz Bazar
Gaur
Berhait
Barahat
Bausi
Farakka
Katuria
Hausdiha
Dhulian
Deoghar
JHARKHAND
Jangipur
Hugli R
Murshidabad
Madhupur
Giridi
Rampurhat
Baharampur
Tarapith
Parsnath
Topchanchi Lake
Maithon Reservoir
Dumri
Suri
Sainthia
Plassey
Bakresvar
Santiniketan
Dhanbad
Kulti
Asanol
Raniganj
Bolpur
Durgapur
NH2
Krishnanagar
Nabadwip
Kalna
Barddhaman
Damodar R
Bankura
Purulia
Naihati
Pandua
Bangaon
Benapole
BANGLADESH
Balarampur
Bishnupur
Tarakeswar
Raipur
Arambagh
Serampore
NH35
Chandil
KOLKATA
WEST BENGAL
NH6
Subarnarekha R
Jaynagar
Diamond Harbour
Canning
Badampahar
Baripada
Haldia
Kakdwip
Talbandh
Joshipur
Jaleswar
Sunderbans NP
Sagardwip Island
Similipal NP
Digha
Chandragiri
Baleshwar

TIBET (CHINA)
ARUNACHAL PRADESH
Mechaka
Along
Roing
Tezu
Lohit
Pasighat
Parasuram Kund
Subansiri
Daporijo
Saikhoa Ghat
Dibru-Saikhowa NP
Miao
Namdapha NP
Sonargaon
Tinsukia
Digboi
Ledo
NH38
Dibrugarh
Margherita
Ziro
Tawang
Kinsa
Lilabari
N Lakhimpur
Brahmaputra R
NH37
Sonari
Bomdila
Dirang
Bhoreli
Itanagar
Naharlagun
Sibsagar
Simalguri
Bhalukpong
Majuli
Majuli
Jorhat
Mon
Nameri NP
NH52
Mariani
Sonairupal NP
Numaligarh
Tezpur
Rowta
NH37
Orang NP
Golaghat
Furkating
Kaziranga NP
Tuensang
Mangaldai
Silghat
Nagaon
Dhing
Nowgong
Mokokchung
Wokha
Hajo
North Guwahati
Sualkuchi
NH36
Dimapur
Guwahati
ASSAM
Diphu
NAGALAND
Dispur
NH40
Lumding
Kohima
Shillong
Garampani
Nartiang
Mawkyrwat
Jowai
NH39
Cherrapunji
Lumshong
NH40
Syndai
Haflong
MANIPUR
Mawmluh Mawsmai
Imphal
Badarpur
NH44
Karimganj
Silchar
NH39
Moirang
Churachandpur
Keibul Lamjao NP
Moreh
MYANMAR (BURMA)
Kailashahar
Dhamnagar
Unakoti
TRIPURA
Aizawl
Reiek
Saitual
Agartala
Champhai
MIZORAM
Udaipur
Neermahal
Pilak
Lunglei
A
B
C
4
5
6
N
50 km
50 miles
The Government of India state that "the external boundaries of India are neither correct nor authenticated"

Map 5
GUJARAT
Gop
Gondal
Hingolgadh
Botad
Jasdan
Gadhada
Velavadhar NP
Porbandar
Ranavav
NH8B
Dhoraji
Jetpur
Derdi
Babra
Bhavnagar
Sihor
Gogha
Vanthali
Junagadh
Bagsara
Amreli
Palitana
Alang
Keshod
Sasan Gir NP
Visavadar
Dhari
Kundla
Talaja
Talala
Sasan Gir
Tulsishyam
Gopnath
Chorwad
Prabhas Patan
Mahuva
Pip-a-Vav
Veraval
Somnath
Una
Jafrabad
Delwada
Kodinar
Diu
Gulf of Khambhat
Jambusar
Karjan
Chandod
Rajpipla
Dahej
Bharuch
Ankleshwar
NH8
Surat
Mandvi
Uchchhal
Dumas
Navsari
Vyara
Ubhrat
Dandi
Chikhli
Vansda
Saputara
Valsad
Tithal
North Sahyadri Range
Daman
Pardi
DADRA & NAGAR HAVELI
Silvassa
Jawhar
Trimbak
Nashik
Deolali
Arabian Sea
N
50 km
50 miles
The Government of India state that "the external boundaries of India are neither correct nor authenticated"
Manor
Vada
Igatpuri
Dahisar
Shahpur
Kalsubai Range
Kanheri Caves
Bhiwandi
Harischandra Range
Bassein
Kalyan
Shivner
Manori
Thane
Marve
Matheran
Neral
Panvel
Karjat
MUMBAI
Khandala
Karla Caves
Kihim
Lonavla
Pen
NH50
NH4
Alibag
NH17
Baja Caves
Kashid
Roha
Murud
Janjira
Pune
Waki
Sinhagarh
Purandhar
Raigad
Mahadeo
Veer
Mahad
Panchgani
Pratapgarh
Wai
Mahabaleshwar
Krishna
Harnai
Khed
Satara
Koyna Sagar
Chiplun
Ganpatipule
Ratnagiri
Hatkamba
Malkapur
Rajapur
Vijayadurg
Talera
NH17
Malvan
Sawantwadi
Vengurla
Redi
GOA
Mapusa
Panjim
Vasco Da Gama
NH4A
Madgaon
Cotigao Sanctuary
Karwar
Map 5a Goa
To Mumbai
<50m
50-100m
100-300m
+300m
10 km
10 miles
Tiracol Fort
Tiracol R
Naibaga
Keri
Pernem
Alorna Fort
MAHARASHTRA
Arambol
Parsi
Dargalim
Colvale
Assonora
Chapora Fort
Mapusa
Bicholim
Anjuna
Mapusa R
Chorao
Carambolin -Brahma
Sanquelim
Calangute
Salim Ali Bird Sanctuary
Kudne R
Valpoi
Divar
Aguada Fort
Banastari
Caranzol
Mandovi R
PANJIM
Old Goa
Savoi-Verem
Bondla Sanctuary
Pilar
Cumbarjua Canal
Mardol
Tambdi Surla
Mormugao
Usgaon
Khandepar
Sancordem
Vasco da Gama
Tisk
Cortalim
Ponda
Bhagwan Mahaveer Sanctuary
Dabolim
Loutolim
Molem
NH4a
Cansaulim
Borlim
Zuari R
Dudhsagar R
Colem
Siroda
Majorda
Rachol
Dudhsagar
Sanguem R
Calem
Colva
Margao
Benaulim
Chandor
Sanvordem
Varca
Quepem
Arabian Sea
Paroda
Sanguem
Damai
Sal R
Paroda R
Cuncolim
Zambaulim
Cumbari
Mobor
Bali
Rivona
Curdi
Betul
Fatorpa
Cabo de Rama Fort
Pirla
Kushavati R
NH17
Netorli
Chaudi (Canacona)
Cotigao Sanctuary
Palolem
Talpona R
Partagal Math
Galibaga
KARNATAKA
To Mangalore
GOA

ANDHRA PRADESH
TAMIL NADU
Bay of Bengal
SRI LANKA
Palk Strait
Gulf of Mannar
CHENNAI
BENGALURU
6
A
B
C
4
5
6
Ahobilam
Allagadda
Kanigi
Udayagiri
Kavali
Gooty
Tadpatri
Badvel
Anantapur
Penar R
Cuddappah
Nellore
Dharmavaram
Puttaparthi
Penukonda
Kadiri
Rajampet
Gudur
Rayachotti
Venkatagiri
Nayudupeta
Tirumalai
Sri Kalahasti
Tirupati
Renigunta
Tada
Chintamani
Chikballapur
Mulbagal
Kolar Gold Fields
Kolar
Palmaner
Chittoor
Arkonam
Poonamallee
Bangrapet
Vellore
Ranipet
Arcot
Kanchipuram
Arani
Palar
Covelong
Chengalpattu
Mahabalipuram
Hosur
Ambur
Vaniyambadi
Tirukkalukundram
Sadras
Vedanthangal Bird Sanctuary
Madurantakam
Krishnagiri
Tiruppattur
Polur
Uttangarai
Gingee
Hogenakkal Falls
Dharmapuri
Sathanur
Tiruvannamalai
Marakkanam
Harur
Kalapettai
Auroville
Ponnaiyar
Pondicherry
Stanley Reservoir
Villupuram
Mettur
Yercaud
Ulundurpettai
Cuddalore
Omalur
Attur
Neyveli
Salem
Shankari Drug
Vriddhachalam
Parangipettai
Chidambaram
Pichchavaram
Bhavani
Gangaikondacholapuram
Erode
Namakkal
Kaveri
Ariyalur
Swamimalai
Poompuhar
Kumbakonam
Tirubvanam
Tranquebar
Karur
Srirangam
Darasuram
Karaikal
Kulittalai
Tiruchirappalli
Thiruvaiyaru
Nagapattinam
Dharapuram
Thanjavur
Tiruvarur
Manapparai
Kiranur
Narthamalai
Tirutturaippundi
Ayilur
Pattukottai
Kodumbalur
Pt Calimere Bird Sanctuary
Palani
Pudukkottai
Dindigul
Kodikkarai
Natham
Chettinad
Kodaikkanal
Kodai Road
Arantangi
Vargai
Melur
Karaikkudi
Usilampatti
Teni
Madurai
Tirumangalam
Sivaganga
Manamadurai
Srivilliputtur
Sivakasi
Virudhunagar
Paramakkudi
Rajapalayam
Ramanathapuram
Ramesvaram
Kilakkarai
Kalugumalai
Mandapam
Adam's Bridge
Talaimannar
Apu Tivu
Kovilpatti
Mariyachchi
Tuticorin
Tirunelveli
Palayamkottai
Tamraparni
Tiruchendur
Nanguneri
Tisayanvilai
Pannakkudi
Nagercoil
Suchindram
Kanniyakumari
NH5
NH7
NH4
NH46
NH47
NH45
NH49
NH7a

Main railways

5
6
7
ARUNACHAL
PRADESH
Murkong Salek
SIKKIM
North Lakhimpur
Tinsukia
Rangapara
Darjeeling
New Jalpaiguri
Jorhat
Furkating
Siliguri
New
Bongaigaon
ASSAM
Guwahati
NAGALAND
Lumding
Darbhanga
Dimapur
Samastipur
MEGHALAYA
Bhagalpur
Katihar
Haflong
Malda
BIHAR
Badarpur
MANIPUR
Barharwa
Hazaribag
Road
Lalaghat
TRIPURA
MIZORAM
Chittaranjan
Bolpur
WEST
BENGAL
Muri
Tatanagar
Kolkata
Kharagpur
Talcher
Cuttack
Bhubaneswar
Khurda Road
Puri

Index

India distance chart

	Ahmedabad	Bengaluru	Bhopal	Bhubaneswar	Chennai	Delhi	Guwahati	Hyderabad	Jaipur	Jaisalmer	Kolkata	Lucknow	Mumbai	Panjim	Shimla	Thiruvananthapuram
Bengaluru	1495															
Bhopal	568	1401														
Bhubaneswar	1810	1440	1192													
Chennai	1826	331	1435	1235												
Delhi	915	2061	744	1745	2095											
Guwahati	2423	2932	1855	1483	2718	1959										
Hyderabad	1208	562	839	1075	688	1499	2370									
Jaipur	657	1985	584	1791	2019	258	1961	1443								
Jaisalmer	595	2094	982	2214	2417	793	2531	1803	570							
Kolkata	1924	1881	1356	441	1676	1461	1081	1516	1462	2032						
Lucknow	1154	1928	678	1265	1962	497	1479	1366	595	1165	980					
Mumbai	545	998	779	1507	1329	1407	2746	711	1202	1140	1987	1365				
Panjim	1068	592	1291	1746	923	1912	3020	747	1725	1663	2187	1877	593			
Shimla	1258	2403	1086	2099	2437	343	2250	1841	601	1013	1751	840	1742	2254		
Thiruvananthapuram	2040	753	2154	1943	708	2814	3426	1315	2697	2635	2384	2681	1543	1001	3156	
Varanasi	1244	1779	676	965	1813	780	1179	1217	782	1352	680	300	1593	1903	1071	2516

Distances in kilometres 1 kilometre = 0.62 miles

Map symbols

- Capital city
- Other city, town
- International border
- Regional border
- Customs
- Contours (approx)
- Mountain, volcano
- Mountain pass
- Escarpment
- Glacier
- Salt flat
- Rocks
- Seasonal marshland
- Beach, sandbank
- Waterfall
- Reef
- Motorway
- Main road
- Minor road
- Track
- Footpath
- Railway
- Railway with station
- Airport
- Bus station
- Metro station
- Cable car
- Funicular
- Ferry
- Pedestrianized street
- Tunnel
- One way-street
- Steps
- Bridge
- Fortified wall
- Park, garden, stadium
- Sleeping
- Eating
- Bars & clubs
- Building
- Sight
- Cathedral, church
- Chinese temple
- Hindu temple
- Meru
- Mosque
- Stupa
- Synagogue
- Tourist office
- Museum
- Post office
- Police
- Bank
- Internet
- Telephone
- Market
- Medical services
- Parking
- Petrol
- Golf
- Archaeological site
- National park, wildlife reserve
- Viewing point
- Campsite
- Refuge, lodge
- Castle, fort
- Diving
- Deciduous, coniferous, palm trees
- Hide
- Vineyard, winery
- Distillery
- Shipwreck
- Historic battlefield
- Detail map
- Related map